Oxford ESL Dictionary

For students of American English

A. S. Hornby

with the assistance of
Christina A. Ruse

American Editors
Dolores Harris
William A. Stewart

Oxford University Press

Calcutta Cape Town Dar es Salaam Delhi
Florence Hong Kong Istanbul Karachi
Kuala Lumpur Madras Madrid Melbourne
Mexico City Nairobi Paris Singapore
Taipei Tokyo Toronto

and associated companies in
Berlin Ibadan

First published 1991
Seventh impression 1996

Originally published as Oxford Student's Dictionary of American English

Filmset in Times New Roman by
Pindar Graphics Origination, Scarborough, North Yorkshire

Printed in Hong Kong

rary of Congress Cataloging in Publication a

in entry under title:
ford ESL Dictionary for Students of
erican English.

Adaptation of: Oxford student's dictionary of current English, 1978.

I. English language—Dictionaries. I. Hornby, Albert Sydney. II. Harris, Dolores. III. Stewart, William A. (William Alexander), 1930. IV.
Oxford student's dictionary of current English.
PE1628.095 1983 423 83-2242.

ISBN 0 19 431403 0

Table of Contents

Acknowledgments

This dictionary is adapted from the *Oxford Student's Dictionary of Current English* by A. S. Hornby with the assistance of Christina A. Ruse. Changes made during the rewriting do not reflect the opinions of contributors to this volume.

I wish to thank the members of the English Language Teaching department of Oxford University Press, New York, who worked with the American editors from the beginning of the project to Americanize the *Oxford Student's Dictionary of Current English* to the final editing: Marilyn Rosenthal, Laurie Likoff, Vicky Bijur, Catherine Clements, and Kathy Kutz, who researched the American photographs. I would like also to thank Norman MacAfee for his proofreading services during the last stage of the Dictionary.

N.Y.C. W.A.S
1983

Illustrations by:
Vantage Art, Inc.
Jack Fetchko for flex, Inc.
From *Oxford Advanced Learner's Dictionary of Current English*
by A. S. Hornby, 3rd edition © 1974
by Oxford University Press, reproduced by arrangement.

The publishers are grateful to the following for permission to reproduce the photographs:
adobe houses–Courtesy of the American Museum of Natural History
Navajo–Courtesy of the Navajo Community College, Shiprock
basketball–New York Knicks
U.S. armed forces–The Department of Defense
aircraft–U.S. Coast Guard; Beech Aircraft Corporation; American Airlines
church architecture–Dick Smith
eclipse–Yerkes Observatory photograph, University of Chicago, Williams Bay, Wis.
football–New York Jets
geyser–Iceland National Tourist Office
U.S. Supreme Court Justices–The Supreme Court Historical Society
Lincoln Memorial–National Park Service, U.S. Department of the Interior
microphone–Photo courtesy of Shure Brothers Inc.
surfing–Hawaii Visitors Bureau
patchwork quilt–The Metropolitan Museum of Art, Gift of Miss Eliza Polhemus Cobb through Mrs. Arthur Bunker, 1952 (52.103)
space capsule–NASA
boardwalk: Coney Island–The Long Island Historical Society
caboose–Association of American Railroads
car (automobile)–Chevrolet Public Relations, General Motors
U.S. Capitol–National Park Service, U.S. Department of the Interior
duplex–Department of Housing and Urban Development
oil tanker–Photo by Bill Ray, Courtesy of Texaco Inc.
telephone booth–American Telephone & Telegraph Co.
tractors and trucks–General Motors, GMC Truck & Coach Division; International Harvester, Truck Group
Washington Monument–National Park Service, U.S. Department of the Interior
U.S. Pentagon–U.S. Air Force
skyscrapers: New York–N.Y. Convention & Visitors Bureau
soccer–Cosmos
Statue of Liberty–Courtesy of the National Park Service, Statue of Liberty National Monument
inside a synagogue–Temple Emanu-El, N.Y.C.
mosque–Turkish Embassy
White House–National Park Service, U.S. Department of the Interior
Uncle Sam–James Montgomery Flagg, *I Want You for U.S. Army*, 1917, Lithograph, $40\frac{1}{4} \times 29\frac{1}{2}''$, Collection, The Museum of Modern Art, New York, acquired by exchange
keyboard instruments–Baldwin Piano & Organ Company; Baldwin Piano & Organ Company; The Metropolitan Museum of Art, Gift of Joseph W. Drexel, 1889; Steinway & Sons; The Metropolitan Museum of Art, The Crosby Brown Collection of Musical Instruments, 1889

Preface

This Dictionary is an American adaptation of the *Oxford Student's Dictionary of Current English*, with some inclusion of advanced level material from the *Oxford Advanced Learner's Dictionary of Current English*, somewhat expanded to serve learners of American English through the Intermediate level. It lists the more usual words, compounds, and idiomatic expressions that the learner is likely to hear in everyday conversation among educated Americans or to see written in letters, newspapers, and documents of the kind that one might be expected to encounter when beginning to work or study in the United States. This Dictionary also contains most of the words used in modern American books and periodicals of all but the most technical or literary kind. For listed words there is information on spelling, pronunciation, grammatical use, and meaning. In addition, there are often example sentences or phrases to illustrate details of usage, and special guidance is given on difficult points of spelling, pronunciation, and meaning.

The exclusive use of American spelling conventions should pose no problem to learners accustomed to British usage if a few general correspondences are kept in mind. These, however, have many exceptions and cannot be taken as a sure guide for converting from British to American spelling, or vice versa.

- American *-er* for British *-re* in some words; *center:centre*, *theater: theatre* (but both American and British *neuter*, *acre*).
- American *-ize* for the more frequently used *-ise* of British English; *organize:organise* (but both American and British *recognize*, *advise*).
- American (-)*e*- for British (-)*ae*-/(-)*æ*- or (-)*oe*-/(-)*œ*-; *anemic:anaemic/anæmic, fetus:foetus/fœtus.*
- American *-or* for British *-our* in many words; *color:colour*, *honor:honour*, *labor:labour* (but both American and British *glamour*).
- American *-l-* for British *-ll-* when certain verbs ending in *-l* are inflected with *-ing*/*-ed*/*-er*; *leveling:levelling*, *reveled:revelled*, *traveler:traveller*.
- Different American and British spellings of individual words; American *jail* for British *gaol*, American *check* for British *cheque*.
- American use of the period (.) after certain kinds of abbreviations which may be without it in British usage; *Mr./Dr.:Mr/Dr*.

As with the spelling, the pronunciation indicated in this Dictionary is fully American. The tradition established in the *Oxford Student's Dictionary of Current English* and the *Oxford Advanced Learner's Dictionary of Current English* of using the phonetic symbols of the International Phonetic Association is continued here, but the shift in focus from British to American pronunciation has prompted some changes in the use of specific symbols as well as in the indication of stress and length. Teachers and learners who may take up the use of this Dictionary after having familiarized themselves with its British counterparts should keep the following changes in mind:

- The symbol /y/ is used instead of /j/ for the beginning sound of *yes*. This is the only true departure from the International Phonetic Association alphabet, but it is a change in line with current American linguistic and pedagogical practice.
- The symbol /ə/ is used for both the unstressed and stressed vowels in *above* /əˈbəv/ (transcribed as /əˈbʌv/ in the British system), the /ə/-/ʌ/ phonetic distinction of British pronunciation being much less evident in the United States, and in any case a function of the degree of stress.
- The symbol /:/, used after a vowel in British transcription to indicate the lengthening of that vowel, is here discarded because of the predictability of vowel length in American pronunciation from the following consonant.
- The symbol /i/ is used instead of /ɪ/ for the final element of the diphthongs /ai, ei, ɔi/ as well as for the final unstressed vowel in, e.g., *alley* /ˈæli/, *funny* /ˈfəni/ as being a more accurate representation of distinctively American usage. For the same reason, the symbol /u/ is used instead of /ʊ/ for the final element in the diphthongs /au, ou/.
- The symbol /o/ is used instead of /ə/ to represent the first element in the diphthong in *note* /nout/, *road* /roud/, etc., as being more representative of American pronunciation.
- Secondary stress, indicated by the symbol /ˌ/ placed before the syllable which it affects, is both frequent and prominent in American English, and is consistently marked throughout this Dictionary.

Learners who wish to pursue on their own the study of American pronunciation, and in particular the interesting details of regional and social variation, should consult one or more of the books available on the subject. Among these, the following are considered standard works:

Arthur J. Bronstein, *The Pronunciation of American English*. Englewood Cliffs, N.J.: Prentice-Hall, 1960.

Laurie Bauer, John M. Dienhart, Hans H. Hartvigson, and Leif Kvistgaard Jakobsen, *American English Pronunciation*. Copenhagen: Gyldendal, 1980.

John S. Kenyon, *American Pronunciation*. 6th edition. Ann Arbor, Mich.: George Wahr, 1935.

Charles K. Thomas, *An Introduction to the Phonetics of American English*. New York: Ronald Press, 1947.

All of these works use the alphabet of the International Phonetic Association, though they differ in some details of its use both among each other and from this Dictionary.

Certain current and more or less permanent slang words have been included in the Dictionary, but there has been no attempt to include the considerable body of slang, which varies from place to place and is always changing. Those interested in a more complete reference can consult the *Dictionary of American Slang* by Harold Wentworth and Stuart Berg Flexner. 2nd supplemental ed. New York: Thomas Y. Crowell, 1975.

Dictionary Workbook

Table of Contents

Introduction

This dictionary was written specially for learners of English as a foreign or second language. It contains an enormous amount of useful information that will help you in speaking, reading and writing English.

This workbook tells you all about the different types of information available. When you have finished the practice exercises, you will know exactly what the dictionary contains and how it can help you in your English studies.

Each short exercise shows you how to develop a particular skill – for example, how to check the spelling of a plural or how to find an idiom in the dictionary.

When you are doing an exercise you must

- read the English instructions carefully.
- look at the example and check our answer in your dictionary.
- find the answers by using the dictionary. Even if you know an answer, check it in your dictionary.

When you have done an exercise you must

- check your answers in the back of the workbook.
- look carefully at your mistakes. Make sure that you understand why your answer is wrong.

Look at the entry for the word **abhor**, shown below. When you look up a word in the dictionary, you will find information on:

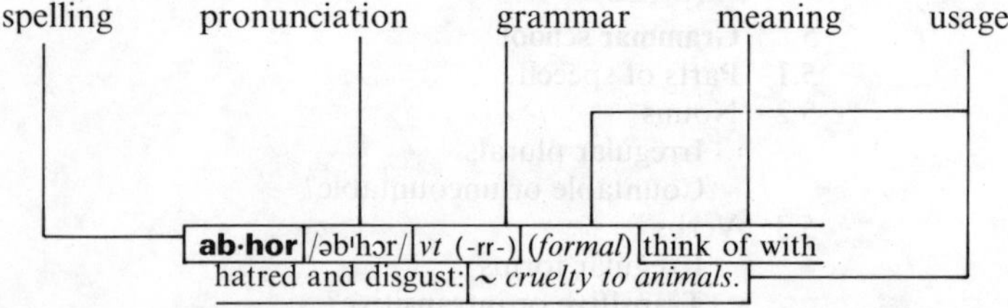

The workbook contains a section on each of these five areas. But first you must know how to *find* the entry you want . . .

1 From A to Z

1.1 Finding a word

How do you find a word in the dictionary? First you must know the English alphabet. Here it is in capital letters …

A B C D E F G H I J K L M N O P Q R S T U V W X Y Z

… and here it is in small letters …

a b c d e f g h i j k l m n o p q r s t u v w x y z

The words that are explained in the dictionary – *entry words* – are arranged in alphabetical order, so words whose first letter is **a** or **A** are at the beginning, and words whose first letter is **z** or **Z** are at the end.

If the alphabet of your own language is like the English alphabet you will find the first three exercises very easy.

Exercise 1 Write down this shopping list in alphabetical order. We have started it for you.

eggs	*apples*
apples	*bread*
cheese	
jam	
kumquats	
fish	
bread	
ice	
margarine	
honey	
dates	
grapes	
lemons	

Exercise 2 Now write down these words in alphabetical order. We have started the list for you.

Venus	*November*
October	*October*
Tuesday	
Yankee	
Ramadan	
November	
Quaker	
Uranus	
Zen	
September	
Xmas	
Pluto	
Wednesday	

What if you have a list of words beginning with the same letter, like **ball, bring, beach** and **bird**? Look at the second letter of each word: **ba** comes before **be**, **be** comes before **bi** and **bi** comes before **br**, so the correct order is **ball, beach, bird, bring**. If the second letter of each word is the same, look at the third letter, and so on.

When you know the alphabet, you can find any word quickly and easily. First decide if the word is near the beginning, middle or end of the dictionary, and open the dictionary at about the right place. Then use the guide words at the top of each page, which tell you the first and last entry word on a page.

1.2 Finding the right entry word

Imagine you want to find the meaning of the words in **bold** type in the following sentence:

The **laziest pupils failed** the exam.

If you look them up in your dictionary, you won't find these words. You will have to look up:

lazy **pupil** **fail**

This is because

- *comparative* and *superlative* forms of *adjectives* (e g *smaller, smallest*);
- *plural* forms of *nouns* (e g *bags, churches*); and
- *inflected* forms of *verbs* (e g *pushes, pushing, pushed*) are not usually listed as entry words in the dictionary.

Exercise 3 Look at each word below in **bold** type. If you want to find its meaning, which entry word do you look for in the dictionary? Write down the entry word in the space.

example	**visited**	*visit*
1	**priests**	______
2	**entered**	______
3	**arranging**	______
4	**daffodils**	______
5	**ripest**	______
6	**oranges**	______
7	**buying**	______
8	**larger**	______

Many words in English can be used as more than one part of speech. For example, **sip** is often used both as a noun and as a verb:

Sip your coffee slowly. (*verb*)
He took a **sip** of his coffee. (*noun*)

Sometimes both parts of speech are dealt with in the same entry in the dictionary, the two sections being separated by the box (□):

sip /sɪp/ *vt,vi* (-pp-) drink, taking a very small quantity at a time: *sip one's coffee.* □ *n* [C] (quantity taken in a) sipping.

However when each part of speech has a number of different meanings the two parts of speech are usually dealt with in separate numbered entries, as in the case of **print**[1] and **print**[2] below:

print[1] /prɪnt/ *n* **1** [C] mark made on a surface by pressure: *ˈfinger ~s; ˈfoot ~s.* **2** [U] **(a)** letters made by printing. **(b)** printed matter. **3** [C] picture, design, etc made by printing on paper, etc: *old Japanese ~s.* **4** [C] photograph printed from a negative.

print[2] /prɪnt/ *vt,vi* **1** press or stamp (letters, a design, etc) onto or into paper, fabric, etc. **2** make books, pictures, etc in this way. **3** publish; cause to be printed: *~ a magazine.* **4** write in printed characters (instead of ordinary, connected handwriting). **5** make (a photograph) from a negative film or plate: *How many copies shall I ~ for you?*

Sometimes words which are completely unrelated in meaning happen to have the same spelling. These are always dealt with in separate entries. For further information on these types of words, see section 2.2.

Exercise 4 Look up each of the following words. Each word may have one entry or several entries in the dictionary. Find the entry that covers the part of speech indicated. (For abbreviations used, see the inside back cover of the dictionary.) Then write the entry word in the space with its raised number if necessary.

example	**show** *v*	*show*[2]
1	**grill** *v*	
2	**primary** *n*	
3	**hold** *n*	
4	**tight** *adv*	
5	**answer** *v*	
6	**crowd** *v*	
7	**ride** *n*	
8	**long** *adj*	

1.3 Finding your way around an entry

Look at the entry for **mark**[2] below. It shows how a typical large dictionary entry is organized. The different meanings of the verb **mark** are divided into sections numbered **1, 2, 3, 4,** etc, while idioms and special verb uses are divided into sections with the letters **(a)** and **(b)**.

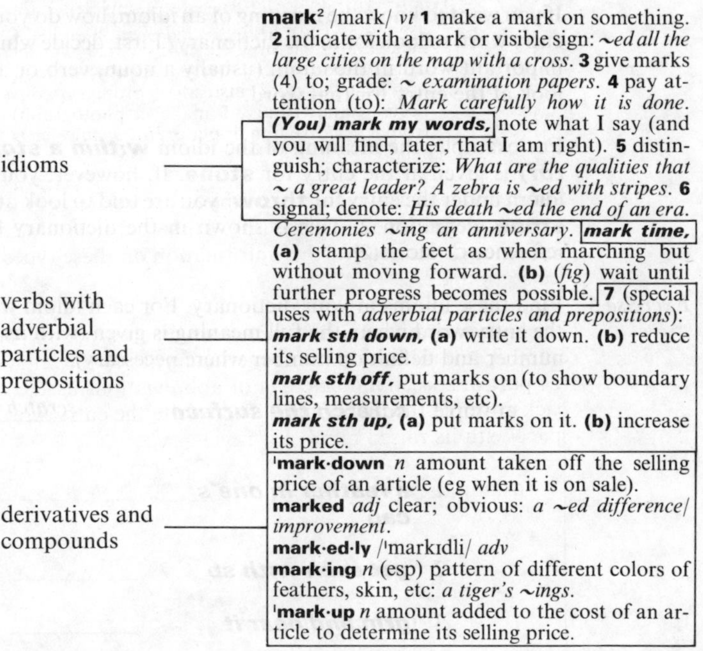

mark[2] /mark/ *vt* **1** make a mark on something. **2** indicate with a mark or visible sign: *~ed all the large cities on the map with a cross.* **3** give marks (4) to; grade: *~ examination papers.* **4** pay attention (to): *Mark carefully how it is done.* ***(You) mark my words,*** note what I say (and you will find, later, that I am right). **5** distinguish; characterize: *What are the qualities that ~ a great leader? A zebra is ~ed with stripes.* **6** signal; denote: *His death ~ed the end of an era. Ceremonies ~ing an anniversary.* ***mark time,*** **(a)** stamp the feet as when marching but without moving forward. **(b)** (*fig*) wait until further progress becomes possible. **7** (special uses with *adverbial particles and prepositions*):

mark sth down, **(a)** write it down. **(b)** reduce its selling price.

mark sth off, put marks on (to show boundary lines, measurements, etc).

mark sth up, **(a)** put marks on it. **(b)** increase its price.

ˈmark·down *n* amount taken off the selling price of an article (eg when it is on sale).

marked *adj* clear; obvious: *a ~ed difference/improvement.*

mark·ed·ly /ˈmarkɪdli/ *adv*

mark·ing *n* (esp) pattern of different colors of feathers, skin, etc: *a tiger's ~ings.*

ˈmark·up *n* amount added to the cost of an article to determine its selling price.

Imagine you want to find the meaning of the words and phrases in **bold** type in the following sentences:

He will just **mark time** in his present job until he retires.
Do car dealers **mark down** last year's models?
This essay shows a **marked** improvement over your last one.
Most stores put a high **mark-up** on jewelry.

You will see that these words and phrases do not have separate entries in your dictionary. They all appear in the entry for **mark**[2] above.

Idioms

An *idiom* is a phrase or sentence of two or more words that has a special meaning of its own, such as ***You mark my words*** or ***mark time*** in the entry for **mark²**. Idioms are printed in ***bold italic*** type and are placed in alphabetical order at the end of the numbered definitions to which they are most closely related.

If you want to know the meaning of an idiom, how do you know which entry word to look for in the dictionary? First, decide which is the most important word in the idiom (usually a noun, verb or adjective) and look at the entry for that word.

For example, the meaning of the idiom ***within a stone's throw (of)*** is given at the entry for **stone**. If, however, you look up this idiom under the entry for **throw²** you are told to look at the entry for **stone**, definition 2. This is shown in the dictionary by the cross-reference ⇨ stone(2).

Exercise 5 Find these idioms in your dictionary. For each idiom write down the entry word where the full meaning is given (with its raised number and definition number where necessary).

example	***scratch the surface***	*scratch² (1)*
1	***a feather in one's cap***	______
2	***get even with sb***	______
3	***grin and bear it***	______
4	***strike it rich***	______
5	***(straight) from the horse's mouth***	______
6	***a skeleton in the closet***	______
7	***spill the beans***	______
8	***a tower of strength***	______

Special verb uses

English contains many phrases made up of a *verb* and an *adverbial particle* or *preposition*, such as **mark sth down**, **mark sth off** and **mark sth up** in the entry for **mark²** (see section 1.3).

When there are several of these phrases in a verb entry they are listed together in a separate numbered section after the definitions of the verb. This section is called "special uses with *adverbial particles* and *prepositions*."

The phrases are printed in ***bold italic*** type, with the particles or prepositions in alphabetical order. So ***[mark sth] down*** comes before ***[mark sth] off***, ***[mark sth] off*** comes before ***[mark sth] up***, and so on.

Exercise 6 The following phrases are all listed in the entry for **put**. Write them down in alphabetical order and then find them in your dictionary. We have started the list for you.

put sth away	*put sth aside*
put in	*put sth away*
put sth out	
put sb up	
put sth to sb	
put sth aside	
put sth down	
put sth on	

Derivatives and compounds

A *derivative* is a word formed by adding an ending to another word, so derivatives of **mark** (see section 1.3) are **marked**, **markedly** and **marking**.

A *compound* is a word or expression formed from two or more separate words. **Markdown** and **markup** are compounds of **mark**.

Derivatives and compounds are listed in **bold** type in a separate section at the end of an entry and are in alphabetical order.

Sometimes, however, a derivative or compound of a word has its own separate entry. It may be that its spelling is very different: compare **adhere** with its derivative **adhesion**. It may also be because its meaning is very different: the meaning of the compound **horseradish**, for example, has no obvious connection with the word **horse**.

Exercise 7 Find the following words in your dictionary. They are all derivatives or compounds of the word **soft**:

soft-boiled, soft drink, soft-hearted, softly, softness, soft option, soft-soled, soft-spoken, software

Now complete each of the sentences below by writing one of the derivatives or compounds in the space. We have done an example sentence for you.

example Those *soft-soled* shoes are not suitable for climbing!

1 How much ________________ is supplied with the computer?

2 He didn't offer us a ________________, let alone a beer!

3 He always speaks too ________________ on the telephone.

4 She's too ________________ – she should be tougher.

5 The ________________ of the baby's skin surprised her.

6 Could I please have a ________________ egg?

7 Is studying literature a ________________?

8 He's always very ________________ on the telephone.

1.4 Finding abbreviations and contractions

An *abbreviation* is a short form of a word or of a group of words, such as **Nov.** for **November** and **NATO** for **North Atlantic Treaty Organization**. Abbreviated forms are often (but not always) written with a period (.).

A *contraction* is also a short form of a word or of a group of words, such as **e'en** for **even** and **I've** for **I have**. Contracted forms are always written with an apostrophe (').

Abbreviations and contractions are listed for easy reference in the main part of the dictionary, just as if they were whole words.

Exercise 8 The list below contains four abbreviations followed by four contractions. Find each item in your dictionary and write its full form in the space. We have done an example for you.

example	**VIP**	*very important person*
1	**Fri.**	
2	**rpm**	
3	**OPEC**	
4	**PTA**	
5	**they're**	
6	**I'm**	
7	**don't**	
8	**we've**	

2 What's the meaning?

2.1 One word, one entry

One of the most important functions of a dictionary is to give the meanings of words. When an entry word has more than one meaning, the dictionary always gives the most common meaning of the word first.

In addition, *example phrases* and *sentences* form a large and very important part of the dictionary. They follow the definitions and are printed in *italic* type. (If an entry word has more than three letters, it is shown by the tilde (~) in example phrases and sentences.) The more important functions of these example phrases and sentences are:

- They show how the entry word, derivative, compound or idiomatic expression is used in different sentence patterns.
- They show the kinds of style or context in which the word or phrase is typically used, including the sorts of words used with it.
- They often include information on where to put the stress when using the entry word in a phrase or sentence.
- They teach the writing conventions of correct punctuation and the use of capital letters, since many of the examples are full, correctly written and punctuated sentences.

Exercise 9 Look at the list of diseases in the example below. If you look these words up in your dictionary you will find that the list contains a word for something that is *not* a disease: **angora** is a fluffy type of wool, and should therefore not be in the list. Use your dictionary to find the word that does not belong in each of the following lists, and underline it.

example (*diseases*)
mumps, typhoid, angora, cholera, malaria

1 (*dogs*)
terrier, poodle, collie, chameleon, bloodhound

2 (*games*)
chess, checkers, baseball, rickets, hockey

3 (*precious stones*)
diamond, aluminum, emerald, ruby, sapphire

4 (*materials*)
linen, cotton, parsley, velvet, denim

Exercise 10 Each of the sentences below describes the job that a person does. However the name of the person who does that job is missing. By checking the meanings of the words below carefully in your dictionary, you will find the missing word. Write this word in the space.

author, tailor, artist, conductor, dentist, engineer, butcher

example An *author* writes books.

1 A ____________ looks after your teeth.

2 A ____________ makes clothes.

3 An ____________ designs machines, bridges, etc.

4 A ____________ tells an orchestra what to do.

5 A ____________ sells meat.

6 An ____________ paints pictures.

2.2 One word, several entries

Exercise 4 gave you practice in finding related words with the same spelling but different parts of speech. However sometimes words happen to have the same spelling but have very different meanings and origins (and often very different pronunciations, as in the case of **tear**[1] and **tear**[2]). These are always listed as separate entries in the dictionary:

tear[1] /tɪr/ *n* [C] drop of salty water coming from the eye: *Her eyes filled with ~s. The sad story moved us to ~s,* made us cry. *The girl burst into ~s,* began to cry.

tear[2] /ter/ *vt,vi* (*pt* tore /tɔr/, *pp* torn /tɔrn/) **1** pull apart or to pieces; make a hole in something, damage, by pulling sharply: *~ a sheet of paper in two/~ it to pieces/to bits. He tore the parcel open.* ***tear sth up,*** tear it into small pieces. **2** cause (something) to be out of place (*down, off, away, etc*) by pulling sharply: *~ a page out of a book. She could scarcely ~ herself away from the scene,* found it difficult to leave. **3** destroy the peace of: *a country torn by civil war; a heart torn by grief.* ***torn between,*** unable to choose between (conflicting demands, wishes, etc). **4** become torn: *This material ~s easily.* **5** go in excitement or at great speed: *The children tore out of the school yard.* □ *n* [C] torn place.

Exercise 11 Each of the words in **bold** type in the following sentences has more than one entry in the dictionary. Look up each word in your dictionary. Then write down the entry word (with its raised number) that covers the meaning of the word *as it is used in the sentence.*

example He works in a gold **mine**. *mine*[2]

1 Don't use that pen – it's **mine**! ______

2 The dog fell through the **ice**. ______

3 How long will it take to **ice** the cake? ______

4 Please **sign** this check. ______

5 What does that traffic **sign** mean? ______

6 Tell the truth – don't **lie**! ______

7 **Lie** down – you look tired. ______

8 That allegation is a **lie**! ______

3 Spelling it out

3.1 Finding a word that you can't spell

How do you find a word in the dictionary when you can't spell it? It may be that you know how to spell most of a word, but are unsure of certain letters. In that case, write down the parts of the word that you *can* spell, and leave gaps for any missing letters, like this:

sep_r_te

Now start looking through the words beginning with **sep-** in the dictionary. You will soon find that **separate** is the correct spelling.

Exercise 12 Each of the following sentences contains a word in **bold** type with a letter missing. Use your dictionary to find the missing letter and write it in the space.

example My brother is studying **med** *i* **cine**.

1 Is it really **ne___essary** for me to go shopping?

2 She bought some **b___nanas**.

3 Today is **Independ___nce** Day!

4 He has a **white-coll___r** job.

5 She **apologi___ed** for arriving late.

6 The scientist **analy___ed** the results of his experiment.

7 The President consulted his **advi___ers**.

8 Do you play a **music___l** instrument?

Exercise 13 Each of the following sentences contains a word in **bold** type that is spelled incorrectly. Use your dictionary to find the correct spelling of the word and write it in the space.

example We had an **arguement**. *argument*

1 Can you give me Mr. Baker's **adress**? ___

2 The **commitee** met to discuss the proposal. ___

3 Acorns **develope** into oak trees. ______

4 There was an **aksident** on the highway. ______

5 The twins are **identicel**. ______

6 She could not hide her **dissappointment**. ______

7 The soldiers were very **couragous**. ______

8 Were you **responsable** for the damage? ______

3.2 Finding an alternative

Sometimes there is more than one correct spelling of a word. For example, **siphon** can also be spelled **syphon**. In these cases, the most common spelling is listed first in the entry for the word. This is the spelling that the dictionary recommends. So if you look up the entry **siphon, syphon** you will see that **siphon** is the recommended spelling. If you look up the entry **syphon** in your dictionary you will find "= siphon." "=" in this case means "is an alternative spelling of."

Exercise 14 Look up each of the words in the list below in your dictionary. Find another possible spelling of the word and write it in the space.

		Another possible spelling
example	**orangutan**	*orangutang*
1	**installment**	______
2	**acknowledgment**	______
3	**pickaxe**	______
4	**encyclopedia**	______
5	**jailer**	______
6	**grannie**	______
7	**lollypop**	______
8	**marvellous**	______

3.3 Breaking your word

When you are writing or typing you often find that you have to divide a word at the end of a line because there is not enough space for the complete word. You show that you have done this by adding a hyphen (-) after the first part of the word at the end of the line.

The recommended places for dividing words are shown in the dictionary by a dot (·). This information is given for all headwords, derivatives and one-word or hyphenated compounds.

Here are five rules to remember:

	Right	Wrong
● Never divide a word within a syllable.*	**punc·ture**	**pu·nctu·re**
● With the exception of *-ly*, never divide a word so that an ending of two letters such as *-ed*, *-er*, *-ic* begins the next line.	**leader**	**lead·er**
● Never divide a word so that one of the parts is a single letter.	**apart**	**a·part**
● Never divide a word of one syllable.	**through**	**thr·ough**
● Never divide a word of less than five letters.	**upon**	**up·on**

Exercise 15 Look up each of the words in the list below in your dictionary. Then write the word in the space, with dots to show where it can be divided, as in the dictionary. If a word cannot be divided, write "no" opposite the word.

example **pepper** *pep·per*

1 **antiseptic** ________

2 **theater** ________

3 **kindness** ________

4 **footstep** ________

5 **nosy** ________

6 **strawberry** ________

7 **water** ________

8 **unauthorized** ________

*A *syllable* is a unit of sound containing a vowel sound on its own, as in **eye** or **you**, or a vowel sound with one or more consonants, as in **but** or **tree**. An English word may consist of one or more syllables.

4 Just say the word

Knowing how to *spell* a word does not always help you to *say* it properly. Many letters of the English alphabet can be pronounced in several ways. For example, the letter **a** is pronounced differently in **hat, came, water, dare** and **ago**.

Phonetic spelling is a way of writing a word so that one symbol always represents only one sound. Two words may be spelled differently in ordinary spelling, but if they sound the same, the phonetic spelling will be the same. For example, **way** and **weigh** have the same phonetic spelling /wei/.

On the other hand, there may be just one ordinary spelling for a word, but if you can say it two different ways it will have two phonetic spellings. If you look up **schedule** in your dictionary, you will find /'skedʒul, -dʒəl/ as the phonetic spelling. This means that both /'skedʒul/ and /'skedʒəl/ are possible. Another way of indicating an alternative pronunciation of a word is to show a phonetic symbol in parentheses, as in /sə(r)'praiz/ for **surprise**. This means that both /sə'praiz/ and /sər'praiz/ are possible.

We give a phonetic spelling for each entry word in the dictionary. Many compounds and derivatives have phonetic spellings too, where this is necessary or helpful.

Inside the front cover of the dictionary is a list of the phonetic symbols used. The following exercises will give you practice in recognizing them.

4.1 Pronouncing vowels

Exercise 16 Each word in the following list contains the sound /i/ or /ɪ/. Find out which sound each word contains and put the word into the correct column. We have done the first word to help you.

sit, seat, ship, sheep, reach, ridge, leap, lip

/i/	/ɪ/
	sit

Exercise 17 Each word in the following list contains the sound /au/ or /ou/. Find out which sound each word contains and put the word into the correct column.

growl, grow, bowl, now, cow, crow, blow, blouse

/au/	/ou/

4.2 Pronouncing consonants

Exercise 18 The letter combination **ch** can be pronounced in several ways in English. Find out how the **ch** is pronounced in each word and put the word into the correct column.

church, schedule, much, chauffeur, school, chemist, lunch, chalet

/tʃ/	/k/	/ʃ/

Exercise 19 The sounds /s/ and /z/ can be spelled with several different letters or combinations of letters. Find out how the underlined letter or pair of letters is pronounced in each word and put the word into the correct column.

city, gaze, news, zoo, psychology, scientific, dress, magnetism

/s/	/z/

4.3 Different spelling, same sound

Exercise 20 In each of the following sentences there is a choice of two words in **bold** type that are spelled differently but sound the same. Only one of the two can be correct in that sentence. Find the correct spelling and underline it.

example Can I have a **peace** / **piece** of cake?

1 Can you **weight** / **wait** five minutes?

2 The car was **stationary**. / **stationery**.

3 We planted the vegetables in **rows**. / **rose**.

4 He **through** / **threw** a brick **threw** / **through** the window.

5 I bought a **pear** / **pair** of gloves.

6 The bride and groom walked up the **aisle** / **isle** to the **alter**. / **altar**.

7 Can you **write** / **right** down your address?

8 There was a strong **currant** / **current** in the river.

4.4 Same spelling, different sound

Exercise 21 In each of the following sentences there is a word in **bold** type that has two possible phonetic spellings. Only one of the two can be correct in that sentence. Find the correct phonetic spelling and write it in the space.

example She tied a **bow** /bou/ in her hair.

1 John and Mary had a **row** /__________/ about money.

2 We were sitting in the front **row** /__________/.

3 **Lead** /__________/ is a heavy metal.

4 Who is going to **lead** /__________/ the expedition?

5 **Wind** /__________/ the string into a ball.

6 My hat blew off in the **wind** /__________/.

7 Can you **close** /__________/ the door?

8 I sat **close** /__________/ to the fire.

4.5 Stressing your point

When an English word has more than one syllable, one of the syllables is spoken with more force than the others. This force is called *stress*. In the dictionary, stress is shown in the phonetic spelling by placing the mark /ˈ/ in front of the stressed syllable, as in /ˈʃouldər/, /ˈnoutɪs/, /ˈwɔtər/.

A word with several syllables may have two of them stressed, one having a stronger stress than the other. In this case the stronger stress is called *primary stress* (still marked /ˈ/). The weaker stress is called *secondary stress* (marked /ˌ/), as in /ˈteləˌvɪʒən/, /ˌklɔstrəˈfoubiə/.

When derivatives and compounds (see section 1.3) come at the end of entries and have no phonetic spellings, the stress pattern is shown in the ordinary spelling in bold type, as in the compound ˈ**bathroom** in the entry for **bath**.

Exercise 22 In each list of words, every word except one has primary stress on the *first* syllable. Use your dictionary to find the word in each list that should not be there, and underline it.

example **music, muscular, musician, mussel**

1 **palace, policy, police, politics**

2 **neutral, neutralize, neutrality**

3 **comfortable, reliable, able, fashionable**

4 **adjective, admit, adequate, additive**

Exercise 23 In each list of words, every word except one has primary stress on the *second* syllable. Use your dictionary to find the word in each list that should not be there, and underline it.

example **avert, avid, avoid, await**

1 **benefit, benevolent, beneath, because**

2 **important, different, reluctant, persistent**

3 **photograph, photographer, photography**

4 **incredible, incapable, incident, include**

4.6 Stressing the difference

Many words in English can be used either as a noun or as a verb. Sometimes the stress does not change:

He sent his **reply** /rɪˈplaɪ/ immediately. (*noun*)
Please **reply** /rɪˈplaɪ/ immediately. (*verb*)

In many cases, however, the noun and verb are stressed differently. The general rule is that for two-syllable words of this kind, nouns are stressed on the first syllable and verbs are stressed on the second syllable:

Thank you for the **present** /ˈprezənt/. (*noun*)
Who is going to **present** /prɪˈzent/ the prize? (*verb*)

Exercise 24 In each of the following sentences, show the stress in the word in **bold** type by placing the mark (ˈ) in front of the stressed syllable.

example The company's profits have **inˈcreased** this year.

1 The travelers died of thirst in the **desert**.

2 I **object** to people smoking in restaurants.

3 I bought a **refill** for my pen.

4 You need a **permit** to enter the laboratory.

5 Can you **refill** my glass?

6 What's the name of this **object**?

7 If you **desert** the army you will be punished.

8 The company president does not **permit** laziness.

5 Grammar school

Look at the entry for the word **dictionary**, shown below:

grammar

dic·tion·ary /ˈdɪkʃəˌneri/ *n* [C] (*pl* -ies) book with words or topics arranged in alphabetical order, that gives a meaning, spelling, pronunciation, etc for each word.

Immediately after the information on pronunciation comes the grammatical information. We are told that **dictionary** is

- a countable noun;
- has the plural **dictionaries**.

The dictionary gives two main types of grammatical information about a word. It tells you

- what its part of speech is;
- how to change its form to make plurals, comparative and superlative forms of adjectives, tenses of verbs, etc.

5.1 Parts of speech

Exercise 25 Look at the list of nouns in the example below. If you look these words up in your dictionary, you will find that the list contains a word which is *not* a noun: **lunar** is an adjective, and should therefore not be in the list. Use your dictionary to find the word that does not belong in each of the following lists and underline it.

example (*nouns*)
scholar, collar, lunar, cigar

1 (*nouns*)
syllable, participle, disciple, probable

2 (*verbs*)
deduct, product, instruct, obstruct

3 (*adjectives*)
ugly, rainy, quickly, lovely

4 (*prepositions*)
too, towards, through, to

5.2 Nouns

Irregular plurals

The dictionary gives you information on the *irregular plurals of nouns* under the entry for the word in its singular form, so if you want to check the plural **cities**, look up the singular form **city**. However, if the plural is spelled very differently from the singular noun it is also listed separately. Therefore **mice** (the plural of **mouse**) is a separate entry word in the dictionary.

Exercise 26 Use your dictionary to fill in the plural form of each of the nouns listed below. Write each plural form in full. Where more than one form is given in the dictionary, fill in both forms.

example **foot** *feet*

1 **hoof** ____________

2 **knife** ____________

3 **potato** __________

4 **diary** __________

5 **buffalo** __________

6 **child** __________

7 **deer** __________

8 **donkey** __________

9 **roof** __________

10 **tooth** __________

Countable or uncountable?

Before you can use a noun correctly in a sentence, you must know whether it is *countable* or *uncountable*. The symbol [C] (countable) means that the noun has both a singular and a plural form. It can be used in the singular with *a, an, another* (as in *a bottle, an apple, another boy*), in the plural with *many* (*many apples*) and in the singular or plural with numbers (*one bottle, six bottles*).

The symbol [U] (uncountable) means that the noun does not have a plural form. It can be used in the singular with words like *some, enough, much, more* (*some information, enough money, much noise*). It cannot normally be used with *a, an, another,* with *many* or with numbers.

The symbols [C, U] mean that the noun can be used either as *countable* or *uncountable*. For example, **coffee** is used as [C] in *Two coffees, please!* and as [U] in *Have some more coffee!*

Exercise 27 Look up these nouns in your dictionary. Are they countable or uncountable? Can they be both? Write "[C]," "[U]" or "both" in the space.

example **leg** [C]

1 **bread** __________

2 **table** __________

3 **information** __________

4 **tennis** ______

5 **cake** ______

6 **student** ______

7 **knowledge** ______

8 **experience** ______

5.3 Verbs

Irregular forms

The dictionary gives you information on the *irregular forms of verbs* under the entry for the verb in the infinitive form. However many irregular verb forms are spelled very differently from the infinitive and are also listed separately. Therefore **swum** (the irregular past participle of the verb **swim**) is a separate entry word in the dictionary.

Exercise 28 Use your dictionary to fill in the form indicated of each of the verbs listed below. (For abbreviations used, see the inside back cover of the dictionary.)

example **swim** *pt* *swam*

1 **hide** *pt* ______

2 **catch** *pp* ______

3 **fry** *pp* ______

4 **bring** *pp* ______

5 **take** *pt* ______

6 **teach** *pt* ______

7 **kneel** *pp* ______

8 **forgive** *pt* ______

Transitive or intransitive?

The dictionary also tells you whether a verb is *transitive* or *intransitive*. A transitive verb is followed by a direct object and is shown by *vt* in the dictionary. An intransitive verb cannot be followed by a direct object and is shown by *vi*.

Sometimes a verb can be used transitively or intransitively. For example, **cook** is used transitively in *Are you cooking dinner?* and intransitively in *Are you cooking?*

Exercise 29 Look up these verbs in your dictionary. Are they transitive or intransitive? Can they be both? Write "vt," "vi" or "both" in the space.

example	**rise**	*vi*
1	**lose**	______
2	**quarrel**	______
3	**complete**	______
4	**obey**	______
5	**protect**	______
6	**drop**	______
7	**complain**	______
8	**ruin**	______

Uses with adverbial particles and prepositions

Exercise 6 gave you practice in *finding* special uses of verbs in long dictionary entries. The following exercise helps you to *choose* the correct adverbial particle or preposition to go with a verb.

First, however, it is important to understand the use in the dictionary of the *diagonal* (/) and *parentheses* (**( )**). Find the entry for **look**[2] in your dictionary. In section 6 you will find phrases such as ***look sth up, look after sb/sth, look out (of sth) (at sth),*** etc. The diagonal shows that the items separated by it are alternatives. For example, in ***look after sb/sth*** the diagonal tells you that you can say sentences like

Can you look after the children? (***look after sb***)
Can you look after my money? (***look after sth***)

Parentheses are used to enclose an optional word or phrase. For example, in ***look out (of sth) (at sth)*** the parentheses tell you that you can say sentences like

He looked out.	(***look out***)
He looked out of the window.	(***look out of sth***)
He looked out at the rain.	(***look out at sth***)
He looked out of the window at the rain.	(***look out of sth at sth***)

Exercise 30 First find the section on "special uses with *adverbial particles* and *prepositions*" at **take**[1] (17).

In each of the following sentences there is a choice of two words in **bold** type. Only one of the two can be used correctly with the verb **take** in that sentence. Find the correct word and underline it.

example He took the washing machine **apart** / **on** to repair it.

1 The airplane took **off** / **up** from John F. Kennedy Airport.

2 John has taken **over** / **up** surfing.

3 Susan is taking **up** / **on** extra responsibilities at work.

4 Peter is taking his girlfriend **away** / **out** to the cinema.

5.4 Adjectives and adverbs

Comparative and superlative forms

Information on the *comparative and superlative forms of adjectives* is given when these are *not* formed by using the words *more* (for the comparative) and *most* (for the superlative). Therefore, in an adjective entry

- (-er, -est) indicates adjectives of the type *cold, colder, coldest*;
- (-r, -st) indicates adjectives ending in *-e*, of the type *late, later, latest*;
- (-ier, -iest) indicates adjectives ending in *-y*, of the type *happy, happier, happiest*.

If an adjective has irregular comparative and superlative forms, these are given in full, for example (worse, worst) in the entry for **bad**[1]. They are also listed as separate entry words in the dictionary.

Adverbs are treated in exactly the same way.

Exercise 31 Use your dictionary to fill in the form indicated of each of the adjectives listed below. Write each comparative or superlative form in full.

example	**white**	*comp*	*whiter*
1	**comfortable**	*superl*	
2	**fast**	*comp*	
3	**good**	*superl*	
4	**young**	*comp*	
5	**gentle**	*superl*	
6	**likely**	*comp*	
7	**arrogant**	*superl*	
8	**tender**	*superl*	

5.5 Doubling consonants

Many verbs that end with a single consonant have this letter doubled in the spelling for the present and past participles and the past tense, as in **drop**: **dropping**, **dropped**. In the same way, some adjectives double the last consonant in the spelling for the comparative and superlative, as in **hot**: **hotter**, **hottest**. If the final consonant of a word is doubled in this way, the dictionary shows this by printing the doubled letter in brackets, for example (-pp-) in the entry for **drop²**.

Exercise 32 Use your dictionary to fill in the form indicated of each of the words listed below. Write each word in full. Where more than one form is given in the dictionary, fill in both forms.

example	**trip**	*pres p*	*tripping*
1	**flat**	*comp*	
2	**stop**	*pt*	
3	**drip**	*pres p*	
4	**cancel**	*pp*	
5	**prefer**	*pp*	

6 **sad**	*superl*	__________
7 **trap**	*pp*	__________
8 **fasten**	*pt*	__________

5.6 Word-endings

In English, new words are often made by adding prefixes – like **in-** and **un-** – or suffixes – like **-able** and **-ment** – to words. These are all listed in the dictionary, with examples.

Exercise 33 Look at the list of adjectives below. Make the opposite of each adjective by adding one of these prefixes:

in-, dis-, un-

Check your answers in your dictionary.

	Adjective	Opposite
example	**tidy**	*untidy*
1	**happy**	__________
2	**honest**	__________
3	**obedient**	__________
4	**convenient**	__________

Exercise 34 Look at the list of verbs below. Make each verb into a noun by adding one of these suffixes:

-ment, -ance, -age

Check your answers in your dictionary.

	Verb	Noun
example	**enjoy**	*enjoyment*
1	**break**	__________
2	**annoy**	__________
3	**avoid**	__________
4	**disappoint**	__________

6 What's the use?

6.1 Styles of speech

Some words may only be used in certain styles of speaking or writing. Information on this (such as the labels *formal* and *informal*) is given in parentheses after the word.

Exercise 35 Look up the entry words listed below. For each word, write down the style label that is given in the dictionary. Where the label is abbreviated (such as *sl* for slang) write it out in full. (For abbreviations used see the inside back cover of the dictionary.)

example	**flunk**	*informal*
1	**taciturn**	____________
2	**cop**	____________
3	**rookie**	____________
4	**e'en**	____________

Some words are used by a certain group of speakers or writers because of the work they do, the sport they are playing, etc. Information on these specialist areas (such as the labels *sport* and *medicine*) is given in parentheses after the word.

Exercise 36 Look up the entry words listed below. Where it is indicated in parentheses, find the right numbered section of the entry word. Then write down the specialist label that is given in the dictionary. Where the label is abbreviated (such as *med* for *medicine*) write it out in full. (For abbreviations used, see the inside back cover of the dictionary.)

example	**prognosis**	*medicine*
1	**pitcher**^{2}	____________
2	**debit**	____________
3	**root**^{1}(6)	____________
4	**battery**(5)	____________

Answers to exercises

Exercise 1

apples
bread
cheese
dates
eggs
fish
grapes
honey
ice
jam
kumquats
lemons
margarine

Exercise 2

November
October
Pluto
Quaker
Ramadan
September
Tuesday
Uranus
Venus
Wednesday
Xmas
Yankee
Zen

Exercise 3

1 priest
2 enter
3 arrange
4 daffodil
5 ripe
6 orange
7 buy
8 large

Exercise 4

1 grill
2 primary
3 hold[1], hold[3]
4 tight
5 answer[2]
6 crowd
7 ride[1]
8 long[1]

Exercise 5

1 feather[1]
2 even[1](3)
3 grin(1)
4 strike[2](3)
5 horse(1)
6 skeleton(1)
7 spill(3)
8 tower(2)

Exercise 6

put sth aside
put sth away
put sth down
put in
put sth on
put sth out
put sth to sb
put sb up

Exercise 7

1 software
2 soft drink
3 softly
4 soft-hearted
5 softness
6 soft-boiled
7 soft option
8 soft-spoken

Exercise 8

1 Friday
2 revolution(s) per minute
3 Organization of Petroleum Exporting Countries
4 Parent-Teacher Association
5 they are
6 I am
7 do not
8 we have

Exercise 9

1 chameleon
2 rickets
3 aluminum
4 parsley

Exercise 10

1 dentist
2 tailor
3 engineer
4 conductor
5 butcher
6 artist

Exercise 11

1 mine[1]
2 ice[1]
3 ice[2]
4 sign[2]
5 sign[1]
6 lie[1]
7 lie[2]
8 lie[1]

Exercise 12

1 necessary
2 bananas
3 Independence
4 white-collar
5 apologized
6 analyzed
7 advisers
8 musical

Exercise 13

1 address
2 committee
3 develop
4 accident
5 identical
6 disappointment
7 courageous
8 responsible

Exercise 14

Another possible spelling

1 instalment
2 acknowledgement
3 pickax
4 encyclopaedia
5 jailor
6 granny
7 lollipop
8 marvelous

Exercise 15

1 anti·sep·tic
2 the·ater
3 kind·ness
4 foot·step
5 no
6 straw·berry
7 no
8 un·auth·or·ized

Exercise 16

/i/	/ɪ/
seat	sit
sheep	ship
reach	ridge
leap	lip

Exercise 17

/au/	/ou/
growl	grow
now	bowl
cow	crow
blouse	blow

Exercise 18

/tʃ/	/k/
church	schedule
much	school
lunch	chemist

/ʃ/
chauffeur
chalet

Exercise 19

/s/	/z/
city	gaze
psychology	news
scientific	zoo
dress	magnetism

Exercise 20

1 wait
2 stationary
3 rows
4 threw, through
5 pair
6 aisle, altar
7 write
8 current

Exercise 21

1 /rau/
2 /rou/
3 /led/
4 /lid/
5 /waind/
6 /wɪnd/
7 /klouz/
8 /klous/

Exercise 22

1 police
2 neutrality
3 reliable
4 admit

Exercise 23

1 benefit
2 different
3 photograph
4 incident

Exercise 24

1 'desert
2 ob'ject
3 'refill
4 'permit
5 re'fill
6 'object
7 de'sert
8 per'mit

Exercise 25

1 probable
2 product
3 quickly
4 too

Exercise 26

1 hoofs or hooves
2 knives
3 potatoes
4 diaries
5 buffaloes or buffalos
6 children
7 deer
8 donkeys
9 roofs
10 teeth

Exercise 27

1 [U] 5 both
2 [C] 6 [C]
3 [U] 7 [U]
4 [U] 8 both

Exercise 28

1 hid
2 caught
3 fried
4 brought
5 took
6 taught
7 knelt
8 forgave

Exercise 29

1 both 5 vt
2 vi 6 both
3 vt 7 vi
4 both 8 vt

Exercise 30

1 off 3 on
2 up 4 out

Exercise 31

1 most comfortable
2 faster
3 best
4 younger
5 gentlest
6 likelier
7 most arrogant
8 tenderest

Exercise 32

1 flatter
2 stopped
3 dripping
4 canceled or cancelled
5 preferred
6 saddest
7 trapped
8 fastened

Exercise 33

1 unhappy
2 dishonest
3 disobedient
4 inconvenient

Exercise 34

1 breakage
2 annoyance
3 avoidance
4 disappointment

Exercise 35

1 formal
2 slang
3 informal
4 poetic

Exercise 36

1 baseball
2 bookkeeping
3 mathematics
4 legal

a

A[1]**, a** /ei/ (*pl* A's, a's /eiz/) the first letter of the English alphabet.
A one /ˌei ˈwən/ *adj* **(a)** (of ships) first class. **(b)** (*informal*) excellent: *feeling A one,* in excellent health.

a[2] /ə *strong form:* ei/, **an** /ən *strong form:* æn/ *indefinite article* (*Note: an* is used before a vowel) ➪ the. **1** one (but no particular one): *I have a pen* (*pl = some pens*). *Do you have a pen* (*pl = any pens*)? *I said ˈa train was coming, not ˈthe train.* **2** (used when speaking or writing about number, quantity, groups, etc): *a lot of money; a little more; a few books; half a dozen; half an hour; a friend of mine,* one of my friends. (*Note:* when several objects, etc are parts of a known group, the *indefinite article* is not repeated: *a knife and fork.*) **3** each: *60 miles an hour; twice a week; $2.50 a yard.* **4** that which is called; every: *A horse is an animal* (*pl = Horses are animals*). **5** another; a kind of: *He thinks he's a Napoleon.* (For use with numbers ➪ App 1.)

A[3] *abbr =* answer.

a-[1] /ei-, ə-, a-/ *prefix* not, without: *amoral; atheist.*

a-[2] /ə-/ *prefix* **1** (a– + *n = adv*) in: *abed;* on, at: *ashore.* **2** (a– + *v = adv*) in the state or process of: *asleep; ablaze.*

ab- /æb-, əb-/ *prefix* (away) from: *absent; abduct.*

aback /əˈbæk/ *adv* ***be ˌtaken aˈback (at/by sth),*** be suddenly surprised or upset: *He was taken ~ by the cost of the repairs.*

aba·cus /ˈæbəkəs/ *n* [C] (*pl* ~es or -ci /ˈæbəˌsai/) frame with beads or balls sliding on rods, for teaching numbers to children or for calculating.

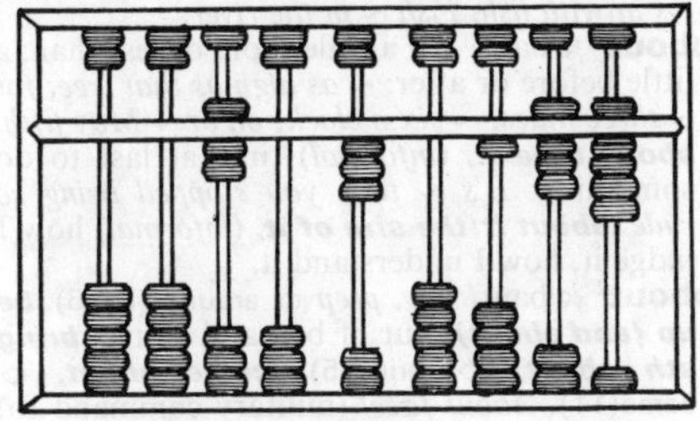

ABACUS

abaft /əˈbæft/ *adv, prep* (*naut*) at, in, toward, the stern half (back part) of a ship; behind.

ab·alo·ne /ˌæbəˈlouni/ *n* [C] edible shellfish found on the Pacific coast of North America.

aban·don[1] /əˈbændən/ *vt* **1** go away from, not intending to return to: *The order was given to ~ ship,* for all on board to leave the (sinking) ship. *He ~ed his wife and child.* **2** give up; stop: *The police ~ed the chase.* **3** ***abandon oneself to,*** allow oneself to feel, act, etc because of extreme emotion, etc: *He ~ed himself to despair.*
aban·doned *adj* left or deserted (with no possibility of being reclaimed): *an ~ed car/wife.*
aban·don·ment *n* [U]

aban·don[2] /əˈbændən/ *n* [U] giving way to emotion or impulse: *dancing with gay ~.*

abase /əˈbeis/ *vt* ***abase oneself,*** lower oneself in dignity or respect.
abase·ment *n* [U]

abashed /əˈbæʃt/ *adj* very embarrassed or ashamed.

abate /əˈbeit/ *vt,vi* (of winds, storms, floods, pain, etc) make or become less: *The ship sailed when the storm ~d.*
abate·ment *n* [U] abating; decrease.

ab·at·toir /ˌæbəˈtwar/ *n* [C] slaughterhouse (for cattle, sheep, etc).

ab·bess /ˈæbɪs/ *n* [C] woman (*Mother Superior*) at the head of a convent or nunnery.

ab·bey /ˈæbi/ *n* [C] (*pl* ~s) **1** building(s) in which monks or nuns live as a community in the service of God; the community. **2** church that once belonged to an abbey.

ab·bot /ˈæbət/ *n* [C] man at the head of an abbey or monastery.

abbr., abbrev. *abbr =* **1** abbreviated. **2** abbreviation.

ab·brevi·ate /əˈbriviˌeit/ *vt* shorten (a word, title, etc): *~ January to Jan.*

ab·brevi·ation /əˌbriviˈeiʃən/ *n* **1** [U] abbreviating or being abbreviated. **2** [C] shortened form (esp of a word).

ABC[1] /ˌei ˌbi ˈsi/ *n* (*pl* ABC's) the alphabet. ***as easy as ABC,*** very easy.

ABC[2] /ˌei ˌbi ˈsi/ *abbr =* American Broadcasting Company.

ab·di·cate /ˈæbdɪˌkeit/ *vt,vi* **1** surrender or renounce a high office, control or responsibility. **2** give up the throne: *King Edward VIII of England ~d in 1936.*

ab·di·ca·tion /ˌæbdɪˈkeiʃən/ *n* **1** [U] abdicating. **2** [C] instance of this.

ab·do·men /ˈæbdəmən/ *n* [C] **1** part of the body that includes the stomach and bowels. **2** last of the three divisions of an insect, spider, etc. ➪ illus at insect, trunk.

ab·domi·nal /æbˈdamənəl/ *adj* in, of, for, the abdomen: *~ pains.*

ab·duct /æbˈdəkt/ *vt* take or lead (a person) away unlawfully, by force or fraud. ⇨ kidnap.
ab·duc·tion /æbˈdəkʃən/ *n* **1** [U] abducting. **2** [C] act of abducting.
abeam /əˈbim/ *adv* on a line at a right angle to the length of a ship or aircraft.
ab·er·rant /æˈberənt/ *adj* turning away from what is normal, expected or right.
ab·er·ra·tion /ˌæbəˈreiʃən/ *n* **1** [U] turning away from what is expected, normal or right. **2** [C] instance of this; defect: *Stealing the pen was a momentary* ~.
abet /əˈbet/ *vt* (-tt-) help or encourage (in vice, crime). ***aid and abet sb,*** (*legal*) help him to do something illegal.
abey·ance /əˈbeiəns/ *n* [U] condition of not being in force or in use for a time. ***in abeyance,*** suspended, eg until more information is obtained. ***fall/go into abeyance,*** (of a law, rule, custom, etc) be suspended; be no longer observed.
ab·hor /əbˈhɔr/ *vt* (-rr-) (*formal*) think of with hatred and disgust: ~ *cruelty to animals*.
ab·hor·rence /əbˈhɔrəns/ *n* [U] hatred and disgust: *hold murder in* ~.
ab·hor·rent /əbˈhɔrənt/ *adj* hateful; causing horror.
abide /əˈbaid/ *vt,vi* **1** ***abide by,*** (*formal*) be faithful to; keep: ~ *by a promise/decision*. **2** ***cannot/can't/couldn't abide,*** cannot/could not tolerate; hate(d): *She can't* ~ *that man/cruelty to children*.
abid·ing /əˈbaidıŋ/ *adj* (*liter*) lasting.
abil·ity /əˈbıləti/ *n* (*pl* -ies) **1** [U] (possible) capacity or power (to do something physical or mental). ***to the best of one's ability,*** as well as one can. **2** [U] cleverness; intelligence: *a man of great* ~. **3** [C] skill; power; talent: *a man of many abilities*.
ab·ject /ˈæbˌdʒekt/ *adj* **1** (of conditions) poor; miserable: *living in* ~ *poverty*. **2** (of a person, his action, behavior) disliked or thought to be worthless because he/it is cowardly or undignified: *an* ~ *apology*.
ab·ject·ly *adv*
ablaze /əˈbleiz/ *adj, adv* **1** on fire: *The whole building was soon* ~. **2** (*fig*) shining; bright; excited: *The streets were* ~ *with lights*.
able /ˈeibəl/ *adj* **1** ***be able to do sth,*** have the power, means or opportunity: *Will you be* ~ *to come?* ⇨ can[2], could. **2** (-r, -st) clever; capable; having or showing knowledge or skill: *an* ~ *lawyer/speech; the* ~*st/most* ~ *man I know*.
ˈable-ˈbodied *adj* physically strong.
-able (also **-ible**) /-əbəl/ *suffix* **1** (*n* + ~ = *adj*) showing qualities of: *fashionable; responsible*. **2** (*v* + ~ = *adj*) that can be; fit to be: *laughable; edible*.
-ably, -ibly /-əbli/ *suffix* (to form an *adv*)
ab·lu·tions /əˈbluʃənz/ *n pl* ceremonial washing of the hands or the body, esp as a religious act.
ably /ˈeibli/ *adv* in an able manner.
ABM /ˌei ˌbi ˈem/ *abbr* = antiballistic missile.
ab·nor·mal /ˌæbˈnɔrməl/ *adj* different from what is normal, ordinary or expected: ~ *behavior*.
ab·nor·mal·ly *adv*
ab·nor·mal·ity /ˌæbnɔrˈmæləti/ *n* **1** [U] quality of being abnormal. **2** [C] (*pl* -ies) something that is abnormal: *physical abnormalities*.
aboard /əˈbɔrd/ *adv, prep* on, in, onto or into a ship, airplane, train or bus: *It's time to go* ~. *All* ~*! Welcome* ~*!*
abode /əˈboud/ *n* [C] home. ***of/with no fixed abode,*** (*legal*) having no permanent home.
abol·ish /əˈbalıʃ/ *vt* put an end to, do away with, eg war, slavery, an old custom.
aboli·tion /ˌæbəˈlıʃən/ *n* [U] abolishing or being abolished (esp of slavery).
aboli·tion·ist /-ıst/ *n* [C] (esp) person who wished to abolish Negro slavery.
A-bomb /ˈei ˌbam/ *n* [C] = atomic bomb.
abom·i·nable /əˈbamənəbəl/ *adj* **1** causing hatred and disgust. **2** (*informal*) unpleasant; bad: ~ *weather/food*.
abom·i·nably /-əbli/ *adv*
abom·i·nate /əˈbaməˌneit/ *vt* (*formal*) feel hatred or disgust for.
abom·ina·tion /əˌbaməˈneiʃən/ *n* (*formal*) **1** [U] horror and disgust: *hold killing in* ~. **2** [C] something that arouses horror and disgust.
abo·rig·inal /ˌæbəˈrıdʒənəl/ *adj* (of people, animals, plants etc) belonging to, existing in, a region from earliest times or from the time when the region was first known. □ *n* [C] earliest inhabitant, plant, etc of a region.
Abo·rig·ine /ˌæbəˈrıdʒəni/ *n* [C] Australian aboriginal person.
abo·rig·ines /ˌæbəˈrıdʒəniz/ *n pl* **the aborigines,** the aboriginal inhabitants.
abort /əˈbɔrt/ *vt,vi* **1** come to nothing; cancel: ~ *a space mission,* stop it prematurely, eg because of mechanical trouble. **2** expel an undeveloped fetus.
abor·tion /əˈbɔrʃən/ *n* **1** [U] expulsion of the fetus from the womb during the first 12 weeks of pregnancy; helping or causing this: *Abortion was once a crime in New York*. **2** [C] instance of this: *have/obtain/get an* ~.
abor·tion·ist /-ıst/ *n* [C] person who brings about an abortion.
abor·tive /əˈbɔrtıv/ *adj* unsuccessful: *plans that proved* ~*; an* ~ *attempt/rebellion*.
abor·tive·ly *adv*
abound /əˈbaund/ *vi* ***abound in/with,*** have, exist, in great numbers or quantities: *The river* ~*s in/with fish. Fish* ~ *in the river*.
about[1] /əˈbaut/ *adv* a little more or less than; a little before or after: ~ *as high as that tree; for* ~ *three miles;* ~ *six o'clock; on or* ~ *May fifth*. ***about time...,*** (*informal*) time at last to do something: *It's* ~ *time you stopped being so rude*. ***about it/the size of it,*** (*informal*) how I judge it, how I understand it.
about[2] /əˈbaut/ *adv, prep* ⇨ around (3,4,5). ***be up (and about),*** out of bed and active. ***bring sth about,*** ⇨ bring(5). ***come about,*** ⇨ come(11). *About face!* (military command to) turn around to face the other way.
aˌbout-ˈface *vi* turn and face the other way. □ *n* [C] complete reversal of opinions, etc: *He did a complete* ~*-face!*
about[3] /əˈbaut/ *prep* **1** concerning; regarding; in connection with: *He is careless* ~ *his personal*

appearance. *What do you know ~ him? Tell me all ~ it.* ***How/What about...,*** (used to ask for information, to make a suggestion or to get an opinion): *How ~ going to Miami for our vacation?* **2** concerned or occupied with: *And while you're ~ it...*, while you're doing that.... ***go/set about sth,*** deal with it: *Do you know how to go ~ it?* **3** = around (the usual word): *She placed the scarf about her neck.* **4** ***be about to,*** just going to (do something): *As I was (just) ~ to say, when you interrupted me...; He was ~ to start, when....* ***not about,*** determined not to (do something): *We're not ~ to quit!*

above[1] /ə'bəv/ *adv* **1** at a higher point; overhead; on high: *My bedroom is just ~. A voice from ~ shouted a welcome.* **2** earlier (in a book, article, etc): *As I mentioned/stated ~.* **3** above zero degrees (Fahrenheit): *It's only ten ~.*

a'bove·board *adv* without deceiving; honorably. ▫ *adj* frank; open[1](11).

a,bove-'mentioned/-'named *adj* mentioned/named earlier in this book, article, etc.

above[2] /ə'bəv/ *prep* **1** higher than: *The sun rose ~ the horizon. The water came ~ our knees. We were flying ~ the clouds.* ⇨ over[2], across[2]. **2** greater in number, price, weight, etc: *The temperature has been ~ average recently. Applicants must be ~ the age of 21.* **3** more than. ***above all,*** more than anything else. ***over and above,*** ⇨ over[2] (6) **4** too great, good, difficult, etc for: *If you want to learn, you must not be ~ asking* (= not be too proud to ask) *questions. He is ~ meanness,* is too generous for meanness. **5** out of reach of (because too great, good, etc): *His heroism was ~* (or *beyond*) *all praise. His conduct has always been ~ reproach/suspicion.* **6** (various uses): *the waterfall ~* (= upstream from) *the bridge; live ~ one's means,* spend more than one's income.

ab·ra·ca·dabra /,æbrəkə'dæbrə/ *n* [U] **1** word used in magic spells. **2** jargon.

ab·ra·sion /ə'breiʒən/ *n* **1** [U] rubbing, scraping, or wearing off. **2** [C] area where something has been worn or scraped away: *an ~ of the skin.*

ab·ra·sive /ə'breisıv/ *n* [C,U] substance (eg emery) used for smoothing or grinding down surfaces. ▫ *adj* **1** causing abrasion. **2** (*fig*) harsh, rough: *an ~ voice/character.*

abreast /ə'brest/ *adv* (of persons, ships, etc) on a level, side by side, and facing the same way: *walking three ~; warships lined up ~.* ***be/keep abreast (of/with),*** be/keep up-to-date: *You should read the newspapers to keep ~ of the times,* to be informed of the latest events, ideas, discoveries, etc.

abridge /ə'brıdʒ/ *vt* make shorter, esp by using fewer words: *an ~d edition of* Moby Dick.

abridg·ment, abridge·ment *n* [U] abridging; [C] thing, eg a book, that is abridged.

abroad /ə'brɔd/ *adv* **1** in or to a foreign country or countries; away from one's own country: *be/go/live/travel ~; visitors who have come from ~.* **2** (*dated*) far and wide; everywhere: *There's a rumor ~ that...*, People are saying that...

abrupt /ə'brəpt/ *adj* **1** unexpectedly sudden: *The road is full of ~ turns.* **2** (of speech, writing, behavior) rough; bad-tempered; unfriendly. **3** (of a slope) steep.

abrupt·ly *adv*

abrupt·ness /-nıs/ *n* [U]

ab·scess /'æb,ses/ *n* [C] collection of thick yellowish-white liquid (called *pus*) in the tissues of the body: *~es on the gums.*

ab·scond /əb'skand/ *vi* go away, suddenly, secretly, esp to avoid arrest: *~ with the money.*

ab·sence /'æbsəns/ *n* **1** [U] being away: *In the ~ of the Supervisor* (= while he is not here) *Mr. Green is in charge of business.* **2** [C] occasion or period of being away: *numerous ~s from school; after an ~ of three months.* **3** [U] non-existence; lack: *in the ~ of definite information. Cold is the ~ of heat.*

leave of absence, ⇨ leave[2].

ab·sent[1] /'æbsənt/ *adj* **1** ***absent from,*** not present at: *~ from school/work.* **2** lost in thought; having one's attention elsewhere: *When I spoke to him he looked at me in an ~ way but did not answer.*

absent·ly *adv*

,ab·sent-'minded *adj* so deep or far away in thought that one is unaware of what one is doing, what is happening, etc.

,ab·sent-'mind·ed·ly *adv*

,ab·sent-'mind·ed·ness /-nıs/ *n* [U]

ab·sent[2] /æb'sent/ *vt* (*formal*) stay away (from): *Why did you ~ yourself from school yesterday?*

ab·sen·tee /,æbsən'ti/ *n* [C] person who is absent, eg a landlord who lives away from his property: (as an *adjective*) *~ voters.*

ab·sen·tee·ism /-,ızəm/ *n* [U] habit of being absent, eg the practice of often being away from work without a good reason.

ab·so·lute /'æbsə,lut/ *adj* **1** complete; perfect: *When giving evidence in a law court, we should tell the ~ truth.* **2** unlimited; having complete power: *An ~ ruler does not need to ask anyone for permission to do anything.* **3** certain; undoubted: *It is an ~ fact. He must not be punished unless you have ~ proof of his guilt.*

ab·so·lute·ly /'æbsə,lutli/ *adv* **(a)** completely: *~ly impossible/right.* **(b)** unconditionally: *He refused ~ly.* **(c)** /,æbsə'lutli/ (*informal*) I agree; (in answer to a question, or as a comment) certainly.

ab·so·lute zero /,æbsə,lut 'zırou/ *n* [U] lowest temperature theoretically possible, = -273.15°C or -459.67°F.

ab·sol·ution /,æbsə'luʃən/ *n* [U] (in the Roman Catholic Church) freeing from guilt or punishment of sin: *grant ~ from sin.*

ab·so·lut·ism /,æbsə'lu,tızəm/ *n* [U] despotism.

ab·solve /əb'zalv/ *vt* declare free (from sin, guilt, a promise, duty, etc): *I ~ you from all blame/from your vows.*

ab·sorb /əb'sɔrb/ *vt* **1** take or suck in, eg a liquid, heat, light: *Dry sand ~s water.* **2** take in, eg facts, information: *The clever student ~ed all the knowledge his teachers could give him.* **3** use up all or a great deal of the attention, interest or time of: *His business ~s him. He is completely ~ed in his work.*

ab·sorb·ent /əb'sɔrbənt/ *adj* able to absorb: *~ cotton.* ▫ *n* [U] absorbent material.

ab·sorp·tion /əb'sɔrpʃən/ *n* [U] absorbing or

being absorbed: *His ~ in the book made him forget the time.*
ab·stain /əbˈstein/ *vi* deliberately avoid using or doing something: *His doctor told him to ~ from alcohol. At the last election he ~ed (from voting).*
ab·stainer *n* [C] person who abstains.
ˌtotal abˈstainer, one who never takes alcoholic drinks.
ab·stemi·ous /əbˈstimiəs/ *adj* taking small amounts of, esp, food and drink.
ab·stemi·ous·ly *adv*
ab·stemi·ous·ness /-nɪs/ *n* [U]
ab·sten·tion /əbˈstenʃən/ *n* [U] abstaining, eg not voting in an election, etc; [C] instance of this: *six votes for, three against and two ~s.*
ab·sti·nence /ˈæbstənəns/ *n* [U] abstaining, eg from food, enjoyment and esp alcoholic drink.
ˌtotal ˈabstinence, not taking any alcoholic drink.
ab·stract[1] /æbˈstrækt, ˈæbˌstrækt/ *adj* **1** separated from what is real or concrete; thought of separately from facts, objects or particular examples: *A flower is beautiful, but beauty itself is ~.* ***in the abstract,*** regarded in an ideal or theoretical way. **2** difficult to understand: *~ arguments.*
ˌabstract ˈart, art which does not represent objects, scenes, etc in an obvious way.
ˌabstract ˈnoun, (*gram*) noun that names a quality or state, eg *length, goodness, virtue.*
ab·stract[2] /ˈæbˌstrækt/ *n* [C] short account, eg of the chief points of a piece of writing, a book, speech, etc.
ab·stract[3] /æbˈstrækt/ *vt* take out; separate: *~ metal from ore.*
ab·stracted /æbˈstræktɪd/ *adj* not paying attention.
ab·stract·ed·ly *adv*
ab·strac·tion /æbˈstrækʃən/ *n* **1** [U] abstracting or being abstracted. **2** [U] absentmindedness: *in a moment of ~.* **3** [C] abstract(**1**) term or idea: *Don't lose yourself in ~s,* be realistic. **4** [U] formation of such an idea or ideas.
ab·struse /əbˈstrus/ *adj* difficult to understand.
ab·struse·ly *adv*
ab·struse·ness /-nɪs/ *n* [U]
ab·surd /əbˈsərd/ *adj* unreasonable; foolish; ridiculous: *What an ~ suggestion!*
ab·surd·ity /-əti/ *n* (*pl* -ies) **1** [U] state of being absurd. **2** [C] absurd act or statement.
ab·surd·ly *adv*
abun·dance /əˈbəndəns/ *n* [U] great plenty: *food and drink in ~.* ***an abundance of,*** more than enough: *an ~ of good things.*
abun·dant /əˈbəndənt/ *adj* more than enough; plentiful: *We have ~ proof of his guilt.*
abuse[1] /əˈbyus/ *n* **1** [U] wrong use; [C] instance of this: *an ~ of trust.* **2** [C] unjust custom or practice. **3** [U] angry or harsh words; bad language; cursing: *shower ~ on her.* **4** [U] cruel, or unjust physical treatment.
abuse[2] /əˈbyuz/ *vt* **1** make a bad or wrong use of: *Don't ~ the confidence they have placed in you.* **2** say severe, cruel or unjust things to or about a person. **3** treat cruelly or unjustly.
abu·sive /əˈbyusɪv/ *adj* **1** using insults or curses: *~ language.* **2** treating cruelly or unjustly.
abu·sive·ly *adv*
abys·mal /əˈbɪzməl/ *adj* **1** bottomless. **2** (*informal*) extreme: *~ ignorance.*
abys·mal·ly *adv*
abyss /əˈbɪs/ *n* [C] hole so deep as to appear bottomless; hell: (*fig*) *the ~ of despair.*
AC, a.c. *abbr* (often spoken as /ˌei ˈsi/) = alternating current.
aca·demic /ˌækəˈdemɪk/ *adj* **1** of teaching, studying; of schools, colleges, etc; scholarly, literary or classical (contrasted with technical or scientific): *~ subjects; the ~ year; ~ freedom,* liberty to teach and to discuss problems without outside, eg government, interference. **2** too concerned with theory and not practical: *The question is ~,* is of no practical importance. **3** formal; conventional: *an ~ style (of writing).* □ *n* [C] professional scholar.
aca·demi·cally /-kli/ *adv*
aca·dem·ician /ˌækədəˈmɪʃən/ *n* [C] **1** member of a society that encourages literature, art or science. **2** academic.
acad·emy /əˈkædəmi/ *n* [C] (*pl* -ies) school for higher learning, usually for a special purpose: *a ˈnaval/ˈmilitary ~; an ~ of music.*
ac·cede /ækˈsid/ *vi* (*formal*) **1** agree, eg to a request. **2** take or succeed to (a position of authority).
ac·cel·er·ate /ɪkˈseləˌreit/ *vt,vi* **1** increase the speed of; cause to move faster or happen earlier. **2** (of a motion or process) become faster.
ac·cel·er·ation /ɪkˌseləˈreiʃən/ *n* [U] making or being made quicker; rate of increase of speed per unit of time: *a car with good ~.*
ac·cel·er·ator /ɪkˈseləˌreitər/ *n* [C] device, eg the pedal in a car, for controlling speed.
ac·cent[1] /ˈækˌsent/ *n* [C] **1** force when speaking (by means of stress or intonation) given to a syllable: *In the word "today" the ~ is on the second syllable.* **2** mark or symbol used in writing and printing to show a vowel sound or syllabic stress. ⇨ acute, circumflex and grave[3]. **3** [sometimes U] individual, local or national way of pronouncing: *speaking English with a foreign ~.* **4** (*informal*) emphasis given to one aspect or detail: *At this year's Auto Show the ~ is on sports cars.*
ac·cent[2] /ækˈsent, ˈækˌsent/ *vt* **1** pronounce with an accent(3). **2** put emphasis on (a syllable or word).
ac·cen·tu·ate /ækˈsentʃuˌeit/ *vt* give more force or importance to; draw attention to.
ac·cen·tu·ation /ækˌsentʃuˈeiʃən/ *n* [U] (system of) stress or intonation of the words of a language.
ac·cept /ɪkˈsept, ækˈsept/ *vt,vi* **1** (agree to) receive or take (something offered): *~ a gift/an invitation.* **2** agree; recognize; approve: *I ~ the fact that the change may take some time. It is an ~ed truth/fact,* something that everyone believes. **3** take responsibility for: *~ delivery of goods.*
ac·cept·able /-əbəl/ *adj* worth accepting; welcome: *if this proposal is ~able to you.*
ac·cept·ance /ɪkˈseptəns, ækˈseptəns/ *n* [U] **1** accepting or being accepted. **2** = approval (the usual word).

ac·cess /ˈækˌses/ *n* [U] **1** way (in) to a place: *The only ~ to the farmhouse is across the fields.* **2** ***access to,*** right, opportunity or means of reaching, using or approaching: *Students must have ~ to good books.*

ac·ces·si·bil·ity /ɪkˌsesəˈbɪləti/ *n* [U]

ac·cess·ible /ɪkˈsesəbəl/ *adj* able to be reached, used, visited, influenced, etc; convenient: *a collection of paintings not ~ible to the public.*

ac·ces·sion /ækˈseʃən/ *n* ***accession to,*** **1** [U] reaching a rank, position, or state: *the mayor's ~to high office.* **2** [C,U] (*informal*) (an) addition; (an) increase: *recent ~s to the school library.*

ac·cess·ory /ɪkˈsesəri/ *n* [C] (*pl* -ies) **1** (*legal*) person who helps in any act, esp a crime. ***accessory after the fact,*** who helps another who has committed a crime. ***accessory before the fact,*** who helps another to commit a crime. **2** something that is extra, helpful, useful, but not an essential part of: *the accessories of a bicycle,* eg the lamp, a pump.

ac·ci·dent /ˈæksədənt/ *n* **1** [C] something that happens unexpectedly or without a cause that can be seen at once, usually something unfortunate and undesirable: *He was killed in a ˈcar ~.* ***have an accident***, be involved in one: *She's had an ~ with a knife,* cut herself. ***Accidents will happen,*** (*prov*) it is probable that unfortunate events will occur. **2** [U] chance; fortune: *by ~ of birth.* ***by accident,*** by chance: *We met by ~.*

accident-prone *adj* tending to have accidents.

ac·ci·den·tal /ˌæksəˈdentəl/ *adj* happening unexpectedly and by chance: *an ~ meeting with a friend.*

ac·ci·den·tally /-t(ə)li/ *adv* ***(do sth) accidentally on purpose***, (*informal*) do it deliberately, but so as to make it appear accidental.

ac·claim /əˈkleim/ *vt* **1** welcome with shouts of approval; applaud loudly: *~ the winner of a race; ~ him as a great actor.* **2** declare by acclamation: *They ~ed him Governor.* □ *n* [U] applause; approval: *The movie received great critical ~.*

ac·cla·ma·tion /ˌækləˈmeiʃən/ *n* [U] loud and enthusiastic approval, eg of a proposal: *elected/carried by ~.*

ac·cli·mat·ize /əˈklaiməˌtaiz/ *vt,vi* get (oneself, animals, plants, etc) used to a new climate, or (*fig*) to a new environment, new conditions, etc: *You will soon become ~d.*

ac·cli·ma·tiz·ation /əˌklaimətəˈzeiʃən/ *n* [U]

ac·co·lade /ˈækəˌleid/ *n* [C] praise; recognition; approval.

ac·com·mo·date /əˈkaməˌdeit/ *vt* **1** have or make room for. **2** provide lodging or space for: *This hotel can ~ 600 guests.* **3** ***accommodate sth to,*** (*formal*) change or adopt something so that it fits in with something else: *I will ~ my plans to yours.*

ac·com·mo·dat·ing /əˈkaməˌdeitɪŋ/ *adj* willing to please others; easy to come to an agreement with.

ac·com·mo·da·tion /əˌkaməˈdeiʃən/ *n* [C] **1** something that gives aid or convenience. **2** (usually *pl*) lodging in a hotel, boardinghouse, etc or a place on a public vehicle: *Hotel ~s were scarce during the Olympic Games.*

ac·com·pani·ment /əˈkəmp(ə)nɪmənt/ *n* [C] **1** something that naturally or often goes with another thing: *Disease is often an ~ of famine.* **2** (*music*) (usually) instrumental part to go with a voice, choir or solo instrument: *a song with a piano ~.*

ac·com·pa·nist /əˈkəmp(ə)nɪst/ *n* [C] musician who plays an accompaniment to a singer or other player(s).

ac·com·pany /əˈkəmp(ə)ni/ *vt* (*pt,pp* -ied) **1** go with: *He was accompanied by his secretary.* **2** occur or do at the same time as: *fever ~ing a headache.* **3** (*music*) play an accompaniment (2) to.

ac·com·plice /əˈkamplɪs/ *n* [C] helper or companion (in doing something illegal).

ac·com·plish /əˈkamplɪʃ/ *vt* succeed in doing; finish successfully: *~ a task; a man who will never ~ anything.*

ac·com·plished *adj* **(a)** clever; well trained; skilled: *an ~ed dancer/~ed in dancing.* **(b)** completed; done.

an accomplished fact, thing already done.

ac·com·plish·ment /əˈkamplɪʃmənt/ *n* **1** [U] completion; finishing: *the ~ of their aims.* **2** [C] thing well done or successfully completed; skill.

ac·cord¹ /əˈkɔrd/ *n* [U] agreement. ***of one's own accord,*** without being asked or forced; willingly. ***in/out of accord (with),*** agreeing/not agreeing (with). ***with one accord,*** everybody agreeing.

ac·cord² /əˈkɔrd/ *vi,vt* (*formal*) **1** be in agreement or harmony: *His behavior does not ~ with his principles.* **2** give; grant: *He was ~ed a warm welcome.*

ac·cord·ance /əˈkɔrdəns/ *n* ***in accordance with,*** in agreement with; as is expected of: *in ~ with your wishes/the regulations.*

ac·cord·ing /əˈkɔrdɪŋ/ ***according to,*** *prep* **(a)** on the authority of: *According to the Bible, God created the world in six days.* **(b)** in proportion to: *He will be punished ~ to the seriousness of his crime.* **(c)** in a manner consistent with: *The books are arranged on the shelves ~ to subject.*

ac·cord·ing·ly *adv* for that reason.

ac·cor·dion /əˈkɔrdiən/ *n* [C] portable musical instrument with a bellows, metal reeds and a keyboard.

ac·cost /əˈkɔst, əˈkast/ *vt* go up to and speak to first, esp a stranger in a public place: *I was ~ed by a beggar/a prostitute.*

ac·count¹ /əˈkaunt/ *n* **1** [C] (*business*) (statement of) money (to be) paid or received (for goods, services, etc): *I have an ~ with the First National Bank,* keep my money at this bank. ***open an account; open a bank/credit union, etc account,*** start to keep one's money at a bank, etc. ***settle one's account (with),*** **(a)** pay what one owes. **(b)** (*fig*) do something to get revenge for an injury, etc. ⇨ also budget, check¹, joint¹ and save¹. **2** [U] benefit; profit. ***give a good account of oneself,*** do well; act in a way that brings credit. ***turn/put sth to (good) account,*** use money, abilities, talent, etc profitably. **3** [C] report; description: *Don't always believe newspaper ~s of events.* ***by one's own account,*** according to what one says oneself. ***by/from all accounts,*** according to what everybody, all the papers, etc say. **4** [U] ***take sth into account; take account of sth,*** note or consider it; pay attention to it. ***take no account of sth,*** pay no attention to it. **5** [U] ***on account of,*** because of. ***on this/that account,*** for this/that reason: *Don't stay away on ~ of John/on John's ~.* ***on no account,*** not for any reason: *Don't leave the baby alone in the house on any ~.* **6** [C] person or business that is a client or customer: *The advertising agency lost its biggest ~.*

ac·count² /ə'kaunt/ *vt,vi* **1** ***account for,*** **(a)** be an explanation of: *His illness ~s for his absence. Ah, that ~s for it!* ***There's no accounting for tastes,*** we cannot explain why people have different likes and dislikes. **(b)** give an explanation of money spent. **2** (*formal*) consider to be: *In the US a man is ~ed innocent until he is proved guilty.*

account·able /-əbəl/ *adj* responsible; expected to give an explanation: *A mental patient is not ~able for his actions.*

ac·count·ancy /ə'kauntənsi/ *n* [U] profession of an accountant.

ac·count·ant /ə'kauntənt/ *n* [C] person whose profession is to keep and examine business accounts.

ac·credit /ə'kredɪt/ *vt* **1** appoint or send a person as an ambassador. **2** give official approval or recognition to: The school has been *~ed by the Board of Education.*

ac·credi·ta·tion /əˌkredɪ'teiʃən/ *n* [U]

ac·crue /ə'kru/ *vi* come as a natural growth or development: *If you keep your money in a savings bank, interest ~s.*

acct. *abbr* = account¹.

ac·cu·mu·late /ə'kyumyəˌleit/ *vt,vi* make or become greater in number or quantity: *This account is accumulating interest. Dust soon ~s if the rooms are not swept or vacuumed.*

ac·cu·mu·la·tion /əˌkyumyə'leiʃən/ *n* [C,U] collection; growth by addition: *the ~ of money/useful knowledge; an ~ of books/evidence/rubbish.*

ac·cu·mu·lat·ive /ə'kyumyəˌleitɪv/ *adj* growing by being added to.

ac·cu·racy /'ækyərəsi/ *n* [U] exactness; correctness.

ac·cu·rate /'ækyərɪt/ *adj* **1** careful and exact: *be ~ in one's work/in what one says.* **2** free from error: *Clocks in airports should be ~.*

ac·cur·ate·ly *adv*

ac·cursed, ac·curst /ə'kərst/ *adj* under a curse; hateful.

ac·cu·sa·tion /ˌækyə'zeiʃən/ *n* **1** [U] accusing or being accused. **2** [C] charge of doing wrong, of having broken the law: *bring an ~ (of theft) against a person.*

ac·cuse /ə'kyuz/ *vt* say that a person has done wrong, broken the law, is to be blamed: *Are you accusing me of stealing?*

the accused, the person(s) charged in a criminal case.

ac·cuser *n* the person who accuses.

ac·cus·ing·ly *adv* in an accusing manner: *He pointed accusingly at me.*

ac·cus·tom /ə'kəstəm/ *vt* make (oneself, somebody) used to: *This is not the kind of treatment I'm ~ed to,* not the kind I usually receive.

ac·cus·tomed *adj* usual: *in his ~ed seat.*

ace /eis/ *n* [C] **1** playing card, domino, etc marked with one spot: *the ace of spades.* ***an ace in the hole,*** (*sl*) any advantage held back until it is needed. **2** (*informal*) person who is first rate or an expert. **3** ***within an ace of,*** very near; on the point of: *within an ace of death/of being killed/of winning.*

acer·bity /ə'sərbəti/ *n* (*formal*) **1** [U] bitterness of speech, manner, temper. **2** [C] (*pl* -ies) instance of this.

ac·etate /'æsəˌteit/ *n* [U] **1** cellulose material, esp in fiber form. **2** textile made from this.

acetic /ə'sitɪk/ *adj* of vinegar.

acety·lene /ə'setələn/ *n* [U] (*chem*) colorless gas (symbol C_2H_2) which burns with a hot flame, used for welding and cutting metal: *an ~ torch.*

ache /eik/ *n* [C] dull continuous pain: *have ~s and pains all over; have a 'head~; suffer from head~s.* (*Note: ache* is only combined with *back, ear, head, heart, stomach, tummy* and *tooth.*) □ *vi* **1** have a steady or continuous dull pain: *My head ~s/is aching.* **2** want very much: *He was aching for freedom.*

achieve /ə'tʃiv/ *vt* **1** get (something) done; carry out successfully: *He will never ~ anything,* will not do anything successfully. **2** gain or reach by effort; win: *achieving success/distinction in public life.*

achiev·able /-əbəl/ *adj* that can be achieved.

achieve·ment /ə'tʃivmənt/ *n* **1** [U] achieving: *the ~ of one's aims.* **2** [C] thing done successfully, with effort and skill: *The inventor was rewarded by the government for his scientific ~.*

Achilles' heel /əˌkɪliz 'hiəl/ *n* (*fig*) (small but) weak part, eg of a person's character.

acid /'æsɪd/ *adj* **1** sour; sharp to the taste: *A lemon is an ~ fruit. Vinegar has an ~ taste.* **2** (*fig*) sarcastic: *an ~ wit; ~ remarks.* □ *n* **1** [C,U] (*chem*) substance that reacts with metals to form a salt: *Some ~s burn holes in wood and cloth.* **2** [U] (*sl*) LSD.

'acid test, (*fig*) difficult test that gives proof of something.

acid·ify /ə'sɪdəˌfai/ *vt,vi* (*pt,pp* -ied) make or become acid.

acid·ity /ə'sɪdəti/ *n* [U] state or quality of being acid.

ac·know·ledge /ɪk'nalɪdʒ/ *vt* **1** admit the truth, existence or reality of: *He refused to ~ defeat/that he was defeated.* **2** make known the fact that one has received (something): *~ (receipt of) a letter.* **3** express thanks for: *We must ~ his services to his country.* **4** show that one recognizes (somebody) by giving a greeting, a smile, a nod of the head, etc: *I met her downtown but she didn't even ~ my wave.*

ac·knowl·edg·ment, ac·knowl·edge·ment /ɪk'nalɪdʒmənt/ *n* **1** [U] act of acknowledging: *We are sending you a gift in ~ of your kindness.* **2** [C] something given or done to acknowledge: *We have had no ~ of our letter,* no reply.

acme /ˈækmi/ *n* [C] ***the acme of,*** highest point of development; point of perfection: *the ~ of politeness/skill.*

acne /ˈækni/ *n* [U] skin disease (common among adolescents) in which there are pimples on the face and neck.

acorn /ˈeiˌkɔrn/ *n* [C] seed or nut of the oak tree.

acous·tic /əˈkustɪk/ *adj* of sound, the science of sound and the sense of hearing. □ *n* [C] studio, hall, etc from the consideration of how well music, speech, etc can be heard.

acous·tics *n* **(a)** (used with a *sing verb*) the scientific study of sound. **(b)** (used with a *pl verb*) the physical qualities of sound; the design of a hall, etc that make it good, poor, etc for hearing music or speeches: *The ~s of the new concert hall are excellent.*

ac·quaint /əˈkweint/ *vt* **1** ***acquaint sb/oneself with,*** cause him/oneself to know: *~ oneself/become ~ed/make oneself ~ed with one's new duties.* **2** ***be acquainted (with sb),*** have met (him) personally: *We are not ~ed.*

ac·quaint·ance /əˈkweintəns/ *n* **1** [U] knowledge or information gained through experience. ***make sb's acquaintance,*** get to know him, eg by being introduced. **2** [C] person whom one knows (but not as close as a friend): *He has a wide circle of ~s.*

ac·quiesce /ˌækwiˈes/ *vi* accept silently or without protest.

ac·qui·escence /-ˈesəns/ *n* [C,U] (act of) acquiescing.

ac·quire /əˈkwaiər/ *vt* get by skill or ability, by one's own efforts or behavior: *acquiring a good knowledge of English.*

an acquired taste, liking that comes when one has tried something often.

ac·qui·si·tion /ˌækwəˈzɪʃən/ *n* **1** [U] (*formal*) gaining; collecting: *He devotes his time to the ~ of knowledge.* **2** [C] person or thing acquired: *Mr. Brown will be a valuable ~ to* (= a valuable new member of) *the teaching staff of our school.*

ac·quis·itive /əˈkwɪzətɪv/ *adj* fond of, in the habit of, collecting, buying, etc.

ac·quit /əˈkwɪt/ *vt* (-tt-) **1** give a legal decision that (a person) is not guilty, eg of an offense. **2** (*formal*) behave, conduct oneself: *He ~ted himself well/like a hero.*

ac·quit·tal /əˈkwɪtəl/ *n* [C,U] judgment that a person is not guilty: *three convictions and two ~s.*

acre /ˈeikər/ *n* [C] measure of land, 4,840 sq. yds. or about 4,000 sq. meters.

acre·age /ˈeikərɪdʒ/ *n* [U] area of land measured in acres.

ac·rid /ˈækrɪd/ *adj* (of smell or taste) sharp; bitter.

ac·ri·moni·ous /ˌækrəˈmouniəs/ *adj* (*formal*) (of arguments, words etc) bitter.

ac·ri·mony /ˈækrəˌmouni/ *n* [U] (*formal*) bitterness of temper, manner, language.

ac·ro·bat /ˈækrəˌbæt/ *n* [C] person who can do clever or unusual gymnastic acts, eg on a tightrope or trapeze.

ac·ro·batic /ˌækrəˈbætɪk/ *adj* of or like an acrobat.

ac·ro·bat·ics *n pl* (used with a *sing verb*) acrobatic tricks or feats.

ac·ro·nym /ˈækrəˌnɪm/ *n* [C] word formed from the initial letters of a name, eg radar /ˈreiˌdar/, *ra*dio *d*etecting *a*nd *r*anging.

acrop·olis /əˈkrapəlɪs/ *n* [C] (*pl* ~es) fortified part of an ancient Greek city, esp **the Acropolis** in Athens.

across[1] /əˈkrɔs/ *adverbial particle* from one side to the other: *Can you swim ~? The river is a mile ~,* wide. ⇨ also come, get, put and run².

across[2] /əˈkrɔs/ *prep* **1** from one side to the other side of: *walk ~ the street; draw a line ~ a sheet of paper.* **2** on the other side of: *My house is just ~ the street.* ***across the border,*** (esp) in(to) Mexico or Canada. ***across the line,*** in(to) an adjacent state. **3** so as to cross or intersect: *He sat with his arms ~ his chest.*

aˌcross-the-ˈboard *adj* including all members of a group, business, etc: *an ~-the-board wage increase.*

a·cryl·ic /əˈkrɪlɪk/ *adj* of a kind of synthetic material. □ *n* [U] fiber or resin of this material.

act[1] /ækt/ *n* [C] **1** thing done: *To kick a dog is a cruel act.* **2** process of, instance of, doing; action. ***(catch sb) in the (very) act (of doing sth),*** while doing it: *The thief was caught in the act of breaking into the house.* **3** law made by a government: *an act of Congress.* **4** main division of a play: *a play in five acts; Hamlet, Act I.* **5** one of a series of short performances in a program: *a circus/variety act.* **6** pretense: *He's not really sorry; it's all just an act.* ***put on an act,*** (*informal*) pretend (in order to get one's own way, etc).

ˌact of ˈGod, something which is the result of uncontrollable natural forces, eg storms, floods, earthquakes.

act[2] /ækt/ *vi,vt* **1** do something: *The time for talking is past; we must act at once.* ***act on/upon*** (*a suggestion/somebody's advice/an order*), do what is suggested, advised, etc. **2** produce an effect: *The drug acted quickly.* **3** do one's professional or official duty: *The police refused to act,* would not interfere. ***act for/on behalf of,*** represent (a person) eg as a lawyer, agent etc. **4** behave: *She acted generously.* ***act one's age,*** behave in a way proper for one's age and maturity. **5 (a)** play a part, eg in a play or movie: *Who is acting* (*the part of*) *Hamlet?* **(b)** pretend: *She's not really crying; she's only acting in order to gain your sympathy.* ***act up,*** (*informal*) behave badly so as to get attention; cause pain, annoyance, etc: *My leg/car/TV has been acting up all week.*

act·ing /ˈæktɪŋ/ *adj* doing the duties of another person for a time: *The ~ superintendent.* □ *n* [U] (art of) performing in a play for the theater, movies, TV, etc: *She did a lot of ~ while she was at college.*

ac·tion /ˈækʃən/ *n* **1** [U] process of doing something; (way of) using energy, influence, etc: *The time has come for ~,* we must act now. ***bring/call (sth) into action,*** cause (it) to act. ***put (sth) out of action,*** cause (it) to stop working; make (it) unfit for use. ***take action,*** begin to act. **2** [C] thing done; act; (usually *pl*) behavior: *We shall judge you by your ~s, not by your promises.*

3 [C] legal process. ***bring an action against sb,*** (*legal*) seek judgment against him in a law court. **4** [C,U] fight(ing) between bodies of troops, between warships, etc: *go into* ~, start fighting. **5** [U] influence of one thing on another: *the* ~ *of acid on wood.*

ˈaction painting, form of abstract painting in which paint is splashed, dribbled, etc onto the canvas.

ac·ti·vate /ˈæktəˌveit/ *vt* make active; cause or speed up a chemical reaction, eg by heat; (*physics*) make radioactive.

ac·tive /ˈæktɪv/ *adj* doing things; able to do things; in the habit of doing things: *He's over 90 and not very* ~. *Mount Vesuvius is an* ~ *volcano,* is one that erupts. ***under active consideration,*** being considered.

ˌactive ˈvoice, (*gram*) *verbal phrase* or *sentence* in which the *noun* or *pronoun* subject of the *verb* refers to the doer of the action: *"The children ate the cake" is in the* ~ *voice.* ⇨ passive.

ac·tive·ly *adv*

ac·tiv·ist /ˈæktəvɪst/ *n* [C] person taking an active part, eg in a political movement.

ac·tiv·ity /ækˈtɪvəti/ *n* (*pl* -ies) **1** [U] being active or lively: *When a man is over 70, his time of full* ~ *is usually past.* **2** [C] thing (to be) done; occupation: *My numerous activities leave me little free time.*

ac·tor /ˈæktər/ *n* [C] person who acts on the stage, TV, in the movies, etc.

ac·tress /ˈæktrɪs/ *n* [C] woman who acts on the stage, TV, in the movies, etc.

ac·tual /ˈæktʃuəl/ *adj* existing in fact; real: *Can you give me the* ~ *figures,* the real figures, not an estimate or a guess?

ac·tu·al·ity /ˌæktʃuˈæləti/ *n* (*pl* -ies) **1** [U] actual existence; reality. **2** [C, usually *pl*] actual conditions or facts.

ac·tu·ally /ˈæktʃuəli/ *adv* **1** really: *the political party* ~ *in power. He looks honest, but* ~ *he's a thief.* **2** in fact; surprising as it may seem: *He not only ran in the race; he* ~ *won it!*

ac·tu·ate /ˈæktʃuˌeit/ *vt* (*formal*) cause to act: *A great statesman is* ~*d by love of his country, not by love of power.*

acu·men /əˈkyumən/ *n* [U] ability to understand quickly and clearly: *business* ~.

acu·punc·ture /ˈækyəˌpəŋktʃər/ *n* [U] (*med*) practice of puncturing the human body with fine needles to relieve pain and as a local anesthetic.

acute /əˈkyut/ *adj* **1** (of the senses, sensations, intellect) keen, quick to react: *A bad tooth can cause* ~ *pain.* **2** (of a disease or condition) lasting for a short time: *She has an* ~ *form of the disease.* ⇨ chronic. **3** of or at a crisis; critical: *The company has an* ~ *shortage of equipment.*

aˈcute accent, mark (´) placed over a vowel to indicate how it is to be sounded (as in *café*).

aˈcute angle, angle of less than 90°.

acute·ly *adv*

acute·ness /-nɪs/ *n* [U]

A.D., AD /ˌei ˈdi/ *abbr* = Anno Domini.

ad /æd/ *n* [C] (*informal*) (short for) advertisement.

ad- /əd-, æd-/ *prefix* to, towards: *advance; adjoin.*

ad·age /ˈædɪdʒ/ *n* [C] old and wise saying.

Adam /ˈædəm/ *n* ***not know sb from Adam,*** have no idea who he is.

ˈAdam's apple, part that projects in the front of the throat, esp in men, and moves up and down when one speaks. ⇨ illus at head.

ada·mant /ˈædəmənt/ *adj* refusing to give in: *On this point I am* ~, nothing can change my decision.

adapt /əˈdæpt/ *vt* make fit or suitable for a new use, need, situation, etc: *When you go to a new country, you must* ~ *(yourself) to new manners and customs. Novels are often* ~*ed for the stage, television and radio.*

adapt·able /-əbəl/ *adj* able to adapt or be adapted: *an* ~*able man can change according to circumstances, etc.*

ad·ap·ta·tion /ˌædæpˈteiʃən/ *n* **1** [U] state of being adapted; adapting. **2** [C] thing made by adapting: *An* ~ *(of a novel) for the stage/for television.*

adapter, adaptor /əˈdæptər/ *n* [C] **1** person who adapts. **2** device that makes it possible for something to be used for a purpose or in a way different from that for which it was designed, eg one for connecting two pipes of different sizes.

add /æd/ *vt,vi* **1** join, unite, put (one thing with another): *If you add 5 and/to 5 you get 10.* ***add to,*** increase: *This adds to our difficulties.* ***add together,*** combine two or more things. ***add sth up,*** find the sum of: *add up a column of figures; add them up.* ***add up (to),*** **(a)** give as a result, when joined: *The figures add up to 365.* **(b)** (*informal*) mean; amount to: *All that this adds up to is that you don't want to help, so why not say so?* **(c)** (*informal*) make sense; be believable: *It just doesn't add up.* **2** say something more; go on to say: *"And I hope you'll come early," he added.*

ˈadding machine, machine for calculating mechanically.

ad·den·dum /əˈdendəm/ *n* [C] (*pl* -da /-də/) something (to be) added to a speech, book, etc.

ad·der /ˈædər/ *n* [C] **1** any of several small poisonous snakes, eg the viper, common in Europe. **2** any of several harmless snakes, eg the *ˈpuff* ~ of North America.

ad·dict /əˈdɪkt/ *vt* ***be addicted to,*** have a habit (and be unable to control or stop it): *He is* ~*ed to alcohol/smoking/lying/drugs.* □ *n* [C] /ˈædɪkt/ person who is addicted: *A ˈdrug* ~.

ad·dic·tion /əˈdɪkʃən/ *n* [C,U] (instance of) being addicted.

ad·dic·tive /əˈdɪktɪv/ *adj* causing addiction: ~*ive drugs.*

ad·di·tion /əˈdɪʃən/ *n* **1** [U] action of adding: *The sign + means* ~. **2** [C] person or thing added: *He will be a useful* ~ *to the school faculty,* a useful new teacher. ***in addition (to),*** as well (as).

ad·di·tional /əˈdɪʃənəl/ *adj* extra; added: ~ *charges.*

ad·di·tion·ally /-ʃənəli/ *adv*

ad·di·tive /ˈædətɪv/ *n* [C] substance added in small amounts for a special purpose: *food* ~*s,* eg to add color.

ad·dress[1] /əˈdres, ˈæˌdres/ *n* **1** [C] (details of the) place where a person, business, etc is and where mail may be delivered: *What's your home/*

business ~? **2** [C] speech or talk (to an audience). **3** [U] (usually /əˈdres/) ***form of address,*** style of writing or speaking: *polite forms of* ~.

ad·dres·see /ˌædreˈsi/ *n* [C] person to whom something is addressed.

ad·dress[2] /əˈdres/ *vt* **1** make a speech to: *Mr. Green will now* ~ *the meeting.* **2** speak to, using a title: *Don't* ~ *me as "Colonel"; I'm only a major.* **3** write the name and address(1) on a letter, etc. **4** ***address sth to,*** send (a remark, complaint, etc) to: *Please* ~ *complaints to the manager, not to me.*

ad·duce /əˈdus/ *vt* (*formal*) put forward (as proof, as an example).

-ade /-eid, -ad/ *suffix* (used to form a *noun*): *blockade; facade.*

ad·en·oids /ˈædənɔidz/ *n pl* soft, sponge-like growth of tissue between the back of the nose and the throat, sometimes making breathing and speech difficult. ⇨ illus at head.

ad·en·oidal /ˌædəˈnɔidəl/ *adj*

adept /æˈdept/ *adj* expert, skilled. □ *n* [C] /ˈædept/ expert (the usual word): *I'm not an* ~ *in photography/at playing chess.*

ad·equacy /ˈædıkwəsi/ *n* [U] (*formal*) state of being adequate: *He often doubts his* ~ *as a husband and father.*

ad·equate /ˈædıkwıt/ *adj* satisfactory; sufficient: *Are you getting* ~ *payment for the work you're doing?*

ad·equate·ly *adv*

ad·here /ədˈhır/ *vi* **1** stick (to): *Glue is used to make one surface* ~ *to another.* **2** remain faithful (to); support firmly: ~ *to one's plans/an opinion/a political party/a promise.*

ad·her·ence /-əns/ *n* [U]

ad·her·ent /ədˈhırənt/ *n* [C] supporter (of a party, etc but not necessarily a member): *The proposal is gaining more and more* ~*s.*

ad·hesion /ədˈhiʒən/ *n* **1** [U] being or becoming attached or united. **2** [C] growing together of body tissues, eg after surgery.

ad·hesive /ədˈhisıv/ *adj* able to stick or join: ~ *tape.* □ *n* [C,U] substance that sticks or joins, eg *glue.*

ad hoc /ˌæd ˈhak/ *adj, adv* (*Lat*) arranged for a particular purpose.

adieu /əˈdu, əˈdyu/ *int, n* [C] (*pl* ~s or ~x /əˈduz, əˈdyuz/) goodbye: *bid her* ~.

adi·pose /ˈædəˌpous/ *adj* of animal fat; fatty: ~ *tissue.*

adj. *abbr* = adjective.

ad·jac·ent /əˈdʒeisənt/ *adj* next (to), lying near (to) but not necessarily touching: ~ *rooms/angles; the room* ~ *to mine.*

ad·jec·tival /ˌædʒıkˈtaivəl/ *adj* (*gram*) of or like an adjective: *an* ~ *phrase/clause.*

ad·jec·tive /ˈædʒıktıv/ *n* [C] (*gram*) word that describes, modifies or limits a noun; eg *green, pretty, bad.*

ad·join /əˈdʒɔin/ *vt,vi* be next or nearest (to): *The two houses* ~.

ad·journ /əˈdʒərn/ *vt,vi* **1** stop, eg discussion at a meeting, etc for a time: *The meeting was* ~*ed for a week.* **2** (of a meeting, etc) stop or be stopped for a time. **3** (*informal*) go to another place: *They* ~*ed to the living room for coffee.*

ad·journ·ment *n* [C,U]

ad·judge /əˈdʒədʒ/ *vt* decide officially, by law.

ad·ju·di·cate /əˈdʒudıˌkeit/ *vt,vi* **1** (*legal*) (of a judge or court) give a judgment or decision: ~ *a claim for damages.* **2** (*formal*) sit in judgment in order to decide: ~ *on/upon a disagreement.*

ad·ju·di·ca·tion /əˌdʒudıˈkeiʃən/ *n* [C,U]

ad·ju·di·ca·tor /əˈdʒudıˌkeitər/ *n* [C] judge (esp in labor–management arbitration).

ad·junct /ˈæˌdʒəŋkt/ *n* [C] **1** = accessory(2). **2** (*gram*) word or phrase that describes or modifies another word in a sentence.

ad·jure /əˈdʒʊr/ *vt* (*formal*) ask earnestly or solemnly; require a person to do something as though on oath or under penalty: *I* ~ *you to tell the truth.*

ad·jur·ation /ˌædʒəˈreiʃən/ *n* (*formal*) [U] adjuring; [C] earnest or solemn request.

ad·just /əˈdʒəst/ *vt* set right; put in order; regulate; make suitable or convenient for use: *The body* ~*s itself to changes in temperature. She will have to* ~ *herself to new conditions,* change her ways of living, thinking, etc.

ad·just·able /-əbəl/ *adj* that can be adjusted.

ad·just·ment *n* [U] adjusting; settling of, eg insurance, claims; [C] act or means of adjusting.

ˌwell-adˈjusted *adj* getting on well with other persons.

ad·ju·tant /ˈædʒətənt/ *n* [C] staff officer who assists a commanding officer with general administration.

ad lib /ˌæd ˈlıb/ *adv* (*informal*) freely.

ad-lib *vi* (-bb-) (*informal*) make up without preparation, eg by making additions to one's part in a play. □ *adj* made by ad-libbing: *ad-lib comments.*

Adm. *abbr* = Admiral.

adman /ˈædmən/ *n* (*pl* admen/-men/) person whose work is preparing or selling advertisements.

admin. *abbr* = administration.

ad·min·is·ter /ədˈmınəstər/ *vt,vi* **1** control, manage, look after the affairs of a business, etc: ~ *a country,* govern it. **2** apply; put into operation; hand out; give: ~ *the law;* ~ *relief/help to people who are suffering from floods.* **3** cause to take: ~ *the medicine,* ie to a sick person.

ad·min·is·tra·tion /ədˌmınəˈstreiʃən/ *n* **1** [U] management of affairs, etc, esp public affairs, government policy, etc. **2** [C,U] (act or process of) administering: *the* ~ *of justice.* **3** [C] group of persons who manage, esp officials of public affairs: *the school* ~. **the Administration,** the executive branch of the US government.

ad·min·is·tra·tive /ədˈmınəˌstreitıv/ *adj* of the management of affairs: *an* ~ *post; lacking in* ~ *ability.*

ad·min·is·tra·tor /ədˈmınəˌstreitər/ *n* [C] **1** person who administers; person with ability to organize. **2** person appointed by law to manage or settle an estate, etc.

ad·mir·able /ˈædmərəbəl/ *adj* excellent; to be admired: *an* ~ *performance.*

ad·mir·ably /-əbli/ *adv*

ad·miral /ˈædmərəl/ *n* [C] commissioned officer in the US navy or coast guard who ranks above a vice admiral and below a fleet admiral.

ad·mir·ation /ˌædməˈreiʃn/ *n* [U] feeling of pleasure, wonder, respect: *She speaks English so well that her friends are filled with ~.*

ad·mire /ˌædˈmaiər/ *vt* **1** look at with pleasure or satisfaction; have a high opinion of: *Visitors to New York usually ~ its skyscrapers.* **2** express admiration of: *They've been admiring your new car.*

ad·mirer *n* [C] person who admires; man who finds a woman attractive: *Mary and her many ~s.*

ad·mir·ing *adj* showing or feeling admiration.

ad·mir·ing·ly *adv*

ad·mis·sible /ˌædˈmɪsəbəl/ *adj* **1** capable or worthy of being admitted. **2** that can be permitted or allowed: *~ evidence,* eg in a law court.

ad·mis·sion /ˌædˈmɪʃən/ *n* **1** [U] admitting, being admitted, to a club, a school, a theater, a museum, etc; fee, charge or condition for this: *Admission to the school is by examination only. Admission free.* **2** [C] statement admitting or confessing something: *make an ~ of guilt.* ***by/on sb's own admission,*** as he himself admitted.

ad·mit /ˌædˈmɪt/ *vt,vi* (-tt-) **1** allow to enter; let in: *The secretary opened the door and ~ted me (into the office).* **2** have room enough for: *The theater is small and ~s only 300 people.* **3** acknowledge; confess; accept as true or valid: *The accused man ~ted his guilt. I ~ my mistake/that I was mistaken. You must ~ that this is difficult.* ***admit to,*** confess: *I must ~ to feeling ashamed of my conduct.*

ad·mit·tance /ˌædˈmɪtəns/ *n* [U] act of admitting, being admitted (esp to a place that is not public); right or permission to enter: *No ~ except on business.*

ad·mit·ted·ly /ˌædˈmɪtɪdli/ *adv* without denial; by general agreement: *Admittedly, he has not misbehaved before, but...*

ad·mix·ture /ˌædˈmɪkstʃər/ *n* [C,U] (mixture that is the result of the) action of mixing.

ad·mon·ish /ædˈmanɪʃ/ *vt* give a mild warning or show disapproval: *The teacher ~ed the students for being lazy.*

ad·mo·ni·tion /ˌædməˈnɪʃən/ *n* [C,U] (act of) admonishing.

ad nauseam /ˌæd ˈnɔziəm/ *adv* (*Lat*) **1** to a disgusting degree. **2** (*informal*) so as to cause (great) annoyance, eg because of continuing for too long.

ado /əˈdu/ *n* [U] fuss: *Without more/much/further ado, he signed the agreement.*

adobe /əˈdoubi/ *n* **1** [U] sun-dried brick of clay and straw: (as an *adjective*) *an ~ house.* **2** [C] building made of adobe bricks.

ado·lescence /ˌædəˈlesəns/ *n* [U] period of life between childhood and maturity; growth during this period.

ado·lescent /ˌædəˈlesənt/ *n* [C], *adj* (person) growing up (age 12 or 13 to 18).

adopt /əˈdapt/ *vt* **1** take legally (a child of other parents) as one's own child: *As they had no children of their own, they ~ed an orphan.* ⇨ foster (2). **2** take, eg an idea or custom, and use as one's own: *European dress has been ~ed by people in many parts of the world.* **3** accept, eg a report or recommendation: *Congress ~ed the new measures.*

ADOBE HOUSES

adop·tion /əˈdapʃən/ *n* [U] adopting or being adopted: *the country of his ~.*

adop·tive /əˈdaptɪv/ *adj* taken by adoption: *his ~ parents.*

ador·able /əˈdɔrəbəl/ *adj* lovable; delightful.

ador·ably /-əbli/ *adv*

ador·ation /ˌædəˈreiʃən/ *n* [U] worship; love: *his ~ for Jane.*

adore /əˈdɔr/ *vt* **1** worship (God); love deeply and respect highly. **2** (*informal*) like very much: *The baby ~s being tickled.*

adorer *n* person who adores (another).

ador·ing *adj* showing love: *adoring looks.*

ador·ing·ly *adv*

adorn /əˈdɔrn/ *vt* add beauty or ornament(s) to; decorate (the usual word): *~ing herself with jewels.*

adorn·ment *n* [U] adorning; [C] (*formal*) ornament; decoration.

ad·renal /əˈdrinəl/ *adj* (*anat*) of or near the kidneys: *~ glands.*

adren·a·lin /əˈdrenəlɪn/ *n* [U] (*med*) hormones from the adrenal glands, made into a drug for treating heart failure, etc.

adrift /əˈdrɪft/ *adv, adj* **1** (of ships and boats) afloat, not under control; loose: *cut a boat ~ from its moorings.* **2** without guidance or direction. ***turn sb adrift,*** (*fig*) send him away, eg from home, without money or means of livelihood.

adroit /əˈdrɔit/ *adj* (*formal*) clever; skilful.

adroit·ly *adv*

adroit·ness /-nɪs/ *n* [U]

ADST *abbr* = Atlantic Daylight Saving Time.

adu·la·tion /ˌædʒəˈleiʃən/ *n* [U] much praise or flattery.

adult /əˈdəlt, ˈæˌdəlt/ *adj* grown to full size or strength; (of persons) intellectually and emotionally mature. □ *n* [C] **1** person, animal or plant grown to full size and strength. **2** (*legal*) person old enough to vote, marry, etc.

adult·hood /əˈdəltˌhʊd/ *n* [U] period or state of being adult.

adul·ter·ate /əˈdəltəˌreit/ *vt* (*formal*) make impure, make poorer in quality, esp by adding something inferior.

adul·ter·ation /əˌdəltəˈreiʃən/ *n* [U]

adul·terer /əˈdəltərər/ *n* [C] man who commits adultery.

adul·ter·ess /əˈdəlt(ə)rɪs/ *n* [C] woman who commits adultery.

adul·ter·ous /əˈdəlt(ə)rəs/ *adj* of adultery.
adul·tery /əˈdəlt(ə)ri/ *n* (*pl* -ies) [U] voluntary sexual intercourse of a married person with a person to whom he or she is not married; [C] instance of this.
adv. *abbr* = adverb.
ad·vance¹ /ədˈvæns/ *n* [C,U] **1** forward movement; progress: *Science has made great ~s during the last fifty years.* ***in advance (of),*** ahead of; before(hand): *Send your luggage in ~. Galileo's ideas were (well) in ~ of the age in which he lived.* **2** (as an *adjective*) before; early: *have ~ notice,* eg of a person's arrival. **3** rise in price, value or amount. **4** offer; approach: *She rejected his ~s.*
ad·vance² /ədˈvæns/ *vi,vt* **1** come or move forward: *Our troops have ~d two miles. Has civilization ~d during this century?* **2** (of costs, values, prices) rise: *Property values continue to ~.* **3** bring forward: *The date of the meeting was ~d from the 10th to the 3rd of June.* **4** help: *Such actions are unlikely to ~ your promotion.* **5** pay (money) before the due date: *He asked his employer to ~ him a month's salary.*
ad·vance·ment *n* [U] promotion; improvement: *The aim of a university should be the ~ment of learning.*
ad·vanced /ədˈvænst/ *adj* far on in life or progress, etc: *~d in years,* very old; *~d courses of study.* ⇨ elementary.
ad·van·tage /ədˈvæntɪdʒ/ *n* **1** [C] something useful, helpful or likely to bring success, esp in competition: *the ~s of a good education.* ***give sb/have an advantage (over),*** give/have a better position or opportunity: *Tom's education gave him an ~ over boys who had not gone to college.* **2** [U] benefit; profit: *He gained little ~ from his visit to New York.* ***take advantage of sb,*** use him selfishly for one's own benefit. ***take (full) advantage of sth,*** use it profitably, for one's own benefit: *He always takes full ~ of every opportunity.* ***to advantage,*** in a way that enables a thing to be seen, used, etc in the best way: *The painting is seen to better ~ from a distance.* ***be/prove to sb's advantage,*** be profitable or helpful to him.
ad·van·tage·ous /ˌædvənˈteidʒəs/ *adj* profitable; helpful.
ad·van·tage·ous·ly *adv*
ad·vent /ˈædˌvent/ *n* **1** coming or arrival (of an important development, season, etc): *Since the ~ of atomic power, there have been great changes in industry.* (*Note:* usually with *the.*) **2 Advent,** (in the Christian religion) the coming of Christ; period of the Christian calendar beginning 4 Sundays before Christmas Day.
Ad·ven·tist /ædˈventɪst/ *n* [C] member of any Christian group which believes that the Advent will soon take place.
ad·ven·ti·tious /ˌædvenˈtɪʃəs/ *adj* (*formal*) obtained or happening by chance: *~ aid.*
ad·ven·ture /ədˈventʃər/ *n* **1** [C] unusual event, esp an exciting or dangerous journey or activity: *The explorer told the boys about his ~s in the Arctic.* **2** [U] risk; danger, eg in travel and exploration: *He's fond of ~.*
ad·ven·turer *n* **(a)** daring or adventurous person. **(b)** person who is ready to make a profit by risky or dishonest methods.
ad·ven·tur·ess /-ɪs/, female adventurer.
ad·ven·tur·ous /ədˈventʃərəs/ *adj* **1** fond of, eager for, adventure. **2** full of danger and excitement: *an ~ voyage.*
ad·verb /ˈædˌvərb/ *n* [C] (*gram*) word that answers questions with *how, when, where* and modifies or limits a verb, adjective or another adverb, eg *quickly, now, here, very.*
ad·ver·bial /ædˈvərbiəl/ *adj* of the nature of an adverb: *In the sentence "I put my hand out of the window," "out of the window" is an ~ phrase.* □ *n* [C] adverb or adverbial phrase.
ad·verbi·ally *adv*
ad·ver·sary /ˈædvərˌseri/ *n* [C] (*pl* -ies) enemy; opponent (in a contest).
ad·verse /ˈædˌvərs/ *adj* unhelpful or unfavorable: *~ weather conditions.*
ad·verse·ly *adv*
ad·ver·sity /ædˈvərsəti/ *n* (*pl* -ies) [C,U] trouble: *Try to be patient/cheerful in ~.*
ad·ver·tise, ad·ver·tize /ˈædvərˌtaiz/ *vt,vi* make known to people (by printing notices in newspapers, announcements on TV, etc: *~ for an assistant.*
ad·ver·tiser, ad·ver·tizer *n* person who advertises.
ad·vert·ise·ment, ad·vert·ize·ment /ˌædvərˈtaizmənt/ *n* **1** [U] advertising: *Advertisement helps to sell goods.* **2** [C] public announcement (in the press, TV, etc): *put an ~ in the newspaper.*
ad·vice /ədˈvais/ *n* [U] (informed) opinion about what to do, how to behave: *You won't get well unless you follow your doctor's ~.* ***act on sb's advice,*** do what he suggests. ***(give sb) a piece/a bit/a word/a few words of advice,*** (give him) an opinion about what to do, etc.
ad·vis·able /ədˈvaizəbəl/ *adj* sensible; to be recommended: *Do you think it ~ to wait?*
ad·vise /ədˈvaiz/ *vt,vi* **1** give advice to; recommend: *The doctor ~d a complete rest. What do you ~ me to do?* **2** (*formal*) inform; notify: *Please ~ us when the goods are ready.*
ad·viser, ad·visor *n* person who gives advice, esp one who is regularly consulted: *an ~r to the Government/on student affairs.*
ˌill-adˈvised, *adj* ⇨ ill.
ˌwell-adˈvised, *adj* ⇨ well-.
ad·vi·sory /ədˈvaizəri/ *adj* of advice; having the power to advise: *an ~ committee.*
ad·vo·cacy /ˈædvəkəsi/ *n* [U] pleading in support.
ad·vo·cate /ˈædvəkət/ *n* [C] **1** person who supports or speaks in favor of a person or thing (esp a cause): *an ~ of equal opportunity for men and women.* **2** person who represents or acts for another, esp a lawyer. □ *vt* /ˈædvəˌkeit/ = support (the usual word): *Do you ~ euthanasia?*
advt. *abbr* = advertisement.
adz, adze /ædz/ *n* [C] carpenter's tool (with a blade at right angles to the handle) for cutting or shaping wood.
aegis, egis /ˈidʒɪs/ *n* ***under the aegis of,*** with the support of.
aer·ate /ˈeˌreit/ *vt* let or put air into: *~ the soil*

by digging.
aer·ation /ˌeˈreiʃən/ *n* [U]
aer·ial[1] /ˈeriəl/ *adj* **1** existing in, moving through, from the air: *an ~ photograph*. **2** of or like air; immaterial.
aer·ial[2] /ˈeriəl/ *n* [C] ⇨ antenna (2).
aero·bat·ics /ˌerəˈbætɪks/ *n* (used with a *sing verb*) [U] performance of acrobatic feats by an aircraft, eg flying upside down.
aero·dy·nam·ics /ˌerədaiˈnæmɪks/ *n* (used with a *sing verb*) [U] science dealing with the flow of air and other gases and the motion of aircraft, bullets, etc through air.
aero·naut·ics /ˌerəˈnɔtɪks/ *n* (used with a *sing verb*) [U] = aviation (the more usual word).
aero·plane /ˈerəˌplein/ *n* [C] = airplane.
aero·sol /ˈerəˌsɔl/ *n* [C] container with compressed gas for spraying a mist of hairspray, paint, etc.
aero·space /ˈerouˌspeis/ *n* [U] the earth's atmosphere and the space beyond: (used as an *adjective*) *an ~ vehicle*.
aes·thete, es·thete /ˈesˌθit/ *n* [C] person who has or claims to have great love of and understanding of what is beautiful, esp in the arts.
aes·thetic, es·thetic /esˈθetɪk/ *adj* of the appreciation of beauty or taste in music, painting, nature etc; (of persons) having such appreciation: *~ standards*.
aes·thet·ics, es·thet·ics *n* (used with a *sing verb*) [U] branch of philosophy which deals with the laws and principles of beauty.
afar /əˈfar/ *adv* far off or away. ***from afar,*** from a distance.
AFB *abbr* = Air Force Base.
aff. *abbr* = affix.
af·fable /ˈæfəbəl/ *adj* polite and friendly: *~ to everybody*.
affa·bil·ity /ˌæfəˈbɪləti/ *n* [U] quality of being affable.
af·fably /-əbli/ *adv*
af·fair /əˈfer/ *n* [C] **1** something (to be) done or thought about; concern: *That's my ~, not yours*. **2** (*pl*) business of any kind: *The President is kept busy with ~s of state,* the task of government. ***mind one's own affairs,*** not ask personal questions. ***state of affairs,*** conditions: *in the present state of ~s,* as things are now. **3** ***have an affair (with sb),*** have an emotional (and sexual) relationship. **4** (*informal*) thing: *The engine was a complicated ~*. **5** (*informal*) event: *The dinner party was a lavish ~*.
af·fect[1] /ˈæˌfekt/ *n* [U] feeling; emotion.
af·fect[2] /əˈfekt/ *vt* **1** influence; have an effect on: *The cold climate ~ed his health,* injured it. **2** produce sad, grateful, etc feelings: *He was much ~ed by the sad news*. **3** (of diseases) cause a particular condition in: *The left lung is ~ed, eg by cancer, tuberculosis*.
af·fect[3] /əˈfekt/ *vt* pretend to have or feel or to do: *He ~ed ignorance*.
af·fec·ted *adj* not natural or genuine: *~ed manners*.
af·fec·ta·tion /ˌæfekˈteiʃən/ *n* [C,U] (kind of) behavior that is not natural or genuine, esp for effect: *The ~s in the way she speaks* (eg her choice of words, diction) *are very annoying*.
af·fec·tion /əˈfekʃən/ *n* [U] kindly feeling; love: *Every mother has ~ for/feels ~ toward her children*. ***gain/win sb's affection(s),*** win the love of.
af·fec·tion·ate /əˈfekʃənɪt/ *adj* loving: *an ~ wife*.
af·fec·tion·ate·ly *adv* ***Yours affectionately,*** used at the close of a letter, eg from a man to his sister.
af·fi·da·vit /ˌæfəˈdeivɪt/ *n* [C] (*legal*) written statement, made under oath, (to be) used as legal proof or evidence: *swear/make/take an ~*.
af·fili·ate /əˈfɪliˌeit/ *vt,vi* (of society or institution, or a member) enter into association: *The College is ~d with the State University System*.
af·fili·ation /əˌfɪliˈeiʃən/ *n* [U] affiliating or being affiliated; [C] connection made by affiliating.
af·fin·ity /əˈfɪnəti/ *n* (*pl* -ies) [C] **1** close connection, relation; structural similarity (between animals and plants, languages, etc or of one thing with another). **2** strong liking or attraction: *She feels a strong ~ to/for him*.
af·firm /əˈfərm/ *vt,vi* declare positively: *~ the truth of a statement/that it is true*.
af·fir·ma·tion /ˌæfərˈmeiʃən/ *n* **1** [U] affirming. ⇨ negation (1). **2** [C] something affirmed.
af·firm·ative /əˈfərmətɪv/ *adj,n* [C] (answering) "yes": *The answer is in the ~,* is "Yes."
af·firm·ative·ly *adv*
af·fix[1] /əˈfɪks/ *vt* fix or attach (the usual words): *~ a seal/stamp to a document*.
af·fix[2] /ˈæˌfɪks/ *n* [C] suffix or prefix, eg *-ly, -able, un-, co-*.
af·flict /əˈflɪkt/ *vt* cause bodily or mental harm: *~ed with rheumatism*.
af·flic·tion /əˈflɪkʃən/ *n* **1** [U] suffering; distress: *help people in ~*. **2** [C] cause or occasion of suffering: *the ~s of old age,* eg deafness, blindness.
af·flu·ence /ˈæˌfluəns/ *n* [U] wealth, *living in ~*.
af·flu·ent /ˈæˌfluənt/ *adj* wealthy: *the ~ society,* society which is wealthy and whose members are concerned with prosperity.
af·ford /əˈfɔrd/ *vt* **1** (usually with *can/could, be able to*) spare or find enough time or money for: *We can't ~ a vacation/to go away this summer*. **2** (with *can/could*) run the risk of: *I can't ~ to neglect my work*. **3** (*formal*) provide: *The trees ~ pleasant shade*.
af·for·est /əˈfɔrɪst/ *vt* make into a forest.
af·for·est·ation /əˌfɔrɪˈsteiʃən/ *n* [U]
af·fray /əˈfrei/ *n* [C] quarrel or fight in a public place: *The men were charged with causing an ~*.
af·front /əˈfrənt/ *vt* insult on purpose, esp in public: *feel ~ed at having one's word doubted*. □ *n* [C] insult; deliberate show of disrespect: *an ~ to his pride*.
afield /əˈfild/ *adv* ***far afield,*** far away from home; to or at a distance.
aflame /əˈfleim/ *adj* (*poet*) in flames; red as if burning: (*fig*) *~ with passion*.
AFL - CIO /ˌei ˌef ˈel ˌsi ˌai ˈou/ *abbr* = (combined) American Federation of Labor (and) Congress of Industrial Organizations.
afloat /əˈflout/ *adj* **1** floating; carried along on

air or water: *The ship crashed on the rocks and we couldn't get it ~ again.* **2** flooded. **3** (of stories, rumors) passing from person to person. **4** (*commerce*) out of debt: *He was not able to keep his company ~ and went bankrupt.*

afoot /əˈfʊt/ *adj* **1** in progress or operation; being prepared: *There's a scheme ~ to improve the roads.* **2** (*old use*) on foot.

afore·said /əˈfɔrˌsed/ *adj* (*legal*) said or written before.

Afr. *abbr* = **1** Africa. **2** African.

afraid /əˈfreid/ *adj* ***afraid (of)/that/to do sth,*** **1** frightened: *There's nothing to be ~ of.* **2** doubtful or anxious about what may happen: *I was ~ of hurting his feelings/that I might hurt his feelings.* **3** ***be afraid,*** (with *that* usually omitted) (a polite way of saying or writing something that may be unwelcome): *I'm ~ (that) we shall be late.*

afresh /əˈfreʃ/ *adv* again; in a new way: *Let's start ~.*

Af·ri·can /ˈæfrɪkən/ *n* [C], *adj* (native) of Africa.

Afri·kaans /ˌæfrɪˈkanz/ *n* [U] language developed from Dutch, one of the two official European languages in the Republic of South Africa. □ *adj* of this language or the people who speak it.

Af·ri·ka·ner /ˌæfrɪˈkanər/ *n* [C] white Afrikaans speaker. □ *adj* of such a person.

Afro /ˈæˌfrou/ *n* (*pl* ~s) hairstyle of rounded, bushy curls.

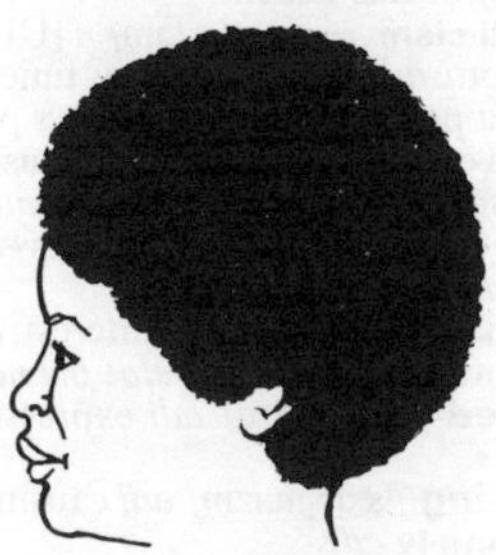

AFRO HAIRSTYLE

Afro- /ˌæfrou-/ *prefix* of Africa or Africans.

ˌAfro-ˈAsian *n, adj* (person) of African and Asian descent.

ˌAfro-Aˈmerican *n, adj* (person) of American and African descent.

aft /æft/ *adv* at or near the rear of a ship or aircraft.

after[1] /ˈæftər/ *adj* **1** later; following: *in ~ years.* **2** toward the rear of a ship or aircraft: *the ˈ~ cabin.*

after[2] /ˈæftər/ *adv* later in time; behind in place: *He fell ill on Monday and died three days ~* (*later* is more usual). *Soon ~* (*afterwards* is more usual)*, he went to live in Texas.*

after[3] /ˈæftər/ *conj* at or during a time later than: *I arrived ~ he (had) left.*

after[4] /ˈæftər/ *prep* **1** following in time; later than: *~ dinner/dark/two o'clock.* ***after that,*** then; next. **2** next in order to; following: *"Against" comes ~ "again" in a dictionary.* **3** behind: *Shut the door ~ you.* **4** as a result of: *I shall never speak to him again ~ what he has said about me.* **5** in spite of: *After all my care, it was broken. He failed ~ all,* in spite of all that had been done, etc. **6** (in the pattern: *noun ~ noun*) repeatedly; very often: *day ~ day. It's one damned thing ~ another,* a succession of unpleasant happenings, etc. **7** in the style of; in imitation of: *a painting ~ Rembrandt.* **8** (with *verbs* of pursuit, search, inquiry): *Did they ask ~ me,* ask for news of me? *The police are ~* (= trying to find and perhaps arrest) *my brother.* ⇨ also look[2], and take[1].

after- /æftər-/ *prefix* second or later.

ˈafter·care *n* [U] further treatment given to a person, eg who has been ill.

ˈafter·effect *n* [C] effect that occurs afterwards, eg a delayed effect of a drug used medically.

(the) ˈafter·life *n* **(a)** the life believed to follow death. **(b)** the later part of a person's lifetime (esp after a particular event).

ˈafter·math /-ˌmæθ/ *n* [U] (*fig*) outcome; consequence: *Misery is usually the ~math of war.*

ˈafter·thought *n* [U] thinking afterwards; [C] thought that comes afterwards.

after·noon /ˌæftərˈnun/ *n* [C] time between morning and evening: *in/during the ~; this/yesterday/tomorrow ~; on Sunday ~;* (as an *adjective*) *an ~ nap.*

after·ward /ˈæftərwərd/ *adv* after; later.

again /əˈgen/ *adv* **1** once more: *If you fail the first time, try ~.* ***now and again,*** occasionally. ***again and again; time and (time) again,*** repeatedly; very often. **2** ***not/never again,*** not any more: *Don't do that ~.* **3** to or in the original condition, position, etc: *You'll soon be well ~. He was glad to be home ~.* **4** ***as many/much again,*** **(a)** the same number or quantity. **(b)** twice as many/much; the same in addition. **5** ***then again,*** **(a)** furthermore, besides: *Then ~, I doubt whether...* **(b)** on the other hand: *It might happen, and then ~ it might not.*

against /əˈgenst/ *prep* **1** (showing opposition or opposite direction): *rowing ~ the current. Public opinion was ~ the proposal.* ***a race against time,*** an attempt to finish before a certain time, before a possible happening, etc. **2** (with *verbs* of protest): *vote/cry out/write ~ a proposal.* **3** (with *verbs* of collision or impact): *The rain was beating ~ the windows.* **4** in contrast to: *The trees were black ~ the morning sky.* **5** in preparation for; to prevent: *have an injection ~ smallpox.* **6** (showing support or closeness) by the side of, near to, and touching: *Place the ladder ~ the tree. Put the piano ~ the wall. He was leaning ~ a post.*

ag·ate /ˈægɪt/ *n* [C,U] **1** (kinds of) very hard stone with bands or patches of color. **2** marble colored like agate for playing games.

age[1] /eidʒ/ *n* **1** [C] length of time a person has lived or a thing has existed: *What's his age,* How old is he? *Their ages are 4, 7 and 9. What's the age of that old church?* ***age of consent,*** age at which the law considers a person old enough to give his consent, eg to marriage. ***be/come of age,*** be/become old enough to be responsible in law. ***over age,*** past a certain age or age limit: *He won't be allowed a child's fare; he's over age.* ***under age,*** too young. **2** [U] later part of life (contrasted with *youth*): *His back was bent with age.* **3** [C] great or long period of time, with special characteristics or events: *the atomic age.* ⇨ also middle, stone. **4** [C] (*informal*) very long time: *We've been waiting for ages/an age.*

ˈage bracket, period of life between two specified ages, eg between 20 and 30.

ˈage group, number of persons of the same age.

ˈage·less *adj* eternal; always young.

ˈage-long *adj* lasting for a very long time.

ˌage-ˈold *adj* that has been known, practiced, etc for a long time: *age-old customs/ceremonies*

age[2] /eidʒ/ *vt,vi* (*present participle* ageing or aging, *pp* aged /eidʒd/) (cause to) grow old: *He's ag(e)ing fast.*

-age /-ɪdʒ, -aʒ/ *suffix* (used to form a *noun*): *breakage; orphanage; sabotage.*

aged[1] /ˈeidʒd/ *adj* of the age of: *a boy ~ ten.*

aged[2] /ˈeidʒɪd/ *adj* very old: *an ~ man.*

age·ing /ˈeidʒɪŋ/ *n* [U] = aging.

agency /ˈeidʒənsi/ *n* (*pl* -ies) **1** [C] business, place of business, of an agent(1): *He found a job through an emˈployment ~.* **2** [U] ***the agency of,*** the action, help or cause of: *Rocks are worn smooth through the ~ of water.* **3** [C] administrative division, esp of government: *a consumer protection ~.*

agenda /əˈdʒendə/ *n* [C] (*pl* ~s) (list of) things to be done, business to be discussed, eg by a committee: *the next item on the ~.*

agent /ˈeidʒənt/ *n* [C] **1** person who acts for, or who manages or arranges the affairs of another or others: *an insurance ~.* **2** person used to achieve something or to get a result. **3** (*science*) substance producing an effect: *Rain and frost are natural ~s that wear away rocks.*

ag·glom·er·ation /əˌglaməˈreiʃən/ *n* **1** [U] action of collecting into a mass. **2** [C] (esp untidy or unplanned) heap or collection.

ag·grand·ize·ment /əˈgrændɪzmənt/ *n* [C] increase in power, wealth, importance: *seeking personal ~.*

ag·gra·vate /ˈægrəˌveit/ *vt* **1** make worse or more serious: *~ an illness/offense.* **2** (*informal*) irritate: *How aggravating!* How annoying!

ag·gra·va·tion /ˌægrəˈveiʃən/ *n* [C,U]

ag·gre·gate /ˈægrɪgət/ *n* [C] total obtained by adding together.

ag·gres·sion /əˈgreʃən/ *n* **1** [U] attack that has no (obvious) cause, often beginning a quarrel or war: *It was difficult to decide which country was guilty of ~.* **2** [C] instance of this.

ag·gres·sive /əˈgresɪv/ *adj* **1** quarrelsome; capable of attacking without a reason: *an ~ man.* **2** of or for attacking: *~ weapons.* **3** forceful; energetic, able to argue powerfully: *A man who goes from door to door selling things has to be ~ if he wants to succeed.*

ag·gres·sive·ly *adv*

ag·gres·sive·ness /-nɪs/ *n* [U]

ag·gres·sor /əˈgresər/ *n* [C] person, country, making an aggressive attack.

ag·grieved /əˈgrivd/ *adj* feeling great sorrow (esp because of unjust treatment).

aghast /əˈgæst/ *adj* filled with fear or surprise; shocked: *He stood ~ at the terrible sight.*

agile ˈædʒəl/ *adj* (of living things) moving, acting, quickly and effortlessly: *an ~ mind.*

agile·ly *adv.*

agil·ity /əˈdʒɪləti/ *n* [U].

ag·ing, age·ing /ˈeidʒɪŋ/ *n* [U] process of growing old; changes that occur as the result of the passing of time.

agi·tate /~ædʒɪteit/ *vt, vi* **1** move or shake (a liquid). **2** cause anxiety to (a person, his mind or feelings): *He was ~d about his wife's health.* **3** ***agitate for,*** argue publicly in favor of, take part in a campaign for: *agitating for higher wages.*

agi·tated *adj* anxious.

agi·ta·tion ˌædʒɪˈteiʃn/ *n* **1** [U] moving or shaking (of a liquid). **2** [U] anxiety: *She was in a state of ~.* **3** [C, U] discussion or debate (for the purpose of bringing about a change); [U] social or political unrest or trouble caused by such discussion: *The labor unions carried on long ~ against the government.*

agi·ta·tor /ˈædʒɪˌteitər/ *n* [C] person who agitates for, esp political, change.

aglow /əˈglou/ *adj* **1** bright with color: *The sky was ~ with the setting sun.* **2** (of persons) showing warmth from exercise or excitement: *~ with pleasure.*

ag·nos·tic /ægˈnastɪk/ *n* [C] person who believes that nothing can be known about God or of anything except things we can see, touch, etc. □ *adj* of this belief.

ag·nos·ti·cism /ægˈnastɪsɪzəm/ *n* [U] this belief.

ago /əˈgou/ *adv* (used to show time measured back to a point in the past; always placed after the word or words it describes and used with the *past tense*): *The train left a few minutes ago/not long ago/a long while ago. It was seven years ago that my brother died.* ⇨ since.

agog /əˈgag/ *pred adj* full of interest; excited: *all ~ for news/to hear the news/at the news.*

ag·on·ized /ˈægəˌnaizd/ *adj* expressing agony: *~ shrieks.*

ag·on·iz·ing /ˈægəˌnaizɪŋ/ *adj* causing agony.

agon·iz·ing·ly *adv*

ag·ony /ˈægəni/ *n* [C] (*pl* -ies) great pain or suffering (of mind or body): *She looked on in ~ at her child's suffering.*

agou·ti /əˈguti/ *n* [C] small rodent with gray-streaked fur found in tropical America.

agrar·ian /əˈgreriən/ *adj* of land (esp farmland) or land ownership: *~ policies.*

agree /əˈgri/ *vi,vt* **1** say "Yes"; consent: *I asked him to help me and he ~d. He ~d to my proposal.* **2** be of the same opinion(s): *We ~d to start early/on making an early start/that we should start early. We could not ~ with her* (*as to*) *how it should be done. Have you ~d about/on the price yet?* **3** (of two or more persons) be happy together; get on well with one another (without arguing, etc): *We shall never ~.* **4** match, be the same: *This bill does not ~ with your original estimate,* the two are different. **5** suit, eg the health of: *The climate doesn't ~ with me.* **6** (*gram*) have the same case, number, person, etc as: *The verb ~s with its subject in number and person.*

agree·able /əˈgriəbəl/ *adj* **1** pleasant (the usual word): *She has an ~ voice.* **2** willing to agree: *Are you ~ to the proposal?*
agree·ably /-əbli/ *adv* pleasantly: *I was ~ably surprised.*

agree·ment /əˈgrimənt/ *n* **1** [U] agreeing. ***be in agreement***, have the same opinion(s): *We are in ~ on that point. I'm quite in ~ with what you say.* **2** [C] arrangement or understanding (spoken or written) made by two or more persons, governments, etc: *sign an ~.* ***come to/ arrive at/make/reach an agreement (with sb),*** agree.

ag·ri·cul·tural /ˌægrɪˈkəltʃərəl/ *adj* of farming.

ag·ri·cul·ture /ˈægrɪˌkəltʃər/ *n* [U] science or practice of farming.

aground /əˈgraund/ *pred adj, adv* (of ships) touching the bottom in shallow water: *The ship went ~.*

ah /a/ *int* cry of surprise, pity, etc.

aha /aˈha/ *int* cry of surprise, triumph, satisfaction, etc.

ahead /əˈhed/ *adv* in front; in advance: *Standard time in New York is two hours ~ of Mountain Standard Time.* ***Full speed ahead!*** Go forward at full speed. ***get ahead,*** succeed: *Hard work helped him to get ~.* ***go ahead,*** (*informal*) continue (with what you're about to say or do). ***look ahead,*** think of and prepare for future needs.

ahem /əˈhem/ *int* (usual spelling for the) noise made when clearing the throat or to give a warning or to call somebody.

ahoy /əˈhɔi/ *int* greeting or warning cry used by seamen.

aid /eid/ *vt* = help (the usual word): *The money will aid us in our work.* □ *n* **1** [U] help: *He came to my aid,* helped me. ⇨ also first aid. **2** [C] something that helps.

aide /eid/ *n* [C] **1** aide-de-camp. **2** helper; assistant: *a presidential ~.*

aide-de-camp /ˌeid də ˈkæmp/ *n* [C] (*pl* aides-de-camp) naval or military officer who helps a superior.

ail /ˈeiəl/ *vt,vi* (-ing, /ˈeilɪŋ/) **1** trouble: *What ails him?* What's wrong with him? **2** be ill: *The children are always ailing,* always in poor health.
ail·ment /ˈeiəlmənt/ *n* [C] = illness (the usual word).

ail·eron /ˈeiləˌran/ *n* hinged flap on the wing of an aircraft that helps to balance the aircraft and control ascent and descent. ⇨ illus at aircraft.

aim¹ /eim/ *vt,vi* **1 (a)** point (a gun, etc) towards: *He aimed (his gun) at the lion, fired and missed.* **(b)** send, direct, eg a blow, object: *Tom got angry with his brother and aimed a heavy book at his head.* **(c)** (*fig*) (of criticism, praise, etc) be meant for: *My remarks were not aimed at you.* **2** have as a plan or intention: *Harry aims to become a doctor.*

aim² /eim/ *n* **1** [U] act of aiming, eg with a gun: *Take careful aim at the target.* **2** [C] purpose; objective: *He has only one aim and object in life —to make a fortune before he is fifty.*
aim·less *adj* having no aim(2).
aim·less·ly *adv.*
aim·less·ness /-nɪs/ *n* [U]

ain't /eint/ (*dial*) = are/is/am not; have/has not: *I ain't going. We ain't done it yet.*

air¹ /er/ *n* **1** [U] the mixture of gases that sur-

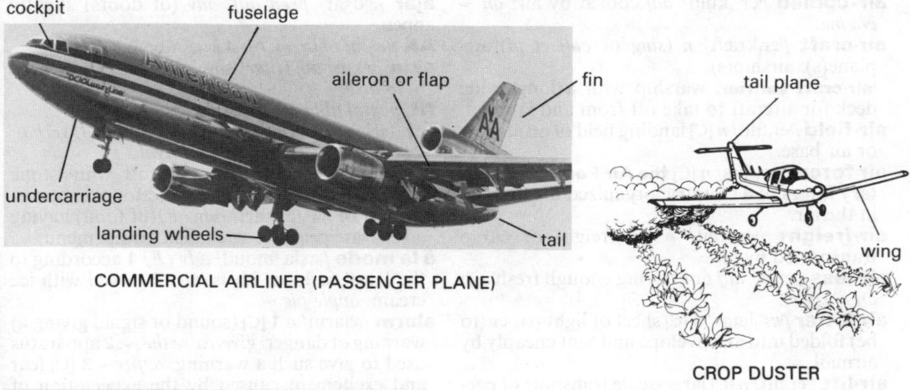

COMMERCIAL AIRLINER (PASSENGER PLANE)

CROP DUSTER

AMPHIBIAN

LIGHT AIRCRAFT

AIRCRAFT

rounds the earth and which we breathe: *Let's go out and enjoy the fresh air.* ***in the air,*** **(a)** uncertain: *My plans are still in the air.* **(b)** (of opinions, etc) passing from one person to another: *There are rumors in the air that....* ***clear the air,*** **(a)** make the air (in a room, etc) fresh again. **(b)** (*fig*) lessen suspicion, doubt, etc by giving facts, etc. ***up in the air,*** uncertain. ⇨ also hot. **2** ***by air,*** in aircraft: *travel/send goods, etc by air.* **3** [U] ***on the air,*** on the radio or television: *The President will be on the air at 9:15pm.* ***go off the air,*** stop broadcasting. **4** [C] (*dated*) tune, melody. **5** [C] appearance; manner: *He has an air of importance,* seems to be, looks, important. ***give oneself/put on airs,*** act in an affected way in the hope of impressing people.

air² /er/ *vt* **1** put (clothing, etc) out in the fresh air: *The blankets need to be aired.* **2** let fresh air into (a room, etc). **3** say publicly; make known: *He likes to air his views.*

ˈair·ing *n* ***give sth an airing,*** **(a)** expose it to the fresh air. **(b)** discuss it.

air base /ˈer ˌbeis/ *n* [C] headquarters for military aircraft.

air·borne /ˈerˌbɔrn/ *adj* **1** carried by air. **2** (of an aircraft) in flight: *We were soon ~.*

air brake /ˈer ˌbreik/ *n* [C] brake with piston(s) driven by compressed air.

air-con·di·tion /ˈer kənˌdɪʃən/ *vt* **1** supply with air that is cleaned and kept at a certain temperature and humidity. **2** install equipment for this.

ˈair-conditioned *adj*

ˈair conditioner, machine for this.

ˈair conditioning, this process.

air-cooled /ˈer ˌkuld/ *adj* cooled by air: *an ~ engine.*

air·craft /ˈerˌkræft/ *n* (*sing* or *collect pl*) airplane(s); airship(s).

ˈair·craft car·rier, warship with a long, wide deck for aircraft to take off from and land on.

air·field /ˈerˌfild/ *n* [C] landing field of an airport or air base.

air force /ˈer ˌfɔrs/ *n* [C] **the Air Force,** the military forces of a country, organized for fighting in the air.

air·freight /ˈerˌfreit/ *n* [U] freight or cargo transported by air.

air·less /ˈerlɪs/ *adj* not having enough fresh air: *an ~ room.*

air letter /ˈer ˌletər/ *n* [C] sheet of light paper (to be) folded into an envelope and sent cheaply by airmail.

air·lift /ˈerˌlɪft/ *n* [C] large-scale transport of persons or supplies by air, esp in an emergency.

air·line /ˈerˌlain/ *n* [C] (company that operates a) regular service of aircraft for public use.

ˈair·liner *n* [C] large, passenger-carrying aircraft. ⇨ illus at aircraft.

air·mail /ˈerˌmeiəl/ *n* [U] mail (to be) carried by air. □ *vt* (-ing /ˈerˌmeilɪŋ/) send by airmail.

air·man /ˈermən/ *n* [C] (*pl* airmen /-men/) enlisted member of the Air Force. ⇨ illus at arm².

air·plane /ˈerˌplein/ (*Note:* The pronunciation /ˈerəˌplein/, transferred from the older form aeroplane, is often used as well.) *n* [C] aircraft heavier than air with one or more engines.

air·port /ˈerˌpɔrt/ *n* [C] place where aircraft can take off and land, usually with a hangar and other buildings for aircraft storage and maintenance.

air pressure /ˈer ˌpreʃər/ *n* [U] pressure that results from the weight of the atmosphere(1), or from confinement of the air in an airtight place.

air raid /ˈer ˌreid/ *n* [C] attack by aircraft that drop bombs.

air·screw /ˈerˌskru/ *n* [C] aircraft propeller. ⇨ screw(4).

air·ship /ˈerˌʃɪp/ *n* [C] flying machine with one or more engines, which is lighter than air. ⇨ balloon.

air space /ˈer ˌspeis/ *n* [C] part of the earth's atmosphere above a country: *violation of our ~ by unauthorized foreign aircraft.*

air speed /ˈer ˌspid/ *n* [C] speed of an aircraft relative to the air through which it is moving.

air·strip /ˈerˌstrɪp/ *n* [C] strip of ground for the use of aircraft, esp one made for use in war or in an emergency.

air·tight /ˈerˌtait/ *adj* **1** not allowing air to enter or escape. **2** (*fig*) leaving no possibility of misunderstanding or not succeeding, etc.

air·way /ˈerˌwei/ *n* [C] route regularly followed by aircraft

airy /ˈeri/ *adj* (-ier, -iest) **1** having plenty of fresh air moving through it: *a nice ~ room.* **2** of or like air. **3** not solid; superficial: *~ promises,* unlikely to be kept.

aisle /ˈaiəl/ *n* [C] **1** passage in a church, esp one that is divided by a row of columns from the nave. **2** passage between any rows of seats, eg in a church, theater, etc.

ajar /əˈdʒar/ *pred adj, adv* (of doors) slightly open.

AK *postal abbr* = Alaska. ⇨ App 6.

akin /əˈkɪn/ *adj* (*liter*) similar; like: *Pity is often ~ to love.*

AL *postal abbr* = Alabama. ⇨ App 6.

-al /-əl/ *suffix* **1** (*n* + -al = *adj*): *magical; verbal.* **2** (*v* + -al = *n*): *recital; survival.*

ala·bas·ter /ˈæləˌbæstər/ *n* [U] soft, white stone like marble in appearance, used for ornaments.

à la carte /ˌa ˌla ˈkart/ *adv (F)* (of food) having a separate price for each dish on the menu.

à la mode /ˌa ˌla ˈmoud/ *adv (F)* **1** according to the latest fashion, ideas, etc. **2** served with ice cream: *apple pie ~.*

alarm /əˈlarm/ *n* **1** [C] (sound or signal giving a) warning of danger: *give/raise the ~.* **2** apparatus used to give such a warning: *a ˈfire~* **3** [U] fear and excitement caused by the expectation of danger: *He jumped up in ~.* □ *vt* **1** warn of danger. **2** cause to feel fear or anxiety: *Everybody was ~ed at the news that war might break out.*

alarm·ing *adj* causing fear or anxiety.

alarm·ist /-ɪst/ *n* [C] person who is easily alarmed.

alas /əˈlæs/ *int* cry of sorrow or regret.

alb /ælb/ *n* [C] white vestment reaching to the feet, worn by some Christian priests at ceremonies.

al·ba·tross /ˈælbəˌtrɔs/ *n* [C] large, white, webfooted seabird, common in the Pacific and Southern Oceans.

al·beit /ˌɔlˈbiət/ *conj* (*formal*) although.
al·bino /ˌælˈbainou/ *n* [C] (*pl* ~s /-nouz/) animal or human being born without natural coloring matter in the skin and hair (which are white) and the eyes (which are pink or blue).
al·bum /ˈælbəm/ *n* [C] **1** blank book in which a collection of photographs, autographs, postage stamps, etc can be kept. **2** holder for a set of records. **3** one or more long-playing records or tape recordings with several pieces.
al·bu·men /ælˈbyumən/ *n* [U] white of egg.
al·chem·ist /ˈælkəmɪst/ *n* [C] (in the Middle Ages) person who studied or practiced alchemy.
al·chemy /ˈælkəmi/ *n* [U] chemistry of the Middle Ages that tried to discover how to change ordinary metals into gold.
al·co·hol /ˈælkəˌhɔl/ *n* [U] (flammable, colorless liquid in) such drinks as beer, wine, brandy, whiskey.
al·co·holic /ˌælkəˈhɔlɪk/ *adj* of or containing alcohol. □ *n* [C] person addicted to alcoholic drink.
al·co·hol·ism /ˈælkəˌhɔˌlɪzəm/ *n* [U] **1** action of alcohol on the human system; diseased condition caused by this. **2** addiction to alcohol.
al·cove /ˈælkouv/ *n* [C] small room or recess that opens into and is part of a larger room.
al·der·man /ˈɔldərmən/ *n* [C] (*pl* -men /-men/) (senior member) of a city or borough council in some cities.
ale /ˈeiəl/ *n* [U] light-colored beer-like drink.
alert /əˈlərt/ *adj* fully awake and ready to act, speak, etc: ~ *in answering questions.* □ *n* **1** ***on the alert,*** ready to act, attack, etc. **2** [C] period of being on the alert. □ *vt* make a person alert; warn.
al·fresco /ˌælˈfreskou/ *adj, adv* in the open air: *lunching* ~.
alga /ˈælgə/ *n* (*pl* ~e /ˈældʒi/) water plant of very simple structure.
al·ge·bra /ˈældʒəbrə/ *n* [U] branch of mathematics in which signs and letters are used to represent quantities.
al·ge·braic /ˌældʒəˈbreiɪk/, **al·ge·braic·al** /-kəl/ *adj*
alias /ˈeiliəs/ *n* [C] (*pl* ~es) name which a person, esp a criminal uses instead of his own. □ *adv* also called: *Harold Smith,* ~ *Harry the Shark.*
alibi /ˈæləˌbai/ *n* [C] (*pl* ~s) **1** (*legal*) plea that one was in another place at the time of an act, esp a crime: *The accused man was able to establish an* ~. **2** (*informal*) excuse (for failure, etc).
alien /ˈeiliən/ *n* [C] person who is not a citizen of the country in which he is living: *An Englishman is an* ~ *in the United States.* □ *adj* **1** foreign: *an* ~ *environment.* **2** (*formal*) different in nature or character: *These principles are* ~ *to our religion.*
alien·ate /ˈeiliəˌneit/ *vt* cause (a person) to become unfriendly or indifferent (by unpopular or unpleasant actions): *The candidate's speeches* ~*d many of his followers.*
alien·ation /ˌeiliəˈneiʃən/ *n* [U]
alight[1] /əˈlait/ *pred adj* **1** on fire; lit. **2** (*fig*) cheerful, bright: *Their faces were* ~ *with happiness.*
alight[2] /əˈlait/ *vi* get down (from a horse, etc); (of a bird) come down from the air and settle (on a branch, etc).
align /əˈlain/ *vt,vi* **1** arrange in a line; bring into alignment. **2** join with others (on some issue): *They* ~*ed themselves with us.*
align·ment *n* [C,U] **(a)** (an) arrangement in a straight line: *The desks are in/out of* ~*ment.* **(b)** grouping together for a common purpose: *There was a new* ~*ment of European powers.*
alike /əˈlaik/ *pred adj* like one another: *The two sisters are very much* ~. □ *adv* in the same way: *treat everybody* ~; the same: *summer and winter* ~.
ali·men·tary /ˌæləˈment(ə)ri/ *adj* of food and digestion.
the ˌaliˈmentary canal, tube or passage (from the mouth to the anus) through which food enters and solid waste leaves the body.
ali·mony /ˈæləˌmouni/ *n* [U] money allowance (to be) paid by a man to his wife, or former wife, by a judge's order, eg after a legal separation or divorce.
alive /əˈlaiv/ *pred adj* **1** living: *Who's the greatest man* ~? **2** in existence: *An awareness of the dangers of air pollution should be kept* ~ *by the press and TV.* ***alive to,*** aware of: *He is fully* ~ *to the dangers of the situation.* ***alive with,*** full of (living or moving things): *The lake was* ~ *with fish.*
al·kali /ˈælkəˌlai/ *n* [C] (*pl* -lies, -lis /-ˌlaiz/) (*chem*) one of a number of substances (such as *soda, potash, ammonia*) that combine with acids to form salts.
al·ka·line /ˈælkəˌlain/ *adj*
all[1] /ɔl/ *adj* **1** (with *pl nouns*) the whole number of: *All horses are animals.* **2** (with *uncountable nouns* and in ***all the ...***) the whole extent or amount: *All hope is lost. They walked all the way home.* ***all ˈget-out,*** (*sl*) (used in comparisons to express the greatest imaginable degree): *He's as strong as/stronger than all get-out*, extremely strong. ***all (of),*** the whole (of): *He spent all (of) that year in Europe.* **3** any: *It's beyond all doubt,* there is no reason for doubt.
all[2] /ɔl/ *adv* **1** entirely: *They were dressed all in black.* **2** (with *comparatives*) much; so much: *You'll be all the better for a holiday.* **3** (special uses with *particles* and *prepositions*):
all alone, without the help or company of others.
all along, **(a)** for the whole length of: *There are trees all along the road.* **(b)** (*informal*) all the time: *But I knew that all along!*
all for, (*informal*) strongly in favor of: *I'm all for accepting the offer.*
all in, (*informal*) exhausted; *He was all in at the end of the race.* ***all out,*** (*informal*) using all possible strength, energy, etc: *He was going all out.*
all over, **(a)** in every part of: *He has traveled all over the world.* **(b)** at an end.
all right, (*alright* is a less accepted spelling) **(a)** satisfactory, satisfactorily; safe and sound; in good order: *I hope they've arrived all right.* **(b)** (as a response to a suggestion, etc) Yes, I consent.
all there, (*informal*) mentally alert. ***not all there,*** (*informal*) not quite sane.
all the same = nevertheless. ***all the same to,*** a

matter of indifference to: *It's all the same to me whether you go or stay.*

all told, altogether; as the total: *There were six people all told* (= in all).

all wet, (*informal*) mistaken.

all[3] /ɔl/ *n* (in such phrases as *my/his/their, etc all*) everything: *He gave his all,* tried as hard as he could.

all[4] /ɔl/ *pron* **1** everything or everybody: *They were all broken. Take it all. We all want to go.*

all of, every one, the whole: *Take all of them/it.* **2** (special uses with *particles* and *prepositions*):

above all, ⇨ above² (3).

all in all, considering all the facts: *All in all he's a nice man.*

in all, ⇨ in² (13).

not all that + *adj/adv,* not to that extent: *It's not all that easy.*

not as/so + *adj/adv* + ***as all that,*** not to that extent: *It's not as easy as all that,* not as easy as it seems.

(not) at all /ə ˈtɔl, æt ˈɔl/ (not) in any way. (*Note:* used in the *negative* and *interrogative.*) *She's not at all suitable. Are you at all worried?*

not at all, polite reply when receiving thanks.

once (and) for all, now and for the last or only time.

all- /ɔl/ *prefix* completely: *ˌall-ˈpowerful.*

ˌall-aˈround, ˌall-ˈround *adj* having various abilities: *an all-around athlete.*

ˈall-star *adj* with many famous actors or outstanding performers: *an all-star cast.*

Allah /ˈalə/ *n* name of God among Moslems.

al·le·ga·tion /ˌæləˈgeiʃən/ *n* **1** [U] alleging. **2** [C] statement, esp one made without proof: *You have made serious ~s, but can you prove that they are true?*

al·lege /əˈledʒ/ *vt* declare; put forward, esp as a reason or excuse, in support of a claim or in denial of a charge: *In your statement you ~ that the accused man was seen at the scene of the crime.*

al·leg·edly /-ɪdli/ *adv*

al·le·giance /əˈlidʒəns/ *n* [U] duty, support, loyalty, due (to a ruler or government): *They took an oath of ~ to the government.*

al·le·gory /ˈæləˌgɔri/ *n* [C] (*pl* -ies) story or description in which ideas such as patience, purity and truth are symbolized by persons who are characters in the story.

al·le·goric /ˌæləˈgɔrɪk/, **al·le·gori·cal** /-kəl/ *adj*

al·ler·gic /əˈlərdʒɪk/ *adj* of allergy. ***allergic to,*** **(a)** having an allergy to. **(b)** (*informal*) having a dislike of; unable to get on well with.

al·lergy /ˈælərdʒi/ *n* [C] (*pl* -ies) (*med*) (condition of) being abnormally sensitive to particular foods, fur, insect stings, etc.

al·levi·ate /əˈliviˌeit/ *vt* make (pain, suffering) less or easier to bear.

al·levi·ation /əˌliviˈeiʃən/ *n* [U]

al·ley /ˈæli/ *n* [C] (*pl* ~s) **1** narrow passage or street. **2** narrow lane for such games as bowling, etc. ***right up/down one's alley,*** just suited to one's taste or ability.

ˌblind ˈalley, (a) narrow street closed at one end. **(b)** (*fig*) profession, career with no opportunity for progress.

al·liance /əˈlaiəns/ *n* **1** [U] association or connection. **2** [C] union, eg of states (by treaty): *enter into an ~ with another country.*

al·lied /əˈlaid, ˈæˌlaid/ *pt, pp* of ally¹.

al·li·ga·tor /ˈæləˌgeitər/ *n* [C] reptile (like a crocodile but with a shorter head) living in the Americas (the southeastern US) and in China. ⇨ illus at reptile.

al·li·ter·ation /əˌlɪtəˈreiʃən/ *n* [U] repetition of the first sound or letter in a series of words, eg *safe and sound.*

al·lit·er·ative /əˈlɪtəˌreitɪv/ *adj*

al·lit·er·ative·ly *adv*

al·lo·cate /ˈæləˌkeit/ *vt* give, put to one side, as a share or for a specific purpose: *~ a sum of money to education.*

al·lo·ca·tion /ˌæləˈkeiʃən/ *n* **1** [U] allocating or distributing. **2** [C] person or thing allocated.

al·lot /əˈlat/ *vt* (-tt-) distribute; give out in shares: *Can we do the work within the time ~ted (to) us?*

al·lot·ment *n* [C] part or share.

al·low /əˈlau/ *vt,vi* **1** permit: *Smoking is not ~ed here.* **2** give, let (a person or thing) have; agree to give: *How much money are you ~ed to have?*

allow for, take into consideration: *It will take an hour to get to the station, ~ing for traffic delays.*

al·low·able /-əbəl/ *adj* that is or can be allowed (by law, the rules, etc).

al·low·ance /əˈlauəns/ *n* **1** [C] sum of money, amount, allowed. **2** ***make allowance(s) for,*** allow for: *We must make ~(s) for his youth,* remember that he is young, etc.

al·loy /ˈæˌlɔi/ *n* [C,U] **1** mixture of metals. **2** metal of low value mixed with a metal of higher value: *Copper is often used as an ~ for gold.*

all·spice /ˈɔlˌspais/ *n* [U] spice made from the dried berries of a West Indian tree called the pimiento.

al·lude /əˈlud/ *vi* ***allude to,*** mention (the more usual word); refer to indirectly: *In your remarks you ~d to certain dangerous developments.*

allur·ing /əˈlʊrɪŋ/ *adj* attractive (the usual word).

al·lu·sion /əˈluʒən/ *n* [C] (*formal*) indirect reference to: *His books are full of classical ~s which few people understand.*

al·lu·sive /əˈlusɪv/ *adj* containing allusions.

al·lu·vial /əˈluviəl/ *adj* made of sand, earth, etc left by rivers or floods: *~ soil.*

ally[1] /əˈlai/ *vt* (*pt, pp* -ied) **1** ***ally (oneself) with/to,*** unite by treaty, marriage, etc: *Great Britain was allied with the United States in both World Wars;* hence: *the Allied* /ˈæˌlaid/ *Powers.* **2** ***be allied to,*** (of things) related to: *The English language is allied to the German language.*

ally[2] /ˈæˌlai/ *n* [C] (*pl* -ies) **1** person, state, etc allied to another. **2** person who gives help or support.

al·ma·nac /ˈɔlmˌənæk, ˈal-, ˈæl-/ *n* [C] annual book or calendar of months and days, with information about the sun, moon, tides, holidays, etc.

Al·mighty /ˌɔlˈmaiti/ *n* **the Almighty,** God.

almond /ˈamənd, ˈæ-/ *n* [C] (long, flat nut inside the) hard seed of a tree similar to the peach and plum.

ˌ**almond-ˈeyed** *adj* having eyes shaped like an almond.

al·most /ˈɔlmoust/ *adv* very nearly: *He slipped and ~ fell. Dinner's ~ ready.* ⇨ nearly. ***almost no/none/no one/nothing/never,*** (= *hardly any/anyone/anything/ever, scarcely any/anything*): *Almost no one believed her. She says ~ nothing of importance.*

alms /amz/ *n* (*sing* or *pl*) money, clothes, food, etc given to the poor: *give ~ to a person.*

aloft /əˈlɔft, əˈlaft/ *adv* high up, esp at the masthead of a ship, or up in the rigging.

alo·ha /əˈlou(h)ə, əˈlouha/ *int* used for greeting or farewell in Hawaii.

alone /əˈloun/ *pred adj, adv* ⇨ lonely. **1** (= *by oneself/itself*) without the company or help of others: *He likes living ~. You can't lift the piano ~,* without help. **2** (*noun/pronoun* + ~) and no other: *Smith ~ knows what happened.* **3** ***be (not) alone in,*** (not) the only persons who are: *We are not ~ in thinking that.* **4** ***let alone,*** without considering: *He cannot afford subway tokens let ~ cigarettes.* ***let/leave sb/sth alone,*** not touch, move, interfere with: *You had better leave that dog ~; it will bite you if you bother it.*

along /əˈlɔŋ/ *adv* **1** (used to show onward movement, often with the same sense as *on*): *Come ~! The dog was running ~ behind its owner.* **2** (*informal*) (used like *over, across, up, down*): *Come ~ to my office.* **3** together (with someone or something); in addition: *They took ~ plenty of warm clothing. The bill came ~ with the package.* **4** ***along about,*** (*informal*) (of time) approximately: *~ about noon.* ***all along,*** ⇨ all²(3). ***get along,*** ⇨ get(16). □ *prep* from one end of to the other end of; through any part of the length of: *We walked ~ the road.*

along·side /əˌlɔŋˈsaid/ *adv, prep* close to, side by side with.

aloof /əˈluf/ *adj* (of a person's character) keeping away, taking no part in: *I find him rather ~.* □ *adv* apart.

aloof·ness /nɪs/ *n* [U]

aloud /əˈlaud/ *adv* **1** in a voice loud enough to be heard, not in a whisper: *Please read the story ~.* **2** loudly, so as to be heard at a distance: *He called ~ for help.*

alp /ælp/ *n* [C] high mountain, esp one of those (**the Alps**) between France and Italy.

al·paca /ælˈpækə/ *n* **1** [C] sheeplike animal found in Peru. **2** [U] cloth woven from its hair.

al·pha /ˈælfə/ *n* the first letter (A, α) of the Greek alphabet: *Alpha and Omega,* the beginning and the end.

al·pha·bet /ˈælfəˌbet/ *n* [C] the letters used in writing a language, arranged in order: *the Greek ~.*

al·pha·beti·cal /ˌælfəˈbetɪkəl/ *adj* in the order of the alphabet: *The words in a dictionary are in ~ical order.*

al·pha·beti·cally /-kli/ *adv*

al·pine /ˈælˌpain/ *adj* of the Alps; of alps: *~ plants.*

al·ready /ɔlˈredi/ *adv* (usually used to show emphasis) **1** by this/that time: *The mailman has ~ been here/has been here ~.* ⇨ yet. **2** (used to show surprise): *You're not leaving us ~, are you?* **3** previously; before now: *I've ~ been there/been there ~.*

Al·sa·tian /ˌælˈseiʃən/ *n* [C] = German shepherd.

also /ˈɔlˌsou/ *adv* too; besides; as well: *Tom has been to Canada. Harry has ~ been to Canada.* ⇨ as well, either. ***not only... but also,*** both... and: *He not only read the book but ~ remembered what he had read.*

ˈ**also-ran** *n* [C] unsuccessful contender, eg in a contest, election campaign, etc.

al·tar /ˈɔltər/ *n* [C] **1** flat-topped table or platform on which offerings are made to a god. **2** (in Christian churches) table for Communion service or for celebrating Mass.

al·ter /ˈɔltər/ *vt,vi* make or become different; change in character, appearance, etc: *These clothes are too large; they must be ~ed. He has ~ed a great deal since I saw him a year ago.*

al·ter·able /-əbəl/ *adj* that alters or that can be altered.

alter·ation /ˌɔltəˈreiʃən/ *n* **1** [U] altering. **2** [C] act of changing; change that is the result of altering: *Alterations to clothes can cost a lot of money.*

al·ter·nate¹ /ˈɔltərnɪt/ *adj* (of things of two kinds) by turns, first the one and then the other: *Tom and Harry do the work on ~ days,* eg Tom on Monday, Harry on Tuesday, Tom on Wednesday, etc.

al·ter·nate·ly *adv*

al·ter·nate² /ˈɔltərˌneit/ *vt,vi* arrange or do by turns; cause to take place, appear, one after the other: *she ~s boiled eggs with fried eggs for breakfast.* ***alternate between,*** pass from one state, etc to a second, then back to the first, etc: *He ~s so easily between happiness and sadness.*

ˌ**alternating** ˈ**current,** electric current that regularly changes to the opposite direction and back, the number of complete changes per second being known as the *frequency.* ⇨ direct¹.

al·ter·na·tive /ɔlˈtərnətɪv/ *adj* (of two things) that may be had, used, etc in place of something else: *There are ~ answers to your question.* □ *n* [C] **1** choice between two things: *You have the ~ of working hard and succeeding or of not working and being unsuccessful.* **2** one of more than two possibilities.

al·ter·na·tive·ly *adv* as a choice: *a fine of $500 or ~ly six weeks imprisonment.*

al·though /ɔlˈðou/ *conj* ⇨ though.

al·ti·tude /ˈæltəˌtud/ *n* **1** (not of living things) height, esp above sea level. **2** (*pl*) place high above sea level: *It is difficult to breathe at these ~s.*

alto /ˈæltou/ *n* [C] (*pl* ~s) **1** (musical part for or a singer having a) range between soprano and tenor. **2** = contralto. **3** instrument with the same range: *an ~ saxophone.*

al·to·gether /ˌɔltəˈgeðər/ *adv* **1** entirely; wholly: *I don't ~ agree with him.* **2** considering everything: *The weather was bad and the trains were crowded; ~, it was a bad journey.*

al·tru·ism /ˈæltruˌɪzəm/ *n* [U] considering the well-being and happiness of others first.

al·tru·ist /ˈæltruɪst/ *n* [C] person who is altruistic.

al·tru·is·tic /ˌæltruˈɪstɪk/ *adj*

al·tru·is·ti·cally /-kli/ *adv*
alum /ˈæləm/ *n* [U] white mineral salt used in medicine, for dyeing, etc.
alu·mi·num /əˈlumənəm/ *n* [U] light white metal, used for cookware, aircraft construction, etc.
al·ways /ˈɔlweiz, -wɪz/ *adv* **1** at all times; without exception: *The sun ~ rises in the east.* (*Note: Always* may be used with *almost, nearly* or *not* : *He's nearly ~ at home in the evening.*) **2** again and again; repeatedly: *He ~ asks for money.*
AM[1]**, am** /ˌei ˈem/ *abbr* (= *Lat* ante meridiem) (in the) morning; between midnight and noon. ⇨ App 2.
AM[2] /ˌei ˈem/ *abbr* = amplitude modulation (radio channel).
am[3] ⇨ be.
AMA /ˌei ˌem ˈei/ *abbr* = American Medical Association.
amal·ga·mate /əˈmælgəˌmeit/ *vt,vi* mix; combine; unite.
amal·ga·ma·tion /əˌmælgəˈmeiʃən/ *n* [C,U] (instance of) mixing; combining.
amass /əˈmæs/ *vt* pile or heap up, collect: *~ a fortune/riches.*
ama·teur /ˈæməˌtʃər, ˈæməˌtər/ *n* [C] **1** person who paints pictures, performs music, plays, etc, for pleasure, not professionally; person playing a game, taking part in sports, without receiving payment. (*Note:* often used as an *adj*): *an ~ painter/photographer.* **2** person who engages in something without enough knowledge or training (contrasting with *professional*).
ama·teur·ish *adj* inexpert; imperfect.
amateur·ism /-ˌɪzəm/ *n* [U]
amaze /əˈmeiz/ *vt* fill with great surprise or wonder: *I was ~d at the news/~d (to hear) that....*
amaze·ment *n* [U] surprise: *I heard with ~ment that....*
amaz·ing *adj*
amaz·ing·ly *adv*: *He's doing amazingly well.*
Ama·zon /ˈæməˌzan/ *n* [C] **1** (*Greek myth*) female warrior. **2 amazon,** tall, strong, active woman.
am·bas·sa·dor /æmˈbæsədər/ *n* [C] **1** minister representing the government of his country in a foreign country: *the American Ambassador to Great Britain.* **2** authorized representative.
am·bas·sa·dor·ial /æmˌbæsəˈdɔriəl/ *adj* of an ambassador or his duties.
am·bas·sa·dress /ˌæmˈbæsədrɪs/ *n* [C] female ambassador.
am·ber /ˈæmbər/ *n* [U] **1** hard, clear yellowish-brown gum used for making ornaments, etc. **2** its color.
ambi- /æmbɪ-, æmbə-/ *combined form* both; double; two: *ambiguous; ambidextrous.*
am·bi·dex·trous /ˌæmbəˈdekstrəs/ *adj* able to use the left hand or the right equally well.
am·bi·dex·trous·ly *adv*
am·bience /ˈæmbiəns/ *n* [U] environment; atmosphere: *a friendly ~.*
am·bient /ˈæmbiənt/ *adj* (of air, etc) on all sides; surrounding.
am·bi·guity /ˌæmbəˈgyuəti/ *n* (*pl* -ies) **1** [U] state of being ambiguous. **2** [C] expression, etc that can have more than one meaning.
am·bigu·ous /æmˈbɪgyuəs/ *adj* uncertain: *"Flying planes can be dangerous" is ~.*
am·bigu·ous·ly *adv*
am·bi·tion /æmˈbɪʃən/ *n* **1** [U] strong desire for fame, success, etc: *A boy who is filled with ~ usually works hard.* **2** [C] particular desire of this kind: *He has great ~s.* **3** [C] object of such a desire: *achieve one's ~(s).*
am·bi·tious /æmˈbɪʃəs/ *adj* **1** full of ambition: *an ~ boy; ~ to succeed in life.* **2** showing or needing ambition: *~ plans; an ~ attempt.*
am·bi·tious·ly *adv*
am·bi·tious·ness /-nɪs/ *n* [U]
am·biva·lence /æmˈbɪvələns/ *n* [U] **1** existence of opposite or conflicting feelings. **2** inability to make up one's mind.
am·biva·lent /æmˈbɪvələnt/ *adj* having conflicting feelings
am·biva·lent·ly *adv*
amble /ˈæmbəl/ *vi* (of a horse) move along without hurrying; (of a person) walk without hurrying. □ *n* slow, gentle, pace.
am·brosia /æmˈbrouʒə/ *n* [U] (*Greek myth*) **1** the food of the gods. **2** (*fig*) anything that has a delightful taste or smell.
am·bu·lance /ˈæmbyələns/ *n* vehicle for carrying people who are sick or injured.
ˈambulance-ˌchaser *n* (*sl*) lawyer who tries to persuade accident victims to sue for damages and become his clients.
am·bush /ˈæmˌbʊʃ/ *n* [C,U] (surprise attack by) troops, etc stationed in a hidden position, lying in wait for the enemy: *be attacked from an ~.* □ *vt* lie in wait and attack.
ameba = amoeba.
ameli·or·ate /əˈmilyəˌreit/ *vt,vi* (*formal*) (cause to) become better.
amen /ˌeiˈmen *in some formal church services:* ˌaˈmen/ *int* word used at the end of a prayer or hymn and meaning "May it be so."
amen·able /əˈminəbəl/ *adj* **1** (of persons) willing to be guided or controlled: *be ~ to kindness/advice/reason.* **2** liable to be called to account; answerable to: *We are all ~ to the law.*
amend /əˈmend/ *vt,vi* **1** improve; correct: *He'll have to ~ his ways,* improve his behavior. **2** make changes, eg in a rule, a proposed law, etc.
amend·able /-əbəl/ *adj*
amend·ment /əˈmendmənt/ *n* **1** [U] correcting. **2** [C] change proposed or made to a rule, etc. **3 Amendment,** (following its number) one of the adopted amendments to the US Constitution: *the Fourteenth Amendment.*
amends /əˈmendz/ *n pl* ***make amends (to sb) (for sth),*** make a suitable payment; apologize: *make ~ to a person for an injury.*
amen·ity /əˈminəti/ *n* (*pl* -ies) **1** (*pl*) things, circumstances, surroundings, that make life easy or pleasant: *a town with many amenities,* eg a park, a public library, etc. **2** [U] pleasantness: *the ~ of the Mediterranean climate.*
Amer. *abbr* = American.
Ameri·can /əˈmerɪkən/ *adj* of America, esp the US. □ *n* [C] native or inhabitant of America; citizen of the US.
Aˈmerican ˌplan, hotel rate which includes meals.

Ameri·can·ism /əˈmerıkəˌnızəm/ *n* **1** [C] word or phrase typical of American English. **2** [U] loyalty to the US or to things typically American.
am·ethyst /ˈæməθıst/ *n* precious stone which is purple or violet.
ami·able /ˈeimiəbəl/ *adj* (formal) friendly; good-natured: *I found him a most ~ person.*
amia·bil·ity /ˌeimiəˈbıləti/ *n* [U]
ami·ably /-əbli/ *adv*
amic·able /ˈæmıkəbəl/ *adj* with a friendly attitude: *They settled their dispute in an ~ way.*
amic·ably /-əbli/ *adv*
amid /əˈmıd/,ˌ æmi:dst /əˈmıdst/ *preps* among, in, the middle of.
amid·ships /əˈmıdˌʃıps/ *adv* (*naut*) halfway between the bow and stern of a ship.
amir, ameer = emir.
amiss /əˈmıs/ *pred adj, adv* wrong(ly); out of order: *He didn't think anything was ~ until he read the bad report.* ***take sth amiss,*** be hurt in one's feelings (esp too strongly): *Don't take it ~ if I point out your errors.*
am·ity /ˈæməti/ *n* [U] (*formal*) = friendship (the usual word).
am·me·ter /ˈæmˌmitər/ *n* [C] meter that measures electric current in amperes.
ammo /ˈæmou/ *n* [U] (*informal*) (short for) ammunition.
am·mo·nia /əˈmounyə/ *n* [U] (solution in water of a) strong, colorless gas (symbol $\mathbf{NH_3}$) with a sharp smell, used for household cleaning, in refrigeration, and for the manufacture of explosives and fertilizers.
am·mu·ni·tion /ˌæmyəˈnıʃən/ *n* [U] **1** explosives (bullets, shells, bombs, etc) for use against an enemy. **2** anything that can be thrown at a target.
am·nesia /æmˈniʒə/ *n* [U] (*med*) partial or total loss of memory.
am·nesty /ˈæmnəsti/ *n* [C] (*pl* -ies) general pardon, esp for political offenses: *The rebels returned home under an ~.*
amoeba /əˈmibə/ *n* [C] (*pl* ~s or ~e /-bi/) microscopic, shapeless form of living matter, found in water, soil, etc.
amoebic /əˈmibık/ *adj* of, caused by, amoebae: *~ dysentery.*
amok, amuck /əˈmək/ *adv* ***run amok,*** run about wildly (eg with a desire to kill people).
among /əˈməŋ/, ˌ æmɒngst /əˈməŋst/ *preps* **1** (showing position) surrounded by: in the middle of: *a village ~ the hills; hiding ~ the bushes.* (*Note:* the *noun* or *pronoun* must be more than two in number.) **2** (showing association, connection): *You are only one ~ many who need help.* **3** (followed by a *superl*) one of: *Detroit is ~ the most important industrial cities of the US.* **4** (showing division, distribution, possession, activity, to, for or by more than two persons): *You must settle the matter ~ yourselves.* ⇨ between. **5** (after a *prep*): *Choose one from ~ these.*
amoral /ˌeiˈmɔrəl/ *adj* not concerned with or having morals.
am·or·ous /ˈæmərəs/ *adj* easily moved to love; showing love; of (esp sexual) love: *~ looks; ~ poetry.*
am·or·ous·ly *adv*
amount /əˈmaunt/ *vi* ***amount to,*** add up to; be equal to: *His debts ~ to $5000. Riding on a bus without paying the fare ~s to* (= is the same thing as) *stealing.* □ *n* [C] **1** total; whole: *He owed me $100 but could pay only half that ~,* could only pay *$50.* **2** quantity: *A large ~ of money is spent on tobacco every year.*
amour /əˈmʊr/ *n* [C] love affair (esp a secret one).
amp /æmp/ *n* [C] (short for) ampere.
am·pere /ˈæmˌpır/ *n* [C] unit for measuring the strength of an electric current.
am·per·sand /ˈæmpərˌsænd/ *n* [C] the sign (&) used in writing and printing to mean "and".
am·phib·ian /æmˈfıbiən/ *n* [C] **1** animal able to live both on land and in water, eg a frog. **2** aircraft designed to take off from and land on either land or water. ⇨ illus at aircraft. **3** vehicle able to move in water and on land.
am·phibi·ous /æmˈfıbiəs/ *adj* adapted for both land and water.
amphi·theater /ˈæmfəˌθiətər/ *n* [C] round or oval building with rows of seats rising behind and above each other round an open space, used for public games and amusements.
am·phora /ˈæmfərə/ *n* [C] (*pl* ~s or ~e /-ri/) two-handled jar, used in ancient Greece and Rome for holding wine or oil.
ample /ˈæmpəl/ *adj* (-r, -st) **1** with plenty of space: *There's ~ room for the children.* **2** plentiful: *He has ~ resources,* is wealthy. **3** sufficient: *$5 will be ~ for my needs.*
am·ply /ˈæmpli/ *adv*
am·plify /ˈæmpləˌfai/ *vt* (*pt,pp* -ied) **1** make larger or fuller, esp give fuller information, more details, etc, about. **2** increase the strength of, esp sound.
am·pli·fi·ca·tion /ˌæmpləfıˈkeiʃən/ *n* [U]
am·pli·fier /ˈæmpləˌfaiər/ *n* [C] appliance for amplifying, esp sound.
am·pli·tude /ˈæmpləˌtud/ *n* [U] (*formal*) breadth; largeness; abundance.
am·pu·tate /ˈæmpyəˌteit/ *vt* cut off, eg an arm, a leg, by surgery.
am·pu·ta·tion /ˌæmpyəˈteiʃən/ *n* [C,U]
amt. *abbr* = amount.
Am·trak /ˈæmˌtræk/ *n* public corporation, officially the National Railroad Passenger Corporation, that provides rail passenger service between major cities in the US.
amuck = amok.
amu·let /ˈæmyəlıt/ *n* [C] thing worn in the belief or hope that it will protect (against evil, etc).
amuse /əˈmyuz/ *vt* **1** make time pass pleasantly for: *Keep the baby ~d with these toys.* **2** make (a person) laugh or smile: *His funny stories ~d all of us.*
amuse·ment /əˈmyuzmənt/ *n* **1** [U] state of being amused: *To the great ~ of everybody, the actor's beard fell off.* **2** [C] something that makes leisure time pass pleasantly: *There are plenty of ~s here — movies, theaters, concerts, sports, and so on.*
amus·ing /əˈmyuzıŋ/ *part adj* causing laughter or smiles: *an ~ story/storyteller.*

an /ən *strong form:* æn/ ➪ a².
an- /æn-, ən-/ *prefix* not; without: *anesthetic; anonymous.*
-an (also **-ian** or **-ean**) /-(i)ən/ *suffix* (*proper n* + -an = *n* or *adj*): *Mexican; Bostonian; European.*
anach·ron·ism /əˈnækrəˌnɪzəm/ *n* [C] **1** something out of date either now or in a description of past events: *In the sentence "Julius Caesar looked at his wristwatch and lifted the telephone receiver" there are two ~s.* **2** person, attitude, etc regarded (unfavorably) as out-of-date: *Is the Electoral College an ~?*
anach·ron·is·tic /əˌnækrəˈnɪstɪk/ *adj*
ana·conda /ˌænəˈkandə/ *n* [C] (*pl* ~s) large South American snake of the boa family.
anae·mia = anemia.
anaemic = anemic.
an·aes·thesia = anesthesia.
an·aes·thetic = anesthetic.
an·aes·the·tist = anesthetist.
an·aes·the·tize = anesthetize.
ana·gram /ˈænəˌgræm/ *n* word made from another by changing the order of the letters (eg *plum—lump*).
anal /ˈeinəl/ *adj* (*anat*) of the anus.
an·al·gesia /ˌænəlˈdʒiziə/ *n* [U] (*med*) condition of not feeling pain, without loss of consciousness.
an·al·gesic /ˌænəlˈdʒizɪk/ *n* [C] substance, eg an ointment, which relieves pain.
anal·og·ous /əˈnæləgəs/ *adj* similar or parallel: *The two processes are not ~ (with each other).*
anal·og·ous·ly *adv*
ana·logue, ana·log /ˈænəˌlɔg/ *n* [C] something that is similar to another thing.
anal·ogy /əˈnælədʒi/ *n* (*pl* -ies) **1** [C] partial likeness or agreement: *The teacher drew an ~ between the human heart and a pump.* **2** [U] process of reasoning between parallel cases: *argue by/from ~; on the ~ of.*
analy·sis /əˈnæləsɪs/ *n* (*pl* -ses /-ˌsiz/) **1** [C,U] (instance of) analyzing, eg a book, a situation, information, etc, possibly with comment and judgment about: *a critical ~ of a poem; an ~ of the news.* **2** [C,U] (*chem*) separation or identification of the ingredients that make up a substance. **3** [C] statement of the result of analyzing. **4** [C,U] = psychoanalysis.
ana·lyst /ˈænəlɪst/ *n* [C] **1** person who analyzes or is skilled in making (esp chemical) analyses: *a food analyst.* **2** = psychoanalyst.
ana·lytic /ˌænəˈlɪtɪk/, **-i·cal** /-kəl/ *adj* of or using analysis.
ana·lyti·cally /-kli/ *adv*
ana·lyze /ˈænəˌlaiz/ *vt* **1** examine (a thing) in order to learn what it is made up of: *If we ~ water, we find that it is made up of two parts of hydrogen and one part of oxygen.* **2** study or examine in order to learn about: *He ~d the situation and told us what we had done wrong.* **3** = psychoanalyze.
an·arch·ism /ˈænərˌkɪzəm/ *n* [U] political theory that government and laws are undesirable.
an·arch·ist /ˈænərkɪst/ *n* [C] person who favors anarchism.
an·archy /ˈænərki/ *n* [U]. **1** absence of government or control. **2** disorder.
an·archic /əˈnarkɪk/ *adj*
an·archi·cally /-kli/ *adv*
anath·ema /əˈnæθəmə/ *n* [C] **1** formal declaration by church authorities excommunicating a person or condemning something as evil. **2** thing that is detested.
anat·omy /əˈnætəmi/ *n* [U] science of the structure of animal bodies; study of their structures by separation into parts.
ana·tomi·cal /ˌænəˈtamɪkəl/ *adj*
anat·om·ist /əˈnætəmɪst/ *n* [C] person who studies or teaches anatomy.
-ance, -ence /-əns/ *suffix* **1** (*v* + ~ = *n*): *assistance; confidence.* **2** (*adj* + ~ = *n*): *brilliance.*
an·ces·tor /ˈænˌsestər/ *n* [C] anyone from whom a person is descended, esp one more remote than a grandparent.
an·ces·tral /ænˈsestrəl/ *adj* belonging to, having come from, one's ancestors: *his ~ home.*
an·ces·tress /ˈænˌsestrɪs/ *n* [C] woman ancestor.
an·ces·try /ˈænˌsestri/ *n* [C] (*pl* -ies) line of ancestors.
an·chor /ˈæŋkər/ *n* [C] **1** heavy piece of iron used for keeping a ship in place. **2** any thing or person that gives stability or security. □ *vt, vi* **1** make (a ship) secure with an anchor. **2** hold in place.
an·chor·age /ˈæŋkərɪdʒ/ *n* [C] place where ships may anchor safely.
an·chor·man /ˈæŋkərˌmæn/ *n* [C] (*pl* -men /-ˌmen/) person broadcasting on radio or television who is in charge of a program and of putting together news stories and information from other reporters.
an·chovy /ˈænˌtʃouvi/ *n* [C] (*pl* -ies) small fish, similar to a herring, with a strong flavor, used for sauces, etc.
ancient /ˈeinʃənt/ *adj* **1** belonging to times long past: *~ Rome and Greece.* **2** (often *hum*) very old: *an ~-looking hat.*
an·cil·lary /ˈænsəˌleri/ *adj* **1** helping, providing a service to those carrying on the main business. **2** secondary: *~ roads/undertakings/industries.*
-ancy /-ənsi/ *suffix* (*adj* + ~ = *n*): *constancy.*
and /*usual forms:* end, en; *strong form:* ænd/ *conj* **1** (connecting words, clauses, sentences): *a table and four chairs; learning to read and write.* (*Note:* when two *nouns* stand for things or persons closely connected, *a* or *the* is not repeated before the second *noun*: *a knife and fork.*) **2** (replacing an *if*-clause): *Work hard and you will pass* (= If you work hard, you will pass) *the examination.* **3** (showing repetition or continuation): *for hours and hours; better and better.* **4** (*informal*, after some *verbs*) to: *Try and come early.*
and·iron /ˈænˌdaiərn/ *n* [C] one of a pair of metal supports for holding wood in a fireplace.
an·ec·dote /ˈænɪkˌdout/ *n* [C] short, usually amusing, story about a real person or event.
anemia /əˈnimiə/ *n* [U] **1** lack of enough blood. **2** poor condition of the blood, causing paleness.
ane·mic /əˈnimɪk/ *adj*
anem·o·ne /əˈneməni/ *n* [C] small star-shaped woodland flower or cultivated varieties of this

flower.
ˈ**sea anemone,** popular name of a creature living in the sea, having flower-like tentacles.
an·es·thesia /ˌænəsˈθiʒə/ *n* [U] state of being unable to feel (pain, heat, cold, etc).
an·es·the·tic /ˌænəsˈθetɪk/ *n* [C] substance, eg ether, chloroform, etc that produces anesthesia. ⇨ local (2).
an·es·the·tist /əˈnesθətɪst/ *n* [C] person trained to give anesthetics.
an·es·the·tize /əˈnesθəˌtaiz/ *vt* make (a person) unable to feel pain, etc.
anew /əˈnu/ *adv* again; in a new or different way.
angel /ˈeindʒəl/ *n* [C] **1** (esp in Christian belief) messenger from God (usually shown in pictures as a human being with wings). **2** person who is lovely or good as an angel. (as a compliment): *Thanks, you're an ~!*
an·gelic /ænˈdʒelɪk/ *adj* of or like an angel.
an·geli·cally /-kli/ *adv*
anger /ˈæŋgər/ *n* [U] strong feeling of displeasure or rage that comes when one has been wronged or insulted, or when one sees cruelty or injustice: *filled with ~; do something in a moment of ~.* □ *vt* make (a person) angry: *He is easily ~ed.*
angle[1] /ˈæŋgəl/ *n* [C] **1** space between two lines or surfaces that meet: *an acute/obtuse ~.* **2** (*fig*) point of view: *What ~ are you using in the story?* □ *vt* **1** move, turn or bend an angle. **2** (of a story, report, etc) tell from a certain point of view.
angle[2] /ˈæŋgəl/ *vi* **1** fish with a hook and bait. **2** (*fig*) use tricks, hints, etc in order to get something: *~ for an invitation to a party.*
angler /ˈæŋglər/ *n* [C] person who angles.
Ang·li·can /ˈæŋglɪkən/ *n* [C], *adj* (member) of the Church of England.
ang·li·cize /ˈæŋgləˌsaiz/ *vt* make English or like English: *~ a French word.*
Anglo /ˈæŋˌglou/ *n* [C] (*informal*) Anglo-American. ⇨ Anglo-.
Anglo- /ˌæŋˌglou-/ *combined form* English; British; of the United Kingdom: *~-French relations,* between the United Kingdom and France.
ˌ**Anglo-A**ˈ**merican** *n* [C] (in the US southwest) American of Anglo-Saxon descent, as opposed to a Mexican-American.
ˌ**Anglo-**ˈ**Saxon** *n* [C], *adj* (person) of English descent; race of people who settled in England before the Norman Conquest; their language (also called *Old English*).
an·gora /æŋˈgɔrə/ *n* [U] fluffy yarn made from the long, silk hair of certain rabbits or goats.
angry /ˈæŋgri/ *adv* (-ier, -iest) **1** filled with, showing anger: *He was ~ at being kept waiting.* **2** (of a cut, sore, wound) red; inflamed. **3** (of the sea, sky, clouds) stormy; threatening.
angri·ly /ˈæŋgrɪli/ *adv*
an·guish /ˈæŋgwɪʃ/ *n* [U] severe mental or physical suffering: *She was in ~ until she knew that her husband's life had been saved.*
an·guished *adj* expressing suffering: *~ed looks.*
angu·lar /ˈæŋgyələr/ *adj* **1** having angles or sharp corners. **2** (of persons) thin and bony. **3** (of a person's nature, etc) rather stiff and awkward.
angu·lar·ity /ˌæŋyəˈlærəti/ *n* [C,U]
ani·mal /ˈænəməl/ *n* [C] **1** living thing that can feel and move about: *Men, horses, birds, flies, fish, snakes are all ~s.* **2** four-footed animal such as a dog or horse. **3** any animal other than man. **4** (as an *adj*) physical, not spiritual; of animals(1).
the ˈ**animal kingdom,** all animals, as contrasted with vegetables or minerals.
ani·mate /ˈænəmət/ *adj* living; lively. □ *vt* /ˈænəˌmeit/ **1** give life to. **2** make lively. **3** inspire; move to action: *~d us to greater efforts.*
animated carˈ**toon,** motion picture film made by photographing a series of drawings.
ani·ma·tion /ˌænəˈmeiʃən/ *n* [U] **(a)** liveliness; spirit. **(b)** process of making animated cartoons.
ani·mos·ity /ˌænəˈmasəti/ *n* (*pl* -ies) **1** [U] strong hatred, active hostility. **2** [C] instance of this.
an·ise /ˈænɪs/ *n* herb with sweet-smelling seeds.

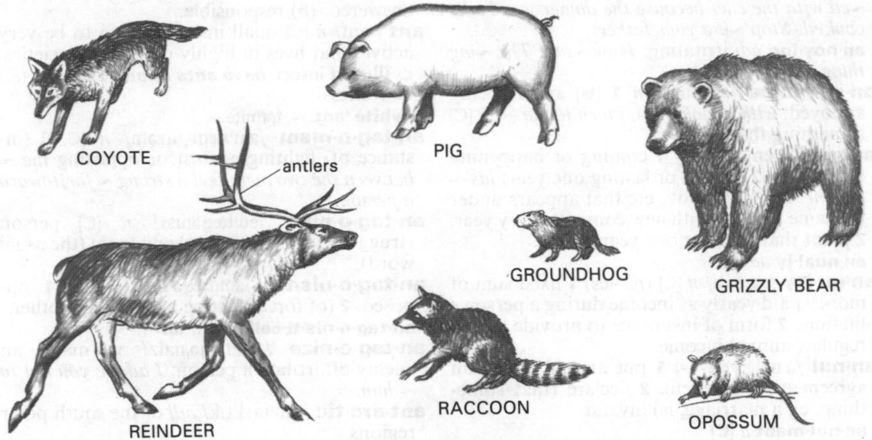

ANIMALS

ani·seed /ˈænɪˌsid/ *n* [U] seed of anise, used for flavoring.

ankle /ˈæŋkəl/ *n* [C] **1** joint connecting the foot with the leg. ➪ illus at leg. **2** thin part of the leg between this joint and the calf.

an·nals /ˈænəlz/ *n pl* **1** story of events year by year. **2** historical records.

an·nex[1] /ˈæˌneks/ *n* [C] something annexed, esp smaller building added to, or situated near, a larger one: *a hotel* ~.

an·nex[2] /əˈneks, ˈæˌneks/ *vt* **1** take possession of (territory, etc). **2** add or join to (something) (as a secondary part).

an·nex·ation /ˌænekˈseiʃən/ *n* [C,U]

an·ni·hi·late /əˈnaiəˌleit/ *vt* destroy completely; end the existence of (eg an army, a fleet): *The invasion force was ~d.*

an·ni·hi·la·tion /əˌnaiəˈleiʃən/ *n* [U] complete destruction.

an·ni·ver·sary /ˌænəˈvərsəri/ *n* [C] (*pl* -ies) (celebration of the) yearly return of the date of an event: *my ˈwedding ~; the ~ of the Declaration of Independence.*

an·no Dom·ini /ˌænou ˈdamənai/ (*Lat, abbr* **AD** /ˌei ˈdi/) in the year of our Lord: *in* AD *250,* 250 years after the birth of Christ. ➪ before[3](1).

an·no·tate /ˈænəˌteit/ *vt* add notes (to a book, etc) explaining difficulties, giving opinions, etc: *an ~d text/version.*

an·no·ta·tion /ˌænəˈteiʃən/ *n* **(a)** [U] annotating. **(b)** [C] note or comment.

an·nounce /əˈnauns/ *vt* **1** make known to the public: *Mr. Green ~d (to his friends) his engagement to Miss White.* **2** make known the arrival of: *The secretary ~d Mr. and Mrs. Brown,* spoke their names as they entered. **3** say that somebody is about to speak, sing, etc.

an·nounce·ment *n* [C] something said, written, or printed to make known what has happened or (more often) what will happen: *An ~ment will be made next week.*

an·nouncer *n* [C] person who makes announcements, esp on radio or TV

an·noy /əˈnɔi/ *vt* irritate; make angry: *He was ~ed with the chef because the dinner was badly cooked. Stop ~ing your father!*

an·noy·ing *adj* irritating: *How ~ing! The ~ing thing about it is that....*

an·noy·ance /əˈnɔiəns/ *n* **1** [U] anger; being annoyed: *with a look of ~; much to our ~.* **2** [C] something that annoys.

an·nual /ˈænyuəl/ *adj* **1** coming or happening every year. **2** of, for, or lasting one year: *his ~ income.* □ *n* [C] **1** book, etc that appears under the same title but with new contents every year. **2** plant that lives for one year or less.

an·nual·ly *adv*

an·nu·ity /əˈnuəti/ *n* [C] (*pl* -ies) **1** fixed sum of money paid yearly as income during a person's lifetime. **2** form of insurance to provide such a regular, annual income.

an·nul /əˈnəl/ *vt* (-ll-) **1** put an end to, eg an agreement, a law, etc. **2** declare (that something, eg a marriage, is) invalid.

an·nul·ment *n* [C]

an·ode /ˈæˌnoud/ *n* [C] (*electr*) **1** positively charged electrode. **2** positive terminal of a battery. ➪ cathode.

anoint /əˈnɔint/ *vt* apply oil or ointment to (eg as a religious act): *~ a person with oil.*

anoint·ment *n* [C,U]

anom·al·ous /əˈnamələs/ *adj* irregular; abnormal.

anom·al·ous·ly *adv*

anom·aly /əˈnaməli/ *n* [C] (*pl* -ies) abnormal thing: *A bird that cannot fly is an ~.*

anon[1] /əˈnan/ *adv* (*old use*) soon.

anon.[2] *abbr* = anonymous.

ano·nym·ity /ˌænəˈnɪməti/ *n* [U] state of being anonymous.

anony·mous /əˈnanəməs/ *adj* without a name, or with a name that is not (made) known: *an ~ letter,* not signed; *an ~ gift,* from a person whose name is not known.

anony·mous·ly *adv*

anoph·eles /əˈnafəˌliz/ *n* (kinds of) mosquito, esp the kinds that spread malaria.

an·other /əˈnəðər/ *adj pron* **1** an additional (one): *Would you like ~ cup of coffee/~ (one)?* **2** a similar (one): *He thinks he's ~ Napoleon,* a man like Napoleon. **3** a different (one): *We can do that ~ time. That's quite ~ matter.*

answer[1] /ˈænsər/ *n* **1** something done in return; reply: *Have you had an ~ to your letter?* ***in answer to,*** as a reply to: *in ~ to your letter.* **2** solution; result of working with numbers, etc: *The ~ to* 3 × 17 *is* 51.

answer[2] /ˈænsər/ *vt,vi* **1** say, write or do in return or reply: *Have you ~ed his letter? No one ~ed.* ***answer the door,*** open the door when somebody has knocked or rung the bell. ***answer the (tele)phone,*** pick up the receiver when it has rung. **2** be suitable or satisfactory for: *Will this ~ your purpose?* **3** (special uses with *adverbial particles* and *prepositions*): ***answer back,*** be impolite, esp when told one has done wrong.

answer for, **(a)** be responsible for: *I can't ~ for his honesty.* **(b)** be punished for: *If the police catch you, you'll have a lot to ~ for.*

answer·able /-əbəl/ *adj* **(a)** that can be answered. **(b)** responsible.

ant /ænt/ *n* [C] small insect, known to be very active, that lives in highly organized societies. ➪ illus at insect. ***have ants in one's pants,*** (*sl*) be restless.

ˌwhite ˈant = termite.

an·tag·o·nism /ænˈtægəˌnɪzəm/ *n* [C,U] (instance of) fighting against or opposing *the ~ between the two men; feel a strong ~ for/toward a person.*

an·tag·o·nist /ænˈtægənɪst/ *n* [C] person struggling against another; opponent (the usual word).

an·tag·o·nis·tic /ænˌtægəˈnɪstɪk/ *adj* **1** opposed. **2** (of forces) acting against each other.

an·tag·o·nis·ti·cally /-kli/ *adv*

an·tag·o·nize /ˌænˈtægəˌnaiz/ *vt* make an enemy of; irritate a person: *I advise you not to ~ him.*

ant·arc·tic /ˌænˈtarktɪk/ *adj* of the south polar regions.

the ˌAntarctic ˈCircle, line of latitude about 23° from the South Pole.

ante- /ˈæntɪ-/ *prefix* **1** in front of: *~room.* **2** before: *~nuptial,* before marriage.
ant·eater /ˈæntˌitər/ *n* [C] any of various animals that live on ants.
ante·bel·lum /ˌæntɪˈbeləm/ *adj* before the war, esp the Civil War (1861-65).
ante·ced·ence /ˌæntəˈsidəns/ *n* [U] (*formal*) priority.
ante·ced·ent /ˌæntəˈsidənt/ *adj* previous (to). □ *n* [C] **1** preceding event or circumstance. **2** (*pl*) ancestors; past history of a person or persons. **3** (*gram*) noun, clause or sentence, to which a following pronoun or adverb refers.
ante·cham·ber /ˈæntɪˌtʃeimbər/ *n* [C] room leading into a larger room or hall.
ante·date /ˌæntɪˈdeit/ *vt* **1** put a date on, eg a letter, document, etc, earlier than the true one; give an earlier date than the true one to (an event). **2** come before in time: *This event ~s the arrival of Columbus by several centuries.*
ante·di·luvian /ˌæntɪdɪˈluviən/ *adj* **1** of the time before the (Biblical) Flood. **2** (*fig*) old-fashioned; out-of-date.
ante·lope /ˈæntəˌloup/ *n* [C] deer-like, fast-running animal with thin legs.
ante·natal /ˌæntɪˈneitəl/ *adj* = prenatal.
an·tenna /ænˈtenə/ *n* [C] (*pl* ~e /-ni/) **1** jointed organ found in pairs on the head of insects, shellfish, etc., used for feeling, etc. ⇨ illus at crustacean, insect. **2** that part of a radio or TV system which receives.
an·ter·ior /ænˈtɪriər/ *adj* coming before (in time or position).
an·them /ˈænθəm/ *n* [C] musical composition to be sung in churches.
ˌnational ˈanthem, song or hymn of a country, eg "The Star-Spangled Banner."
an·ther /ˈænθər/ *n* [C] part of a flower containing pollen. ⇨ illus at flower.
ant·hill /ˈæntˌhɪl/ *n* [C] pile of earth, etc over an underground nest of ants.
an·thol·ogy /ænˈθalədʒi/ *n* [C] (*pl* -ies) collection of poems or pieces of prose, or of both, by different writers, or a selection from the work of one writer.
an·thra·cite /ˈænθrəˌsait/ *n* [U] very hard form of coal that burns with little smoke or flame.
anthrop(o)- /ænθrəp(ə)-/ *combined form* of man(kind): *anthropology.*
an·thro·poid /ˈænθrəˌpɔid/ *adj* man-like. □ *n* [C] man-like animal, eg a gorilla.
an·thro·po·logi·cal /ˌænθrəpəˈladʒɪkəl/ *adj* of anthropology.
an·thro·pol·ogist /ˌænθrəˈpalədʒɪst/ *n* [C] expert in, student of anthropology.
an·thro·pol·ogy /ˌænθrəˈpalədʒi/ *n* [U] science of man, esp of his beginnings, development, customs and beliefs.
anti- /ˌæntai-, ˌæntɪ-/ *prefix* against: ˌ~ˈ*Russian.*
anti·air·craft /ˌæntɪˈerˌkræft/ *adj* used against enemy aircraft: *~ guns.*
anti·biotic /ˌæntɪbaiˈatɪk/ *n* [C], *adj* (substance produced by molds and bacteria, eg penicillin) capable of destroying or preventing the growth of bacteria.
anti·body /ˈæntɪˌbadi/ *n* [C] (*pl* -ies) (kinds of) substance formed in the blood tending to inhibit or destroy harmful bacteria, etc.
an·tici·pate /ænˈtɪsəˌpeit/ *vt* **1** do, make use of, before the right or natural time. **2** do before somebody else does it: *It is said that Columbus discovered America, but he was probably ~d by sailors from Norway who reached Labrador 500 years earlier.* **3** see what needs doing, what is likely to happen, etc and do what is necessary: *He tries to ~ all my needs,* satisfy them before I mention them. **4** expect: *We are anticipating a large crowd.*
an·tici·pa·tion /ænˌtɪsəˈpeiʃən/ *n* [C,U] (action of) anticipating; expectation, esp of something pleasant.
anti·cli·max /ˌæntɪˈklaiˌmæks/ *n* [C] sudden fall from something serious and important to the trivial and unimportant; descent that contrasts with a previous rise.
anti·cli·mac·tic /ˌæntɪklaiˈmæktɪk/ *adj*
an·tics /ˈæntɪks/ *n pl* **1** unusual or clever tricks, acts, etc intended to amuse, eg by a clown at a circus. **2** odd behavior.
anti·cyc·lone /ˌæntɪˈsaiˌkloun/ *n* [C] area in which atmospheric pressure is high compared with that of surrounding areas, giving cool, dry weather.
anti·dote /ˈæntɪˌdout/ *n* [C] **1** medicine used against a poison: *an ~ against/for/to snakebite.* **2** any remedy against evil.
anti·freeze /ˈæntɪˌfriz/ *n* [U] substance added to another liquid (eg in the radiator of a motor vehicle) to prevent freezing.
anti-hero /ˈæntɪˌhɪrou/ *n* [C] (*pl* ~es) (in fiction and drama) leading character lacking the traditional characteristics of a hero, such as courage and dignity.
an·tipa·thy /ænˈtɪpəθi/ *n* (*pl* -ies) **1** [U] strong dislike. **2** [C] instance or object of this: *feel/show a strong ~ to a place/toward a person.*
an·tipo·des /ænˈtɪpəˌdiz/ *n pl* **the antipodes,** (two) place(s) on the opposite sides of the earth, eg the North and South Poles.
anti·quated /ˈæntɪˌkweitɪd/ *adj* obsolete; out-of-date; (of persons) having old-fashioned ideas and ways.
an·tique /ˌænˈtik/ *adj* belonging to the distant past; existing since old times; in the style of past times. □ *n* [C] object (eg a piece of furniture, a work of art) of a past period.
an·tiquity /ˌænˈtɪkwəti/ *n* **1** [U] ancient times, esp before the Middle Ages: *the heroes of ~; a city of great ~,* eg Athens. **2** [C] (*pl* -ies) buildings, ruins, works of art, remaining from ancient times: *Greek and Roman antiquities.*
anti-Sem·ite /ˌæntɪˈseˌmait/ *n* [C], *adj* (person) hostile to or discriminating against Jews.
anti-Sem·itic /ˌæntɪsəˈmɪtɪk/ *adj*
anti-Semi·tism /ˌæntɪˈseməˌtɪzəm/ *n* [U]
anti·sep·tic /ˌæntəˈseptɪk/ *n* [C] *adj* (substance) preventing disease, esp by destroying germs.
anti·so·cial /ˌæntɪˈsouʃəl/ *adj* **1** opposed to social laws or to organized societies. **2** (*informal*) against the general welfare: *It is ~ to leave litter in public places.* **3** unsociable.
an·tith·esis /ænˈtɪθəsɪs/ *n* (*pl* -ses /-ˌsiz/) **1** [U] direct opposite. **2** [U] opposition: *the ~ of good to evil.* **3** [C] instance of this; balanced contrast

of ideas, as in "Give me liberty, or give me death."

anti·toxin /ˌæntɪˈtaksɪn/ *n* [C] substance, formed in the blood, that helps in overcoming a disease.

ant·ler /ˈæntlər/ *n* [C] branch of a horn (of a stag or other deer). ⇨ illus at animal.

an·to·nym /ˈæntəˌnɪm/ *n* [C] word that is opposite in meaning to another: *Hot is the ~ of cold.* ⇨ synonym.

anus /ˈeinəs/ *n* [C] (*anat*) opening at the end of the alimentary canal, through which solid waste matter passes out.

an·vil /ˈænvəl/ *n* [C] **1** large, heavy block of iron on which heated metal is hammered into shape. **2** (*anat*) bone in the ear. ⇨ illus at ear.

anxiety /æŋˈzaiəti/ *n* (*pl* -ies) **1** [U] emotional condition in which there is fear and uncertainty about the future: *We waited with ~ for news of her safe arrival.* **2** [C] instance of such a feeling: *All these anxieties made him look pale and tired.* **3** [U] keen desire: *~ to please his employers.*

anxious /ˈæŋkʃəs/ *adj* **1** feeling anxiety; troubled: *I am very ~ about my son's health.* **2** causing anxiety: *We have had an ~ time.* **3** ***anxious to/for/about/that,*** strongly wishing: *He was ~ to meet you/~ for his brother to meet you. We were ~ that help should be sent /~ for help to be sent.*

anxious·ly *adv*

anxious·ness /-nɪs/ *n* [U]

any[1] /ˈeni/ *adj* **1** one or some (of an amount, quantity or a number, usually more than two): *Have you any milk? They haven't any children. Are there any flowers left?* (*Note: any* is used in questions and in negative sentences; with verbs such as *prevent, doubt*, etc; after *without, hardly*, etc): *We did it without any help. I've hardly any left.* **2** (used for *every*): *Any child knows better.* **3** one or another, no matter which: *Come any day you like.* **4** (in negative sentences): a, one: *This is useless — it hasn't any handle.*

at ˈany rate, = in any case.

in ˈany case, whatever happens; even considering the facts: *It's too late now, in any case.*

any[2] /ˈeni/ *adv* at all; to even a little extent: *Is he feeling any better? We can't go any further.* (*Note: any* is used in questions, negative sentences and with *comparatives.*)

any[3] /ˈeni/ *pron* = some.

any·body /ˈeniˌbadi, -ˌbədi/ *n, pron* **1** a person, but not a particular one: *Is ~ there? We couldn't see ~.* (*Note:* used in questions and negative sentences.) ⇨ somebody, someone. **2** (in statements, etc) no matter who: *Anybody will tell you where the bus stop is.* **3** person of importance: *You must work harder if you wish to be ~.*

anybody else, ⇨ else[1].

any·how /ˈeniˌhau/ *adv* **1** in any possible way; by any possible means: *The house was empty, and I couldn't get in ~ I tried.* **2** = in any case: *It's too late now, ~.*

any·one /ˈeniˌwən/ *n, pron* = anybody.

any·thing /ˈeniˌθɪŋ/ *n, pron* **1** an event, happening, but not a particular one: *Has ~ unusual happened?* (*Note:* used in questions, negative sentences, etc.) ⇨ something. **2** no matter what: *I want something to eat; ~ will do. He is ~ but mad,* far from being mad. **3** (used to intensify a meaning): *The thief ran like ~ when he saw the policeman. It's* (*as*) *easy as anything,* (*informal*) very easy.

APES AND MONKEYS

any·way /ˈeniˌwei/ *adj* = anyhow.

any·where /ˈeniˌ(h)wer/ *adv* **1** to any place: *I'm not going ~ without you. Are we going ~ (in) particular?* (*Note:* used in questions, negative sentences, etc. ⇨ somewhere.) **2** a place, but not a particular one: *That leaves me without ~ to keep all my books.* **3** no matter where: *Put the box down ~. We'll go ~ you like.*

A one /ˌei ˈwən/ *adj* ⇨ A[1].

aorta /eiˈɔrtə/ *n* [C] (*pl* ~s) chief bloodvessel through which blood is carried from the left side of the heart. ⇨ illus at respiratory.

AP /ˌei ˈpi/ *abbr* = Associated Press.

apart /əˈpart/ *adv* **1** distant; not together: *The two houses are 500 yards ~. The negotiating sides are still miles ~,* show no signs of agreeing. **2** to or on one side (the usual words). ***joking apart,*** speaking seriously. **3** separate(ly): *He was standing with his feet wide ~.* ***apart from,*** independently of; leaving on one side: *~ from these reasons.* ***tell/know two things or persons apart,*** distinguish one from the other. ⇨ also come(11), take[1](17).

apart·heid /əˈpartˌheit/ *n* (South African policy of) racial segregation; separate development of Europeans and non-Europeans.

apart·ment /əˈpartmənt/ *n* [C] **1** room or set of rooms, for living in. **2** apartment house.

aˈpartment house, building divided into apartments(1).

apa·thetic /ˌæpəˈθetɪk/ *adj* showing or having apathy.

apa·theti·cally /-kli/ *adv*

apa·thy /ˈæpəθi/ *n* [U] absence of concern or interest.

ape /eip/ *n* [C] **1** tailless monkey (gorilla, chimpanzee, orangutan, gibbon). **2** person who copies the behavior of others. **3** (*informal*) large, clumsy person. □ *vt* copy (a person's behavior, etc), often badly or clumsily.

aperi·tif /əˌperəˈtɪf/ *n* [C] alcoholic drink, (eg vermouth) taken as an appetizer.

ap·er·ture /ˈæpərˌtʃʊr/ *n* [C] opening, esp one that admits light, eg to a camera lens.

apex /ˈeiˌpeks/ *n* [C] (*pl* ~es or apices /ˈeipəˌsiz/) top or highest point: *the ~ of a triangle/his career/fortunes.*

apiece /əˈpis/ *adv* to, for or by, each one of a group: *They cost a nickel ~,* each.

apish /ˈeipɪʃ/ *adj* of or like an ape; foolishly imitative.

aplomb /əˈplam/ *n* [U] self-confidence (in speech or behavior): *He answered with perfect ~.*

apoca·lypse /əˈpakəˌlɪps/ *n* revelation (esp of knowledge from God).

the Apocalypse, the last book in the New Testament.

Apoc·ry·pha /əˈpakrəfə/ *n* (used with a *sing verb*) those books of the Old Testament considered of doubtful authorship, as well as certain early Christian writings, that are not included in the Jewish and Protestant Bibles.

apoc·ry·phal /əˈpakrəfəl/ *adj* of doubtful authority or authorship.

apolo·getic /əˌpaləˈdʒetɪk/ *adj* making an apology; excusing a fault or failure: *He was ~ for arriving late.*

apolo·geti·cally /-kli/ *adv*

apolo·gize /əˈpaləˌdʒaiz/ *vi* ***apologize (to sb) (for sth),*** make an apology; say one is sorry: *You must ~ to your sister for being so rude.*

apol·ogy /əˈpalədʒi/ *n* [C] (*pl.* -ies) statement of being sorry (for doing wrong, hurting someone's feelings): *make one's apologies (to a person),* eg for being late, for not being able to come. ***poor apology for,*** a poor example of, eg a dinner/letter.

apo·plec·tic /ˌæpəˈplektɪk/ *adj* **1** causing or suffering from apoplexy. **2** (*informal*) red in the face; easily made angry.

apo·plexy /ˈæpəˌpleksi/ *n* [U] loss of the ability to feel, move, etc caused by the breaking of a blood vessel in the brain or by a clot in a blood vessel.

a pos·teri·ori /ˌei ˌpastɪriˈɔˌrai/ *adv, adj phrase* (*Lat*) (reasoning) from effects to causes, eg saying, *"The boys are tired so they must have walked a long way."* ⇨ a priori.

apostle /əˈpasəl/ *n* [C] **1** (in Christian belief) one of the twelve men chosen by Christ to spread His teaching, also St. Barnabas and St. Paul. **2** leader or teacher of reform, of a new faith or movement.

apos·tolic /ˌæpəˈstalɪk/ *adj* **1** of the apostles(1) or the times when they lived. **2** of the Pope.

apos·trophe /əˈpastrəfi/ *n* [C] the sign (') used to show omission of letter(s) or number(s), (as in *can't, I'm, '05,* for *cannot, I am, 1905*), for the possessive (as in *boy's, boys'*), and for the plurals of letters and numbers (as in *There are two l's in "bell"*).

apoth·ecary /əˈpaθəˌkeri/ *n* [C] (*pl* -ies) (*old use*) person who prepares and sells medicines and medical goods.

app. *abbr* = appendix.

ap·pall, ap·pal /əˈpɔl/ *vt* (-ll-) fill with fear or dismay; shock deeply: *They were ~ed at the news.*

ap·pal·ling *adj*

ap·pa·ratus /ˌæpəˈrætəs, -ˈreitəs/ *n* [C] (*pl* ~es) **1** set of tools, instruments or machinery for a particular purpose. **2** group of organs of the body by which natural processes are carried on: *your digestive ~.*

ap·parel /əˈpærəl/ *n* [U] dress; clothing.

ap·par·ent /əˈpærənt/ *adj* **1** clearly seen or understood: *It was ~ to all of us that he was lying,* we all saw clearly that he was lying. **2** appearing but not necessarily true or genuine: *the ~ cause but not the real one.*

ap·par·ent·ly *adv*

ap·pa·rition /ˌæpəˈrɪʃən/ *n* [C] strange or unexpected sight, esp of a ghost or the spirit of a dead person.

ap·peal /əˈpiəl/ *vi* (-ing /əˈpilɪŋ/) ***appeal (to sb) for/from (against),*** **1** make an earnest request: *The prisoner ~ed to the judge for mercy.* **2** (*legal*) take a case to a higher court for review. **3** attract; move the feelings of: *Do these paintings ~ to you?* □ *n* **1** [C] an earnest call for: *make an ~ for help.* **2** [C] act of appealing(2). **3** (power of) attraction: *That sort of music hasn't much ~ for me/has lost its ~.* **4** [U] asking for help or sympathy: *with a look of ~ on her face.*

ap·peal·ing /əˈpilɪŋ/ *adj* **(a)** moving; touching the feelings or sympathy. **(b)** attractive.

ap·peal·ing·ly *adv*

ap·pear /əˈpɪr/ *vi* **1** come into view, become visible: *When we reached the top of the hill, the town ~ed below us. The ship ~ed on the horizon.* **2** arrive: *He promised to come at 4 but didn't ~ until 6.* **3 (a)** (of an actor, singer, lecturer, etc) come before the public: *He has ~ed in every large concert hall in Europe.* **(b)** (of a book) be published: *When will your new novel ~?* **(c)** (*legal*) present oneself: *The defendant failed to ~ before the court.* **4** look; seem: *Why does she ~ so sad?*

ap·pear·ance /əˈpɪrəns/ *n* [C] **1** act of appearing: *make one's first ~,* (of an actor, singer, etc) appear in public for the first time. **2** that which shows or can be seen; what a thing or person appears to be: *The child had the ~ of being* (= looked as if it were) *half-starved.*

ap·pease /əˈpiz/ *vt* make quiet, calm, or less angry.

ap·pease·ment *n* [U]

ap·pel·late /əˈpelɪt/ *adj* (*legal*) authorized to review (lower) court decisions on appeal: *~ court.*

ap·pend /əˈpend/ *vt* (*formal*) add to something larger: *~ a signature to a document.*

ap·pend·age /əˈpendɪdʒ/ *n* [C] something added to, fastened to or forming a natural part of, a larger thing.

ap·pen·di·ci·tis /əˌpendəˈsaitɪs/ *n* [U] diseased condition of the appendix(2).

ap·pen·dix /əˈpendɪks/ *n* [C] (*pl* ~es or -dices /-dɪˌsiz/) **1** something added, esp at the end of a book. **2** small outgrowth on a bodily organ, esp the large intestine.

ap·per·tain /ˌæpərˈtein/ *vi* (*formal*) belong to as a right: *the duties ~ing to his office.*

ap·pe·tite /ˈæpəˌtait/ *n* **1** [C,U] physical desire, esp for food: *The long walk gave him a good ~.* **2** (*fig*) enthusiasm: *He had no ~ for the fight.*

ap·pe·tizer /ˈæpəˌtaizər/ *n* [C] something that encourages the appetite(1).

ap·pe·tiz·ing *adj* exciting the appetite: *an appetizing smell from the kitchen.*

ap·plaud /əˈplɔd/ *vi,vt* **1** show approval (of) by clapping the hands: *The audience ~ed (the singer) for five minutes. He was loudly ~ed.* **2** express approval of; agree with: *I ~ your decision.*

ap·plause /əˈplɔz/ *n* [U] loud approval; handclapping.

apple /ˈæpəl/ *n* [C] (tree with a) round fruit with firm juicy flesh and a thin skin. ⇨ illus at fruit. ***the apple of one's eye,*** thing or person dearly loved.

ˈAdam's apple, ⇨ Adam.

ap·pli·ance /əˈplaiəns/ *n* [C] piece of equipment or apparatus: *an ~* (= tool) *for opening tin cans; household ~s,* eg a washing-machine.

ap·pli·cable /ˈæplɪkəbəl/ *adj* that can be applied; that is suitable and proper: *Is the rule ~ to this case?*

ap·pli·cant /ˈæplɪkənt/ *n* [C] person who applies, eg for work: *There were no ~s for the job.*

ap·p·li·ca·tion /ˌæpləˈkeiʃən/ *n* **1** [U] putting one thing on to another: *He suggests an ~ of this cream to small cuts only.* [C,U] substance used: *This ~ is for burns and cuts.* **2** [U] putting to a special or practical use: *the ~ of a new technical process to industry.* **3** [U] effort; close attention: *If you show ~ in your studies* (= If you work hard) *you will succeed.* **4** [C] request (esp in writing): *We made an ~ to the manager for an interview.*

ˌappliˈcation form, one to be filled in when asking for a job, membership, etc.

ap·pli·ca·tor /ˈæpləˌkeitər/ *n* [C] device for applying, eg medicine, paint, polish, etc.

ap·plied /əˈplaid/ *adj* put to practical use: *~ mathematics.*

ap·ply /əˈplai/ *vt,vi* (*pt,pp* -ied) **1** ask for: *~ to the Consul for a visa.* **2 (a)** lay one thing on or in another: *~ a plaster to a cut.* **(b)** put into operation: *We intend to ~ economic sanctions.* **3** (cause to) have a bearing (on); concern: *What I have said does not ~ to you.* **4 *apply oneself/one's energies (to sth/to doing sth),*** give all one's thought, energy or attention to: *~ yourself to your work.* **5** make practical use of (research, a discovery).

ap·point /əˈpɔint/ *vt* **1** fix or decide: *The time ~ed for the meeting was 8:30pm.* **2** name to an office or position: *They ~ed White (to be) manager. We must ~ a committee.*

ap·poin·tee /əˌpɔinˈti/ *n* [C] person appointed.

ap·point·ment /əˈpɔintmənt/ *n* **1** [U] act of appointing: *meet by ~,* after fixing a time and place. **2** [C] arrangement to meet: *make/fix an ~; keep/break an ~.* **3** [C] position or office: *He got the ~ as manager.*

ap·por·tion /əˈpɔrʃən/ *vt* divide; distribute (the usual words): *This sum of money is to be ~ed among the survivors.*

ap·po·site /ˈæpəzɪt/ *adj* strikingly apt (2): *an ~ remark.*

ap·praisal /əˈpreizəl/ *n* [C,U] opinion, judgment of how good, valuable, etc somebody or something is.

ap·praise /əˈpreiz/ *vt* fix a price or value for; *~ property (at a certain sum) for taxation.*

ap·praiser *n*

ap·preci·able /əˈpriʃəbl/ *adj* large enough to be seen or felt: *an ~ change in the temperature.*

ap·preci·ably /-əbli/ *adv*

ap·preci·ate /əˈpriʃiˌeit/ *vt,vi* **1** judge rightly the value of; understand and enjoy: *We all ~ a vacation after a year of hard work.* **2** put a high value on: *We greatly ~ all your help.* **3** (of land, goods, etc) increase in value: *The land has ~d greatly since the new highway was built.*

ap·preci·ation /əˌpriʃiˈeiʃən/ *n* **1** [C,U] (statement giving) judgment, valuation. **2** [U] understanding and recognition: *in sincere ~ of your valuable help.* **3** [U] rise in value, eg of land, stocks.

ap·preci·ative /əˈpriʃətɪv, -ʃɪətɪv/ *adv* feeling or showing appreciation(2): *an ~ audience.*

ap·pre·hend /ˌæprɪˈhend/ *vt* **1** seize; arrest: *~ a thief.* **2** (*formal*) understand. **3** (*formal*) fear.

ap·pre·hen·sion /ˌæprɪˈhenʃən/ *n* **1** [U] understanding: *a lack of ~.* **2** [U] (also *pl*) fear; unhappy feeling about the future: *feel ~ for*

somebody's safety. **3** seizing: *the ~ of a thief.*
ap·pre·hen·sive /ˌæprɪˈhensɪv/ *adj* uneasy; worried: *~ for his safety.*
ap·pren·tice /əˈprentɪs/ *n* [C] learner of a trade who has agreed to work for a number of years in return for being taught. □ *vt* put into training as an apprentice: *The boy was ~d to a carpenter.*
ap·pren·tice·ship /-ˌʃɪp/ *n* [C,U] (time of) being an apprentice.
ap·proach /əˈproutʃ/ *vt,vi* **1** come near(er) (to): *As winter ~ed the weather became colder. Few writers can even ~ Shakespeare in greatness.* **2** go to (a person) with a request or offer: *When is the best time to ~ him about an increase in salary?* □ *n* **1** [C,U] (act of) approaching: *The enemy ran away at our ~.* **2** [C] way, path, road: *All the ~es to the embassy were guarded by soldiers.*
ap·proach·able /-əbəl/ *adj* (of a person or place) that can be approached; accessible.
ap·pro·pri·ate¹ /əˈproupriɪt/ *adj* **1** suited to: *That dress is not ~ for a formal wedding.* **2** in keeping with: *Write in a style ~ to your subject.*
ap·pro·pri·ate·ly *adv*
ap·pro·pri·ate² /əˈproupriˌeit/ *vt* **1** put on one side for a special purpose: *$20,000 has/have been ~d for the new buildings.* **2** take and use as one's own: *He often ~s my ideas.*
ap·pro·pri·ation /əˌproupriˈeiʃən/ *n* **1** [C,U] (instance of) appropriating or being appropriated. **2** [C] thing, esp a sum of money, that is appropriated: *make an ~ for payment of debts.*
ap·proval /əˈpruvəl/ *n* [U] feeling, showing or saying, that one is satisfied, that something is right, that one agrees: *Your plans have my ~. Does what I have done meet with your ~?* ***on approval,*** to be returned if not satisfactory: *sent out goods to customers on ~.*
ap·prove /əˈpruv/ *vt,vi* **1** give one's approval of: *Her father will never ~ of her marriage to you.* **2** agree to: *The minutes (of the meeting) were read and ~d.* **3** accept (something) as being satisfactory: *our expenses have been ~d.*
ap·prov·ing *adj*
ap·prov·ing·ly *adv*
approx. *abbr* = **1** approximate. **2** approximately.
ap·proxi·mate¹ /əˈpraksəmɪt/ *adj* very near (to); about right: *The ~ speed was 30 miles an hour.*
ap·proxi·mate·ly *adv*
ap·proxi·mate² /əˈpraksəˌmeit/ *vt* come near to (esp in quality or number): *His description of the event ~d the truth but there were a few errors.*
ap·proxi·ma·tion /əˌpraksəˈmeiʃən/ *n* **1** [C] almost correct amount or estimate. **2** [U] being or getting near (in number or quality).
appt. *abbr* = appointment.
Apr. *abbr* = April.
apri·cot /ˈæprəˌkat, ˈeiprəˌkat/ *n* **1** [C] (tree with) round, orange-yellow or orange-red fruit with soft flesh and a hard stone-like seed. ⇨ illus at fruit. **2** [U] color of this fruit when ripe.
April /ˈeiprəl/ *n* fourth month of the year.
ˌApril ˈfool, person who has a practical joke played on him on ˌApril ˈFools' Day (April 1).
a priori /ˌei ˌpraiˈɔri/ *adv, adj phrase* (*Lat*) (reasoning) from cause to effect, eg saying, *"The boys have walked a long way so they must be tired."* ⇨ a posteriori.
apron /ˈeiprən/ *n* [C] loose garment worn over the front part of the body to keep clothes clean; any similar covering.
ˈapron stage, (in some theaters) part of the front of a stage extending into the audience.
apro·pos /ˌæprəˈpou/ *adv, adj* well-suited (to what is being said or done): *His suggestion is very much ~.* ***apropos of,*** concerning, with reference to.
apse /æps/ *n* [C] semicircular or many-sided recess, with an arched or domed roof, esp at the east end of a church.
apt¹ /æpt/ *adj* (-er, -est) **1** intelligent: *apt at picking up a new subject.* **2** well-suited: *an apt remark.* **3** having a tendency, likely (to do something): *He's a clever boy but apt to get into mischief.*
apt·ly *adv* suitably: *aptly named.*
apt·ness /-nɪs/ *n* [U]
apt.² *abbr* = apartment.
ap·ti·tude /ˈæptəˌtud/ *n* [C,U] natural or acquired talent: *He shows an ~ for languages.*
aqua·lung /ˈækwəˌləŋ/ *n* [C] breathing device used for underwater swimming or diving.
aqua·mar·ine /ˌækwəməˈrin/ *n* [C] **1** bluish-green semiprecious stone. **2** (often as an *adj*) bluish-green color.
aqua·naut /ˈækwəˌnɔt/ *n* [C] person who lives in an underwater shelter to study marine life, etc.
aqua·plane /ˈækwəˌplein/ *n* [C] wide board that is towed behind a motorboat and is ridden by a person who stands on it.
aquar·ium /əˈkweriəm/ *n* [C] (*pl* ~s, -ria /-riə/) (building with an) artificial pond or tank for keeping and showing living fish, water animals and water plants.
Aquar·ius /əˈkweriəs/ *n* the Water Carrier, the eleventh sign of the zodiac. ⇨ illus at zodiac.
aquatic /əˈkwætɪk/ *adj* **1** (of plants, animals, etc) growing or living in or near water. **2** (of sports) taking place on or in water, eg rowing, swimming.
aque·duct /ˈækwəˌdəkt/ *n* artificial channel for supplying water, esp one built of stone or brick and higher than the surrounding land.
aqui·line /ˈækwəˌlain/ *adj* curved like an eagle's beak: *an ~ nose.*
AR *postal abbr* = Arkansas. ⇨ App 6.
-ar /-ər/ *suffix* (used to form an *adj*) of, relating to or like: *spectacular; polar.*
Arab /ˈærəb/ *n* [C] member of a Semitic people who speak Arabic.
Arabian /əˈreibiən/ *adj* of Arabia or the Arabs.
Ara·bic /ˈærəbɪk/ *adj* of the Arabs: *~ numerals,* the signs 0, 1, 2, 3, etc. □ *n* language of the Arabs.
Ara·bist /ˈærəbɪst/ *n* [C] expert or student of Arabic culture, language, etc.
ar·able /ˈærəbəl/ *adj* (of land) suitable for plowing.
ar·bi·ter /ˈarbətər/ *n* [C] = arbitrator.
ar·bi·trary /ˈarbəˌtreri/ *adj* **1** based on opinion, accident or sudden decision only, not on reason. **2** using unlimited power.
ar·bi·trate /ˈarbəˌtreit/ *vt,vi* decide by arbitra-

tion: *Mr. Smith has been asked to ~ between the employers and their workers.*

ar·bi·tra·tion /ˌarbəˈtreiʃən/ *n* [U] settlement of a dispute by the decision of a person or persons chosen and accepted as judges: *The labor union agreed to (go to) ~*, ie for a settlement of their claims.

ar·bi·tra·tor /ˈarbəˌtreitər/ *n* [C] person appointed by law or by two parties to settle a dispute.

ar·bor /ˈarbər/ *n* [C] shady place among trees. **ˈArbor Day,** day set aside for planting trees.

ar·bor·vi·tae /ˌarbərˈvaiti/ *n* [C] evergreen tree with spreading branches, often planted for hedges, etc.

ar·bu·tus /arˈbyutəs/ *n* [C] trailing plant of North America with clusters of fragrant pink or white flowers.

arc /ark/ *n* [C] **1** part of the circumference of a circle or other curved line. ⇨ illus at circle. **2** light caused by electric current flowing from one conductor to another.

ar·cade /arˈkeid/ *n* [C] covered passage, usually with an arched roof, eg a passage with shops or market stalls along one or both sides; covered market.

arch[1] /artʃ/ *n* **1** curved structure supporting the weight of what is above it, as in bridges, gateways, etc. **2** (also **ˈarch·way**) passageway under an arch, built as an ornament or gateway: *a triumphal ~*. **3** any curve in the shape of an arch, eg the curved part under the foot. ⇨ illus at leg. □ *vt,vi* **1** form into an arch: *The cat ~ed its back when it saw the dog.* **2** be like an arch: *The trees ~ over the river.*

arch[2] /artʃ/ *adj* mischievous in an innocent or playful way (esp of women and children): *an ~ glance/smile.*

arch·ly *adv*

arch- /artʃ-/ *prefix* chief; notable: *my ~enemy.*

ar·chae·ologi·cal, ar·che- /ˌarkiəˈladʒɪkəl/ *adj* of archaeology.

ar·chae·ol·ogist, ar·che- /ˌarkiˈalədʒɪst/ *n* [C] expert in archaeology.

ar·chae·ol·ogy, ar·che- /ˌarkiˈalədʒi/ *n* [U] study of past human life and esp of remains of prehistoric times.

ar·chaic /ˌaˈkeiɪk/ *adj* **1** (of languages, words) not now used except for special purposes. **2** of ancient times.

ar·chaism /ˌarˈkeiˌɪzəm/ *n* **1** [C] archaic word or expression. **2** [U] use or imitation of what is archaic.

arch·angel /ˌarˈkeindʒəl/ *n* [C] angel of highest rank.

arch·bishop /ˌartʃˈbɪʃəp/ *n* [C] chief bishop.

arch·bishop·ric *n* [C] position, rank or district of an archbishop.

archer /ˈartʃər/ *n* [C] person who shoots with a bow and arrows.

arch·ery /ˈartʃəri/ *n* [U] (art of) shooting with a bow and arrows.

archi·pel·ago /ˌarkəˈpeləgou/ *n* [C] (*pl* ~es, ~s) (sea with a) group of many islands.

archi·tect /ˈarkəˌtekt/ *n* [C] person who designs (and supervises the construction of) buildings.

archi·tec·tural /ˌarkəˈtektʃərəl/ *adj* of architecture: *the ~ beauties of a city.*

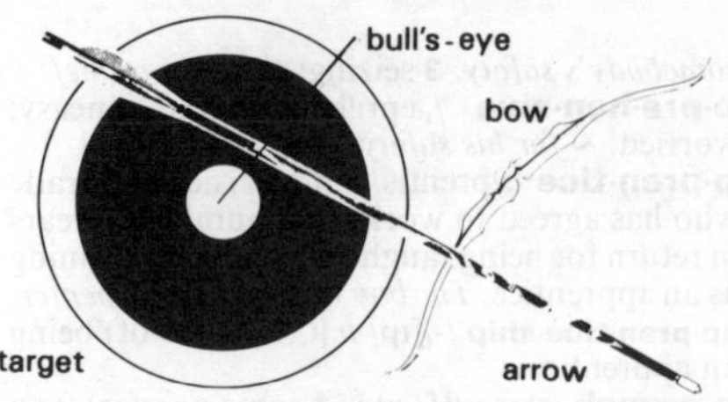

ARCHERY

archi·tec·ture /ˈarkəˌtektʃər/ *n* [U] **1** art and science of building. **2** design or style of building(s).

ar·chives /ˈarˌkaivz/ *n pl* (place for keeping) public or government records or other historical records.

archi·vist /ˈarkəvɪst/ *n* [C] person in charge of archives.

arch·way /ˈartʃˌwei/ *n* ⇨ arch[1](2).

arc·tic /ˈarktɪk/ *adj* of the north polar regions: *the Arctic Ocean; ~ weather,* very cold weather. **the ˌArctic ˈCircle,** line of latitude about 23° from the North Pole.

ar·dent /ˈardənt/ *adj* very enthusiastic: *~ supporters of the new movement.*

ar·dent·ly *adv*

ar·dor /ˈardər/ *n* [C,U] = enthusiasm (the more usual word).

ar·du·ous /ˈardʒuəs/ *adj* needing and using up much energy; difficult.

ar·du·ous·ly *adv*

are ⇨ be.

area /ˈeriə/ *n* [C] **1** surface measure: *If a room measures 10 × 15 feet, its ~ is 150 square feet/it is 150 square feet in ~.* **2** region of the earth's surface: *desert ~s of North Africa.* **3** (*fig*) field of activity: *The ~s of disagreement were clearly indicated at the Board Meeting.*

ˈarea code, number used in addition to the regular telephone number when making direct long-distance calls. ⇨ App 1.

arena /əˈrinə/ *n* [C] (*pl* ~s) **1** central part, for games and fights, of a Roman amphitheater. **2** place for public contests and shows. **3** (*fig*) any scene of competition or struggle: *the political ~.*

aren't /arnt/ = are not. ⇨ be.

ar·gon /ˈarˌgan/ *n* [U] colorless gas (Symbol **Ar**) used in making light bulbs.

ar·gu·able /ˈarˌgyuəbəl/ *adj* that can be supported by facts; that can be disagreed with.

ar·gu·ably /-əbli/ *adv*

ar·gue /ˈarˌgyu/ *vi,vt* **1** ***argue (with sb) (about/over sth),*** express disagreement; quarrel: *Don't ~ with me; my decision is final.* **2** ***argue (for/against/that...),*** give reasons (in support of, for, against, esp with the aim of persuading a person): *You can ~ either way, for or against. He was arguing that poverty may be a blessing.* **3** debate: *The lawyers ~d the case for hours.*

ar·gu·ment /ˈargyəmənt/ *n* **1** [C] (perhaps serious) disagreement; quarrel: *endless ~s about money; an ~ with the referee.* **2** [C,U] discussion giving reasons for agreeing or disagreeing: *It is beyond ~ that....*

ar·gu·men·ta·tive /ˌargyəˈmentətɪv/ *adj* fond

of arguing(1).

Ar·gus /ˈargəs/ *n* (*Greek myth*) monster with a hundred eyes.

aria /ˈariə/ *n* [C] (*pl* ~s) melody for a single voice in an opera, etc.

-arian /-eriən/ *suffix* practicer of: *disciplinarian*.

arid /ˈærɪd/ *adj* **1** (of soil, land) dry, barren. **2** (of climate, regions) without enough rainfall to support plants, etc.

Aries /ˈeˌriz/ *n* the Ram, the first sign of the zodiac. ⇨ illus at zodiac.

arise /əˈraiz/ *vi* (*pt* arose /əˈrouz/, *pp* arisen /əˈrɪzən/) **1** come into existence; be noticed: *A new difficulty has ~n*. **2** result from: *Serious consequences may ~ from your mistakes*. **3** (*old use*) get up; stand up.

ar·is·toc·racy /ˌærɪˈstakrəsi/ *n* (*pl* -ies) **1** [C,U] (country or state with a) government by persons of the highest social rank. **2** [C] **(a)** ruling body of nobles. **(b)** the social class from which these nobles come. **3** group considered superior because of eg intelligence, culture, etc.

a·ris·to·crat /əˈrɪstəˌkræt/ *n* [C] **1** member of an aristocracy. **2** person who is like an aristocrat.

a·ris·to·cratic /əˌrɪstəˈkrætɪk/ *adj* of the aristocracy; like an aristocrat: *with an ~ walk*.

a·ris·to·crati·cally /-kli/ *adv*

arith·me·tic /əˈrɪθməˌtɪk/ *n* [U] science of numbers; working with numbers.

ar·ith·meti·cal /ˌærɪθˈmetɪkəl/ *adj* of arithmetic.

ark /ark/ *n* [C] **1** (in the Bible) covered ship in which Noah and his family were saved from the Flood. **2** cabinet in a synagogue for holding the scrolls of the Torah.

Ark of the Covenant, wooden chest in which writings of Jewish law were kept.

arm[1] /arm/ *n* [C] **1** either of the two upper limbs of the human body, from the shoulder to the hand: *She was carrying a child in her arms*. ***keep sb at arm's length,*** avoid becoming familiar

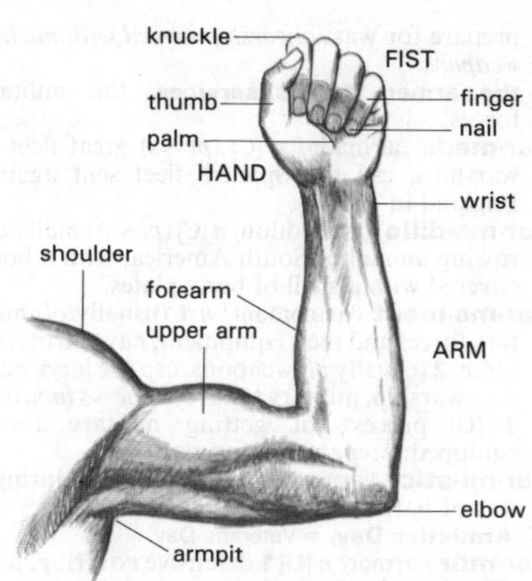

ARM AND HAND

with him. ***(welcome sb/sth) with open arms,*** (accept or greet) warmly, with enthusiasm. ***walk ˌarm-in-ˈarm,*** (of two persons) walk side by side, with the arms linked. **2** sleeve: *The arms of this coat are too long*. **3** anything shaped like or suggesting an arm: *the arms of a chair*. ***4 the arm of the law,*** the authority or power of the law.

ˈarm·chair *n* [C] chair with supports for the arms.

ˈarm·ful /-ˌfʊl/ *n* [C] as much as one arm or both arms can hold: *an armful of books*.

ˈarm·hole *n* [C] hole (in a shirt, jacket, etc) through which the arm is put.

ˈarm·pit *n* [C] hollow under the arm near the shoulder.

arm[2] /arm/ *vt,vi* supply, fit, weapons and armor;

U.S. ARMED FORCES

prepare for war: *a warship armed with nuclear weapons.*

the armed ˈforces/ˈservices, the military forces.

ar·mada /arˈmadə/ *n* [C] (*pl* ~s) great fleet of warships, esp the Spanish fleet sent against England in 1588.

ar·ma·dillo /ˌarməˈdɪlou/ *n* [C] (*pl* ~s) small burrowing animal of South America, with a body covered with a shell of bony plates.

ar·ma·ment /ˈarməmənt/ *n* **1** (usually *pl*) military forces and their equipment; navy, army, air force. **2** (usually *pl*) weapons, esp the large guns on a warship, military tank, etc: *the ~s industry.* **3** [U] process of getting military forces equipped; preparation for war.

ar·mi·stice /ˈarməstɪs/ *n* [C] agreement during a war or battle to stop fighting for a time.

ˈArmistice Day, = Veterans Day.

ar·mor /ˈarmər/ *n* [U] **1** defensive covering, usually metal, for the body, worn in fighting: *a suit of ~.* **2** metal covering for warships, tanks, motor vehicles, etc. **3** (*collect*) tanks, motor vehicles, etc protected with armor(2).

ar·mored *adj* **(a)** covered with armor: *an ~ed car.* **(b)** equipped with tanks, vehicles, guns, etc, that are protected with armor: *an ~ed column.*

ar·morer *n* [C] manufacturer or repairer of arms and armor.

ar·mory /ˈarməri/ *n* [C] (*pl* -ies) place where arms are kept.

arms /armz/ *n pl* **1** weapons: *The soldiers had plenty of ~ and ammunition.* (*Note: firearm* is used in the *sing.*) ***lay down (one's) arms,*** stop fighting. ***take up arms; rise up in arms (against),*** (*liter* or *fig*) get ready to fight. ***(be) up in arms (about/over),*** (be) protesting strongly. **2** (*heraldry*) pictorial design used by a noble family, town, university, etc.

ˈarms race, competition among nations for military strength.

ˌcoat of ˈarms, arms(2) eg on a shield in heraldry.

ˈsmall arms, weapons that can be carried by hand, eg guns, rifles.

army /ˈarmi/ *n* [C] (*pl* -ies) **1** (often **the Army**) the military forces of a country, organized for fighting on land: *be in the ~,* be a soldier. **2** large number: *an ~ of workmen/officials/ants.*

aroma /əˈroumə/ *n* [U] pleasant smell: *the ~ of bread being baked.*

aro·matic /ˌærəˈmætɪk/ *adj* fragrant; spicy: *the ~ bark of the cinnamon tree.*

arose /əˈrouz/ *pt* of arise.

around /əˈraund/ *adv, prep* **1** in a circle. **2** on every side (of), in every direction: *She put a scarf ~ her neck.* **3** somewhere nearby; here and there: *I'll be ~* (= not far away) *if you should want me. There was no one ~,* no one to be seen. **4** (with *verbs* of position or movement) here and there, in no particular place or direction: *The children were running ~. The boys were climbing ~ on the rocks. There were books lying ~ on the floor.* **5** approximately: *~ $10.*

arouse /əˈrauz/ *vt* **1** awaken: *behavior that might ~ suspicion.* **2** cause (somebody) to become active: *fully ~d.*

arr. *abbr* = **1** arrival. **2** arrive.

ar·raign /əˈrein/ *vt* (*legal*) bring a criminal charge against (a person) in a court: *~ed on a charge of theft.*

ar·range /əˈreindʒ/ *vt,vi* **1** put in order: *She's good at arranging flowers.* **2** make plans in advance; see to the details of: *I have ~d to meet her at ten o'clock. The meeting ~d for tomorrow has been postponed.* **3** come to an agreement *I've ~d a loan with Harry for the car.* **4** adapt (a piece of music): *~ a piece of music for the violin.*

ar·range·ment /əˈreindʒmənt/ *n* **1** [U] putting in order; arranging or being arranged: *The ~ of the furniture in our new house took a long time.* **2** [C] (*pl*) plans; preparations: *Have you made ~s for your trip to Hawaii?* **3** [U] agreement; settlement: *We can come to some sort of ~ over expenses.* **4** [C] result or manner of arranging: *an ~* (eg of orchestral music) *for the piano. I have an ~ by which I can cash my checks at banks anywhere in the US.*

ar·ray /əˈrei/ *vt* (*liter*) **1** position (esp armed forces, troops) in order for battle. **2** dress: *~ed in ceremonial robes.* □ *n* [C] (*liter*) **1** order: *troops in battle ~.* **2** clothes: *in military ~.* **3** display (of): *an impressive ~ of statistics.*

ar·rears /əˈrɪrz/ *n pl* **1** money that is owing and that ought to have been paid: *~ of rent/wages.* ***be in/fall into arrears (with),*** be late in paying. **2** work still waiting to be done.

ar·rest /əˈrest/ *vt* **1** seize (somebody) by the authority of the law: *The police ~ed the thief and put him in prison.* **2** put a stop to (a process or movement): *Poor food ~s the natural growth of children.* **3** catch and hold: *The bright colors of the flowers ~ed the child's attention.* □ *n* [C] act of arresting (a wrongdoer, etc): *The police made several ~s.* ***be/place/put under arrest,*** be (made) a prisoner.

ar·rest·ing *adj* likely to hold the attention.

ar·riv·al /əˈraivəl/ *n* **1** [U] act of arriving: *waiting for the ~ of news; to await ~,* (on a letter, parcel, etc) to be kept until the addressee arrives. **2** [C] person or thing that arrives: *The new ~* (*informal* = The newborn child) *is a boy.*

ar·rive /əˈraiv/ *vi* **1** reach a place, esp the end of a journey: *~ home.* **2** come: *At last the day ~d. Her baby ~d* (= was born) *yesterday.* **3** ***arrive at,*** reach (a decision, a price, the age of 40, manhood, etc). **4** establish one's position or reputation: *The publicity he received at the airport proved he'd ~d.*

ar·ro·gance /ˈærəgəns/ *n* [U] arrogant behavior, manner.

ar·ro·gant /ˈærəgənt/ *adj* **1** (of persons) behaving in a proud, superior manner. **2** (of behavior, etc) showing too much pride in oneself and too little consideration for others: *speaking in an ~ tone.*

ar·ro·gant·ly *adv*

ar·row /ˈærou/ *n* **1** thin, pointed stick (to be) shot from a bow. ⇨ illus at archery. **2** mark or sign (→) used to show direction or position, eg on a map or as a road sign.

ˈarrow·head *n* [C] pointed end of an arrow.

ar·row·root /ˈærouˌrut/ *n* [U] starch made from

the potatolike root of a tropical American plant.
ar·senal /ˈarsənəl/ *n* [C] place where weapons and ammunition are made or stored.
ar·senic /ˈars(ə)nɪk/ *n* [U] poisonous chemical element (symbol **As**), used in glass-making, dyes, etc.
ar·son /ˈarsən/ *n* [U] crime of starting a fire intentionally.
art[1] /art/ *n* **1** [U] the creation or expression of what is beautiful, esp in visual form; fine skill or aptitude in such expression: *the art of the Renaissance; children's art; an art historian.* **2** [C] something in which imagination and personal taste are more important than exact measurement and calculation: *History and literature are among the arts* (contrasted with the sciences). **3** [C,U] trickery; trick: *In spite of all her arts, the young man was not attracted to her.* ⇨ also bachelor, black, fine[1], master, work[1].
ˈart gallery, one for the display of paintings, etc.
ˈart school, one where painting, sculpture, etc are taught.
art[2] /art/ *v* (*archaic*) *present tense* form of *be* used with *thou*: *thou art,* you are.
art.[3] *abbr* = article.
ar·te·fact = artifact.
ar·te·rial /arˈtɪriəl/ *adj* **1** of or like an artery: *~ blood.* **2** (*fig*) *~ roads,* important main roads.
ar·tery /ˈartəri/ *n* [C] (*pl* -ies) **1** one of the tubes carrying blood from the heart to all parts of the body. ⇨ illus at respiratory. **2** main road or river; chief channel in a system of communications, etc.
ar·te·sian well /arˌtiʒən ˈwel/ *n* [C] bored well, esp one in which water flows up without pumping.
art·ful /ˈartfəl/ *adj* cunning; deceitful; clever in getting what one wants.
art·fully /-fəli/ *adv*
art·ful·ness /-nɪs/ *n* [U]
ar·thrit·ic /arˈθrɪtɪk/ *adj* of arthritis.
ar·thri·tis /ˌarˈθraitɪs/ *n* [U] inflammation of a joint or joints.
ar·ti·choke /ˈartəˌtʃouk/ *n* [C] **1 globe artichoke,** plant like a large thistle, with a head of thick, leaf-like scales used as a vegetable. **2 Jerusalem artichoke,** plant like a sunflower, with roots used as a vegetable.
ar·ticle /ˈartɪkəl/ *n* [C] **1** particular or separate thing: *~s of clothing,* eg shirts, coats; *toilet ~s,* eg soap, toothpaste. **2** piece of writing, complete in itself, in a newspaper or other periodical. **3** separate clause or item in an agreement, treaty, etc: *~s of confederation.* **4** (*gram*) word that limits or makes definite (a noun): *definite ~,* "the"; *indefinite ~,* "a," "an".
ar·ticu·late[1] /arˈtɪkyəlɪt/ *adj* **1** (of speech) in which the separate sounds and words are clear. **2** (of a person) able to put thoughts and feelings into clear speech: *That man is not very ~.*
ar·ticu·late·ly *adv*
ar·ticu·late[2] /arˈtɪkyəˌleit/ *vt,vi* **1** speak (distinctly). **2** connect by joints: *bones that ~/are ~d with others.*
ar·ticu·la·tion /arˌtɪkyəˈleiʃən/ *n* [U] **1** production of speech sounds: *The speaker's ideas were good but his ~ was poor.* **2** (connection by a) joint.
ar·ti·fact, ar·te·fact /ˈartəˌfækt/ *n* [C] something made by human being(s), eg a simple tool.
ar·ti·fice /ˈartəfɪs/ *n* (*formal*) **1** [C] skillful way of doing something. **2** [U] cunning; ingenuity; trickery. **3** [C] trick.
ar·ti·fi·cial /ˌartəˈfɪʃəl/ *adj* not natural or real; made by the art of man: *~ flowers/light; ~ respiration,* method of forcing air into the lungs, eg of a man nearly drowned.
ar·ti·fi·cial·ly /-ʃəli/ *adv*
ar·til·lery /arˈtɪləri/ *n* [U] **1** big guns (mounted on wheels, etc). **2** branch of an army that uses these.
ar·ti·san /ˈartɪzən/ *n* [C] skilled workman in industry or trade.
art·ist /ˈartɪst/ *n* [C] **1** person who practices one of the fine arts, esp painting. **2** person who performs with skill and good taste: *an ~ in words.*
art·iste /arˈtist/ *n* [C] professional singer, actor, dancer, etc.
ar·tis·tic /arˈtɪstɪk/ *adj* **1** done with skill and good taste, esp in the arts. **2** having or showing good taste. **3** of art or artists.
ar·tis·ti·cally /-kli/ *adv*
art·istry /ˈartəstri/ *n* [U] qualities of taste and skill possessed by an artist.
art·less /ˈartlɪs/ *adj* **1** natural. **2** without deceit.
arty /ˈarti/ *adj* (*informal*) pretending or falsely claiming to be artistic.
-ary /-ˌeri/ *suffix* **1** (used to form an *adj*): *planetary.* **2** (*pl* -ies) (used to form a *noun*): *dictionary.*
Aryan /ˈeriən/ *adj* (*dated*) **1** of the family of languages called Indo-European, ie related to Sanskrit, Persian, Greek, Latin and the Germanic and Slavonic languages. **2** of a people using an Aryan language. □ *n* [C] person whose mother tongue is one of the Aryan languages.
as[1] /əz *strong form:* æz/ *adv* in the same degree: *a room three times as long.* **as** (*adv*) + *adj/adv* + **as** (*conj*): *I'm as tall as you.* (*Note:* In a negative sentence *as* is often replaced by *so*: *It's not so/as difficult as we expected.*)
as[2] /əz *strong form:* æz/ *conj* **1** when; while: *I saw him as he was getting off the bus. As he grew older he became less active.* **2** since; because: *as he wasn't ready in time, we went without him.* **3** (in comparisons): *I want a box twice as large as this. It's as easy as ABC.* **4** (usually replaceable by a clause with *although*): *Much as I like you* (= Although I like you very much) *I will not marry you.* **5** in the way in which: *Do as I do. Do it as I do it. Leave it as it is.* **6** like: *Why is he dressed as a woman?* ***as if/though,*** **(a)** (with a *past tense* in the clause) the way it would be if: *He talks as if he knew all about it. It isn't as though he were poor.* **(b)** (followed by *to*+*infinitive*): *He opened his lips as if to say something.* **7** (used to avoid repetition): *Harry is unusually tall, as are his brothers,* and his brothers are also unusually tall. **8** in the position or character of: *He was respected both as a judge and as a man.* **9** (used after *regard, treat, acknowledge, etc*): *Most people regarded him* (= looked upon him) *as a fool.* ***such as,*** for

example: *Countries in the north of Europe, such as Finland, Norway, Sweden,....* **as for,** /ˌæz fər/ with reference to (sometimes suggesting indifference or contempt): *as for you, I never want to see you here again.* **10** (usually after *same* and *such*): *You must do the same things as he does. We left the country by the same road as we came in.* **11** (introducing a clause equal to a relative clause): *Cyprus, as* (= which fact) *you all know, is in the Mediterranean. To shut your eyes to facts, as many of you do, is foolish.* **so as to,** /ˌsou əz tə/ **(a)** *He stood up so as to* (= in order to) *see better.* **(b)** *It is foolish to behave so as to annoy* (= in ways that annoy) *your neighbors.* **as/so long as, (a)** on condition that: *You can go where you like so long as you get back before dark.* **(b)** while: *You will never enter this house as long as I live in it.* **as much,** so: *I thought as much.* ⇨ also far²(2), soon(3,4), well³(5,8), yet(5).

as·bes·tos /æsˈbestəs, æz-/ *n* [U] soft, gray, mineral substance used to make fireproof articles.

as·cend /əˈsend/ *vt,vi* (*formal*) go or come up; climb: *We watched the mists ~ing from the valley. The path ~s here.* **ascend the throne,** become king or queen.

as·cen·dancy, as·cen·dency /əˈsendənsi/ *n* [U] influence; power.

as·cen·sion /əˈsenʃən/ *n* act of ascending. **the Ascension,** (*Christianity*) the ascent of Jesus Christ from the earth to heaven.

as·cent /əˈsent/ *n* [C] **1** act of ascending; upward movement: *The ~ of the mountain was not difficult.* **2** way up.

as·cer·tain /ˌæsərˈtein/ *vt* find out for certain; make sure of: *~ the facts; ~ what really happened.*

as·cer·tain·able /-əbəl/ *adj* that can be found.

as·cetic /əˈsetɪk/ *adj* self-denying; leading a life of severe self-discipline. □ *n* [C] person who (often for religious reasons) leads a severely simple life without ordinary pleasures.

ascor·bic acid /eiˌskɔrbɪk ˈæsɪd/ *n* [U] (also known as *vitamin C*) vitamin found in citrus fruits and vegetable products.

as·cribe /əˈskraib/ *vt* **ascribe to, (a)** consider to be the cause, origin, reason or author of: *He ~d his failure to bad luck.* **(b)** consider as belonging to: *He has ~d a wrong meaning to a word.*

asep·tic /əˈseptɪk/ *adj* (of wounds, dressings, etc) free from bacteria; surgically clean.

asex·ual /ˌeiˈsekʃuəl/ *adj* without sex or sex organs: *~ reproduction.*

a·sex·ual·ity /ˌeiˌsekʃuˈæləti/ *n* [U]

ash¹ /æʃ/ *n* **1** [C] forest-tree with silver-gray bark, hard, tough wood and winged seeds. **2** [U] wood of this tree.

ash² /æʃ/ *n* [U] (also as *collective pl* ashes) **1** powder that is left after something has burned: *Don't drop cigarette ash(es) on the carpet. The house was burned to ashes.* **2** (*pl*) burnt remains, eg of a cremated human body.

ˈash·tray *n* small (metal, glass, etc) receptacle for tobacco ash.

ˈAsh Wednesday, (*Christianity*) first day of Lent.

ashamed /əˈʃeimd/ *adj* feeling shame: *You should be ~ of yourself/of what you have done. He was ~ to admit his mistake. They were ~ that they had behaved so rudely.*

asham·ed·ly /əˈʃeimɪdli/ *adv*

ashen /ˈæʃən/ *adj* **1** of ashes. **2** pale; ash-colored: *His face turned ~ at the news.*

ashore /əˈʃɔr/ *pred adj, adv* on, on to, the shore. **go ashore,** (of a sailor, etc) leave a ship to go on land.

ashy /ˈæʃi/ *adj* **1** = ashen. **2** covered with ashes.

Asian /ˈeiʒən/ *n* [C], *adj* (native) of Asia.

Asi·atic /ˌeiʒiˈætɪk/ *n* [C], *adj* = Asian (the preferred word).

aside /əˈsaid/ *adv* on or to one side: *He laid the book ~,* put it down and stopped reading it. *Please put this ~ for me,* reserve it. *Joking ~,* Speaking seriously, ... □ *n* [C] word(s) spoken, esp (on the stage) words that other persons (on the stage) are supposed not to hear.

as·i·nine /ˈæsəˌnain/ *adj* **1** of asses¹. **2** (*informal*) stupid.

ask /æsk/ *vt,vi* (*pt,pp* asked) **1** call for an answer to; request information or service: *Did you ask the price? We must ask him about it. I will ask (him) how to get there. Please ask (her) when she will be back.* **2** invite: *Mr. Brown is at the door; should I ask him (to come) in?* **ask for trouble,** behave in such a way that trouble is likely. **3** request to be allowed: *I must ask you to excuse me/ask to be excused.* **for the asking,** on request: *It's yours for the asking,* just ask for it and you will get it. **4** demand as a price: *What are they asking for the house?*

askance /əˈskæns/ *adv* (used only in) **look askance at (sb/sth),** look at with suspicion.

askew /əˈskyu/ *adv, pred adj* out of the straight or usual (level) position: *have one's hat on ~.*

aslant /əˈslænt/ *adv, prep* in a slanting direction: *The wrecked railroad car lay ~ the track.*

asleep /əˈslip/ *pred adj* **1** sleeping: *He was fast ~. He fell ~ during the lecture.* **2** (of the arms or legs) without feeling (as when under pressure).

asp /æsp/ *n* [C] small poisonous snake of Egypt and Libya.

as·para·gus /əˈspærəgəs/ *n* [U] **1** plant whose stalks are cooked and eaten as a vegetable. **2** the stalks of this plant.

as·pect /ˈæˌspekt/ *n* [C] **1** look or appearance (of a person or thing): *a man of fierce ~; a man with a serious ~.* **2** front that faces a particular direction: *a house with a southern ~.* **3** particular way in which something appears or may be looked at: *study every ~ of a subject,* study it from every point of view.

as·pen /ˈæspən/ *n* [C] poplar tree with leaves that move in the slightest wind.

as·per·ity /əˈsperəti/ *n* [U] (*formal*) roughness; harshness (of manner): *speak with ~.*

as·per·sion /əˈspərʒən/ *n* **cast aspersions (up)on sb/sth's honor, etc,** say false or damaging things about him.

as·phalt /ˈæsˌfɔlt/ *n* [U] black, sticky substance like coal-tar used for making waterproof cement, road surfaces, etc. □ *vt* surface (a road) with asphalt.

as·phyxia /æsˈfɪksiə/ *n* [U] condition caused by lack of enough air in the lungs; suffocation.
as·phyxi·ate /æsˈfɪksiˌeit/ *vt* make ill, cause the death of, through lack of sufficient air in the lungs: *The men in the coal mine were* ~*d*.
as·phyxi·ation /æsˌfɪksiˈeiʃən/ *n* [U] suffocation.
as·pic /ˈæspɪk/ *n* [U] clear jelly of fish or meat stock: *chicken in* ~.
as·pir·ant /ˈæspərənt/ *n* [C] person who is ambitious for fame, etc: *an* ~ *to high office*.
as·pir·ate¹ /ˈæspərɪt/ *n* [C] **1** the sound of "h." **2** sound with an "h" in it.
as·pir·ate² /ˈæspəˌreit/ *vt* say with an "h" sound: *The "h" in "honor" is not* ~*d*.
as·pir·ation /ˌæspəˈreiʃən/ *n* [C,U] desire; ambition: *his* ~*(s) for fame; his* ~ *to be an actor; the* ~*s of the developing countries*.
as·pire /əˈspaiər/ *vi* be filled with ambition or desire for: ~ *after knowledge;* ~ *to become an author*.
as·pirin /ˈæsp(ə)rən/ *n* **1** [U] medicine used to relieve pain and reduce fever. **2** [C] tablet of this: *Take two* ~*s for a headache*.
ass¹ /æs/ *n* [C] **1** animal of the horse family with long ears; donkey. **2** stupid person.
ass² /æs/ *n* [C] (⚠ *vulg*) buttocks.
ass·hole /ˈæsˌhoul/ *n* [C] **1** (⚠ *vulg*) anus. **2** (⚠ *sl*) fool.
as·sail /əˈseiəl/ *vt* (-ing) /əˈseilɪŋ/) = attack (the usual word) ~ *them with questions/insults; be* ~*ed with doubts*.
as·sail·able /əˈseiləbəl/ *adj* that can be attacked.
as·sail·ant /əˈseilənt/ *n* [C] = attacker (the usual word).
as·sas·sin /əˈsæsən/ *n* [C] person, often one hired by others, who assassinates.
as·sas·si·nate /əˈsæsəˌneit/ *vt* kill a person (esp an important public figure), for political reasons.
as·sas·si·nation /əˌsæsəˈneiʃən/ *n* [C,U] (instance of) murder of this kind.
as·sault /əˈsɔlt/ *n* [C] violent and sudden attack: *They made an* ~ *on the enemy's positions*. ***assault and battery,*** (*legal*) verbal and physical attack on a person. □ *vt* make an assault on.
as·semble /əˈsembəl/ *vt,vi* **1** gather together; collect: *The pupils* ~*d/were* ~*d in the school hall*. **2** fit or put together (the parts of): ~ *a car*.
as·sem·bly /əˈsembli/ *n* [C] (*pl* -ies) **1** number of persons who have come together: *the school* ~, the daily meeting of staff and pupils. **2** act or process of assembling: *the* ~ *of men and materials*. **3** collection of parts making a complete unit: *the tail* ~ *of a plane*. **4 Assembly,** the lower branch of a state legislature.
asˈsembly hall, one where eg a school meets.
asˈsembly line, line of workers and machines along which work moves until the final product is put together.
as·sem·bly·man /əˈsemblimən/ *n* [C] (*pl* -men /-men/) member of an assembly(4).
as·sent /əˈsent/ *n* [C] (official) agreement, eg to a proposal: *by common* ~, everybody agreeing. □ *vi* (*formal*) give agreement (to eg a proposal).
as·sert /əˈsərt/ *vt* **1** make a claim to: ~ *one's rights*. **2** declare firmly: ~ *one's innocence/that one is innocent*.
as·ser·tion /əˈsərʃən/ *n* **1** [U] insisting on one's rights. **2** [C] strong statement; claim: *make an* ~.
as·ser·tive /əˈsərtɪv/ *adj* having or showing (often excessive) confidence: *speaking in an* ~ *tone*.
as·ser·tive·ly *adv*
as·sess /əˈses/ *vt* **1** decide or fix the amount of (eg a tax or a fine): *Damages were* ~*ed at $100*. **2** fix or decide the value of (eg property), the amount of (eg income), for purposes of taxation. **3** (*fig*) decide the value or importance of: ~ *a speech at its true worth*.
as·sess·ment *n* **(a)** [U] assessing. **(b)** [C] amount assessed.
as·ses·sor /əˈsesər/ *n* [C] person who assesses property, income, taxes, etc.
as·set /ˈæˌset/ *n* [C] **1** (usually *pl*) anything owned by a person, company, etc that has money value and that may be sold to pay debts. ⇨ liability. **2** valuable or useful quality or skill: *Good health is a great* ~.
as·sign /əˈsain/ *vt* **1** give for use or enjoyment, or as a share or part in, eg of work, duty: *Those rooms have been* ~*ed to us. Your teacher* ~*s you work to be done at home*. **2** name, put forward as a time, place, reason, etc: *Has a day been* ~*ed for the trial? Can one* ~ *a cause to these events?* **3** appoint: *Assign your best man to the job. Two pupils were* ~*ed to sweep the classroom*. **4** (*legal*) transfer property, rights, etc to.
as·sign·able /-əbəl/ *adj* that can be assigned: ~*able to several causes*.
as·sign·ment *n* **(a)** [U] assigning. **(b)** [C] that which is assigned.
as·simi·late /əˈsɪməˌleit/ *vt,vi* **1** take in; absorb (eg food into the body after digestion); be absorbed: *We* ~ *some kinds of food more easily than others*. **2** (cause people to) become part of another social group or state: *The USA has* ~*d people from many countries,* has absorbed them, so that they are Americans.
as·simi·la·tion /əˌsɪməˈleiʃən/ *n* [U] assimilating or being absorbed.
as·sist /əˈsɪst/ *vt,vi* (*formal*) help: ~ *him in filling out the forms*.
as·sis·tance /əˈsɪstəns/ *n* [U] help: *give/lend* ~ *(to a person)*.
as·sis·tant /əˈsɪstənt/ *n* [C] helper: *an* ~ *to the Manager*.
assn. *abbr* = association.
assoc. *abbr* = **1** associate. **2** association.
as·so·ci·ate¹ /əˈsouʃɪt/ *adj* closely connected (eg in position, duties, etc): *an* ~ *judge*. □ *n* [C] **1** person joined with others in work, business or crime; colleague. **2** companion.
as·so·ci·ate² /əˈsouʃiˌeit/ *vt,vi* **1** ***associate with,*** join or connect: ~ *one thing with another. We* ~ *New York with the Statue of Liberty*. **2** be often in the company of: *Don't* ~ *with dishonest people*.
as·so·ci·ation /əˌsouʃiˈeiʃən/ *n* **1** [U] associating; being associated; companionship (with): *I benefited much from my* ~ *with him/from our* ~. ***in association (with),*** together. **2** [C] group of persons joined together for some common purpose: *the Aˈmerican ˈAutomobile Association*.
as·sorted /əˈsɔrtɪd/ *adj* of various sorts; mixed:

a pound of ~ chocolates.
as·sort·ment /əˈsɔrtmənt/ *n* [C] assorted collection of different examples or types: *This store has a good ~ of merchandise to choose from.*
asst. *abbr* = assistant.
as·sume /əˈsum/ *vt* **1** take for granted, without proof: *You ~ his innocence/him to be innocent/that he is innocent before hearing the evidence against him.* **2** undertake: *~ office,* begin to govern. **3** take on; pretend to have: *~ a new name.*
as·sump·tion /əˈsəmpʃən/ *n* **1** [C] something regarded as likely or true even though not proved: *Their ~ that the war would end quickly was proved wrong. I am going on the ~ that...,* I am supposing that.... **2** [C] ***assumption of,*** **(a)** the act of assuming(2): *his ~ of office/power/the presidency.* **(b)** pretense: *with an ~ of indifference,* pretending not to be interested. **3 the Assumption,** (*Christianity*) **(a)** reception into Heaven in bodily form of the Virgin Mary. **(b)** Church feast commemorating this.
as·sur·ance /əˈʃʊrəns/ *n* **1** [U] (often **self-assurance**) self-confidence; belief and trust in one's own powers: *He answered all the questions with ~.* **2** [C] promise; statement made to give confidence: *He gave me his ~ that the repairs would be finished by Friday.*
as·sure /əˈʃʊr/ *vt* **1** say positively, with confidence: *I ~ you (that) there's no danger.* **2** cause (a person) to be sure, to feel certain: *We tried to ~ the nervous old lady that flying was safe.*
as·sured *adj* sure; confident.
as·sur·ed·ly /əˈʃʊrədli/ *adv* surely; confidently.
AST *abbr* = Atlantic Standard Time.
as·ter /ˈæstər/ *n* [C] garden plant with flowers that have white, pink or purple petals round a yellow center.
as·ter·isk /ˈæstərɪsk/ *n* the sign (*) used to call attention to something or (*dated*) to show that letters are omitted, as in *Mr. J***s,* for *Mr. Jones.*
astern /əˈstərn/ *adv* (*naut*) in or at the stern of a ship.
as·ter·oid /ˈæstəˌrɔid/ *n* [C] any of many small planets between the orbits of Mars and Jupiter.
asthma /ˈæzmə/ *n* [U] chronic chest disease marked by difficulty in breathing.
asth·matic /ˌæzˈmætɪk/ *adj* **(a)** having asthma. **(b)** of asthma.
astir /əˈstər/ *adv, pred adj* out of bed; up and about.
as·ton·ish /əˈstanɪʃ/ *vt* surprise greatly: *The news ~ed everybody. Everybody was ~ed to hear the news.*
as·ton·ish·ing *adj* very surprising.
as·ton·ish·ment *n* [U] great surprise: *I heard to my ~ment that...; He looked at me in ~ment.*
astound /əˈstaund/ *vt* = shock (the usual word).
as·tral /ˈæstrəl/ *adj* of or from the stars.
astray /əˈstrei/ *adv, pred adj* out of, off, the right path, esp (*fig*) into doing wrong: *The boy was led ~ by bad friends.*
astride /əˈstraid/ *adv, pred adj, prep* with one leg on each side (of): *sitting ~ his father's knee.*
as·trin·gent /əˈstrɪndʒənt/ *n* [C] (kind of) substance that shrinks soft tissues and contracts blood vessels. □ *adj* of or like an astringent.
astr(o)- /æstr(ə)-/ *combined form* of the stars, of outer space: *astronomy.*
as·trol·oger /əˈstralədʒər/ *n* [C] expert in, student of, astrology.
as·tro·logi·cal /ˌæstrəˈladʒɪkəl/ *adj* of astrology.
as·trol·ogy /əˈstralədʒi/ *n* [U] art of observing the positions of the stars in the belief that they influence human affairs.
as·tro·naut /ˈæstrəˌnɔt/ *n* [C] person who travels in a spacecraft.
as·tron·omer /əˈstranəmər/ *n* [C] expert in, student of, astronomy.
as·tro·nomi·cal /ˌæstrəˈnamɪkəl/ *adj* **1** of the study of astronomy. **2** (*informal*) enormous: *an ~ sum.*
as·tron·omy /əˈstranəmi/ *n* [U] science of the sun, moon, stars and planets.
as·tute /əˈstut/ *adj* quick at seeing how to gain an advantage; clever: *an ~ lawyer/businessman.*
as·tute·ly *adv*
as·tute·ness /-nɪs/ *n* [U]
asy·lum /əˈsailəm/ *n* **1** [C,U] (place of) refuge or safety. **2** [C] place for the care of persons (eg orphans, the mentally ill, etc) unable to care for themselves. **3** [U] protection given by one country to persons from another: *ask for political ~.*
at /æt *strong form:* æt/ *prep* **1** **(a)** (in or near): *at my uncle's; at the station.* (*Note: in* is used for countries and large towns.) **(b)** (towards; in the direction of): *look at him; laugh at the joke; throw it at her.* **(c)** (indicating an attempt to get or reach something): *He had to guess at the meaning.* **(d)** (indicating distance): *It looks better at a distance.* **2** **(a)** (indicating a point of time): *at 2 o'clock; at sunset; at any moment.* **(b)** (of age): *He left school at (the age of) 15.* **(c)** (indicating order): *at the third attempt; at first; at last.* **(d)** (indicating the rate of occurrence): *at (all) times; at regular intervals.* **3** **(a)** (indicating occupation): *at work; at play.* ***hard ˈat it,*** working hard. **(b)** (after *adjectives*): *good at translation.* **(c)** (state, condition): *at war.* **4** **(a)** (rate): *at full speed; at a snail's pace.* **(b)** (value, cost, etc): *buy articles at 20 cents and sell them at 25 cents.* **(c)** (with *superlatives*): *at least; at the worst.* **5** (cause): *The pupils were shocked at the news. She was delighted at the idea of going to England.*
ate *pt* of eat.
-ate *suffix* **1** /-ɪt/ (used to form a *noun*): *electorate.* **2** /-eɪt/ (used to form a *verb*): *stimulate.*
athe·ism /ˈeiθiˌɪzəm/ *n* [U] belief that there is no God.
athe·ist /ˈeiθiɪst/ *n* [C] person who believes that there is no God.
athe·is·tic /ˌeiθiˈɪstɪk/ *adj* of atheism or atheists.
ath·lete /ˈæθˌlit/ *n* [C] person trained for competing in physical exercises and games, eg running, jumping, swimming, boxing.
ath·letic /æθˈletɪk/ *adj* **1** of athletes or athletics. **2** physically strong, with a well-balanced body: *an ~-looking young man.*
ath·let·ics *n pl* (usually with *sing verb*) practice

of physical exercises and sports, esp competitions in running, jumping, etc.

-ation *suffix* ⇨ -tion.

-ative /-ətɪv/ *suffix* (used to form an *adjective* from an *-ate* verb): *illustrative.*

-atively *suffix* (used to form an *adverb*).

At·lan·tic Time /ət'læntɪk ˌtaim/ *n* time zone covering eastern Canada.

at·las /'ætləs/ *n* [C] book of maps.

at·mos·phere /'ætməsˌfɪr/ *n* [U] **1** esp **the atmosphere,** mixture of gases surrounding the earth. **2** air in any place. **3** feeling, eg of good, evil, from a place, conditions, etc: *There is an ~ of peace and calm in the country quite different from the ~ of a big city.*

at·mos·pheric /ˌætməs'fɪrɪk/ *adj* of, connected with, the atmosphere: *~ conditions.*

atoll /'æˌtɔl/ *n* [C] ring of coral reef(s) around a lagoon.

atom /'ætəm/ *n* [C] **1** smallest unit of an element that can take part in a chemical change: *A molecule of water* (H_2O) *is made up of two ~s of hydrogen and one ~ of oxygen.* ⇨ electron, neutron, nucleus, proton. **2** very small bit: *There's not an ~ of truth* (= no truth at all) *in what he said.*

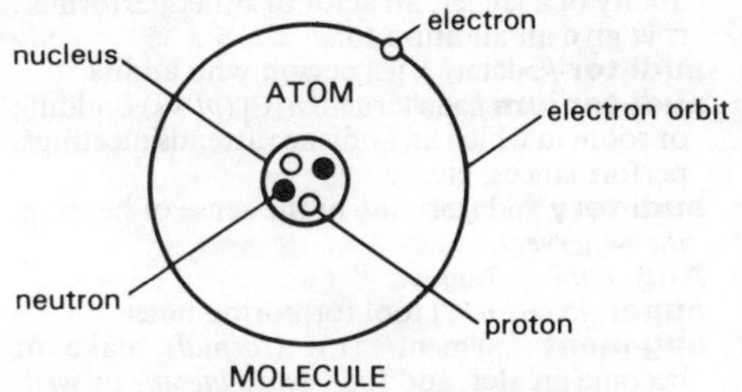

ATOMIC STRUCTURE

atomic /ə'tamɪk/ *adj* of an atom, or atoms.

aˌtomic 'bomb, 'atom ˌbomb, bomb whose destructive power comes from atomic energy.

aˌtomic 'energy, energy obtained as the result of splitting an atom.

at·om·izer /'ætəˌmaizər/ *n* [C] device for spraying a liquid in very small drops: *a perfume ~.*

atone /ə'toun/ *vi* make repayment: *How can I ~ for hurting your feelings?*

atone·ment *n* [U] atoning: *make ~ment for a fault.*

the Atonement, (*Christianity*) the sufferings and death of Jesus Christ.

Day of Atonement, (*Judaism*) day of the year in which one atones for one's sins.

-ator /-ˌeitər/ *suffix* object or person performing an *-ate* verb: *illustrator.*

atro·cious /ə'trouʃəs/ *adj* **1** very wicked or cruel: *an ~ crime.* **2** (*informal*) very bad: *an ~ dinner; ~ weather.*

atro·cious·ly *adv*

atroc·ity /ə'trasəti/ *n* (*pl* -ies) **1** [U] wickedness. **2** [C] wicked or cruel act: *Shooting prisoners of war is an ~.*

at·tach /ə'tætʃ/ *vt,vi* **1** fasten or join (one thing to another): *~ labels to the luggage; a house with a garage ~ed. Attached you will find/Attached please find. . .,* (*business style*) you will find, ~ed to this letter. . .. **2** tied by affection. ***be attached to***: *She is deeply ~ed to her young brother.* **3** consider to have; connect with: *Do you ~ much importance to what he says?* **4** go with; be joined (to): *No suspicion/blame ~es to him,* He cannot be suspected/blamed. **5** join as a member: *I am ~ed to the Sixth battalion/to the US European Command.*

at·taché /ˌætə'ʃei/ *n* [C] person who is attached to the staff of an ambassador: *the naval/military/press ~*

attaché case /ˌætə'ʃei ˌkeis/ *n* [C] small, flat suitcase for papers.

at·tach·ment *n* **1** [U] act of joining; being attached. **2** [C] something attached. **3** [C] affection; friendship: *have an ~ for her.*

at·tack /ə'tæk/ *n* [C] **1** violent attempt to hurt, overcome, defeat: *make an ~ upon the enemy.* ***be/come under attack,*** be or become the object of an attack: *The enemy came under ~.* **2** hostile criticism in speech or writing: *a strong ~ against/on the government's policy.* **3** start, eg of disease: *an ~ of fever; a 'heart ~,* pain in the region of the heart, with irregular beating. □ *vt* make an attack on: *~ the enemy; a disease that ~s children. Rust ~s metals.*

at·tacker *n* [C] person who ~s.

at·tain /ə'tein/ *vt,vi* (*formal*) **1** = achieve (the usual word): *~ one's hopes.* **2** arrive at: *~ the top of the mountain.*

at·tain·able /-əbəl/ *adj* that can be attained.

at·tain·ment *n* **(a)** [U] act of attaining: *for the ~ment of* (= in order to achieve) *his purpose.* **(b)** [C] (usually *pl*) skill; accomplishment: *legal ~ments.*

at·tempt /ə'tempt/ *vt* make an effort to do something; try: *The prisoners ~ed to escape but failed. Don't ~ impossibilities,* Don't try to do impossible things. □ *n* [C] **1** act or instance of attempting. ***attempt to do sth/attempt at doing sth***: *They made no ~ to escape/at escaping.* ***attempt on/upon***: *make an ~ on the world speed record.* **2** ***attempt at,*** thing not very well done: *Her ~ at a birthday cake had to be thrown away.*

at·tend /ə'tend/ *vi,vt* **1** give care and thought to: *~ to one's work. You're not ~ing,* not listening, not paying attention. **2** wait (*upon*); serve; look after: *Which doctor is ~ing you?* **3** go to; be present at: *~ school/church; ~ a meeting/lecture.*

at·tend·ance /ə'tendəns/ *n* **1** [C,U] being present, at school etc: *The boy was given a prize for perfect ~,* for attending school every day. **2** [U] number of persons present: *The ~ at church was poor.* **3** [U] act of attending(2): *Now that the patient is out of danger, the doctor is no longer in ~.*

at·tend·ant /ə'tendənt/ *n* [C] servant or companion. □ *adj* = accompanying (the usual word): *famine and its ~ diseases.*

at·ten·tion /ə'tenʃən/ *n* **1** [U] act of directing one's thoughts closely upon something: *Pay ~ to what you're doing. He shouted to attract ~,* to make people notice him. **2** (often *pl*) kind or polite act: *A pretty girl usually receives more ~s* *than a plain girl,* finds men more willing to do things for her. **3** [U] drill position in which a man stands straight and still: *come to/stand at ~;* (as a military command): *Attention!* (informally shortened to **'shun** /ʃən/).

at·ten·tive /əˈtentɪv/ *adj* **1** giving or paying attention: *A speaker likes to have an ~ audience.* **2** thoughtful; polite.

at·ten·tive·ly *adv*: *They listened ~ly to the teacher.*

at·test /əˈtest/ *vt,vi* **1** be or give clear proof of: *These papers ~ the fact that....* **2** declare on oath; put (a person) on oath; cause (a person) to declare solemnly: *I have said nothing that I am not ready to ~,* to say on oath. **3** ***attest to,*** bear witness to: *feats which ~ to his strength of will.*

at·tic /ˈætɪk/ *n* [C] space just under the roof of a house: *two small rooms in the ~.*

at·tire /əˈtaiər/ *n* [U] (*formal*) dress: *in holiday ~.* □ *vt* (*old use*) dress: *~d in white/satin.*

at·ti·tude /ˈætəˌtud/ *n* [C] **1** way of feeling, thinking or behaving: *What is your ~ toward this question,* What do you think about it? **2** manner of placing or holding the body: *He stood there in a threatening ~.*

attn. *abbr* = attention.

at·tor·ney /əˈtərni/ *n* [C] (*pl* ~s) **1** person with legal authority to act for another in business or law: *power of ~,* authority so given. **2** lawyer.

atˌtorney ˈgeneral, (a) chief law officer of a state, etc. **(b) the Attorney General,** legal adviser to the US President and head of the Department of Justice.

at·tract /əˈtrækt/ *vt* **1** draw or pull towards: *A magnet ~s steel.* **2** get the attention or liking of: *Bright lights ~ moths. He shouted to ~ attention. Do you feel ~ed to her,* do you like her?

at·trac·tion /əˈtrækʃən/ *n* **1** [U] power of pulling towards: *He cannot resist the ~ of the sea on a hot day/of a pretty girl.* **2** [C] that which attracts: *the ~s of a big city,* eg concerts, theaters, department stores.

at·trac·tive /əˈtræktɪv/ *adj* having the power to attract; pleasing: *a most ~ girl; ~ prices.*

at·trac·tive·ly *adv*

at·tribut·able /əˈtrɪbyətəbəl/ *adj* that can be attributed.

at·tribute[1] /əˈtrɪbyut/ *vt* consider as a quality of, as being the result of, as coming from: *He ~s his success to hard work.*

at·tribute[2] /ˈætrəˌbyut/ *n* [C] **1** quality considered to be naturally or necessarily belonging to a person or thing: *Mercy is an ~ of God.* **2** object recognized as a symbol of a person or his position: *The crown is an ~ of kingship.*

at·tune /əˈtun/ *vt* make used to: *ears ~d to the sound of gunfire.*

atty. *abbr* = attorney.

auburn /ˈɔbərn/ *adj* (usually of hair) reddish-brown.

auc·tion /ˈɔkʃən/ *n* [C,U] public sale at which goods are sold to the persons making the highest bids or offers: *sale by ~.* □ *vt* sell by auction.

auc·tion·eer /ˌɔkʃəˈnɪr/ *n* [C] person in charge of an auction.

au·dacious /ɔˈdeiʃəs/ *adj* **1** daring; bold. **2** impudent.

au·dacious·ly *adv*

au·dac·ity /ɔˈdæsəti/ *n* [U] **1** daring. **2** impudence.

au·dible /ˈɔdəbəl/ *adj* loud enough to be heard: *The speaker was barely ~.*

au·dibly /-əbli/ *adv*

audi·ence /ˈɔdiəns/ *n* **1** gathering of persons for the purpose of hearing a speaker, singer, etc: *There was a large ~ at the pop concert.* **2** persons listening, watching, reading: *That television program has an ~ of several million. His book has reached a wide ~.* **3** formal interview given by a ruler, the Pope, etc: *The Pope granted him an ~.*

audio- /ˌɔdiou-/ *combined form* of hearing, of sound: *~-visual.*

audio-vis·ual /ˌɔdiouˈvɪʒuəl/ *adj* of hearing and seeing.

ˌaudio-visual ˈaids, teaching aids such as recordings, filmstrips, etc.

audit /ˈɔdɪt/ *n* [C] official examination of accounts to see that they are in order. □ *vt* examine accounts officially.

au·dition /ɔˈdɪʃən/ *n* [C] trial hearing to test the ability of a singer, an actor or other performer. □ *vt* give an audition to.

audi·tor /ˈɔdətər/ *n* [C] person who audits.

audi·tor·ium /ˌɔdəˈtɔriəm/ *n* [C] (*pl* ~s) building or room in which an audience attends meetings, performances, etc.

audi·tory /ˈɔdəˌtɔri/ *adj* of the sense of hearing: *the ~ nerve.*

Aug. *abbr* = August.

auger /ˈɔgər/ *n* [C] tool for boring holes.

aug·ment /ɔgˈment/ *vt,vi* (*formal*) make or become greater; add to: *~ one's income by writing short stories.*

augur /ˈɔgər/ *n* [C] person claiming to foretell future events. □ *vi,vt* foretell; be a sign of.

augury /ˈɔgyəri/ *n* [C] (*pl* -ies) omen; sign.

august /ɔˈgəst/ *adj* majestic; causing feelings of respect or awe.

August /ˈɔgəst/ *n* the eighth month.

auk /ɔk/ *n* [C] northern seabird with short wings.

auld lang syne /ˌɔld ˌlæŋ ˈzain/ (*Scot*) good times long ago.

aunt /ænt/ *n* [C] sister of one's father or mother; wife of one's uncle.

aun·tie, aun·ty /ˈænti/ *n* [C] (*informal*) aunt.

aura /ˈɔrə/ *n* [C] (*pl* ~s) atmosphere surrounding a person or object and thought to come from him or it: *There seemed to be an ~ of holiness about the Indian saint.*

aural /ˈɔrəl/ *adj* of the organs of hearing: *an ~ surgeon.*

aure·ole /ˈɔrˌioul/ *n* [C] = halo (the usual word).

au re·voir /ˌou rəˈvwar/ *int* (*F*) till we meet again; good-bye.

au·ricle /ˈɔrəkəl/ *n* [C] (*anat*) **1** the external part of the ear. ⇨ illus at ear. **2** either of the two upper cavities of the heart. ⇨ illus at respiratory.

au·rora aus·tra·lis /əˌrɔrə ɔˈstreiləs/ *n* bands of colored light, usually red and green, seen in the sky in the regions of the South Pole.

au·rora bor·ea·lis /əˌrɔrə ˌbɔriˈæləs/ *n* bands of

colored light, usually red and green, seen in the sky in the regions of the North Pole.

aus·pices /ˈɔspəsəz/ *n pl* ***under the auspices of,*** helped and favored by.

aus·pi·cious /ɔˈspɪʃəs/ *adj* **1** showing signs, giving promise, of future success; favorable. **2** fortunate; prosperous.

aus·pi·cious·ly *adv*

Aus·sie /ˈɔsi/ *n* [C] (*sl*) Australian.

aus·tere /ɔˈstɪr/ *adj* **1** (of a person, his behavior) severely moral and strict. **2** (of a way of living, of places, styles) simple and plain; without ornament or comfort.

aus·tere·ly *adv*

aus·ter·ity /ɔˈsterəti/ *n* (*pl* -ies) **1** [U] quality of being austere. **2** (*pl*) austere practices, eg fasting, living in a cell, for religious reasons.

Aus·tra·lian /ɔˈstreiliən/ *n* [C], *adj* (native) of Australia.

au·then·tic /ɔˈθentɪk/ *adj* **1** genuine; known to be true: *an* ~ *signature.* **2** correct; reliable.

au·then·ti·cally /-kli/ *adv*

au·then·ti·cate /ɔˈθentəˌkeit/ *vt* prove beyond doubt the origin, authorship, etc of.

au·then·ti·ca·tion /ɔˌθentəˈkeiʃən/ *n* [U]

au·then·tic·ity /ɔˌθenˈtɪsəti/ *n* [U] **1** quality of being genuine: *feel confident of the* ~ *of a signature.* **2** reliability: *doubt the* ~ *of his report.*

author /ˈɔθər/ *n* [C] **1** writer of a book, play, etc: *Faulkner is his favorite* ~. **2** person who creates or begins something.

author·ess /ˈɔθərɪs/ *n* [C] woman author.

au·thori·tar·ian /əˌθɔrəˈteriən/ *adj* supporting or requiring obedience to authority, esp that of the state. □ *n* [C] supporter of this principle.

au·thori·tat·ive /əˈθɔrəˌteitɪv/ *adj* **1** having, given with, authority: ~ *orders.* **2** having an air of authority; commanding: *in an* ~ *manner.* **3** that can be trusted because from a reliable source: *an* ~ *report.*

au·thori·tat·ive·ly *adv*

au·thor·ity /əˈθɔrəti/ *n* (*pl* -ies) **1** [U] power or right to give orders and make others obey: Who is in ~ here? *Only the treasurer has* ~ *to make payments.* **2** [C] person or (*pl*) group of persons having authority: *the legal authorities.* **3** [C] **(a)** person with special knowledge; expert. **(b)** book, etc that supplies reliable information or evidence: *The Oxford English Dictionary is the best* ~ *on English words.*

au·thor·iz·ation /ˌɔθərəˈzeiʃən/ *n* **1** [C,U] (act of) authorizing. **2** legal right or permission given.

au·thor·ize /ˈɔθəˌraiz/ *vt* **1** give authority to: *I have* ~*d him to act for me while I am abroad.* **2** give authority for: *The Finance Committee* ~*d the spending of $10,000 on a new playground.*

ˌAuthorized ˈVersion, the English translation of the Bible, first published 1611.

author·ship /ˈɔθərˌʃɪp/ *n* [U] **1** occupation of an author. **2** origin of a book, etc: *Nothing is known of the* ~ *of the book.*

auto /ˈɔtou/ *n* [C] (*informal*) (short for) automobile.

auto- /ˌɔtou-, ˌɔtə-/ *combined form* **1** of oneself: *autobiography.* **2** without help, independently: *automatic.*

auto·bio·graphi·cal /ˌɔtəˌbaiəˈgræfɪkəl/, **-graphic** /-ˈgræfɪk/ *adj* of, engaged in, autobiography.

auto·bi·ogra·phy /ˌɔtəbaiˈagrəfi/ *n* [C] (*pl* -ies) story of a person's life written by himself.

autoc·racy /ɔˈtakrəsi/ *n* (*pl* -ies) **1** [U] government by a ruler who has unlimited power. **2** [C] (country with a) government of this kind.

auto·crat /ˈɔtəˌkræt/ *n* [C] ruler with unlimited power.

auto·cratic /ˌɔtəˈkrætɪk/ *adj* of or like an autocrat: *Don't be so* ~*ic!*

auto·crati·cally /-kli/ *adv*

auto·graph /ˈɔtəˌgræf/ *n* [C] person's own handwriting, esp his signature. □ *vt* write one's name on or in: *a book* ~*ed by the author.*

auto·mate /ˈɔtəˌmeit/ *vt* convert to, control by, automation.

auto·matic /ˌɔtəˈmætɪk/ *adj* **1** (of a machine) able to work or be worked without attention: ~ *weapons,* weapons that continue firing until pressure on the trigger is released. **2** (of actions) done without thought; unconscious: *Breathing is* ~. □ *n* [C] small automatic gun.

auto·mati·cally /-kli/ *adv*

auto·ma·tion /ˌɔtəˈmeiʃən/ *n* [U] (use of) methods and machines to save labor.

auto·mo·bile /ˈɔtəməˌbiəl/ *n* [C] motor-driven passenger vehicle. ⇨ illus at car.

auton·omous /ɔˈtanəməs/ *adj* (of states) self-governing.

auton·omy /ɔˈtanəmi/ *n* [C,U] (*pl* -ies) (right of) self-government.

au·topsy /ˈɔˌtapsi/ *n* [C] (*pl* -ies) (*med*) examination of a body (by cutting it open) to learn the cause of death.

autumn /ˈɔtəm/ *n* [C] fall; third season of the year, between summer and winter (Sept., Oct. and Nov. in the northern hemisphere).

autum·nal /ˌɔˈtəmnəl/ *adj* of autumn.

AUX[1] *abbr* = auxiliary.

aux.[2] *abbr* = auxiliary.

aux·il·iary /ɔgˈzɪlyəri/ *adj* helping; supporting: ~ *troops.* □ *n* [C] (*pl* -ies) (*gram*) verb (as *have, be, do, can, shall, will,* etc) that is used with other verbs to form tenses, voices, etc.

av. *abbr* = average.

avail /əˈveiəl/ *vt,vi* (-ing /əˈveilɪŋ/) ***avail oneself of,*** (*formal*) make use of, profit by, take advantage of: *You should* ~ *yourself of every opportunity to practice speaking English.* □ *n* ***of no/little avail,*** not helpful; not effective: *His intervention was of little* ~. ***without avail; to no avail,*** without result; unsuccessfully: *We pulled him out of the river and tried to revive him, but to no* ~.

avail·able /əˈveiləbəl/ *adj* that may be used or obtained: *There were no tickets* ~ *for Friday's performance.*

avail·abil·ity /əˌveiləˈbɪləti/ *n* [U]

ava·lanche /ˈævəˌlæntʃ/ *n* [C] **1** great mass of snow and ice at a high altitude, caused by its own weight to slide down a mountain side, often carrying with it thousands of tons of rock: **2** (*fig*) great many: *an* ~ *of words/letters/questions.*

av·a·rice /ˈævərɪs/ *n* [U] = greed (the usual word); great eagerness to get or keep.

av·a·ricious /ˌævəˈrɪʃəs/ *adj* greedy.
av·a·ricious·ly *adv*

Ave. *abbr* = Avenue.

avenge /əˈvendʒ/ *vt* get or take revenge for: ~ *an insult*.

av·enue /ˈævəˌnu/ *n* [C] **1** wide street with buildings on one or both sides. **2** (*fig*) way (to an object or aim): ~*s to success/promotion*.

av·er·age /ˈæv(ə)rɪdʒ/ *n* [C] **1** result of adding several quantities together and dividing the total by the number of quantities: *The* ~ *of 4, 5 and 9 is 6*. **2** standard or level regarded as ordinary or usual: *Tom's work at school is above/below* ~. □ *adj* **1** found by making an average: *The* ~ *age of the students in this class is fifteen*. **2** of the ordinary or usual standard: *students of* ~ *ability*. □ *vt,vi* **1** find the average of: *If you* ~ *7, 14 and 6, you get 9*. **2** amount to as an average; do as an ~: ~ *200 miles a day during a journey*.

averse /əˈvərs/ *adj* opposed, unwilling: *He is* ~ *to hard work/working hard*.

aver·sion /əˈvərʒən/ *n* **1** [C,U] strong dislike: *showed her* ~ *for him by leaving the room whenever he entered*. ***aversion to***: *He has a strong* ~ *to getting up early*. **2** [C] thing or person disliked: *my pet* ~, thing I specially dislike.

avert /əˈvərt/ *vt* **1** turn away: ~ *one's eyes/gaze from a terrible scene*. **2** prevent, avoid: ~ *an accident*.

avg. *abbr* = average.

avi·ary /ˈeiviˌeri/ *n* [C] (*pl* -ies) place for keeping birds, eg in a zoo.

avi·ation /ˌeiviˈeiʃən, ˌæv-/ *n* [U] (art and science of) flying in aircraft.

avi·ator /ˈeiviˌeitər, ˈæv-/ *n* [C] person who flies an aircraft.

avid /ˈævɪd/ *adj* (*formal*) eager, greedy: ~ *for fame/applause*.
avid·ity /əˈvɪdəti/ *n* [U]
avid·ly /ˈævɪdli/ *adv*

avo·cado /ˌævəˈkadou/ *n* [C] (*pl* ~s) pear-shaped tropical fruit.

avoid /əˈvɔid/ *vt* keep or get away from; escape: *Try to* ~ *danger. He* ~*ed looking at her*.
avoid·able /-əbəl/ *adj* that can be avoided.
avoid·ance /-əns/ *n* [U] avoiding.

avoir·du·pois /ˌævərdəˈpɔiz/ *n* [U] pre-metric system of weights used in most English-speaking countries (1 pound = 16 ounces) for all goods except medicines and precious metals and stones.

avow /əˈvau/ *vt* (*formal*) admit; declare openly: ~ *a fault. He* ~*ed himself* (*to be*) *a Christian*.
avowal /-əl/ *n* **(a)** [U] free and open confession. **(b)** [C] instance of this.

await /əˈweit/ *vt* **1** (of persons) wait for: *I* ~ *your instructions*. **2** be in store for; be waiting for: *Death* ~*s all men*.

awake[1] /əˈweik/ *vi* (*pt* awoke /əˈwouk/, *pp* awoken or ~d) **1** = wake (the usual word). **2** become conscious of, realize: *He awoke to his opportunities*.

awake[2] /əˈweik/ *pred adj* roused from sleep: *Is he* ~ *or asleep?* ***awake to,*** aware of: *be* ~ *to danger*.

awaken /əˈweikən/ *vt* = wake[1].

awaken·ing /əˈweikənɪŋ/ *n* [C] act of becoming aware, of realizing: *It was a rude* ~*ing when he was told that he was to be dismissed*.

award /əˈwɔrd/ *vt* give or grant (by official decision): *He was* ~*ed first prize*. □ *n* [C] thing awarded eg a prize in a contest.

aware /əˈwer/ *adj* ***aware of/that,*** having knowledge: *We are* ~ *of the seriousness of this matter/that this matter is serious*.
aware·ness /-nɪs/ *n* [U]

awash /əˈwɔʃ, əˈwaʃ/ *pred adj* washed over by, level with, the waves: *rocks* ~ *at high tide. The ship's deck was* ~.

away /əˈwei/ *adv* **1** to or at a distance (from a place, person, etc): *The sea is two miles* ~. *Take these things* ~, Remove them. **2** ***away with,*** (used in exclamations without a verb): *Away with them!* Take them away! **3** continuously; constantly: *He was working* ~. **4** (used to indicate loss, lessening, weakening, exhaustion): *The water has all boiled* ~, there is no water left. **5** ***far and away,*** very much: *This is far and* ~ *the best*. ***right/straight away,*** at once, without delay.

awe /ɔ/ *n* [U] respect combined with fear: *He had a feeling of awe as he was taken before the judge*.
ˈawe-inspiring *adj* filling with awe: *an awe-inspiring sight*.
ˈawe·some /-səm/ *adj* causing awe.
ˈawe-stricken, ˈawe-struck *adj* struck with awe.

aw·ful /ˈɔfəl/ *adj* **1** terrible; dreadful: *He died an* ~ *death*. **2** (*informal*) very bad; very great; extreme of its kind: *What an* ~ *nuisance! What* ~ *handwriting/weather!*

aw·fully /ˈɔfli/ *adv* very: *It has been* ~ *hot this week. I'm* ~ *sorry*.

awhile /əˈ(h)waiəl/ *adv* for a short time: *Please stay* ~.

awk·ward /ˈɔkwərd/ *adj* **1** (of objects, places, circumstances, etc) likely to cause inconvenience or difficulty: *The big piano was* ~ *to move*. ***an awkward customer,*** (*informal*) person difficult or dangerous to deal with. **2** (of living things) clumsy; having little skill: *Some animals are* ~ *on land but able to move easily in the water*. **3** embarrassed: *an* ~ *silence/pause*.
awk·ward·ly *adv*
awk·ward·ness /-nɪs/ *n* [U]

awl /ɔ:l/ *n* [C] small pointed tool for making holes, esp in leather.

awn·ing /ˈɔnɪŋ/ *n* [C,U] canvas covering (against rain or sun), eg over a ship's deck, over windows, etc.

awoke *pp* of awake[1].

awry /əˈrai/ *adv, pred adj* crooked(ly); wrong(-ly): *Our plans have gone* ~, have gone wrong.

ax, axe /æks/ *n* [C] (*pl* axes /ˈæksɪz/) tool for felling trees or splitting wood. ***ˌhave an ˈaxe to grind,*** **(a)** have special reasons for being interested. **(b)** have reasons to quarrel. ***give someone the ax,*** (*sl*) fire, dismiss him, ***get the ax,*** (*sl*) be fired or dismissed.

ax·iom /ˈæksiəm/ *n* [C] statement accepted as true without argument.
axio·matic /ˌæksiəˈmætɪk/ *adj* obviously true: *It is* ~*atic that a whole is greater than any of its*

parts.

axis /ˈæksɪs/ *n* [C] (*pl* axes /ˈækˌsiz/) **1** line round which a turning object spins. **2** line that divides a figure into two symmetrical parts, eg the diameter of a circle.

the earth's axis, the imaginary line joining the North and South Poles through the center of the earth, on which the earth rotates once in twenty-four hours.

axle /ˈæksəl/ *n* [C] **1** rod on or with which a wheel turns. **2** bar or rod that passes through the centers of a pair of wheels: *the back ~ of a bus.*

aye /ai/ *int, adv* yes; (*naval*) usual reply to an order: *aye, aye, sir!* □ *n* [C] vote in favor of a proposal: *The ayes have it,* Those for it are in the majority.

AZ *postal abbr* = Arizona. ⇨ App 6.

aza·lea /əˈzeiəlyə, əˈzeiliə/ *n* [C] kinds of flowering shrub like the rhododendron.

az·ure /ˈæʒər/ *adj, n* (*poet*) bright blue: *an ~ sky.*

b

B, b /bi/ (*pl* B's, b's /biz/) the second letter of the English alphabet.

b. *abbr* (before a date) = born.

BA /ˌbi ˈei/ *abbr* = Bachelor of Arts (degree).

baa /ba, bæ/ *n* [C] cry of a sheep or lamb. □ *vi* make this cry; bleat.

babble /ˈbæbəl/ *vi,vt* **1** make unclear or meaningless sounds like a baby, a brook, etc. **2** talk too much; chatter: *~ nonsense/secrets.* □ *n* [U] **1** childish or foolish talk; talk not easily understood (as when many people are talking at once). **2** gentle sound of water flowing over stones, etc.

babe /beib/ *n* [C] (*liter* and *informal*) = baby.

babel /ˈbeibəl/ *n* **1 the Tower of Babel,** (in the Bible) tower built to try to reach heaven and left unfinished when the builders' language became mixed and confused. **2** [U] scene of noisy and confused talking.

ba·boon /bæˈbun/ *n* large monkey (of Africa and southern Asia) with a dog-like face. ⇨ illus at ape.

baby /ˈbeibi/ *n* [C] (*pl* -ies) **1** very young child: *She has a ˌ~ ˈboy/ˈgirl. Which of you is the ~* (= the youngest member) *of the family?* **2** person who acts like a baby. **3** (*sl*) girl; sweetheart.

ˈbaby buggy/carriage four-wheeled carriage for babies, designed to be pushed.

ˈbaby-face(d) *n, adj* (of an adult) (having a) youthful face.

ˈbaby ˈgrand, small grand piano.

ˈbaby·hood *n* [U] state, period of being a baby.

ˈbaby·ish *adj* of, like a baby: *~ish behavior.*

ˈbaby·sit *vi* (*pt,pp* -sat) look after a baby for a short time (eg while the parents are at the movies).

ˈbaby-sitter *n* [C] person paid to do this.

bach·elor /ˈbætʃlər/ *n* [C] **1** unmarried man. ⇨ spinster. **2** (as an *adj*) of, suitable for, an unmarried person: *~ apartments.* **3** (man or woman who has taken the) first college or university degree: *Bachelor of Arts/Science.*

ba·cil·lus /bəˈsɪləs/ *n* [C] (*pl* -cilli /-lai/) any of the types of long bacterium, some of which cause disease.

back[1] /bæk/ *n* [C] **1** (of the human body) surface of the body from the neck to the buttocks: *If you lie on your ~, you can look up at the sky.* ***do/say sth behind sb's back,*** without his knowledge (always in connection with something unpleasant, such as slander). ***be on/get off sb's back,*** be/stop being a burden or nuisance. ***have/with one's back to the wall,*** in a difficult position, forced to defend oneself. ***put/get sb's back up,*** make him angry. ***turn one's back on sb,*** abandon him. **2** upper surface of an animal's body: *Fasten the saddle on the horse's ~.* **3** that part of a chair or seat on which a person's back rests. **4** that surface of an object that is less used, less visible or important: *the ~ of one's hand.* **5** that part of a thing that is farthest from the front: *a room at the ~ of the house.* ***in back of,*** at the back of. **6** (*sport*) player whose position is behind the front line of players.

ˈback·ache *n* [U,C] pain in the back.

ˈback·bite *vt,vi* say things to damage a person's reputation.

ˈback·bone *n* [C,U] **(a)** line of bones down the middle of the back; spine. ⇨ illus at skeleton. **(b)** (*fig*) strength of character.

ˈback·breaking *adj* (of work) exhausting.

ˈback·date *vt* put an earlier date on a document (esp a check) than that of its actual writing.

ˈback·less *adj* (of a dress) not covering the back.

ˈback·stroke *n* [U] style of swimming on one's back.

back[2] /bæk/ *adverbial particle* **1** to or at the rear; away from the front: *Stand ~, please! Sit ~ in your chair and be comfortable.* ***back and forth,*** first one way and then the other: *walked ~ and forth restlessly.* ***go back on one's word,*** fail to keep a promise. **2** in (to) an earlier position or condition: *Throw the ball ~ to me. We shall be ~* (= home again) *before dark. How far is it there and ~?* **3** in return: *If I hit you, would you hit me ~?* **4** (of time) ago; into the past: *a few years ~.* **5** from in the past: overdue: *~ dues/pay.*

ˈback·country *n* (esp uninhabited) land away from the coast or from a populated area.

ˈback·field *n* (*sport*) the area of eg a football field on which the backs(6) play.

ˈback·fire *n* [U] sound caused by the pistons in an engine when gas explodes. □ *vi* **(a)** produce this sound. **(b)** (*fig*) fail; have an unpleasant result.

ˈback·ground *n* **(a)** that part of a view, scene, etc at the back. **(b)** existing or relevant conditions: *the political ~ground.* **(c)** person's past experiences, education, etc. **(d)** ***in the background,*** away from publicity; not being clearly seen or heard.

ˈback·hand *n* [C] stroke (in tennis, etc) made with the back of the hand turned outward.

back·ˈhanded *adj* (*fig*) not direct, sarcastic: *a ~handed compliment.*

ˈ**back·lash** *n* (*fig*) (in social or race relations) unpleasant or violent reaction.
ˈ**back·log** *n* business affairs (eg correspondence) still to be attended to.
ˈ**back·pack** *n* [C] kind of knapsack with a metal frame for carrying esp camping gear on the back. □ *vi* hike with a backpack.
ˈ**back·packer** *n* [C] person who goes hiking with a backpack.
ˈ**back·packing** *n* [U] activity of hiking with backpack.
back ˈseat, (of a car, etc) seat at the back. ***take a back seat,*** (*fig*) stay in the background.
ˌ**back-seat ˈdriver,** (*informal*) passenger who gives the driver unwanted advice on driving.
ˈ**back·side** *n* (*informal*) buttocks.
ˈ**back·slide** *vi* (of one who has reformed or improved his behavior) relapse into bad behavior.
ˈ**back·slider** *n* [C] one who relapses into bad behavior.
ˈ**back·space** *vt,vi* (cause a typewriter carriage to) move back one space.
back·ˈstage *adv* (in a theater, etc) behind the stage.
ˈ**back·track** *vi* retrace one's steps (eg on a trail).
ˈ**back·woods** *n pl* wooded land away from a settled area.
back·ˈyard *n* [C] small area or garden at the back of a terraced house.

back[3] /bæk/ *vt,vi* **1** go or cause to go back: *He ~ed the car into/out of the garage.* ***back up***, (cause to) go back or backward. **2** support: *~ a friend in an argument or quarrel.* ***back sb up,*** support him in every way. **3** bet money on (a horse, etc). **4** ***back down (from),*** give up a claim, etc: *I see he has ~ed down from the position he took last week.* ***back out (of),*** withdraw (from a promise or undertaking): *He's trying to ~ out* (*of his bargain*), escape from the agreement. **5** put or be a lining to; put on as a surface at the back: *~ed with sheet iron.*
ˈ**back·down** *n* [C] act of giving up a claim or retreating from a position.
backer *n* [C] **(a)** person who bets on a horse. **(b)** person who gives support or help (eg to a person, movement, etc).
ˈ**back·ing** *n* **(a)** help; support; body of supporters: *The new leader has a large ~ing.* **(b)** material used to form a support or lining to something.
ˈ**back·up** *n* [C] **(a)** support. **(b)** accumulation (of cars in traffic, liquid in a pipe, etc) extending backward from a stoppage.

back·gam·mon /ˈbækˌgæmən/ *n* [U] game for two players, played on a board with counters and dice.

back·ward /ˈbækwərd/ *adj* **1** towards the back or the starting point: *a ~ glance/movement.* **2** having made, making, less than the usual or normal progress: *This part of the country is still ~; there are no roads and no electricity.* **3** shy; reluctant; hesitating: *He is ~ in giving his views.*

back·ward(s) /ˈbækwərd(z)/ *adv* **1** away from one's front; toward the back: *He looked ~ over his shoulder.* **2** with the back or the end first: *Can you say the alphabet ~,* ie ZYXWV, etc? ***know sth backward(s)/(and forward(s))*** know it perfectly. ***backward(s) and forward(s),*** back and forth.

bacon /ˈbeikən/ *n* [U] salted or smoked meat from the back or sides of a pig.

bac·terial /bækˈtɪriəl/ *adj* of bacteria: *~ diseases.*

bac·terium /bækˈtɪriəm/ *n* [C] (*pl* -ria /-riə/) (kinds of) simplest and smallest form of plant life, existing in air, water and soil, and in living and dead creatures and plants, essential to animal life and sometimes a cause of disease.

bad[1] /bæd/ *adj* (worse, worst) **1** wicked, evil, immoral: *It is bad to steal.* ***call sb bad names,*** call him insulting names. **2** unpleasant; disagreeable; unwelcome: *We've had bad news. What bad weather we're having!* **3** (of things that are unpleasant) serious; noticeable: *That was a bad mistake. He's had a bad accident.* **4** inferior; worthless; incorrect; of poor quality: *His pronunciation of English is bad. What a bad drawing!* ***be in a bad way,*** be very ill or unfortunate; be in trouble or difficulty. ***go from bad to worse,*** get worse every day. ***with bad grace,*** showing unwillingness. ***not (so) bad,*** (*informal*) quite good. ***not half bad,*** (*informal*) very good. **5** unfit to eat; rotten: *bad eggs/meat.* ***go bad,*** become unfit to eat. **6** ***bad for,*** hurtful or injurious to; unsuitable for: *Smoking is bad for the health.* **7** in ill health, diseased: *a bad* (= sore) *back.* **8** ***too bad*** (*informal*) unfortunate: *It's too bad she's so ill.* **9** (*informal*) sorry: *I feel so bad about not being able to help you.*
bad debt, one that is unlikely to be paid.
ˈ**bad·lands** *n pl* (in certain parts of the western US) wild regions, esp one difficult to live in, cross through, etc.
bad language, swearwords; improper use of words connected with holy or sacred things.
bad·ly *adv* (worse, worst) **(a)** in a bad manner; roughly; untidily, etc: *badly made/dressed/wounded.* **(b)** by much: *badly beaten at football.* **(c)** ***want/need badly,*** very much: *She wants it badly.* **(d)** ***badly off,*** poor.
bad·ness /-nɪs/ *n* [U]
bad word, swearword; obscenity.

bad[2] /bæd/ *n* [U] that which is bad: *take the bad with the good,* take bad fortune with good fortune. ***in bad (with),*** (*informal*) in disfavor: *got in bad with the boss.*

bade /bæd/ *pt* of bid[3].

badge /bædʒ/ *n* [C] something (eg a design on cloth, metal, etc) worn to show a person's occupation, rank, etc or membership in a society.

badger[1] /ˈbædʒər/ *n* [C] small, gray animal living in holes in the earth and going about at night.

badger[2] /ˈbædʒər/ *vt* worry or annoy (with questions, requests, etc): *Tom has been ~ing his uncle to buy him a camera/for a camera.*

bad·min·ton /ˈbædˌmɪntən/ *n* [U] game played with rackets and shuttlecocks across a high, narrow net.

baffle[1] /ˈbæfəl/ *vt* hinder or prevent (a person) from doing something, by being too hard to understand, etc *One of the examination questions ~d me completely.*

baffle[2] /ˈbæfəl/ *n* [C] plate, board, screen, etc used to prevent or control the flow of a gas, liquid or sound.

bag[1] /bæg/ *n* [C] **1** container made of flexible material (paper, cloth, leather) with an opening at the top, used for carrying things from place to place: *a ˈtraveling bag; a ˈhandbag.* ***hold the bag,*** (*informal*) left to take the blame. ***in the bag,*** (*informal*) certain; assured: *the outcome of the election was in the bag.* ***let the cat out of the bag,*** tell a secret (without intending to do so). **2** base in baseball. **3** (*sl*) ugly or old woman.

bag[2] /bæg/ *vt,vi* (-gg-) **1** put into a bag or bags: *to bag groceries.* **2** kill or catch in hunting: *They bagged nothing except a couple of rabbits.* **3** (*informal*) take; seize. **4** hang loosely: *pants that bag at the knees.*

ba·gel /ˈbeigəl/ *n* [C] ring-shaped unsweetened roll.

bag·gage /ˈbægɪdʒ/ *n* [U] **1** luggage. **2** tents, bedding, equipment, etc, of an army: *a ˈ~ train.*

baggy /ˈbægi/ *adj* (-ier, -iest) hanging in loose folds: *~ pants.*

bag·pipes /ˈbægˌpaips/ *n pl* musical instrument with air stored in a bag of wind held under one arm and pressed out through pipes in which there are reeds.

bah /ba/ *int* used as a sign of contempt.

bail[1] /ˈbeiəl/ *n* [U] sum of money demanded by a law court, paid by or for a person accused of wrongdoing, as security that he will appear for his trial, until which time he is allowed to go free. □ *vt* (-ing /ˈbeilɪŋ/) ***bail sb out,*** obtain his freedom until trial by payment of bail.

bail[2] /ˈbeiəl/ *n* [C] curved handle of a pail or bucket.

bail[3] /ˈbeiəl/ *vt,vi* (-ing /ˈbeilɪŋ/) **1** throw water out of a boat with buckets, etc: *~ing water (out).* **2** ***bail out,*** jump with a parachute from an airplane.

bail·iff /ˈbeilɪf/ *n* [C] law officer who helps a sheriff.

bail·i·wick /ˈbeilɪˌwɪk/ *n* [C] area of one's authority, knowledge, skill, etc.

bait[1] /beit/ *n* [U] **1** anything, esp food, put on a hook to catch fish, or in nets, traps, etc to attract prey. **2** (*fig*) anything that attracts or tempts.

bait[2] /beit/ *vt,vi* **1** put bait (on a hook, etc) to catch fish, etc: *~ a hook with a worm.* **2** torment by making cruel or insulting remarks.

baize /beiz/ *n* [U] thick woolen cloth, usually green, used for covering (tables, etc): *green ~ for the card table.*

bake /beik/ *vt,vi* **1** cook, be cooked, by dry heat in an oven: *~ bread/cakes.* **2** make or become hard by heating: *The sun ~d the ground hard.*

baker *n* [C] person who bakes bread, etc.

baker's dozen, thirteen.

bak·ery *n* [C] place where bread and cakes are baked or sold.

ˈbake·shop *n* [C] = bakery.

baking powder /ˈbeikɪŋ ˌpaudər/ *n* [U] mixture of powders used to make bubbles of gas in cakes, etc and so cause them to be light.

baking soda /ˈbeikɪŋ ˌsoudə/ *n* [U] bicarbonate of soda.

bal. *abbr* = balance.

bala·laika /bæləˈlaikə/ *n* [C] stringed musical instrument (triangular, with three strings), popular in Russia and other countries in eastern Europe. ⇨ illus at string.

bal·ance[1] /ˈbæləns/ *n* **1** [C] apparatus for weighing, with two scales or pans. ***(be/hang) in the balance,*** (*fig*) (of a result) (be) still uncertain. **2** [U] condition of being steady; condition that exists when two opposing forces are equal. ***keep one's balance,*** keep steady, remain upright: *A small child has to learn to keep its ~ before it can walk far.* ***lose one's balance,*** become unsteady; fall. ***balance of power,*** condition in which no one country or group of countries is much stronger than another. **3** [U] (in art) harmony of design and proportion: *a picture lacking in ~.* **4** (*business*) difference between two columns of an account (money received and money paid out, etc). ***on balance,*** taking everything into consideration. **5** amount still owed after a part payment: *~ to be paid within one week.* **6 the balance,** (*informal*) the remainder of anything; what is left.

ˈbalance sheet, (*business*) written statement of financial condition showing credit and debit.

BALANCE

bal·ance[2] /ˈbæləns/ *vt,vi* **1** keep or put (something, oneself) in a state of balance: *Can you ~ a stick on the end of your nose?* **2** (of accounts) compare debits and credits and record the sum needed to make them equal; (of the two sides of a balance sheet) be equal: *My accounts ~.* **3** compare (two objects, plans, arguments, etc) (in order to judge the relative weight, value, truth, etc). ***a balanced diet,*** one with the quantity and variety of food needed for good health.

bal·cony /ˈbælkəni/ *n* [C] (*pl* -ies) **1** platform (with a wall or rail) built on an outside wall of the upper floor of a building. **2** (in a theater or concert hall) gallery or platform above orchestra level with rows of seats (usually) rising one above the other.

bald /bɔld/ *adj* (-er, -est) **1** (of men) having no or not much hair on the scalp; (of animals) hairless; (of birds) featherless; (of trees) leafless; (of land, hills, etc) without trees or bushes. **2** (*fig*) plain; without ornament: *a ~ statement of the facts,* one that gives the bare facts.

bald·ly *adv* (*fig*): *speaking ~ly; to put it ~ly,* plainly, without trying to soften what one says.

bald·ness /-nɪs/ *n* [U]

bald eagle /ˌbɔld ˈigəl/ *n* [C] common North American eagle, the national bird of the US, with white head and neck feathers when adult. ⇨ illus at bird.

bale /ˈbeiəl/ *n* [C] heap of material pressed

together and tied with rope or wire: *~s of cloth*. □ *vt* (-ing /ˈbeilɪŋ/) make into, pack in, bales.

balk /bɔk/ *vt,vi* **1** purposely get in the way of or prevent: *~ somebody's plans*, prevent him from carrying them out. **2** stop and refuse to go forward; *The horse ~ed at the high hedge. His boss ~ed at his expenses claim.*

ball[1] /bɔl/ *n* [C] **1** any solid or hollow sphere. **2** round or oval object, as used in games: (*ˈfoot~, ˈbase~, ˈbasket~, ˈtennis~*, etc). ***be on the ball,*** be alert, competent (in what one is doing). ***keep the ball rolling,*** keep the conversation, etc going. **3** (*informal*) the game of baseball. ***play ball,*** (*informal*) cooperate: *The management refused to play ~.* **4** material gathered, rolled or wound, into a round mass: *a ~ of wool/string; a ˈsnow~; a ˈmeat~,* of ground meat. **5** metal missile to be fired from a gun. **6** round part: *the ~ of the thumb,* near the palm; *the ~ of the foot,* near the base of the big toe. **7**⚠ (*vulg*) testicle. □ *int* ⚠ (*pl, vulg*) Nonsense! □ *vi* form into a ball; wind or squeeze into a ball.

ˈball game, the game of baseball.

ball[2] /bɔl/ *n* [C] **1** large, formal party for dancing. **2** (*informal*) a good time: *had a ~.*

ˈball·room *n* [C] large room where balls are held.

bal·lad /ˈbæləd/ *n* [C] song or poem, esp one that tells a story.

bal·last /ˈbæləst/ *n* [U] **1** heavy material (eg rock, iron, sand) loaded into a ship to keep it steady. **2** sand or other material carried in a balloon, to be thrown out to make the balloon go higher. **3** gravel, crushed rock, etc used to make a roadbed, esp for a railroad. □ *vt* supply with ballast.

ball bearing /ˌbɔl ˈberɪŋ/ *n* [C] bearing in which the revolving part turns on smooth metal balls in a groove.

bal·ler·ina /ˌbæləˈrinə/ *n* [C] woman ballet dancer.

bal·let /ˈbæˌlei/ *n* [C,U] **1** dramatic performance, without dialogue or singing, illustrating a story by a group of dancers. **2** the dancers: *a member of the ~.*

the ballet, this kind of stage performance as an art.

ˈballet dancer, person who dances in ballets.

bal·lis·tic /bəˈlɪstɪk/ *adj* of rockets, bullets, etc: *intercontinental ~ missiles,* long-range rockets for use in war.

bal·lis·tics *n pl* (with *sing verb*) science of projectiles.

bal·loon /bəˈlun/ *n* [C] **1** bag or envelope filled with heated air, or with gas lighter than air so that it will float above the ground. **2** toy, made of rubber, that can be filled with air or gas. □ *vi* swell out like a balloon.

bal·loon·ist *n* [C] person who goes up in balloons.

bal·lot /ˈbælət/ *n* **1** [C] piece of paper ticket, etc used in secret voting. **2** [C, U] (act of) secret voting. **3** total number of votes. □ *vi* vote or decide by ballot.

ˈballot box, box into which ballots are dropped by voters.

ball·point pen /ˌbɔlˌpɔint ˈpen/, **ball·point** /ˈbɔlˌpɔint/ *n* [C] pen that writes with a tip made of a small ball around which ink flows.

bally·hoo /ˈbæliˌhu/ *n* (*informal*) overstated, usually sensational advertising. □ *vt,vi* (*pt,pp* -ooed) advertise (something) in this way: *The company ~ed its product on bright, garish billboards.*

balm /bam/ *n* [U] **1** sweet-smelling oil or ointment obtained from certain kinds of trees, used, for soothing pain or healing. **2** (*fig*) that which gives peace of mind; consolation.

balmy *adj* (-ier, -iest) **1** (of air) soft and warm. **2** healing; fragrant.

ba·loney /bəˈlouni/ *n* [U] **1** (*sl*) nonsense. **2** = bologna.

balsa /ˈbɔlsə/ *n* [C,U] (light-weight wood of a) tropical American tree.

bal·sam /ˈbɔlsəm/ *n* **1** = balm(1). **2** plant or tree that gives balsam. **3** flowering plant grown in gardens.

balsam ˈfir, evergreen tree that is widely used as a Christmas tree.

bal·us·ter /ˈbæləstər/ *n* [C] **1** one of the upright posts supporting a handrail. **2** (*pl*) banisters.

bal·us·trade /ˈbæləˌstreid/ *n* [C] row of posts with a rail on top, round a balcony, terrace, flat roof, etc.

bam·boo /ˌbæmˈbu/ *n* (*pl* ~s) [U] tall plant with hard, hollow, jointed stems, of the grass family.

bam·boozle /ˌbæmˈbuzəl/ *vt* (*informal*) **1** bewilder: *You can't ~ me.* **2** cheat, trick: *~ him into paying too much; ~d them out of their fair share.*

ban /bæn/ *vt* (-nn-) order with authority that a thing must not be done, said, etc. *The school administration banned the textbook.* □ *n* [C] order that bans something.

ba·nal /bəˈnal, ˈbeinəl/ *adj* dull, ordinary and uninteresting: *~ remarks.*

ba·nana /bəˈnænə/ *n* [C] long, finger-shaped, thick-skinned (yellow when ripe) fruit growing in bunches on the banana tree in tropical and semitropical countries. ⇨ illus at fruit.

band /bænd/ *n* [C] **1** flat, thin strip of material, esp for fastening things together or for placing round an object to strengthen it: *papers kept together with a rubber ~.* **2** flat, thin strip of material forming part of an article of clothing: *waist~.* **3** strip or line, different from the rest in color or design, on something: *a white plate with a blue ~ round the edge.* **4** group of persons under a leader and with a common purpose: *a ~ of robbers.* **5** group of persons who play popular or light music together: *a ˈdance ~; a ˈjazz ~; a ˈsteel ~.* **6** particular range of wavelengths in radio broadcasting. **7** ring for a finger: *She wore a gold wedding ~.* □ *vt,vi* **1** put a band, strip or line on. **2** unite in a group: *They ~ed together to protest.*

ˈBand-Aid *n* [U] (*P*) pre-packaged adhesive bandage with a gauze pad.

ˈband·stand *n* [C] raised, open-air platform for a band(5).

ˈband·wagon *n* vehicle carrying the band(5) in a procession. ***jump on the bandwagon,*** join in, but only because success is guaranteed.

ban·dage /ˈbændɪdʒ/ *n* [C] strip of material as used for binding round a wound or injury. □ *vt* tie up with a bandage.

ban·danna /bænˈdænə/ *n* [C] large, brightly-colored handkerchief often worn around the neck or head.

ban·dit /ˈbændɪt/ *n* [C] robber, one of an armed band (eg attacking travelers in forests or mountains).

bandy[1] /ˈbændi/ *adj* (of the legs) curving outwards at the knees.

bandy[2] /ˈbændi/ *vt* exchange (words, blows). ***have one's name bandied about,*** be talked about in an unfavorable way, be a subject for gossip.

bang[1] /bæŋ/ *n* [C] **1** violent blow: *He fell and got a nasty ~ on the head.* **2** sudden, loud noise: *He always shuts the door with a ~.* □ *vt,vi* **1** hit violently or shut with a noise: *He ~ed at the door. He ~ed his fist on the table. Don't ~ the lid down. The door ~ed shut.* **2** make a loud noise: *The guns ~ed away.* □ *adv, int*: *go ~,* burst with a loud noise.

bang[2] /bæŋ/ *n* [C] (usu *pl*) fringe of hair cut short over the forehead.

bangle /ˈbæŋgəl/ *n* [C] ornamental rigid band worn as jewelry.

ban·ish /ˈbænɪʃ/ *vt* **1** send away, esp out of the country, as a punishment: *He was ~ed from the realm.* **2** put away from, out of (the mind): *~ care.*

banish·ment *n* [U]

ban·is·ter /ˈbænəstər/ *n* [C] **1** post supporting the handrail of a staircase. **2** (*pl*) posts and handrail together.

banjo /ˈbændʒou/ *n* [C] (*pl* ~s, ~es) musical instrument played by plucking the strings with the fingers or a pick. ⇨ illus at string.

bank[1] /bæŋk/ *n* [C] **1** land along each side of a river or canal: *A river flows between its ~s.* **2** mound or heap of earth. **3** (also ˈ**sandbank**) part of the seabed higher than its surroundings, but covered with enough water for ships except at low tide. **4** flat-topped mass of clouds, snow, etc, esp one formed by the wind: *The sun went down behind a ~ of clouds. The snow ~ completely blocked the driveway.* **5** inward slope along a curve, eg to enable a car to go round a curve with less risk.

bank[2] /bæŋk/ *vt,vi* **1** ***bank up,*** **(a)** make or form into banks, ⇨ 4 above: *The snow has ~ed up.* **(b)** heap up (the fire in a fireplace or furnace) with coal, etc so that the fire burns slowly for a long time. **2** (of a motorcycle or aircraft) travel with one side higher than the other (eg when turning).

bank[3] /bæŋk/ *n* [C] **1** establishment for lending, paying out and taking care of money: *have money in the ~,* have savings. **2** small container for holding coins, etc. **3** (place for storing) reserve supplies: *a ˈblood ~.*

ˈ**bank account,** arrangement for keeping money in a bank.

ˌ**bank ˈholiday,** day (except Sundays) when banks are closed by law.

ˈ**bank·note** *n* [C] piece of paper money.

ˈ**bank·roll,** *n* [C] (person's) ready cash. □ *vt* (*informal*) finance.

bank[4] /bæŋk/ *vt,vi* **1** place (money) in a bank[3] (1): *He ~s half his salary every month.* **2** keep money in a bank. **3** ***bank on,*** base one's hopes on: *I'm ~ing on your help.*

banker *n* [C] person who has to do with the business of running a bank.

bank·ing *n* [U] business of keeping a bank.

bank·rupt /ˈbæŋkˌrəpt/ *n* (*legal*) person judged by a law court to be unable to pay his debts in full, his property being divided among his creditors. □ *adj* **1** unable to pay one's debts. ***go bankrupt,*** become unable to pay one's debts. **2** completely without: *~ in ideas.* □ *vt* make bankrupt.

bank·ruptcy /ˈbæŋkˌrəpsi/ *n* (*pl* -ies) **1** [U] bankrupt condition. **2** [C] instance of this: *There were ten bankruptcies last year.*

ban·ner /ˈbænər/ *n* [C] **1** flag: *the ~ of freedom.* **2** flag or announcement, sometimes on two poles, on which there is a design, slogans, etc. **3** (also ˌ**banner ˈheadline**) (in a newspaper) prominent headline in large type.

ˈ**banner year,** one that is outstanding.

banns /bænz/ *n pl* public announcement in church that two persons are to be married: *put up/publish the ~.*

ban·quet /ˈbæŋkwɪt/ *n* [C] elaborate meal, usually for a special event, at which speeches are made: *a ˈwedding ~.* □ *vt,vi* give or take part in a banquet.

ban·tam /ˈbæntəm/ *n* [C] kind of small domestic fowl, of which esp the cock is a fighter.

bantam·weight *n* [C] boxer weighing between 112 and 118 lbs (50.8 and 53.5 kg).

ban·ter /ˈbæntər/ *vt,vi* tease in a playful way. □ *n* [U] good-humored teasing.

Bantu /ˈbænˌtu/ *adj, n* **1** one of a group of Central and South African Negro tribes. **2** their languages.

bao·bab /ˈbeiəˌbæb/ *n* [C] tree of tropical Africa with a trunk that grows to an enormous size.

bap·tism /ˈbæpˌtɪzəm/ *n* **1** [U] ceremony of sprinkling a person with, or immersing a person in, water, accepting him as a member of the Christian Church and (usually) giving him a name or names (in addition to the family name). **2** [C] instance of this: *There were six ~s at this church last week.* **3** (*fig*) first experience, often an ordeal: *a soldier's ~ of fire,* his first experience of warfare.

bap·tis·mal /bæpˈtɪzməl/ *adj* of baptism: *~al water.*

Bap·tist /ˈbæptɪst/ *n* [C] member of a Protestant church believing that baptism should be by immersion and at an age when a person is old enough to understand the meaning of the ceremony.

bap·tize /bæpˈtaiz, ˈbæpˌtaiz/ *vt* **1** give baptism to: *He had been ~d a Roman Catholic.* **2** give a name to: *was ~d Charles.*

bar[1] /bar/ *n* [C] **1** piece of hard, stiff material (eg metal, wood, soap, chocolate) longer than it is wide. **2** rod or rail, rigid length of wood or metal, across a door, window or gate, etc: *He was placed behind prison bars,* put into a prison cell. **3** (in a hotel, etc) room, counter, where drinks (such as beer and spirits) are served. **4** counter at which meals, etc are served and also eaten: *a ˈcoffee bar*. **5** bank or ridge of sand, etc across the mouth of a river or the entrance to a bay: *The ship crossed the bar safely*. **6** (*fig*) barrier or obstacle; thing that hinders or stops progress: *Poor health may be a bar to success in life*. **7** narrow band (of color, light, etc): *As the sun went down, there was a bar of red across the western sky*. **8** (*music*) (also **ˈbar line**) vertical line across the staff marking divisions of equal value in time; one of these divisions and the notes in it: *the opening bars of the Star-Spangled Banner*. ⇨ illus at notation. **9** railing or barrier in a law court, separating the part where the business is carried on from the part for spectators. ***the prisoner at the bar,*** the accused person.

the bar, (a) profession of law. **(b)** (*collect*) lawyers. ***be admitted to the bar,*** be received as a member of the bar.

ˈbar·fly *n* [C] (*sl*) steady drinker who frequents a bar[1](3).

ˈbar·girl *n* [C] = B-girl.

ˈbar·maid *n* [C] waitress at a bar.

ˈbar·ten·der *n* [C] person who mixes drinks at a bar[1](3).

bar[2] /bar/ *vt* (-rr-) **1** fasten (a door, gate, etc) with a bar or bars[1](2). **2** keep in or out: *He barred himself in,* fastened doors, windows, etc so that no one could enter the building. **3** obstruct: *Soldiers were barring the way and we couldn't go any farther*. **4** keep from: *bar a person from a competition,* order that he shall not take part.

bar[3] /bar/, **bar·ring** /ˈbarɪŋ/ *prep* except: *We shall arrive at noon barring accidents,* unless there are accidents. ***bar none,*** without exception. ***bar one,*** except one.

barb /barb/ *n* [C] curving point of an arrow, spear, fish hook, etc.

barbed *adj* having a barb or barbs: *~ed wire,* wire with short, sharp points, used for fences, etc.

bar·bar·ian /barˈbæriən/ *adj* uncivilized or uncultured. □ *n* [C] barbarian person.

bar·baric /barˈbærɪk/ *adj* of or like barbarians; rough and rude (esp in art and taste).

bar·ba·rism /ˈbarbəˌrɪzəm/ *n* **1** [U] state of being uncivilized, ignorant, or rude: *living in ~*. **2** [C] instance of this.

bar·bar·ity /barˈbærəti/ *n* (*pl* -ies) **1** [U] savage cruelty. **2** [C] instance of this: *the barbarities of modern warfare,* eg the bombing of cities.

bar·ba·rize /ˈbarbəˌraiz/ *vt* make barbarous.

bar·ba·rous /ˈbarbərəs/ *adj* **1** uncivilized; unrefined in taste, conduct, or habits. **2** cruel; savage.

bar·ba·rous·ly *adv*

bar·be·cue /ˈbarbɪˌkyu/ *n* [C] **1** grill, iron framework, for cooking meat, fish, etc. **2** animal (hog, steer, etc) roasted whole or in large pieces over an open fire. **3** (outdoor) social occasion at which meat cooked over a charcoal fire is eaten. □ *vt* **1** roast (meat, etc) in this way. **2** cook (meat, fish) in a spicy sauce.

bar·ber /ˈbarbər/ *n* [C] person whose trade is shaving men's beards and cutting men's hair.

bar·bitu·rate /barˈbɪtʃərɪt/ *n* [C,U] **1** (*chem*) (kinds of) substance causing sleep. **2** pill for settling the nerves or inducing sleep.

bard /bard/ *n* [C] (*liter*) poet: *the ~ of Avon,* Shakespeare.

bard·ic *adj* of bards or their songs.

bare[1] /ber/ *adj* **1** without clothing, covering, protection, or decoration: *fight with ~ hands,* without boxing gloves; *in his ~ skin,* naked; *~ floors,* without carpets, rugs, etc; *a ~ hillside,* without shrubs or trees. ***lay bare,*** uncover, expose, make known (something secret or hidden). **2** not more than: *the ~ necessities of life,* things needed just to keep alive; *earn a ~ living,* only just enough money to live on; *approved by a ~ majority,* a very small one.

ˈbare·back *adv* (of a horse) without a saddle: *ride ~back*.

ˈbare·faced *adj* insolent; shameless; undisguised: *It's ~faced robbery to ask $75 for such an old bicycle! He told me a ~faced lie*.

ˈbare·foot, bare·ˈfooted *adj, adv* without shoes and socks. ***be/go/walk barefoot.***

ˌbare·ˈheaded *adj* not wearing a hat.

ˌbare·ˈlegged *adj* with the legs bare; not wearing stockings or tights.

bare·ly *adv* only just; scarcely: *We ~ly had time to catch the train. I ~ly know her*.

bare·ness *n* [U]

bare[2] /ber/ *vt* uncover; reveal: *~ one's head,* take one's hat off. ***bare one's heart,*** make known one's deepest feelings. ***bare its teeth,*** (of an animal) show them in anger.

bar·gain /ˈbargən/ *n* [C] **1** agreement to buy, sell or exchange something, made after discussion. ***a good/bad bargain,*** one that favors/does not favor oneself. ***into the bargain,*** as well; in addition; moreover. ***drive a hard bargain,*** force an agreement favorable to oneself. ***make/strike a bargain,*** reach agreement. **2** thing offered, sold or bought cheap: *ˈ~-basement,* lowest floor of a store, where goods are offered at reduced prices; *~ price,* low price. □ *vi,vt* **1** talk for the purpose of reaching an agreement (about buying or selling, doing a piece of work, etc): *We ~ed with the farmer for a supply of milk and butter*. **2** ***bargain away,*** give up in return for something; sacrifice: *~ away one's freedom,* give it up in return for some advantages or other. ***bargain for,*** be ready or willing to accept or agree to: *He got more than he ~ed for,* (*informal*) was unpleasantly surprised. *I didn't ~ for John arriving so soon,* didn't expect it.

barge[1] /bardʒ/ *n* [C] large flat-bottomed boat for carrying goods and people on rivers and canals.

barge[2] /bardʒ/ *vi* (*informal*) move clumsily, without proper control of one's movements or without care. ***barge in/into,*** intrude; rudely interrupt: *Stop barging into our conversation*.

bari·tone /ˈbærəˌtoun/ *n* [C], *adj* (musical part for, or a male singer) having a range between tenor and bass.

bark[1] /bark/ *n* [U] outer covering or skin on the trunks, boughs and branches of trees. □ *vt* **1** take the bark off (a tree). ⇨ illus at tree. **2** scrape the skin off (one's knuckles, knee, etc) (by falling, etc).

bark[2] /bark/ *n* [C,U] **1** the cry made by dogs and

foxes. **2** (*fig*) harsh sound, eg of a cough. ***His bark is worse than his bite,*** he is not as dangerous as he seems. □ *vi,vt* **1** (of dogs, etc) give a bark or barks: *The dog ~s at strangers.* ***bark up the wrong tree,*** be mistaken. **2** say (something) in a fierce, commanding voice: *The officer ~ed (out) his orders.*

barker, *n* [C] person who calls out or announces wares for sale, acts at a circus, etc.

bar·ley /ˈbarli/ *n* [U] grass-like plant and its seed (called *grain*), used for food and for making beer and whiskey. ⇨ illus at cereal.

bar mitz·vah /ˌbar ˈmɪtsvə/ *n* [C] **1** ceremony held when a Jewish boy reaches the age of 13, recognizing that he has reached the age of religious responsibility. **2** boy who celebrates his bar mitzvah. ⇨ bas mitzvah.

barn /barn/ *n* [C] covered building for storing hay, grain, etc on a farm.

ˈbarn dance, dance formerly held in a barn.

ˈbarn owl, type of owl which is commonly found living in barns, where it eats rats, etc.

ˈbarn·yard *n* [C] area around a barn.

bar·nacle /ˈbarnəkəl/ *n* [C] small saltwater shellfish that fastens itself to objects under water, rocks, the bottoms of ships, etc.

barn·storm /ˈbarnˌstɔrm/ *vi* tour through the countryside giving stage performances or political speeches.

ba·rom·eter /bəˈramətər/ *n* [C] **1** instrument for measuring the pressure of the atmosphere in order to forecast the weather. **2** (*fig*) something which measures changes (eg in public opinion, market prices).

baro·met·ric /ˌbærəˈmetrɪk/ *adj*

bar·on /ˈbærən/ *n* [C] **1** (in Britain) member of a low rank of nobility. **2** powerful person; leader: *ˈoil ~s; a ˈcattle ~.*

bar·on·ess /ˈbærənɪs/ *n* [C] **1** (in Britain) baron's wife. **2** (in Britain) woman holding the rank of a baron in her own right.

bar·onet /ˌbærəˈnet/ *n* (in Britain) man lower in rank than a baron but above a knight.

bar·o·nial /bəˈrouniəl/ *adj* of, suitable for, noblemen.

ba·roque /bəˈrouk/ *n* [U], *adj* (of the) ornamental or extravagant style in the arts (esp architecture) in Europe in the 17th and 18th centuries.

bar·rack /ˈbærək/ *n* (usually *pl*) large building(s) for soldiers to live in.

bar·rage /bəˈraʒ/ *n* [C] **1** (*mil*) barrier made by heavy, continuous gunfire directed onto a given area. **2** large number of eg letters, words, etc, coming quickly, one after the other: *a ~ of questions.*

barred *pt,pp* of bar[2]

bar·rel /ˈbærəl/ *n* [C] **1 (a)** round container, made of curved strips of wood with bands or hoops, or of metal or plastic. **(b)** the amount that a barrel holds. **2** metal tube of a rifle, revolver or pistol. □ *vi, vt* (-l- or -ll-) **1** put in a barrel or barrels. **2** ***barrel along,*** (*sl*) travel at a high speed: *was ~ing along the highway.*

bar·reled, bar·relled *adj* stored in a barrel: *~ed beer.*

ˈbarrel organ, instrument from which music is produced by turning a cylinder to make it act mechanically on keys.

bar·ren /ˈbærən/ *adj* **1** (of land) not able to produce crops. **2** (of plants, trees) not producing fruit or seeds. **3** (of women, female animals) unable to have young ones. **4** (*fig*) without value, interest, or result: *a ~ discussion.*

bar·ren·ness *n* [U]

bar·rette /bəˈret/ *n* [C] clasp or bar with a pin, used by women and girls for holding the hair in place.

bar·ri·cade /ˈbærəˌkeid/ *n* [C] barrier of objects (eg sacks of sand, barbed wire, overturned cars) across or in front of something as a defense. □ *vt* block (a street, doorway, etc): *They ~d themselves in.*

bar·rier /ˈbæriər/ *n* [C] **1** something (eg a rail, gate, turnstile) that prevents, hinders, or controls progress or movement: *The Sahara Desert is a natural ~ that separates North and Central Africa.* **2** limit or boundary: *the ˈsound ~.* **3** (*fig*) hindrance: *Poor health and lack of money may both be ~s to educational progress.*

bar·ring ⇨ bar[3].

bar·row /ˈbærou/ *n* **1** = wheelbarrow. **2** small cart with two wheels, pulled or pushed by hand.

bar·ter /ˈbartər/ *vt,vi* exchange (goods, property, etc) (for other goods, etc): *~ wheat for machinery;* (*fig*) *~ away one's rights/honor/freedom.* □ *n* [U] exchange made in this way.

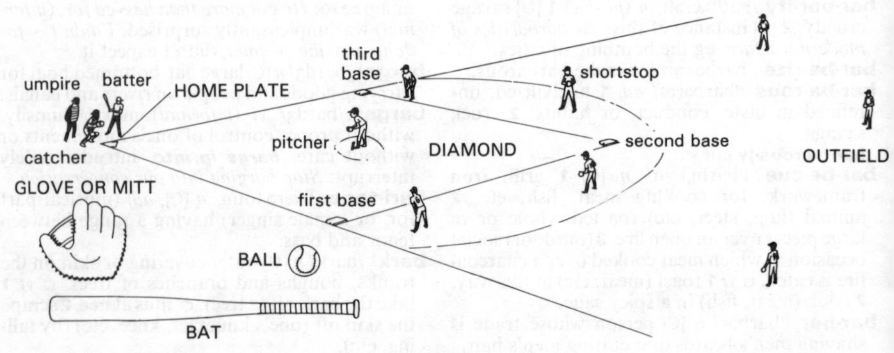

BASEBALL

bar·terer *n* [C]

base[1] /beis/ *n* [C] **1** lowest part of anything, esp the part on which a thing rests or is supported: *the ~ of a pillar*. **2** place at which armed forces, expeditions, etc have their stores, hospitals, etc: *a ˈnaval ~; a ~ camp,* eg for an Everest expedition. **3** (*geometry*) line or surface on which a figure stands or can stand. **4** (*math*) the number (usually 10) which is the starting point for a numerical system. **5** (*chem*) substance capable of combining with an acid to form a salt and water only. **6** one of four positions a runner in baseball must touch in order to score. ⇨ illus at baseball. ***off base,*** (*informal*) wrong, mistaken.

base·less *adj* without cause or reason: *~less fears*.

base[2] /beis/ *vt* ***base on/upon,*** use as a basis for: *Direct taxation is usually ~d on income*.

base[3] /beis/ *adj* **1** (of persons, their behavior, thoughts, etc) dishonorable: *acting from ~ motives*. **2** of low value or quality: *~ metals,* non-precious metals.

base·ball /ˈbeisˌbɔl/ *n* **1** [U] game played with a bat and ball by two teams of nine players on a field with four bases. **2** [C] ball used in this game. **ˈbaseball bat,** used for hitting the ball in this game.

base·board /ˈbeisˌbɔrd/ *n* [C] line of boards around the walls of a room, next to the floor.

base·ment /ˈbeismənt/ *n* [C] lowest part of a building, partly or wholly below ground level.

bases **1** /ˈbeiˌsiz/ *pl* of basis. **2** /ˈbeisɪz/ *pl* of base[1].

bash /bæʃ/ *vt* (*informal*) strike heavily so as to break or injure: *~ in the lid of a box; ~ him on the head with a stick; ~ one's head in the dark*. □ *n* [C] **1** violent blow or knock: *I gave somebody a ~ on the nose*. **2** (*informal*) party.

bash·ful /ˈbæʃfəl/ *adv* = shy (the usual word).

bash·fully /-fəli/ *adv*

basic /ˈbeisɪk/ *adj* of or at the base or start; fundamental: *the ~ vocabulary of a language,* the words that must be known.

ba·si·cally /-kli/ *adv* fundamentally.

basil /ˈbæzəl, ˈbeizəl/ *n* [U] sweet-smelling herb like mint, used in cooking.

ba·sil·ica /bəˈsɪlɪkə/ *n* [C] (*pl* ~s) **1** oblong hall divided by rows of columns (used in ancient Rome as a law court). **2** building of this type used as a church: *the ~ of St. Peter's in Rome*.

basin /ˈbeisən/ *n* [C] **1** round, open dish for holding liquids. ⇨ washbasin. **2** as much as a basin can hold. **3** hollow place where water collects (eg a stone structure at the base of a fountain, a deep pool at the base of a waterfall, deep part of a harbor). **4** area of country drained by a river and its tributaries: *the Mississippi ~*.

basis /ˈbeisɪs/ *n* [C] (*pl* -ses /-ˌsiz/) foundation; base: *arguments that have a firm ~,* that are easily supported by facts; *On the ~ of our sales forecasts* (ie from what these show) *we may make a profit next year*.

bask /bæsk/ *vi* enjoy warmth and light: *sitting in the garden, ~ing in the sunshine;* (*fig*) *~ing in her favor/approval*.

bas·ket /ˈbæskɪt/ *n* [C] **1** container, usually made of materials that bend and twist easily (canes, rushes): *a ˈshopping ~; a ˌwaste ˈpaper ~*. **2** as much as a basket can hold: *They gathered a ~ of plums*.

bas·ket·ball /ˈbæskɪtˌbɔl/ *n* **1** [U] indoor game played by two teams of five players who try to throw a large ball into baskets fixed 10 ft. above the ground at each end of the court. **2** [C] ball used in this game.

BASKETBALL

bas mitz·vah /ˌbas ˈmɪtsvə/ *n* [C] **1** ceremony held when a Jewish girl reaches the age of 13, recognizing that she has reached the age of religious responsibility. **2** girl who celebrates her bas mitzvah. ⇨ bar mitzvah.

bas-relief /ˌbarɪˈlif/ *n* **1** [U] (= *low relief*) sculpture in which a flat surface of metal or stone is cut away so that a design or picture stands out. **2** [C] example of this.

bass[1] /ˈbæs/ *n* (*pl* unchanged) kinds of fish used as food, caught in rivers, lakes and in the sea. ⇨ illus at fish.

bass[2] /beis/ *n* [C], *adj* **1** deep-sounding; low in tone; (musical part for, or singer) having the lowest adult male voice. **2** instrument with the same range. ⇨ illus at notation.

bas·soon /ˈbəˈsun/ *n* [C] musical wind instrument with double reeds made of wood, giving very low notes. ⇨ illus at brass.

bass·wood /bæsˌwʊd/ *n* **1** [C] linden tree of North America. **2** [U] wood of this tree.

bas·tard /ˈbæstərd/ *n* [C] **1** illegitimate child: *a ~ child/daughter/son*. **2** ⚠ (also as *int*) ruthless insensitive person, esp a male (used as a term of abuse): *He's a real ~, leaving his wife in that way*. **3** (*informal*) (mock abusively, between friends); *Harry, you old ~, imagine meeting you here!* **4** ⚠ unfortunate fellow: *Poor ~! He's been fired and he won't find another job very easily*. **5** (of things) not genuine or authentic.

bas·tard·ize /ˈbæstərˌdaiz/ *vt* **1** (of things) counterfeit. **2** (of languages) speak incorrectly, esp because of imperfect learning: *~d French*.

baste[1] /beist/ *vt* sew cloth with long temporary stitches (tacks(2)).

baste[2] /beist/ *vt* moisten meat with its own juices, fat, etc while cooking.

bas·tion /ˈbæstʃən/ *n* [C] **1** (often five-sided) part of a fortification that stands out from the rest. **2** (*fig*) stronghold near hostile territory.

bat[1] /bæt/ *n* [C] small mouse-like, winged animal that flies at night and feeds on fruit and insects. ***as blind as a bat,*** unable to see, not seeing, clearly.

bat[2] /bæt/ *n* [C] **1** shaped wooden implement for striking the ball in games, esp baseball. ***go to bat for sb,*** (*informal*) support him. ***right off the bat,*** (*informal*) immediately: *did it right off the bat.* **2** ***(be) at bat,*** take one's turn batting. □ *vi,vt* (-tt-) hit; hit with a bat.

batter *n* [C] baseball player who bats. ⇨ illus at baseball.

ˈ**batting average,** measure of a baseball player's performance at bat, determined by dividing the number of sucessful hits by the number of turns at bat.

bat[3] /bæt/ *vt* (-tt-) ***not bat an eyelid,*** not show any surprise.

batch /bætʃ/ *n* [C] **1** number of persons or things treated as a group: *a ~ of letters to be answered.* **2** number of loaves, cakes, etc baked together: *baked in ~es of twenty.*

ba·teau, bat·teau /bæˈtou, ˈbæˌtou/ rowboat with a flat bottom and blunt ends.

bath /bæθ/ *n* (*pl* ~s /bæðz/) **1** [C] washing of the body, by sitting or lying in water: *I shall have a hot ~ and go to bed.* **2** [U] water for a bath: *Your ~ is ready.* **3** [C] (container for) liquid in which something is washed or dipped.

ˈ**bath·room** *n* [C] **(a)** room in which there is a bath. **(b)** room in which there is a toilet.

ˈ**bath·tub** *n* [C] oblong vessel in which baths are taken.

bathe /beið/ *vt,vi* **1** apply water to; soak in water; put in water: *The doctor told him to ~ his eyes twice a day.* **2** go into the sea, a river, lake, etc for sport, swimming, to get cool, etc. **3** ***be bathed in,*** be covered or surrounded: *Her face was ~d in tears.* ⇨ also sun[1].

bather /ˈbeiðər/ *n* [C]

bath·ing suit /ˈbeiðiŋ ˌsut/ *n* [C] garment worn for swimming.

bathos /ˈbeiˌθas/ *n* [U] sudden change (in writing or speech) from what is deeply moving or sublime to what is foolish or unimportant.

ba·tik /bəˈtik/ *n* **1** [U] method of printing colored designs on textiles by waxing the parts not to be dyed. **2** [C] piece of cloth dyed in this way.

baton /bəˈtan/ *n* [C] **1** staff carried as a symbol of office. **2** short, thin stick as used by the conductor of a band or an orchestra.

bats /bæts/ *adj* (*sl*) mad; eccentric. ***go bats,*** go crazy.

bat·tal·ion /bəˈtælyən/ *n* [C] **1** army unit made up of several companies and commanded by a lieutenant colonel. **2** large group of persons acting together.

bat·ten /ˈbætən/ *n* [C] **1** long board, eg one used to keep other boards in place, or to which other boards are nailed. **2** (on a ship) strip of wood or metal used to fasten down covers or tarpaulins over a hatch. □ *vt* ***batten down,*** make secure with battens.

bat·ter[1] /ˈbætər/ *vt,vi* strike hard and often; beat out of shape: *It's no good — we'll have to ~ the door down. He was driving a badly ~ed old car.*

ˈ**battering ram,** (*mil*) big, heavy log with an iron head (formerly) used for knocking down walls.

bat·ter[2] /ˈbætər/ *n* [U] beaten mixture of flour, eggs, milk, etc for cooking.

bat·ter[3] ⇨ bat[2].

bat·tery /ˈbætəri/ *n* [C] (*pl* -ies) **1** group of connected electric cells from which current will flow: *This radio has four small batteries.* **2** army unit of big guns, with men and vehicles. **3** group of big guns on a warship, or for coastal defense. **4** set of similar utensils or instruments used together: *a ~ of lenses/ovens.* **5** (*legal*) attack on or threatening touch. ⇨ assault.

battle /ˈbætəl/ *n* **1** [C,U] fight, esp between organized and armed forces. **2** (*fig*) any struggle: *the ~ of life.* ***die in battle,*** die fighting. ***be half the battle,*** be a great advantage: *Youth is half the ~,* youthful strength brings likelihood of success. □ *vi* struggle: *battling against poverty. They ~d with the winds and waves.*

ˈ**battle-ax, battle-axe** *n* [C] **(a)** heavy ax(e) with a long handle, formerly used as a weapon. **(b)** (*informal*) quarrelsome woman.

ˈ**battle cruiser,** large, fast cruiser with heavy guns and lighter armor than a battleship.

ˈ**battle·field** *n* [C] place where a battle is or was fought.

ˈ**battle·ship** *n* [C] large warship, with big guns and heavy armor.

battle·ments /ˈbætəlmənts/ *n pl* low wall at the top of a tower or castle with openings through which to shoot.

batty /ˈbæti/ *adj* (-ier, -iest) (*sl*) crazy; slightly mad. ***go batty,*** go crazy.

bauble /ˈbɔbəl/ *n* [C] pretty, bright and pleasing ornament of little value.

baux·ite /ˈbɔkˌsait/ *n* [U] clay-like substance from which aluminum is obtained.

bawdy /ˈbɔdi/ *adj* (-ier, -iest) (of talk, persons) vulgar; using obscene, indecent subjects to laugh at, etc: *~ talk/stories.*

bawd·ily /ˈbɔdəli/ *adv*

bawl /bɔl/ *vt,vi* shout or cry loudly: *The frightened child ~ed for help.*

bay[1] /bei/ *n* **1** kind of tree or shrub with leaves that are used in cooking and are spicy when crushed. **2** (*pl*) **(a)** laurel wreath given in ancient times to poets and heroes, victors in war and athletic contests. **(b)** (*fig*) honor; glory.

bay[2] /bei/ *n* [C] part of the sea or of a large lake, enclosed by a wide curve of the shore.

bay[3] /bei/ *n* [C] **1** space between pillars that divide a wall, building etc. **2** recess. **3** part of a ship, etc for those who are ill or injured: *the ˈsick-bay.* **4** compartment in an aircraft, warehouse, barn, etc for storing things: *the ˈbomb bay; Clear No. 3 bay to make room for new stock.*

bay ˈwindow, window(s) in a recess that extends outward from the wall of a building.

bay[4] /bei/ *n* [C] long, deep bark, esp of hounds while hunting. ***keep/hold sb at bay,*** keep an enemy, etc at a distance; prevent him from coming too near. □ *vi* (esp of large dogs, hounds) bark with a deep note, esp continuously, when hunting.

bay[5] /bei/ *adj, n* [C] reddish-brown (horse): *He was riding a dark bay.*
bay·onet /ˈbeiənɪt, -ˌnet/ *n* [C] dagger-like blade that fits on to the muzzle of a rifle. □ *vt* stab with a bayonet.
ba·zaar /bəˈzar/ *n* [C] **1** shop for the sale of many different kinds of goods. **2** (place where there is a) sale of goods for charitable purposes: *a church* ~. **3** (in Asian countries) street of workshops and shops; that part of a town where the markets and shopping streets are.
ba·zoo·ka /bəˈzukə/ *n* [C] (*pl* ~s) portable weapon for firing armor-piercing rockets.
BB /ˈbibi/ *n* (*pl* BB's) small pellet for shooting in an air rifle.
ˈBB ˌgun, air rifle for firing BB's.
B.C., BC /ˌbiˈsi/ *abbr* = Before Christ. ⇨ before[3].
bdrm. *abbr* = bedroom.
BBC /ˌbi ˌbi ˈsi/ *abbr* = British Broadcasting Corporation.
be[1] /bi/ *vi* (*present tense* am /*after "I":* m *otherwise:* əm, *strong form:* æm/, is /z *but* s *after* p, t, k, f, θ, *strong form:* ɪz/, are /ər *strong form:* ar/; *pt* was /wəz/, were /wər/ *contracted forms,* I'm /aim/, he's /hiz/, she's /ʃiz/, it's /ɪts/, we're /wə *strong form:* wɪr/, you're /yər, yʊər/, they're /ðer/; *negatives* isn't /ɪzənt/, aren't /arnt/, wasn't /wəzənt/, weren't /wərnt/; *present participle* being /ˈbiɪŋ/, *pp* been /bɪn/) **1** (with a *noun* or *pronoun*, identifying or asking about the subject): *Today is Monday. Is Peter a teacher/a Catholic?* **2** (with an *adjective,* etc, in descriptions): *The world is round. He is ten years old.* **3** (with a *prepositional phrase* or *adverb*, indicating place): *The lamp is on the table. Mary's upstairs.* **4** (with a *prep,* indicating possession): *The parcel is for you.* **5** (indicating a change from one quality, place, etc to another): *He wants to be* (= become) *a fireman when he grows up. You can be* (= get) *there in five minutes.* **6** go; come (esp the *pp* been): *I've been to see my uncle. He has been to Paris.* **7** exist; live (with *there*): *There's a bus stop down the road. There were six of us. Is there a God?* ***for the time being,*** until some other arrangement, etc is made. ⇨ also being.
be[2] /bi/ *auxiliary verb* (used with other verbs) (for pronunciations, etc ⇨ be[1]) **1** (used with *present participles* to form the progressive or continuous tenses): *They are/were reading. I shall be seeing him soon. What have you been doing this week?* **2** (used with a *pp* to form the passive voice): *He was killed in the war.* **3** (used with a *to*-infinitive) **(a)** (= *must* or *ought*, indicating duty, necessity, etc): *You are to be congratulated. At what time am I to be there?* **the** ***n*****-to-ˈbe,** the future...: *the bride-to-ˈbe.* **(b)** (intention): *They are to be married in May.* **(c)** (mutual arrangement): *Every member of the party was to pay his own expenses.* **(d)** (indicating future time): *We are to see him next Monday.*
be- /bi-/ *prefix* **1** (be- + *v* = *v*) all over; all around; in all directions: *bestrew.* **2** (be- + *n* or *adj* = *v*) make; become: *befriend.* **3** (be- + *vi* = *vt*): *bemoan.*
beach /bitʃ/ *n* [C] shore of an ocean, sea or lake, covered with sand or pebbles. □ *vt* push or pull (a boat, a ship) up on to the shore or beach.
ˈbeach ball, very large light-weight ball used for games on the beach.
ˈbeach·comber /-ˌkoumər/ *n* [C] **(a)** long wave rolling in from the sea. **(b)** man who makes a poor living on the waterfront.
ˈbeach·head *n* fortified position established on a beach by an invading army. ⇨ bridgehead.
ˈbeach·wear *n* [U] clothes for sunbathing, swimming, etc on the beach.
beach plum /ˈbitʃ ˌpləm/ *n* [C,U] fruit of a shrubby plum growing on the Atlantic coast of the northern US and Canada.
bea·con /ˈbikən/ *n* [C] **1** fire lit on a hill-top as a signal. **2** light on a hill or mountain, or on the coast, in a lighthouse, etc to give warning of danger or for the guidance of ships, etc. ⇨ illus at lighthouse. **3** radio transmitter that sends out beams to guide aircraft.
bead /bid/ *n* [C] **1** small ball of wood, glass, etc with a hole through it, for threading with others on a string or wire. **2** (*pl*) necklace of beads. **3** drop of liquid: *His face was covered with* ~*s of sweat.*
beady /ˈbidi/ *adj* (-ier, -iest) (of eyes) small, round and bright.
beagle /ˈbigəl/ *n* [C] small, short-legged dog used for hunting. ⇨ illus at dog.
beak /bik/ *n* [C] hard, horny part of bird's mouth, esp when curved. ⇨ illus at bird.
beaker /ˈbikər/ *n* [C] **1** open glass vessel with a lip (as used for chemical experiments, etc). **2** similar vessel, used as a drinking glass.
beam /bim/ *n* [C] **1** long horizontal piece of squared timber, steel, etc used to carry the weight of a building, etc. **2 (a)** ray or stream of light (eg from a lamp or lighthouse, the sun or moon). **(b)** (*fig*) bright look or smile, showing happiness, etc: *with a* ~ *of delight.* **(c)** radio signal used to direct an aircraft on its course. **3** crosspiece of a balance, from which the scales hang. □ *vt,vi* **1** (of the sun, etc) send out light and warmth. **2** (*fig*) smile happily and cheerfully: *~ing on his friends; ~ing with satisfaction.* **3** send (a radio program, etc) in a particular direction: *~ed from the US to South America.*
bean /bin/ *n* [C] **1** (any of several plants with) seed in long pods (all used as vegetables): *ˈgreen* ~*s, ˈkidney* ~*s, ˈsoy* ~*s.* **2** seed shaped like a bean *ˈcoffee* ~*s.* ***full of beans,*** lively; in high spirits. ***spill the beans,*** make a secret known. **3** (*sl*) head. **4** (*pl*) (*sl*) the smallest amount: *doesn't know* ~*s about the subject.*
ˈbean·stalk *n* stalk of tall-growing varieties of bean.
bear[1] /ber/ *n* [C] **1** large, heavy animal with thick fur. **2** rough, clumsy ill-mannered person. **3** speculator (esp on the stock exchange) who sells shares in anticipation of a drop in prices.
bear·ish *adj* (of investors, speculators, etc, esp on the stock market) having a belief that prices will fall rapidly.
ˌbear ˈmarket, condition (on the stock exchange) when stock prices are falling rapidly.
ˌGreat/ˌLittle ˈBear, names of two constellations in the northern hemisphere.

bear[2] /ber/ *vt,vi* (*pt* bore /bɔr/, *pp* borne /bɔrn/) **1** carry: *~ a heavy load.* **2** have; show: *~ the marks/signs of blows/wounds/punishment; a document that ~s your signature.* **3** have; be known by: *a family that bore an ancient and honored name.* **4** feel: *the love/hatred she bore him,* felt towards him. **5** support; sustain: *The ice is too thin to ~ your weight. Who will ~ the responsibility/expense?* **6** (with *can/could*) endure; tolerate; put up with: *I can't ~ (the sight of) that evil man. The pain was almost more than he could ~. How can you ~ to look at her?* **7** be fit for: *His language doesn't ~ repeating.* **8** give birth to: *~ a child. She has borne him six sons.* (*Note: born: The eldest son was born in 1932.*) **9** turn: *When you reach the top of the hill, ~ (to the) right.* **10** (special uses with *adverbial particles* and *prepositions*):

bear on/upon, be connected; have influence on: *These are matters that ~ on the welfare of the community.* ***bring to bear on/upon,*** make (a thing) relate to, have influence on: *bring pressure to ~ on a person.* ⇨ bearing(2).

bear (sth/sb) out, confirm (something); support (somebody): *John will ~ me out/will ~ out what I've said.*

bear up (against/under sth), be strong in the face of (sorrow, etc): *Tell her to ~ up,* to have courage, not give way.

bear with (sb), treat patiently: *Please ~ with me* (ie listen patiently to me) *a little longer.*

bear·able /ˈberəbəl/ *adj* (from bear[2](6)) that can be endured.

beard /bɪrd/ *n* [C] **1** hair of the lower part of the face (excluding the mustache): *a man with a ~.* **2** similar growth of hair on an animal: *a goat's ~.* □ *vt* defy openly, oppose.

bearded *adj* having a beard.

bearer /ˈberər/ *n* [C] **1** person who brings a letter or message: *the ~ of good news; the ~ of this letter.* **2** person who helps to carry a coffin to a grave, who carries a stretcher, flag, etc. **3** person who presents a check at a bank.

bear·ing /ˈberɪŋ/ *n* **1** [U] way of behaving; way of standing, walking, etc: *a man of military ~.* **2** [C,U] relation, aspect: *What he said has no/not much ~ on* (= is not connected with) *the subject.* **3** [C] direction in which a place, etc, lies: *take a compass ~ on a lighthouse.* **4** (*pl*) relative position; direction. ***find/lose one's bearings,*** (*fig*) find/lose one's sense of direction or purpose in life, etc. **5** (in a machine) part on or in which another part turns.

beast /bist/ *n* [C] **1** four-footed, usually large, animal (*animal* is the usual word). ***beast of burden,*** animal used for heavy work or for carrying heavy loads. **2** (*informal*) cruel or disgusting person.

beast·ly *adj* like a beast.

beat[1] /bit/ *n* [C] **1** regular repeated stroke, or sound of this: *We heard the ~ of a drum. His heart ~s were getting weaker.* **2** recurring emphasis marking rhythm in music or poetry. **3** route over which a person (eg a policeman) goes regularly.

beat[2] /bit/ *vt,vi* (*pt* ~, *pp* ~en /ˈbitən/, sometimes *pp* ~ in sense(5)) **1** hit repeatedly (eg with a stick): *He was ~ing a drum. The boy was ~en until he was black and blue,* covered with bruises. *Somebody was ~ing at/on the door.* ***beat a retreat,*** **(a)** give the signal (by drum) to retreat. **(b)** (*fig*) go back, retire. **2** (of the sun, rain, wind, etc) strike: *The rain was ~ing against the windows.* **3** mix thoroughly and let air into by using a fork or similar utensil: *~ eggs.* **4** hammer, change the shape of by blows: *~ something flat.* **5** defeat; do better than: *Our army was ~en. He ~ me at chess.* ***beat the record,*** make a new and better record. **6** be too difficult for: *That problem has ~en me.* **7** move up and down regularly: *His heart was still ~ing.* ***beat time,*** measure time (in music) by making regular movements (with the hands, etc). **8** ***beat about the bush,*** talk about something without coming to the point. ***beat it,*** (*sl*) go away. **9** (special uses with *adverbial particles* and *prepositions*):

beat down (on), *The sun was ~ing down on our heads,* shining with great heat. ***beat sb/sth down:*** *He wanted $800 for the car but I ~ him down* (= made him lower his price) *to $600.*

beat sb/sth off, repel: *The attacker/attack was ~en off.*

beat sth out, **(a)** (of a fire) put out. **(b)** (of rhythm, etc) be played: *He ~ out* (= drummed) *a tune on a tin can.*

beat sb up, fight and hurt badly.

beat[3] /bit/ *adj* (*sl*) **1** exhausted: *I really feel ~.* **2** of an unconventional lifestyle, esp of the type which first developed on the West Coast in the late 1950's: *the ~ generation.*

beat·nik /ˈbitnɪk/ *n* [C] person with a beat lifestyle.

beaten /ˈbitən/ *adj* (esp) **1** shaped by beating: *~ silver.* **2** (of a path) worn hard by use: *a well-~ path.* ***go off/keep to the beaten track,*** do something/not do anything unusual.

beater /ˈbitər/ *n* [C] utensil used for beating: *an ˈegg ~.*

bea·tif·ic /biəˈtɪfɪk/ *adj* showing great happiness.

be·ati·fi·ca·tion /biˌætəfəˈkeiʃən/ *n* [C,U] beatifying or being beatified; first step before canonization.

be·atify /biˈætəˌfai/ *vt* (*pt,pp* -fied) (in the Catholic Church) announce that a dead person is among the blessed.

beat·ing /ˈbitɪŋ/ *n* [C] (esp punishment by hitting or striking repeatedly) defeat: *give him a good ~ing.*

be·ati·tude /biˈætəˌtud/ *n* [U] great happiness.

beau /bou/ *n* [C] (*pl* ~x, ~s /bouz/) **1** (*old use*) rather old man who is greatly interested in fashion of his clothes. **2** (now usu *hum*) girl's admirer or lover.

beau·te·ous /ˈbyutiəs/ *adj* (*poet*) beautiful.

beau·ti·cian /byuˈtɪʃən/ *n* [C] person who works in a beauty shop.

beau·ti·ful /ˈbyutəfəl/ *adj* giving pleasure or delight to the mind or senses: *a ~ face/flower/voice; ~ weather/music.*

beau·ti·fully /-f(ə)li/ *adv* in a beautiful manner: *She plays the piano ~ly.*

beau·tify /ˈbyutəˌfai/ *vt* (*pt,pp* -fied) make

beautiful.

beauty /ˈbyuti/ *n* (*pl* -ies) **1** [U] combination of qualities that give pleasure to the senses (esp the eye and ear) or to the moral sense or the intellect: *the ~ of a sunlit rose garden.* **2** [C] person, thing that is beautiful or particularly good: *Isn't she a ~! Look at this horse. Isn't it a ~!*

ˈbeauty parlor = beauty shop.

ˈbeauty queen, girl voted the most beautiful in a contest.

ˈbeauty shop, place for the care of women's figure, skin, hair, etc.

ˈbeauty sleep, sleep before midnight.

ˈbeauty spot, (a) place with beautiful scenery. **(b)** birthmark.

bea·ver /ˈbivər/ *n* **1** [C] fur-coated animal that lives both on land and in water, with strong teeth with which it cuts down trees and makes dams across rivers. **2** [U] its fur.

ˈbeaver dam, made by beavers of twigs, etc in a stream to create a pond for their lodges.

ˈbeaver lodge, underwater dwelling of twigs, etc made by beavers in a pond.

ˈbeaver pond, created by beavers for their lodges.

be·bop /ˈbiˌbap/ *n* [U] fast style of jazz music.

be·calmed /biˈkamd/ *adj* (of a sailing ship) stopped because there is no wind.

be·came *pt* of become.

be·cause /bɪˈkɔz, -ˈkəz/ *conj* **1** for the reason that: *I did it ~ they asked me to do it.* (*Note:* when the reason is obvious, or is thought to be known, it is preferable to use *as* or *so: As it's raining, you'd better take a taxi. It's raining, so you'd...* After the noun *reason, that* is preferred to *because: The reason why we were late is that...*) **2** ***because of,*** *prep* by reason of; on account of: *Because of his bad leg, he couldn't walk so fast as the others.*

beckon /ˈbekən/ *vt,vi* get a person's attention by a movement of the hand or arm, usually to show that he is to come nearer or to follow.

be·come /bɪˈkəm/ *vi,vt* (*pt* became /bɪˈkeim/, *pp* become) **1** come or grow to be; begin to be: *He became a doctor. It's becoming much more expensive to travel abroad.* **2** ***become of,*** happen to: *What will ~ of the children if their father dies?* **3** be right or fitting: *He used language* (eg vulgar language) *that does not ~ a man of his education.*

be·com·ing *adj* attractive; suitable: *a becoming hat/dress; with a modesty becoming to his low rank.*

be·com·ing·ly *adv*

bed¹ /bed/ *n* [C] **1** piece of furniture, or other arrangement, on which to sleep (*Note:* the example sentences show when the *articles* are used.): *go to bed; get into/out of bed; put the children to bed; sit on the bed; find a bed for her.* ***bed and board,*** food and lodging. ***get out of bed on the wrong side,*** be bad-tempered. ***make the bed,*** put the bedclothes (sheets, blankets, etc) in order, ready for use. **2** flat base on which something rests: *The dam is built on a bed of concrete.* **3** bottom of the sea, a river, lake, etc: *the ˈsea bed.* **4** layer of rock, stone, etc as a foundation for a road or railway; layer of clay, rock, etc, below the surface soil: *If you dig here, you will find a bed of clay.* **5** garden plot, piece of ground (for flowers, vegetables, etc): *ˈflower beds.*

ˈbed·bug *n* [C] small, bloodsucking insect sometimes found in houses, and esp in beds. ⇨ illus at insect.

ˈbed·clothes *n pl* sheets, blankets, etc for a bed.

ˈbed·pan *n* [C] vessel for urine, etc, used by an invalid in bed.

ˈbed·rid·den *adj* confined to bed by weakness or old age.

ˈbed·rock *n* [U] (layer of) solid rock underneath soil.

ˈbed·room *n* [C] room for sleeping in.

ˈbed·side *n* [C] side of a sick person's bed: (as an *adjective*) *Dr. Green has a good bedside manner,* knows how to win his patients' confidence in himself.

ˈbed·sore *n* [C] sore on the back, etc of an invalid, caused by lying in bed for a long time.

ˈbed·spread *n* [C] covering spread over a bed during the day.

ˈbed·stead *n* [C] framework of wood and metal to support the mattress.

ˈbed·time *n* [C] time for going to bed: *His usual bedtime is eleven o'clock.*

bed² /bed/ *vt* (-dd-) **1** make or find a bed for: *The farmer bedded the animals in the barn.* ***bed down sb/sth,*** make or arrange a bed for: *bed down a soldier/traveler/horse, etc.* **2** embed; place or fix in a foundation: *The bullet bedded itself in* (= went deep into) *the wall.* **3** plant or set (seedlings etc): *She bedded the tulips by the front sidewalk.*

bed·ding /ˈbedɪŋ/ *n* [U] **1** bedclothes. **2** straw, etc for animals to sleep on.

be·decked /biˈdekt/ *adj* adorned, decorated (with flowers, jewels, etc).

be·dev·il /biˈdevəl/ *vt* (-l-, -ll-) **1** trouble; torment. **2** confuse; complicate: *The issue is ~ed by Smith's refusal to cooperate with us.*

be·dev·il·ment *n* [U]

be·dewed /biˈdud/ *pred adj* (*liter*) sprinkled with, made wet with: *a face ~ with tears.*

be·dimmed /biˈdɪmd/ *pred adj* (*liter*) (of the eyes, the mind) made dim: *eyes ~ with tears; a mind ~ with sorrow.*

bed·lam /ˈbedləm/ *n* [C] **1** (*old use*) asylum for mad people. **2** scene of noisy confusion: *When the teacher was called away the classroom was a regular ~.*

be·drag·gled /biˈdrægəld/ *adj* made wet or dirty, eg by being dragged in mud.

bee¹ /bi/ *n* [C] small, four-winged, stinging insect that lives in colonies and produces wax and honey. ⇨ illus at insect. ***have a bee in one's bonnet,*** be obsessed by an idea. ***make a ˈbee line for,*** go toward by the shortest way, go quickly toward.

ˈbee·bread *n* [U] pollen mixed with honey, used as food for young bees.

ˈbee·hive *n* [C] ⇨ hive.

bee² /bi/ *n* [C] gathering of people to accomplish some task or to compete in a contest: *ˈsewing/ˈspelling bee.*

beech /bitʃ/ *n* **1** [C] forest tree with smooth bark

and shiny dark-green leaves and small triangular nuts. **2** [U] its wood.

beef /bif/ *n* **1** [U] flesh of a steer, bull or cow, used as meat. **2** [C] (*sl*) complaint. □ *vi* (*sl*) complain: *Stop ~ing so much!*

ˈbeef·steak *n* [U] ⇨ steak.

beefy /ˈbifi/ *adj* (-ier, -iest) (of a person) well covered with flesh; strong.

been *pp* of be[1].

beep /bip/ *n* [C] repeated signal or note (as during a phone conversation, indicating that it is being recorded).

beer /bɪr/ *n* [U] **1** alcoholic drink made from malt and flavored with hops. **2** soft drink made from roots, etc: *ˈroot ~; ˌginger ˈ~.*

ˈbeer belly, (*informal*) protruding abdomen, supposed to be caused by heavy beer drinking.

beery *adj* (-ier, -iest) like beer in taste or smell; (eg of a person) smelling of beer.

bees·wax /ˈbizˌwæks/ *n* [U] wax made by bees for honeycomb.

beet /bit/ *n* [C] leafy plant with a sweet, juicy root, of which both leaves and roots are eaten as a vegetable.

ˈsugar beet, white beet used for making sugar.

beetle /ˈbitəl/ *n* [C] insect with hard, shiny wing covers. ⇨ illus at insect.

be·fall /biˈfɔl/ *vt,vi* (*pt* befell /biˈfel/ *pp* ~en /biˈfɔlən/) (*liter*) (used only in the 3rd person) happen (to): *What has ~en him?*

be·fit /biˈfɪt/ *vt* (-tt-) (used only in the 3rd person) be fitted for; be right and suitable for: *It does not ~ a man in your position to....*

be·fit·ting *adj* right and proper.

be·fogged /biˈfɔgd, -ˈfagd/ *adj* (*fig*) (of a person) puzzled.

be·fore[1] /biˈfɔr/ *adv* **1** in front; ahead: *went on ~.* **2** at an earlier time; in the past; already: *I've seen that film ~. You should have told me so ~,* earlier.

be·fore[2] /biˈfɔr/ *conj* **1** previous to the time when: *I must finish my work ~ I go home. Do it now ~ you forget.* **2** rather than: *He would starve ~ he would beg.*

be·fore[3] /biˈfɔr/ *prep* **1** earlier than: *the day ~ yesterday; the year ~ last; two days ~ Christmas.* ***before Christ*** (*abbr* **BC**): *in 55* BC, 55 years before the birth of Christ. ⇨ anno Domini. ***before long,*** soon. **2** in front of (esp with reference to order or arrangement): *B comes ~ C.* (*Note:* Except in a few phrases, *in front of* is preferred to *before* when referring to position, eg There are some trees *in front of* the house.) **3** in the presence of; face to face with: *He was brought ~ the judge.* **4** in preference to: *Death ~ dishonor.*

be·fore·hand /biˈfɔrˌhænd/ *adv* earlier; before[3] (1): *I knew what he would need, so I made preparations ~,* in advance, in readiness. □ *pred adj* early; in advance: *She's always ~ with the rent,* pays it, or is ready to pay it, before it is due.

be·friend /biˈfrend/ *vt* make a friend of; be kind and helpful to (eg a younger person who needs help).

beg /beg/ *vt,vi* (-gg-) **1** ask for (food, money, clothes, etc) as charity; ask for money (esp in the streets, etc): *He made a living by begging from door to door.* **2** ask earnestly, or with deep feeling: *They begged us not to punish them. I beg (of) you not to take any risks.* ***go begging,*** (of things) be unwanted: *If these things are going begging* (= if nobody wants them), *I'll take them.* **3** (*formal*) take the liberty of (saying or doing something): *I beg to differ.*

be·gan *pt* of begin.

be·gat *pt* of beget.

be·get /biˈget/ *vt* (-tt-), (*pt* begot /biˈgat/, *archaic* begat /biˈgæt/, *pp* begotten /biˈgatən/) **1** give existence to (as father): *Abraham begat Isaac.* **2** (*liter*) be the cause of: *War ~s misery and ruin.*

beg·gar /ˈbegər/ *n* [C] **1** person who lives by begging, esp for money, food; poor person. ***Beggars can't be choosers,*** (*prov*) people asking for help must take whatever is offered them. **2** (*informal*) (playful or friendly use) person; fellow: *You lucky ~!* □ *vt* make poor, ruin.

beg·gar·ly *adj* very poor; mean; deserving contempt.

be·gin /biˈgɪn/ *vt,vi* (-nn-, *pt* began /biˈgæn/, *pp* begun /biˈgən/) (For notes on the use of *begin* and *start,* ⇨ start[2].) **1** start: *It's time to ~ work. The meeting will ~ at seven o'clock.* **2** (used of activities and states that come into existence): *She began to feel dizzy/afraid. I'm ~ning to understand. The water is ~ning to boil. She began crying/to cry.* **3** ***begin at,*** start from: *Today we ~ at page 30, line 12.* ***to begin with,*** in the first place: *We can't appoint Smith: to ~ with, he's too young; secondly, I want my son to have the job.*

be·gin·ner *n* [C] (esp) person still learning and without much experience.

be·gin·ning *n* [C,U] starting point: *I've read the book from ~ning to end.*

be·gone /biˈgɔn/ *v* (*imperative* only) (*liter*) go away!

be·gonia /bɪˈgounyə/ *n* [C] garden plant with small, waxy flowers and richly colored leaves.

be·got, be·got·ten *pt, pp* of beget.

be·grudge /biˈgrədʒ/ *vt* (intensive form of *grudge*) feel or show dissatisfaction or envy at: *We don't ~ your going to Italy.*

be·guile /biˈgaiəl/ *vt* (-ing /biˈgailɪŋ/) cheat, deceive: *They were ~d into forming an unwise alliance.*

be·gun *pp* of begin.

be·half /biˈhæf/ *n* ***on behalf of,*** for, in the interest of, on account of, as the representative of. ***on my/his/our/John's, etc behalf,*** for me/him/us/John, etc: *On ~ of my colleagues and myself,* speaking for them and me.

be·have /biˈheiv/ *vi* **1** act; conduct oneself: *Can't you make your little boy ~ (himself),* show good manners, be polite? **2** (of machines, etc) work; function: *How's your new car behaving?*

ˌwell-/ˌbadly-be·ˈhaved *adj* behaving well/badly.

be·hav·ior /biˈheivyər/ *n* [U] way of behaving, manners (good or bad): *His ~ towards me shows that he does not like me. Tom won a prize for good ~ at school.* ***be on one's best behavior,*** take great care to behave well.

be·head /biˈhed/ *vt* execute by cutting off the

head. ⇨ decapitate.

be·held *pt, pp* of behold.

be·hest /biˈhest/ *n* (*archaic*) (only in) ***at one's behest,*** on a person's orders: *at the commander's ~.*

be·hind[1] /biˈhaind/ *adv* **1** in the rear: *The dog came running ~. The others are a long way ~.* ***stay/remain behind,*** stay after others have left. **2** ***be behind in/with,*** be in arrears with: *He was ~ in his payments,* had not made payments (eg of rent) when they were due.

be·hind[2] /biˈhaind/ *n* (*informal*) buttocks: *He fell on his ~.*

be·hind[3] /biˈhaind/ *prep* **1** to the rear of: *The boy was hiding ~ a tree. The sun was ~* (= hidden by) *the clouds.* **2** not having made so much progress as: *~ other boys of his age; a country far ~ its neighbors.* **3** remaining after, when one has left a place: *The storm left a trail of destruction ~ it.* **4** (of time): *Your schooldays will soon be far ~ you.*

be·hind·hand /biˈhaindˌhænd/ *pred adj* **1** in arrears: *be ~ with the rent.* **2** late; after others: *He did not want to be ~ in generosity.*

be·hold /biˈhould/ *vt* (*pt,pp* beheld /biˈheld/) (*archaic* or *liter*) observe.

be·hol·den /biˈhouldən/ *adj* under an obligation; owing thanks: *We are much ~ to you for your help.*

beige /beiʒ/ *n* [U] **1** soft fabric of undyed and unbleached wool. **2** color of sand. □ *adj* sand-colored.

be·ing /ˈbiɪŋ/ *n* **1** [U] existence. ***come into being,*** begin to exist: *We do not know when this world came into ~.* **2** [C] creature: *Men, women and children are human ~s.*

be·jew·eled, be·jew·elled /biˈdʒuəld/ *adj* decorated, adorned, with jewels.

be·la·bor /biˈleibər/ *vt* **1** beat hard, give hard blows to: *The robbers ~ed him soundly.* **2** discuss something excessively: *Stop ~ing the point!*

be·lated /biˈleitɪd/ *adj* coming very late or too late: *a ~ apology.*

belch /beltʃ/ *vt,vi* **1** send out, eg smoke, flames: *A volcano ~es out smoke and ashes.* **2** send out gas from the stomach noisily through the mouth. □ *n* [C] **1** act or sound of belching. **2** thing belched out (eg smoke from a chimney).

be·leaguer /biˈligər/ *vt* surround with an army.

bel·fry /ˈbelfri/ *n* [C] (*pl* -ies) tower for bells; part of a church tower in which bells hang.

be·lie /biˈlai/ *vt* **1** give a wrong or untrue idea of: *His cheerful appearance ~d his feelings.* **2** fail to justify or be equal to (what is hoped for or promised).

be·lief /biˈlif/ *n* **1** [U] the feeling that something is real and true; trust; confidence: *My ~ in his honesty/that he is honest. He has lost his ~ in God,* no longer accepts the existence of God as true. ***to the best of my belief,*** in my genuine opinion. **2** [C] something accepted as true or real. **3** [C] something taught and accepted as a religious truth: *He lives according to his ~s.*

be·lieve /biˈliv/ *vt,vi* **1** feel sure of the truth of something, that somebody is telling the truth: *I ~ that man. I ~ what that man says. They ~d that he was insane.* **2** think; suppose: *Will they be ready tomorrow? Yes, I ~ so. No, I ~ not.* **3** ***believe in,*** **(a)** have trust in: *I ~ in that man.* **(b)** feel sure of the existence of: *~ in God.* **(c)** feel sure of the value or worth of: *He ~s in getting plenty of exercise.* **4** ***make believe,*** pretend: *The boys made ~ that they were pioneers in the Wild West.*

be·liever *n* [C] person who believes, esp in a religious faith.

be·liev·ing *n* ***seeing is believing,*** ⇨ see[1].

ˈmake-believe *n* [C] pretense: *Don't be frightened, it's all make-~.*

be·little /biˈlɪtəl/ *vt* cause to seem unimportant or of small value: *Don't ~ yourself,* be too modest about your abilities, etc.

bell /bel/ *n* [C] **1** hollow vessel of cast metal, usually shaped like a cup, that makes a ringing sound when struck. ***as sound as a bell,*** (*fig*) in first-rate condition. ***ring a bell,*** (*informal*) recall to memory something half forgotten. **2** (*naut*) ***one to eight bells,*** bells sounded every half hour.

ˈbell buoy /ˈbel ˌbɔi/ *n* [C] one equipped with a bell, so it can be located in foggy weather.

bell-bottoms /ˈbelˌbatəmz/ *n pl* pants having legs that flare at the bottom.

ˈbell-bottom(ed) *adj*

bell·boy /ˈbelˌbɔi/ *n* [C] man or boy who carries luggage, runs errands, etc for the guests of a hotel or club.

belle /bel/ *n* [C] beautiful girl or woman. ***the belle of the ball,*** the most beautiful woman present.

bell·hop /ˈbelˌhap/ *n* [C] (*informal*) = bellboy.

bel·li·cose /ˈbelɪˌkous/ *adj* fond of fighting; anxious to fight.

bel·liger·ency /bəˈlɪdʒərənsi/ *n* [U] being warlike; state of being at war.

bel·liger·ent /bəˈlɪdʒərənt/ *adj, n* (state, party, nation) eager to be at war.

bel·low /ˈbelou/ *vi,vt* **1** make a loud, deep noise (like a bull); roar; shout: *He began to ~ even before the dentist had started.* **2** sing, shout loudly or angrily: *They ~ed out a drinking song.*

bel·lows /ˈbelouz/ *n pl* (often ***a pair of bellows,*** sometimes ***a bellows***) apparatus for blowing or forcing air into something, eg a fire, an accordion, the pipes of an organ, etc.

belly[1] /ˈbeli/ *n* [C] (*pl* -ies) **1** (*informal*) = abdomen. ⇨ illus at trunk. **2** stomach: *have a ~ache.* **3** bulging part (concave or convex) of anything, eg the surface of a violin across which the strings pass.

ˈbelly·ache *vi* (*informal*) grumble or complain, esp without a good reason.

ˈbelly·button *n* (*informal*) = navel.

belly·ful /ˈbeliˌfʊl/ *n* as much as one wants of anything: *He's had his ~ful of fighting,* doesn't want any more.

ˈbelly·landing *n* landing of an aircraft without its undercarriage in position.

ˈbelly·laugh *n* [C] loud, coarse laugh.

belly[2] /ˈbeli/ *vi,vt* (*pt,pp* -ied) (cause to) swell out: *The wind bellied* (*out*) *the sails.*

be·long /biˈlɔŋ/ *vi* **1** ***belong to,*** **(a)** be the property of: *These books ~ to me,* are mine. **(b)**

be a member of, be connected with: *Which union do you ~ to?* **2** have as a right or proper place. *Do you ~ here?*

be·long·ings /bɪˈlɔŋɪŋz/ *n pl* movable possessions (eg luggage, furniture; not land, buildings, a business, etc): *I hope you've left none of your personal ~ in the hotel.*

be·loved /bɪˈləvd, bɪˈləvɪd/ *adj, n* [C] (person) dearly loved: *~ by all.*

be·low[1] /bɪˈlou/ *adv* **1** at or to a lower level: *From the hilltop we saw the blue ocean ~. We heard voices from ~.* **2** at the foot of a page, etc; later (in a book, article, etc): *see paragraph six ~.* **3** ***down below,*** in the lower part of a building, in a ship's hold, etc (according to context). ***here below,*** on earth. **4** below zero degrees (Fahrenheit): *It got to twenty below, yesterday.*

be·low[2] /bɪˈlou/ *prep* (*Note*: *Below* can sometimes be replaced by *under*; when *under* is possible, it is given in the examples) **1** lower than: *Skirts this year reach just ~ the knees. Your work is ~ average. Shall I write my name on, above or ~ the line? The Dead Sea is ~ sea level. There is nothing ~/under a dollar*, costing less than this. *He can't be much ~/under sixty* (years of age). **2** down stream from: *a few yards ~ the bridge.*

belt /belt/ *n* **1** band or strip of cloth, leather, etc worn round the waist to support or keep clothes in place: *He ate so much that he had to loosen his ~.* ***hit below the belt,*** give an unfair blow, fight unfairly. **2** similar strip of leather, etc worn over the shoulder to support weapons, etc. **3** endless strap, used to connect wheels and so drive machinery: *a ˈfan~,* in the engine of a car. **4** any wide strip or band, surrounding area, etc. □ *vt* **1** fasten with a belt: *The officer ~ed his sword on.* **2** hit with a belt. **3** (*informal*) hit hard: *if you don't shut up, I'll ~ you.*

belt·ing *n* [C] beating.

ˈbelt·way *n* [C] expressway running completely around a city, to allow bypassing the downtown section or access from different directions.

be·moan /bɪˈmoun/ *vt* (*liter*) moan for; show great sorrow for: *~ one's sad fate.*

be·mused /bɪˈmyuzd/ *adj* **1** confused; stupid. **2** deeply interested; preoccupied

bench /bentʃ/ *n* [C] **1** long seat of wood or stone, eg in a public park. **2** worktable at which a shoemaker, carpenter, etc, works. **3 the bench,** **(a)** (*collect*) judges. **(b)** judge's seat. **(c)** position of a judge. **(d)** law court.

bend[1] /bend/ *n* [C] **1** curve or turn: *a sharp ~ in the road.* **2** sailor's knot (in a rope). **3 the bends,** (*informal*) pains in the joints, caused, eg by coming to the surface too fast after diving with a breathing apparatus.

bend[2] /bend/ *vt,vi* (*pt,pp* bent /bent/) **1** cause (something rigid) to be out of a straight line or surface; force into a curve or angle: *Bend the end of the wire up/down/back. Her head was bent over her book.* ***bend a rule,*** (*informal*) interpret it loosely (to suit the circumstances). **2** become curved or angular; bow down: *The branches were ~ing (down) with the weight of the fruit. Can you ~ down and touch your toes without ~ing your knees? The road ~s to the left here.* **3** direct: *All eyes were bent on me,* everyone was looking at me. **4** submit: *~ to somebody's will;* make (a person) submit: *~ somebody to one's will.* **5** ***be bent on,*** have the mind set on, have as a fixed purpose: *He is bent on mastering English,* determined to learn it thoroughly.

be·neath /bɪˈniθ/ *prep, adv* **1** under(neath), below. **2** not worthy of: *His accusations are ~ contempt/notice,* should be ignored.

ben·edic·tion /ˌbenəˈdɪkʃən/ *n* [C] blessing (esp one given by a priest at the end of a church service): *pronounce the ~.*

ben·efac·tion /ˌbenəˈfækʃən/ *n* **1** [U] doing good. **2** [C] good deed (esp the giving of money for charity); charitable gift.

ben·efac·tor /ˈbenəˌfæktər/ *n* [C] person who has given help, esp financial help, to a school, hospital or charitable institution.

ben·efac·tress /ˈbenəˌfæktrɪs/ *n* [C] woman benefactor.

be·nefi·cence /bəˈnefisəns/ *n* [U] (*formal*) doing good; active kindness.

be·nefi·cent /bəˈnefisənt/ *adj* (*formal*) doing good; kind.

ben·efi·cial /ˌbenəˈfɪʃəl/ *adj* having good effect; helpful: *Fresh air and good food are ~ to the health.*

ben·efici·ary /ˌbenəˈfɪʃiˌeri/ *n* [C] (*pl* -ries) person who receives a benefit, esp one who receives money, property, etc under a will.

bene·fit /ˈbenəˌfɪt/ *n* **1** [U] advantage; profit; help: *Did you get much ~ from your holiday?* Did you feel better afterward? *The money is to be used for the ~ of the poor,* to help poor people. ***give sb the benefit of the doubt,*** assume that he is innocent because there is insufficient evidence that he is guilty. **2** [C] entertainment, etc to raise money for a charity, a cause, a person, etc. **3** [C] act of kindness; favor; advantage: *the ~s of a good education.* **4** [C] money paid to a person (as by an insurance company or government agency) because of sickness, unemployment, etc: *medical/unemployment/sickness ~.* □ *vt,vi* **1** do good to: *The sea air will ~ you.* **2** get help or advantage from: *You will ~ by a holiday.*

ben·ev·ol·ence /bəˈnevələns/ *n* **1** [U] wish to do good. **2** [C,U] activity in doing good: *His ~ made it possible for many poor boys to attend college.*

ben·ev·ol·ent /bəˈnevələnt/ *adj* kind and helpful (toward, to).

ben·ev·ol·ent·ly *adv*

be·nign /bɪˈnain/ *adj* **1** (of persons) kind and gentle. **2** (of soil, climate) mild, favorable. **3** (of a disease, tumor) not dangerous.

bent[1] /bent/ *n* ***bent (for),*** inclination or aptitude; natural skill in and liking: *She has a ~ for sewing/music.*

bent[2] *pt,pp* of bend[2].

be·numbed /bɪˈnəmd/ *adj* made numb: *My fingers were ~ with cold.*

be·queath /bɪˈkwiθ, -ð/ **1** give (property, etc) by means of a will: *He has ~ed me his gold watch.* **2** hand down to those who come after: *discoveries ~ed to us by the scientists of the last* century.

be·quest /bi'kwest/ *n* **1** [U] bequeathing. **2** [C] thing bequeathed: *He left ~s of money to all his staff.*

be·reave /bə'riv/ *vt* **1** (*pt, pp* bereft /bə'reft/) rob or take away from: *bereft of hope,* without hope; *bereft of reason,* mad. **2** (of death) leave sad and alone: *the ~d husband,* the man whose wife had died.

be·reave·ment *n* **(a)** [U] being bereaved; loss by death. **(b)** [C] instance of this.

be·reft *pt, pp* of bereave.

be·ret /bə'rei/ *n* [C] flat, round cap of felt or cloth.

berg /bərg/ *n* = iceberg.

beri·beri /ˌberi'beri/ *n* [U] disease caused by lack of vitamin B_1.

berry /'beri/ *n* [C] (*pl* -ies) **1** kinds of small fruit with seeds: *straw~; black~; rasp~.* **2** coffee bean.

ber·serk /bər'sərk/ *adj* ***be/go/send sb berserk,*** be, go, etc uncontrollably wild: *He went completely ~.*

berth /bərθ/ *n* [C] **1** sleeping place in a train, ship, etc. **2** place at a wharf, etc where a ship can be tied up. **3** job; position. □ *vt,vi* **1** find, have, a sleeping place (for). **2** (of a ship) come or bring into a berth.

beryl /'berəl/ *n* [C] precious (usually green) stone.

be·seech /bi'sitʃ/ *vt* (*pt,pp* besought /bi'sɔt/) (*archaic* or *liter*) ask earnestly or urgently: *Spare him, I ~ you.*

be·seech·ing *adj* (of a person's look, tone of voice, etc) appealing.

be·set /bi'set/ *vt* (-tt-, *pt,pp* ~) attack or surround on all sides: *a problem ~ with difficulties; ~ by doubts,* troubled by doubts.

be·side /bi'said/ *prep* **1** at the side of; close to: *Come and sit ~ me.* **2** ***beside the point/mark/question,*** having nothing to do with (what is being discussed, etc). **3** ***beside oneself,*** at the end of one's self-control: *He was ~ himself with joy/rage.*

be·sides /bi'saidz/ *adv* moreover; also: *I don't like that new dictionary; ~, it's too expensive.* □ *prep* in addition to; as well as: *I have three other brothers ~ John.*

be·siege /bi'sidʒ/ *vt* **1** surround (a place) with armed forces; lay seige to: *Troy was ~d by the Greeks for ten years.* **2** ***besiege with,*** crowd around (with requests, etc): *The teacher was ~d with questions. He was ~d by his fans.*

be·sieger *n* [C]

be·smirch /bi'smərtʃ/ *vt* make dirty: (*fig*) *His reputation was ~ed.*

be·sot·ted /bi'satɪd/ *adj* stupefied (by alcoholic drink, drugs, love, etc).

be·sought *pt,pp* of beseech.

be·spat·tered /bi'spætərd/ *adj* covered with: *~ with mud.*

best[1] /best/ *adj* of the most excellent kind: *the ~ poetry/poets; the ~* (= quickest, most convenient, etc) *way from New York to Montreal.* ***make the best use of one's time, etc,*** use one's time, etc in the most useful way. ***put one's best foot forward,*** ⇨ foot[1] (1). ***with the best will in the world,*** even making every effort to be fair, etc. ⇨ good[1], better[1].

ˌbest 'man, bridegroom's friend, supporting him at his wedding.

best[2] /best/ *adv* in the most excellent way: *He works ~ in the morning. Do as you think ~. She was the ~-dressed woman at the party.* ⇨ well[3], better[2].

ˌbest-'seller *n* [C] book that is sold in very large numbers.

best[3] /best/ *n* the outstanding person, thing, etc among several; the most excellent part, aspect: *We're the ~ of friends,* very close friends. ***be (all) for the best,*** be good in the end (although not at first seeming to be good). ***at best,*** taking the most hopeful view: *We can't arrive before Friday at ~.* ***at its/their/his, etc best,*** in the best condition: *The garden is at its ~ this month.* ***(even) at the best of times,*** (even) when circumstances are most favorable. ***with the best of intentions,*** intending only to help. ***do one's best/the best one can,*** do one's utmost. ***(do sth) to the best of one's ability,*** use all one's ability when doing it. ***make the best of it/things,*** be contented (although things are not satisfactory). ***to the best of my knowledge, etc,*** so far as I know (though my knowledge, etc may be imperfect).

best[4] /best/ *vt* (*informal*) get the better of; defeat.

bes·tial /'bistʃəl, 'bestʃəl/ *adj* of or like a beast; brutish; savage.

be·stir /bi'stər/ *vt* (-rr-) rouse to action; stir up.

be·stow /bi'stou/ *vt* give as an offering: *~ an honor/a title on him.*

be·stowal *n* [U]

be·strew /bi'stru/ *vt* (*pt* ~ed, *pp* ~n /bi'strun/ or ~ed) (*formal*) scatter (things) about.

be·stride /bi'straid/ *vt* (*pt* bestrode /bi'stroud/, *pp* bestridden /bi'strɪdən/) sit, stand, with one leg on each side of: *~ a horse.* ⇨ astride.

bet /bet/ *vt,vi* (-tt-, *pt,pp* bet or betted) **1** risk money on a race or on some other event of which the result is doubtful: *He bet me a dollar that he would win.* **2** (*informal*) be certain: *I bet I win.* □ *n* [C] **1** agreement to bet. **2** the money, etc offered: *make a bet; win/lose a bet.*

be·tray /bi'trei/ *vt* **1** be disloyal to; act treacherously toward: *He ~ed his principles.* **2** allow (a secret) to become known, either by accident or on purpose. **3** be or give a sign of; show: *His accent at once ~ed the fact that he was a foreigner.*

be·trayal /bi'treiəl/ *n* **(a)** [U] betraying or being betrayed. **(b)** [C] instance of this.

be·trayer *n* [C]

be·trothed /bi'trouðd/ *adj* (*liter*) engaged. □ *n* person engaged to be married.

be·trothal *n* [C] engagement to be married.

bet·ter[1] /'betər/ *adj* **1** having higher qualities or abilities: *This is good but that is ~. He's a ~ man than his brother.* ***no better than,*** practically the same as: *He's no ~ than a fool.* ***see better days,*** be not so poor or unfortunate as at present. ***his better half,*** (*jocular*) his wife. **2** (of health) improving: *He feels ~ today but is still not well enough to get up.* ***quite better,*** recovered: *I'm* *quite ~ now.* ⇨ good[1], best[1].

bet·ter[2] /ˈbetər/ *adv* **1** in a more excellent or desirable way: *You would write ~ if you had a good pen. You play tennis ~ than I do. You'll like it ~* (= more) *when you understand it more.* ***be better off,*** in a better condition: *They're much ~ off now that he's found a job. We'd be ~ off without all that noise.* ***know better,*** **(a)** know enough not to do something: *You ought to know ~ than to go out with wet hair.* **(b)** refuse to accept a statement (because one knows it is not true): *He says he didn't cheat, but I know ~,* feel sure that he did. **2** ***had better,*** ought to: *You had ~ mind your own business. You'd ~ not say that,* I advise you not to say that. *Hadn't you ~ take an umbrella?* ⇨ best[2], well[3].

bet·ter[3] /ˈbetər/ *n* ***one's (elders and) betters,*** older, wiser, more experienced people. ***get the better of sb/sth,*** overcome; defeat; win (an argument, etc): *She always gets the ~ of these quarrels/him.* ***for better or worse,*** whether one has good or bad fortune.

bet·ter[4] /ˈbetər/ *vt* improve; do better than: *Your work last year was good; I hope you will ~ it this year. She hopes to ~ herself* (= earn more, etc) *in the civil service.*

bet·ter·ment *n* [U] improvement.

bet·tor, bet·ter[5] /ˈbetər/ *n* [C] person who bets.

be·tween[1] /biˈtwin/ *adv* in or into a place or time that is between: *We visited the Museum in the morning and the Art Gallery later, with a quick lunch ~.* ***few and far between,*** few and widely scattered or separate: *In this part of Wyoming houses are few and far ~.* ***in between,*** spaced out among.

be·tween[2] /biˈtwin/ *prep* **1** (of place): *The letter B comes ~ A and C.* (*Note: Between* usually involves only two limits, but when boundaries are concerned, there may be more than two limits: *Switzerland lies ~ France, Italy, Austria and Germany.* ⇨ among.) **2** (of order, rank, etc): *An army major ranks ~ a captain and a colonel.* **3** (of time): *~ the two world wars; ~ 1 o'clock and 2 o'clock.* **4** (of distance, amount, etc): *~ five and six miles; somewhere ~ thirty and forty years old.* **5** to and from: *This liner sails ~ New York and Southampton.* **6** (showing connection): *after all there has been ~ us,* in view of our past friendship, the experiences we have shared, etc. **7** (to show sharing; used of two only): *Divide/Share the money ~ you.* ***between you, me and the gatepost/you and me,*** in confidence. **8** (to show combination, used of two, or more than two to show several independent relationships): *We* (two or more) *saved up for a year and bought a second-hand car ~ us.* **9** (showing relationship): *the distinction ~ right and wrong; wars ~ nations.*

bevel /ˈbevəl/ *n* [C] sloping edge; surface with such a slope, eg at the side of a picture frame. □ *vt* (-l-, -ll-) give a bevel to.

bev·er·age /ˈbev(ə)rɪdʒ/ *n* [C] any sort of drink except water, eg milk, tea, wine, beer.

be·ware /biˈwær/ *vi,vt* (usually *imperative* or *infinitive*) be on guard, take care: *Beware of the dog! Beware of pickpockets!*

be·whisk·ered /biˈ(h)wɪskərd/ *adj* having whiskers.

be·wil·der /biˈwɪldər/ *vt* puzzle; confuse: *The old woman from the country was ~ed by the crowds and traffic in the big city.*

be·wilder·ing *adj*

be·wilder·ment *n* [U]

be·witch /biˈwɪtʃ/ *vt* **1** work magic on; put a magic spell on. **2** charm; delight very much: *She danced so well that she ~ed all the young men.*

be·witch·ing *adj*: *a ~ing smile.*

be·witch·ing·ly *adv*

be·yond[1] /biˈyand/ *adv* at or to a distance; farther on: *India and the lands ~.*

be·yond[2] /biˈyand/ *prep* **1** at, on or to, the farther side of: *The house is ~ the bridge.* **2** (of time) later than: *Don't stay out ~ 6 o'clock* (*after* is more usual). **3** surpassing, exceeding; out of reach of: *That's going ~ a joke,* passes the limits of what is reasonable as a joke. *He lives ~ his income,* spends more than he earns. *It's quite ~ me,* is more than I can understand.

B-girl /ˈbi-ˌgərl/ *n* [C] (*sl*) female working in a bar[1](3) as a prostitute, or employed to encourage customers to buy drinks.

bi- /ˌbai-/ *prefix* **1** happening twice (in one period): *bimonthly; biannual.* **2** happening every two: *bicentennial.* **3** having two: *bilingual; biped.*

bias /ˈbaiəs/ *n* [C] (*pl* ~es) **1** particular inclination or tendency: *He has a ~ toward/against the plan,* is in favor of it/opposed to it without having full knowledge of it. **2** ***cut on the bias,*** (dressmaking, etc) cut at a slant across. □ *vt* give a bias to; influence (usually unfairly): *The government used newspapers and the radio to ~ the opinions of the people.*

bib /bɪb/ *n* [C] **1** piece of cloth tied under a child's chin. **2** upper part of an apron.

Bible /ˈbaibəl/ *n* sacred writings of the Jews and the Christian Church.

bib·li·cal /ˈbɪblɪkəl/ *adj* of, concerning, contained in, the Bible.

bib·li·ogra·pher /ˌbɪbliˈagrəfər/ *n* [C] person who writes or studies bibliographies.

bib·li·ography /ˌbɪbliˈagrəfi/ *n* (*pl* -ies) **1** [C] list of books and writings of one author or about one subject. **2** [U] study of the authorship, editions, etc of books.

bi·car·bon·ate of soda /baiˌkarbənɪt əv ˈsoudə/ *n* [U] crystalline salt used in cooking and medicine.

bi·cen·ten·ary /ˌbaisenˈtenəri/ *n* [C] (*pl* -ies) = bicentennial.

bi·cen·ten·nial /ˌbaisenˈteniəl/ *n* [C], *adj* (date) of a 200th anniversary: *The USA celebrated its ~ in 1976.*

bi·ceps /ˈbaiˌseps/ *n* (*pl* unchanged) large muscle in the front part of the upper arm.

bicker /ˈbɪkər/ *vi* quarrel over something small or unimportant.

bi·cus·pid /baiˈkəspɪd/ *n* [C] one of the eight double-pointed teeth that grind and tear food.

bi·cycle /ˈbaisɪkəl/ *n* two-wheeled machine propelled by using pedals, for riding on. □ *vi* ride a bicycle (to).

bid[1] /bɪd/ *n* [C] **1** (at an auction sale) offer of a price: *Are there no bids for this very fine painting?* **2** ***make a bid for,*** try to get: *make a bid for*

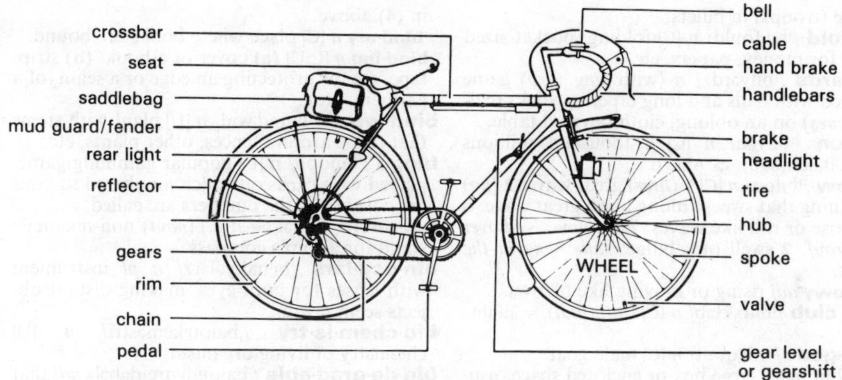

BICYCLE

popular support. **3** (in card games, esp bridge) statement of the number of tricks a player proposes to win: *a bid of 2 hearts*.

bid² /bɪd/ *vt,vi* (-dd-, *pt, pp* bid) **1** (at an auction sale) make an offer of money; offer (a certain price): *Will anyone bid $500 for this painting?* **2** (playing certain card games) make a bid: *bid 2 hearts*. ⇨ bid¹, outbid.

bid³ /bɪd/ *vt,vi* (-dd-, *pt* bade /bæd/, *pp* bidden /ˈbɪdən/, bid) (*old use*) **1** command; tell: *He bade me (to) come in*. **2** say (as a greeting, etc): *bid him good morning*.

bid·der /ˈbɪdər/ *n* [C] person who bids.

bid·ding /ˈbɪdɪŋ/ *n* [U] **1** ***do sb's bidding,*** do what he commands. **2** act of offering a price at an auction sale: ~ *was brisk*, there were many bids, quickly made. **3** (at cards) the making of bids¹(3).

bien·nial /baiˈeniəl/ *n* [C], *adj*(something) lasting for, happening, or done every two years.

bier /bɪr/ *n* [C] movable wooden stand for a coffin or a dead body.

bi·focal /ˌbaiˈfoukəl/ *adj* (esp of lenses in eyeglasses) designed for both distant and near vision.

bi·focals *n pl* eyeglasses with bifocal lenses.

big /bɪg/ *adj* (-ger, -gest) (opposite = *little*; ⇨ large, small) of large size, extent, capacity, importance, etc: *big feet/ideas/gardens/cups; a big day*, an important one; *big-hearted*, (*informal*) generous, kind; *to think big*, have big ideas.

ˌbig ˈbusiness, industry or business thought of as one large and powerful group.

ˈbig·head *n* [C] (*informal*) conceited person.

ˈbig·mouth *n* [C] (*sl*) loudmouthed, talkative person.

ˈbig·shot *n* [C] (*sl*) = bigwig.

the ˈbig time, (*sl*) highly profitable situation.

ˈbig·wig *n* [C] (*sl*) important person.

big·am·ist /ˈbɪgəmɪst/ *n* [C] person guilty of bigamy.

big·am·ous /ˈbɪgəməs/ *adj* guilty of, involving, bigamy.

big·amy /ˈbɪgəmi/ *n* [U] illegally having two wives or husbands.

bight /bait/ *n* [C] curve in a coast, larger than, or with not so much curve as, a bay.

bigot /ˈbɪgət/ *n* [C] person who stubbornly and unreasonably holds an opinion or belief and is intolerant of the views of others.

big·oted *adj* intolerant and narrow-minded.

bike /baik/ *n* (*informal*) (short for) bicycle. ☐ *vi* = bicycle.

bi·kini /bəˈkini/ *n* [C] scanty two-piece bathing suit worn by girls and women.

bi·lat·eral /ˌbaiˈlætərəl/ *adj* **1** of, on, with two sides. **2** (of an agreement, etc) made between two (persons, governments).

bi·lat·er·ally /-rəli/ *adv*

bile /ˈbaiəl/ *n* [U] greenish-yellow bitter liquid produced by the liver to help in digesting food.

bilge /bɪldʒ/ *n* [U] **1** ship's bottom, inside or outside. **2** (also **ˈbilgewater**) the dirty water that collects here. **3** (*informal*) foolish or worthless talk or writing.

bi·lin·gual /ˌbaiˈlɪŋgwəl/ *adj* **1** speaking, using, two languages. **2** written, printed, in two languages.

bil·ious /ˈbɪlyəs/ *adj* feeling sick, because of too much bile: *a* ~ *attack;* ~ *patients*.

bill¹ /bɪl/ *n* [C] horny part of the mouth of some birds. ⇨ illus at bird. ☐ *vi* ***bill and coo,*** exchange caresses.

bill² /bɪl/ *n* [C] **1** written statement of charges for goods delivered or services given: *There are some* ~*s to pay/to be paid*. ***foot the bill,*** ⇨ foot². **2** written or printed notice, poster, etc. ***fill the bill,*** be, do, all that is required or expected. **3** (*legal*) proposed law, presented to a lawmaking body for approval. **4** piece of paper money: *a ten-dollar* ~. ☐ *vt* **1** make known by means of bills²(2); announce, put in, a program: *Several rock groups were* ~*ed to appear*. **2** ***bill sb for sth,*** give or send a bill²(1) to.

Bill of ˈRights, the first ten amendments to the US Constitution, stating the fundamental rights of citizens.

bill of ˈsale, statement that transfers ownership of personal property from seller to buyer.

bill·board /ˈbɪlˌbɔrd/ *n* [C] structure, usually outdoors, with a large, flat surface for advertisements, posters, etc.

bil·let /ˈbɪlɪt/ *n* [C] place (usually a private house) where soldiers are boarded and lodged. ☐ *vt* place (troops) in billets.

bill·fold /ˈbɪlˌfould/ *n* [C] folding, pocket-sized case for money, papers, etc.

bil·liards /ˈbɪlyərdz/ *n* (with *sing verb*) game played with balls and long tapering sticks (called *cues*) on an oblong, cloth-covered table.

bil·lion /ˈbɪlyən/ *n* [C] a thousand millions (1,000,000,000). ⇨ App 1.

bil·low /ˈbɪlou/ *n* [C] **1** (*liter*) great wave. **2** (*fig*) anything that sweeps along like a great wave. □ *vi* **1** rise or roll like waves: *The flames ~ed over the roof.* **2** swell out; bulge: *sails ~ing in the wind.*

bil·lowy *adj* rising or moving like billows.

billy club /ˈbɪli ˌkləb/ *n* [C] (*informal*) = nightstick.

billy·goat /ˈbɪliˌgout/ *n* [C] male goat.

bin /bɪn/ *n* [C] large box or enclosed space, usually with a lid, for storage: *ˈcoal bin.*

bi·nary /ˈbainəri, -ˌneri/ *adj* of or involving a pair or pairs.

ˈbinary star, two stars revolving round each other.

ˈbinary system, (*math*) number system with only two digits, 0 and 1, ie 1 = 1, 2 = 10, 3 = 11, 4 = 100, etc.

bind /baind/ *vt,vi* (*pt,pp* bound /baund/) **1** tie or fasten, with rope, etc: *They bound his legs (together) so that he couldn't escape.* ***in a bind***, (*informal*) in a predicament. **2** secure the edge of something with tape, etc: *~ the cuffs of a jacket with leather.* **3** tie or wind something around: *~ up a wound.* **4** fasten (sheets of paper) together within a cover: *a book bound in leather.* **5** (*fig*) link closely: *We are bound to him by gratitude/by a close friendship.* **6** hold (a person) to a legal agreement, a promise, etc: *~ somebody to secrecy*, make him promise to keep a secret. ***bind sb over,*** order that he must appear before the judge again (if he fails to keep the peace, etc). ⇨ bound[4] for special uses of the *pp*.

binder *n* [C] person or thing that binds, esp as in (4) above.

ˈbind·ery *n* [C] place where books are bound.

bind·ing *n* [C,U] **(a)** cover of a book. **(b)** strip, tape, etc for protecting an edge or a seam (of a garment, etc).

bind·weed /ˈbaindˌwid/ *n* [U] plant with stems that twine around fences, other plants, etc.

bingo /ˈbɪŋgou/ *n* [U] popular gambling game, played with cards on which numbered squares are covered as the numbers are called.

bin·nacle /ˈbɪnəkəl/ *n* [C] (*naut*) non-magnetic stand for a ship's compass.

bin·ocu·lars /bɪˈnakyələrz/ *n pl* instrument with lenses for both eyes, making distant objects seem nearer.

bio·chem·is·try /ˌbaiouˈkeməstri/ *n* [U] chemistry of living organisms.

bio·de·grad·able /ˌbaioudiˈgreidəbəl/ *adj* that can be broken down by the action of bacteria.

bi·ogra·pher /baiˈagrəfər/ *n* [C] person who writes a biography.

bio·graphi·cal, bio·graphic /ˌbaiəˈgræfɪkəl, ˌbaiəˈgræfɪk/ *adj* of biography.

bi·ogra·phy /baiˈagrəfi/ *n* (*pl* -ies) **1** [C] person's life history written by another. **2** [U] branch of literature dealing with the lives of persons.

bio·logi·cal /ˌbaiəˈladʒɪkəl/ *adj* of biology.

ˌbioˌlogical ˈwarfare, the deliberate use of germs, etc for spreading disease.

bi·ol·ogist /ˈbaiˈalədʒɪst/ *n* [C] student of, expert in, biology.

bi·ol·ogy /baiˈalədʒi/ *n* [U] science of the physical life of animals and plants.

bi·par·ti·san /ˌbaiˈpartɪzən/ *adj* of, supported by, consisting of, two otherwise opposed (esp political) parties: *a ~ foreign policy.*

bi·ped /ˈbaiˌped/ *n* [C] two-footed animal, eg a man or a bird.

bi·plane /ˈbaiˌplein/ *n* [C] aircraft with two pairs of wings, one above the other.

birch /bərtʃ/ *n* **1** [C] (kinds of) forest tree growing in northern countries; it has a smooth bark

BIRDS

and slender branches. **2** [U] its wood.

ˈ**birch·bark** *n* [U] bark of the birch tree, formerly used for making canoes, etc.

bird /bərd/ *n* [C] **1** feathered creature with two legs and two wings, usually able to fly. ***A bird in the hand is worth two in the bush,*** (*prov*) something which one has, though small, is better than anything larger which one does not or cannot have. ***kill two birds with one stone,*** achieve two aims at the same time. ***(be) for the birds*** (*sl*) (be) worthless. **2** (*sl*) person: *He's an odd ~.*

ˈ**bird·bath** *n* [C] shallow basin with water, for birds to bathe in.

ˈ**bird·cage** *n* [C] cage for birds.

ˌ**bird's-**ˌ**eye** ˈ**view, (a)** wide view seen from high up. **(b)** (*fig*) general survey without details.

ˈ**bird·house** *n* [C] **(a)** small house or box for birds to nest in. **(b)** building for exhibiting live birds.

ˈ**bird of** ˈ**prey,** flesh-eating bird, eg the eagle, owl, hawk, etc.

ˈ**bird·watcher** *n* [C] one who studies the habits of birds in their natural surroundings.

birth /bərθ/ *n* **1** [C,U] (process of) being born, coming into the world: *The baby weighed seven pounds at ~,* when it was born. ***give birth to,*** produce (a child). **2** [U] origin, descent: *She is Russian by ~ and American by marriage.*

ˈ**birth control,** (method of) preventing unwanted conception(3).

ˈ**birth·day** *n* [C] (anniversary of the) day of one's birth.

ˈ**birth·mark** *n* [C] mark on the body at or from birth.

ˈ**birth·place** *n* [C] house or district in which one was born.

ˈ**birth·rate** *n* [C] number of births in one year for every 1,000 persons.

bis·cuit /ˈbɪskɪt/ *n* [C] **1** small cake of bread dough, made by rolling and cutting or dropping from a spoon. **2** = cookie.

bi·sect /ˈbaiˌsekt/ *vt* cut or divide into two (usually equal parts).

bi·sec·tion /ˌbaiˈsekʃən/ *n* [U] division into two (equal) parts.

bi·sex·ual /ˌbaiˈsekʃuəl/ *adj* **1** individual plant or animal with both male and female reproductive organs. **2** person who is sexually attracted to both males and females.

bishop /ˈbɪʃəp/ *n* [C] **1** Christian clergyman of high rank. **2** piece in the game of chess.

bishop·ric /-rɪk/ *n* office, district, etc of a bishop.

bi·son /ˈbaisən/ *n* [C] (*pl* ~) **1** European wild ox. **2** American buffalo.

bisque /bɪsk/ *n* [U] soup of shellfish purée: *shrimp/lobster ~.*

bit[1] /bɪt/ *n* **1** mouthpiece (metal bar) forming part of a horse's bridle. **2** part of a tool that cuts or grips when twisted; tool for boring or drilling holes.

bit[2] /bɪt/ *n* [C] **1** small piece or amount of anything: *He ate every bit of* (= all) *his dinner.* ***a bit,*** a little: *She's feeling a bit tired.* ***not a bit,*** not at all; not in the least: *He doesn't care a bit.* ***wait a bit,*** a short time. ***bit by bit,*** slowly, gradually. ***every bit as good, etc as,*** equally (good, etc). ***to bits,*** into small pieces. **2** old unit of reckoning US currency, equivalent to 12 cents, and now used only in the combinations *two bits* (25 cents), *four bits* (50 cents), and occasionally *six bits* (75 cents). ⇨ App 4. **3** unit of information in computer programing.

bit[3] *pt* of bite[2].

bitch /bɪtʃ/ *n* [C] **1** female dog, wolf or fox. **2** (*sl*) spiteful woman or girl. □ *vi* (*sl*) complain bitterly.

bite[1] /bait/ *n* **1** [C] act of biting. **2** [C] injury resulting from a bite or sting: *His face was covered with insect ~s.* **3** [C] piece (of food) cut off by biting: *I haven't had a ~ since morning,* have eaten nothing. **4** [C] catching of a fish on a hook: *He had been fishing all morning but hadn't had a ~.* **5** [U] sharpness; sting: *There's a ~ in the air this morning.* **6** [U] grip; hold: *a file/screw with plenty of ~.*

bite[2] /bait/ *vt,vi* (*pt* bit /bɪt/, *pp* bitten /ˈbɪtən/). **1** cut into with the teeth: *The dog bit me in the leg.* ***bite off more than one can chew,*** attempt too much. ***bite the dust,*** (*sl*) **(a)** fall to the ground. **(b)** be killed. **2 (a)** (of fleas, mosquitoes, etc) sting. **(b)** (of fish) accept the bait: *The fish wouldn't ~.* **3** cause a smarting pain to; injure: *His fingers were bitten by the frost/were* ˈ*frost-bitten.* **4** take strong hold of; grip: *The roads were covered with sand and the wheels did not ~.*

bit·ing /ˈbaitɪŋ/ *adj* sharp; cutting: *a biting wind; biting words.*

bit·ing·ly *adv*

bit·ten /ˈbɪtən/ *pp* of bite[2].

bit·ter /ˈbɪtər/ *adj* **1** (opposite = *sweet*) tasting sharp and unpleasant. **2** unwelcome to the mind; unpleasant; causing sorrow: *~ disappointments/memories.* **3** filled with, showing, caused by, envy, hate, or disappointment: *~ quarrels/enemies.* **4** extremely sharp and cold: *a ~ wind.* **5** ***to the bitter end,*** **(a)** until the very last moment. **(b)** until death.

bit·ter·ly *adv*

bit·ter·ness /-nɪs/ *n* [U]

bit·tern /ˈbɪtərn/ *n* [C] any of several kinds of wading birds that live on marshes.

bit·ter·sweet /ˈbɪtərˌswit/ *n* [U] **1** vine with purple flowers and poisonous red berries. **2** climbing vine with orange seedcases and red seeds. □ *adj* sweet and bitter at the same time.

bitu·men /bəˈtumən/ *n* [U] black, sticky substance (from petroleum), used for making roads, etc.

bi·tu·mi·nous coal /bəˌtumənəs ˈkoul/ *n* [U] soft coal that burns with a heavy smoke.

bi·valve /ˈbaiˌvælv/ *n* [C] water animal with a hinged double shell, eg an oyster, a mussel, a clam.

biv·ou·ac /ˈbɪvˌwæk/ *n* [C] makeshift camp. □ *vi* (*pt,pp* ~ked; *pres part* ~king) camp in a makeshift way; make a temporary camp.

bi·week·ly /ˌbaiˈwikli/ *adj* **1** happening every other week. **2** happening twice a week.

bi·zarre /bəˈzar/ *adj* very odd or unusual.

blab /blæb/ *vt,vi* (-bb-) talk foolishly or indiscreetly; tell (a secret).

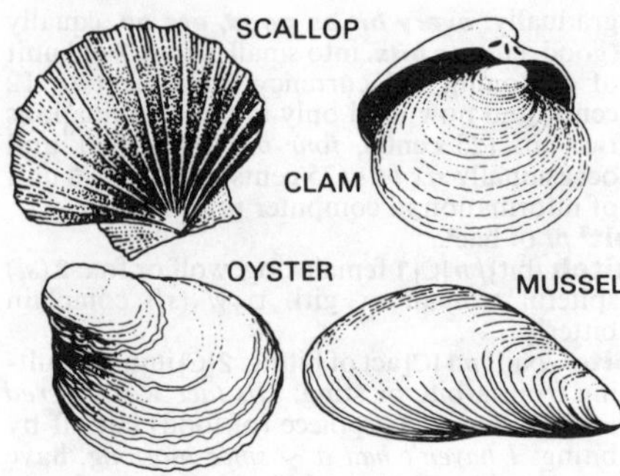

BIVALVES

ˈ**blabber·mouth** *n* [C] person who talks excessively or indiscreetly; one who tells secrets.

black /blæk/ *adj* (-er, -est) **1** without light or almost without light; the color of this printing-ink; opposite to white. ***in black and white,*** written down. **2** (various uses, mostly to intensify the meaning of the *noun*) **(a)** gloomy: ~ *despair/moods*. **(b)** evil. **(c)** angry; sullen: ~ *looks*. **3** having to do with Negroes: ~ *literature*. □ *n* **1** [U] black color. **2** [C] Negro. □ *vt* **1** make black; clean and shine (boots, etc), with black polish. **2** ***black out,*** **(a)** make dark, by putting out lights in buildings, etc as a protection against air raids in wartime. **(b)** lose one's memory or consciousness for a short period.

ˌ**black-and-**ˈ**blue** *adj* discolored because of bruises.

ˌ**black** ˈ**art** = black magic.

ˈ**black·berry** *n* [C] small berry, black when ripe, growing wild on bushes (called *brambles*). ➪ illus at fruit.

ˈ**black·bird** *n* [C] North American bird, of which the male is all or mostly black in color.

ˈ**black·board** *n* [C] board used in schools for writing and drawing on with chalk.

ˌ**black** ˈ**magic,** evil magic; witchcraft.

ˈ**black·out** *n* (instance or period of) blacking out.

ˌ**black** ˈ**sheep,** worthless person.

blackball /ˈblækˌbɔl/ *vt* prevent (a person) from being elected a member of a club by voting against him at a secret ballot.

blacken /ˈblækən/ *vt,vi* **1** make or become black. **2** say harmful things about (a person).

black·jack /ˈblækˌdʒæk/ *n* **1** [U] kind of card game. **2** [C] small, weighted and flexible club.

black·list /ˈblækˌlɪst/ *n* [C] list of persons who are considered dangerous or who are to be punished. □ *vt* enter a person's name on such a list.

black·mail /ˈblækˌmeiəl/ *vt,* (-ing -ˌmeilɪŋ/), *n* [U] (force a person to make a) payment of money for not making known something to harm his character.

ˈ**black·mailer** *n* [C]

black market /ˌblæk ˈmarkɪt/ *n* [U] unlawful buying and selling of goods, currencies, etc that are officially controlled; place where such trading is carried on.

Black Mus·lim /ˌblæk ˈməzləm/ *n* [C] member of a US Negro sect of the Islamic religion.

Black Pan·ther /ˌblæk ˈpænθər/ *n* [C] member of a militant US Negro group.

black power /ˌblæk ˈpauər/ *n* [U] (program of) political and economic power for Negroes, to gain equality.

black·smith /ˈblækˌsmɪθ/ *n* [C] man who makes and repairs things of iron, and esp shoes horses.

black·top /ˈblækˌtap/ *n* [U] black material used as a surface for roads, parking lots, airport runways, etc.

black widow /ˌblæk ˈwɪdou/ (also **black widow spider**) *n* [C] poisonous, glossy black spider of the (esp western) US.

BLACK WIDOW SPIDER

blad·der /ˈblædər/ *n* [C] **1** bag of skin in which urine collects in human and animal bodies. ➪ illus at kidney. **2** bag of rubber, etc that can be filled with air, eg in a football.

blade /bleid/ *n* [C] **1** sharp cutting part of a knife, sword, chisel, etc: ˈ*razor*~, thin, flat piece of steel with a sharp edge for shaving. **2** sword. **3** flat wide part of, eg, an oar (the part that goes into the water), propeller, etc. **4** flat, long, narrow leaf, esp of grass and cereals (wheat, barley, etc).

blame /bleim/ *vt* hold a person responsible for something bad: *He ~d the teacher for his failure/his failure on the teacher*. ***(be) to blame,*** responsible: *I am not to ~*. □ *n* [U] **1** responsibility for failure, etc: *Where does the ~ lie for our failure*, who or what is responsible? **2** expression of disapproval: *received a great deal of ~*.

blame·less *adj* free from responsibility or faults; innocent.

blame·less·ly *adv*

blame·worthy *adj* deserving blame.

blanch /blæntʃ/ *vt,vi* **1** make or become pale or white, eg by taking the skin off almonds. **2** make or become pale with fear, cold, etc. **3** put (esp vegetables, fruit) in boiling water for a very short time.

bland /blænd/ *adj* **1** gentle or polite in manner or talk. **2** (of air, food, drink) mild; comforting.

bland·ly *adv*

bland·ness /-nɪs/ *n* [U]

blank /blæŋk/ *adj* **1** (of paper) with nothing written, printed or drawn on it: *a ~ sheet of paper*. **2** (of a document) with spaces in which details, signature, etc are to be filled in: *a ~ form*. **3** empty; without interest or expression: *There was a ~ look on his face*, he seemed not to be interested, not to understand, etc. *My mind went ~*, I could not recall things, esp things I needed to be aware of. □ *n* [C] **1** space left empty or to be filled (in an application form, etc). **2** empty surface; emptiness: *His mind/memory was a complete* ~, he could remember nothing. **3** cartridge without a bullet.

ˌblank ˈcartridge, ⇨ blank *n* (3).

ˌblank ˈcheck, (a) signed but with no amount stated. **(b)** freedom to do anything one wishes.

blank·ly *adv*

ˌblank ˈverse, poetry without rhyme, esp the ten-syllable verse common in English epic and dramatic poems.

blan·ket /ˈblæŋkɪt/ *n* [C] **1** thick, woven covering as used on beds. **2** (*fig*) similar covering or layer: *a* ~ *of snow*. □ *vt* covered thickly with: *The valley was* ~*ed with fog*.

ˌwet ˈblanket, (*informal*) gloomy person who stops others from enjoying themselves.

blare /bler/ *n* [U] sound or noise (as of trumpets or horns). □ *vi,vt* make or produce such sounds: *The trumpets* ~*d (forth). He* ~*d out a warning*, shouted.

blasé /blaˈzei/ *adj* tired of pleasure; bored.

blas·pheme /blæsˈfim/ *vi,vt* speak in an irreverent way about God and sacred things: ~ *the name of God*.

blas·phemer *n* [C]

blas·phe·mous /ˈblæsfəməs/ *adj* (of persons) using blasphemy; (of language) containing blasphemy.

blas·phe·mous·ly *adv*

blas·phemy /ˈblæsfəmi/ *n* **1** [U] contemptuous or irreverent talk about sacred things. **2** [C] instance of this.

blast /blæst/ *n* [C] **1** strong, sudden rush of wind: *A* ~ *of hot air came from the oven*. **2** strong rush of air or gas spreading outwards from an explosion: *Thousands of windows were broken by the ˈbomb*~. ***full blast,*** (*informal*) with the maximum activity. **3** sound made by a wind instrument: *The hunter blew a* ~ *on his horn*. **4** quantity of explosive (eg dynamite) used at one time (eg in a quarry). **5** strong criticism; verbal attack. **6** (of plants) blight; disease. **7** (*sl*) wild party or celebration. □ *vt* **1** blow up (rocks, etc) with explosives. **2** destroy; injure: *The tree had been* ~*ed by lightning. His hopes were* ~*ed*. **3** criticize strongly; attack verbally. **4** ***blast off,*** (of spacecraft, etc) take off.

blasted *adj* (*informal*) (used to avoid swearing): *He wrecked the whole* ~*ed thing*.

ˈblast furnace, for melting iron ore by forcing heated air into it.

ˈblast-off *n* (time of) launching of a space craft. ⇨ blast *v* (4).

bla·tant /ˈbleitənt/ *adj* **1** noisy and rough. **2** too obvious, esp in a vulgar way.

bla·tant·ly *adv*

blaze[1] /bleiz/ *n* [C] **1** bright flame or fire: *We could see the* ~ *of a fire through the window*. **2** fire; burning building: *It took the firemen two hours to put the* ~ *out*. **3** (*pl*) hell: *Go to* ~*s!* **4** glow of color; bright light: *The red tulips made a* ~ *of color in the garden*. **5** violent outburst: *in a* ~ *of anger*.

blaze[2] /bleiz/ *vi,vt* **1** burn with flame: *When the firemen arrived the whole building was blazing*. **2** be bright with color; shine brightly or with warmth: *The sun* ~*d down on us*. **3** burst out with strong feeling: *He was blazing with anger/indignation*. **4** fire continuously with rifles, etc: *They* ~*d away at the enemy*.

blaz·ing *adj*

blaze[3] /bleiz/ *n* [C] **1** white mark on a horse's or an ox's face. **2** mark made on a tree by cutting the bark. □ *vt* mark (a tree) by cutting off part of the bark. ***blaze a trail,*** **(a)** mark trees to show a path through a forest. **(b)** (*fig*) do something for the first time for others to follow.

blaze[4] /bleiz/ *vt* make known far and wide: ~ *the news (abroad)*.

blazer /ˈbleizər/ *n* [C] loose-fitting jacket (often made of flannel, sometimes in the colors of a school, club, team, etc).

bla·zon /ˈbleizən/ *n* coat of arms, esp on a shield.

bleach /blitʃ/ *n* [U] chemical used for bleaching or sterilizing. □ *vt,vi* make or become white (by chemical action or sunlight): ~ *linen; bones of animals* ~*ing on the desert sand*.

bleak /blik/ *adj* (-er, -est) **1** (of the weather) cold and miserable. **2** (of a place) bare, swept by cold winds: *a* ~ *hillside*. **3** (*fig*) gloomy: ~ *prospects*.

bleak·ly *adv*

bleary /ˈblɪri/ *adj* (-ier, -iest) dim; blurred.

ˈbleary-eyed *adj* unable to see clearly because one is tired, ill, etc.

bleat /blit/ *n* [C,U] cry of a sheep, goat or calf. □ *vi,vt* make a cry of this kind.

bleed /blid/ *vi,vt* (*pt,pp* bled /bled/) **1** lose, send out, blood; suffer wounds (for a cause, etc): *If you cut your finger it will* ~. **2** feel great distress: *Our hearts* ~ *for homeless people during this cold winter*.

blem·ish /ˈblemɪʃ/ *n* [C,U] mark, etc that spoils the beauty or perfection; defect: *without* ~, faultless. □ *vt* spoil the perfection of.

blench /blentʃ/ *vi* make a quick movement of fear.

blend /blend/ *vt,vi* **1** mix together thoroughly, eg coffee, tobacco, spirits, etc to get a certain quality. **2** mix, form a mixture: *Oil does not* ~ *with water*. **3** go well together; have no sharp or unpleasant contrast; (esp of colors) pass by degrees into each other: *These two colors* ~ *well. How well their voices* ~! □ *n* [C] mixture made of various sorts (of tea, tobacco, etc): *This coffee is a* ~ *of Java and Brazil*.

bless /bles/ *vt* (*pt,pp* ~ed, blest /blest/) **1** ask God's favor for: *They brought the children to Jesus and he* ~*ed them*. **2** wish happiness or favor to: *Bless you, sir!* **3** consecrate; make sacred or holy: *bread* ~*ed at the altar*. **4** ***be blessed with,*** be fortunate in having: *May you always be* ~*ed with good health*. **5** (*informal*) (in exclamations): *Bless my soul! Bless you!* (said to a person who has sneezed.)

bles·sed /ˈblesɪd/ *adj* **1** holy, sacred: *the Blessed Virgin*, the mother of Jesus; *the Blessed Sacrament*, Holy Communion. **2** fortunate: *Blessed are the poor in spirit*. **3 the Blessed,** those who are believed to be with God in paradise. **4** (*informal*) (used to avoid swearing): *He didn't do a* ~ *thing all day*.

bless·ing /ˈblesɪŋ/ *n* [C] **1** the favor of God;

prayer for God's favor; thanks to God before or after a meal: *ask a* ~. **2** something that one is glad of, that brings comfort or happiness: *What a ~ it is you didn't get caught in the storm yesterday!* ***a blessing in disguise,*** something that seemed unfortunate, but that is seen later to be fortunate.

blest *pt,pp* of bless.

blew *pt* of blow².

blight /blait/ *n* **1** [U] (kinds of) plant disease; mildew. **2** [C] evil influence of obscure origin: *a ~ on his hopes.* □ *vt* injure; ruin: *His hopes were ~ed. Her life was ~ed by constant illness.*

blimp /blɪmp/ *n* [C] small airship shaped like a cigar.

blind¹ /blaind/ *adj* **1** without the power to see: *Tom helped the ~ man across the road.* ***turn a blind eye (to sth),*** pretend not to see it. **2** unable to see effects, to judge or understand well: *Mothers are sometimes ~ to the faults of their children.* **3** reckless; thoughtless: *In his ~ haste he almost ran into the river.* **4** not having a purpose: *Some people think that the world is governed by ~ forces.*

ˌblind ˈalley, ⇨ alley.

ˌblind ˈdate, ⇨ date¹(4).

ˌblind·ˌman's ˈbuff, game in which a person is blindfolded and tries to catch and identify others.

ˈblind spot, (a) point on the retina insensible to light. **(b)** (*fig*) something one does not seem able to understand or know in spite of having information.

blind² /blaind/ *vt* **1** make blind: *a ~ing light.* **2** (*fig*) take away the power of judgment: *His feelings for her ~ed him to her faults.*

blind·ly *adv*

blind·ness /-nɪs/ *n* [U]

blind³ /blaind/ *n* [C] **1** something (a window shade, shutter etc) that keeps out light: *pull down/lower, draw up/raise the ~s.* **2** (*fig*) deception: *It was only a ~.*

blind·ers /ˈblaindərz/ *n pl* flaps to prevent a horse from seeing sideways.

blind·fold /ˈblaindˌfould/ *vt* cover the eyes of (a person) with a bandage, scarf, etc so that he cannot see. □ *n* such a cover. □ *adj* with the eyes bandaged, etc.

blink /blɪŋk/ *vi,vt* **1** shut and open the eyes quickly: *~ the eyes; ~ away a tear.* **2** (of lights, esp when in the distance) come and go; shine in an unsteady way: *We saw the lighthouse ~ing on the horizon.* □ *n* [C] blinking. ***on the blink,*** not working properly.

blip /blɪp/ *n* [C] spot of light on a radar screen.

bliss /blɪs/ *n* [U] perfect happiness; great joy.

ˈbliss·ful /-fəl/ *adj*

ˈbliss·fully /-fəli/ *adv*

blis·ter /ˈblɪstər/ *n* [C] **1** small swelling under the skin, filled with liquid (caused by rubbing, a burn, etc): *If your shoes are too tight, you may get ~s on your feet.* **2** similar swelling on the surface of metal, painted or varnished wood, etc. □ *vt,vi* cause, get, a blister or blisters on.

blithe /blaið/ *adj* cheerful and happy; gay.

blitz /blɪts/ *n* [C] rapid, violent attack (esp from the air). □ *vt* attack or destroy in this way.

bliz·zard /ˈblɪzərd/ *n* [C] violent and heavy snowstorm.

bloated /ˈbloutɪd/ *adj* swollen; fat and large in an unhealthy way: *a ~ face.*

blob /blab/ *n* [C] drop of liquid, eg paint; small round mass, eg of wax; spot of color.

bloc /blak/ *n* [C] combination of parties, groups, states, etc with a special interest.

block¹ /blak/ *n* [C] **1** large, solid piece of wood, stone, etc: *A butcher cuts up his meat on a large ~ of wood.* **2** mass of buildings (shops, offices, apartments, etc) joined together. **3** area bounded by four streets; the length of one side of such an area: *To reach the post office, walk two ~s east and then turn left.* **4** number of things of the same kind, thought of as a unit or group: *a ~ of seats in the theater.* **5** obstruction: *There was a ~ in the pipe and the water couldn't flow away.* **6 the block,** (formerly) large piece of wood on which a person put his neck to have his head cut off as a punishment. **7** ***block and tackle,*** pulley, or system of pulleys, in a wooden case. **8** piece of wood or metal with designs, etc cut (engraved) on it for printing. **9** (*sl*) (person's) head: *I'll knock your ~ off!*

ˈblock·buster *n* [C] (*informal*) expensively produced, often sensational movie, book, etc for the mass market.

ˈblock·busting *n* [U] strategy of acquiring real estate at low prices by starting a rumor that previous racial, etc restrictions on residence will be broken.

ˌblock ˈletters, with each letter separate and in capitals: *Write your name in ~ letters.*

block² /blak/ *vt* **1** make movement difficult or impossible; obstruct: *All roads were ~ed by the heavy snowfall.* **2** make (action) difficult or impossible: *The general succeeded in ~ing the enemy's plans.* **3** ***block in/out,*** make a rough sketch or plan of the general arrangement (of objects in a drawing, etc).

block·ade /blaˈkeid/ *n* [C] the enclosing or surrounding of a place, eg by armies or warships, to keep goods or people from entering or leaving. ***run the blockade,*** get through it. □ *vt* put, eg a town, fort, etc under a blockade.

block·age /ˈblakɪdʒ/ *n* [C] **1** state of being blocked. **2** thing that blocks: *There's a ~ in the drain-pipe.*

block·head /ˈblakˌhed/ *n* [C] (*sl*) slow and stupid person.

block·house /ˈblakˌhaus/ *n* [C] small fort with openings to shoot from.

blond, blonde /bland/ *n* [C], *adj* (person) having fair complexion and hair.

blood /bləd/ *n* [U] **1** red liquid flowing throughout the body. ***make one's blood boil,*** make one very angry. ***in cold blood,*** when one is not feeling angry or excited; deliberately. ***make one's ˈblood run cold,*** fill one with fear or horror. **2** relationships; family: *They are of the same ~*, have ancestors in common. ***one's own flesh and blood,*** one's relations. ***Blood is thicker than water,*** (*prov*) the ties of one's family are the most important.

ˈblood·bath *n* [C] large-scale slaughter of people.

ˈ**blood count,** (counting of the) number of red and white corpuscles in a certain volume of blood.
ˈ**blood·curdling** *adj* horrible.
ˈ**blood donor,** person who gives blood for transfusions.
ˈ**blood group/type,** any of several distinct classes of human blood.
blood·less /lɪs/ *adj* **1** without bloodshed: *a ~less victory*. **2** pale; unfeeling and cold-hearted.
blood·less·ly *adv*
ˈ**blood poisoning,** condition that results when poisonous germs enter the blood, esp through a cut or wound.
ˈ**blood pressure,** the force exerted by blood within the arteries.
ˈ**blood·shed** *n* [U] killing or wounding of people; putting to death.
ˈ**blood·shot** *adj* (of the white of the eyes) red.
ˈ**blood·thirsty** *adj* cruel and taking pleasure in killing.
ˈ**blood transfusion,** ⇨ transfusion.
ˈ**blood vessel,** tube (vein or artery) through which blood flows in the body.

blood·hound /ˈblədˌhaund/ *n* [C] large dog able to trace a person by scent. ⇨ illus at dog.

bloody /ˈblədi/ *adj* (-ier, -iest) **1** bleeding; covered with blood: *a ~ nose*. **2** with much bloodshed: *a ~ battle*.

bloom /blum/ *n* **1** [C] flower, esp of plants admired chiefly for their flowers (eg roses, tulips, chrysanthemums): *The tulips are in full ~ now*. **2** (*sing* only) (time of) greatest beauty or perfection: *She was in the ~ of youth*. □ *vi* **1** be in flower; bear flowers: *The roses have been ~ing all summer*. **2** (*fig*) be in full beauty and perfection.
bloom·ing /ˈblumɪŋ/ *adj*

bloom·ers /ˈblumərz/ *n pl* **1** short, full pants, gathered at knee, formerly worn by girls and women for games, cycling, etc. **2** underpants of a similar design worn by girls and women.

blos·som /ˈblasəm/ *n* **1** [C] flower, esp of a fruit tree. **2** [U] time or state of flowering: *The apple trees are in ~*. □ *vi* **1** open into flowers: *The cherry trees will ~ next month*. **2** develop: *He ~ed out as a first-rate athlete*.

blot /blat/ *n* [C] **1** mark or stain, esp of ink. **2** fault; disgrace: *a ~ on his character; a ~ on the landscape*, eg an ugly building or advertisement. □ *vt* (-tt-) **1** make a blot or blots on (paper with ink). **2** dry up (wet ink) with blotting paper. **3** ***blot out,*** **(a)** make a blot over (words that have been written): *Several words in his letter had been ~ted out*. **(b)** hide from view: *The mist came down and ~ted out the view*.
blot·ter *n* [C] piece or pad of blotting paper.
ˈ**blotting paper,** absorbent paper used to dry up wet ink.

blotch /blatʃ/ *n* [C] large, discolored mark (eg on the skin).

blouse /blaus/ *n* [C] outer garment from neck to waist, worn by women and girls, sailors, etc.

blow[1] /blou/ *n* [C] **1** hard stroke (given with the hand, a stick, etc): *He struck his enemy a heavy ~ on the head*. ***come to/exchange blows,*** fight. ***(strike) a blow for,*** (perform) an act of support for. **2** shock; disaster: *His wife's death was a great ~ to him*.

blow[2] /blou/ *vi,vt* (*pt* blew /blu/, *pp* ~n /bloun/) **1** (of air, wind, etc) move along, flow as a current of air: *The wind was ~ing round the street corners*. **2** (of the wind) cause to move: *The wind blew my hat off. I was almost ~n over by the wind*. **3** (of objects, etc) be moved or carried by the wind or other air current: *The door blew open*. **4** send or force a strong current of air on, into or through: *~ (on) one's food,* (to cool it); *~ one's nose,* in order to clear it. **5** make by blowing: *~ bubbles*. **6** produce sound from (a trumpet, etc) by sending air into it; (of a wind instrument, etc) produce sound: *The referee blew his whistle. We heard the bugles ~ing*. **7** breathe hard and quickly: *The old man was puffing and ~ing when he got to the top of the hill*. **8** (of a fuse) melt because the electric current is too strong; cause to do this: *The fuse has ~n*. **9** (*sl*) spend (money) recklessly or extravagantly: *~ $50 on a dinner with a girl friend*. ***blow a fuse/gasket/stack/one's top,*** (*sl*) lose one's temper. **10** (special uses with *adverbial particles* and *prepositions*):
blow off steam, release tension by arguing, being noisy, etc: *Parents must let children ~ off steam sometimes*.
blow (sth) out, (be) put out by blowing: *The candle was ~n out by the wind*. ***blow one's brains out,*** kill oneself by shooting in the head.
blow over, pass by; be forgotten: *The storm/scandal will soon ~ over*.
blow up, **(a)** explode: *The barrel of gunpowder blew up*. **(b)** lose one's temper: *I'm sorry I blew up at you*. ***blow sth up,*** **(a)** break or destroy by explosion: *The soldiers blew up the bridge*. **(b)** inflate with air or gas: *~ up a tire*. **(c)** enlarge greatly: *~ up a photograph*. **(d)** exaggerate: *His abilities have been greatly ~n up by the newspapers*.
ˈ**blow·out** *n* [C] **(a)** sudden (often violent) escape of air, steam, etc; (esp) bursting of a tire. **(b)** blowing out of an electric fuse. **(c)** (*sl*) big meal; feast.
ˈ**blow·pipe** *n* [C] (esp) tube for increasing the heat of a flame by forcing air into it.
ˈ**blow·torch** *n* [C] for directing an intensely hot flame on to a surface.
ˈ**blow·up** *n* [C] **(a)** greatly enlarged photograph. **(b)** (*informal*) argument; burst of anger.

blow[3] /blou/ *n* [C] blowing: *Give your nose a good ~*, clear it thoroughly.

blow[4] /blou/ *vi* (*pp* ~n /bloun/) bloom; blossom: (chiefly in *pp* as) *full-~n roses,* wide open.

blower /ˈblouər/ *n* [C] **1** apparatus for forcing air, etc into or through something. **2** person who makes things by blowing (eg *a* ˈ*glass~*).

blown *pp* of blow[2]. ⇨ also blow[4].

blowsy, blowzy /ˈblauzi/ *adj* (-ier, -iest) (of a woman) **1** red-faced and coarse. **2** untidy.

BLT /ˌbi ˌel ˈti/ (also **BLT sandwich**) *abbr*, *n* [C] sandwich made of bacon, lettuce and tomatoes.

blub·ber[1] /ˈbləbər/ *n* [U] fat of whales and other sea animals from which oil is obtained.

blub·ber[2] /ˈbləbər/ *vi* weep noisily.

bludgeon /ˈblədʒən/ *n* [C] short, thick stick with a heavy end, used as a weapon. □ *vt* **1** strike with a stick: *He had been ~ed to death.* **2** (*fig*) force or bully somebody into doing something.

blue[1] /blu/ *adj* (-r, -st) of or like the color blue: *His face was ~ with cold.* ***once in a blue moon,*** very rarely.

blue[2] /blu/ *n* **1** color of the sky on a clear day: *dark/light ~.* **2** (the) sky. ***out of the blue,*** unexpectedly. ***a bolt from the blue,*** something unexpected. **3** (*poet*) (the) sea. **4 the blues, (a)** (*music*) melancholy songs composed in a style that originated among Negroes in the southern US. **(b)** (*informal*) condition of being sad, melancholy.

blue[3] /blu/ *vt* make blue.

blue·bell /ˈbluˌbel/ *n* [C] plant with blue, bell-shaped flowers.

blue·berry /ˈbluˌberi/ *n* [C] (*pl* -ies) round, sweet berry, similar to the huckleberry, but with smaller seeds.

blue·bird /ˈbluˌbərd/ *n* [C] small North American bird with blue feathers on the back and wings.

blue-blooded /ˈbluˌblədɪd/ *adj* of aristocratic birth.

blue·bottle /ˈbluˌbatəl/ *n* [C] large blue fly with a hairy body.

blue-collar /ˌbluˈkalər/ *adj* manual: *~ workers in factories.* ⇨ white-collar.

blue·fish /ˈbluˌfɪʃ/ *n* [C] large, saltwater fish used as food.

blue·grass /ˈbluˌgræs/ *n* [U] **1** grass with bluish-green stems, used for pasture, lawns, etc. **2** kind of music, between popular and folk, originating esp in Kentucky and Tennessee.

blue·jacket /ˈbluˌdʒækɪt/ *n* [C] (*sl*) sailor in the US Navy.

blue·jay /ˈbluˌdʒei/ *n* [C] bird of North America, having a crest and bright blue feathers.

blue·print /ˈbluˌprɪnt/ *n* [C] **1** photographic print, white on blue paper, usually of building plans. **2** (*fig*) plan, scheme.

bluff[1] /bləf/ *n* [C] headland with a broad and very steep face. □ *adj* **1** (of headlands, cliffs, a ship's bows) with a broad, perpendicular front. **2** (of a person, his manner, etc) abrupt; rough but honest and kind, simple and good-natured.

bluff·ly *adv*

bluff·ness /-nɪs/ *n* [U]

bluff[2] /bləf/ *vt,vi* deceive by pretending to have strength that one does not really have. ***bluff it out,*** survive a difficult situation by a pretense of strength. □ *n* [U] deception of this kind; (the use of) threats that are intended to get results without being carried out. ***call sb's bluff,*** challenge him to carry out his threats.

bluff·er *n* [C]

blu·ing /ˈbluɪŋ/ *n* [U] material giving a bluish tint, used in washing to make white clothes, etc seem whiter.

blu·ish /ˈbluɪʃ/ tending towards blue: *~ green.*

blun·der /ˈbləndər/ *vi,vt* **1** move about uncertainly, as if blind: *~ into a wall.* **2** make foolish mistakes: *Our leaders have ~ed again.* □ *n* [C] stupid or careless mistake.

blunt /blənt/ *adj* (-er, -est) **1** without a point or sharp edge: *a ~ knife.* **2** (of a person, what he says) plain; not troubling to be polite: *He's a ~ man.* □ *vt* make blunt: *If you try to cut stone with a knife, you will ~ the edge.*

blunt·ly *adv*: *to speak ~ly,* frankly.

blunt·ness /nɪs/ *n* [U]

blur /blər/ *n* [C] **1** dirty spot or mark; smear of ink. **2** confused or indistinct effect: *If, when you read, you see only a ~, you may need glasses.* □ *vt,vi* (-rr-) **1** make a dirty mark or smear on. **2** make or become unclear in appearance: *Tears ~red her eyes. The writing was ~red.*

blurb /blərb/ *n* [C] description of the contents of a book, usually full of praise, printed on the dust jacket, etc.

blurt /blərt/ *vt* ***blurt sth out,*** tell, eg a secret, suddenly, often thoughtlessly.

blush /bləʃ/ *vi* **1** become red (in the face) from shame or confusion: **2** be ashamed: *~ to admit that....* □ *n* [C] reddening of the face, eg from shame, etc: *She turned away to hide her ~es.*

blus·ter /ˈbləstər/ *vi,vt* **1** (of the wind, waves, etc) storm; be rough or violent. **2** (of persons) act and speak in a noisy, often rather boastful way. **3** utter in this way: *~ out threats.* □ *n* [U] **1** noise of violent wind or waves. **2** boastful, noisy talk, behavior, threats.

blus·tery *adj* (of the weather) rough and windy.

Blvd *abbr* = Boulevard.

boa /ˈbouə/ *n* [C] (also **ˈboa constrictor**) large non-poisonous snake that kills by crushing its prey. ⇨ illus at snake.

boar /bɔr/ *n* [C] **1** wild male pig. **2** uncastrated male domestic pig.

board[1] /bɔrd/ *n* **1** [C] long, thin, flat piece of wood with squared edges, used in building walls, floors, boats, ship's decks, etc. **2** [C] flat piece of wood or other material for a special purpose: *a ˈbulletin ~; a ˈdiving ~* (at a swimming pool). **3** [C] flat surface with patterns, etc on which games, eg chess, are played. **4** [U] (from the boards that form the deck of a ship) ***be/go on board,*** be/go in a ship, train, airplane, etc. ***go by the board,*** (*fig*) (of plans, hopes, etc) be given up or abandoned. **5** [C] committee; group of persons managing a business, or a government department: *the ˌBoard of ˈTrade; a ˈschool ~.* ***across the board,*** ⇨ across[2]. **6** [U] food served at table, esp meals supplied by the week or month (eg at a rooming house) or as part payment for service: *Board and lodging $75 weekly.* ⇨ also cardboard.

ˈboard·walk *n* [C] footpath or sidewalk made of boards(1), esp at a beach resort.

board[2] /bɔrd/ *vt,vi* **1** make or cover with boards (1): *~ up a window.* **2** get, supply with, meals for a fixed weekly/monthly, etc payment: *In a university town, many people make a living by ~ing students* (⇨ board[1](6)). **3** get on or into (a ship, train, bus, etc).

boarder *n* [C] **(a)** person who boards with somebody. ⇨ 2 above. **(b)** schoolboy or girl at a boarding school (⇨ below).

board·ing *n* [U] (structure of) boards(1).

ˈboarding·house *n* [C] house that provides board and lodging.

ˈboarding school, one at which pupils live.

BOARDWALK
CONEY ISLAND

boast /boust/ *n* [C] words used in praise of oneself, one's acts, belongings, etc; cause for satisfaction or pride: *It was his ~ that he had never failed in an examination.* □ *vt,vi* **1** make a boast or boasts: *He ~s of being/~s that he is the best tennis player in the town.* **2** possess with pride: *Our school ~s a fine swimming pool.*

ˈboast·ful *adj* (of persons) fond of boasting.

ˈboast·fully *adv*

boat /bout/ *n* [C] small open vessel for traveling in on water, esp the kind moved with oars (*ˈrow ~*), sails (*ˈsail ~*), engines (*ˈmotor~*); also used of fishing vessels and small steamers: *We crossed the river by ~/in a ~.* ⇨ illus at ship. ***be (all) in the same boat,*** have the same problems to face. □ *vi* travel in a boat, esp for pleasure: *We ~ed down the river.* ⇨ also ferry, house[1], life.

ˈboat·house *n* [C] shed in which boats are stored.

ˈboat·man *n* [C] man who rows or sails a small boat for pay; man from whom boats may be hired.

ˈboat race, race between boats.

boat·swain /ˈbousən/ *n* [C] officer who is in charge of a ship's rigging, boats, anchors, etc.

bob[1] /bab/ *vi* (-bb-) move up and down: *The cork on his fishing line was bobbing on the water.* □ *n* [C] quick up and down movement.

bob[2] /bab/ *vt* (-bb-) cut (a woman's or child's hair) so that it is short and even: *She wears her hair bobbed.* □ *n* [C] child's or woman's short haircut.

bob·bin /ˈbabɪn/ *n* [C] small roller or spool for holding thread, yarn, wire, etc in a machine.

bobby pin /ˈbabi ˌpɪn/ *n* [C] flat metal hairpin for holding hair tightly in place.

bobby socks /ˈbabi ˌsaks/ *n pl* (esp girls') ankle socks.

bob·cat /ˈbabˌkæt/ *n* [C] small lynx of North America, having rust-colored fur with black spots.

bob·o·link /ˈbabəˌlɪŋk/ *n* [C] North American songbird.

bob·sled /ˈbabˌsled/ *n* [C] racing sled for two or more persons. □ *vi* ride in a bobsled.

bob·tail /ˈbabˌteiəl/ *n* [C] **1** short tail; tail that is cut short. **2** animal with a short tail.

bob·white /ˈbabˌ(h)wait/ *n* [C] North American quail whose call is like its name.

bock /bak/ (also ˌ**bock** ˈ**beer**) *n* [U] dark, sweet kind of beer.

bode /boud/ *vt,vi* ***bode well/ill for,*** be a good/bad sign of: *His idle habits ~ ill for his future,* suggest that his future career will be a failure.

bod·ice /ˈbadɪs/ *n* [C] close-fitting part of a woman's dress from the shoulders to the waist.

bod·ily /ˈbadəli/ *adj* of or in the human body or physical nature: *~* (= physical) *assault.* □ *adv* **1** as a whole or mass; completely: *The class rose ~ when the famous professor entered the room.* **2** in person; in the body.

bod·kin /ˈbadkɪn/ *n* [C] blunt, thick needle.

body /ˈbadi/ *n* [C] (*pl* -ies) **1** The whole physical structure of a man or animal: *We wear clothes to keep our bodies warm.* **2** dead body; corpse: *His ~ was brought back for burial.* **3** main portion of a man or animal without the head, arms and legs: *He received one wound in the left leg and another in the ~.* **4** main part of anything: *the ~ of a car; the ~ of a letter.* **5** group of persons who do something together or who are united in some way: *Large bodies of unemployed men marched through the streets demanding work.* ***in a body,*** all together; as a whole: *The staff resigned in a ~.* **6** mass, quantity, collection: *A lake is a ~ of water.* **7** piece of matter; *the heavenly bodies,* the sun, moon and stars. **8** person: *a kind old ~.* ⇨ also anybody, everybody, nobody, somebody.

ˈbody·guard *n* [C] man or men guarding an important person.

ˈbody·work *n* [U] body of (esp) a motor-vehicle.

bog /bag, bɔg/ *n* [C] (area of) soft, wet, spongy ground (chiefly decayed or decaying vegetable matter). □ *vt,vi* (-gg-) ***bog down,*** (cause to) be stuck fast, unable to make progress: *The tanks were bogged down in the mud.*

boggy *adj* (-ier, -iest) (of land) soft and wet.

bo·gey, bogy /ˈbougi/ *n* [C] (*pl* ~s, -ies) **1** evil spirit. **2** anything that one fears.

boggle /ˈbagəl/ *vi* be unwilling, hesitate, to do something: *The mind/imagination ~s* (*at the idea*), is overwhelmed by the idea.

bo·gus /ˈbougəs/ *adj* not genuine.

boil[1] /ˈbɔiəl/ *n* [C] hard (usu red, often painful) infected swelling under the skin, which bursts when ripe.

boil[2] /ˈbɔiəl/ *n* [U] boiling point. ***bring sth to a boil,*** heat it until it boils. ***come to a boil,*** **(a)** begin to boil. **(b)** (*fig*) reach a crisis.

boil[3] /ˈbɔiəl/ *vi,vt* (-ing /ˈbɔilɪŋ/) **1** (of water or other liquid, also of the container that holds a liquid) heat or be heated to the temperature at which change to gas occurs; bubble up: *When water ~s it changes into steam. The kettle is ~ing.* **2** (of the sea, of a person's feelings, etc) be agitated: *He was ~ing (over) with rage.* **3** cook or be cooked in boiling water: *Please ~ my egg for three minutes.* **4** (special uses with *adverbial particles* and *prepositions*):

boil away, **(a)** continue to boil: *The kettle was ~ing away merrily on the fire.* **(b)** boil until nothing remains: *The water had all ~ed away and the kettle was empty.*

boil down, be reduced in quantity: *It all ~s down to this...,* (*informal*) the statement, proposal, etc amounts to this....

boil over, flow over the side: *The milk had ~ed over.*

ˈboiling ˈhot *adj* (*informal*) very hot: *a ~ing hot day.*

ˈboiling point, (a) temperature at which a liquid boils. **(b)** (*fig*) height of excitement, anger, etc.

boiler /ˈbɔilər/ *n* [C] metal container in which water, etc is heated, eg for producing steam in an engine, for supplying hot water.

bois·ter·ous /ˈbɔist(ə)rəs/ *adj* (of a person, his behavior) noisy and cheerful.

bold /bould/ *adj* (-er, -est) **1** without fear; showing absence of fear. **2** without feelings of shame. ***as bold as brass,*** daring. **3** well marked; clear: *the ~ outline of a mountain.*

bold·ly *adv*

bold·ness /-nɪs/ *n* [U]

boll /boul/ *n* [C] pod for seeds (of cotton and flax).

ˈboll weevil, small destructive insect in cotton plants.

bo·logna /bəˈlouni/ *n* [U] large smoked sausage made of beef, veal and pork.

bol·ster[1] /ˈboulstər/ *n* [C] long pillow or cushion.

bol·ster[2] /ˈboulstər/ *vt* give (greatly needed encouragement or) support to, eg a person, theory, etc: *She'll need ~ing up if you want her to win the race.*

bolt[1] /boult/ *n* [C] **1** metal fastening for a door or window, consisting of a sliding pin or rod and a staple into which it fits. **2** metal pin with a head at one end and a thread (as on a screw) at the other, used with a nut for holding things together. **3** discharge of lightning. ⇨ thunderbolt. □ *vt,vi* fasten with a bolt or bolts(1): *~ the doors and windows.*

bolt[2] /boult/ *vi,vt* **1** run away quickly; (esp of a horse) run off out of control: *As soon as I came downstairs the burglar ~ed through the back door.* **2** swallow (food) quickly: *We ~ed a few mouthfuls of food and hurried on.* □ *n* act of running away. ***make a bolt for it,*** run off quickly.

bolt[3] /boult/ *adv* (only in) ***bolt upright,*** suddenly and completely upright.

bomb /bam/ *n* [C] **1** hollow metal ball or shell filled either with explosive or with smoke, gas, etc. **2** dispenser with paint, insecticide, etc stored under pressure. **3** (*sl*) failure. □ *vt,vi* **1** attack with bombs(1). **2** (*sl*) fail.

bomber *n* [C] aircraft used for bombing; person who sets bombs.

ˈbomb·shell *n* (*fig*) thing that causes great surprise or shock.

bom·bard /bamˈbard/ *vt* **1** attack with shells from big guns. **2** (*fig*) worry with questions, requests, complaints, etc.

bom·bard·ment *n* [C,U]

bond /band/ *n* [C] **1** agreement or engagement that a person is bound to observe, esp one that has force in law; document, signed and sealed, containing such an agreement. **2** (usually *fig*) something that joins or unites: *the ~(s) of affection.* **3** printed paper issued by a government or a corporation acknowledging that money has been lent to it and will be paid back with interest.

bond·age /ˈbandɪdʒ/ *n* [U] slavery, servitude: *in hopeless ~ to his master.*

bone /boun/ *n* **1** [U] hard material that makes up the skeleton of most animals. **2** [C] one of the parts that make up the framework of an animal's body: *This fish has a lot of ~s in it.* ***feel in one's bones that,*** feel certain that. ***have a bone to pick with sb,*** have something to argue or complain about. ***make no bones about doing sth,*** not hesitate to do it. □ *vt* **1** take bones out of (a chicken, a piece of meat, etc). **2** ***bone up,*** (*sl*) study hard: *~d up on geometry.*

ˈbone·head *n* (*sl*) stupid person.

bon·fire /ˈbanˌfaiər/ *n* [C] large fire made outdoors either to celebrate some event or to burn up rubbish, etc

bongo /ˈbaŋgou/ *n* [C] (*pl* unchanged or ~es) small hand drum, usually connected with another of a different pitch, used for Cuban-style dance music: (also as an *adjective*) ˈ*~ beat/drum(s).* ⇨ illus at percussion.

bon·net /ˈbanɪt/ *n* [C] **1** head covering, usually tied under the chin, worn by women and children. **2** headdress of an American Indian.

bo·nus /ˈbounəs/ *n* [C] (*pl* ~es) payment in addition to what is usual, necessary or expected, eg an extra payment to workers.

bony /ˈbouni/ *adj* (-ier, -iest) **1** of bone. **2** full of bones: *a ~ fish,* eg a herring. **3** having big or prominent bones: *~ fingers.*

boo /bu/ *int* **1** sound made to show disapproval or contempt. **2** exclamation used to surprise or startle. □ *vt,vi* make such sounds: *The speaker was booed off the platform.*

boob[1] /bub/ *n* [C] (*informal*) stupid person; dunce.

boob[2] /bub/ *n* [C] (*sl* ⚠) woman's breast.

boo·boo /ˈbuˌbu/ *n* [C] (*sl*) mistake.

booby /ˈbubi/ *n* [C] (*pl* -ies) silly or stupid person.

ˈbooby prize, prize given as a joke, eg to the person who is last in a race or competition.

ˈbooby trap, apparently harmless object that will kill or injure when picked up or interfered with.

book[1] /bʊk/ *n* [C] **1** number of sheets of paper, either printed or blank, fastened together inside a cover; literary composition that would fill such a set of sheets: *write a ~.* ***the Good Book,*** (*informal, dated*) the Bible. ***throw the book at sb,*** (*informal*) charge or punish him to the full extent of the law. **2** main division of a large work, eg the Bible: *the Book of Genesis.* **3** packet of similar items fastened together, eg postage stamps, matches. **4** (*informal*) record of bets kept by a bookmaker. ***make book,*** take and keep records of bets. **5** (*pl*) business accounts, records, etc.

ˈbook·case *n* [C] piece of furniture with shelves for books.

ˈbook·club *n* [C] organization that sells books at a discount to members who agree to buy a minimum number.

ˈbook·ends *n pl* pair of props used to keep books upright.

ˈbook·mark *n* [C] something in a book to mark

the place.
ˈ**book·seller** *n* [C] person who sells books.
ˈ**book·worm** *n* [C] **(a)** small maggot that eats holes in books. **(b)** person who is very fond of reading.
book[2] /bʊk/ *vt* **1** write down (orders, etc) in a notebook. ***(be) booked up***, (have) all possible orders or reservations filled. **2** record a police charge against (a person): *be ~ed for speeding*. **3** give or receive an order for, eg tickets for a journey. **4** engage (a person) as a speaker, entertainer, etc.
bookie /ˈbʊki/ *n* [C] (*informal*) = bookmaker.
book·keeper /ˈbʊkˌkipər/ *n* [C] person who keeps accounts, eg of a business, public office.
book·keep·ing /ˈbʊkˌkipɪŋ/ *n* [U] (work of) keeping (business) accounts.
book·let /ˈbʊklɪt/ *n* [C] thin book, pamphlet.
book·maker /ˈbʊkˌmeikər/ *n* [C] person whose business is taking bets on horse races, etc.
boom[1] /bum/ *n* [C] **1** long pole used to keep the bottom of a sail stretched out. ⇨ illus at ship. **2** long, movable arm for a microphone. **3** pole fastened to a crane(2), used for (un)loading cargo. **4** heavy chain, mass of floating logs, etc held in position across a river or harbor entrance. ***lower the boom,*** punish or regulate: *The government lowered the ~ on profiteers.*
boom[2] /bum/ *vt,vi* **1** (of big guns, etc) make deep, hollow sounds. **2** ***boom out,*** say in a loud deep voice: *~ing out Shakespearean verses.* □ *n* [C] deep, hollow sound: *the ~ of supersonic aircraft.*
boom[3] /bum/ *n* [C] sudden increase in trade activity, esp a time when money is being made quickly. □ *vi* have a boom: *Business is ~ing.*
boom·er·ang /ˈbuməˌræŋ/ *n* [C] **1** curved stick of hard wood (originally used for hunting by Australian Aborigines) which returns to the thrower if it fails to hit its target. **2** (*fig*) argument or scheme that comes back and harms its user. □ *vi* (of a scheme) cause harm in this way.
boon /bun/ *n* [U] advantage; blessing, comfort: *Parks are a great ~ to people in big cities.*
boor /bʊr/ *n* [C] rough, ill-mannered person.
boor·ish *adj* of or like a boor.
boost /bust/ *vt* increase the value, reputation, etc of: *Seeing him there ~ed my morale.* □ *n* [C] act of boosting.
booster /ˈbustər/ *n* [C] **1** thing that boosts: *His work got a welcome ~.* **2** (also ˈ**booster shot**) supplementary dose of vaccine to strengthen the effect of an earlier dose. **3** rocket used to give initial speed to a missile, after which it drops and leaves the missile to continue under its own power.
boot[1] /but/ *n* [C] **1** outer covering for the foot and leg, made of leather or rubber. ***get the boot,*** (*sl*) be dismissed, be kicked out. ***give sb the boot,*** (*sl*) dismiss him from his job. **2** recruit in basic training in the US Marines or Navy. □ *vt* **1** kick. **2** dismiss (a person): *He was ~ed out of office.*
ˈ**boot camp,** camp at which boots(2) are trained.
boot[2] /but/ *n* (only in) ***to boot,*** as well; in addition.
bootee, bootie /ˈbuti/ *n* [C] baby's knitted wool sock.
booth /buθ/ *n* [C] **1** shelter of boards, canvas or other light materials, esp one where goods are sold at a market or a fair. **2** small compartment: *a telephone ~; a voting ~.*
boot·jack /ˈbutˌdʒæk/ *n* [C] device used for pulling off boots.
boot·leg /ˈbutˌleg/ *vt* (-gg-) make, transport or sell goods (esp alcoholic drinks) illegally. □ *n* [U], *adj* something that is bootlegged.
booty /ˈbuti/ *n* [U] what is taken by robbers or captured from the enemy in war.
booze /buz/ *n* [U] (*informal*) **1** alcoholic drink. **2** period of drinking alcoholic drink. □ *vi* drink (too much) alcoholic drink.
boozy /ˈbuzi/ *adj* (-ier, -iest) (*sl*) drunk; fond of boozing.
bor·der /ˈbɔrdər/ *n* [C] **1** edge; part near the edge: *We camped on the ~ of a lake. There is a ~ of flowers around the lawn.* **2** (land near the) line dividing two states or countries: *The criminal escaped over the ~.* □ *vt,vi* **1** put or be an edge to: *Our garden is ~ed by a stream.* **2** ***border on/upon,*** **(a)** be next to: *My land ~s on yours.* **(b)** be almost the same as: *The proposal ~s on the absurd.*
ˈ**border·land** *n* **(a)** district on either side of a boundary. **(b)** condition between: *the ~land between sleeping and waking.*
ˈ**border·line** *n* line that marks a boundary. ***a borderline case,*** one that is doubtful, eg a person who may or may not pass an examination.
bore[1] /bɔr/ *vt,vi* make a narrow, round deep hole with a revolving tool; make (a hole, one's way) by doing this or by digging out soil, etc: *~ a hole in wood/a tunnel through a mountain.* □ *n* [C] **1** hole made by boring. **2** hollow inside of a gun barrel; its diameter.
bore[2] /bɔr/ *vt* make (a person) feel tired by being dull or tedious: *I hope you're not getting ~d listening to me.* □ *n* [C] person or thing that bores.
bore·dom /-dəm/ *n* [U] state of being bored.
bor·ing *adj*: *a boring evening.*
bore[3] *pt* of bear[2].
born /bɔrn/ (one of the *pp's* of bear[2]) **1** ***be born,*** come into the world by birth. **2** destined to be: *He was ~ a poet.*
borne *pp* of bear[2].
bor·ough /ˈbərou/ *n* [C] **1** self-governing town or village (in some states of the US). **2** one of the five political divisions of New York City.
bor·row /ˈbarou/ *vt,vi* **1** get something, or its use, on the understanding that it is to be returned: *May I ~ your pen?* ⇨ lend. **2** take and use as one's own: *~ somebody's ideas/methods.*
bor·rower *n* [C] person who borrows.
bo'sn /ˈbousən/ *n* [C] = boatswain.
bosom /ˈbʊzəm/ *n* **1** (*old use*) person's breast; part of dress covering this. **2** center or inmost part, where one feels joy or sorrow: *a ~ friend,* one who is dear and close.
boss /bɔs/ *n* [C] **1** person who supervises workmen; foreman. **2** master; person who controls or gives orders: *Who's the ~ in this house?* **3** person who controls a political organization. □

vt be in charge of: *He wants to ~ the show,* to make all the arrangements. ⇨ show[1](6). ***boss sb around,*** give them orders.

bossy *adj* (-ier, -iest) fond of being in authority.

bo'sun /ˈbousən/ *n* [C] = boatswain.

botan·ical /bəˈtænɪkəl/ *adj* of botany: *~ gardens.*

bot·an·ist /ˈbatənɪst/ *n* [C] student, expert, of botany.

bot·any /ˈbatəni/ *n* [U] science of the structure of plants.

botch /batʃ/ *vt* repair badly; spoil by poor, clumsy work: *a ~ed piece of work.* □ *n* piece of clumsy, badly done work: *make a ~ of it.*

both[1] /bouθ/ *adj* (opposite = *neither*) (of two things, persons, etc) the two; the one and also the other: *I want ~ books. I saw him on ~ occasions.* (*Note:* Compare *both* and *each*: *There are shops on ~ sides of the street. There is a butcher's shop on each side of the street.*)

both[2] /bouθ/ *pron* (opposite = *neither*) the two; not only the one: *Both are good. Both of them are good. We ~ want to go.* ⇨ all, each.

bother /ˈbaðər/ *vt,vi* **1** be or cause trouble to; worry: *Don't ~ me with foolish questions.* **2** take trouble: *Don't ~ about getting/~ to get dinner for me today; I'll eat out.* □ *n* **1** [U] worry, trouble: *Don't put yourself to any ~,* inconvenience yourself. **2** (*sing* only) person or thing that gives trouble: *His lazy son is quite a ~ to him. This drawer won't shut; isn't it a ~!*

ˈbother·some /-səm/ *adj* troublesome or annoying.

bottle /ˈbatəl/ *n* [C] **1** container with a narrow neck, for liquids. **2** its contents: *Mary drinks two ~s of wine a day.* □ *vt* **1** put into bottles: *~ beer.* **2** ***bottle up,*** (*fig*) hold in, keep under control, eg anger.

ˈbottle-fed *adj* (of a child) given milk from a bottle, not fed from its mother's breast.

ˈbottle·neck *n* [C] **(a)** narrower strip of road, between two wide parts, where traffic is slowed down or held up. **(b)** person, thing, or situation that slows down progress.

bot·tom /ˈbatəm/ *n* [C] **1** lowest part of anything, inside or outside: *We were glad to reach the ~* (= foot) *of the mountain.* **2** bed of the sea, a lake, river, etc: *The ship went to the ~,* sank. **3** (also **ˈbottom land**) region of low, flat land along the side(s) of a river. **4** seat (of a chair, etc.): **5** (*informal*) buttocks: *She smacked the child's ~.* **6** lowest, last, (level); foundation: *Put it on the ~ shelf. We must get to the ~ of this mystery,* find out how it began. ***from the bottom of my heart,*** genuinely, deeply.

bot·tom·less *adj* very deep: *a ~less pit.*

bough /bau/ *n* [C] large branch coming from the trunk of a tree. ⇨ illus at tree.

bought *pt,pp* of buy.

boul·der /ˈbouldər/ *n* [C] large piece of rock or stone, esp one that has been rounded by water or weather.

bounce /ˈbauns/ *vi,vt* **1** (of a ball, etc) (cause to) move away and then back when sent against something hard: *The ball ~ed over the wall. She was bouncing a ball.* **2** (cause to) move up and down violently or noisily; rush noisily or angrily: *The boy was bouncing* (*up and down*) *on the bed. He ~d into/out of the room.* **3** (*informal*) (of a check) be returned by a bank because there is no money in the account. **4** (*sl*) order someone to leave, or throw someone out of, a social gathering, place of business, etc for misbehavior. □ *n* [C] (of a ball) bouncing: *catch the ball on the ~.*

bouncer *n* [C] (*sl*) man employed by a night club, bar, etc to throw out rowdy customers.

bounc·ing /ˈbaunsɪŋ/ *adj* strong, healthy: *a ~ baby boy.*

bound[1] /baund/ *vt* jump, spring, bounce; move or run in jumping movements: *His dog came ~ing to meet him.* □ *n* [C] jumping movement upward or forward: *at one ~.* ***by leaps and bounds,*** very rapidly.

bound[2] /baund/ *adj* (*liter*) ready to start; on the way: *Where are you ~* (*for*), where are you headed?

bound[3] /baund/ *vt* set limits to; be the boundary of: *Mexico is ~ed on the north by the US.*

bound[4] /baund/ *pp* of bind. (special uses) certain, destined, obliged: *~ to win; ~ to come.* ***bound up in,*** much interested in, very busy with: *He is ~ up in his work.*

bound·ary /ˈbaund(ə)ri/ *n* [C] (*pl* -ies) line that marks a limit; dividing line: *This stream forms a ~ between my land and his.*

bound·less /ˈbaundlɪs/ *adj* without limits: *his ~ generosity.*

bound·less·ly *adv*

bounds /baundz/ *n pl* limit: *It is beyond the ~ of human knowledge,* man can know nothing about it. ***out of bounds,*** outside the limits of areas that one is allowed to enter.

boun·te·ous /ˈbauntiəs/ *adj* **1** generous; giving or given freely. **2** abundant: *a ~ harvest.*

boun·ti·ful /ˈbauntɪfəl/ *adj* = bounteous.

bounty /ˈbaunti/ *n* (*pl* -ies) **1** [U] freedom in giving; generosity. **2** [C] something given out of kindness (esp to the poor). **3** [C] reward or payment offered (usually by a government) to encourage something (eg an increase in production, kill dangerous animals).

bou·quet /buˈkei/ *n* [C] **1** bunch of flowers (to be) carried in the hand. **2** fragrance of wine.

bour·bon /ˈbərbən/ *n* **1** [U] kind of whiskey distilled chiefly from corn. **2 Bourbon,** (esp in the southern US) conservative, landholding member of the Democratic party.

bour·geois /ˌburˈʒwa/ *n, adj* **1** (person) of the class that owns property or engages in trade. **2** (person) concerned chiefly with material prosperity and social status.

the bour·geoisie /ˌburʒwaˈzi/ (*collect*) bourgeois(1) persons as a class.

bout /baut/ *n* [C] **1** period of exercise, work or other activity: *a ˈwrestling ~; a ~ of drinking.* **2** fit (of illness): *a ~ of influenza.*

bou·tique /buˈtik/ *n* [C] small shop selling articles (clothes, cosmetics, hats, etc) of the latest fashion.

bov·ine /ˈbouˌvain/ *adj* of, like, an ox or cow.

bow[1] /bou/ *n* [C] **1** piece of wood curved by a tight string, used for shooting arrows. ⇨ illus at archery. **2** rod of wood with horsehair stretched from end to end, used for playing the violin, etc. ⇨ illus at string. **3** something curved like a bow: *a rainbow*. **4** knot made with a loop or loops; ribbon, etc, tied in this way: *She had a bow of pink ribbon in her hair*. ⇨ illus at knot. □ *vt* use a bow on (a violin, etc).

bow·legged /ˈbouˌlegɪd/ *adj* with the legs curved outwards at the knees; bandy.

ˌbow ˈtie, one made into a bow(4).

bow² /bau/ *vi,vt* **1** bend the head or body (as a greeting, or in submission or respect, or to show agreement); bend (the head or body): *They bowed their heads in prayer.* ***bow to sb's opinion, etc,*** submit to it. **2** bend: *The branches were bowed down with the weight of the snow.* □ *n* [C] bending of the head or body (in greeting, etc): *He answered with a low bow.*

bow³ /bau/ *n* [C] **1** (often *pl*) front or forward end of a boat, ship or aircraft, from where it begins to curve. ⇨ illus at ship. **2** (in a rowboat) oarsman nearest the bow.

bowel /ˈbauəl/ *n* **1** (usu *pl*) division of the food canal below the stomach; intestine. ***move the/one's bowels***, pass waste from the bowels; defecate. **2** (always *pl*) innermost part: *in the ~s of the earth*, deep underground.

ˈbowel movement, (act of) passing waste from the bowels; defecation.

bower /ˈbauər/ *n* [C] **1** = arbor. **2** summerhouse in a garden.

bow·ie knife /ˈboui ˌnaif/ *n* [C] large knife for hunting and fighting, used esp in the early southwestern US.

bowl¹ /boul/ *n* [C] **1** deep, round, hollow dish: *a ˈsalad/ˈsugar ~*. **2** contents of such a dish: *She ate three ~s of rice*. **3** thing shaped like a bowl: *the ~ of a spoon/pipe*.

bowl² /boul/ *vi,vt* **1** throw or roll a ball in bowling. **2** ***bowl along,*** go quickly and smoothly on wheels: *Our car ~ed along over the smooth roads*. **3** ***bowl (sb) over,*** **(a)** knock down. **(b)** make helpless, overcome: *He was ~ed over by the news*.

bowler¹ /ˈboulər/ *n* person who bowls.

bowler² /ˈboulər/ *n* (also ˌ**bowler** ˈ**hat**) = derby(3).

bowl·ing /ˈboulɪŋ/ *n* [U] indoor game in which balls are rolled so as to knock down wooden pins at the far end of an alley.

bow·man /ˈboumen/ *n* [C] (*pl* bowmen /-men/) archer.

bow·sprit /ˈbauˌsprɪt/ *n* [C] large pole or spar projecting forward from the bow of a ship, to which ropes that support sails, etc are fastened.

bow·string /ˈbouˌstrɪŋ/ *n* [C] cord connecting two ends of a bow(1).

bow·wow /ˌbau ˈwau/ *int* imitation of a dog's bark.

box¹ /baks/ *n* **1** container, usually with a lid, made of wood, cardboard, plastic, metal, etc used for holding solids: *a box of matches; a ˈtoolbox*. **2** separate compartment, with seats for several persons, in a theater, concert hall, etc. **3** compartment in a law court for a special purpose: *a ˈjury box*. **4** small hut or shelter, eg for a sentry or railway signalman. **5** separate compartment in a stable or railway truck for a horse. ⇨ also mailbox. □ *vt* put into a box. ***box in/up,*** shut up in a small space.

box·ful /-ˌfʊl/ *n* [C] as much as a box(1) can hold.

ˈbox number, number used in an advertisement as an address to which answers may be sent.

ˈbox office, office in a theater, auditorium, etc where admission tickets are sold.

box² /baks/ *vt,vi* fight with the fists, usually with thick gloves, for sport. ***box sb's ears,*** give him a blow with the open hand on the ears.□ *n* slap or blow with the open hand (on the ear(s).

ˈboxing glove, padded glove for use in boxing.

ˈboxing match, fight between two boxers.

box³ /baks/ *n* [U] **1** evergreen shrub, used for hedges. **2** (also **ˈbox·wood**) wood of this shrub.

box·car /ˈbaksˌkar/ *n* [C] railroad freight car with a roof and sliding doors on either side.

boxer /ˈbaksər/ *n* [C] **1** person who boxes. **2** breed of bulldog.

boy /bɔi/ *n* [C] **1** male child up to the age of 17 or 18. **2** son of any age: *He has two boys and one girl*. **3** (*dated*) male servant (any age).

ˈboy·friend *n* [C] favored male companion of a girl or young woman.

ˈboy·hood *n* [U] state or time of being a boy.

boy·ish *adj* of, for, like, a boy.

boy·cott /ˈbɔiˌkat/ *vt* (join with others and) refuse to have anything to do with, to trade with (a person, business firm, country, etc); refuse to handle (goods, etc). □ *n* [C] treatment of this kind.

boy scout /ˈbɔi ˌskaut/ *n* [C] member of an organization for developing character, self-reliance, good citizenship, etc.

bra /bra/ *n* [C] (*informal*) (short for) brassiere.

brace¹ /breis/ *n* [C] **1** thing used to clasp, tighten or support, eg the roof or walls of a building. **2** revolving tool for holding another tool, eg a bit for boring holes, etc. **3** (often *pl*) appliance of bands and wires to straighten crooked teeth. **4** pair; couple: *a ~ of quail*.

brace² /breis/ *vt,vi* **1** support; give firmness to: *The struts are firmly ~d*. **2** steady oneself; stand firm: *He ~d himself to meet the blow*.

brace·let /ˈbreislɪt/ *n* [C] ornamental band or chain of metal for the wrist or arm.

brac·ing /ˈbreisɪŋ/ *adj* stimulating: *a ~ climate*.

bracken /ˈbrækən/ *n* [U] **1** large fern that grows on hillsides, waste land, etc. **2** mass of such fern.

bracket /ˈbrækɪt/ *n* [C] **1** wood or metal support for a shelf, etc. **2** either of the two symbols ([]) used in writing and printing. **3** grouping; classification: *income ~*, eg of incomes of $10,000 to $20,000. □ *vt* **1** put inside, join with, brackets. **2** put together to imply connection or equality: *Jones and Smith were ~ed together at the top of the list*.

brack·ish /ˈbrækɪʃ/ *adj* (of water) slightly salty.

bract /brækt/ *n* [C] leaflike part of a plant, often highly colored, situated below a flower or cluster of flowers.

brad /ˈbræd/ *n* [C] **1** small, thin nail. **2** rivet.

brag /bræg/ *vi* (-gg-) boast: *~ of what one has done*.

brag·gart /ˈbrægərt/ *n* [C] person who brags.

Brah·man, Brah·min /ˈbramən/ *n* [C] **1** member of the highest Hindu priestly caste. **2** (*fig*) aristocrat. **3** (also /ˈbreimɪn/) kind of cattle bred in southwestern US.

braid /breid/ *n* **1** [C] number of strands of hair woven together: *She wears her hair in ~s.* **2** [U] silk, linen, etc woven into a band, used for edging or decorating cloth or garments: *gold/silver ~.* □ *vt* **1** make into braids. **2** trim with braid.

braille /ˈbreiəl/ *n* [U] system of writing and reading (using raised dots) for blind people, to enable them to read by touch. □ *vt,vi* (*pres p* -ing /ˈbreilɪŋ/) write in braille.

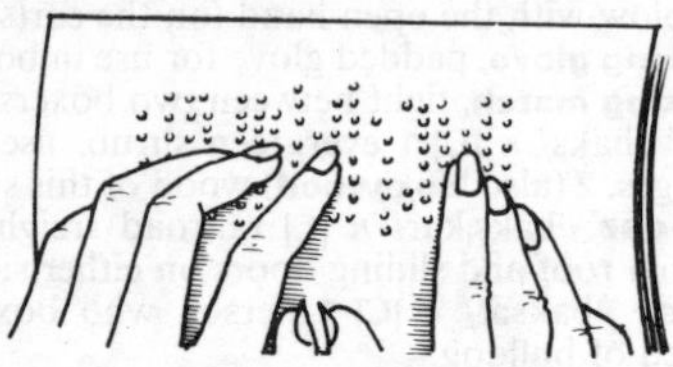

READING BRAILLE

brain /brein/ *n* [C] **1** (*sing*) (in man and animals) the mass of soft gray matter in the head, center of the nervous system: *The human ~ is a complex organ.* (*informal* and usually *pl*) *I'll knock your ~s out if you do it again!* ⇨ illus at head. **2** (*informal*) mind; intellect: *have a good ~; use your ~s.* ***have sth on the brain,*** think constantly about it. ***pick sb's brain(s),*** learn and use his ideas. **3** clever, brilliant person: *He's the ~ of the school staff.* □ *vt* kill by a heavy blow on the head.

brain·less *adj* stupid.

ˈbrain·storm *n* [C] **(a)** mental upset with uncontrolled emotion, eg weeping, and violence. **(b)** (*informal*) sudden inspiration or bright idea.

ˈbrain·teaser *n* [C] difficult problem; puzzle.

ˈbrain·washing *n* [U] process of forcing a person to reject old beliefs and accept new beliefs by use of extreme mental pressure.

ˈbrain wave, (a) (pattern of) electric current in the brain, produced by the process of thought. **(b)** (*informal*) = brainstorm(b).

brainy *adj* (-ier, -iest) clever.

braise /breiz/ *vt* cook (meat, vegetables) slowly with a little water in a covered pot: *~d beef/chicken.*

brake[1] /breik/ *n* [C] **1** device for reducing speed or stopping motion, eg of a bicycle, motor vehicle, train, etc. **2** ***act as a brake on,*** hamper or stop progress, initiative, etc. □ *vt,vi* use the brake(1): *The driver ~d suddenly.*

brake[2] /breik/ *n* [U] = bracken.

bramble /ˈbræmbəl/ *n* [C,U] **1** rough shrub with long prickly shoots. **2** blackberry bush.

bran /bræn/ *n* [U] outer covering (husks) of grain (wheat, rye, etc) separated from flour by grinding and sifting.

branch /bræntʃ/ *n* [C] **1** armlike part of a tree, growing out from the trunk; smaller division growing from a bough: *He climbed up the tree and hid among the ~es.* ⇨ illus at tree. **2** division or subdivision of a river, road, railway, mountain range, etc; division or subdivision of a family, subject of knowledge, organization, etc: *The bank has ~es in all parts of the country.* □ *vi* send out, divide into, branches: *The road ~es here.* ***branch off,*** (of a car, road, train, etc) leave a main route and take a minor one. ***branch out,*** (of a person, business firm, etc) expand in a new direction, open new departments or lines of activities.

brand /brænd/ *n* [C] **1** trademark or tradename; particular kind of goods with such a mark: *the best ~s of cigars; an excellent ~ of coffee.* **2** piece of burning wood (in a fire). **3** (also **ˈbranding iron**) iron used red-hot, for burning a mark into a surface. **4** mark made with a branding iron. **5** (*fig*) mark of guilt or disgrace. □ *vt* **1** mark (cattle, goods, etc) with a branding iron. **2** give (a person) a bad name: *She has been ~ed as a thief.*

ˌbrand-ˈnew *adj* completely new.

bran·dish /ˈbrændɪʃ/ *vt* wave about (to display, threaten, etc): *~ing a sword.*

brandy /ˈbrændi/ *n* [C,U] strong alcoholic drink distilled from wine of grapes: *Two brandies, please.*

brash /bræʃ/ *adj* (*informal*) **1** saucy; impudent. **2** hasty; rash.

brass /bræs/ *n* **1** [U] bright yellow metal made by mixing copper and zinc. ***get down to brass tacks,*** consider the essential facts only. **2** ([U] or *pl*) thing(s) made of brass, eg ornaments. **3** (often *pl*) wind instruments made of brass. **4** **the brass** (also **ˌtop ˈbrass**) (*informal*) senior officials, eg high-ranking officers in the armed forces. **5** (*sl*) impudence. ⇨ brazen.

ˌbrass ˈband, group of musicians with brass instruments.

brassy *adj* (-ier, -iest) **(a)** like brass in color or sound. **(b)** (*sl*) impudent.

brass·iere /brəˈzɪr/ *n* [C] woman's close-fitting support for the breasts. ⇨ bra.

brat /bræt/ *n* [C] badly behaved child.

bratty *adj* (-ier, -iest)

bra·vado /brəˈvadou/ *n* (*pl* ~es, ~s) **1** [U] display of boldness or daring, often a pretense: *do something out of ~,* in order to show one's courage. **2** [C] instance of this.

brave /breiv/ *adj* (-r, -st) **1** ready to face danger, pain or suffering; having no fear: *as ~ as a lion.* **2** needing courage: □ *n* [C] American Indian warrior. □ *vt* face, go into, meet, without showing fear: *He had ~d death a hundred times.*

brave·ly *adv*

brav·ery /ˈbreivəri/ *n* [U] courage.

bravo /ˈbravou/ *int, n* [C] (*pl* ~es, ~s) (cry of approval) Well done! Excellent!

brawl /brɔl/ *n* [C] noisy quarrel or fight. □ *vi* quarrel noisily; take part in a brawl.

brawler *n* [C]

brawn /brɔn/ *n* [U] muscle; strength.

brawny *adj* (-ier, -iest) muscular.

bray /brei/ *n* [C] **1** cry of a donkey. **2** any harsh sound like this. □ *vt* make a cry or sound of this kind.

brazen /ˈbreizən/ *adj* **1** made of brass; like brass: *a ~ voice; the ~ notes of a trumpet.* **2** (often *ˈ~-faced*) shameless.

braz·ier /ˈbreiʒər/ *n* [C] portable open metal framework for holding a charcoal or coal fire.

Brazil nut /brəˈzɪl ˌnət/ *n* [C] three-sided nut

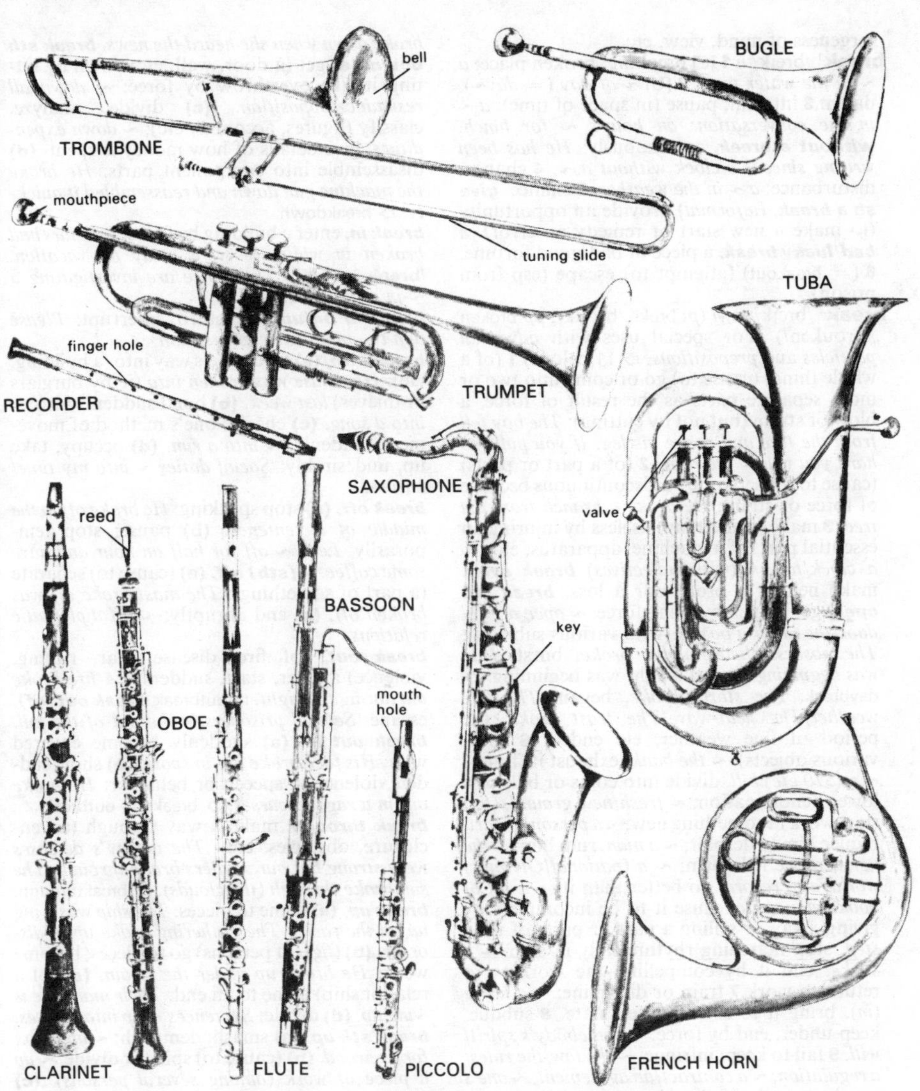

BRASS AND WOODWIND INSTRUMENTS

with an oily, edible kernel.

breach /britʃ/ *n* [C] **1** breaking or neglect (of a rule, duty, agreement, etc): *a ~ of the peace*, unlawful fighting in a public place, eg the streets; *a ~ of promise* (esp of a promise to marry). **2** opening, eg one made in a defensive wall, etc by artillery; gap: The waves made a ~ in the sea wall. ***step into/fill the breach,*** come forward to help. □ *vt* make an opening in, break through (a defensive wall, etc).

bread /bred/ *n* [U] **1** food made by mixing flour with water and usually yeast, kneading, and baking in an oven: *a loaf/slice/piece of ~*. **2** food. **3** (*sl*) money.

bread and butter, (a) slice(s) of bread spread with butter. **(b)** (*informal*) means of living: *earn one's ~ and butter by writing.*

ˈ**bread·crumb** *n* [C] tiny bit of bread, esp for use in cooking.

ˈ**bread·board** *n* [C] wooden board on which bread is sliced.

ˈ**bread·fruit** *n* tree with starchy fruit, grown in the South Sea Islands and West Africa.

ˈ**bread knife** *n* [C] one for slicing bread.

ˈ**bread·line** *n* [C] line of people waiting for food given as charity or relief.

ˈ**bread·win·ner** *n* [C] person who works to support a family.

breadth /bredθ/ *n* **1** distance or measure from side to side; width: *ten feet in ~*. ⇨ broad¹(2). **2**

largeness of mind, view, etc.

break[1] /breik/ *n* **1** [C] breaking; broken place: *a ~ in the water pipes* **2** [U] *~ of day* (= *day~*), dawn. **3** interval; pause (in space of time): *a ~ in the conversation; an hour's ~ for lunch.* ***without a break,*** continuously: *He has been writing since 2 o'clock without a ~.* **4** change, disturbance: *a ~ in the weather.* **5** chance. ***give sb a break,*** (*informal*) provide an opportunity (to make a new start or remedy an error). ***a bad/lucky break,*** a piece of bad/good fortune. **6** (= breakout) (attempt to) escape (esp from prison).

break[2] /breik/ *vt,vi* (*pt* broke /brouk/, *pp* broken /ˈbroukən/) (For special uses with *adverbial particles* and *prepositions,* ➪ 11 below.) **1** (of a whole thing) (cause to) go or come into two or more separate parts as the result of force, a blow or strain (but not by cutting): *The boy fell from the tree and broke his leg. If you pull too hard you will ~ the rope.* **2** (of a part or parts) (cause to) be separate or discontinuous because of force or strain: *He broke a branch from the tree.* **3** make (something) useless by injuring an essential part (of a machine, apparatus, etc): *~ a clock/toy.* **4** (with *adjectives*) ***break even,*** make neither a profit nor a loss. ***break sth open,*** get it open by using force: *~ open a safe/door/the lid of a box.* **5** (with various subjects): *The abscess/blister/bubble broke*, burst. *Day was beginning to ~*, daylight was beginning. ➪ daybreak. *The storm broke*, began. *The fine weather/The heat-wave/The frost broke*, the period of fine weather, etc ended. **6** (with various objects): *~ the bank,* exhaust its funds; *~ a* (*$10 etc*) *bill,* divide into coins or bills of a lower denomination; *~ fresh/new ground,* (*fig*) start work at something new; *~ a person's heart,* reduce him to despair; *~ a man,* ruin him; *~ the news,* make it known; *~ a* (*national/Olympic/world, etc*) *record,* do better than it; *~ a set of books/china, etc,* cause it to be incomplete by giving away or selling a part or parts of it; *~ step,* stop marching rhythmically in step; *~ a strike,* end it by compelling the workers to return to work.**7** train or discipline: *~ a horse* (*in*), bring it to a disciplined state. **8** subdue, keep under, end by force: *~ somebody's spirit/will.* **9** fail to keep; infringe: *~ the law/the rules/a regulation; ~ a contract/an agreement; ~ one's word/a promise*, fail to keep a promise; *~ an appointment*, fail to keep it. **10** interrupt or end: *~* (*the*) *silence; ~ one's journey; a broken night's sleep*, one that is disturbed or interrupted. ***break for coffee/lunch,*** interrupt work, a meeting, etc to drink coffee/have lunch. **11** (special uses with *adverbial particles* and *prepositions*):

break away (from), **(a)** go away suddenly or abruptly. **(b)** give up (habits, belief): *About twenty members of the Party have broken away.*

break down, **(a)** collapse: *Negotiations have broken down.* **(b)** become disabled or useless: *The car/engine/machinery broke down.* **(c)** suffer a physical or mental weakening: *His health broke down.* ➪ breakdown. **(d)** be overcome by emotion, eg by bursting into tears: *She broke down when she heard the news.* ***break sth down,*** **(a)** get (a door, wall, etc) down by hitting it. **(b)** overthrow by force: *~ down all resistance/opposition.* **(c)** divide, analyze, classify (figures, accounts, etc): *~ down expenditure*, give details of how money is spent. **(d)** disassemble into component parts: *He broke the machine gun down and reassembled it quickly.* ➪ breakdown.

break in, enter a building by force: *Burglars had broken in while we were away on vacation.* **ˈbreak-in** *n* [C]: *The police are investigating a ~-in at the local bank.*

break in on/upon, disturb; interrupt: *Please don't ~ in on our conversation.*

break into, **(a)** force one's way into (a building, etc): *His house was broken into* (ie by burglars or thieves) *last week.* **(b)** burst suddenly into: *~ into a song.* **(c)** change one's method of movement suddenly: *~ into a run.* **(d)** occupy, take up, undesirably: *Social duties ~ into my time/leisure.*

break off, **(a)** stop speaking: *He broke off in the middle of a sentence.* **(b)** pause; stop temporarily: *Let's ~ off for half an hour and have some coffee.* ***~ (sth) off,*** **(a)** (cause to) separate (a part of something): *The mast broke off/was broken off.* **(b)** end abruptly: *~ off diplomatic relations.*

break out, (of fire, disease, war, rioting, violence) appear, start, suddenly: *A fire broke out during the night.* ➪ outbreak. ***break out (of),*** escape: *Several prisoners broke out of the jail.*

break out in, **(a)** suddenly become covered with: *His face broke out in spots.* **(b)** show sudden violence in speech or behavior: *He broke out in a rage/in curses.* ➪ breakout, outbreak.

break through, make a way through (an enclosure, obstacles, etc): *The enemy's defenses were strong but our soldiers broke through. The sun broke through* (*the clouds*). ➪ breakthrough.

break up, **(a)** come to pieces: *The ship was ~ing up on the rocks. The gathering broke up in disorder.* **(b)** (*fig*) (of persons) go to pieces; become weak: *He broke up under the strain.* **(c)** (of a relationship) come to an end: *Their marriage is ~ing up.* **(d)** divide: *Sentences ~ up into clauses.*

break sth up, **(a)** smash; demolish: *~ up a box for firewood.* **(b)** (cause to) split, or divide: *~ up a piece of work* (*among several persons*). **(c)** (cause to) disperse: *The police broke up the crowd/meeting.* **(d)** bring to an end: *They broke up the alliance.*

break with, **(a)** end a friendship with: *~ with an old friend.* **(b)** give up; make an end of: *~ with old habits.*

ˈbreak·up *n* [C] end (of a marriage, coalition, etc).

break·able /ˈbreikəbəl/ *adj* easily broken.

break·age /ˈbreikɪdʒ/ *n* [C] **1** act of breaking. **2** broken articles; loss by breaking: *The hotel allows $150 a year for ~.*

break·down /ˈbreikˌdaun/ *n* [C] **1** failure in machinery: *A ~ on the highway caused a huge traffic jam.* **2** collapse of physical or mental health: *He had a nervous ~.* **3** analysis of figures: *a ~ of expenses.*

breaker /ˈbreikər/ *n* [C] **1** large wave breaking into foam as it advances towards the shore; wave breaking against a rock, etc. **2** person or thing that breaks.
break·fast /ˈbrekfəst/ *n* [C] first meal of the day. □ *vi* have breakfast.
break·neck /ˈbreikˌnek/ *adj* ***at (a) breakneck speed,*** at a dangerously fast speed.
break·out /ˈbreikˌaut/ *n* [C] escape from jail, prison, etc.
break·through /ˈbreikˌθru/ *n* [C] **1** movement through or beyond the enemy's defenses. **2** major discovery or achievement in science, medicine, technology, etc.
break·water /ˈbreikˌwɔtər/ *n* [C] structure built out into the sea to shelter (part of) a harbor.
bream /brim/ *n* (*pl* unchanged) **1** freshwater fish of the carp family. **2** (also **ˈseabream**) saltwater fish of the porgy family.
breast /brest/ *n* [C] **1** either of the milk-producing parts of a woman's chest. **2** chest; upper front part of the human body, or of a garment covering this. ⇨ illus at trunk. **3** feelings; heart: *a troubled* ~, a sad, anxious, etc feeling. ***make a clean breast of,*** confess. **4** part of an animal corresponding to the human breast.
ˈbreast·bone *n* [C] sternum. ⇨ illus at skeleton.
ˈbreast pocket, one in the breast of a jacket, etc.
ˈbreast·stroke *n* [U] stroke (in swimming) in which both the arms are brought at the same time from in front of the head to the sides of the body.
breath /breθ/ *n* **1** [U] air taken into and sent out of the lungs. **2** [C] single act of taking in and sending air out: *take a deep* ~, fill the lungs with air. ***catch/hold one's breath,*** stop breathing for a moment (from fear, excitement, etc). ***in the same breath,*** at the same time or in the same way: *They are not to be mentioned in the same* ~, cannot be compared. ***out of breath,*** unable to breathe quickly enough. ***take sb's breath away,*** surprise or amaze him: *The beautiful sunset took his* ~ *away.* ***waste one's breath,*** talk in vain. **3** [C] air in movement; light breeze: *There wasn't a* ~ *of air/wind*, the air was quite still. **4** [C] (*fig*) suggestion: *not a* ~ *of suspicion/scandal.*
breath·less *adj* **1** out of breath; likely to cause a shortness of breath. **2** unstirred by wind: *a* ~*less* (= calm) *evening.*
breath·less·ly *adv*
ˈbreath·taking *adj* exciting; amazing.
breathe /brið/ *vi,vt* **1** take air into the lungs and send it out again: ~ *in/out. He's still breathing*, is still alive. **2** utter; send out, eg a scent, feeling: *Don't* ~ *a word of this*, keep it secret.
breather *n* [C] short pause for rest or excercise: *take/go for a* ~*r.*
breath·ing /ˈbriðɪŋ/ *n* [U] **1** act of one who breathes. **2** single breath.
ˈbreathing space, time to pause, rest.
bred *pt,pp* of breed.
breech /britʃ/ *n* [C] back part of a rifle or gun barrel, where the cartridge or shell is placed.
breeches (also **britches**) /ˈbrɪtʃɪz/ *n pl* **1** pants. ***be/get too big for one's britches,*** (*informal*) be, become arrogant. **2** (also **riding britches**) pants covering the hips and thighs, buttoned below the knee, worn by men and women for riding on horseback.
breed /brid/ *vt,vi* (*pt,pp* bred /bred/) **1** keep (animals, etc) for the purpose of producing young, esp by selection of parents: ~ *horses/cattle.* **2** give birth to young; reproduce: *Rabbits* ~ *quickly.* **3** train, educate, bring up: *a well-bred boy*, one who has been trained to behave well. **4** be the cause of: *Dirt* ~*s disease.* □ *n* [C] kind or variety (of animals, etc) with hereditary qualities: *a good* ~ *of cattle.*
breeder *n* [C] person who breeds animals.
breed·ing *n* [U] **(a)** (in senses of verbs): *the* ~*ing of horses; the* ~*ing season for birds.* **(b)** knowledge of how to behave resulting from training: *a man of good* ~*ing.*
breeze /briz/ *n* [C,U] wind, esp a soft, gentle wind. □ *vi* ***breeze in/out,*** (*informal*) come in/go out in high spirits, or unexpectedly.
breez·ily /-əli/ *adv*
breezi·ness /-inɪs/ *n* [U]
breezy /-i/ *adj* (-ier, -iest) **1** pleasantly windy: *breezy weather.* **2** (of persons) lively: good-humored.
breth·ren /ˈbreðrɪn/ *n pl* (*archaic*) ⇨ brother(4).
brev·ity /ˈbrevəti/ *n* [U] shortness (of time, speech and other nonmaterial things).
brew /bru/ *vt,vi* **1** prepare (beer, tea, etc). **2** (*fig*) bring about; gather, be forming: *A storm is* ~*ing*, gathering force. *There's trouble* ~*ing between them*, they are likely to quarrel. □ *n* [C] result of brewing: *a good, strong* ~ (*of tea*).
brew·ery /ˈbru(ə)ri/ place where beer is brewed.
briar *n* = brier.
bribe /braib/ *n* [C] something given, offered or promised to a person in order to influence or persuade him dishonestly: *offer/take* ~*s.* □ *vt* offer, give, a bribe to: ~ *a judge/witness.*
bri·bery *n* [U] giving or taking of bribes.
bric-a-brac /ˈbrɪkəˌbræk/ *n* [U] bits of old furniture, china, ornaments, etc esp of no great value.
brick /brɪk/ *n* **1** [C,U] (usually rectangular block of) clay molded and baked by fire or sun, used for building purposes. **2** [C] rectangular block, eg of ice cream. □ *vt* ***brick up/in,*** block (an opening) with bricks.
ˈbrick·layer *n* [C] workman who builds with bricks.
ˈbrick·work *n* [U] (part of a) structure made of bricks.
bri·dal /ˈbraidəl/ *adj* of a bride or wedding.
bride /ˈbraid/ *n* [C] woman on her wedding day; newly married woman.
bride·groom /ˈbraidˌgrum/ *n* [C] man on his wedding day; newly married man.
brides·maid /ˈbraidzˌmeid/ *n* [C] girl or young unmarried woman attending a bride at her wedding. ⇨ best man.
bridge[1] /brɪdʒ/ *n* [C] **1** structure of wood, stone, brickwork, steel, concrete, etc providing a way across a river, canal, railroad track, etc. **2** platform over and across the deck of a ship for the use of the captain and officers. **3** upper, bony

part of the nose. ⇨ illus at head. **4** arched part over which the strings of a violin, etc are stretched. ⇨ illus at string. □ *vt* join by means of a bridge.

bridge·head *n* [C] fortified position established on the enemy's side of a river, etc; any military position occupied in the face of the enemy.

bridge[2] /brɪdʒ/ *n* [U] card game in which two players (partners) play to win a certain number of tricks against another two players acting as defenders.

bridle /ˈbraidəl/ *n* [C] that part of a horse's harness that goes on its head, including the metal bit for the mouth, the straps and the reins. □ *vt,vi* **1** put a bridle on (a horse). **2** (*fig*) control, check: *Try to ~ your passions*. **3** throw back the head and pull in the chin (showing pride, contempt, vanity, etc): *~ at somebody's remarks*.

brief[1] /brif/ *adj* (-er, -est) (of time, events, writing, speaking) lasting only for a short time. ***in brief,*** in a few words.

ˈbrief·ly *adv*

brief[2] /brif/ *n* [C] summary of the facts of a case to be presented in court. □ *vt* **1** give a briefing to. **2** summarize the facts for: *~ed reporters on the details of the new tax program*.

ˈbrief·case *n* [C] flat case of leather or other material, for documents, etc.

brief·ing /ˈbrifɪŋ/ *n* [C] **1** information, instructions, advice, etc given in advance, eg to an aircraft crew before a combat mission. **2** summary of facts, information, etc.

briefs /brifs/ *n pl* close-fitting pants without legs, held up by an elastic waistband.

brier /ˈbraiər/ *n* **1** [U] hard wood (root of a bush) used esp for making tobacco pipes. **2** [C] pipe made of this wood. **3** thorny bush, esp the wild rose.

brig·ade /brɪˈgeid/ *n* [C] **1** army unit, of one or more units, forming part of an army division; corresponding armored unit. **2** organized body of persons with special duties: *the ˈfire ~*.

briga·dier gen·eral /brɪgəˌdɪr ˈdʒenərəl/ *n* [C] (*pl* ~s) commissioned officer in the US army, air force or marine corps who ranks above a colonel and below a major general.

brig·and /ˈbrɪgənd/ *n* [C] member of a band of robbers, esp one that attacks travelers in forests or mountains.

bright /brait/ *adj* (-er, -est) **1** giving out or reflecting much light; shining: *Sunshine is ~*. **2** glowing; vivid: *The leaves on the trees are ~ green in spring*. **3** cheerful and happy; lit up with joy or hope: *~ faces; a ~ smile*. **4** clever: *A ~ person learns quickly*. □ *adv* (usually with *shine*) = brightly.

brighten *vt,vi* make or become brighter, lighter or more cheerful, etc: *These flowers ~en up the classroom*.

bright·ly *adv*

bright·ness /-nɪs/ *n* [U]

bril·liance /ˈbrɪlyəns/ *n* [U] **1** radiance, splendor. **2** intelligence; great ability.

bril·liant /ˈbrɪlyənt/ *adj* **1** sparkling; very bright (1): *a week of ~ sunshine*. **2** very clever: *a ~ scientist!*

bril·liant·ly *adv*

brim /brɪm/ *n* [C] **1** edge of a cup, bowl, glass, etc: *full to the ~*. **2** out-turned part (rim) of a hat. □ *vi* (-mm-) ***brim over,*** **(a)** be so full that some spills over the top. **(b)** (*fig*) = overflow(2).

brim·stone /ˈbrɪmˌstoun/ *n* [U] (*dated*) sulphur.

brine /brain/ *n* [U] salt water, esp for pickling.

bring /brɪŋ/ *vt* (*pt,pp* brought /brɔt/) **1** cause to come towards the speaker, writer, etc carrying something or accompanying somebody: *Take this empty box away and ~ me a full one*. **2** cause to come; produce: *Spring ~s warm weather and flowers. The sad news brought tears to her eyes.* **3** ***bring sb/oneself to do sth,*** persuade, induce, lead: *She couldn't ~ herself to speak about the matter*. **4** (*legal*) start, put forward: *~ an action against her*. **5** (special uses with *adverbial particles* and *prepositions*):

bring about, **(a)** cause to happen: *~ about a war/reforms*. **(b)** (*naut*) cause (a sailing ship) to change direction: *The helmsman brought us about*.

bring around, **(a)** cause (somebody) to regain consciousness after fainting. **(b)** convert to one's views, etc: *He wasn't keen on the plan, but we managed to ~ him around*.

bring back, **(a)** return: *Please ~ back the book tomorrow*. **(b)** call to mind; cause to remember: *Seeing you brought back many memories*. **(c)** restore; reintroduce: *~ back hanging*.

bring down, **(a)** cause to fall; cause to be down: *~ down a hostile aircraft*, shoot it down; *~ down prices*, lower them; **(b)** kill or wound: *He aimed, fired and brought down the antelope*.

bring forward, **(a)** cause to be seen, discussed, etc: *Please ~ the matter forward at the next meeting*. **(b)** (*bookkeeping*) carry the total of a column of figures at the foot of one page to the top of the next page.

bring in, **(a)** yield; produce as profit: *He does odd jobs that ~ him in a few dollars a month*. **(b)** introduce: *~ in a new fashion*. **(c)** admit (as a partner, adviser, etc): *They've brought in experts to advise on the scheme*. **(d)** arrest or bring to a police station for questioning, etc: *Two suspicious characters were brought in*. **(e)** (of a jury) pronounce (a verdict): *~ in a verdict of guilty*.

bring sth off, manage to do it successfully: *It was a difficult task but we brought it off*.

bring on, lead to, (help to) produce: *He was out all day in the rain and this brought on a bad cold*.

bring out, **(a)** cause to appear, show clearly: *~ out the meaning of a passage of prose*. **(b)** publish (a book, etc): *When are the publishers ~ing out his new book?* **(c)** call forth (a quality): *Danger ~s out the best in him*.

bring to, = bring around(a).

bring up, **(a)** educate; rear: *She has brought up five children*. **(b)** vomit: *~ up one's dinner*. **(c)** call attention to: *These are matters that you can ~ up in committee*.

brink /ˈbrɪŋk/ *n* [C] **1** upper edge of a steep place, a sharp slope, etc; border (of water, esp when deep): *He stood shivering on the ~*, hesitating to plunge into the water. **2** (*fig*) edge of something unknown, dangerous or exciting: *on the ~ of war/an exciting discovery*.

brisk /brɪsk/ *adj* (-er, -est) (of persons and movement) active; lively; quick-moving: *a ~ walk. Business is ~.*
brisk·ly *adv*
bristle /ˈbrɪsəl/ *n* [C] one of the short stiff hairs on an animal; one of the short stiff hairs in a brush: *a toothbrush with stiff ~s.* □ *vi* **1** (of hair) stand up, rise on end: *The dog was angry and its hair ~d.* **2** (*fig*) show rage, indignation, etc: *~ with anger.*
britches /ˈbrɪtʃɪz/ *n pl* = breeches.
Brit·ish /ˈbrɪtɪʃ/ *n pl* (used with *the*) British people. □ *adj* of Great Britain, the British Commonwealth or its inhabitants: *British citizenship; a Jamaican with a British passport.*
Briton /ˈbrɪtən/ *n* [C] native or subject of Great Britain.
brittle /ˈbrɪtəl/ *adj* hard but easily broken (eg coal, ice, glass).
broach[1] /broutʃ/ *n* [C] = brooch.
broach[2] /broutʃ/ *vt* bring up (a topic) for discussion.
broad[1] /brɔd/ *adj* (-er, -est) **1** wide: *The river grows ~er as it nears the sea.* **2** (after a phrase indicating width) from side to side: *a river fifty feet ~.* **3** extending in various or all directions: *the ~ ocean.* **4** full and complete. ***in broad daylight,*** when it is completely light. **5** general, not minute or detailed: *a ~ distinction.* ***in broad outline,*** a general impression, without details. **6** (of the mind and ideas) liberal; not kept within narrow limits: *a man of ~ views,* a tolerant man.
broad·ly *adv*
ˌbroad-ˈminded *adj* having a liberal and tolerant mind.
broad[2] /brɔd/ *n* [C] **1** the wide part: *the ~ of the back.* **2** (*sl*) woman or girl.
broad·cast /ˈbrɔdˌkæst/ *vt,vi* (*pt,pp* ~) send out, speak, etc in all directions, esp by radio or TV: *~ the news/a speech/a concert.* □ *n* [C] **1** act of broadcasting. **2** radio/TV program: *a ~ of a football game.*
broad·side /ˈbrɔdˌsaid/ *n* [C] **1** the whole of a ship's side above the water. **2** (the firing on the same target of) all the guns on one side of a ship. **3** (*fig*) strong attack of any kind made at one time against one person or group.
bro·cade /brouˈkeid/ *n* [C,U] woven material richly ornamented with designs (eg in raised gold or silver thread). □ *vt* decorate (cloth) with raised patterns.
broc·coli /ˈbrak(ə)li/ *n* [C] (*pl* unchanged) hardy kind of cauliflower with green stalks and sprouts (flower-heads), eaten as a vegetable.
bro·chure /brouˈʃʊr/ *n* [C] short, usually illustrated booklet: *travel/holiday ~s.*
brogue[1] /broug/ *n* [C] strong, thick-soled shoe.
brogue[2] /broug/ *n* strong accent(3), esp the Irish pronunciation of English: *My grandfather had a strong Irish ~.*
broil /ˈbrɔiəl/ *vt,vi* (-ing /ˈbrɔilɪŋ/) **1** cook, be cooked, by direct contact with fire; grill. **2** (*fig*) be very hot: *sit ~ing in the sun.*
broke /brouk/ *pt* of break. □ *adj* ***stone/flat broke,*** (*sl*) penniless.
bro·ken /ˈbroukən/ *pp* of break □ *adj*: *a ~ marriage,* one that has failed; *a ~ home,* one in which the parents have separated or are divorced; ~ (= imperfect) *English;* ~ (= disturbed) *sleep.*
ˌbroken-ˈhearted *adj* filled with grief.
bro·ker /ˈbroukər/ *n* [C] person who buys and sells (business shares, etc) for others.
bron·chi /ˈbraŋˌkai/ *n pl* (*sing* bronchus) two main branches into which the windpipe divides before entering the lungs, also called *bronchial tubes.* ⇨ illus at respiratory.
bron·chial /ˈbraŋkiəl/ *adj* of or affecting the bronchi: *~al asthma.*
bron·chi·tis /braŋˈkaitɪs/ *n* [U] inflammation of the bronchi.
bron·co, bron·cho /ˈbraŋkou/ *n* [C] (*pl* ~s) small wild or partly tamed horse of western North America.
ˈbronco buster, professional tamer of wild horses.
ˈbronco busting, (act or job of) taming wild horses.
bronze /branz/ *n* **1** [U] alloy of copper and tin: *a ~ statue.* **2** [U] reddish brown color. **3** [C] work of art made of bronze: *Benin ~.* □ *vt,vi* make or become bronze color: *faces ~d by the sun and wind.*
the ˈBronze Age, prehistoric period when men used tools and weapons made of bronze (between the Stone Age and the Iron Age).
brooch, broach /broutʃ/ *n* [C] ornamental pin for a woman's dress.
brood /brud/ *n* [C] **1** all the young birds hatched at one time in a nest. **2** (*informal*) family of children. □ *vi* **1** (of a bird) sit on eggs to hatch them. **2** (*fig*) think about (troubles, etc) for a long time: *~ing over/on his misfortunes.*
ˈbrood·er *n* [C] closed place that can be heated, used for raising young chicks, etc.
brook[1] /brʊk/ *n* [C] small stream.
brook[2] /brʊk/ *vt* (*formal*) put up with; tolerate: *He cannot ~ interference.* (*Note:* Usually used in the *negative* or in *questions.*)
broom /brum/ *n* [C] **1** long-handled brush for sweeping floors, etc. **2** shrub with long branches and yellow or white flowers growing.
Bros. *abbr* = Brothers.
broth /brɔθ/ *n* [U] soup made from water in which meat, vegetables, etc have been boiled.
broth·el /ˈbraθəl/ *n* [C] house of prostitution.
brother /ˈbrəðər/ *n* [C] **1** son of the same parents as another person. **2** person of the same family, country, etc as another. **3** fellow member of a society, profession, organization, trade union, etc. **4** (*pl* brethren /ˈbreðrən/) fellow member of a religious group.
ˈbrother·hood *n* **(a)** [U] feeling (as) of brother for brother. **(b)** [C] (members of an) association of men with common interests and aims, esp a religious society or socialist organization.
ˈbrother-in-law /ˈbrəðər-ɪn-ˌlɔ/ *n* [C] (*pl* ~s-in-law) brother of one's husband or wife; husband of one's sister.
ˈbrother·ly *adj*
brought *pt,pp* of bring.
brow /brau/ *n* **1** (usually *pl*; also **ˈeye·brow**) arch of hair above the eye. **2** forehead. ⇨ high[1],

low[1]. **3** edge or top of a slope: *the ~ of a hill.*

brow·beat /ˈbraʊˌbit/ *vt* (*pt* ~, *pp* ~en) frighten by shouts, threats, etc; bully: *She was ~en into doing what he wanted.*

brown /braʊn/ *n, adj* (-er, -est) (having the) color of toasted bread, or coffee mixed with milk. □ *vt,vi* make or become brown.

brownie /ˈbraʊni/ *n* [C] **1** small, good-natured fairy or elf. **2** member of the junior program of the Girl Scouts. **3** cake-like chocolate cookie, usually with nuts.

browse /braʊz/ *vi* **1** feed, as animals do (on grass, etc): *cattle browsing in the fields.* **2** read parts of a book or books: *browsing among books in the public library.* **3** inspect articles on display or for sale in a museum, antique shop, etc.

bruise /bruz/ *n* [C] injury by a blow or knock to the body, or to a fruit, so that the skin is discolored but not broken: *He was covered with ~s after falling off his bicycle.* □ *vt,vi* **1** cause a bruise on: *Handle the peaches carefully so that you don't ~ them.* **2** show the effects of a blow or knock: *A child's flesh ~s easily.*

brunch /brəntʃ/ *n* [C] late morning meal instead of breakfast and lunch.

bru·net, bru·nette /bruˈnet/ *n* [C] person (of one of the white races) with dark skin and dark-brown or black hair.

brunt /brənt/ *n* [U] chief stress or strain: *bear the ~ of an attack.*

brush[1] /brəʃ/ *n* **1** [C] implement of bristles, hair, wire, etc fastened in wood, bone, or other material, used for scrubbing, sweeping, cleaning, painting, etc: *a ˈtooth~; a ˈnail~; a ˈhair~; ˈpaint~.* **2** (*sing* only) (act of) using a brush: *He gave his clothes a good ~.* **3** (*sing* only) light stroke or touch. **4** [U] rough, low-growing bushes; undergrowth: *a ~ fire.* ⇨ bush(2). **5** [C] short fight or encounter: *a ~ with the enemy.*

brush[2] /brəʃ/ *vt,vi* **1** use a brush on; clean, polish, make tidy or smooth: *~ your hat/clothes/shoes/hair/teeth.* **2** ***brush off,*** **(a)** come off as the result of being brushed: *The mud will ~ off when it dries.* **(b)** (*informal*) refuse to see or listen to; dismiss: *~ed him off without giving him a chance to explain.* ***brush sth aside,*** (*fig*) pay no or little attention to (difficulties, objections, etc). ***brush up (on),*** study or practice in order to get back skill that has been lost: *If you're going to France you'd better ~ up (on) your French.* **3** touch lightly: *He ~ed past/by/against me.*

brusque /brəsk/ *adj* (of speech or behavior) rough and abrupt.

brusque·ly *adv*

brusque·ness /-nɪs/ *n* [U]

Brus·sels sprouts /ˈbrəsəl(z) ˌspraʊts/ *n pl* small, green, cabbagelike heads growing on a plant of the cabbage family, that are eaten as a vegetable. ⇨ illus at vegetable.

bru·tal /ˈbrutəl/ *adj* savage; cruel.

bru·tal·ity /bruˈtæləti/ *n* (*pl* -ies) **(a)** [U] cruelty; savagery. **(b)** [C] cruel or savage act.

bru·tally *adv*

brute /brut/ *n* [C] **1** animal (except man). **2** stupid, savage or cruel person. □ *adj* **1** cruel, savage. **2** unthinking and physical: *~ strength.*

brut·ish /ˈbrutɪʃ/ *adj* of or like a brute: *~ appetites.*

brut·ish·ly *adv*

B.S., BS /ˌbi ˈes/ *abbr* = Bachelor of Science (degree).

BSA *abbr* = Boy Scouts of America.

bubble /ˈbəbəl/ *n* [C] **1** (in air) floating ball formed of liquid and containing air or gas: *soap ~s.* **2** (in liquid) ball of air or gas that rises to the surface, eg in boiling water, in sparkling wines. **3** air-filled cavity in a solidified liquid, eg glass. □ *vi* **1** send up, rise in bubbles. **2** make the sound of ~s: *She was bubbling with joy/laughter.*

ˈbubble gum, chewing gum which can be blown into bubbles.

bub·bly /ˈbəbli/ *adj* (-ier, -iest) full of bubbles.

buc·ca·neer /ˌbəkəˈnɪr/ *n* [C] pirate.

buck[1] /bək/ *n* [C] male deer, rabbit or hare. ⇨ doe.

buck[2] /bək/ *vi,vt* **1** (of a horse) jump up with the four feet together and the back arched; throw (the rider) to the ground by doing this. **2** (*informal*) resist, (esp in:) ***buck the system,*** resist pressure to conform.

buck[3] /bək/ *n* [C] (*sl*) US dollar.

buck[4] /bək/ *n* ***pass the buck (to sb),*** (*sl*) shift the responsibility (to).

buck·a·roo /ˈbəkəˌru/ *n* [C] (*informal*) cowboy.

bucket /ˈbəkɪt/ *n* [C] **1** pail of wood, plastic, etc for holding or carrying water, etc. **2** (also **ˈbucket·ful**) as much as a bucket can hold.

buckle /ˈbəkəl/ *n* [C] metal, plastic, etc fastener, with one or more spikes made to go through a hole in a belt, etc □ *vt,vi* **1** fasten, be fastened with a buckle: *~ a belt; ~on a sword.* **2** ***buckle to/down to,*** begin (work, etc) in earnest: *The sooner he ~s down to it, the better.* **3** (of metal work, etc) bend, become twisted, etc from strain or heat.

buck·shot /ˈbəkˌʃat/ *n* [U] large lead shot used in shotgun shells.

buck·skin /ˈbəkˌskɪn/ *n* [U] soft yellowish or grayish leather made from the skin of a sheep or deer.

buck·wheat /ˈbəkˌ(h)wit/ *n* [U] **1** (plant with) small triangular seed used for feeding horses and poultry. **2** flour made from these seeds.

ˈbuck·wheat cakes, pancakes made with buckwheat flour.

bud /bəd/ *n* [C] **1** leaf, flower or branch, at the beginning of its growth. ⇨ illus at flower. ***in bud,*** having buds or sending out buds: *The trees are in bud.* **2** (in some animals or plants) small swelling from which a new individual of the same kind develops. ***nip sth in the bud,*** put an end to, eg a plot, while it is in the beginning stage. □ *vi* (-dd-) put out buds.

bud·ding *adj* beginning to develop: *a ~ lawyer/poet.*

Bud·dhism /ˈbuˌdɪzəm/ *n* the religion founded by Gautama Buddha /ˌgaʊtəmə ˈbudə/.

Bud·dhist /ˈbudɪst/ *n* [C] follower of Buddha. □ *adj* of Buddhism.

buddy /ˈbədi/ *n* [C] (*pl* -ies) (*informal*) chum; companion.

ˈbuddy system, used during dangerous

activities (eg scuba diving, military reconnaissance, etc) when participants work in pairs for greater safety.

budge /bədʒ/ *vt,vi* (usually in *negative* and with *can, could* or with *won't, wouldn't*) **1** (cause to) move very little, make the slightest movement. **2** (*fig*) (cause to) change a position or attitude: *I won't ~ an inch.*

bud·geri·gar /ˈbədʒəriˌgar/ *n* [C] kind of (originally Australian) parakeet.

budget /ˈbədʒɪt/ *n* [C] estimate of probable future income and expenses made by a government, business company, society, private person, etc. □ *vi* ***budget for,*** allow or arrange for: *~ for the coming year.*

ˈbudget account, system of buying goods by making regular monthly payments.

budgie /ˈbədʒi/ *n* [C] (*informal*) (short for) budgerigar.

buff /bəf/ *n* [U] **1** thick, strong, soft leather. **2** dull yellow color. **3** bare skin, esp in: *stripped to the ~*, naked. **4** (*informal*) person devoted to an activity, hobby etc: *She is an auto ~.* □ *vt* polish (metal) with buff.

buf·falo /ˈbəf(ə)ˌlou/ *n* [C] (*pl* ~es, ~s) **1** kinds of ox in India, Asia, Europe and Africa. **2** North American bison.

BUFFALO

buf·fer /ˈbəfər/ *n* [C] thing or person helping to lessen the effect of a blow, collision, confrontation, etc.

buf·fet[1] /bəˈfei/ *n* [C] **1** counter where food and drink may be bought and consumed, eg in a railroad station or on a train. **2** sideboard or table for holding silverware, dishes, etc.

buf·fet[2] /ˈbəfɪt/ *n* [C] blow, generally one given with the hand; □ *vt,vi* give a blow to: *flowers ~ed by rain and wind.*

buf·foon /bəˈfun/ *n* [C] clown; fool.

bug /bəg/ *n* [C] **1** any small insect. **2** (*informal*) germ; virus infection: *You've got the Asian flu bug.* **3** (*sl*) defect, snag, eg in a computer program. **4** small hidden microphone (for listening to conversations, etc). □ *vt* (-gg-) **1** (*informal*) hide a small microphone (in a room, etc) in order to listen secretly to conversations. **2** (*sl*) annoy: *That man really bugs me.*

buga·boo /ˈbəgəˌbu/ *n* [C] = bogey.

bug·bear /ˈbəgˌber/ *n* [C] thing feared or disliked, with or without good reason: *the ~ of rising prices.*

buggy /ˈbəgi/ *n* [C] (*pl* -ies) **1** light carriage, usually pulled by one horse. **2** baby carriage.

bugle /ˈbyugəl/ *n* [C] musical wind instrument of copper or brass (like a small trumpet but without keys or valves), used for military signals. ⇨ illus at brass.

bugler /ˈbyuglər/ *n* [C] person who plays a bugle.

build[1] /bɪld/ *vt,vi* (*pt,pp* built /bɪlt/) **1** make by putting parts, materials, etc together: *~ a house/railway.* **2** put parts together to form a whole: *He has built these scraps of metal into a very strange-looking sculpture.* **3** base (hopes, etc) on; rely on: *Don't ~ too many hopes on his helping you.* **4** ***build up,*** develop; increase gradually: *Traffic is ~ing up* (= the number of vehicles is increasing steadily) *along the roads to the coast. Their pressure on the enemy is ~ing up.* ***build sb/sth up,*** **(a)** try to increase a person's, an institution's reputation (through publicity, praise): *Don't ~ me up too much; I may disappoint you.* **(b)** make, acquire, steadily and gradually: *He has built up a good business.* **(c)** become covered with buildings: *The district has been built up since I was last there.*

builder *n* [C] **(a)** person who builds, esp houses. **(b)** (*fig*) person who builds up(b): *a great empire ~er.*

ˈbuild·up *n* **(a)** increase: *a ~up of forces/pressure.* **(b)** flattering publicity, etc: *The press gave him a tremendous ~up.*

build[2] /bɪld/ *n* [U] general shape or structure; (of the human body) general characteristics of shape and proportion: *a man of powerful ~.*

build·ing /ˈbɪldɪŋ/ *n* **1** [C] house or other structure: *Houses, schools, churches, factories and sheds are all ~s.* **2** [U] (art of) constructing houses, etc: *~ materials.*

bulb /bəlb/ *n* [C] **1** almost round, thick, underground part of a plant sending roots downwards and leaves upwards. **2** thing like a bulb in shape, eg the swollen end of a glass tube: *the ~ of a thermometer; an electric light ~.*

bul·bous /ˈbəlbəs/ *adj* of or like a bulb.

bulge /ˈbəldʒ/ *n* [C] **1** irregular swelling; place where a swelling or curve shows. **2** temporary increase in volume or numbers. □ *vi,vt* (cause to) swell beyond the usual size; curve outwards: *His pockets were bulging with apples.*

bulk /bəlk/ *n* [U] quantity, volume, esp when large. ***in bulk,*** **(a)** in large amounts: *buy in ~.* **(b)** loose, not packed in boxes, tins, etc. ***the bulk of,*** the greater part or number of: *He left the ~ of his property to his brother.* □ *vi* appear large or important.

bulky *adj* (-ier, -iest) taking up much space; clumsy to move or carry.

bulk·head /ˈbəlkˌhed/ *n* [C] watertight or airtight division or partition in a ship or tunnel, spacecraft, etc.

bull[1] /bʊl/ *n* **1** uncastrated male of any animal of the ox family: *a man with a neck like a ~*, with a thick neck. ***a bull in a china shop,*** person who is rough and clumsy where skill and care are needed. ***take the bull by the horns,*** meet a difficulty boldly instead of trying to escape from it. **2** male of the whale, elephant and other large animals. **3** (of investors, speculators, etc, esp on the stock market) having a belief that prices will rise rapidly.

ˈbull·dog *n* [C] large, powerful breed of dog,

with a short, thick neck, noted for its strong grip and its courage.

ˈbull·fight *n* [C] fight between men and a bull for public entertainment, as in Spain.

ˌbull-ˈheaded *adj* clumsy, impetuous, obstinate.

bull·ish *adj* (of the stock exchange) characterized by rapidly rising prices.

ˌbull ˈmarket, condition (on the stock exchange) when stock prices are rising rapidly.

ˈbull's-eye *n* **(a)** center of target (for archers, etc). ⇨ illus at archery. **(b)** shot that hits the center of a target.

bull[2] /bʊl/ *n* [C] official order from the Pope.

bull·doze *vt* /ˈbʊlˌdouz/ **1** remove earth, flatten obstacles with a bulldozer. **2** force a person into doing something by using one's strength or by intimidating him.

bull·dozer *n* [C] powerful tractor with a broad steel blade in front, used for shifting large quantities of earth, etc.

bul·let /ˈbʊlɪt/ *n* [C] shaped piece of lead, usually coated with another metal, (to be) fired from a rifle or revolver. (*Note: shells* are fired from large guns.)

ˈbullet-proof *adj* able to stop bullets: *a ∼-proof jacket*.

bull·etin /ˈbʊlətɪn/ *n* [C] **1** official statement of news: *The doctors issued ∼s twice a day*. **2** printed sheet with official news or announcements.

ˈbulletin board, board for putting up bulletins and other notices.

bull·finch /ˈbʊlˌfɪntʃ/ *n* [C] small European songbird with rounded beak and colored feathers.

bull·frog /ˈbʊlˌfrɔg, -ˌfrag/ *n* [C] large American frog that makes a loud, booming sound.

bul·lion /ˈbʊlyən/ *n* [U] gold or silver in bulk or bars, before manufacture.

bul·lock /ˈbʊlək/ *n* [C] castrated bull.

bull·pen /ˈbʊlˌpen/ *n* [C] **1** area or structure for temporarily holding prisoners in a police station, courthouse, etc. **2** (*baseball*) place where relief pitchers warm up while a game is in progress.

bully /ˈbʊli/ *n* [C] (*pl* -ies) person who uses his strength or power to frighten or hurt those who are weaker. □ *vt* use strength, etc in this way.

bul·rush /ˈbʊlˌrəʃ/ *n* [C] (kinds of) tall rush or reed with a thick head.

bul·wark /ˈbʊlˌwərk/ *n* [C] **1** wall, esp one built of earth, against attack. **2** (*fig*) thing that defends or protects: *Law is the ∼ of society*, gives us security. **3** (usu *pl*) wall around (esp a sailing) ship's deck.

bum[1] /bəm/ *adj* (*informal*) **1** worthless. **2** disabled: *a bum arm*.

bum[2] /bəm/ *n* (*sl*) habitual beggar or loafer. ***give sb the bum's rush***, (*sl*) forcibly expel (usually for misbehavior) from a social gathering, place of business, etc. ***on the bum,*** (*sl*) broken; out of order. □ *vt,vi* (-mm-) **1** (*sl*) get by begging: *bummed a ride*. **2** ***bum around,*** (*sl*) wander about doing nothing.

bumble·bee /ˈbəmbəlˌbi/ *n* [C] large kind of hairy bee.

bump /bəmp/ *vt,vi* **1** come against with a blow or knock: *The room was dark and I ∼ed* (*my head*) *against the door. The blind man ∼ed into me*. **2** move with a jerky, jolting motion (like a cart on a bad road): *The heavy bus ∼ed along the rough mountain road*. **3** ***bump sb off,*** (*sl*) murder him. □ *n* [C] **1** blow or knock; dull sound made by a blow (as when two things come together with force). **2** swelling on the body as caused by such a blow **3** irregularity on a road surface.

bumpy *adj* (-ier, -iest) with many bumps: *a ∼y road/ride*.

bump·er[1] /ˈbəmpər/ *n* [C] steel bar on a bus, motor vehicle (front and rear) to lessen the effect of a collision.

bump·er[2] /ˈbəmpər/ *adj* unusually large or abundant: *∼ harvest*.

bump·kin /ˈbəmpkɪn/ *n* [C] awkward person with unpolished manners, esp one from the country.

bump·tious /ˈbəmpʃəs/ *adj* conceited: *∼ officials*.

bun /bən/ *n* [C] **1** small round, sweet cake. **2** twisted knot of hair above the back of the neck.

bunch /bəntʃ/ *n* [C] **1** number of small, similar things naturally growing together: *a ∼ of grapes/bananas*. **2** collection of things of the same sort placed or fastened together: *a ∼ of flowers*. □ *vt,vi* ***bunch up,*** form into a bunch.

bundle /ˈbəndəl/ *n* [C] number of things fastened, tied or wrapped together: *The books were tied up in ∼s of twenty*. □ *vt,vi* **1** ***bundle up,*** **(a)** make into a bundle. **(b)** dress warmly. **2** put together or away in a confused heap; *We ∼d everything into a drawer*. **3** send or go in a hurry or without ceremony: *They ∼d him into a taxi*.

bung /bəŋ/ *n* [C] large (usually rubber, cork or plastic) stopper for closing a hole in a cask or barrel. □ *vt* put a bung into.

bun·ga·low /ˈbəŋgəˌlou/ *n* [C] small house with only one story.

bungle /ˈbəŋgəl/ *vt,vi* do (a piece of work) badly and clumsily; spoil (a task, etc) by lack of skill.

bun·ion /ˈbənyən/ *n* [C] inflamed swelling, esp on the large joint of the big toe.

bunk[1] /bəŋk/ *n* [C] **1** narrow bed fixed on the wall, eg in a ship. **2** one of two narrow beds built one above the other, usually for children.

ˈbunk·house *n* [C] dormitory with bunks for workers on a job, crewmen, etc.

bunk[2] /bəŋk/ *n* [U] (*informal*) bunkum.

bunker /ˈbəŋkər/ *n* [C] **1** that part of a ship where coal or fuel oil is stored. **2** sandy hollow, made as an obstacle, on a golf course. **3** fortified underground shelter.

bun·kum /ˈbəŋkəm/ *n* [U] senseless or purposeless talk: *That's all ∼!*

bunny /ˈbəni/ *n* [C] (*pl* -ies) (child's word for a) rabbit.

Bun·sen burner /ˈbənsən ˌbərnər/ *n* [C] burner for gas, as used in a chemistry laboratory with an air valve.

bunt /bənt/ *vt, vi* (esp in baseball) make the ball rebound a short distance by holding the bat in the path of the ball without swinging it. □ *n* [C] instance of bunting.

bunt·ing *n* act of bunting.

bun·ting[1] /ˈbəntɪŋ/ *n* [U] (flags or decorations made of) loosely woven, thin cloth.

bun·ting[2] /ˈbəntɪŋ/ *n* [C] small, brightly colored bird of the finch family.

buoy /bui, bɔi/ *n* [C] **1** floating object, anchored to the bottom, used to show a navigable channel or to indicate reefs, submerged wrecks, etc. **2** = life buoy. □ *vi* **1** mark the position of with a buoy: *~ a wreck/channel.* **2** ***buoy up,*** **(a)** keep afloat. **(b)** (*fig*) keep up hopes, etc.

buoy·ancy /ˈbɔiənsi/ *n* [U] **1** power to float or keep things floating. **2** (*fig*) lightness of spirits; cheerfulness.

buoy·ant /ˈbɔiənt/ *adj* **1** able to float or to keep things floating. **2** (*fig*) cheerful: *a ~ disposition.*

buoy·ant·ly *adv*

bur, burr /bər/ *n* [C] (plant with a) seed case or flower head that clings to the hair or fur of animals.

burble /ˈbərbəl/ *vi* make a gentle murmuring or bubbling sound: *burbling with happiness.*

bur·den /ˈbərdən/ *n* **1** [C] load (esp one that is heavy). **2** [C] (*liter* and *fig*) something difficult to bear: *the ~ of taxation on industry.* ***beast of burden,*** ⇨ beast. **3** [U] ship's carrying capacity, tonnage: *a ship of 3,000 tons ~.* **4** ***burden of proof,*** obligation to prove. □ *vt* load; put a burden on: *~ oneself with a heavy overcoat/with useless facts.*

bur·den·some /-səm/ *adj* hard to bear; making tired.

bureau /ˈbyʊrou/ *n* [C] (*pl* ~s, ~x /-rouz/) **1** chest of drawers, often with a mirror. **2** government or municipal department or office: *the ˌInforˈmation Bureau.*

bureauc·racy /byʊˈrakrəsi/ *n* **1** [U] government by bureaucrats, esp when thought of as being slow and inefficient, because of too many rules, official forms, etc. **2** [C] (*pl* -ies) **(a)** this system of government. **(b)** the officials as a body.

bureau·crat /ˈbyʊrəˌkræt/ *n* [C] government official who is appointed or hired and not elected, esp one who obeys the rules of his department rigidly.

bureau·cratic /ˌbyʊrəˈkrætɪk/ *adj* **1** of or like a bureaucrat. **2** too much attached to rules.

bureau·crati·cally *adv*

bur·glar /ˈbərglər/ *n* [C] person who breaks into a house at night in order to steal.

ˈburglar alarm *n* [C] device to give warning of burglars.

ˈburglar·proof *adj* made so that burglars cannot break in or into.

bur·glary /ˈbərgləri/ *n* (*pl* -ies) **1** [U] crime of breaking into a house by night to steal. **2** [C] instance of this.

burial /ˈberiəl/ *n* **1** [U] burying. **2** [C] instance of this.

ˈburial ground, = cemetery.

bur·lap /ˈbərˌlæp/ *n* [U] coarse fabric (usually made from jute or hemp) used for bags, wrappings, etc.

bur·lesque /bərˈlesk/ *n* **1** [C] imitation, eg of a book, speech, person's behavior, for the purpose of making fun of it or of amusing people. **2** [U] entertainment, with vulgar comedy, dancing, etc.

burly /ˈbərli/ *adj* (-ier, iest) (of a person) big and strong; solidly built.

burn[1] /bərn/ *n* [C] injury, mark, made by fire, heat or acid: *He died of the ~s he received in the fire.*

burner *n* [C] **1** person who burns something. **2** (that part of an) apparatus from which the light or flame comes: *an ˈoil ~er.*

burn·ing *adj* intense; exciting: *a ~ing thirst/desire/question.*

burn[2] /bərn/ *vt,vi* (*pt,pp* ~ed /bərnd/ ~t /bərnt/) (*Note: burnt* is used most often to modify a *noun.*) **1** use for the purpose of lighting or heating: *Most large steamships now ~ oil instead of coal.* **2** (cause to) be or become damaged, hurt, destroyed by fire, heat, etc: *Be careful not to ~ the meat. I dislike ~t toast. Wood ~s easily.* **3** make by heat: *~ a hole in a carpet,* eg by dropping a cigarette end. **4** be or feel warm or hot: *She is ~ing with fever.* **5** (*fig*) be filled with strong feeling: *He was ~ing with anger/enthusiasm.* **6** (special uses with *adverbial particulars* and *prepositions*):

burn away, **(a)** continue to burn: *The fire was ~ing away cheerfully.* **(b)** make, become less, by burning: *Half the candle had ~ed away.*

burn down, be destroyed, destroy to the foundations, by fire: *The house (was) ~ed down.*

burn out, **(a)** become extinguished: *The fire ~ed (itself) out.* **(b)** (of a rocket) use up its fuel. **(c)** be destroyed by fire: *~t-out factories/tanks.*

burn sb/sth up, **(a)** get rid of, by burning: *We ~ed up all the garden rubbish.* **(b)** (*informal*) make (a person) angry: *He really ~s me up.*

bur·nish /ˈbərnɪʃ/ *vt,vi* polish by, or as if by, rubbing.

burp /bərp/ *n* [C] (*informal*) belch □ *vi* make a burp.

burr[1] *n* = bur.

burr[2] /bər/ *n* [C] whirring sound made by parts of machines that turn quickly.

bur·ro /ˈbərou/ *n* [C] donkey, usually a small one, used for carrying loads.

bur·row /ˈbərou/ *n* [C] hole made in the ground (by foxes, rabbits, etc). □ *vi,vt* make a burrow.

bur·sar /ˈbərsər/ *n* treasurer (esp of a college or university).

burst[1] /bərst/ *n* [C] **1** bursting explosion: *the ~ of a shell/bomb; a ~ in the water main.* **2** brief, violent effort: *a ~ of energy/speed.* **3** outbreak: *a ~ of applause; a ~ of gunfire.*

burst[2] /bərst/ *vi,vt* (*pt,pp* ~) **1** (of a bomb, shell, etc) (cause to) fly or break violently apart from within; explode. **2** (of river banks, a dam, an abscess, a boil) (cause to) break outwards; (of a bubble) break; (of leaf and flower buds) open out. ***be bursting to,*** be eager to: *He was ~ing to tell us the news.* **3** be full to overflowing; be able to contain with difficulty: *They were ~ing with happiness/impatience/health.* **4** make a way or entry suddenly or by force: *He ~ into the room. The sun ~ through the clouds.* **5** (special uses with *adverbial particles* and *prepositions*):

burst in (on/upon), **(a)** interrupt: *He ~ in on our conversation.* **(b)** appear or arrive suddenly.

burst into, send out suddenly; break out into. (*Note: burst into* is followed by a *noun.*): *The coat fell in the fire and ~ into flames;* (*fig*) *~ into* tears/laughter/song, etc, suddenly begin to cry/laugh, etc; ~ *into blossom*, begin to bloom. ***burst out,*** ⇨burst into. (*Note: burst out* is followed by an *-ing* form.): ~ *out laughing/crying*.

bury /ˈberi/ *vt* (*pt,pp* -ied) **1** place (a dead body) in the ground, in a grave or in the sea: *He's dead and buried*. **2** put underground; cover with earth, leaves, etc; cover up; hide from view: *buried treasure. She buried* (= hid) *her face in her hands*.

bus[1] /bəs/ *n* (*pl* busˈes, busses) public motor vehicle that travels along a fixed route and takes up and sets down passengers at fixed points: *Should we walk or take the bus? **miss the bus,*** (*sl*) be too late to use an opportunity. □ *vi,vt* (-s-, -ss-) **1** go, take, by bus. **2** transport children to their schools.

ˈbus stop, fixed stopping place for buses.

ˈbus·(s)ing *n* [U] (esp) the transportation of children beyond their neighborhood school to achieve racial integration.

bus.[2] *abbr* = business.

bush /bʊʃ/ *n* **1** [C] low-growing plant with several or many woody stems coming up from the root: *a ˈrose* ~. **2** [U] (often **the bush**) wild, uncleared land in Africa and Australia. **3** [C] hairstyle of rounded, bushy curls. ⇨ Afro.

ˈbush·man /-mən/ *n* [C] (*pl* -men /-men/) member of certain tribes in the South African bush.

ˈbushy *adj* (-ier, -iest) **1** covered with bushes. **2** growing thickly; thick and rough: ~*y eyebrows*.

bushed /bʊʃt/ *adj* (*sl*) exhausted.

bushel /ˈbʊʃəl/ *n* [C] **1** measure for grain and fruit (= 8 gallons). **2** container that holds a bushel.

bush·whack /ˈbʊʃˌ(h)wæk/ *vt,vi* **1** chop or clear one's way through brush or words. **2** live in the woods, esp in hiding. **3** ambush.

ˈbush·whacker *n* [C] **(a)** one who lives (esp in hiding) in the woods. **(b)** person who ambushes.

busier, busiest ⇨ busy.

busi·ly /ˈbɪzəli/ *adv* in a busy way: ~ *engaged in working*.

busi·ness /ˈbɪznɪs/ *n* **1** [U] buying and selling; commerce; trade: *We do not do much* ~ *with them*. ***on business,*** for the purpose of doing business: *Are you here on* ~ *or for pleasure?* **2** [C] commercial or industrial enterprise, etc: *He is the manager of three different* ~*es*. **3** [U] task, duty, concern: *It is a teacher's* ~ *to help his pupils*. ***get down to business,*** start the work that must be done. ***give sb the business,*** (*sl*) treat him roughly (for a particular purpose). **4** affair; matter. ***mind one's own business,*** attend to one's own duties and not interfere with those of others.

ˈbusiness-like *adj* using, showing, system, promptness, care, etc.

ˈbusiness·man /-ˌmæn/ (*pl* -men /ˌmen/) man who is engaged in buying and selling, etc (not a lawyer, doctor, etc).

bust[1] /bəst/ *n* [C] **1** sculpture of the head and shoulders of a person in stone, bronze, etc. **2** upper front part of the body, esp a woman's breasts. **3** measurement round the chest and back.

bust[2] /bəst/ *vt,vi* **1** (*informal*) = burst. **2** (*informal*) break; smash. **3** (*sl*) (of police) raid; catch in the act of doing something illegal; arrest. □ *n* **1** (*sl*) wild party. **2** (*sl*) police raid; arrest.

bustle[1] /ˈbəsəl/ *vi,vt* (cause to) move quickly and excitedly: *Everyone was bustling about/in and out*. □ *n* [U] excited activity.

bustle[2] /ˈbəsəl/ *n* [C] pad on frame formerly used to puff out a woman's skirt at the back.

busy /ˈbɪzi/ *adj* (-ier, -iest) **1** working; occupied; having much to do: *The doctor is a* ~ *man*. **2** full of activity: *a* ~ *day;* (of places) filled with active people, traffic, etc: *The stores are* ~ *before Christmas*. **3** (of a telephone line) in use. □ *vt* keep busy, occupy oneself with: *He busied himself with all sorts of little tasks*.

busy·work *n* [U] work assigned or done merely to keep one busy.

busy·body /ˈbɪziˌbadi/ *n* [C] (*pl* -ies) meddlesome person.

but[1] /bət/ *adv* = only (the usual word): *We can but try. He's but a boy*.

but[2] /bət/ *conj* **1** (coordinating): *Tom was not there but his brother was*. **2** (subordinating): *Never a month passes but she writes* (= in which she does not write) *to her old parents*. **3** (*formal*) (with *cannot* or *could not*): *I could not choose but go* (= had no alternative).

but[3] /bət/ *prep* (with *negatives,* eg *no one, none, nothing,* and *interrogatives,* eg *who,* and such words as *all, every one*) except, excluding: *Nothing but disaster would come from such a plan. No one but he/him showed much interest in the proposal*. ***but for,*** except for, without: *but for your help we should not have finished in time*. ***but then,*** on the other hand: *New York is a noisy place, but then it's also a place where there is a great deal of excitement*.

bu·tane /ˈbyuˌtein/ *n* [U] colorless gas, used as a fuel.

ˈbutane lighter, cigarette lighter which uses butane.

butcher /ˈbʊtʃər/ *n* [C] **1** person who kills, cuts up and sells animals for food. **2** person who kills savagely and needlessly. □ *vt* **1** prepare meat for selling as food. **2** kill violently, esp with a knife. **3** spoil; bungle.

butch·ery *n* [U] (esp) needless and cruel killing of people.

but·ler /ˈbətlər/ *n* [C] head manservant (in charge of the wine cellar, pantry, etc).

butt[1] /bət/ *n* [C] large barrel for wine or ale.

butt[2] /bət/ *n* [C] **1** thicker, larger end (esp of a fishing rod or rifle). **2** unburned end, eg of a smoked cigar or cigarette.

butt[3] /bət/ *n* **1** target and the mound of earth behind it (used for practice in firing rifles). **2** person who is a target for ridicule, jokes, etc: *He is the* ~ *of the whole school*.

butt[4] /bət/ *vt,vi* **1** push with the head (as a goat does): ~ *a man in the stomach*. **2** ***butt in,*** (*informal*) force oneself into the conversation or company of others. □ *n* [C] push or sudden blow.

butte /byut/ *n* [C] steep hill with a flat top, standing alone.

but·ter /ˈbətər/ *n* [U] **1** solid, yellowish fat made from cream, used on bread, in cooking, etc: *She looks as if ~ would not melt in her mouth*, has an innocent appearance. **2** substance similar to butter, made from other materials: *peanut ~*. □ *vt* **1** spread with butter. **2** ***butter sb up,*** flatter him.

ˈbut·ter·cup *n* wild plant with yellow flowers.

ˈbut·ter·fat *n* [U] fatty substance in milk.

ˈbut·ter·fin·gers *n* person unable to hold or catch things well

ˈbut·ter·milk *n* [U] **(a)** liquid that remains after butter has been separated from milk. **(b)** cultured milk made from sweet milk.

ˈbut·ter·scotch *n* [U] sweet substance made by boiling sugar and butter together.

but·ter·fly /ˈbətərˌflai/ *n* [C] (*pl* -ies) insect with four wide wings, often brightly colored.

but·ter·nut /ˈbətərˌnət/ *n* [C] **1** oily kind of edible walnut. **2** North American tree that bears this nut.

but·tock /ˈbətək/ *n* [C] either side of that part of the body on which a person sits: *an injection of penicillin in the left ~*. (*Note:* usually *pl* in form with a *sing indef art* and *verb* when the entire structure is referred to: *She has a big ~s. Her ~s sticks out.*)

but·ton /ˈbətən/ *n* [C] **1** small, usually round, bit of plastic, metal, etc for fastening articles of clothing. **2** small, round object, esp one that, when pushed, makes an electrical contact, eg for a bell: *press/push/touch the ~*. **3** usually round bit of plastic, metal, etc incorporating a design or slogan, pinned on to articles of clothing. **4** small, young mushroom. □ *vt,vi* fasten with a button: *~ (up) one's coat*. ***on the button,*** (*informal*) precisely.

ˈbutton·hole *n* [C] hole or loop through which a button is passed. □ *vt* stop a person and hold him in conversation.

but·tress /ˈbətrɪs/ *n* [C] **1** support built against a wall. **2** (*fig*) prop; thing that supports: *the ~es of society/the constitution*. □ *vt* strengthen, support: *~ up an argument*.

buxom /ˈbəksəm/ *adj* (of women) large and healthy-looking.

buy /bai/ *vt,vi* (*pt,pp* bought /bɔt/) **1** get in return for money, get by paying a price: *Can money buy happiness? I bought this car from Mr Green.* **2** obtain at a sacrifice: *Victory was dearly bought.* □ *n* [C] (*informal*) purchase: *a good buy*, a bargain.

buyer *n* [C] person who buys.

buzz /bəz/ *vi,vt* **1** make a humming sound (as of bees or machinery in rapid motion). **2** move rapidly or excitedly. ***buzz off,*** (*sl*) go away. **3** be filled with a low murmer or with a buzzing noise: *My ears ~. The room ~ed with gossip.* **4** (of an aircraft) fly near to or low over: *Two fighters ~ed the airliner.* **5** summon with a buzzer. □ *n* [U] **1** sound of people talking, of whirling machinery, etc. **2** humming (of bees or other insects).

buzzer *n* [C] electrical bell that produces a buzzing note when the current flows.

ˈbuzz saw, (*informal*) = circular saw.

buz·zard /ˈbəzərd/ *n* [C] **1** any of several large, slow-moving hawks. **2** (also **ˈturkey buzzard)** American vulture.

by[1] /bai/ *adverb* **1** near: *He hid the money when nobody was standing by* **2** past: *He hurried by without a word.* ***by and by,*** later on. ***by and large,*** on the whole.

by[2] /bai/ *prep* **1** near; at or to the side of: *Come and sit by me/by my side.* ***stand by sb,*** support him. **2** (showing direction of movement) through, along, across, over: *We came by the path through the woods.* **3** past: *He walked by me without speaking.* **4** (of time, esp to indicate conditions and circumstances) during: *The enemy attacked by night.* **5** (of time) as soon as; not later than: *Can you finish the work by tomorrow?* **6** (in phrases indicating a unit of time, length, weights, measurements, etc): *rent a house by the year; sell cloth by the yard, eggs by the dozen, etc.* **7** through the agency or means of: *He makes a living by teaching. He was killed by lightning.* **8** (indicating means of travel, transport, conveyance): *travel by land/sea/air; by bus/car/boat, etc.* **9** (indicating a part of the body that is touched, etc): *grab him by the arm.* **10** according to: *By my watch it is 2 o'clock.* **11** to the extent of: *the bullet missed me by two inches.* **12** ***know/learn sth by heart,*** so that one can repeat it from memory. ***by accident/mistake/chance,*** not on purpose or intentionally. ***by oneself,*** **(a)** alone: *He was (all) by himself.* **(b)** without help: *She learned it by herself*

bye-bye /ˌbai ˈbai/ *int* (*informal*) goodbye.

by·gone /ˈbaiˌgɔn/ *adj* past: *in ~ days*, in the time now past. □ *n* (*pl*) ***Let bygones be bygones,*** forgive and forget the past.

by·law, bye·law /ˈbaiˌlɔ/ *n* [C] law or regulation made by authority (eg a town, an organization, etc) for the conduct of its own affairs.

by·pass /ˈbaiˌpæs/ *n* [C] new, wide road passing round a heavily populated urban area or village, to take through traffic. □ *vt* **1** provide with, make a bypass. **2** (*fig*) ignore.

by-prod·uct /ˈbai-ˌpradəkt/ *n* [C] substance obtained during the manufacture of some other substance.

by·stander /ˈbaiˌstændər/ *n* [C] person standing near but not taking part in an event or activity.

by·way /ˈbaiˌwei/ *n* [C] side road or path, esp one that is little used.

by·word /ˈbaiˌwərd/ *n* [C] person, event, etc regarded and spoken of as a notable or typical example.

C

C¹, c /si/ (*pl* C's, c's /siz/) **1** the third letter of the English alphabet. **2** Roman numeral for 100.
C² *abbr* = **1** Cape. **2** Celsius. **3** centigrade. **4** (often inside a circle) copyright.
CA¹ *postal abbr* = California. ⇨ App 6.
ca.² *abbr* (= *Lat* circa) about.
C.A.B., CAB *abbr* = Civil Aeronautics Board.
cab /kæb/ *n* [C] **1** (also **taxicab**) automobile with a driver, that may be hired for short journeys, usually in towns: *Shall we go by bus or take a cab?* **2** compartment of a railroad engine, truck, tractor, etc for the driver. **3** horse-drawn carriage formerly hired in towns.
cabbie, cabby /ˈkæbi/ *n* [C] (*informal*) driver of a (taxi)cab.
cab·aret /ˌkæbəˈrei/ *n* [C] (esp European) restaurant that serves liquor and provides entertainment (songs, dancing, etc).
cab·bage /ˈkæbɪdʒ/ *n* [C,U] (kinds of) plant with a round head of thick green leaves used as a vegetable. ⇨ illus at vegetable.
cabin /ˈkæbɪn/ *n* [C] **1** room in a ship or aircraft, esp (in a ship) one for sleeping in. **2** small house, roughly built.

LOG CABIN

ˈcabin cruiser, large motorboat with a cabin.
cabi·net /ˈkæb(ə)nɪt/ *n* [C] **1** piece of furniture with drawers or shelves for storing or displaying things: *a ˈmedicine ~; a ˈfiling ~,* for storing letters, documents. **2** plastic, wooden or metal container for radio or record-playing equipment. **3** (sometimes **Cabinet**) group of persons chosen by the head of the government to advise on government administration and policy: *The Secretary of State is a member of the President's Cabinet.*
cable /ˈkeibəl/ *n* **1** [C,U] (length of) thick, strong rope (of fiber or wire), used on ships, bridges, etc. **2** protected bundle of insulated wires for carrying electrical power or messages by electric telegraph. **3** ⇨ cablegram. □ *vt,vi* **1** tie or fasten with a cable. **2** send (a message) by cable.
ˈcable car, one up a steep slope, pulled by a cable(1).

CABLE CAR: SAN FRANCISCO

ˈcable·gram *n* [C] message sent by cable(2).
cable ˈtelevision, cable T.ˈV. *n* [U] system of broadcasting television programs by cable(2).
ca·boose /kəˈbus/ *n* [C] small car, usually at the end of a freight train, for the workmen or crew.

CABOOSE

ca·cao /kəˈkau/ *n* [C] (*pl* ~s) **1** (also **caˈcao bean**) seed of a tropical tree from which cocoa and chocolate are made. **2** (also **caˈcao tree**) the tree.
cache /kæʃ/ *n* [C] **1** hiding or storage place for food, supplies, etc. **2** something stored or hidden. □ *vt* store or hide.
cackle /ˈkækəl/ *n* **1** [U] noise made by a hen after laying an egg. **2** [C] loud laugh. **3** [U] foolish talk. □ *vi* **1** (of a hen) make this noise. **2** (of a person) talk or laugh noisily.
cac·tus /ˈkæktəs/ *n* [C] (*pl* ~es, cacti /ˈkækˌtai/) (kinds of) plant from hot, dry climates with a thick, fleshy stem, with spines or prickles instead of leaves.
caddie, caddy /ˈkædi/ *n* [C] (*pl* -ies) person who carries a golf player's clubs. □ *vi* serve as a caddie.
ca·dence /ˈkeidəns/ *n* [C] rhythm in sound; the rise and fall of the voice in speaking.

CACTUSES

ca·det /kəˈdet/ *n* [C] **1** student at a naval, military or air force college. **2** young person under training for a profession: ˈ*police* ~*s*.

cadge /kædʒ/ *vt,vi* (*informal*) beg; (try to) get by begging: *be always cadging*.

cad·ger *n* [C] person who cadges.

Caesar /ˈsizər/ *n* [C] **1** title of the Roman emperors from Augustus to Hadrian. **2** any Roman emperor.

Caesar·ean /sɪˈzæriən/ *n* [C] = Cesarean.

café /ˌkæˈfei/ *n* [C] **1** restaurant. **2** bar room.

cafe·teria /ˌkæfəˈtɪriə/ *n* [C] restaurant at which customers serve themselves.

caf·feine /ˈkæˌfin/ *n* [U] stimulating substance found in tea and coffee.

caf·tan /ˈkæftən/ *n* [C] **1** long tunic with a cord at the waist, worn by men in the Near East. **2** woman's loosely hanging dress.

cage /keidʒ/ *n* [C] **1** framework, fixed or portable, with wires or bars, in which birds or animals may be kept. **2** camp for prisoners of war. **3** structure with bars or beams that encloses or supports. **4** (*baseball*) fence behind home plate for stopping pitched balls. □ *vt* put, keep in a cage.

cagey /ˈkeidʒi/ *adj* (-ier, -iest) shrewd; cautious.

cais·son /ˈkeiˌsan/ *n* [C] **1** chest for ammunition, usually mounted on a two-wheeled wagon. **2** watertight box or chamber in which men can work under water (to dig foundations, build tunnels, etc).

ca·jole /kəˈdʒoul/ *vt* use flattery or deceit to persuade or soothe, or to get information, etc.

cake /keik/ *n* **1** [C,U] sweet mixture of flour, eggs, butter, etc baked in an oven: *a piece of* ~. ***take the cake,*** (*sl*) rank or stand first: *that takes the* ~ *for stupidity*. **2** [C] small shaped mixture of other kinds of food: ˈ*fish* ~*s*. **3** [C] shaped piece of other materials or substances: *a* ~ *of soap*. □ *vt,vi* coat thickly, become coated (with mud, etc).

cala·bash /ˈkæləˌbæʃ/ *n* [C] (tree with a) fruit or gourd of which the hard outer skin (or shell) is used as a container or ornament.

ca·lam·ity /kəˈlæməti/ *n* [C] (*pl* -ies) great and serious misfortune or disaster (eg a big earthquake or flood).

cal·cium /ˈkælsiəm/ *n* [U] soft white metal (symbol **Ca**), the chemical basis of many compounds essential to life which occurs in bones and teeth, and forms part of limestone, marble and chalk.

cal·cu·lable /ˈkælkyələbəl/ *adj* that may be measured, reckoned or relied on.

cal·cu·late /ˈkælkyəˌleit/ *vt,vi* **1** find out by working with numbers: ~ *the cost of a journey*. **2** plan or intend: *This advertisement is* ~*d to attract the attention of young people*. **3** consider and be confident (that something will happen, etc).

cal·cu·lat·ing *adj* scheming; crafty.

cal·cu·la·tion /ˌkælkyəˈleiʃən/ *n* **1** [U] act of calculating; careful thought. **2** [C] result of this: *I'm off in my* ~*s*, have made a mistake in them.

cal·cu·la·tor /ˈkælkyəˌleitər/ *n* [C] **1** person who calculates. **2** machine that calculates automatically.

cal·cu·lus /ˈkælkyələs/ *n* [C] (*pl* -li /-lai/ or ~es) **1** branch of higher mathematics that deals with variable quantities. **2** (*med*) stone formed in some part of the human body.

cal·dron /ˈkɔldrən/ *n* [C] large kettle or open pot.

cal·en·dar /ˈkæləndər/ *n* [C] **1** list or table of the days, weeks, months, of a particular year. **2** system by which time is divided into days, weeks, months and years: *the Moslem* ~. **3** list or schedule: *an engagement* ~.

calf[1] /kæf/ *n* **1** [C] (*pl* calves /kævz/) young of the domestic cow; young of the seal, whale and some other animals for the first year. **2** [U] (also ˈ**calfskin**) leather from the skin of a calf.

calf[2] /kæf/ *n* [C] (*pl* calves /kævz/) fleshy part of the back of the human leg, between the knee and the ankle. ⇨ illus at leg.

cal·iber /ˈkæləbər/ *n* **1** [C] inside diameter of a tube/gun/barrel, etc. **2** [U] quality of mind or character: *a man of high* ~.

cali·brate /ˈkæləˌbreit/ *vt* determine or correct the scale of a thermometer, gauge or other graduated instrument.

cali·bra·tion /ˌkæləˈbreiʃən/ *n* degree marks, etc on a measuring instrument.

cal·ico /ˈkælɪˌkou/ *n* [U] cotton cloth, usually with a colored pattern printed on one side.

cali·pers, cal·lipers /ˈkæləpərz/ *n pl* instrument for measuring the diameter or thickness of something.

ca·liph, ca·lif /ˈkeilɪf/ *n* title once used by rulers who were descendants and successors of Mohammad; chief civil and religious ruler: *the Caliph of Baghdad*.

ˈ**cal·iph·ate** /ˈkeilɪˌfeit/ *n* rank, territory of a caliph.

call[1] /kɔl/ *n* **1** shout; cry: *a* ~ *for help*. **2** characteristic cry of a bird. **3** military signal (on a bugle, etc). **4** short visit (to a house, etc); short stop (at a place): *Pay a* ~ *on a friend. I have several* ~*s to make*. **5** message; summons: *telephone* ~*s*. ***on call,*** (of doctors, nurses, etc) prepared to go on duty if asked. **6** [U] (chiefly *negative* or *interrogative*) need; occasion: *There's no* ~ *for you to worry*.

ˈ**call girl** *n* [C] (*informal*) (esp high-class) prostitute.

ˈ**call house,** (*informal*) house of prostitution.

ˈ**call sign,** identification signal of a radio transmitter.

call[2] /kɔl/ *vt,vi* **1** say in a loud voice; cry; speak or shout to attract attention: *She* ~*ed to her* *father for help.* **2** name; describe as: *His name is Richard but we all ~ him Dick.* ***call sb names,*** abuse or insult him. ***call it a day,*** ⇨ day(3). **3** consider; regard as: *I ~ that a shame.* ***call it quits,*** (*informal*) give up (a job, task etc). **4** summon; wake; send a message to: *Please ~ a doctor. Please ~ me* (= wake me up) *at 6 tomorrow morning. Please ~ me a taxi/~ a taxi for me.* **5** stop; end: *~ed the game because of rain.* **6** (special uses with *nouns*) ***call attention to,*** require (a person) to give his attention to. ***call a meeting,*** announce that one will be held and summon people to attend. ***call a strike,*** order workers to come out on strike. **7** (special uses with *adverbial particles* and *prepositions*):

call (sb) down, (*informal*) scold (him): *~ed down for sloppy work.*

call for, **(a)** stop to get: *I'll ~ for you at 6 o'clock, and then we'll go to the movies.* **(b)** demand, require: *You must take such steps as seem* (*to be*) *~ed for.*

call sth in, order or request the return of: *The librarian has ~ed in all books.*

call (sb/sth) off, **(a)** tell (it/him/them) to go/come away: *Please ~ your dog off.* **(b)** cancel; stop: *The strike/attack was ~ed off.*

call on/upon, **(a)** make a short visit: *I ~ed on Mr. Green.* **(b)** appeal to; invite; require: *I ~ed* (*up*)*on him to keep his promise. I now ~ on* (= invite) *Mr. Grey to address the meeting.*

call out, **(a)** shout for help, or with surprise, pain, etc. **(b)** summon, esp to an emergency: *The fire brigade was ~ed out twice yesterday.*

call sb/sth up, **(a)** telephone to: *I'll ~ you up this evening.* **(b)** bring back to the mind: *~ up scenes of childhood.* **(c)** summon for (military, etc) service: *If war breaks out, we shall be ~ed up at once.*

ˈcall-up *n* summons for military service.

cal·ler /ˈkɔlər/ *n* [C] person who makes a visit.

cal·ligra·phy /kəˈlɪgrəfi/ *n* [U] **1** handwriting. **2** (art of) beautiful handwriting.

cal·ling /ˈkɔlɪŋ/ *n* [C] (esp) occupation, profession or trade.

cal·liope /kəˈlaiəpi/ *n* [C] musical instrument with steam whistles, played by pressing keys.

cal·li·pers *n pl* = calipers.

cal·lous /ˈkæləs/ *adj* **1** (of the skin) made hard (by rough work, etc). **2** (*fig*) hard-hearted; unsympathetic.

cal·low /ˈkælou/ *adj* young; inexperienced: *a ~ youth.*

cal·lus /ˈkæləs/ *n* [C] (*pl* ~es) area of thick, hardened skin.

calm /kam/ *adj* (-er, -est) **1** (of the weather) quiet; not windy; (of the sea) still; without large waves. **2** not excited; untroubled; quiet: *keep ~.* □ *n* [U] quiet; peacefulness. □ *vt,vi* make or become calm: *He asked the workers to ~ down.*

calm·ly *adv*

calm·ness /-nɪs/ *n* [U]

cal·orie /ˈkæləri/ *n* [C] **1** unit of heat. **2** unit of energy supplied by food: *An ounce of sugar supplies about 100 ~s.*

cal·or·ific /ˌkæləˈrɪfɪk/ *adj* producing heat: *calorific value*, (of food or fuel) quantity of heat produced by a given quantity.

cal·umny /ˈkæləmni/ *n* **1** [C] (*pl* -ies) false statement about a person, made to damage his character. **2** [U] slander.

ca·lyp·so /kəˈlɪpsou/ *n* [C] (*pl* ~s) improvised popular song, of a style originating in the West Indies, on a subject of current interest.

ca·lyx /ˈkeilɪks/ *n* [C] (*pl* ~es or calyces /ˈkeiləˌsiz/) ring of leaves (called *sepals*) forming the outer support of the petals of an unopened flower bud. ⇨ illus at flower.

cama·raderie /ˌkæməˈrædəri/ *n* (*F*) [U] friendliness and mutual trust of comrades and friends.

cam·bi·um /ˈkæmbiəm/ *n* [U] soft tissue, between the bark and wood in trees, from which new bark and wood grows.

came *pt* of come.

camel /ˈkæməl/ *n* [C] long-necked animal, with either one or two humps on its back, used in desert countries for riding and for carrying goods.

cameo /ˈkæmiou/ *n* [C] (*pl* ~s) piece of hard stone with a raised design, often of a different color, used as a jewel or ornament.

cam·era /ˈkæm(ə)rə/ *n* [C] apparatus for taking single photographs or moving pictures, etc: *ˈmovie camera; ˈTV camera.*

cam·ou·flage /ˈkæməˌflaʒ/ *n* [U] **1** anything which hides or disguises something or makes it less noticeable: *The white fur of the polar bear is a natural ~,* because the bear is not easily seen in the snow. **2** (in war) the use of paint, netting, branches, etc to change the appearance of military equipment so as to deceive the enemy. □ *vt* conceal by means of camouflage.

camp /kæmp/ *n* [C] **1** place where people (eg people on vacation, soldiers, explorers) live in tents, huts or outdoors. **2** number of people with the same ideas (esp on politics or religion): *We're in the same ~,* are in agreement, are working together. □ *vi* make, live in a camp: *Where shall we ~ tonight?* ***go camping,*** spend a vacation in tents, etc: *The boys have decided to go ~ing next summer.*

camper *n* [C] **(a)** person who camps, esp on a vacation. **(b)** portable structure, fitted and equipped for camping, that can be attached to the rear of an automobile or small truck.

ˈcamp·ground *n* [C] place for camping.

ˈcamp·site *n* [C] = campground.

cam·paign /kæmˈpein/ *n* [C] **1** group of military operations with a set purpose, usually in one area. **2** program of activities (esp advertisements, public speeches, etc) intended to win votes for a candidate for an elected office. **3** series of planned activities to gain any special object: *an ˈadvertising ~.* □ *vi* take part in, go on, a campaign.

cam·paigner *n* [C] person who campaigns, esp for (re)election.

cam·pa·nile /ˌkæmpəˈnili/ *n* [C] bell tower, usually as a separate building.

cam·phor /ˈkæmfər/ *n* [U] strong-smelling white substance used in medicine and to protect clothes from moths.

cam·pus /ˈkæmpəs/ *n* [C] (*pl* ~es) grounds of a school, college or university.

can[1] /kæn/ *n* [C] **1** metal container for liquids, etc: *an ˈoil can.* **2** tin-plated airtight container (for food, etc). **3** contents of such a container: *a can of beer*. ***(open a) can of worms,*** (*informal*) (attempt to deal with) a difficult, perhaps unsolvable, problem. **4** (*sl*) prison. □ *vt* (-nn-) preserve (food, etc) by putting in a can(2) or jar.

can·nery /ˈkænəri/ *n* [C] (*pl* -ies) place where food is canned.

can[2] /kən *strong form:* kæn/ *auxiliary verb* (*negative* cannot /ˈkæˌnat, kæˈnat/ can't /kænt/, *pt* could /kəd *strong form:* kʊd/, *negative* couldn't /ˈkʊdənt/) **1** be able to; know how to: *Can you lift this box? She can speak French.* **2** (used with *verbs* of perception): *I can hear people talking in the next room. We could hear someone singing in the bathroom.* **3** (*informal*) (used to indicate permission; *may* is more formal): *You can go home now. The children asked whether they could go for a swim. You can't smoke in here.* **4** (used to indicate possibility or likelihood): *That couldn't be true. It can be very cold here, even in May.* **5** (when used in questions to indicate surprise, doubt, etc., the *strong forms* are used): *What ˌcan he ˈmean?*

Can·a·da goose /ˌkænədə ˈgus/ *n* [C] (*pl* Canada geese) wild goose of North America, with a black head and neck and a gray or brown body.

ca·nal /kəˈnæl/ *n* [C] **1** channel cut through land for use of boats or ships (eg *the Suez Canal*) or to carry water to fields for irrigation. **2** tube or pipe (or system of these) in a plant or animal body for food, air, etc: *the alimentary ~.*

ca·nary /kəˈneri/ *n* (*pl* -ies) **1** [C] small, yellow-feathered songbird. **2** [U] its color, light yellow.

can·cel /ˈkænsəl/ *vt,vi* (-l-, -ll-) **1** cross out, draw a line through (words or figures); make a mark on something, (eg postage stamps, to prevent re-use). **2** say that something already arranged or decided will not be done, will not take place, etc: *The sports meeting was ~ed.*

can·cel·la·tion /ˌkænsəˈleiʃən/ *n* **(a)** [U] canceling or being canceled. **(b)** [C] instance of this. **(c)** mark(s) used to cancel.

can·cer /ˈkænsər/ *n* [C,U] diseased growth in the body, often causing death: *lung ~.*

can·cer·ous /ˈkænsərəs/ *adj* of, like, having, cancer.

Can·cer /ˈkænsər/ *n* **1 Tropic of Cancer,** the parallel of latitude 23½° north of the equator. **2** the Crab, the fourth sign of the zodiac. ⇨ illus at zodiac.

can·de·la·brum /ˌkændəˈlabrəm/ *n* (*pl* -bra /-brə/) candlestick with branches for candles.

can·did /ˈkændɪd/ *adj* frank, straightforward: *I will be quite ~ with you: I think you acted foolishly.*

can·did·ly *adv*

can·di·date /ˈkændɪˌdeit/ *n* [C] person who wishes, or who is put forward by others, to take an office or position (eg for election to Congress): *The Independent ~ was elected.*

candle /ˈkændəl/ *n* [C] round stick of wax, etc with a string (*wick*) through it, burned to give light.

ˈcandle·light *n* [U] light of candles.

ˈcandle·stick *n* [C] holder or support for a candle.

can·dor /ˈkændər/ *n* [U] quality of saying freely what one thinks.

candy /ˈkændi/ *n* **1** [U] sugar or sugar syrup, cooked and flavored, and then cooled. **2** [C] (*pl* -ies) piece of this. □ *vt,vi* preserve (eg fruit) by boiling or cooking in sugar: *candied lemon peel.*

cane /kein/ *n* **1 (a)** [C] long, hollow, jointed stem of tall reeds and grass-like plants (eg bamboo). **(b)** [U] this material: *a chair with a ~ seat.* **2** [C] length of cane or wood used as a walking stick. □ *vt* **1** beat with a cane(2). **2** make, repair with cane(1).

ca·nine /ˈkeiˌnain/ *n* [C] **1** (*formal*) dog. **2** pointed tooth, such as dogs have, found in man and other mammals. ⇨ illus at mouth. □ *adj* of or like a dog or dogs.

can·is·ter /ˈkænɪstər/ *n* [C] **1** small box (usually metal) with a lid, used for holding tea, etc. **2** cylinder which, when thrown, or fired from a gun, bursts and scatters its contents.

can·ker /ˈkæŋkər/ *n* [U] **1** disease that destroys the wood of trees. **2** ulcer or sore, esp one in the mouth. **3** (*fig*) evil influence or tendency that causes decay. □ *vt* destroy by canker.

can·ker·ous /ˈkæŋkərəs/ *adj* of, like, causing, canker.

can·na·bis /ˈkænəbɪs/ *n* [U] dried flowering tops of the hemp plant, from which marijuana and hashish are made. ⇨ hemp.

can·nery ⇨ can[1].

can·ni·bal /ˈkænəbəl/ *n* [C] **1** person who eats human flesh. **2** animal that eats its own kind.

can·ni·bal·ism /-bəˌlɪzəm/ *n* [U] practice of eating the flesh of one's own kind.

can·ni·bal·is·tic /ˌkænəbəˈlɪstɪk/ *adj* of or like cannibals.

can·non /ˈkænən/ *n* [C] **1** (*pl* often unchanged) large, heavy gun, fixed to the ground or to a gun carriage, esp the old kind that fired a solid ball of metal (called a ˈ~ *ball*). (*Gun* and *shell* are the words used for modern weapons.) **2** heavy, automatic gun, firing explosive shells, used in modern aircraft.

can·non·ade /ˌkænəˈneid/ *n* [C] continued firing of big guns.

can·not ⇨ can[2].

canny /ˈkæni/ *adj* (-ier, -iest) shrewd.

ca·noe /kəˈnu/ *n* [C] light boat moved by one or more paddles. □ *vt* travel by canoe.

ca·noe·ist *n* [C] person who paddles a canoe.

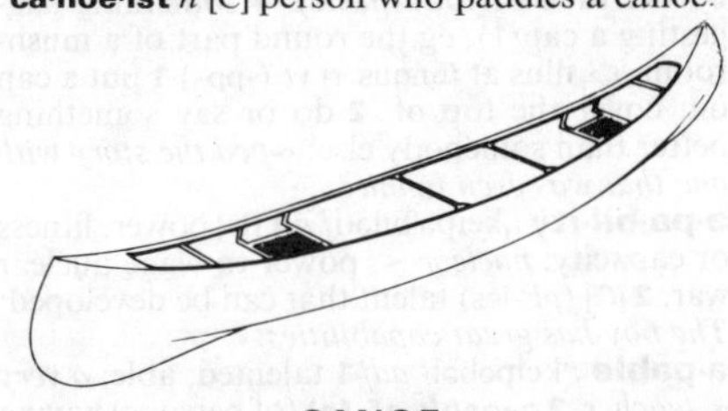

CANOE

canon /ˈkænən/ *n* [C] **1** church law. **2** general standard or principle by which something is judged: *the ~s of conduct/good taste*. **3** musical composition for two or more voices, in which the different parts repeat the same melody. **4** priest who is one of a group with duties in a cathedral.

ca·noni·cal /kəˈnanɪkəl/ *adj* **1** according to church law. **2** authorized; accepted.

canon·ize /ˈkænəˌnaiz/ *vt* declare (a person) to be a saint.

can·opy /ˈkænəpi/ *n* [C] (*pl* -ies) **1** (usually cloth) covering over a bed, throne, etc or held (on poles) over a person. **2** any overhanging shelter.

cant /kænt/ *n* [U] **1** insincere talk; hypocrisy. **2** special talk, words, used by a particular class of people.

can't /kænt/ = cannot.

can·ta·loupe, can·te·lope /ˈkæntəˌloup/ *n* [C] kind of melon.

can·tank·er·ous /kænˈtæŋkərəs/ *adj* bad-tempered; quarrelsome.

can·tata /kənˈtatə/ *n* short musical work to be sung by soloists and a choir, that is usually a dramatic story, but not acted.

can·teen /ˌkænˈtin/ *n* [C] **1** place (esp in factories, offices, barracks) where food, drink and other articles are sold and meals bought and eaten. **2** place of recreation for servicemen. **3** small container for carrying drinking water.

can·te·lope *n* [C] = cantaloupe.

can·ter /ˈkæntər/ *n* [C] (of a horse) slow gallop. □ *vt,vi* (cause to) go at a canter.

can·ticle /ˈkæntəkəl/ *n* [C] short hymn.

can·ti·lever /ˈkæntəˌlivər/ *n* [C] long, large bracket or beam extending from a wall or base (eg to support a balcony).

canto /ˈkæntou/ *n* [C] (*pl* ~s) chief division of a long poem.

can·vas /ˈkænvəs/ *n* **1** [U] strong, coarse cloth used for tents, sails, bags, etc and by artists for oil paintings. **2** [C] (piece of this for an) oil painting.

can·vas·back /ˈkænvəsˌbæk/ *n* [C] North American wild duck.

can·vass /ˈkænvəs/ *vt,vi* go from person to person and ask for votes, orders for goods, subscriptions, etc or learn about people's views on a question. □ *n* [C,U] canvassing.

can·yon /ˈkænyən/ *n* [C] deep gorge (usually with a river flowing through it).

cap /kæp/ *n* [C] **1** soft head covering, worn by boys and men, without a brim, but often with a visor. **2** indoor headdress worn by nurses and formerly by old women. **3** cover (eg on a milk bottle, tube of toothpaste). **4** something suggesting a cap(1), eg the round part of a mushroom. ⇨ illus at fungus. □ *vt* (-pp-) **1** put a cap on; cover the top of. **2** do or say something better than somebody else: *~ped the story with one that was even funnier*.

ca·pa·bil·ity /ˌkeipəˈbɪləti/ *n* **1** [U] power, fitness or capacity: *nuclear ~*, power to wage nuclear war. **2** [C] (*pl* -ies) talent that can be developed: *The boy has great capabilities*.

ca·pable /ˈkeipəbəl/ *adj* **1** talented; able: *a very ~ teacher*. **2** ***capable of*,** **(a)** (of persons) having the power, ability or inclination: *He's ~ of any crime*. **(b)** (of things, situations, etc) ready for; open to: *The situation is ~ of improvement*.

ca·pably *adv*

ca·pac·ity /kəˈpæsəti/ *n* (*pl* -ies) **1** [U] ability to hold, contain, get hold of, learn: *The hall has a seating ~ of 500*, has seats for 500 people. **2** [C] position; character: *I am your friend, but in my ~ as your manager I must ask you to resign*.

cape[1] /keip/ *n* [C] loose sleeveless garment, hanging from the shoulders.

cape[2] /keip/ *n* [C] high point of land going out into the sea: *the Cape of Good Hope*.

cap·il·lary /ˈkæpəˌleri/ *n* [C] (*pl* -ies) small, narrow tube, esp a minute blood vessel. ⇨ illus at respiratory.

capi·tal /ˈkæpətəl/ *n* (often as an *adjective*) **1** [C] town or city where the government of a country, state or county is carried on: *Sacramento is the ~ of California. London, Paris and Rome are ~ cities*. **2** [C] (of letters of the alphabet) not small: *Write your name in ~ letters/in ~s*. **3** [U] amount of money or property with which a business, etc is started and operated: *The company has ~ amounting to $5 million*. □ *adj* punishable by death: *~ offenses*.

capi·tal·ism /ˈkæpətəˌlɪzəm/ *n* [U] economic system in which trade and industry are privately owned, in which free competition determines prices, production, etc for goods and services.

capi·tal·ist /ˈkæpətəˌlɪst/ *n* [C] **(a)** supporter of capitalism. **(b)** person who controls much capital(3).

capi·tal·is·tic /ˌkæpətəˈlɪstɪk/ *adj*

capi·tal·ize /ˈkæpətəˌlaiz/ *vt,vi* **1** write or print with a capital letter. **2** convert into, use as, capital(3). **3** ***capitalize on*,** take advantage of; use to one's advantage or profit.

Capi·tol /ˈkæpətəl/ *n* building in which the United States Congress meets.

U.S. CAPITOL

ca·pitu·late /kəˈpɪtʃəˌleit/ *vi* surrender (on stated conditions).

ca·pitu·la·tion /kəˌpɪtʃəˈleiʃən/ *n* [U]

ca·pon /ˈkeiˌpan/ *n* [C] rooster castrated and fattened for eating.

ca·price /kəˈpris/ *n* [C] (tendency towards a) sudden change of mind without an apparent cause.

ca·pri·cious /kəˈprɪʃəs/ *adj* often changing; irregular; unreliable.

ca·pri·cious·ly *adv*

Cap·ri·corn /ˈkæprɪˌkɔrn/ *n* **1 Tropic of**

Capricorn, the parallel of latitude 23½° south of the equator. **2** the Goat, the tenth sign of the zodiac. ⇨ illus at zodiac.

cap·size /ˈkæpˌsaiz/ *vt,vi* (esp of a boat in the water) (cause to) overturn, upset.

cap·stan /ˈkæpstən/ *n* [C] upright device to which a rope is fastened, that is turned to raise anchors, sails, etc and for pulling a ship to a wharf, etc.

cap·sule /ˈkæpsəl/ *n* [C] **1** seedcase that opens when the seeds are ripe. **2** tiny soluble container for a dose of medicine. **3** (recoverable or non-recoverable) compartment which can be ejected from a spacecraft.

SPACE CAPSULE

Capt. *abbr* = Captain.

cap·tain /ˈkæptən/ *n* [C] **1** leader or chief commander: *the ~ of a ship/football team.* **2** commissioned officer in the US army, air force or marine corps who ranks above a first lieutenant and below a major. **3** commissioned officer in the US navy or coastguard who ranks above a commander and below a rear admiral. □ *vt* act as captain.

cap·tion /ˈkæpʃən/ *n* [C] **1** short title or heading of an article in a periodical, etc. **2** words printed with a photograph or illustration.

cap·ti·vate /ˈkæptɪˌveit/ *vt* fascinate: *He was ~d by his new girl friend.*

cap·tive /ˈkæptɪv/ *n, adj* (person, animal) taken or kept as a prisoner.

ˌcaptive ˈaudience, one that cannot get away easily.

cap·tiv·ity /kæpˈtɪvəti/ *n* [U] state of being held captive: *Some birds will not sing in ~.*

cap·tor /ˈkæptər/ *n* [C] someone who takes or holds a person captive.

cap·ture /ˈkæptʃər/ *vt* **1** make a prisoner of; take or obtain by force, trickery, skill, etc: *Our army ~d 500 of the enemy.* **2** hold; attract: *~d everyone's attention.* □ *n* **1** [U] act of capturing: *the ~ of a bank robber.* **2** [C] thing that is caught.

car /kar/ *n* [C] **1** automobile. **2** vehicle that runs on tracks: *streetcar; dining car; cable car.* **3** that part of an elevator, balloon, etc that carries passengers.

ˈcar·hop *n* [C] (*informal*) waiter, waitress at a drive-in restaurant.

ˈcar pool, system of getting to and from work in which several employees share a single car.

ˈcar port, open-sided shelter for a motor vehicle.

ˈcar·sick *adj* suffering from motion sickness as a result of riding in a car, train, etc.

ˈcar·sick·ness /-nɪs/ *n* [U]

cara·mel /ˈkærəməl/ *n* **1** [U] burnt sugar used for coloring and flavoring. **2** [C] small, chewy piece of candy flavored with caramel.

CAR (AUTOMOBILE)

cara·pace /ˈkærəˌpeis/ *n* [C] shell on the back of a turtle, lobster, etc.

carat /ˈkærət/ *n* [C] **1** unit of weight (about three and one-fifth grains) for precious stones. **2** = karat.

cara·van /ˈkærəˌvæn/ *n* [C] **1** company of persons (eg pilgrims, merchants) making a journey together for safety, usually across desert country. **2** covered cart or wagon used for living in, eg by gypsies.

car·bine /ˈkarˌbain, -ˌbin/ *n* [C] short, light rifle.

carbo·hy·drate /ˌkarbouˈhaiˌdreit/ *n* [C,U] (kinds of) organic compound including sugars and starches.

car·bolic acid /karˌbalɪk ˈæsɪd/ *n* [U] strong-smelling, powerful liquid used as an antiseptic and disinfectant.

car·bon /ˈkarbən/ *n* **1** [U] non-metallic element (symbol **C**) that occurs in all living matter, in its pure form as diamonds and graphite and in an impure form in coal and charcoal. **2** [C,U] (also **ˈcarbon paper**) (sheet of) thin paper coated with colored matter, used between sheets of writing paper for making copies. **3** [C] copy made by the use of a carbon(2).

car·bon di·oxide /ˌkarbən daiˈakˌsaid/ *n* [U] colorless, odorless gas (symbol **CO_2**) produced eg in breathing out from the lungs, used to make carbonated beverages, in fire extinguishers, etc.

car·bon mon·oxide /ˌkarbən məˈnakˌsaid/ *n* [U] colorless, odorless, poisonous gas (symbol **CO**), present in the exhaust gases of automobile engines, etc.

car·buncle /ˈkarˌbəŋkəl/ *n* [C] (esp) red (usually painful) inflamed swelling under the skin.

car·bu·re·tor /ˈkarbəˌreitər/ *n* [C] that part of an internal combustion engine, eg in a car, in which gasoline and air are mixed to make an explosive mixture.

car·cass /ˈkarkəs/ *n* [C] **1** dead body of an animal. **2** (*hum*) human body.

card /kard/ *n* [C] **1** (usually small, oblong-shaped) piece of stiff paper, plastic or thin cardboard, as used for various purposes, eg *a ˈcredit ~; ˈChristmas/ˈNew Year/ˈBirthday ~,* sent with greetings at Christmas, etc. *ˈ~ index,* index on cards. ⇨ also postcard. **2** program, esp for a sporting event, with details, and space for marking results: *a ˈscore~.* **3** (often **playing card**) (esp) one of the 52 cards used for various games (whist, bridge, poker, etc) and for telling fortunes. ***in the cards,*** (*informal*) likely or possible. ***put one's cards on the table,*** make one's plans, intentions, etc, known. **4** (*pl*) **(a)** game(s)

played with playing cards. **(b)** card playing.
ˈcard·sharp *n* [C] one skilled at cheating in card games for money.

HEART CLUB DIAMOND SPADE

PLAYING CARD SYMBOLS

car·da·mom /ˈkardəməm/ *n* [U] aromatic spice from various East Indian plants.

card·board /ˈkardˌbɔrd/ *n* [U] thick, stiff kind of paper or pasteboard, used for making boxes, etc.

car·diac /ˈkardiˌæk/ *adj* of the heart: ~ *muscle.*

car·di·gan /ˈkardɪgən/ *n* [C] sweater or jacket that buttons up the front, made with sleeves.

car·di·nal[1] /ˈkard(ə)nəl/ *adj* chief; most important; on which something depends: *the ~ virtues.*
ˌcardinal ˈnumber, any number eg 2, 5, 17, . . . (contrasted with *second, fifth,* etc). ⇨ ordinal.
ˌcardinal ˈpoints, the four chief points of the compass (North, South, East and West).

car·di·nal[2] /ˈkard(ə)nəl/ *n* **1** [C] member of the Sacred College of the Roman Catholic Church, which elects Popes. **2** [U] bright red. **3** [C] North American songbird, having a crest and bright red feathers.

care[1] /ker/ *n* **1** [U] serious attention or thought: *She devotes much ~ to her work.* ***take care of,*** (*informal*) deal with, be responsible for. **2** [U] protection; charge; responsibility: *The child was left in its sister's ~.* ***care of,*** (often written **c/o**) used in addresses before the name of the person(s) to whose house, office, etc a letter is sent. **3** [U] sorrow; anxiety; troubled state of mind caused by doubt or fear: *Care has made him look ten years older.* **4** [C] (usually *pl*) cause of sorrow and anxiety: *He was poor and troubled by the ~s of a large family.*
ˈcare·free *adj* free from care(3).
ˈcare·taker *n* [C] person in charge of the property, goods, etc of another.
ˈcare·worn *adj* showing the effects of care and anxiety.

care[2] /ker/ *vi* **1** feel interest, anxiety or sorrow: *He failed in the examination but I don't think he ~s very much/he doesn't seem to ~.* **2** (only in the *negative* or in *questions*): like; be willing: *Would you ~ to go for a walk?* **3** ***care for,*** **(a)** like (to have): *Would you ~ for a drink?* **(b)** have a taste for; like: *Do you ~ for modern music?* **(c)** look after, provide food, attendance, etc: *Who will ~ for the children if their mother dies?*

CARE /ker/ *abbr* = Cooperative for American Relief Everywhere.

ca·reer /kəˈrɪr/ *n* **1** [C] course or progress through life: *We can learn much by reading about the ~s of great men.* **2** [C] way of making a living; profession: *All ~s should be open to women.* **3** [U] quick or violent forward movement: *in full ~,* at top speed. ▫ *vi* rush wildly: *~ about/past.*

care·ful /ˈkerfəl/ *adj* **1** (of a person) cautious; thinking of, paying attention to, what one does, says, etc: *Be ~ not to break the eggs. Be more ~ with your work.* **2** done with, showing care: *a ~ piece of work.*
care·fully *adv*
care·ful·ness /-nɪs/ *n* [U]

care·less /ˈkerlɪs/ *adj* **1** (of a person) not taking care; thoughtless: *A ~ driver is a danger to the public.* **2** done or made without care: *a ~ mistake.* **3** unconcerned about: *He is ~ of his reputation.*
care·less·ly *adv*
care·less·ness /-nɪs/ *n* [U]

ca·ress /kəˈres/ *n* [C] loving or affectionate touch; kiss. ▫ *vt* give a caress to.

cargo /ˈkargou/ *n* [C,U] (*pl* ~es) goods carried in a ship, aircraft or other vehicle.

cari·bou /ˈkærəˌbu/ *n* [C] (*pl* ~, ~s) reindeer of Greenland and the northern regions of North America.

cari·ca·ture /ˈkærɪkəˌtʃʊr/ *n* **1** [C] picture, imitation of a person's voice, behavior, etc stressing certain features in order to cause amusement or ridicule. **2** [U] art of doing this. ▫ *vt* make, give, a caricature of.

car·ies /ˈkæˌriz/ *n* [U] decay (of bones or teeth): *dental ~.*

car·il·lon /ˈkærəˌlan/ *n* [C] set of bells played by machinery or by a keyboard.

car·nage /ˈkarnɪdʒ/ *n* [U] killing of many people; slaughter.

car·nal /ˈkarnəl/ *adj* of the body or flesh; sensual: *~ desires.*

car·na·tion /karˈneiʃən/ *n* [C] **1** garden plant with sweet-smelling white, pink or red flowers. **2** the flower.

car·ne·lian /karˈnilyən/ *n* [U] hard, reddish stone used in jewelry.

car·ni·val /ˈkarnəvəl/ *n* **1** [U] public merrymaking and feasting, usually with processions of persons in fancy dress. **2** [C] festival of this kind. **3** [C] traveling show with games, amusement rides etc.

car·ni·vore /ˈkarnəˌvɔr/ *n* [C] flesh-eating animal.
car·ni·vor·ous /karˈnɪvərəs/ *adj* flesh-eating. ⇨ herbivorous.

carol /ˈkærəl/ *n* [C] song of joy or praise, esp a Christmas hymn. ▫ *vt* (-l-, -ll-) **1** sing joyfully. **2** sing carols.

ca·rouse /kəˈrauz/ *vt* drink heavily and be merry (at a noisy feast, etc).

carp[1] /karp/ *n* [C] (*pl* unchanged) freshwater fish that lives in lakes and ponds.

carp[2] /karp/ *vi* make unnecessary complaints about small matters: *They're always ~ing at each other.*

car·pal /ˈkarpəl/ *n* [C] (*med*) bone of the wrist. ⇨ illus at skeleton.

car·pen·ter /ˈkarpəntər/ *n* [C] workman who makes and repairs (esp) the wooden parts of buildings and other structures of wood.
car·pen·try *n* [U] work of a carpenter.

car·pet /ˈkarpɪt/ *n* [C] **1** thick covering for floors or stairs. ***(call sb) on the carpet,*** (*sl*) (summon, esp an employee, to) be reprimanded. **2** something suggesting a carpet: *a ~ of moss.* □ *vt* cover (as) with a carpet: *to ~ the stairs.*

car·riage /ˈkærɪdʒ/ *n* **1** [C] vehicle, esp one with four wheels, pulled by a horse or horses, for carrying people. **2** [U] (cost of) carrying of goods from place to place. **3** [C] wheeled support on which a heavy object may move or be moved (eg a ˈ*gun~*). **4** [C] moving part of a machine, changing the position of other parts (eg on typewriter). **5** [U] manner of holding the head or the body (when walking, etc): *She has a graceful ~.*

car·rier /ˈkæriər/ *n* [C] **1** person or company that carries goods or people for payment. **2** person, animal, etc that carries or transmits a disease without catching it. **3** vehicle, ship, etc used for the transport of troops, aircraft, tanks, etc: *an aircraft ~.*

ˈ**carrier pigeon,** pigeon used to carry messages because it can find its way home from a distant place.

car·rion /ˈkæriən/ *n* [U] dead and decaying flesh.

car·rot /ˈkærət/ *n* [C] (plant with) yellow or orange root used as a vegetable. ⇨ illus at vegetable.

carry /ˈkæri/ *vt,vi* (*pt,pp* -ied) **1** support the weight of and move from place to place; take a person, a message, etc from one place to another: *He was ~ing a box on his shoulder. Some kinds of seeds are carried by the wind for great distances. The police seized the spy and carried him off to prison.* (*Note:* commonly used in the southern US, of people, in the sense of *take*): *Will you ~ the children to school?* ***carry a lot of weight,*** (*fig*) be important. ***carry the torch for sb,*** (*informal*) be devotedly in love with him/her (usually without the love being returned). **2** have with one; wear; possess: *Do you always ~ an umbrella? Can you ~ all these figures in your head,* remember them without writing them down? **3** support: *These pillars ~ the weight of the roof.* **4** involve; have as a result: *The loan carries 10% interest.* **5** (of pipes, wires, etc) conduct; take: *Water carries sound. Copper carries electricity.* **6** make longer; extend; take (in a particular direction, to a particular point): *The motif carries throughout the building.* ***carry (a joke, plan, etc) too far,*** overdo it. **7** win; capture; persuade; overcome: *The bill/motion/resolution* (*was*) *carried,* there were more votes for it than against it. ***carry the day,*** be victorious. **8** hold oneself, one's head, etc in a particular way: *He carries himself like a soldier,* stands and walks like one. **9** (of sounds, projectiles, etc) (have the ability to) go to: *Their voices carried over a mile.* **10** (of newspapers, the radio, TV) publish; broadcast: *News of the murder was carried in the newspaper/on TV.* **11** (special uses with *adverbial particles* and *prepositions*):

be carried away, lose self-control: *He was carried away by his enthusiasm,* was so enthusiastic that he was unable to judge calmly, etc.

carry back, take back in the memory: *an incident that carried me back to my schooldays,* made me remember them.

carry forward, transfer (a total of figures on a page) to the head of a new column or page.

carry off, (of a prize, honors, etc) win: *The little-known runner carried off First Prize.* ***carry it off (well),*** succeed in a difficult situation; cover a mistake, etc.

carry on, **(a)** conduct; manage: *Rising costs made it hard to ~ on the business.* **(b)** talk loud and complainingly; behave strangely or suspiciously: *Did you notice how they were ~ing on?*

carry over, transfer, extend, continue, from one place or condition to another.

carry through, **(a)** help (through difficulties, etc): *Their courage will ~ them through.* **(b)** complete something: *Having made a promise, you must ~ it through.*

ˈ**carry-on** *n* piece of luggage small enough to be carried on board an airplane; (also as an *adjective*): *~-on bag/luggage.*

ˈ**carry-out** *adj* (of food) prepared for being taken away and eaten elsewhere.

ˈ**carry-out** ˌ**shop,** one specializing in preparing carry-out food.

ˈ**carry-over** *n* thing or condition carried over.

cart /kart/ *n* [C] two-wheeled vehicle pulled by a horse, used in farming and for delivery of goods by tradesmen (now usually replaced by motor vehicles). ***put the cart before the horse,*** do or put things in the wrong order. □ *vt* **1** carry in a cart: *~ing away the trash.* **2** (*informal*) carry in the hands, etc: *Do you really have to ~ these parcels around for the rest of the day?*

ˈ**cart·horse** *n* [C] strong horse for heavy work.

ˈ**cart·load** *n* [C] as much as a cart can hold.

carte blanche /ˌkart ˈblanʃ/ *n* (*F*) full authority or freedom (to use one's own judgment about how to proceed, etc).

car·tel /karˈtel/ *n* [C] (esp international) combination of large business organizations: ˈ*oil ~.*

car·ti·lage /ˈkartəlɪdʒ/ *n* [C,U] (structure, part, of) tough, white tissue attached to the joints in animal bodies; gristle.

car·togra·pher /karˈtɔgrəfər, karˈta-/ *n* [C] person who draws maps and charts.

car·togra·phy /karˈtɔgrəfi, karˈta-/ *n* [U] the drawing of maps and charts.

car·ton /ˈkartən/ *n* [C] cardboard box for holding goods: *a ~ of cigarettes.*

car·toon /karˈtun/ *n* [C] **1** drawing dealing with contemporary (esp political) events in an amusing way. **2** full-size preliminary drawing on paper, used as a model for a painting, etc. **3** (also **animated cartoon**) moving picture made by photographing a series of drawings: *a Walt Disney ~.* □ *vt* represent (a person, etc) in a cartoon.

car·toon·ist *n* [C] person who draws cartoons (1).

car·tridge /ˈkartrɪdʒ/ *n* [C] **1** case containing explosive (for blasting), or explosive with bullet or shot (for firing from a rifle or shot gun). **2** unit (on a record player) that holds the needle. **3** cassette.

carve /ˈkarv/ *vt,vi* **1** form by cutting away material from a piece of wood or stone: *~ a statue out of wood; a figure ~d from marble;* (*fig*) *~ out a career for oneself,* achieve one by great effort. **2** inscribe by cutting on a surface: *~ one's* *initials.* **3** cut up (cooked meat) into pieces or slices at or for the table: ~ *a leg of lamb.*

carver *n* [C] **(a)** carving knife. **(b)** person who carves.

carv·ing *n* [C] something carved (in wood, etc): *a* ˈ*wood*~.

cary·atid /ˌkæriˈætɪd/ *n* [C] draped statue of a female figure used as a support (eg a pillar) in a building.

cas·cade /kæsˈkeid/ *n* [C] **1** waterfall. **2** similar fall of lace, cloth, etc. □ *vi* fall like a cascade.

case[1] /keis/ *n* [C] **1** instance or example of something: *It's a clear* ~ *of cheating,* is clear that cheating has taken place. **2** actual state of affairs; *If that's the* ~ (= if that is true), *you'll have to work much harder. No, that's not the* ~, is not true. **3** circumstances or special conditions relating to a person or thing: *I can't make an exception in your* ~. ***(just) in case,*** if it should happen that; because of a possibility: *It may rain; you'd better take an umbrella* (*just*) *in* ~. *In* ~ *I forget, please remind me of my promise.* ***in any case,*** whatever happens or may have happened. ***in this/that case,*** if this/that happens, has happened, should happen. **4 (a)** person suffering from a disease. **(b)** instance of this: *There were five* ~*s of influenza.* **5** (*legal*) question to be decided in a law court. **6** the facts, arguments, etc used on one side in a law court. ***make out a case (for),*** give arguments in favor of. **7** (*gram*) form of a noun, pronoun, etc that shows its relation to another word: *The first person pronoun has three* ~*s, "I," "me" and "my."*

case[2] /keis/ *n* [C] **1** box, bag, covering, container: *a* ˈ*pillow*~, of cloth for covering a pillow: ⇨ also suitcase, bookcase. **2** (*printing*): ˈ*upper* ~, capital letters; ˈ*lower* ~, small letters. □ *vt* enclose in a case or casing.

ca·sein /ˈkeiˌsin/ *n* [U] protein found in milk, that is the basis of cheese.

case·ment /ˈkeismənt/ *n* [C] window that opens outwards or inwards like a door, not up or down or from side to side.

cash /kæʃ/ *n* [U] **1** money in coin or bills: *I have no* ~ *with me; may I pay by check?* ⇨ credit[1](2). **2** money in any form: *be short of* ~, without money. □ *vt,vi* **1** give or get cash for: *Can you* ~ *this check for me/*~ *me a check?* **2** take advantage of; benefit from: *storekeepers who* ~ *in on shortages by raising prices.*

ˈ**cash bar,** arrangement for the voluntary purchase of alcoholic drinks at a conference, banquet, etc.

ˈ**cash crop,** crop grown to be sold for cash (not for use by the growers).

ˈ**cash register,** cash box with a device for recording and storing cash received.

cash·ew /ˈkæʃu/ *n* [C] (tropical American tree with) small kidney-shaped nut (ˈ~ *nut*).

cash·ier /kæˈʃɪr/ *n* [C] person who receives and pays out money in a bank, store, hotel, restaurant, etc.

cash·mere /ˈkæʒmɪr/ *n* [U] fine soft wool of Kashmir goats of India.

cas·ing /ˈkeisɪŋ/ *n* [C,U] covering; protective wrapping: *copper wire with a plastic* ~.

ca·sino /kəˈsinou/ *n* [C] (*pl* ~s) public room or building for music, dancing, etc and (usually) for gambling.

cask /kæsk/ *n* [C] **1** barrel for liquids. **2** amount that a cask holds.

cas·ket /ˈkæskɪt/ *n* [C] **1** small box to hold letters, jewels, etc. **2** coffin.

cas·sava /kəˈsavə/ *n* [C,U] (tropical plant with) starchy roots eaten as food.

cas·ser·ole /ˈkæsəˌroul/ *n* [C] **1** heat-proof dish with a lid in which food is cooked. **2** food so cooked: *a lamb-and-rice* ~.

cas·sette /kəˈset/ *n* [C] sealed container for magnetic tape or for photographic film.

casˈ**sette deck** ⇨ deck[1](5).

cas·sock /ˈkæsək/ *n* [C] long, close-fitting outer garment, worn by some priests.

cast[1] /kæst/ *n* [C] **1** act of throwing (eg a net or fishing line). **2** thing made by casting(3) or by pressing soft material into a mold: *His leg was in a plaster* ~. **3** mold for a casting. **4** set of actors in a play: *a play with an all-star* ~. **5** type or quality: ~ *of/mind.* **6** eye disorder in which the two eyes are not able to focus on the same thing.

cast[2] /kæst/ *vt,vi* (*pt,pp* ~) **1** throw; allow to fall or drop: *The fisherman* ~ *his net into the water.* ***be cast down,*** be depressed, unhappy. ⇨ downcast. ***cast a vote,*** give a vote. **2** turn or send in a particular direction. ***cast one's eye over sth,*** look at, examine, it. **3** pour (liquid metal) into a mold; make in this way: *a figure* ~ *in bronze.* **4** give (an actor) a part in a play, film, etc: *He was* ~ *for the part of Hamlet.* ⇨ casting. **5** ***cast sb/sth aside,*** abandon; throw away as useless or unwanted. ***cast off,*** **(a)** unloose (a boat) and let go. **(b)** (*fig*) abandon; throw away as unwanted. **(c)** remove the last row of stitches from a knitting needle. ***cast on,*** make the first row of stitches when knitting.

casting vote, one given (eg by the chairman) to decide a question when votes on each side are equal.

ˈ**cast iron** *n* [U] iron in a hard, brittle form, made in molds after melting the ore in a blast furnace.

ˈ**cast-iron** *adj* **(a)** made of cast iron. **(b)** (*fig*) hard; strong; unyielding: *a man with a* ~*-iron will/constitution.*

cas·ta·nets /ˌkæstəˈnets/ *n pl* instruments of hardwood, etc used in pairs on the fingers to make rattling sounds as a rhythm for dancing.

cast·away /ˈkæstəˌwei/ *n* [C] shipwrecked person, esp one reaching a strange country or lonely island.

caste /kæst/ *n* **1** [C] one of the Hindu hereditary social classes; any exclusive social class. **2** [U] this system.

cas·tel·lated /ˈkæstəˌleitɪd/ *adj* having turrets or battlements (like a castle).

cas·ter, cas·tor /ˈkæstər/ *n* [C] **1** wheel (on a swivel) fixed to the legs of furniture (so that it may be moved easily). **2** bottle or metal pot, with holes in the top, for sugar, salt, etc.

cas·ti·gate /ˈkæstəˌgeit/ *vt* punish severely with blows or by criticizing.

cas·ti·ga·tion /ˌkæstəˈgeiʃən/ *n* [C,U] (instance

of) severe punishment.
cast·ing /ˈkæstɪŋ/ *n* **1** [C] thing made by being poured into a mold. ⇨ cast²(3). **2** [U] job of casting actors in plays, films, etc: *Whoever was responsible for the ~ in that film did a very good job!* ⇨ cast²(4).
castle /ˈkæsəl/ *n* [C] **1 (a)** large building or group of buildings fortified against attack, esp as in olden times. **(b)** house that was once such a fortified building. **2** = rook³. □ *vi* (in chess) move the king sideways two squares and place the rook on the square the king moved across.
cas·tor oil /ˈkæstər ˌɔiəl/ *n* [U] thick oil, used as a laxative.
cas·trate /ˈkæˌstreit/ *vt* **1** make (a male animal) useless for breeding purposes by removing the testicles. **2** (*fig*) treat a man so as to make him feel that he has lost his manhood.
cas·tra·tion /kæˈstreiʃən/ *n* [C,U] castrating.
cas·ual /ˈkæʒuəl/ *adj* **1** happening by chance: *a ~ meeting*. **2** careless; informal: *a ~ glance; ~ clothes,* for informal occasions, etc. **3** irregular; not continued: *~ laborers*, not permanently engaged by one employer.
cas·ual·ly *adv*
casu·alty /ˈkæʒu(ə)lti/ *n* [C] (*pl* -ies) **1** accident, esp one involving loss of life or serious injury. **2** person killed or seriously injured in war or an accident: *The enemy suffered heavy casualties.*
cat /kæt/ *n* [C] **1** small, fur-covered animal often kept as a pet, to catch mice, etc. ***not room to swing a cat (in),*** very small, narrow space. **2** any animal of the group that includes cats, tigers, lions, panthers and leopards.
several scaleless fishes having feelers around the mouth that resemble a cat's whiskers.
ˈcat·gut *n* [U] = gut(3).
ˈcat·nap *n* [C] short sleep or doze (in a chair, etc not in bed).
ˌcat-o'-ˈnine-tails, knotted whip formerly used to punish offenders.
ˌcat's ˈcradle, game played by looping string over the fingers of both hands.
ˈcat·walk *n* [C] narrow footway along a bridge, or through a mass of machinery, engines, etc.
cata·clysm /ˈkætəˌklɪzəm/ *n* [C] sudden and violent event (eg an earthquake, a political or social revolution).
cata·clys·mic /ˌkætəˈklɪzmɪk/ *adj*
cata·combs /ˈkætəˌkoumz/ *n pl* series of underground galleries with openings along the sides for the burial of the dead (as in ancient Rome).
cata·falque /ˈkætəˌfælk/ *n* [C] decorated stand or stage for a coffin at a funeral.
cata·logue, cata·log /ˈkætəˌlɔg/ *n* [C] list of names, places, goods, etc in a special order: *a library ~*. □ *vt* make, put in, a catalogue.
ca·tal·pa /kəˈtælpə/ *n* [C] tree of America and Asia, bearing clusters of flowers and long pods.
cata·maran /ˈkætəməˌræn/ *n* [C] boat with twin hulls.
cat·a·pult /ˈkætəpəlt/ *n* [C] **1** = slingshot. **2** (in ancient times) machine for throwing heavy stones in war. **3** apparatus for launching aircraft without a runway (eg from the deck of a carrier). □ *vt* **1** shoot (as) from a catapult. **2** launch (aircraft) with a catapult.
cata·ract /ˈkætəˌrækt/ *n* [C] **1** large, steep waterfall. **2** eye disorder in which the lens becomes cloudy and progressively obscures sight.

WILD CATS

ˈcat·bird *n* [C] grayish North American songbird that makes a sound like a cat.
ˈcat·bird ˌseat, position of power or advantage: *The young Chairman of the board was in the catbird seat.*
ˈcat·boat *n* [C] sailboat having a single mast that is set far forward.
ˈcat·call *vi, n* [C] (make a) loud, shrill whistle or noise expressing disapproval (eg at a performance).
ˈcat·fish *n* [C] (*pl* catfish or catfishes) any of
ca·tarrh /kəˈtar/ *n* [U] inflammation, esp in the nose and throat, causing flow of liquid, as when one has a cold.
ca·tas·trophe /kəˈtæstrəfi/ *n* [C] sudden event causing great suffering and destruction (eg a flood).
cata·strophic /ˌkætəˈstrafɪk/ *adj*
catch¹ /kætʃ/ *n* [C] **1** act of catching (esp a ball): *That was a difficult ~*. **2** that which is caught or

worth catching: *a fine ~ of fish*. **3** something intended to trick or deceive: *There's a ~ in it somewhere*. **4** device for fastening or securing a lock, door, etc.

catch[2] /kætʃ/ *vt,vi* (*pt,pp* caught /kɔt/) **1** grasp or lay hold of (something in motion) (eg with the hands, by holding out something into which it may come): *I threw the ball to him and he caught it*. **2** capture; seize; intercept: *~ a thief. How many fish did you ~?* **3** surprise a person doing something: *I caught the boys stealing apples from my garden*. **4** get to in time for: *~ a train/ the bus, etc*. **5** ***catch up with sb,*** **(a)** come up to a person who is going in the same direction; overtake. **(b)** do all the work that has not yet been done: *Tom has got to work hard to ~ up with the rest of the class*. **6** (cause to) become fastened or hooked; (cause to) be entangled: *I caught my fingers in the door*, trapped them between the door and the frame. **7** get (the meaning of); hear (the sound): *I don't quite ~ your meaning. I didn't ~ the end of the sentence*. ***catch on,*** **(a)** come to understand. **(b)** become popular. ***catch sight/a glimpse of,*** see for a short time. **8** become infected with: *~ a disease/ a cold*. **9** (try to) grasp: *A drowning man will ~ at a straw. He caught hold of my arm*. **10** hit: *Her blow caught him on the cheek*. **11** ***catch one's breath,*** fail to breathe regularly for a moment (from surprise, etc). ***catch fire,*** begin to burn. ***catch it,*** receive punishment, blame, etc: *You'll ~ it!*

catcher *n* [C] (*baseball*) player who catches the ball when missed by the batter. ⇨ illus at baseball.

ˈ**catch·word** *n* [C] phrase or slogan in frequent current use.

catch·ing /ˈkætʃɪŋ/ *adj* (esp of diseases) infectious.

catchy /ˈkætʃi/ *adj* (-ier, -iest) **1** (of a tune, etc) easily remembered. **2** tricky, deceptive.

cat·echism /ˈkætəˌkɪzəm/ *n* **1** [U] instruction (esp about religion) by question and answer. **2** [C] set of questions and answers designed for this purpose.

cat·echize /ˈkætəˌkaiz/ *vt* teach or examine by asking many questions.

cat·egori·cal /ˌkætəˈgɔrɪkəl/ *adj* (of a statement) unconditional; absolute: *the ~ truth*.

cat·egori·cally /-kli/ *adv*

cat·egor·ize /ˈkætəgəˌraiz/ *vt* place in a category.

cat·egory /ˈkætəˌgɔri/ *n* [C] (*pl* -ies) division or group in a system of classification.

ca·ter /ˈkeitər/ *vt, vi* **1** provide food, drink, etc for: *Who shall we get to cater the banquet?* **2** ***cater for,*** provide food: *Weddings and parties ~ed for*. **3** ***cater for/to,*** supply what is wanted or needed: *TV programs usually ~ to all tastes*.

ca·terer *n* [C]

cater·cor·ner /ˈkætərˌkɔrnər/ (also **catty-corner** /ˈkæti-/, **kitty-corner** /ˈkɪti-/) *adv, adj* diagonal(ly).

cat·er·pil·lar /ˈkætərˌpɪlər/ *n* [C] **1** larva of a butterfly or moth. **2** (also **caterpillar tractor**) tractor with treaded belts over the wheels, for moving over rough ground.

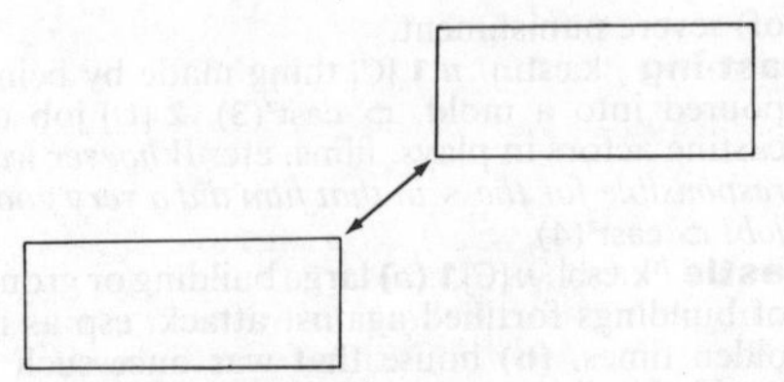

CATERCORNER

ca·thar·tic /kəˈθartɪk/ *adj, n* [C] (medicine that is) strongly laxative.

ca·the·dral /kəˈθidrəl/ *n* [C] chief church in a diocese.

cath·ode /ˈkæˌθoud/ *n* [C] (*electr*) **1** electrode which releases negative electrons, eg in a ˈ*~-ray tube*. **2** negative terminal of a battery. ⇨ anode.

cath·olic /ˈkæθ(ə)lɪk/ *adj* **1** liberal; general; including many or most things: *a man with ~ tastes and interests*. **2** **Catholic,** ⇨ Roman(2). □ *n* [C] **Catholic,** member of the Roman Catholic Church.

Ca·tholi·cism /kəˈθaləˌsɪzəm/ *n* [U] teaching, beliefs, etc of the Roman Catholic Church.

cat·kin /ˈkætkɪn/ *n* [C] spike of soft, downy flowers hanging down from twigs of such trees as willows and birches.

cat·nip /ˈkætˌnɪp/ *n* [U] plant of the mint family, with leaves that are attractive to cats.

cat·sup /ˈketʃəp/ *n* [U] sauce for meat, fish, etc: *tomato ~*.

cat·tail /ˈkætˌteiəl/ *n* [C] tall marsh plant with brown, furry spikes.

catty /ˈkæti/ *adj* (-ier, -iest) (esp) sly and spiteful.

catty-cor·ner /ˈkætiˌkɔrnər/ *adv* = catercorner.

cattle /ˈkætəl/ *n pl* bulls, steers, cows: *twenty head of ~*.

ˈ**cattle baron/king,** owner of a large cattle ranch.

ˈ**cattle car,** railroad car especially designed for transporting cattle.

ˈ**cattle ranch,** one devoted to the raising of cattle.

ˈ**cattle range,** large area of land used for grazing cattle.

Cau·casian /kɔˈkeiʒən/ *n* [C], *adj* (member) of the light-skinned race of people.

cau·cus /ˈkɔkəs/ *n* [C] (*pl* ~es) meeting of the members of a political party (making plans, decisions, etc).

cau·dal /ˈkɔdəl/ *adj* of or at the tail.

caught *pt,pp* of catch[2].

caul·dron = caldron.

cauli·flower /ˈkɔləˌflauər/ *n* [C,U] (cabbagelike plant with a) large, white flower head, used as a vegetable. ⇨ illus at vegetable.

caulk /kɔk/ *vt* make (seams between planks, etc) tight with fiber or a sticky substance.

cau·sal /ˈkɔzəl/ *adj* of cause and effect; of, expressing, cause.

cau·sal·ity /kɔˈzæləti/ *n* [C] (*pl* -ties) relation of cause and effect; the principle that nothing can happen without a cause.

cau·sa·tive /ˈkɔzətɪv/ *adj* acting as, expressing, cause.

cause /kɔz/ *n* **1** [C,U] person, thing, etc that

makes something happen: *The ~ of the fire was carelessness.* **2** [U] reason: *You have no ~ for complaint/no ~ to complain.* **3** [C] purpose for which efforts are being made: *fight in the ~ of justice.* □ *vt* be the cause of: *What ~d his death?*
cause·less *adj* without any natural or known reason.
cause·way /ˈkɔzˌwei/ *n* [C] raised road or footpath, esp across wet land or water.
caus·tic /ˈkɔstɪk/ *adj* **1** able to burn or destroy by chemical action: *~ soda.* **2** (*fig*) sarcastic: *~ remarks.*
caus·ti·cally /ˈkɔstɪkli/ *adv*
cau·ter·ize /ˈkɔtəˌraiz/ *vt* burn (eg a snakebite) with a caustic substance or with a hot iron (to destroy infection).
cau·tion /ˈkɔʃən/ *n* **1** [U] great care or prudence; paying attention (to avoid danger or making mistakes): *When crossing a busy street we must use ~.* **2** [C] warning: *The judge gave the prisoner a ~ (against repeating the offense) and set him free.* □ *vt* give a caution to: *I ~ed him against being late. The judge ~ed the prisoner.*
cau·tion·ary /ˈkɔʃəˌneri/ *adj* conveying advice or warning: *~ tales.*
cau·tious /ˈkɔʃəs/ *adj* having or showing caution.
cau·tious·ly *adv*
cau·tious·ness /-nɪs/ *n* [U]
cav·al·cade /ˌkævəlˈkeid/ *n* [C] procession of persons on horseback or in carriages. ➪ motorcade.
cava·lier /ˌkævəˈlɪr/ *n* [C] horseman or knight. □ *adj* **1** carefree; offhand. **2** scornful and proud.
cav·alry /ˈkævəlri/ *n* (*collect*) (branch of an army made up of) soldiers who fight on horseback.
cave /keiv/ *n* [C] hollow place in the side of a cliff or hill; large natural hollow under the ground. □ *vi,vt* ***cave in,*** (cause to) fall in, give way to pressure: *The roof of the tunnel ~d in.*
ˈcave·man /-ˌmæn/ (*pl* ~men /-ˌmen/) *n* [C] **(a)** cave dweller. **(b)** (*informal*) crude, rough man.
cav·ern /ˈkævərn/ *n* [C] (*liter*) cave.
caviar, cavi·are /ˈkæviˌar/ *n* [U] salted eggs of the sturgeon or certain other large fish.
cav·ity /ˈkævəti/ *n* [C] (*pl* -ies) empty space; small hole, within a solid body: *a ~ in a tooth.*
ca·vort /kəˈvort/ *vi* (*informal*) prance or jump about.
caw /kɔ/ *n* [C] harsh cry of a raven, rook or crow. □ *vi,vt* make this cry.
cay·enne /keiˈen/ *n* [U] (also **cayenne pepper**) very hot kind of red pepper.
cay·use /ˈkaiˌyus/ *n* [C] (western US) horse or pony, esp an Indian pony.
CB /ˌsi ˈbi/ *abbr* = citizens' band (radio).
CBC /ˌsi ˌbi ˈsi/ *abbr* = Canadian Broadcasting Corporation.
CBS /ˌsi ˌbi ˈes/ *abbr* = Columbia Broadcasting System.
cc *abbr* = carbon copy (to somebody).
CDST *abbr* = Central Daylight Saving Time.
cease /sis/ *vt,vi* = stop (the usual word): *The controls ~d to function.*
cease·less /-lɪs/ *adj* never ending.
cease·less·ly *adv*

cedar /ˈsidər/ *n* [C,U] (evergreen tree with) hard, red, sweet-smelling wood.
cede /sid/ *vt* ***cede to,*** give up (rights, land, etc to another state, etc).
ce·dilla /sɪˈdɪlə/ *n* [C] mark (,) placed under a vowel or consonant to indicate how it is to be sounded (as in French *façade*).
ceil·ing /ˈsilɪŋ/ *n* [C] **1** upper or overhead surface of a room. **2** highest level at which an aircraft can operate: *a plane with a ~ of 20,000 ft.* **3** maximum height, limit or level: *price ~s; wage ~s.*
cel·ebrate /ˈseləˌbreit/ *vt* **1** do something to show that a day or an event is important, or an occasion for rejoicing: *~ Christmas/one's birthday.* **2** perform publicly, with the proper forms: *~ Mass.* **3** praise and honor: *The names of many heroes are ~d by the poets.*
ˈcel·ebrated *adj* famous: *a ~d painter.*
cel·ebra·tion /ˌseləˈbreiʃən/ *n* [C,U] (the act of, an occasion of) celebrating.
ce·leb·rity /səˈlebrəti/ *n* (*pl* -ies) **1** [U] being celebrated; fame and honor. **2** [C] famous person.
ce·ler·ity /səˈlerəti/ *n* [U] (*formal*) speed.
cel·ery /ˈsel(ə)ri/ *n* [U] garden plant of which the white stems are eaten as a vegetable: *~ soup.*
ce·lesta /səˈlestə/ *n* [C] musical instrument that makes a tinkling sound by means of hammers striking steel plates.
ce·lestial /səˈlestʃəl/ *adj* **1** of the sky; of heaven: *~ bodies,* eg the sun and the stars. **2** divinely good or beautiful.
celi·bacy /ˈseləbəsi/ *n* [U] state of living unmarried, esp as a religious obligation.
celi·bate /ˈseləbɪt/ *n* [C], *adj* (of an) unmarried person (esp for religious reasons).
cell /sel/ *n* [C] **1** small room for one person (esp in a prison or a monastery). **2** compartment in a larger structure, esp in a honeycomb. **3** unit of an apparatus for producing electric current by chemical action. **4** microscopic unit of living matter. **5** small group of persons forming a unit of a (usually revolutionary) organization: *communist ~s in an industrial town.*
cel·lar /ˈselər/ *n* [C] underground rooms for storing coal, wine, etc.
cel·list /ˈtʃelɪst/ *n* [C] cello player.
cello /ˈtʃelou/ *n* [C] (*pl* ~s) (short for violoncello) stringed instrument like the violin, but much larger and with a deeper tone. ➪ illus at string.
cel·lu·lar /ˈselyələr/ *adj* consisting of cells(4): *~ tissue.*
Cel·sius /ˈselsiəs/ *adj* (of thermometers) = centigrade.
Celt /selt/ *n* [C] member of the last group of immigrants to settle in Britain before the coming of the Romans, now represented by some of the Irish, Welsh, Cornish and Highland Scots.
Cel·tic *n* [U], *adj* (language) of the Celts.
ce·ment /sɪˈment/ *n* [U] **1** gray powder (made by burning lime and clay) which, after being mixed with water, sand, etc, becomes hard like stone and is used for building, etc. ➪ concrete *n.* **2** any similar soft substance that sets firm and holds things together. □ *vt* **1** put on or in, join with

cement. **2** (*fig*) strengthen; unite firmly: ~ *a friendship.*
ce'ment mixer, (vehicle with a) revolving drum in which concrete is mixed.
cem·etery /'semə,teri/ *n* [C] (*pl* -ies) area of land used for burying the dead.
ceno·taph /'senə,tæf/ *n* [C] monument put up in memory of a person or persons buried elsewhere.
cen·sor /'sensər/ *n* [C] (esp) official with authority to examine letters, books, periodicals, plays, motion pictures, etc and to cut out or change anything regarded as immoral, undesirable, or, in time of war, helpful to the enemy. □ *vt* examine or make changes in as a censor.
'cen·sor·ship /-,ʃɪp/ *n* [U] office, duties, etc of a censor.
cen·sure /'senʃər/ *vt* ***censure sb (for),*** criticize unfavorably: ~ *a pupil for being lazy.* □ *n* **1** [U] rebuke; disapproval: *pass a vote of* ~. **2** [C] expression of disapproval.
cen·sus /'sensəs/ *n* [C] (*pl* ~es) official counting of the population of a country, city, etc.
cent /sent/ *n* [C] **1** the 100th part of a dollar and some other metric units of currency. **2** metal coin of this value; penny. ⇨ App 4.
cen·taur /'sen,tɔr/ *n* [C] (*Greek myth*) creature, half man and half horse.
cen·ten·ar·ian /,sentə'neriən/ *n* [C], *adj* (person who is) (more than) 100 years old.
cen·ten·ary /'sentə,neri/ *adj, n* [C] (*pl* -ies) = centennial.
cen·ten·nial /sen'teniəl/ *adj, n* [C] (having to do with a) period of 100 years or (with a) 100th anniversary.
cen·ten·nially *adv*
cen·ter /'sentər/ *n* [C] **1** middle part or point: *the* ~ *of town.* ***center of gravity,*** that point in an object about which the weight is evenly balanced in any position. **2** place of great activity, of special interest, etc: *a 'health* ~; *the 'shopping* ~ *of a town.* **3** person or thing that attracts interest, attention etc: *She loves to be the* ~ *of attraction.* **4** that which occupies a middle position, eg in politics, persons with moderate views. **5** player on a team who holds the middle position on the court, field, etc. □ *vt,vi* **1** place in, pass to, come to, be at, the center: *The defender* ~*ed the ball.* **2** ***center on/upon***: *Our thoughts* ~ *on one idea.*
cen·ti·grade /'sentə,greid/ *adj* in or of the temperature scale that has 0° as the freezing point and 100° as the boiling point of water: *100°* ~ (212° F).
cen·ti·gram /'sentə,græm/ *n* [C] the 100th part of a gram.
cen·ti·meter /'sentə,mitər/ *n* [C] the 100th part of a meter.
cen·ti·pede /'sentə,pid/ *n* [C] small, wormlike creature with many legs.
cen·tral /'sentrəl/ *adj* **1** of, at, from or near, the center: *My house is very* ~, is in or near the middle of the town. **2** chief; most important: *the* ~ *idea of an argument.*
,central 'heating, system of heating a building from a central source through radiators, etc.
Central In'telligence ,Agency, (*abbr* **,CI'A**) US government agency responsible for coordinating intelligence activities.
cen·tral·ly *adv*
'Central ,Time, one of four official time zones of the continental US.
cen·tral·ize /'sentrə,laiz/ *vt,vi* bring to the center; come, put, bring, under central control.
cen·tral·iz·ation /,sentrələ'zeiʃən/ *n* [U]
cen·trifu·gal /sen'trɪfyəgəl/ *adj* moving, tending to move, away from the center or axis: ~ *force,* the force which causes a body spinning around a center to tend to move outwards.
cen·tury /'sentʃəri/ *n* [C] (*pl* -ies) **1** period of 100 years. **2** one of the periods of 100 years before or since the birth of Jesus Christ: *in the 20th* ~, AD 1901-2000.
ce·ramic /sə'ræmɪk/ *adj* of the art of pottery.
ce·ram·ics *n* **1** art of making and decorating pottery. **2** (with a *pl verb*) articles made of porcelain, clay, etc.
cer·eal /'sɪriəl/ *n* [C] (usually *pl*) **1** any kind of grain used for food. **2** food prepared from cereals: *breakfast* ~*s.*
ce·rebral /sə'ribrəl/ *adj* of the brain: ~ *hemorrhage.*
cer·emo·nial /,serə'mouniəl/ *adj* formal; as used for ceremonies: ~ *dress.* □ *n* [C,U] special order of ceremony, formality, for a special event, etc.
cer·emo·nial·ly *adv*
cer·emo·ni·ous /,serə'mouniəs/ *adj* fond of, marked by, formality.
cer·emo·ni·ous·ly *adv*
cer·e·mo·ny /'serə,mouni/ *n* (*pl* -ies) **1** [C] special act(s), religious service, etc on an

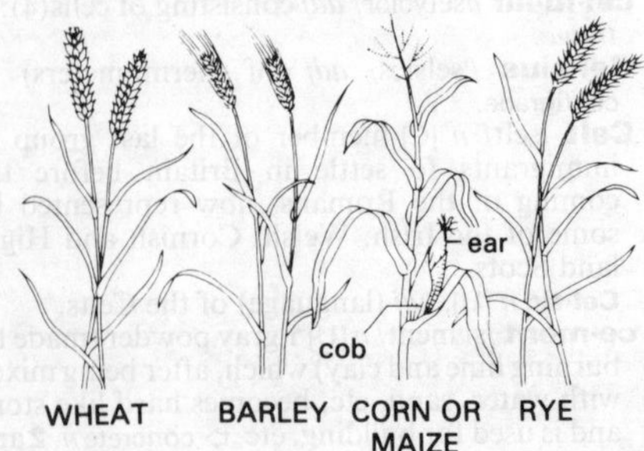

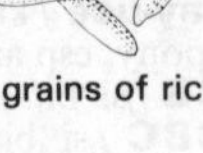

CEREALS

occasion such as a wedding, funeral, the opening of a new public building, etc. **2** [U] very polite and formal behavior required by social customs: *There's too much ~ on official occasions.*

ce·rise /sə'ris/ *adj, n* [U] (of a) light, pinkish red.

cer·tain /'sərtən/ *adj* **1** settled; of which there is no doubt: *It is ~ that two and two make four.* **2** convinced; having no doubt; confident: *I'm ~ (that) he saw me.* ***for certain,*** without doubt: *I cannot say for ~* (= with complete confidence) *when he will arrive.* ***make certain,*** **(a)** inquire in order to be sure: *I think there's a train at 8:20 but you ought to make ~.* **(b)** do something in order to be assured: *I'll go and make ~ of our seats.* **3** reliable; sure to come or happen: *There is no ~ cure for this disease.* **4** not named, stated or described, although it is possible to do so: *on ~ conditions; a ~ person I met yesterday.*

cer·tain·ly *adv* **(a)** without doubt: *He will ~ly die if you don't get a doctor.* **(b)** (in answer to questions) yes: *Will you pass me the towel, please? Certainly!*

cer·tain·ty *n* (*pl* -ies) **(a)** [C] thing that is certain: *Prices have gone up—that's a ~ty.* **(b)** [U] state of being sure: freedom from doubt: *We can have no ~ty of success.*

cer·ti·fi·able /ˌsərtə'faiəbəl/ *adj* that can be certified.

cer·tifi·cate /sər'tɪfəkɪt/ *n* [C] written or printed statement, that may be used as proof or evidence: *a 'birth/'marriage ~.*

cer·tify /'sərtəˌfai/ *vt,vi* (*pt,pp* -ied) declare (sometimes by giving a certificate) that one is certain, that something is true, correct, in order: *I ~ (that) this is a true copy of....*

cer·ti·tude /'sərtəˌtud/ *n* [U] = certainty (the more usual word).

cer·vix /'sərvɪks/ *n* [C] (*anat*) necklike part of an organ, esp the narrow outer end of the uterus.

cer·vi·cal /'sərvəkəl/ *adj*

Cesar·ean /sɪ'zæriən/ *n* [C], *adj* delivery of a child by cutting the walls of the abdomen and uterus: *~ section.*

ces·sa·tion /se'seiʃən/ *n* [U] (*formal*) ceasing: *the ~ of hostilities.*

ces·sion /'seʃən/ *n* [U] act of ceding or giving up lands/rights etc by agreement; [C] thing ceded.

cess·pool /'sesˌpul/ *n* (usually covered) hole, pit or underground tank into which drains empty (esp for sewage).

cf. *abbr* = confer (ie, compare).

ch. *abbr* = chapter(1).

chafe /tʃeif/ *vi,vt* **1** rub (the skin, one's hands) to get warmth. **2** make or become rough or sore by rubbing: *Her skin ~s easily.* **3** feel irritation or impatience: *~ at the delay/inefficiency; ~ under restraints.*

chaff[1] /tʃæf/ *n* [U] **1** outer covering (husks) of grain, removed before the grain is used as human food. **2** something worthless.

chaff[2] /tʃæf/ *n* [U] good-humored teasing or joking. □ *vt* tease.

chaf·finch /'tʃæˌfɪntʃ/ *n* [C] small European songbird.

chag·rin /ʃə'grɪn/ *n* [U] disappointment or annoyance (at having failed, made a mistake, etc): *Much to his ~, he did not win the race.* □ *vt* cause to feel disappointment, etc.

chain /tʃein/ *n* [C] **1** flexible line of connected rings or links for connecting, continuing, restraining, ornament, etc. ***in chains,*** kept as a prisoner or slave. **2** number of connected things, events, etc: *a ~ of mountains/ideas/events/proof.* **3** surveyors' measure of length (66 ft). □ *vt* make fast with a chain.

'chain armor/mail, armor made of metal rings linked together.

'chain gang, gang of prisoners in chains while at work outside their prison.

'chain reaction, (a) chemical change forming products that themselves cause more changes so that the process is repeated again and again. **(b)** (*fig*) series of events related to each other, so that each one causes the next to happen.

'chain smoker, person who smokes cigarettes one after the other.

'chain stitch, kind of sewing in which each stitch makes a loop through which the next stitch is taken.

'chain store, one of many shops owned and controlled by the same company.

chair /tʃer/ *n* [C] **1** separate seat for one person, usually with a back and in some cases with arms (*'arm~*): *Won't you take a ~,* sit down? **2** seat of office, dignity, rank, etc. ***be in/take the chair,*** preside at a meeting. **3** office or position of authority, dignity, etc: *the Chair of Philosophy.* □ *vt* **1** place in a chair. **2** conduct as chairman: *~ a meeting.*

'chair·man/·woman/·person *n* [C] (*pl* ~men /-men/, ~women/-ˌwɪmɪn/, ~persons/-ˌpərsənz/) one presiding at a meeting.

chalet /ʃæ'lei/ *n* [C] **1** Swiss mountain hut or cottage built of wood and with a sharply sloping and overhanging roof. **2** cottage built in the same style.

chal·ice /'tʃælɪs/ *n* [C] wine cup, esp that used for the Communion service in Christian churches.

chalk /tʃɔk/ *n* **1** [U] soft, white substance (a kind of limestone) used for making lime. **2** [C,U] this material, or a material similar in texture, white or colored, made into sticks for writing and drawing. □ *vt* write, draw, mark, whiten, with chalk.

chalky *adj* (-ier, iest) of, containing, like, chalk.

chal·lenge /'tʃæləndʒ/ *n* [C] **1** invitation or call to play a game, run a race, have a fight, etc to see who is better, stronger, etc. **2** order given by a sentry to stop and explain who one is: *"Who goes there?" is the ~.* □ *vt* **1** give, send, be, a challenge to. **2** question; ask for facts (to support a statement, etc): *~ a person's right to do something.*

chal·lenger *n* [C] person who challenges.

cham·ber /'tʃeimbər/ *n* **1** (*old use*) room, esp a bedroom. **2** (*pl*) judge's office. **3** (sometimes **Chamber**) (hall used by a) group of legislators: *the 'Upper Chamber; the 'Lower Chamber.* **4** (sometimes **Chamber**) group of persons organized for purposes of trade: *a Chamber of Commerce.* **5** enclosed compartment or space in the body of an animal or plant, in a gun.

'chamber·maid *n* [C] housemaid who keeps

bedrooms in order (now chiefly in hotels). ˈ**chamber music,** music for a small number of players (eg a string quartet).

cha·meleon /kəˈmiliən/ *n* [C] **1** small lizard with a long tongue, whose color changes according to its background. ⇨ illus at reptile. **2** person who changes his voice, manner, etc to match his surroundings.

cham·ois /ˈʃæmi/ *n* (*pl* unchanged) **1** [C] small animal like a goat that lives in the high mountains of Europe and Southwestern Asia. **2** (also **chammy**) [U] soft leather made from the skin of the chamois or from sheepskin.

champ[1] /tʃæmp/ *vt,vi* (of horses) bite (food, the bit) noisily. ***champ at the bit,*** (*fig*) be impatient to start something.

champ[2] /tʃæmp/ *n* [C] (*informal*) (short for) champion(2).

cham·pagne /ʃæmˈpein/ *n* [C,U] (kinds of) white sparkling French wine.

cham·pion /ˈtʃæmpiən/ *n* [C] **1** person who fights, argues or speaks in support of another or of a cause: *a ~ of free speech/of woman's rights.* **2** person, team, animal, etc taking the first place in a competition: *a ˈboxing/ˈtennis ~.* □ *vt* support; defend.

cham·pion·ship *n* **(a)** [U] act of championing. **(b)** [C] position of a champion.

chance[1] /tʃæns/ *n* **1** [U] the happening of events without any cause that can be seen or understood; the way things happen; fortune or luck: *Let's leave it to ~.* ***by chance,*** unexpectedly, not by design or on purpose. ***take one's chance(s),*** trust to luck, take whatever happens to come. **2** [C,U] possibility: *He has no/not much ~/a poor ~ of winning. The ~s are that you'll lose.* **3** [C] opportunity: *It's the ~ of a lifetime,* a favorable opportunity that is unlikely ever to come again. ***stand a (good, fair) chance (of...),*** have a (fair) hope (of...). □ *adj* coming or happening by chance (1): *a ~ meeting.*

chance[2] /tʃæns/ *vi,vt* **1** find, happen or meet by chance: *I ~d to be there.* **2** risk. ***chance it,*** (*informal*) take a risk.

chan·cel /ˈtʃænsəl/ *n* [C] eastern part of a church, around the altar, used by the priest(s) and choir.

chan·cel·lor /ˈtʃæns(ə)lər/ *n* [C] **1** (in some countries, eg Germany) chief minister of state. **2** (in some countries) high state official. **3** (of some universities) head or president.

chancy /ˈtʃænsi/ *adj* (-ier, -iest) (*informal*) risky; uncertain.

chan·de·lier /ˌʃændəˈlɪr/ *n* [C] branched support for a number of lights.

chan·dler /ˈtʃændlər/ *n* [C] **1** person who makes or sells candles, paint, etc. **2** **ship's ˈchandler,** dealer in canvas, ropes and other supplies for ships.

change[1] /tʃeindʒ/ *n* **1** [C] changed or different condition(s); thing used in place of another or others: *a welcome ~ from town to country life. Take a ~ of clothes with you,* extra clothes to put on. ***a change of air/climate,*** eg a holiday away from home. **2** [U] money in small(er) units; money that is the difference between the cost and the amount given: *Can you give me ~ for a dollar? Don't leave your ~ on the counter!* **3** [C,U] alteration; changing: *Let's hope there will be a ~ in the weather.* ***for a change,*** for the sake of variety; to be different from one's routine: *Why not pay for me for a ~?*

change[2] /tʃeindʒ/ *vt,vi* **1** make or become different: *That has ~d my ideas. The wind has ~d from north to east.* ***change one's mind,*** decide on a new plan, have a new opinion, etc. **2** take off something and put something else on: *It won't take me five minutes to ~,* to put on different clothes. **3** give and receive in return; exchange: *He ~d his Italian money before leaving Rome. I ~d places with her.* **4** transfer from one train, bus, etc to another: *~d planes in Chicago.*

change·able *adj* likely to alter; able to be changed: *~able weather.*

chan·nel /ˈtʃænəl/ *n* [C] **1** stretch of water joining two seas; *the English Channel,* between France and England. **2** natural or artificial bed of a stream of water; passage along which a liquid may flow. **3** (*fig*) any way by which news, ideas, etc may travel: *He gets his information through secret ~s.* **4** band of radio or TV frequencies within which signals from a transmitter must be kept. □ *vt* (-l-, -ll-) **1** form a channel in; cut out (a way): *The river had ~led its way through the soft rock.* **2** cause to go through channels.

chant /tʃænt/ *n* [C] **1** melody in which several syllables or words are sung on one note (as in a psalm or prayer). **2** rhythmic way of speaking. □ *vi,vt* sing; sing or intone a chant.

chan·ti·cleer /ˈtʃæntəˌklɪr/ *n* [C] (*liter*) rooster.

chaos /ˈkeiˌas/ *n* [U] complete absence of order or shape; confusion: *The room was in complete ~ when the burglars had left.*

cha·otic /keiˈatɪk/ *adj* in a state of chaos; confused.

cha·oti·cally /-kli/ *adv*

chap[1] /tʃæp/ *vt,vi* (-pp-) **1** (of the skin) become sore, rough, cracked: *My skin soon ~s in cold weather.* **2** cause to become cracked or rough: *hands and face ~ped by the cold.* □ *n* [C] crack, esp in the skin.

chap[2] *abbr* = chapter(1).

chapel /ˈtʃæpəl/ *n* [C] **1** place (not a parish church) used for Christian worship, eg in a school, prison, etc. **2** small place within a Christian church, used for private prayer, with an altar. **3** service held in a chapel.

chap·er·on /ˈʃæpəˌroun/ *n* [C] married or elderly person (usually a woman) in charge of a girl or young unmarried woman on social occasions. □ *vt* act as a chaperon to.

chap·lain /ˈtʃæplən/ *n* [C] priest or clergyman, esp in the armed forces.

chaps /ʃæps/ *n pl* leather leggings worn esp by cowboys or ranch hands. ⇨ illus at cowboy.

chap·ter /ˈtʃæptər/ *n* [C] **1** (usually numbered) division of a book. ***chapter and verse,*** exact reference. **2** period: *the most brilliant ~ in our history.* **3** group, branch, organization or assembly: *a ~ of a fraternity at the college; a ~ of canons at a cathedral.*

char /tʃar/ *vt,vi* (-rr-) make or become black by

burning: *~red wood.*
char·ac·ter /ˈkærɪktər/ *n* **1** [U] nature; features or qualities that make a person, country, etc different from others: *a woman of fine/strong/noble, etc ~; the ~ of the French.* ***in/out of character,*** appropriate/inappropriate to a person's known character. **2** [U] moral strength; reputation: *a man of ~.* **3** person in a novel, play, etc: *the ~s in the novels of Henry James.* **4** odd or unusual person. **5** [C] letter, sign, mark, etc used in a system of writing or printing: *Greek/Chinese ~s.*
char·ac·ter·less /-lɪs/ *adj* undistinguished; ordinary.
char·ac·ter·is·tic /ˌkærɪktəˈrɪstɪk/ *adj* forming part of, showing, the known character of: *It's so ~ of him.* □ *n* [C] special mark or quality.
ˌchar·ac·ter·ˈis·ti·cally /-kli/ *adv*
char·ac·ter·ize /ˈkærɪktəˌraiz/ *vt* show or mark in a special way: *Your work is ~d by lack of attention to detail.*
cha·rade /ʃəˈreid/ *n* [C] game in which a word is guessed by the onlookers after each syllable of it has been suggested by acting a little play.
char·coal /ˈtʃarˌkoul/ *n* [U] black substance, used as fuel, for drawing, etc, made by burning wood slowly in an oven with little air.
charge[1] /tʃardʒ/ *n* [C] **1** accusation; statement that a person has done wrong, esp that he has broken a law. ***bring a charge against sb,*** accuse him of (a crime). **2** sudden and violent attack at high speed (by soldiers, animals, a football player, etc). **3** price asked for goods or services: *hotel ~s.* **4** amount of powder, etc (to be) used in a gun or for causing an explosion; quantity of energy (to be) contained in an electrical battery, etc: *a positive/negative ~.* **5** [C,U] care, responsibility. ***in charge (of),*** having control (over) or responsibility (for): *In the supervisor's absence, his assistant is in ~. Mary was in ~ of the baby.* ***take charge of,*** be responsible for. **6** instructions: *the judge's ~ to the jury,* instructions concerning their duty (in reaching a verdict).
charge[2] /tʃardʒ/ *vt,vi* **1** accuse; bring a charge (1) against: *He was ~d with murder.* **2** rush forward (and attack): *The wounded lion suddenly ~d at me.* **3** ask in payment: *He ~d me fifty cents for it.* **4** record or put down as a debt to be paid later: *Charge the shoes to my account.* **5** load (a gun); fill, put a charge(4) into: *~ a battery.* **6** ***charge with,*** give as a task or duty: *He was ~d with an important mission.* **7** (*formal*) command; instruct: *I ~ you not to forget what I have said.*
charge·able /ˈtʃardʒəbəl/ *adj*
ˈcharge account *n* [C] account kept by a seller (eg a department store) to which a customer may charge(4) goods.
char·iot /ˈtʃæriət/ *n* [C] horse-drawn vehicle with two wheels, used in ancient times in fighting and racing.
char·io·teer /ˌtʃæriəˈtɪr/ *n* [C] driver of a chariot.
cha·risma /kəˈrɪzmə/ *n* [C] (*pl* ~s) **1** spiritual grace. **2** (of a political leader, etc) great power to inspire devotion and popular enthusiasm. **3** charm; appeal.
char·is·matic /ˌkærɪzˈmætɪk/ *adj*
chari·table /ˈtʃærɪtəbəl/ *adj* showing, having, for, charity: *~ trusts.*
ˈchari·tably *adv*
char·ity /ˈtʃærəti/ *n* (*pl* -ies) **1** [U] (kindness in giving) help to the poor; money, food, etc so given. **2** [C] society or organization for helping the poor. **3** [U] willingness to judge other persons with kindness or love.
char·la·tan /ˈʃarlətən/ *n* [C] person who claims to have more skill, knowledge or ability than he really has.
charm /tʃarm/ *n* **1** [U] attractiveness; power to give pleasure. **2** [C] pleasing quality or feature: *Among her ~s were her beauty and grace.* **3** [C] thing believed to have magic power, good or bad: *a good-luck ~.* □ *vt,vi* **1** attract; give pleasure to: *We were ~ed with the scenery.* **2** use magic on; influence or protect as if by magic: *She ~ed away his sorrow.*
charm·ing *adj* delightful: *a ~ing young lady.*
charm·ing·ly *adv*
chart /tʃart/ *n* [C] **1** map used by sailors, showing the coasts, depth of the sea, position of rocks, lighthouses, etc. **2** sheet of paper with information, in the form of tables, diagrams, etc: *a ˈweather ~.* □ *vt* make a chart of; show on a chart.
char·ter /ˈtʃartər/ *n* [C] **1** (written or printed statement of) rights, permission esp from a ruler or government (eg to a town, city or university). **2** hiring or engagement (of an aircraft, a ship, etc): *a ˈ~ flight.* □ *vt* **1** give a charter to. **2** hire (space on) a ship, an aircraft, etc for an agreed time, purpose and payment.
char·woman /ˈtʃarˌwʊmən/ *n* [C] (*pl* -women /-ˌwɪmɪn/) woman who is hired to clean homes, offices, etc.
chary /ˈtʃæri/ *adj* (-ier, iest) cautious; careful: *~ of catching cold.*
char·ily /ˈtʃærəli/ *adv*
chase[1] /tʃeis/ *vt,vi* **1** run after in order to capture, kill, overtake or drive away: *Dogs like to ~ rabbits. Chase those boys off the grass.* **2** (*informal*) follow a strong alcoholic drink with a weaker one, to get rid of the taste of the first: *He drank straight vodka, chasing it with beer.* □ *n* [C] **1** act of chasing: *After a long ~, we caught the thief.* **2** hunted animal, person or thing being pursued.
chaser *n* [C] (*informal*) mildly alcoholic or non-alcoholic drink taken after a strong one.
chase[2] /tʃeis/ *vt* cut patterns or designs on; engrave: *~d silver.*
chasm /ˈkæzəm/ *n* [C] **1** deep opening or crack in the ground. **2** (*fig*) wide difference (of feeling or interests, between persons, groups, nations, etc).
chas·sis /ˈʃæsi/ *n* [C] (*pl* unchanged) framework of a motor vehicle, aircraft, etc on which the body is fastened or built.
chaste /tʃeist/ *adj* **1** virtuous in word, thought and deed. **2** (esp) abstaining from unlawful or immoral sexual intercourse. **3** (of style, taste) simple; refined.
chaste·ly *adv*
chas·ten /ˈtʃeisən/ *vt* **1** punish in order to correct. **2** make chaste(3).

chas·tise /tʃæˈstaiz/ *vt* punish severely.
chas·tise·ment *n* [U] punishment.
chas·tity /ˈtʃæstəti/ *n* [U] state of being chaste.
chat /tʃæt/ *n* [C] friendly, informal talk: *I had a long ~ with him.* □ *vi,vt* (-tt-) have a chat: *They were ~ting (away) in the corner.*
chatty *adj* (-ier, -iest) fond of chatting.
châ·teau /ʃæˈtou/ *n* [C] (*pl* ~s, ~x /-touz/) castle or large country house in France.
chat·tel /ˈtʃætəl/ *n* [C] (*legal*) article of personal movable property (eg a chair, a car).
chat·ter /ˈtʃætər/ *vi* **1** (of a person) talk quickly or foolishly; talk too much. **2** (of the cries of monkeys and some birds) make quick, indistinct sounds. **3** (of the teeth) strike together and rattle from cold or fear. □ *n* [U] sounds of the kind noted above: *the ~ of children.*
ˈchat·ter·box *n* person who chatters(1).
chauf·feur /ˌʃouˈfər/ *n* [C] man paid to drive a car.
chau·vin·ism /ˈʃouvəˌnɪzəm/ *n* [U] unreasoning enthusiasm for one's country, its military glory, one's sex, etc.
ˈchau·vin·ist *n* [C] person with such enthusiasm: *a male ~.*
chau·vin·is·tic /ˌʃouvəˈnɪstɪk/ *adj*
cheap /tʃip/ *adj* (-er, -est) **1** costing little money: *travel by the ~est route.* **2** worth more than the cost. **3** of poor quality: *The book's ~ binding soon fell apart.* **4** of little value: *~ emotion.*
cheap·ly *adv*
cheap·ness /-nɪs/ *n* [U]
cheapen /ˈtʃipən/ *vt,vi* make or become cheap; lower the price or quality of: *Don't ~ yourself.*
cheat /tʃit/ *vi,vt* act in a dishonest way to win an advantage or profit: *~ a person out of his money; ~ on an examination.* □ *n* [C] **1** person who cheats. **2** dishonest trick.
check¹ /tʃek/ *n* [C] **1** control; person or thing that checks or restrains: *Wind acts as a ~ on speed.* **2** examination to make certain of accuracy. **3** mark (usually written) to show that something has been proved to be correct. **4** written order to a bank to pay money: *a ~ for $10; pay by ~.* **5** receipt given temporarily in return for something handed over. **6** bill in a restaurant.
ˈcheck·book, number of blank checks fastened together.
ˈchecking account, account(1) with a bank from which the depositor can pay out money for bills, etc by writing a check.
check² /tʃek/ *vt,vi* **1** examine in order to learn whether something is correct: *Will you please ~ these figures?* ***check up on sb/sth,*** examine to see whether he/it is what is claimed. **2** hold back; cause to go slow or stop: *He couldn't ~ his anger.* **3** threaten an opponent's king in chess. **4** ***check in,*** arrive and register at a hotel, etc. ***check out,*** **(a)** pay one's bill and leave. **(b)** (of a store employee) add up cost of purchases and collect payment. **(c)** (*informal*) investigate whether a story etc is true or not. **(d)** (*informal*) (of a story etc) agree with the true facts.
checker *n* [C] **(a)** person who checks, esp an employee who checks out purchases in a store. **(b)** ⇨ checkers.
ˈcheck·out *n* [C] (esp) place (eg in a supermarket) where a cashier collects payment for one's purchases.
ˈcheck·up *n* [C] (esp a medical) examination.
check³ /tʃek/ *n* **1** pattern of crossed lines forming squares (often of different shades or colors); cloth with such a pattern.
checkers /ˈtʃekərz/ *n pl* (with a *sing verb*) game for two players with twelve pieces each (called ~), played on a board with sixty-four squares (called a *ˈcheckerboard*).
check·mate /ˈtʃekˌmeit/ *vt* **1** make a move in chess that prevents the opponent's king from being moved away from a direct attack (and so win the game). **2** (*fig*) obstruct and defeat (a person, his plans). □ *n* [C] complete defeat.
cheek /tʃik/ *n* **1** [C] either side of the face below the eye. ⇨ illus at head. **2** [U] impudence: *He had the ~ to ask me to do his work for him!*
ˈcheek·bone *n* [C] bone below the eye.
cheek·ily /ˈtʃikəli/ *adv*
cheeky *adj* (-ier, -iest) impudent.
cheep /tʃip/ *vi, n* (make a) weak, shrill note (as young birds do).
cheer¹ /tʃɪr/ *n* **1** [U] state of hope, gladness: *words of ~,* of encouragement. **2** [C] shout of joy or encouragement.
cheer² /tʃɪr/ *vt,vi* **1** fill with gladness, hope, high spirits; comfort: *Your visit has really ~ed me (up).* **2** take comfort, become happy: *He ~ed up when I promised to go.* **3** give shouts of joy, approval or encouragement: *The speaker was loudly ~ed.*
cheer·ing *n* [U] *The ~ing could be heard half a mile away.* □ *adj: That's ~ing news.*
cheer·ful /ˈtʃɪrfəl/ *adj* **1** bringing or suggesting happiness: *a ~ day/room/smile.* **2** happy and contented; willing: *~ workers.*
cheer·ful·ly *adv*
cheer·ful·ness /-nɪs/ *n* [U]
cheer·less /ˈtʃɪrlɪs/ *adj* without comfort; gloomy; miserable: *a wet and ~ day.*
cheery /ˈtʃɪri/ *adj* (-ier, -iest) lively; merry: *a ~ smile/greeting.*
cheer·ily /ˈtʃɪrəli/ *adv*
cheese /tʃiz/ *n* **1** [C,U] kinds of solid food made from milk curds. **2** [C] cut or shaped portion of this.
ˈcheese·cloth *n* thin cotton cloth (gauze) put round some kinds of cheese.
chee·tah /ˈtʃitə/ *n* [C] kind of leopard.
chef /ʃef/ *n* [C] (*pl* ~s) head male cook in a hotel, restaurant, etc.
chemi·cal /ˈkemɪkəl/ *adj* of, made by, chemistry: *~ warfare,* using poison gas, smoke, etc. □ *n* [C] (often *pl*) substance used in, or obtained by, chemistry.
chem·ical·ly /-kli/ *adv*
chem·ist /ˈkemɪst/ *n* [C] person who is expert in chemistry.
chem·is·try /ˈkemɪstri/ *n* [U] branch of science that deals with what substances are made of, how they (their elements) combine, how they act under different conditions.
cher·ish /ˈtʃerɪʃ/ *vt* **1** care for tenderly. **2** keep alive (hope, ambition, feelings, etc) in one's heart: *For years she ~ed the hope that her hus-*

band might still be alive.

Cher·o·kee /ˈtʃerəki/ *n* [C,U], *adj* (*pl* unchanged or ~s) **1** (member) of a tribe of American Indians originally from Tennessee and North Carolina. **2** (of) the language of these people.

cherry /ˈtʃeri/ *n* [C] (*pl* -ies) (tree with) soft, small, round fruit, red, yellow or black when ripe and with a stone-like seed in the middle. ⇨ illus at fruit. □ *adj* bright red: *~ lips*.

cherub /ˈtʃerəb/ *n* [C] **1 (a)** (*pl* ~s) small beautiful child. **(b)** (in art) such a child with wings. **2** (*pl* ~im /-bɪm/) one of the second highest order of angels.

chess /tʃes/ *n* [U] game for two players with sixteen pieces each (called ˈ*~men* /-ˌmen/), on a board with sixty-four squares (called a ˈ*~board*).

chest /tʃest/ *n* [C] **1** large, strong (usually wooden) box with a lid for storing things. **2** upper front part of the body, enclosed by the ribs, containing the heart and lungs. ⇨ illus at trunk. ***get sth off one's chest,*** (*sl*) say what one is anxious to say.

ˌchest of ˈdrawers, large chest (1) with drawers for clothes.

chest·nut /ˈtʃesˌnət/ *n* **1** [C,U] tree with smooth, bright reddish-brown nut (some being edible). **2** color of the nut. **3** [C] the nut of this tree. **4** [U] its wood. **5** [C] horse of this color. □ *adj* reddish-brown.

chew /tʃu/ *vt,vi* crush or grind (food, etc) esp with the teeth: *Chew your food well before you swallow it*. ***chew sb out,*** (*sl*) reprimand (esp somebody of lower rank or position, eg in the military service). ***chew the fat/rag,*** (*sl*) chat, gossip at length. □ *n* act of chewing; thing to chew.

ˈchewing gum, sticky substance sweetened and flavored for chewing.

ˌchewing ˈout, (*sl*) reprimand: *The Captain gave him a ~ing out*.

chewy /ˈtʃui/ *adj* (-ier, -iest) (of food) having a firmness between hard and soft; capable of being chewed.

chic /ʃik/ *n* [U] (of clothes, their wearer) style that gives an air of superior excellence. □ *adj* stylish.

Chi·cano /tʃiˈkanou/ *n* [C] (*pl* ~s) American of Mexican descent.

chick /tʃɪk/ *n* [C] **1** young bird, esp a young chicken. **2** small child. **3** (*sl*) girl.

chick·a·dee /ˈtʃɪkəˌdi/ *n* [C] small grayish bird with, usually, black feathers on its head.

chicken /ˈtʃɪkən/ *n* **1** [C] young bird, esp a young hen. ***(Don't) count one's chickens before they are hatched,*** (*prov*) (don't) be too hopeful of one's chances of success, etc. **2** [U] its flesh as food. □ *adj* (*sl*) cowardly.

ˈchicken·hearted *adj* lacking in courage.

ˈchicken pox, disease producing red spots on the skin.

chicle /ˈtʃɪkəl/ *n* [U] gummy substance that is the chief ingredient of chewing gum.

chic·ory /ˈtʃɪkəri/ *n* [U] **1** plant used as a vegetable and in salads. **2** the root roasted and made into a powder (used with or instead of coffee).

chide /tʃaid/ *vt,vi* (*pt* ~d or chid /tʃɪd/, *pp* ~d) scold; blame.

chief /tʃif/ *n* [C] **1** leader or ruler: *the ~ of the tribe*. ⇨ chieftain. **2** head of a department; highest official. □ adj **1** principal; most important: *the ~ thing to remember*. **2** first in rank: *the Chief Justice*.

chief·ly *adv* **1** above all; first of all. **2** mostly; mainly.

-in-ˈchief *adj* supreme: *the Commander-in-~*.

chief·tain /ˈtʃiftən/ *n* [C] chief of esp an Indian tribe.

chig·ger /ˈtʃɪgər/ *n* [C] larva of certain mites that sucks blood and causes severe itching.

chi·gnon /ˈʃinˌyan/ *n* [C] (*F*) knot or roll of hair worn at the back of the head by women.

child /ˈtʃaiəld/ *n* [C] (*pl* children /ˈtʃɪldrən/) **1** young human being. **2** son or daughter (of any age).

ˈchild·birth *n* [U] the process of giving birth to a child.

ˈchild·hood *n* [U] state or time of being a child.

ˈchild·ish *adj* of, behaving like, suitable for, a child: *~ish games/arguments*.

child·less *adj* having no child(ren).

ˈchild·like *adj* simple, innocent.

ˈchild's play, something very easily done.

chili /ˈtʃɪli/ *n* [C,U] **1** dried pod of red pepper, often made into powder and used to give a hot flavor. **2** (also **chili con carne** /ˌtʃɪli kan ˈkarni/) dish of chopped meat cooked with chili and, usually, kidney beans.

chill /tʃɪl/ *n* **1** (*sing* only) unpleasant feeling of coldness: *There's quite a ~ in the air this morning*. **2** (*sing* only) (*fig*) something that causes a downhearted feeling: *The bad news cast a ~ over the gathering*. **3** [C] illness caused by cold and damp, with shivering of the body. □ adj unpleasantly cold: *a ~ breeze; a ~ greeting*. □ *vt,vi* make or become cold or cool: *He was ~ed to the bone*, very cold.

chilly *adj* (-ier, -iest) **1** rather cold: *feel ~y*. **2** (*fig*) unfriendly: *a ~y welcome*.

chime /tʃaim/ *n* [C] (series of notes sounded by a) tuned set of bells. □ *vi,vt* **1** (of bells, a clock) (make) ring: *The bells are chiming*. **2** ***chime in,*** break in on or join in the talk of others: *"Of course," he ~d in*.

chim·ney /ˈtʃɪmni/ *n* [C] **1** structure through which smoke from a fire is carried away from a building. **2** glass tube around the flame of an oil lamp.

ˈchimney·pot *n* [C] pipe fitted to the top of a chimney(1).

ˈchimney sweep, man or boy who sweeps soot from chimneys.

ˈchimney swift, small North American bird with long, narrow wings, that nests in unused chimneys.

chimp /tʃɪmp/ *n* (*informal*) (short for) chimpanzee.

chim·pan·zee /ˌtʃɪmpænˈzi/ *n* [C] African ape, smaller than a gorilla. ⇨ illus at ape.

chin /ˈtʃɪn/ *n* [C] part of the face below the mouth; front of the lower jaw. ⇨ illus at head. □ *vt, vi* (-nn-) pull oneself up when hanging by one's hands (as from an overhead bar) until the chin is level with the hands.

china /ˈtʃainə/ *n* [U] **1** baked and glazed fine white clay. **2** articles (eg cups, saucers, plates) made from this.

chin·chilla /tʃɪnˈtʃɪlə/ *n* **1** [C] small South American animal that looks like a squirrel. **2** [U] its soft gray fur.

chink[1] /tʃɪŋk/ *n* [C] narrow opening or crack.

chink[2] /tʃɪŋk/ *vt,vi, n* [U] (make or cause the) sound of coins, glasses, etc striking together.

chintz /tʃɪnts/ *n* [U] cheap kind of printed cloth, usually in gaudy colors.

chintzy *adj* (*informal*) **(a)** gaudy, cheap looking. **(b)** (*sl*) stingy.

chip /tʃɪp/ *n* [C] **1** small piece cut or broken off (from wood, stone, china, glass, etc). ***a chip off the old block,*** (*informal*) similar in looks, actions, etc to one's parent(s). ***have a chip on one's shoulder,*** resent or exaggerate prejudice against oneself. ***in the chips,*** (*sl*) suddenly or temporarily wealthy. **2** thin slice of food: *potato ~s.* **3** place (eg in a cup) from which a chip has come. **4** flat plastic counter used as money (esp in gambling). □ *vt,vi* (-pp-) **1** cut or break (a piece off or from): *He ~ped the ice off the steps.* **2** break off in chips: *These cups ~ easily.* **3** ***chip in,*** (*informal*) contribute money (to a fund).

chip·munk /ˈtʃɪpˌmənk/ *n* [C] small striped animal resembling a squirrel, found in North America.

chip·per /ˈtʃɪpər/ *adj* lively, vigorous (esp of old people).

chip·ping spar·row /ˈtʃɪpɪŋ ˌspærou/ *n* [C] small North American sparrow.

chi·rop·odist /kəˈrapədɪst/ *n* [C] person who is expert in the treatment of the feet.

chi·rop·ody /kəˈrapədi/ *n* [U] work of a chiropodist.

chi·ro·prac·tor /ˈkairəˌpræktər/ *n* [C] person who performs physical therapy by manipulating the spine and joints.

chirp /tʃərp/ *vi,vt, n* [C] (make) short, sharp note(s) or sound(s) (as of small birds or insects).

chir·rup /ˈtʃɪrəp/ *vt, n* [C] (make a) series of chirps.

chisel /ˈtʃɪzəl/ *n* [C] steel tool used for shaping wood, stone or metal. □ *vt* (-l-, -ll-) **1** cut or shape with a chisel. **2** (*informal*) cheat.

chisel·er *n* [C] (*informal*) cheat(er).

chit /tʃɪt/ *n* [C] **1** young child. **2** young saucy woman.

chit-chat /ˈtʃɪtˌtʃæt/ *n* [U] light, informal conversation.

chit·terlings, chit·lins /ˈtʃɪtlɪnz/ *n pl* small intestines of the pig, cooked as a food.

chiv·alry /ˈʃɪvəlri/ *n* [U] **1** laws and customs (religious, moral and social) of the knights in the Middle Ages. **2** qualities of a knight (such as courage, honor, courtesy, loyalty, devotion to the weak and helpless, to the service of women).

chiv·al·rous /ˈʃɪvəlrəs/ *adj*

chloro·form /ˈklɔrəˌfɔrm/ *n* [U] thin, colorless liquid given as an anesthetic. □ *vt* give chloroform to.

chloro·phyll /ˈklɔrəˌfɪl/ *n* [U] green coloring matter in the leaves of plants.

choc·olate /ˈtʃaklɪt, ˈtʃɔk-/ *n* **1** [U] substance (powder or bar) made from the crushed seeds of the cacao tree. **2** [C,U] drink made by mixing this with hot water or milk. **3** [C,U] candy made from this: *a bar of ~; a box of ~s.* **4** the color of this substance, dark brown. □ *adj* dark brown.

choice /tʃɔis/ *n* **1** [C] act of choosing: *take your ~.* **2** [U] power or possibility of choosing: *I have no ~ in the matter,* must act in this way. **3** [C] variety from which to choose: *This shop has a large ~ of bags.* **4** [C] person or thing chosen: *This is my ~.* □ *adj* unusually good: *~ fruit.*

choir /ˈkwaiər/ *n* [C] **1** company of persons trained to sing together, esp to lead the singing in church. **2** part of a church building for the choir.

choke[1] /tʃouk/ *vi,vt* **1** (cause to) stop breathing or breathe with difficulty because of something blocking the windpipe, because of emotion, by squeezing the throat, or by making the air unfit to breathe: *~ over one's food; ~ with anger. Heavy black smoke ~d the firemen.* **2** fill, partly or completely, a passage, space, etc that is usually clear: *a drain ~d (up) with dirt.* **3** ***choke sth back/down,*** hold or keep back/down: *~ back one's tears.* **4** cut off or lower the air intake of a gasoline engine.

choke[2] /tʃouk/ *n* [C] valve in a gasoline engine to control the intake of air.

choke·cherry /ˈtʃoukˌtʃeri/ *n* [C,U] (*pl* -ies) North American shrub or small tree that bears clusters of white flowers and bitter wild cherries.

chol·era /ˈkalərə/ *n* [U] infectious and often fatal disease, common in hot countries.

choose /tʃuz/ *vt,vi* (*pt* chose /tʃouz/, *pp* chosen /ˈtʃouzən/) pick out from a greater number; select: *She took a long time to ~ a new dress.* decide; be pleased or determined: *He chose to stay where he was.*

choosy /ˈtʃuzi/ *adj* (-ier, -iest) (*informal*) (of persons) careful and cautious in choosing; difficult to please.

chop[1] /tʃap/ *n* [C] **1** chopping blow. **2** thick slice of meat with the bone in it. **3** short, quick movement.

chop[2] /tʃap/ *vt,vi* (-pp-) cut into pieces by blow(s) with an axe, etc: *Meat is often ~ped up before being cooked. I'm going to ~ that tree down.*

chop·per /ˈtʃapər/ *n* [C] **1** heavy tool with a sharp edge for chopping meat, wood, etc. **2** (*sl*) helicopter.

choppy /ˈtʃapi/ *adj* (-ier, -iest) **1** (of the sea) moving in short, broken irregular waves. **2** (of the wind) continually changing.

chops /tʃaps/ *n pl* jaws and the flesh that covers them.

chop·sticks /ˈtʃapˌstɪks/ *n pl* pair of sticks (of wood, ivory, etc) used by Chinese and Japanese for lifting food to the mouth.

choral /ˈkɔrəl/ *adj* of, for, sung by or together with, a choir: *a ˈ~ society.*

chorale /kəˈræl/ *n* [C] simple hymn tune, usually sung in unison.

chord /ˈkɔrd/ *n* [C] **1** straight line that joins two points on the circumference of a circle or the ends of an arc. ⇨ illus at circle. **2** combination

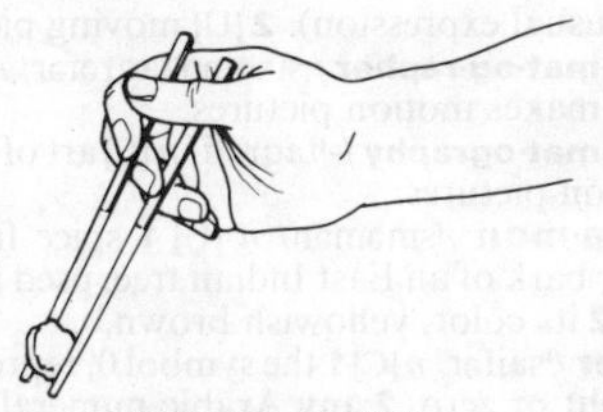

CHOPSTICKS

of three or more musical notes sounded together in harmony.

chore /tʃɔr/ *n* [C] **1** small duty or piece of work, esp an ordinary everyday task (eg in the home). **2** unpleasant task.

chor·eogra·phy /ˌkɔriˈagrəfi/ *n* [U] art of designing ballet and other dance patterns.

chor·eogra·pher *n* [C]

cho·ris·ter /ˈkɔrəstər/ *n* [C] member of a chorus.

chorus /ˈkɔrəs/ *n* [C] (*pl* ~es) **1** (music for a) group of singers. **2** (part of a) song for all to sing (after solo verses): *Mr. White sang the verses and everybody joined in the* ~. **3** something said or cried by many people together: *The proposal was greeted with a* ~ *of approval.* □ *vt* sing, speak, in chorus.

chose, chosen *pt,pp* of choose.

chow /tʃau/ *n* [U] (*sl*) food.

chow·der /ˈtʃaudər/ *n* [U] thick soup or stew made of fish, clams, or vegetables, usually cooked with milk.

christen /ˈkrɪsən/ *vt* **1** = baptize. **2** give a name to (a new ship when it is launched).

CHURCH ARCHITECTURE

ˈchristen·ing *n* [C] ceremony of baptizing or naming.

Christen·dom /ˈkrɪsəndəm/ *n* [U] all Christian people and Christian countries.

Chris·tian /ˈkrɪstʃən/ *adj* **1** of Jesus Christ and his teaching. **2** of the religion, beliefs, church, etc based on this teaching. □ *n* [C] person believing in the religion of Christ.

ˈChristian name, name given at baptism; forename.

Chris·ti·an·ity /ˌkrɪstʃiˈænəti/ *n* [U] the Christian faith, religion, or character.

Christ·mas /ˈkrɪsməs/ *n* [C] (also **ˌChristmas ˈDay**) yearly celebration of the birth of Jesus Christ, Dec. 25: *the* ~ *holidays*.

ˈChristmas card, sent as a greeting to friends at Christmas.

ˈChristmas tree, (usually evergreen) tree set up and decorated at Christmas.

chrome /kroum/ *n* [U] **1** coloring matter used in paints, etc. **2** = chromium.

chro·mium /ˈkroumiəm/ *n* [U] element (symbol **Cr**) used to plate other metals and in making stainless steel, etc.

chro·mo·some /ˈkrouməˌsoum/ *n* [C] one of the tiny threads in every nucleus in animal and plant cells, carrying genes.

chronic /ˈkranɪk/ *adj* (of a disease or condition) continual, lasting for a long time: ~ *rheumatism; a* ~ *illness.* ⇨ acute(2)

chroni·cally /-kli/ *adv*

chron·icle /ˈkranɪkəl/ *n* [C] record of events in the order of their happening. □ *vt* make a chronicle of; record.

chrono·logi·cal /ˌkranəˈladʒɪkəl/ *adj* in order of time: *Shakespeare's plays in* ~ *order*, in the order in which they were written.

chrono·logi·cal·ly /-kli/ *adv*

chron·ol·ogy /krəˈnalədʒi/ *n* (*pl* -ies) **1** [U] science of fixing dates. **2** [C] arrangement or list of events in the order of their occurrence.

chro·nometer /krəˈnamətər/ *n* [C] kind of watch that keeps very accurate time.

chrysa·lis /ˈkrɪsəlɪs/ *n* [C] (*pl* ~es) **1** form taken by an insect between the time when it creeps or crawls as a larva and the time when it flies as a

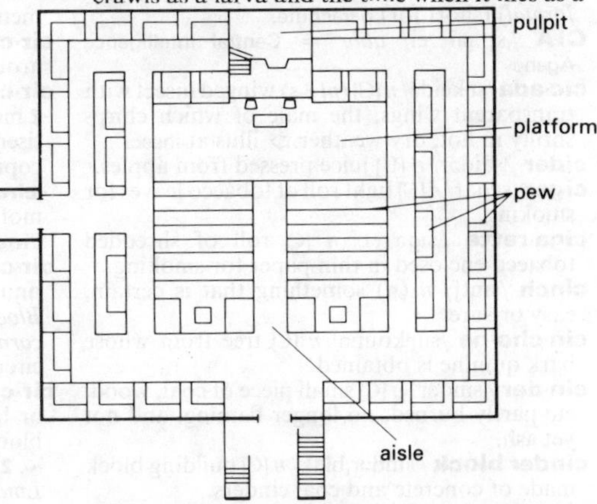

CONGREGATIONALIST CHURCH

moth, butterfly, etc. **2** the sheath or case that covers it during this time.

chry·san·the·mum /krɪˈsænθəməm/ *n* [C] (*pl* ~s) (flower of a) garden plant blooming in late summer and autumn.

chubby /ˈtʃəbi/ *adj* (-ier, -iest) plump: *~ cheeks.*

chuck[1] /tʃək/ *vt* (*informal*) **1** throw: *Let's ~ out* (= throw away) *the old cooker.* **2** pat: *~ed the baby under the chin.*

chuck[2] /tʃək/ *n* [C] part of a lathe which grips the work to be operated on; part which grips the bit on a drill.

chuck·hole /ˈtʃəkˌhoul/ *n* [C] hole or rut in a road.

chuckle /ˈtʃəkəl/ *n* [C] low, quiet laugh (indicating satisfaction or amusement). □ *vt* laugh in this way: *He was chuckling to himself.*

chuck wagon /ˈtʃəkˌwægən/ *n* [C] wagon made into a kitchen, for feeding cowhands, lumberjacks, etc at their place of work.

chug /tʃəg/ *vi* (-gg-) make the short explosive sound (of an engine running slowly): *The boat ~ged along.* □ *n* [C] this sound.

chum /tʃəm/ *n* [C] close friend (esp among boys). □ *vi* (-mm-) ***chum around (with sb),*** to be close friends (with).

chummy *adj* (-ier, -iest) friendly.

chump /tʃəmp/ *n* [C] (*sl*) fool.

chunk /tʃəŋk/ *n* [C] thick, solid piece or lump of bread, meat, cheese etc.

chunky *adj* (-ier, -iest) short and thick.

church /tʃərtʃ/ *n* **1** [C] building for public Christian worship. **2** [U] service in such a building: *What time does ~ begin?* **3** [C] organized group of Christians: *the Methodist Church.*

ˈchurch·goer *n* [C] person who goes to church regularly.

ˈchurch·yard *n* [C] yard around a church, often used as a cemetery.

churn /tʃərn/ *n* [C] container in which cream is shaken or beaten to make butter. □ *vt,vi* **1** make (butter) in a churn. **2** stir or move about violently: *The ship's propellers ~ed up the waves.*

chute /ʃut/ *n* [C] **1** long, narrow, steep slope down which things may slide: *a mail ~.* **2** smooth, rapid fall of water over a slope. **3** (*informal*) (short for) parachute.

CIA /ˌsi ˌai ˈei/ *abbr* = Central Intelligence Agency.

cic·ada /sɪˈkeidə/ *n* [C] (*pl* ~s) winged insect with transparent wings, the male of which chirps shrilly in hot, dry weather. ⇨ illus at insect.

cider /ˈsaidər/ *n* [U] juice pressed from apples.

cigar /sɪˈgar/ *n* [C] tight roll of tobacco leaves for smoking.

ciga·rette /ˌsɪgəˈret/ *n* [C] roll of shredded tobacco enclosed in thin paper for smoking.

cinch /sɪntʃ/ *n* (*sl*) something that is certain, easy or sure.

cin·cho·na /sɪŋˈkounə/ *n* [C] tree from whose bark quinine is obtained.

cin·der /ˈsɪndər/ *n* [C] small piece of coal, wood, etc partly burned, no longer flaming, and not yet ash.

cinder block /ˈsɪndərˌblak/ *n* [C] building block made of concrete and coal cinders.

cin·ema /ˈsɪnəmə/ *n* **1** [C] motion picture theater (the usual expression). **2** [U] moving pictures.

cin·emat·og·rapher /ˌsɪnəməˈtagrəfər/ *n* [C] one who makes motion pictures.

cin·emat·ography /-ˈtagrəfi/ *n* [C] art of making motion pictures.

cin·na·mon /ˈsɪnəmən/ *n* [U] **1** spice from the inner bark of an East Indian tree, used in cooking. **2** its color, yellowish brown.

cipher /ˈsaifər/ *n* [C] **1** the symbol 0, representing nought or zero. **2** any Arabic numeral, 1 to 9. **3** (*fig*) person or thing of no importance. **4** (method of, key to) secret writing: *a message in ~.* □ *vt,vi* put into secret writing.

circa /ˈsərkə/ *prep* (*Lat*) = about (before a date) (usually shortened to **ca.**): *born ~ 150* BC.

circle /ˈsərkəl/ *n* [C] **1** space enclosed by a curved line, every point on which is the same distance from the center; the line enclosing this space. **2** ring: *a ~ of trees; standing in a ~.* **3** set of seats in curved rows in a theater or hall. **4** number of persons bound together by having the same or similar interests: *He has a large ~ of friends.* □ *vt,vi* move in a circle; go around: *The aircraft ~d (over) the landing field.*

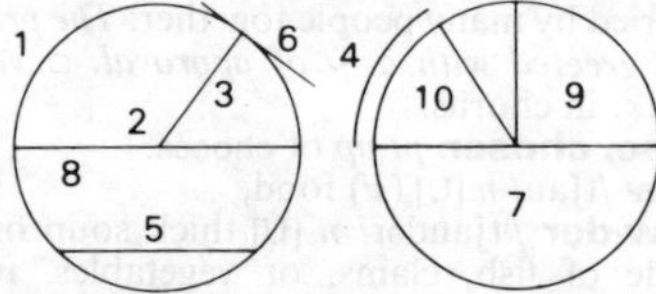

1 CIRCUMFERENCE 2 CENTER 3 RADIUS
4 ARC 5 CHORD 6 TANGENT 7 SEMICIRCLE
8 DIAMETER 9 QUADRANT 10 SECTOR

PARTS OF A CIRCLE

cir·cuit /ˈsərkɪt/ *n* [C] **1** boundary or distance around an area: *The ~ of the racing track is three miles.* **2** motion around in a circular path: *the ~ of the planets around the sun.* **3** travel along a regular route in the performance of one's duties: *a ~ judge.* **4** closed path for an electrical current; apparatus for using an electric current: *~ diagram,* one that shows the connections in such an apparatus. ⇨ short[1]. **5** chain of theaters, etc under a single management.

cir·cu·itous /sərˈkyuətəs/ *adj* going a long way around; indirect: *a ~ route.*

cir·cu·lar /ˈsərkyələr/ *adj* **1** round like a circle. **2** moving around. □ *n* [C] printed letter, advertisement, announcement, etc of which many copies are made and sent around.

ˌcircular ˈsaw, saw with the cutting edge on a motor-driven disc. ⇨ illus at saw.

cir·cu·lar·ize /ˈsərkyələˌraiz/ *vt* send circulars to.

cir·cu·late /ˈsərkyəˌleit/ *vi,vt* **1** go around continuously; move from place to place freely: *Blood ~s through the body. Don't stand in the corner—~ among the other guests.* **2** cause to circulate: *I'll ~ this book among you.*

cir·cu·la·tion /ˌsərkyəˈleiʃən/ *n* **1** [U] circulating or being circulated, esp the movement of the blood from and to the heart: *He has good/poor ~.* **2** [U] state of being circulated: *When were the Lincoln pennies put into ~?* **3** [C] number of copies of a newspaper or other periodical sold to the public during a certain time.

cir·cum·cise /ˈsərkəmˌsaiz/ *vt* remove the foreskin of (a male).

cir·cum·ci·sion /ˌsərkəmˈsɪʒən/ *n* [C,U]

cir·cum·fer·ence /sərˈkəmf(ə)rəns/ *n* [C] **1** line that marks out a circle or other curved figure. ⇨ illus at circle. **2** distance around: *The ~ of the earth is almost 25,000 miles.*

cir·cum·flex /ˈsərkəmˌfleks/ *n* [C] mark (ˆ) placed over a vowel to indicate how it is to be sounded (as in French *rôle*).

cir·cum·navi·gate /ˌsərkəmˈnævəˌgeit/ *vt* sail around (esp the world).

cir·cum·navi·ga·tion /ˌsərkəmˌnævəˈgeiʃən/ *n* [C,U]

cir·cum·stance /ˈsərkəmˌstæns/ *n* [C] **1** (usually *pl*) conditions, facts, etc connected with an event or person: *Don't judge the crime until you know the ~s.* ***in/under the circumstances,*** such being the state of affairs. ***in/under no circumstances,*** never. **2** fact or detail: *He has plenty of money, which is a fortunate ~.* **3** (*pl*) financial condition.

cir·cum·stan·tial /ˌsərkəmˈstænʃəl/ *adj* **1** (of a description) giving full details. **2** (of evidence) based on or consisting of details that suggest strongly but do not provide direct proof.

cir·cum·vent /ˌsərkəmˈvent/ *vt* **1** gain advantage over; defeat (a person's plans). **2** prevent (a plan) from being carried out; find a way to get around (a law, rule, etc).

cir·cum·ven·tion /ˌsərkəmˈvenʃən/ *n* [C,U]

cir·cus /ˈsərkəs/ *n* [C] (*pl* ~es) **1** (round or oval) place, often covered by a tent, with seats on all sides for (in modern times) a show of performing animals, acrobats, etc. **2** persons and animals giving such a show.

cir·rus /ˈsɪrəs/ *n* [C] filmy cloud, formed in the highest cloud region of the sky.

cis·tern /ˈsɪstərn/ *n* [C] (often underground) tank for storing water.

cita·del /ˈsɪtədəl, -ˌdel/ *n* [C] **1** fortress. **2** strong, safe place.

ci·ta·tion /saiˈteiʃən/ *n* **1** [U] citing. **2** [C] (esp) a statement, that is cited.

cite /sait/ *vt* **1** give or mention as an example (esp by quoting from a book, to support an argument, etc). **2** (*legal*) summon to appear before a court. **3** mention or refer to, esp to praise: *She was ~d as an outstanding example.*

citi·zen /ˈsɪtəzən, -sən/ *n* [C] **1** person who has full rights in a state or nation, either by birth or by gaining such rights: *immigrants who have become ~s of the United States.* **2** person who lives permanently in a place: *the ~s of Paris.*

ˈciti·zen·ry *n* (*collect*) (*pl* -ries) citizens as a group or body.

ˈcitizen·ship *n* [U] being, rights and duties of, a citizen.

cit·ric acid /ˌsɪtrɪk ˈæsɪd/ *n* [U] acid from such fruits as lemons and limes.

cit·ron /ˈsɪtrən/ *n* **1** [C] (tree with) pale yellow fruit like a lemon but larger. **2** [U] its candied rind, used in fruitcake, pudding, etc.

cit·rous /ˈsɪtrəs/ *adj* of the citrus fruits.

cit·rus /ˈsɪtrəs/ *n* [C] (*pl* ~es) kinds of tree including the lemon, lime, citron, orange and grapefruit. □ *adj* of these trees: *ˈ~ fruit.*

city /ˈsɪti/ *n* [C] (*pl* -ies) **1** large and important town. **2** town given special rights in self-government. **3** people living in a city.

civic /ˈsɪvɪk/ *adj* of the official life and affairs of a town or a citizen: *~ pride; a ~ center.*

civ·ics /ˈsɪvɪks/ *n pl* (used with a *sing verb*) study of city government, the rights and duties of citizens, etc.

civil /ˈsɪvəl/ *adj* **1** of citizens. **2** of human society; of people living together: *We all have ~ rights and ~ duties.* **3** not of the armed forces. **4** polite: *Can't you be more ~?*

ˌcivil ˌengiˈneering, the design and building of roads, railways, canals, docks, etc.

ˌcivil ˈlaw, law dealing with private rights of citizens, not with crime.

civil·ly *adv* politely.

ˌcivil ˈrights, rights of a citizen to political, racial, legal, social freedom or equality.

ˌcivil ˈservant, official in the civil service.

the ˌcivil ˈservice, all government departments except the armed forces.

civil ˈwar, (a) war between opposing groups of the same country. **(b) the Civil War,** war (1861-1865) between the northern and southern states of the US.

ci·vil·ian /sɪˈvɪlyən/ *n* [C], *adj* (person) not serving with the armed forces: *In modern wars ~s as well as soldiers are killed.*

ci·vil·ity /sɪˈvɪləti/ *n* (*pl* -ies) **1** [U] politeness. **2** (*pl*) polite acts.

civi·li·za·tion /ˌsɪvəlɪˈzeiʃən/ *n* **1** [U] civilizing or being civilized; state of being civilized: *The ~ of mankind has taken thousands of years.* **2** [C] system, stage of, social development: *the ~s of ancient Egypt, Babylon and Persia.* **3** [U] civilized states collectively: *acts that horrified ~.*

civi·lize /ˈsɪvəˌlaiz/ *vt* **1** bring out of a savage or ignorant state (by education, moral teaching, etc). **2** improve and educate.

clack /klæk/ *vi, n* [U] (make the) short, sharp sound of objects struck together.

claim[1] /kleim/ *n* **1** [C] act of claiming(1,2): *His ~ to own the house is invalid.* **2** [C] sum of money demanded, eg under an insurance agreement: *make/put in a ~ (for a refund).* **3** [U] right to ask for: *You have no ~ on my sympathies.* **4** [C] something claimed; piece of land given to a miner, settler, etc. ***lay claim to,*** claim.

claim[2] /kleim/ *vt,vi* **1** demand recognition of the fact that one is, or owns, or has a right to (something): *He ~ed to be the owner of/~ed that he owned the land.* ***claim damages,*** ⇨ damage[2]. **2** say that something is a fact: *He ~ed to be the best tennis player in the school.* **3** (of things) need; deserve: *There are several matters that ~ my attention.*

claim·ant /ˈkleimənt/ *n* [C] person who makes a claim, esp in law.

clair·voy·ance /klerˈvɔiəns/ *n* [U] abnormal power of seeing in the mind what is happening or what exists beyond the normal range of the senses.

clair·voy·ant /-ənt/ *n* [C] person with such power.

clam /klæm/ *n* [C] large shellfish, with a shell in

two halves, used for food. ⇨ illus at bivalve. □ *vi* ***clam up*** (*sl*) refuse to speak (esp to give revealing information).

clam·bake /ˈklæmˌbeik/ *n* [C] party at which clams and other food (as chicken, lobster, corn, etc) are steamed, usually in a pit lined with heated rocks and seaweed.

clam·ber /ˈklæmbər/ *vi* climb with difficulty, using the hands and feet: *~ up/over a wall.* □ *n* [C] awkward or difficult climb.

clammy /ˈklæmi/ *adj* (-ier, -iest) damp and sticky to the touch: *~ hands.*

clam·or /ˈklæmər/ *n* [C,U] loud confused noise or shout, esp of people complaining angrily or making a demand. □ *vi,vt* make a clamor: *The foolish people were ~ing for war.*

clamp /klæmp/ *n* [C] **1** appliance for holding things together tightly by means of a screw. **2** band of iron, etc for strengthening or tightening. □ *vt,vi* **1** put a clamp on; put in a clamp. **2** ***clamp down (on),*** (*informal*) put pressure on or against (in order to stop something): *They ~ed down on drug pushers.*

ˈclamp·down *n* [C]

clan /klæn/ *n* [C] large family group, as found in tribal communities, eg Scottish Highlanders.

clan·nish *adj* showing family feeling; in the habit of supporting one another against outsiders.

clan·des·tine /klænˈdestın/ *adj* secret; done secretly; kept secret: *a ~ marriage.*

clang /klæŋ/ *vt,vi, n* (make a) loud ringing sound: *The ~ of the firebell alarmed the village.*

clangor /ˈklæŋər/ *n* [U] continued clanging noise.

clank /klæŋk/ *vt,vi, n* (make a) ringing sound (not so loud as a clang): *Prisoners ~ing their chains.*

clap /klæp/ *vt,vi* (-pp-) **1** show approval, by striking the palms of the hands together; do this as a signal (eg to summon a waiter, etc): *When the violinist finished the audience ~ped for five minutes.* **2** strike or slap lightly with the open hand, usually in a friendly way: *~ someone on the back.* **3** put quickly or energetically: *~ped in prison.* ***clap eyes on sb,*** (*informal*) catch sight of: *I haven't ~ped eyes on him since 1960.* □ *n* **1** [C] loud explosive noise (of thunder). **2** [C] sound of the palms of the hands brought together. (*Note: Clapping* is the usual word for applause, not *claps.*) **3** [U] (*sl*) venereal disease.

clap·board /ˈklæbərd/ *n* [C] narrow board that overlaps the one below it, used for covering the outside of a wooden building.

clap·trap /ˈklæpˌtræp/ *n* [U] silly or insincere ideas, remarks, that are intended merely to impress or win applause.

claret /ˈklærıt/ *n* [U] **1** (kind of) red table wine from Bordeaux. **2** its color. □ *adj* dark red.

clar·ify /ˈklærəˌfai/ *vt,vi* (*pt,pp* -ied) **1** make or become clear or intelligible. **2** make (a liquid, etc) free from impurities.

clari·fi·ca·tion /ˌklærəfəˈkeiʃən/ *n* [U] being clarified.

clari·net /ˌklærəˈnet/ *n* [C] woodwind instrument, with finger holes and keys. ⇨ illus at brass.

clari·net·ist *n* [C] clarinet player.

clar·ion /ˈklæriən/ *n* [C] loud, shrill call made to rouse and excite.

clar·ity /ˈklærəti/ *n* [U] clearness: *~ of thought.*

clash /klæʃ/ *vi,vt* **1** make a loud, broken, confused noise (as when metal objects strike together): *The cymbals ~ed.* **2** come suddenly together; meet in conflict: *The two armies ~ed outside the town.* **3** (of events) interfere with each other because they are (to be) at the same time on the same date: *It's a pity the two concerts ~, I want to go to both.* **4** be in disagreement with: *I ~ed with him/We ~ed at the last meeting of the Council. The* (*colors of the*) *curtains ~ with* (*the colors of*) *the carpet.* □ *n* [C] **1** clashing noise. **2** disagreement; conflict: *a ~ of views/colors.*

clasp /klæsp/ *n* [C] **1** device with two parts that fasten together, (eg on the ends of a necklace or belt). **2** firm hold (with the fingers or arms). □ *vt,vi* **1** hold tightly or closely: *~ed in each other's arms; with his hands ~ed behind him.* **2** fasten with a clasp(1).

class /klæs/ *n* **1** [C] group having qualities of the same kind; kind, sort or division: *As an actor A is not in the same ~ with B,* is not so good as B. **2** [U] system of ranks in society: *It will be difficult to abolish ~; the ~ struggle.* **3** [C] all persons in one of these ranks: *Should society be divided into upper, middle and lower ~es?* **4** group of persons taught together. **5** meeting of such a group. **6** group of pupils or students who enter school or college in the same year and leave together: *the ~ of 1973.* **7** (*informal*) distinction; excellence; style: *There's not much ~ about her.* □ *vt* place in a class(1): *a ship ~ed A one.*

class·less *adj* without distinctions of class(2): *Is a ~less society possible?*

class·room *n* [C] room where a class(4) is taught.

classy *adj* (*informal*) stylish, elegant.

clas·sic /ˈklæsık/ *adj* **1** of the highest quality; having a recognized value or position recognized. **2** of the standard of ancient Greek and Latin literature, art and culture. **3** famous because of a long history: *The Kentucky Derby* (horse race) *is a ~ event.* **4** (of fashion) traditional: *a ~ suit.* □ *n* [C] **1** writer, artist, book, etc of the highest class: *Robinson Crusoe is a ~.* **2** ancient Greek or Latin writer. **3** (*pl*) **(the) classics,** (literature of the) ancient languages of Greece and Rome: *He majored in ~s.* **4** classic(3) event.

clas·si·cal /ˈklæsıkəl/ *adj* **1** in, of, the best (esp ancient Greek and Roman) art and literature: *a ~ education.* **2** of proved value because of having passed the test of time: *~ music,* usually taking traditional form as a symphony, etc, eg of Mozart. ⇨ light[2](6).

clas·si·cal·ly /-kli/ *adv*

clas·si·cist /ˈklæsəsıst/ *n* [C] **1** follower of classic style. **2** classical scholar: *Milton was a ~.*

clas·si·fi·ca·tion /ˌklæsəfəˈkeiʃən/ *n* **1** [U] classifying or being classified. **2** [C] group into which something is put.

clas·sify /ˈklæsəˌfai/ *vt* (*pt,pp* -ied) arrange in

classes or groups; put into a class(1): *In a library, books are usually classified by subjects.*
clas·si·fied *adj* **(a)** arranged in classes(1): *classified advertisements.* **(b)** officially secret: *classified information.*
clat·ter /ˈklætər/ *n* [U] **1** long, continuous, resounding noise (as of hard things falling or knocking together): *the ~ of cutlery.* **2** noisy talk: *The boys stopped their ~ when the teacher came into the classroom.* □ *vi,vt* make a clatter (1): *Pots and pans were ~ing in the kitchen.*
clause /klɔz/ *n* [C] **1** (*gram*) part of a sentence, with its own subject and predicate. **2** complete paragraph in an agreement, legal document, etc.
claus·tro·pho·bia /ˌklɔstrəˈfoubiə/ *n* [U] abnormal fear of confined places (eg of being in an elevator).
clavi·chord /ˈklævəˌkɔrd/ *n* [C] early stringed instrument with a keyboard, like the piano.
clav·icle /ˈklævəkəl/ *n* [C] collar bone. ⇨ illus at skeleton.
claw /klɔ/ *n* **1** one of the pointed nails on the feet of some animals and birds. ⇨ illus at bird. **2** pincers of a shellfish (eg a lobster). ⇨ illus at crustacean. **3** instrument or device like a claw (eg a steel hook on a machine for lifting things). □ *vt* get hold of, pull, scratch, with claws or hands.
clay /klei/ *n* [U] stiff, sticky earth that becomes hard when baked, from which bricks, pots, earthenware, etc are made.
clean¹ /klin/ *adj* (-er, -est) **1** free from dirt: *~ hands. Wash it ~.* **2** not yet used; fresh: *Give me a ~ sheet of paper.* **3** pure; innocent; free from offense or indecency: *a ~ joke; He has a ~ record,* is not known to have done wrong. **4** even; regular; with a smooth edge or surface: *A sharp knife makes a ~ cut.* **5** having clean habits: *a ~ waitress.* **6** fit for food: *~/un~ animals,* those that are/are not considered fit for food (by religious custom). **7** thorough, complete. ⇨ sweep²(1), breast(3) and slate(2). □ *adv* completely; entirely: *I ~ forgot about it.* ***come clean,*** make a full confession.
ˌclean-ˈcut *adj* **(a)** sharply outlined. **(b)** neat and wholesome looking.
cleanly /ˈklinli/ *adv* (*Note:* not to be confused in pronunciation with the *adj* of the same form. ⇨ cleanly *adj*) **(a)** in a clean manner. **(b)** exactly, sharply, neatly; *He performed the feat ~,* without clumsiness.
ˌclean-ˈshaven *adj* with the hair of the face shaved off.
clean² /klin/ *vt,vi* **1** make clean (of dirt, etc): *I must have this suit ~ed,* sent to the dry cleaner's. ⇨ dry¹. **2** (special uses with *adverbial particles* and *prepositions*):
clean sb out, win or take all the money of. ***clean sth out,*** clean the inside of: *It's time you ~ed out your bedroom.*
clean up, **(a)** make things clean or tidy; put things in order: *You should always clean up after a picnic,* collect litter, empty bottles, etc. **(b)** (*informal*) make a large amount of money. ***clean sth up,*** **(a)** get rid of criminal and immoral elements, etc: *The mayor has decided to ~ up the city,* end corruption, etc. **(b)** (*informal*) finish.
cleaner /ˈklinər/ *n* [C] **1** person or thing that cleans. **2** tool, machine, substance, etc for cleaning: *send/take a suit to the (ˌdry) ˈ~'s; ˈvacuum ~.*
clean·ly /ˈklenli/ *adj* (-ier, -iest) (*Note:* not to be confused in pronunciation with the *adv* of the same form. ⇨ clean¹) having clean habits; usually clean: *Are cats ~ animals?*
clean·li·ness /-nɪs/ *n* [U]
cleanse /ˈklenz/ *vt* make thoroughly clean or pure: *~ the heart of/from sin.*
ˈcleans·er *n* [C,U] substance used for cleaning.
clear¹ /klɪr/ *adj* (-er, -est) **1** easy to see (through): *the ~ water of a mountain lake; a ~ sky/light.* **2** free from guilt or blame: *a ~ conscience.* **3** (of sounds, etc) easily heard; distinct; pure: *the ~ note of a bell.* **4** (of and to the mind) free from doubt or difficulty: *It was ~ (to everyone) that the war would not end quickly.* ***make oneself/one's meaning clear,*** make oneself understood. **5** free from obstacles, dangers, etc: *Is the road ~?* **6** confident; certain: *I am not ~ as to what you expect me to do.* **7** free: *I wish I were ~ of debt.* □ *n* [U] ***in the clear,*** free from suspicion, danger, etc.
ˌclear-ˈheaded *adj* having good understanding.
ˌclear-ˈsighted *adj* able to see, think, understand well.
clear² /klɪr/ *adv* **1** distinctly: *speak loud and ~.* **2** quite; completely: *The prisoner got ~ away.* **3** apart; without touching; at or to a distance: *He jumped three inches ~ of the bar.*
clear·ness /nɪs/ *n* [U]
clear³ /klɪr/ *vt,vi* **1** remove, get rid of, what is unwanted or unwelcome: *~ the streets of snow; ~ oneself (of a charge),* prove one's innocence. ***clear the air,*** ⇨ air¹(1). ***clear one's throat,*** eg by coughing. **2** get past or over without touching: *Our car only just ~ed the gatepost.* **3** make as a net gain or profit: *~ $500.* **4** get (a ship or its cargo) free by doing what is necessary (signing papers, paying dues, etc) on entering or leaving a port: *~ goods through customs.* **5** authorize somebody esp to handle diplomatic or military secrets, after determining his reliability. **6** (special uses with *adverbial particles* and *prepositions*):
clear away, **(a)** take away, get rid of: *~ away the plates.* **(b)** pass away: *The clouds have ~ed away.*
clear off, **(a)** make clean and tidy: *Clear off the table!* **(b)** (*informal*) go away: *This is my garden, so ~ off!*
clear out, **(a)** empty; make clear by taking out the contents of: *~ out a drain/a cupboard.* **(b)** (*informal*) go away; leave: *The police are after you, you'd better ~ out!*
clear up, become clear: *The weather/The sky is ~ing up.* ***clear sth up,*** **(a)** put in order; make tidy: *Who's going to ~ up the mess?* **(b)** make clear; solve (a mystery, etc): *~ up a misunderstanding.* **(c)** get rid of: *~ up a debt.*
clear·ance /ˈklɪrəns/ *n* **1** [C] clearing up, removing, making tidy. **2** [C,U] free space; space between, for moving past: *There is not much/not*

enough ~ for large trucks passing under this bridge. **3** [C] sale (of goods) at lowered prices. **4** [U] authorization, approval, esp to handle diplomatic or military secrets.

clear·ing /ˈklɪrɪŋ/ *n* [C] open space from which trees have been cleared in a forest.

ˈclearing house, (a) office at which banks exchange checks, etc and settle accounts. **(b)** governmental or private agency which functions to exchange information on a particular subject.

clear·ly /ˈklɪrli/ *adv* **1** distinctly: *speak/see ~.* **2** undoubtedly: *He was ~ly mistaken.*

cleat /klit/ *n* [C] **1** device around which a rope or line may be wound in order to fasten it. **2** strip or piece of wood, metal, etc fastened to something to prevent slipping: *~s on a pair of golf shoes.*

cleav·age /ˈklivɪdʒ/ *n* [C] **1** split or division. **2** the cleft between a woman's breasts as seen above the low neckline of a dress.

cleave /kliv/ *vt,vi* (*pt* cleaved /klivd/, clove /klouv/, cleft /kleft/, *pp* cleaved, cleft or cloven /klouvən/) **1** cut or split; come apart: *~ a block of wood in two.* **2** make by cutting: *~ one's way through the jungle.*

cleav·er /ˈklivər/ *n* [C] person or thing that cleaves, esp a heavy knife with a large blade, used for cutting meat.

clef /klef/ *n* [C] musical symbol placed at the beginning of a staff to show the pitch of the notes. ⇨ illus at notation.

cleft[1] *pp* of cleave.

cleft[2] /kleft/ *n* [C] opening; split or crack. □ *adj* divided; split.

ˌcleft ˈpalate, division in the roof of the mouth present at birth.

clema·tis /ˈklemətɪs/ *n* [U] (kinds of) climbing plant with clusters of white, yellow or purple flowers.

clem·ency /ˈklemənsi/ *n* [U] **1** mercy. **2** mildness (of temper or weather).

clem·ent /ˈklemənt/ *adj* **1** showing mercy. **2** (of the weather, a person's temper) mild.

clench /klentʃ/ *vt* press or clasp firmly together, close tightly: *~ one's teeth/fists.*

clergy /ˈklərdʒi/ *n* (*collect*) persons ordained as priests, ministers, rabbis, mullahs, etc.

ˈclergy·man *n* [C] (*pl* ~men /-men/) member of the clergy.

cleric /ˈklerɪk/ *n* [C] = clergyman.

cleri·cal /ˈklerɪkəl/ *adj* **1** of the clergy: *~ dress; a ~ collar.* **2** of, for a clerk or clerks(1): *a ~ error,* one made in copying or writing.

clerk /klərk/ *n* [C] **1** person employed in a bank, office, store, etc to keep records and accounts, copy letters, etc: *a ˈbank ~.* **2** officer in charge of records, etc: *the town ~.* **3** saleswoman or salesman in a store.

clever /ˈklevər/ *adj* (-er, -est) **1** quick in learning and understanding things; skillful: *He's ~ at arithmetic/at making excuses.* **2** (of things done) showing ability and skill: *a ~ speech/book.*

clever·ly *adv*

clever·ness /-nɪs/ *n* [U]

cliché /kliˈʃei/ *n* [C] idea or expression that has been used too much.

click[1] /klɪk/ *vi, n* [C] (make a) short, light sound (like that of a key turning in a lock): *The door ~ed shut.*

click[2] /klɪk/ *vi* **1** agree; be in harmony. **2** succeed.

cli·ent /ˈklaiənt/ *n* [C] person who gets help or advice from a lawyer or any professional man: *a successful lawyer with hundreds of ~s.*

cli·en·tele /ˌklaiənˈtel/ *n* (*collect*) customers.

cliff /klɪf/ *n* [C] steep face of rock.

ˈcliff-hanger *n* (*informal*) episode in a story or contest with an uncertain end leaving the reader or spectator in suspense.

cli·mac·tic /klaiˈmæktɪk/ *adj* forming a climax; of a climax.

cli·mate /ˈklaimɪt/ *n* [C] **1** weather conditions of a place or area; conditions of temperature, rainfall, wind, etc. **2** area or region with certain weather conditions: *A drier ~ would be good for her health.* **3** current condition: *the political ~,* general political attitudes.

cli·mat·ic /klaiˈmætɪk/ *adj* of climate.

cli·mati·cally /kli/ *adv*

cli·max /ˈklaiˌmæks/ *n* [C] (*pl* ~es) event, point, of greatest interest or excitement (eg in a story or drama): *bring matters to a ~.* □ *vt,vi* bring or come to a climax.

climb /klaim/ *vt,vi* **1** go or get up (a tree, wall, rope, mountain, etc) or down. **2** (of aircraft) go higher. **3** (of plants) grow upwards. **4** rise by effort in social rank, position, etc. □ *n* [C]

climber *n* [C] **(a)** person who climbs. **(b)** climbing plant.

clinch /klɪntʃ/ *vt,vi* **1** settle (a bargain, an argument) conclusively: *That ~es the argument.* **2** make (a nail or rivet) fast by hammering sideways the end that protrudes. **3** put one or both arms round a person's body: *The boxers/lovers ~ed.* □ *n* [C] instance of clinching.

cling /klɪŋ/ *vi* (*pt,pp* clung /kləŋ/) ***cling to/together,*** hold tight; resist separation: *~ to a hope of being rescued. They clung together when the time came to part.*

clinic /ˈklɪnɪk/ *n* [C] **1** class in which medical advice and treatment are given and in which students are taught through observation of cases. **2** place where people can get treatment for medical problems, often at a low cost.

clini·cal /ˈklɪnɪkəl/ *adj*

clink[1] /klɪŋk/ *vi,vt, n* [U] (make the) sound of small bits of metal, glass, etc knocking together: *the ~ of keys/glasses.*

clink[2] /klɪŋk/ *n* [C] (*sl*) prison: *be (put) in the ~.*

clip[1] /klɪp/ *n* [C] (esp) wire or metal device for holding things (eg papers) together. □ *vt* (-pp-) put or keep together with a clip: *~ papers together.*

clip[2] /klɪp/ *vt* (-pp-) **1** cut with scissors or shears; make short or neat: *~ a hedge.* **2** (seem to) shorten words (eg by saying *shootin'* /ˈʃutən/ instead of *shooting* /ˈʃutɪŋ/). **3** (*informal*) hit or punch sharply: *~ him on the jaw.* **4** (*informal*) cheat or rob, esp by overcharging. □ *n* [C] **1** instance of clipping. **2** (*informal*) smart blow: *a ~ on the jaw.* **3** rapid pace: *went at quite a ~.*

ˈclip joint, (*informal*) bar, nightbar, etc where the customers are overcharged or cheated.

clip·ping *n* [C] (esp) something cut from a newspaper, etc.
clip·per /ˈklɪpər/ *n* **1** (*pl*) (also ***a pair of clippers***) instrument for clipping: *ˈhair ~s; ˈnail ~s.* **2** large, fast sailing ship.
clique /klik/ *n* [C] small group of persons united by common interests.
cloak /klouk/ *n* [C] **1** loose outer garment, without sleeves. **2** (*fig*) something used to hide or keep secret: *under the ~ of darkness.* □ *vt* hide (thoughts, purposes, etc).
ˈcloak·room *n* [C] place where coats, etc may be left for a short time (eg in a theater).
clock /klak/ *n* [C] instrument (not carried or worn like a watch) for measuring and showing the time. ***around the clock,*** all day and night. □ *vt,vi* **1** do something (eg run a race) in a measured period of time: *He ~ed 9.6 seconds for the 100 meters.* **2** ***clock in/out,*** record the time of one's arrival/departure on a time clock.
ˈclock·face *n* [C] surface of a clock showing figures marking the hours, etc.
ˈclock tower, tall structure (forming part of a building, eg a church) with a clock high up on an outside wall.
ˈclock·wise *adv* moving in the same direction as the hands of a clock.
clock·work /ˈklakˌwərk/ *n* [U] **1** machinery (as wheels, springs, etc) that makes a clock run. **2** similar machinery that operates eg a mechanical toy. ***like clockwork,*** smoothly and regularly.
clod /klad/ *n* [C] lump (of earth, etc).
clog¹ /klag/ *n* [C] shoe with a wooden sole.
clog² /klag/ *vt,vi* (-gg-) **1** (cause to) be or become blocked with dirt, grease, etc so that movement, flow of liquid, etc is difficult or prevented. **2** (*fig*): *Don't ~ your memory with useless facts.*
clois·ter /ˈklɔistər/ *n* [C] **1** covered walk, usually along the walls of a building around an open courtyard with columns or arches on the courtyard side. **2** (life in a) convent or monastery. □ *vt* put in, live in, a cloister(2).
close¹ /klous/ *adj* (-r, -st) **1** near (in space or time): *fire a gun at ~ range.* ***close at hand; close to/by,*** near. **2** with little or no space in between: *The soldiers advanced in ~ order,* with little space between them. **3** strict; severe: *be (kept) under ~ arrest.* ***keep a close watch on,*** watch carefully. **4** thorough: *paid ~ attention.* **5** intimate: *a ~ friend/friendship.* **6** nearly even; almost equal: *a ~ contest/election.* **7** (of the weather or air) uncomfortably heavy. **8** (of a room, etc) having little fresh air. **9** hidden; secret; not in the habit of talking about one's affairs: *keep/lie ~ for a while,* keep one's whereabouts secret, not show oneself. □ *adv* in a close manner; near together; tightly: *stand/sit ~ against the wall; come ~r together.* ⇨ closely below.
ˌclose ˈcall/ˈshave, narrow escape.
ˌclose-ˈfisted *adj* stingy.
close·ly *adv* in a close manner: *listen ~ly. She ~ly resembles her mother.*
ˌclose-ˈmouthed *adj* talking very little; secretive.
close·ness /-nɪs/ *n* [U]
ˈclose-up *n* [C] **(a)** photograph, taken near to an object, etc and showing it in large scale. **(b)** close view.
close² /klouz/ *vt,vi* **1** = shut: *If you ~ your eyes, you can't see. This box/The lid of this box doesn't ~ properly.* **2** (not usually replaceable by *shut*) bar access to: *This road is ~d to heavy traffic.* **3** bring or come to an end: *~ a discussion; the closing* (= last, final) *day for applications.* **4** bring or come together by making less space or fewer spaces between. **5** (special uses with *adverbial particles* and *prepositions*):
close down, stop; shut completely.
close in on/upon, **(a)** envelop: *Darkness ~d in on us.* **(b)** come near(er) and attack: *The enemy ~d in upon us.*
close with, accept (an offer); make a bargain with.
close³ /klouz/ *n* [U] **1** end (of a period of time): *towards the ~ of the century.* **2** conclusion (of an activity, etc): *brought the game to a ~.*
closet /ˈklɔzɪt/ *n* [C] cupboard set in a recess in a room for storing things. □ *vt* shut up (as if) in a closet.
clo·sure /ˈklouʒər/ *n* [C] act of closing(2).
clot /klat/ *n* [C] semi-solid lump formed from liquid, esp blood. □ *vt,vi* (-tt-) form into clots: *~ted cream.*
cloth /klɔθ/ *n* (*pl* ~s /klɔðz, klɔθs/) **1** [U] material made by weaving (cotton, wool, etc): *three yards of ~.* **2** [C] piece of this material for special purpose: *a ˈdish~.*
clothe /klouð/ *vt* dress; put clothes on, supply clothes for: *He has to work hard in order to ~ his family.*
clothes /klouz/ *n pl* coverings for a person's body; dress: *ˈbaby ~; a ˈ~ brush.*
ˈclothes·line *n* [C] line for hanging clothes to dry.
ˈclothes·pin *n* [C] clip used for fastening clothes to a clothesline.
cloth·ing /ˈklouðɪŋ/ *n* [U] (*collective*) clothes: *articles of ~.*
cloud /klaud/ *n* **1** [C,U] (mass of) visible water vapor floating in the sky: *The top of the mountain was hidden under ~.* **2** similar mass of smoke, etc in the air: *a ~ of insects.* **3** vague patch on or in a liquid or a transparent object. **4** something that causes unhappiness or fear: *the ~s of war.* ***under a cloud,*** under suspicion, in disgrace. □ *vi,vt* become, make, indistinct (as) through cloud: *Her eyes were ~ed with tears.*
ˈcloud·burst *n* [C] sudden heavy shower of rain.
cloudy *adj* (-ier, -iest) **(a)** covered with clouds: *a ~y sky.* **(b)** (esp of liquids) not clear.
clove¹ *pt* of cleave¹.
clove² /klouv/ *n* [C] dried, unopened flower bud of a tropical tree, used as a spice.
clove³ /klouv/ *n* [C] one of the small, separate sections of some bulbs: *a ~ of garlic.*
clo·ver /ˈklouvər/ *n* [U] low-growing plant with (usually) three leaves on each stalk.
ˈclover·leaf *n* [C] (*pl* -leafs /-lifs/ or -leaves /-livz/) highway intersection with ramps, etc forming the pattern of a four-leaf clover.
clown /klaun/ *n* [C] **1** person (esp in a circus or

carnival) who makes a living by dressing up and performing foolish tricks and antics for fun. **2** person acting like a clown. □ *vt* behave like a clown: *Stop all this ~ing.*

cloy /klɔi/ *vt,vi* make or become weary by too much of something (as food, pleasure, etc): *~ed with pleasure.*

club[1] /kləb/ *n* [C] **1** heavy stick with one thick end, used as a weapon. **2** stick with a curved head for playing golf and hockey. □ *vt* (-bb-) hit with a club: *He had been ~bed to death.*

ˌclub·ˈfoot *n* [C] (*pl* -feet /fit/) foot that is (from birth) thick and badly formed.

ˌclub·ˈfooted *adj*

club[2] /kləb/ *n* [C] one of the thirteen playing cards with black leaf-like shapes printed on it. ⇨ illus at card.

club[3] /kləb/ *n* [C] **1** society of persons who pay money to provide themselves with sport, social entertainment, etc. **2** the rooms or building(s) used by such a society. □ *vi* (-bb-) ***club together,*** join or act (together, with others) for a common purpose: *The staff ~bed together to buy a present for the Manager.*

cluck /klək/ *vi, n* [C] (make the) noise made by a hen, eg when calling her chicks.

clue /klu/ *n* [C] fact, idea, etc that suggests a possible answer to a problem.

clump[1] /kləmp/ *n* [C] group or cluster (of trees, shrubs or plants): *growing in ~s.* □ *vt* (cause to) form a clump.

clump[2] /kləmp/ *vi* tread heavily: *~ about*, eg walk in heavy boots. □ *n* [U] sound of clumping.

clumsy /ˈkləmzi/ *adj* (-ier, -iest) **1** ungraceful in movement or construction; not well designed for its purpose: *The ~ man put his elbow through the window and broke it.* **2** tactless; unskillful: *a ~ apology/remark.*

ˈclum·sily /-zəli/ *adv*

ˈclum·si·ness /-nɪs/ *n* [U]

clung /kləŋ/ *pt,pp* of cling.

clunk /kləŋk/ *vi, n* [C] (make the) sound of heavy metals striking together.

clus·ter /ˈkləstər/ *n* [C] **1** number of things of the same kind growing closely together: *a ~ of flowers/curls.* **2** number of persons, animals, objects, etc in a small, close group: *a ~ of spectators/islands; consonant ~,* eg *str* in *strong.* □ *vi* be in, form, a close group around.

clutch[1] /klətʃ/ *vt,vi* seize; (try to) take hold of tightly with the hand(s): *He ~ed* (*at*) *the rope we threw to him.* □ *n* [C] **1** act of clutching. **2** (esp in *pl*) control; power: *He's in his son-in-law's ~es.* **3** device, eg a pedal, in a machine or engine for connecting and disconnecting working parts: *let the ~ in/out.*

clutch[2] /klətʃ/ *n* [C] **1** set of eggs placed under a hen to hatch at one time. **2** number of chicks hatched from these.

clut·ter /ˈklətər/ *vt* make untidy or confused: *a desk ~ed up with papers.* □ *n* [U] disorder.

CO[1] *postal abbr* = Colorado. ⇨ App 6.

Co.[2] *abbr* = **1** Company. **2** County.

c/o[3] *abbr* = care of. ⇨ care[1] (2).

co- /ˌkou-/ *prefix* together, jointly, equally: *coauthor; coeducation.*

coach[1] /koutʃ/ *n* [C] **1** bus. **2** railroad car. **3** four-wheeled carriage pulled by four or more horses, formerly used to carry passengers and mail.

coach[2] /koutʃ/ *n* [C] **1** teacher, esp one who gives private lessons to prepare students for an examination. **2** person who trains athletes for contests: *a ˈfootball ~.* □ *vt,vi* teach or train.

co·agu·late /kouˈægyəˌleit/ *vt,vi* (of liquids) change to a thick and solid state, as blood does in air.

co·agu·lation /kouˌægyəˈleiʃən/ *n* [U]

coal /koul/ *n* **1** [U] black mineral that burns and supplies heat. **2** [C] piece of this material.

ˈcoal gas, the mixture of gases made from coal, used for lighting and heating.

ˈcoal mine, mine from which coal is dug.

ˈcoal tar, thick, black, sticky substance produced when coal gas is made.

co·alesce /ˌkouəˈles/ *vi* come together and unite into one substance, group, etc.

co·ales·cence /ˌkouəˈlesəns/ *n* [U]

co·ali·tion /ˌkouəˈlɪʃən/ *n* **1** [U] uniting. **2** [C] union of political parties for a special purpose: *a ~ government; form a ~.*

coarse /kɔrs/ *adj* (-r, -st) **1** (of substances) not fine and small; rough, lumpy: *~ sand/sugar; ~ cloth; a ~ skin/complexion.* **2** (of behavior, language, etc) vulgar; not delicate or refined. **3** (of food) common; inferior.

coarse·ly *adv*

coarsen /ˈkɔrsən/ *vt,vi* make or become coarse.

coarse·ness /-nɪs/ *n* [U]

coast[1] /koust/ *n* [C] seashore and land near it: *There are numerous islands off the ~.*

ˈcoast guard, (a) military force that patrols a coast (to prevent or detect smuggling, report passing ships, etc). **(b)** member of the coast guard.

ˈcoast·line *n* shoreline, esp when referring to its shape: *a rugged ~line.*

coast[2] /koust/ *vi,vt* **1** go in, sail, a ship along the coast. **2** move or slide along or down a hill or slope without using power (eg without pedaling a bicycle). **3** (*fig*) make progress without effort: *The student ~ed through school without studying.*

coastal /ˈkoustəl/ *adj* of the coast: *~ waters/fishing.*

coat /kout/ *n* [C] **1** outer garment with sleeves, buttoned in the front. **2** any covering that is compared to a garment, eg an animal's hair or wool. **3** layer of paint or other substance put on a surface: *The woodwork has had its final ~ of paint.* □ *vt* cover with a layer: *furniture ~ed with dust.*

ˌcoat of ˈarms /ˌkout əv ˈarmz/ *n* ⇨ arms.

coat·ing /ˈkoutɪŋ/ *n* **1** [C] thin layer or covering: *two ~s of paint.* **2** [U] cloth for coats(1).

coax /ˈkouks/ *vt,vi* **1** get a person or thing to act by kindness or patience: *~ a child to take its medicine; ~ a fire to burn.* **2** get by coaxing; *~ a smile from the baby.*

co·axi·al cable /kouˌæksiəl ˈkeibəl/ *n* [C] insulated cable for transmitting many telephone, telegraph and television signals at the same time.

cob /kab/ *n* [C] **1** male swan. **2** strong short-legged horse for riding. **3** = corncob.

co·balt /ˈkouˌbɔlt/ *n* [U] **1** hard, silvery-white metal (symbol **Co**) used in many alloys. **2** dark blue coloring matter made from this.

cobble[1] /ˈkabəl/ *n* (also ˈ**cobblestone**) stone worn round and smooth by the water and used for paving. □ *vt* pave with these stones: *~d streets.*

cobble[2] /ˈkabəl/ *vt* (*dated*) mend (esp shoes), or put together roughly.

cob·bler /ˈkablər/ *n* [C] **1** (*dated*) person who makes or repairs shoes. **2** deep-dish fruit pie, usually having only a top crust.

co·bra /ˈkoubrə/ *n* [C] poisonous snake of esp Asia and Africa. ⇨ illus at snake.

cob·web /ˈkabˌweb/ *n* [C] fine network or single thread made by a spider.

co·caine /kouˈkein/ *n* [U] drug used as a local anesthetic and (illegally) for pleasure.

cochi·neal /ˈkatʃəˌniəl/ *n* [U] bright red coloring matter.

coch·lea /ˈkakliə/ *n* [C] spiral-shaped part of the inner ear. ⇨ illus at ear.

cock[1] /kak/ *n* [C] **1** adult male chicken. (*Note:* now chiefly replaced by *rooster* in even *formal* usage in the US because of cock(3).) ⇨ rooster. **2** (in compounds) male of other kinds of bird: *a* ˈ*pea~.* **3** (*vulg* ⚠) penis.

ˈ**cock·crow** *n* **(a)** rooster's cry. **(b)** early dawn.

cock[2] /kak/ *n* [C] **1** valve or faucet for controlling the flow of a liquid or a gas, eg from a pipe. **2** hammer of a gun. **3** position of this hammer when it is raised and ready to be released by the trigger.

cock[3] /kak/ *vt* **1** turn upwards, cause to be erect (showing attention, inquiry, defiance, etc): *The horse ~ed its ears.* **2** raise the hammer of (a gun) ready for firing. ⇨ cock[2](2). ***go off half-cocked,*** act prematurely.

cock-a-doodle-doo /ˌkakəˌdudəlˈdu/ *n* imitation of a rooster's crow.

cocka·too /ˈkakəˌtu/ *n* [C] crested parrot.

cock·erel /ˈkak(ə)rəl/ *n* [C] young cock[1] (1).

cock·er spaniel /ˌkakər ˈspænyəl/ *n* [C] small dog with a silky coat and drooping ears. ⇨ illus at dog.

cock·eyed /ˈkaˌkaid/ *adj* (*sl*) **1** squinting; crooked; turned or twisted to one side. **2** foolish; crazy: *a ~ scheme.*

cockle /ˈkakəl/ *n* [C] **1** edible shellfish. **2** (also ˈ**cockleshell**) its shell.

cock·pit /ˈkakˌpɪt/ *n* [C] compartment in an airplane for the pilot. ⇨ illus at aircraft.

cock·roach /ˈkakˌroutʃ/ *n* [C] large, dark-brown insect that comes out at night in kitchens and places where food is kept. ⇨ illus at insect.

cock·sure /ˌkakˈʃʊr/ *adj* offensively sure or confident.

cock·tail /ˈkakˌteiəl/ *n* [C] **1** mixed alcoholic drink, esp one taken before a meal. **2** mixture of fruit, fruit juices, small quantities of shellfish, etc served as an appetizer.

cocky /ˈkaki/ *adj* (-ier, -iest) (*informal*) = cocksure.

co·coa /ˈkoukou/ *n* **1** [U] powder of crushed cacao seeds. **2** [C,U] drink made by mixing this with hot water or milk.

coco·nut, co·coa·nut /ˈkoukəˌnət/ *n* [C,U] large hard-shelled fruit (of the ˈ*~-palm*) filled with milky juice and with pulpy white meat.

co·coon /kəˈkun/ *n* [C] silky covering made by a caterpillar to protect itself while it is a chrysalis.

C.O.D, COD /ˌsi ˌou ˈdi/ *abbr* = cash on delivery.

cod /kad/ *n* **1** [C] (*pl* unchanged) (also ˈ **codfish**) large saltwater fish. **2** [U] its flesh as food.

cod-liver ˈ**oil,** used as a source of vitamins A and D.

coddle /ˈkadəl/ *vt* **1** treat with great care and tenderness: *~ a child because it is in poor health.* **2** cook, eg eggs, in water just below boiling point.

code /koud/ *n* [C] **1** collection of laws arranged in a system. **2** system of rules and principles that has been accepted by society or a class or group of people: *a high moral ~; a ~ of honor.* **3** system of signs, secret writing, etc used for a computer, or to keep a message short or secret: *the Morse ~.* ***break a code,*** discover how to interpret a code(3). □ *vt* = encode.

co·deine /ˈkouˌdin/ *n* [U] drug from opium used as a medicine.

codi·fy /ˈkadəˌfai, ˈkoudəˌfai/ *vt* put into the form of a code(1): *~ the laws.*

coed /ˈkouˌed/ *n* [C] (*informal*) (student at a) coeducational school.

coedu·ca·tion /ˌkouˌedʒəˈkeiʃən/ *n* [U] education of boys and girls together.

coedu·ca·tional /-nəl/ *adj*

co·erce /kouˈərs/ *vt* force (a person) to do something: *~d him into carrying out their orders.*

co·ercion /kouˈərʃən/ *n* [U] coercing or being coerced.

co·ercive /kouˈərsɪv/ *adj*

co·exist /ˌkouɪgˈzɪst/ *vi* exist together or at the same time.

co·exist·ence /-təns/ *n* [U] (esp) peaceful coexisting of opposing states.

cof·fee /ˈkɔfi/ *n* **1** [U] bush or shrub with berries containing seeds (called *beans*) used for making a drink. **2** (ground) beans of this plant. **3** [C,U] the drink.

ˈ**coffee break,** short intermission or break[1](3) in the work routine for resting and taking coffee or other refreshments.

ˈ**coffee grounds, (a)** ground coffee beans, ready for brewing. **(b)** the used residue of ground coffee, after brewing.

ˈ**coffee shop,** small, quick-order restaurant.

ˈ**coffee table,** living room table for serving coffee, etc to guests.

cof·fer /ˈkɔfər/ *n* [C] (esp) large, strongbox, esp one for holding money or other valuables.

cof·fin /ˈkɔfɪn/ *n* [C] box or case for a dead person to be buried in.

cog /kag/ *n* [C] one of a series of teeth on the rim of a wheel which transfers motion by locking into the teeth of a similar wheel.

co·gency /ˈkoudʒənsi/ *n* [U] force or strength (of arguments).

co·gent /ˈkoudʒənt/ *adj* (of arguments) strong and convincing.

cogi·tate /ˈkadʒəˌteit/ *vi,vt* meditate; think over.

cognac /ˈkounˌyæk/ *n* [U] fine French brandy.
cog·nate /ˈkagˌneit/ *adj* **1** having the same source or origin: *Dutch is ~ with German.* **2** related: *Physics and astronomy are ~ sciences.* □ *n* [C] word, etc that is cognate with another.
co·habit /kouˈhæbɪt/ *vi* (of an unmarried couple) live together as husband and wife.
co·habi·ta·tion /ˌkouˌhæbəˈteiʃən/ *n* [U]
co·here /kouˈhɪr/ *vi* **1** stick together; be or remain united. **2** (of arguments, etc) be consistent.
co·her·ence /-rəns/, **co·her·en·cy** /-rənsi/ *n* [U]
co·her·ent /-rənt/ *adj*
co·her·ent·ly *adv*
coif·fure /kwaˈfyʊr/ *n* [C] style of hairdressing.
coil /ˈkɔiəl/ *vt,vi* (-ing /ˈkɔilɪŋ/) wind or twist into a continuous circular or spiral shape; curl round and round: *The snake ~ed (itself) round the branch.* □ *n* [C] **1** something coiled; a single turn of something coiled: *the thick ~s of a python.* **2** length of wire wound in a spiral to conduct electric current. **3** series of connected pipes (as in a refrigerator) arranged in a roll, coil, or layer: *a freezing ~.*
coin /kɔin/ *n* [C,U] (piece of) metal money: *a small heap of ~(s).* □ *vt* **1** make (metal) into coins. **2** invent (esp a new word or phrase).
coin·age /ˈkɔinɪdʒ/ *n* **1** [U] making coins. **2** the coins made. **3** [C] system of coins in use: *a decimal ~.* **4** [U] inventing (of a new word). **5** [C] newly invented word.
co·incide /ˌkouənˈsaid/ *vi* **1** (of two or more objects) correspond in area and outline. **2** (of events) happen at the same time; occupy the same period of time: *His free time never ~d with hers.* **3** (of ideas, etc) be in harmony or agreement: *His tastes and habits ~ with those of his wife.*
co·inci·dence /kouˈɪnsədəns/ *n* **1** [U] the condition of coinciding. **2** [C] instance of this, happening by chance: *by a curious ~.*
co·inci·dent /-dənt/ *adj* coinciding.
co·inci·den·tal /kouˌɪnsəˈdentəl/ *adj*
co·inci·den·tal·ly *adv*
coke /kouk/ *n* [U] fuel made by heating soft coal until some of its gases have been removed. □ *vt* turn (coal) into coke.
Col. *abbr* = Colonel.
col·an·der /ˈkələndər/ *n* [C] vessel with many small holes, used to drain off water from vegetables, etc in cooking.
cold[1] /kould/ *adj* (-er, -est) **1** of low temperature, esp when compared with the human body: *~ weather; a ~ wind; feel ~.* ***have cold feet,*** feel afraid or reluctant. ***in cold blood; make one's blood run cold,*** ⇨ blood(2). **2** (*fig*) unkind; unfriendly: *a ~ greeting/welcome, etc.* **3** (of colors) suggesting cold, eg gray and blue.
ˈcold-blooded *adj* **(a)** having blood that varies with the temperature (eg fish, reptiles). **(b)** (*fig*) of persons, their actions) without emotion.
ˈcold cream, ointment for cleansing and softening the skin.
ˈcold cuts, (servings of) slices of meat that has been cooked and cooled.
ˈcold ˌfront, ⇨ front(5).
ˌcold-ˈhearted *adj* without sympathy; indifferent.
cold·ness /-nɪs/ *n* [U]
ˌcold ˈshoulder, (*informal*) deliberately unfriendly treatment. □ *vt* snub, ignore.
ˈcold ˌsnap, short period of cold weather.
ˈcold ˌwar, struggle for superiority using propaganda, economic measures, etc without actual fighting.
cold[2] /kould/ *n* **1** [U] relative absence of heat; low temperature (esp in the atmosphere): *He was shivering with ~. He disliked both the heat of summer and the ~ of winter. Don't stay outside in the ~, come indoors by the fire.* ***(be left) out in the cold,*** (*fig*) (be) ignored or neglected. (*Note:* often used with *the*). **2** [C,U] inflammation of the nose or throat, usually accompanied with sneezing, coughing, etc: *have a ~; catch (a) ~.*
cole·slaw /ˈkoulˌslɔ/ *n* [U] salad of finely sliced or chopped raw cabbage.
colic /ˈkalɪk/ *n* [U] sharp pain in the stomach and bowels.
col·lab·o·rate /kəˈlæbəˌreit/ *vi* **1** work in partnership: *~ on writing a biography.* **2** ***collaborate with,*** act treasonably, esp with enemy forces occupying one's country.
col·lab·o·ration /kəˌlæbəˈreiʃən/ *n* [U] collaborating: *working in collaboration with others.*
col·lab·o·rator /kəˈlæbəˌreitər/ *n* person who collaborates.
col·lage /kəˈlaʒ/ *n* [C] picture made by a combination of bits of paper, cloth, photographs, etc.
col·lapse /kəˈlæps/ *vi,vt* **1** fall down or in; come or break to pieces suddenly: *The roof ~d under the weight of the snow.* **2** lose physical strength, courage, mental powers, etc: *If you work too hard you may ~.* **3** (of apparatus, eg a chair) close or fold up. □ *n* [C] **1** collapsing: *the ~ of a table/tent/tower, etc.* **2** breakdown: *the ~ of their plans/hopes; suffer a nervous ~.*
col·ˈlaps·ible *adj* that can be collapsed(3) (for packing, etc): *a collapsible chair.*
col·lar /ˈkalər/ *n* [C] **1** part of a garment that fits around the neck; turned-over neckband of a shirt, dress, etc. ⇨ white-collar, blue-collar. **2** separate article of clothing (linen, lace, etc) worn around the neck. **3** band of leather, etc put around the neck of a dog, horse or other animal. **4** metal band joining two pipes, rods or shafts, eg in a machine. □ *vt* seize (roughly) by the collar: *The policeman ~ed the thief.*
ˈcol·lar·bone *n* [C] bone joining the shoulder blade and the breastbone. ⇨ illus at skeleton.
col·lat·eral /kəˈlætərəl/ *adj* **1** secondary or subordinate but from the same source: *~ evidence.* **2** descended from a common ancestor but in a different line, ie through different sons or daughters. □ *n* [U] property (as a mortgage, stocks, bonds) pledged as security for a loan.
col·league /ˈkaˌlig/ *n* [C] person working with another or others: *When he left the company, his ~s bought him a present.*
col·lect[1] /ˈkaˌlekt/ *n* [C] short prayer in the mass or the Communion Service to be read on certain appointed days.
col·lect[2] /kəˈlekt/ *vt,vi* **1** bring or gather

together; get from a number of persons or places: *Please ~ all the empty bottles and put them over here.* **2** obtain specimens of (books, stamps, etc), eg as a hobby or in order to learn things: *~ foreign stamps.* **3** come together: *A crowd soon ~s when there's an accident.* **4** receive payment for: *~ed all the taxes due.* **5** get or recover control of (one's thoughts, energies, oneself): *Before you begin to make a speech, you should ~ your thoughts and ideas.* □ *adj, adv* paid for by the receiver: *a ~ call; sent the telegram ~.*

col·lected /kəˈlektəd/ *adj* (esp of a person) calm; not distracted.

col·lec·tion /kəˈlekʃən/ *n* **1** [U] collecting. **2** [C] instance of this: *How many ~s of letters are there every day?* **3** [C] group of objects that have been collected and that belong together: *a fine ~ of paintings.* **4** heap of materials or objects that have come together: *a ~ of dust/junk.* **5** [C] money collected (at a meeting, a church service, etc).

col·lec·tive /kəˈlektɪv/ *adj* of a group or society (of persons, nations, etc) as a whole: *~ leadership,* (emphasis on) government by a group rather than an individual.

ˌcollective ˈnoun, (*gram*) one that is singular in form but stands for many individuals, as *cattle, crowd, audience.*

col·lec·tor /kəˈlektər/ *n* [C] person who collects: *a ˈtax ~; a ˈticket ~.*

col·lege /ˈkalɪdʒ/ *n* [C] **1** school for higher or professional education: *go to ~.* **2** body of teachers and students forming part of a university: *the Columbia and Harvard ~s.* **3** the building(s) used for this purpose. *go to ~; be at ~.* **4** union of persons with common purposes and duties: *the College of Cardinals,* who elect and advise the Pope.

col·le·giate /kəˈlidʒɪt/ *adj* of or like a college (student): *collegiate life.*

col·lide /kəˈlaid/ *vi* **1** come together violently; meet and strike: *As the bus came round the corner, it ~d with a truck. The ships ~d in the fog.* **2** be opposed; be in conflict: *If the aims of two countries ~, there may be war.*

col·lie /ˈkali/ *n* [C] (kind of) sheepdog with shaggy hair. ⇨ illus at dog.

col·li·sion /kəˈlɪʒən/ *n* **1** [U] colliding. **2** [C] instance of this: *an automobile ~.*

collocate /ˈkaləˌkeit/ *vt* arrange or place together (words): *"Weak" ~s with "coffee"* (ie *weak coffee* is acceptable) *but "feeble" does not* (ie *feeble coffee* is not good English).

col·lo·ca·tion /ˌkaləˈkeiʃən/ *n* [C,U]

col·loquial /kəˈloukwiəl/ *adj* (of words, phrases, style) suitable for ordinary conversation; not formal or literary.

col·loquial·ism /-ˌlɪzəm/ *n* [C] colloquial word or phrase.

col·loquial·ly *adv*

col·lu·sion /kəˈluʒən/ *n* [U] secret agreement or understanding for a dishonest purpose: *act in ~ with a thief.*

co·lon[1] /ˈkoulən/ *n* [C] lower and greater part of the large intestine.

co·lon[2] /ˈkoulən/ *n* [C] punctuation mark (:) used in writing and printing.

co·lonel /ˈkərnəl/ *n* [C] commissioned officer in the US army, air force or marine corps who ranks above a lieutenant colonel and below a brigadier general.

co·lo·nial /kəˈlouniəl/ *adj* **1** of a colony or colonies(1). **2** in the style of architecture, etc of the British colonies of North America: *~ furniture/architecture.* □ *n* [C] inhabitant of a colony(1), esp one who helps or helped to found and develop it.

co·lo·nial·ism /-ˌlɪzəm/ *n* [U] policy of having colonies(1) and keeping them dependent.

co·lo·nial·ist *n* [C] supporter of colonialism.

col·o·nist /ˈkalənɪst/ *n* [C] pioneer settler in a colony(1).

col·o·nize /ˈkaləˌnaiz/ *vt* establish a colony; establish in a colony: *The ancient Greeks ~d many parts of the Mediterranean.*

col·o·niz·ation /ˌkalənɪˈzeiʃən/ *n* [U]

col·on·nade /ˌkaləˈneid/ *n* [C] row of columns (1).

col·ony /ˈkaləni/ *n* [C] (*pl* -ies) **1** country or territory settled by migrants from a mother country, and, for a time, controlled by it, eg (formerly) Australia. **2** such a settlement. **3** any of the thirteen British colonies in North America which became the original thirteen states of the US. **4** country, territory, controlled, administered, and (often) developed by another, eg Hong Kong and (formerly) Sierra Leone. **5** group of people from another country, or of people with the same trade, profession or occupation, living together: *a ~ of artists.* **6** number of animals or plants, living or growing together: *a ~ of ants.*

col·or[1] /ˈkələr/ *n* **1 (a)** [U] effect or sensation produced in the eye by waves of decomposed light. **(b)** [C] quality or characteristic of an object, apart from its size or shape, produced by light rays of a particular wavelength: *Red, blue, and yellow are ~s. There isn't enough ~ in the picture.* **2** [U] complexion, esp of the tint or coloring considered healthy, etc: *Her ~ is poor.* **3** [C] paint or other material used to give color: *water ~s.* **4** [U] outward appearance of truth: *details that gave his lies the ~ of truth.* ***local color,*** details of a particular place, time, etc used to make a description realistic. **5** (*pl*) flag, ensign, or pennant as the symbol of a country, its armed forces, etc: *salute the ~s.* ***(come off) with flying colors,*** (do something) successfully. ***show one's true colors,*** show what one really is. **6** [U] skin color associated with one's race.

ˈcolor-blind *adj* **(a)** unable to see or distinguish between certain colors. **(b)** not conscious of racial differences.

color·ful *adj* **(a)** full of color. **(b)** vivid; exciting.

color·less *adj* **(a)** without color. **(b)** dull; uninteresting.

col·or[2] /ˈkələr/ *vt, vi* **1** give color to; put color on: *~ a wall green.* **2** take on or change color; blush: *She ~s whenever she is embarrassed.* **3** change, distort, or misrepresent: *~ed his account so that he seemed to be a hero.*

col·ored /ˈkələrd/ *adj* **1** having color; (esp in compounds) having a specified color: *cream-~.*

2 of (partially) Negro race.

col·or·ing /ˈkələrɪŋ/ *n* [U] **1** something that colors. **2** way in which something is colored; complexion. **3** way in which something is described.

co·los·sal /kəˈlasəl/ *adj* immense.

co·los·sus /kəˈlasəs/ *n* [C] (*pl* -si /-ˌsai/, ~es) **1** immense statue (esp of a man). **2** immense person or thing.

colt /koult/ *n* [C] male horse up to the age of four years. ⇨ filly.

ˈcolt·ish *adj* like a colt; frisky.

col·um·bine /ˈkaləmˌbain/ *n* [C] plant related to the buttercup, having flowers with spur-shaped petals.

col·umn /ˈkaləm/ *n* [C] **1** tall, upright pillar, usually of stone, either supporting or decorating part of a building, or standing alone as a monument. **2** something shaped like or suggesting a column: *a ~ of smoke; the spinal ~*, the backbone. **3** vertical division of a printed page, (eg of this page or of a newspaper). **4** long row or line: *add up a long ~ of figures; a ~ of soldiers*. **5** department of a newspaper dealing with a special subject: *the sports ~*.

Com. *abbr* = Commander.

coma /ˈkoumə/ *n* [C] ***in a coma,*** in an unnatural deep sleep usually from injury or illness.

comb /koum/ *n* [C] **1** implement of metal, rubber, plastic, etc with teeth for making the hair tidy, keeping it in place, or as an ornament. **2** part of a machine like a comb, esp for tidying and straightening wool, cotton, etc for manufacture. **3** = honeycomb. **4** fleshy crest on the head of the chicken and some related birds. □ *vt,vi* **1** use a comb on (the hair). **2** prepare (wool, flax, etc) with combs for manufacture. **3** search thoroughly: *The police ~ed the whole city in their efforts to find the murderer*. **4** ***comb out,*** (*fig*) take out (unwanted things, persons) from a group: *~ out a government department*, get rid of officials who are not really needed.

com·bat[1] /ˈkamˌbæt/ *n* [C] fight; struggle.

com·bat[2] /kəmˈbæt/ *vt,vi* fight; struggle (against): *~ the enemy; ~ing with inflation*.

com·bat·ant /kəmˈbætənt/ *adj* fighting. □ *n* [C] one who fights: *In modern wars both ~s and non~s are killed in air attacks*.

com·bi·na·tion /ˌkambəˈneiʃən/ *n* **1** [U] joining or putting together; state of being joined: *in ~ with*. **2** [C] number of persons or things that are joined: *The college is supported by a ~ of grants from the government and fees from students*. **3** (also **combination lock**) formula, complicated arrangement, for the lock of a safe, etc: *How did the thieves learn the ~?*

com·bine[1] /kəmˈbain/ *vt,vi* ***combine (with),*** (cause to) join together; possess at the same time: *We can't always ~ work with pleasure. Hydrogen and oxygen ~/Hydrogen ~s with oxygen to form water*.

com·bine[2] /ˈkamˌbain/ *n* [C] **1** group of persons, trading companies, etc joined for a purpose (such as controlling prices). **2** machine that both reaps and threshes (grain).

combo /ˈkamˌbou/ *n* [C] (*informal*) small dance band.

com·bus·tible /kəmˈbəstɪbəl/ *adj* catching fire and burning easily.

com·bus·tion /kəmˈbəstʃən/ *n* [U] process of burning; destruction by fire.

come /kəm/ *vi* (*pt* came /keim/, *pp* ~) **1** approach; move towards the speaker: *Are you coming to my party this evening? He's ~ to get/~ for his book. The children came running to meet us. Come in out of the rain. Can you ~ out with me for a walk? The sunshine came streaming through the windows*. **2** arrive: *When will the train ~?* **3** reach; extend to (a particular level, figure, point): *Your bill ~s to $20. When it ~s to helping his wife with the housework, John never grumbles*. ***come to an agreement,*** agree. ***come into flower,*** begin to have flowers. ***come to a decision,*** decide. ***come to light,*** become known; be revealed or discovered. ***come to one's notice/attention,*** be noticed. ***come into view,*** appear. (*Note:* In phrases of this kind *come* indicates that the state or condition of the *noun* has been reached. For similar phrases ⇨ the *noun* entries.) **4** ***come to sb (from sb),*** be left or willed: *The farm came to him on his father's death*. **5** ***come to sb,*** occur to, happen to: *The idea came* (= occurred) *to him in his bath*. **6** reach a point where one sees, understands, etc: *He came to realize that he was mistaken. How did you ~ to find out where she's living? Now that I ~* (= happen) *to think of it....* ***how come,*** (*informal*) why; for what reason(s): *How ~ the lights aren't working?* **7** occur; be found; have as its place: *May ~s between April and June*. **8** (often with *adjectives* prefixed with *un-*) be; become; prove to be: *The handle has ~ loose. My shoelaces have ~ untied*. ***come clean,*** confess; tell everything. ***come true,*** (of wishes, dreams) be realized. **9** ***to come,*** (indicating future): *in years to ~; the life to ~*, life in the next world; *for some time to ~*, for a period of time in the future. **10** (*sl*, ⚠) have an orgasm; ejaculate. **11** (special uses with *adverbial particles* and *prepositions*):

come about, happen: *It came about in this way....*

come across (sb/sth), **(a)** find or meet by chance: *I came across this old brooch in a curio shop*. **(b)** be easily understood or readily acceptable: *His warnings didn't ~ across to them*. **(c)** (*sl*) do something as promised or expected: *They didn't ~ across with the money*.

come along, **(a)** progress: *The garden is coming along quite nicely*. **(b)** appear; arrive: *When the right opportunity ~s along, he'll take it*.

come apart, fall to pieces: *It just came apart in my hands*.

come around, **(a)** come by an indirect route: *The roads were blocked, so we had to ~ around through the fields*. **(b)** change views, etc: *He has ~ around to our way of thinking*. **(c)** = come to.

come back, return; (of fashions) become popular again: *Will pointed shoes ~ back?* ⇨ comeback. ***come back at,*** answer: *He came back at me with a cutting remark*. ***come back (to one),*** return to the memory: *Their names are all coming back to me now*.

come between, **(a)** interfere with a relation-

ship: *It is not advisable to ~ between a man and his wife.* **(b)** prevent a person from having, doing something: *He never lets anything ~ between him and his evening paper.*
come by sth, obtain by effort; become possessed of: *Jobs were hard to ~ by.*
come down, **(a)** collapse: *The ceiling came down on our heads.* **(b)** (of rain, snow, hail) fall: *The rain came down heavily.* **(c)** (of prices, temperature, etc) fall. ***come down in the world,*** lose social position; become poor. ⇨ comedown. ***come down to,*** **(a)** reach to: *Her hair ~s down to her waist.* **(b)** can be reduced to: *Your choices in the matter ~ down to these.* **(c)** (of traditions, etc) be handed down: *legends that have ~ down to us* from our ancestors. ***come down to earth,*** return to reality: *Now that his money has all been spent, he's had to ~ down to earth.*
come forward, offer or present oneself; volunteer: *Will no one ~ forward as a candidate?*
come in, **(a)** (of the tide) rise: *The tide is coming in.* **(b)** become fashionable: *When did miniskirts first ~ in?* **(c)** be received as income, etc: *There's not much money coming in at present.* ***come in handy/useful,*** happen to be useful, serve a purpose: *Don't throw it away; it may ~ in handy one day.* ***come in on,*** join; take part in: *If you want to ~ in on the scheme, you must decide now.*
come of, **(a)** be descended from: *She ~s of a good family.* **(b)** be the result of: *He promised his help, but I don't think anything will ~ of it.* ***come of age,*** ⇨ age[1](1).
come off (sth), **(a)** become detached or separated (from): *A button has ~ off my coat.* **(b)** get down (from): *Come off that wall before you fall off (it).* ***come off,*** **(a)** take place: *Did your holiday in Italy ever ~ off?* **(b)** (of plans, attempts) succeed: *The experiment did not ~ off.*
come on, **(a)** follow: *You go first, I'll ~ on later.* **(b)** (used to urge a person to do something): *Come on! Let's race to the bottom of the hill.* **(c)** make progress; develop: *How's your garden coming on?* **(d)** (of rain, the seasons, night, illness, etc) start; arrive: *He said he felt a cold coming on*, beginning.
come out, **(a)** appear; become visible: *The sun/stars came out.* **(b)** become known: *If the truth ever ~s out....* **(c)** be published: *When will his new book ~ out?* **(d)** declare oneself: *come out for/in favor of election reform.* **(e)** end up; turn out: *Did everything ~ out all right?* **(f)** (of stains, dyes, etc) be removed; disappear: *These ink stains won't ~ out. Will the color ~ out if the material is washed?* ***come out with,*** say: *He came out with a most extraordinary story.*
come over, **(a)** come from a distance: *Won't you ~ over to our house?* **(b)** change sides or opinions: *He will never ~ over to our side.* **(c)** ***come over sb,*** (of feelings, influences) take possession of: *What has ~ over you?*
come through, **(a)** recover from a serious illness or injury: *With such a weak heart, he was lucky to ~ through.* ⇨ pull[2](8). **(b)** arrive (by telephone, radio, etc): *Listen; a message is just coming through.*
come to, recover consciousness: *Pour some water on his face. He'll soon ~ to.*
come under sth, **(a)** be in (a certain category, etc): *What heading does this ~ under?* **(b)** be subjected to: *~ under her notice/influence.*
come up, **(a)** (of seed, etc): show above the ground: *The seeds/snowdrops haven't ~ up yet.* **(b)** arise: *The question hasn't ~ up yet. We shall write to you if a vacancy ~s up.* ***come up against,*** meet (difficulties, opposition). ***come up (to),*** **(a)** reach: *The water came up to my waist.* **(b)** equal: *Your work has not ~ up to my expectations.* ***come up with,*** produce; find: *~ up with a solution.*
come upon, = come across(a).
ˈcome·back *n* (eg of actors, politicians, athletes, etc) successful return to a former position: *Can he stage a ~back?*
ˈcome·down *n* fall in social position: *He has had to sell his house and furniture. What a ~down for him!*

co·median /kəˈmidiən/ *n* [C] **1** actor who plays comic parts in plays, etc. **2** person who behaves in a comic way and who cannot be taken seriously.

co·medienne /kəˌmidiˈen/ *n* [C] female comedian.

com·edy /ˈkamədi/ *n* (*pl* -ies) **1** [U] branch of drama that deals with everyday life and humorous events: *He prefers ~ to tragedy.* **2** play for the theater, of a light, amusing kind. **3** [C,U] amusing incidents in real life: *There's not much ~ in modern war.*

come·ly /ˈkəmli/ *adj* (-ier, -iest) (of a person) pleasant to look at.

co·mest·ible /kəˈmestəbəl/ *n* (*formal*) (usually *pl*) thing to eat.

comet /ˈkamɪt/ *n* [C] heavenly body (looking like a star with a bright center and a less bright tail) that moves round the sun.

com·fort /ˈkəmfərt, -fɔrt/ *n* **1** [U] state of being free from suffering, anxiety, pain, etc: *living in great ~.* **2** [U] help or kindness to a person who is suffering: *a few words of ~.* **3** [C] person or thing that brings relief or help: *Your letters/You have been a great ~ to me.* □ *vt* give comfort to: *~ those who are in trouble.*

com·fort·able /ˈkəmfərtəbəl, ˈkəmfɔrt-/ *adj* **1** giving comfort to the body: *a ~ chair/bed.* **2** having or providing comfort: *a ~ life/income.* **3** at ease; free from (too much) pain, anxiety, etc: *to be/feel ~.*
com·fort·ably /-əbli/ *adv* in a comfortable manner: *a car that holds six people comfortably.*

comic /ˈkamɪk/ *adj* **1** causing people to laugh; intended to amuse: *a ~ song.* **2** of comedy: *~ opera.* □ *n* [C] **1** comic book. **2** (*pl*) section of the newspaper with comic strips. **3** comedian.
ˈcomic book, magazine with comic strips.
ˈcomic strip, series of drawings, telling a story, as printed in newspapers, etc.

comi·cal /ˈkamɪkəl/ *adj* amusing: *a ~ act.*

com·ing /ˈkəmɪŋ/ *n* [C] arrival. □ *adj* which is to come or which will come: *in the coming years; the coming generation.*
ˌcomings and ˈgoings, arrivals and departures.

comma /ˈkamə/ *n* [C] punctuation mark (,) used to show a slight pause or break between parts of a sentence.

com·mand[1] /kəˈmænd/ *n* **1** [C] order: *His ~s were quickly obeyed.* **2** [U] authority; power (to control): *General X is in ~ of the army.* ***have/take command (of),*** have/take authority: *When the major was killed, the captain took ~ (of the company).* **3** [U] possession and skill: *He has a good ~ of the English language,* is able to use it well.

com·mand[2] /kəˈmænd/ *vt,vi* **1** order (usually with the right to be obeyed): *Do as I ~ (you). The officer ~ed his men to fire.* **2** have authority over; be in control of: *The captain of a ship ~s all the officers and men.* **3** be in a position to use; have at one's service: *He ~s great sums of money,* is able to use them if he so wishes. **4** demand and get: *Great men ~ our respect.* **5** (of a place) be in a position that overlooks (and may control): *The fort ~s the entrance to the valley.*

com·mand·ing *adj*: *the ~ing officer; in a ~ing tone/position.*

com·man·dant /ˈkamənˌdænt, -ˌdant/ *n* [C] officer in command of a fort or other military establishment.

com·man·deer /ˌkamənˈdɪr/ *vt* seize (provisions, etc) esp for military purposes.

com·man·der /kəˈmændər/ *n* [C] **1** person in command: *the ~ of the expedition; ˌ~-in-ˈchief,* commander of all the military forces of a state. **2** commissioned officer in the US navy or coast guard who ranks above a lieutenant commander and below a captain.

com·mand·ment /kəˈmændmənt/ *n* [C] **1** command. **2** (in the Bible) one of the ten laws given by God to Moses.

com·mando /kəˈmændou/ *n* (*pl* ~s or ~es) (member of a) military group trained to make surprise raids in enemy territory.

com·mem·o·rate /kəˈmeməˌreit/ *vt* **1** keep or honor the memory of (a person or event). **2** (of things) be in memory of: *A monument was built to ~ the victory.*

com·mem·o·ration /kəˌmeməˈreiʃən/ *n* **1** [U] act of commemorating: *in ~ of the victory.* **2** [C] ceremony or service in memory of a person or event.

com·mem·o·rative /kəˈmemərətɪv, -ˌreitɪv/ *adj* serving to commemorate: *~ stamps/medals.*

com·mence /kəˈmens/ *vt,vi* (*formal*) begin; start (the more usual words).

com·mence·ment *n* **(a)** beginning. **(b)** graduation ceremonies.

com·mend /kəˈmend/ *vt* (*formal*) **1** praise; speak favorably of: *His work was highly ~ed.* **2** ***commend sb/sth to,*** give for safekeeping to.

com·mend·able *adj* worthy of praise.

com·men·su·rable /kəˈmenʃərəbəl/ *adj* that can be measured by the same standard: *Their achievements are not ~.*

com·men·su·rate /kəˈmenʃərɪt/ *adj* in the right proportion: *Was the pay you received ~ with the work you did?*

com·ment /ˈkaˌment/ *n* **1** [C,U] opinion given briefly in speech or writing about an event, or in explanation or criticism: *Have you any ~s to make on my story?* **2** [C] remark. □ *vi* give or make a comment; *~ on an essay.*

com·men·tary /ˈkamənˌteri/ *n* [C] (*pl* -ies) **1** collection of comments, eg on a book: *a Bible ~.* **2** series of continuous comments (on an event): *a radio ~ on a football game.*

com·men·tate /ˈkamənˌteit/ *vi* give a commentary (on).

com·men·ta·tor /ˈkamənˌteitər/ *n* [C] person who gives a radio or TV commentary or who writes on an event.

com·merce /ˈkamərs/ *n* [U] trade (esp between countries); exchange and distribution of goods: *a Chamber of Commerce.*

com·mer·cial /kəˈmərʃəl/ *adj* of commerce: *~ traveler,* traveling salesman. □ *n* [C] advertisement broadcast on TV or radio.

comˌmercial TˈV/ˈradio, financed by charges made for commercial advertising.

com·mer·cial·ly *adv*

com·mer·cial·ize /kəˈmərʃəˌlaiz/ *vt* manage in order to make money out of: *Many sports have been ~d.*

com·miser·ate /kəˈmɪzəˌreit/ *vt,vi* feel or express pity for: *~ (with) a friend on his misfortunes.*

com·miser·ation /kəˌmɪzəˈreiʃən/ *n* [C,U] (expression of) pity or sympathy.

com·mis·sion /kəˈmɪʃən/ *n* **1** [U] the giving of authority to a person to act for another. **2** [C] instance of this; action or piece of business that is done: *He has got two ~s to design buildings for the city.* **3** [U] payment for selling goods, etc: *He receives a ~ of 10 percent on sales, as well as a salary.* **4** [C] written order appointing an officer in the armed services. **5** [C] body of persons given the duty and authority to perform certain tasks: *a special ~ to report on betting and gambling.* **6** [C] act of committing. ***out of commission,*** (*fig*) not working, not available. □ *vt* **1** give a commission to: *~ an artist to paint a portrait.* **2** put (a ship) into service.

comˌmissioned ˈofficer *n* [C] officer in the armed forces with a rank of second lieutenant or ensign or higher.

com·mis·sioner /kəˈmɪʃənər/ *n* [C] **1** member of a commission(4), esp one with particular duties: *the Federal Trade Commissioners.* **2** official in charge of a government department: *the Commissioner of Public Health.*

com·mit /kəˈmɪt/ *vt* (-tt-) **1** perform (a crime, etc): *~ murder/suicide/an offense.* **2** give up, hand over to, for guarding or treatment: *~ a man to prison; ~ a patient to a mental hospital.* ***commit to memory,*** learn by heart. **3** ***commit oneself (to...),*** pledge oneself (to do something); undertake: *He has ~ted himself to support his brother's children.*

com·mit·ment *n* [C] (esp) something to which one is committed(3): *If you have to support your parents, and two children in college, you have quite a lot of ~ments.*

com·mit·tee /kəˈmɪti/ *n* [C] group of persons appointed or elected to attend to special business: *to attend a ˈ~ meeting; to be/sit on the ~.*

com·mod·ity /kəˈmadəti/ *n* [C] (*pl* -ies) useful thing, esp an article of trade: *household commodities,* eg pots and pans.

com·mo·dore /ˈkaməˌdɔr/ *n* [C] **1** (formerly) officer having rank above a captain and below a rear admiral. **2** senior captain of a shipping line. **3** president or head of a yacht club.

com·mon[1] /ˈkamən/ *adj* (-er, -est) **1** belonging to, used by, coming from, done by, affecting, all or nearly all members of a group or society: *the ~ welfare; a ~ language*. **2** usual and ordinary; happening or found often and in many places: *a ~ experience. Is this word in ~ use?* **3** ordinary or average: *the ~ people*. **4** vulgar; coarse: *~ manners*. **5** (*math*) belonging to two or more quantities: *12 is a ~ multiple of 2, 3, 4, and 6*.

ˌcommon ˈground, (*fig*) shared opinions, point of view, etc as a basis for discussion, dispute, etc.

ˌcommon ˈknowledge, what is generally known: *It is ~ knowledge that you are dating Mary*.

ˌcommon ˈlaw, unwritten law based on customs and earlier legal decisions.

ˌcommon-law ˈmarriage, living together as husband and wife without a legal marriage ceremony.

com·mon·ly *adv* **1** usually: *That very ~ly happens. Thomas, ~ly called Tom*. **2** in a common (4) way: *~ly dressed*.

the ˌCommon ˈMarket, (officially the *European Economic Community*) economic association of various European countries.

ˌcommon ˈsense, practical good sense from general experience of life, not by special study.

com·mon[2] /ˈkamən/ *n* **1** [C] area of land for all to use: *a gathering on the town ~*. **2** ***in common,*** shared by all (of a group): *They have nothing in ~ with one another*, have no shared interests, etc.

com·moner /ˈkamənər/ *n* [C] one of the common people, not a member of the nobility.

com·mon·place /ˈkamənˌpleis/ *adj* ordinary or usual.

com·mon·wealth /ˈkamənˌwelθ/ *n* [C] **1** body of people of a nation or state. **2** union of states: *the Commonwealth of Australia*. **3** state of the US, esp Kentucky, Massachusetts, Pennsylvania, and Virginia. **4 the Commonwealth,** free association of independent states which were formerly colonies and dominions of Great Britain.

com·mo·tion /kəˈmouʃən/ *n* **1** [U] noisy confusion; excitement. **2** [C] instance of this; uprising or disturbance. **3** [C] complaint: *You're making a great ~ about nothing*.

com·mu·nal /kəˈmyunəl/ *adj* **1** of or for a community: *~ facilities*. **2** for common use: *~ land/kitchens*.

com·mune[1] /kəˈmyun/ *vi* feel at one with; feel, be, in close touch with; talk with in an intimate way: *communing with nature/God in prayer*.

com·mune[2] /ˈkaˌmyun/ *n* [C] **1** (in France, Belgium, Italy, Spain) smallest territorial district for purposes of administration, with a mayor and council. **2** organized group of people promoting local interests. **3** group of people living together and sharing property and responsibilities.

com·muni·cable /kəˈmyunɪkəbəl/ *adj* that can be communicated or passed on: *~ diseases*.

com·muni·cant /kəˈmyunɪkənt/ *n* **1** one who receives Holy Communion. **2** (*formal*) informer.

com·muni·cate /kəˈmyunɪˌkeit/ *vt,vi* **1** pass on (news, information, feelings, an illness, etc). **2** ***communicate with,*** share or exchange (news, etc): *We can ~ with people in most parts of the world by telephone*. **3** (of rooms, gardens, roads, etc) be connected (which is more usual): *My garden ~s with the garden next door by a gate*.

com·muni·ca·tion /kəˌmyunɪˈkeiʃən/ *n* **1** [U] the act of communicating: *Among the deaf ~ is often by means of sign language and the finger alphabet*. **2** [C] that which is communicated (eg news): *This ~ is confidential*. **3** [C,U] means of communicating; roads, railways, telephone or telegraph lines connecting places, radio and TV: *All ~ with the north has been stopped by snowstorms*.

com·muni·cat·ive /kəˈmyunɪˌkeitɪv/ *adj* ready and willing to talk and give information.

com·mu·nion /kəˈmyunyən/ *n* **1** [U] sharing in common; communication (with). **2** [U] exchange of thought and feelings. **3** [C] group of persons with the same religious beliefs: *We belong to the same ~*. **4 Communion** (also **ˌHoly Comˈmunion**) Christian service or sacrament in which bread and wine are shared to commemorate the Last Supper of Jesus Christ.

com·muniqué /kəˈmyunɪˌkei/ *n* [C] official announcement, eg as issued to the press.

com·mu·nism /ˈkamyəˌnɪzəm/ *n* [U] **1** (belief in a) social system in which property is owned by the community and used for the good of all its members. **2** (usually **Communism**) political and social system in which all power is held by the highest members of the Communist Party, which controls the land and its resources, the means of production, transport, etc and directs the activities of the people.

com·mu·nist *n* [C] (sometimes **Communist**) believer in, supporter of, communism. □ *adj* of communism.

com·mu·nity /kəˈmyunəti/ *n* (*pl* -ies) **1** [C] the people living in one place, district or country, considered as a whole: *work for the good of the ~*. **2** [C] group of persons having the same religion, race, occupation, etc or with common interests: *a ~ of monks; the Jewish ~ in Los Angeles*. **3** [U] condition of sharing, having things in common, being alike in some way: *~ of religion/interests*.

community ˈcollege, public junior college.

com·mu·ta·tion /ˌkamyəˈteiʃən/ *n* **1** [U] commuting; making one kind of payment instead of another, eg money instead of service. **2** [C] payment made in this way. **3** [C] reduced punishment: *a ~ of the death sentence to life imprisonment*.

com·mute /kəˈmyut/ *vt,vi* **1** exchange one thing (esp one kind of payment) for another: *~ one's weekly payment for a single, large payment*. **2** reduce the severity of a punishment: *~ a death sentence (to one of life imprisonment)*. **3** travel regularly, eg by train or car, between one's work in a town and one's home in the country

or suburbs.
com·muter *n* [C] person who commutes(3).
com·pact[1] /ˈkamˌpækt/ *n* [C] agreement between parties; contract; covenant.
com·pact[2] /kəmˈpækt/ *adj* **1** closely packed together. **2** neatly fitted so as to save space. **3** brief. □ *vt* **1** join firmly together. **2** condense.
com·pact·ly *adv*
com·pact·ness /-nɪs/ *n* [U]
com·pact[3] /ˈkamˌpækt/ *n* [C] **1** small, flat container for face powder. **2** small car, esp one made by a company which also manufactures large cars.
com·pan·ion /kəmˈpænyən/ *n* [C] **1** person who goes with, or is often or always with, another; comrade: *my ~s on the journey*. **2** one of two things that go together; thing that matches another or is one of a pair: *the ~ volume*.
com·pan·ion·ship *n* state of being companions: *a ~ship of many years*.
com·pan·ion·way /kəmˈpænyənˌwei/ *n* [C] staircase from the deck of a ship to the saloon or cabins below.
com·pany /ˈkəmpəni/ *n* (*pl* -ies) **1** [U] being together with another or others: *I shall be glad of your ~* (= to have you with me) *on the journey. He came in ~ with* (= together with) *a group of boys*. ***part company (with),*** separate: *It's sad that we have to part ~*. **2** [U] group of persons; number of guests: *We're expecting ~* (= guests, visitors) *next week*. **3** [U] associates; companions: *You may know a man by the ~ he keeps*, judge his character by his friends. **4** [C] number of persons united for business or commerce: *a steamship ~*. **5** [C] number of persons working together: *a theatrical ~*. **6** [C] military unit, commanded by a captain or major.
com·par·able /ˈkamp(ə)rəbəl/ *adj* (often with *to* or *with*) that can be compared: *His achievements are ~ with the best/to yours*.
com·para·tive /kəmˈpærətɪv/ *adj* **1** having to do with comparison or comparing: *~ religion*. **2** measured or judged by comparing: *living in ~ comfort*, eg comfortably compared with others, or with one's own life at an earlier period. **3** (*gram*) (of the form of) an adjective or adverb expressing "more", as in *smaller, worse, more likely, more prettily*. □ *n* [C] comparative form of an *adjective* or *adverb*: *"Better" is the ~ of "good"*.
com·para·tive·ly *adv*
com·pare /kəmˈpær/ *vt,vi* **1** examine, judge to what extent persons or things are similar or not similar: *~ two translations*. **2** point out the likeness or relation between: *Poets have ~d sleep to death*. ***3 compare with,*** worthy of being compared: *He cannot ~ with Shakespeare*. **4** (*gram*) make the comparative and superlative form (of adjectives and adverbs).
com·pari·son /kəmˈpærəsən/ *n* **1** [U] ***by/in comparison (with),*** when compared (with): *The tallest buildings in Los Angeles are small in ~ with those of New York*. **2** [C] act of comparing; instance of this: *It is often useful to make a ~ between two things*. **3** ***stand comparison with,*** be able to be compared favorably with: *That's a good dictionary, but it won't/can't stand ~ with this*. **4** (*gram*) positive, comparative and superlative (of adjectives and adverbs), eg *good, better, best*.
com·part·ment /kəmˈpartmənt/ *n* [C] one of several separate divisions of a structure: *The desk has a secret ~*.
com·pass /ˈkəmpəs/ *n* [C] **1** device for determining direction, with a needle that points to the magnetic north: *the points of the ~* (N, NE, E, SE, S, etc). **2** similar device, eg *a radio ~*, for determining direction. **3** (*pl*) (also **a pair of ˈcompasses**) V-shaped instrument with two arms joined by a hinge, used for drawing circles, measuring distances on a map or chart, etc. **4** extent; range: *outside the ~* (= range) *of her voice*.
com·pas·sion /kəmˈpæʃən/ *n* [U] pity; feeling for the sufferings of others; sympathy: *be filled with ~ for the refugees*.
com·pas·sion·ate /kəmˈpæʃənɪt/ *adj* showing or feeling compassion.
com·pat·ible /kəmˈpætəbəl/ *adj* suited to, in accord with, able to exist together with: *driving a car at a speed ~ with safety*.
com·pati·bil·ity /kəmˌpætəˈbɪləti/ *n* [U] the state of being compatible.
com·pat·ibly *adv*
com·pa·triot /kəmˈpeitriət/ *n* [C] person born in or citizen of the same country as another.
com·pel /kəmˈpel/ *vt* (-ll-) force (a person or thing to do something); get, bring about, by force: *His conscience ~led him to confess. Can they ~ obedience from us*, force us to obey?
com·pen·sate /ˈkampənˌseit/ *vt,vi* make a suitable payment, give something, to make up (for loss, injury, etc): *Nothing can ~ for the loss of one's health*.
com·pen·sa·tion /ˌkampənˈseiʃən/ *n* **1** [U,C] compensating. **2** [C] something that compensates: *He received $5,000 in ~/by way of ~ for the loss of his right hand*.
com·pen·sa·tory /kəmˈpensəˌtori/ *adj* compensating.
com·pete /kəmˈpit/ *vi* take part in a race, contest, examination, etc: *to ~ against/with other countries in trade*.
com·pet·ence /ˈkampətəns/ *n* **1** [U] being competent; ability: *his ~ in handling money/to handle money*. **2** (of a court, etc) legal capacity: *business that is within/beyond the ~ of the court*.
com·pet·ent /ˈkampətənt/ *adj* **1** (of persons) able, fit or qualified (to do what is needed): *Is Mr. X ~ in his work/as a teacher/to teach French?* **2** (of qualities) sufficient, adequate: *Does she have a ~ knowledge of French?*
com·pet·ent·ly *adv*
com·pe·ti·tion /ˌkampəˈtɪʃən/ *n* **1** [U] competing; activity in which persons compete: *At the Olympic Games we were in ~* (= were competing) *with the best athletes from all parts of the world*. **2** [C] instance of competing; contest; meeting(s) at which skill, strength, knowledge, etc is tested: *swimming ~s*.
com·peti·tive /kəmˈpetətɪv/ *adj* in or for which there is competition: *We offer ~ prices*, prices that match those of other firms (and are therefore good value).

com·peti·tor /kəmˈpetətər/ *n* [C] person, firm, etc that competes.
com·pi·la·tion /ˌkampəˈleiʃən/ *n* **1** [U] compiling. **2** [C] thing that is compiled.
com·pile /kəmˈpaiəl/ *vt* (-ing /kəmˈpailıŋ/) collect (information) and arrange (in a book, list, report, etc): ~ *a dictionary*.
com·piler *n* [C]
com·pla·cence /kəmˈpleisəns/ *n* [U] self-satisfaction; feeling of quiet contentment.
com·pla·cency /-sənsi/ *n* [U] = complacence.
com·pla·cent /kəmˈpleisənt/ *adj* pleased with oneself, one's ability (usually in an annoying way): *with a ~ smile/air*.
com·pla·cent·ly *adv*
com·plain /kəmˈplein/ *vi* say that one is not satisfied, that something is wrong, that one is suffering: *We have nothing to ~ of/about. He ~ed that the noise kept him awake.*
com·plain·ant /kəmˈpleinənt/ *n* [C] (*legal*) person who makes a complaint (4).
com·plaint /kəmˈpleint/ *n* **1** [U] complaining. **2** [C] statement of, grounds for, dissatisfaction: *Some children are full of ~s about their food.* **3** [C] illness; disease: *a heart/liver ~*. **4** (*legal*) formal charge against a person.
com·plai·sance /kəmˈpleisəns/ *n* [U] readiness and willingness to do what pleases others.
com·plai·sant /-sənt/ *adj* obliging; ready to please: *a complaisant employee*.
com·ple·ment /ˈkampləmənt/ *n* [C] **1** something that completes or makes perfect; the full number or quantity needed. **2** (*gram*) word(s) esp *adjectives* and *nouns*, used after verbs such as *be* and *become* and qualifying the subject. □ *vt* complete; form the complement to.
com·ple·men·tary /ˌkampləˈment(ə)ri/ *adj* that complements.
compleˌmentary ˈangles, two angles that together form an angle of 90°.
com·plete[1] /kəmˈplit/ *adj* **1** having all its parts; whole: *a ~ edition of Shakespeare's plays.* **2** finished; ended: *When will the work be ~?* **3** thorough; in every way: *It was a ~ surprise to me*, I wasn't expecting it and hadn't even thought of it.
com·plete·ly *adv* wholly; in every way: *~ly charming*.
com·plete·ness /-nıs/ *n* [U]
com·plete[2] /kəmˈplit/ *vt* finish; bring to an end; make perfect: *I need one more volume to ~ my set of Henry James.*
com·ple·tion /kəmˈpliʃən/ *n* [U] act of completing; state of being complete: *The house is near ~.*
com·plex[1] /kamˈpleks/ *adj* **1** made up of two or more closely connected parts. **2** difficult to understand or explain: *a ~ argument/proposal/situation*.
com·plex·ity /kəmˈpleksəti/ *n* [C,U]
com·plex[2] /ˈkamˌpleks/ *n* [C] **1** a whole made up of different parts intricately related: *The hospital consisted of a ~ of low buildings.* **2** (abnormal) mental state which is the result of past experiences or suppressed tendencies. **3** (*informal*) unreasonable concern or fear. ⇨ inferiority.
com·plexion /kəmˈplekʃən/ *n* [C] **1** natural color, appearance, etc of the skin, esp of the face: *a good/dark/fair ~*. **2** general character or aspect (of conduct, affairs, etc): *This victory changed the ~ of the war.*
com·pli·ance /kəmˈplaiəns/ *n* [U] action of complying: *in ~ with your wishes*, as you wish(ed) us (to do).
com·pli·ant /kəmˈplaiənt/ *adj* ready to comply.
com·pli·cate /ˈkampləˌkeit/ *vt* make complex; make difficult to do or understand: *This ~s matters.*
com·pli·cated *adj* **1** made up of many parts: *a ~d machine/business deal.* **2** hard to understand or explain.
com·pli·ca·tion /ˌkampləˈkeiʃən/ *n* [C] state of being complex, confused, difficult; something that adds new difficulties (eg of a person who is ill): *Here are further ~s to worry us. She'll live; if no further ~s set in.*
com·plic·ity /kəmˈplısəti/ *n* [U] taking part with another person (in doing wrong).
com·pli·ment /ˈkampləmənt/ *n* [C] **1** act or expression of admiration, approval, etc. **2** (*pl*) greetings: *My ~s to your wife*, Please give her a greeting from me. □ *vt* express admiration, etc: *I ~ed him on his skill.*
com·pli·men·tary /ˌkampləˈment(ə)ri/ *adj* **1** expressing admiration, praise, etc. **2** given free, out of courtesy or kindness: *a ~ ticket*.
com·ply /kəmˈplai/ *vt* (*pt,pp* -ied) act in accordance (with a request, command, a wish, etc): *He refused to ~.*
com·po·nent /kəmˈpounənt/ *adj* helping to form (a complete thing): *~ parts*. □ *n* [C] part of a larger or more complex object: *the ~s of a camera*.
com·port /kəmˈpɔrt/ *vt,vi* (*formal*) **1** (usually *reflex*) behave; conduct: *~ oneself with dignity.* **2** ***comport with,*** suit, be in harmony with: *His conduct did not ~ with his high position.*
com·pose /kəmˈpouz/ *vt,vi* **1** (of elements) make up: *the parts that ~ the whole; Our party was ~d of teachers, pupils and their parents.* **2** put together (words, musical notes, etc) in literary, musical, etc form: *~ a poem/a song/a speech.* **3** (printing) set up (type) to form pages, etc. **4** get under control; calm: *~ one's thoughts/passions.*
com·posed *adj* calm; with feelings under control.
com·posed·ly *adv*
com·pos·er /kəmˈpouzər/ *n* [C] (esp) person who composes music.
com·pos·ite /kəmˈpazıt/ *adj* made up of different parts or materials: *a ~ illustration*, made by putting together two or more drawings, etc.
com·po·si·tion /ˌkampəˈzıʃən/ *n* **1** [U] act or art of composing, eg a piece of writing or music. **2** [C] that which is composed, eg a piece of music, an arrangement of objects to be painted or photographed. **3** [C] (esp) exercise in writing. **4** [U] the parts of which something is made up: *Scientists study the ~ of the soil.* **5** [C] substance composed of more than one material, esp an artificial substance: *~ floors*.
com·posi·tor /kəmˈpazətər/ *n* [C] person who sets type for printing.

com·pos men·tis /kampəs ˈmentɪs/ *adj* (*Lat*) of sound mind and therefore legally responsible.
com·post /ˈkamˌpoust/ *n* [U] prepared mixture, esp of rotted food, leaves, manure, etc for use as a fertilizer. □ *vt* make into compost.
com·po·sure /kəmˈpouʒər/ *n* [U] calmness: *behave with great* ~.
com·pound[1] /ˈkamˌpaund/ *n* [C], *adj* **1** (thing) made up of two or more combined parts: *Common salt is a* ~ *of sodium and chlorine.* **2** (*gram*) word made up of two or more parts, themselves usually words, eg *long-legged.*
ˌcompound ˈfracture, breaking of a bone so as to make an open wound in the skin.
ˌcompound ˈinterest, on capital and on accumulated interest.
com·pound[2] /kəmˈpaund/ *vt,vi* (*formal*) **1** mix together: ~ *a medicine.* **2** settle (a quarrel, a debt) by mutual agreement; agree to terms: *He ~ed with his creditors for a remission of what he owed.* **3** add to, increase the seriousness of (an offense or injury): *That simply ~s the offense.*
com·pound[3] /ˈkamˌpaund/ *n* [C] enclosed area with buildings, etc, eg a number of houses.
com·pre·hend /ˌkampriˈhend/ *vt* (*formal*) **1** understand fully. **2** include; consist of.
com·pre·hen·sible /ˌkampriˈhensəbəl/ *adj* that can be understood fully: *a book that is* ~ *only to specialists.*
com·pre·hen·si·bil·ity /ˌkampriˌhensəˈbɪləti/ *n* [U]
com·pre·hen·sion /ˌkampriˈhenʃən/ *n* [U] **1** act or power of understanding: *The problem is beyond my* ~. **2** power of including: *a term of wide* ~, that has many meanings, uses, etc.
com·pre·hen·sive /ˌkampriˈhensɪv/ *adj* that comprehends(2): *a* ~ *description.*
comprehensive·ly *adv*
com·pre·hen·sive·ness /-nɪs/ *n* [U]
com·press[1] /kəmˈpres/ *vt* press, get into a small(er) space: *~ed air; ~ed his ideas into a few words.*
com·press[2] /ˈkamˌpres/ *n* [C] pad or cloth pressed on to a part of the body (to stop bleeding, reduce fever, etc): *a cold/hot* ~.
com·pres·sion /kəmˈpreʃən/ *n* [U] compressing; being compressed.
com·pres·sor /kəmˈpresər/ *n* [C] (esp) machine for compressing gas, air, etc.
com·prise /kəmˈpraiz/ *vt* be composed of; have as parts or members: *The committee ~s men of widely different views.*
com·pro·mise /ˈkamprəˌmaiz/ *n* **1** [U] settlement of a dispute by which each side gives up something it has asked for. **2** [C] instance of this; settlement reached in this way: *A* ~ *agreement was at last arrived at.* □ *vt,vi* **1** settle a dispute, etc, by making a compromise: *if they agree to* ~. **2** run the risk of danger, suspicion, etc: *You will* ~ *yourself/your reputation if you stay in that hotel. The battalion's safety was ~d by the lieutenant colonel's poor judgment.*
com·pul·sion /kəmˈpəlʃən/ *n* [U] compelling or being compelled.
com·pul·sive /kəmˈpəlsɪv/ *adj* **1** having a tendency or the power to compel. **2** caused by an obsession: *a* ~ *eater/liar.*
com·pul·sive·ly *adv*
com·pul·sory /kəmˈpəlsəri/ *adj* that must be done; required: *Is English a* ~ *subject?*
com·punc·tion /kəmˈpəŋkʃən/ *n* [U] uneasiness of conscience; feeling of regret for one's action: *She kept me waiting without the slightest* ~.
com·pu·ta·tion /ˌkampyəˈteiʃən/ *n* **1** [U] computing; calculation. **2** [C] result of computing.
com·pute /kəmˈpyut/ *vt* reckon; count; calculate.
com·pu·ter /kəmˈpyutər/ *n* [C] electronic device which computes, stores information, etc.
com·rade /ˈkamˌræd/ *n* [C] **1** trusted companion; loyal friend: *~s in arms*, fellow soldiers. **2** fellow member of a trade union, a (left-wing) political party, etc.
com·rade·ship /ˈkamˌrædˌʃɪp/ *n* [U]
con[1] /kan/ *n* [C] (*sl*) convict: *ex-con*, former convict.
con[2] /kan/ *vt* (*sl*) swindle.
ˈcon-man *n* [C] (*pl* conmen /kanmen/) (*sl*) confidence man; swindler.
con[3] /kan/ *adv* against: *argued pro and con.*
con- (also **col-, com-, cor-**) /kan-, kən- (etc)/ *prefix* with; together: *conspire; collaborate; combine; correlate.*
con·cave /kanˈkeiv/ *adj* (of an outline or surface) curved inwards like the inside of a sphere or circle. ⇨ illus at convex.
con·cav·ity /kanˈkævəti/ *n* **1** [U] concave condition. **2** [C] (*pl* -ies) concave surface.
con·ceal /kənˈsiəl/ *vt* (-ing /kənˈsilɪŋ/) hide; keep secret: *He tried to* ~ *the truth from me.*
con·ceal·ment *n* [U] (state) of being concealed: *Stay in ~ment until the danger has passed.*
con·cede /kənˈsid/ *vt* admit; grant; allow: *~d a point in an argument/that he was right. We cannot* ~ *any of our territory,* allow another country to have it.
con·ceit /kənˈsit/ *n* [U] too high opinion of, too much pride in, oneself or one's abilities, etc: *He's full of* ~.
con·ceited *adj*
con·ceited·ly *adv*
con·ceiv·able /kənˈsivəbəl/ *adj* that can be thought of or believed: *It is hardly* ~ *(to me) that....*
con·ceiv·ably *adv*
con·ceive /kənˈsiv/ *vt,vi* **1** form (an idea, plan, etc) in the mind: *Who first ~d the idea of the wheel?* **2** (of a woman) become pregnant (with): ~ *a child.*
con·cen·trate /ˈkasənˌtreit/ *vt,vi* **1** bring or come together at one point: *to* ~ *soldiers in a town.* **2** keep one's attention: *You'll solve the problem if you* ~ *on it.* **3** increase the strength of (a solution) by reducing its volume (eg by boiling it down). □ *n* [C] product made by concentrating(3).
con·cen·trated *adj* **(a)** intense: *~d hate.* **(b)** increased in strength or value by evaporation of liquid: *~d orange juice.*
con·cen·tra·tion /ˌkansənˈtreiʃən/ *n* **1** [C] that which is concentrated: *~s of enemy troops.* **2** [U] concentrating or being concentrated: *a book*

that requires great ~.

ˌ**concenˈtration camp,** camp where civilian political prisoners, prisoners of war, etc are held.

con·cen·tric /kənˈsentrɪk/ *adj* (of circles) having a common center.

CONCENTRIC CIRCLES

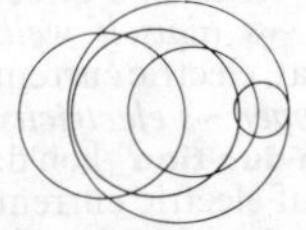
CIRCLES NOT CONCENTRIC

con·cept /ˈkanˌsept/ *n* [C] idea underlying a class of things; general notion.

con·cep·tion /kənˈsepʃən/ *n* **1** [U] conceiving of an idea or plan. **2** [C] idea or plan that takes shape in the mind: *A good novelist needs great powers of* ~. **3** conceiving(2).

con·cern[1] /kənˈsərn/ *vt* **1** have relation to; affect; be of importance to: *Does this* ~ *me? So/As far as I'm* ~*ed*..., so far as the matter is important to me, or affects me.... **2** ***concern oneself,*** be busy with, interest oneself in: *He has* ~*ed himself with the details of committee work.* **3** make unhappy or troubled: *Her safety has concerned all of us.*

con·cern·ing *prep* = about[3](1).

con·cern[2] /kənˈsərn/ *n* **1** [C] relation or connection; something in which one is interested or which is important: *It's no* ~ *of mine*, I have nothing to do with it. **2** [C] business or undertaking: *The shop has now become a paying* ~, is making profits. **3** [U] anxiety: *There is some cause for* ~.

con·cerned *adj* **1** anxious: *with a* ~*ed look.* **2** involved.

con·cert /ˈkanˌsərt/ *n* **1** [C] musical entertainment, esp one given in a public hall by players or singers. **2** [U] agreement; harmony: *working in* ~ *with his colleagues.*

con·cert·ed /kənˈsərtɪd/ *adj* planned, performed, agreed on (by two or more together): *to make a* ~ *effort.*

con·cer·tina /ˌkansərˈtinə/ *n* [C] (*pl* ~s) small musical instrument similar to an accordion.

con·cer·to /kənˈtʃertou/ *n* [C] (*pl* ~s, -ti /-ti/) musical composition for one or more solo instruments supported by an orchestra: *a ˈpiano* ~.

con·ces·sion /kənˈseʃən/ *n* **1** [U] conceding. **2** [C] that which is conceded, esp after discussion, an argument, etc: *As a* ~ *to public opinion, the government reduced the tax on gas.* **3** [C] (esp) right given by owner(s) of land, or by a government, to do something (eg take minerals from land): *American oil* ~*s in the Middle East.*

conch /kantʃ, kaŋk/ *n* (*pl* ~es /ˈkantʃɪz/ or ~s /kaŋks/) shellfish with a large spiral shell. ⇨ illus at mollusk.

con·cili·ate /kənˈsɪliˌeit/ *vt* **1** win the support, goodwill or friendly feelings of. **2** calm the anger of; soothe.

con·cili·atory /kənˈsɪliəˌtɔri/ *adj* tending or likely to conciliate: *a conciliatory act/spirit.*

con·cili·ation /kənˌsɪliˈeiʃən/ *n* [U] conciliating or being conciliated: *The dispute is being dealt with by a* ~ *board*, a group of persons who arbitrate, etc.

con·cise /kənˈsais/ *adj* (of a person, his speech or style, of writings, etc) giving much information in few words.

con·cise·ly *adv*

con·cise·ness /-nɪs/ *n* [U]

con·clave /ˈkanˌkleiv/ *n* [C] private or secret meeting (eg of cardinals to elect a Pope).

con·clude /kənˈklud/ *vt,vi* **1** come or bring to an end: *He* ~*d by saying that*.... **2** arrange; bring about: *to* ~ *a treaty with*.... **3** arrive at a belief or opinion: *The jury* ~*d, from the evidence, that the accused man was not guilty.*

con·clu·sion /kənˈkluʒən/ *n* [C] **1** end: *at the* ~ *of his speech.* ***in conclusion,*** lastly. **2** arrangement; decision; settlement: *the* ~ *of a peace treaty.* **3** belief or opinion which is the result of reasoning: *to come to/reach the* ~ *that*....

con·clu·sive /kənˈklusɪv/ *adj* (of facts, evidence, etc) convincing; ending doubt: ~ *evidence/proof of his guilt.*

con·clus·ive·ly *adv*

con·coct /kənˈkakt/ *vt* **1** prepare by mixing together: *to* ~ *a new kind of soup.* **2** make up, invent (a story, an excuse, a plot for a novel, etc).

con·coc·tion /kənˈkakʃən/ *n* **1** [U] mixing. **2** [C] mixture.

con·cord /ˈkanˌkɔrd/ *n* **1** [U] agreement or harmony (between persons or things): *live in* ~ *(with...).* **2** [C] instance of this.

con·cor·dance /kənˈkɔrdəns/ *n* **1** [U] agreement. **2** [C] arrangement in alphabetical order of the important words used by an author or in a book: *a ˈShakespeare* ~.

con·course /ˈkanˌkɔrs/ *n* [C] **1** coming or moving together of things, persons, etc: *an unforeseen* ~ *of circumstances.* **2** place where crowds come together.

con·crete /kanˈkrit/ *adj* **1** of material things; existing in material form; that can be touched, felt, etc: *A lamp is* ~ *but light is abstract.* **2** definite; positive: ~ *proposals/evidence/proof.* □ /ˈkanˌkrit/ *n* [U] building material made by mixing cement with sand, gravel, etc: *a ˈ~ mixer.* □ /ˈkanˌkrit/ *vt* cover with concrete: ~ *a road.*

con·cu·bine /ˈkaŋkyəˌbain/ *n* [C] (in some countries, where polygamy is legal) lesser wife.

con·cur /kənˈkər/ *vi* (-rr-) **1** agree in opinion: *I* ~ *with the speaker in condemning what has been done.* **2** (of circumstances, etc) happen together: *Everything* ~*red to produce a successful result.*

con·cur·rence /kənˈkərəns/ *n* [U] **1** agreement. **2** coming together.

con·cur·rent /kənˈkərənt/ *adj* **1** happening together. **2** cooperating.

con·cur·rent·ly *adv*

con·cuss /kənˈkəs/ *vt* injure (the brain) by concussion.

con·cus·sion /kənˈkəʃən/ *n* [C,U] (an) injury or (a) violent shaking or shock esp to the brain (as caused by a blow, knock or fall).

con·demn /kənˈdem/ *vt* **1** declare to be wrong; express disapproval of: *We all* ~ *cruelty to* *children.* **2** declare that something is unfit to use: *The surveyor ~ed the building as unsafe.* **3** (*legal*) give judgment against; sentence: *~ a murderer to life imprisonment.* **4** take for public use by law: *The block has been ~ed to make way for the new road.*

con·dem·na·tion /ˌkandemˈneiʃən/ *n* [U]

con·den·sa·tion /ˌkandenˈseiʃən/ *n* **1** [U] condensing or being condensed: *the ~ of steam to water.* **2** [C,U] (mass of) drops of liquid formed when vapor condenses: *A cloud is a ~ of vapor.*

con·dense /kənˈdens/ *vt,vi* **1** (of a liquid) (cause to) increase in density or strength, to become thicker: *~ed milk.* **2** (of a gas or vapor) (cause to) change to a liquid. **3** (of light) focus; concentrate (by passing through a lens). **4** put into fewer words: *a ~d account of an event.*

con·dens·er /kənˈdensər/ *n* [C] **1** apparatus for cooling gas or vapor and condensing it to liquid. **2** apparatus for receiving and accumulating static electricity.

con·de·scend /ˌkandɪˈsend/ *vi* **1** do something that one's rank, importance, etc does not require one to do: *The famous actor has graciously ~ed to support our cause.* **2** lower oneself: *He occasionally ~ed to trickery/to take bribes.* **3** do something in a way that shows one's feeling of superiority: *Mrs. Hope doesn't like being ~ed to.*

con·de·scend·ing *adj*

con·di·ment /ˈkandəmənt/ *n* [C,U] (*formal*) = seasoning.

con·di·tion[1] /kənˈdɪʃən/ *n* **1** [C] something on which another thing depends: *Ability is one of the ~s of success in life.* ***on condition that,*** only if; provided that: *You can go on ~ that you come home early.* **2** [U] the state, nature, quality, character of: *The ~ of my health prevents me from working. He's in no ~ to travel,* is not well or strong enough. **3** (*pl*) circumstances: *under existing/favorable ~s.*

con·di·tion[2] /kənˈdɪʃən/ *vt* **1** determine; govern; regulate: *My expenditure is ~ed by my income.* **2** bring into a desired state or condition: *We'll never ~ the workers to a willing acceptance of a wage freeze.*

con·di·tioned *adj* **1** subject to certain provisions or conditions. **2** put into a specified condition.

con·di·tional /kənˈdɪʃənəl/ *adj* depending on, containing, a condition: *a ~ clause,* beginning with "if" or "unless."

con·di·tionally *adv*

con·do·lence /kənˈdouləns/ *n* (often *pl*) expression of sympathy: *Please accept my ~s.*

con·do·min·i·um /ˌkandəˈmɪniəm/ *n* [C] (*pl* ~s) **1** apartment building with privately owned units. **2** individual apartment in such a building.

con·done /kənˈdoun/ *vt* overlook or forgive (an offense): *~ a child's bad behavior.*

con·dor /ˈkandər, -ˌdɔr/ *n* [C] large American vulture with a white neck ruff and a bare head.

con·du·cive /kənˈdusɪv/ *adj* helping to produce: *Good health is ~ to happiness.*

con·duct[1] /ˈkanˌdəkt/ *n* [U] **1** way a person acts; behavior: *good/bad ~.* **2** manner of directing or managing affairs: *People were not at all satisfied with the ~ of the war,* the way in which the leaders were directing it.

con·duct[2] /kənˈdəkt/ *vt,vi* **1** lead or guide: *Mr. Young ~ed the visitors around the museum.* **2** control; direct; manage: *to ~ a meeting/negotiations.* **3** direct (an orchestra). **4** behave: *He ~s himself well.* **5** (of substances) allow (heat, electric current) to pass along or through: *Copper ~s electricity.*

con·duc·tion /kənˈdəkʃən/ *n* [U] transmission, eg of electric current, sound, heat, etc.

con·duc·tive /kənˈdəktɪv/ *adj* able to transmit (heat, electric current, etc).

con·duc·tor /kənˈdəktər/ *n* [C] **1** person who conducts esp a group of singers, a band, an orchestra. **2** person in charge of bus, train, etc. **3** substance that conducts heat or electric current.

con·duc·tress /kənˈdəktrɪs/ *n* [C] woman conductor(2). (*Note:* Less common than *conductor* or *lady/woman conductor*).

cone /koun/ *n* [C] **1** solid body which narrows to a point from a round, flat base. ⇨ illus at geometry. **2** something of this shape whether solid or hollow. **3** fruit of certain evergreen trees (fir, pine, cedar). ⇨ illus at tree.

con·fec·tion /kənˈfekʃən/ *n* (*formal*) **1** [C] sweet mixture, eg preserves, candy, cake, etc. **2** [U] mixing; compounding.

con·fec·tioner *n* [C] (*formal*) person who makes and sells pastry, pies, cakes, etc.

con·fec·tion·ery /kənˈfekʃəˌneri/ *n* **(a)** [U] candy, cakes, pies, pastry, etc. **(b)** [C] (*pl* -ies) place, business, of a confectioner.

con·fed·er·acy /kənˈfedərəsi/ *n* **1** [C] (*pl* -ies) union of states, parties or persons. **2 the Confederacy** (also the **Confederate States of America**) the eleven States that separated from the Union in 1860-61.

con·fed·er·ate[1] /kənˈfedərɪt/ *adj* **1** joined together by an agreement or treaty. **2 Confederate**, of the Confederacy *the Confederate Army.* □ *n* **1 Confederate,** soldier, citizen, etc of the Confederacy (2). **2** ally, accomplice (in a plot, etc).

con·fed·er·ate[2] /kənˈfedəˌreit/ *vt,vi* bring into or come into alliance.

con·fed·er·ation /kənˌfedəˈreiʃən/ *n* **(a)** [U] confederating or being confederated. **(b)** [C] alliance; league.

con·fer /kənˈfər/ *vt,vi* (-rr-) **1** ***confer sth on/upon,*** give or grant (a degree, title, favor): *The University ~red honorary degrees on several distinguished writers.* **2** consult or discuss: *~ with one's lawyer.*

con·fer·ment *n* [C,U]

con·fer·ral *n* [C,U]

con·fer·ence /ˈkanf(ə)rəns/ *n* [C,U] (meeting for) discussion; exchange of views: *The Director is in ~/holding a ~.*

con·fess /kənˈfes/ *vt,vi* **1** acknowledge or admit (guilt, a fault or weakness, etc): *He ~ed that he had stolen the money. I ~ to having a fear of spiders.* **2** make known one's sins, esp to a priest. **3** (of a priest) listen to a person telling his sins.

con·fess·edly /kənˈfesɪdli/ *adv* as, by one's own

confession.

con·fes·sion /kən'feʃən/ *n* **1** [U] confessing. **2** [C] instance of this: *The accused man made a full* ~. *She is a good Catholic and goes to* ~ *regularly*. **3** [C] declaration (of religious beliefs, or of principles of conduct, etc): *a* ~ *of faith*.

con·fes·sional /kən'feʃənəl/ *n* [C] private place in a church where a priest sits to hear confessions.

con·fetti /kən'feti/ *n* [U] bits of colored paper showered on people at weddings. etc.

con·fi·dant /'kanfəˌdænt, -ˌdant/ *n* [C] person who is trusted with private affairs or secrets (esp about love affairs).

con·fide /kən'faid/ *vt,vi* **1** tell a secret; give to be looked after; give (a task or duty to a person): *He* ~*d his troubles to a friend*. **2** ***confide in,*** have trust or faith in: *Can I* ~ *in his honesty?*

con·fid·ing *adj* truthful; trusting: *She's of a confiding nature*.

con·fi·dence /'kanfədəns/ *n* **1** [U] (act of) confiding in or to. ***in strict confidence,*** expecting something to be kept secret. **2** [C] secret, confidential information, which is confided to a person: *The two girls sat in a corner exchanging* ~*s about the young men they knew*. **3** [U] belief in oneself or others or in what is said, reported, etc; belief that one is right or that one is able to perform: *to have/lose* ~ *in oneself/her*. *He answered the questions with* ~.

'confidence man, swindler who is entrusted with valuables by his victim.

con·fi·dent /'kanfədənt/ *adj* feeling or showing confidence; certain: *He feels fairly* ~ *of passing/that he will pass the examination*.

con·fi·dent·ly *adv*

con·fi·den·tial /ˌkanfə'denʃəl/ *adj* **1** (to be kept) secret: ~ *information*. **2** trusted with secrets, etc: *a* ~ *secretary*.

con·fi·den·tially *adv*

con·fine /kən'fain/ *vt* **1** ***confine to,*** keep or hold, restrict, within limits: *Please* ~ *your remarks to the subject we are debating*. **2** keep shut up: *Is it cruel to* ~ *a bird in a cage?* **3** ***be confined,*** give birth to a child.

con·fined *adj* (of space) limited; narrow; restricted.

con·fine·ment *n* **(a)** [U] being confined; imprisonment: *He was placed in* ~*ment*. **(b)** [U] giving birth to a child. **(c)** [C] instance of this.

con·fines /'kanˌfainz/ *n pl* limits; borders; boundaries: *beyond the* ~ *of human knowledge/this valley*.

con·firm /kən'fərm/ *vt* **1** make (power, ownership, opinions, rights, feelings, etc) firmer or stronger; make sure of the truth of: *The report of an earthquake in Greece has now been* ~*ed*, we now know that the report was true. **2** agree definitely to (a treaty, an appointment, etc). **3** admit to full membership of the Christian Church: *She was baptized when she was a month old and* ~*ed when she was thirteen*.

con·firmed *adj* (esp) unlikely to change or be changed: *a* ~*ed invalid*.

con·fir·ma·tion /ˌkanfər'meiʃən/ *n* [C,U] confirming or being confirmed (all senses): *We are waiting for* ~ *of the news*.

con·fis·cate /'kanfəˌskeit/ *vt* (as punishment or in enforcing authority) take (private property) without compensation or payment: *If you try to smuggle goods into the country, they may be* ~*d by the customs authorities*.

con·fis·ca·tion /ˌkanfə'skeiʃən/ *n* **1** [U] confiscating or being confiscated. **2** [C] instance of this.

con·flict[1] /'kanˌflɪkt/ *n* [C] **1** fight; struggle; quarrel: *a bitter* ~ *between employers and workers*. **2** (of opinions, desires, etc) opposition; difference: *the* ~ *between duty and desire*.

con·flict[2] /kən'flɪkt/ *vi* be in opposition or disagreement: *His account of the war* ~*s with mine*.

con·flict·ing *adj*

con·form /kən'fɔrm/ *vi,vt* **1** ***conform to,*** be in agreement with, comply with (generally accepted rules, standards, etc): *You should* ~ *to the rules/to the wishes of others*. **2** make similar to; adapt oneself to.

con·form·ist /kən'fɔrmɪst/ *n* [C] one who conforms.

con·form·ity /kən'fɔrməti/ *n* [U] **1** action, behavior, in agreement with what is usual, accepted or required by custom, etc: *Conformity to fashion* (= Having things of the latest fashions) *is not essential to the happiness of all women*. **2** agreement: *Was his action in* ~ *with the law?*

con·found /kən'faund/ *vt* **1** fill with, throw into, confusion: *His behavior amazed and* ~*ed her*. **2** mix up, confuse (ideas, etc): *Don't* ~ *the means with the ends*.

con·front /kən'frənt/ *vt* bring, come, be face to face: *When* ~*ed with the evidence of his guilt, he confessed at once. A soldier has to* ~ *danger*.

con·fron·ta·tion /'kanfrən'teiʃən/ *n* [C,U] **1** (instance of) being face to face. **2** conflict: *Fairy-tales often depict the* ~ *between the forces of good and evil*.

con·fuse /kən'fyuz/ *vt* **1** put into disorder; mix up in the mind: *They asked so many questions that they* ~*d me/I got* ~*d*. **2** mistake one thing for another: *Don't* ~ *Austria with/and Australia*.

con·fus·edly /kən'fyuzɪdli/ *adv* in a confused manner.

con·fu·sion /kən'fyuʒən/ *n* [U] being confused; disorder: *His unexpected arrival threw everything into* ~. *There has been some* ~*; it was Mr. Smythe who came not Mr. Smith*.

con·fute /kən'fyut/ *vt* (*formal*) **1** prove (a person) to be wrong. **2** show (an argument) to be false.

Cong. *abbr* = **1** Congress. **2** Congressional.

con·geal /kən'dʒiəl/ *vt,vi* (*pres part* ~ing /kən'dʒilɪŋ/) make or become stiff or solid: ~*ed blood*.

con·gen·ial /kən'dʒinyəl/ *adj* **1** (of persons) having the same or a similar nature, common interests, etc: *In this small town he found few persons* ~ *to him*. **2** (of things, occupations, etc) in agreement with one's tastes, nature: *a* ~ *climate;* ~ *work*.

con·gen·ial·ly *adv*

con·geni·tal /kən'dʒenətəl/ *adj* (of diseases,

etc) present, belonging to one, from or before birth.

con·ger eel /ˈkaŋgər ˌiəl/ *n* [C] saltwater eel of large size.

con·gested /kənˈdʒestɪd/ *adj* **1** too full; overcrowded: *streets ~ with traffic.* **2** (of parts of the body, eg the brain, the lungs) having an abnormal accumulation of blood, mucus, etc.

con·ges·tion /kənˈdʒestʃən/ *n* [U] being congested: *~ of the lungs/ of traffic in town.*

con·glom·er·ate¹ /kənˈglamərɪt/ *adj, n* [C,U] (made up of a) number of things or parts (eg rock made up of small stones held together).

con·glom·er·ate² /kənˈglaməˌreit/ *vt,vi* collect into a mass.

con·glom·er·ation /kənˌglaməˈreiʃən/ *n* **1** [U] conglomerating or being conglomerated. **2** [C] mass of conglomerated things.

con·gratu·late /kənˈgrætʃəˌleit/ *vt* tell (a person) that one is pleased about his success, happiness, etc: *~ him on his marriage/for winning the election. I ~d myself on my escape/on having escaped unhurt.*

con·gratu·la·tory /kənˈgrætʃələˌtori/ *adj* that congratulates: *a congratulatory telegram.*

con·gratu·la·tion /kənˌgrætʃəˈleiʃən/ *n* [C] (often *pl*) words that congratulate.

con·gre·gate /ˈkaŋgrəˌgeit/ *vi,vt* come or bring together: *People quickly ~d round the speaker.*

con·gre·ga·tion /ˌkaŋgrəˈgeiʃən/ *n* **1** [U] congregating. **2** [C] gathering of people, esp for religious worship.

con·gre·ga·tional *adj* of a congregation(2).

con·gress /ˈkaŋgrɪs/ *n* **1** [C] meeting, series of meetings, of representatives (of societies, etc) for discussion: *a medical ~.* **2** [C] lawmaking body of a nation, esp of a republic. **3 Congress,** chief lawmaking body of the US, consisting of the Senate and the House of Representatives. **4** a session of Congress.

con·gres·sion·al /kanˈgreʃənəl/ *adj* of Congress.

con·gress·man /-mən/ *n* (*pl* ~men /-men/) male member of Congress.

con·gress·woman /-ˌwʊmən/ *n* (*pl* ~women /-ˌwɪmən/) female member of Congress.

con·gru·ent /kənˈgruənt/ *adj* **1** suitable; agreeing (with). **2** (*geom*) having the same size and shape: *~ triangles.*

con·gru·ous /ˈkaŋgruəs/ *adj* fitting; proper; harmonious (with).

conic /ˈkanɪk/ *adj* of a cone: *~ sections.*

coni·cal /ˈkanɪkəl/ *adj* cone-shaped.

coni·fer /ˈkanəfər/ *n* [C,U] tree of the kind (eg *pine, fir*) that bears cones.

co·nifer·ous /kəˈnɪfərəs/ *adj*

con·jec·ture /kənˈdʒektʃər/ *vi,vt* guess; put forward an opinion formed without facts as proof: *It was just as I ~d.* □ *n* [C] guess; guessing: *I was right in my ~s.*

con·jec·tural /kənˈdʒektʃərəl/ *adj* involving, inclined to conjecture.

con·ju·gal /ˈkandʒəgəl/ *adj* of marriage and wedded life; of husband and wife: *~ happiness/ infidelity.*

con·ju·gal·ly *adv*

con·ju·gate /ˈkandʒəˌgeit/ *vt* give the forms of a verb (for number, tense, etc).

con·ju·ga·tion /ˌkandʒəˈgeiʃən/ *n* **(a)** [C,U] scheme or system of verb forms. **(b)** [C] class of verbs conjugated alike.

con·junc·tion /kənˈdʒəŋkʃən/ *n* **1** [C] (*gram*) word that joins other words, clauses, etc, eg *and, but, or.* **2** [U] joining; state of being joined: *the ~ of skill and imagination in planning a garden.* ***in conjunction with,*** together with. **3** [C] combination (of events, etc): *an unusual ~ of circumstances.*

con·junc·tive /kənˈdʒəŋktɪv/ *adj* serving to join; connective. □ *n* [C] = conjunction(1).

con·junc·ture /kənˈdʒəŋktʃər/ *n* [C] combination of events or circumstances.

con·jure /ˈkandʒər/ *vt,vi* **1** do clever tricks which appear magical: *~ a rabbit out of a hat.* **2** ***conjure up,*** **(a)** cause to appear as if from nothing, or as an image in the mind: *~ up visions of the past.* **(b)** compel (a spirit) to appear by invocation: *~ up the spirits of the dead.* **(c)** (*informal*) make appear or happen as if by magic: *~ up a stew.*

con·jurer, con·juror /ˈkandʒərər/ *n* [C] person who conjures.

con·nect /kəˈnekt/ *vt,vi* **1** join, be joined (by things, by personal or business relationships, etc): *The two towns are ~ed by a railway. Mr. Smith has been ~ed with this firm since 1950.* **2** think of (different things or persons) as being related to each other: *to ~ Malaya with rubber and tin.*

con·nec·tion /kəˈnekʃən/ *n* **1** [C,U] connecting or being connected: *How long will the ~ of the new telephone take?* How long will it take to connect the house by telephone? **2** [C] thing which connects: *What is the ~ between the two ideas?* **3** [C] train, boat, airline flight, etc arranged to leave a station, port, etc soon after the arrival of another, so that passengers can change from one to the other: *The train was late and I missed my ~.* **4** [C] rich or important friend, associate, etc: *He had powerful ~s to help him in his career.*

con·nect·ive /kəˈnektɪv/ *adj* serving to connect. □ *n* [C] (esp) word that connects (eg a conjunction).

con·nive /kəˈnaiv/ *vi* **1** ***connive at,*** take no notice of (what is wrong, what ought to be opposed) (suggesting consent or approval): *~ at an escape from prison.* **2** cooperate secretly: *was conniving with the enemy.*

con·niv·ance /-əns/ *n* [U] conniving (at or in a crime): *done with the connivance of/in connivance with....*

con·nois·seur /ˌkanəˈsər/ *n* [C] person with good judgment on matters in which (artistic) taste is needed: *a ~ of painting/wine.*

con·note /kəˈnout/ *vt* (of words) suggest something in addition to the basic meaning: *"Whiteness" ~s purity.*

con·no·ta·tion /ˌkanəˈteiʃən/ *n* [C] that which is suggested.

con·quer /ˈkaŋkər/ *vt* **1** defeat or overcome enemies, bad habits, etc. **2** take possession of by force: *~ a country.*

con·queror *n* [C] person who conquers.

con·quest /ˈkanˌkwest/ *n* **1** [U] conquering (eg a country and its people). **2** [C] something got by conquering. **3** [C] person whose affections have been won .

con·science /ˈkanʃəns/ *n* [C,U] the consciousness within oneself of the choice one ought to make between right and wrong: *have a clear/guilty* ~. ***have no conscience (about),*** be as ready to do wrong as right. ***(have sth/sb) on one's conscience,*** (feel) troubled about something one has done, or failed to do.

con·scien·tious /ˌkanʃiˈenʃəs/ *adj* **1** (of persons) guided by one's sense of duty: *a ~ obˈjector*, person who objects to doing something (eg serving in the armed forces) because he thinks it is morally wrong. **2** (of actions) done carefully and honestly: ~ *work*.

con·scien·tious·ly *adv*

con·scien·tious·ness /-nɪs/ *n* [C]

con·scious /ˈkanʃəs/ *adj* **1** awake; aware; knowing things because one is using the bodily senses and mental powers: *They were ~ of being/that they were being watched.* **2** (of actions, feelings, etc) realized by oneself: *He spoke/acted with ~ superiority.*

con·scious·ly *adv*

con·scious·ness /ˈkanʃəsnɪs/ *n* [U] **1** being conscious; awareness: *We have no ~ during sleep. He didn't recover/regain ~ until two hours after the accident.* **2** all the ideas, thoughts, feelings, wishes, intentions, recollections, of a person or persons: *the moral ~ of a political party.*

con·script /kənˈskrɪpt/ *vt* compel by law, summon, to serve in the armed forces: *~ed into the army.* ⇨ draft[1](3). □ *n* [C] /ˈkanˌskrɪpt/ person who is conscripted.

con·scrip·tion /kənˈskrɪpʃən/ *n* [U]

con·se·crate /ˈkansəˌkreit/ *vt* set apart as sacred or for a special purpose; make sacred: *to ~ one's life to the service of God/to the relief of suffering. He was ~d Archbishop last year.*

con·se·cra·tion /ˌkansəˈkreiʃən/ *n* **1** [U] consecrating or being consecrated. **2** [C] instance of this: *the ~ of a church.*

con·secu·tive /kənˈsekyətɪv/ *adj* coming one after the other in regular order: *on five ~ days.*

con·secu·tive·ly *adv*

con·sen·sus /kənˈsensəs/ *n* [C] (*pl* ~es) general agreement: *a ~ of opinion.*

con·sent /kənˈsent/ *vi* give agreement or permission: *The patient would not ~ to the operation.* □ *n* [U] agreement; permission: *He was chosen leader by general ~,* everyone agreed.

ˌage of conˈsent, age at which the law recognizes a girl's responsibility for agreeing to sexual intercourse, a person's right to marry, etc.

con·se·quence /ˈkansəˌkwens/ *n* **1** [C] result; effect: *If you behave so foolishly you must be ready to take the ~s,* accept what happens as a result. **2** [U] importance: *It's of no ~.*

con·se·quent /ˈkansəˌkwənt/ *adj* (*formal*) following as a consequence: *the drought and the ~ failure of the crops.*

con·se·quent·ly *adv*

conse·quen·tial /ˌkansəˈkwenʃəl/ *adj* **1** = consequent. **2** (of a person) self-important.

con·ser·va·tion /ˌkansərˈveiʃən/ *n* [U] preservation; prevention of loss, waste, damage, etc: *the ~ of forests/fuel.*

con·ser·va·tion·ism /-ˌnɪzəm/ *n* [U] position, movement, in support of preserving the natural environment.

con·ser·va·tion·ist /-nɪst/ *n* [C] one who advocates conservationism.

con·serva·tism /kənˈsərvəˌtɪzəm/ *n* [U] tendency to maintain a state of affairs (esp in politics) without great or sudden change.

con·serva·tive /kənˈsərvətɪv/ *adj* **1** opposed to great or sudden change: *Old people are usually more ~ than young people.* **2** cautious; moderate: *a ~ estimate of one's future income.* □ *n* [C] **1** conservative person. **2 Conservative,** member, supporter, of a conservative political party.

con·serva·tive·ly *adv*

con·serva·tory /kənˈsərvəˌtori/ *n* [C] (*pl* -ies) **1** building, or part of a building, with glass walls and roof in which plants are protected from cold. **2** school of music or art.

con·serve /kənˈsərv/ *vt* keep from change, loss or destruction: *~ one's strength/energies/health.* □ /ˈkanˌsərv/ *n* [U] jam (the usual word) made of two or more kinds of fruit.

con·sider /kənˈsɪdər/ *vt* **1** think about: *Please ~ my suggestion. We are ~ing going to Canada.* **2** take into account; make allowances for: *We must ~ the feelings of other people/what other people feel.* **3** be of the opinion; regard as: *They ~ed themselves very important. Do you ~ it wise to interfere?*

con·sider·able /kənˈsɪdərəbəl/ *adj* great; much; important: *bought at a ~ expense.*

con·sider·ably *adv* much; a great deal: *It's considerably colder this morning.*

con·sider·ate /kənˈsɪdərət/ *adj* thoughtful (of the needs, etc of others): *It was ~ of you to bring me flowers.*

con·sider·ate·ly *adv*

con·sider·ation /kənˌsɪdəˈreiʃən/ *n* **1** [U] act of considering, thinking about: *Please give the matter your careful ~.* ***take sth into consideration,*** (esp) make allowances for: *When marking the examination, I took Tom's long illness into ~.* **2** [U] quality of being considerate; thoughtful attention to the wishes, feelings, etc, of others: *in ~ of/out of ~ for his youth.* **3** [C] something which must be thought about; fact, thing, etc thought of as a reason: *Time is an important ~ in this case.*

con·sider·ing /kənˈsɪdərɪŋ/ *prep* in view of; having regard to: *She's very active, ~ her age.*

con·sign /kənˈsain/ *vt* **1** send (goods, etc) for delivery: *The goods have been ~ed by rail.* **2** hand over, give up: *~ a child to its uncle's care.*

con·sign·ment *n* **(a)** [U] consigning. **(b)** [C] goods consigned.

con·sist /kənˈsɪst/ *vi* **1** ***consist of,*** be made up of: *The committee ~s of ten members.* **2** ***consist in,*** have as a basis: *The happiness of a country ~s in the freedom of its citizens.*

con·sist·ence /kənˈsɪstəns/ *n* = consistency.

con·sis·tency /kənˈsɪstənsi/ *n* (*pl* -ies) **1** [U] the state of always being the same in thought, behavior, etc; keeping to the same principles: *His actions lack* ~. **2** [C,U] degree of thickness, firmness or solidity (esp of a thick liquid, or of something made by mixing with a liquid): *mix flour and milk to the right* ~.

con·sis·tent /kənˈsɪstənt/ *adj* **1** (of a person, his behavior, principles, etc) having a regular pattern or style: *The ideas in his various speeches are not* ~. **2** in agreement (with): *What you say now is not* ~ *with what you said last week.*

con·sis·tent·ly *adv*

con·so·la·tion /ˌkansəˈleiʃən/ *n* **1** [U] consoling or being consoled: *a few words/a letter of* ~. **2** [C] person, thing, event that consoles: *Your company has been a great* ~ *to me.*

con·sola·tory /kənˈsouləˌtɔri/ *adj* intended to give comfort: *a* ~ *letter.*

con·sole[1] /kənˈsoul/ *vt* give comfort or sympathy to: ~ *him in his disappointment;* ~ *oneself with the thought that it might have been worse.*

con·sol·able *adj* that can be comforted.

con·sole[2] /ˈkanˌsoul/ *n* [C] **1** bracket to support a shelf. **2** frame containing the keyboards, stops, etc of an organ. **3** panel for the controls of electronic or mechanical equipment. **4** cabinet (for a phonograph, radio, etc) designed to stand on the floor.

con·soli·date /kənˈsaləˌdeit/ *vt,vi* **1** make or become (more) solid or strong: ~ *one's position/influence.* **2** unite or combine into one: ~ *debts/business companies.*

con·soli·da·tion /kənˌsaləˈdeiʃən/ *n* **1** [U] consolidating or being consolidated. **2** [C] instance of this.

con·sommé /ˌkansəˈmei/ *n* [C] (*F*) clear meat soup.

con·son·ance /ˈkansənəns/ *n* [U] (*formal*) **1** agreement. **2** harmony.

con·so·nant /ˈkansənənt/ *n* [C] **1** speech sound produced by a complete or partial stoppage of the breath. **2** letter of the alphabet or symbol (eg phonetic) for such a sound: *b, c, d, f, are* ~*s.*

con·sort[1] /ˈkanˌsɔrt/ *n* [C] **1** husband or wife, esp of a ruler: *the prince* ~, the reigning queen's husband. **2** ship sailing with another (esp for safety during a war). **3** associate.

con·sort[2] /kənˈsɔrt/ *vi* ***consort with,*** **1** pass time in the company of: ~ *with criminals.* **2** (*formal*) be in harmony, go well: *His behavior does not* ~ *with his beliefs.*

con·spicu·ous /kənˈspɪkyuəs/ *adj* easily seen; attracting attention: ~ *for his bravery. Traffic signs should be* ~. ***make oneself conspicuous,*** attract attention by unusual behavior, wearing unusual clothes, etc.

con·spicu·ous·ly *adv*

con·spir·acy /kənˈspɪrəsi/ *n* (*pl* -ies) **1** [U] act of conspiring. **2** [C] plan made by conspiring: *a* ~ *to overthrow the government.*

con·spira·tor /kənˈspɪrətər/ *n* [C] person who conspires.

con·spira·tor·ial /kənˌspɪrəˈtɔriəl/ *adj* of conspirators or a conspiracy: *in a conspiratorial manner.*

con·spire /kənˈspaiər/ *vi,vt* **1** make secret plans (with others, esp to do wrong): ~ *against the Government.* **2** (of events) act together; combine: *events that* ~*d to bring about his ruin.*

con·stable /ˈkanstəbəl/ *n* [C] (*dated*) law enforcing officer, esp in a small town or rural area of the US.

con·stancy /ˈkanstənsi/ *n* [U] quality of being firm, faithful, unchanging: ~ *of purpose.*

con·stant /ˈkanstənt/ *adj* **1** going on all the time; frequently recurring: ~ *complaints.* **2** firm; faithful; unchanging: *a* ~ *friend.*

con·stant·ly *adv* continuously; frequently.

con·stel·la·tion /ˌkanstəˈleiʃən/ *n* [C] named group of fixed stars (eg *Ursa Major,* the most visible stars of which form *the Big Dipper*).

con·ster·na·tion /ˌkanstərˈneiʃən/ *n* [U] surprise and fear; dismay: *filled with* ~.

con·sti·pate /ˈkanstəˌpeit/ *vt* cause constipation.

con·sti·pated /ˈkanstəˌpeitɪd/ *adj* having bowels that are emptied infrequently or only with difficulty.

con·sti·pa·tion /ˌkanstəˈpeiʃən/ *n* [U] difficult or infrequent emptying of the bowels.

con·stitu·ency /kənˈstɪtʃuənsi/ *n* [C] (*pl* -ies) (body of voters living in a) town or district that is entitled to send a representative to a legislative body.

con·stitu·ent /kənˈstɪtʃuənt/ *adj* **1** having the power or right to make or alter a political constitution: *a* ~ *assembly.* **2** forming or helping to make a whole: *a* ~ *part.* □ *n* [C] **1** member of a constituency; voter. **2** part (of something else); element: *the* ~*s of happiness.*

con·sti·tute /ˈkanstəˌtut/ *vt* **1** establish; set up. **2** make up (a whole); amount to; be the components of: *Twelve months* ~ *a year.* **3** (*formal*) appoint to a position, etc: *They* ~*d him chief adviser.*

con·sti·tu·tion /ˌkanstəˌtuʃən/ *n* [C] **1** system of government; laws and principles according to which a state is governed: *The United States has a written* ~. **2** general physical structure and condition of a person's body: *Only people with strong* ~*s should climb in the Himalayas.* **3** general structure of a thing; act or manner of constituting: *the* ~ *of the solar spectrum.*

con·sti·tu·tional /ˌkanstətuʃənəl/ *adj* **1** of a constitution(1): ~ *government/reform.* **2** of a person's constitution(2): *a* ~ *weakness.* □ *n* [C] walk taken for exercise: *his morning* ~.

con·sti·tu·tive /ˈkanstəˌtutɪv/ *adj* (*formal*) **1** constructive; formative. **2** essential.

con·strain /kənˈstrein/ *vt* force; compel: *I feel* ~*ed to write and ask for your forgiveness.*

con·strained *adj* (of manner, etc) forced; uneasy; unnatural.

con·straint /kənˈstreint/ *n* [U] constraining or being constrained: *to act under* ~, because one is forced to do so.

con·strict /kənˈstrɪkt/ *vt* make tight or smaller; inhibit; cause (a vein or muscle) to become tight or narrow: *a* ~*ed outlook*, one that is limited.

con·stric·tion /kənˈstrɪkʃən/ *n* **(a)** [U] tightening. **(b)** [C] thing that constricts. **(c)** [C] feeling of being constricted: *a* ~*ion in the chest.*

con·struct /kənˈstrəkt/ *vt* build: *to* ~ *a factory/a sentence/a theory.*

con·struc·tor /-tər/ *n* [C]

con·struc·tion /kən'strəkʃən/ *n* **1** [U] act or manner of constructing; being constructed: *The new railway is still under ~.* **2** [C] structure; building. **3** [C] meaning; sense in which words, statements, acts, etc are taken: *Please do not put a wrong ~ on his action,* misunderstand its purpose. **4** [C] arrangement and relationships of words in a sentence: *This dictionary gives the meanings of words and also gives examples to illustrate their ~s.*

con·struc·tive /kən'strəktɪv/ *adj* **1** of or relating to construction **2** helpful: *~ criticism/proposals.*

con·struc·tive·ly *adv*

con·strue /kən'stru/ *vt,vi (formal)* **1** translate or explain the meaning of words, sentences, acts: *His remarks were wrongly ~d,* were misunderstood. **2** analyze (a sentence).

con·sul /'kansəl/ *n* [C] **1** government official living in a foreign town to help and protect his countrymen there. **2** (in ancient Rome) either of the two heads of the state before Rome became an empire.

con·su·lar /'kansələr/ *adj* of a consul or his work.

consu·late /'kansəlɪt/ *n* [C] consul's position or offices.

con·sult /kən'səlt/ *vt,vi* **1** go to a person, a book, etc for information, advice, opinion, etc: *to ~ one's lawyer/a map/the dictionary.* **2** ***consult with,*** take advice, opinion, from: *~ with one's fellow workers.*

con·sul·tant /kən'səltənt/ *n* [C] person who gives expert advice (eg in medicine, business): *a ~ surgeon; a firm of ~s.*

con·sul·ta·tion /ˌkansəl'teiʃən/ *n* **1** [U] consulting or being consulted: *in ~ with the director.* **2** [C] meeting for consulting: *The doctors held a ~ to decide whether an operation was necessary.*

con·sul·ta·tive /kən'səltətɪv/ *adj* of, for the purpose of, consulting: *a ~ committee.*

con·sume /kən'sum/ *vt,vi (formal)* **1** eat or drink. **2** use up; get to the end of: *~ all one's energies. This is 'time-consuming work.* **3** destroy by fire or wastefulness.

con·sum·ing *adj* possessing or dominating: *a consuming ambition.*

con·sumer /kən'sumər/ *n* [C] person who uses (esp manufactured) goods: *~ research.*

con·sum·mate /'kansəˌmeit/ *vt* **1** *(formal)* accomplish; make perfect: *Her happiness was ~d when her father took her to Paris.* **2** make complete (esp marriage by sexual intercourse).

con·sum·ma·tion /ˌkansə'meiʃən/ *n* [C,U] completion; fulfillment: *the ~ of one's ambitions/a marriage.*

con·sump·tion /kən'səmpʃən/ *n* [U] **1** using up, consuming (of food, energy, materials, etc). **2** the quantity consumed: *The ~ of beer did not go down when the tax was raised.* **3** (esp) pulmonary tuberculosis.

con·sump·tive /kən'səmptɪv/ *n* [C], *adj* (person) suffering from, having a tendency to, consumption(3).

cont. *abbr* = **1** content(s). **2** continued.

con·tact /'kanˌtækt/ *n* **1** [U] (state of) touching or communication; (process of) coming together. ***be in/out of, come/bring into, contact (with)***: *Our troops are in ~ with the enemy. A steel cable came into ~ with an electric power line.* ***make contact (with),*** (esp after searching, striving, etc): *I finally made ~ with him in Paris.* **2** [C] business or social connection: *He made many business ~s while he was in Canada.* **3** [C] **(a)** connection (for electric current). **(b)** device for making this connection. □ *vt* get into touch with: *Where can I ~ Mr. Green?*

'contact lens, one of thin plastic made to fit over the eyeball to improve vision.

con·ta·gion /kən'teidʒən/ *n* **1** [U] the spreading of disease by contact or close association. **2** [C] disease that can be spread by contact. **3** *(fig)* the spreading of any influence (as ideas, false rumors, feelings, etc): *A ~ of fear swept through the crowd.* ⇨ infection.

con·ta·gi·ous /kən'teidʒəs/ *adj* **1** (of disease) spreading by contact: *Scarlet fever is ~.* **2** (of a person) causing the spread of disease. **3** *(fig)* spreading easily by example: *~ laughter/enthusiasm.* ⇨ infection.

con·ta·gi·ous·ly *adj*

con·tain /kən'tein/ *vt* **1** have or hold within itself: *The atlas ~s forty maps.* **2** be equal to: *A dollar ~s 100 cents.* **3** be capable of holding: *How much can this bottle ~?* **4** keep feelings, etc under control: *Can't you ~ your enthusiasm?*

con·tainer /kən'teinər/ *n* [C] box, bottle, etc designed to contain something, esp one for transporting goods.

con·tami·nate /kən'tæməˌneit/ *vt* make dirty, impure or diseased (by touching, or adding something impure): *Flies ~ food.*

con·tami·na·tion /kənˌtæmə'neiʃən/ *n* **1** [U] contaminating or being contaminated: *the ~ of the water supply.* **2** [C] that which contaminates.

cont'd. *abbr* = continued.

con·tem·plate /'kantəmˌpleit/ *vt* **1** look at; think about: *She stood contemplating herself in the mirror.* **2** have in view as a purpose, intention or possibility: *She was contemplating a visit to England.*

con·tem·pla·tion /ˌkantəm'pleiʃən/ *n* [U] **1** contemplating; deep thought. **2** intention; expectation.

con·tem·pla·tive /kən'templətɪv/ *adj (formal)* thoughtful.

con·tem·po·raneous /kənˌtempə'reiniəs/ *adj* originating, existing, happening, during the same period of time: *~ events.*

con·tem·po·rary /kən'tempəˌreri/ *adj* **1** of the time or period to which reference is being made; belonging to the same time: *Thoreau was ~ with Emerson.* **2** of the present time; modern: *~ music.* □ *n* [C] *(pl* -ies) person of the same age, belonging to the same period, etc as another: *Thoreau and Emerson were contemporaries.*

con·tempt /kən'tempt/ *n* [U] **1** condition of being looked down on or despised: *A man who is cruel to his children should be held in ~.* **2** mental attitude of despising: *We feel ~ for liars.* **3** disregard or disrespect: *in ~ of all rules and regulations.* **4** (short for) contempt of court or Congress: *He was held in ~.*

con'tempt of 'court/'Congress, disobedience

or disrespect shown to a judge, court, or legislative body.

con·tempt·ible /kənˈtemptəbəl/ *adj* worthy of contempt.

con·temptu·ous /kənˈtemptʃuəs/ *adj* showing contempt: *~ of public opinion.*

con·tend /kənˈtend/ *vi,vt* **1** struggle, be in rivalry or competition: *~ing with difficulties/for a prize.* **2** argue, assert: *~ed that she was wrong.*
con·tender *n* [C] competitor, rival, eg one who challenges the holder of a boxing title.

con·tent¹ /kənˈtent/ *adj* not wanting more; satisfied: *Are you ~ with your present salary? I am ~ to remain where I am now.* □ *n* [U] the condition of being satisfied: *to one's heart's ~,* to one's complete satisfaction. □ *vt* satisfy: *Since there's no milk we have to ~ ourselves* (= be satisfied) *with black coffee.*
con·tented *adj* satisfied; showing or feeling satisfaction, happiness: *with a ~ed look/smile.*
con·tent·ed·ly *adv*
con·tent·ment *n* [U] state of being content.

con·tent² /ˈkanˌtent/ *n* [C] **1** (*pl*) that which is contained: *the ~s of a room/a book/a pocket.* **2** (*pl*) the amount which a vessel will hold: *the ~s of this bottle.* **3** substance (of a book, speech, etc as opposed to its form): *Do you approve of the ~ of the article/speech?*

con·ten·tion /kənˈtenʃən/ *n* **1** [U] quarreling or disputing: *This is not a time for ~.* **2** [C] argument used in contending: *My ~ is that....*

con·ten·tious /kənˈtenʃəs/ *adj* quarrelsome; likely to cause argument: *a ~ clause in a treaty.*

con·test¹ /ˈkanˌtest/ *n* [C] struggle; fight; competition: *a ~ for the prize; a ~ of skill; heavyweight ~.*
con·test·ant /kənˈtestənt/ *n* [C] person who contests.

con·test² /kənˈtest/ *vt,vi* **1** argue; debate; dispute: *~ a statement/point,* try to show that it is wrong. **2** = contend (1).

con·text /ˈkanˌtekst/ *n* [C,U] **1** what comes before and after a word, phrase, etc helping to fix the meaning: *Can't you guess the meaning of the word from the ~?* **2** circumstances in which an event occurs.
con·tex·tual /kənˈtekstʃuəl/ *adj* of the context.

con·ti·nent /ˈkantənənt/ *n* [C] **1** one of the seven main land masses (Europe, Asia, Africa, North America, South America, Australia, Antarctica) of the world. **2 the Continent,** the mainland of Europe.

con·ti·nen·tal /ˌkantəˈnentəl/ *adj* **1** belonging to, typical of, a continent: *a ~ climate.* **2 Continental,** of the mainland of Europe: *~ breakfast,* of bread rolls and coffee only. □ *n* [C] **Continental,** inhabitant of the mainland of Europe.

con·tin·gency /kənˈtɪndʒənsi/ *n* (*pl* -ies) **1** [U] uncertainty of occurrence. **2** [C] event that is possible but uncertain. **3** [C] event that happens by chance: *to be prepared for all contingencies; ~ plans.*

con·tin·gent /kənˈtɪndʒənt/ *adj* **1** uncertain. **2** accidental. **3** ***contingent on/upon,*** dependent on (something that may or may not happen). □ n [C] **1** body of troops, number of ships, lent or supplied to form part of a larger force. **2** group of persons forming part of a larger group.

con·tin·ual /kənˈtɪnyuəl/ *adj* going on all the time without stopping, or with only short breaks: *Aren't you tired of this ~ rain?*
con·tin·ually *adv* again and again; without stopping.

con·tin·uance /kənˈtɪnyuəns/ *n* [U] **1** = duration (the more usual word): *during the ~ of the war.* **2** remaining; staying: *a ~ of prosperity.*

con·tinu·ation /kənˌtɪnyuˈeiʃən/ *n* **1** [U] continuing. **2** [U] starting again after a stop. **3** [C] something continued: *The next issue will contain an exciting ~ of the story.*

con·tinue /kənˈtɪnyu/ *vi,vt* **1** go farther; go on (being or doing); stay at/in; remain at/in: *The desert ~d as far as the eye could reach. I hope this wet weather will not ~. How long shall you ~ working/to work?* **2** start again after stopping: *The story will be ~d in next month's issue.* **3** retain (in office, etc): *The Secretary of Commerce was ~d in office.*

con·ti·nu·ity /ˌkantəˈnuəti/ *n* [U] **1** the state of being continuous: *There is no ~ of subject in a dictionary.* **2** (in movies, TV) arrangement of the parts of a story: *Films are often made out of ~,* eg a scene near the end may be filmed before a scene near the beginning. **3** comments, announcements, etc made between (parts of) broadcast programs.

con·tinu·ous /kənˈtɪnyuəs/ *adj* going on without a break: *a ~ performance, 1:00pm to 11:30pm,* eg at a motion picture theater.
con·tinu·ous·ly *adv*

con·tort /kənˈtɔrt/ *vt* force or twist out of the usual shape or appearance: *a face ~ed with pain.*

con·tor·tion /kənˈtɔrʃən/ *n* **1** [U] contorting or being contorted (esp of the face or body). **2** [C] instance of this; contorted condition: *the ~s of an acrobat.*

con·tour /ˈkanˌtʊr/ *n* [C] **1** outline (of a coast, a human figure, etc). **2** = contour line. □ *vt* **1** mark with contour lines. **2** make (a road) along the contour of a hill, etc.
ˈcontour line, line (on a map) joining points at the same height above sea level.

contra- /ˌkantrə-/ *prefix* against; opposite to: *contraception; contradict.*

contra·band /ˈkantrəˌbænd/ *n* [U] **1** illegal import or export of goods; smuggling. **2** smuggled goods.

contra·cep·tion /ˌkantrəˈsepʃən/ *n* [U] practice, method, of preventing conception(3).

contra·cep·tive /ˌkantrəˈseptɪv/ *n* [C] device or drug intended to prevent conception(3). □ *adj* preventing conception: *~ pills/devices.*

con·tract¹ /ˈkanˌtrækt/ *n* [C,U] binding agreement (between persons, groups, states); agreement to supply goods, do work, etc at a fixed price: *enter into/make a ~ with an agent for the purchase of a house/to purchase a house, work to be done by private ~; a breach of ~.* (*Note: the* or *a* is not used in the last two examples.)

con·tract² /kənˈtrækt/ *vt,vi* **1** be bound, bind, by agreement: *~ a marriage; ~ an alliance with another country.* **2** become liable (for debts). **3** catch (an illness): *~ measles.* **4** form; acquire (eg bad habits).

con·trac·tor /ˈkanˌtræktər/ *n* [C] person, business firm, that enters into contracts: *building ~ors.*

con·trac·tual /kənˈtræktʃuəl/ *adj* of (the nature of) a contract.

con·tract[3] /kənˈtrækt/ *vt,vi* **1** make or become smaller or shorter: *"I will" can be ~ed to "I'll."* **2** make or become tighter or narrower: *to ~ a muscle.*

con·tract·ible *adj* that can be contracted.

con·trac·tion /kənˈtrækʃən/ *n* **1** [U] contracting or being contracted: *the ~ of a muscle.* **2** [C] something contracted, eg a shortened word-form, such as *can't* for *cannot.*

con·tra·dict /ˌkantrəˈdɪkt/ *vt* **1** deny the truth of (something said or written); deny (the words of a person): *to ~ a statement. Don't ~ me.* **2** (of facts, statements, etc) be contrary to: *The reports ~ each other.*

con·tra·dic·tion /ˌkantrəˈdɪkʃən/ *n* **1(a)** [U] contradicting. **(b)** [C] instance of this. **2(a)** [U] absence of agreement: *Your statements today are in ~ with what you said yesterday.* **(b)** [C] instance of this.

con·tra·dic·tory /ˌkantrəˈdɪktəri/ *adj* contradicting: *~ statements/reports.*

contra·dis·tinc·tion /ˌkantrədɪˈstɪŋkʃən/ *n* (*formal*) distinction by contrast: *flying across the Atlantic in a few hours, in ~ to the longer journey by steamer.*

con·tralto /kənˈtræltou/ *n* [C] (*pl ~s*) = alto(1).

con·trap·tion /kənˈtræpʃən/ *n* [C] (*informal*) strange-looking apparatus or device.

con·trary[1] /ˈkanˌtreri/ *adj* **1** ***contrary to,*** opposite (in nature or tendency): *What you have done is ~ to the doctor's orders.* **2** (of the wind and weather) unfavorable (for sailing). **3** (*informal*) (usually /kənˈtreri/) obstinate; self-willed.

con·trar·ily /ˈkanˌtrerɪli/ *adv.*

con·trari·ness /ˈkanˌtrerinɪs/ *n* [C]

con·trary[2] /ˈkanˌtreri/ *n* (*pl* -ies) **1** opposite: *The ~ of "wet" is "dry."* ***on the contrary,*** (denying or contradicting what has been said, written): *"You've nothing to do now, I think."—"On the ~, I have piles of work."* ***to the contrary,*** to the opposite effect: *I will come on Monday unless you write me to the ~,* telling me not to come. **2** ***by contraries,*** opposite to expectation: *Many things in our lives go by contraries. She said that dreams go by contraries.*

con·trast[1] /kənˈtræst/ *vt,vi* **1** compare so that differences are made clear: *Contrast these imported goods (with/and the domestic product).* **2** show a difference when compared: *His actions ~ sharply with his promises.*

con·trast[2] /ˈkanˌtræst/ *n* **1** [U] the act of contrasting: *Contrast may make something appear more beautiful than it is when seen alone.* **2** [C] difference which is clearly seen when unlike things are put together: *The ~ between the two brothers is remarkable.* **3** person, thing showing such a difference.

con·trib·ute /kənˈtrɪbyut/ *vt,vi* **1** join with others in giving help, money, ideas, suggestions, etc: *~ money to a charity/new information on a scientific problem.* **2** have a share in; help to bring about: *Drink ~d to his ruin.* **3** write (articles, etc) and send in (to): *Mr. Green has ~d (poems) to the magazine for several years.*

con·tribu·tor /-tər/ *n* [C]

con·tri·bu·tion /ˌkantrəˈbyuʃən/ *n* **1** [U] act of contributing. **2** [C] something contributed: *~s to the relief fund.*

con·tribu·tory /kənˈtrɪbyəˌtəri/ *adj* **1** helping to bring about: *~ negligence,* eg that helped to cause an accident. **2** for which contributions are to be made: *a ~ pension plan.*

con·trite /kənˈtrait/ *adj* filled with, showing, deep sorrow for doing wrong.

con·tri·tion /kənˈtrɪʃən/ *n* [U] deep sorrow (for sins, etc); repentance.

con·triv·ance /kənˈtraivəns/ *n* **1** [U] act or manner of contriving. **2** [U] capacity to invent: *Some things are beyond human ~.* **3** [C] something contrived; invention.

con·trive /kənˈtraiv/ *vt,vi* **1** invent; design. **2** find a way of doing or causing (something): *to ~ a means of escape from prison.*

con·trol /kənˈtroul/ *n* **1** [U] power or authority to direct, order, or restrain: *some children lack parental ~,* are not kept in order by parents. ***be in control (of),*** be in command, in charge. ***be/get out of control,*** in a state where authority, etc is lost: *The children are/have got out of ~.* ***have/get/keep control (over/of),*** have, get, keep authority, power, etc: *That teacher has no ~ over his class.* ***lose control (of),*** be unable to manage or contain: *lose ~ of one's temper.* ***take control (of),*** take authority: *We must find someone to take ~ of the situation.* **2** [U] management; guidance: *~ of traffic/traffic ~.* **3** [C] means of regulating, restraining, keeping in order: *government ~s on trade and industry.* **4** [C] standard of comparison for results of an experiment: *The tests were given to three groups, one being used as a ~.* **5** (usually *pl*) means by which a machine, etc is operated or regulated: *the ~s of an aircraft,* for direction, altitude, etc. □ *vt* (-ll-) **1** have control of; check: *to ~ expenditure/one's temper.* **2** regulate (prices, etc).

ˈbirth control, ⇨ birth.

con·trol·lable *adj* that can be controlled.

con·trol·ler /kənˈtroulər/ *n* [C] **1** person who controls expenditure and accounts for a business, institution, etc. **2** (also **ˌair-traffic conˈtroller**) person who controls the movement of aircraft while in flight, landing/or taking off.

con·tro·ver·sial /ˌkantrəˈvərʃəl/ *adj* **1** likely to cause controversy: *a ~ speech.* **2** (of persons) fond of controversy.

con·tro·ver·sially *adv*

con·tro·versy /ˈkantrəˌvərsi/ *n* [C,U] (*pl* -ies) prolonged argument, esp over social, moral or political matters: *engage in (a) ~ with him; a question that has given rise to much ~.*

con·tro·vert /ˌkantrəˈvərt/ *vt* (*formal*) **1** dispute about. **2** deny; oppose.

co·nun·drum /kəˈnəndrəm/ *n* [C] puzzling question, esp one asked for fun; riddle.

con·va·lesce /ˌkanvəˈles/ *vi* regain health and strength after an illness: *She is convalescing by the sea.*

con·va·les·cence /ˌkanvəˈlesəns/ *n* [U] (time of) gradual recovery of health and strength after an illness.

con·va·les·cent /ˌkanvəˈlesənt/ *n* [C], *adj* (person who is) recovering from illness.

con·vec·tion /kənˈvekʃən/ *n* [U] the conveying of heat from one part of a liquid or gas to another by the movement of the heated substance.

con·vene /kənˈvin/ *vt,vi* **1** call (persons) to come together (for a meeting, etc). **2** come together (for a meeting, council, etc).
con·vener *n* [C]

con·ven·ience /kənˈvinyəns/ *n* **1** [U] the quality of being convenient or suitable; freedom from difficulty or worry: *I keep my reference books near my desk for* ~. *Please come at your earliest* ~, at the earliest time suitable to you. **2** [C] appliance, device, arrangement, etc that is useful, helpful or convenient: *The house has all modern* ~*s*, eg central heating and air conditioning, a dishwasher, etc

con·ven·ient /kənˈvinyənt/ *adj* **1** easy to use: handy **2** easy to do: *Will it be* ~ *for you to start work tomorrow?* **3** easy to get to: *a* ~ *location.*
con·veni·ent·ly *adv*

con·vent /ˈkanvənt, -ˌvent/ *n* [C] **1** society of women (*nuns*) living apart from others in the service of God. ⇨ monastery. **2** building(s) in which they live and work: *enter a* ~, become a nun.

con·ven·tion /kənˈvenʃən/ *n* **1** [C] conference of members of a society, political party, etc or of persons in business, commerce, etc: *the Democratic Convention.* **2** [C] agreement between states, rulers, etc (less formal than a treaty): *the Geneva Conventions,* about the treatment of prisoners of war, etc. **3** [C] accepted practice or custom: *It is silly to be a slave to* ~.

con·ven·tional /kənˈvenʃənəl/ *adj* **1** based on convention(3): ~ *greetings.* **2** following what has been customary; traditional: *a* ~ *design for a carpet.*
con·ven·tionally *adv*

con·verge /kənˈvərdʒ/ *vi,vt* (of lines, moving objects, opinions) come, cause to come, towards each other and meet at a point; tend to do this: *armies converging on the capital.*
con·ver·gent *adj*

con·ver·sant /kənˈvərsənt/ *adj* ***conversant with,*** having a knowledge of: ~ *with all the rules.*

con·ver·sa·tion /ˌkanvərˈseiʃən/ *n* **1** [U] talking: *I saw him in* ~ *with a friend.* **2** [C] talk: *I've had several* ~*s with him.*
con·ver·sa·tional *adj*

con·verse[1] /kənˈvərs/ *vi* (*formal*) talk.

con·verse[2] /ˈkanˌvərs/ *n, adj* (idea, statement which is) opposite (to another).
con·verse·ly *adv*

con·ver·sion /kənˈvərʒən/ *n* **1** [U] converting or being converted: *the* ~ *of cream into butter/of pagans to Christianity.* **2** [C] instance of this. **3** [C] extra point(s) scored after a touchdown in football.

con·vert[1] /ˈkanˌvərt/ *n* [C] person converted, esp to a religion, or to different principles: *a* ~ *to socialism.*

con·vert[2] /kənˈvərt/ *vt, vi* **1** change (from one form, use, etc into another): *to* ~ *dollars into francs.* **2** cause (a person) to change his beliefs, etc: *to* ~ *a person to Christianity.* **3** make a conversion(3).
con·verted *adj*

con·vert·ible /kənˈvərtəbəl/ *adj, n* [C] **1** (something) that can be converted; **2** (automobile) having a folding or removable top.

con·vex /kanˈveks/ *adj* (of an outline or surface) curved outwards like the outer surface of a sphere or ball: *a* ~ *lens.* ⇨ concave.

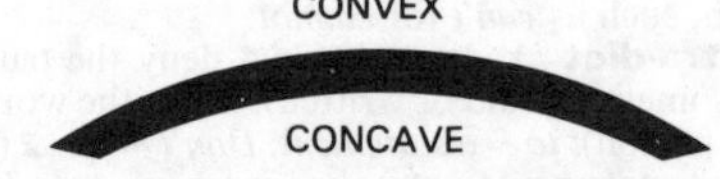

con·vey /kənˈvei/ *vt* **1** take, carry: *Pipes* ~ *hot water from this boiler to every part of the building.* **2** make known ideas, views, feelings, etc to another person: *This picture will* ~ *to you some idea of the beauty of the scenery.* **3** ***convey to,*** (*legal*) give full legal rights (in land or property): *The land was* ~*ed to his brother.*
con·veyer, con·veyor /-ˈveiər/ *n* [C] **1** person or thing that conveys. **2** (usually **conveyor**) band or chain moving over wheels for carrying packages, etc.

con·vey·ance /kənˈveiəns/ *n* **1** [U] conveying. **2** [C] something which conveys.

con·vict[1] /ˈkanˌvɪkt/ *n* [C] person convicted of crime and being punished.

con·vict[2] /kənˈvɪkt/ *vt* **1** (esp declare in a law court) that (a person) is guilty: *He was* ~*ed of murder.* **2** cause (a person) to be certain that he has done wrong, made a mistake: *to* ~ *him of his errors.*

con·vic·tion /kənˈvɪkʃən/ *n* **1** [U] the convicting of a person for a crime: *The* ~ *of the accused man surprised us.* **2** [C] instance of this: *He has had six previous* ~*s.* **3** [U] the act of convincing, of bringing certainty to the mind. **4** [C,U] firm or assured belief: *He spoke with such* ~.

con·vince /kənˈvɪns/ *vt* make (a person) feel certain; cause (a person) to believe: *I am* ~*d of his honesty. We couldn't* ~ *him of his mistake/that he was mistaken. He* ~*d me to try again.*
con·vinc·ing *adj* that convinces: *a convincing speaker/argument.*
con·vin·cing·ly *adv*

con·viv·ial /kənˈvɪviəl/ *adj* gay; fond of, marked by drinking and merry making: ~ *companions; a* ~ *evening.*

con·vo·ca·tion /ˌkanvəˈkeiʃən/ *n* **1** [U] calling together. **2** [C] formal academic or school assembly.

con·voke /kənˈvouk/ *vt* call together, summon (to a meeting): *to* ~ *the academic senate.*

con·vo·luted /ˈkanvəˌlutɪd/ *adj* coiled; twisted (eg like a ram's horn).

con·vo·lution /ˌkanvəˈluʃən/ *n* [C] coil; twist: *the* ~*s of a snake.*

con·voy[1] /ˈkanˌvɔi/ *n* **1** [U] convoying or being convoyed; protection: *The supply ships sailed under* ~. **2** [C] protecting force (of warships,

troops, etc). **3** [C] ship(s), supplies under escort: *The ~ was attacked by submarines.*
con·voy² /ˈkanˌvɔi/ *vt* (esp of a warship) go with, escort (other ships) to protect (them): *The troopships were ~ed across the Atlantic.*
con·vulse /kənˈvəls/ *vt* shake or disturb violently: *~d with laughter; a country ~d by civil war.*
con·vul·sion /kənˈvəlʃən/ *n* [C] **1** violent disturbance: *a ~ of nature,* eg an earthquake. **2** (usually *pl*) violent irregular movement of a limb or limbs, or of the body, caused by contraction of muscles: *The child's ~s filled us with fear.* **3** (*pl*) fit of laughter: *The story was so funny that we were all in ~s.*
con·vul·sive /kənˈvəlsɪv/ *adj* having or producing convulsions: *~ movements.*
coo /ku/ *vi,vt, n* (make a) soft, murmuring sound (as of doves).
cook /kʊk/ *vt,vi* **1** prepare (food) by heating (eg boiling, baking, roasting, frying). **2** be cooked: *These apples ~ well.* **3** ***cook up,*** (*informal*) invent; make up: *~ed up a wild story.* ▫ *n* [C] person who cooks food.
cook·ing *n* [U]
cook·book /ˈkʊkˌbʊk/ *n* [C] book with recipes.
cook·ery /ˈkʊkəri/ *n* [U] art and practice of cooking.
cookie /ˈkʊki/ *n* [C] (*pl* ~s) small, flat, crisp sweet pastry.
cool¹ /kul/ *adj* (-er, -est) **1** between warm and cold: *~ autumn weather. The coffee's not ~ enough to drink.* **2** calm; unexcited: *Keep ~! He was always ~ in the face of danger. He has a ~ head,* is not easily excited, etc. **3** unfriendly; not showing interest or enthusiasm: *They gave the prime minister a ~ reception.* **4** (of colors) giving an effect of coolness: *blue is a ~ color.* **5** (*informal*) (used for emphasis): *a ~ million dollars.* **6** (*sl*) street-wise; sophisticated; elegant. ▫ *n* [U] cool air or place; coolness: *in the ~ of the evening; the ~ of the forest.*
cool-ˈheaded *adj* not easily excited.
coolly *adv*
cool·ness /-nɪs/ *n* [U]
cool² /kul/ *vt,vi* make or become cool: *The rain has ~ed the air. Has his anger ~ed yet?* ***cool down/off,*** (*fig*) become calm, less excited or enthusiastic: *I told him to ~ down.*
coon /kun/ (*informal*) *n* [C] (short for) raccoon.
coop /kup/ *n* [C] cage, esp for poultry. ▫ *vt* ***coop up,*** put in a coop; confine (a person): *How long are we going to stay ~ed up in here?*
co-op /ˈkou-ˌap/ *n* [C] (*informal*) (short for) cooperative (1, 2).
cooper /ˈkupər/ *n* [C] maker of tubs, barrels, casks, etc.
coop·er·ate /kouˈapəˌreit/ *vi* work or act together in order to bring about a result: *~ with friends in starting a social club.*
coop·er·ator *n* [C]
coop·er·ation /kouˌapəˈreiʃən/ *n* [U] working or acting together for a common purpose: *The workers, in ~ with the management, have increased output by 10 percent.*
coop·er·ative /kouˈapərətɪv/ *adj* of cooperation; willing to cooperate. ▫ *n* [C] **1** association or group in which the profits and losses are shared by all its members: *agricultural ~s in India and China.* **2** (also **cooperative apartment**) **(a)** apartment building owned in common by the residents. **(b)** individual apartment in such a building.
co-opt /kou-ˈapt/ *vt* (of a committee) add (a person) as a new member.
coor·di·nate¹ /kouˈɔrdənɪt/ *adj* equal in importance. ▫ *n* [C] coordinate thing or person.
coor·di·nate² /kouˈɔrdəˌneit/ **1** *vt* make coordinate. **2** bring or put into proper relation; harmonize: *to ~ the movements of the arms and legs.*
coor·di·na·tion /kouˌɔrdənˈeiʃən/ *n* [C] act of coordinating; state of being coordinate.
coot /kut/ *n* [C] name of several kinds of swimming and diving birds. ***as bald as a coot,*** very bald.
cop¹ /kap/ *n* [C] (*sl*) policeman.
cop² /kap/ *vi* (-pp-) ***cop out,*** (*sl*) back out of (a promise, responsibility, etc).
cope /koup/ *vi* manage successfully; be equal to: *coping with difficulties.*
copi·ous /ˈkoupiəs/ *adj* plentiful: *a ~ supply.*
copi·ous·ly *adv*
cop·per¹ /ˈkapər/ *n* **1** [U] common reddish-brown metal (symbol **Cu**): *~ wire/cable/alloy.* **2** [C] coin made of copper (alloy). ▫ *adj* reddish-brown.
ˈcop·per·head *n* [C] poisonous copper-colored snake of the eastern US.
ˈcopper·plate *n* [U] polished copper plate on which designs, etc, are engraved.
ˈcopper·smith *n* [C] person who makes articles of copper.
cop·per² /ˈkapər/ *n* [C] (*sl*) policeman.
cop·pice /ˈkapɪs/ *n* [C] small area of shrubs and small trees.
copra /ˈkouprə/ *n* [U] dried meat of coconuts, from which oil is extracted for making soap, etc.
copse /kaps/ *n* [C] = coppice.
copu·late /ˈkapyəˌleit/ *vi* unite in sexual intercourse.
copu·la·tion /ˌkapyəˈleiʃən/ *n* [C,U] act or process of copulating.
copy¹ /ˈkapi/ *n* (*pl* -ies) **1** [C] thing made to be like another; reproduction of a letter, picture, etc: *Make three carbon copies of the letter.* **2** [C] one example of a book, newspaper, etc of which many have been made: *If you can't buy a ~ of the book, perhaps you can borrow one from the library.* **3** [U] material to be sent to a printer: *The printers are waiting for more ~.*
copy·cat *n* (*informal*) slavish imitator.
copy² /ˈkapi/ *vt,vi* **1** make a copy of: *~ notes (out of a book, etc); ~ an address down* (eg from a bulletin-board). **2** do, try to do, the same as; imitate: *You should ~ his good points, not his bad points.*
copy·right /ˈkapiˌrait/ *n* [U] sole legal right, granted by the government to reproduce, perform, a literary, artistic, or musical work. ▫ *vt* protect in this way.
coral /ˈkɔrəl/ *n* [U] **1** hard, red, pink or white substance formed by the skeletons of small sea

creatures. **2** deep red or pink color. □ *adj* deep red or pink: *~ lips.*

ˌcoral ˈisland, one formed by the growth of coral.

ˈcoral reef, one of coral.

cord /kɔrd/ *n* **1** [C,U] (length of) twisted strands, thicker than string, thinner than rope. **2** [C] anything like a cord, esp the cable used with electrical appliances. **3** [C] part of the body like a cord: *the spinal ~; the vocal ~s.* **4** [C] unit of measure for cut firewood that is 4 × 4 × 8 feet (= 128 cubic feet). □ *vt* **1** put a cord around. **2** pile up (firewood) in a cord.

ˈcord·less *adj* powered or run by batteries: *a ~less shaver.*

cor·dial /ˈkɔrdʒəl/ *adj* **1** deep and sincere (in feeling, behavior); heartfelt: *a ~ smile; ~ dislike.* **2** (of food, drink, or medicine) strengthening; stimulating. □ *n* [C] **1** stimulant. **2** liqueur.

cord·ially *adv*

cor·don /ˈkɔrdən/ *n* [C] **1** line or circle, persons, military posts, etc acting as guards: *a poˈlice ~.* **2** ornamental ribbon of an order¹(10) (usually worn across the shoulder). □ *vt* ***cordon off,*** separate or enclose by means of a cordon(1).

cor·du·roy /ˈkɔrdəˌrɔi/ *n* **1** [U] sturdy cotton cloth with raised lines or ribs. **2** (*pl*) trousers made of this cloth.

core /kɔr/ *n* [C] **1** (usually hard) center, with seeds, of such fruits as the apple and pear. ➪ illus at fruit. **2** central or most important part of anything: *the ~ of an electromagnet.* ***to the core,*** right to the center: *rotten to the core,* (*fig*) thoroughly bad. □ *vt* take out the core of: *to ~ an apple.*

cork /kɔrk/ *n* **1** [U] light, brown, tough outer bark of the tree called the *ˈcork oak.* **2** [C] round piece of this material used as a stopper for a bottle. □ *vt* stop with, or as with a cork: *to ~ up one's feelings.*

ˈcork·screw *n* [C] tool for pulling corks from bottles.

corm /kɔrm/ *n* [C] bulblike underground stem of certain plants, from which buds sprout.

cor·mo·rant /ˈkɔrmərənt/ *n* [C] large black sea bird with a long neck, hooked beak, and webbed feet.

corn¹ /kɔrn/ *n* **1** [U] any of various grain plants, esp maize or Indian corn; such plants while growing: *a field of ~; a ˈ~field.* **2** [U] the grains or kernels of maize, on or off the ear, cooked and eaten as a vegetable when ripe and as a cereal when dried. ➪ illus at cereal, vegetable. **3** [C] single grain (of wheat, pepper, etc): *ˈpepper~.*

ˈcorn·bread *n* [U] yellow-colored bread, like a cake in texture, made from Indian corn.

ˈcorn·cob *n* [C] long, woody core of an ear of Indian corn, on which the kernels grow.

ˌcorncob ˈpipe, tobacco pipe with the bowl made from a corncob.

ˈcorn·meal *n* [U] coarsely ground corn.

ˈcorn pone, flat loaf of pudding-like corn bread.

ˈcorn·silk *n* ➪ silk(2).

ˈcorn·starch *n* [U] starch, in the form of flour, made from Indian corn.

corn² /kɔrn/ *n* [C] small area of hardened skin on the foot, esp on a toe, often with a painful center and root.

corn³ /kɔrn/ *vt* preserve (meat) with salt: *~ed beef.*

corn·ball /ˈkɔrnˌbɔl/ *n* [C] (*sl*) person who likes outdated jokes, overly sentimental songs, etc. ➪ corny.

cor·nea /ˈkɔrniə/ *n* [C] (*pl* ~s) tough transparent covering for the iris of the eyeball. ➪ illus at eye.

cor·ner /ˈkɔrnər/ *n* **1** angle; place where two lines, sides, edges or surfaces meet: *a shop on/at the corner; sitting in the ~ of the room.* ***cut corners,*** **(a)** drive across them in order to travel fast. **(b)** (*fig*) cut down on expenses, time, etc: *We've had to cut a few ~s to stay within our budget.* ***turn the corner,*** (*fig*) pass a critical point in an illness, a period of difficulty, etc. ***just round the corner,*** very near (in position, time, etc.). ***in a tight corner,*** in an awkward or difficult situation. **2** hidden, secret, place: *money hidden in odd ~s.* **3** region; quarter: *to the four ~s of the earth.* □ *vt,vi* **1** force into a corner; put into a difficult position: *The escaped prisoner was ~ed at last.* **2** turn a corner (on a road, etc): *My new car ~s well.* **3** get control over (the supply of) a commodity, so as to control its price: *~ed the market in gold.*

ˈcorner·stone *n* **(a)** stone forming a corner of a foundation for a building. **(b)** (*fig*) foundation: *Charm was the ~stone of his success.*

cor·net /kɔrˈnet/ *n* [C] **1** small musical instrument of brass, like a trumpet. **2** piece of paper, etc twisted into the shape of a cone, to hold candy, etc.

cor·nice /ˈkɔrnɪs/ *n* [C] **1** projecting part above the frieze in a column(1). **2** ornamental molding (eg in plaster) round the walls of a room, just below the ceiling. **3** horizontal strip of carved wood or stone along the top edge of a building.

corny /ˈkɔrni/ *adj* (-ier, -iest) (*sl*) outdated; often heard or repeated; overly sentimental: *~ jokes/music.*

co·rolla /kəˈralə/ *n* [C] ring of petals forming the base of a flower. ➪ illus at flower.

co·rol·lary /ˈkɔrəˌleri/ *n* [C] (*pl* -ies) natural result or outcome.

co·rona /kəˈrounə/ *n* [C] (*pl* ~s, ~e /-ni/) ring of light seen round the sun or moon, eg during an eclipse. ➪ illus at eclipse.

cor·o·nary /ˈkɔrəˌneri/ *adj* of arteries supplying blood to the heart. □ *n* [C] (*pl* -ies) (*informal*) = coronary thrombosis.

ˌcoronary thromˈbosis, formation of a clot in a coronary artery.

cor·o·nation /ˌkɔrəˈneiʃən/ *n* [C] ceremony of crowning a king, queen or other sovereign ruler.

cor·oner /ˈkɔrənər/ *n* [C] official who inquires into the cause of any death thought to be from violent or unnatural causes; *~'s inquest,* such an inquiry (held with a jury).

cor·onet /ˌkɔrəˈnet/ *n* [C] **1** small crown . **2** circle or band of precious materials, flowers, etc worn around the head.

Corp. = **1** Corporation. **2** Corporal.
cor·poral[1] /ˈkɔrp(ə)rəl/ *adj* of the body: *~ punishment*, eg whipping, beating.
cor·poral[2] /ˈkɔrp(ə)rəl/ *n* [C] lowest-ranking noncommissioned officer (below a sergeant) in the US army or marine corps.
cor·po·rate /ˈkɔrp(ə)rɪt/ *adj* **1** of or belonging to a corporation(2): *~ property*. **2** of, shared by persons united as a whole or a group: *~ responsibility/action*.
cor·po·ration /ˌkɔrpəˈreiʃən/ *n* [C] group of persons authorized to act as an individual, eg for business purposes.
cor·po·real /kɔrˈpɔriəl/ *adj* (*formal*) **1** of or for the body. **2** physical (contrasted with *spiritual*).
corps /kɔr/ *n* [C] (*pl* ~ /kɔrz/) **1** one of the technical branches of a military force: *the ˈMedical Corps*. **2** military force made up of two or more divisions.
corpse /kɔrps/ *n* [C] dead body (esp of a human being).
cor·pu·lent /ˈkɔrpyələnt/ *adj* (*formal*) (of a person or his body) fat and heavy.
cor·pus /ˈkɔrpəs/ *n* [C] (*pl* corpora /ˈkɔrpərə/) complete collection, esp of writings on a specified subject.
cor·puscle /ˈkɔrˌpəsəl/ *n* [C] one of the red or white cells in the blood.
cor·ral /kəˈræl/ *n* [C] enclosure for horses and cattle or the capture of wild animals. □ *vt* (-ll-) drive (cattle, etc) into, shut up in, a corral.
cor·rect[1] /kəˈrekt/ *adj* **1** true; right: *the ~ time*. **2** (of conduct, manners, dress, etc) proper; in accord with good taste or convention: *the ~ dress for a ceremony*.
cor·rect·ly *adv*
cor·rect·ness /-nɪs/ *n* [U]
cor·rect[2] /kəˈrekt/ *vt* **1** make right; take out mistakes from: *Please ~ my pronunciation*. **2** point out the faults of; punish: *~ a child for disobedience*.
cor·rec·tion /kəˈrekʃən/ *n* **1** [U] correcting: *the ~ of schoolchildren's work*. **2** [C] something that corrects a mistake: *a written exercise with ~s in red ink*.
cor·rec·tive /kəˈrektɪv/ *n, adj* (something) serving to correct: *~ training*, eg for young offenders.
cor·re·late /ˈkɔrəˌleit/ *vt,vi* ***correlate with,*** show the relation between; bring (one thing) into a systematic connection (with another): *Research workers find it hard to ~ the two sets of figures/to ~ one set with the other*.
cor·re·la·tion /ˌkɔrəˈleiʃən/ *n* [C] mutual relationship: *the ~ between climate and vegetation*.
cor·re·spond /ˌkɔrəˈspand/ *vi* **1** be in harmony: *His actions do not ~ with his words*. **2** ***correspond to,*** be equal (to); be similar (in position, etc) (to): *The British Parliament ~s to the American Congress*. **3** exchange letters: *We've been ~ing with each other for years*.
cor·re·spond·ing *adj* agreeing or matching: *Imports for July 1-10 this year are higher by 10 percent than for the ~ing period last year*.
cor·re·spond·ing·ly *adv*
cor·re·spon·dence /ˌkɔrəˈspandəns/ *n* **1** [C,U] agreement; similarity: *There is not much ~ between their ideals and ours*. **2** [U] letter writing; letters: *I have been in ~ with him about the problem*.
cor·re·spon·dent /ˌkɔrəˈspandənt/ *n* [C] **1** person with whom one exchanges letters: *He's a good/bad ~,* writes regularly/seldom. **2** person regularly contributing local news or special articles to a newspaper: *a ˈwar ~*.
cor·ri·dor /ˈkɔrədər, -ˌdɔr/ *n* [C] long narrow passage from which doors open into rooms or compartments.
cor·rob·o·rate /kəˈrabəˌreit/ *vt* give support or certainty to (a statement, belief, theory, etc).
cor·rob·o·ra·tive /kəˈrabəˌreitɪv/ *adj* tending to corroborate: *~ evidence*.
cor·rode /kəˈroud/ *vt,vi* wear away, destroy slowly (as by chemical action or disease): *Rust ~s iron*.
cor·rosion /kəˈrouʒən/ *n* [U] corroding or being corroded.
cor·ro·sive /kəˈrousɪv/ *n* [C], *adj* (substance) that corrodes: *Rust and acids are ~*.
cor·ru·gate /ˈkɔrəˌgeit/ *vt,vi* make into folds, wrinkles or furrows: *~d cardboard*, used for packing fragile goods.
cor·ru·ga·tion /ˌkɔrəˈgeiʃən/ *n* [C,U] fold(s); wrinkle(s).
cor·rupt[1] /kəˈrəpt/ *adj* **1** (of persons, their actions) immoral; dishonest (esp through taking bribes): *~ practices*, (esp) the offering and accepting of bribes. **2** impure: *~ air/blood*.
cor·rupt·ly *adv*
cor·rupt·ness /-nɪs/ *n* [U]
cor·rupt[2] /kəˈrəpt/ *vt,vi* make or become corrupt: *young persons whose morals have been ~ed*.
cor·rupt·ible *adj* that can be corrupted: *~ible government officials*.
cor·rup·tion /kəˈrəpʃən/ [U] corrupting or or being corrupt; decay: *the ~ of the body after death*.
cor·sage /kɔrˈsaʒ/ *n* [C] **1** upper part of a woman's dress (around the bust). **2** arrangement of flowers to be worn usually at a woman's shoulder.
cor·set /ˈkɔrsɪt/ *n* [C] close-fitting reinforced undergarment confining the waist and hips, to shape or support the body.
cor·tege, cor·tège /kɔrˈteʒ/ *n* (*F*) procession, eg at the funeral of a king or president.
cor·tex /ˈkɔrˌteks/ *n* [C] (*pl* cortices /ˈkɔrtəˌsiz/). **1** outer layer of gray matter of the brain. **2** outer shell or covering (eg the bark of a tree).
cor·ti·cal /ˈkɔrtɪkəl/ *adj* of the cortex.
cos·metic /kazˈmetɪk/ *adj, n* [C] (preparation, substance) designed to make the skin or hair beautiful, eg face powder, lipstick.
cos·mic /ˈkazmɪk/ *adj* of the whole universe or cosmos: *~ rays*, radiations that reach the earth from outer space.
cos·mo·naut /ˈkazməˌnɔt/ *n* [C] = astronaut.
cos·mo·poli·tan /ˌkazməˈpalətən/ *adj* **1** of or from all, or many different parts of, the world: *the ~ gatherings at the United Nations Assembly*. **2** free from a narrow, national outlook: *a statesman with a ~ outlook*. □ *n* [C] cos-

mopolitan(2) person.

cos·mos /ˈkazməs/ *n* **1 the cosmos,** the universe, all space, considered as a well-ordered system. **2** tall garden plant with pinkish or white flowers blooming in late summer or early fall.

cost[1] /kɔst/ *n* **1** [C,U] price (to be) paid for a thing: *the ~ of living. He built his house without regard to ~,* without considering how much money would be needed. **2** that which is used, needed or given to obtain something: *The battle was won at a great ~ in human lives.* ***at all costs,*** whatever the cost(2) may be. **3** (*pl*) (*legal*) expense of having an action settled in a law court: *He had to pay a $10 fine and $3 ~s.*

cost[2] /kɔst/ *vi* (*pt,pp* ~) **1** have as the price of; require the payment of: *The house ~ him $20,000.* **2** cause (a person) to spend, sacrifice, or lose: *Careless driving may ~ you your life. The boy's bad behavior ~ his mother many sleepless nights.* □ *vt* (*pt,pp* ~ed) estimate the price to be charged for an article based on the expense of producing it.

co-star /ˈkou-ˌstar/ *n* [C] star in a motion picture or play who is equal in importance to another star. □ *vi, vt* (-rr-) present or appear as a co-star: *The film ~red John Wayne. Meryl Streep ~red with Dustin Hoffman in this film.*

cost·ly /ˈkɔstli/ *adj* (-ier, -iest) of great value; costing much: *~ jewels; (fig) a ~ mistake.*

cos·tume /ˈkaˌstum/ *n* **1** [U] style of dress: *actors wearing historical ~,* clothes in the style of a period in the past. **2** [C] complete suit or set of outer garments.

cosy = cozy.

cot /kat/ *n* [C] narrow bed sometimes made of canvas stretched on a folding frame.

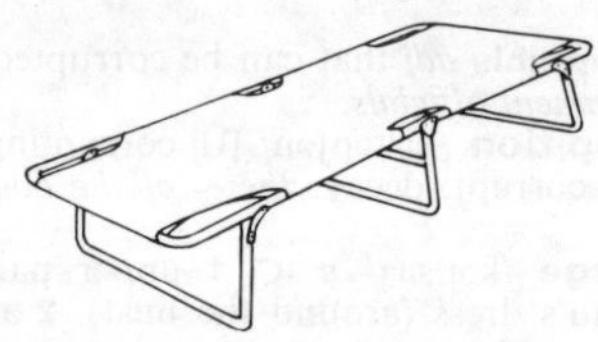

COT

cote /kout/ *n* [C] shed or shelter for domestic animals or birds: *a ˈdove ~.*

cot·tage /ˈkatɪdʒ/ *n* [C] small house, esp in the country: *farm ~s; ~ industries,* those that can be carried on in ~s, eg knitting, pottery, some kinds of weaving.

cot·ton /ˈkatən/ *n* [U] **1** soft, white fibrous substance round the seeds of the ˈcottonplant, used for making thread, cloth, etc. **2** thread spun from cotton. **3** cloth made of cotton. □ *vi* ***cotton to,*** (*informal*) take a liking to: *~ed to her from the beginning.*

ˈcotton gin, machine that removes the seeds from cotton.

cot·ton-pick·ing, cot·ton-pickin' /ˈkatənˌpɪkɪn; only rarely -ɪŋ/ *adj* (*informal*) worthless; damned; darned: *(It's) none of your ~ business!*

cot·ton·tail /ˈkatənˌteiəl/ *n* [C] any of several North American wild rabbits with a white tail.

cot·ton·wood /ˈkatənˌwʊd/ *n* **1** [C] tree related to the poplar, having seeds with cottonlike tufts of hair. **2** [U] wood of this tree.

couch[1] /kautʃ/ *n* [C] **1** long bed-like seat for sitting on or lying on: *a studio ~.* **2** (*liter*) bed.

couch[2] /kautʃ/ *vt,vi* **1** lie down (as if) on a couch. **2** (of animals) lie flat (either in hiding, or ready for a jump forward). **3** (*formal*) put in words; express: *His answer was ~ed in insulting language.*

cou·gar /ˈkugər/ *n* [C] (*pl* ~s or ~.) large wild cat, also called a *puma, mountain lion,* or *panther.*

cough[1] /kɔf/ *n* [C] **1** act or sound of coughing: *He gave me a warning ~.* **2** condition, illness, that causes a person to cough often: *to have a bad ~.*

cough[2] /kɔf/ *vi,vt* send out air from the lungs violently and noisily. ***cough up,*** **(a)** get out of the throat by coughing. **(b)** (*sl*) pay; give: *Jones refused to ~ up the money.*

could /kəd, *strong form* kʊd/ (neg ~n't /ˈkʊdənt/) *auxiliary verb pt* of *can,* used in indirect speech in place of *can* if the main verb is *pt*; to express doubt or possibility, and to express polite requests. ⇨ can[2].

couldn't /ˈkʊdənt/ = could not.

coun·cil /ˈkaunsəl/ *n* [C] group of persons appointed, elected or chosen to give advice, make rules, and carry out plans, manage affairs, etc, esp of government: *a city/county ~; the municipal ~.*

coun·cil·or, coun·cil·lor /ˈkaunsələr/ *n* [C] member of a council.

coun·sel[1] /ˈkaunsəl/ *n* **1** [U] advice; consultation; opinions; suggestions. **2** [C] (*pl* unchanged) lawyer(s), giving advice in a law case: *when the jury had heard ~ on both sides,* the lawyers for the prosecution and the defense.

coun·sel[2] /ˈkaunsəl/ *vt* (-l-, -ll-) (*formal*) advise: *~ed us to be patient.*

coun·sel·or, coun·sel·lor /ˈkaunsələr/ *n* [C] adviser.

count[1] /kaunt/ *n* [C] **1** act of counting: *Four ~s were necessary before we were certain of the total.* **2** number got by counting; amount. **3** (*legal*) one of a number of things of which a person has been accused: *He was found guilty on all ~s.*

count[2] /kaunt/ *vt,vi* **1** say or name (the numerals) in order: *to ~ from 1 to 10. He can't ~ yet.* **2** find the total of: *Don't forget to ~ your change.* **3** include, be included, in the calculation: *fifty people, not ~ing the children.* **4** consider to be: *I ~ myself fortunate in being here.* **5** be of value: *Every person's vote ~s.* ***count (sth) against sb,*** be considered, consider to the disadvantage of: *Please don't ~ his youth against him.* **6** (special uses with *adverbial particles* and *prepositions*):

count down, count seconds backwards (eg 10, 9, 8, 7...) as when launching a rocket, etc into space.

count in, include: *If you're all going for a drink, you can ~ me in.*

count on/upon, expect with confidence; rely on: *We are ~ing on you to help.*

count out, **(a)** count things (slowly), one by one: *The old lady ~ed out fifteen dollars and* *passed it to the salesgirl.* **(b)** count up to ten over a boxer who is down: *The referee ~ed him out in the first round.* **(c)** not include: *If it's going to be a drunken party, ~ me out.*

count up, find the total of: *Just you ~ up the number of times he has failed to keep a promise!*

ˈcount·down *n* [C] counting of seconds backwards: *The mission was aborted 30 seconds from ~down.*

count[3] /kaunt/ *n* [C] (in Europe) member of the nobility similar in rank to a British earl.

count·able /ˈkauntəbəl/ *adj* that can be counted.

coun·ten·ance /ˈkauntənəns/ *n* (*formal*) **1** [C] face, including its appearance and expression: *a woman with a fierce ~.* **2** [U] support; approval: *to give ~ to a person/a plan.* □ *vt* (*formal*) give support or approval to: *to ~ a fraud.*

coun·ter[1] /ˈkauntər/ *n* [C] table or flat surface on which goods are shown, customers served, food is prepared, etc. ***under the counter,*** in a dishonest and secret way.

coun·ter[2] /ˈkauntər/ *n* [C] **1** small (round) flat piece of plastic, etc used for keeping count in games, etc. **2** person or thing that counts.

coun·ter[3] /ˈkauntər/ *adv* ***counter to,*** in the opposite direction (to); in opposition (to): *to act ~ to a person's wishes.*

coun·ter[4] /ˈkauntər/ *vt,vi* oppose; meet an attack (with a return attack): *They ~ed our proposal with one of their own.*

coun·ter-[5] /ˌkauntər-/ *prefix* **1** opposite in direction: *~productive.* **2** made in answer to: *ˈ~attack.* **3** corresponding: *ˈ~part.*

coun·ter·act /ˌkauntərˈækt/ *vt* act against and make (action, force) of less or no effect: *~ (the effects of) a poison.*

coun·ter·at·tack /ˈkauntərəˌtæk/ *n* [C] attack made in reply to an attack. □ *vt,vi* make such an attack.

coun·ter·bal·ance /ˈkauntərˌbæləns/ *n* [C] weight, force, equal to another and balancing it. □ /ˌkauntərˈbæləns/ *vt* act as a counterbalance to.

coun·ter·clock·wise /ˌkauntərˈklakˌwaiz/ *adv* in a direction opposite to the one in which the hands of a clock move.

coun·ter·espion·age /ˌkauntərˈespiəˌnaʒ/ *n* [U] spying directed against the enemy's spying.

coun·ter·feit /ˈkauntərˌfɪt/ *n* [C], *adj* (something) made or done in imitation of another thing in order to deceive: *~ money.* □ *vt* copy, imitate (coins, handwriting, etc) in order to deceive.

coun·ter·foil /ˈkauntərˌfɔiəl/ *n* [C] section of a check, receipt, etc kept as a record.

coun·ter·in·tel·li·gence /ˌkauntərɪnˈtelədʒəns/ *n* [U] = counterespionage.

coun·ter·mand /ˌkauntərˈmænd/ *vt* take back, cancel, a command already given.

coun·ter·march /ˈkauntərˌmartʃ/ *vi,vt,n* (cause to) march in the opposite direction.

coun·ter·offer /ˈkauntərˌɔfər/ *n* [C] offer made in reply to an offer.

coun·ter·pane /ˈkauntərˌpein/ *n* [C] bedspread.

coun·ter·part /ˈkauntərˌpart/ *n* [C] person or thing exactly like, or closely corresponding to, another.

coun·ter·plot /ˈkauntərˌplat/ *n* plot made to defeat another plot. □ *vt,vi* (-tt-) make such a plot.

coun·ter·rev·ol·ution /ˌkauntərˌrevəˈluʃən/ *n* [C] political movement directed against a revolution.

coun·ter·rev·o·lution·ary *adj* characteristic of a counterrevolution. □ *n* [C] (*pl* -ies) supporter of counterrevolution(s).

coun·ter·sign /ˈkauntərˌsain/ *n* [C] password; secret word(s) to be given, on demand, to a sentry: *"Advance and give the ~."* □ *vt* add another signature to (a document) to give it authority.

coun·ter·tenor /ˈkauntərˌtenər/ *n* [C], *adj* (musical part for, or adult male singer) having a range above that of a tenor.

count·ess /ˈkauntɪs/ *n* [C] **1** wife or widow of a count or earl. **2** woman holding an earldom in her own right.

count·less /ˈkauntlɪs/ *adj* too many to count.

coun·tri·fied /ˈkəntrɪˌfaid/ *adj* rural; having the unsophisticated ways, habits, outlook, etc of those who live in the country(4).

coun·try /ˈkəntri/ *n* (*pl* -ies) **1** [C] land occupied by a nation: *European countries.* **2** [C] land of a person's birth or citizenship: *to return to one's own ~.* **3 the country,** the people of a country (1); the nation as a whole: *Does the ~ want war?* **4 the country,** land used for farming; rural area as opposed to the town or city: *to live in the ~.* **5** [U] area of land; region: *We passed through miles of densely wooded ~.* (*Note:* used without *a* or *the.*) **6** (as an *adjective*) of or in the country (4): *~ life; ~ roads.*

coun·try·man/·woman *n* [C] (*pl* ~men /-men/, ~women /-ˌwɪmən/) **(a)** person living in the country(4). **(b)** person of one's own (or a specified) country(1).

country ˈmusic *n* [U] music in the folk style of the southern or western US.

ˈcoun·try·side *n* [U] rural area(s) (contrasted with urban areas): *New England ~side looks its best in the fall.*

ˌcountry ˈstore *n* [C] small, often rustic store offering general merchandise in rural areas.

county /ˈkaunti/ *n* (*pl* -ies) subdivision of a state.

ˌcounty ˈseat *n* [C] town or city in which a county government is located.

coup /ku/ *n* [C] (*pl* ~s /kuz/) (*F*) sudden action taken to get power, obtain a desired result, etc: *He made/pulled off a great ~,* succeeded in what he attempted.

coup d'état /ˌku deiˈta/ *n* [C] (*pl* ~s /ˌku deiˈtaz/ or coups d'état /ˌku deiˈta/) (*F*) violent or unconstitutional change in government.

coupé /kuˈpei/ *n* [C] (*pl* ~s) **1** (often /kup/) roofed two-door automobile with a sloping back. **2** closed horse-drawn carriage with one inside seat for two people and an outside seat for the driver.

couple[1] /ˈkəpəl/ *n* [C] **1** two persons or things, seen together or associated: *He came back with a ~ of rabbits and a hare.* ***go/hunt/run in ~s,*** in pairs; two together. **2** man and woman paired in marriage, for a dance, etc: *They make a hand* *some* ~. **3** few: *a* ~ *of weeks ago*.

couple[2] /ˈkəpəl/ *vt,vi* **1** fasten, join (two things) together: *We* ~ *the name of Harvard with the idea of learning*. **2** come together; unite.

coup·let /ˈkəplɪt/ *n* [C] two successive lines of verse, esp two that rhyme and are equal in length.

coup·ling /ˈkəplɪŋ/ *n* **1** [U] act of joining. **2** [C] link, etc that joins two parts, esp two railroad cars or other vehicles.

cou·pon /ˈkuˌpan/ *n* [C] **1** ticket, part of a document, paper, bond, etc, which gives the holder the right to receive or do something, eg a voucher given with a purchase to be exchanged for goods. **2** entry form for a competition; form (7) in a newspaper, etc for buying by mail, obtaining brochures, etc: *Fill in the* ~ *below and send it to*....

cour·age /ˈkərɪdʒ/ *n* [U] quality that enables a person to control fear in the face of danger, pain, misfortune, etc.

cou·rageous /kəˈreidʒəs/ *adj* brave; fearless: *It was* ~ *of him to chase the gunman*.

cou·rageous·ly *adv*

cour·ier /ˈkʊriər/ *n* [C] messenger carrying news or important government papers.

course[1] /kɔrs/ *n* **1** [U] forward movement in space or time; progress: *a river in its* ~ *to the sea; the* ~ *of events*. ***in due course,*** in the natural order; at the normal time: *Sow the seed now and in due* ~ *you will have the flowers*. ***in the course of,*** during: *in the* ~ *of conversation*. **2** [C] direction of movement or progress: *a map that shows the* ~*s of the chief rivers; The ship is on/off her right* ~, is going/not going in the right direction. *The* ~ *of the argument suddenly changed*, went in a different direction. *The disease must run its* ~. ***of course,*** **(a)** as naturally expected: *You needn't ask him to come; he'll come as a matter of* ~. **(b)** naturally; certainly: *"Do you study hard?" "Of* ~ *I do."* **3** [C] ground laid out for games: *a ˈgolf* ~*; a ˈrace*~. **4** [C] series of talks, treatments, etc: *a* ~ *of lectures; a* ~ *of X-ray treatment*. **5** [C] continuous layer of brick, stone, etc in a wall. **6** [C] one of the several parts of a meal, eg soup, fish, dessert: *five-*~ *dinner; the main* ~.

course[2] /kɔrs/ *vt,vi* **1** chase game with dogs. **2** move quickly; run over or through: *The blood* ~*d through his veins*.

court[1] /kɔrt/ *n* **1** [C] place where legal cases are held. **2** [C] the judges, magistrates, and other officers who administer justice: *The prisoner was brought before the* ~. **3** [C] (residence of a) great ruler, king, queen, emperor, his family and officials, councilors, etc. **4** [U] state gathering or reception given by a ruler. **5** [C] space marked out for certain games: *a ˈtennis* ~. **6** = courtyard. **7** [C] short street. **8** [U] attention given to win favor: *paid* ~ *to those in power*.

court[2] /kɔrt/ *vt,vi* **1** try to win the affections of, engage in activities, with a view to marriage: *He had been* ~*ing Jane for six months*. **2** try to win or obtain: *to* ~ *a person's approval/support*. **3** act so as to get (something disagreeable): *That would be* ~*ing disaster*.

cour·teous /ˈkərtiəs/ *adj* having, showing, good manners; polite and kind (to).

cour·teous·ly *adv*

cour·tesy /ˈkərtəsi/ *n* (*pl* -ies) **1** [U] courteous behavior. **2** [C] courteous act. ***3 by courtesy of,*** by favor or permission, usually free of charge: *a radio program presented by* ~ *of*....

court·house /ˈkɔrtˌhaus/ *n* [C] (*pl* ~s /-ˌhauzɪz/) building for holding courts of law or for housing the offices of a county government.

court·ier /ˈkɔrtiər/ *n* [C] person in attendance at the court of a sovereign: *the king and his* ~*s*.

court·ly /ˈkɔrtli/ *adj* (-ier, -iest) (*formal*) polite and dignified.

court-mar·tial /ˈkɔrt-ˌmarʃəl/ *n* [C] (*pl* courts-martial) **1** court for trying offenses against military law. **2** trial by such a court. □ *vt* (-l-, -ll-) try (a person) in a court of this kind.

court·room /ˈkɔrtˌrum/ *n* [C] room in which a court of law is held.

court·ship /ˈkɔrtˌʃɪp/ *n* [C,U] (period of time of) courting(1): *after a brief* ~.

court·yard /ˈkɔrtˌyard/ *n* [C] unroofed space with walls or buildings around it.

cousin /ˈkəzən/ *n* [C] child of one's uncle or aunt.

cove /kouv/ *n* [C] small bay[2].

cov·e·nant /ˈkəvənənt/ *n* [C] **1** (*legal*) formal agreement that is legally binding. **2** solemn agreement. □ *vt,vi* make a covenant.

cover[1] /ˈkəvər/ *n* **1** [C] thing that covers: *Some chairs are fitted with loose* ~*s*. **2** [C] binding of a book, magazine, etc; either half of this: *The book needs a new* ~. ***from cover to cover,*** from beginning to end: *The child read the book from* ~ *to* ~. **3** [C] wrapper or envelope. ***under separate cover,*** in a separate parcel or envelope. **4** [U] anything that shelters or protects: *The underbrush was a good* ~ *for small animals*. ***take cover,*** place oneself where one is concealed, or protected: *There was nowhere we could take* ~. **5** [U] ***under cover of,*** under the disguise or protection of: *under* ~ *of friendship/darkness*. **6** [U] force of aircraft protecting a military operation: *give an operation fighter* ~.

cover[2] /ˈkəvər/ *vt* **1** place (one substance or thing) over or in front of (another); hide or protect (something) in this way; lie or extend over; occupy the surface of: *Cover the table with a cloth. Snow* ~*ed the ground. He laughed to* ~ (= hide) *his nervousness*. ***cover up,*** **(a)** wrap up: *Cover yourself up well*, Put on warm clothes, etc. **(b)** hide; conceal: *How can we* ~ *up our tracks/our mistakes?* **2** lie thickly over the surface of. ***be covered with,*** **(a)** have a great number or amount of: *trees* ~*ed with blossom/fruit*. **(b)** have as a natural coat: *Cats are* ~*ed with fur and dogs are* ~*ed with hair*. **(c)** be overcome by: ~*ed with shame/confusion*. **3** bring upon oneself: ~ *oneself with glory/honor/disgrace*. **4** protect or guard: *Are you* ~*ed* (= insured) *against fire and theft?* **5** travel (a certain distance): *By sunset we had* ~*ed thirty miles*. **6** keep a gun aimed at a person (so that he cannot shoot or escape). **7** (of guns, fortresses, etc) command[2](5); dominate: *Our heavy artillery* ~*ed every possible approach to the town*. **8** (of money) be enough for: *We have only just* ~*ed* *our expenses*, made enough for our expenses, but no profit. **9** include; extend over; be adequate for: *His researches ~ed a wide field. This book does not fully ~ the subject*, does not deal with all aspects of it. **10** (*sport*) guard (a player) to stop or prevent a play: *The shortstop ~ed second base.* **11** (of a journalist) gather and report the news about (an event): *~ the annual conference on public education.*

ˈcover-up *n* [C] (*informal*) concealment of a crime or wrongdoing, esp by a public official.

cover·age /ˈkəvərɪdʒ/ *n* [U] **1** insurance against loss, damage, etc: *Does your policy provide adequate ~ against fire?* **2** covering of events, etc: *TV ~ of the election campaign*, eg by televising political meetings, interviews with candidates and voters. ⇨ cover²(11).

covered wagon /ˌkəvərd ˈwægən/ *n* [C] wagon with an arched canvas top (as used by the pioneers for traveling across the prairies).

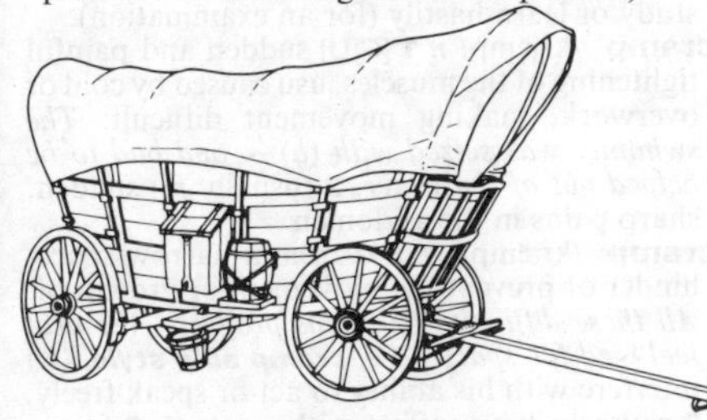

COVERED WAGON

cover·ing /ˈkəvərɪŋ/ *n* [C] thing that covers: *a leafy ~*, the trees. □ *adj*: *~ letter*, one sent with a document, or with goods, etc.

cover·let /ˈkəvərlɪt/ *n* [C] bedspread.

cov·ert¹ /ˈkəvərt, ˈkouv-/ *adj* half-hidden; secret.

cov·ert·ly *adv*

cov·ert² /ˈkəvərt, ˈkouv-/ *n* [C] area of thick undergrowth in which animals hide.

covet /ˈkəvɪt/ *vt* desire eagerly (esp something belonging to somebody else).

covet·ous /ˈkəvətəs/ *adj* (*formal*) ***covetous of***, eagerly desirous (esp of things belonging to somebody else).

covet·ous·ly *adv*

covet·ous·ness /-nɪs/ *n* [U].

cow¹ /kau/ *n* [C] fully grown female of any animal of the ox family, esp the domestic kind kept by farmers for producing milk; also female elephant, rhinoceros, whale, etc.

ˈcow·ˌbird *n* [C] small North American blackbird found near cattle, that usually lays its eggs in another bird's nest.

ˈcow·boy *n* [C] man (usually on horseback) who looks after cattle on a ranch.

ˈcowboy ˌhat, with a large brim, worn typically by cowboys.

ˈcow·ˌcatcher *n* [C] metal frame on the front of a locomotive, that can clear obstacles from the track.

ˈcow·girl *n* [C] woman or girl who works on a ranch or in a rodeo.

ˈcow·hand *n* [C] = cowboy.

ˈcow·herd *n* [C] person who looks after grazing cattle.

ˈcow·hide *n* leather (or a strip of leather as a whip) made from a cow's hide.

ˈcow·poke *n* [C] (*sl*) cowboy.

ˈcow·pox *n* [C] contagious disease of cattle which is the source of vaccine for smallpox.

ˈcow·puncher *n* [C] (*sl*) cowboy.

ˈcow·town *n* [C] town or small city serving primarily as a center for the cattle business.

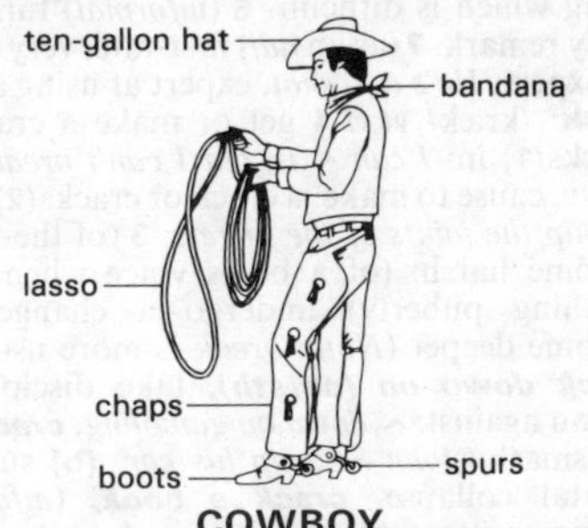

COWBOY

cow² /kau/ *vt* frighten (a person) into submission: *The child had a cowed look*, looked frightened because of threats of violence, etc.

cow·ard /ˈkauərd/ *n* [C] person unable to control his fear; person who runs away from danger.

cow·ard·ly *adj* **(a)** not brave. **(b)** of or like a coward: *~ly behavior*.

cow·ard·ice /ˈkauərdɪs/ *n* [U] feeling, behavior, of a coward.

cower /ˈkauər/ *vi* crouch or shrink back because of cold, misery, fear, shame: *The dog ~ed under the table when its master raised the whip.*

cowl /kaul/ *n* [C] **1** long, loose gown (as worn by monks) with a hood that can be pulled over the head; the hood itself. **2** metal cap for a chimney, ventilating pipe, etc, made to improve the draft (4).

cox·swain /ˈkaksən/ *n* [C] **1** person who steers a row boat, esp in races. **2** person in charge of a ship's boat and crew.

coy /kɔi/ *adj* (-er, -est) (esp of a girl) (pretending to be) shy, modest.

coy·ly *adv*

coy·ote /ˈkaiˌout, kaiˈouti/ *n* [C] prairie wolf of western North America. ⇨ illus at animal.

cozy /ˈkouzi/ *adj* (-ier, -iest) warm and comfortable: *a ~ room with a fireplace*.

coz·ily *adv*

cozi·ness *n*

CPA /ˌsi ˌpi ˈei/ *abbr* = Certified Public Accountant. □ *n* [C] (*pl* CPA's).

CPI *abbr* = Consumer Price Index.

CPO, C.P.O. *abbr* = Chief Petty Officer.

crab¹ /kræb/ *n* [C] broad, flat shellfish with four pairs of legs and one pair of pincers. ⇨ illus at crustacean.

crab² /kræb/ *n* [C] ill-tempered person. □ *vi* (*informal*) complain; find fault.

ˈcrab·by *adj* (-ier, -iest) ill-natured; cross.

crab apple /ˈkræb ˌæpəl/ *n* [C] wild apple tree;

its hard, sour fruit.

crab·bed /ˈkræbɪd/ *adj* **1** bad-tempered; easily irritated. **2** (of handwriting) difficult to read; (of writings, authors) difficult to understand.

crack[1] /kræk/ *n* [C] **1** line of division where something is broken, but not into separate parts: *a cup with bad ~s in it*. **2** sudden, sharp noise (as of a rifle or whip): *the ~ of thunder*. **3** sharp blow which can be heard: *give/get a ~ on the head*. **4** ***have a crack at sth,*** try to do something which is difficult. **6** (*informal*) funny or witty remark. **7** (as an *adj*) first-rate; very clever or expert: *He's a ~ shot*, expert at using a rifle.

crack[2] /kræk/ *vt,vi* **1** get or make a crack or cracks(1) in: *I can ~ it, but I can't break it*. **2** make, cause to make, a crack or cracks(2): *to ~ a whip/the joints of the fingers*. **3** (of the voice) become harsh; (of a boy's voice when he is reaching puberty) undergo a change and become deeper (*Note: break* is more usual). **4** ***crack down on (sb/sth),*** take disciplinary action against: *~ down on gambling*. ***crack up,*** **(a)** smash: *John ~ed up his car*. **(b)** suffer a mental collapse. ***crack a book,*** (*informal*) (begin or attempt to) study. ***crack a joke,*** make one. ***get cracking,*** (*informal*) get busy (with work waiting to be done).

cracker[1] /ˈkrækər/ *n* [C] thin, flaky, dry biscuit (as eaten with cheese).

cracker[2] /ˈkrækər/ *n* [C] (*informal*) US southern poor white: *Georgia ~*.

crackle /ˈkrækəl/ *vi* make a series of small cracking sounds, as when one steps on dry twigs, or when dry sticks burn: *A cheerful wood fire was crackling on the hearth*. □ *n* [U] small cracking sounds, as described above: *the distant ~ of machine gun fire*.

crack·ling /ˈkræklɪŋ/ *n* **1** [U] crackle. **2** (usually *pl*) crisp, well-cooked skin of roast pork.

crack·pot /ˈkrækˌpat/ *n* [C] (*informal*) eccentric person with strange ideas.

cradle /ˈkreidəl/ *n* [C] **1** small, low bed sometimes mounted on rockers, for a newborn baby. ***from the cradle to the grave,*** from birth to death. **2** (*fig*) place where something is born or begins: *Greece, the ~ of Western culture*. **3** framework resembling a cradle or which is used like a cradle, eg a structure on which a ship is supported while being built or repaired; part of a telephone that holds the receiver. □ *vt* place, hold, in or as in a cradle: *~ a child in one's arms*.

CRADLE

craft /kræft/ *n* **1** [C] occupation, esp one in which skill in the use of the hands is needed; such a skill or technique: *the potter's ~*. **2** (*collect*) those engaged in such an occupation, organized into a guild or union: *the ~ of masons*. **3** [C] (*pl* unchanged) boat(s), ship(s): *a handy and useful little ~. The harbor was full of all kinds of ~*. ⇨ also aircraft, spacecraft. **4** [U] cunning; trickery; skill in deceiving: *Be careful when you do business with that man: he's full of ~*.

crafts·man /ˈkræftsmən/ *n* [C] (*pl* -men /-men/) skilled workman who practices a craft.

crafty /ˈkræfti/ *adj* (-ier, -iest) cunning; showing skill in trickery or deceit.

craft·ily /ˈkræftəli/ *adv*

crafti·ness /-inɪs/ *n* [U]

crag /kræg/ *n* [C] high, steep, sharp or rugged mass of rock.

craggy *adj* (-ier, -iest) having many crags.

cram /kræm/ *vt,vi* (-mm-) **1** ***cram into/with,*** make too full; put, push, very much or too much into: *to ~ food into one's mouth/~ one's mouth with food; to ~ papers into a drawer*. **2** study or learn hastily (for an examination).

cramp[1] /kræmp/ *n* **1** [C,U] sudden and painful tightening of the muscles, usu caused by cold or overwork, making movement difficult: *The swimmer was seized with (a) ~ and had to be helped out of the water*. **2** (usually *pl*) sudden, sharp pains in the abdomen.

cramp[2] /kræmp/ *vt* **1** keep in a narrow space; hinder or prevent the movement or growth of: *All these difficulties ~ed his progress. We are/feel ~ed for space here*. ***cramp sb's style,*** (*sl*) interfere with his ability to act or speak freely. **2** cause to have, affect with, cramp[1]. **3** fasten with a cramp[3].

cramp[3] /kræmp/ *n* [C] **1** metal bar with the ends bent, used for holding together masonry or timbers. **2** clamp.

cram·pon /ˈkræmpən/ *n* [C] (usually *pl*) iron plate with spikes, worn on shoes for walking or climbing on ice.

cran·berry /ˈkrænˌberi/ *n* [C] (*pl* -ies) **1** small, red, tart berry of a shrub, used for making jelly and sauce. **2** creeping evergreen shrub that bears this berry.

crane[1] /krein/ *n* [C] **1** large wading bird with long legs and neck. **2** machine with a long arm that can be swung around, used for lifting and moving heavy weights.

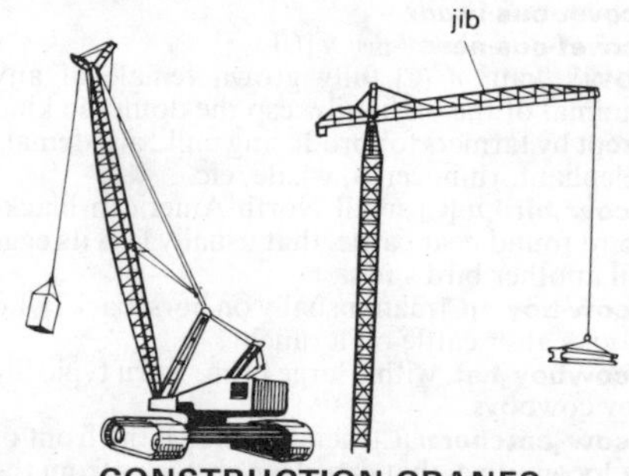

CONSTRUCTION CRANES

crane[2] /krein/ *vt,vi* stretch (the neck): *craning one's neck in order to see*.

crane fly /ˈkrein ˌflai/ *n* [C] (*pl* -ies) kind of fly with very long legs.

cran·ial /ˈkreiniəl/ *adj* of the skull.

cran·ium /ˈkreiniəm/ *n* [C] bony part of the head enclosing the brain.

crank[1] /kræŋk/ *n* L-shaped arm and handle for transmitting rotary motion. □ *vt* move, cause to move, by turning a crank: *to ~ up an engine*.

ˈcrank·shaft *n* shaft that turns or is turned by a crank.

crank[2] /kræŋk/ *n* [C] person with fixed (and often strange) ideas, esp on one matter: *The newspaper often gets letters from ~s.*

cranky *adj* (-ier, -iest) **1** cross; irritable. **2** odd; eccentric.

cranny /ˈkræni/ *n* [C] (*pl* -ies) small crack or opening, eg in a wall.

crap /kræp/ *n* [U] **1** (*sl*) nonsense. **2** (*vulg*⚠) feces. □ *vi* (*vulg*⚠) defecate.

crash[1] /kræʃ/ *n* [C] **1** (noise made by a) violent fall, blow or breaking: *The tree fell with a great ~. He was killed in an ˈairplane ~.* **2** ruin; collapse (eg in trade, finance): *The great ~ on Wall Street in 1929 ruined international trade.*

ˈcrash helmet, hard helmet worn, eg by a motorcyclist, to protect the head in a crash.

ˈcrash-land *vi,vt* (of aircraft) land, be landed in an emergency.

ˌcrash ˈlanding *n* [C]

ˈcrash ˌprogram/project, one requiring immediate action and involving an all-out effort.

crash[2] /kræʃ/ *vt,vi* **1** fall or strike suddenly, violently, and noisily (esp of things that break): *The bus ~ed into a tree. The airplane ~ed.* **2** cause to crash: *to ~ an airplane.* **3** force or break through violently: *elephants ~ing through the jungle.* ***crash the gate,*** ⇨ gate, party. **4** (of a business company, government, etc) come to ruin; meet disaster: *His great financial scheme ~ed.*

crass /kræs/ *adj* gross; insensitive.

crate /kreit/ *n* [C] large frame or case of wood for goods in transport. □ *vt* put in a crate.

cra·ter /ˈkreitər/ *n* [C] **1** mouth of a volcano. **2** hole in the ground made by the explosion of a bomb, shell, etc.

cra·vat /krəˈvæt/ *n* [C] necktie.

crave /kreiv/ *vt,vi* **1** ask earnestly for: *to ~ forgiveness.* **2** have a strong desire for: *to ~ a drink.*

crav·ing /ˈkreiviŋ/ *n* [C] strong desire: *a ~ for strong drink.*

craw /krɔ/ *n* [C] **1** crop of a bird. **2** stomach of an animal.

craw·dad /ˈkrɔˌdæd/ *n* [C] = crayfish.

craw·fish /ˈkrɔˌfiʃ/ *n* [C] (*pl* unchanged) = crayfish.

crawl /krɔl/ *vi* **1** move slowly, pulling the body along the ground or other surface (as worms and snakes do); (of human beings) move in this way, or on the hands and knees: *The wounded soldier ~ed into a shell hole.* **2** go very slowly: *Our train ~ed over the damaged bridge.* **3** be full of, covered with, things that crawl: *The ground was ~ing with ants.* **4** (of the flesh) feel as if covered with crawling things: *She says that the sight of snakes makes her flesh ~.* □ *n* **1** [U] crawling movement: *Traffic on Broadway was reduced to a ~ during the rush hours.* **2 the crawl,** high-speed swimming stroke in which the head is kept low in the water.

crawler *n* **(a)** person or thing that ~s. **(b)** (*pl*) overall garment made for a baby to crawl about in.

cray·fish /ˈkreiˌfiʃ/ *n* [C] (*pl* unchanged) freshwater lobster-like shellfish.

crayon /ˈkreiˌan/ *n* [C] stick or pencil of soft colored chalk, wax or charcoal. □ *vt* draw with crayons.

craze /kreiz/ *vt* make wildly excited or mad: *a ~d look/expression; a half-~d prophet.* (*Note:* usually used as a *pp*.) □ *n* [C] enthusiastic interest lasting only for a short time; the object of such interest: *the modern ~ for rock music.*

crazy /ˈkreizi/ *adj* (-ier, -iest) **1** wildly excited or enthusiastic: *I'm ~ about/for you, darling.* **2** suffering from mental disorder; foolish: *You were ~ to lend that man your money.* **3** (of buildings, etc) unsafe; likely to collapse. **4** (*sl, dated*) wonderful.

craz·ily /ˈkreizəli/ *adv*

crazi·ness /ˈkreizinis/ *n* [U]

crazy quilt /ˈkreizi ˌkwilt/ *n* [C] quilt made up of irregularly shaped pieces of cloth fitted together with no definite pattern.

creak /krik/ *n, vi* (make a) sound like that of an unoiled hinge.

creaky *adj* (-ier, -iest) making creaking sounds: *~y stairs.*

cream /krim/ *n* [U] **1** fatty or oily part of milk which rises to the surface and can be made into butter. **2** kind of food containing or resembling cream: *~ sauce; ice ~.* **3** thick substance like cream in appearance or consistency, used for polishing, as a cosmetic, etc: *~ polish; ˈface ~.* **4** best part of anything: *the ~ of society*, those of highest rank. **5** yellowish-white color. □ *adj* yellowish-white. □ *vt* **1** take cream from (milk). **2** add cream or cream sauce to: *~ed potatoes.* **3** beat until creamy.

cream·ery *n* [C] (*pl* -ies) **1** place where milk, cream, butter, cheese, etc are sold. **2** place where butter and cheese are made.

ˌcream of ˈtartar *n* [U] white powder used esp in making baking powder.

creamy *adj* (-ier, -iest) **1** smooth and rich like cream. **2** containing much cream.

crease /kris/ *n* line made (on cloth, paper, etc) by crushing, folding or pressing: *~-resisting cloth.* □ *vt,vi* make, get a crease in: *This material ~s easily.*

cre·ate /kriˈeit/ *vt* **1** cause something to exist; make (something new or original): *God ~d the world. James Fenimore Cooper ~d many wonderful characters in his novels.* **2** give rise to; produce: *His behavior ~d a bad impression.*

cre·ation /kriˈeiʃən/ *n* **1** [U] the act of creating (eg the world): *the ~ of great works of art/of an empire.* **2** [U] all created things. ***all creation,*** (*informal*) the entire world. **3 the Creation,** creating of the world or universe by God. **4** [C] something created, esp by human intelligence and imagination: *the ~s of poets, artists, composers and dramatists. The women were wearing the newest ~s of the Paris designers.*

cre·ative /kriˈeitiv/ *adj* having power to create;

of creation: *useful and ~ work,* ie requiring intelligence and imagination.

cre·ative·ly *adv*

cre·ativ·ity /ˌkrieiˈtɪvəti/ *n* [U].

cre·ator /kriˈeitər/ *n* **1** [C] one who creates. **2** (in the Christian religion) **the Creator,** God.

crea·ture /ˈkritʃər/ *n* [C] **1** animal. **2** human being. **3** person who is influenced or dominated by another: *mere ~s of the dictator.*

ˈcreature comforts, material needs such as food and drink.

crèche /ˈkreʃ/ *n* [C] representation (as in a church at Christmas) of the birth of Christ.

cre·dence /ˈkridəns/ *n* [U] belief. ***give/attach credence to,*** (*formal*) believe (gossip, what is said, etc).

cre·den·tials /krɪˈdenʃəlz/ *n pl* letters or papers showing that a person is what he claims to be: *A police detective always carries his ~ with him.*

cred·ible /ˈkredəbəl/ *adj* that can be believed: *~ witnesses.*

cred·ibly *adv*

credi·bil·ity /ˌkredəˈbɪləti/ *n* [U]

credit[1] /ˈkredɪt/ *n* **1** [U] belief of others that a person, business company, etc can pay debts, or will keep a promise to pay: *His ~ is good.* **2** [U] right to charge (4) goods or services: *No ~ is given at this store*, payment must be in cash. **3** [U] money shown as owned by a person, company, etc in a bank account: *You have a ~ balance of $250.* **4** [C] sum of money advanced or loaned (by a bank, etc): *The bank refused further ~ to the company.* **5** (*bookkeeping*) record of payments received: *Does this item go among the ~s or the debits?* **6** [C] entry on a record to show that a course of study has been completed: *~s in history and geography.* **7** [U] honor, approval, good name or reputation: *a man of the highest ~.* ***get/take credit (for sth),*** get/take praise, recognition, etc: *He got all the ~.* **8** addition to a person's reputation: *The work does you ~.* ***be a credit to sb/sth,*** add to the good name of: *The pupils are a ~ to their teacher.* **9** [U] belief; trust; confidence; credence: *The rumour is gaining ~.* **10** [C] list of the persons who acted in or helped to produce a play, motion picture, etc.

ˈcredit card, one that entitles the holder to buy goods on credit(2).

credit[2] /ˈkredɪt/ *vt* **1** believe. ***credit sb/sth with sth,*** believe that a person or thing has a trait or quality: *Until now I've always ~ed you with more sense. The relics are ~ed with miraculous powers.* **2** enter as money paid on an account: *~ a customer with $10; ~ $10 to a customer/to his account.*

credi·table /ˈkredɪtəbəl/ *adj* that brings credit (7): *a ~ attempt.*

credi·tably /-əbli/ *adv*

credi·tor /ˈkredɪtər/ *n* [C] person to whom one owes money: *run away from one's ~s.*

cre·du·lity /krəˈd(y)uləti/ *n* [U] too great a readiness to believe things.

credu·lous /ˈkredʒələs/ *adj* (too) ready to believe things: *~ people who accept all the promises of the politicians.*

credu·lous·ly *adv*

creed /krid/ *n* **1** [C] (system of) beliefs or opinions, esp on religious doctrine. **2 the Creed,** formal statement of the fundamentals of Christian belief.

creek /krik/ *n* [C] small stream.

creep /krip/ *vi* (*pt,pp* crept /krept/) **1** move along with the body close to the ground or floor: *The cat crept silently toward the bird.* **2** move slowly, quietly or secretly: *The thief crept along the corridor. Old age ~s up on one unawares.* **3** (of plants, etc) grow along and cling to the ground, the surface of a wall, etc: *Ivy had crept over the ruined castle walls.* **4** (of the flesh) have the feeling that things are creeping over it (as the result of fear, repugnance, etc): *The sight of the rats made her flesh ~.* □ *n* **1** [C] (*informal*) distasteful or repulsive person: *He's a real ~.* **2 the creeps,** (*informal*) feeling of fear, distaste, etc: *He gives me the ~s.*

creeper /ˈkripər/ *n* [C] **1** insect, bird, etc that creeps. **2** plant that creeps along the ground, over rocks, walls, etc.

creepy /ˈkripi/ *adj* (-ier, -iest) having or causing fear: *The ghost story made us all ~.*

cre·mate /ˈkriˌmeit/ *vt* burn (a corpse) to ashes: *He says he wants to be ~d, not buried.*

cre·ma·tion /kriˈmeiʃən/ *n* **1** [U] cremating. **2** [C] instance of this.

cre·ma·tor·ium /ˌkriməˈtɔriəm/ *n* [C] = crematory.

cre·ma·tory /ˈkriməˌtɔri/ *n* [C] (*pl* -ies) (building with a) furnace for cremating corpses.

Cre·ole /ˈkriˌoul/ *n, adj* **1** (of a) person or thing native to the New World, esp descending from the original French and Spanish settlers in southern Louisiana. **2** (of a) person of mixed Negro and French or Spanish ancestry, esp in Louisiana. **3** (of a) language showing both European and non-European, esp African, influences: *Creole French/French Creole.*

crêpe, crepe /kreip/ *n* **1** [U] light, crinkled fabric. **2** [C] thin pancake.

ˌcrêpe ˈpaper, thin paper with a wavy or wrinkled surface.

ˌcrêpe ˈrubber, rubber which has a wrinkled surface, used for the soles of shoes, etc.

crept *pt, pp* of creep.

cres·cendo /krɪˈʃendou/ *n* [C] (*pl* ~s) **1** gradual increase in loudness, esp in music. **2** (*fig*) climax.

cres·cent /ˈkresənt/ *n* [C] (something shaped like) the curve of the moon in the first quarter. □ *adj* **1** shaped like the moon in the first quarter. **2** growing; increasing.

cress /kres/ *n* [U] any of various plants of the mustard family (used in salads and sandwiches).

crest /krest/ *n* [C] **1** tuft of feathers on a bird's head. **2** decoration like a crest formerly worn on the top of a helmet. **3** design over the shield of a coat of arms, also used separately (eg on a seal, or on notepaper): *the family ~*, one used by a family. **4** top of a slope or hill; white top of a large wave. □ *vt* reach the crest of a hill, a wave.

crest·fallen /ˈkrestˌfɔlən/ *adj* very disappointed.

cre·tin /ˈkritən/ *n* [C] person who is physically

and mentally retarded because of a deficiency of the thyroid gland.

cre·vasse /krɪ'væs/ *n* [C] deep, open crack, esp in the ice of a glacier.

crev·ice /'krevɪs/ *n* [C] narrow opening or crack (in a rock, wall, etc).

crew[1] /kru/ *n* [C] **1** all the persons working on a ship or aircraft; all these except the officers: *officers and ~.* **2** group of persons working together; gang.

crew cut /'kru ˌkət/ *n* **1** [U] style of close haircut popular in the military service. **2** [C] haircut done in this style.

crib[1] /krɪb/ *n* [C] **1** wooden framework (manger) from which animals can pull out fodder. **2** bed with high sides for a newborn baby.

crib[2] /krɪb/ *n* [C] **1** something copied dishonestly from the work of another. **2** word-for-word translation of a foreign text used by students of the language. □ *vt,vi* (-bb-) **1** use a crib(2). **2** copy (another's work) dishonestly.

cricket /'krɪkɪt/ *n* [C] small, brown jumping insect, the male of which makes a shrill noise by rubbing its front wings together: *the chirping of ~s.* ⇨ illus at insect.

cried *pt,pp* of cry[1]

crier /'kraiər/ *n* [C] **1** officer who makes public announcements in a court of law. **2** person (esp a young child) who cries(1).

cries *pres t* of cry[1]; *pl* of cry[2]

crime /kraim/ *n* **1** [C] serious offense against the law: *to commit a serious ~.* **2** [U] serious lawbreaking; criminal activity: *It is the business of the police to prevent and detect ~.* **3** foolish or wrong act, not necessarily an offense against the law: *It would be a ~ to send the boy out on such a cold, wet night.*

crimi·nal /'krɪmənəl/ *adj* of crime or wrongdoing: *a ~ act.* □ *n* [C] person who commits a crime or crimes.

crimi·nally *adv*

crimi·nol·ogy /ˌkrɪmə'nalədʒi/ *n* [U] the study of crime.

crim·son /'krɪmzən/ *adj, n* [U] deep red (color). □ *vt,vi* make or become crimson; blush.

cringe /krɪndʒ/ *vi* **1** shrink back or down in fear: *The dog ~d at the sight of the whip.* **2** behave (toward a superior) in a way that shows lack of self-respect; be too humble: *cringing to/before a policeman.*

crinkle /'krɪŋkəl/ *n* [C] small, narrow wrinkle (in material such as foil or paper). □ *vt,vi* make or get crinkles in: *~d paper,* eg crêpe paper.

cripple /'krɪpəl/ *n* [C] person unable to walk or move properly, through injury or weakness in the spine or legs; lame person. □ *vt* **1** make a cripple of: *~d soldiers.* **2** damage or weaken seriously: *activities ~d by lack of money.*

cri·sis /'kraisɪs/ *n* [C] (*pl* -ses /-ˌsiz/) **1** turning point in an illness, life, history, etc. **2** time of difficulty, danger or anxiety about the future: *a cabinet/financial ~.*

crisp /krɪsp/ *adj* (-er, -est) **1** (esp of food) firm, crunchy, and easily broken: *~ toast/lettuce.* **2** (of the air, the weather) frosty, cold: *the ~ air of an autumn morning.* **3** (of hair) tightly curled. **4** (of style, manners) quick, precise and decided; showing no doubts or hesitation: *a man with a ~ manner of speaking.* □ *vt,vi* make or become crisp.

crisp·ly *adv*

crisp·ness /-nɪs/ *n* [U]

criss·cross /'krɪsˌkrɔs/ *adj* with crossed lines: *a ~ pattern/design.* □ *adv* crosswise. □ *vt,vi* **1** move crosswise; come and go across. **2** mark with lines that cross.

cri·terion /krai'tɪriən/ *n* [C] (*pl* -ria /-riə/ or ~s) standard or rule for making a judgment: *The ability to make money is not always a good ~ of real success in life.*

critic /'krɪtɪk/ *n* [C] **1** person who forms and gives judgments, esp about literature, art, music, etc: *music/drama/literary, etc ~s.* **2** person who finds fault, points out mistakes, etc: *I am my own most severe ~.*

criti·cal /'krɪtɪkəl/ *adj* **1** of or at a crisis: *We are at a ~ time in our history. The patient's condition is ~,* he is dangerously ill. **2** of the work of a critic: *~ opinions on art and literature.* **3** faultfinding: *~ remarks.*

criti·cal·ly /-kli/ *adv*

criti·cism /'krɪtɪˌsɪzəm/ *n* **1** [U] the work of a critic; the art of making judgments (concerning art, literature, etc). **2** [C] judgment or opinion on literature, art, etc. **3** [U] faultfinding. **4** [C] remark, etc that finds fault.

criti·cize /'krɪtɪˌsaiz/ *vt,vi* **1** form and give a judgment of. **2** find fault with: *~ somebody for being late/for lateness.*

cri·tique /krɪ'tik/ *n* [C] critical essay or review.

croak /krouk/ *n* [C] deep, hoarse sound (as made by frogs). □ *vt,vi* **1** speak with or make this kind of sound. **2** express dismal views about the future. **3** (*sl*) = die[2](1).

cro·chet /krou'ʃei/ *vt,vi* make (lace, knitting, etc) with a thread by looping with the help of a small hooked needle (called a *~ hook*). □ *n* [U] lace, etc (being) made in this way.

crock /krak/ *n* [C] pot or jar made of baked earth, eg for containing water.

crock·ery /'krakəri/ *n* [U] pots, plates, cups, dishes and other utensils (made of baked clay).

croco·dile /'krakəˌdaiəl/ *n* [C] large river reptile with a long body and tail, covered with a hard skin. ⇨ illus at reptile.

'crocodile ˌtears, insincere sorrow.

cro·cus /'kroukəs/ *n* [C] (*pl* ~es) (kind of) small plant growing from a corm, bearing colored flowers early in spring.

crony /'krouni/ *n* [C] (*pl* -ies) close friend; companion.

crook /krʊk/ *n* [C] **1** stick or staff with a rounded hook at one end, esp such a stick used by a shepherd. **2** bend or curve, eg in a river or path. **3** (*informal*) dishonest person. □ *vt,vi* bend into the shape of a crook: *to ~ one's finger/arm.*

crooked /'krʊkɪd/ *adj* **1** not straight or level; twisted; bent: *You've got your hat on ~.* **2** (*informal*) dishonest; not straightforward.

crook·ed·ly *adv*

croon /krun/ *vt,vi* hum or sing in a low voice: *~ a lullaby.*

crop[1] /krap/ *n* [C] **1** yearly (or season's) produce of grain, grass, fruit, etc: *the potato ~.* **2** (*pl*) agricultural plants: *to get the ~s in.* **3** batch: *The President's statement produced a ~ of questions.*

crop[2] /krap/ *n* [C] **1** baglike part of a bird's throat where food is broken up for digestion before passing into the stomach. **2** very short haircut.

crop[3] /krap/ *vt,vi* (-pp-) **1** (of animals) bite off the tops of (grass, plants, etc); graze: *The sheep had ~ped the grass short.* **2** cut short (a person's hair, a horse's tail or ears). **3** sow or plant: *to ~ ten acres with wheat.* **4** bear a crop: *The beans ~ped well this year.* **5** ***crop up/out,*** (of rock, minerals) show up above the earth's surface. **6** ***crop up,*** appear or arise (esp unexpectedly): *All sorts of difficulties ~ped up.*

cro·quet /krouˈkei/ *n* [U] game played on short grass with wooden balls which are knocked with wooden mallets through hoops.

cro·quette /krouˈket/ *n* [C] small roll or cake of chopped meat, fish, etc, that has been coated in crumbs and fried: *chicken ~s.*

cro·sier, cro·zier /ˈkrouʒər/ *n* [C] bishop's staff, usually shaped like a shepherd's crook.

cross[1] /krɔs/ *adj* **1** (*informal*) bad-tempered; easily or quickly showing anger: *Don't be ~ with the child for being late.* **2** contrary; opposing: *Strong ~-winds made it difficult for the yachts to leave harbor.*

cross·ly *adv*

cross·ness /-nɪs/ *n* [U]

cross[2] /krɔs/ *n* [C] **1** mark made by drawing one line across another, thus: ×, +: *The place is marked on the map with a ~.* **2 (a)** stake or post with another piece of wood across it like T,†, or X. **(b) the Cross,** that on which Christ was crucified. **3** model of a cross as a religious emblem. **4** (*fig*) suffering; affliction; burden of sorrow: *to bear one's ~.* **5** emblem or badge in the form of a cross, esp one awarded for bravery: *the Distinguished Service Cross.* **6** offspring of animals or plants of different sorts or breeds: *A mule is a ~ between a horse and a donkey.*

cross[3] /krɔs/ *vt,vi* **1** go across; pass from one side to the other side of: *to ~ a road/river/bridge/the sea/the Sahara.* ***cross one's mind,*** (of ideas, etc) occur to one: *The idea has just ~ed my mind that....* **2** remove by drawing a line or lines across or through: *Two of the words had been ~ed out. I ~ed his name off the list.* **3** put or place across or over: *to ~ one's legs.* ***keep one's fingers crossed,*** (*fig*) hope for the best, that nothing will happen to upset one's plans, etc. **4** ***cross oneself,*** make a cross with one's right hand on or over oneself as a religious act. **5** (of persons traveling, letters in the post) meet and pass: *We ~ed each other on the way. Our letters ~ed in the mail.* **6** oppose or obstruct (somebody, his plans, wishes, etc): *He was angry at having his plans ~ed.* **7** produce a cross (6) by mixing breeds.

cross·bar /ˈkrɔsˌbar/ *n* [C] bar going across, eg the bar joining the front and rear ends of a bicycle frame.

cross·beam /ˈkrɔsˌbim/ *n* [C] beam placed across, esp one that supports parts of a structure.

cross·bones /ˈkrɔsˌbounz/ *n pl* (design of) two large bones laid across each other, usually under a skull, as an emblem of death.

cross·bow /ˈkrɔsˌbou/ *n* [C] old kind of bow placed across a grooved wooden support, used for shooting arrows, bolts, stones, etc.

cross·bred /ˈkrɔsˌbred/ *adj* produced by crossing breeds: *~ sheep.*

cross·breed /ˈkrɔsˌbrid/ *n* [C] (in farming, etc) animal, plant, etc, produced by crossing breeds.

cross-country /ˌkrɔs-ˈkəntri/ *adj, adv* across the country or fields, not along roads: *a ~ race.*

cross·cur·rent /ˈkrɔsˌkərənt/ *n* [C] (*fig*) contrary or opposing tendency.

cross-exam·ine /ˌkrɔs-ɪgˈzæmɪn/ *vt* question (a witness) closely, esp to test answers already given to someone else, as in a law court.

ˌcross-eˈxam·iner *n* [C]

ˌcross-eˌxam·i·ˈna·tion *n* [C]

cross-eyed /ˈkrɔs-ˌaid/ *adj* with one or both eyeballs turned towards the nose.

cross-fer·til·ize /ˌkrɔs-ˈfərtəˌlaiz/ *vt* fertilize by carrying pollen from one plant to another.

ˌcross-ˌfer·tili·ˈza·tion *n* [U]

cross·fire /ˈkrasˌfaiər/ *n* [U] **1** gunfire from two or more points so that the lines of fire cross. **2** (*fig*) situation in which questions, comment, etc come from different directions.

cross-grained /ˈkrɔs-ˌgreind/ *adj* **1** (of wood) with the grain in crossing directions. **2** (*fig*) difficult to please or get along with.

cross·ing /ˈkrɔsɪŋ/ *n* [C] **1** the act of going across, esp by sea: *We had a rough ~ during the storm.* **2** place where two roads, two railroads, or a road and a railroad cross. **3** place at which a street, river, etc may be crossed.

cross-legged /ˈkrɔs-ˌlegɪd/ *adv* with one leg placed across the other.

cross-pur·poses /ˌkrɔs-ˈpərpəsɪz/ *n pl* ***be at cross-purposes,*** (of two persons or groups) misunderstand one another; have different and conflicting purposes.

cross-ref·er·ence /ˌkrɔs-ˈrefrəns/ *n* [C] reference from one part of a book, index, file, etc to another, for further information.

cross·road /ˈkrɔsˌroud/ *n* **1** road that crosses another. **2** (*pl*, used with *sing v*) place where two or more roads meet: *We came to a ~s.* ***at the crossroads,*** at a point where a decision must be made.

cross sec·tion /ˈkrɔs ˌsekʃən/ *n* [C] **1** (drawing of a) piece or slice made by cutting across, eg a tree trunk. **2** (*fig*) typical or representative sample of the whole: *a ~ of the voters.*

cross-stitch /ˈkrɔs-ˌstɪtʃ/ *n* [C] (needlework using a) stitch formed of two stitches that cross.

cross·walk /ˈkrɔsˌwɔk/ *n* [C] specially marked path for pedestrians to use in crossing a street.

cross·wise /ˈkrɔsˌwaiz/ *adv* across; so as to cross.

cross·word puzzle /ˈkrɔsˌwərd ˌpəzəl/ *n* [C] puzzle consisting of groups of squares in which words are (to be) written across and down in the numbered squares that match up with numbered clues.

crotch /kratʃ/ *n* [C] **1** place where a branch forks from a tree: *The child was sitting in a ~ of a tree.* **2** place where a pair of trousers or a person's legs fork from the trunk.

crotchet /ˈkratʃɪt/ *n* strange, unreasonable idea.

crotchety *adj* unreasonably bad tempered.

crouch /krautʃ/ *vi* ***crouch (down),*** lower the body with the legs bent (like an animal ready to spring). □ *n* [C] crouching position.

croup[1] /krup/ *n* [U] children's disease in which there is inflammation of the windpipe, with coughing and difficulty in breathing.

croup[2] /krup/ *n* [C] rump or buttocks of certain animals.

crow[1] /krou/ *n* [C] (kinds of) large, black bird with a harsh cry. ⇨ illus at bird. ***as the ˈcrow flies,*** in a straight line; by the shortest way.

ˈcrow's-feet *n pl* small wrinkles that may form at the outer corners of a person's eyes.

ˈcrow's nest, enclosed platform on the mast of a ship for the lookout man.

crow[2] /krou/ *vi* **1** (of a rooster) make a loud, shrill cry. **2** (of persons) express gleeful triumph: *to ~ over an unsuccessful rival.* □ *n* [C] crowing sound.

crow·bar /ˈkrouˌbar/ *n* [C] straight, iron bar, often wedge-shaped at the end, used as a lever for moving heavy objects.

crowd /kraud/ *n* [C] **1** large number of people together, but without order or organization: *He pushed his way through the ~.* **2** (*informal*) group of persons with something in common; set of persons: *I can't afford to go around with that ~; they're too extravagant.* **3** large number (of things, usually without order): *a desk covered with a ~ of books.* □ *vt,vi* **1** come together in a crowd: *People quickly ~ around when there is a street accident.* **2** (cause to) move through, etc in a crowd; fill with: *They ~ed through the gates into the stadium. They ~ed everyone into the buses.* **3** (*informal*) put pressure on: *Don't ~ me; give me time to think!*

crowded *adj* having large numbers of people: *~ed cities/trains.*

crown[1] /kraun/ *n* [C] **1** ornamental headdress of gold, jewels, etc worn by a sovereign ruler; royal power: *succeed to the ~,* become the sovereign ruler. **2** circle or wreath of flowers or leaves worn on the head, esp as a sign of victory, or as a reward: *a martyr's ~.* **3** top of the head or of a hat. **4** part of a tooth that shows. **5** (*fig*) perfection; highest state: *the ~ of one's labors.*

ˌcrown ˈprince, heir to a throne.

crown[2] /kraun/ *vt* **1** make someone king or queen by the ceremony of putting a crown on his/her head: *the ~ed heads* (= kings and queens) *of Europe.* **2** reward; give honor to: *efforts that were ~ed with success.* **3** be or have at the top of: *The hill is ~ed with a wood.* **4** put a happy finishing touch to: *to open a bottle of wine to ~ a feast.* ***to crown (it) all,*** to complete good or bad fortune: *It rained, we had no umbrellas, and, to ~ all, we missed the last bus and had to walk home.* **5** put an artificial cover on a broken tooth.

crown·ing *adj* completing; making perfect: *Her ~ing glory is her hair.*

cro·zier = crosier.

cru·cial /ˈkruʃəl/ *adj* decisive; critical: *the ~ test/question; at the ~ moment.*

cru·cial·ly *adv*

cru·cible /ˈkrusəbəl/ *n* [C] pot in which metals are melted (eg in a chemistry laboratory).

cru·ci·fix /ˈkrusəˌfɪks/ *n* [C] cross with the figure of Jesus on it.

cru·ci·fixion /ˌkrusəˈfɪkʃən/ *n* [C,U] **1** (instance of) crucifying or being crucified. **2 the Crucifixion,** that of Jesus.

cru·ci·form /ˈkrusəˌfɔrm/ *adj* cross-shaped.

cru·cify /ˈkrusəˌfai/ *vt* (*pt,pp* -ied) **1** put to death by nailing or binding to a cross. **2** treat with cruelty; torture.

crude /krud/ *adj* (-r, -st) **1** (of materials) in a natural state; not refined or manufactured: *~ oil,* petroleum. **2** not having grace, taste or refinement; coarse: *~ manners.* **3** not finished properly; badly worked out: *~ schemes/methods/ideas.*

crude·ly *adv*

cru·dity /ˈkrudəti/ *n* **1** [U] the state or quality of being crude. **2** [C] (*pl* -ies) instance of this; crude act, remark, etc.

cruel /ˈkru(ə)l/ *adj* (-er, -est) **1** (of persons) taking pleasure in or indifferent to the suffering of others; prepared to give pain to others: *a man who is ~ to animals.* **2** causing pain or suffering: *a ~ blow/punishment/disease/war.*

cruel·ly /ˈkruəli/ *adv*

cruel·ty /ˈkru(ə)lti/ *n* (*pl* -ies) **1** [U] readiness to give needless pain or cause suffering to others: *Cruelty to children should be severely punished.* **2** [C] cruel act.

cruet /ˈkruɪt/ *n* [C] small glass bottle for vinegar, oil, etc, for use at the table.

cruise /kruz/ *vi* **1** sail about, either for pleasure, or, in war, looking for enemy ships. **2** travel at the speed at which an automobile, aircraft, etc operates best: *The car has a cruising speed of 50 miles an hour.* □ *n* [C] cruising voyage: *to go on/for a ~.*

cruiser /ˈkruzər/ *n* [C] **1** fast warship. **2** (also *ˈcabin ~*) motorboat (with sleeping accommodation, etc) designed for pleasure cruises.

crul·ler /ˈkrələr/ *n* [C] sweet cake made of a twisted strip of dough fried in deep fat.

crumb /krəm/ *n* [C] **1** very small piece of dry food, esp a bit of bread or cake rubbed or broken off from a large piece: *sweep up the ~s.* **2** (*fig*) small amount: *a few ~s of information/comfort.* **3** (*sl*) contemptible person.

crumble /ˈkrəmbəl/ *vt,vi* **1** break, rub or fall into very small pieces: *crumbling walls,* that are falling into ruin. **2** (*fig*) be destroyed, decay: *hopes that ~d to dust,* came to nothing.

crum·bly /ˈkrəmbli/ *adj* (-ier, -iest) easily crumbled.

crum·my /ˈkrəmi/ *adj* (-ier, -iest) (*informal*) worthless; cheap.

crumple /ˈkrəmpəl/ *vt,vi* **1** press or crush into wrinkles: *to ~ one's clothes,* eg by packing them carelessly. **2** become full of wrinkles: *Some kinds of material ~ more easily than others.* **3** ***crumple up,*** **(a)** crush: *to ~ a sheet of paper into a ball.* **(b)** collapse.

crunch /krəntʃ/ *vt,vi* **1** crush noisily with the teeth when eating: *People who ~ nuts at the* *movies can be very annoying*. **2** crush, be crushed, noisily: *The frozen snow ~ed under the wheels of our car*. □ *n* [C] the act of, noise made by, crunching.

crunchy *adj* (-ier, -iest) (of food) having a brittle kind of hardness, capable of being crunched with the teeth.

cru·sade /kruˈseid/ *n* [C] **1** any one of the military expeditions made by the Christian rulers and people of Europe during the Middle Ages to recover the Holy Land from the Moslems. **2** any struggle or movement in support of something believed to be good or against something believed to be bad: *a ~ against racial intolerance*. □ *vi* take part in a crusade.

cru·sader *n* [C] person taking part in a crusade.

crush[1] /krəʃ/ *n* **1** [U] crowd of people pressed together: *There was an awful ~ at the gate into the stadium*. **2** ***have a crush on sb,*** (*informal*) be, imagine oneself to be, in love with.

crush[2] /krəʃ/ *vt,vi* **1** press, be pressed, so that there is breaking or injury: *Wine is made by ~ing grapes*. **2** (cause to) become full of wrinkles; lose shape: *Her dresses were badly ~ed when she took them out of the suitcase*. **3** subdue; overwhelm: *He was not satisfied until he had ~ed his enemies*. **4** press or push in, etc: *They all tried to ~ into the front seats*.

crust /krəst/ *n* **1** [C,U] (piece of the) hard-baked surface of a loaf of bread; outer covering (pastry) of a pie or tart. **2** [C,U] hard surface: *a thin ~ of ice/frozen snow; the earth's ~*, the surface. □ *vt,vi* ***crust over,*** cover, become covered, with a crust; form into a crust: *The snow ~ed over* (= froze hard on top) *during the night*.

crus·ta·cean /krəˈsteiʃən/ *n* [C] shellfish.

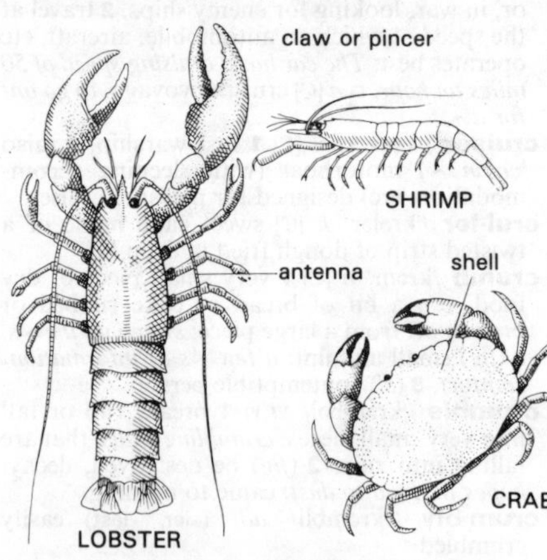

CRUSTACEANS

crusty /ˈkrəsti/ *adj* (-ier, -iest) **1** having a crust; hard like a crust: *~ bread*. **2** quick to show irritation, etc.

crutch /krətʃ/ *n* [C] **1** stick used as a support under the arm to help a lame person to walk: *a pair of ~es*. **2** support that is like a crutch in shape or use; (*fig*) any moral support.

crux /krəks/ *n* [C] (*pl* ~es) part (of a problem) that is the most difficult to solve: *The ~ of the matter is this...*

cry[1] /krai/ *vi,vt* (*pt,pp* cried) **1** (of persons) make loud sounds; call out; exclaim: *"Help! Help!" he cried. He cried out with pain when the dentist pulled the tooth out*. **2** (of persons) weep; shed tears (with or without sounds): *A baby can cry as soon as it is born. The boy was crying because he had lost his money*. ***cry one's ˈeyes/ˈheart out,*** weep very bitterly. ***cry oneself to sleep,*** cry until one falls asleep. **3** (of an animal or bird) make its particular call. **4** beg; ask earnestly for: *cried for mercy*. **5** make known by calling out: *to cry the news all over the town*.

cry[2] /krai/ *n* [C] (*pl* cries) **1** loud sound of fear, pain, grief, etc; words spoken loudly: *a cry for help; the cry of an animal in pain; angry cries from the mob*. ***a ˈfar/ˈlong cry,*** a long way from; very different from: *Being a junior clerk in a law firm is a far cry from being one of the partners*. **2** characteristic sound made by a bird or animal. **3** watchword or slogan: *"Asia for the Asians" was their cry*. **4** fit of weeping: *have a good cry*.

ˈcry·baby *n* young person who cries often or easily without good or apparent cause.

cry·ing /ˈkraiŋ/ *adj* very bad; demanding attention: *a ~ shame/evil/need*.

crypt /krɪpt/ *n* [C] underground room, esp of a church.

cryp·tic /ˈkrɪptɪk/ *adj* secret; with a hidden meaning, or a meaning not easily seen: *a ~ remark*.

cryp·ti·cally /-kli/ *adv*

crys·tal /ˈkrɪstəl/ *n* **1** [U] transparent, natural substance like quartz. **2** [C] piece of this, esp as an ornament: *a necklace of ~s*. **3** [U] glassware of best quality, made into bowls, vases, etc: *The dining table shone with silver and ~*. **4** [C] flat, angular and regular shape taken naturally by the molecules of certain substances: *sugar and salt ~s; snow and ice ~s*. **5** [C] glass covering over the face of a watch.

cry·stal·line /ˈkrɪstəlɪn/ *adj* **1** like or made of crystal(s). **2** like crystal; very clear.

cry·stal·lize /ˈkrɪstəˌlaiz/ *vt,vi* **1** form, cause to form, into crystals (4). **2** cover (fruit, etc) with sugar crystals: *~d ginger*. **3** (*fig*) (of ideas, plans) become, cause to be, clear and definite: *His vague ideas ~d into a definite plan*.

crys·tal·li·za·tion /ˌkrɪstələˈzeiʃən/ *n* [U]

CST *abbr* = Central Standard Time.

CT *postal abbr* = Connecticut. ⇨ App 6.

ct. *abbr* = **1** cent. **2** county. **3** court[1] (esp 1, 7).

cu. *abbr* = cubic.

cub /kəb/ *n* [C] **1** young lion, bear, fox, tiger. **2** (esp) inexperienced newspaper reporter.

ˈcub scout *n* [C] member of the junior program of the Boy Scouts.

cubby·hole /ˈkəbiˌhoul/ *n* [C] small enclosed space.

cube /kyub/ *n* [C] **1** solid body having six equal square sides; block of something so shaped or similarly shaped. **2** (*math*) third power of a number: *The ~ of 5* (5^3) *is* $5 \times 5 \times 5$ *(125)*. □ *vt* **1** raise a number to the third power: *10 ~d is 1,000*. **2** cut or shape into cubes.

cu·bic /ˈkyubɪk/ *adj* having the shape of a cube; of a cube: *one ~ foot,* volume of a cube whose side is one foot.
cu·bi·cal /ˈkyubɪkəl/ *adj* = cubic.
cu·bicle /ˈkyubɪkəl/ *n* [C] small division of a larger room, walled or curtained to make a separate compartment, eg for sleeping in.
cuckoo /ˈkuˌku/ *n* [C] bird whose call is like its name. □ *adj* (*informal*) crazy; silly.
ˈcuckoo clock, one that strikes the hours with notes like the call of a cuckoo.
cu·cum·ber /ˈkyuˌkəmbər/ *n* [C,U] (creeping plant with) long, green-skinned fleshy fruit, that is sliced and eaten in salads, or made into pickles. ⇨ illus at vegetable. ***as cool as a cucumber,*** unexcited.
cud /kəd/ *n* [U] food which cattle, etc bring back from the first stomach and chew again. ***chew the cud,*** (*fig*) reflect; ponder.
cuddle /ˈkədəl/ *vt,vi* **1** hold close and lovingly in one's arms: *She likes to ~ her doll.* **2** lie close and comfortably: *The children ~d up* (*together*) *under the blankets.* □ *n* [C] act of cuddling; hug.
cud·dly /ˈkədli/ *adj* suitable for, inviting, cuddling: *a nice cuddly doll.*
cud·gel /ˈkədʒəl/ *vt, n* [C] (-l-, -ll-) (hit with a) short, thick stick or club.
cue[1] /kyu/ *n* [C] **1** word(s) or action in a play showing when somebody else is to do or say something. **2** hint about how to behave, what to do, etc. ***take one's cue from sb,*** observe what he does as a guide to one's own action.
cue[2] /kyu/ *n* [C] long, tapering, leather-tipped rod, for striking the ball in pool or billiards.
ˈcue ball, that which the player strikes with the cue in billiards and pool.
cuff[1] /kəf/ *n* [C] **1** band at the wrist, on the end of a sleeve. ***off the cuff,*** (*sl*) without previous thought or preparation. ***on the cuff,*** (*sl*) on credit. **2** turned-back hem around the bottom of a trouser leg.
ˈcuff link, used for fastening the cuff on a sleeve.
cuff[2] /kəf/ *vt, n* [C] (give a) light blow with the open hand.
cui·sine /kwɪˈzin/ *n* [U] style of cooking; cooking: *a hotel where the ~ is excellent.*
cul-de-sac /ˈkəl-dɪ-ˌsæk/ *n* [C] dead-end street.
cu·li·nary /ˈkələˌneri/ *adj* of cooking or a kitchen: *~ plants,* suitable for cooking.
cull /kəl/ *vt* pick out; select: *extracts ~ed from the best authors.* □ *n* [C] something that is culled.
cul·len·der /ˈkələndər/ *n* = colander.
cul·mi·nate /ˈkəlməˌneit/ *vt* ***culminate in,*** (of efforts, hopes, careers, etc) reach the highest point: *misfortunes that ~d in bankruptcy.*
cul·mi·na·tion /ˌkəlməˈneiʃən/ *n* [C] highest point: *the culmination of his career.*
cul·pable /ˈkəlpəbəl/ *adj* (*legal*) blameworthy; guilty: *hold a person ~.*
cul·pably /ˈkəlpəbli/ *adv*
cul·prit /ˈkəlprɪt/ *n* [C] person who has done wrong.
cult /kəlt/ *n* [C] **1** system of religious worship. **2** devotion to a person, practice or idea: *the ~ of archery; the ~ of Whitman.* **3** (group of persons devoted to a) popular fashion or craze.
cul·ti·vate /ˈkəltəˌveit/ *vt* **1** prepare (land) for crops by plowing, etc; help (crops) to grow (eg by breaking up the soil around them, destroying weeds, etc). **2** give care, thought, time, etc in order to develop something: *to ~ the mind/a person's friendship.*
cul·ti·vated /ˈkəltəˌveitɪd/ *adj* **1** produced by cultivating; not wild. **2** having good manners; refined; educated.
cul·ti·va·tion /ˌkəltəˈveiʃən/ *n* [U] **1** cultivating or being cultivated: *the ~ of the soil; land that is under ~.* **2** refinement.
cul·ti·va·tor /ˈkəltəˌveitər/ *n* [C] **1** person who cultivates. **2** machine for breaking up ground, destroying weeds, etc.
cul·tural /ˈkəltʃ(ə)rəl/ *adj* having to do with culture: *~ studies,* eg art, literature.
cul·ture /ˈkəltʃər/ *n* **1** [U] advanced development of the human powers; development of the body, mind and spirit by training and experience: *Physical ~ is important, but we must not neglect the ~ of the mind.* **2** [U] refinement that is the result of the development of the mind, taste, etc: *a man of ~.* **3** [C,U] (particular form of the) civilization characteristic of a nation, community, tribe, etc: *we owe much to Greek ~.* **4** [U] cultivating; the rearing of bees, silkworms, etc. **5** [C] growth of bacteria in a special medium for medical or scientific study: *a ~ of cholera germs.*
cul·tured *adj* cultivated; refined.
cul·vert /ˈkəlvərt/ *n* [C] sewer or drain that crosses under a road, or railroad.
cum·ber·some /ˈkəmbərsəm/ *adj* heavy and awkward to carry: *a ~ parcel.*
cumu·lat·ive /ˈkyumyəˌleitɪv/ *adj* increasing in amount by one addition after another.
cumu·lus /ˈkyumyələs/ *n* [C] (*pl* -li /-ˌlai/) cloud made up of rounded masses on a flat base.
cunei·form /kyuˈniəˌfɔrm/ *adj* wedge-shaped: *~ characters,* as used in old Persian and Assyrian writing.
cun·ning[1] /ˈkənɪŋ/ *adj* **1** clever at deceiving; artful; sly: *a ~ old fox; a ~ trick.* **2** attractive; cute: *a ~ child.*
cun·ning·ly *adv*
cun·ning[2] /ˈkənɪŋ/ *n* [U] quality of being cunning(1): *The boy showed a great deal of ~ in getting what he wanted.*
cup[1] /kəp/ *n* [C] **1** small bowl, with a handle, used with a saucer: *a ˈteacup.* **2** contents of a cup: *a ˌcup of ˈcoffee.* ***not my cup of tea,*** (*informal*) not what I like, not what suits me. **3** unit of measurement, in cooking, of one-half pint or eight fluid ounces. **4** = chalice. **5** vessel (usually of gold or silver) given as a prize in competitions. **6** thing shaped like a cup; *the cup of a flower; an ˈeggcup; the cups of a bra.*
cup·ful /ˈkəpˌfʊl/ *n* [C] (*pl* ~s) **(a)** as much as a cup can hold. **(b)** = cup[1](3).
cup[2] /kəp/ *vt* (-pp-) **1** put into the shape of a cup: *to cup one's hands,* eg to catch a ball. **2** put around or over like a cup: *with her chin cupped in her hand.*
cup·board /ˈkəbərd/ *n* [C] cabinet or closet, either built into a room as a fixture, or a separate piece of furniture, used for dishes, provisions, clothes, etc.

cup·cake /ˈkəpˌkeik/ *n* [C] small, sweet cake baked in a cup-shaped pan.

Cu·pid /ˈkyupɪd/ *n* **1** Roman god of love. **2 cupid** [C] (picture or statue of a) beautiful boy (with wings and a bow and arrows).

cu·pid·ity /kyuˈpɪdəti/ *n* [U] greed, esp for money or property.

cu·pola /ˈkyupələ/ *n* [C] (*pl* ~s) **1** small dome or tower on top of a roof. **2** ceiling of a dome.

cur /kər/ *n* [C] **1** bad-tempered or worthless dog (esp lowbred). **2** low worthless person.

cur·able /ˈkyʊrəbəl/ *adj* that can be cured.

cura·bil·ity /ˌkyʊrəˈbɪləti/ *n* [U]

cur·acy /ˈkyʊrəsi/ *n* [C] (*pl* -ies) office and work of a curate.

curate /ˈkyʊrɪt/ *n* [C] clergyman who helps the rector or vicar of a church.

cura·tive /ˈkyʊrətɪv/ *adj* helping to, able to, cure (disease or ill health): *the ~ value of sunshine and sea air.*

cu·ra·tor /kyʊˈreitər, ˈkyʊˌreitər/ *n* [C] official in charge of a museum, art gallery, zoo, etc.

curb /kərb/ *n* [C] **1** chain or leather strap passing under a horse's jaw, used to control it. **2** (*fig*) something that holds one back or restrains: *put/keep a ~ on one's anger/passions.* **3** border or edging of stone, etc, esp on a sidewalk. □ *vt* **1** control (a horse) by means of a curb. **2** keep (feelings, etc) under control: *to ~ one's impatience.*

curd /kərd/ *n* [C] (often *pl*) thick, almost solid substance (formed when milk turns sour) used to make cheese.

curdle /ˈkərdəl/ *vi,vt* **1** form, cause to form, into curds: *The milk has ~d.* **2** (*fig*): *What a blood-curdling* (= horrifying) *yell!*

cure[1] /kyʊr/ *n* [C] **1** curing or being cured(1): *The doctor cannot guarantee a ~.* **2** substance or treatment which cures(1): *Is there a ~ for cancer yet?*

cure[2] /kyʊr/ *vt,vi* **1** bring (a person) back to health; provide and use successfully a remedy for a disease, ill health, suffering; get rid of (an evil): *to ~ a man of a disease; to ~ a child of bad habits.* **2** treat meat, fish, skin, tobacco, etc in order to keep it in good condition by salting, smoking, drying, etc: *ˈwell-~d bacon.*

cur·few /ˈkərˌfyu/ *n* [C] (*modern use*) time or signal for people to remain indoors: *to impose a ~ on a town; to lift/end the ~.*

curio /ˈkyʊriˌou/ *n* [C] (*pl* ~s) object of a rare or unusual character.

curi·os·ity /ˌkyʊriˈasəti/ *n* (*pl* -ies) **1** [U] being curious(1,2): *to be dying of/burning with ~ to know what was happening.* **2** [C] curious(3) thing; strange or rare object.

curi·ous /ˈkyʊriəs/ *adj* **1** eager (to learn, know): *I'm ~ to know what he said.* **2** having or showing too much interest in the affairs of others: *~ neighbors.* **3** strange; unusual: *What a ~ mistake! Isn't he a ~-looking person!*

curi·ous·ly *adv*

curl[1] /kərl/ *n* **1** [C] something shaped like a coil or spiral, esp a ringlet of hair: *~s (of hair) falling over a girl's shoulders; a ~ of smoke rising from a cigarette.* **2** [U] the state of being curly: *How do you keep your hair in curl?*

curl[2] /kərl/ *vt,vi* **1** make or grow in curls; twist: *Does her hair ~ naturally?* **2** curve; twist: *The dog ~ed (itself) up on the rug.*

cur·lew /ˈkərˌlu/ *n* [C] wading bird with a long, slender, down-curved bill.

curly /ˈkərli/ *adj* (-ier, -iest) having curls; arranged in curls: *~ hair; a ˈ~ headed girl.*

cur·rant /ˈkərənt/ *n* [C] **1** small, sweet, seedless raisin (grown in Greece and neighboring countries) used in buns, cakes, puddings, etc. **2** (cultivated bush with) small black, red or white juicy fruit growing in clusters.

cur·rency /ˈkərənsi/ *n* (*pl* -ies) **1** [U] the state of being in common or general use: *The rumor soon gained ~,* was repeated until many people were aware of it. **2** [C,U] money that is in use in a country: *foreign currencies; a decimal ~.*

cur·rent[1] /ˈkərənt/ *adj* **1** in common or general use; generally accepted: *~ opinions/beliefs; words that are no longer ~.* **2** now passing; of the present time: *the ~ year,* this year; *a newsreel showing ~ events.*

cur·rent·ly *adv*

cur·rent[2] /ˈkərənt/ *n* [C] **1** stream of water, air, gas, esp one flowing through slower moving or still water, etc: *A cold ~ of air came in when the door was opened. Although he was a strong swimmer he was swept away by the ~ and was drowned.* **2** flow of electricity through something or along a wire or cable. **3** course or movement (of events, opinions, thoughts, etc): *The government used the radio to influence the ~ of thought.*

cur·ricu·lum /kəˈrɪkyələm/ *n* [C] (*pl* ~s or -la /-lə/) course of study in a school, college, etc.

curry[1] /ˈkəri/ *n* (*pl* -ies) **1** [U] (also **curry powder**) mixture of hot-tasting spices. **2** [C,U] (dish of) meat, fish, eggs, etc, cooked with curry powder. □ *vt* prepare with curry.

curry[2] /ˈkəri/ *vt* **1** rub down and clean (a horse). **2** prepare (tanned leather) by soaking, scraping, etc. ***curry favor (with sb),*** try to win favor or approval (by using flattery, etc).

curse[1] /kərs/ *n* **1** word(s) calling down punishment, injury or destruction upon someone. **2** cause of misfortune or ruin: *Gambling is often a ~. The rabbits are a ~* (ie do a lot of damage to crops, etc) *in this part of the country.* **3** word(s) used in cursing.

curse[2] /kərs/ *vt,vi* **1** use a curse against; use violent language against. **2** utter curses: *to ~ and swear; to ~ at a stupid mistake.* **3** ***be cursed with,*** suffer misfortune, trouble, etc because of: *to be ~d with a violent temper.*

cursed /kərst, ˈkərsɪd/ *adj* damnable; hateful; (*informal*) very bad: *This work is a ~ nuisance.*

cur·sive /ˈkərsɪv/ *adj* (of handwriting) with the letters rounded and joined together.

cur·sory /ˈkərsəri/ *adj* (of work, reading, etc) quick; hurried; done without attention to details: *a ~ glance/inspection.*

cur·sor·ily /ˈkərsərəli/ *adv*

curst /kərst/ *adj* = cursed.

curt /kərt/ *adj* rudely brief, abrupt: *gave him a ~ answer.*

curt·ly *adv*

curt·ness /-nɪs/ *n* [U]

cur·tail /kər'teiəl/ *vt* (*pres part* -ing /kər'teilɪŋ/) make shorter than was at first planned; cut off a part of: *to ~ a speech/one's holidays.*

cur·tail·ment *n* [C,U]

cur·tain /'kərtən/ *n* [C] **1** piece of cloth, etc as hung up at a window: *Please draw the ~s,* pull them across the window(s). **2** sheet of heavy material to draw or lower across the front of the stage in a theater before and after each scene of a play. ***be/look like curtains,*** (*sl*) (appear to) be death (for someone): *If you don't slow down when you get to that curve, then it'll be ~s (for you).* **3** something that covers or hides like a curtain: *A ~ of mist hid the view.* □ *vt* **1** furnish or cover with curtains: *enough material to ~ all the windows.* **2** ***curtain off,*** separate or divide with curtains: *to ~ off part of a room.*

curt·sy, curt·sey /'kərtsi/ *n* [C] (*pl* ~s, -ies) bow made by women and girls (eg to a king or queen). □ *vi* (*pt,pp* ~ed, curtsied) make this gesture.

cur·va·ture /'kərvətʃər/ *n* [C,U] curving; the state of being curved: *to suffer from ~ of the spine; the ~ of the earth's surface.*

curve /kərv/ *n* [C] line which has no straight part and which changes direction without angles: *a ~ in the road.* □ *vt,vi* have, cause to have, the form of a curve: *The river ~s round the hill.*

cushion /'kʊʃən/ *n* [C] **1** pillow or pad filled with feathers or other soft material, to sit on, to kneel on, etc. **2** something soft and like a cushion in shape or function: *a ~ of moss; a 'pin-~.* □ *vt* **1** supply with cushions. **2** protect from shock with cushions: *~ed seats.* **3** (*fig*) protect from shock or injury: *farmers who are ~ed against falls in prices,* eg by subsidies.

cusp /kəsp/ *n* [C] point (esp on a tooth).

cusp·id /'kəspɪd/ *n* [C] sharp-pointed tooth that is next to the front teeth; canine tooth.

cuss /kəs/ *n* [C] (*informal*) **1** curse. **2** worthless person: *a strange old ~.*

cus·tard /'kəstərd/ *n* [C,U] (dish of) mixture of eggs and milk, sweetened and flavored, baked or boiled.

cus·tod·ian /kə'stoudiən/ *n* [C] **1** person in charge of something or somebody. **2** caretaker of a building.

cus·tody /'kəstədi/ *n* [U] **1** watchful care; guarding: *A father has the ~ of his children while they are young.* **2** imprisonment. ***(be) in custody,*** in prison. ***take into custody,*** arrest.

cus·tom /'kəstəm/ *n* **1** [U] usual and generally accepted behavior or practice among members of a social group; tradition: *Don't be a slave to ~,* do not do things merely because most people do them and have always done them. **2** [C] particular way of behaving: *Social ~s vary in different countries. It was his ~ to take a walk before breakfast.* ⇨ habit(1,2). **3** [U] regular business given to a tradesman by his customers: *We should very much like to have your ~.* **4** (*pl*) **(a)** taxes due to the government on goods imported into a country; import duties. **(b)** (with *sing v*) department of government that collects such duties: *How long will it take us to get through ~s?* □ *adj* (also ˌ**custom-'made**) made to order.

cus·tom·ary /'kəstəˌmeri/ *adj* in agreement with, according to, custom(1,2): *There was the ~ vote of thanks to the chairman.*

cus·tom·ar·ily /ˌkəstə'merəli/ *adv*

cus·tomer /'kəstəmər/ *n* [C] **1** person who buys things, esp one who buys regularly from a store, business, etc: *Mr. Jones has lost some of his best ~s.* **2** (*informal*) person or fellow: *a strange/awkward ~,* person who is difficult to deal with.

cut[1] /kət/ *n* [C] **1** act of cutting; stroke with a sword, whip, etc; result of such a stroke; opening made by a knife or other sharp-edged tool, etc: *a deep cut in the leg.* **2** reduction in size, amount, length, etc: *a cut in prices/salaries/expenditure.* **3** a cutting out; part that is cut out: *There were several cuts in the film,* parts of it had been deleted. **4** something obtained by cutting: *a nice cut of beef.* **5** style in which clothes, hair, etc are made by cutting. **6** remark, etc that wounds a person's feelings: *That remark was a cut at me.* **7** refusal to recognize a person. **8** a way from one place to another that shortens the distance: *Let's take a 'shortcut.* **9** ***a cut above,*** (*informal*) rather superior to: *She's a cut above the other girls in the office.*

cut[2] /kət/ *vt,vi* (-tt-; *pt,pp* cut) **1** make a cut (with a sharp-edged instrument, eg a knife, a pair of scissors, or other edged tool). **(a)** make a mark or wound: *He cut his face/himself while shaving.* **(b)** shorten; trim: *I'm having my hair cut tomorrow.* **(c)** harvest; reap: *Has the wheat been cut yet?* **(d)** remove from something larger: *Please cut a slice of cake for me/cut me a slice of cake. Two scenes/episodes were cut* (deleted) *by the film editor.* **(e)** reduce: *Was your salary cut?* **(f)** make by cutting: He cut a tunnel through a hill. **2 (a)** (of a sharp tool, instrument, etc) be suitable to use: *This knife does not cut well.* **(b)** (of a material) be capable of being cut: *Sandstone cuts easily.* **3** stay away from, be absent from: *to cut a class/a lecture.* **4** cross: *Let the point where AB cuts CD be called E.* **5** (*sport*) strike (a ball) so that it spins or is deflected; hit the edge of (a ball). **6** (used with *nouns* or *pronouns*) ***cut the cards/pack,*** lift part of a pack of playing-cards lying face downwards and turn it up to decide something (eg who is to deal). ***cut corners,*** ⇨ corner(1). ***cut a disc/record,*** record music, etc on to a phonograph record. ***cut the ground from under sb/from under sb's feet,*** leave him in a weak or illogical position; destroy the foundation of his plan, argument, etc. ***cut no/not much ice (with sb),*** (*sl*) have little or no effect or influence (on). ***cut one's losses,*** abandon a scheme before one loses any more. ***cut both ways,*** (of an action or argument) have an effect both for and against. **7** (used with *adjectives*) ***cut sb dead,*** pretend not to have seen somebody; treat as a complete stranger: *She cut me dead in the street,* ignored me completely. ***cut sb/sth loose (from),*** make loose or separate by cutting: *cut oneself loose from one's family,* live an independent life. ***cut sth open,*** make an opening or split in: *He fell and cut his head open.* ***cut sth short,*** shorten, often prematurely: *to cut a long story short; a career cut short by illness.* **8** (special uses with *adverbial* *particles* and *prepositions*):

cut across sth, **(a)** take a shorter route across (a field, etc). **(b)** be contrary to; rise above: *The desire to end inflation cuts clean across normal political loyalties.*

cut sth away, remove by cutting: *We cut away all the dead wood from the tree.*

cut sth back, **(a)** (of shrubs, bushes, etc) prune close to the stem. **(b)** reduce: *cut back production.*

cut sth/sb down, **(a)** cause to fall by cutting: *to cut down a tree.* **(b)** kill or injure with a weapon. **(c)** deprive of life or health (by disease, etc): *He was cut down in his prime.* **(d)** reduce in quantity, amount, etc: *I won't have a cigarette, thanks —I'm trying to cut down*, reduce the number of cigarettes I smoke. **(e)** reduce the length of: *cut down a pair of trousers.* ***cut down on,*** reduce one's consumption of: *He's trying to cut down on cigarettes and beer.*

cut in, **(a)** return too soon to a line of traffic (with possibility of collision, etc): *Accidents are often caused by drivers who cut in.* **(b)** interrupt (a conversation, etc).

cut sb/sth off (from), **(a)** remove by cutting: *He cut off a yard of cloth from the roll.* **(b)** stop; interrupt; isolate: *be cut off while talking on the telephone; cut off the gas/electricity supply; be cut off from all possibility of help.*

cut out, (*sl*) leave; depart: *He picked up his check and cut out.* ***cut sth out,*** **(a)** remove by cutting (eg from a periodical): *That's an interesting article—I'll cut it out.* **(b)** make by cutting: *cut out a path through the jungle.* **(c)** shape (a garment) by cutting the outlines of the parts on cloth: *cut out a dress.* **(d)** leave out; omit: *Let's cut out unimportant details.* **(e)** stop doing or using: *My doctor told me I must cut out smoking/tobacco*, stop smoking/using tobacco. ***cut sb out,*** defeat, eliminate (a rival, esp in a competition). ***(not) be cut out for,*** (not) have the qualities and abilities needed for: *He's not cut out for that sort of work.*

cut up (*informal*) act humorously; engage in pranks; *He's always cutting up on the job.* ***cut sth/sb up,*** **(a)** cut into pieces: *cut up one's meat.* **(b)** destroy: *cut up the enemy's forces.* **(c)** (*informal*) cause mental suffering to: *He was badly cut up by the news of his son's death.*

cut-and-dried *adj* already formed and unlikely to be changed.

ˈcut·back *n* [C] reduction.

ˌcut ˈglass, glassware with designs cut or engraved in it.

ˈcut·out *n* [C] **(a)** article, etc cut out of a newspaper, etc. **(b)** device that disconnects an electric circuit.

ˈcut-rate *adj* at a reduced price.

ˈcut·up *n* [C] (*informal*) prankster.

ˈcut·ˌworm *n* [C] night-feeding caterpillar that cuts off the stalks of young plants.

cute /kyut/ *adj* (-r, -st) **1** sharp-witted; quick-thinking. **2** (*informal*) attractive; pretty and charming.

cute·ly *adv*

cute·ness /-nɪs/ *n* [U]

cu·ticle /ˈkyutɪkəl/ *n* [C] outer layer of hardened skin at the base of a fingernail or toenail.

cut·lass /ˈkətləs/ *n* [C] (sailor's) short, one-edged sword with a slightly curved blade.

cut·ler /ˈkətlər/ *n* [C] man who makes and repairs knives and other cutting tools and instruments.

cut·lery /ˈkətləri/ *n* [U] **1** implements used at meals (knives, forks, spoons, etc). **2** trade of things made or sold by cutlers.

cut·let /ˈkətlɪt/ *n* [C] slice of meat or fish for broiling or frying: *a veal ~.*

cut·ter /ˈkətər/ *n* [C] **1** person or thing that cuts: *a tailor's ~,* who cuts out cloth; *ˈwire ~s.* **2** sailing vessel with one mast; ship's boat, for use between ship and shore. **3** small sleigh.

cut·throat /ˈkətˌθrout/ *n* [C] murderer. □ *adj* murderous: *~ competition*, likely to ruin the weaker competitors.

cut·ting¹ /ˈkətɪŋ/ *adj* **1** sharp; piercing: *a ~ wind.* **2** sarcastic: *a ~ remark.*

cut·ting² /ˈkətɪŋ/ *n* **1** [C] short piece of the stem of a plant, to be used for growing a new plant: *chrysanthemum ~s.* **2** [U] process of editing moving picture films, tape recordings, etc, by cutting out unwanted parts.

cuttle·fish /ˈkətəlˌfɪʃ/ *n* [C] sea animal with long arms (tentacles) which sends out a black liquid when attacked. ⇨ illus at mollusk.

cy·an·ide /ˈsaiəˌnaid/ *n* [U] poisonous compound substance: *potassium ~; sodium ~.*

cycle /ˈsaikəl/ *n* [C] **1** series of events taking place in a regularly repeated order: *the ~ of the seasons.* **2** complete set or series: *a song ~ by Schubert.* **3** (short for) bicycle or motorcycle. □ *vi* ride a bicycle.

cy·clist /ˈsaiklɪst/ *n* [C] person who cycles.

cy·clone /ˈsaiˌkloun/ *n* [C] violent wind rotating around a calm central area; violent windstorm.

cy·clonic /saiˈklanɪk/ *adj* of or like a cyclone.

cyg·net /ˈsɪgnɪt/ *n* [C] young swan.

cyl·in·der /ˈsɪlɪndər/ *n* [C] **1** solid or hollow body shaped like a pole or log. ⇨ illus at geometry. **2** cylinder-shaped chamber (in an engine) in which gas or steam works a piston: *a six-~ engine/automobile.*

cy·lin·dri·cal /sɪˈlɪndrɪkəl/ *adj*

cym·bal /ˈsɪmbəl/ *n* [C] one of a pair of round brass plates struck together to make clanging sounds. ⇨ illus at percussion.

cynic /ˈsɪnɪk/ *n* [C] person who believes that selfishness and self-interest are the only motives for people's actions.

cyni·cism /ˈsɪnəˌsɪzəm/ *n* **1** [U] cynic's opinions or attitude of mind. **2** [C] cynical remark.

cyni·cal /ˈsɪnɪkəl/ *adj* of or like a cynic; sneering or contemptuous: *a ~ smile/remark.*

cyni·cally /-kli/ *adv*

cy·press /ˈsaiprəs/ *n* [C] (kinds of) evergreen tree with dark leaves and hard wood.

cyst /sɪst/ *n* [C] abnormal, saclike growth in the body containing liquid matter.

czar /zar/ *n* [C] **1** (also **tsar**) emperor (of Russia before 1917). **2** person with power and authority in some activity: *a ~ in the publishing business.*

cza·rina /zaˈrinə/ *n* [C] (also **tsarina**) Russian empress.

d

D[1], **d** /di/ (*pl* D's, d's /diz/) **1** the fourth letter of the English alphabet. **2** Roman numeral for 500.

d.[2] *abbr* (before a date) = died.

'd, used for *had* or *would* (esp after *I, we, you, he, she, they, who*).

DA /ˌdi ˈei/ *abbr* = District Attorney. □ *n* [C] (*pl* DA's).

dab /dæb/ *vt,vi* (-bb-) touch, put on, lightly and gently: *~ one's eyes with a handkerchief.* □ *n* [C] **1** small quantity (of paint, etc). **2** slight tap; pat.

dabble /ˈdæbəl/ *vt,vi* **1** splash (the hands, feet, etc) about in water; put in and out of water. **2** engage in, study without serious effort: *~ in philosophy.*

dachs·hund /ˈdaksˌhʊnd/ *n* [C] small short-legged dog with a long body and drooping ears.

Da·cron /ˈdeiˌkran, ˈdæˌkran/ *n* [U] (*P*) artificial fiber or fabric used to make dresses, shirts, sheets, etc.

dad /dæd/ *n* [C] (*informal*) father.

daddy /ˈdædi/ *n* [C] (*pl* -ies) (*informal*) father.

ˌdaddy ˈlong·legs, spiderlike insect with a round body and long, thin legs.

daf·fo·dil /ˈdæfəˌdɪl/ *n* [C] yellow flower with long narrow leaves, growing from a bulb. ⇨ illus at flower.

daf·fy /ˈdæfi/ *adj* (-ier, -iest) (*informal*) crazy; foolish.

daft /dæft/ *adj* (-er, -est) (*informal*) silly; foolish; reckless.

daft·ly *adv*

dag·ger /ˈdægər/ *n* [C] **1** short weapon with a pointed blade. **2** mark (†) used in printing.

da·hlia /ˈdælyə/ *n* [C] (*pl* ~s) garden plant with brightly colored flowers.

daily /ˈdeili/ *adj, adv* (happening, done, appearing) every day (or every weekday); of, for, or lasting a day: *Most newspapers appear ~. Thousands of people cross this bridge ~.* □ *n* [C] (*pl* -ies) newspaper published every day or every weekday.

dainty /ˈdeinti/ *adj* (-ier, -iest) **1** (of persons) pretty, neat and delicate(1,3): *a ~ little girl.* **2** (of persons and animals) particular; difficult to please: *She's ~ about her food.* **3** (of things) delicate(3); easily injured or broken: *~ cups and saucers; ~ spring flowers.* **4** (of food) delicate(5) and delicious: *~ cakes.*

dain·tily /ˈdeintɪli/ *adv*

dainti·ness /-nɪs/ *n* [U]

dai·qui·ri /ˈdaikəri, ˈdækəri/ (also sometimes **daquiri**) *n* [C] cocktail made of rum, crushed ice, and a fruit flavoring, usually lime juice.

dairy /ˈderi/ *n* [C] (*pl* -ies) **1** store where milk, butter, eggs, etc, are sold. **2** place where milk and milk products are prepared. **3** (also **dairy farm**) farm that produces milk, cream, etc.

ˈdairy cattle, cows raised to produce milk, not meat.

ˈdairy·maid *n* [C] woman who works in a dairy.

ˈdairy·man *n* [C] (*pl* ~men /-ˌmen/) dealer in milk, etc.

dais /ˈdeiɪs/ *n* [C] (*pl* ~es /-sɪz/) platform (esp at the end of a hall) or large room.

daisy /ˈdeizi/ *n* [C] (*pl* -ies) (plant having a) small white or pink flower with a yellow center.

dale /deiəl/ *n* [C] (*poet*) valley.

dal·li·ance /ˈdæliəns/ *n* [U] **1** trifling behavior. **2** flirtation.

dally /ˈdæli/ *vi* **1** trifle; think idly about: *~ with an idea or proposal.* **2** waste time: *Don't ~ over your work.*

dam[1] /dæm/ *n* [C] **1** barrier built to keep back water (eg to form a reservoir). **2** body of water kept back by a dam. □ *vt* (-mm-) **1** make a dam across (a narrow valley, etc); hold back by means of a dam: *dam up a river.* **2** (*fig*) hold back: *to dam up one's feelings.*

dam[2] /dæm/ *n* [C] female parent of an animal. ⇨ sire (2).

dam·age /ˈdæmɪdʒ/ *n* **1** [U] harm or injury that causes loss of value: *The insurance company will pay for the ~ to my car.* **2** (*pl*) (*legal*) money claimed from or paid by a person causing loss or injury: *He claimed $10,000 ~s from his employers for the loss of his finger.* □ *vt* cause damage(1) to: *furniture ~d by fire.*

dame /deim/ *n* **1** (title of a) woman holding a knighthood, certain traditional offices, etc. **2** (*sl*) woman.

damn /dæm/ *vt* **1** condemn to punishment, esp (in religion) to hell. **2** condemn; say that something or somebody is worthless, bad, etc: *The book was ~ed by the critics.* **3** (used to express anger, annoyance, impatience, etc): *I'll be ~ed if I'll go,* I absolutely refuse to go. *Oh ~! Damn you!* □ *n* ***not give a damn,*** not care in the least. ***not (be) worth a damn,*** (be) worthless. □ *adj* = damned.

dam·nable /ˈdæmnəbəl/ *adj* **1** hateful; deserving to be damned. **2** (*informal*) very bad: *~ weather.*

dam·nably /ˈdæmnəbli/ *adv*

dam·na·tion /dæmˈneiʃən/ *n* [U] being damned; ruin: *to suffer eternal ~.* □ *int* (*dated*) (used as a curse).

damned /dæmd/ *adj* **1** **the damned,** souls in

hell. **2** (*informal*) deserving to be damned: *You ~ fool!* □ *adv* (*informal*) extremely: *~ hot/funny*.

damp¹ /dæmp/ *adj* (-er, -est) not thoroughly dry; moist; slightly wet: *~ clothes*. □ *n* [U] state of being damp; damp atmosphere; moisture on the surface of, or existing throughout, something: *The ~ rising from the ground caused the walls to stain badly*.

damp·ish *adj* rather damp.

damp·ness /-nɪs/ *n* [U]

damp² /dæmp/ *vt,vi* **1** (also ˈ**dampen**) make damp. **2** (also ˈ**dampen**) make sad or dull: *Nothing could ~ his spirits*. **3** ***damp down,*** make (a fire) burn more slowly (eg by heaping ashes on it, or by controlling the draft of air entering a stove, etc).

dampen /ˈdæmpən/ *vt,vi* = damp²(1,2).

damper /ˈdæmpər/ *n* [C] **1** movable metal plate that regulates the flow of air into a fire in a stove or furnace. **2** person or thing that checks or discourages: *His complaints were a ~ on the evening*.

dam·sel /ˈdæmzəl/ *n* [C] (*old use*) girl; young unmarried woman.

dam·son /ˈdæmzən/ *n* [C] (tree producing a) small dark-purple plum.

dance¹ /dæns/ *n* [C] **1** (series of) movements and steps in time with music. **2** particular set of movements and steps (eg a waltz). **3** tune, piece of music, for such dancing. **4** round or turn of dancing: *May I have the next ~?* **5** social gathering for dancing.

dance² /dæns/ *vi,vt* **1** perform, take part in a dance, alone, with a partner, or in a group: *to ~ a waltz; went on dancing until after midnight*. **2** move in a lively way, quickly, up and down, etc: *The leaves were dancing in the wind*. **3** cause to dance: *to ~ a baby on one's knee*.

dancer *n* [C] person who dances.

danc·ing *adj* who or that dances. □ *n* [U] (in compounds): ˈ*dancing teacher*, professional teacher of dancing; ˈ*dancing partner*, person with whom one (usually) dances; ˈ*ballet dancing;* ˈ*tap dancing*.

dan·de·lion /ˈdændəˌlaiən/ *n* [C] small wild plant with bright yellow flowers.

dandle /ˈdændəl/ *vt* move (a baby) up and down on one's knees or in one's arms.

dan·druff /ˈdændrəf/ *n* [U] dead skin that comes off the scalp in small whitish scales.

dandy /ˈdændi/ *n* [C] (*pl* -ies) **1** man who pays too much care to his clothes and personal appearance. **2** (*informal*) something excellent or first-rate. □ *adj* (-ier, -iest) (*informal*) very good; excellent.

dan·ger /ˈdeindʒər/ *n* **1** [U] chance of harm; exposure to injury or loss of life: *Is there any ~ of fire?* ***in danger (of):*** *His life was in ~. He was in ~ of losing his life*. ***out of danger:*** *He has been very ill, but the doctors say that he is now out of ~,* not likely to die. **2** [C] something or somebody that may cause danger: *That man is a ~ to society*.

dan·ger·ous /ˈdeindʒ(ə)rəs/ *adj* likely to cause harm; unsafe: *a ~ bridge/journey/illness. The river is ~ to swim in*.

dan·ger·ous·ly *adv*

dangle /ˈdæŋgəl/ *vi,vt* **1** hang or swing loosely; carry (something) so that it hangs or swings loosely: *a bunch of keys dangling at the end of a chain*. **2** ***keep sb dangling (around),*** keep near (as an admirer) in uncertainty: *She likes to keep her men dangling (around her)*.

Dan·ish pas·try /ˌdeiniʃ ˈpeistri/ *n* [C] (*pl* -ries) (also **Danish**) rich, flaky yeast-raised pastry.

dank /dæŋk/ *adj* (-er, -est) damp in an unpleasant or unhealthy way: *a ~ and chilly cave*.

daphne /ˈdæfni/ *n* [C] kinds of flowering shrub.

dapple /ˈdæpəl/ *vt* mark, become marked with spots of different color or shades of color: *a ~d horse; ~d shade,* as when sunlight comes through the leaves of trees. (*Note:* usually used as a *pp*.)

da·qui·ri /ˈdækəri/ *n* = daiquiri.

dare¹ /der/ *auxiliary verb* (*3rd person sing* is *dare*, not *dares*) have the courage or boldness to: *He wanted to fight me but he didn't ~. How ~ he say such rude things about me!*

dare² /der/ *vt,vi* **1** be brave enough to: *They wouldn't ~ (to be so rude)!* **2** take the risk of; face: *He will ~ any danger*. **3** suggest that somebody has not the courage or ability to do something: *I ~ you (to say that again)!* □ *n* (only in) ***do sth for/on a dare,*** do something because one is dared(3) to do it.

dare·devil /ˈderˌdevəl/ *n* [C] person who is foolishly bold or reckless: *What a ~ he is!*

dar·ing /ˈderɪŋ/ *n* [U] adventurous courage: *the ~ of the commandos*. □ *adj* bold and adventurous: *a ~ robbery. What a ~ thing to do!*

dar·ing·ly *adv*

dark¹ /dark/ *adj* (-er, -est) **1** with no or very little light: *a ~, moonless night. It's getting too ~ to take photographs*. **2** (of color) not reflecting much light; closer to black than to white: *~ blue/green/brown;* ˈ*~-brown eyes*. **3** (of the skin) not fair: *a ~ complexion*. **4** (*fig*) hidden, mysterious: *a ~ secret*. ***a dark horse,*** (*fig*) **(a)** winner who is little known. **(b)** unexpected candidate in politics. **5** hopeless; sad; cheerless: *Don't look on the ~ side of things*. **6** without culture, knowledge, etc: *the* ˈ*Dark Ages*, (in European history) from the 5th to the 10th centuries.

dark·ly *adv*

dark·ness /-nɪs/ *n* [U]

dark² /dark/ *n* [U] **1** absence of light: *All the lights went out and we were left in the ~.* ***before/after dark,*** before/after the sun goes down. **2** (*fig*) ignorance: *We were completely in the ~ about his movements*.

dark·en /ˈdarkən/ *vt,vi* make or become dark(er): *His face ~ed with anger*.

dar·ling /ˈdarlɪŋ/ *n* [C] person or object very much loved. □ *adj* **1** dearly loved. **2** charming.

darn¹ /darn/ *vt,vi* mend (esp something knitted, eg a sock) by passing thread in and out and in two directions: *My socks have been ~ed again and again*. □ *n* [C] place mended by darning.

ˈ**darning needle,** large sewing needle used for darning.

darn² /darn/ *vt* (*informal*) (used as a mild substitute for) damn(3).

dart¹ /dart/ *n* [C] **1** quick, sudden, forward

movement: *The child made a sudden ~ across the road.* **2** small, sharp-pointed missile, feathered and pointed: *a poison ~.*

dart² /dart/ *vi,vt* (cause to) move forward suddenly and quickly; send suddenly and quickly: *The deer ~ed away when it saw us. She ~ed into the shop.*

dash¹ /dæʃ/ *n* **1** [C] sudden rush; violent movement: *to make a ~ for shelter/freedom.* **2** [C] (sound of) liquid splashing: *the ~ of the waves on the rocks.* **3** [C] small amount of something added or mixed: *water with a ~ of whiskey in it; red with a ~ of blue.* **4** [C] stroke of the pen or a mark (—) used in printing. **5** short race: *the 100-meter(s) ~.* **6** [U] (capacity for) vigorous action; energy: *an officer famous for his skill and ~.*

dash² /dæʃ/ *vt,vi* **1** send or throw violently; move or be moved violently: *The huge waves ~ed over the rocks.* **2** ***dash sb's hopes,*** destroy, discourage, them.

dash·ing *adj* impetuous; lively; full of, showing, energy: *a ~ing cavalry charge.*

dash·board /ˈdæʃˌbɔrd/ *n* [C] panel beneath the windshield of an automobile, motorboat, etc, with the speedometer, various controls, etc.

da·shi·ki /dæˈʃiki/ *n* [C] (*pl* ~s) loose, African-style pullover shirt, usually brightly colored.

data /ˈdeitə, ˈdætə/ *n* (*pl* of Latin *datum*) **1** (*collective pl*) facts; things certainly known (and from which conclusions may be drawn): *unless sufficient ~ are/is available.* **2** (*sing*) [U] information prepared for and operated on a computer program: *The ~ is ready for processing.* ⇨ datum.

ˈdata bank, collection of data, esp for use in a computer.

ˌdata ˈprocessing, the performing of operations on data to obtain information, solutions to problems, etc.

date¹ /deit/ *n* [C] **1** (statement of the) day, month, or year of an event: *Date of birth, April 20, 1974; the ~ of the discovery of America by Columbus (1492). What's today's ~?* **2** period of time to which something belongs: *Many ruins of Roman ~* (= of the time of ancient Rome) *are to be seen in the south of France.* ***(be/go) out of date,*** no longer used; old-fashioned: *ideas that are out of ~.* ***to date,*** so far; until now. ***up to date,*** **(a)** modern: *His methods are up to ~.* **(b)** up to the present time: *to bring a catalogue up to ~.* **3** (*informal*) social meeting arranged at a certain time and place; appointment: *I have a ~ with her next month.* **4** (*informal*) person of the other sex with whom one has a date(3). ***blind date,*** date between two people who have never met before.

date·less *adj* **(a)** endless. **(b)** timeless.

date² /deit/ *vt,vi* **1** have or put a date(1) on: *Don't forget to ~ your letters.* **2** give a date(2) to: *to ~ old coins. That suit ~s you,* shows your age (because it is old-fashioned). ⇨ 4 below. **3** ***date from/back to,*** belong to a certain period: *The castle ~s back to the 14th century,* was built then. **4** become out of date: *Isn't this textbook beginning to ~?* **5** make or go on a date(3) with.

dated *adj* out of fashion; not in current use.

date³ /deit/ *n* [C] small, brown, sweet, edible fruit of the ˈ~ *palm.*

da·tive /ˈdeitɪv/ *n* (*gram*) (in Latin and other inflected languages) form of a word showing that it is an indirect object of the verb.

datum /ˈdeitəm, ˈdætəm/ *n* (always *sing*) single bit or item of information. ⇨ data.

daub /dɔb/ *vt,vi* **1** put (paint, clay, plaster, etc) roughly on a surface: *to ~ a wall with paint.* **2** paint (pictures) without skill or artistry. **3** make dirty: *trousers ~ed with paint.* □ *n* [C,U] (covering of) soft, sticky material, eg clay.

daugh·ter /ˈdɔtər/ *n* [C] one's female child.

daughter-in-law /ˈdɔtər-ɪn-ˌlɔ/ (*pl* ~s-in-law) *n* [C] wife of one's son.

daunt /dɔnt/ *vt* discourage; make afraid.

daunt·less /ˈdɔntlɪs/ *adj* not discouraged or afraid.

davit /ˈdævɪt/ *n* [C] one of a pair of small cranes (2), curved at the top, for supporting, lowering and raising a ship's boat.

dawdle /ˈdɔdəl/ *vi,vt* be slow; waste time: *Stop dawdling and do something useful!*

daw·dler *n* [C]

dawn¹ /dɔn/ *n* [C] **1** first light of day; daybreak: *We must start at ~.* **2** (*fig*) beginning; birth: *the ~ of civilization.*

dawn² /dɔn/ *vi* **1** begin to grow light: *The day was just ~ing.* **2** begin to be seen or understood: *The truth began to ~ on him.*

day /dei/ *n* **1** [U] time between sunrise and sunset: *He has been working all (the) day. We traveled day and night/night and day without stopping.* ***by day,*** during daylight: *We traveled by day and stayed at hotels every night.* ***pass the time of day (with sb),*** exchange greetings, chat. **2** [C] period of twenty-four hours (from midnight): *There are seven days in a week.* ***day after day,*** every day, for many days together. ***day in, day out,*** continuously. ***one day,*** on a day (past or future). ***the other day,*** a few days ago. ***some day,*** some time in the future. ***one of these (fine) days,*** some day before long. **3** [C] the hours of the day given to work: *I've done a good day's work.* ***call it a day,*** stop working. **4** [C] (often *pl*) time; period. ***see better days,*** ⇨ better¹(1). ***the present day,*** the time we are now living in: *writers of the present day; in these days* (= nowadays); *in those days* (= then); *in the days of Prohibition; in days to come,* in future times. **5** ***his/her, etc day,*** lifetime; period of success, prosperity, power, etc: *Colonialism has had its day.* **6** **the day,** contest: *We've won/carried/lost the day.*

ˈday·break *n* dawn.

ˈday camp, summer camp, usually set up in the city, which children can attend during the day while sleeping home at night.

ˈday·dream *vi, n* [C] (have) idle and pleasant thoughts.

ˈday·long *adj, adv* (lasting) for the whole day.

ˈday nursery, place where small children may be left (while their mothers are at work).

ˈday school, private school at which the pupils do not board.

ˈday shift, (workers working a) period during the day.

ˈ**day·time** *n* period of daylight.

day·light /ˈdeiˌlait/ *n* [U] **1** light of day: *Can we reach our destination in* ~, before it gets dark? **2** dawn: *We must leave before* ~.

ˌ**Daylight** ˈ**Saving** ˌ**Time,** system of setting the time of day (usually) one hour ahead of Standard Time in esp the summer in order to have the use of more daylight.

daze /deiz/ *vt* make (a person) feel stupid or unable to think clearly: *He looked* ~*d with drugs/was in a* ~*d state.* □ *n* ***in a daze,*** in a bewildered condition.

dazzle /ˈdæzəl/ *vt* make (a person) unable to see clearly or act normally because of too much light, brilliance, splendor, etc; bewilder: ~*d by bright lights; dazzling opportunities.*

DC[1], **D.C.** *postal abbr* (postal usage now without periods; as *informal* name often spoken as /ˌdi ˈsi/) = District of Columbia. ➪ App 6.

DC[2], **d.c.** *abbr* (often spoken as /ˌdi ˈsi/) = direct current.

DD *abbr* = Doctor of Divinity.

DDT /ˌdi ˌdi ˈti/ *abbr* (kind of) chemical used to kill insects.

DE *postal abbr* = Delaware. ➪ App 6.

de- /di-, dɪ-/ *prefix* (used with a *v*) the negative, reverse, or opposite of: *defrost; depopulate.*

dea·con /ˈdikən/ *n* [C] **1** clergyman or layman who assists a minister or priest. **2** clergyman ranking below a bishop or priest.

dea·con·ess /ˈdikənɪs/ *n* [C] woman deacon.

dea·con·ry *n* [C] (*pl* -ies) (office of) deacons.

dead /ded/ *adj, n* **1** (of plants, animals, persons) no longer living: ~ *flowers/leaves. The hunter fired and the tiger fell* ~. ***dead duck*** (*sl*) person or thing in a failing condition or hopeless situation; goner. **2** never having had life: ~ *matter,* eg rock. **3** without movement or activity: *in the* ~ *hours of the night*, when everything is quiet. **4** (of languages, customs, etc) no longer used or observed: *a* ~ *language*. **5** (of the hands, etc) numbed, eg by cold; unable to feel anything: ~ *fingers*. ***dead to,*** unconscious of, hardened against: ~ *to the world,* (*fig*) fast asleep. **6** complete; abrupt; exact: *a* ~ *stop;* ~ *silence;* ~ *center; a* ~ *loss.* **7** that can no longer be used: *The telephone went* ~, did not transmit sounds. **8** (of sound) dull, heavy. **9** (of colors) lacking brilliance. **10** out of play: *a* ~ *ball.* □ *adv* completely; absolutely; thoroughly: ~ˈ*tired;* ~ ˈ*certain*/ˈ*sure;* ~ˈ*drunk*; ~ *ahead,* directly ahead. *You're* ~ *right!*

ˌ**dead** ˈ**end, (a)** street that is closed at one end. **(b)** point beyond which progress is impossible.

dead-end *adj*

ˌ**dead** ˈ**heat,** (*sl*) tie; even finish (esp in racing).

ˌ**dead** ˈ**letter,** one which cannot be delivered by the postal service because of a faulty address, etc.

ˈ**dead·line** *n* [C] fixed date for finishing (doing) something.

ˈ**dead·pan** *adj* (of a face) showing no emotion.

ˌ**dead** ˈ**ringer,** (*sl*) exact look-alike: *He's a* ~ *ringer for my uncle.*

dead·beat /ˈdedˌbit/ *n* [C] (*informal*) person who fails to pay his debts.

deaden /ˈdedən/ *vt* take away, deprive of, strength, feeling, etc: *drugs to* ~ *the pain; thick walls that* ~ *the noise.*

dead·lock /ˈdedˌlak/ *n* [C,U] stop or standstill because of failure to reach an agreement, to settle a quarrel or grievance.

dead·ly /ˈdedli/ *adj* (-ier, -iest) **1** causing, likely to cause, death: ~ *weapons/poison.* **2** filled with hate: ~ *enemies.* **3** that may result in damnation: *the seven* ~ *sins.* **4** like that of death: *a* ~ *paleness.* □ *adv* like that of death: ~ *pale.*

deaf /def/ *adj* (-er, -est) **1** partly or completely unable to hear: *to become* ~. **2** unwilling to listen: ~ *to all advice/entreaty. He turned a* ~ *ear to* (= refused to listen to) *our requests for help.*

ˈ**deaf-mute** *n* [C] deaf person who has not learned to speak.

deaf·ness /-nɪs/ *n* [U]

deafen /ˈdefən/ *vt* **1** make deaf. **2** make so much noise that hearing is difficult or impossible: *We were almost* ~*ed by the uproar. There were* ~*ing cheers when the speaker finished.*

deal[1] /diəl/ *n* [U] large or considerable quantity; quite a lot: *He has had to spend a good* ~ *of money on medicines. I have taken a great* ~ *of trouble over the work.* □ *adv* very much, often: *They see each other a great* ~.

deal[2] /diəl/ *n* [C] **1** (in games) distribution of playing cards: *It's your* ~. ***a raw deal,*** ➪ raw(6). **2** business transaction or agreement; (*informal*) bargain: *I'll make a* ~ *with you,* make a bargain. ***No deal!*** (*informal*) I/We refuse your offer!

deal[3] /diəl/ *vt,vi* (*pres p* -ing /ˈdilɪŋ/) (*pt,pp* ~t /delt/) **1** give out (shares) to a number of persons: *The money must be* ~*t out fairly. Who* ~*t the cards?* **2** give: *to* ~ *a fatal blow*. **3** do business: *Do you* ~ *with Smith, the butcher?* ***deal in sth,*** stock, sell: *a store that* ~*s in goods of all sorts.* **4** ***deal with,*** **(a)** have relations with: *That man is easy/difficult/impossible to* ~ *with.* **(b)** behave toward: *How would you* ~ *with an armed burglar?* **(c)** (of affairs) manage; attend to: *How shall we* ~ *with this problem?* **(d)** be about; be concerned with: *a book* ~*ing with West Africa.*

dealer /ˈdilər/ *n* [C] **1** person who deals out playing cards. **2** trader: *a* ˈ*car* ~.

deal·ing /ˈdilɪŋ/ *n* **1** [U] conduct; behavior towards others: *He is well known for fair* ~. **2** (*pl*) business relations: *I've always found him honest in his* ~*s with me.*

dealt *pt,pp* of deal[3].

dean /din/ *n* [C] **1** clergyman at the head of a cathedral chapter. **2** (in a school, college or university) faculty member in charge of students. **3** head of a division, college, etc of a university.

dear /dɪr/ *adj* (-er, -est) **1** loved; lovable: *What a* ~ *little child!* **2** (used as a form of address at the beginning of letters): *Dear Madam/Sir; Dear Mr. Green.* **3** high in price; expensive: *Everything is getting* ~*er.* **4** precious (to); greatly valued: *He lost everything that was* ~ *to him.* □ *adv* at a high cost: *If you want to make money, you must buy cheap and sell* ~. □ *n* [C] **1** lovable person: *Isn't she a* ~*!* **2** (used to address a person): *"Yes,* ~*."* □ *int* (used to express surprise, impatience, wonder, dismay, etc): *Oh* ~*! Dear me!*

dear·ly *adv* **1** very much: *He would ~ly love to see his mother again. He loves his mother ~ly.* **2** at great cost: *Victory was ~ly bought*, eg when hundreds of soldiers were killed.
dear·ness /-nɪs/ *n* [U]
dearth /dərθ/ *n* [U] scarcity; too small a supply: *a ~ of food.* ⇨ shortage, the usual word.
death /deθ/ *n* [C,U] **1** dying; ending of life: *There have been several ~s from drowning here this summer. Two children were burnt to ~ in the fire.* ***to death,*** to a very great degree: *bored him to death,* bored him extremely. **2** killing or being killed: *The murderer was sentenced to ~,* to be executed. ***put to death,*** kill. **3** [U] state of being dead: *lie still in ~.* ***(a fate) worse than death,*** to be greatly dreaded. **4** ***be the death of sb,*** be the cause of his death: *That old motorcycle will be the ~ of you.* **5** (*fig*) destruction; end: *the ~ of one's hopes/plans.*
ˈdeath·bed *n* on which one dies: *She's on her ~bed,* is dying.
the ˈdeath penalty, punishment by death.
ˌdeath ˈrow, part of a prison holding those condemned to death.
death·ly /ˈdeθli/ *adj* like death: *a ~ stillness.* □ *adv* like death: *~ pale.*
deb /deb/ *n* [C] *informal* (short for) debutante.
de·bar /diˈbar/ *vt* (-rr-) shut out; prevent a person (from doing or having something): *~ persons who have been convicted of crime from voting at elections.*
de·bark /diˈbark/ *vt,vi* = disembark.
de·bar·kation /ˌdibarˈkeiʃən/ *n* [C,U] = disembarkation.
de·base /diˈbeis/ *vt* make lower in value, poorer in quality, character, etc: *to ~ the coinage*, eg by reducing the percentage of silver.
de·base·ment *n* [U]
de·bat·able /diˈbeitəbəl/ *adj* open to question or debate.
de·bate /diˈbeit/ *n* [C,U] **1** formal discussion, eg at a public meeting, in which arguments for and against a question are given. **2** contest between two speakers, or two groups of speakers, to show skill and ability in arguing. □ *vt,vi* have a debate about; think over in order to decide: *We were debating whether to go to the mountains or to the seaside.*
de·bater *n* [C] one who debates.
de·bauch /diˈbɔtʃ/ *vt* cause a person to lose virtue, to act immorally; □ *n* [C] occasion of excessive drinking, immoral behavior: *a drunken ~.*
de·bauch·ery /diˈbɔtʃəri/ *n* **(a)** [U] excessive eating, drinking, etc: *a life of ~ery.* **(b)** [C] (*pl* -ies) instances of this.
de·bili·tate /diˈbɪləˌteit/ *vt* make (a person, his constitution) weak: *a debilitating climate.*
de·bil·ity /diˈbɪləti/ *n* [U] weakness (of health, purpose): *After her long illness she is suffering from general ~.*
debit /ˈdebɪt/ *n* **1** (*bookkeeping*) entry (in an account) of a sum owing. **2** (also **ˈdebit side**) left-hand side of an account, on which such entries are made. □ *vt* put on the debit side of an account: *~ a person's account* (*with $10*).
de·brief /ˌdiˈbrif/ *vt* question (a diplomat, spy, former hostage, etc) to get esp tactical information.
de·brief·ing *n* [C]
de·bris /dəˈbri/ *n* [U] scattered broken pieces; wreckage: *searching among the ~ after the explosion.*
debt /det/ *n* [C,U] something owed; obligation: *If I pay all my ~s I shall have no money left. I owe him a ~ of gratitude for all he has done for me.* ***in/out of debt,*** owing/not owing money to others.
debtor /-tər/ *n* [C] person who is in debt to another.
de·bunk /diˈbəŋk/ *vt, vi* expose (a fraud, fallacy, etc).
debut /ˈdeiˌbyu, deiˈbyu/ *n* [C] (of an actor, musician, etc) first appearance on a public stage: *to make one's ~.*
debu·tante /ˈdebyʊˌtant/ *n* [C] upper-class girl making her first appearance in society.
Dec. *abbr* = December.
dec·ade /ˈdeˌkeid/ *n* [C] period of ten years: *the first ~ of the 20th century*, ie 1900-1909 or 1901-1910.
deca·dence /ˈdekədəns/ *n* [U] falling to a lower level (in morals, art, literature, etc, esp after a period at a high level).
deca·dent /ˈdekədənt/ *adj* in a state of decadence. □ *n* [C] person in this state.
deca·dent·ly *adv*
de·camp /diˈkæmp/ *vi* go away suddenly (and often secretly).
de·cant /diˈkænt/ *vt* pour (wine, etc) from a bottle into another vessel slowly so as not to disturb the sediment.
de·canter *n* [C] vessel, usually of glass with a stopper, used for serving wine, etc.
de·capi·tate /diˈkæpəˌteit/ *vt* behead.
de·cay /diˈkei/ *vi* go bad; lose power, health: *~ing teeth/vegetables.* □ *n* [U] decaying. ***in decay,*** in a state of decay: *The house is in ~.*
de·cease /dɪˈsis/ *n* (esp *legal*) (a person's) death. □ *vi* die.
the deceased, person(s) recently dead.
de·ceit /dɪˈsit/ *n* **1** [U] causing a person to accept as true or genuine something that is false: *She is incapable of ~,* would never tell lies, etc. **2** [C] lie; dishonest trick.
de·ceit·ful /dɪˈsitfəl/ *adj* **1** in the habit of deceiving. **2** intended to deceive; misleading in appearance, etc: *~ words/acting.*
de·ceit·fully *adv*
de·ceit·ful·ness /-nɪs/ *n* [U]
de·ceive /dɪˈsiv/ *vt* cause a person to believe something that is false; play a trick on; mislead (on purpose): *You can't pass the examination without working hard, so don't ~ yourself.*
de·ceiver *n* [C] person who deceives.
De·cem·ber /diˈsembər/ *n* twelfth month of the year.
de·cency /ˈdisənsi/ *n* [U] (the quality of) being decent; conforming to the general opinion as to what is decent: *an offense against ~,* eg appearing naked in public.
de·cent /ˈdisənt/ *adj* **1** right and suitable; respectful: *Put on some ~ clothes before you call on the Smiths.* **2** modest; not likely to shock or

embarrass others: *~ language and behavior.* (*Note:* this is the only sense for which *indecent* is the opposite.) **3** fairly good; satisfactory: *He earns a ~ salary. Lending me the money was very ~ of her.*

de·cent·ly *adv*

de·cen·tra·lize /diˈsentrəˌlaiz/ *vt* give greater powers (for self-government, etc) to (places, branches, etc away from the center).

de·cen·tra·liz·ation /diˌsentrəlɪˈzeiʃən/ *n* [U]

de·cep·tion /dɪˈsepʃən/ *n* **1** [U] deceiving; being deceived: *to practice ~ on the public.* **2** [C] trick intended to deceive: *a gross ~.*

de·cep·tive /dɪˈseptɪv/ *adj* deceiving: *Appearances are often ~.*

de·cep·tive·ly *adv*

deci·bel /ˈdesəˌbel, ˈdesəbəl/ *n* [C] unit for measuring the relative loudness of sounds.

de·cide /dɪˈsaid/ *vt,vi* **1** settle (a question or a doubt); give a judgment: *The judge ~d the case. It's difficult to ~ between the two. The judge ~d for/in favor of/against the plaintiff.* **2** think about and come to a conclusion; make up one's mind: *The boy ~d not to/~d that he would not become a pilot. In the end she ~d to buy it. We ~d against going/~d not to go.* **3** cause to decide (2): *What ~d you to give up your job?*

de·cided *adj* **1** clear; definite: *There is a ~d difference between them.* **2** (of persons) determined: *He's quite ~d about it.*

de·cid·ed·ly *adv* definitely; undoubtedly: *~dly better.*

de·cidu·ous /dɪˈsɪdʒuəs/ *adj* (of trees) losing their leaves annually (esp in autumn). ⇨ evergreen.

deci·mal /ˈdesəməl/ *adj* of tens or one-tenths: *the ˈ~ system,* for money, weights, etc; *a ~ fraction,* eg 0.091; *the ~ point,* the point in 15.61.

deci·mate /ˈdesəˌmeit/ *vt* kill or destroy one-tenth or a large part of: *a population ~d by disease.*

de·cipher /dɪˈsaifər/ *vt* find the meaning of (something written in code, bad handwriting, etc).

de·cipher·able *adj*

de·ci·sion /dɪˈsɪʒən/ *n* **1 (a)** [U] deciding; judging. **(b)** [C] result of this; settlement of a question: *give a ~ on a case. Have they reached/come to/arrived at/made a ~ yet?* **2** [U] ability to decide and act accordingly; determination: *He lacks ~,* hesitates, cannot decide questions.

de·cis·ive /dɪˈsaisɪv/ *adj* **1** having the ability or power to decide; *a ~ battle,* deciding which side wins the war. **2** showing decision(2); definite: *He gave a ~ answer.*

de·cis·ive·ly *adv*

deck[1] /dek/ *n* [C] **1** any of the floors of a ship, in or above the hull: *My cabin is on E ~. Shall we go up on ~?* **2** any similar surface, eg the floor of an aircraft. **3** pack of playing cards. **4** level, layer (esp where there is more than one). ⇨ decker below. **5** (also **casˈsette deck** or **ˈtape deck**) cassette or tape recorder (without speakers or amplifiers) as a component in a hi-fi system.

ˈdeck chair, collapsible chair of canvas or plastic on a wooden or metal frame, used out of doors, eg in parks, on the beach.

-decker *n* (in compounds) with a specified number of decks: *a three-~er,* ship with three ~s; *single/double-ˈ~er bus; double-/triple-decker sandwiches.*

ˈdeck·hand *n* [C] member of a ship's crew who works on deck.

deck[2] /dek/ *vt* **1** decorate: *streets ~ed with flags.* **2** cover, provide (a boat, ship) with a deck.

de·claim /diˈkleim/ *vi,vt* speak in the manner of addressing an audience or reciting poetry.

dec·la·ma·tion /ˌdekləˈmeiʃən/ *n* **1** [U] declaiming. **2** [C] formal speech.

de·clama·tory /dɪˈklæməˌtɔri/ *adj*

dec·lar·ation /ˌdekləˈreiʃn/ *n* **1** [U] declaring. **2** [C] that which is declared: *a ~ of war; a ~ of income.*

ˌDeclaration of Indeˈpendence, that made by the North American colonies of Great Britain, on July 4, 1776, that they were politically independent.

de·clare /dɪˈklær/ *vt,vi* **1** make known clearly or formally; announce: *to ~ the results of an election. I ~ this meeting closed.* ***declare war (on/against),*** announce that a state of war exists. **2** say solemnly; say in order to show that one has no doubt: *The accused man ~d that he was not guilty.* **3** ***declare for/against,*** say that one is/is not in favor of. **4** make a statement (to government officials) of one's dutiable goods or of one's income: *Have you anything to ~?*

de·clar·able /dɪˈklærəbəl/ *adj* that must be declared(4).

de·class·ify /ˌdiˈklæsəˌfai/ *vt* (*pt, pp* -ied) remove from a particular (esp security) classification: *~ information concerning nuclear weapons.*

de·class·ifi·cation /ˌdiˌklæsəfɪˈkeiʃən/ *n* [U]

de·clen·sion /dɪˈklenʃən/ *n* (*gram*) **1** [U] varying the endings of *nouns, pronouns,* and *adjectives* according to their use in a sentence. **2** [C] class of nouns, etc whose endings for the different cases are of the same type.

de·cline[1] /dɪˈklain/ *n* [C] declining; gradual and continued loss of strength: *the ~ of the Roman Empire; a ~ in prices/prosperity.*

de·cline[2] /dɪˈklain/ *vt,vi* **1** say "No" (to); refuse (something offered): *to ~ an invitation to dinner; ~d to attend the meeting.* **2** become smaller, weaker, lower: *a declining birthrate; declining sales.* **3** (of the sun) go down. **4** give the cases of (a noun, etc).

de·code /ˌdiˈkoud/ *vt* decipher (a code).

de·com·pose /ˌdikəmˈpouz/ *vt,vi* **1** separate (a substance, light, etc) into its parts: *A prism ~s light.* **2** become bad or rotten; decay.

de·com·po·si·tion /diˌkampəˈzɪʃən/ *n* [U]

de·cor /deiˈkɔr/ *n* [C] (usually *sing*) decorating arrangement, eg of a room or the stage setting of a theater.

dec·o·rate /ˈdekəˌreit/ *vt* **1** put ornaments on; make (more) beautiful by placing adornments on or in, or by furnishing, painting, papering, etc the rooms (of a building): *to ~ a street with flags/the house with antiques.* **2** give (a person) an honor or award (eg a medal): *Several soldiers were ~d for bravery.*

dec·o·ra·tion /ˌdekəˈreiʃən/ *n* **1** [U] decorating or being decorated. **2** [C] thing used for decorating: *Christmas ~s.* **3** [C] medal, ribbon, etc given and worn as an honor or award.

dec·o·rative /ˈdekəˌreitɪv/ *adj* suitable for decorating(1): *Holly, with its bright red berries, is very ~.*

dec·o·rator /ˈdekəˌreitər/ *n* [C] person who decorates(1), esp the interiors of buildings.

dec·o·rous /ˈdekərəs/ *adj* correct; proper; dignified.

de·co·rum /dɪˈkɔrəm/ *n* [U] proper behavior; dignity.

de·coy /ˈdiˌkɔi/ *n* [C] **1** (real or imitation) bird (eg a duck) or animal used to attract others so that they may be shot or caught. **2** (*fig*) person or thing used to lure somebody into a trap. □ *vt* /diˈkɔi/ trick or trap by means of a decoy: *He had been ~ed across the frontier and arrested as a spy.*

de·crease /diˈkris/ *vt,vi* (cause to) become shorter, smaller, less: *The population of the town has ~d from 1,000 to 500.* □ *n* /ˈdiˌkris/ **1** [U] decreasing. **2** [C] amount by which something decreases: *There has been a ~ in our imports this year.*

de·cree /diˈkri/ *n* [C] **1** order given by a ruler or authority and having the force of a law: *issue a ~; rule by ~.* **2** judgment or decision of some law courts: *a ~ of divorce.* □ *vt,vi* command or order by decree: *It had been ~d that....*

de·crepit /diˈkrepɪt/ *adj* made weak by old age or hard use: *a ~ horse.*

de·cry /diˈkrai/ *vt* (*pt,pp* -ied) **1** try, by speaking against something, to make it seem less valuable, useful, etc. **2** condemn.

dedi·cate /ˈdedɪˌkeit/ *vt* **1** give up, devote (one's time, energy, etc, to a noble cause or purpose): *He ~d his life to the service of his country.* **2** devote with solemn ceremonies (to God, to a sacred use). **3** (of an author) write (or print) a person's name at the beginning of a book (to show gratitude or friendship to).

dedi·ca·tion /ˌdedɪˈkeiʃən/ *n* **(a)** [U] dedicating: *the dedication of a church.* **(b)** [C] words used in dedicating a book.

de·duce /diˈdus/ *vt* arrive at (knowledge, a theory, etc) by reasoning; reach a conclusion: *If you saw a doctor leaving a house, you might ~ the fact that someone in the house was ill.*

de·duct /diˈdəkt/ *vt* take away (an amount or part) from a total.

de·duc·tion /diˈdəkʃən/ *n* **1** [U] deducting. **2** [C] amount deducted: *~s from pay for insurance and taxes.* **3** [U] deducing. **4** [C] conclusion reached by reasoning from general laws to a particular case. ⇨ induction.

de·duc·tive /dɪˈdəktɪv/ *adj* (of reasoning) based on deduction (3).

deed /did/ *n* [C] **1** something done; act: *Deeds are better than promises.* **2** (*legal*) written or printed signed document, esp about ownership.

dee·jay /ˈdiˌdʒei/ (originally and sometimes still **DJ**) *n* [C] (*sl*) disc jockey. ⇨ disc.

deep[1] /dip/ *adj* (-er, -est) **1** going a long way down from the top: *a ~ well/river.* **2** going a long way from the surface or edge: *a ~ wound.* **3** (*fig*) serious; not superficial: *a ~ thinker; ~ insight.* **4** placed or extending down, back or in (with words to indicate extent): *a hole two feet ~; to be ~ in debt.* **5** (of sounds) low: *in a ~ voice.* **6** (of sleep) profound: *in a ~ sleep,* from which one is not easily awakened. **7** (of colors) strong; intense: *a ~ red.* **8** brought from far down: *a ~ sigh,* strongly felt. *~ sorrow/feelings/sympathy.* **9** ***deep in,*** absorbed in; having all one's attention centered on: *~ in thought/study/a book.* **10** (*fig*) difficult to understand or learn about: *a ~ mystery.*

deepen /ˈdipən/ *vt,vi* make or become deep.

deep·ly *adv* intensely: *He is ~ly interested in the subject.*

deep·ness /-nɪs/ *n* [U]

deep[2] /dip/ *adv* far down or in: *We had to dig ~ to find water.*

ˌdeep-ˈfreeze *vt* (*pt* ~froze /-ˈfrouz/, *pp* ~frozen /-ˈfrouzən/) freeze (food) quickly in order to preserve it for long periods: *~-frozen fish.*

ˈdeep-rooted, not easily removed; firmly established: *his ~-rooted dislike of hard work.*

ˈdeep-seated, = deep-rooted: *The causes of the trouble are ~-seated.*

deep[3] /dip/ *n* **the deep,** (*poet*) the sea.

deer /dɪr/ *n* [C] (*pl* unchanged) (kinds of) graceful, quick-running animal, the male of which has horns.

ˈdeer·skin *n* (leather made of) deer's skin.

de-esca·late /ˌdi-ˈeskəˌleit/ *vt* decrease the area or intensity of, eg a war.

def. *abbr* = definition(2).

de·face /diˈfeis/ *vt* spoil the appearance of (by marking or damaging the surface of).

de·face·ment *n* [C,U]

de·fame /diˈfeim/ *vt* attack the good reputation of; say evil things about.

defa·ma·tion /ˌdefəˈmeiʃən/ *n* [C,U] (act of) defaming or being defamed.

de·fama·tory /dɪˈfæməˌtɔri/ *adj*

de·fault[1] /dɪˈfɔlt/ *n* [U] defaulting: *to win a case/a game by ~,* because the other party (team, player, etc) does not appear. ***in default of,*** in the absence of.

de·faulter *n* [C]

de·fault[2] /dɪˈfɔlt/ *vi* fail to perform a duty, or to appear (eg in a law court) when required to do so, or to pay a debt.

de·feat /dɪˈfit/ *vt* **1** overcome; win a victory over: *to ~ another school at football.* **2** make useless; cause to fail: *Our hopes were ~ed.* □ *n* **1** [U] defeating or being defeated: *Our team has not yet suffered ~.* **2** [C] instance of this: *six victories and two ~s.*

def·e·cate /ˈdefəˌkeit/ *vt,vi* pass waste from the bowels.

def·e·ca·tion, /ˌdefəˈkeiʃən/ *n* [U]

de·fect[1] /ˈdifekt/ *n* [C] fault; imperfection; lack of something required for completeness or perfection: *~s in a system of education.*

de·fect[2] /diˈfekt/ *vi* desert one's country, one's allegiance, etc: *the ballerina who ~ed to the West,* eg by asking for political asylum.

de·fec·tion /diˈfekʃən/ *n* [C,U]

de·fec·tor /-tər/ *n* [C]

de·fec·tive /dɪˈfektɪv/ *adj* imperfect; faulty: *~ in workmanship/moral sense.*
de·fec·tive·ly *adv*
de·fec·tive·ness /-nɪs/ *n* [U]
de·fend /dɪˈfend/ *vt* **1** guard; protect from danger: *to ~ one's country against enemies.* **2** speak or write in support of: *~* (= uphold) *a claim; ~ an accused person in court.*
de·fen·dant /dɪˈfendənt/ *n* [C] person against whom a legal action is brought. ⇨ plaintiff.
de·fender /dɪˈfendər/ *n* **1** person who defends. **2** (*sport*) player who guards his area against attacks from the other side.
de·fense /dɪˈfens/ **1** [U] defending from attack; fighting against attack: *money needed for national ~.* **2** [C] something that defends or protects; means of defending: *People used to build strong walls around their towns as a ~ against enemies.* **3** [C,U] (*legal*) **(a)** argument(s) used to contest an accusation: *The accused man made no ~.* **(b)** (*collect*) the lawyer(s) acting for an accused person.
de·fense·less *adj* without defense; unprotected.
de·fense·less·ly *adv*
de·fense·less·ness /-nɪs/ *n* [U]
de·fen·sible /dɪˈfensəbəl/ *adj* able to be defended.
de·fen·sive /dɪˈfensɪv/ *adj* used for, intended for, defending: *~ warfare/measures.* □ *n* ***be on the defensive,*** state or position of defense.
de·fen·sive·ly *adv*
de·fer[1] /dɪˈfər/ *vt* (-rr-) **1** put off to a later time: *to ~ one's departure for a week.* **2** grant a delay in being drafted(2).
de·fer·ment *n* [C] act of deferring(2).
de·fer[2] /dɪˈfər/ *vi* (-rr-) give way; yield (often to show respect): *to ~ to one's elders/to his opinions.*
de·fer·ence /ˈdef(ə)rəns/ *n* [U] giving way to the wishes, accepting the opinions or judgments, of another or others; respect: *to show ~ to a judge.* ***in deference to,*** out of respect for.
de·fer·en·tial /ˌdefəˈrenʃəl/ *adj* showing respect.
de·fer·en·tially *adv*
de·fiance /dɪˈfaiəns/ *n* [U] open disobedience or resistance; refusal to recognize authority; defying. ***in defiance of,*** showing contempt or disregard: *to act in ~ of orders.*
de·fiant /dɪˈfaiənt/ *adj* showing defiance; openly disobedient.
de·fiant·ly *adv*
de·fi·ciency /dɪˈfɪʃənsi/ *n* (*pl* -ies) **1** [U] the state of being short of, less than, what is correct or needed. **2** [C] instance of this: *suffering from a ~ of food.* **3** [C] amount by which something is short of what is required or needed: *a ~ of $15.* **4** [C] something imperfect: *Cosmetics do not always cover up the deficiencies of nature.*
de·ficient /dɪˈfɪʃənt/ *adj* not having enough of: *~ in courage; a mentally ~ person,* one who is mentally subnormal.
defi·cit /ˈdefəsɪt/ *n* [C] amount by which something, esp a sum of money, is too small; amount by which expenses exceed income.
de·file /dɪˈfaiəl/ *vt* (*pres p* defiling /dɪˈfailɪŋ/) make dirty or impure: *rivers ~d by waste from factories; to ~ one's mind.*
de·fine /dɪˈfain/ *vt* **1** state the meaning of (eg words). **2** state or show clearly: *The powers of a judge are ~d by law.* **3** fix or mark the limits of.
de·fin·able *adj*
defi·nite /ˈdefənɪt/ *adj* **1** clear; not doubtful or uncertain: *I want a ~ answer: "Yes" or "No."* **2** having distinct limits: *a ~ period of time.* **the ˌdefinite ˈarticle,** the word *"the."*
defi·nite·ly *adv* **(a)** in a definite manner. **(b)** (*informal*) (in answer to a question) yes, certainly.
defi·ni·tion /ˌdefəˈnɪʃən/ *n* **1** [U] defining. **2** [C] statement that defines: *To give a ~ of a word is more difficult than you think.* **3** [U] clearness of outline. **4** [U] (action or power of) making clear and distinct.
de·fini·tive /dɪˈfɪnətɪv/ *adj* decisive; without the need for, or possibility of, change or addition: *a ~ offer/answer.*
de·flate /dɪˈfleit/ *vt* **1** make (a tire, balloon, etc) smaller by letting out air or gas. **2** (*fig*) lessen the conceit of: *~ a pompous politician.* **3** take action to lower or keep steady the prices of salable goods. ⇨ inflate.
de·fla·tion /diˈfleiʃən/ *n* [U] **(a)** act of deflating; state of being deflated. **(b)** continuing decrease in the price of goods and services.
de·fla·tion·ary /-əˌneri/ *adj* of, caused by, deflation.
de·flect /dɪˈflekt/ *vt,vi* (cause to) turn aside (from): *The bullet struck a wall and was ~ed from its course.*
de·flec·tion /dɪˈflekʃən/ *n* [C,U]
de·foli·ate /diˈfouliˌeit/ *vt* cause (a tree, plant) to lose its leaves, esp by chemical means.
de·form /dɪˈfɔrm/ *vt* spoil the form or appearance of; put out of shape.
de·formed *adj* badly or unnaturally shaped: *The boy has a ~ed foot and cannot play games.*
de·form·ity /dɪˈfɔrməti/ *n* **1** [U] being deformed. **2** [C] (*pl* -ies) deformed part (esp of the body).
de·fraud /dɪˈfrɔd/ *vt* trick (a person) out of what is rightly his.
de·fray /dɪˈfrei/ *vt* supply the money needed; pay (the expenses) for something.
de·frayal *n* [U]
de·frost /dɪˈfrɔst/ *vt,vi* **1** remove, get rid of, ice, frost, or condensation (eg in a refrigerator, on the windshield of an automobile, etc). **2** thaw out.
de·froster *n* [C] mechanism, etc that defrosts.
deft /deft/ *adj* quick and clever (esp with the fingers).
deft·ly *adv*
deft·ness /-nɪs/ *n* [U]
de·funct /dɪˈfəŋkt/ *adj* dead; no longer in existence.
de·fuse /diˈfyuz/ *vt* remove or make useless the fuse of eg an unexploded bomb or shell.
defy /diˈfai/ *vt* (*pt,pp* -ied) **1** resist openly; refuse to obey or show respect to: *to ~ one's superiors.* **2** have the power to resist; withstand: *The problem defied solution,* could not be solved. **3** = dare[2](3) (the usual word).
deg. *abbr* = degree(1,2).

de·gen·er·ate[1] /dɪˈdʒenərɪt, di-/ *adj* having been degraded: *He didn't let riches and luxury make him ~.* □ *n* [C] degenerate person or animal.

de·gen·er·ate[2] /dɪˈdʒenəˌreit, di-/ *vi* pass from a higher to a lower state; decline or grow worse in physical, moral or mental qualities: *Young people of today are not degenerating*, eg not becoming less hardworking, less honest, than those of earlier times.

de·grade /dɪˈgreid, di-/ *vt* **1** reduce in rank or status. **2** cause to be less moral or less deserving of respect: *to ~ oneself by cheating and telling lies.*

degra·da·tion /ˌdegrəˈdeiʃən/ *n* [U] degrading or being degraded.

de·gree /dɪˈgri/ *n* [C] **1** unit of measurement for angles: *an angle of ninety ~s,* (90°) a right angle; *a ~ of latitude*, about 69 miles. **2** unit of measurement for temperature: *Water freezes at 32 ~s Fahrenheit* (32°F) *or zero Centigrade* (0°C). **3** step or stage in a scale or process: *The students showed various ~s of skill in their use of carpentry tools. He was not in the slightest ~ interested*, was completely uninterested. ***by degrees,*** gradually: *Their friendship grew by ~s into love.* ***to a high/the highest degree,*** intensively; exceedingly. **4** position in society: *persons of high ~.* **5** academic title; rank or grade given by a university to one who has finished a certain course of study: *studying for a ~; the ~ of Master of Arts* (MA). **6** (*music*) interval from one note to another on a staff. **7** (*gram*) each of the three levels of comparison of an *adjective* or *adverb*: *"Good," "better," and "best" are the positive, comparative, and superlative ~s of "good."*

ˌthird deˈgree, severe and long examination (eg by the police) of an accused person to get information or a confession.

de·hu·mid·ify /ˌdi(h)yuˈmɪdəˌfai/ *vt* (*pt,pp* -ied) remove moisture from (the air, etc).

de·hy·drate /diˈhaiˌdreit/ *vt* remove water or moisture from (a substance): *~d vegetables.*

de·ice /ˌdiˈais/ *vt* free, eg the surfaces of an aircraft, from ice.

de·icer *n* [C] mechanism, etc that deices.

de·ify /ˈdiəˌfai/ *vt* make a god of; worship as a god.

deign /dein/ *vi* (*liter*) consider fit or suitable to one's dignity: *He passed by without ~ing to look at me.*

de·ity /ˈdiəti/ *n* (*pl* -ies) **1** [U] divine quality or nature of a god or goddess. **2** [C] god or goddess: *Roman deities,* eg Neptune, Minerva. **3 the Deity,** God.

de·ject·ed /dɪˈdʒektɪd/ *adj* sad or gloomy: *Why is she looking so ~*, in such low spirits?

de·ject·ed·ly *adv*

de·jec·tion /dɪˈdʒekʃən/ *n* [U] dejected state; low spirits: *He left in ~.*

de·lay /dɪˈlei/ *vt,vi* **1** make or be slow or late: *The train was ~ed two hours.* **2** put off until later: *Why have they ~ed opening the new school?* □ *n* **1** [U] delaying or being delayed: *We must leave without ~.* **2** [C] instance, time, of this: *after a ~ of three hours.*

de·lec·table /dɪˈlektəbəl/ *adj* delightful; pleasant.

del·egate[1] /ˈdelɪgɪt, ˈdelɪˌgeit/ *n* [C] person to whom something is delegated (eg an elected representative sent to a conference or convention).

del·ega·tion /ˌdelɪˈgeiʃən/ *n* **(a)** [U] delegating or being delegated. **(b)** [C] group of delegates.

del·egate[2] /ˈdelɪˌgeit/ *vt* **1** appoint and send as a representative to a meeting. **2** entrust (one's duties, rights, etc) to another: *to ~ her to perform a task.*

de·lete /dɪˈlit/ *vt* strike or take out (something written or printed): *Several words had been ~d by the editor.*

de·le·tion /dɪˈliʃən/ *n* **(a)** [U] deleting. **(b)** [C] instance of this.

deli, delly /ˈdeli/ *n* [C] (*informal*) (short for) delicatessen.

de·lib·er·ate[1] /diˈlɪb(ə)rɪt/ *adj* **1** done on purpose; intentional: *a ~ lie/insult.* **2** slow and cautious (in action, speech, etc): *He entered the room with ~ steps.*

de·lib·er·ate·ly *adv*

de·lib·er·ate[2] /diˈlɪbəˌreit/ *vt,vi* (*formal*) consider, talk about, carefully: *We were deliberating what to do/whether to buy a new automobile.*

de·lib·er·ation /diˌlɪbəˈreiʃən/ *n* (*formal*) **1** [C,U] careful consideration and discussion; debate: *After long ~, she decided to go to medical school.* **2** [U] being deliberate(2); slowness of movement: *to speak/take aim with great ~.*

deli·cacy /ˈdelɪkəsi/ *n* (*pl* -ies) **1** [U] quality of being delicate (all senses): *The political situation is one of great ~*, requires very careful handling. **2** [C] rare and choice kind of food: *all the delicacies of the season.*

deli·cate /ˈdelɪkɪt/ *adj* **1** soft; tender; of fine or thin material: *the ~ skin of a young baby.* **2** fine; exquisite: *jewelry of ~ workmanship.* **3** easily injured; becoming ill easily; needing great care: *~ china/plants; a ˈ~-looking child.* **4** requiring careful treatment or skillful handling: *a ~ surgical operation.* **5** pleasing to the senses; mild, soft; not strong: *a ~ shade of pink. Some kinds of fish have a more ~ flavor than others.* **6** able to sense very small changes or differences: *the ~ instruments needed by scientists*, eg for weighing or measuring. **7** considerate; taking great care not to hurt the feelings of others.

deli·cate·ly *adv*

deli·ca·tes·sen /ˌdelɪkəˈtesən/ *n* [C,U] (shop selling) prepared foods ready for serving (esp cooked meat, salads, etc).

de·li·cious /dɪˈlɪʃəs/ *adj* giving delight (esp to the senses of taste and smell): *a ~ cake.*

de·li·cious·ly *adv*

de·light[1] /dɪˈlait/ *n* **1** [U] great pleasure; joy: *To his great ~ he passed the examination.* ***take delight in,*** find pleasure in: *The mean boy took great ~ in pulling the cat's tail.* **2** [C] cause or source of great pleasure: *Dancing is her chief ~.*

de·light·ful *adj* giving pleasure: *a ~ful holiday.*

de·light[2] /dɪˈlait/ *vt,vi* **1** give great pleasure to; please greatly: *Her singing ~ed everyone.* ***be delighted***, be greatly pleased: *I was ~ed to hear the news of your success/~ed at the news. . ./~ed* *that you were successful.* **2** take or find great pleasure: *He* ~*s in teasing his young sister.*

de·lin·quency /dɪˈlɪŋkwənsi/ *n* (*pl* -ies) **1** [U] wrongdoing: *juvenile* ~, wrongdoing by young persons. **2** [U] neglect of duty or obligation. **3** [C] instance of wrongdoing or neglect of duty.

de·lin·quent /dɪˈlɪŋkwənt/ *n* [C], *adj* (person) doing wrong, failing to perform a duty.

de·liri·ous /dɪˈlɪriəs/ *adj* suffering from, showing, delirium; wildly excited: *The patient's temperature went up and he became* ~. *We were* ~ *with joy.*

de·liri·ous·ly *adv*

de·lirium /dɪˈlɪriəm/ *n* [U] violent mental disturbance, often accompanied by wild talk, esp during feverish illness; wild excitement.

de·liver /dɪˈlɪvər/ *vt* **1** give or hand over; convey: *Did you* ~ *my message? The sofa was* ~*ed yesterday.* **2** ***deliver from,*** (*formal*) rescue, save, set free: *May God* ~ *us from all evil.* **3** give forth in words: *to* ~ *a sermon/a course of lectures.* **4** help (a woman) to give birth. **5** surrender; give up: *to* ~ *up stolen goods; to* ~ *over one's property to one's son.* **6** send against; throw: *to* ~ *a blow in the cause of freedom.*

de·liverer *n* [C] one who delivers; rescuer.

de·liver·ance /dɪˈlɪvərəns/ *n* [U] delivering(2); rescue; being set free.

de·liv·ery /dɪˈlɪv(ə)ri/ *n* (*pl* -ies) **1** [C,U] (instance of) delivering (of letters, goods, etc): *We guarantee prompt* ~. *How many deliveries are there in your town* (= How often does the mailman deliver letters) *every day?* **2** rescue. **3** [U] manner of speaking (in lectures, etc): *His sermon was good, but his* ~ *was poor.* **4** act of giving birth. **5** act or style of throwing.

deˈlivery boy, one who works for a business, delivering purchases, etc to customers.

deˈlivery truck, = panel truck.

dell /del/ *n* [C] small valley, usually with trees.

delly /ˈdeli/ = deli.

delta /ˈdeltə/ *n* [C] (*pl* ~s) **1** the fourth letter (Δ, δ) of the Greek alphabet. **2** land in this shape (Δ) at the mouth of a river between two or more branches: *the Nile Delta.*

de·lude /dɪˈlud/ *vt* deceive; mislead (on purpose): *to* ~ *oneself with false hopes; to* ~ *him/oneself into believing that....*

del·uge /ˈdelyudʒ/ *n* [C] **1** great flood; heavy rush of water; violent rainfall. **2** anything coming in a heavy rush: *a* ~ *of words/questions/protests.* □ *vt* flood: *He was* ~*d with questions.*

de·lu·sion /dɪˈluʒən/ *n* **1** [U] deluding or being deluded. **2** [C] false opinion or belief, esp one that may be a symptom of madness: *to be under a* ~*/under the* ~ *that...; to suffer from* ~*s.*

de·lu·sive /dɪˈlusɪv/ *adj* not real; deceptive.

de·lu·sive·ly *adv*

de·luxe /diˈlʊks, diˈləks/ *adj* of very high quality, high standards of comfort, etc: *a* ~ *edition of a book.*

delve /delv/ *vt,vi* ***delve into,*** make a careful search into, eg old manuscripts: *to* ~ *into his past.*

Dem. *abbr* = **1** Democrat. **2** Democratic.

dema·gogue /ˈdeməˌgag/ *n* [C] political leader who stirs up the people by appealing to prejudices and feelings instead of to reason.

de·mand[1] /dɪˈmænd/ *n* **1** [C] **(a)** act of demanding(1). **(b)** something demanded(1): *The workers'* ~*s* (eg for higher pay) *were refused by the employers.* ***on demand,*** when demanded: *a check payable on* ~. **2** [U] (*Note:* sometimes used with *a* and an *adjective*) desire, by people ready to buy, employ, etc: *There is a great* ~ *for typists but not much* ~ *for clerks. Our goods are in great* ~.

de·mand[2] /dɪˈmænd/ *vt* **1** ask for as if ordering, or as if one has a right to: ~ *an apology from her.* **2** need; require: *This sort of work* ~*s great patience.*

de·mar·cate /ˈdimarˌkeit/ *vt* mark or fix the limits of, eg a frontier.

de·mar·ca·tion /ˌdimarˈkeiʃən/ *n* [U] marking of a boundary or limit; separation: *a line of* ~.

de·mean /dɪˈmin/ *vt* (*formal*) lower oneself in dignity, social esteem.

de·mean·or /dɪˈminər/ *n* [U] way of behaving: *I dislike his pompous* ~.

de·mented /dɪˈmentɪd/ *adj* mad; insane.

de·mented·ly *adv*

de·mer·it /diˈmerɪt/ *n* [C] **1** fault. **2** mark against a person's record because of poor work, bad behavior, etc.

de·mili·ta·rized /diˈmɪlətəˌraizd/ *adj* (of a country, or part of it) required, by treaty or agreement, to have no military forces or installation in it.

de·mise /diˈmaiz/ *n* [C] (*formal*) death.

demi·tasse /ˈdemiˌtæs, -ˌtas/ *n* [C] very small cup (of or for) black coffee.

de·mo·bi·lize /diˈmoubəˌlaiz/ *vt* discharge from military service.

de·mo·bi·liz·ation /diˌmoubələˈzeiəʃn/ *n* [U]

democ·racy /dɪˈmakrəsi/ *n* [C,U] (*pl* -ies) **1** (country with principles of) government in which all adult citizens share either directly or through their elected representatives. **2** (country with a government based on the) political power of the common people. **3** (society in which there is) treatment of citizens as equals and absence of class feeling: *Iceland has a long history of* ~.

demo·crat /ˈdeməˌkræt/ *n* [C] **1** person who favors or supports democracy. **2 Democrat,** member of the Democratic Party.

demo·cratic /ˌdeməˈkrætɪk/ *adj* **1** of, relating to, supporting the principles of a democracy (1,2). **2** (esp) of, supporting, democracy(3); treating other people as equals.

demo·crati·cally /-kli/ *adv*

the ˈDemocratic Party, one of the two main political parties in the US. ⇨ republican.

de·moc·ra·tize /dɪˈmakrəˌtaiz/ *vt* make democratic.

de·mol·ish /dɪˈmalɪʃ/ *vt* **1** pull or tear down, eg old buildings. **2** destroy, eg an argument; make an end of.

demo·li·tion /ˌdeməˈlɪʃən/ *n* **1** [U] demolishing or being demolished. **2** [C] instance of this.

de·mon /ˈdimən/ *n* [C] **1** evil, wicked or cruel supernatural being or spirit. **2** (*informal*) fierce or energetic person: *He's a* ~ *for work.*

de·mon·strable /dɪˈmanstrəbəl/ *adj* that can

be shown or proved.

de·mon·strably *adv*

dem·on·strate /ˈdemənˌstreit/ *vt,vi* **1** show clearly, esp by giving proof(s) or evidence: *How would you ~ that the world is round?* **2** take part in a demonstration(2): *The workers marched through the streets carrying banners to ~ against the rising cost of living.*

dem·on·stra·tion /ˌdemənˈstreiʃən/ *n* [C,U] **1** demonstrating(1): *a ~ of affection*, eg when a child puts its arms round its mother's neck. **2** public gathering, meeting, etc to display feeling for a cause: *a ~ that ended in violence.*

de·mon·stra·tive /dɪˈmanstrətɪv/ *adj* **1** showing or marked by open expression of the feelings: *Some children are more ~ than others. ~ behavior.* **2** serving to point out.

de·mon·stra·tive·ly *adv*

deˌmonstrative ˈpronoun, word such as "this," "these," "that," "those."

dem·on·stra·tor /ˈdemənˌstreitər/ *n* [C] **1** person who demonstrates(2): *The ~s were dispersed by the police.* **2** person who teaches or explains by demonstration(1). **3** object (machine, etc) used in demonstrations, eg by a salesman.

de·moral·ize /diˈmɔrəˌlaiz/ *vt* **1** hurt or weaken the morals of: *drugs that have a demoralizing effect.* **2** weaken the courage, confidence, self-discipline, etc of, eg an army.

de·moral·i·za·tion /diˌmɔrələˈzeiʃən/ *n* [U]

de·mote /diˈmout/ *vt* reduce to a lower rank or grade.

de·motion /diˈmouʃən/ *n* [U]

de·mur /dɪˈmər/ *vi* (-rr-) (*formal*) raise an objection: *to ~ to a demand; to ~ at working on Sundays.* □ *n* [C] objection: without ~.

de·mure /dɪˈmyʊr/ *adj* **1** quiet and serious: *a ~ young lady.* **2** pretending to be, suggesting that one is, demure: *She gave him a ~ smile.*

de·mure·ly *adv*

den /den/ *n* [C] **1** animal's hidden resting-place, eg a cave. **2** secret place; hideout: *an ˈopium den; a den of thieves.* **3** dirty, miserable room or dwelling place. **4** cozy room in which a person works and studies without being disturbed.

de·na·tured /diˈneitʃərd/ *adj* (esp) made unfit to eat or drink (but still useful for other purposes): *~ alcohol.*

de·nial /dɪˈnaiəl/ *n* **1** [U] denying; refusing a request. **2** [C] instance of this: *the ~ of justice/a request for help.* **3** [C] statement that something is not true: *the prisoner's repeated ~s of being involved in the robbery.*

denim /ˈdenɪm/ *n* **1** [U] (usually pale blue) cotton cloth (used for jeans, overalls, etc). **2** (*pl*) (*informal*) jeans made from denim.

de·nomi·na·tion /dɪˌnaməˈneiʃən/ *n* [C] **1** name, esp one for a class of things. **2** religious group or sect: *The Protestant ~s include the Methodists, Presbyterians and Baptists.* **3** class or unit (in weight, length, numbers, money, etc): *The US coin of the lowest ~ is the cent.*

de·nomi·na·tional /-ˈneiʃənəl/ *adj* of religious groups.

de·nomi·na·tor /dɪˈnaməˌneitər/ *n* [C] number or quantity below the line in a fraction, eg 4 in $\frac{3}{4}$. ⇨ numerator.

de·note /dɪˈnout/ *vt* (*formal*) **1** be the sign or symbol of: *In algebra the sign* x *usually ~s an unknown quantity.* **2** mean; be the name for: *In American slang the term "windbag" ~s a talkative person.*

de·nounce /dɪˈnauns/ *vt* **1** speak publicly against; give information against: *to ~ him as a spy.* **2** give notice that one intends to end (a treaty or agreement).

dense /dens/ *adj* (*-r, -st*) **1** (of liquids, vapor) not easily seen through: *a ~ fog; ~ smoke.* **2** (of people and things) crowded together in great numbers: *a ~ crowd/forest.* **3** stupid; dull; thick-headed.

dense·ly *adv*: *a ~ly populated country.*

dense·ness /-nɪs/ *n* [U]

den·sity /ˈdensəti/ *n* (*pl* -ies) **1** [U] the quality of being dense: *the ~ of a forest; population ~.* **2** [C,U] (*phys*) relation of weight to volume.

dent /dent/ *n* [C] hollow, depression, in a hard surface made by a blow or by pressure. (*fig*): *a ~ in one's pride.* □ *vt,vi* make or get a dent in: *a car badly ~ed in a collision.*

den·tal /ˈdentəl/ *adj* of or for the teeth: *a ~ surgeon.*

den·tist /ˈdentɪst/ *n* [C] person whose work is filling, cleaning, taking out teeth and fitting artificial teeth.

den·tistry *n* [U] work of a dentist.

den·ture /ˈdentʃər/ *n* [C] (usually *pl*) set of artificial teeth.

de·nunci·ation /dɪˌnənsiˈeiʃən/ *n* [C,U] denouncing: *the ~ of a traitor.*

deny /dɪˈnai/ *vt* (*pt,pp* -ied) **1** say that (something) is not true: *The accused man denied the charge/denied that he was guilty. It cannot be denied that.../There is no ~ing the fact that...,* everyone must admit that.... **2** disown; refuse to acknowledge: *He denied the signature,* said that it was not his. **3** say "no" to a request; refuse to give (something asked for or needed): *He denies himself/his wife nothing.*

de·odor·ant /diˈoudərənt/ *n* [C] substance that disguises or absorbs unpleasant (esp body) odors.

de·odor·ize /diˈoudəˌraiz/ *vt* remove bad smells from.

dep. *abbr* = **1** depart. **2** departure.

de·part /dɪˈpart/ *vi* **1** go away; leave: *The train ~s at 3:30pm.* **2** turn or go away from: *~ from routine/the truth.*

(the) de·parted, *n* **(a)** (*sing*) person who has recently died. **(b)** (*pl*) those who have died: *pray for the souls of the ~ed.*

de·part·ment /dɪˈpartmənt/ *n* [C] **1** one of several divisions of a government, business, university, etc: *the Education Department/Department of Education.* **2** division of a department store: *the shoe ~.*

de·part·mental /ˌdipartˈmentəl/ *adj* of a department (contrasting with the whole): *~al duties/administration.*

deˈpartment store, large store in which many kinds of goods are sold in different departments.

de·par·ture /dɪˈpartʃər/ *n* **1** [U] departing; going

away. **2** [C] instance of this: *His ~ was unexpected. There are notices showing arrivals and ~s of trains over there.* **3** [C,U] turning away or aside; changing: *a ~ from old custom; a new ~ in physics*, eg the discovery of nuclear fission.

de·pend /dɪˈpend/ *vi* **1** need, rely on (the support, etc of) in order to exist or to be true or to succeed: *Children ~ on their parents for food and clothing.* ***that/it all depends,*** the result depends on something else. **2** trust; be certain about: *You can always ~ (up)on John to be there when he is needed.*

de·pend·able *adj*

de·pend·ence /dɪˈpendəns/ *n* [U] **1** the state of depending; being supported by others: *Why don't you find a job and end this ~ (up)on your parents?* **2** confident trust; reliance: *He's not a man you can put much ~ on,* you can't rely on him. **3** the state of being determined or conditioned by: *the ~ on drugs.*

de·pen·dency /dɪˈpendənsi/ *n* (*pl* -ies) **1** [C] country governed or controlled by another: *The Hawaiian Islands are no longer a ~ of the USA.* **2** [U] = dependence(1).

de·pend·ent /dɪˈpendənt/ *adj* depending: *Promotion is ~ (up)on your record of success.* □ (also **dependant**) *n* [C] person who depends on another or others for a home, food, etc.

de·pict /dɪˈpɪkt/ *vt* **1** show in the form of a picture: *Mediterranean scenes ~ed in these photographs.* **2** describe in words.

de·pic·tion /dɪˈpɪkʃən/ *n* [C, U]

de·plete /dɪˈplit/ *vt* use up, empty until little or none remains: *to ~ a lake of fish; ~d supplies.*

de·ple·tion /dɪˈpliʃən/ *n* [U]

de·plore /dɪˈplɔr/ *vt* show, say, that one is filled with sorrow or regret for.

de·plor·able /dɪˈplɔrəbəl/ *adj* that is, or should be, deplored: *deplorable conduct.*

de·plor·ably /dɪˌplɔrəbli/ *adv*

de·ploy /dɪˈplɔi/ *vt,vi* (cause to) spread out into position, eg into the line of battle.

de·popu·late /ˌdiˈpapyəˌleit/ *vt* lessen the number of people living in a place: *a country ~d by war/famine.*

de·popu·la·tion /ˌdiˌpapyəˈleiʃən/ *n* [U]

de·port[1] /dɪˈpɔrt/ *vt* expel (an unwanted person) from a country: *The spy was imprisoned for two years and then ~ed.*

de·por·ta·tion /ˌdɪpɔrˈteiʃən/ *n* [C,U]

de·port[2] /dɪˈpɔrt/ *vt* (*formal*) behave: *to ~ oneself with dignity.*

de·port·ment *n* [U] behavior; way of acting: *Young ladies used to have lessons in ~ment.*

de·pose /dɪˈpouz/ *vt,vi* remove, esp a ruler such as a king, from a position of authority.

de·posit[1] /dɪˈpazɪt/ *n* [C] **1** money that is deposited(2,3): *The sales clerk promised to hold my purchases for me if I left/paid/made a ~.* **2** mass or layer of matter deposited(4): *A thick ~ of mud covered the fields after the floods went down.* **3** layer of solid matter (often buried in the earth): *Valuable new ~s of tin have been found in Bolivia.*

de·posit[2] /dɪˈpazɪt/ *vt* **1** lay or put down: *Some insects ~ their eggs in the ground.* **2** put or store for safekeeping: *to ~ money in a bank/papers with one's lawyer.* **3** make part payment of money that is or will be owed: *We should like you to ~ a tenth of the price of the house.* **4** (esp of a river) leave (a layer of material on): *When the Nile rises it ~s a layer of mud on the land.*

de·posi·tor /dɪˈpazɪtər/ *n* [C] person who deposits, eg money in a bank.

de·pot /ˈdipou/ *n* [C] **1** (also /ˈdepou/) storehouse, esp for military supplies; warehouse. **2** railway or bus station.

de·praved /dɪˈpreivd/ *adj* morally bad; corrupt: *~ children; ~* (= vicious or perverted) *tastes.*

de·prav·ity /dɪˈprævəti/ *n* (*pl* -ies) **1** [U] depraved state. **2** [C] vicious act.

de·pre·ci·ate /diˈpriʃiˌeit/ *vt,vi* make or become less in value: *Shares in this company have ~d.*

de·preci·ation /diˌpriʃiˈeiʃən/ *n* [U]

de·press /dɪˈpres/ *vt* **1** press, push or pull down: *to ~ a lever/the keys of a piano.* **2** (usually /dɪˈpres/) make sad, low in spirits: *The newspapers are full of ~ing news nowadays,* eg of war, crime, natural disasters, rising prices. **3** make less active: *When business is ~ed there is usually an increase in unemployment.* **4** cause (prices) to be lower.

de·pression /dɪˈpreʃən/ *n* **1** [U] being depressed (2); low spirits: *He commited suicide during a fit of ~.* **2** [C] hollow, sunk place, in the surface of something, esp the ground: *It rained heavily and every ~ in the bad road was soon filled with water.* **3** [C] time when business is depressed(3).

depri·va·tion /ˌdeprəˈveiʃən/ *n* **1** [U] depriving or being deprived. **2** [C] something of which one is deprived: *~ of one's rights as a citizen.*

de·prive /dɪˈpraiv/ *vt* take away from; prevent from using or enjoying: *trees that ~ a house of light.*

de·prived *adj* underprivileged.

dept. *abbr* = department.

depth /depθ/ *n* **1** [C,U] being deep; distance from the top down, from the front to the back, from the surface inwards: *Water was found at a ~ of 10 feet. The snow is three feet in ~.* ***be out of one's depth,*** **(a)** be in water too deep to stand in: *If you can't swim, don't go out of your ~.* **(b)** (*fig*) be beyond one's ability to understand: *When people start talking about nuclear physics I'm out of my ~.* **2** [C] deep learning, thought, feeling, etc: *She showed a ~ of feeling that surprised us.* **3 the depth(s),** deepest or most central part(s): *in the ~ of winter; in the ~s of despair.*

ˈdepth charge, explosive charge for use under water, esp against submarines.

ˈdepth gauge, instrument for measuring the depth, esp in water (as in a submarine, worn by a skin diver, etc).

depu·ta·tion /ˌdepyəˈteiʃən/ *n* [C] group of representatives; number of persons given the right to act or speak for others.

de·pute /dəˈpyut/ *vt* give (one's work, authority, etc) to a substitute; give (another person) authority to act as one's representative.

depu·tize /ˈdepyəˌtaiz/ *vt, vi* appoint as deputy, act as deputy.

deputy /ˈdepyəti/ *n* [C] (*pl* -ies) **1** person to whom work, authority, etc is given: *The Sheriff* *had three deputies to help him recapture the escaped prisoners.* **2** (in some countries, eg France) member of a legislative assembly.

de·rail /dɪˈreiəl/ *vt* (*pres p* ~ing /diˈreilɪŋ/) cause (a train, etc) to run off the rails: *The locomotive was ~ed.*

de·rail·ment *n* [C,U]

de·range /dɪˈreindʒ/ *vt* put out of working order; put into confusion; disturb: *He is mentally ~d,* insane.

derby /ˈdərbi/ *n* [C] (*pl* -ies) **1** important horse race, usually taking place every year: *the Kentucky Derby.* **2** race or contest, open to all: *soapbox ~.* **3** man's hat with a stiff, rounded crown and a narrow brim.

der·e·lict /ˈderəlɪkt/ *adj* **1** abandoned; deserted and left to fall into ruin: *a ~ house.* **2** neglectful (of one's duty).

der·el·ic·tion /ˌderəˈlɪkʃn/ *n* **1** abandonment. **2** (deliberate) neglect of duty.

de·ride /dɪˈraid/ *vt* laugh scornfully at: *They ~d his efforts as childish.*

de·ri·sion /dɪˈrɪʒən/ *n* [U] deriding or being derided: *be/become an object of ~.*

de·ri·sive /dɪˈraisɪv/ *adj* showing or deserving derision: *a ~ offer,* eg $200 for a car that is worth $1,000.

de·ri·sory /dɪˈraisəri/ *adj* = derisive.

deri·va·tion /ˌderəˈveiʃən/ *n* **1** [U] deriving or being derived. **2** origin; descent: *the ~ of words from Latin; a word of Latin ~.* **3** [C] (statement of the) way in which a word is formed: *to study the ~s of words.*

de·riva·tive /dɪˈrɪvətɪv/ *adj, n* [C] (thing, word, substance) derived from another; not original or primitive: *"Assertion" is a ~ of "assert".*

de·rive /diˈraiv/ *vt,vi* **1** get: *to ~ great pleasure from one's studies.* **2** have as a source or origin: *Thousands of English words are ~d from/~ from Latin.*

der·ma·tol·ogist /ˌdərməˈtalədʒɪst/ *n* [C] expert in skin diseases.

der·ma·tol·ogy /ˌdərməˈtalədʒi/ *n* [U] medical study of the skin, its diseases, etc.

dero·gate /ˈderəˌgeit/ *vi* (*formal*) take away (a merit, good quality, right).

dero·ga·tion /ˌderəˈgeiʃən/ *n* [U] lessening (of authority, dignity, reputation, etc).

de·roga·tory /dɪˈragəˌtɔri/ *adj* tending to damage or take away from (one's credit, etc): *Is the slang word "cop" as ~ as "pig" for "policeman"?*

der·rick /ˈderɪk/ *n* [C] **1** large crane for moving or lifting heavy weights, esp on a ship. **2** framework over an oil well, to hold the drilling machinery, etc.

des·cant /ˈdeˌskænt/ *n* [C] (*music*) additional independent accompaniment (often improvised) to a melody.

de·scend /dɪˈsend/ *vi,vt* **1** (*formal*) come or go down: *On turning the corner, we saw that the path ~ed steeply.* **2** ***be descended from,*** have as ancestors: *According to the Bible, we are all ~ed from Adam.* **3** (of property, qualities, rights) pass by inheritance; come from earlier times. **4** attack suddenly: *The bandits ~ed (up)on the defenseless village.* **5** lower oneself: *You would never ~ to fraud/cheating.*

de·scend·ant /dɪˈsendənt/ *n* [C] person who is descended from (the person or persons named): *the ~s of Thomas Jefferson.*

de·scent /dɪˈsent/ *n* **1** [C,U] coming or going down: *The ~ of the mountain took two hours.* **2** [U] ancestry: *of French ~,* having French ancestors. **3** [C] sudden attack: *The Danes made numerous ~s upon the English coast during the 10th century.* **4** [U] handing down, eg of property, titles, qualities, etc by inheritance.

de·scribe /dɪˈskraib/ *vt* **1** say what (a person or thing) is like: *Words cannot ~ the beauty of the scene. He ~s himself as a doctor.* **2** mark out, draw (esp a geometric figure): *It is easy to ~ a circle if you have a pair of compasses.*

de·scrip·tion /dɪˈskripʃən/ *n* **1** [C,U] describing; picture in words: *The scenery was beautiful beyond ~. Can you give me a ~ of the thief?* **2** [C] sort: *The harbor was crowded with vessels of every ~.*

de·scrip·tive /dɪˈskrɪptɪv/ *adj* serving to describe.

des·ecrate /ˈdesəˌkreit/ *vt* use (a sacred thing or place) in an unworthy or wicked way.

des·ecra·tion /ˌdesəˈkreiʃən/ *n* [U] desecrating or being desecrated.

de·seg·re·gate /ˌdiˈsegrɪˌgeit/ *vt* abolish (esp racial) segregation in: *~ schools in Springfield.*

de·seg·re·ga·tion /ˌdɪˌsegrɪˈgeiʃən/ *n* [U]

de·sert[1] /dɪˈzərt/ *vt,vi* **1** leave; go away from: *The streets were ~ed,* no people were to be seen. **2** leave without help or support, esp in a wrong or cruel way: *He ~ed his wife and children and went abroad.* **3** run away from; leave (esp service in the armed forces) without authority or permission: *A soldier who ~s his post in time of war is punished severely.* **4** fail: *His courage ~ed him.*

de·serter *n* [C] person who deserts, esp in the sense of (3) above.

de·ser·tion /dɪˈzərʃən/ *n* **1** [U] deserting or being deserted. **2** [C] instance of this.

des·ert[2] /ˈdezərt/ *n* [C,U] (large area of) barren land, waterless and treeless, often sand-covered: *the Sahara Desert.* □ *adj* **1** barren; uncultivated: *the ~ areas of North Africa.* **2** uninhabited: *wrecked on a ~ island.*

de·serts /dɪˈzərts/ *n pl* what a person deserves: *to be rewarded/punished according to one's ~.*

de·serve /dɪˈzərv/ *vt,vi* worthy of (because of actions, conduct, qualities): *He ~s to be sent to prison.*

de·serv·ed·ly /dɪˈzərvɪdli/ *adv* according to what is deserved; rightly: *to be ~dly punished.*

de·serv·ing /dɪˈzərvɪŋ/ *adj* having merit; worthy (of): *to give money to a ~ cause; to be ~ of sympathy.*

de·sign /dɪˈzain/ *n* **1** [C] drawing or outline from which something may be made: *~s for a dress/garden.* **2** [U] art of making such drawings, etc: *a school of ~.* **3** [U] general arrangement or planning (of a picture, book, building, machine, etc): *The building seats 2,000 people, but is poor in ~.* **4** [C] pattern; arrangement of lines, shapes, details, as ornament: *a vase with a ~ of flowers on it.* **5** [C,U] purpose; intention; mental plan: *Was it by accident or ~ that he arrived too late* *to help us?* ***have designs against/on,*** plot against for one's own advantage, gain, etc: *That man has ~s on your money/your life; He has ~s on that young girl,* wants to be intimate with her. □ *vt,vi* **1** prepare a plan, sketch, etc (of something to be made): *~ a dress/garden. He ~s for a large firm of carpet manufacturers.* **2** intend, plan: *This course is ~ed to help those wishing to teach abroad. This room was ~ed for the children.*

de·sign·er /dɪˈzainər/ *n* [C]

des·ig·nate[1] /ˈdezɪgˌneit, ˈdezɪgnɪt/ *adj* appointed to an office (but not yet installed): *the bishop ~.*

des·ig·nate[2] /ˈdezɪgˌneit/ *vt* **1** mark or point out clearly: *The Hudson River ~s the boundary between Manhattan and New Jersey.* **2** give a name or title to: *The head of the company is ~d chairman of the board.* **3** appoint to a position or office: *He ~d Smith as his successor.*

des·ig·na·tion /ˌdezɪgˈneiʃən/ *n* **1** [U] appointing to an office. **2** [C] name, title or description.

de·sign·ing /dɪˈzainɪŋ/ *adj* (esp) artful and cunning; fond of intrigue.

de·sir·able /dɪˈzairəbəl/ *adj* to be desired; worth having: *This is a ~ piece of property.*

de·sir·abil·ity /dɪˌzairəˈbɪləti/ *n* [U]

de·sire[1] /dɪˈzaiər/ *n* **1** [U] strong longing: *He has no/not much ~ for wealth.* **2** [C] thing that is wished for: *I hope you will get your heart's ~,* thing you wish for the most. **3** request: *at the ~ of the President.*

de·sire[2] /dɪˈzaiər/ *vt* (*formal*) **1** long for; wish; have a desire(1) for: *We all ~ happiness and health.* **2** request: *It is ~d that this rule shall be brought to the attention of the staff.*

de·sir·ous /dɪˈzaiərəs/ *adj* (*formal*) feeling desire: *~ of peace.*

de·sist /dɪˈsɪst, dɪˈzɪst/ *vi* (*formal*) stop: *~ from gossiping.*

desk /desk/ *n* [C] **1** piece of furniture (not a table) with a flat or sloping top and drawers at which to read, write or do business, eg one for office use. **2** division or department of an organization: *the reception/information ~.*

deso·late /ˈdesəlɪt, ˈdezəlɪt/ *adj* **1** in a ruined, neglected state: *a ~ house.* **2** barren or deserted: *a ~, wind-swept plain.* **3** friendless; wretched; lonely and sad: *a ˈ~-looking child.* □ *vt* /ˈdesəˌleit/ make desolate.

deso·late·ly /ˈdesəlɪtli/ *adv*

deso·la·tion /ˌdesəˈleiʃən/ *n* [U] making or being desolate: *the desolation caused by war.*

des·pair[1] /dɪˈsper/ *n* [U] **1** the state of having lost all hope: *You will drive me to ~. He gave up in ~. He was filled with ~ when he read the examination questions.* ***2 the despair of,*** the cause of hopelessness: *This boy is the ~ of all his teachers,* they no longer hope to teach him anything.

des·pair[2] /dɪˈsper/ *vi* be in despair: *to ~ of success/of ever succeeding.*

des·pair·ing·ly *adv*

des·patch /dɪˈspætʃ/ *n, v* = dispatch.

des·per·ado /ˌdespəˈradou/ *n* [C] (*pl* ~es or ~s) reckless outlaw.

des·per·ate /ˈdesp(ə)rɪt/ *adj* **1** (of a person) filled with despair and ready to do anything, regardless of danger: *The prisoners became ~ in their attempts to escape. They are all ~ criminals.* **2** extremely serious or dangerous: *The economic state of the country is ~.* **3** giving little hope of success; tried when all else has failed: *~ remedies.*

des·per·ate·ly *adv*

des·per·ation /ˌdespəˈreiʃən/ *n* [U] the state of being desperate(1): *The people rose in ~ against their rulers.*

des·pic·able /dɪˈspɪkəbəl/ *adj* deserving to be despised; contemptible.

des·pic·ably *adv*

des·pise /dɪˈspaiz/ *vt* feel contempt for; consider worthless: *Strikebreakers are ~d by their fellow workers.*

des·pite /dɪˈspait/ *prep* in spite of: *~ what she says....*

de·spon·dency /dɪˈspandənsi/ *n* [U] loss of hope; discouragement: *to fall into ~.*

de·spon·dent /dɪˈspandənt/ *adj* discouraged; having lost hope: *Don't become too despondent.*

de·spon·dent·ly *adv*

des·pot /ˈdespət/ *n* [C] ruler with unlimited powers, esp one who uses these powers wrongly or cruelly.

des·potic /dɪˈspatɪk/ *adj*

des·pot·ism /despətɪzəm/ *n* [U]

des·sert /dɪˈzərt, di-/ *n* [C] course of fruit, cake, cheese, etc at the end of a meal.

des·ti·na·tion /ˌdestəˈneiʃən/ *n* [C] place to which a person or thing is going or is being sent.

des·tine /ˈdestɪn/ *vt* **1** settle, decide in advance: *Their plan was ~d to fail.* ***2 destined for,*** bound for; intending to go to: *a ship ~ed for the Orient.*

des·tiny /ˈdestəni/ *n* (*pl* -ies) **1** [U] power believed to control events: *tricks played on human beings by ~.* **2** [C] that which happens to a person, thought of as determined in advance by fate, etc: *It was his ~ to die in a foreign country, far from his family.*

des·ti·tute /ˈdestəˌtut/ *adj* without food, clothes and other things necessary for life; very poor: *When Mr. Hill died, his wife and children were left ~.*

des·ti·tu·tion /ˌdestəˈtuʃən/ *n* [U] being destitute: *a war that brought desolation and ~.*

de·stroy /dɪˈstrɔi, di-/ *vt* **1** break to pieces; make useless: *Don't ~ that box—it may be useful.* **2** put an end to: *All his hopes were ~ed.*

de·stroyer /dɪˈstrɔiər, di-/ *n* [C] **1** person or thing that destroys. **2** a small, fast warship armed with guns, torpedoes, etc.

de·struc·tible /dɪˈstrəktəbəl/ *adj* that can be destroyed.

de·struc·ti·bil·ity /dɪˌstrəktəˈbɪləti/ *n* [U]

de·struc·tion /dɪˈstrəkʃən/ *n* [U] **1** destroying or being destroyed: *the ~ of a town by an earthquake.* **2** that which ruins or destroys: *Gambling was his ~.*

de·struc·tive /dɪˈstrəktɪv/ *adj* causing destruction; tending to destroy: *Are all small children ~?*

de·tach /dɪˈtætʃ/ *vt* **1** unfasten and take apart; separate: *to ~ a coach from a train.* **2** send (a party of soldiers, ships, etc) away from the main

body: *A number of men were ~ed to guard the right flank.*
de·tached *adj* **1** (of the mind, opinions, etc) not influenced by others: *to take a ~ed view of an event.* **2** (of a house) not joined to another on either side.
de·tach·able *adj* that can be separated: *a ~able lining in a coat.*
de·tach·ment /dɪˈtætʃmənt/ *n* **1** [U] detaching or being detached: *the ~ of a letter from a file.* **2** [U] the state of being detached; being uninfluenced by prejudices, opinions, etc. **3** [U] being indifferent and uninterested. **4** [C] group of men, ships, etc, detached(2) for a special duty, etc.
de·tail[1] /dɪˈteiəl, ˈdiˌteiəl/ *n* **1** [C] small, particular fact or item: *Please give me all the ~s.* ***in detail,*** item by item; thoroughly: *We intend to go into the matter in ~.* **2** [C] collection of such small facts or items. **3** [U] (*art*) the smaller or less important parts considered collectively: *The composition of the picture is good but there is too much ~.* **4** [C] group assigned to special duty.
de·tail[2] /dɪˈteiəl, ˈdiˌteiəl/ *vt* (*pres p* ~ing /dɪˈteilɪŋ, ˈdiˌteilɪŋ/) **1** describe fully: *a ~ed description.* **2** appoint for special duty: *Three soldiers were ~ed to guard the bridge.* ⇨ detail[1] (4).
de·tain /dɪˈtein/ *vt* delay; keep back; prevent from leaving or going forward: *He told his wife that he had been ~ed at the office.*
de·tainee /ˌdɪˌteiˈni/ *n* [C] person who is detained (esp by the authorities, who is suspected of doing wrong, etc).
de·tect /dɪˈtekt/ *vt* discover (the existence or presence of, etc): *The dentist could ~ no sign of decay in her teeth.*
de·tect·able *adj*
de·tec·tor /-tər/ *n* [C] device for detecting, eg changes of pressure, temperature or a radio signal.
de·tec·tion /dɪˈtekʃən/ *n* [U] detecting: discovering: *He tried to escape ~ by disguising himself as an old man.*
de·tec·tive /dɪˈtektɪv/ *n* [C] person whose business it is to solve crime, gather information, etc.
deˈtective story/novel, one in which the main interest is crime and the process of solving it.
de·ten·tion /dɪˈtenʃən/ *n* [U] detaining or being detained, eg detaining a pupil in school after ordinary hours, as a punishment.
de·ter /dɪˈtər/ *vt* (-rr-) discourage, hinder: *Failure did not ~ him from trying again.*
de·ter·gent /dɪˈtərdʒənt/ *n* [U,C], *adj* (substance) that removes dirt: *Most synthetic ~s are in the form of powder or liquid.*
de·terio·rate /dɪˈtɪriəˌreit/ *vt,vi* make or become of less value, or worse (in quality): *Health quickly ~s in a cold, damp house.*
de·terio·ra·tion /dɪˌtɪriəˈreiʃən/ *n* [U]
de·ter·mi·nate /dɪˈtərmənɪt/ *adj* (*formal*) definite; fixed.
de·ter·mi·na·tion /dɪˌtərməˈneiʃən/ *n* [U] **1** determining or being determined; deciding. **2** calculation or finding out. **3** firmness of purpose; resolution: *his ~ to learn English.*
de·ter·mine /dɪˈtərmən/ *vt,vi* **1** decide; fix; settle: *to ~ a date for a meeting.* **2** calculate; find out precisely: *to ~ the speed of light* **3** decide firmly, resolve, make up one's mind: *When did he ~ to study medicine?* **4** cause to decide: *What ~d you to accept the offer?* **5** be the fact that decides: *The size of your feet ~s the size of your shoes.*
de·ter·min·able *adj* that can be determined.
de·ter·rent /dɪˈtərənt/ *n* [C] *adj* (thing) tending to, intended to, deter: *Do you believe that nuclear weapons are a ~,* that they will discourage countries from making war?
de·test /dɪˈtest/ *vt* hate strongly: *to ~ dogs.*
de·test·able *adj* hateful: deserving to be hated.
de·throne /diˈθroun/ *vt* **1** remove (a ruler) from the throne. **2** (*fig*) remove from a position of authority or influence.
de·throne·ment *n* [U]
det·o·nate /ˈdetəˌneit/ *vt,vi* (cause to) explode with a loud noise.
det·o·nation /ˌdetəˈneiʃən/ *n* [C,U] explosion; noise of an explosion.
det·o·nator /ˈdetəˌneitər/ *n* [C] part of a bomb or shell that explodes first, causing the substance in the bomb, etc to explode.
de·tour /ˈdiˌtʊr/ *n* [C] roundabout way, eg a way used when the main road is blocked: *to make a ~.* □ *vt,vi* (cause to) make a detour.
de·tract /dɪˈtrækt/ *vi* take away (from the credit, value, etc of): *to ~ from his merit,* make it less.
de·trac·tor /-tər/ *n* [C]
det·ri·ment /ˈdetrəmənt/ *n* [U] damage; harm: *I know nothing to his ~,* nothing against him.
det·ri·men·tal /ˌdetrəˈmentəl/ *adj* harmful: *activities that would be ~al to our interests.*
det·ri·men·tally *adv*
deuce /dus/ *n* [C] **1** the two on playing cards or dice. **2** (in tennis) the score of 40 all, after which either side must gain two successive points to win the game.
de·value /diˈvælyu/ *vt* make less in worth or value: *to ~ the dollar/pound.*
de·valu·ation /diˌvælyuˈeiʃən/ *n* [C]
dev·as·tate /ˈdevəˌsteit/ *vt* ruin; destroy: *towns ~d by fire/floods/war.*
dev·as·ta·tion /ˌdevəˈsteiʃən/ *n* [U]
de·velop /dɪˈveləp/ *vt,vi* **1** (cause to) grow larger, fuller or more mature, organized: *Plants ~ from seeds. We must ~ the natural resources of our country. Amsterdam ~ed into one of the greatest ports in the world.* **2** (of something not at first active or visible) come or bring into a state in which it is active or visible: *He ~ed a cough.* **3** treat (an exposed film or plate) with chemicals so that the photographed image can be seen. **4** make (land) more usable.
de·vel·oper *n* [C] person, thing that develops, esp a chemical used to develop photographic film.
de·vel·op·ment /dɪˈveləpmənt/ *n* **1** [U] developing or being developed (all senses): *He is engaged in the ~ of his business. The ~ of photographic films requires great care.* **2** [C] new stage which is the result of developing: *The latest ~s in medical research.*
de·vi·ate /ˈdiviˌeit/ *vi* turn away, leave (what is usual, customary, right, etc): *to ~ from the*

truth/a rule/one's custom.

de·vi·ation /ˌdiviˈeiʃən/ *n* **1** [U] turning aside or away: *~ from the rules.* **2** [C] instance or amount or degree of this: *slight ~s of the magnetic needle,* in a compass.

de·vice /dɪˈvais/ *n* [C] **1** plan; scheme; trick: *a ~ to put the police off the scent.* ***leave sb to his own devices,*** let him do as he wishes. **2** apparatus, piece of equipment, etc, invented or adapted, for a special purpose: *a nuclear ~,* eg an atomic or hydrogen bomb. **3** sign, symbol or figure used in a decoration, eg a crest on a shield.

devil /ˈdevəl/ *n* [C] **1** the spirit of evil; wicked spirit; cruel or mischievous person. **the Devil,** the supreme spirit of evil, Satan. **2** ***poor ˈdevil,*** wretched or unfortunate person: *Oh, you poor ~!* **3** (*informal*) used in exclamations: *What/Who/Where/Why the ~...?*

ˈdevil-may-ˌcare *adj* without thinking of the consequences.

devil·ment /ˈdevəlmənt/ (also **dev·il(t)ry** /ˈdevəl(t)ri/) *n* **1** [C] mischief: *She's up to some ~ or other.* **2** [U] high spirits: *full of ~.*

de·vi·ous /ˈdiviəs/ *adj* **1** winding; roundabout: *to take a ~ route to avoid busy streets.* **2** cunning, deceitful: *to get rich by ~ means.*

de·vi·ous·ly *adv*

de·vi·ous·ness /-nɪs/ *n* [U]

de·vise /dɪˈvaiz/ *vt* think out; plan: *to ~ a scheme for making money.*

de·void /dɪˈvɔid/ *adj* ***devoid of,*** without; empty of: *~ of shame/sense.*

de·volve /dɪˈvalv/ *vi,vt* (*formal*) **1** (of work, duties) be transferred or passed to: *When the President is ill, his duties ~ upon the Vice-President.* **2** pass, transfer (work, duties).

de·vote /dɪˈvout/ *vt* give up (oneself, one's time, energy, etc) to: *to ~ one's life to sport. He ~d himself to mission work in Africa.*

de·voted *adj* very loving or loyal: *a ~d friend.*

de·vot·ed·ly *adv*

devo·tee /ˌdevəˈti, ˌdevouˈti/ *n* [C] person who is devoted to something: *a ~ of sport/music.*

de·vo·tion /dɪˈvouʃən/ *n* **1** [U] deep, strong love: *the ~ of a mother for her children.* **2** [U] devoting or being devoted: *~ to duty.* **3** (*pl*) prayers: *The priest was at his ~s.*

de·vo·tional *adj* of, used in devotions(3): *~al literature,* for use in worship.

de·vour /dɪˈvauər/ *vt* **1** eat hungrily or greedily: *The hungry boy ~ed his dinner.* **2** (*fig*) absorb, use up, destroy, occupy, etc completely: *She ~ed the new detective novel. The fire ~ed twenty square miles of forest.*

de·vout /dɪˈvaut/ *adj* **1** paying serious attention to religious duties: *a ~ old lady.* **2** serious; sincere: *a ~ supporter; ~ wishes for your success.*

de·vout·ly *adv* eagerly; sincerely.

de·vout·ness /-nɪs/ *n* [U]

dew /du/ *n* [U] tiny drops of moisture formed at night on cool surfaces from water vapor in the air: *The grass was wet with ~.*

ˈdew·drop *n* [C] small drop of dew.

dewy *adj* (-ier, -iest) wet with dew.

dex·ter·ity /ˌdekˈsterəti/ *n* [U] skill, esp in handling things.

dex·ter·ous, dex·trous /ˈdekstrəs/ *adj* clever, skillful with the hands.

dex·ter·ous·ly *adv*

dhow /dau/ *n* [C] single-masted ship, esp as used by Arab sailors for coastal voyages.

dia·betes /ˌdaiəˈbitiz/ *n* [U] disease of the pancreas in which sugar and starchy foods cannot be properly absorbed.

dia·betic /ˌdaiəˈbetɪk/ *adj* of diabetes. □ *n* [C] person suffering from diabetes.

dia·bolic /ˌdaiəˈbalɪk/ (also **diabolical** /-kəl/) *adj* **1** of or like a devil. **2** very cruel or wicked.

dia·boli·cally /-kli/ *adv*

dia·dem /ˈdaiəˌdem/ *n* [C] crown, worn as a sign of royal power; wreath of flowers or leaves worn round the head.

di·aer·esis, di·er·esis /daiˈerəsɪs/ *n* [C] (*pl* -eses /-əˌsiz/) mark (̈) placed over a vowel to show that it is sounded separately from a preceding vowel (as in *naïve*).

di·ag·nose /ˌdaiɪgˈnous, -ˈnouz/ *vt* determine the nature of (esp a disease) from observation of symptoms: *The doctor ~d the illness as diphtheria.*

di·ag·nosis /ˌdaiɪgˈnousɪs/ *n* (*pl* -noses /-ˈnouˌsiz/) **1** [U] diagnosing. **2** [C] (statement of the) result of this.

di·ag·nos·tic /ˌdaiɪgˈnastɪk/ *adj* of diagnosis.

di·ag·onal /daiˈægənəl/ *n* [C], *adj* **1** (straight line) going across a straight-sided figure, eg an oblong, from corner to corner. ⇨ illus at geometry. **2** line running in a slanting direction.

di·ag·onal·ly *adv*

dia·gram /ˈdaiəˌgræm/ *n* [C] drawing, design or plan to explain or illustrate something.

dia·gram·matic /ˌdaiəgrəˈmætɪk/ *adj*

dia·gram·mati·cally /-kli/ *adv*

dial /ˈdaiəl/ *n* [C] **1** marked face or flat plate with a pointer for measuring (weight, volume, pressure, consumption of gas, etc). **2** plate, disc, etc on a radio set with names or numbers, for tuning into broadcasting stations. **3** part of a telephone, with numbers and/or letters, used to make a connection. **4** face (of a clock or watch). □ *vt* (-l-, -ll-; *pres p* ~ing /ˈdailɪŋ/) telephone: *to ~ a number.*

ˈdial tone, electronic tone, in a telephone set, indicating that the line is clear for dialing.

dia·lect /ˈdaiəˌlekt/ *n* [C,U] form of a language (grammar, vocabulary and pronunciation) used in a certain part of a country or by a particular class of people: *the ~ of the mountaineers.*

dia·lec·tal /ˌdaiəˈlektəl/ *adj* of dialects.

dia·logue, dia·log /ˈdaiəˌlɔg/ *n* **1** [U] (writing in the form of a) conversation or talk: *Plays are written in ~.* **2** [C] exchange of views; talk: *a ~ between the two Heads of State.*

di·am·eter /daiˈæmətər/ *n* [C] measurement across any geometric figure or body; (length of a) straight line drawn from side to side through the center, esp of a circular, spherical or cylindrical form: *the ~ of a tree trunk.* ⇨ illus at circle.

dia·metri·cally /ˌdaiəˈmetrɪkli/ *adv* completely; entirely: *~ opposed views.*

dia·mond /ˈdai(ə)mənd/ *n* **1** [C, U] brilliant

precious stone, the hardest substance known; piece of this cut as a gem, or for industrial use in drills, etc: *a ring with a ~ in it*. **2** [C] figure with four equal sides whose angles are not right angles. **3** [C] one of the thirteen playing cards with red diamond shapes printed on it: *the ten of ~s*. ⇨ illus at card. **4** [C] (*baseball*) **(a)** the inner part of the playing field. **(b)** the whole field. ⇨ illus at baseball.

ˌdiamond ˈwedding, 60th wedding anniversary.

dia·per /ˈdai(ə)pər/ *n* [C] piece of soft cloth, folded and fastened about the waist, serving as underpants for a baby.

dia·phragm /ˈdaiəˌfræm/ *n* [C] **1** wall of muscle between the chest and the abdomen. ⇨ illus at respiratory. **2** device that controls the amount of light let in, eg through a camera lens. **3** vibrating disc or cone in some instruments, eg a telephone receiver. **4** device placed over the cervix to prevent conception.

di·ar·rhea, di·ar·rhoea /ˌdaiəˈriə/ *n* [U] too frequent and too watery emptying of the bowels.

diary /ˈdaiəri/ *n* [C] (*pl* -ies) (book for a) daily record of events, thoughts, etc: *keep a ~*.

dia·rist /ˈdaiərɪst/ *n* [C] person who keeps a diary.

dice /dais/ *n pl* (*sing* die /dai/ which is rarely used) (game played with) small cubes of wood, bone, etc marked with spots: *to play ~*. ***No dice!*** (*sl*) = No deal! ⇨ deal²(2). □ *vi,vt* **1** play dice. **2** cut (food, eg carrots) into small cubes.

di·chot·omy /daiˈkatəmi/ *n* [C] (*pl* -ies) division into two (usually contradictory classes or mutually exclusive pairs): *the ~ of truth and falsehood*.

dickey /ˈdɪki/ *n* [C] separate shirt collar or sweater neck and front, to be worn under a jacket to give the appearance of a shirt, or for warmth.

dic·tate /ˈdɪkˌteit/ *vt,vi* **1** say or read aloud (words to be written down by another or others): *to ~ a letter to a secretary*. **2** state with the force of authority: *to ~ terms to a defeated enemy*. **3** give orders: *I won't be ~d to*, I refuse to accept orders from you. □ *n* [C] (usually *pl*) direction or order: *the ~s of common sense*.

dic·ta·tion /dɪkˈteiʃən/ *n* **1** [U] dictating; being dictated to: *The pupils wrote at their teacher's ~*. **2** [C] passage, etc that is dictated.

dic·ta·tor /ˈdɪkˌteitər/ *n* [C] ruler who has absolute authority, esp one who has obtained such power by force.

dic·ta·torial /ˌdɪktəˈtɔriəl/ *adj* **(a)** of or like a dictator: *~ial government*. **(b)** fond of giving orders: *his ~ial manner*.

dic·ta·tori·ally *adv*

dic·ˈta·tor·ship [C,U] (country with) government by a dictator.

dic·tion /ˈdɪkʃən/ *n* [U] choice and use of words; style or manner of speaking and writing.

dic·tion·ary /ˈdɪkʃəˌneri/ *n* [C] (*pl* -ies) book with words or topics arranged in alphabetical order, that gives a meaning, spelling, pronunciation, etc for each word.

did *pt* of do.

didn't /dɪdənt/ = did not.

di·dac·tic /daiˈdæktɪk/ *adj* **1** intended to teach: *~ poetry*. **2** having the manner of a teacher.

die¹ /dai/ *n* **1** (*pl* dice) ⇨ dice. **2** (*pl* dies) block of hard metal with a design, etc cut in it, used for shaping coins, type¹(3), medals, etc or for stamping paper, leather, etc.

die² /dai/ *vi* (*pt,pp* died, *pres p* dying) **1** come to the end of life: *Flowers soon die if they are left without water. She died of a fever. He died by violence/from a wound/in battle*. **2** have a strong wish: *We're all dying for a drink. She's dying to know where you've been*. **3** pass from human knowledge; be lost: *His fame will never die. His secret died with him*, He died without telling it to anyone. **4** (special uses with *adverbial particles* and *prepositions*):

die away, lose strength, become faint or weak: *The breeze/noise died away*.

die down, **(a)** (of a fire) burn with less heat. **(b)** (of excitement, etc) become less violent. **(c)** (of noise, etc) become less loud.

die off, die one by one: *The leaves of this plant are dying off*.

die out, become extinct; come to a complete end: *Many old customs are gradually dying out*.

die·sel (engine) /ˈdizəl (ˌendʒɪn)/ *n* [C] oil-burning engine (as used for buses, locomotives) which burns its fuel by means of the heat of highly compressed air.

diet¹ /ˈdaiɪt/ *n* [C] **1** sort of food usually eaten (by a person, community, etc): *Too rich a ~* (= Too much rich food) *is not good for you*. **2** sort of food to which a person is limited, eg in order to lose weight: *The doctor put her on a ~*. □ *vt,vi* restrict, be restricted, to a diet(2): *Is he still ~ing?*

die·tary /ˈdaiəˌteri/ *adj*

diet² /ˈdaiɪt/ *n* [C] series of meetings for discussion of national, international or church affairs: *the Japanese Diet*, legislative assembly.

die·titian, die·tician /daiəˈtɪʃən/ *n* [C] person whose work is planning a balanced diet, esp in a hospital, school, etc.

dif·fer /ˈdɪfər/ *vi* **1** be unlike: *They look like each other but ~ widely in their tastes. How does American football ~ from English football?* **2** disagree; have another opinion: *I'm sorry to ~ from you about/on/upon that question*.

dif·fer·ence /ˈdɪfrəns/ *n* [C,U] **1** the state of being unlike: *the ~ between summer and winter*. **2** amount, degree, manner, in which things are unlike: *The ~ between 7 and 18 is 11. I can't see much ~ between/in them*. **3** ***make a/some/no/any/not much (etc) difference,*** be of some/no, etc importance: *It won't make much ~ whether you go today or tomorrow*. **4** disagreement: *Why can't you settle your ~s and be friends again?*

dif·fer·ent /ˈdɪfrənt/ *adj* **1** not the same; unlike: *They are ~ people with the same name. She wears a ~ dress every time I see her. How ~ life is now than it was! Life today is ~ from life long ago*. **2** separate; distinct: *I called three ~ times, but he was out*.

dif·fer·ent·ly *adv*

dif·fer·en·tial /ˌdɪfəˈrenʃəl/ *adj* of, showing, depending on, a difference: *~ taxes*, that differ according to circumstances. □ *n* (also **wage differential**) difference (expressed in a percentage) in wages between skilled and unskilled workers in the same industry: *The increase for all workers would upset the wage ~.*

dif·fer·en·ti·ate /ˌdɪfəˈrenʃiˌeit/ *vt* **1** see as different; show to be different: *to ~ varieties of plants; to ~ one variety from another.* **2** treat as different: *It is wrong to ~ between pupils according to their family background.*

dif·fi·cult /ˈdɪfə(ˌ)kəlt/ *adj* **1** not easy; hard to understand or do: *a ~ problem/language. The sound is ~ to pronounce. It is a ~ sound to pronounce.* **2** (of persons) not easily pleased or satisfied; easily offended: *He's a ~ man to get along with.*

dif·fi·culty /ˈdɪfəˌkəlti/ *n* (*pl* -ies) **1** [U] the state or quality of being difficult: *The ~ of the work exhausted her.* **2** [U] great or unusual effort: *read poorly and with ~.* **3** [C] something hard to do or understand: *A ~ came up which almost prevented them from finishing on time.* **4** [C] problem; difficult situation: *to be in financial difficulties,* short of money, in debt, etc.

dif·fi·dence /ˈdɪfədəns/ *n* [U] lack of self-confidence; shyness.

dif·fi·dent /ˈdɪfədənt/ *adj* not having, not showing, much belief in one's own abilities: *to be ~ about doing something.*

dif·fi·dent·ly *adv*

dif·fuse[1] /dɪˈfyuz/ *vt,vi* **1** send out, spread, in every direction: *to ~ knowledge/light/heat.* **2** (of gases and liquids) (cause to) mix slowly.

dif·fu·sion /dɪˈfyuʒən/ *n* [U] diffusing or being diffused.

dif·fuse[2] /dɪˈfyus/ *adj* **1** using too many words: *a ~ writer/style.* **2** spread out; scattered: *~ light.*

dif·fuse·ly *adv*

dif·fuse·ness /-nɪs/ *n* [U]

dig[1] /dɪg/ *n* [C] (*informal*) **1** push or thrust: *give somebody a dig in the ribs.* **2** cutting or sarcastic remark. *That was a dig at me,* a remark directed against me.

dig[2] /dɪg/ *vt,vi* (*pt,pp* dug /dəg/) (-gg-) **1** use a tool (eg a spade), to break up and move earth, to make a way (through, into, etc), or to make (a hole, etc) by doing this: *It is difficult to dig the ground when it is frozen hard. They are digging a tunnel through the hill.* **2** get (something) by digging: *dig potatoes; dig for gold.* **3** (*sl*) **(a)** enjoy; appreciate. **(b)** understand; follow: *I don't dig modern jazz.* **4** (special uses with *adverbial particles* and *prepositions*):

dig sth in/into sth, push, thrust, poke: *to dig a fork into a pie/a potato.*

dig sb/sth out (of sth), **(a)** get out by digging: *He was buried by the avalanche and had to be dug out.* **(b)** get by searching: *to dig information out of books and reports.*

dig sth up, **(a)** remove from the ground by digging: *We dug the tree up by the roots.* **(b)** bring to light (what has been buried or hidden) by digging: *An old Greek statue was dug up here last month.* (*fig*): *The newspapers love to dig up scandals.*

di·gest[1] /ˈdaiˌdʒest/ *n* [C] short, condensed account; summary: *a ~ of the week's news.*

di·gest[2] /dɪˈdʒest/ *vt,vi* **1** (of food) change, be changed, in the stomach and bowels, so that it can be used in the body: *Some foods ~/are ~ed more easily than others.* **2** take into the mind; make part of one's knowledge; reduce (a mass of facts, etc) to order: *Have you ~ed everything that is important in the book?*

di·gest·ible *adj* that can be digested.

di·ges·tion /dɪˈdʒestʃən, dai-/ *n* [U] **1** digesting. **2** ability to digest food.

di·ges·tive /dɪˈdʒestɪv, dai-/ *adj*

the diˈgestive system, the alimentary canal.

dig·ger /ˈdɪgər/ *n* [C] person or thing that digs.

digit /ˈdɪdʒɪt/ *n* [C] **1** any one of the ten Arabic numerals 0 to 9: *The number 57,306 contains five ~s.* **2** finger or toe.

digi·tal /ˈdɪdʒɪtəl/ *adj*

digital ˈclock/ˈwatch, one that shows time by displaying a row of numbers.

dig·nify /ˈdɪgnəˌfai/ *vt* (*pt,pp* -ied) cause to appear worthy or honorable; give dignity to.

dig·ni·fied *adj* having or showing dignity: *a dignified old lady.*

dig·ni·tary /ˈdɪgnəˌteri/ *n* [C] (*pl* -ies) person holding a high office or rank, eg a bishop.

dig·nity /ˌdɪgnəti/ *n* [U] **1** true worth; the quality that earns or deserves respect: *A man's ~ depends on his character, not his wealth.* **2** calm and serious manner or style: *He's afraid of losing his ~* (eg of being made to look foolish) *and won't speak a foreign language.*

di·gress /daiˈgres/ *vi* (esp in speaking or writing) turn or wander away (from the main subject).

di·gres·sion /daiˈgreʃən/ *n* **(a)** [U] digressing. **(b)** [C] instance of this.

dike, dyke /daik/ *n* [C] **1** ditch (for carrying away water from land). **2** long wall of earth, etc (to keep back water and prevent flooding). □ *vi* make dikes.

dil·api·dated /dɪˈlæpəˌdeitɪd/ *adj* falling to pieces; in a state of disrepair: *a ~ old house.*

dil·api·da·tion /dɪˌlæpəˈdeiʃən/ *n* [U]

di·late /daiˈleit/ *vi,vt* **1** (cause to) become wider, larger, further open: *The pupils of your eyes ~ when you enter a dark room.* **2** (*formal*) speak or write at length about: *If there were time, I could ~ on this subject.*

di·la·tion /daiˈleiʃən/ *n* [U]

dila·tory /ˈdɪləˌtɔri/ *adj* slow in doing things; causing delay.

di·lemma /dəˈlemə/ *n* [C] (*pl* ~s) situation in which one has to choose between two things, two courses of action, etc which seem equally undesirable; difficult choice.

dili·gence /ˈdɪlədʒəns/ *n* [U] steady effort; and care.

dili·gent /ˈdɪlədʒənt/ *adj* hardworking; showing care and effort.

dili·gent·ly *adv*

dill /dɪl/ *n* [U] herb with spicy seeds, eg as used for flavoring pickles.

dilly-dally, dilly·dally /ˈdɪliˌdæli/ *vt* dawdle; waste time (by not making up one's mind).

di·lute /daiˈlut, dɪ-/ *vt* **1** make (a liquid or color) weaker or thinner (by adding water or other liquid): *to ~ wine with water.* **2** (*fig*) weaken the strength, purity, etc of (by mixing). □ *adj* (of acids, etc) weakened by diluting.

di·lu·tion /daiˈluʃən, dɪ-/ *n* **(a)** [U] diluting or being diluted. **(b)** [C] something that is diluted.

dim /dɪm/ *adj* (-mmer, -mmest) **1** not bright; dull. **2** faint; not (to be) seen or perceived clearly: *the dim outline of buildings on a dark night; dim memories/recollections of my childhood.* **3** (of the eyes, eyesight) not able to see clearly: *His eyesight is getting dim.* ***take a dim view of,*** (*informal*) **(a)** disapprove of. **(b)** have no faith or belief in. □ *vt,vi* (-mm-) make or become dim: *eyes dimmed by tears.*

dim·ly *adv*

dim·ness /-nɪs/ *n* [U]

dime /daim/ *n* [C] coin of the US and Canada worth ten cents. ⇨ App 4.

di·men·sion /dɪˈmenʃən/ *n* **1** [C] measurement of any sort (breadth, length, thickness, height, etc): *What are the ~s of the room?* **2** (*pl*) size; extent: *the ~s of the problem.*

di·men·sional *adj*: ˌ*two-*, ˌ*three-ˈ~al*, having two, three, dimensions.

di·min·ish /dɪˈmɪnɪʃ/ *vt,vi* make or become less: *~ing food supplies.*

di·minu·tive /dɪˈmɪnyətɪv/ *adj* **1** unusually or remarkably small. **2** (*gram*) (of a *suffix*) indicating smallness. □ *n* [C] word formed by the use of a *suffix* of this kind, eg *streamlet*, a small stream; *lambkin*, a small lamb.

dimple /ˈdɪmpəl/ *n* [C] **1** small natural hollow in the chin or cheek (either permanent, or which appears, for example, when a person smiles). **2** slight hollow or dent (made, for example, by a breeze on water). □ *vt,vi* make, form, dimples.

din /dɪn/ *n* [U] loud, confused noise that continues: *The children were making such a din that I couldn't study.* □ *vi,vt* (-nn-) **1** make a din. **2** ***din sth in/into sb,*** cause him to learn something by repetition: *dinned good manners into his students.*

dine /dain/ *vi,vt* **1** have dinner: *to ~ on/off roast beef.* ***dine out,*** eat outside one's home (eg at the house of friends, or at a restaurant). **2** give a dinner for.

ˈdining car, railroad car in which meals are served.

ˈdining room, room in which meals are eaten.

ˈdining table, table used for dining.

diner /ˈdainər/ *n* [C] **1** person who dines. **2** dining car on a train. **3** restaurant shaped like a diner (2).

ding-dong, ding·dong /ˈdɪŋˌdɔŋ/ *n* [U] *adv* (with the) sound of bells striking repeatedly.

din·ghy /ˈdɪŋi/ *n* [C] (*pl* -ies) **1** (kinds of) small open boat. ⇨ illus at ship. **2** inflatable rubber boat (eg for use in an emergency).

dingy /ˈdɪndʒi/ *adj* (-ier, -iest) dirty-looking; not fresh or bright: *a ~ room.*

ding·ily /ˈdɪndʒəli/ *adv*

dingi·ness /ˈdɪndʒinɪs/ *n* [U]

din·ing /ˈdainɪŋ/ ⇨ dine.

dinky /ˈdɪŋki/ *adj* (-ier, -iest) (*informal*) small and unimportant.

din·ner /ˈdɪnər/ *n* [C] main meal of the day, whether eaten at midday or in the evening: *It's time for ~. Did you see her at ~? Should we ask him to ~?* (*Note: a* and *the* are rarely used with *dinner* after *have* or *preps.*)

dino·saur /ˈdainəˌsɔr/ *n* [C] large extinct reptile.

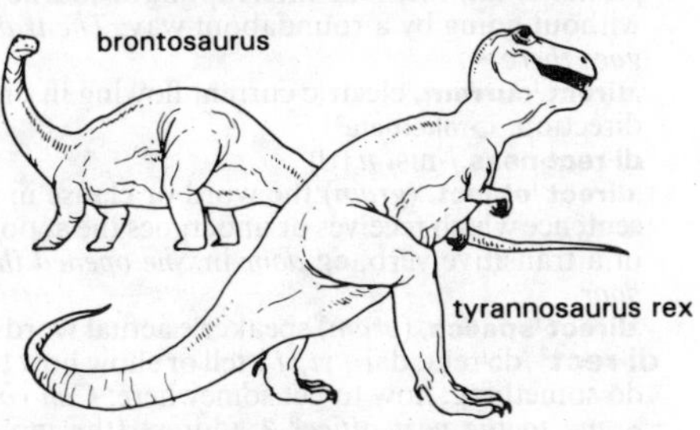

DINOSAURS

dint /dɪnt/ *n* **1** [U] force; strength. ***by dint of,*** because of. **2** [C] dent.

di·ocesan /daiˈasisən/ *adj* of a diocese.

dio·cese /ˈdaiəsɪs/ *n* [C] (*pl* ~s /-səsəz/) bishop's district.

dip[1] /dɪp/ *n* [C] **1** act of dipping. **2** (*informal*) quick bath or swim: *to have/take/go for a dip.* **3** downward slope, usually turning up again; *a dip in the road.*

dip[2] /dɪp/ *vt,vi* (-pp-) **1** put, lower, into a liquid for a short time: *to dip one's pen into the ink.* **2** reach into and take out with one's hand, a spoon, ladle, etc: *dipped water from the well.* ***dip into,*** (*fig*): *dip into one's purse*, spend money; dip *into a book/an author*, read for a short time. **3** go below a surface or level: *The sun dipped below the horizon.* **4** lower and then raise: *to dip the wing of a plane.* **5** slope downward: *The land dips gently to the south.*

diph·theria /dɪfˈθɪriə/ *n* [U] serious disease of the throat causing difficulty in breathing.

diph·thong /ˈdɪfˌθɔŋ/ *n* [C] speech sound which is the union of two vowel sounds, eg /ai/ in *pipe* /paip/.

di·ploma /dɪˈploumə/ *n* [C] (*pl* ~s) certificate from a school, college, etc saying that one has graduated or completed a course of study: *a ~ in architecture.*

di·plo·macy /dɪˈplouməsi/ *n* [U] **1 (a)** management of the official business and relations between countries. **(b)** skill in this. **2** art of, skill in, dealing with people so that business is done smoothly.

diplo·mat /ˈdɪpləˌmæt/ *n* [C] person engaged in diplomacy for his country (eg an ambassador).

diplo·matic /ˌdɪpləˈmætɪk/ *adj* **1** of diplomacy: *the ~ service.* **2** tactful; having diplomacy(2): *a ~ answer; to be ~ in dealing with people.*

diplo·mati·cally /-kli/ *adv*

dip·so·mania /ˌdɪpsəˈmeiniə/ *n* [U] uncontrollable desire for alcoholic drink.

dip·so·maniac /ˌdɪpsəˈmeiniˌæk/ *n* [C] alcoholic.

dir. *abbr* = director.

dire /ˈdaiər/ *adj* **1** dreadful; terrible: *~ news.* **2** extreme: *to be in ~ need of help.*

di·rect[1] /dəˈrekt, dai-/ *adj* **1** (going) straight; not curved or crooked; not turned aside: *in a ~ line.* **2** with nothing or no one in between; in an unbroken line: *as a ~ result of this decision. He's* *a ~ descendant of John Adams.* **3** straightforward; going straight to the point: *He has a ~ way of speaking/doing things.* **4** exact: *the ~ opposite.* □ *adv* without interrupting a journey; without going by a roundabout way: *The train goes there ~.*

ˌdirect ˈcurrent, electric current flowing in one direction. ⇨ alternate².

di·rect·ness /-nɪs/ *n* [U]

ˌdirect ˈobject, (*gram*) the word or clause in a sentence which receives or undergoes the action of a transitive verb, eg *door* in *She opened the door.*

ˌdirect ˈspeech, (*gram*) speaker's actual words.

di·rect² /dəˈrekt, dai-/ *vt,vi* **1** tell or show how to do something, how to get somewhere: *Can you ~ me to the post office?* **2** address (the more usual word): *Should I ~ the letter to his office or to his home?* **3** speak or write to: *My remarks were not ~ed to all of you.* **4** manage; control: *Who is ~ing the play?* **5** turn to: *Our energies must be ~ed toward higher productivity.* **6** order: *The officer ~ed his men to advance slowly.*

di·rec·tion /dəˈrekʃən, dai-/ *n* **1** [C] course taken by a moving person or thing; point toward which a person or thing looks or faces: *Tom went off in one ~ and Harry in another* (~). **2** [U] ***have a good/poor sense of direction,*** be able/unable to determine well one's position when there are no known or visible landmarks. **3** [C] (often *pl*) information or instructions about what to do, where to go, how to do something, etc: *Directions for putting the parts together are printed on the card.* **4** [U] management; control; guidance: *He did the work under my ~.*

di·rec·tional *adj*

di·rec·tive /dəˈrektɪv, dai-/ *n* [C] order or instruction (usually given by someone in a position of authority).

di·rect·ly /dəˈrektli, dai-/ *adv* **1** in a direct manner: *He was looking ~ at us.* **2** at once; without delay: *Come in ~.* **3** in a short time: *I'll be there ~.*

di·rec·tor /dəˈrektər, dai-/ *n* [C] **1** person who directs, esp one of a group (called *the Board of Directors*) who manage the affairs of a business company. **2** person who supervises and instructs actors and actresses, the lighting, camera crew, etc for plays and motion pictures.

di·rec·tor·ate /dəˈrektərət, dai-/ *n* [C] **1** office or position of a director. **2** board of directors.

di·rec·tory /dəˈrektəri, dai-/ *n* [C] (*pl* -ies) (book with a) list of persons, business firms, etc in a district, with their addresses, usually in alphabetical order: *a telephone ~.*

dirge /dərdʒ/ *n* [C] song sung at a burial or for a dead person.

diri·gible /ˈdɪrədʒəbəl/ *n* [C] airship.

dirt /dərt/ *n* [U] **1** unclean matter (eg dust, soil, mud) esp when it is where it is not wanted (eg on the skin, clothes, in buildings): *His clothes were covered with ~.* **2** loose earth or soil: *a ~ road.* ***treat sb like dirt,*** treat him as if he were worthless. **3** obscene, unclean talk or action.

ˌdirt ˈcheap, very cheap.

dirty¹ /ˈdərti/ *adj* (-ier, -iest) **1** not clean; covered with dirt: *~ hands/clothes.* **2** causing one to be dirty: *~ work.* **3** obscene: *scribble ~ words on lavatory walls.* **4** (*informal*) mean, dishonorable: *play a ~ trick on her; ~ look,* one of severe disapproval or disgust.

dirt·ily /ˈdərtəli/ *adv*

dirty² /ˈdərti/ *vt,vi* (*pt,pp* -ied) make or become dirty: *Don't ~ your new dress.*

dis- /dɪs-/ *prefix* the negative, reverse, opposite of: *disorder; disagree; disbelieve.*

dis·abil·ity /ˌdɪsəˈbɪləti/ *n* (*pl* -ies) **1** [U] state of being disabled. **2** [C] something that disables or disqualifies a person.

dis·able /dɪˈseibəl/ *vt* make unable to do something, esp take away the power of using the limbs: *He was ~d in the war.*

dis·able·ment *n* [U]

dis·abuse /ˌdɪsəˈbyuz/ *vt* (*formal*) free (a person, his mind) from false ideas; put (a person) right (in his ideas): *to ~ a man of silly prejudices.*

dis·ad·van·tage /ˌdɪsədˈvæntɪdʒ/ *n* **1** [C] unfavorable condition; something that stands in the way of progress, success, etc: *It is a ~ to be small when you're standing in a crowd at a football game.* **2** [U] loss; injury: *rumors to his ~,* that hurt his reputation, etc.

dis·ad·van·tageous /ˌdɪˌsædvənˈteidʒəs/ *adj* causing a disadvantage (to): *in a ~ position.*

dis·ad·van·tageous·ly *adv*

dis·af·fected /ˌdɪsəˈfektɪd/ *adj* (*formal*) unfriendly; (inclined to be) disloyal.

dis·af·fec·tion /ˌdɪsəˈfekʃən/ *n* [U] discontent; disloyalty.

dis·agree /ˌdɪsəˈgri/ *vt* **1** be unlike or different, fail to agree: *the two reports ~.* **2** have different opinions; not agree; quarrel with: *I'm sorry to ~ with you/with your statement/with what you say.* **3** (of food, climate) have bad effects on; be unsuitable: *The climate/That fish ~s with me.*

dis·agree·able *adj* unpleasant: *~able weather; a ~able fellow.*

dis·agree·ably *adv*

dis·agree·ment /ˌdɪsəˈgrimənt/ *n* **1** [U] act of disagreeing; absence of agreement: *to be in ~ with him/the plan.* **2** [C] instance of this; difference of opinion; slight quarrel: *~s between husbands and wives.*

dis·al·low /ˌdɪsəˈlau/ *vt* refuse to allow or accept as correct: *The judge ~ed the claim.*

dis·ap·pear /ˌdɪsəˈpɪr/ *vi* go out of sight; be seen no more: *Let's hope our difficulties will soon ~.*

dis·ap·pear·ance /-rəns/ *n* [C,U]

dis·ap·point /ˌdɪsəˈpɔint/ *vt* **1** fail to do or be equal to what is hoped for or expected: *The book ~ed me.* **2** prevent a hope, plan, etc from being realized: *I'm sorry to ~ your expectations.*

dis·ap·pointed *adj* sad at not getting what was hoped for, etc: *We were ~ed to hear/~ed when we heard that you couldn't come. What are you looking so ~ed about?*

dis·ap·point·ed·ly *adv*

dis·ap·point·ing *adj* causing disappointment: *Our vacation was very ~ing.*

dis·ap·point·ment /ˌdɪsəˈpɔintmənt/ *n* **1** [U] being disappointed: *To her great ~, it rained on the day of the picnic.* **2** [C] person or thing that disappoints: *He had suffered many ~s in love.*

dis·ap·pro·ba·tion /ˌdɪˌsæprəˈbeiʃən/ *n* [U]

(*formal*) disapproval.

dis·ap·proval /ˌdɪsəˈpruvəl/ *n* [U] disapproving; failure to approve: *He shook his head in* ~, to show that he disapproved.

dis·ap·prove /ˌdɪsəˈpruv/ *vi,vt* have, express, an unfavorable opinion: *She wants to become an actress but her parents* ~ *(of her intentions).*

dis·ap·prov·ing·ly *adv* in a way that shows disapproval: *When John told the joke, his wife looked at him disapprovingly.*

dis·arm /dɪˈsarm/ *vi,vt* **1** take away weapons from: *Five hundred rebels were captured and* ~*ed.* **2** (of nations) reduce the size of, give up the use of, armed forces: *It is difficult to persuade the major powers to* ~. **3** make (a person) feel friendly; remove suspicion or doubt: *I felt angry, but her smiles* ~*ed me.*

dis·arma·ment /dɪˈsarməmənt/ *n* [U] disarming or being disarmed(2): ~*ament conferences.*

dis·ar·range /ˌdɪsəˈreindʒ/ *vt* disturb; upset; put into disorder: *The wind* ~*d her hair.*

dis·array /ˌdɪsəˈrei/ *vt n* [U] (put into) disorder: *The troops were in* ~.

dis·as·sociate /ˌdɪsəˈsouʃiˌeit/ *vt* = dissociate.

dis·as·ter /dɪˈzæstər/ *n* [C] great or sudden misfortune; terrible accident (eg a great flood or fire, an earthquake, a serious defeat in war, the loss of a large sum of money).

diˈsaster ˌarea *n* [C] area officially declared to be in a state of emergency because of a disaster, and therefore eligible for aid from the government.

dis·as·trous /dɪˈzæstrəs/ *adj* causing disaster: ~ *floods; a defeat that was* ~ *to the country.*

dis·as·trous·ly *adv*

dis·avow /ˌdɪsəˈvau/ *vt* (*formal*) deny belief in, approval or knowledge of: *He* ~*ed any share in the plot.*

dis·avowal *n* [C,U]

dis·band /dɪsˈbænd/ *vt,vi* (of organized groups) break up: *The army (was)* ~*ed when the war ended.*

dis·band·ment *n* [U]

dis·be·lief /ˌdɪsbɪˈlif/ *n* [U] lack of belief; refusal to believe.

dis·be·lieve /ˌdɪsbɪˈliv/ *vt,vi* refuse to believe; be unable or unwilling to believe in.

dis·burse /dɪsˈbərs, dɪˈspərs/ *vt,vi* pay out (money).

dis·burse·ment *n* **(a)** [U] paying out (of money). **(b)** [C] sum of money paid out.

disc /dɪsk/ *n* [C] **1** = disk. **2** phonograph record.

ˈdisc jockey, radio or TV broadcaster who introduces performers and comments on records and tapes (esp) of light and popular music. ⇨ deejay.

dis·card /dɪˈskard/ *vt* **1** throw out or away; put aside, give up (something useless or unwanted): *to* ~ *one's vest when the weather gets warm; to* ~ *old beliefs.* **2** remove a playing card from those in one's hand. □ *n* /ˈdɪˌskard/ [C] something discarded.

dis·cern /dɪˈsərn/ *vt* (*formal*) **1** see clearly (with the eyes or with the mind). **2** make out; recognize: *It is often difficult to* ~ *the truth of what we are told.*

dis·cern·ible *adj* that can be discerned.

dis·cern·ing *adj* able to see and understand well.

dis·cern·ment *n* [U] keenness in judging, forming opinions.

dis·charge[1] /ˈdɪsˌtʃardʒ/ *n* [C,U] **1** (act of) discharging or being discharged (all senses). **2** something that is discharged: *The* ~ *of water is carefully controlled.* **3** something (eg a document) that discharges: *received an honorable* ~ *from the army.*

dis·charge[2] /dɪsˈtʃardʒ/ *vt,vi* **1** unload (cargo from) a ship. **2** give or send out (liquid, gas, electric current, etc): *Where do the sewers* ~ *their contents? Lightning is caused by clouds discharging electricity.* **3** fire (a gun, etc); let fly (an arrow or other missile). **4** send (a person) away; allow (a person) to leave: *to* ~ *a patient from hospital. The accused man was found not guilty and was* ~*d.* **5** dismiss: *The typist was* ~*d for being dishonest.* **6** pay (a debt); perform (a duty).

dis·ciple /dɪˈsaipəl/ *n* [C] **1** follower of any leader of religious thought, art, learning, etc. **2** (usually **Disciple**) one of the twelve personal followers of Jesus Christ.

dis·ci·pli·nar·ian /ˌdɪsəplɪˈneriən/ *n* [C] person who maintains discipline[1](2): *a good/strict/poor* ~.

dis·ci·plin·ary /ˈdɪsəplɪˌneri/ *adj* of or for discipline: *to take* ~ *action;* ~ *punishment.*

dis·ci·pline[1] /ˈdɪsəplɪn/ *n* **1** [U] training, esp of the mind and character, to produce self-control, habits of obedience, etc: *school* ~*; military* ~. **2** [U] the result of such training; orderly behavior (eg among soldiers): *The soldiers showed perfect* ~ *under the fire of the enemy.* **3** [C] set rules for conduct; method by which training may be given: *Pronunciation drill and question and answer work are good* ~*s for learning a foreign language.* **4** [U] punishment. **5** [C] branch of knowledge; subject of instruction.

dis·ci·pline[2] /ˈdɪsəplɪn/ *vt* **1** apply discipline(1) to; train and control the mind and character of. **2** punish: *to* ~ *badly behaved children.* **3** bring under control.

dis·claim /dɪˈskleim/ *vt* say that one has no connection with: *to* ~ *responsibility for his behavior; to* ~ *all knowledge of an incident.*

dis·claimer *n* [C] denial of a claim on something or of responsibility for something.

dis·close /dɪˈsklouz/ *vt* **1** uncover; allow to be seen. **2** make known: *to* ~ *a secret.*

dis·clos·ure /dɪˈsklouʒər/ *n* **(a)** [U] disclosing or being disclosed. **(b)** [C] that which is disclosed (esp a secret).

disc·og·raphy /dɪsˈkagrəfi/ *n* [C] (*pl* -ies) list of phonograph records of a particular kind of music, of a particular composer, recorded by a particular artist, etc.

dis·color /dɪsˈkələr/ *vt,vi* change in color; stain: *walls* ~*ed by damp; paper that* ~*s in strong sunlight.*

dis·color·ation /dɪsˌkələˈreiʃən/ *n* [C,U]

dis·com·fit /dɪsˈkəmfɪt/ *vt* confuse; upset.

dis·comfi·ture /dɪsˈkəmfɪtʃər/ *n* [U]

dis·com·fort /dɪsˈkəmfərt/ *n* **1** [U] absence of

comfort; uneasiness of mind or body. **2** [C] something that causes uneasiness; hardship: *the ~s endured by explorers in the Antarctic.*

dis·con·cert /ˌdɪskənˈsɜrt/ *vt* **1** upset the calmness or self-possession of: *The Director was ~ed to discover a stranger in his office.* **2** spoil or upset (plans).

dis·con·nect /ˌdɪskəˈnekt/ *vt* separate; take (two things) apart: *You should ~ the toaster* (eg by pulling out the plug) *before you clean it.*

dis·con·nected *adj* (of speech or writing) having the ideas, etc badly ordered.

dis·con·so·late /dɪˈskansəlɪt/ *adj* unhappy; forlorn; without hope or comfort.

dis·con·so·late·ly *adv*

dis·con·tent /ˌdɪskənˈtent/ *n* [U] dissatisfaction; absence of contentment.

dis·con·tent·ed *adj* dissatisfied: *to be ~ with one's job.*

dis·con·tent·ed·ly *adv*

dis·con·tinue /ˌdɪskənˈtɪnyu/ *vt,vi* (*formal*) stop; give up; put an end to; come to an end: *I'm so busy that I shall have to ~ (paying) these weekly visits.*

dis·con·tinu·ance /-ˈtɪnyuəns/ *n* [U]

dis·con·tinu·ous /ˌdɪskənˈtɪnyuəs/ *adj* not continuous.

dis·cord /ˈdɪˌskɔrd/ *n* **1** [U] disagreement; quarreling; conflict: *What has brought ~ into the family*, caused its members to be quarrelsome? **2 (a)** [U] lack of harmony between sounds, notes, etc sounded together. **(b)** [C] instance of this.

dis·cor·dance /dɪˈskɔrdəns/ *n* [U] lack of harmony; disagreement.

dis·cor·dant /dɪˈskɔrdənt/ *adj* **1** not in agreement: *~ant opinions.* **2** (of sounds) not harmonious: *the ~ant noises of automobile horns.*

dis·cor·dant·ly *adv*

dis·co·theque /ˈdɪskəˌtek/ *n* [C] nightclub where people dance to recorded music.

dis·count[1] /ˈdɪˌskaunt/ *n* [C] amount of money which may be taken off the regular price of goods or off a bill if it is paid promptly.

ˈdiscount house, store that sells merchandise for less than the regular price.

dis·count[2] /ˈdɪˌskaunt, dɪˈskaunt/ *vt* **1** subtract a certain percentage from a bill, price, etc. **2** believe only part of a piece of news, a story, etc: *Some reporters like sensational news, so you should ~ a great deal of what appears in the popular press.*

dis·coun·ten·ance /dɪˈskauntənəns/ *vt* (*formal*) refuse to approve of.

dis·cour·age /dɪˈskərɪdʒ/ *vt* **1** lessen, take away, the courage or confidence of: *Don't let one failure ~ you; try again.* **2** put difficulties in the way of; try to keep from doing: *The wet weather is discouraging people from going to the meeting.*

dis·cour·age·ment *n* **(a)** [U] discouraging or being discouraged. **(b)** [C] something that does this.

dis·course /ˈdɪˌskɔrs/ *n* (*formal*) **1** [C] long speech or essay on a subject. **2** [U] conversation: *in ~ with.* □ *vi* /dɪˈskɔrs/ (*formal*) *talk, or write at length on a subject.*

dis·cour·teous /dɪsˈkɜrtiəs/ *adj* = impolite (the usual word): *It was ~ of you to arrive late.*

dis·cour·teous·ly *adv*

dis·cour·tesy /dɪsˈkɜrtəsi/ *n* [C,U]

dis·cover /dɪˈskəvər/ *vt* find out; see or learn of for the first time: *Columbus ~ed America, but did not explore the new continent.*

dis·cov·er·er *n* [C] person who has made a discovery.

dis·covery /dɪˈskəvəri/ *n* (*pl* -ies) **1** [U] discovering or being discovered: *a voyage of ~; the ~ of new chemical elements.* **2** [C] something that is discovered: *He made wonderful scientific discoveries.*

dis·credit[1] /dɪsˈkredɪt/ *vt* refuse to believe; cause the truth of (something) to seem doubtful: *The judge instructed the jury to ~ the testimony of one of the witnesses.*

dis·credit·able *adj*

dis·credit·ably *adv*

dis·credit[2] /dɪsˈkredɪt/ *n* **1** [U] loss of credit or reputation: *If you continue to behave in this way, you will bring ~ on yourself.* **2** [C] ***a discredit to,*** person, thing, causing such a loss: *a ~ to the school.* **3** [U] doubt; disbelief.

dis·creet /dɪˈskrit/ *adj* careful, tactful, in what one says and does: *to maintain a ~ silence.*

dis·creet·ly *adv*

dis·crep·ancy /dɪˈskrepənsi/ *n* [C,U] (*pl* -ies) (of statements and accounts) difference; absence of agreement: *There was considerable ~/There were numerous discrepancies between the two accounts of the fighting.*

dis·cre·tion /dɪˈskreʃən/ *n* [U] **1** being discreet: *You must show more ~ in choosing your friends.* **2** freedom to make one's own judgment or decision: *Use your ~.*

dis·cre·tion·ary /-ʃəˌneri/ *adj* having discretion (2): *~ary powers.*

dis·crimi·nate /dɪˈskrɪməˌneit/ *vt,vi* be, make, see, a difference between: *Can you ~ good books from bad/~ between good and bad books?* ***discriminate against,*** treat with less favor, usually unfairly: *laws which do not ~ against anyone*, that treat all people in the same way. ***discriminate in favor of,*** treat with special favor, often unfairly so.

dis·crimi·nat·ing *adj* **(a)** able to see or make small differences: *He isn't very discriminating in his choice of television programs.* **(b)** giving special or different treatment to certain people, countries, etc.

dis·crim·i·na·tory /dɪˈskrɪmənəˌtɔri/ *adj* discriminating(b): *discriminatory legislation.*

dis·crimi·na·tion /dɪˌskrɪməˈneiʃən/ *n* [U] **1** discriminating (a); ability to discriminate: *Some people do not show much ~ in their choice of books.* **2** (esp) unfair difference in the way people are treated: *Is there racial ~ in your country?*

dis·cur·sive /dɪˈskərsɪv/ *adj* wandering from one point or subject to another.

dis·cur·sive·ly *adv*

dis·cus /ˈdɪskəs/ *n* [C] (*pl* ~es) heavy, round plate of stone, metal or wood, thrown in ancient and in modern athletic contests (eg the Olympic Games).

dis·cuss /dɪˈskəs/ *vt* examine and argue about (a subject): *to ~ (with one's friends) what to do/how to do it/how something should be done.*
dis·cussion /dɪˈskəʃən/ *n* **1** [U] discussing or being discussed: *after much ~.* ***under discussion,*** being discussed: *The question is still under ~.* **2** [C] talk or argument on a subject: *after several ~s.*
dis·dain /dɪsˈdein/ *vt* (*formal*) look on with contempt; think (it) dishonorable, be too proud, (to do something): *A good man should ~ flattery. He ~ed (to accept) my offer of help.* □ *n* [U] contempt; scorn: *No one likes to be treated with ~.*
dis·dain·ful *adj* showing contempt: *~ful looks.*
dis·dain·fully /-fəli/ *adv*
dis·ease /dɪˈziz/ *n* **1** [U] illness; disorder of the normal functioning of an animal or plant. **2** [C] particular kind of illness or disorder.
dis·eased /dɪˈzizd/ *adj* suffering from, injured by, disease.
dis·em·bark /ˌdɪsɪmˈbark/ *vt,vi* put, go, on shore: *~ from the liner.*
dis·em·bar·ka·tion /ˌdɪsɪmbarˈkeiʃən/ *n* [C,U]
dis·en·chant /ˌdɪsɪnˈtʃænt/ *vt* free from enchantment or illusion: *He is quite ~ed with the Administration.*
dis·en·chant·ment *n* [C,U]
dis·en·fran·chise /ˌdɪsɪnˈfrænˌtʃaiz/ *vt* = disfranchise.
dis·en·gage /ˌdɪsɪnˈgeidʒ/ *vt,vi* free (oneself or something) from anything that engages or holds: *to ~ the gears of a car.*
dis·en·tangle /ˌdɪsɪnˈtæŋgəl/ *vt,vi* **1** free, from complications, tangles or confusion: *to ~ truth from falsehood.* **2** become clear of tangles.
dis·favor /dɪsˈfeivər/ *n* [U] (*formal*) state of being out of favor; disapproval: *to be in ~; to fall into ~.*
dis·fig·ure /dɪsˈfɪgyər/ *vt* spoil the appearance or shape of: *beautiful scenery ~d by ugly advertising signs; a face ~d by a broken nose/an ugly scar.*
dis·fig·ure·ment *n* [C,U]
dis·fran·chise /dɪsˈfrænˌtʃaiz/ *vt* deprive of a legal right or privilege; (esp) deprive (a citizen) of the right to vote.
dis·gorge /dɪsˈgɔrdʒ/ *vt* throw up or out from, or as from, the throat. **2** (*fig*) give up (esp unwillingly).
dis·grace[1] /dɪsˈgreis/ *n* **1** [U] loss of respect, favor, reputation: *A man who commits a crime and is sent to prison brings ~ on himself and his family.* **2** [U] state of having lost respect, etc: *He told a lie and is in ~.* **3** [C] (usually *sing*) cause of shame or discredit: *These slums are a ~ to the city.*
dis·grace·ful *adj* bringing or causing disgrace: *~ful behavior.*
dis·grace·fully *adv*
dis·grace[2] /dɪsˈgreis/ *vt* **1** bring disgrace on; be a disgrace to: *Don't ~ the family name.* **2** cause (a person) to lose favor.
dis·gruntled /dɪsˈgrəntəld/ *adj* discontented; in a bad mood.
dis·guise[1] /dɪsˈgaiz, dɪˈskaiz/ *vt* **1** change the appearance, etc of, in order to deceive or to hide the identity of: *He ~d his looks but he could not ~ his voice.* **2** conceal: *He ~d his sorrow beneath a cheerful appearance/by appearing cheerful.*
dis·guise[2] /dɪsˈgaiz, dɪˈskaiz/ *n* **1** [U] disguising; disguised condition: *He went among the enemy in ~.* **2** [C,U] dress, actions, manner, etc used for disguising: *He had tried all sorts of ~s.*
dis·gust[1] /dɪsˈgəst, dɪˈskəst/ *n* [U] strong feeling of dislike or distaste (eg caused by a bad smell or taste, a horrible sight, evil conduct): *He turned away in ~.*
dis·gust[2] /dɪsˈgəst, dɪˈskəst/ *vt* cause disgust in: *We were ~ed at/by/with what we saw.*
dis·gust·ing *adj*
dis·gust·ing·ly *adv*
dish[1] /dɪʃ/ *n* [C] **1** shallow, flat-bottomed vessel, of earthenware, glass, metal, etc from which food is served. **2** (*pl*) all the plates, bowls, cups and saucers, etc used for a meal: *to do/wash the ~es,* clean them after a meal. **3** (kind of) food prepared in a certain way: *His favorite ~ is fried chicken.* **4** contents of a dish: *a ~ of ice cream.* **5** (*sl*) attractive girl: *She's quite a ~!*
ˈdish·cloth *n* [C] cloth for washing dishes, etc.
ˈdish·ful /-ˌfʊl/ *n* [C] as much as a dish can hold.
ˈdish towel, cloth for drying dishes, etc that have been washed.
ˈdish·washer *n* [C] machine for washing dishes, cutlery, etc.
ˈdish·water *n* [U] water in which dishes are to be or have been washed.
dish[2] /dɪʃ/ *vt* **1** put on or into a dish: *to ~ up dinner.* **2** (*fig*) prepare, serve up: *to ~ up the usual arguments in a new form.* ***dish sth out,*** (*informal*) distribute it; give it out.
dis·hearten /dɪsˈhartən/ *vt* cause to lose courage or confidence: *Don't be ~ed by what he says.*
di·shev·eled, di·shev·elled /dɪˈʃevəld/ *adj* (of the hair and clothes) untidy.
dis·hon·est /dɪˈsanəst/ *adj* not honest; intended to cheat, deceive or mislead.
dis·hon·est·ly *adv*
dis·honesty /dɪˈsanəsti/ *n* (*pl* -ies) **(a)** [U] being dishonest. **(b)** [C] dishonest act, etc.
dis·hon·or /dɪˈsanər/ *n* [U] **1** disgrace or shame; loss, absence, of honor and self-respect: *to bring ~ on one's family.* **2** person or thing that brings dishonor: *He was a ~ to his regiment.* □ *vt* **1** bring shame, discredit. **2** refuse to take or pay a bill or check.
dis·hon·or·able *adj* without honor; shameful.
dis·hon·or·ably *adv*
dis·il·lu·sion /ˌdɪsəˈluʒən/ *vt* set free from mistaken beliefs: *They had thought that the vacation would be restful, but they were soon ~ed.* □ *n* [U] = disillusionment.
dis·il·lu·sion·ment *n* [U] freedom from illusions: *in a state of complete ~ment.*
dis·in·cli·na·tion /ˌdɪˌsɪnkləˈneiʃən/ *n* [U] unwillingness: *Some students have a strong ~ for study.*
dis·in·clined /ˌdɪsɪnˈklaind/ *adj* (*formal*) reluctant or unwilling: *He was ~ to help me.*
dis·in·fect /ˌdɪsɪnˈfekt/ *vt* make free of bacteria which might cause disease: *The house was ~ed after Tom had had scarlet fever.*

dis·in·fec·tant /ˌdɪsɪnˈfektənt/ *adj, n* [C] disinfecting (chemical).

dis·in·herit /ˌdɪsɪnˈherɪt/ *vt* take away the right to inherit.

dis·in·heri·tance /ˌdɪsɪnˈherɪtəns/ *n* [C,U] (act of) disinheriting.

dis·in·te·grate /dɪˈsɪntəˌgreit/ *vt,vi* (cause to) break up into small parts or pieces: *rocks ~d by frost and rain.*

dis·in·te·gra·tion /dɪˌsɪntəˈgreiʃən/ *n* [U]

dis·in·ter /ˌdɪsɪnˈtər/ *vt* (-rr-) dig up (a body) from the earth (eg from a grave).

dis·in·ter·ment *n* [C,U]

dis·in·ter·est /dɪˈsɪntrəst/ *n* [U] **1** absence of selfish interest. **2** lack of interest.

dis·in·ter·ested /dɪˈsɪntrəstɪd/ *adj* **1** not influenced by personal feelings or interests: *His action was not altogether ~.* **2** uninterested.

dis·in·ter·est·ed·ly *adv*

dis·jointed /dɪsˈdʒɔintɪd/ *adj* (eg of speech and writing) not connected; not orderly.

dis·jointed·ly *adv*

dis·jointed·ness /-nɪs/ *n* [U]

disk /dɪsk/ *n* [C] **1** flat, round plate, eg a coin. **2** round surface that appears to be flat: *the sun's ~.* **3** (*anat*) layer of cartilage between vertebrae of the spine. **4** (*comp*) circular plate coated with magnetic material, used to store computer programs, data, etc.

dis·like /dɪsˈlaik/ *vt* not like: *to ~ getting up early/being disturbed.* □ *n* [C] feeling of not liking; feeling against: *to have a ~ of/for cats; to take a ~ to him,* begin to dislike him.

dis·lo·cate /ˈdɪslouˌkeit/ *vt* **1** put (esp a bone in the body) out of position: *He fell off a ladder and ~ his shoulder.* **2** put (a functioning system) in disorder: *Traffic was badly ~d by the heavy snowfall.*

dis·lo·cation /ˌdɪslouˈkeiʃən/ *n* [U].

dis·lodge /dɪsˈladʒ/ *vt* move, force, from the place occupied: *to ~ a stone from a building/the enemy from their positions.*

dis·loyal /dɪsˈlɔiəl/ *adj* not loyal (to).

dis·loyal·ly *adv*

dis·loyal·ty *n* [C,U]

dis·mal /ˈdɪzməl/ *adj* sad, gloomy; miserable; comfortless: *~ weather; in a ~ voice.*

dis·mal·ly *adv*

dis·mantle /dɪsˈmæntəl/ *vt* **1** take away fittings, furnishings, etc from: *The old warship was ~d,* its guns, armor, engines, etc were taken out. **2** take to pieces: *to ~ an engine.*

dis·may /dɪˈsmei/ *n* [U] feeling of fear and discouragement: *The news that the enemy was near filled them with ~.* □ *vt* fill with dismay: *We were ~ed at the news.*

dis·mem·ber /dɪsˈmembər/ *vt* **1** tear or cut the limbs from: *He was ~ed by the lion.* **2** break up into pieces.

dis·miss /dɪˈsmɪs/ *vt* **1** send away (from one's employment, from service): *He was ~ed for being lazy and dishonest.* **2** allow to go: *The teacher ~ed her class when the bell rang.* **3** stop thinking or talking about: *to ~ all thoughts of revenge.*

dis·mis·sal *n* [C,U]

dis·mount /dɪsˈmaunt/ *vi,vt* **1** get down (from a horse, bike etc). **2** remove (something) from its mount: *to ~ a gun* (from the gun carriage). **3** cause to fall (from a horse, etc): *The knight ~ed his opponent.*

dis·obedi·ence /ˌdɪsəˈbidiəns/ *n* [U] failure or refusal to obey: *acts of ~; ~ to orders.*

dis·obedi·ent /ˌdɪsəˈbidiənt/ *adj* not obedient (to).

dis·obedi·ent·ly *adv*

dis·obey /ˌdɪsəˈbei/ *vt* pay no attention to orders; not obey a person, a law, etc.

dis·order /dɪˈsɔrdər/ *n* **1** [U] absence of order; confusion: *The burglars left the room in great ~.* **2(a)** [U] absence of order caused by political troubles. **(b)** [C] riot: *Troops were called out to deal with the ~s in the capital.* **3** [C,U] abnormal state of the body or mind: *suffering from mental ~.* □ *vt* put into disorder: *a ~ed mind.*

dis·order·ly /dɪˈsɔrdərli/ *adj* **1** in disorder: *a ~ room/desk.* **2** causing disturbance; unruly; lawless: *~ crowds/behavior.*

dis·or·gan·ize /ˌdɪˈsɔrgəˌnaiz/ *vt* throw into confusion; upset the working or system of: *The train service was ~d by fog.*

dis·or·gan·iz·ation /dɪˌsɔrgənəˈzeiʃən/ *n* [U]

dis·orient /dɪˈsɔriənt/ (also **dis·orien·tate** /dɪˈsɔriənˌteit/) *vt* cause (a person) to lose his sense of direction, time, etc.

dis·own /dɪˈsoun/ *vt* say that one does not know, that one does not have, or no longer wishes to have, any connection with (a person or thing): *The man was so cruel that his friends ~ed him.*

dis·par·age /dɪˈspærɪdʒ/ *vt* belittle (a person or thing); speak slightingly of.

dis·par·age·ment *n* [U]

dis·par·ag·ing·ly *adv* in a disparaging manner.

dis·par·ate /ˈdɪspərɪt/ *adj* too different or unlike to be compared.

dis·par·ity /dɪˈspærəti/ *n* **1** [U] inequality; difference. **2** [C] (*pl* -ies) instance or degree of this.

dis·pas·sion·ate /dɪsˈpæʃənɪt/ *adj* free from feeling or prejudice; not taking sides, not showing favor (in a quarrel, etc between others).

dis·pas·sion·ate·ly *adv*

dis·patch[1] /dɪˈspætʃ/ *n* **1** [U] dispatching or being dispatched (all senses): *Please hurry up the ~ of these messages.* **2** [C] message, report, esp a government, military or newspaper report: *Large newspapers receive ~es from all parts of the world.* **3** [U] (*formal*) speed: *to act with ~.*

dis·patch[2] /dɪˈspætʃ/ *vt* **1** send off, to a destination, on a journey, for a special purpose: *to ~ letters/telegrams/a messenger.* **2** finish, get through, business, etc quickly. **3** kill: *The executioner quickly ~ed the condemned man.*

dis·pel /dɪˈspel/ *vt* (-ll-) drive away; scatter: *The wind soon ~led the fog. How can we ~ their doubts and fears?*

dis·pens·able /dɪˈspensəbəl/ *adj* that can be done without; not necessary.

dis·pens·ary /dɪˈspensəri/ *n* [C] (*pl* -ies) place where medicines, medical care, etc are given out.

dis·pen·sa·tion /ˌdɪspənˈseiʃən/ *n* **1** [U] the act of dispensing(1) or distributing: *the ~ of justice/*

medicine/food. **2** [C,U] permission to disregard a rule or law, esp an ecclesiastical law: *to be granted ~ from fasting during a journey.*

dis·pense /dɪˈspens/ *vt,vi* **1** deal out; distribute; administer: *to ~ charity/justice.* **2** mix; prepare, give out (medicines): *to ~ a prescription.* **3** ***dispense with,*** **(a)** do without: *He is not yet well enough to ~ with the doctor's services.* **(b)** make unnecessary: *The new engine design ~s with gears.*

dis·penser *n* [C] **(a)** person who dispenses, esp medicines. **(b)** container from which something can be obtained without removing a cover, lid, etc: *a ~r for liquid soap/paper cups.*

dis·perse /dɪˈspərs/ *vt,vi* (cause to) go in different directions; scatter: *The police ~d the crowd. The crowd ~d when the police arrived.*

dis·per·sal /dɪˈspərsəl/ *n* [U] dispersing or being dispersed.

dis·per·sion /dɪˈspərʒən/ *n* [U] = dispersal, esp of light into its different colors.

dis·pirited /dɪˈspɪrɪtɪd/ *adj* discouraged; disheartened.

dis·place /dɪsˈpleis/ *vt* **1** put out of the right or usual position. **2** take the place of: *Tom has ~d Harry in Mary's affections.*

dis·place·ment /dɪsˈpleismənt/ *n* [U] **1** displacing or being displaced: *the ~ of human labor by machines.* **2** weight of the amount of water displaced by a solid body in it, or floating in it: *a ship of 10,000 tons ~.*

dis·play[1] /dɪˈsplei/ *n* [C,U] displaying; show or exhibition: *a ~ of bad temper.*

dis·play[2] /dɪˈsplei/ *vt* **1** show; place or spread out for viewing: *Department stores ~ their goods in the windows.* **2** allow to be seen; show signs of: *to ~ one's ignorance. She ~ed no sign of emotion.*

dis·please /dɪsˈpliz/ *vt* offend; annoy; make indignant or angry: *to be ~d with her for acting silly; to be ~d at her conduct.*

dis·pleas·ing *adj* not pleasing (to a person).

dis·pleas·ing·ly *adv*

dis·pleasure /dɪsˈpleʒər/ *n* [U] displeased feeling; dissatisfaction: *He incurred his father's ~.*

dis·pos·able /dɪˈspouzəbəl/ *adj* made so that it may be (easily) disposed of after use: *~ diapers.*

dis·posal /dɪˈspouzəl/ *n* [U] **1** the act of disposing(1,2): *the ~ of rubbish,* getting rid of it; *a ˈbomb ~ squad,* group of men who, when unexploded bombs are found, try to make them harmless and remove them. **2** control; management. ***at one's disposal,*** to be used as one wishes: *My desk is at your ~.*

dis·pose /dɪˈspouz/ *vi,vt* **1** ***dispose of,*** finish with; get rid of; deal with: *to ~ of rubbish. He doesn't want to ~ of* (eg sell) *the land.* **2** place (persons, objects) in good order or in suitable positions: *The cruisers were ~d in a single line.* **3** (*formal*) be willing or inclined: *I'm not ~d/ don't feel ~d to help that lazy fellow.*

dis·po·si·tion /ˌdɪspəˈzɪʃən/ *n* [C] **1** = arrangement (the more usual word): *the ~ of furniture in a room.* **2** person's natural qualities of mind and character: *a man with a cheerful ~.* **3** inclination: *There was a general ~ to leave early,* most people seemed to wish to leave early. **4** power of ordering and disposing: *Who has the ~ of this property,* the power or authority to dispose of it?

dis·pos·sess /ˌdɪspəˈzes/ *vt* take away (property, esp land) from; compel (a person) to give up (the house or land he occupies): *The nobles were ~ed of their property after the revolution.*

dis·pro·por·tion·ate /ˌdɪsprəˈpɔrʃənɪt/ *adj* out of proportion; relatively too large or small, etc: *to give a ~ amount of one's time to games.*

dis·pro·por·tion·ate·ly *adv*

dis·prove /ˌdɪsˈpruv/ *vt* prove to be wrong or false.

dis·put·able /dɪˈspyutəbəl/ *adj* that may be disputed; questionable.

dis·pu·tant /dɪˈspyutənt/ *n* [C] person who disputes.

dis·pute[1] /dɪˈspyut/ *n* **1** [U] debate, argument: *The matter in ~* (= being disputed) *is the ownership of a house.* **2** [C] quarrel; controversy: *Religious ~s in England during the 17th century caused many people to flee to America.*

dis·pute[2] /dɪˈspyut/ *vi,vt* **1** argue, debate, quarrel. **2** discuss, question the truth or validity of: *to ~ a statement/a claim/a decision.* **3** oppose; resist: *to ~ an advance by the enemy.*

dis·qual·ify /dɪsˈkwaləˌfai/ *vt* (*pt,pp* -ied) make or declare unfit: *As he was a professional, he was disqualified from taking part in the Olympic Games.*

dis·quali·fi·ca·tion /dɪsˌkwaləfɪˈkeiʃən/ *n* [C,U]

dis·quiet /dɪsˈkwaiɪt/ *vt* (*formal*) make, anxious, uneasy: *~ed by fears of illness.* □ *n* [U] anxiety: *The President's speech caused considerable ~ in some European capitals.*

dis·quiet·ing *adj* causing anxiety: *~ing news.*

dis·re·gard /ˌdɪsriˈgard/ *vt* pay no attention to; show no respect for: *to ~ a warning.* □ *n* [U] inattention; indifference; neglect: *~ of a rule; ~ for one's teachers.*

dis·re·pair /ˌdɪsriˈper/ *n* [U] the state of needing repair: *The building was in a state of ~.*

dis·repu·table /dɪsˈrepyətəbəl/ *adj* having a bad reputation; not respectable: *a ~ appearance.*

dis·repu·tably *adv*

dis·re·pute /ˌdɪsriˈpyut/ *n* [U] condition of being disreputable; discredit. ***fall into disrepute,*** no longer have a good reputation.

dis·re·spect /ˌdɪsriˈspekt/ *n* [U] rudeness; lack of respect: *He meant no ~ by that remark,* did not intend to be impolite.

dis·re·spect·ful *adj* showing disrespect.

dis·re·spect·fully *adv*

dis·rupt /dɪsˈrəpt/ *vt* break up, split, separate by force a state, an empire, communications, etc: *Their quarrels seem likely to ~ the meeting.*

dis·rup·tion /dɪsˈrəpʃən/ *n* [U] disrupting or being disrupted: *the ~ion of the Roman Empire.*

dis·rup·tive /dɪsˈrəptɪv/ *adj* causing disruption: *~ive forces.*

dis·sat·is·fac·tion /dɪ(s)ˌsætɪsˈfækʃən/ *n* [U] state of being dissatisfied.

dis·sat·isfy /dɪ(s)ˈsætɪsˌfai/ *vt* (*pt,pp* -ied) fail to satisfy; make discontented: *to be dissatisfied with one's salary.*

dis·sect /dɪˈsekt, dai-/ *vt* cut up (an animal body, plant, etc) into parts in order to study its structure.
dis·sec·tion /dɪˈsekʃən, dai-/ *n* [C,U]

dis·semi·nate /dɪˈsemə,neit/ *vt* distribute or spread widely.
dis·semi·na·tion /dɪ,seməˈneiʃən/ *n* [U]

dis·sen·sion /dɪˈsenʃən/ *n* **1** [U] angry quarreling. **2** [C] instance of this.

dis·sent[1] /dɪˈsent/ *n* [U] dissenting; (expression of) disagreement: *to express strong ~.*

dis·sent[2] /dɪˈsent/ *vi* **1** refuse to consent. **2** have a different opinion (from); disagree: *I strongly ~ from what the last speaker has said.* **3** (esp) refuse to accept the religious doctrine of an established church.
dis·sen·ter *n* [C] (often **Dissenter**) person who dissents(3).

dis·ser·ta·tion /,dɪsərˈteiʃən/ *n* [C] long written or spoken account (eg as submitted for a higher university degree): *a ~ on/upon/concerning ....*

dis·ser·vice /,dɪsˈsərvɪs/ *n* [U] harmful or unhelpful action: *You are doing her a great ~ in spreading such rumors.*

dis·si·dent /ˈdɪsədənt/ *adj* disagreeing. □ *n* [C] person who disagrees.

dis·simi·lar /,dɪsˈsɪmələr/ *adj* different; not similar: *people with ~ tastes.*
dis·simi·lar·ity /,dɪs,sɪməˈlærəti/ *n* **(a)** [U] lack of similarity. **(b)** [C] (*pl* -ies) point of difference.

dis·si·pate /ˈdɪsə,peit/ *vt,vi* **1** (cause to) disperse, go away: *to ~ fear/doubt/ignorance.* **2** waste time, leisure, money foolishly: *Don't ~ your efforts.*
dis·si·pated *adj* behaving in a wasteful and often harmful way: *to lead a ~d life.*

dis·si·pa·tion /,dɪsəˈpeiʃən/ *n* [U] dissipating or being dissipated: *a life of ~.*

dis·sociate /dɪˈsouʃi,eit/ *vt* separate or disconnect from: *A politician's public and private life should be ~d. I wish to ~ myself from what has just been said.*
dis·socia·tion /dɪ,souʃiˈeiʃən/ *n* [U]

dis·sol·uble /dɪˈsalyəbəl/ *adj* that can be dissolved.
dis·solu·bil·ity /dɪ,salyəˈbɪləti/ *n*

dis·so·lute /ˈdɪsə,lut/ *adj* (of persons, their behavior) immoral, evil; vicious: *to lead a ~ life.*
dis·so·lute·ly *adv*

dis·sol·ution /,dɪsəˈluʃən/ *n* [C,U] breaking up; undoing or ending (of a marriage, partnership, etc).

dis·solve /dɪˈzalv/ *vt,vi* **1** (of a solid) become or cause to become liquid; melt: *Salt ~s in water. He ~d the salt in water.* **2** disappear; fade away: *The view ~d in mist.* **3** bring to, come to, an end: *to ~ a business partnership/a marriage.*

dis·son·ance /ˈdɪsənəns/ *n* **1** [U] discord. **2** [C] combination of notes that is discordant.

dis·son·ant /ˈdɪsənənt/ *adj* harsh or discordant in tone.

dis·suade /dɪˈsweid/ *vt* advise against: *I tried to ~ her from marrying him.*
dis·sua·sion /dɪˈsweiʒən/ *n* [U]

dis·taff /ˈdɪ,stæf/ *n* [C] stick for holding wool, flax, etc in spinning.

dis·tance /ˈdɪstəns/ *n* [C,U] **1** measure of space, between two points, places, etc: *In most English-speaking countries ~ is measured in miles, not in kilometers. The town is a great ~ off,* a long way off. ***in the distance,*** far away: *A ship could be seen in the ~.* **2** space of time: *to look back over a ~ of fifty years.*

dis·tant /ˈdɪstənt/ *adj* **1** far away in space or time: *We had a ~ view of Mt. Everest.* **2** far off in family relationship: *She's a ~ cousin of mine.* **3** (of degree of similarity) not easily seen: *There is a ~ resemblance between the cousins.* **4** reserved; not warm or friendly: *She's always very ~ with strangers.*
dis·tant·ly *adv*

dis·taste /dɪsˈteist/ *n* [U] dislike: *a ~ for hard work.*
dis·taste·ful *adj* disagreeable; unpleasant: *It is ~ful to me to have to say this, but....*
dis·taste·fully *adv*

dis·tend /dɪˈstend/ *vt,vi* (cause to) swell out (by pressure from within): *a ~ed stomach/vein.*

dis·till, dis·til /dɪˈstɪl/ *vt,vi* (-ll-) **1** change (a liquid) to vapor by heating, cool the vapor and collect the drops of liquid that condense from the vapor, as in purifying water, making whiskey, etc: *Salt water can be ~ed and made into drinking water.* **2** fall, let fall, in drops: *flowers that ~ nectar.*
dis·til·la·tion /,dɪstəˈleiʃən/ *n* **1** [U] distilling or being distilled. **2** [C,U] substance obtained by distilling.

dis·til·ler /dɪˈstɪlər/ *n* [C] person who distills (esp whiskey).
dis·til·lery *n* [C] place where liquids (eg gin, whiskey) are distilled.

dis·tinct /dɪˈstɪŋkt/ *adj* **1** easily heard, seen, understood; clearly marked: *a ~ pronunciation. There is a ~ improvement in her typing.* **2** different; separate: *Keep the two ideas ~,* the one from the other.
dis·tinct·ly *adv*

dis·tinc·tion /dɪˈstɪŋkʃən/ *n* **1 (a)** [U] distinguishing, being distinguished, as different. **(b)** [C] instance of this: *It is difficult to make exact ~s between all the meanings of a word.* **2** [C] something which distinguishes or marks as different: *The ~ between poetry and prose is obvious.* **3** [U] quality of being superior, excellent, distinguished: *a writer/novel of ~.* **4** [C] mark of honor: *academic ~s,* eg a doctor's degree.

dis·tinc·tive /dɪˈstɪŋktɪv/ *adj* serving to mark a difference or make distinct: *Soldiers often have ~ insignias on their lapels.*
dis·tinc·tive·ly *adv*

dis·tin·guish /dɪˈstɪŋgwɪʃ/ *vt,vi* **1** see, hear, recognize, understand as different: *The twins were so alike that it was impossible to ~ one from the other.* **2** make out by looking, listening, etc: *A person with good eyesight can ~ distant objects.* **3** mark as different: *Speech ~es man from the animals.* **4** behave so as to bring credit or distinction: *to ~ oneself in an examination.*
dis·tin·guish·able /-əbəl/ *adj* that can be distinguished between: *Tom is hardly ~able from his twin brother.*

dis·tin·guished /dɪˈstɪŋgwɪʃt/ *adj* famous; well known; remarkable; showing distinction(3):

He is ~ for his knowledge of economics/*~ as an economist.*

dis·tort /dɪˈstɔrt/ *vt* **1** pull, twist, out of the usual shape: *a face ~ed by pain.* **2** give a false or inaccurate account of: *Newspaper accounts of international affairs are sometimes ~ed.*

dis·tor·tion /dɪˈstɔrʃən/ *n* **1** [U] distorting or being distorted. **2** [C] instance of this; something that is distorted.

dis·tract /dɪˈstrækt/ *vt* draw away a person's attention, concentration, etc: *The noise in the street ~ed me from my reading.*

dis·trac·tion /dɪˈstrækʃən/ *n* **1** [U] distracting or being distracted. **2** [C] something (annoying and unwelcome) that distracts: *Noise is a ~ when you are trying to study.* **3** [C] something that amuses and entertains: *He complained that there were not enough ~s in the town.* **4** [U] wildness or confusion of mind: *He loves her to ~. You'll drive me to ~ with your silly questions.*

dis·traught /dɪˈstrɔt/ *adj* extremely upset: *~ with grief.*

dis·tress[1] /dɪˈstres/ *n* [U] **1** (cause of) great pain, discomfort or sorrow: *He was a great ~ to his mother.* **2** (suffering caused by) great need; or lack of money. **3** serious danger or difficulty: *a ship in ~; a ~ signal.*

dis·tress[2] /dɪˈstres/ *vt* cause distress(2) to: *the news of her illness ~ed him.*

dis·tress·ing *adj* causing or experiencing distress.

dis·trib·ute /dɪˈstrɪbyut/ *vt* **1** give or send out: *The teacher ~d the books to the class.* **2** spread out (over a larger area): *to ~ fertilizer over a field.* **3** divide into groups or classes.

dis·tribu·tion /ˌdɪstrəˈbyuʃən/ *n* [U] distributing or being distributed; manner of being distributed; [C] instance or occasion of distributing: *They could not agree about the ~ of the profits.*

dis·tribu·tive /dɪˈstrɪbyət̬ɪv/ *adj* **1** of distribution. **2** (*gram*) of each individual, each member of a class: *"Each," "every," "either" and "neither" are ~ pronouns.*

dis·tribu·tive·ly *adv*

dis·tri·bu·tor /dɪˈstrɪbyətər/ *n* [C] **1** person who distributes. **2** part of the engine (in a motor vehicle) that sends electricity to the spark plugs.

dis·trict /ˈdɪstrɪkt/ *n* [C] **1** part of a country or area: *a mountainous ~.* **2** part of a town or country marked out or used for a special purpose: *voting ~s; the garment ~ in New York City.*

district atˈtorney, chief prosecuting attorney of esp a city government, often elected.

dis·trust /dɪsˈtrəst/ *n* [U] doubt or suspicion; want of trust or confidence: *The child looked at the big stranger with ~.* □ *vt* have no trust in; be doubtful about: *He ~ed his own eyes.*

dis·trust·ful *adj* suspicious; not trusting: *I was ~ful of his motives.*

dis·trust·fully *adv*

dis·turb /dɪˈstərb/ *vt* break the quiet, calm, peace or order of; put out of the right or usual position: *She opened the door quietly so as not to ~ the sleeping child. He was ~ed to hear of your illness*/*was ~ed by the news of your illness.*

dis·turb·ance /dɪˈstərbəns/ *n* **1** [U] disturbing or being disturbed. **2** [C] instance of this; something that disturbs; disorder (esp social or political): *Don't cause any more ~s. Were there many political ~s in the country last year?*

dis·unity /dɪsˈyunəti/ *n* [U] lack of unity; dissension.

dis·use /dɪsˈyus/ *n* [U] state of no longer being used: *machines that have fallen into ~.*

dis·used /dɪsˈyuzd/ *adj* no longer used.

ditch /dɪtʃ/ *n* [C] narrow channel dug in or between fields, or at the sides of a road, etc to hold or carry off water. □ *vt* **1** send or throw into a ditch. **2** (*fig*) abandon: *The pilot had to ~ his plane,* make a forced landing on water. *He's ~ed his girlfriend,* (*informal*) stopped seeing her.

dither /ˈdɪðər/ *n* (*informal*) disturbed or excitable state.

dithery *adj*

ditto /ˈdɪtou/ *n* [C] (*pl* ~s) **1** the same (used in lists to avoid writing words again): *One hat at $25; ~ at $50.* **2** mark (") used as a symbol for *ditto.*

ditty /ˈdɪti/ *n* [C] (*pl* -ies) short, simple song.

di·van /ˈdaiˌvæn, ˌdaiˈvæn/ *n* [C] long, low, soft, backless seat or bed.

dive[1] /daiv/ *n* [C] **1** act of diving, esp into water: *a graceful ~.* **2** (*sl*) disreputable bar or nightclub.

dive[2] /daiv/ *vi* (*pt* ~d also dove /douv/) **1** go head first into water: *He ~d from the bridge and rescued the drowning child.* **2** (of a submarine, divers) go under water. *to ~ for pearls.* **3** go quickly to a lower level: *The aircraft ~d steeply.* **4** move (eg the hand) quickly and suddenly downwards (into something): *He ~d into his pocket and pulled out a handful of coins.*

diver *n* [C] person who dives (1,2), esp a person who works under water in a diving suit.

ˈdiving board, from which to dive (esp into a swimming pool).

ˈdiving suit, suit with heavy boots and a helmet worn by a diver.

di·verge /dɪˈvərdʒ, dai-/ *vi* lie or move apart from a common point turn or branch away from: *to ~ from the beaten track; diverging views*/*opinions.*

di·ver·gence /dɪˈvərdʒəns, dai-/ *n* **(a)** [U] diverging. **(b)** [C] instance of this.

di·ver·gent /-dʒənt/ *adj*

di·vers /ˈdaivərz/ *adj* (*old use*) several; more than one.

di·verse /daiˈvərs, dɪ-/ *adj* of different kinds: *The wild life in Africa is extremely ~.*

di·verse·ly *adv*

di·ver·sify /dɪˈvərsəˌfai/ *vt* (*pt,pp* -ied) make diverse; give variety to.

di·ver·si·fi·ca·tion /dɪˌvərsəfəˈkeiʃən/ *n* [U]

di·ver·sion /dɪˈvərʒən, dai-/ *n* **1** **(a)** [U] diverting; the act of turning something aside or giving it a different direction. **(b)** [C] instance of this. **2** [C] something amusing or which gives rest or amusement: *Chess and tennis are his favorite ~s.* **3** [C] attack made to draw the enemy's attention from one place to another: *to create*/*make a ~.*

di·ver·sionary /dɪˈvərʒəˌneri, dai-/ *adj*

di·ver·sity /dɪˈvərsəti, dai-/ *n* [U] the state of

being diverse; variety.

di·vert /dɪˈvərt, dai-/ *vt* **1** turn in another direction: *to ~ a river from its course.* **2** amuse; entertain: *Some people are easily ~ed.*

di·vest /daiˈvest, dɪ-/ *vt* (*formal*) **1** take off (clothes): *to ~ a king of his robes.* **2** take away from; deprive: *to ~ an official of power and authority.*

di·vide[1] /dɪˈvaid/ *vt,vi* **1** separate, be separated (into); split or break up: *We ~d the money equally. They ~d the money between/among themselves. The road ~s at this point.* **2** find out how often one number is contained in another: *If you ~ 6 into 30/~ 30 by 6, the answer is 5.* **3** arrange in groups: *The teacher ~d the boys from the girls.* **4** differ; disagree: *Opinions are ~d on the question.*

di·vide[2] /dɪˈvaid/ *n* [C] something that divides, eg a line of high land that separates two different river systems.

divi·dend /ˈdɪvəˌdend/ *n* [C] **1** (usually periodical) payment of a share of profit, to shareholders in a business company, to a policy holder in a mutual insurance company, etc: *to pay a ~ of 10 percent.* **2** number to be divided by another: *When 30 is divided by 6, 30 is the ~.*

di·vid·ers /dɪˈvaidərz/ *n pl* pair of measuring compasses, used for dividing lines or angles, measuring or marking distances, etc.

di·vine[1] /dɪˈvain/ *adj* **1** of, from, or like God or a god: *Divine Will,* the will of God. **2** (*informal*) excellent; very good: *~ weather. She looks ~ in that new dress.*

di·vine·ly *adv*

di·vine[2] /dɪˈvain/ *n* [C] clergyman.

di·vine[3] /dɪˈvain/ *vt,vi* discover or learn (something) about future events, hidden things, etc by means not based on reason: *to ~ what the future has in store.*

di·viner *n* [C]

div·ing ⇨ dive.

di·vin·ing rod /dɪˈvainɪŋ ˌrad/ *n* [C] Y-shaped stick or rod that is supposed to have the power to find underground water, metal, etc.

di·vin·ity /dɪˈvɪnəti/ *n* **1** [U] the quality of being divine: *the ~ of Christ.* **2** [C] (*pl* -ies) divine being. **3** [U] the study of theology: *a doctor of ~.*

di·vis·ible /dɪˈvɪzəbəl/ *adj* that can be divided: *8 is ~ by 2.*

di·vision /dɪˈvɪʒən/ *n* **1** [U] (action of) dividing or being divided: *the ~ of time into months, weeks and days; a simple problem in ~* (eg 50 ÷ 5). **2** [C] the effect of dividing; one of the parts into which something is divided: *Is that a fair ~ of the money?* **3** [C] large military unit usually commanded by a major general. **4** [C] something that divides: *A hedge forms the ~ between his land and mine.* **5** [C] disagreement; separation in thought, feeling, etc: *Agitators who stir up ~s in society are dangerous.*

diˈvision ˌsign, sign (÷) used to indicate division.

di·vi·sor /dɪˈvaizər/ *n* [C] number by which another number is to be divided: *When 30 is divided by 6, 6 is the ~.*

di·vorce[1] /dɪˈvɔrs/ *n* **1** [U] legal ending of a marriage so that husband and wife are free to marry again; [C] instance of this: *to sue for a ~; to take/start ~ proceedings; to obtain a ~ (from...).* **2** [C] separation: *the ~ between religion and science.*

di·vorce[2] /dəˈvɔrs/ *vt* **1** put an end to a marriage by law: *Did Mr. Hill ~ his wife or did she ~ him?* **2** (*fig*) separate (things usually together): *How would this sculpture look if it were ~d from its surroundings?*

di·vor·c·ee /dɪˌvɔrˈsi/ *n* [C] divorced woman.

di·vulge /dɪˈvəldʒ/ *vt* (*formal*) make known (a secret).

divvy /ˈdɪvi/ *vt* (*sl*) divide: *They wanted him to ~ up the loot.*

Dixie(·land) /ˈdɪksi(ˌlænd)/ *n* (*sing* only) the South of the US, esp in the cultural or political sense.

ˈDixie·crat *n* [C] conservative southern democrat.

ˌDixie·land ˈjazz, traditional kind of jazz originating in New Orleans.

dizzy /ˈdɪzi/ *adj* (-ier, -iest) **1** (of a person) feeling as if everything were turning round, as if unable to balance; mentally confused. **2** causing such a feeling: *a ~ height.* □ *vt* (*pt,pp* -ied) make dizzy.

diz·zily /ˈdɪzəli/ *adv*

diz·zi·ness /ˈdɪzinɪs/ *n* [U]

DNA /ˌdi ˌen ˈei/ *abbr* (name of) basic material in the gene.

do[1] /də *strong form:* du/ *auxiliary verb* (*present tense* negative don't /dount/, *3rd person sing present tense* does /dəz/, negative doesn't /ˈdəzənt/, *pt* did /dɪd/, negative didn't /ˈdɪdənt/, *pp* done /dən/) **1** used with the main verb **(a)** for negative sentences with *not*: *He didn't go. Don't go yet.* **(b)** for *questions: Does/Did he want it?* **(c)** for emphasis: *That's exactly what he ˈdid say.* **2** used in place of a main verb **(a)** in comparisons: *She plays the piano better now than she did* (ie played) *last year.* **(b)** in question phrases: *He lives by himself, doesn't he?* **(c)** in answers, comments, etc: *"Who broke the window?"—"I did!"*

do[2] /du/ *vt,vi* (For pronunciations, etc ⇨ do[1], except that do[2] is never pronounced /də/) **1** perform, carry out (an action): *What are you doing now? What does he do for a living?* What is his job? *I have nothing to do. It's easier said than done,* easier to talk about than to do. ***do it yourself,*** (esp) do house decorating, repairs, etc oneself (instead of paying professional workers). **2** (used with *nouns* in many senses) **(a)** produce; make: *I have done* (ie made) *six copies.* **(b)** work at; be busy with: *She's doing her knitting.* **(c)** perform: *do your duty.* **(d)** find the answer to: *I can't do this math problem.* **(e)** put in order; arrange: *Go and do your hair.* **(f)** clean, sweep, etc: *Have you done* (ie cleaned) *your bedroom?* **(g)** deal with, attend to: *I have a lot of correspondence to do.* **(h)** use, exert: *do one's best/all one can to help.* **3** (as a *pp*) bring to an end; finish: *It's done. I've done it. A housekeeper's work is never done.* **4** ***do (for),*** be good, satisfactory or convenient, enough: *These shoes won't do* (ie are not strong enough) *for mountain climbing.* **5** be fitting, suitable, tolerable: *This will never do!* (=cannot be accepted or allowed). *It doesn't do to be rude to your father.* **6** (*informal*) happen: *He came to ask what was doing*. (= being done, happening). **7 (a)** get on: *Everything in the garden is doing* (= growing) *well. He's doing well at school.* **(b)** (esp of health) make progress: *The patient is doing quite well.* **(c) *How do you do?*** (formula used when people are formally introduced). **8** complete (a journey); travel (a distance); go (at a certain speed): *How many miles a day did you do? We did the journey in six hours.* **9** play the part of: *He does Hamlet well.* **10** cheat, swindle, get the better of: *He once tried to do me out of my job.* **11** cook to the right degree: *How would you like your steak done?* **12 *have to do with,*** be connected with: *I know he behaves badly—It all has to do with the way he was brought up.* ***have sth/nothing/not much/a great deal, etc to do with,*** be/not be connected or concerned with: *Hard work had a great deal to do with* (= contributed greatly to) *his success.* **13** (special uses with *adverbial particles* and *prepositions*):

do away with, **(a)** abolish, get rid of: *That department was done away with two years ago.* **(b)** put to death: *Everyone suspected he had done away with his opponents*, had them put to death.

do by, treat; behave towards: *They did very well by her.*

do for, (*informal*) **(a)** manage: *What/How will you do for water* (= manage to have supplies of water) *while you're crossing the desert?* **(b)** ruin; destroy; kill: *The country's done for*, ruined.

do sb in, (*sl*) kill him. ***be done in,*** exhausted: *The horse was done in after the race.*

do sb out of sth, ⇨ 10 above.

do sth up, **(a)** tie or wrap up; make into a bundle or parcel: *Please do up these books and mail them to Mr. Smith.* **(b)** fasten (a dress or other garment) with buttons, hooks and eyes, etc: *Please do your coat up. This dress does up at the back.*

do with, **(a)** (meanings as in the examples): *What did you do with my umbrella?* Where did you put it, leave it, etc? *What are we to do with* (= How shall we deal with) *this bad boy? She didn't know what to do with herself*, how to occupy her time. **(b)** (with *can, could*) expressing a need or wish: *You look as if you could do with* (= as if you need) *a good night's sleep.*

do without, manage without: *We shall have to do without a vacation this summer.*

do[3] /du/ *n* [C] (*pl* dos or do's /duz/) **1** (*informal*) entertainment; party: *We're going to a big do at the Greens' this evening.* **2** customs, rules: *Some teachers have too many do's and don'ts.*

do[4], **doh** /dou/ *n* [C] (*music*) syllable used for the first note of a scale.

doc, **Doc** /dak/ *n* [C] (*informal*) (short for) doctor (esp as form of address).

doc·ile /ˈdasəl/ *adj* easily trained or controlled: *a ~ child/horse.*

do·cil·ity /daˈsɪləti/ *n* [U] the quality of being docile.

dock[1] /dak/ *n* [C] **1** place in a harbor, river, etc with gates through which water may be let in and out, where ships are (un)loaded or repaired: *to be in ~.* **2** wharf; platform built out from the shore for (un)loading ships.

ˈdock·yard *n* [C] place with docks and facilities for building and repairing ships.

dock[2] /dak/ *vi,vt* **1** (of a ship) come or go into a dock. **2** bring, take, (a ship) into a dock. **3** join together (two or more spacecraft) in space.

dock[3] /dak/ *n* [C] enclosure in a criminal court for the prisoner: *to be in the ~.*

dock[4] /dak/ *vt* (esp) cut or lessen wages: *to ~ a workman's wages; to have one's salary ~ed.*

docket /ˈdakɪt/ *n* [C] **1** list of cases to be tried in a court of law. **2** list of matters to be considered or acted on. □ *vt* enter in or write on a docket.

doc·tor /ˈdaktər/ *n* [C] **1** person who has received the highest university degree: *Doctor of Laws/Divinity, etc.* **2** person who has been trained in medical science. ⇨ physician, surgeon. □ *vt* **1** (*informal*) give medical treatment to: *~ a cold/a child.* **2** change, usually by adding something to: *~ed the drinks so that they were too strong.* **3** (*fig*) falsify accounts, evidence.

doc·tor·ate /ˈdaktərɪt/ *n* [C] doctor's (1) degree.

doc·tri·nal /ˈdaktrənəl/ *adj* of doctrine(s).

doc·trine /ˈdaktrən/ *n* [C,U] body of teaching; beliefs and teachings of a church, political party, school of scientists, etc: *the ~s of the Christian religion.*

docu·ment /ˈdakyəmənt/ *n* [C] something written or printed, to be used as a record or in evidence (eg birth, marriage and death certificate). □ *vt* (also /-yuˌment/) prove by, supply with, documents: *to be well ~ed.*

doc·u·men·ta·tion /ˌdakyəmənˈteiʃən/ *n* [U]

doc·u·men·tary /ˌdakyəˈmentəri/ *adj* consisting of documents: *~ proof/evidence.* □ *n* [C] (*pl* -ies) motion picture television program that presents factual information about social topics, the natural world, science, etc.

dod·der /ˈdadər/ *vi* (*informal*) walk, move, in a shaky way, as from weakness or old age: *to ~ along.*

dod·der·ing *adj* trembling; weak and uncertain in movement.

dodge[1] /dadʒ/ *n* [C] **1** quick movement to one side in order to avoid something. **2** (*informal*) trick: *He's on to all the ~s*, knows them all.

dodge[2] /dadʒ/ *vt,vi* **1** move quickly to one side, change position or direction, in order to escape or avoid something: *I ~d behind a tree so that he wouldn't see me.* **2** get around or avoid (duties, etc) by cunning or trickery: *to ~ military service.*

dodger *n* [C] **(a)** person who dodges, esp an artful or cunning person: *ˈtax ~r; ˈdraft ~r.* **(b)** cake or bread made of cornmeal and fried or baked.

dodo /ˈdouˌdou/ *n* [C] (*pl* ~es, ~s) extinct, large, flightless bird of Mauritius.

doe /dou/ *n* [C] female deer, rabbit or hare. ⇨ buck.

ˈdoe·skin *n* (esp) soft leather made from this skin.

doer /ˈduər/ *n* [C] person who does things (contrasted with persons who merely talk, etc): *He's a ~, not a talker.* (*Note:* also used in compounds, *evil-~*).

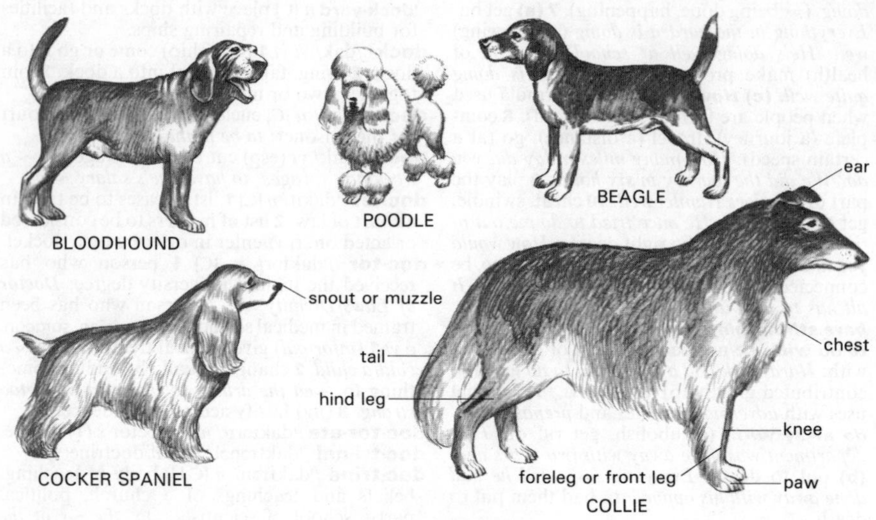

DOGS

does ⇨ do[1].

doesn't /ˈdəzənt/ = does not.

doff /daf, dɔf/ *vt* (*formal*) take off (an article of clothing).

dog[1] /dɔg/ *n* [C] **1 (a)** common domestic animal related to the wolf and the fox. **(b)** male dog, fox or wolf. ***go to the dogs,*** be ruined. ***lead a dog's life,*** be troubled all the time. ***lead sb a dog's life,*** give him no peace; worry him all the time. ***let sleeping dogs lie,*** leave something alone; not look for trouble. ***be top dog,*** (*sl*) be in a position where one rules. **2** (*informal*) person: *He's a dirty/sly/lucky dog.*

ˈdog-like *adj* like or as of a dog, esp *dog-like devotion*, the kind of devotion given by a dog to its master.

dog[2] /dɔg/ *vt* (-gg-) **1** keep close behind, in the footsteps of: *dog a suspected thief.* **2** (*fig*) follow: *dogged by misfortune*.

dog·cart /ˈdɔgˌkart/ *n* [C] **1** small cart drawn by dogs. **2** light one-horse carriage with two seats placed back to back.

dog·catcher /ˈdɔgˌkætʃər/ *n* [C] official catcher of stray dogs in a town or city.

dog days /ˈdɔgˌdeiz/ *n pl* hot part of summer, during July and August.

dog-eared /ˈdɔgˌɪrd/ *adj* (of a book) having the corners of the pages folded down.

dog·fight /ˈdɔgˌfait/ *n* [C] **1** fight between dogs. **2** combat between two fighter planes.

dog·fish /ˈdɔgˌfɪʃ/ *n* [C] kind of small shark.

dog·ged /ˈdɔgɪd/ *adj* stubborn.

dog·ged·ly *adv*

dog·ged·ness /-nɪs/ *n* [U]

dog·gone /ˈdɔ(g)ˌgɔn/ *adj* (*informal*) = darned. ⇨ darn[2].

doggy, doggie /ˈdɔgi/ *n* [C] (*pl* -ies) (used as a pet name or child's word for a) dog.

dog·house /ˈdɔgˌhaus/ *n* [C] small outdoor shelter for a dog, usually shaped like a house. ***in the doghouse,*** (*sl*) (temporarily) in disfavor.

dogma /ˈdɔgmə, ˈdag-/ *n* (*pl* ~s) **1** [C] (esp a religious) belief stated by an authority and accepted as true without question. **2** [U] system or collection of such beliefs.

dog·matic /dɔgˈmætɪk, dag-/ *adj* **1** of, relating to dogma: ~ *theology*. **2** (of persons, statements) holding or expressing opinions as if they were dogmas, esp in an arrogant way.

dog·mati·cally /-kli/ *adv*

dog·ma·tism /ˈdɔgməˌtɪzəm, ˈdag-/ *n* [U] (the quality of) being dogmatic: *His ~ was unbearable.*

dog tag /ˈdɔg ˌtæg/ *n* [C] **1** metal identification tag for a dog's collar. **2** *pl* (*sl*) pair of metal identification tags worn by soldiers and sailors on a chain around their necks.

dog·wood /ˈdɔgˌwʊd/ *n* [U] tree or shrub bearing white or pinkish flowers in the spring and red berries in the fall.

doily /ˈdɔili/ *n* [C] (*pl* -ies) small mat of linen, lace, paper, etc.

do·ings /ˈduɪŋz/ *n pl* (*informal*) things done or being done: *Tell me about all your ~ in Boston.*

dol·drums /ˈdouldrəmz/ *n pl* **1** area of the ocean near the equator with little or no wind. **2** ***in the doldrums,*** (fig) miserable, depressed.

dole /doul/ *vt* distribute food, money, etc in small amounts: *The cook ~d out the remaining food to the men.* □ *n* [C] something distributed.

dole·ful /ˈdoulfəl/ *adj* miserable, depressed.

dole·fully *adv*

doll[1] /dal/ *n* [C] **1** small figure of a baby or person, usually for a child to play with. **2** (*sl*) pretty but empty-headed girl or woman.

doll[2] /dal/ *vt,vi* (*informal*) ***doll up,*** dress

(oneself) up smartly: *She was all* ~*ed up for the party.*

dol·lar /ˈdalər/ *n* [C] unit of money (symbol **$**) used in the US and in Canada, Australia and other countries. ⇨ App 4.

ˌdollar ˈbill, US or Canadian bank note valued at one dollar.

dol·lop /ˈdaləp/ *n* [C] (*informal*) shapeless portion of food, etc: *a* ~ *of ice cream.*

dolly /ˈdali/ *n* [C] (*pl* -ies) **1** (used as a child's word for a) doll. **2(a)** small wheeled frame or platform for moving heavy objects. **(b)** mobile platform for a heavy camera.

dol·phin /ˈdalfən/ *n* [C] long-nosed sea animal like a porpoise.

dolt /doult/ *n* [C] stupid person.

do·main /douˈmein/ *n* [C] (*formal*) **1** lands under the rule of a government, ruler, etc. **2** (*fig*) area or topic of thought, knowledge, activity: *in the* ~ *of science.*

dome /doum/ *n* [C] **1** rounded roof with a circular base. **2** something shaped like a dome: *the rounded* ~ (= top) *of a hill.*

domed /doumd/ *adj* rounded: *a man with a* ~*d forehead.*

do·mes·tic /dəˈmestɪk/ *adj* **1** of the home, family, household: *He has had a good many* ~ *troubles.* **2** not foreign; native; of one's own country: *This newspaper provides more foreign news than* ~ *news.* **3** (of animals, etc) kept by, living with man; tame: *Horses, cows and sheep are* ~ *animals.* ⇨ wild. □ *n* person who is employed in household work.

do·mes·ti·cate /dəˈmestɪˌkeit/ *vt* **1** make able to do, interested in, household work and duties: *She's not at all* ~*d*, is not good at, interested in, cooking, housekeeping, etc. **2** tame (animals).

do·mes·ti·ca·tion /dəˌmestɪˈkeiʃən/ *n* [U]

do·mes·tic·ity /ˌdouˌmeˈstɪsəti/ *n* [U] home or family life.

domi·cile /ˈdaməˌsaiəl/ *n* [C] **1** (*formal*) home. **2** (*legal*) place where a person lives permanently.

domi·nance /ˈdamənəns/ *n* [U] being dominant.

domi·nant /ˈdamənənt/ *adj* **1** having control or authority; dominating; most important or influential; *the* ~ *partner in a business.* **2** (of heights) overlooking others: *a* ~ *cliff.*

domi·nant·ly *adv*

domi·nate /ˈdaməˌneit/ *vt,vi* **1** have control, authority or influence: *The strong usually* ~ (*over*) *the weak. Mary* ~*d the conversation.* **2** (of a place, esp a height) overlook: *The whole valley is* ~*d by this mountain.*

domi·na·tion /ˌdaməˈneiʃən/ *n* [U] dominating or being dominated.

domi·neer /ˌdaməˈnɪr/ *vi* act, speak, in a dominating manner; be overbearing: *Big boys sometimes* ~ *over their small friends.*

domi·neer·ing *adj*: *He's a very* ~*ing sort of man.*

Do·mini·can /dəˈmɪnɪkən/ *adj* **1** of St. Dominic (/ˈdamɪnɪk/) or the order of friars he founded in 1215. **2** of the Dominican Republic. □ *n* [C] friar of the Dominican order.

do·min·ion /dəˈmɪnyən/ *n* **1** [U] authority to rule; control (over). **2** [C] territory of a sovereign government. **3** [C] **Dominion,** one of the self-governing territories of the British Commonwealth: *the Dominion of Canada.*

dom·ino /ˈdaməˌnou/ *n* [C] (*pl* ~es or ~s) **1** small, flat, oblong piece of wood or bone, marked with spots. **2** (*pl*) game played with 28 of these. (*Note:* used with a *sing verb.*) **3** loose cloak and a half mask, worn as a disguise or costume.

don /dan/ *vt* (-nn-) (*formal*) put on (a piece of clothing).

do·nate /ˈdouˌneit/ *vt* give (eg money, to a charity, etc); contribute.

do·na·tion /douˈneiʃən/ *n* **(a)** [U] giving. **(b)** [C] something given: ~*s to the refugee fund.*

done *pp* of do[1]

don·key /ˈdaŋki, ˈdɔŋki/ *n* [C] (*pl* ~s) **1** (the usual word for an) ass (1). **2** silly or stupid person.

do·nor /ˈdounər/ *n* [C] person who gives something: a ˈ*blood* ~, person who gives his own blood for transfusion.

don't = do not.

do·nut = doughnut.

doodle /ˈdudəl/ *vi, n* [C] (*informal*) (make) meaningless scrawls or scribbles.

doodle·bug /ˈdudəlˌbəg/ *n* [C] larva of an insect (sometimes called an *ant lion*) which traps and eats ants, etc in a pit dug in sand or loose soil.

doom[1] /dum/ *n* [U] **1** judgment; sentence. **2** ruin; death; something evil that is to come: *to send a man to his* ~.

doom[2] /dum/ *vt* condemn (esp in *pp*): ~*ed to disappointment;* ~*ed to die.*

dooms·day /ˈdumzˌdei/ *n* = Judgment Day.

door /dɔr/ *n* [C] **1** that swinging or sliding part which opens and closes the entrance to a building, room, cupboard, etc: *The* ~ *opened/was opened and a man came out.* ***next door,*** (in, to) the next house: *I'm just going next* ~ *to see Mrs. Jones.* ***out of doors,*** in the open air: *It's cold out of* ~*s; put an overcoat on.* ***at death's door,*** near death. **2** (*fig*) means of obtaining or approaching something: *a* ~ *to success.*

ˈback door, door at the back of the house (to the yard, garden, etc).

ˈfront door, main door from a house to the street or road.

ˈdoor·bell *n* [C] bell inside a building, operated by a button, etc outside by somebody seeking admittance.

ˈdoor·man *n* [C] (*pl* ~men /-men/) uniformed attendant at the entrance to a hotel, theater, etc.

ˈdoor·mat *n* [C] rough mat by a door on which shoes may be wiped.

ˈdoor·step *n* [C] step before an outer door.

ˈdoor·way *n* [C] opening into which a door fits.

dope /doup/ *n* **1** [U] (*informal*) harmful drug (eg opium). **2** [U] (*sl*) information. **3** [C] (*informal*) stupid person. □ *vt* **1** give dope(1) to; make unconscious, stimulate, with a drug. **2** ***dope out,*** (*informal*) = figure out.

dopey, dopy /ˈdoupi/ *adj* (-ier, -iest) (*sl*) **(a)** half asleep; (as if) drugged. **(b)** stupid.

dor·mant /ˈdɔrmənt/ *adj* inactive but capable of development or activity: *a* ~ *volcano; plants which are* ~/*lie* ~ *during the winter*, are alive but not growing.

dor·mer /ˈdɔrmər/ *n* [C] **1** (also **ˈdormer win-**

dow) upright window built from a sloping roof. **2** built-out part of a roof containing such a window.

dor·mi·tory /ˈdɔrməˌtɔri/ *n* [C] (*pl* -ies) **1** sleeping room with several or many beds, esp in a school or institution. **2** building that contains many sleeping rooms.

dor·mouse /ˈdɔrˌmaus/ *n* [C] (*pl* dormice /ˈdɔrˌmais/) small animal (like a mouse) that sleeps during cold weather in winter.

dor·sal /ˈdɔrsəl/ *adj* of, on, near, the back(1,2): *the ~ fin,* eg of a shark.

dos·age /ˈdousɪdʒ/ *n* [U] **1** giving of medicines in doses. **2** quantity of a single dose.

dose /dous/ *n* [C] **1** amount (of medicine) to be taken at one time: *The bottle contains six ~s.* **2** (*fig*) portion or amount of a usually unpleasant experience: *He needs a good ~ of hard work.* □ *vt* give medicine to: *to ~ oneself with aspirin.*

dos·sier /ˈdasiˌei/ *n* [C] set of papers giving information, esp about a person.

dot /dat/ *n* **1** small round mark (as over the letters *i* and *j*). ***on the dot,*** (*informal*) at the precise moment. **2** thing like a dot in appearance: *We watched the ship until it was a mere dot on the horizon.* □ *vt* (-tt-) **1** mark with a dot. **2** cover (as if) with dots: *a dotted line,* eg on a document, for a signature; *dotted about,* scattered here and there.

dot·age /ˈdoutɪdʒ/ *n* [U] weakness of mind caused by old age: *He's in his ~,* fails to remember or notice things, etc.

dot·ard /ˈdoutərd/ *n* [C] person in his dotage.

dote /dout/ *vi* be too fond of: *She ~s on her grandson. He's a doting* (= very loving) *husband.*

doth /dəθ/ *v* (*archaic*) *present tense* form of *does,* used with *he, she* or *it*: *he ~,* he does.

dotty /ˈdati/ *adj* (-ier, -iest) (*informal*) mad; idiotic; eccentric.

double[1] /ˈdəbəl/ *adj* **1** twice as much, large, good, etc: *His income is ~ what it was five years ago.* **2** having two like things or parts: *a railway with a ~ track; a man with a ~ chin,* with a fold of loose flesh below the chin. **3** made for two persons or things: *a ~ bed.* **4** combining two things, qualities, etc: *a piece of furniture that serves a ~ purpose,* eg one that is a sofa and can be opened out to make a bed.

ˌdouble-ˈbarreled *adj* (of a gun) having two barrels, side-by-side.

ˌdouble ˈbass, largest and lowest-pitched instrument in the violin family. ⇨ illus at string.

ˌdouble ˈboiler, combination of two saucepans, one fitted inside the other so that boiling water in the lower one cooks food in the upper one.

ˌdouble-ˈbreasted *adj* (of a coat or waistcoat) having two rows of buttons down the front.

ˌdouble ˈbunk, combination of two bunks or narrow beds, one placed above the other.

ˌdouble-ˈcheck *vt* check[2] (1) twice in order to be certain.

ˌdouble-ˈcross *vt* (*informal*) cheat or betray.

ˌdouble-ˈdealer *n* [C] person who says one thing and does another.

ˌdouble-ˈdealing *n* [U], *adj* deceit(ful).

ˌdouble-ˈdecker *n* [C] **(a)** bus with two decks. ⇨ deck[1]. **(b)** sandwich with two layers of filling.

ˌdouble ˈheader, (a) train pulled by two engines. **(b)** one of two (esp baseball) games that are played right after the other on the same day.

ˌdouble-ˈjointed *adj* having joints that allow the fingers (or arms, legs) to move or bend in unusual ways.

ˌdouble-ˈpark *vi* park a car in the street, next to a car parked at the curb.

ˈdouble·speak *n* [U] deliberately misleading rhetoric.

ˌdouble ˈtake, (*informal*) (used with *do*) quick second look, usually to double-check a first impression: *He did a ~ take.*

ˈdouble-talk *n* [U] talk that appears to have meaning, but is a mixture of sense and nonsense.

double[2] /ˈdəbəl/ *adv* **1** twice (as much): *Many things now cost ~ what they did a few years ago.* **2** in twos, in pairs or couples: *to see ~,* to see two things when there is only one.

double[3] /ˈdəbəl/ *n* [C] **1** twice the quantity: *Ten is the ~ of five.* **2** person or thing that looks exactly, or almost exactly, like another: *She's the ~ of her sister.* **3** (*baseball*) hit that gets a batter safely to second base. **4** (*pl*) (*sport*) game with two people on each side: *mixed ~s,* a man and woman against another man and woman.

double[4] /ˈdəbəl/ *vt,vi* **1** multiply by two: *to ~ one's income. Money earning good interest will ~ itself in time.* **2** bend or fold in two: *If you are cold, ~ the blanket.* **3** ***double back,*** **(a)** turn or fold back. **(b)** retrace one's steps (on a trail, etc): *The fox ~d back on its tracks.* ***double up,*** **(a)** fold (something) up: *He ~d up his legs and kicked out,* eg when swimming. **(b)** (of persons) (cause to) bend the body: *He ~d up with laughter/pain.* **(c)** share a room, bed, etc with another. **4** act in two capacities; serve two purposes: *He ~s as cook and waiter. The couch ~s as sofa and bed.*

doub·let /ˈdəblɪt/ *n* [C] close-fitting garment for the upper part of the body, worn by men (about 1400-1600).

dou·bloon /dəˈblun/ *n* [C] Spanish gold coin no longer in use.

doubly /ˈdəbli/ *adv* to twice the extent or amount: *to be ~ careful/sure.* (*Note:* used before an *adjective.*)

doubt[1] /daut/ *n* [C,U] (feeling of) uncertainty; uncertain state of things: *I have no ~ that you will succeed/no ~ of your ability. I have my ~s about his honesty. When in ~* (= uncertain) *about the meaning of a word, consult a dictionary.* ***no doubt,*** **(a)** certainly. **(b)** very probably: *He meant to help, no ~, but in fact he forgot to come.*

doubt[2] /daut/ *vt,vi* feel doubt about; question the truth of: *Can you ~ that he will win? Do you ~ my word?* (= think I am not telling the truth?) *I ~ that he will come.*

doubt·ful /ˈdautfəl/ *adj* **1** feeling doubt: *I am/feel ~ about what I ought to do.* **2** causing doubt: *The future/weather looks very ~.*

doubt·fully *adv*

doubt·less /ˈdautlɪs/ *adv* **1** without doubt. **2**

(*informal*) very probably.

dough /dou/ *n* [U] **1** thick, soft mixture of flour, water, etc (for making bread, pastry, etc). **2** (*sl*) money.

ˈdough·nut, do·nut /ˈdouˌnət/ *n* [C] small round or ring-shaped cake of sweetened dough fried in deep fat.

doughy *adj* (-ier, -iest) of or like dough; soft.

dour /ˈdauər/ *adj* gloomy; severe; stern: *~ looks/ silence.*

dour·ly *adv*

douse, dowse /daus/ *vt* **1** put into water. **2** throw water over. **3** put out (a light).

dove[1] /dəv/ *n* **1** kind of pigeon (often used as a symbol of peace). **2** (*informal*) (in foreign affairs) person who favors a policy of peace and negotiation rather than military force. ⇨ hawk[1] (2).

ˈdove·cote *n* [C] small shelter or house with nesting-boxes for doves.

dove[2] *pt of* dive[2].

dove·tail /ˈdəvˌteiəl/ *n* [C] joint for two pieces of wood. □ *vt,vi* (*pres p* ~ing /ˈdəvˌteilɪŋ/) **1** join together with these joints. **2** (*fig*) fit (together): *My plans ~ed with his.*

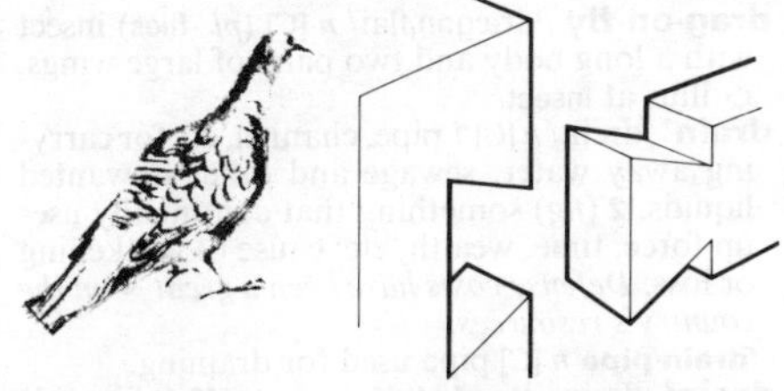

DOVE DOVETAILING

dowa·ger /ˈdauədʒər/ *n* [C] **1** woman with property or a title from her dead husband: *the ~ duchess.* **2** dignified older woman.

dowdy /ˈdaudi/ *adj* (-ier, -iest) shabby or unfashionable: *~ clothes.*

dow·di·ly /ˈdaudəli/ *adv*

dow·di·ness /ˈdaudinɪs/ *n* [U]

dowel /ˈdauəl/ *n* [C] headless pin or peg for keeping two pieces of wood, metal, stone, etc together.

down[1] /daun/ *n* [U] **1** fluffy, soft feathers of (young) birds. **2** similar fine soft hair, eg on a boy's face, on some plants and seeds.

downy *adj* (-ier, -iest)

down[2] /daun/ *adverbial particle* **1** (used with *verbs* indicating motion) **(a)** from a high(er) level to a low(er) level: *The sun went ~. If you can't jump ~, climb ~. Some kinds of food go ~* (= can be swallowed) *more easily than others.* **(b)** from an upright position to a horizontal position): *He was knocked ~ by a bus. If you're tired, go and lie ~.* **2** (used with *verbs* indicating change of position to or in a lower position or direction): *Sit ~, please. The tall man bent ~ to speak to me.* **3(a)** in a southerly direction: *We went ~ to Atlanta* (eg from Washington) *for the weekend.* **(b)** toward the coast, from (usually higher) inland: *We went ~ to Savannah* (eg from Atlanta). ***down East*** ⇨ east. ***down Easter*** ⇨ Easter[2]. ***down South*** ⇨ south(1). **4** (used with *verbs* to indicate reduction to a smaller volume, a lower degree, a state of less activity, etc): *The heels of my shoes have worn ~. The wind died ~. The temperature has gone ~. The factory was closed ~* (= Work was stopped) *because of a steel shortage.* **5** (used with reference to writing): *to write something ~; Put me ~/Put my name ~ for a dollar,* eg as willing to give this sum. **6** from an earlier time (to a later time): *the history of Europe ~ to 1914.* **7** including the lower limit in a series: *everyone, from the Director ~ to the janitor.* ***Down with,*** let us get rid of: *Down with grammar!* ***down under,*** (*informal*) in Australia or New Zealand. ***get down to sth,*** start work, etc in real earnest. ***come down in the world,*** fall to a lower social position. □ *adj* **1 (a)** in a lower position; at a lower level: *The price of fruit is ~. All the telephone lines are ~,* eg as the result of a storm. **(b)** (of a computer system) not working: *We can't determine your bank balance at the moment because our computer is ~.* **2** going down: *a ~ staircase/ escalator.* **3** sad; depressed: *felt ~ after hearing the bad news.* **4** sick: *He's ~ with a cold.* ***be down and out,*** (*informal*) be without money, friends, etc. ***be down in the dumps/mouth,*** (*informal*) sad; depressed. ***be down on one's luck,*** having suffered misfortune. ***be down on sb,*** be angry at him; have a grudge against him.

ˌdown ˈpayment, partial payment made at the time when an article is bought.

ˌdown-to-ˈearth *adj* realistic; practical (contrasted with *impractical, vague, idealistic*): *He's a ~-to-earth person.*

down[3] /daun/ *prep* **1** from a high(er) to a low(er) level: *to run ~ a hill. The tears ran ~ her face.* **2** at a lower part of: *New Orleans is farther ~ the river.* **3** along (not necessarily with reference to a lower level): *I was walking ~ the street.*

down[4] /daun/ *vt* (*informal*) bring, put, knock, down: *to ~ a glass of beer,* drink it.

down[5] /daun/ *n* **1** ***ups and downs,*** changes in fortune, prosperity, etc: *have one's ups and ~s.* **2** [C] (*football*) one of four plays made in an attempt to advance the ball by a distance of 10 yards.

down·beat /ˈdaunˌbit/ *n* [C] first beat of a bar in music (when the conductor's hand moves down).

down·cast /ˈdaunˌkæst/ *adj* **1** (of a person) depressed; discouraged; sad. **2** (of eyes) looking downwards.

down·fall /ˈdaunˌfɔl/ *n* [C] **1** heavy fall (of rain, etc). **2** ruin; fall from fortune or power: *His ~ was caused by gambling and drink.*

down·grade /ˈdaunˌgreid/ *vt* make lower in grade, reputation, etc.

down·hearted /ˈdaunˌhartɪd/ *adj* sad; depressed.

down·hill /ˌdaunˈhɪl/ *adv* in a downward direction. ***go downhill,*** (*fig*) go from bad to worse (in health, fortune, etc).

down·pour /ˈdaunˌpɔr/ *n* [C] heavy fall of rain.

down·right /ˈdaunˌrait/ *adj* **1** honest; frank: *He is a ~ sort of person.* **2** thorough; complete: *It's* *a ~ lie.* □ *adv* thoroughly: *He was ~ rude.*

down·stairs /ˌdaunˈsterz/ *adv* **1** to, at, on, of, a lower floor; down the stairs: *Your brother is waiting ~.* **2** (used as an *adjective*): *the ~ rooms.*

down·town /ˌdaunˈtaun/ *adv* to or in the main business district of a city or town: *went ~ to buy a new coat.* □ *adj*: *the ~ shopping mall.*

down·trod·den /ˈdaunˌtradən/ *adj* oppressed; treated badly.

down·ward[1] /ˈdaunwərd/ *adj* moving, leading, going, pointing, to what is lower: *a ~ slope; prices with a ~ tendency.*

down·ward[2], **down·wards** /ˈdaunwərd, -wərdz/ *adv* toward what is lower: *He laid the picture face ~ on the table.*

dowry /ˈdau(ə)ri/ *n* [C] (*pl* -ies) property, money, brought by a bride to her husband.

dowse /daus/ *vt* = douse.

doz. *abbr* = dozen.

doze /douz/ *vi* sleep lightly; be half asleep: *He ~d off during the sermon.* □ *n* [C] short, light sleep.

dozen /ˈdəzən/ *n* (*pl* ~, ~s) (group of) twelve: *Eggs are a dollar a ~. I want three ~ of these.* ⇨ App 1. ***dozens of,*** a large number of: *I've been there ~s of times.*

Dr. *abbr* = Doctor.

drab /dræb/ *adj* (~ber, ~best) dull; uninteresting; monotonous: *a ~ existence.*

drab·ly *adv*

drab·ness /-nɪs/ *n* [U]

draft[1], **draught** /dræft/ *n* **1** [C] outline (usually in the form of rough notes) of something to be done: *a ~ for a speech/letter.* **2** [C] written order for payment of money by a bank: *a ~ for $500.* **3(a)** method of selecting persons from a group (esp for military service). **(b)** group of persons so selected. **4** [C,U] current of air in a room, chimney or other enclosed place: *You'll catch cold if you sit in a ~.* **5** [C] device that controls the supply of air in a furnace, stove, etc. **6** [C] the pulling in of a net of fish. **7** [U] depth of water needed to float a ship: *a ship with a ~ of ten feet.* **8** [U] drawing of liquid from a container (eg a barrel): *~ beer.* **9** (amount drunk during) one continuous process of swallowing: *a ~ of water.* **10** act of drawing or pulling: *a ˈ~ horse*, one that pulls heavy loads.

draft[2], **draught** /dræft/ *vt* make a draft(1) of: *to ~ a speech.* **2** select (a man) for the armed forces.

ˈdraft ˌdodger/reˌsister, person who tries to escape being drafted(2).

draf·tee /ˌdræfˈti/ *n* [C] one who has been drafted(2).

draft·ing *n* [C,U] the act, method, of drafting (all senses).

drafts·man /ˈdræftsmən/ *n* (*pl* -men /-men/) person who draws plans and designs, esp for machines and buildings.

drafty /ˈdræfti/ *adj* (-ier, -iest) in or having a draft(4).

drag[1] /dræg/ *n* **1** [C] something that is dragged, eg a net pulled over the bottom of a river to catch fish, a heavy harrow pulled over the ground to break up the soil. **2** [C] (*informal*) person or thing that slows down progress because dull, etc: *Do we have to take your sister with us? She's such a ~.* ⇨ drag[2](3). **3** [U] (*sl*) woman's clothes worn by a man: *"As you Like It" performed in ~,* with the women's parts acted by men dressed as women. **4** [C] (*sl*) puff at a cigarette or cigar. **5** [C] short race between stock cars or hot rods, on either a racing strip or a roadway. **6** [C] (*sl*) bore: *the party was a ~.* **7** [U] (*sl*) influence: *He has a lot of ~ with the new mayor.*

ˈdrag race, = drag(5).

ˈdrag strip, paved course for a drag race.

drag[2] /dræg/ *vt,vi* (-gg-) **1** pull along (esp with effort and difficulty): *to ~ a heavy box out of a cupboard.* **2** (allow to) move slowly and with effort; (allow to) trail: *He could scarcely ~ himself along.* ***drag one's feet,*** deliberately act slowly: *We suspect the Government of ~ging its feet.* **3** (of time, work, an entertainment) go on slowly in a dull manner: *Time seemed to ~.* **4** use nets, tools, etc to search the bottom of a river, lake, etc: *They ~ged the river for the missing child.* **5** engage in a drag race. ⇨ drag[1](5).

dragon /ˈdrægən/ *n* [C] fictional creature like a crocodile or snake, but with wings and claws, able to breathe out fire, often guarding a treasure.

drag·on·fly /ˈdrægənˌflai/ *n* [C] (*pl* -flies) insect with a long body and two pairs of large wings. ⇨ illus at insect.

drain[1] /drein/ *n* [C] **1** pipe, channel, etc for carrying away water, sewage and other unwanted liquids. **2** (*fig*) something that continually uses up force, time, wealth, etc; cause of weakening or loss: *Defense costs have been a great ~ on the country's resources.*

ˈdrain·pipe *n* [C] pipe used for draining.

drain[2] /drein/ *vt,vi* **1** ***drain away/off,*** (of liquid) (cause to) run or flow away: *The water will soon ~ away/off.* **2** make, become dry as water flows away: *Land must be well ~ed for some crops. Leave the dishes to ~.* **3** (*fig*) (cause to) lose (strength, wealth, etc) by degrees: *The country was ~ed of its manpower and wealth by war.*

ˈdrain·board *n* [C] board at the side of a sink, on which dishes, etc are placed to drain.

drain·age /ˈdreinɪdʒ/ *n* [U] **1** draining or being drained. **2** system of drains(1). **3** that which is drained away or off.

drake /dreik/ *n* [C] male duck.

dram /dræm/ *n* [C] **1** unit of weight. **2** small drink of alcoholic spirits: *He's fond of his ~,* eg of whiskey.

drama /ˈdramə, ˈdræmə/ *n* **1** [C] play for the theater, radio or TV. **2** [U] composition, presentation and performance of such plays: *a student of (the) ~; to be interested in (the) ~.* **3** [C,U] series of exciting or interesting events.

dra·matic /drəˈmætɪk/ *adj* **1** of drama(1): *~ performances/criticism.* **2** sudden or exciting: *~ changes in the international situation.* **3** (of a person, his speech, behavior) showing feelings or character in a lively way.

dra·mati·cally /-kli/ *adv*

dra·mat·ics *n pl* **(a)** dramatic works or performances: *Are you interested in amateur ~s?* **(b)** (*informal*) dramatic behavior.

drama·tist /ˈdræmətɪst/ *n* [C] writer of plays.

drama·tize /ˈdræməˌtaiz/ *vt* **1** put a story, novel, etc into the form of a drama. **2** present in an exaggerated or dramatic way.
drama·ti·za·tion /ˌdræmətɪˈzeiʃən/ *n* [C,U]
drank *pt* of drink².
drape /dreip/ *vt* **1** hang curtains, cloth, a cloak, etc in folds around or over something: *to ~ curtains over a window; to ~ a flag over the coffin.* **2 *drape with,*** cover or decorate: *walls ~d with flags.* **3** allow to rest loosely: *He ~d his legs over the arms of his chair.* □ *n* [C] curtain.
drap·ery *n* [C] (*pl* -ies) (materials draped and used esp for) curtains.
dras·tic /ˈdræstɪk/ *adj* having a strong or violent effect: *~ measures to cure inflation/an illness.*
dras·ti·cally /-kli/ *adv*
draught = draft.
draw¹ /drɔ/ *n* [C] **1** the act of drawing (in various senses): *the ~ for the fourth round of the tennis tournament.* ***be quick/slow on the draw,*** quick/slow at pulling out a gun, sword, etc. **2** tie: *The game ended in a ~,* neither side won. **3** person or thing that attracts attention, ⇨ draw²(4): *Mr. A is always a great ~ at political meetings,* is a popular speaker.
draw² /drɔ/ *vt,vi* (*pt* drew /dru/, *pp* ~n /drɔn/) **1** move by pulling: *to ~ a boat (up) out of the water/on to the beach; to ~ one's chair up to the table; to ~ a curtain across a window. The fisherman drew in his net.* **2** take or get out by pulling; extract: *to ~ a cork,* out of a bottle; *to ~ nails from a plank/a sword from its sheath; to ~ a chicken* (*etc*), remove the entrails before cooking it; *to ~ cards from a pack; to ~ the winner,* get a ticket, etc at a lottery, on which there is a payment, prize, etc; *to ~ a gun* (*on* somebody), take it from its holster, ready for use. ***draw a blank,*** find nothing. ***draw lots,*** ⇨ lot(1). **2** (esp of horses, etc) pull by being attached at the front of: *The wagon was ~n by two horses.* ⇨ draft¹ (10). **3** obtain; get: *to ~ water from a well; to ~ beer from a barrel; to ~ one's salary; to ~ money from the bank/from one's account; to ~ inspiration from nature. What moral are we to ~ from this story?* **4** attract: *Street accidents always ~ crowds. He drew* (= called) *my attention to a point I had overlooked.* **5** take in: *to ~ a deep breath.* **6** allow a current of air to flow through: *This chimney/cigar does not ~ well.* **7 *draw sb out,*** cause, persuade, him to talk, show his feelings, etc: *He has many interesting stories of his travels if you can ~ him out.* **8** stretch; (cause to) become longer: *The discussion was ~n out for hours.* **9** (cause to) move; come (in the direction indicated by the *adverb,* etc): *Christmas is ~ing near. The day drew to its close. The two ships drew level. The horse quickly drew away from the others,* went ahead of them. *Everyone drew back in alarm. The taxi drew up at* (= reached and stopped at) *the station entrance.* ***draw back,*** (*fig*) show unwillingness: *~ back from a proposal.* **10(a)** make a picture with a pen, pencil, chalk, etc: *to ~ a picture/straight line/a circle.* **(b)** (*fig*) describe in words: *The characters in Edith Wharton's novels are well ~n.* ***draw the line (at),*** set limits; refuse to permit or do: *This noisy behavior cannot be allowed; we must ~ the line somewhere.* **11** write out: *to ~ a check for $100: to ~ up* (= compose) *a contract/an agreement.* **12 *draw on,*** take or use as a source: *If newspaper men cannot get facts for their stories, they sometimes ~ on their imaginations. We mustn't ~ on our savings.* **13** (of a ship) require (a certain depth of water) in order to float, ⇨ draft¹(7): *The ship ~s 20 feet of water.* **14** end (a game, etc) without either side winning or losing: *to ~ a football game.* **15** (usually in *pp*) (of the features) pull out of shape: *a face ~n with pain/anxiety.*
draw·back /ˈdrɔˌbæk/ *n* [C] something which lessens one's satisfaction; disadvantage.
draw·bridge /ˈdrɔˌbrɪdʒ/ *n* [C] bridge made so that all or part of it can be drawn up or down or moved to one side (eg to allow ships to pass).
drawer /drɔr/ *n* [C] **1** box-like container (with a handle or handles) which slides in and out of a piece of furniture, etc. **2** (*pl*) undergarment for the lower part of the body. **3** /ˈdrɔər/ person who draws pictures, a check, etc.
ˌchest of ˈdrawers, ⇨ chest.
draw·ing /ˈdrɔɪŋ/ *n* **1** [U] the art or act of representing objects, scenes, etc by lines, with a pencil, chalk, etc. **2** [C] sketch, picture, plan, etc.
ˈdrawing board, flat board on which to fasten paper for drawing: *still on the ~ board,* (*fig*) in the planning stage.
draw·ing-room /ˈdrɔɪŋˌrum, -ˌrʊm/ *n* [C] room in which guests are received.
drawl /drɔl/ *vi,vt* speak more slowly than usual: *The speaker ~ed on.* □ *n* [U] slow way of speaking, esp by lengthening the vowels as in some dialects: *a Southern ~.*
drawn *pp* of draw². also ⇨ draw²(15).
dread /dred/ *n* [U] (or with *a*) great fear and anxiety: *to live in constant ~ of poverty. Cats have a ~ of water.* □ *vt,vi* fear greatly: *to ~ a visit to/~ having to visit the dentist.*
dreaded *adj* greatly feared.
dread·ful /-fəl/ *adj* **1** causing anxiety: *a ~ful dream.* **2** very unpleasant: *What ~ful weather!*
dread·fully *adv* extremely: *It was ~fully hot.*
dream¹ /drim/ *n* [C] **1** something which one seems to see or experience during sleep: *to have a ~ (about...); to awake from a ~.* **2** state of mind in which things going on around one seem unreal: *to live/go about in a ~.* **3** mental picture(s) of the future: *to have ~s of wealth and happiness.* **4** beautiful or pleasing person, thing, experience, etc: *His new car went like a ~. She looked like a ~.*
ˈdream·land/·world *n* unreal place, as experienced in sleep or in the imagination.
dream·less *adj*
ˈdream·like *adj*
dream² /drim/ *vi,vt* (*pt,pp* ~ed or ~t /dremt/) **1** have dreams; see, experience, in a dream; imagine; suppose: *The soldier often ~ed/~t of/about home. I wouldn't ~ of doing such a thing,* the idea would never occur to me. **2 *dream away one's time/the hours, etc,*** pass one's time idly. **3 *dream sth up,*** (*informal*) imagine, conceive (a plan, etc).
dreamer *n* [C] **(a)** person who dreams. **(b)** per-

son with impractical ideas, plans, etc.

dreamy /ˈdrimi/ *adj* (-ier, -iest) **1** (of a person) with thoughts far away from his surroundings or work. **2** (of things, experiences) vague; unreal: *a ~ recollection of what happened.*

dream·ily /ˈdrimɪli/ *adv*

dreary /ˈdrɪri/ *adj* (-ier, -iest) dull; gloomy; causing depression: *~ work/weather.*

drear·ily /ˈdrɪrəli/ *adv*

dredge[1] /dredʒ/ *n* [C] apparatus for bringing up mud, removing earth, etc from the bed of the sea, rivers, etc. □ *vt,vi* bring up, clean, (as if) with a dredge: *to ~ (up) mud; to ~ a channel/harbor.*

dredger *n* [C] boat carrying a dredge.

dredge[2] /dredʒ/ *vt* sprinkle or scatter: *to ~ meat with flour; to ~ sugar over a cake.*

dregs /dregz/ *n pl* **1** bits of worthless matter which sink to the bottom of a glass, bottle, barrel, etc of liquid, esp of wine. **2** (*fig*) worst or useless part: *the ~ of society/humanity.*

drench /drentʃ/ *vt* make wet all over or all through: *to be ~ed with rain/~ed to the skin.*

drench·ing *n* thorough wetting: *We got a ~ing.*

dress[1] /dres/ *n* **1** [C] one-piece outer garment with a top part and skirt worn by a woman or girl. **2** [U] clothing in general (for both men and women), esp outer garments: *He doesn't care much about ~*, is not much interested in clothes.

ˈevening dress, clothing worn at formal social occasions (eg dinners, receptions).

ˌfull ˈdress, kind of clothes worn on special occasions: *ambassadors, naval and military officers, all in full ~.*

ˈdress·maker *n* [C] person who makes dresses.

ˈdress rehearsal, final rehearsal of a play, at which actors wear the costumes to be worn at actual performances.

dress[2] /dres/ *vt,vi* **1** put on (clothes): *Mary was ~ing her doll. Jimmy isn't old enough to ~ himself. Have you finished ~ing?* ***dress up,*** **(a)** put on special clothes, as for a play, for fun, etc: *The children ~ed (themselves) up as pirates.* **(b)** put on one's best clothes. **2** put on evening dress: *We don't ~ for dinner nowadays.* **3** (of what is habitual) wear clothes: *He has to ~ well in his position.* ***be dressed in,*** be wearing: *She was ~ed in white.* **4** provide clothes for: *How much does it cost him to ~ his wife and daughters?* **5** make ready to use; prepare: *to ~ leather*, make it soft and smooth; *to ~ a salad*, put dressing on it, ⇨ dressing(3). **6** brush and comb, arrange (one's hair). ***dress sb down/give sb a dressing-down,*** (*fig*) scold him severely. **7** clean and bandage a wound, etc. **8** make cheerful and attractive: *to ~ a store window.*

dresser[1] /ˈdresər/ *n* [C] **1** person who dresses: *a stylish ~.* **2** person who helps actors and actresses to dress ready for the stage.

dresser[2] /ˈdresər/ *n* [C] **1** piece of furniture with shelves for dishes, and cupboards below, often with drawers for cutlery, etc. **2** piece of furniture having drawers for clothing, etc; bureau.

dress·ing /ˈdresɪŋ/ *n* **1** [U] process of dressing (putting on clothes, cleaning and bandaging a wound, etc). **2** [C,U] something used for dressing wounds, eg an ointment, bandage, etc. **3** [C,U] mixture of oil, vinegar, etc used as a sauce for salads and other dishes. **4** [U] stuffing for chicken, turkey, etc.

ˈdressing gown, loose gown worn over pajamas, etc.

ˈdressing table, one with a mirror, used in a bedroom.

drew *pt* of draw[2].

dribble /ˈdrɪbəl/ *vt,vi* **1** (of liquids) flow, allow to flow, drop by drop or slowly (esp from the side of the mouth): *Babies often ~ on their bibs.* **2** (of a ball) take forward by means of quick, short bounces.

drib·bler *n* [C]

dribs and drabs /ˌdrɪbz ən ˈdræbz/ *n pl* (*informal*) small amounts.

dried *pt,pp* of dry[2].

drier[1] /ˈdraiər/ *adj* ⇨ dry[1].

drier[2] /ˈdraiər/ *n* [C] **1** substance that speeds up drying (when mixed with oil, paint, varnish, etc). **2** ⇨ dryer.

drift[1] /drɪft/ *n* **1** [U] drifting movement; being carried along by currents: *the ~ of the tide.* **2** [C] something caused by drifting: *Big ~s of snow /ˈsnow~s made progress slow and difficult.* **3** [U] general tendency or meaning: *Did you get/catch the ~ of the argument?* **4** [U] the way in which events, etc tend to move: *The general ~ of affairs was towards war.* **5** [U] the state of being without purpose or direction; aimlessness: *Is the government's policy one of ~?*

drift·age /-ɪdʒ/ *n* (of a ship) general movement off course due to currents, winds, tides, etc.

ˈdrift·wood *n* [U] wood carried along by currents and washed up on beaches.

drift[2] /drɪft/ *vi,vt* **1** be carried along by, or as by, a current of air or water: *The boat ~ed out to sea.* **2** (*fig,*) (of persons, etc) be without aim, purpose or self-control: *Is the government/the country ~ing towards bankruptcy? She ~s from one job to another.* **3** cause to drift: *The logs were ~ed down the stream to the saw-mills.*

drifter *n* [C] person who drifts(2) or moves from place to place.

drill[1] /drɪl/ *n* [C] instrument with a pointed end or cutting edges for making holes in hard substances: *a dentist's ~.* □ *vt,vi* make a hole with a drill.

drill[2] /drɪl/ *n* [C,U] **1** army training in handling weapons, marching, etc: *bayonet ~; a marching ~ on the parade ground.* **2** thorough training by means of practice and repetition: *~s in the English vowel sounds; fire ~; lifeboat ~.* □ *vt,vi* train, be trained, by means of drills: *to ~ troops.*

drill[3] /drɪl/ *n* [C] **1** long channel where seeds are to be sown. **2** machine for making these, sowing seeds in them, and covering the seeds. □ *vt* sow (seeds) in drills.

drily *adv* = dryly. ⇨ dry[1].

drink[1] /drɪŋk/ *n* [C,U] **1** liquid for drinking: *We have plenty of bottled ~s*, beer, lemonade, etc in bottles. **2** alcoholic liquor: *He's too fond of ~.* **3 the drink,** (*sl*) the sea.

drink[2] /drɪŋk/ *vt,vi* (*pt* drank /dræŋk/, *pp* drunk /drəŋk/) **1** take (liquid) into the mouth and swallow: *to ~ a pint of milk. Drink (up) your coffee.* **2** (of plants, the soil, etc) take in, absorb (liquid): *The thirsty plants drank (up) the water I gave them.* ***drink sth in,*** (*fig*) take in eagerly: *The children drank in every word of the story.* **3** take alcoholic liquors, beer, wine, etc, esp too much: *He ~s far too much. He'll ~ himself to death.* **4** wish good (to a person) while raising one's glass: *to ~ (to) a person's health.*

drink·able /-əbəl/ *adj* suitable, fit, for drinking.

drinker *n* [C] (esp) person who drinks(3) too often or too much: *He's a heavy ~er.*

drink·ing *n* [U] process or habit of taking liquid(s), esp alcoholic liquor: *He's too fond of ~ing.*

drip /drɪp/ *vi,vt* (-pp-) (of a liquid) fall, allow to fall, in drops: *The tap was ~ping. Blood was ~ping from his hand/His hand was ~ping blood.* ***dripping wet,*** very wet. □ *n* [C] **1** sound of the falling of a liquid drop by drop: *the ~s of the rain.* **2** (*sl*) a dull, foolish person.

ˈdrip-ˌdry *adj* made of washable fabric that needs little or no ironing: *~-dry shirts.* □ *vt* dry a garment by letting it drip until dry.

drip·pings *n pl* liquid that drips or has dripped, esp fat and juices from roasted meat.

drive[1] /draiv/ *n* **1** [C] journey (in a car, etc, not in a public bus, etc): *to go for a ~. The station is an hour's ~ away.* **2** [C] **(a)** (also **ˈdriveway**) private road to a house or garage. **(b)** public road eg in a park. **3** (of a ball) **(a)** [U] force given to a ball when it is struck. **(b)** [C] stroke or hit: *a ~ to the boundary.* **4** [U] energy; capacity to get things done: *The new headmaster is lacking in ~.* **5** basic need; motivation: *the ˈsex ~.* **6** [C] organized effort or campaign: *a ~ to raise money for a new school building.* **7** apparatus for driving a machine: *a four-wheel ~*, with four wheels connected to the source of power.

drive[2] /draiv/ *vt,vi* (*pt* drove /drouv/, *pp* ~n /ˈdrɪvən/) **1** move, push, urge along or onward: *to ~ cattle to market. The gale drove the ship on to the rocks. The wind was driving the rain against the windowpanes.* ***drive sb into a corner,*** (*fig*) force him (eg during an argument) into a position from which escape will be difficult. **2** operate, direct the course of an automobile or other vehicle; control, direct the course of an animal or animals drawing a cart, plow, etc: *to ~ a taxi; to take driving lessons.* **3** travel or go in a car, carriage, etc.: *Shall we ~ home or walk?* (*Note: ride* is used of buses, trains, etc.) **4** carry, convey, (a person) in a car, etc (not a public vehicle): *He drove me to the station.* **5** set or keep in motion; be the power to operate: *The machinery is ~n by steam.* **6** go or move along fast or violently: *The ship drove/was ~n on the rocks.* **7** hit so as to force into: *With one blow he drove the nail into the plank.* **8** hit or strike with force: *to ~ a golf ball on to the putting green.* ***drive sth home,*** (*fig*) use great force or effort to be believed or understood. **9** bring (a person) to a certain state: *Failure drove him to despair/to drink. You'll ~ me mad.* **10** force (a person) to act: *He was ~n by fear to tell a lie.* **11** (cause to) work very hard: *He ~s himself very hard.* **12** make by digging, excavating, etc: *to ~ a tunnel/a railroad track across a hilly district.* **13** carry on: ***drive a hard bargain,*** not give way easily to another person in a business deal. **14** ***drive at,*** mean, intend: *What's he driving at?*

drive-in /ˈdraivˌɪn/ *n* [C] motion picture theater, restaurant, etc to which customers drive in and remain in their automobiles while being entertained or served.

drivel /ˈdrɪvəl/ *vt* (-l-, -ll-) talk nonsense; talk childishly: *What's he ~ling (on) about?* □ *n* [U] silly nonsense; foolish talk.

drivel·er /ˈdrɪv(ə)lər/ *n* [C]

driven /ˈdrɪvən/ *pp* of drive[2].

driver /ˈdraivər/ *n* [C] **1** (esp) person who drives (vehicles): *a taxi ~; a bus ~.* ⇨ chauffeur. **2** (*old use*) boss of a gang of laborers: *ˈslave ~.* **3** specially-shaped club used in golf to hit the ball straight over long distances.

drizzle /ˈdrɪzəl/ *vt* rain (in many small fine drops): *It ~d all day.* □ *n* [U] fine rain.

driz·zly /ˈdrɪz(ə)li/ *adj* (-ier, -iest) drizzling: *drizzly weather.*

drom·edary /ˈdraməˌderi/ *n* [C] (*pl* -ies) fast, one-humped camel.

drone /droun/ *n* **1** [C] male bee that does not gather honey. **2** [C] person who does no work and lives on others. **3** [U] low humming sound (as) made by bees: *the ~ of distant traffic.* □ *vi,vt* **1** make a drone(3). **2** talk or sing in a low, boring way: *The minister ~d out the psalm.*

drool /drul/ *vi* **1** let saliva run from the mouth. **2** = drivel.

droop /drup/ *vi,vt* **1** bend or hang downward (through tiredness or weakness): *The flowers were ~ing for lack of water. His spirits ~ed*, he became sad. **2** let (the head, face, eyes) hang down. □ *n* [C] bending position.

drop[1] /drap/ *n* [C] **1** very small quantity of liquid, usually with a rounded shape: *ˈrain~s.* **2** (*pl*) liquid medicine taken in drops: *ˈear/eye/nose ~s.* **3** very small quantity: *There isn't a ~ of milk left.* ***a drop in the bucket,*** a very small and unimportant quantity. **4** something like a drop in shape or appearance: *chocolate ~s.* **5** movement from a higher to a lower level, esp distance of a fall: *a sudden ~ in the temperature*, eg from 30°C to 20°C; *a ~ in the price of meat.* ***at the drop of a hat,*** **(a)** as soon as a signal is given. **(b)** at once; readily or willingly. **6** thing that drops or is dropped(1).

ˈdrop·kick *n* [C] (*football*) one in which the ball is dropped and kicked as it falls.

drop[2] /drap/ *vt,vi* (-pp-) **1** (of liquids) fall, cause to fall, in drops. ⇨ drip. **2** (allow to) fall: *She ~ped the teapot.* ***drop anchor,*** lower the anchor. ***drop a stitch,*** (in knitting) let it slip off the needle. **3** (allow to) become weaker or lower: *The wind/temperature has ~ped. His voice ~ped/He ~ped his voice to a whisper.* **4** (cause to) fall or sink to the ground, etc: *They were ready to ~ with fatigue. He ~ped (on)to his knees*, knelt down. *Supplies were ~ped by parachute.* **5(a)** say casually: *to ~ him a hint*, give him one; *to ~ a word in her ear.* **(b)** send: *Drop me a postcard/a few lines/a short note.* **6** omit; fail to pronounce, write or insert: *He ~s his g's*, eg by saying *singin'* /ˈsɪŋən/ instead of *singing* /sɪŋɪŋ/. **7** stop (a car, etc) to allow a person to get out: *Please ~ me (off) at the post* *office*. **8** stop associating with: *He seems to have ~ped most of his friends*. **9** give up: *to ~ a bad habit*. **10** (cause to) come to an end; no longer deal with or discuss: *Let's ~ the subject*. **11** (special uses with *adverbial particles* and *prepositions*):

drop away, = drop off(a).

drop back/behind, not keep up with: *They ~ped behind the rest of the party*.

drop by, pay a casual visit to: *They dropped by for a drink*.

drop in (on sb), pay an unexpected visit: *Some friends ~ped in on me*.

drop off, **(a)** become fewer or less: *The doctor's practice has ~ped off*, he now has fewer patients. **(b)** fall asleep: *He ~ped off during the sermon*.

drop out, **(a)** not take part; withdraw: *Three of the runners ~ped out*. *Smith has ~ped out of the team*. **(b)** withdraw from conventional society.

ˈdrop·out *n* [C] **(a)** person who withdraws from a course of instruction: *the high number of ~outs in a language course*. **(b)** person who deliberately lives in an unconventional style.

drop·pings /drapɪŋz/ *n pl* dung of animals.

dross /drɔs, dras/ *n* [U] waste matter.

drought /draut/ *n* [C,U] continuous (period of) dry weather causing distress.

drove[1] *pt* of drive[2].

drove[2] /drouv/ *n* [C] **1** large number of animals (sheep, cattle) being driven together. **2** crowd of people moving together: *~s of sightseers; visitors in ~s*.

drover *n* [C] man who drives cattle, sheep, etc to market.

drown /draun/ *vt,vi* **1** (cause to) die in water because unable to breathe: *a ~ing man. He ~ed the kittens*. **2** (*fig*) drenched: *~ed in tears*. **3** (of sound) be loud enough to prevent another sound from being heard: *The noises in the street ~ed* (*out*) *the teacher's voice*.

drowse /drauz/ *vi,vt* be half asleep: *to ~ away a hot afternoon*.

drowsy /ˈdrauzi/ *adj* (-ier, -iest) **1** feeling sleepy. **2** making one feel sleepy.

drows·ily /ˈdrauzəli/ *adv*

drow·si·ness /ˈdrauzinɪs/ *n* [U]

drudge /drədʒ/ *n* [C] person who must work hard and long at unpleasant tasks. □ *vi* work as a drudge does.

drudg·ery /ˈdrədʒəri/ *n* [U] hard, unpleasant, uninteresting work.

drug /drəg/ *n* [C] **1** substance used for medical purposes, either alone or in a mixture. **2** substance that changes the state or function of cells, organs or organisms. **3** (often habit-forming) substance: *a ˈ~ addict; ˈ~ addiction*. □ *vt* (-gg-) **1** add harmful drugs to (food and drink): *His wine had been ~ged*. **2** give drugs to, esp in order to make unconscious: *They ~ged the guard and then robbed the bank*.

drug·gist /ˈdrəgɪst/ *n* [C] **1** pharmacist. **2** person who operates a drugstore.

drug·store /ˈdrəgˌstɔr/ *n* [C] pharmacy; place where medicines, cosmetics, and sometimes food and drink may be bought.

drum[1] /drəm/ *n* [C] **1** musical instrument made of a hollow cylinder or hemisphere with parchment stretched over the open side(s). ⇨ illus at percussion. **2** sound (as) of a drum or drums. **3** thing shaped like a drum, eg a container for oil.

ˈdrum·stick *n* [C] **(a)** stick for beating a drum. ⇨ illus at percussion. **(b)** lower part of the leg of a cooked chicken, turkey, etc.

drum[2] /drəm/ *vt,vi* (-mm-) **1** play a drum. **2** beat or tap continuously on something: *to ~ on the table with one's fingers*. **3** ***drum up,*** (*fig*) get by repeated efforts; *~med up a lot of new business*. **4** cause a person to remember something by using repetition: *~ the spelling into his head*.

drum·mer *n* [C] person who plays a drum.

drunk /drəŋk/ *adj* (*pp* of drink[2]) ***be drunk***, be overcome by drinking alcoholic liquor: *He was dead/blind/half ~*. ***get drunk,*** **(a)** become intoxicated: *It's easy to get ~ on brandy*. **(b)** (*fig*) become greatly excited: *He was ~ with joy/success*. □ *n* [C] person who is drunk.

drunk·ard /ˈdrəŋkərd/ *n* [C] person who is habitually drunk.

drunken /ˈdrəŋkən/ *adj* **1** in the habit of drinking; often drunk: *a ~ and destitute man*. **2** caused by drinking; showing the effects of drinking: *a ~ spree/stupor*.

drunken·ly *adv*

drunken·ness /-nɪs/ *n* [U]

dry[1] /drai/ *adj* (-ier, -iest) **1** not wet; free from moisture: *Is this wood dry enough to burn?* ***dry as a bone; ˌbone-ˈdry,*** quite dry. **2(a)** not rainy: *dry weather*. **(b)** having a small rainfall: *a dry climate*. **3(a)** not supplying water: *a dry well*. **(b)** not supplying milk: *The cows are dry*. **4** solid, not liquid. **5** without butter, etc: *dry toast*. **6** (of drink) not sweet, not fruity in flavor: *dry wines*. **7** thirsty: *to feel dry*. **8** uninteresting; dull: *a dry lecture*. **9** plain; undisguised: *dry facts*. **10** without mucus: *a dry cough*. **11** prohibiting or restricting the sale of alcoholic liquor: *a dry county*.

ˌdry-ˈclean *vt* clean (clothes, etc) by using chemicals instead of water.

ˌdry-ˈcleaner *n* [C]

ˌdry-ˈcleaning *n* [U]

ˈdry goods, textiles, clothing, etc as contrasted with groceries, etc: *dry goods store*.

dryly /ˈdraili/ *adv*

dry·ness /-nɪs/ *n* [U]

ˌdry ˈrot, decay of wood (causing it to crumble to powder), occurring when there is no movement of air over its surface.

ˌdry ˈrun, (a) practice attack, without use of ammunition. **(b)** practice session; rehearsal.

dry[2] /drai/ *vt,vi* (*pt,pp* dried) **1** make or become dry: *Dry your hands on this towel. We were drying our clothes in front of the fire. Our clothes soon dried.* ***dry out/up,*** make or become completely dry: *The stream dries up during the hot summer*. (*fig*) *His imagination seems to have dried up. Let the clothes dry out*. **2** (usually in *pp*) preserve by extracting moisture: *dried fruit/mushrooms*.

dryer /ˈdraiər/ *n* [C] something that dries: *a ˈhair ~*; a *ˈclothes ~*.

DST *abbr* = Daylight Saving Time.

dual /ˈduəl/ *adj* of two; double; divided in two:

~ *ownership;* ˌ~-ˈ*purpose*, adapted to, intended or used for two purposes.

dub /dəb/ *vt* (-bb-) **1** make (a person) a knight by touching him on the shoulder with a sword. **2** give (a person) a pet name: *They dubbed him "Shorty" because he was so tall.* **3** replace or add to the sound track of a film or magnetic tape, esp one in a different language.

du·bi·ous /ˈdubiəs/ *adj* **1** feeling doubt: *I feel ~ of/about his honesty.* **2** causing doubt; of doubtful worth or value: *He's a ~ character. a ~ compliment.*

du·bi·ous·ly *adv*

du·bi·ous·ness /-nɪs/ *n* [U]

duch·ess /ˈdətʃɪs/ *n* [C] **1** wife or widow of a duke. **2** woman holding the rank of duke in her own right.

duchy /ˈdətʃi/ *n* [C] (*pl* -ies) (also **dukedom**) land ruled by a duke or duchess.

duck[1] /dək/ *n* (*pl* ~s, but often unchanged when collective) **1** [C] **(a)** common water bird, both wild and domestic. **(b)** female duck. ⇨ drake. ***(take to sth) like a duck to water,*** (take it up) naturally, without fear, hesitation or difficulty. ***like water off a duck's back,*** without producing any effect. **2** [U] its flesh as food.

ˌ**duck** ˈ**soup,** (*sl*) task which is easily carried out: *that test was ~ soup (to me).*

duck[2] /dək/ *vt,vi* **1** move quickly down (to avoid being seen or hit): *to ~ one's head.* **2** go, push (a person), quickly under water for a short time: *The big boy ~ed all the small boys in the swimming pool.* □ *n* [C] **1** quick downward or sideways movement of the head or body. **2** quick dip below water (when bathing in the sea, etc).

duck·ing *n* thorough wetting.

duck·bill(ed) platypus /ˌdəkˌbɪl(d) ˈplætɪpəs/ *n* [C] small Australian egg-laying water mammal with webbed feet and a beak like a duck.

duck·ling /ˈdəklɪŋ/ *n* [C] young duck: *ugly ~,* plain or stupid child who grows up to be attractive or brilliant.

duck·weed /ˈdəkˌwid/ *n* [C] small, stemless water plant.

duct /dəkt/ *n* [C] **1** tube or canal through which liquid in the body flows: ˈ*tear ~s.* **2** metal tube and outlet for air, liquid, etc: *air ~s in a heating system.*

dud /dəd/ *n* [C], *adj* (*sl*) (thing or person) which has proven useless, eg a shell or bomb that fails to explode or a check of no value.

dude /dud/ *n* [C] **1** man who pays too much attention to his dress. **2** (esp) Easterner in the western US. **3** (*sl*) man.

ˈ**dude ranch,** western(-style) ranch set up as a resort for vacationing Easterners.

dudg·eon /ˈdədʒən/ *n* ***in high dudgeon,*** feeling offended and angry.

due[1] /du/ *adj* **1** owing; to be paid: *When is the rent due? The wages due to him will be paid tomorrow.* **2** suitable; right; proper: *after due consideration; in due course,* at the right and proper time. **3** (to be) expected; appointed or agreed (for a certain time or date): *The train is due (in) at 1:30.* **4** ***due to,*** **(a)** that may be attributed to: *The accident was due to careless driving.* **(b)** because of: *Due to his careless driving, we had a bad accident.* □ *adv* (of points of the compass) exactly: *due east/north.*

due[2] /du/ *n* **1** (*sing* only) that which must be given to a person because it is right or owing: *give the man his due.* **2** (*pl*) sums of money to be paid, eg for membership of a club; fees; charges.

duel /ˈduəl/ *n* [C] **1** (illegal) fight (usually with swords or pistols) between two persons, esp to decide a point of honor, in the presence of two other persons called *seconds.* **2** any two-sided contest: *a ~ of wits.* □ *vi* (-l-, -ll-) fight a duel.

duel·ist *n* [C] person who fights a duel.

duet /duˈet/ *n* [C] piece of music for two voices or for two players.

duffel /ˈdəfəl/ *n* [U] coarse thick woolen cloth: *a* ˈ*~ coat,* one of this material, with toggles instead of buttons.

ˈ**duffel bag,** large cylindrical bag made of canvas, used for carrying clothing, etc.

dug[1] *pt,pp* of dig.

dug[2] /dəg/ *n* [C] udder or teat of a female mammal.

dug·out /ˈdəˌgaut/ *n* [C] **1** rough covered shelter made by digging, esp by soldiers for protection in war. **2** canoe made by hollowing a tree trunk.

duke /duk/ *n* [C] **1** member of the nobility ranking below a prince. **2** (in some parts of Europe) independent sovereign ruler of a small state.

duke·dom /ˈdukdəm/ *n* **(a)** position, duties, rank of a duke. **(b)** = duchy.

dul·cet /ˈdəlsɪt/ *adj* (of sounds) sweet; pleasing.

dull /dəl/ *adj* (-er, -est) **1** not clear or bright: *a ~ color/sound/mirror/day/sky; ~ weather* **2** slow in understanding: *~ pupils; a ~ mind.* **3** monotonous; not exciting or appealing: *a ~ book/speech/sermon/play.* **4** not sharp: *a ~ knife.* **5** (of pain) not felt distinctly: *a ~ ache.* **6** (of trade) not active. □ *vt,vi* make or become dull: *to ~ the edge of a razor; drugs that ~ pain.*

dull·ness /-nɪs/ *n* [U]

dully /ˈdəlli/ *adv*

duly /ˈduli/ *adv* in a right or suitable manner; at the right time.

dumb /dəm/ *adj* (-er, -est) **1** unable to speak: *~ from birth; ~ animals,* animals other than human beings. **2** unwilling to speak; silent: *The class remained ~ when the teacher asked a difficult question.* ***strike dumb,*** make unable to talk because of surprise, fear, etc: *He was struck ~ with horror.* **3** (*informal*) stupid; dull.

dumb·ly *adv*

dumb·ness /-nɪs/ *n* [U]

dumb·bell /ˈdəmˌbel/ *n* [C] **1** short bar of wood or iron with a weighted ball at each end, used for exercising the muscles of the arms and shoulders. **2** (*informal*) stupid person.

dumb·waiter /ˈdəmˌweitər/ *n* [C] **1** stand with (usually revolving) shelves for food, dishes, etc used at a dining table. **2** box with shelves, pulled up and down a shaft, to carry food, etc from one floor to another, eg in a restaurant.

dum·found, dumb·found /ˌdəmˈfaund/ *vt* astonish; strike dumb with surprise.

dummy /ˈdəmi/ *n* [C] (*pl* -ies) **1** object made to look like and serve the purpose of the real person or thing: *a tailor's ~,* for fitting clothes. **2(a)** (in card games, esp bridge) player whose cards are placed upwards on the table and played by his partner. **(b)** the cards so placed. **3** person who is thought to be acting for himself but who is really acting for someone else. **4** stupid person.

dump /dəmp/ *n* [C] **1 (a)** place where rubbish, etc may be unloaded and left. **(b)** heap of rubbish, etc. **2** (place where there is a) temporary store of military supplies: *an ˌammunition ~.* **3** (*sl*) poorly cared for, dirty or ugly place: *I should hate to live in a ~ like this.* □ *vt* **1** put on or into a dump (1); put or throw out. **2** let fall in a mass or heap: *Where can I ~ this rubbish? They ~ed the coal outside the shed instead of putting it inside.*
ˈdump truck, vehicle with a bin that can be tilted, for carrying and emptying soil, rubble, etc (eg for road building).

dump·ling /ˈdəmplɪŋ/ *n* [C] **1** small round mass of dough steamed or boiled with meat and vegetables. **2** dessert made of dough baked with an apple or other fruit inside it.

dumps /dəmps/ *n pl* ***(down) in the dumps,*** (*informal*) depressed; feeling gloomy.

dumpy /ˈdəmpi/ *adj* (-ier, -iest) short and fat.

dunce /dəns/ *n* [C] stupid person.
ˈdunce cap, pointed cap formerly given to wear in class as a punishment for a slow learner.

dune /dun/ *n* [C] mound of loose, dry sand formed by the wind, esp near the coast.
ˈdune buggy, automobile esp built for driving on sand.

dung /dəŋ/ *n* [U] excrement dropped by animals (esp cattle), used on fields as manure.

dunga·rees /ˌdəŋgəˈriz/ *n pl* overalls or trousers (usually) of coarse cotton.

dun·geon /ˈdəndʒən/ *n* [C] dark underground cell used (in olden times) as a prison.

dunk /dəŋk/ *vt* dip (a piece of food) into a liquid: *~ a doughnut in coffee.*

duo·denal /ˌduəˈdinəl/ *adj* of the duodenum: *a ~ ulcer.*

duo·denum /ˌduəˈdinəm/ *n* [C] (*pl ~s*) first part of the small intestine immediately below the stomach.

dupe /dup/ *vt* cheat; make a fool of. □ *n* [C] person who is duped.

du·plex /ˈduˌpleks/ *adj* double; with two parts. □ *n* [C] **1** house built to hold two families. **2** two-level apartment for one family.

du·pli·cate[1] /ˈduplɪkɪt/ *adj* **1** exactly like: *~ keys for the front door of a house.* **2** with two corresponding parts; doubled; twofold. □ *n* [C] thing that is exactly like another. ***in duplicate,*** (of documents, etc) with a copy.

du·pli·cate[2] /ˈduplɪˌkeit/ *vt* **1** make an exact copy of (a letter, etc); produce copies of. **2** multiply by two.
du·pli·ca·tion /ˌduplɪˈkeiʃən/ *n* **(a)** [U] duplicating or being duplicated. **(b)** [C] copy.
du·pli·ca·tor /ˈduplɪˌkeitər/ *n* [C] (esp) machine, etc that makes copies

du·plic·ity /duˈplɪsəti/ *n* [U] (*formal*) deliberate deception.

du·rable /ˈdurəbəl/ *adj* likely to last for a long time: *a ~ pair of shoes.* □ *n pl* durable goods (eg vacuum cleaners).

DUPLEX

dura·bil·ity /ˌdurəˈbɪləti/ *n* [U]

du·ration /dəˈreiʃən/ *n* [U] time during which something lasts or exists: *for the ~ of the war; of short ~.*

du·ress /dəˈres/ *n* [U] threats, or force, used to compel a person to do something: *under ~,* compelled by such means.

dur·ing /ˈdurɪŋ/ *prep* **1** throughout the continuance of: *The sun gives us light ~ the day.* **2** at some point of time in the course of: *He called to see me ~ my absence.*

dusk /dəsk/ *n* [U] time just before it gets quite dark: *scarcely visible in the ~.*

dusky /ˈdəski/ *adj* (-ier, -iest) **1** somewhat dark-colored. **2** dim.

dust[1] /dəst/ *n* **1** [U] dry earth or other matter in the form of fine powder, lying on the ground or the surface of objects, or blown about by the wind: *The ~ was blowing in the streets.* **2** (*fig*) what is left of a dead body.
ˈdust bowl, drought area that has frequent dust storms.
ˈdust jacket/wrapper, removable paper cover to protect the binding of a book.
ˈdust·pan *n* [C] pan into which dust is swept from the floor.
ˈdust storm *n* [C] strong wind carrying clouds of dust.

dust[2] /dəst/ *vt* **1** remove dust from by wiping, brushing, etc: **2** sprinkle with powder: *to ~ a cake with sugar.*
duster *n* [C] cloth for removing dust from furniture, etc.

dusty /dəsti/ *adj* (-ier, -iest) **1** covered with dust; full of dust. **2** like dust; dry as dust.

Dutch /dətʃ/ *n* **1** the Dutch language. **2** (*pl*) (used with *the*) Dutch people. □ *adj* **1** of the Netherlands (Holland), its language or its people: *~ cheese.* ***go Dutch (with sb),*** pay one's own expenses. ⇨ Dutch treat.
ˈDutch·man/·woman /-mən, -ˌwumən/ *n* [C] (*pl* ~men /-men/, ~women /-ˌwɪmɪn/) male/female native of the Netherlands (Holland).
ˌDutch ˈtreat *n* [C] meal, entertainment for which each person pays his own expenses.

duti·able /ˈdutiəbəl/ *adj* on which customs duties must be paid: *~ goods.* ⇨ duty(3).

duti·ful /ˈdutɪfəl/ *adj* having a sense of duty;

showing respect and obedience: *a ~ son.*
duti·fully /ˈdutɪfli/ *adv*
duty /ˈduti/ *n* (*pl* -ies) **1** [C,U] conduct expected of one or task that one is obliged to do by custom, law, one's work, etc: *Do not forget your ~ to your parents. His duties at the hospital take up most of his time.* ***on/off duty,*** engaged/not engaged in one's regular work: *He goes on ~ at 8am and comes off ~ at 5pm.* **2** force of moral obligation: *the call of ~.* **3** [C,U] government tax, esp on exported or imported goods.
dwarf /dwɔrf/ *n* [C] (*pl* ~s, dwarves /dwɔrvz/) **1** person, animal or plant much below the usual size. **2** (in fairy tales) small being with magic powers. □ *vt* **1** prevent from growing to full size. **2** cause to appear small by contrast or distance: *The big steamer ~ed our little motorboat.*
dwell /dwel/ *vt* (*pt,pp* dwelt /dwelt/) **1** live, have as one's home. **2** ***dwell (up)on,*** think, speak or write at length about: *She ~s too much on her past.*
dwel·ler *n* (in compounds) inhabitant: *ˈcity-~ers.*
dwell·ing *n* place of residence (a house, apartment, etc).
dwindle /ˈdwɪndəl/ *vi* become less or smaller by degrees.
dye[1] /dai/ *vt,vi* (*3rd person sing present tense,* dyes, *pt,pp* dyed, *present participle* dyeing) **1** color, usually by dipping in a liquid: *to dye a white dress blue; to have a dress dyed.* **2** give color to: *Deep blushes dyed her cheeks.* **3** take color from dyeing: *This material does not dye well.*
ˌdyed-in-the-ˈwool *adj* (*fig*) complete, deep-rooted: *a dyed-in-the-wool conservative.*
dye[2] /dai/ *n* [C,U] substance used for dyeing cloth; color given by dyeing.
dyer *n* [C] one who dyes cloth.
dy·ing *pres p of* die[1].
dyke *n* = dike.
dy·namic /daiˈnæmɪk/ *adj* **1** of physical power and forces producing motion. ➪ static[1]. **2** (of a person) having great energy or force. □ *n pl* (with *sing verb*) branch of physics dealing with matter in motion.
dy·nami·cally /daiˈnæmɪkli/ *adv*
dyna·mite /ˈdainəˌmait/ *n* [U] powerful explosive (as used in mining and quarrying). □ *vt* blow up with dynamite.
dy·namo /ˈdainəˌmou/ *n* [C] (*pl* ~s) **1** machine for changing steam power, water power, etc into electrical energy. **2** (*fig*) energetic person.
dyn·asty /ˈdainəsti/ *n* [C] (*pl* -ies) succession of rulers belonging to one family: *the Tudor ~* (in England).
dyn·astic /daiˈnæstɪk/ *adj*
dys·en·tery /ˈdɪsənˌteri/ *n* [U] painful disease of the bowels, with discharge of mucus and blood.
dys·pep·sia /dɪsˈpepʃə, -ˈpepsiə/ *n* [U] indigestion (the usual word).
dys·pep·tic /dɪsˈpeptɪk/ *adj* of indigestion. □ *n* [C] person suffering from indigestion.
dz. *abbr* = dozen.

e

E, e /i/ (*pl* E's, e's /iz/) the fifth letter of the English alphabet.
E. *abbr* = East.
ea. *abbr* = each.
each /itʃ/ *adj* (of two or more) every one, thing, group, person, etc taken separately or individually: *He was sitting with a child on ~ side of him.* ***each and every 'one***, each one. □ *adv* to, for, every one of a group: *He gave the boys a dollar ~.* □ *pron* **1** every thing, person, group, etc: *Each of them wants to try.* **2** each one, taken separately: *We ~ took a big risk. Tom, Dick and Harry ~ put forward a different scheme.* **3 *each other***, one another: *We see ~ other* (= each of us sees the other) *at the office every day*. (*Note: one another* is often used when referring to more than one.)
eager /ˈigər/ *adj* full of, showing, strong desire: *~ for success/to succeed.*
ˌeager ˈbeaver, (*sl*) person who shows more than the usual willingness to do something: *He's an ~ beaver for work.*
eager·ly *adv*
eager·ness /-nɪs/ *n* [U]
eagle /ˈigəl/ *n* [C] **1** large, strong bird of prey of the hawk family with keen sight. ⇨ illus at bird. **2** (formerly) gold coin of the US, worth ten dollars.
eag·let, /ˈiglɪt/ *n* [C] young eagle(**1**).
ear[1] /ɪr/ *n* [C] **1** organ of hearing. ***be all ears,*** be listening eagerly. ***fall on deaf ears,*** pass unnoticed; be ignored. ***go in one ear and out the other,*** make no impression. ***have an ear to the ground,*** be well informed about what is or may be happening. ***(put) a word in sb's ear,*** say something in confidence. ***lend an ear (to),*** listen. ***turn a deaf ear (to),*** refuse to listen, help. ***up to one's ears (in),*** extremely busy or involved (with). ***the walls have ears,*** someone may be listening. ***wet behind the ears,*** naïve; immature. **2** sense of hearing. ***have a good ear,*** be able to discriminate sounds. ***have a bad/tin ear,*** be poor at discriminating sounds. ***(play sth) by ear,*** **(a)** (play it) without printed music. **(b)** (*fig*) (do something) without planning or preparing in advance. **3** something that is like an ear in shape or position.
ˈear·ache *n* [U,C] pain in the ear.
ˈear·drum *n* thin membrane (in the inner ear) which vibrates when sound waves strike it.
ˈear·muff *n* pad of fur, etc worn over the ear as protection from the cold: ˈ*~muffs*, pair of these, usually with connecting band.
ˈear·phone *n* small speaker (attached esp to a radio) that plugs into the ear.
ˈear·ring *n* [C] ornament worn in or on the lobe of the ear.
ˈear·shot *n* hearing distance: *within/out of earshot.*
ˈear·wax *n* [U] material, like wax, which accumulates in the ear.
ear[2] /ɪr/ *n* [C] seed-bearing part of corn, barley, etc. ⇨ illus at cereal, vegetable.
-eared /ɪrd/ *adj* (used in compounds): *long-*

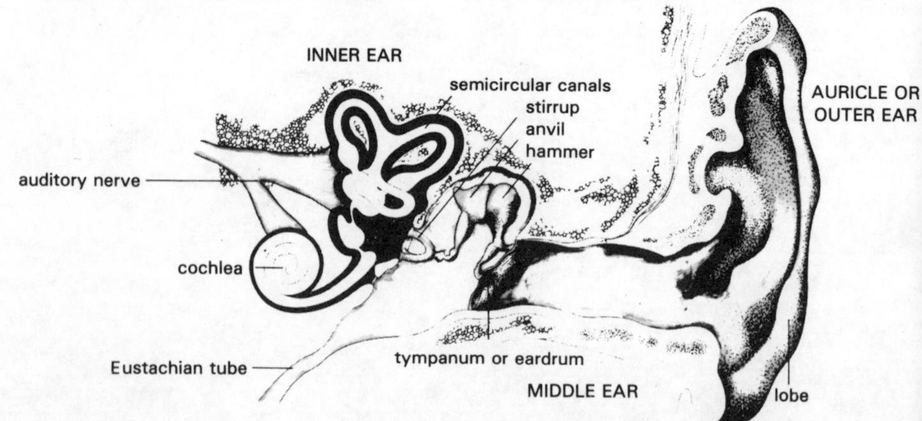

EAR

eared, having long ears; *dog-eared*.

earl /ˈərl, ˈərəl/ *n* [C] high-ranking member of the nobility (feminine = *countess*).

ˈearl·dom /ˈərldəm, ˈərəl-/ *n* rank, lands, of an earl.

early /ˈərli/ (-ier, -iest) *adj, adv* **1** near to the beginning of a period of time: *in the ~ part of this century; in ~ spring.* **2** before the usual time: *He's an ~ riser*, gets up early.

ˈearly bird, person who gets up earlier or who arrives before others.

ear·mark /ˈɪrˌmark/ *vt* set aside for a special purpose: *~ a sum of money for research.*

earn /ərn/ *vt* get in return for work or as a reward for one's qualities or in payment for a loan: *to ~ $25,000 a year. His achievements ~ed him respect and admiration. I enjoyed a well-~ed rest.*

earn·ings *n pl* money earned: *He has spent all his ~ings.*

ear·nest /ˈərnɪst/ *adj* serious; determined: *an ~ worker/pupil.* □ *n* ***in dead earnest,*** serious(ly): *I'm telling you in dead ~*, I'm not joking at all.

earn·est·ly *adv*

earn·est·ness /-nɪs/ *n* [U]

earth /ərθ/ *n* **1** (sometimes **Earth**) this world; the planet on which we live: *The ~ goes around the sun. Who do you think was the greatest man on ~?* ⇨ illus at planet. **2** [U] land surface of the world; land contrasted with the sea and air. ***come down/back to earth,*** return to practical realities. ***move heaven and earth (to do sth)***, make every possible effort. **3** [U] soil: *to cover the roots of a plant with ~.* **4** [C] hole of a fox, badger or other wild animal. ***run sth/sb to earth,*** (*fig*) discover by searching.

ˈearth·ling /-lɪŋ/ *n* [C] inhabitant of earth; mortal.

ˈearth satellite, one which orbits the earth.

ˈearth·worm *n* [C] common kind of worm that lives in the soil.

earthy *adj* (-ier, -iest) **(a)** of or like soil: *an ~y smell.* **(b)** (*fig*) coarse, unrefined.

earthen·ware /ˈərθənˌwer/ *n* [U] dishes, etc made of baked clay: *an ~ casserole.*

earth·ly /ˈərθli/ *adj* **1** of this world, not of heaven: *~ joys/possessions.* **2** (*informal*) possible; conceivable: *You haven't an ~ chance*, no chance at all. ***no earthly use,*** quite useless, pointless.

earth·quake /ˈərθˌkweik/ *n* [C] sudden, violent movements of the earth's surface.

ear·wig /ˈɪrˌwɪg/ *n* [C] small insect with pincers at the rear end. ⇨ illus at insect.

ease¹ /iz/ *n* [U] freedom from work, discomfort, trouble, difficulty, anxiety: *a life of ~; with ~*, without difficulty. ***(be/feel) ill at ease,*** anxious or embarrassed. ***at ease,*** **(a)** (as a military command) with the legs apart and the hands behind the back. **(b)** comfortable.

ease² /iz/ *vt,vi* **1** give relief to (the body or mind) from pain, discomfort, anxiety: *~ his anxiety; ~ him of his pain/trouble.* **2** make looser, less tight: *~ a coat under the armpits.* **3** move slowly and with care: *~ a desk through a narrow door.* **4** become less tense or troublesome: *the easing of tension between the two countries. The situation has ~d (off).*

easel /ˈizəl/ *n* [C] wooden frame to hold a blackboard or a picture upright.

eas·ily /ˈiz(ə)li/ *adv* **1** with ease. **2** without doubt: *~ the best TV program.*

east /ist/ *n* **1 the east,** point of the horizon where the sun rises; part of any country, etc, lying farther in this direction than other parts: *Pennsylvania is to the ~ of Illinois.* **2 the East, (a)** the Orient. **(b)** the eastern part of the USA, esp New York and New England. *adj* □ **1** coming from the east: *an ~ wind.* **2** toward, at, in the direction of the east: *on the ~ coast.* □ *adv* toward the east: *to travel/face ~.* ***down East,*** (*old use*) to, in the northeastern US. (*Note:* unless Maine is specifically meant, (*in the*) *East* is now the usual term.)

east·ward /ˈistwərd/ *adj, adv* toward the east.

east·wards /-wərdz/ *adv*

Easter¹ /ˈistər/ *n* anniversary of the resurrection of Christ, observed on the first Sunday after the full moon that falls on or after March 21: *the ~ holidays.*

ˈEaster egg, egg with a painted or dyed shell, or an egg made of chocolate, used as an Easter gift.

Easter² /ˈistər/ *n* ***down Easter,*** (*old use*) native of the northeastern US. (*Note:* unless a native of Maine is meant, *easterner* is now the usual term.)

east·er·ly /ˈistərli/ *adj* in an eastern direction or position; (of the wind) coming from the east.

east·ern /ˈistərn/ *adj* of, from, living in, the east part of the world: *~ religions.*

the ˌEastern ˈChurch, the Greek Orthodox Church.

east·erner *n* [C] native or resident of the northeastern part of the US.

the ˌEastern ˈHemisphere, part of the world that includes Europe, Asia, Africa, and Australia.

east·ern·most /-moust/ *adj* farthest east.

ˈEastern Time, one of the four official time zones of the continental US.

easy /ˈizi/ (-ier, -iest) *adj* **1** not difficult: *an ~ book. The place is ~ to reach.* **2** free, from pain, discomfort, anxiety, trouble, etc: *to lead an ~ life; an ˈ~ chair*, one that is soft and restful. **3** not strict or severe: *She is an ~ teacher.* **4** relaxed; natural; pleasant: *an ~ manner.* □ *adv* easily. ***take it easy,*** (*informal*) **(a)** not work too hard or too energetically. **(b)** not get excited. **(c)** (as *informal* phrase for taking one's leave from another): = good-bye. ***go easy on,*** (*informal*) be careful or moderate with: *Go ~ on the wine—it's the last bottle!* ***easier said than done,*** it is easier to say one will do it than to do it.

ˈeasy chair, large comfortable chair.

ˈeasy-ˌgoing *adj* (of persons) pleasant; tolerant; casual.

eat /it/ *vt,vi* (*pt* ate /eit/ *pp* eaten /ˈitən/) **1** take (solid food, also soup) into the mouth and swallow it: *to eat one's dinner; to eat up* (= finish eating) *one's food.* ***eat one's heart out,*** suffer; be very sad. ***eat one's words,*** take a statement back, say that one was wrong. **2** destroy as if by eating: *Acids eat into metals. He is eaten up with pride. The river had eaten away the banks.* ***What's eating you/him/her?*** (*informal*) What's bothering you/him/her?

eat·able /-əbəl/ *adj* capable of being eaten. = edible.

eaves /ivz/ *n pl* overhanging edge of a roof: *icicles hanging from the* ~.

eaves·drop /ˈivzˌdrap/ *vi* (-pp-) listen secretly to private conversation.

ˈeaves·drop·per *n* [C] person who does this.

ebb /eb/ *vi* **1** (of the tide) flow back from the land to the sea. **2** (*fig*) grow less; become weak or faint: *His fortune's beginning to ebb.* □ *n* [U] **1** the flowing out of the tide: *the ebb and flow of the sea/the tide.* **2** (*fig*) low state; decline or decay: *at the ebb.*

ˈebb·ˌtide *n* = ebb (1).

eb·ony /ˈebəni/ *n* [U] **1** hard, black wood. **2** the color of this. □ *adj* made of, black as, ebony.

ebul·lience /ɪˈbʊlyəns/ *n* (*formal*) [U] excitement, enthusiasm.

ebul·lient /ɪˈbʊlyənt/ *adj* very excited, enthusiastic.

ec·cen·tric /ɪkˈsentrɪk/ *adj* **1** (of a person, his behavior) odd; not normal. **2** (of circles) not having the same center. **3** (of orbits) not perfectly circular. □ *n* [C] (esp) eccentric person.

ec·cen·tric·ity /ˌekˌsenˈtrɪsəti/ *n* (*pl* -ies) **1** [U] quality of being eccentric; strangeness of behavior, etc: ~ *in dress.* **2** [C] instance of this; strange or unusual act or habit: *One of his eccentricities is wearing bright red socks with his black suit.*

ec·clesi·as·tic /ɪˌklizi'æstɪk/ *n* [C] clergyman.

ec·clesi·as·ti·cal (a) *adj* of a church. **(b)** of clergymen.

ec·clesi·as·ti·cally /-kli/ *adv*

eche·lon /ˈeʃəˌlan/ *n* [C] **1** formation of troops, aircraft, ships, etc in lines to the side of the one in front, like steps: *flying in* ~. **2** (*fig*) level of authority or command: *an order from the upper* ~ *of the company.*

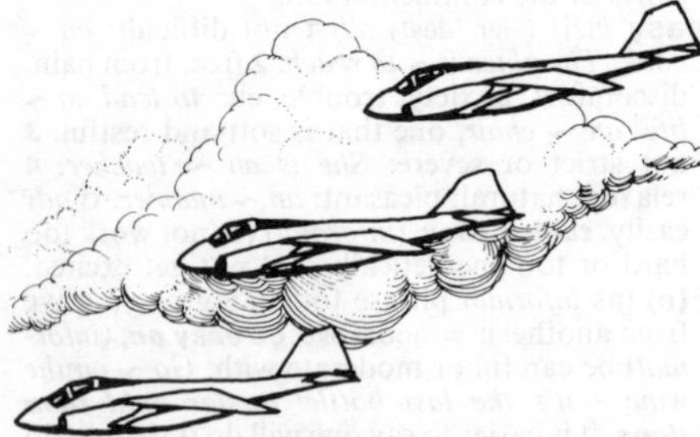

FLYING IN ECHELON (FORMATION)

echo¹ /ˈekou/ *n* (*pl* ~es) [C,U] repetition of a sound caused by reflection (eg from a wall of rock).

echo² /ˈekou/ *vi,vt* **1** (of places, sounds) make an echo: *The valley* ~*ed as he sang. The shot* ~*ed through the woods.* **2** repeat the words, actions etc of another: *They* ~*ed every word of their leader.*

éclair /eiˈkler/ *n* [C] oblong pastry iced on top and filled with cream: *chocolate* ~*s.*

eclipse /ɪˈklɪps/ *n* [C] **1** total or partial cutting off of the light of the sun (when the moon is between it and the earth), or of the reflected light of the moon (when the earth's shadow falls on it). **2** (*fig*) loss of brilliance, power, reputation, etc: *After suffering an* ~ *he is now again famous.* □ *vt* **1** (of a planet, etc) cause an eclipse; cut off the light from. **2** (*fig*) make (a person or thing) appear dull by comparison: *She was so beautiful that she* ~*d every other woman in the room.*

ECLIPSE

eco·logi·cal /ˌikəˈladʒɪkəl, ˌek-/ *adj* of ecology: *the* ~ *effects of industry*, eg the pollution of the atmosphere, of rivers, etc.

eco·logi·cally /-kli/ *adv*

ecol·ogy /iˈkalədʒi/ *n* [U] branch of biology that deals with the habits of living things, esp their relation to their environment.

eco·nomic /ˌikəˈnamɪk, ˌek-/ *adj* **1** of economics: *the government's* ~ *policy.* **2** connected with commerce, systems of production, etc.

eco·nomi·cal /ˌikəˈnamɪkəl, ˌek-/ *adj* careful in the spending of money, time, etc and in the use of goods: *an* ~ *fire*, one that does not waste fuel.

econ·omi·cally /-kli/ *adv*

eco·nomics /ˌikəˈnamɪks, ˌek-/ *n* [U] (used with a *sing verb*) science of the production, distribution and using up of goods.

econ·om·ist /iˈkanəmɪst/ *n* [C] expert in economics.

econ·o·mize /iˈkanəˌmaiz/ *vt,vi* use or spend less than before: *He* ~*d by using buses instead of taking taxis.*

econ·omy /iˈkanəmi/ *n* (*pl* -ies) **1** [C,U] (instance of) economical use of money, strength or anything else of value: *By various little economies, she managed to save enough money for a vacation.* **2** [C] economic system of a country or region: an *agricultural* ~.

eˈconomy class, cheapest class of travel (esp by air).

ec·stasy /ˈekstəsi/ *n* [C,U] (*pl* -ies) (feeling of) great joy and emotional uplift: *in an* ~ *of delight; to be in/go into ecstasies* (*over something*).

ec·static /ekˈstætɪk/ *adj* of, in, ecstasy.

ec·stati·cally /-kli/ *adv*

ecu·meni·cal /ˌekyəˈmenɪkəl/ *adj* **1** of or representing the whole Christian Church: *an* ~ *council*, eg as summoned by the Pope. **2**

promoting unity, esp of the Christian churches: *the ~ movement*.

ec·zema /ˈeksəmə, ɪgˈzimə, eg-/ *n* [U] itching skin disease.

ed. *abbr* = **1** edition. **2** editor. **3** education.

-ed (also **-d**) (after p, k, f, θ, s, ʃ, tʃ) /-t/; (after t, d) /-ɪd/; (otherwise) /-d/. Exception ⇨ use². *suffix* (used to form the *pt* and *pp* of regular *verbs*): *laughed; acted; judged.*

Ed.D. *abbr* = Doctor of Education.

eddy /ˈedi/ *n* [C] (*pl* -ies) current (of wind, mist, water, etc) having esp a circular or spiral movement: *Eddies of mist rose from the valleys.* □ *vi* move in small circles; whirl.

edge[1] /edʒ/ *n* [C] **1** sharp, cutting part of a knife, sword or other tool or weapon: *a knife with a sharp ~.* ***on edge,*** excited or anxious. ***set one's teeth on edge,*** upset or irritate him. **2** (line marking the) outer limit or boundary of a (flat) surface: *a cottage on the ~ of a forest/a lake. He fell off the ~ of the cliff.* **3** advantage: *Being older gave him an ~ over the other boys.*

edgy /ˈedʒi/ *adj* (-ier, -iest) excited, nervous.

edge[2] /edʒ/ *vt,vi* **1** give a border or edge to: *to ~ a garden path with plants; a road ~d with grass.* **2** (cause to) move slowly forward or along: *~ one's way through a crowd; ~ along a narrow ledge of rock.*

edge·wise, edge·ways /ˈedʒˌwaiz, -ˌweiz/ *adv* with the edge outward or forward. ***not get a word in edgewise/edgeways,*** be unable to say anything when a very talkative person is speaking.

edg·ing /ˈedʒɪŋ/ *n* [C] narrow border: *an ~ of lace on a dress.*

ed·ible /ˈedəbəl/ *adj* fit to be eaten. □ *n* [C] (usually *pl*) things fit to be eaten.

edict /ˈidɪkt/ *n* [C] order or proclamation issued by authority; decree.

edi·fi·ca·tion /ˌedəfəˈkeiʃən/ *n* [U] (*formal*) mental or moral improvement.

edi·fice /ˈedəfɪs/ *n* [C] (*formal* **1** building (esp a large or imposing one). **2** (*fig*) something built up in the mind: *The whole ~ of his hopes was destroyed.*

edify /ˈedəˌfai/ *vt* (*pt,pp* -ied) improve morally or spiritually: *~ing books.*

edit /ˈedɪt/ *vt* **1** prepare (another person's writing) for publication: *~ a newspaper.* **2** do the work of planning and directing the publication of a newspaper, magazine, book, encyclopedia, etc. **3** prepare a film, tape recording, etc by putting together parts in a suitable order.

edi·tion /ɪˈdɪʃən/ *n* [C] **1** form in which a book is published: *a paperback ~.* **2** total number of copies (of a book, newspaper, etc) issued from the same type: *the first/a revised ~.* ⇨ impression (2).

edi·tor /ˈedətər/ *n* [C] **1** person who edits (eg a newspaper, a manuscript or a TV or radio program) or who is in charge of part of a newspaper: *the sports/financial ~.* **2** person who writes editorials.

edi·to·rial /ˌedəˈtɔriəl/ *adj* of an editor: *~ work.* □ *n* [C] special article in a newspaper, etc usually written by the editor and giving his opinions.

edi·to·ri·alize *vi* express an opinion (on an issue) in the form of (esp) an editorial.

EDST *abbr* = Eastern Daylight Saving Time.

educ. *abbr* = education; educational.

edu·cate /ˈedʒəˌkeit/ *vt* **1** give intellectual and moral training to; teach: *You should ~ your children to behave well.* **2** provide schooling for: *They have three children to ~.*

edu·ca·tion /ˌedʒəˈkeiʃən/ *n* [U] **1** systematic training and instruction: *No country can afford to neglect ~.* **2** knowledge and abilities, development of character and mental powers, resulting from such training. **3** study of the methods of teaching and learning.

edu·ca·tional *adj* of, connected with, education: *~al books.*

eel /iəl/ *n* [C] long, snakelike fish.

e'en /in/ *adv* (*poet*) = even.

e'er /er/ *adv* (*poet*) = ever.

eerie, eery /ˈɪri/ *adj* (-ier, -iest) causing a feeling of mystery and fear: *an ~ shriek.*

eer·ily /ˈɪrəli/ *adv*

eeri·ness /ˈɪrinɪs/ *n* [U]

ef·face /ɪˈfeis/ *vt* **1** rub or wipe out; make indistinct: *~ an inscription.* (*fig*) *~ unpleasant memories of the past.* **2** ***efface oneself,*** keep in the background in order to escape being noticed; make oneself appear to be unimportant. ⇨ self-effacing.

ef·face·ment *n*

ef·fect /ɪˈfekt/ *n* **1** [C,U] result; outcome: *the ~ of heat on metals. The children were suffering from the ~s of the hot weather. Did the medicine have any ~/a good ~?* ***of no effect,*** not doing what was intended or hoped for. ***in effect,*** **(a)** in fact, really. **(b)** in operation: *The rule/law is still in ~.* ***take effect,*** **(a)** produce the result intended or required. **(b)** come into force; operate; become active. **2** [C, U] **(a)** impression produced on the mind of a spectator, hearer, reader, etc: *Everything he says and does is calculated for (its) ~,* done to impress. **(b)** something that produces an impression: *ˈsound ~s,* sounds that imitate those made, eg by a train, a galloping horse, etc, as required for a play, TV program, etc. **3** [U] meaning: *That is what he said, or words to that ~,* words with the same general meaning. **4** (*pl*) goods; property: *The hotel keeper seized her personal ~s because she could not pay her bill.* □ *vt* bring about: *~ a cure.*

ef·fec·tive /ɪˈfektɪv/ *adj* **1** having an effect; able to bring about the result intended: *~ measures to cure unemployment.* **2** making a striking impression: *an ~ scheme of decoration.* **3** actual or existing: *the ~ membership of the society; the ~ strength of the army.*

ef·fec·tive·ly *adv*

ef·fec·tive·ness /-nɪs/ *n*

ef·fec·tual /ɪˈfektʃuəl/ *adj* (not used of persons) bringing about the result required; answering its purpose: *an ~ remedy/punishment.*

ef·fec·tual·ly *adv*

ef·femi·nate /ɪˈfemənɪt/ *adj* unmanly; having qualities more suited to a woman.

ef·fer·vesce /ˌefərˈves/ *vi* **1** give off bubbles of gas; bubble. **2** (*fig*) (of persons) be excited.

ef·fer·vescence /-əns/ *n* [U]

ef·fer·vescent /-ənt/ *adj*

ef·fi·ciency /ɪˈfɪʃənsi/ *n* [U] state or quality of being efficient.

ef·fi·cient /ɪˈfɪʃənt/ *adj* capable of producing a desired result or of performing duties without waste of time, effort, etc: *an ~ secretary/staff of teachers; ~ methods of teaching.*

ef·fic·ient·ly *adv*

ef·figy /ˈefədʒi/ *n* [C] (*pl* -ies) image or representation of a person (in wood, stone, etc).

ef·flu·ent /ˈefluənt/ *n* [C] **1** stream flowing from a larger stream or from a lake. **2** discharge of waste liquid matter, sewage, etc, eg from a factory.

ef·fort /ˈefərt/ *n* **1** [C,U] (instance of) trying hard; use of strength and energy (to do something): *Please make an ~ to arrive early. I will make every ~* (= do all I can) *to help you. His ~s at clearing up the mystery failed.* **2** [C] result of, something done with, effort: *That's a pretty good ~.*

ef·fort·less /-lɪs/ *adj* needing no effort; easy: *done with ~less skill.*

ef·front·ery /ɪˈfrəntəri/ *n* [U] shameless boldness: *How can you have the ~ to ask for another loan?*

ef·fu·sion /ɪˈfyuʒən/ *n* (*formal*) **1 (a)** [U] sending or pouring out (of liquid, eg blood). **(b)** [C] liquid that pours out. **2** [C] (esp unrestrained) outpouring of thought or feeling: *~s in love letters.*

ef·fu·sive /ɪˈfyusɪv/ *adj* too demonstrative; expressing emotion too freely: *~ thanks.*

ef·fu·sive·ly *adv*

ef·fu·sive·ness /-nɪs/ *n* [U]

e.g. /ˌi ˈdʒi/ *abbr* (*Lat* = exempli gratia) for example.

egali·tar·ian /ɪˌgæləˈteriən/ *n* [C], *adj* (person) favoring equal rights, benefits and opportunities for all people.

egg[1] /eg/ *n* [C] **1** embryo enclosed in a rounded or oval shell, that is produced by a bird (eg a hen) and often used as food: *Birds, reptiles and insects come from eggs. Do you want your eggs boiled or fried?* ***put all (of) one's eggs in one basket,*** risk everything one has in a single venture, eg by investing all one's money in one business. **2** female germ cell.

ˈegg beater, utensil for beating eggs.

ˈegg·cup *n* [C] small cup for holding a boiled egg.

ˈegg·head *n* (*sl*) intellectual person.

egg·nog /ˈegˌnag, -ˌnɔg/ *n* [C,U] (portion of) drink made of eggs, milk, and usually rum or whiskey.

ˈegg·roll *n* [C] Chinese food snack of vegetables rolled in batter and fried.

ˈegg·shell *n* [C] shell of an egg.

egg[2] /eg/ *vt* ***egg sb on,*** urge him (to do something, usually bad).

egg·plant /ˈegˌplænt/ *n* [C] (plant that bears an) egg-shaped vegetable with a shiny purple skin. ⇨ illus at vegetable.

ego /ˈigou/ *n* (*pl* egos) **1** [C] one's self. **2** [U] conceit.

ego·cen·tric /ˌigouˈsentrɪk/ *adj* interested chiefly in oneself; self-centered.

ego·ism /ˈigouˌɪzəm/ *n* [U] **1** state of mind in which one is always thinking of oneself. **2** conceit.

ego·ist /ˈigouɪst/ *n* [C]

ego·istic /ˌigouˈɪstɪk/, **ego·isti·cal** /-kəl/ *adj*

ego·tism /ˈigəˌtɪzəm/ *n* [U] **1** practice of talking too often or too much about oneself; selfishness. **2** (*informal*) = egoism.

ego·tist /ˈigətɪst/ *n* [C]

ego·tis·tic /ˌigəˈtɪstɪk/, **ego·tis·ti·cal** /-kəl/ *adj*

egret /ˈigrɪt/ *n* [C] kind of heron with beautiful long feathers in the tail and on the back.

eh /ei, e/ *int* (used to express surprise or doubt, or to invite agreement.)

eider /ˈaidər/ *n* [C] large, wild sea duck with very soft down.

eider·down /ˈaidərˌdaun/ *n* [C] quilt filled with down from the eider.

eight /eit/ *adj, n* [C] (of) the number 8.

eighth /eitθ/ *adj, n* [C](of) one of 8 (parts) or the next after seven.

eight·een /ˌeiˈtin/ *adj, n* (of) 18.

eight·eenth /-ˈtinθ/ *adj, n* [C] (of) one of 18 (parts), or the next after 17.

eighty /ˈeiti/ *adj, n* (of) 80.

the eighties, (a) (of a person's age, temperature, etc) between 79 and 90. **(b)** (of a period) the years from 80 to 89 inclusive of a century.

eight·ieth /ˈeitiəθ/ *adj, n* [C] (of) one of 80 (parts), or the next after 79.

either /ˈiðər, ˈaiðər/ *adj, pron* **1** one or the other (of): *Take ~ half; they're exactly the same. Either of them/Either one will be satisfactory.* (*Note:* compare the use of *any* (*one of*) when the number is greater than two.) **2** one and the other (of two): *There was an armchair at ~ end of the long table.* □ *adv* (used in statements after *not*): *I don't like the red one, and I don't like the pink one, ~.* ⇨ neither. □ *conj* (used to introduce the first of two or more alternatives, followed by *or*): *He must be ~ mad or drunk.*

ejacu·late /ɪˈdʒækyəˌleit/ *vt* **1** (*formal*) say suddenly and briefly. **2** discharge (esp semen) from the body.

ejacu·la·tion /ɪˌdʒækyəˈleiʃən/ *n* [C]

eject /ɪˈdʒekt/ *vt,vi* **1** compel (a person) to leave (a place) by force: *They were ~ed because they made too much noise.* **2** send out (liquid, etc): *lava ~ed from a volcano.*

ejec·tion /ɪˈdʒekʃən/ *n* [C,U]

eˈjection seat, one in an airplane for ejecting the occupant so that he may descend by parachute.

ejec·tor /-ər/ *n* [C]

eke /ik/ *vt* **1** ***eke out,*** add to with great effort or strain: *eke out one's allowance by selling one's books after use.* **2** make (eg a living) with great effort.

elabo·rate[1] /ɪˈlæb(ə)rɪt/ *adj* **1** worked out with much care and in great detail: *~ designs.* **2** carefully prepared and finished: *~ plans.*

elabo·rate[2] /ɪˈlæbəˌreit/ *vt,vi* **1** work out in detail: *He is elaborating their plans.* **2** give additional details: *~d upon her statement.*

elabo·ra·tion /ɪˌlæbəˈreiʃən/ *n* [C,U]

elapse /ɪˈlæps/ *vi* (of time) pass.

elas·tic /ɪˈlæstɪk/ *adj* **1** tending to go back to its original size or shape after being pulled or pressed: ~ *bands*. *Rubber is* ~. **2** (*fig*) not firm, fixed or unalterable; able to be adapted: ~ *rules*. □ *n* [U] cord or material made elastic by weaving rubber into it: *a piece of* ~.

elas·tic·ity /ɪˌlæˈstɪsəti/ *n* [U] the quality of being elastic.

elate /ɪˈleit/ *vt* make happy, proud, etc: *He was* ~*d at the news/by his success.*

ela·tion /ɪˈleiʃən/ *n* [U] great happiness, etc: *filled with elation.*

el·bow /ˈelˌbou/ *n* [C] **1** (outer part of the) joint between the two parts of the arm. ***at one's elbow,*** close to; near by. ⇨ illus at arm. **2** bend (eg in a pipe or chimney) shaped like an elbow. □ *vt* push or force (one's way through, forward, etc) with the elbows: *to* ~ *one's way through a crowd.*

ˈelbow grease, (*sl*) hard work.

ˈelbow room, space to move freely.

el·der¹ /ˈeldər/ *adj* older; senior: *My* ~ *brother is in India.* □ *n* [C] **1** person of greater age: *Should we always follow the advice of our* ~*s and betters?* **2** official in some Christian churches. **3** older of two persons: *He is my* ~ *by several years.*

ˌelder ˈstatesman, one whose unofficial advice is sought and valued because of his long experience.

el·der² /ˈeldər/ = elderberry.

el·der·berry /ˈeldərˌberi/ (also **el·der**) *n* [C] (kinds of) bush or small tree with clusters of white flowers and red or black berries.

el·der·ly /ˈeldərli/ *adj* rather old.

el·dest /ˈeldɪst/ *adj* first-born or oldest (member of a family): *my* ~ *son/brother.*

elect¹ /ɪˈlekt/ *adj* (used after the *noun*) chosen, but not yet in office: *the president-*~. □ *n* **the elect,** those persons specially chosen, or considered to be the best.

elect² /ɪˈlekt/ *vt* **1** choose by vote: *to* ~ *a president.* **2** choose; decide: *He had* ~*ed to become a lawyer.*

elec·tion /ɪˈlekʃən/ *n* **1** [U] choosing or selection (of candidates for an office, etc) by vote. **2** [C] instance of this: ~ *results.*

elec·tion·eer /ɪˌlekʃəˈnɪr/ *vi* work in an election for a party or candidate.

elec·tive /ɪˈlektɪv/ *adj* **1** having the power to elect: *an* ~ *assembly.* **2** chosen or filled by election: *an* ~ *office.* **3** not required: ~ *subjects in college.*

elec·tor /ɪˈlektər/ *n* [C] **1** person having the right to vote in an election. **2** member of the electoral college in the US.

elec·toral /ɪˈlektərəl/ *adj* of an election or an elector.

EˌIectoral ˈCollege, (system of having a) group of electors chosen by the voters to elect formally the President and Vice-President of the US.

elec·tor·ate /-ɪt/ *n* whole body of people having the right to vote.

elec·tric /ɪˈlektrɪk/ *adj* **1** of, worked by, charged with, produced by electricity: *an* ~ *current/torch/iron/shock.* **2** (*fig*) thrilling; exciting.

ˌelectric ˈchair, chair in which condemned criminals are electrocuted.

ˌelectric guiˈtar, one with a built-in microphone to amplify the sound.

elec·tri·cal /ɪˈlektrɪkəl/ *adj* relating to electricity: ~ *engineering.*

elec·tri·cally /-kli/ *adv*

elec·tri·cian /ɪˌlekˈtrɪʃən/ *n* [C] expert in setting up, repairing and operating electrical apparatus.

elec·tric·ity /ɪˌlekˈtrɪsəti/ *n* [U] **1** form of energy found in nature (as in lightning) or produced by chemical action, friction, etc, that is composed of electrons (negative charge) and protons (positive charge), either in motion or at rest. **2** electric current. **3** science or study of electricity.

elec·trify /ɪˈlektrəˌfai/ *vt* (*pt,pp* -ied) **1** charge with electricity. **2** equip (a railroad, etc) for the use of electric power. **3** (*fig*) excite, shock, as if by electricity: *to* ~ *an audience with an unexpected announcement.*

elec·tri·fi·ca·tion /ɪˌlektrəfɪˈkeiʃən/ *n* [U]

elec·tro- /ɪˈlektrou-/ *combined form* of electricity: *electromagnet.*

elec·tro·car·dio·gram /ɪˌlektrouˈkardiəˌgræm/ *n* [C] tracing made by an electrocardiograph, used in the diagnosis of heart disease.

elec·tro·car·dio·graph /ɪˌlektrouˈkardiəˌgræf/ *n* [C] apparatus which detects and records the action of the heart.

elec·tro·cute /ɪˈlektrəˌkyut/ *vt* kill by means of an electrical current.

elec·tro·cu·tion /ɪˌlektrəˈkyuʃən/ *n* [C,U]

elec·trode /ɪˈlekˌtroud/ *n* [C] solid conductor by which an electric current enters or leaves a vacuum tube, etc. ⇨ anode, cathode.

elec·troly·sis /ɪˌlekˈtraləsɪs/ *n* [U] **1** separation of a substance into its chemical parts by electric current. **2** removal of hair by means of an electrical current that destroys the roots.

elec·tro·mag·net /ɪˌlektrouˈmægnɪt/ *n* [C] piece of soft iron that becomes magnetic when an electric current is passed through wire coiled around it.

elec·tron /ɪˈlekˌtran/ *n* [C] particle of matter, smaller than an atom, having a negative electric charge. ⇨ illus at atom.

elec·tronic /ˌɪlekˈtranɪk/ *adj* of electrons or electronics.

ˌelectronic ˈmusic, consisting of sounds produced or altered by electronic means.

ˈelec·tron·ics *n* (used with a *sing verb*) the science and technology of electrons and electronic devices and systems, as in radio, TV, tape recorders, computers, etc.

el·egance /ˈelɪgəns/ *n* [U] elegant quality or style.

el·egant /ˈelɪgənt/ *adj* showing, having, done with, good taste; graceful: *an* ~ *young man;* ~ *manners.*

el·egant·ly *adv*

el·egy /ˈelədʒi/ *n* [C] (*pl* -ies) poem or song of sorrow, esp for the dead.

el·ement /ˈeləmənt/ *n* [C] **1** (*science*) substance which has not so far been split up into a simpler form by ordinary chemical methods: *Water is a compound containing the* ~*s hydrogen and oxygen.* **2** (according to the ancient philosophers) one of the four elements, earth, air, fire and water (out of which the material universe was thought to be composed). ***in/out of one's element,*** in/not in suitable or satisfying surroundings: *He's in his ~ when people start talking about economics.* **3** (*pl*) the forces of nature, the weather, etc: *exposed to the ~s,* to the winds, storms, etc. **4** (*pl*) beginnings or outlines of a subject of study; parts that must be learned first: *the ~s of geometry.* **5** necessary or basic feature: *Justice is an important ~ in good government.* **6** very small amount or part; trace: *There's an ~ of truth in his account of what happened.* ⇨ atom(2). **7** resistance wire in an electrical appliance (eg a heater).

el·emen·tal /ˌeləˈmentəl/ *adj* of the elements (2,3).

ele·men·tary /ˌeləˈment(ə)ri/ *adj* of or in the beginning stage(s); not developed; simple: *an ~ course; ~ arithmetic.*

eleˈmentary school, level of school through the sixth (in some systems the eighth) grade.

el·eph·ant /ˈeləfənt/ *n* [C] largest four-footed animal now living, with curved ivory tusks and a long trunk.

ˌwhite ˈelephant, costly or troublesome possession useless to its owner.

el·ev·ate /ˈeləˌveit/ *vt* **1** lift up; raise to a higher level. **2** raise in rank or social position: *~d to the rank of colonel.* **3** (*fig*) make (the mind, morals) higher and better: *an elevating book/sermon.*

el·ev·ation /ˌeləˈveiʃən/ *n* **1** [U] elevating or being elevated: *~ to higher office.* **2** [U] nobility or dignity: *~ of thought/style/language.* **3** [C] **(a)** height (esp above sea level). **(b)** hill or high place: *an ~ of 5,000 feet.* **4** [C] plan (drawn to scale) of one side of a building. ⇨ plan(1).

el·ev·ator /ˈeləˌveitər/ *n* [C] **1** cage or platform for carrying people and equipment from one level to another of a building, mine, etc. **2** machine like a continuous belt with buckets at intervals, used for raising grain, etc. **3** storehouse for grain. **4** device on an aircraft that is used to make the aircraft go up or down.

eleven /ɪˈlevən/ *adj, n* **1** (of) the number 11. **2** [C] team of eleven players for football or hockey.

elev·enth /ɪˈlevənθ/ *adj, n* [C] (being) one of 11 (parts), or the next after 10. ***at the eleventh hour,*** at the latest possible time.

elf /elf/ *n* [C] (*pl* elves /elvz/) small, usually mischievous fairy.

elfin /ˈelfɪn/ *adj* of elves: *elfin dances/laughter.*

elf·ish /ˈelfɪʃ/ *adj* mischievous.

elicit /ɪˈlɪsɪt/ *vt* bring out: *to ~ the truth/a reply.*

eli·gible /ˈelədʒəbəl/ *adj* fit, suitable, to be chosen; having the right qualifications: *~ for promotion/a pension/membership in a society.*

el·igi·bil·ity /ˌelədʒəˈbɪləti/ *n* [U]

elim·in·ate /ɪˈlɪməˌneit/ *vt* do away with; get rid of (because unnecessary or unwanted): *a campaign to ~ poverty.*

elim·in·ation /ɪˌlɪməˈneiʃən/ *n* [U]

elite /ˌeiˈlit/ *n* [C] group in society considered to be superior because of the power, privileges, etc of its members: *the diplomatic ~.*

elit·ism /-ˌtɪzəm/ *n* [U] advocacy of an elite.

elit·ist /-tɪst/ *n* [C] *adj* (person) advocating elitism.

elixir /ɪˈlɪksər/ *n* [C] **1** preparation formerly thought to change metals into gold or to prolong life indefinitely. **2** remedy that cures all ills.

Eliza·bethan /ɪˌlɪzəˈbiθən/ *adj* of the time of Queen Elizabeth I of England: *the ˈ~ age; ~ drama.* □ *n* [C] English person who lived during her reign, eg Shakespeare.

elk /elk/ *n* [C] **1** one of the largest kinds of living deer with broad antlers, that is found in Europe and Asia. **2** large deer of North America with branched antlers.

el·lipse /ɪˈlɪps/ *n* [C] regular oval. ⇨ illus at geometry.

el·lip·tic /ɪˈlɪptɪk/, **el·lip·ti·cal** /-kəl/ *adj* shaped like an ellipse.

elm /elm/ *n* **1** [C] common deciduous tree that grows to a great size and height. **2** [U] its hard, heavy wood.

elo·cu·tion /ˌeləˈkyuʃən/ *n* [U] art or style of speaking well, esp in public.

elo·cu·tion·ist *n* [C]

elon·gate /ɪˈlɔŋˌgeit/ *vt,vi* make or become long(er).

elope /ɪˈloup/ *vi* run away in order to get married.

elope·ment *n* [C,U]

elo·quence /ˈeləkwəns/ *n* [U] **1** skillful use of language to persuade or to appeal. **2** fluent speaking.

elo·quent /-ənt/ *adj*

elo·quent·ly *adv*

else /els/ *adj* **1** besides; in addition: *Did you see anybody ~,* any other person(s)? *Have you anything ~ to do?* **2** different: *Ask somebody ~ to help you. We went nowhere ~,* to no other place. *How ~* (= In what other way) *would you do it?* **3** otherwise; if not: *Run or ~ you'll be late.*

else·where /ˈelsˌ(h)wer/ *adv* somewhere else; in, at or to some other place.

eluci·date /ɪˈlusəˌdeit/ *vt* (*formal*) make clear; explain; throw light on (a problem, difficulty).

eluci·da·tion /ɪˌlusəˈdeiʃən/ *n* [C,U]

elude /ɪˈlud/ *vt* (*formal*) escape capture by (esp by means of a trick); avoid: *~ one's enemies.*

elu·sive /ɪˈlusɪv/ *adj* **1** tending to elude: *an ~ criminal.* **2** not easy to understand: *an ~ word.*

elves *pl* of elf.

'em /əm/ *pron* (*informal*) = them.

em·aci·ate /ɪˈmeiʃiˌeit/ *vt* (*formal*) make thin or lean: *~d by long illness.*

emaci·a·tion /ɪˌmeiʃiˈeiʃən/ *n* [U]

ema·nate /ˈeməˌneit/ *vi* (*formal*) come, flow, proceed from.

ema·na·tion /ˌeməˈneiʃən/ *n* [C,U]

eman·ci·pate /ɪˈmænsəˌpeit/ *vt* set free from restraint or slavery: *an ~d young woman,* one who is free from the conventions or restrictions of the community to which she belongs.

eman·ci·pa·tion /ɪˌmænsəˈpeiʃən/ *n* [U] **1** emancipating or being emancipated. **2 Emancipation,** the formal abolition of slavery, eg in the US by presidential proclamation in 1863.

em·balm /emˈbam/ *vt* **1** preserve (a dead body) from decay by using spices or chemicals. **2** (*fig*) preserve (eg in the memory). **3** fill with fragrance.

em·balmer *n* [C]

em·bank·ment /ɪmˈbæŋkmənt/ *n* [C] raised bank or mound of earth, stone, etc to hold back water or support a road, etc.

em·bargo /ɪmˈbargou/ *n* [C] (*pl* ~es) **1** government order that forbids the movement of merchant ships, etc. **2** legal restriction of (a branch) of commerce: *lift/raise/remove an* ~. □ *vt* (*pt,pp* ~ed) put an embargo on (ships or goods).

em·bark /ɪmˈbark/ *vi,vt* **1** go, put or take on board a ship: *The soldiers ~ed for Europe. The ship ~ed passengers and cargo.* **2** start, take part in: ~ *on/upon a new business undertaking.*

em·bar·ka·tion /ˌembarˈkeiʃən/ *n* [C,U]

em·bar·rass /ɪmˈbærəs/ *vt* disconcert, cause mental discomfort or anxiety to: *~ing questions; ~ed by lack of money.*

em·bar·rass·ing·ly *adv*

em·bar·rass·ment *n* [C,U]

em·bassy /ˈembəsi/ *n* [C] (*pl* -ies) **1** duty or position of an ambassador. **2** official residence of an ambassador: *attended a reception at the French* ~. **3** ambassador and his staff: ~ *officials.*

em·bed /ɪmˈbed/ *vt* (-dd-) fix firmly (in a surrounding mass): *stones ~ded in rock;* (*fig*) *facts ~ded in one's memory.*

em·bel·lish /ɪmˈbelɪʃ/ *vt* make beautiful; add ornaments or details to: ~ *a story*, eg by adding amusing but perhaps untrue details.

em·bel·lish·ment *n* [C,U]

em·ber /ˈembər/ *n* [C] **1** small piece of burning wood or coal in a dying fire. **2** (*pl*) ashes of a dying fire.

em·bezzle /ɪmˈbezəl/ *vt* take (money or property placed in one's care) dishonestly for one's own benefit.

em·bezzle·ment *n* [C,U]

em·bit·ter /ɪmˈbɪtər/ *vt* make (even more) bitter (3): *~ed by repeated failures.*

em·bit·ter·ment *n* [U]

em·blem /ˈembləm/ *n* [C] symbol; device that represents something: *an ~ of peace*, eg a dove.

em·blem·atic /ˌembləˈmætɪk/ *adj*

em·body /ɪmˈbadi/ *vt* (*pt,pp* -ied) (*formal*) **1** give form to ideas, feelings, etc: ~ *one's ideas in a speech.* **2** bring together; include: *The latest commercial airplanes ~ many new features.*

em·bodi·ment /ɪmˈbadimənt/ *n* [C] that which embodies or in which something is embodied: *She is the embodiment of kindness.*

em·bold·en /ɪmˈbouldən/ *vt* make bold; give courage to.

em·boss /ɪmˈbɔs/ *vt* cause a pattern, writing, etc to stand out on (the surface of something); raise the surface of something into a pattern: *~ed notepaper; a silver vase ~ed with a design of flowers.*

em·brace /ɪmˈbreis/ *vt,vi* **1** take (a person, etc) into one's arms, as a sign of affection: *embracing a child. They ~d.* **2** (*formal*) accept; take up gladly: ~ *an offer/opportunity.* **3** (*formal*) include: ~ *many colors in a single design.* □ *n* [C] act of embracing: *He held her to him in a warm* ~.

em·bro·ca·tion /ˌembrəˈkeiʃən/ *n* [U] lotion or liniment for rubbing a bruised or aching part of the body.

em·broider /ɪmˈbrɔidər/ *vt,vi* **1** ornament (cloth) with needlework: *a design ~ed in gold thread.* **2** (*fig*) add untrue details to a story for a better effect.

em·broi·dery *n* [U] embroidered needlework.

em·bryo /ˈembriˌou/ *n* [C] (*pl* ~s) **1** human or animal in the early stage of development before birth (or before coming out of an egg). **2** underdeveloped plant contained within a seed. **3** (*fig*) something in its very early stage of development.

em·bry·onic /ˌembriˈanɪk/ *adj*

em·cee /ˈemˌsi/ *n* [C] (originally and sometimes still **MC**) master of ceremonies. □ *vt,vi* act as master of ceremonies: *~d a talk show on television.*

emend /ɪˈmend/ *vt* take out errors from: ~ *a passage in a book.*

em·er·ald /ˈem(ə)rəld/ *n* **1** [C] bright green precious stone. **2** [U] (often as an *adjective*) bright green color.

emerge /ɪˈmərdʒ/ *vi* **1** come into view; (esp) come out (from water, etc): *The moon ~d from behind the clouds.* **2** (of facts, ideas) appear; become known: *No new ideas ~d during the talks.*

emer·gence /-dʒəns/ *n* [U]

emer·gent /-dʒənt/ *adj*

emer·gency /ɪˈmərdʒənsi/ *n* (*pl* -ies) **1** [C] serious happening or situation needing quick action: *This fire extinguisher is to be used only in an ~.* **2** (as an *adjective*): *an ˌ~ ˈexit.*

em·ery /ˈem(ə)ri/ *n* [U] mineral used (esp in powdered form) for grinding and polishing.

e·metic /ɪˈmetɪk/ *n* [C], *adj* (medicine capable of) causing vomiting.

emi·grate /ˈeməˌgreit/ *vi* go away from one's own country to settle in another.

emi·grant /ˈeməgrənt/ *n* [C] person who emigrates: *emigrants to Canada.*

emi·gra·tion /ˌeməˈgreiʃən/ *n* [C,U]

émi·gré /ˈeməˌgrei/ *n* [C] person who has left his own country, esp for political reasons.

emi·nence /ˈemənəns/ *n* **1** [U] high standing; superiority of position; *win ~ as a scientist.* **2** [C] high place or natural elevation. **3** *His/Your Eminence*, title used of/to a cardinal in the Roman Catholic Church.

emi·nent /ˈemənənt/ *adj* (*formal*) **1** (of a person) distinguished: ~ *as a sculptor.* **2** (of qualities) remarkable in degree: *a man of ~ goodness.*

emi·nent·ly *adv*

emir /ɪˈmɪr/ *n* [C] **1** Arab prince or governor. **2** title given to a male descendant of Mohammed.

emir·ate /ɪˈmɪˌreit/ *n* [C] rank, lands, etc of an emir.

emission /ɪˈmɪʃən/ *n* **1** [U] emitting: *an ~ of light/heat.* **2** [C] something which is emitted; discharge[1](2).

emit /ɪˈmɪt/ *vt* (-tt-) give or send out: *A volcano ~s smoke and ashes.*

Emmy /ˈemi/ *n* [C] (*pl* ~s or -ies) small statue awarded annually for outstanding contributions to the television industry.

emo·tion /ɪˈmouʃən/ *n* **1** [U] excitement of the mind or (more usually) the feelings: *He thought* *of his dead child with deep ~.* **2** [C] strong feeling of any kind: *Love, joy, hate, fear and grief are ~s.*

emo·tional /-əl/ *adj* **(a)** of, directed to, the emotions: *an ~al appeal.* **(b)** easily affected by emotion: *an ~al actor/nature.*

emo·tion·ally *adv*

em·peror /ˈempərər/ *n* [C] ruler of an empire.

em·pha·sis /ˈemfəsɪs/ *n* [C,U] (*pl* -ases /-əsiz/) **1** force or stress put on a word or group of words to make their meaning clear, or to show their importance. **2** (the placing of) special value or importance: *Some schools lay/put special ~ on language study.*

em·pha·size /ˈemfəˌsaiz/ *vt* give emphasis to: *He ~d the importance of careful driving.*

em·phatic /ɪmˈfætɪk/ *adj* having, showing, using, emphasis: *an ~ opinion/person.*

em·phati·cally /-kli/ *adv*

em·pire /ˈemˌpaiər/ *n* **1** [C] group of countries under a single sovereign authority: *the Roman Empire.* **2** [U] supreme political power: *the responsibilities of ~.*

em·piri·cal /ɪmˈpɪrɪkəl/ *adj* relying on observation and experiment, not on theory.

em·piri·cally /-kli/ *adv*

em·ploy[1] /ɪmˈplɔi/ *vt* **1** give work to, usually for payment: *He is ~ed in a bank.* **2** (*formal*) make use of: *How do you ~ your spare time?*

em·ploy·able *adj*

em·ployer *n* [C] person who employs others.

em·ploy[2] /ɪmˈplɔi/ *n* [U] (*formal*) employment: *He's in the ~ of foreign powers.*

em·ployee /ˌemplɔiˈ(y)i/ *n* [C] person who is employed.

em·ploy·ment /ɪmˈplɔimənt/ *n* [U] **1** employing or being employed. **2** one's regular work or occupation.

emˈployment agency, business establishment which helps a person (for a fee) to find a job.

em·por·ium /ɪmˈpɔriəm/ *n* [C] (*pl* ~s) **1** center of commerce; market. **2** large retail store.

em·power /ɪmˈpauər/ *vt* give power or authority to act.

em·press /ˈemprɪs/ *n* [C] **1** wife or widow of an emperor. **2** woman who rules an empire in her own right.

empty[1] /ˈempti/ *adj* (-ier, -iest) **1** having nothing inside; containing nothing: *an ~ box; ~ promises/words,* not meaning anything, not giving satisfaction. **2** unoccupied: *an ~ building.* □ *n* [C] (*pl* -ies) box, bottle, crate, etc that is empty.

ˌempty-ˈhanded *adj* bringing back nothing; carrying nothing away.

ˌempty-ˈheaded *adj* lacking in common sense.

emp·ti·ly /ˈemptəli/ *adv*

emp·ti·ness /ˈemptinɪs/ *n* [U]

empty[2] /ˈempti/ *vt,vi* (*pt,pp* -ied) make or become empty, remove what is inside: *~ one's glass,* drink everything in it; *~ (out) a drawer; ~ the garbage; ~ one's pockets. The tank empties* (= becomes empty) *in five minutes.*

emu /ˈimyu, ˈimu/ *n* [C] large, flightless Australian bird.

emu·late /ˈemyəˌleit/ *vt* try to do as well as or better than.

emu·la·tion /ˌemyəˈleiʃən/ *n* [U]

emul·sion /ɪˈməlʃən/ *n* [C,U] (kinds of) creamy liquid in which particles of oil, fat, etc are suspended: *~ paint.*

en- /ɪn-, en-/ *prefix* (used to form a *verb*) **1** put in or on: *enthrone; encase.* **2** cause to be: *enrich; enlarge.*

-en /-ən/ *suffix* **1** (used to form the *pp* of some *verbs*): *broken; hidden.* **2** (used to form an *adj*): *wooden; golden.*

en·able /ɪˈneibəl/ *vt* make able, give authority or means: *The collapse of the strike ~d the company to resume normal bus services.*

en·act /ɪˈnækt/ *vt* **1** make (a law); decree; ordain. **2** perform on, or as though on, the stage of a theater (*act* is more usual).

en·act·ment *n* **(a)** [U] enacting or being enacted. **(b)** [C] law.

enam·el /ɪˈnæməl/ *n* [U] **1** glasslike substance used for coating metal, porcelain, etc, for decoration or as a protection. **2** paint which dries to make a hard, glossy surface. **3** hard outer covering of teeth. □ *vt* (-l-, -ll-) cover, decorate, with enamel

en·amor /ɪˈnæmər/ *vt* (*liter*) (usu in passive) ***be enamored of,*** in love with, delighted with: *~ed of one's own voice.*

enc. *abbr* = enclosure(2).

en·camp /ɪnˈkæmp/ *vi* make or set up a camp.

en·camp·ment *n* **(a)** [U] encamping. **(b)** [C] camp.

en·case /ɪnˈkeis/ *vt* **1** put into a case. **2** surround or cover as with a case: *a broken arm ~d in a plaster cast.*

-ence ⇨ -ance.

en·chant /ɪnˈtʃænt/ *vt* **1** charm; delight: *She was ~ed with/by the flowers you sent her.* **2** use magic on; put under a magic spell: *the ~ed palace,* eg in a fairy tale.

en·chanter *n* [C] man who enchants.

en·chant·ing *adj* charming; bewitching.

en·chant·ing·ly *adv*

en·chant·ment *n* **(a)** [U] being enchanted. **(b)** [C] something which enchants; magic spell. **(c)** [U] charm; delight: *the ~ment of moonlight.*

en·chant·ress /ɪnˈtʃæntrɪs/ *n* [C] woman who enchants.

en·circle /ɪnˈsərkəl/ *vt* surround; form a circle around: *a lake ~d by trees.*

en·circle·ment *n* [C,U]

encl. *abbr* = enclosure(2).

en·close /ɪnˈklouz/ *vt* **1** put a wall, fence, etc around; shut in on all sides: *~ a garden with a wall.* **2** put in an envelope, parcel, etc: *A check for $5 is ~d.*

en·clos·ure /ɪnˈklouʒər/ *n* **1** **(a)** [U] enclosing: *~ of public land.* **(b)** [C] instance of this. **2** [C] something enclosed (esp with a letter).

en·code /ɪnˈkoud/ *vt* put (a message) into code.

en·com·pass /ɪnˈkəmpəs/ *vt* **1** encircle; envelop. **2** include.

en·core /ˈanˌkɔr/ *int* Repeat! Again! □ *vt, n* [C] (call for a) repetition (of a song, etc) or further performance by the same person(s): *They ~d the violinist twice. The singer gave three ~s.*

en·coun·ter /ɪnˈkauntər/ *vt* **1** find oneself faced by (danger, difficulties, etc). **2** meet (an enemy or enemies). **3** meet (a friend, etc) unexpectedly. □ *n* [C] **1** sudden or unexpected meeting. **2** (esp) unfriendly meeting; fight: *an ~ with the bank manager.*

en·cour·age /ɪnˈkərɪdʒ/ *vt* give hope, courage or confidence to; support: *~ a man to work harder; ~ a boy in his studies.*

en·cour·age·ment *n* **(a)** [U] encouraging: *words of ~ment.* **(b)** [C] something that encourages: *Praise acts as an ~ment to the young.*

en·croach /ɪnˈkroutʃ/ *vi* **1** go beyond what is right or usual: *The sea is ~ing on the land.* **2** trespass or intrude on: *~ on/upon his rights/time/land.*

en·croach·ment *n* [C,U]

en·crust /ɪnˈkrəst/ *vt,vi* **1 (a)** cover with a crust. **(b)** put on (a surface) a layer of ornamental or costly material: *a gold vase ~ed with precious stones.* **2** form into a crust.

en·cum·ber /ɪnˈkəmbər/ *vt* **1** get in the way of, be a burden to: *be ~ed with a large family.* **2** crowd; fill up: *a room ~ed with old and useless furniture.*

en·cum·brance /ɪnˈkəmbrəns/ *n* [C] thing that encumbers; burden: *An idle grown-up daughter may be an ~ to her parents.*

en·cyc·li·cal /ɪnˈsɪklɪkəl/ *n* [C], *adj* (letter written by the Pope) for wide circulation.

en·cy·clo·pedia, -pædia /ɪnˌsaikləˈpidiə/ *n* [C] (*pl* ~s) book, or set of books, giving information about every branch of knowledge, or about just one subject, with articles in alphabetical order.

en·cy·clo·pedic, -pædic /ɪnˌsaikləˈpidɪk/ *adj*

end[1] /end/ *n* [C] **1** farthest or last part: *the end of a road/stick/line, etc; the house at the end of the street; the west/east end of a town,* the parts in the west/east. ***begin/start at the wrong end,*** in the wrong way, at a wrong point. ***get/have hold of the wrong end of the stick,*** have a completely mistaken idea of what is intended or meant. ***go off the deep end,*** lose control of oneself. ***make (both) ends meet,*** live within one's income. ***at loose ends,*** having nothing important or interesting to do. ***on end,* (a)** upright: *Place the barrel/box on (its) end. His hair stood on end.* **(b)** continuously: *for two hours on end.* ***end to end,*** in a line with the ends touching: *Arrange the tables end to end.* **2** small piece that remains: *a cigarette end; odds and ends.* **3** finish; conclusion: *at the end of the day/the century. We shall never hear the end of it/the matter,* it will be talked about for a long time to come. ***(be) at an end,*** finished: *The war was at an end.* ***be at the end of sth,*** have none left: *She was at the end of her patience.* ***come to an end,*** finish: *The meeting came to an end at last.* ***put an end to sth,*** stop it: *You must put an end to your bad behavior.* ***in the end,*** finally, at last: *He tried many ways of earning a living; in the end he became a farm laborer.* ***no end of,*** (*informal*) very many or much, very great, etc: *We met no end of interesting people.* ***without end,*** never reaching an end: *We had trouble without end.* **4** death: *He's nearing his end,* is dying. **5** purpose, aim: *gain/win/achieve one's end(s); with this end in view; for/to this end.*

end[2] /end/ *vi,vt* (cause to) come to an end; reach an end: *The road ends here,* goes no farther. *How does the story end?* ***end up,*** finish: *If you continue to steal, you'll end up in prison,* will one day be sent to prison. *We started with soup, and had fruit to end up with.*

end·ing *n* [C] end, esp of a word or a story.

en·dan·ger /ɪnˈdeindʒər/ *vt* put in danger; cause danger to: *~ one's chances of success.*

en·dear /ɪnˈdɪr/ *vt* make dear or precious: *~ oneself to everyone; an ~ing smile.*

en·dear·ing·ly *adv*

en·dear·ment *n* [C,U] act, word, expression, of affection: *a term of ~ment,* eg *darling.*

en·deav·or /ɪnˈdevər/ *n* [C] (*formal*) effort (the usual word): *Please make every ~ to be early.* □ *vi* try: *~ to please one's boss.*

en·demic /ɪnˈdemɪk/ *adj* regularly found in a country or area, or among a particular group of people: *an ~ disease.* ⇨ epidemic.

en·dive /ˈenˌdaiv/ *n* **1** [C] kind of curly-leaved chicory, used as salad. **2** [U] = escarole.

end·less /ˈendlɪs/ *adj* having no end; never stopping: *a woman with ~ patience.*

end·less·ly *adv*

en·dorse /ɪnˈdɔrs/ *vt* **1** write one's name on the back of (a check or a document). **2** approve, support.

en·dorse·ment *n* **(a)** [U] endorsing. **(b)** [C] instance of this.

en·dow /ɪnˈdau/ *vt* **1** give money, property, etc to provide a regular income for (eg a college). **2** ***be endowed with,*** be born with (qualities, etc): *be ~ed by nature with great talents.*

en·dow·ment *n* **(a)** [U] endowing. **(b)** [C] money, property, etc given to provide an income. **(c)** [C] (*formal*) talent: *natural ~ments,* eg a good ear for music.

en·dur·ance /ɪnˈdʊrəns/ *n* [U] ability to endure: *He showed remarkable powers of ~.* ***past/beyond endurance,*** to an extent that can no longer be endured.

en·dure /ɪnˈdʊr/ *vt,vi* **1** suffer; bear²(6). **2** last; continue in existence: *fame that will ~ forever.*

en·dur·able /-rəbəl/ *adj* able to endure.

en·dur·ing *adj* lasting: *an ~ peace.*

en·dur·ing·ly *adv*

end·ways /ˈendˌweiz/ (also **end·wise** /-ˌwaiz/) *adj,adv* **1** with the end forward. **2** end to end.

en·ema /ˈenəmə/ *n* [C] injection of liquid into the rectum to clear the bowels.

en·emy /ˈenəmi/ *n* [C] (*pl* -ies) **1** one who hates another and who tries or wishes to harm or attack him: *A successful man often has many enemies.* **2 the enemy,** armed forces of a nation with which one's country is at war: *The ~ was forced to retreat.* **3** (as an *adjective*) of the enemy: *~ aircraft/ships.* **4** anything that harms or injures: *Laziness is his chief ~.*

en·er·getic /ˌenərˈdʒetɪk/ *adj* full of, done with, energy(1).

en·er·geti·cally /-kli/ *adv*

en·ergy /ˈenərdʒi/ *n* (*pl* -ies) **1** [U] force, strength; capacity to do things and get things done: *He had so much ~ that he did the work of three men. He's full of ~.* **2** (*pl*) (person's) powers available for working, or as used in working: *apply/devote all one's energies to a task.* **3** [U] capacity for, power of, doing work: *electrical ~.*

en·er·vate /ˈenərˌveit/ *vt (formal)* cause to lose physical, moral strength: *a country with an enervating climate.*

en·fold /ɪnˈfould/ *vt* **1** wrap up in. **2** embrace.

en·force /ɪnˈfɔrs/ *vt* **1** cause to be obeyed: *~d the law.* **2** force; compel: *~ discipline/silence.* **3** give strength to: *Have you any statistics that would ~ your argument?*

en·force·able /-əbəl/ *adj*

en·force·ment *n* [U]

en·fran·chise /ɪnˈfrænˌtʃaiz/ *vt* **1** give political rights to (esp, the right to vote). **2** set free (slaves).

Eng. *abbr* = English.

en·gage /ɪnˈgeidʒ/ *vt,vi* **1** hire; employ: *~ him as a guide/an interpreter.* **2** promise; pledge: *~ to do all we can to help.* **3** ***engage in,*** take part in; busy oneself with: *~ in politics.* **4** ***be engaged (in),*** be busy (with), be occupied; take part in: *be ~d in conversation/in writing a novel.* **5** promise, agree, to marry: *Tom and Anne are ~d. Tom is ~d to Anne.* **6** *(formal)* attract; hold: *Nothing ~s his attention for long.* **7** attack; begin fighting with: *The general did not ~ the enemy.* **8** (of parts of a machine) lock together; (cause to) fit into: *The teeth of one wheel ~ with those of the other.*

en·ˈgag·ing *adj* attractive; charming: *an engaging smile/manner.*

en·ˈgag·ingly *adv*

en·gage·ment /ɪnˈgeidʒmənt/ *n* [C] **1** agreement to marry: *Their ~ was announced in the papers.* **2** appointment: *I can't come because of another ~.* **3** (time of) work or employment. **4** battle: *The admiral tried to bring about an ~,* to make the enemy fight.

enˈgagement ring, one given by a man to a woman when they agree to marry.

en·gen·der /ɪnˈdʒendər/ *vt (formal)* produce; cause: *Crime is often ~ed by poverty.*

en·gine /ˈendʒɪn/ *n* [C] **1** machine that converts energy into power or motion: *a ˈsteam ~; a new ~ for an automobile.* **2** any mechanical device. **3** locomotive; railroad engine.

en·gin·eer /ˌendʒəˈnɪr/ *n* [C] **1** person who designs machines, bridges, railways, docks, etc: *a civil/electrical ~.* **2** skilled and trained person in control of an engine or engines: *the chief ~ of a ship.* **3** member of a military unit that builds roads and bridges, controls communications, etc. □ *vt,vi* **1** act, construct or control as an engineer. **2** arrange or bring about skillfully: *~ a scheme/plot.*

en·gin·eer·ing *n* [U] the science, work or profession of an engineer.

Eng·lish[1] /ˈɪŋglɪʃ/ *n* **1** the English language. **2** (used with *the*) English people. □ *adj* **1** of England, its language or people.

English·man/·woman /-mən, -ˌwʊmən/ *(pl* ~men /-mən/, ~women /-ˌwɪmɪn/) *n* [C] male/female native of England.

English[2] /ˈɪŋglɪʃ/ *n* [U] spinning motion given to a ball in certain games while throwing it (as in bowling) or striking it at an angle (as in billiards or pool): *put English on a ball.*

Eng·lish horn /ˌɪŋglɪʃ ˈhɔrn/ *n* [C] musical instrument similar to an oboe, but larger and lower in pitch.

en·grave /ɪnˈgreiv/ *vt* **1** cut or carve (lines, words, designs, on or upon) a hard surface: *a name ~d on a tombstone.* ***engrave with,*** cut into a surface with (an inscription, etc): *~ a bracelet with initials.* **2** print from an engraved plate. **3** *(fig)* impress deeply (on the memory or mind).

en·graver *n* [C]

en·grav·ing *n* **(a)** [U] art of cutting or carving designs on metal, stone, etc. **(b)** [C] copy of a picture, design, etc printed from an engraved plate.

en·gross /ɪnˈgrous/ *vt* take up all the time or attention of: *He's ~ed in his work/a book.*

en·gulf /ɪnˈgəlf/ *vt* swallow up: *a boat ~ed by waves.*

en·hance /ɪnˈhæns/ *vt* add to the value, importance, etc of.

enigma /ɪˈnɪgmə/ *n* [C] *(pl ~s)* question, person, thing, circumstance, that is puzzling.

enig·matic /ˌenɪgˈmætɪk/ *adj* difficult to understand; mysterious.

enig·mati·cally /-kli/ *adv*

en·join /ɪnˈdʒɔin/ *vt (formal)* order; urge; command: *~ silence/obedience.*

en·joy /ɪnˈdʒɔi/ *vt* **1** get pleasure from; take delight in: *~ one's dinner.* **2** have as an advantage or benefit: *~ good health/a good income.* **3** ***enjoy oneself,*** have a good time; be happy.

en·joy·able /-əbəl/ *adj* giving joy; pleasant.

en·joy·ably *adv*

en·joy·ment /ɪnˈdʒɔimənt/ *n* **1** [U] pleasure; joy; satisfaction: *to think only of/live for ~.* **2** [U] *(formal)* possession and use: *be in the ~ of good health.* **3** [C] something that gives joy and pleasure.

en·large /ɪnˈlardʒ/ *vt,vi* **1** make or become larger: *~ a photograph/one's house.* **2** ***enlarge on,*** *(formal)* say or write more about: *I need not ~ on this matter; you all know my views.*

en·large·ment *n* [C] (esp) photographic print that has been made larger than the negative.

en·lighten /ɪnˈlaitən/ *vt* give more knowledge to; free from ignorance, misunderstanding or false beliefs: *Can you ~ me on this subject?* (= help me to understand it better?)

en·light·ened *adj* free from ignorance, prejudice, superstition, etc: *in these ~ed days.*

en·lighten·ment *n* [U] enlightening or being enlightened.

en·list /ɪnˈlɪst/ *vt,vi* **1** enrol in the armed forces, esp voluntarily: *~ in the army.* **2** obtain; get the support of: *Can I ~ your sympathy in a charitable cause?*

en·list·ment *n* [C,U]

en·liven /ɪnˈlaivən/ *vt* make (more) lively: *How can we ~ the party?*

en·mity /ˈenməti/ *n* [U] hatred.

enor·mity /ɪˈnɔrməti/ *n (pl -ies) (formal)* **1** [U] great wickedness: *Does he realize the ~ of his offense?* **2** [C] serious crime. **3** immense size: *the ~ of the problem of feeding the world's population in AD 2000.*

enor·mous /ɪˈnɔrməs/ *adj* very great; immense:

an ~ sum of money.
enor·mous·ly *adv*
enough /ɪˈnəf/ *adj* as great as is needed; as much or as many as necessary: *There's ~ food/food ~ for everybody.* (*Note:* as an *adjective "enough"* may either precede or follow a *noun.*) □ *adv* **1** to the right or necessary degree; sufficiently: *The meat is not cooked ~. You're old ~ to know better.* **2** adequately (but sometimes used to suggest something could be better, etc): *She sings well ~, but...* **3** quite: *oddly/curiously/strangely ~*, in a way that is quite odd, etc. □*n* sufficient amount or number: *Have you had ~ to eat? I can't judge her ability because I haven't seen ~ of her work.*
en·quire, en·quiry *v, n* = inquire, inquiry.
en·rage /ɪnˈreidʒ/ *vt* fill with rage: *~d at/by his stupidity.*
en·rap·ture /ɪnˈræptʃər/ *vt* (*formal*) fill with great delight or joy.
en·rich /ɪnˈrɪtʃ/ *vt* **1** make rich: *knowledge ~es the mind.* **2** improve in quality, flavor, etc: *~ed bread*, with added vitamins. **3** make more fertile: *~ soil with manure.*
en·rich·ment *n* [C,U]
en·roll, en·rol /ɪnˈroul/ *vt,vi* **1** enter on a list. **2** (cause to) enter or join: *to ~ in night school; to ~ (a person) as a member of a society/club.*
en·roll·ment, en·rol·ment *n* **(a)** [U] enrolling or being enrolled. **(b)** [C] number enrolled: *a school with an ~ment of 800 pupils.*
en route /ˌan ˈrut/ *adv* on the way: *We stopped in Providence ~ from New York to Boston.*
en·semble /anˈsambəl/ *n* [C] **1** something viewed as a whole; general effect. **2** (*music*) **(a)** passage of music in which all the performers unite. **(b)** small group of musicians or dancers performing together.
en·shrine /ɪnˈʃrain/ *vt* (*formal*) place or keep in, or as in, a shrine; serve as a shrine for: *basic human rights ~d in the Constitution.*
en·sign /ˈensən/ *n* [C] **1** flag or banner. **2** badge or symbol of rank, office, authority, etc. **3** lowest-ranking commissioned officer in the US navy or coast guard.
en·slave /ɪnˈsleiv/ *vt* make a slave of.
en·slave·ment *n* [U]
en·snare /ɪnˈsnær/ *vt* catch in, or as in, a snare or trap.
en·sue /ɪnˈsu/ *vi* happen later or as a result: *in the ensuing* (= following) *year.*
en·sure /ɪnˈʃʊr/ *vt,vi* make sure or safe; guarantee: *I can't ~ that he will be there in time. We ~d (ourselves) against possible disappointment. These documents ~ to you the authority you need.*
-ent ⇨ -ant.
en·tail /ɪnˈteiəl/ *vt* (*pres p* ~ing /ɪnˈteilɪŋ/) **1** make necessary: *That will ~ an early start.* **2** (*legal*) leave, settle, (land) to a line of heirs so that none of them can give it away or sell it. □ *n* **1** [U] settlement of landed property in this way. **2** [C] the property so settled.
en·tangle /ɪnˈtæŋgəl/ *vt* **1** catch in a trap; tangle: *My fishing line got ~d in weeds.* **2** (*fig*) put or get into difficulties: *become ~d with the law.*
en·tangle·ment *n* [C,U]
en·ter /ˈentər/ *vt,vi* **1** come or go into: *~ a room. The train ~ed a tunnel.* **2** become a member of; join: *~ college/the army.* **3** ***enter into sth (with sb),*** begin, open: *~ into negotiations with a business firm.* **4** (esp) make a start on: *~ on/upon a new career/another term of office.* **5** write, record names, details, etc in a book, etc: *~ an item in the accounts.* **6** enroll as a member or a competitor, etc: *~ed his son in a private school; ~ a horse for the Derby.*
en·ter·prise /ˈentərˌpraiz/ *n* **1** [C] undertaking, esp one that needs courage or boldness. **2** [U] courage and willingness to engage in such projects: *He is a man of great ~.* **3** [U] (esp commercial) undertaking or activity: *Do you prefer private ~ to government control of commerce and industry?*
en·ter·pris·ing *adj* having, showing, enterprise (2).
en·ter·tain /ˌentərˈtein/ *vt* **1** receive (people) as guests, esp in one's home: *The Smiths ~ a great deal/do a great deal of ~ing*, often give parties, etc. **2** amuse, interest: *We were all ~ed by his tricks.* **3** consider; have in mind: *~ a proposal; ~ ideas/doubts, etc.*
en·ter·tainer *n* [C] person who entertains(2), eg a singer, comedian.
en·ter·tain·ing *adj* pleasing; amusing.
en·ter·tain·ment /ˌentərˈteinmənt/ *n* **1** [U] entertaining or being entertained(1,2): *a hotel famous for its ~. He fell into the water, much to the ~ of the onlookers.* **2** [C] public performance (at a theater, circus, etc).
en·thrall, en·thral /ɪnˈθrɔl/ *vt* (-ll-) **1** take the whole attention of; please greatly: *~ed by an exciting story.* **2** greatly attracted: *~ed by a woman's beauty.*
en·throne /ɪnˈθroun/ *vt* place a person (as if) on a throne.
en·throne·ment *n* [C,U]
en·thuse /ɪnˈθuz/ *vi* (*informal*) show great enthusiasm for: *~ over the new carpets.*
en·thusi·asm /ɪnˈθuziˌæzəm/ *n* [U] strong feeling of admiration or interest: *arouse ~ in him; feel no ~ for/about the play; an outburst of ~.*
en·thusi·ast /ɪnˈθuziˌæst/ *n* [C] person filled with enthusiasm: *a sports enthusiast; an enthusiast for/about politics.*
en·thusi·astic /ɪnˌθuziˈæstɪk/ *adj* full of enthusiasm: *~ admirers of a movie star.*
en·thusi·asti·cally /-kli/ *adv*
en·tice /ɪnˈtais/ *vt* tempt or persuade: *~ her into doing something/to do something wrong.*
en·tice·ment *n* [C,U]
en·tire /ɪnˈtaiər/ *adj* whole, complete; unbroken: *She was paid for the ~ day, even though she left early.*
en·tire·ly *adv* completely: *~ly unnecessary/different.*
en·tirety /ɪnˈtairəti, ɪnˈtaiərti/ *n* [U] completeness. ***in its entirety***, as a whole, completely: *He read the report in its ~.*
en·title /ɪnˈtaitəl/ *vt* **1** give as a title: *He ~d the book* The Europeans. **2** give a right (to): *If you fail three times, you are not ~d to try anymore.*
en·title·ment *n* [U]
en·tity /ˈentəti/ *n* (*pl* -ies) **1** [C] something that

exists or is thought to exist. **2** [U] being; existence.

ento·mol·ogy /ˌentəˈmalədʒi/ *n* [U] the study of insects.

en·to·mo·logi·cal /ˌentəməˈladʒɪkəl/ *adj*

en·to·mol·ogist /ˌentəˈmalədʒɪst/ *n* [C] expert in entomology.

en·trails /ˈentrəlz, ˈenˌtreiəlz/ *n pl* bowels; intestines.

en·trance[1] /ˈentrəns/ *n* **1** [C] opening, gate, door, passage, etc by which one enters: *The ~ to the cave had been blocked up.* **2** [C] act of entering: *made a dramatic ~.* **3** [C,U] right or permission to enter: *to be refused ~.*

en·trance[2] /ɪnˈtræns/ *vt* overcome, carry away as in a dream, with pleasure: *~d with the music. She stood ~d at the sight.*

en·trant /ˈentrənt/ *n* [C] person who enters, esp a competition, race, etc.

en·treat /ɪnˈtrit/ *vt* ask earnestly: *I ~ you to show mercy.*

en·treaty /ɪnˈtriti/ *n* [C] (*pl* -ies) earnest request or appeal: *He was deaf to all entreaties.*

en·trée /ˈanˌtrei/ *n* **1** [U] right or permission to enter. **2** [C] main dish of a meal.

en·trench /ɪnˈtrentʃ/ *vt* **1** surround or protect with a trench or trenches. **2** establish firmly: *customs ~ed by tradition.*

en·trust /ɪnˈtrəst/ *vt* (*formal*) give something into a person's care or trust: *Can I ~ the task to you/~ you with the task?*

en·try /ˈentri/ *n* [C] (*pl* -ies) **1** coming or going in: *Thieves had forced an ~ into the building.* **2** (place of) entrance. **3** right or permission to enter. **4** item in a list, an account book, etc: *dictionary entries; make an ~ in the accounts.* **5** person, etc entering for a competition: *a large number of entries for the race.*

en·twine /ɪnˈtwain/ *vt* twist together or around.

enu·mer·ate /ɪˈnuməˌreit/ *vt* count or name (a list of articles) one by one.

enu·mer·ation /ɪˌnuməˈreiʃən/ *n* **(a)** [U] enumerating. **(b)** [C] list.

enun·ci·ate /ɪˈnənsiˌeit/ *vt,vi* **1** say, pronounce (words): *He ~s (his words) clearly.* **2** state clearly or definitely; announce.

enun·ci·ation /ɪˌnənsiˈeiʃən/ *n* [U]

env. *abbr* = envelope.

en·velop /ɪnˈveləp/ *vt* wrap up, cover, on all sides: *hills ~ed in mist.*

en·velop·ment *n* [U]

en·vel·ope /ˈenvəˌloup, ˈan-/ *n* [C] paper wrapper or covering for a letter, usually having a gummed edge that can be folded over and sealed.

en·venom /ɪnˈvenəm/ *vt* (*formal*) **1** put poison on or in, eg a weapon. **2** (*fig*) fill with bitter hate: *~ed quarrels/tempers.*

en·vi·able /ˈenviəbəl/ *adj* worthy of envy: *an ~ school record*, one of great success, etc.

en·vi·ous /ˈenviəs/ *adj* full of, feeling, expressing, envy: *~ of her success; ~ looks; looking at it with ~ eyes.*

en·vi·ous·ly *adv*

en·vi·ron·ment /ɪnˈvairənmənt, ɪnˈvaiərnmənt/ *n* (*collective* with *sing verb*) surroundings, circumstances, influences affecting a person, animal or plant: *His home ~ is very poor.*

en·vi·ron·mental /ɪnˌvairənˈmentəl, ɪnˌvaiərnˈ-/ *adj*

en·virons /ɪnˈvairənz/ *n pl* districts surrounding a town, etc: *Berlin and its ~.*

en·vis·age /ɪnˈvɪzɪdʒ/ *vt* = envision.

en·vi·sion /ɪnˈvɪʒən/ *vt* visualize, picture in the mind: *~ed seeing her again.*

en·voy /ˈenˌvɔi/ *n* [C] **1** messenger, esp one sent on a special mission. **2** diplomatic representative next in rank below an ambassador.

envy[1] /ˈenvi/ *n* [U] **1** feeling of disappointment and ill will because another person has something which one would like to have: *He was filled with ~ at my success.* **2** object of such feeling: *His splendid new car was the ~ of all his friends/an object of ~ to all his friends.*

envy[2] /ˈenvi/ *vt* (*pt,pp* -ied) feel envy of: *I ~ you. I ~ your good fortune.*

en·zyme /ˈenˌzaim/ *n* [C] organic chemical substance formed in living cells, able to cause changes in other substances without being changed itself.

eon, aeon /ˈiən, ˈiˌan/ *n* [C] very long period of time.

ep·aulet, ep·aul·ette, /ˈepəˌlet/ *n* [C] shoulder ornament on a military uniform.

ephem·er·al /ɪˈfemərəl/ *adj* living, lasting, for a very short time.

epic /ˈepɪk/ *n* [C] long poem in a dignified style, telling of the deeds of one or more great heroes, eg Homer's *Iliad*. □ *adj* of or like an epic: *an ~ hero.*

epi·demic /ˌepəˈdemɪk/ *n* [C], *adj* (disease) spreading rapidly among many people in the same place for a time: *an influenza ~.* ⇨ endemic.

epi·demi·ologist /-dʒɪst/ *n* [C] one specializing in epidemiology.

epi·demi·ology /ˌepəˌdimiˈalədʒi/ *n* [U] scientific study of the spread and control of disease in a population.

epi·der·mis /ˌepəˈdərmɪs/ *n* [U] outer layer of the skin.

epi·glot·tis /ˌepəˈglatɪs/ *n* [C] structure of tissue at the root of the tongue, lowered during swallowing to prevent food, etc from entering the windpipe. ⇨ illus at head.

epi·gram /ˈepəˌgræm/ *n* [C] short poem or saying expressing an idea in a clever and amusing way.

epi·gram·matic /ˌepəgrəˈmætɪk/ *adj*

epi·lepsy /ˈepəˌlepsi/ *n* [U] disorder of the nervous system, usually causing unconsciousness and jerky, involuntary movements.

epi·lep·tic /ˌepəˈleptɪk/ *adj* of epilepsy: *an ~ seizure.* □ *n* [C] person suffering from epilepsy.

epi·logue, epi·log /ˈepəˌlɔg, -ˌlag/ *n* [C] last part of a literary work, esp a speech or poem spoken by an actor at the end of a play.

epi·sode /ˈepəˌsoud/ *n* [C] one event in a series of events.

epi·sodic /ˌepəˈsadɪk/ *adj*

epistle /ɪˈpɪsəl/ *n* [C] **1** letter, esp in formal or elegant language. **2 the Epistles,** letters included in the New Testament, written by the Apostles.

epi·taph /ˈepəˌtæf/ *n* [C] words (describing a dead person), usually cut on a tombstone.

epi·thet /ˈepəˌθet/ *n* [C] adjective or descriptive phrase used to indicate the character of a person or thing, as in "Alfred *the Great*."

epit·ome /ɪˈpɪtəmi/ *n* [C] **1** short summary of a book, speech, etc. **2** something which is a typical example.

epit·om·ize /ɪˈpɪtəˌmaiz/ *vt* make or be an epitome of.

ep·och /ˈepək/ *n* [C] (beginning of a) period of time in history, life, etc marked by special events or characteristics: *Einstein's theory marked a new ~ in physics*.

ep·oxy /eˈpaksi/ *n* [U] (also **epoxy cement**) (kind of) resin used for cementing. □ *vt* (*pt,pp* -ied) glue together with epoxy cement.

equal /ˈikwəl/ *adj* **1** the same in size, amount, number, degree, value, etc: *~ pay for ~ work; ~ opportunity; divide a cake into two ~ parts; two boys of ~ height*. **2** evenly balanced: *an ~ match*. **3** ***equal to,*** having strength, courage, ability, etc for: *He was ~ to the occasion*, was able to deal with it. □ *n* [C] person or thing equal to another: *Is he your ~ in strength?* □ *vt* (-l-, -ll-) be equal to: *He ~s me in strength but not in intelligence*.

equal·ity /iˈkwaləti/ *n* [U] the state of being equal.

equally /ˈikwəli/ *adv* in an equal manner; in equal shares: *~ly clever. Divide it ~ly*.

equal·ize /ˈikwəˌlaiz/ *vt* make equal.

equal·iz·ation /ˌikwələˈzeiʃən/ *n* [U]

equa·nim·ity /ˌikwəˈnɪməti, ˌekwə-/ *n* [U] calmness of mind or temper: *bear misfortune with ~*.

equate /iˈkweit, ɪ-/ *vt* consider, treat (two or more things) as being equal or identical: *I ~ happiness with health*.

equa·tion /iˈkweiʒən, ɪ-/ *n* **1** [C] statement of equality between two mathematical expressions by the sign (=) as in: $2x + 5 = 11$. **2** [U] equating or being equated.

equa·tor /iˈkweitər, ɪ-/ *n* [C] (often **Equator**) imaginary line around the earth that is at an equal distance from the north and south poles.

equa·tor·ial /ˌekwəˈtɔriəl/ *adj* of or near the equator: *~ Africa*.

eques·trian /iˈkwestriən, ɪ-/ *adj* of horses or horseback riding: *~ skill*. □ *n* [C] person who rides or performs on horseback.

equi- *pref* equal; the same: *equivalent*.

equi·dis·tant /ˌikwəˈdɪstənt/ *adj* equally distant (constructed with *from*).

equi·lat·eral /ˌikwəˈlætərəl/ *adj* having all sides equal: *an ~ triangle*.

equi·lib·rium /ˌikwəˈlɪbriəm/ *n* [U] state of being balanced: *maintain/lose one's ~*.

equine /ˈiˌkwain/ *adj* of, like, a horse; of horses.

equi·nox /ˈikwəˌnaks, ˈekwə-/ *n* [C] time of the year at which the sun crosses the equator and when day and night are of equal length: *the spring* (= vernal) *~*, about March 21; *the autumnal ~*, about September 23.

equip /iˈkwɪp, ɪ-/ *vt* (-pp-) supply with what is needed for a special purpose; fit out: *~ oneself for a task; ~ a ship for a voyage; ~ soldiers with uniforms and weapons*.

equip·ment *n* [U] **(a)** equipping or being equipped: *The ~ment of his laboratory took time and money*. **(b)** (*collect*) things needed for a particular purpose: *ˈradar ~ment*.

equi·table /ˈekwətəbəl/ *adj* fair; just; reasonable.

equi·tably /-bli/ *adv*

equity /ˈekwəti/ *n* [U] **1** fairness; justice. **2** (*legal*) system of law, used in circumstances in which common law and statute law do not adequately protect a person's rights.

equiv. *abbr* = equivalent.

equiv·a·lent /iˈkwɪvələnt, ɪ-/ *adj* equal in value, amount, meaning: *What is $5 ~ to in French francs?* □ *n* [C] thing that is equivalent: *Is there a French word that is the exact ~ of the English word "home"?*

equi·va·lence /iˈkwɪvələns, ɪ-/ *n* [U] condition or state of being equivalent.

equivo·cal /iˈkwɪvəkəl, ɪ-/ *adj* having two or more meanings; uncertain; doubtful: *an ~ reply*.

-er[1] /-ər/ (also **-ier** /-iər/ and **-yer** /-yər/) *suffix* (*v* + er = *n*) person, thing that carries out the action of the *verb: runner; sleeper*.

-er[2] (also **-r**) /-ər/ *suffix* (used to form the *comp* of an *adj*): *stronger; rarer; thinner*.

era[1] /ˈɪrə, ˈerə/ *n* [C] **1** period in history, starting from a particular time or event: *the Christian era*. **2** important historical period: *era of industrial expansion*.

ERA[2] /ˌi ˌar ˈei, or ˈerə/ *abbr* = Equal Rights Amendment.

eradi·cate /ɪˈrædəˌkeit/ *vt* **1** pull up by the roots. **2** destroy or put an end to: *~ crime/typhoid fever*.

eradi·ca·tion /ɪˌrædəˈkeiʃən/ *n* [U]

erase /ɪˈreis/ *vt* **1** rub or scrape out: *~ pencil marks*. **2** remove; blot out.

eraser *n* [C] thing, usually of rubber, used to erase.

ere /er/ *conj, prep* (*old use*) before.

erect[1] /ɪˈrekt/ *adj* upright; straight up: *stand ~*.

erect·ly *adv*

erect·ness /-nɪs/ *n* [U]

erect[2] /ɪˈrekt/ *vt* **1** build, set up; establish: *~ a statue* (*to somebody*); *~ a tent*. **2** set upright: *~ a flagstaff/a mast*.

erec·tion /ɪˈrekʃən/ *n* **1** [U] act of erecting; state of being erected. **2** [C] building, or other structure erected. **3** [C] erect state of the penis.

er·mine /ˈərmən/ *n* **1** [C] small animal whose fur is brown in summer and white (except for its black-tipped tail) in winter. **2** [U] its fur: *dressed in ~; a gown trimmed with ~*.

erode /ɪˈroud/ *vt* (of acids, rain, etc) wear away; eat into: *Metals are ~d by acids*.

ero·sion /ɪˈrouʒən/ *n* [U] eroding or being eroded: *soil erosion,* by wind and rain.

ero·sive /ɪˈrousɪv/ *adj*

erotic /ɪˈratɪk/ *adj* of sexual love or desire.

err /ər/ *vi* **1** make a mistake: *It is better to ~ on the side of mercy*, be too merciful than too severe. **2** do or be wrong.

er·rand /ˈerənd/ *n* [C] **1** short trip to do something, eg carry a message, pay a bill: *to go on/run ~s for him*. **2** purpose of such a trip.

er·rant /ˈerənt/ *adj* **1** erring; mistaken: *an ~ husband*, one who is unfaithful to his wife. **2** (often after the *noun*) traveling in search of adventure: *a knight ~*.

er·ratic /ɪˈrætɪk/ *adj* **1** (of a person, his behavior) likely to do unusual or unexpected things; odd. **2** (of things) uncertain; irregular.

er·rati·cally /-kli/ *adv*

er·roneous /ɪˈrouniəs/ *adj* incorrect; mistaken.

er·roneous·ly *adv*

er·ror /ˈerər/ *n* **1** [C] mistake: *spelling ~s; an ~ of judgment*. **2** [U] condition of being wrong in belief or conduct: *do something in ~*, by mistake.

eru·dite /ˈerəˌdait/ *adj* (*formal*) having, showing, great learning; scholarly.

eru·dite·ly *adv*

erupt /ɪˈrəpt/ *vi* **1** (of a volcano) burst forth (with hot lava, etc). **2** break out suddenly or violently: *~ with anger; a painful rash ~ed on her arms*.

erup·tion /ɪˈrəpʃən/ *n* [C,U] **(a)** outbreak of a volcano: *~ions of ashes and lava*. **(b)** (*fig*) outbreak of war, disease, anger, etc.

es·ca·late /ˈeskəˌleit/ *vt,vi* increase in intensity or extent.

es·ca·la·tion /ˌeskəˈleiʃən/ *n* [U]

es·ca·la·tor /ˈeskəˌleitər/ *n* [C] moving stairway carrying people up or down between floors or different levels.

es·ca·pade /ˈeskəˌpeid/ *n* [C] daring, mischievous or adventurous act, often one causing gossip or trouble.

es·cape[1] /ɪˈskeip/ *n* **1** [C,U] (act of) escaping; fact of having escaped: *There have been very few successful ~s from this prison*. **2** [C] means of escape: *a ˈfire ~*. **3** relief or distraction from difficulties or dull routine.

es·cap·ism /-ˌɪzəm/ *n* [U] avoidance of something unpleasant by means of daydreaming, amusements, etc.

es·cap·ist /-ɪst/ *n* [C] person who engages in escapism.

es·cape[2] /ɪˈskeip/ *vi,vt* **1** get free; get away: *Two prisoners have ~d*. **2** (of steam, fluids, etc) find a way out; leak: *The gas has ~ed from this hole*. **3** avoid; keep free or safe from: *You were lucky to ~ punishment/being punished*. **4** be forgotten or unnoticed by: *His name ~s me for the moment*.

es·ca·role /ˈeskəˌroul/ *n* [U] kind of salad plant with broad, smooth leaves, that is related to chicory.

es·carp·ment /ɪˈskarpmənt/ *n* [C] steep slope or cliff separating two areas of different levels.

es·chew /ɪsˈtʃu/ *vt* (*formal*) = avoid (the usual word): *~ wine/evil*.

es·cort[1] /ˈeˌskɔrt/ *n* [C] **1** person(s) going with another or others, as protection, or as an honor: *an ~ of soldiers; under police ~*. **2** one or more ships, aircraft, etc, esp as protection: *an ~ of ten destroyers; a motorcycle ~*. **3** man who escorts a woman on a date.

es·cort[2] /ɪˈskɔrt/ *vt* go with as an escort: *a convoy of merchant ships ~ed by destroyers. Who will ~ this young lady home?*

Es·ki·mo /ˈeskəˌmou/ *n* **1** [C] (*pl* ~, ~s) one of a group of people of the Arctic regions of North America and eastern Siberia. **2** [U] the language of the Eskimos.

ˌEskimo ˈdog *n* [C] one of a breed of dogs with a thick coat of fur, used by the Eskimos for drawing sleds.

esopha·gus /ɪˈsafəgəs/ *n* [C] (*pl* -gi /-ˌdʒai/) passage from the pharynx to the stomach; gullet. ⇨ illus at head.

eso·teric /ˌesəˈterɪk/ *adj* understood by, intended for, only a small circle of disciples or followers.

ESP /ˌi ˌes ˈpi/ *abbr* = extrasensory perception.

esp. *abbr* = especially.

es·pec·ially /ɪˈspeʃəli/ *adv* to an exceptional degree; in particular: *She likes the country, ~ in spring*.

espion·age /ˈespiəˌnaʒ/ *n* [U] practice of spying or using spies.

es·pouse /ɪˈspauz/ *vt* (*formal*) **1** take up; support (a cause, theory, etc). **2** (*old use*) (of a man) marry.

Esq. *abbr* = Esquire.

Es·quire /ˈeˌskwaiər/ *n* title of courtesy for a lawyer or justice of the peace, written *Esq.*, after the family name instead of *Mr.*, etc before it).

es·say[1] /ˈeˌsei/ *n* [C] **1** usually short piece of writing on any one subject. **2** (*formal*) attempt.

es·say·ist *n* [C] writer of essays(1).

es·say[2] /eˈsei/ *vt,vi* (*formal*) try; attempt: *~ a task*.

es·sence /ˈesəns/ *n* **1** [U] basic, necessary or most important quality of a thing: *Caution is the ~ of that man's character*. **2** [C,U] substance having all the important qualities of a fruit, plant, etc in concentrated form: *~ of peppermint*. **3** perfume.

es·sen·tial /ɪˈsenʃəl/ *adj* **1** necessary; most important: *Is wealth ~ to happiness?* **2** of an essence(2): *~ oils*. **3** fundamental; basic: *Being reserved is said to be an ~ part of the English character*. □ *n* [C] fundamental element: *the ~s of English grammar*.

es·sen·tial·ly /ɪˈsenʃəli/ *adv* in an essential(3) manner: *We are an ~ly peace-loving people*.

EST *abbr* = Eastern Standard Time.

es·tab·lish /ɪˈstæblɪʃ/ *vt* **1** set up, put on a firm foundation: *~ a new state/government/business*. **2** settle, place a person, oneself in a position, office, place, etc: *We are now comfortably ~ed in our new house*. **3** cause people to accept a belief, claim, custom, etc: *He succeeded in ~ing a claim to the title*. **4** make (a church) national by law.

es·tab·lish·ment /ɪˈstæblɪʃmənt/ *n* **1** [U] establishing or being established: *the ~ of a new state*. **2** [C] that which is established, eg a business firm, a residence, etc. **3 the Establishment,** group of persons in positions of power and authority, who control and influence a nation, organization, etc.

es·tate /ɪˈsteit/ *n* **1** [C] large piece of property in the form of land: *He owns a large ~ in Maryland*. **2** [U] a person's possessions or property. **3** [C] political or social group or class. **4** (*old use*) condition; state in life: *the holy ~ of matrimony*.

es·teem /ɪˈstim/ *vt* (*formal*) **1** have a high opinion of; respect greatly: *No one can ~ your father more than I do.* **2** consider; regard: *I shall ~ it a favor if...* □ *n* [U] high regard: *We all hold him in great ~.*
es·thetic = aesthetic.
es·ti·mable /ˈestəməbəl/ *adj* (*formal*) worthy of esteem.
es·ti·mate[1] /ˈestəmɪt/ *n* [C] **1** judgment; opinion: *formed an ~ of his abilities.* **2** approximate calculation (of size, cost, etc): *I hope the builders don't exceed their ~.*
es·ti·mate[2] /ˈestəˌmeit/ *vt,vi* **1** judge the worth, value, etc of. **2** calculate roughly the cost, value, size, etc of: *They ~d the cost at $8,000.*
es·ti·ma·tion /ˌestəˈmeiʃən/ *n* [U] **1** judgment; regard; opinion: *in my ~; in the ~ of most people.* **2** esteem; respect.
es·trange /ɪˈstreindʒ/ *vt* (*formal*) bring about a separation: *foolish behavior that ~d all his friends.*
es·trange·ment *n* [C,U]
es·tu·ary /ˈestʃuˌeri/ *n* [C] (*pl* -ies) mouth of a river into which the tide flows: *the Delaware ~.*
ETA /ˌi ˌti ˈei/ *abbr* = estimated time of arrival.
et al /ˌet ˈæl, ˌet ˈal/ *abbr* (= *Lat* et alii, et alia) and others.
etc. *abbr* = et cetera.
et cet·era /et ˈset(ə)rə/ (*Lat*) (usually shortened to **etc.**) and other things; and so on.
etch /etʃ/ *vt,vi* **1** (of acids or other strong chemicals) eat into the surface of metal, glass, etc: corrode: *the aluminum trimming has been badly ~ed by the sea air.* **2** use a needle and acid to make a picture, etc on a metal plate from which copies may be printed; make (pictures, etc) in this way.
etcher *n* [C] one who etches(2).
etch·ing *n* **(a)** [U] the art of etching(2). **(b)** [C] picture made by etching(2).
ETD /ˌi ˌti ˈdi/ *abbr* = estimated time of departure.
eter·nal /ɪˈtərnəl, ɪ-/ *adj* **1** without beginning or end; lasting for ever: *The Christian religion promises ~ life.* **2** constant; continual: *Stop this ~ bickering.*
eter·nally *adv*
eter·nity /ɪˈtərnəti, ɪ-/ *n* (*pl* -ies) **1** [U] time without end. **2** [U] endless time after death: *send a man to ~,* to his death. **3** [C] period of time that seems endless: *It seemed an ~ before news of his safety reached her.*
ether /ˈiθər/ *n* [U] **1** upper regions of space; clear sky. **2** strong-smelling inflammable liquid used esp as an anesthetic.
ethe·real /iˈθɪriəl, ɪ-/ *adj* **1** of ether (1). **2** delicate; light and airy.
ethi·cal /ˈeθɪkəl/ *adj* **1** of ethics. **2** morally right. **3** agreeing with accepted standards of professional conduct.
ethi·cally /-kli/ *adv*
eth·ics /ˈeθɪks/ *n pl* **1** (used with a *sing verb*) study of morals: *Ethics is a branch of philosophy.* **2** (used with a *pl verb*) (esp professional) rules of conduct: *medical ~.*
eth·nic /ˈeθnɪk/ *adj* **1** of race or culture, or the races and cultures of mankind. **2** having to do with a minority group whose members share a common descent, customs and traits: *won the ~ vote in the last election.* □ *n* [C] (*informal*) member of a minority group.
eth·ni·cally /-kli/ *adv*
eth·no·logi·cal /ˌeθnəˈladʒɪkəl/ *adj* of ethnology.
eth·nol·ogist /eθˈnalədʒɪst/ *n* [C] student of, expert in, ethnology.
eth·nol·ogy /eθˈnalədʒi/ *n* [U] science of the races and cultures of mankind, their relations to one another, etc.
eti·quette /ˈetɪkɪt/ *n* [U] rules for behavior among people in a social group, a profession, etc: *medical/legal ~.*
etude /ˈeiˌtud/ *n* [C] (*music*) piece of music, esp for practice or to develop skill.
ety·mo·logi·cal /ˌetəməˈladʒɪkəl/ *adj* of etymology.
ety·mol·ogist /ˌetəˈmalədʒɪst/ *n* [C] student of, expert in, etymology.
ety·mol·ogy /ˌetəˈmalədʒi/ *n* (*pl* ies) **1** [U] science of the origin and history of words. **2** [C] account of the origin and history of a word.
euca·lyptus /ˌyukəˈlɪptəs/ *n* [C] (*pl* ~es) sorts of tall evergreen tree (including the Australian gum tree) from which oil, wood, and gum are obtained.
Eu·cha·rist /ˈyukərɪst/ *n* **the Eucharist,** Holy Communion; the bread and wine taken at this.
eu·logize /ˈyuləˌdʒaiz/ *vt* (*formal*) praise highly in speech or writing.
eu·logy /ˈyulədʒi/ *n* [C,U] (*pl* -ies) (speech or writing full of) high praise.
eu·phe·mism /ˈyufəˌmɪzəm/ *n* [C,U] (example of the) use of less harsh words or phrases in place of unpleasant and more accurate expressions: *"Pass away" is a ~ for "die."*
eu·phe·mis·tic /ˌyufəˈmɪstɪk/ *adj*
eu·phe·mis·ti·cally /-kli/ *adv*
eu·phoria /yuˈfɔriə/ *n* [U] state of well-being and pleasant excitement.
eu·phoric /yuˈfɔrɪk/ *adj*
Euro·pean /ˌyʊrəˈpiən/ *n* [C], *adj* (native) of Europe: *~ countries.*
Euroˈpean ˌplan, hotel rate which excludes meals.
Eu·sta·chian tube /yuˈsteiʃən ˌtub/ *n* [C] tube connecting the middle ear with the throat. ⇨ illus at ear.
eu·tha·nasia /ˌyuθəˈneiʒə/ *n* = mercy killing.
evacu·ate /ɪˈvækyuˌeit/ *vt* **1** (esp of soldiers) withdraw from; leave empty: *~ a fort/town.* **2** remove (a person) from a place of danger: *The women and children were ~d to the country.*
evacu·ation /ɪˌvækyuˈeiʃən/ *n* **(a)** [U] evacuating or being evacuated. **(b)** [C] instance of this.
evacuee /ɪˌvækyuˈi/ *n* [C] person who is evacuated(2).
evade /ɪˈveid/ *vt* **1** get or keep out of the way of: *~ a blow/one's enemies/an attack.* **2** find a way of not doing something; avoid: *~ paying income tax; ~ a question.*
evalu·ate /ɪˈvælyuˌeit/ *vt* find out, decide, the amount or value of.
evalu·ation /ɪˌvælyuˈeiʃən/ *n* [C,U]
evan·geli·cal /ˌivænˈdʒelɪkəl/ *adj* **1** of, according to, the teachings of the Gospel: *~ preaching.*

2 of those Protestant sects which stress the importance of the atoning death of Jesus Christ and of salvation by faith.

evan·gel·ist /ɪˈvændʒəlɪst/ *n* [C] **1** one of the writers (Matthew, Mark, Luke or John) of the Gospels. **2** preacher of the Gospel, esp one who travels, preaching to any who are willing to listen.

evan·gel·is·tic /ɪˌvændʒəˈlɪstɪk/ *adj*

evap·o·rate /ɪˈvæpəˌreit/ *vt,vi* **1** (cause to) change into vapor: *Heat ~s water. The water soon ~d.* **2** remove liquid from a substance, eg by heating: *~d milk.* **3** disappear; die: *His hopes ~d.*

evap·o·ration /ɪˌvæpəˈreiʃən/ *n* [U]

eva·sion /ɪˈveiʒən/ *n* **1** [U] evading: *an ~ of responsibility.* **2** [C] statement, excuse, etc made to evade something; act of evading: *His answers to my questions were all ~s.*

evas·ive /ɪˈveisɪv/ *adj* tending, trying, to evade: *an ~ answer; take ~ action,* do something in order to evade danger, etc.

evas·ive·ly *adv*

evas·ive·ness /-nɪs/ *n* [U]

eve /iv/ *n* [C] **1** day or evening before a Church festival or any special date or event; time just before an event: *Christmas Eve,* December 24; *New Year's Eve,* December 31. **2** (*poet*) evening.

even[1] /ˈivən/ *adj* **1** level; smooth: *The best lawns are perfectly ~.* **2** regular; steady; of unchanging quality: *His ~ breathing showed that he was asleep. The quality of work is not very ~.* **3** (of amounts, distances, values) equal: *Our scores are now ~.* ***be/get even with sb,*** have one's revenge on him. ***break even,*** ⇨ break[2] (4). **4** (of numbers) that can be divided by two without a remainder: *The pages on the left side of a book have ~ numbers.* **5** fair, equally balanced. **6** (of temper, etc) not easily disturbed or made angry: *an ~-tempered wife.* □ *vt* make even or equal.

even·ly *adv*

even·ness /ˈivənnɪs/ *n* [U]

even[2] /ˈivən/ *adv* **1** (used to stress or indicate something that is unexpected): *He never ~ opened the letter* (so he certainly did not read it). *It was cold there ~ in July* (so you may imagine how cold it was in winter). *Even a child can understand the book* (so adults certainly can). **2** ***even if/though,*** (used to stress the extreme case of what follows) although: *She won't leave the TV set, ~ though she ought to study for her exams.* **3** (used for stress with *comparatives*) still, yet: *You know ~ less about it than I do. You seem ~ busier than usual today.*

even as, just at the time when: *Even as I gave the warning the car skidded.*

even now/then, in spite of these or those circumstances, etc: *Even now he won't believe me. Even then he would not admit his mistake.*

even so, though that is the case: *It has many omissions; ~ so, it is quite a useful reference book.*

eve·ning /ˈivnɪŋ/ *n* [C] **1** that part of the day between afternoon and nightfall: *two ~s ago; this/tomorrow/yesterday ~; in the ~; on Sunday ~;* (as an *adjective*) *an ~ paper,* published after the morning papers. **2** last part: *the ~ of life.*

ˈevening dress, dress as worn for formal occasions.

even·song /ˈivənˌsɔŋ/ *n* vespers.

event /ɪˈvent/ *n* [C] **1** something (usually important) that happens or has happened: *the chief ~s of 1901. It was quite an ~* (often used to suggest that what happened was unusual, memorable, etc). **2** fact of a thing happening: *in the ~ of his death,* if he dies; *in that ~,* if that happens, if that is the case. ***in any event,*** whatever happens. **3** outcome; result. **4** one of the races, competitions, etc in a sports program: *Which ~s have you entered for?*

event·ful /-fəl/ *adj* full of notable events: *He had had an ~ful life.*

even·tide /ˈivənˌtaid/ *n* (*liter*) evening.

even·tual /ɪˈventʃuəl/ *adj* coming at last as a result: *his foolish behavior and ~ failure.*

even·tually /-tʃ(u)əli/ *adv* in the end: *After several attempts he ~ly swam across.*

even·tual·ity /ɪˌventʃuˈæləti/ *n* [C] (*pl* -ies) possible event.

ever /ˈevər/ *adv* **1** (usually in *negative* sentences and questions, and in sentences expressing doubt or conditions) at any time: *Nothing ~ happens in this town. If you ~ visit Europe.... Have you ~ been in an airplane?* (*Note: ever* is not used in the answer; use either "Yes, I have" or "No, never," etc.) **2** (used after a *comparative* or *superlative*): *It is raining harder than ~,* than it has been doing so far. *This is the best work you have ~ done.* **3** at all times; always: *~ after; for ~ (and ~); ~ since I was a boy.* **4** (used to stress surprise, uncertainty, etc): *When/Where/How ~ did you lose it? What ~ do you mean?*

ever·green /ˈevərˌgrin/ *n* [C], *adj* (tree, shrub) having green leaves throughout the year: *The pine, cedar and spruce are ~s.* ⇨ deciduous.

ever·last·ing /ˌevərˈlæstɪŋ/ *adj* **1** eternal: *~ fame/glory.* **2** (*informal*) repeated too often: *I'm tired of his ~ complaints.*

ever·more /ˌevərˈmɔr/ *adv* forever.

every /ˈevri/ *adj* **1** all or each one of: *I have read ~ book* (= all the books) *on that shelf. Not ~ horse* (= Not all horses) *can run fast.* ⇨ all[1] (1). (*Note:* when *every* is used attention is directed to the whole; when *each* is used, attention is directed to the unit or individual: *Every boy in the class* (= All the boys) *passed the examination.* **2** each one of an indefinite number (the emphasis being on the unit, not on the total or whole): *Such things do not happen ~ day.* (*Note:* not replaceable by *all.*) ***every last/single ˈone,*** each one, without exception. **3** all possible: *You have ~ reason to be satisfied.* **4** (used with numbers and with *other* and *few,* to indicate recurrence, or intervals in time or space): *Write on ~ other line,* on alternate lines. *There are buses to the station ~ ten minutes,* at ten minute intervals. *I go there ~ other day/~ three days/~ few days, etc.* ***every now and then/again,*** from time to time. ***every time,*** **(a)** always: *Our football team wins ~ time.* **(b)** whenever: *Every time I meet him, he tries to borrow money from me.* ***in every way,*** in all respects: *This is in ~ way better than that.*

every·body /ˈevriˌbadi, -ˌbədi/ *pron* every person: *In a small town ~ knows ~ else.*

every·day /ˈevriˌdei/ *adj* happening or used daily; common and familiar: *an ~ occurrence; in his ~ clothes.*

every·one /ˈevriˌwən/ *pron* everybody.

every·thing /ˈevriˌθɪŋ/ *pron* **1** all things: *Tell me ~ about it.* **2** thing of the greatest importance: *Money means ~ to him.*

every·where /ˈevriˌ(h)wer/ *adv* in, at, to, every place: *I've looked ~ for it.*

evict /iˈvɪkt, ɪ-/ *vt* expel (a tenant) (from a house or land) by authority of the law: *They were ~ed for not paying the rent.*

evic·tion /iˈvɪkʃən, ɪ-/ *n* [C,U]

evi·dence /ˈevədəns/ *n* [U] **1** proof; anything that makes clear what is true and what is not: *There wasn't enough ~ to prove him guilty. The scientist must produce ~ in support of his theories.* **2** indication, mark, trace: *There was ~ of glacial action on the rocks.* ***in evidence***, clearly or easily seen.

evi·dent /ˈevədənt/ *adj* plain and clear (to the eyes or mind): *It must be ~ to all of you that...*

evi·dent·ly /ˈevədəntli, ˌevəˈdentli/ *adv*

evil /ˈivəl/ *adj* **1** wicked, sinful, bad, harmful: *~ men/thoughts.* **2** likely to cause trouble; bringing trouble or misfortune: *an ~ tongue.* □ *n* **1** [U] sin; wrong-doing: *the spirit of ~.* **2** [C] misfortune; disaster: *War, famine and flood are terrible ~s.* ***be/choose the lesser of two evils,*** the less harmful of two bad choices.

ˈevil·doer /ˈivəlˌduər/ *n* [C] person who does evil.

evil·ly *adv*

evil-minded /ˌivəlˈmaindɪd/ *adj* having evil thoughts and desires.

evince /ɪˈvɪns/ *vt* (*formal*) show that one has a feeling, quality, etc: *a child who ~s great intelligence.*

evoca·tive /ɪˈvakətɪv/ *adj* that evokes, or tends to evoke.

evoke /ɪˈvouk/ *vt* call up, bring out: *~ admiration/surprise/a smile/memories of the past.*

evo·ca·tion /ˌivəˈkeiʃən/ *n* [C,U]

evol·ution /ˌevəˈluʃən/ *n* [U] **1** process of growth or development: *the ~ of a plant from a seed.* **2** (theory of the) development of the existing forms of plant and animal life from earlier and simpler forms by means of a series of gradual changes.

evolve /iˈvalv, ɪ-/ *vi,vt* develop or be developed, naturally and (usually) gradually: *The American constitution was planned; the British constitution ~d.*

ewe /yu/ *n* [C] female sheep.

ewer /ˈyuər/ *n* [C] large wide-mouthed pitcher or jug for holding water.

ex. *abbr* = example.

ex- /ˈeks-/ *prefix* former; at one time: *ex-wife; ex-president.*

exact¹ /ɪgˈzækt/ *adj* **1** correct in every detail; free from error: *Give me his ~ words. What is the ~ size of the room?* **2** strictly accurate; precise: *~ sciences; an ~ memory.*

exacti·tude /ɪgˈzæktəˌtud/ *n* [U] = exactness.

exact·ly *adv* **(a)** precisely; quite: *Your answer is ~ly right. That's ~ly* (= just) *what I expected.* **(b)** (as an answer or confirmation) quite so; just as you say.

exact·ness /-nɪs/ *n* [U] state of being exact; precision.

exact² /ɪgˈzækt/ *vt* **1** demand and get: *~ taxes (from* people)*; ~ obedience.* **2** (*formal*) require urgently; make necessary: *work that ~s care and attention.*

exact·ing *adj* making great demands; severe; strict: *an ~ing piece of work.*

exag·ger·ate /ɪgˈzædʒəˌreit/ *vt,vi* make something seem larger, better, worse, etc than it really is: *You ~ the difficulties. If you always ~, people will no longer believe you.*

exag·ger·ation /ɪgˌzædʒəˈreiʃən/ *n* **(a)** [U] exaggerating or being exaggerated. **(b)** [C] exaggerated statement: *a story full of exaggerations.*

exalt /ɪgˈzɔlt/ *vt* **1** make high(er) in rank, great(er) in power or dignity. **2** praise highly; glorify.

exal·ta·tion /ˌegˌzɔlˈteiʃən/ *n* [U] **(a)** exalting or being exalted. **(b)** (*fig*) elation; state of spiritual delight.

exalted *adj*

exam /ɪgˈzæm/ *n* (*informal*) (short for) examination(2).

exam·i·na·tion /ɪgˌzæməˈneiʃən/ *n* **1** [C,U] examining or being examined; *On ~, it was found that the signature was not genuine. The prisoner is still under ~,* being examined; *an ~ of business accounts; an ~ of one's eyes.* **2** [C] test of knowledge or ability: *an ~ in mathematics; ~ questions/papers; an oral ~.* **3** questioning by a lawyer in a law court: *the ~ of a witness.*

exam·ine /ɪgˈzæmən/ *vt* **1** look at carefully in order to learn; inspect: *~ old records; have one's teeth/eyes ~d.* **2** put questions to in order to test knowledge or get information: *~ a pupil's grammar; ~ a witness in a law court.*

exam·iner, person who examines.

example /ɪgˈzæmpəl/ *n* [C] **1** sample, specimen, etc which represents others in the same group or of the same kind: *This dictionary has many ~s of how words are used in sentences.* ***for example,*** using this or these as typical: *Many great men have risen from poverty—Lincoln and Edison, for ~.* **2** (esp) problem to be solved that illustrates a general rule: *ten ~s in math.* **3** model to be copied or imitated: *follow her ~; set him a good ~.* **4** warning: *Let her sorrow be an ~ to you.* ***make an example of sb,*** punish him as a warning to others.

exas·per·ate /ɪgˈzæspəˌreit/ *vt* irritate; make angry: *~d by/at his stupidity. It is exasperating to miss a flight by a few minutes.*

exas·per·ation /ɪgˌzæspəˈreiʃən/ *n* [U] state of being irritated: *"Stop that noise," he cried out in ~.*

ex·ca·vate /ˈekskəˌveit/ *vt* make, uncover, by digging: *~ a trench/a buried city.*

ex·ca·va·tion /ˌekskəˈveiʃən/ *n* [C,U]

ex·ca·vator /ˈekskəˌveitər/ *n* [C]

ex·ceed /ɪkˈsid/ *vt* **1** be greater than: *Their success ~ed all expectations.* **2** go beyond what is allowed, necessary or advisable: *~ the speed limit,* drive faster than is allowed.

exceed·ing·ly *adv* extremely; to an unusual

degree: *an ~ingly difficult problem.*

ex·cel /ɪkˈsel/ *vi,vt* (-ll-) **1** do better than others, be very good: *He ~s in courage/as a writer.* **2** do better than: *He ~s all of us in/at tennis.*

ex·cel·lence /ˈeksələns/ *n* **1** [U] the quality of being excellent: *a prize for ~ in French.* **2** [C] thing or quality in which a person excels: *They do not recognize her many ~s.*

ex·cel·lency /ˈeksələnsi/ *n* [C] (*pl* -ies) **1** [U] excellence. **2** ***Your/His/Her Excellency***, title for ambassadors, bishops, etc.

ex·cel·lent /ˈeksələnt/ *adj* very good; of the highest quality.

ex·cel·lent·ly *adv*

ex·cept[1] /ɪkˈsept/ *prep* **1** not including; but not: *He gets up early every day ~ Sunday. Nobody was late ~ me.* (*Note: except* does not occur with *negatives.* ⇨excepting.) **2** other than: *You can't get there ~ by plane.* ***except for,*** apart from: *Your essay is good ~ for the spelling.* □ *conj* but. ***except that,*** apart from the fact that: *She knew nothing ~ that he was likely to be late.*

ex·cept[2] /ɪkˈsept/ *vt* exclude (from); leave out (from a number or group): *When I say that those fellows are lazy, I ~ Tom.*

ex·cept·ing *prep, conj* (used after *not, always* and *without*) leaving out; excluding: *the whole staff, not ~ing the heads of departments.*

ex·cep·tion /ɪkˈsepʃən/ *n* **1** [C] person or thing that is left out: *You must all be here at 8am; I can make no ~s. I enjoyed all his novels with the ~ of his last.* **2** [C] something that does not follow the rule: *~s to a rule of grammar.* **3** [U] objection. ***take exception to,*** object to, protest against; be offended by: *He took great ~ to what I said.*

ex·cep·tional /ɪkˈsepʃənəl/ *adj* unusual: *weather that is ~ for June.*

ex·cep·tion·ally *adv* unusually: *an ~ly clever boy.*

ex·cerpt /ˈekˌsərpt/ *n* [C] extract from a book etc.

ex·cess /ɪkˈses/ *n* **1** [U] (and in *sing* with *an*) fact of being more than enough, or more than is expected or proper: *an ~ of enthusiasm.* ***to excess,*** to an extreme degree: *She is generous to ~.* **2** [U] amount that is more than enough: *We'll give the ~ away.* **3** (*pl*) personal acts which go beyond the limits of good behavior, morality or humanity: *The ~es* (= acts of cruelty, etc) *committed by the troops when they occupied the capital will never be forgotten.*

ex·cess /ˈekˌses/ *adj* extra; additional: *~ fare/baggage/postage.*

ex·ces·sive /ɪkˈsesɪv/ *adj* too much; too great; extreme: *~ive charges.*

ex·ces·sive·ly *adv*

ex·change[1] /ɪksˈtʃeindʒ/ *n* **1** [C,U] (act of) exchanging: *He is giving her French lessons in ~ for English lessons.* **2** [U] **(a)** the giving and receiving of the money of one country for that of another. **(b)** relation in value between kinds of money used in different countries: *the rate of ~ between the dollar and the pound.* **3** [C] place where merchants or financiers meet for business: *the ˈStock Exchange,* for the buying and selling of shares, etc. **4** [C] control office where telephone lines are connected.

ex·change[2] /ɪksˈtʃeindʒ/ *vt,vi* trade (one thing) for another: *~ greetings/glances. Mary ~d seats with Anne.*

ex·change·able /-əbəl/ *adj* that may be exchanged (*for*).

ex·cise[1] /ˈekˌsaiz/ *n* [U] government tax on certain goods manufactured, sold or used within a country: *the ~ on beer/tobacco.*

ex·cise[2] /ekˈsaiz/ *vt* (*formal*) remove by, or as if by cutting (a part of the body, a passage from a book, etc).

ex·ci·sion /ekˈsɪʒən/ *n* [C,U]

ex·cite /ɪkˈsait/ *vt* **1** stir up the feelings of: *Everybody was ~d by the news of the victory.* **2** move or stir to action: *Extremists were exciting the people to rebellion/to rebel against their rulers.* **3** arouse: *~d the admiration/envy of all his friends.*

ex·cit·able /ɪkˈsaitəbəl/ *adj* easily excited.

ex·cite·ment /ɪkˈsaitmənt/ *n* **1** [U] state of being excited: *news that caused great ~.* **2** [C] exciting incident, etc: *He kept calm amid all these ~s.*

ex·claim /ɪkˈskleim/ *vt,vi* say or cry out suddenly and loudly from pain, anger, surprise, etc: *"What!" he ~ed, "Are you leaving without me?"*

ex·cla·mation /ˌekskləˈmeiʃən/ *n* **1** [U] crying out or exclaiming. **2** [C] sudden short cry, expressing surprise, pain, etc. *"Oh!" "Look out!" and "Hurrah!" are ~s.*

ˌexclaˈmation point, the punctuation mark (!) used in writing.

ex·clama·tory /ɪkˈsklæməˌtɔri/ *adj* using, containing, in the nature of, an exclamation: *an ~ sentence.*

ex·clude /ɪkˈsklud/ *vt* **1** shut or keep out; bar: *~ him from taking part; facts that ~ all doubt on our part; heavy curtains excluding light and air.* **2** ignore; disregard: *We can ~ the possibility that the money won't arrive.*

ex·clu·sion /ɪkˈskluʒən/ *n* [U] excluding or being excluded (*from*).

ex·clu·sive /ɪkˈsklusɪv/ *adj* **1** tending to exclude others (esp those considered to be inferior in social position, education, etc): *He belongs to the most ~ clubs.* **2** fashionable and usually expensive: *~ shops.* **3** not shared with others: *have ~ rights to manufacture and sell his designs; an ~ story/interview,* eg given to only one newspaper. **4** ***exclusive of,*** not including: *The ship had a crew of 57 ~ of officers.* **5** excluding everything else; sole: *Teaching has not been his ~ employment.*

ex·clu·sive·ly *adv*

ex·com·muni·cate /ˌekskəˈmyunəˌkeit/ *vt* exclude (as a punishment) from membership in a church.

ex·com·muni·ca·tion /ˌekskəˌmyunəˈkeiʃən/ *n* [C,U]

excre·ment /ˈekskrəmənt/ *n* [U] solid waste matter discharged from the bowels.

ex·creta /ekˈskritə/ *n pl* waste (excrement, urine, sweat) expelled from the body.

ex·crete /ekˈskrit/ *vt* (of an animal or plant) discharge from the system, eg waste matter, sweat.

ex·cre·tion /ekˈskriʃən/ *n* **(a)**[U] excreting. **(b)**

[C,U] that which is excreted.

ex·cru·ciat·ing /ɪkˈskruʃiˌeitɪŋ/ *adj* very painful.

ex·cru·ciat·ing·ly *adv*

ex·cur·sion /ɪkˈskərʒən/ *n* [C] **1** short journey, esp one made by a number of people together for pleasure: *go on/make an ~ to the mountains.* **2** trip made at a lower fare than usual.

ex·cuse[1] /ɪkˈskyus/ *n* [C] reason given (true or invented) to explain or defend one's conduct: *He's always making ~s for being late.* ***without excuse***: *Those who are absent without ~ will be punished.*

ex·cuse[2] /ɪkˈskyuz/ *vt* **1** give reasons showing, or intended to show, that a person or his action is not to be blamed: *She tried to ~ her mistakes on the test by saying that she had not been given enough time.* **2** set free from a duty, punishment, etc: *He was ~d from attending the lecture.* **3** forgive: *Please ~ my coming late/~ me for being late/~ my late arrival.* ***Excuse me,*** (used as an apology when one interrupts, disagrees, etc): *Excuse me, but is this seat vacant?*

ex·cus·able /ɪkˈskyuzəbəl/ *adj* that may be excused: *an excusable mistake.*

exec. *abbr* (sometimes spoken in *informal style* as /ɪgˈzek/) = executive.

ex·ecute /ˈeksəˌkyut/ *vt* **1** carry out: *~ a plan/a command/a purpose.* **2** give effect to: *~ a will/a legal document,* by having it signed, witnessed, etc. **3** carry out punishment by death: *~ a murderer.* **4** perform on the stage, at a concert, etc: *The piano sonata was badly ~d.*

ex·ecu·tion /ˌeksəˈkyuʃən/ *n* **1** [U] the carrying out or performance of a piece of work, etc: *His ~ of the plan was unsatisfactory.* **2** [U] skill in performing. **3** [C,U] (act of) putting to death as a legal punishment: *~ by hanging; five ~s last year.*

ex·ecu·tioner *n* [C] person who executes(3).

execu·tive /ɪgˈzekyətɪv/ *adj* **1** having to do with managing or executing(1): *~ duties.* **2** having authority to carry out decisions, laws, decrees, etc: *the ~ branch of the government.* □ *n* [C] **1 the executive,** the executive branch of a government. **2** person in an organization who has administrative or managerial powers. **the ˌChief Exˈecutive,** the President of the United States.

execu·tor /ɪgˈzekyətər/ *n* [C] person who is appointed to carry out the terms of a will.

execu·trix /ɪgˈzekyətrɪks/ *n* [C] woman executor.

exemp·lary /ɪgˈzempləri, ˈegzəmˌpleri/ *adj* serving as an example or a warning: *~ conduct/punishment.*

exem·plify /ɪgˈzempləˌfai/ *vt* (*pt,pp* -ied) illustrate by example; be an example of.

exemp·lifi·ca·tion /ɪgˌzempləfəˈkeiʃən/ *n* [C,U]

exempt /ɪgˈzempt/ *vt* free from (an obligation): *Poor eyesight will ~ you from military service.* □ *adj* not liable to; free (*from*): *~ from tax.*

exemp·tion /ɪgˈzempʃən/ *n* [C,U]

ex·er·cise[1] /ˈeksərˌsaiz/ *n* **1** [U] use or practice (of mental or physical powers, of rights): *Walking, running, rowing and cycling are all healthy forms of ~. The ~ of patience is essential in diplomatic negotiations.* **2** [C] activity, drill, etc designed for bodily, mental or spiritual training: *vocal/gymnastic ~s; ~s for the harp/flute, etc; ~s in English composition.* **3** (*pl*) ceremony; program: *graduation ~s.*

ex·er·cise[2] /ˈeksərˌsaiz/ *vt,vi* **1** take exercise; give exercise to, ⇨ exercise[1] (1): *We get fat and lazy if we don't ~ enough.* **2** employ; make use of: *~ patience/one's rights.* **3** trouble; worry the mind of: *The problem that is exercising our minds. . .*

exert /ɪgˈzərt/ *vt* **1** put forth; bring into use: *~ all one's energy/influence, etc.* **2** make an effort: *~ oneself to arrive early.*

exer·tion /ɪgˈzərʃən/ *n* **(a)** [U] exerting. **(b)** [C] instance of this.

ex·hale /eksˈheiəl/ *vt,vi* (*pres p* -ing /eksˈheilɪŋ/) **1** breathe out. **2** give off gas, vapor; be given off (as gas or vapor).

ex·ha·la·tion /ˌeks(h)əˈleiʃən/ *n* [C,U]

ex·haust[1] /ɪgˈzɔst/ *n* [C,U] (outlet, in an engine or machine, for the) escape of steam, vapor, etc that has done its work.

exˈhaust pipe, for releasing gases from a motor vehicle engine.

ex·haust[2] /ɪgˈzɔst/ *vt* **1** use up completely: *~ one's patience/strength.* **2** make empty: *~ a well;* **3** tire out: *The long trip ~ed us.* **4** say, find out, all there is to say about (something): *~ a subject.*

ex·haus·tion /ɪgˈzɔstʃən/ *n* [U] **1** exhausting or being exhausted. **2** extreme weariness: *They were in a state of ~ after climbing the mountain.*

ex·haus·tive /ɪgˈzɔstɪv/ *adj* thorough; complete: *an ~ inquiry.*

ex·hib·it[1] /ɪgˈzɪbɪt/ *n* [C] **1** object or collection of objects, shown publicly, eg in a museum: *Do not touch the ~s.* **2** document, object, etc produced in a law court and referred to in evidence, eg a weapon said to have been used by the accused person.

ex·hib·it[2] /ɪgˈzɪbɪt/ *vt* **1** show publicly for sale, in a competition, etc: *~ paintings. The artist ~s in several galleries.* **2** give clear evidence of (a quality): *The girls ~ed great courage during the climb.*

ex·hi·bi·tor *n* [C] person who exhibits at a show of pictures, etc.

ex·hi·bi·tion /ˌeksɪˈbɪʃən/ *n* **1** [C] public display or show (eg of works of art, commercial or industrial goods, etc). **2** (*sing* with *the* or *an*) act or instance of showing: *an ~ of bad manners; an opportunity for the ~ of one's knowledge.*

ex·hil·a·rate /ɪgˈzɪləˌreit/ *vt* fill with high spirits; make lively or glad: *exhilarating news.*

ex·hil·a·ration /ɪgˌzɪləˈreiʃən/ *n* [U]

ex·hort /ɪgˈzɔrt/ *vt* (*formal*) urge: *~ her to do good/to work harder/to give up bad ways.*

ex·hor·ta·tion /ˌekˌsɔrˈteiʃən/ *n* **(a)** [U] exhorting. **(b)** [C] earnest request, sermon, etc.

ex·hume /ɪgˈzum/ *vt* dig out (a dead body) of the earth (for examination).

ex·hum·ation /ˌeksuˈmeiʃən/ *n* [C,U]

ex·ile /ˈegˌzaiəl/ *n* **1** [U] being sent away from one's country or home, esp as a punishment: *be/live in ~; go/be sent into ~; a place of ~; after an ~ of ten years.* **2** [C] person who is banished in this way. □ *vt* (*pres p* exiling /ˈegˌzailɪŋ/) send into exile.

ex·ist /ɪgˈzɪst/ *vi* **1** be; have being; be real: *The idea ~s only in the minds of poets. Does life ~ on Mars?* **2** continue living: *We cannot ~ without food and water.* **3** occur; be found: *a bird that no longer ~s in this country.*

ex·ist·ence /-əns/ *n* **(a)** [U] (state of) being: *Do you believe in the ~ence of ghosts? This is the oldest skull in ~ence.* **(b)** manner of living: *lead a happy ~ence.*

ex·ist·ent /-ənt/ *adj* existing.

exit /ˈegzɪt, ˈeksɪt/ *n* [C] **1** departure of an actor from the stage: *make one's ~*, go out or away. **2** way out, eg from a theater or other public building. □ *vi* **1** leave. **2** as a stage direction: *Exit the King.*

ex·on·er·ate /ɪgˈzanəˌreit/ *vt* free, clear from blame.

ex·on·er·ation /ɪgˌzanəˈreiʃən/ *n* [U]

ex·or·bi·tant /ɪgˈzɔrbətənt/ *adj* (of a price, charge or demand) much too high or great.

ex·or·bi·tant·ly *adv*

ex·or·cise, exorcize /ˈekˌsɔrˌsaiz/ *vt* drive out, eg an evil spirit, by prayers or magic.

ex·otic /ɪgˈzatɪk/ *adj* **1** (of plants, fashions, words, ideas) introduced from another country. **2** unusual in style; striking or pleasing because colorful, unusual: *~ birds.*

ex·pand /ɪkˈspænd/ *vt,vi* **1** make or become larger: *Metals ~ when they are heated. Our foreign trade has ~ed during recent years.* **2** unfold or spread out: *The petals of many flowers ~ in the sunshine.*

ex·pand·able /-əbəl/ *adj*

ex·panse /ɪkˈspæns/ *n* [C] wide and open area: *the broad ~ of the Pacific; the blue ~ of the sky.*

ex·pan·sion /ɪkˈspænʃən/ *n* [U] expanding or being expanded(1): *the ~ of gases when heated.*

ex·pan·sive /ɪkˈspænsɪv/ *adj* **1** able, tending, to expand. **2** (of persons, speech) high-spirited, good-humored.

ex·patri·ate /eksˈpeitriˌeit/ *vt* leave one's own country to live abroad; renounce one's citizenship. □ *n* /-rɪt/ [C] person living outside his own country: *American ~s in Paris.*

ex·pect /ɪkˈspekt/ *vt* **1** think or believe that something will happen; wait for and look forward to with confidence: *We ~ed you (to arrive) yesterday.* **2** (*informal*) suppose: *I ~ that he will write soon.* **3** require; consider necessary: *They ~ me to work on Saturdays.*

ex·pect·ancy /-ənsi/ *n* [U] **(a)** the state of expecting: *with a look/an air of ~ancy.* **(b)** expected amount: *life ~ancy,* years a person is expected to live.

ex·pect·ant /-ənt/ *adj* expecting: *an ~ant mother*, woman who is pregnant.

ex·pec·ta·tion /ˌekˌspekˈteiʃən/ *n* **1** [U] expecting: *He ate a light lunch in ~ of a good dinner.* **2** (often *pl*) thing that is expected. **3** (*pl*) future prospects, esp something to be inherited: *a young man with great ~s.*

ex·pedi·ent /ɪkˈspidiənt/ *adj* useful or helpful for a purpose; advantageous though often contrary to principle: *In times of war governments do things because they are ~.* □ *n* [C] necessary plan, action, device, etc.

ex·pedi·ence /-əns/, **ex·pedi·ency** /-ənsi/ *n* [U] suitability for a purpose; self-interest: *act from expediency, not from principle.*

ex·pedi·ently *adv*

ex·pedite /ˈekspəˌdait/ *vt* (*formal*) help the progress of; speed up (business, etc).

ex·pedi·tion /ˌekspəˈdɪʃən/ *n* **1** [C] (men, ships, etc making a) journey or voyage for exploration, to wage war, etc: *send a party of men/go on an ~ to the Antarctic.* **2** [U] (*formal*) promptness; speed.

ex·pedi·tion·ary /-ˌeri/ *adj* of, making up, an expedition.

ex·pedi·tious /ˌekspəˈdɪʃəs/ *adj* (*formal*) acting quickly; prompt and efficient.

ex·pedi·tious·ly *adv*

ex·pel /ɪkˈspel/ *vt* (-ll-) **1** send out or away by force: *~ a boy from school.* **2** force out: *~ air from the lungs.*

ex·pend /ɪkˈspend/ *vt* **1** spend: *~ time and care in doing something.* **2** use up: *They had ~ed all their ammunition.*

ex·pend·able /-əbəl/ *adj* (esp) that may be sacrificed to achieve a purpose: *The general considered that these troops were ~able.*

ex·pen·di·ture /ɪkˈspendɪtʃər/ *n* **1** [U] spending or using: *the ~ of money on armaments.* **2** [C,U] amount expended: *an ~ of $900 on new furniture.*

ex·pense /ɪkˈspens/ *n* **1** [U] spending (of money, time, energy, etc); cost: *I want the best you can supply; you need spare no ~*, you need not try to economize. ***at the expense of,*** at the cost of: *He became a brilliant scholar, but only at the ~ of his health.* **2** (usually *pl*) money used or needed: *traveling ~s. The doctor's bills and other ~s reduced his bank balance to almost nothing.*

ex·pen·sive /ɪkˈspensɪv/ *adj* costing a great deal: *an ~ dress; too ~ for me to buy.*

ex·pen·sive·ly *adv*

ex·peri·ence /ɪkˈspɪriəns/ *n* **1** [U] process of gaining knowledge or skill by doing and seeing things; knowledge or skill so gained: *We all learn by ~. Has he had much ~ in work of this sort?* **2** [C] event, activity, which has given one experience(1). **3** [C] event that affects one in some way: *an unpleasant/unusual ~.* □ *vt* have experience of: *~ pleasure/pain/difficulty.*

ex·peri·enced *adj* having knowledge or skill as the result of experience: *an ~d nurse/teacher.*

ex·peri·ment /ɪkˈsperəmənt/ *n* [C] test or trial carried out carefully in order to study what happens and gain new knowledge: *perform/carry out an ~ in chemistry.* □ *vi* make experiments: *~ with new methods.*

ex·peri·men·ta·tion /ɪkˌsperəmənˈteiʃən/ *n* [U]

ex·peri·men·tal /ɪkˌsperəˈmentəl/ *adj* of, used for, based on, experiments: *~ methods; an ~ farm.*

ex·pert /ˈekˌspərt/ *n* [C] person with special knowledge, skill or training: *an agricultural ~; an ~ in economics.* □ *adj* trained, skilled, by practice: *according to ~ advice/opinions.*

ex·pert·ly *adv*

ex·pert·ness /-nɪs/ *n* [U]

ex·pi·ration /ˌekspəˈreiʃən/ *n* [U] **1** ending: *at the*

~ *of the lease.* **2** breathing out (of air).

ex·pire /ɪkˈspaɪər/ *vi* **1** come to an end: *When does your driving license ~?* **2** (*formal*) die. **3** breathe out.

ex·plain /ɪkˈsplein/ *vt* **1** make plain or clear; show the meaning of: *A dictionary tries to ~ the meanings of words. He ~ed the problem very carefully. She ~ed that it was difficult to save money out of her salary.* **2** account for; give reasons for: *Can you ~ his behavior? That ~s his absence/why he was absent.*

ex·pla·na·tion /ˌekspləˈneiʃən/ *n* **1** [U] (process of) explaining: *Not much ~ will be needed.* **2** [C] statement, fact, circumstances, etc that explains: *an ~ of his conduct/of a mystery.*

ex·plana·tory /ɪkˈsplænəˌtɔri/ *adj* serving or intended to explain.

ex·ple·tive /ˈeksplətɪv/ *n* [C] (often meaningless) exclamation, eg "My goodness," or an oath such as "Damn."

ex·plic·able /ekˈsplɪkəbəl/ *adj* that can be explained.

ex·pli·cit /ɪkˈsplɪsɪt/ *adj* (of a statement, etc) clearly and fully expressed: *His orders were ~,* left no doubt about what he meant.

ex·pli·cit·ly *adv*

ex·pli·cit·ness /-nɪs/ *n* [U]

ex·plode /ɪkˈsploud/ *vt,vi* **1** (cause to) burst with a loud noise: *~ a charge of gunpowder/a bomb. The bomb ~d.* **2** (of feelings) burst out; (of persons) show violent emotion: *At last his anger ~d. He ~d with rage.* **3** destroy, expose (the incorrectness of) an idea, a theory, etc: *~ a superstition; an ~d idea.*

ex·ploit¹ /ˈekˌsplɔit/ *n* [C] bold or adventurous act.

ex·ploit² /ɪkˈsplɔit/ *vt* **1** use, work or develop for profit: *~ the natural resources of a country.* **2** use selfishly, or for one's own profit: *~ child labor.*

ex·ploi·ta·tion /ˌekˌsplɔiˈteiʃən/ *n* [U]

ex·plore /ɪkˈsplɔr/ *vt* **1** travel into or through (a country, etc) for the purpose of learning about it: *~ the Arctic regions.* **2** examine thoroughly problems, possibilities, etc in order to test, learn about, them.

ex·plo·ra·tion /ˌekspləˈreiʃən/ *n* **(a)** [U] exploring: *the ~ of the ocean depths.* **(b)** [C] instance of this.

ex·plora·tory /ɪkˈsplɔrəˌtɔri/ *adj* for the purpose of exploring.

ex·plorer *n* [C]

ex·plo·sion /ɪkˈsplouʒən/ *n* [C] **1** (loud noise caused by a) sudden and violent bursting: *a ˈbomb ~. The ~ was heard a mile away.* **2** outburst or outbreak of anger, laughter, etc. **3** great and sudden increase: *a ˈpopulation ~.*

ex·plo·sive /ɪkˈsplousɪv/ *n* [C,U], *adj* (substance) tending to or likely to explode: *a shell filled with high ~s. That's an ~ issue,* one likely to cause anger, etc.

ex·plo·sive·ly *adv*

ex·po·nent /ɪkˈspounənt/ *n* [C] person who explains, interprets, or advocates: *Huxley was an ~ of Darwin's theory of evolution.*

ex·port¹ /ˈekˌspɔrt/ *n* **1** [U] (business of) exporting: *a ban on the ~ of gold; the ˈ~ trade.* **2** [C] thing exported: *Last year ~s exceeded imports in value.*

ex·port² /ɪkˈspɔrt/ *vt* send (goods) to another country: *~ cotton goods.*

ex·porter *n* [C]

ex·port·able /-əbəl/ *adj*

ex·pose /ɪkˈspouz/ *vt* **1** uncover; leave uncovered or unprotected: *~ one's body to the sunlight; ~ soldiers to unnecessary risks.* **2** display: *~ merchandise in a store window.* **3** disclose, make known: *~ a plot/villain.* **4** (in photography) allow light to reach (camera film, etc): *~ 30 feet of motion picture film.*

ex·po·si·tion /ˌekspəˈzɪʃən/ *n* **1** [U] expounding or explaining. **2** [C] instance of this; explanation or interpretation of a theory, plan, etc. **3** [C] exhibition of manufactured articles, etc: *an industrial ~.*

ex·po·sure /ɪkˈspouʒər/ *n* **1** [U] exposing or being exposed (all senses): *The climbers lost their way on the mountain and died of ~. The ~ of the plot against the President probably saved his life.* **2** [C] instance of exposing or being exposed (all senses): *How many ~s have you made?* How many pictures have you taken on the (camera) film? **3** position with respect to sea and wind: *a house with a southern ~.*

ex·pound /ɪkˈspaund/ *vt* explain or set forth in detail.

ex·press¹ /ɪkˈspres/ *adj* **1** clearly stated; explicit: *It was his ~ wish that you were to finish his work.* **2** special: *went for the ~ purpose of meeting her train.* **3** quick; designed for high speed: *an ~ letter; and ~ bus/train,* one that makes few or no stops along its way.

ex·press² /ɪkˈspres/ *n* [C] **1** train, bus, etc making few or no stops on its way. **2** (company operating a) system for the rapid transport of goods: *sent the packages by ~.* **3** goods sent by express.

ex·press³ /ɪkˈspres/ *vt* **1** make known, show by words, looks, actions: *I find it difficult to ~ my meaning. A smile ~ed her joy at the good news.* **2** send a letter, goods, etc by express: *The letter is urgent; you had better ~ it.* **3** press or squeeze out juices/oil (construction with *from/out of*): *juice ~ed* (*pressed* is more usual) *from grapes.*

ex·pression /ɪkˈspreʃən/ *n* **1** [U] (way of) expressing(1): *read* (aloud) *with ~,* in a way that shows feeling for the meaning. **2** [C] word or phrase: *"Shut up"* (= Stop talking) *is not a polite ~.* **3** (*math*) symbol(s) expressing a quantity, eg $3xy^2$. **4** [C] appearance; look: *a discontented ~.*

ex·pression·less *adj* without expression(1): *an ~less face.*

ex·pres·sive /ɪkˈspresɪv/ *adj* **1** serving to express: *looks ~ of despair.* **2** full of expression or feeling: *an ~ smile.*

ex·pres·sive·ly *adv*

ex·press·ly /ɪkˈspresli/ *adv* **1** plainly; definitely: *You were ~ forbidden to touch my papers.* **2** especially: *went there ~ to use the library.*

ex·press·way /ɪkˈspresˌwei/ *n* [C] highway built for travel at high speeds.

ex·pul·sion /ɪkˈspəlʃən/ *n* **1** [U] expelling or being expelled. **2** [C] instance of this: *the ~ of a student from college.*

ex·punge /ɪkˈspəndʒ/ *vt* (*formal*) wipe or rub out completely; erase.

ex·pur·gate /ˈekspərˌgeit/ *vt* take out objectionable parts, esp from a book: *an ~d edition of a novel.*

ex·pur·ga·tion /ˌekspərˈgeiʃən/ *n* [U]

ex·quis·ite /ekˈskwɪzɪt/ *adj* **1** of great excellence, a high state of perfection: *~ workmanship.* **2** (*formal*) (of pain, pleasure, etc) keenly felt. **3** delicate; lovely: *What ~ flowers!*

ex·quis·ite·ly *adv*

ext. *abbr* = extension.

ex·tant /ˈekˌstænt, ekˈstænt/ *adj* still in existence: *the earliest ~ manuscript of this poem.*

ex·tem·po·raneous /ˌekˌstempəˈreiniəs/ *adj* spoken or done without previous thought or preparation: *an ~ speech.*

ex·tem·po·raneous·ly *adv*

ex·tem·pore /ekˈstempəri/ *adj, adv* extemporaneous(ly): *speak ~*, without notes.

ex·tend /ɪkˈstend/ *vt,vi* **1** make longer (in space or time); enlarge: *~ a railroad/the city boundaries.* **2** lay or stretch out the body, a limb, or limbs at full length: *~ one's hand to her.* **3** offer, grant: *~ an invitation/a warm welcome to him.* **4** (of space, land, etc) reach, stretch: *a road that ~s for miles and miles.* **5** cause to reach or stretch: *~ a cable between two posts.*

ex·ten·sion /ɪkˈstenʃən/ *n* **1** [U] extending or being extended: *the ~ of useful knowledge.* **2** [C] additional part; enlargement: *an ~ of one's summer vacation; build an ~ to a hospital; get an ~ of time*, eg for paying a debt. **3** [C] additional telephone connected to the main line.

ex·ten·sive /ɪkˈstensɪv/ *adj* extending far; far-reaching: *~ repairs/inquiries.*

ex·ten·sive·ly *adv*

ex·tent /ɪkˈstent/ *n* [U] **1** size; range: *I was amazed at the ~ of his knowledge.* **2** degree or limit: *to a certain ~*, partly; *will go to any ~ to get what he wants.*

ex·tenu·ate /ɪkˈstenyuˌeit/ *vt* make (wrongdoing) seem less serious (by finding an excuse): *There are extenuating circumstances in this case.*

ex·tenu·ation /ɪkˌstenyuˈeiʃən/ *n* [C,U]

ex·ter·ior /ekˈstɪriər/ *adj* outer; of, on or for the outside: *the ~ wall of a building.* ⇨ interior(1). □ *n* [C] outside; outward appearance: *a good man with an unpleasant ~.*

ex·ter·mi·nate /ɪkˈstərməˌneit/ *vt* get rid of by killing; destroy completely.

ex·ter·mi·na·tion /ɪkˌstərməˈneiʃən/ *n* [C,U]

ex·ter·nal /ekˈstərnəl/ *adj* outside; situated on the outside; of or for the outside. □ *n* [C] (usually *pl*) (*formal*) external part or feature.

ex·ter·nally *adv*

ex·tinct /ɪkˈstɪŋkt/ *adj* **1** no longer active: *an ~ volcano.* **2** no longer in existence; dead: *an ~ species; become ~.*

ex·tinc·tion /ɪkˈstɪŋkʃən/ *n* [U] **1** making, being, becoming, extinct: *a people threatened by ~.* **2** act of extinguishing: *the ~ of a fire.*

ex·tin·guish /ɪkˈstɪŋwɪʃ/ *vt* **1** put out a light, fire. **2** destroy; make an end of: *His enthusiasm was ~ed by the lack of encouragement from his friends.*

ex·tin·guisher *n* [C] (kinds of) apparatus for discharging a jet of liquid chemicals for putting out a fire.

ex·tol /ɪkˈstoul/ *vt* (-ll-) praise highly: *~ him as a hero.*

ex·tort /ɪkˈstɔrt/ *vt* obtain by violence, threats, etc: *~ money from him.*

ex·tor·tion /ɪkˈstɔrʃən/ *n* [C,U]

ex·tor·tion·ate /ɪkˈstɔrʃənɪt/ *adj* **1** in the nature of extortion. **2** (of demands, prices) exorbitant.

ex·tor·tion·ate·ly *adv*

ex·tra /ˈekstrə/ *adj* additional; beyond what is usual, expected or arranged for: *~ pay for ~ work.* □ *adv* **1** more than usually: *~ fine quality.* **2** in addition: *$2.50, postage and handling ~.* □ *n* [C] **1** special issue of a newspaper. **2** additional thing; something for which an extra charge is made: *The bike costs $100; the pump and saddlebag are ~s.* **3** (in a motion picture, TV program, etc) person employed for a minor part, eg in a crowd scene.

ex·tract[1] /ɪkˈstrækt/ *vt* **1** take or get out (usually with effort): *have a tooth ~ed; ~ a bullet from a wound;* (*fig*) *~ money/information from a person,* who is unwilling to give it. **2** obtain (juices etc) by pressing, crushing, boiling, etc: *~ oil from olives.* **3** select and copy out words, examples, passages, etc (from a book).

ex·tract[2] /ˈekˌstrækt/ *n* **1** [C,U] that which has been extracted(2): *beef ~.* **2** [C] passage extracted(3): *~s from a long poem.*

ex·trac·tion /ɪkˈstrækʃən/ *n* **1** [U] extracting or being extracted(1): *the ~ion of a tooth.* **2** [U] descent: *Is he of French ~ion?* **3** [C] something extracted.

extra·cur·ricu·lar /ˌekstrəkəˈrɪkyələr/ *adj* outside the regular course of academic work or studies: *~ activities*, eg a dramatic society.

ex·tra·dite /ˈekstrəˌdait/ *vt* **1** give up, hand over (an alleged criminal) from one state or country to another for trial or punishment. **2** obtain (such a person) for trial.

ex·tra·di·tion /ˌekstrəˈdɪʃən/ *n* [U]

ex·traneous /ɪkˈstreiniəs/ *adj* **1** not related (to an object); coming from outside. **2** not belonging (to what is being dealt with); irrelevant.

extra·ordi·nary /ɪkˈstrɔrdəˌneri/ *adj* **1** beyond what is usual or ordinary; remarkable: *a man of ~ genius; ~ weather.* **2** (of officials) additional; specially employed: *envoy ~.*

ex·tra·ordi·nar·ily /ɪkˌstrɔrdəˈnerəli/ *adv*

ex·tra·ter·res·tri·al /ˌekstrətəˈrestriəl/ *adj* coming from or existing outside the earth or its atmosphere.

ex·trava·gance /ɪkˈstrævəgəns/ *n* **1** [U] being extravagant: *His ~ explains why he is always in debt.* **2** [C] extravagant statement, act, etc.

ex·trava·gant /ɪkˈstrævəgənt/ *adj* **1** (in the habit of) wasting (money, etc): *an ~ man; ~ tastes and habits.* **2** (of ideas, speech, behavior) going beyond what is reasonable; excessive: *~ praise/behavior.*

ex·trava·gant·ly *adv*

ex·treme /ɪkˈstrim/ *n* **1** either end of anything; (*pl*) qualities, etc as wide apart, as widely different, as possible: *the ~s of heat and cold. Love and hate are ~s.* **go/be driven to extremes**, to do more than is usually considered right or desirable. **2** highest degree: *annoying in the ~*, very annoying. □ *adj* **1** at the end(s); farthest possible: *in ~ old age*. **2** reaching the highest degree: *~ patience/kindness*. **3** (of persons, their ideas) going to great lengths in views or actions: *the ~ left*, (in politics) those who are farthest to the left.

ex·treme·ly *adv*

ex·trem·ist /ɪkˈstrimɪst, ɪkˈstremɪst/ *n* [C] person who holds extreme views (esp in politics).

ex·trem·ity /ɪkˈstreməti/ *n* [C] (*pl* -ies) **1** extreme point, end or limit. **2** (*pl*) hands and feet. **3** (*sing* only) extreme degree (of joy, misery, esp of misfortune): *an extremity of pain*. **4** extreme measures: *The retreating army was forced to the ~ of burning crops.*

ex·tri·cate /ˈekstrəˌkeit/ *vt* set (a person) free from a difficulty: *~ oneself from a trying situation.*

ex·tri·cable /ekˈstrɪkəbəl/ *adj* that can be freed.

ex·tri·ca·tion /ˌekstrəˈkeiʃən/ *n* [U]

ex·tro·vert /ˈekstrəˌvərt/ *n* [C] **1** person more interested in what goes on around him than in his own thoughts and feelings. **2** (*informal*) lively, cheerful person. ⇨ introvert.

ex·tro·ver·sion /ˌekstrəˈvərʒən/ *n* [U]

ex·uber·ant /ɪgˈzubərənt/ *adj* **1** growing vigorously; luxuriant: *plants with ~ foliage*. **2** full of life and vigor; high-spirited: *an ~ imagination.*

ex·uber·ance /-rəns/ *n* [U] state or quality of being exuberant: *The speaker's ~ won over an apathetic audience.*

ex·uber·ant·ly *adv*

ex·ude /ɪgˈzud/ *vt,vi* **1** (*formal*) (of drops of liquid) come or pass out slowly: *Sweat ~s through the pores*. **2** (*fig*) (of a person) give an impression of some attitude or quality: *The salesman ~s confidence.*

ex·ult /ɪgˈzəlt/ *vi* rejoice greatly: *~ at/in a success; ~* (= triumph) *over a defeated rival.*

ex·ult·ant /-ənt/ *adj* joyful; triumphant.

ex·ul·ta·tion /ˌegzəlˈteiʃən/ *n* [U] great joy (*at*); triumph (*over*).

eye[1] /ai/ *n* **1** organ of sight: *We see with our eyes.* ***an eye for an eye,*** punishment as severe as the injury suffered. ***in the eyes of the law,*** from the point of view of the law. ***under/before one's very eyes,*** **(a)** in one's presence, in front of one. **(b)** with no attempt at concealment. ***up to one's eyes in,*** very busy with (work, etc). ***with an eye to,*** with a view to, hoping for. ***be in the public eye,*** be often seen in public. ***close/shut one's eyes to,*** refuse to see or take notice of. ***have an eye for,*** be a good judge of. ***keep an eye on,*** (*liter, fig*) keep a watch on. ***keep one's eyes open/peeled (for),*** be alert. ***make eyes at,*** flirt with. ***open sb's eyes to,*** cause him to realize. ***see eye to eye (with),*** agree entirely (with), have identical views. ***set/lay eyes on,*** meet, see: *I hope I shall never set eyes on her again.* **2** thing like an eye: *the eye of a needle*, the hole for the thread; *a hook and eye*, fastening with a hook and loop for a dress; *the eye of a potato*, pit from which a new bud develops. ⇨ illus at vegetable. **3** center: *the eye of a hurricane.* **4** (*sl*) (also **private eye**) private detective.

ˈeye·ball *n* [C] the eye within the lids and socket. ***eyeball to eyeball,*** (*informal*) face to face. □ *vt* (*sl*) eye².

ˈeye·brow *n* [C] arch of hair above the eye. ***raise one's eyebrows,*** express surprise, doubt, etc. ⇨ illus at head.

ˈeye·lash *n* [C] hair, row of hairs, on the edge of the eyelid.

ˈeye·lid *n* [C] upper or lower skin covering of the eye when blinking.

ˈeye-opener *n* circumstance, etc (often surprising) that makes one realize, understand something.

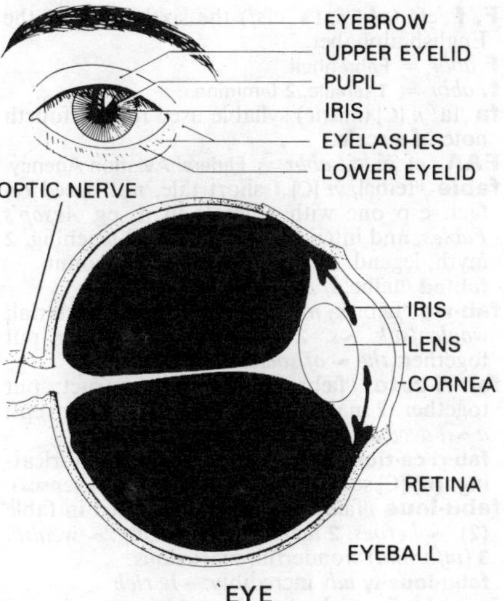

EYE

ˈeye·sight *n* [U] power, faculty, of seeing: *to have good/poor eyesight.*

ˈeye socket *n* [U] opening in the skull for the eye. ⇨ illus at skeleton.

ˈeye·sore *n* something unpleasing to look at.

ˈeye·strain *n* [U] tired or strained condition of the eyes (as caused, for example, by reading very small print).

ˈeye·tooth *n* [C] canine tooth. ⇨ illus at mouth.

ˈeye·witness *n* [C] person who can report what he has himself seen: *an eyewitness account of a crime.*

eye² /ai/ *vt* observe, watch: *He eyed me with suspicion. They were eyeing us jealously.*

-eyed /aid/ *adj* (used in compounds) having the type or number of eyes mentioned: *one-eyed; blue-eyed.*

eye·glass /ˈaiˌglæs/ *n* [C] **1** lens worn to improve faulty eyesight. **2** (*pl*) pair of lenses in a frame, that is used to correct poor eyesight; glasses; spectacles.

eye·hole /ˈaiˌhoul/ *n* [C] **1** eye socket. ⇨ eye¹. **2** peephole. **3** eyelet.

eye·let /ˈailɪt/ *n* [C] small hole in cloth, etc for a rope, etc to go through; metal ring round such a hole, to strengthen it.

f

F, f /ef/ (*pl* F's, f's /efs/) the sixth letter of the English alphabet.

F *abbr* = Fahrenheit.

f. *abbr* = **1** female. **2** feminine.

fa /fa/ *n* [C] (*music*) syllable used for the fourth note of a scale.

FAA /ˌef ˌei ˈei/ *abbr* = Federal Aviation Agency.

fable /ˈfeibəl/ *n* [C] **1** short tale, not based on fact, esp one with animals in it, eg *Aesop's Fables*, and intended to give moral teaching. **2** myth; legend. **3** false statement or account.

fabled /ˈfeibəld/ *adj* legendary.

fab·ric /ˈfæbrɪk/ *n* [C,U] **1** cloth; textile material; *woolen/silk ~s*. **2** structure; something put together: *the ~ of society*.

fab·ri·cate /ˈfæbrəˌkeit/ *vt* **1** construct; put together. **2** make up (something false); invent: *a ~d account of adventures*.

fab·ri·ca·tion /ˌfæbrəˈkeiʃən/ *n* **(a)** [U] fabricating. **(b)** [C] something fabricated (both senses).

fabu·lous /ˈfæbyələs/ *adj* **1** celebrated in fable (2): *~ heroes*. **2** incredible; amazing: *~ wealth*. **3** (*informal*) wonderful; marvelous.

fabu·lous·ly *adv* incredibly: *~ly rich*.

fa·cade, fa·çade /fəˈsad/ *n* [C] **1** front or face of a building (toward a street or open place). **2** (*fig*) false appearance: *a ~ of indifference*.

face[1] /feis/ *n* [C] **1** the front part of the head (eyes, nose, mouth, cheeks, chin): *He fell on his ~*. ***face to face,*** (of persons) in each other's presence: *The two politicians were brought ~ to ~ in a TV interview*. ***in one's face,*** **(a)** straight against: *The sun was shining in our ~s*. **(b)** with no attempt at concealment: *She'll only laugh in your ~*. ***to one's face,*** openly; boldly: *I'll tell him so to his ~*, I'm not afraid to tell him. ***fly in the face of sth,*** openly defy, disregard. ***show one's face,*** appear, let oneself be seen: *How can you show your ~ here after the way you behaved last time?* **2** look; expression: *a sad ~; smiling ~s*. ***make a face,*** twist the face, esp to express dislike: *made a ~ at the bitter taste*. ***on the face of it,*** judging by appearances: *On the ~ of it, his story seems unconvincing*. ***keep a straight face,*** hide one's amusement (by not smiling or laughing). ***lose/save face,*** suffer/avoid suffering loss of credit or reputation. ***put a good/bold face on sth,*** make it look well; show courage in dealing with it. **3** surface; facade (of a building); front: *the ~ of a clock. He laid the cards ~ down on the table. The team climbed the north ~ of the mountain*.

ˈface card, king, queen, or jack.

ˈface·cloth *n* [C] (esp) small square towel for washing the face and hands.

face·less *adj* (*fig*) unknown; unidentified: *the ~less men who have power in commerce and industry*.

ˈface·lift *n* [C] operation to smooth out wrinkles and make the face look younger.

ˈface powder, cosmetic powder for the face.

face[2] /feis/ *vt,vi* **1** have or turn the face to, or in a certain direction; be opposite to: *Turn round and ~ me. Who's the man facing us?* **2** meet confidently or defiantly: *~ the enemy; ~ dangers*. ***face the music,*** meet a danger, difficulty. **3** recognize the existence of: *~ facts*, be realistic. ***face up to (sth),*** recognize and deal with, honestly and bravely: *Face up to the fact that you are no longer young*. **4** present itself to: *the problem that ~s us*. **5** cover with a layer of different material: *~ a wall with concrete*.

facet /ˈfæsɪt/ *n* [C] **1** one of the many sides of a cut stone or jewel. **2** one view, aspect, eg of a problem.

fac·eted /ˈfæsɪtɪd/ *adj* having facets (1, 2): *a multiˈ~ problem*, one with many aspects or points of view.

fa·cetious /fəˈsiʃəs/ *adj* (intended to be, trying to be) humorous; fond of, marked by, joking: *a ~ remark/young man*.

fa·cetious·ly *adv*

fa·cetious·ness /-nɪs/ *n* [U]

fa·cial /ˈfeiʃəl/ *adj* of or for the face: *a ~ massage*. □ *n* [C] facial massage or treatment.

facile /ˈfæsəl/ *adj* **1** easily done or obtained: *a ~ victory*. **2** (of a person) able to do things easily. **3** made or done easily but sometimes without enough thought or care: *a ~ remark/decision*.

fa·cili·tate /fəˈsɪləˌteit/ *vt* make easy; lessen the difficulty of: *Modern inventions have ~d housework*.

fa·cil·ity /fəˈsɪləti/ *n* (*pl* -ies) **1** [U] quality which makes learning or doing things easy or simple; skill: *have great ~ in learning languages*. **2** (*pl*) aids, circumstances, which make it easy to do things: *facilities for travel*, eg buses, trains, air services.

fac·ing /ˈfeisɪŋ/ *n* **1** coating of different material, eg on a wall. **2** (*pl*) material of a different color on a military garment, eg on the cuffs, collar. ⇨ face[2] (5).

fac·sim·ile /fækˈsɪməli/ *n* [C] exact copy or reproduction of writing, printing, a picture, etc.

fact /fækt/ *n* **1** [C] something that has happened or been done. ***accessory after/before the fact,*** ⇨ accessory. **2** [C] something known to be true or accepted as true: *No one can deny the ~*

that fire burns. **3** (*sing* without *a*) reality; what is true; what exists: *It is important to distinguish ~ from fiction.* ***in fact; as a matter of fact; in point of fact,*** really: *I think so; in ~, I'm certain.*

fac·tion /ˈfækʃən/ *n* **1** [C] group of persons within a political party, social group, etc who act together: *The party split into petty ~s.* **2** [U] quarreling among such groups; party strife.

fac·tious /ˈfækʃəs/ *adj* of, caused by, inclined to faction(2): *a factious spirit.*

fac·tor /ˈfæktər/ *n* [C] **1** whole number (except 1) by which a larger number can be divided exactly: *2, 3, 4 and 6 are ~s of 12.* **2** fact, circumstance, etc helping to bring about a result: *evolutionary ~s*, environmental influences, etc; *an unknown ~*, something unknown, likely to influence a result. **3** agent; person or organization, eg a bank, acting for another in a business transaction.

fac·tory /ˈfækt(ə)ri/ *n* [C] (*pl* -ies) building(s) where goods are made (esp by machinery); workshop: *~ workers.*

fac·tual /ˈfæktʃuəl/ *adj* of, based on, fact.

fac·ulty /ˈfækəlti/ *n* (*pl* -ies) [C] **1** ability; power to do, learn, etc: *the mental faculties*, reason; *have a great ~ for learning languages.* **2** (in a university) department or grouping of related departments: *the Faculty of Law/Science.* **3** all the teachers, lecturers, professors, etc in a school, college, etc: *a member of the ~.*

fad /fæd/ *n* [C] fashion, interest, enthusiasm, unlikely to last: *Will Tom continue to collect foreign stamps or is it only a passing fad?*

fade /feid/ *vt,vi* **1** (cause to) lose color, freshness or vigor: *The strong sunlight had ~d the curtains. Flowers soon ~ when cut.* **2** go slowly out of view, hearing or the memory: *Daylight ~d away. His hopes ~d.* **3** (in filming, broadcasting) (cause to) decrease or increase gradually in strength: *~ one scene into another; ~ a conversation out/in.*

faeces *n pl* = feces.

fag[1] /fæg/ *n* [C] (*sl*) male homosexual.

fag[2] /fæg/ *vt* (-gg-) (of work) make very tired: *I'm fagged out by all the work.*

fag·ot, fag·got /ˈfægət/ *n* [C] bundle of sticks or twigs tied together for burning as fuel.

Fahr·en·heit /ˈfærənˌhait/ *adj* in or of the temperature scale that has 32° as the freezing point and 212° as the boiling point of water.

fail[1] /ˈfeiəl/ *n* (only in) ***without fail,*** for certain, no matter what difficulties, etc there may be: *I'll be there at two o'clock without ~.*

fail[2] /ˈfeiəl/ *vi,vt* (*pres p* ~ing /ˈfeilɪŋ/) **1** be unsuccessful: *~ (in) an examination; ~ to pass an examination. All our plans/attempts ~ed.* **2** grade (a student) as failing in a course, an examination, etc: *Students not taking the final exam will be ~ed.* **3** be not enough; come to an end while still needed or expected: *The crops ~ed because of drought. Words ~ me*, I cannot find words (to describe my feelings, etc). **4** (of health, eyesight, etc) become weak: *His eyesight is ~ing.* **5** omit; neglect: *He never ~s to write* (= always writes) *to his mother every week.* **6** become bankrupt: *Several of the biggest banks ~ed during the depression.*

fail·ing[1] /ˈfeilɪŋ/ *n* [C] weakness or fault (of character): *We all have our little ~s.*

fail·ing[2] /ˈfeilɪŋ/ *prep* in the absence of: *~ this*, if this does not happen; *~ an answer*, if no answer is received.

fail·ure /ˈfeiəlyər/ *n* **1** [U] lack of success: *All his efforts ended in ~*, were unsuccessful. **2** [C] instance of failing; person, attempt, or thing that fails: *Success came after many ~s.* **3(a)** [U] state of not being adequate. **(b)** [C] instance of this: *ˈheart ~. Crop ~ often results in famine.* **4** [C] bankruptcy: *many bank ~s.* **5** [C,U] neglect, omission, inability: *His ~ to help us was disappointing.*

faint[1] /feint/ *adj* (-er, -est) **1** (of things known by the senses) weak; indistinct; not clear: *The sounds of the music grew ~er in the distance. There was a ~ smell of burning.* **2** (of things in the mind) weak; vague: *There is a ~ hope that she may be cured.* **3** (of the body's movements and functions) weak; failing: *His breathing became ~.* **4** (of persons) likely to lose consciousness: *She looks/feels ~.* **5** (of persons) weak, exhausted: *~ with hunger and cold.* **6** (of actions, etc) unlikely to have much effect: *make a ~ attempt to do something.*

ˌfaint-ˈhearted *adj* lacking in courage.

faint·ly *adv*

faint[2] /feint/ *vi* lose consciousness (because of loss of blood, the heat, shock, etc): *He ~ed from hunger.* □ *n* [C] act, state, of fainting: *She keeled over in a ~.*

fair[1] /fer/ *adj* (-er, -est) **1** just; acting in a just and honorable manner; in accordance with justice or the rules (of a game, etc): *Everyone must have a ~ share.* ***give sb/get a fair hearing,*** an opportunity to defend his conduct, etc, eg in a law court. ***fair play,*** justice. **2** average; passable: *a ~ chance of success.* **3** (of the weather) good; dry and fine: *hoping for ~ weather.* **4** (of the skin, hair) pale; light in color; blond: *a ˈ~-haired girl; a ~ complexion.* **5** (*old use*) beautiful: *the ~ sex*, women.

fair[2] /fer/ *adv* in a fair(1) manner: *play ~.* ***fair enough,*** (*informal*) (response used to indicate that a person has acted reasonably, made a reasonable suggestion, etc.)

fair[3] /fer/ *n* [C] **1** exhibition (esp of livestock, farm products, etc) held periodically in a particular place, often with entertainment, sideshows, etc: *the state/county ~.* **2** large-scale exhibition of commercial and industrial goods for sale: *a trade ~.* **3** entertainment and sale, usually for charity: *a church ~.*

ˈfair·ground *n* [C] open space for fairs(1).

fair·ly /ˈferli/ *adv* **1** justly; honestly: *treat him ~.* **2** (*informal*) utterly; completely: *He was ~ beside himself with rage.* **3** moderately: *This is a ~ easy book.*

fair·way /ˈferˌwei/ *n* [C] **1** navigable channel for ships. **2** part of a golf course, between a tee and a green, free from hazards.

fairy /ˈferi/ *n* [C] (*pl* -ies) small imaginary being with magical powers, able to help or harm human beings.

ˈfairy·land *n* **(a)** home of fairies. **(b)** enchanted place.

ˈ**fairy tale, (a)** tale about fairies. **(b)** obviously untrue account.

faith /feiθ/ *n* **1** [U] trust; unquestioning confidence: *have/put one's ~ in God. I haven't much ~ in this medicine.* **2** [U] belief in divine truth without proof. **3** [C] particular religion: *the Christian, Jewish and Muslim ~s.* **4** loyalty; faithfulness, esp in keeping promises. ***in bad/good faith,*** with/without the intention of deceiving. ***keep/break faith with sb,*** be loyal/disloyal.

ˈ**faith healing,** (belief in) healing (of disease, etc) by prayer, etc.

faith·ful /ˈfeiθfəl/ *adj* **1** loyal and true: *a ~ friend; ~ to one's promise.* **2** true to the facts: *a ~ copy/description/account.* **3 the faithful,** (*pl*) the true believers, esp of Islam and Christianity.

faith·fully *adv*

faith·ful·ness /-nɪs/ *n* [U]

faith·less /ˈfeiθlɪs/ *adj* false; disloyal.

faith·less·ly *adv*

fake /feik/ *n* [C] **1** story, work of art, etc that is made to deceive; fraud. **2** person who tries to deceive by claiming falsely to be or have something. □ *vt* **1** make (eg a work of art, a story) in order to deceive: *~ an oil painting by Rembrandt.* **2** pretend: *~d a headache to get out of work early.* ***fake it,*** (*informal*) bluff.

fakir /fəˈkɪr/ *n* [C] Moslem or Hindu holy man.

fal·con /ˈfælkən/ *n* [C] small hawk, esp one trained to hunt and kill other birds and small animals.

fal·con·ry *n* [U] hunting with, art of training, falcons.

fall[1] /fɔl/ *n* [C] **1** act of falling: *a ~ from a horse; a ~ in (the) temperature; a ~ in prices.* **2(a)** amount of rain that falls. **(b)** distance by which something falls or comes down: *The ~ of the river here is six feet.* **3** (often *pl*) place where a river falls over cliffs, etc: *Niagara Falls.* **4** autumn: *in the ~ of 1970.*

fall[2] /fɔl/ *vi,vt* (*pt* fell /fel/, *pp* ~en /ˈfɔlən/) **1** come or go down freely (by force of weight, loss of balance, etc): *He fell into the water. The rain was ~ing steadily.* ***fall on one's feet,*** (*fig*) be fortunate; get out of a difficulty successfully. ***fall short of,*** fail to equal; be inferior to: *Your work ~s short of my expectations.* **2** no longer stand; come to the ground; collapse; be overthrown: *He fell over and broke his left leg. He fell on his knees* (= knelt down) *and begged for mercy.* ***fall flat,*** (*fig*) fail to have the intended effect: *His best jokes all fell flat,* did not amuse his listeners. **3** hang down: *Her hair fell over her shoulders.* **4** come or go to a lower level or point; become lower or less: *The barometer is ~ing. The temperature fell rapidly.* **5** become: *His horse fell lame. He fell silent. The old man fell asleep.* ***fall in love (with),*** become filled with love (for): *He fell in love with an actress. I've ~en in love with your beautiful house.* **6** descend; come as if by falling: *Darkness fell upon the scene,* it became dark. *Not a word fell from his lips,* he didn't speak at all. **7** sin; give way to doing wrong: *Eve tempted Adam and he fell.* **8** be overcome or defeated; (of a city, fort, etc) be captured: *The city has ~en to the enemy.* **9** be killed or wounded: *fell in battle.* **10 *fall on,*** take a direction or position: *A shadow fell on the wall. His eye fell on* (= He suddenly saw) *a curious object. In "adult" the stress may ~ on either the first or the second syllable.* **11 *fall on,*** come to by chance, design, or right: *All the blame fell on me.* **12** (of land) slope: *The ground ~s toward the river.* **13** occur, have as date: *Easter ~s early next year.* **14** separate or divide naturally: *The samples ~ into three groups.* **15** (special uses with *adverbial particles* and *prepositions*):

fall away, **(a)** desert: *His supporters began to ~ away.* **(b)** = fall off.

fall back, move or turn back: *Our attack was so successful that the enemy fell back.* ***fall back on,*** turn to for support: *It's always useful to have savings to ~ back on.*

fall behind (with), fail to keep up with: *He always ~s behind when we're going uphill. Don't ~ behind with your rent, or you'll be evicted.*

fall for, (*informal*) **(a)** fall in love with: *He ~s for every pretty face he sees.* **(b)** be deceived by: *He fell for one of their schemes and lost all his money.*

fall in, **(a)** collapse; give way: *The roof fell in.* **(b)** (*mil*) take a place in formation: *The sergeant ordered the men to ~ in.* ***fall in with,*** **(a)** happen to meet or join: *He fell in with bad company.* **(b)** agree to: *He fell in with my plans.*

fall into line (with), agree to (what others are doing or wish to do).

fall off, become smaller, fewer or less: *Attendance at church has ~en off this summer.*

fall on/upon, attack; assault (the enemy).

fall out, (*mil*) leave one's place in a formation.

fall out (with), quarrel (with): *He has ~en out with the girl he was going to marry.*

fall through, fail; come to nothing: *His scheme fell through.*

fall to, begin to eat, fight, attack, etc: *They fell to with a good appetite.*

fall under, be classifiable under: *The results ~ under three heads.*

ˈ**fall·out** *n* [U] radioactive dust in the atmosphere, after a nuclear explosion.

fal·lacy /ˈfæləsi/ *n* (*pl* -ies) **1** [C] false or mistaken belief. **2** [U] false reasoning; error: *a statement based on ~.*

fal·lacious /fəˈleiʃəs/ *adj* misleading; based on error.

fallen *pp* of fall[2].

fal·lible /ˈfæləbəl/ *adj* liable to error.

fal·li·bil·ity /ˌfæləˈbɪləti/ *n* [U] (state of) being fallible.

Fal·lo·pian tube /fəˌloupiən ˈtub/ *n* either of a pair of tubes in a female through which the egg passes from the ovary to the uterus.

fal·low /ˈfælou/ *adj, n* [U] (land) plowed but not sown or planted: *allow land to lie ~.*

fal·low deer /ˈfælouˌdɪr/ *n* [C] (*pl* unchanged) small deer with a reddish-yellow coat with, in the summer, white spots.

false /fɔls/ *adj* **1** wrong; incorrect: *a ~ alarm.* **2** deceitful; lying: *give a ~ impression; give ~ witness,* tell lies or deceive (eg in a law court). **3** not genuine; artificial: *~ teeth.*

false·ly *adv*
false·ness /-nɪs/ *n* [U]
false·hood /ˈfɔlsˌhʊd/ *n* **1** [C] = lie (the usual word); untrue statement: *How can you utter such ~s?* **2** [U] telling lies; lying: *guilty of ~.*
fal·setto /fɔlˈsetou/ *n* [C] (*pl* ~s) unnaturally high-pitched voice in men.
falsies /ˈfɔlsiz/ *n pl* (*sl*) woman's breast pads, worn with a brassiere to make the breasts appear larger.
fal·sify /ˈfɔlsəˌfai/ *vt* (*pt,pp* -ied) **1** make false: *~ records/accounts.* **2** misrepresent: *~ an issue.*
falsi·fi·ca·tion /ˌfɔlsəfəˈkeiʃən/ *n* [C,U]
fals·ity /ˈfɔlsəti/ *n* (*pl* -ies) **1** [U] state of being false. **2** [C] false act, statement, etc.
fal·ter /ˈfɔltər/ *vi,vt* **1** move, walk or act in an uncertain or hesitating manner, from either weakness or fear. **2** (of the voice) waver; (of a person) speak in a hesitating way or with a broken voice: *His voice ~ed as he tried to speak.*
fal·ter·ing·ly *adv*
fame /feim/ *n* [U] **1** (condition of) being known or talked about by all. **2** (esp good) reputation: *His ~ as a poet did not come until after his death.*
famed *adj* famous: *~d for their courage.*
fa·mil·iar /fəˈmɪlyər/ *adj* **1** ***familiar with,*** having a good knowledge of: *I am not very ~ with European history.* **2** ***familiar to,*** well known to: *facts that are ~ to everyone.* **3** common; usual; often seen or heard: *the ~ voices of one's friends.* **4** close; personal; intimate: *Are you on ~ terms with Mr. Green?* **5** forward; more friendly than is proper: *He made himself much too ~ with my wife.* □ *n* [C] intimate friend.
fa·mil·iar·ly *adv*
fa·mili·ar·ity /fəˌmɪlˈyærəti/ *n* (*pl* -ies) **1** [U] (the state of) being familiar: *His ~ with the languages used in Nigeria surprised me. You should not treat her with such ~.* ⇨ familiar(4,5). **2** (*pl*) instance of familiar behavior: *She dislikes such familiarities as the use of her first name by men she has only just met.*
fa·mil·iar·ize /fəˈmɪlyəˌraiz/ *vt* **1** make well acquainted (with): *~ oneself with the rules of a game.* **2** make well known: *Television has ~d the word "newscast."*
fam·ily /ˈfæm(ə)li/ *n* (*pl* -ies) **1** [C] **(a)** parents and their children. (*Note:* used with a *sing verb* when *family* is a *collective noun*: *Almost every ~ in town has a man in the army,* and used with a *pl verb* when *family* means members of a family: *My ~ are early risers.*) **(b)** (as a *collective noun*) children: *He has a large ~.* **2** [C] all of the people in a household. **3** [C] **(a)** all those persons descended from a common ancestor: *families that have been in the US for two hundred years.* **(b)** all one's relatives. **4** [U] famous or distinguished ancestry: *a man of good ~.* **5** [C] (*biol*) group of related plants or animals: *animals of the cat ~,* eg lions and tigers. **6** (as an *adjective*) of or for a family: *a ~ likeness; a ~ man,* one who is fond of home life with his family.
ˈfamily name, surname.
ˌfamily ˈplanning, (use of one of the means of birth control for) planning the number of children, intervals between births, etc in a family.
ˌfamily ˈtree, genealogical tree or chart.
fam·ine /ˈfæmɪn/ *n* **1** [U] extreme scarcity (esp of food) in a region: *Parts of India have often suffered from ~.* **2** [C] particular occasion when there is such a shortage: *a water/coal ~.*
fam·ish /ˈfæmɪʃ/ *vi,vt* **1** suffer from extreme hunger: *They were ~ing for food.* **2** cause (a person) to suffer from hunger: *The child looked half ~ed.* (*Note:* usually passive.)
fa·mous /ˈfeiməs/ *adj* known widely; having fame; celebrated: *a ~ scientist.*
fa·mous·ly *adv* excellently: *getting on ~ly.*
fan[1] /fæn/ *n* [C] **1** object (waved in the hand, or operated mechanically, eg by an electric motor) for making a breeze of air (eg to cool a room). **2** something that is or can be spread out flat, eg the tail of a peacock.
ˈfan belt, rubber belt used to turn the cooling fan of an engine.
ˈfan·light *n* fan-shaped window over a door.
fan[2] /fæn/ *vt,vi* (-nn-) **1** move a current of air with a fan: *fan oneself.* **2** blow on (as if) with a fan: *The breeze fanned our faces.* **3** open or spread out like a fan: *The troops fanned out across the fields.*
fan[3] /fæn/ *n* [C] (*informal*) fanatical supporter or admirer: *ˈfootball fans.*
ˈfan mail, letters from fans, eg to a pop singer.
fa·natic /fəˈnætɪk/ *n* [C] person filled with excessive enthusiasm: *chess ~s.* □ *adj* (also **fa·nati·cal** /-kəl/) excessively enthusiastic: *~(al) beliefs.*
fa·nati·cally /-kli/ *adv*
fa·nati·cism /-ˌsɪzəm/ *n* **(a)** [U] extreme, unreasoning enthusiasm. **(b)** [C] instance of this.
fan·cier /ˈfænsiər/ *n* [C] person with special knowledge of and love for some plant, animal, etc: *a ˈrose ~.*
fan·ci·ful /ˈfænsɪfəl/ *adj* **1** of based on, or using fancy instead of reason and experience: *a ~ writer.* **2** curiously designed: *~ drawings.*
fan·ci·fully /-fli/ *adv*
fancy[1] /ˈfænsi/ *n* (*pl* -ies) **1** [U] power of creating images in the mind. **2** [C] something supposed; unfounded opinion or belief: *It may be just a ~ of mine, but I believe the winters are getting colder.* **3** [C] fondness, liking, desire (*for*): *a ~ for some wine with my dinner.* ***take a fancy to,*** become fond of: *The children have taken quite a ~ to you.*
ˌfancy-ˈfree *adj* not committed to anything or anyone, esp not in love.
fancy[2] /ˈfænsi/ *adj* (-ier, -iest) **1** highly decorated; made to please the eye: *~ cakes.* **2** not plain or ordinary: *~ dress,* ie unusual costume, often historical or exotic, as worn at parties. **3** requiring skill: *~ diving.* **4** superior in quality: *"Fancy Crab"* (on a label, etc).
fancy[3] /ˈfænsi/ *vt* (*pt,pp* -ied) **1** picture in the mind; imagine: *Can you ~ me as a mother?* **2** think or believe without good reason: *I ~ (that) he won't come.* **3** have a fancy(3) for: *What do you ~ for your dinner?*
fan·fare /ˈfænˌfær/ *n* **1** [C] flourish of trumpets or bugles. **2** [U] showy publicity for an event, activity, etc.
fang /fæŋ/ *n* [C] **1** long, sharp tooth (esp of dogs and wolves). **2** snake's poison tooth.

fanny /ˈfæni/ *n* [C] (*pl* -ies) (*sl*) buttocks.
fan·tas·tic /fænˈtæstɪk/ *adj* **1** wild and strange: ~ *dreams/shapes/fashions*. **2** extremely fanciful; extravagant: ~ *plans/ideas*. **3** (*informal*) marvelous; wonderful: *She's a really ~ girl!*
fan·tas·ti·cally /-kli/ *adv*
fan·tasy /ˈfæntəsi/ *n* (*pl* -ies) **1** [U] fancy(1); imagination, esp when extravagant. **2** [C] wild or strange product of the imagination.
far¹ /far/ *adj* (farther, farthest, further, furthest). **1** (usually *liter*) distant: *a far country*. ***a far cry,*** ⇨ cry² (1). **2** (= farther) more remote: *on the far bank of the river*.
the ˌFar ˈEast, countries of Eastern and Southeastern Asia.
the ˌFar ˈWest, part of the US that lies between the Rocky Mountains and the Pacific Ocean.
far² /far/ *adv* (farther, farthest, further, furthest). **1** (indicating distance in space or time): *How far did you go? We didn't go far*. (*Note:* usually used in the *negative* and *interrogative*.) **2** (used with other *adverbs* and *prepositions*) to an advanced point, degree, etc: *far beyond the bridge/above the clouds/into the night/back in history*. ***by far,*** by a great deal: *He is by far the best writer of our time*. ***far and away,*** = by far. ***few and far between,*** ⇨ between¹. ***far from,*** not at all: *Your work is far from (being) satisfactory. Far from* (= Instead of) *admiring his paintings, I dislike them intensely*. ***go far,*** **(a)** (of persons) be successful; do much: *He's clever and intelligent, and will go far*. **(b)** (of money) buy goods, services, etc: *A dollar does not go ~ nowadays*. ***go/carry sth too far,*** go beyond the limits of what is considered reasonable: *You've gone too far this time!* ***far and near/wide,*** everywhere: *They searched far and wide for the missing child*. ***so far,*** until now: *So far the work has been easy*. ***So far, so good,*** up to now everything has gone well. ***as/so far as,*** **(a)** to the place mentioned: *He walked as far as the post office*. **(b)** the same distance: *We didn't go as/so far as the others*. **(c)** to the extent that: *So far as I know he will be away for three months*. **3** (by) much; considerably; to a great extent: *It fell far short of our expectations*.
ˈfar·away *adj* **(a)** distant, remote: *faraway places/times*. **(b)** (of a look in a person's eyes) dreamy: *a faraway look in his eyes*.
ˌfar-ˈfetched *adj* (of a comparison, an idea, etc) forced; unnatural.
ˈfar-flung *adj* widely spread or extended.
ˌfar ˈgone, very ill, mad, drunk, etc.
ˌfar-ˈreaching *adj* having a wide influence on application: *far-reaching proposals*.
ˈfar·sighted *adj* **(a)** able to see distant objects more clearly than near objects. **(b)** (*fig*) having good judgment of future needs, etc. ⇨ near-sighted, short-sighted.
far-sight·ed·ness /-nɪs/ *n* [U]
farce /fars/ *n* **1** [C] play for the theater, full of ridiculous situations intended to make people laugh. **2** [U] kind of humor found in this style of drama. **3** [C] series of actual events like a farce; ridiculous or absurd action: *The trial was a ~*.
far·ci·cal /ˈfarsɪkəl/ *adj*
far·ci·cally /-kli/ *adv*

fare¹ /fær/ *n* [C] **1** money charged for a journey by bus, ship, taxi, etc. **2** passenger in a hired vehicle: *The taxi driver had only six ~s all day*.
fare² /fær/ *n* [U] food provided at table: *simple/homely ~*.
fare³ /fær/ *vi* progress; get on: *How did you ~ during your journey?*
fare·well /ˌfærˈwel/ *int* good-bye. □ *n* [C] leave-taking: *make one's ~s;* (as an *adjective*) *a ~ speech*.
farm¹ /farm/ *n* [C] area of land and buildings for growing crops, raising animals, etc: *working on the ~*.
ˈfarm·hand *n* [C] worker on a farm.
ˈfarm·house *n* [C] dwelling house on a farm.
ˈfarm·yard *n* [C] space enclosed by farm buildings (shed, barns, etc).
farm² /farm/ *vt,vi* **1** use (land) for growing crops, raising animals, etc: *He ~s 200 acres*. **2** ***farm out,*** send work out to be done by others.
farmer *n* [C] man who owns or manages a farm.
far·ther /ˈfarðər/ *adv* (*comparative* of *far*): *We can't go any ~ without a rest. They went ~ into the forest*. (*Note:* usually refers to physical distance although *further* is now often used.) □ *adj* more distant: *on the ~ bank of the river*.
far·thest /ˈfarðəst/ *adj* (*superlative* of *far*) most distant: *Which state is ~ north?* □ *adv* to or at the greatest distance. (*Note:* ⇨ farther.)
fas·ci·nate /ˈfæsəˌneit/ *vt* **1** charm or attract greatly: *The children were ~d by the exhibition*. **2** take away the power to move through fear, etc.
fas·ci·nat·ing *adj* having strong charm or attraction: *a fascinating smile/idea/girl*.
fas·ci·nat·ing·ly *adv*
fas·ci·na·tion /ˌfæsəˈneiʃən/ *n* [C,U]
fas·cism, Fas·cism /ˈfæˌʃɪzəm/ *n* [U] philosophy, movement, or government (as that in Italy 1922-1943) that advocates militarism, nationalism and a dictatorial form of government with the power to control economic and social matters and to suppress the opposition.
fas·cist, Fas·cist /ˈfæʃɪst/ *n* [C] supporter of fascism. □ *adj* of fascism; extreme right-wing; reactionary.
fashion /ˈfæʃən/ *n* **1** (*sing* with *a, an* or *the*) manner of doing or making something: *He was behaving in a strange ~*. ***after a fashion,*** somehow or other, but not particularly well: *He can speak and write English, after a ~*. **2** [C,U] custom, style, etc which is most admired and imitated in a particular period or place: *dressed in the latest ~*. ***in fashion,*** fashionable. ***come into/go out of fashion,*** become/no longer be in fashion: *When did miniskirts come into/go out of ~?* □ *vt* give form or shape to: *~ a lump of clay into a bowl*.
fashion·able /ˈfæʃənəbəl/ *adj* **1** following the fashion(2). **2** used by, of, people who follow the current fashions or trends: *a ~ summer resort*.
fashion·ably /-əbli/ *adv*
fast¹ /fæst/ *adj* (-er, -est) **1** firmly fixed; not easily moved: *Make the boat ~*, Make it secure. ***hard and fast rules,*** rigid rules. **2** steady; loyal. **3** (of colors) unfading. □ *adv* firmly, securely, tightly: *She was ~ asleep*, in a deep sleep.

fast[2] /fæst/ *adj* (-er, -est) **1** quick; rapid: *a ~ train/horse.* **2** (of a watch or clock) showing time later than the true time: *My watch is five minutes ~,* eg showing 2:05 at 2:00. **3** (of a surface) promoting quick motion: *a ~ track.* **4** (of photographic film) suitable for very brief exposures. **5** wild; loose in morals: *went around with a ~ crowd.* ***play fast and loose with,*** be tricky and unreliable: *play ~ and loose with a girl's affections.* ***pull a ˈfast one (on sb),*** (*sl*) trick, deceive.

fast[3] /fæst/ *adv* quickly: *Don't speak so ~.*

fast[4] /fæst/ *vi* go without food, or without certain kinds of food, esp as a religious duty: *days devoted to ~ing,* eg in Lent. □ *n* [C] (period of) going without food: *a ~ of three days.*

fas·ten /ˈfæsən/ *vt,vi* **1** fix firmly; tie or join together: *Have you ~ed all the doors and windows?* **2** become fast[1] (1) or secured: *This dress ~s down the back,* has buttons, etc down the back. **3** direct one's looks, thoughts, attention, etc on: *He ~ed his eyes on/upon me.* **4** ***fasten (up)on,*** seize; take hold of: *He ~ed (up)on the idea.*

fas·tener *n* [C] thing that fastens things together: *a paper ~er; a ˈsnap ~er.*

fas·ten·ing *n* [C] thing that fastens, eg a bolt.

fas·tid·ious /fæˈstɪdiəs/ *adj* hard to please; quick to find fault: *He is ~ about his food.*

fa·stid·ious·ly *adv*

fast·ness /ˈfæstnɪs/ *n* [U] the quality of being fast[1] (3): *We guarantee the ~ of these dyes.*

fat[1] /fæt/ *adj* (-tter, -ttest) **1** plump; fleshy: *a fat man.* **2** containing fat; greasy: *fat meat.* **3** thick; well filled: *a fat wallet,* one stuffed with bills. **4** rich, fertile: *fat lands.*

ˌfat ˈcat, (*sl*) financier, esp one who uses his money to obtain power and special privileges.

ˈfat·head *n* (*informal*) dull, stupid person.

fat·ness /-nɪs/ *n* [U]

fat[2] /fæt/ *n* [C,U] **1** (kinds of) white or yellow substance, oily or greasy, found in animal bodies. **2** oily substance in seeds, etc. **3** this substance purified for cooking purposes: *Fried potatoes are cooked in deep fat.* ***live on/off the fat of the land,*** have the best of everything.

fa·tal /ˈfeitəl/ *adj* **1** causing, ending in, death or disaster (*to*): *a ~ accident.* **2** important; decisive: *the ~ day.*

fa·tally /ˈfeitəli/ *adv*: *~ly injured/wounded.*

fa·tal·ism /ˈfeitəˌlɪzəm/ *n* [U] belief that events are decided by fate(1).

fatal·ist /ˈfeitəlɪst/ *n* [C] believer in fatalism.

fatal·is·tic /ˌfeitəlˈɪstɪk/ *adj* believing that all that happens is inevitable: *a fatalistic attitude.*

fa·tal·ity /feiˈtæləti/ *n* (*pl* -ies) **1** [C] misfortune, disaster, esp one that causes death and destruction: *floods, earthquakes and other fatalities.* **2** [C] death by accident, in war, etc. **3** [U] state of being subject to fate(1) or destiny. **4** [U] fatal infuence; deadliness: *the ~ of certain diseases,* eg cancer.

fate /feit/ *n* **1** [U] power looked on as controlling all events in a way that cannot be opposed: *He had hoped to live to 80 but ~ decided otherwise.* **2** [C] the future as decided by fate: *They left/abandoned the men to their ~.* **3** (*sing*) death; destruction. **4** what becomes of a person: *decide a person's ~,* what will happen to him. □ *vt* ***be fated to/that,*** be destined to/that: *He was ~d to be hanged. It was ~d that we should fail.*

fate·ful /ˈfeitfəl/ *adj* **1** controlled by, showing the power of, fate(1). **2** important and decisive: *a ~ decision; on this ~ day.* **3** prophetic.

fate·fully /-fəli/ *adv*

fa·ther[1] /ˈfaðər/ *n* [C] **1** male parent: *You have been like a ~ to me. The property had been handed down from ~ to son for many generations.* **2** **(the) Father,** God: *Our* (*Heavenly*) *Father.* **3** (usually *pl*) ancestor(s). **4** (usually **Father**) founder or first leader: *the Father of English poetry,* Chaucer. **5** (usually **Father**) *(used as a title for a) priest.* **6** (usually **Father**) title used in personifications: *Father Time.*

the Holy Father, the Pope.

ˈfather·hood /-ˌhʊd/ *n* [U] state of being a father.

father-in-law /ˈfaðər-ɪn-ˌlɔ/ *n* [C] (*pl* ~s-in-law) father of one's wife or husband.

ˈfather·land /-ˌlænd/ *n* [C] one's native country (*mother country* is more usual, ⇨ mother).

father·less *adj* without a living or known father.

father·ly *adj* having, showing the qualities of a father.

ˈFather's Day, third Sunday in June that is set aside in the US to honor fathers.

fa·ther[2] /ˈfaðər/ *vt* **1** become the father of. **2** act as a father to. **3** be the founder, originator or author of: *~ed a new political movement.*

fathom /ˈfæðəm/ *n* [C] measure (six feet or 1.8 meters) of depth of water: *The ship sank in six ~s.* □ *vt* **1** measure the depth of. **2** get to the bottom of; understand fully: *I cannot ~ his meaning.*

fathom·less *adj* too deep to fathom.

fa·tigue /fəˈtig/ *n* [U] **1** condition of being very tired as a result of work: *Several men dropped with ~ during the long march.* **2** weakness in metals caused by prolonged stress. **3** (also **fatigue duty**) non-military duty of soldiers, such as cleaning, cooking, etc. □ *vt* cause fatigue to: *fatiguing work.*

fa·tigues /fəˈtigz/ *n pl* loose-fitting uniform worn by soldiers for fatigue duty. ⇨ fatigue(3).

fat·ten /ˈfætən/ *vt,vi* make or become fat: *~ cattle.*

fatty /ˈfæti/ *adj* (-ier, -iest) **1** like, consisting of, fat: *~ bacon.* **2** greasy; oily.

fau·cet /ˈfɔsɪt/ *n* [C] device for controlling the flow of liquid from a pipe, tank, etc.

fault /fɔlt/ *n* **1** [C] something that makes a person, thing, etc imperfect; defect; blemish; flaw: *She loves me in spite of all my ~s. There is a ~ in the electrical connections.* ***at fault,*** in the wrong; worthy of blame: *My memory was at ~.* ***find fault with,*** complain about: *I have no ~ to find with your work.* **2** (*sing* only) responsibility for being wrong: *It's your own ~.* **3** [C] break in the earth's crust that displaces layers of rock, etc. □ *vt* find fault with: *No one could ~ his performance.*

ˈfault·finder *n* [C] person who tends to criticize or find fault.

ˈ**fault·finding** *adj, n* [U]
fault·less *adj* without fault.
fault·less·ly *adv*
faulty *adj* (-ier, -iest) having a fault or faults.

faun /fɔn/ *n* [C] (*Roman myth*) god of the woods and fields, represented as part goat and part man.

fauna /ˈfɔnə/ *n* [U] all the animals of an area or a period: *the ~ of East Africa.*

fa·vor[1] /ˈfeivər/ *n* **1** [U] friendly regard; kindness; approval: *win a person's ~; look on a plan with ~*, approve of it. ***be in/out of favor (with sb),*** have/not have his friendship, etc. **2** [U] aid; support. ***in favor of,*** in sympathy with; on the side of: *Are you in ~ of women's lib?* ***in sb's favor,*** to the advantage of: *The exchange rate is in our ~.* **3** [U] treatment that is more than fair; partiality: *He obtained his position more by ~ than by merit or ability.* **4** [C] act of kindness: *May I ask you a ~? Would you do me a ~?* **5** [C] small token or gift, eg one given out at a party. **6** (*old use*) *by your ~*, with your permission.

fa·vor[2] /ˈfeivər/ *vt* **1** show favor to; support: *Fortune ~s the brave.* **2** show more favor to one person, group, etc than to another: *A teacher should not ~ any of his/her pupils.* **3** (*formal*) do something for: *Will you ~ me with an interview?* **4** (*formal*) (of circumstances) make possible or easy: *The weather ~ed our voyage.* **5** resemble in features: *The child ~s its father.*

fa·vor·able /ˈfeiv(ə)rəbəl/ *adj* **1** giving or showing approval: *a ~ report on one's work.* **2** promising; helpful: *~ winds.*
fa·vor·ably /-əbli/ *adv*

fa·vor·ite /ˈfeiv(ə)rɪt/ *adj, n* [C] **1** (person or thing) preferred above all others: *He is a ~ with his uncle/a ~ of his uncle's/his uncle's ~.* **2 the favorite,** contestant that is generally expected to win: *The ~ came in third.* **3** person who is favored unfairly.
fa·vor·it·ism /-ˌtɪzəm/ *n* [U] (practice of) having favorites(3).

fawn[1] /fɔn/ *n* **1** [C] young deer less than one year old. **2** [U] light yellowish-brown color. □ *adj* light yellowish-brown.

fawn[2] /fɔn/ *vi* **1** (of dogs) show pleasure and affection by jumping about, tail-wagging, etc. **2** ***fawn on sb,*** try to win his favor by flattery, etc.

FBI /ˌef ˌbi ˈai/ *abbr* = Federal Bureau of Investigation.

FCC /ˌef ˌsi ˈsi/ *abbr* = Federal Communications Commission.

FD *abbr* = Fire Department.

FDA /ˌef ˌdi ˈei/ *abbr* = Food and Drug Administration.

feal·ty /ˈfiəlti/ *n* [U] (*liter*) loyalty.

fear[1] /fɪr/ *n* **1** [U] (state of) being afraid because of the feeling that danger is near: *They stood there trembling in ~*, shaking from fright. *He was overcome with/by ~.* **2** [C] instance of being afraid. **3** [U] concern, worry, or anxiety about: *He lives in ~ of losing his job.* ***for fear of,*** because of anxiety about: *She asked us not to be noisy, for ~ of waking the baby.* **4** [U] cause for fear; chance of danger: *There's not much ~ of my losing the money.* **5** [U] awe and reverence: *~ of God.*
fear·ful /-fəl/ *adj* **(a)** causing fear; terrible: *a ~ful accident.* **(b)** (*informal*) annoying; very great: *What a ~ful mess!* **(c)** frightened; apprehensive: *~ful of waking the baby.*
fear·fully /-fəli/ *adv*
fear·less *adj* without fear: *~less of the consequences.*
fear·less·ly *adv*
fear·less·ness /-nɪs/ *n* [U]

fear[2] /fɪr/ *vt,vi* **1** feel fear (of), be afraid (of): *~ death.* **2** be uneasy or anxious about: *~ed that he would miss his train.* ***fear for,*** feel anxiety about: *We ~ed for his life/safety.*

fea·sible /ˈfizəbəl/ *adj* **1** that can be done or carried out: *His plan is ~.* **2** (*informal*) plausible; likely: *a ~ explanation.*
feasi·bil·ity /ˌfizəˈbɪləti/ *n* [U]

feast /fist/ *n* [C] **1** religious anniversary or festival, eg Christmas or Easter. **2** splendid meal with many good things to eat and drink. □ *vt,vi* **1** take part in, give a feast: *~ one's friends; ~ all evening.* **2** give pleasure to: *~ one's eyes on beautiful scenes.*

feat /fit/ *n* [C] act or deed, esp one showing skill, strength or daring: *brilliant ~s of engineering.*

feather[1] /ˈfeðər/ *n* [C] one of the light coverings that grow from a bird's skin. ⇨ illus at bird. ***a feather in one's cap,*** an honor. ***as light as a feather,*** very light. ***birds of a feather,*** people of the same sort.
ˌ**feather ˈbed,** (bed with a) feather mattress.
ˈ**feather·bed** *vi* (esp of a labor union) require an employer to create more jobs than necessary.
ˈ**feather·bedding** *n* [U]
ˈ**feather·weight** *n* [C] boxer weighing between 118 and 126 lbs (53.5 and 57 kg).
feathery *adj* **(a)** light and soft like feathers: *~y snow.* **(b)** having feathers.

feather[2] /ˈfeðər/ *vt* supply with feathers: *~ an arrow.* ***feather one's nest,*** make things comfortable for oneself.

fea·ture /ˈfitʃər/ *n* [C] **1** one of the parts of the face: *Her eyes are her best ~.* **2** (*pl*) the face as a whole: *a man with handsome ~s.* **3** characteristic or striking part: *geographical ~s.* **4** prominent article or subject in a newspaper. **5** chief motion picture on a program, etc. □ *vt* be or make a feature(3,4,5) of; have a prominent part for: *a film that ~s a new French actress.*
fea·ture·less *adj* uninteresting; with no obvious features(3).

Feb. *abbr* = February.

Feb·ru·ary /ˈfebyuˌeri, ˈfebru-/ *n* the second month of the year.

feces /ˈfiˌsiz/ *n pl* bodily waste discharged from the bowels.

fed /fed/ *pt,pp* of feed[2]. ***be fed up with,*** be tired of or disgusted with: *I'm fed up with your grumbling.*

fed·er·al /ˈfed(ə)rəl/ *adj* **1** of, based on, federation: *In the US foreign policy is decided by the ~* (ie central) *government, and ~ laws are made by Congress.* **2** relating to, supporting, central (as distinct from state) government.
Federal Bureau of Investiˈgation, (*abbr* **FBI**) government agency of the US responsible for

investigating violations of federal law.
fed·er·al·ism /-ˌlɪzəm/ *n* [U]
fed·er·al·ist /-lɪst/ *n* [C] supporter of federal union or power.
fed·er·ate /ˈfedəˌreit/ *vt,vi* (of states, societies, organizations) combine, unite, into a federation.
fed·er·ation /ˌfedəˈreiʃən/ *n* **1** [C] political system in which a union of states leave foreign affairs, defense, etc to the central government but keep powers of government over local affairs. **2** [C] such a union of states (eg the USA) or societies, trade unions, etc. **3** [U] act of federating.
fee /fi/ *n* [C] **1** charge or payment for professional advice or services, eg doctors, lawyers, etc. **2** entrance money for an examination, club, etc. □ *vt* pay a fee to.
feeble /ˈfibəl/ *adj* (-r, -st) weak; faint; without energy or force: *a ~ old man; a ~ cry/argument.*
ˌfeeble-ˈminded *adj* subnormal in intelligence.
feebly /ˈfibli/ *adv*
feed[1] /fid/ *n* **1** [C] (chiefly of animals; jokingly of persons) meal: *We stopped to let the horses have a ~.* **2** [U] food for farm animals: *There isn't enough ~ left for the hens.* (*Note:* Referring to dogs and cats, *food* is used instead.) **3 (a)** [C] pipe, channel, etc through which material is carried to a machine. **(b)** [U] material supplied.
feed[2] /fid/ *vt,vi* (*pt,pp* fed /fed/) **1** give food to: *Have the pigs been fed yet?* **2** (chiefly of animals, but *informally* or jokingly of persons) eat: *The cows were ~ing in the meadows.* (*Note:* Referring to dogs and cats, *eat* is used instead.) ***feed on,*** take as food: *Cattle ~ chiefly on grass.* **3** supply with material; supply (material) to: *This moving belt ~s the machine with raw material/~s raw material into the machine.*
feed·back /ˈfidˌbæk/ *n* [U] **1** return of part of the output of a system to its source (eg to correct it). **2** information, etc (eg about a product) given by the user to the supplier, maker, etc: *interesting ~ from our customers.*
feeder /ˈfidər/ *n* [C] **1** one that feeds. **2** (often as an *adjective*) branch railway line, airline, canal, etc linking outlying areas with the main line, etc.
feel[1] /ˈfiəl/ *n* (*sing* only) **1** feeling; touch. **2** quality of something as sensed by touching: *the smooth ~ of silk.*
feel[2] /ˈfiəl/ *vt,vi* (*pres p* ~ing /ˈfilɪŋ/; *pt,pp* felt /felt/) **1** learn about, examine, by touching, handling, etc: *Blind persons can usually recognize objects by ~ing them.* ***feel one's way,*** go forward carefully, as in the dark, or as a blind man does. **2** search for (something) with the hand(s) (or the feet, a stick, etc): *He felt in his pocket for a penny.* **3** be aware of (through contact): *I can ~ a nail in my shoe.* **4** be aware of (not through contact): *He felt his heart beating wildly. She felt concern for them all.* **5** be in a certain physical, moral or emotional state: *~ cold/hungry/happy, etc. How are you ~ing today? He felt cheated. Please ~ free* (= consider yourself welcome) *to come whenever you like.* **6** be capable of sensation: *The dead cannot ~.* **7** ***feel for/with,*** have sympathy, compassion: *I ~ with you in your sorrow. I ~ for you.* **8** ***feel as if/though,*** have, give, the impression that: *She felt as if her head were splitting.* **9** give the sensation of being; seem: *This new suit doesn't ~ right.* **10** ***feel like,*** (of persons) be in the mood for: *I don't ~ like (eating) a big meal now.* **11** be sensitive to; suffer because of: *He doesn't ~ the heat at all,* is not troubled by it. **12** have the opinion; think or believe: *He felt* (= was confident) *that he would succeed.*
feeler /ˈfilər/ *n* [C] **1** part (of an animal) used for testing things by touch, eg whiskers, antennae. ⇨ illus at insect. **2** proposal, suggestion, made to find out about the opinions or feelings of others.
feel·ing /ˈfilɪŋ/ *n* **1** [U] power and capacity to feel: *He had lost all ~ in his legs.* **2** [C] physical or mental awareness; emotion: *a ~ of hunger/gratitude/joy.* **3** [C] idea or belief not based wholly on reason: *a ~ of danger.* **4** (usually *sing*) general opinion: *The ~ of those present was that he had behaved properly.* **5** (*pl*) sensitive, emotional side of a person's nature (contrasted with the intellect): *Have I hurt your ~s?* (= offended you?) **6** [U] sympathy: *He doesn't show much ~ for the sufferings of others.* **7** [U] ability to feel emotion; sensibility: *She plays the piano with ~.* □ *adj* sympathetic; showing emotion: *a ~ remark.*
feel·ing·ly *adv* so as to express feeling: *speak ~ly on a subject.*
feet *pl of* foot[1].
feign /fein/ *vt, vi* pretend: *~ sickness.*
feint /feint/ *n* [C] **1** = pretense (the more usual word). **2** pretended attack made to draw attention away from the place where a real attack is intended. □ *vi* pretend.
fel·ic·ity /fəˈlɪsəti/ *n* (*formal*) **1** [U] great happiness or contentment. **2** [U] pleasing manner of speaking or writing: *express oneself with ~.*
fe·line /ˈfiˌlain/ *adj* **1** of or like a cat: *walk with ~ grace.* **2** belonging to the animal family that includes cats, tigers, lions, leopards, and panthers. □ *n* [C] any animal of the cat family.
fell[1] *pt* of fall[2].
fell[2] /fel/ *vt* cause to fall; strike down; cut down (a tree): *He ~ed his enemy with a single blow.*
fel·low /ˈfelou/ *n* [C] **1** (*informal*) (in this sense also sometimes /ˈfelə/) man or boy: *He's a pleasant ~.* **2** (usually *pl*) comrade, companion: *ˈschool ~s.* **3** person of the same class, kind, etc: (as an *adjective*) *ˌ~ ˈcitizen.* **4** one of a pair; mate. **5** member of a learned society.
ˌfellow ˈtraveler, person who sympathizes with the philosophy of the Communist Party, but is not a member.
fel·low·ship /ˈfelouˌʃɪp/ *n* **1** [U] friendly association; companionship: *enjoy ~ with people.* **2 (a)** [C] number of persons associated together; group or society. **(b)** [U] membership in such a group: *admitted to the ~.* **3** [C] position or money given by a college or university to an advanced student to permit him to continue his studies.
felon /ˈfelən/ *n* [C] person guilty of felony; criminal.
fe·loni·ous /fəˈlouniəs/ *adj* criminal.
fel·ony /ˈfeləni/ *n* [C,U] (*pl* -ies) major serious

crime, eg murder, armed robbery, arson.

felt[1] *pt,pp* of feel[2].

felt[2] /felt/ *n* [U] cloth made of wool, hair or fur, that has been compressed and rolled flat: (as an *adjective*) *~ hats/slippers*.

fem. *abbr* = feminine.

fe·male /ˈfiˌmeiəl/ *adj* **1** of the sex that gives birth to offspring: *a ~ child/giraffe*. **2** (*bot*) fruit-bearing. **3** of or relating to women: *~ suffrage*. **4** (*mech*) having a hollow part designed to receive an inserted part, eg a plug. □ *n* [C] **1** woman or girl. **2** female animal or plant.

femi·nine /ˈfemənɪn/ *adj* **1** of, like, women: *~ intuition,* said to be characteristic of women. **2** (*gram*) of the female gender: *"Actress" and "lioness" are ~. "She" and "her" are ~ pronouns*.

fem·i·nin·ity /ˌfeməˈnɪnəti/ *n* [U] quality of being feminine.

fem·i·nism /ˈfeməˌnɪzəm/ *n* [U] movement for recognition of the claims of women for rights (legal, political, etc) equal to those possessed by men.

fem·in·ist /-nɪst/ *n* [C] supporter of feminism.

fe·mur /ˈfimər/ *n* [C] thigh bone. ⇨ illus at skeleton.

fence[1] /fens/ *n* [C] barrier made of wood or metal, eg one put around a field, garden, etc. ***sit/be on/straddle the fence,*** be undecided or hesitant. □ *vt* surround, divide, provide with a fence: *Farmers ~ their fields. The land is ~d off/in*.

fenc·ing /ˈfensɪŋ/ *n* [U] material for making fences.

fence[2] /fens/ *vt* **1** practice the art of fighting with long slender swords or foils. **2** (*fig*) avoid giving a direct answer to a question(er).

fencer *n* [C] person who fences.

fenc·ing /ˈfensɪŋ/ *n* [U] art, sport, of fighting with swords.

fence[3] /fens/ *n* [C] **1** person who buys stolen goods. **2** his place of business. □ *vt* sell (stolen goods) to a fence.

fend /fend/ *vt,vi* **1** ***fend off,*** defend oneself from: *~ off a blow*. **2** ***fend for oneself,*** look after oneself: *When his father died, Tom had to ~ for himself*.

fend·er /ˈfendər/ *n* [C] **1** metal frame bordering an open fireplace (to prevent burning coal, etc from rolling on to the floor). **2** metal frame over the wheel of a vehicle.

fer·ment[1] /ˈfərˌment/ *n* [C] **1** substance, eg yeast, that causes other substances to ferment. **2** ***in a ferment,*** (*fig*) in a state of, eg social, political, excitement.

fer·ment[2] /fərˈment/ *vt,vi* **1** (cause to) undergo chemical changes through the action of organic bodies (esp yeast): *When wine is ~ed, it gives off bubbles of gas*. **2** (*fig*) (cause to) become excited.

fer·men·ta·tion /ˌfərmənˈteiʃən/ *n* [U]

fern /fərn/ *n* [C] kinds of feathery, green-leaved flowerless plant.

ferny *adj*

fe·rocious /fəˈrouʃəs/ *adj* fierce, cruel, savage: *a ~ temper*.

fe·rocious·ly *adv*

fe·roc·ity /fəˈrasəti/ *n* **1** [U] fierceness; savage cruelty. **2** [C] (*pl* -ies) fierce, savage or cruel act.

fer·ret /ˈferɪt/ *n* [C] small animal of the weasel family, used for driving rabbits from their burrows, killing rats, etc. □ *vt,vi* **1** hunt with ferrets. **2** discover by searching; search: *~ out a secret; ~ about for a lost book*.

Ferris wheel /ˈferəs ˌ(h)wiəl/ *n* [C] large, upright, power-driven wheel carrying swinging seats around its rim, that is used in amusement parks, at carnivals, etc.

ferry /ˈferi/ *n* [C] (*pl* -ies) (place where there is a) boat, that carries people and goods across a river, channel, etc. □ *vt,vi* take, go, across in a ferry: *~ people/a boat across a river*.

ˈferry·boat *n* [C] one used for ferrying.

ˈferry·man *n* [C] /-mən/ (*pl* ~men /-ˌmen/) person who runs a ferry.

fer·tile /ˈfərtəl/ *adj* **1** (of land, plants, etc) producing much: *~ soil*. **2** (of a person, his mind, etc) full of ideas, plans, etc: *a ~ imagination*. **3** able to produce fruit, young. **4** capable of developing: *~ seeds/eggs*. ⇨ sterile.

fer·til·ity /fərˈtɪləti/ *n* [U] state of being fertile.

fer·til·ize /ˈfərtəˌlaiz/ *vt* make fertile or productive: *~ the soil* (by using manure).

fer·tili·za·tion /ˌfərtələˈzeiʃən/ *n* [U]

fer·t·ilizer *n* [C,U] substance (as chemical plant food or manure) that makes soil more productive.

fer·vent /ˈfərvənt/ *adj* showing warmth of feeling; intense; passionate: *~ love/hatred*.

fer·vent·ly *adv*

fer·vor /ˈfərvər/ *n* [U] strength or warmth of feeling.

fes·tal /ˈfestəl/ *adj* (*liter*) = festive (the usual word).

fes·ter /ˈfestər/ *vi* **1** (of a cut or wound) (cause to) fill with poisonous matter (pus): *If the cut gets dirty, it will probably ~*. **2** (*fig*) act like poison in the mind: *The insult ~ed in his mind*.

fes·ti·val /ˈfestəvəl/ *n* [C] **1** (day or season for) rejoicing; public celebrations: *Christmas and Easter are Christian ~s*. **2** series of performances (of music, ballet, drama, etc) given periodically, eg once a year: *a ~ of music*.

fes·tive /ˈfestɪv/ *adj* of a feast or festival; joyous: *a ˈ~ season*, eg Christmas.

fes·tiv·ity /feˈstɪvəti/ *n* (*pl* -ies) **1** [U] rejoicing; merrymaking. **2** (*pl*) events that celebrate a joyful occasion: *wedding festivities*.

fes·toon /feˈstun/ *n* [C] chain of flowers, leaves, ribbons, etc hanging in a curve or loop between two points, as a decoration. □ *vt* decorate with festoons: *~ed with tinsel*.

fetch /fetʃ/ *vt,vi* **1** go for and bring back; get (the usual word). **2** cause to come out; draw forth; produce (the usual word).

fete, fête /feit, fet/ *n* [C] festival or large party, often held outdoors. □ *vt* /feit/ honor, esp by giving a fete: *The hero was ~d wherever he went*.

fetid /ˈfetɪd/ *adj* stinking.

fet·ish, fe·tich /ˈfetɪʃ/ *n* [C] **1** object worshiped by pagan people because of its magical power. **2** anything to which foolishly excessive respect or attention is given: *Some people make a ~ of clothes*.

fet·lock /ˈfetˌlak/ *n* [C] (tuft of hair on the) part

of a horse's leg above and behind the hoof.

fet·ter /ˈfetər/ *n* [C] **1** chain for the ankles of a prisoner or the leg of a horse. **2** (*fig* usually *pl*) something that hinders progress. □ *vt* put in chains; (*fig*) restrain.

fe·tus /ˈfitəs/ *n* [C] human or animal embryo, in the womb or in the egg, esp in the later stages of its development.

fe·tal /ˈfitəl/ *adj*

feud /fyud/ *n* [C] bitter quarrel between two persons, families or groups, over a long period of time.

feu·dal /ˈfyudəl/ *adj* of feudalism.

feu·dal·ism /ˈfyudəˌlɪzəm/ *n* [U] system of government during the Middle Ages in Europe in which land was held by a subject as a gift from the king or a lord in return for military services, etc.

fe·ver /ˈfivər/ *n* **1** [U] condition of the human body in which the temperature is higher than usual, esp as a sign of illness: *He has a high* ~. **2** [U] one of a number of diseases in which there is high fever: *yellow/typhoid/rheumatic* ~. **3** (usually *sing* with *a*) state of excitement or nervous activity: *in a* ~ *of impatience*.

fe·vered *adj* affected by a fever: *a* ~*ed* (= highly excited) *imagination*.

fe·ver·ish *adj* having symptoms of, caused by, causing a fever.

fe·ver·ish·ly *adv*

few /fyu/ *adj* (-er, -est) **1** (with a *pl noun*) not many: *Few people live to be 100 and fewer still live to be 110. Such occasions are few.* ***no fewer than,*** as many as: *No fewer than twenty workers were absent through illness.* **2** (with *a* or *an*) a small number (of): *I know a few of these people. We are going away for a few days.* ***3 every few days, etc,*** ⇨ every(4). □ *pron* (with a *pl verb*) not many persons or things: *Few* (*of his friends*) *have helped him.*

the few, the minority.

few·ness /-nɪs/ *n* [U]

fez /fez/ *n* [C] red felt hat with a flat top and no brim, worn by some Moslem men.

FHA /ˌef ˌeitʃ ˈei/ *abbr* = Federal Housing Administration.

fi·ancé /ˌfianˈsei/ *n* [C] man to whom one is engaged to be married.

fi·ancée /ˌfianˈsei/ *n* [C] woman to whom one is engaged to be married.

fi·asco /fiˈæskou/ *n* [C] (*pl* ~s, ~es) complete failure: *The new play was a* ~.

fib /fɪb/ *n* [C] (*informal*) lie (esp about something unimportant). □ *vi* (-bb-) tell a fib.

fib·ber *n* [C]

fib·bing *n* [U] telling fibs.

fiber, fibre /ˈfaibər/ **1** [C] one of the very thin threads of which many animal and vegetable growths are formed, eg cotton, wood, nerves, muscles. **2** [U] substance formed of a mass of fibers, for manufacture into various materials. **3** [U] structure; texture: *material of coarse* ~. **4** [U] (*fig*) character: *a person of strong moral* ~.

ˈfiber·glass *n* [U] material of glass fibers in resin, used in making yarns, insulating material, and made into structural materials.

fi·brous /ˈfaibrəs/ *adj* made of, like, fibers.

fib·ula /ˈfɪbyələ/ *n* [C] (*pl* ~s) outer of the two bones between the knee and the foot. ⇨ illus at skeleton.

fickle /ˈfɪkəl/ *adj* (of moods, the weather, etc) often changing; not constant.

fickle·ness /-nɪs/ *n* [U]

fic·tion /ˈfɪkʃən/ *n* **1** [C] something invented or imagined (as contrasted with fact). **2** [U] (branch of literature consisting of) stories, novels and romances.

fic·ti·tious /fɪkˈtɪʃəs/ *adj* untrue; imagined or invented: *The account he gives of his movements is quite* ~.

fiddle /ˈfɪdəl/ *n* [C] (*informal*) violin. ***fit as a fiddle,*** very well; in good health. ***play second fiddle (to),*** take a less important part (than). □ *vt* **1** (*informal*) play a tune, etc on the fiddle. **2** make aimless movements; play nervously with: *He was fiddling* (*around*) *with a piece of string*.

fid·dler /ˈfɪdlər/ *n* [C] **(a)** (*informal*) violinist. **(b)** person who fiddles.

ˈfid·dler crab, (kind of) small sand crab.

fi·del·ity /fɪˈdeləti/ *n* [U] **1** loyalty, faithfulness: ~ *to one's principles/wife*. **2** accuracy; exactness: *translate with the greatest* ~.

ˌhigh fiˈdelity, ⇨ high[1].

fidget /ˈfɪdʒɪt/ *vi,vt* (cause to) move the body (or part of it) about restlessly or nervously: *The boy was* ~*ing while he waited* □ *n* [C] **1** (usually *pl*) fidgeting movements: *Having to sit still for a long time often gives small children the* ~*s*. **2** person who fidgets.

fidgety *adj*

fief /fif/ *n* [C] piece of land given to a subject by a feudal lord.

field[1] /ˈfiəld/ *n* [C] **1** area of land, usually enclosed by means of hedges, fences, etc: *working in the* ~*s*. **2** area or expanse; open space: *an ˈice* ~, eg around the North Pole; *a ˈfootball* ~. **3** area of land from which minerals, etc are obtained: *ˈgold* ~*s; a new ˈoil* ~*; ˈcoal* ~*s*. **4** place, area, where a battle or war is or was fought: *the* ~ *of battle* (*ˈbattle* ~). **5** area or department of study or activity: *the* ~ *of politics/medical research. That is outside my* ~, is not something that I have studied. **6** range (of operation, activity, use); area or space in which forces can be felt: *a magnetic* ~, around a magnet: *a wide* ~ *of vision*. **7** (*sport*) all those taking part.

ˈfield day, (a) day on which military operations are practiced. **(b)** day for athletic contests and outdoor sports. **(c)** (*fig*) great or special occasion: *having a* ~ *day,* having great fun, success, etc.

ˈfield event, athletic event such as jumping or throwing which does not take place on a track.

ˈfield glasses, binoculars for outdoor use.

ˈfield goal, (*football*) score of three points made by a dropkick or a placekick.

ˈfield hockey, ⇨ hockey.

ˈfield hospital, temporary one near the scene of fighting.

ˈfield ˌmarshal, army officer of highest rank in the British and some European armies.

ˈfield officer, major, lieutenant colonel or colonel.

ˈfield trip, trip made for the purpose of first-hand observations, interviews, etc.

ˈfield·work *n* [U] **(a)** research done in the field, eg by a geologist. **(b)** work done in the field in order to gain practical experience.

field[2] /ˈfiəld/ *vt,vi* **1** (esp *baseball*) throw, catch or stop (the ball): *He* ~*s well.* **2** put into the field: *The school is* ~*ing a strong team in their next football match.*

fielder *n* [C] (esp *baseball*) player who fields[2] (1).

fiend /find/ *n* [C] **1** devil. **2** very wicked or cruel person. **3** (*informal*) person devoted to or addicted to something: *a ˌfresh-ˈair* ~*; a ˈdrug* ~.

fiend·ish *adj* savage and cruel.

fiend·ish·ly *adv*

fierce /firs/ *adj* (-r, -st) **1** violent; cruel; angry: ~ *dogs/winds; look* ~*; have a* ~ *look.* **2** (of heat, desire, etc) intense: ~ *hatred.*

fierce·ly *adv*

fierce·ness /-nɪs/ *n* [U]

fiery /ˈfaiəri/ *adj* (-ier, -iest) **1** flaming; on fire. **2** hot as if on fire: *a* ~ *sunset;* ~ *eyes*, angry and glaring. **3** quickly or easily made angry; passionate: *a* ~ *temper/speech.*

fieri·ness /-nɪs/ *n* [U]

fi·esta /fiˈestə/ *n* [C] (*pl* ~s) **1** religious festival; saint's day. **2** holiday, festival.

fife /faif/ *n* [C] small musical wind instrument like a flute, used with drums in military music.

fif·teen /ˌfɪfˈtin/ *adj, n* [C] (of) 15.

fif·teenth /ˌfɪfˈtinθ/ *adj, n* [C] (of) one of 15 (parts) or the next after 14.

fifth /fɪfθ/ *adj, n* [C] (of) one of 5 (parts) or the next after 4. ▫ *n* [C] (bottle holding) one fifth of a gallon, esp of whiskey, rum, etc.

fifth·ly *adv*

fifty /ˈfɪfti/ *adj, n* [C] (of) 50. ***ˌfifty-ˈfifty,*** **(a)** equally shared. **(b)** having an equal chance.

the fifties (*pl*) **(a)** (of a person's age, temperature, etc) between 49 and 60 **(b)** (of a century) the years from 50 to 59 inclusive.

fif·ti·eth /ˈfɪftiəθ/ *adj, n* [C] (of) one of 50 (parts) or the next after 49.

fig[1] /fɪg/ *n* [C] (broad-leaved tree having a) soft, sweet, pear-shaped fruit full of small seeds. ***not care/give a fig (for),*** not care or value in the least.

fig[2] *abbr* = **1** figure. **2** figurative.

fight[1] /fait/ *n* **1** [C] act of fighting; struggle: *a* ~ *between two dogs; the* ~ *against poverty.* **2** [U] desire, spirit or ability for fighting: *The news that their leader had surrendered took all the* ~ *out of them.*

fight[2] /fait/ *vi,vt* (*pt,pp* fought /fɔt/) **1** struggle with the hands or with weapons; use physical force against (as in war): ~ *a battle/war. The dogs were* ~*ing over a bone.* ***fight to the finish,*** until there is a decision. ***fight shy of,*** keep away from, not get mixed up with. **2** oppose; struggle with: ~ *ignorance/crime;* ~ *a fire.* ***fight sth down,*** repress; overcome: ~ *down a feeling of jealousy.* ***fight sb/sth off,*** drive away; struggle against: ~ *off a cold*, eg by taking aspirin. ***fight it out,*** fight until a dispute is settled.

fighter *n* [C] **(a)** person or thing that fights. **(b)** boxer. **(c)** fast aircraft designed for attacking bombers etc: (as an *adjective*) *a ˈ*~*er pilot/squadron.*

fight·ing *n* [U]: *ˈstreet* ~*ing.* ▫ *adj* ***a fighting chance,*** a possibility of success if great efforts are made.

fig·ment /ˈfɪgmənt/ *n* [C] something invented or imagined: ~*s of the imagination.*

fig·urat·ive /ˈfɪgyərətɪv/ *adj* (of words and language) used not in the literal sense but in an imaginative way, eg ⇨ bait[1](2).

fig·ura·tive·ly *adv*

fig·ure /ˈfɪgyər/ *n* [C] **1** symbol for a number, esp 0 to 9: *He has an income of six figures*, somewhere between $100,000 and $999,000. **2** price; value given in figures: *sold for a high* ~. **3** arithmetic: *Are you good at* ~*s?* **4** diagram; illustration: *The blackboard was covered with geometrical* ~*s*, ie squares, triangles, etc. **5** person's figure drawn or painted, or carved, etc; drawing, painting, image, of the body of an animal, etc. **6** shape; appearance: *I'm dieting to keep my* ~, in order not to grow fat. **7** person, esp his influence: *Einstein, one of the greatest* ~*s of his era.* ▫ *vt,vi* **1** (*informal*) believe; think; conclude: ~*d that it would happen.* **2** appear; have an important part; be prominent: ~ *in history/in a play.* **3** calculate; compute. ***figure sth/sb out,*** think about until one understands: *I can't* ~ *that man out*, he puzzles me.

ˈfigure·head *n* [C] **(a)** carved image (either bust or full-length) placed for ornament at the prow of a sailing ship. **(b)** person in high position but with no real authority.

ˌfigure of ˈspeech, expression, eg a simile or metaphor, that gives variety or force, using words out of their literal meaning.

fila·ment /ˈfɪləmənt/ *n* [C] slender thread, eg of wire in an electric light bulb.

fil·bert /ˈfɪlbərt/ *n* [C] hazelnut.

filch /fɪltʃ/ *vt* (*informal*) steal (something of small value).

file[1] /ˈfaiəl/ *n* [C] metal tool with roughened surface(s) for cutting or smoothing hard substances. ▫ *vt* (*pres p* filing /ˈfailɪŋ/) use a file on; make smooth, remove, cut through, with a file: *filing one's fingernails.*

fil·ings /ˈfailɪŋz/ *n pl* bits removed by filing.

file[2] /ˈfaiəl/ *n* [C] holder, cover, case, box, drawer etc for keeping papers, etc together and in order for reference purposes. ***on file,*** in a file. ▫ *vt* (*pres p* filing /ˈfailɪŋ/) place on or in a file: *Please* ~ (*away*) *these letters.*

file[3] /ˈfaiəl/ *n* [C] line of persons or things one behind the other: *in single* ~. ***the rank and file,*** **(a)** common soldiers (corporals and below). **(b)** (*fig*) ordinary, undistinguished persons. ▫ *vi* march in file: *The men* ~*d in/out*, came or went in/out in a row.

fi·let *n* [C] = fillet.

fil·ial /ˈfiliəl/ *adj* of a son or daughter: ~ *duty.*

fill[1] /fɪl/ *n* [U] full supply; as much as is wanted: *eat/drink one's* ~. ***have (had) one's fill of sth,*** (*informal*) have had as much as one can bear.

fill·ing *n* [C] something put in to fill something: *a* ~*ing in a tooth.*

fill[2] /fɪl/ *vt,vi* **1** make or become full; occupy all the space in: ~ *a hole with sand/a tank with gasoline. Tears* ~*ed her eyes. I was* ~*ed with* *admiration.* **2** hold a position and do the necessary work; put a person in a position: *The vacancy has already been ~ed.* ***fill sb's shoes,*** take his place. **3** supply what is needed or wanted. ***fill the bill,*** (*informal*) do or be what is wanted. **4** stop up a crack; plug: *~ a tooth.* **5** (special uses with *adverbial particles* and *prepositions*):

fill in, **(a)** add what is necessary to make complete: *~ in an application form,* write one's name, etc; *~ in an outline,* add details, etc. **(b)** substitute for, esp for a short time: *~ed in for the manager during the emergency.*

fill out, **(a)** make or become larger, rounded or fatter: *Her cheeks began to ~ out.* **(b)** = fill in (a).

fill up, make or become quite full: *~ up a tank. The channel of the river ~ed up with mud.*

fil·let, fi·let /fɪˈlei/ *n* [C] slice of fish or meat without bones. □ *vt* cut into fillets: *~ed sole.*

fill·ing sta·tion /ˈfɪlɪŋ ˌsteɪʃən/ *n* [C] = service station.

fil·lip /ˈfɪlɪp/ *n* [C] **1** quick blow or stroke given with a finger. **2** (*fig*) something that revives or stimulates: *an advertising campaign that gave a fresh ~ to sales.*

filly /ˈfɪli/ *n* [C] (*pl* -ies) female horse of less than four years. ⇨ colt.

film[1] /fɪlm/ *n* **1** [C] thin coating or covering: *a ~ of dust/mist.* **2** [C,U] roll or sheet of thin flexible material for use in photography: *a roll of ~.* **3** [C] motion picture.

filmy *adj* (-ier, -iest) like a film(1): *~y clouds.*

film[2] /fɪlm/ *vt,vi* **1** cover, become covered, with a film(1): *The scene ~ed over.* **2** make a motion picture of: *~ a play.* **3** be well, badly suited for filming: *She ~s well.*

fil·ter /ˈfɪltər/ *n* [C] **1** apparatus for holding back solid substances, impurities, etc in a liquid or gas passed through it: *a coffee ~.* **2** colored glass (as used on a camera lens) which allows light of certain wavelengths to pass through. **3** (in radio) device which separates alternating current of one frequency from others. □ vt,vi **1** (cause to) flow through a filter. **2** (*fig*) make a way, pass or flow as if through a filter: *new ideas ~ing into people's minds.*

ˈfilter tip, cigarette with a filter (for nicotine, etc).

ˈfilter-ˌtipped, having a filter tip.

filth /fɪlθ/ *n* [U] **1** disgusting dirt. **2** obscenity; vileness.

filthy *adj* (-ier, -iest)

fin /fɪn/ *n* [C] **1** movable part (like a wing) of a fish, used in swimming. ⇨ illus at fish. **2** thing shaped like or used in the same way as a fin: *the ˈtail fin of an aircraft.*

fi·nagle /fəˈneigəl/ *vt,vi* (*informal*) use trickery (to get something).

fi·nal /ˈfainəl/ *adj* **1** coming at the end: *the ~ chapter of a book.* **2** putting an end to doubt or argument; not to be changed: *a ~ decision/judgment.* □ *n* [C] (often *pl*) last of a series: *take one's ~s,* last examinations; *the tennis ~s,* deciding game, match, etc at the end of a series.

fi·nal·ist *n* [C] player who takes part in the last of a series of contests, games, etc.

fi·nally /-nəli/ *adv* **(a)** lastly; in conclusion. **(b)** once and for all: *settle a matter ~ly.*

fi·na·le /fɪˈnæli/ *n* [C] end; last part.

fi·nal·ity /faiˈnæləti/ *n* [U] state or quality of being final: *speak with an air of ~,* as if there is nothing more to be said or done.

fi·nal·ize /ˈfainəˌlaiz/ *vt* give a final form to.

fi·nance /ˈfaiˌnæns, fəˈnæns/ *n* **1** [U] (science of) the management of (esp public) money: *an expert in ~.* **2** (*pl*) money (esp of a government or a business company): *Are the country's ~s sound?* □ *vt* provide money for (a scheme, etc).

fi·nan·cial /fəˈnænʃəl/ *adj* of finance: *in ~ difficulties,* short of money; *the ~ year,* the annual period for which accounts are made up.

fi·nan·cially /-ʃəli/ *adv*

fin·an·cier /ˌfɪnənˈsɪr/ *n* [C] person skilled in finance.

finch /fɪntʃ/ *n* [C] kinds of small seed-eating bird, eg sparrows, canaries, etc.

find[1] /faind/ *n* [C] act of finding; something (esp valuable or pleasing) found: *I made a great ~ in a secondhand bookstore yesterday.*

find[2] /faind/ *vt* (*pt,pp* found /faund/) **1** look for and get back, after a search: *Did you ever ~ that pen you lost? The missing child has not been found yet.* **2** get or discover after search, experience or effort: *~ a cure/remedy (for something); ~ a solution/an answer (to a problem). They couldn't ~ the way in/out/back.* ***find fault (with),*** ⇨ fault(1). **3** arrive at; reach: *Water always ~s its own level.* **4** discover by chance; come across: *He was found dead at the foot of a cliff.* **5** become informed or aware of, by experience or trial: *We found the beds quite comfortable. I ~ it difficult to understand him/~ him difficult to understand/~ that it is difficult to understand him.* **6** learn by study, calculation, inquiry (often ***find out***): *Please ~ (out) when the train leaves.* **7** (= *there is/are,* the subject being *one* or *you*): *One doesn't/You don't ~* (= There isn't) *much sunshine in this area.* **8** supply; furnish; provide: *Who will ~ the money for the expedition?* **9** (*legal*) decide and declare; give as a verdict: *How do you ~ the accused? The jury found the accused man guilty.*

finder *n* [C] **(a)** person who finds something: *Lost—a diamond ring: ~er will be rewarded.* **(b)** (also **ˈviewfinder**) lens in a camera that shows what is being photographed.

find·ing *n* (usually *pl*) what has been decided by a jury, learned as the result of an inquiry, etc.

fine[1] /fain/ *adj* (-r, -st) **1** (of weather) bright; clear; not raining: *It rained all morning, but it's ~ now.* **2** in good health; very well: *I'm feeling ~.* **3** excellent; pleasing; very good: *a ~ view; have a ~ time. That's a ~ excuse,* (*ironic*) a very poor excuse. **4** delicate; carefully made and easily injured: *~ silk.* **5** of very small particles: *Sand is ~r than gravel.* **6** slender; thin; sharp: *a pencil with a ~ point.* **7** (of metals) refined; pure: *~ gold.* **8** (to be) seen only with difficulty or effort; subtle: *a ~ distinction.* □ *adv* (*informal*) very well: *That will suit me just ~.*

the ˌfine ˈarts, arts that have to do with the creation of beautiful things, esp music, painting and sculpture.

fine·ly *adv* **(a)** splendidly: *~ly dressed.* **(b)** into small particles or pieces: *carrots ~ly chopped up.*

fine·ness /-nɪs/ *n* [U]

fine[2] /fain/ *n* [C] sum of money (to be) paid as a penalty for breaking a law or rule. □ *vt* punish by a fine: *~ him $25.*

fin·ery /ˈfainəri/ *n* [U] gay and elegant dress or appearance: *young ladies in their Sunday ~,* smart clothes.

fi·nesse /fɪˈnes/ *n* [U] artful or delicate way of dealing with a situation: *show ~ in dealing with people.*

fin·ger /ˈfɪŋgər/ *n* [C] **1** one of the slender divisions at the end of the hand: *There are five ~s* (or *four ~s and one thumb*) *on each hand.* ***have a finger in every pie,*** ⇨ pie. ***keep one's fingers crossed,*** ⇨ cross[3](3). ***not lift a finger (to help sb),*** do nothing to help when help is needed. ***put one's finger on sth,*** find it and point it out: *put his ~ on the problem as soon as I explained what was going on.* ***slip through one's fingers,*** ⇨ slip[2](3). ⇨ illus at arm. **2** part of a glove that covers a finger. **3** something like a finger in shape or function. □ *vt* touch with the fingers: *~ a piece of cloth.*

ˈ**fin·ger·nail** *n* [C] nail at the tip of the finger.

ˈ**fin·ger·print** *n* [C] mark made by a finger when pressed on a surface, used for identification. ⇨ illus at whorls.

ˈ**fin·ger·tip** *n* [C] end of a finger. ***have sth at one's fingertips,*** be thoroughly familiar with it.

fin·icky /ˈfɪnɪki/ *adj* fussy.

fin·ish /ˈfɪnɪʃ/ *vt,vi* **1** bring or come to an end; complete: *~ one's work; ~ reading a book. Have you ~ed with that dictionary?* Are you still using it? **2** make complete or perfect; polish: *The woodwork is beautifully ~ed,* smoothed and polished. *He gave the picture a few ~ing touches.* □ *n* (*sing* only) **1** last part: *the ~ of a race.* ***fight to the finish,*** ⇨ fight[2] (1). **2** manner of being finished: *a table with a shiny ~.* **3** polish, esp in manners and speech: *His manners lack ~.*

fi·nite /ˈfaiˌnait/ *adj* **1** limited: *Human understanding is ~.* **2** (*gram*) showing person, number and tense in a verb: *In "He runs," "runs" is the ~ form of "run"; in "the running dog," "running" is the ˈnon ~ form.*

fiord *n* [C] = fjord.

fir /fər/ *n* **1** [C] evergreen tree of the pine family with needle-like leaves. **2** [U] wood of this tree.

fire[1] /ˈfaiər/ *n* **1** [U] burning with flames, heat and light: *Fire burns.* ***on fire,*** burning: *The house was on ~.* ***catch fire,*** begin to burn: *Paper catches ~ easily.* ***set sth on fire/set fire to sth,*** cause it to begin burning: *He set his hair on ~.* **2** [U] destructive burning: *Have you insured your house against ~?* **3** [C] instance of destructive burning: *forest ~s.* **4** [C] burning fuel in a grate, etc to heat a building, for cooking, etc: *Can you chop the wood for the ~?* **5** [U] shooting (from guns). ***open/cease fire,*** start/stop shooting. ***under fire,*** being shot at. **6** [U] strong emotion; angry or excited feeling; enthusiasm: *a speech that lacks ~,* is uninspiring.

ˈ**fire alarm,** apparatus (bell, etc) for making known the outbreak of a fire.

ˈ**fire·arm** *n* rifle, gun, pistol or revolver.

ˈ**fire·break** *n* strip of cleared land, through a wooded area, to stop the spread of fire.

ˈ**fire chief,** head of a fire department or fire station.

ˈ**fire·cracker** *n* [C] paper roll or tube filled with explosive, that is exploded as an amusement.

ˈ**fire department,** organization (usually part of a city or town government) trained and equipped to put out fires.

ˈ**fire drill,** practice of the routine to be followed when fire breaks out.

ˈ**fire engine,** (motor truck with an) apparatus for putting out a fire.

ˈ**fire escape,** outside staircase for leaving a burning building.

FIRE ESCAPE

ˈ**fire extinguisher,** (esp) portable cylinder with chemical substance, etc inside, for putting out a small fire.

ˈ**fire·fighter** *n* [C] = fireman(b).

ˈ**fire·fly** *n* [C] (*pl* -ies) beetle that makes flashes of light when flying around at night.

ˈ**fire·house** *n* [C] = fire station.

ˈ**fire hydrant,** valve of a high-volume water outlet on the street, for the use of firefighters.

ˈ**fire·man** /-mən/ (*pl* ~men /-men/) **(a)** man who looks after the fire in a furnace, etc. **(b)** member of an organized team trained to put out fires.

ˈ**fire·place** *n* place for a fire in a room.

ˈ**fire·plug** *n* = fire hydrant.

ˈ**fire·proof** *adj* that does not burn; that does not crack or break when heated.

ˈ**fire sale,** special sale, at bargain prices, of merchandise allegedly damaged by smoke, etc from a fire.

ˈ**fire·side** *n* (*sing* with *the*) part of a room round the fireplace: *sitting at/by the ~side;* (as an *adjective*) *a ~side chair.*

ˈ**fire station,** building where the apparatus for putting out fires is kept and where firemen usually live when they are on duty.

ˈ**fire·wood** *n* [U] wood prepared for lighting fires or as fuel.

ˈ**fire·work** *n* **(a)** [C] device containing gunpowder and chemicals, used for making a display at night, or as a signal. **(b)** (*pl*) display of such devices. **(c)** (*pl*) (*fig*) display of temper.

fire[2] /ˈfaiər/ *vt,vi* **1** set fire to with the intention of destroying; cause to burn: *~ a heap of leaves.* **2** use heat on; dry by heat: *~* (= bake) *pottery in a kiln.* **3** supply (a furnace) with fuel: *an ˈoil-~d furnace.* **4** excite or stimulate: *~d his hearers* *with enthusiasm.* **5** send (a bullet, etc) from a gun; explode (a charge of explosive); shoot: ~ *a gun/six rounds of ammunition. The police ~d into the crowd.* **fire away,** (*fig*) go ahead; begin: *I'm ready to answer questions; ~ away.* **6** (*sl*) discharge or dismiss (an employee) from a job, esp for bad work, theft, etc.

ˈfiring line, front line where soldiers fire at the enemy. ***in the firing line,*** (*fig*) exposed to attack, criticism, etc.

ˈfiring squad, number of soldiers ordered to fire volleys at a military funeral or to carry out a military execution.

firm[1] /fərm/ *adj* (-er, -est) **1** solid; hard; not yielding when pressed: ~ *flesh/muscles.* **2** not easily changed or influenced; showing strength of character and purpose: *be ~ with children,* insist upon obedience and discipline; *be ~ in one's beliefs.* **3** (of a person, his body, its movements, characteristics, etc) steady, stable: *walk with ~ steps. He spoke in a ~ voice.* □ *vt,vi* make or become firm.

firm·ly *adv* in a firm manner.

firm·ness /-nɪs/ *n* [U]

firm[2] /fərm/ *n* [C] **1** (two or more) persons carrying on a business. **2** any business organization: *John works for a big law ~.*

fir·ma·ment /ˈfərməmənt/ *n* **the firmament,** the expanse, the heavens; sky.

first[1] /fərst/ *adj* (*abbr* **1st**) before all others in time, order, importance, etc: *January, the ~ month of the year; at the ~* (= earliest) *opportunity; not know the ~ thing* (= not even one thing) *about it.* ***at first sight,*** initially: *It seemed easy at ~ sight, but ...*

ˌfirst ˈaid, treatment given at once to a sick or injured person before a doctor comes.

ˌfirst ˈbase, (*baseball*) (position of the player defending the) base that must be touched first by a runner. ⇨ illus at baseball.

ˌfirst ˈclass, best accommodation in a train, liner, airplane, etc.

ˈfirst-class *adj* of the best class: *~-class hotels;* □ *adv* by the best class: *travel ˌ~-ˈclass.*

ˌfirst ˈfloor, ground floor.

ˌfirst·ˈhand *adj, adv* (obtained) directly from the source: *~hand information; learn something ˌ~ˈhand.*

ˌFirst ˈLady *n* [C] (*pl* -ies) wife or hostess of the President of the US, of the governor of a state, etc.

first·ly *adv* in the first place.

first ˈmate, ⇨ mate[1](2).

ˈfirst name, given name (contrasted with family name).

ˌfirst ˈnight, evening on which a play, etc is presented for the first time.

ˌfirst ofˈfender, one against whom no previous conviction has been recorded.

ˌfirst ˈperson, (*gram*) the *pronouns I, me, we, us* (and the *verb* forms used with them).

ˌfirst-ˈrate *adj* of the best class; excellent: *~-rate acting.*

first[2] /fərst/ *adv* **1** before anyone or anything else (often, for emphasis, *~ of all, ~ and foremost*): *Which horse came in ~,* won the race? **2** for the first time: *When did you ~ see him/see him ~?* **3** before some other (specified or implied) time: *I must finish this work ~,* before starting something else. **4** in preference: *He said he would resign ~.*

ˈfirst·born *n, adj* oldest (child).

first[3] /fərst/ *n* **1** ***at first,*** at the beginning. ***from the first,*** from the start. ***from first to last,*** from beginning to end; throughout. **2** [C] winning place in a race, contest, etc: *We took four*

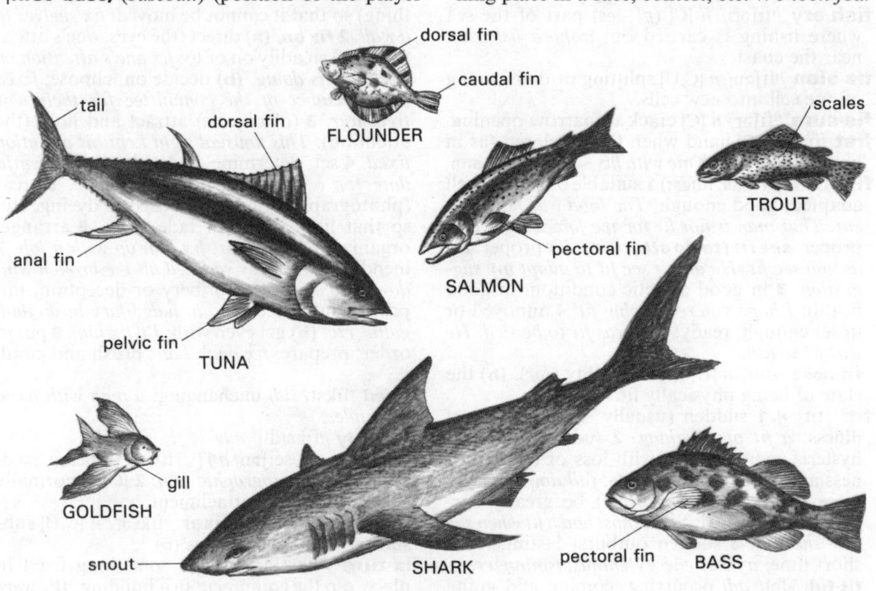

FISH

~s at the track meet.

fis·cal /ˈfɪskəl/ *adj* of public revenue.

fish[1] /fɪʃ/ *n* (*pl* ~ or ~es) **1** [C] cold-blooded animal living wholly in water and breathing through gills: *catch a ~/two ~es/a lot of ~.* ***have ˈother fish to fry,*** more important business to attend to. **2** [U] fish as food.

ˈfish·cake *n* [C] shredded fish mixed with mashed potatoes, made into a cake or ball and then fried.

ˈfish fry, (esp outdoor) social gathering at which fish are fried and eaten.

ˈfish·hook *n* [C] metal hook used for catching fish.

ˈfish·net *n* [C] net for catching fish.

fishy *adj* (-ier, -iest) **(a)** smelling or tasting like fish: *a ~y smell.* **(b)** (*informal*) causing a feeling of doubt: *a ~y story.*

fish[2] /fɪʃ/ *vi,vt* **1** try to catch fish: *go ~ing.* **2** (*fig*) try to get, by indirect methods: *~ for information/compliments.* **3** draw or pull forth: *~ out a coin from one's pocket; ~ up a dead cat out of a canal.*

fish·ing *n* [U] catching fish for a living or for pleasure.

ˈfishing bank, underwater shelf (eg off the northeastern coast of the US) where fish can be caught in large numbers.

ˈfishing hole, (a) depression in a river or lake shore where fish are commonly caught. **(b)** hole cut in the ice of a frozen lake for fishing.

ˈfishing line, line[1](1) with a fishhook attached for fishing.

ˈfishing pole/rod, rod to which a fishing line is fastened.

ˈfishing tackle, things needed for fishing.

fisher·man /ˈfɪʃərmən/ *n* [C] (*pl* -men, /-men/) (esp) man who earns a living by fishing.

fish·ery /ˈfɪʃəri/ *n* [C] (*pl* -ies) part of the sea where fishing is carried on: *inshore fisheries,* near the coast.

fis·sion /ˈfɪʃən/ *n* [C,U] splitting or division, eg of one cell into new cells.

fis·sure /ˈfɪʃər/ *n* [C] crack or narrow opening.

fist /fɪst/ *n* [C] hand when tightly closed (as in boxing): *He struck me with his ~.* ⇨ illus at arm.

fit[1] /fɪt/ *adj* (fitter, fittest) **1** suitable or suited; well adapted; good enough: *The food was not fit to eat. That man is not fit for the job.* **2** right and proper. ***see fit (to do sth),*** consider proper: *Do as you see fit. He didn't see fit to adopt my suggestion.* **3** in good athletic condition; in good health: *I hope you're keeping fit.* **4** annoyed or upset enough; ready: *She was fit to be tied. He was fit to kill.*

fit·ness /-nɪs/ *n* [U] **(a)** suitability (*for*). **(b)** the state of being physically fit.

fit[2] /fɪt/ *n* **1** sudden (usually short) attack of illness: *a fit of coughing.* **2** sudden attack of hysteria, paralysis, eg with loss of consciousness and violent movements: *fall down in a fit.* ***have/throw a fit,*** (*informal*) be greatly surprised or outraged: *She almost had a fit when she saw the bill.* **3** sudden outburst lasting for a short time: *a fit of energy/enthusiasm/anger.*

fit·ful /-fəl/ *adj* occurring, coming and going irregularly.

fit·fully /-fəli/ *adv*

fit[3] /fɪt/ *vt,vi* (*pt,pp* fit or fitted; -tt-) **1** be the right measure, shape and size for: *shoes that fit well.* **2** (cause to) be the right size, shape, etc: *have a new coat fitted.* **3** put into place and adjust properly: *fit a new lock on a door.* **4** make (a person, oneself, a thing) suitable or competent: *fit ourselves for the struggle. We should fit the punishment to the crime.* **5** ***fit in (with),*** (cause to) be in a suitable or harmonious relation (with); agree; belong: *I must fit my vacations in with yours. She just doesn't fit in.* ***fit sb/sth out,*** supply with what is needed; equip: *fit out a ship for a long voyage.* ***fit sb/sth up,*** supply: *a hotel fitted up with modern comforts.* □ *n* (usually *sing* with *a* or *an* and an *adjective*) style, manner, in which something, eg a garment, fits: *The coat is a tight/good/excellent fit.*

fit·ter /ˈfɪtər/ *n* [C] **1** person who fits and alters garments. **2** workman who fits and adjusts parts of an engine, machine, etc.

fit·ting /ˈfɪtɪŋ/ *adj* proper; right; suitable. □ *n* [C] **1** act of fitting: *go to the tailor's for a ~.* **2** small accessory part: *pipe ~s.* **3** (*pl*) furnishings: *office ~s,* eg desks, filing cabinets.

five /faiv/ *adj, n* [C] (of) 5.

five-and-ten(-cent store) *n* (usually chain) store featuring a wide variety of inexpensive, usually small dry goods, and sometimes containing a luncheon counter.

ˈfive·fold *adj* **(a)** with 5 parts. **(b)** 5 times as much.

fix[1] /fɪks/ *n* [C] **1** ***be in/get oneself into a fix,*** a dilemma, an awkward situation. **2** finding of a position, position found, by taking bearings, observing the stars, etc. **3** (*sl*) injection of a narcotic drug, eg heroin.

fix[2] /fɪks/ *vt,vi* **1** make firm or fast; fasten (something) so that it cannot be moved: *fix shelves to a wall.* **2** ***fix on,*** **(a)** direct (the eyes, one's attention, etc) steadily on or to: *fix one's attention on what one is doing.* **(b)** decide on; choose: *fixed on a member of the committee for their new treasurer.* **3** (of objects) attract and hold (the attention): *This unusual sight kept his attention fixed.* **4** set; determine or decide: *fix the rent/a date for a meeting; fixed the blame.* **5** treat (photographic film, colors used in dyeing, etc) so that light does not fade them. **6** arrange; organize, provide for: *fix him up with a job.* **7** mend; repair: *They've fixed all the broken windows.* **8** (*sl*) **(a)** use bribery or deception, improper influence: *fix a judge/jury/basketball game, etc.* **(b)** get even with: *I'll fix him.* **9** put in order; prepare: *fix one's hair,* brush and comb it.

fixed /fɪkst/ *adj* unchanging: *a man with fixed principles.*

fix·ed·ly /ˈfɪksɪdli/ *adv*

fix·ation /fɪkˈseiʃən/ *n* **1** [U] fixing or being fixed: *the ~ of a photographic film.* **2** [C] abnormally strong emotional attachment.

fixa·tive /ˈfɪksətɪv/**, fixer** /ˈfɪksər/ *n* [C,U] substance which sets or fixes[2](5).

fix·ture /ˈfɪkstʃər/ *n* [C] **1** something fixed in place, esp the equipment in a building: *We were charged for the electric light ~s.* **2** (*informal*) person or thing that appears unlikely to move from or leave a place: *Professor Green seems to be a ~ in the college.*

fizz /fɪz/ *vi* make a bubbly hissing sound (as when gas escapes from a liquid). □ *n* [U] this sound.

fizzy *adj* (-ier, -iest)

fizzle /ˈfɪzəl/ *vi* hiss or splutter feebly. ***fizzle out,*** come to a weak, unsatisfactory end.

fjord, fiord /fiˈɔrd/ *n* [C] long narrow arm of the sea, between high cliffs.

FL *postal abbr* = Florida. ⇨ App 6.

fl. *abbr* = **1** floor[1](2). **2** fluid.

flabby /ˈflæbi/ *adj* (-ier, -iest) **1** (of the muscles, flesh) soft; not firm: *A man who never takes exercise is likely to have ~ muscles.* **2** (*fig*) weak; without force: *a ~ will/character.*

flab·bily /-əli/ *adv*

flab·bi·ness /-nɪs/ *n* [U]

flag[1] /flæg/ *n* [C] (usually oblong) piece of cloth, often attached by one edge to a rope, used as the distinctive symbol of a country, or as a signal: *A red ~ means danger.* □ *vt* (-gg-) **1** place a flag on; decorate with flags: *streets ~ged to celebrate a victory.* **2** signal to stop a train, car, etc by moving one's outstretched arm up and down or waving a flag: *~ down the next car.*

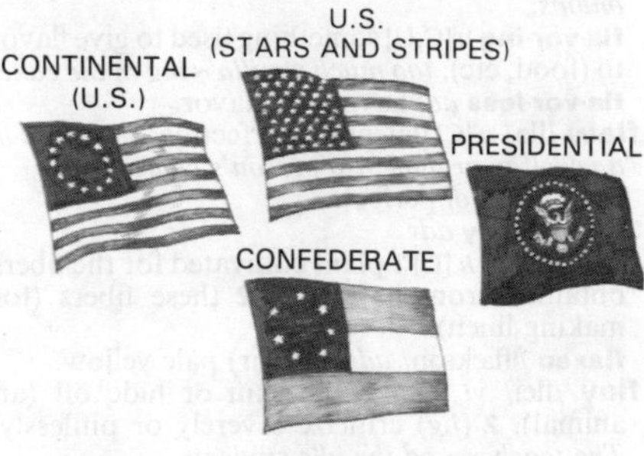

FLAGS

ˈflag·pole *n* [C] pole on which a flag is displayed.

ˈflag·ship *n* [C] warship of the commander of a fleet or squadron.

ˈflag·staff *n* [C] = flagpole.

flag[2] /flæg/ *vi* (-gg-) **1** droop, hang down, become limp. **2** (*fig*) become tired or weak: *His strength/interest in his work was ~ging.*

flagel·late /ˈflædʒəˌleit/ *vt* whip; flog.

flagel·la·tion /ˌflædʒəˈleiʃən/ *n* [U]

flagon /ˈflægən/ *n* [C] vessel for liquids with a handle, spout, and lid.

fla·grant /ˈfleigrənt/ *adj* openly and obviously wicked; glaring; scandalous: *~ offenses/sinners.*

fla·grant·ly *adv*

flag·stone /ˈflægˌstoun/ *n* [C] flat, square or oblong piece of stone for a floor, path or paving.

flail /ˈfleiəl/ *n* [C] hand tool for threshing grain. □ *vt* (*pres p* ~ing /ˈfleilɪŋ/) beat (as) with a flail.

flair /fler/ *n* [C] (usually *sing*) natural or instinctive ability (to do something well, to select or recognize what is best, most useful, etc): *have a ~ for languages,* be quick at learning them.

flake /fleik/ *n* [C] small, light, leaf-like piece: *ˈsnow~s; ˈsoap ~s.* □ *vt,vi* separate or fall off in(to) flakes: *I ~d the cooked fish into the bowl.*

flaki·ness /-nɪs/ *n* [U]

flaky *adj* (-ier, -iest) **(a)** made up of flakes: *flaky pastry.* **(b)** (sl) very odd; eccentric: *flaky behavior.*

flam·boy·ance /flæmˈbɔiəns/ *n* [U] being flamboyant.

flam·boy·ant /flæmˈbɔiənt/ *adj* **1** brightly colored and highly decorated. **2** showy; given to display.

flam·boy·ant·ly *adv*

flame[1] /fleim/ *n* **1** [C,U] glowing part of a fire: *He put a match to the papers and they burst into ~(s).* **2** [C] blaze of light or brilliant color that is like a flame: *the ~s of sunset.* **3** [C] passion: *a ~ of anger/indignation/enthusiasm.* **4** [C] (*informal*) sweetheart: *She's an old ~ of his.*

flame[2] /fleim/ *vi* **1** burn with, send out, flames. **2** be or become like flames in color: *hillsides flaming with the colors of autumn.*

flam·ing *adj* **(a)** burning; very hot: *a flaming sun.* **(b)** violent: *in a flaming rage.*

fla·mingo /fləˈmɪŋgou/ *n* [C] (*pl* ~s, ~es) large long-legged, long-necked wading bird with pink feathers. ⇨ illus at bird.

flam·mable /ˈflæməbəl/ *adj* easily set on fire and capable of burning rapidly.

flange /flændʒ/ *n* [C] projecting or outside rim, eg of a wheel.

flank /flæŋk/ *n* [C] **1** fleshy part of the side of a human being or animal between the last rib and the hip. **2** side of a building or mountain. **3** right or left side of a body of troops: *attack the left ~.* □ *vt* **1** be situated at or on the flank of. **2** go around the flank of (the enemy).

flan·nel /ˈflænəl/ *n* **1** [U] soft woolen or cotton cloth. **2** (*pl*) flannel trousers or underwear.

flap[1] /flæp/ *n* [C] **1** (sound of a) flapping blow or movement. **2** flat piece of material that hangs loose: *the ~ of a pocket; the gummed ~ of an envelope.* **3** movable, hinged part of the wing of an aircraft used to help in landing or taking off. ⇨ illus at aircraft. **4** ***be in/get into a flap,*** (*sl*) state of nervous excitement or confusion.

flap[2] /flæp/ *vt,vi* (-pp-) **1** (cause to) move up and down or from side to side: *The sails were ~ping against the mast. The bird was ~ping its wings.* **2** give a light blow to with something soft and flat: *~ the flies off/away.*

flap·jack /ˈflæpˌdʒæk/ *n* [C] pancake. ⇨ illus at pancake.

flap·per /ˈflæpər/ *n* [C] something broad and flat (eg as used to swat flies, etc).

flare[1] /fler/ *vi* **1** burn with a bright, unsteady flame: *flaring torches.* **2** ***flare up,*** **(a)** burst into bright flame. **(b)** (*fig*) burst into rage; (of violence) suddenly break out: *She ~s up at the least thing. Rioting ~d up again later.* □ *n* **1** [U] flaring light: *the ~ of torches.* **2** [C] device for producing a flaring light, used as a signal, etc: *The wrecked ship was using ~s to attract the attention of the coast guards.*

ˈflare-up *n* [C] sudden outburst.

flare[2] /fler/ *vi,vt* (cause to) spread gradually outward; become, make, wider at the bottom: *the flaring sides of a ship; trousers that ~ at the* *bottom.* □ *n* [C] gradual widening or spreading outward.

flash[1] /flæʃ/ *n* [C] **1** sudden burst of flame or light: *a ~ of lightning*. **2** (*fig*) sudden outburst; sudden idea, realization, etc: *a ~ of inspiration*. ***in a flash,*** instantly, at once. ***a flash in the pan,*** a single, sudden effort that fails. **3** (also **ˈnews-flash**) brief item of news on the radio, TV, etc. **4** (as an *adjective*) starting suddenly and lasting only a short time: *a ~ fire/flood*.

ˈflash·back *n* [C] part of a motion picture, etc that shows a scene earlier in time than the rest.

ˈflash·bulb *n* [C] bulb used in photography giving a momentary bright light.

ˈflash·cube *n* [C] cube containing four flash-bulbs, that can be attached to a camera for taking pictures, one right after the other.

ˈflash·gun *n* [C] device attached to a camera, for holding and setting off flashbulbs.

ˈflash·light *n* **(a)** light used for signals, in light-houses, etc. **(b)** brilliant, artificial flash of light for taking a photograph indoors or when natural light is too weak. **(c)** small, portable electric light that is operated by batteries.

flash[2] /flæʃ/ *vi,vt* **1** send, give out, a sudden bright light: *The lightning ~ed across the sky*. **2** come suddenly (into view, into the mind): *The idea ~ed into/through his mind*. **3** send suddenly or instantly: *~ a light in his eyes; ~ news across the world* (by radio or TV). **4** send or reflect like a flash: *Her eyes ~ed defiance*. **5** show quickly or briefly: *~ed his badge*.

flashy /ˈflæʃi/ *adj* (-ier, -iest) brilliant and attractive but rather vulgar: *~ clothes/jewelry*.

flash·ily /-əli/ *adv*

flask /flæsk/ *n* [C] **1** narrow-necked bottle, esp as used in laboratories, etc. **2** (also **ˈhip flask**) flat-sided bottle of metal or (often leather-covered) glass for carrying liquor in the pocket.

flat[1] /flæt/ *adj* (-tter, -ttest) **1** smooth and level; even; having an unbroken surface: *The top of a table is ~. One of the tires is ~*, has no or not enough air in it. **2** spread out; (lying) at full length: *He fell ~ on his back*. **3** with a broad level surface and little depth: *A phonograph record is ~*. **4** lacking air or gas: *a ~ tire*. **5** dull; uninteresting; monotonous: *The party/conversation was rather ~*. **6** (*music*) below the true pitch; (of a note) lowered half a tone in pitch: *A ~*. ⇨ sharp (9). **7** absolute; positive: *give her a ~ denial/refusal*. **8** (of paints, painted surfaces) not shiny: *~ black*. □ *adv* **1** in a flat manner: *sing ~*. ***fall flat*** ⇨ fall[2](2). **2** positively. ***flat broke,*** (*informal*) with no money at all. **3** exactly: *ran the mile in four minutes ~*.

ˈflat·boat *n* [C] large, flat-bottomed boat, formerly used for transporting goods.

ˈflat·fish *n* (kinds of) fish (sole, flounder, etc) having a flat body and swimming on one side.

ˈflat-footed *adj* **(a)** having feet with flat soles. **(b)** (*informal*) forthright: *a~-footed refusal*.

ˈflat·iron *n* [C] iron for pressing clothes.

flat·ly *adv* in a flat(7) manner: *He ~ly refused to join us*.

flat·ness /-nɪs/ *n* [U]

flat·top *n* (*informal*) aircraft carrier.

flat[2] /flæt/ *n* **1** flat part of anything: *the ~ of his sword*. **2** stretch of low level land, esp near water: *ˈmud ~s*. **3** (*music*) flat note; the symbol ♭ used to show this. ⇨ illus at notation. **4** deflated tire, eg after a puncture. **5** piece of stage scenery on a movable frame.

flat·ten /ˈflætən/ *vt,vi* make or become flat: *a field of wheat ~ed by storms; ~ oneself against a wall*.

flat·ter /ˈflætər/ *vt* **1** praise too much or insincerely (in order to please). ***flatter oneself that…,*** be pleased with one's belief that…. **2** give a feeling of pleasure to: *I'm ~ed by your invitation*. **3** (of a picture, artist, etc) show (a person) as better looking than he is: *This photograph ~s you*.

flat·terer *n* [C] person who flatters.

flat·tery *n* **(a)** [U] insincere praise. **(b)** [C] act of flattering: *Don't be deceived by her flatteries*.

flaunt /flɔnt/ *vt,vi* **1** show off in order to attract attention to: *~ oneself/one's riches, etc*. **2** wave proudly: *flags and banners ~ing in the breeze*.

flau·tist /ˈflɔtɪst, ˈflau-/ *n* [C] = flutist.

fla·vor /ˈfleivər/ *n* **1** [U] sensation of taste and smell: *Some food has very little ~*. **2** [C] special or distinctive taste: *various ~s of ice cream*. **3** [C] special quality: *a newspaper story with a ~ of romance*. □ *vt* give a flavor to: *~ a sauce with onions*.

fla·vor·ing *n* [C,U] something used to give flavor to (food, etc): *too much vanilla ~ing in the cake*.

fla·vor·less *adj* having no flavor.

flaw /flɔ/ *n* [C] defect; imperfection; fault: *~s in a jewel/an argument/a person's character*.

flaw·less *adj* perfect.

flaw·less·ly *adv*

flax /flæks/ *n* [U] **1** plant cultivated for the fibers obtained from its stems. **2** these fibers (for making linen).

flaxen /ˈflæksən/ *adj* (of hair) pale yellow.

flay /flei/ *vt* **1** take the skin or hide off (an animal). **2** (*fig*) criticize severely or pitilessly: *The teacher ~ed the idle students*.

flea /fli/ *n* [C] small wingless jumping insect that feeds on the blood of human beings and some animals. ⇨ illus at insect.

ˈflea market, open-air market selling cheap and secondhand goods.

fleck /flek/ *n* [C] **1** small spot or patch: *~s of color on a bird's breast*. **2** small particle (of dust, etc). □ *vt* mark with flecks: *a sky ~ed with clouds*.

fled *pt,pp* of flee.

fledged /fledʒd/ *adj* (of birds) with fully grown wing feathers; able to fly.

fledg(e)·ling /ˈfledʒlɪŋ/ *n* [C] **(a)** young bird just able to fly. **(b)** (*fig*) young inexperienced person.

ˌfull-ˈfledged *adj* fully developed; experienced: *a full-~ engineer*.

flee /fli/ *vi,vt* (*pt,pp* fled /fled/) **1** run or hurry away (as from danger): *He killed his enemy and fled the country*. **2** pass away; vanish.

fleece /flis/ *n* [C,U] woolly covering of a sheep or similar animal; quantity of wool cut from a sheep in one operation: *a coat lined with ~*. □ *vt* **1** cut the fleece from; shear. **2** rob (a person) by trickery: *He was ~d of his money*.

fleecy *adj* (-ier, -iest) like fleece: *~ snow*.

fleet[1] /flit/ *n* [C] **1 (a)** number of warships under one commander. **(b)** all the warships of a country. **2** number of ships, aircraft, buses, etc moving or working under one command or ownership.

ˈ**fleet admiral,** admiral of the highest rank in the US navy.

fleet[2] /flit/ *adj* (*poet*) quick-moving.

fleet·ness /-nɪs/ *n* [U]

fleet·ing /ˈflitɪŋ/ *adj* passing quickly: *a ~ visit*, a short one; *~ happiness*, lasting for a short time.

flesh /fleʃ/ *n* [U] **1 (a)** soft substance, esp muscle, between the skin and bones of animal bodies: *Tigers are ~-eating animals.* ***flesh and blood,*** human nature with its emotions, weaknesses, etc: *more than ~ and blood can stand*, more than human nature can bear. ***one's own flesh and blood,*** one's near relatives. ***in the flesh,*** alive and in person. **(b)** this substance as food. **2 the flesh,** physical or bodily desires; the body (contrasted with the *mind* and *soul*): *The spirit is willing but the ~ is weak. the sins of the ~*. **3** pulpy part of fruits and vegetables.

fleshy *adj* (-ier, -iest) fat; of flesh.

fleur-de-lis, -lys /ˌflərdəˈli/ *n* [C] (*pl* fleurs-de-lis, -lys pronunciation unchanged) heraldic lily; royal arms of France.

flew *pt* of fly[2].

flex /fleks/ *vt* bend, stretch, eg a limb, one's muscles.

flex·ible /ˈfleksəbəl/ *adj*. **1** easily bent without breaking. **2** (*fig*) easily changed to suit new conditions; adaptable.

flexi·bil·ity /ˌfleksəˈbɪləti/ *n* [U]

flick /flɪk/ *n* [C] **1** quick light blow, eg with a whip or the tip of a finger. **2** sound of such a short sudden movement. □ *vt* strike with a flick, **the flick(s),** (*sl*) cinema (films).

flicker[1] /ˈflɪkər/ *vi* **1** (of a light) burn or shine unsteadily: *The candle ~ed and then went out*. **2** (*fig*) appear fitfully or briefly: *A faint hope still ~ed in her breast*. **3** move back and forth, wave to and fro: *~ing shadows*. □ *n* [C] (usually *sing*) flickering movement: *a ~ of interest*.

flicker[2] /ˈflɪkər/ *n* [C] large, insect-eating woodpecker of North America.

flier /ˈflaiər/ *n* [C] **1** person who flies; aviator. **2** train that travels with exceptional speed. **3** small printed notice given out esp as an advertisement. **4** (*informal*) reckless business venture.

flight[1] /flait/ *n* **1** [U] flying through the air: *the science of ~; study the ~ of birds*, how they fly. ***in flight,*** while flying. **2** [C] journey made by air; distance covered: *a nonstop ~ from Paris to New York*. **3** [U] movement (and path) through the air: *the ~ of an arrow*. **4** [C] number of birds or objects moving together through the air: *a ~ of swallows*. **5** [U] swift passing: *the ~ of time*. **6** [C] going beyond the ordinary: *a ~ of the imagination/fancy*. **7** [C] series (*of* stairs, etc without change of direction); stairs between two landings: *My bedroom is two ~s up*. **8** [C] group of aircraft in a country's air force.

flight·less *adj* (of birds) unable to fly.

flight[2] /flait/ *n* [C,U] (act, instance, of) fleeing of running away (from danger, etc): *seek safety in ~*. ***take (to) flight,*** run away.

flighty /flaiti/ *adj* (-ier, -iest) **1** impulsive and frivolous: *The ~ young girl thought only of boys and parties*. **2** irresponsible: *He was a ~ person who could never hold down a job*.

flimsy /ˈflɪmzi/ *adj* (-ier, -iest) **1** (of material) light and thin. **2** (of objects) easily injured and destroyed. **3** (*fig*) poor; feeble: *a ~ excuse/argument*.

flims·ily /ˈflɪmzəli/ *adv*

flim·si·ness /ˈflɪmzinɪs/ *n* [U]

flinch /flɪntʃ/ *vi* draw or move back, esp from pain, danger, etc: *have a tooth pulled out without ~ing*.

fling /flɪŋ/ *vt,vi* (*pt,pp* flung /flәŋ/) **1** throw violently: *~ a stone; ~ the doors and windows open*, open them quickly and forcibly; *be flung into prison*. **2** move oneself, one's arms, etc violently, hurriedly, impulsively or angrily: *~ one's arms up/about; ~ one's clothes on,* dress hurriedly. □ *n* [C] **1** act, movement, of flinging. **2** kind of lively dance: *the Highland ~*, as danced in Scotland. **3** time of doing as one pleases: *We've had our ~; now let's get to work*.

flint /flɪnt/ *n* **1 (a)** [U] hard grayish quartz that makes a spark with steel. **(b)** [C] piece of this used with steel to produce sparks. **2** [C] piece of hard alloy used in a cigarette lighter to produce sparks. **3** [U] something very hard and unyielding.

flinty *adj* (-ier, -iest)

flint·lock /ˈflɪntˌlak/ *n* [C] old-fashioned gun using a flint and steel to make the sparks for exploding the gunpowder.

flip /flɪp/ *vt,vi* (-pp-) **1** put (something) into motion by a snap of the finger and thumb: *~ a coin (down) on the counter*. **2** turn over suddenly or quickly: *The acrobat ~ped onto the mat*. ***flip over:*** *The car ~ped over while going around the sharp curve*. ***flip through sth,*** look at hurriedly: *She ~ped through the magazine*. **3** (*informal*) get excited: *She really ~ped over him*. □ *n* [C] **(a)** quick, light blow. **(b)** sudden complete turn; somersault: *The young gymnast did a ~*. □ *adj* (-pper, -ppest) flippant.

ˈ**flip side,** (*informal*) the reverse side (of a phonograph record).

flip·pancy /ˈflɪpənsi/ *n* **1** [U] being flippant. **2** [C] flippant remark, etc.

flip·pant /ˈflɪpənt/ *adj* not showing deserved respect or seriousness: *a ~ answer/remark*.

flip·pant·ly *adv*

flip·per /ˈflɪpər/ *n* [C] **1** broad, flat limb of certain sea animals (not fish) used in swimming: *Seals, turtles and penguins have ~s*. ⇨ illus at seal. **2** similar device, usually of rubber, worn on the feet to aid swimming.

flirt /flərt/ *vi* **1** try to attract a person; play at showing attraction, affection, etc. *She ~s with every handsome man she meets*. **2** think about, but not seriously: *He's been ~ing with the idea of going to Moscow*. **3** move quickly about. □ *n* [C] man or girl who flirts(1).

flir·ta·tion /flərˈteiʃən/ *n* **(a)** [U] flirting. **(b)** [C] instance of flirting (1): *carry on a ~ation*.

flir·ta·tious *adj*

flit /flɪt/ *vi* (-tt-) **1** fly or move lightly and quickly: *bees* ~*ting from flower to flower*. **2** (*fig*) pass quickly: *fancies that* ~ *through one's mind*. □ *n* [C] quick, light movement.

float[1] /flout/ *n* [C] **1** piece of cork or other light material used on a fishing line (to show when the bait has been taken) or to support the edge of a fishnet. **2** hollow ball, etc eg to regulate the level of water in a tank or cistern. **3** low flat car, as used for showing things in a procession. **4** drink of soda, etc with a scoop of ice cream floating in it.

float[2] /flout/ *vi,vt* **1** be held on the surface of a liquid, or up in air, gas: *Wood* ~*s on water. A balloon* ~*ed across the sky*. **2** cause to float: *There wasn't enough water to* ~ *the ship*. **3** move or drift aimlessly.

float·ing *adj* not fixed or settled: *the* ~*ing population*.

flock[1] /flak/ *n* [C] **1** number of birds or animals (usually sheep, goats) of one kind, either kept together or feeding and traveling together. **2** crowd of people: *Visitors came in* ~*s to see the new bridge*. **3** church group or congregation: *a priest and his* ~. □ *vi* gather, come or go together in great numbers: *The children* ~*ed around their teacher*.

flock[2] /flak/ *n* **1** [C] tuft of wool or hair. **2** [U] wool or cotton waste for stuffing mattresses, etc.

floe /flou/ *n* [C] sheet of floating ice.

flog /flag/ *vt* (-gg-) beat severely with a rod or whip. ***flog a dead horse,*** waste one's efforts.

flog·ging *n* [C,U]

flood[1] /flәd/ *n* [C] **1** (coming of a) great quantity of water over a place that is usually dry: *The rainstorms caused* ~*s in the low-lying areas*. **2** great outpouring or outburst: ~*s of rain/tears; a* ~ *of anger/letters*. **3** flowing in at the tide.

ˈflood·gate *n* [C] gate in a canal, river, etc, that is opened and closed to admit or keep out water.

ˈflood tide, rising tide. ⇨ ebb.

flood[2] /flәd/ *vt,vi* **1** cover or fill (as) with a flood: *The meadows were* ~*ed. The soldiers* ~*ed the countryside. We have been* ~*ed with requests*. **2** fill to overflowing.

floor[1] /flɔr/ *n* **1** [C] part of a room on which one walks or stands: *a bare* ~, one with no carpet, etc. **2** [C] number of rooms, etc on the same level in a building: *offices on the first* ~. **3** [C] bottom of the sea, of a cave, etc. **4** [C] part of a legislative chamber, eg Congress, where members sit. **5** [U] right to speak from the floor of a lawmaking body, at a meeting, etc: *The chairman will decide who has the* ~. **6** [C] lower limit (of prices).

ˈfloor·board *n* [C] plank of a wooden floor.

floor·ing *n* [U] material, eg boards, used for making floors.

ˈfloor show, entertainment in a nightclub.

ˈfloor·walker *n* [C] person employed in a large shop or store to direct the staff and help customers.

floor[2] /flɔr/ *vt* **1** put (a floor) in a building. **2** knock down: ~ *a man in a boxing match*. **3** puzzle, defeat: *Tom was* ~*ed by two questions in the examination*.

flop /flap/ *vi,vt* (-pp-) **1** move, fall, clumsily or helplessly: *The fish were* ~*ping around in the boat. He* ~*ped down on his knees*. **2** put down or drop clumsily or roughly: ~ *down a heavy bag*. **3** (*informal*) fail. □ *n* [C] **1** act or sound of flopping. **2** (*informal*) failure of a book, play, etc.

floppy *adj* (-ier, -iest) hanging down loosely: *a* ~*py hat*.

flop house /ˈflap ˌhaus/ *n* [C] mission house or very low-class hotel where derelicts sleep.

flora /ˈflɔrә/ *n* [U] all the plants of an area or period.

floral /ˈflɔrәl/ *adj* of flowers: ~ *designs*.

florid /ˈflɔrɪd/ *adj* **1** (too) rich in ornament and color: *a* ~ *style*, eg of writing. **2** (of a person's face) naturally red: *a* ~ *complexion*.

flor·id·ly *adv*

florin /ˈflɔrɪn/ *n* [C] old coin formerly used in various countries of Europe.

flor·ist /ˈflɔrɪst/ *n* [C] person who grows or sells flowers.

floss /flɔs, flas/ *n* [U] **1** untwisted silk thread, as used for embroidery. **2** soft, silky substance.

flo·tilla /flouˈtɪlә/ *n* [C] (*pl* ~s) fleet of small ships.

flot·sam /ˈflatsәm/ *n* [U] parts of a wrecked ship or its cargo floating in the sea. ***flotsam and jetsam,*** **(a)** wreckage and cargo found on the sea or on shore. **(b)** useless odds and ends.

flounce /flauns/ *vi* move, go, with quick, troubled or impatient movements: ~ *out of/about the room*. □ *n* [C] sudden impatient movement of the body.

floun·der[1] /ˈflaundәr/ *vi* **1** make wild and usually useless efforts (as when one is in deep water and unable to swim). **2** (*fig*) act clumsily and make mistakes.

floun·der[2] /ˈflaundәr/ *n* [C] (*pl* ~, ~s) flatfish. ⇨ illus at fish

flour /ˈflauәr/ *n* [U] fine powder, made from grain, used for making bread, cakes, pastry, etc. □ *vt* cover or sprinkle with flour.

flour·ish /ˈflәrɪʃ/ *vi,vt* **1** grow in a healthy manner; be well and active; prosper: *His business is* ~*ing. I hope you are all* ~*ing*, keeping well. **2** wave about and show: ~ *a sword*. **3** be alive and active (at the time indicated): *Socrates* ~*ed about 400 BC*. □ *n* [C] **1** flourishing movement. **2** curve or decoration, ornament eg on a signature. **3** showy passage of music; fanfare: *a* ~ *of trumpets*.

flout /flaut/ *vt* scorn; treat with contempt: ~*ed his uncle's wishes/advice*.

flow /flou/ *vi* (*pt, pp* ~ed) **1** move along or over in a stream; move smoothly: *Rivers* ~ *into the sea. The tears* ~*ed from her eyes*. **2** (of hair, garments, etc) hang down loosely: ~*ing robes; hair* ~*ing down her back*. **3** come from: *Wealth* ~*s from industry and economy*. **4** (of the tide) come in; rise: *The tide began to* ~. ⇨ ebb. □ *n* (*sing* only) flowing movement; quantity that flows: *a good* ~ *of water; a* ~ *of angry words; the ebb and* ~ *of the sea*.

flower /ˈflauәr/ *n* [C] **1** blossom; part of a plant that produces seeds. ***in*** ~, blooming. **2** (*sing* only) (*fig*) finest part: *in the* ~ *of one's youth*. □ *vi* produce flowers: ~*ing plants*.

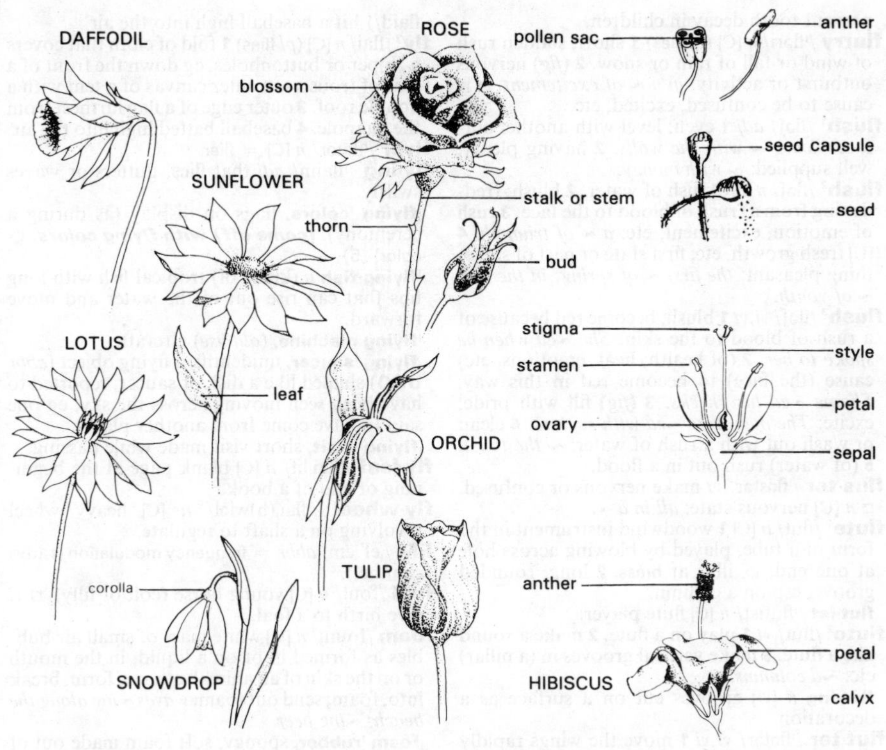

FLOWERS

flow·ered *adj* decorated with floral patterns: *~ed cloth*.

flower·less *adj* not having, not producing, flowers: *~less plants*.

flow·ery *adj* (-ier, -iest) **(a)** having many flowers: *~y fields*. **(b)** (*fig*) having an elaborate style: *~y language*.

flown *pp* of fly².

flt. *abbr* = flight¹(2).

flu /flu/ *n abbr* = influenza.

fluc·tu·ate /ˈflәktʃuˌeit/ *vi* (of levels, prices, etc) move up and down; change continually: *fluctuating prices*.

fluc·tu·ation /ˌflәktʃuˈeiʃәn/ *n* **(a)** [U] fluctuating. **(b)** [C] fluctuating movement: *fluctuations of temperature*.

flue /flu/ *n* [C] pipe or tube for carrying heat, hot air or smoke, esp to the outside.

flu·ency /ˈfluәnsi/ *n* [U] the quality of being fluent.

flu·ent /ˈfluәnt/ *adj* **1** (of a person) able to speak smoothly and easily: *a ~ speaker*. **2** (of speech) coming smoothly and easily: *speak ~ French*.

flu·ent·ly *adv*

fluff /flәf/ *n* **1** [U] soft, feathery stuff that comes from blankets or other soft woolly material. **2** [C] (*informal*) small error in reading, speaking, etc. ⇨ 2 below. □ *vt* **1** shake, puff or spread out: *~ out a pillow. The bird ~ed (out) its feathers*. **2** (*informal*) make an error (esp in speaking one's lines in a play, etc).

fluffy *adj* (-ier, -iest) of or like, covered with, fluff.

fluid /ˈfluid/ *adj* **1** able to flow (as gases and liquids do). **2** not fixed; capable of being changed: *~ opinions/plans*. □ *n* [C,U] substance that flows, eg a liquid or a gas.

flu·id·ity /fluˈidәti/ *n* [U] quality of being fluid.

ˌfluid ˈounce, one sixteenth of a pint.

fluke¹ /fluk/ *n* [C] fortunate accident; instance of good luck.

fluke² /fluk/ *n* [C] **1** broad, triangular flat end of each arm of an anchor, that fastens in the ground. **2** barbed head of an arrow, harpoon, etc. **3** (either lobe of a) whale's tail. ⇨ illus at whale.

fluke³ /fluk/ *n* [C] **1** flatfish. **2** parasite, a kind of flat worm, found in a sheep's liver.

flung *pt,pp* of fling.

flunk /flәŋk/ *vt, vi* (*informal*) **1** fail (a test, course, etc). **2** give a failing grade to: *~ed half the students in the class*.

flunky, flunkey /ˈflәŋki/ *n* [C] apprentice, employee; etc. who does odd jobs, often without understanding their purpose.

flu·o·rescent light /flʊˌresәnt ˈlait/ *adj* electric light, usually in the form of a tube, which gives off a cool white light.

flu·ori·da·tion /ˌflʊrәˈdeiʃәn/ *n* [U] addition of small amounts of fluoride to a water supply to prevent tooth decay in children.

flurry /ˈflɚri/ *n* [C] (*pl* -ies) **1** short, sudden rush of wind or fall of rain or snow. **2** (*fig*) nervous outburst or activity: *in a ~ of excitement.* □ *vt* cause to be confused, excited, etc.

flush[1] /flǝʃ/ *adj* **1** even; level with another surface: *doors ~ with the walls.* **2** having plenty; well supplied: *~ with money.*

flush[2] /flǝʃ/ *n* **1** [C] rush of water. **2** blush; (reddening from a) rush of blood to the face. **3** rush of emotion, excitement, etc: *a ~ of triumph.* **4** [U] fresh growth, etc; first state or part of something pleasant: *the first ~ of spring; in the first ~ of youth.*

flush[3] /flǝʃ/ *vi,vt* **1** blush; become red because of a rush of blood to the skin: *She ~ed when he spoke to her.* **2** (of health, heat, emotions, etc) cause (the face) to become red in this way: *Shame ~ed his cheeks.* **3** (*fig*) fill with pride; excite: *The men were ~ed with success.* **4** clean or wash out with a rush of water: *~ the toilet.* **5** (of water) rush out in a flood.

flus·ter /ˈflǝstǝr/ *vt* make nervous or confused. □ *n* [U] nervous state: *all in a ~.*

flute[1] /flut/ *n* [C] **1** woodwind instrument in the form of a tube, played by blowing across hole at one end. ⇨ illus at brass. **2** long, rounded groove, esp on a column.

flut·ist /ˈflutɪst/ *n* [C] flute player.

flute[2] /flut/ *vt* **1** play on a flute. **2** make a sound like a flute. **3** make vertical grooves in (a pillar) etc: *~d columns.*

flut·ing *n* [U] grooves cut on a surface as a decoration.

flut·ter /ˈflǝtǝr/ *vt,vi* **1** move the wings rapidly without flying, or in short flights only; cause (the wings) to move in this way: *The wounded bird ~ed to the ground.* **2** (cause to) move about in a quick, irregular or restless way: *curtains ~ing in the breeze.* **3** (of the heart, pulse) beat irregularly. □ *n* **1** (usually *sing*) fluttering movement. **2** (*sing* with *a*) state of nervous excitement; flurry: *in a ~.*

flux /flǝks/ *n* **1** [U] series of changes: *in a state of ~.* **2** (*sing* only) flowing; flowing out.

fly[1] /flai/ *n* [C] (*pl* flies) **1** two-winged insect, esp the common housefly. ⇨ illus at insect. **2** artificial fly, used as a bait in fishing for trout, etc.

fly·paper *n* sticky paper, hung in strips to attract flies in a house.

ˈfly·swatter *n* [C] ⇨ swat.

ˈfly·weight *n* [C] boxer weighing 112 lbs (50.8 kg) or less.

fly[2] /flai/ *vi,vt* (*pt* flew /flu/, *pp* flown /floun/) **1** travel or move through the air as a bird does, or in an aircraft: *birds flying in the air; fly from New York to London.* **2** operate an aircraft. **3** transport goods/passengers in aircraft: *Five thousand passengers were flown to Florida during Easter weekend.* **4** go or move quickly; rush along; pass quickly: *He flew down the road. The door flew open.* ***fly off the handle,*** lose one's temper or self-control. ***fly into a rage/temper,*** become suddenly angry. **5** cause (a kite) to rise and float or wave in the air: *fly a kite.* **6** flee from: *fly the country.* **7** (*pt,pp* flied /flaid/) hit a baseball high into the air.

fly[3] /flai/ *n* [C] (*pl* flies) **1** fold of cloth that covers a zipper or buttonholes, eg down the front of a pair of trousers. **2** outer canvas of a tent with a double roof. **3** outer edge of a flag farthest from the flagpole. **4** baseball batted high into the air.

flyer /ˈflaiǝr/ *n* [C] = flier.

fly·ing /ˈflaiɪŋ/ *adj* that flies, flutters or waves swiftly.

ˌflying ˈcolors, flags on display (as during a ceremony). ***(come off) with flying colors,*** ⇨ color[1] (5).

ˈflying·fish *n* (kinds of) tropical fish with long fins that can rise out of the water and move forward.

ˈflying machine, (*old use*) aircraft.

ˌflying ˈsaucer, unidentified flying object (*abbr* **UFO**) shaped like a disk or saucer, reported to have been seen moving across the sky, eg one said to have come from another planet.

ˌflying ˈvisit, short visit made while passing.

fly·leaf /ˈflaiˌlif/ *n* [C] blank page at the beginning or end of a book.

fly·wheel /ˈflaiˌ(h)wiǝl/ *n* [C] heavy wheel revolving on a shaft to regulate.

FM /ˌefˈem/ *abbr* = frequency modulation (radio channel).

foal /foul/ *n* [C] young horse (colt or filly). □ *vi* give birth to a foal.

foam /foum/ *n* [U] white mass of small air bubbles as formed in or on a liquid, in the mouth or on the skin of an animal, etc. □ *vi* form, break into, foam; send out foam: *waves ~ing along the beach; ~ing beer.*

ˌfoam ˈrubber, spongy, soft foam made out of rubber, that is used in upholstery.

foamy *adj* (-ier, -iest)

fob /fab/ *vt* (-bb-) ***fob sth off on sb***, get a person to accept something of little or no value. *He fobbed his broken-down car off on me.*

fo·cal /ˈfoukǝl/ *adj* of or at a focus: *the ~ length/distance of a lens*, from the surface of a lens to its focus.

fo·cus /ˈfoukǝs/ *n* [C] (*pl* ~es or foci /ˈfouˌsai/) **1** meeting point of rays of light, heat, etc. **2** point, distance, at which the sharpest outline is given (to the eye, through a telescope, through a lens on a camera, etc): *The image is in/out of ~.* **3** center of interest, activity, etc: *the ~ of attention.* □ *vt,vi* (-s- or -ss-) **1** (cause to) come together at a focus. **2** adjust (an instrument, etc) so that it is in focus: *~ the lens of a microscope.* **3** concentrate: *~ one's attention/efforts on a problem.*

fod·der /ˈfadǝr/ *n* [U] dried food, hay, etc for farm animals, horses, etc.

foe /fou/ *n* [C] (*poet*) enemy.

foe·tal *adj* = fetal.

foe·tus *n* [C] = fetus.

fog /fɔg, fag/ *n* **1** [U] very fine drops of water suspended in the atmosphere near the earth's surface, thicker than mist and difficult to see through. **2** [C] period of fog; abnormal darkened state of the atmosphere: *London used to have bad fogs in winter.* **3** [C,U] mental confusion; puzzled state. □ *vt* (-gg-) cover with, as with, fog; bewilder.

ˈ**fog·bound** *adj* unable to proceed safely because of fog.

foggy *adj* (-ier, -iest) **(a)** filled with fog; not clear, because of fog: *a foggy evening*. **(b)** confused: *have only a foggy idea.*

ˈ**fog·horn** *n* [C] instrument used for warning ships in fog.

foible /ˈfɔibəl/ *n* [C] slight peculiarity or defect of character, often one of which a person is wrongly proud.

foil[1] /ˈfɔiəl/ *n* **1** [U] very thin, flexible metal sheet: *aluminum* ~. **2** [C] person or thing that contrasts with, and makes another seem more attractive: *A plain old woman acts as a* ~ *to her beautiful daughter*.

foil[2] /ˈfɔiəl/ *n* [C] light sword with a button on the point, for fencing.

foil[3] /ˈfɔiəl/ *vt* (*pres p* ~ing /ˈfɔiliŋ/) frustrate or prevent from carrying out plans: *He was* ~*ed in his attempt to deceive the girl.*

foist /fɔist/ *vt* trick a person into accepting (a useless article, etc).

fold[1] /fould/ *vt,vi* **1** bend or double one part of a thing back on itself: ~ *up a newspaper;* ~ *back the sheets.* **2** become, be able to be, folded: ~*ing doors. The window shutters* ~ *back.* **3** collapse; fail: *The business finally* ~*ed* (*up*) *last week.* **4** bend until close against the body. ***fold one's arms,*** cross them over the chest. **5** cover; enclose; embrace: ~ *something* (*up*) *in paper; hills* ~*ed in mist.* **6** (in cooking) gently mix (an ingredient, eg beaten eggs) into another. □ *n* [C] **1** part that is folded. **2** line made by folding.

folder *n* [C] **(a)** holder (made of cardboard, etc) for loose papers. **(b)** booklet made of folded paper: *travel* ~.

fold[2] /fould/ *n* [C] **1** enclosure for sheep. **2** (*fig*) group of people (as members of a church, political party, etc) sharing the same beliefs.

fo·li·age /ˈfouliidʒ/ *n* [U] all the leaves of a tree or plant.

fo·lio /ˈfouliˌou/ *n* [C] (*pl* ~s) **1** sheet of paper folded only once making four pages in a book. **2** very large book made of such sheets.

folk /fouk/ *n* **1** (*pl* ~s) people in general: *Some* ~*s are never satisfied.* **2** (*pl* ~, ~s) certain kind of people: *They are honest* ~. *Young* ~*s like to have a good time.* **3** (*pl* ~s) (*informal*) one's family; relatives: *visited the* ~*s back home.* □ *adj* of or traditional with the common people of a country: *Paul Bunyan is an American* ~ *hero.*

ˈ**folk dance,** (music for a) traditional dance.

ˈ**folk·lore** *n* [U] beliefs, legends, customs, etc handed down by a people from generation to generation.

ˈ**folk music/song,** traditional music/song handed down from the past.

folksy /ˈfouksi/ *adj* (-ier, -iest) (*informal*) **1** simple; casual. **2** friendly and sociable.

fol·low /ˈfalou/ *vt,vi* **1** come, go, have a place, after (in space, time or order): *You go first and I will* ~ (*you*). *Monday* ~*s Sunday.* ***as follows,*** as now to be stated. ***follow through,*** complete a task, carry out a plan to the end. **2** go along, keep to (a road, etc): *Follow this road for six miles.* **3** keep up with; understand: *He spoke so fast that I couldn't* ~ *him*/~ *what he said.* **4** engage in as a business, trade, etc: ~ *the sea*, be a seaman. **5** take or accept as a guide, an example, etc: ~ *somebody's advice*/*the latest fashion.* ***follow suit,*** do what has just been done by somebody else. **6** come as a result: *It* ~*s from what you say that….* **7** ***follow sth up,*** work at it further: ~ *up an inquiry.*

fol·lower *n* [C] **(a)** supporter; disciple: *the football team and their* ~*ers.* **(b)** pursuer.

fol·low·ing *adj* next: *the* ~*ing day.* ***the following,*** the one or ones about to be mentioned. □ *n* [C] body of supporters: *a political leader with a large* ~*ing.*

folly /ˈfali/ *n* (*pl* -ies) **1** [U] foolishness. **2** [C] foolish act, idea or practice; ridiculous thing.

fo·ment /fouˈment/ *vt* stir up (disorder, discontent, ill feeling, etc).

fond /fand/ *adj* **1** ***be fond of,*** like, be full of love for, take pleasure in: ~ *of music.* **2** loving and kind: *a* ~ *mother;* ~ *looks.*

fond·ly *adv* **(a)** lovingly: *look* ~*ly at her.* **(b)** foolishly: *He* ~*ly imagined that he could learn French in six weeks.*

fond·ness /-nɪs/ *n* [U]

fondle /ˈfandəl/ *vt* touch or stroke lovingly: ~ *a baby*/*a kitten.*

font /fant/ *n* [C] basin or vessel (often in carved stone) to hold water for baptism; basin for holy water.

food /fud/ *n* **1** [U] that which can be eaten by people or animals, or used by plants, to keep them living and for growth: (as an *adjective*) ~ *poisoning.* (*Note:* Food for farm animals is usually called *feed.*) **2** [U] solid nourishment as contrasted with liquid: ~ *and drink.* **3** [C] particular kind of food: *baby* ~. ***food for thought,*** something to think about.

ˈ**food stamp,** (usually in the *pl*) coupon, issued to needy people by the US Government, to be exchanged for value in food.

ˈ**food·stuff** *n* material used as food.

fool /ful/ *n* [C] person without much sense; person whose conduct one considers silly: *What* ~*s we were not to see the joke! She was* ~ *enough* (= enough of a fool) *to believe him.* ***make a fool of sb,*** trick him; cause him to seem like a fool. ***play the fool,*** behave stupidly. □ *adj* (*informal*) foolish; silly: *a scheme devised by some* ~ *politician.* □ *vi,vt* **1** behave like a fool; be idle and silly: *If you go on* ~*ing with that gun, there'll be an accident.* ***fool around,*** act foolishly; waste time: *Stop* ~*ing around!* **2** play a joke or trick or deceive: *You can't* ~ *me!*

ˌ**April** ˈ**fool,** ⇨ April.

fool·ery /ˈfuləri/ *n* (*pl* -ies) **1** [U] foolish behavior. **2** [C] foolish acts, ideas or words.

fool·hardy /ˈfulˌhardi/ *adj* taking unnecessary risks.

fool·hardi·ness /-nɪs/ *n* [U]

fool·ish /ˈfulɪʃ/ *adj* senseless; stupid; silly: *It would be* ~ *for us to quarrel.*

fool·ish·ly *adv*

fool·ish·ness /-nɪs/ *n* [U]

foot[1] /fʊt/ *n* (*pl* feet /fit/) **1** part forming the lower end of the leg, beginning at the ankle: *I've been on my feet* (= standing) *all day.* ***on foot,*** walking, not riding. ***put one's best foot for-***

ward, try to make a good impression. ***put one's foot down,*** (*informal*) take a firm stand. ***put one's foot in it/in one's mouth,*** (*informal*) say or do something wrong or stupid. ***sweep sb off his feet,*** fill him with strong enthusiasm. ⇨ illus at leg. **2** (*sing* only) way of walking; tread: *light of* ~. **3** lowest part; bottom: *at the* ~ *of the page/ladder/wall/mountain.* **4** lower end where the feet usually rest: *the* ~ *of a bed.* **5** measure of length, 12 inches: *George is very tall —he's six* ~ *two* (6′ 2″). (*Note: pl* feet or unchanged.) **6** division or unit of verse, each with one strong stress and one or more weak stresses, as in: *for mén/may cóme/and mén/may gó.*

ˌfoot-and-ˈmouth disease, disease of cattle and other cloven-hoofed animals.

ˈfoot·ball *n* [U] game played by two teams of eleven players each. [C] ball used in this game.

FOOTBALL

ˈfoot·fall *n* sound of a footstep.

ˈfoot·hill *n* low hill lying at the foot of a mountain or a range of mountains.

ˈfoot·hold *n* **(a)** secure place for the foot, eg when climbing on rocks or ice. **(b)** (*fig*) secure position.

ˈfoot·lights *n pl* lights at the front of the stage floor in a theater.

ˈfoot·man /fʊtmən/ *n* [C] (*pl* ~men /-men/) manservant who admits visitors, waits at table, etc.

ˈfoot·note *n* [C] one at the foot of a page.

ˈfoot·path *n* [C] path for the use of persons on foot.

ˈfoot·print *n* [C] impression left on a soft surface by a foot.

ˈfoot·sore *adj* having sore feet, esp because of walking.

ˈfoot·step *n* [C] (sound of a) step of a person walking. ***follow in sb's footsteps,*** do as he did.

ˈfoot·stool *n* [C] low stool for resting the feet on.

ˈfoot·wear *n* [U] boots, shoes, etc.

ˈfoot·work *n* [U] manner of using the feet, eg in boxing, dancing.

foot[2] /fʊt/ *vt,vi* (*informal*) ***foot it,*** walk: *We've missed the last bus, so we'll have to* ~ *it.* ***foot the bill,*** (agree to) pay it.

foot·age /ˈfʊtɪdʒ/ *n* [C] length measured in feet, eg of moving picture film.

-footed /ˈfʊtɪd/ *adj* (used in compounds) having the (kind of) feet indicated: *ˈflat-footed; ˈfour-footed.*

foot·ing /ˈfʊtɪŋ/ *n* [C] **1** placing of the feet: *He lost his* ~ *and fell.* **2** = foothold(a). **3** (*sing* only) position or state, esp in relation to other people, groups, nations, etc: *be on a friendly* ~ *with their neighbors; on a peace/war* ~.

fop /fap/ *n* [C] (*dated*) man who pays too much attention to his clothes and personal appearance.

fop·pish /-ɪʃ/ *adj* of or like a fop.

for[1] /fər *strong form:* fɔr/ *prep* **1** (showing a destination or goal) **(a)** after *verbs*: *set out for home. The ship was making for* (= sailing toward) *the open sea.* **(b)** after *nouns*: *the train for New Haven.* **2** (showing the aim or object of a feeling, desire, activity, etc) **(a)**: *He felt that he was destined for something great.* **(b)** (showing eventual possession): *Here's a letter for you.* **(c)** (showing preparation): *prepare for an examination; get ready for school.* **(d)** (showing purpose) in order to be, do, have, get, etc: *go for a walk/ride/swim; a cry for help; a prayer for peace. What's this tool for? What did you do that for? It's a machine for cutting steel.* **(e)** (showing an object of hope, liking, etc): *hope for the best; a taste for art; no regret for the past.* **(f)** (showing suitability; fitness, etc): *a good ear for music; bad/good for your health. It is for him to decide.* **3** (with *too* and *enough*: *too beautiful for words; quite risky enough for me.* **4** as being: *They left him for dead. They chose him for* (= as, to be) *their leader.* ***take sb/sth for,*** mistakenly think that he or it is: *He took me for my brother.* ***for certain,*** ⇨ certain(2). **5** considering (the circumstances, etc); in view of: *It's quite warm for January. She's tall for her age.* **6** representing; in place of: *B for Benjamin.* ***stand for,*** represent: *The letters MP stand for Military Police in the US and for Member of Parliament in Great Britain.* **7** in defense or support of; in favor of: *Are you for or against the proposal? Three cheers for the team!* **8** with regard to; so far as concerns: *anxious for his safety.* **9** because of; on account of: *for this reason; for my sake; win a medal for bravery.* (after a *comparative*) *Are you any the better for your long sleep?* **10** in spite of: *for all his wealth, he is unhappy.* **11** to the amount or extent of: *Put my name down for $5.* **12** in exchange for: *I paid 50 cents for the book. He did the job for nothing.* **13** in contrast with: *For one enemy he has fifty friends.* **14** (showing extent in time): *I'm going away for a few days.* ***for good,*** ⇨ good[2] (2). **15** (showing extent in space): *We walked* (*for*) *three miles. The road is lined with trees for ten miles.* **16** (in the pattern *for* + noun or pronoun + *to inf*) **(a)** : *For a woman to divorce her husband is impossible in some countries. I am anxious for you and my sister to become acquainted. There's no need for anyone to know.* **(b)** (showing purpose, design, determination, etc): *I have brought the books for you to examine. I'd have given anything for this not to have happened.*

for[2] /fər *strong form:* fɔr/ *conj* (*formal*) (rare in spoken English; not used at the beginning of a sentence) the reason, proof, etc being that: *I asked her to stay awhile, for I had something to tell her.*

for·age /ˈfɔrɪdʒ/ *n* [U] food for horses and cattle. □ *vi* search for food, etc.

foray /ˈfɔˌrei/ *n* [C] raid; sudden attack (esp to get food, animals, etc): *make/go on a* ~. □ *vi* make a foray.

for·bade, for·bad *pt* of forbid.

for·bear[1] /fɔrˈber/ *vt,vi* (*pt* forbore /fɔrˈbɔr/, *pp* forborne /fɔrˈbɔrn/) (*formal*) **1** refrain (from); not use or mention: *I cannot* ~ *from going into details.* **2** be patient; show self-control.

for·bear·ance /-rəns/ *n* [U] patience; self-control: *show* ~*ance in dealing with people.*

for·bear[2] *n* [C] = forebear.

for·bid /fərˈbɪd, fɔr-/ *vt* (*pt* forbade or forbad /fərˈbeid, -ˈbæd/, *pp* ~den /fərˈbɪdən/ or ~) order (a person) not to do something; order that something shall not be done: *I* ~ *you to use that word.*

for·bid·ding *adj* stern; uninviting; threatening: *a* ~*ding appearance.*

for·bore, for·borne *pt,pp* of forbear[1].

force[1] /fɔrs/ *n* **1** [U] strength; power of body or mind: *the* ~ *of a blow/an explosion/argument. The enemy attacked in* (*great*) ~. **2** [C] person or thing that makes great changes; strong influence: *the* ~*s of nature*, eg storms, earthquakes. *Fascism and Communism have been powerful* ~*s in world affairs.* **3** [C] organized body of armed or disciplined men and women: *the armed* ~*s of a country; the ˈAir Force; the poˈlice* ~. ***join forces (with),*** unite (with). **4** [C,U] (intensity of, measurement of) pressure or influence: *the* ~ *of gravity.* **5** ***in force,*** (of a regulation, etc) taking effect: *The law is no longer in* ~.

force[2] /fɔrs/ *vt* **1** compel, oblige; use force to (make somebody) get or do something: ~ *one's way through a crowd; She* ~*d him to tell the truth.* **2** break open by using force: ~ (*open*) *a door.* **3** cause plants, etc to mature earlier than is normal, eg by giving them extra warmth. **4** produce through effort: ~ *a smile*, eg when one is unhappy.

force·ful /ˈfɔrsfəl/ *adj* convincing, believable: *a* ~ *speaker/style of writing.*

force·fully /-fəli/ *adv*

for·ceps /ˈfɔrsəps/ *n pl* (also ***a pair of forceps***) small pincers or tongs used by dentists and by doctors for gripping things: *pulled the tooth with* (*a pair of*) ~.

forc·ible /ˈfɔrsəbəl/ *adj* **1** done by, involving the use of, physical force: *a* ~ *entry into a building.* **2** (of a person) = forceful.

forc·ibly /-əbli/ *adj*

ford /fɔrd/ *n* [C] shallow place in a river where it is possible to walk or drive across. □ *vt* cross (a body of water) by wading.

ford·able /-əbəl/ *adj* that can be forded.

fore /fɔr/ *n* (*sing* only) **1** front part (of a ship). **2** ***to the fore,*** forward; to an important position. □ *adv* (*naut*) in front. ***fore and aft,*** at both the bow and stern of a ship; lengthwise in a ship.

fore- /fɔr-/ *prefix* before; in front of: *foretell; foreground.*

fore·arm[1] /ˈfɔrˌarm/ *n* [C] arm from the elbow to the wrist or fingertips. ⇨ illus at arm and hand.

fore·arm[2] /ˌfɔrˈarm/ *vt* arm beforehand; prepare for trouble in advance: *To be forewarned is to be* ~*ed.*

fore·bear /ˈfɔrˌber/ *n* [C] ancestor.

fore·bode /fɔrˈboud/ *vt* (*formal*) **1** be a sign of warning of: *These black clouds* ~ *a storm.* **2** have a feeling that something evil is going to happen.

fore·bod·ing *n* [C,U] feeling that trouble is coming.

fore·cast /ˈfɔrˌkæst/ *vt* (*pt,pp* ~ or ~ed) say in advance what is likely to happen. □ *n* [C] such a statement: *inaccurate weather* ~*s.*

fore·court /ˈfɔrˌkɔrt/ *n* [C] enclosed space in front of a building.

fore·doom /ˌfɔrˈdum/ *vt* destine (to): ~*ed to failure.*

fore·father /ˈfɔrˌfaðər/ *n* ancestor.

fore·fin·ger /ˈfɔrˌfɪŋgər/ *n* [C] index finger.

fore·front /ˈfɔrˌfrənt/ *n* (*sing* with *the*) most forward part: *in the* ~ *of the battle.*

fore·gather, = forgather.

forego = forgo.

fore·going /ˈfɔrˌgouɪŋ/ *adj* preceding, already mentioned.

fore·gone /ˈfɔrˌgɔn/ *adj*: *a* ~ *conclusion,* ending that can be seen or could have been seen from the start.

fore·ground /ˈfɔrˌgraund/ *n* [C] part of a view nearest to the observer. ***in the foreground,*** in the most noticeable position: *keep oneself in the* ~.

fore·hand /ˈfɔrˌhænd/ *n* [C] stroke (in tennis, etc) made with the palm turned forward.

fore·head /ˈfɔrɪd, ˈfɔrˌhed, ˈfar-/ *n* [C] part of the face above the eyes. ⇨ illus at head.

foreign /ˈfɔrɪn, ˈfar-/ *adj* **1** of, in, from, another country, not one's own: ~ *languages/countries.* **2** ***foreign to,*** not natural to, unconnected with: *Lying is* ~ *to his nature.* **3** coming or introduced from outside: *a* ~ *body in the eye*, eg a bit of dirt.

foreigner *n* [C] person born in or from a foreign country.

fore·leg /ˈfɔrˌleg/ *n* [C] one of the front legs of a four-footed animal.

fore·lock /ˈfɔrˌlak/ *n* [C] lock of hair growing just above the forehead.

fore·man /ˈfɔrmən/ *n* [C] (*pl* -men /-men/) **1** workman in authority over others. **2** chief member and spokesman of a jury.

fore·mast /ˈfɔrˌmæst/ *n* [C] mast that is nearest the bow of a ship.

fore·most /ˈfɔrˌmoust/ *adj* first; most important; chief: *the* ~ *painter of his period.* □ *adv* first in position.

fore·name /ˈfɔrˌneim/ *n* [C] (as used, eg on forms) first name.

fore·noon /ˈfɔrˌnun/ *n* [C] early part of the day from sunset to noon.

for·en·sic /fəˈrensɪk/ *adj* of, used in, courts of law.

fore·part /ˈfɔrˌpart/ *n* [C] part in front.

fore·run·ner /ˈfɔrˌrənər/ *n* [C] **1** sign of what is to follow: *swallows, the* ~*s of spring.* **2** person who foretells and prepares for the coming of another.

fore·see /fɔr'si/ *vt* (*pt* foresaw /fɔr'sɔ/, *pp* foreseen /fɔr'sin/) see in advance: ~ *trouble*.

fore·shadow /fɔr'ʃædou/ *vt* be a sign or warning of.

fore·shorten /fɔr'ʃɔrtən/ *vt* (in drawings) show (an object) with a shortening of lines to give an impression of depth or distance.

fore·sight /'fɔr,sait/ *n* [U] **1** ability to see future needs. **2** care in preparing for these; prudence: *With more* ~, *you would have saved yourself a lot of trouble*.

fore·skin /'fɔr,skɪn/ *n* [C] fold of skin covering the end of the penis.

for·est /'fɔrɪst, 'far-/ *n* **1** [C,U] large area of land covered with trees and underbrush: (as an *adjective*) ~ *fires*. **2** the trees growing in a forest. **3** (*fig*) something like a forest: *a* ~ *of masts*, eg in a harbor.

'forest ranger, person in charge of a forest (protecting wild animals, watching for fires, etc).

forestry *n* [U] (science of) planting and caring for forests.

fore·stall /fɔr'stɔl/ *vt* act first and so prevent another from doing something.

fore·swear /fɔr'swer/ *vt* = forswear.

fore·taste /'fɔr,teist/ *n* [C] taste (of something) in advance.

fore·tell /fɔr'tel/ *vt* (*pt,pp* foretold /fɔr'tould/) tell beforehand; predict: ~ *her future*.

fore·thought /'fɔr,θɔt/ *n* [U] careful thought or planning for the future.

fore·told *pt,pp* of foretell.

for·ever /fə'revər/ *adv* **1** always; at all times. **2** endlessly.

for·ever·more /fə,revər'mɔr/ *adv* (*liter*) forever.

fore·warn /fɔr'wɔrn/ *vt* warn in advance.

fore·woman /'fɔr,wʊmən/ *n* [C] (*pl* -women /-,wɪmɪn/) woman in authority over other workers.

fore·word /'fɔr,wərd/ *n* [C] introduction or preface to a book.

for·feit /'fɔrfɪt/ *vt* lose (the right to) something because of a fault, error, etc. □ *n* [C] something (to be) forfeited: *His health was the* ~ *he paid for overworking*.

for·feit·ure /'fɔrfɪtʃər/ *n* [U]

for·gather /fɔr'gæðər/ *vi* come together.

for·gave *pt* of forgive.

forge[1] /fɔrdʒ/ *n* [C] **1** workshop with a fire and anvil where metals are heated and shaped, esp one used by a blacksmith for making shoes for horses, etc. **2** (workshop with a) furnace or hearth for melting or refining metal.

forge[2] /fɔrdʒ/ *vt* **1** shape (metal) by heating and hammering. **2** (*fig*) form or make: *Their friendship was* ~*d by poverty*. **3** make or write falsely, in order to deceive: ~ *a check/a ten-dollar bill*.

forger *n* [C] person who forges(3).

forg·ery /'fordʒəri/ *n* **(a)** [U] forging(3) of a document, signature, etc. **(b)** [C] (*pl* -ies) forged document, signature, etc.

forge[3] /fɔrdʒ/ *vi* ***forge ahead,*** make steady progress; take the lead (in a race, etc).

for·get /fər'get, fɔr-/ *vt,vi* (*pt* forgot /fər'gat, fɔr-/, *pp* forgotten /fər'gatən, fɔr-/) **1** fail to keep in the memory; fail to recall: *I* ~*/I've forgotten her name. I shall never* ~ *your kindness to me. I forgot all about it*. **2** neglect or fail (to do something): *Don't* ~ *to mail the letters*. **3** put out of the mind; stop thinking about: *Let's* ~ *our quarrels*.

for·get·ful /-fəl/ *adj* in the habit of forgetting: *Old people are sometimes* ~*ful*.

for·get·fully /-fəli/ *adv*

for·get·ful·ness /-nɪs/ *n* [U]

for·give /fər'gɪv, fɔr-/ *vt,vi* (*pt* forgave /fər'geiv, fɔr-/, *pp* ~n /fər'gɪvən, fɔr-/) **1** say that one no longer has the wish to punish somebody for an offense, a sin; pardon or show mercy to (a person): ~ *him for being rude*/~ *his rudeness*. **2** not demand repayment of (a debt).

for·giv·able /-əbəl/ *adj*

for·give·ness /-nɪs/ *n* [U] forgiving or being forgiven: *ask for/receive* ~*ness*.

for·giv·ing *adj* ready or willing to forgive: *a forgiving nature*.

forgo /fɔr'gou/ *vt* (*pt* forwent /fɔr'went/, *pp* forgone /fɔr'gɔn/) do without; give up: ~ *pleasures in order to study hard*.

for·got, for·got·ten *pt,pp* of forget.

fork /fɔrk/ *n* [C] **1** implement with two or more prongs used for holding food, lifting it to the mouth, etc. **2** farm or gardening tool like a fork (1). **3** place where a road, tree, etc divides or branches. **4** one of the branches into which a road, etc divides: *took the left-hand* ~. □ *vt,vi* **1** lift, move, carry, with a fork: ~ *the ground over*, turn the soil over with a fork. **2** (of a road, river, etc) divide into branches: *The road* ~*s at the church*. **3** (*informal*) hand over, pay: *I've got to* ~ *out a lot in taxes this year*.

forked *adj* branching; shaped like a fork: *the* ~*ed tongue of a snake*.

for·lorn /fər'lɔrn/ *adj* (*liter*) unhappy; deserted.

for·lorn·ly *adv*

form[1] /fɔrm/ *n* **1** [U] shape; structure; outward or visible appearance: *without shape or* ~; *take* ~, begin to have a (recognizable) shape. **2** [C] person or animal as it can be seen or touched: *A dark* ~ *could be seen in the distance*. **3** [C,U] general arrangement or structure; way in which parts are put together to make a whole or a group: *literary* ~ (as contrasted with subject matter). **4** [C] particular kind of arrangement or structure; manner in which a thing exists; type, kind or variety: ~*s of government. Ice, snow and steam are* ~*s of water*. **5** (*gram*) [C] one of the shapes taken by a word (in sound or spelling): *The word "brother" has two plural* ~*s, "brothers" and "brethren."* **6** [U] acceptable manner of behaving or speaking fixed, required or expected by custom or etiquette: *say "Good morning" as a mere matter of* ~, ie not because one is really pleased to see the person to whom the words are spoken. **7** [C] printed paper with spaces to be filled in: *application* ~*s*. **8** [U] condition for performing some activity: *Jack was in great* ~ *at the dinner party*, in high spirits, lively.

form·less *adj* without shape.

form[2] /fɔrm/ *vt,vi* **1** give shape or form to; make, produce: ~ *the plural of a noun by adding* -s or

-es. **2** develop, build up, conceive: ~ *good habits;* ~ *ideas/conclusions.* **3** organize: *They* ~*ed themselves into a committee.* **4** be (the material of): *This series of lectures* ~*s part of a complete course on French history.* **5** (*mil*) (cause to) move into a particular order: ~ *into line.* **6** come into existence; become solid; take shape: *The idea* ~*ed in his mind.*

for·mal /ˈfɔrməl/ *adj* **1** strictly in accordance with established rules, customs and convention: *pay a* ~ *call on the Ambassador.* **2** (of style, vocabulary, etc) chosen and used in formal(1) situations. **3** regular or geometric in design. **4** of the outward shape or appearance (not the reality or substance): *a* ~ *resemblance between two things.*

for·mally /-məli/ *adv*

for·mal·ity /fɔrˈmæləti/ *n* (*pl* -ies) **1** [U] strict attention to rules, forms and convention: *There was too much* ~ *in the governor's household.* **2** [C] action required by custom or rules: *legal formalities.* ***a mere formality,*** something one is required or expected to do, but which has little meaning or importance.

for·ma·tion /fɔrˈmeiʃən/ *n* **1** [U] forming or shaping: *the* ~ *of character/of ideas in the mind;* [C] that which is formed: *Clouds are* ~*s of condensed water vapor.* **2** [C,U] structure or arrangement: *troops/warships in ˈbattle* ~*; rock* ~*s.*

for·ma·tive /ˈfɔrmətɪv/ *adj* giving, or tending to give, shape to: ~ *influences,* eg on a child's character; *the* ~ *years of a child's life.*

for·mer /ˈfɔrmər/ *adj* **1** of an earlier period: *in* ~ *times; my* ~ *students.* **2** first-mentioned: *I prefer the* ~ *alternative to the latter.*

for·mer·ly *adv* in earlier times.

for·mi·dable /ˈfɔrmɪdəbəl/ *adj* **1** causing fear or dread: *a man with a* ~ *appearance.* **2** requiring great effort to deal with or overcome: ~ *obstacles/opposition/enemies/debts.*

for·mi·dably /-əbli/ *adv*

for·mula /ˈfɔrmyələ/ *n* [C] (*pl* ~s, or, in scientific usage, ~e /-li/) **1** set form of words used regularly (as "How do you do?" "Excuse me," "Thank you") or used in legal documents, etc. **2** statement of a rule, fact, etc esp one in signs or numbers, eg "Water = H_2O." **3** set of directions, usually in symbols, as for a medical preparation.

for·mu·late /ˈfɔrmyəˌleit/ *vt* express clearly and exactly: ~ *one's thoughts/a doctrine.*

for·mu·la·tion /ˌfɔrmyəˈleiʃən/ *n* **1** [U] formulating. **2** [C] exact and clear statement.

for·ni·cate /ˈfɔrnəˌkeit/ *vi* commit fornication.

for·ni·ca·tion /ˌfɔrnəˈkeiʃən/ *n* [U] voluntary sexual intercourse between unmarried persons.

for·sake /fərˈseik/ *vt* (*pt* forsook /fərˈsʊk/, *pp* ~n /fərˈseikən/) give up; abandon; desert: ~ *one's wife and children.*

for·swear /fɔrˈswer/ *vt* (*pt* forswore /fɔrˈswɔr/, *pp* forsworn /fɔrˈswɔrn/) give up doing or using (something): ~ *bad habits.*

for·syth·ia /fərˈsɪθiə, fɔr-/ *n* [C] shrub with yellow bell-shaped flowers blooming in early spring.

fort /fɔrt/ *n* [C] building or group of buildings specially erected or strengthened for military defense.

forte[1] /ˈfɔrt, ˈfɔrˌtei/ *n* [C] something a person does particularly well: *Singing is not my* ~.

forte[2] /ˈfɔrˌtei/ *adj, adv* (*music*) loud(ly).

forth /fɔrθ/ *adv* **1** (*liter*) out (which is more usual). **2** onward; forward: *from this day* ~*; and so* ~ (= and so on). ***back and forth,*** to and fro (which is more usual). **3** ***hold forth,*** ⇨ hold² (14).

forth·com·ing /fɔrθˈkəmɪŋ/ *adj* **1** about to appear: ~ *books.* **2** ready when needed: *The money/help we hoped for was not* ~*,* We did not receive it.

forth·right /ˈfɔrθˌrait/ *adj* outspoken; straightforward.

forth·right·ly *adv*

forth·right·ness /-nɪs/ *n* [U]

forth·with /fɔrθˈwɪθ/ *adv* at once; without losing time.

for·ti·eth /ˈfɔrtiəθ/ ⇨ forty.

for·tify /ˈfɔrtəˌfai/ *vt* (*pt,pp* -ied) strengthen (a place) against attack (with walls, trenches, guns, etc); support or strengthen oneself, one's courage, etc: ~ *a town against the enemy;* ~ *oneself against the cold.*

for·ti·fi·ca·tion /ˌfɔrtəfɪˈkeiʃən/ *n* **(a)** [U] fortifying. **(b)** [C] (often *pl*) defensive wall(s), tower(s), etc.

for·ti·tude /ˈfɔrtəˌtud/ *n* [U] (*formal*) calm courage, self-control, in the face of pain, danger or difficulty.

fort·night /ˈfɔrtˌnait/ *n* [C] any period of two weeks.

fort·night·ly *adj, adv* (happening) once a fortnight; of, for or lasting a fortnight.

for·tress /ˈfɔrtrɪs/ *n* [C] fortified building or town.

for·tu·itous /fɔrˈtuətəs/ *adj* happening by chance: *a* ~ *meeting.*

for·tu·itous·ly *adv*

for·tu·nate /ˈfɔrtʃənət/ *adj* favored by fortune; lucky; prosperous; having, bringing, brought by, good fortune: *You were* ~ *to escape being injured.*

for·tu·nate·ly *adv*

for·tune /ˈfɔrtʃən/ *n* **1** [C,U] chance; chance looked on as a power deciding or influencing; fate; good or bad luck coming to a person or undertaking: *have* ~ *on one's side,* be lucky. ***tell sb's fortune,*** foretell what will happen to him. **2** [C,U] prosperity; success; great sum of money: *a man of* ~. ***come into a fortune,*** inherit a lot of money. ***make a fortune,*** make a lot of money.

ˈfortune hunter, person seeking a rich person to marry.

ˈfortune teller, person who claims to be able to tell a person's fortune.

forty /ˈfɔrti/ *adj, n* [C] (of) 40: *under/over* ~.

the forties (*pl*) (a) (of a person's age, temperature etc) between 39 and 50. (b) (of a century) the years from 40 to 49 inclusive.

for·ti·eth /ˈfɔrtiəθ/ *adj, n* [C] (of) one of 40 (parts) or the next after 39.

fo·rum /ˈfɔrəm/ *n* [C] (*pl* ~s) **1** (in ancient Rome) public place for meetings. **2** any place for public discussion: *TV is an accepted* ~ *for the* *discussion of public affairs.*

for·ward[1] /ˈfɔrwərd/ *adj* **1** directed toward the front; situated in front; moving on, advancing: *a ~ march/movement.* **2** eager or impatient; ready and willing; too eager or bold: *a ~ young girl.* **3** advanced or extreme: *~ opinions.* **4** for the future: *~ buying,* buying in advance. □ *n* [C] (*sport*) one of the front-line players in football, hockey, etc.

for·ward·ness /-nɪs/ *n* [U]

for·ward[2] /ˈfɔrwərd/ *vt* **1** help or send forward; help to advance: *~ his plans.* **2** send a letter, parcel, etc after a person to a new address: *Please ~ my letters to this address.*

for·ward(s) /ˈfɔrwərd(z)/ *adv* (*Note: forwards* is rare or not much used except as in 4 below.) **1** onward so as to make progress: *rush/step ~; go ~.* **2** toward the future; onward in time: *from this time ~; look ~,* think ahead, think about the future. **3** to the front; into view: *bring ~* (= call attention to) *new evidence.* ***come forward,*** offer oneself for a task, a post, etc. **4** ***backwards and forwards,*** ⇨ backward.

fos·sil /ˈfasəl/ *n* [C] recognizable (part, trace or imprint of a) prehistoric animal or plant once buried in earth, now hardened like rock.

fos·sil·ize /ˈfasəˌlaiz/ *vt,vi* change or turn into a fossil.

fos·ter /ˈfɔstər/ *vt* **1** help the growth and development of: *~ good relations/evil thoughts.* **2** take into one's home and care for as a parent, but without legal guardianship: *~ a child.* ⇨ adopt(1).

ˈfoster-brother/-sister *n* [C] one fostered by one's parents.

ˈfoster-child *n* [C] one brought up by foster-parents.

ˈfoster-parent/-mother/-father *n* [C] one who acts as a parent in place of a natural parent.

fought *pt,pp* of fight[2].

foul[1] /faul/ *adj* (-er, -est) **1** causing disgust; having a bad smell or taste. **2** dirty; filthy. **3** wicked; evil. **4** (of language) vulgar; obscene. **5** (of the weather) stormy; rough. ***fall/run foul of,*** (*fig*) get entangled or into trouble with: *fall ~ of the law.* **6** (*sport*) unfair; against the rules. □ *n* **1** [C] (*sport*) something contrary to the rules. **2** [U] ***through fair and foul,*** through good and bad fortune.

foul·ly /ˈfau(l)li/ *adv*

foul·ness /-nɪs/ *n* [U]

ˌfoul ˈplay, treachery; dishonesty; violent crime, esp murder: *Is ~ play suspected?*

foul[2] /faul/ *vt,vi* **1** make or become foul: *chimneys that ~ the air with smoke.* **2** collide (with); (cause to) become entangled: *The rope ~ed the anchor chain.* **3** (*sport*) commit a foul(1) against: *~ an opponent.*

found[1] *pt,pp* of find[2].

found[2] /faund/ *vt* **1** start the building of; lay the base of; establish: *The Methodist Church was ~ed by John Wesley.* **2** base on: *arguments ~ed upon facts.*

foun·da·tion /faunˈdeiʃən/ *n* **1** [U] founding or establishing (of a town, school, church, etc). **2** [C] **(a)** fund of money given for charity, research, etc: *the Ford Foundation.* **(b)** institution founded with such money. **3** [C] (often *pl*) strong base of a building, on which it is supported: *the ~(s) of an apartment house.* **4** [C,U] that on which an idea, belief, etc is based; starting point: *the ~s of religious beliefs; a story that has no ~ in fact/is without ~,* is untrue.

founder[1] /ˈfaundər/ *n* [C] person who founds or establishes a school, etc.

foun·der[2] /ˈfaundər/ *vi,vt* **1** (of a ship) (cause to) fill with water and sink. **2** fall or stumble; (esp of a horse) go lame.

found·ling /ˈfaundlɪŋ/ *n* [C] (*dated*) deserted or abandoned child of unknown parents.

found·ry /ˈfaundri/ *n* [C] (*pl* -ies) place where metal is melted and molded.

fount /faunt/ *n* [C] (*liter*) **1** source. **2** fountain.

foun·tain /ˈfauntən/ *n* [C] **1** spring of water, esp one made artificially with water forced through holes in a pipe or pipes for ornamental purposes. **2** device, esp in a public place, that supplies a small stream of water: *a drinking ~.* **3** (*fig*) source or origin: *the ~ of wisdom.*

ˈfountain·head *n* original source.

ˈfountain pen, pen with a supply of ink inside the holder.

four /fɔr/ *adj, n* [C] (of) 4: *a child of ~,* four years old; *an income of ~ figures.* ***on all fours,*** on the hands and knees.

four-ˈposter *n* [C] bed with tall corner posts that were originally to support curtains, etc.

ˈfour·score *adj, n* (of) 80. ⇨ score[1](7).

ˈfour·square *adj* **(a)** square-shaped. **(b)** (*fig*) steady; firm.

fourth /fɔrθ/ *adj, n* [C] (of) one of 4 (parts) or the next after 3.

fourth·ly *adv* in the 4th place.

four·teen /ˌfɔrˈtin/ *adj, n* [C] (of) 14.

four·teenth /ˌfɔrˈtinθ/ *adj, n* [C] (of) one of 14 (parts) or the next after 13.

fowl /faul/ *n* (*pl* ~, ~s) **1** [C] any bird: *ˈwild~.* **2** [C] domestic rooster or hen. **3** [U] flesh of fowl as food. □ *vi* catch, hunt, wildfowl: *go ~ing.*

fox /faks/ *n* [C] wild animal of the dog family, with pointed ears and a bushy tail: *as cunning as a fox.* □ *vt* deceive by cunning; confuse; puzzle: *He was completely foxed.*

ˌfox ˈterrier, small and lively short-haired dog.

foxy *adj* (-ier, -iest) crafty.

fox·fire /ˈfaksˌfaiər/ *n* [U] phosphorescent light given out in woods and swamps by kinds of fungus.

fox·hole /ˈfaksˌhoul/ *n* [C] shallow hole used for protection in a battle, etc.

fox·trot /ˈfaksˌtrat/ *n* [C] kind of two-step ballroom dance.

foyer /ˈfɔiər/ *n* [C] entrance hall, esp in a public building.

Fr. *abbr* = **1** French. **2** Father ⇨ father[1](5).

fra·cas /ˈfreikəs/ *n* [C] noisy quarrel.

frac·tion /ˈfrækʃən/ *n* [C] **1** small part or bit of something. **2** number that is not a whole number (eg $\frac{1}{3}$, 0.76).

frac·tional /-nəl/ *adj* of or in fractions.

frac·ture /ˈfræktʃər/ *n* **1** [U] breaking or being broken, eg of a bone, a pipeline. **2** [C] instance of this: *compound/simple ~s,* with/without skin wounds. □ *vt,vi* break; crack: *~ one's leg.*

frag·ile /ˈfrædʒəl/ *adj* easily injured, broken or destroyed: ~ *china/health/happiness.*
fra·gil·ity /frəˈdʒɪləti/ *n* [U]
frag·ment /ˈfrægmənt/ *n* [C] part broken off; separate or incomplete part: *overhear ~s of conversation.* □ *vi* /ˈfrægˌment/ break into pieces.
frag·men·tary /ˈfrægmənˌteri/ *adj* incomplete; disconnected: *a ~ary report of an event.*
fra·grance /ˈfreigrəns/ *n* [U] sweet or pleasing smell.
fra·grant /ˈfreigrənt/ *adj* sweet-smelling: ~ *flowers.*
fra·grant·ly *adv*
frail /freiəl/ *adj* (-er, -est) weak; fragile: *a ~ child.*
frailty /ˈfreiəlti/ *n* **(a)** [U] the quality of being frail: *the ~ty of human life.* **(b)** [C] (*pl* -ies) fault; moral weakness: *He loved her in spite of her little frailties.*
frame[1] /freim/ *n* [C] **1** skeleton or main structure (as of steel girders, pieces of wood) that gives shape and support to a ship, building, etc, esp in the process of building. **2** border in which a picture, photograph, window or door is enclosed or set. **3** structure that holds the lenses of a pair of eyeglasses. **4** human or animal body: *a girl of slender ~.* **5** ***frame of mind,*** temporary mental state or attitude: *in a cheerful ~ of mind.* **6** single exposure on a roll of movie film.
ˈ**frame·work** *n* frame (1): *a bridge with a steel ~work; the ~work of a government.*
frame[2] /freim/ *vt,vi* **1** put together; shape; build up: ~ *a plan/theory/sentence.* **2** put a frame(2) around; enclose in a frame: *have a painting ~d.* **3** (*sl*) arrange or set up evidence so as to make (an innocent person) appear guilty of something: *The accused man said he had been ~d.*
ˈ**frame-up** *n* (*sl*) scheme to make an innocent person appear guilty.
franc /fræŋk/ *n* [C] unit of money used in France, Belgium, Switzerland, etc.
fran·chise /ˈfrænˌtʃaiz/ *n* [C] **1** usually **the franchise,** right to vote at elections. **2** special right or privilege given to a person or company for selling a product or providing a service in an area: *a ~ for a bus service.*
Franco- /ˌfræŋkou-/ *combined form* French: *the Franco-ˈGerman/Prussian War.*
frank[1] /fræŋk/ *adj* (-er, -est) showing clearly the thoughts and feelings: *a ~ look; make a ~ confession of one's guilt; be quite ~ with him* (*about something*).
frank·ly *adv*
frank·ness /nɪs/ *n* [U]
frank[2] *abbr* = frankfurter.
frank[3] /fræŋk/ *vt* mark mail as free or prepaid.
frank·furter /ˈfræŋkfərtər/ *n* [C] **1** seasoned and smoked sausage made of beef and pork. **2** = hot dog.
frank·in·cense /ˈfræŋkənˌsens/ *n* [U] kind of gum obtained from trees, giving a sweet smell when burned.
fran·tic /ˈfræntɪk/ *adj* wildly excited with pain, anxiety, etc: ~ *cries for help.*
fran·ti·cally /-kli/ *adv*
fra·ter·nal /frəˈtərnəl/ *adj* brotherly: ~ *love.*
fra·ter·nally /-nəli/ *adv*
fra·ter·nity /frəˈtərnəti/ *n* (*pl* -ies) **1** [U] brotherly feeling. **2** [C] society of men who are joined together esp by common interests. **3** [C] society of students, with branches in various colleges, usually with names made up of Greek letters. ⇨ sorority.
frat·er·nize /ˈfrætərˌnaiz/ *vi* become friendly (construction with *with*).
frat·er·niz·ation /ˌfrætərnəˈzeiʃən/ *n* [U]
fraud /frɔd/ *n* **1 (a)** [U] criminal deception. **(b)** [C] act of this kind: *get money by ~.* **2** [C] person or thing that deceives.
fraudu·lent /ˈfrɔdʒələnt/ *adj* acting with, obtained by, fraud; deceitful.
fraudu·lent·ly *adv*
fraught /frɔt/ *adj* **1** involving; attended by; threatening (unpleasant consequences): *an expedition ~ with danger.* **2** filled with: ~ *with meaning.*
fray[1] /frei/ *n* [C] fight; battle.
fray[2] /frei/ *vt,vi* **1** (of cloth, rope, etc) become worn, make worn, by rubbing so that there are loose threads. **2** (*fig*) strain (3): *~ed nerves.*
freak /frik/ *n* [C] **1** abnormal or very unusual idea, act or happening: (as an *adjective*) *a ~ storm.* **2** person, animal or plant that is abnormal in form or behavior. **3** (*sl*) fan; enthusiast: *a movie ~.* □ *vt,vi* ***freak out,*** (*informal*) (cause to) be in a state of great excitement or anxiety, esp as a result of taking drugs.
freak·ish /-ɪʃ/ *adj* abnormal: *~ish behavior.*
freak·ish·ly *adv*
freaky *adj* (-ier, -iest) = freakish.
freckle /ˈfrekəl/ *n* [C] one of the small light-brown spots on the human skin. □ *vt,vi* (cause to) become covered with freckles: ~ *more easily than others.*
free[1] /fri/ *adj* (-r, -st) **1** (of a person) not a slave; not in the power of another person or other persons. **2** not in prison; having personal rights and social and political liberty: *The prisoners were set ~.* **3** (of a state, its citizens, and institutions) not controlled by a foreign government: *a ~ country.* **4** not fixed or held back; able to move about; not controlled by rules, regulations or conventions: *You are ~ to go or stay as you please.* ***free from/of,*** **(a)** without: ~ *from blame/error/anxiety; ~ of charge. At last I am ~ of her,* have escaped from her. **(b)** not liable; exempt from: ~ *from the ordinary regulations.* **5** without payment; costing nothing: ~ *tickets for the theater; admission ~.* **6** not occupied or engaged: *Her afternoons are usually ~/She is usually ~ in the afternoon(s).* **7** coming or given readily: *a ~ flow of water; ~ with his money/advice.*
ˈ**free-for-all** *n* dispute, quarrel, etc in which all take part.
ˈ**free·hand** *adj* (of drawings) done by hand, no compasses or other drawing instruments being used: *a ~hand sketch.*
ˈ**free lance,** writer, artist, etc who works from his own office or studio and does work for a variety of contractors.
ˈ**free-lance** *adj, vi*
ˈ**free-lancer** *n* [C] = free lance.
ˈ**free·load** *vi* eat, drink, be entertained, etc at another's expense, excessively and without

apology.

ˈ**free·loader** *n* [C] one who engages in freeloading.

ˈ**free·loading** *n* [U]

free·ly *adv* in a free manner; readily.

ˌ**free ˈverse,** without regular meter.

ˈ**free·way** *n* [C] expressway with several lanes and no intersections.

ˌ**free ˈwill,** individual's power of guiding and choosing his actions: *do something of one's own ~ will*, without being required or compelled.

free[2] /fri/ *vt* (*pt,pp* ~d /frid/) make free (*from*): *~ an animal (from a trap); ~ oneself from debt.*

free·dom /ˈfridəm/ *n* [U] **1** condition of being free or independent; liberty. **2** ease: *A full skirt gives great ~ of movement.* **3** frankness; boldness: *spoke with too much ~ about his employer.*

freeze /friz/ *vt,vi* (*pt* froze /frouz/, *pp* frozen /ˈfrouzən/) **1** (of water) make or become ice; (of other substances) make or become hard or stiff from cold: *The lake froze over*, became covered with ice. **2** be or become very cold: *I'm freezing.* **3** preserve (food) by keeping it very cold: *frozen food.* **4** fix or set prices, wages: *ˈprice-/ˈwage-ˌfreezing.* **5** become motionless, eg of an animal that stands quite still to avoid attracting attention. □ *n* [C] **1** period of freezing weather. **2** severe control of prices, wages, etc: *a ˈwage-~.*

ˈ**freeze-dried** *adj* (of esp coffee, tea, spices, etc) dehydrated by freezing to preserve the flavor: *~-dried coffee.*

freezer *n* machine, room, etc for freezing food or for storing frozen food.

ˈ**freezing point,** temperature at which a liquid (esp water) freezes.

freight /ˈfreit/ *n* [C] **1** (money charged for) the carrying of goods from place to place. **2** the goods carried. □ *vt* load (a ship) with cargo; send or carry (goods): *~ a boat with fruit.*

freighter *n* [C] ship or aircraft that carries cargo.

French /frentʃ/ **1** the French language. **2** (*pl*) (used with *the*) French people. □ *adj* of France, its language or its people.

ˌ**French ˈfries,** thin strips of potato cooked in deep fat.

ˌ**French ˈhorn,** brass wind instrument. ⇨ illus at brass.

French·man/·woman /-mən, -ˌwʊmən/ *n* [C] (*pl* ~men /-men/, ~women /-ˌwɪmɪn/) male/female native of France.

fren·etic /frəˈnetɪk/ *adj* frantic.

frenzy /ˈfrenzi/ *n* [U] violent excitement: *in a ~ of despair/enthusiasm.*

fren·zied *adj* wildly excited.

fre·quency /ˈfrikwənsi/ *n* (*pl* -ies) **1** [U] frequent occurrence: *the ~ of earthquakes in Italy.* **2** [C] rate of occurrence; number of repetitions (in a given time): *the ~ of a sound wave/an alternating electric current.*

fre·quent[1] /ˈfrikwənt/ *adj* happening often; numerous: *Hurricanes are ~ here in autumn. He's a ~ visitor.*

fre·quent·ly *adv*

fre·quent[2] /friˈkwent/ *vt* go often to (a place): *Frogs ~ wet places.*

fresco /ˈfreskou/ *n* [C] (*pl* ~es, ~s) **1** [U] (method of) painting moist plaster surfaces: *painting in ~.* **2** [C] picture painted in this way.

fresh /freʃ/ *adj* (-er, -est) **1** newly made, produced, gathered, grown, arrived, etc; (of food) not stale or bad. **2** not canned, smoked or frozen: *~ butter/meat.* **3** new or different: *Is there any ~ news?* **4** (of the air, wind, weather) cool; refreshing: *go out for some ~ air.* **5** bright and clean: *~ colors.* **6** (of water) not sea water: *ˈ~water fish.* **7** (*informal*) bold; forward.

freshen /ˈfreʃən/ *vt,vi* make or become fresh. ***freshen up,*** make fresh by washing.

fresh·ly *adv* (only with a *pp*) recently: *~ly gathered fruit.*

fresh·man /ˈfreʃmən/ *n* [C] (*pl* ~men /-men/) first-year student in a high school or college.

fresh·ness /-nɪs/ *n* [U]

fret[1] /fret/ *vi,vt* (-tt-) **1** (cause to) be worried or bad-tempered: *What are you ~ting about?* **2** wear away as by rubbing: *a stream ~ting a channel through rock.* □ *n* [U] irritated or worried state of mind: *in a ~.*

fret·ful /-fəl/ *adj* irritable: *a ~ful baby.*

fret·fully /-fəli/ *adv*

fret[2] /fret/ *n* (-tt-) decorative pattern often made by cutting or sawing wood.

ˈ**fret·saw** *n* very narrow saw, fixed in a frame, for cutting designs in thin sheets of wood.

ˈ**fret·work** *n* [U] **(a)** work in decorative patterns. **(b)** wood cut with such patterns by using a fret saw.

fret[3] /fret/ *n* [C] one of the ridges across the neck of a guitar, banjo, etc.

Fri. *abbr* = Friday.

friar /ˈfraiər/ *n* [C] man who is a member of one of certain Roman Catholic religious orders.

fric·tion /ˈfrɪkʃən/ *n* **1** [U] the rubbing of one thing against another. **2** [C,U] (instance of a) difference of opinion leading to argument and quarreling: *political ~ between two countries.*

Fri·day /ˈfraidi, ˈfraiˌdei/ *n* sixth day of the week.

ˌ**Good ˈFriday,** the one before Easter Sunday.

fried *pt,pp* of fry.

friend /frend/ *n* [C] **1** person, not a relation, whom one knows and likes well; *He has been a good ~ to me.* **2** helpful thing or quality: *Among gossips silence can be your best ~.* **3** helper or sympathizer: *a good ~ of the poor.*

friend·less *adj*

friend·less·ness /-nɪs/ *n* [U]

friend·ly /ˈfrendli/ *adj* (-ier, -iest) acting, or ready to act, as a friend; showing or expressing kindness: *be ~ with/be on ~ terms with her.*

friend·li·ness /-nɪs/ *n* [U]

friend·ship /ˈfren(d)ʃɪp/ *n* **1** [U] being friends; the feeling or relationship that exists between friends: *my ~ for her.* **2** [C] instance or period of this feeling: *a ~ of twenty years.*

frieze /friz/ *n* [C] ornamental band or strip along (usually the top of) a wall.

frig·ate /ˈfrɪgɪt/ *n* [C] **1** fast sailing ship formerly used in war. **2** (*modern use*) fast escort vessel.

fright /frait/ *n* **1** [U] great and sudden fear: *die of ~.* **2** [C] instance of this.

frighten /ˈfraitən/ *vt* fill with fright; alarm suddenly: *Did the noise ~ you?*

fright·ened *adj* **(a)** afraid: *be ~ed of him or it.*

(b) alarmed: *~ed at the idea of that happening.*
fright·en·ing *adj* causing fright: *a ~ing experience.*
fright·en·ing·ly *adv*
fright·ful /ˈfraitfəl/ *adj* **1** causing fear; dreadful: *a ~ accident.* **2** (*informal*) very great; extreme.
fright·fully /-fəli/ *adv*
frigid /ˈfrɪdʒɪd/ *adj* **1** cold: *a ~ climate.* **2** unfriendly: *a ~ manner.*
frigid·ity /frɪˈdʒɪdəti/ *n* [U]
frigid·ly *adv*
frill /frɪl/ *n* [C] **1** ornamental border on a dress, etc. **2** (*pl*) unnecessary adornments, eg to speech or writing.
frilly *adj* (-ier, -iest)
fringe /frɪndʒ/ *n* [C] **1** ornamental border of loose threads, eg on a rug. **2** edge (of a crowd, forest, etc): *on the ~(s) of the desert.* □ *vt* put on, serve as, a fringe: *a roadside ~d with trees.*
frisk /frɪsk/ *vi,vt* **1** jump and run about playfully. **2** pass the hands over (a person) to search for concealed weapons.
frisky *adj* (-ier, -iest) lively: *as ~y as a kitten.*
frit·ter[1] /ˈfrɪtər/ *vt* waste on useless things: *~ away one's time/energy/money.*
frit·ter[2] /ˈfrɪtər/ *n* [C] piece of fried batter with sliced fruit, meat, in it.
fri·vol·ity /frɪˈvaləti/ *n* (*pl* -ies) **1** [U] frivolous behavior or character. **2** [C] frivolous act or statement.
friv·o·lous /ˈfrɪvələs/ *adj* **1** not serious or important: *~ remarks/behavior.* **2** (of persons) not serious.
friv·o·lous·ly *adv*
frizz, friz /frɪz/ *vt* (of hair) form into masses of small curls.
frizzy *adj* (-ier, -iest) (of hair) frizzed.
frizzle[1] /ˈfrɪzəl/ *vt,vi* cook, be cooked, with a spluttering noise: *bacon frizzling in the pan.*
frizzle[2] /ˈfrɪzəl/ *vt,vi* (of hair) frizz, twist in small, crisp curls.
fro /frou/ *adv* (only in) ***to and fro,*** back and forth: *to and fro between New York and Washington.*
frock /frak/ *n* [C] **1** woman's or girl's dress (the usual word). **2** monk's long gown with loose sleeves.
frog /frɔg, frag/ *n* [C] **1** small, cold-blooded, jumping animal living in water and on land. **2** ornamental fastener on a coat, dress, etc. **3** (*informal*) hoarseness caused by a swelling in the throat. **4** weighted base with holes for holding cut flowers upright.
frog·man /ˈfrɔgˌmæn, ˈfrag-/ (*pl* ~men /-men/) person skilled in swimming under water with the aid of flippers on the feet and a breathing apparatus.
frolic /ˈfralɪk/ *vi* (*pt,pp* ~ked) play about in a gay, lively way. □ *n* [C] time of gaiety or merrymaking.
ˈfrolic·some /-səm/ *adj*
from /frəm *strong form:* ˈfram, ˈfrəm/ *prep* **1** (used to indicate a starting point): *jump (down) ~ a wall; travel ~ Houston to Dallas.* **2** (showing the beginning of a period of time): *~ the first of May; ~ childhood; ~ beginning to end.* **3** (showing the place, object, etc from which distance, absence, etc is stated): *ten miles ~ the coast; stay away ~ school.* **4** (showing the giver, sender, etc): *a letter ~ my brother.* **5** (showing the lower limit): *There were ~ ten to fifteen boys absent.* **6** (showing the source from which something is taken): *quotations ~ Lincoln; ~ this point of view.* **7** (showing the material, etc used to make something): *Wine is made ~ grapes.* **8** (showing separation, removal, prevention, escape, avoidance, etc: *When were you released ~ prison?* **9** (showing change): *Things are going ~ bad to worse.* **10** (showing reason, cause or motive): *suffer ~ starvation and disease.* **11** (showing distinction or difference): *How would you know an Englishman ~ an American?*
frond /frand/ *n* [C] leaf part of a fern or palm tree.
front /frənt/ *n* **1** (usually *sing* with *the*) foremost or most important side: *the ~ of a building; sitting in the ~ of the class;* (as an *adjective*) *the ~ page of a newspaper*, page 1. ***in front,*** *adv*: *Please go in ~.* ***in front of,*** *prep: There are some trees in ~ of the house.* **2** [C] (in war) part where the fighting is taking place: *go/be sent to the ~.* **3** [C] road, etc bordering the sea, a lake, etc: *have a walk along the ocean ~.* **4** [U] outer appearance. ***put on/show/present a bold front,*** face a situation with (apparent) boldness. **5** [C] boundary between masses of cold and warm air: *a cold ~/warm ~.* □ *vt,vi* face: *hotels that ~ the sea; windows ~ing the street.* ⇨ also seafront.
front·age /ˈfrəntɪdʒ/ *n* [C] extent of a piece of land or a building along its front: *a building site with a road ~ of 500 feet.*
frontal /ˈfrəntəl/ *adj* of, on or to, the front: *a ~ attack.*
fron·tier /frənˈtɪr/ *n* [C] **1** part of a country bordering on another country; (land on each side of a) boundary. **2** area of a country that is farthest from its settled or developed part. **3** (*fig*) undeveloped area or field: *the ~s of knowledge.*
frost /frɔst/ *n* **1 (a)** [U] weather condition with temperature below the freezing point of water. **(b)** [C] occasion or period of such weather. **2** [U] frozen, powdery coating on the ground, roofs, plants, etc. □ *vt,vi* **1** cover or become covered with frost(2): *~ed window panes.* **2** give a roughened surface to (glass) to make it opaque: *~ed glass.* **3** cover (a cake, etc) with frosting.
ˈfrost·bite *n* [U] injury to tissue in the body from freezing.
ˈfrost·bitten *adj* having, suffering from, frostbite.
frost·ing /ˈfrɔstɪŋ/ *n* [U] **1** icing; creamy covering for cakes made with sugar, etc. **2** dull, rough surface on glass.
frosty /ˈfrɔsti/ *adj* (-ier, -iest) **1** cold with frost: *~ weather.* **2** (*fig*) unfriendly; without warmth of feeling: *a ~ welcome.*
froth /frɔθ/ *n* [U] **1** creamy mass of small bubbles; foam: *a glass of beer with a lot of ~ on it.* **2** (*fig*) something that is light and of little value. □ *vi* have, give off, froth (1): *A mad dog may ~ at the mouth.*
frothy *adj* (-ier, -iest) of, like, covered with, froth: *~y beer.*

frown /fraun/ *vi* draw the eyebrows together, wrinkle the forehead (to express displeasure, puzzlement, deep thought, etc). ***frown on/upon,*** disapprove of: *Gambling is ~ed on here.* □ *n* [C] frowning look: *There was a deep ~ on his brow.*

froze, frozen *pt,pp* of freeze.

fru·gal /ˈfrugəl/ *adj* not wasteful; economical (esp of food, expenditure): *a ~ meal.*

fru·gal·ity /fruˈgæləti/ *n* [C,U]

fru·gal·ly /-gəli/ *adv*

fruit /frut/ *n* **1** (usually *sing* as a *collective noun*) that part of a plant or tree that contains the seeds and is used as food, eg apples, bananas: *Do you eat much ~?* **2** [C] that part of any plant in which the seed is formed. **3** (*pl*) any plant or vegetable products used for food: *the ~s of the earth.* **4** (*fig*) (often *pl*) profit, result or reward (of labor, study, etc): *the ~s of industry.* □ *vi* (of trees, bushes, etc) bear fruit.

ˈfruit fly, (kinds of a) common small fly that hatches out and feeds on fruit.

fruit·ful /-fəl/ *adj* **(a)** producing fruit. **(b)** (*fig*) producing good results: *a ~ful career.*

fruit·ful·ness /-nɪs/ *n* [U]

fruit·less *adj* **(a)** without fruit. **(b)** (*fig*) without results or success: *~less efforts.*

fruit·less·ly *adv*

ˌfruit ˈsalad, various kinds of fruit cut up and mixed in a bowl.

fruity *adj* (-ier, -iest) of or like fruit.

fru·ition /fruˈɪʃən/ *n* [U] getting what was wanted or hoped for: *aims brought/that come to ~.*

frus·trate /ˈfrəˌstreit/ *vt* prevent (a person) from doing something; prevent (plans) from being carried out: *~ an enemy in his plans.*

frus·tra·tion /frəˈstreiʃən/ *n* [C,U]

frwy. *abbr* = freeway.

fry /frai/ *vt,vi* (*3rd person sing pres tense* fries /fraiz/, *pt,pp* fried /fraid/) cook, be cooked, in

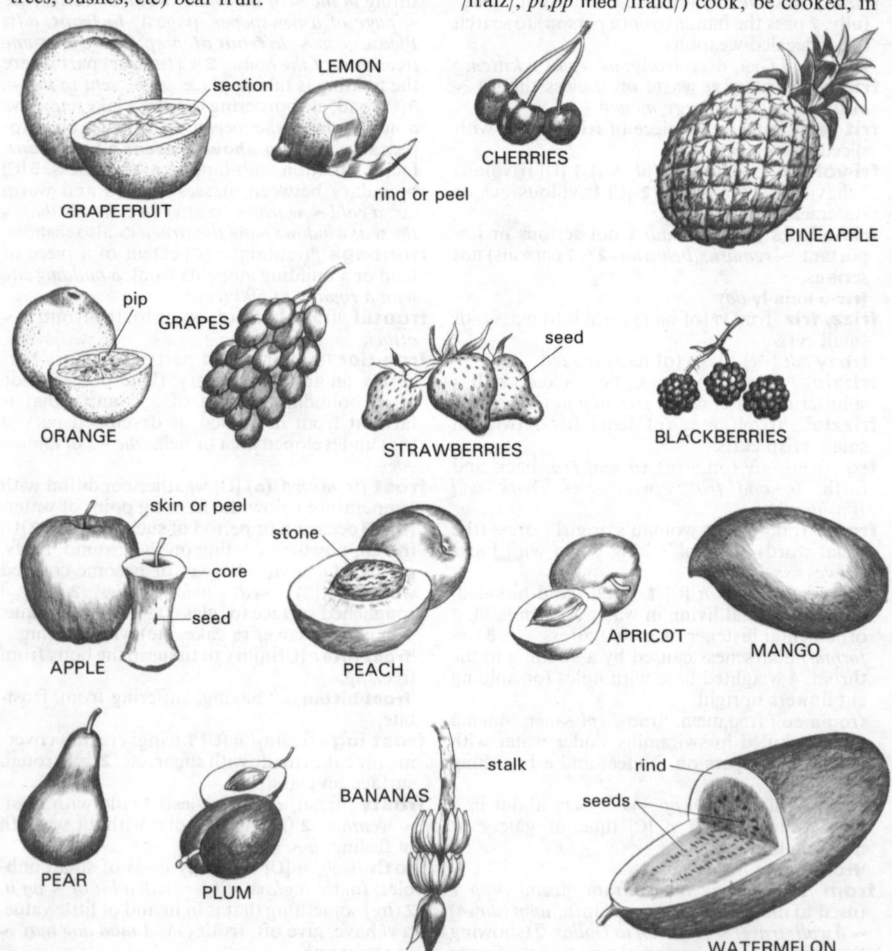

FRUIT

boiling fat: *fried chicken.*
ˈfrying pan, shallow pan with a long handle used for frying.

ft. *abbr* = foot¹(5).

fudge¹ /fədʒ/ *n* [U] sort of soft candy made with milk, sugar, chocolate, etc.

fudge² /fədʒ/ *vi* (used with *on*) cheat slightly; hedge: *He ~d on his age.*

fuel /ˈfyuəl/ *n* **1** material for producing heat or energy, eg coal, oil. **2** (*fig*) something that inflames the passions. □ *vt,vi* (-l-, -ll-) supply with fuel: *a power station ~ed by uranium.*

fugi·tive /ˈfyudʒətɪv/ *n* [C] person running away from justice, danger, etc: *~s from justice.* □ *adj* **1** of a fugitive. **2** of temporary interest or value; lasting a short time only.

-ful /-fəl/ *suffix* **1** full of; having the quality of: *peaceful; eventful.* **2** amount that fills: *mouthful; handful.*

ful·crum /ˈfʊlkrəm/ *n* [C] point on which a lever turns.

ful·fill, ful·fil /fʊlˈfɪl/ *vt* (-ll-) perform or carry out a task, duty, promise, etc: *~ one's duties/an obligation/his hopes.*
ful·fill·ment *n* [U]

full /fʊl/ *adj* (-er, -est) **1** holding or having plenty or as much or as many (*of*); completely filled: *The room was ~ of people.* **2** ***full of,*** completely occupied with thinking of: *She was ~ of the news.* **3** plump; rounded: *a ~ figure; rather ~ in the face.* **4** (of clothes) having a great deal of material; not tight or narrow: *a ~ skirt.* **5** reaching the usual or the specified extent, limit, length, etc: *wait a ~ hour*, not less than an hour. ***in full,*** without omitting or shortening anything: *write one's name in ~*, eg John Henry Smith, not J.H. Smith. ***at full speed,*** at the highest possible speed. ***to the full,*** to the utmost extent: *enjoy oneself to the ~.* **6** (with *comp* and *superl*) complete: *A ~er account will be given later. This is the ~est account yet received.*
ˈfull·back *n* [C] **(a)** (*football*) offensive player who lines up between the halfbacks. **(b)** (*soccer*) player (defender) placed nearest the goal.
ˌfull-ˈlength *adj* **(a)** covering the whole figure. **(b)** of standard or usual length: *a ~-length novel.*
ˌfull ˈmoon, a complete disk.
ˈfull-scale *adj* (of drawings, plans, etc) of the same size, area, etc of the object itself.
ˈfull-time *adj, adv* occupying all normal working hours: *a ~-time worker; working ~-time.*
fully /ˈfʊli/ *adv* **(a)** to the full; completely: *~y satisfied.* **(b)** altogether; at least: *The journey will take ~y two hours.*

fumble /ˈfəmbəl/ *vi,vt* **1** feel about uncertainly with the hands; use the hands awkwardly: *~ in one's pockets for a key.* **2** handle or deal with clumsily: *~ a ball*, eg in baseball. □ *n* [C] act of fumbling.

fume /fyum/ *n* (often *pl*) strong-smelling smoke, gas or vapor: *gasoline ~s.* □ *vi,vt* **1** give off fumes. **2** (*fig*) show anger or irritation: *fuming at her incompetence.*

fu·mi·gate /ˈfyuməˌgeit/ *vt* treat with fumes to kill germs, insects, etc: *~ a room.*
fu·mi·ga·tion /ˌfyuməˈgeiʃən/ *n* [U]

fun /fən/ *n* [U] **1** amusement, sport; playfulness: *What fun the children had!* ***make fun of, poke fun at,*** ridicule; cause people to laugh at: *It is wrong to make fun of a cripple.* ***for/in fun,*** as a joke, for amusement; not seriously: *He did it for fun.* **2** that which causes merriment or amusement: *Paul is great fun*, is very amusing. *Sailing is good fun.* **3** (as an *adjective*): *a ˈfun car/fur*, used, worn for amusement.

func·tion /ˈfəŋkʃən/ *n* [C] **1** special activity or purpose of a person or thing: *the ~s of a judge/of education.* **2** public or formal ceremony or event: *the numerous ~s that the mayor must attend.* □ *vi* fulfill a function(1); operate; act: *The telephone was not ~ing*, was out of order.
func·tional /-nəl/ *adj* having, designed to have, functions(1).

fund /fənd/ *n* [C] **1** store or supply (of non-material things): *a ~ of amusing stories.* **2** (often *pl*) sum of money for a particular purpose: *a reˈlief ~*, eg to help in a disaster. **3** (*pl*) money: *run off with the ~s.* □ *vt* provide money for: *~ an arts festival.*

fun·da·men·tal /ˌfəndəˈmentəl/ *adj* of or forming a foundation; of basic importance; serving as a starting point: *the ~ rules of arithmetic.* □ *n* [C] (usually *pl*) basic or most important rule or principle; essential part: *the ~s of mathematics.*
fun·da·men·tally /-təli/ *adv*

fu·neral /ˈfyunərəl/ *n* [C] burial or cremation of a dead person with the usual ceremonies.
ˈfuneral march, sad and solemn piece of music.
fu·ner·eal /fyuˈnɪriəl/ *adj* of or like a funeral; gloomy; dark.

fun·gus /ˈfəŋgəs/ *n* (*pl* -gi /-ˌdʒai/) plant without leaves, flowers or green coloring matter, growing on other plants or on decaying matter, eg old wood: *Mushrooms, toadstools and mildew are all fungi.*

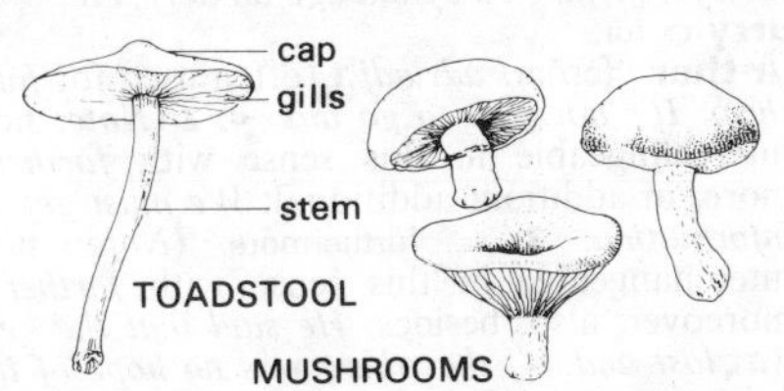

FUNGI

fun·gi·cide /ˈfəndʒəˌsaid/ *n* [U,C] substance that destroys fungi.
fun·goid /ˈfəŋˌgɔid/ *adj* of or like fungi.
fun·gous /ˈfəŋgəs/ *adj* of or like, caused by, fungi.

funnel /ˈfənəl/ *n* [C] **1** tube or pipe wide at the top and narrowing at the bottom, for pouring liquids or powders through small openings. **2** outlet for smoke of a steamer, railway engine, etc. □ *vt,vi* (-l-, -ll-) (cause to) move (as if) through a funnel.

funny /ˈfəni/ *adj* (-ier, -iest) **1** causing fun or amusement: *~ stories.* **2** strange; queer; odd: *There's something ~ about him/the affair*, perhaps not quite honest or straightforward.
fun·nily /ˈfənəli/ *adv* in a funny way: *funnily* (=

strangely) *enough*.

ˈfunny bone, (*informal*) part of the elbow over which a very sensitive nerve passes.

fur /fər/ *n* **1** [U] soft thick hair covering certain animals, eg cats, rabbits. **2** [C] animal skin with the fur on it, esp when made into garments: (as an *adj*) *a fur coat*. **3** [U] coating that is like fur.

furry /ˈfəri/ *adj* (-ier, -iest) of or like fur; covered with fur.

furi·ous /ˈfyʊriəs/ *adj* violent; full of fury: *a ~ struggle/storm/quarrel*.

furi·ous·ly *adv*

furl /fərl/ *vt,vi* (of sails, flags, umbrellas, etc) roll up and fasten: *~ the sails of a yacht*.

fur·long /ˈfərˌlɔŋ/ *n* [C] measure of 220 yards (= 201 meters) or one eighth of a mile.

fur·lough /ˈfərlou/ *n* [C,U] vacation or leave of absence from duty (esp in the armed forces). ⇨ leave².

furn. *abbr* = furnished(2).

fur·nace /ˈfərnɪs/ *n* [C] **1** enclosed fireplace for heating buildings with hot water or steam in pipes. **2** enclosed space for heating metals, making glass, etc.

fur·nish /ˈfərnɪʃ/ *vt* **1** supply or provide: *~ a library with books*. **2** equip with furniture: *~ a room/an office*.

fur·nish·ings *n pl* furniture and equipment.

fur·ni·ture /ˈfərnɪtʃər/ *n* [U] all those movable things such as chairs, beds, desks, etc needed in a house, office, etc.

fu·ror /ˈfyʊˌrɔr/ *n* [C] outburst of feeling, eg disapproval, enthusiasm, etc; uproar: *The new play at the National Theater created a ~*.

fur·rier /ˈfəriər/ *n* [C] person who prepares, or who deals in, furs.

fur·row /ˈfərou/ *n* [C] **1** long cut or groove in the ground, as made by a plow: *newly turned ~s*. **2** wrinkle, esp in the forehead. □ *vt* make furrows in: *a forehead ~ed by old age/anxiety, etc*.

furry ⇨ fur.

fur·ther /ˈfərðər/ *adv,adj* **1** (often used for *farther*): *It's not safe to go any ~*. **2** (*Note:* not interchangeable in this sense with *farther*) more; in addition; additional: *We must get ~ information*. **3** = furthermore. (*Note:* not interchangeable in this sense with *farther*); moreover; also; besides: *He said that the key was lost and, ~, that there was no hope of its being found*. □ *vt* help forward; promote: *~ the cause of peace*.

fur·ther·ance /-rəns/ *n* [U] advancement: *in ~ance of your aims*.

fur·ther·more /ˈfərðərˌmɔr/ *adv* moreover; in addition.

fur·ther·most /-ˌmoust/ *adj* most distant; farthest.

fur·thest /ˈfərðɪst/ *adj, adv* = farthest.

fur·tive /ˈfərtɪv/ *adj* done secretly so as not to attract attention: *a ~ glance; ~ behavior*.

fur·tive·ly *adv*

fur·tive·ness /-nɪs/ *n* [U]

fury /ˈfyʊri/ *n* (*pl* -ies) **1** [U] violent excitement, esp anger; *filled with ~*. **2** [C] outburst of wild feelings: *He flew into a ~*.

fuse¹ /fyuz/ *n* [C] tube, cord, etc for carrying a spark to explode powder, etc, eg in a firework, bomb.

fuse² /fyuz/ *vt,vi* **1** make or become liquid as the result of great heat. **2** join, become joined, (as if) by melting: *~ two pieces of wire together*. □ *n* [C] device made of a piece of wire which melts when the electric current passing through becomes too strong.

fu·se·lage /ˈfyusəˌlaʒ, ˈfyuzə-/ *n* [C] body of an aircraft which holds the passengers and to which the wings and tail are attached. ⇨ illus at aircraft.

fu·sil·lade /ˌfyusəˈleid, ˌfyuzə-/ *n* [C] continuous discharge of firearms.

fusion /ˈfyuʒən/ *n* [C,U] mixing or uniting of different things into one: *the ~ of copper and tin; a ~ of races/political parties*.

fuss /fəs/ *n* [U] **1** unnecessary nervous activity; commotion: *a lot of ~ and excitement*. **2** show of anxiety, concern, distress, etc, esp about unimportant things: *made a ~ about being first in line*. **3** display of attention or excessive affection: *Don't make such a big ~ over the children*. □ *vt,vi* get into, (cause to) be in a fuss: *Stop ~ing. Don't ~ over the children so much*.

ˈfuss·budget *n* (*informal*) very fussy person.

fussy /ˈfəsi/ *adj* (-ier, -iest) **1** full of, showing, nervous excitement; too concerned with unimportant details: *be too ~ about one's clothes*. **2** (of dress, style, etc) too elaborate.

fuss·ily /ˈfəsəli/ *adv*

fussi·ness /ˈfəsinɪs/ *n* [U]

fu·tile /ˈfyutəl/ *adj* **1** (of actions) of no use; without result: *a ~ attempt*. **2** (of persons) unlikely to accomplish much.

fu·til·ity /fyuˈtɪləti/ *n* [C,U]

fu·ture /ˈfyutʃər/ *adj* **1** coming after the present. **2** of or in the future: *the ~ life*, after death of the body; *his ~ wife*, the woman he will marry; *the ~ tense*. □ *n* [C] time, event, coming after the present: *I hope you have a happy ~ before you*. ***in the future,*** from this time onward: *Try to live a better life in the ~*.

fu·ture·less *adj*

fuze /fyuz/ = fuse¹.

fuzz /fəz/ *n* [U] **1** fluff; mass of short fibers. **2 the fuzz,** (*sl*) police.

fuzzy /fəzi/ *adj* (-ier, -iest) **1** blurred; indistinct (in shape or outline). **2** of, like, or covered with fuzz.

fwd. *abbr* = forward¹(1)

FYI *abbr* = for your information.

g

G, g /dʒi/ (*pl* G's, g's /dʒiz/) the seventh letter of the English alphabet.
GA *postal abbr* = Georgia. ⇨ App 6.
gab·ar·dine /ˈgæbərˌdin/ *n* [U] hard material of wool, cotton or silk with slanting ribs.
gabble /ˈgæbəl/ *vt,vi* talk quickly and indistinctly: *The little girl ~d her prayers and jumped into bed.* □ *n* [U] fast, confused, unintelligible talk.
gab·er·dine = gabardine.
gable /ˈgeibəl/ *n* [C] three-cornered part of an outside wall between two sloping sides of a roof.
gabled /ˈgeibəld/ *adj*
gad /gæd/ *vi* (-dd-) go from place to place for excitement or pleasure.
ˈgad·about *n* person who does this.
gad·fly /ˈgædˌflai/ *n* [C] (*pl* -ies) **1** fly that bites horses, cattle, etc. **2** (*fig*) person who annoys or arouses others.
gadget /ˈgædʒɪt/ *n* (*informal*) small (usually mechanical) device: *a new ~ for opening tin cans.*
gadgetry /ˈgædʒɪtri/ *n* [U] (*collect*) gadgets.
gaff /gæf/ *n* [C] iron hook with a handle, that is used to pull or lift a large fish out of the water.
gag /gæg/ *n* [C] **1** something put in or over a person's mouth to prevent him from speaking or crying out. **2** joke, funny story, esp as part of a comedian's act. □ *vt,vi* (-gg-) **1** put a gag(1) into or over the mouth of. **2** (*fig*) prevent (a person) from speaking freely. **3** choke or retch: *gagged on a large piece of meat.*
gage = gauge.
gai·ety /ˈgeiəti/ *n* (*pl* -ies) **1** [U] being gay; cheerfulness; bright appearance: *flags and scarves that added to the ~ of the scene.* **2** (*pl*) merrymaking; joyful, festive occasions: *the gaieties of the Christmas season.*
gaily /ˈgeili/ *adv* in a gay manner.
gain¹ /gein/ *n* **1** [U] increase of possessions; acquiring of wealth: *interested only in ~*, in becoming rich. **2** [C] increase in amount or power: *a ~ in weight/health.*
gain·ful /-fəl/ *adj* providing wealth: *~ful occupations.*
gain·fully /-fəli/ *adv*
gain² /gein/ *vt,vi* **1** obtain (something wanted or needed): *~ experience; ~ an advantage over a competitor.* ***gain time,*** improve one's chances by delaying something, making excuses, etc. ***gain the upper hand,*** be victorious. **2** increase in weight, speed, etc: *The baby ~ed five pounds.* **3** (of a watch or clock) run fast, ahead of the correct time: *The clock ~s three minutes a day.* **4** ***gain on/upon,*** get closer to (the person or thing pursued); catch up with: *~ on the other runners in a race; ~ on one's pursuers.* **5** reach, arrive at (a desired place, esp with effort): *The swimmer ~ed the shore.*
gait /geit/ *n* [C] manner of walking or running: *an awkward ~.*
gai·ter /ˈgeitər/ *n* [C] cloth or leather covering for the leg from knee to ankle, or for the ankle: *a pair of ~s.*
gal /gæl/ *n* (*dated informal*) = girl.
gal. *abbr* = gallon.
gala /ˈgeilə, ˈgælə/ *n* [C] festive occasion: (as an *adjective*) *a ~ performance*, eg at a theater, with special guests.
ga·lac·tic /gəˈlæktɪk/ *adj* of the galaxy.
gal·axy /ˈgæləksi/ *n* [C] (*pl* -ies) **1** any of the large-scale clusters of stars in outer space. **2 the Galaxy,** the one containing our solar system, visible as a luminous band known as *the Milky Way.* **3** (*fig*) collection of persons: *a ~ of beautiful women.*
gale /geiəl/ *n* [C] **1** strong and violent wind: *The ship lost her masts in the ~.* **2** noisy outburst: *~s of laughter.*
gall¹ /gɔl/ *n* [U] **1** bitter liquid produced by the liver. ⇨ bile. **2** bitter feeling. **3** (*informal*) impudence: *Of all the ~!*
ˈgall·bladder *n* vessel attached to the liver containing gall.
ˈgall·stone *n* hard mass that forms in the gallbladder.
gall² /gɔl/ *n* [C] painful swelling on an animal caused by rubbing. □ *vt* **1** make sore by rubbing. **2** (*fig*) hurt the feelings of; humiliate: *It was ~ing to have to ask for a loan.*
gall³ /gɔl/ *n* [C] swelling on a plant.
gal·lant /ˈgælənt/ *adj* **1** = brave (now the usual word): *~ deeds.* **2** (*dated*) fine; stately: *a ~-looking ship.* **3** (also /gəˈlænt/) showing special respect and courtesy to women: *He was very ~ at the ball.*
gal·lant·ly *adv*
gal·lant·ry *n* [U] **1** bravery. **2** devotion, chivalrous attention, to women.
gal·leon /ˈgæliən, ˈgælyən/ *n* [C] large Spanish sailing ship of the 15th to 17th centuries.
gal·lery /ˈgæləri/ *n* [C] (*pl* -ies) **1** room or building for the display of works of art. **2** (people in the) highest and cheapest seats in the balcony of a theater. **3** balcony of a hall, church, etc. **4** covered walk or corridor, partly open at one side. **5** long, narrow room: *a ˈshooting ~*, for indoor target practice. **6** horizontal under-

ground passage in a mine.
gal·ley /ˈgæli/ *n* [C] (*pl* ~s) **1** low, flat ship used in ancient times and in the Middle Ages for war, trading, etc, that was often rowed by slaves or criminals. **2** ship's kitchen.
gal·li·vant /ˈgæləˌvænt/ *vi* = gad.
gal·lon /ˈgælən/ *n* [C] measure for liquids, four quarts.
gal·lop /ˈgæləp/ *n* [C] (of a horse, etc) fastest pace with all four feet off the ground at each stride: *He rode away at a ~/at full ~.* □ *vi,vt* **1** (cause to) go at a gallop: *He ~ed across the field.* **2** hurry: *~ through one's work/lecture.*
gal·lows /ˈgælouz/ *n* [C] (*pl* ~, ~es) (usually with a *sing verb*) wooden framework on which to put criminals to death by hanging: ***send sb to the gallows,*** condemn him to be hanged.
ga·loot /gəˈlut/ *n* [C] (*sl*) clumsy or odd-looking person.
ga·lore /gəˈlɔr/ *adj* in abundance: *a meal with beef and beer ~.* (*Note: galore* always follows the noun(s) it modifies.)
ga·losh /gəˈlaʃ/ *n* [C] (usually *pl*) rubber overshoe worn in wet weather: *a pair of ~es.*
gal·va·nize /ˈgælvəˌnaiz/ *vt* **1** coat (iron or steel) with zinc to prevent rust. **2** stir up or excite to action: *His speech ~d his hearers into voting at the elections.*
gam·bit /ˈgæmbɪt/ *n* [C] **1** (kinds of) opening move in chess. **2** (*fig*) any initial move: *His opening ~ at the debate was a direct attack on Administration policy.*
gamble /ˈgæmbəl/ *vi,vt* **1** play games of chance for money; bet. **2** take great risks for the chance of winning something or making a profit. **3** ***gamble sth away,*** lose by gambling: *He has ~d away half his fortune.* □ *n* [C] uncertain undertaking; risk.
gam·bler /ˈgæmblər/ *n* [C] person who gambles.
gamb·ling /ˈgæmblɪŋ/ *n* [U] **(a)** playing games for money. **(b)** taking risks for possible advantage: *fond of gambling.*
gam·bol /ˈgæmbəl/ *n* [C] (usually *pl*) quick, playful, jumping or skipping movements, eg of lambs, children. □ *vi* (-l-, -ll-) make such movements.
game¹ /geim/ *adj* (-r,-st) **1** brave; ready to go on fighting. **2** ready and willing: *Are you ~ for a 10-mile walk?*
game² /geim/ *n* **1** [C] form of play, esp with rules, eg tennis, football, cards: *play ~s.* ***play the game,*** **(a)** keep the rules. **(b)** (*fig*) be straightforward and honest. **2** [C] apparatus, etc needed for a game, eg one played by children with a board and dice and counters. **3** (*pl*) athletic contests: *the Olympic Games.* **4** single round in some contests, eg tennis: *win four ~s in the first set.* **5** [C] scheme, plan or undertaking; trick: *I wish I knew what his ~ is,* what he is trying to do. *None of your little ~s!* ***ˌgive the ˈgame away,*** reveal a secret trick, scheme, etc. **6** [U] (flesh of) animals and birds hunted for sport and food. ***big game,*** the larger animals (elephants, lions, tigers). ***fair game,*** **(a)** what may be lawfully hunted or shot. **(b)** (*fig*) person or institution that may with reason be attacked or criticized.
ˈgame·cock *n* [C] rooster that has been trained for fighting.
ˈgame warden, officer appointed to enforce fishing and hunting regulations.
gamma ray /ˈgæmə ˌrei/ *n* [C] ray of very short wavelength from radioactive substances.
gamut /ˈgæmət/ *n* [C] **1** whole range of musical notes. **2** (*fig*) complete extent or scope of anything: *the whole ~ of feeling,* eg from the greatest joy to the depths of despair or misery.
gan·der /ˈgændər/ *n* [C] male goose.
gang /gæŋ/ *n* [C] **1** number of unskilled laborers working together. **2** group of persons associating for esp criminal purposes. ⇨ gangster. **3** (*sl*) group of close friends or associates: *Let's invite the ~ over for drinks.* □ *vi* ***gang up on/against sb,*** attack him as a gang(2): *They ~ed up on/against me.*
gang·land /ˈgæŋˌlænd/ *n* [U] (usually as an *adj*) (of) the criminal world: *a ~ slaying.*
gan·gling /ˈgæŋglɪŋ/ *adj* (of a person) tall, thin and awkward.
gang·plank /ˈgæŋˌplæŋk/ *n* [C] movable plank placed between a ship or boat and the land.
gan·grene /ˈgæŋˌgrin/ *n* [U] death and decay of tissue in the body, eg because the supply of blood to it has been stopped. □ *vt,vi* affect, become affected, with gangrene.
gan·gre·nous /ˈgæŋgrənəs/ *adj*
gang·ster /ˈgæŋstər/ *n* [C] member of a gang of criminals.
gang·way /ˈgæŋˌwei/ *n* [C] **1** gangplank. **2** passage into or out of an enclosed space.
gan·net /ˈgænɪt/ *n* [C] large, fish-eating sea bird that nests along rocky coasts.
gan·try /ˈgæntri/ *n* [C] (*pl* -ies) **1** structure of steel bars to support a traveling crane, etc. **2** movable structure used for assembling or servicing a rocket.
gap /gæp/ *n* [C] **1** break or opening in a wall, hedge, etc: *The cow got out of the field through a gap in the fence.* **2** unfilled space; opening; wide separation (of ideas, etc): *a gap in a conversation.* **3** gorge or pass between mountains. **ˌgeneˈration gap,** differences between the younger and older generations that make it hard for them to understand one another.
gape /geip/ *vi* **1** open the mouth wide. **2** stare openmouthed and in surprise: *country visitors gaping at the neon lights.* **3** open or be opened wide: *a gaping hole,* an obvious one. □ *n* [C] act of gaping.
garage /gəˈraʒ/ *n* [C] **1** building in which to keep a car or cars. **2** repair shop for motor vehicles. □ *vt* put (a motor vehicle) in a garage.
garb /garb/ *n* [U] (style of) dress (esp as worn by a particular kind of person): *a man in clerical ~.* □ *vt* (*dated*) dress: *~ed in black.*
gar·bage /ˈgarbɪdʒ/ *n* [U] **1** waste food thrown out, or fed to pigs, etc. **2** rubbish, refuse (of any kind). **3** (*informal*) nonsense.
ˈgarbage can, container for garbage.
ˈgarbage disposal (unit), grinder, installed under the kitchen sink, for liquefying garbage.
ˈgarbage ˌtruck, truck which goes from house to house to collect garbage.
garble /ˈgarbəl/ *vt* change or twist the form or meaning of statements, facts, etc: *a ~d report of*

a speech.

gar·den /ˈgardən/ *n* **1** [C,U] (piece of) ground used for growing flowers, fruit, vegetables, etc. **2** [C] public park, often with animals or plants on display: *zoological ~s*. □ *vi* work in or make a garden: *He's been ~ing all day*.

gar·dener /ˈgard(ə)nər/ *n* [C] person who works in a garden.

gar·den·ing /ˈgard(ə)nɪŋ/ *n* [U] cultivating of gardens: *fond of ~ing;* (as an *adjective*) *~ing tools*.

gar·de·nia /garˈdinyə/ *n* [C] **1** (kind of) plant with large, sweet-smelling yellow or white flowers. **2** flower of this plant.

gargle /ˈgargəl/ *vt,vi* wash the throat with liquid kept in motion by a stream of breath. □ *n* [C] **1** liquid used for this purpose. **2** act of gargling.

gar·goyle /ˈgarˌgɔiəl/ *n* [C] stone or metal water-spout, usually in the form of a grotesque human or animal creature.

gar·ish /ˈgærɪʃ/ *adj* too brightly colored; gaudy, over-decorated: *~ clothes*.

gar·ish·ly *adv*

gar·land /ˈgarlənd/ *n* [C] circle or rope of flowers or leaves as an ornament or decoration, as a prize for victory, etc. □ *vt* decorate, crown, with a garland.

gar·lic /ˈgarlɪk/ *n* [U] onionlike plant with strong taste and smell, used in cooking.

gar·ment /ˈgarmənt/ *n* [C] article of clothing.

the ˈgarment industry/trade, manufacturing and selling clothing.

gar·net /ˈgarnɪt/ *n* [C] semiprecious gem of deep transparent red.

gar·nish /ˈgarnɪʃ/ *vt* decorate, esp food for the table: *fish ~ed with slices of lemon*. □ *n* [C] something used to garnish.

gar·ret /ˈgærɪt/ *n* [C] attic.

gar·ri·son /ˈgærəsən/ *n* [C] military force stationed in a town or fort. □ *vt* **1** supply a town, etc with a garrison. **2** place, troops, etc on garrison duty.

gar·rote, ga·rotte /gəˈrat/ *vt* **1** execute (a condemned person), by strangling. **2** strangle, esp in order to rob. □ *n* [C] (apparatus for) this method of killing.

gar·ru·lous /ˈgærələs/ *adj* (*formal*) talking too much about unimportant things.

gar·ru·lity /gəˈrulətі/ *n* [U]

gar·ter /ˈgartər/ *n* [C] (elastic) band worn around the leg to keep a stocking in place.

gar·ter snake /ˈgartərˌsneik/ *n* [C] nonpoisonous snake of North America, having stripes along the back.

gas /gæs/ *n* (*pl* gases) **1** [C,U] any airlike substance (used chiefly of those that do not become liquid or solid at ordinary temperatures): *Air is a mixture of gases*. **2** [U] one of the gases or mixtures of gases used for lighting and heating: *ˈcoal gas*. **3** [U] poisonous gas: *tear gas*. **4** (*informal*) (short for) gasoline. □ *vt,vi* (-ss-) **1** poison or overcome by gas. **2** (*informal*) talk for a long time without saying much that is useful.

ˈgas chamber, airtight room for using poison gas to execute condemned criminals.

ˈgas mask, breathing apparatus to protect the wearer against poison gas.

ˈgas meter, one for registering the amount of gas that passes through it.

ˈgas station, = service station.

ˈgas tank, on motor vehicle, for holding gasoline. (*Note:* more common than *gasoline tank*.)

ˈgas·works *n pl* (often used with a *sing verb*) factory where gas is made.

gas·eous /ˈgæsiəs/ *adj* of or like gas: *a ~ mixture*.

gash /gæʃ/ *n* [C] long deep cut or wound. □ *vt* make a gash in.

gas·ket /ˈgæskɪt/ *n* [C] strip or soft, flat piece of material used for packing a piston, pipe joints, etc to prevent steam, gas, etc from escaping.

gas·o·hol /ˈgæsəˌhɔl/ *n* [U] mixture of gasoline and alcohol, as fuel for motor vehicles.

gaso·line /ˈgæsəˌlin/ *n* [U] inflammable liquid used esp as a motor fuel.

ˈgasoline tank, = gas tank. ⇨ gas.

gasp /gæsp/ *vi,vt* **1** struggle for breath; take short, quick breaths: *~ing for breath; ~ing* (= breathless) *with rage/surprise*. **2** say in a breathless way: *He ~ed out a few words*. □ *n* [C] catching of the breath through pain, surprise, etc.

gassy /ˈgæsi/ *adj* (-ier, -iest) of or like gas; full of gas.

gas·tric /ˈgæstrɪk/ *adj* of the stomach: *a ~ ulcer; ~ juices*.

gas·tron·omy /gæˈstranəmi/ *n* [U] (*formal*) art and science of choosing, preparing and eating good food.

gas·tron·omic /ˌgæstrəˈnamɪk/ *adj* of gastronomy.

gate /geit/ *n* [C] **1** opening in the wall of a city, hedge, fence or other enclosure, capable of being closed by means of a barrier: *He opened/jumped over the garden ~*. **2** barrier that closes such an opening; barrier used to control the passage of water, eg into or out of a lock on a canal.

ˈgate·way *n* [C] **(a)** way in or out that can be closed by a gate. **(b)** (*fig*) means of approach: *a ~way to fame/knowledge*.

gate-crash /ˈgeitˌkræʃ/ *vt* (*sl*) enter and attend a private party or public entertainment without being invited or paying admission.

ˈgate-crasher *n* [C]

gather /ˈgæðər/ *vt,vi* **1** get, come or bring together: *A crowd soon ~ed around him*. **2** pick (flowers, etc); collect: *~ one's papers and books together*. **3** obtain gradually; gain little by little: *~ information*. **4** understand; conclude: *What did you ~ from his statement?* **5** (in sewing) pull together into small folds by putting a thread through: *a skirt ~ed at the waist*.

gather·ing *n* [C] coming together of people; meeting.

gator /ˈgeitər/ *n* [C] (*informal*) (short for) alligator.

gauche /gouʃ/ *adj* socially awkward.

gau·cho /ˈgautʃou/ *n* [C] (*pl* ~s) cowboy of South America.

gaudy /ˈgɔdi/ *adj* (-ier, -iest) too bright and showy; gay or bright in a tasteless way: *cheap and ~ jewels*.

gaud·ily /-əli/ *adv*

gauge, gage /geidʒ/ *n* [C] **1** standard measure;

extent. **2** distance between rails (or between opposite wheels of a vehicle that runs on rails). **3** (instrument for measuring the) thickness of wire, sheet metal, etc; diameter of a bullet, etc. **4** instrument for measuring, eg rainfall, strength of wind. □ *vt* **1** measure accurately: ~ *the diameter of wire/the strength of the wind.* **2** (*fig*) make an estimate, form a judgment, of: ~ *a person's character*.

gaunt /gɔnt/ *adj* **1** (of a person) lean as from hunger, illness or suffering. **2** (of a place) grim or desolate: *a* ~ *hillside.*

gaunt·ness /-nɪs/ *n* [U]

gaunt·let /ˈgɔntlɪt/ *n* [C] **1** glove with metal plates worn by soldiers in the Middle Ages. ***throw down/pick up/take up the gauntlet,*** give/accept a challenge to a fight. **2** strong glove with a wide, flaring cuff.

gauze /gɔz/ *n* [U] thin, netlike material of cotton, etc (for bandages).

gave *pt* of give¹.

gavel /ˈgævəl/ *n* [C] hammer used by an auctioneer or a chairman as a signal for order or attention.

gawky /ˈgɔki/ *adj* (-ier, -iest) (of persons) awkward, shy.

gay /gei/ *adj* (gayer, gayest) **1** light-hearted; cheerful; happy and full of fun: ~ *voices/looks/laughter*. **2** suggesting happiness and joy: *gay colors.* **3** (*informal*) homosexual. □ *n* [C] homosexual person.

gay·ness /-nɪs/ *n* [U]

gaze /geiz/ *n* (*sing* only) long, steady look: *with a bewildered* ~. □ *vi* look long and steadily: *What are you gazing at?*

ga·zelle /gəˈzel/ *n* [C] small, graceful kind of antelope.

ga·zette /gəˈzet/ *n* [C] **1** official journal or periodical. **2** newspaper (*Note:* dated, except in titles): *The Centerville Gazette.*

ga·zet·teer /ˌgæzəˈtɪr/ *n* [C] index of geographical names, eg at the end of an atlas.

G.B. *abbr* = Great Britain.

gear /gɪr/ *n* **1** [C] set of toothed wheels working together in a machine, eg to connect the engine of a motor vehicle with the road wheels. **2** [C] apparatus, appliance, mechanism, arrangement, of wheels, levers, etc for a special purpose: *the ˈlanding* ~ *of an aircraft*. **3** [U] equipment, clothes for a special purpose: *ˈhunting* ~. □ *vt,vi* adjust one thing to the working of another: *The country's economics must be* ~*ed to wartime requirements.*

ˈgear·shift *n* device for engaging or disengaging gears.

gecko /ˈgekou/ *n* [C] (*pl* ~s, ~es) kind of small house lizard, found in warm countries.

gee /dʒi/ *int* exclamation of wonder or surprise.

geese *pl* of goose.

geisha /ˈgeiʃə/ *n* [C] Japanese girl or woman trained to entertain men by singing and dancing at parties, etc.

gel /dʒel/ *n* [C,U] semisolid substance like a jelly. □ *vi* (-ll-) set into a jelly.

gela·tin, gela·tine /ˈdʒelətən/ *n* [U] clear, tasteless substance, obtained from the tissue, bones, etc of animals, that is used to make jelly.

ge·lati·nous /dʒəˈlætənəs/ *adj* of or like gelatin; jellylike in consistency, etc.

geld /geld/ *vt* castrate.

geld·ing *n* [C] gelded animal, esp a horse.

gem /dʒem/ *n* [C] **1** precious stone or jewel, esp one that is cut or polished. **2** something valued, eg because of great beauty: *the gem of the collection.* □ *vt* (-mm-) (*liter*) adorn with, or as with, gems: *the night sky gemmed with stars.*

Gemini /ˈdʒeməˌnai/ *n* the Twins, third sign of the zodiac. ⇨ illus at zodiac.

Gen. *abbr* = General.

gen·der /ˈdʒendər/ *n* [C] (*gram*) **1** class (as masculine, feminine or neuter) into which words (*nouns* and *pronouns*) are divided. **2** sex.

gene /dʒin/ *n* [C] biological unit controlling heredity.

genea·logi·cal /ˌdʒiniəˈladʒɪkəl/ *adj* of genealogy: *a* ~ *tree*, a diagram (like a tree) showing the descent of a family or person.

genea·logi·cally /-kli/ *adv*

gen·eal·ogy /ˌdʒiniˈalədʒi/ *n* (*pl* -ies) **1** [C] (diagram illustrating the) descent of a family, etc from an ancestor or ancestors. **2** [U] study of family history.

gen·era *pl* of genus.

gen·eral /ˈdʒenərəl/ *adj* **1** of, affecting, all or nearly all; not special, local or particular: *a matter of* ~ *interest*, one in which all or most people are likely to be interested; *a* ~ *meeting*, one to which all members (of a society, etc) are invited; *a good* ~ *education*, in all the chief subjects; *a word that is in* ~ *use*, used by all people. ***as a general rule; in general,*** in most cases; usually. **2** not in detail; not definite: *a* ~ *outline of a scheme; have a* ~ *idea of what a book is about*. **3** (after an official title) chief: *ˌPostmaster ˈGeneral; the Atˈtorney ˈGeneral*~. □ *n* [C] commissioned officer in the US army, air force or marine corps who ranks above a lieutenant general.

ˌgeneral eˈlection, one for the whole country.

ˌgeneral ˈknowledge, of a wide variety of subjects.

ˌgeneral of the ˈair force, general of the highest rank in the US air force.

ˌgeneral of the ˈarmy, general of the highest rank in the US army.

ˌgeneral pracˈtitioner, doctor who is not a specialist.

ˌgeneral ˈstore, = country store.

gen·er·al·ity /ˌdʒenəˈræləti/ *n* (*pl* -ies) **1** [C] general rule or statement, esp one that is vague or imprecise: *I wish you would go from generalities to particulars.* **2** [U] quality of being general: *a rule of great* ~, one with few exceptions.

gen·er·al·i·zation /ˌdʒenərələˈzeiʃən/ *n* **1** [U] generalizing: *It is unwise to be hasty in* ~. **2** [C] generality (1): *Her* ~*s about people are usually wrong.*

gen·er·al·ize /ˈdʒen(ə)rəˌlaiz/ *vi,vt* **1** draw a general conclusion; make a general statement. **2** state in general terms or principles: ~ *a conclusion from a collection of instances or facts.* **3** bring into general use; make general: ~ *the use of a new invention.*

gen·er·ally /ˈdʒen(ə)rəli/ *adv* **1** usually; as a general rule: *I ~ get up at six o'clock.* **2** widely; for the most part: *The new plan was ~ welcomed,* was welcomed by most people. **3** in a general sense; without paying attention to details: *~ speaking.*

gen·er·ate /ˈdʒenəˌreit/ *vt* cause to exist or occur; produce: *~ heat/electricity; hatred ~d by cultural differences.*

gen·er·ation /ˌdʒenəˈreiʃən/ *n* **1** [U] generating; bringing into existence: *the ~ of electricity by steam or water power.* **2** [C] single stage or step in family descent: *three ~s,* children, parents, grandparents. **3** [C] average period (regarded as 30 years) in which children are born, grow up, marry, and have children: *a ~ ago.* **4** [C] all persons born about the same time, and, therefore, of about the same age: *the younger ~.*
ˌgeneˈration gap, ⇨ gap.

gen·er·at·ive /ˈdʒenərətɪv/ *adj* able to produce; productive.
ˌgenerative ˈgrammar/phoˈnology, linguistic theory in which sentences/speech sounds are generated by rules operating on basic syntactic structures/phonological elements.

gen·er·ator /ˈdʒenəˌreitər/ *n* [C] machine or apparatus that generates (electricity, gas, etc).

gen·eric /dʒəˈnerɪk/ *adj* of a genus; common to a whole group or class, not special.
gen·eri·cally /-kli/ *adv*

gen·er·os·ity /ˌdʒenəˈrasəti/ *n* (*pl* -ies) **1** [U] the quality of being generous; greatness of heart: *show ~ in dealing with a defeated enemy.* **2** [C] generous act, etc.

gen·er·ous /ˈdʒen(ə)rəs/ *adj* **1** giving, ready to give, given, freely: *He is ~ with his money/~ in giving help.* **2** plentiful: *a ~ helping of meat and vegetables.*
gen·er·ous·ly *adv*

gen·esis /ˈdʒenəsɪs/ *n* [C] (*pl* -eses /-ˌsiz/) **1** beginning; starting point: *the ~ of civilization.* **2 Genesis,** the first book of the Old Testament.

gen·etic /dʒəˈnetɪk/ *adj* of genes or genetics.
gen·eti·cist /dʒəˈnetəsɪst/ *n* [C] specialist in genetics.
gen·etics *n pl* (used with a *sing verb*) branch of biology dealing with heredity, the ways in which characteristics are passed on from parents to offspring.

ge·nial /ˈdʒiniəl/ *adj* **1** kindly, sympathetic; cheerful: *a ~ old man; ~ smiles.* **2** favorable to growth; mild; warm: *a ~ climate.*
ge·ni·ally *adv*
ge·nial·ity /ˌdʒiniˈæləti/ *n* [C,U]

ge·nie /ˈdʒini/ *n* [C] (*pl* ~s, genii /ˈdʒiniˌai/) (in Arabic stories) spirit or goblin with magical powers.

geni·tal /ˈdʒenətəl/ *adj* **1** of generation(1) or reproduction. **2** of animal reproductive organs.
geni·tals *n pl* (esp the external) sex organs.

geni·tive /ˈdʒenətɪv/ *n* (*gram*) (in Latin and other inflected languages) form of a word showing source or possession.

gen·ius /ˈdʒinyəs/ *n* (*pl* ~es) **1** [U] great and exceptional capacity of the mind or imagination: *men of ~.* **2** [C] person having this capacity: *Einstein was a mathematical ~.* **3** (usually *sing* with *a,* followed by *for*) strong natural ability: *have a ~ for languages/acting/making friends.* **4** (usually *sing* with *the*) special spirit or character of a nation, a language, a period of time, etc: *the ~ of the Renaissance period in Italy.* **5** (*pl* genii /ˈdʒiniˌai/) spirit; supernatural being. ⇨ genie.

geno·cide /ˈdʒenəˌsaid/ *n* [U] deliberate murder or elimination of a race, religious group, etc.

gent /dʒent/ *n* (*informal*) gentleman.

gen·tile /ˈdʒenˌtaiəl/ *n, adj* **1** (person) not of the Jewish religion. **2** (person) not of the Mormon religion.

gentle /ˈdʒentəl/ *adj* (-r, -st) kind, friendly; not rough or violent: *a ~ nature/heart/look/voice/call/touch; a ~ breeze; a ~ slope,* ie not steep.
gentle·ness /-nɪs/ *n* [U]

gentle·man /ˈdʒentlmən/ *n* [C] (*pl* ~men /-men/) **1** man who shows consideration for the feelings of others, who is honorable and well-bred: *a fine old ~; a true ~.* **2** (corresponding to *lady*) man of good family, superior social position, etc. **3** (used courteously) any man: *A ~ has called to see you.* **4** (*pl* only) polite form of address (3) to male members of an audience: *Gentlemen! Ladies and Gentlemen!* Also sometimes used instead of *Sirs* or *Dear Sirs* when writing to a business firm, etc.
gentle·man·ly *adj* of or like a gentleman: *a ~ly appearance.*

gen·tly /ˈdʒentli/ *adv* in a gentle manner: *Hold it ~,* carefully. *The road slopes ~* (= gradually) *to the sea.*

gen·try /ˈdʒentri/ *n* (*collective pl,* usually with *the*) people of good social position (next below the nobility, in some societies).

genu·flect /ˈdʒenyəˌflekt/ *vi* bend the knee, esp in worship.
genu·flec·tion /ˌdʒenyəˈflekʃən/ *n* [C]

genu·ine /ˈdʒenyuɪn, ˈdʒenyuˌain/ *adj* true; really what it is said to be: *a ~ picture by Rubens; ~ pearls; a ~ signature.*
genu·ine·ly /ˈdʒenyuɪnli/ *adv*
genu·ine·ness /ˈdʒenynɪnnɪs/ *n* [U]

ge·nus /ˈdʒinəs/ *n* [C] (*pl* genera /ˈdʒenərə/) **1** (*science*) division of animals or plants within a family. **2** sort; kind; class.

ge(o)- /dʒi(ə- *etc*)/ *pref* of the earth: *geology.*

ge·ogra·pher /dʒiˈagrəfər/ *n* [C] student, expert, in geography.

geo·graphi·cal /ˌdʒiəˈgræfɪkəl/ *adj* of geography.
geo·graphi·cally /-kli/ *adv*

ge·ogra·phy /dʒiˈagrəfi/ *n* [U] science of the earth's surface, physical features, divisions, climate, products, population, etc.

geo·logi·cal /ˌdʒiəˈladʒɪkəl/ *adj* of geology.
ge·o·logi·cally /-kli/ *adv*

ge·ologist /dʒiˈalədʒɪst/ *n* [C] expert, student, in geology.

ge·ol·ogy /dʒiˈalədʒi/ *n* [U] science of the earth's history as shown by its rocks, etc.

geo·met·ric, -met·ri·cal /ˌdʒiəˈmetrɪk, -ˈmetrɪkəl/ *adj* of geometry; of or like the lines, figures, etc used in geometry: *~ patterns.*
geo·met·ri·cally /-kli/ *adv*

ge·ometry /dʒiˈamətri/ *n* [U] science of the properties and relations of lines, angles, sur-

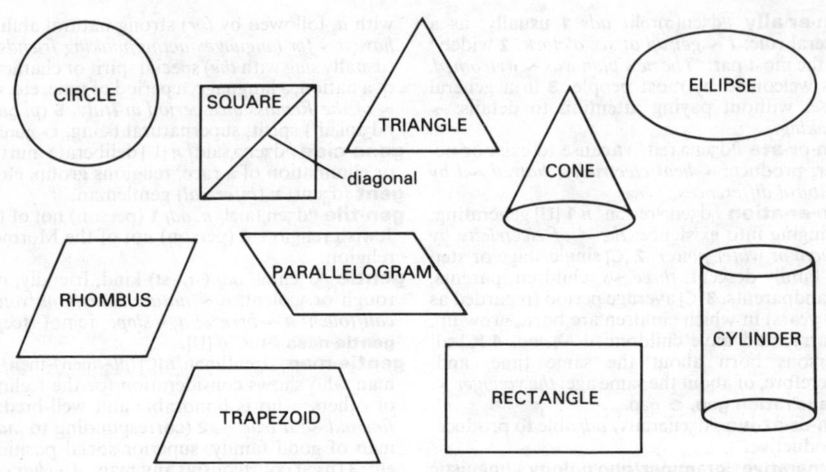

GEOMETRIC FIGURES

faces and solids.

Geor·gian /ˈdʒɔrdʒən/ *adj* **1** of the time of any of the first four Georges, Kings of England (1714-1830). **2** of the people or the state of Georgia in the US. **3** of the Georgian Soviet Socialist Republic in the USSR or of its people.

Ger. *abbr* = German.

ge·ranium /dʒəˈreiniəm/ *n* [C] (*pl* ~s) kind of plant with red, pink or white flowers.

geri·atrics /ˌdʒeriˈætrɪks/ *n pl* (with a *sing verb*) medical care of old people.

geri·atric *adj*

germ /dʒərm/ *n* [C] **1** portion of a living organism capable of becoming a new organism; seed. **2** (*fig*) beginning or starting point (of an idea, etc). **3** microbe or bacillus, esp one causing disease.

Ger·man /ˈdʒərmən/ *n* **1** the German language. **2** native of Germany. □ *adj* of Germany, its language or its people.

Ger·manic /dʒərˈmænɪk/ *adj* of the group of languages now including German, English and Dutch.

ˌGerman ˈshepherd, breed of working dog often used for police work and as a guide for blind people.

ger·mi·cide /ˈdʒərməˌsaid/ *n* [U] substance used for killing germs.

ger·mi·nate /ˈdʒərməˌneit/ *vi,vt* (of seeds) (cause to) start growth.

ger·mi·na·tion /ˌdʒərməˈneiʃən/ *n* [U]

ger·und /ˈdʒerənd/ *n* [C] the *-ing* form of an English verb when used as a noun (as in "fond of *swimming*").

ges·ta·tion /dʒeˈsteiʃən/ *n* [U] (period of) development in the womb between conception and birth.

ges·ticu·late /dʒeˈstɪkyəˌleit/ *vi* make gestures, esp when speaking.

ges·ticu·la·tion /dʒeˌstɪkyəˈleiʃən/ *n* [C,U]

ges·ture /ˈdʒestʃər/ *n* **1** [C] movement of the hand or head to show or illustrate an idea, feeling, etc: *a ~ of refusal*. **2** [C] something done to show friendship, etc: *give money as a ~ of support*. **3** [U] use of expressive movements: *an actor who is a master of the art of ~*. □ *vi* make gestures.

get /get/ *vt,vi* (*pt* got /gat/, *pp* got or gotten /ˈgatən/) **1** (cause to) be or become; (cause to) pass from one state to another or to be in a certain condition: *get wet/tired/drunk. You'll soon get used to the climate here. She soon got the children ready for school.* ***get even (with sb),*** ⇨ even¹(3). **2** reach the stage where one is doing something: *We should get going*, make a start. **3** bring a person or thing to the point where he/it is doing something: *Can you really get that old car going again?* (= restart or repair it?) **4** reach the stage where one knows, feels, etc something: *When you get to know him you'll like him.* **5** bring, persuade, cause to do or act in a certain way: *You'll never get him to understand. I can't get this old radio to work.* **6** receive; have; obtain; acquire: *I got* (= now have) *your telegram. I'll come as soon as I get time. If we divide 12 by 4, we get 3.* ***get control (over/of),*** ⇨ control(1). ***get sb's goat,*** (*informal*) annoy, irritate him: *Those simple-minded TV commercials really get my goat!* ***get the sack,*** ⇨ sack¹(3). ***get one's own way,*** ⇨ way¹(4). ***get wind of,*** ⇨ wind¹(4). ***get the worst of,*** ⇨ worst. **7** catch (an illness): *get the measles*. **8** receive as a penalty: *get six months*, be sentenced to six months' imprisonment. ***get it,*** (*informal*) receive a punishment, scolding, etc: *You'll really get it when he finds out that you're to blame.* ***get told off,*** ⇨ tell (6). **9** (*informal*) understand: *I don't get you/your meaning. She didn't get my jokes.* **10** puzzle: *Ah! That's got him!* **11** ***has/have got*** (*Note: present perfect* only) (*informal*) have (*present tense* only), eg as a possession or characteristic: *What ugly teeth he's got!* **12** ***has/have/had got to,*** must, be compelled or obliged: *It has got to* (= must) *be done today.* **13** be able: *Do you ever get to see him*, have opportunities of seeing him? **14** (non-idiomatic uses with *adverbial particles* and *prepositions;* for idiomatic uses, ⇨ 16 below) move to or from a specified point or in a particular direction: *When did you get here*, arrive? *A car makes it easier to get around. Did you manage to get away* (= have a vacation) *this Easter? She got back into bed. I'm getting off* (= leaving the train) *at the next station. Get out!* **get somewhere/anywhere/nowhere,** obtain some/any/no result; make some/any/no progress. **15** (non-idiomatic uses with *adverbial particles* and *prepositions;* for idiomatic uses, ⇨ 16 below) cause to move to or from a point, or be in a particular direction: *It was nailed to the wall and I couldn't get it off. Get* (= Put) *your hat and coat on. I can't get the lid on/off.* **16** (special uses with *adverbial particles* and *prepositions*):

get (sth) across (to sb), (*informal*) (cause something to) be understood: *I spoke slowly, but my meaning didn't get across.*

get ahead (of sb), go forward and pass others; make progress: *Tom got ahead of all the other boys in the class.*

get along, **(a)** manage: *We can't get along without money.* **(b)** make progress: *How is he getting along with his French?* **(c) get along (with sb),** work or live in a sociable way: *The new boss is easy to get along with.*

get around sb, persuade somebody into some action or to agree to something to which he was at first opposed or indifferent: *Alice knows how to get around her father.* **get around sth,** evade, eg a law or regulation, but without committing a legal offense: *A clever person might find ways of getting around that rule.* **get around to sth/to doing sth,** deal with it (when more important matters have been dealt with): *I'm very busy this week but I hope to get around to (answering) your letter next week.*

get at sb/sth, reach; gain access to: *The books are locked up and I can't get at them.* **get at sb,** bribe, influence: *They got at one of the witnesses.* **be getting at,** (*informal*) (be trying to) say or suggest: *What are you getting at?*

get away, manage to leave; escape: *Two of the prisoners got away.* **get away with sth,** pursue successfully a course of action which might usually be expected to result in blame, punishment or misfortune: *The thieves got away with the contents of the safe. If I cheat in the examination, do you think I might get away with it?*

get back at sb, have one's revenge on him: *He tricked me this time but I'll get back at him someday.*

get by, **(a)** (*fig*) pass; be accepted, without comment or criticism: *I have no formal clothes for this occasion; perhaps I can get by in a dark suit.* **(b)** manage; survive: *She can't get by without him.*

get sb down, (*informal*) depress: *Don't let this wretched weather get you down.* **get sth down,** **(a)** swallow: *The medicine was horrid, and she couldn't get it down.* **(b)** write down: *Did you get that telephone message down?* **get down to sth,** deal (seriously) with: *get down to one's work after a vacation.*

get in, **(a)** arrive: *The train got in five minutes early.* **(b)** enter: *The theater was so crowded we were lucky to get in.* **get sth in,** collect; gather: *get in the crops/the harvest.*

get into, **(a)** fit into: *I can't get into these shoes.* **(b)** reach a certain state or a particular condition: *get into trouble/a rage/a temper; get into debt; get into bad habits.*

get off, start: *We got off immediately after breakfast.* **get off lightly,** escape severe punishment, suffering, etc. ***tell sb where to get off/where he gets off,*** (*informal*) tell that his misbehavior, impudence, etc will no longer be tolerated. **get sb off,** save from punishment or a penalty: *His youth and inexperience got him off.* **get off with sth,** escape more severe punishment or misfortune: *He got off with only a fine*, eg instead of possible imprisonment.

get on, make progress; advance: *He's sure to get on in life.* **get on sth,** mount: *He got on his bike/horse/the train.* **get on one's nerves,** ⇨ nerve(2). **get on (with sth),** continue: *Please get on with your work.*

get out, become known: *The secret got out. If the news gets out there'll be trouble.* **get out of (sth/doing sth),** **(a)** (*fig*) avoid; escape (from): *I wish I could get out of going to that wedding.* **(b)** (*fig*) abandon gradually: *get out of bad habits.* **get sth out of sb,** extract by force: *The police will get a confession out of him.*

get over sb/sth, (*informal*) **(a)** recover from, eg illness, surprise, a loss: *I can't get over his rudeness. He never got over Jane, you know,* She stayed in his memory. **(b)** overcome: *She can't get over her shyness.* **get sth over,** make it clear.

get through, reach a person: *I rang you several times yesterday but couldn't get through.* **get through sth,** reach the end of; finish: *He got through all his work before he left the office.*

get to, reach a particular state. **get down to business,** ⇨ business(3). **get to the point,** ⇨ point[1](9). **get to work,** ⇨ work[1](1).

get together, come or meet together, eg for discussion or social purposes: *Let's get together one evening and talk about old times.* **get people/things together,** collect; organize, put in order: *The rebel leader couldn't get an army together.*

get under way, ⇨ way[1](7).

get up, **(a)** rise: *What time do you get up*, ie from bed? *He got up* (= stood up) *to ask a question.* **(b)** mount: *get up behind me*, eg on a horse. **get sb/oneself up,** **(a)** cause to rise, be out of bed: *get the children up and dressed for school.* **(b)** dress in a certain style: *get oneself up as a sailor.* **get up to sth,** reach: *We got up to page seventy-two in the last lesson.*

get with it, (*informal*) become aware, alert, etc.

ˈget·away *n* ***make one's getaway,*** escape; (as an *adjective*): *The get-away car had been stolen.*

ˈget-together *n* [C] social gathering.

ˈget·up *n* (unusual) style of dress.

gey·ser /ˈgaizər/ *n* [C] natural spring[1](2) sending up a column of hot water and steam from time to time.

ghast·ly /ˈgæstli/ *adj* (-ier, -iest) **1** deathlike; pale and ill: *looking* ~; (also as an *adverb*): ~ *pale.* **2** causing horror or fear: *a* ~ *accident.* **3**

GEYSER

(*informal*) very bad; unpleasant: *a ~ dinner.*

gher·kin /ˈgərkən/ *n* [C] small, green cucumber for pickling.

ghetto /ˈgetou/ *n* (*pl* ~s, ~es) **1** (formerly, in some countries) Jewish quarter of a town. **2** section of a town, lived in by people who are members of a racial, ethnic or religious minority.

ghost /goust/ *n* [C] **1** spirit of a dead person appearing to a person still living: *He looked as if he had seen a ~*, looked frightened. **2** (*old use*) spirit of life. ***give up the ghost,*** die. **3** something shadowy or without substance. ***not have a ghost of a chance,*** no chance at all.

ghost·ly *adj* (-ier, -iest) of, like, suggesting, a ghost.

ˈghost town, one now abandoned, eg an area where gold was once mined.

ˈghost·writer *n* [C] person who does writing for another person who takes the credit.

the ˌHoly ˈGhost, (in Christian theology) the Third Person of the Trinity.

GI, G.I. /ˌdʒi ˈai/ *n* [C] (*pl* GI's, G.I.'s) (*informal*) US Army enlisted man. □ *adj* of the US Army: *GI rations.*

gi·ant /ˈdʒaiənt/ *n* [C] **1** (in fairy tales) man of very great height and size. **2** man, animal or plant much larger than normal. **3** (*fig*) person of extraordinary ability or genius. **4** (as an *adjective*) of great size or force: *a ~ cabbage.*

gi·ant·ess /ˈdʒaiəntɪs/ *n* [C] female giant.

gib·ber·ish /ˈdʒɪb(ə)rɪʃ/ *n* [U] confused, meaningless talk.

gib·bet /ˈdʒɪbɪt/ *n* [C] **1** wooden post on which corpses of executed criminals were formerly displayed as a warning. **2** gallows. □ *vt* put to death by hanging.

gib·bon /ˈgɪbən/ *n* [C] kinds of small, tailless ape. ⇨ illus at ape.

gib·bous /ˈgɪbəs/ *adj* (of the moon) having the bright part greater than a semicircle and less than a circle. ⇨ illus at phase.

gibe /dʒaib/ *vi* make fun of; sneer: *~ at a fellow student's mistakes.* □ *n* [C] sneering remark.

gib·lets /ˈdʒɪblɪts/ *n pl* heart, liver, gizzard, etc of a turkey, hen, etc.

giddy /ˈgɪdi/ *adj* (-ier, -iest) **1** causing, having, a feeling of dizziness. **2** silly; frivolous; not serious: *a ~ young girl.*

gid·dily /ˈgɪdəli/ *adv*

gid·di·ness /-nɪs/ *n* [U]

gift /gɪft/ *n* **1** [C] something given; present: *~s to charities.* **2** [C] natural ability or talent: *have a ~ for art/languages.* **3** [U] right or power to give.

gifted *adj* talented.

gig /gɪg/ *n* [C] **1** small, light two-wheeled carriage pulled by one horse. **2** narrow, small boat for the captain of a ship.

gi·gan·tic /dʒaiˈgæntɪk/ *adj* of immense size, strength, etc.

giggle /ˈgɪgəl/ *vi* laugh in a nervous and silly way. □ *n* [C] laugh of this kind.

Gila monster /ˈhilə ˌmanstər/ *n* [C] large, poisonous lizard of the southwestern US.

gild /gɪld/ *vt* cover with gold leaf or gold-colored paint: *~ a picture frame.*

gilder *n* [C]

gill[1] /gɪl/ *n* [C] organ with which a fish breathes. ⇨ illus at fish.

gill[2] /dʒɪl/ *n* [C] liquid measure, one quarter of a pint.

gilt /gɪlt/ *n* [U] very thin layer of gold.

gim·let /ˈgɪmlət/ *n* [C] small tool for boring holes in wood, etc.

gim·mick /ˈgɪmɪk/ *n* [C] **1** clever trick, catchword, article of wear, etc used to attract attention, customers, etc. **2** gadget.

gin[1] /dʒɪn/ *n* [U] colorless alcoholic drink.

gin[2] /dʒɪn/ *n* [C] machine for separating the seeds from cotton. □ *vt* (-nn-) use a gin to take the seeds out of cotton.

gin·ger /ˈdʒɪndʒər/ *n* [U] **1** (plant with a) hot-tasting root used in cooking. **2** liveliness; energy. **3** (also as an *adjective*) light reddish-brown color: *~ hair.* □ *vt* make more vigorous or lively: *~ the supporters up.*

ˌginger ˈale/ˈbeer, non-alcoholic drink flavored with ginger.

ˈgin·ger·bread *n* [U] cake flavored with ginger and molasses.

gin·ger·ly /ˈdʒɪndʒərli/ *adv* with great care to avoid harming oneself, what one touches, making a noise, etc. □ *adj* cautious; careful: *in a ~ fashion.*

ging·ham /ˈgɪŋəm/ *n* [U] cotton or linen cloth, usually woven in stripes or checks.

gin·seng /ˈdʒɪnˌseŋ/ *n* [U] **1** flavorful root of an Asian and North American plant used as a medicine. **2** beverage made from this root.

gipsy /ˈdʒɪpsi/ *n* [C] (*pl* -ies) = gypsy.

gi·raffe /dʒəˈræf/ *n* [C] African animal with a very long neck and legs and a spotted coat.

gird /gərd/ *vt* (*pt,pp* girded, girt /gərt/) **1** put around or fasten, eg with a belt. **2** prepare (oneself) for a struggle.

girder /ˈgərdər/ *n* [C] wood, iron or steel beam to support the joists of a floor or to form the frame of a bridge, roof, etc.

girdle /ˈgərdəl/ *n* [C] **1** cord or belt fastened around the waist to keep clothes in position. **2** light corset. **3** something that encircles like a girdle: *a ~ of green fields round a town.* □ *vt* encircle: *a lake ~d with trees.*

girl /gərl/ *n* [C] **1** female child; (esp young) unmarried woman. **2** daughter. **3** (*dated*) girl or woman working in a shop, office, etc (irrespective of age): *ˈoffice ~s.* **4** (*informal*) = girl friend (b).

ˈgirl friend, (a) female friend. **(b)** (*informal*) female lover.

ˈgirl·hood *n* [U] state or time of being a girl.

girl·ish *adj* of, for, like a girl.

girl·ish·ly *adv*
girl·ish·ness /-nɪs/ *n* [U]
ˈ**Girl Scout,** member of an organization for girls similar to the Boy Scouts.
girt *pt,pp* of gird.
girth /gərθ/ *n* [C] **1** leather or cloth band tightened round the body of a horse to keep the saddle in place. **2** measurement around the body of a person or thing: *a tree 10 yards in ~.*
gist /dʒɪst/ *n* **the gist,** real or main point(s); general sense: *Tell/Give me the ~ of what he said.*
give[1] /gɪv/ *vt,vi* (*pt* gave /geiv/, *pp* ~n /ˈgɪvən/) **1** hand over (to a person) without payment or exchange, eg as a present or gift: *I gave David a book. Give one to me.* **2** pay: *How much will you ~ me for my old car?* ***give sth (in order) to*** *+inf, I would ~ a lot to know where she is.* **3** hand over (a person or thing) into the care or safekeeping or custody of: *Give the porter your bags.* **4** allow, eg time; agree to; grant: *You'd better ~ yourself half an hour for the trip. They gave me a week to make up my mind.* **5** furnish; supply; provide: *The sun ~s us warmth and light.* **6** cause to have: *You've ~n me your cold.* **7** devote; dedicate: *He gave his life to the cause of peace.* **8** (used with a *noun*) make or do; produce: *~ a groan/yell*, groan, yell; *~ him a kick*, kick him; *~ her a ring*, telephone her. **9** (in fixed phrases) ***give it to sb,*** attack, scold, etc: *She really gave it to me for being late.* ***give or take...,*** plus or minus: *She'll be here at 4 o'clock, ~ or take a few minutes.* ***give way,*** **(a)** retire, retreat: *Our troops had to ~ way.* **(b)** fail to support: *The rope gave way*, broke. ***give way (to sth/sb),*** **(a)** yield to: *Give way to traffic coming in from the right.* **(b)** be replaced by: *Sorrow gave way to smiles.* **(c)** abandon oneself to: *Don't ~ way to despair.* **(d)** make concessions (to): *We mustn't ~ way to these impudent demands.* **10** lose firmness; bend; yield to pressure: *The branch gave* (eg bent) *but did not break. His knees seemed to ~*, to feel weak (so that he fell down). **11** (special uses with *adverbial particles* and *prepositions*):
give sb away, (esp) hand over (the bride) to the bridegroom at a wedding. ***give sth away,*** **(a)** allow somebody else to have; sacrifice: *You've ~n away a good chance of winning the match.* **(b)** give freely, not expecting anything in return: *He gave away all his money.* **(c)** reveal, intentionally or unintentionally: *His accent gave him away.* ˌ***give the*** ˈ***game away,*** ⇨ game[2] (5).
give sth back (to sb); give sb back sth, restore; return: *~ it back to its rightful owner.*
give in (to sb), surrender; submit: *The rebels were forced to ~ in.*
give sth off, send out, eg smoke, vapor, etc: *This chemical ~s off a terrible smell!*
give out, come to an end; be exhausted: *Our food supplies began to ~ out. His strength gave out.* ***give sth out,*** distribute; send out: *~ out books.*
give up, abandon the attempt to do something, find the answer: *I can do nothing more; I ~ up. I can't answer that puzzle; I ~ up.* ***give sb up,*** **(a)** say that one regards him as hopeless: *The doctors have ~n him up*, say that they cannot cure him. **(b)** no longer expect a person: *She was so late that we had ~n her up.* ***give sb up for lost,*** no longer expect him to be found or saved. ***give sb/oneself/sth up,*** surrender; part with: *~ up one's seat to another person*, eg on a crowded bus. The escaped prisoner gave himself up. ***give sth up,*** stop (doing something): *I wish I could ~ up smoking.*
ˈ**give-away** *n* **(a)** something given without charge, expected returns. **(b)** something revealed, intentionally or unintentionally: *The expression on the thief's face was a ~-away*, showed his guilt.
give[2] /gɪv/ *n* [U] **1** quality of being elastic, of yielding to pressure: *A stone floor has no ~ in it.* **2** (*fig*) (of a person) quality of yielding. ***give and take,*** compromise; willingness on both sides to give way: *There must be ~ and take if the negotiations are to succeed.*
given /ˈgɪvən/ *pp* of give[1]. □ *adj* **1** granting or assuming that one has, eg as a basis for reasoning: *Given good health, I hope to finish the work this year.* **2** agreed on: *They were to meet at a ~ time and place.* ⇨ given name below. **3** ***given to (doing) sth,*** devoted or addicted to; having as a habit or inclination: *He's ~ to boasting.*
ˈ**given name,** = first name.
giver /ˈgɪvər/ *n* [C] one who gives.
giz·zard /ˈgɪzərd/ *n* [C] bird's second stomach for grinding food.
glacé /glæˈsei/ *adj* **1** (of fruits) candied or glazed with sugar. **2** (of leather, cloth) smooth, polished.
gla·cial /ˈgleiʃəl/ *adj* of ice, esp of glaciers.
gla·cier /ˈgleiʃər/ *n* [C] mass of ice, formed by packed snow, moving slowly along a wide area.
glad /glæd/ *adj* (-dder, -ddest) **1** pleased: *be/look/feel ~ about something. I'm ~ to see you.* **2** causing or bringing joy; joyful: *Have you heard the ~ news?*
glad·den /ˈglædən/ *vt* make glad.
glad·ly *adv*
glad·ness /-nɪs/ *n* [U]
glade /gleid/ *n* [C] clear, open space in a forest.
gladi·ator /ˈglædiˌeitər/ *n* [C] (in ancient Rome) slave, prisoner, etc who fought with weapons at public shows in an arena.
gladi·olus /ˌglædiˈouləs/ *n* (*pl* -li /-ˌlai/ or ~es) plant with sword-shaped leaves and spikes of brightly colored flowers.
glam·or·ize /ˈglæməˌraiz/ *vt* make glamorous: *newspapers glamorizing the lives of rock musicians.*
glam·or·ous /ˈglæmərəs/ *adj* full of glamour: *~ movie stars.*
glam·our, glam·or /ˈglæmər/ *n* [U] exciting charm that fascinates and attracts: *a scene full of ~; the ~ of a beautiful woman.*
glance /glæns/ *vi* **1** take a quick look: *~ at the clock; ~ over/through a letter; ~ around a room. He ~d down the column of classified ads.* **2** ***glance off,*** hit and fly off at an angle: *The bullet ~d off his helmet.* **3** (of bright objects, light) flash: *Their helmets ~d in the sunlight.* □ *n* [C] **1** quick look: *take a ~ at the newspaper headlines;*

see something at a ~, at once. *loving* ~*s*. **2** flash of light: *a* ~ *of spears in the sunlight*.

gland /glænd/ *n* [C] simple or complex organ that produces substances that are to be used by or expelled from the body: *sweat* ~*s*.

glandu·lar /ˈglændʒələr/ *adj* of or like a gland: ~*ular fever*.

glare[1] /glær/ *n* **1** [U] strong, fierce, unpleasant light: *the* ~ *of the sun on the water*. (*fig*) *in the full* ~ *of publicity*, with public attention directed toward one. **2** [C] angry or fixed stare: *look at someone with a* ~.

glare[2] /glær/ *vi,vt* **1** shine in a dazzling or disagreeable way: *The tropic sun* ~*d down on us all the day*. **2** stare angrily or fiercely: *They stood glaring at each other*.

glar·ing /ˈglærɪŋ/ *adj* **1** dazzling: *a car with* ~ *headlights*. **2** angry; fierce: ~ *eyes*. **3** obvious; conspicuous: *a* ~ *mistake;* ~ *injustice*. **4** (of colors) too bright and showy.

glass /glæs/ *n* **1** [U] hard, brittle, usually transparent substance (as used in windows): *made of* ~. **2** [C] article made of this substance. **(a)** glass drinking vessel or its contents: *a* ~ *of milk*. **(b)** mirror. **(c)** telescope: *The sailor looked through his* ~. **(d)** barometer: *The* ~ *is falling*. **(e)** (*pl*) eyeglasses: *She can't read without* ~*es*. **(f)** (*pl*) binoculars. ⇨ looking glass, magnifying glass. □ *vt* fit with glass; glaze.

ˈglass·blower *n* [C] workman who blows molten glass to shape it into bottles, etc.

glass·ful /-ˌfʊl/ *n* [C] as much as a drinking glass can hold.

ˈglass·ware *n* [U] articles made of glass.

ˈglass wool, fine glass fibers used for filters, insulation, etc.

ˈglass·works *n pl* (often used with a *sing verb*) factory where glass is made.

glassy *adj* (-ier, -iest) **(a)** like glass in appearance: *a* ~*y shine*. **(b)** lifeless, expressionless, fixed: *a* ~*y stare*.

glaze /gleiz/ *vt,vi* **1** fit glass into: ~ *a window*. **2** cover with a glasslike surface: ~ *pottery*. **3** (of the eyes) become glassy: *His eyes* ~*d over*. □ *n* [C,U] (substance used for, surface obtained by giving, a) thin glassy coating.

gla·zier /ˈgleiʒər/ *n* [C] workman who fits glass into the frames of windows, etc.

gleam /glim/ *n* [C] **1** beam or ray of soft light, esp one that comes and goes: *the* ~*s of the morning sun*. **2** (*fig*) brief show or faint trace: *an essay with an occasional* ~ *of intelligence*. □ *vi* send out gleams: *reflectors* ~*ing in the highway*.

glean /glin/ *vi, vt* **1** pick up grain left in a harvest field by the workers. **2** (*fig*) gather news, facts in small quantities.

gleaner *n* [C] person who gleans.

glean·ings *n pl* (usually *fig*) small items of knowledge gathered little by little.

glee /gli/ *n* [U] feeling of joy caused by success or triumph: *shout with* ~.

glee·ful /-fəl/ *adj* full of glee; joyous.

glee·fully /-fəli/ *adv*

glen /glen/ *n* [C] narrow valley.

glib /glɪb/ *adj* (-bber, -bbest) (of a person, his speech) ready and fluent, but not sincere: *a* ~ *talker;* ~ *excuses*.

glib·ly *adv*

glib·ness /-nɪs/ *n* [U]

glide /glaid/ *vi* move along smoothly and continuously: *The pilot* ~*d skillfully down to the landing field*. □ *n* [C] gliding movement: *The dance consists of a series of* ~*s*.

glider *n* [C] aircraft without an engine, eg the kind towed behind a powered aircraft.

glim·mer /ˈglɪmər/ *vi* send out a weak, uncertain light: *lights* ~*ing in the distance*. □ *n* [C] weak, faint, unsteady light: *a* ~ *of light through the curtains;* (*fig*) *a* ~ *of hope*.

glimpse /glɪmps/ *n* [C] quick look or view: *get/catch a* ~ *of something from the window of a train*. □ *vt* catch a glimpse of.

glint /glɪnt/ *vi* gleam. □ *n* [C] gleam or flash: ~*s of gold in her hair*.

glis·ten /ˈglɪsən/ *vi* shine brightly; sparkle: *eyes* ~*ing with tears*.

glit·ter /ˈglɪtər/ *vi* shine brightly with flashes of light: ~*ing with jewels*. □ *n* [U] brilliant, sparkling light: *the* ~ *of the decorations*.

glit·ter·ing *adj* brilliant; attractive.

gloat /glout/ *vi* look at or think about with selfish delight: ~ *over one's wealth*.

gloat·ing·ly *adv*

glob·al /ˈgloubəl/ *adj* **1** worldwide: ~ *war*. **2** like a globe.

globe /gloub/ *n* [C] **1** object shaped like a ball, esp a model of the earth. **2** the earth. **3** any spherical or round object, as a lampshade or a fishbowl.

ˈglobe-trotter *n* [C] person who makes frequent trips to distant parts of the world.

glob·ule /ˈglabyul/ *n* [C] tiny, round drop.

globu·lar /ˈglabyələr/ *adj* **1** globe-shaped. **2** made up of globules.

glock·en·spiel /ˈglakənˌspiəl/ *n* [C] musical instrument consisting of metal bars which are struck with two light hammers. ⇨ illus at percussion.

gloom /glum/ *n* [U] **1** total or partial darkness. **2** feeling of sadness and hopelessness: *The news filled everyone with* ~.

gloomy /ˈglumi/ *adj* (-ier, -iest) **1** dark, unlit. **2** depressed; sad: *feeling* ~ *about the future*. **3** causing gloom; depressing.

gloom·ily /-əli/ *adv*

glo·rify /ˈglɔrəˌfai/ *vt* (*pt,pp* -ied) **1** give adoration and thanksgiving to (God); worship. **2** give honor and glory to (a hero). **3** make (a person or thing) seem better, more important, etc than is actually the case: *His weekend cottage is only a glorified barn*.

glori·fi·ca·tion /ˌglɔrəfəˈkeiʃən/ *n* [U]

glori·ous /ˈglɔriəs/ *adj* **1** splendid; magnificent: *a* ~ *sunset/view*. **2** possessing or giving glory: *a* ~ *victory*. **3** (*informal*) very enjoyable: *have a* ~ *time;* ~ *fun*.

glori·ous·ly *adv*

glory /ˈglɔri/ *n* [U] **1** high fame and honor won by great achievements. **2** adoration and praise offered to God: *"Glory to God in the highest."* **3** splendid or magnificent state: *the* ~ *of a sunset*. **4** (sometimes [C]) (*pl* -ies) reason for pride; something deserving respect and honor: *the glories of ancient Rome*. □ *vi* ***glory in,*** rejoice in, take great pride in: ~ *in one's strength/in her success.*

gloss[1] /glas, glɔs/ *n* **1** [U] smooth, bright surface: *the ~ of silk and satin.* **2** (*fig*) (usually *sing* with *a* or *an*) deceptive appearance: *a ~ of respectability.* □ *vt* ***gloss over,*** cover up or explain away (an error, etc): *~ over his faults.*

glossy *adj* (-ier, -iest) smooth and shiny.

gloss[2] /glas, glɔs/ *n* [C] explanation (in a footnote, etc) of a word, phrase, etc in a text. □ *vt* glosses for (a text).

glos·sary /ˈglasəri, ˈglɔsəri/ *n* [C] (*pl* -ies) **1** collection of glosses. **2** list and explanations of special or unusual works.

glot·tis /ˈglatɪs/ *n* opening between the vocal chords. ⇨ illus at head.

glove /gləv/ *n* [C] **1** covering of leather, knitted wool, etc for the hand, esp one with a division for each finger. ***fit like a glove,*** fit perfectly. ***be hand in glove (with...),*** be in close relations (with...). **2** padded leather covering for the hand, used by baseball players. ⇨ illus at baseball. **3** boxing glove.

glow /glou/ *vi* **1** send out light or heat without flame: *~ing embers/charcoal.* **2** (*fig*) be, look, feel, warm or flushed (as after exercise or when excited): *~ing with enthusiasm/health/pride.* **3** show strong or warm colors: *trees ~ing with autumn tints.* □ *n* (*sing* only, with *the, a* or *an*) glowing state; warm or flushed look; warm feeling: *in a ~ of enthusiasm; the ~ of the sky at sunset.*

glow·ing *adj* showing warm color or (*fig*) enthusiasm: *give a ~ing account of what happened.*

glow·ing·ly *adv*

ˈ**glow-worm** *n* [C] wingless female insect or insect larva that gives off light.

glower /ˈglauər/ *vi* look in an angry or threatening way: *~ at her.*

glu·cose /ˈgluˌkous/ *n* [U] sugar that occurs in plant and animal tissue.

glue /glu/ *n* [U] substance used for joining (esp wooden) things. □ *vt* (*pt,pp* ~d) **1** stick, make fast, with glue: *gluing two pieces of wood together; ~ a piece of wood on to something.* **2** fasten closely or firmly: *His eyes were/His ear was ~d to the keyhole. Why must you always be ~d to the TV?* Why do you always watch it?

gluey /ˈglui/ *adj* (gluier, gluiest) sticky, like glue.

glum /gləm/ *adj* (-mmer, -mmest) gloomy; sad.

glum·ly *adv*

glum·ness /-nɪs/ *n* [U]

glut /glət/ *vt* (-tt-) **1** supply too much to: *~ the market (with fruit, etc).* **2** overeat; satisfy to the full; fill to excess: *~ one's appetite; ~ted with pleasure.* □ *n* [C] oversupply: *a ~ of pears on the market.*

glu·ten /ˈglutən/ *n* [U] sticky substance (protein) that is found esp in wheat flour.

glu·ti·nous /ˈglutənəs/ *adj* of or like gluten; sticky.

glut·ton /ˈglətən/ *n* [C] person who eats too much: *You've eaten the whole pie, you ~! He's a ~ for work,* (*fig*) is always willing and ready for more work.

glut·ton·ous /ˈglətənəs/ *adj* very greedy.

glut·ton·ous·ly *adv*

glut·tony /-təni/ *n* [U] habit or practice of eating too much.

gly·cer·in, gly·cer·ine /ˈglɪsərɪn/ *n* [U] thick, sweet, colorless liquid made from fats and oils, used in medical and toilet preparations and explosives.

gm. *abbr* = gram(s).

G-man /ˈdʒi-ˌmæn/ *n* [C] (*pl* G-men /-ˌmen/) agent of the Federal Bureau of Investigation.

GMT *abbr* = Greenwich Mean Time.

gnarled /narəld/ *adj* (of tree trunks) twisted and rough; covered with knobs: *a ~ old oak; ~* (= knotty, deformed) *fingers.*

gnash /næʃ/ *vt* grind or strike together, eg in rage.

gnat /næt/ *n* [C] small two-winged fly that stings.

gnaw /nɔ/ *vt,vi* **1** bite steadily at: *The dog was ~ing (at) a bone.* **2** torment; waste away: *fear and anxiety ~ing (at) the heart.*

gnome /noum/ *n* [C] (in tales) dwarf living under the ground.

GNP *abbr* = gross national product.

go[1] /gou/ *vi* (*3rd person, present tense* goes /gouz/, *pt* went /went/, *pp* gone /gɔn/) **1 (a)** (with a *prep* or *adv* of place or direction; ⇨ come) move, pass, from one point to another and away from the speaker, etc: *He has gone to see his sister. Go and get your hat. Let's go to the movies.* **(b)** leave; depart: *They came at six and went* (= left) *at nine. I wish this pain would go (away).* ***to go,*** to be taken out or away: *a roast beef sandwich to go.* **2 (a)** belong; have as a usual or proper position: *Where do you want your piano to go?* Where shall we put it? **(b)** fit: *My clothes won't go into this small suitcase. 7 into 15 won't go,* 15 does not contain exact multiples of 7. **3** reach, extend; last: *This road goes to Springfield.* ***go a long way,*** last: *She makes a little money go a long way.* ***go (very) far,*** **(a)** last: *A dollar doesn't go far nowadays.* **(b)** (of a person) succeed: *He will go far in the diplomatic service,* will win promotion, etc. **4** follow a particular course; reach a certain limit. ***go too far,*** go beyond acceptable limits: *That's going too far,* saying or doing more than is right. ***go to great lengths/trouble/pains (to do sth),*** take care to do something well: *He went to great trouble to make his guests comfortable.* ***go to one's head,*** ⇨ head[1](20). **5** ***go on a journey/trip/outing,*** make a journey, take a trip, have an outing, etc. ***go for a walk, etc,*** go out in order to walk, etc. ***go swimming/shopping, etc,*** take part in the activity of swimming, etc. **6** ***go*** + ***prep*** + ***noun,*** **(a)** pass into/from the state described by the *noun*: *go from bad to worse; go out of fashion; go to pieces; go to sleep.* ⇨ the *noun* entries. **(b)** go to the place, etc described by the *noun* for the purpose associated with it: *go to church,* attend a church service; *go to school/college/university,* attend school, etc in order to learn or study. **7** ***go to sb,*** pass into somebody's possession; be allotted to: *The first prize went to Mr. Hill.* **8** become; pass into a specific condition: *go blind/mad, etc.* ***go bad,*** ⇨ bad[1](5). **9** be moving, working, etc: *This clock doesn't go. Is your* *watch going?* **10** be or live habitually in a specific state or condition: *Refugees often go hungry. They went barefoot.* **11** (showing manner of progress; sometimes after "How"): *How's everything going* (= progressing)? *How's your work going? Things went better than had been expected.* ***be going strong,*** be proceeding vigorously; be still flourishing: *He's ninety and/but still going strong.* **12** work; operate: *This machine goes by electricity.* **13** ***go for,*** **(a)** try to get: *She is going for her doctorate.* **(b)** be sold (to a person) for: *The house went for too little money. I won't let mine go* (= sell it) *for less than $95,000.* **(c)** like; favor; support: *He really goes for her,* likes her very much. *The committee didn't go for his suggestion.* **(d)** (of money) be spent on: *Most of her income goes for food and rent.* **14** be given up, abandoned, lost: *I'm afraid the car must go. My sight is going,* I'm losing my ability to see. **15** ***as men/things, etc go,*** considering what is usual or general: *They're good workers, as workers go nowadays.* **16** fail; collapse; give way; break off: *First the sails and then the mast went in the storm.* ***let oneself go,*** relax, enjoy oneself, etc. **17** pass away: *He's dead and gone,* dead and buried. **18** be decided: *The case* (ie in a law court) *went against him,* he lost. *How did the election go in Chicago,* Who was elected? **19** (various phrases) ***go bail (for sb),*** ⇨ bail[1]. ***go shares/halves (with sb in sth),*** ⇨ share[1](1), half(1). ***go to bat for sb,*** actively support him. **20** have a certain wording or tune: *I'm not quite sure how the tune goes.* **21** make a specific sound or gesture: *The clock goes "tick-tock, tick-tock." "Bang! went the gun."* **22** begin an activity: *One, two, three, go!* (eg as a signal for competitors in a race to start). *Well, here goes!* (used to call attention to the fact that one is about to start to do something). **23** ***be going to do sth,*** **(a)** (showing what is intended, determined or planned): *We're going to spend our vacation in Miami this year. We're going to buy a house.* **(b)** (showing what is considered likely or probable): *Look at those black clouds — we're going to have/there's going to be a storm.* **(c)** about to: *I'm going to tell you a story. I'm going to be twenty next month.* **24** (special uses with *adverbial particles* and *prepositions*):

go about sth, set to work at: *You're not going about that job in the right way.*

go after sb/sth, try to win or obtain.

go ahead, proceed without hesitation: *"May I start now?" "Yes, go ahead."*

go along, proceed: *You may have some difficulty first but you'll find it easier as you go along.* ***go along with sb,*** **(a)** accompany: *I'll go along with you as far as the corner.* **(b)** agree with: *I can't go along with you on that point.*

go around, **(a)** be enough, in number or amount, for everyone to have a share: *There aren't enough apples/isn't enough whiskey to go around.* **(b)** travel to a place by an indirect route: *The main road to Tampa was flooded, and we had to go (the long way) around.*

go at sb/sth, **(a)** rush at; attack: *They went at each other for nearly an hour.* **(b)** deal with something energetically: *They were going at the job for all they were worth,* making the greatest effort.

go away, leave.

go back, **(a)** return. **(b)** extend backwards in space or time: *His family goes back for hundreds of years.* ***go back on,*** fail to keep; break or withdraw from, eg a promise: *He's not the sort of man who would/to go back on his word.*

go behind sb's back, do or say something without his knowledge.

go by, pass: *Time went by slowly. We waited for the procession to go by.* ˈ***go by sth,*** be guided or directed by: *That's a good rule to go by,* to be guided by.

go down, **(a)** (of a ship, etc) sink. **(b)** (of the sun, moon, etc) set. **(c)** (of food and drink) be swallowed. **(d)** (of prices) go lower: *The price of eggs/The cost of living has gone down.* ***go down (in sth),*** be written, recorded or remembered in: *It all goes down in his notebook. He'll go down in history as a great statesman.* ***go down to,*** be continued or extended as far as: *This History of Europe goes down to 1970.* ***go for sb,*** **(a)** go to fetch: *Shall I go for a doctor?* **(b)** (*informal*) like; enjoy: *He really goes for Dixieland jazz.*

go in, **(a)** enter: *The key won't go in (the lock). She went in (the house, kitchen) to cook the dinner.* **(b)** (of the sun, moon, etc) be obscured by clouds: *The sun has gone in and it is rather cold.* ***go in for sth,*** **(a)** enter a competition: *go in for the hurdles.* **(b)** have an interest in, etc: *go in for golf.*

go into sth, **(a)** enter: *go into the army/the Church/politics.* **(b)** busy or occupy oneself with: *go into (the) details/particulars; go into the evidence. This problem will need a lot of going into,* will need thorough investigation. **(c)** pass into (a certain state): *go into fits of laughter.*

go off, **(a)** explode; be fired: *The gun went off by accident.* **(b)** (of events) proceed well, etc: *The performance/concert went off well.* **(c)** go away; depart: *He's gone off to Boston with his friends.*

go on, **(a)** (of time) pass: *As the months went on, he became impatient.* **(b)** continue: *If you go on* (= continue to act) *like this you'll be expelled.* **(c)** happen; take place; be in progress: *What's going on here?* ***go on about sth,*** talk too much about: *I wish you'd stop going on about your problems.* ***go on to sth/to do sth,*** do or say next: *Let's now go on to the next item on the agenda.* ***go on (with sth/doing sth),*** continue, persevere, with: *Go on with your work.*

go out, **(a)** leave the room, building, etc: *She was (all) dressed to go out. Out you go!* **(b)** go to social functions, parties, dances, etc: *She still goes out a great deal, even at seventy-five.* **(c)** become extinguished: *The fire/lights went out.* **(d)** become unfashionable: *Have miniskirts gone out?* ***go out with sb,*** (*informal*) be regularly in a person's company: *How long has Jane been going out with David? How long have Jane and David been going out together?*

go over sth, **(a)** examine carefully: *We must go over the accounts carefully before we settle them. We should like to go over the house before deciding whether we want to buy it.* **(b)** study or review carefully: *Let's go over this chapter/lesson/the main facts again.* ***go over to sb/sth,*** change one's political party, side, a preference, etc: *Has he gone over to the Democrats?*

go through, **(a)** (= get through) be passed or approved: *The bill* (ie in Congress) *did not go through.* **(b)** be concluded: *The deal did not go through.* ***go through sth,*** **(a)** discuss in detail: *Let's go through the arguments again.* **(b)** search: *The police went through his pockets.* **(c)** perform; take part in: *They went through both a civil and religious wedding.* **(d)** undergo; suffer: *If you only knew what she has to go through with that husband of hers!* **(e)** reach the end of; spend: *go through a fortune/all one's money.* ***go through with sth,*** do it: *He's determined to go through with the marriage in spite of his parents' opposition.*

go together, be suitable for each other; harmonize: *These curtains and rugs don't go together.*

go under, **(a)** sink. **(b)** (*fig*) fail; become bankrupt: *The firm will go under unless business improves.*

go up, **(a)** rise: *The temperature is going up. Everything went up in the budget except pensions.* **(b)** be erected: *New office buildings are going up everywhere.* **(c)** be destroyed by explosion or fire: *The whole building went up in flames.*

go with sb/sth, **(a)** accompany: *I'll go with you.* **(b)** be a normal accompaniment of: *That belt goes with the blue dress.* **(c)** match; be fitting and suitable with: *These new curtains don't go well with your rugs*, don't suit them.

go without (sth), endure the lack of: *There's no money for a vacation this year; we'll just have to go without.* ***go without saying,*** be understood without actually being stated: *It goes without saying that she's a good cook.*

ˈgo-ahead *n* permission to proceed: *Give them the go-ahead.*

ˈgo-getter, (*informal*) ambitious, enterprising person.

ˌgoing-ˈover *n* (*pl* goings-over) **(a)** inspection; examination: *The document will need a careful going-over before we can make a decision.* **(b)** beating: *The thugs gave him a thorough going-over.*

go[2] /gou/ *n* (*pl* goes /gouz/) (*informal*) **1** [U] energy; vigor. ***be on the go,*** be very busy, active: *She's been on the go all day.* **2** [C] try; attempt. ***have a go (at sth),*** make an attempt: *I'd like to have a go at it.* ***at one go,*** at one attempt: *He blew out all the candles on his birthday cake at one go.* **3** success: *made a go of the shop all by herself.* ***no go,*** useless.

goad /goud/ *n* [C] **1** pointed stick for driving or prodding cattle. **2** (*fig*) something urging a person to action. □ *vt* urge; incite: *~ him on; ~ him into stealing.*

goal /goul/ *n* [C] **1** point marking the end of a race. **2** (*sport*) **(a)** place, object to which the ball or puck is to be driven in order to score. **(b)** point(s) made by doing this: *score/kick a ~; win by three ~s to one.* **3** (*fig*) object of efforts or ambition: *one's ~ in life.*

goal·ie /ˈgouli/ *n* [C] (*informal*) goalkeeper.

ˈgoal·keeper *n* [C] player whose duty is to keep the ball or puck out of the goal.

goat /gout/ *n* [C] small horned animal with a beard, raised for milk, meat, etc: *ˈnanny ~*, female goat: *ˈbilly ~*, male goat. ⇨ kid[1](1). ***get sb's goat*** ⇨ get(6).

ˈgoat·herd *n* [C] person who looks after a flock of goats.

ˈgoat·skin *n* (leather made from the) skin of a goat.

gob /gab/ *n* [C] **1** lump or piece. **2 gobs,** (*informal*) a large amount: *gobs of money.*

gobble[1] /ˈgabəl/ *vt,vi* eat fast, noisily and greedily: *~ up an ice-cream cone.*

gobble[2] /ˈgabəl/ *vi* (of a turkey) make the characteristic sound in the throat □ *n* [U] this sound.

gob·bler /ˈgablər/ *n* [C] male turkey.

gob·let /ˈgablɪt/ *n* [C] drinking vessel with a stem and base and no handle.

gob·lin /ˈgablɪn/ *n* [C] mischievous demon; ugly evil spirit.

god /gad/ *n* [C] **1** being regarded or worshiped as having power over nature and control over human affairs. **2** image in wood, stone, etc to represent such a being. **3 God,** (*Judaism, Christianity*) the Supreme Being, creator and ruler of the universe. ***God willing,*** if circumstances permit. **4** person greatly adored or admired; something to which excessive attention is paid.

ˈgod-awful *adj* (*informal*) extremely disagreeable or unpleasant: *a god-awful mess.*

ˈgod·child/·daughter/·son *n* [C] person for whom a godparent acts as sponsor at baptism.

ˈgod·father *n* [C] **(a)** male godparent. **(b)** head of a family-based criminal organization, esp in the Mafia.

ˈgod-fearing *adj* living a good life and sincerely religious.

ˈgod·for·saken *adj* dismal; wretched.

ˈgod·mother *n* [C] female godparent.

ˈgod·parent *n* [C] person who promises, when a child is baptized, to see that it receives (Christian) religious training.

ˈgod·send *n* something (unexpected and) welcome because it is a great help in time of need.

god·dess /ˈgadɪs/ *n* [C] female god, esp in Greek and Latin mythology: *Venus, the ~ of love.*

god·less /ˈgadlɪs/ *adj* not having belief in God; not recognizing God.

god·like /ˈgadˌlaik/ *adj* like God or a god in some quality; divine.

god·ly /ˈgadli/ *adj* (-ier, -iest) loving and obeying God; deeply religious.

god·li·ness /-nɪs/ *n* [U]

goggle /ˈgagəl/ *vi* roll the eyes about (or *at* something): *He ~d at her in surprise.*

goggles /ˈgagəlz/ *n pl* large round glasses with special rims to protect the eyes from the wind, dust, etc (worn by motorcyclists, etc).

go·ing /ˈgouɪŋ/ *n* ⇨ also go[1]. **1** [U] condition of the ground, a road, a race track, etc, for walking, riding, etc: *The ~ is hard over this mountain road.* **2** [U] method or speed of working or traveling: *For a car this old, 50 miles an hour is good ~.* **3** departure. ***comings and goings,*** (*literally* or *fig*) arrivals and departures: *the* *comings and ~s in the corridors of power.* □ *adj* **1** operating successfully: *a ~ concern.* **2** now existing or now available: *the ~ price for an ounce of gold.*

goi·ter, goi·tre /ˈgɔitər/ *n* [C] swelling of the thyroid gland (in the neck).

gold /gould/ *n* [U] **1** precious yellow metal (symbol **Au**) used for coins, ornaments, jewelry, etc: *$500 in ~, in ~ coins;* (as an *adjective*) *a ~ watch/bracelet.* **2** money in large sums; wealth. **3** (*fig*) brilliant or precious things or qualities: *a heart of ~.* **4** (as an *adjective*) the color of gold.

ˌgold ˈleaf, gold beaten into thin sheets.

ˈgold mine, (a) place where gold is mined. **(b)** (*fig*) source of wealth, eg a business that is very successful in making money.

ˈgold rush, rush of people to newly discovered gold fields (eg to California starting in 1849).

ˈgold·smith *n* [C] manufacturer of gold articles; merchant who sells these.

ˈgold standard, system in which the value of money is based on gold.

golden /ˈgouldən/ *adj* **1** of gold or like gold in value or color: *~ hair.* **2** precious; excellent; important: *a ~ opportunity.*

the ˌgolden ˈrule, important rule of conduct, esp a rule which says that one should treat other people as one would like others to treat him.

ˌgolden ˈwedding, 50th wedding anniversary.

gold·en·rod /ˈgouldənˌrad/ *n* [C] (*pl* unchanged) North American plant blooming in late summer and early fall, with clusters of small yellow flowers.

gold·finch /ˈgouldfɪntʃ/ *n* [C] small songbird related to the canary, with a yellow body and black wings.

gold·fish /ˈgouldˌfɪʃ/ *n* [C] (*pl* unchanged) small, yellow-orange fish, often kept as a pet. ⇨ illus at fish.

ˈgoldfish ˌbowl, (a) glass bowl, usually with flat sides, for keeping and viewing goldfish. **(b)** (*informal*) place, esp a dwelling, lacking privacy.

golf /galf, gɔlf/ *n* [U] game in which a player uses *ˈgolf clubs* to drive a ball with as few strokes as possible into a series of 9 or 18 holes spread out over a stretch of land called a *ˈgolf course.* □ *vi* play golf.

golfer *n* [C] person who plays golf.

golly /ˈgali/ *int* (*sl*) used to express surprise.

gon·dola /ˈgandələ/ *n* [C] long, flat-bottomed boat with high peaks at each end, used on canals in Venice.

gon·do·lier /ˌgandəˈlɪr/ *n* [C] man who propels a gondola.

gone *pp* of go[1].

goner /ˈgɔnər/ *n* [C] (*sl*) person or thing in a desperate or hopeless situation.

gong /gaŋ, gɔŋ/ *n* [C] metal disc with a turned rim giving a resonant note when struck with a stick.

gon·or·rhea,-rhœa /ˌganəˈriə/ *n* [U] contagious venereal disease which causes an inflammatory discharge from the genital organs.

goo /gu/ *n* [U] (*informal*) (any) thick, sticky substance.

goo·ey /ˈgui/ *adj* (gooier, gooiest) like, or covered with, goo.

good[1] /gʊd/ *adj* (better, best) **1** having the right or desired qualities; giving satisfaction: *a ~* (eg sharp) *knife; ~* (= fertile) *soil; a woman of ~ family,* of a family with high social position; well born. **2** beneficial; wholesome: *Milk is ~ for children. Exercise is ~ for you.* **3** efficient; competent; able to do satisfactorily what is required: *a ~ teacher/driver/worker; ~ at mathematics/languages.* **4** pleasing; agreeable; advantageous: *~ news. It's ~ to be home again.* ***be a good thing,*** be something that one approves, enjoys: *Do you think lower taxes are a ~ thing?* ***put in/say a good word for sb,*** say something in his favor. ***have a good time,*** enjoy oneself. **5** kind; benevolent; willing to help others: *It was ~ of you to help them.* **6** (in exclamations of surprise, shock, etc): *ˌGood ˈGod! ˌGood ˈGracious! ˌGood ˈHeavens!* **7** thorough; sound; complete: *give her a ~ beating/scolding; find a ~ excuse.* ***have a good mind to do sth,*** feel a strong desire to: *I've a ~ mind to report you to the police.* **8** strong; vigorous: *His eyesight is still ~.* **9** fresh; eatable: *Fish does not stay ~ in hot weather.* **10** reliable; safe; sure: *a car with ~ brakes.* ***good for,*** **(a)** safely to be trusted for (the amount stated): *His credit is ~ for $5,000.* **(b)** having the necessary strength, inclination, etc: *My car is ~ for another five years.* **(c)** valid: *The return half of the ticket is ~ for three months.* **11** (esp of a child) well behaved; not giving trouble: *Try to be a ~ boy. She's as ~ as gold,* very good. **12** morally excellent; virtuous: *live a ~ life.* **13** (used in forms of greeting and farewell): *Good morning/afternoon/evening/night.* **14** considerable in number, quantity, etc: *a ~ deal of money; a ~ many people. We've come a ~ way,* quite a long way. **15** not less than; rather more than: *We waited for a ~ hour.* **16** ***as good as,*** practically, almost: *He as ~ as said I was a liar,* suggested that I was a liar without actually using the word "liar." *My car is as ~ as new, even though I've had it a year.* **17** ***make good,*** be successful; prosper: *He went to California, where he soon made ~.*

ˈgood-for-nothing *adj, n* worthless (person).

ˌgood ˈhumor, cheerful mood; happy state of mind.

ˌgood-ˈhumored *adj*

ˌgood-ˈlooking *adj* attractive; handsome.

ˌgood-ˈnatured *adj* kind; ready and willing to help others.

ˌgood ˈsense, soundness of judgment.

ˌgood-ˈtempered *adj* not easily irritated or made angry.

good[2] /gʊd/ *n* [U] **1** that which is good; what is morally right, beneficial, advantageous, profitable, etc; what has use, worth, value: *It's no ~ (my) talking to him. Was his advice ever any ~? What ~ was it? This gadget isn't much ~.* ***do good,*** help (through charitable works, etc). ***(do sth) for the good of,*** in order to benefit: *He works for the ~ of the country.* ***for sb's own good,*** for his benefit: *Is it right to deceive people, even if it's for their own ~?* ***do (sb) good,*** help or benefit him: *Eat more fruit: it will do you ~.* **2** ***for good (and all),*** forever; finally: *He says* *that he's leaving the country for* ~, intending never to return to it. **3** (with a *pl verb*) good or virtuous persons: *Good and bad alike respected him.*

good-bye /ˌgʊdˈbai/ *int, n* [C] (saying of) farewell.

goodie = goody.

good·ness /ˈgʊdnɪs/ *n* [U] **1** quality of being good; excellence. **2** kindness: ~ *of heart.* **3** (in exclamations): *Goodness Gracious! Goodness me! For* ~*' sake! Thank* ~*!*

goods /gʊdz/ *n pl* **1** movable property. **2** merchandise: *He buys and sells leather* ~. **3** fabric; cloth. ***dry goods,*** ⇨ dry¹.

good·will /ˌgʊdˈwɪl/ *n* [U] **1** friendly feeling: *a policy of* ~ *in international relations.* **2** favor or good reputation of a well-established business which has a value that is in addition to the value of its goods, etc: *The* ~ *is to be sold with the business.*

goody, goodie /ˈgʊdi/ *n* [C] (*pl* -ies) (*informal*) something which is pleasant to eat, own, etc.

goody-goody /ˌgʊdi-ˈgʊdi/ *adj, n* [C] (*pl* -ies) (person who is) affectedly good or proper.

goof /guf/ *n* [C] (*sl*) **1** careless mistake. **2** stupid person. □ *vi* **1** made a careless mistake. **2** ***goof off,*** (*sl*) waste time.

goofy /ˈgufi/ *adj* (-ier, -iest) (*sl*) silly.

goon /gun/ *n* [C] (*informal*) ruffian employed esp by a criminal boss to carry out violence and intimidation.

goop /gup/ *n* [U] (*sl*) (any) thick, sticky substance.

goose /gus/ *n* (*pl* geese /gis/) **1** [C] **(a)** water bird larger than a duck. **(b)** female of this, ⇨ gander. **2** [U] its flesh as food. **3** [C] (*informal*) mildly foolish person.

ˈgoose flesh, (also **goose bumps, goose pimples**), rough bristling skin caused by cold or fear.

goose·berry /ˈgusˌberi/ *n* [C] (*pl* -ies) (bush with a) green, hairy berry.

GOP /ˌdʒi ˌou ˈpi/ *abbr* = Grand Old Party. ⇨ grand.

gore¹ /gɔr/ *vt* pierce, wound, with the horns or tusks: ~*d to death by a bull.*

gore² /gɔr/ *n* [U] (esp dried or clotted) blood.

gorge /gɔrdʒ/ *n* [C] **1** narrow opening, usually with a stream, between hills or mountains. **2** gullet; contents of the stomach: *His* ~ *rose at the sight/It made his* ~ *rise,* He was sickened or disgusted. □ *vi,vt* eat greedily: ~ *on rich food;* ~ *oneself with meat.*

gor·geous /ˈgɔrdʒəs/ *adj* **1** richly colored; magnificent: *a* ~ *sunset.* **2** very beautiful: ~ *weather; a* ~ *dress.*

gor·geous·ly *adv*

go·rilla /gəˈrɪlə/ *n* [C] man-sized, tree-climbing African ape. ⇨ illus at ape.

gory /ˈgɔri/ *adj* (-ier, -iest) covered with blood.

gosh /gaʃ/ *int* (*sl*) exclamation of surprise.

gos·ling /ˈgazlɪŋ/ *n* [C] young goose.

gos·pel /ˈgaspəl/ *n* **1 the Gospel, (a)** (the life and teachings of Jesus Christ as recorded in the) first four books of the New Testament. **(b)** any one of these four books. **2** thing accepted as true; principle or set of principles that one acts upon or believes in: *the* ~ *of health.*

ˌGospel ˈmusic, (esp Negro) style of religious singing.

ˌGospel ˈoath, oath sworn on the Gospels.

ˌGospel ˈtruth, something as true as the Gospels are believed to be.

gos·sa·mer /ˈgasəmər/ *n* **1** [C,U] (thread of the) fine silky substance of webs made by small spiders. **2** [U] soft, light, delicate material: *a* ~ *veil.*

gos·sip /ˈgasɪp/ *n* **1** [U] idle, often critical, talk about the affairs of other people: *Don't believe all the* ~ *you hear.* **2** [U] informal writing about persons and social happenings, eg in letters or in newspapers: (as an *adjective*) *the* ˈ~ *column,* of a newspaper; *a* ˈ~ *writer.* **3** [C] instance of gossip: *have a good* ~ *with a neighbor over the back fence.* **4** [C] person who is fond of gossip (1): *She's an old* ~. □ *vi* (-pp-) talk or write gossip.

got *pt,pp* of get.

Gothic /ˈgaθɪk/ *adj* **1** of the style of architecture common in Western Europe in the 12th to 16th centuries, characterized by pointed arches, clusters of columns, etc. **2** of the 18th century style of romantic literature: ~ *novels.*

got·ten *pp* of get.

gouge /gaudʒ/ *n* [C] tool with a sharp semicircular edge for cutting grooves in wood. □ *vt* **1** cut, shape, force out (as) with a gouge: ~ *out a person's eye with one's thumb.* **2** charge more for something than is fair or legal.

goug·er *n* [C] seller who gouges(2): ˈ*ticket* ~*r.*

goug·ing *n* [U] act, instance of gouging(2): ˈ*price-gouging.*

gou·lash /ˈguˌlaʃ/ *n* [U] stew of meat and vegetables, seasoned with paprika.

gourd /gɔrd, gʊrd/ *n* [C] **1** (large, hard-skinned fleshy fruit of) kinds of climbing or trailing plant. **2** bottle or bowl consisting of the dried skin of this fruit.

gour·mand /ˈgʊrˌmand/ *n* [C] lover of food.

gour·met /ˈgʊrˌmei/ *n* [C] person who enjoys, and is expert in the choice of, delicate food, wines, etc.

gout /gaut/ *n* [U] disease causing painful swellings in joints, esp toes, knees and fingers.

gov·ern /ˈgəvərn/ *vt,vi* **1** rule (a country, etc). **2** control or direct the public affairs of (a city, country, etc). **3** control: ~ *one's temper.* **4** (usually passive) determine; influence: *be* ~*ed by the opinions of others.* **5** (*gram*) (esp of a *verb* or *prep*) require, make necessary (a certain case or form of another word).

gov·ern·ing *adj* having the power or right to govern: *the* ~*ing body of a school/college, etc.*

gov·ern·ess /ˈgəvərnɪs/ *n* [C] woman who is employed to teach young children in a private family.

gov·ern·ment /ˈgəvər(n)mənt/ *n* **1** [U] act or process of governing. **2** [U] method or system of governing: *We prefer democratic* ~. **3** [C] body of persons governing a state: *The* ~ *has decided to raise taxes.*

gov·ern·mental /ˌgəvərnˈmentəl/ *adj* connected with government.

gov·ernor /ˈgəvə(r)nər/ *n* [C] **1** person who

governs a province or colony. **2** chief executive of a state: *the Governor of New York State*. **3** member of the governing body of an institution (eg a school, a college, a hospital): *the board of ~s*. **4** device that controls or regulates a machine.

govt. *abbr* = government.

gown /gaun/ *n* [C] **1** woman's dress, esp one for special occasions: *an ˈevening ~; a ˈnight ~*. **2** loose, flowing robe worn by members of a university, judges, etc.

grab /græb/ *vt,vi* (-bb-) take roughly, selfishly or eagerly: *The dog ~bed the bone and ran off with it. He ~bed at the opportunity of going abroad*. □ *n* [C] **1** sudden snatch: *make a ~ at something*. **2** mechanical device for taking up and holding something to be lifted or moved.

grace /greis/ *n* **1** [U] quality of being pleasing, attractive or beautiful, esp in form or movement: *She danced with ~/with a ~ that surprised us*. **2** (usu *pl*) pleasing accomplishment or quality: *the social ~s*. **3** [U] favor; goodwill. ***do sth with a good/bad grace,*** do it willingly/reluctantly. **4** extra time allowed before requiring a person to fulfill an obligation: *a week's ~*. **5** short prayer of thanks before or after a meal: *say ~*. **6** [U] (*Christianity*) God's mercy and favor toward mankind. □ *vt* add grace to; confer honor or dignity on; be an ornament to: *The occasion was ~d by the presence of the governor's wife*.

grace·ful /ˈgreisfəl/ *adj* having or showing grace(1): *a ~ dancer; a ~ letter of thanks*.

grace·fully /-fəli/ *adv*

grace·less /ˈgreislɪs/ *adj* **1** without grace(1). **2** without a sense of what is right and proper: *~ behavior*.

grace·less·ly *adv*

gra·cious /ˈgreiʃəs/ *adj* **1** (of persons and their behavior) pleasant; kind; polite: *It was ~ of her to come*. **2** (in exclamations) expressing surprise: *Good(ness) Gracious!*

gra·cious·ly *adv*

gra·cious·ness /-nɪs/ *n* [U]

grackle /ˈgrækəl/ *n* [C] large blackbird with shiny feathers and a harsh cry.

gra·da·tion /greiˈdeiʃən/ *n* **1** [C] step, stage, degree in development. **2** [U] gradual change from one thing to another or from one state to another.

grade[1] /greid/ *n* [C] **1** step, stage or degree in rank, quality, value, etc: *The rank of major is one ~ higher than that of captain*. **2** **(a)** division of the school course; one year's work. **(b)** pupils in such a division. **3** the mark, eg 80% or "B," or rating, eg "Excellent" or "Fair," given to a pupil for his work in school. ***make the grade,*** (*informal*) succeed; do as well as is required. **4** (degree of) slope.

ˌGrade ˈA, (*sl*) of the highest quality: *a Grade A job*.

grade[2] /greid/ *vt* **1** arrange in order in grades or classes: *~d by size*. **2** make land (esp for roads) more level by reducing the slope.

gradi·ent /ˈgreidiənt/ *n* [C] = grade(4).

grad·ual /ˈgrædʒuəl/ *adj* **1** taking place by degrees. **2** (of a slope) not steep.

grad·ually /-dʒ(u)əli/ *adv* by degrees; very slowly.

grad·uate[1] /ˈgrædʒuɪt/ *n* [C] person who has completed a course at an educational institution: *high school/college ~s*.

grad·uate[2] /ˈgrædʒuˌeit/ *vt,vi* **1** mark with degrees for measuring: *a ruler ~d in both inches and centimeters*. **2** arrange according to grade. **3** take an academic degree: *He ~d from Yale*.

grad·u·ation /ˌgrædʒuˈeiʃən/ *n* [C,U] **1** graduating or being graduated. **2** ceremony at which degrees are conferred.

graf·fiti /grəˈfiti/ *n pl* (*I*) drawing, words, written or scratched esp on a wall.

graft[1] /græft/ *n* [C] **1** shoot from a branch or twig of a living tree, fixed in another tree to form a new growth. **2** (in surgery) piece of skin, bone, etc from a living person or animal, transplanted on another body or another part of the same body. □ *vt,vi* put a graft in or on: *~ one variety on/upon/in/into another; ~ new skin*.

graft[2] /græft/ *n* [U] **1** (instance of) getting business advantages, profit-making, etc by dishonestly using connections in politics, municipal business, etc. **2** money or profit gained in this way.

grain /grein/ *n* **1** [U] (*collective sing*) small, hard seeds of food plants such as wheat and rice: *a cargo of ~*. **2** [C] single seed of such a plant: *eat up every ~ of rice*. **3** [C] tiny, hard bit: *~s of sand/sugar*. **4** (*fig*) small amount: *a boy without a ~ of intelligence*. **5** smallest unit of weight, 1/7,000 lb. or 0.065 grams. **6** [U] natural arrangement or pattern of the lines of fiber in wood, etc as seen on a surface that has been sawn or cut: *woods of fine/coarse ~*. ***be/go against the grain,*** (*fig*) be unnatural or against one's inclination.

grainy *adj* (-ier, -iest)

gram /græm/ *n* [C] metric unit of weight equal to 0.035 of an ounce.

gram·mar /ˈgræmər/ *n* **1** [U] study or science of, rules for, the combination of words into sentences (*syntax*), and the forms of words. **2** [U] way of using language according to established rules of usage: *His ~ is bad*. **3** [C] book about the grammar of a language: *an English ~*.

gram·mar·ian /grəˈmæriən/ *n* [C] expert in grammar.

ˈgrammar school, school that includes the first six or the first eight grades.

gram·mati·cal /grəˈmætɪkəl/ *adj* of, conforming to, the rules of grammar: *a ~ error*.

gram·mati·cally /-kli/ *adv*

gramo·phone /ˈgræməˌfoun/ *n* (*dated*) = record player.

Grammy /ˈgræmi/ *n* [C] (*pl* ~s or -ies) small statue awarded annually for outstanding contributions to the recording industry.

gran·ary /ˈgreinəri, ˈgræn-/ *n* [C] (*pl* -ies) storehouse for grain.

grand /grænd/ *adj* (-er, -est) **1** (in official titles) chief; most important: *Grand Master*, eg of some orders or societies; *a ~ master*, chess champion. **2** of most or greatest importance: *the ~ finale*. **3** magnificent; splendid: *living in ~ style*. **4** self-important; proud: *He puts on a very ~ manner/air*. **5** very fine or enjoyable: *We had* *a ~ time. What ~ weather!* **6** full; complete: *the ~ total,* including everything. □ *n* **1** [C] grand piano. **2** (*pl* ~) (*sl*) a thousand dollars: *The car cost ten ~.*

grand·ly *adv*

Grand Old Party, (*informal*) (name for) the Republican Party.

ˌgrand piˈano, large piano with horizontal strings.

grand·aunt /ˈgrændˌænt, -ˌant/ *n* [C] aunt of one's father or mother.

grand·child /ˈgræn(d)ˌtʃaiəld/ *n* [C] (*pl* -children /-ˌtʃɪldrən/) child of one's son or daughter.

grand·dad /ˈgrænˌdæd/ *n* [C] (*informal*) grandfather.

grand·daugh·ter /ˈgrænˌdɔtər/ *n* [C] daughter of one's son or daughter.

gran·deur /ˈgrændʒər, ˈgrænˌd(y)ʊr/ *n* [U] greatness; magnificence: *the ~ of the Swiss Alps.*

grand·father /ˈgræn(d)ˌfaðər/ *n* [C] father of one's father or mother.

ˈgrandfather('s) clock, clock worked by weights in a tall wooden case.

gran·di·ose /ˈgrændiˌous/ *adj* **1** planned on an impressive scale; imposing. **2** exaggeratedly or affectedly great.

grand·ma /ˈgrænˌma, ˈgræmˌma/ *n* [C] (*informal*) grandmother.

grand·mother /ˈgræn(d)ˌməðər/ *n* [C] mother of one's father or mother.

grand·nephew /ˈgræn(d)ˌnefyu/ *n* [C] son of one's nephew or niece.

grand·niece /ˈgræn(d)ˌnis/ *n* [C] daughter of one's nephew or niece.

grand·pa /ˈgrænˌpa, ˈgræmˌpa/ *n* [C] (*informal*) grandfather.

grand·son /ˈgræn(d)ˌsən/ *n* [C] son of one's son or daughter.

grand·stand /ˈgrændˌstænd/ *n* [C] rows of roofed seats for spectators at races, sports events, etc.

grand·uncle /ˈgrændˌəŋkəl/ *n* [C] uncle of one's father or mother.

grange /greindʒ/ *n* [C] **1** country house with farm buildings attached. **2** (branch of an) association of farmers.

gran·ite /ˈgrænɪt/ *n* [U] hard, usually gray, stone used for building.

granny, grannie /ˈgræni/ *n* [C] (*pl* -ies) (*informal*) grandmother.

grant /grænt/ *vt* **1** consent to give or allow (what is asked for): *~ a favor/request.* **2** give formally: *rights that are ~ed by law.* **3** agree (that something is true): *He's a nice person, I'll ~ you that.* ***take sth for granted,*** accept it as true or as certain without discussion. □ *n* [C] **1** act of granting. **2** something granted, eg money from a government toward the cost of a university education, for research, etc.

granu·lar /ˈgrænyələr/ *adj* of or like grains.

granu·late /ˈgrænyəˌleit/ *vt,vi* form into grains; make or become grainy.

ˌgranulated ˈsugar, sugar in the form of small grains.

gran·ule /ˈgrænˌyul/ *n* [C] small grain.

grape /greip/ *n* [C] **1** green or purple berry growing in clusters on vines, often used for making wine: *a bunch of ~s.* ⇨ illus at fruit. **2** = grapevine(a).

ˈgrape·vine *n* [C] **(a)** kind of vine on which grapes grow. **(b)** means by which news gets around, eg in an office, school or a group of friends: *I heard through the ~vine that Jill is to be promoted.*

grape·fruit /ˈgreipˌfrut/ *n* [C] (*pl* ~, ~s) large, yellow-skinned fruit with an acid taste, that is related to the orange and the lemon. ⇨ illus at fruit.

graph /græf/ *n* [C] diagram that shows by means of lines or dots the relationship between two quantities, eg the temperature at each hour.

ˈgraph paper, paper with small squares of equal size, used for graphs.

graphic /ˈgræfɪk/ *adj* **1** of visual symbols (eg lettering, diagrams, drawings): *a ~ artist.* **2** described in clear and vivid images: *a ~ account of the battle.* □ *n* (*pl*) lettering, drawings, etc.

graphi·cally /-kli/ *adv* **(a)** by writing or diagrams. **(b)** vividly.

graph·ite /ˈgræˌfait/ *n* [U] soft, black substance (a form of carbon) as used in making lead pencils.

grap·nel /ˈgræpnəl/ *n* **1** small anchor with many hooks. **2** instrument like this for seizing and holding something.

grapple /ˈgræpəl/ *vi* **1** seize firmly. **2** struggle with at close quarters: *~ with an enemy.* **3** (*fig*) try to deal with (a problem, etc): *grappling with staff problems.*

ˈgrappling iron, grapnel.

grasp /græsp/ *vt,vi* **1** seize firmly with the hand(s) or arm(s): *~ a person's hand/a rope.* **2** understand: ~ an argument/her meaning. **3** ***grasp at,*** try to seize; accept eagerly: *~ at an opportunity.* □ *n* [C] (usually *sing*) firm hold or grip; (power of) grasping: *in the ~ of a wicked enemy; have a thorough ~ of the problem; a problem within/beyond my ~,* that I can/cannot understand.

grasp·ing *adj* eager to grasp; greedy (for money, etc): *a ~ing rascal.*

grass /græs/ *n* **1** [U] kinds of low-growing, green plant often with narrow leaves, that are used for grazing animals. **2** [C] (*pl* ~es) any species of this plant (including cereals, reeds and bamboos). **3** [U] land covered with grass, eg a lawn or pasture. **4** (*sl*) marijuana.

ˈgrass·land *n* area of land covered with grass where there are few trees.

ˌgrass ˈroots, ordinary people of a country, esp those who are remote from political centers: *got support from the ~ roots.*

grassy *adj* (-ier, -iest) covered with grass.

grass·hopper /ˈgræsˌhapər/ *n* [C] plant-eating insect with strong hind legs for jumping. ⇨ illus at insect.

grate¹ /greit/ *n* [C] metal frame for holding wood, etc in a fireplace.

grate² /greit/ *vt,vi* **1** rub into small pieces, usually against a rough surface; rub small bits off: *~ cheese.* **2** make a harsh noise by rubbing: *The gate ~s on its hinges.* **3** (*fig*) have an irritating effect (on a person, his nerves): *His bad manners*

~*d on everyone.*

grater *n* [C] device with a rough surface for grating food, etc.

grat·ing·ly *adv*

grate·ful /ˈgreitfəl/ *adj* feeling or showing thanks: *We are ~ to you for your help.*

grate·fully /-fəli/ *adv*

grat·ify /ˈgrætəˌfai/ *vt* (*pt,pp* -ied) **1** give pleasure or satisfaction to: *He was gratified by his success.* **2** give what is desired to: *~ a child's curiosity.*

grati·fi·ca·tion /ˌgrætəfɪˈkeiʃən/ *n* [C,U]

grat·ify·ing *adj* pleasing: *It is very ~ing to learn that.*

grat·ing /ˈgreitɪŋ/ *n* [C] framework of wooden or metal bars, either parallel or crossing one another, placed across an opening, eg a window, to keep out burglars or to allow air to flow through.

gra·tis /ˈgrætɪs/ *adv, adj* free of charge: *be admitted ~.*

grati·tude /ˈgrætəˌtud/ *n* [U] being grateful.

gra·tu·itous /grəˈtuətəs/ *adj* **1** given, obtained or done, without cost; free: *~ service/information/help/advice.* **2** done or given, acting, without good reason: *a ~ insult.*

gra·tu·itous·ly *adv*

gra·tu·ity /grəˈtuəti/ *n* [C] (*pl* -ies) gift (of money); tip (for service).

grave[1] /greiv/ *adj* (-r, -st) serious; requiring careful consideration: *~ news.*

grave·ly *adv*

grave[2] /greiv/ *n* [C] **1** hole dug in the ground for burying a dead body. ***have one foot in the grave,*** be nearing death, be very old. **2** any burial place: *The ocean was his ~.* **3** (*fig*) death.

ˈgrave·stone *n* [C] stone over a grave, with the name, etc of the person buried there.

ˈgrave·yard *n* [C] burial ground; cemetery.

ˈgraveyard shift, the working shift, in a factory operating 24 hours a day, which begins at slightly after midnight.

grave[3] /greiv/ *n* [C] (also **grave accent**) mark (`) placed over a vowel to indicate how it is to be sounded (as in French *mère*).

gravel /ˈgrævəl/ *n* [U] small stones and small pieces of rock, as used for roads and paths. □ *vt* (-l-, -ll-) cover with gravel.

graven /ˈgreivən/ *adj* (only in) ***a graven image,*** an idol carved from wood, stone, etc.

gravi·tate /ˈgrævəˌteit/ *vi* move or be attracted: *~ toward the cities.*

gravi·ta·tion /ˌgrævəˈteiʃən/ *n* [U] **(a)** process of gravitating. **(b)** gravity(1).

grav·ity /ˈgrævəti/ *n* [U] **1** force of attraction between any two objects, esp that force which attracts objects toward the center of the earth. **2** weight: *center of ~.* **3** importance; seriousness: *the ~ of the international situation.*

gravy /ˈgreivi/ [U] **1** juice which comes from meat while it is cooking; sauce made from this. **2** (*sl*) extra, easy money or profit.

ˈgravy boat, vessel in which gravy is served at the table.

ˈgravy train, (*informal*) easy and well-paying situation: *He used to have it hard, but now he's on the ~ train.*

gray /grei/ *adj* (-er, -est) of the color made by mixing black and white, colored like ashes: *His hair has turned ~.* □ *n* gray color: *dressed in ~,* gray clothes. □ *vt,vi* make or become gray.

ˈgray matter, (*informal*) **(a)** nervous tissue of the brain. **(b)** intelligence.

gray·ish /ˈgreiɪʃ/ *adj* somewhat gray.

graze[1] /greiz/ *vi,vt* **1** (of cattle, sheep, etc) eat growing grass: *cattle grazing in the fields.* **2** put (cattle, etc) in fields to graze.

graze[2] /greiz/ *vt,vi* touch or scrape lightly in passing; rub the skin from: *The bullet ~d his cheek.* □ *n* [C] place where the skin is grazed.

grease /gris/ *n* [U] **1** animal fat, esp when soft. **2** any thick, semisolid oily substance. □ *vt* put or rub grease on or in (esp parts of a machine).

ˈgrease gun, (a) device for forcing grease into the parts of an engine, machine, etc. **(b)** (*sl*) automatic pistol; submachine gun.

greasy /ˈgrisi, ˈgrizi/ *adj* (-ier, -iest) covered with grease; slippery: *~ fingers; a ~ road.*

greas·ily /ˈgrisəli, ˈgrizəli/ *adv*

greasi·ness /ˈgrisinɪs, ˈgrizinɪs/ *n* [U]

greasy spoon /ˌgrizi ˈspun/ (*Note:* /z/ in *greasy* in this term, even by those who use /s/ in *greasy* otherwise) cheap, esp somewhat dirty, restaurant.

great /greit/ *adj* (-er, -est) **1** well above the average in size, quantity or degree: *take ~ care of; a ~ friend of mine,* one for whom I feel more than ordinary friendship. **2** of remarkable ability or character: *~ men/woman; a ~ painter/musician.* **3** important; noted; of high rank or position: *a ~ occasion; Alexander the Great.* **4** used with words showing quantity, etc: *a ~ deal,* very much; *a ~ number.* **5** (*informal*) excellent, wonderful: *We had a ~ time in Paris.* ***great at,*** clever or skillful at. **6** (used in compounds for family relationships) removed by one generation: *ˌ~-ˈaunt,* = grandaunt; *ˌ~-ˈgrandfather,* father of any of one's grandmothers or grandfathers.

ˌGreat ˈBritain, (*abbr* **GB**) England, Wales and Scotland.

ˌGreat ˈLakes, group of five large lakes (Erie, Huron, Michigan, Ontario, and Superior) in North America along the boundary between Canada and the US.

great·ly *adv* much; by much: *~ly amused.*

great·ness /-nɪs/ *n* [U]

the ˌGreat ˈWar, (*dated*) World War I, 1914-1918.

grebe /grib/ *n* [C] kinds of diving bird.

Gre·cian /ˈgriʃən/ *adj* (eg of architecture, pottery, culture, etc) Greek.

greed /grid/ *n* [U] strong desire for more food, wealth, etc, esp for more than is right or reasonable.

greedy /ˈgridi/ *adj* (-ier, -iest) filled with greed: *He's not hungry, just ~. He's ~ for gain/honors.*

greed·ily /ˈgridəli/ *adv*

greedi·ness /ˈgridinɪs/ *n* [U]

Greek /grik/ *n* **1** [C] member of the Greek race, either of ancient Greece or modern Greece. **2** the Greek language. ***be (all) Greek to sb,*** be beyond his understanding. □ *adj* of Greece, its language, or its people.

green[1] /grin/ *adj* (-er, -est) **1** of the color between blue and yellow in the spectrum, the color of growing grass. **2 (a)** (of fruit) not yet ripe: *~ apples*. **(b)** (of wood) not yet dry enough for use: *Green wood does not burn well*. **3** inexperienced; undeveloped; untrained: *a boy who is still ~ at his job*. **4** (*fig*) flourishing; full of vigor: *keep a person's memory ~*, not allow it to fade. **5** (of the complexion) pale; sickly looking. ***green with envy,*** jealous.

ˈgreen·back *n* [C] (*sl*) US banknote or bill of paper currency.

green·gage /-ˌgeidʒ/ *n* [C] kind of plum with greenish-yellow skin and flesh.

ˈgreen·horn *n* [C] inexperienced person who is easily tricked or cheated.

ˈgreen·house *n* [C] building with sides and roof of glass, used for growing plants that need protection from the weather.

ˌgreen ˈpepper, unripe red pepper, used as a vegetable. ⇨ illus at vegetable.

ˌgreen ˈthumb, (*informal*) skill in making plants grow.

green[2] /grin/ *n* **1** [C,U] green color: *a girl dressed in ~; a picture in ~s and blues*. **2** (*pl*) green leaf vegetables, eg cabbage, spinach, before or after cooking. **3** area of land with growing grass. **(a)** public or common land: *the village ~*. **(b)** grassy, smooth area surrounding a hole on a golf course: *a ˈputting ~*.

greenery /ˈgrinəri/ *n* [U] green foliage: *the ~ of the woods in spring*.

green·ish /ˈgriniʃ/ *adj* somewhat green: (used in compounds) *ˌ~-ˈyellow; ˌ~-ˈbrown*.

Green·wich /ˈgrenitʃ/ *n* suburb of London, England, east and west of which longitude is measured.

ˌGreenwich (ˈmean) time, (*abbr* **GMˈT**), mean[2] time for the meridian of Greenwich, used as a basis for calculating time in most parts of the world.

greet /grit/ *vt* **1** say words of welcome to; express one's feelings on receiving (news, etc); write (in a letter) words expressing respect, friendship, etc: *~ a friend by saying, "Good morning!"; ~ someone with a smile*. **2** (*formal*) (of sights and sounds) meet the eyes and ears: *the view that ~ed us at the hilltop*.

greet·ing *n* [C,U] first words or act used on seeing a person or in writing to a person; this expression or act: *"Good morning" and "Dear Sir" are ~ings*.

gre·gari·ous /griˈgæriəs/ *adj* **1** living in groups or societies. **2** liking the company of others.

gre·gari·ous·ly *adv*

gre·gari·ous·ness /-nis/ *n* [U]

Gre·gor·ian cal·en·dar /griˌgɔriən ˈkæləndər/ *n* the calendar introduced by Pope Gregory XIII (1502-85), with the days and months arranged as now.

grem·lin /ˈgremlin/ *n* [C] goblin jokingly said to trouble airmen during World War II (by causing mechanical trouble).

gre·nade /griˈneid/ *n* [C] small bomb as thrown by hand.

grew *pt* of grow.

grey = gray.

grey·hound /ˈgreiˌhaund/ *n* [C] slender, long-legged dog, able to run fast, used in hunting hares and in racing.

grid /grid/ *n* [C] **1** network of squares on maps, numbered for reference. **2** grating. **3** metal plate in a storage battery.

griddle /ˈgridəl/ *n* [C] flat metal pan used for cooking pancakes, etc.

ˈgriddle·cake *n* [C] pancake.

grid·iron /ˈgridˌaiərn/ *n* [C] **1** framework of metal bars used for broiling meat or fish. **2** (*informal*) football field.

grief /grif/ *n* **1** [U] deep or violent sorrow: *die of ~*. **2** [C] something causing grief: *His failure was a great ~ to his parents*. **3** ***come to grief,*** meet with misfortune, injury or ruin.

griev·ance /ˈgrivəns/ *n* [C] **1** real or imagined cause for complaint or protest (*against*). **2** complaint.

grieve /griv/ *vt,vi* (cause to) feel grief: *~ for the dead/over his death*.

griev·ous /ˈgrivəs/ *adj* **1** causing grief or suffering: *~ wrongs*. **2** severe: *~ pain*.

griev·ous·ly *adv*

grif·fin, grif·fon, gry·phon /ˈgrifən/ *n* [C] (*Gk myth*) creature with the head and wings of an eagle and a lion's body.

grill /gril/ *n* [C] **1** = grating; grille; gridiron. **2** dish of meat, etc cooked directly over or under great heat. □ *vt,vi* **1** cook, be cooked, under or over great heat. **2** question closely and severely.

grille /gril/ *n* [C] screen of parallel bars used to close an open space, eg a window, door, etc.

grim /grim/ *adj* (-mmer, -mmest) **1** stern; severe; without mercy: *a ~ struggle; a ~ smile/expression*. **2** very firm; unyielding: *~ determination*.

grim·ly *adv*

grim·ness /-nis/ *n* [U]

gri·mace /ˈgriməs, griˈmeis/ *n* [C] ugly, twisted expression of pain, disgust, etc. □ *vi* make grimaces.

grime /graim/ *n* [U] dirt, esp a coating on the surface of something or on the body: *a face covered with ~ and sweat*. □ *vt* make dirty with grime: *~d with dust*.

grimy /ˈgraimi/ *adj* (-ier, -est) covered with grime.

grin /grin/ *vi,vt* (-nn-) **1** smile broadly so as to show the teeth: *~ning with delight; ~ from ear to ear*. ***grin and bear it,*** endure pain, disappointment, etc, uncomplainingly. **2** express by grinning: *He ~ned his approval*. □ *n* [C] act of grinning.

grind /graind/ *vt,vi* (*pt,pp* ground /graund/) **1** crush to grains or powder between millstones, the teeth, etc: *~ coffee beans; ~ corn into flour*. **2** be capable of grinding: *This wheat ~s well*. **3** (*fig*) oppress or crush: *people who were ground (down) by poverty*. **4** polish or sharpen by rubbing on or with a rough, hard surface: *~ a knife/lens*. **5** rub harshly together, esp with a circular motion: *~ one's teeth (together); ~ one's heel into the ground*. **6** work by turning; produce by turning: *~ a barrel organ*. ***grind to a halt,*** (*fig*) (of a process) stop slowly: *The strikes brought industry ~ing to a halt*. **7** work or study hard and long: ~ *away at one's studies.* □ *n* **1** act, noise of grinding. **2** [U] (*informal*) long, monotonous task: *Do you find learning English a ~?* **3** [C] (*informal*) person who studies very hard.

grinder /ˈgraindər/ *n* [C] thing or person that grinds, eg an apparatus for grinding coffee.

grind·stone /ˈgraindˌstoun/ *n* [C] stone shaped like a wheel, turned on an axle, used for sharpening tools. ***keep one's nose to the grindstone,*** work hard without rest.

grip /grɪp/ *vt,vi* (-pp-) **1** take and keep a firm hold of; seize firmly: *The frightened child ~ped its mother's hand.* **2** hold the attention of: *The speaker ~ped the attention of his audience. The film is a ~ping story of love and hate.* □ *n* **1** (*sing* only except as shown) act, manner, or power of gripping: *let go one's ~ of a rope; have a good ~* (*fig* = understanding) *of a problem; have a good ~ on an audience*, hold their attention and interest. ***come to grips with,*** try to deal with or solve: *He came to ~s with his problem.* **2** [C] part for gripping, as a handle. **3** [C] small bag for traveling: *a leather ~.*

gripe /graip/ *vt,vi* **1** grip. **2** (cause to) feel a sharp pain in the bowels. **3** (*informal*) annoy. **4** (*informal*) complain: *He's always griping about the food.* □ *n* [C] **1** (*pl*) sharp pains in the bowels. **2** (*informal*) complaint.

grippe /grɪp/ *n* [U] (*old use*) influenza.

gris·ly /ˈgrɪzli/ *adj* (-ier, -iest) causing horror or terror.

grist /grɪst/ *n* [U] grain for grinding or that has already been ground. ***grist for the/sb's mill,*** (*fig*) something which one can use to his own advantage.

gristle /ˈgrɪsəl/ *n* [U] tough, elastic tissue in animal bodies, esp in meat.

grit /grɪt/ *n* [U] **1** (collective *sing*) tiny, hard bits of stone, sand, etc. **2** (*informal*) quality of courage and endurance: *have plenty of ~.* □ *vt* (-tt-) ***grit one's teeth,*** clamp one's teeth tight together, esp in anger, determination, etc.

gritty *adj* (-ier, -iest)

grits /grɪts/ (also **ˈhominy ˌgrits**) *n pl* (with *pl* or *sing* verb) ground hominy, prepared as a mush, commonly eaten in the Southern US.

grizzled /ˈgrɪzəld/ *adj* streaked or mixed with gray.

griz·zly bear /ˈgrɪzli ˌber/ *n* [C] large, grayish bear of North America. ⇨ illus at animal.

groan /groun/ *vi,vt* **1** make a deep sound expressing pain, despair or distress: *The wounded men lay there ~ing. The teacher ~ed with dismay.* **2** (of things) make a noise like that of groaning: *The ship's timbers ~ed during the storm.* **3** express with groaning: *He ~ed out a sad story.* □ *n* [C] deep sound of groaning: *~s of disapproval.*

grocer /ˈgrousər/ *n* [C] person who sells food and household supplies.

grocery /ˈgrous(ə)ri/ *n* (*pl* -ies) **(a)** [U] grocer's trade: *a ˈ~y business.* **(b)** (*pl*) things sold by a grocer.

ˈgrocery store, store specializing in groceries.

groggy /ˈgragi/ *adj* (-ier, -iest) unsteady; likely to collapse or fall: *You look rather ~.*

groin /grɔin/ *n* [C] **1** part of the body at the top of the thigh. ⇨ illus at trunk. **2** curved edge where two vaults meet (in a roof). □ *vt* build with groins.

groom /grum/ *n* [C] **1** person in charge of horses. **2** = bridegroom. □ *vt* **1** clean, brush and in other ways look after an animal. **2** (of apes, monkeys) clean the fur of: *apes ~ing each other.* **3** (of persons) make neat: *well/badly ~ed,* well/badly cared for (esp of the hair and clothes). **4** (*informal*) prepare a person (for a career, etc).

groove /gruv/ *n* [C] **1** long, hollow channel in the surface of hard material, esp one made to guide the motion of something that slides along it, eg a sliding door or window. **2** spiral cut on a phonograph record (in which the needle or stylus moves). **3** way of living that has become a habit. ***get into/be stuck in a groove,*** become set in one's ways. □ *vt* make grooves in: *a ~d shelf.*

groovy *adj* (-ier, -iest) (*sl*) very good; first-rate: *groovy clothes/people.*

grope /group/ *vi,vt* feel about, search, as one does in the dark: *He ~d for the doorknob.*

gross[1] /grous/ *n* [C] (*pl* unchanged) twelve dozen; 144. ⇨ App 1.

gross[2] /grous/ *adj* **1** vulgar; coarse in mind or morals: *~ language/behavior.* **2** (of the senses) heavy and dull. **3** glaring; clearly seen: *~ injustice/negligence.* **4** (of vegetation) luxuriant: *the ~ vegetation of the tropical rain forest.* **5** (of persons) extremely fat. **6** (opposite of *net*) total, whole: *his ~ income.* □ *vt* earn as a total amount: *His last film ~ed five million dollars.*

gross·ly *adv*

gross·ness /-nɪs/ *n* [U]

gro·tesque /grouˈtesk/ *adj* **1** absurd; laughable because strange and incongruous: *a ~ appearance; ~ manners.* **2** (*art*) combining human, animal and plant forms in a fantastic way; made up of distorted figures and designs. □ *n* [C] grotesque person, animal, style or design.

gro·tesque·ly *adv*

grotto /ˈgratou/ *n* (*pl* ~es, ~s) cave, esp one made artificially as a garden shelter.

grouch /grautʃ/ *vi* (*informal*) complain. □ *n* [C] **1** fit of ill temper. **2** bad-tempered person.

ground[1] /graund/ *n* **1** (*sing* with *the*) solid surface of the earth: *lie on/sit on/fall to the ~.* ***get off the ground,*** **(a)** (of an aircraft) rise into the air. **(b)** (*fig*) (of an undertaking or scheme) pass from the planning stage and make a start. ***above ground,*** **(a)** on or above the surface of the earth. **(b)** alive. ***below ground,*** **(a)** below the surface of the earth. **(b)** dead and buried. **2** [U] position, area or distance on the earth's surface. ***cover (much, etc) ground,*** **(a)** travel: *We've covered a great deal of ~ today*, have come a long way. **(b)** (*fig*) (of a lecture, report, inquiry, etc) deal with a variety of subjects: *The committee's report covers much new ~*, deals with many new matters. ***gain ground,*** **(a)** make progress. **(b)** win a success or an advantage. ***give/lose ground,*** fail to keep one's position or advantage. ***hold/stand/keep one's ground,*** stand firm; not yield; maintain one's claim, intention, argument, etc. ***common ground,***

subject on which two or more persons or parties are in agreement or on which they have similar views. **3** [U] soil; earth: *The frost has made the ~ hard.* **4** [C] area or piece of land for a special purpose or a particular use: *a pa'rade ~; a 'play ~.* **5** (always *pl*) land, gardens, around a building, often enclosed with walls, hedges or fences: *the White House ~s.* **6** (*pl*) particles of solid matter that sink to the bottom of a liquid: *'coffee ~s.* **7** (*pl* or [U]) reason(s) for saying, doing or believing something: *On what ~s do you suspect him?* ***be/have/give grounds for,*** be, have, give a cause or reason for: *I have good ~s for believing him. What are the ~s for the divorce?* **8** [C] background; surface on which a design is painted, printed, cut, etc: *a design on a white ~.* **9** something that makes an electrical connection with the earth.

ˌground 'floor, the floor of a building level with the ground.

'ground·nut *n* [C] = peanut (the usual word).

'ground speed, speed of an airborne aircraft as measured by its progress along the ground below it.

'ground·work *n* [U] (usually *fig*) foundation; basis.

ground[2] /graund/ *vt,vi* **1** (of a ship) (cause to) run aground. **2** (of aircraft, airmen) compel to stay on the ground: *All airplanes at Kennedy Airport were ~ed by fog yesterday.* **3** base (the more usual word) (a belief, etc) on: *His argument is ~ed on facts.* **4** give good teaching or basic training in: *The teacher ~ed his pupils in arithmetic.* **5** connect to a ground(9).

ground·ing *n* [U] thorough teaching of the elements of a subject: *a good ~ing in grammar.*

ground[3] *pt,pp* of grind.

ground·hog /'graundˌhag, -ˌhɔg/ *n* [C] woodchuck. ⇨ illus at animal.

'Groundhog Day, February 2, the day in winter when the groundhog is supposed to leave his hole. If he is frightened back to his hole by his shadow, then it is said winter will last for six more weeks.

ground·less /'graundlɪs/ *adj* without foundation or good reason: *~ fears.* ⇨ ground[1](7).

group /grup/ *n* [C] number of persons or things gathered or placed together, or naturally associated: *a ~ of girls/trees/houses.* □ *vt,vi* form into, gather in, a group or groups.

grouse[1] /graus/ *n* [C] (*pl* unchanged) (kinds of) bird with feathered feet, shot for sport and food.

grouse[2] /graus/ *vi* (*informal*) grumble; complain.

grove /grouv/ *n* [C] group of trees; small wood.

grovel /'grəvəl/ *vi* (-l-, -ll-) **1** lie down on one's face, crawl, in fear, (as if) begging for mercy. **2** (*fig*) humble oneself; behave in a way that shows one has no self-respect.

groveler *n* [C] person who grovels.

grow /grou/ *vi,vt* (*pt* grew /gru/, *pp* ~n /groun/) **1** develop; increase in size, height, length, etc: *Rice ~s in warm climates. How tall you've ~n!* ***grow out of,*** **(a)** become too big for: *~ out of one's clothes.* **(b)** become too old for; cease to practice; abandon: *He has ~n out of playing with toys.* **(c)** have as a source: *His troubles grew out of his bad temper.* ***grow up,*** **(a)** (of persons, animals) become adult or mature: *When the boys ~ up,...* **(b)** develop: *A warm friendship grew up between them.* **2** become: *~ older. It began to ~ dark.* **3** ***grow to be/like, etc,*** reach the point or stage where one is/likes, etc: *He grew to like his mother-in-law.* **4** cause or allow to grow: *~ roses. He's ~ing a beard.* **5** **grow on, (a)** become more deeply rooted: *a habit that ~s on you.* **(b)** come to have a greater attraction for; win the liking of: *a book/a piece of music that ~s on you.*

grower *n* [C] **(a)** person who grows things: *a 'fruit ~er; 'rose ~ers.* **(b)** plant, etc that grows in a certain way: *a fast ~er.*

'grown·up *n* [C] adult person (contrasted with children).

growl /graul/ *vi,vt* **1** (of animals, men, thunder) make a low, threatening sound: *The dog ~ed at me. We heard thunder ~ing in the distance.* **2** say in a growling manner: *He ~ed (out) his answer.* □ *n* [C] low threatening sound; angry complaint.

growl·ing·ly *adv*

grown /groun/ *adj* mature: *a ~ man.*

growth /grouθ/ *n* **1** [U] growing; development; process of growing: *the rapid ~ of our economy.* **2** [U] cultivation: *apples of foreign ~,* grown abroad. **3** [C] something that grows or has grown: *a three-days' ~ of beard.* **4** [C] diseased formation in the body, on a plant, etc, eg a cancer.

grub[1] /grəb/ *n* **1** [C] larva of an insect. **2** [U] (*sl*) food.

grub[2] /grəb/ *vt,vi* (-bb-) dig in or turn over the soil, esp in order to get something: *~bing around in the ground.*

grubby /'grəbi/ *adj* (-ier, -iest) dirty; unwashed.

grudge /grədʒ/ *vt* be unwilling to give or allow: *I don't ~ him his success.* □ *n* [C] feeling of ill-will, resentment, envy or spite: *I bear him no ~. He has a ~ against me.*

grudg·ingly *adv* unwillingly.

gruel /'gruəl/ *n* [U] liquid food of oatmeal, etc boiled in milk or water.

gruel·ing /'gruəlɪŋ/ *adj* severe; exhausting: *a ~ race.*

grue·some /'grusəm/ *adj* filling one with horror or disgust.

grue·some·ly *adv*

gruff /grəf/ *adj* (-er, est) **1** (of a person, his behavior) rough and abrupt. **2** harsh; rough: *a ~ voice.*

gruff·ly *adv*

grumble /'grəmbəl/ *vi,vt* **1** complain or protest, say, in a bad-tempered way: *He's always grumbling. He ~d (out) a reply.* **2** make a low, growling sound: *thunder grumbling in the distance.* □ *n* [C] complaint or protest: *All you hear from him is ~s.*

grum·bler *n* [C] person who grumbles.

grumpy /'grəmpi/ *adj* (-ier, -iest) bad-tempered.

grump·ily *adv*

grumpi·ness /-nɪs/ *n* [U]

grunt /grənt/ *vi,vt* **1** (of animals, esp pigs) make a low, short sound. **2** (of persons) make a similar sound expressing disagreement,

boredom, irritation, etc. □ *n* [C] **1** low, short sound. **2** ocean fish related to the snapper, that makes such a sound.
gry·phon *n* = griffin.
GSA *abbr* = **1** General Services Administration. **2** Girl Scouts of America.
guar·an·tee[1] /ˌgærənˈti/ *n* [C] **1** promise or undertaking that certain conditions agreed to in a transaction will be fulfilled: *under ~; a year's ~ with a watch.* **2** undertaking given by one person to another that he will be responsible for something, eg payment of a debt, by a third person. **3** person who gives such an undertaking: *be ~ for a friend's good behavior.* **4** something offered, as security for the fulfilling of conditions in a guarantee(1,2): *"What ~ can you offer?"* **5** something that seems to make an occurrence likely: *Blue skies are not always a ~ of fine weather.*
guar·an·tee[2] /ˌgærənˈti/ *vt* **1** give a guarantee[1] (1,2,4) for: *~ a man's debts; ~ to pay a man's debts. We can't ~ our workers regular employment.* **2** promise (without legal obligation): *Many storekeepers ~ satisfaction to customers.*
guar·an·tor /ˈgærənˌtɔr/ *n* = guarantee[1](3).
guar·an·ty /ˈgærənti/ *n* = guarantee[1].
guard[1] /gard/ *n* **1** [U] state of watchfulness against attack, danger or surprise: *The sentry/soldier is on ~/was ordered to keep ~.* **2** [U] attitude of readiness to defend oneself, eg in fencing, boxing, etc. ***off/on (one's) guard,*** unprepared/prepared to meet an attack. **3** [C] soldier or party of soldiers keeping guard; sentry. **4** [C] body of soldiers with the duty of protecting, honoring or escorting a person: *a ~ of honor.* **5** [C] (esp in compounds) (part of) an article or apparatus designed to prevent injury or loss: *a ˈmud~,* over the wheel of a bicycle, etc. **6** [C] **(a)** (*football*) one of two players on either side of the center. **(b)** (*basketball*) one of two players usually playing toward the center of the court, who is responsible esp for moving and passing the ball to other players on his team.
ˈguard·house *n* [C] building for a military guard or one in which soldiers who are prisoners are kept.
ˈguard·room *n* [C] room for soldiers on guard.
guard[2] /gard/ *vt,vi* **1** protect; keep from danger: *~ a camp; ~ one's life/one's reputation.* **2** use care and caution to prevent: *~ against disease.*
guarded *adj* (of statements, etc) cautious: *a ~ed answer.*
guard·ian /ˈgardiən/ *n* [C] **1** (official or private) person who guards. **2** (*legal*) person who is responsible for the care of another person (esp a child) and his property.
guard·ian·ship /-ˌʃɪp/ *n* [U] position of a guardian.
guava /ˈgwavə/ *n* [C] (tropical tree with) acid fruit used for making jelly.
gu·ber·na·to·ri·al /ˌgubərnəˈtɔriəl/ *adj* of a governor or his office.
guer·rilla, gue·rilla /gəˈrɪlə/ *n* [C] person sometimes not part of a regular army, who carries out sudden raids, ambushes, etc against an enemy, often with the help of the local population.
guess /ges/ *vt,vi* **1** form an opinion without careful thought, calculation or definite knowledge: *Can you ~ my weight/what my weight is/how much I weigh?* **2** arrive at the correct answer by guessing: *We ~ed the right answer to his question.* **3** believe; suppose: *~ he won't be there.* □ *n* [C] opinion formed by guessing.
ˈguess·work *n* [U] (result of) guessing.
guest /gest/ *n* [C] **1** person at another's house for a visit or a meal: *We're expecting ~s to dinner.* **2** customer in a hotel, inn, restaurant, etc.
ˈguest room, bedroom kept for guests.
guf·faw /gəˈfɔ/ *vi, n* [C] (give a) noisy laugh.
guid·ance /ˈgaidəns/ *n* [U] guiding or being guided; leadership.
ˈguidance system, mechanism for steering eg a missile.
guide /gaid/ *n* [C] **1** person who shows others the way, esp a person employed to point out interesting sights on a journey or visit. **2** something that directs or influences (conduct, etc): *Instinct is not always a good ~.* **3** (also **ˈguide·book**) book for travelers, tourists, etc with information about a place: *a ~ to the National Gallery.* **4** book of information; manual: *a ~ to growing roses.* □ *vt* act as guide to: *~ a person to a place. You must be ~d by common sense.*
ˌguided ˈmissile, rocket (for use in war) which can be directed while in flight by electronic devices.
guild /gɪld/ *n* [C] society of persons for helping one another, forwarding common interests, eg trade, social welfare.
guile /gaiəl/ *n* [U] deceit; cunning: *full of ~.*
guile·less *adj* free of deceit.
guillo·tine /ˈgɪləˌtin/ *n* [C] machine, with a sliding blade, for beheading criminals. □ *vt* execute with a guillotine.
guilt /gɪlt/ *n* [U] **1** feeling or condition of having done wrong. **2** responsibility for wrongdoing: *The ~ of the accused man was in doubt.*
guilt·ily /-əli/ *adv*
guilt·less *adj* innocent.
guilty *adj* (-ier, -iest) **(a)** having done wrong: *plead ~y to a crime; be ~y of a crime.* **(b)** showing or feeling guilt: *a ~y conscience.*
guinea fowl /ˈgɪni ˌfaul/ *n* [C] domestic fowl of the pheasant family.
guinea pig /ˈgɪni ˌpɪg/ *n* [C] **1** short-eared animal like a big rat, often used in experiments. **2** person or thing used in medical or other experiments.
guitar /gɪˈtar/ *n* [C] stringed musical instrument, plucked with the fingers or a plectrum. ⇨ illus at string.
gulch /gəltʃ/ *n* [C] ravine.
gulf /gəlf/ *n* **1** part of the sea almost surrounded by land: *the Gulf of Mexico.* **2** deep hollow; chasm; abyss. **3** (*fig*) wide separation or division (*between* opinions, etc).
gull[1] /gəl/ *n* [C] (kinds of) large, long-winged seabird.
gull[2] /gəl/ *vt* cheat; deceive: *~ a fool out of his money.* □ *n* [C] person easily gulled.
gul·let /ˈgəlɪt/ *n* [C] food passage from the mouth to the stomach; throat. ⇨ illus at head.
gull·ible /ˈgələbəl/ *adj* easily deceived.

gulli·bil·ity /ˌgələˈbɪləti/ *n* [U]
gully /ˈgəli/ *n* [C] (*pl* -ies) narrow channel cut or formed by rainwater, eg on a hillside.
gulp /gəlp/ *vt,vi* **1** swallow (food or drink) quickly or greedily: *~ down a cup of tea.* **2** hold back or suppress (as if swallowing). **3** gasp; draw in air. □ *n* [C] **1** act of gulping. **2** amount that is gulped.
gum[1] /gəm/ *n* [C] (usually *pl*) firm, pink flesh round the teeth. ⇨ illus at mouth.
gum·boil /ˈgəmˌbɔiəl/ *n* [C] boil or abscess on the gums.
gum[2] /gəm/ *n* **1** [U] sticky substance obtained from some trees, used for sticking things together. **2** [U] gum that has been specially prepared for chewing: *chewing gum.* **3** [C] (also ˈ**gum tree**) (kinds of) eucalyptus tree. **4** [U] rubber. □ *vt* (-mm-) stick together with gum; spread gum on the surface of: *gum two things together.*
ˈ**gum·drop** *n* [C] soft, clear kind of candy, made in the shape of a hemisphere.
gummy *adj* (-ier, -iest) sticky.
gump·tion /ˈgəmpʃən/ *n* [U] (*informal*) **1** common sense; good judgment. **2** initiative; energy.
gun /gən/ *n* [C] **1** any kind of firearm that sends shells or bullets from a metal tube: *maˈchine gun.* ***stick to one's guns,*** maintain one's position against attack or argument. **2** shooting of a gun, as a salute or signal. ***jump the gun,*** begin (eg a race) before the signal to start. □ *vt* ***gun sb (down),*** shoot with a gun.
ˈ**gun·boat** *n* [C] small warship carrying heavy guns, or long-range missiles.
ˈ**gun carriage,** wheeled support of a big gun, or part on which a gun slides when it recoils.
ˈ**gun·fight** *n* [C] fight using guns, esp pistols.
ˈ**gun·fighter** *n* [C] person (esp in the early West) skilled in the use of pistols.
ˈ**gun·man** /-man/ (*pl* gunmen /-men/) *n* [C] man who uses a gun to rob or kill people.
ˈ**gun·metal** *n* alloy of copper and tin or zinc.
ˈ**gun moll,** (*sl*) **(a)** girl friend of a criminal. **(b)** (esp gun-carrying) female criminal.
ˈ**gun·powder** *n* [U] explosive powder used in guns, fireworks, blasting, etc.
ˈ**gun·runner** *n* [C] person engaged in gunrunning.
ˈ**gun·running** *n* [U] introduction of firearms, secretly and illegally, into a country, eg to help a revolt.
ˈ**gun·shot** *n* range of a gun: *be out of/within gunshot.*
ˈ**gun·slinger** *n* [C] (*sl*) = gunfighter.
ˈ**gun·smith** *n* [C] person who makes and repairs small firearms.
gunk /gəŋk/ *n* [U] (*sl*) (any) thick, sticky substance.
gun·ner /ˈgənər/ *n* [C] **1** soldier, sailor, or airman who operates a large or stationary gun. **2** (in the navy) warrant officer in charge of a ship's guns.
gun·nery *n* construction and management or firing of large guns.
gunny /ˈgəni/ *n* [U] loose-woven material, used esp for making sacks.
ˈ**gunny bag/sack,** sack made of gunny or similar material.
gun·wale /ˈgənəl/ *n* [C] upper edge of the side of a boat or a small ship.
guppy /ˈgəpi/ *n* [C] (*pl* -ies) small tropical fish often kept in home aquariums.
gurgle /ˈgərgəl/ *n* [C,U] bubbling sound as of water flowing from a narrow-necked bottle: *~s of delight.* □ *vi* make this sound: *The baby was gurgling happily.*
guru /ˈgʊru, gəˈru/ *n* [C] Hindu spiritual teacher.
gush /gəʃ/ *vi* **1** burst, flow, out suddenly: *oil ~ing from a new well; blood ~ing from a wound.* **2** talk with excessive enthusiasm: *girls who ~ over handsome movie stars.* □ *n* [C] sudden outburst or outflow: *a ~ of oil/anger/enthusiasm.*
gush·er *n* [C] (esp) oil well with an abundant natural flow.
gush·ing *adj*: *~ing compliments.* ⇨ 2 above.
gus·set /ˈgəsɪt/ *n* [C] (usually triangular or diamond-shaped) piece of cloth inserted in a garment, boot or shoe to strengthen or enlarge it.
gust /gəst/ *n* [C] **1** sudden, violent rush of wind; burst of rain, hail, fire or smoke. **2** (*fig*) outburst of feeling: *a ~ of rage.*
gusty *adj* (-ier, -iest) stormy.
gut /gət/ *n* [C] **1** (*pl*) intestines; bowels. ***hate sb's guts,*** (*sl*) hate him intensely. **2** (*pl*) (*informal*) courage and determination: *a man with plenty of ~s.* **3** [U] (also **catgut**) strong cord made from the intestines of animals, used for the strings of violins, etc. □ *vt* (-tt-) **1** take the guts(1) out of (a fish, etc). **2** destroy the inside of or the contents of: *a building ~ted by fire.*
gut·ter /ˈgətər/ *n* [C] **1** channel or trough fixed under the edge of a roof to carry away rainwater; channel at the side of a road for the same purpose. **2** (*fig*) streets, esp of a poor district: *the language of the ~,* low and vulgar language.
ˈ**gut·ter·ˌsnipe** *n* [C] poor, badly dressed child.
gut·tural /ˈgətərəl/ *n* [C], *adj* (sound) produced in the throat.
guy[1] /gai/ *n* [C] rope or chain used to keep something steady or secured, eg to hold a tent in place.
guy[2] /gai/ *n* [C] (*sl*) man.
guy[3] /gai/ *vt* (*pt,pp* guyed) ridicule.
guzzle /ˈgəzəl/ *vi,vt* eat or drink greedily: *guzzling beer.*
gym /dʒɪm/ *n* [C] (*informal*) (short for) gymnasium.
ˈ**gym shoes,** sneakers.
gym·nasium /dʒɪmˈneiziəm/ *n* [C] (*pl* ~s) room or hall with apparatus for physical training.
gym·nast /ˈdʒɪmˌnæst/ *n* [C] expert in gymnastics.
gym·nas·tic /dʒɪmˈnæstɪk/ *adj* of bodily training.
gym·nas·tics *n pl* (forms of) exercises for physical training.
gyne·col·ogy /ˌgainəˈkalədʒi/ *n* [U] science of the diseases of women and of pregnancy.
gyne·co·logi·cal /ˌgainəkəˈladʒɪkəl/ *adj*
gyne·colo·gist /ˌgainəˈkalədʒɪst/ *n* [C] expert in gynecology.
gyp /dʒɪp/ *n* [C] (*sl*) **1** swindler. **2** swindle. □ *vt* cheat, swindle.

ˈ**gyp joint**, place of business which overcharges.

gypsy /ˈdʒɪpsi/ *n* [C] (*pl* -ies) **1** member of a wandering group of people who originally came to Europe from India. **2** person who lives like a gypsy.

gy·rate /ˈdʒaiˌreit/ *vi* move around in circles or spirals; revolve.

gy·ra·tion /ˌdʒaiˈreiʃən/ *n* [C,U] revolving; revolution.

gyro·scope /ˈdʒairəˌskoup/ *n* heavy wheel which, when spinning fast, keeps steady the object in which it is fixed.

h

H, h /eitʃ/ (*pl* H's, h's /ˈeitʃız/) the eighth letter of the English alphabet.

ha /ha(h)/ *int* used to express surprise, joy, triumph, suspicion, etc. When repeated in print (*"Ha! Ha! Ha!"*) it indicates laughter.

hab·er·dasher /ˈhæbərˌdæʃər/ *n* [C] dealer who sells men's clothing and accessories.

hab·er·dash·ery /-əri/ *n* [U] (articles sold in a) haberdasher's store.

habit /ˈhæbıt/ *n* **1** [C] person's usual or normal practice, esp something that cannot easily be given up: *the ~ of smoking*. ***fall/get into bad habits,*** acquire them. ***get out of a habit,*** abandon it. **2** [U] usual behavior: *Are we all creatures of ~?* Do we do things because of habit? **3** [C] dress worn by members of a religious order: *a monk's ~*.

hab·it·able /ˈhæbətəbəl/ *adj* fit to be lived in: *The old house is no longer ~*.

habi·tat /ˈhæbəˌtæt/ *n* [C] (of plants, animals) usual natural place and conditions of growth.

habi·ta·tion /ˌhæbəˈteiʃən/ *n* **1** [U] living in: *houses that were not fit for ~*. **2** [C] dwelling; place to live in.

ha·bit·ual /həˈbıtʃuəl/ *adj* **1** regular, usual: *He took his ~ seat in the train.* **2** acting by habit; having a regular habit: *a ~ liar*.

ha·bit·ually /-tʃuəli/ *adv* as a habit: *~ly late for school*.

ha·bitu·ate /həˈbıtʃuˌeit/ *vt* accustom; make used to: *~ oneself to hard work*.

habi·tude /ˈhæbəˌtud/ *n* [U] custom; habitual way of acting or doing things.

haci·enda /ˌhasiˈendə/ *n* (*pl* ~s) (in Latin American countries and southwest US) large landed estate with a dwelling house.

hack¹ /hæk/ *vt,vi* **1** cut roughly or clumsily; chop: *He ~ed at the branch until it fell to the ground.* **2** cough roughly. □ *n* [C] rough cough.

ˈhack·saw *n* [C] one with a replaceable blade in a frame, for cutting through metal.

hack² /hæk/ *n* [C] **1** horse that may be hired. **2** person paid to do hard and uninteresting work as a writer. **3** (*sl*) taxicab.

hackles /ˈhækəlz/ *n pl* **1** long feathers on the neck of a rooster or other bird. **2** hairs on a dog's neck and back, that rise when he is angry or afraid. ***raise sb's hackles,*** make him angry, ready to fight.

hack·ney /ˈhækni/ *n* [C] **1** kind of horse for riding or driving. **2** vehicle, eg a taxi, that may be hired.

hack·neyed /ˈhæknid/ *adj* (esp of sayings) too common; repeated too often.

had *pt,pp* of have².

had·dock /ˈhædək/ *n* [C] (*pl* unchanged) seafish much used for food.

Hades /ˈheiˌdiz/ *n* (*Gk myth*) place where the spirits of the dead go.

hadn't /ˈhædənt/ = had not.

hæ·mo·glo·bin *n* = hemoglobin.

hæ·mo·philia *n* = hemophilia.

hæm·or·rhage *n* = hemorrhage.

hæm·or·rhoids *n* = hemorrhoids.

haft /hæft/ *n* [C] handle of an axe, knife, dagger, etc.

hag /hæg/ *n* [C] **1** witch. **2** ugly old woman.

hag·gard /ˈhægərd/ *adj* (of a person, his face) looking tired and lined, esp from worry, lack of sleep.

haggle /ˈhægəl/ *vi* argue, dispute: *haggling with the boss over/about an increase in salary*.

hail¹ /ˈheiəl/ *n* **1** [U] frozen raindrops falling from the sky. **2** (usually with *a* or *an*) something coming down in great numbers and force: *a ~ of blows*. □ *vi,vt* (*pres p* ~ing /ˈheilıŋ/) **1** (of hail) come down: *It ~ed during the morning.* **2** (of blows, etc) come, send down: *They ~ed curses down on us.*

ˈhail·stone *n* [C] small ball of ice.

ˈhail·storm *n* [C] storm with a fall of hail.

hail² /ˈheiəl/ *vt,vi* (*pres p* ~ing /ˈheilıŋ/) **1** greet: *He was ~ed as their leader.* **2** call out to (so as to attract attention): *Let's ~ a taxi, shall we?* **3** ***hail from,*** come from: *They ~ from Indiana.* □ *n* [C] greeting. ***within hail,*** close enough to hear a call or greeting. □ *int* used to express greeting or approval.

hair /her/ *n* **1** [U] (*collective sing*) all the thread-like growths on the skin of animals, esp on the human head; thread-like growth as on the stems and leaves of some plants: *brush one's ~; have one's ˈ~ cut.* ***let one's ˈhair down,*** (*fig*) relax after a period of being formal. ***make one's ˈhair stand on end,*** fill one with fright or horror. **2** [C] single thread of hair: *find a ~ in the soup*. ***split hairs,*** make very fine distinctions, etc, so small as to be unimportant. ***not turn a hair,*** give no sign of being troubled. **3** (*sing* only) very small distance or amount: *won the race by a ~*.

ˈhair('s)breadth *n* very small distance: *escape by a ~('s)breadth*.

ˈhair·brush *n* [C] toilet brush for the hair.

ˈhair·cut *n* [C] act or style of cutting the hair: *have/get a ~cut*.

ˈhair·do *n* [C] style of a woman's hair.

ˈhair·dresser *n* [C] person who cuts or styles a

woman's hair.
hair·less *adj* bald.
ˈ**hair·line** *n* **(a)** line where the hair begins or ends on the forehead. **(b)** width of a hair: (as an *adjective*) *a ~line fracture.*
ˈ**hair·net** *n* [C] net for keeping the hair in place.
ˈ**hair·pin** *n* [C] (woman's) U-shaped pin for keeping the hair in place: (as an *adj*) *a ~pin ˈcurve/turn,* sharp turn in a road.
ˈ**hair-raising** *adj* terrifying.
ˈ**hair·spring** *n* very delicate spring in a watch, controlling the balance wheel.
hairy *adj* (-ier, -iest) of or like, covered with, hair: *a ~y chest.*

hale /ˈheiəl/ *adj* ***hale and hearty,*** strong and healthy.

half /hæf/ *n* (*pl* halves /hævz/) *adj, adv* **1** one of two equal or corresponding parts into which a thing is divided: *Half of 6 is 3. Two halves make a whole. Two pounds and a ~/Two and a ~ pounds.* ***half a ˈdollar,*** fifty cents. ***half a dozen,*** six. ***half past (the hour/nine, etc),*** thirty minutes after, eg nine o'clock, etc. ⇨ App 2. **2** one of two equal time periods in some games. □ *adj* **1** being a half of: *a ~ cup of milk.* **2** partial; not complete. □ *adv* **1** to the extent of a half: *meat that is only ~ cooked.* **2** partially: *~ starved.* ***not half bad,*** (*informal*) not at all bad; quite good.
ˈ**half·back** *n* [C] **(a)** (*football*) player who lines up on either flank. **(b)** (*soccer, field hockey*) player stationed behind the forward line.
ˌ**half-ˈbaked** *adj* (*informal*) foolish; not fully worked out.
ˈ**half-breed** *n* [C] **(a)** person with parents of different races (esp American Indian and Caucasian). **(b)** offspring of two plants or animals of different kinds.
ˈ**half brother/sister** *n* [C] brother/sister by one parent only.
ˈ**half-caste** *n* [C] (esp) person with one European and one Asian parent.
ˌ**half-ˈcocked** *adj* (*informal*) unprepared: *Don't go off ~-cocked,* don't speak/act without adequate thought/preparation.
ˌ**half-ˈdollar** *n* [C] US fifty-cent coin.
half-ˈhearted *adj* done with, showing, little interest or enthusiasm: *a ~hearted attempt.*
ˌ**half-ˈhearted·ly** *adv*
ˈ**half ˌhitch,** kind of knot. ⇨ illus at knot.
ˌ**half-ˈhourly** *adj, adv* (done, occurring) every half hour.
ˌ**half-ˈmast** *n* (of a flag) the position, near the middle of a mast, to indicate mourning: *Flags were at ~-mast on the day of the President's funeral.*
ˌ**half-ˈprice** *adv* at half the usual price: *Children admitted ~-price.*
ˈ**half time,** interval between the two halves of a game of football, etc: *The score at ~ time was 2-2.*
ˈ**half-truth** *n* [C] statement that conveys only a part of the truth.
ˌ**half-ˈway** *adj* **(a)** at an equal distance between two points. **(b)** partial; not thorough: *In an emergency ~way measures are usually unsatisfactory.* □ *adv* to or at half the distance: *meet a person ~way,* be ready to make a compromise.
ˈ**half-wit** *n* [C] foolish or feeble-minded person.
ˌ**half-ˈwitted** *adj*
ˌ**half-ˈyearly** *adj, adv* (done, occurring) every half year.

hal·i·but /ˈhæləbət/ *n* [C] (*pl* ~, ~s) large flatfish used as food, found both in the Atlantic and Pacific Oceans.

hall /hɔl/ *n* [C] **1** (building with a) large room for meetings, concerts, public business, etc: *Symphony Hall,* for concerts, eg in Boston; ˌ*city* ˈ~. **2** building of a university or college: *a ~ of residence.* **3** passage, space, into which the main entrance or front door of a building opens: *Leave your hat and coat in the ~.*
ˌ**Hall of ˈFame,** hall or building serving as a monument to famous people (eg in sports).
ˈ**hall·way** *n* = hall(3).

hal·le·lu·jah /ˌhæləˈluyə/ *n, int* praise to God.

hall·mark /ˈhɔlˌmark/ *n* **1** [C] mark used (originally in England) for marking the standard of gold and silver in articles (as a guarantee of quality). **2** any mark that indicates excellence, quality, etc. □ *vt* stamp a hallmark on.

hal·low /ˈhælou/ *vt* (usually passive) make holy; regard as holy: *~ed ground.*

Hal·low·een /ˌhæləˈwin, ˌhalə-/ *n* October 31, observed by children (usually dressed in masks and costumes) as an evening for tricks and merrymaking.

hal·luci·na·tion /həˌlusəˈneiʃən/ *n* [C,U] (instance of) seeming to see something not actually present: *Drugs sometimes cause ~s.*
hal·luci·na·tory /həˈlusənəˌtɔri/ *adj*

halo /ˈheilou/ *n* [C] (*pl* ~s, ~es) **1** circle of light round the sun or moon. **2** (in paintings) ring around or above the heads of Christ and other figures, indicating holiness.

halt[1] /hɔlt/ *n* [C] stop or pause: *The train came to a ~.* ***call a halt (to),*** **(a)** order a short stop on a march or journey. **(b)** (*fig*) order an end: *It's time to call a ~ to vandalism.* □ *vi,vt* **1** stop marching. **2** bring to an end.

halt[2] /hɔlt/ *vi* hesitate; act in a hesitating way: *speak in a ~ing voice.*
halt·ing·ly *adv* in a hesitating way.

hal·ter /ˈhɔltər/ *n* [C] **1** rope or leather strap put round a horse's head (for leading or fastening the horse). **2** rope used for hanging a person. **3** woman's blouse, held in place by a strap or band around the neck, that leaves the arms, back and shoulders bare.

halve /hæv/ *vt* **1** divide into two equal parts: *~ an apple.* **2** lessen by one half: *The supersonic plane has ~d the time needed for crossing the Atlantic.*

halves *pl* of half.

hal·yard /ˈhælyərd/ *n* [C] rope for raising or lowering a sail or flag.

ham /hæm/ *n* **1** **(a)** [C] upper part of a pig's hind leg, salted and dried or smoked. **(b)** [U] this as meat: *a ham sandwich.* **2** [C] (of animals) back of the thigh; thigh and buttock. **3** [C] (*sl*) poor actor or performer who plays in an affected or exaggerated fashion. **4** [C] (*informal*) amateur radio operator. □ *vt,vi* (-mm-) (*informal*) overact.

ˌham-ˈhanded/-ˈfisted *adj* clumsy in using the hands.
ham·burger /ˈhæmbərgər/ *n* [C] **1** ground beef made into round flat cakes and fried. **2** sandwich or bread roll filled with this.

HAMBURGER

ham·let /ˈhæmlɪt/ *n* [C] small village.
ham·mer /ˈhæmər/ *n* [C] **1** handtool with a heavy metal head used for driving in nails, etc. ***be/go at it hammer and tongs,*** fight, argue, etc with great energy and noise. **2** heavy metal ball thrown in an athletic competition. **3** (in a piano, etc) part like a hammer that strikes the strings. **4** part of a gun that strikes and explodes the charge. **5** wooden mallet used by an auctioneer. ***be/come under the hammer,*** be sold by auction. **6** small bone in the ear. ⇨ illus at ear. □ *vt,vi* **1** strike, beat or drive in (as if) with a hammer: *~ in a nail/~ a nail in; ~ at the door*, eg with a stick or one's fists; *~ at the keys*, play the piano loudly; (*fig*) *~ an idea into his head.* **2** (*fig*) work hard and steadily: *~ away at a problem.* **3** (*fig*) make; shape: *~ed out a new program for the schools.*
ham·mock /ˈhæmək/ *n* [C] hanging bed of canvas or rope network.
ham·per[1] /ˈhæmpər/ *n* [C] basket, etc with a lid, esp one used for carrying food: *a picnic ~.*
ham·per[2] /ˈhæmpər/ *vt* prevent free movement or activity: *~ed by heavy boots.*
ham·ster /ˈhæmstər/ *n* [C] rodent like a large rat, often kept as a pet.
ham·string /ˈhæmˌstrɪŋ/ *vt* (*pt, pp* -strung /ˈhæmˌstrəŋ/) **1** cripple (a person or animal) by cutting the tendon(s) at the back of the knee(s). **2** (*fig*) destroy the power or efficiency of.
hand[1] /hænd/ *n* **1** [C] part of the human arm below the wrist. ⇨ illus at arm. ***at hand,*** near; within reach: *He lives close at ~.* ***at first/second hand,*** directly/indirectly. ***by hand,*** with hands: *Are your socks knitted by ~?* ***from hand to hand,*** from one person to another: *pass buckets of water from ~ to ~.* ***hand in hand,*** **(a)** holding hands: *walk ~ in ~.* **(b)** close together; closely related: *War and misery go ~ in ~.* ***hands down,*** easily: *won the race ~s down.* ***Hands off!*** Don't touch or interfere! ***have one's hands full,*** be very busy. ***live from hand to mouth,*** live poorly, with nothing to spare. ***on hand,*** available: *had plenty of food on ~.* ***shake hands (with sb),*** grasp his hand as a greeting, to show agreement, etc. ***wait on sb hand and foot,*** do whatever he asks. **2** (usually *pl*) control; possession; responsibility: *The matter is in your ~s*, you must decide how to deal with it. ***change hands,*** pass to another owner. ***in the hands of,*** being looked after, managed by: *evidence in the ~s of the police.* ***in good hands,*** being well cared for. ***off one's hands,*** free from one's responsibility. ***on one's hands,*** being one's responsibility or burden: *have too many children on my ~s.* ***out of hand,*** out of control: *He has got out of ~.* **3** help. ***give/lend a hand,*** help with, take part in, doing something: *Please give me a ~ with this suitcase.* ***not lift a hand,*** make no attempt (to help). ***have/get the upper hand,*** have/get control, an advantage, over. ***take sb/sth in hand,*** accept control of: *These noisy children must be taken in hand.* ***wash one's hands of,*** refuse to be involved, responsible, any longer. **4** (*sing* only) part or share. ***have a hand in,*** be involved: *Did he have a ~ in the burglary?* ***take a hand (in),*** take part in. **5** promise, esp of marriage: *asked for her ~.* **6** (*sing* only) skill in using one's hands: *Why don't you try your ~ at embroidery?* ***keep one's hand in,*** practice in order to keep one's skill: *practice the piano every day to keep one's ~ in.* **7** (esp a skilled or experienced) person: *He's an old ~ at this sort of work*, has long experience of it. **8** workman; member of a ship's crew: *The factory has taken on 200 extra ~s. All ~s on deck!* All seamen are needed on deck! **9** pointer or indicator on the dial of a watch, clock or other instrument: *the ˈhour/ˈminute/ˈsecond ~ of a watch.* **10(a)** position or direction (to right or left): *a small table at the right hand of the chair.* **(b)** ***on the one hand ..., on the other hand ...,*** (used to indicate contrasted points of view, arguments, etc). **11** (*sing* only) handwriting: *He writes a good/legible ~.* **12** (in card games, eg bridge) **(a)** (number of) cards dealt to, held by, a player at one time: *a good/bad/poor hand.* **(b)** player at cards: *We have only three players — we need a fourth ~.* **(c)** one round in a game of cards: *Let's play one more ~.* **13** [C] unit of measurement, about four inches (10.16 cm), used for the height of a horse (from the ground to the top of the shoulder). **14** (*informal*) applause by clapping. ***give sb a hand,*** applaud him.
ˈhand·bag *n* [C] woman's bag for money, keys, etc.
ˈhand·cart *n* [C] small cart pushed or pulled by hand.
ˈhand·cuff *n* (usu *pl*) one of a pair of metal rings joined by a chain, fastened round a prisoner's wrists. □ *vt* put handcuffs on.
ˈhand·ful *n* [C] **(a)** as much or as many as can be held in one hand. **(b)** small number: *Only a ~ful of persons came to the meeting.* **(c)** (*informal*) person or animal difficult to control: *That young boy of hers is quite a ~ful.*
ˌhand-ˈmade *adj* made by hand (contrasted with *machine-made*).
ˌhand-ˈpicked *adj* carefully selected.
ˈhand·rail *n* railing along the edge of a staircase, etc.
ˈhand·shake *n* greeting given by grasping a person's hand with one's own.
ˈhand·stand *n* acrobatic feat of supporting oneself in an upright position on the hands: *do a ~stand.*
ˈhand·writing *n* [U] (person's style of) writing by hand.

hand[2] /hænd/ *vt* give or pass (to a person); help with the hand(s): *Please ~ me that book/~ that book to me.* ***hand sth down (to sb),*** pass by tradition, inheritance, etc: *We cannot always observe the traditions ~ed down to us from the past.* ***hand sth on (to sb),*** send, give, to another: *Please ~ on the magazine to your friends.* ***hand sth out,*** distribute. ***hand sb/sth over (to sb),*** deliver or give up a person/thing: *~ him over to the police. Hand over that knife at once.* ***hand it to sb,*** (*informal*) give him the credit that is his due: *He's done well! You've got to ~ it to him.*

ˈhand·out *n* [C] **(a)** printed statement, leaflet, eg political, distributed free of charge. **(b)** something given free of charge, eg money, clothes.

handi·cap /ˈhændiˌkæp/ *n* [C] **1** (competition, race, in which there is a) disadvantage imposed on a more skilled or experienced competitor to make the chances of success more equal for all. **2** anything likely to lessen one's chance of success; hindrance: *Poor eyesight is a ~ to a student.* □ *vt* (-pp-) give or be a handicap to: *~ped children*, suffering from a disability.

handi·craft /ˈhændiˌkræft/ *n* [C] art or craft needing skill with the hands, eg needlework, pottery.

handi·work /ˈhændiˌwərk/ *n* **1** [U] work done or something made. **2** [C] thing made, by the hands. **3** [U] something done by a single person: *That's some of Smith's ~.*

hand·ker·chief /ˈhæŋkərtʃɪf, -ˌtʃif/ *n* [C] **1** square piece of cotton, etc for blowing the nose into or wiping the face. **2** similar square worn, eg round the neck.

handle /ˈhændəl/ *n* [C] part of a tool, cup, bucket, door, drawer, etc by which it may be held in the hand. ***fly off the handle,*** (*informal*) get into a rage and lose self-control. □ *vt* **1** touch with, take up in, the hands: *Please ~ that dish carefully.* **2** manage; deal with: *Can you ~ the situation*, deal with it? **3** treat: *The speaker was roughly ~d by the crowd.* **4** buy and sell: *This store does not ~ imported goods.* **5** behave or act in a certain way when handled: *This truck ~s well.*

ˈhandle·bar *n* (often *pl*) bar with a handle at each end, for steering a bicycle, etc.

han·dler *n* [C] (esp) person who trains and controls an animal, eg a police dog.

hand·some /ˈhænsəm/ *adj* **1** of fine appearance; (of men) good-looking; (of women, *dated*) having a fine bearing: *What a ~ old building it is! He's so ~.* **2** (of gifts, behavior) generous: *He said some very ~ things about you.*

hand·some·ly *adv* in a generous manner.

handy /ˈhændi/ *adj* (-ier, -iest) **1** (of persons) clever with the hands. **2** convenient to handle; easily used: *A good toolbox is a ~ thing to have in the house.* ***come in handy,*** be useful some time or other: *Don't throw that plastic bag away; it may come in ~.* **3** not far away; available for use: *Always keep a first-aid kit ~.*

hand·ily /-əli/ *adv*

handy·man /ˈhændiˌmæn/ *n* [C] person who does odd jobs of various kinds.

hang[1] /hæŋ/ *n* (*sing* only) **1** way in which a thing hangs: *the ~ of a coat/skirt.* **2** ***get the hang of sth,*** **(a)** see how something works or is managed: *I've been trying to get the ~ of this new typewriter.* **(b)** see the meaning or significance of something: *I don't quite get the ~ of your argument.*

hang[2] /hæŋ/ *vt,vi* (*pt,pp* hung /həŋ/ or, for 2 below, also ~ed) **1** support, be supported, from above so that the lower end is free: *~ a lamp from the ceiling. Hang your coat on that hook.* **2** (*pt,pp* hung or ~ed) put, be put, to death by hanging with a rope around the neck: *He was ~ed for murder.* **3** (cause to) droop or bend downward: *~ one's head.* **4** (various uses) *~ wallpaper*, attach it to a wall with paste: *~ a door*, fasten it on hinges. **5** depend: *The outcome ~s on the decision of one man.* ***hang by a hair/a single thread,*** (of a person's fate, etc) be in a delicate or critical state. ***hang fire,*** (of events) be slow in developing. **6** (special uses with *adverbial particles* and *prepositions*):

hang around, be standing around, doing nothing definite: *boys ~ing around on street corners.*

hang back, show unwillingness to act or advance: *When volunteers were asked for, not one man hung back.*

hang in, (*informal*) = hang on (b).

hang on, **(a)** hold tight: *He hung on until the rope broke.* **(b)** persevere: *It's hard work, but if you ~ on long enough you'll succeed.*

hang out, hang around (a particular place).

hang sth out, **(a)** hang (wet clothes, etc) out to dry. **(b)** display: *~ out flags for the President's visit.*

hang together, **(a)** (of persons) support one another; act in unison: *If we all ~ together, our plan will succeed.* **(b)** fit well together: *Their accounts don't ~ together*, are inconsistent.

hang up, replace the receiver at the end of a telephone conversation. ***be hung up,*** (*informal*) **(a)** be delayed: *He telephoned his wife to tell her he was hung up at the office with an important client.* **(b)** be frustrated or troubled: *I'm hung up on a problem I just can't solve.* **(c)** be filled with a foolish love for a person: *He's really hung up on her.*

ˈhang·man /-mən/ (*pl* ~men /-men/) executioner who hangs criminals.

ˈhang·out *n* place where one spends time.

ˈhang·over *n* **(a)** unpleasant after-effects of excessive drinking. **(b)** survival of out-of-date news, rules, etc.

ˈhang·up *n* **(a)** problem, esp one that causes continuing worry, concern, etc. **(b)** (*informal*) irrational feeling (about something).

han·gar /ˈhæŋər/ *n* [C] building for aircraft.

hang·er /ˈhæŋər/ *n* [C] device, loop, etc to, on or by which something is hung: *a coat ~*, device on which clothes, etc are hung.

hanger-on /ˌhæŋər-ˈan/ *n* [C] (*pl* hangers-on) person who forces his company on another or others in the hope of profit or advantage.

hang·ing /ˈhæŋɪŋ/ *n* **1** [C,U] (instance of) death by hanging: *There were three ~s here last month.* **2** (usually *pl*) curtains, etc with which walls are hung.

hank /hæŋk/ *n* [C] (twisted) coil of wool, silk,

etc.

han·ker /ˈhæŋkər/ *vi* have a strong desire: *~ for/after sympathy/after wealth.*

han·ker·ing *n*: *have a ~ing for/after fame.*

hanky /ˈhæŋki/ *n* [C] (*pl* -ies) (*informal*) handkerchief.

hanky-panky /ˈhæŋkiˌpæŋki/ *n* [U] (*sl*) deception, dishonesty.

hap·haz·ard /ˌhæpˈhæzərd/ *adj, adv* accidental; (by) chance.

hap·pen /ˈhæpən/ *vi* **1** take place; come about: *How did it ~? If anything ~s to him* (= If he meets with an accident) *let me know.* **2** chance; have the fortune: *I ~ed to be out when he called.* **3** find by chance: *I ~ed on just the thing I'd been looking for.*

hap·pen·ing *n* **(a)** (often *pl*) event: *There have been strange ~ings here lately.* **(b)** (*informal*) spontaneous entertainment often involving the audience.

happy /ˈhæpi/ *adj* (-ier, -iest) **1** fortunate; lucky: *Meeting them was a ~ accident.* **2** feeling or expressing pleasure, contentment, satisfaction, etc: *Their marriage has been a ~ one.* **3** (in polite formulas) pleased: *We shall be ~ to accept your kind invitation.* **4** (of language, conduct, suggestions) well suited to the situation: *a ~ thought/idea, etc.*

hap·pily /-pəli/ *adv*

hap·pi·ness /-nɪs/ *n* [U]

ˌhappy-go-ˈlucky *adj* carefree.

ha·rangue /həˈræŋ/ *n* [C] long, loud (often scolding) talk or speech. □ *vt,vi* make such a speech (to).

ha·rass /həˈræs/ *vt* **1** trouble; worry: *~ed by the cares of a large family.* **2** make repeated attacks on: *The town was continually ~ed by pirates.*

ha·rass·ment *n* [U]

harbor /ˈharbər/ *n* [C] **1** place of shelter for ships: *a natural ~*, eg an inlet of the sea. **2** (*fig*) any place of safety or shelter. □ *vt,vi* **1** give refuge or shelter to; protect; conceal: *~ an escaped criminal.* **2** hold in the mind: *~ thoughts of revenge.* **3** take shelter (as) in a harbor.

hard[1] /hard/ *adj* (-er, -est) **1** (contrasted with *soft*) firm; not yielding to the touch; not easily cut; solid: *as ~ as rock.* **2** (contrasted with *easy*) difficult (to do): *She found it ~ to make up her mind. That man is ~ to please/He is a ~ man to please.* **3** causing unhappiness, discomfort, or pain; difficult to bear: *have/be given a ~ time*, experience difficulties, misfortunes, etc. ***learn sth the hard way,*** by suffering, making a tiring effort, etc. **4** severe; harsh: *a ~ father*, one who is severe; *~ words*, harsh; showing lack of sympathy. **5** (of the body) having hard muscles and not much fat: *Exercises soon made the boys ~.* **6** requiring much effort or force; strenuous: *Digging ditches is ~ labor.* **7** diligent; energetic: *a ~ worker.* **8** (of the weather) severe: *a ~ winter/frost.* **9** (of sounds) the letters "c" and "g" when pronounced /k, g/. **10** (various uses) ***hard and fast (rules, etc),*** that cannot be altered. ***hard of hearing,*** rather deaf.

ˈhard·back *n* [C] book bound in a hard (= stiff) cover (contrasted with *paperback*).

ˈhard·board *n* [U] board made of compressed wood chips.

ˌhard-ˈboiled *adj* **(a)** (of an egg) boiled until hard. **(b)** (of a person) hard-hearted.

ˌhard ˈcash, coins and bills, not a check or a promise to pay.

ˌhard ˈdrugs, those likely to lead to addiction, eg heroin.

ˌhard-ˈheaded *adj* **(a)** not sentimental; business-like. **(b)** stubborn.

ˌhard-ˈhearted *adj* lacking in sympathy.

ˌhard ˈliquor, liquor with a high alcoholic content, eg whiskey.

ˌhard ˈpalate, hard part of the roof of the mouth. ⇨ illus at mouth.

ˌhard ˈsell, act, instance of selling aggressively, with much psychological pressure on the prospective buyer.

ˌhard ˈup, short of money.

ˈhard·ware *n* [U] **(a)** metal goods for domestic use, eg pans. **(b)** (*mil*) weapons and equipment, eg armored vehicles. **(c)** (*comp*) mechanical equipment, not data and programs. ⇨ software.

ˈhard·wood *n* heavy, close-grained wood, eg oak, teak.

hard[2] /hard/ *adv* **1** with great energy; strenuously; with all one's force: *try ~ to succeed.* **2** severely; heavily: *freezing/raining ~.* **3** with difficulty; with a struggle; painfully: *my ˈ~-earned money.* **4** so as to be hard(1), solid: *The water was frozen ~.* **5** closely; immediately: *follow ~ after/upon/behind someone.*

harden /ˈhardən/ *vt,vi* make or become hard, strong, hardy, etc: *a ~ed criminal*, one who shows no signs of shame or repentance.

hard·ly /ˈhardli/ *adv* **1** only just; scarcely: *I ~ know her. I'm so tired I can ~ walk.* **2** (used to suggest that something is improbable, unlikely or unreasonable): *You can ~ expect me to lend you money again.* **3** (negative in meaning) almost no, not, never: *He ~ ever goes to bed before midnight. I need ~ say* (= It is almost unnecessary for me to say) *that I am innocent. There's ~ any coal left. Hardly anybody* (= Very few people) *came to the meeting.*

hard·ship /ˈhardˌʃɪp/ *n* **1** [C] something that causes discomfort or suffering: *the ~s of war.* **2** [U] severe suffering: *bear ~ without complaining.*

hardy /ˈhardi/ *adj* (-ier, -iest) **1** strong; able to endure suffering or hardship: *A few ~ men broke the ice on the lake and had a swim.* **2** (of plants) able to survive frost: *~ annuals.* **3** bold; ready to face danger.

hardi·ness /-nɪs/ *n* [U]

hare /her/ *n* [C] fast-running field animal with long ears and a divided upper lip, like but larger than a rabbit.

ˈhare·brained *adj* rash; wild.

ˈhare·lip *n* person's upper lip divided (from birth) like that of a hare.

harem /ˈherəm/ *n* [C] **1** women's part of a Moslem household. **2** women living in a harem.

hark /hark/ *vi* **1** listen to. **2** ***hark back (to),*** refer to something done or said earlier.

harken = hearken.

har·le·quin /ˈharləkwɪn/ *n* [C] **1** character as in Italian comedy or English pantomime. **2** clown.

har·lot /ˈharlət/ *n* [C] (*liter*) prostitute.

harm /harm/ *n* [U] damage; injury: *It will do you no ~. He meant no ~.* ***out of harm's way,*** safe. □ *vt* cause harm to.

harm·ful *adj* causing harm (*to*).

harm·fully *adv*

harm·less *adj* **(a)** not doing harm: *~less snakes.* **(b)** uninvolved (esp in a fight): *Several ~less bystanders were hurt.*

harm·less·ly *adv*

har·mon·ica /har'manıkə/ *n* [C] small, rectangular instrument played by breathing through its metal reeds; mouth-organ.

har·moni·ous /har'mouniəs/ *adj* **1** pleasingly or satisfactorily arranged: *a ~ group of buildings.* **2** in agreement; free from ill feeling: *~ families.* **3** tuneful; pleasing to the ear.

har·moni·ous·ly *adv*

har·mon·ize /'harməˌnaiz/ *vt,vi* **1** bring (one thing) into, be in, harmony (with another). **2** (*music*) add notes (to a melody) to make chords.

har·moni·za·tion /ˌharmənı'zeiʃən/ *n* [U]

har·mony /'harməni/ *n* (*pl* -ies) **1** [U] agreement (of feeling, interests, opinions, etc): *racial ~.* **2** [C,U] (instance or example of) pleasing combination of related things: *the ~ of color in nature.* **3** [C,U] pleasing combination of musical notes sounded together to make chords.

har·ness /'harnıs/ *n* [C] arrangement of leather straps and metal fastenings by which a horse is controlled and fastened to the cart, wagon, plow, etc, that it pulls. □ *vt* **1** put a harness on (a horse). **2** put to work: *~ a river to produce electric power.*

harp /harp/ *n* [C] upright musical instrument with vertical strings played with the fingers. ⇨ illus at string. □ *vi* **1** play the harp. **2** ***harp on,*** talk repeatedly or tiresomely about: *She is always ~ing on her misfortunes.*

harp·ist /-ıst/ *n* [C] player on the harp.

har·poon /ˌhar'pun/ *n* [C] spear on a rope, thrown by hand or fired from a gun, used in hunting whales and large fish. □ *vt* strike with a harpoon.

harp·si·chord /'harpsəˌkɔrd/ *n* [C] keyboard instrument similar to a piano. ⇨ illus at keyboard.

har·ri·dan /'hærıdən/ *n* [C] bad-tempered old woman.

har·row /'hærou/ *n* [C] heavy frame with metal teeth or discs for breaking up the soil after plowing. □ *vt* use a harrow. **2** (*fig*) distress (the feelings): *a ~ing tale of misfortunes.*

harry /'hæri/ *vt* (*pt,pp* -ied) **1** attack frequently: *The Indians ~ed the outpost.* **2** annoy or worry: *mischievous students ~ing their teachers.*

harsh /harʃ/ *adj* (-er, -est) **1** rough and disagreeable: *a ~ voice.* **2** stern, cruel, severe: *a ~ judge/punishment.*

harsh·ly *adv*

harsh·ness /-nıs/ *n* [U]

har·vest /'harvıst/ *n* [C] **1** **(a)** (season for) cutting and gathering in of grain and other food crops. **(b)** quantity obtained in this way. **2** (*fig*) result of action or behavior: *reap the ~ of one's hard work.* □ *vt* cut, gather, dig up, a crop: *~ rice.*

ˌharvest 'moon, full moon occurring nearest to the beginning of autumn.

har·ves·ter *n* [C] **(a)** person who harvests. **(b)** machine for cutting and gathering grain.

has ⇨ have[1].

has-been /'hæz-ˌbın/ *n* [C] (*informal*) person who has lost former importance, wealth, fame, etc.

hash /hæʃ/ *vt* chop (meat) into small pieces. □ *n* **1** [U] (dish of) cooked chopped meat and vegetables. **2** (*sing* only) jumble; mess. ***make a hash of sth,*** (*fig*) do it very badly, make a mess of it. **3** [U] (*sl*) hashish.

hash·ish, hash·eesh /'hæˌʃiʃ/ *n* [U] extract of the hemp plant, that is smoked or chewed.

hasn't /'hæzənt/ = has not.

hasp /hæsp/ *n* [C] metal fastening of a padlock used with a staple.

hassle /'hæsəl/ *n* (*informal*) **1** [C] fight; argument. **2** [U] trouble.

has·sock /'hæsək/ *n* [C] cushioned footstool.

haste /heist/ *n* [U] quickness of movement; hurry: *Why all this ~?*

hasten /'heisən/ *vi,vt* **1** move or act with speed: *~ to tell someone the good news.* **2** cause to or to be done, to happen quickly or earlier: *Artificial heating ~s the growth of plants.*

hasty /'heisti/ *adj* (-ier, -iest) said, made or done (too) quickly: *~ preparations.*

hast·ily /-əli/ *adv*

hasti·ness /'heistinıs/ *n* [U]

hat /hæt/ *n* [C] covering for the head worn out of doors. ***pass the hat,*** (*informal*) collect donations of money (as by passing around an upturned hat). ***take one's hat off to,*** (*fig*) express admiration for. ***talk through one's hat,*** (*sl*) talk foolishly.

hat·ter *n* [C] man who makes, repairs or sells hats.

hatch[1] /hætʃ/ *n* [C] (movable covering over an) opening in a door or floor, esp (**'hatch·way**) one in a ship's deck through which cargo is lowered and raised.

hatch[2] /hætʃ/ *vt,vi* **1** (cause to) break out (of an egg): *~ chickens.* **2** think out and produce (a plan, etc).

hatch·ery *n* [C] place for hatching (esp fish): *a 'trout ~ery.*

hatchet /'hætʃıt/ *n* [C] light, short-handled ax. ***bury the hatchet,*** stop quarreling or fighting. **'hatchet man,** (*sl*) professional killer (esp for a gang).

hatch·way /'hætʃˌwei/ *n* ⇨ hatch[1].

hate /heit/ *vt* **1** have a great dislike of or for: *My cat ~s dogs.* **2** regret: *I ~ to trouble you.* □ *n* [U] extreme dislike.

hate·ful /'heitfəl/ *adj* exciting hatred or strong dislike: *a ~ person/act.*

hate·fully *adv*

hath /hæθ/ *v* (*archaic*) *present tense* form of *has* used with *he, she,* or *it*: *he ~,* he has.

hatred /'heitrıd/ *n* [U] hate: *He looked at me with ~.*

hat·ter /'hætər/ *n* ⇨ hat.

haughty /'hɔti/ *adj* (-ier, -iest) having or showing a high opinion of oneself: *treating the staff with ~ contempt.*

haught·ily /-əli/ *adv*

haugh·ti·ness /'hɔtinıs/ *n* [U]

haul /hɔl/ *vt,vi* pull (with effort or force): *They ~ed the boat up the beach.* □ *n* [C] **1** act of hauling. **2** distance along which something is hauled. **3** amount gained, esp of fish hauled up in a net. **4** (*fig*) catch: *The thief made a good ~,* What he stole was valuable.

haunch /hɔntʃ, hantʃ/ *n* [C] (in man and animals) fleshy part of the buttock or thigh: *a dog sitting on its ~es.*

haunt /hɔnt, hant/ *vt* **1** visit, be with, habitually or repeatedly. **2** (esp of ghosts and spirits) appear repeatedly in. **3** return to the mind repeatedly: *constantly ~ed by fear of discovery.* □ *n* [C] place frequently visited: *a ~ of criminals.*

have[1] /*usual form after "I, we, you, they"* v; *elsewhere* həv, əv; *strong form* hæv/ *auxiliary verb* (*3rd person sing* has /həz, əz; *strong form* hæz/, *pp* had /*usual form after "I, we, you, they"* d; *elsewhere* həd, əd; *strong form* hæd/; negative forms haven't /ˈhævənt/, hasn't /ˈhæzənt/, hadn't /ˈhædənt/; inverted with the subject in the negative and interrogative) **1** (used in forming the perfect tenses and the perfect infinitive): *I ~/I've finished. He has/He's gone. Have you done it? Yes, I ~. No, I ~n't. I shall ~ done it by next week.* **2** (inverted with *subject*, as an equivalent of an *if*-clause): *Had I* (= If I had) *known* ... ⇨ if(1).

have[2] /hæv/ *vt* (*3rd person sing* has /hæz/, *pp* had /hæd/; negative forms ⇨ have[1]; used in the negative and interrogative with the *aux v do*) **1** own; possess: *He has a house in the country/five dollars. Will/Would you ~ the kindness/goodness, etc* (= Please be kind or good enough) *to hand me that book. Does she ~ blue eyes?* (*Note:* In *informal* style, the *pp got* with *aux v have* is common: *He's only got five dollars. Has she got blue eyes?*) **2** be related to: *How many sisters does he ~?* **3** be the parent of: *They're having a baby in June.* **4** (often with *got*) hold or keep in the mind: *Do you~/Have you got any idea where he lives?* **5** (always stressed) allow; permit: *I won't ˈ~ such conduct.* **6** (before *to* have /hæf/, has /hæs/) (expressing obligation or necessity): *You don't ~ to go to school today, do you? We had to leave early.* **7** suffer from: *Do you ~ a cold?* **8** take; receive; accept; obtain: *What shall we ~ for dinner?* **9** (used with a noun where the meaning is the same as the use of the *noun* as a *verb*): *~ a swim/walk. Let me ~ a try/look.* **10** experience; undergo: *We didn't ~ much difficulty. Did you ~ a good holiday?* ***have ˈhad it,*** (*informal*) have had enough; be through: *I put up with those restrictions for years, but now I've had it!* ***let sb ˈhave it,*** (*sl*) punish him. **11** cause to do or be done *I must ~ these shoes repaired.* ⇨ get(1). **12 (a)** (*informal*) trick; deceive: *I'm afraid you've been had.* **(b)** beat; win an advantage over: *You had me there!* **13** state; maintain: *Rumor has it* (= There is a rumor) *that the chairman is going to resign.* **14** (special uses with *adverbial particles* and *prepositions*):

have sth on, **(a)** be wearing: *He had nothing on,* was naked. **(b)** be busy, engaged: *I ~ nothing on tomorrow evening,* I am free.

have it out with sb, argue about or discuss a matter with him until an understanding is reached.

ha·ven /ˈheivən/ *n* [C] **1** harbor. **2** (*fig*) place of safety or rest.

hav·er·sack /ˈhævərˌsæk/ *n* [C] canvas bag for supplies carried on the back by soldiers, hikers, etc

havoc /ˈhævək/ *n* [U] widespread damage; destruction: *The floods caused terrible ~.*

Ha·wai·ian /həˈwaiən/ *adj* of Hawaii /həˈwai(y)i/, and esp its original Polynesian people, their language, culture, etc. □ *n* member, language, of Hawaii's Polynesian people.

Haˈwaii(an) Time, one of the official time zones of the US (also including part of Alaska, and sometimes called **Alaska-Hawaii Time**).

hawk[1] /hɔk/ *n* [C] **1** strong, swift, keen-sighted bird of prey. **2** (*informal*) (in foreign affairs) person who favors the use of military force. ⇨ dove[1](2).

hawk[2] /hɔk/ *vt* offer goods for sale in the streets by calling out.

hawker *n* [C] person who hawks goods.

haw·ser /ˈhɔzər/ *n* [C] **1** thick, heavy rope. **2** thin steel cable used for towing or mooring ships.

haw·thorn /ˈhɔˌθɔrn/ *n* [C] thorny shrub or tree with white, red or pink blossoms and small red berries.

hay /hei/ *n* [U] grass cut and dried for use as animal food. ***make hay while the sun shines,*** (*prov*) make the best use of one's opportunities.

ˈhay·cock /-ˌkak/ *n* [C] cone-shaped pile of hay.

ˌhay ˈfever, disease affecting the nose and throat, caused by pollen (dust) from various plants.

ˈhay·fork *n* [C] **(a)** long-handled two-pronged fork for turning and lifting hay. **(b)** mechanical device for loading and unloading hay.

ˈhay·loft /-ˌlɔft/ *n* [C] upper part of a barn, used for storing hay.

ˈhay·seed n (*sl*) bumpkin.

ˈhay·stack *n* [C] large pile of hay.

ˈhay·wire *n* [U] wire for tying up bales of hay. □ *adj* (*informal*) **(a)** out of order. **(b)** excited or confused. ***go haywire,*** **(a)** (of persons) become upset, excited etc. **(b)** (of eg a plan) become badly disorganized. **(c)** (of a device, piece of equipment, etc.) become out of order.

haz·ard /ˈhæzərd/ *n* [C] risk; danger: *ˈhealth ~s,* eg smoking cigarettes. □ *vt* **1** take the risk of; expose to danger: *Mountain climbers sometimes ~ their lives.* **2** take a chance at: *~ a guess.*

haz·ard·ous *adj* risky: *a ~ous climb.*

haze /heiz/ *n* [U] **1** thin mist. **2** (*fig*) mental confusion or uncertainty.

hazel /ˈheizəl/ *n* **1**[C] small shrub or tree with edible nuts. **2** [U] (esp of eyes) color of the shell of the nut, reddish brown. □ *adj* reddish-brown.

hazy /ˈheizi/ *adj* (-ier, -iest) **1** misty: *~ weather.* **2** (*fig*) vague; slightly confused; uncertain: *~ about what to do next.*

haz·ily /ˈheizəli/ *adv*

hazi·ness /ˈheizinɪs/ *n* [U]

H-bomb /ˈeitʃ-ˌbam/ *n* [C] hydrogen bomb.

HDST *abbr* = Hawaii(an) Daylight Saving Time.

he (usually **He** when referring to God) /hi; often i when after another word in rapid speech/ *per-*

(1) hair
(2) forehead
(3) eyebrow
(4) bridge
(5) temple
(6) eye
(7) ear
(8) cheek
(9) nose
(10) nostril
(11) mouth
(12) jaw
(13) chin
(14) nape
(15) neck
(16) throat

ANTERIOR VIEW

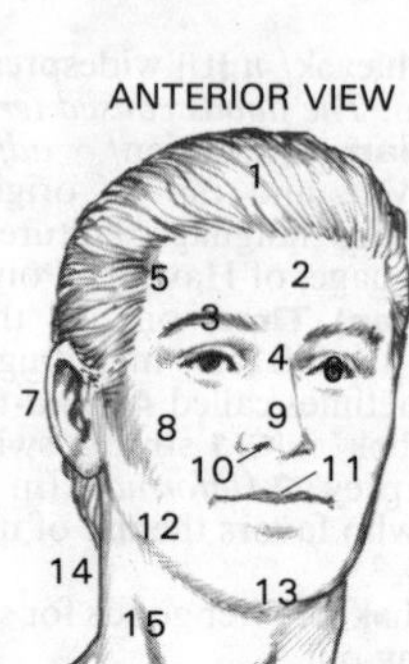

CROSS SECTION

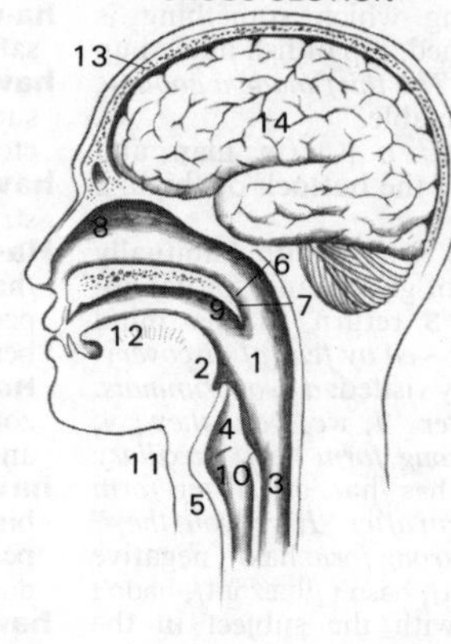

(1) glottis
(2) epiglottis
(3) esophagus or gull
(4) vocal cords
(5) thyroid
(6) tonsil
(7) pharynx
(8) adenoids
(9) tonsil
(10) larynx
(11) Adam's apple
(12) tongue
(13) skull
(14) brain

HEAD AND NECK

sonal pron male person or animal previously referred to: *Where's your brother? He's in Paris.* ⇨ him, object form. □ *n* [C](often used in compounds) male: *Is it a he or a she? a ˈhe-goat.*

ˈhe-man /-ˌmæn/ *n* [C] (*pl* he-men /-ˌmen/) (*informal*) strong, active man.

head¹ /hed/ *n* **1** that part of the body which contains the eyes, nose, mouth, brain etc: *They cut his ~ off.* **2** (as a measure) head's length: *The dark horse won by a ~.* **3** that side of a coin on which a head appears, the other side being the *tail*. ***be unable to make head or tail of sth,*** be unable to understand it at all. **4** person: *50 dinners at $6.50 a ~.* **5** (*pl* unchanged) unit of a flock or herd: *50 ~ of cattle.* **6** intellect; imagination; power to reason: *He made the story up out of his own ~.* ***carry/keep sth in one's head,*** have it memorized. **7** natural aptitude or talent: *He has a good ~ for business.* **8** something like a head in form or position, eg the part that is pressed, struck, etc: *the ~ of a pin/nail.* **9** top: *at the ~ of the page/staircase; at the ~ of the class,* having gained the highest marks. **10** upper end: *the ˈ~waters of the Nile,* its sources and upper streams; *the ~ of a bed,* where a person's head rests. **11** (of plants) mass of leaves or flowers at the top of a stem or stalk: *a fine ~ of cabbage.* **12** (often as an *adjective*) ruler; chief; position of command: *~s of government,* eg the President of the US; *the ~ office,* the chief or most important office; the ~master/mistress of a (private preparatory) school; the ~waiter of a large restaurant. **13** front; front part: *at the ~ of the procession.* **14** (chiefly in proper names) projecting part, cape: *Hilton Head.* ⇨ headland. **15** body of water kept at a certain height (eg for a hydroelectric power station). **16** pressure or force (per unit of area) of a confined body of steam, etc: *They kept up a good ~ of steam.* **17** main division in a discourse, essay, etc: *a speech arranged under five ~s.* ⇨ heading. **18** foam which forms on the top of a liquid that has been poured out, esp a fermented beverage: *the ~ on a glass of beer.* **19** point rising from a boil or other swelling on the flesh: *The boil came to a ~.* **20** (various phrases) ***bite sb's head off,*** scold him angrily. ***bring/come to a head,*** (*fig*) cause to reach/reach a crisis: *Affairs have come to a ~.* ***give sb his head,*** (*fig*) *leave him to act freely.* ***go to one's head,*** **(a)** (of liquor) intoxicate: *The whiskey went to his ~.* **(b)** make conceited: *His successes have gone to his ~.* ***have a ˌgood ˈhead on one's shoulders,*** have practical ability, common sense, etc. ***head over heels,*** **(a)** upside down; headlong. **(b)** (*fig*) deeply or completely: *~ over heels in love.* ***keep one's head,*** keep calm. ***lose one's head,*** become confused or excited. ***(go) out of one's ~,*** **(a)** (become) crazy; mad. **(b)** (become) wildly excited. ***one's head off,*** excessively; to an extreme degree: *laughed our ~s off.* ***put our/your, etc heads together,*** consult together. ***turn sb's head,*** make them conceited. ***(be) weak in the head,*** (be) not very intelligent.

ˈhead·ache *n* [C,U] **(a)** continuous pain in the head: *have a bad ~ache.* **(b)** (*informal*) troublesome problem: *more ~aches for the Administration.*

ˈhead·dress *n* [C] (ornamental) covering for the head.

ˈhead·hunter *n* [C] **(a)** savage who cuts heads off and keeps them as trophies. **(b)** (*sl*) person or employment agency that seeks executives: *The company used a ~hunter to locate a new president.*

ˈhead·land *n* land projecting from the coastline. ⇨ head¹(14).

ˈhead·less *adj* having no head.

ˈhead·light *n* [C] large lamp on the front of a motor vehicle, etc.

ˈhead·line *n* newspaper heading.

ˈhead·man /-ˌmæn/ n [C] (*pl* ~men /-ˌmen/) chief man of a tribe, etc.

ˈhead-on *adj, adv* (of collisions) with the front

parts (of vehicles) meeting: *a ~-on collision.*
ˈ**head·phones** *n pl* receivers fitting over the head (for radio, etc).
ˈ**head·quarters** *n* (*sing* or *pl*) place from which (eg police, army) operations are controlled.
ˈ**head·rest** *n* [C] something that supports the head.
ˈ**head·room** *n* [U] = clearance(2).
ˈ**head·set** *n* [C] = headphones.
ˈ**head·stone** *n* [C] stone set up at the head of a grave.
ˈ**head·waters** *n pl* source of a stream or river.
ˈ**head·way** *n* [U] progress.
ˈ**head·wind** *n* [C] one that blows directly into one's face, or against the course of a ship, etc.
ˈ**head·word** *n* [C] word used as a heading, eg the first word of a dictionary entry.

head[2] /hed/ *vt,vi* **1** be at the head or top of: *~ a procession; Smith's name ~ed the list.* **2** ***head sth/sb off,*** get in front of, so as to turn back or aside: *~ off a flock of sheep* (to prevent them from going the wrong way). **3** move in the direction indicated: *~ south; ~ straight for home;* (*fig*) *be ~ing for disaster*.

-headed /hedɪd/ *adj* (used in compounds) having the type or number of heads mentioned: *three-ˈheaded.*

header /ˈhedər/ *n* [C] (only in:) **double/triple header** (*baseball, football*) two/three games played by the same teams on the same day.

head·first /ˌhedˈfərst/ *adv* headlong.

head·ing /ˈhedɪŋ/ *n* [C] word or words printed at the top of a section of written material (to show the subject of what follows).

head·long /ˈhedˌlɔŋ/ *adv, adj* **1** with the head first: *fall ~.* **2** thoughtless(ly) and hurried(ly): *rush ~ into a decision.*

heads·man /ˈhedzmən/ *n* [C] (*pl* -men /-men/) executioner who beheads people.

head·strong /ˈhedˌstrɔŋ/ *adj* self-willed; obstinate.

heady /ˈhedi/ *adj* (-ier, -iest) **1** acting, done, on impulse; headstrong. **2** (of alcoholic drink) tending to make one dizzy. **3** (*fig*) (eg of sudden success) having an exciting effect.

heal /hiəl/ *vt,vi* (*pres p* ~ing /ˈhilɪŋ/) **1** (esp of wounds) (cause to) become healthy and sound: *The wound soon ~ed up/over.* ⇨ also faith healing. **2** (*fig*) set right: *~ a quarrel*, end it.
healer /ˈhilər/ *n* [C] person or thing that heals: *Time is a great ~er.*

health /helθ/ *n* [U] **1** condition of the body or the mind: *in poor ~.* **2** (esp) state of being well and free from illness: *get one's ~ back*, recover.

healthy /helθi/ *adj* (-ier, -iest) **1** having good health; well, strong and able to resist disease: *The children look very ~.* (*Note: well* is the usual word in polite references, eg *I hope you're quite well*). **2** likely to produce good health: *a ~ climate.* **3** showing good health: *a ~ appetite.*
health·ily /-əli/ *adj*

heap /hip/ *n* [C] **1** number of things, mass of material, piled up: *a ~ of sand.* **2** (*informal*) large number; plenty: *We have ~s of books/time.* □ *vt* **1** put in a heap: *~ (up) stones.* **2** fill; load: *heap a plate with food; a ~ing teaspoon*, more than a level teaspoon.

hear /hɪr/ *vt,vi* (*pt,pp* ~d /hərd/) **1** become aware of (sound, etc) with the ears: *I ~d someone laughing.* **2** be told or informed: *Have you ~d the news? I've just ~d about his dismissal/illness.* ***hear from sb,*** receive a letter, news, etc: *How often do you ~ from your sister?* ***hear of sb/sth,*** have knowledge of: *I've never ~d of her/the place*, know nothing of her/the place. **3** listen to; pay attention to: *You'd better ~ what they have to say.* ***hear sb out,*** listen to the end: *Don't judge me before I've finished my explanation. Hear me out, please.* **4** (of a judge, committee, etc.) listen to (evidence, an argument, etc) in an official capacity.
hearer *n* [C] person who hears.

hear·ing /ˈhɪrɪŋ/ *n* **1** [U] becoming aware by sound: *Her ~ is poor*, she is rather deaf. ***hard of hearing,*** ⇨ hard[1](10). **2** [U] distance within which one can hear: *in the ~ of strangers*, where strangers may hear. ***within/out of hearing,*** near enough/not near enough to hear or be heard. **3** [C] chance to be heard (esp in self-defense). ***a fair hearing,*** an opportunity of being listened to impartially. **4** (legal) trial or an examination of witnesses, esp before a judge.
ˈ**hearing aid,** electronic device to improve hearing.

hearken /ˈharkən/ *vi* (constructed with *to*) (*liter*) listen.

hear·say /ˈhɪrˌsei/ *n* [U] rumor; what one has heard another person or other persons say: *I don't believe it; it's merely ~.*

hearse /hərs/ *n* [C] vehicle for carrying a coffin at a funeral.

heart /hart/ *n* [C] **1** that part of the body which pumps blood through the system: *When a man's ~ stops beating, he dies.* ⇨ illus at respiratory. **2** center of the emotions, esp love; deepest part of one's nature: *a man with a kind ~.* ***at heart,*** deep down; basically. ***from (the bottom of) one's heart,*** sincerely. ***to one's heart's content,*** as much as, for as long as, etc one wishes. ***with all one's heart,*** completely and willingly: *I love you with all my ~.* ***heart and soul,*** completely: *I'm yours ~ and soul.* ***break a person's heart,*** make him very sad. ***(learn/know sth) by heart,*** from memory. ***(have) a change of heart,*** change that makes one a better person. ***have a heart,*** have sympathy or consideration. ***have one's heart in one's mouth,*** be anxious, badly frightened. ***have one's heart in the right place,*** have true or kind feelings. ***have one's heart set on sth,*** desire it greatly. ***lose heart,*** be discouraged. ***set one's heart on sth/having sth/doing sth, etc,*** be bent on, very anxious (to have, to do, etc). ***take sth to heart,*** be much affected by it. **3** central part: *in the ~ of the forest.* ***the heart of the matter,*** the essence. **4** (of a vegetable, etc) the central part: *a lettuce ~.* **5** heart-shaped thing. **6** one of the thirteen playing cards with red heart shapes printed on it: *the ten/queen/etc of ~s.* ⇨ illus at card. **7** (as a term of endearment to a person): *ˈsweet~.*
ˈ**heart·ache** *n* [U] deep sorrow.
ˈ**heart·beat** *n* [C] movement of the heart (about 70 beats a minute).
ˈ**heart·break** *n* overwhelming sorrow.

ˈ**heart·break·ing** *adj* causing deep sorrow.
ˈ**heart·broken** *adj* overwhelmed by sorrow.
ˈ**heart·burn** *n* [U] burning sensation in the lower part of the chest, caused by indigestion.
ˈ**heart·felt** *adj* sincere: *~felt emotion/thanks.*
heart·less *adj* unkind; without pity.
heart·less·ly *adv*
-hearted /hartɪd/ *adj.* (used in compounds) having a heart(2) of a particular kind: *ˌkind-ˈhearted;ˌbroken-ˈhearted,* heart-broken.
hearten /ˈhartən/ *vt* give courage to; cheer: *~ing news.*
hearth /harθ/ *n* [C] **1** floor of a fireplace. **2** (*fig*) fireside as representing the home.
heart·ily /ˈhartəli/ *adv* **1** with goodwill, courage or appetite: *eat ~.* **2** very: *~ sick of this wet weather.*
heart·wood /ˈhartˌwʊd/ *n* [U] dark-colored wood in the center of a tree.
hearty /ˈharti/ *adj* (-ier, -iest) **1** (of feelings) sincere: *give her a ~ welcome.* **2** strong; in good health: *still hale and ~ at eighty-five.* **3** (of meals, appetites) big: *a ~ meal.*
heat[1] /hit/ *n* **1** [U] hotness: the opposite of cold: *the ~ of the sun's rays.* **2** [U] (*fig*) intense feeling: *in the ~ of the debate/argument.* **3** [C] single stage or a round in a competition the winners of which take part in (further competitions leading to) the finals: *trial/preliminary ~s.* ***dead heat,*** race that ends in a tie, without a winner. **4** [U] ***in heat,*** (of female mammals) ready for mating.
ˈ**heat·stroke** *n* [U] sudden illness, caused by excessive heat.
ˈ**heat wave,** unbroken period of unusually hot weather.
heat[2] /hit/ *vt,vi* **1** make or become hot: *~ (up) some water.* **2** (*fig*) become excited: *a ~ed discussion,* one during which feelings are roused.
heat·ed·ly *adv* in an excited manner.
heater *n* [C] device for supplying warmth to a room, or for heating water, etc: *an oil ~er.*
hea·then /ˈhiðən/ *n* **1** [C] (*pl* without *s* when used as a *collective pl*) believer in a religion other than the chief world religions: *The enslavement of Africans and Indians was originally justified on the grounds that they were ~s. Missionaries went abroad to save the ~.* **2** [C] person whose morals, etc are disapproved of: *a young ~,* wild, ill-mannered young person. □ *adj ~ cults/tribes.*
hea·then·ish /-ɪʃ/ *adj*
heather /ˈheðər/ *n* [U] shrub with small light-purple or white flowers.
heave /hiv/ *vt,vi* (*pt, pp* ~d or hove /hoʊv/) **1** raise, lift up (something heavy): *~ the anchor.* **2** utter with effort: *~ a sigh/groan.* **3** lift and throw: *~ a brick through a window.* **4** pull (*at* a rope, etc). **5** rise and fall regularly; move up and down. **6** (of a ship) move or turn in a certain direction or manner (*pt, pp* usually *hove* in this sense): *The ship hove into sight.* □ *n* [C] act of heaving: *with a mighty ~.*
heaven /ˈhevən/ *n* [C] **1** (in some religions) home of God and the saints: *die and go to ~.* **2** (usually *Heaven*) God, Providence: *Thank Heaven you were not killed.* **3** (as an exclamation): *Good Heavens!* **4** place, state, of supreme happiness. **5** (often *pl*) the sky. ***move heaven and earth,*** do one's utmost.
ˈ**heaven-sent** *adj* opportune, fortunate: *a ~-sent opportunity.*
ˈ**heaven·ward(s)** /-ˌwərd(z)/ *adj, adv* toward heaven.
heav·en·ly /ˈhevənli/ *adj* **1** of, from, like, heaven: *a ~ angel/vision.* **2** of more than earthly excellence. **3** (*informal*) very pleasing (esp taste, smell or sound): *What a ~ aroma!*
ˌ**heavenly ˈbody,** sun, moon, planet, etc.
heavy /ˈhevi/ *adj* (-ier, -iest) **1** having (esp great) weight; difficult to lift, carry or move: *It's too ~ for me to lift.* **2** of more than usual size, amount, force, etc: *~ rain/work; a ~ heart,* made sad; *a ~* smoker; *~ food,* rich, difficult to digest. **3** (of persons) slow in speech or thought; (of writing or painting) dull, tedious. **4** (of bodily states) inactive: *~ with sleep/wine.* □ *adv* heavily: *The crime lies ~ on his conscience.*
ˌ**heavy ˈgoing,** difficult or boring.
heav·ily /ˈhevəli/ *adv*
heavi·ness /ˈhevinɪs/ *n* [U]
ˌ**heavy·ˈhearted** *adj* sad.
ˈ**heavy·weight** *n* [C] boxer weighing 175 lbs (79.3 kg) or more.
He·braic /hɪˈbreɪɪk/ *adj* Hebrew.
He·brew /ˈhiˌbru/ *n* [C] **1** Jew (esp of Ancient Israel); Israelite. **2 (a)** (also **Ancient Hebrew**) language used by the ancient Hebrews (as in the Old Testament). **(b)** (also **Modern Hebrew**) language now spoken by the people of Israel. □ *adj* of the Hebrew language or people.
heck /hek/ *n* (*sl*) (used as a mild oath): *Oh! What the ~!*
heckle /ˈhekəl/ *vt* interrupt and ask questions, ie at a meeting: *~ the candidate.*
heck·ler /ˈheklər/ *n* [C]
hec·tare /ˈhekˌtær, -ˌtar/ *n* [C] metric measure of area, 10,000 square meters (= 2.471 acres).
hec·tic /ˈhektɪk/ *adj* **1** unnaturally red; feverish: *~ cheeks.* **2** full of excitement and without rest: *lead a ~ life.*
hecto- /ˈhektou-/ *prefix* hundred: *ˈ~gram,* 100 grams.
he'd /hid/ = he had; he would.
hedge /hedʒ/ *n* [C] **1** row of bushes, shrubs or tall plants, etc forming a boundary for a field, garden, etc. **2** (*fig*) means of protection or defense. □ *vt,vi* **1** put a hedge or (*fig*) barrier around: *~ a garden; ~ a person in/around with rules and regulations.* **2** avoid giving a definite answer to a question: *Answer "yes" or "no"—don't ~!*
ˈ**hedge·row** *n* row of bushes forming a hedge.
hedge·hog /ˈhedʒˌhɔg, -ˌhag/ *n* [C] insect-eating animal covered with spines.
heed /hid/ *vt* pay attention to: *~ a warning.* □ *n* [U] pay attention, notice: *pay no ~ to a warning.*
heed·ful *adj* giving heed: *be more ~ful of advice.*
heed·less *adj: ~less of danger.*
hee·haw /ˈhiˌhɔ/ *n* [U] **1** (*sing* only) ass's bray. **2** rude laugh.
heel[1] /hiəl/ *n* [C] **1(a)** back part of the human foot. ⇨ illus at leg. **(b)** part of a sock, stocking,

etc covering this. part of a shoe, boot, etc supporting this. ***at/(up)on sb's heel(s),*** close behind him: *Famine often follows on the ~s of war*. ***down at the heels,*** untidy and poor. ***head over heels,*** ⇨ head[1](20). ***come to heel,*** **(a)** (of a dog) come, walk, close behind its master. **(b)** (*fig*) submit to discipline and control. ***cool one's heels,*** (*sl*) stop, stay for a while: *He cooled his ~s in jail for a year*. ***take to one's heels,*** run away. **2** (*sl*) worthless person.

heel[2] /hiəl/ *vt, vi* (*pres p* ~ing /ˈhilɪŋ/) **1** put a heel on (esp a shoe, boot, etc). **2** (esp of a dog) follow at somebody's heels.

ˌwell-ˈheeled *adj* (*informal*) very rich.

heel[3] /hiəl/ *vi,vt* (*pres p* ~ing /ˈhilɪŋ/) ***heel over,*** (of a ship) lean over to one side.

hef·ty /ˈhefti/ *adj* (-ier, -iest) big, strong: *a ~ increase/farm worker*.

heifer /ˈhefər/ *n* [C] young cow that has not yet had a calf.

height /hait/ *n* [C] **1** measurement from bottom to top; distance to the top of something, esp from sea level: *the ~ of a mountain*. *What is your ~?* How tall are you? **2** high place: *on the mountain ~s*. **3** utmost degree: *the ~ of his ambition/of fashion*.

heighten /ˈhaitən/ *vt,vi* **1** make or become high(er). **2** make greater in degree: *~ a person's anger*.

hei·nous /ˈheinəs, ˈhi-/ *adj* (of crime) extremely bad; terrible.

hei·nous·ly *adv*

heir /er/ *n* [C] person who receives or has the legal right to receive a title, property, etc when the owner dies: *He is ~ to a large fortune*.

heir·ess /ˈerɪs/ *n* [C] female heir.

heir·loom /ˈerˌlum/ *n* [C] personal property handed down in a family for several generations.

heist /haist/ *vt* (*sl*) rob, □ *n* [C] act, instance of armed robbery.

held *pt,pp* of hold[2].

heli·cop·ter /ˈhelɪˌkaptər/ *n* [C] kind of aircraft with horizontal revolving blades (*rotors*).

he·lio·trope /ˈhiliəˌtroup/ *n* [C] plant with small, sweet-smelling purple flowers; color of these.

heli·port /ˈhelɪˌpɔrt/ *n* [C] airport for helicopters.

he·lium /ˈhiliəm/ *n* [U] light, colorless gas (symbol **He**) that does not burn, used to inflate balloons and airships.

hell /hel/ *n* [C] **1** (in some religions) place of punishment after death. **2** place, condition, of great suffering or misery: *suffer ~ on earth*. **3** (*informal*) (used in exclamations, to express anger, or to intensify a meaning): *What the ~ do you want? He ran like ~*, very fast. *I like him a ~ of a lot*. ***for the hell of it,*** for no particular reason.

hell·ish /-ɪʃ/ *adj* horrible.

he'll /hiəl/ = he will; he shall.

hello /heˈlou, hə-/ *int* used as a greeting.

helm /helm/ *n* [C] handle (also called *tiller*) or wheel for moving the rudder of a boat or ship. ***at the helm,*** in control.

helms·man /ˈhelmzmən/ (*pl* ~smen /-men/) man at the helm.

hel·met /ˈhelmət/ *n* [C] protective covering for the head as worn by soldiers, police, motorbike riders, etc.

hel·meted *adj* wearing, provided with, a helmet.

helot /ˈhelət/ *n* [C] **1** one of a class of slaves in ancient Sparta. **2** slave; serf.

help[1] /help/ *n* **1** [U] act of helping: *Thank you for your ~*. **2** (*sing* with *a* or *an*) person or thing that helps: *Your advice was a great ~*. **3** [U] remedy: *There's no ~ for it*. **4** [C] person(s) paid to give help: *hired ~*.

helper *n* [C] person who helps.

help·ful /-fəl/ *adj* giving help.

help·fully /-fəli/ *adv*

help·ful·ness /-fəlnɪs/ *n* [U]

help·ing *n* [C] (esp) portion of food served at a meal: *three ~ings of pie*.

help·less /-lɪs/ *adj* **(a)** not receiving help. **(b)** dependent on others: *a ~less invalid*.

help·less·ly *adv*

help[2] /help/ *vt,vi* **1** aid; give assistance or support to; make it easier for (a person) to do something or for (something) to happen: *I can't lift this box by myself, please ~ me. The money ~ed him to complete his education*. ***help out,*** give help (esp in a crisis). **2** serve with food, drink, etc: *Help yourself to the fruit*. **3** (with *can/cannot/can't*) avoid; refrain; prevent: *I can't ~*, can't avoid, *thinking he's still alive. She burst out crying; she couldn't ~ herself*, couldn't refrain from it. *It can't be ~ed*, is inevitable.

hel·ter-skel·ter /ˌheltər-ˈskeltər/ *adv* in disorderly haste.

hem[1] /hem/ *n* [C] border or edge of cloth, esp one on an article of clothing, when turned and sewn down. □ *vt* (-mm-) **1** make a hem on. **2** enclose; confine; surround: *hemmed in by the enemy*.

ˈhem·line *n* [C] (esp) lower edge of a skirt or dress.

hem[2] (also **h'm**) /hem, həm/ *int* used to indicate doubt, etc or to get attention.

hemi·sphere /ˈhemɪˌsfɪr/ *n* [C] **1** half a sphere. **2** half the earth.

the ˌEastern ˈhemisphere, Europe, Asia, Africa and Australia.

the ˌNorthern/ˌSouthern ˈhemisphere, north/south of the equator.

the ˌWestern ˈhemisphere, North and South America.

hem·lock /ˈhemˌlak/ *n* [C,U] **1** (plant which produces a) poison. **2** evergreen tree related to the pine.

he·mo·glo·bin /ˌhiməˈgloubən/ *n* [U] protein that gives color to the red corpuscles of the blood and acts in supplying oxygen to the bodily tissues.

he·mo·philia /ˌhiməˈfɪliə/ *n* [U] (usually hereditary) tendency of blood (from a wound, etc) not to clot, so that bleeding continues.

he·mo·phil·iac /ˌhiməˈfɪliˌæk/ *n* [C] person having hemophilia.

hem·or·rhage /ˈhem(ə)rɪdʒ/ *n* **1** [U] heavy bleeding. **2** [C] instance of this.

hem·or·rhoids /ˈheməˌrɔidz/ *n pl* mass of swollen veins, esp at or near the anus.

hemp /hemp/ *n* [U] **1** (kinds of) plant from which

coarse fibers are obtained for the manufacture of rope and cloth. **2** (also **Indian hemp**) narcotic from the flowering tops, seed and resin of such plants, eg hashish, marijuana.

hempen /ˈhempən/ *adj* made of, like, hemp: *a ~en rope*.

hem·stitch /ˈhemˌstɪtʃ/ *vt, n* [C] (ornament the hem of a dress, etc with a) decorative stitch made by pulling out some of the threads and tying the cross-threads in groups.

hen /hen/ *n* [C] **1** female of the common domestic fowl. ⇨ cock[1](1). **2** female (of the bird named): ˈ*guinea hen*, ˈ*peahen*.

ˈ**hen party,** (*informal*) party for women only. ⇨ stag party.

ˈ**hen·pecked** *adj* (of a man) ruled by a nagging wife.

hence /hens/ *adv* **1** from here; from now: *a week ~*, in a week's time. **2** for this reason.

ˌ**hence·ˈforth,** ˌ**hence·ˈforward** *adv* from this time on; in the future.

hench·man /ˈhentʃmən/ *n* [C] (*pl* -men /-men/) faithful supporter, esp one who obeys without question the orders of his leader.

henna /ˈhenə/ *n* [U] (plant producing) reddish-brown dye for coloring leather, the hair, etc.

hepa·titis /ˌhepəˈtaitɪs/ *n* [U] inflammation of the liver.

hep·ta·gon /ˈheptəˌgan/ *n* [C] flat figure with seven (esp equal) sides.

hep·tag·onal /hepˈtægənəl/ *adj* seven-sided.

her /hər; often ər when after another word in rapid speech/ *personal pron* (used as the object form of *she*): *Give her the book*. □ *adj* of, relating to, or belonging to her: *That's her hat, not yours*.

hers /hərz/ *possessive pron* belonging to her: *Is that his or hers?*

her·ald /ˈherəld/ *n* [C] **1** person (formerly) making public announcements for, and carrying messages from, a ruler. **2** person or thing foretelling the coming of a person or thing: *In New England the robin is a ~ of spring*. **3** official who keeps records of families that have coats of arms. □ *vt* announce.

he·ral·dic /heˈrældɪk/ *adj* of heralds or heraldry.

her·aldry /ˈherəldri/ *n* [U] branch of knowledge dealing with the coats of arms, descent, and history of old families.

herb /ərb/ *n* [C] **1** low-growing, soft-stemmed flowering plant. **2** plant of this kind whose leaves or seeds are used in medicine or for flavoring food, eg sage, mint.

herb·age /-ɪdʒ/ *n* [U] grass and other field plants.

herbal /-əl/ *adj n* of (esp) medicinal herbs; book describing useful herbs and herbal remedies.

herb·al·ist /-ɪst/ *n* [C] person who grows or sells herbs.

her·ba·ceous /hərˈbeiʃəs/ *adj* (of plants) having stems that are not woody: *a ~ border*, border with plants which grow and flower year after year.

her·bivor·ous /hərˈbɪvərəs/ *adj* (of animals) feeding on grass, etc. ⇨ carnivorous.

her·cu·lean /ˌhərkyəˈliən/ *adj* having, needing, great powers of body or mind: *a ~ task*.

herd /hərd/ *n* [C] number or company of animals, esp cattle, feeding or going about together: *a ~ of cattle/deer/elephants*. □ *vi,vt* **1** (cause to) gather (as) into a herd: *We were ~ed together like cattle*. **2** look after a herd.

herds·man /ˈhərdzmən/ *n* [C] (*pl* ~smen /-men/) keeper of a herd.

here /hɪr/ *adv* **1** in, at, to, towards, this point of place: *Come ~. I live ~. Here comes the bus! Here you are/it is! Do you live near ~?* **2** at this point (in a series of events, in a process, etc): *Here the speaker paused to take a drink*. ***Here goes!*** Now I'm going to make a start, have a go! **3** ***here and there,*** in various places. ***here, there and everywhere,*** in all parts; all round. ***neither here nor there,*** (*informal*) irrelevant. **4** (used to call attention): *My friend ~ was a witness of the accident. Look/See ~*, pay attention. **5** (when answering a roll call) present. **6** (used when drinking to a person's health, etc): *Here's to the bride and bridegroom!*

ˈ**here·abouts** *adv* near or about here.

here·ˈafter *adv, n* [U] (in the) future; the life to come.

ˈ**here·by** *adv* (*legal*) by reason of this.

ˌ**here·ˈin** *adv* (*legal*) in this.

here·ˈof *adv* (*legal*) of or about this.

here·ˈto *adv* (*legal*) to this document.

ˈ**here·to·fore** *adv* (*legal, archaic*) until now; formerly.

ˌ**here·ˈwith** *adv* with this.

he·red·itary /həˈredəˌteri/ *adj* passed on from parent to child, from one generation to following generations: *~ rulers/diseases*.

he·red·ity /həˈredəti/ *n* [U] **1** tendency to pass characteristics on to offspring, etc. **2** characteristics, etc so passed on.

here's /hɪrz/ = here is.

her·esy /ˈherəsi/ *n* [C,U] (*pl* -ies) belief or opinion contrary to what is generally accepted, esp in religion: *be guilty of ~*.

her·etic /ˈherətɪk/ *n* [C] person guilty of, supporting, heresy; person who holds an unorthodox opinion.

he·reti·cal /həˈretɪkəl/ *adj* of heresy or heretics: *~al beliefs*.

heri·tage /ˈherətɪdʒ/ *n* [C] something given or received by inheritance.

her·maph·ro·dite /hərˈmæfrəˌdait/ *n* [C] animal or other creature, eg an earthworm, which has both male and female sexual organs or characteristics.

her·metic /hərˈmetɪk/ *adj* completely airtight.

her·meti·cally /-kli/ *adv*: *~ally sealed*.

her·mit /ˈhərmɪt/ *n* [C] **1** person living in isolation from others. **2** molasses cookie.

her·mit·age /-ɪdʒ/ *n* [C] dwelling place of a hermit.

ˈ**hermit crab,** soft-shelled sea crab which lives in the shells of (dead) sea snails.

her·nia /ˈhərniə/ *n* [U] rupture, esp of part of the bowel through the muscle wall of the abdomen.

hero /ˈhɪrou, ˈhirou/ *n* [C] (*pl* ~es) **1** boy or man respected for bravery or noble qualities. **2** chief male character in a poem, story, play, etc.

ˈ**hero·ism** /ˈherouˌɪzəm, ˈhɪrou-/ *n* [U] quality of being a hero; courage.

he·roic /hɪˈrouɪk/ *adj* **1** of, like, fit for, a hero: ~ *deeds/tasks*. **2** of a size larger than life: *a statue on a ~ scale*. **3** (of poetry) dealing with heroes. **4** (of language) grand; attempting great things.
he·roi·cally /-kli/ *adv*
he·roics *n pl* excessively grand talk or sentiments.

her·oin /ˈherouɪn/ *n* [U] narcotic drug prepared from morphine.

her·oine /ˈherouɪn/ *n* [C] female hero.

heron /ˈherən/ *n* [C] long-legged wading bird living in marshy places.

her·ring /ˈherɪŋ/ *n* [C] (*pl* ~, ~s) seafish used as food (fresh, salted, or dried).
ˈher·ring·bone *n* zigzag pattern (esp in cloth) like the spine and bones of a herring.
ˌred ˈherring, ⇨ red(3).

hers ⇨ her.

her·self /hərˈself; often ərˈself when after another word in rapid speech/ *pron* **1** (*possessive pron* used as a *reflexive*): *She hurt ~. She ought to be ashamed of ~.* ***(all) by herself,*** **(a)** alone. **(b)** without help. **2** (used for emphasis): *She told me the news ~* (she, and no one else). **3** her normal or healthy self: *She's not quite ~ today*.

he's /hiz/ = he is; he has.

hesi·tant /ˈhezətənt/ *adj* tending to hesitate.
hesi·tant·ly *adv*
hes·i·tance /-əns/, **hes·i·tancy** /-ənsi/ *n* [U]

hesi·tate /ˈhezəˌteit/ *vi* show signs of uncertainty or unwillingness in speech or action: *He's still hesitating about joining*.
hesi·tat·ing·ly *adv*

hesi·ta·tion /ˌhezəˈteiʃən/ *n* **1** [U] state of hesitating. **2** [C] instance of this: *His doubts and ~s were tedious*.

het·ero·gen·eous /ˌhetərəˈdʒiniəs/ *adj* mixed; made up of different kinds: *the ~ population of the USA*, of many different races. ⇨ homogeneous.

het·ero·sex·ual /ˌhetərouˈsekʃuəl/ *adj* sexually attracted to/by the opposite sex.

het up /ˌhet ˈəp/ *adj* (*informal*) upset; excited: *She's all het up about the wedding*.

hew /(h)yu/ *vt,vi* (*pt* hewed, *pp* hewed or, esp when used as an *adjective,* hewn) **1** cut (by striking or chopping); aim cutting blows (*at, among*): *hew down a branch*. **2** shape by cutting or chopping: *hewn timber*. (*fig*) *hew out a career for oneself*.
hewer *n* [C] person who hews: *hewers of coal*.

hexa·gon /ˈheksəˌgan/ *n* [C] flat figure with six (esp equal) sides.
hex·ag·onal /heksˈægənəl/ *adj* six-sided.

hey /hei/ *int* used to call attention, to express surprise, etc.

hey·day /ˈheiˌdei/ *n* (*sing* only) time of greatest prosperity or power: *in the ~ of the steam engine*.

hf[1] *abbr* = half.

hf[2] *abbr* = high frequency.

hgt. *abbr* = height.

hgwy *abbr* = highway.

HI[1] *postal abbr* = Hawaii. ⇨ App 6.

hi[2] /hai/ *int* (*informal*) (used esp as a greeting): *Hi, Tom!*

hi·atus /haiˈeitəs/ *n* [C] (*pl* ~es) gap in space or time, or in a series, where a part is missing.

hi·ber·nate /ˈhaibərˌneit/ *vi* (of some animals) pass the whole of the winter in a state like sleep.
hi·ber·na·tion /ˌhaibərˈneiʃən/ *n* [U]

Hi·ber·nian /ˌhaiˈbərniən/ *adj* (*liter*) of Ireland; Irish.

hi·bis·cus /haiˈbɪskəs/ *n* [C,U] (usually tropical) plant or shrub with brightly colored flowers. ⇨ illus at flower.

hic·cup, hic·cough /ˈhɪˌkəp/ *n* [C] sudden stopping of the breath with a cough-like sound. □ *vi* (-p; -pp-) make a hiccup.

hick /hɪk/ *n* [C] (*sl*) unsophisticated rural person.

hick·ory /ˈhɪkəri/ *n* [C,U] (*pl* -ies) (hard wood of a) North American tree with edible nuts.

hid, hidden *pt, pp* of hide[1].

hide[1] /haid/ *vt,vi* (*pt* hid /hɪd/, *pp* hidden /ˈhɪdən/ or hid) **1** put or keep out of sight; prevent from being seen, found or known: *Quick, ~!/~ yourself! The sun was hidden by the clouds*. **2** be or become hidden: *Where is he hiding?*
ˈhide·out/·away *n* [C] hiding place: *a guerrilla ~ out in the mountains*.
hid·ing *n* ***be in/go into hiding,*** be hidden/hide oneself. ***come out of hiding,*** show oneself.
ˈhiding place, place where a person or thing is or could be hidden.

hide[2] /haid/ *n* **1** [C] animal's skin. **2** (*informal*) human skin. □ *vt* give a beating to.
hid·ing *n* [C] beating: *give/get a good hiding*.

hide·bound /ˈhaidˌbaund/ *adj* having, showing, too much respect for rules and traditions.

hid·eous /ˈhɪdiəs/ *adj* very ugly; horrible: *a ~ crime/sight*.
hid·eous·ly *adv*

hi·er·archy /ˈhaiərˌarki/ *n* [C] (*pl* -ies) organization with grades of authority from lowest to highest.

hi·ero·glyph /ˈhai(ə)rəˌglɪf/ *n* [C] **1** picture or figure of an object, representing a word, syllable or sound, as used in the writing of the ancient Egyptians and Mexicans. **2** (*fig*) any secret or illegible written symbol.
hi·ero·glyphic /ˌhai(ə)rəˈglɪfɪk/ *adj* of hieroglyphs. □ *n* [C] = hieroglyph.

hi-fi /ˌhai-ˈfai/ *n* **1** [U] = high fidelity. **2** [C] equipment for reproducing sound with high fidelity.

hig·gledy-pig·gledy /ˌhɪgəldi-ˈpɪgəldi/ *adj, adv* mixed up; in confusion.

high[1] /hai/ *adj* (-er, -est) **1** extending far upwards; measuring (the distance given) from the base to the top: *There was an airplane ~ in the sky. How ~ is Mt. Everest?* (*Note: tall* is used for human beings and for a few things which have great height in relation to breadth, eg a tall building/tower.) ***high and dry,*** stranded; abandoned. **2** chief; important: *a ~ official; the ~ altar*, in a church. **3** (of sounds) at or near the top of the scale; shrill; sharp: *speak in a ~ tone/key*. **4** extreme; intense; great: *~ prices/temperatures; have a ~ opinion of her; in ~ spirits; have a ~* (= joyous) *time; ~* (= luxurious) *living; ~ noon/summer*, at or near its peak. **5** noble; virtuous: *~ aims/ideals; a ~ calling*, eg that of a priest, doctor or nurse. **6** (*informal*) intoxicated; under the influence of alcohol or hallucinatory drugs.

ˈ**high·ball** *n* mixed (alcoholic) drink, esp when served in a tall glass.
ˈ**high·born** *adj* of noble birth.
ˈ**high·brow** *n* [C], *adj* (person) with intellectual tastes and interests considered to be superior.
ˈ**high chair,** one on high legs for an infant.
ˌ**high-ˈclass** *adj* first-class.
ˌ**High ˈCourt,** supreme court of justice.
ˌ**high fiˈdelity** *n* [U] faithful reproduction of sound by the use of a wide range of sound waves.
ˌ**high-ˈflown** *adj* pompous; pretentious.
ˌ**high ˈfrequency** *n* (*abbr* **hf**) radio frequency between 3 and 30 megacycles per second.
ˈ**high-grade** *adj* of superior quality.
ˌ**high-ˈhanded** *adj* using power or authority without consideration for the feelings of others.
ˈ**high-hat(ter)** *n* (*sl*) snob.
ˈ**high·jack** *vt* = hijack.
ˈ**high jump,** athletic contest for jumping over an adjustable horizontal bar.
high·land /ˈhailənd/ *n* mountainous region; (*pl*) mountainous parts of a country.
ˈ**high life,** fashionable and luxurious style of living.
ˈ**high·light** *n* **(a)** (usually *pl*) luminous area on a photograph, picture, etc which shows reflected light; reflection or contrast of light, color. **(b)** (*fig*) most conspicuous or prominent part: *the ~lights of the week's events.* □ *vt* give prominence or emphasis to.
ˌ**high-ˈminded** *adj* having high morals, ideals or principles.
ˌ**high-ˈpowered** *adj* **(a)** having, using, great power: *a ~-powered engine.* **(b)** (of optical instruments) giving great magnitude. **(c)** (of persons) important; energetic.
ˌ**high ˈpriest,** chief priest.
ˈ**high-rise** *adj* of tall buildings with many stories or levels. *~-rise apartment buildings.*
ˈ**high school,** secondary school including from the 9th or 10th to the 12th grades.
ˌ**high ˈseas,** (with *the*) all parts of the seas and oceans beyond territorial waters.
ˈ**high sign,** (esp secret) signal or gesture.
ˌ**high soˈciety,** upper classes.
ˈ**high-sounding** *adj* (of style) pretentious.
ˌ**high-ˈspirited** *adj* bold; lively.
ˈ**high spot,** outstanding feature, memory, event, etc.
ˌ**high-ˈstrung** *adj* very nervous and sensitive.
ˌ**high ˈtide,** (time of) tide at its highest level.
ˈ**high time,** time when something should be done at once: *It's ~ time you started,* You should start at once.
ˌ**high ˈtreason,** ⇨ treason.
ˌ**high ˈwater,** = high tide.
ˈ**high·way** *n* [C] main public road; main route (by air, sea or land).
ˈ**high·way·man** /-mən/ (*pl* ~waymen /-men/) (formerly) man who robbed travelers on highways by using or threatening, violence.

high[2] /hai/ *adv* in or to a high degree: *climb ~.* ***hold one's head high,*** proudly. ***run high,*** **(a)** (of the sea) have a strong current with a high tide. **(b)** (of the feelings) be very excited. ***high and low*** everywhere: *looked for the book ~ and low.*

high[3] /hai/ *n* **1** high level: *from* (*on*) *~,* from Heaven; *reach a new ~,* highest known level. **2** (*informal*) state of intoxication by alcohol or hallucinatory drugs.

high·ly /ˈhaili/ *adv* in or to a high degree: *a ~ paid official; a ~ amusing film.* ***think highly of sb,*** have a high opinion of him.

high·ness /ˈhainıs/ *n* **1** [U] (opposite of *lowness*) state or quality of being high. **2** [C] used as a title for kings, princes, etc: *His*/*Her*/*Your*/(*Royal*) *Highness.*

high·tail /ˈhaiˌteiəl/ *vi* (-ing /-ˌteilıŋ/) ***hightail it,*** (*sl*) leave in haste: *He ~ed it out of town.*

hi·jack, high·jack /ˈhaiˌdʒæk/ *vt* **1** steal goods from, eg a truck, by stopping it in transit. **2** force those in control of an aircraft or vehicle to go where one wishes.
hi·jacker *n* [C]

hike /haik/ *vi, n* [C] **1** (go for a) long walk in the country, taken for pleasure or exercise. ⇨ hitchhike. **2** (*informal*) increase; raise; rise: *a wage-~/a ~in wages.*
hiker *n* [C] person who hikes.

hi·lari·ous /hıˈlæriəs/ *adj* marked by or causing noisy merriment.
hi·lari·ous·ly *adv*
hi·lar·ity /hıˈlærəti/ *n* [U] cheerfulness; loud laughter.

hill /hıl/ *n* [C] **1** mass of high land, lower than a mountain. **2** slope, eg on a road: *drive up a steep ~.* ***(be) over the hill.*** (*fig*) beyond the more difficult stages in a task or experience. **3** heap of earth: *ˈant~s.*
ˈ**hill·side** *n* side, slope, of a hill.
hilly *adj* (-ier, -iest) having many hills.

hill·bil·ly /ˈhılˌbıli/ *n* [C] (*pl* -ies) person from a remote, mountainous area,

hill·ock /ˈhılək/ *n* [C] small hill(1).

hilt /hılt/ *n* [C] handle of a sword or dagger. ***(up) to the hilt,*** completely: *His guilt was proved to the ~.*

him (usually **Him** when referring to God) /hım; often ım when after another word in rapid speech/ *personal pron* (used as the object form of *he*): *Give ~ the money.*

him·self (usually **Himself** when referring to God) /hımˈself; often ımˈself when after another word in rapid speech/ *pron* **1** (used as a *reflexive*): *He cut ~. He ought to be ashamed of ~.* ***(all) by himself,*** **(a)** alone. **(b)** without help. **2** (used for emphasis): *Did you see the manager ~?* **3** his normal or healthy self: *He's not quite ~ today.*

hind[1] /haind/ *adj* located at the back: *the ~ legs of a horse.* ⇨ fore-.
ˈ**hind·most** *adj* farthest behind or back.
ˈ**hind·ˌquarters** *n pl* back part of the halved carcass of lamb, beef, etc.
ˈ**hind·sight** *n* [U] looking back and becoming aware of the true meaning, etc of an event after its occurrence.

hind[2] /haind/ *n* [C] **1** female of (esp the red) deer. **2** (kinds of) ocean fish.

hind·er /ˈhındər/ *vt* obstruct; get in the way of: *Don't ~ me in my work.*

Hindi /ˈhındi/ *n, adj* (one of the official languages) of Northern India.

hin·drance /ˈhɪndrəns/ *n* [C] person or thing that hinders: *You are more of a ~ than a help.*

Hindu /ˈhɪndu/ *n* [C] person, esp of Northern India, whose religion is Hinduism. □ *adj* of the Hindus.

Hin·du·ism /-ˌɪzəm/ *n* [U] religion involving the worship of many gods, a belief in reincarnation, and a divinely ordained caste system.

hinge /hɪndʒ/ *n* [C] **1** joint on which a lid, door or gate turns or swings. **2** (*fig*) central principle on which something depends. □ *vt,vi* **1** support, attach with, a hinge or hinges. **2** ***hinge on/upon,*** depend on.

hint /hɪnt/ *n* [C] slight or indirect indication or suggestion: *He didn't say anything, but his expression gave me a ~.* □ *vt,vi* **1** suggest; give a hint: *I ~ed that he ought to work harder.* **2** refer indirectly to: *He ~ed at my indiscretion.*

hin·ter·land /ˈhɪntərˌlænd/ *n* [C] **1** area that is remote from cities and towns. **2** area inland from the coast.

hip[1] /hɪp/ *n* [C] part below the waist on either side of the body, where the bone of a person's leg is joined to the trunk: *He stood there with his hands on his hips.* ⇨ illus at trunk.

ˈhip flask, small flask (for brandy, etc).

hip[2] /hɪp/ *n* [C] (also **rose hip**) fruit (red when ripe) of the wild rose.

hip[3] /hɪp/ *adj* (-pper, -ppest) (*sl*) informed, aware of new ideas and developments.

hippie, hippy /ˈhɪpi/ *n* [C] (*pl* -ies) usually young person who behaves, dresses, etc in an unconventional way.

hip·po·pota·mus /ˌhɪpəˈpatəməs/ *n* [C] (*pl* ~es or -mi /-ˌmai/) large, thick-skinned African river animal.

hire /ˈhaiər/ *vt* obtain or allow the use or services of in return for fixed payment: *~ a horse/car.* □ *n* [U] (money paid for) hiring: *bicycles for ~, two dollars an hour.*

his (usually **His** when referring to God) /hɪz; often ɪz when after another word in rapid speech/ *adj, possessive pron* of, relating to, or belonging to him: *He hurt his hand. Are you a friend of his? That desk is his.*

hiss /hɪs/ *vi,vt* **1** make a sound like /s/, eg the noise heard when water falls on a very hot surface: *The steam escaped with a ~ing sound.* **2** show disapproval by making a prolonged /s/ sound: *~ (at) an actor.* □ *n* [C] hissing sound: *The speaker ignored the ~es.*

his·tor·ian /hɪˈstɔriən/ *n* [C] writer, student of, expert in, history.

his·toric /hɪˈstɔrɪk/ *adj* notable or memorable in history; associated with past times: *a ~ event.*

his·tori·cal /hɪˈstɔrɪkəl/ *adj* **1** belonging to history (as contrasted with legend and fiction): *a ~ novel/play/film, etc,* one dealing with real events in history. **2** having to do with history: *~ studies.*

his·tori·cally /-kli/ *adv*

his·tory /ˈhɪst(ə)ri/ *n* (*pl* -ies) **1** [U] branch of knowledge dealing with past events. ***make history,*** do something which will be recorded in history **2** [C] description of past events (of a country, etc): *a new ~ of Europe.* **3** [C] events connected with a person or thing: *a house with a strange ~.*

ˌancient ˈhistory, (a) to AD 476, when the Western Roman Empire was destroyed. **(b)** (*fig*) a matter of no further interest or importance.

ˌmedieval ˈhistory, to 1453, when Constantinople was taken by the Turks.

ˌmodern ˈhistory, since 1453.

ˌnatural ˈhistory, science, study, of all objects in nature.

his·tri·onic /ˌhɪstriˈanɪk/ *adj* **1** of drama, the theater or acting. **2** artificial; theatrical.

his·tri·on·ics *n pl* **1** (*formal*) theatrical performances. **2** exaggerated manners, behavior, etc, to create an effect.

hit /hɪt/ *vt,vi* (-tt-; *pt,pp* hit) **1** give a blow or stroke to (something) with force: *hit a man on the head; be hit by a falling stone.* ***hit the nail on the head,*** guess, say or do exactly the right thing. ***hit it off (with sb),*** get on well. **2** strike a target or something aimed at. **3** ***hit sb hard,*** cause him to suffer: *He was hard hit/hit hard by his financial losses.* **4** get to; find; reach: *~ a bumpy stretch of the road.* **5** ***hit on/upon,*** find by chance or unexpectedly: *~ on an idea.* **6** (*baseball*) *score by striking the ball with a bat: hit 3 home runs.* □ *n* [C] **1** blow; stroke: *three hits and five misses.* **2** successful attempt or performance: *The new play is quite a hit.* **3** (*baseball*) struck ball that permits a batter to get to at least first base safely.

hitch /hɪtʃ/ *vt,vi* **1** pull up with a quick movement: *~ up one's trousers.* **2** fasten, become fastened, on or to a hook, etc: *~ a horse to a fence.* ***hitch a ride*** (*informal*) = hitchhike. □ *n* [C] **1** sudden pull or push. **2** kind of noose or knot used for a temporary fastening. **3** temporary stoppage or difficulty: *a technical ~.* ***go off without a hitch,*** without difficulty.

hitch·hike /ˈhɪtʃˌhaik/ *vi* get a free ride by asking for one (from the driver of a car, truck, etc).

hitch·hiker *n* [C]

hither /ˈhɪðər/ *adv* (*old use*) (to) here.

ˌhither·ˈto *adv* until now.

hive /haiv/ *n* [C] **1 (a)** container or place for bees to live in. **(b)** the bees living in a hive. **2** (*fig*) place full of busy people: *What a ~ of industry!* □ *vt,vi* **1** cause (bees) to go into a hive. **2** (of bees) store (honey) in a hive. **3** live close together as bees do.

hives /haivz/ *n pl* itching rash on the skin caused by an allergy.

ho /hou, hə/ *int* used to express surprise, admiration, etc.

hoard /ˈhɔrd/ *n* [C] carefully saved and guarded store or collection of money, coins, food or other treasured or valuable things. □ *vt,vi* save and store: *~ (up) gold.*

hoarder *n* [C] person who hoards.

hoar·frost /ˈhɔr ˌfrɔst/ *n* [U] white frost; frozen dew on grass, leaves, etc.

hoarse /hɔrs/ *adj* (-r, -st) **1** (of the voice) rough and harsh. **2** (of a person) having a hoarse voice: *He shouted himself ~.*

hoarse·ly *adv*

hoarse·ness /-nɪs/ *n* [U]

hoary /ˈhɔri/ *adj* (-ier, -iest) gray or white, esp

with age.
hoari·ness /-nɪs/ *n* [U]
hoax /houks/ *n* [C] mischievous or humorous trick. □ *vt* deceive in this way.
hoaxer *n* [C]
hob /hab/ *n* [C] flat metal shelf at the side of a fireplace where pots and pans can be kept warm or a kettle boiled.
hobble /ˈhabəl/ *vi,vt* **1** walk as when lame, limp: *The old man ~d along with the aid of his stick.* **2** tie two legs of a horse or donkey to prevent it from going far away. □ *n* [C] stumbling or limping way of walking.
hobby /ˈhabi/ *n* [C] (*pl* -ies) occupation, not one's regular business, for one's leisure time, eg stamp collecting.
hobby·ist /ˈhabiɪst/ *n* [C]
hobby·horse /ˈhabiˌhɔrs/ *n* [C] **1** wooden horse on rockers as a child's toy. **2** long stick with a horse's head.
hob·gob·lin /ˈhabˌgablɪn/ *n* [C] mischievous imp; ugly and evil spirit.
hob·nail /ˈhabˌneiəl/ *n* [C] short nail with a heavy head used for the soles of heavy shoes and boots, eg for mountain-climbing.
hob·nailed *adj*
hob·nob /ˈhabˌnab/ *vi* (-bb-) associate in a friendly way: *Mrs. Green, happily ~bing with the boss.*
ho·bo /ˈhouˌbou/ *n* [C] (*pl* ~s, ~es) tramp.
hock[1] /hak/ *n* [C] middle joint of an animal's hind leg.
hock[2] /hak/ *vt* (*informal*) pawn. □ *n* ***in hock,*** pawned.
ˈhock shop, pawn shop.
hockey /ˈhaki/ *n* [U] **ˈfield hockey,** game played with sticks and a rubber ball on a field by two teams of players. **ˈice hockey,** similar game played on ice by two teams of skaters, using sticks and a rubber disc (a *puck*).
ˈhockey stick, long curved or angled stick used to hit the ball or puck.
ho·cus-po·cus /ˌhoukəs-ˈpoukəs/ *n* [U] meaningless or nonsensical talk, used to confuse or deceive.
hod /had/ *n* [C] box with a long handle used by workmen for carrying bricks, etc on the shoulder.
hodge·podge /ˈhadʒˌpadʒ/ *n* [U] jumbled mixture.
hoe /hou/ *n* [C] implement with a flat blade, used for loosening soil, etc. □ *vt,vi* (*pt,pp* hoed) work with a hoe: *hoeing up weeds.*
hoe·down /ˈhouˌdaun/ *n* [C] lively rural dance or party.
hog /hɔg, hag/ *n* [C] **1** (esp castrated male) pig reared for meat. **2** (*fig*) greedy, dirty, selfish person. ***go (the) whole hog,*** do something thoroughly. □ *vt* take or keep greedily and selfishly.
hog·gish /-ɪʃ/ *adj* greedy and selfish.
ˈhog-tie *vt* **(a)** tie the legs of an animal together to keep it from moving. **(b)** (*fig*) keep someone from doing something.
ˈhog·wash *n* (*informal*) nonsense.
ho·gan /ˈhougən/ *n* [C] dwelling of logs and earth, as built by the Navajo Indians.

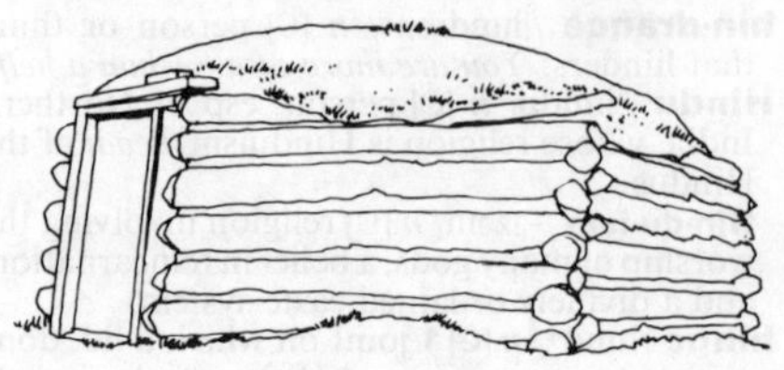

HOGAN

hogs·head /ˈhɔgzˌhed, ˈhagz-/ *n* [C] **1** large barrel. **2** liquid measure (= 62 US gallons or about 234.5 liters).
hoist /hɔist/ *vt* lift with an apparatus of ropes and pulleys or a kind of elevator: *~ a flag/sail; ~ crates aboard.* □ *n* [C] **1** apparatus for hoisting. **2** (*informal*) push up: *give him a ~,* eg when he is climbing a wall.
hoity-toity /ˌhɔiti-ˈtɔiti/ *adj* (*informal*) snobbish and haughty.
hold[1] /hould/ *n* **1** [C,U] act, manner, power of holding: *Take ~ of the wheel,* grasp it. *Be sure to get a firm ~* (= grip) *on the branch before climbing further. He has a great ~* (= influence) *over his younger brother.* **2** [C] something that may be used for holding on to: *The rock face provides few ~s to climbers.* ⇨ foothold. **3** (in wrestling) (kinds of) grip: *wrestling, with no ~s barred.*
hold[2] /hould/ *vt,vi* (*pt,pp* held /held/) **1** have or keep in one's possession, keep fast or steady, in or with the hand(s), arm(s) or other part of the body, eg the teeth, or with a tool: *The girl was ~ing her father's hand. He held the knife in his teeth as he climbed the tree.* ***hold the line,*** keep a telephone connection (eg while the person at the other end goes away temporarily). **2** restrain; keep back; control: *The police held back the crowd.* ***hold one's breath,*** eg from excitement or fear: *The watchers held their breath as the acrobat crossed the tightrope.* ***hold one's tongue/peace,*** be quiet. **3** keep or maintain in a specified position, manner, attitude or relationship: *Hold your head up.* **4** maintain a grip of: *This new car ~s the road well,* is stable, eg when turning a corner. **5** support; bear the weight of: *Come down—that branch won't ~ you!* **6** be filled by; have the capacity to contain or accommodate: *Will this suitcase ~ all your clothes? What does the future ~ for us?* ***(not) hold water,*** (not) be sensible, valid, logical: *Your argument doesn't ~ water.* **7** keep the interest or attention of: *The speaker held his audience spellbound.* **8** consider; regard; believe; affirm: *He does not ~ himself responsible for his wife's debts.* **9** defend; keep possession of: *They held the city against all attacks.* ***hold the fort,*** (*fig*) be in charge during a person's absence. ***hold one's ground/own,*** not give way: *The patient is still ~ing his own,* maintaining his strength. *Our soldiers held their ground bravely.* **10** possess; own: *~ shares/stock.* **11** occupy;

have the position of: *The Democrats held office then.* **12** have; conduct; cause to take place: *~ a meeting. We ~ a presidential election every four years.* **13** remain unbroken, unchanged, etc; persist: *How long will this fine weather ~*, continue? **14** (special uses with *adverbial particles* and *prepositions*):
hold sth against sb, allow something to influence one's opinions unfavorably: *Don't ~ his criminal convictions against him.*
hold back, hesitate; show unwillingness: *Buyers are ~ing back*, making few or no offers.
hold sb/sth back, **(a)** ⇨ 2 above. **(b)** hinder the progress of: *His poor education is ~ing him back.* ***hold sth back,*** keep secret or to oneself: *~ back information.*
hold sb/sth down, **(a)** keep or maintain in a low position. **(b)** keep down or under: *We must ~* (= keep) *prices down.* ***hold a job down,*** (*informal*) have and keep it.
hold forth, speak at length.
hold in, check, restrain; control one's feelings.
hold off, **(a)** remain at a distance: *The storm held off.* **(b)** keep from: *Hold off firing for a minute.*
hold on, **(a)** stand firm when there is danger, difficulty, etc: *How much longer do they think we can ~ on?* **(b)** (usually imperative) stop: *Hold on a minute!* Don't go further in what you're doing. ***hold on to,*** **(a)** keep one's grip on; not let go: *~ on to one's hat on a windy day.* **(b)** not give up the ownership of: *You should ~ on to your oil shares.* ***hold sth on,*** keep in position: *These bolts and nuts ~ the wheels on.*
hold out, **(a)** not give way: *How long can we ~ out against these attacks?* **(b)** last: *How long will our food supplies ~ out?* ***hold out for,*** refuse compromise: *The workers are still ~ing out for higher wages.* ***hold out on,*** **(a)** keep back; refuse to give: *He's ~ing out on us,* won't tell us what he knows. **(b)** refuse to deal with: *The baseball players continued to ~ out on the team owner and refused to sign the new contract.*
hold sth over, defer; postpone: *The matter was held over until the next meeting.*
hold to sth, **(a)** remain loyal or steadfast to: *He held to his convictions.* **(b)** keep to: *The ship held to a southerly course.* ***hold sb to sth,*** make him keep, eg a promise: *We must ~ the contractors to their estimates*, not allow them to exceed them.
hold together, **(a)** be and continue whole: *an old car that hardly ~s together*, is falling apart. **(b)** remain united: *~ together in times of crisis.*
hold sb/sth together, cause to remain together: *a leader who will ~ the nation together.*
hold sb/sth up, **(a)** ⇨ 1,2 above. **(b)** delay: *They were held up by fog.* **(c)** stop by the use or threat of force, for the purpose of robbery: *The travelers were held up by bandits.* **(d)** put forward as an example: *Don't ~ me up as a model husband.*
hold with sth, approve of: *Do you ~ with free enterprise?*

hold³ /hould/ *n* [C] part of a ship or airplane where cargo is carried.

holder /ˈhouldər/ *n* [C] person or thing that holds: *a ˈcigarette ~; the ~ of the contract.*

hold·ing /ˈhouldɪŋ/ *n* [C] land or property held or owned.

hold·up /ˈhoulˌdəp/ *n* [C] **1** delay. **2** robbery at the point of a gun.

hole /houl/ *n* [C] **1** opening or hollow place in or through a solid body: *a ~ in a tooth; roads full of ~s.* ***pick holes in,*** find fault with, eg an argument. ***a square peg in a round hole,*** person not fitted for the position he occupies. **2** (*informal*) awkward situation: *I'm in something of/kind of a ~.* **3** animal's burrow: *a mouse's ~.* **4** (*fig*) small, dark, wretched place: *What a wretched little ~ he lives in!* **5** (*golf*) hollow into which the ball must be hit: *the first ~.* □ *vt,vi* **1** make a hole in or through: *~ a ship*, eg by striking a rock. **2** hit (a golf ball) into a hole.

holi·day /ˈhaləˌdei/ *n* [C] day of rest from work: *Sunday is a ~ in Christian countries.* ⇨ bank holiday.

holi·ness /ˈhoulinɪs/ *n* **1** [U] being holy or sacred. **2 His/Your Holiness,** title used of or to the Pope.

hol·ler¹ /ˈhalər/ *vi,vt* (*informal*) yell: *Stop ~ing!*

hol·ler² /ˈhalər/ *n* [C] = hollow *n* (2).

hol·low /ˈhalou/ *adj* **1** not solid; with a hole or empty space inside: *a ~ tree.* **2** (of sounds) as if coming from something hollow: *a ~ groan.* **3** (*fig*) unreal; false; insincere: *a ~ laugh; a ~ victory*, one without real value. **4** sunken: *~ cheeks.* □ *n* [C] **1** hole: *a ~ in the ground.* **2** small valley: *a wooded ~.* □ *vt* make a hollow in: *river banks ~ed out by rushing water.*

holly /ˈhali/ *n* [U] evergreen shrub with shiny, spiny leaves and, in winter, red berries.

holly·hock /ˈhaliˌhak/ *n* [C] plant with tall stiff stems bearing clusters of large showy flowers.

holo·caust /ˈhaləˌkɔst/ *n* [C] large-scale destruction, esp of human lives: *a nuclear ~; the Holocaust,* (new usage) the destruction of European Jewish society by the Nazis.

hol·ster /ˈhoulstər/ *n* [C] leather case for a gun. ⇨ illus at police.

holy /ˈhouli/ *adj* (-ier, -iest) **1** of God; associated with God or with religion: *the Holy Bible; the Holy Land*, where Jesus lived; the *Holy City*, Jerusalem; *ˈHoly Week*, the week before Easter Sunday; *Holy Communion; the Holy Father*, the Pope. ***Holy Cats/Cow/Moses!*** *int* (*informal*) expression of surprise. **2** devoted to religion: *live a ~ life.* □ *n* **the ˌHoly of ˈHolies, (a)** most sacred and innermost chamber in a Jewish temple. **(b)** (*fig*) any sacred place.

hom·age /ˈ(h)amɪdʒ/ *n* [U] expression of respect. ***do/pay homage (to sb)***: *Many came to do the dead man ~.*

home¹ /houm/ *adv* **1** at, in or to one's home or country: *Is he ~ yet?* **2** to the point aimed at; so as to be in the right place: *drive a nail ~*, strike it so that it is completely in. ***drive a point/an argument home,*** cause its full force to be understood.

home² /houm/ *n* [C] **1** place where one lives or has lived, esp with one's family: *He left ~ at the age of 16.* ***at home,*** **(a)** in the house: *I've left my* *books at* ~. **(b)** (*sport*) in the town, etc to which the team belongs: *Is our next game at ~ or away?* **(c)** ready to receive visitors: *Mrs. Hill is not at ~ to anyone except relatives.* ***make oneself/be/feel at home,*** as if in one's own house; at one's ease: *The boy did not feel at ~ in such a splendid house.* ***nothing to write home about,*** (*informal*) nothing remarkable. **2** institution or place (for the care of children, old or sick people, etc): *a 'nursing ~.* **3** (often as an *adjective*) family or domestic life: *the pleasures of ~; ~ life.* **4** place where an animal or plant is native or most common: *the ~ of the tiger and the elephant*, eg the jungle. **5** (*sport, games*) goal; place where a player is safe and cannot be caught, etc. ⇨ illus at baseball. **6** (as an *adjective*) of one's own country (= *domestic,* contrasted with *foreign*): *~ industries.*

home 'base, (a) = home(5). **(b)** permanent home or central office from which one travels on business or pleasure trips.

'home·coming *n* arrival at home.

the 'home front, the civilians (in a country at war).

ˌhome-'grown *adj* (of food, etc) produced in the country (contrasted with what is imported).

'home·land *n* native land; country from which one's ancestors came.

home·less *adj* having no home.

home·like *adj* like home: *a hotel with a ~like atmosphere.*

ˌhome-'made *adj* made at home (not bought in a store).

'home·room *n* (class)room to which assigned pupils report at the opening of each school day for roll call, etc.

ˌhome 'rule, government of a city, country, etc by its own citizens.

'home·sick *adj* sad because away from home.

'home·sick·ness /-nɪs/ *n* [U]

'home·spun *n, adj* (clothes made of) hand-woven cloth.

'home·stead *n* (esp) farmhouse with the land and outbuildings round it.

home 'town, city or town of one's birth or where one has lived a long time.

ˌhome 'truth *n* unpleasant one which is obvious.

home·ward /-ˌwərd/ *adv* going toward home.

'home·work *n* [U] work which a pupil is required to do at home.

home[3] /houm/ *vi* go, return, straight home, esp from a distance.

home 'in ˌon, move selectively and directly toward: *The missile ~d in on its target.*

'hom·ing pigeon, one trained to fly home from a great distance.

home·ly /'houmli/ *adj* (-ier, -iest) **1** simple and plain; of the sort used every day. **2** not beautiful or handsome: *a ~ child.*

home·li·ness /-nɪs/ *n* [U]

homi·cide /'haməˌsaid/ *n* **1** [U,C] (instance of) killing of a human being. **2** [C] person who kills a human being.

homi·cidal /ˌhamə'saidəl/ *adj* of homicide: *homicidal tendencies.*

hom·ily /'haməli/ *n* [C] (*pl* -ies) [C] sermon; long and tedious moralizing talk.

hom·i·ny /'hamənі/ *n* [U] hulled corn that is cooked and eaten as food.

'hominy grits ⇨ grits.

ho·mo·gene·ous /ˌhoumə'dʒiniəs/ *adj* (formed of parts) of the same kind.

hom·ogen·ize /hə'madʒəˌnaiz/ *vt* **1** make homogeneous. **2** (esp) make milk more uniform in consistency by breaking down and blending the particles of fat.

homo·graph /'haməˌgræf/ *n* [C] word spelled like another but with a different meaning.

homo·nym /'haməˌnɪm/ *n* [C] word that is the same in form or sound as another but different in meaning, eg pale, pail.

homo·phone /'haməˌfoun/ *n* [C] word pronounced like another but different in meaning, spelling or origin, eg sum/some, new/knew.

homo·sex·ual /ˌhoumə'sekʃuəl/ *adj* sexually attracted to/by persons of one's own sex. □ *n* [C] homosexual person.

homo·sex·ual·ity /ˌhouməˌsekʃu'æləti/ *n* [U]

Hon. *abbr* = (the) Honorable.

hone /houn/ *n* [C] stone used for sharpening tools. □ *vt* sharpen on a hone.

hon·est /'anɪst/ *adj* **1** not telling lies; not cheating or stealing: *an ~ man; ~ in business; give an ~ opinion.* **2** showing, resulting from, an honest person: *an ~ face; an ~ piece of work.*

hon·est·ly *adv* in an honest manner; truthfully: *Honestly, that's all the money I have.*

hon·esty *n* [U] the quality of being honest.

honey /'həni/ *n* **1** [U] sweet, sticky yellowish substance made by bees from nectar. **2** [C] (*pl* ~s) (*informal*) sweetheart; darling.

'honey·bee *n* [C] bee that produces honey.

hon·eyed /'hənid/ *adj* sweet as honey.

'honey·suckle *n* [U] climbing shrub with sweet-smelling yellow or reddish flowers.

honey·comb /'həniˌkoum/ *n* [C,U] **1** (container with) wax structure of six-sided cells made by bees for honey and eggs. **2** something that is like a honeycomb. □ *vt* fill with holes, tunnels, etc.

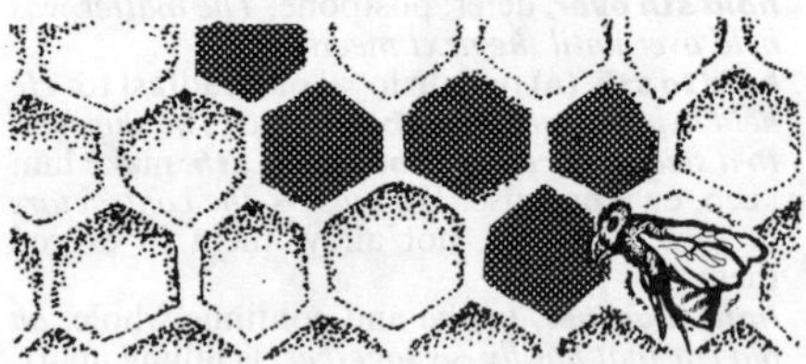

HONEYCOMB

honey·moon /'həniˌmun/ *n* [C] **1** vacation taken by a newly married couple. **2** (*fig*) period of harmony at the start of an undertaking, etc. □ *vi* go on a honeymoon: *They will ~ in Paris.*

honk /hɔŋk/ *n* [C] **1** cry of a goose. **2** sound made by a horn. □ *vi* make a honk.

honky-tonk /'haŋkiˌtaŋk, 'hɔŋkiˌtɔŋk/ *n* [C] **1** low-class nightclub. **2** kind of music (originally) played at a honky-tonk(1).

hon·or[1] /'anər/ *n* **1** [U] great respect; high public regard: *win ~ in war; a ceremony in ~ of those killed in battle.* **2** [U] good personal character;

reputation for good behavior, loyalty, truthfulness, etc. ***be/feel honor bound to do sth,*** required to do it as a moral duty, but not by law. ***give/on one's word of honor,*** guarantee to fulfill an obligation, keep a promise, etc. **3** [U] sense of what is right or moral; integrity. **4** (in polite formulas): *May I have the ~ of your company at dinner? I have the ~ to inform you that....* **5 Your/His Honor,** title of respect used to or of some judges. **6** (with *a* or *an*) person or thing bringing credit: *He is an ~ to his school/family.* **7** (*pl*) marks of respect, distinction, etc: *military ~s.* **8** (*pl*) special distinction for high grade or extra proficiency in school: *graduate with high ~s.*

ˌguard of ˈhonor, number of soldiers chosen as an escort, eg for a distinguished person as a mark of respect.

hon·or[2] /ˈanər/ *vt* **1** respect highly, feel honor for; confer honor on: *I feel highly ~ed by the kind things you say about me.* **2** accept and pay when due: *~ a bill/check/draft, etc.*

hon·or·able /ˈan(ə)rəbəl/ *adj* **1** possessing or showing the principles of honor; consistent with honor(1,2): *~ conduct.* **2 the Honorable ...** (*abbr* **Hon**) title given to judges and some other officials.

hon·or·ary /ˈanəˌreri/ *adj* **1** (of a position) unpaid: *the ~ secretary.* **2** (of a degree, rank) given as an honor: *an ~ degree/doctorate.*

hooch, hootch /hutʃ/ *n* [U] (*sl*) (esp homemade) whiskey.

hood /hʊd/ *n* [C] **1** bag-like covering for the head and neck, often fastened to a coat, etc so that it can hang down at the back when not in use. **2** anything like a hood in shape or use, eg the folding metal cover over an automobile engine. □ *vt* (chiefly in *pp*) cover with, or as with, a hood: *a ~ed falcon.*

-hood /-ˌhʊd/ *suffix* state; rank; condition: *boyhood.*

hood·lum /ˈhudləm/ *n* [C] **1** gangster; criminal. **2** wild young rowdy.

hood·wink /ˈhʊdˌwɪŋk/ *vt* deceive; trick.

hoof /hʊf, huf/ *n* (*pl* ~s or hooves /hʊvz, huvz/) horny part of the foot of a horse, ox or deer. □ *vi* (*sl*) **1 *hoof it,*** walk. **2** dance.

hook[1] /hʊk/ *n* [C] **1** curved or bent piece of metal or other material, for catching hold, or for hanging something on: *a ˈfish~.* ***by hook or by crook,*** by whatever means possible. ***off the hook,*** out of trouble. **2** something shaped like a hook, eg a narrow point of land, part of a cape. **3** (*boxing*) short blow with the elbow bent: *a left ~.* □ *vt,vi* **1** fasten, be fastened, hold with a hook: *a dress that ~s/is ~ed at the back.* **2** catch or grab (as) with a hook: *~ a fish.* **3** make into the form of a hook: *~ one's finger.* **4** (*informal*) steal. **5 *hook up,*** set up and connect a device or piece of equipment: *~ up a telephone.*

hooked *adj* **(a)** hook-shaped: *a ~ed nose.* **b** (*sl*) addicted to; completely committed to: *be/get ~ed on heroin.*

hookah /ˈhʊkə, ˈhukə/ *n* [C] tobacco pipe with a long flexible tube through which smoke is drawn through water in a vase and so cooled.

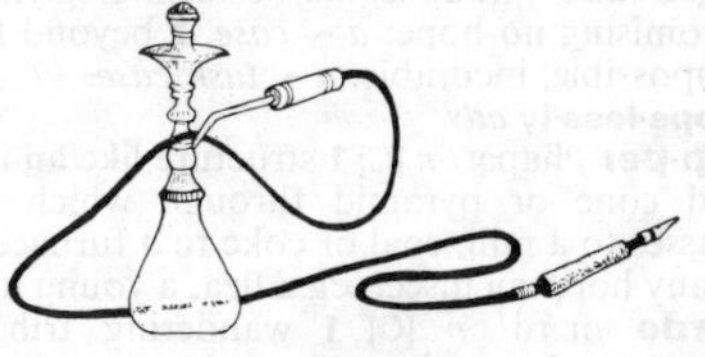

HOOKAH

hooky /ˈhʊki/ *n* ***play hooky,*** (*informal*) stay away from school without permission.

hoo·li·gan /ˈhulɪgən/ *n* [C] person making disturbances in the streets or other public places.

hoo·li·gan·ism /-ˌnɪzəm/ *n* [U]

hoop /hup/ *n* [C] **1** circular band of wood or metal as for a barrel, etc. **2** large ring used as a toy. □ *vt* bind (a barrel, etc) with hoops.

hoop·la /ˈhupˌla/ *n* [U] (*informal*) noisy excitement.

hoo·ray /hʊˈrei, hu-/ = hurrah.

hoot /hut/ *n* [C] **1** cry of an owl. **2** sound made by an automobile horn, foghorn, etc. **3** shout or cry expressing disapproval or scorn. ***not care/give a hoot/two hoots,*** (*informal*) not care at all. □ *vi,vt* make a hoot (at): *an owl ~ing in the tree. The crowd ~ed at the speaker.*

hooves *pl* of hoof.

hop[1] /hap/ *n* [C] **1** plant with flower clusters like small pine cones. **2** (*pl*) dried flower clusters of this plant which are used for giving a bitter flavor to beer, etc.

hop[2] /hap/ *vi,vt* (-pp-) **1** jump on one foot. **2** jump in short leaps or with a springing motion: *Sparrows were hopping about on the lawn.* ***hopping mad,*** (*informal*) very angry. **3** jump on; *~ a bus.* □ *n* [C] **1** the action of hopping. **2** short jump. **3** (*dated, informal*) dance. **4** short trip esp in a plane: *It's just a hop from New York to Washington.*

ˈhop·scotch *n* children's game of throwing a stone into numbered squares marked on the ground, and hopping from square to square to collect it.

hope[1] /houp/ *n* **1** [C,U] feeling that what one wishes or expects will happen: *There is not much ~ that they are alive.* ***hold out some/no/little/not much hope (of sth),*** give some, etc encouragement or expectation: *The doctors could hold out no ~ of recovery.* ***(be) past/beyond hope,*** without possibility of success, recovery, etc. ***raise sb's hopes,*** encourage him to expect better fortune, etc: *Don't raise his ~s too much.* **2** [C] person, thing, circumstance, etc on which hope is based: *You are my last ~,* if you can't help, I'm ruined.

hope[2] /houp/ *vt,vi* expect and desire: *We ~ to see you soon. We ~ that he will go. We've had no news from him but we're still hoping.*

hope·ful /ˈhoupfəl/ *adj* **1** having hope: *be/feel ~ about the future.* **2** giving hope; promising: *The future does not seem very ~.* □ *n* [C]: *a young ~,* boy or girl who wants or seems likely to succeed.

hope·fully *adv*

hope·ful·ness /-nɪs/ *n* [U]

hope·less /ˈhouplɪs/ *adj* **1** feeling, giving or promising no hope: *a ~ case.* **2** beyond hope; impossible; incurable: *a ~ task/case.*

hope·less·ly *adv*

hop·per /ˈhapər/ *n* [C] **1** structure like an inverted cone or pyramid through which grain passes to a mill, coal or coke to a furnace, etc. **2** any hopping insect, eg a flea, a young locust.

horde /hɔrd/ *n* [C] **1** wandering tribe (of nomads). **2** crowd; great number: *~s of people/locusts.*

hor·izon /həˈraizən/ *n* [C] **1** line at which the earth or sea and sky seem to meet: *The sun sank below the ~.* **2** (*fig*) limit of one's knowledge, experience, thinking, etc.

hori·zon·tal /hɔrəˈzantəl, ˌhar-/ *adj* (of a line or plane) parallel to the horizon; flat or level. □ *n* [C] horizontal line, bar, etc. ➪ vertical.

hori·zon·tally *adv*

hor·mone /ˈhɔrˌmoun/ *n* [C] (kinds of) internal secretion that passes into the blood and stimulates the bodily organs.

horn /hɔrn/ *n* **1** [C] one of the hard, pointed, usually curved, outgrowths on the heads of cattle, deer, and some other animals. **2** [U] hard, smooth substance of which horns are made: *a ~ spoon.* **3** [C] article made from this substance (or a modern substitute): *a ˈpowder ~.* **4** [C] kinds of musical wind instrument: *a French ~.* ➪ illus at brass. **5** device for making warning sounds: *a ˈfog~; an ˈautomobile ~.* **6** horn-like part, eg on the head of a snail. □ *vi* ***horn in (on),*** (*sl*) join in without being invited.

horned *adj* having horns(1): *~ed cattle.*

horny *adj* (-ier, -iest) made of, like, horn: *hands ~y from hard work.*

hor·net /ˈhɔrnɪt/ *n* [C] large wasp.

horn·pipe /ˈhɔrnˌpaip/ *n* [C] (music for a) lively dance (usually for one person, esp a sailor).

ho·rol·ogy /həˈralədʒi/ *n* [U] art of designing and constructing clocks.

hor·oscope /ˈhɔrəˌskoup/ *n* [C] **1** diagram of, positions of the planets at a certain time, eg a person's birth, for the purpose of forecasting future events. **2** such a forecast.

hor·rible /ˈhɔrəbəl, ˈhar-/ *adj* **1** exciting horror: *~ cruelty/crimes.* **2** (*informal*) unpleasant: *~ weather.*

hor·ribly /-əbli/ *adv*

hor·rid /ˈhɔrɪd, ˈharɪd/ *adj* **1** frightful; terrible. **2** unpleasant: *~ weather.*

hor·rid·ly /-li/*adv*

hor·rific /həˈrɪfɪk/ *adj* horrifying.

hor·rify /ˈhɔrəˌfai, ˈhar-/ *vt* (*pt,pp* -ied) **1** fill with horror. **2** shock: *We were horrified by what we saw.*

hor·ror /ˈhɔrər, ˈharər/ *n* **1**[U] extreme fear, dread or dislike: *To her ~ she saw her husband knocked down by a bus.* **2** [C] something that causes horror: *We have all read about the ~s of modern warfare.*

ˈhorror-struck/-stricken *adj* (of persons) filled with horror.

hors d'œuvres /ˌɔr ˈdərv/ *n pl* food served as an appetizer at the beginning of a meal.

horse /hɔrs/ *n* **1** [C] four-legged solid-hoofed animal used from early times to carry loads, for riding, etc. ➪ colt, filly, foal, mare, stallion. ***back/bet on the wrong horse,*** support the loser in a contest. ***be/get on one's high horse,*** become conceited, arrogant, etc. ***hold one's horses,*** hesitate; hold back. ***horse of another/different color,*** something entirely different. ***look a gift horse in the mouth,*** examine a gift critically for faults. ***(straight) from the horse's mouth,*** (of tips, advice, information) from a first-hand source. **2** (*collective sing*) cavalry. **3** [C] framework, often with legs, on which something is supported: *a ˈsaw~.* **4** piece of equipment used in a gymnasium for vaulting or jumping over.

ˈhorse·back *n* (only in) ***on horseback,*** on a horse.

ˈhorse·fly *n* [C] large insect which bites horses and cattle.

ˈhorse·man/ˌ·woman /-mən, -wʊmən/ *n* [C] (*pl* ~men /-men/, ~women /-wɪmɪn/) (skilled) man/woman who rides a horse.

ˈhorse·play *n* [U] rough, noisy fun or play.

ˈhorse sense, practical common sense.

ˈhorse·shoe *n* [C] U-shaped metal shoe for a horse.

ˈhorse·whip *n* [C] whip for horses. □ *vt* (-pp) flog or thrash with a horsewhip.

horse·power /ˈhɔrsˌpauər/ *n* (*pl* unchanged) (*abbr* hp) unit for measuring the power of an engine etc.

horse·radish /ˈhɔrsˌrædɪʃ/ *n* [U] **1** plant with a hot-tasting root which is ground or scraped to make a sauce. **2** this sauce.

hor·ti·cul·tural /ˌhɔrtəˈkəltʃərəl/ *adj* of horticulture: *a ~ show.*

hor·ti·cul·ture /ˈhɔrtəˌkəltʃər/ *n* [U] (art of) growing flowers, fruit and vegetables.

hose[1] /houz/ *n* [C,U] (length of) flexible tubing (of rubber, plastic, etc) for directing water on to fires, gardens, etc. □ *vt* water (a garden, etc) with a hose; wash (a car, etc) by using a hose.

hose[2] /houz/ *n* [C] (*pl* ~) **1** stockings and socks: *six pairs of ~.* **2** garment from the waist to the knees or feet formerly worn by men: *dressed in doublet and ~.*

ho·siery /ˈhouʒəri/ *n* [U] stockings and socks.

hosp. *abbr* = hospital.

hos·pi·table /haˈspɪtəbəl/ *adj* giving, liking to give, hospitality: *a ~ man.*

hos·pit·ably /-əbli/ *adv*

hos·pi·tal /ˈhaˌspɪtəl/ *n* [C] place where sick or injured people are cared for.

hos·pi·tal·ity /ˌhaspəˈtæləti/ *n* [U] friendly and generous reception and entertainment of guests, esp in one's own home.

hos·pi·tal·ize /ˈhaˌspɪtəˌlaiz/ *vt* cause to go into a hospital for treatment.

hos·pi·tal·iza·tion /ˌhaˌspɪtəlɪˈzeiʃən/ *n* [C,U]

host[1] /houst/ *n* [C] great number: *He has ~s of friends.*

host[2] /houst/ *n* [C] **1** person who entertains guests. **2** inn keeper; hotel keeper. **3** (*biol*) living plant or animal on which a parasite lives. □ *vt* act as host to or at.

host[3] /houst/ *n* [C] bread or wafer which has been consecrated.

hos·tage /ˈhastɪdʒ/ *n* [C] person given or left as

a guarantee of protection or that demands will be satisfied: *The hijackers demanded that one of the travelers should stay with them as a* ~.

hos·tel /ˈhastəl/ *n* [C] building in which board and lodging are provided esp for young people: *a youth* ~.

hos·tel·er *n* [C] traveler who stops at hostels.

host·ess /ˈhoustɪs/ *n* [C] **1** woman who acts as a host. **2** woman who greets guests in a restaurant, hotel, etc. **3** airline stewardess.

hos·tile /ˈhastəl/ *adj* **1** of an enemy: *a* ~ *army*. **2** unfriendly: *a* ~ *crowd/look*.

hos·tile·ly *adv*

hos·til·ity /haˈstɪləti/ *n* (*pl* -ies) **1** [U] unfriendly feeling; hatred: *feelings of* ~. **2** (*pl*) (acts of) war.

hot /hat/ *adj* (-tter, -ttest) **1** having great heat or a high temperature: *hot weather; feel hot*. **2** producing a burning sensation to the taste: *Pepper and mustard are hot*. **3** intense; violent; excited: *a man with a hot temper*. **4** (of music, esp jazz) performed with strong rhythms, improvisation, etc. **5** (*sl*) recently stolen. **6** fresh: *news that is hot off the press; a hot trail*. ***blow hot and cold,*** (*fig*) change one's mind often about something; be by turns favorable and unfavorable.

ˌhot ˈair, (*informal*) meaningless talk, promises, etc.

ˈhot·bed *n* (*fig*) place favorable to growth, esp of something evil: *a hotbed of vice/crime*.

ˌhot-ˈblooded *adj* passionate.

ˈhot dog, heated frankfurter served usually in a long split roll.

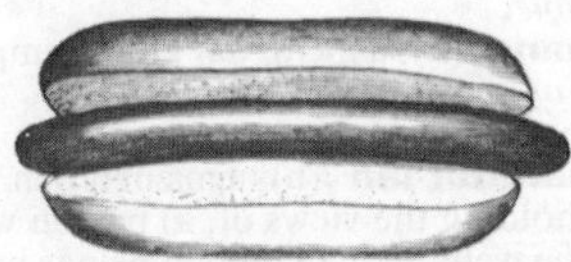

HOT DOG

ˈhot·foot *adv* eagerly; in great haste: *follow the enemy hotfoot*. □ *vi* go hastily: *hotfoot it down to the library*.

ˈhot·head *n* person acting on impulse.

ˌhot-ˈheaded *adj* quick to become excited; rash.

ˈhot·house *n* [C[heated building, usually made of glass, for growing plants.

ˈhot line, direct telephone line for speedy communication between heads of governments.

hot·ly *adv* passionately; excitedly: *a hotly contested match*.

ˈhot·plate *n* [C] small, portable stove for cooking, etc.

ˈhot rod, automobile that has been altered or rebuilt for high speed.

ˌhot ˈspring, (often *pl*) naturally heated spring[1] (2).

ˌhot-ˈtempered *adj* easily angered.

ˌhot ˈwater, (*informal*) trouble: *be/get into hot water*.

ˌhot-ˈwater bottle, container (often of rubber) to be filled with hot water for warmth in bed.

ho·tel /houˈtel/ *n* [C] building where meals and rooms are provided for travelers.

ho·tel·ier /ˌouteIˈyei/ *n* [C] person who manages a hotel.

hound /haund/ *n* [C] (kinds of) dog used esp for hunting and racing: *ˈblood*~. □ *vt* **1** chase or hunt with hounds. **2** trouble; worry: *be* ~*ed by one's creditors*.

hour /ˈauər/ *n* [C] **1** twenty-fourth part of a day; 60 minutes: *walk for* ~*s (and* ~*s); a three* ~ *journey*. ***at the eleventh hour,*** when almost too late. **2** time of day; point or period of time: *They disturb me at all* ~*s of the day and night*, constantly. **3** (*pl*) fixed periods of time, esp for work: *ˈOffice* ~*s, 9am to 5pm*. **4** particular time: *in the* ~ *of danger*.

ˈhour hand, small hand on a clock or watch, pointing to the hour.

hour·ly /ˈauərli/ *adv* **1** every hour; once every hour: *This medicine is to be taken* ~. **2** at any hour: *We're expecting news* ~. □ *adj* **1** done or occurring every hour: *an* ~ *bus service*. **2** frequent or continual: *live in* ~ *fear of discovery*.

house[1] /haus/ *n* [C] (*pl* ~s /ˈhauzɪz/) **1** building made for people to live in: *New* ~*s are going up everywhere*. ⇨ home[2](1). ***get on like a ˈhouse on fire,*** (of people) quickly become friendly. **2** (often in compounds) building made or used for some particular purpose or occupation: *a ˈware*~. **3** (building used by an) assembly: *the House of Representatives*. **4(a)** household. **(b)** family line; dynasty: *the House of Orange*. **5** spectators, audience, in a theater: *a full* ~, every seat occupied. ***bring the ˈhouse down,*** win very great applause and approval.

ˈhouse·boat *n* [C] boat fitted up as a place to live in.

ˈhouse·bound *adj* having to stay at home (eg because of bad weather).

ˈhouse·fly *n* [C] common fly found in and around houses. ⇨ illus at insect.

ˈhouse·hold *n* [C] all persons (family, lodgers, etc) living in a house.

ˈhouse·keeper *n* [C] woman employed to look after a household.

ˈhouse·mother *n* [C] woman in charge of children esp a boarding school.

ˈhouse·wares *n pl* small articles of household use.

ˈhouse·warm·ing *n* [C] party to celebrate moving into a new home.

ˈhouse·wife *n* [C] (*pl* ~wives /-waivz/) woman head of a family, who runs the home, brings up the family, etc.

ˈhouse·work *n* [U] work done in a house, eg cleaning, sweeping, etc.

house[2] /hauz/ *vt* provide a home, room or shelter for: *We can* ~ *you and your friends if the hotels are full*.

hous·ing /ˈhauzɪŋ/ *n* **1** [U] (accommodation in) houses, etc: *More* ~ *is needed for old people*. **2** [C] something that covers or protects: *a motor* ~.

hove *pt,pp* of heave.

hovel /ˈhəvəl/ *n* [C] small, wretched house or hut.

hover /ˈhəvər/ *vi* **1** (of birds) remain in the air at one place: *a hawk* ~*ing overhead*. **2** remain at or near. **3** be in a state of uncertainty; waver: ~ *between life and death*.

ˈ**Hover·craft** *n* [C] (*P*) craft capable of moving over land or water while supported on a cushion of air made by jet engines.

how /hau/ *adv* **1** in what way or manner; by what means: *How is that word spelled? Tell me how to spell the word.* **2** (in questions and exclamations) to what extent; in what degree: *how old is he? How kind you are!* **3** in what state of health: *How are you?* ***How do you do?*** (used as a conventional greeting, esp when persons are formally introduced.) **4** (used in asking for an opinion, decision, explanation, etc): *How's that?* What's the explanation of that? ***how about,*** what do you think of: *How about* (*going for*) *a walk?*

howdy /ˈhaudi/ *int* (used as a greeting, esp in rural areas).

how·ever /hauˈevər/ *adv* **1** in whatever way or degree: *He will never succeed, ~ hard he tries.* **2** all the same; nevertheless: *Later, ~, he decided to go.*

howl /haul/ *n* [C] **1** long, loud cry, eg of a wolf. **2** long cry of pain, scorn, amusement, etc: *~s of derision.* □ *vi,vt* (of the wind, etc) make such a noise; utter such cries (at): *The wind ~ed through the trees. They ~ed with laughter/~ defiance at the enemy.*

howl·ing *adj* **(a)** making such a noise: *a ~ing gale.* **(b)** (*sl*) extreme; glaring: *a ~ing error.*

how's /hauz/ = how is; how has.

hp *abbr* = horsepower.

HQ *abbr* = headquarters.

hr(s). *abbr* = hour(s).

HST *abbr* = Hawaii(an) Standard Time.

ht. *abbr* = height.

Hts. *abbr* = Heights.

hub /həb/ *n* [C] **1** central part of a wheel from which the spokes radiate. **2** (*fig*) central point of activity or importance: *a hub of industry/commerce.*

ˈ**hub·cap** *n* [C] metal disc covering the hub of a car wheel.

hub·bub /ˈhəˌbəb/ *n* [U] confused noise, eg of voices.

hubby /ˈhəbi/ *n* [C] (*pl* -ies) (*informal*) husband.

huckle·berry /ˈhəkəlˌberi/ *n* [C] (*pl* -ies) (shrub bearing a) blackish berry that is related to the blueberry.

huddle /ˈhədəl/ *vt,vi* **1** crowd together: *sheep huddling together for warmth.* **2** curl or coil up against: *Tom was cold, so he ~d up against his brother in bed.* **3** gather or come together in a huddle: *~ things together.* □ *n* [C] **1** number of things or persons close together without order or arrangement. **2** close gathering, esp of football players to plan their play, etc.

hue¹ /(h)yu/ *n* [C] (shade of) color: *the dark hue of the ocean.*

hue² /(h)yu/ *n* [C] (only in) ˌ***hue and*** ˈ***cry,*** general outcry of alarm (as when a criminal is being pursued) or protest: *raise a hue and cry against new tax proposals.*

huff /həf/ *n* ***be in/get into a huff,*** be/become bad-tempered.

huffy /ˈhəfi/ *adj* (-ier, -iest) touchy; easily made angry.

hug /həg/ *vt* (-gg-) **1** put the arms round tightly, esp to show love: *The child was hugging her doll.* **2** cling to: *hug cherished beliefs.* **3** ***hug the shore,*** (of a ship) keep close to it. □ *n* [C] tight embrace: *She gave her mother a big hug.*

huge /(h)yudʒ/ *adj* (-r, -st) very large; very great.

huge·ly *adv* enormously; very much.

hula /ˈhulə/ *n* [C,U] kind of Polynesian dance, esp as done in Hawaii. □ *vi* dance a/the hula.

ˈ**hula skirt,** one, usually of grass, worn by hula dancers.

hulk /həlk/ *n* [C] **1** old ship no longer in use or used only as a storehouse. **2** big, clumsy person or object.

hulk·ing *adj* clumsy; awkward.

hull /həl/ *n* [C] **1** outer covering of certain kinds of fruits and seeds, esp the pods of peas and beans. **2** body or frame of a ship. ⇨ illus at ship. □ *vt* remove the hulls(1) from: *~ peas.*

hul·la·ba·loo /ˈhələbəˌlu/ *n* [C] uproar; disturbance: *What's all this ~ about?*

hum¹ /həm/ *vi,vt* (-mm-) **1** make a continuous sound like that made by bees. **2** sing with closed lips: *She was humming a song to herself.* **3** be in a state of activity: *a factory humming with activity.* □ *n* [U] humming noise: *the hum of bees/of distant traffic/of voices.*

hum.² *abbr* = humorous.

hu·man /ˈ(h)yumən/ *adj* **1** of man or mankind (contrasted with animals, God): *a ~ being; ~ nature.* **2** having, showing, the form, qualities, etc that distinguish man: *His cruelty shows that he is less than ~.* □ *n* [U] human being.

hu·man·ly *adv* (esp) by human means; without divine help: *The doctors have done all that is ~ly possible.*

hu·mane /(h)yuˈmein/ *adj* kind; sympathetic: *a man of ~ character.*

hu·mane·ly *adv*

hu·mani·tar·ian /(h)yuˌmænɪˈteriən/ *adj, n* [C] (of, holding the views of, a) person who works for the welfare of all human beings by reducing suffering, reforming laws about punishment, etc.

hu·man·ity /(h)yuˈmænɪti/ *n* [U] **1** the human race; mankind: *crimes against ~.* **2** human nature. **3** quality of being humane: *treat people and animals with ~.*

the humanities, the branches of learning, eg art, literature, history and philosophy as contrasted with the sciences.

hu·man·ize /ˈ(h)yuməˌnaiz/ *vt,vi* make or become human or humane.

humble /ˈhəmbəl/ *adj* (-r, -st) **1** having or showing a modest opinion of oneself, one's position, etc: *He is very ~ toward his superiors.* **2** (of persons) low in rank or position; obscure and unimportant. **3** (of things) poor in appearance. □ *vt* make lower in rank or self-opinion: *~ one's enemies.*

hum·bly *adv* in a humble way: *beg most humbly for forgiveness.*

hum·bug /ˈhəmˌbəg/ *n* **1** [C,U] (instance of) dishonest and deceiving behavior or talk. **2** (*dated*) [C] dishonest, deceitful person. □ *vt* (-gg-) (*dated*) deceive or trick: *Don't try to ~ me!* □ *int* (*dated*) Nonsense!

hum·drum /ˈhəmˌdrəm/ *adj* dull; ordinary: *live*

a ~ *life*.

hu·merus /ˈ(h)yumərəs/ *n* [C] bone of the upper arm in man. ⇨ illus at skeleton.

hu·mid /ˈ(h)yumɪd/ *adj* (esp of air, climate) damp; moist.

hu·mid·ify /(h)yuˈmɪdəˌfai/ *vt* (*pt,pp* -ied) make humid.

hu·mid·ity /(h)yuˈmɪdəti/ *n* [U] (degree of) moisture (in the air).

hu·mili·ate /(h)yuˈmɪliˌeit/ *vt* cause to feel ashamed; lower the dignity or self-respect of: *humiliating peace terms*.

hu·mili·ation /(h)yuˌmɪliˈeiʃən/ *n* [C,U]

hu·mil·ity /(h)yuˈmɪləti/ *n* [U] humble condition or state of mind.

hum·ming·bird /ˈhəmɪŋˌbərd/ *n* [C] any of a family of small, brightly-colored birds with a long bill, whose wings move so rapidly that they make a humming sound.

hum·mock /ˈhəmək/ *n* [C] hillock; small mound.

hu·mor /ˈ(h)yumər/ *n* [U] **1** (capacity to cause or feel) amusement: *a good sense of* ~. **2** person's state of mind (esp at a particular time); temper: *I was in a good/bad* ~ *that day*. □ *vt* give way to someone's wishes: *Is it wise to always* ~ *a child?*

hu·mor·ist /ˈ(h)yumərɪst/ *n* [C] humorous talker or writer.

hu·mor·ous /ˈ(h)yumərəs/ *adj* having or showing a sense of humor; funny: ~ *remarks*.

hu·mor·ous·ly *adv*

hump /həmp/ *n* [C] **1** round lump, eg on a camel's back or (as a deformity) on a person's back. **2** (*informal*) ***over the hump,*** past a critical time or point. □ *vt* make hump-shaped: *The cat* ~*ed* (*up*) *her back when she saw the dog*.

hu·mus /ˈ(h)yuməs/ *n* [U] substance formed by the decay of vegetable matter (dead leaves, plants).

hunch /həntʃ/ *n* [C] **1** thick piece; hunk; hump. **2** (*informal*) suspicion; vague feeling: *I had a* ~ *that she was the person who wrote the letter*. □ *vt* arch to form a hump: *with his shoulders* ~*ed up*.

ˈhunch·back *n* [C] (person having a) back with a hump.

ˈhunch·backed *adj*

hun·dred /ˈhəndrɪd/ *adj, n* [C] **1** of the number 100: *two* ~ *and five*, 205. **2** (in *pl*) large number: ~*s of people*.

ˈhundred·fold *adv* one hundred times as much or as many.

hun·dredth /ˈhəndrɪdθ/ *adj, n* [C] (of) one of a hundred (parts) or the next after 99.

hung *pt,pp* of hang[2].

hun·ger /ˈhəŋgər/ *n* **1** [U] need, desire for food: *die of* ~. **2** (*fig*) any strong desire: *a* ~ *for excitement*. □ *vi* **1** feel, suffer from, hunger. **2** have a strong desire: ~ *for news*.

ˈhunger strike, refusal to take food as a protest.

hun·gry /ˈhəŋgri/ *adj* (-ier, -iest) feeling, showing signs of, hunger: *be/go* ~. *The young orphan was* ~ *for affection*.

hun·grily /ˈhəŋgrəli/ *adv*

hunk /həŋk/ *n* [C] thick piece; chunk: *a* ~ *of bread*.

hunt[1] /hənt/ *n* **1** (*sing* with *the, a* or *an*) act of hunting; search: *find something after a long* ~. **2** group of persons who hunt together.

hunt·ing *n* [U] the act of hunting, esp for game: *He's fond of* ~*ing*.

hunt[2] /hənt/ *vi,vt* **1** go after (wild animals) for food or sport: ~ *deer/elephants*. **2** ***hunt down,*** look for, track and find: ~ *down a criminal/an escaped prisoner*. **3** search; try to find: ~ *for a lost book*. ***hunt high and low,*** search everywhere.

hunter, huntress *n* [C] male/female who hunts.

hurdle /ˈhərdəl/ *n* **1** [C] light frame to be jumped over in a race. **2** (*fig*) difficulty to be overcome. □ *vt* **1** jump over (something) while running. **2** overcome difficulties.

hur·dler *n* [C] person who runs in hurdle races.

hurl /hərl/ *vt* throw with force: ~ *a spear at a tiger*. □ *n* [C] violent throw.

hurly-burly /ˌhərli-ˈbərli/ *n* [U] noisy commotion.

hur·rah, hur·ray /həˈra, həˈrei, hʊ-, hu-/ *int* expressing joy, approval, etc. □ *vi* cheer (the usual word).

hur·ri·cane /ˈhərəˌkein/ *n* [C] violent, usually tropical storm, with winds of over 75 miles per hour.

ˈhurricane lamp, kind with a glass chimney to protect the light from the wind.

hurry /ˈhəri/ *n* [U] eager haste; wish to get something done quickly: *Why all this* ~? ***in a hurry,*** in a rush; acting, anxious to act, quickly: *He was in a* ~ *to leave*. □ *vt,vi* (*pt,pp* -ied) (cause to) move or do something (too) quickly: *It's no use* ~*ing her/trying to make her* ~. ***Hurry up!*** Make haste.

hur·ried /ˈhərid/ *adj* done, etc in a hurry; showing haste: *a hurried meal*.

hur·ried·ly /ˈhərɪdli/ *adv*

hurt /hərt/ *vt,vi* (*pt,pp* ~) **1** cause bodily injury or pain to: *He* ~ *his back when he fell*. **2** cause a person mental pain: *He was rather* ~ *by their criticisms*. **3** suffer injury; have a bad effect (on): *It won't* ~ *to wait for a few days*. □ *n* [U] (or with *a, an*) harm; injury: *I intended no* ~ *to his feelings*.

hurt·ful *adj*

hurtle /ˈhərtəl/ *vi* (cause to) rush or be flung violently: *During the earthquake the bricks came hurtling down*.

hus·band /ˈhəzbənd/ *n* [C] man to whom a woman is married.

hush /həʃ/ *vt,vi* make or become silent or quiet: *Hush!* Be silent! ***hush sth up,*** prevent it from becoming public knowledge: *She tried to* ~ *up the fact that her husband was an ex-convict*. □ *n* [U] silence; stillness: *in the* ~ *of night*.

ˈhush-hush *adj* (*informal*) secret.

ˈhush puppy, kind of dumpling made of cornmeal and fried in deep fat.

husk /həsk/ *n* [C] dry outer covering of seeds, esp of grain: *rice in the* ~. ⇨ illus at cereal. □ *vt* remove husks from.

husky[1] /ˈhəski/ *adj* (-ier, -iest) **1** (dry) like husks. **2** (of a person, his voice) hoarse; with a dry and almost whispering voice: *a* ~ *voice/cough*. □ *n* [C] (*pl* -ies) thick-coated dog of North American Eskimos.

husk·ily /-əli/ *adv*
huski·ness /ˈhəskinɪs/ *n* [U]
husky[2] /ˈhəski/ *adj* (ier, -iest) big and strong; rugged.
hussy /ˈhəsi, ˈhəzi/ *n* [C] (*pl* -ies) **1** impudent, ill-mannered, girl. **2** immoral woman.
hustle /ˈhəsəl/ *vt,vi* **1** push or shove roughly: *The police ~d the thief into their van.* **2** (cause to) act quickly and with energy: *I don't want to ~ you into a decision.* **3** (*informal*) sell or obtain something by energetic (and sometimes illegal) activity. □ *n* (*sing* only) quick and energetic activity: *Get a ~ on!* Hurry up! ***hustle and bustle,*** busy preparations or other purposeful moving about.
hus·tler /ˈhəslər/ *n* [C] person who hustles.
hut /hət/ *n* [C] small, roughly made house or shelter; shack.
hutch /hətʃ/ *n* [C] **1** box or cage, esp one used for rabbits. **2** low cabinet with open shelves above.
hwy *abbr* = highway.
hya·cinth /ˈhaiəˌsɪnθ/ *n* [C] **1** plant growing from a bulb with spikes of colored flowers. **2** its sweet-smelling flowers.
hy·brid /ˈhaibrɪd/ *n* [C] **1** animal or plant that is the offspring of two parents belonging to different species, varieties, etc. **2** anything of mixed origin.
hy·drangea /haiˈdreindʒə/ *n* [C] (kinds of) shrub with large bunches of white, blue or pink flowers.
hy·drant /ˈhaidrənt/ *n* [C] pipe from a water main (esp in a street) with an opening to which a hose can be attached for putting out fires, etc.
hy·drau·lic /haiˈdrɔlɪk/ *adj* of or by the pressure of a fluid, esp water: *~ brakes*, in which the braking force is transmitted by compressed fluid.
hy·drau·lics *n pl* science of the behavior and use of water and other liquids, in motion and at rest.
hy·dro·car·bon /ˈhaidrəˌkarbən/ *n* [C] substance made up of only hydrogen and carbon, eg benzene.
hy·dro·chloric acid /ˌhaidrəˌklɔrɪk ˈæsɪd/ *n* [U] acid (symbol **HCl**) containing hydrogen and chlorine, used widely in industrial processes.
hy·dro·elec·tric /ˌhaidrourˈlektrɪk/ *adj* of electricity produced by water power or steam.
hy·dro·foil /ˈhaidrəˌfɔiəl/ *n* [C] boat with plates or fins which, when the boat is in motion, raise the hull out of the water so as to increase speed.
hy·dro·gen /ˈhaidrɪdʒɪn/ *n* [U] colorless gas (symbol **H**), an element, that combines with oxygen to form water.
ˈhydrogen bomb, bomb with a force much greater than an atomic bomb.
hy·dro·pho·bia /ˌhaidrəˈfoubiə/ *n* [U] **1** rabies. **2** (illness marked by a) great fear of water.
hy·ena /haiˈinə/ *n* [C] flesh-eating wild animal of Africa and Asia, with a laughing cry.
hy·giene /ˈhaiˌdʒin/ *n* [U] science of, rules for, healthy living; cleanliness.
hy·gienic /ˌhaidʒiˈenɪk, -ˈdʒenɪk/ *adj* **1** of hygiene. **2** free from disease germs: *hygienic conditions.*
hy·gieni·cally /-kli/ *adv*
hy·gro·graph /ˈhaigrəˌgræf/ *n* [C] instrument that records changes in the amount of moisture in the air.
hy·grom·eter /haiˈgramətər/ *n* [C] instrument that measures the amount of moisture in the air.
hymn /hɪm/ *n* [C] song of praise, esp to God. □ *vt* praise in hymns.
hym·nal /ˈhɪmnəl/ *n* [C] book of hymns.
hy·per·bole /haiˈpərbəli/ *n* **1** [U] (use of) exaggerated statement(s) made for effect and not intended to be taken literally. **2** [C] instance of this, eg waves as high as a mountain.
hy·per·criti·cal /ˌhaipərˈkrɪtɪkəl/ *adj* too critical, esp of small faults.
hy·per·tension /ˌhaipərˈtenʃən/ *n* [U] illness marked by high blood pressure.
hy·phen /ˈhaifən/ *n* [C] the mark (-) used in a compound (as in *Anglo-American*), or between syllables, esp of a word that is divided at the end of a line. □ *vt* join (words) with a hyphen.
hy·phen·ate /-ˌneit/ *vt* join or divide (a word) with a hyphen.
hyp·no·sis /hɪpˈnousɪs/ *n* [C] (*pl* -ses /-ˌsiz/) (artificially produced) state like deep sleep in which a person's acts may be controlled by another person.
hyp·notic /hɪpˈnatɪk/ *adj* of hypnosis: *in a ~ state.*
hyp·no·tism /ˈhɪpnəˌtɪzəm/ *n* [U] (production of) hypnosis.
hyp·not·ist /-ɪst/ /ˈhɪpnətɪst/ *n* [C] person able to produce hypnosis.
hyp·no·tize /-ˌtaiz/ *vt* produce hypnosis in (a person).
hy·po·chon·dria /ˌhaipəˈkandriə/ *n* [U] mental depression due to unnecessary anxiety about one's health.
hy·po·chon·driac /-ˌæk/ *adj* of, affected by, hypochondria. □ *n* [C] sufferer from hypochondria.
hy·poc·risy /hɪˈpakrəsi/ *n* [C,U] (*pl* -ies) (instance of) falsely making oneself appear to be virtuous or good; insincerity.
hyp·o·crite /ˈhɪpəˌkrɪt/ *n* [C] person guilty of hypocrisy.
hyp·o·criti·cal /ˌhɪpəˈkrɪtɪkəl/ *adj* of hypocrisy or a hypocrite.
hyp·o·criti·cally /-kli/ *adv*
hy·po·der·mic /ˌhaipəˈdərmɪk/ *adj* (of drugs, etc) injected beneath the skin: *~ injections.* □ *n* [C] syringe (also *~ needle/syringe*) for giving hypodermic injections.
hy·pot·en·use /haiˈpatəˌnus/ *n* [C] side of a right-angled triangle opposite the right angle.
hy·poth·esis /haiˈpaθəsɪs/ *n* [C] (*pl* -ses /-ˌsiz/) idea, suggestion, not proved as true, but put forward as a starting point for an argument or explanation.
hy·po·theti·cal /ˌhaipəˈθetɪkəl/ *adj* of, based on, a hypothesis.
hys·teria /hɪˈsteriə/ *n* [U] **1** disturbance of the nervous system, with outbursts of emotion, often uncontrollable. **2** uncontrolled excitement.
hys·teri·cal /hɪˈsterɪkəl/ *adj* caused by, suffering from, hysteria: *~ laughter*.
hys·teri·cally /-kli/ *adv*
hys·ter·ics /hɪˈsterɪks/ *n pl* (with *sing* or *pl verb*) attack of hysteria: *go into hysterics.*

I

I¹, i /ai/ (*pl* I's i's /aiz/) **1** the ninth letter of the English alphabet. **2** Roman numeral for one, as I (= 1), iii (= 3), IX (= 9).

I² /ai/ *personal pron* used by a speaker or writer to refer to himself. ⇨ me, object form, and ⇨ we, us, plural forms.

I³ *abbr* (usually before a number) = Interstate Highway.

I.⁴ *abbr* = Island.

IA *postal abbr* = Iowa. ⇨ App 6.

ibex /ˈaiˌbeks/ *n* [C] (*pl* ~, ~es) wild goat with large, backward-curving horns that is found in Europe, Asia and Africa.

ibid. *abbr* (*Lat* = ibidem) in the same place.

ibis /ˈaibɪs/ *n* [C] large bird (like a stork or heron) found in lakes and swamps in warm climates.

-ible ⇨ -able.

ICBM /ˌai ˌsi ˌbi ˈem/ *abbr* = intercontinental ballistic missile.

ice¹ /ais/ *n* **1** [U] frozen water; water made solid by cold: *Is the ice thick enough for skating?* ***break the ice,*** overcome strangeness or formality (eg at a first meeting). **2** [C,U] frozen sweetened fruit juice or syrup; differing from *ice cream* in containing no milk or cream: *lemon ice.*

ˈIce Age, time when much of the northern hemisphere was covered with glaciers.

ˈice·berg *n* [C] mass of ice floating in the sea.

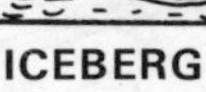
ICEBERG

ICICLES

ˈice·boat *n* [C] **(a)** frame on runners, fitted with sails for moving over the ice. **(b)** = icebreaker.

ˈice·bound *adj* (of harbors, etc) obstructed by ice.

ˈice·box *n* **(a)** box in which ice is used to keep food cool. **(b)** = refrigerator.

ˈice·breaker *n* [C] **(a)** ship, equipped with a special bow, used for breaking up ice in shipping channels, etc. **(b)** action, etc which overcomes strangeness or formality.

ˌice ˈcream *n* [C,U] (portion of) cream or custard, flavored and frozen.

ˈice-ˌcream ˌcone, (a) pastry cone in which portions of ice cream are sold. **(b)** portion of ice cream, served in a cone.

ˈice cube, cube of ice, used for chilling drinks, etc.

ˈice hockey, ⇨ hockey.

ˈice skate, thin metal runner or blade on a boot for skating on ice.

ˈice-skate *vi* skate on ice.

ˈice tray, one in a refrigerator, for making cubes of ice.

ˈice water, water (esp for drinking) that has been chilled in a refrigerator or by adding ice cubes.

ice² /ais/ *vt,vi* **1** make very cold: *iced tea.* **2** cover, become covered, with a coating of ice: *The pond is icing over.* **3** cover (a cake) with icing.

icicle /ˈaisɪkəl/ *n* [C] pointed piece of ice formed by the freezing of dripping water.

icing /ˈaisɪŋ/ *n* [U] = frosting(1).

icon /ˈaiˌkan/ *n* [C] (in the Eastern Church) religious painting, usually on a wooden panel.

icy /ˈaisi/ *adj* (-ier, -iest) **1** very cold, like ice: *icy winds.* **2** covered with ice: *icy roads.* **3** (*fig*) unfriendly: *an icy welcome.*

icily /ˈaisəli/ *adv*

ID¹ *postal abbr* = Idaho. ⇨ App 6.

ID² /ˌai ˈdi/ *abbr* = identification. **ID bracelet/card/tag,** one with a name, etc on it, worn or carried for identification.

I'd /aid/ = had; I would.

idea /aiˈdiə/ *n* [C] **1** thought; picture in the mind: *have a good ~ of life in ancient Greece.* **2** plan; scheme; design; purpose: *He's full of new ~s.* **3** opinion: *You shouldn't force your ~s on other people.* **4** vague belief, feeling that something is probable: *I have an ~ that she will be late.* **5** conception: *You have no ~ (of) how anxious we have been.*

ideal /aiˈdiəl/ *adj* **1** satisfying one's idea of what is perfect: *~ weather for a holiday.* **2** existing only in the imagination; not likely to be achieved: *~ happiness.* □ *n* [C] idea, example, looked on as perfect: *She's looking for a husband but hasn't found her ~ yet.*

ideal·ist /-ɪst/ *n* [C] person who pursues (often impractical) ideals.

ideal·istic /aiˌdiəˈlɪstɪk/ *adj*

ideally /aiˈdiəli/ *adv*

ideal·ize /aiˈdiəˌlaiz/ *vt* see, think of, as perfect.

ideal·iz·ation /aiˌdiəlɪˈzeiʃən/ *n* [U]

iden·tical /aiˈdentɪkəl/ *adj* **1** the same: *This is* *the ~ knife with which the murder was committed.* **2** exactly alike: *Our views of what should be done are ~.*

i͵dentical ˈtwins, twins from one single fertilized ovum.

iden·tically /-kli/ *adv*

iden·tify /aiˈdentə͵fai/ *vt* (*pt,pp* -ied) **1** say, show, prove, who or what a person or thing is: *Could you ~ your umbrella among a hundred others?* **2** ***identify with,*** treat (something) as identical (with another). ***identify oneself with,*** be associated with: *He refused to ~ himself with the new political party.*

identi·fi·ca·tion /ai͵dentəfəˈkeiʃən/ *n* [U]

iden·tity /aiˈdentəti/ *n* (*pl* -ies) **1** [U] state of being identical; exact likeness. **2** [C,U] who a person is; what something is: *He was arrested because of mistaken ~.*

ideo·gram /ˈɪdiə͵græm/ *n* [C] written or printed character that symbolizes the idea of a thing, eg as used in Chinese writing.

ideo·graph /ˈɪdiə͵græf/ *n* [C] = ideogram.

ideol·ogy /͵aidiˈalədʒi/ *n* [C] (*pl* -ies) manner of thinking, ideas, characteristic of a person, group, etc, esp as forming the basis of an economic or political system.

ideo·logi·cal /͵aidiəˈladʒɪkəl/ *adj*

ideo·logi·cally /-kli/ *adv*

idi·ocy /ˈɪdiəsi/ *n* (*pl* -ies) **1** [U] state of being an idiot; extreme stupidity. **2** [C] extremely stupid act, remark, etc.

id·iom /ˈɪdiəm/ *n* [C] **1** form of language as used in a particular area or by a particular group: *He spoke the local ~,* the local dialect. *Some young people adopt the ~ of jazz musicians* (their slang, etc). **2** succession of words whose meaning is not obvious through knowledge of the individual words but must be learned as a whole, eg *give up, in order to, be all ears.*

idio·matic /͵ɪdiəˈmætɪk/ *adj*

idi·om·ati·cally /-kli/ *adv*

idio·syn·crasy /͵ɪdiəˈsɪŋkrəsi/ *n* [C] (*pl* -ies) way of thinking or behaving that is peculiar to a person.

idio·syn·cratic /͵ɪdiəsɪŋˈkrætɪk/ *adj*

id·iot /ˈɪdiət/ *n* [C] **1** person suffering severe mental handicap and incapable of rational conduct. **2** (*informal*) fool: *"I left my umbrella on the bus. What an ~ I am!"*

idi·otic /͵ɪdiˈatɪk/ *adj* very stupid.

idi·oti·cally /-kli/ *adv*

idle /ˈaidəl/ *adj* (-r, -st) **1** doing no work; not active or in use: *~ workers.* **2** (of time) not spent in doing something: *We spent many ~ hours during the holidays.* **3** (of persons) lazy (the more usual word for this sense): *an ~, worthless girl.* **4** useless; worthless: *Don't listen to ~ gossip.* □ *vi,vt* **1** be idle: *Don't ~ (about).* **2** spend in a lazy manner: *idling away your time.* **3** (of a car engine) run slowly in neutral gear.

idler /ˈaidlər/ *n* [C] person who is habitually idle.

idly /ˈaidli/ *adv*

idol /ˈaidəl/ *n* [C] **1** image in wood, stone, etc of a god; such an image used as an object of worship. **2** person or thing greatly loved or admired: *He was an only child, and the ~ of his parents.*

idol·ater /aiˈdalətər/ *n* [C] **1** worshiper of idols. **2** devoted admirer of a person or thing: *an ~ of wealth.*

idol·atress /-trɪs/ *n* [C] woman idolater.

idol·atrous /aiˈdalətrəs/ *adj* **1** (of a person) worshiping idols. **2** of the worship of idols.

idol·atrous·ly *adv*

idol·atry /aiˈdalətri/ *n* [U] **1** the worship of idols. **2** excessive devotion to or admiration of (a person or thing).

idol·ize /ˈaidə͵laiz/ *vt* **1** make an idol of. **2** love or admire to excess.

idol·iz·ation /͵aidələˈzeiʃən/ *n* [U]

idyll /ˈaidəl/ *n* [C] **1** short description, usually in verse, of a simple scene or event. **2** scene, etc suitable for this.

idyl·lic /aiˈdɪlɪk/ *adj* suitable for, like, an idyll.

i.e. /͵ai ˈi/ *abbr* (*Lat* = id est) that is.

if /ɪf/ *conj* **1** on the condition that; supposing that: **(a)** (of something that is possible, probable, or likely): *If you ask him, he will help you.* **(b)** (of an event that is unlikely or improbable): *If anyone should call, please let me know.* **(c)** of a condition that cannot be, or is unlikely to be realized, or is one put forward for consideration): *If I asked him/If I were to ask him for a loan, would he agree?* **(d)** (of a condition that was not fulfilled, eg because it was an impossible one, or through failure to act): *If they'd started earlier, they would have arrived in time.* **2** when; whenever: *If you mix yellow and blue you get green. If she wants the steward she rings the bell.* **3** granting or admitting that: *Even if he did say that, I'm sure he didn't intend to hurt your feelings.* ***(even) if,*** (may mean "although"): *I'll do it, even if it takes me all the afternoon.* **4** even though: *an enjoyable if lazy day.* **5** (*informal*) whether: *Do you know if Mr. Smith is at home?* **6** ***as if,*** as it would be if. (*It isn't as if* suggests that the contrary of what follows is true): *It isn't as if we were rich,* ie We are *not* rich. **7** ***if only,*** (often introducing a wish, or of an unfulfilled condition, especially in exclamations): *if only he had arrived in time!*

if·fy /ˈɪfi/ *adj* (*informal*) uncertain: *I don't like his offer; it's too ~,* too many conditions are attached.

ig·loo /ˈɪglu/ *n* [C] (*pl* ~s) winter hut of blocks of hard snow, used by the Eskimos.

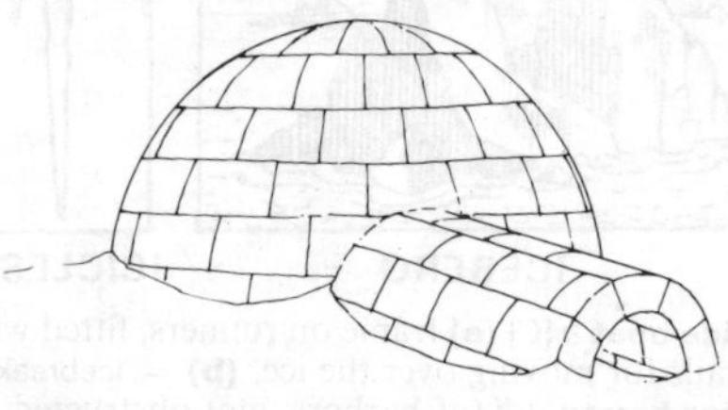

IGLOO

ig·neous /ˈɪgniəs/ *adj* (of rocks) formed by volcanic action.

ig·nite /ɪgˈnait/ *vt,vi* set on fire.

ig·ni·tion /ɪgˈnɪʃən/ *n* **1** [U] igniting or being ignited. **2** [C] (in an engine) electrical mechanism for igniting the fuel mixture.

ig·no·mini·ous /ˌɪgnəˈmɪniəs/ *adj* bringing contempt, disgrace, shame: *an ~ defeat.*

ig·no·mini·ous·ly *adv*

ig·no·miny /ˈɪgnəˌmɪni/ *n* (*pl* -ies) **1** [U] public dishonor or shame. **2** [C] dishonorable or disgraceful act. **3** [U] dishonorable behavior.

ig·no·ramus /ˌɪgnəˈreiməs/ *n* [U] (*pl* ~es) unusually ignorant person.

ig·no·rance /ˈɪgnərəns/ *n* [U] the state of being ignorant; lack of knowledge: *We are in complete ~ of his plans.*

ig·no·rant /ˈɪgnərənt/ *adj* **1** (of persons) knowing little or nothing; not aware: *I am quite ~ of his plans.* **2** showing ignorance; resulting from ignorance: *~ conduct.*

ig·no·rant·ly *adv*

ig·nore /ɪgˈnɔr/ *vt* take no notice of; refuse to take notice of: *~ rude remarks.*

iguana /ɪˈgwanə/ *n* [C] large, tree-climbing lizard of tropical America.

IL *postal abbr* = Illinois. ⇨ App 6.

I'll /ˈaiəl/ = I will; I shall.

ill /ɪl/ *adj* **1** in bad health; sick: *She was seriously ill.* ***fall/be taken ill,*** become ill. **2** bad: *in an ill temper/humor; in ill health.* □ *n* **1** [U] evil; injury: *do ill.* **2** [C] misfortune; trouble: *the various ills of life.* □ *adv* badly; imperfectly; unfavorably: *We could ill* (= not well, not easily) *afford the time and money.* ***be/feel ill at ease,*** uncomfortable, embarrassed.

ˌill-adˈvised *adj* unwise; imprudent.

ˌill-ˈbred *adj* badly brought up; rude.

ˌill-disˈposed (toward) *adj* **(a)** wishing to do harm (to). **(b)** unfavorable (toward a plan, etc).

ˌill-ˈmannered *adj* having bad manners; rude.

ˌill-ˈtimed *adj* done at a wrong or unsuitable time.

ˌill-ˈtreat/-ˈuse *vt* treat badly or cruelly.

ˌill ˈwill *n* [U] enmity; unkind feeling.

il·legal /ɪˈligəl/ *adj* not legal.

il·legally *adv*

il·legal·ity /ˌɪliˈgæləti/ *n* [C,U]

il·leg·ible /ɪˈledʒəbəl/ *adj* difficult or impossible to read.

il·leg·ibly /-əbli/ *adv*

il·leg·ibil·ity /ɪˌledʒəˈbɪləti/ *n* [U]

il·legit·imacy /ˌɪləˈdʒɪtəməsi/ *n* [U] state of being illegitimate.

il·legit·imate /ˌɪlɪˈdʒɪtəmɪt/ *adj* **1** not authorized by law; contrary to law. **2** born of parents who were not married to each other: *an ~ child.*

il·legit·imate·ly *adv*

il·lib·eral /ɪˈlɪbrəl/ *adj* **1** narrow-minded; intolerant. **2** (*archaic*) ungenerous; mean.

il·lib·erally /-rəli/ *adv*

il·licit /ɪˈlɪsɪt/ *adj* unlawful; forbidden: *the ~ use of drugs.*

il·licit·ly *adv*

il·lit·er·acy /ɪˈlɪtərəsi/ *n* [U] state of being illiterate.

il·lit·er·ate /ɪˈlɪtərɪt/ *adj* **1** with little or no education. **2** unable to read or write. □ *n* [C] illiterate person.

ill·ness /ˈɪlnɪs/ *n* **1** [U] state of being ill: *no/not much/a great deal of ~ this winter.* **2** [C] specific kind of, occasion of, illness: *She had one ~ after another.*

il·logi·cal /ɪˈladʒɪkəl/ *adj* without, contrary to, logic.

il·logi·cally /-kli/ *adv*

il·logi·cal·ity /ɪˌladʒɪˈkæləti/ *n* [U]

il·lumi·nate /ɪˈluməˌneit/ *vt* **1** give light to: *a street ~d by street lights.* **2** make clear; help to explain: *~ a difficult passage in a book.* **3** decorate (a book, manuscript) with designs and pictures.

il·lumi·na·tion /ɪˌluməˈneiʃn/ *n* **(a)** [U] lighting or being lit. **(b)** [C] something that illuminates. **(c)** [U] amount or kind of illumination. **(d)** [U] decoration of a book or manuscript in gold and colors.

illus. *abbr* = **1** illustration(s). **2** illustrated. **3** illustrator.

il·lu·sion /ɪˈluʒən/ *n* **1** [C] (the seeing of) something that does not really exist; false or misleading impression: *an optical ~.* **2** [U] mistaken idea: *childish ~s.*

il·lu·sive /ɪˈlusɪv/ *adj* = illusory.

il·lu·sive·ly *adv*

il·lu·sory /ɪˈlusəri/ *adj* unreal; deceptive.

illust. *abbr* = **1** illustration(s). **2** illustrated. **3** illustrator.

il·lus·trate /ˈɪləˌstreit/ *vt* **1** explain by examples, pictures, etc. **2** supply a book, article, lecture, etc with pictures, diagrams, etc: *a well-~d textbook.*

il·lus·tra·tor /-tər/ *n* [C] person who illustrates books, etc.

il·lus·tra·tion /ˌɪləˈstreiʃən/ *n* **1** [U] illustrating or being illustrated: *Illustration is often more useful than definition for giving the meanings of words.* **2** [C] something that illustrates, eg a picture, diagram, etc.

il·lus·tra·tive /ɪˈləstrətɪv/ *adj* serving to explain, as an explanation or example (*of*).

il·lus·tri·ous /ɪˈləstriəs/ *adj* celebrated; famous.

il·lus·tri·ous·ly *adv*

I'm /aim/ = I am.

im·age /ˈɪmɪdʒ/ *n* [C] **1** likeness or copy of a shape, esp one made in wood, stone, etc: *an ~ of the Virgin Mary.* **2** close likeness; counterpart: *Did man create God in his own ~?* **3** mental picture or idea. **4** impression presented to the public, eg of a politician, political party, commercial firm, product: *How can we improve our ~?* **5** likeness seen in a mirror or through the lens of a camera. □ *vt* **1** make an image of, portray. **2** reflect.

imagery /ˈɪmɪdʒri/ *n* [U] **(a)** making or using images, esp in art or literature. **(b)** the occurrence of images in the mind.

im·agi·nable /ɪˈmædʒɪnəbəl/ *adj* that can be imagined: *Every ~ difficulty arose to keep us from getting here on time.*

im·agi·nary /ɪˈmædʒəˌneri/ *adj* existing only in the mind; unreal.

im·agi·nation /ɪˌmædʒəˈneiʃən/ *n* [C,U] **1** power of the mind to imagine: *He hasn't much ~.* **2** what is imagined: *You didn't really see a ghost —it was only* (*your*) *~.*

im·agi·native /ɪˈmædʒənətɪv/ *adj* of, having, using, imagination.

im·ag·ine /ɪˈmædʒɪn/ *vt* **1** form a picture of in the mind: *Can you ~ life without electricity?* **2** think of as probable: *Don't ~ that I can lend you money every time you ask!*

imam /ɪˈmam/ *n* [C] **1 Imam,** title of various Moslem leaders claiming descent from Mohammed. **2** prayer leader in a mosque.

im·bal·ance /ɪmˈbæləns/ *n* [C] lack of balance: *the increasing ~ between rich and poor countries.*

im·be·cile /ˈɪmbəsəl/ *adj* **1** mentally weak. **2** stupid: *~ remarks.* □ *n* [C] **1** feeble-minded person. **2** stupid person; fool.

im·be·cil·ity /ˈɪmbəˈsɪləti/ *n* [C,U]

im·bue /ɪmˈbyu/ *vt* (*pt,pp* ~d) (*formal*) fill, inspire: *~d with patriotism/hatred.*

IMF /ˌai ˌem ˈef/ *abbr* = International Monetary Fund.

imi·tate /ˈɪməˌteit/ *vt* **1** copy the behavior of; take as an example: *You should ~ great and good men.* **2** mimic (consciously or not): *Parrots imitating human speech.* **3** be like; make a likeness of: *wood painted to ~ marble.*

imi·ta·tor /-tər/ *n* [C]

imi·ta·tion /ˌɪməˈteiʃən/ *n* **1** [U] imitating: *I~ is the sincerest form of flattery.* **2** [C] something made or done like something else. **3** (as an *adjective*) not real: *~ leather.*

imi·ta·tive /ˈɪməˌteitɪv/ *adj* following the model or example of: *as ~ as a monkey.*

im·macu·late /ɪˈmækyələt/ *adj* **1** pure; faultless: *~ conduct.* **2** perfectly clear.

im·macu·late·ly *adv*: *~ly dressed.*

im·ma·terial /ˌɪməˈtɪriəl/ *adj* **1** unimportant: *That's quite ~ to me.* **2** not having physical substance: *as ~ as a ghost.*

im·ma·ture /ˌɪməˈtʃʊr, -ˈtʊr/ *adj* not yet fully developed: *an ~ girl.*

im·ma·tu·rity /ˌɪməˈtʃʊrəti, -ˈtʊr-/ *n* [U]

im·measur·able /ɪˈmeʒərəbəl/ *adj* that cannot be measured; without limits.

im·medi·ate /ɪˈmidiət/ *adj* **1** without anything coming between; nearest: *my ~ neighbors.* **2** occurring, done, at once: *take ~ action.*

im·medi·ate·ly *adv* **(a)** at once; without delay. **(b)** directly or closely.

im·mem·o·rial /ˌɪməˈmoriəl/ *adj* beyond the reach of memory, history, etc. ***from time immemorial,*** going back beyond memory.

im·mense /ɪˈmens/ *adj* very large.

im·mense·ly *adv* (*informal*) very much: *They enjoyed themselves ~ly.*

im·men·sity /ɪˈmensəti/ *n* [C,U] extreme largeness.

im·merse /ɪˈmərs/ *vt* **1** put under the surface of (water or other liquid): *~ one's head in the water.* **2** absorb(3): *be ~d in one's work.*

im·mer·sion /ɪˈmərʒən/ *n* [C,U]

im·mi·grant /ˈɪmɪgrənt/ *n* [C] person who immigrates: *His grandfather came over as an ~.*

im·mi·grate /ˈɪməˌgreit/ *vi* come as a settler (into another country), not as a tourist or visitor.

im·mi·gra·tion /ˌɪməˈgreiʃən/ *n* [C,U]

im·mi·nent /ˈɪmənənt/ *adj* (of events, esp dangers) likely to come or happen soon: *A storm is ~.*

im·mi·nence /-əns/ *n* [U] the state of being imminent.

im·mi·nent·ly *adv*

im·mo·bile /ɪˈmoubəl/ *adj* not able to move or be moved; motionless.

im·mo·bil·ity /ˌɪmouˈbɪləti/ *n* [U] state of being immobile.

im·mo·bi·lize /ɪˈmoubəˌlaiz/ *vt* make immobile.

im·mo·bi·liz·ation /ɪˌmoubəlɪˈzeiʃən/ *n* [U]

im·mod·er·ate /ɪˈmadərɪt/ *adj* excessive: *~ eating and drinking.*

im·mod·er·ate·ly *adv*

im·mod·est /ɪˈmadɪst/ *adj* **1** lacking in modesty; conceited. **2** indecent or indelicate: *~ behavior.*

im·mod·est·ly *adv*

im·mod·esty *n* [C,U]

im·moral /ɪˈmɔrəl/ *adj* not moral; wicked and evil: *~ conduct.*

im·mo·ral·ity /ˌɪmɔˈræləti/ *n* [C,U]

im·mor·ally *adv*

im·mor·tal /ɪˈmɔrtəl/ *adj* **1** living forever: *the ~ gods.* **2** never forgotten: *~ fame.* □ *n* [C] immortal being.

the immortals, the gods of ancient Greece and Rome; the saints of ancient China.

im·mor·tal·ity /ˌɪmɔrˈtæləti/ *n* [U] endless life or fame.

im·mor·tal·ize /ɪˈmɔrtəˌlaiz/ *vt* give endless life or fame to.

im·mov·able /ɪˈmuvəbəl/ *adj* **1** that cannot be moved: *~ property*, eg buildings, land. **2** incapable of being affected or changed.

im·mov·ably /-əbli/ *adv*

im·mune /ɪˈmyun/ *adj* **1** safe, secure: *~ from attack.* **2** protected against disease: *~ to smallpox.*

im·mun·ity /ɪˈmyunəti/ *n* [U]

im·mu·nize /ˈɪmyəˌnaiz/ *vt* make immune (against).

im·mu·niz·ation /ˌɪmyənɪˈzeiʃən/ *n* [C,U]

imp /ɪmp/ *n* [C] **1** little devil or demon. **2** mischievous child.

im·pact /ˈɪmˌpækt/ *n* **1** [C] collision. **2** [U] force exerted by one object when striking against another. **3** (*sing* only) strong influence or effect: *the ~ of his speech on the audience.* □ *vt* /ɪmˈpækt, ˈɪmˌpækt/ **1** pack, drive or wedge firmly into. **2** influence or affect strongly.

im·pacted *adj* driven together; wedged in(to): *an ~ed tooth,* one kept from emerging properly by being wedged in between another tooth and the bone.

im·pair /ɪmˈper/ *vt* weaken; damage: *~ one's health by overwork.*

im·pair·ment *n* [U]

im·pale /ɪmˈpeiəl/ *vt* (*pres p* impaling /ɪmˈpeilɪŋ/) pierce through, pin down, with a sharp, pointed object.

im·pale·ment *n* [U]

im·pal·pable /ɪmˈpælpəbəl/ *adj* **1** that cannot be touched or felt. **2** not easily grasped by the mind.

im·part /ɪmˈpart/ *vt* (*formal*) give, pass on, a secret, news, etc.

im·par·tial /ɪmˈparʃəl/ *adj* just; not favoring one more than another.

im·par·tially *adv*

im·par·tial·ity /ɪmˌparʃiˈæləti/ *n* [U]
im·pass·able /ɪmˈpæsəbl/ *adj* (of roads, etc) impossible to travel across or on.
im·passe /ˈɪmˌpæs/ *n* [C] position from which there is no way out.
im·pas·sioned /ɪmˈpæʃənd/ *adj* full of, showing, deep feeling: *an ~ speech.*
im·pas·sive /ɪmˈpæsɪv/ *adj* showing no sign of feeling; unmoved.
im·pas·sive·ly *adv*
im·pa·tience /ɪmˈpeiʃəns/ *n* [U] lack of patience; intolerance.
im·pa·tient /ɪmˈpeiʃənt/ *adj* not patient: *The children were ~ to start.*
im·pa·tient·ly *adv*
im·peach /ɪmˈpitʃ/ *vt* **1** (*formal*) question, raise doubts about (a person's character, etc). **2** (*legal*) charge or accuse a public official of doing wrong while in office: *~ a judge for taking bribes.*
im·peach·ment *n* [C,U]
im·pec·cable /ɪmˈpekəbəl/ *adj* (*formal*) faultless; incapable of doing wrong: *an ~ character/record.*
im·pe·cuni·ous /ˌɪmpɪˈkyuniəs/ *adj* (*formal*) having little or no money.
im·pede /ɪmˈpid/ *vt* get in the way of: *What is impeding an early start?*
im·pedi·ment /ɪmˈpedəmənt/ *n* [C] **1** physical defect esp in speech, eg a stammer. **2** something that hinders; obstacle.
im·pel /ɪmˈpel/ *vt* (-ll-) force, urge: *He said he had been ~led to commit the crime by poverty.*
im·pend /ɪmˈpend/ *vi* (*formal*) be about to come or happen: *her ~ing arrival.*
im·pen·etrable /ɪmˈpenətrəbəl/ *adj* that cannot be entered or penetrated: *~ forests.*
im·pera·tive /ɪmˈperətɪv/ *adj* **1** urgent; essential: *Is it ~ that they have/for them to have two cars?* **2** expressing a command: *an ~ gesture.* **3** (*gram*) form of a *verb* and sentence expressing commands, eg *Listen! Go away!*
im·pera·tive·ly *adv*
im·per·cep·tible /ˌɪmpərˈseptəbəl/ *adj* that cannot be perceived; unnoticeable; very slight or gradual.
im·per·cep·tibly /-əbli/ *adv*
im·per·fect /ɪmˈpərfɪkt/ *adj* **1** not perfect or complete. **2** (*gram*): *~ tense,* denoting (usu past) action in progress and not yet completed, eg *I was thinking about it.* □ *n* [C] imperfect tense.
im·per·fect·ly *adv*
im·per·fec·tion /ˌɪmpərˈfekʃən/ *n* **1** [U] state of being imperfect. **2** [C] fault: *the little ~ions in her character.*
im·pe·rial /ɪmˈpɪriəl/ *adj* **1** of an empire or its ruler(s): *~ trade.* **2** (*formal*) majestic; magnificent: *with ~ generosity.*
im·pe·rially /-riəli/ *adv*
im·peri·al·ism /ɪmˈpɪriəˌlɪzəm/ *n* [U] (political system using a) policy of extending a country's empire and influence, by acquiring colonies, etc.
im·pe·rial·ist /-əlɪst/ *n* [C] supporter of, believer in, imperialism.
im·per·ial·is·tic /ɪmˌpɪriəˈlɪstɪk/ *adj*
im·peril /ɪmˈperəl/ *vt* (-l-, -ll-) put or bring into danger.
im·peri·ous /ɪmˈpɪriəs/ *adj* (*formal*) **1** dictatorial; arrogant: *~ commands/looks.* **2** urgent; imperative.
im·peri·ous·ly *adv*
im·peri·ous·ness /-nɪs/ *n* [U]
im·per·ish·able /ɪmˈperɪʃəbəl/ *adj* (*formal*) that will never die or pass away: *~ fame/glory.*
im·per·ma·nent /ɪmˈpərmənənt/ *adj* (*formal*) not permanent.
im·per·ma·nence /-nəns/ *n* [U]
im·per·sonal /ˌɪmˈpərsənəl/ *adj* **1** not influenced by personal feeling; not referring to any particular person: *an ~ discussion.* **2** having no existence as a person: *~ forces,* eg those of nature. **3** (of *verbs*) used after "it" to make statements such as *"It is raining."*
im·per·sonally /-nəli/ *adv*
im·per·son·ate /ɪmˈpərsəˌneit/ *vt* **1** act the part of; pretend to be. **2** personify.
im·per·son·ation /ɪmˌpərsəˈneiʃən/ *n* [C,U]
im·per·ti·nence /ɪmˈpərtənəns/ *n* **1** [U] rudeness; impudence. **2** [C] impudent remark or act.
im·per·ti·nent /ɪmˈpərtənənt/ *adj* **1** not showing proper respect; impudent: *~ remarks.* **2** not pertinent; irrelevant.
im·per·ti·nent·ly *adv*
im·per·turb·able /ˌɪmpərˈtərbəbəl/ *adj* (*formal*) not capable of being excited; calm.
im·per·vi·ous /ɪmˈpərviəs/ *adj* **1** (of materials) not allowing (water, etc) to pass through. **2** (*fig*) not moved or influenced by: *~ to criticism.*
im·petu·ous /ɪmˈpetʃuəs/ *adj* **1** acting, inclined to act, on impulse, with insufficient thought or care: *~ remarks.* **2** moving quickly or violently.
im·petu·ous·ly *adv*
im·petu·os·ity /ɪmˌpetʃuˈasəti/ *n* [C,U]
im·pe·tus /ˈɪmpətəs/ *n* (*pl* ~es) **1** [U] force with which a body moves. **2** [C] stimulus; driving force: *The treaty will give an ~ to trade between the two countries.*
im·pinge /ɪmˈpɪndʒ/ *vi* (*formal*) **1** make an impact (*on/upon*). **2** trespass; encroach.
im·pinge·ment *n* [U]
im·pi·ous /ˈɪmpiəs/ *adj* (*formal*) not pious; irreverent (the more usual word).
im·pi·ous·ly *adv*
imp·ish /ˈɪmpɪʃ/ *adj* of or like an imp.
imp·ish·ly *adv*
im·pla·cable /ɪmˈplækəbəl/ *adj* (*formal*) that cannot be easily calmed or appeased; relentless: *an ~ enemy.*
im·plant /ɪmˈplænt/ *vt* establish firmly; fix or put ideas, feelings, etc (in): *deeply ~ed hatred.*
im·ple·ment[1] /ˈɪmpləmənt/ *n* [C] tool or instrument for working with: *farm ~s.*
im·ple·ment[2] /ˈɪmpləˌment/ *vt* carry out an undertaking, agreement, promise: *~ a scheme.*
im·ple·men·ta·tion /ˌɪmpləmənˈteiʃən/ *n* [U]
im·pli·cate /ˈɪmpləˌkeit/ *vt* **1** show that (a person) is or was involved (*in* a crime, etc). **2** imply.
im·pli·ca·tion /ˌɪmpləˈkeiʃən/ *n* **1** [U] implicating or being implicated (*in* a crime, etc). **2** [C] what is implied: *What are the ~s of this statement?*
im·plic·it /ɪmˈplɪsɪt/ *adj* (*formal*) **1** implied or understood though not plainly expressed: *an ~*

threat. **2** unquestioning: ~ *belief*.
im·plic·it·ly *adv*

im·plore /ɪmˈplɔr/ *vt* request earnestly; beg: *imploring a judge for mercy*.
im·plor·ing·ly *adv*

im·ply /ɪmˈplai/ *vt* (*pt,pp* -ied) **1** say indirectly; suggest (*that*): *Are you ~ing that I am not telling the truth?* **2** involve as logically necessary: *A fever implies an illness*.

im·po·lite /ˌɪmpəˈlait/ *adj* not polite.
im·po·lite·ly *adv*
im·po·lite·ness /-nɪs/ *n* [U]

im·port /ɪmˈpɔrt/ *vt* **1** bring in, introduce, from a foreign country: ~ *coffee from Brazil*. **2** (*formal*) mean: *What does this ~?* □ *n* /ˈɪmˌpɔrt/ **1** (often *pl*) goods imported: *food ~s*. **2** [U] act of importing goods. **3** [U] (*formal*) meaning: *What is the ~ of his statement?* **4** [U] (*formal*) importance: *questions of great ~*.
im·porter /ɪmˈpɔrtər/ *n* [C] person who imports goods.

im·por·tation /ˌɪmpɔrˈteiʃən/ *n* [C,U]

im·por·tance /ɪmˈpɔrtəns/ *n* [U] being important: *The matter is of great/no/not much/little ~ to us*.

im·por·tant /ɪmˈpɔrtənt/ *adj* **1** of great influence; to be treated seriously; having a great effect: ~ *decisions/books*. **2** (of a person) having fame, authority, etc.
im·por·tant·ly *adv*

im·por·tu·nate /ɪmˈpɔrtʃənɪt/ *adj* (*formal*) **1** (of persons) making repeated and inconvenient requests: *an ~ beggar*. **2** (of affairs, etc) urgent: ~ *demands*.

im·por·tune /ɪmpərˈtun/ *vt* (*formal*) beg urgently and repeatedly: *importuning for more money*.

im·por·tun·ity /ɪmpərˈtunəti/ *n* **1** [U] persistence in making urgent or inconvenient requests. **2** [C] (*pl* -ies) (*Note:* usually *pl* in this sense) repeated, nagging requests.

im·pose /ɪmˈpouz/ *vt,vi* **1** lay or place a tax, duty, etc on: *New duties were ~d on wines and spirits*. **2** force (something, oneself, one's company) on others. **3** take advantage of: ~ *on/upon someone's good nature*.
im·pos·ing *adj* impressive because of size, character, appearance: *an imposing old lady*.
im·pos·ing·ly *adv*

im·po·si·tion /ɪmpəˈzɪʃən/ *n* **1** [U] the act of imposing(1): *the ~ of new taxes*. **2** [C] something imposed, eg tax, burden, punishment. **3** [C] fraud; trick; deception.

im·pos·sible /ɪmˈpasəbəl/ *adj* **1** not possible: *It is ~ to get there by train*. **2** intolerable; that cannot be endured: *It's an ~ situation!*
im·pos·sibly /-əbli/ *adv*
im·possi·bil·ity /ɪmˌpasəˈbɪləti/ *n* [C,U]

im·pos·tor /ɪmˈpastər/ *n* [C] person pretending to be somebody else.

im·pos·ture /ɪmˈpastʃər/ *n* [C,U] (act of) deception by an impostor.

im·po·tence /ˈɪmpətəns, ɪmˈpoutəns/ *n* [U] state of being impotent.

im·po·tent /ˈɪmpətənt, ɪmˈpoutənt/ *adj* lacking sufficient strength (to do something).
im·po·tent·ly *adv*

im·pound /ɪmˈpaund/ *vt* take possession of by law or by authority.

im·pov·er·ish /ɪmˈpav(ə)rɪʃ/ *vt* (*formal*) **1** cause to become poor: *~ed by doctors' fees*. **2** reduce the strength, fertility, etc of: *~ed farm land*.
im·pov·er·ish·ment /-mənt/ *n* [U]

im·prac·ti·cable /ɪmˈpræktɪkəbəl/ *adj* that cannot be put into practice or carried out: *an ~ scheme*.
im·prac·ti·cably /-əbli/ *adv*

im·prac·ti·cal /ɪmˈpræktɪkəl/ *adj* not practical.

im·preg·nable /ɪmˈpregnəbəl/ *adj* that cannot be overcome or taken by force: ~ *defenses/arguments*.
im·preg·nably /-əbli/ *adv*

im·preg·nate /ɪmˈpregˌneit/ *vt* **1** make pregnant; fertilize, eg an ovum. **2** fill, saturate: *water ~d with salt*.

im·pre·sario /ˌɪmprɪˈsariou/ *n* [C] (*pl* ~s) manager of an operatic or concert company.

im·press /ɪmˈpres/ *vt* **1** press (one thing on or with another); make (a mark, etc) by doing this: ~ *a design on metal*. **2** have a strong influence on; fix deeply (on the mind, memory): *The book/He did not ~ me at all*. □ *n* /ˈɪmˌpres/ [C] impression(1), mark made by pressure.

im·pres·sion /ɪmˈpreʃən/ *n* **1** [C] mark made by pressing: *the ~ of a seal on wax*. **2** [C] (product of) any one printing operation: *a first ~ of 5,000 copies*. **3** [C,U] effect produced on the mind or feelings: *It's my ~ that he doesn't want to come*. ***be under the impression that,*** have a vague idea, think, that.
im·pres·sion·ism /-ˌnɪzəm/ *n* [U] method of painting or writing so as to give the general effect without elaborate detail.
im·pres·sion·ist /-ɪst/ *n* [C] person who uses this method.
im·pres·sion·is·tic /ɪmˌpreʃənˈɪstɪk/ *adj* of, characteristic of, impressionism.

im·pres·sion·able /ɪmˈpreʃənəbəl/ *adj* easily influenced or affected: *children are very ~*.

im·pres·sive /ɪmˈpresɪv/ *adj* making a deep impression on the mind and feelings: *an ~ ceremony*.
im·pres·sive·ly *adv*

im·print /ɪmˈprɪnt/ *vt* print; stamp firmly: (*fig*) *ideas ~ed on the mind*. □ *n* /ˈɪmˌprɪnt/ [C] mark made by imprinting: *the ~ of suffering on her face*.

im·prison /ɪmˈprɪzən/ *vt* put or keep in prison.
im·prison·ment *n* [U]

im·prob·able /ɪmˈprabəbəl/ *adj* not likely to be true or to happen: *an ~ story/result*.
im·prob·ably /-əbli/ *adv*
im·prob·abil·ity /ɪmˌprabəˈbɪləti/ *n* [C,U]

im·promptu /ɪmˈprampˌtu/ *adj, adv* without preparation: *an ~ speech*. □ *n* [C] musical composition that seems to have been improvised.

im·proper /ɪmˈprapər/ *adj* **1** not suited for the purpose, situation, circumstances, etc: *Laughing is ~ at a funeral*. **2** incorrect: *an ~ diagnosis of disease*. **3** indecent: ~ *stories*.
im·proper·ly *adv*

im·proper frac·tion /ɪmˌprapər ˈfrækʃən/ *n* [C] fraction, as 32/8, in which the numerator is larger than the denomenator.

im·pro·pri·ety /ˌɪmprəˈpraiəti/ *n* (*pl* -ies) (*formal*) **1** [U] incorrectness; unsuitability. **2** [C] improper act, remark, etc.

im·prove /ɪmˈpruv/ *vt,vi* make or become better: *His health is improving.*

im·prove·ment *n* **1** [U] improving or being improved: *There is need for ~ment in your handwriting.* **2** [C] something which adds to beauty, usefulness, value, etc: *an ~ment in the weather.*

im·provi·dent /ɪmˈpravədənt/ *adj* (*formal*) wasteful; not looking to future needs.

im·pro·vise /ˈɪmprəˌvaiz/ *vt,vi* **1** compose music while playing, compose verse while reciting, etc: *If an actor forgets his words, he has to ~.* **2** provide, make or do something quickly, using whatever happens to be available: *an ~d meal.*

im·pro·vis·ation /ɪmˌpravɪˈzeiʃən/ *n* [C,U]

im·prud·ent /ɪmˈprudənt/ *adj* rash; unwise: *an ~ act/remark.*

im·pru·dent·ly *adv*

im·prud·ence /-əns/ *n* [C,U]

im·pu·dence /ˈɪmpyədəns/ *n* [U] (act of) being impudent: *The father punished the child because of her ~.*

im·pu·dent /ˈɪmpyədənt/ *adj* shamelessly rude, disrespectful: *What an ~ rascal he is!*

im·pu·dent·ly *adv*

im·pulse /ˈɪmˌpəls/ *n* **1** [C] push or thrust: *give an ~ to trade/education.* **2** [C] sudden inclination to act without thought about the consequences: *feel an irresistible ~ to jump out of a window; a man who acts on ~.*

im·pul·sive /ɪmˈpəlsɪv/ *adj* **1** (of persons, their conduct) acting on impulse; resulting from impulse: *a girl with an ~ nature.* **2** (of a force) tending to impel or drive forward.

im·pul·sive·ly *adv*

im·pul·sive·ness /-nɪs/*n* [U]

im·pun·ity /ɪmˈpyunəti/ *n* [U] (esp) ***with impunity,*** without risk of injury or punishment.

im·pure /ɪmˈpyʊr/ *adj* not pure: *~ motives.*

im·pu·rity /-əti/ *n* [C,U]

im·pute /ɪmˈpyut/ *vt* (*formal*) consider responsible for; charge with responsibility for: *He was innocent of the crime ~d to him.*

im·pu·ta·tion /ˌɪmpyəˈteiʃən/ *n* [C,U]

in[1] /ɪn/ *adv* (contrasted with *out*) **1** (used with many verbs, such as *come in* (= enter), *give in* (= surrender); ⇨ the *verb* entries for these) **2** ***be in,*** **(a)** at home: *Is there anyone in?* **(b)** arrive: *Is the train in yet?* **(c)** (of crops) harvested: *The wheat crop is safely in.* **(d)** in season; obtainable: *Strawberries are in now.* **(e)** in fashion: *Long skirts are in again.* **(f)** elected; in power; in office: *The Democrats are in.* ***be in on,*** (*informal*) participate in; have a share in: *I'd like to be in on this scheme.* **3** ***in for,*** likely to have or experience (often something unpleasant): *I'm afraid we're in for a storm.* ***have it in for sb,*** have a grudge against him.

in[2] /ɪn/ *prep* **1** (of place; ⇨ at): *in Africa; children playing in the street; not a cloud in the sky; lying in bed. He was wounded in the leg. I read about it in the newspapers.* **2** (of direction): *in this/that direction; in all directions.* **3** (of direction of motion or activity) into: *He put his hands in his pockets. Cut/break it in two.* **4** (of time when) during: *in 1970; in spring/summer.* ***in the end,*** finally. **5** (of time) in the course of; at/by the conclusion of: *They built the house in a month. I'll be back in a few days.* **6** (indicating inclusion): *seven days in a week; a man in his thirties,* ie between 29 and 40 years of age. **7** (of ratio): *Not one in ten of the boys could spell well.* **8** (of dress, etc): *dressed in white,* wearing white clothes; *in uniform.* **9** (of physical surroundings, circumstances, etc): *go out in the rain.* **10** (of a state or condition): *in good order; in poor health; in a hurry; in love; in public.* **11** (of form, shape, arrangement): *words in alphabetical order; dancing in a ring.* **12** (of form, means, etc): *speaking/writing in English; payment in cash.* **13** (of degree or extent): *in large/small quantities.* ***in all,*** as the total: *We were fifteen in all.* **14** (of identity): *We have lost a first-rate teacher in Mr Hill,* Mr Hill, who has left us, was a first-rate teacher. **15** (of relation, reference, respect): *in every way; blind in the left eye; my equal in strength.* **16** (of occupation, activity, etc): *He's in the army/in the civil service. How much time do you spend in reading?* **17** (used in numerous prepositional phrases of the pattern *in + noun + prep;* ⇨ the *noun* entries, eg): *in defense of; in exchange for.* **18** ***in that,*** since, because: *A high income tax is harmful in that it may discourage people from trying to earn more.* ***in as/so far as,*** to the extent that: *He is a Russian in so far as he was born there.* ***in itself,*** considered apart from other things: *Playing cards is not harmful in itself, but gambling may be.*

in[3] /ɪn/ *n* (only in) ***have an ˈin to/with sb,*** (*informal*) have privileged access, an inside connection, etc., esp to or with an important individual or organization. ***the ins and (the) outs,*** all the details and complexities: *know all the ~s and outs of a problem.*

IN[4] *postal abbr* = Indiana. ⇨ App 6.

in.[5] *abbr* = inch(es).

-in /-ˌɪn/ *suff* added to another word (usually a *verb*) to indicate participation in a group activity, etc: *ˈsit-ˌin, ˈteach-ˌin.*

in-[1]**, il-, im-, ir-** /ɪn-, ɪl-, ɪm-, ɪr-/ *prefix* **1** in; on: *intake, imprint.* **2** not: *indefinite; immoral; irreverent.*

in-[2] /ˈɪn-/ *prefix* (before a *noun*): *ˈinpatient,* one who lives in hospital while being treated (contrasted with *outpatient*).

in·abil·ity /ˌɪnəˈbɪləti/ *n* [U] being unable; lack of power or means: *an ~ to pay one's debts.*

in·ac·ces·sible /ˌɪnəkˈsesəbəl/ *adj* (*formal*) not accessible.

in·ac·cessi·bil·ity /ˌɪnəkˌsesəˈbɪləti/ *n* [U]

in·ac·cu·racy /ɪˈnækyərəsi/ *n* **1** [U] being inaccurate. **2** [C] (*pl* -ies) inaccurate statement, etc.

in·ac·cu·rate /ɪˈnækyərɪt/ *adj* not accurate.

in·ac·cur·ate·ly *adv*

in·ac·tion /ɪˈnækʃən/ *n* [U] doing nothing; lack of activity.

in·ac·tive /ɪˈnæktɪv/ *adj* **1** not active. **2** not available for duty or service.

in·ac·tiv·ity /ˌɪnækˈtɪvəti/ *n* [U]

in·ad·equate /ɪˈnædɪkwɪt/ *adj* **1** not adequate; insufficient. **2** not capable.

in·ad·equate·ly *adv*
in·ad·equacy /ɪˈnædɪkwəsi/ *n* [U]
in·ad·mis·sible /ˌɪnədˈmɪsəbəl/ *adj* that cannot be admitted or allowed: ~ *evidence*.
in·ad·ver·tent /ˌɪnədˈvərtənt/ *adj* (*formal*) **1** not paying or showing proper attention. **2** (of actions) done thoughtlessly or not on purpose.
in·ad·ver·tent·ly *adv*
in·alien·able /ɪˈneiliənəbəl/ *adj* (*formal*) (of rights, etc) that cannot be given away or taken away.
in·ane /ɪˈnein/ *adj* silly; senseless: *an* ~ *remark*.
in·ane·ly *adv*
in·an·ity /ɪˈnænəti/ *n* [C,U]
in·ani·mate /ɪˈnænəmɪt/ *adj* **1** lifeless: ~ *rocks and stones*. **2** spiritless; dull.
in·ap·pli·cable /ɪˈnæplɪkəbəl/ *adj* not applicable (*to*).
in·ap·preci·able /ˌɪnəˈpriʃəbəl/ *adj* not worth reckoning; too small or slight to be perceived: *an* ~ *difference*.
in·ap·pro·pri·ate /ˌɪnəˈproupriɪt/ *adj* not appropriate or suitable.
in·ar·ticu·late /ˌɪnarˈtɪkyəlɪt/ *adj* (of speech) not clear or distinct; (of a person) not speaking distinctly, clearly or fluently: ~ *rage*.
in·ar·tis·tic /ˌɪnærˈtɪstɪk/ *adj* not artistic.
in·as·much as /ˌɪnəzˈmətʃ əz/ *adv* since; because.
in·at·ten·tion /ˌɪnəˈtenʃən/ *n* lack of, failure to pay, attention.
in·at·ten·tive /ˌɪnəˈtentɪv/ *adj* not attentive.
in·aud·ible /ɪˈnɔdəbəl/ *adj* that cannot be heard.
in·audi·bil·ity /ɪˌnɔdəˈbɪləti/ *n* [U]
in·aug·ural /ɪˈnɔgyərəl/ *adj* of or for an inauguration: *an* ~ *address*. □ *n* [C] **1** inaugural speech. **2** = inauguration.
in·au·gu·rate /ɪˈnɔgyəˌreit/ *vt* **1** install a new official, professor, etc (in office with) at a special ceremony: ~ *a president*. **2** open for public use, esp with a ceremony. **3** begin: *The invention of the internal combustion engine* ~*d a new era in travel*.
in·au·gur·ation /ɪˌnɔgyəˈreiʃən/ *n* [C,U]
in·aus·pi·cious /ˌɪnɔˈspɪʃəs/ *adj* not auspicious; unfavorable.
in·aus·pi·cious·ly *adv*
in·born /ˈɪnˌbɔrn/ *adj* innate; present in a person or animal at birth: *an* ~ *talent*.
in·bound /ˈɪnˌbaund/ *adj* inward or homeward bound; ~ *traffic over the George Washington bridge*, traffic coming into the city.
in·bred /ˈɪnˌbred/ *adj* **1** inborn; innate: ~ *courtesy*. **2** bred for several or many generations from ancestors closely related.
in·breed·ing /ˈɪnˌbridɪŋ/ *n* [U] breeding from closely related ancestors, stocks, etc.
Inc. *abbr* = Incorporated.
in·cal·cu·lable /ɪnˈkælkyələbəl/ *adj* **1** too great to be calculated: *This has done* ~ *harm to our reputation*. **2** that cannot be reckoned beforehand. **3** (of a person, his character, etc) uncertain: *a lady of* ~ *moods*.
in·can·descent /ˌɪnkənˈdesənt/ *adj* giving out, able to give out, light when heated: *an* ~ *filament*, eg in an electric-light bulb.
in·can·descence /-səns/ *n* [U] being or becoming incandescent.
in·can·ta·tion /ˌɪnˌkænˈteiʃn/ *n* [C,U] (the use of) (a form of) words used in magic; charm or spell.
in·capable /ɪnˈkeipəbəl/ *adj* ***incapable (of)***, not capable: ~ *of telling a lie*, too honest to do so.
in·capa·bil·ity /ˌɪnˌkeipəˈbɪləti/ *n* [U]
in·ca·paci·tate /ˌɪnkəˈpæsəˌteit/ *vt* **1** make incapable or unfit: *His poor health* ~*d him for work/from working*. **2** disqualify.
in·ca·pac·ity /ˌɪnkəˈpæsəti/ *n* [U] ***incapacity (for sth/for doing sth/to do sth),*** inability; powerlessness.
in·car·cer·ate /ɪnˈkarsəˌreit/ *vt* (*formal*) imprison.
in·car·cer·ation /ɪnˌkarsəˈreiʃən/ *n* [U]
in·car·nate /ɪnˈkarnɪt/ *adj* **1** having a body; (esp) in human form: *That prison officer is a devil* ~. **2** (of an idea, ideal, etc) appearing in human form: *Liberty* ~. □ *vt* /ɪnˈkarˌneit/ **1** make incarnate. **2** (of a person) embody (a quality): *a wife who* ~*s all the virtues*.
in·car·na·tion /ˌɪnkarˈneiʃən/ *n* **the Incarnation,** (in Christian belief) the taking of bodily form by Jesus.
in·cen·di·ary /ɪnˈsendiˌeri/ *n* [C] (*pl* -ies), *adj* **1** (person) setting fire to property unlawfully. **2** (person) tending to excite, stir up violence, etc: *an* ~ *speech*. **3** (bomb) causing fire.
in·cense[1] /ˈɪnˌsens/ *n* [U] (smoke or perfume of a) substance producing a sweet smell when burning.
in·cense[2] /ɪnˈsens/ *vt* make angry: ~*d by his conduct/at her remarks*.
in·cen·tive /ɪnˈsentɪv/ *n* [C,U] that which incites or encourages a person: *He hasn't much* ~ *to work hard/to hard work*.
in·cep·tion /ɪnˈsepʃən/ *n* [C] (*formal*) start; beginning.
in·ces·sant /ɪnˈsesənt/ *adj* continual; often repeated: *a week of* ~ *rain*.
in·ces·sant·ly *adv*
in·cest /ˈɪnˌsest/ *n* [U] sexual intercourse between two people who are so closely related (eg brother and sister) that they cannot legally marry.
in·ces·tuous /ɪnˈsestʃuəs/ *adj*
inch /ɪntʃ/ *n* [C] **1** measure of length, one-twelfth of a foot. **2** small amount. □ *vt,vi* make one's way very slowly or gradually: ~ *along a ledge on a cliff*.
in·ci·dence /ˈɪnsədəns/ *n* [C] range or extent of something which occurs or affects things: *the* ~ *of a disease*.
in·ci·dent[1] /ˈɪnsədənt/ *adj* forming a natural or expected part of; naturally connected with: *the risks* ~ *to the life of a racing driver*.
in·ci·dent[2] /ˈɪnsədənt/ *n* [C] **1** event, esp one of less importance than others: *frontier* ~*s*, eg disputes between forces on a frontier. **2** happening which attracts general attention.
in·ci·den·tal /ˌɪnsəˈdentəl/ *adj* **1** accompanying but not forming a necessary part: ~ *music to a film*. **2** small and comparatively unimportant: ~ *expenses*.
in·ci·den·tally /-tli/ *adv* by chance; by the way.
in·cin·er·ate /ɪnˈsɪnəˌreit/ *vt* burn to ashes;

destroy by burning.
in·cin·er·ation /ɪnˌsɪnəˈreiʃən/ *n* [U]
in·cin·er·ator /ɪnˈsɪnəˌreitər/ *n* [C] furnace, etc for burning rubbish, etc.
in·cipi·ent /ɪnˈsɪpiənt/ *adj* in an early stage; just beginning to show: *~ decay of the teeth.*
in·cise /ɪnˈsaiz/ *vt* make a cut in; engrave.
in·ci·sion /ɪnˈsɪʒən/ *n* **1** [U] cutting (into something). **2** [C] clean, narrow cut, eg in surgery.
in·ci·sive /ɪnˈsaisɪv/ *adj* **1** sharp and cutting. **2** (of a person's mind, remarks) clear-cut: *~ criticism.*
in·cis·ive·ly *adv*
in·cisor /ɪnˈsaizər/ *n* [C] (in human beings) any one of the sharp-edged front cutting teeth. ⇨ illus at mouth.
in·cite /ɪnˈsait/ *vt* stir up: *insults inciting resentment.*
in·cite·ment *n* [C,U]
incl. *abbr* = **1** including. **2** inclusive.
in·clem·ent /ɪnˈklemənt/ *adj* (*formal*) (of weather or climate) severe; cold and stormy.
in·clem·ency /-ənsi/ *n* [U]
in·cli·na·tion /ˌɪnkləˈneiʃən/ *n* **1** [C] bending; bowing; slope; slant: *the ~ of a roof*, its degree of slope. **2** [C,U] liking or desire: *He showed no ~ to leave.*
in·cline[1] /ɪnˈklain/ *vt,vi* **1** (cause to) lean, slope or slant. **2** bend (the head, body, oneself) forward or downward: *~ the head in prayer.* **3** tend: *He ~s to leanness.* ***be inclined to,*** have a willingness; have a tendency: *I am ~d to think that he is opposed to the plan. He's ~d to be lazy.*
in·cline[2] /ˈɪnˌklain/ *n* [C] slope; sloping surface: *a steep ~.*
in·close, in·clos·ure = enclose, enclosure.
in·clude /ɪnˈklud/ *vt* bring in, reckon, as part of the whole: *ten competitors, including two from California.*
in·clu·sion /ɪnˈkluʒən/ *n* [U]
in·clu·sive /ɪnˈklusɪv/ *adj* **1** including: *from May 1 to June 3 ~*, May 1 and June 3 being included. **2** including much or all: *a price ~ of tax.*
in·clu·sive·ly *adv*
in·cog·nito /ˌɪnkagˈnitou/ *adj* disguised; with an assumed name. □ *adv* with one's name, character, etc concealed: *travel ~.*
in·co·her·ent /ˌɪnkouˈhɪrənt/ *adj* not coherent.
in·co·her·ence /-əns/ *n* [U]
in·co·her·ent·ly *adv*
in·come /ˈɪnˌkəm/ *n* [C] money received during a given period (as salary, receipts from trade, interest from investments, etc): *live within/beyond one's ~*, spend less/more than one receives.
ˈincome tax, tax imposed on income.
in·com·ing /ˈɪnˌkəmɪŋ/ *adj* coming in: *the ~ tide/tenant.*
in·com·men·su·rate /ˌɪnkəˈmenʃərɪt/ *adj* **1** not comparable (*to*). **2** not adequate or equal when compared (*with*).
in·com·mode /ˌɪnkəˈmoud/ *vt* (*formal*) cause trouble or inconvenience to.
in·com·par·able /ɪnˈkamp(ə)rəbəl/ *adj* not to be compared; without equal: *~ beauty.*
in·com·pat·ible /ˌɪnkəmˈpætəbəl/ *adj* opposed in character; unable to exist in harmony: *Excessive drinking is ~ with good health.*
in·com·pati·bil·ity /ˌɪnkəmˌpætəˈbɪləti/ *n* [U]
in·com·pe·tent /ɪnˈkampətənt/ *adj* not qualified or able: *an ~ teacher.*
in·com·pe·tent·ly *adv*
in·com·pe·tence /-əns/, **in·com·pe·tency** /-ənsi/ *n* [U] being incompetent.
in·com·plete /ˌɪnkəmˈplit/ *adj* not complete.
in·com·plete·ly *adv*
in·com·pre·hen·sible /ˌɪnˌkamprɪˈhensəbəl/ *adj* (*formal*) that cannot be understood.
in·com·pre·hen·si·bil·ity /ˌɪnˌkamprɪˌhensəˈbɪləti/ *n* [U]
in·com·pre·hen·sion /ˌɪnˌkamprɪˈhenʃən/ *n* [U] failure to understand.
in·con·ceiv·able /ˌɪnkənˈsivəbəl/ *adj* **1** that cannot be imagined. **2** hard to believe; very remarkable.
in·con·clu·sive /ˌɪnkənˈklusɪv/ *adj* not decisive or convincing; not leading to a definite result: *~ actions.*
in·con·clu·sive·ly *adv*
in·con·gru·ous /ɪnˈkaŋgruəs/ *adj* not in harmony or agreement; out of place.
in·con·gru·ity /ˌɪnkənˈgruəti/ *n* [C,U]
in·con·gru·ous·ly *adv*
in·con·sequen·tial /ɪnˌkansəˈkwenʃəl/ *adj* (esp) unimportant.
in·con·sid·er·able /ˌɪnkənˈsɪdərəbəl/ *adj* not worth considering; of small size, value, etc.
in·con·sid·er·ate /ˌɪnkənˈsɪdərɪt/ *adj* (of a person, his actions) thoughtless: *~ children/remarks.*
in·con·sid·er·ate·ly *adv*
in·con·sist·ent /ˌɪnkənˈsɪstənt/ *adj* **1** not in harmony; contradictory; having parts that do not agree: *The two stories were ~.* **2** changeable, esp in one's actions, beliefs, etc: *an ~ person.*
in·con·sist·ency /-ənsi/ *n* [C,U]
in·con·sist·ent·ly *adv*
in·con·sol·able /ˌɪnkənˈsouləbəl/ *adj* that cannot be consoled: *~ grief. The widow was ~.*
in·con·spicu·ous /ˌɪnkənˈspɪkyuəs/ *adj* not striking or obvious: *dressed in ~ colors.*
in·con·spicu·ous·ly *adv*
in·con·stant /ɪnˈkanstənt/ *adj* (*formal*) (of persons) changeable in feelings, intentions, purpose, etc: *an ~ lover.*
in·con·stancy /-ənsi/ *n* [C,U]
in·con·test·able /ˌɪnkənˈtestəbəl/ *adj* that cannot be disputed or questioned.
in·con·ti·nent /ɪnˈkantənənt/ *adj* lacking in self-control or self-restraint.
in·con·ti·nence /-əns/ *n* [U]
in·con·tro·vert·ible /ˌɪnˌkantrəˈvərtəbəl/ *adj* that cannot be disputed.
in·con·ven·ience /ˌɪnkənˈvinyəns/ *n* **1** [U] discomfort or trouble: *I suffered great ~.* **2** [C] something that causes inconvenience. □ *vt* cause inconvenience to.
in·con·ven·ient /ˌɪnkənˈvinyənt/ *adj* causing discomfort, trouble or annoyance.
in·con·ven·ient·ly *adv*
in·cor·po·rate /ɪnˈkərpəˌreit/ *vt,vi* **1** make, become, united in one body or group: *Hanover was ~d into Prussia in 1886.* **2** (*legal*) form into,

become, a corporation: *The firm finally ~d.*
in·cor·po·ration /ɪnˌkɔrpəˈreiʃən/ *n* [U]
in·cor·rect /ˌɪnkəˈrekt/ *adj* not correct.
in·cor·rect·ly *adv*
in·cor·rect·ness /-nɪs/ *n* [U]
in·cor·ri·gible /ɪnˈkɔrɪdʒəbəl, -ˈkar-/ *adj* (of a person, his faults, etc) that cannot be corrected or reformed: *an ~ liar.*
in·cor·rupt·ible /ˌɪnkəˈrəptəbəl/ *adj* **1** that cannot decay or be destroyed. **2** honest; that cannot be corrupted, esp by being bribed.
in·cor·rupti·bil·ity /ˌɪnkəˌrəptəˈbɪləti/ *n* [U]
in·crease[1] /ˈɪnˌkris/ *n* **1** [U] increasing; growth. **2** [C] amount by which something increases.
in·crease[2] /ɪnˈkris/ *vt,vi* make or become greater in size, number, degree, etc: *Our difficulties are increasing.*
in·creas·ing·ly /ɪnˈkrisɪŋli/ *adv* more and more.
in·cred·ible /ɪnˈkredəbəl/ *adj* **1** that cannot be believed. **2** difficult to believe; very surprising.
in·credi·bil·ity /ɪnˌkredəˈbɪləti/ *n* [U]
in·cred·ibly /-əbli/ *adv*
in·credu·lous /ɪnˈkredʒələs/ *adj* **1** unbelieving. **2** showing disbelief: *~ looks.*
in·cred·ul·ity /ˌɪnkrɪˈduləti/ *n* [U]
in·credu·lous·ly *adv*
in·cre·ment /ˈɪnkrəmənt/ *n* **1** [U] increase. **2** [C] amount of increase: *yearly salary ~s of $500.*
in·crimi·nate /ɪnˈkrɪməˌneit/ *vt* say, show, that (a person) is guilty of a crime or of doing wrong.
in·cu·bate /ˈɪŋkyəˌbeit/ *vt,vi* **1** hatch (eggs) by natural heat (as of a hen's body) or by artificial warmth. **2** keep in a state favorable to development or growth.
in·cu·ba·tion /ˌɪŋkyəˈbeiʃən/ *n* [U]
in·cu·ba·tor /ˈɪŋkyəˌbeitər/ *n* [C] **(a)** apparatus for hatching eggs by artificial warmth. **(b)** apparatus that controls warmth, moisture, etc, used for small, weak babies.
in·cul·cate /ɪnˈkəlˌkeit/ *vt* teach by frequent repetition; instill.
in·cum·bent /ɪnˈkəmbənt/ *adj* (*formal*) **1** required as a duty: *It is ~ on you to warn him not to smoke.* **2** currently holding an office, position, etc. □ *n* [C] holder of any position or appointment.
in·cum·bency /-ənsi/ *n* [C] (*pl* -ies) position of an incumbent.
in·cur /ɪnˈkər/ *vt* (-rr-) bring on oneself: *~ debts/hatred/great expense.*
in·cur·able /ɪnˈkyurəbəl/ *adj* that cannot be cured: *~ diseases/habits.* □ *n* [C] person who is incurable.
in·cur·ably /-əbli/ *adv*
in·cur·sion /ɪnˈkərʒən/ *n* [C] sudden attack or invasion: (*fig*) *~s on my leisure time.*
ind. *abbr* = independent.
in·debted /ɪnˈdetɪd/ *adj* owing money or gratitude: *I am ~ to you for your help.*
in·de·cent /ɪnˈdisənt/ *adj* **1** (of behavior, talk, etc) not decent(2); obscene. **2** improper.
in·de·cency /-ənsi/ *n* [C,U]
in·de·cent·ly *adv*
in·de·cision /ˌɪndɪˈsɪʒən/ *n* [U] the state of being unable to decide; hesitation.
in·de·ci·sive /ˌɪndɪˈsaisɪv/ *adj* not decisive.
in·de·ci·sive·ly *adv*
in·deed /ɪnˈdid/ *adv* **1** really; as you say; as you may imagine: *"Are you pleased at your son's success?"—"Yes, ~."* **2** (used to intensify): *It is ~ a surprise.* **3** (used as a comment to show interest, surprise, etc): *"He spoke to me about you."—"Oh, ~!"*
in·de·fen·sible /ˌɪndɪˈfensəbəl/ *adj* that cannot be defended, justified or excused.
in·de·fin·able /ˌɪndɪˈfainəbəl/ *adj* that cannot be defined.
in·defi·nite /ɪnˈdefənɪt/ *adj* **1** vague: *an ~ answer,* eg neither "Yes" nor "No." **2** not limited or fixed: *an ~ period of time.*
the ˌindefinite ˈarticle, the word *"a"* or *"an".*
in·defi·nite·ly *adv*
in·del·ible /ɪnˈdeləbəl/ *adj* that cannot be washed or rubbed out or removed: *~ ink.*
in·del·ibly /-əbli/ *adv*
in·deli·cate /ɪnˈdelɪkɪt/ *adj* (of a person, his speech, behavior, etc) coarse; lacking in refinement: *~ remarks.*
in·deli·cacy /-kəsi/ *n* [C,U]
in·dem·nify /ɪnˈdemnəˌfai/ *vt* (*pt,pp* -ied) **1** (*legal, comm*) make safe; insure: *~ a person against harm/loss.* **2** repay (a person) for loss, injury, etc: *The company will ~ you for any medical expenses.*
in·dem·nity /ɪnˈdemnəti/ *n* (*pl* -ies) **1** [U] insurance against damage or loss. **2** [C] compensation for damage or loss.
in·dent /ɪnˈdent/ *vt,vi* **1** make notches in the edge or surface of. **2** start (a line of print or writing) farther from the margin than the others: *You must ~ the first line of each paragraph.*
in·den·ta·tion /ˌɪndenˈteiʃən/ *n* **1** [U] indenting or being indented. **2** [C] deep recess, as in a coastline. **3** [C] space left at the beginning of a line of print or writing.
in·de·pen·dence /ˌɪndɪˈpendəns/ *n* [U] state of being independent: *colonies obtaining ~ from European countries.*
Indeˈpendence Day, July 4, (US national holiday on) the anniversary of the signing in 1776 of the *Declaration of Independence.*
in·de·pen·dent /ˌɪndɪˈpendənt/ *adj* **1** not dependent on or controlled by (other persons or things): *Campers are ~ of hotels.* **2** not depending on others for a living: *~ means,* private wealth. **3** self-governing: *when the colony became ~.* **4** acting or thinking freely: *an ~ witness.* □ *n* [C] (esp) voter, candidate, etc who does not belong to a political party.
in·de·pen·dent·ly *adv*
in·de·scrib·able /ˌɪndɪˈskraibəbəl/ *adj* that cannot be described.
in·de·struct·ible /ˌɪndɪˈstrəktəbəl/ *adj* that cannot be destroyed: *~ concrete buildings.*
in·de·ter·mi·nate /ˌɪndɪˈtərmənɪt/ *adj* not fixed; vague or indefinite.
in·de·ter·min·able /ˌɪndɪˈtərmənəbəl/ *adj* that cannot be determined, decided or (eg of a dispute) settled.
in·de·ter·min·ably /-əbli/ *adv*
in·dex /ˈɪnˌdeks/ *n* [C] (*pl* ~es, indices /ˈɪndəˌsiz/) **1** something that points to or indicates, esp on a scale of degree or proportion: *increasing*

unemployment was an ~ of the country's poverty. **2** list of names, subjects, references, etc in alphabetical order, at the end of a book, or on cards (*a 'card ~*) in a library, etc. □ *vt* make an index for a book, collection of books, etc.

in·dexer *n* [C] person who prepares an index.

the 'index 'finger, the forefinger, next to the thumb, used for pointing.

In·dia ink /ˈɪndiə ˌɪŋk/ *n* [U] heavy, black ink used esp for lettering and artwork.

In·dian /ˈɪndiən/ *n* [C], *adj* **1** (native) of the Republic of India. **2** (one) of the original inhabitants of the Western Hemisphere.

SIOUX

NAVAJO

INDIANS OF NORTH AMERICA

Indian reser'vation, = reservation(2).

Indian 'summer, period of calm, dry weather in late autumn.

American 'Indian, = Indian(2).

West 'Indian, (native) of the West Indies.

In·dian corn /ˌɪndiən ˈkɔrn/ *n* [U] **1** (plant of North America bearing) seeds or kernels growing on long narrow ears; maize. **2** this as food.

in·di·cate /ˈɪndəˌkeit/ *vt* **1** point to; make known; be a sign of: *a sudden rise in temperature indicating pneumonia.* **2** say or state briefly: *He ~d that the interview was over.*

in·di·ca·tion /ˌɪndəˈkeiʃən/ *n* **1** [U] indicating or being indicated. **2** [C] sign: *I had no indication of his decision.*

in·dica·tive /ɪnˈdɪkətɪv/ *adj* **1** (*gram*) stating a fact or asking questions of fact: *the ~ mood.* **2** giving indications: *Is a high forehead ~ of intelligence?*

in·di·ca·tor /ˈɪndəˌkeitər/ *n* [C] person, thing, that points out or gives information.

in·di·ces *pl* of index.

in·dict /ɪnˈdait/ *vt* (*legal*) charge with or accuse (a person) of a crime.

in·dict·able /-əbəl/ *adj*

in·dict·ment *n* [C,U]

in·dif·fer·ence /ɪnˈdɪf(ə)rəns/ *n* [U] lack of interest or feeling: *It is a matter of ~ to me whether you go or stay,* I don't care which you do.

in·dif·fer·ent /ɪnˈdɪf(ə)rənt/ *adj* **1** impartial; having no interest; neither for nor against: *Justice should be ~ to wealth and power.* **2** unsympathetic: *He was ~ to our pleas.* **3** not of good quality or ability: *an ~ player.*

in·dif·fer·ent·ly *adv*

in·dige·nous /ɪnˈdɪdʒənəs/ *adj* native, belonging naturally to: *Kangaroos are ~ to Australia.*

in·di·gest·ible /ˌɪndəˈdʒestəbəl/ *adj* difficult or impossible to digest.

in·di·ges·tion /ˌɪndəˈdʒestʃən/ *n* [U] (pain from) difficulty in digesting food: *an attack of ~.*

in·dig·nant /ɪnˈdɪgnənt/ *adj* angry, esp at injustice or because of undeserved blame, etc.

in·dig·nant·ly *adv*

in·dig·na·tion /ˌɪndɪgˈneiʃən/ *n* [U] anger caused by injustice, misconduct, etc.

in·dig·nity /ɪnˈdɪgnəti/ *n* (*pl* -ies) **1** [U] rude or insulting treatment causing shame or loss of respect. **2** [C] something said or done that humiliates a person: *subjected to all sorts of indignities.*

in·digo /ˈɪndɪˌgou/ *n* [U] artificially made deep blue dye (formerly obtained from plants).

ˌindigo 'blue, dark blue-violet (color).

in·di·rect /ˌɪndəˈrekt/ *adj* **1** not straight or direct: *an ~ answer to a question.* **2** not coming as a direct result; secondary: *~ benefits.*

in·dir·ect·ly *adv*

ˌindirect 'object, (*gram*) referring to the secondary person, etc affected by the *verb*, eg *him* in *Give him the money.*

ˌindirect 'speech, (*gram*) speech as it is reported with the necessary changes of pronouns, tenses, etc, eg *He said he would come* for *He said "I will come."*

in·dis·creet /ˌɪndɪˈskrit/ *adj* not wise, cautious or careful.

in·dis·creet·ly *adv*

in·dis·cre·tion /ˌɪndɪˈskreʃən/ *n* **1** [U] indiscreet conduct. **2** [C] indiscreet remark or act.

in·dis·crimi·nate /ˌɪndɪˈskrɪmənɪt/ *adj* lacking care or taste: *~ praise.*

in·dis·crimi·nate·ly *adv*

in·dis·pens·able /ˌɪndɪˈspensəbəl/ *adj* absolutely essential: *Air, food and water are ~ to life.*

in·dis·posed /ˌɪndɪˈspouzd/ *adj* (*formal*) **1** unwell. **2** unwilling: *He seems ~ to help us.*

in·dis·put·able /ˌɪndɪˈspyutəbəl/ *adj* that cannot be disputed.

in·dis·sol·uble /ˌɪndɪˈsalyəbəl/ *adj* (*formal*) that cannot be dissolved or broken up; firm and lasting: *The Roman Catholic Church regards marriage as ~.*

in·dis·tinct /ˌɪndɪˈstɪŋkt/ *adj* not distinct: *~ sounds/memories.*

in·dis·tinct·ly *adv*

in·dis·tinct·ness /-nɪs/ *n* [U]

in·dis·tin·guish·able /ˌɪndɪˈstɪŋgwɪʃəbəl/ *adj* that cannot be clearly distinguished.

in·di·vid·ual /ˌɪndɪˈvɪdʒuəl/ *adj* **1** (opposite of *general*) specially for one person or thing: *~ attention.* **2** characteristic of a single person, animal, plant or thing: *an ~ style of speaking.* **3**

single; separate. □ *n* [C] any one human being, animal, or thing (contrasted with a group or with society): *the rights of the* ~.
in·di·vid·ually *adv* separately; one by one: *be interviewed* ~*ly*.
in·di·vidual·ism /ˌɪndɪˈvɪdʒuəˌlɪzəm/ *n* [U] **1** personal independence; principle of following one's own ideas. **2** theory that the individual is more important than the state, community, etc.
in·di·vidual·ist *n* [C]
in·di·vidu·al·ity /ˌɪndɪˌvɪdʒuˈæləti/ *n* (*pl* -ies) **1** [U] all the characteristics that belong to an individual and that distinguish him from others. **2** [C] state of separate existence.
in·di·vis·ible /ˌɪndɪˈvɪzəbəl/ *adj* that cannot be divided.
in·doc·tri·nate /ɪnˈdaktrəˌneit/ *vt* fill the mind of (a person) (with ideas or beliefs).
in·doc·tri·na·tion /ɪnˌdaktrəˈneiʃən/ *n* [U]
Indo-Euro·pean /ˌɪndou-ˌyʊrəˈpiən/ *adj* of the prehistoric people who spoke the language(s) which gave rise to Sanskrit, Greek, Latin, and most of the modern languages of Europe and India.
in·do·lent /ˈɪndələnt/ *adj* (*formal*) lazy; inactive.
in·dol·ence /-əns/ *n* [U]
in·do·lent·ly *adv*
in·domi·table /ɪnˈdamətəbəl/ *adj* that cannot be subdued or conquered; unyielding: ~ *courage*.
in·door /ˈɪnˌdɔr/ *adj* belonging to, carried on, situated, inside a building: ~ *games*.
in·doors /ˌɪnˈdɔrz/ *adv* in or into a building: *go/stay* ~*; kept* ~ *all week by bad weather*.
in·dorse /ɪnˈdɔrs/ = endorse.
in·dubi·table /ɪnˈdubətəbəl/ *adj* (*formal*) that cannot be doubted.
in·duce /ɪnˈdus/ *vt* **1** persuade or influence; cause: *What* ~*d you to do such a thing?* **2** bring about; produce: *illness* ~*d by overwork*. **3** reach a conclusion by reasoning from particular facts.
in·duce·ment *n* [C,U] that which induces; incentive: *He hasn't much* ~*ment to study English*.
in·duct /ɪnˈdəkt/ *vt* **1** introduce, install, formally in a position or appointment. **2** draft into military service.
in·duc·tion /ɪnˈdəkʃən/ *n* [U] **1** inducting or being inducted. **2** method of reasoning which obtains general laws from particular facts or examples; production of facts to prove a general statement. ⇨ deduction(3,4).
in·duc·tive /ɪnˈdəktɪv/ *adj* (of reasoning) based on induction(2).
in·dulge /ɪnˈdəldʒ/ *vt,vi* **1** give way to and satisfy (desires, etc): *to* ~ *a sick child*. **2** ***indulge in,*** allow oneself the pleasure of: *He occasionally* ~*s in the luxury of a good cigar*.
in·dul·gent /-ənt/ *adj* inclined to indulge: *indulgent parents*.
in·dul·gent·ly *adv*
in·dul·gence /ɪnˈdəldʒəns/ *n* **1** [U] indulging; the state of being indulged: *Constant* ~ *in gambling brought about his ruin*. **2** [C] something in which a person indulges: *Wine and cigarettes are his only* ~*s*. **3** [C] (in the Roman Catholic Church) granting of freedom from punishment still due for sin after sacramental forgiveness.
in·dus·trial /ɪnˈdəstriəl/ *adj* **1** of industries: *an* ~ *park,* area of land planned and used for factories. **2** with highly developed industries: *an* ~ *nation*.
in·dus·trial·ism /-əˌlɪzəm/ *n* [U] social system in which large-scale industries have an important part.
in·dus·trial·ist /-əlɪst/ *n* [C] owner or manager of a large-scale industrial undertaking.
the Inˌdustrial Revoˈlution, the social and economic changes brought about by mechanical inventions in the 18th and early 19th centuries.
in·dus·tri·ous /ɪnˈdəstriəs/ *adj* hardworking.
in·dus·try /ˈɪndəstri/ *n* (*pl* -ies) **1** [U] quality of being hard-working; being always employed usefully. **2** [C,U] (branch of) trade or manufacture (contrasted with distribution and commerce): *the cotton and woolen industries*.
in·ebri·ate /ɪˈnibriˌeit/ *vt* make drunk. □ *n* [C], *adj* /ɪnˈibriɪt/ (person who is habitually) drunk.
in·ed·ible /ɪˈnedəbəl/ *adj* not suitable to be eaten.
in·ef·fable /ɪˈnefəbəl/ *adj* too great to be described in words: ~ *joy/beauty*.
in·ef·fably /-əbli/ *adv*
in·ef·fec·tive /ˌɪnɪˈfektɪv/ *adj* **1** not producing the effect(s) desired. **2** not capable; incompetent.
in·ef·fec·tive·ly *adv*
in·ef·fec·tive·ness /-nɪs/ *n* [U]
in·ef·fec·tual /ˌɪnɪˈfektʃuəl/ *adj* ineffective: *an* ~ *teacher/leader;* ~ *efforts*.
in·ef·fec·tually /-tʃuəli/ *adv*
in·ef·fi·cient /ˌɪnɪˈfɪʃənt/ *adj* **1** (of persons) wasting time, energy, etc in their work or duties: *an* ~ *management/administration*. **2** (of machines, processes, etc) wasteful; not producing adequate results.
in·ef·fi·cient·ly *adv*
in·ef·fi·ciency /-ənsi/ *n* [U]
in·el·egant /ɪˈneləgənt/ *adj* not graceful or refined.
in·el·egant·ly *adv*
in·el·egance /-əns/ *n* [U]
in·eli·gible /ɪˈnelədʒəbəl/ *adj* not suitable or qualified: ~ *for the position*.
in·eli·gi·bil·ity /ɪˌnelədʒəˈbɪləti/ *n* [U]
in·ept /ɪˈnept/ *adj* **1** lacking skill or competence. **2** unsuitable; inappropriate: ~ *remarks*.
in·ept·ly *adv*
in·ep·ti·tude /ɪˈneptəˌtud/ *n* [C,U]
in·e·qual·ity /ˌɪniˈkwaləti/ *n* (*pl* -ies) **1** [U] want of, absence of, equality in size, degree, circumstances, etc. **2** [C] instance of this; difference in size, rank, wealth, etc: *Great inequalities in wealth cause social unrest*.
in·equi·table /ɪˈnekwətəbəl/ *adj* (*formal*) unjust; unfair: *an* ~ *division of the profits*.
in·equity /ɪˈnekwəti/ *n* [C,U] (*pl* -ies) (instance of) injustice or unfairness.
in·ert /ɪˈnərt/ *adj* **1** without power to move or act: ~ *matter*. **2** without active chemical properties: ~ *gases*. **3** heavy and slow to move (in mind or body).
in·er·tia /ɪˈnərʃə/ *n* [U] **1** state of being inert(3).

2 tendency of matter to remain in a state of rest or, if it is in motion, to continue in the same direction and in a straight line unless it is acted on by an external force.

in·es·cap·able /ˌɪnəˈskeipəbəl/ *adj* not to be escaped from: *an ~ conclusion that he is a thief.*

in·es·ti·mable /ɪˈnestəməbəl/ *adj* too great, precious, etc to be estimated.

in·evi·table /ɪˈnevətəbəl/ *adj* that cannot be avoided, that is sure to happen.

in·evi·ta·bil·ity /ɪˌnevətəˈbɪləti/ *n* [U]

in·ex·act /ˌɪnɪgˈzækt/ *adj* not exact.

in·ex·acti·tude /ˌɪnɪgˈzæktəˌtud/ *n* [C,U]

in·ex·cus·able /ˌɪnɪkˈskyuzəbəl/ *adj* that cannot be excused: *~ conduct/delays.*

in·ex·haust·ible /ˌɪnɪgˈzɔstəbəl/ *adj* that cannot be exhausted or used up: *My patience is not ~.*

in·exo·rable /ɪˈneksərəbəl/ *adj* (*formal*) relentless; unyielding: *~ demands/pressures.*

in·exo·rably /-əbli/ *adv*

in·ex·pedi·ent /ˌɪnɪkˈspidiənt/ *adj* not expedient.

in·ex·pedi·ency /-ənsi/ *n* [U].

in·ex·pen·sive /ˌɪnɪkˈspensɪv/ *adj* not expensive; low priced.

in·ex·pen·sive·ly *adv*

in·ex·pe·ri·ence /ˌɪnɪkˈspɪriəns/ *n* [U] lack of experience or of the knowledge gained by experience.

in·ex·pe·ri·enced *adj*

in·ex·plic·able /ˌɪnɪkˈsplɪkəbəl/ *adj* that cannot be explained.

in·ex·pres·sible /ˌɪnɪkˈspresəbəl/ *adj* that cannot be expressed in words: *~ sorrow/anguish.*

in·ex·tri·cable /ɪˈnekstrɪkəbəl/ *adj* that cannot be solved or escaped from: *~ confusion.*

in·fal·lible /ɪnˈfæləbəl/ *adj* **1** incapable of making mistakes or doing wrong: *None of us is ~.* **2** never failing: *~ cures.*

in·fal·li·bil·ity /ɪnˌfæləˈbɪləti/ *n* [U].

in·fa·mous /ˈɪnfəməs/ *adj* wicked; shameful; disgraceful: *~ behavior; an ~ plot/traitor.*

in·famy /ˈɪnfəmi/ *n* (*pl* -ies) **1** [U] being infamous. **2** [U] bad reputation. **3** [C] infamous act.

in·fancy /ˈɪnfənsi/ *n* [U] **1** state of being, period when one is, an infant. **2** early stage of development or growth: *when space travel was still in its ~.*

in·fant /ˈɪnfənt/ *n* **1** [C] child during the first few years of its life. **2** (as an *adjective*): *~ voices.*

in·fan·ti·cide /ɪnˈfæntəˌsaid/ *n* [U] crime of killing an infant.

in·fan·tile /ˈɪnfənˌtaiəl/ *adj* characteristic of infants: *~ behavior.*

ˌinfantile paˈralysis, poliomyelitis.

in·fan·try /ˈɪnfəntri/ *n* (*collective*) (branch of an army made up of) foot soldiers: *an ~ regiment.*

in·fatu·ate /ɪnˈfætʃuˌeit/ *vt* ***be infatuated with/by sb,*** be filled with a wild and foolish love for: *He's ~d with that girl.*

in·fatu·ation /ɪnˌfætʃuˈeiʃən/ *n* [C,U]

in·fect /ɪnˈfekt/ *vt* **1** contaminate; affect with disease. **2** (*fig*) cause to share one's feelings, ideas, etc: *Mary's high spirits ~ed the whole class.*

in·fec·tion /ɪnˈfekʃən/ *n* **1** [U] infecting or being infected; communication of disease, esp through the atmosphere or water. **2** [C] disease spread in this way. **3** (*fig*) influence that spreads from one person to another. ⇨ contagion.

in·fec·tious /ɪnˈfekʃəs/ *adj* **1** infecting with disease. **2** (of disease) that can be spread by means of bacteria carried in the atmosphere or in water. **3** (*fig*) likely to spread to others: *~ humor/laughter.* ⇨ contagious.

infer /ɪnˈfər/ *vt* (-rr-) reach an opinion or conclusion (from facts or reasoning): *Am I to ~ from your remarks that you think I am a liar?*

in·fer·ence /ˈɪnf(ə)rens/ *n* **1** [U] process of inferring. ***by inference,*** as the result of drawing a conclusion. **2** [C] that which is inferred.

in·fe·rior /ɪnˈfɪriər/ *adj* **1** low(er) in rank, social position, importance, quality, etc: *make a person feel ~.* **2** located below; lower. □ *n* [C] person who is low(er) (in rank, ability, etc).

in·fe·rior·ity /ɪnˌfɪriˈɔrəti/ *n* [U] state of being inferior.

inferiˈority complex, feeling of being an inferior or worthless person.

in·fer·nal /ɪnˈfərnəl/ *adj* of hell; devilish; abominable: *the ~ regions; ~ cruelty.*

in·ferno /ɪnˈfərnou/ *n* [C] (*pl* ~s) hell or a place like hell, eg a blazing building in which people are trapped.

in·fer·tile /ɪnˈfərtəl/ *adj* not fertile.

in·fer·til·ity /ˌɪnfərˈtɪləti/ *n* [U]

in·fest /ɪnˈfest/ *vt* be present in large numbers so as to be troublesome: *warehouses ~ed with rats.*

in·fes·ta·tion /ˌɪnˌfeˈsteiʃən/ *n* [C,U]

in·fi·del /ˈɪnfədəl/ *n* [C] person with no belief in a particular religion.

in·fi·del·ity /ˌɪnfəˈdeləti/ *n* (*pl* -ties) **1** [U] disloyalty; unfaithfulness, esp to one's husband or wife. **2** [C] act of disloyalty or unfaithfulness.

in·field /ˈɪnˌfiəld/ *n* [C] (*baseball*) **1** part of a baseball field that is enclosed by the three bases and home plate. **2** players (first baseman, second baseman, third baseman, and shortstop) who are the infielders of a team.

in·field·er *n* [C] (*baseball*) defensive player whose position is in the infield(**1**).

in·fight·ing /ˈɪnˌfaitɪŋ/ *n* [U] animosity and conflict between the members of an organization.

in·fil·trate /ɪnˈfɪlˌtreit/ *vt,vi* **1** (cause to) pass through or into by filtering. **2** pass through or enter secretly or gradually. **3** (of ideas) pass into people's minds.

in·fil·tra·tion /ˌɪnfɪlˈtreiʃən/ *n* [U]

in·fi·nite /ˈɪnfənɪt/ *adj* endless; without limits; that cannot be measured, calculated, or imagined: *~ space. Such ideas may do ~ harm.*

in·fi·nite·ly *adv* in an infinite degree: *She is ~ patient with her children.*

in·fini·tesi·mal /ˌɪnˌfɪnəˈtesəməl/ *adj* infinitely small.

in·fini·tive /ɪnˈfɪnətɪv/ *adj, n* [C] (*gram*) (in English) verb form without person. number, or tense that is used with or without *to*, eg let him *go*; allow him *to go*.

in·fin·ity /ɪnˈfɪnəti/ *n* [U] infinite quantity (expressed by the symbol ∞).

in·firm /ɪnˈfərm/ *adj* **1** physically weak (esp

through age): *walk with ~ steps.* **2** mentally or morally weak.

in·fir·mity /ɪnˈfərməti/ *n* [C,U] (*pl* -ties) (particular form of) weakness.

in·fir·mary /ɪnˈfərməri/ *n* [C] (*pl* -ies) place¹(3) (esp in an institution, etc) used to care for people who are ill or injured.

in·flame /ɪnˈfleim/ *vt,vi* **1** (cause to) become red, angry, overheated: *~d eyes;* (*fig*) *~d with passion.* **2** (cause to) become affected with inflammation.

in·flam·mable /ɪnˈflæməbəl/ *adj* **1** easily set on fire. (*Note:* now usually replaced by *flammable*, esp on public notices.) **2** (*fig*) easily excited.

in·flam·ma·tion /ˌɪnfləˈmeiʃən/ *n* **1** [U] redness, pain, etc (esp of some part of the body) resulting from injury, etc: *~ of the eyes.* **2** [C] instance of this.

in·flam·ma·tory /ɪnˈflæməˌtɔri/ *adj* **1** tending to excite strong feelings: *~ speeches.* **2** of, tending to produce, inflammation(1).

in·flate /ɪnˈfleit/ *vt* **1** fill (a tire, balloon, etc) with air or gas; (cause to) swell. **2** (*fig*) puff up: *~d with pride.* **3** increase the amount of money in circulation so that prices rise. ⇨ deflate.

in·flat·able /-əbəl/ *adj* that can be inflated: *an inflatable rubber raft.*

in·fla·tion /ɪnˈfleiʃən/ *n* [U] **(a)** act of inflating; state of being inflated. **(b)** continuing rise in the price of goods and services.

in·fla·tion·ary /ɪnˈfleiʃəˌneri/ *adj* of, caused by, inflation.

in·flect /ɪnˈflekt/ *vt* **1** (*gram*) change the ending or form of (a word) to show number, gender, tense, etc. **2** adapt, change the pitch of one's voice in speaking.

in·flec·tion /ɪnˈflekʃən/ *n* **1** [U] inflecting. **2** [C] inflected form of a word suffix used to inflect, eg *-ed, -ing.* **3** [U] rise and fall of the voice in speaking.

in·flec·tional /-ʃənəl/ *adj*

in·flex·ible /ɪnˈfleksəbəl/ *adj* **1** that cannot be bent or turned. **2** (*fig*) unyielding: *an ~ will.*

in·flexi·bil·ity /ɪnˌfleksəˈbɪləti/ *n* [U]

in·flex·ibly -əbli/ *adv*

in·flict /ɪnˈflɪkt/ *vt,* **1** give as by striking: *~ a blow/a severe wound on him.* **2** cause to suffer; impose: *I'm sorry to ~ my company upon you.*

in·flic·tion /ɪnˈflɪkʃən/ *n* [C,U]

in·flow /ˈɪnˌflou/ *n* **1** [U] flowing in; influx. **2** [C,U] that which flows in.

in·flu·ence /ˈɪnˌfluəns/ *n* **1** [U] act or power of producing an effect or change, often by indirect means: *had a great ~ on her brother; the ~ of climate (on vegetation).* **2** [C] person, fact, etc that exercises such power: *He's an ~ for good in the town.* **3** [U] power due to wealth, position, etc: *Will you use your ~ to get me a job?* □ *vt* exert an influence on; have an effect on: *Don't be ~d by what she says.*

in·flu·ential /ˌɪnfluˈenʃəl/ *adj* having influence.

in·flu·en·tially /-ʃəli/ *adv*

in·flu·enza /ˌɪnfluˈenzə/ *n* [U] infectious disease with fever, muscular pain, a running nose, etc.

in·flux /ˈɪnˌfləks/ *n* (*pl* ~es) **1** [U] flowing in. **2** [C] constant inflow of large numbers or quantities: *an ~ of wealth.*

info /ˈɪnˌfou/ *n* [C] (*informal*) (short for) information.

in·form /ɪnˈfɔrm/ *vt,vi* **1** give knowledge to: *Keep me ~ed of fresh developments.* **2** give information that accuses (or incriminates a person).

in·for·mant /-ənt/ *n* [C] person who gives information.

in·former *n* [C] person who informs(2), esp against a criminal.

in·for·mal /ɪnˈfɔrməl/ *adj* not formal(1,2); without ceremony or formality: *an ~ visit; ~ dress.*

in·for·mal·ity /ˌɪnfɔrˈmæləti/ *n* [C,U] (*pl* -ies)

in·for·mally /-məli/ *adv*

in·for·ma·tion /ˌɪnfərˈmeiʃən/ *n* [U] **1** informing or being informed. **2** news or knowledge given: *That's a useful piece/bit of ~.*

in·for·ma·tive /ɪnˈfɔrmətɪv/ *adj* giving information; instructive: *~ books; an ~ talk.*

in·for·ma·tive·ly *adv*

in·fra·red /ˌɪnfrəˈred/ *adj* (of radiation) rays lying outside the visible end of the spectrum.

in·fre·quent /ɪnˈfrikwənt/ *adj* not frequent; rare.

in·fre·quency /ɪnˈfrikwənsi/ *n* [U]

in·fre·quent·ly *adv*

in·fringe /ɪnˈfrɪndʒ/ *vt,vi* **1** break (a rule, etc). **2** ***infringe on/upon,*** intrude or encroach on: *Be careful not to ~ on/upon the rights of other people.*

in·fringe·ment *n* [C,U]

in·furi·ate /ɪnˈfyʊriˌeit/ *vt* fill with fury or rage: *infuriating delays.*

in·fuse /ɪnˈfyuz/ *vt,vi* (*formal*) **1** put, pour (a quality, etc *into*); fill (a person with): *~ fresh courage/new life into soldiers.* **2** soak (leaves, herbs, etc) in very hot water without boiling: *Let the tea ~ for three minutes.*

in·fu·sion /ɪnˈfyuʒən/ *n* **1** [U] infusing or being infused. **2** [C] liquid made by infusing.

-ing /-ɪŋ/ *suffix* **1** (used to form a *present participle*): *talking.* **2** (used to form a *noun* from a *verb*): *thinking.*

in·ge·nious /ɪnˈdʒinyəs/ *adj* **1** (of a person) very clever and skillful (at making or inventing). **2** (of things) skillfully made: *an ~ tool.*

in·ge·nious·ly *adv*

in·ge·nuity /ˌɪndʒɪˈnuəti/ *n* [U] cleverness and skill; originality in design.

in·gest /ɪnˈdʒest/ *vt* take in (food) for digestion.

in·got /ˈɪŋgət/ *n* [C] (usually brick-shaped) lump of metal (esp gold and silver), cast in a mold.

in·grained /ˈɪnˌgreind/ *adj* **1** (of habits, tendencies, etc) deeply fixed: *~ prejudices.* **2** going deep: *~ dirt.*

in·grate /ˈɪnˌgreit/ *n* [C] ungrateful person.

in·grati·ate /ɪnˈgreiʃiˌeit/ *vt* work oneself into favor, esp in order to gain an advantage: *an ingratiating smile.*

in·grati·at·ing·ly *adv*

in·grati·tude /ɪnˈgrætəˌtud/ *n* [U] lack of gratitude.

in·gredi·ent /ɪnˈgridiənt/ *n* [C] one of the parts of a mixture: *the ~s of a cake.*

in·gress /ˈɪnˌgres/ *n* [U] **1** way or means of entering. **2** (instance of) entering.

in·habit /ɪnˈhæbɪt/ *vt* live in; occupy.
in·hab·it·able /-əbəl/ *adj* that can be lived in.
in·habit·ant /-ənt/ *n* [C] person living in a place.

in·ha·la·tor /ˈɪn(h)əˌleitər/ *n* [C] (esp) device for inhaling medicine, oxygen, etc.

in·hale /ɪnˈheiəl/ *vt,vi* (*pres p* -ing /ɪnˈheilɪŋ/) draw into the lungs: *~ air*.
in·ha·lant /ɪnˈheilənt/ *n* [C,U] something (as a medicine) that is inhaled.
in·ha·la·tion /ˌɪn(h)əˈleiʃən/ *n* [C,U] (instance of) inhaling.
in·haler /ɪnˈheilər/ *n* [C] (esp) inhalator.

in·her·ent /ɪnˈhɪrənt/ *adj* existing as a natural and permanent part or quality of: *He has an ~ love of beauty*.

in·herit /ɪnˈherɪt/ *vt,vi* **1** receive property, a title, etc as heir: *The eldest son will ~ the title*. **2** receive (qualities, etc) from one's ancestors: *She ~ed her mother's good looks*.
in·heri·tance /-əns/ *n* **(a)** [U] inheriting: *receive money by ~ance*. **(b)** [C] what is inherited: (*fig*) *an ~ance of ill-feeling*.

in·hibit /ɪnˈhɪbɪt/ *vt* hinder, restrain; suppress: *an ~ed person*, one who is unable or unwilling to express his feelings.
in·hi·bi·tion /ˌɪnəˈbɪʃən/ *n* **(a)** [U] restraint or suppression of emotion, impulse or desire. **(b)** [C] instance of this.
in·hibi·tory /ɪnˈhɪbəˌtɔri/ *adj* tending to inhibit; of an inhibition.

in·hos·pi·table /ˌɪnhaˈspɪtəbəl/ *adj* not hospitable.

in·hu·man /ɪnˈ(h)yumən/ *adj* **1** lacking human qualities. **2** cruel; without feeling: *~ treatment*.
in·hu·man·ity /ˌɪn(h)yuˈmænəti/ *n* [C,U] (*pl* -ies): *man's ~ity to man*.
in·hu·man·ly *adv*

in·hu·mane /ˌɪn(h)yuˈmein/ *adj* not humane; cruel; without pity.
in·hu·mane·ly *adv*

in·iqui·tous /ɪˈnɪkwətəs/ *adj* (*formal*) very wicked or unjust.
in·iqui·tous·ly *adv*
in·iquity /ɪnˈɪkwəti/ *n* [C,U] (*pl* -ies)

in·itial /ɪˈnɪʃəl/ *adj* of or at the beginning: *the ~ letter of a word*. □ *n* [C] first letter, esp (*pl*) first letters of a person's names, as *J.F.K.* (for *John Fitzgerald Kennedy*). □ *vt* (-l-, -ll-) mark, sign, with one's initials.
in·itially /-ʃəli/ *adv* at the beginning.

in·iti·ate /ɪˈnɪʃiˌeit/ *vt* **1** set (a scheme, etc) working: *~ a plan*. **2** admit or introduce a person (to membership of a group, etc). **3** give a person elementary instruction, or secret knowledge of. □ *n* [C], *adj* /ɪˈnɪʃiət/ (person) who has been initiated(2,3).
in·iti·ation /ɪˌnɪʃiˈeiʃən/ *n* [C,U]

in·iti·at·ive /ɪˈnɪʃətɪv/ *n* [U] **1** first or introductory step or move. ***act/do sth on one's own initiative,*** without an order or suggestion from others. ***have/take the initiative,*** (be in the position to) make the first move, eg in war. **2** capacity to see what needs to be done and the will to do it: *A statesman must show ~*.

in·ject /ɪnˈdʒekt/ *vt* **1** drive or force a liquid, drug, etc (into something) with, or as with, a syringe; fill by injecting: *~ penicillin into the bloodstream*. **2** (*fig*) put into: *His appointment may ~ some new life into the committee*.
in·jec·tion /ɪnˈdʒekʃən/ *n* **(a)** [U] injecting. **(b)** [C] something injected.

in·ju·di·cious /ˌɪndʒʊˈdɪʃəs/ *adj* (*formal*) unwise: *~ remarks*.

in·junc·tion /ɪnˈdʒəŋkʃən/ *n* [C] order, esp a written order from a law court, demanding that something shall or shall not be done.

in·jure /ˈɪndʒər/ *vt* hurt; damage.
in·jured *adj* wounded; wronged; offended: *~d looks*.

in·juri·ous /ɪnˈdʒʊriəs/ *adj* (*formal*) causing, likely to cause, injury: *habits that are ~ to health*.

in·jury /ˈɪndʒəri/ *n* (*pl* -ies) **1** [U] harm; damage; wrongful treatment. **2** [C] place (in the body) that is hurt or wounded: *a ˈback ~*. **3** [C] act that injures: *a severe ~ to his reputation*.

in·jus·tice /ɪnˈdʒəstɪs/ *n* **1** [U] lack of justice; unfairness. **2** [C] unjust act, etc.

ink /ɪŋk/ *n* [U] **1** colored liquid used for writing and printing. **2** black liquid ejected by cuttlefish, etc. □ *vt* mark or cover with ink: *~ one's fingers*.
inky *adj* (-ier, -iest)

ink·ling /ˈɪŋklɪŋ/ *n* [C] vague idea: *have/get/give an ~ (of the truth)*.

ink·well /ˈɪŋkˌwel/ *n* [C] container for ink.

in·land /ˈɪnlənd, ˈɪnˌlænd/ *adj* situated in the interior of a country, far from the sea or border: *~ towns*. □ *adv* /ɪnˈlænd/ in or toward the interior.

in-law /ˈɪnˌlɔ/ *n* [C] (*informal*) relative by marriage.

in·lay /ɪnˈlei/ *vt* (*pt,pp* inlaid /-ˈleid/) set pieces of wood, metal, etc into a surface to form a design. □ /ˈɪnˌlei/ *n* **1** [U] inlaid work; materials used for this. **2** [C] molded pieces of gold, porcelain, etc made to fit a cavity in a tooth and cemented in place.

in·let /ˈɪnˌlet, ˈɪnlɪt/ *n* [C] **1** strip of water extending into the land from a larger body of water (the sea, a lake), or between islands. **2** way of entering or going in.

in·mate /ˈɪnˌmeit/ *n* [C] one of a number of persons living together, esp in a prison or other institution.

in·most /ˈɪnˌmoust/ *adj* = innermost.

inn /ɪn/ *n* [C] **1** public house where lodgings, drink and meals may be had. **2** restaurant; tavern.
ˈinn·keeper *n* [C] person who keeps an inn.

in·nards /ˈɪnərdz/ *n pl* (*informal*) **1** stomach and bowels. **2** any inner parts as of a machine.

in·nate /ɪˈneit/ *adj* **1** (of a quality, etc) in one's nature. **2** inborn; possessed from birth: *her ~ courtesy*.
in·nate·ly *adv*

in·ner /ˈɪnər/ *adj* inside; of the inside: *an ~ room*. ⇨ outer.
in·ner·most /-ˌmoust/ *adj* **1** farthest from the surface. **2** (*fig*) most private or secret: *my ~ feelings*.

in·ning /ˈɪnɪŋ/ *n* [C] (*baseball*) division of a game in which each team bats.

in·no·cence /ˈɪnəsəns/ *n* [U] quality or state of

being innocent.

in·no·cent /ˈɪnəsənt/ *adj* **1** not guilty: *~ of the charge*. **2** harmless: *~ amusements*. **3** knowing nothing of evil or wrong: *as ~ as a newborn babe*. **4** unsophisticated; foolishly simple: *Don't be so ~ as to believe everything he says*. □ *n* [C] innocent person, esp a young child.

in·no·cent·ly *adv*

in·nocu·ous /ɪˈnakyuəs/ *adj* causing no harm.

in·no·vate /ˈɪnəˌveit/ *vi* introduce new things; make changes.

in·no·va·tion /ˌɪnəˈveiʃən/ *n* **(a)** [U] innovating. **(b)** [C] change; something new that is introduced: *technical innovations in industry*.

in·no·va·tor /-tər/ *n* [C] person who innovates.

in·nu·endo /ˌɪnyuˈendou/ *n* [C] (*pl* ~es) indirect reference (usually unfavorable to a person's reputation).

in·numer·able /ɪˈnumərəbəl/ *adj* too many to be counted.

in·ocu·late /ɪˈnakyəˌleit/ *vt* inject a serum or vaccine into (a person or animal) in order to prevent or cure disease: *inoculating against cholera*.

in·ocu·la·tion /ɪˌnakyəˈleiʃən/ *n* [C,U]

in·of·fen·sive /ˌɪnəˈfensɪv/ *adj* not giving offense; not objectionable: *an ~ remark/person*.

in·op·er·able /ɪˈnapərəbəl/ *adj* **1** not working. **2** not suitable for correction or cure by surgery.

in·op·er·at·ive /ɪˈnapərətɪv/ *adj* (of laws, rules, etc) not working or taking effect; invalid.

in·op·por·tune /ɪˌnapərˈtun/ *adj* not right or appropriate; inconvenient: *at an ~ time*.

in·op·por·tune·ly *adv*

in·or·di·nate /ɪˈnɔrdənɪt/ *adj* (*formal*) not properly restrained or controlled; excessive: *~ tax demands*.

in·or·di·nate·ly *adv*

in·or·ganic /ˌɪnɔrˈgænɪk/ *adj* **1** neither animal nor vegetable; not organic; mineral: *Rocks and metals are ~ substances*. **2** (*chem*) of or dealing with substances that do not contain carbon. ⇨ organic.

in·or·gani·cally /-kli/ *adv*

in-pa·tient /ˈɪnˌpeiʃənt/ *n* ⇨ in-².

in·put /ˈɪnpʊt/ *n* [U] what is put in or supplied, eg data for processing in a computer, power supplied to a machine. ⇨ output.

in·quest /ˈɪnˌkwest/ *n* [C] official inquiry to learn facts, esp concerning a death which may not be the result of natural causes.

in·quire /ɪnˈkwaiər/ *vt,vi* **1** ask to be told; ask for information (about): *~ about what a person wants/where to stay*. *~ about buses to Chicago*. ***inquire after sb,*** ask about (his health, welfare). **2** ***inquire into,*** investigate.

in·quirer *n* [C] person who inquires.

in·quir·ing *adj* in the habit of asking for information: *an inquiring mind*.

in·quir·ing·ly *adv*

in·quiry /ɪnˈkwaiəri, ˈɪnkwəri/ *n* (*pl* -ies) **1** [U] asking; inquiring. **2** [C] investigation: *hold an official ~ into the incident*.

in·qui·si·tion /ˌɪnkwəˈzɪʃən/ *n* **1** [U] thorough search or investigation. **2** [C] instance of this, esp a judicial or official inquiry. **3 the Inquisition,** court formerly appointed by the Roman Catholic Church to suppress heresy.

in·quisi·tive /ɪnˈkwɪzətɪv/ *adj* (esp) too fond of inquiring into other people's affairs.

in·quisi·tive·ly *adv*

in·quisi·tive·ness /-nɪs/ *n* [U]

in·road /ˈɪnˌroud/ *n* [C] **1** sudden attack (into a country, etc); raid. **2** (*fig*) something that trespasses on or encroaches on: *make ~s on one's savings*.

in·rush /ˈɪnˌrəʃ/ *n* [C] rushing in: *an ~ of water/tourists*.

INS /ˌai ˌen ˈes/ *abbr* = Immigration and Naturalization Service.

in·sane /ɪnˈsein/ *adj* **1** mentally ill; crazy. **2** (*informal*) senseless.

in·sane·ly *adv*

in·san·ity /ɪnˈsænəti/ *n* [U] **(a)** madness; mental illness. **(b)** foolishness.

in·sani·tary /ɪnˈsænəˌteri/ *adj* not sanitary: *living under ~ conditions*.

in·sa·tiable /ɪnˈseiʃəbəl/ *adj* (*formal*) that cannot be satisfied; very greedy: *~ appetites*.

in·sa·tiably /-ʃəbli/ *adv*

in·scribe /ɪnˈskraib/ *vt* **1** mark, carve (words, one's name, etc) in or on a surface: *a monument ~d with the names of the dead*. **2** write in or on: *~ one's name in a book*. **3** impress deeply. **4** (*geom*) draw one figure within another so as to touch in as many points as possible.

in·scrip·tion /ɪnˈskrɪpʃən/ *n* [C] (esp) words inscribed, eg on a monument, or stamped on a coin or medal.

in·scru·table /ɪnˈskrutəbəl/ *adj* not easily understood or known; mysterious: *the ~ ways of fate*.

in·sect /ˈɪnˌsekt/ *n* [C] sorts of small animal, eg ant, fly, wasp, having six legs and no backbone and a body divided into three parts (head, thorax, abdomen).

in·sec·ti·cide /ɪnˈsektəˌsaid/ *n* [C,U] something used for killing insects, eg DDT.

in·sec·tivo·rous /ˌɪnsekˈtɪvərəs/ *adj* eating insects as food: *Swallows are ~*.

in·se·cure /ˌɪnsɪˈkyʊr/ *adj* **1** not safe. **2** not providing good support; not to be relied on: *an ~ job*. **3** feeling unsafe lacking confidence.

in·se·cure·ly *adv*

in·se·cur·ity /ˌɪnsɪˈkyurəti/ *n* [U]

in·sen·si·bil·ity /ɪnˌsensəˈbɪləti/ *n* [U] (*formal*) lack of mental feeling or emotion; state of being unable to know, recognize, understand or appreciate: *~ to pain/beauty*.

in·sen·sible /ɪnˈsensəbəl/ *adj* **1** unconscious as the result of injury, illness, etc. **2** unaware (of): *~ of danger*. **3** without feeling: *When your hands are frozen they become ~*, numb. **4** unsympathetic; emotionless. **5** too small or gradual to be perceived: *by ~ degrees*.

in·sen·sibly /-əbli/ *adv*

in·sen·si·tive /ɪnˈsensətɪv/ *adj* not sensitive (to touch, light, the feelings of other people).

in·sen·si·tive·ly *adv*

in·sen·si·tiv·ity /ɪnˌsensəˈtɪvəti/ *n* [U]

in·sep·ar·able /ɪnˈsepərəbəl/ *adj* that cannot be separated: *~ friends*.

in·sert /ɪnˈsərt/ *vt* put, fit, place (*in, into, between,* etc): *~ a key in a lock*. □ *n* /ˈɪnˌsərt/ [C]

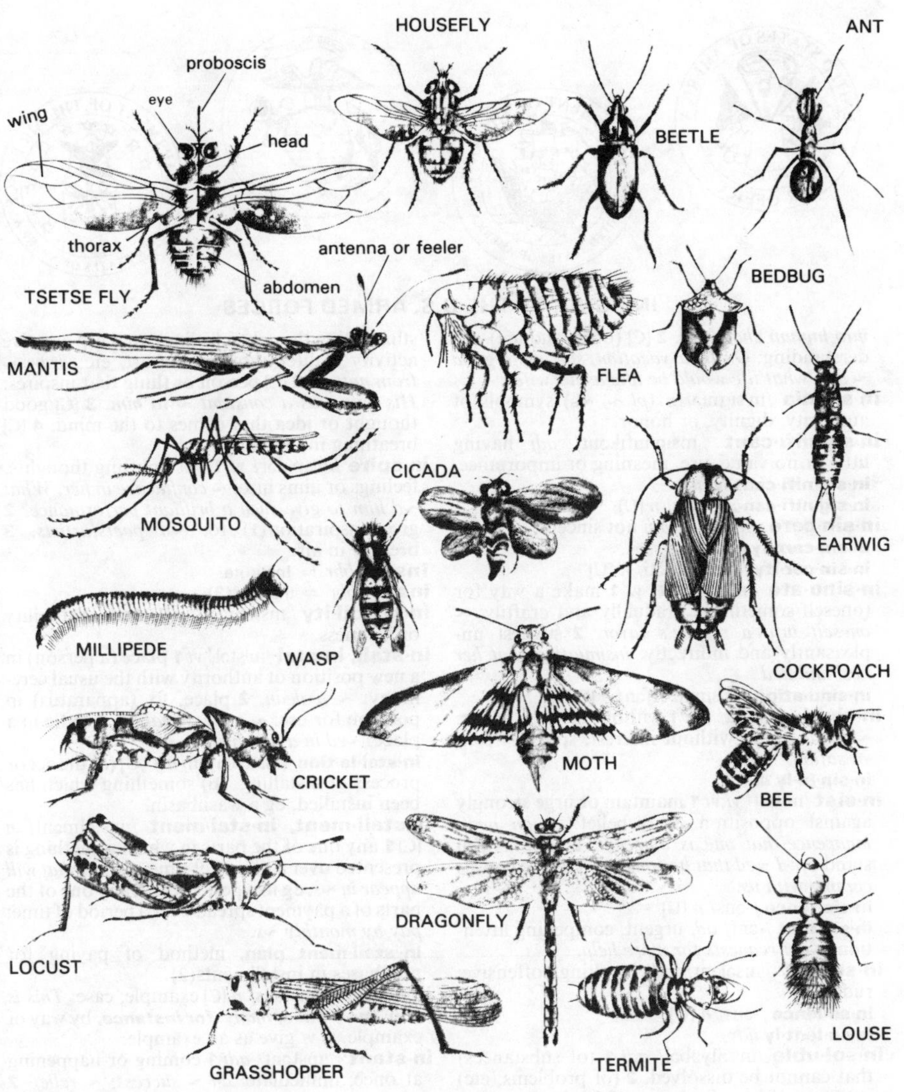

INSECTS

something inserted, eg in a book.

in·ser·tion /ɪnˈsɜrʃən/ *n* [C,U]

in·set /ˈɪnˌset/ *n* [C] **1** small map, diagram, etc within the border of a larger one. **2** piece of material let into a dress. □ *vt* put in; insert.

in·shore /ˈɪnˌʃɔr/ *adj, adv* close to the shore: *an ~ current; ~ fisheries.*

in·side /ɪnˈsaid/ *n* [C] **1** inner side or surface; part(s) within: *the ~ of a box.* ˌ***inside ˈout,*** **(a)** with the inner side out: *He put his socks on ~ out.* **(b)** thoroughly: *He knows the subject ~ out.* **2** part of a road, track, etc on the inner edge of a curve; part of a pavement or footpath farthest from the road. **3** (*informal*) (usually *pl*) stomach and bowels: *a pain in his ~s.* □ *adj* situated on or in, coming from the inside: *the ~ pages of a newspaper.* □ *adv* on or in the inside: *Look ~. There's nothing ~.* □ *prep* on the inner side of: *Don't let the dog come ~ the house.*

in·sider *n* [C] person who, because he is a member of some society, organization, etc can obtain facts and information, or has advantages over others.

in·sidi·ous /ɪnˈsɪdiəs/ *adj* **1** treacherous. **2** doing harm secretly, unseen: *an ~ enemy/disease.*

in·sidi·ous·ly *adv*

in·sight /ˈɪnˌsait/ *n* **1** [U] understanding; power of seeing the real nature of something: *show ~*

INSIGNIA OF THE U.S. ARMED FORCES

into human character. **2** [C] (often sudden) understanding: *On their vacation, she had a good ~ into what life would be like as his wife.*

in·sig·nia /ɪnˈsɪgniə/ *n* (*pl* ~, ~s) symbols of authority, dignity, or honor.

in·sig·nifi·cant /ˌɪnsɪgˈnɪfɪkənt/ *adj* having little or no value, use, meaning or importance.
in·sig·nifi·cant·ly *adv*
in·sig·nifi·cance /-əns/ *n* [U]

in·sin·cere /ˌɪnsɪnˈsɪr/ *adj* not sincere.
in·sin·cere·ly *adv*
in·sin·cer·ity /ˌɪnsɪnˈserəti/ *n* [U]

in·sinu·ate /ɪnˈsɪnyuˌeit/ *vt* **1** make a way for (oneself/something) gradually and craftily: *~ oneself into a person's favor.* **2** suggest unpleasantly and indirectly: *insinuating that her husband lied.*
in·sinu·ation /ɪnˌsɪnyuˈeiʃən/ *n* [C,U]

in·sipid /ɪnˈsɪpɪd/ *adj* **1** without taste or flavor: *~ food.* **2** (*fig*) without interest, spirit: *~ conversation.*
in·sip·id·ly *adv*

in·sist /ɪnˈsɪst/ *vi,vt* **1** maintain or urge strongly against opposition or disbelief: *~ on one's innocence/that one is innocent.* **2** take a firm stand on: *I ~ed that he come with us/~ed on his coming with us.*
in·sis·tence /-əns/ *n* [U]
in·sis·tent /-ənt/ *adj* urgent; compelling attention: *~ent requests for more help.*

in·so·lent /ˈɪnsələnt/ *adj* insulting; offensive; rude.
in·so·lence /-əns/ *n* [U]
in·so·lent·ly *adv*

in·sol·uble /ɪnˈsalyəbəl/ *adj* **1** (of substances) that cannot be dissolved. **2** (of problems, etc) that cannot be solved or explained.

in·sol·vent /ɪnˈsalvənt/ *n* [C], *adj* (person) unable to pay debts; bankrupt.
in·sol·vency /-ənsi/ *n* [U]

in·som·nia /ɪnˈsamniə/ *n* [U] habitual inability to sleep.
in·som·niac /ɪnˈsamniˌæk/ *n* [C] person suffering from insomnia.

in·spect /ɪnˈspekt/ *vt* **1** examine carefully. **2** visit and examine officially to see that work is done properly, etc.
in·spec·tion /ɪnˈspekʃən/ *n* [C,U]

in·spec·tor /ɪnˈspektər/ *n* [C] **1** person who inspects, eg schools, factories, mines. **2** police officer who is, in rank, below a superintendent.

in·spi·ra·tion /ˌɪnspəˈreiʃən/ *n* **1** [U] influence(s) stimulating thoughts, feelings, and esp creative activity in literature, music, art, etc: *draw ~ from nature.* **2** [C] person or thing that inspires: *His wife was a constant ~ to him.* **3** [C] good thought or idea that comes to the mind. **4** [C] breathing in; inhaling.

in·spire /ɪnˈspaiər/ *vt* **1** put uplifting thoughts, feelings or aims into: *~ confidence in her. What ~d him to give such a brilliant performance?* **2** give inspiration(1) to: *~d poets/artists.* **3** breathe in air.

Inst.[1] *abbr* = Institute.

inst.[2] *abbr* = instant²(3).

in·sta·bil·ity /ˌɪnstəˈbɪləti/ *n* [U] lack of stability or firmness.

in·stall, in·stal /ɪnˈstɔl/ *vt* **1** place (a person) in a new position of authority with the usual ceremony: *~ a dean.* **2** place, fix (apparatus) in position for use: *~ central heating.* **3** settle in a place: *~ed in a new home.*
in·stal·la·tion /ˌɪnstəˈleiʃən/ *n* [C,U] **(a)** the act or process of installing. **(b)** something which has been installed, eg a washbasin.

in·stall·ment, in·stal·ment /ɪnˈstɔlmənt/ *n* [C] **1** any one of the parts in which something is presented over a period of time: *a story that will appear in ~s*, eg in a periodical. **2** any one of the parts of a payment spread over a period of time: *pay by monthly ~s.*
in·ˈstall·ment plan, method of paying for purchases in installments(2).

in·stance /ˈɪnstəns/ *n* [C] example; case: *This is only one ~ out of many.* ***for instance,*** by way of example. □ *vt* give as an example.

in·stant[1] /ˈɪnstənt/ *adj* **1** coming or happening at once; immediate: *an ~ success; ~ relief.* **2** urgent: *in ~ need of help.* **3** (of food, drink) made to be prepared quickly and easily: *~ coffee.*
in·stant·ly *adv* at once.

in·stant[2] /ˈɪnstənt/ *n* **1** particular point of time: *Come here this* (*very*) *~!* at once! *I sent you the news the ~* (*that*) (= as soon as) *I heard it.* **2** moment: *Help arrived not an ~ too soon.* **3** (in business correspondence, usually abbreviated *inst.*) the present month: *I refer to your letter of the 5th inst.*

in·stan·taneous /ˌɪnstənˈteiniəs/ *adj* happening, done in, an instant: *Death was ~*, eg in an accident.
in·stan·taneous·ly *adv*

in·stead /ɪnˈsted/ *adv* as an alternative or substitute: *If Harry is not well enough to go with you, take me ~.* **instead of,** in place of; as an alternative to or substitute for: *I will go ~ of you. Instead of reading, she wrote some letters.*

in·step /ˈɪnˌstep/ *n* [C] **1** upper surface of the human foot between the toes and the ankle. ⇨ illus at leg. **2** part of a shoe, etc covering this.

in·sti·gate /ˈɪnstəˌgeit/ *vt* incite; stir up (something): *~ a strike.*

in·sti·ga·tor /-tər/ *n* [C] person who instigates.

in·sti·ga·tion /ˌɪnstəˈgeiʃən/ *n* [U]

in·still, in·stil /ɪnˈstɪl/ *vt* (-ll-) introduce (ideas, etc) gradually.

in·stinct /ˈɪnˌstɪŋkt/ *n* **1** [U] natural tendency to behave in a certain way without reasoning or training: *Birds learn to fly by ~.* **2** [C] instance of this: *an ~ for always saying the right thing.*

in·stinc·tive /ɪnˈstɪŋktɪv/ *adj* based on instinct, not coming from training or teaching.

in·stinc·tive·ly *adv*

in·sti·tute[1] /ˈɪnstəˌtut/ *n* [C] **1** society or organization for a special (usually a social or educational) purpose. **2** its office(s) or building(s).

in·sti·tute[2] /ˈɪnstəˌtut/ *vt* **1** establish, get started an inquiry, custom, rule, etc: *~ legal proceedings.* **2** appoint (a person *to, into,* an office, esp a church office).

in·sti·tu·tion /ˌɪnstəˈtuʃən/ *n* **1** [U] instituting or being instituted: *the ~ of customs/rules, etc.* **2** [C] established law, custom or practice, eg of a group, community, society, etc: *the ~ of marriage.* **3** (building of) organization with charitable purposes or for social welfare, eg an orphanage, a home for old people.

in·sti·tu·tional /-ʃənəl/ *adj*

in·sti·tu·tion·al·ize /-əˌlaiz/ *vt* **(a)** establish as (part of) an institution: *The ceremony soon became ~alized.* **(b)** send (a person) to an institution, eg for health care.

in·struct /ɪnˈstrəkt/ *vt* **1** teach a school subject, a skill: *~ a class in history.* **2** give orders or directions to: *~ him to start early.* **3** inform: *I have been ~ed by my bank to pay the deposit.*

in·struc·tor /-tər/ *n* [C] person who teaches; trainer.

in·struc·tress /-trɪs/ *n* [C] woman who teaches or trains.

in·struc·tion /ɪnˈstrəkʃən/ *n* **1** [U] instructing or being instructed: *~ in chemistry.* **2** (*pl*) directions; orders: *give ~s to arrive early.*

in·struc·tional /-ʃənəl/ *adj* educational: *~al films.*

in·struc·tive /ɪnˈstrəktɪv/ *adj* giving or containing instruction: *~ books.*

in·stru·ment /ˈɪnstrəmənt/ *n* [C] **1** implement, apparatus, used in performing an action, esp for delicate or scientific work: *optical ~s,* eg a microscope. **2** apparatus for producing musical sounds, eg a piano, violin, flute or drum: *musical ~s.* **3** means of doing something, esp a person used by another for his own purposes: *be made the ~ of another's crime.* **4** legal document.

in·stru·men·tal /ˌɪnstrəˈmentəl/ *adj* **1** serving as an instrument or means: *be ~ in finding well-paid work for a friend.* **2** of or for musical instruments: *~ music.*

in·stru·men·tal·ist /-təlɪst/ *n* [C] player of a musical instrument.

in·stru·men·tal·ity /ˌɪnstrəmenˈtæləti/ *n* [U] agency: *by the ~ity of,* by means of.

in·stru·men·ta·tion /ˌɪnstrəmenˈteiʃən/ *n* [U] arrangement of music for instruments.

in·sub·or·di·nate /ˌɪnsəˈbɔrdənɪt/ *adj* disobedient; rebellious.

in·sub·or·di·na·tion /ˌɪnsəˌbɔrdəˈneiʃən/ *n* **(a)** [U] being disobedient. **(b)** [C] instance of this.

in·sub·stan·tial /ˌɪnsəbˈstænʃəl/ *adj* **1** not solid or real; lacking substance: *an ~ vision.* **2** without good foundation: *an ~ accusation.*

in·suf·fer·able /ɪnˈsəfrəbl/ *adj* intolerable; unbearable: *~ insolence.*

in·suf·fi·cient /ˌɪnsəˈfɪʃənt/ *adj* not sufficient: *~ evidence.*

in·suf·fi·ciency /-ʃənsi/ *n* [U]

in·suf·fi·cient·ly *adv*

in·su·lar /ˈɪnsələr/ *adj* **1** of an island. **2** of or like islanders. **3** narrow-minded: *~ habits and prejudices.*

in·su·lar·ity /ˌɪnsəˈlærəti/ *n* [U] state of being insular.

in·su·late /ˈɪnsəˌleit/ *vt* **1** cover or separate (something) with nonconducting materials to prevent loss of heat, passage of electricity, etc: *ˈinsulating tape.* **2** separate; isolate: *children carefully ~d from harmful experiences.*

in·su·la·tion /ˌɪnsəˈleiʃən/ *n* [U] **(a)** insulating or being insulated. **(b)** materials used for this.

in·su·la·tor /-tər/ *n* [C] substance, device, for insulating.

in·su·lin /ˈɪnsəlɪn/ *n* [U] hormone produced by the pancreas, that controls the amount of sugar in the blood.

in·sult /ɪnˈsəlt/ *vt* speak or act in a way that hurts or is intended to hurt a person's feelings or dignity. □ *n* /ˈɪnˌsəlt/ [C,U] remark or action that insults.

in·sult·ing /ɪnˈsəltɪŋ/ *adj*

in·su·per·able /ɪnˈsupərəbəl/ *adj* (of difficulties, etc) that cannot be overcome: *~ barriers.*

in·sup·port·able /ˌɪnsəˈpɔrtəbəl/ *adj* unbearable.

in·sur·ance /ɪnˈʃʊrəns/ *n* **1** [C,U] (contract, made by a company or the state, to provide) safeguard in the form of money in case of loss, sickness, accident, death, etc in return for regular payments. **2** [U] payment made to or by such a company, etc: *When her husband died, she received $20,000 ~.* **3** (*sing* only) any measure taken as a safeguard against loss, failure, etc.

in·sure /ɪnˈʃʊr/ *vt* **1** cover by insurance(1): *~ one's house against fire.* **2** make safe or certain. **the insured,** the person to whom payment will be made. **the insurer,** the person or company undertaking to make payment in case of loss, etc.

in·sur·gent /ɪnˈsərdʒənt/ *adj* rebellious: *~ troops.* □ *n* [C] rebel.

in·sur·mount·able /ˌɪnsərˈmauntəbəl/ *adj* (of obstacles, etc) that cannot be surmounted or overcome.

in·sur·rec·tion /ˌɪnsəˈrekʃən/ *n* **1** [U] rebellion; rising of people in open resistance to the government. **2** [C] instance of this.

int. *abbr* = **1** international. **2** interchange²(2). **3** intersection. **4** interest¹(6). **5** internal. **6** intransitive. **7** interjection.

in·tact /ɪnˈtækt/ *adj* untouched; undamaged; complete.

in·take /ˈɪnˌteik/ *n* **1** [C] place where water, gas, etc is taken into a pipe, channel, etc. **2** [C,U] quantity, number, etc entering or taken in (during a given period): *an annual ~ of 200 students.* **3** act of taking in.

in·tan·gible /ɪnˈtændʒəbəl/ *adj* that cannot be touched or grasped by the mind: *~ ideas.*

in·tan·gi·bil·ity /ɪnˌtændʒəˈbɪləti/ *n* [U]

in·te·ger /ˈɪntɪdʒər/ *n* [C] whole number (contrasted with *fractions*).

in·te·gral /ˈɪntəgrəl/ *adj* **1** necessary for completeness: *The arms and legs are ~ parts of a human being.* **2** whole; having or containing all parts that are necessary for completeness. **3** (*math*) (made up) of integers.

in·te·grally /-grəli/ *adv*

in·te·grate /ˈɪntəˌgreit/ *vt, vi* **1** combine (parts) into a whole; complete by adding parts. **2** join with different ethnic groups or different races: *The schools have (been) ~d.*

in·te·gra·tion /ˌɪntəˈgreiʃən/ *n* [U]

in·teg·rity /ɪnˈtegrəti/ *n* [U] **1** quality of being honest and upright in character: *commercial ~.* **2** state or condition of being complete: *Wasn't this treaty supposed to guarantee our territorial ~?*

in·tel·lect /ˈɪntəˌlekt/ *n* **1** [U] power of the mind to reason (contrasted with feeling and instinct): *Intellect distinguishes man from other animals.* **2** [C] person of good understanding, reasoning power, etc: *the ~(s) of the age.*

in·tel·lec·tual /ˌɪntəˈlektʃuəl/ *adj* **1** of the intellect: *~ pursuits.* **2** having or showing superior reasoning power: *~ people.* □ *n* [C] intellectual person.

in·tel·lec·tual·ly /-tʃuəli/ *adv*

in·tel·li·gence /ɪnˈtelədʒəns/ *n* [U] **1** the power of seeing, learning, understanding and knowing; mental ability: *The children were given an ~ test.* **2** news; information, esp with reference to important events: *have secret ~ of the enemy's plans.*

in·tel·li·gent /-ənt/ *adj* having, showing, intelligence.

in·tel·li·gent·ly *adv*

in·tel·li·gible /ɪnˈtelədʒəbəl/ *adj* that can be understood.

in·tel·li·gi·bil·ity /ɪnˌtelədʒəˈbɪləti/ *n* [U]

in·tel·li·gibly /-əbli/ *adv*

in·tem·per·ance /ɪnˈtemp(ə)rəns/ *n* [U] lack of moderation or self-restraint.

in·tem·per·ate /ɪnˈtemp(ə)rɪt/ *adj* not moderate; showing intemperance: *~ language.*

in·tend /ɪnˈtend/ *vt* **1** have in mind as a purpose or plan: *What do you ~ to do/~ doing today?* **2** mean for a particular use, receiver, etc: *What do you ~ by this word? Who was the package ~ed for?*

in·tense /ɪnˈtens/ *adj* **1** (of qualities) high in degree: *~ heat.* **2** (of persons, their feelings, etc) ardent: *an ~ young lady.*

in·tense·ly *adv*

in·ten·sify /ɪnˈtensəˌfai/ *vt,vi* (*pt,pp* -ied) make or become (more) intense.

in·ten·sity /ɪnˈtensəti/ *n* [U] **1** state or quality of being intense. **2** quantity, degree of strength or depth (of feeling, etc).

in·ten·sive /ɪnˈtensɪv/ *adj* **1** deep and thorough: *make an ~ study of a subject.* **2** (*gram*) giving force and emphasis: *In "a terribly hot day," "terribly" is used as an ~ word.*

in·ten·sive·ly *adv*

in·tent¹ /ɪnˈtent/ *adj* **1** with eager attention; earnest: *an ~ look.* **2** determined: *He was ~ on success/succeeding.*

in·tent·ly *adv*

intent² /ɪnˈtent/ *n* **1** [U] purpose; intention: *shoot with ~ to kill.* **2** (*pl*) ***to all intents and purposes,*** in all essential points.

in·ten·tion /ɪnˈtenʃən/ *n* [C,U] intending; thing intended; aim; purpose: *He hasn't the least ~ of marrying yet.*

ˌwell-in·ˈten·tioned *adj* having good intentions.

in·ten·tional /ɪnˈtenʃənəl/ *adj* done on purpose: *If I hurt your feelings, it was not ~.*

in·ten·tion·ally /-ʃənəli/ *adv* on purpose.

in·ter /ɪnˈtər/ *vt* (-rr-) (*formal*) bury.

inter- /ˈɪntər-/ *prefix* between; from one to another: *international.*

in·ter·act /ˌɪntərˈækt/ *vi* act on each other.

in·ter·ac·tion /-ˈækʃən/ *n* [C,U]

in·ter·cede /ˌɪntərˈsid/ *vi* plead on behalf of another, esp to bring about an agreement or to settle differences: *~ with the father for/on behalf of the daughter.*

in·ter·ces·sion /ˌɪntərˈseʃən/ *n* [C,U]

in·ter·cept /ˌɪntərˈsept/ *vt* **1** stop, catch (a person or thing) between the starting-point and destination: *~ a letter/a messenger.* **2** (*math*) intersect.

in·ter·cep·tion /ˌɪntərˈsepʃən/ *n* [U]

in·ter·cep·tor /-tər/ *n* [C] person or thing that intercepts.

in·ter·change¹ /ˌɪntərˈtʃeindʒ/ *vt* **1** (of two persons, etc) give and receive: *~ views.* **2** put (each of two things) in the other's place.

in·ter·change·able /-əbəl/ *adj* that can be interchanged: *True synonyms are ~able.*

in·ter·change² /ˈɪntərˌtʃeindʒ/ *n* **1** [U] interchanging. **2** [C] intersection of highways, with separate levels so as to permit each stream of traffic to move freely.

in·ter·col·legi·ate /ˌɪntərkəˈlidʒet/ *adj* carried on, etc between colleges: *~ sports/debates.*

in·ter·com /ˈɪntərˌkam/ *n* [C,U] (*informal*) radio or telephone intercommunication system, esp one linking different parts of a building, ship, etc.

in·ter·con·ti·nen·tal /ˌɪntərˌkantəˈnentəl/ *adj* carried on, etc between continents: *~ ballistic missiles,* that can be fired from one continent to another.

in·ter·course /ˈɪntərˌkɔrs/ *n* [U] **1** relations, dealings, between individuals, societies, nations, etc. **2** sexual relations.

in·ter·de·nomi·na·tional /ˌɪntərdɪˌnaməˈneiʃənəl/ *adj* common to, shared by, or involving different religious denominations, eg Methodist, Baptist.

in·ter·de·pen·dent /ˌɪntərdɪˈpendənt/ *adj* depending on each other.

in·ter·de·pen·dence /-əns/ *n* [U]

in·ter·dict /ˌɪntərˈdɪkt/ *vt* (*formal*) prohibit (an action). □ *n* /ˈɪntərdɪkt/ [C] formal or authoritative prohibition, esp (Roman Catholic Church) an order debarring a person or place from church services, etc: *lay a priest/a town under an* ~.

in·ter·est[1] /ˈɪntrɪst/ *n* **1** [U] condition of wanting to know or learn about a person or thing: *feel/take no/not much/a great* ~ *in politics*. **2** [U] quality that causes concern or curiosity: *of considerable/not much* ~. **3** [C] something with which one concerns oneself: *His two great* ~*s in life are music and painting*. **4** [C] (often *pl*) advantage; profit; well-being: *work in the* ~*(s) of humanity*. **5** [C] legal right to a share in something, esp in its profits: *have an* ~ *in a brewery*. **6** [U] money charged or paid for the use of money, usually a percentage of the amount that is borrowed: *rate of* ~*; an* ˈ~ *rate of 5%*. **7** (often *pl*) group of persons engaged in the same trade, etc: *business* ~*s*, large business firms collectively.

in·ter·est[2] /ˈɪntrɪst/ *vt* **1** cause (a person) to feel curious about or to give his attention to: *His story* ~*ed everyone in the room*. **2** cause (a person) to become involved or concerned in: *tried to* ~ *us in working for his candidate*.

in·ter·ested *adj* **(a)** involved in. **(b)** having or showing interest(1): *an* ~*ed look*.

in·ter·est·ing *adj* holding the attention; causing interest(1): *an* ~*ing conversation*.

in·ter·fere /ˌɪntərˈfɪr/ *vi* **1** (of persons) break in on (another person's affairs) without right or invitation; meddle; *Please don't* ~ *in my business*. **2** (of events, circumstances, etc) get in the way of; act as an obstacle to: *Do you ever allow pleasure to* ~ *with duty?*

in·ter·fer·ence /ˌɪntərˈfɪrəns/ *n* [U]

in·terim /ˈɪntərɪm/ *n* **1** ***in the interim,*** meanwhile; during the time that comes between. **2** (as an *adjective*) temporary: *an* ~ *report*, one that precedes the final report.

in·te·rior /ɪnˈtɪriər/ *adj* **1** situated inside; of the inside. **2** inland; away from the coast. □ *n* [C] **1** the inside: ~ *decorators*, those who decorate the inside of a building. **2** inland areas. **3** domestic affairs of a country (as contrasted with foreign affairs): *Department of the Interior*.

in·ter·ject /ˌɪntərˈdʒekt/ *vt* put in suddenly (a remark, etc) between other things; insert.

in·ter·jec·tion /ˌɪntərˈdʒekʃən/ *n* [C] (*gram*) (esp) word or phrase used as an exclamation, eg *Oh! Good! Indeed!*

in·ter·lace /ˌɪntərˈleis/ *vt,vi* join, be joined (as if) by weaving or lacing together: *interlacing branches*.

in·ter·linear /ˌɪntərˈlɪniər/ *adj* written, printed, between the lines.

in·ter·lock /ˌɪntərˈlak/ *vt,vi* lock or join together; clasp firmly together.

in·ter·lo·per /ˈɪntərˌloupər/ *n* [C] person who, esp for profit or personal advantage, pushes himself in where he has no right.

in·ter·lude /ˈɪntərˌlud/ *n* [C] **1** interval between two events or two periods of time: ~*s of bright weather*. **2** interval between two parts of a play, etc. **3** music played during the interval of a play, two longer pieces of music, etc.

in·ter·marry /ˌɪntərˈmæri/ *vi* (*pt,pp* -ied) marry with members of other tribes, races, ethnic groups, etc.

in·ter·mar·riage /ˌɪntərˈmærɪdʒ/ *n* [U]

in·ter·medi·ary /ˌɪntərˈmidiˌeri/ *n* [C] (*pl* -ies), *adj* **1** (person or thing) acting as a mediator between others. **2** (something) intermediate.

in·ter·medi·ate /ˌɪntərˈmidiɪt/ *adj* situated or coming between in time, space, degree, etc: *an* ~ *school*, between primary and secondary schools. □ *n* [C] something that is intermediate.

in·ter·medi·ate·ly *adv*

in·ter·ment /ɪnˈtərmənt/ *n* [C] burial.

in·ter·mi·nable /ɪnˈtərmɪnəbəl/ *adj* (seeming) endless; tedious because too long: *an* ~ *debate*.

in·ter·mi·nably /-əbli/ *adv*

in·ter·mingle /ˌɪntərˈmɪŋgəl/ *vt,vi* mix or mingle together.

in·ter·mission /ˌɪntərˈmɪʃən/ *n* [C] pause; interval, eg between the acts of a play: *without* ~*/with a short* ~.

in·ter·mit·tent /ˌɪntərˈmɪtənt/ *adj* pausing or stopping at intervals: ~ *fever*.

in·ter·mit·tent·ly *adv*

in·tern[1] /ɪnˈtərn/ *vt* compel (persons, esp aliens during a war) to live in a certain place, eg a camp, etc.

in·tern·ment *n* [U]

in·tern[2]**, in·terne** /ˈɪnˌtərn/ *n* young doctor who has graduated from medical school and is completing his practical training in a hospital.

in·ter·nal /ɪnˈtərnəl/ *adj* **1** of or in the inside: *suffer* ~ *injuries*. **2** domestic; of the home affairs of a country: ~ *trade*.

in·ter·nally *adv*

in·ter·na·tional /ˌɪntərˈnæʃənəl/ *adj* existing, carried on, between nations: ~ *trade*.

in·ter·na·tion·al·ize /-ˌlaiz/ *vt* put or bring under international control or protection: *Should the Panama Canal be* ~*ized?*

in·terne *n* = intern[2].

in·ter·necine /ˌɪntərˈneˌsin/ *adj* (of war) causing destruction to both sides.

in·ter·plan·etary /ˌɪntərˈplænəˌteri/ *adj* between planets: *an* ~ *journey in a spacecraft*.

in·ter·play /ˈɪntərˌplei/ *n* [U] operation, effect, of two things on each other: *the* ~ *of colors*.

in·ter·po·late /ɪnˈtərpəˌleit/ *vt* make additions to a book, text, etc.

in·ter·po·la·tion /ɪnˌtərpəˈleiʃən/ *n* [C,U]

in·ter·pose /ˌɪntərˈpouz/ *vt,vi* **1** put or come between two parts. **2** break in with (a question, comment, etc). **3** come between; mediate: ~ *between two persons who are quarreling*.

in·ter·pret /ɪnˈtərprɪt/ *vt,vi* **1** make clear, explain, the meaning: ~ *a difficult passage in a book*. **2** bring out the meaning of, as in a performance: ~ *the role of Hamlet*. **3** consider to be the meaning of: *We* ~*ed his silence as a refusal*. **4** act as interpreter, esp when translating(1).

in·ter·pre·ta·tion /ɪnˌtərprəˈteiʃən/ *n* [C,U]

in·ter·preter *n* [C] person who gives an oral translation of words spoken in another language.

in·ter·racial /ˌɪntərˈreiʃəl/ *adj* between, involving, different races.

in·ter·reg·num /ˌɪntərˈregnəm/ *n* [C] (*pl* ~s, -na /-nə/) **1** period between the end of one reign or regime and the beginning of another. **2** pause or interval.

in·ter·re·late /ˌɪntərɪˈleit/ *vt,vi* bring or come together in mutual relationship: *~d studies,* of separate but related subjects.

in·ter·re·la·tion·ship /-rɪˈleiʃənˌʃɪp/ *n* [C,U]

in·ter·ro·gate /ɪnˈterəˌgeit/ *vt* question thoroughly or formally: *~ a prisoner.*

in·ter·ro·ga·tion /ɪnˌterəˈgeiʃən/ *n* **(a)** [U] asking questions. **(b)** [C] instance of interrogating: *interrogations by police officers.*

in·ter·ro·ga·tor /-tər/ *n* [C] person who does this.

in·ter·roga·tive /ˌɪntəˈragətɪv/ *adj* **1** asking a question: *an ~ look/glance; in an ~ tone.* **2** (*gram*) used in asking questions: *~ pronouns/adverbs,* eg who, why. □ *n* [C] interrogative word or construction.

in·ter·roga·tive·ly *adv*

in·ter·roga·tory /ˌɪntəˈragəˌtɔri/ *adj* of inquiry: *in an ~ tone.*

in·ter·rupt /ˌɪntəˈrəpt/ *vt,vi* **1** break the continuity of: *The war ~ed trade between the two countries.* **2** break in on (a person speaking, doing something, etc): *Don't ~ (me) while I'm reading.*

in·ter·rup·tion /ˌɪntəˈrəpʃən/ *n* [C,U]

in·ter·sect /ˌɪntərˈsekt/ *vt,vi* **1** divide by cutting across, or passing through. **2** (of lines) cross each other.

in·ter·sec·tion /ˌɪntərˈsekʃən/ *n* **(a)** [U] intersecting. **(b)** place where two or more things (esp streets) intersect.

in·ter·sperse /ˌɪntərˈspərs/ *vt* place, scatter, here and there.

in·ter·state /ˌɪntərˈsteit/ *adj* of or between two or more states, esp of the US: *an ~ highway.*

in·ter·stel·lar /ˌɪntərˈstelər/ *adj* between the stars: *~ communications.*

in·ter·twine /ˌɪntərˈtwain/ *vt,vi* twine or twist together: *a lattice ~d with vines.*

in·ter·ur·ban /ˌɪntərˈərbən/ *adj* between cities or towns.

in·ter·val /ˈɪntərvəl/ *n* [C] **1** time between two events or two parts of an action. **2** space between (two objects or points): *arranged at ~s of six feet/at six foot ~s.* **3** (*music*) difference of pitch between two notes on a given scale.

in·ter·vene /ˌɪntərˈvin/ *vi* **1** come between (two events, two points) in time, etc: *I shall leave on Sunday if nothing ~s; during the years that ~d.* **2** (of persons) interfere (so as to try to stop something): *~ in a dispute; ~ between people who are quarreling.*

in·ter·ven·tion /ˌɪntərˈvenʃən/ *n* [C,U]

in·ter·view /ˈɪntərˌvyu/ *n* [C] **1** meeting face to face for discussion or conference: *a job ~.* **2** meeting (of a reporter, etc) with a person in order to get facts, news, etc: *He refused to give any newspaper ~s.* **3** account of such a meeting. □ *vt* have an interview with.

in·ter·weave /ˌɪntərˈwiv/ *vt* (*pt* -wove /-ˈwouv/, *pp* -woven /-ˈwouvən/) weave together (one with another).

in·tes·tate /ɪnˈteˌsteit/ *adj* not having made a legal will before death occurs: *die ~.*

in·tes·tine /ɪnˈtestɪn/ *n* [C] (usually *pl* unless referring to a specific section, eg *large/small ~.*) lower part of the food canal from below the stomach to the anus, that helps to digest food and discharge waste matter.

in·tes·ti·nal /ɪnˈtestɪnəl/ *adj*

in·ti·macy /ˈɪntəməsi/ *n* (*pl* -ies) [U] the state of being intimate; close personal friendship or relationship.

in·ti·mate[1] /ˈɪntəmɪt/ *adj* **1** close and familiar: *~ friends.* **2** innermost; private and personal: *the ~ details of one's life.* **3** resulting from close study or great familiarity: *an ~ knowledge of Greek.* □ *n* [C] close friend.

in·ti·mate·ly *adv*

in·ti·mate[2] /ˈɪntəˌmeit/ *vt* **1** make known. **2** hint; suggest: *~ one's approval.*

in·ti·ma·tion /ˌɪntəˈmeiʃən/ *n* [C,U]

in·timi·date /ɪnˈtɪməˌdeit/ *vt* frighten, esp in order to force a person into doing something: *~ a witness,* eg by threatening him.

in·timi·da·tion /ɪnˌtɪməˈdeiʃən/ *n* [U]

into /ˈɪntə *strong form:* ˈɪnˌtu/ *prep* **1** (indicating motion or direction to a point within): *Come ~ the house/garden.* **2** (indicating change of condition, result): *She burst ~ tears. The rain changed ~ snow.* **3** against: *ran ~ the fence.* **4** (*math*) (to express division): *5 ~ 25* (= 25 divided by 5). **5** (*informal*) interested in: *Are you ~ classical music?*

in·tol·er·able /ɪnˈtalərəbəl/ *adj* that cannot be tolerated or endured: *~ heat/insolence.*

in·tol·er·ably /-əbli/ *adv*

in·tol·er·ant /ɪnˈtalərənt/ *adj* not tolerant.

in·tol·er·ance /-əns/ *n* [U]

in·tol·er·ant·ly *adv*

in·ton·ation /ˌɪntəˈneiʃən/ *n* [U] (esp) the rise and fall of the pitch of the voice in speaking.

in·toxi·cant /ɪnˈtaksɪkənt/ *adj, n* [C] intoxicating (liquor).

in·toxi·cate /ɪnˈtaksɪˌkeit/ *vt* **1** make drunk; cause to lose self-control as the result of taking alcoholic drink. **2** (*fig*) excite greatly: *be ~d with joy.*

in·toxi·ca·tion /ɪnˌtaksɪˈkeiʃən/ *n* [U]

intra- /ˈɪntrə-/ *prefix* inside; within: *intravenous.*

in·trac·table /ɪnˈtræktəbəl/ hard to control.

in·tra·mu·ral /ˌɪntrəˈmyʊrəl/ *adj* within the limits of a school: *~ sport.*

in·tran·si·gent /ɪnˈtrænsədʒənt/ *adj* (*formal*) unwilling to compromise; obstinate.

in·tran·si·tive /ɪnˈtrænsətɪv/ *adj* (*gram*) (of a verb) that cannot take a direct object (*Note:* marked *vi* in this dictionary).

in·tran·si·tive·ly *adv*

intra·uter·ine /ˌɪntrəˈyutərain/ *adj* within the womb.

ˌintraˌuterine deˈvice, (*abbr* **IUˈD**) placed inside the womb to prevent conception.

in·tra·venous /ˌɪntrəˈvinəs/ *adj* within a vein or veins: *~ injections.*

in·treat = entreat.
in·trepid /ɪnˈtrepɪd/ *adj (formal)* fearless.
in·trep·id·ly *adv*
in·tri·cacy /ˈɪntrɪkəsi/ *n* (*pl* -ies) **1** [U] state or quality of being intricate. **2** [C] something intricate.
in·tri·cate /ˈɪntrɪkɪt/ *adj* complicated; difficult to follow or understand: *an ~ piece of machinery.*
in·tri·cate·ly *adv*
in·trigue /ɪnˈtrig/ *vi,vt* **1** make and carry out secret plans or plots: *intriguing with Smith against Robinson.* **2** arouse the interest or curiosity of: *The news ~d all of us.* □ *n* /ˈɪnˌtrig/ **1** [U] secret plotting. **2** [C] secret plan, plot. **3** [C] secret love affair.
in·trin·sic /ɪnˈtrɪnsɪk/ *adj* (of value, quality) belonging naturally; inherent; existing within, not coming from outside: *a man's ~ worth.*
in·trin·si·cally /-kli/ *adv*
intro /ˈɪnˌtrou/ *n* [C] (*pl* ~s) (*informal*) (short for) introduction. (Compare the following entry.)
intro(d). *abbr* = introduction. (Compare the preceding entry.)
in·tro·duce /ˌɪntrəˈdus/ *vt* **1** bring in or forward: *~ a new topic.* **2** bring into use or operation for the first time: *~ new ideas into a business.* **3** make (persons) known by name (to one another): *He ~d me to his parents.* **4** insert; put in: *~ foreign matter into the body.*
in·tro·duc·tion /ˌɪntrəˈdəkʃən/ *n* **1** [U] introducing or being introduced. **2** [C] introducing of persons to one another. **3** [C] opening paragraph of a letter, essay, speech, etc; explanatory article at or before the beginning of a book. **4** [C] elementary textbook: *"An Introduction to Greek Grammar."*
in·tro·duc·tory /ˌɪntrəˈdəktəri/ *adj* serving to introduce: *an ~ chapter.*
in·tro·spec·tion /ˌɪntrəˈspekʃən/ *n* [U] looking inside oneself to examine one's thoughts, feelings, etc.
in·tro·spec·tive /-tɪv/ *adj*
in·tro·vert /ˈɪntrəvərt/ *n* [C] **1** person who is more interested in his own thoughts and feelings than in things outside himself. **2** (*informal*) shy, reserved person. ⇨ extrovert.
in·tro·ver·sion /ˌɪntrəˈvərʒən/ *n* [U]
in·trude /ɪnˈtrud/ *vt,vi* force (something, oneself, on a person, into a place); enter without invitation: *I hope I'm not intruding.*
in·truder, person or thing that intrudes.
in·tru·sion /ɪnˈtruʒən/ *n* **1** [U] intruding. **2** [C] instance of this: *numerous ~s on one's privacy.*
in·tru·sive /ɪnˈtrusɪv/ *adj* intruding; tending to intrude.
in·tu·ition /ˌɪntuˈɪʃən/ *n* **1** [U] (power of) the immediate understanding of something without conscious reasoning or study. **2** [C] piece of knowledge gained by this power.
in·tu·itive /ɪnˈtuətɪv/ *adj*
in·tu·itive·ly *adv*
in·un·date /ˈɪnənˌdeit/ *vt* **1** flood; cover (with water) by overflowing. **2** (*fig*) (esp passive) overwhelm: *be ~d with requests for help.*
in·un·da·tion /ˌɪnənˈdeiʃən/ *n* [C,U]
in·vade /ɪnˈveɪd/ *vt* **1** enter (a country) with armed forces in order to attack. **2** (*fig*) crowd into; enter in great numbers: *a city ~d by tourists.* **3** violate; interfere with: *~ a person's rights.*
in·vader *n* [C] person, thing, that invades.
in·valid[1] /ɪnˈvælɪd/ *adj* not valid: *~ arguments.*
in·vali·date /ɪnˈvæləˌdeit/ *vt* make invalid.
in·vali·da·tion /ɪnˌvæləˈdeiʃən/ *n* [C,U]
in·va·lid[2] /ˈɪnvəlɪd/ *n* [C] weak or disabled person. □ *vt* (esp of members of the armed forces) remove from active service as an invalid: *be ~ed home.*
in·valu·able /ɪnˈvælyəbəl/ *adj* of value too high to be measured: *Her services are ~ to me.*
in·vari·able /ɪnˈveriəbəl/ *adj* unchanging; constant: *an ~ temperature.*
in·vari·ably /-əbli/ *adv*
in·va·sion /ɪnˈveiʒən/ *n* **1** [U] invading or being invaded. **2** [C] instance of this: *an ~ of privacy.*
in·vec·tive /ɪnˈvektɪv/ *n* [U] harsh, abusive language: *speeches filled with ~.*
in·veigh /ɪnˈvei/ *vi* (*formal*) protest or complain bitterly: *~ed against the government.*
in·veigle /ɪnˈveigəl/ *vt* persuade by flattery, deception, etc: *~d them into lending him the money.*
in·vent /ɪnˈvent/ *vt* **1** create or design (something not existing before): *When was television ~ed?* **2** make up: *~ an excuse.*
in·ven·tive /ɪnˈventɪv/ *adj* able to invent: *an ~ive mind.*
in·ven·tor /-tər/, person who invents things.
in·ven·tion /ɪnˈvenʃən/ *n* **1** [U] inventing: *the ~ of the telephone.* **2** [C] something invented: *the many ~s of Edison.* **3** [U] power of inventing: *a man of great ~.*
in·ven·tory /ˈɪnvənˌtɔri/ *n* [C] (*pl* -ies) **1** detailed list, eg of assets, goods, furniture, etc. **2** process of making such a list. **3** stock or goods on hand.
in·verse /ɪnˈvərs/ *adj* opposite; reversed in position, direction or relations.
in·verse·ly *adv*
in·ver·sion /ɪnˈvərʒən/ *n* **1** [U] inverting or being inverted. **2** [C] instance of this; something inverted.
in·vert /ɪnˈvərt/ *vt* **1** put upside down. **2** put in the opposite order, position or arrangement.
in·ver·tebrate /ɪnˈvərtəbrɪt, -ˌbreit/ *adj* not having a backbone or spinal column, eg insects, worms. □ *n* [C] invertebrate animal.
in·vest /ɪnˈvest/ *vt,vi* **1** put money into property, a business, etc in order to make a profit: *~$5,000 in a business.* **2** spend in order to get a future benefit: *~ time in training a new clerk.* **3** give authority: *~ed with full military power.* **4** place in office with a formal ceremony. **5** fill or surround with a certain quality.
in·ves·tor /-tər/ *n* [C] person who invests money.
in·ves·ti·gate /ɪnˈvestəˌgeit/ *vt* examine, inquire closely into; make a careful study of: *~ a crime/the market for sales of a product.*
in·ves·ti·ga·tor /-tər/ *n* [C] person who investigates.
in·ves·ti·ga·tion /ɪnˌvestəˈgeiʃən/ *n* [C,U]
in·vest·ment /ɪnˈvestmənt/ *n* **1** [U] investing money: *careful ~ of capital.* **2** [C] sum of money that is invested; that in which money is invested: *profitable ~s.*

in·vet·er·ate /ɪnˈvetərɪt/ *adj* habitual; long-established: *an ~ liar*.

in·vidi·ous /ɪnˈvɪdiəs/ *adj* likely to cause anger, resentment (because of real or apparent injustice).

in·vidi·ous·ly *adv*

in·vig·o·rate /ɪnˈvɪgəˌreit/ *vt* give strength, energy or courage to: *an invigorating climate*.

in·vin·cible /ɪnˈvɪnsəbəl/ *adj* too strong to be overcome or defeated: *an ~ will*.

in·vin·cibly /-əbli/ *adv*

in·viol·able /ɪnˈvaiələbəl/ *adj* too sacred to be violated: *an ~ oath*.

in·viol·ate /ˌɪnˈvaiələt/ *adj* kept sacred; held in respect; not violated.

in·vis·ible /ɪnˈvɪzəbəl/ *adj* that cannot be seen: *stars that are ~ to the naked eye*.

in·visi·bil·ity /ɪnˌvɪzəˈbɪləti/ *n* [U]

in·vis·ibly /-əbli/ *adv*

in·vite /ɪnˈvait/ *vt* **1** ask (a person to do something, come somewhere, etc): *~ a friend to one's house*. **2** encourage: *~ questions*. **3** tempt; attract: *Don't leave the windows open—it's inviting thieves to enter*.

in·vit·ing *adj* tempting; attractive.

in·vit·ing·ly *adv*

in·vi·ta·tion /ˌɪnvəˈteiʃən/ *n* **1** [U] inviting or being invited: *admission by ~ only*. **2** [C] request to come or go somewhere, or do something: *send out ~s to a party*.

in·vo·ca·tion /ˌɪnvəˈkeiʃən/ *n* **1** [U] invoking or being invoked. **2** [C] prayer or appeal that invokes.

in·voice /ˈɪnˌvɔis/ *vt, n* [C] (make a) list of goods sold with the price(s) charged.

in·voke /ɪnˈvouk/ *vt* **1** call on God, the power of the law, etc for help or protection. **2** request earnestly: *~ vengeance on one's enemies*. **3** summon up (by magic): *~ evil spirits*.

in·vol·un·tary /ɪnˈvalənˌteri/ *adj* done without intention; done unconsciously: *an ~ movement of fear*.

in·vol·un·tar·ily /ɪnˌvalənˈterəli/ *adv*

in·volve /ɪnˈvalv/ *vt, vi* **1** cause (a person or thing) to be caught or mixed up (in trouble, a difficult condition, etc): *The robbers ~d the guard in their crime*. **2** ***(be) involved in/with sth/sb,*** devote much time and attention to it/him: *He is ~d in politics. Mary was very ~d with John*, in love with him. **3** require; have as a necessary consequence: *a job involving a lot of extra work*. **4** take in; include: *The new law ~s everyone who owns a car*.

in·volved *adj* complicated in form, etc: *an ~d sentence/style*.

in·volve·ment *n* [C,U]

in·vul·ner·able /ɪnˈvəln(ə)rəbəl/ *adj* that cannot be wounded, hurt, attacked: *an ~ position*.

in·ward /ˈɪnwərd/ *adj* **1** situated within; inner: *one's ~* (ie mental or spiritual) *nature*. **2** turned toward the inside: *an ~ curve*.

in·ward·ly *adv* in mind or spirit: *suffer ~ly*, ie so as not to show one's grief.

in·ward(s) *adv* **(a)** toward the inside. **(b)** into or toward the mind or soul.

io·dine /ˈaiəˌdain/ *n* **1** [U] nonmetallic element used in medicine, in photography and in the manufacture of some dyes. **2** substance made of iodine dissolved in alcohol, widely used as an antiseptic.

ion /ˈaiən/ *n* [C] electrically charged particle formed as a result of losing or gaining electrons.

ion·ize /ˈaiəˌnaiz/ *vt,vi* **(a)** convert into ions. **(b)** break apart into ions.

iono·sphere /aiˈanəˌsfɪr/ *n* **the ionosphere,** set of layers of the earth's atmosphere containing ionized particles, which transmit radio waves around the earth.

iota /aiˈoutə/ *n* [C] (*pl* ~s) **1** the ninth letter (I, ι) of the Greek alphabet. **2** smallest amount; minute part: *not an ~ of truth in the story*, no truth at all.

I.O.U, IOU /ˌai ˌou ˈyu/ (the pronounciation of the letters being the same as the phrase *I owe you*.) *n* [C] (*informal*) note given as a promise to pay a personal debt.

-ious ⇨ -ous.

IPA /ˌai ˌpi ˈei/ *abbr* = **1** International Phonetic Alphabet. **2** International Phonetic Association.

IQ /ˌai ˈkyu/ *abbr* = intelligence quotient.

I.R.A., IRA /ˌai ˌar ˈei/ *abbr* = Irish Republican Army.

irate /aiˈreit/ *adj* angry.

irate·ly *adv*

ire /ˈaiər/ *n* (*poet or formal*) anger.

iri·descent /ˌɪrəˈdesənt/ *adj* (*formal*) showing colors like those of the rainbow; changing color as light falls from different directions.

iri·descence /-ˈdesəns/ *n* [U]

iris /ˈairɪs/ *n* [C] **1** colored part around the pupil of the eye. ⇨ illus at eye. **2** kinds of flowering plant with sword-shaped leaves.

Irish /ˈairɪʃ/ *n* **1** the Irish language. **2** (*pl*) (used with *the*) Irish people. □ *adj* of Ireland, its language or its people.

Irish·man/-woman /-mən, -wʊmən/ *n* [C] (*pl* ~men /-men/, ~women /ˌ-wɪmɪn/) male/female native of Ireland.

irk /ərk/ *vt* trouble; annoy.

irk·some /-səm/ *adj* tiresome; annoying.

iron¹ /ˈaiərn/ *n* **1** [U] commonest of all metallic elements (symbol **Fe**), used in various forms. **2** [C] tool, etc made of iron, esp a flat-bottomed implement heated and used for pressing clothes, etc. **3** (*pl*) fetters: *put him in ~s*.

the ˈIron Age, prehistoric period when men used tools and weapons made of iron (after the Stone Age and the Bronze Age).

ˈiron·clad *adj* **(a)** (*old use*) (of fighting ships, during the US Civil War) protected with a covering of iron plates. **(b)** (*fig*) resistant to attack or alteration.

ˌIron ˈCurtain, (esp) barrier of censorship, lack of contact etc dividing USSR and allied countries from other countries.

ˌiron ˈlung, apparatus fitted over the whole body, except the head, to provide artificial respiration.

iron² /ˈaiərn/ *vt,vi* smooth cloth/clothes with an iron: *She's been ~ing all afternoon*. ***iron out,*** **(a)** remove by ironing: *~ out wrinkles*. **(b)** (*fig*) work out and remove difficulties, etc: *~ out misunderstandings*.

ˈironing board, padded board on which to iron

clothes, etc.

ironic /aiˈranɪk/, **ironi·cal** /aiˈranɪkəl/ *adj* of, using, expressing, irony: *an ~ smile.*

ironi·cally /-kli/ *adv*

iron·wood /ˈaiərnˌwʊd/ *n* [U] exceptionally hard, tough wood from various kinds of trees and shrubs.

irony /ˌairəni/ *n* (*pl* -ies) **1** [U] sarcastic or humorous use of words to express the direct opposite of their literal meaning, in order to make one's remarks forceful. **2** [C] event, situation, etc which is the opposite of what one would expect or desire: *Inheriting a large fortune and dying a month later might be called one of life's ironies.*

Ir·o·quois /ˈɪrəˌkwɔi/ *n* [C] (*pl* unchanged, or ~s /ˈɪrəˌkwɔiz/) any member of a group of North American Indian tribes that formed a confederacy known as the Five Nations.

ir·ra·di·ate /ɪˈreidiˌeit/ *vt* **1** shine upon; illuminate. **2** treat with radiation.

ir·ration·al /ɪˈræʃənəl/ *adj* **1** not being able to reason: *an ~ animal.* **2** absurd; illogical: *~ fears/behavior.*

ir·ration·ally *adv*

ir·rec·on·cil·able /ˌɪˌrekənˈsailəbəl/ *adj* that cannot be reconciled or brought into harmony.

ir·re·cover·able /ˌɪrɪˈkəvərəbəl/ *adj* that cannot be recovered: *~ losses.*

ir·re·fut·able /ˌɪrɪˈfyutəbəl, ɪˈrefyətəbəl/ *adj* that cannot be proved false: *an ~ argument.*

ir·regu·lar /ɪˈregyələr/ *adj* **1** contrary to rules, to what is normal and established: *~ attendance.* **2** uneven; not regular in shape, arrangement, etc: *a coast with an ~ outline.* **3** (*gram*) (of words), not having the usual endings or forms in a sentence: *"Child" has an ~ plural.*

ir·regu·lar·ity /ˌɪˌregyəˈlærəti/ *n* [C,U]

ir·regu·lar·ly *adv*

ir·rel·evant /ɪˈreləvənt/ *adj* not to the point; having nothing to do with: *~ remarks.*

ir·re·li·gious /ˌɪrɪˈlɪdʒəs/ *adj* opposed to, showing no interest in, religion: *~ acts/persons.*

ir·re·me·di·able /ˌɪrɪˈmidiəbəl/ *adj* that cannot be remedied, corrected, cured, etc.

ir·re·mov·able /ˌɪrɪˈmuvəbəl/ *adj* that cannot be removed.

ir·rep·ar·able /ɪˈrep(ə)rəbəl/ *adj* (of a loss, injury, etc) that cannot be put right or restored: *~ damage.*

ir·re·place·able /ˌɪrɪˈpleisəbəl/ *adj* that cannot be replaced.

ir·re·proach·able /ˌɪrɪˈproutʃəbəl/ *adj* free from blame or fault: *~ conduct.*

ir·re·sist·ible /ˌɪrɪˈzɪstəbəl/ *adj* too strong, convincing, delightful, etc to be resisted: *~ temptations.*

ir·re·spec·tive /ˌɪrɪˈspektɪv/ *adj* not taking into account; regardless of: *~ of the danger.*

ir·re·spon·sible /ˌɪrɪˈspansəbəl/ *adj* (esp) without a proper sense of responsibility: *~ behavior.*

ir·re·spon·si·bil·ity /ˌɪrɪˌspansəˈbɪləti/ *n* [U]

ir·re·spon·sib·ly *adv*

ir·re·triev·able /ˌɪrɪˈtrivəbəl/ *adj* that cannot be retrieved or remedied: *an ~ loss.*

ir·rev·er·ent /ɪˈrev(ə)rənt/ *adj* feeling or showing no respect for sacred things.

ir·rev·er·ent·ly *adv*

ir·rev·er·ence /-əns/ *n* [U]

ir·re·vers·ible /ˌɪrɪˈvərsəbəl/ *adj* that cannot be reversed or revoked: *an ~ decision.*

ir·revo·cable /ɪˈrevəkəbəl/ *adj* final and unalterable: *an ~ legal decision.*

ir·revo·cably *adv*

ir·ri·gate /ˈɪrəˌgeit/ *vt* **1** supply (land, crops) with water (by means of rivers, pipes, etc): *~ desert areas to make them fertile.* **2** wash or flush out (eg a wound) with liquid.

ir·ri·ga·tion /ˌɪrəˈgeiʃən/ *n* [U]

ir·ri·table /ˈɪrətəbəl/ *adj* easily annoyed or made angry.

ir·ri·ta·bil·ity /ˌɪrətəˈbɪləti/ *n* [U]

ir·ri·tably /-əbli/ *adv*

ir·ri·tant /ˈɪrətənt/ *adj* causing irritation. □ *n* [C] irritating substance.

ir·ri·tate /ˈɪrəˌteit/ *vt* **1** make angry or annoyed: *irritating delays.* **2** cause discomfort to (part of the body); make sore or inflamed: *The smoke ~d her eyes.*

ir·ri·ta·tion /ˌɪrəˈteiʃən/ *n* [C,U]

IRS /ˌai ˌar ˈes/ *abbr* = Internal Revenue Service.

is[1] ⇨ be[1].

Is.[2] *abbr* = Island.

-ish /-ɪʃ/ *suffix* **1** (used to form an *adj* of nationality): *Irish; Spanish.* **2** resembling; in the manner of: *devilish.* **3** somewhat; near to: *reddish; twentyish.*

Isl. *abbr* = Island.

Is·lam /ɪsˈlam, ɪz-, -ˈlæm/ *n* **1** faith, religion, proclaimed by the prophet Mohammed. **2** all Moslems as a group. **3** all the Moslem nations.

Is·lamic /ɪsˈlæmɪk, ɪz-/ *adj*

is·land /ˈailənd/ *n* [C] **1** piece of land surrounded by water. **2** something like an island because it is detached or isolated: *a ˈtraffic ~,* in a busy street.

is·lander *n* [C] person born on or living on an island.

isle /ˈaiəl/ *n* [C] island (not much used, except in poetry and proper names): *the British Isles.*

is·let /ˈailɪt/ *n* [C] small island.

-ism /-ˌɪzəm/ *suff* **1** showing qualities typical of: *heroism.* **2** act, process, or practice: *criticism.* **3** specific doctrine, system or principle: *Buddhism.*

isn't = is not.

iso·bar /ˈaisəˌbar/ *n* [C] line on a map, esp a weather chart, joining places with the same atmospheric pressure at a particular time.

iso·late /ˈaisəˌleit/ *vt* separate, put or keep apart from others: *isolating the infected children.*

iso·la·tion /ˌaisəˈleiʃən/ *n* [U] isolating or being isolated: *an ˈ~ ward,* one for persons with infectious diseases.

isos·celes /aiˈsasəˌliz/ *adj* (of a triangle) having two sides equal.

iso·therm /ˈaisəˌθərm/ *n* [C] line on a map joining places having the same average temperature.

iso·tope /ˈaisəˌtoup/ *n* [C] form of a chemical element having an atomic mass and physical properties different from other forms of the same element.

Is·rae·li /ɪzˈreili/ *adj* of modern Israel or its people. □ *n* [C] (*pl* ~s) native or inhabitant of modern Israel.

Is·ra·e·lite /ˈɪzriəˌlait/ *adj* of ancient Israel or its people. □ *n* [C] native or inhabitant of ancient Israel.

issue /ˈɪʃu/ *vi,vt* **1** come, go, flow, out: *blood issuing from a wound.* **2** give out; distribute for use or consumption: ~ *travel tickets to the passengers.* **3** publish (books, etc). **4** put stamps, banknotes, shares[1](3), etc into circulation. □ *n* **1 (a)** [U] outgoing; outflowing. **(b)** [C] the act of flowing out; that which flows out: *an ~ of blood.* **2** [U] putting out; distributing. **3** [C] publication: *the most recent ~s of a periodical.* **4** [C] question that arises for discussion: *argue political ~s.* **5** [C] result; outcome; consequence: *await the ~.* **6** [U] (*legal*) children; offspring: *die without ~*, ie childless.

-ist /-ɪst/ *suffix* **1** person who performs a certain action: *dramatist; motorist.* **2** person who believes in a certain doctrine, principle, etc: *socialist.* **3** person who specializes in a particular art, field of knowledge, etc: *flutist; physicist.*

isth·mus /ˈɪsməs/ *n* (*pl* ~es) strip of land joining two larger bodies of land: *the Isthmus of Panama.*

it[1] /ɪt/ *personal pron* (*pl* they /ðei/, them /ðem/) **1** that one previously spoken about (used of lifeless things, animals and of a baby or small child when the sex is unknown or unimportant): *Where's my book?—Have you seen it? Where's the cat?—It's in the garden. She's expecting another baby and hopes it will be a boy.* **2** (used as the grammatical subject, followed by a word, phrase or clause which is the logical subject): *Is it difficult to learn Chinese? It was hard for him to live on his pension. It's no use trying to do that. Does it matter what you do next? "Who's that at the door?"—"It's the mailman."* **3** (used as the subject in expressions of weather, time, distance, etc): *It is raining. It's six o'clock. It's ten miles to town.* **4** (used to bring emphasis to one part of a sentence): *It was work that exhausted him. It's the red book that I want. It was John I gave the book to, not Harry.* **5** (used to refer to a general condition, state of affairs, etc): *How is it going?* □ *n* (*Note:* always stressed: /ˈɪt/): (esp in children's games) player who has to perform a certain action, as catching or finding other players: *Now Bobby is ˈit.*

It.[2] *abbr* = Italian.

Ital·ian /ɪˈtaljən/ *n* **1** the Italian language. **2** native of Italy □ *adj* of Italy, its language or its people.

italic /ɪˈtælɪk/ *adj* (of printed letters) sloping: *This is ~ type.* □ *n* [C] italic letter: *written in ~s.*

itch /ɪtʃ/ *n* [C] **1** (rarely *pl*) feeling of irritation on the skin, causing a desire to scratch: *have an ~.* **2** restless desire or longing: *an ~ to travel.* □ *vi* **1** have an itch(1): *scratch where it ~es.* **2** have a strong desire: *~ing to go on vacation.*

itchy *adj* (-ier, -iest)

it'd /ɪtəd, ɪtɪd/ = it had; it would.

item /ˈaitəm/ *n* [C] **1** single article or unit in a list, etc: *the first ~ on the program.* **2** detail or paragraph (of news): *interesting ˈnews ~s/~s of news in the paper.*

item·ize /-ˌmaiz/ *vt* list every item of: *an ~ized account.*

i·tin·er·ant /aiˈtɪnərənt/ *adj* (*formal*) traveling from place to place: ~ *circus performers.*

i·tin·er·ary /aiˈtɪnəˌreri/ *n* [C] (*pl* -ies) schedule for, details or records of, a journey.

it'll /ˈɪtəl/ = it will; it shall.

it's /ɪts/ = it is; it has.

its /ɪts/ *adj* of, relating to, or belonging to it: *The dog wagged ~ tail.*

itself /ɪtˈself/ *pron* **1** (used as a *reflexive*): *The dog got up and stretched ~.* ***by itself,*** **(a)** automatically: *The machine works by ~.* **(b)** alone. **2** (used for emphasis): *The thing ~ is not valuable.*

-ity /-əti/ *suffix* (used to form a *noun*): *crudity; ability.*

IUD /ˌai ˌyu ˈdi/ *abbr* = intrauterine device.

IV /ˌai ˈvi/ *abbr* = intravenous.

I've /aiv/ = I have.

ivory /ˈaiv(ə)ri/ *adj, n* [U] **1** (of the) white, bone-like substance forming the tusks of elephants, used for ornaments, piano keys, etc. **2** (of the) color of ivory; yellowish white (color).

ivy /ˈaivi/ *n* [U] climbing, clinging, evergreen plant with dark, shiny leaves.

Ivy League /ˌaivi ˈlig/ *n* (*sing* only) league of (esp football) teams belonging to the older, more traditional universities of the north-eastern US.

ˌivy-ˈleague *adj* (in the style) of universities belonging to the Ivy League: *ivy-league clothing.*

-ize /-ˌaiz/ *suffix* (used to form a *verb*) **1** become; cause to become: *dramatize; industrialize:* **2** take part in a certain activity: *criticize.*

J

J, j /dʒei/ (*pl* J's, j's /dʒeiz/) the tenth letter of the English alphabet.

jab /dʒæb/ *vt,vi* (-bb-) **1** poke or push (*at, into*): *He jabbed at the lid with a knife. He jabbed his elbow into my side.* **2** force or push out by jabbing: *Don't jab my eye out with your umbrella!* □ *n* [C] sudden blow or thrust.

jabber /ˈdʒæbər/ *vi,vt* talk rapidly or indistinctly: *Listen to those children ~ing away!* □ *n* [U] chatter: *the ~ of monkeys.*

jack¹ /dʒæk/ *n* [C] **1** (usually portable) device for raising heavy weights off the ground, esp one for raising the axle of a car so that a wheel may be changed. **2** playing card with the picture of a man, that ranks below the queen. **3 (a)** small, six-pointed metal piece. **(b)** (*pl*) children's game played with a set of these pieces and a small rubber ball. **4** (small) flag flown by a ship to show its nationality. **5** male donkey. **6** socket into which a plug is inserted to make an electrical connection: *a telephone ~.*

jack² /dʒæk/ *vt* **1** lift with a jack(1): *Jack (up) the car and change the tire.* **2** ***jack up,*** (*informal*) raise: *~ up prices.*

jackal /ˈdʒækəl/ *n* [C] wild animal like a dog.

jack·ass /ˈdʒæˌkæs/ *n* [C] **1** male donkey. **2** foolish person.

jack·daw /ˈdʒækˌdɔ/ *n* [C] **1** European bird of the crow family. **2** = grackle.

jacket /ˈdʒækɪt/ *n* [C] **1** short, sleeved coat. **2** outer covering round a tank, pipe, etc. **3** skin (of a potato): *baked in their ~s.* **4** (also **ˈdust jacket**) loose paper cover on a hardback book.

Jack Frost /ˌdʒæk ˈfrɔst/ *n* frost personified.

jack-in-the-box /ˈdʒæk-ɪn-ðə-ˌbaks/ *n* [C] (*pl* jacks-) toy consisting of a small box out of which a figure springs up when the lid is raised.

jack-in-the-pul·pit /ˌdʒæk-ɪn-ðə-ˈpʊlpɪt, -ˈpəlpɪt/ *n* [C] (*pl* jacks-) North American plant bearing a small flower which is protected by a hood-shaped leaf.

jack·knife /ˈdʒækˌnaif/ *n* [C] (*pl* -knives /-ˌnaivz/) **1** large pocketknife with a folding blade. **2** dive in which the diver bends over so as to touch his toes and then straightens out before entering the water. □ *vi* fold and double back.

jack-o'-lantern /ˈdʒæk-ə-ˌlæntərn/ *n* [C] lantern made of a pumpkin that has been hollowed out and carved to look like a human face.

jack·pot /ˈdʒækˌpat/ *n* [C] accumulated stake(3) or big prize in various games, increasing in value until won. ***hit the jackpot,*** **(a)** win the prize in a game of chance or skill. **(b)** enjoy unexpected success in an effort.

JACK-O'-LANTERN

jack·rab·bit /ˈdʒækˌræbɪt/ *n* [C] large hare of North America, having long ears and long hind legs.

jade /dʒeid/ *n* [U] hard, usually green stone, carved into ornaments, etc.

jaded /dʒeidɪd/ *adj* worn out; overworked: *She looks ~d.*

jag¹ /dʒæg/ *n* [C] sharp projection, eg of rock.

jaggy *adj* (-ier, -iest) having jags.

jag² /dʒæg/ *vt* (-gg-) cut or tear unevenly.

jag·ged /ˈdʒægɪd/ *adj* notched; with rough, uneven edges: *jagged rocks.*

jag³ /dʒæg/ *n* [C] (*sl*) bout; spree: *a crying jag.*

jag·uar /ˈdʒægˌwar/ *n* [C] large, fierce, flesh-eating animal of the cat family found in Central and South America. ⇨ illus at cat.

jail /ˈdʒeiəl/ *n* [C] building in which persons are confined, esp while awaiting trial; prison. □ *vt* (*pres p* ~ing /ˈdʒeilɪŋ/) put or keep in jail.

jailer, jailor /ˈdʒeilər/ *n* [C] keeper of a jail.

ja·lop·y /dʒəˈlapi/ *n* [C] (*pl* -ies) (*informal*) battered, worn-out automobile, barely in running condition.

jam¹ /dʒæm/ *n* [U] fruit boiled with sugar until it is thick, and often preserved in jars, pots, cans, etc.

jam² /dʒæm/ *vt,vi* (-mm-) **1** crush, be crushed, between two surfaces or masses; squeeze, be squeezed: *a piano jammed in the doorway.* **2** (of parts of a machine, etc) (cause to) become fixed so that movement or action is prevented: *jammed the keys of the adding machine.* **3** push with a hard and sudden effort: *jam the brakes on/jam on the brakes.* **4** crowd or pack into tightly: *jam clothes into a suitcase. The crowd jammed onto the bus.* **5** make (eg a radio broadcast) impossible or difficult to receive by broadcasting that deliberately interferes: *jam the enemy's stations during a war.* □ *n* [C] **1** number of things or people crowded together so that movement is difficult or impossible: *ˈtraffic jams in our big towns.* **2** (*sl*) awkward position; difficult situation: *be in/get into a jam.*

jam·boree /ˌdʒæmbəˈri/ *n* [C] **1** merry, noisy party. **2** large rally or gathering, esp of Boy Scouts.
jam-packed /ˈdʒæm-ˌpækt/ *vt* (*informal*) crowded to capacity: *a stadium ~ with spectators.*
Jan. *abbr* = January.
jangle /ˈdʒæŋgəl/ *vt,vi* (cause to) give out a harsh metallic noise. □ *n* [U] harsh noise.
jani·tor /ˈdʒænətər/ *n* [C] person hired to clean and take care of a building, offices, etc. (*Note:* now considered impolite, and replaced by *custodian* in formal style.)
Jan·uary /ˈdʒænyuˌeri/ *n* the first month of the year.
ja·pan /dʒəˈpæn/ *vt* (-nn-), n [U] (cover with a) hard, shiny black varnish.
jar[1] /dʒar/ *n* [C] **1** (usually harsh) sound or vibration: *We felt a jar when the train started to move.* **2** shock: *an unpleasant jar to my nerves.* □ *vi,vt* (-rr-) **1** make a harsh unpleasant sound. **2** have an unpleasant effect: *The way he laughs jars on my nerves.* **3** send a shock through (the nerves): *He was badly jarred by the blow.* **4** conflict; be out of harmony: *His opinions jar with mine.*
jar·ring *adj* causing disharmony; harsh: *a jarring note.*
jar·ring·ly *adv*
jar[2] /dʒar/ *n* [C] **1** tall vessel, usually round, with a wide mouth of glass, stone or earthenware. **2** its contents: *a jar of jam.*
jar·ful /-ˌfʊl/ *n* [C] as much as a jar can hold.
jar·gon /ˈdʒargən/ *n* [U] **1** language difficult to understand, because it differs from the norm: *a baby's ~.* **2** the simplified form of a language, used for trade, etc: *Chinook Jargon,* used to and between Indians in the northwestern US. **3** language full of technical or special words: *scientific ~.*
jas·mine /ˈdʒæzmɪn/ *n* [U] kinds of shrub with white or yellow sweet-smelling flowers.
jas·per /ˈdʒæspər/ *n* [U] opaque quartz, usually red, yellow or brown.
jaun·dice /ˈdʒɔndɪs/ *n* [U] **1** disease marked by yellowness of the skin and the whites of the eyes. **2** (*fig*) state of mind in which one is jealous, spiteful, envious and suspicious.
jaun·diced *adj* affected with jaundice: *take a ~d view,* one influenced by jealousy, etc.
jaunt /dʒɔnt/ *n* [C] short journey for pleasure. □ *vi* make such a journey.
jaunty /ˈdʒɔnti/ *adj* (-ier, -iest) feeling or showing self-confidence and self-satisfaction.
jaunt·ily /-əli/ *adv*
jav·elin /ˈdʒævəlɪn/ *n* [C] light spear thrown for distance in an athletic contest.
jaw /dʒɔ/ *n* [C] **1** either of the two bone structures containing the teeth. **2** (*pl*) framework of the mouth, including the teeth; (*sing*) lower part of the face: *a man with a strong jaw.* ⇨ illus at head. **3** (*pl*) narrow mouth of a valley, channel, etc. **4** (*fig*) something similar to a jaw or jaws (2): *the jaws of death.* **5** (*pl*) parts of a tool, machine, etc, eg a vise, between which things are gripped or crushed. □ *vi* (*sl*) talk, esp at tedious length.
ˈjaw·bone *n* [C] one in which the teeth are set.
jay /dʒei/ *n* (kinds of) noisy bird with brightly colored feathers (such as the *North American bluejay*).
jay·walk /ˈdʒeiˌwɔk/ *vi* cross a street without paying attention to the traffic rules.
ˈjay·walker *n* [C] person who jaywalks.
jazz /dʒæz/ *n* [U] **1** American music, first played by Negro musicians, which developed from ragtime and blues and is characterized by improvisation and strong rhythms. **2** (esp worthless) stuff or talk. □ *vt* **1** play or arrange in the style of jazz. **2** ***jazz up,*** (*sl*) liven up: *~ up a party.*
jazzy *adj* (-ier, -iest) (*informal*) **(a)** of or like jazz. **(b)** showy: *a ~y sports car.*
jct. *abbr* = junction.
J.D. /ˌdʒei ˈdi/ *abbr* (= *Lat* Juris/Jurum Doctor) Doctor of Law(s).
jeal·ous /ˈdʒeləs/ *adj* **1** fearful of the loss of love: *a ~ husband.* **2** envious or unhappy because of the better fortune, etc of others: *~ of her success.* **3** taking watchful care (*of*): *~ of one's rights.* **4** suspicious; watchful: *~ looks.*
jeal·ous·ly *adv*
jeal·ousy /ˈdʒeləsi/ *n* (*pl* -ies) **1** [U] being jealous: *a lover's ~.* **2** [C] instance of this; jealous act or utterance.
jeans /dʒinz/ *n* **1** (*pl*) trousers made of a coarse, heavy cotton cloth. **2** (as an *adjective*) any other article of clothing of the same cloth, made to go with the trousers: *a ˈ~-jacket.*
jeep /dʒip/ *n* [C] small, rugged military motor vehicle with great freedom of movement.
jeer /dʒɪr/ *vi,vt* mock, laugh rudely: *a ~ing crowd.* □ *n* [C] jeering remark.
jeer·ing·ly *adv*
Je·ho·vah /dʒɪˈhouvə/ *n* name of God used in the Old Testament and by some religious sects (eg the Jehovah's Witnesses).
Jehovah's ˈWitness, member of an evangelical religious sect.
jell /dʒel/ *vi,vt* (*informal*) take shape: *My ideas are beginning to ~.*
jello /ˈdʒelou/ *n* [U] (*P* = Jell-O) fruit jelly prepared in a mold and flavored and colored, as a sweet dish.
jelly /ˈdʒeli/ *n* (*pl* -ies) **1** [U] soft, semisolid food substance made from gelatin, from meat juices, or from fruit juice and sugar. **2** = jello. **3** [U] substance like jelly. □ *vt,vi* (cause to) turn into jelly.

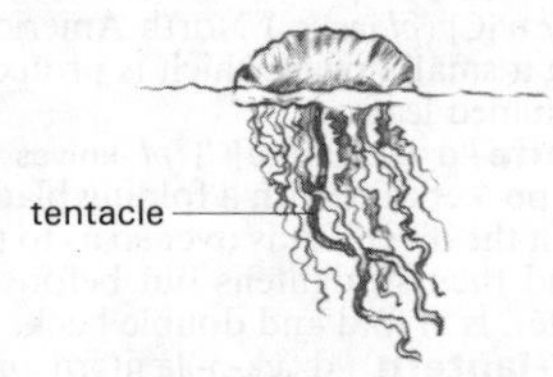

JELLYFISH

ˈjelly·fish *n* kinds of sea animal with a jellylike body.
jeop·ard·ize /ˈdʒepərˌdaiz/ *vt* put in danger.
jeop·ardy /ˈdʒepərdi/ *n* [U] danger.
jerk /dʒərk/ *n* [C] **1** sudden movement, as a push,

pull, twist, etc: *The train stopped with a ~.* **2** sudden involuntary twitch of a muscle or muscles. **3** (*sl*) stupid person; fool. □ *vt,vi* move with a jerk: *He ~ed the fish out of the water.*
jerky *adj* (-ier, -iest) moving with jerks: *a ~y ride in an old bus.*

jer·kin /ˈdʒərkɪn/ *n* [C] short, close-fitting jacket usually without sleeves.

jerry-built /ˈdʒeriˌbɪlt/ built cheaply, hastily or badly.

jer·sey /ˈdʒərzi/ *n* (*pl* ~s) **1** [U] soft, fine knitted fabric used for clothes. **2** [C] garment, eg a sweater, made of jersey. **3 Jersey,** breed of cow, usually light brown, that is raised for its milk.

jes·sa·mine /ˈdʒesəmɪn/ *n* = jasmine.

jest /dʒest/ *n* [C] joke. ***in jest,*** as a joke; in fun. □ *vi* make jokes: *He's not a man to ~ with.*

jest·er /ˈdʒestər/ *n* [C] person who jests, esp (formerly) a man employed to make jokes to amuse a court or noble household.

jet[1] /dʒet/ *n* [C] **1** fast, strong stream of gas, liquid, steam or flame, forced out of a small opening: *a jet of water.* **2** narrow opening from which a jet comes out: *a ˈgas jet.* **3 (a)** jet airplane. **(b)** jet engine. □ *vi,vt* (-tt-) **1** come, send out, in a jet or jets. **2** travel by jet airplane.
ˌjet ˈairplane, one operated by jet engines.
ˌjet ˈengine, one that is used to propel an aircraft by sending out gases through jets at the back.
ˌjet proˈpulsion, method of producing movement by using jets of air or water.
ˈjet stream, narrow current of high speed winds several miles above the earth.

jet[2] /dʒet/ *adj, n* [U] (made of a) hard, black mineral that takes a brilliant polish.
ˌjet ˈblack, deep, glossy black.

jet·sam /ˈdʒetsəm/ *n* [U] goods thrown overboard from a ship at sea to lighten it, eg in a storm. ⇨ flotsam.

jet·ti·son /ˈdʒetəsən/ *vt* **1** throw (goods) overboard in order to lighten a ship, eg during a storm. **2** abandon, discard (what is unwanted).

jetty /ˈdʒeti/ *n* [C] (*pl* -ies) structure built out into a body of water as a breakwater or as a landing place for ships and boats.

Jew /dʒu/ *n* [C] **1** descendant of the Hebrew people of the Bible. **2** person whose religion is Judaism.
Jew·ess /ˈdʒuɪs/ *n* (*dated*) female Jew.
Jew·ish /ˈdʒuɪʃ/ *adj* of the Jews.

jewel /ˈdʒuəl/ *n* [C] **1** precious stone, eg a diamond or a ruby. **2** ornament with jewels set in it. **3** gem used in a watch as a bearing: *This watch has 15 ~s.* **4** (*fig*) highly valued person or thing: *His wife is a ~.* □ *vt* (-l-, -ll-) adorn with jewels: (usually in *pp*) *a ~ed ring.*
jew·eler, jew·el·ler /ˈdʒu(ə)lər/ *n* [C] dealer in jewelry.
jew·elry /ˈdʒuəlri/ *n* [U] (*collect*) jewels.

Jew's harp /ˈdʒuz ˌharp/ *n* [C] simple musical instrument played, usually as a toy, while holding it against the teeth.

Jeze·bel /ˈdʒezəˌbel/ *n* [C] (esp) shameless, immoral woman.

jib /dʒɪb/ *n* [C] **1** small triangular sail (in front of the mainsail). **2** projecting arm of a crane or derrick. ⇨ illus at crane, ship.

jibe[1] /dʒaib/ *vi* agree.

jibe[2] /dʒaib/ *vi* = gibe.

jiffy /ˈdʒɪfi/ *n* [C] (*pl* -ies) (*informal*) moment (esp in) ***in a jiffy,*** very soon.

jig /dʒɪg/ *n* [C] **1** (music for a) quick, lively dance. **2** device that holds a piece of work and guides the tools that are used on it. □ *vi,vt* (-gg-) **1** dance a jig. **2** move up and down in a quick, jerky way: *jigging up and down in excitement.*

jigger /ˈdʒɪgər/ *n* [C] (contents of a) small, usually metal cup of about 1 ounce (or 2 ounces for a ˈ*double jigger*) for measuring whiskey, etc.

jiggle /ˈdʒɪgəl/ *vt,vi* move with short, quick jerks. □ *n* [C] jiggling motion.

jig·saw /ˈdʒɪgˌsɔ/ *n* [C] **1** saw with a narrow blade used for cutting curved or irregular lines. **2** (also **jigsaw puzzle**) picture, map, etc pasted on cardboard or wood and cut in irregularly shaped pieces which are to be fitted together again.

jilt /dʒɪlt/ *vt* get rid of a sweetheart: *When he lost his job, she ~ed him.* □ *n* [C] person who jilts.

Jim Crow /dʒɪm ˈkrou/ *n* [U] (*informal*) practice of discriminating against Negroes.

jim·son·weed /ˈdʒɪmsənˌwid/ *n* [U] poisonous plant with large trumpet-shaped flowers and prickly seed pods.

jingle /ˈdʒɪŋgəl/ *n* [C] **1** metallic clinking or ringing sound (as of coins, keys or small bells). **2** short verse or song designed to attract the attention: *advertising ~s.* □ *vt,vi* (cause to) make a light, ringing sound: *He ~d his keys.*

jinks /ˈdʒɪŋks/ *n* (only in) ***high jinks,*** noisy merrymaking; uncontrolled fun.

jin·rik·i·sha, jin·rick·sha /dʒɪnˈrɪkˌshɔ/ *n* [C] = ricksha.

jinx /dʒɪŋks/ *n* [C] (*sl*) person or thing that brings bad luck.

jit·ters /ˈdʒɪtərz/ *n pl* (sl) extreme nervousness: *have/get/give her the ~.*
jit·tery /ˈdʒɪtəri/ *adj* nervous; frightened.

jiu·jitsu /ˌdʒuˈdʒɪtsu/ *n* = jujitsu.

jive /dʒaiv/ *n* **1** [C] style of popular music with a strong beat; dancing to this. **2** [U] (*sl*) misleading or foolish talk. □ *vi* dance to jive music.

job /dʒab/ *n* [C] **1** piece of work, either to be done, or completed: *odd jobs,* separate tasks, not related to one another. ***on the job,*** (*informal*) at work; busy. ***make the best of a bad job,*** do what one can in spite of difficulties. ***have a hard job doing sth,*** be/have (great) difficulty. **2** (*informal*) employment; position: *He has lost his job.* **3** duty: *It's his job to see that supplies are ordered.*

job lot /ˈdʒab ˌlat/ *n* [C] collection of miscellaneous articles, bought together.

jockey /ˈdʒaki/ *n* [C] (*pl* ~s) professional rider in horse races. ⇨ also disc jockey. □ *vt,vi* trick; cheat: *He ~ed Green out of his job.*

jo·cose /dʒouˈkous/ *adj* (*formal*) humorous.

jocu·lar /ˈdʒakyələr/ *adj* (*formal*) joking; playful.
jocu·lar·ity /ˌdʒakyəˈlærəti/ *n* [C,U]
jocu·lar·ly *adv*

joc·und /ˈdʒakənd/ *adj* (*formal*) merry; cheerful.
joc·und·ity /dʒaˈkəndəti/ *n* [C,U]

jodh·purs /ˈdʒadpərz/ *n pl* breeches for horseback riding, close-fitting from the knee to the ankle.

jog /dʒag/ *vt,vi* (-gg-) **1** give a slight knock or push to: *He jogged my elbow*, touched it, eg to attract my attention. ***jog sb's memory,*** (try to) make him remember something. **2** move up and down with a shaking motion. **3** run at a slow pace, eg for exercise: *I jog for an hour every afternoon.* □ *n* [C] **1** slight push, shake or nudge. **2** (also **ˈjog trot**) slow walk or trot.

joggle /ˈdʒagəl/ *vt,vi* shake, move, by or as if by repeated jerks. □ *n* [C] slight shake.

john /dʒan/ *n* (*sl*) = toilet(3).

join /dʒɔin/ *vt,vi* **1** bring together in close contact; fasten together: *~ one thing to another; ~ two things together.* ***join hands,*** clasp each other's hands. ***join forces (with...),*** unite in action; work together. **2** come together: *Parallel lines never ~.* **3** become a member of: *~ the Army.* ***join up,*** (*informal*) join one of the branches of military service. **4** come into the company of; associate with: *I'll ~ you in a few minutes. May I ~ in (the game)?* □ *n* [C] place or line where two things are joined.

joiner /ˈdʒɔinər/ *n* [C] skilled workman who makes the inside woodwork of buildings, etc.

joint[1] /dʒɔint/ *adj* held or done by, belonging to, two or more persons together: *~ responsibility.* **ˈjoint account,** bank account in the name of more than one person, eg a husband and wife.

joint·ly *adv*

joint[2] /dʒɔint/ *n* [C] **1** place where two movable bones in the body of an animal come together. **2** place, line or surface at which two or more things are joined: *Can you see the ~s?* **3** device or structure by which things, eg lengths of pipe, bones, are joined together: *ˈfinger ~s.* **4** larger piece of meat for roasting, cut from the shoulder, leg, etc of an animal: *a ~ of beef/lamb.* **5** (*informal*) shabby or makeshift place, esp a restaurant, bar, etc: *ˈhamburger ~*, small shop (differing from a *stand* in having seats for the customers) where esp hamburgers are sold. **6** (*sl*) marijuana cigarette.

joint[3] /dʒɔint/ *vt* **1** provide with a joint or joints(3): *a ~ed doll.* **2** divide into joints(4).

joist /dʒɔist/ *n* [C] small beam laid crosswise for supporting a floor or ceiling.

joke /dʒouk/ *n* [C] something said or done to cause amusement. ***play a joke on sb,*** make him the victim of a joke. ***It's no joke,*** it's serious. □ *vi* make jokes: *I was only joking.*

jok·ing·ly *adv* in a joking manner.

joker /ˈdʒoukər/ *n* [C] **1** person who jokes. **2** extra playing card which is used in some games as the highest card. **3** (*informal*) (often hidden) catch in an agreement, how, etc: *Membership in the club is open to all, but the ~ is that dues are $1000 per year.*

jolly /ˈdʒali/ *adj* (-ier, -iest) joyful; gay; merry.

ˌJolly ˈRoger, pirate's black flag (with skull and crossbones).

jolt /dʒoult/ *vt,vi* **1** give a jerk or jerks to; shake up. **2** move along by jerks: *The old bus ~ed along.* □ *n* [C] sudden bump or shake.

jon·quil /ˈdʒankwɪl/ *n* [C] (plant bearing a) yellow flower similar to the daffodil.

jostle /ˈdʒasəl/ *vt,vi* push roughly (against); bump: *We were ~d by the crowd.*

jot[1] /dʒat/ *n* [C] small amount: *not a jot of truth in it*, no truth at all.

jot[2] /dʒat/ *vt* (-tt-) write quickly and briefly: *jot down your name and address.*

jour·nal /ˈdʒərnəl/ *n* [C] **1** newspaper: *The Providence Journal.* **2** periodical: *the Economic Journal.* **3** daily record of news, events, business accounts, etc.

jour·nal·ism /-ˌlɪzəm/ *n* [U] work of writing for, editing, or publishing journals.

jour·nal·ist /-ɪst/ *n* [C] person engaged in journalism.

jour·nal·is·tic /ˌdʒərnəˈlɪstɪk/ *adj*

jour·ney /ˈdʒərni/ *n* [C] (*pl* ~s) (distance traveled in) going to a place, esp a distant place: *go on a ~ around the world.* □ *vi* make a long trip.

jour·ney·man /ˈdʒərnimən/ *n* [C] (*pl* -men /-men/) skilled workman who works for another person.

joust /dʒaust/ *vi, n* [C] (engage in a) fight on horseback with lances (as between knights in the Middle Ages).

jov·ial /ˈdʒouviəl/ *adj* full of fun and good humor; merry: *in a ~ mood.*

jov·ially /-iəli/ *adv*

jov·ial·ity /ˌdʒouviˈæləti/ *n* [C,U]

jowl /dʒaul/ *n* [C] jaw, esp the lower jaw: *a man with a heavy ~.*

joy /dʒɔi/ *n* **1** [U] deep pleasure; great gladness: *I wish you great/much joy.* **2** [C] something that gives joy: *the joys and sorrows of life.*

joy·ful /-fəl/ *adj* filled with, showing, causing, joy.

joy·fully /-fəli/ *adv*

joy·ful·ness /-nɪs/ *n* [U]

joy·less *adj* without joy; gloomy; sad.

joy·ous /ˈdʒɔiəs/ *adj* full of joy.

joy·ous·ly *adv*

Jr. *abbr* = Junior.

ju·bi·lant /ˈdʒubələnt/ *adj* rejoicing.

ju·bi·lant·ly *adv*

ju·bi·la·tion /ˌdʒubəˈleiʃən/ *n* [U] great rejoicing.

ju·bi·lee /ˈdʒubəˌli/ *n* [C] (celebration of a) special anniversary of some event, eg a wedding: *diamond/golden/silver ~*, 60th/50th/25th anniversary.

Ju·daic /dʒuˈdeiɪk/ *adj* of Jews and Judaism.

Ju·da·ism /ˈdʒudiˌɪzəm/ *n* [U] **1** the religion of the Jewish people. **2** culture, history, way of life, etc of the Jews.

judge[1] /dʒədʒ/ *n* [C] **1** public official with authority to hear and decide cases in a law court. **2** person who decides in a contest, competition, dispute, etc. **3** person qualified to give opinions on merits and values: *a good ~ of horses.*

judge[2] /dʒədʒ/ *vt,vi* **1** act as a judge(1). **2** give a decision (in a competition, etc). **3** estimate; consider; form an opinion about: *Judging from what you say, he ought to succeed.*

judg·ment, judge·ment /ˈdʒədʒmənt/ *n* **1** [U] judging or being judged: *sit in ~ on a case,* (in

a law court); *pass ~ on a prisoner*, give a decision after trial. **2** [C] decision of a judge or court: *The ~ was in his favor*. **3** [U] process of judging: *an error of ~*. **4** [U] good sense; ability to judge(2,3): *He showed excellent ~ in choosing a wife*. **5** [C,U] opinion: *in the ~ of most people*.
ˈJudgment Day, the ˌDay of ˈJudgment, the day when, according to some religions, God will judge all men.

ju·di·cial /dʒuˈdɪʃəl/ *adj* of or by a court of law; of a judge or of judgment.
ju·di·cially /-ʃəli/ *adv*

ju·dici·ary /dʒuˈdɪʃiˌeri, -ˈdɪʃəri/ *n* [C] (*pl* -ies) **1** (*collect*) the judges of a country. **2** the system of law courts in a country.

ju·di·cious /dʒuˈdɪʃəs/ *adj* (*formal*) showing or having good sense; prudent.
ju·di·cious·ly *adv*

judo /ˈdʒudou/ *n* [U] Japanese art of wrestling and self-defense developed from jujitsu, in which an opponent's own weight and strength are used against him.

jug /dʒəg/ *n* [C] **1** deep vessel for liquids with a handle, a narrow neck, and a lip. **2** the contents of such a vessel: *a jug of milk*. **3** (*sl*) prison.
jug·ful /-ˌfʊl/ *n* [C] as much as a jug can hold.

jug·ger·naut /ˈdʒəgərˌnɔt/ *n* [C] (*fig*) force, machine, etc which crushes anything that is in its way: *the ~ of war*.

juggle /ˈdʒəgəl/ *vi,vt* **1** keep two or more balls, plates, etc in motion in the air at the same time. **2** play tricks (with facts, figures, etc) to deceive people.
jug·gler *n* [C] person who juggles.

jugu·lar /ˈdʒəgyələr/ *adj* of the neck or throat: *~ veins*.

juice /dʒus/ *n* [C,U] **1** fluid part of fruits, vegetables and meat: *a glass of ˈorange ~*. **2** fluid in organs of the body: *gastric ~s*. **3** (*informal*) electricity, gasoline or other source of power.

juicy /ˈdʒusi/ *adj* (-ier, -iest) **1** containing much juice: *~ oranges*. **2** (*informal*) interesting (esp because scandalous, etc).
juici·ness /-nɪs/ *n* [U]

ju·jitsu /ˌdʒuˈdʒɪtsu/ *n* [U] Japanese art of self-defense from which judo was developed.

juke·box /ˈdʒukˌbaks/ *n* [C] coin-operated record player.

Jul. *abbr* = July.

July /dʒuˈlai, dʒə-/ *n* seventh month of the year.

jumble /ˈdʒəmbəl/ *vi,vt* mix, be mixed, in a confused way: *toys ~d up together in the cupboard*. □ *n* [C] confused mixture; muddle.

jumbo /ˈdʒəmbou/ *adj* unusually large: *~ jets*.

jump[1] /dʒəmp/ *n* [C] **1 (a)** act of jumping. ***get the jump on sb,*** get an early lead on him (in a race, contest, etc). **(b)** distance or height jumped: *a ~ of four feet*. **2** sudden movement. **3** sudden rise in amount, price, value, etc: *a ~ in car exports*.
ˈjump suit, light-weight, single-piece suit (similar to the kind) worn by pilots and for sporting activities.
jumpy *adj* (-ier, -iest) excited and nervous.

jump[2] /dʒəmp/ *vi,vt* **1** leap or spring into the air: *~ to one's feet/over a fence*. **2** (cause to) pass over by moving in this way: *~ a ditch; ~ a horse over a fence*. **3** (*fig*) move, act, suddenly or aimlessly: *~ from one subject to another in a speech*. **4** leap on: *~ a bus* (to catch it). *The thieves ~ed the stroller* (to rob him). ***jump down sb's throat,*** answer, interrupt, him with sudden anger. **5** move with a jerk; start suddenly: *~ for joy; ~ up and down in excitement*. **6** rise suddenly in price: *Gold shares ~ed on the Market yesterday*. **7** ***jump at,*** accept eagerly: *~ at an offer*. ***jump on sb,*** (*informal*) reprimand, criticize: *The boss really ~ed on me for that mistake*. ***jump to conclusions,*** reach them hastily. **8** ***jump bail,*** forfeit one's bail by not appearing in court. ***jump sb's claim,*** take another person's rightful property. ***jump the gun,*** ⇨ gun(2).

jumper /ˈdʒəmpər/ *n* [C] **1** dress without sleeves, that is often worn with a blouse. **2** person, animal or insect, that jumps.

Jun. *abbr* = June.

junc·tion /ˈdʒəŋkʃən/ *n* **1 (a)** [U] joining or being joined. **(b)** [C] instance of this. **2** [C] place where roads, railway lines or sections of an electrical circuit meet or diverge.

junc·ture /ˈdʒəŋktʃər/ *n* [C] (*formal*) **1** junction (1). **2** (esp critical) point of time: *at this juncture*, at this time.

June /dʒun/ *n* sixth month of the year.

jungle /ˈdʒəŋgəl/ *n* [C] (land covered with) thickly growing underbrush and tangled vegetation: *cut a path through the ~*. ***the law of the jungle,*** (*fig*) ruthless competition or exploitation.
jun·gly /ˈdʒəŋgli/ *adj*

jun·ior /ˈdʒunyər/ *n* [C], *adj* **1** (person) younger, lower in rank, than another: *He is my ~ by two years. Thomas Brown, Junior*, used of a son having the same first name as his father. **2** student in his third year (of four) at school or college.

jun·ior col·lege /ˌdʒunyər ˈkalɪdʒ/ *n* [C] school offering two years of undergraduate courses after high school.

jun·ior high school /ˌdʒunyər ˈhai ˌskul/ *n* [C] secondary school that usually includes the 7th, 8th, and 9th grades. (also called *middle school* in some states. ⇨ middle)

ju·ni·per /ˈdʒunəpər/ *n* [C] evergreen tree or shrub related to the pine.

junk[1] /dʒəŋk/ *n* [U] old, discarded things of little or no value: *a ˈ~ shop*.

junk[2] /dʒəŋk/ *n* [C] flat-bottomed Chinese ship with sails and a high stern.

junket /ˈdʒəŋkɪt/ *n* [C] trip taken by an official at public expense, claimed to be in line of duty but actually for his own enjoyment. □ *vi* go on a junket.
junke·teer /ˌdʒəŋkəˈtɪr/ *n* [C] official who goes on a junket.

junkie, junky /ˈdʒəŋki/ *n* [C] (*pl* -ies) (*sl*) drug addict.

junta /ˈhʊntə, ˈdʒəntə/ *n* [C] (*pl ~s*) group of leaders who control a government, esp after seizing power in a revolution.

Ju·pi·ter /ˈdzupətər/ *n* (*astron*) largest planet of the solar system, fifth in order from the sun. ⇨ illus at planet.

ju·ridi·cal /dʒʊˈrɪdɪkəl/ *adj* of law or legal proceedings.

ju·ris·dic·tion /ˌdʒʊrɪsˈdɪkʃən/ *n* [U] **1** authority or right to interpret or administer the law. **2** extent of this: *This matter does not come/fall within our ~*, we have no authority to deal with it. **3** [C] area or territory under such a legal authority.

ju·ris·pru·dence /ˌdʒʊrɪsˈprudəns/ *n* [U] **1** science and philosophy of human law. **2** branch of law.

jur·ist /ˈdʒʊrɪst/ *n* [C] expert in law.

juror /ˈdʒʊrər/ *n* [C] member of a jury.

jury /ˈdʒʊri/ *n* [C] (*pl* -ies) **1** body of persons who swear to give a true decision (a *verdict*) on issues of fact in a case in a court of justice: *The ~ found the prisoner not guilty*. **2** body of persons chosen to give a decision or make an award in a competition.

ˈjury box, enclosure for a jury in court.

ˈjury·man/·woman /-mən, -wʊmən/ *n* [C] (*pl* ~men /-men/, ~women /ˌwɪmɪn/) male/female juror.

just[1] /dʒəst/ *adj* **1** fair; in accordance with what is right: *a ~ man; be ~ to a person*. **2** well deserved; fairly earned: *get/receive one's ~ reward*. **3** reasonable; based on reasonable grounds: *~ suspicions*.

just·ly *adv*

just[2] /dʒəst/ *adv* **1** (of an immediate past): *I('ve) ~ had dinner*. **2** exactly; precisely: *It's ~ two o'clock. This is ~ what I wanted. Just my luck!* ***just as,*** **(a)** exactly as: *Leave everything ~ as* (*tidy as*) *you find it*. **(b)** when: *He arrived ~ as I was leaving*. **(c)** in the same way as: *Just as you hate Mr. Green, so I dislike his wife*. **3** at this, that very moment: *We're ~ going/about to start*. ***just now,*** **(a)** at this moment: *I'm busy ~ now*. **(b)** a very short time ago: *Tom came in ~ now*. **4** barely: *We ~ caught the train*, almost missed it. **5** only; merely: *He's ~ an ordinary man. Would you walk five miles ~ to see a movie?* (used informally, esp with imperatives, for emphasis): *Just listen to him! Just a moment, please*, Please wait a moment. **6** very; quite: *The concert was ~ wonderful*. **7** ***just about,*** nearly; almost: *I've ~ about finished the book*. ***just the same,*** nevertheless: *I may not have much of a chance; I intend to try hard, ~ the same*.

jus·tice /ˈdʒəstɪs/ *n* **1** [U] just conduct; the quality of being right and fair: *treat all men with ~*. **2** [U] the law and its administration: *a court of ~*. **3** [C] judge of the Supreme Courts: *the Chief Justice*.

U.S. SUPREME COURT JUSTICES

ˌJustice of the ˈPeace, a local magistrate who can perform marriages, administer oaths, etc.

Deˌpartment of ˈJustice, executive department in the US Government, headed by the Attorney General, supervising internal security, naturalization, immigration, etc.

jus·tify /ˈdʒəstəˌfai/ *vt* (*pt,pp* -ied) **1** show that (a person, statement, act, etc) is right or just: *You can hardly ~ such conduct*. **2** be a good reason for: *Only a shortage can ~ such high prices*.

jus·ti·fi·able /ˌdʒəstəˈfaiəbəl/ *adj* that can be justified.

jus·ti·fi·ably /-əbli/ *adv*

jus·ti·fi·ca·tion /ˌdʒəstəfəˈkeiʃən/ *n* [U]

jut /dʒət/ *vi* (-tt-) ***jut out,*** stand out from; be out of line (from what is around): *The balcony juts out over the garden*.

jute /dʒut/ *n* [U] fiber from a tropical plant, used for making canvas, rope, etc.

ju·ve·nile /ˈdʒuvənəl, -ˌnaiəl/ *n* [C] young person. □ *adj* of, characteristic of, suitable for, juveniles: *a ~ court*.

ˌjuvenile deˈlinquency, law-breaking by young people usually under the age of 18.

ˌjuvenile deˈlinquent, young person guilty of juvenile delinquency.

jux·ta·pose /ˌdʒəkstəˈpouz/ *vt* place side by side.

jux·ta·po·si·tion /ˌdʒəkstəpəˈzɪʃən/ *n* [U]

K

K¹, k /kei/ (*pl* K's, k's /keiz/) the eleventh letter of the English alphabet.

K² *abbr* = **1** Kelvin. **2** kindergarten. **3** karat(s).

k. *abbr* = karat(s).

ka·bob /kə'bab/ *n* [C] dish of small pieces of meat, fish, vegetables, etc seasoned and roasted on skewers.

kale /keiəl/ *n* [C,U] kind of curly-leaved cabbage.

ka·leido·scope /kə'laidəˌskoup/ *n* [C] **1** tube containing small, loose pieces of colored glass and mirrors which reflect changing patterns as the tube is turned. **2** (*fig*) frequently changing pattern or scenes: *a ~ of color in the landscape.*

ka·leido·scopic /kəˌlaidə'skapɪk/ *adj*

kan·ga·roo /ˌkæŋgə'ru/ *n* [C] Australian animal that jumps along on its strong hind legs. The female has a pouch in which its young are carried.

kangaroo court, one set up without authority by workers, prisoners, etc to try someone whom they consider to have acted against their interests.

kao·lin /'keiələn/ *n* [U] fine white clay used in making porcelain, etc.

ka·pok /'keiˌpak/ *n* [U] soft silky material (from seeds of a tropical tree) used for filling cushions, etc.

karat /'kærət/ unit of measure of the purity of gold, pure gold being 24 karats: *14 ~ gold,* consisting of 14 parts of pure gold to 10 parts of alloy.

ka·rate /kə'rati/ *n* [U] Japanese method of unarmed combat using blows made with the sides of the hands, feet, head or elbow.

karma /'karmə/ *n* [C] (in Buddhism) person's acts in one of his successive existences, looked upon as deciding his fate in his next existence.

ka·ty·did /'keitiˌdid/ *n* [C] large green, long-horned grasshopper of North America.

kayak /'kaiˌæk/ *n* [C] **1** Eskimo canoe of light wood completely covered with skins except for a small opening for the paddler(s). **2** any rigid, canvas-covered canoe.

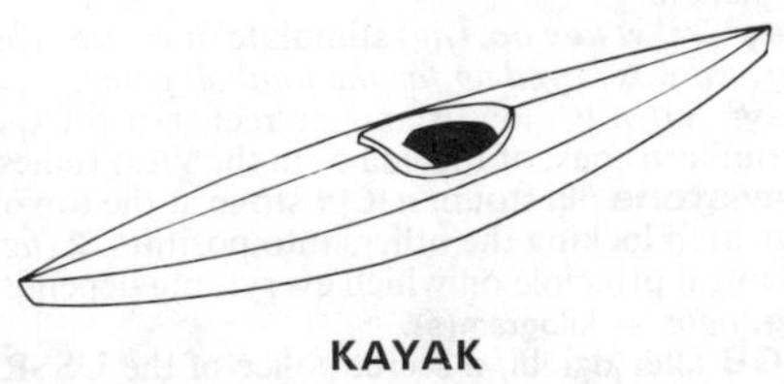

KAYAK

kc *abbr* = kilocycle(s).

keel /'kiəl/ *n* [C] timber or steel structure on which the framework of a ship is built up. ⇨ illus at ship. ***on an even keel,*** steady. □ *vt,vi* (*pres p* ~ing /'kilɪŋ/) **1** turn (a ship) over on one side to repair it, etc. **2** ***keel over,*** fall in a faint.

keen /kin/ *adj* (-er, -est) **1** (of points and edges) sharp: *a knife with a ~ edge.* **2** (*fig*) sharp: *a ~* (= cutting) *wind.* **3** (of interest, the feelings) strong; deep: *He has a ~ interest in his work.* **4** (of the mind, the senses) active; sensitive: *~ eyesight.* **5** eager; enthusiastic: *a ~ sportsman.* ***keen on,*** (*informal*) enthusiastic about: *~ on camping.*

keen·ly *adv*

keen·ness /-nɪs/ *n* [U]

keep¹ /kip/ *vt,vi* (*pt,pp* kept /kept/) (For *keep* and *nouns* not given here, ⇨ the *noun* entries, eg ***keep pace/step (with sb), keep watch.***) **1** (cause to) remain in a specified state or position: *~ the children quiet/happy. The cold weather kept us indoors. Please ~ quiet! ~ fit,* remain in good health. ***keep an eye on,*** (*informal*) watch over closely: *Please ~ an eye on the baby.* ***keep sth in mind,*** remember it. **2** (cause to) continue doing something: *Please ~ the fire burning. Keep smiling! Why does she ~ (on) giggling?* ***keep going,*** not stop; not give up: *This is exhausting work, but I manage to ~ going.* **3** ***keep sb/sth from doing sth,*** prevent, hold back: *What kept you (from joining me)?* **4** ***keep sth (back) from,*** **(a)** not let others know about it: *She can ~ nothing (back) from her friends.* **(b)** hold back; withhold: *They ~ back $10 a month from my salary for insurance.* ***keep sth to oneself,*** **(a)** not express, eg comments, views, etc: *Keep/You may ~ your remarks to yourself,* I don't want to hear them. **(b)** refuse to share: *He kept the good news to himself.* ***keep a secret,*** ⇨ secret. **5** pay proper respect to; be faithful to; observe; fulfill: *~ a promise/a treaty/an appointment/the law.* **6** celebrate: *~ Christmas.* **7** continue to have; have in one's possession and not give away: *Keep the change,* ie from money offered in payment. *Please ~ these things for me while I'm away.* **8** support; take care of; provide what is needed for; maintain: *Does he earn enough to ~ himself and his family?* **9** have habitually on sale or in stock: *"Do you sell batteries for transistor radios?"—"Sorry, but we don't ~ them."* **10** ***keep house,*** be responsible for the housework, cooking, shopping, etc. ⇨ housekeeper. **11** own or manage; take care of: *~ hens; ~ a boat.* **12** make entries in, records of: ~ *a diary*. ⇨ bookkeeper. **13** continue in a particular direction; remain in a particular relationship to a place, etc: *Keep straight on until you get to the church. Traffic in the United States* ~*s* (*to the*) *right*. **14** (of food) remain in good condition: *Will this meat* ~ *till tomorrow?* **15** (special uses with *adverbial particles* and *prepositions*):

keep after sb, speak to or remind him again and again: *I kept after him not to forget his promise*.

keep 'at sth, persist at it: *Keep at it*, don't give up!

keep away (from), avoid, prevent coming/going near (to): *Keep away from the water's edge*.

keep back, remain in the rear, at the back. ***keep sb back,*** prevent him from advancing. ***keep sth back,*** ⇨ 4 above.

keep sb down, prevent from making progress or succeeding: ~ *down all his rivals*. ***keep sth down,*** limit: *We must* ~ *down expenses*.

keep from, refrain: *It was hard to* ~ *from laughing*.

keep 'in with sb, remain on good terms with, continue to be friendly with: *You must* ~ *in with your customers*, retain their good will.

keep 'off sth, stay away from: *Please* ~ *off that subject*, say nothing about it. ***keep sb/sth off,*** hold, cause to remain, at a distance: *Keep your hands off*. Don't touch it, me, etc.

keep 'on (doing sth), continue; persist: ~ *on* (*working*) *although one is tired*. ⇨ also 2 above. ***keep sth 'on,*** continue to wear: ~ *one's hat on*. ***keep sb 'on,*** continue to employ him/her.

keep 'out (of), remain outside: *Danger! Keep out! Keep out of their quarrels*, Don't get involved in them. ***keep sb/sth 'out (of),*** prevent from entering: *Keep that dog out of the kitchen*.

'keep to sth, **(a)** do what one has agreed to do: *He always* ~*s to his promises*. **(b)** limit oneself to: ~ *to the subject*. ***keep to oneself,*** avoid meeting people.

keep 'up (with), go at the same pace or speed as: *Harry couldn't* ~ *up with the class. I can't* ~ *up with you*, walk as fast as you. ***keep sb 'up,*** delay a person from going to bed. ***keep sth 'up,*** **(a)** continue: *They kept up the attack all day*. **(b)** maintain in proper condition: *How much does it cost you to* ~ *up your large house and garden?* ***keep it 'up,*** continue without slackening: *He works far too hard; he'll never be able to* ~ *it up*.

keep² /kip/ *n* **1** [U] (food needed for) support: *The dog doesn't earn his* ~, is not worth the cost of keeping him. **2** [C] stronghold of a fortress, etc: *the castle* ~. **3** ***for keeps,*** (*informal*) permanently.

keeper /ˈkipər/ *n* [C] **1** guard, eg a person who looks after animals in a zoo. **2** (in compounds) person with special duties: *ˈinn*~*; ˈshop*~.

keep·ing /ˈkipɪŋ/ *n* [U] **1** care. ***in safe keeping,*** being kept carefully. **2** (in verbal senses of keep (12)): *the* ~ *of bees*. **3** agreement: *His actions are not in* ~ *with his promises*.

keep·sake /ˈkipˌseik/ *n* [C] something kept in memory of the giver.

keg /keg/ *n* [C] small barrel, usually of less than 10 gallons: *a keg of brandy*.

kelp /kelp/ *n* [U] large brown seaweed.

Kelvin /ˈkelvɪn/ *adj* in or of the temperature scale on which 0° is equivalent to absolute zero (−273·15° C).

ken /ken/ *n* [U] (*liter*) **1** sight. **2** understanding: *beyond the ken of man*.

ken·nel /ˈkenəl/ *n* [C] **1** hut to shelter a dog. **2** place where dogs are bred, cared for, etc. □ *vt,vi* (-l-, -ll-) put, keep, live, in a kennel.

kept /kept/ *pt, pp* of keep¹.

ker·chief /ˈkərtʃɪf/ *n* [C] **1** square piece of cloth or lace used by women as a head covering. **2** handkerchief.

ker·nel /ˈkərnəl/ *n* [C] **1** softer, inner part of a nut, seed, or fruit stone. **2** grain or seed, eg of wheat, within the husk. **3** (*fig*) central or important part of a subject, problem, etc.

kero·sene /ˈkerəˌsin/ *n* [U] oil used as a fuel in lamps, stoves, etc.

ketch /ketʃ/ *n* [C] small two-masted sailing vessel.

ketch·up /ˈketʃəp/ *n* [U] = catsup.

kettle /ˈketəl/ *n* [C] (esp) metal vessel with lid, spout and handle, for boiling water.

kettle·drum /ˈketəlˌdrəm/ *n* [C] drum shaped like a hemisphere with parchment over the top. ⇨ illus at percussion.

key¹ /ki/ *n* [C] **1** metal instrument, with rounded or winged grip, used for moving the bolt of a lock. **2** key-like instrument for turning a shaft, e.g. to wind the spring of a clock or tighten the clamp which holds roller skates on shoes. **3** (*fig*) something that provides an answer or an explanation, eg a set of answers to exercises or problems. **4** operating part (lever or button) of a typewriter, piano, organ, flute, etc pressed down by a finger. **5** winged fruit of some trees, eg the ash and elm. **6** (*music*) scale of notes arranged in relationship to a particular note called the *ˈkeynote*: *the key of C major*. **7** (*fig*) tone or style of thought or expression: *in a minor key*, sadly. **8** means of entrance, control, or possession: (as an *adjective*) *a key position*. **9** essential; basic; fundamental: (as an *adjective*) *key industry; a key man/position*.

ˈkey·board *n* [C] row of arrangement of keys(4) (on a piano, organ, typewriter).

key·less *adj* not having or needing a key.

ˈkey·note *n* [C] **(a)** note on which a key(6) is based. **(b)** (*fig*) basic tone or idea: *The keynote of the President's speech was the need for higher productivity*.

ˈkey ring, ring on which to keep keys.

ˈkey signature, symbols (sharps and flats), in musical notation, showing the key(6). ⇨ illus at notation.

key² /ki/ *vt* ***key up,*** (*fig*) stimulate or excite: *The crowd was keyed up for the football game*.

key³ /ki/ *n* [C] low island or reef, esp off the southern coast of Florida or in the West Indies.

key·stone /ˈkiˌstoun/ *n* [C] **1** stone at the top of an arch locking the others into position. **2** (*fig*) central principle on which everything depends.

kg. *abbr* = kilogram(s).

KGB /ˌkei ˌdʒi ˈbi/ *n* secret police of the USSR.

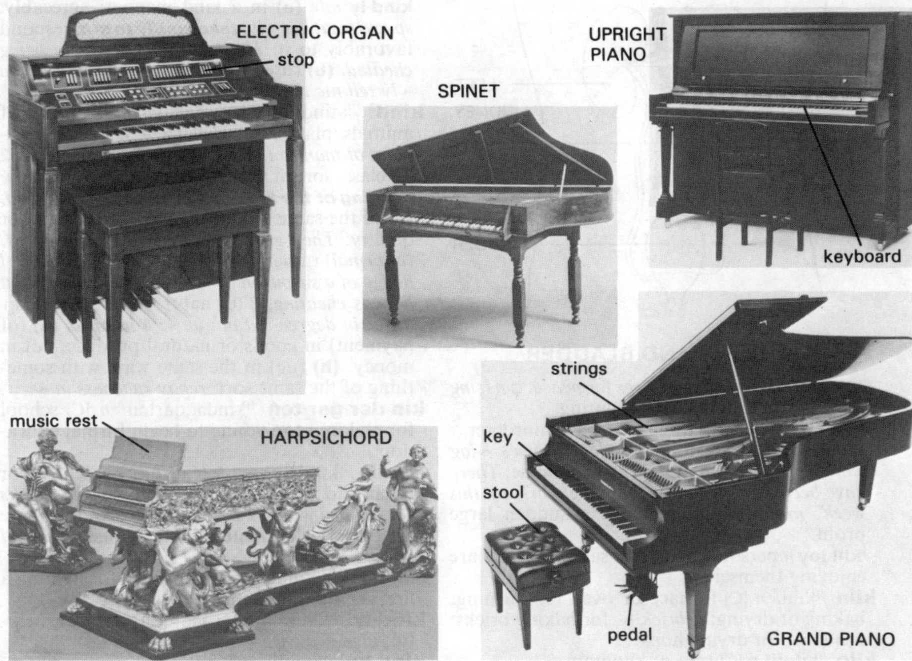

KEYBOARD INSTRUMENTS

khaki /ˈkæki/ *n* [U], *adj* (cloth, military uniform, of a) dull yellowish-brown.

khan /kan/ *n* [C] courtesy title given to some rulers and officials in Central Asia, Afghanistan, etc.

kick¹ /kɪk/ *n* **1** [C] act of kicking: *The bruise was caused by a ~*. **2** [C] (*sl*) thrill of pleasure or excitement: *I get a big ~ out of racing. He did it for ~s.* **3** [U] (*informal*) strength: *Add some liquor to the punch to give it more ~.*

kick² /kɪk/ *vt,vi* **1** hit with the foot; strike out with the foot: *~ a ball; ~ a hole in the door; ~ off one's slippers.* ***kick the bucket,*** (*sl*) die. **2** (of a gun) recoil when fired: *This old rifle ~s badly.* **3** (*informal*) express annoyance; protest: *He ~ed because he was treated badly.* **4** (*football*) score by kicking. **5** (special uses with *adverbial particles* and *prepositions*):

kick around, (*informal*) **(a)** treat roughly. **(b)** consider or discuss at length: *~ed his ideas around with the staff.*

kick in, (*informal*) pay one's share: *Is she going to ~ in for the office party?*

kick off, **(a)** (*football*) start the game. **(b)** (*sl*) begin.

kick sb out, (*informal*) dismiss; expel; turn out: *They ~ed him out of the club for insulting another member.*

kick up, (*informal*) raise or stir up trouble: *The angry man ~ed up a fuss.*

kick·back /ˈkɪkˌbæk/ *n* [C] (*sl*) payment paid to another person from money which he has helped one to earn or receive.

kicker /ˈkɪkər/ *n* **1** someone who kicks. **2** (*sl*) unexpected or ironic happening, ending, etc.

kick·off /ˈkɪkˌɔf/ *n* [C] **1** (*football*) start of the game. **2** (*sl*) beginning.

kid¹ /kɪd/ *n* **1** [C] young goat. **2** [U] leather made from skin of this: *kid gloves.* ***handle sb with kid gloves,*** (*fig*) deal with him gently. **3** (*informal*) child or young person: *college kids.*

kiddy *n* [C] (*pl* -dies) (*informal*) child.

kid² /kɪd/ *vt,vi* (-dd-) (*informal*) **1** deceive; fool: *Stop trying to kid me!* **2** tease playfully: *His friends kidded him about his bright necktie.* ***kid (around) (with sb),*** engage in teasing or horseplay: *They kidded (around) with him all day. Stop kidding around!*

kid·nap /ˈkɪdˌnæp/ *vt* (-p-, -pp-) steal or carry off (a person, esp a child) usually in order to obtain a ransom.

kid·nap·per *n* [C] person who kidnaps.

kid·ney /ˈkɪdni/ *n* [C] (*pl* ~s) **1** one of a pair of organs in the body that separate waste matter from the blood and pass it from the body as urine. **2** kidney of sheep, cattle, etc as food: *~ casserole.*

ˈkidney bean, (plant with pod containing a) reddish-brown kidney-shaped bean.

ˈkidney machine, one which purifies the blood when one's own kidneys are diseased.

kill /kɪl/ *vt,vi* **1** put to death; cause the death of: *~ animals for food.* ***kill sb/sth off,*** get rid of: *The frost ~ed off most of the insect pests.* ***kill time,*** find ways of passing spare time waiting for something. **2** ruin; destroy; cause to fail: ~

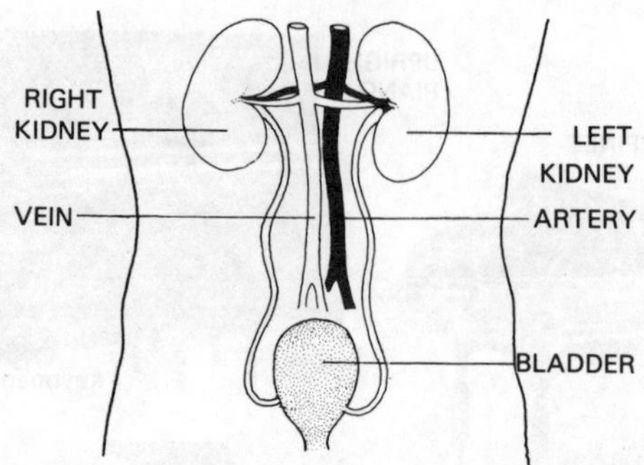

KIDNEYS AND BLADDER

a proposal; ~ed all our hopes for peace. □ *n* (*sing* only) act of killing, esp in hunting.

killer *n* [C] person, thing that kills; murderer.

kill·ing *adj* exhausting: *His job involves ~ing work.* □ *n* **(a)** act of killing, esp homicide: *There have been three ~ings in that neighborhood this week.* ***make a killing,*** make a sudden large profit.

'kill·joy *n* person who makes sad those who are enjoying themselves.

kiln /ˈkɪln/ *n* [C] furnace or oven for burning, baking or drying: *a 'brick ~*, for baking bricks; *a 'hop ~*, for drying hops.

kilo /ˈkilou/ *n* [C] (*pl* ~s) kilogram.

kilo- *prefix* 1,000.

kilo·cycle /ˈkɪləˌsaikəl/ *n* [C] unit of frequency of vibration, used of radio waves.

kilo·gram /ˈkɪləˌgræm/ *n* [C] 1,000 grams.

kilo·liter /ˈkɪləˌlitər/ *n* [C] 1,000 liters.

kilo·meter /kɪˈlamətər/ *n* [C] 1,000 meters.

kilo·watt /ˈkɪləˌwat/ *n* [C] 1,000 watts.

kilt /kɪlt/ *n* [C] **1** pleated skirt, usually of tartan cloth, worn as part of male dress in the Scottish Highlands. **2** similar skirt worn by women and children.

ki·mono /kɪˈmounou, kɪˈmounə/ *n* [C] (*pl* ~s) **1** wide-sleeved long flowing gown with a broad sash, characteristic of Japanese traditional costume. **2** dressing gown that is similar to a kimono.

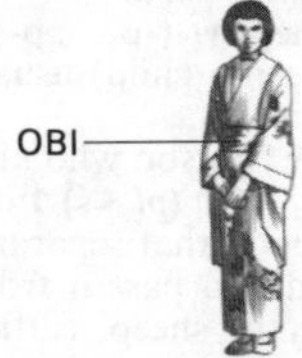

KIMONO

kin /kɪn/ *n* (*pl* unchanged) **1** (*pl*) (*collect*) family; relations. ***next of kin,*** nearest relation(s). **2** (*sing*) relative.

kind[1] /kaind/ *adj* (-er, -est) having, showing, thoughtfulness, sympathy or love for others: *be ~ to animals. It was ~ of you to help us.*

'kind·hearted *adj* being kind.

kind·ly *adv* **(a)** in a kind manner; agreeably: *speak/treat her ~ly.* ***take kindly to sth,*** respond favorably to it: *He doesn't take ~ly to being cheated.* **(b)** (used in polite formulas) *Will you ~ly tell me the time?*

kind[2] /kaind/ *n* **1** [C] race, natural group, of animals, plants, etc: *The dog preferred the company of man to that of its own ~.* ⇨ mankind. **2** [C] class, sort or variety: *What ~ of tree is this?* ***nothing of the kind,*** not at all like it. ***of a kind,*** **(a)** of the same kind: *two of a ~.* **(b)** of a poor quality: *They gave us coffee of a ~.* ***kind of,*** (*informal*) rather; somewhat: *She's ~ of tired. I had ~ of a suspicion* (= I rather suspected) *that he was cheating.* **3** [U] nature; character: *They differ in degree but not in ~.* **4** ***in kind,*** **(a)** (of payment) in goods or natural produce, not in money. **(b)** (*fig*) in the same way; with something of the same sort: *repay rudeness in ~.*

kin·der·gar·ten /ˈkɪndərˌgartən/ *n* [C] school for children too young to begin formal education.

kindle /ˈkɪndəl/ *vt,vi* **1** (cause to) catch fire or burst into flames or flaming color: *The sparks ~d the dry wood.* **2** rouse, be roused, to a state of strong feeling, interest, etc: *~ the interest of an audience.*

kind·ling /ˈkɪndlɪŋ/ *n* [U] material for lighting a fire, esp light, dry sticks of wood.

kind·ly[1] /ˈkaindli/ *adj* (-ier, -iest) friendly; helpful: *give ~ advice.*

kind·ly[2] /ˈkaindli/ *adv* ⇨ kind[1].

kind·ness /ˈkaindnɪs/ *n* **1** [U] kind nature; being kind: *do something out of ~.* **2** [C] kind act: *He has done/shown me many ~es.*

kin·dred /ˈkɪndrɪd/ *n* (*sing* only) (used with a *pl verb*) group of related persons; all one's relatives: *His ~ are still living in Ireland.* □ *adj* **1** related; having a common source: *~ languages*, eg English and Dutch. **2** similar: *a ~ spirit*, person whom one feels to be congenial, sympathetic.

ki·netic /kɪˈnetɪk/ *adj* of, relating to, produced by, motion.

kinetic 'energy, energy of a moving body because of its motion.

ki·netics *n* [U] (used with a *sing verb*) science of the relations between the motions of bodies and the forces acting on them.

kin·folk /ˈkɪnˌfouk/ *n pl* relatives.

king /kɪŋ/ *n* [C] **1** male sovereign ruler or monarch. **2** man of greatest importance in a certain field or line of business: *the 'diamond ~.* **3** principal piece in the game of chess. **4** playing card with the picture of a king, that ranks above the queen: *the ~ of spades.* **5** most prominent or powerful member of a group, category, etc: *the ~ of beasts*, the lion; *the ~ of the forest*, the oak. **6** checker that has moved all the way across the board and has the power to move backwards and forwards.

king·ly *adj* (-ier, -iest) of, like, suitable for, a king.

king·ship *n* [U] state, office, of a king.

'king-size, 'king-sized *adj* extra large: *~-size cigarettes.*

king·dom /ˈkɪŋdəm/ *n* [C] **1** country ruled by a

king or a queen. **2** the spiritual reign of God: *Thy Kingdom come*, may the rule of God be established. **3** any one of the three divisions of the natural world: *the animal, vegetable and mineral ~s.* **4** realm or region in which a person, quality, etc is dominant: *the ~ of thought*, the mind.

king·fisher /ˈkɪŋˌfɪʃər/ *n* [C] small brightly colored bird feeding on fish in rivers, etc.

king·pin /ˈkɪŋˌpɪn/ *n* [C] **1** vertical bolt used as a pivot. **2** (*fig*) indispensable or essential person or thing.

kink /kɪŋk/ *n* [C] **1** twist or curl in a length of wire, pipe, cord, etc. **2** cramp or stiffness in a muscle. **3** peculiarity; odd notion or idea. **4** slight flaw: *worked out the ~s in our plan.* □ *vt,vi* make, form, a kink: *This hose ~s easily.*

kinky *adj* (ier, -iest).

kin·ship /ˈkɪnˌʃɪp/ *n* [U] relationship by blood; similarity in character.

kins·man /ˈkɪnzmən/ *n* [C] (*pl* -men /-men/) male relative.

kins·woman /ˈkɪnzˌwʊmən/ *n* [C] (*pl* -women /-ˌwɪmɪn/) female relative.

kiosk /ˈkiˌask/ *n* [C] small structure used as a newsstand, etc.

kip·per /ˈkɪpər/ *vt* cure (esp fish) by salting and drying or smoking. □ *n* [C] kippered herring.

kiss /kɪs/ *vt,vi* touch with the lips to show affection or as a greeting: *~ the children goodnight.* □ *n* [C] **1** touch, caress, given with the lips. **2** small piece of candy: *chocolate ~es.*

kisser *n* [C] **(a)** person that kisses. **(b)** (*sl, dated*) mouth.

kit /kɪt/ *n* [C] **1** collection of equipment or articles for personal use. **2** equipment for a special purpose, eg as needed by a workman for his trade: *a tool kit; a first-ˈaid kit.* **3** set of parts, material, etc: to be put together to make something *a ˌmodel ˈcar kit.* **4** container for such a collection or set.

kitch·en /ˈkɪtʃən/ *n* [C] room in which meals are cooked or prepared.

kitchen ˈsink, ⇨ sink¹(1).

kitch·en·ette /ˌkɪtʃəˈnet/ *n* [C] tiny room or alcove used as a kitchen.

kite /kait/ *n* [C] **1** bird of prey of the hawk family. **2** framework of wood, etc covered with paper or cloth, made to fly in the wind at the end of a long string.

kith /kɪθ/ *n* (only in) ***kith and kin,*** friends and relations.

kit·ten /ˈkɪtən/ *n* [C] young cat.

kit·ten·ish *adj* like a kitten; playful.

kitty¹ /ˈkɪti/ *n* [C] (*pl* -ies) (*informal*) cat.

kitty² /ˈkɪti/ *n* [C] (*pl* -ies) **1** (in some card games) pool of stakes (money) to be played for. **2** (*informal*) any joint pool or fund, for a special purpose.

kit·ty-corner /ˈkɪti-ˌkɔrnər/ *adv* = catercorner.

kiwi /ˈkiˌwi/ *n* [C] New Zealand bird with undeveloped wings.

KKK *abbr* = Ku Klux Klan.

Kleenex /ˈkliˌneks/ *n* [U] (*P*) ⇨ tissue(3).

klep·to·mania /ˌkleptəˈmeiniə/ *n* [U] abnormal and irresistible wish to steal, not necessarily because of poverty.

klep·to·maniac /-niˌæk/ *n* [C] person with kleptomania.

km. *abbr* = kilometer.

knack /næk/ *n* [C] (rarely *pl*) natural or learned skill at doing something: *It's quite easy when you have/get the ~ of it. He has a ~ for making furniture.*

knap·sack /ˈnæpˌsæk/ *n* [C] canvas, nylon or leather bag, strapped to the back and used (by soldiers, hikers, etc) for carrying clothing, food, etc.

knave /neiv/ *n* [C] **1** (*old use*) dishonest man. **2** = jack¹(2).

knav·ery /ˈneivəri/ *n* [C,U]

knead /nid/ *vt* **1** work and press (eg dough, clay) into a firm paste with the hands. **2** massage (muscles, etc) as if making dough.

knee /ni/ *n* [C] **1** joint between the thigh and the lower part of the leg in man; corresponding part in animals. ⇨ illus at leg. ***bring sb to his knees,*** force him to submit. **2** part of a garment covering the knees: *the ~s of a pair of trousers.* □ *vt* strike with the knee. ⇨ illus at skeleton.

ˈknee breeches /ˈni ˌbrɪtʃɪz/ *n pl* pants reaching down to or just below the knees.

ˈknee·cap *n* flat, movable bone at the front of the knee.

ˌknee-ˈdeep *adj, adv* so deep as to reach the knees: *The water was ~-deep.*

kneel /niəl/ *vi* (*pt,pp* knelt /nelt/; *pres p* ~ing /ˈnilɪŋ/) go down on the knee(s); rest on the knee(s): *Everyone knelt in prayer.*

knell /nel/ *n* [C] (usually *sing* with *a* or *the*) sound of a bell, as rung esp for a death or at a funeral. □ *vi* **1** ring slowly, toll, as for a death. **2** announce as by a knell.

knelt *pt, pp* of kneel.

knew *pt* of know¹.

knicker·bock·ers /ˈnɪkərˌbakərz/ *n pl* knickers.

knickers /ˈnɪkərz/ *n pl* loose pants gathered at the knee.

knick·knack /ˈnɪkˌnæk/ *n* [C] small ornament, trinket, etc.

knife /naif/ *n* [C] (*pl* knives /naivz/) instrument with a sharp blade and a handle, used for cutting or as a weapon: *a ˈpocket ~*, one with hinged blade(s). □ *vt* **1** stab (a person) with a knife. **2** move through (as) with a knife: *knifing quickly through the water.* **3** (*informal*) betray.

knight /nait/ *n* [C] **1** (in the Middle Ages) man, usually of noble birth, raised to honorable military rank. **2** man on whom a title (lower than that of baronet) or honor is conferred in some countries as a reward for services to the state or for artistic achievements, etc. **3** piece in the game of chess. □ *vt* make (a person) a knight (2).

knight·hood /ˈnaitˌhʊd/ *n* **(a)** [C,U] rank, character or dignity of a knight. **(b)** (*collective*) knights as a group: *the ~hood of France.*

knight·ly *adj* chivalrous; brave and gentle.

knit /nɪt/ *vt,vi* (*pt,pp* ~ or ~ted; -tt-) **1** make (an article of clothing, etc) by interlacing thread or yarn in loops on long needles: *She often ~s while watching TV.* **2** unite firmly or closely: *The two families are ~ together by common interests.* **3** wrinkle: *~ one's brows,* frown.

knit·ter *n* [C] person who knits.
knit·ting *n* [U] **(a)** action of one who knits. **(b)** material being knitted.
ˈknitting needle, long slender rod of steel, wood, etc used to knit.
ˈknit·wear [U] knitted garments.
knives *pl* of knife.
knob /nab/ *n* [C] **1** round handle of a door, drawer, etc. **2** control, eg of a radio, television set, etc. **3** round swelling or mass on a surface, eg of a tree trunk.
knob·by /ˈnabi/ *adj* (-ier, -iest) like knobs(3): *~by knees.*
knock¹ /nak/ *n* [C] **1** (short, sharp sound of a) blow: *He got a nasty ~ on the head when he fell. I heard a ~ at the door.* **2** sound of knocking in an engine. ⇨ knock²(3). **3** (*informal*) misfortune: *He's suffered a lot of hard ~s.*
knocker *n* [C] **(a)** person that knocks. **(b)** (esp) a hinged metal device on a door for use in knocking.
knock² /nak/ *vt,vi* **1** hit; strike; make a noise by hitting: *Someone is ~ing at the door. He ~ed the bottom out of the box. He ~ed* (= accidentally hit) *his head on/against the wall.* **2** make or produce by hitting: *~ a hole in the wall.* ***knock flat,*** (*sl*) surprise; shock: *I was ~ed flat by the news.* ***knock sb for a loop,*** (*sl*) **(a)** strike him so as to knock him over. **(b)** surprise or shock him greatly. **3** (of an engine) make a tapping or pounding noise. **4** (*informal*) criticize: *Why do you always have to ~ American wines?* **5** (special uses with *adverbial particles* and *prepositions*):
knock about/around, (*informal*) wander or go from place to place.
knock sb/sth down, strike to the ground or floor: *He was ~ed down by a bus.* ***knock sth down,*** take to pieces: *The machines will be ~ed down before being packed for shipment.*
knock off, (*informal*) stop work: *We all ~ed off for the day at noon.*
knock sb out, **(a)** (in boxing) strike (an opponent) so that he cannot rise to his feet before the count of ten. **(b)** (*fig*) shock: *She was ~ed out by the news.*
knock sth together, make roughly or hastily: *The bookshelf had obviously been ~ed together.*
knock-kneed /ˈnak-ˌnid/ *adj* having legs curved inward at the knee.
knock·out /ˈnaˌkaut/ *n* [C] **1** blow that knocks a boxer out. **2** person or thing that is very impressive or attractive: *Isn't she a ~!*
ˈknockout drop, (*informal*) drug (to be) put in a person's drink (usually without his knowledge) to make him become unconscious.
knoll /noul/ *n* [C] small hill.
knot /nat/ *n* [C] **1** parts of one or more pieces of string, rope, etc twisted together to make a fastening: *tie/make a ~.* **2** (*fig*) something that ties together: *the ˈmarriage~.* **3** piece of ribbon, etc twisted and tied as an ornament. **4** difficulty; hard problem. **5** hard, dark spot in wood where a branch grew out from a bough or trunk. **6** lump in the tissue of the body. **7** group of persons or things: *People were standing about in ~s, anxiously waiting for news.* **8** measure of speed for ships, one nautical mile per hour. ▫

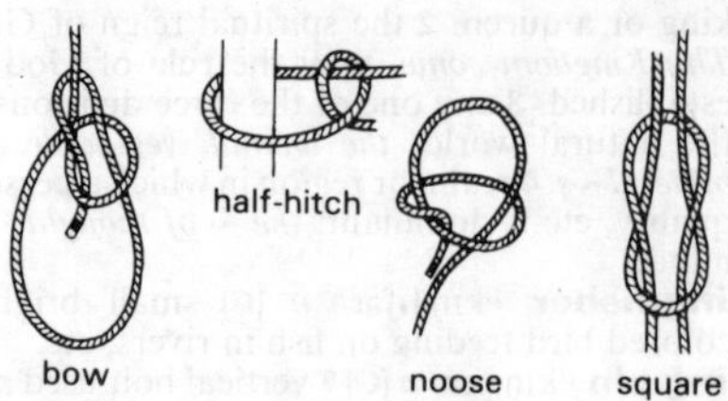

KNOTS

vt,vi (-tt-) make a knot in; tie with knots: *~ two ropes together.*
ˈknot·hole *n* [C] hole (in a board) from which a knot(5) has come out.
knotty *adj* (-ier, -iest) **(a)** full of knots. **(b)** difficult: *a ~ problem.*
know¹ /nou/ *vt,vi* (*pt* knew /nu/, *pp* ~n /noun/) **1** have the facts about; be sure of the truth of: *Every child ~s that two and two make four.* **2** have experience or skill in: *Do you ~ how to play chess?* **3** have in the mind because one has learned: *She ~s the poem by heart. At your age you should ~ better.* **4** be acquainted or familiar with: *Do you ~ Mr. Hill? I ~ Mr. White by sight but have never spoken to him. He's ~n better days,* has not always been so poor, etc. **5** recognize: *He ~s a good play when he sees one. They're twins and it's almost impossible to ~ one from the other.* ***not know sb from Adam,*** have no idea who he is. **6** ***know about/of,*** have information concerning; be aware of: *I knew about that last week.*
ˈknow-how *n* [U] practical knowledge (contrasted with theoretical knowledge).
ˈknow-it-all *n* person who knows, or claims to know, everything.
know² /nou/ *n* (only in) ***in the know,*** (*informal*) having information not shared by all or not available to all.
know·ing /ˈnouŋ/ *adj* **1** having or showing knowledge, information, etc: *~ looks.* **2** shrewd.
know·ing·ly *adv*
knowl·edge /ˈnalɪdʒ/ *n* [U] **1** understanding; awareness: *A baby has no ~ of good and evil.* **2** (range of) information: *It has come to my ~* (= I have been informed) *that you have been spreading gossip about me. To the best of my ~* (= As far as I know) *he is honest and reliable.* **3** learning: *a woman of great ~.*
knowl·edge·able /-əbəl/ *adj* having or showing much knowledge.
knuckle /ˈnəkəl/ *n* [C] **1** bone at a finger joint. ⇨ illus at arm. **2** (esp in animals used as food) knee joint, or part joining leg to foot. ▫ *vi* **1** ***knuckle down to,*** (of a task, etc) apply oneself earnestly. **2** ***knuckle under,*** submit, yield.
KO /ˌkei ˈou/ *abbr* = knockout. ▫ *vt* (*informal*) knock (somebody) out: *He was KO'ed in the second round of the fight.*
ko·ala /kouˈalə/ *n* [C] Australian tree-climbing mammal, like a small bear.
kohl·rabi /koulˈrabi/ *n* [C] (*pl* -bies) plant related to the cabbage, having a turnip-shaped stem that is eaten as a vegetable.
kook /kuk/ *n* [C] (*sl*) crazy or strange person.

kooky /ˈkuki/ *adj* (-ier, -iest) (*sl*) crazy; strange.

Ko·ran /kɔˈræn/ *n* sacred book of the Moslems, containing the Prophet Mohammed's oral revelations.

Ko·ranic *adj*

ko·sher /ˈkouʃər/ *adj* **1** fulfilling the requirements of Jewish dietary laws. **2** (*sl*) legitimate.

kow·tow /ˌkauˈtau/ *vi* show exaggerated humility.

k.p.h., kph *abbr* = kilometers per hour.

KS *postal abbr* = Kansas. ⇨ App 6.

kt. *abbr* = karat(s).

ku·dos /ˈkuˌdous/ *n* [U] (*informal*) glory; credit.

Ku Klux Klan /ˌku ˌkləks ˈklæn/ *n* secret organization, originating in the southern US after the Civil War, opposed to civil rights for Negroes.

kum·quat /ˈkəmˌkwat/ *n* [C] (tree bearing an) edible citrus fruit resembling a small orange.

kw, kW *abbr* = kilowatt(s).

KY *postal abbr* = Kentucky. ⇨ App 6.

l

L[1], **l** /el/ (*pl* L's l's /elz/) **1** the twelfth letter of the English alphabet. **2** Roman numeral for 50.
l[2] *abbr* = liter(s).
L.[3] *abbr* = **1** Lake. **2** Latin.
l.[4] *abbr* = **1** left. **2** line.
LA[1] *postal abbr* = Louisiana. ⇨ App 6.
LA[2] /ˌel ˈei/ *abbr* (*informal*) = Los Angeles (California).
la[3] /la/ *n* [C] (*music*) syllable used for the sixth note of a scale.
lab[1] /læb/ *n* [C] (*informal*) (short for) laboratory. (Compare the following entry.)
lab.[2] *abbr* = laboratory. (Compare the preceding entry.)
label /ˈleibəl/ *n* [C] **1** piece of paper, cloth, metal, wood or other material used for describing or identifying something: *put ~s on one's luggage*. **2** short word or phrase describing a person or thing: *the ~ of thief*. □ *vt* (-l-, -ll-) **1** put a label on: *properly ~ed luggage*. **2** name or describe: *~ed as untruthful*.
la·bial /ˈleibiəl/ *adj* of, made with, the lips: *~ sounds*, eg m, p, b.
la·bor /ˈleibər/ *n* **1** [U] bodily or mental work: *A great deal of ~ went into making that chair*. **2** [C] task; piece of work. ***a labor of love,*** task gladly undertaken. **3** [U] particular kind of work, esp work done with the hands: *manual ~*. **4** [U] workers as a class (contrasted with the owners of capital, etc): *skilled and unskilled ~*. **5** [U] process of childbirth: *a woman in ~*. □ *vi,vt* **1** work hard: *~ in the cause of peace*. **2** move or act with great effort: *The old man ~ed up the hillside*. **3** ***labor under,*** be burdened with, suffer because of: *~ under a disadvantage/illusion*. **4** work out in detail; treat at great length: *There's no need to ~ the point*.
la·bored *adj* **(a)** produced with great effort: *~ed breathing*. **(b)** not easy or natural; showing too much effort: *a ~ed style of writing*.
la·borer *n* [C] (esp) worker who does heavy unskilled work: *ˈfarm ~ers*.
ˈlabor-saving *adj* designed to save human labor.
lab·ora·tory /ˈlæbrəˌtɔri/ *n* [C] (*pl* -ies) room, building, for scientific experiments, research, etc. ⇨ language laboratory.
la·bori·ous /ləˈbɔriəs/ *adj* **1** (of work, etc) requiring great effort: *a ~ task*. **2** showing signs of great effort: *a ~ style of writing*. **3** (of persons) hardworking.
la·bori·ous·ly *adv*
la·bur·num /ləˈbərnəm/ *n* [C] (*pl* ~s) small tree with hanging clusters of yellow flowers.
lab·y·rinth /ˈlæbəˌrɪnθ/ *n* [C] **1** network of winding paths, roads, etc which it is difficult to get through. **2** (*fig*) anything that is difficult and complex like a labyrinth.
lace /leis/ *n* **1** [U] delicate material with the threads making patterns: *a ~ collar*. **2** [C] string or cord put through small holes in shoes, etc to fasten edges together: *ˈshoe~s*. **3** ornamental braid of gold or silver. □ *vt,vi* **1** fasten or tighten with laces(2): *~ (up) one's shoes*. **2** weave or twine together.
lac·er·ate /ˈlæsəˌreit/ *vt* **1** tear (the flesh). **2** (*fig*) hurt the feelings.
lac·er·ation /ˌlæsəˈreiʃən/ *n* [C,U]
lack /læk/ *vt,vi* **1** be without; not have: *He's ~ing in/He ~s courage*. ***lack for,*** (*formal*) need: *They ~ed for nothing*, had everything. **2** have less than enough. ***be lacking,*** be in short supply: *Money was ~ing to complete the building*. □ *n* [U] **1** condition of being without. **2** shortage: *~ of water*. **3** something that is needed or lacking.
lacka·daisi·cal /ˌlækəˈdeizɪkəl/ *adj* appearing tired, unenthusiastic.
lacka·daisi·cally /-kli/ *adv*
lack·luster /ˈlækˌləstər/ *adj* = dull(3).
la·conic /ləˈkanɪk/ *adj* (*formal*) using, expressed in, few words: *a ~ person/reply*.
la·coni·cally /-kli/ *adv*
lac·quer /ˈlækər/ *n* [C,U] (sorts of) varnish used to give a hard, bright coating to metal or wood. □ *vt* coat with lacquer.
la·crosse /ləˈkrɔs/ *n* [U] outdoor game, played with a ball which is caught in, carried in, and thrown from, a long-handled racket.
lac·tic /ˈlæktɪk/ *adj* of milk.
lacy /ˈleisi/ *adj* (-ier, -iest) of or like lace(1).
lad /læd/ *n* [C] boy; young man.
lad·der /ˈlædər/ *n* [C] **1** two lengths of wood, metal or rope, with crosspieces (*rungs*), used in climbing up and down. **2** anything like a ladder: *climb the social ~*.
laden /ˈleidən/ *adj* weighted or burdened (with): *trees ~ with apples*.
lad·ing /ˈleidɪŋ/ *n* [U] cargo; freight: *ˌbill of ˈlading*, details of a ship's cargo.
ladle /ˈleidəl/ *n* [C] large, deep, spoon for serving liquids: *a ˈsoup ~*. □ *vt* serve with a ladle: *~ out soup*.
lady /ˈleidi/ *n* [C] (*pl* -dies) **1** woman who has good manners. **2** (used courteously) any woman. **3** (corresponding to *gentleman*) woman of good family, superior social position, etc. **4** (*pl* only) polite form of address (3) to female members of an audience: *Ladies!*

Ladies and Gentlemen! **5 Lady,** (in some countries) used of and to the wives and daughters of some nobles. **6 the First Lady,** wife of the President of the United States.

ˈlady·like /-ˌlaik/ *adj* behaving as a lady(1,2).

ˈLady·ship /-ˌʃɪp/, used in speaking to or of a Lady(5): *Your/Her Ladyship.*

lady·bug /ˈleidiˌbəg/ *n* [C] small reddish beetle with a rounded back and often with black spots.

lady's slipper /ˈleidiz ˌslɪpər/ *n* [C] North American wild orchid with a flower thought to resemble a slipper.

lag /læg/ *vi* (-gg-) **1** go too slow, not keep up with: *lag behind.* **2** become weaker. □ *n* [C] **1** act of lagging. **2** amount of lagging: *a lag of thirty years.*

la·ger /ˈlagər/ *n* **1** [U] kind of light beer. **2** [C] bottle or glass of this.

lag·gard /ˈlægərd/ *n* [C] person who lags behind.

la·goon /ləˈgun/ *n* [C] (usually shallow) lake separated from the sea by a sandbank or coral reef.

laid *pt,pp* of lay².

lain *pp* of lie².

lair /ler/ *n* [C] den or dwelling place of a wild animal.

laity /ˈleiəti/ *n* [C] (usually with *the*) **1** all laymen. **2** those outside a particular profession, eg used by professionals of those not trained in their particular profession.

lake /leik/ *n* [C] large area of water enclosed by land: *the Great Lakes.*

lam /læm/ *n* (only in) ***on the lam,*** (*sl*) running away from the law.

lama /ˈlamə/ *n* [C] (*pl* ~s) Buddhist priest of Tibet or Mongolia.

lama·sery /ˈlaməˌseri/ *n* [C] (*pl* -ies) monastery of lamas.

lamb /læm/ *n* **1 (a)** [C] young of the sheep. **(b)** [U] its flesh as food: *roast* ~. **2** [C] innocent, mild person. ***like a lamb,*** without resistance or protest. □ *vi* give birth to lambs: *the* ~*ing season.*

ˈlamb·kin *n* little lamb.

ˈlamb·skin *n* **(a)** [C] skin of a lamb with the wool on it. **(b)** [U] leather made from this.

lam·baste /ˌlæmˈbeist/ *vt* (*informal*) **1** beat. **2** scold.

lame /leim/ *adj* (-r, -st) **1** not able to walk normally because of an injury or defect. **2** weak: unsatisfactory: *a* ~ *excuse.* □ *vt* make lame.

lame ˈduck *n* [C] (esp) public official who has been defeated in an election, but still has a part of his term to serve.

lame·ly *adv*

lame·ness /-nɪs/ *n* [U]

lamé /ˌlæˈmei/ *n* [U] fabric woven with gold or silver threads.

la·ment /ləˈment/ *vt,vi* show, feel, express, great sorrow or regret: ~ (*over*) *the death of a friend.* □ *n* [C] **1** expression of grief. **2** song or poem expressing grief: *a funeral* ~.

lam·en·table /ˈlæməntəbəl, ləˈmentəbəl/ *adj* regrettable: *a* ~*able* (= poor, unsatisfying) *performance.*

lam·en·tably /-əbli/ *adv*

lam·en·ta·tion /ˌlæmənˈteiʃən/ *n* [C,U]

lami·nate /ˈlæməˌneit/ *vt,vi* **1** beat or roll (metal, wood, etc) into thin layers. **2** make material strong by putting these layers together.

lamp /læmp/ *n* [C] **1** apparatus for giving light (from gas, electricity, etc). **2** apparatus for heating or for giving a particular kind of light: *an infrared* ~.

ˈlamp·black *n* [U] black coloring matter made from the soot of burning oil, as used in paint and ink.

ˈlamp·light *n* [U] light from a lamp: *read by* ~ *light.*

ˈlamp·post *n* [C] post for a street light.

ˈlamp·shade *n* [C] shade of glass, plastic, etc placed around or over a lamp to soften or direct light.

lam·poon /læmˈpun/ *n* [C] piece of writing, drawing, etc attacking and ridiculing someone. □ *vt* ridicule with a lampoon.

lance¹ /læns/ *n* [C] **1** weapon with a long shaft and a pointed steel head used by a horseman. **2** similarly shaped instrument, eg as used by surgeons.

ˈlance corporal, noncommissioned officer ranking below a corporal in the US Marine Corps.

lancer *n* [C] soldier of a cavalry regiment originally armed with lances.

lance² /læns/ *vt* **1** stab with a lance. **2** cut open with a lancet: ~ *an abscess.*

lan·cet /ˈlænsɪt/ *n* [C] pointed, two-edged knife used by surgeons.

land¹ /lænd/ *n* **1** [U] solid part of the earth's surface (contrasted with *sea, water*): *travel over* ~ *and sea.* ***by land,*** (traveling) by train, car, etc; not by plane, ship, etc. **2** [U] surface of the moon, a planet, etc. **3** [U] ground, earth, as used for farming, etc: *working* (*on*) *the* ~. **4** [U] (sometimes *pl*) property in the form of land: *Do you own much* ~ *here?* **5** [C] country (which is the usual word) and its people: *my native* ~. **6** domain: *the* ~ *of dreams.*

ˈland·holder *n* [C] owner or tenant of land(4).

ˈland·lady *n* [C] woman landlord.

ˈland·locked *adj* **(a)** (of a country) with no frontier at the sea. **(b)** (of a bay, harbor, etc) almost or completely surrounded by land.

ˈland·lord *n* [C] **(a)** man who leases property to a tenant. **(b)** owner, manager, of an inn, lodging house, etc.

ˈland·lubber *n* [C] person not used to the sea and ships.

ˈland·mark *n* [C] **(a)** object that marks the boundary of a piece of land. **(b)** object, etc that is easily seen and that can be used as a guide. **(c)** (*fig*) event, discovery, change, etc that marks a stage or turning point: ~*marks in the course of social history.*

ˈland mine, device put in the ground so as to be exploded by vehicles, footsteps, etc.

ˈland·owner *n* [C] owner of land(4).

land² /lænd/ *vt,vi* **1** go, come, put, on land (from a ship, aircraft, etc): *The airliner* ~*ed safely. The pilot* ~*ed the airliner safely.* ***land on one's feet,*** (*fig*) be lucky; escape injury. **2** (cause to) arrive: *You'll* ~ *in prison one day.* **3** (*informal*) get; ob-

tain; catch: ~ *a good job*. **4** (*informal*) hit: *She ~ed him one in the eye*.
landed *adj* **(a)** consisting of land: *~ed property*. **(b)** owning land: *the ~ed gentry*.
land·less *adj*
land·ing /ˈlændıŋ/ *n* [C] **1** act of coming or bringing to land: *The pilot made an emergency ~*. **2** place where people and goods may be landed from a ship, etc. **3** level area at the top or bottom of a flight of stairs.
ˈlanding craft, ship designed to allow soldiers, vehicles, etc to get ashore easily.
ˈlanding field/strip, place for aircraft to take off from and land on.
ˈlanding gear, part of an aircraft that supports it on land or water.
land·scape /ˈlændˌskeip/ *n* [C] (picture of) inland scenery. □ *vt* improve or make (land) more beautiful by planting and arranging trees, flowers, etc.
land·slide /ˈlændˌslaid/ *n* [C] **1** sliding down of a mass of earth, rock, etc from the side of a cliff, hillside, etc. **2** overwhelming number of votes for one side in an election: *a Democratic ~*.
lane /lein/ *n* [C] **1** narrow road or path. **2** (marked) division of a road for a single line of vehicles: *the inside/outside ~*. **3** marked division to guide competitors in a race (eg on a running track or a swimming pool). **4** route regularly used by ships or aircraft. **5** narrow wooden passageway down which a bowling ball is rolled.
lang. *abbr* = language.
lan·guage /ˈlæŋgwıdʒ/ *n* **1** [U] (product of) human communication by means of ordered signs (usually speech sounds, but sometimes other kinds of signs): *spoken/written ~, sign ~* (eg of the deaf). **2** [C] particular form of this used by a nation or ethnic group: *the ~s of the world*. **3** [U] special words, phrases, etc used by a profession or class: *medical/legal ~*. **4** [C] system of signs or symbols with use similar to human language: *computer ~*. **5** particular form or style of speech or writing: *poetical ~*.
ˈlanguage laboratory, place where students can practice speaking and listening to foreign languages by using tape recorders, etc.
lan·guid /ˈlæŋgwıd/ *adj* having no energy; slow.
lan·guid·ly *adv*
lan·guish /ˈlæŋgwıʃ/ *vi* **1** lose health and strength. **2** suffer neglect: ~ *in prison for ten years*. **3** long for: ~ *for love and sympathy*.
lan·guor /ˈlæŋgər/ *n* (*formal*) [U] **1** loss of strength, energy; weakness; weariness. **2** laziness; indolence: *the ~ of a summer day*.
lan·guor·ous /-əs/ *adj*
lan·guor·ous·ly *adv*
lank /læŋk/ *adj* **1** (of hair) straight and limp. **2** tall and lean.
lank·ly *adv*
lank·ness /-nıs/ *n* [U]
lanky /ˈlæŋki/ *adj* (-ier, -iest) tall, thin, and awkward: *a ~ girl*.
lank·i·ness /-nıs/ *n* [U]
lano·lin /ˈlænəlın/ *n* [U] fat from sheep's wool used in soaps, ointments for the skin, etc.
lan·tern /ˈlæntərn/ *n* [C] apparatus for enclosing a flame to protect it from the wind, with an opening to give light.
ˈlantern-jawed *adj* having long, thin jaws and hollow cheeks.
lan·yard /ˈlænyərd/ *n* [C] **1** cord worn around the neck, eg for a whistle or knife. **2** short rope used on a ship for fastening the rigging.
lap[1] /læp/ *n* [C] **1** part of anything that overlaps or extends over another. **2** one complete journey around a track or race course. **3** one stage or part of a journey. □ *vt, vi* (-pp-) **1** fold over or wrap around something. **2** put or extend partly over something; overlap: *The builder lapped the shingles over one another*.
lap[2] /læp/ *n* [C] front part of a person from the waist to the knees, when sitting: *The mother had the baby on her lap*. ***the lap of luxury,*** fortunate, wealthy, state or condition.
lap[3] /læp/ *vi,vt* (-pp-) **1** drink by taking up with the tongue, as a cat does. ***lap up,*** (*fig*) take in quickly or eagerly: *lap up compliments*. **2** (of water) move with a sound like the lapping up of liquid: *waves lapping on the shore*. □ *n* [C] **1** act of lapping up. **2** sound of lapping: *the lap of the the waves against the side of the boat*.
la·pel /ləˈpel/ *n* [C] flap of a coat or jacket folded back against the chest.
la·pis la·zuli /ˌlæpıs ˈlæʒəli/ *adj, n* **1** [C] (of a) bright blue semiprecious stone. **2** [U] (of) its color.
lapse /læps/ *n* [C] **1** small error in speech, behavior, memory, etc. **2** fall from a higher or better state: *a moral ~*. **3** passage of time; interval: *a long ~ of time*. **4** ending of a right, custom, etc because of failure to use it or observe it. □ *vi* **1** make a lapse(1). **2** fall or change from an earlier, and sometimes better, state: *lapsing into bad habits*. **3** (of rights, privileges, etc) come to an end or be lost because not used or observed.
lar·ceny /ˈlarsəni/ *n* (*pl* -ies) **1** [U] stealing; theft. **2** [C] instance of this.
larch /lartʃ/ *n* **1** [C] deciduous tree with small cones and light-green leaves. **2** [U] its wood.
lard /lard/ *n* [U] fat of pigs used in cooking. □ *vt* put lard or other fat on or in. ***lard with,*** fill with: *a speech ~ed with boring quotations*.
lar·der /ˈlardər/ *n* [C] room, cupboard, for storing meat and other kinds of food.
large /lardʒ/ *adj* (-r, -st) **1** of considerable size; taking up much space; able to contain much: *A man with a ~ family needs a ~ house. He is a ~ man and weighs more than 300 pounds*. **2** generous; tolerant: *He has a ~ heart*. **3** broad; extensive: *give an official ~ powers*. □ *n* (only in) ***at large,*** **(a)** free: *The escaped prisoner is still at ~*. **(b)** in general: *Did the people at ~ approve of the government's policy?* **(c)** representing a whole country, area, etc; not confined to just one district: *delegate-at-~ to the convention*. □ *adv* ***by and large,*** ⇨ by[1](2).
large·ly *adv* to a great extent: *His success was ~ly due to luck*.
large·ness /-nıs/ *n* [U]
ˈlarge-scale *adj* **(a)** extensive: *~-scale operations*. **(b)** made or drawn to a large scale: *a ~-scale map*.
lar·iat /ˈlæriət/ *n* [C] lasso.

lark[1] /lark/ *n* [C] **1** (kinds of) small European and African songbird: *the sky~.* **2** (kinds of) medium-sized North American bird: *the meadow~.*

lark[2] /lark/ *n* [C] bit of fun; merry adventure: *He did it for a ~,* in fun.

lark·spur /ˈlarkˌspər/ *n* [C] tall garden plant with blue, white or pink flowers.

larva /ˈlarvə/ *n* (*pl* ~e /-vi/, ~s) **1** often wormlike form of an insect in the first stage of its development after coming out of the egg. **2** earliest stage of any animal with a form different from its adult appearance: *The tadpole is the ~ of the frog.*

lar·val /ˈlarvəl/ *adj*

lar·yn·gi·tis /ˌlærɪnˈdʒaitɪs/ *n* [U] inflammation of the larynx that sometimes causes a temporary loss of the voice.

lar·ynx /ˈlærɪŋks/ *n* [C] (*pl* larynges /ləˈrɪnˌdʒiz/, ~es) upper part of the windpipe where the vocal cords are. ⇨ illus at head.

las·civ·ious /ləˈsɪviəs/ *adj* (*formal*) feeling, causing, showing, lust.

las·civ·ious·ly *adv*

laser /ˈleizər/ *n* [C] device for generating, amplifying and concentrating light waves into one intense beam going only in one direction.

lash[1] /læʃ/ *n* [C] **1** (flexible part of a) whip. **2** blow or stroke given with a lash: *twenty ~es.* **3** = eyelash.

lash[2] /læʃ/ *vt,vi* **1** whip; strike violently; make a sudden movement: *The rain was ~ing (against) the windows. The tiger ~ed its tail angrily. He ~ed the horse across the back with his whip.* **2** drive as if with a whip: *The speaker ~ed his listeners into a fury.* **3** ***lash out (against/at sb/sth),*** attack violently with blows or words: *He ~ed out against the government.* **4** fasten tightly together with rope, etc.

lash·ing /ˈlæʃɪŋ/ *n* [C] **1** cord or rope used for binding or fastening. **2** whipping or beating: *ˈtongue ~ing,* a scolding.

lass /læs/ *n* [C] girl.

las·si·tude /ˈlæsəˌtud/ *n* (*formal*) [U] **1** tiredness; exhaustion. **2** languor.

lasso /ˈlæˌsou, -ˌsu, læˈsu/ *n* (*pl* ~s, ~es) long rope with a noose, used esp by cowboys for catching horses and cattle. ⇨ illus at cowboy. □ *vt* catch with a lasso.

last[1] /læst/ *adj* **1** (contrasted with *first*) coming after all others in time or order; final: *the ~ Sunday in June; the ~ time I saw you.* ***last but not least,*** coming at the end, but not least in importance. ***the last word,*** ⇨ word(2). **2** just past; latest; most recent: *~ night/year; his ~ speech.* **3** only remaining: *This is our ~ hope. I ate the ~ cookie.* **4** least likely, suitable, etc: *That's the ~ thing I would expect him to do.* □ *adv* **1** (contrasted with *first*) after all others: *I am to speak ~ at the meeting.* **2** (contrasted with *next*) most recently: *She was quite well when I saw her ~/when I ~ saw her.* □ *n* **1** person or thing that comes at the end: *These are the ~ of our apples.* **2** end: *cheerful to the ~.* ***at (long) last,*** in the end; after a long time: *At (long) ~ we reached our destination.* ***see the last of sb,*** not see him again: *I hope we've seen the ~ of them.*

last·ly *adv* (as in making a list) finally: *Lastly I must explain that...*

last[2] /læst/ *vi* **1** go on; continue: *How long will the good weather ~?* **2** be enough for: *These supplies should ~ for a month.*

last·ing *adj* continuing for a long time.

last[3] /læst/ *n* [C] block of wood shaped like a foot, used for making or repairing shoes.

Lat.[1] *abbr* = Latin.

lat.[2] *abbr* = latitude.

latch /lætʃ/ *n* [C] fastening for a door or gate, having a movable bar that falls into a slot or notch. □ *vt,vi* **1** fasten with a latch. **2** ***latch on (to),*** (*informal*) get hold of: *~ed on to the latest fad.*

late[1] /leit/ (-r /-ər/, -st /-əst/) ⇨ last[1], latter. *adj* **1** (contrasted with *early*) after the right, fixed or usual time: *Am I ~?* **2** far on in the day or night, in time, in a period or season: *in the ~ afternoon.* **3** recent; that recently was: *the ~st news/fashions.* **4** recently dead: *her ~ husband.* **5** ***of late,*** recently. ***at the latest,*** before or not later than: *Be here on Monday at the latest.*

late·ness /-nɪs/ *n* [U]

late[2] /leit/ *adv* (-r /-ər/, -st /-əst/) **1** (contrasted with *early*) after the usual, right, fixed or expected time: *get up/go to bed/arrive home ~.* ***later on,*** at a later time; afterwards. ***sooner or later,*** some time or other. **2** recently: *I saw him as ~ as/no ~r than yesterday.*

late·ly /ˈleitli/ *adv* in recent times; recently: *Have you gone to the movies ~? We haven't been there ~. It is only ~ that she has been well enough to go out.*

latent /ˈleitənt/ *adj* present but not yet active, developed or visible: *~ energy.*

lat·eral /ˈlætərəl/ *adj* of, at, from, to, the side(s).

la·tex /ˈleiˌteks/ *n* [U] **1** milky, sticky sap produced by certain plants and trees, eg the rubber tree. **2** artificial substance similar to this, used in paints, adhesives, etc.

lath /læθ/ *n* [C] (*pl* ~s /læðz/) long, thin strip of wood, esp as used as a base for plaster walls and ceilings.

lathe /leið/ *n* [C] machine for holding and turning pieces of wood or metal while they are being shaped by a tool. □ *vt* work wood or metal on a lathe.

lather /ˈlæðər/ *n* [U] **1** soft mass of white froth from soap and water. **2** frothy sweat on a horse. **3** (*informal*) agitated state. □ *vt,vi* **1** cover with lather: *~ one's chin before shaving.* **2** form a lather or foam.

Latin /ˈlætən/ *adj, n* **1** (of the) language of ancient Rome. **2** (of the) peoples whose language and culture derive from ancient Rome, esp Spanish and Portuguese.

ˌLatin Aˈmerica, countries of South and Central America in which Spanish and Portuguese are spoken.

lati·tude /ˈlætəˌtud/ *n* **1** [C] distance north or south of the equator measured in degrees. **2** (*pl*) geographical region or district: *warm ~s.* **3** [U] freedom in action or opinion: *was given a certain ~ in his choice of a chairman.*

lati·tudi·nal /ˌlætəˈtudənəl/ *adj*

la·trine /ləˈtrin/ *n* [C] pit dug in the earth for use

as a toilet.

lat·ter /ˈlætər/ *adj* **1** recent; belonging to the end (of a period): *the ~ half of the year*. **2 the latter,** (contrasted with *the former*) the second of two things or persons already mentioned: *Of these two men the former is dead, but the ~ is still alive.*

ˈlatter-ˌday *adj* modern.

ˌLatter-Day ˈSaint, (official term for) member of the Mormon religion or *Church of Jesus Christ of Latter-Day Saints.*

lat·ter·ly *adv* (*formal*) lately.

lat·tice /ˈlætɪs/ *n* [C] framework of crossed laths or metal strips as a screen, fence or door, or for climbing plants to grow over: *a ~ window.*

lat·ticed *adj*

laud /lɔd/ *vt* (*liter*) praise highly.

laud·able /-əbəl/ *adj* deserving praise.

laud·ably /-əbli/ *adv*

lauda·tory /ˈlɔdəˌtɔri/ *adj* expressing praise.

laugh /læf/ *vi,vt* **1** make sounds and movements of the face and body, showing amusement, joy, contempt, etc: *The jokes made everyone ~.* **2** ***laugh at,*** **(a)** be amused by: *~ at a joke.* **(b)** make fun of: *It's unkind to ~ at a person who is in trouble.* **(c)** disregard; treat with indifference: *~ at difficulties.* ***laugh in sb's face,*** show contempt for; defy. ***laugh up one's sleeve,*** be secretly amused. **3** arrive at a state, obtain a result, by laughing: *~ oneself silly/helpless.* □ *n* [C] **1** sound, act, of laughing: *We've had a good many ~s over his foolishness.* ***have the last laugh,*** finally win after appearing to lose. **2** something that causes laughter; joke. ***good for laughs,*** expected or likely to amuse.

laugh·able /-əbəl/ *adj* amusing; ridiculous: *a ~able mistake.*

laugh·ably /-əbli/ *adv*

laugh·ter /ˈlæftər/ *n* [U] action or sound of laughing: *burst into ~.*

launch[1] /lɔntʃ, lantʃ/ *vt,vi* **1** set (a ship, esp one newly built) afloat: *~ a new passenger liner.* **2** set in motion; send; aim: *~ an attack; ~ a missile/spacecraft.* **3** (*fig*) get started; set going: *~ a new business enterprise.* **4** make or start (on): *~ out into a new career; ~ed forth on his favorite subject.* □ *n* [C] act of launching (a ship or spacecraft).

ˈlaunching pad, base or platform from which spacecraft, etc are launched.

launch[2] /lɔntʃ, lantʃ/ *n* [C] open motorboat (used on rivers and lakes, in harbors).

laun·der /ˈlɔndər, ˈlan-/ *vt,vi* wash and press (clothes): *Send these sheets to be ~ed.*

laun·der·ette /ˌlɔndəˈret, ˌlan-/ *n* [C] self-service laundry with coin-operated automatic washing machines and dryers.

laun·dress /ˈlɔndrɪs, ˈlan-/ *n* [C] woman who earns money by washing and ironing clothes.

laun·dro·mat /ˈlɔndrəˌmæt, ˈlan-/ *n* [C] = launderette.

laun·dry /ˈlɔndri, ˈlan-/ *n* (*pl* -ies) **1** [C] place where clothes, sheets, etc are sent to be laundered. **2** [U] clothes (to be) laundered: *Has the ~ come back yet?*

laur·eate /ˈlɔriɪt/ *n* [C] person who has won the highest honors for achievements in science, literature, etc.

laurel /ˈlɔrəl, ˈlarəl/ *n* [C] evergreen shrub with smooth, shiny leaves, used by ancient Romans and Greeks as an emblem of victory, success and distinction. ***look to one's laurels,*** be on the lookout for possible rivals. ***rest on one's laurels,*** be content with past or present achievements.

lava /ˈlavə/ *n* [U] **1** hot melted rock flowing from a volcano: *a stream of ~.* **2** this substance which has cooled and hardened.

lava·tory /ˈlævəˌtɔri/ *n* [C] (*pl* -ies) **1** toilet. **2** room for washing the hands and face in.

lav·en·der /ˈlævəndər/ *adj, n* [U] **1** (of the) plant with pale purple scented flowers. **2** (of) a pale purple color.

ˈlavender water, scent from lavender.

lav·ish /ˈlævɪʃ/ *adj* **1** giving or producing freely, liberally or generously: *~ in giving money to charity.* **2** (of what is given) given abundantly; excessive: *~ praise.* □ *vt* spend or give generously: *~ care on an only child.*

lav·ish·ly *adv*

law /lɔ/ *n* **1** [C] rule made by authority for the proper regulation of a community or society or for correct conduct in life. **2 the law,** (*collective*) system of laws of a society, etc: *If a man breaks the law he can be punished.* ***lay down the law,*** **(a)** give orders and demand obedience to them. **(b)** talk as if one is certain of being right. **3 the law** (*collective sing*) (*informal*) the police: *Here comes the law!* **4** [U] controlling influence of the law: *maintain law and order,* see that the laws are respected. **5** [U] study or profession of the law: *study law; law students.* **6** [U] special branch of the law: *commercial/international law.* **7** [U] trial in a court; operation of the law (as providing a remedy for wrongs): *go to law.* ***take the law into one's own hands,*** try to get justice for oneself outside the law(2). **8** [C] rule or principle: *the laws of perspective.* **9** (also **law of nature** or **natural law**) factual statement of what always happens in certain circumstances; regularity in nature, eg the order of the seasons: *the laws of gravity.*

ˈlaw-abid·ing *adj* obeying the law(2).

ˈlaw·breaker *n* [C] person who disobeys the law (2).

ˈlaw court, court of justice.

law·ful /-fəl/ *adj* **(a)** allowed by law; according to law: *lawful acts.* **(b)** recognized by law; rightful: *the lawful heir.*

law·fully /-fəli/ *adv*

law·less *adj* **(a)** not according to, not conforming to, the law. **(b)** having no laws.

law·less·ly *adv*

law·less·ness /-nɪs/ *n* [U]

ˈlaw·maker *n* [C] legislator.

ˈlaw·suit *n* [C] case in a law court.

lawn[1] /lɔn/ *n* [C] area of grass cut short and smooth, eg in a yard around a house or park.

ˈlawn mower, machine for cutting grass.

ˌlawn ˈtennis, tennis played on a grass court.

lawn[2] /lɔn/ *n* [U] kind of fine, thin cotton or linen.

law·yer /ˈlɔyər/ *n* [C] person whose profession is to advise clients about legal matters and to represent them in a court of law.

lax /læks/ *adj* **1** negligent; careless. **2** not strict or severe: *lax discipline.*

lax·ity /ˈlæksəti/ *n* [C,U]

lax·ly *adv*

laxa·tive /ˈlæksətɪv/ *n* [C], *adj* (medicine, drug) causing the bowels to empty.

lay[1] /lei/ *adj* **1** of, for, done by, persons who are not ordained as clergy. ⇨ laity. **2** without specialized professional training, eg in law, medicine, science, etc: *lay opinion*, what non-professional people think.

ˈlay·man /-mən/ *n* [C] (*pl* laymen /-men/) lay person.

lay[2] /lei/ *vt,vi* (*pt,pp* laid /leid/) **1** put on a surface: *lay a carpet*. **2** put in a certain position: *He laid his hand on my shoulder*. **3** place; put: *lay emphasis on neatness*. ***lay (one's) hands on sth/sb,*** (*fig*) **(a)** seize; get possession of: *He keeps everything he can lay (his) hands on.* **(b)** find: *The book is somewhere, but I can't lay my hands on it just now.* ***lay the blame (for sth) on sb,*** say that he is responsible for what is wrong, etc. **4** cause to be in a certain state, condition, or situation. ***lay sb to rest,*** bury him. ***lay sth*** (eg a fear, rumor, etc) ***to rest*** (*fig*) dispose of. ***lay claim to sth,*** ⇨ claim[1](4). ***lay siege to,*** ⇨ siege. ***lay sth bare,*** show; reveal: *lay bare one's heart*, reveal one's inmost feelings, etc. ***lay sth flat,*** cause to be flat: *crops laid flat by heavy rainstorms.* ***be laid low,*** be ill in bed: *I've been laid low by influenza.* ***lay sth open,*** (esp) expose, reveal: *lay open a plot*. ***lay oneself open to sth,*** expose oneself to criticism, etc. ***lay sth waste,*** ravage, destroy: *a countryside laid waste by invading armies.* **5** cause to settle: *sprinkle water on the roads to lay the dust.* **6** place or arrange (ready for use, etc): *lay the table (for a meal)*, put out plates, knives, etc; *lay a fire*, make it ready for lighting. **7** put down (a sum of money) as a bet: *I'll lay you a hundred to one that...* **8** (of birds and insects) produce (an egg): *Are your hens laying yet?* **9** set (a story, etc) in time and place: *The scene is laid in Athens, in the third century BC.* **10** cover; coat: *lay paint on canvas.* **11** knock or strike down. **12** (special uses with *adverbial particles* and *prepositions*):

lay sth aside, **(a)** save; keep for future use: *lay aside money for one's old age.* **(b)** put down: *He laid his book aside to listen to me.*

lay sth away, put it aside for use or delivery in the future.

lay sth by, = lay something aside (a).

lay sb/oneself down, place in a lying position. ***lay down one's arms,*** put one's weapons down as a sign of surrender. ***lay down the law,*** ⇨ law(2). ***lay down one's life,*** sacrifice it: *He laid down his life for his country.*

lay sth in, provide oneself with a stock of: *lay in provisions/stores.*

lay into sb, (*informal*) **(a)** beat. **(b)** scold.

lay off, (*informal*) stop doing something which annoys: *You've been seeing my sister again. — Well, you can just lay off.* ***lay sb off,*** dismiss temporarily: *lay off workmen*, eg because of a shortage of materials.

lay it on (thick/with a trowel), use exaggerated praise, flattery, etc.

lay sth out, **(a)** spend (money): *lay out $200 for a new suit.* **(b)** make a plan for: *laid out a national advertising campaign.*

lay sth up, save; store for the future: *lay up provisions.* ***be laid up,*** forced to stay in bed because of sickness or injury: *He's laid up with a broken leg.*

ˈlay·away *n* (holding of) merchandise reserved for a customer who has made partial payment on it.

ˈlay-off *n* [C] temporary dimissal of a worker.

lay[3] /lei/ *vi* (*pt, pp* laid /leid/) = lie[2] (*Note:* while not even considered correct in *informal* usage, *lay* for *lie* is usual in the first and common in the second of the following idioms:) ***lay for sb***, lie (hiding) in wait for him. ***lay low*** = lie low ⇨ low[1] (1).

layer /ˈleiər/ *n* [C] **1** thickness of material (esp one of several) laid or lying on or spread over a surface, or forming one horizontal division: *a ~ of clay.* **2** person who lays something: *a brick ~.* **3** (of hens): *good/bad ~s*, laying eggs in large/small numbers.

lay·ette /leiˈet/ *n* [C] outfit for a newborn baby.

lay·man ⇨ lay[1].

lay·out /leiˌaut/ *n* [C] plan; arrangement: *Their house has a good ~.*

laze /leiz/ *vi* be lazy: *lazing away the afternoon.*

lazy /ˈleizi/ *adj* (-ier, -iest) **1** unwilling to work; doing little work: *a ~ fellow.* **2** suitable for, causing, inactivity: *a ~ afternoon.* ⇨ idle.

lazi·ly /ˈleizəli/ *adv*

lazi·ness /ˈleizinɪs/ *n* [U]

ˈlazy·bones *n* (*informal*) lazy person.

lb(s). *abbr* (= *Lat* libra) pound(s).

l.c. *abbr* = lower case.

lea /li/ *n* (*poet*) stretch of open grassland.

lead[1] /led/ *n* **1** [U] soft, heavy, easily melted metallic element (symbol **Pb**) used for pipes, etc. **2** [U] graphite as used in a pencil. **3** [C] lump of lead(1) on a line marked in fathoms, for measuring the depth of the sea from ships. **4** strip of metal used in printing to separate the lines of type.

leaded *adj* secured with strips of lead: *~ed windows.*

leaden /ˈledən/ *adj* **(a)** made of lead. **(b)** having the dull gray color of lead: *~en clouds.* **(c)** dull and heavy: *a ~en heart.*

lead ˈpencil, one with a lead(2), or core of graphite.

ˌlead ˈpoisoning, diseased condition caused by taking lead(1) into the system.

lead[2] /lid/ *n* **1** (*sing* with *the* or *a, an*) action of guiding or setting an example; leadership. **2(a)** first place or position: *have/gain/take the ~ in a race.* **(b)** distance by which one leads: *an actual ~ of ten feet.* **3** [C] hint; something that guides or gives information. **4** [C] opening section of a news story. **5** [C] cord, leather strap, for leading a dog. **6** [C] chief role or part in a play, motion picture, etc. **7** [C] conductor conveying electrical current.

lead[3] /lid/ *vt,vi* (*pt,pp* led /led/) **1** guide or take, esp by going in front. ***lead the way (to),*** go first; show the way. **2** guide the movement of (a person, etc) by the hand, by touching him, or by a rope, etc: ~ *a blind man/a horse*. ***lead sb astray,*** (*fig*) tempt him to do wrong. ***lead sb on,*** mislead; cause (a person) to do something unwise or to believe something that is untrue. **3** act as head; direct; manage: ~ *an army/an expedition/a political party*. **4** have the first place in; go first: *Which horse is ~ing*, eg in a race? **5** guide the actions and opinions of; influence; persuade: *What led you to think that?* **6** be a path, way or road to: *Where does this road ~?* **7** (*fig*) have as a result: *The change of plan led to great confusion.* ***lead up to,*** prepare the way for, esp gradually: *That's just what I was ~ing up to.* **8** (cause a person to) pass, spend (his life, etc): ~ *a miserable existence*. **9** make the first move. ***lead off,*** begin; start.

leader /ˈlidər/ *n* [C] person who leads: *the ~ of an army/an expedition/the Republican Party.*

leader·less *adj*

leader·ship *n* [U] **(a)** position of being a leader. **(b)** ability or power to lead.

lead·ing /ˈlidɪŋ/ *adj* **1** first. **2** chief; most important: *the ~ men of the day; the ~ lady*, the actress with the chief part in a play. □ *n* [U] act of leading.

ˌ**leading** ˈ**question,** one formed to suggest the answer that is hoped for.

leaf /lif/ *n* (*pl* leaves /livz/) **1** [C] one of the parts (usually green and flat) growing from the side of a stem or branch or direct from the root of a tree, bush, plant, etc: *burned all the dead leaves*. ⇨ illus at tree, vegetable. ***in leaf,*** with all the leaves green and growing: *The trees will soon be in ~.* **2** [C] petal. **3** [C] single sheet of paper forming two pages of a book. ***turn over a new leaf,*** (*fig*) make a new and better start. **4** [C] hinged flap, etc of a table (used to make it larger). **5** [U] very thin sheet of metal, esp of gold or silver: *gold ~.* □ *vi* **1** produce leaves. **2** ***leaf through,*** turn over the pages of a book, etc.

leafy *adj* (-ier, -iest) covered with, having, made by, leaves: *a ~y shade.*

leaf·let /ˈliflɪt/ *n* [C] **1** small leaf or part of a leaf. **2** printed sheet (sometimes folded) with announcements, etc.

league[1] /lig/ *n* [C] former measure of distance (about three miles or 4.8 kms).

league[2] /lig/ *n* [C] **1** association or alliance of persons, groups or nations for their common welfare, eg to work for peace. ***in league with,*** having made an agreement with. **2** group of sports clubs or teams playing games among themselves: *the* ˈ*football ~; the National League.* □ *vt,vi* form into, become, a league: *countries that are ~d together.*

the League of Nations, that formed in 1919 after the First World War, dissolved in 1946. ⇨ United Nations.

leak /lik/ *n* [C] **1** hole, crack, etc caused by wear, injury, etc through which a liquid, gas, etc may wrongly get in or out: *a ~ in the roof.* **2** instance of leaking: (*fig*) *a ~ of secret information.* **3** substance that leaks out or in: *a gas ~.* □ *vi,vt* **1** (allow to) pass out or in through a leak: *The rain is ~ing in.* **2** (of news, secrets, etc) (cause to) become known by chance or deliberately: *Who ~ed the news to the press?*

ˈ**leak·age** /-ɪdʒ/ *n* [C,U]

leaky *adj* (-ier, -iest) having a leak.

lean[1] /lin/ *adj* (-er, -est) **1** not fat; thin. **2** (of meat) containing little or no fat. **3** not productive or plentiful: *a ~ harvest.* □ *n* [U] meat with little or no fat.

lean·ness /-nɪs/ *n* [U]

lean[2] /lin/ *vi,vt* **1** be or put in a sloping position: ~ *backwards;* ~ *out of a window.* ***lean over backward(s) (to do sth),*** (*informal*) make too great an effort. **2** (cause to) rest against in a sloping position for support: ~ *on one's elbows.* ~ *a ladder against a wall.* **3** ***lean toward,*** have a tendency: *Does the radical element ~ toward anarchy?* **4** depend on: ~ *on a friend's advice.*

lean·ing *n* [C] tendency (*toward*): *He has pacifist ~ings.*

lean-to /ˈlinˌtu/ *n* [C] (*pl* ~s) **1** shed with a sloping roof that is built against the wall of another building. **2** simple shelter with a slope reaching to the ground.

leap /lip/ *vi,vt* (*pt,pp* ~ed or ~t /lipt, lept/) **1** = jump (the usual word): *He ~t at the opportunity*, seized it eagerly. ***Look before you leap,*** ⇨ look[2](1). **2** (cause to) jump over: ~ *a wall.* □ *n* [C] sudden upward or forward movement: *a great ~ forward,* (*fig*) a great advance. ***by leaps and bounds,*** very rapidly.

ˈ**leap·frog** *n* [U] game in which players jump with parted legs over others who stand with bent backs. □ *vt* (-gg-) jump over in this way.

ˈ**leap year,** in which February has 29 days.

learn /lərn/ *vt,vi* (*pt,pp* ~ed or ~t /lərnt/) **1** gain knowledge of or skill in, by study, practice or being taught: ~ *a foreign language;* ~ *to swim/how to ride a horse.* ***learn sth by heart,*** ⇨ heart(2). **2** find out: *We haven't yet ~ed if he arrived safely. She ~ed that everyone had left.*

learned /ˈlərnɪd/ *adj* having or showing much knowledge: *~ed men/books/societies.*

learn·ed·ly /ˈlərnɪdli/ *adv*

learner *n* [C] person who is learning; beginner.

learn·ing *n* [U] (knowledge gained by) study or education.

lease /lis/ *n* [C] **1** written contract by which the owner of land or a building agrees to let another have the use of it for a certain time for a fixed money payment. **2** period of time specified in such a contract: *When does the ~ expire?* ***a new lease on life,*** a better chance of living longer, or of being happier, etc. □ *vt* give, take a lease on; rent.

leash /liʃ/ *n* [C] leather strap or thong for holding or controlling an animal.

least /list/ *adj, n* [U] (contrasted with *most*; ⇨ less, little) **1** smallest in size, amount, extent, etc: *A has little, B has less, and C has (the) ~. That's the ~ of my anxieties.* ***at least,*** **(a)** not less than: *It will cost at ~ twenty dollars.* **(b)** in any case: *At ~ she's happy.* ***not in the least,*** not at all: *It doesn't matter in the ~.* ***to say the least,*** without saying more: *It's not a very good record, to say the ~.* □ *adv* to the smallest extent: *This is the ~ useful of the four books.* ***least of all***: *None of you can complain, Charles ~ of all,* Charles has the least reason for complaining.

leather /ˈleðər/ *n* [U] material from cleaned and

tanned animal skins, used for making shoes, bags, etc.

leathery *adj* like leather: *~y meat*, hard, tough.

leave[1] /liv/ *vt,vi* (*pt,pp* left /left/) **1** go away from: *It's time for us to ~/time we left.* ***leave for,*** go away to: *We're leaving for Europe next week.* **2** go away finally or permanently; no longer live (in a place); cease to belong to a school, society, etc; give up working for (an employer, etc): *When did you ~ school?* **3** permit or cause to remain behind: *I left my books on the table.* **4** allow or cause to remain in a certain place or condition: *Who left that window open? Don't ~ her waiting outside in the rain.* ***leave sb/sth alone,*** not touch, spoil or interfere with: *Leave me alone.* ***leave off,*** stop: *Has the rain left off yet?* ***leave sb/sth out,*** omit; fail to include: *Don't ~ me out, please!* **5** (cause to) remain; allow to remain: *Three from seven ~s four* (7 − 3 = 4). *When I've paid all my debts, there'll be nothing left/I'll have nothing left.* **6** hand over (before going away): *Did the mailman ~ anything for me?* **7** entrust; commit; hand over: *I'll ~ the matter in your hands/~ it to you. He left his assistant in charge of the store.* **8** bequeath by will: *He left me $2,000.*

leave[2] /liv/ *n* **1** [U] permission: *give him ~ to do as he wished.* **2** official permission to be absent from duty or work: *You have my ~ to stay away from the office tomorrow.* ***on leave,*** absent with permission: *He went home on ~.* **3** [C] period, occasion, of such absence. **4** (*sing* only) departure. ***take (one's) leave (of sb),*** (*formal*) say goodbye. ***take leave of one's senses,*** become mentally disordered.

ˌleave of ˈabsence, official permission to be absent from work, school, etc.

leaven /ˈlevən/ *n* [U] **1** substance, eg yeast, used to make dough rise before it is baked to make bread. **2** any trait or quality that changes or modifies: *a ~ of humor.* □ *vt* **1** add leaven to. **2** act like leaven on.

leaves *pl* of leaf.

leavings /ˈlivɪŋz/ *n pl* what is left over, eg unwanted food.

lecher /ˈletʃər/ *n* [C] lecherous man.

lech·ery /ˈletʃəri/ *n* [C,U] excessive sexual activity.

lech·er·ous /ˈletʃərəs/ *adj* having, giving way to, strong sexual desires.

lec·tern /ˈlekˌtərn/ *n* [C] tall, sloping reading desk.

lec·ture /ˈlektʃər/ *n* [C] **1** talk for the purpose of teaching: *philosophy ~s.* **2** scolding or reproof. □ *vi,vt* **1** give a lecture (to): *~ on modern drama.* **2** scold, reprove: *~d them for being lazy.*

lec·turer *n* [C]

led *pt, pp* of lead[3].

ledge /ledʒ/ *n* [C] **1** narrow shelf coming out from a wall, cliff or other upright surface: *a ˈwindow ~.* **2** ridge of rocks under water, esp near the shore.

ledger /ˈledʒər/ *n* [C] book in which a business firm's accounts are kept.

ledger line, leger line /ˈledʒər ˌlain/ *n* [C] short line added above or below the staff for outside notes in musical notation. ⇨ illus at notation.

lee /li/ *n* [C,U] (place giving) protection against wind. □ *adj* of or on the side away from the wind.

leech /litʃ/ *n* [C] **1** small bloodsucking worm living in fresh water. **2** (*fig*) person who tries to get advantage or profit out of others.

leek /lik/ *n* [C] vegetable, like an onion, with a long, slender white bulb. ⇨ illus at vegetable.

leer /lɪr/ *n* [U] sly, lustful, or unpleasant look. □ *vi* look with a leer: *~ing at his neighbor's wife.*

leery /ˈlɪri/ *adj* (-ier, -iest) (*informal*) suspicious: *~ of strangers.*

lee·ward /ˈliwərd, among sailors ˈluərd/ *adj, adv, n* [U] (on or to the) side (esp of a ship) away from the wind (contrasted with *windward*).

lee·way /ˈliˌwei/ *n* [U] **1** sideways drift (of a ship) in the direction toward which the wind is blowing. **2** extra amount of space, time, etc allowed for the unexpected: *gave a few days' ~ on the deadline for finishing the job.*

left[1] *pt,pp* of leave[1].

left[2] /left/ *adj* (contrasted with *right*) of the side of the body which is toward the west when a person faces north: *~ arm. adv* to the left hand or side: *turn ~ at the end of the road.* □ *n* **1** [U] side or direction on one's left hand: *In England people drive on the ~.* **2 the Left,** group holding radical or liberal political views; (as an *adjective*) *the ~ wing of the party.* **3** [C] blow given (esp in boxing) with the left fist.

ˌleft-ˈhand *adj* of, situated on, the left side: *a house on the ~-hand side of the street.*

ˌleft-ˈhanded *adj* **(a)** (of a person) using the left hand more easily or with more skill than the right. **(b)** (of a blow, etc) given with the left hand. **(c)** having a counterclockwise turn or twist; awkward; clumsy. **(d)** of doubtful sincerity: *a ~-handed compliment.*

ˈleft·ist /-ɪst/ *n* [C], *adj* (supporter) of liberalism or radicalism.

left·over /ˈleftˌouvər/ *n* [C] something, esp food prepared for a meal, that remains unused.

lefty /ˈlefti/ *n* [C] (*sl*) left-handed person.

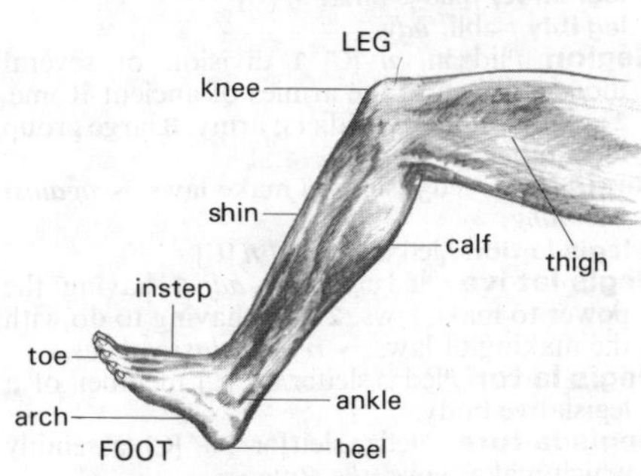

LEG AND FOOT

leg /leg/ *n* [C] **1** one of the parts of an animal's or a person's body used for walking, esp (of a human body) the part above the foot. ***be on one's last legs,*** exhausted; ready to collapse, die, etc. ***pull sb's leg,*** deceive him for fun. ***not have a leg to stand on,*** have nothing to support one's opinion, defense, etc. ***stretch one's legs,***

go for a walk. **2** that part of a garment that closely covers a leg: *the legs of a pair of pants.* **3** support of a chair, table, etc: *a chair with four legs.* **4** one stage or portion of a trip, esp by air: *the first leg of an around-the-world flight.* **5** one stage of a relay race.

leg·less *adj* having no legs.

ˈleg·room *n* [U] room for the legs (esp in front of a seat, under a table, etc).

leg·acy /ˈlegəsi/ *n* [C] (*pl* -ies) **1** money, etc left to a person under the will of another person. **2** (*fig*) something handed down: *a* ~ *of good government.*

legal /ˈligəl/ *adj* connected with, in accordance with, authorized or required by, the law: ~ *affairs.*

legally /ˈligəli/ *adv*

ˌlegal ˈtender, form of money which must legally be accepted as payment.

legal·ity /lɪˈgæləti/ *n* [C,U] state or quality of being legal: *the* ~ *of an act.*

legal·ize /ˈligəˌlaiz/ *vt* make legal: ~ *the sale of alcoholic drinks.*

legal·i·zation /ˌligələˈzeiʃən/ *n* [U]

le·gation /lɪˈgeiʃən/ *n* [C] (house, offices, etc, of a) diplomatic mission that ranks below an embassy.

leg·end /ˈledʒənd/ *n* **1** [C] old story handed down from the past, esp one of doubtful truth: *the Greek* ~*s.* **2** [U] literature of such stories: *heroes who are famous in* ~. **3** [C] inscription on a coin or medal; explanatory words on a map, a picture, etc.

leg·end·ary /ˈledʒənˌderi/ *adj* of or like a legend.

leger line = ledger line.

leg·gings /ˈlegɪŋz/ *n pl* outer covering for the leg up to the knee, or up to the waist: *a pair of* ~*s.*

leggy /ˈlegi/ *adj* (-ier, -iest) **1** (esp of young children, colts, etc) having long legs. **2** having long, attractive legs.

leg·ible /ˈledʒəbəl/ *adj* (of handwriting, print) that can be read.

legi·bil·ity /ˌledʒəˈbɪləti/ *n* [U]

leg·ibly /-əbli/ *adv*

legion /ˈlidʒən/ *n* [C] **1** division of several thousand men in the armies of ancient Rome. **2** great number of soldiers; army. **3** large group or number.

legis·late /ˈledʒəˌsleit/ *vi* make laws: ~ *against gambling.*

legis·la·tion /ˌledʒəˈsleiʃən/ *n* [U]

legis·lat·ive /ˈledʒəˌsleitɪv/ *adj* **1** having the power to make laws. **2** of or having to do with the making of laws: ~ *reforms/assemblies.*

legis·la·tor /ˈledʒəˌsleitər/ *n* [C] member of a legislative body.

legis·la·ture /ˈledʒəˌsleitʃər/ *n* [C] assembly which makes laws: *the state* ~.

le·git·imacy /lɪˈdʒɪtəməsi/ *n* [U] being legitimate.

le·git·imate /lɪˈdʒɪtəmɪt/ *adj* **1** lawful, regular: *the* ~ *king.* **2** reasonable; that can be justified: *a* ~ *reason for being absent from work.* **3** born of persons legally married to one another: *of* ~ *birth.* □ *vt* /lɪˈdʒɪtəˌmeit/ make legitimate.

le·git·imate·ly *adv*

le·git·ima·tize /lɪˈdʒɪtəməˌtaiz/ *vt* make legitimate.

le·git·imize /lɪˈdʒɪtəˌmaiz/ = legitimatize.

leg·ume /ˈleˌgyum/ *n* [C] **1** any of a family of plants that bears its seeds in pods (as peas, beans, etc). **2** part of a legume used as food.

le·gumi·nous /lɪˈgyumənəs/ *adj* of or like the legume family.

lei /lei/ *n* [C] (*pl* leis) necklace or wreath of flowers, given as a sign of friendship in Hawaii and other parts of Polynesia.

lei·sure /ˈliʒər, ˈleʒər/ [U] spare time; time free from work.

lei·sure·ly *adv* without hurrying: *work* ~*ly.* □ *adj* unhurried: ~*ly movements.*

lem·ming /ˈlemɪŋ/ *n* [C] small, short-tailed rodent of the arctic regions, that sometimes migrates in great numbers.

lemon /ˈlemən/ *n* [C] (tree with a) pale yellow citrus fruit with acid juice used for drinks and flavoring. ⇨ illus at fruit.

lem·on·ade /ˌleməˈneid/ *n* [C,U] drink made from lemon juice, sugar and water.

ˌlemon ˈcurd, sweet mixture made of lemons, eggs, sugar and butter, used as a pie filling or spread(5).

lemur /ˈlimər/ *n* [C] (kinds of) nocturnal animal related to the monkey, with a face like a fox and large eyes.

lend /lend/ *vt* (*pt,pp* lent /lent/) **1** give (a person) the use of (something) on the understanding that it or its equivalent will be returned: *I will* ~ *you $100.* ***lend a hand (with sth),*** help. **2** contribute: *facts that* ~ *probability to a theory.* **3** ***lend itself/oneself to,*** serve; be suitable for: *This hot weather* ~*s itself to sleeping.*

lender *n* [C]

length /leŋ(k)θ/ *n* [C] **1** measurement from end to end (of space or time): *a river 300 miles in* ~; *the* ~ *of time needed for the work.* ***at length,*** **(a)** at last; finally. **(b)** for a long time: *speak at (great)* ~. **(c)** in detail; thoroughly: *treat a subject at* ~. **2** measurement of a particular thing from end to end, taken as a unit of measurement: *The horse won by a* ~, by its own length. **3** extent; extreme. ***go to any length(s),*** do anything necessary to get what one wants. **4** piece of material long enough for a particular purpose, usually cut from a larger piece: *a ˈdress* ~; *a* ~ *of tubing/pipe.*

lengthen /ˈleŋ(k)θən/ *vt,vi* make or become longer: ~*en a skirt. The days* ~*en in March.*

ˈlength·wise /-ˌwaiz/, **ˈlength·ways** /-ˌweiz/ *adv, adj* in the direction of the length; from end to end.

lengthy *adj* (-ier, -iest) (of speech, writing) very long; too long.

leni·ent /ˈliniənt/ *adj* not severe (esp in punishing people): ~ *toward juvenile offenders.*

le·ni·ence /-əns/, **le·ni·ency** /-ənsi/ *n* [U] being lenient.

leni·ent·ly *adv*

lens /lenz/ *n* [C] (*pl* ~es) **1** piece of glass or substance like glass with one or both sides curved, for use in eyeglasses, cameras, telescopes and other optical instruments. **2** transparent part of the eye that focuses light. ⇨ illus at eye.

lent *pt,pp* of lend.
Lent /lent/ *n* annual period of forty weekdays between Ash Wednesday and Easter, observed by Christians as a period of fasting and penitence.
Lenten /ˈlentən/ *adj* of Lent: *~en services.*
len·til /ˈlentəl/ *n* [C] **1** kind of legume. **2** flat, edible seed of this: *~ soup.*
Leo /ˈliou/ *n* the Lion, the fifth sign of the zodiac. ⇨ illus at zodiac.
leop·ard /ˈlepərd/ *n* [C] large African and South Asian animal of the cat family with a yellow coat and dark spots. ⇨ illus at cat.
leop·ard·ess /ˈlepərdɪs/ *n* [C] female leopard.
leper /ˈlepər/ *n* [C] person who has leprosy.
lep·rosy /ˈleprəsi/ *n* [U] skin disease that forms sores on the skin, causes loss of feeling and the destruction of tissue.
lep·rous /ˈleprəs/ *adj* of, having, leprosy.
les·bian /ˈlezbiən/ *n* [C] homosexual woman.
lesion /ˈliʒən/ *n* [C] **1** wound. **2** harmful change in the tissues of a bodily organ, caused by injury or disease.
less /les/ *adj* (contrasted with *more*) not so much; a smaller quantity of: *~ butter/food/speed.* ***less than,*** not so much as: *I have ~ money than you.* □ *adv* to a smaller extent or degree; not so much: *Eat ~, drink ~, and sleep more. Tom is ~ clever than his brother. He won no ~ than $200* (expressing surprise at the amount). ***much/still less,*** especially not: *I don't even suspect him of robbery, much ~ of robbery with violence.* □ *n* smaller amount, quantity, time, etc: *in ~ than an hour; ~ than $10.* □ *prep* minus; without: *$800 a month ~ $300 for the rent.*
-less /-lɪs/ *suffix* without: *treeless; homeless.*
les·see /leˈsi/ *n* [C] tenant who holds a lease.
less·en /ˈlesən/ *vt,vi* make or become less: *to ~ the impact/effect.*
less·er /ˈlesər/ *adj* **1** not so great as the other; smaller: *choose the ~ evil.* **2** lower, smaller, in range, importance, value, etc.
les·son /ˈlesən/ *n* [C] **1** something to be learned or taught. **2** period of time given to learning or teaching: *ˈEnglish ~s.* **3** something serving as an example or a warning: *Let his fate be a ~ to you all!* **4** passage from the Bible read aloud during a church service.
les·sor /ˈleˌsɔr/ *n* [C] person that leases property to another.
lest /lest/ *conj* (*dated*) **1** for fear that; in order that... not: *He ran away ~ he should be seen.* **2** (after *fear, be afraid/anxious*) that: *We were afraid ~ he arrive too late.*
let[1] /let/ *vt,vi* (*pt,pp* let) (-tt-) **1** allow (to): *Her father will not let her go to the dance. Her father won't let her (go).* ***let alone,*** not to mention: *There were five people in the car, let alone the luggage and the two dogs!* ***let oneself go,*** no longer hold back one's feelings, desires, etc. ***let it go at that,*** say or do no more about it: *I disagree but we'll let it go at that.* ***let sb know,*** inform him. ***live and let live,*** ⇨ live[2](2). ***let sb/sth loose,*** release him/it. ***let sth pass,*** disregard it. **2** (used to express a request, proposal, or order). (*Note: let us* in this sense is often shortened to *let's* /lets/ in *informal* speech or writing.): *Let's go! Let's not/Don't let's start yet! Let her do it at once. Let me be!* Leave me alone! **3** suppose; assume: *Let AB be equal to CD.* **4** allow to move or pass in a certain direction: *Let them through, please. Windows let in the light and air. Who let you into the building?* **5** (special uses with *adverbial particles* and *prepositions*):
let sth down, lower; put or take down: *Please let the window down. This skirt needs letting down,* lengthening by lowering the hemline. ***let sb down,*** (*fig*) disappoint; fail to help: *Harry will never let you down.*
let sb/oneself in for, involve in loss, difficulty, hard work, etc: *He didn't realize how much work he was letting himself in for when he became secretary of the society.*
let sb in on, allow to share (a secret): *She has been let in on* (= told) *the secret.*
let sb off, excuse; not punish (severely): *He was let off with a fine instead of being sent to prison.*
let ˈon (that), (*informal*) reveal a secret: *He knew where the boy was but he didn't let on.*
let sth out, make (a garment, etc) looser, larger, etc: *He's getting so fat that his trousers need to be let out round the waist.*
let up, become less strong, etc: *Will the rain never let up?*
ˈlet·down *n* [C] disappointment.
ˈlet·up *n* [U] lessening or slowing down in force, speed, etc.
let[2] /let/ *vt* (*archaic*) hinder; obstruct. □ *n* [C] **1** hindrance, esp in the legal phrase: *without let or hindrance.* **2** (in tennis) ball which, when served, hits the net before dropping into the opponent's court.
lethal /ˈliθəl/ *adj* (capable of) causing death: *a ~ dose of poison.*
leth·argy /ˈleθərdʒi/ *n* [U] (state of) being tired; indifference.
leth·ar·gic /lɪˈθardʒɪk/ *adj*
leth·ar·gi·cally /-kli/ *adv*
let's /lets/ = let us. ⇨ let[1](2).
let·ter /ˈletər/ *n* [C] **1** character or sign representing a sound, of which words in writing are formed: *capital ~s* (A, B, C, etc) *and small ~s* (a, b, c, etc). **2** written message, request, account of events, etc sent by one person to another: *I have some ~s to write.* **3** exact meaning: *carry out an order to the ~.* **4** (*pl*) literature and learning: *a man of ~s.* □ *vt* mark with letters.
let·ter·ing /ˈletərɪŋ/ *n* [U] letters, words, esp in a title, on a poster, etc: *the ~ing on a book cover.*
letter·head /ˈletərˌhed/ (sheet of paper with a) printed name and address, eg of a business firm.
let·tuce /ˈletəs/ *n* **1** [C] garden plant with crisp green leaves used in salads. ⇨ illus at vegetables. **2** [U] these leaves as food.
leu·ke·mia /luˈkimiə/ *n* [U] (usually fatal) disease in which there are too many white blood cells in the blood.
lev·ee /ˈlevi/ *n* [C] **1** bank (as of earth) built along a river to prevent flooding. **2** landing place or pier on a river.
level[1] /ˈlevəl/ *adj* **1** having a flat, smooth surface: *~ ground.* **2** horizontal. **3** of an equal rank,

position, height, etc: *draw ~ with the other runners.*

level-'headed, sensible; having good judgment.

level² /ˈlevəl/ *n* **1** [C] horizontal line or surface, esp as a reference point from which height can be measured: *5,000 feet above sea ~; eye ~.* **2** grade or stage in rank, education, etc: *He is taking courses at an advanced ~,* ***one's own level,*** one's natural or right position. **3** [C] device that shows whether or not a surface is level: *a carpenter's ~.* **4** ***on the level,*** (*informal*) honest(ly); straightforward(ly): *Is he on the ~?*

level³ /ˈlevəl/ *vt,vi* (-l-, -ll-) **1** make or become level or flat: *~ the ground before planting.* ***level off/out,*** come to a level or steady position: *Inflation seems to have ~ed off at 10%.* **2** knock down to the ground: *houses ~ed by a hurricane.* **3** make (two or more things, persons) equal in status, etc. **4** aim (a weapon, criticism, at): *~ a gun at a tiger; ~ed an accusation against his brother.* **5** ***level with sb,*** (*informal*) be honest or frank with him.

lever /ˈlevər/ *n* [C] **1** bar or other tool used to lift something or to force something open. **2** switch or control bar, swiveled at the base and sticking up or out: *an adjustment ~.* **3** (*fig*) any means by which force may be exerted. □ *vt* move, raise, etc with a lever(1).

lever·age /-ɪdʒ/ *n* [U] action of a lever or the advantage gained by using a lever(1).

Le·vis /ˈliˌvaiz/ *n pl* (*P*) pants of heavy denim.

lev·ity /ˈlevəti/ *n* [U] (*formal*) lack of proper respect or seriousness.

levy /ˈlevi/ *vt,vi* (*pt,pp* -ied) **1** impose; collect by authority or force: *~ a tax/a fine.* **2** ***levy war on/upon/against,*** declare, make, war on. **3** draft for military service: *~ troops.* □ *n* [C] (*pl* -ies) act, amount, of levying.

lewd /lud/ *adj* **1** indecent; obscene. **2** lustful.

lewd·ly *adv*

lewd·ness /nɪs/ *n* [U]

lexi·cal /ˈleksɪkəl/ *adj* of the vocabulary of a language.

lexi·cally /-kli/ *adv*

lexi·cogra·phy /ˌleksɪˈkagrəfi/ *n* [U] dictionary writing.

lexi·cogra·pher /ˌleksɪˈkagrəfər/ *n* [C] person who writes a dictionary.

lexi·con /ˈleksɪˌkan/ *n* [C] dictionary (esp of Greek, Latin or Hebrew).

lg. *abbr* = large.

lia·bil·ity /ˌlaiəˈbɪləti/ *n* (*pl* -ies) **1** [U] the state of being liable: *~ to pay taxes.* **2** (*pl*) obligations; debts (contrasted with *assets*). **3** [C] handicap; disadvantage: *The team's goalkeeper is more of a ~ than an asset.*

liable /ˈlaiəbəl/ *adj* **1** responsible according to law: *Is a man ~ for his wife's debts in your country?* **2** ***be liable to sth,*** be subject to: *be ~ to a heavy fine.* **3** ***be liable to do sth,*** have a tendency to, be likely to. (*Note:* usually pronounced /ˈlaibəl/ in this sense): *We are all ~ to make mistakes occasionally.*

li·aison /ˈliəˌzan, liˈeizan/ *n* **1** [U] connection between two different groups or parts of an army or other organization. **2** [C] illicit sexual relationship.

liar /ˈlaiər/ *n* [C] person who tells lies.

lib /lɪb/ *n* [U] (*informal*) (short for) liberation: *women's lib* (from inequality of the sexes).

li·bel /ˈlaibəl/ *n* **1** [U,C] (the publishing of a) written or printed statement that unjustly damages a person's reputation: *sue for ~.* **2** [C] anything that is false and brings discredit on. □ *vt* (-l-, -ll-) publish or utter a libel against.

li·bel·ous /ˈlaibələs/ *adj* **(a)** containing, in the nature of, a libel: *~ous reports.* **(b)** publishing or uttering libels: *a ~ous person/periodical.*

lib·eral /ˈlɪb(ə)rəl/ *adj* **1** giving or given freely; generous: *a ~ supply of food and drink.* **2** having, showing, a broad mind, free from prejudice. **3** (of education) based on the liberal arts. **4** having political views and opinions which favor progress, protection of civil liberties, and democratic reform. □ *n* [C] person holding liberal views.

ˌliberal ˈarts *n pl* studies, as philosophy, history, languages and literature, directed chiefly toward broadening the mind rather than toward professional or technical training.

lib·er·al·ism /-ˌlɪzəm/ *n* [U] liberal views, opinions and principles.

lib·er·al·ize /ˈlɪbrəˌlaiz/ *vt* make liberal.

lib·er·al·iz·ation /ˌlɪbrələˈzeiʃən/ *n* [U]

lib·er·al·ity /ˌlɪbəˈræləti/ *n* (*formal*) [U] **1** generosity. **2** broad-mindedness; freedom from prejudice.

lib·er·ate /ˈlɪbəˌreit/ *vt* set free: *~ the slaves.*

lib·er·ation /ˌlɪbəˈreiʃən/ *n* [U]

lib·er·ator /-tər/ *n* [C]

lib·erty /ˈlɪbərti/ *n* (*pl* -ies) **1** [U] state of being free (from captivity, slavery, imprisonment, despotic control, government by others). **2** right or power to decide for oneself what to do, how to live, etc: *They fought to defend their ~.* ***at liberty,*** **(a)** (of a person) free; not imprisoned. **(b)** permitted: *You are now at ~ to leave any time.* **(c)** not busy. **3** [C,U] (act of) bold and sometimes improper familiarity or disrespect: *I took the ~ of borrowing your lawn mower while you were away on vacation. You must stop taking liberties with the truth,* stop lying. **4** (*pl*) privileges or rights granted by authority: *civil liberties.* **5** permission for a sailor to go ashore when he is not on duty.

Libra /ˈlibrə/ *n* the Scales or Balance, the seventh sign of the zodiac. ⇨ illus at zodiac.

li·brary /ˈlaiˌbreri/ *n* [C] (*pl* -ies) **1** collection of books, manuscripts, etc for public or private use. **2** room or building for such a collection: *a public ~; a ˈreference ~,* one in which books may be consulted but not taken away. (as an *adjective*): *a ˈ~ book.*

li·brar·ian /laiˈbreriən/ *n* [C] person in charge of a library(1).

li·bretto /lɪˈbretou/ *n* [C] (*pl* ~s or -ti /-ti/) text of an opera or musical play.

li·bret·tist /lɪˈbretɪst/ *n* [C] writer of a libretto.

lice *pl* of louse.

li·cense /ˈlaisəns/ *n* **1** [C,U] (written or printed statement giving) legal permission to do something: *a ~ to drive a car/a ˈdriver's ~.* **2** [U] excessive freedom of action; lack of restraint: *The ~ shown by the troops when they entered enemy* *territory disgusted everyone.* □ *vt* give a license to: *stores* ~*d to sell tobacco.*

li·cen·tious /lɪˈsenʃəs/ *adj* immoral (esp in sexual matters).

li·cen·tious·ly *adv*

li·cen·tious·ness /-nɪs/ *n* [U]

li·chee, li·chi /ˈlitʃi/ = litchi.

li·chen /ˈlaikən/ *n* [C] small plant with a dry, scaly appearance and without stems or leaves, that grows on rocks, tree trunks, etc.

licit /ˈlɪsɪt/ *adj* (*informal*) lawful; permitted.

lick /lɪk/ *vt,vi* **1** pass the tongue over or under: *The cat was* ~*ing its paws.* ***lick sb's boots,*** be abject, servile. ***lick one's lips,*** show eagerness or satisfaction. **2** (esp of waves, flames) touch lightly: *The flames* ~*ed at the dry grass.* **3** (*informal*) overcome, defeat. **4** (*informal*) beat; strike repeatedly. □ *n* [C] **1** act of licking with the tongue. **2** (*informal*) bit; very small amount: *not a* ~ *of truth in his story.* **3** (*informal*) chance; try: *wanted a* ~ *at the job.* ***give sth a lick and a promise,*** a hasty attempt to clean, polish, etc. **4** (also ˈ**salt lick**) place to which animals go for salt. **5** blow.

lick·ing *n* [C] (*informal*) beating; defeat: *Our football team got/took a* ~*ing yesterday.*

licor·ice /ˈlɪk(ə)rɪʃ, -rɪs/ *n* [U] **1** (plant whose root yields a) sweet, black extract used as a flavoring. **2** chewy black candy flavored with this extract.

lid /lɪd/ *n* [C] **1** movable cover (hinged or detachable) for an opening, esp at the top of a container: *the lid of a box.* **2** eyelid.

lid·less *adj*

lie[1] /lai/ *n* [C] statement that the maker knows to be untrue: *What a pack of lies!* □ *vi* (*pt,pp* lied, *present participle* lying /ˈlaiɪŋ/) **1** tell a lie. **2** give a false impression: *Figures can sometimes lie.*

ˈ**lie detector,** device which records physical changes (eg in blood pressure, pulse rate, etc) that may indicate whether a person is lying.

lie[2] /lai/ *vi* (*pt* lay /lei/, *pp* lain /lein/, *present participle* lying /ˈlaiɪŋ/) **1** be in, take up, a horizontal or resting position; be at rest: *lie on one's back/side. He lay on the grass enjoying the sunshine.* ***(not) take sth lying down,*** (not) submit or give in without protest. ***lie in,*** (*dated*) remain in bed to give birth to a child: *The time had come for her to lie in.* ***lie low,*** ⇨ low[1](1). **2** (of things) be resting flat on something: *The book lay open on the table.* **3** be kept, remain, in a certain state or position: *money lying idle in the bank.* ***lie heavy on sth,*** cause discomfort, trouble, distress: *The theft lay heavy on his conscience.* **4** be situated: *ships lying at anchor. Many small towns lay along the coast.* **5** (of abstract things) exist: *The trouble lies* (= is) *in the engine.* □ *n* **1** (*sing* only) the way something lies. **2** [C] hiding place of an animal.

lieu /lu/ *n* (only in) ***in lieu of,*** instead of.

lieu·ten·ant /luˈtenənt/ *n* [C] **1** commissioned officer in the US army, air force or marine corps who ranks below a captain. **2** commissioned officer in the US navy or coast guard who ranks below a lieutenant commander. **3** chief deputy or assistant; one who acts for a superior.

ˈ**first lieutenant,** higher grade of lieutenant (1).

ˈ**second lieutenant,** lower grade of lieutenant (1), the lowest commissioned rank.

lieu,tenant ˈcolonel, commissioned officer in the US army, air force or marine corps, who ranks above a major and below a colonel.

lieu,tenant comˈmander, commissioned officer in the US navy or coast guard, who ranks above a lieutenant and below a commander.

lieu,tenant ˈgeneral, commissioned officer in the US army, air force or marine corps, who ranks above a major general and below a general.

lieu,tenant ˈgovernor, executive in a state government, ranking below the governor and assuming authority in the governor's absence.

lieu,tenant ˈjunior grade, commissioned officer in the US navy or coast guard, who ranks above an ensign and below a lieutenant.

life /laif/ *n* (*pl* lives /laivz/) **1** [U] condition that distinguishes animals and plants from earth, rock, etc, such as the ability to grow, reproduce, etc: *How did* ~ *begin?* **2** [U] living things in general; plants, animals, people: *Is there any* ~ *on the planet Mars?* **3** [U] state of existence: *great loss of* ~ *in war.* ***bring to life,*** **(a)** cause to live. **(b)** cause to recover consciousness. ***come to life,*** recover consciousness. ***for one's/for dear life,*** (as if) to save one's life. ***a matter of life and death,*** **(a)** one on which continued existence depends. **(b)** matter of great importance. ***a new lease on life,*** ⇨ lease(2). **4** [C] person; living being: *How many lives were lost in the disaster?* ***take sb's life,*** kill him. ***take one's own life,*** commit suicide. ***for the life of me,*** if my life depended on it: *For the* ~ *of me I couldn't recall her name.* ***Not on your life!*** (*informal*) Definitely not! **5** [C] period of being alive: *He spent his entire* ~ *abroad. The murderer received a* ~ *sentence/was sentenced to imprisonment for* ~. ***early/late in life,*** during the early/late part of one's life. ***have the time of one's life,*** enjoy oneself immensely. **6** [U] human existence; the pleasures, business and social activities, etc, of the world: *There is not much* ~ (eg social activity) *in our small town.* ***true to life,*** (of a story, drama, etc) giving a true description of how people live. **7** [C,U] way of living: *Which do you prefer, city* ~ *or country* ~*?* **8** [C] biography: *He has written a new* ~ *of Thoreau.* **9** [U] liveliness; spirit: *The children are full of* ~. ***the life of the party,*** person who is the most lively and amusing member of a social gathering. **10** [C] period during which something is active or useful: *the* ~ *of a ship/a government.*

ˈ**life belt,** belt of cork or other buoyant material to keep a person afloat in water.

ˈ**life·blood** *n* (*fig*) (esp) something that gives strength and energy.

ˈ**life·boat** *n* [C] **(a)** boat specially built for going to the help of persons in danger at sea. **(b)** boat carried on a ship for use in case the ship is in danger of sinking, etc. ⇨ illus at ship.

ˈ**life buoy,** device to keep a person afloat in water.

ˈlife cycle, progression through different stages of development: *the ~ cycle of a frog.*

ˈlife·guard *n* [C] expert swimmer hired to protect the safety of bathers at a beach or pool.

ˈlife jacket, one of cork or other buoyant material or that can be inflated to keep a person afloat in water.

life·less *adj* **(a)** dead; without life: *~less stones.* **(b)** incapable of supporting life. **(c)** dull; not lively: *answer in a ~less manner.*

life·less·ly *adv*

ˈlife·like *adj* **(a)** resembling real life. **(b)** looking like the person represented: *a ~like portrait.*

ˈlife·line *n* [C] **(a)** rope used for saving life. **(b)** (*fig*) any chain of communication, provisions, etc on which one's life depends.

ˈlife·long *adj* continuing or lasting for a lifetime.

ˈlife preserver, (a) float (usually in the shape of a ring) carried on board a boat or ship. **(b)** = life belt, life jacket.

ˈlife-size(d) *adj* (of pictures, statues, etc) having the same size as the person, animal, etc represented.

ˈlife·time *n* period of an existence or being alive: *the chance of a ~time,* an opportunity that comes only once.

ˈlife·work *n* task to which one devotes all one's life.

lift /lɪft/ *vt,vi* **1** raise, be raised to a higher level; move upward: *~ a child out of his crib. This box is too heavy for me to ~.* ***not lift a finger,*** ⇨ finger(1). ***lift off,*** (of a spacecraft) rise from the launching site. **2** make louder: *~ (up) one's voice.* **3** raise in rank, condition, mental state, etc: *The good news ~ed her spirits.* **4** (of clouds, fog, etc) rise and pass away: *The mist began to ~.* **5** (*informal*) steal: *~ articles in a supermarket.* **6** (*informal*) copy without permission or proper acknowledgment: *long passages ~ed from other authors.* **7** end (a ban, prohibition, blockade, siege). □ *n* [C] **1** act of lifting. **2** (esp free) ride in a vehicle: *Can you give me a ~ to the station?* **3** influence that makes a person more cheerful, contented: *The salary increase was a tremendous ~.* **4** moving cable (often with seats) for taking people up or down the side of a mountain: *a ski ~.*

ˈlift·off *n* [C] moment of rising of a spacecraft from the launching site.

liga·ment /ˈlɪgəmənt/ *n* [C] band of tough, strong tissue that holds two or more bones together.

light[1] /lait/ *adj* (-er, -est) (opposite of *dark*) **1** bright; having light[3] (1): *It's beginning to get ~.* **2** pale in color: *~ blue/green/brown.*

light[2] /lait/ *adj* (-er, -est) **1** not heavy; not having much weight (for its size): *as ~ as air/as a feather; ~ clothes for the summer.* **2** gentle; delicate: *give her a ~ touch on the shoulder.* **3** small in strength, amount, etc: *a ~ meal; a ~ sleep; a ~ snowfall.* **4** not containing much alcohol: *a ~ wine.* **5** not easily disturbed or awakened. **6** primarily for amusement, not for serious entertainment or study: *~ reading/music.* **7** nimble; moving with ease: *a ~ footstep.* **8** not difficult to bear. **9** (of work) easily done. ***make light work of sth,*** do it without much effort. **10** not serious or important: *a ~ attack of flu.* ***make light of,*** treat as of no or little importance. **11** cheerful; happy: *~ spirited.*

ˌlight-ˈfingered *adj* skillful in using the fingers, esp as a shoplifter or pickpocket.

ˌlight-ˈfooted *adj* moving with light(2), easy steps.

ˌlight-ˈhanded *adj* having a light(2) hand.

ˌlight-ˈheaded *adj* **(a)** dizzy; delirious. **(b)** frivolous; silly.

ˌlight-ˈhearted *adj* cheerful; gay.

light·ly *adv:* ***get off lightly,*** escape with little or no punishment.

light·ness /-nɪs/ *n* [U]

ˈlight·weight *n* [C], *adj* **1** (person, animal, thing) light in weight. **2** (boxer) weighing between 126 and 135 lbs (57 and 61 kg). **3** (*informal*) (person) of little influence or importance.

light[3] /lait/ *n* (opposite of *darkness*) **1** [U] **(a)** that which makes it possible to see. **(b)** electromagnetic radiation, esp in a form that is visible to the eye: *the ~ of the sun/a lamp/the fire; ˈmoon~; ˈsun~.* ***see the light,*** (esp) realize the truth of something for the first time. **2** [C] something that gives light, eg a candle or lamp: *street/traffic/signal ~s; turn/switch the (house/automobile) ~s on/off.* **3** [C] (something used for producing a) spark or flame, esp to light[4] (1) a cigarette: *Can you give me a ~, please?* **4** [U] brightness or glow in a person's face or eyes, suggesting happiness or other emotion. **5** [U] public knowledge or view. ***bring sth to light,*** cause it to become known. ***come to light,*** become visible or known: *Much new evidence has come to ~ in recent years.* ***shed/throw (a new) light on sth,*** make something clearer, provide new information. ***in the light of,*** with the help given by or gained from. **6** [C] way in which something is seen or appears: *I've never viewed the matter in that ~.* ***in a good/bad/false, etc light,*** (esp) so as to make a good/bad/inaccurate, etc impression: *Press reports always show him in a bad ~.* **7** [C] famous or outstanding person: *one of the shining ~s of our age.* **8** [C] window or opening for letting in light: *a ˈsky~.* **9** bright part of a picture: *~ and shade.* ⇨ highlight(a). **10** traffic light.

LIGHTHOUSE

ˈlight·house *n* [C] tower or other tall structure containing a strong, flashing light for warning or guiding ships at sea.

ˈ**light·ship** *n* [C] ship provided with a light, that is anchored in a dangerous place to warn and guide ships.

ˈ**light year,** the distance traveled by light in one year (about 6 trillion miles).

light[4] /lait/ *vt,vi* (*pt,pp* ~ed, lit /lɪt/) **1** cause to begin burning or to give out light: *~ a cigarette/fire*. **2** provide lights(2) to or for: *Our streets are lit by electricity*. **3** cause to become bright: *The burning building lit up the whole district*. **4** ***light up (with),*** (of a person's face or expression) (cause to) become bright: *Her face lit up with pleasure*.

light[5] /lait/ *vi* (*pt,pp* ~ed, lit /lɪt/) **1** alight; land on. **2** find by chance: *~ on/upon a rare book in the library*.

lighten[1] /ˈlaitən/ *vt,vi* make or become less heavy; reduce the weight of: *~ a ship's cargo. Her heart ~ed when she heard the news*.

lighten[2] /ˈlaitən/ *vt,vi* **1** make (more) light or bright: *A solitary candle ~ed the darkness of the cellar*. **2** become light or bright: *The eastern sky ~ed*.

lighter[1] /ˈlaitər/ *n* [C] **1** device for lighting[4] (1) cigarettes or cigars. **2** (chiefly in compounds) person or thing that lights: *a* ˈ*lamp~*, man who used to light gas-burning street lamps.

lighter[2] /ˈlaitər/ *n* [C] shallow boat used esp for loading and unloading ships.

light·ning /ˈlaitnɪŋ/ *n* [U] flash of bright light produced by a discharge of natural electricity between clouds or between a cloud and the ground: *be struck/killed by ~*.

ˈ**lightning bug,** = firefly.

ˈ**lightning rod,** metal rod fixed on the top of a high building, etc and connected to the earth, to prevent damage by lightning.

light·weight /ˈlaitˌweit/ *n* [C], *adj* **1** (person, animal, thing) light in weight. **2** (boxer) weighing between 126 and 135 lbs (57 and 61 kg). **3** (*informal*) (person) of little influence or importance.

lik·able, like·able /ˈlaikəbəl/ *adj* pleasing; easily liked: *He's a very ~ fellow*.

like[1] /laik/ *adj* similar; having the same or similar qualities, etc: *After John showed off his new camera Harry went out and bought a ~ one*, an identical or similar one. ***Like father, like son,*** as the one is, so the other will be. □ *conj* as: *She can't cook ~ her mother* (*does*). □ *n* similar person(s) or thing(s); that which is equal or similar to something else: *Music, painting and the ~,* and the other arts. □ *prep* **1** such as; similar to: *What is he ~?* What sort of person is he? *She was clever ~ her mother and kind ~ her father*. ***nothing like,*** nothing to be compared with: *There's nothing ~ walking as a means of keeping fit*. ***something like,*** nearly; about: *The cost will be something ~ five dollars*. **2** ˈ***feel like,*** be in a suitable state or mood for: *She felt ~ crying. We'll go for a walk if you feel ~ it*. ˈ***look like,*** look inclined to or likely to: *It looks ~ rain*. **3** characteristic of: *Isn't that just ~ a woman!* **4** in the manner of; to the same degree as: *Don't talk ~ an idiot. It fits him ~ a glove,* closely, tightly. *He drinks ~ a fish*. **5** ***like anything/crazy/mad/hell, etc,*** (*informal*) with as much energy, force, speed, etc as can be imagined: *She works ~ anything when she's interested. He complains ~ mad when things go wrong. He ran ~ hell for the bus*. ***like fun/hell,*** (*int*): *"But you were there, weren't you?" "Like hell, I was!"* I certainly wasn't!

ˌ**like-**ˈ**minded** *adj* having the same tastes, aims, etc.

like[2] /laik/ *vt,vi* **1** be fond of; enjoy; find satisfactory or agreeable: *Do you ~ fish? She ~s him but she doesn't love him*. **2** (used with *how*) feel about: *How do you ~ your new car?* **3** want; wish (often used with *would/should*): *She would ~ a cup of tea*. **4** prefer; choose: *Come whenever you ~*. ***if you like,*** (used to express consent to a request or suggestion): *I'll come if you ~*. □ *n* (*pl*) (only in) ˌ***likes and*** ˈ***dislikes,*** things a person prefers or hates.

like·li·hood /ˈlaikliˌhʊd/ *n* [U] probability: *There is a strong ~ of rain tomorrow*.

like·ly /ˈlaikli/ *adj* (-ier, -iest) **1** that seems reasonable or suitable for a purpose: *What do you think is the likeliest/the most ~ time to find him at home?* **2** seeming to be true; believable: *That's a ~ story/excuse* (often used ironically). **3** to be expected; probable: *He is very ~ to succeed. It's (very) ~ that he will succeed*. □ *adv* ***most/very likely,*** probably: *I shall very ~ be here again next month*.

liken /ˈlaikən/ *vt* ***liken sth to sth,*** point out the likeness of one thing to another; compare: *~ the heart to a pump*.

like·ness /ˈlaiknɪs/ *n* **1** [U] resemblance; similarity: *I can't see much ~ between the two boys*. **2** [C] detail, instance, of being like: *There's a family ~ in all of them*. **3** [C] copy; picture, photograph, etc: *The portrait is a good ~*.

like·wise /ˈlaikˌwaiz/ *adv* **1** in the same or a similar way: *Watch him and do ~*. **2** also; moreover.

lik·ing /ˈlaikɪŋ/ *n* [U] **1** fondness: *His feeling for her grew from a ~ to love*. ***have a liking for,*** be fond of. ***to one's liking,*** as one likes it. **2** taste; preference: *Is everything to your ~?* ***take a liking to,*** become fond of.

li·lac /ˈlailək, -lak/ *n* **1** [C] shrub with clusters of sweet-smelling pale purple or white blossoms. **2** [U] pale purple color: (as an *adjective*) *a ~ dress*.

lilt /lɪlt/ *n* [C] (lively song or tune with a) well-marked rhythm. □ *vt,vi* go, sing with a lilt: *a ~ing waltz*.

lily /ˈlɪli/ *n* [C] (*pl* -ies) (kinds of) plant having large, usually trumpet-shaped flowers.

ˌ**lily-**ˈ**white** *adj* **(a)** pure white. **(b)** innocent; pure.

lima bean /ˈlaimə ˌbin/ *n* [C] (plant bearing an) edible, flat green bean that grows in pods. ⇨ illus at vegetable.

limb /lɪm/ *n* [C] **1** leg, arm or wing of an animal body: *escape with life and ~*, without serious injury. **2** large branch of a tree. ***out on a limb,*** in a vulnerable or dangerous position.

lim·ber /ˈlɪmbər/ *adj* flexible; bending with ease. □ *vt,vi* ***limber up,*** make or become pliant, flexible.

limbo /ˈlɪmbou/ *n* [C] (*pl* ~s) **1** [U] condition,

place of neglect and confinement for forgotten and unwanted things. **2** (usually **Limbo**) region for souls of unbaptized infants and pre-Christian righteous persons.

lime[1] /laim/ *n* [U] white substance (calcium oxide, symbol **CaO**) used in making cement and mortar.

lime[2] /laim/ *n* [C] European linden tree.

lime[3] /laim/ *n* [C] (tree with) round greenish fruit similar to the lemon.

lime·light /ˈlaimˌlait/ **1** [C] intense white light produced by heating a rod of lime[1] in a very hot flame, formerly used for lighting the stage in theaters. **2** [U] center of public attention.

lim·er·ick /ˈlɪmərɪk/ *n* [C] humorous poem of five lines.

lime·stone /ˈlaimˌstoun/ *n* [U] rock consisting chiefly of lime, that is used for building and in making cement.

limit[1] /ˈlɪmɪt/ *n* [C] **1** line or point that may not or cannot be passed: *within a ~ of five miles/a five-mile ~. We must set a ~ to the expense of the trip. She has reached the ~ of her patience.* ***within limits,*** in moderation: *I'm willing to help you, within ~s.* **2** greatest or smallest amount, number, etc that is allowed: *What is the speed ~?*

limit[2] /ˈlɪmɪt/ *vt* put a limit or limits to: *We must ~ our spending to what we can afford.*

lim·ited *pp* small; restricted; narrow: *Accommodation is very ~ed. He seems to have only a ~ed intelligence.*

lim·it·less *adj* without limit: *~less ambitions.*

limi·ta·tion /ˌlɪməˈteiʃən/ *n* **1** [U] limiting; condition of being limited. **2** [C] condition, fact or circumstance that limits; disability or inability: *He knows his ~s,* knows the extent of his ability.

limn /lɪm/ *vt* (*old use*) **1** paint or draw. **2** describe.

limou·sine /ˈlɪməˌzin/ *n* [C] large automobile with the front seats separated from the back seats by means of a partition (as in some taxis).

limp[1] /lɪmp/ *adj* not stiff or firm; lacking strength: *The flowers looked ~ in the heat.*

limp·ly *adv*

limp·ness /-nɪs/ *n* [U]

limp[2] /lɪmp/ *vi* **1** walk lamely or unevenly as when one leg or foot is hurt: *The wounded soldier ~ed off the battlefield.* **2** move slowly and with difficulty, as from a disability: *The damaged ship ~ed into port.* □ *n* [U] (usually with *a, an*) lame walk: *have/walk with a bad ~.*

lim·pet /ˈlɪmpɪt/ *n* [C] small shellfish that fastens itself tightly to rocks. ⇨ illus at mollusk.

lim·pid /ˈlɪmpɪd/ *adj* clear; transparent: *a ~ pool of water.*

lim·pid·ity /lɪmˈpɪdəti/ *n* [U]

lim·pid·ly *adv*

linch·pin /ˈlɪntʃˌpɪn/ *n* [C] iron pin passed through the end of an axle to keep the wheel on.

lin·den /ˈlɪndən/ *n* **1** [C] tree with heart-shaped leaves and sweet-smelling yellowish flowers. **2** [U] wood of this tree.

line[1] /lain/ *n* [C] **1** piece or length of thread, string, rope or wire for various purposes: *ˈfishing/ˈtelephone ~s. The ~ is busy,* (used of a telephone line) already in use. ⇨ hot line. **2 (a)** (*math*) path taken by a moving point. **(b)** long, narrow mark made on a surface: *Draw a ~ from A to B.* **3** system of pipes for carrying a liquid: *plumbing ~s.* **4** (*sport*) mark made to show the limits of play on a court, ground, etc: *Did the ball cross the foul ~?* **5** crease in the skin, esp of the face or hand; furrow or wrinkle. **6** (*pl*) contour; outline: *a dress with flattering ~s.* **7** row of persons or things: *a ~ of trees/chairs/people; manufactured goods on the asˈsembly ~.* ***in line for,*** next in order for: *He's in ~ for promotion.* ***stand in/on line,*** form a line for the purpose of taking one's turn. **8** edge, boundary, that divides: *cross the ~ into the US* (ie from Canada or Mexico). ***draw the line (at),*** ⇨ draw[2] (10). **9** single track of railroad: *the main ~; a ˈbranch ~.* ***the end of the line,*** (*fig*) point where something ends. **10** (firm operating an) organized system of transport: *an ˈair~.* **11** direction; course; track: *~ of flight.* **12** attitude; way of behavior, dealing with a situation, etc: ***the line of least resistance,*** the easiest way of doing things. ***take a strong/firm line (over sth),*** deal with a problem, etc in a firm(2) manner: *Should the Administration take a stronger ~ over inflation?* **13** alignment; agreement. ***in/out of line (with),*** in agreement/disagreement (with). ***come/fall into line (with),*** conform; agree. ***the party line,*** official policy of a political party. ***toe the line,*** (*fig*) ⇨ toe(2). **14** connected series of persons following one another in time; (esp) lineage; ancestry: *a long ~ of great kings.* **15 (a)** row of words on a page of writing or in print: *page 5, ~ 10.* ***read between the lines,*** (*fig*) find more meaning than the words suggest. **(b)** (*pl*) actor's part in a drama: *The leading actor was not sure of his ~s.* **(c)** short letter: *Drop us a ~.* **16** series of connected military defense posts, trenches, etc: *the front/enemy ~(s).* **17** business; occupation: *He's in the ˈgrocery ~.* **18** extent of activity or knowledge: *That's out of my ~,* (*fig*) I don't know much about it. **19** class of commercial goods: *a cheap ~ of denim jeans.* **20** (*informal*) account, story, etc that is false or exaggerated: *They were completely fooled by the ~ he gave them.*

line[2] /lain/ *vt,vi* **1** mark with lines: *~d paper,* with lines printed on it. **2** cover with lines: *a face ~d with anxiety.* **3** ***line up,*** (cause to) be in a line, get into a line: *The soldiers quickly ~d up.* **4** form, be placed, in a line or lines along: *a road ~d with trees/spectators.*

line[3] /lain/ *vt* **1** cover the inside surface of (eg bags, boxes, etc) with a layer of material: *She lined the drawers with paper.* **2** serve as a lining for: *Paintings ~d the walls of the room.* ⇨ lining below.

lin·eage /ˈlɪniɪdʒ/ *n* [U] (*formal*) (group of persons who share) direct descent from a common ancestor.

lin·eal /ˈlɪniəl/ *adj* **1** in the direct line of descent (from father to son, etc): *a ~ descendant/heir.* **2** linear.

lin·eal·ly /-iəli/ *adv*

lin·ear /ˈlɪniər/ *adj* **1** of or in lines: *a ~ design.* **2** of length: *~ measurement.*

line·man /ˈlainmən/ *n* [C] (*pl* -men /-men/)

person who works on telephone, electrical, etc lines.

linen /ˈlɪnən/ *n* **1** [U] yarn or cloth made of flax. **2** (*pl*) household articles, esp sheets, tablecloths, etc, made from linen or some other fabric. ***wash one's dirty linen in public,*** discuss family quarrels, unpleasant personal affairs, etc in the presence of other people.

liner /ˈlainər/ *n* [C] **1** ship or airplane of a line (10): *jet ˈair~; ocean ~.* **2** = lining.

lines·man /ˈlainzmən/ *n* [C] (*pl* -men /-men/) (*sport*) person who helps the umpire or referee by saying whether a ball is out-of-bounds.

line·up /ˈlainˌəp/ *n* (usu *sing*) **1** row of persons placed side-by-side for identification: *police ~.* **2** (list of) players taking part in a game. **3** way in which persons, states, etc are allied: *~ of Third World powers.*

ling. *abbr* = linguistics.

lin·ger /ˈlɪŋgər/ *vi* **1** be late or slow in leaving a place: *~ around.* **2** be slow to act.

ˈling·erer *n* [C]

ling·er·ing *adj* long; prolonged: *a ~ing illness; a few ~ing* (= remaining) *doubts.*

ling·er·ing·ly *adv*

linge·rie /landʒəˈri, -ˈrei/ *n* [U] (*F*) women's underwear.

lingo /ˈlɪŋgou/ *n* [C] (*pl* ~es) **1** language, esp one that one does not know. **2** jargon; way of talking, vocabulary, of a special subject or class of people: *the strange ~ used by disc jockeys.*

lin·gua franca /ˌlɪŋgwə ˈfræŋkə/ *n* [C] (*pl* lingua francas) language adopted as a common language in an area in which several languages are spoken, eg Swahili in East Africa.

lin·guist /ˈlɪŋgwɪst/ *n* [C] **1** person skilled in foreign languages: *She's a good ~.* **2** person who makes a scientific study of language(s).

lin·guis·tic /lɪŋˈgwɪstɪk/ *adj* of (the scientific study of) languages.

lin·guis·tics *n* (used with a *sing verb*) the science of language, eg of its structure, development, etc.

lini·ment /ˈlɪnəmənt/ *n* [C,U] (kind of) liquid for rubbing on stiff or aching parts of the body.

lin·ing /ˈlainɪŋ/ *n* [C] material used to line something: *a fur ~.* ***Every cloud has a silver lining,*** (*prov*) there is a possibility of good out of every evil.

link /lɪŋk/ *n* [C] **1** one ring or loop of a chain. **2** person or thing that unites or connects two others: *the ~ between the past and the future.* **3** measure of length, one hundredth of a chain (= 7.92 inches or about 20 centimeters). □ *vt,vi* join, be joined, with, or as with, a link: *~ things together; two towns ~ed by a canal.*

links /lɪŋks/ *n* (often used with a *sing verb*) golf course.

li·noleum /lɪˈnouliəm/ *n* [U] strong floor covering made of canvas, powdered cork and linseed oil.

lin·seed /ˈlɪnˌsid/ *n* [U] seed of the flax and plant. **ˈlinseed oil,** oil used in making paint, varnish, linoleum, etc.

lint /lɪnt/ *n* [U] fluff or short fibers from yarn or fabric.

lin·tel /ˈlɪntəl/ *n* [C] horizontal piece of wood or stone over the top of a door or window, that supports the weight of the structure above.

lion /ˈlaiən/ *n* [C] large, strong, flesh-eating animal of the cat family found in Africa and South Asia. ⇨ illus at cat. ***the lion's share,*** the larger or largest part.

lion·ess /-ɪs/ *n* [C] female lion. ⇨ illus at cat.

lip /lɪp/ *n* **1** [C] one or other of the fleshy edges of the opening of the mouth: *the lower/upper lip.* ⇨ illus at mouth. ***bite one's lip,*** hide one's feelings. ***curl one's lip,*** show scorn. ***give/pay ˈlip service to sth,*** speak insincerely. ***lick/smack one's lips,*** show (anticipation of) enjoyment. **2** [C] edge of a container or opening: *the lip of a bowl/crater.* **3** [U] (*informal*) impudence: *That's enough of your lip!*

lip·read /ˈlɪpˌrid/ *vt,vi* understand speech by watching a speaker's lip movements.

ˈlip·reading *n* [U] method (taught to deaf people) of understanding speech from lip movements.

lip·stick /ˈlɪpˌstɪk/ *n* [C] stick of cosmetic material for coloring the lips.

liq. *abbr* = liquid.

liquefy /ˈlɪkwəˌfai/ *vt,vi* (*pt,pp* -ied) make or become liquid.

lique·fac·tion /ˌlɪkwəˈfækʃən/ *n* [U] (*formal*).

li·queur /lɪˈkər/ *n* [C] (kinds of) sweet alcoholic drink often served after dinner.

liquid /ˈlɪkwɪd/ *n* [C,U] substance like water or oil that flows freely and is neither a solid nor a gas. □ *adj* **1** in the form of a liquid: *~ food,* soft, easily swallowed, suitable for sick people. **2** clear and bright: *~ eyes,* bright and shining. **3** (of sounds) clear; pure: *the ~ notes of a goldfinch.* **4** easily sold or changed into cash: *~ assets.*

liqui·date /ˈlɪkwəˌdeit/ *vt,vi* **1** pay or settle (a debt). **2** bring (esp an unsuccessful business company) to an end by dividing up its property to pay debts. **3** put an end to; kill: *gangsters who ~ their rivals.*

liqui·da·tion /ˌlɪkwəˈdeiʃən/ *n* [U] liquidating or being liquidated.

liquor /ˈlɪkər/ *n* [U] **1** distilled alcoholic drinks: *He can't drink ~, especially gin.* **2** liquid produced eg by cooking food.

lisp /lɪsp/ *vi,vt* pronounce the sounds /s/ and /z/ as /θ/ and /ð/. □ *n* [C] lisping way of speaking: *The child has a bad ~.*

lis·some, lis·som /ˈlɪsəm/ *adj* quick and graceful in movement.

list[1] /lɪst/ *n* [C] number of names (of persons, items, things, etc) written or printed: *a ˈshopping ~.* □ *vt* **1** make a list of. **2** put on a list. **ˈlist price,** published or advertised price.

list[2] /lɪst/ *vi* (esp of a ship) lean over to one side: *The ship ~ed to starboard.* □ *n* [C] listing (of a ship).

lis·ten /ˈlɪsən/ *vi* **1** try to hear: *We ~ed but heard nothing.* ***listen in (on),*** **(a)** listen to a broadcast: *Did you ~ in on the concert yesterday evening?* **(b)** listen secretly to a conversation, eg by using an extension telephone receiver. **2** pay attention: *Don't ~ to him; he wants to get you into trouble.*

lis·tener *n* [C]

list·less /ˈlɪstlɪs/ *adj* tired; lethargic.
list·less·ly *adv*
list·less·ness /-nɪs/ *n* [U]
lit.[1] *abbr* = **1** literary. **2** literature.
lit[2] *pt,pp* of light[4].
lit·any /ˈlɪtəni/ *n* [C] (*pl* -ies) **1** form of prayer recited by a priest with responses from the congregation. **2** (*fig*) monotonous (reciting of a) series of items: *a ~ of complaints*.
lit·chi /ˈlitʃi/ *n* [C] (*pl* ~s) (tree bearing a) sweet, thin-shelled fruit.
liter[1] /ˈlitər/ *n* [C] unit of capacity in the metric system equal to about 1.057 liquid quarts or 0.908 of a dry quart.
liter.[2] *abbr* = **1** literary. **2** literature.
lit·er·acy /ˈlɪtərəsi/ *n* [U] ability to read and write.
lit·eral /ˈlɪtərəl/ *adj* **1** connected with, expressed in, letters of an alphabet. **2** corresponding word for word to the original: *a ~ translation*. **3** taking words in their usual and obvious sense, without exaggeration, etc: *the ~ sense of a word*. **4** (of a person) lacking in imagination: *He has a rather ~ mind*.
lit·er·ally /ˈlɪtərəli/ *adv*
lit·er·ary /ˈlɪtəˌreri/ *adj* of literature or authors: *a ~ man*, either an author or a man interested in literature; *a ~ style*, as used in literature.
lit·er·ate /ˈlɪtərɪt/ *adj* **1** able to read and write. **2** cultured; well-read: *Ben's a remarkably ~ young man*. □ *n* [C] literate person.
lit·era·ture /ˈlɪtərətʃər/ *n* [U] **1** (the writing or the study of) books, etc valued as works of art (drama, fiction, essays, poetry, biography, contrasted with technical books and journalism). **2** body of writings of a country, a period, or on a special subject: *travel ~; French ~, 18th century ~*. **3** printed material describing or advertising something: *political ~; ~ about our package tours*.
lithe /laið/ *adj* bending, twisting or turning easily: *a ~ body*.
lith·i·um /ˈlɪθiəm/ *n* [U] soft, silvery element (symbol **Li**) that is the lightest metal known.
lith·o·graph /ˈlɪθəˌgræf/ *n* [C] (esp) picture produced from a plate which has been treated so that ink sticks only to certain parts.
liti·gate /ˈlɪtəˌgeit/ *vi,vt* make a claim in a law court; contest in a lawsuit.
liti·ga·tion /ˌlɪtəˈgeiʃən/ *n* [U]
lit·mus /ˈlɪtməs/ *n* [U] coloring matter that is turned red by acid solutions and blue by alkaline solutions: *ˈ~ paper*, used as a test for acids and alkalis.
li·totes /ˈlaitəˌtiz/ *n* [C] (*pl* unchanged) understatement used ironically, esp using a negative to express the contrary, as "I won't be sorry when it's over" meaning "I will be very glad".
Litt.D. *abbr* (= *Lat* Litterarum Doctor) Doctor of Letters.
lit·ter[1] /ˈlɪtər/ *n* [C] **1** couch or bed (often with a covering and curtains) in which a person may be carried around. **2** sort of stretcher for carrying a sick or wounded person.
lit·ter[2] /ˈlɪtər/ *n* **1** [U] bits of paper, wrappings, bottles, etc left lying around: *Pick up your ~ after a picnic*. **2** [U] straw, hay, etc, used as bedding for animals. **3** [C] all the young ones of an animal born at one time: *a ~ of puppies*. □ *vt,vi* **1** make untidy with litter(1): *~ a desk with papers; ~ up one's room*. **2** (of animals, esp dogs and pigs) bring forth a litter(3).
ˈlitter·bug *n* [C] (*informal*) person who litters (1).
little[1] /ˈlɪtəl/ *adj* (*Note: little* has no formal *comparative* and *superlative; ~r* and *~st* are informally used with *countable nouns* and less and least are used with *uncountable nouns.*) **1** small, or small in comparison: *the ~ finger/toe*. **2** (often used with a preceding *adjective* to show affection, tenderness): *What a pretty ~ house! That poor ~ girl!* **3** brief; short (in time, distance, etc): *Won't you stay a ~ time with me?* **4** young: *How are the ~ ones*, the children? **5** not much: *I have very ~ time for reading*. **6** (with *a*) some but not much; a small quantity of: *He knows a ~ French. Will you have a ~ cake?* □ *adv* **1** not much; hardly at all; only slightly: *He is ~ known. She slept very ~ last night. I see him very ~* (= rarely) *nowadays. He is ~ better than* (= is almost as bad as) *a thief*. ***a little,*** rather; somewhat: *a ~ afraid; a ~ too big*. ***not a little,*** very: *not a ~ annoyed*. **2** (with such *verbs* as *know, think, imagine, guess, suspect, realize*, and always placed before the *verb*) not at all: *He ~ knows/Little does he know that the police are about to arrest him.*
little·ness /-nɪs/ *n* [U]
little[2] /ˈlɪtəl/ *n* [U] **1** not much; only a small amount: *You have done very ~ for us. I see very ~ of him. I got ~ out of it*, not much advantage or profit. *He did what ~ he could*. ***little by little,*** gradually; by degrees. ***little or nothing,*** hardly anything. ⇨ less, least. **2** (with *a*) a small quantity; something (*a ~* is positive; *~* is negative): *He knows a ~ of everything. Please give me a ~*. ***after/for a little,*** after/for a short time or distance. ⇨ less, least.
lit·urgy /ˈlɪtərdʒi/ *n* [C] (*pl* -ies) fixed form of public worship used in a church.
li·turgi·cal /lɪˈtərdʒɪkəl/ *adj*
liv·able /ˈlɪvəbəl/ *adj* **1** (of a house, room, climate, etc) fit to live in. **2** tolerable.
live[1] /laiv/ *adj* **1 (a)** having life: *~ fish*. **(b)** lively. **2** burning or glowing: *~ coals*. **3** unexploded: *a ~ bomb*, not used. **4** charged with electricity: *a ~ rail*, carrying current for trains. **5** (of a broadcast) not recorded in advance (on tape or records). **6** of current interest, importance, etc: *a ~ question/issue*. □ *adv* (⇨ 5 above): *The concert will be broadcast ~*.
live wire, (*fig*) lively, energetic, person.
live[2] /lɪv/ *vi,vt* **1** exist(1); be alive. **2** continue to be, remain, alive: *She's very ill—the doctors don't think she will ~*. ***live ˈon,*** continue to live: *The old people died but the young people ~d on in the village*. ***live through,*** experience and survive: *He has ~d through two wars and three revolutions*. ***live and let live,*** be tolerant. **3** support or maintain oneself: *~ on fruit; ~ on one's salary*. ***live off the land,*** use its agricultural products for one's food needs. **4** dwell; reside; make one's home: *~ in the United States/abroad. Where do you ~?* ***live together,*** **(a)** live

in the same house, etc. **(b)** live as if married: *I hear that Jane and Bill are living together.* **5** spend, pass, one's life: *He ~d and died a bachelor.* **6** conduct oneself; pass one's life in a specified way: *~ honestly/happily; ~ like a saint.* ***7 live sth down,*** live in such a way that something damaging (past guilt, scandal, foolishness, etc) is forgotten: *He hopes to ~ down the scandal caused by the divorce proceedings.* ***live up to sth,*** **(a)** act in accordance with: *~ up to a promise.* **(b)** reach the standard that may be expected: *He didn't ~ up to his reputation.* ***(learn to) live with sth,*** put up with it; learn to endure it: *I don't like commuting, but I've learned to ~ with it.* **8** enjoy life intensely: *"I want to ~," she said, "I don't want to spend my days looking after babies."* ***live it up,*** have great fun: *Let's go into town and ~ it up a little.*

live·li·hood /ˈlaivliˌhʊd/ *n* [C] way in which one earns one's living: *earn/gain one's ~ by teaching.*

live·long /ˈlɪvˌlɔŋ/ *adj* (only in) ***the livelong day/night,*** all day/night.

live·ly /ˈlaivli/ *adj* (-ier, -iest) **1** full of life and spirit; gay and cheerful: *The patient seems a little livelier/a little more ~ this morning. He has a ~ imagination.* **2** (of color) bright; gay. **3** moving quickly or causing quick movement: *a ~ ball.* **4** lifelike; realistic: *a ~ description of a football game.*

live·li·ness /-nɪs/ *n* [U]

liven /ˈlaivən/ *vt,vi* make or become lively: *How can we ~ things up?*

liver[1] /ˈlɪvər/ *n* **1** [C] large, reddish-brown organ in the body which secretes bile and cleans the blood of waste matter. **2** [U] animal's liver as food.

liver[2] /ˈlɪvər/ *n* [C] person who lives in a specified way: *a clean/loose ~.*

liv·ery /ˈlɪvəri/ *n* [C] (*pl* -ies) **1** special dress or uniform worn by the male servants of a household (esp of a king or noble). **2** (*poet*) dress; covering: *birds in their winter ~.* **3** stabling and care of horses for payment: *ˈlivery stable,* stable from which horses may be hired. **4** (service of providing) vehicles to be hired for transportation.

liv·er·ied /ˈlɪvərid/ *adj* wearing livery(1).

lives *pl* of life.

live·stock /ˈlaivˌstak/ *n* [U] (esp) farm animals kept for use or profit, eg cattle, sheep, pigs.

livid /ˈlɪvɪd/ *adj* **1** discolored, as from a bruise. **2** pale: *~ with rage.*

liv·id·ly *adv*

liv·ing[1] /ˈlɪvɪŋ/ *adj* **1** alive, esp now existent: *~ languages.* ***within/in living memory,*** within the memory of people now alive. **2** (of a likeness) true to life: *He's the ~ image of* (= is exactly like) *his father.* **3** (as an intensifier): *scare the ~ daylights out of him.* □ *n* **the living,** (used with a *pl verb*) those now alive: *He's still in the land of the ~.*

liv·ing[2] /ˈlɪvɪŋ/ *n* **1** [C] means of keeping alive, of earning what is needed for life: *earn/gain/get/make a ~ as a car salesman.* **2** [U] manner of life: *a high standard of ~.*

ˈliving room, room for general use such as relaxing, entertaining.

liz·ard /ˈlɪzərd/ *n* [C] (kinds of) small, creeping, long-tailed four-legged reptile. ⇨ illus at reptile.

llama /ˈlamə/ *n* [C] South American animal with a thick woolly coat, used for carrying loads.

LL.B. /ˌelˌel ˈbi/ *abbr* (= *Lat* Legum Baccalaurens) Bachelor of Laws.

LL.D. /ˌelˌel ˈdi/ *abbr* (= *Lat* Legum Doctor) Doctor of Laws.

lo /lou/ *int* Look! See!: *Lo and behold!*

load[1] /loud/ *n* [C] **1** weight which is (to be) carried or supported, esp if heavy. ***loads of,*** (*informal*) a large number or amount. **2** (*fig*) weight of care, responsibility, etc: *a heavy ~ on one's shoulders.* ***take a load off sb's mind,*** relieve him of anxiety, etc. **3** amount which a vehicle can carry: *a ˈfull ~ of passengers.* **4** amount of work that a machine or person can do. **5** amount of current supplied by a generating station or carried by an electric circuit.

load[2] /loud/ *vt,vi* **1** put a load in or on: *~ sacks onto a truck; a poor old woman ~ed (down) with her shopping.* ***load (sth) up,*** fill with goods, materials, etc: *Have you finished ~ing up (the van) yet?* **2** put ammunition into (a gun). **3** put a length of film into (a camera). **4** add extra weight to dice, so as to gain an unfair advantage. **5** (*baseball*) put base runners on the three bases.

loaded *adj* (*sl*) **(a)** having a lot of money; rich. **(b)** drunk.

ˌloaded ˈquestion, one that is intended to trap a person into making an admission which may be harmful.

loaf[1] /louf/ *n* (*pl* loaves /louvz/) **1** [C] bread shaped and cooked as a separate mass: *a two-pound ~.* ***Half a loaf is better than none,*** (*prov*) it is better to take a small amount that one is sure of getting than to run the risk of having nothing. **2** [C,U] (quantity of) food shaped and cooked: *(a) meat ~,* made of ground meat, eggs, etc: *ˈmeat ~.*

loaf[2] /louf/ *vi,vt* waste time; idle: *Don't ~ about while there's so much work to be done.*

loafer *n* [C] **(a)** one who habitually loafs. **(b)** kind of shoe for leisure dress, with an upper part like a moccasin. ⇨ illus at moccasin.

loam /loum/ *n* [U] fertile soil of sand and clay, often with much decayed vegetable matter in it.

loamy *adj* (-ier, -iest).

loan /loun/ *n* **1** [C] something lent, esp a sum of money: *a ˈbank ~.* **2** [U] lending or being lent: *I have the book out on ~ from the library.* □ *vt* = lend.

ˈloan·word *n* [C] word taken from another language.

loath, loth /louθ/ *adj* ***loath to do sth,*** unwilling.

loathe /louð/ *vt* feel disgust for; dislike greatly: *She was seasick, and ~d the smell of greasy food. He ~s traveling by air.*

loath·ing *n* [U] disgust.

loath·some /-səm/ *adj* disgusting; detestable: *a loathsome disease.*

loaves *pl* of loaf[1].

lob /lab/ *vi,vt* (-bb-) strike or throw (a ball) in a high arc (as in tennis). □ *n* [C] ball that is lobbed.

lobby /ˈlabi/ *n* [C] (*pl* -ies) **1** porch, entrance hall, corridor: *the ~ of a hotel/theater.* **2** group of people who try to influence lawmakers to support or oppose proposed legislation. □ *vt,vi* try to influence the members of a lawmaking body to pass laws in favor of a special interest.

ˈlobby·ist /-ɪst/ *n* [C] person who lobbies.

lobe /loub/ *n* [C] projecting rounded part, esp of an organ: *an ˈearˌ~.* ⇨ illus at ear, respiratory.

lobed *adj* having lobes.

lob·ster /ˈlabstər/ *n* **1** [C] shellfish having five pairs of legs (and in some kinds) with two large claws on the front pair, whose shell turns scarlet after cooking. ⇨ illus at crustacean. **2** [U] its flesh as food.

lo·cal /ˈloukəl/ *adj* **1** of, special to, a place or district: *the ~ doctor; ~ customs; ~ government.* **2** affecting a part, not the whole: *a ~ pain/injury/anesthetic.* **3** (of a train, bus, etc) making all stops on a route. □ *n* [C] **1** local train, bus, elevator, etc. **2** branch or chapter, esp of a labor union.

ˌlocal ˈcolor *n* [U] details in a story, drama, etc.

lo·cally /-kəli/ *adv*

lo·cale /louˈkæl/ *n* [C] scene of an event; locality, etc.

lo·cal·ity /louˈkæləti/ *n* (*pl* -ies) [C] position, particular place, and location in which an event occurs.

lo·cal·ize /ˈloukəˌlaiz/ *vt* make local, not general; confine within a particular part or area: *There is little hope of localizing the disease.*

lo·cal·iz·ation /ˌloukələˈzeiʃən / *n* [U]

lo·cate /ˈlouˌkeit/ *vt* **1** discover, show, the locality of: *~ a town on a map.* **2** establish in a place: *Where is the new factory to be ~d?*

lo·ca·tion /louˈkeiʃən/ *n* **1** [U] locating or being located. **2** [C] position or place: *suitable ~s for new factories.* **3** place outside the studio, where (part of) a motion picture is photographed. ***(be) on location,*** (be) filming at a location.

lock[1] /lak/ *n* [C] portion of hair that naturally hangs or clings together.

lock[2] /lak/ *n* [C] **1** device by which a door, lid, etc may be fastened with a bolt that needs a key to work it. ***under lock and key,*** locked up securely. **2** mechanism by which a gun is fired. ***lock, stock and barrel,*** completely. **3** section of a canal or river at a point where the water level changes, that can be closed off by gates so that water can be pumped in or out to raise or lower a ship. **4** hold in wrestling.

ˈlock·smith *n* [C] maker and mender of locks.

lock[3] /lak/ *vt,vi* **1** fasten (a door, box, etc) with a lock. ***lock sth away.*** **(a)** put it away in a locked box, drawer, etc. **(b)** (*fig*) keep securely: *have a secret safely ~ed (away) in one's heart.* ***lock sb in/out,*** keep him from leaving/entering, by locking the gate or door. ***lock sth/sb up,*** **(a)** make safe by locking it/him away: *Lock up your jewelry before you go away.* **(b)** shut up a house, etc by locking all the doors. **(c)** put (a person) in prison, a mental home, etc. **2** have a lock; become locked: *This door doesn't ~,* has no lock or has a lock that does not work. **3** (cause to) become fixed, unable to move: *He ~ed the wheels of the car to prevent its being stolen. They were ~ed in each other's arms. He ~ed his gaze/His gaze was ~ed on the distant object.* ***lock on to,*** (of a missile, etc) find and automatically follow (a target) by radar.

ˈlock·out *n* act of closing down a plant by an employer until the employees agree to his terms.

ˈlock·up *n* (*informal*) jail.

locker /ˈlakər/ *n* [C] compartment used for storing clothes, food, etc.

locket /ˈlakɪt/ *n* [C] small (often gold or silver) case for a portrait, a lock of hair, etc, usually worn around the neck on a chain.

lock·jaw /ˈlakˌdʒɔ/ *n* [U] **1** tetanus, a serious and sometimes fatal disease. **2** symptom of tetanus in which the muscles of the jaw tighten so that the jaw is held tightly closed.

loco /ˈlouˌkou/ *adj* (*sl*) crazy.

loco·mo·tion /ˌloukəˈmouʃən/ *n* [U] moving, ability to move, from place to place.

loco·mo·tive /ˌloukəˈmoutɪv/ *adj* of, having, causing, locomotion. □ *n* [C] self-propelled engine used for moving other cars on a railroad track.

lo·cust /ˈloukəst/ *n* **1** [C] (kinds of) grasshopper which flies in great swarms and destroys crops and vegetables. ⇨ illus at insect. **2** [C] cicada. **3** [C] (kind of) hard-wooded American tree with beanlike pods. **4** [U] wood of a locust tree.

lode /loud/ *n* [C] vein of metal ore.

lode·star /ˈloudˌstar/ *n* [C] guiding star by which a ship may be steered, esp the North Star.

lode·stone /ˈloudˌstoun/ *n* **1** [U] magnetized iron ore. **2** [C] any person or thing that attracts strongly.

lodge[1] /ladʒ/ *n* [C] **1** small house, esp one on an estate, occupied by a gardener or other employee. **2** house for temporary use: *a ˈhunting ~; a ˈski ~.* **3** inn or resort hotel. **4** (meeting place for) members of a branch of a society (such as the Freemasons). **5** animal den or lair. ⇨ beaver lodge.

lodge[2] /ladʒ/ *vt,vi* **1** supply (a person) with a room or shelter: *The shipwrecked sailors were ~d in the school.* **2** live, esp in rented quarters: *Where are you lodging now?* **3** ***lodge in,*** be or become fixed in: *The bullet ~d in his jaw.* **4** lay (a charge, etc) before the proper authorities: *~ a complaint against one's noisy neighbors with the police.*

lodger *n* [C] person lodging(2) in a house.

lodg·ing /ˈladʒɪŋ/ *n* [C,U] **1** (usually *pl*) room or rooms (not in a hotel) rented to live in. **2** temporary place to stay or sleep in: *Where can we find (a) ~ for the night?*

loft[1] /lɔft/ *n* [C] **1** attic. **2** large, undivided space under the roof of a warehouse. **3** hayloft. **4** gallery in a church or hall: *the ˈorgan ~.*

loft[2] /lɔft/ *vt* (*sport*) hit (a ball) high: *~ a ball over the fielders' heads.*

lofty /ˈlɔfti/ *adj* (-ier, -iest) **1** (not used of persons) of great height: *a ~ mountain/tower.* **2** high or elevated in spirit; noble: *~ sentiments; a ~ style.* **3** haughty; proud; consciously superior: *in a ~ manner.*

loft·ily /-əli/ *adv*

lofti·ness /ˈlɔftinɪs/ *n* [U]

log[1] /lɔg, lag/ *n* [C] **1** rough length of tree trunk that has fallen or been cut down. **2** cut piece of this; (as an *adjective*) *a ˌlog ˈcabin,* cabin made of logs. ***sleep like a log,*** sleep soundly. □ *vt* (*pt, pp* logged /lɔgd, lagd/, *present part* logging /ˈlɔgɪŋ, ˈlagɪŋ/) **1** cut down (trees) for lumber. **2** clear (land) of trees.

logger /ˈlɔgər, ˈlagər/ *n* [C] person who logs as a profession; lumberjack ⇨ lumber[1].

log·ging /ˈlɔgɪŋ, ˈlagɪŋ/ *n* [U] work of cutting down forest trees for lumber.

log[2] /lɔg, lag/ *n* [C] **1** device attached to a knotted line, trailed from a ship, to measure its speed through the water. **2** official record of events kept during a trip, esp of the position, speed, etc of a ship or aircraft. **3** any journal or record of performance. □ *vt* (-gg-) **1** enter (facts) in the log of a ship or aircraft. **2** travel (a certain distance) or reach (a certain speed).

log[3] /lɔg, lag/ *n* (short for) logarithm.

lo·gan·berry /ˈlougənˌberi/ *n* [C] (*pl* -ies) (large dark-red berry from a) plant that is related to the blackberry and the raspberry.

log·ar·ithm /ˈlɔgəˌrɪðəm, ˈlag-/ *n* [C] (*math*) number which indicates the power to which another number (called the *base*) must be raised in order to produce a specified result: *The ~ of 100 to the base 10 is 2.*

log·ger·head /ˈlɔgərˌhed, ˈlag-/ *n* [C] **1** large sea turtle found in the western parts of the Atlantic Ocean. **2** ***at loggerheads,*** disagreeing or disputing: *He's constantly at ~ with his wife.*

logic /ˈladʒɪk/ *n* [U] **1** study of the science, principles and rules of sound reasoning. **2** (esp correct or sound) reasoning: *argue with ~.*

logi·cal /-kəl/ *adj* **(a)** in accordance with the rules of logic. **(b)** able to reason correctly. **(c)** reasonable: *~al behavior.*

logi·cally /-kli/ *adv*

lo·gician /louˈdʒɪʃən/ *n* [C] person skilled in or using logic.

loin /lɔin/ *n* **1** (*pl*) the lower part of the body on both sides of the spine between the ribs and the hip bones. **2** [C] joint of meat which includes the loins: *~ of pork.* **3** (*pl*) **(a)** thighs and pubic area. **(b)** organs of reproduction.

ˈloin·cloth *n* [C] piece of cloth covering the loins (3).

loi·ter /ˈlɔitər/ *vi* **1** go slowly and stop frequently on the way somewhere: *~ on one's way home.* **2** hang around or stand about idly.

loi·terer *n* [C]

loll /lal/ *vi,vt* **1** rest, move or stand (*about/around*) in a lazy way. **2** (allow to) hang out loosely: *The dog's tongue was ~ing out.*

lol·li·pop, lol·ly·pop /ˈlaliˌpap/ *n* [C] lump of candy on a stick, held in the hand and sucked.

lone /loun/ *adj* **1** solitary; without companions. **2** unfrequented. (*Note:* occurs only before a *noun.*)

lone·ly /ˈlounli/ *adj* (-ier, -iest) **1** alone; without companions: *a ~ traveler.* **2** sad or melancholy because one is alone: *feel ~.* **3** (of places) not often visited; far from inhabited places or towns: *a ~ mountain village.*

lone·li·ness /-nɪs/ *n* [U] state of being lonely.

lone·some /ˈlounsəm/ *adj* = lonely(2,3).

long[1] /lɔŋ/ *adj* (-er /ˈlɔŋgər/, -est /ˈlɔŋgəst/) **1** (of extent in space) not short; of great length: *How ~ is the Mississippi River? She wore a ~ dress for the occasion.* ***the long arm of the law,*** its far-reaching power. **2** of great duration or extent in time: *He was ill for a ~ time. He won't be ~ (in) making up his mind,* will soon do so. **3** (of sounds) taking more time to utter than others: *"Feel" has a ~ vowel.* **4** extending into the future. ***take the long view,*** consider events, situations, etc in terms of the future, rather than the present situation, etc. ***in the ˈlong run,*** ⇨ run[1] (12). ***a ˈlong shot,*** **(a)** shot taken at a target standing at a great distance. **(b)** (*fig*) risk or gamble with little hope of success. ***not by a ˈlong shot,*** not at all.

long[2] /lɔŋ/ *adv* (-er /ˈlɔŋgər/, -est /ˈlɔŋgəst/) **1** for a long time: *Stay (for) as ~ as you like.* ***as/so long as,*** on condition that, provided that: *You may borrow the book so ~ as you return it.* ***before long,*** soon. **2** a long time before or after a certain time, event, etc: *~ before/after the party.* **3** for the duration of the specified time: *all day ~,* throughout the whole day. **4** ***longer than,*** after a certain point of time: *I can't wait any/much ~er than noon.* ***no longer,*** not now: *He's no ~er living here.* **5** ***so long,*** (*informal*) goodbye.

long[3] /lɔŋ/ *n* (only in) ***the long and the short of it,*** main idea or substance of something; the general effect or result.

long[4] /lɔŋ/ *vi* desire earnestly; wish for very much: *She ~ed for him to say something. I'm ~ing to see you.*

long·ing *n* [C,U] strong or earnest desire: *a ~ing to be home.* □ *adj* having or showing an earnest desire: *with ~ing eyes.*

long·ing·ly *adv*

long.[5] *abbr* = longitude.

long·boat /ˈlɔŋˌbout/ *n* [C] largest boat on a ship.

long-distance /ˌlɔŋ-ˈdɪstəns/ *adj, adv* **1** covering a long distance: *a ~ race.* **2** (of a telephone call) connecting with a point beyond the *local* range, and for which a special charge is usually made.

lon·gev·ity /lanˈdʒevəti/ *n* [U] long life.

long·hand /ˈlɔŋˌhænd/ *n* [U] ordinary handwriting (contrasted with printing and typing).

long·horn /ˈlɔŋˌhɔrn/ *n* [C] any of a breed of cattle with long horns, formerly common in the Southwestern US.

longi·tude /ˈlandʒəˌtud/ *n* [C] distance east or west (measured in degrees) from the prime meridian(1) at Greenwich, England.

longi·tudi·nal /ˌlandʒəˈtudənəl/ *adj* **(a)** of longitude. **(b)** of length. **(c)** running lengthwise: *longitudinal stripes.*

long-playing /ˌlɔŋ-ˈpleiɪŋ/ *adj* (of a record) turning at a rate of $33\frac{1}{3}$ revolutions a minute or less.

long-range /ˌlɔŋ-ˈreindʒ/ *adj* of long periods or distances: *a ~ weather forecast,* eg for one month ahead.

long·shore·man /ˌlɔŋˈʃɔrmən/ *n* [C] (*pl* -men /-men/) man employed at a wharf to load and unload cargo.

long-standing /ˌlɔŋ-ˈstændɪŋ/ *adj* that has

existed for a long time: *a ~ promise.*

long-suf·fer·ing /ˌlɔŋ-ˈsəfərɪŋ/ *adj* enduring long and patiently.

long-term /ˌlɔŋ-ˈtərm/ *adj* involving a long period of time.

long-winded /ˌlɔŋ-ˈwɪndɪd/ *adj* (*fig*) boring: tedious: *a ~ lecturer.*

look[1] /lʊk/ *n* [C] **1** act of looking: *Let me have a ~ at your new car.* ***take a look at,*** examine (briefly). **2** aspect; form in which something appears or is seen: *The town has a European ~.* **3** (*pl*) person's physical appearance: *She's beginning to lose her ~s,* her beauty. **4** expression, esp of the face: *He gave her an angry ~.*

look[2] /lʊk/ *vi,vt* **1** use one's eyes in order to see: *~ (up) at the ceiling; ~ (down) at the floor. We ~ed but saw nothing.* ***Look before you leap,*** (*prov*) do not act without considering the possible consequences. **2** seem to be, have a certain appearance: *~ sad/ill/tired.* ***(not) look oneself,*** (not) have one's normal appearance, health etc. ***look one's age,*** have an appearance that conforms to one's age: *You don't ~ your age,* look younger than you are. ***look one's best,*** appear most attractive, to the greatest advantage: *She ~s her best in black.* ***look blue,*** appear sad or discontented. ***look well,*** **(a)** (of persons) be healthy in appearance: *He's ~ing very well.* **(b)** (of things, a person) be attractive, pleasing: *Does this hat ~ well on me? He ~s well in naval uniform.* **3** ***look like/as if,*** appear, seem (to be); probably will: *It ~s like (it will) rain. You ~ as if you've seen a ghost!* **4** direct the eyes or attention to: *Look at your room; it's a mess!* **Look. . .!** (used to call attention or for emphasis): *Look, I'd really like to do it, but right now it's impossible.* **5** face; point toward: *The windows ~ north.* **6** (special uses with *adverbial particles* and *prepositions*):

look after sb/sth, **(a)** take care of; attend to: *He needs a wife to ~ after him.* **(b)** follow with the eyes: *They ~ed after the train as it left the station.*

look away (from sth), turn the eyes away.

look back (on sth), (*fig*) think about something in the past.

look down on sb, consider oneself superior to.

look down one's nose at sb, (*informal*) consider him to be inferior.

look for sb/sth, search for; try to find: *Are you still ~ing for a job?* ***be looking for trouble,*** behave in a way that will get one into trouble.

look forward to sth, think about something which will happen in the future (usually with pleasure): *We're ~ing forward to seeing you again.*

look in (on sb), make a short visit: *Won't you ~ in (on me) next time you're in town?*

look into sth, **(a)** investigate; examine: *~ into a question.* **(b)** look at (the inside of): *He ~ed into the box/the mirror/her eyes.*

look on, watch: *Why don't you play football instead of just ~ing on?*

look out (of sth) (at sth): *He stood and ~ed out (of the window) (at the view).* ***look out (for sb/sth),*** be prepared (for), be on the watch for: *Look out for reckless drivers.*

look over sth, inspect; examine: *Look over a house before buying it.*

look through, study; examine: *Look through your notes before the examination.*

look to sth, be careful of or about: *The country must ~ to its defenses.* ***look to sb for sth/to do sth,*** rely on: *They are all ~ing to you for help.*

look to/toward, ⇨look(5) above: *a house ~ing toward the river/to the south.*

look up, **(a)** raise the eyes: *Don't ~ up.* **(b)** (*informal*) improve; get better: *Business is ~ing up.* ***look sth up,*** search for (a word in a dictionary, facts in a guide, etc): *Please ~ up that information for me.* ***look sb up,*** visit: *Look me up next time you're in town.* ***look sb up and down,*** look at him coldly or critically.

look·ing glass /ˈlʊkɪŋ ˌglæs/ *n* [C] (*dated*) mirror.

look·out /ˈlʊˌkaut/ *n* **1** [C] place from which to watch. **2** [C] person who has the duty of watching. **3** [C] high place from which one can watch. **4** (*sing* only) prospect; what seems likely to happen.

loom[1] /lum/ *n* [C] machine for weaving cloth.

loom[2] /lum/ *vi* **1** appear indistinctly and in a threatening way: *The dark outline of another ship ~ed (up) through the fog.* **2** (*fig*) appear great and fill the mind: *The threat of nuclear weapons ~ed large in their minds.*

loon /lun/ *n* [C] **1** large fish-eating diving bird that has a loud, wild cry. **2** stupid person.

loony /ˈluni/ *n* [C] (*pl* -ies), *adj* (-ier, -iest) (*informal*) (person who is) crazy or foolish.

ˈloony bin, (*sl*) insane asylum.

loop /lup/ *n* [C] **1** (shape produced by a) curve crossing itself. **2** part of a length of string, wire, ribbon, metal, etc in such a shape, eg as a knot, fastening, or handle. **3** complete turn in the form of a loop, made by an aircraft. **4** closed or complete electric circuit. □ *vt,vi* **1** form or bend into a loop. **2** fasten with a loop: *~ things together.* **3** execute a loop in an airplane.

loop·hole /ˈlupˌhoul/ *n* [C] **1** narrow vertical opening in a wall (as in old forts, stockades, etc). **2** (*fig*) means of escape, esp one provided by unclear wording: *find a ~ in the law.*

loose[1] /lus/ *adj* (-r, -st) **1** not held, tied up, fastened, packed, or confined: *That dog is too dangerous to be left ~.* ***break/get loose,*** escape confinement: *One of the tigers in the zoo has broken/gotten ~.* **2** not close-fitting: *~ clothes.* **3** not tightly attached or fastened: *a ~ tooth.* ***come/work loose,*** become unfastened or insecure. **4** not tightly stretched or tense: *a ~ belt.* ***at loose ends,*** (*fig*) (of a person) having nothing to do. **5** not controlled; immoral: *~ conduct* **6** inexact; indefinite: *a ~ estimate.* **7** not compact; not closely packed: *~ soil; cloth with a ~ weave.*

loose·ly *adv*

loose[2] /lus/ *vt* **1** loosen (which is more usual): *Wine ~d his tongue,* made him talk freely. **2** discharge (esp an arrow).

loosen /ˈlusən/ *vt,vi* make or become loose or looser: *Loosen the screw. I must exercise and ~ up my muscles.*

loot /lut/ *n* [U] goods (esp private property) stolen, eg by thieves, or by soldiers in time of war. □ *vt,vi* carry off loot from.

looter *n* [C]

lop /lap/ *vt* (-pp-) cut off, chop (branches, etc from a tree).

lop-sided /ˈlapˌsaidid/ *adj* with one side lower than the other; unbalanced.

lope /loup/ *vi* move along with long, easy steps or strides. □ *n* [C] loping step, stride.

lord /lɔrd/ *n* [C] **1** supreme male ruler: *our sovereign ~ the King*. **2 Lord, (a)** God. **(b)** Christ. **3** (used in exclamations of surprise, etc): *Good Lord!* **4** (in some countries) nobleman (used as a title): *Lord Derby*. ***My Lord,*** (translation of) respectful formula for addressing certain noblemen and (in some countries) judges and bishops. **5** man in a position of authority. **6** (in feudal times) man of superior rank: *the ~ of the manor*, man from whom other men received land and to whom they owed service.

ˌLord's ˈPrayer, prayer taught by Christ to his followers.

ˌLord's ˈsup·per, = communion(4).

lord·ly /ˈlɔrdli/ *adj* (-ier, -iest) **1** arrogant; feeling superior. **2** like, suitable for, a lord.

lord·ship /ˈlɔrdˌʃip/ *n* **1** [U] rule, authority (*over*). **2 Lordship,** used in speaking to or of a Lord(4): *Your/His Lordship*.

lore /lɔr/ *n* [U] knowledge, esp as handed down from past times: *ˈfolk~*.

lose /luz/ *vt,vi* (*pt,pp* lost /lɔst/) **1** have taken away from one by accident, carelessness, misfortune, death, etc: *She has lost her husband*, he is dead. *He has lost his job*, has been dismissed. **2** fail to keep or maintain. ***lose one's balance,*** fall over. ***lose one's head,*** ⇨ head[1](20). ***lose interest (in sb/sth),*** cease to be interested in, attracted by. ***lose one's temper,*** become angry. **3** be unable to find: *I've lost the keys of my car*. ***lose one's place,*** be unable to find the page, paragraph, etc where one stopped reading. ***lose sight of,* (a)** fail to take account of: *We mustn't ~ sight of the fact that....* **(b)** no longer be able to see: *We lost sight of him in the crowd*. ***lose track of sth,*** ⇨ track(1). **4** miss or stray from: *~ one's way*. **5** fail to hear, see, etc: *They lost what was said in the applause that greeted him*. **6** cause (a person) the loss of: *Lateness will ~ you your job*. **7** fail to win, be defeated: *~ a game/a battle/a lawsuit*. ***lose out,*** fail to win or get: *lost out in the race for seats*. **8** (of a watch or clock) go too slowly; fail to keep correct time because of this: *My watch ~s two minutes a day*. **9** spend time, opportunity, efforts to no purpose; waste: *There's not a moment to ~. He lost no time in doing it*, did it at once. **10** ***lose oneself in sth,*** become deeply interested in it so that one is unaware of other things: *She lost herself in a book*.**11** get rid of: *I lost ten pounds on my diet*.

loser *n* [C] *He's a good/bad ~r*, is cheerful/discontented when he loses.

loss /lɔs/ *n* **1** [U] act or fact or process of losing: *Loss of health is more serious than ~ of money*. **2** [U] (and with *a, an*) failure to keep, maintain or use: *an enormous ~. There was a temporary ~ of power*. **3** [U] failure to win or obtain: *the ~ of a game/contract*. **4** [C] that which is lost: *suffer heavy ~es in war*, men killed, wounded, captured; ships and aircraft put out of action. ***a total loss,*** from which nothing can be saved: *The ship was wrecked and became a total ~*. **5** (*sing* only) disadvantage or deprivation: *Such a man is no great ~*, We need not regret losing his services. **6** ***(be) at a loss for sth/to do sth,*** be uncertain: *He was at a ~ for words, did not know how to express himself*.

lost /lɔst/ (*pt,pp* of lose) □ *adj* **1** misplaced; missing. **2** having gone astray. **3** not won. ***a lost cause,*** cause for which there is no hope of success. **4** ruined; destroyed: *~ hopes*. **5** gone; passed away: *~ youth*. **6** absorbed: *~ in thought*. **7** bewildered: *had a ~ look on his face*.

lot /lat/ *n* **1** [U] (one of a set of objects used in) the making of a selection or decision by methods depending on chance: *divide property by lot*. ***draw/cast lots,*** eg by taking pieces of paper marked in some way from a box: *They drew lots to decide who should begin*. **2** (*sing* only) decision or choice resulting from this: *The lot came/fell to me*. **3** (*sing* only) person's fortune or destiny: *His lot has been a hard one*. ***cast/throw in one's lot with sb,*** decide to share work, interests, money, etc. **4** [C] number of persons or things, thought of as a group: *We have received a new lot of coats from Paris*. **5** ***a lot of/lots of,*** a great amount or number (of): *What a lot of time you take to dress! I saw quite a lot of her* (= saw her often) *when I was in Houston last month*. ***a lot/lots*** (used *adverbially*) very much: *He's feeling a lot/lots better today*. **6** ***a bad lot,*** a bad sort or kind (of person, thing). **7** [C] plot of land: *a vacant lot*, a building site.

loth = loath.

lo·tion /ˈlouʃən/ *n* [C,U] (kind of) medicinal or cosmetic liquid for use on the skin: *~ for the face; soothing ~s for insect bites*.

lot·tery /ˈlatəri/ *n* [C] (*pl* -ies) contest in which the winner is determined by drawing lots.

lo·tus /ˈloutəs/ *n* [C] (*pl* -ses) **1** (kinds of) water lily, esp the Egyptian and Asiatic kinds. ⇨ illus at flower. **2** (*Gk myth*) fruit that caused forgetfulness and dreamy idleness.

ˈlotus-eater *n* person who engages in idle daydreaming.

loud /laud/ *adj* (-er, -est) **1** not quiet or soft; easily heard: *~ voices/cries/laughs*. **2** showy; forcing itself on the attention; □ *adv* in a loud manner: *Don't talk so ~*.

loud·ly *adv* in a loud manner: *Someone knocked ~ly at the door*.

loud·ness /-nis/ *n* [U]

loud·mouth /ˈlaudˌmauθ/ *n* [C] (*informal*) **1** person who talks loudly and too much. **2** one who does not keep secrets.

loud·speak·er /ˈlaudˌspikər *n* [C] (often shortened to **speaker**) part of a radio receiving apparatus that converts electric impulses into sounds and amplifies them.

lounge /laundʒ/ *vi* **1** sit, stand about or lie in a lazy way: *~d comfortably in a hammock*. **2** pass time idly; loaf: *lounging at street corners*. □ *n* [C] **1** comfortable sitting room, eg in a club or

hotel. **2** long couch.
ˈlounge chair, comfortable chair.
louse /laus/ *n* [C] (*pl* lice /lais/) **1** (kinds of) small insect living as a parasite on the bodies of animals and human beings. ⇨ illus at insect. **2** (*sl*) contemptible person: *He's an absolute ~.* □ *vt* ***louse up,*** (*sl*) make a mess of; bungle.
lousy /ˈlauzi/ *adj* (-ier, -iest) **1** infested with lice. **2** (*informal*) nasty; bad: *a ~ film.* **3** (*sl*) well provided (*with*): *He's ~ with money.*
lout /laut/ *n* [C] clumsy, stupid man.
ˈlout·ish /-ɪʃ/ *adj*
lov·able /ˈləvəbəl/ *adj* worthy of love: *a ~ child.*
love[1] /ləv/ *n* **1** [U] warm, kind feeling; fondness; affectionate and tender devotion: *a mother's ~ for her children; ~ of (one's) country.* ***not (to be had) for love or money,*** impossible (to get) for any price. ***There's no love lost between them,*** they dislike each other. ***a labor of love,*** ⇨ labor (2). **2** [U] sexual passion or desire for another person: *My ~ for you is deeper than the sea.* ***be/fall in love (with sb),*** feel/begin to feel love and desire (for). ***make love (to sb),*** **(a)** pay attention, to kiss, etc. **(b)** have sexual intercourse. **3** [C] **(a)** person or thing that is loved. **(b)** used to address someone who is loved: *Come here, my ~.* **4** [U] fondness; strong liking: *~ of adventure.* **5** (in games) no score: *~ all,* no score for either side.
ˈlove affair, ⇨ affair(3).
ˈlove·bird *n* [C] small brightly colored parrot which seems very fond of its mate.
ˈlove knot, bow of ribbon, tied in a special way, formerly given or worn as a pledge of love.
love·less *adj* without love: *a ~less marriage.*
ˈlove·lorn /-ˌlɔrn/ *adj* unhappy because one's love is not returned.
ˈlove·sick *adj* suffering because of (unreturned) love.
love[2] /ləv/ *vt* **1** have strong affection or deep tender feelings for: *loving one's parents/one's country.* **2** feel passion or desire for. **3** be very fond of; like; find pleasure in: *~ ice cream/new clothes/going to parties. "Will you come with me?"—"I'd ~ to."*
love·ly /ˈləvli/ *adj* (-ier, -iest) **1** beautiful; attractive; pleasing: *a ~ view; a ~ woman; ~ hair/weather.* **2** pleasant; enjoyable: *We had a ~ vacation. It's ~ and warm here,* pleasant because warm. **3** lovable: *Oh, she's a ~ person.*
love·li·ness /-nɪs/ *n* [U]
lover /ˈləvər/ *n* [C] **1** person who is fond of or devoted to (something): *a ~ of music/horses/good wine.* **2** (*pl*) two persons in love with each other: *happy ~s.* **3** (esp) man who loves a woman who is not his wife and has a sexual relationship with her.
lov·ing /ˈləvɪŋ/ *adj* feeling or showing love: *a ~ friend; ~ parents.*
lov·ing·ly *adv* in a loving way.
low[1] /lou/ *adj* (-er, -est) **1** not extending far upward; not high or tall: *a low wall/ceiling/shelf/hills. She was wearing a dress cut low in the neck/a ˈlow-necked dress,* one leaving shoulders and part of the breasts visible. ***lie low,*** (*fig*) keep hidden or quiet (and wait): *The escaped prisoners had to lie low for months.* **2** below the usual or normal level or intensity: *low pressure,* eg of the atmosphere, of gas or water. *The rivers were low during the dry summer.* **3** (of sounds) **(a)** not loud: *speak in a low voice.* **(b)** not high in pitch: *the low notes of a cello.* **4** lowly: *men of low birth/rank.* **5** commonplace; coarse; vulgar: *low manners/tastes.* ***bring sb/sth low,*** reduce in position, wealth, etc. **6** **(a)** feeble; lacking in strength of body or mind: *in a low state of health.* **(b)** unhappy; depressed: *feel low/in low spirits.* **7** of small amount as measured by a scale or by degrees: *a low temperature; low prices/wages/rates of pay.* ***have a low opinion of sb/sth,*** think very little of him, his work, etc. **8** short in supply; nearly exhausted: *The sugar is low.* **9** not highly developed: *low forms of life.* **10** **(a)** near the horizon: *The sun was low.* **(b)** near the equator.
ˈlow·born *adj* of humble birth.
ˈlow·bred *adj* having coarse manners.
ˈlow·brow *n* [C] *adj* (person) showing little interest in or taste for intellectual things.
ˈlow-down *adj* (*informal*) dishonorable: *low-down behavior/tricks.*
ˈlow·down *n* [U] (*sl*) truth; accurate information: *Let's get the low-down on that business.*
ˈlower case, (in printing) small letters, not capitals.
Lower Chamber/House, lower branch of a legislative assembly, eg the House of Representatives in US.
low·ness *n* [U]
low ˈtide/ˈwater, time when the tide is farthest from the shore or river bank.
low[2] /lou/ *adv* (-er, -est) in or to a low position, point, degree, etc; in a low manner; *aim/shoot low; bow low to the audience; buy low* (= at low prices) *and sell high. The coal is running low.*
low[3] /lou/ *n* [C] low level or figure: *Several industrial shares reached new lows yesterday.*
low[4] /lou/ *n* [U] sound made by cows. □ *vi* (of cows) make this sound.
low·boy /ˈlouˌbɔi/ *n* [C] low chest of drawers on long legs.
lower[1] /ˈlouər/ *vt,vi* **1** let or bring down: *~ the sails/a flag.* **2** make or become less in value, amount, etc: *~ the rent of a house.* **3** ***lower oneself,*** degrade, disgrace: *He would never ~ himself by taking bribes.* **4** drop, become less in volume: *She ~ed her voice to a whisper.*
lower[2] /ˈlauər/ *vi* **1** frown; look bad-tempered. **2** (of the sky, clouds) look dark, stormy.
lower·most /ˈlouərˌmoust/ *adj* = lowest.
low·land /ˈloulənd/ *n* [C] country or area that is low and usually flat.
low·ly /ˈlouli/ *adj* (-ier, -iest) humble; modest.
low·li·ness /-nɪs/ *n* [U]
loyal /ˈlɔiəl/ *adj* true and faithful (*to*): *~ supporters; ~ to one's country.*
ˈloyal·ist /-ɪst/ *n* [C] person who is loyal to his ruler and government, esp during a revolt.
loy·ally /ˈlɔiəli/ *adv*
loy·alty *n* [U] being loyal; loyal conduct.
loz·enge /ˈlazɪndʒ/ *n* [C] **1** four-sided, diamond-shaped figure. **2** piece of medicated candy, often of this shape: *ˈcough ~s.*
LP /ˌel ˈpi/ *n* [C] *abbr* = long-playing record: *I*

bought three new LPs yesterday. □ *adj* long-playing; *an LP-recording.*

LSD /ˌelˌesˈdi/ *n* [U] drug that causes hallucinations and other disturbances like those of mental illness.

Lt. *abbr* = Lieutenant.

Ltd. *abbr* = Limited.

lu·au /ˈluˌau/ *n* [C] Hawaiian feast.

lu·bri·cant /ˈlubrəkənt/ *n* [U] substance that lubricates.

lu·bri·cate /ˈlubrəˌkeit/ *vt* **1** put oil or grease into (machine parts) to make (them) work easily. **2** (*fig*) do something that makes action, etc easier.

lu·bri·ca·tion /ˌlubrəˈkeiʃən/ *n* [U]

lu·cid /ˈlusɪd/ *adj* **1** clear; easy to understand: *a ~ explanation.* **2** mentally sound: *~ intervals,* periods of sanity between periods of insanity.

lu·cid·ity /luˈsɪdəti/ *n* [U]

lu·cid·ly *adv*

luck /lək/ *n* [U] **1** chance; fortune (good or bad); something considered to come by chance: *have good/bad ~.* **2** good fortune: *He had beginner's ~.* ***Good Luck!*** (used to encourage, express hopes of good fortune, etc). ***in/out of luck,*** fortunate/unfortuate.

luck·less *adj* unfortunate; turning out badly: *a ~less day/attempt.*

lucky /ˈləki/ *adj* (-ier, -iest) having, bringing, resulting from, good luck: *a ~ man/guess/escape. You are ~ to be alive after being in that accident.*

luck·ily /ˈləkəli/ *adv* fortunately: *Luckily, the train was late, so I just caught it.*

lu·cra·tive /ˈlukrətɪv/ *adj* profitable.

lu·di·crous /ˈludəkrəs/ *adj* ridiculous; absurd.

lu·di·crous·ly *adv*

lug[1] /ləg/ *vt* (-gg-) pull or drag roughly and with much effort: *lugging two heavy suitcases up the stairs.*

lug[2] /ləg/ *n* [C] **1** projecting, earlike part used as a handle. **2** (*sl*) clumsy, stupid person.

lug·gage /ˈləgɪdʒ/ *n* [U] bags, trunks, etc and their contents taken on a journey; baggage: *six pieces of ~.*

lu·gu·bri·ous /lʊˈgubriəs/ *adj* (*formal*) dismal; mournful.

lu·gu·bri·ous·ly *adv*

luke·warm /ˌlukˈwɔrm/ *adj* **1** neither very warm nor cold. **2** (*fig*) not enthusiastic; indifferent: *give only ~ support to a cause.*

lull /ləl/ *vt,vi* cause to sleep or rest: *~ a baby to sleep,* eg by rocking it and singing to it. □ *n* [C] interval of quiet or calm: *a ~ in the storm/in the conversation.*

lul·laby /ˈləlәˌbai/ *n* [C] (*pl* -ies) song for lulling a child to sleep.

lum·bago /ləmˈbeigou/ *n* [U] muscular pain in the lumbar regions.

lum·bar /ˈləmbər, ˈləmbar/ *adj* of the loins: *the ~ regions,* the lower part of the back.

lum·ber[1] /ˈləmbər/ *n* [U] wood that has been sawed into planks, boards, etc. □ *vi* cut trees for lumber.

ˈlum·ber·jack *n* [C] person who fells trees, saws or transports lumber.

lum·ber[2] /ˈləmbər/ *vi* move in a heavy, clumsy, noisy way: *The tanks ~ed along/by/past.*

lu·min·ary /ˈluməˌneri/ *n* [C] (*pl* -ies) **1** something that gives light, as the sun or moon. **2** (*fig*) famous or outstanding person.

lu·mi·nous /ˈlumənəs/ *adj* **1** giving out light; bright: *~ paint,* as used on road signs, clocks and watches, visible in the dark. **2** (*fig*) easily understood.

lu·mi·nos·ity /ˌluməˈnasəti/ *n* [U]

lump[1] /ləmp/ *n* [C] **1** hard or compact mass, usually without a regular shape: *a ~ of coal/sugar.* ***a lump ˈsum,*** one payment for a number of separate sums that are owed. **2** abnormal swelling or bump: *He has a bad ~ on the forehead.* ***have a lump in one's throat,*** a feeling of pressure (as caused by strong emotion). □ *vt* form into lumps. ***lump together,*** put together in one group or mass: *Can we ~ all these items together under the heading "incidental expenses"?*

lumpy *adj* (-ier, -iest) full of, covered with, lumps: *~y gravy.*

lump[2] /ləmp/ *vt* (only in) ***lump it,*** (*informal*) put up with something unpleasant or unwanted: *If you don't like it you can ~ it.*

lu·nacy /ˈlunəsi/ *n* [U] **1** insanity. **2** foolishness.

lu·nar /ˈlunər/ *adj* of the moon.

ˌlunar ˈmodule, detachable section of a spacecraft, designed to land on the surface of the moon and to return to the spacecraft.

ˌlunar ˈmonth, average time between successive new moons, about 29½ days.

lu·na·tic /ˈlunəˌtɪk/ *n* [C] insane person (the preferred term). □ *adj* **1** insane; extremely foolish: *a ~ proposal.* **2** of or for insane persons.

ˈlunatic asylum, (*dated*) mental home or hospital.

lunch /ləntʃ/ *n* [C] **1** meal taken in the middle of the day: *They were at ~ when I called.* **2** food for this. □ *vi* eat lunch.

lunch·eon /ˈləntʃən/ *n* [C] (esp formal) lunch.

lung /ləŋ/ *n* [C] either of the two breathing organs in the chest of man and other animals. ⇨ illus at respiratory.

lunge /ləndʒ/ *n* [C] sudden forward movement, eg with a sword, or forward movement of the body (eg when aiming a blow). □ *vi* make a lunge: *lunging out suddenly.*

lu·pine, lu·pin /ˈlupɪn/ *n* [C] plant with tall spikes of flowers of various colors.

lurch[1] /lərtʃ/ *n* (only in) ***leave sb in the lurch,*** leave him without help in a difficult situation.

lurch[2] /lərtʃ/ *n* [C] sudden movement to one side; sudden roll or pitch: *The ship gave a ~ to starboard.* □ *vi* move along with a lurch: *The drunken man ~ed across the street.*

lure /lʊr/ *n* [C] **1** bait or decoy to attract wild animals. **2** (*fig*) something that attracts or entices: *the ~ of the sea; the ~s used by a pretty woman.* □ *vt* attract, tempt: *~ him away from his duty.*

lu·rid /ˈlʊrɪd/ *adj* **1** highly colored, esp suggesting flame and smoke: *a ~ sky/sunset; ~ thunderclouds.* **2** (*fig*) sensational; shocking: *~ details of a railway accident.*

lurid·ly *adv*

lu·rid·ness /-nɪs/ *n* [U]

lurk /lərk/ *vi* **1** be, keep, out of view, lying in wait or ready to attack: *a man ~ing in the shadows. Some suspicion still ~ed in his mind.* **2** move furtively; sneak.

luscious /ˈləʃəs/ *adj* **1** rich and sweet in taste and smell; delicious: *~ peaches.* **2** pleasing to the eye, ear, etc; delightful: *~ lips.*

lush[1] /ləʃ/ *adj* **1** (esp of grass and vegetation) growing luxuriantly: *~ meadows.* **2** (*fig*) luxuriously comfortable.

lush[2] /ləʃ/ *n* [C] (*sl*) alcoholic.

lust /ləst/ *n* **1** [U] great desire or longing. **2** [U] strong sexual desire (*for*): *filled with ~.* **3** [C] instance of this: *a ~ for power/gold; the ~s of the flesh.* □ *vi* have lust for: *~ for/after gold.*

ˈlust·ful /-fəl/ *adj* full of lust.

ˈlust·fully /-fəli/ *adv*

luster /ˈləstər/ *n* [U] **1** bright, soft light as reflected from a smooth or polished surface: *the ~ of pearls.* **2** (*fig*) glory; distinction: *add ~ to one's name.*

lus·trous /ˈləstrəs/ *adj* glossy; having luster: *~ pearls/eyes.*

lusty /ˈləsti/ *adj* (-ier, -iest) healthy and strong; vigorous: *a ~ girl; ~ cheers.*

ˈlust·ily /-əli/ *adv*

lute /lut/ *n* [C] stringed musical instrument with a pear-shaped body, played by plucking the strings.

lux·uri·ant /ləgˈʒʊriənt/ *adj* **1** strong in growth; abundant: *the ~ vegetation of the tropics.* **2** richly ornamented; very elaborate.

lux·uri·ance /-əns/ *n* [U]

lux·uri·ant·ly *adv*

lux·uri·ate /ləgˈʒʊriˌeit/ *vi* (*formal*) take great delight (in): *~ in the warm spring sunshine.*

lux·uri·ous /ləgˈʒʊriəs/ *adj* supplied with luxuries; characterized by luxury: *a ~ hotel; ~ habits.*

lux·uri·ous·ly *adv*

lux·ury /ˈləkʃəri, ˈləgʒəri/ *n* (*pl* -ies) **1** [U] way of life in which one has and uses things that please the senses (good food and drink, clothes, comfort, beautiful surroundings): *live in ~; a life of ~;* (as an *adjective*) *a ~ hotel.* **2** [C] something not essential but which gives enjoyment and pleasure, esp something expensive, out of season, etc: *His salary is low and he gets few luxuries.*

-ly /-li/ *suffix* **1** (*n* + -ly = *adj*) having the qualities of: *cowardly.* **2** (*n* + -ly = *adj* or *adv*) at a regular interval: *hourly.* **3** (*adj* + -ly = *adv*) in the manner of: *stupidly.*

ly·chee = litchi.

lye /lai/ *n* [U] strong alkali used in making soap, paper, etc.

ly·ing /ˈlaiɪŋ/ *pres participle* of lie[1], lie[2].

lymph /lɪmf/ *n* [U] colorless fluid in the tissues of the body, consisting of white blood cells and a liquid similar to blood plasma.

lym·phatic /lɪmˈfætɪk/ *adj* of or carrying lymph.

lynch /lɪntʃ/ *vt* put to death (esp by hanging) without a lawful trial.

lynx /lɪŋks/ *n* [C] short-tailed wild animal of the cat family, noted for its keen sight. ⇨ illus at cat.

ˈlynx-ˌeyed *adj* keen-sighted.

lyre /ˈlaiər/ *n* [C] kind of harp with strings fixed in a U-shaped frame, used by the ancient Greeks.

lyric /ˈlɪrɪk/ *adj* **1** of or like a song. **2** of poetry that expresses the poet's emotions about love, death, etc. □ *n* [C] **1** lyric poem. **2** (*pl*) words of a song.

lyri·cal /ˈlɪrɪkəl/ *adj* **1** = lyric. **2** full of emotion; enthusiastic.

lyri·cally /-kli/ *adv*

m

M[1], **m** /em/ (*pl* M's, m's /emz/) **1** the thirteenth letter of the English alphabet. **2** Roman numeral for 1000.

M[2] *abbr* = Mach.

m[3] *abbr* = **1** mile(s). **2** meter(s).

m.[4] *abbr* = **1** minute(s). **2** male. **3** masculine. **4** married.

MA[1] *postal abbr* = Massachusetts. ⇨ App 6.

M.A.[2] /ˌem ˈei/ *abbr* = Master of Arts. □ *n* [C] (*pl* M.A.'s) (one who has a) Master of Arts degree.

ma[3] /ma/ *n* [C] (*informal*) (short for) mamma, mother.

ma'am /mæm/ *n* [C] madam (only when used as a form of address).

ma·cabre /məˈkabrə, -bər/ *adj* gruesome; suggesting death.

mac·adam /məˈkædəm/ *n* [C,U] (road of) finely crushed rock or stone, packed down in a layer and rolled hard before the next layer is put down.

mac·adam·ize *vt* make or pave (a road) with macadam.

maca·roni /ˌmækəˈrouni/ *n* [U] (*I*) pasta made in the form of hollow tubes (often chopped into short pieces).

maca·roon /mæk(ə)ˈrun/ *n* [C] small cookie made of sugar, white of egg, and ground almonds or coconut.

ma·caw /məˈkɔ/ *n* large, long-tailed parrot of tropical America.

mace[1] /meis/ *n* [C] **1** large, heavy club, usually with a metal head covered with spikes, used as a weapon in the Middle Ages. **2** ceremonial rod or staff carried by or before an official, as a symbol of authority.

mace[2] /meis/ *n* [U] spice made from the dried outer covering of nutmegs.

Mach /mak/ *n* (also ˈ**Mach number**) ratio of the air speed of an aircraft to the speed of sound: *~ two*, twice the speed of sound.

ma·chete /məˈʃeti, məˈtʃeti/ *n* [C] broad, heavy knife used in Latin America as a tool and weapon.

Machi·a·vel·lian /ˌmækiəˈveliən/ *adj* showing or having no scruples in gaining what is wanted.

machi·na·tion /ˌmækəˈneiʃən/ *n* [C] evil plot or scheme.

ma·chine /məˈʃin/ *n* [C] **1** appliance or mechanical device with parts working together to perform some desired task: *a sewing ~*. **2** device (as a lever or pulley) that is used to apply or change the direction of power, force, etc. **3** (*dated*) vehicle, esp an automobile. **4** group of persons controlling a political party: *the party ~*. □ *vt* cut, shape, make (something) with, a machine.

ma·chin·ist /məˈʃinɪst/ *n* [C] **(a)** person who makes, repairs or runs machine tools. **(b)** person who runs a machine.

ma·chine gun /məˈʃin ˌgən/ *n* [C] gun that fires repeatedly while the trigger is pressed.

ma·chin·ery /məˈʃinəri/ *n* [U] **1** moving parts of a machine. **2** (*collect*) machines: *How much new ~ has been installed?* **3** any system or organization for getting something done: *the ~ of government*.

ma·chine tool /məˈʃin ˌtul/ *n* [C] automatic tool (as a lathe) that cuts and shapes materials.

mack·erel /ˈmækrəl/ *n* [C] (*pl* ~) kind of ocean fish used as food.

mack·i·naw /ˈmækəˌnɔ/ *n* [C] short coat made of heavy woolen cloth usually in a plaid pattern.

mad /mæd/ *adj* (-dder, -ddest) **1** crazy; insane. ***drive sb mad,*** cause him to become mad. ***go mad,*** become mad, crazy. **2** (*informal*) filled with great enthusiasm: *mad about pop music*. **3** frantic; wildly excited: *in a mad rush*. **4** (*informal*) angry: *They were mad about missing the train. Dad got mad at/with me for coming home late*. **5** (of a dog, etc) rabid.

mad·ly *adv* **(a)** in a mad manner. **(b)** (*informal*) extremely: *madly excited/in love*.

ˈ**mad·man/-woman** /-ˌmæn, -ˌwʊmən/ (*pl* madmen /-ˌmen/, madwomen /-ˌwɪmɪn/) one who is mad(1).

mad·ness /-nɪs/ *n* [U]

madam /ˈmædəm/ *n* **1** (used alone as a respectful form of address to a woman whether married or unmarried): *Can I help you, ~?* **2** (used in formal letters): *Dear Madam*. **3** (used with a title of office): *Madam Chairman*. **4** (usually older) woman in charge of the prostitutes in a house of prostitution: *Then she went to San Francisco, where she set herself up as a ~*.

mad·cap /ˈmædˌkæp/ *n* [C] wild, reckless person.

mad·den /ˈmædən/ *vt* **1** make mad or insane. **2** make angry; irritate.

mad·den·ing *adj* infuriating: *~ing delays*.

made *pt,pp* of make[1].

Ma·donna /məˈdanə/ *n* **the Madonna,** (picture or statue of) Mary, Mother of Jesus Christ.

mad·ras /məˈdræs/ *n* [U] fine cotton cloth, usually of a striped or checked pattern.

mad·ri·gal /ˈmædrɪgəl/ *n* [C] song for several voices without instrumental accompaniment.

mael·strom /ˈmeiəlstrəm/ *n* [C] **1** great whirlpool. **2** (*fig*) similarly violent or destructive force: *the ~ of war*.

maes·tro /ˈmaistrou/ *n* [C] (*pl* ~s, maestri /ˈmaistri/) (*I*) distinguished or eminent musical composer, teacher, or conductor.

Mafia /ˈmafiə/ *n* [U] (usually **the Mafia**) family-based criminal organization, said to be derived from Italy.

maga·zine /ˌmægəˈzin, ˈmægəˌzin/ *n* [C] **1** store for arms, ammunition, explosives, etc. **2** chamber for holding cartridges in a gun. **3** place for rolls or cartridges of film in a camera. **4** (weekly or monthly) periodical, with stories, articles, etc by various writers.

ma·genta /məˈdʒentə/ *adj, n* [U] bright purplish red (color).

mag·got /ˈmægət/ *n* [C] larva, eg of the housefly.

mag·goty *adj* having maggots: *~y cheese*.

Magi /ˈmeiˌdʒai/ *n pl* **the Magi,** in the Bible, the three wise men from the East who brought offerings to the infant Jesus.

magic /ˈmædʒɪk/ *adj* done by, or as if by, magic; possessing magic; used in magic: *~ arts/words; a ~ touch*. □ *n* [U] **1** art of controlling events by the supposed use of supernatural forces. ***as if by/like magic,*** in a mysterious manner. **2** art of obtaining mysterious results by tricks: *use ~ to produce a rabbit*. **3** (*fig*) mysterious charm; quality that enchants: *the ~ of poetry*.

ˌblack ˈmagic, ⇨ black.

magi·cal /-kəl/ *adj* = magic.

magi·cally /-kli/ *adv*

ma·gician /məˈdʒɪʃən/ *n* [C] **1** person who uses magic(1); wizard. **2** person who entertains with magic(2).

magis·ter·ial /ˌmædʒəˈstɪriəl/ *adj* **1** of, relating to, a magistrate or his duties. **2** having or showing authority: *a ~ manner*.

magis·ter·ially /-iəli/ *adv*

magis·tracy /ˈmædʒəstrəsi/ *n* [C] (*pl* -ies) **1** position of a magistrate. **2** (with *the*) magistrates collectively.

magis·trate /ˈmædʒəˌstreit/ *n* [C] **1** official with the power to administer the law. **2** minor official, as a judge in a police court or a justice of the peace.

mag·nani·mous /mægˈnænəməs/ *adj* having, showing, generosity and unselfishness.

mag·na·nim·ity /ˌmægnəˈnɪməti/ *n* [C,U]

mag·nani·mous·ly *adv*

mag·nate /ˈmægˌneit/ *n* [C] influential and powerful leader of business or industry.

mag·nesia /mægˈniʒə/ *n* [U] white, tasteless powder (symbol **MgO**) used in medicine and in industry.

mag·nesium /mægˈniziəm/ *n* [U] silver-white metallic element (symbol **Mg**) used in the manufacture of aluminum and other alloys, and in photography: *~ light*, bright light obtained by burning magnesium.

mag·net /ˈmægnɪt/ *n* [C] **1** piece of iron able to attract iron, either naturally (as in lodestone) or by means of an electric current. **2** (*fig*) person or thing that attracts.

mag·net·ic /mægˈnetɪk/ *adj* **1** of a magnet or magnetism. **2** having the properties of a magnet: *the ~ field*, area in which a magnetic force may be detected. **3** of or relating to the magnetism of the earth. **4** having the power to attract: *a ~ smile/personality*.

mag·neti·cally /-kli/ *adv*

ˌmagnetic ˈneedle, narrow, magnetized steel rod used in a magnetic compass to indicate the direction of the earth's magnetism.

ˌmagnetic ˈnorth, the point indicated by the north-seeking pole of a magnetic needle.

ˌmagnetic ˈpole, either of the two points on the earth's surface at which the earth's magnetic field is strongest.

ˌmagnetic ˈtape, kind of tape coated with iron oxide used for recording sounds and images.

mag·net·ism /ˈmægnəˌtɪzəm/ *n* [U] **1** (the science of) magnetic phenomena and properties. **2** (*fig*) personal charm and attraction.

mag·net·ize /ˈmægnəˌtaiz/ *vt* **1** give magnetic properties to. **2** (*fig*) attract; charm.

mag·ne·to /mægˈnitou/ *n* [C] (*pl* ~s) small generator in some engines, that uses magnets to produce an electrical current.

mag·nifi·cent /mægˈnɪfəsənt/ *adj* **1** splendid; grand: *a ~ cathedral*. **2** outstanding; remarkable: *his ~ generosity*.

mag·nifi·cence /-səns/ *n* [U]

mag·nifi·cent·ly *adv*

mag·nify /ˈmægnəˌfai/ *vt* (*pt,pp* -ied) **1** make (a person or thing) appear larger (as with a lens or microscope). **2** exaggerate: *~ dangers*.

mag·ni·fi·ca·tion /ˌmægnəfəˈkeiʃən/ *n* [U] (esp) power of magnifying, eg of a lens, a pair of binoculars.

mag·ni·fier /-ˌfaiər/ *n* [C] instrument, etc that magnifies.

ˈmagnifying glass, lens for making objects look larger than they really are.

mag·ni·tude /ˈmægnəˌtud/ *n* [C] (*formal*) **1** size. **2** greatness of size, importance, etc. **3** comparative brightness of stars.

mag·no·lia /mægˈnouliə/ *n* [C] (tree or shrub bearing a) large, showy, usually white or pink flower, common to the southern US, blooming in early spring.

mag·pie /ˈmægˌpai/ *n* [C] **1** noisy black and white bird which is attracted by, and often takes away, small, bright objects. **2** (*fig*) person who chatters a great deal.

ma·hog·any /məˈhagəni/ *n* [C,U] (tropical tree with) reddish-brown wood used for making furniture.

maid /meid/ *n* **1** (*liter*) girl. **2** (*old use*) young, unmarried woman. **3** woman servant: *It's the ~'s day off*.

ˌold ˈmaid, elderly unmarried woman.

ˌmaid of ˈhonor, (a) unmarried woman who is the chief attendant of a bride at a wedding. **(b)** unmarried noble woman attending a queen or princess.

maiden /ˈmeidən/ *n* [C] (*liter*) unmarried girl or woman. □ *adj* **1** of a maiden. **2** first or earliest: *a ship's ~ voyage*. **3** (of an older woman) unmarried: *my ~ aunt*.

ˈmaiden·hood *n* [U] state, period, of being a maiden.

ˈmaiden·ly *adj* gentle; modest; of, like, or suitable to a maiden.

ˌmaiden ˈname, family name of a woman before marriage.

mail¹ /ˈmeiəl/ *n* [U] flexible body armor of metal rings or plates: *a coat of ~; ˈchain-~.*

mail² /ˈmeiəl/ *n* **1** [U] government system of collecting, carrying and delivering letters and parcels: *send a letter by ˈair~.* **2** [C,U] **(a)** letters, parcels, etc, sent or delivered by post. **(b)** the letters, etc, sent collected or delivered at one time: *Is there any ~ this morning?* □ *vt* (*pres p* ~ing /ˈmeiliŋ/) send by mail.

ˈmail·box *n* [C] **(a)** public box for the collection of mail. **(b)** private box for the delivery of mail.

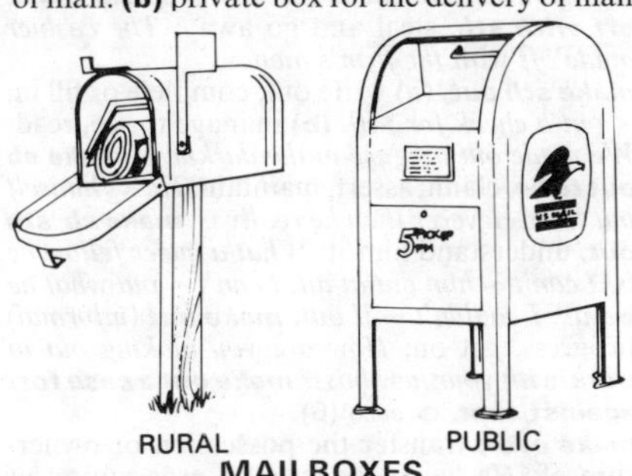

MAILBOXES

ˈmail·man /-ˌmæn/ *n* [C] (*pl* ~men /-ˌmen/) person who delivers mail; postman.

ˈmail ˌorder, order for goods to be delivered by mail.

maim /meim/ *vt* wound or injure so that some part of the body is useless; cripple: *He was seriously ~ed in the war.*

main¹ /mein/ *adj* chief; most important: *the ~ thing to remember; the ~ street of a town; the ~ point of my argument; the ~ course of a meal.* (*Note: main* is used only before a *noun.*)

main·ly *adv* chiefly; for the most part: *You are ~ly to blame.*

main² /mein/ *n* **1** [C] principal pipe bringing water or gas, principal wire transmitting electric current, from the source of supply into a building: *My new house is not yet connected to the water ~.* **2** ***in the main,*** for the most part; on the whole. **3** (only in) ***with might and main,*** physical force; strength. **4** (*poet*) sea, esp a wide expanse of sea.

main·land /ˈmeinlənd, -ˌlænd/ *n* [C] country, continent or land mass, without its islands.

main·mast /ˈmeinˌmæst, among sailors ˈmeinməst/ *n* [C] chief mast of a sailing ship.

main·sail /ˈmeinˌseiəl, among sailors ˈmeinsəl/ *n* [C] principal sail on a mainmast. ⇨ illus at ship.

main·spring /ˈmeinˌspriŋ/ *n* [C] **1** principal spring of a clock or watch. **2** (*fig*) driving force or motive.

main·stay /ˈmeinˌstei/ *n* [C] (*fig*) chief support.

main·stream /ˈmeinˌstrim/ *n* [C] dominant trend, tendency, etc: *the ~ of political thought.*

main·tain /meinˈtein/ *vt* **1** keep up; retain; continue: *~ friendly relations with one's neighbors; ~ law and order; ~ a speed of 60 miles an hour.* **2** support: *~ a son at college.* **3** assert as true: *~ one's innocence/that one is innocent.* **4** keep in good repair or working order: *~ the roads.* **5** defend: *~ one's rights.*

main·tain·able /-əbəl/ *adj* that can be maintained.

main·te·nance /ˈmeintənəns/ *n* [U] **1** maintaining or being maintained. **2** work of keeping or maintaining in good repair. **3** means of supporting life.

maize /meiz/ *n* [U] = Indian corn. ⇨ illus at cereal.

Maj. *abbr* = Major.

ma·jes·tic /məˈdʒestik/ *adj* having, showing, majesty.

ma·jes·ti·cally /-kli/ *adv*

maj·esty /ˈmædʒəsti/ *n* (*pl* -ies) **1** [U] impressive appearance; grandeur. **2** [U] royal power or dignity. **3 His/Her/Your Majesty; Their/Your Majesties,** (form used when speaking of or to a sovereign ruler or rulers).

ma·jor¹ /ˈmeidʒər/ *adj* **1** (contrasted with *minor*) greater or more important: *~ roads; a ~ operation,* (in surgery) one that may be dangerous to the person's life. **2** greater in number or amount: *got the ~ share of the money.* **3** (*music*) of or based on a major scale. □ *vi* ***major in sth,*** specialize in a certain field of study: *Brian ~ed in economics.*

ma·jor² /ˈmeidʒər/ *n* [C] **1** commissioned officer in the US army, air force, or marine corps, who ranks above a captain and below a lieutenant colonel. **2(a)** student's chief field of study. **(b)** student specializing in a particular field: *an ˈEnglish ~.*

ˌmajor ˈgeneral, commissioned officer in the US army, air force, or marine corps who ranks above a brigadier general and below a lieutenant general.

ˌmajor ˈleague, sports league or association ranking among the highest class of professional sports in the US.

ˌmajor ˈscale, (*music*) scale with half steps after the third and seventh notes.

ma·jor·ity /məˈdʒɔrəti/ *n* [C] (*pl* -ies) **1** (used with a *sing* or *pl verb*) greater number or part (*of*): *The ~ were/was in favor of the proposal.* **2** number by which votes for one side exceed those for the other side: *He was elected by a large ~/by a ~ of 3,749.* **3** (*sing* only) age of legal responsibility: *He will reach his ~ next month.*

make¹ /meik/ *vt,vi* (*pt,pp* made /meid/) **1** construct or produce by combining parts or putting materials together; form or shape from material: *~ bread. Cloth is made of cotton, wool, nylon and other materials.* **2** cause to exist: *I don't want to ~ any trouble for you. John and Mary seem to have been made for each other,* eg because they get on so well together. *~ a hole in the ground/a gap in a hedge.* **3** enact; establish: *Who made this ridiculous rule?* **4** execute: *A treaty has been made with our former enemies.* **5** prepare; set up: *made a lunch/dinner; ~ a bed.* **6** frame or form in the mind: *~ plans for a trip.* **7** carry out; engage in: *~ war.* **8** cause to be or become: *The news made her happy. He soon made himself understood. She was made head of the department.* ***make it worth sb's while (to do sth),*** pay or reward him: *If you will help me* *with this job, I'll ~ it worth your while.* ***make*** + *noun* + ***of (sth/sb); make sth/sb (into) sth,*** cause a person or thing to be or become: *His parents want to ~ a doctor of him*, want him to be educated for the medical profession. *Don't ~ a habit of it/~ it a habit*, don't let it become a habit. ***make an ass/a fool of oneself,*** behave stupidly. **9** earn; win; gain; acquire: *~ a profit of $500. He first made his reputation as a state senator.* ***make one's living (as/at/by/from),*** earn one's livelihood: *He ~s his living as a teacher/from teaching/by giving piano lessons.* **10** cause the success of: *That one experience made the trip.* ***make it,*** (*informal*) succeed: *Couldn't ~ it as an actor.* ***make or break,*** cause to achieve success or ruin. **11** score: *~ 10 points in a game.* **12** (*informal*) win or achieve a certain rank, status, etc: *He made colonel by the end of the war.* **13** compel; force; persuade; cause (sth) to happen: *Can you ~ this old car start? He made them agree to his terms. His jokes made us all laugh.* ***make believe (that),*** pretend: *The boys made believe that they were pioneers in the Wild West.* ⇨ make-believe. ***ˌmake one's ˈblood boil/one's ˈhackles rise,*** make one furious. ***make ends meet,*** make one's income cover all one's expenses: *I don't know how she ~s ends meet.* ***make sth do; make do with sth,*** manage with it although it may not be really adequate or satisfactory: *You'll have to ~ do with cold meat for dinner.* ***ˌmake one's ˈhair stand on end,*** ⇨ hair(1). **14** have the necessary qualities for: *Cheese ~s a good snack. This box ~s a comfortable seat.* **15** estimate or reckon (to be): *I ~ the distance to be about 70 miles.* **16** come to, equal; add up to; amount to (in significance): *5 and 7 ~ 12. This ~s the fifth time you're failed the examination.* ***make (good/much/little) sense,*** seem sensible: *His arguments have never made much sense.* **17** turn into; turn out to be; prove to be: *She will ~ him a good wife.* **18** travel: *We've made 80 miles since noon.* **19** catch: *The train leaves at 7:13; can we ~ it?* **20** reach: *When does the ship ~ port?* **21** ***make as if,*** behave as if about to (do something): *He made as if to hit me.* **22** (used with many *nouns* where *make* and the *noun* together have the same meaning as a *verb* related in form to the *noun*). ***make allowance(s) (for),*** ⇨ allowance(2). ***make an application (to sb) (for sth),*** apply (to somebody) (for something). ***make arrangements for,*** arrange for. ***make an attempt,*** attempt. ***make a decision,*** decide. ***make a demand,*** demand. ***make an offer,*** offer. ***make a success of (sth),*** succeed in/with. For other phrases of this kind, ⇨ the *noun* entries. **23** (used with *nouns* in special senses. The examples below are a selection only; for definitions ⇨ the entry for the *noun* in the example): *~ an* appointment; *~ the* bed(1); *~ the* best *of; ~ a* bid *for; ~ an* effort*; ~ an* excuse; *~* eyes *at; ~ a* face; *~* fun *of; ~ a* fuss; *~ a* go²(3) *of sth; ~* head *or tail of; ~* love*(to); ~ a* man *of; ~ the* most *of; ~* much *of; ~ a* name *for oneself; ~ a* night *of it; ~ a* pass *at; ~ a* point *of; ~* room *(for); ~ one's* way *in life.* **24** (used with *adjectives* in special senses; for definitions ⇨ the entry for the *adjective* in the example): *~* certain; *~* good; *~* light *of; ~* sure. **25** (special uses with *adverbial particles* and *prepositions*):

make away with sb/sth, **(a)** carry off; steal. **(b)** kill.

make for sb/sth, (*informal*) move in the direction of: *It's late; we'd better ~ for home.*

make sth/sb into sth, ⇨8 above: *The huts can be made into temporary houses.*

make of, understand, interpret: *What are we to ~ of his behavior?*

make off, hurry away (esp in order to escape): *The getaway car made off at top speed.* ***make off with sth,*** steal and go away: *The cashier made off with the firm's money.*

make sth out, **(a)** write out; complete or fill in: *~ out a check for $10.* **(b)** manage to see, read: *We made out a figure in the darkness.* ***make sb out to be,*** claim; assert; maintain: *He ~s himself out to be cleverer than he really is.* ***make sb/sth out,*** understand him/it: *What a queer fellow he is! I can't ~ him out at all. I can't ~ out what he wants. I couldn't ~ it out.* ***make out*** (*informal*) progress, get on: *How are you making out at work/with your new boss?* ***make out a case for/against/that,*** ⇨ case¹(6).

make over, transfer the possession or ownership of: *He has made over his property to his children.*

make sth up, **(a)** complete: *We still need $5 to ~ up the sum we asked for.* **(b)** give or do something in payment for a loss, deficiency, etc: *I'm sorry you can't come to the party but I'll ~ it up to you.* **(c)** take a test in place of one which has been failed or missed. **(d)** invent (esp to deceive): *Stop making things up!* **(e)** form; compose; constitute: *Are all animal bodies made up of cells?* **(f)** prepare; put together. ***make sb/oneself up,*** prepare (an actor/oneself) by applying cosmetics to the face: *It takes him more than an hour to ~ up for the part of Othello.* ***make up one's mind,*** come to a decision: *I've made up my mind. My mind's made up.* ***make up for sth,*** compensate for: *He worked much harder than anyone else, to ~ up for arriving late.* ***make up for lost time,*** hurry, work hard, etc after losing time, starting late, etc. ***make up (with sb),*** end a quarrel, dispute or misunderstanding: *Why don't you ~ up with her?*

make² /meik/ *n* [C,U] **1** way a thing is made: *a skirt of stylish ~.* **2** kind; brand: *cars of all ~s. Is this your own ~*, made by you? **3** ***on the make,*** (*sl*) **(a)** constantly concerned with making a profit, gaining an advantage. **(b)** seeking sexual conquests.

make-believe /ˈmeik biˌliv/ *n* [U] pretense: *Don't be frightened, it's all ~.* □ *adj* pretended. ⇨ make¹ (13).

maker /ˈmeikər/ *n* **1 the/our Maker,** the Creator; God. **2** [C] (esp in compounds) person or thing that makes: *ˈdress~.*

make·shift /ˈmeikˌʃɪft/ *n* [U], *adj* (something) used for a time until the right thing is available: *use an empty crate as a ~ for a table/as a ~ table.*

make·up /ˈmeikˌəp/ *n* [U] **1** way in which something is constructed or arranged. **2** cosmetics,

esp for the face. **3** character, temperament: *people of that ~.*
mak·ing /ˈmeikɪŋ/ *n* ***be the making of,*** cause to develop well: *The two years he served in the Army were the ~ of him.* ***have the makings of,*** have the necessary qualities for becoming: *He has in him the ~s of a great man.*
mala·chite /ˈmæləˌkait/ *n* [U] green mineral, a kind of stone used for ornaments, decoration, etc.
mal·adjusted /ˌmæləˈdʒəstɪd/ *adj* (esp of a person) poorly adjusted to one's environment or situation.
mal·adjust·ment *n* [U]
mal·ady /ˈmælədi/ *n* [C] (*pl* -ies) **1** (esp chronic) disease; illness. **2** disorder: *a social ~.*
ma·laria /məˈlæriə/ *n* [U] disease with chills, caused by mosquitoes, characterized by sweating and fever.
ma·lar·ial /-iəl/ *adj*
male /ˈmeiəl/ *adj* **1** of the sex that does not give birth to offspring: *a ~ voice.* **2** (*bot*) which does not bear fruit. **3** of or relating to men. **4** (*mech*) having a protruding part designed to be inserted into a corresponding hollow part. □ *n* [C] **1** man or boy. **2** male animal or plant.
mal·edic·tion /ˌmæləˈdɪkʃən/ *n* [C] (*formal*) curse, esp as a prayer for harm to fall on another person.
ma·levo·lent /məˈlevələnt/ *adj* wishing harm to another; spiteful.
ma·levo·lence /-ləns/ *n* [U]
ma·levo·lent·ly *adv*
mal·for·ma·tion /ˌmælfɔrˈmeiʃən/ *n* **1** [U] state of being badly or abnormally formed. **2** [C] malformed part: *a ~ of the spine.*
mal·formed /ˌmælˈfɔrmd/ *adj* abnormally or badly formed.
mal·ice /ˈmælɪs/ *n* [U] active hatred; desire to harm others. ***bear sb malice,*** feel hatred for him.
ma·li·cious /məˈlɪʃəs/ *adj* feeling, showing, caused by, malice: *~ gossip.*
ma·li·cious·ly *adv*
ma·lign /məˈlain/ *adj* evil or injurious: *a ~ influence.* □ *vt* speak badly of; slander: *~ an innocent person.*
ma·lig·nancy /məˈlɪgnənsi/ *n* (*pl* -ies) **1** [U] the state of being malignant. **2** [C] malignant tumor.
ma·lig·nant /məˈlɪgnənt/ *adj* **1** (of persons, their actions) filled with, showing, a desire to hurt: *~ glances.* **2** harmful to life: *a ~ disease.*
ma·lig·nant·ly *adv*
ma·lig·nity /məˈlɪgnəti/ *n* (*pl* -ies) **1** [U] deep-rooted hatred. **2** [C] instance of this; hateful act, remark, etc.
ma·lin·ger /məˈlɪŋgər/ *vi* pretend to be ill in order to escape duty or work.
ma·lin·gerer *n* [C]
mall /mɔl/ *n* [C] **1** shaded public walk. **2** grassy center strip on a road. **3** shopping center with stores arranged around covered walks.
mal·lard /ˈmælərd/ *n* [C] kind of wild duck.
mal·leable /ˈmæliəbəl/ *adj* **1** (of metals) that can be hammered or pressed into new shapes. **2** (*fig*) (eg of a person's character) easily trained or adapted.
mal·lea·bil·ity /ˌmæliəˈbɪləti/ *n* [U]
mal·let /ˈmælɪt/ *n* [C] **1** hammer with a wooden head and a short handle. **2** hammer with a long handle and wooden head for striking a croquet or polo ball.
mal·nu·tri·tion /ˌmælnuˈtrɪʃən/ *n* [U] condition caused by not getting (enough of) (the right kind(s) of) food.
mal·prac·tice /ˌmælˈpræktɪs/ *n* [U] **1** wrong treatment or neglect of a patient by a doctor. **2** any professional or official misconduct.
malt /mɔlt/ *n* **1** [U] grain (usually barley) allowed to sprout, used for making beer, whiskey, etc. **2** [C] (*informal*) malted milk. □ *vt,vi* **1** make (grain) into malt; (of grain) become malt. **2** prepare or mix with malt.
ˌmalted ˈmilk (also **malted, malt**) *n* [C,U] (drink made by mixing milk with a) powder made from dried milk and malted grains.
mal·treat /mælˈtrit/ *vt* (*formal*) treat roughly or cruelly.
mal·treat·ment *n* [U]
mama, mamma = momma.
mam·mal, /ˈmæməl/ *n* [C] any of the class of animals which feed their young with milk from the breast.
mam·moth /ˈmæməθ/ *n* [C] large kind of hairy elephant now extinct. □ *adj* huge: *a ~ task.*
mammy /ˈmæmi/ *n* [C] (*pl* -ies) (*old use*) black woman put in charge of white children in the Old South.
man[1] /mæn/ *n* [C] (*pl* men /men/) **1** adult male human being: *The man of the house,* the male head of the family. **2** human being; person: *All men must die.* ***the man in the street,*** person regarded as representing the interests and opinions of ordinary people. ***as one man,*** in complete agreement. ***to a man,*** without exception. **3** (*sing* only, without *the, a* or *an*) the human race; all mankind: *Man is mortal.* **4** (in the military) enlisted man: *officers and men.* **5** male person having the qualities (eg strength, confidence) associated with men: *How can we make a man of him?* **6** husband, lover, etc: *man and wife.* **7** (*dated*) *male servant, employee, etc.* **8** piece in chess, checkers, etc.
ˈman·hood *n* [U] **(a)** state of being a man. **(b)** male qualities, eg virility, courage. **(c)** (*collect*) men in general.
ˈman-hour *n* [C] work done by one person in one hour.
man-ˈmade *adj* made by humans; artificial; synthetic.
ˈman·servant *n* [C] male servant.
ˈman-sized *adj* of a size suitable for or needing a (large or strong) man; *a man-sized steak/job.*
ˌman-to-ˈman *adj* frank, not holding back: *a man-to-man discussion.*
man[2] /mæn/ *vt* (-nn-) supply with men for service or defense: *~ a fort/a ship/the barricades.*
man·acle /ˈmænəkəl/ *n* [C] (usually *pl*) chains for the hands or feet. □ *vt* **1** put in chains. **2** (*fig*) restrain.
man·age /ˈmænɪdz/ *vt,vi* **1** control; operate; direct: *managing a business.* **2** succeed in doing: *I ~d to attract their attention in spite of the crowd.* **3** (often with *can, could, be able to*) get

along; make do or make progress with. (*Note: manage* is often used in this sense without a following *verb*; meaning is supplied by the other words in the sentence.) *Can you* ~ (*to eat*) *another slice of cake? We can't* ~ (*to do our work*) *with these poor tools. I don't know how he* ~*s* (*to live, pay his bills, etc*) *on his salary.*

man·age·abil·ity /ˌmænɪdʒəˈbɪləti/ *n* [U]

ˈman·age·able /-əbəl/ *adj* that can be managed.

man·age·ment /ˈmænɪdʒmənt/ *n* **1** [U] managing or being managed. **2** [U] skillful treatment or handling: *It needed a good deal of* ~ *to persuade them to give me the job.* **3** [C,U] (*collect*) all those persons managing an industry, enterprise, etc: *joint consultation between workers and* ~.

man·ager /ˈmænɪdʒər/ *n* [C] person who manages a business, household affairs, etc, esp in a certain way: *My wife is an excellent* ~. *She is a hotel* ~.

mana·ge·rial /ˌmænɪˈdʒɪriəl/ *adj* of managers or management.

man·date /ˈmænˌdeit/ *n* [C] **1** command or order from an authority. **2(a)** authority to administer a territory given by the League of Nations after the First World War. **(b)** territory given in this way. **3** authority given to representatives, esp by voters: *the* ~ *of the people.* □ *vt* put (a territory) under a mandate(2): *the* ~*d territories.*

man·da·tory /ˈmændəˌtɔri/ *adj* **(a)** of, conveying, a command. **(b)** required: *a mandatory safety test for all cars.*

man·dible /ˈmændəbəl/ *n* [C] **1** lower jaw in mammals and fishes. ⇨ illus at skeleton. **2** either part of a bird's beak. **3** (in insects) either half of the upper pair of jaws, used for biting and seizing.

man·do·lin /ˌmændəˈlɪn/ *n* [C] musical instrument with 6 or 8 metal strings and a pear-shaped body.

mane /mein/ *n* [C] long hair on the neck of a horse, male lion, etc. ⇨ illus at cat.

man-eater /ˈmæn-ˌitər/ *n* [C] **1** cannibal. **2** man-eating tiger or shark.

ma·neu·ver /məˈnuvər/ *n* [C] **1** planned movement (eg of armed forces, of a ship or airplane, etc). **2** (*pl*) series of such movements, eg as training exercises: *army* ~*s.* **3** clever move or trick, made to deceive, to evade, or to gain something: *the desperate* ~*s of some politicians.* □ *vi,vt* (cause to) perform maneuvers: ~*ing a car into a difficult space.*

ma·neu·ver·abil·ity /məˌnuvərəˈbɪləti/ *n* [U]

ma·neu·ver·able /-vərəbəl/ *adj* that can be maneuvered.

man·ful /ˈmænfəl/ *adj* brave; determined.

man·fully /-fəli/ *adv*

man·ga·nese /ˈmæŋgəˌniz/ *n* [U] hard, brittle, light-gray metallic element (symbol **Mn**) used in making steel, glass, etc.

mange /meindʒ/ *n* [U] contagious skin disease, esp of dogs and cats.

manger /ˈmeindʒər/ *n* [C] long open box or trough for horses or cattle to feed from.

mangle[1] /ˈmæŋgəl/ *n* [C] machine with rollers for pressing or smoothing clothes, etc. □ *vt* put (clothes, etc) through a mangle.

mangle[2] /ˈmæŋgəl/ *vt* cut up, tear, damage, badly: *be badly* ~*d in an automobile accident.*

mango /ˈmæŋgou/ *n* [C] (*pl* ~es or ~s) (tropical tree bearing) pear-shaped fruit with sweet yellow flesh. ⇨ illus at fruit.

man·grove /ˈmæŋˌgrouv/ *n* [C] tropical tree growing in swamps, that sends down new roots from its branches.

mangy /ˈmeindʒi/ *adj* (-ier, -iest) **1** having or seeming to have mange. **2** shabby.

man·handle /ˈmænˌhændəl/ *vt* **1** move by physical strength. **2** handle roughly: ~*d by the police.*

man·hole /ˈmænˌhoul/ *n* [C] opening through which one may enter (an underground sewer, boiler, tank, etc).

ˈmanhole cover, round, heavy metal lid covering manholes in the street.

mania /ˈmeiniə/ *n* **1** [U] madness shown by great excitement, delusions, violence. **2** [C] extreme enthusiasm: *a* ~ *for powerful motorcycles.*

maniac /ˈmeiniˌæk/ *n* [C] insane person.

ma·niacal /məˈnaiəkəl/ *adj* violently insane; raving.

ma·niacally /-kli/ *adv*

mani·cure /ˈmænəˌkyʊr/ *n* [C] beauty treatment and care of the hands and fingernails. □ *vt* cut, clean and polish the fingernails.

ˈmani·cur·ist /-ɪst/ *n* [C] person who gives manicures.

mani·fest /ˈmænəˌfest/ *adj* clear and obvious: *a* ~ *truth.* □ *vt* show clearly; display; reveal: ~ *the truth of a statement. She doesn't* ~ *much desire to marry him. No disease* ~*ed itself during the long voyage.* □ *n* [C] list of passengers and cargo (eg for a ship or plane).

mani·fes·ta·tion /ˌmænəfɪˈsteiʃən/ *n* [C,U]

mani·fest·ly *adv*

mani·festo /ˌmænəˈfestou/ *n* [C] (*pl* ~s or ~es) public declaration of principles, policy, purposes, etc, esp by a political party.

mani·fold /ˈmænəˌfould/ *adj* **1** of many kinds. **2** having many parts. □ *n* [C] pipe or fitting with many openings for making connections with other pipes, etc.

mani·kin /ˈmænəkɪn/ *n* [C] **1** little man; dwarf. **2** = mannequin.

ma·nipu·late /məˈnɪpyəˌleit/ *vt* **1** operate, handle, esp with skill: ~ *machinery.* **2** manage or control dishonestly or craftily: *A clever politician knows how to* ~ *his supporters/public opinion.*

ma·nipu·la·tion /məˌnɪpyəˈleiʃən/ *n* [C,U]

man·kind *n* [U] **1** /ˌmænˈkaind/ the human species. **2** /ˈmænˌkaɪnd/ the male sex; all men (contrasted with *ˈwomankind*).

man·like /ˈmænˌlaik/ *adj* having the qualities (good or bad) of a man.

man·ly /ˈmænli/ *adj* (-ier, -iest) **1** having the strong qualities expected of a man. **2** of or suitable for a man.

man·li·ness /-nɪs/ *n* [U]

manna /ˈmænə/ *n* [U] **1** (in the Bible) food provided by God for the Israelites during their forty years in the desert. **2** (*fig*) something needed that is unexpectedly supplied.

man·ne·quin /ˈmænəkɪn/ *n* [C] **1** = model(4) (the usual word). **2** life-size figure of a human

body, as used to display clothes.
man·ner /ˈmænər/ *n* [C] **1** way in which a thing is done or happens: *Do it in this ~.* **2** (*sing* only) person's way of behaving: *I don't like his ~.* **3** (*pl*) habits and customs. **4** (*pl*) **(a)** social behavior: *good/bad ~s.* **(b)** polite behavior: *The child has no ~s.* **5** style in literature or art: *a painting in the ~ of Raphael.* **6** kind, sort: *What ~ of man is he?* ***all manner of,*** every kind of.
-man·nered *adj* (used in compounds): *ˈill-mannered,* having bad manners(4).
man·ner·ism /ˈmænəˌrɪzəm/ *n* [C] peculiarity of behavior, speech, etc, esp one that is affected.
man·ner·ly /ˈmænərli/ *adj* courteous, polite.
man·nish /ˈmænɪʃ/ *adj* (of a woman) like a man; more suitable for a man than for a woman: *a ~ style of dress.*
manor /ˈmænər/ *n* [C] **1** unit of land under the feudal system, part of which was used directly by the lord of the manor and the rest occupied and farmed by tenants who paid rent in crops and service. **2** landed estate. **3** main house of an estate (also called the *ˈ~ house*).
ma·nor·ial /məˈnɔriəl/ *adj* of a manor.
man·power /ˈmænˌpauər/ *n* [U] **1** power supplied by human strength. **2** number of men available for military service, work, etc: *a shortage of ~ in the coal mines.*
man·sion /ˈmænʃən/ *n* [C] large and stately house.
man·slaughter /ˈmænˌslɔtər/ *n* [U] (act of) killing a human being unlawfully but without meaning to do so.
man·tel /ˈmæntəl/ *n* [C] **1** structure of wood, marble, etc above and around a fireplace. **2** mantelpiece.
ˈmantel·piece *n* shelf over a fireplace.
man·tilla /mænˈtiə, mænˈtɪlə/ *n* [C] (*pl* ~s) large veil or scarf worn esp by Spanish and Latin American women to cover the hair and shoulders.
man·tis /ˈmæntɪs/ *n* [C] (kinds of) long-legged insect related to the grasshopper, which holds its front legs lifted. ⇨ illus at insect.
mantle /ˈmæntəl/ *n* [C] **1** loose, sleeveless cloak. **2** (*fig*) covering: *hills with a ~ of snow.* **3** lace-like cover around the flame in certain kinds of lamps, which glows and gives off light. □ *vt,vi* cover in, or as in, a mantle: *an ˈivy-~d wall.*
man·ual /ˈmænyuəl/ *adj* of, done with, the hands: *~ labor.* □ *n* [C] book of instructions or information esp about a particular subject.
man·ually /-yuəli/ *adv*
manu·fac·ture /ˌmænyəˈfæktʃər/ *vt* **1** make, produce (goods, etc), esp by machinery: *manufacturing industries; ~d goods.* **2** invent (a story, an excuse, etc). □ *n* [U] process or act of manufacturing: *the ~ of plastic.*
manu·fac·turer *n* [C] person, firm, etc that manufactures things.
ma·nure /məˈnuər/ *n* [U] animal waste, collected eg from stables, cow barns, etc, and used as a fertilizer. □ *vt* put manure in or on (land or soil).
manu·script /ˈmænyəˌskrɪpt/ *n* **1** [C] handwritten or typed book, article, etc: *sent the ~ to his publisher.* **2** [U] handwriting as contrasted with printing.

many /ˈmeni/ *adj* (⇨ more, most) **1** (used with *pl nouns*) numerous; being a large number: *Many people think so. How ~ books do you want?* ***one too many,*** one more than the correct or needed number. **2** (*liter*) (used with *a(n)* and a *sing noun*) being one of a large number: *Many a man* (= Many men) *would welcome the opportunity.* □ *n* large number: *Many of the students were eager to help.* □ *pron* large number of people or things: *We had to borrow records for the party because we didn't have ~.*
map /mæp/ *n* [C] drawing or representation on paper, etc of the earth's surface or a part of it, showing countries, oceans, rivers, mountains, etc; representation of the sky showing positions of the stars, etc. ***put sth on the map,*** (*fig*) cause it to be considered important, to be reckoned with. ***off the map,*** (*informal*) (of a place) inaccessible. ***wipe sth off the map,*** destroy it. □ *vt* (-pp-) **1** make a map of. **2** ***map out,*** plan or arrange in detail: *map out one's time.*
maple /ˈmeipəl/ *n* **1** [C] (kinds of) tree of the northern hemisphere, grown for timber and ornament. ⇨ illus at tree. **2** [U] wood of this tree.
ˈmaple sugar/syrup, [U] sugar/syrup that is obtained from the sap of one kind of maple.
mar[1] /mar/ *vt* (-rr-) injure; spoil; damage: *Nothing marred their happiness.*
Mar.[2] *abbr* = March.
mara·thon /ˈmærəˌθan/ *n* [C] **1** long-distance race on foot (about 26 miles or 41.8 kilometers at modern sports meetings). **2** (*fig*) test of endurance.
ma·raud /məˈrɔd/ *vi* go about in search of loot or prey.
ma·rauder *n* [C] person, animal that marauds.
marble /ˈmarbəl/ *n* **1** [U] (kinds of) hard limestone used, when cut and polished, for building and sculpture: (as an *adjective*) *a ~ statue/tomb.* **2** [C] small ball of glass, clay or stone used in games played by children. **3** (*pl*) children's game played with these. ***lose one's marbles,*** (*sl*) go crazy.
March[1] /martʃ/ *n* the third month of the year.
march[2] /martʃ/ *n* **1** [U] act of marching (by soldiers, etc). **2** [C] instance of marching. **3** [C] distance traveled or time required for a march: *a ~ of ten miles.* ***steal a march on sb,*** get ahead of him without being noticed. **4** progress: *the ~ of events/time.* **5** [C] piece of music for marching to: *military ~es.*
march[3] /martʃ/ *vi,vt* **1** (cause to) walk as soldiers do, with regular and measured steps: *The troops ~ed by/past/in/out/off/away. He was ~ed off to prison.* **2** move forward steadily; progress.
mar·chion·ess /ˈmarʃənɪs/ *n* [C] **1** wife or widow of a marquess. **2** woman holding the rank of a marquess in her own right.
Mardi Gras /ˈmardi ˌgra/ (*F*) *n* feast and celebration held on last Tuesday before Lent in certain southern US cities, esp New Orleans.
mare /ˈmær/ *n* [C] female horse or donkey.
mar·gar·ine /ˈmardʒərɪn/ *n* [U] food substance, used like butter, made chiefly from vegetable fats.
mar·gin /ˈmardʒɪn/ *n* [C] **1** blank space around the printed or written matter on a page. **2** edge

or border: *the ~ of a lake*. **3** extra amount (of time, money, etc) beyond what is estimated as necessary. **4** amount or degree: *He escaped defeat by a ~ of three votes*.

mar·ginal /-nəl/ *adj* **(a)** of or in a margin(1): *~al notes*. **(b)** of a margin(4): *a ~al victory*, victory won by a narrow margin.

mar·gin·ally /-nəli/ *adv*

mari·gold /ˈmærəˌgould/ *n* [C] (plant bearing a) bright orange or yellow rounded flower.

mari·juana, mari·huana /ˌmærəˈ(h)wanə/ *n* [U] **1** hemp plant. **2** dried leaves and flowers of this plant smoked in cigarettes for its intoxicating effect.

ma·rim·ba /məˈrɪmbə/ *n* [C] (kind of) Central and South American xylophone.

ma·rina /məˈrinə/ *n* [C] (*pl* ~s) place with docks, moorings, and other facilities for small boats, yachts, cabin cruisers, etc.

mari·nade /ˌmærəˈneid/ *n* [C,U] liquid, as wine or vinegar with various spices, for soaking fish or meat before cooking.

mari·nate /ˈmærəˌneit/ *vt* soak in (a) marinade.

ma·rine /məˈrin/ *adj* **1** of, by, found in, produced by, the sea: *~ fishing*. **2** of ships, shipping, the navy, etc: *~ transport*. □ *n* **1** [U] shipping in general. **2** [C] soldier serving on a ship. **3 Marine,** member of the US Marine Corps. ⇨ illus at arm². **4 the Marines** (*informal*) the US Marine Corps.

Ma·rine Corps /məˈrin ˌkɔr/ *n* branch of the US armed forces whose members are trained for operations on land and sea.

mari·ner /ˈmærənər/ *n* [C] sailor.

mari·on·ette /ˌmæriəˈnet/ *n* [C] puppet moved with strings or by the hands.

mari·tal /ˈmærətəl/ *adj* of or relating to marriage.

mari·time /ˈmærəˌtaim/ *adj* **1** connected with the sea or shipping: *~ law*. **2** situated or found near the sea: *the ~ provinces of Canada*.

mark¹ /mark/ *n* **1** [C] line, scratch, cut, stain, etc made on a surface: *Who made these dirty ~s on my new book?* **2** [C] sign or indication (of a quality, etc): *~s of old age/suffering*. **3** [C] **(a)** written or printed symbol: *ˌpunctuˈation ~s*. **(b)** cross or other symbol made in place of a signature by someone who cannot write. **4** [C] grade or rating: *He got the best ~s in his class*. **5** target. ***be/fall wide of the mark,*** be inaccurate, imprecise: *Your guess/calculation is wide of the ~*. ***beside the mark,*** irrelevant. **6** [U] strong or lasting impression. ***make one's mark,*** become famous. **7** (*sing* only) standard. ***up to/below the mark,*** equal to/below the required or normal standard. ***not be/feel (quite) up to the mark,*** not in one's usual health. **8** [C] (in athletics) line showing the starting point of a race: *On your ~, get set, go!* (words used by the starter). **9** [C] label, brand, seal, etc used for identification or as an indication of quality.

mark² /mark/ *vt* **1** make a mark on something. **2** indicate with a mark or visible sign: *~ed all the large cities on the map with a cross*. **3** give marks (4) to; grade: *~ examination papers*. **4** pay attention (to): *Mark carefully how it is done*. ***(You) mark my words,*** note what I say (and you will find, later, that I am right). **5** distinguish; characterize: *What are the qualities that ~ a great leader? A zebra is ~ed with stripes*. **6** signal; denote: *His death ~ed the end of an era. Ceremonies ~ing an anniversary*. ***mark time,*** **(a)** stamp the feet as when marching but without moving forward. **(b)** (*fig*) wait until further progress becomes possible. **7** (special uses with *adverbial particles and prepositions*):

mark sth down, **(a)** write it down. **(b)** reduce its selling price.

mark sth off, put marks on (to show boundary lines, measurements, etc).

mark sth up, **(a)** put marks on it. **(b)** increase its price.

ˈmark·down *n* amount taken off the selling price of an article (eg when it is on sale).

marked *adj* clear; obvious: *a ~ed difference/improvement*.

mark·ed·ly /ˈmarkɪdli/ *adv*

mark·ing *n* (esp) pattern of different colors of feathers, skin, etc: *a tiger's ~ings*.

ˈmark·up *n* amount added to the cost of an article to determine its selling price.

marker /ˈmarkər/ *n* [C] **1** something that makes marks. **2** thing that marks or indicates, eg a flag or post on a playing field.

mar·ket¹ /ˈmarkɪt/ *n* [C] **1 (a)** public place (an open space or a building) where people meet to buy and sell goods: *She went to (the) ~ to buy food for the family*. **(b)** gathering or meeting for such a purpose: *The next ~ is on the 15th*. **2** store esp of a particular kind: *a fruit ~*. **3** trade in a particular type of goods: *the ˈcoffee ~*. **4** state of trade as shown by prices: *The ~ rose/fell/was steady*, Prices rose/fell/did not change much. ***play the market,*** buy and sell to make the most profit. **5** demand: *There's no/not much/only a poor ~ for these goods*. **6** (*sing* only) buying and selling. ***be in the market for sth,*** be ready to buy something. ***be on/come on (to)/put on the market,*** be offered/offer for sale: *This house will probably come on the market next month*. **7** **(a)** area, country, in which goods may be sold: *We must find new ~s for our manufacturers*. **(b)** buyers of a particular class or kind: *the teenage ~*.

ˈmarket ˌgarden, one where vegetables are grown for market.

ˈmarket·place *n* **(a)** open place in a town where a market is held. **(b) the marketplace,** (*fig*) the world of business.

mar·ket² /ˈmarkɪt/ *vi,vt* **1** buy or sell in a market. **2** prepare and offer for sale in a market.

ˈmar·ket·able /-əbəl/ *adj* that can be, fit to be, sold.

ˈmar·ket·ing *n* [U] theory and practice of (large-scale) selling.

marks·man /ˈmarksmən/ *n* [C] (*pl* -men /-men/) person skilled in aiming at a mark, esp with a rifle.

mar·ma·lade /ˈmarməˌleid, ˌmarməˈleid/ *n* [U] preserve made from the rind and pulp of citrus fruit: *orange ~*.

mar·mo·set /ˈmarməˌset/ *n* [C] small, tropical American monkey with soft, thick fur and a bushy tail. ⇨ illus at ape.

mar·mot /ˈmarmət/ *n* [C] small animal of the squirrel family.

ma·roon[1] /məˈrun/ *adj, n* [U] brownish-red (color).

ma·roon[2] /məˈrun/ *vt* put (a person) on a desert island, uninhabited coast, etc, and abandon him there. □ *n* [C] (sometimes **Maroon**) person who has fled (esp from enslavement) to the wilds to live in isolation: *the Jamaican Maroons*.

mar·quee /marˈki/ *n* [C] **1** large tent (as used for flower shows, a circus, etc). **2** structure or canopy projecting over an entrance: *a theater ~*.

mar·quess, mar·quis /ˈmarkwɪs/ *n* **1** (in Great Britain) member of the nobility next in rank above an earl and below a duke. **2** (in other countries) member of the nobility next in rank above a count.

mar·quise /marˈkiz/ *n* [C] = marchioness.

mar·riage /ˈmærɪdʒ/ *n* **1** [C,U] **(a)** (instance of a) legal union of a man and woman as husband and wife. **(b)** state of being married. **2** wedding (the usual word). **3** any close or intimate union.

ˈmar·riage·able /-əbəl/ *adj* suitable for marriage: *a girl of ~able age*.

mar·ried /ˈmærid/ *adj* **1** united in marriage. *~ couples*. **2** of or relating to marriage: *~ life*.

mar·row /ˈmærou/ *n* [U] **1** soft, fatty substance that fills the hollow parts of bones. ***chilled to the marrow,*** cold through and through. **2** (*fig*) essence; essential part.

marry /ˈmæri/ *vt,vi* (*pt,pp* -ied) **1** take as a husband or wife; become married. **2** (of a clergyman, a civil official) join as husband or wife: *Which priest is going to ~ them?* **3** (sometimes with *off*) give in marriage: *He married (off) both his daughters to rich Hollywood producers*.

Mars /marz/ *n* (*astron*) planet fourth in order from the sun. ⇨ illus at planet.

marsh /marʃ/ *n* [C] area of low-lying, wet land.

marshy *adj* (-ier, -iest) of or like a marsh.

mar·shal[1] /ˈmarʃəl/ *n* [C] **1** officer of the highest rank in the military forces of some countries. **2** official in charge of important public events or ceremonies: *grand ~ of the parade*. **3** federal official with functions similar to those of a sheriff. **4** head of a fire or police department in some US cities.

mar·shal[2] /ˈmarʃəl/ *vt* (-l-, -ll-) **1** arrange in proper order: *~ facts/military forces*. **2** guide or lead (a person) with ceremony: *~ persons into the presence of the Ambassador*.

mar·su·pial /marˈsupiəl/ *n* [C] one of the class of animals (eg kangaroos) in which the females have a pouch for carrying their young.

mart /mart/ *n* [C] (*liter*) marketplace; trading center.

mar·ten /ˈmartən/ *n* **1** [C] slender, flesh-eating mammal related to the mink and the weasel. **2** [U] its thick, soft, brown fur.

mar·tial /ˈmarʃəl/ *adj* **1** of, associated with, war: *~ music*. **2** brave: *~ spirit*.

ˌmartial ˈlaw, military rule, as imposed during an emergency or in wartime.

mar·tial·ly /-ʃəli/ *adv*

mar·tin /ˈmartən/ *n* [C] bird of the swallow family, having long wings and a forked tail.

mar·ti·net /ˈmartəˌnet/ *n* [C] strict disciplinarian.

mar·tyr /ˈmartər/ *n* [C] **1** person who chooses to die or to suffer greatly for his religious beliefs or for a great cause or principle: *the early Christian ~s in Rome*. **2** person who suffers or pretends to suffer greatly. ***be a martyr to sth,*** suffer greatly from: *He's a ~ to rheumatism*. □ *vt* put to death, cause to suffer, as a martyr.

ˈmar·tyr·dom /-dəm/ *n* [U] state of being a martyr: *His wife's never-ending complaints made his life one long ~dom*.

mar·vel /ˈmarvəl/ *n* [C] something causing great surprise, wonder, astonishment: *the ~s of modern science*. □ *vi* (-l-, -ll-) be greatly surprised (at); be filled with wonder: *~ at her*.

mar·vel·ous, mar·vel·lous /ˈmarvələs/ *adj* astonishing; wonderful.

mar·vel·ous·ly, mar·vel·lous·ly *adv*

Marx·ism /ˈmarkˌsɪzəm/ *n* [U] (esp) economic theory of Karl Marx (1818-83), German economist, that class struggle has been the major force behind historical change and that capitalism will give way to socialism and a classless society.

Marx·ist /ˈmarksɪst/ *n* [C] follower of Marxism.

mar·zi·pan /ˈmarzəˌpæn/ *n* [U] thick paste of ground almonds, sugar, etc, often made into small cakes.

masc. *abbr* = masculine.

mas·cara /mæˈskærə/ *n* [U] cosmetic for the eyelashes and eyebrows.

mas·cot /ˈmæˌskat/ *n* [C] person, animal or object believed to bring good luck.

mas·cu·line /ˈmæskyəlɪn/ *adj* **1** of, like, men: *a ~ style*. **2** (*gram*) of the male gender: *"He" and "him" are ~ pronouns*.

mas·cu·lin·ity /ˌmæskyəˈlɪnəti/ *n* [U] quality of being masculine.

mash /mæʃ/ *n* [U] **1** grain, bran, etc cooked in water as food for poultry, cattle or pigs. **2** any substance (eg boiled potatoes) softened and crushed. **3** mixture of malt and hot water used in brewing. □ *vt* beat or crush into a mash: *~ed potato(es)*.

mask[1] /mæsk/ *n* [C] **1** covering for all or part of the face, with openings for the eyes, worn as a disguise. **2** likeness of the face made from wax, wood, ivory, etc. **3** pad of sterile gauze worn over the mouth and nose by doctors and nurses. **4** any covering for the face worn as protection: *a ˈgas ~*. **5** (*fig*) anything that conceals or disguises like a mask.

mask[2] /mæsk/ *vt* **1** cover (the face) with a mask: *a ~ed rider*. **2** conceal: *~ one's hatred under an appearance of friendliness*.

maso·chism /ˈmæsəˌkɪzəm/ *n* [U] **1** mental disorder in which a person gets pleasure and satisfaction (esp sexual) from pain or humiliation inflicted by another person. **2** pleasure in suffering pain and humiliation.

maso·chist /-ɪst/ *n* [C] person guilty of masochism.

maso·chis·tic /ˌmæsəˈkɪstɪk/ *adj* of masochism.

ma·son /ˈmeisən/ *n* [C] **1** worker who builds or works with stone. **2 Mason** (also ˈ**Freemason**) member of the Free and Accepted Masons, an international secret society.

ma·son·ry /ˈmeisənri/ **(a)** stonework; that part of a building made of stone and mortar. **(b) Masonry** (also **ˈFreemasonry**) beliefs and practices of the Masons.

mas·quer·ade /ˌmæskəˈreid/ *n* [C] **1** party at which masks and other disguises are worn. **2** (*fig*) false show or pretense. □ *vi* appear, be, in disguise: *a prince masquerading as a peasant.*

mass[1] /mæs/ *n* **1** [C] lump, quantity of matter, without regular shape: *a large ~ of dough.* **2** [C] large number or amount: *~es of dark clouds in the sky.* **3** (*sing* only) **the mass,** greater part; majority: *The ~ of voters favor reform.* **4** (*pl* only) **the masses,** the common people. **5** [U] bulk or size. **6** [U] (*science*) quantity of material in a body measured by its resistance to change of motion. □ *vt,vi* form or collect into a mass: *Troops are ~ing/are being ~ed on the frontier.* □ *adj* **1** of or involving the masses(4). **2** of or having to do with large numbers of people: *a ~ meeting.* **3** on a large scale: *~ production.*

ˌmass comˌmuniˈcations/ˈmedia, means (as newspapers, radio, TV) of reaching or communicating with large numbers of people.

ˈmass noun, noun having *some* as an indefinite modifier rather than *a* or *an*, which denotes a substance (as *sugar* or *butter*) or a notion (as *love* or *patriotism*) that is not usually divided or numbered.

ˌmass-proˈduce *vt* make in large quantities, esp by machinery.

Mass[2] /mæs/ *n* [C] **1** in the Roman Catholic and some Protestant churches, (ceremony or service that includes the) celebration of the Eucharist. **2** musical setting for certain parts of the Mass.

mas·sacre /ˈmæsəkər/ *n* [C] cruel killing of large numbers of people (or sometimes, animals). □ *vt* kill violently and cruelly.

mas·sage /məˈsaʒ/ *n* [C,U] (instance of) pressing and rubbing the body with the hands, esp the muscles and joints, in order to lessen pain, stiffness, etc. □ *vt* give a massage to.

mas·seur /mæˈsər/ *n* [C] man who gives massages.

mas·seuse /mæˈsus/ *n* [C] woman who gives massages.

mas·sive /ˈmæsɪv/ *adj* **1** large, heavy and solid: *a ~ monument; a ~ forehead.* **2** (*fig*) substantial; impressive.

mas·sive·ly *adv*

mas·sive·ness /-nɪs/ *n* [U]

mast /mæst/ *n* [C] **1** upright pole for a ship's sails, rigging, etc. ⇨ illus at ship. **2** tall pole (for a flag).

mas·ter[1] /ˈmæstər/ *n* [C] **1** man who has others working for him or under him. ***be one's own master,*** be free and independent. **2** male head of a household: *the ~ of the house.* **3** captain of a merchant ship. **4** male owner of an animal. **5** male teacher. **6** person who has control or authority: *He is ~ of the situation,* has it under control. **7 Master,** (title sometimes used with a name, when speaking of or to a boy up to about the age of 14): *Master Charles Smith.* **8** (person holding the) academic degree next above the bachelor's degree: *Master of Science.* **9** person having great skill, learning, artistic gifts, etc: *old ~s,* the great painters of the 13th to 17th centuries. **10** original record, document, etc used for making copies. □ *adj* **1** having or showing professional skill: *a ~ builder/carpenter.* **2** being the chief one or the one that controls all others: *a ~ key.*

ˌMaster of ˈCeremonies, person at a public banquet entertainment, etc, who is in charge of the program and introduces the speakers and performers.

ˈmaster sergeant, noncommissioned officer of second highest rank in the US army, air force, or marine corps.

mas·ter[2] /ˈmæstər/ *vt* **1** become the master(6) of: *~ one's feelings.* **2** become skilled at: *~ a foreign language.*

mas·ter·ful /ˈmæstərfəl/ *adj* **1** fond of controlling others: *speak in a ~ manner.* **2** = masterly.

mas·ter·fully /-fəli/ *adv*

mas·ter·ly /ˈmæstərli/ *adj* very skillful: *with a few ~ strokes of the brush.*

master·mind /ˈmæstərˌmaind/ *n* [C] person, esp of superior intelligence who plans or directs a scheme that is usually carried out by others. □ *vt* be the mastermind of (a plan, etc).

master·piece /ˈmæstərˌpis/ *n* [C] something made or done with very great skill.

mas·tery /ˈmæstəri/ *n* [U] **1** great skill or knowledge of a master: *his ~ of the violin.* **2** control; domination: *Which side will get the ~?*

mast·head /ˈmæstˌhed/ *n* [C] **1** highest part of a mast. **2** part of a newspaper or magazine that gives its title and a list of its owners, editors, etc.

mas·ti·cate /ˈmæstəˌkeit/ *vt* (*formal*) chew; soften, grind up (food) with the teeth.

mas·ti·ca·tion /ˌmæstəˈkeiʃən/ *n* [U]

mas·tiff /ˈmæstɪf/ *n* [C] large, strong dog with a smooth coat and a deep chest, much used as a watchdog.

mas·to·don /ˈmæstəˌdan/ *n* [C] extinct large animal related to the elephant.

mas·toid /ˈmæˌstɔid/ *n* [C] bone of the skull located behind the ear.

mas·tur·bate /ˈmæstərˌbeit/ *vi* achieve sexual pleasure by means of rubbing or touching the genital organs, esp with the hand.

mas·tur·ba·tion /ˌmæstərˈbeiʃən/ *n* [U]

mat[1] /mæt/ *n* [C] **1** piece of material used for a floor covering or as a pad. **2** piece of material for wiping dirty shoes on. **3** small piece of material placed under vases, dishes, etc, for ornament or protection. **4** thick pad used for gymnastics, wrestling, etc. **5** anything thickly tangled or twisted together: *a mat of weeds.* □ *vt,vi* (-tt-) **1** cover or supply with mats. **2** (cause to) be or become tangled or knotted: *matted hair.*

mat[2] /mæt/ *n* [C] **1** dull finish. ⇨ gloss[1](1). **2** border (often of cardboard) placed around a picture, print, etc. □ *vt* place a mat around a picture.

mata·dor /ˈmætəˌdɔr/ *n* [C] man whose task is to fight and kill the bull in a bullfight.

match[1] /mætʃ/ *n* [C] short piece of wood, waxed paper, etc, with a top made of material that bursts into flame when rubbed on a rough or

specially prepared surface.
ˈmatch·book *n* [C] cardboard folder containing paper matches.
ˈmatch·box *n* [C] box for holding matches.
match[2] /mætʃ/ *n* [C] **1** contest; game: *a ˈwrestling ~.* **2** person or thing equal to another in strength, skill, etc: *You are no ~ for him,* are not strong, clever, etc enough to compete with him. **3** marriage: *a love ~.* **4** person considered as a possible husband or wife: *He's a good ~,* is considered satisfactory or desirable. **5** person or thing exactly like, similar to, or combining well with, another: *colors/materials that are a good ~.*
ˈmatch·maker *n* [C] (esp) person who arranges matches(3) for others.
match[3] /mætʃ/ *vt,vi* **1** enter in competition (with): *I'm ready to ~ my strength with/against yours.* **2** be equal to: *a well-~ed pair,* eg boxers about equal in skill. **3** go with or be suitable for (in quality, color, design, etc): *The carpets should ~ the curtains.* **4** find a match(5) for (another): *Can you ~ this silk?* **5** join (one person *with* another) in marriage.
match·less *adj* unequaled: *~less beauty.*
mate[1] /meit/ *n* **1** companion; associate (used mostly in compounds): *room~.* **2** ship's officer below the rank of captain. **3** one of a pair of birds or animals: *the lioness and her ~.* **4** either of a matched pair: *the ~ to a slipper.* **5** husband or wife.
mate[2] /meit/ *vt,vi* **1** join or fit together; pair. **2** marry. **3** (of birds or animals) (cause to) unite for the purpose of producing young.
the ˈmating season, spring, when most animals mate.
mate[3] /meit/ *n, v* = checkmate.
ma·terial[1] /məˈtɪriəl/ *adj* **1** (contrasted with *spiritual*) physical; made of, connected with, matter or substance: *the ~ world.* **2** of the body; of physical needs: *~ needs,* eg food and warmth. **3** important; essential.
ma·teri·ally /-iəli/ *adv* essentially.
ma·terial[2] /məˈtɪriəl/ *n* **1** [C,U] substance from which something is or can be made or for performing a certain task: *raw ~s,* not yet used in manufacture; *ˈwriting ~s,* pen, ink, paper, etc. **2** [C,U] cloth; fabric: *ˈdress ~s,* cloth; **3** [U] (*fig*) elements (as facts, happenings, ideas, etc): *the ~ from which history is made.*
ma·teri·al·ism /məˈtɪriəˌlɪzəm/ *n* [U] **1** theory, belief, that only physical matter exists and that everything is or comes from matter. **2** tendency to value material things (wealth, bodily comforts, etc) too much and spiritual and intellectual things too little.
ma·teri·al·ist /-ɪst/ *n* [C] believer in materialism; person who ignores religion, art, music, etc.
ma·teri·al·is·tic /məˌtɪriəˈlɪstɪk/ *adj*
ma·teri·al·is·ti·cally /-kli/ *adv*
ma·teri·al·ize /məˈtɪriəˌlaiz/ *vi* take material form; (cause to) become fact: *Our plans did not ~,* came to nothing, were not carried out.
ma·teri·al·iz·ation /məˌtɪriələˈzeiʃən/ *n* [U]
ma·ter·nal /məˈtərnəl/ *adj* **1** of or like a mother: *~ care/instincts.* **2** related through one's mother: *my ~ grandfather/aunt, etc.* **3** inherited or received from one's mother.
ma·ter·nally /-nəli/ *adv*
ma·tern·ity /məˈtərnəti/ *n* [U] being a mother: (as an *adjective*) *a ˈ~ ward/hospital,* for women who are about to become mothers.
math[1] /mæθ/ *n* (*informal*) (short for) mathematics. (Compare next entry.)
math.[2] *abbr* = mathematics. (Compare preceding entry.)
mathe·mat·ics /ˌmæθəˈmætɪks/ *n* [U] (used with a *sing* or *pl verb*) science of numbers (of which arithmetic, algebra, trigonometry and geometry are branches).
math·emat·ical /ˌmæθəˈmætɪkəl/ *adj*
math·emat·ically /-kli/ *adv*
math·ema·ti·cian /ˌmæθəməˈtɪʃən/ *n* [C] specialist in mathematics.
mati·née /ˌmætəˈnei/ *n* [C] afternoon performance of a movie, play, concert, etc.
ma·tri·arch /ˈmeitriˌark/ *n* [C] woman who rules a family or tribe.
ma·tri·ar·chal /ˌmeitriˈarkəl/ *adj*
ma·tri·archy /-ˌarki/ *n* [C] social organization in which women hold most of the authority.
ma·trices *pl* of matrix.
mat·ri·cide /ˈmætrɪˌsaid/ *n* **1** [C,U] act or instance of killing one's own mother. **2** [C] person guilty of this.
ma·tricu·late /məˈtrɪkyəˌleit/ *vt,vi* (allow to) enroll as a student, esp in a college or a university.
ma·tricu·la·tion /məˌtrɪkyəˈleiʃən/ *n* [C,U]
mat·ri·mony /ˈmætrəmouni/ *n* [U] state of being married; marriage.
mat·ri·mo·nial /ˌmætrəˈmouniəl/ *adj*
ma·trix /ˈmeitrɪks/ *n* (*pl* matrices /ˈmeitrəˌsiz/, or ~es) **1** mold into which eg hot metal is poured to be shaped. **2** substance in which a mineral, etc is embedded or enclosed.
ma·tron /ˈmeitrən/ *n* [C] **1** woman housekeeper in a school or other institution. **2** woman who is in charge of the women prisoners in a jail. **3** married woman or widow, esp one of middle age or older.
ma·tronly *adj*
matt /mæt/ *n* = mat[2] (1).
mat·ter[1] /ˈmætər/ *n* **1** [U] substance(s) of which a physical thing is made and which occupies space and has weight: *organic/inorganic ~.* **2** content or substance of a book, speech, etc, as contrasted with the form or style. **3** [U] something printed or written: *ˈreading ~,* books, periodicals, etc. **4** [C] something to which attention is given; piece of business; affair: *ˈmoney ~s. That's a ~ of opinion,* something about which opinions may differ. ***a matter of course,*** expected in the natural course of events. ***as a matter of fact,*** actually (although you may not know it). ***for ˈthat matter,*** so far as that is concerned. ***no laughing matter,*** a serious affair. **5** [U] importance. ***no matter,*** regardless: *No ~ whether you arrive early or late, they won't be ready.* ***no matter ˈwho/ˈwhat/ˈwhere, etc,*** whoever (it is), whatever (happens, etc). **6** [U] trouble; difficulty: *What's the ~ with it?* **7** ***a matter of,*** not (much) more or less than: *a ~ of 20 weeks/10 miles; within a ~ of hours.*

ˌ**matter-of-ˈcourse** *adj* to be expected.
ˌ**matter-of-ˈfact** *adj* (of a person, his manner) unimaginative; keeping to the facts.
mat·ter² /ˈmætər/ *vi* be of importance: *It doesn't ~ much, does it?*
mat·ting /ˈmætɪŋ/ *n* [U] rough woven material used esp for floor covering.
mat·tock /ˈmætək/ *n* [C] tool used for breaking up hard ground, etc, with a flat metal blade at a right angle to the handle.
mat·tress /ˈmætrɪs/ *n* [C] thick, flat, pad of wool, hair, feathers, foam rubber, etc on which to sleep.
matu·rate /ˈmætʃəˌreit/ *vi* (*formal*) become mature.
matu·ra·tion /ˌmætʃəˈreiʃən/ *n* [U]
ma·ture /məˈtʊr, məˈtʃʊr/ *vt,vi* **1** come or bring to full development or to a state ready for use: *His character ~d during these years.* **2** (of bills, etc) become due. □ *adj* **1** fully grown or developed; ripe; adult: *persons of ~ years.* **2** carefully thought out; perfected: *~ plans.* **3** (of bills, etc) due for payment.
ma·ture·ly *adv*
ma·tur·ity /məˈtʊrəti, məˈtʃʊrəti/ *n* [U] the state of being mature.
mat·zo /ˈmatsə/ *n* [C] (*pl* -zoth /-sout/, ~s) flat piece of unleavened bread, as eaten during the Jewish feast of Passover.
maud·lin /ˈmɔdlɪn/ *adj* sentimental or self-pitying in a silly or tearful way.
maul /mɔl/ *n* [C] heavy hammer used for driving stakes, posts, etc. □ *vt* hurt or injure by rough or brutal handling: *~ed by a tiger.*
Maundy Thurs·day /ˌmɔndi ˈθərzdi/ *n* Thursday before Easter.
mau·so·leum /ˌmɔsəˈliəm/ *n* [C] magnificent and monumental tomb.
mauve /mouv/ *adj, n* [U] bright but delicate pale purple (color).
mav·er·ick /ˈmæv(ə)rɪk/ *n* [C] **1** unbranded calf or colt. **2** independent person who will not go along with the other members of a group, political party, etc.
maw /mɔ/ *n* [C] mouth, throat, or gullet, esp of a flesh-eating animal.
maw·kish /ˈmɔkɪʃ/ *adj* maudlin.
max. *abbr* = maximum.
maxim /ˈmæksɪm/ *n* [C] widely accepted rule of conduct or general truth briefly expressed, eg *"Waste not, want not."*
maxi·mize /ˈmæksəˌmaiz/ *vt* raise to a maximum: *~ educational opportunities.*
maxi·mi·za·tion /ˌmæksəməˈzeiʃən/ *n* [U]
maxi·mum /ˈmæksəməm/ *n* [C] (*pl* ~s or -ma /-mə/) (opp of *minimum*) greatest possible or recorded degree, quantity, etc: *The plane flies at a ~ of 350 miles per hour.* □ *adj* largest; highest; greatest possible: *the ~ temperature recorded in Dallas. The ~ load is one ton.*
may¹ /mei/ *auxiliary verb* (*pt* might /mait/) **1** (used of possibility or probability): *That may or may not be true. He may have* (= Perhaps he has) *missed his train. This might have cured your cough,* if you had taken it. **2** (used to request or grant permission): *May I come in? You may.* **3** (used to express politeness when asking for information or making a request): *Well, who might you be? Might I make a suggestion?* **4** (used to suggest "There is good reason"): *We may/might as well stay where we are,* It seems reasonable to do so. **5** (used to express wishes and hopes): *May you both be happy!* **6** (in clauses of purpose, result, etc): *He died so that others might live.*
May² /mei/ *n* the fifth month of the year.
ˈ**May Day,** 1st of May, celebrated as a spring festival and also, in some countries, as a holiday for labor.
Ma·ya /ˈmaiə/ *n* [C] (*pl* ~, ~s) member of an ancient Indian civilization of Mexico and Central America.
Ma·yan *adj*
may·be /ˈmeibi/ *adv* perhaps; possibly.
may·fly /ˈmeiˌflai/ *n* [C] (*pl* -ies) short-lived insect with transparent wings.
may·hem /ˈmeiˌhem/ *n* [U] **1** (*legal*) crime of willfully and permanently injuring or crippling a person. **2** state of violent disorder and confusion.
may·on·naise /ˈmeiəˌneiz/ *n* [U] thick dressing of eggs, cream, oil, vinegar, etc used on cold foods, esp salads.
mayor /ˈmeiər/ *n* [C] highest official of a city or borough.
maze /meiz/ *n* [C] **1** (often confusing) network of lines, paths, etc; labyrinth: *a ~ of narrow roads.* **2** state of confusion or bewilderment.
ma·zurka /məˈzərkə/ *n* [C] (piece of music for a) lively Polish dance for four or eight couples.
MC¹ *abbr* = Medical Corps.
mc² *abbr* = megacycle(s).
M.C.³ *abbr* = **1** Master of Ceremonies (*Note:* often spoken as /ˈemˌsi/, ⇨ emcee). **2** Member of Congress.
MD¹ *postal abbr* = Maryland. ⇨ App 6.
M.D.² /ˌem ˈdi/ *abbr* Doctor of Medicine (*Lat* = Medicinae Doctor). □ *n* [C] (*pl* M.D.'s) (one who has a) Doctor of Medicine degree.
ME¹ *postal abbr* = Maine. ⇨ App 6.
me² /mi/ *personal pron* (used as the object form of *I*): *He saw me. Give me one. It's me,* (*informal*) it is I.
mead¹ /mid/ *n* [U] alcoholic drink made from fermented honey and water.
mead² /mid/ *n* [C] (*archaic*) meadow.
meadow /ˈmedou/ *n* [C] area, field, of grassland, esp one kept for hay.
meadow·lark *n* North American songbird found in open, grassy fields.
mea·ger /ˈmigər/ *adj* **1** thin; lacking in flesh: *a ~ face.* **2** insufficient; poor; scanty: *a ~ meal.*
mea·ger·ly *adv*
mea·ger·ness /-nɪs/ *n* [U]
meal¹ /ˈmiəl/ *n* [C] **1** act or time of eating: *three ~s a day.* **2** food that is prepared or eaten at one time: *have a good ~.*
ˈ**meal·time** *n* usual time for taking a meal.
meal² /ˈmiəl/ *n* [U] grain coarsely ground: ˈ*corn-~.*
mealy /ˈmili/ *adj* (-ier, -iest) of, like, containing, covered with, meal².
mealy·bug /ˈmiliˌbəg/ *n* [C] insect that infests vines, etc.

mealy·mouthed /ˈmiliˌmauθt/ *adj* tending to avoid straightforward, frank, language because of shyness, hypocrisy, etc.

mean[1] /min/ *adj* (-er, -est) **1** poor in appearance; shabby: *a ~ house in a ~ street.* **2** unkind; spiteful; cruel: *That was a ~ trick! Don't be so ~ to your little brother*, don't tease him, treat him unkindly, etc. **3** of low rank or humble birth: *We offer justice even to the ~est citizens.* **4** (of the understanding, the natural powers) inferior; poor: *This should be clear even to the ~est intelligence.* **5** lacking in generosity; stingy; miserly: *Her husband is so ~ about money.* **6** (*informal*) nasty; ill-tempered: *He's a ~, sullen person.* **7** (*sl*) excellent: *plays a ~ game of tennis.*
mean·ly *adv*
mean·ness /-nɪs/ *n* [U]

mean[2] /min/ *adj* occupying the middle position between two extremes: *the ~ annual temperature in Hawaii.*

mean[3] /min/ *n* [C] **1** condition, quality, course of action, etc that is halfway between two extremes. **2** (*math*) (also **arithˈmetic mean**) average; term obtained by adding all the members in a series and then dividing that total by the number of members: *The ~ of 3, 5 and 7 is 5* (because 3 + 5 + 7 = 15 and 15 ÷ 3 = 5).

mean[4] /min/ *vt,vi* (*pt,pp* ~t /ment/) **1** (of words, sentences, etc) signify; have the sense of: *A dictionary tries to tell you what words ~.* **2** be a sign of; be likely to result in: *These new orders will ~ working overtime.* **3** intend to express or to refer to: *What do you ~ by saying that? Do you ~* (= refer to) *Miss Ann Smith or Miss Angela Smith? Is this figure ~t to be a 1 or a 7?* **4** have as a purpose: *He ~s you no harm*, does not intend to hurt you. *He ~s to succeed.* ***mean business,*** (*informal*) be in earnest, ready to act (not merely to talk). ***mean well,*** have good intentions (though perhaps not the will or capacity to carry them out): *Of course he ~s well.* **5** design for a particular purpose; determine: *a room ~t for storage.* **6** be of importance or value to: *Your friendship ~s a great deal to me. $50 ~s a lot to her.*
mean·ing *n* [C,U] what is meant or intended: *a word with many distinct ~ings. What's the ~ing of this?* (asked, for example, by a person who thinks he has been badly treated, etc). □ *adj* full of meaning; expressive: *a ~ing look.*
mean·ing·ful /-fəl/ *adj* (esp) significant; full of meaning.
mean·ing·fully /-fəli/ *adv*
mean·ing·less *adj* without meaning or motive.

me·ander /miˈændər/ *vi* **1** follow a winding course. **2** wander here and there: *The brook ~ed through the fields in an aimless way.*

means[1] /minz/ *n pl* (often used with a *sing verb*, as in examples) method, process, by which a result may be obtained: *There is/are no ~ of learning what is happening. Does the end always justify the ~?* If the aim or purpose is good, may any methods, even if bad or immoral, be used? ***by means of,*** through; with the help of: *Thoughts are expressed by ~ of words.* ***by all means,*** certainly. ***by no means,*** not at all.

means[2] /minz/ *n pl* money; wealth; resources: *a man of ~*, a rich man. ***live beyond/within one's means,*** spend more/less than one's income.

meant *pt,pp* of mean[4].

mean·time /ˈminˌtaim/ *adv, n* (*sing* only) (in the) interval between.

mean·while /ˈminˌ(h)waiəl/ *adv, n* (*sing* only) meantime.

meas. *abbr* = measure.

measles /ˈmizəlz/ *n* [U] (used with a *sing verb*) contagious disease, marked by fever and small red spots that cover the whole body.

measly /ˈmizli/ *adj* (-ier, -iest) (*informal*) of little value; of poor quality; of small size or amount: *What a ~ helping of ice cream!*

measure[1] /ˈmeʒər/ *n* **1** [U] size, quantity, degree, weight, etc as determined by a standard or unit. **2** [C] unit, standard or system used in stating size, quantity, or degree: *liquid/dry ~.* ***for good measure,*** in addition to the necessary amount. **3** [C] something with which to test size, quantity, etc: *a pint ~; ˈtape ~,* ⇨ tape. **4** extent, (esp in) ***in great/large measure,*** to a large extent: *Their success was in large ~/in great ~ the result of thorough preparation.* **5** knowledge of the extent or limitations of something or somebody, (esp in) ***beyond measure,*** very great(ly): *Her joy was beyond ~.* ***take the measure of somebody,*** determine his strengths, weaknesses, etc: *He took the ~ of his opponent.* **6** [C] legislative bill; law: *~s to halt inflation.* **7** [C] proceeding; step: *They took strong ~s against dangerous drivers.* **8** [C] (*music*) rests and notes between two bars on a musical staff. ⇨ illus at notation.

measure[2] /ˈmeʒər/ *vt,vi* **1** find the size, extent, volume, degree, etc of: *~ an area of ground/the strength of an electric current/the speed of a car/the length of my arm.* **2** have as a measurement: *This room ~s 10 yards across.* **3** give or mark a measured quantity: *~ out a dose of medicine; ~ off 2 yards of cloth.* **4** ***measure up to,*** meet a certain standard: *His work has not ~d up to our expectations.*
measur·able /ˈmeʒərəbəl/ *adj*
measur·ably /-əbli/ *adv*
meas·ured *adj* **(a)** carefully chosen or considered: *~d words.* **(b)** in slow and regular rhythm: *with a ~d tread.*
measure·less *adj* limitless.
measure·ment *n* **(a)** [U] measuring: *the metric system of ~ment.* **(b)** (usu *pl*) figures about length, breadth, depth, etc: *the ~ments of a room.*
ˈmeasur·ing cup, with measurement marks on the inside or outside and usually with a pouring spout, esp for kitchen use.

meat /mit/ *n* **1** [U] flesh of animals used as food, excluding fish and poultry. **2** (*archaic*) food: *~ and drink.* **3** fleshy, edible part inside the shell or husk of a nut, fruit, etc. **4** (*fig*) substance: *There's not much ~ in his argument.*
ˈmeat·ball *n* [C] small ball of ground meat.
meaty *adj* (-ier, -iest) **(a)** fleshy. **(b)** (*fig*) full of substance.

me·chanic /mɪˈkænɪk/ *n* [C] skilled workman, esp one who repairs or adjusts machinery and tools.

me·chan·ical /mɪˈkænɪkəl/ *adj* **1** of, connected with, produced by, machines: ~ *engineering*. **2** (of persons, their actions) like machines; automatic; as if done without thought or feeling: ~ *movements*.

me·chan·ically /-kli/ *adv*

me·chan·ics /mɪˈkænɪks/ *n* (usually used with a *sing verb*) **1** science of motion and force: *Mechanics is taught by Dr. Hill.* **2** technical knowledge having to do with machinery. **3** (used with a *pl verb*) (method of) construction or operation: *the ~ of producing plays.*

mech·an·ism /ˈmekəˌnɪzəm/ *n* [C] **1** working parts of a machine collectively. **2** structure or arrangement of parts that work together as the parts of a machine do: *the ~ of government.* **3** way in which something works or is constructed.

mech·an·ize /ˈmekəˌnaiz/ *vt* **1** use machines in or for. **2** make mechanical.

mech·an·iz·ation /ˌmekənəˈzeiʃən/ *n* [U]

med. *abbr* = **1** medical. **2** medicine.

medal /ˈmedəl/ *n* [C] flat piece of metal, often round and stamped with a design, given as an award for bravery, for a great achievement, etc.

me·dal·lion /məˈdælyən/ *n* [C] **1** large medal. **2** flat, circular, ornamental design.

meddle /ˈmedəl/ *vi* become involved without being asked to do so; interfere: *Don't ~ in my affairs. Who's been meddling with my papers?*

med·dler *n* [C]

ˈmeddle·some /-səm/ *adj* tending to meddle.

me·dia *pl* of medium.

medi·aeval = medieval.

me·dial /ˈmidiəl/ *adj* **1** situated, placed, in the middle. **2** of average size.

me·di·ally /-iəli/ *adv*

me·di·ate /ˈmidiˌeit/ *vi,vt* **1** act as go-between or peacemaker: ~ *between employers and their workers.* **2** bring about by doing this: ~ *a settlement/a peace.*

me·dia·tion /ˌmidiˈeiʃən/ *n* [U]

me·dia·tor /ˈmidiˌeitər/ *n* [C]

medic /ˈmedɪk/ *n* (*informal*) **1** doctor. **2** medical student. **3** person who is in a medical corps of the armed forces.

Medi·caid /ˈmedɪˌkeid/ *n* program providing medical benefits for the poor and the disabled sponsored by the federal and state governments.

medi·cal /ˈmedɪkəl/ *adj* **1** of the study or practice of medicine: *a ~ practitioner*, a qualified doctor; *a ˈ~ school.* **2** of medicine (as contrasted with *surgery*): *The hospital has a ~ ward and a surgical ward.* □ *n* [C] medical examination.

medi·cally /-kli/ *adv*

Medi·care /ˈmedɪˌker/ *n* government program that provides medical care esp for the aged.

medi·cate /ˈmedəˌkeit/ *vt* **1** treat with medicine. **2** add a medicinal substance to: *~d soap.*

medi·ca·tion /ˌmedəˈkeiʃən/ *n* [C,U]

me·dici·nal /məˈdɪsənəl/ *adj* able to heal or cure: ~ *preparations; for ~ use.*

medi·cine /ˈmedəsən/ *n* **1** [U] **(a)** the art and science of the prevention and cure of disease. **(b)** branch of this that treats disease by methods other than surgery. **2** [C,U] (kind of) substance, esp one taken through the mouth, used to treat disease: *He's always taking ~(s).* **3** [U] (esp among American Indians) (object believed to have) magical power.

ˈmedicine ˌman, member of an American Indian tribe believed to have the ability to cure diseases by means of potions and magic.

medi·eval /ˌmidiˈivəl/ *adj* of the Middle Ages (about AD 500-1500).

me·di·ocre /ˌmidiˈoukər/ *adj* not very good; neither very good nor very bad; ordinary.

me·di·oc·rity /ˌmidiˈakrəti/ *n* [U] quality of being mediocre.

medi·tate /ˈmedəˌteit/ *vt,vi* **1** plan; consider at length: ~ *revenge/mischief.* **2** give oneself up to serious thought; think deeply about: *He sat there meditating on his misfortunes.* ~ *on world peace.*

medi·ta·tion /ˌmedəˈteiʃən/ *n* **1** [U] meditating: *deep in ~.* **2** [C] instance of this.

medi·tat·ive /ˈmedəˌteitɪv/ *adj*

medi·tat·ive·ly *adv*

Medi·ter·ra·nean /ˌmedətəˈreiniən/ *adj* of, characteristic of, the Mediterranean Sea or the countries, etc bordering it: *a ~ climate.*

me·dium /ˈmidiəm/ *n* [C] (*pl* ~s or media /ˈmidiə/) **1 (a)** means of expression: *Oil paint is a ~ for the artist.* **(b)** method of communication. ***the media,*** (often with a *sing verb*) television, radio, the press, etc: *the ˌmass ˈmedia,* ⇨ mass. **2** middle quality or degree. ***the happy medium,*** something, as a course of action, between two extremes, eg being neither very lax nor very strict in maintaining discipline. **3** (*pl* often media) substance, surroundings, in which something exists or moves: *Air is the ~ of sound.* **4** any means by which something is done, brought about, etc: *used gold coins as a ~ of exchange.* **5** (*pl* usually mediums) person who claims to be able to receive messages from the spirits of the dead. □ *adj* coming halfway between; not extreme: *a man of ~ height; a ~-sized firm.*

ˈmedium frequency, radio-wave frequency between 300 to 3000 kilocycles per second.

med·ley /ˈmedli/ *n* [C] (*pl* ~s) **1** mixture of different kinds of things or persons. **2** musical composition or arrangement made up of (parts of) other melodies.

me·dul·la /məˈdələ/ *n* (*pl* ~s, -lae /-li/) **1** [U] marrow. **2** [C] mass of nerve tissue at the base of the brain, which controls breathing, circulation, etc.

meek /mik/ *adj* (-er, -est) mild and patient; unprotesting: *as ~ as a lamb.*

meek·ly *adv*

meek·ness /-nɪs/ *n* [U]

meet[1] /mit/ *vt,vi* (*pt,pp* met /met/) **1** come face to face with, from the opposite or a different direction; come together from different points or directions: *The two trucks met on a narrow road.* **2** come together by arrangement: *The Debating Society ~s every Friday at 8pm.* **3** come into the presence of; encounter, esp by chance: ~ *an old friend at a party.* ***meet with,*** experience: ~ *with misfortune/an accident.* **4** make the acquaintance of; become acquainted: *I know Mrs. Hill by sight, but have never met* *her/we've never met. Pleased to ~ you,* as a formal introduction. **5** go to a place and await the arrival of: *I'll ~ you at the station/~ your train.* **6** satisfy (a demand, etc): *~ his wishes,* do what he wants. ***meet sb halfway,*** (*fig*) give way to some extent in order to satisfy him or reach agreement. **7** pay: *met all his bills.* **8** come into contact; join; connect: *Their hands met. The roads should ~ about a mile away.* ***make ends meet,*** ⇨ make[1](13). **9** ***meet the eye(s)/ear(s),*** become noticed. ***more to sb/sth than meets the eye,*** person, thing, situation, etc is more complicated than it seems to be at first. **10** come together as opponents or face a person in a contest, struggle, etc: *met the champion in the finals. The teams met on the playing field.*

meet[2] /mit/ *n* [C] athletic meeting or contest: *a ˈtrack ~.*

meet·ing /ˈmitɪŋ/ *n* [C] **1 (a)** coming together of a number of persons at a certain time and place, esp for discussion: *political ~s.* **(b)** people present at such a gathering. **2** any coming together.

ˈmeeting house, building for worship, esp for certain Protestant religions.

mega·cycle /ˈmegəˌsaikəl/ *n* [C] million cycles per second.

mega·lith /ˈmegəˌlɪθ/ *n* [C] large stone, esp one used in a prehistoric monument.

mega·lithic /ˌmegəˈlɪθɪk/ *adj* made of, marked by, the use of megaliths.

mega·lo·ma·nia /ˌmeg(ə)louˈmeiniə/ *n* [U] mental disorder in which a person has exaggerated ideas of his importance, power, wealth, etc: *The dictator was obviously suffering from ~.*

mega·lo·ma·niac /-niˌæk/ *n* [C] person suffering from megalomania.

mega·phone /ˈmegəˌfoun/ *n* [C] cone-shaped device for magnifying or directing sound.

mega·ton /ˈmegəˌtən/ *n* [C] explosive force equal to one million tons of TNT.

mel·an·cholic /ˌmelənˈkalɪk/ *adj* (with a tendency to) being in a state of melancholy.

mel·an·choly /ˈmelənˌkali/ *n* [U] sad and depressed state or atmosphere. □ *adj* **1** sad; depressed. **2** causing sadness or depression: *a ~ occasion,* eg a funeral.

mel·an·cholia /ˌmelənˈkouliə/ *n* [U] mental illness marked by melancholy.

melba toast /ˌmelbə ˈtoust/ very thin, crisp toast, usually bought ready-made in a box.

melio·rate /ˈmiliəˌreit/ *vt,vi* (*formal*) make or become better.

melio·ration /ˌmiliəˈreiʃən/ *n* [U]

mel·low /ˈmelou/ *adj* (-er, -est) **1** soft and sweet in taste; ripe and full in flavor. **2** soft, pure and rich in color or sound. **3** made wise and gentle by age or experience. **4** kindly; genial. **5** soft, loamy, and moist: *~ soil.* □ *vt,vi* make or become mellow.

mel·low·ly *adv*

mel·low·ness /-nɪs/ *n* [U]

me·lodic /məˈladɪk/ *adj* of melody; melodious.

me·lodi·ous /məˈloudiəs/ *adj* of, producing, melody; sounding sweet: *the ~ notes of a thrush.*

me·lodi·ous·ly *adv*

me·lodi·ous·ness /-nɪs/ *n* [U]

melo·drama /ˈmeləˌdramə/ *n* **1** [C] play with exciting and often sensational events, usually having a happy ending. **2** [U] plays of this kind as a group. **3** [U] events, language, behavior, suggestive of plays of this kind.

melo·dra·matic /ˌmelədrəˈmætik/ *adj*

melo·dra·mati·cally /-kli/ *adv*

mel·ody /ˈmelədi/ *n* (*pl* -ies) **1** [U] sweet music; tunefulness. **2** [C] song or tune: *old Irish melodies.* **3** [C] principal part or voice in harmonized music; theme: *The ~ is next taken up by the flutes.* **4** [U] musical quality of any series of pleasing sounds.

melon /ˈmelən/ *n* [C] (kinds of) large, juicy round fruit with a hard rind, that grows on a vine.

melt /melt/ *vt,vi* (*pt,pp* ~ed) **1** change from a solid to a liquid, esp through heating: *The ice will ~ when the sun shines on it.* ***melt sth down,*** melt metals (eg articles of gold and silver) in order to use the metal as raw material. **2** (of a solid in a liquid) dissolve (the usual word). **3** (of a person, heart, feelings) soften, be softened: *Her heart ~ed with pity.* **4** fade; go (slowly) away: *One color ~ed into another,* eg in the sky at sunset. ***melt away,*** become less, disappear, (as) by melting: *The snow soon ~ed away when the sun came out. Her money seemed to ~ away in Paris.*

ˈmelt·ing point, temperature at which a solid melts.

ˈmelt·ing pot, (a) pot in which metals, etc are melted. **(b)** place in which people of many different races, nationalities, etc live together and make one community.

mem·ber /ˈmembər/ *n* [C] **1** person belonging to a group, society, etc: *Every ~ of her family came to her wedding.* **2** part of a human or animal body.

ˈmem·ber·ship *n* **(a)** [U] the state of being a member (of a society, etc). **(b)** [C] total number of members: *a ~ship of 80.*

mem·brane /ˈmemˌbrein/ *n* [C] soft, thin, pliable layer esp of animal, vegetable or synthetic tissue.

mem·bra·nous /ˈmembrənəs/ *adj*

mem·ento /məˈmentou/ *n* [C] (*pl* ~s, ~es) something that serves to remind one of a person or event; souvenir.

memo /ˈmemou/ *n* [C] (*pl* ~s) (*informal*) (short for) memorandum.

mem·oir /ˈmemˌwar/ *n* [C] **1** biography. **2** (*pl*) account of the proceedings of a learned society. **3** (*pl*) autobiography. **4** author's account of something he has experienced.

mem·or·able /ˈmemərəbəl/ *adj* deserving to be remembered; remarkable.

mem·or·ably /-əbli/ *adv*

mem·or·an·dum /ˌmeməˈrændəm/ *n* [C] (*pl* -da /-də/ or ~s) **1** note written as a reminder. **2** informal business communication. **3** report of the terms of an agreement.

me·mor·ial /məˈmɔriəl/ *n* [C] **1** something made or done to remind people of an event, person, etc: *a ˈwar ~.* **2** petition sent to a government, legislature, etc. □ *adj* serving to keep in mind: *a ~ service.*

LINCOLN MEMORIAL

Me'morial Day, legal holiday in honor of persons in military service who were killed in war, observed in most of the US on the last Monday in May.

mem·or·ize /ˈmeməˌraiz/ *vt* commit to memory; learn by heart.

mem·ory /ˈmem(ə)ri/ *n* (*pl* -ies) **1** [U] ability to remember; power of retaining and recalling what has been learned, experienced, etc. ***commit sth to memory,*** learn it by heart. **2** [C] ability of an individual to retain and remember: *He has a bad ~ for dates.* **3** [U] period of time over which the memory can go back. ***within living memory,*** within the years that people now alive can remember. **4** [C] something remembered; recollection: *memories of childhood.* ***in memory of sb,*** in honor of someone remembered with love: *gave to charity in ~ of his father.* **5** [C] unit of a computer which stores data or information for future use.

men *pl* of man¹(1).

men·ace /ˈmenəs/ *n* **1** [C,U] danger; threat: *a ~ to world peace.* **2** [C] annoying person: *That woman is a ~.* □ *vt* threaten: *countries ~d by/with war.*

men·ac·ing·ly *adv*

mé·nage /meiˈnaʒ/ *n* [C] household; domestic establishment.

me·nag·erie /məˈnædʒəri/ *n* [C] collection of wild animals in captivity.

mend /mend/ *vt,vi* **1** remake, repair (something broken, worn out or torn); restore to good condition or working order: *~ shoes/a broken window.* **2** correct faults or errors: *That won't ~* (= improve) *matters.* ***mend one's ways,*** reform or improve one's behavior. **3** regain health; heal. □ *n* [C] part that has been mended: *The ~s were almost invisible.* ***on the mend,*** improving in health or condition.

ˈmend·ing *n* [U] **(a)** (esp) work of repairing (clothes, etc). **(b)** clothing that is to be mended.

men·da·cious /menˈdeiʃəs/ *adj* (*formal*) false; untruthful: *~ newspaper reports.*

men·dac·ity /menˈdæsəti/ *n* (*pl* -ies) (*formal*) **1** [U] untruthfulness. **2** [C] lie; untrue statement.

men·folk /ˈmenˌfouk/ *n pl* (*informal*) men, esp the men of a family: *The ~ have all gone fishing.*

men·ha·den /menˈheidən/ *n* [C] (*pl* ~, ~s) (kind of) fish found off the Atlantic coast of the US, that is used as bait and as a source of oil and fertilizer.

me·nial /ˈminiəl/ *adj* suitable for, to be done by, a household servant: *~ tasks such as washing pots and pans.* □ *n* [C] servant.

me·ni·ally /-iəli/ *adv*

men·in·gi·tis /ˌmenınˈdʒaitıs/ *n* [U] serious illness caused by inflammation of any or all of the membranes enclosing the brain and spinal cord.

meno·pause /ˈmenəˌpɔz/ *n* [C] final stopping of the menses at the age of about 50.

men·ses /ˈmenˌsiz/ *n pl* discharge of blood and dead tissue from the uterus, usually occurring about once a month in human females between the ages of 12 and 50.

men·strual /ˈmenstruəl/ *adj* of the menses.

men·stru·ate /ˈmenstruˌeit/ *vi* discharge the menses.

men·stru·ation /ˌmenstruˈeiʃən/ *n* [U]

-ment /-mənt/ *suffix* **1** process or action: *development.* **2** means or result of an action: *government.* **3** condition or state: *amusement.*

men·tal /ˈmentəl/ *adj* **1** of or in the mind: *~ aˈrithmetic,* done in the mind without using written figures or a mechanical device. **2** of, having, or for the care of mental illnesses or disorders: *a ˈ~ hospital.*

men·tally /ˈmentəli/ *adv*

men·tal·ity /menˈtæləti/ *n* (*pl* -ies) **1** [U] general intelligence; degree of intellectual power: *persons of average ~.* **2** [C] characteristic attitude of mind: *a war ~.*

men·thol /ˈmenˌθɔl/ *n* [U] solid white substance obtained from oil of peppermint, used medicinally and as a flavoring (eg in cigarettes).

men·tho·lated /ˈmenθəˌleitıd/ *adj*

men·tion /ˈmenʃən/ *vt* speak or write about briefly; refer to: *I'll ~ it to him. She ~ed that he called.* ***Don't mention it,*** phrase used after being thanked. □ *n* **1** [U] mentioning or being mentioned: *He made no ~ of your request.* **2** [C] brief notice or reference. **3** [U,C] formal notice of achievement in a race, contest, etc: *received (an) honorable ~ at the state fair.*

-men·tioned *adj* (with an *adverb* prefixed): *ˌabove-/ˌbelow-ˈ~ed,* referred to above/below.

men·tor /ˈmenˌtɔr/ *n* [C] wise and trusted adviser and teacher.

menu /ˈmenyu/ *n* [C] **1** list of courses or dishes at a meal or of dishes available in a restaurant. **2** food that is served.

me·ow /miˈau/ *vi, n* [C] (make the) sound or cry of a cat.

mer·can·tile /ˈmərkənˌtaiəl/ *adj* of trade, commerce and merchants.

mer·ce·nary /ˈmərsəˌneri/ *adj* concerned only about money or other reward; inspired by love of money: *~ politicians; act from ~ motives.* □ *n* [C] (*pl* -ies) soldier hired for pay to serve in a foreign army.

mer·chan·dise /ˈmərtʃənˌdaiz, -ˌdais/ *n* [U] goods bought and sold; commercial wares. □ *vt,vi* **1** buy and sell (goods). **2** promote or increase sales by the use of advertising, attractive displays, etc.

mer·chant /ˈmərtʃənt/ *n* [C] **1** trader, esp one doing business with foreign countries. **2** person who keeps a retail store. □ *adj* **1** having to do with trade or commerce: ~ *ships*. **2** of or relating to the merchant marine.

mer·chant ma·rine /ˌmərtʃənt məˈrin/ *n* **1** commercial ships of a nation. **2** persons who serve on such ships.

mer·ci·ful /ˈmərsɪfəl/ *adj* having, showing, feeling mercy (to).

mer·ci·fully /-fli/ *adv*

mer·ci·less /ˈmərsɪlɪs/ *adj* showing no mercy.

mer·ci·less·ly *adv*

mer·cur·ial /mərˈkyʊriəl/ *adj* **1** clever; quick-witted. **2** changeable; inconstant: *a ~ temperament.*

mer·cury[1] /ˈmərkyəri/ *n* [U] heavy, silver-colored metallic element (symbol **Hg**) usually liquid at room temperature, as used in thermometers and barometers.

Mer·cury[2] /ˈmərkyəri/ *n* (*astron*) planet nearest the sun. ⇨ illus at planet.

mercy /ˈmərsi/ *n* (*pl* -ies) **1** [U] willingness to forgive or to keep from punishing a guilty person or a person who is in one's power. ***show (sb) mercy,*** act with mercy (toward him): *We were shown no ~.* ***at the mercy of,*** in the power of; without defense against: *The ship was at the ~ of the waves.* **2** [U] gentle and kindly treatment of those who are in trouble. **3** [C] piece of good fortune; blessing: *We must be thankful for small mercies.*

ˈmercy killing, killing considered as an act of mercy, eg to keep an incurably ill person from suffering further pain.

mere /mɪr/ *adj* (no *comp*, -st) not more than: *She's a ~ child. It's a ~/the ~st trifle,* nothing at all important, nothing of any value, etc.

mere·ly *adv* only; simply: *I ~ly asked his name. I said it ~ly as a joke.*

mer·etri·cious /ˌmerəˈtrɪʃəs/ *adj* (*formal*) attractive on the surface but of little value.

mer·gan·ser /mərˈgænsər/ *n* [C] wild duck with a narrow, hooked beak and a usually crested head.

merge /mərdʒ/ *vt,vi* **1** (cause to) become one: *The small banks ~d/were ~d into one large organization.* **2** ***merge into,*** fade or change gradually into: *Twilight ~d into darkness.*

merger *n* [C] (esp) act of merging or uniting two or more companies into one.

me·rid·ian /məˈrɪdiən/ *n* [C] **1** (either half of an imaginary) circle around the globe, passing through a given place and the north and south poles: *Every place on the same ~ has the same longitude.* **2** highest point above the horizon reached by the sun or other star as viewed from a point on the earth's surface; zenith. **3** (*fig*) point of highest development.

me·ringue /məˈræŋ/ *n* **1** [U] beaten whites of an egg and sugar baked as a covering for pies, tarts, etc: *lemon ~ pie,* lemon curd or custard topped with meringue. **2** [C] small shell made of this mixture, used for fruit, ice cream, etc.

me·ri·no /məˈrinou/ *n* (*pl* ~s) **1** [C] sheep with long, fine wool. **2** [U] cloth or yarn made from the wool of this breed of sheep.

merit /ˈmerɪt/ *n* **1** [U] value; worth; excellence: *a certificate of ~; Do men of ~ always win recognition?* **2** [C] quality, fact, action, etc that deserves reward or praise: *has both ~s and faults.* **3** [C] actual facts or qualities, whether good or bad: *We must decide the case on its ~s.* □ *vt* deserve; be worthy of: *~ reward.*

meri·tori·ous /ˌmerəˈtɔriəs/ *adj* (*formal*) praiseworthy; deserving reward: *a prize for ~ conduct.*

meri·tori·ous·ly *adv*

mer·maid /ˈmərˌmeid/ *n* [C] imaginary creature with the upper body of a woman and with a fish's tail in place of legs.

merry /ˈmeri/ *adj* (-ier, -iest) happy; cheerful; bright and gay: *a ~ laugh. I wish you a ~ Christmas.*

mer·rily /ˈmerəli/ *adv*

mer·ri·ment /ˈmerɪmənt/ *n* [U]

merry·go·round /ˈmerigouˌraund/ *n* [C] **1** revolving circular platform with seats, often in the form of animals, on which people ride for amusement. **2** rapid round of events, activities, etc: *The days before the wedding were a ~.*

merry·mak·ing /ˈmeriˌmeikɪŋ/ *n* **1** [U] festive activity, gaiety. **2** [C] festive party or occasion.

me·sa /ˈmeisə/ *n* [C] flat-topped hill or plateau with steep sides, as found in the southwestern US.

MESA

mesh /meʃ/ *n* **1** [C] one of the spaces in material such as a net or wire screen: *a net with half-inch ~es.* **2** [U] fabric knit or woven with small, even spaces between the threads. **3** (*pl*) network: *the ~es of a spider's web.* **4** (*fig*) trap; snare: *the ~es of political intrigue.* □ *vt,vi* **1** catch or entangle, as in a net. **2** (of gears) engage or come together with others. **3** (*fig*) fit together properly; harmonize: *Our ways of looking at these problems don't ~.*

mess /mes/ *n* [C] **1** (rarely *pl*) state of confusion; dirt or disorder: *The workmen cleaned up the ~ before they left.* **2** person or thing that is dirty, disorderly, etc: *My room is a ~!* **3** troublesome or confused situation: *He got us into another ~.* **4** portion of (esp soft) food: *a ~ of cereal.* **5** amount of a particular food gathered or prepared at one time: *a ~ of fried chicken.* **6** group of persons (as soldiers, sailors, etc.) regularly taking meals together. **7** meal taken by or served to such a group. **8** place where such a group has its meals: *the officers' ~.* □ *vt,vi* **1** make dirty or disorderly. ***mess up,*** **(a)** put into disorder or confusion: *~ed up the kitchen.* **(b)** spoil; bungle: *The late arrival of the train ~ed up all our* *plans.* **2** ***mess around,*** (*informal*) pass time aimlessly. **3** ***mess in/with,*** (*informal*) meddle or interfere with: *Don't ~ in my affairs!* **4** take meals with a group of people forming a mess (6).

mes·sage /ˈmesɪdʒ/ *n* [C] **1** communication sent to a person, group, etc. *Will you take this ~ to my brother?* **2** inspired teaching: *the ~ of Christianity.* **3** moral lesson or theme: *a book with a ~.*

mes·sen·ger /ˈmesɪndʒər/ *n* [C] person carrying a message.

mes·siah /məˈsaiə/ *n* **1** **Messiah,** person expected by the Jews to come and set them free. **2** **Messiah,** Jesus Christ. **3** any person considered to be a savior or liberator.

mes·ti·zo /meˈstizou, -sou/ *n* [C] (*pl* ~s) person of mixed European and American Indian ancestry.

met *pt, pp* of meet[1].

me·tab·olism /məˈtæbəˌlɪzəm/ *n* [U] all the processes by which a living thing uses food and living matter to provide energy for the vital activities and to build new cells and tissues.

meta·bolic /ˌmetəˈbalɪk/ *adj*

meta·car·pal /ˌmetəˈkarpəl/ *adj, n* [C] (of a) bone extending either from the wrist to the finger, or from the ankle to the toe. ⇨ illus at skeleton.

metal /ˈmetəl/ *n* **1** [C,U] any of a class of mineral substances which have a shiny appearance, conduct heat and electricity, can be melted, and can usually be drawn into a wire: *Iron, gold and copper are ~s. Is the tray made of wood or ~?* **2** (as an *adjective*): *~ containers.* **3** = mettle (the usual spelling).

me·tal·lic /məˈtælɪk/ *adj* **1** of or like metal: *a ~ gleam.* **2** harsh in sound: *a ~, grating noise.*

meta·mor·pho·sis /ˌmetəˈmɔrfəsɪs/ *n* [C] (*pl* -ses /-ˌsiz/) **1** sudden and striking change in appearance, character, etc. **2** change of form or character, eg by natural growth or development: *the ~ from a tadpole to a frog.*

meta·phor /ˈmetəˌfɔr/ *n* [C] figure of speech which implies or suggests a likeness between two different objects, notions, etc. as in, "Snow blanketed the hills," ie snow covered the hills as if it were a blanket.

meta·phori·cal /ˌmetəˈfɔrɪkəl/ *adj* of, like, containing or using a metaphor.

meta·phori·cally /-kli/ *adv*

meta·tar·sal /ˌmetəˈtarsəl/ *adj, n* [C] (of a) bone which is one of five extending from the ankle to the toe and forming the instep of the foot. ⇨ illus at skeleton.

mete /mit/ *vt* ***mete out,*** allot; measure: *Justice was ~d out to them.*

me·teor /ˈmitiər/ *n* [C] (streak of light produced by a) small body that falls from outer space into the earth's atmosphere and burns up.

me·teoric /ˌmitiˈɔrɪk/ *adj* **1** of or having to do with meteors. **2** (*fig*) swift, brilliant, and usually brief: *a ~ career; a ~ rise to fame.*

me·teor·ite /ˈmitiəˌrait/ *n* [C] meteor that reaches the earth's surface.

me·teor·ol·ogy /ˌmitiəˈralədʒi/ *n* [U] science and study of the earth's atmosphere and its changes, and their effect on weather conditions.

me·teoro·logi·cal /ˌmitiərəˈladʒɪkəl/ *adj*

me·teor·ol·ogist /ˌmitiəˈralədʒɪst/ *n* [C] specialist in meteorology.

me·ter[1] /ˈmitər/ *n* [C] **1** apparatus which measures, esp one that records amounts, speed, distance etc. **2** = parking meter.

ˈmeter maid, policewoman assigned to patrol parking meters and give citations for violations.

me·ter[2] /ˈmitər/ *n* [C] basic unit of length in the metric system equal to 39.37 inches.

me·ter[3] /ˈmitər/ *n* [C,U] (kind of) basic, systematic rhythm in verse or music.

method /ˈmeθəd/ *n* **1** [U] system, order: *He's a man of ~.* **2** [C] regular way of doing something: *modern ~s of teaching arithmetic.*

me·thodi·cal /məˈθadɪkəl/ *adj* **(a)** arranged, done, carried out, with order or method: *~ical work.* **(b)** having orderly habits: *a ~ical worker.*

me·thodi·cally /-kli/ *adv*

Meth·od·ism /ˈmeθəˌdɪzəm/ *n* [U] beliefs and worship of the Protestant denomination started by John Wesley.

Meth·od·ist /ˈmeθədɪst/ *n* [C], *adj* (member) of this denomination.

meth·yl al·co·hol /ˌmeθəl ˈælkəˌhɔl/ *n* [U] colorless, flammable alcohol used as a fuel, solvent, and antifreeze.

me·ticu·lous /məˈtɪkyələs/ *adj* **1** giving, showing, great attention to detail. **2** careful and exact.

me·ticu·lous·ly *adv*

met·ric /ˈmetrɪk/ **1** *adj* of, relating to, or using the metric system. **2** = metrical(1). **3** having to do with measurement.

ˈmetric system, the decimal measuring system based on the meter as the unit of length, the kilogram as the unit of mass or weight and the liter as the unit of volume.

met·ri·cal /ˈmetrɪkəl/ *adj* **1** of, composed in, meter[3] (contrasted with ordinary prose): *a ~ translation of the Iliad.* **2** connected with measurement: *~ geometry.*

met·ri·cally /-kli/ *adv*

met·ro·nome /ˈmetrəˌnoum/ *n* [C] device which can be set to make a certain number of beats per minute, in order to provide a steady beat for practicing music.

me·trop·olis /məˈtrapəlɪs/ *n* [C] (*pl* ~es) **1** chief or capital city of a country, region etc. **2** large, important city.

metro·poli·tan /ˌmetrəˈpalɪtən/ *adj* **1** of or having to do with a metropolis: *the ~ police.* **2** including a large city and its surrounding suburbs: *~ Washington.* □ *n* [C] **1** person who lives in a metropolis. **2** **Metropolitan,** bishop having authority over his province.

mettle /ˈmetəl/ *n* [U] **1** quality of character; temperament. **2** spirit; daring. ***be/put sb on his mettle,*** rouse him to do his best, put him in a position that tests him.

mew /myu/ *vi, n* = meow (esp of a kitten).

mews /myuz/ *n pl* (used with a *sing verb*) former square or street of stables behind a residential street; now often converted to houses, apartments, etc: *a Boston ~.*

Mex·ican /ˈmɛksɪkən/ *n* [C] native of Mexico. □ *adj* of Mexico or its people.
mezza·nine /ˈmɛzəˌnin/ *n* [C] **1** floor, often like a balcony, between the ground floor and first floor (esp in a department store). **2** (first few rows of the) lowest balcony in a theater.
mfg. *abbr* = manufacturing.
mg *abbr* = milligram(s).
mgr. *abbr* = manager.
mi[1] /mi/ *n* [C] (*music*) syllable used for the third note of a scale.
MI[2] *postal abbr* = Michigan. ⇨ App 6.
MI[3] *abbr* = Military Intelligence.
mi.[4] *abbr* = mile(s).
mice *pl* of mouse.
micro- /ˌmaikrou, ˈmaikrə-/ (*pref*) very small: *microfilm*.
mi·crobe /ˈmaiˌkroub/ *n* [C] germ, esp one causing disease; microorganism.
micro·bi·ol·ogy /ˌmaikroubaiˈalədʒi/ *n* [U] study of microorganisms.
micro·film /ˈmaikrəˌfɪlm/ *n* [C,U] (roll, section, of) photographic film for reproduction of written or printed material in greatly reduced size. □ *vt* photograph on microfilm.
mi·crom·eter /maiˈkramətər/ *n* [C] device for measuring very small objects.
mi·cron /ˈmaiˌkran/ *n* [C] unit of length (symbol X) equal to one millionth of a meter.
micro·or·gan·ism /ˌmaikrouˈɔrgəˌnɪzəm/ *n* [C] organism so small that it can only be seen under a microscope.

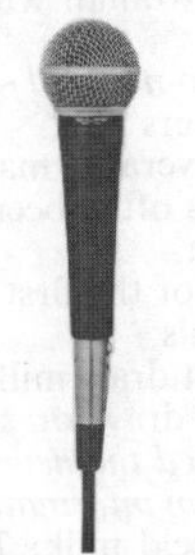

MICROPHONE

micro·phone /ˈmaikrəˌfoun/ *n* [C] instrument for changing sound waves into electrical waves, used to magnify or transmit sound, as in a telephone, radio, etc.

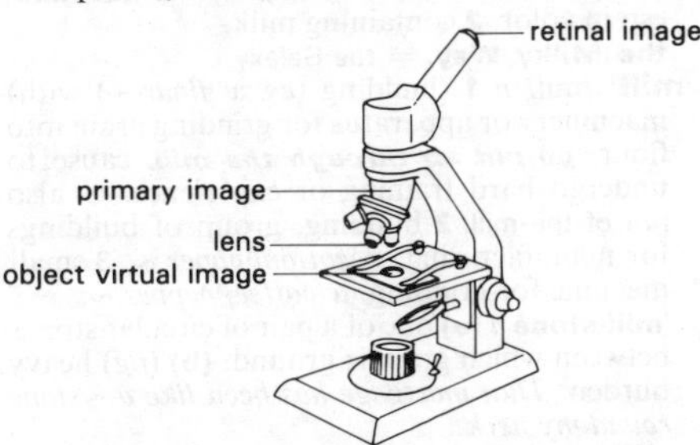

MICROSCOPE

micro·scope /ˈmaikrəˌskoup/ *n* [C] instrument with lenses for making very small objects appear larger.
micro·scopic /ˌmaikrəˈskapɪk/ *adj* **(a)** of or having to do with a microscope. **(b)** like a microscope; able to see very small objects. **(c)** very small; capable of being seen only through a microscope.
micro·scopi·cally /-kli/ *adv*
micro·wave /ˈmaikrouˌweiv/ *n* [C] very short radio wave (as used in radar).
ˌmicro·wave ˈoven, one using microwaves to heat the food.
mid[1] /mɪd/ *adj* in the middle of; middle: *from mid-June to mid-August;* (used in compounds) *a midmorning cup of coffee.*
the ˌMidˈwest, area of the US which extends west of the Appalachian Mountains, east of the Rocky Mountains, and as far south as Kansas, Missouri and the Ohio River.
mid[2] /mɪd/ *prep* (*poet*) among.
mid.[3] *abbr* = middle.
mid·day /ˈmɪdˌdei/ *n* (*sing* only) noon: (as an *adjective*) *the ~ meal.*
middle /ˈmɪdəl/ *n* **1 the middle,** point, position or part, which is at an equal distance from two or more points, etc or between the beginning and the end: *the ~ of a room. They were in the ~ of dinner* (= were having dinner) *when I called.* **2** [C] waist. □ *adj* in the middle: *the ~ house in the row. The ~ finger.*
ˌmiddle ˈage, the period between youth and old age.
ˌmiddle-ˈaged *adj*
the ˌMiddle ˈAges, the period in European history from about AD 500-1500.
ˌmiddle ˈclass, class of society between the lower and upper classes (eg business men, professional workers).
ˈmiddle-ˌclass *adj*
the ˌMiddle ˈEast, area in Asia and Africa extending from Libya in the west to Iran in the east.
ˈmiddle·man /-mən/ *n* [C] (*pl* ~men /-men/) any trader through whose hands goods pass between the producer and the consumer.
middle name, name between one's first name and family name, eg *Allan* in *Edgar Allan Poe*.
middle-of-the-ˈroad *adj* not extreme; moderate, esp in politics.
ˈmiddle school, type of school between primary school and high school. ⇨ junior high school.
ˈmiddle·weight, *n* [C] boxer weighing between 147 and 160 lbs (66.6 and 72.5 kg).
mid·dling /ˈmɪdlɪŋ/ *adj* of middle or medium size, quality, grade, etc: *a town of ~ size.* ***fair to middling,*** (*informal*) fairly good but not very good health.
mid·dy /ˈmɪdi/ *n* [C] (*pl* -ies) **1** (*informal*) midshipman. **2** loose blouse worn by women and children, that has a wide square collar.
midge /mɪdʒ/ *n* [C] small winged insect like a gnat.
midget /ˈmɪdʒɪt/ *n* [C] extremely short person. □ *adj* very small: *a ~ submarine.*
mid·land /ˈmɪdlənd/ *adj, n* [C] (of the) middle

part of a country.
mid·most /ˈmɪdˌmoust/ *adj* in the exact middle.
mid·night /ˈmɪdˌnait/ *n* (*sing* only) 12 o'clock at night: *at/before/after* ~. □ *adj* during the middle of the night; at midnight.
mid·riff /ˈmɪdrɪf/ *n* [C] **1** diaphragm. **2** middle region of the human body, from about the middle of the chest to the waist.
mid·ship·man /ˈmɪdˌʃɪpmən/ *n* [C] (*pl* -men /-men/) student training to be commissioned as an officer in the Navy.
mid·ships /ˈmɪdˌʃɪps/ *adv* = amidships.
midst /mɪdst/ *adv, n* (*liter* or *archaic*) (in the) middle part.
mid·stream /ˈmɪdˌstrim/ *n* [U] **1** middle of a stream. **2** middle of a period of time.
mid·sum·mer /ˈmɪdˌsəmər/ *n* (*sing* only) **1** the middle of summer. **2** summer solstice.
mid·way /ˈmɪdˌwei/ *adj, adv* halfway. □ *n* [C] place for rides, games, etc at an amusement park, fair, or carnival.
mid·wife /ˈmɪdˌwaif/ *n* [C] (*pl* midwives /-ˌwaivz/) person trained to help women in childbirth.
mid·win·ter /ˈmɪdˌwɪntər/ *n* (*sing* only) **1** the middle of the winter. **2** winter solstice.
mien /min/ *n* [U] (*liter*) person's appearance or bearing, esp as showing a mood: *with a sorrowful* ~.
might[1] *pt* of may[1].
might[2] /mait/ *n* [U] great power; strength: *work with all one's* ~.
mightn't /ˈmaitənt/ = might not.
mighty /ˈmaiti/ *adj* (-ier, -iest) **1** having or showing great power: *a* ~ *nation*. **2** great: *the* ~ *ocean*. ***high and mighty,*** very proud. □ *adv* (*informal*) very: *think oneself* ~ *clever*.
might·ily /-əli/ *adv*
mi·graine /ˈmaiˌgrein/ *n* [C] severe, frequently recurring, headache.
mi·grant /ˈmaigrənt/ *n* [C] person, bird, animal, etc that migrates. □ *adj* migrating: ~ *workers*.
mi·grate /ˈmaiˌgreit/ *vi* **1** move from one place to another (to live there). **2** move regularly from one region to another, esp at a particular season of the year.
mi·gra·tion /maiˈgreiʃən/ n [C,U]
mi·gra·tory /ˈmaigrəˌtori/ *adj* of, having to do with or marked by migrating: *migratory birds*.
mike /maik/ *n* [C] (*informal*) (short for) microphone.
mil. *abbr* = military.
milch /mɪltʃ/ *adj* giving milk: *a* ~ *cow*.
mild /ˈmaiəld/ *adj* (-er, -est) **1** soft; gentle; not severe: ~ *weather; a* ~ *answer*. **2** not sharp or strong in taste or flavor: ~ *cheese; a* ~ *cigar*.
mild·ly *adv* in a mild manner. ***to put it mildly,*** to speak without exaggeration.
mild·ness /-nɪs/ *n* [U]
mil·dew /ˈmɪlˌdu/ *n* [U] (usually destructive whitish coating produced by) tiny fungi growing on plants, leather, food, etc in warm and damp conditions: *roses ruined by* ~. □ *vt,vi* affect, become affected, with mildew.
mile /ˈmaiəl/ *n* [C] **1** (also **ˈstatute mile**) unit of length equal to 5,280 feet. **2 ˈnautical mile,** unit of length equal to about 6,076 feet, used in air and sea navigation. **3** race of a mile: *He ran the* ~ *in 4 minutes/a 4-minute* ~. **4** (*pl*) (*informal*) any long distance: *walk for* ~*s* (*and* ~*s*). *There's no one within* ~*s of him as a tennis player*, no one who can rival him.
ˈmile·stone *n* **(a)** stone at the side of a road showing places and distances. **(b)** (*fig*) (important) stage or event in history, research, etc.
mile·age /ˈmailɪdʒ/ *n* [U] **1** distance traveled, measured in miles: *a used car with a low* ~. **2** allowance for traveling expenses at a fixed rate a mile. **3** = miles per gallon.
mili·tant /ˈmɪlətənt/ *adj* **1** making war; fighting actively. **2** struggling or working, esp for a cause: ~ *students/workers*. □ *n* [C] militant person.
ˈmili·tancy /-ənsi/ *n* [U]
mili·tary /ˈmɪləˌteri/ *adj* of or for soldiers, an army, war on land: ~ *training;* ~ *government*. □ *n* **the military,** the armed forces.
mili·tate /ˈmɪləˌteit/ *vi* work; operate: *Several factors combined to* ~ *against the success of our plan*.
mi·litia /məˈlɪʃə/ *n* [C] (usually **the militia**) force of civilians trained as soldiers but not part of the regular army.
milk[1] /mɪlk/ *n* [U] **1 (a)** white liquid produced by female mammals as food for their young. **(b)** (esp) milk of cows, used as food by human beings. ***cry over spilt milk,*** waste time in regretting something which is done and cannot be corrected or changed. **2** liquid like milk: *coconut* ~*;* ~ *of magnesia*.
ˈmilk·maid *n* [C] woman who milks cows and works in a dairy.
ˈmilk·man /-ˌmæn/ *n* [C] (*pl* ~men /-ˌmen/) man who sells or delivers milk.
ˈmilk shake, beverage made of milk with flavoring that has often been mixed or shaken up with ice cream.
ˈmilk tooth, one of the first (temporary) teeth in young mammals.
milk[2] /mɪlk/ *vt,vi* **1** draw milk from a cow/ewe/goat, etc. **2** (*fig*) draw or squeeze something valuable from: ~*ed the newspapers and magazines for every bit of information; to* ~ *a business of its profits*. **3** yield milk: *The cows are* ~*ing well*.
milk·sop /ˈmɪlkˌsap/ *n* [C] (*dated*) man or boy who is timid and lacking in spirit.
milk·weed /ˈmɪlkˌwid/ *n* [C] plant with milky juice and large seed pods.
milky /ˈmɪlki/ *adj* (-ier, -iest) **1** of or like milk, esp in color. **2** containing milk.
the ˌMilky ˈWay, = the Galaxy.
mill[1] /mɪl/ *n* **1** (building (eg a ˈ*flour*-~) with) machinery or apparatus for grinding grain into flour. ***go/put sb through the mill,*** cause to undergo hard training or experience. ⇨ also run-of-the-mill. **2** building, group of buildings for manufacturing: *a ˈcotton/ˈpaper* ~. **3** small machine for grinding: *a ˈcoffee/ˈpepper* ~.
ˈmill·stone *n* **(a)** one of a pair of circular stones between which grain is ground. **(b)** (*fig*) heavy burden: *That mortgage has been like a* ~*stone round my neck*.
mill[2] /mɪl/ *vt,vi* **1** put through a machine for grinding; produce by doing this: ~ *grain/flour*.

2 produce regular markings on the edge of a coin: *silver coins with a ~ed edge*. **3** ***mill about/around,*** (of crowds) move in a disorganized or confused way.

mil·len·nium /mɪˈleniəm/ *n* [C] (*pl* -nia /-niə/, ~s) **1** period of 1,000 years. **2** (*fig*) future time of (imagined) great happiness and prosperity for everyone.

mil·ler /ˈmɪlər/ *n* [C] owner or operator of a mill, esp a flour mill.

mil·let /ˈmɪlɪt/ *n* [U] **1** cereal plant growing 3 to 4 feet high. **2** seeds of this plant as food.

milli- /mɪlə-/ *combined form* one-thousandth part of: *ˈmillimeter*.

mil·li·bar /ˈmɪləˌbar/ *n* [C] unit of atmospheric pressure.

mil·liner /ˈmɪlənər/ *n* [C] person who makes and sells women's hats, and sells lace, trimmings, etc for hats.

mil·li·nery /-ˌneri/ *n* [U] (the business of making and selling) women's hats.

mil·lion /ˈmɪlyən/ *n* [C] **1** one thousand thousand (1,000,000). (*Note:* the *pl* is rarely used after a number: *six ~*.) **2** (*pl*) any indefinitely large number: *has ~s of ideas*. □ *adj*: *a ~ people*.

mil·lion·aire /ˌmɪlyəˈner/ person whose wealth exceeds a million dollars; extremely rich man.

mil·lionth /ˈmɪlyənθ/ *adj, n* [C] (of) the next after 999,999 or one part of a million.

mil·li·pede /ˈmɪləˌpid/ *n* [C] small wormlike creature similar to a centipede, having a segmented body and a pair of legs at each segment. ➪ illus at insect.

mime /maim/ *n* **1** [C] (in ancient Greece and Rome) simple kind of drama in which real persons and events were made fun of. **2** [U] acting without speech, using only facial expressions and gestures to tell a story; pantomime. **3** [C] act in such drama. □ *vi,vt* act without speaking.

mim·eo·graph /ˈmɪmiəˌgræf/ *n* [C] (machine for producing a) copy of written or printed material made from a stencil.

mimic /ˈmɪmɪk/ *adj* imitated or pretended: *~ warfare*, as in peacetime maneuvers. □ *n* [C] person who is clever at imitating others, esp in order to make fun of their habits, appearance, etc. □ *vt* (*pt,pp* ~ked) **1** ridicule by imitating: *He was ~king his uncle's voice*. **2** imitate closely: *wood painted to ~ marble*.

ˈmim·icry *n* [U]

min. *abbr* = **1** minimum. **2** minute(s).

min·aret /ˈmɪnəˌret/ *n* [C] tall, slender spire on a mosque, from which people are called to prayer. ➪ illus at mosque.

mince /mɪns/ *vt,vi* **1** cut or chop (meat, etc) into small pieces. **2** speak in an affected, unnatural way in an attempt to appear delicate or refined.

mince·meat /ˈmɪnsˌmit/ *n* [U] mixture of currants, raisins, sugar, candied peel, apples, suet, etc, used esp for filling pies. ***make mincemeat of,*** (*informal*) destroy a person, an argument, etc.

mind[1] /maind/ *n* **1** [U] person's capacity to think, know, feel, perceive, etc. ***the mind's eye,*** imagination. **2** [U] intellect; intelligence; ability to reason: *He has a good ~*. ***presence of mind,*** ability to think or act quickly and calmly when necessary. **3** [U] sanity; healthy mental state: *lost his ~*. ***blow sb's mind,*** (*sl*) cause him to feel great wonder, amazement, etc. ***out of one's mind,*** **(a)** insane. **(b)** wild; extremely excited. **4** [U] memory; remembrance. ***bear/keep sth in mind,*** ➪ keep[1] (1). ***bring/call sth to mind,*** remember it. **5** [U] desire; purpose; intention: *Nothing was further from his ~*. ***have a good mind to do sth,*** ➪ good[1](7). ***have half a mind to do sth,*** be almost decided to do it. ***know one's own mind,*** know what one wants; have no doubts. ***make up one's mind,*** ➪ make[1](25). **6** [U] attention. ***have sth on one's mind,*** keep thinking or worrying about it. ***keep one's mind on sth,*** continue to pay attention to it: *Keep your ~ on what you're doing*. ***take sb's mind off sth,*** distract his attention from something (often disagreeable). **7** [U] opinion: *To my ~, he is talking nonsense*. ***give sb a piece of one's mind,*** ➪ piece[1](2). ***speak one's mind,*** say plainly what one thinks. **8** [C] person who has intelligence: *No two ~s think alike. That is a problem which the greatest ~s have not been able to solve*.

mind[2] /maind/ *vt,vi* **1** take care of; attend to: *Who's ~ing the baby?* ***ˌmind your ˌown ˈbusiness,*** do not interfere in the affairs of others/my affairs. **2** be troubled by; feel objection to: *He doesn't ~ the cold weather at all. Do you ~ if I smoke? Would you ~ opening the window?* Will you please do this? *I wouldn't ~ a glass of beer*, I would like one. ***Never mind,*** **(a)** It doesn't matter. **(b)** Don't worry about it. **3** obey: *Children should ~ their parents*. **4** be careful about: *Mind that broken step!* ***mind one's P's and Q's,*** be careful what one says or does. **5** take notice; pay attention to: *He made many mistakes because he didn't ~ what he was doing*.

minded /ˈmaindɪd/ *adj* **1** (usually with an *adj* or *adv* prefixed): having a certain kind of mind: *a ˈstrong-~ man; ˈhigh-~ leaders*. **2** inclined: *When ~ to, he can be very firm*.

mind·ful /ˈmaindfəl/ *adj* ***mindful of,*** giving thought and attention to: *~ of one's duties/the nation's welfare*.

mind·less /ˈmaindlɪs/ *adj* **1** ***mindless of,*** paying no attention to; forgetful of: *~ of danger*. **2** lacking in or not requiring intelligence: *~ idiots*.

mind·less·ly *adv*.

mind·less·ness /-nɪs/ *n* [U]

mine[1] /main/ *possessive pron* belonging to me: *Is this book yours or ~? He's an old ˈfriend of ~*, one of my old friends.

mine[2] /main/ *n* [C] **1** hole, pit, or tunnel dug/made in the earth from which coal, mineral ores, etc, are extracted: *a ˈcoal ~*. **2** (*fig*) rich or abundant source: *A good encyclopedia/My grandmother is a ~ of information*. **3** tunnel made under an enemy position for the purpose of setting off explosives; bomb or explosive device placed in the ground and exploded by contact with a vehicle, a person etc: *The truck was destroyed by a ˈland ~*. **4** similar explosive device placed in a body of water as a weapon against ships.

mine[3] /main/ *vt,vi* **1** dig (for coal, ores, etc) from the ground; obtain (coal, etc) from mines. **2** lay explosive mines in or under: ~ *the entrance to a harbor*.

miner /ˈmainər/ *n* [C] person who works in a mine and takes minerals from the earth: ˈ*coal* ~*s*.

min·eral /ˈmɪnərəl/ *n* [C] **1** natural substance obtained from the earth by mining. **2** substance that is neither animal nor vegetable. □ *adj* of, containing, mixed with, minerals: ~ *ores*.

ˈmineral oil *n* [U] (esp) colorless, odorless oil refined from petroleum, that is used as a laxative.

min·er·al·ogy /ˌmɪnəˈralədʒi/ *n* [U] the study and science of minerals.

min·er·al·ogist /ˌmɪnəˈralədʒɪst/ *n* [C] specialist in mineralogy.

mingle /ˈmɪŋgəl/ *vt,vi* **1** mix: ~ *sorrow with joy*. **2** associate closely with: ~ *with the crowds*.

mini- /ˈmɪni-, ˈmɪnɪ-/ *combined form* of small size, length, etc: ˈ~*bus; a* ˈ~*skirt*.

minia·ture /ˈmɪniətʃər/ *n* [C] **1** very small painting of a person. ***in miniature,*** on a small scale. **2** small-scale copy or model of any object. □ *adj* on a small scale: *a* ~ *railroad*.

minia·tur·ize /ˈmɪniətʃəˌraiz/ *vt* design or make in a very small size.

minim /ˈmɪnəm/ *n* [C] unit of liquid measure equal to one-sixtieth of a dram.

mini·mal /ˈmɪnəməl/ *adj* smallest in amount or degree: *On these cliffs vegetation is* ~.

mini·mize /ˈmɪnəˌmaiz/ *vt* **1** reduce to the smallest possible amount or degree: ~ *the chance of an error*. **2** belittle; cause to seem of little importance: ~*d her contribution to his success*.

mini·mum /ˈmɪnəməm/ *n* [C] (*pl* ~s or -ma /-mə/) (opp of *maximum*) least possible or recorded degree, quantity, etc: *reduce something to a* ~. □ *adj* smallest, lowest: *the* ~ *temperature; a* ~ *wage*, lowest wage that regulations allow to be paid.

min·ing /ˈmainɪŋ/ *n* [U] the process of getting minerals, etc from mines.

min·ion /ˈmɪnyən/ *n* [C] **1** favorite. **2** slavish follower or servant.

min·is·ter[1] /ˈmɪnəstər/ *n* **1** person at the head of a department of some governments (and often a member of the cabinet): *the Prime Minister*, eg of Great Britain, Canada. **2** diplomat of some governments, who is of lower rank than an ambassador. **3** Protestant clergyman.

min·is·ter[2] /ˈmɪnəstər/ *vi* give help or service: ~ *to the wants of a sick man*.

min·is·ter·ial /ˌmɪnəˈstɪriəl/ *adj* of or relating to a minister or ministry.

min·is·ter·ially /-iəli/ *adv*

min·is·tra·tion /ˌmɪnəˈstreiʃən/ *n* **1** [U] ministering or serving. **2** [C] act of this kind.

min·is·try /ˈmɪnəstri/ *n* [C] (*pl* -ies) **1** department of government under a minister(1): ˌ*Ministry of* ˈ*Defense*, eg of Great Britain. **2** office, duties, term of service, of a minister. **3 the ministry,** (*collect*) the ministers of (esp Protestant) religion as a body; clergymen. ***enter the ministry,*** become a minister of religion.

mink /mɪŋk/ *n* **1** [C] small weasel-like animal. **2** [U] fur of this animal: (as an *adjective*) *a* ~ *coat*.

min·now /ˈmɪnou/ *n* [C] (kinds of) very small fresh water fish.

mi·nor /ˈmainər/ *adj* **1** (contrasted with *major*) smaller or less important: ~ *repairs/alteration; the* ~ *poets; play only a* ~ *part in the play; a* ~ *operation*. **2** (*music*) of or based on a minor scale. □ *n* [C] **1** (*legal*) person not yet legally of age. **2** academic subject on which a student spends less time than on his major subject of study.

ˌminor ˈleague sports league or association ranking below the major leagues.

ˌminor ˈscale (*music*) scale with half steps after the second, fifth, and sometimes the sixth notes.

mi·nor·ity /məˈnɔrəti, -ˈnar-/ *n* (*pl* -ies) **1** [U] (*legal*) the state of being a minor. **2** the smaller number or part, esp of a total of votes. ***be in the minority,*** be in the smaller of two groups. **3** [C] small group in a community, nation, etc that differs from the larger part of the population in race, religion etc.

Mino·taur /ˈmɪnəˌtɔr/ *n* [C] (*Greek myth*) monster, half man and half bull, kept in the labyrinth in Crete.

min·strel /ˈmɪnstrəl/ *n* [C] **1** (in the Middle Ages) traveling musician, who sang songs and ballads, recited poems, etc. **2** performer or entertainer in a minstrel show.

ˈminstrel show, one in which plantation songs are sung by Negroes or by whites done up as Negroes, esp popular in 19th century America.

mint[1] /mɪnt/ *n* **1** [U] (kinds of) plant whose leaves are used for flavoring. **2** [C] mint-flavored piece of candy.

mint[2] /mɪnt/ *n* [C] **1** place where coins are made. **2** (*informal*) a large amount: *a* ~ *of money*. □ *adj* as if new or freshly made. ***in mint condition,*** in perfect condition. □ *vt* **1** make (a coin) by stamping metal. **2** (*fig*) make up; invent; originate.

min·uet /ˌmɪnyuˈet/ *n* [C] (piece of music for a) slow, graceful dance.

minus /ˈmainəs/ *adj* **1** negative; less than zero: *a* ~ *quantity*, eg $-2x$. **2** slightly less than: *a grade of B* ~. □ *prep* **1** less; with the deduction of: *7* ~ *3 is 4*. **2** (*informal*) without: *He came back from the war* ~ *a leg*. □ *n* [C] **1** (also **ˈminus sign**) sign (−) used to indicate subtraction. **2** minus number or quantity.

min·us·cule /ˈmɪnəˌskyul/ *adj* tiny; small.

min·ute[1] /ˈmɪnɪt/ *n* [C] **1** sixtieth part of an hour (indicated by the mark ′): *seven* ~*s to six; arrive ten* ~*s early*. ***the minute (that),*** as soon as: *I'll give him your message the* ~ (*that*) *he arrives.* **2** sixtieth part of a degree (in an angle): *37° 30′*, 37 degrees 30 minutes. **3** moment; short time. ***in a minute,*** soon: *I'll come in a* ~. **4** (*pl*) official record of the meeting of an organization.

ˈminute hand, long hand on a watch or clock pointing to the minute.

ˈminute·man /-ˌmæn/ (*pl* ~men /-ˌmen/) member of the militia or an armed civilian during the American Revolutionary War, who was ready to fight at a minute's notice.

mi·nute[2] /maiˈnut, -ˈnyut/ *adj* (-r, -st) **1** very small: ~ *particles of dust*. **2** giving small details; careful and exact: ~*inspection*.

mi·nute·ly *adv*
mi·nute·ness /-nɪs/ *n* [U]
mir·acle /ˈmɪrəkəl/ *n* [C] **1** (esp a welcome) act or event which does not follow the known laws of nature, sometimes considered as an act of God's power: *work/accomplish ~s*. **2** remarkable example; outstanding achievement: *It's a ~ of ingenuity.*
mi·racu·lous /mɪˈrækyələs/ *adj*
mi·racu·lous·ly *adv*
mi·rage /məˈraʒ/ *n* [C] illusion, produced by air conditions, causing something distant to become visible (or upside down), eg the appearance of a sheet of water in the desert.
mire /ˈmaiər/ *n* [U] **1** swampy ground; bog. **2** soft, deep mud. □ *vt,vi* **1** (cause to) sink, or stick, in mud. **2** (*fig*) entangle in difficulties.
mir·ror /ˈmɪrər/ *n* [C] **1** polished surface (usually of silver-coated glass) that reflects images. **2** (*fig*) something that gives a likeness or picture: *Pepys's Diary is a ~ of the times he lived in.* □ *vt* reflect (as) in a mirror: *The still water of the lake ~ed the hillside.*
mirth /mərθ/ *n* [U] (*formal*) gaiety, merriment; laughter.
mis- /mɪs-/ *prefix* **1** used to indicate error: *miscalculate*. **2** used to indicate badness: *misconduct*. **3** used to indicate absence or lack: *mistrust*.
mis·ad·ven·ture /ˌmɪsədˈventʃər/ *n* [C,U] (event caused by) bad luck; misfortune.
mis·an·thrope /ˈmɪsənˌθroup/ *n* [C] person who hates mankind.
mis·an·thropic /ˌmɪsənˈθrapɪk/ *adj*
mis·an·thropy /mɪsˈænθrəpi/ *n* [U] hatred of mankind.
mis·apply /ˌmɪsəˈplai/ *vt* (*pt,pp* -ied) use or apply wrongly.
mis·ap·pli·ca·tion /ˌmɪsˌæpləˈkeiʃən/ *n* [C,U]
mis·ap·pre·hend /ˌmɪsˌæprɪˈhend/ *vt* (*formal*) misunderstand.
mis·ap·pre·hen·sion /ˌmɪsˌæprɪˈhenʃən/ *n* [C,U]
mis·ap·pro·pri·ate /ˌmɪsəˈproupriˌeit/ *vt* take (money) esp dishonestly, for one's own use: *The treasurer ~d the society's funds.*
mis·ap·pro·pri·ation /ˌmɪsəˌproupriˈeiʃən/ *n* [C,U]
mis·be·got·ten /ˌmɪsbɪˈgatən/ *adj* illegitimate.
mis·be·have /ˌmɪsbiˈheiv/ *vt,vi* behave badly or improperly.
mis·be·hav·ior /ˌmɪsbiˈheivyər/ *n* [U]
mis·cal·cu·late /ˌmɪsˈkælkyəˌleit/ *vt,vi* calculate wrongly.
mis·cal·cu·la·tion /ˌmɪsˌkælkyəˈleiʃən/ *n* [C,U]
mis·car·riage /ˈmɪsˌkærɪdʒ/ *n* **1** [C,U] (instance of a) failure to administer justice properly: *a ~ of justice*. **2** [C,U] (instance of a) failure to deliver to, or arrive at, the destination. **3** [C] accidental expulsion of a fetus or embryo from the womb before it can live: *have a ~.*
mis·carry /ˌmɪsˈkæri/ *vt* (*pt,pp* -ied) **1** fail; have a result different from what was hoped for. **2** (of a woman) have a miscarriage(3).
mis·cast /ˌmɪsˈkæst/ *vt* (*pt,pp* ~) cast an actor badly or unsuitably: *She was badly ~ as Juliet.*
mis·cel·laneous /ˌmɪsəˈleiniəs/ *adj* of different sorts; having various qualities and characteristics: *a ~ collection of goods.*
mis·cel·lany /ˈmɪsəˌleini/ *n* [C] (*pl* -ies) collection of different items, eg of writings on various subjects by various authors.
mis·chance /ˌmɪsˈtʃæns/ *n* [C,U] (piece of) bad luck: *by ~.*
mis·chief /ˈmɪstʃɪf/ *n* [U] **1** injury; damage; harm: *a storm that did much ~ to shipping. Such wild speeches may work great ~.* **2** foolish or thoughtless behavior likely to cause trouble: *Boys are fond of ~*, of playing tricks, etc. **3** lighthearted tendency or desire to tease: *Her eyes were full of ~.*
mis·chie·vous /ˈmɪstʃɪvəs/ *adj* **1** causing mischief; harmful: *a ~ letter/rumor*. **2** filled with, fond of, engaged in, mischief: *~ looks/tricks; as ~ as a monkey.*
mis·chie·vous·ly *adv*
mis·con·ceive /ˌmɪskənˈsiv/ *vt,vi* understand wrongly; misjudge.
mis·con·cep·tion /ˌmɪskənˈsepʃən/ *n* [C,U]
mis·con·duct /mɪsˈkanˌdəkt/ *n* [U] **1** improper behavior. **2** bad management.
mis·con·strue /ˌmɪskənˈstru/ *vt* get a wrong idea of; mistake the meaning of: *You have ~d my words/meaning.*
mis·count /ˌmɪsˈkaunt/ *vt,vi* count wrongly. □ *n* [C] /ˈmɪsˌkaunt/ wrong count, esp of votes at an election.
mis·cre·ant /ˈmɪskriənt/ *n* [C] (*dated*) scoundrel.
mis·deal /ˌmɪsˈdiəl/ *vt,vi* (*pt,pp* ~t /-ˈdelt/) deal (playing cards) wrongly. □ *n* [C] error in dealing cards.
mis·deed /mɪsˈdid/ *n* [C] immoral act; crime: *be punished for one's ~s.*
mis·de·mean·or /ˌmɪsdɪˈminər/ *n* [C] (*legal*) offense less serious than a felony.
mis·di·rect /ˌmɪsdɪˈrekt/ *vt* **1** direct wrongly: *~ a letter*, by failing to put the full or correct address on it. **2** direct toward a bad or unworthy goal: *~ one's energies or abilities.*
mis·di·rec·tion /ˌmɪsdɪˈrekʃən/ *n* [C,U]
mis·doing /ˌmɪsˈduɪŋ/ *n* [C] misdeed.
miser /ˈmaizər/ *n* [C] stingy person who hoards money and spends as little as possible.
mi·ser·ly *adj*
mis·er·able /ˈmɪzərəbəl/ *adj* **1** wretched; very unhappy: *feeling ~; the ~ lives of refugees.* **2** causing wretchedness and unhappiness: *~ weather*. **3** poor in quality: *a ~ attempt/meal.*
mis·er·ably /-əbli/ *adv*
mis·ery /ˈmɪzəri/ *n* (*pl* -ies) **1** [U] state of being miserable; great suffering (of mind or body): *be in ~ because of a toothache.* **2** [C] something which causes misery: *the miseries of mankind.*
mis·fire /ˌmɪsˈfaiər/ *vi* **1** (of a gun) fail to go off. **2** fail to have the intended effect. □ *n* /ˈmɪsˌfaiər/ [C] example of such a failure.
mis·fit /ˈmɪsˌfɪt/ *n* [C] **1** article of clothing which does not fit well. **2** (*fig*) person who does not fit in with his job or his associates.
mis·for·tune /ˌmɪsˈfɔrtʃən/ *n* **1** [U] bad luck: *suffer ~.* **2** [C] instance of bad luck: *He bore his ~s bravely.*
mis·giv·ing /ˌmɪsˈgɪvɪŋ/ *n* [C] feeling of doubt, suspicion, distrust: *a heart/mind full of ~s.*

mis·gov·ern /ˌmɪsˈgəvərn/ *vt* govern badly.
mis·gov·ern·ment *n* [U]

mis·guided /mɪsˈgaidɪd/ *adj* mistaken; misdirected.
mis·guided·ly *adv*

mis·handle /ˌmɪsˈhændəl/ *vt* **1** deal with roughly. **2** manage inefficiently.

mis·hap /ˈmɪsˌhæp/ *n* [C] unlucky accident: *meet with a slight* ~.

mish·mash /ˈmɪʃˌmæʃ, -ˌmaʃ/ *n* [U] confused mixture; jumble.

mis·in·form /ˌmɪsɪnˈfɔrm/ *vt* give wrong information to.

mis·in·ter·pret /ˌmɪsɪnˈtərprɪt/ *vt* interpret wrongly: *He ~ed her silence as giving consent.*

mis·judge /ˌmɪsˈdʒədʒ/ *vt,vi* judge or estimate wrongly; form a wrong opinion of: *He ~d the distance and fell into the stream.*

mis·lay /ˌmɪsˈlei/ *vt* (*pt,pp* mislaid /-ˈleid/) put something away and then forget where it is; lose: *I've mislaid my passport.*

mis·lead /ˌmɪsˈlid/ *vt* (*pt,pp* misled /-ˈled/) **1** lead wrongly. **2** lead into doing wrong. **3** cause to have a wrong impression: *This information is rather ~ing.*
mis·lead·ing *adj*

mis·man·age /ˌmɪsˈmænɪdʒ/ *vt* manage badly or wrongly.
mis·man·agement *n* [U]

mis·nomer /ˌmɪsˈnoumər/ *n* [C] wrong use of a name or word: *It's a ~ to call this place a first-class hotel.*

mi·sogyn·ist /mɪˈsadʒənɪst/ *n* [C] hater of women.

mis·place /ˌmɪsˈpleis/ *vt* **1** put in a wrong place. **2** lose; mislay. **3** give wrongly or unwisely: *~d confidence.*

mis·print /ˈmɪsprɪnt/ *n* [C] printing error: *The newspaper article has many ~s.*

mis·pro·nounce /ˌmɪsprəˈnauns/ *vt* pronounce wrongly.
mis·pro·nun·ci·ation /ˌmɪsprəˌnənsiˈeiʃən/ *n* [C,U]

mis·quote /ˌmɪsˈkwout/ *vt* quote wrongly.
mis·quo·ta·tion /ˌmɪskwouˈteiʃən/ *n* [C,U]

mis·read /ˌmɪsˈrid/ *vt* (*pt,pp* ~ /-ˈred/) **1** read incorrectly: *~ one's instructions.* **2** misinterpret.

mis·rep·re·sent /ˌmɪsˌreprɪˈzent/ *vt* represent wrongly; give a false account of.
mis·rep·re·sen·ta·tion /ˌmɪsˌreprɪzenˈteiʃən/ *n* [C,U]

mis·rule /ˌmɪsˈrul/ *n* [U] **1** bad government. **2** disorder.

miss[1] /mɪs/ *n* [C] failure to hit, catch, reach, etc: *ten hits and one ~.* □ *vt,vi* **1** fail to hit, hold, catch, reach, etc: *~ the target. He ~ed the 9:30 train* (= was too late and did not catch it). **2** fail to find, notice, see, etc: *The house is at the next corner; you can't ~ it,* you'll certainly see it. **3** fail to understand: *He ~ed the point of my joke.* **4** escape: *just ~ed being hurt.* **5** notice, feel regret at, the absence of: *He's so rich that he wouldn't ~ $100. She'd ~ her husband if he died.* **6** fail to attend: *~ed the first day of the meeting.* **7** ***miss out (on sth),*** lose an opportunity to benefit, enjoy oneself: *If you don't come, you'll be ~ing out on the fun.*
miss·ing *adj* absent; lacking: *a book with two pages ~ing; ~ing persons.*

miss[2] /mɪs/ *n* **1** [C] **Miss,** title for an unmarried woman or girl, and used before her (last) name: *Miss Smith.* **2** (*sing* only) used without a name in speaking to an unmarried woman or girl: *Excuse me, ~, can you tell me the time?* **3** [C] unmarried woman or girl: *dresses for the junior ~.*

mis·sal /ˈmɪsəl/ *n* [C] book containing the order of service for Roman Catholic Mass.

mis·shapen /ˌmɪsˈʃeipən/ *adj* badly shaped; deformed.

mis·sile /ˈmɪsəl/ *n* [C] object or weapon that is thrown (eg a stone), shot (eg an arrow) or projected (eg a rocket).

mis·sion /ˈmɪʃən/ *n* [C] **1** special task or assignment given to a person or group of persons: *a ˈtrade ~ to South America.* **2** permanent diplomatic establishment in a foreign country. **3** place where the religious, charitable or medical work of missionaries is carried on, eg as established by the Spanish in the southwestern US to convert and educate the Indians. **4** special work which a person considers to be his chief purpose: *She thinks her ~ in life is to reform juvenile delinquents.* **5** special task, assigned to an individual or a unit of the armed forces: *The group has carried out twenty bombing ~s.*
mission Indian, native American raised under the influence of a mission(3).

mis·sion·ary /ˈmɪʃəˌneri/ *n* [C] (*pl* -ies) person sent to do religious and charitable work, esp in a foreign country. □ *adj* of missions(3) or missionaries.

mis·sive /ˈmɪsɪv/ *n* [C] (*formal*) message; letter.

mis·spell /ˌmɪsˈspel/ *vt* (*pt,pp* ~ed or misspelt /-ˈspelt/) spell wrongly.
mis·spell·ing *n* [C,U]

mis·spent /ˌmɪsˈspent/ *adj* used wrongly or foolishly; wasted: *a ~ youth.*

mist /mɪst/ *n* **1** [C,U] mass of fine drops of water vapor in the air, at or near the earth's surface: *Hills hidden/shrouded in ~.* **2** [C,U] drops of any liquid in the air. **3** something which blurs or obscures the vision: *a ~ of tears;* (*fig*) *hidden by the ~s of time.* □ **1** *vi,vt* cover, be covered, with mist: *The scene ~ed over.* **2** rain in fine drops.
mist·ily /-əli/ *adv*
misti·ness -nɪs/ *n*
misty *adj* (-ier, iest) **(a)** with mist: *a ~y evening; ~y weather.* **(b)** not clear: *have only a ~y idea.*

mis·take[1] /mɪˈsteik/ *n* [C] wrong opinion, idea or act: *spelling ~s. We all make ~s occasionally.*
by mistake, as the result of carelessness, forgetfulness, etc; in error: *I took your umbrella by ~.*

mis·take[2] /mɪˈsteik/ *vt,vi* (*pt* mistook /mɪˈstʊk/, *pp* ~n /mɪˈsteikən/) **1** be wrong, have a wrong idea, about: *We mistook his intentions.* **2** ***mistake sb/sth for,*** identify wrongly: *She is often ~n for her twin sister.*
mis·taken *adj* in error; wrong: *a case of ~n identity; ~n ideas. If I'm not ~n, there's the man we met on the train. ~n kindness/zeal.*
mis·tak·en·ly *adv*

mis·ter /ˈmɪstər/ *n* **1** (always written **Mr.**; *pl*

Messrs) title used before a man's (last) name: *Mr. Green.* **2** (*sing* only) title used without a name in speaking to a man: *Please, ~, can I have my ball back?*

mis·timed /ˌmɪsˈtaimd/ *adj* said or done at a wrong or unsuitable time: *a ~d intervention.*

mistle·toe /ˈmɪsəlˌtou/ *n* [U] evergreen plant with small white berries that grows as a parasite on trees and is used as a Christmas decoration.

mis·took *pt* of mistake².

mis·tress /ˈmɪstrɪs/ *n* [C] **1** woman at the head of a household or family: *Is your ~ at home?* ➪ master¹(2). **2** woman in a position of authority or control: *She is ~ of the situation.* **3** female owner of an animal. **4** woman who is not married to a man with whom she has regular sexual relations.

mis·trial /ˈmɪsˌtraiəl/ *n* [C] (*legal*) **1** trial which is invalid because of some error in the proceedings. **2** trial in which the jury cannot agree on a verdict.

mis·trust /ˌmɪsˈtrəst/ *vt* feel no trust in: *~ one's own powers.* □ *n* [U] lack of confidence or trust: *a strong ~ of anything new.*

mis·trust·ful /-fəl/ *adj*

misty /ˈmɪsti/ ➪ mist.

mis·un·der·stand /ˌmɪsˌəndərˈstænd/ *vt,vi* (*pt,pp* -stood /-ˈstʊd/) **1** understand wrongly: *His intentions were misunderstood.* **2** fail to understand: *She had always felt misunderstood.*

mis·un·der·stand·ing *n* **(a)** [C,U] failure to understand rightly: *clear up ~ings between nations that may lead to war.* **(b)** [C] quarrel.

mis·use *vt* /ˌmɪsˈyuz/ **1** use wrongly; use for a wrong purpose. **2** abuse; treat badly. □ *n* /ˌmɪsˈyus/ **1** [U] using wrongly: *the ~ of power.* **2** [C] instance of this.

mite¹ /mait/ *n* [C] **1** very small or modest contribution or offering: *offer a ~ of comfort.* **2** tiny object, esp a small child: *Poor little ~!*

mite² /mait/ *n* [C] small parasitic creature related to the spider.

mi·ter /ˈmaitər/ *n* [C] **1** tall, pointed headdress worn by the pope, bishops, etc. **2** (also **miter joint**) joint made by fitting two boards together so as to form a right angle.

miti·gate /ˈmɪtəˌgeit/ *vt* make less severe, violent or painful.

miti·ga·tion /ˌmɪtəˈgeiʃən/ *n* [U]

mitt /mɪt/ *n* [C] **1** mitten. **2** baseball glove. ➪ illus at baseball. **3** (*sl*) hand; fist.

mit·ten /ˈmɪtən/ *n* [C] **1** kind of glove covering four fingers together and the thumb separately. **2** glove that leaves the thumb and fingers bare.

mix¹ /mɪks/ *vt,vi* **1** (of different substances, people, etc) put, bring or come together so that the substances, etc are no longer distinct: *mix flour and water. We can sometimes mix business with pleasure. Oil and water do not mix.* **2** make or prepare by doing this: *mix a cake.* **3** (of persons) come or be together in society: *He doesn't mix well*, doesn't get on well with people. **4** ***mix up,*** **(a)** involve: *Don't get yourself mixed up in politics.* **(b)** confuse (esp one thing with another): *He's mixed up all the dates.*

ˈmix-up *n* [C] confused situation.

mix² /mɪks/ *n* [C] ingredients for making something, mixed and sold together: *a ˈcake mix.*

mixed /mɪkst/ *adj* **1** of different sorts. **2** made up of or involving members of both sexes. **3** involving different races or religions: *a ~ marriage.* **4** involving or made up of different and often opposing elements: *They have ~ feelings about leaving their old home.*

mixer /ˈmɪksər/ *n* [C] person or thing that mixes: *a ceˈment ~.* ***a good/poor mixer,*** one who is at ease/not at ease with others on social occasions. ➪ mix¹(3).

mix·ture /ˈmɪkstʃər/ *n* **1** [U] mixing or being mixed. **2** [C] something made by mixing: *Air is a ~ of gases.*

miz·zen·mast /ˈmɪzənˌmæst/ *n* [C] mast nearest the stern on a three-masted ship.

mkt. *abbr* = market.

mm *abbr* = millimeter(s).

MN *postal abbr* = Minnesota. ➪ App 6.

MO¹ *postal abbr* = Missouri. ➪ App 6.

mo.² *abbr* = month(s).

moan /moun/ *n* [C] low, drawn-out sound (as) of pain, suffering or regret: *the ~s of the wounded; the ~ of the wind on a winter evening.* □ *vi,vt* **1** utter moans. **2** complain: *What's she ~ing about now?*

moat /mout/ *n* [C] deep, wide ditch usually filled with water, surrounding a castle, etc as a defense.

mob /mab/ *n* [C] **1** disorderly crowd, esp one that has gathered for mischief or attack. **2 the mob,** the common people. **3** (usually with *the*) gang of criminals. □ *vt* (-bb-) (of people) crowd round in great numbers, either to attack or to admire: *The pop singer was mobbed by teenagers.*

mo·bile /ˈmoubəl, -ˌbiəl/ *adj* **1** moving, able to be moved, easily and quickly from place to place: *~ troops/artillery.* **2** easily and often changing. □ *n* [C] ornamental structure with parts that move in currents of air.

ˌmobile ˈhome, (usually metal) living quarters, built on wheels (to be pulled by a vehicle) or on the bed of a small truck.

mo·bil·ity /mouˈbɪləti/ *n* [U] being mobile.

mo·bi·lize /ˈmoubəˌlaiz/ *vt,vi* organize for service or action, esp in war.

mo·bi·liz·ation /ˌmoubələˈzeiʃən/ *n* [U]

moc·ca·sin /ˈmakəsɪn/ *n* [C] **1** kind of soft leather shoe, originally worn by North American Indians, having a prominent toe-ridge and with the bottom being a single piece of leather. **2** modern style of shoe similar to this, esp having the toe-ridge. **3** (also **ˈwater moccasin**) poisonous snake of the southern US.

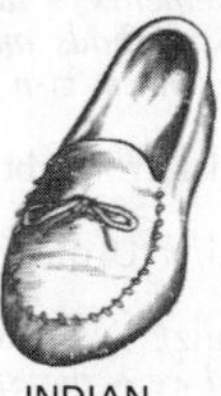

INDIAN

LOAFER

MOCCASINS

mock /mak/ *vt,vi* **1** make fun (of) (esp by imitating in an insulting way): *The rude boys* ~*ed the blind man.* **2** defy: *The heavy steel doors* ~*ed the attempts of the thieves to open the safe.* □ *adj* false; not real or genuine: *a* ~ *battle; a* ~ *turtle soup*, without turtle meat.
mock·ing·ly *adv*

mock·ery /ˈmakəri/ *n* (*pl* -ies) **1** [U] mocking; ridicule: *hold a person up to* ~. **2** [C] person or thing that is mocked. **3** [C] ridiculous imitation: *His trial was a* ~ *of justice.* ***make a mockery of,*** ridicule.

mock·ing·bird /ˈmakɪŋˌbərd/ *n* [C] American bird that mimics other birds.

mod. *abbr* = modern.

mo·dal /ˈmoudəl/ *adj* (*gram*) related to the mood of a verb: ~ *auxiliaries*, eg *can, may*.

mode /ˈmoud/ *n* [C] **1** way in which something is done; way of speaking or behaving. **2** fashion; style. **3** value that occurs most frequently in a set of data.

model[1] /ˈmadəl/ *n* [C] **1** small-scale reproduction or representation: ~ *of an ocean liner*. (as an adjective): ~ *aircraft/trains.* **2** person or thing that sets an example to be copied: *He's a* ~ *of kindness.* (as an *adjective*): *a* ~ *wife*. **3** person who poses for sculptors, painters or photographers. **4** person employed to display clothing or other goods as in a fashion show or magazine advertisement. **5** design; style: *the latest* ~ *of car.*

model[2] /ˈmadəl/ *vt,vi* (-l-, -ll-) **1** shape (in some soft substance): ~ *her head in clay.* **2** work as a model(3,4): *She earns a living by* ~*ing clothes/hats.* **3** take as an example to copy: ~ *oneself on one's father*.
mod·eler *n* [C] person who models(1).

mod·er·ate[1] /ˈmad(ə)rɪt/ *adj* **1** not extreme; limited; having reasonable limits: *a* ~ *appetite.* **2** medium or average in amount: *a* ~ *profit*. **3** reasonable in one's demands. □ *n* [C] person who holds moderate opinions, eg in politics.
mod·er·ate·ly *adv*

mod·er·ate[2] /ˈmadəˌreit/ *vt,vi* **1** make or become less violent or extreme: ~ *one's enthusiasm/demands.* **2** act as a moderator.

mod·er·ation /ˌmadəˈreiʃən/ *n* [U] quality of being moderate. ***in moderation,*** in a moderate manner or degree: *Will alcoholic drinks be harmful if taken in* ~*?*

mod·er·ator /ˈmadəˌreitər/ *n* [C] **1** person presiding over a meeting, discussion group etc. **2** material used for slowing down neutrons in a nuclear reactor.

mod·ern /ˈmadərn/ *adj* **1** of the present or recent times: ~ *technical achievements;* ~ *languages.* **2** new and up-to-date: ~ *methods and ideas; a house with all* ~ *conveniences.* □ *n* [C] person living in modern times.
ˌModern ˈEnglish, English from about 1475 to the present.

mo·dern·ity /maˈdərnəti/ *n* [U] quality of being modern.

mod·ern·ize /ˈmadərˌnaiz/ *vt* make modern; bring up to date: *Should we* ~ *our spelling?*
mod·ern·iz·ation /ˌmadərnɪˈzeiʃən/ *n* [U]

mod·est /ˈmadɪst/ *adj* **1** not vain or boastful; not having too high an opinion of one's merits, abilities, etc: *be* ~ *about one's achievements.* **2** moderate; not large in size or amount: *a* ~ *house. My needs are quite* ~. **3** decent; pure: ~ *in speech, dress and behavior.*
mod·est·ly *adv*
mod·esty /ˈmadɪsti/ *n* [U] quality of being modest (all senses).

modi·cum /ˈmadɪkəm/ *n* (*sing* only) small or moderate amount: *a* ~ *of effort.*

modi·fier /ˈmadəˌfaiər/ (*gram*) word (as an *adjective* or *adverb*) that modifies.

mod·ify /ˈmadəˌfai/ *vt* (*pt,pp* -ied) **1** make changes in; make different: *The industrial revolution modified the whole structure of English society.* **2** make less severe, extreme, etc: *You'd better* ~ *your demands.* **3** (*gram*) qualify or limit the meaning of (a word): *In "red shoes" "red" modifies "shoes."*
modi·fi·ca·tion /ˌmadəfɪˈkeiʃən/ *n* [C,U]

mod·ish /ˈmoudɪʃ/ *adj* fashionable.
mod·ish·ly *adv*

modu·late /ˈmadʒəˌleit/ *vt,vi* **1** regulate; adjust; adapt. **2** (*music*) change or pass from one key to another. **3** vary the frequency, amplitude or other characteristics of a wave or signal for radio, television, etc.

modu·la·tion /ˌmadʒəˈleiʃən/ *n* **1** [U] process of modulating, esp the amplitude, frequency or phase of a wave so that it is suitable for the radio, etc. **2** (*music*) **(a)** [U] passing from one key to another. **(b)** [C] passage of music in which this occurs.

mod·ule /ˈmaˌdʒul/ *n* [C] **1** standard or unit of measurement. **2** standard unit used in the structure of a building. **3** unit component used to make up a larger system, as a computer. **4** independent and self-contained unit of a spacecraft: *a* ˈ*lunar module.*
modu·lar /ˈmadʒələr/ *adj*

mo·hair /ˈmouˌher/ *n* [U] (thread, cloth, made from the) fine, silky hair of the Angora goat.

Mo·ham·medan /mouˈhæmədən, mə-/ *n* [C] believer in Islam. □ *adj* Islamic.

moist /mɔist/ *adj* slightly wet: *eyes* ~ *with tears.*
moisten /ˈmɔisən/ *vt,vi* make or become moist: ~*en the lips.*
mois·ture /ˈmɔistʃər/ *n* [U] condensed vapor on a surface; liquid in the form of vapor.

mo·lar /ˈmoulər/ *n* [C], *adj* (one) of the back teeth used for grinding food. ⇨ illus at mouth.

mo·las·ses /məˈlæsɪz/ *n pl* (used with a *sing verb*) thick, dark syrup drained from raw sugar during the refining process.

mold[1] /mould/ *n* [C] **1** hollow shape or form into which molten metal or glass, plaster, gelatin, etc is poured so that it will take a desired shape. **2** something shaped in a mold: *a gelatin* ~. **3** character; type: *men of the same* ~. □ *vt* **1** make or shape (as) in a mold: ~ *a head out of clay.* **2** guide or influence in a particular way: ~ *a person's character and beliefs.*
molder *n* [C] person that molds: *an iron* ~*er.*

mold[2] /mould/ *n* [U] furry growth of fungus that appears on moist or decaying matter, eg cheese or fruit. □ *vi* become covered with mold.
moldy /ˈmouldi/ *adj* (-ier, -iest) **(a)** covered with

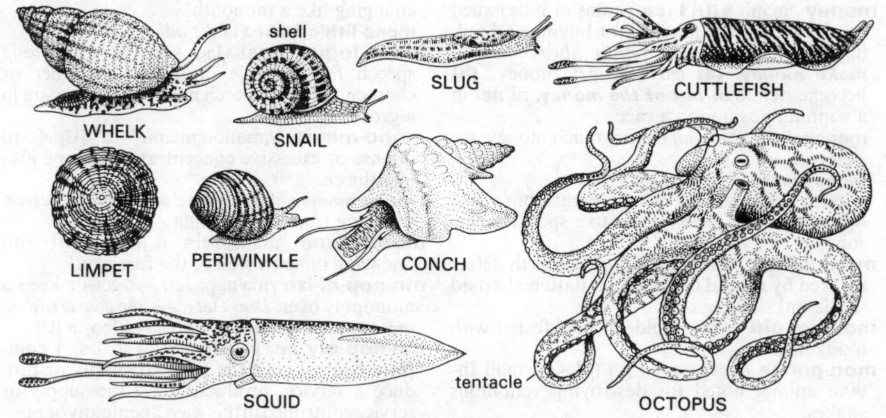

MOLLUSKS

mold. **(b)** of or like mold.

mold[3] /mould/ *n* [U] soft, fine earth that is rich in decayed animal or vegetable matter: *leaf* ~.

molder[1] /ˈmouldər/ *vi* crumble into dust: *old buildings ~ing away*.

molder[2] /ˈmouldər/ ⇨ mold[1].

mold·ing /ˈmouldıŋ/ *n* **1** [U] process or act of molding. **2** [C] anything produced by molding. **3** [C] ornamental strip of shaped wood, plaster, etc used to decorate a wall, a piece of furniture, etc.

mole[1] /moul/ *n* [C] permanent, small dark spot on the human skin.

mole[2] /moul/ *n* [C] small, fur-covered animal living in tunnels or burrows.

ˈmole·hill *n* [C] pile of earth thrown up by a mole while burrowing. ***make a mountain out of a molehill,*** treat a trivial matter as important.

mole[3] /moul/ *n* [C] stone wall built in the sea as a breakwater or causeway.

mol·ecule /ˈmalə,kyul/ *n* [C] smallest unit (usually of a group of atoms) into which a substance could be divided without a change in its chemical nature. ⇨ illus at atom.

mol·ecu·lar /məˈlekyələr/ *adj*

mo·lest /məˈlest/ *vt* **1** trouble or annoy intentionally. **2** make indecent sexual advances to.

moll /mal/ *n* [C] (*sl*) girlfriend (esp of a gangster).

mol·lify /ˈmalə,fai/ *vt* (*pt,pp* -ied) make (a person, his feelings) calmer or quieter: *~ing remarks; ~ his anger*.

mol·li·fi·ca·tion /,maləfəˈkeiʃən/ *n* [U]

mol·lusk, mol·lusc /ˈmaləsk/ *n* [C] one of a class of animals with soft bodies (and often hard shells), eg oysters, mussels, cuttlefish, snails, slugs.

molt /moult/ *vt,vi* shed (feathers, skin, shell, etc) for replacement by a new growth. □ *n* [C] process, act, or time of molting.

mol·ten /ˈmoultən/ *adj* (of metals) melted or made liquid by heat: *~ steel*.

mom /mam/ *n* [C] (*informal*) (short for) momma, mommy.

mo·ment /ˈmoumənt/ *n* [C] **1** point or very brief period of time: *It was all over in a few ~s. Just at that ~ the bell rang*. ***at the moment,*** at present; just now: *At the moment she's very busy*. **2 the moment,** as soon as; at the time when: *The ~ I saw you I knew you were angry with me*. **3** [U] importance: *a matter of ~*.

mo·men·tary /ˈmoumən,teri/ *adj* lasting for, done in, a moment.

mo·men·tar·ily /,moumənˈterəli/ *adv* **(a)** for a moment or instant. **(b)** at any moment: *They are expected momentarily*.

mo·men·tous /mouˈmentəs/ *adj* important; serious.

mo·men·tum /mouˈmentəm/ *n* [U] **1** (*physics*) the product of mass and velocity of a moving body: *Do falling objects gain ~?* **2** (*fig*) force (as) gained by movement; impetus: *lose/gain ~*.

momma, mama, mamma /ˈmamə/ *n* [C] (*informal*) mother.

mommy, mommie /ˈmami/ *n* [C] (*informal*) mother.

Mon. *abbr* = Monday.

mon·arch /ˈmanərk, ˈma,nark/ *n* [C] **1** supreme ruler (a king, queen, emperor or empress). **2** large orange and black butterfly.

mo·nar·chic /məˈnarkık/ *adj*

mon·ar·chism /ˈmanər,kızəm/ *n* [U] **(a)** system of government by a monarch. **(b)** belief in such a system.

mon·ar·chist /ˈmanərkıst/ *n* [C] supporter of monarchism.

mon·archy /ˈmanərki, ˈma,narki/ *n* (*pl* -ies) **(a)** [U] government by a monarch. **(b)** [C] state ruled by a monarch.

mon·as·tery /ˈmanə,steri/ *n* [C] (*pl* -ies) place in which monks live as a community.

mo·nas·tic /məˈnæstık/ *adj* of monks or monasteries: *~ vows*, ie of poverty, chastity, and obedience.

mon·aural /,maˈnɔrəl/ *adj* **1** of or involving one ear. **2** using only one channel to reproduce sound; monophonic.

Mon·day /ˈməndi, -,dei/ *n* second day of the week.

mo·net·ary /ˈmanə,teri/ *adj* of money or coins: *The ~ unit in the US is the dollar*.

money /ˈməni/ *n* [U] **1** (esp) coins or bills issued by a government and used for buying and selling, etc. **2** wealth: *His family always had* ~. ***make money,*** **(a)** earn or get money. **(b)** become rich. **3** ***in/out of the money,*** in/not in a winning position in a race.

moneyed /ˈmənid/ *adj* having much money: *the ~ed classes.*

money·less *adj* having no money.

ˈ**money order,** official order bought from a post office, bank etc for payment to a specified person.

mon·gol·ism /ˈmaŋgəˌlɪzəm/ *n* [U] birth defect marked by mental deficiency, a flattened broad skull, and slanting eyes.

mon·gol·oid /ˈmaŋgəˌlɔid/ of or affected with mongolism.

mon·goose /ˈmaŋˌgus/ *n* [C] (*pl* ~s) small Indian animal noted for destroying venomous snakes.

mon·grel /ˈməŋgrəl, ˈmaŋ-/ *n* [C] any plant or animal (esp a dog) of mixed origin or breed.

moni·tor /ˈmanətər/ *n* [C] **1** pupil, faculty member, in a school who is appointed to help keep order, take attendance, etc. **2** person who advises and instructs others. **3** apparatus for testing, observing, or controlling a process, for detecting activity, etc. **4** one of a group of large lizards found in Asia, Africa, and Australia. □ *vt,vi* watch over or supervise, esp with a monitor(3).

monk /məŋk/ *n* [C] member of a group of men who have taken religious vows and live together as a community in a monastery.

monk·ish /-ɪʃ/ *adj*

mon·key /ˈməŋki/ *n* [C] (*pl* ~s) **1** one of the group of animals most closely resembling man, esp one of the smaller, long-tailed kinds as contrasted with the large apes. ⇨ illus at ape. **2** (*informal*) mischievous person, esp a child: *You little ~!* **3** (*informal*) person who has been made to look foolish: *She made a ~ out of me!* □ *vi* ***monkey around (with),*** play mischievously: *Stop ~ing around with those tools!*

monkey wrench /ˈməŋki ˌrentʃ/ *n* [C] tool with a jaw that can be adjusted for nuts and bolts of various sizes. ⇨ illus at wrench.

mono·chrome /ˈmanəˌkroum/ *n* [C] painting in (different tints of) one color. □ *adj* having only one color.

mono·chro·matic /ˌmanəkrouˈmætɪk/ *adj* = monochrome.

mon·ocle /ˈmanəkəl/ *n* [C] eyeglass for one eye, kept in position by the muscles around the eye.

mon·og·amy /məˈnagəmi/ *n* [U] custom or state of being married to only one person at a time. ⇨ polygamy.

mon·og·amous /məˈnagəməs/ *adj* of, relating to, or practicing monogamy.

mono·gram /ˈmanəˌgræm/ *n* [C] design made usually of a person's initials. □ *vt* (-mm-) mark with a monogram.

mono·graph /ˈmanəˌgræf/ *n* [C] book, article, etc on one particular subject.

mono·lith /ˈmanəˌlɪθ/ *n* [C] **1** single, large block of stone (esp as a monument). **2** government, institution, etc thought of as rigid and unchanging like a monolith.

mono·lithic /ˌmanəˈlɪθɪk/ *adj*

mono·logue /ˈmanəˌlɔg -ˌlag/ *n* [C] **1** long speech for a single dramatic performer or character. **2** long speech made by one person in a group.

mono·mania /ˌmanouˈmeiniə/ *n* [U] (esp) intense or excessive concentration on one idea or subject.

mono·maniac /ˌmanouˈmeiniˌæk/ *n* [C] person suffering from monomania.

mono·plane /ˈmanəˌplein/ *n* [C] aircraft with one wing on each side of the fuselage.

mo·nop·ol·ize /məˈnapəˌlaiz/ *vt* get or keep a monopoly over: *Don't let me ~ the conversation.*

mo·nop·ol·iz·ation /məˌnapələˈzeiʃən/ *n* [U]

mo·nop·oly /məˈnapəli/ *n* [C] (*pl* -ies) **1** complete control over the right to supply or produce a service, product, etc. **2** the supply or service controlled in this way. **3** company or business that possesses such control: *a shipping ~.*

mo·nop·ol·ist /-lɪst/ person, group, etc holding a monopoly.

mo·nop·ol·is·tic /məˌnapəˈlɪstɪk/ *adj*

mono·rail /ˈmanəˌreiəl/ *n* [C] **1** single rail serving as a track for vehicles. **2** railroad system using such a rail.

mono·sodium glu·ta·mate /manəˌsoudiəm ˈglutəmɪt/ *n* [U] (*abbr* **MSG**) chemical used to flavor food.

mono·syl·lable /ˈmanəˌsɪləbəl/ *n* [C] word of one syllable.

mono·syl·labic /ˌmanəsɪˈlæbɪk/ *adj* of or made up of monosyllables.

mo·not·on·ous /məˈnatənəs/ *adj* (uninteresting because) unchanging, without variety: *a ~ voice; ~ work.*

mo·not·on·ous·ly *adv*

mo·not·ony /məˈnatəni/ *n* [U] the state of being monotonous.

mon·soon /manˈsun/ *n* [C] **1** seasonal winds of southern Asia, blowing from the SW from April to October to produce the wet season, and from NE during the other months to produce the dry season. **2** the rainy season that comes with the SW monsoon.

mon·ster /ˈmanstər/ *n* [C] **1** abnormally formed animal or plant. **2** person or thing of extraordinary size, shape, etc. **3** (in stories) imaginary creature (eg half animal, half human): *dragons are ~s.* **4** extremely cruel or evil person: *a ~ of cruelty.* □ *adj* huge.

mon·stros·ity /manˈstrasəti/ *n* (*pl* -ies) **1** [U] state of being monstrous. **2** [C] monster; hideous object, building, etc.

mon·strous /ˈmanstrəs/ *adj* **1** of or like a monster. **2** enormous; of great size. **3** ugly; horrible: *~ crimes.* **4** absurd; incredible; scandalous: *It's absolutely ~ that men should be paid more than women for the same job.*

mon·strous·ly *adv*

mon·tage /ˌmanˈtaʒ/ *n* [C,U] **1** (technique of selecting and arranging a) series of short, rapid scenes on motion-picture film. **2** (process of arranging) pictures, designs, objects, etc, next to or on top of each other to make a composite picture.

month /mənθ/ *n* [C] **1** (also **calendar month**) **(a)** any of the twelve parts into which the year is divided. **(b)** period of time from a day in one month to the corresponding day in the next (eg January 2–February 2): *a baby of three ~s; a three-month-old baby.* **2** (also **lunar month**) time taken by the moon to make a complete revolution, about 28 days.

month·ly *adj, adv* (happening) once a month, every month; of, for, or lasting a month: *a ~ly pass.* □ *n* [C] (*pl* -ies) periodical published once a month.

monu·ment /ˈmanyəmənt/ *n* [C] **1** building, column, statue, etc in memory of a person or event: *a ~ in the town square to a Confederate general.* **2** work of scholarship, literature, science, etc that deserves to be remembered because it is of lasting value: *a ~ of learning.* **3** place, area, or site preserved by a government because of its special beauty, historic significance, etc. **4** marker, stone, etc that marks an important spot.

WASHINGTON MONUMENT

monu·men·tal /ˌmanyəˈmentəl/ *adj* **1** of, serving for, a monument: *a ~ inscription.* **2** of lasting value: *a ~ production*, eg the Oxford English Dictionary. **3** very great: *~ ignorance.*

moo /mu/ *n* [C] sound made by a cow or ox. □ *vi* make this sound.

mood[1] /mud/ *n* [C] state of mind or spirits: *not in the ~ for serious music.*

mood·ily /-əli/ *adv*

moodi·ness /-nɪs/ *n* [U]

moody *adj* (-ier, -iest) **(a)** having moods that often change **(b)** gloomy; bad-tempered.

mood[2] /mud/ *n* [C] (*gram*) group of verb forms that shows whether the action expressed by the verb is regarded as certain, possible, doubtful, etc: *the indicative/imperative ~.*

moon /mun/ *n* [C] **1** **(a)** ***the moon,*** the body which moves round the earth once in a month and shines at night by light reflected from the sun. **(b)** this body at a particular time: *Is it a new ~ or a full ~?* ⇨ illus at phase. **2** satellite of other planets: *How many ~s has the planet Jupiter?* **3** (*poet*) month. ***once in a blue moon,*** (*informal*) rarely or never.

moon·beam /ˈmunˌbim/ *n* [C] ray of moonlight.

moon·light /ˈmunˌlaɪt/ *n* [U] light of the moon □ *vi* (*pt,pp* -lighted) hold a second job in addition to one's regular job.

ˈmoon·light·er *n* [C]

moon·shine /ˈmunˌʃain/ *n* [U] **1** light of the moon. **2** foolish or idle talk, ideas, etc. **3** (esp illegal) home-distilled whiskey.

moon·stone /ˈmunˌstoun/ *n* [C] pearly kind of mineral used as a gem.

moon·struck /ˈmunˌstrək/ *adj* **1** crazy. **2** romantic and sentimental.

Moor[1] /mʊr/ *n* **1** member of a Moslem people who now live in northwestern Africa. **2** one of the Moslem Arabs who invaded Spain in the 8th century.

moor[2] /mʊr/ *vt,vi* secure or make fast (a boat, ship, etc) by means of cables, etc.

moor·ing /ˈmʊrɪŋ/ *n* [C] **(a)** (*pl*) cables, anchors and chains, etc, by which a ship or boat is moored. **(b)** place where a ship is moored.

moose /mus/ *n* [C] (*pl* ~ or ~s /-sɪz/) large sort of deer with coarse fleece and palm-shaped horns, found in the forests of North America, and in northern Europe.

moot /mut/ *adj* ***a moot point/question,*** one which is undecided. □ *vt* raise or bring forward for debate or discussion: *This question has been ~ed before.*

mop /map/ *n* [C] **1** device for cleaning floors, etc made of sponge, a bundle of yarn or cloth, etc attached to a handle. **2** thick, tangled mass: *a mop of hair.* □ *vt* (-pp-) clean or wipe (as) with a mop: *mop the floor; mop one's brow; mop up a mess.* ***mop up,*** **(a)** clean up. **(b)** (*informal*) finish: *a few details to mop up before I leave.*

mope /moup/ *vi* be dull and in low spirits: *~ (about) in the house all day.* □ *n* **1** dull, listless person. **2 the mopes,** low spirits.

mo·ped /ˈmouˌped/ *n* [C] pedal bicycle fitted with a small engine.

mo·raine /məˈrein/ *n* [U] heap or mass of earth, gravel, rock, etc carried down and deposited by a glacier.

moral[1] /ˈmɔrəl/ *adj* **1** concerning principles of right and wrong: *~ standards/law.* **2** good and virtuous: *a ~ life/man.* **3** able to understand the difference between right and wrong: *At what age do we become ~ beings?* **4** teaching or illustrating good or ethical behavior: *a ~ talk.* **5** psychological (contrasted with *physical* or *practical*): *a ~ victory*, actual defeat with which the losing side is nevertheless satisfied because the justness of its position has been clearly demonstrated. ***give sb moral support,*** help by saying that he has justice and right on his side.

mor·ally /-rəli/ *adv* **(a)** from a moral point of view: *Morally he is all that can be desired.* **(b)** according to what is most probable: *~ly bound to fail.*

moral[2] /ˈmɔrəl/ *n* [C] **1** lesson which a story, event or experience teaches: *And the ~ is that a young girl should not speak to strange men.* **2** (*pl*) moral conduct or behavior. **3** (*pl*) principles of right and wrong: *a man without ~s.*

mo·rale /məˈræl/ *n* [U] state of mind and spirit of a person or group, as shown in courage, enthusiasm, etc: *The army recovered its ~ and fighting power.*

mor·al·ist /ˈmɔrəlɪst/ *n* [C] **1** person who teaches or points out moral principles. **2** person who wants to regulate the moral behavior of others.

mor·al·is·tic /ˌmɔrəlˈɪstɪk/ *adj* **1** concerned with morals(2). **2** self-righteous in moral conduct and beliefs.

mor·al·ity /məˈræləti/ *n* (*pl* -ies) **1** [U] (standards, principles, of) good behavior: *standards of commercial ~.* **2** [C] particular system of morals: *Christian ~.*

mor·al·ize /ˈmɔrəˌlaiz/ *vt,vi* **1** talk or write on questions of morality: *~ about/on the failings of the younger generation.* **2** draw a moral(1) from.

mo·rass /məˈræs/ *n* [C] **1** stretch of low, soft, wet land; marsh. **2** (*fig*) difficult, complicated situation: *a ~ of problems.*

mora·tor·ium /ˌmɔrəˈtɔriəm/ *n* [C] (*pl* ~s or -ria /-riə/) [C] **1** (period of) legal authorization to delay payment of debts. **2** temporary ban or delay.

mor·bid /ˈmɔrbɪd/ *adj* **1** diseased: *a ~ growth.* **2** not wholesome; marked by gloomy or unhealthy ideas: *a ~ imagination.*

mor·bid·ity /mɔrˈbɪdəti/ *n* [U]

mor·bid·ly *adv*

more /mɔr/ (contrasted with *less* and *fewer;* ⇨ many, most[1], much[1]) *adj* **1** greater in number, quantity, quality, degree, size, etc. **2** additional: *We need ~ men/help, etc.* □ *n* [U] **1** a greater amount, number, etc: *Ask for ~ next time.* **2** an additional amount: *There are still a few ~.* □ *adv* **1** (used to form the comparative degree of *adjectives* and *adverbs*) to a greater extent or degree: *~ beautiful/useful/interesting/serious (than...). You need to sleep ~,* ie more than you sleep now. **2** again: *I shall not go there any ~,* ever again. **3** ***more and more,*** increasingly: *Food is becoming ~ and ~ expensive.* ***more or less,*** about: *It's an hour's journey, ~ or less.*

more·over /mɔrˈouvər/ *adv* further; besides; in addition (to this).

morgue /mɔrg/ *n* [C] **1** place in which bodies of persons found dead are kept until they are identified or claimed. ⇨ mortuary. **2** department of a newspaper where reference materials and old issues are kept.

mori·bund /ˈmɔrəˌbənd/ *adj* at the point of death; about to come to an end: *~ civilizations.*

morn /mɔrn/ *n* [C] (*poet*) morning.

morn·ing /ˈmɔrnɪŋ/ *n* **1** [C] early part of the day between dawn and noon or between midnight and noon: *in/during the ~; this ~; yesterday/tomorrow ~; every ~; on Sunday/Monday, etc ~; a few ~s ago.* **2** (as an *adjective*) *a ~ walk; an early ~ swim.*

ˈmorning sickness, nausea and vomiting upon rising in the morning, esp during the first few months of pregnancy.

the ˌmorning ˈstar, Venus, or other bright star seen about dawn.

morn·ing glo·ry /ˈmɔrnɪŋ ˌglɔri/ *n* [C] (*pl* -ies) twining vine with showy trumpet-shaped flowers that usually close by the middle of the day.

mo·rocco /məˈrakou/ *n* [U] soft leather made from goatskin.

mo·ron /ˈmɔˌran/ *n* [C] **1** adult with an intelligence that is equal to that of a child between 8 and 12 years of age. **2** stupid person.

mo·ronic /məˈranɪk/ *adj*

mo·rose /məˈrous/ *adj* gloomy; bad-tempered.

mo·rose·ly *adv*

mo·rose·ness /-nɪs/ *n* [U]

mor·pheme /ˈmɔrˌfim/ *n* [C] smallest meaningful part into which a word can be divided: *"Run-s" contains two ~s and "un-friend-ly" contains three.*

mor·phine /ˈmɔrˌfin/ *n* [U] narcotic drug made from opium and used for relieving pain.

mor·phol·ogy /mɔrˈfalədʒi/ *n* [U] **1(a)** branch of biology dealing with the form and structure of animals and plants. **(b)** form and structure of an organism. **2** (*gram*) study of the morphemes of a language and of how they are combined to make words. ⇨ syntax.

mor·row /ˈmarou, ˈmɔrou/ *n* **1** (*liter*) the next or following day. **2** (*archaic*) morning: *Good ~!*

Morse code /ˌmɔrs ˈkoud/ *n* code in which a system of dots and dashes, short and long sounds, or flashes of light, represents the letters of the alphabet and numbers.

mor·sel /ˈmɔrsəl/ *n* [C] tiny piece (esp of food); mouthful: *not a ~ of food anywhere.*

mor·tal /ˈmɔrtəl/ *adj* **1** (contrasted with *immortal*) destined to die; subject to death: *Man is ~.* **2** fatal; causing death: *a ~ wound.* **3** lasting until death: *~ hatred.* **4** of, relating to, or accompanying death: *in ~ agony.* **5** extreme; very great or intense: *in ~ fear.* **6** causing the death of the soul according to the views of the Roman Catholic Church: *a ~ sin.* **7** characteristic of mortals; human. □ *n* [C] human being.

mor·tally /-təli/ *adv* **(a)** so as to cause death: *~ly wounded.* **(b)** extremely: *~ly offended.*

mor·tal·ity /mɔrˈtæləti/ *n* [U] **1** state of being mortal. **2** death in large numbers (caused eg by a disaster or disease): *an epidemic with a heavy ~.* **3** death rate.

mor·tar[1] /ˈmɔrtər/ *n* [U] mixture of lime, sand and water used to hold together bricks, stones, etc. □ *vt* join (bricks, etc) with mortar.

ˈmortar·board *n* **(a)** small board with a short handle underneath, used for holding mortar. **(b)** square cap sometimes worn as part of academic costume.

mor·tar[2] /ˈmɔrtər/ *n* [C] **1** bowl of hard material in which substances are crushed or ground with a pestle. **2** muzzle-loading cannon for firing shells at high angles.

mort·gage /ˈmɔrgɪdʒ/ *vt* give a person a claim on (property) as a security for payment of a debt or loan. □ *n* [C] **1** act of mortgaging. **2** document or agreement about this.

mort·ga·gee /ˌmɔrgɪˈdʒi/ *n* [C] person to whom property is mortgaged.

mort·ga·gor, mort·ga·ger /ˈmɔgɪdʒər/ *n* [C] person who mortgages his property.

mor·tify /ˈmɔrtəˌfai/ *vt,vi* (*pt,pp* -ied) **1** cause to be ashamed, humiliated, or hurt: *a ~ing defeat.* **2** subdue; overcome: *~ the flesh,* overcome bodily desires. **3** become affected with gangrene.

mor·ti·fi·ca·tion /ˌmɔrtəfɪˈkeiʃən/ *n* [U]

mor·tise /ˈmɔrtɪs/ *n* [C] hole cut in a piece of wood, etc to form a joint by receiving the end of another piece (the *tenon*). □ *vt* **1** join or fasten in this way: *~ two beams together*. **2** cut a mortise in.

mor·tu·ary /ˈmɔrtʃuˌeri/ *n* [C] (*pl* -ies) place (eg part of a hospital) in which dead bodies are kept until burial.

mo·saic /mouˈzeiɪk/ *n* **1** [C] design, picture, etc made by fitting together differently colored bits of stone, etc. **2** [U] virus disease of plants which causes the leaves to become spotted and wrinkled.

Mos·lem /ˈmazləm/ *n* [C] believer in Islam. □ *adj* of Islam.

mosque /mask/ *n* [C] building in which Moslems worship.

MOSQUE

mos·quito /məˈskitou/ *n* [C] (*pl* ~es, ~s) small, flying, blood-sucking insect that sometimes spreads diseases such as yellow fever and malaria. ⇨ illus at insect.

moss /mɔs, mas/ *n* [U] kinds of low green or yellow plant without flowers, growing in thick masses or patches. ***A rolling stone gathers no moss,*** (*prov*) a person who never settles down in one place, job, etc will not succeed in life.

mossy *adj* (-ier, -iest) covered with, like, moss: *~y green.*

Spanish moss, silver-gray plant which grows on trees in coastal regions of the southern US.

most[1] /moust/ (contrasted with *least* and *fewest;* ⇨ many, more, much[1]) *adj* **1** (used as an independent superlative) greatest in number, quantity, degree, etc: *Which of you has made the ~ mistakes?* ***at the (very) most,*** not more than: *I can pay only $10 at the ~.* ***make the most of,*** use to the best advantage: *We have only a few hours so we must make the ~ of them.* ***for the ˈmost part,*** usually; on the whole: *Japanese cameras are, for the ~ part, of excellent quality.* **2** (without *the*) the majority of; the greater part of: *Most people think so.* □ *n* the greatest number, amount, degree, etc: *He ended up with the ~.*

most[2] /moust/ *adv* **1** (used to form the superlative degree of *adjectives* and *adverbs*): *the ~ beautiful/interesting/useful.* **2** to the greatest extent; in the greatest degree: *What is troubling you ~?* **3** (*formal*) very; exceedingly: *This is a ~ useful book. He was ~ polite to me.*

most·ly /ˈmoustli/ *adv* chiefly; almost all; generally: *The medicine was ~ sugar and water. We are ~ out on Sundays.*

mote /mout/ *n* [C] particle (of dust, etc).

mo·tel /ˌmouˈtel/ *n* [C] motorists' hotel with rooms that usually open directly on to the parking area.

moth /mɔθ/ *n* [C] (*pl* ~s /mɔðz, mɔθs/) kinds of winged insect that are related to the butterfly but have a stouter body and fly chiefly at night: *ˈclothes ~,* kind whose grubs feed on and make holes in clothing. ⇨ illus at insect.

moth·ball /ˈmɔθˌbɔl/ *n* [C] **1** small ball (of camphor, etc) used to keep moths out of clothing. **2** (*pl*) long-term protective storage: *ships in ~s.*

moth-eaten /ˈmɔθˌitən/ *adj* **1** eaten or destroyed by clothes moths. **2** (*fig*) shabby; out-of-date.

mother /ˈməðər/ *n* [C] **1** female parent. **2** cause; origin: *Necessity is the ~ of invention.* **3** head of a female religious community: *~ superior* □ *vt* be or act as a mother does (toward someone).

ˈmother country, one's native country.

ˈmother·hood /-ˌhʊd/ *n* [U] state of being a mother.

mother-in-law /ˈməðər-ɪn-ˌlɔ/ *n* [C] (*pl* mothers-in-law) mother of one's wife or husband.

mother·less *adj* without a living or known mother.

mother·li·ness /-nɪs/ *n* [U]

mother·ly *adj* having, showing, the qualities of a mother.

Mother's Day /ˈməðərz ˌdei/ *n* second Sunday in May that is set aside in the US to honor mothers.

ˈmother tongue, one's native language.

mother-of-pearl /ˌməðər-əv-ˈpərl/ *n* [U] hard, shiny rainbow-colored lining of some shells, as the pearl oyster, used for ornaments, etc.

mo·tif /mouˈtif/ *n* [C] **1** (*music*) melodic fragment or theme, esp one which recurs. **2** repeated figure or design in a decoration. **3** main feature in a work of art.

mo·tion /ˈmouʃən/ *n* **1** [U] (process of) moving. ***put/set sth in motion,*** cause it to start moving or working. **2** [C] gesture; particular movement: *All her ~s were graceful.* ***go through the motions,*** **(a)** pretend to do something. **(b)** do something in a mechanical manner. **3** [C] proposal to be discussed and voted on at a meeting: *The ~ was adopted/carried/rejected.* □ *vt,vi* direct by a motion or gesture: *He ~ed me into the room.*

mo·tion·less *adj* not moving; still.

mo·tion pic·ture /ˌmouʃən ˈpɪktʃər/ *n* [C] **1** series of pictures projected on a screen, one following after another with such great speed that people and objects seem to move. **2** story or narrative told by means of motion pictures.

mo·ti·vate /ˈmoutəˌveit/ *vt* give a motive to; encourage.

mo·tiv·ation /ˌmoutəˈveiʃən/ *n* [C,U]

mo·tive /ˈmoutɪv/ *adj* causing motion: *~ power/force,* eg steam, electricity. □ *n* [C] that which causes action: *do it from ~s of kindness.*

mo·tive·less *adj*

mot·ley /ˈmatli/ *adj* **1** of various colors. **2** of mixed or various sorts: *a ~ crowd,* eg people of many different occupations, social classes, etc.

□ *n* **1** mixture or jumble of colors. **2** mixture of things which do not normally go together: *The speakers on the program were a ~ of political views.*

mo·tor /ˈmoutər/ *n* [C] **1** device which produces or uses power (esp electric power) to produce motion (but not used of a steam engine): *electric ~s.* **2** device that produces power from fuel; internal combustion engine. □ *adj* **1** driven by a motor. **2** of or relating to motors or engines. **3** of or relating to vehicles which are powered by motors. **4** of or having to do with muscular movement.

mo·tor·boat /ˈmoutərˌbout/ *n* [C] boat powered by a motor.

mo·tor·cade /ˈmoutərˌkeid/ *n* [C] procession of motor vehicles.

mo·tor·car /ˈmoutərˌkar/ *n* [C] small railroad car with its own motor for transporting workmen, etc.

mo·tor·cycle /ˈmoutərˌsaikəl/ *n* [C] motor vehicle with two wheels that is similar to, but much larger and heavier than a bicycle.

mo·tor·ist /ˈmoutərɪst/ *n* [C] (*formal*) person who drives a car.

mo·tor·ize /ˈmoutəˌraiz/ *vt* **1** equip with a motor. **2** equip or supply with motor vehicle.

mottled /ˈmatəld/ *adj* marked with spots or areas of different colors without a regular pattern.

motto /ˈmatou/ *n* [C] (*pl* ~es or ~s) **1** short sentence or phrase used as a guide or rule of behavior (eg "Every man for himself"). **2** short sentence or phrase written or inscribed (eg on a coat of arms) expressing a suitable sentiment.

mould = mold.

moul·der = molder.

mould·ing = molding.

mouldy = moldy.

moult = molt.

mound /maund/ *n* [C] **1** mass of piled up earth. **2** small hill. **3** any pile or mass. **4** (*baseball*) elevated area on which a pitcher stands.

mount[1] /maunt/ *n* [C] **1** (*liter*) mountain, hill: *Christ's sermon on the ~.* **2** (shortened to **Mt.** in proper names): *Mt. Everest.*

mount[2] /maunt/ *vt,vi* **1** climb or go up (a hill, a ladder, etc). **2** get up on (a horse, etc): *He ~ed his horse and rode away.* **3** supply with a horse. **4** rise; ascend. **5** become greater in amount: *Our expenses are ~ing (up).* **6** put and fix in position for display, study, etc: *~ pictures.* **7** station or post (a guard): *~ sentries at the gates.* **8** plan and carry out: *~ an offensive,* attack. **9** furnish costumes, scenery, etc for a play or other theatrical performance. □ *n* [C] **1** structure which holds or supports something. **2** horse for riding on.

moun·tain /ˈmauntən/ *n* [C] **1** mass of very high land, usually going up to a peak: *Everest is the highest ~ in the world.* **2** (*fig*) very large amount or pile: *a ~ of debts/letters.*

moun·tain·eer /ˌmauntəˈnɪr/ *n* [C] climber, inhabitant, of mountains. □ *vi* climb mountains as a sport.

ˈmountain ˌgoat *n* [C] goatlike animal with short black horns and thick white hair, that is found in the Rocky Mountains of the US.

ˈmountain ˌlion *n* [C] cougar.

moun·tain·ous *adj* **(a)** having a great many mountains: *~ country.* **(b)** huge: *~ waves.*

ˈMountain ˌTime *n* [C] one of the four official time zones of the continental US.

mourn /mɔrn/ *vi,vt* feel or show sorrow or grief: *~ for a dead child; ~ over the child's death.*

mourner *n* [C]

mourn·ful /-fəl/ *adj* sad.

mourn·fully /-fəli/ *adv*

mourn·ing /ˈmɔrnɪŋ/ *n* [U] **1** expression of grief. **2** black clothes worn as a sign of grief: *wore ~ for three weeks.*

mourn·ing dove /ˈmɔrnɪŋ ˌdəv/ *n* [C] North American wild dove with a hollow, mournful cry.

mouse /maus/ *n* [C] (*pl* mice /mais/) **1** (kinds of) small rodent with a long, slender tail: *a ˈfield ~.* **2** (*fig*) shy, timid person. □ *vi* hunt for, catch, mice.

mouser /ˈmausər/ *n* [C] cat which is good at catching mice.

ˈmouse·trap *n* [C] trap for catching mice.

mousse /mus/ *n* [C,U] (dish of) sweetened, flavored cream whipped and chilled: *chocolate ~.*

mous·tache = mustache.

mousy /ˈmausi/ *adj* (-ier, -iest) **1** (esp of hair) dull brown. **2** (of a person) timid, shy.

mouth[1] /mauθ/ *n* [C] (*pl* ~s /mauðz, mauθs/) **1 (a)** opening through which animals take in food. **(b)** cavity or space behind this containing the teeth, tongue, etc. ***by word of mouth,*** (of news, etc) orally (not in writing, etc). ***down in the mouth,*** sad, dejected. ***look a gift horse in the mouth,*** look for faults or flaws in a gift. ***take the words out of sb's mouth,*** say what he was about to say. **2** opening or outlet (of a bag,

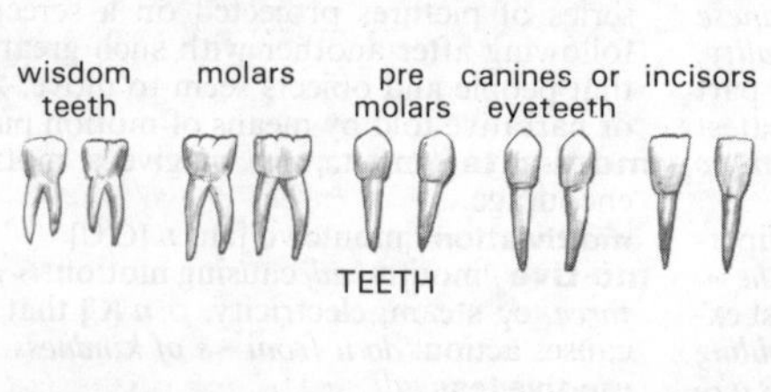

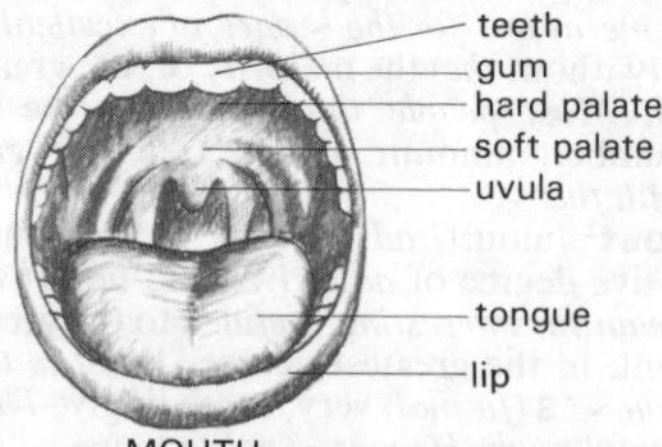

MOUTH AND TEETH

bottle, tunnel, cave, river, etc).

mouth·ful /-ˌfʊl/ *n* [C] (*pl* ~s) **(a)** as much as can be put into the mouth at one time: *have only a ~ful of food.* **(b)** word or phrase which is difficult to pronounce: *That Russian name is really a ~ful.* **(c)** (*informal*) remark or statement that is especially appropriate or significant: *You said a ~ful!*

mouth[2] /mauð/ *vt,vi* **1** speak insincerely or pompously: *He always ~s other people's ideas.* **2** take (food) into, touch with, the mouth.

mouth or·gan /ˈmauθ ˌɔrgən/ *n* [C] harmonica.

mouth·piece /ˈmauθˌpis/ *n* [C] **1** that part of a tobacco pipe, musical instrument, etc placed at or between the lips. **2** person, newspaper, etc that expresses the opinions of others. **3** (*sl, dated*) lawyer.

mov·able /ˈmuvəbəl/ *adj* **1** that can be moved; (of property) that can be taken from place to place (eg furniture). ⇨ portable. **2** (of holidays, etc) changing each year from one date to another (contrasting with fixed): *Christmas is fixed but Easter is a ~ feast.* □ *n* (*pl*) personal property; articles that can be moved from place to place.

move[1] /muv/ *n* [C] **1** act of moving. **2 (a)** act of moving a piece in chess, checkers, etc. **(b)** player's turn to do this: *Whose ~ is it?* **3** act that is calculated to achieve a purpose: *What's our next ~?* **4** ***on the move,*** moving about: *Large enemy forces are on the ~.* ***get a move on,*** (*informal*) **(a)** get started. **(b)** hurry up. ***make a move,*** begin to act: *Unless we make a ~ soon, we shall never get to the top of the mountain.*

move[2] /muv/ *vt,vi* **1** (cause to) change position; put, cause to be, in a different place or attitude; (cause to) be in motion: *Move your chair nearer to the fire. It was calm and not a leaf ~d.* ***move heaven and earth,*** use every possible means (to do something). **2** change one's residence or place of business. ***move in/out,*** take possession of/give up a house, apartment, etc: *We ~d out on Monday and the new tenants ~d in on Tuesday.* **3** go away; depart: *"Move on, please."* **4** affect with feelings of pity, sorrow, etc: *be ~d to tears. The story of their sufferings ~d us deeply.* **5** cause to do something: *What moved him to act so quickly?* **6** propose formally, as at a meeting: *Mr. Chairman, I ~ that the money be used for library books.* ⇨ motion(3). **7** make progress; go forward: *Time is moving on.* **8** take action: *Nobody seems willing to ~.* **9** change (a piece) to another position in chess, checkers, etc. **10** be socially active in: *They ~ in the best society.* **11** empty (the bowels).

move·ment /ˈmuvmənt/ *n* **1** [U] moving or being moved: *His arm was less capable of ~ after the accident.* **2** [C] act of moving or changing position: *~s of troops in the Far East.* **3** [C] group or arrangement of moving parts of a machine or mechanism: *the ~ of a clock or a watch.* **4** [C] united actions and efforts of a group of people for a special purpose: *the ~ to abolish nuclear armaments.* **5** [C] (*music*) principal division of a musical work with a distinctive structure of its own: *the final ~ of the Ninth Symphony.* **6** [C] emptying of the bowels. **7** [U] activity: *not many signs of life or ~.*

mover /ˈmuvər/ *n* [C] (esp) person or company hired to move one's belongings, furniture, equipment, etc from one place to another.

movie /ˈmuvi/ *n* [C] **1** motion picture. **2** (*pl*) showing of a motion picture: *went to the ~s.* **3** (*pl*) motion-picture industry.

movie·goer /ˈmuviˌgouər/ *n* [C] one who goes to the movies, esp frequently out of continued interest.

mov·ing pic·ture /ˌmuvɪŋ ˈpɪktʃər/ *n* [C] = motion picture.

mow[1] /mou/ *vt* (*pt* mowed *pp* mown /moun/ or mowed) **1** cut down (grass, etc) with a scythe, machine, etc. **2** cut the grass from: *mow the lawn.* **3** ***mow down,*** destroy, kill, as if by mowing: *Our men were mowed down by the enemy's machine gun fire.*

mower /ˈmouər/ *n* [C] person or machine that mows: *a ˈlawn mower.*

mow[2] /mau/ *n* [C] **1** pile of hay, straw, grain, etc, esp in a barn. **2** part of a barn where such a pile of hay, etc is stored.

MP /ˌem ˈpi/ *abbr* = military police. □ *n* (*pl* MP's) military policeman.

m.p.g., mpg *abbr* = miles per gallon.

m.p.h., mph *abbr* = miles per hour.

Mr. *abbr* = mister.

Mrs. /ˈmɪsɪz/ (*pl* unchanged) title used before the (last) name of a married woman.

MS[1] *abbr* (*pl* MSS) = manuscript.

MS[2] *postal abbr* = Mississippi. ⇨ App 6.

Ms.[3] /mɪz/ (*abbr* based on *Miss* and *Mrs.*) sometimes used as a title before the (last) name of a woman whether or not she is married.

MSG[1] /ˌem ˌes ˈdʒi/ *abbr* = monosodium glutamate.

msg.[2] *abbr* = message.

Msgt. *abbr* = master sergeant.

MST *abbr* = Mountain Standard Time.

MT[1] *abbr* = Mountain Time.

MT[2] *postal abbr* = Montana. ⇨ App 6.

Mt.[3] *abbr* = Mount.

mtn. *abbr* = mountain.

much[1] /mətʃ/ (⇨more, most.) *adj* (*Note: much* is used with *sing uncountable nouns.* It occurs usually in negative and interrogative sentences, and in affirmative sentences with *too, so,* or *as.* In other affirmative sentences, the same meaning is often expressed by *plenty* (*of*)*, a lot* (*of*)*, a large quantity* (*of*)*, a good/great deal* (*of*)) great in degree, extent, or amount: *There isn't ~ food in the house. You have given me too ~ sugar.* ***how much,*** **(a)** what quantity: *Tell me how ~ flour* (= what amount) *you want.* **(b)** what price: *How ~ is that dress?* ***ˈso much,*** nothing but: *His essays are ˈso ~ nonsense.* □ *n* [U] **1** great quantity, amount, extent, etc: *Much of what you say is true. The bill didn't come to ~.* **2** something important, remarkable, or impressive: *The movie didn't amount to ~.* ***make much of,*** treat as important; pay great attention to: *He makes* (*too*) *~ of his connections with rich people.* ***not think much of,*** have a poor opinion of: *I don't think ~ of the new teacher.* ***not much of a,*** not a good: *He's not ~ of a singer.*

much[2] /mətʃ/ *adv* **1** to a great amount, degree, or extent (used to modify a *comparative*): *You must work ~ harder*. (used often with *very* to modify a *passive participle* or *pred adjective* such as *afraid*): *I am very ~ afraid that... I was ~ annoyed.* (used to modify a *verbal phrase*) *It doesn't ~ matter. I enjoyed it very ~. He doesn't like beef ~.* **2** (used before *the* and *a* following *comparative* or *superlative*) by far: *This is ~ the best. He is ~ the worse since his fall.* **3** ***much as,*** although: *Much as I would like to go, I can't.* ***how much,*** to what extent: *How ~ does losing your job really matter?* ***much less,*** (used to emphasize the phrase, statement, etc that follows) and certainly not; and even less: *I didn't even speak to him, ~ less discuss your problems.* ***much the same,*** about the same: *The patient's condition is ~ the same.* ***much to one's surprise/regret/delight, etc,*** (used to indicate a feeling of great surprise/regret/delight, etc caused by an event or occurrence): *Much to her surprise, forty people showed up.*

mu·ci·lage /ˈmyusəlɪdʒ/ *n* [U] sticky substance used as an adhesive.

muck /mək/ *n* [U] **1** moist animal dung used as a fertilizer. **2** dirt; filth. **3** dark soil that contains decaying vegetable matter.

muck·rake /ˈməkˌreik/ *vi* search out and expose dishonesty and corruption in government, business, etc.

ˈmuck·rak·er *n* [C]

mu·cous /ˈmyukəs/ *adj* **1** of, like, mucus. **2** producing or containing mucus.

the mucous ˈmembrane, tissue rich in glands that secrete mucus, that lines the nose, mouth, food canal, and other cavities of the body that open to the outside.

mu·cus /ˈmyukəs/ *n* [U] thick, slimy liquid (as) produced by the mucous membrane.

mud /məd/ *n* [U] soft, wet earth: *Rain turns soil into mud.* ***his/her/your, etc name is mud,*** he/she/you, etc are in disgrace. ⇨ stick-in-the-mud.

ˈmud-slinger *n* [C] politician who uses malicious gossip against an opponent.

ˈmud-slinging *n* [U] (act of) spreading malicious gossip about a political opponent.

muddle /ˈmədəl/ *vt,vi* **1** make a mess of: *You've ~d the scheme completely.* **2** (cause to) act in a confused way. ***muddle through,*** reach the end of an undertaking in spite of one's mistakes, inefficiency, etc. □ *n* [C] (usually *sing* with *a*) confused or muddled state: *Everything was in a ~ and I couldn't find what I wanted. You have made a ~ of it,* mismanaged it, bungled it.

ˈmuddle-headed *adj* confused; stupid.

muddy /ˈmədi/ *adj* (-ier, -iest) **1** full of, covered with, mud: *~ roads/shoes.* **2** dull, thick, or cloudy like mud: *~ coffee.* **3** muddled and confused: *~ prose.* □ *vt* (*pt,pp* -ied) **1** fill, cover, stain, with mud: *You've muddied the carpet.* **2** make cloudy or dull (as) with mud. **3** obscure; confuse.

mu·ez·zin /muˈezən/ *n* [C] man who calls Moslems to prayer.

muff[1] /məf/ *vt* **1** fail to catch (a ball): *~ an easy catch.* **2** bungle.

muff[2] /məf/ *n* [C] fur or cloth covering in the form of a tube that is open at both ends, used to keep the hands warm.

muf·fin /ˈməfən/ *n* [C] small, round bread, usually eaten hot with butter.

muffle /ˈməfəl/ *vt* **1** wrap or cover for warmth, protection, etc: *~d up in a heavy overcoat.* **2** make (a sound) less loud or clear: *~d voices.*

muf·fler /ˈməflər/ *n* [C] **1** cloth, scarf, worn round the neck for warmth. **2** something used to muffle sound, esp the device on the exhaust of an automobile to muffle engine noise.

mufti /ˈməfti/ *n* [U] civilian clothes worn by someone who is usually dressed in a uniform.

mug[1] /məg/ *n* [C] **1** large cup with a handle, often for use without a saucer. **2** its contents: *a mug of coffee.* **3** (*sl*) face; mouth.

ˈmug shot, (*sl*) photograph of a person's face, esp for police identification.

mug[2] /məg/ *vt* (-gg-) (*sl*) attack (a person) in order to rob him.

mug·ger *n* [C]

muggy /ˈməgi/ *adj* (-ier, -iest) (of the weather, etc) very warm and damp, with no breeze.

muggi·ness /-nɪs/ *n* [U]

Mu·ham·madan /məˈhæmədən/ *adj, n* = Mohammedan.

mu·latto /məˈlatou, məˈlætou, mʊ-/ *n* [C] (*pl* ~s, ~es) **1** person who has one white parent and one Negro parent. **2** person of (esp) equal proportions of white and Negro ancestry.

mul·berry /ˈməlˌberi/ *n* (*pl* -ies) **1** [C] tree with broad, dark-green leaves. **2** [C] purple or white fruit of this tree. **3** [U] dark purplish red color.

mulch /məltʃ/ *n* [U] covering of leaves, sawdust, etc, spread to protect the roots of trees and bushes. □ *vt* cover with mulch.

mulct /məlkt/ *vt* **1** punish by means of a fine. **2** swindle: *be ~ed of one's money.*

mule[1] /myul/ *n* [C] animal that is the offspring of a donkey and a mare. ***as obstinate/stubborn as a mule,*** very obstinate/stubborn.

mul·ish /-ɪʃ/ *adj* obstinate; stubborn.

mu·lish·ly *adv*

mu·lish·ness /-nɪs/ *n* [U]

mule[2] /myul/ *n* [C] slipper or shoe that leaves the heel bare.

mule skin·ner /ˈmyul ˌskɪnər/ *n* [C] (*informal*) muleteer.

mu·le·teer /ˌmyuləˈtɪr/ *n* [C] driver of mules.

mull[1] /məl/ *vt* heat (wine, beer, etc) with sugar, spices, etc: *~ed cider.*

mull[2] /məl/ *vt* ***mull sth over,*** think about it.

mul·lah /ˈmələ/ *n* [C] Moslem priest.

mul·let /ˈməlɪt/ *n* [C] (*pl* ~, ~s) kind of fish used as food: *red/gray ~.*

multi- /ˈməltɪ-, ˌməltɪ-/ *combined form* many: *~colored; ˌ~ˈracial.*

multi·col·ored /ˈməltɪˌkələrd/ *adj* having many colors.

multi·fac·eted /ˌməltɪˈfæsətɪd/ *adj* ⇨ faceted.

multi·far·ious /ˌməltɪˈfæriəs/ *adj* (*formal*) many and various: *his ~ duties.*

multi·lat·eral /ˌməltɪ ˈlætərəl/ *adj* (of an agreement, etc) of, on, affecting, done by, several sides or parties: *~ nuclear disarmament.*

multi·lat·er·ally /-rəli/ *adv*

multi·mil·lion·aire /ˌməltɪˈmɪlyəˌner/ *n* [C] per-

son whose wealth amounts to several million dollars.
multiple /ˈmәltәpәl/ *adj* having more than one part or element. ▫ *n* [C] quantity which contains another quantity an exact number of times: *28 is a ~ of 7.*
multiple scle·ro·sis /ˌmәltәpәl sklәˈrousıs/ *n* [U] disease of the nervous system which often causes paralysis, muscle tremors, etc.
multi·plex /ˈmәltәˌpleks/ *adj* having many parts or forms; of many elements.
mul·ti·pli·cand /ˌmәltәplıˈkænd/ *n* [C] number which is to be multiplied by another number: *10 is the ~ in the problem 10 × 3.*
multi·pli·ca·tion /ˌmәltәplıˈkeiʃәn/ *n* [U] **1** action of multiplying or being multiplied: *The symbol × stands for ~.* **2** (*math*) operation that consists of adding the number of multiplicands specified by the multiplier.
multipliˈcation ˌsign, sign (×) used to indicate multiplication.
multi·plic·ity /ˌmәltәˈplısәti/ *n* [U] (*formal*) a great number: *a ~ of duties.*
mul·ti·pli·er /ˈmәltәˌplaiәr/ *n* [C] number by which another number is to be multiplied: *In 10 × 3, 3 is the ~.*
multi·ply /ˈmәltәˌplai/ *vt,vi* (*pt,pp* -ied) **1** add a quantity or number to itself a specified number of times: *~ 3 by 5; 6 multiplied by 5 is 30,* 6 × 5 = 30. **2** increase in number or amount, eg by giving birth: *Rabbits ~ rapidly.*
multi·tude /ˈmәltәˌtud/ *n* **1** [C] great number (esp of people gathered together). **2 the multitude,** the common people; the masses: *policies which appeal to the ~.*
multi·tud·in·ous /ˌmәltәˈtudәnәs/ *adj* great in number.
mum[1] /mәm/ *adj* silent. ***keep mum,*** say nothing.
mum[2] /mәm/ *n* [C] (*informal*) (short for) chrysanthemum.
mumble /ˈmәmbәl/ *vt* speak indistinctly: *The old man was mumbling away to himself.*
mumbo-jumbo /ˌmәmbou-ˈdʒәmbou/ *n* [U] (*fig*) meaningless or confusing language.
mum·mify /ˈmәmәˌfai/ *vt* (*pt,pp* -ied) embalm and dry (a dead body) as a mummy.
mum·mi·fi·ca·tion /ˌmәmәfәˈkeiʃәn/ *n* [C,U]
mummy /ˈmәmi/ *n* [C] (*pl* -ies) **1** dead body embalmed for burial, as in ancient Egypt. **2** dead body dried and preserved from decay by nature.
mumps /mәmps/ *n* [U] (with *sing verb*) contagious disease marked by painful swellings, esp of the glands in the neck.
munch /mәntʃ/ *vt,vi* chew steadily and noisily: *~ing (away at) a hard apple.*
mun·dane /ˈmәnˌdein/ *adj* **1** worldly (contrasted with spiritual or heavenly). **2** ordinary; practical: *~ jobs in factories.*
mun·dane·ly *adv*
mu·nici·pal /myuˈnısәpәl/ *adj* of or relating to a municipality: *~ buildings,* eg the town hall, public library.
mu·ni·ci·pally /-pli/ *adv*
mu·ni·ci·pal·ity /myuˌnısәˈpælәti/ *n* [C] (*pl* -ies) town, city, district, with local self-government.
mu·nifi·cence /myuˈnıfәsәns/ *n* [U] (*formal*) great generosity.
mu·nifi·cent /myuˈnıfәsәnt/ *adj* (*formal*) extremely generous.
mu·ni·tions /myuˈnıʃәnz/ *n pl* military supplies, esp guns, shells, bombs, etc: *The war was lost because of a shortage of ~s.*
mural /ˈmyurәl/ *n* [C] large picture or painting applied directly to a wall.
mur·der /ˈmәrdәr/ *n* **1** [U] unlawful and intentional killing of a human being. ***get away with murder,*** violate laws, customs, etc without being caught or criticized. **2** [C] instance of this: *commit ~; guilty of ~.* ▫ *vt* **1** kill (a human being) unlawfully and on purpose. **2** (*informal*) spoil by lack of skill or knowledge: *~ a piece of music,* play it very badly.
mur·derer *n* [C] person guilty of murder.
mur·der·ess /-ıs/ *n* [C] female murderer.
mur·der·ous /-әs/ *adj* **(a)** planning, intending, murder. **(b)** of or having to do with murder.
mur·der·ous·ly *adv*
murk /mәrk/ *n* [U] darkness; gloom.
murk·ily /-әli/ *adv*
murky *adj* (-ier, -iest) dark; gloomy.
mur·mur /ˈmәrmәr/ *n* [C] **1** low, continuous, indistinct sound: *the ~ of a brook; the ~ of distant traffic/conversation from the next room.* **2** muttered complaint: *They paid the higher taxes without a ~.* **3** abnormal sound that is caused by a disorder in the function of the heart. ▫ *vi,vt* **1** make a murmur(1): *a ~ing brook.* **2** complain in a murmur(2): *~ against new taxes.* **3** say in a low voice: *~ a prayer.*
muscle /ˈmәsәl/ *n* **1** [U] body tissue that contracts or relaxes to produce movement. **2** [C] organ or structure made up of a band or mass of such tissue: *the large ~s of the body.* **3** [U] strength; power. ▫ *vi* ***muscle ˈin (on),*** (*sl*) use force to get a share of something.
ˈmuscle-bound *adj* having stiff muscles as the result of too much exercise.
mus·cu·lar /ˈmәskyәlәr/ *adj* **1** of or relating to the muscles. **2** having strong muscles: *a ~ man.*
Muse[1] /myuz/ *n* [C] **1** (*Greek myth*) any one of the nine sisters who were the goddesses of art and learning. **2 muse,** spirit that inspires a poet, painter or other artist.
muse[2] /myuz/ *vi* ***muse over/on/upon,*** think deeply about; consider at length: *musing over memories of the past.*
mu·seum /myuˈziәm/ *n* [C] building in which objects of interest or importance in art, history, science, etc are displayed.
mush /mәʃ/ *n* [U] **1** corn boiled in water. **2** anything soft, thick, or spongy like mush. **3** (*informal*) weak or foolish sentimentality.
mushy *adj* (-ier, -iest) like mush.
mush·room /ˈmәʃˌrum, -ˌrʊm/ *n* [C] fast-growing, umbrella-shaped fungus of which some kinds are edible. ⇨ illus at fungus. ▫ *vi* spread or grow rapidly: *Fancy French restaurants are ~ing in Washington DC.*
mu·sic /ˈmyuzık/ *n* [U] **1** art of making pleasing combinations of sounds in rhythm and harmony. **2** the sounds and composition so made. **3** written or printed signs representing these sounds: (as an *adjective*) *a ~ lesson/teacher.* ⇨

illus at notation. **4** any pleasing or melodious sounds: *the ~ of nature*. ***face the music,*** face one's critics, difficulties, boldly. ***set sth to music,*** ⇨ set²(12).

ˈ**music stand,** stand for holding sheets of printed music.

mu·si·cal /ˈmyuzɪkəl/ *adj* **1** of, fond of, skilled in, music: *She's not at all ~*, does not enjoy or understand music. **2** melodious; pleasing to hear. □ *n* [C] **(a)** musical comedy. **(b)** dramatic play, often serious, with songs and dancing.

ˌ**musical** ˈ**comedy,** motion picture or play with songs and dances.

mu·si·cally /-kli/ *adv*

mu·si·cian /myuˈzɪʃən/ *n* [C] person skilled in performing or composing music.

musk /məsk/ *n* [U] **1** strong-smelling substance that is produced by the glands of some male deer and used in the manufacture of perfumes. **2** odor of musk.

musky *adj* (-ier, -iest) having the smell of musk.

mus·ket /ˈməskɪt/ *n* [C] gun, with a smooth bore, used by foot soldiers before the invention of the rifle.

mus·ket·eer /ˌməskəˈtɪr/ *n* [C] soldier armed with a musket.

musk·mel·on /ˈməskˌmelən/ *n* [C] small melon with sweet green or orange flesh.

musk ox /ˈməsk ˌaks/ *n* [C] wild ox with a shaggy coat, found in North America and Greenland.

musk·rat /ˈməskˌræt/ *n* **1** [C] large rodent of North America, with webbed hind feet, a flat, scaly tail, and brown fur. **2** [U] glossy fur of this animal.

Mus·lim /ˈməzlɪm, ˈmʊz-/ *n* [C], *adj* = Moslem.

mus·lin /ˈməzlɪn/ *n* [U] thin, fine, cotton cloth, used for dresses, curtains, etc.

muss /məs/ *n* [U] disorder; confusion. □ *vt* (often with *up*) **1** make untidy: *The children ~ed (up) her dress with their sticky hands*. **2** rain: *~ed (up) all our plans*.

mus·sel /ˈməsəl/ *n* [C] (sorts of) mollusk with a black shell in two parts. ⇨ illus at bivalve.

must /məst/ *auxiliary verb* (no infinitive, no participles, no inflected forms; *must not* may be contracted to *mustn't* /ˈməsənt/.) **1** (used to express obligation or necessity; *must not* expresses a prohibition): *You ~ do as you're told. Cars ~ not be parked in front of the entrance. Man ~ have water in order to live*. **2** (used to express emphasis, determination, insistence, etc): *I ~ ask you not to do that again*. **3** (used to express certainty): *If the light is on, he ~ be home*. **4** (used to express strong probability): *You ~ be joking!* You can't be serious! □ *n* [C] (*informal*) something required or necessary; something that must be done, seen, heard, etc: *Shepard's new play is a ~*.

mus·tache /ˈməˌstæʃ, məˈstæʃ/ *n* [C] hair growing on the upper lip.

mus·tachio /məˈstæʃiˌou/ *n* [C] (*pl* ~s) (esp) large and full mustache.

mus·tang /ˈməˌstæŋ/ *n* [C] small wild horse of the Western plains of North America.

mus·tard /ˈməstərd/ *n* [U] **1** herb with yellow flowers and seeds (black or white) in long, slender pods. **2** fine, yellow powder made from the seeds of this plant. **3** sharp, spicy paste made from this powder and eaten with meat, cheese, etc.

mus·ter /ˈməstər/ *n* [C] assembly or gathering of persons, esp for review or inspection. ***pass muster,*** be considered satisfactory. □ *vt,vi* **1** call, collect or gather together: *Go and ~ all the men you can find. They ~ed (up) all their courage*. **2** ***muster out,*** discharge (a person) from military service.

mustn't /ˈməsənt/ = must not.

musty /ˈməsti/ *adj* (-ier, -iest) stale; smelling or tasting moldy: *a ~ room/book*.

musti·ness /ˈməstinɪs/ *n* [U]

mu·table /ˈmyutəbəl/ *adj* (*formal*) able or likely to change.

mu·ta·bil·ity /ˌmyutəˈbɪləti/ *n* [U]

mu·ta·tion /myuˈteiʃən/ *n* **1** [U] change; alteration. **2** [C] change eg in the genes of a plant or animal which can be inherited by its offspring: *Are ~s in plants caused by cosmic rays?* **3** [C] animal or plant that is the result of this.

mute /myut/ *adj* **1** silent; making no sound: *staring at me in ~ amazement*. **2** unable to speak. **3** (of a letter in a word) not sounded: *The "b" in "dumb" is ~*. □ *n* [C] **1** person who does not speak. **2** device used to soften, change or muffle the sounds produced by a musical instrument. □ *vt* muffle the sound of (esp a musical instrument).

mute·ly *adv*

mu·ti·late /ˈmyutəˌleit/ *vt* damage by breaking, tearing or cutting off a limb or other necessary part.

mu·ti·la·tion /ˌmyutəˈleiʃən/ *n* [U] mutilating or being mutilated.

mu·ti·nous /ˈmyutənəs/ *adj* guilty of mutiny; rebellious: *~ sailors*.

mu·tiny /ˈmyutəni/ *n* (*pl* -ies) **1** [U] open rebellion (esp by soldiers and sailors) against lawful authority. **2** [C] instance of this. □ *vi* (*pt,pp* -ied) rebel.

mu·tin·eer /ˌmyutəˈnɪr/ *n* [C] person who mutinies.

mut·ter /ˈmətər/ *vt,vi* **1** speak in a low voice not meant to be heard. **2** complain; grumble: *He was ~ing about his large tax bill*. □ *n* [C] muttered utterance or sound.

mutterer *n* [C]

mut·ton /ˈmətən/ *n* [U] flesh of full-grown sheep eaten as food.

mu·tual /ˈmyutʃuəl/ *adj* **1** (of love, friendship, respect, etc) shared; (of feelings, opinions, etc) held in common with others: *~ suspicion/affection*. **2** each to the other(s); *~ aid*. **3** common to two or more persons: *our ~ friend Smith*, ie a friend of both of us.

mu·tual·ly /-tʃuəli/ *adv*

muzzle /ˈməzəl/ *n* [C] **1** nose and mouth of an animal (eg dog or fox). ⇨ illus at dog. **2** guard of straps or wires placed over this to prevent biting, etc. **3** open end or mouth of a firearm: *a ~-loading gun*. □ *vt* **1** put a muzzle on (a dog, etc). **2** (*fig*) prevent (a person, group, etc) from expressing opinions freely.

my /mai/ *adj* **1** of, relating to, or belonging to me: *Where's my hat?* **2** (*dated*) (as a part of a form of address): *Yes, my dear. My dear Anne,...!* **3** (used in exclamations): *My goodness!* □ *int: Oh, my!*

my·col·ogy /maiˈkalədʒi/ *n* [U] science or study of fungi.

my·na, my·nah /ˈmainə/ *n* [C] (kinds of) starling of southeastern Asia, known for their ability to mimic human speech.

my·opia /maiˈoupiə/ *n* [U] nearsightedness.

my·opic /maiˈapɪk/ *adj* nearsighted.

myr·iad /ˈmɪriəd/ *n* [C] very great number (*of*). □ *adj* very numerous.

myrrh /mər/ *n* [U] sweet-smelling, bitter-tasting kind of gum or resin obtained from certain trees or shrubs, used for making incense and perfumes.

myrtle /ˈmərtəl/ *n* [C] **1** (kinds of) evergreen shrub with shiny leaves and sweet-smelling white flowers. **2** low, trailing vine with small, glossy leaves and blue or white flowers.

my·self /maiˈself/ *pron* **1** (used as a *reflexive*): *I hurt* ~. ***(all) by myself,*** **(a)** alone. **(b)** without help. **2** (used for emphasis): *I said so* ~. **3** my normal state of health or mind: *I'm not* ~ *today.*

mys·teri·ous /mɪˈstɪriəs/ *adj* full of, suggesting, mystery: *a* ~ *visitor; a* ~*-looking parcel.*

mys·teri·ous·ly *adv*

mys·tery /ˈmɪst(ə)ri/ *n* (*pl* -ies) **1** [C] something which is obscure or impossible to understand or explain: *The murder remained an unsolved* ~. **2** [U] condition of being secret or obscure: *The origin of this tribe is lost in* ~, It has been impossible to learn anything about it. **3** novel or story in which a crime is described and treated as a puzzle to be solved.

ˈ**mystery play,** medieval drama based on episodes from the Bible.

mys·tic /ˈmɪstɪk/ *adj* **1** mystical. **2** causing feelings of awe and wonder: ~ *rites and ceremonies.* □ *n* [C] person who seeks union with God or the realization of truth by means of meditation, intuition, etc.

mys·ti·cal /ˈmɪstɪkəl/ *adj* of or relating to mystics or mysticism.

mys·ti·cism /ˈmɪstɪˌsɪzəm/ *n* [U] **1** beliefs, practices, of a mystic. **2** teaching and belief that knowledge of God or of real truth may be obtained through meditation or spiritual insight, inspiration, etc.

mys·tify /ˈmɪstɪˌfai/ *vt* (*pt,pp* -ied) puzzle; bewilder.

mys·ti·fi·ca·tion /ˌmɪstɪfəˈkeiʃən/ *n* **(a)** [U] mystifying or being mystified. **(b)** [C] something that mystifies.

myth /mɪθ/ *n* **1** [C] story, handed down by tradition, containing eg ideas or beliefs about the early history of a race, explanations of natural events, etc. **2** [U] such stories collectively: *famous in* ~ *and legend.* **3** [C] person, thing, etc that is imaginary or invented: *That rich uncle of whom he boasts is only a* ~.

mythi·cal /ˈmɪθɪkəl/ *adj* **(a)** of, existing only in, myth: ~*ical heroes.* **(b)** imaginary: ~*ical wealth.*

myth·ol·ogy /mɪˈθalədʒi/ *n* (*pl* -ies) **1** [U] study or science of myths. **2** [C] body or collection of myths: *Roman* ~*; the mythologies of primitive cultures.*

mytho·logi·cal /ˌmɪθəˈladʒɪkəl/ *adj* **(a)** of mythology. **(b)** imaginary; unreal.

n

N[1], **n** /en/ (*pl* N's, n's /enz/) **1** the fourteenth letter of the English alphabet. **2** (*math*) unspecified number.

nth /enθ/ *adj* (usually in:) ***to the nth degree***, to the greatest extent possible.

N[2] *abbr* = north.

n.[3] *abbr* = **1** noun. **2** neuter.

N.A. *abbr* = **1** not applicable. **2** not available.

NAACP /ˌenˌeiˌeiˌsiˈpi, ˌenˌdəbəlˌeiˌsiˈpi/ *abbr* = National Association for the Advancement of Colored People.

nab /næb/ *vt* (-bb-) (*sl*) **1** catch (eg a thief, etc): *be nabbed by the police.* **2** grab; seize suddenly: *nab a seat before everyone else.*

na·celle /nəˈsel/ *n* [C] outer casing or shelter on an aircraft for the engine, crew, etc.

na·dir /ˈneidər, ˈneiˌdɪr/ *n* [C] **1** part of the sky directly below the zenith. **2** (*fig*) lowest, weakest, point: *at the ~ of one's hopes.*

nag[1] /næg/ *n* [C] horse, esp one that is old and worn-out.

nag[2] /næg/ *vt,vi* (-gg-) **1** find fault with continuously: *She nagged (at) him all day long.* **2** (of a pain) annoy by continuous or frequent hurting: *a nagging toothache.* □ *n* [C] person who nags.

nag·ger *n* [C] = nag (*n*).

naiad /ˈneiəd/ *n* [C] (*pl* ~s, -des /-ˌdiz/) (*Greek myth*) water nymph.

nail /neiəl/ *n* [C] **1** layer of hard substance over the outer tip of a finger (ˈ*fingernail*) or toe (ˈ*toenail*). ⇨ illus at arm. ***fight tooth and nail,*** make every possible effort to win. **2** slender piece of metal, pointed at one end and with a head at the other, (to be) hammered into articles as a fastener. ***as hard as nails,*** very tough; without feeling or sympathy. ***hit the nail on the head,*** pick out the real or most important point. □ *vt* (*pres p* -ing /ˈneilɪŋ/) **1** fasten (as) with a nail: *~ a lid on a box; ~ down a carpet.* ***nail sth down,*** (*fig*) settle it definitely. **2** (*informal*) grab; catch (a person, his attention, etc): *He ~ed me in the corridor.*

ˈnail brush, brush for cleaning the (finger)nails.

ˈnail file, small, flat file for shaping the (finger)nails.

ˈnail polish, polish for shining or coloring the (finger)nails.

ˈnail scissors, scissors for trimming the (finger)nails.

naive, naïve /na(i)ˈiv/ *adj* natural and innocent in speech and behavior (eg because of youth or lack of experience): *a ~ girl; ~ remarks.*

naive·ly *adv*

naiveté, naïveté /na(i)ˌivˈtei/ *n* **(a)** [U] being naive. **(b)** [C] naive remark, etc.

naked /ˈneikɪd/ *adj* **1** without clothes on; bare: *as ~ as the day he was born.* **2** without protection or covering: *a ~ sword,* without its sheath; *a ~ light,* without a lampshade, etc. ***with the naked eye,*** without a microscope, telescope or other aid to seeing. ***the naked truth,*** not disguised.

naked·ly *adv*

naked·ness /-nɪs/ *n* [U]

name[1] /neim/ *n* **1** [C] word(s) by which a person, animal, place, thing, etc is known and spoken to or of: *The teacher knows all the pupils in his class by ~.* ***in the name of,*** **(a)** with the authority of: *Stop! in the ~ of the law!* **(b)** in the cause of; for the sake of (used when making an appeal): *In the ~ of truth and justice, tell us what you know.* ***call sb names,*** call him bad or insulting names (eg liar, coward). ***not have a penny to one's name,*** be without money. ***have sb's name on it,*** (said esp of a bullet which has struck somebody) be destined by fate or circumstances to hit him. **2** (*sing* only) reputation; fame: *has a bad ~.* ***make/win a name for oneself,*** become well-known. **3** [C] famous person: *the big ~s of the screen/the great ~s of history.*

ˈname·sake *n* [C] person or thing with the same name as another.

name[2] /neim/ *vt* **1** give a name to: *They ~d the child John.* ⇨ first name. **2** identify by name: *Can you ~ all the plants and trees in this garden?* **3** specify: *Name your price,* say what price you want. **4** select: *Please ~ a day for the wedding.* **5** nominate for, appoint to, a position: *He has been ~d secretary of the association.*

name·less /ˈneimlɪs/ *adj* **1** not having a name: *a ~ grave, an unmarked one.* **2** having an unknown name; anonymous: *a well-known person who shall be ~.* **3** too bad to be named: *~ vices.*

name·ly /ˈneimli/ *adv* that is to say: *Only one boy was absent, ~ Harry.*

nanny goat /ˈnæni ˌgout/ *n* [C] female goat.

nap[1] /næp/ *n* [C] short sleep (esp during the day, not necessarily in bed): *have/take a nap after lunch.* □ *vi* (-pp-) sleep for a short time, esp during the day.

nap[2] /næp/ *n* [U] fuzzy or hairy surface on cloth, felt, etc.

na·palm /ˈneiˌpam/ *n* [U] jellied gasoline used in making fire bombs.

nape /neip/ *n* [C] back of the neck. ⇨ illus at head.

nap·kin /ˈnæpkɪn/ *n* [C] piece of cloth or paper used for protecting clothing, for wiping the lips, etc.
nar·cissus /narˈsɪsəs/ *n* [C] (*pl* ~es or -cissi /-ˈsɪˌsai/) garden plant related to the daffodil, bearing heavily scented white or yellow flowers in the spring.
nar·cotic /narˈkatɪk/ *n* [C] drug that produces sleep, dulls pain, and can cause addiction if taken regularly: *Opium is a ~.* □ *adj* **1** causing sleep or insensibility. **2** of or having to do with narcotics.
nar·rate /ˈnæˌreit, næˈreit/ *vt* tell (a story); give an account of: *~ one's adventures.*
nar·rator /-tər/ *n* [C] person who narrates.
nar·ra·tion /næˈreiʃən/ *n* **(a)** [U] the telling of a story, etc. **(b)** [C] story; account of events, etc.
nar·ra·tive /ˈnærətɪv/ *n* [C] story or tale; account of events. □ *adj* in the form of a story: *~ poems.*
nar·row /ˈnærou/ *adj* (-er, -est) (contrary to *wide*) **1** small or slender in width: *a ~ bridge.* **2** small, limited: *a ~ circle of friends.* **3** with a small margin: *a ~ escape from death; elected by a ~ majority.* **4** strict; exact: *What does the word mean in the ~est sense?* **5** limited in outlook; having little sympathy for the ideas, etc, of others. □ *n* (*usu pl*) narrow strait or channel between two larger bodies of water; narrow place in a river or pass. □ *vt,vi* (cause to) become narrow.
nar·row·ly *adv.*
nar·row·ness /-nɪs/ *n* [U]
narrow-minded /ˌnærou-ˈmaindɪd/ *adj* not easily seeing or sympathizing with the ideas of others; prejudiced.
ˌnarrow-ˈminded·ly *adv*
ˌnarrow-ˈminded·ness /-nɪs/ *n* [U]
NASA /ˈnæsə/ *abbr* = National Aeronautics and Space Administration.
na·sal /ˈneizəl/ *adj* **1** of or relating to the nose. **2** produced with resonance in the nasal cavity: *~ sounds,* eg /m, n, ŋ/.
nasal ˈcavity, space behind the nose and above the roof of the mouth.
ˈnasal sound, vowel or consonant pronounced with resonance in the nasal cavity.
na·sal·ly *adv*
nas·tur·tium /nəˈstərʃəm/ *n* [C] (*pl* ~s) garden plant with red, orange or yellow flowers, and edible leaves and seeds.
nasty /ˈnæsti/ *adj* (-ier, -iest) **1** dirty; disgusting; unpleasant: *medicine with a ~ smell and a nastier taste.* **2** immoral; indecent: *a man with a ~ mind.* **3** unpleasant; disagreeable: *a ~ temper/look in his eye. Did he get ~ when you said you wouldn't pay him?* **4** troublesome; awkward: *That's a ~ question.* **5** dangerous; bad: *a ~ accident.*
nas·tily /-əli/ *adv*
nas·ti·ness /ˈnæstinɪs/ *n* [U]
na·tal /ˈneitəl/ *adj* of or having to do with birth.
na·tion /ˈneiʃən/ *n* [C] **1** large community of people associated with a particular territory usually speaking a single language and having one government: *the United Nations.* **2** people forming a federation, tribe, etc: *the Navajo Nation.* **3** territory of a nation.
ˈnation·wide *adj* extending or ˌspreading throughout a nation.
nation·al /ˈnæʃənəl/ *adj* of or relating to a (whole) nation: *~ pride.* □ *n* [C] citizen of a particular nation: *Mexican ~s in the US.*
na·tion·ally /ˈnæʃənəli/ *adv*
nation·al·ism /ˈnæʃənəˌlɪzəm/ *n* [U] **1** patriotic devotion and loyalty to a particular nation. **2** desire for or a belief in the political, economic, etc independence of one's own country.
nation·al·ist /ˈnæʃənəlɪst/ *n* [C] supporter of nationalism(2).
nation·al·ist·ic /ˌnæʃənəˈlɪstɪk/ *adj*
nation·al·ity /ˌnæʃəˈnæləti/ *n* [C,U] (*pl* -ies) being a member of a nation: *What is your ~?*
nation·al·ize /ˈnæʃənəˌlaiz/ *vt* **1** transfer from private to State ownership: *~ the railroads.* **2** make into a nation.
nation·al·iz·ation /ˌnæʃənələˈzeiʃən/ *n* [U]
na·tive /ˈneitɪv/ *n* [C] **1** person born in a place, country, etc and associated with it by right of birth: *a ~ of Ireland/El Paso.* **2** original inhabitant. **3** animal or plant natural to and having its origin in a certain area: *The kangaroo is a ~ of Australia.* □ *adj* **1** born in a certain place, country, etc: *~ Americans.* **2** associated with the place and circumstances of one's birth: *my ~ land.* **3** of or characteristic of the natives of a place, esp those thought to be less civilized: *~ customs.* **4** (of qualities) belonging to one by nature, not acquired through training, by education, etc; inborn: *~ ability/charm.* **5** ***native to,*** (of plants, animals, etc) having their origin in: *One of the animals ~ to India is the tiger.* **6** found in a pure state, uncombined with other substances: *~ gold.*
na·tiv·ity /nəˈtɪvəti/ *n* [C] (*pl* -ies) birth. **the Nativity,** the birth of Jesus Christ.
NATO /ˈneitou/ *abbr* = North Atlantic Treaty Organization.
natty /ˈnæti/ *adj* (-ier, -iest) trim; smart: *~ clothes.*
natu·ral /ˈnætʃ(ə)rəl/ *adj* **1** of, concerned with, produced, by nature: *animals living in their ~ (=wild) state; a country's ~ resources,* its minerals, forests, etc. **2** of, in agreement with, the nature(4) of a living thing: *~ gifts/abilities.* **3** born with certain qualities or powers: *He's a ~ orator,* makes speeches easily. **4** ordinary; normal; to be expected: *It is ~ for a bird to fly.* **5** not artificial; unaffected: *speak in a ~ voice.* **6** (*music*) (of a note) neither sharp nor flat. ⇨ sharp(9), flat²(6). **7** born of parents who are not married to each other; illegitimate: *a ~ child/son/daughter.* □ *n* [C] **1** (*music*) natural(6) note; the symbol ♮ used to show this. ⇨ illus at notation. **2** ***a natural (for sth),*** (*informal*) person naturally expert or qualified: *He's a ~ for the job/the part.*
ˌnatural ˈgas, gas occurring with petroleum deposits, used as fuel.
ˌnatural ˈhistory, scientific study of plants, animals, minerals, their origins and their relationships.
ˌnatural seˈlection, process in nature by which those animals and plants that are best adapted to their environment tend to survive.

natu·ral·ist /ˈnætʃ(ə)rəlɪst/ *n* [C] person who makes a special study of animals or plants, esp in their natural settings.

natu·ral·ize /ˈnætʃ(ə)rəˌlaiz/ *vt,vi* **1** give (a person from another country) rights of citizenship: *~ immigrants as US citizens.* **2** take (a word) from one language into another: *English sporting terms have been ~d in many languages.* **3** introduce and accustom (an animal or plant) to another (part of a) country.

natu·ral·iz·ation /ˌnætʃ(ə)rəlɪˈzeiʃən/ *n* [U]

nat·ur·ally /ˈnætʃ(ə)rəli/ *adv* **1** by nature(4): *She's ~ musical.* **2** of course; as might be expected: *"Did you answer her letter?"—"Naturally!"* **3** without artificial help, special cultivation, etc: *Her hair curls ~.* **4** without exaggeration, pretense, etc: *She speaks and behaves ~.*

na·ture /ˈneitʃər/ *n* **1** [U] the physical universe and everything in it except those things made by man: *Is ~ at its best in spring?* **2** [U] (often **Nature**) force(s) controlling the physical world: *Miracles are contrary to ~.* **3** [U] simple state of life without civilization: *a return to ~,* to the simple and primitive life before mankind became civilized. **4** [C,U] qualities and characteristics which naturally belong to a person or thing: *It is (in) the ~ of a dog to bark. Chemists study the ~ of gases.* **5** temperament; disposition: *has a kind ~.* **6** sort; kind: *Things of this ~ do not interest me.*

naught, nought /nɔt/ *n* **1** [U] (*liter*) nothing, esp in the phrases: ***care naught for,*** have no interest in. ***come to naught,*** fail. **2** [C] the symbol 0 or zero. ⇨ App 1.

naughty /ˈnɔti/ *adj* (-ier, -iest) mischievous; disobedient; causing trouble.

naught·ily /-əli/ *adv*

naughti·ness /ˈnɔtinɪs/ *n* [U]

nausea /ˈnɔziə, ˈnɔʃə, ˈnɔʒə/ *n* [U] **1** feeling of sickness often with the desire to vomit: *overcome by/with ~ as soon as he set foot on the ship.* **2** disgust.

nau·seate /ˈnɔziˌeit, ˈnɔʒ-/ *vt* cause to feel nausea: *a nauseating sight.*

nau·seated *adj* = nauseous(2).

nau·seous /ˈnɔʃəs, ˈnɔziəs, ˈnɔʒəs/ *adj* **1** causing nausea. **2** feeling nausea. (*Note:* many Americans now use only *nauseated* in this sense.)

naut. *abbr* = nautical.

nauti·cal /ˈnɔtɪkəl/ *adj* of ships, sailors or navigation.

ˈnautical mile, ⇨ mile.

Na·va·jo, Na·va·ho /ˈnævəˌhou, ˈna-/ *n* [C] (*pl* ~s, ~es), *adj* **1** (member) of a group of North American Indians living in New Mexico, Arizona, and Utah. **2** the language of these people. ⇨ illus at Indian.

na·val /ˈneivəl/ *adj* **1** of a navy or of warships: *~ officers/battles.* **2** having a navy: *~ power.*

nave /neiv/ *n* [C] central part of a church.

na·vel /ˈneivəl/ *n* [C] depression (sometimes protrusion) in the surface of the abdomen where the umbilical cord was attached before birth. ⇨ illus at trunk.

navi·gable /ˈnævɪgəbəl/ *adj* **1** deep or wide enough for ships: *The Mississippi is ~ by ocean vessels to New Orleans.* **2** (of ships, etc) that can be steered: *not in a ~ condition.*

navi·ga·bil·ity /ˌnævɪgəˈbɪləti/ *n* [U]

navi·gate /ˈnævɪˌgeit/ *vt,vi* **1** plot or control the course of a ship or aircraft, using charts and instruments. **2** sail on or over (a body of water). **3** (*fig*) manage to move about: *had trouble navigating after a few drinks.*

navi·gator /-tər/ *n* [C] **(a)** person who navigates (1). **(b)** person who makes or leads voyages of exploration.

navi·ga·tion /ˌnævɪˈgeiʃən/ *n* [U] **1** the act, science of navigating. **2** the making esp of commercial voyages.

navy /ˈneivi/ *n* [C] (*pl* -ies) **1** a country's warships. **2** the officers and men of a country's warships. **3** (often **the Navy**) the military forces of a country, organised for fighting at sea. **4** (also **navy ˈblue**) dark blue.

nay /nei/ *adv* no: *voted nay.* □ *n* [C] **1** negative vote. **2** person who casts a negative vote.

Nazi /ˈnatsi/ *n* [C], *adj* (member) of the German National Socialist Party led by Hitler.

Nazism, Naziism /ˈnatˌsɪzəm, ˈnatsiˌɪzəm/ *n* [U] beliefs and doctrines of the Nazi party, which include state control of all industry, totalitarian government, and official anti-Semitism.

NBA /ˌen ˌbi ˈei/ *abbr* = **1** National Basketball Association. **2** National Boxing Association.

NBC /ˌen ˌbi ˈsi/ *abbr* = National Broadcasting Company.

NBS /ˌen ˌbi ˈes/ *abbr* = National Bureau of Standards.

NC *postal abbr* = North Carolina. ⇨ App 6.

NCO /ˌen ˌsi ˈou/ *abbr* = noncommissioned officer.

ND[1] *postal abbr* = North Dakota. ⇨ App 6.

n.d.[2] *abbr* = no date (of publication).

NE[1] *abbr* = northeast.

NE[2] *postal abbr* = Nebraska. ⇨ App 6.

neap tide /ˈnip ˌtaid/ *n* [C] tide occuring twice a month in which there is the least difference between the water levels at high and low tide.

Ne·an·der·thal /niˈændərˌθɔl/ *adj* of a prehistoric period of the Stone Age: *~ man.*

near[1] /nɪr/ *adj* (-er, -est) **1** not far from; close in space, time, position, etc: *The post office is quite ~.* **2** close in relation or affection: *a ~ relation,* eg a mother, a son; *friends who are ~ and dear to us.* **3** being the closer of two: *She's the one sitting on the ~ side of the table.* **4** coming close; avoided by a narrow margin: *a ~ miss.* □ *vt,vi* come or draw near (to); approach: *The ship was ~ing land. He's ~ing his end,* is dying.

near·ness /-nɪs/ *n* [U]

near[2] /nɪr/ *adv* not far; to or at a short distance in space, time, etc: *We searched far and ~* (= everywhere) *for the missing child.* ***as near as,*** as closely as: *As ~ as I can guess there were forty people present.* ***near at hand,*** **(a)** within easy reach: *Always have your dictionary ~ at hand.* **(b)** not far distant in the future: *The examinations are ~ at hand.* ***nowhere near,*** far from: *She's nowhere ~ as old as her husband.*

ˌNear ˈEast = Middle East.

near[3] /nɪr/ *prep* close to (in space, time, relationship, etc): *Come and sit ~ me.*

near·by /nɪrˈbai/ *adj, adv* not far away: *a ~ restaurant.*
near·ly /ˈnɪrli/ *adv* **1** almost: *It's ~ one o'clock. I'm ~ ready.* ⇨ hardly, scarcely. **2** closely: *We're ~ related,* are near relations. **3** ***not nearly,*** nowhere near: *I have $20, but that isn't ~ enough for my fare.*
near·sight·ed /ˈnɪrˌsaitɪd/ *adj* unable to see distant things clearly. ⇨ farsighted, shortsighted.
ˈnear·sight·ed·ness /-nɪs/ *n* [U]
neat /nit/ *adj* (-er, -est except 4 below) **1** clean and tidy; orderly: *a ~ worker; ~ writing.* **2** simple and well-designed: *a ~ dress.* **3** clever; skillful: *a ~ reply/conjuring trick.* **4** (of wines and spirits) undiluted: *a ~ brandy.* **5** (*sl*) fine: *had the ~est time!*
neat·ly *adv*
neat·ness /-nɪs/ *n* [U]
neath, 'neath /niθ/ *prep* (*poet*) beneath.
neb·ula /ˈnebyələ/ *n* [C] (*pl* ~s, -lae /-li/) group of very distant stars, mass of gas or dust, sometimes seen as a bright or dark patch in space.
nebu·lar /-lər/ *adj* of nebulas.
nebu·lous /ˈnebyələs/ *adj* **1** of or like a nebula. **2** (*fig*) formless; vague: *a ~ argument.*
necess·ar·ily /ˌnesəˈserəli/ *adv* as a necessary result: *Big men are not ~ strong men.*
necess·ary /ˈnesəˌseri/ *adj* **1** which must be done; required; essential: *It is ~ for him to work very hard. It is ~ that he work very hard. Sleep is ~ to health. Is that really ~?* **2** logically certain; inevitable: *a ~ result.* □ *n* [C] (*pl* -ies) something which is necessary: *bought some necessaries for her trip.*
necessi·tate /nəˈsesəˌteit/ *vt* (*formal*) make necessary: *The increase in population ~s a greater food supply.*
necess·ity /nəˈsesəti/ *n* (*pl* -ies) **1** [U] urgent need: *He was driven by ~ to steal food for his starving children.* **2** [U] condition or state of being necessary. **3** [C] something that is indispensable; requirement; need: *the necessities of life,* food, clothing and shelter. **4** [C] something which cannot be changed or avoided: *Is it a logical ~ that prices go up if wages go up?* ***of necessity,*** unavoidably.
neck¹ /nek/ *n* [C] **1** part of the body that connects the head and the shoulders: *wrap a scarf round one's ~.* ⇨ illus at head. ***neck and neck,*** side by side, level, in a race or struggle. ***a pain in the neck,*** (*informal*) annoying person, thing, or situation. ***break one's neck,*** (*sl*) work extremely hard (to achieve something). ***stick one's neck out,*** (*sl*) do or say something at the risk of severe criticism, pain, etc. **2** something like a neck in shape or position: *the ~ of a bottle; a narrow ~ of land.*
neck² /nek/ □ *vi* (*sl, dated*) exchange kisses, caresses and hugs: *~ing in the dark.*
neck·er·chief /ˈnekərˌtʃɪf, -ˌtʃif/ *n* [C] square of cloth worn around the neck.
neck·lace /ˈneklɪs/ *n* [C] string of beads, pearls, etc worn round the neck as an ornament.
neck·line /ˈnekˌlain/ *n* [C] outline of a garment at the opening for the neck.
neck·tie /ˈnekˌtai/ *n* [C] (*tie* is the usual word) band of material worn round the neck and tied in front.
nec·tar /ˈnektər/ *n* [U] **1** (*Greek myth*) the drink of the gods. **2** sweet liquid in flowers, collected by bees. **3** any delicious drink.
nec·tar·ine /ˌnektəˈrin/ *n* [C] kind of peach with thin, smooth skin.
née, nee /nei/ *adj* born (put after the name of a married woman and before her maiden name): *Mrs. Jane Smith, née Brown.*
need¹ /nid/ *n* **1** [U] necessity: *There's no ~ (for you) to start yet.* ***if need be,*** if necessary. **2** [U] lack of something necessary, desirable, etc: *felt a ~ for fresh air.* **3** (*pl*) something felt to be necessary: *My ~s are few.* **4** [U] poverty; misfortune; adversity: *He helped me in my hour of ~.*
needy *adj* (-ier, -iest) very poor: *help the poor and ~y.*
need² /nid/ *auxiliary verb* (no infinitive, no participles, inflected forms; *need not* may be contracted to needn't /ˈnidənt/) be obliged; be required: *Need you go yet? Need it have happened? We ~n't have hurried,* We hurried but now we see that this was unnecessary. (*Note:* These uses of *need* without a following *to + infinitive* are more likely to occur in *formal* style; ⇨ need³ (3) for the more common usage.)
need³ /nid/ *vt,vi* **1** be in need. **2** want; require: *Does he ~ any help? I'm here if you ~ me.* **3** be required or obliged: *I agree that he ~s to be told about the arrangement. Do you ~ to ask any more questions? We didn't ~ to hurry.*
need·ful /ˈnidfəl/ *adj* = necessary (the usual word).
need·fully /-fəli/ *adv* = necessarily (the usual word).
needle /ˈnidəl/ *n* [C] **1** small, thin piece of polished steel, pointed at one end and with a small hole at the other end for thread, used in sewing and darning. ***look for a needle in a haystack,*** search hopelessly. **pins and ˈneedles,** ⇨ pin¹(1). **2** long, thin piece of polished wood, bone or metal (without an eye), with a pointed end (for knitting) or a hook (for crocheting). **3** thin steel pointer in a compass, or other instrument. **4** something like a needle(1) in shape, appearance or use: *~s of a pine tree.* ⇨ illus at tree. **5** stylus used on a phonograph. **6** slender, pointed tube, as used for giving injections. ⇨ illus at syringe □ *vt* (*informal*) annoy, make angry.
need·less /ˈnidlɪs/ *adj* unnecessary: *~ work/trouble. Needless to say...,* It is unnecessary to say....
need·less·ly *adv*
needn't /ˈnidənt/ = need not.
needs /nidz/ *adv* (now used only with *must*) ***must needs,*** (*formal*) must necessarily.
ne'er /ner/ *adv* (*poet*) never.
ne'er-do-well /ˈner-du-ˌwel/ *n* [C] useless person.
neg. *abbr* = negative.
ne·gate /nɪˈgeit/ *vt* (*formal*) **1** deny. **2** make null and void.
ne·ga·tion /nɪˈgeiʃən/ *n* [U] **1** act of denying, refusing: *Shaking the head is a sign of ~.* ⇨ affirmation(1). **2** opposite of something positive.

nega·tive /ˈnegətɪv/ *adj* **1** (of words and answers) showing *no* or *not: give a ~ answer.* ⇨ affirmative. **2** not positive in character; not constructive: *~ criticism,* that is not helpful. ⇨ positive(3). **3** (*math*) of a number or quantity that is less than zero, or that is to be subtracted (eg, $-x^2y$). **4** of that kind of electricity carried by electrons: *the ~ plate in a battery.* **5** (in photography) having the light parts and dark parts of the actual scene, etc reversed. **6** indicating that a particular disease, condition, etc is absent: *~ results.* □ *n* [C] **1** word or statement that denies: *"No," "not" and "neither" are ~s. The answer is in the ~,* is "no." **2** (*math*) minus quantity (eg, *-5x*). **3** image, esp on photographic film or plate, in which light parts and dark parts are reversed. □ *vt* **1** deny. **2** reject; refuse to accept. **3** vote against.

nega·tive·ly *adv*

ne·glect /nɪˈglekt/ *vt* **1** pay no attention to; give little or not enough care to: *~ing one's studies/children/health.* **2** omit or fail (*to do* something): *He ~ed to say "Thank you."* □ *n* [U] neglecting or being neglected: *~ of duty. The garden was in a state of ~.*

ne·glect·ful /-fəl/ *adj* in the habit of neglecting things: *~ful of her appearance.*

ne·glect·fully /-fəli/ *adv*

ne·glect·ful·ness /-nɪs/ *n* [U]

neg·li·gee, neg·li·gé /ˌnegləˈʒei/ *n* [C] woman's flowing, loose, informal, dressing gown.

neg·li·gence /ˈneglɪdʒəns/ *n* [U,C] **1** carelessness; failure to take proper care or precautions: *The accident was due to ~.* **2** negligent act.

neg·li·gent /ˈneglɪdʒənt/ *adj* taking too little care; guilty of neglect: *He was ~ in his work/of his duties.*

neg·li·gent·ly *adv*

neg·li·gible /ˈneglɪdʒəbəl/ *adj* of little or no importance or size: *a ~ quantity.*

ne·go·ti·able /nɪˈgouʃəbəl/ *adj* **1** that can be negotiated(1): *Is the dispute ~?* **2** that can be passed from one person to another as payment, etc: *~ securities,* eg bonds. **3** (of roads, rivers, etc) that can be passed over or along.

ne·go·ti·ate /nɪˈgouʃiˌeit/ *vi,vt* **1** discuss, confer, in order to come to an agreement: *We've decided to ~ with the employers about our wage claims.* **2** get past or through successfully: *This is a difficult corner for a large car to ~.*

ne·go·ti·ator /-tər/ *n* [C]

ne·go·ti·ation /nɪˌgouʃiˈeiʃən/ *n* [C,U] (act of) negotiating: *enter into/start/carry on ~s with him. Price is a matter of ~.*

Ne·gro /ˈnigrou/ *n* [C] (*pl* ~es) **1** member of one of the black-skinned peoples that include esp the natives of central and southern Africa. **2** person of Negro ancestry. □ *adj* of or relating to Negroes.

Ne·groid /ˈniˌgrɔid/ *adj* of Negroes or the Negro race. □ *n* [C] Negroid person.

NEH /ˌen ˌi ˈeitʃ/ *abbr* = National Endowment for the Humanities.

neigh /nei/ *vi, n* [C] (make the) cry of a horse.

neigh·bor /ˈneibər/ *n* [C] **1** person living in a house, street, etc near another: *We're next-door ~s,* our houses are side by side. **2** person, thing or country that is near(est) another: *Great Britain's nearest ~ is France.* **3** fellow human.

neigh·bor·ing *adj* near to: *~ing countries; in the ~ing village.*

neigh·bor·li·ness /-nɪs/ *n* [U]

neigh·bor·ly *adj* kind; friendly.

neigh·bor·hood /ˈneibərˌhʊd/ *n* [C] **1** (people living in a) district or area near a certain place: *There's some beautiful scenery in our ~. He wants to live in a good ~.* **2** ***in the neighborhood of,*** about; approximately: *He lost in the ~ of $5000.*

nei·ther /ˈniðər, ˈnaiðər/ *adj* (used with a *sing noun* or *pron*) not one nor the other (of two): *Neither statement is true. In ~ case can I agree.* ⇨ either. □ *pron* not one nor the other: *Neither of the two girls knew the answer.* □ *adv, conj* **1** ***neither... nor...,*** not one nor the other: *He ~ knows nor cares what happened. Neither you nor I could do it.* **2** (after a negative *if* clause, etc): *If you don't go, ~ will I. A: "I don't like it."—B: "Neither do I."*

neo- /ˌniou-, ˌniə-, ˈniə-/ *combined form* new; revived; later: *Neolithic.*

Neo·lithic /ˌniəˈlɪθɪk/ *adj* of the new or later Stone Age: *~ man.*

neon /ˈniˌan/ *n* [U] element (symbol **Ne**) which is a colorless gas occurring in small proportions in the earth's atmosphere.

neon ˈlamp/ˈlight, tube filled with neon, which produces an orange-red light when an electric current is passed through it.

neon ˈsign, advertisement, etc in which neon light is used.

ne·o·phyte /ˈniəˌfait/ *n* [C] **1** new convert to a religion, member of a religious order, etc. **2** novice.

ne·o·prene /ˈniəˌprin/ *n* [U] (kind of) synthetic rubber.

nephew /ˈnefyu/ *n* [C] son of one's brother or sister.

nep·ot·ism /ˈnepəˌtɪzəm/ *n* [U] the giving of special favor (esp employment) by a person in high position to his relatives.

Nep·tune /ˈnepˌtun/ *n* (*astron*) planet eighth in order from the sun. ⇨ illus at planet.

nerve /nərv/ *n* **1** [C] fiber or bundle of fibers carrying impulses of feeling and motion between the nervous system and the muscles, organs, glands, etc of the body. **2** (*pl*) condition of being easily excited, worried, irritated: *He is suffering from ~s.* ***a bundle of nerves,*** very nervous person. ***get on one's nerves,*** worry or annoy: *That noise/man gets on my ~s.* **3** [U] daring; courage: *A test pilot needs plenty of ~.* ***have the nerve to do sth,*** **(a)** have the necessary courage etc. **(b)** (*informal*) be impudent enough: *He had the ~ to suggest that I was cheating.* **4** [U] (*informal*) boldness; impudence: *He's got ~, going to work dressed like that!* ***(have) ˈsome/a ˈlot of ˈnerve,*** be very impudent: *He has/He's got some ~, asking for that much!* □ *vt* summon up one's strength or courage in order to do something: *~ oneself for a task.*

ˈnerve cell, cell that transmits impulses in nerves(1).

nerve·less *adj* **(a)** confident, not nervous. **(b)** lacking in vigor or courage; weak: *The knife fell from his ~less hand.*

nerve·less·ly *adv*

ˈnerve-racking/-wracking *adj* irritating.

nerv·ous /ˈnərvəs/ *adj* **1** of the nerves(1): *the ~ system.* **2** easily excited; jumpy. **3** afraid, timid: *Are you ~ in the dark?*

ˌnervous ˈbreakdown, disorder marked by exhaustion, tension, and depression.

ner·vous·ly *adv*

ner·vous·ness /-nɪs/ *n* [U]

ˈnervous system, system of nerves(1) and nerve centers (as the brain and spinal cord) of the body.

nervy /ˈnərvi/ *adj* (-ier, -iest) (*informal*) boldly impudent.

-ness /-nɪs/ *suffix* state; quality; condition: *goodness.*

nest /nest/ *n* [C] **1** place made or chosen by a bird for its eggs. ⇨ illus at bird. **2** place in which certain living things have and keep their young: *a ˈwasps' ~.* **3** comfortable place or shelter: *make oneself a ~ of cushions.* **4** number of like things (esp boxes, tables) fitting one inside another. **5** (*fig*) hiding place or den, usually of bad persons or things: *a ~ of crime/vice/pirates.* □ *vi* **1** make or use a nest: *The swallows are ~ing in the woodshed.* **2** fit snugly together or within one another.

ˈnest egg, (*fig*) sum of money saved for future use.

nestle /ˈnesəl/ *vt,vi* **1** settle comfortably and warmly: *~ (down) among the cushions.* **2** press oneself to: *The child was nestling closely against/~d up to her mother.*

nest·ling /ˈnestlɪŋ/ *n* [C] bird too young to leave the nest.

net[1] /net/ *n* **1** [U] material with regular openings, made of knotted string, hair, wire, etc. **2** [C] such material made up for a special purpose: *a ˈhairnet, ˈfishnet, ˈtennis net.* **3** [C] trap; snare. □ *vt* (-tt-) **1** catch (fish, animals, etc) with or in a net. **2** cover (as) with a net or nets.

net[2] /net/ *adj* remaining when no more charges or deductions are to be taken away: *net profit,* profit after all working expenses have been deducted. □ *vt* (-tt-) gain as a net profit: *He netted $50 from the deal.*

nether /ˈneðər/ *adj* (*archaic*) lower: *the ˈ~ regions/world,* the world of the dead; hell.

nether·most /-ˌmoust/ *adj* lowest.

net·ting /ˈnetɪŋ/ *n* [U] net.

nettle /ˈnetəl/ *n* [C] common wild plant which has hairs that sting and redden the skin when touched. □ *vt* make angry; annoy: *She looked ~d by my remarks.*

net·work /ˈnetˌwərk/ *n* [C] **1** complex system of lines that cross: *a ~work of railways/canals.* **2** connected system: *an intelligence/spy ~work.*

neu·ral /ˈnʊrəl/ *adj* of the nerves(1).

neu·ral·gia /nʊˈrældʒə/ *n* [U] sharp pain occurring along the course of a nerve.

neu·ral·gic /-dʒɪk/ *adj*

neu·rol·ogist /nʊˈralədʒɪst/ *n* [C] physician who specializes in neurology.

neu·rol·ogy /nʊˈralədʒi/ *n* [U] branch of medical science that is concerned with the nervous system.

neu·rosis /nʊˈrousɪs/ *n* [C] (*pl* -ses /-ˌsiz/) disorder which may cause depression, abnormal fears, etc.

neu·rotic /nʊˈratɪk/ *adj* **1** (of a person) suffering from a neurosis. **2** of or relating to a neurosis: *~fears.* □ *n* [C] neurotic person.

neu·ter /ˈnutər/ *adj* **1** (*gram*) neither feminine nor masculine in gender. **2** without functional sex organs. □ *n* [C] **1** neuter word or gender. **2** neuter animal, plant, or insect. □ *vt* castrate: *a ~ed cat.*

neu·tral /ˈnutrəl/ *adj* **1** taking neither side in a war or quarrel: *~ nations.* **2** of or belonging to a country that remains neutral in war: *~ territory/ships.* **3** having no definite characteristics; not clearly one or another: *a ~ color.* **4** (*chemistry*) neither acid nor alkaline. **5** not having an electrical charge. **6** of a gear position in which no power is transmitted: *leave a car in ~ gear.* □ *n* **1** [C] neutral person, country, etc. **2** [U] neutral position of gears: *put the car into ~.* **3** [U] neutral color.

neu·tral·ity /nuˈtræləti/ *n* [U] state of being neutral, esp in time of war.

neu·tral·ize /ˈnutrəˌlaiz/ *vt* **1** declare or keep (a country, territory, etc) neutral in time of war. **2** cancel the effect or force of, by means of an opposite effect or force: *~ize a poison.*

neu·tral·iz·ation /ˌnutrələˈzeiʃən/ *n* [U]

neu·tron /ˈnuˌtran/ *n* [C] particle carrying no electric charge, of about the same mass as a proton, and forming part of the nucleus of an atom. ⇨ illus at atom.

never /ˈnevər/ *adv* **1** at no time; on no occasion: *He has ~ been abroad. N~ in all my life have I heard such nonsense! Such a display has ~ been seen before.* **2** not at all; to no degree; in no way: *That will ~ do.* ***Never mind!*** Don't worry! Don't trouble about it!

never·more /ˌnevərˈmɔr/ *adv* never again.

never·the·less /ˌnevərðəˈles/ *adv, conj* however; in spite of that; still: *There was no news; ~, she went on hoping.*

new /nu/ *adj* (-er, -est) **1** not existing before; seen, heard of, introduced, for the first time; of recent origin, growth, manufacture, etc: *a new idea/film/novel/invention; the newest* (= latest) *fashions.* ***as good as new,*** in very good condition. **2** already in existence, but only now seen, discovered, etc: *learn new words in a foreign language.* **3** unfamiliar: *ideas that were new to him.* **4** not yet accustomed to: *I am new to this town.* **5** taking up a place, position, etc for the first time: *our new typist.* **6** up-to-date; modern. **7** fresh: *felt like a new man after his vacation.* **8** beginning again: *a new life after a divorce.* **9** additional: *found out new information.* □ *adv* (preceding the word it qualifies) recently: *a ˈnewborn baby.*

new·comer /ˈnuˌkəmər/ *n* [C] person who has recently arrived in a place.

ˌnew ˈdeal, improved transaction, agreement, relationship, etc.

the ˌNew ˈDeal, (slogan and popular term for) administration and policies of Franklin Delano

Roosevelt as President of the US, 1933-45.
ˈnew·fangled *adj* recently in use or fashion (and, for this reason, disliked by some): *newfangled ideas.*
the ˌNew ˈLook, the latest style (in clothing fashions, automobile design, etc).
new·ness /-nɪs/ *n* [U] state or condition of being new.
ˌnew ˈmoon, (period of the) moon seen as a crescent after being invisible.
ˌNew ˈTestament, second part of the Christian Bible, containing the life and teachings of Jesus.
ˌNew ˈWorld, western hemisphere; North and South America.
ˌNew Year's ˈDay, the first day of the year, January 1.
ˌNew Year's ˈEve, the last day of the year, December 31.
New·burg, New·burgh /ˈnuˌbərg/ *adj* (*Note:* usually following the *noun*, in imitation of French) (of seafoods) served with, of, a garnish of cream, sherry, and egg yolk: *lobster/shrimp ~; sauce ~.*
new·el /ˈnuəl/ *n* [C] upright post that supports the railing of a stairway.
new·ly /ˈnuli/ *adv* **1** recently: *a ~ married couple.* **2** in a new, different way: *~ arranged furniture.*
ˈnewly·wed /ˈnuliˌwed/ *n* [C] newly married person.
news /nuz/ *n pl* (used with a *sing verb*) information or reports of recent events: *What's the latest ~? Here are the ~ headlines. Here are some interesting pieces/bits of ~. That's no ~ to me,* I already know that. ***break the news,*** ⇨break²(6).
ˈnews·boy *n* [C] boy who delivers and sells newspapers.
ˈnews·cast *n* [C] radio or television broadcast of news.
ˈnews·caster *n* [C] person who presents the news on radio or television.
ˈnews·let·ter *n* [C] printed letter or report sent out to members of a society, etc.
ˈnews·pa·per *n* [C] printed publication, usually issued daily, with news, advertisements, etc.
ˈnews·print *n* [U] paper for printing newspapers on.
ˈnews·reel *n* [C] short motion picture that shows current happenings and news events.
ˈnews·stand *n* [C] stall for the sale of newspapers, etc.
ˈnews·wor·thy *adj* (-ier, iest) sufficiently interesting for reporting, eg in a newspaper.
newsy *adj* (-ier, -iest) (*informal*) full of news.
newt /nut/ *n* [C] (kinds of) small salamander which lives mostly in the water.
next /nekst/ *adj* nearest in time, order, or space: *Take the ~ right turn. Miss Green was the ~ (person) to arrive. I plan to leave ~ Friday/week/month.* ***next to nothing,*** scarcely anything; almost nothing: *She earns ~ to nothing.* □ *adv* **1** in the time immediately after: *What are you going to do ~?* ***come next,*** follow. **2** in the nearest position, rank, place, etc. ***the next best thing,*** something which is immediately after the first choice: *There are no tickets left for the circus; the ~ best thing is the zoo.*
next door /ˌneksˈdɔr, ˌnekˈstɔr/ the next house, apartment, etc: *He lives ~ door (to me).*
ˈnext-door *adj*
ˌnext of ˈkin, nearest relation(s).
Nez Percé /ˌnez ˈpərs/ *n* [C], *adj* (member of) a group of North American Indians living in Oregon, Washington and Utah.
NFL /ˌen ˌef ˈel/ *abbr* = National Football League.
NH *postal abbr* = New Hampshire. ⇨ App 6.
nib /nɪb/ *n* [C] **1** point of a pen. **2** any sharp point or tip. **3** bill or beak of a bird.
nibble /ˈnɪbəl/ *vt,vi* eat with repeated tiny bites: *rabbits nibbling carrots.* □ *n* [C] act of nibbling: *I felt a ~ at the bait.*
nice /nais/ *adj* (-r, -st) **1** (contrary to *nasty*) pleasant; agreeable; *a ~ day; ~ weather; a ~ little girl.* ***nice and quiet/snug/warm, etc,*** (used to intensify the following *adjective*): *~ and warm by the fire.* **2** fine; good: *a ~ lunch.* **3** needing care and exactness; sensitive; subtle: *~ shades of meaning.* well-bred; refined: *comes from a ~ family.* **4** skillful: *a ~ piece of work.*
nice·ly *adv*
nice·ness /-nɪs/ *n* [U]
nicety /ˈnaisəti/ *n* (*pl* -ies) **1** [U] accuracy; exactness: *~ of judgment.* **2** [C] delicate distinction; fine detail. **3** [C] something elegant or refined: *used to linen napkins, fine china, and other niceties.*
niche /nɪtʃ/ *n* [C] **1** alcove or recess in a wall, eg for a statue or ornament. **2** (*fig*) suitable or fitting position: *He found the right ~ for himself in the civil service.*
nick /nɪk/ *n* [C] **1** small notch or cut. **2** ***in the nick of time,*** only just in time; just at the right moment. □ *vt* make a nick(1) in.
nickel /ˈnɪkəl/ *n* **1** [U] hard, silver-white metallic element (symbol **Ni**) used esp in alloys. **2** [C] coin of the US and Canada worth 5 cents. ⇨ App 4.
nick·name /ˈnɪkˌneim/ *n* [C] **1** (often descriptive) name used instead of a person's real name (eg *Fatty* for a fat boy). **2** shortened or altered form of a proper name, as "Chris" (instead of "Christopher") or "Smitty" (instead of "Smith"). □ *vt* give a nickname to.
nic·otine /ˈnɪkəˌtin/ *n* [U] poisonous substance found in tobacco.
NIE /ˌen ˌai ˈi/ *abbr* = National Institute of Education.
niece /nis/ *n* [C] daughter of one's brother or sister, or of the brother or sister of one's spouse.
nifty /ˈnɪfti/ *adj* (*informal, dated*) smart; fine.
nig·gard·ly /ˈnɪgərdli/ *adj* **1** stingy; miserly. **2** small; scanty.
nig·ger /ˈnɪgər/ *n* [C] ⚠ (impolite and offensive word for) Negro.
nigh /nai/ *adv, prep* (-er, -est) (*archaic; poet*) near (to).
night /nait/ *n* **1** [C,U] dark hours between sunset and sunrise or twilight and dawn: *in/during the ~; on Sunday ~; on the ~ of Friday, the 13th of June.* ***night after night,*** for many nights in succession. ***all night (long),*** throughout the whole night. ***night and day,*** continuously: *travel ~ and day for a week.* ***at night,*** during the night. ***by night,*** during the night: *travel by ~.* ***have a***

good/ bad night, sleep well/badly. ***make a night of it,*** spend all night in merrymaking, eg at a party. **2** [U] nightfall. **3** [U] darkness of night.

ˈnight·club *n* [C] place open at night for dancing, supper, entertainment, etc.

ˈnight·fall *n* the coming of night; evening.

ˈnight·gown *n* [C] loose gown for sleeping, worn by a woman or child.

ˈnight·hawk *n* [C] **(a)** insect-eating bird related to the whippoorwill. **(b)** person who habitually stays up late.

night·ly *adj, adv* (taking place, happening, existing) in the night or every night.

ˈnight·mare *n* [C] **(a)** terrible, frightening dream. **(b)** horrible experience: *Traveling on those bad mountain roads was a ~.*

ˈnight·stick *n* [C] club carried by policemen and policewomen on patrol. ⇨ illus at police.

ˈnight·time *n* time of darkness, between evening and morning.

night·in·gale /ˈnaitənˌgeiəl/ *n* [C] **1** small tan bird with white throat, found mostly in eastern North America. **2** small, reddish-brown European migratory bird that sings sweetly, esp at night.

NIH /ˌen ˌai ˈeitʃ/ *abbr* = National Institutes of Health.

nil /nɪl/ *n* [U] nothing; zero.

nimble /ˈnɪmbəl/ *adj* (-r, -st) **1** quick-moving; agile: *as ~ as a goat.* **2** clever; quick to understand.

nim·bly /ˈnɪmbli/ *adv*

nim·bus /ˈnɪmbəs/ *n* [C] (*pl* ~es, -bi /-ˌbai/) **1** bright disc or halo around or over the head of a saint in a painting, etc. **2** gray rain cloud.

nin·com·poop /ˈnɪnkəmˌpup, ˈnɪŋ-/ *n* [C] foolish, stupid person.

nine /nain/ *adj, n* [C] (of) 9: *He's ~ (years old).*

ninth /nainθ/ *adj, n* [C] (of) one of 9 (parts) or the next after 8.

nine·pins /ˈnainˌpɪnz/ *n pl* (used with a *sing verb*) game in which a ball is rolled along the floor at nine bottle-shaped pieces of wood.

nine·pin *n* (*sing*) one of these pins.

nine·teen /ˌnainˈtin/ *adj, n* [C] (of) the number 19.

nine·teenth /ˌnainˈtinθ/ *adj, n* [C] (of) one of 19 parts or the next after 18.

nine·ty /ˈnainti/ *adj, n* [C] (of) 90.

the nine·ties *n pl* **(a)** (of a person's age, temperature, etc) between 89 and 100. **(b)** (of a century) the years from 90 to 99 inclusive.

nine·ti·eth /ˈnaintiəθ/ *adj, n* [C] (of) the next in order after 89 or one of 90 parts.

ninny /ˈnɪni/ *n* [C] (*pl* -ies) fool.

nip[1] /nɪp/ *vt,vi* (-pp-) **1** bite; pinch; press hard or squeeze between two edges or points such as the claws of a crab or the teeth of a dog. **2** take or cut off in this way: *The gardener was nipping off the small twigs on the tree.* **3** stop the growth of; damage. ***nip sth in the bud,*** stop its (bad) development. **4** chill; sting with the cold: *fingers and toes nipped by frost.* □ *n* [C] **1** sharp pinch or bite. **2** sharp chill. **3** small drink (esp of liquor): *a nip of brandy.*

nip·per /ˈnɪpər/ *n* [C] **1** (*pl*) pincers, forceps or other tool for gripping. **2** claw of a crab, etc.

nipple /ˈnɪpəl/ *n* [C] **1** small projection on the breast through which a baby sucks its mother's milk. ⇨ illus at trunk. **2** rubber mouthpiece on a baby's nursing bottle. **3** something like a nipple.

nippy /ˈnɪpi/ *adj* (-ier, -iest) biting; sharp.

nir·vana /nɪrˈvanə/ *n* [U] **1** (in Buddhism) ideal state in which the individual self is united with the supreme spirit. **2** state of harmony, bliss, etc.

nit /nɪt/ *n* [C] egg or young of a louse (esp as found in human hair).

ˈnit-picker *n* [C] (*informal*) fussy person who continually looks for slight errors.

ˈnit-picking (*informal*) *n* [U] action of seeking unimportant errors. □ *adj*

ˈnit·wit /ˈnɪtˌwɪt/ *n* [C] silly or stupid person.

ni·ter /ˈnaitər/ *n* [U] white salt used in making gunpowder, fertilizer, etc.

ni·trate /ˈnaiˌtreit/ *n* [C,U] salt formed by the chemical reaction of nitric acid with an alkali, esp *potassium nitrate* and *sodium nitrate*, used as fertilizers.

ni·tric /ˈnaitrɪk/ *adj* of, containing, nitrogen.

ˌnitric ˈacid, clear colorless, powerful acid (symbol **HNO_3**) used to make fertilizer, explosives, etc.

ni·tro·gen /ˈnaitrədʒən/ *n* [U] gaseous element (symbol **N**) without color, taste or smell, forming about four-fifths of the earth's atmosphere.

ni·tro·glycer·in, ni·tro·glycer·ine /ˌnaitrouˈglɪsərɪn/ *n* [U] powerful explosive made by adding glycerin to a mixture of nitric and sulphuric acids.

nit·wit ⇨ nit.

nix /nɪks/ *n* [U] (*sl*) nothing. □ *adv* (*sl*) no. □ *vt* (*sl*) deny; reject.

NJ *postal abbr* = New Jersey. ⇨ App 6.

NM *postal abbr* = New Mexico. ⇨ App 6.

no[1] /nou/ *adj* **1** not one; not any: *She had no money. No two men think alike. No other man could do the work.* ***no end of,*** (*informal*) a large number or quantity of; very great: *He spends no end of money on clothes.* **2** (used for emphasis) certainly not a/an: *He's no friend of mine.* **3** ***There's no denying/saying, etc,*** it is impossible to deny/say (what he'll be doing next, etc). **4** (in commands, etc): *No smoking*, smoking is not allowed. ***no good/use,*** useless: *It's no good worrying about her now.* ***by ˈno ˈmeans,*** ⇨ means[1]. ***in ˈno time (at all),*** very soon, quickly.

no[2] /nou/ *adv* **1** (used with *comparatives*) not at all; to no degree: *We went no farther than* (= only as far as) *the bridge. I have no more money.* **2** (contrasted with *yes*) (used to express refusal or disagreement): *Is it Monday today? —No it isn't.* □ *n* [C] (*pl* noes) **1** word or answer no; refusal. ***not take no for an answer,*** persist. **2** negative vote or voter: *The noes have it*, Those voting "no" are in the majority.

ˈno-fault *adj* (of insurance claims, divorce settlements, etc) being awarded without assessing blame to any of the parties involved.

ˈno-frills *adj* without luxuries.

ˈno-good *adj* worthless.

No.[3] *abbr* (*pl* Nos.) = number.

no·bil·ity /nouˈbɪləti/ *n* [U] **1** quality of being noble in character, mind, birth or rank. **2** (often **the nobility**) nobles as a class: *a member of the* ~.

noble /ˈnoubəl/ *adj* (-r, -st) **1** of high rank, title or birth: *a* ~ *family*. **2** having a high moral character and qualities; worthy; virtuous: *a* ~ *leader;* ~ *sentiments*. **3** splendid; grand; magnificent: *a building planned on a* ~ *scale*. □ *n* [C] person of noble rank or birth.

ˈnoble·man /-mən/ (*pl* ~men /-men/) *n* [C] man who is a noble.

nobly /ˈnoubli/ *adv*

no·body /ˈnouˌbədi/ *pron* not anybody; no person: *We saw* ~ *we knew. Nobody was there.* ***nobody else,*** no other person. □ *n* [C] (*pl* -ies) unimportant or unimpressive person: *Don't marry a* ~ *like James.*

noc·tur·nal /nakˈtərnəl/ *adj* **1** of or happening in the night. **2** active at night: ~ *birds*, eg owls.

noc·turne /ˈnakˌtərn/ *n* [C] dreamy piece of music.

nod /nad/ *vi,vt* (-dd-) **1** move the head down and up quickly as a sign of agreement or as a familiar greeting: *He nodded to me as he passed.* **2** express by such a movement: *nodded his approval.* **3** let the head fall forward as when sleepy or falling asleep: *She sat nodding by the fire.* ***nod off,*** fall asleep. **4** sway or move up and down gently: *nodding flowers.* □ *n* [C] gesture of nodding(1): *He agreed with a nod.*

node /noud/ *n* [C] **1** enlargement or swelling. **2** enclosed mass of body tissue: *a lymph* ~. **3** point on the stem of a plant where a leaf or bud grows out.

nod·ule /ˈnaˌdʒul/ *n* [C] small rounded lump, knob or swelling.

nod·u·lar /ˈnadʒələr/ *adj*

Noel /nouˈel/ *n* Christmas.

nog·gin /ˈnagɪn/ *n* [C] **1** mug. **2** small quantity, usually equal to a quarter of a pint, of liquor. **3** (*informal*) head.

noise /nɔiz/ *n* [C,U] **1** loud and unpleasant sound(s), esp when unwanted: *the* ~ *of jet aircraft. Don't make so much* ~/*such a loud* ~! **2** any kind of sound: *the* ~ *of the waves breaking on the shore.* **3** fuss: *made quite a* ~ *about the poor service.* □ *vt* make public: *It was* ~*d abroad that he had been arrested.*

noise·less *adj*

noise·less·ly *adv*

noise·less·ness /-nɪs/ *n* [U]

noi·some /ˈnɔisəm/ *adj* offensive or disgusting, esp to the sense of smell.

noisy /ˈnɔizi/ *adj* (-ier, -iest) **1** making, accompanied by, much noise: ~ *children*/*games*. **2** full of noise: *a* ~ *classroom.*

nois·ily /-əli/ *adv*

noisi·ness /ˈnɔizinɪs/ *n* [U]

no·mad /ˈnouˌmæd/ *n* [C] **1** member of a tribe that wanders from place to place, looking for food, water, or pasture for their cattle. **2** any wanderer.

no·madic /nouˈmædɪk/ *adj* of nomads: *a* ~*ic society.*

nom de plume /ˌnam də ˈplum/ *n* [C] (*pl* noms de plume) (*F*) pen name.

no·men·cla·ture /ˈnoumənˌkleitʃər/ *n* [C] (*formal*) system of naming: *botanical* ~.

nom·inal /ˈnamənəl/ *adj* **1** existing, etc, in name or word only, not in fact: *the* ~ *ruler of the country.* **2** very small or low in relation to the real value: *a* ~ *rent.* **3** (*gram*) of a noun or nouns.

nom·inally /-nəli/ *adv*

nomi·nate /ˈnaməˌneit/ *vt* **1** propose for election to a position: ~ *a man for the Presidency.* **2** appoint to office: *was* ~*d for a position in the Cabinet.*

nomi·na·tion /ˌnaməˈneiʃən/ *n* **1** [U] nominating. **2** [C] instance of this: *How many* ~*s have there been so far?* **3** [U] being nominated.

nomi·na·tive /ˈnamənətɪv/ *adj, n* [C] (*gram*) (of the) form of a word that is the grammatical subject: *the* ~ *case*, eg the pronoun *we*.

nomi·nee /ˌnaməˈni/ *n* [C] person who is nominated for an office or appointment.

non- /ˌnan-/ *prefix* not; absence of.

non·cha·lance /ˈnanʃəˌlans/ *n* [U] coolness; unconcern.

non·cha·lant /ˈnanʃəˌlant/ *adj* not having, not showing, interest or concern.

non·cha·lant·ly *adv*

non·com /ˈnanˌkam/ *n* [C] (*informal*) noncommissioned officer.

non·com·bat·ant /ˌnankəmˈbætənt/ *n* [C] **1** person in the armed forces (eg a surgeon or chaplain) who does not take part in the fighting. **2** civilian.

non·com·mis·sioned of·fi·cer /ˌnankəˌmɪʃənd ˈɔfəsər/ *n* [C] officer in the armed forces (such as a sergeant) who is taken from the enlisted ranks and does not hold a commission(4).

non·com·mit·tal /ˌnankəˈmɪtəl/ *adj* not committing oneself to a definite course or to either side (in a dispute, etc): *give a* ~ *answer.*

non com·pos men·tis /ˌnan ˌkampəs ˈmentɪs/ *adj* (*Lat*) not legally responsible because not of sound mind.

non·con·duc·tor /ˌnankənˈdəktər/ *n* [C] substance that does not conduct heat, electricity, or sound.

non·con·form·ist /ˌnankənˈfɔrmɪst/ *n* [C] person who does not conform to accepted customs or conventions.

non·con·form·ity /ˌnankənˈfɔrməti/ *n* [U]

non·de·nom·i·na·tion·al /nandiˌnamɪˈneiʃənəl/ *adj* (of esp religious worship) not restricted to the ritual, beliefs, or membership of any one religion.

non·de·script /ˈnandɪˌskrɪpt/ *adj* not easily classed, and so not easily described.

non·dis·crim·i·na·tory /ˌnandɪˈskrɪmɪnəˌtɔri/ *adj* not discriminating against any person because of race, creed, etc.

none /nən/ *pron* **1** not any, not one: *I wanted some string but there was* ~ *in the house. "Is there any flour left?" "No,* ~ *at all." None of them has*/*have come back yet.* ***none but,*** only: *They chose* ~ *but the best.* ***none other than,*** no one or nothing else but: *The new arrival was* ~ *other than the President* (= the President himself). **2** (in constructions equal to an imperative): *None of that!* Stop that! □ *adv* by no means; in no degree; not at all: *I hope you're ~ the worse for that accident. He was ~ too happy at the result.*

non·en·tity /ˌnanˈentəti/ *n* [C] (*pl* -ties) **1** unimportant person or thing. **2** thing that does not really exist or that exists only in the imagination.

none·the·less /ˌnənðəˈles/ *adv* nevertheless.

non·fic·tion /ˌnanˈfɪkʃən/ *n* [U] literature based on fact (not novels, stories, plays which deal with fictitious events and persons).

non·flam·mable /ˌnanˈflæməbəl/ *adj* not (in-) flammable.

non·in·ter·ven·tion /ˌnanˌɪntərˈvenʃən/ *n* [U] principle or practice of keeping out of the affairs of another country.

non·pareil /ˈnanpəˌrel/ *adj, n* [C] (*formal*) unique or unrivaled (person or thing).

non·par·ti·san /ˌnanˈpartəzən/ *adj* not partisan; free of the influence or ties of a particular political party.

non·pay·ment /ˌnanˈpeimənt/ *n* [C] failure or neglect to pay (a debt, etc).

non·plus /nanˈpləs/ *vt* (-s-, -ss-) (often passive) surprise or puzzle (a person) so much that he does not know what to do or say: *I was completely ~ed when she said "No" to my proposal of marriage.*

non·profit /ˌnanˈprafɪt/ *adj* (of an organization) not created for the purpose of making money.

non·pro·lif·er·a·tion /ˌnanprəˌlɪfəˈreiʃən/ *n* [U] policy of setting limits to the production of (esp nuclear) weapons.

non·resi·dent /ˌnanˈrezədənt/ *adj* not residing in a particular place. □ *n* [C] nonresident person.

non·sense /ˈnanˌsens/ *n* [U] foolish talk, ideas, behavior: *Nonsense! I don't believe a word of it. His ideas are just a lot of ~!*

non·sen·si·cal /nanˈsensɪkəl/ *adj* not making sense: *~ remarks.*

non se·qui·tur /ˌnan ˈsekwɪtər/ *n* [C] (*Lat*) conclusion which does not follow logically from the premises or the evidence.

non·stand·ard /ˌnanˈstændərd/ *adj* (of a word, grammatical usage, dialect, etc) not considered correct.

non·stop /ˌnanˈstap, ˈnanˌstap/ *adj, adv* without a stop: *a ~ flight; fly ~ from New York to Paris.*

non·union /ˌnanˈyunyən/ *adj* not belonging to, not of, a trade union: *~ labor.*

non·vi·o·lence /ˌnanˈvaiələns/ *n* [U] policy of rejecting violence to gain one's goals.

noodle /ˈnudəl/ *n* **1** (usu *pl*) pasta made of flour and eggs and often cut in long, narrow strips for use in soups, etc. **2** (*sl*) head.

nook /nʊk/ *n* [C] **1** alcove; corner. **2** hidden, cozy, or sheltered spot: *search every ~ and cranny,* look everywhere.

noon /nun/ *n* (*sing* only) middle of the day; 12 o'clock in the daytime.

ˈnoon·day /-ˌdei/, **ˈnoon·tide** /-ˌtaid/ (*liter*) noon.

no one /ˈnou ˌwən/ *pron* = nobody.

noose /nus/ *n* [C] **1** loop of rope with a slip knot that becomes tighter when the rope is pulled: *the hangman's ~.* ⇨ illus at knot. **2** (*fig*) trap; snare.

nope /noup/ *adv* (*informal*) no.

nor /nɔr/ *conj* and not: *I have neither the time nor the money for such foolishness. He doesn't know the answer, nor does anybody else.*

Nor·dic /ˈnɔrdɪk/ *adj* northwestern European, esp in physical type (blond hair, blue eyes, etc).

norm /nɔrm/ *n* standard; pattern; average (as typical of the members of a group).

nor·mal /ˈnɔrməl/ *adj* typical, usual, or standard: *the ~ temperature of the human body.* □ *n* (*sing* only) usual state, level, etc: *above/below ~.*

nor·mally /ˈnɔrməli/ *adv*

nor·mal·ize /ˈnɔrməˌlaiz/ *vt* make normal.

Nor·man /ˈnɔrmən/ *n* [U], *adj* **1** (native) of Normandy. **2** (of the) style of architecture which first appeared in Normandy in the 10th century.

north /nɔrθ/ *n* **1 the north,** one of the four cardinal points of the compass, lying to the left of a person facing the sunrise. **2** (often **the North**) **(a)** part of any country, etc lying farther in this direction than other parts: *the ~ of England; cold winds from the ~.* **(b)** (in the US) the states which remained part of the Union during the Civil War. ***up North***, to or in the northern part of the US. □ *adj* in, of, from, or toward the north: *a ~ wind; North Carolina.* □ *adv* to or toward the north.

north·east /ˌnɔrθˈist/ *n, adj, adv* (regions) midway between north and east.

ˌnorth·ˈeaster·ly /-ˈisterli/ *adj* **(a)** (of wind) from the northeast. **(b)** (of direction) toward the northeast.

ˌnorth·ˈeastern /-ˈistərn/ *adj* of, from, or in the northeast.

north·er·ly /ˈnɔrðərli/ *adj, adv* from the north; toward the north; in or to the north.

north·ern /ˈnɔrðərn/ *adj* of, from, in, the north part of the world, a country, etc: *the ~ hemisphere; Northern California.*

north·erner *n* [C] **(a)** person born in or living in the north of a country. **(b) Northerner,** person from the North of the US.

northern lights, = aurora borealis.

ˈnorth·ern·most /-ˌmoust/ *adj* farthest north.

north·ward, north·wards /ˈnɔrθwərd, -wərdz/ *adj* toward the north: *in a ~ direction.*

north·west /ˌnɔrθˈwest/ *n, adj, adv* (regions) midway between north and west: *the Pacific Northwest,* (in the US) the coastal regions of Oregon, Washington, and (sometimes) Northern California.

ˌnorth·ˈwester·ly /-ˈwestərli/ *adj* **(a)** (of wind) from the northwest. **(b)** (of direction) toward the northwest.

ˌnorth·ˈwestern /-ˈwestərn/ *adj* of, from or in the northwest.

ˌNorthwest ˈPassage, once presumed water route across North America.

Nos. *abbr* ⇨ No.[3].

nose[1] /nouz/ *n* **1** [C] part of the face above the mouth, containing the nostrils, and serving as the organ of smell. ⇨ illus at head. ***as plain as the nose on one's face,*** very obvious. ***by a nose,*** by a very small amount. ***on the nose,*** exactly on the target. ***(right) under sb's nose,***

directly in front of him. ***cut off one's nose to spite one's face,*** do something that hurts only one's own interests. ***follow one's nose,*** go straight forward. ***lead sb by the nose,*** control him completely. ***look down one's nose at sb,*** treat or regard him with scorn. ***pay through the nose,*** pay too much for something. ***poke/stick one's nose into (sb else's business),*** meddle; interfere. ***turn one's nose up at,*** show contempt for. **2** (*sing* only) sense of smell: *a dog with a good* ~. **3** (*sing* only) (*fig*) good sense for finding out about things: *a reporter with a ~ for news/scandal/a story.* **4** [C] something like a nose in shape or position, eg the pointed, forward part of an aircraft. ⇨ illus at aircraft.

nose² /nouz/ *vt,vi* **1** go forward carefully, push (one's way): *The ship ~d its way slowly through the ice.* ***nose around*** (*sl*) snoop. **2** ***nose sth out,*** discover by smelling: *The dog ~d out a rat.* **3** (*fig*) pry or search for: *~ out a scandal; nosing into other people's affairs/nosing around for information.*

nose·bleed /ˈnouzˌblid/ *n* [C] bleeding from the nose.

nose·cone /ˈnouzˌkoun/ *n* [C] most forward section of a rocket or guided missile. ⇨ illus at capsule.

-nosed *adj* (in compounds) having the kind of nose indicated: *red-/long-nosed.*

nose dive /ˈnouz ˌdaiv/ *n* [C] **1** sharp vertical descent made by an aircraft. **2** sudden drop.

nose-dive *vi* perform a nose dive.

nose·gay /ˈnouzˌgei/ *n* [C] small bunch of cut flowers.

nosey /ˈnouzi/ *adj* = nosy.

no·show /ˈnouˌʃou/ *n* [C] person who fails to show up (eg, for an air flight) after having made a reservation.

nos·tal·gia /naˈstældʒə/ *n* [U] **1** longing for something in the past. **2** homesickness.

nos·tal·gic /naˈstældʒɪk/ *adj* of, feeling or causing, nostalgia.

nos·tal·gi·cally /-kli/ *adv*

nos·tril /ˈnastrəl/ *n* [C] either of the two outer openings of the nose. ⇨ illus at head.

nosy, nosey /ˈnouzi/ *adj* (-ier, -iest) (*informal*) inquisitive; prying.

not /nat/ *adv* **1** used to express a negative: *She did not answer my letter. He warned me not to be late. It's blue, not brown.* **2** (used after certain verbs, esp *think, suppose, believe, expect, fear, fancy, trust, hope, seem, appear,* and the phrase *be afraid* as the equivalent to a negative *that* clause): *"Can you come next week?"—"I'm afraid not."* I'm afraid that I cannot come. *"Will it rain this afternoon?"—"I hope not."* (*Note: not* is often contracted to *-n't* /-(ə)nt/ and suffixed to *be* and to *auxiliary verbs: hasn't* /ˈhæzənt/.) ***not at all,*** ⇨ all⁴(2).

no·table /ˈnoutəbəl/ *adj* deserving to be noticed; remarkable: ~ *events.* □ *n* [C] well-known or eminent person.

no·tably /-əbli/ *adv*

no·ta·rize /ˈnoutəˌraiz/ *vt* certify (a document) as a notary public.

no·tary pub·lic /ˌnoutəri ˈpəblɪk/ *n* [C] (*pl* notaries public) (also just **ˈnotary**) official with authority to do certain kinds of legal business, such as to certify that he has witnessed the signing of legal documents.

no·ta·tion /nouˈteiʃən/ *n* **1** [C] system of signs or symbols representing numbers, amounts, mu-

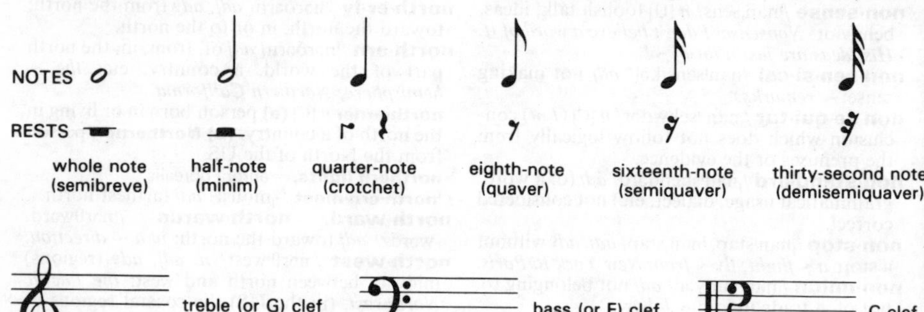

MUSICAL NOTATION

sical notes, etc. **2** [U] action of representing of numbers, etc by such signs or symbols. **3** [U] noting. **4** [C] note; record.

notch /natʃ/ *n* [C] **1** V-shaped cut in a surface. **2** deep gap or pass between mountains. **3** (*informal*) step; degree: *a ~ below the other students in ability.* □ *vt* make or cut a notch in.

note[1] /nout/ *n* [C] **1** short record (of facts, etc) made to help the memory: *He spoke for an hour without ~s.* **2** short letter: *a ~ of thanks.* **3** short comment on or explanation of a word or passage in a book, etc: *a new edition of "Moby Dick," with ~s at the back.* ⇨ footnote. **4** observation (not necessarily written). ***compare notes,*** exchange views; compare experiences. **5** written or printed promise to pay money. **6** piece of paper money. **7 (a)** musical sound of a certain pitch and duration. **(b)** symbol used to represent such a sound in manuscript or printed music. ⇨ illus at notation. **8** (usually *sing* with *a,* or *an*) quality or tone (esp of voice) showing feelings, attitude, etc: *There was a ~ of self-satisfaction in his speech.* **9** [U] distinction; importance: *a family of ~.* **10** [U] notice; attention: *worthy of ~. Take ~ of what he says,* Pay attention to it.

note[2] /nout/ *vt* **1** notice; pay attention to: *Note how I did it.* **2** make a note of; write (*down*) in order to remember: *The policeman ~d down every word I said.*

note·book /ˈnoutˌbʊk/ *n* [C] book with blank pages in which to write notes.

noted /ˈnoutɪd/ *adj* celebrated; well known: *a town ~ for its pottery/as a health resort.*

note·worthy /ˈnoutˌwərði/ *adj* deserving to be noted; remarkable.

noth·ing[1] /ˈnəθɪŋ/ *adv* not at all; in no way: *She looks ~ like her mother.*

noth·ing[2] /ˈnəθɪŋ/ *n* not anything: *He's had ~ to eat yet. Nothing ever pleases her. There's ~ like leather* (= Nothing is as good as leather) *for shoes.* ***for nothing,*** **(a)** free; without payment. **(b)** without a reward or result; to no purpose: *The work of three years was all for ~.* ***next to nothing,*** ⇨ next. ***come to nothing,*** fail; be without result. ***nothing doing,*** (*informal*) certainly not. ***think nothing of,*** consider as ordinary, usual or unremarkable: *He thinks ~ of a twenty-mile walk.*

no·tice /ˈnoutɪs/ *n* **1** [C] written or printed sign or announcement of an event: *put up a ~.* **2** [U] warning; announcement (of what is going to happen): *give the typist a month's ~,* tell her that she must leave her job at the end of one month. ***on short notice,*** with little warning, time for preparation, etc. **3** [U] attention. ***take notice (of),*** pay attention to: *Don't take ~ of them/of what they're saying about you.* **4** [C] short review of a new book, play, etc in a periodical. □ *vt,vi* pay attention; observe: *Noticing that she seemed tired, he asked her to sit down. I didn't ~ you.*

ˈno·tice·able /-əbəl/ *adj* **(a)** easily seen or noticed. **(b)** worth noticing.

ˈno·tice·ably /-əbli/ *adv*

no·tify /ˈnoutəˌfai/ *vt* (*pt,pp* -ied) give notice of; report: *~ the police of a loss; notified the authorities that he could not be present.*

no·ti·fi·ca·tion /ˌnoutəfəˈkeiʃən/ *n* [C,U]

no·tion /ˈnouʃən/ *n* [C] **1** idea; opinion: *has the ~ that people are usually honest.* **2** understanding: *I have no ~ of what he means.* **3** fancy; impulse: *had a good ~ to shake him.* ***take a notion (to sb/sth),*** take a liking to him/her/it. ⇨ liking(2). ***take a notion (to do sth),*** have a sudden desire to do it. **4** (*pl*) small, useful article, eg buttons, thread, pins, etc.

no·to·riety /ˌnoutəˈraiəti/ *n* [U] state of being notorious.

no·tori·ous /nouˈtɔriəs, nə-/ *adj* widely known (esp for something bad): *a ~ criminal.*

no·tori·ous·ly *adv*

not·with·stand·ing /ˌnatwɪθˈstændɪŋ, -wɪð-/ *adv* nevertheless; all the same. □ *conj* although. □ *prep* in spite of.

nou·gat /ˈnugət/ *n* [U] candy made of sugar, nuts, etc.

nought /nɔt/ *n* [C] = naught.

noun /naun/ *n* [C] (*gram*) word which can function as the subject or object of a verb, or the object of a preposition and may take a plural or possessive ending.

nour·ish /ˈnərɪʃ/ *vt* **1** feed; provide with food in order to keep alive and well. **2** improve; promote the development of: *~ the soil.* **3** support; keep alive; maintain: *~ hope in one's heart.*

nour·ish·ment *n* [U] (*formal*) food.

Nov. *abbr.* = November.

nova /ˈnouvə/ *n* [C] (*pl* ~s or -vae /-vi/) star that suddenly increases in brightness and then grows dim again.

novel[1] /ˈnavəl/ *adj* new; strange; of a kind not previously known: *~ ideas.*

novel[2] /navəl/ *n* [C] story in prose, long enough to fill one or more volumes, about either imaginary or historical people: *the ~s of Hemingway.*

novel·ette /ˌnavəˈlet/ *n* [C] novella.

novel·ist /ˈnavəlɪst/ *n* [C] writer of novels.

no·vel·la /nouˈvelə/ *n* [C] short novel.

nov·elty /ˈnavəlti/ *n* (*pl* -ies) **1** [U] newness; strangeness; quality of being novel: *the ~ of his surroundings.* **2** [C] new and unusual thing, idea, etc. **3** (*pl*) small manufactured goods of low cost, eg toys, decorations.

No·vem·ber /nouˈvembər/ *n* the eleventh month of the year.

nov·ice /ˈnavɪs/ *n* [C] **1** person with no earlier experience in a field. **2** person who is preparing to become a monk or a nun, but has not taken final vows.

no·vi·ti·ate /nouˈvɪʃiət/ *n* [C] **1** novice. **2** period of being a novice.

NOW[1] /nau/ *abbr* = National Organization for Women.

now[2] /nau/ *adv* **1** at the present time: *Where are you living now? Now is the best time to see the Grand Canyon.* **2** (used after a *prep*): *Up to/Till/Until now we have been lucky.* ***(every) now and then/again,*** occasionally; from time to time: *We go to the opera now and then.* **3** at once; immediately: *Do it (right) now!* ***just now,*** ⇨ just[2] (3). **4** (used without reference to time, to emphasize or call attention to): *Now stop quarreling and listen to me. Now then, what have you*

been up to? □ *conj* since: *Now (that) you're grown up, you must stop this childish behavior.*
now·a·days /ˈnauəˌdeiz/ *adj* at the present time (often used in contrasts): *Nowadays children are much healthier.*
no·where /ˈnouˌ(h)wer/ *adv* not anywhere: *The boy was ~ to be found.* ***nowhere near,*** not nearly: *50 is ~ near enough.*
nox·ious /ˈnakʃəs/ *adj* harmful: *~ gases.*
nox·ious·ly *adv*
nox·ious·ness /-nɪs/ *n*
nozzle /ˈnazəl/ *n* [C] projecting part of a hose, etc through which a stream of liquid or air is directed.
NP[1] *abbr* = **1** notary public. **2** noun phrase.
n.p.[2] *abbr* = no place (of publication given).
NRA /ˌen ˌar ˈei/ *abbr* = National Rifle Association.
NSF /ˌen ˌes ˈef/ *abbr* = National Science Foundation.
nth /enθ/ *adj* ⇨ N[1].
nu·ance /ˈnuˌans/ *n* [C] small shade of meaning, feeling, color, etc; very subtle difference.
nu·clear /ˈnukliər/ *adj* **1** of a nucleus. **2** of, relating to, or using nuclear energy.
ˌnuclear ˈenergy, great energy produced by changes in the nucleus of an atom.
nu·cleus /ˈnukliəs/ *n* [C] (*pl* nuclei /-kliˌai/) **1** positively charged, central part of an atom, consisting of protons and neutrons. ⇨ illus at atom. **2** central part, around which other parts are grouped. **3** structure in a living cell that controls its growth, reproduction, heredity, etc.
nude /nud/ *adj* naked. □ *n* [C] nude human figure (esp in art). ***in the nude,*** naked.
nu·dity /-əti/ *n* [U] nakedness.
nudge /nədʒ/ *vt* touch or push slightly esp with the elbow in order to attract a person's attention. □ *n* [C] push given in this way.
nug·get /ˈnəgɪt/ *n* [C] lump of metal, esp gold, as found in the earth.
nui·sance /ˈnusəns/ *n* [C] thing, person, act, etc that causes trouble or offense: *These flies are a ~.*
null /nəl/ *adj* **1** of no effect or force; without legal effect; invalid. **2** of no value; amounting to nothing.
nul·lify /ˈnələˌfai/ *vt* (*pt,pp* -ied) make null; negate; annul.
nul·li·fi·ca·tion /ˌnələfəˈkeiʃən/ *n* [U]
numb /nəm/ *adj* without ability to feel or move: *~ with cold/shock.* □ *vt* make numb.
numb·ly *adv*
numb·ness /-nɪs/ *n* [U]
num·ber /ˈnəmbər/ *n* [C] **1** unit which belongs to a mathematical system and is subject to such laws as addition and multiplication: *3, ¼, 9, 6, and −103 are ~s.* **2** quantity or amount: *a large ~ of people.* ***a number of,*** some; an unspecified but usually large number: *A ~ of books are missing from the library.* ***in number,*** as a total: *They were fifteen in ~,* There were fifteen of them. ***beyond/without number,*** too many to be counted. **3 (a)** word or symbol(s) used to represent a number; numeral. **(b)** number used as a means of identification, reference, etc: *a social security ~.* ***have somebody's number,*** (*informal*) be aware of his real character or intensions: *You can't fool her any more; she's got your ~.* ***have somebody's number on it,*** (said esp of a bullet which has struck somebody) be destined by fate or circumstances to hit him. **4** one of a numbered series, as one issue of a periodical, newspaper, etc. **5** one dance, song, musical selection, etc on a program. **6** (*pl*) a large group; many: *There is safety in ~s.* **7** (*pl*) arithmetic: *He's not good at ~s.* □ *vt* **1** count. **2** give a number to: *Let's ~ them from 1 to 10.* **3** amount to; add up to: *We ~ed 20 in all.* **4** include; place in a certain group: *~ her among one's friends.* **5** limit or restrict in number: *His days are ~ed,* He does not have long to live.
nu·mer·able /ˈnumərəbəl/ *adj* that can be numbered or counted.
nu·meral /ˈnumərəl/ *n* [C], *adj* figure(s) or symbol(s) standing for a number: *Arabic ~s,* 1, 2, 3, etc; *Roman ~,* I, II, IV, etc.
nu·mer·ation /ˌnuməˈreiʃən/ *n* [C] **1** method or process of numbering or calculating. **2** expression in words of numbers written in figures.
nu·mer·ator /ˈnuməˌreitər/ *n* [C] number or quantity above the line in a fraction, eg 3 in ¾. ⇨ denominator.
nu·meri·cal /nuˈmerɪkəl/ *adj* of, in, denoting, numbers: *~ symbols.*
nu·meri·cally /-kli/ *adv*
nu·mer·ous /ˈnumərəs/ *adj* great in number; very many: *her ~ friends.*
num·skull /ˈnəmˌskəl/ *n* [C] stupid person.
nun /nən/ *n* [C] woman who is a member of a religious order.
nun·nery /ˈnənəri/ *n* [C] (*pl* -ies) convent.
nup·tial /ˈnəpʃəl/ *adj* (*formal*) of marriage or weddings.
nup·tials *n pl* (*formal*) wedding.
nurse[1] /nərs/ *n* [C] **1** person who has been trained to take care of people who are ill or injured. **2** (also **ˈnursemaid**) woman or girl employed to look after babies and small children. **3** (also **ˈwet nurse**) woman employed to nurse (2) another's baby.
nurse[2] /nərs/ *vt* **1** take care of sick or injured persons. **2** feed (a baby) at the breast. **3** give special care to: *~ young plants.* **4** keep in mind; think about a great deal: *~ feelings of revenge.*
nurs·ery /ˈnərs(ə)ri/ *n* [C] (*pl* -ies) **1** room for the special use of babies or small children. **2** place where young plants and trees are raised for sale. **3** place where mothers who go out to work may leave babies and young children.
ˈnurs·ery·man /-mən/ *n* [C] (*pl* ~men /men/) man who owns or works in a nursery(2).
ˈnursery rhyme, poem or song (usually traditional) for young children.
ˈnursery school, school for children of 2 to 5.
nursing home /ˈnərsɪŋ ˌhoum/ *n* [C] establishment, usually privately owned, not a hospital, for the care of sick or aged.
nur·ture /ˈnərtʃər/ *n* [U] (*formal*) **1** training; upbringing. **2** nourishment. □ *vt* **1** bring up; train. **2** nourish.
nut /nət/ *n* [C] **1** fruit consisting of a hard shell enclosing a kernel that can be eaten. ***a hard nut to crack,*** a difficult problem to solve. **2** small

piece of metal with a threaded hole for screwing on to a bolt. **3** (*sl*) **(a)** crazy person. **(b)** enthusiast; fan.

nut·cracker /ˈnətˌkrækər/ *n* [C] device for cracking nuts.

nut·meg /ˈnətˌmeg/ *n* **1** [C] hard, small, round, sweet-smelling seed of an East Indian evergreen. **2** [U] spice consisting of this seed grated or ground to powder.

nu·tri·ent /ˈnutriənt/ *adj* (*formal*) serving as or providing nourishment.

nu·tri·ment /ˈnutrəmənt/ *n* [C,U] (*formal*) food.

nu·tri·tion /nuˈtrɪʃən/ *n* [U] the process of supplying and receiving nourishment.

nu·tri·tious /nuˈtrɪʃəs/ *adj* having high value as food.

nu·tri·tive /ˈnutrətɪv/ *adj* (*formal*) nutritious.

nuts /nəts/ *adj* (*sl*) **1** crazy; insane. **2** very enthusiastic: *~ about music.* □ *int: Nuts!* Forget it!

nut·shell /ˈnətˌʃel/ *n* [C] hard outside covering of a nut. ***in a nutshell,*** in the fewest possible words.

nutty /ˈnəti/ *adj* (-ier, -iest) **1** tasting like or full of nuts. **2** (*sl*) foolish; crazy.

nuzzle /ˈnəzəl/ *vt,vi* press, rub or push the nose against: *The horse ~d (up against) my shoulder.*

NV *postal abbr* = Nevada. ⇨ App 6.

NW *abbr* = northwest.

NY *postal abbr* = New York. ⇨ App 6.

NYC *abbr* = New York City.

ny·lon /ˈnaiˌlan/ *n* **1** [U] synthetic fiber used for hosiery, rope, brushes, etc. **2** (*pl*) stockings made of nylon.

nymph /nɪmf/ *n* [C] **1** (*myth*) one of the lesser goddesses, living in rivers, trees, hills, etc. **2** immature form of certain insects, eg the larva of the dragonfly, resembling the adult form, but often without wings.

O

O[1], **o** /ou/ (*pl* O's, o's /ouz/) **1** the fifteenth letter of the English alphabet. **2** zero (esp when saying telephone numbers).

O[2] *abbr* = **1** ohm. **2** old.

O[3] *abbr* = **1** ocean **2** Ohio. ⇨ OH.

O[4], oh /ou/ *int* cry of surprise, fear, pain, sudden pleasure, etc.

o' /ə/ *prep* **1** (*liter*) of. **2** ⇨ o'clock.

oak /ouk/ *n* **1** [C] kinds of large tree with tough, hard wood, common in many parts of the world. **2** [U] the wood of this tree.

oaken /ˈoukən/ *adj* made of oak.

oar /ɔr/ *n* [C] **1** long pole with a flat blade at one end, used to row or steer a boat through the water. **2** oarsman.

oar·lock /ˈɔrˌlak/ *n* [C] U-shaped device for holding an oar in place while rowing.

oars·man /ˈɔrzmən/ *n* [C] (*pl* -men /-men/) rower.

OAS /ˌou ˌei ˈes/ *abbr* = Organization of American States.

oasis /ouˈeisɪs/ *n* [C] (*pl* -ses /-ˌsiz/) **1** fertile place, with water and trees, in a desert. **2** (*fig*) pleasant, refreshing spot in a dull or barren region.

oat /out/ *n* [C] (usually *pl*) **1** cereal plant grown in cool climates as food both for human beings and for livestock. ⇨ illus at cereal. ***sow one's wild oats,*** lead a life of pleasure and gaiety while young before settling down seriously. **2** (*pl*) seeds of this plant.

oath /ouθ/ *n* [C] (*pl* ~s /ouðz, ouθs/) **1** solemn promise or vow, often made with God or some other holy person called on as a witness. **2** solemn declaration that something is true. ***on/under oath,*** (*legal*) sworn to tell the truth. **3** irreverent use of God's name or of sacred words to express strong feeling; curse.

oat·meal /ˈoutˌmiəl/ *n* [U] **1** meal made from oats. **2** porridge made from oatmeal.

OAU /ˌou ˌei ˈyu/ *abbr* = Organization of African Unity.

ob·du·racy /ˈabdərəsi/ *n* [U] (*formal*) state or quality of being obdurate.

ob·du·rate /ˈabdərɪt/ *adj* (*formal*) **1** stubborn; obstinate. **2** hard-hearted; not showing regret.

ob·dur·ate·ly *adv*

obedi·ence /ouˈbidiəns/ *n* [U] being obedient: *Soldiers act in ~ to the orders of their superior officers.*

obedi·ent /ouˈbidiənt/ *adj* doing, willing to do, what one is told to do: *~ children.*

obedi·ent·ly *adv*

ob·elisk /ˈabəˌlɪsk/ *n* [C] pointed, tapering, four-sided stone pillar, often set up as a monument or landmark.

obese /ouˈbis/ *adj* (*formal*) (of persons) very fat.

obe·sity /ouˈbisəti/ *n* [U] (*formal*) excessive or extreme fatness.

obey /ouˈbei/ *vt,vi* **1** do what one is told to do; carry out a command: *~ an officer/orders.* **2** follow; act in accordance with.

obi /ˈoubi/ *n* [C] (*pl* obis) sash worn with a kimono. ⇨ illus at kimono.

obitu·ary /ouˈbɪtʃuˌeri/ *n* [C] (*pl* -ies) printed notice of a person's death, often with a short account of his life: (as an *adjective*) *the ~ page,* eg in a newspaper.

obj. *abbr* = object[1].

ob·ject[1] /ˈabdʒɪkt/ *n* [C] **1** something that can be seen or touched; material thing: *Tell me the names of the ~s in this room.* **2** person or thing to which action or feeling or thought is directed: *an ~ of pity/admiration.* **3** purpose; goal: *with no ~ in life; fail/succeed in one's ~.* **4** (*gram*) noun, pronoun, clause, etc that receives or is affected by the action of a verb, or to which a preposition indicates some relation: In the sentence "*I gave him the money*", *money* is the *direct object* and *him* is the *indirect object*, while *the treasurer* is a *prepositional object* in "*I gave the money to the treasurer*".

ob·ject[2] /əbˈdʒekt/ *vt,vi* **1** say that one is not in favor of something; be opposed (to); make a protest against: *I ~ to all this noise/to being treated like a child.* **2** give as an objection: *They ~ed that they were not given enough time to finish the exam.*

ob·jec·tor /-tər/ *n* [C]

ob·jec·tion /əbˈdʒekʃən/ *n* **1** [C] statement of dislike, disapproval or opposition: *He made no ~ to getting up early.* **2** [U] feeling of disapproval: *I have no ~ to him.* **3** [C] reason for objecting.

ob·jec·tion·able /-əbəl/ *adj* likely to cause objection; unpleasant: *~able smell/~able remarks.*

ob·jec·tion·ably /-əbli/ *adv*

ob·jec·tive /əbˈdʒektɪv/ *adj* **1** existing outside the mind; real. ⇨ subjective. **2** impartial; not influenced by personal feelings or opinions. **3** (*gram*) of or relating to the case which indicates the object(4) of a verb or preposition. □ *n* [C] **1** object aimed at; purpose. **2** objective case.

ob·ject·ive·ly *adv* in an objective(2) manner.

ob·jec·tiv·ity /ˌabdʒekˈtɪvəti/ *n* [U] state of being impartial or unprejudiced.

ob·li·gate /ˈabləˌgeit/ *vt* bind (a person) morally or legally (to do something): *His promise ~d* *him to help.*

ob·li·ga·tion /ˌabləˈgeiʃən/ *n* [C] **1** promise, duty, custom or legal requirement that binds a person to do something. **2** binding power of law, duty, etc: *the* ~*s of conscience*. **3** debt owed for a favor, an act of kindness. **4** debt: *met all his* ~*s on time*.

ob·li·ga·tory /əˈblɪgəˌtɔri/ *adj* required by law, rule or custom: *Is attendance at the meeting* ~*?*

ob·lige /əˈblaidʒ/ *vt* **1** compel because of custom, law, circumstances, a promise, etc: *The law* ~*s parents to send their children to school. They were* ~*d to sell their house in order to pay their debts.* **2** cause (a person) to feel grateful because of a service or favor: *We are much* ~*d to him because of his generosity.* **3** do something as a favor or in answer to a request: *Please* ~ *me by closing the door.*

oblig·ing *adj* ready to help: *obliging neighbors.*

oblig·ing·ly *adv*

ob·lique /əˈblik/ *adj* **1** sloping; slanting. **2** indirect; not straightforward: *an* ~ *answer.*

oblique angle, acute or obtuse angle.

ob·lique·ly *adv*

ob·lit·er·ate /əˈblɪtəˌreit/ *vt* rub or blot out; remove all signs of; destroy.

ob·lit·er·ation /əˌblɪtəˈreiʃən/ *n* [U]

ob·liv·ion /əˈblɪviən/ *n* [U] **1** state of being completely forgotten. **2** state of being oblivious.

ob·livi·ous /əˈblɪviəs/ *adj* **1** unaware; inattentive: ~ *to one's surroundings/of what was happening.* **2** forgetful.

ob·long /ˈabˌlɔŋ/ *adj* longer in one direction than in the other, with four parallel sides and four 90° angles; rectangular. □ *n* [C] oblong figure or object.

ob·nox·ious /əbˈnakʃəs/ *adj* offensive; very disagreeable.

ob·nox·ious·ly *adv*

oboe /ˈoubou/ *n* [C] woodwind instrument with a double-reed mouthpiece. ⇨ illus at brass.

ˈobo·ist /-ɪst/ *n* [C] oboe player.

ob·scene /əbˈsin/ *adj* impure, indecent; offensive to modesty.

ob·scene·ly *adv*

ob·scen·ity /əbˈsenəti/ *n* (*pl* -ies) **1** [U] being obscene; offensive language, etc. **2** [C] obscene word, act, etc.

ob·scure /əbˈskyʊr/ *adj* **1** dark; hidden: *an* ~ *view/corner.* **2** difficult to understand: *an* ~ *book.* **3** not well known: *an* ~ *village/poet.* **4** not clear; faint; indistinct: ~ *marks.* □ *vt* make obscure: *The moon was* ~*d by clouds.*

ob·scure·ly *adv*

ob·scur·ity /əbˈskyʊrəti/ *n* (*pl* -ies) **1** [U] (state of) being obscure: *content to live in* ~. **2** [C] something that is obscure: *a philosophical essay full of obscurities.*

ob·sequi·ous /əbˈsikwiəs/ *adj* slavish; too eager to obey or serve (esp from hope of reward or advantage): ~ *to rich or important customers.*

ob·sequi·ous·ly *adv*

ob·sequi·ous·ness /-nɪs/ *n* [U]

ob·serv·able /əbˈzərvəbəl/ *adj* **1** that can be seen or noticed. **2** deserving to be observed.

ob·serv·ably /-əbli/ *adv*

ob·serv·ance /əbˈzərvəns/ *n* **1** [U] the keeping or observing(2,3) of a law, custom, holiday, etc: *the* ~ *of Thanksgiving Day.* **2** [C] customary act or practice: *religious* ~*s.*

ob·serv·ant /əbˈzərvənt/ *adj* **1** quick at noticing things: *an* ~ *boy.* **2** careful to observe(2,3) laws, customs, etc: ~ *of the rules.*

ob·serv·ant·ly *adv*

ob·ser·va·tion /ˌabzərˈveiʃən/ *n* **1** [U] observing or being observed: ~ *of the stars.* **2** [U] ability to take notice: *The writer's skill lay in her painstaking* ~ *of people.* **3** (usually *pl*) information obtained by observing: ~*s on bird life in the Antarctic.* **4** [C] remark; comment: *made some witty* ~*s about the people at the party.*

ob·serv·atory /əbˈzərvəˌtɔri/ *n* [C] (*pl* -ies) place equipped for the observation of the sun and the stars, marine life, weather, etc.

ob·serve /əbˈzərv/ *vt,vi* **1** see and notice; watch carefully: ~ *the behavior of birds. The accused man was* ~*d entering the bank.* **2** obey, act in accordance with (rules, etc). **3** keep and celebrate (festivals, birthdays, anniversaries, etc): *Do they* ~ *Christmas Day in that country?* **4** remark; comment: *He* ~*d that the house seemed to be too small.*

ob·server *n* [C]

ob·sess /əbˈses/ *vt* continually occupy the mind of; haunt: ~*ed by fear of unemployment.*

ob·ses·sion /əbˈseʃən/ *n* **1** [U] state of being obsessed. **2** [C] feeling, fixed idea, etc that continually occupies one's mind.

ob·ses·sive /əbˈsesɪv/ *adj* of or like an obsession.

ob·so·lescence /ˌabsəˈlesəns/ *n* [U] being obsolescent.

ob·so·lescent /ˌabsəˈlesənt/ *adj* becoming out-of-date; passing out of use.

ob·so·lete /ˌabsəˈlit/ *adj* no longer used; out-of-date.

ob·stacle /ˈabstəkəl/ *n* [C] something that stops progress or makes it difficult; hindrance: ~*s to world peace.*

ob·ste·tri·cian /ˌabstəˈtrɪʃən/ *n* [C] physician who is a specialist in obstetrics.

ob·stet·rics /abˈstetrɪks/ *n pl* (used with a *sing verb*) branch of medicine and surgery connected with childbirth.

ob·sti·nacy /ˈabstənəsi/ *n* [U] being obstinate; stubbornness.

ob·sti·nate /ˈabstənɪt/ *adj* **1** stubborn; not easily giving way to argument or persuasion: ~ *children.* **2** not easily overcome: *an* ~ *disease.*

ob·sti·nate·ly *adv*

ob·struct /əbˈstrəkt/ *vt* **1** put an obstacle in the way of. **2** block or cut off from view: *Trees* ~*ed the view.* **3** interfere with in order to hinder: ~ *justice.*

ob·struc·tion /əbˈstrəkʃən/ *n* **1** [U] obstructing or being obstructed. **2** [C] something that obstructs: ~*s on the road,* eg trees blown down in a gale.

ob·struc·tive /əbˈstrəktɪv/ *adj* likely or tending to obstruct.

ob·struc·tive·ly *adv*

ob·tain /əbˈtein/ *vt,vi* **1** acquire or get, usually as a result of effort: ~ *what one wants. Where can I* ~ *the book?* **2** (*formal*) be established or in use:

The custom still ~s in some districts.
ob·tain·able /-əbəl/ *adj* that can be obtained.
ob·trude /əbˈtrud/ *vt,vi* **1** force (oneself, one's opinions, etc) on another esp when unasked or unwanted. **2** push out.
ob·trus·ive /əbˈtrusɪv/ *adj* **1** intruding; forward. **2** unduly noticeable.
ob·trus·ive·ly *adv*
ob·tuse /əbˈtus/ *adj* **1** dull; slow in understanding; unintelligent. **2** (of an angle) between 90° and 180°.
obtuse·ly *adv*
ob·tuse·ness /-nɪs/ *n* [U]
ob·vi·ate /ˈabviˌeit/ *vt* make unnecessary; prevent by acting beforehand: *to ~ war by mutually disarming.*
ob·vi·ous /ˈabviəs/ *adj* easily seen or understood; clear; plain.
ob·vi·ous·ly *adv*
oc·ca·sion /əˈkeiʒən/ *n* **1** [C] time at which a particular event takes place or should take place: *on the ~ of our last meeting.* ***on occasion,*** now and then. **2** event; occurrence. **3** special event or happening: *Her party was quite an ~.* **4** [U] opportunity; chance: *I've had no ~ to visit him recently.* **5** [C] reason; cause: *His error was the ~ of a great deal of embarrassment.* □ *vt* (*formal*) bring about; cause: *The boy's behavior ~ed his parents much anxiety.*
oc·ca·sional /əˈkeiʒənəl/ *adj* **1** occurring from time to time, but not regularly: *He pays me ~ visits.* **2** used or meant for a special event, time, purpose, etc: *~ verses,* eg written to celebrate an anniversary.
oc·ca·sion·ally *adv* now and then; at times.
oc·cu·pancy /ˈakyəpənsi/ *n* [C] (*pl* -ies) act of occupying a house, land, etc by being in possession.
oc·cu·pant /ˈakyəpənt/ *n* [C] person who occupies.
oc·cu·pa·tion /ˌakyəˈpeiʃən/ *n* **1** [U] act of occupying(1); taking and holding possession of: *the ~ of a house by a family.* **2** [U] period during which land, a building, etc is occupied. **3** [C] business, trade, etc; that which occupies one's time, either permanently or as a hobby, etc.
oc·cu·pa·tional /-nəl/ *adj* arising from, connected with, a person's job.
oc·cupy /ˈakyəˌpai/ *vt* (*pt,pp* -ied) **1** live in, be in possession of (a house, farm, etc). **2** take and keep possession of (towns, countries, etc) in war: *~ the enemy's capital.* **3** take up, fill (space, time, attention, the mind): *Many anxieties ~ my mind.* **4** hold (a job or position): *She occupies an important position in the Department of Justice.*
oc·cur /əˈkər/ *vi* (-rr-) **1** take place; happen: *When did the accident ~?* **2** ***occur to,*** come to mind: *Did it ever ~ to you that...?* Did you ever have the idea that...? **3** exist; be found: *Misprints ~ on every page.*
oc·cur·rence /əˈkərəns/ *n* **1** [C] happening; event: *an unfortunate ~.* **2** [U] fact or process of occurring: *of frequent/rare ~.*
ocean /ˈouʃən/ *n* [C] **1** the great body of water that surrounds the land masses of the earth. **2** one of the main divisions of this: *the Atlantic/Pacific Ocean.* **3** (*informal*) great number or quantity: *~s of time.*
oceanic /ˌouʃiˈænɪk/ *adj* of, living in, the ocean.
oc·e·lot /ˈasəˌlat/ *n* [C] wild cat, found in Texas, Mexico, Central and South America, that has a yellowish coat spotted with black.
ocher /ˈoukər/ *n* [U] **1** sorts of earth used for making pigments varying from light yellow to brown. **2** pale brownish-yellow color.
o'clock /əˈklak/ *adv* (used in expressions of time) according to the clock: *He left at five ~.*
Oct. *abbr* = October.
oc·ta·gon /ˈaktəˌgan/ *n* [C] flat figure with eight sides and eight angles.
oc·tag·onal /ˌakˈtægənəl/ *adj* eight-sided.
oc·tane /ˈakˌtein/ *n* [U] hydrocarbon occurring in gasoline, the amount serving as basis for rating the fuel: *high/low ~ gasoline.*
oc·tave /ˈaktɪv, ˈakˌteiv/ *n* [C] **1** (*music*) **(a)** interval between two tones, one of which has twice as many vibrations per second as the other. **(b)** either one of the tones or notes separated by such an interval. **(c)** series of tones within this interval. **2** group of eight.
oc·tet, oc·tette /akˈtet/ *n* [C] **1** (piece of music for) eight singers or players. **2** = octave(2).
Oc·to·ber /akˈtoubər/ *n* the tenth month of the year.
oc·to·pus /ˈaktəpəs/ *n* [C] (*pl* ~es, -pi /-ˌpai/) sea animal with a soft body and eight arms or tentacles which have suckers for holding objects. ⇨ illus at mollusk.
ocu·lar /ˈakyələr/ *adj* (*formal*) of, for, by, the eyes; of seeing: *~ proof/demonstration.*
ocu·list /ˈakyəlɪst/ *n* [C] **1** ophthalmologist. **2** optometrist.
OD /ˌou ˈdi/ *abbr* = **1** officer of the day. **2** olive drab (uniform). **3** overdose (esp of a narcotic). **4** overdraft.
odd /ad/ *adj* **1** (of numbers) not even; not exactly divisible by two: *1, 3, 5 and 7 are odd numbers.* **2** being the only one of a pair or one(s) of a set which is incomplete: *an odd shoe/glove; two odd volumes of an encyclopedia.* **3** a little more than the number specified: *ˈthirty odd years.* **4** not regular, habitual or fixed; occasional: *make a living by doing odd jobs; knit at odd times/moments.* **5** (-er, -est) strange; peculiar: *He's an odd old man. How odd!*
odd·ly *adv* in an odd(5) manner.
odd·ball /ˈadˌbɔl/ *n* [C] (*sl*) queer, eccentric person.
odd·ity /ˈadəti/ *n* (*pl* -ies) **1** [U] quality of being odd(5); strangeness: *~ of behavior/dress.* **2** [C] queer act, thing or person.
odd·ment /ˈadmənt/ *n* [C] something left over; spare piece: *The chair was sold as an ~ at the end of the auction.* ⇨ odds and ends, below.
odds /adz/ *n pl* **1** the chances in favor of one thing and against another: *The ~ are in our favor/against us,* We are likely/unlikely to succeed. **2** probability that a particular event will occur: *~ of ten to one.* **3** ***at odds (with sb) (over sth),*** in a state of disagreement.
ˌodds and ˈends, small articles, bits and pieces of various sorts and usually of small value.
ode /oud/ *n* [C] poem that usually expresses noble feelings.

odi·ous /ˈoudiəs/ *adj* hateful: repulsive.
odi·ous·ly *adv*
odium /ˈoudiəm/ *n* [U] (*formal*) **1** general or widespread hatred. **2** disgrace; blame.
odor /ˈoudər/ *n* **1** [C] smell. **2** [U] repute; favor.
odor·less *adj*
od·ys·sey /ˈadəsi/ *n* [C] (*pl* ~s) long, adventurous journey.
o'er /ˈouər, ɔr/ *adv, prep* (*poet*) over.
of /əv; in rapid speech sometimes ə, esp before consonants/ *prep* **1(a)** (used to indicate distance away from in space): *fifty miles south of Newark.* **(b)** (used in expressions of time) before: *ten minutes of 6.* **2** (used to indicate origin, authorship): *of American Indian descent; the works of Thomas Wolfe.* **3** (used to indicate reason or cause): *die of grief/hunger.* **4** (used to indicate relief, separation, etc): *cure her of a disease/a bad habit; rid a warehouse of rats; free of customs duty.* **5** (used to indicate the material from which something is made): *a dress of silk; built of brick.* **6** (used to name, describe, characterize, etc): *the state of Rhode Island; a man of honor. Where's that fool of an assistant,* that assistant who is a fool? **7** (used to indicate the object of an action that is denoted or implied): *the writer of this letter; loss of power/appetite; fond of music; afraid of being killed.* **8** (used to indicate connection, possession, or belonging): *the mayor of our city; the leg of the table,* the table leg; *the help of my family.* **9** about; concerning: *We talked of him for hours.* **10** (used to indicate selection from a total number or amount): *most of my friends; a volume of Keats's poetry.* **11** on the part of: *How kind of you to help!* **12** in; during: *Of recent years she has been very busy with her research.* ***of late,*** ⇨ late[1](5).
off[1] /ɔf/ *adj* **1** (contrasted with *near*) more distant; far (the usual word): *the off side of the building.* **2** remote; slight: *has only an off chance of succeeding.* **3** inactive; dull: *the ˈoff season.* **4** poor; below what is usual or normal: *Business is off.* **5** not working; not on duty: *He's off on Wednesdays.* **6** not connected or operating: *The stove was off.* **7** canceled: *The whole deal is off.* **8** not accurate; incorrect: *His estimate was off.*
off[2] /ɔf/ *adv* (For special uses of *off* in expressions such as *go off, turn something off,* ⇨ the *verb* entries.) **1** so as to be distant in space or time; so as to be removed, separated, etc; away from a place, position, etc: *The town is five miles off. The holidays are not far off. He drove off in a rush. I must be off now,* I must leave now. *Take your coat off.* **2** (used as an intensifier) completely; thoroughly: *Their engagement was broken off six months ago. I've paid off the loan. Clear off your desk.* **3** so as to be no longer connected or operating: *The power is shut off every night at 10 o'clock.* **4** away or free from work or duty: *The manager gave the staff a day off.* **5** ***on and off/off and on,*** from time to time; irregularly: *It rained on and off all day.* **6** in a certain state: *was left well off.* ***better/worse off,*** ⇨ better[2](1), worse *adv*(1).
off[3] /ɔf/ *prep* **1** not on; away from: *fall off a ladder/a tree/a horse. Keep off the grass.* ***ˌoff ˈside,*** (*football, hockey, soccer*) illegally ahead of the ball. **2** (of a road or street) extending or branching from: *a narrow lane off the main road.* **3** seaward from: *an island off the coast.* **4** below the usual standard: *She's off her game.* **5** free or relieved. ***off duty,*** ⇨ duty (1).
ˌoff-track ˈbetting, system of betting on races from distant agencies connected electronically with the track.
off.[4] *abbr* = **1** office. **2** officer.
of·fal /ˈɔfəl/ *n* [U] **1** waste parts of an animal, eg heart, head, kidneys. **2** rubbish.
off·beat /ˈɔfˌbit/ *adj* (*informal*) unusual; unconventional: *an ~ sort of person.*
of·fence = offense.
of·fend /əˈfend/ *vi,vt* **1** do wrong; commit an offense: *~ against good manners/the law/traditions, etc.* **2** hurt the feelings of: *I'm sorry if I've ~ed you/if you were ~ed by my remarks.* **3** displease; annoy: *ugly buildings that ~ the eye.*
of·fender *n* [C]
of·fense /əˈfens/ *n* **1** [C] crime; sin; breaking of a rule or law: *an ~ against God/the law/good manners.* **2** [U] offending or being offended: *He is quick to take ~,* is easily offended. *I didn't mean to give ~,* I did not intend to hurt your feelings. **3** [U] attack: *They say that the most effective defense is ~.* **4** [C] something which annoys or offends: *That dirty house is an ~ to the neighborhood.*
of·fense·less *adj* without, not giving offense.
of·fen·sive /əˈfensɪv/ *adj* **1** causing offense to the mind or senses; disagreeable: *fish with an ~ smell; ~ language.* **2** used for, connected with, attacking: *~ weapons/wars.* □ *n* [C] **1** attack. **2** attitude or position of attack. ***take the offensive,*** attack.
of·fen·sive·ly *adv*
of·fen·sive·ness /-nɪs/ *n* [U]
of·fer /ˈɔfər/ *vt,vi* **1** hold out, put forward, to be accepted or refused: *They ~ed a reward. I have been ~ed a job in Chile. He ~ed to help me. He ~ed me his help.* **2** present as an act of worship: *~ (up) prayers to God.* **3** show; give signs of: *~ no resistance to the enemy.* **4** occur; arise: *Take the first opportunity that ~s.* □ *n* [C] **1** act of offering. **2** something which is offered: *an ~ of help.* **3** bid; proposed payment or price: *I've had an ~ of $30,000 for the house.*
of·fer·ing /ˈɔfərɪŋ/ *n* **1** [U] act of offering. **2** [C] something offered or presented, eg the money collected during a church service. ***a ˈpeace offering,*** something offered in the hope of restoring friendship after a quarrel, etc.
of·fer·tory /ˈɔfərˌtɔri/ *n* [C] (*pl* -ies) **1 Offertory,** offering to God of the bread and wine before they are consecrated at Communion. **2** money collected at a church service.
off·hand /ˈɔfˌhænd, ˌɔfˈhænd/ *adj, adv* without previous thought or preparation: *~ remarks. I can't say ~ whether I agree.*
of·fice /ˈɔfɪs/ *n* [C] **1** room(s) where business or professional work is done: *a lawyer's/business ~.* **2** the staff working in such a place: *invited the ~ to his wedding.* **3** major administrative department of a government. **4** special position of trust or authority, as in government: *ran suc-*

cessfully for the ~ of mayor. **5** duty: *the ~ of hostess at the governor's mansion.* **6** (*pl*) favors; services; help: *through the good ~s of a friend.*

of·fi·cer /ˈɔfɪsər/ *n* [C] **1 (a)** person appointed to command others in the armed forces, esp one holding a commission: *~s and men.* **(b)** master or mate of a passenger ship, merchant ship, etc. **2** person with a position of authority or trust, eg in the government. **3** policeman.

of·fi·cial /əˈfɪʃəl/ *adj* **1** of a position of trust or authority: *~ responsibilities/records.* **2** holding a certain position or office. **3** approved by authority; authorized: *~ statements. The news is not ~.* **4** characteristic of, suitable for, persons holding office; formal: *written in ~ style.* □ *n* [C] person holding an office (4).

of·fi·cially /-ʃəli/ *adv*

of·fici·ate /əˈfɪʃiˌeit/ *vi* **1** perform the duties of an office or position: *~ as chairman.* **2** perform a ceremony: *~ at a wedding.*

of·fi·cious /əˈfɪʃəs/ *adj* (*formal*) too eager or ready to offer advice, help, etc; meddlesome.

of·fi·cious·ly *adv*

of·fi·cious·ness /-nɪs/ *n* [U]

off·ing /ˈɔfɪŋ/ *n* **1** part of the sea distant but still visible from the shore: *a steamer in the ~.* ***2 in the offing,*** in the immediate future: *promotion is in the ~.*

off·ish /ˈɔfɪʃ/ *adj* (*informal*) distant in manner. ⇨ standoffish.

off·set /ˈɔfˌset/ *vt* (*pt,pp ~, pres p* -tt-) balance; make up for: *In sports, a player's speed and skill can sometimes ~ another player's greater strength.* □ *n* [C] method of printing in which the ink is transferred from a plate to a rubber surface and then onto paper.

off·shoot /ˈɔfˌʃut/ *n* [C] **1** stem or branch growing from a main stem. **2** (*fig*) branch (of a family, mountain range, etc).

off·shore /ˈɔfˌʃɔr/ *adj* **1** in a direction away from the shore or land: *~ breezes.* **2** at a short way out to sea: *~ islands/fisheries.*

off·spring /ˈɔfˌsprɪŋ/ *n* [C] (*pl ~, ~s*) child; children; young of animals: *He is the ~ of a scientist and a ballet dancer.*

off-white /ˌɔfˈ(h)wait/ *adj* not pure white, with a pale grayish or yellowish tinge.

oft /ɔft/ *adv* (*poet*) often.

ˈoft·times *adv* (*archaic*) often.

of·ten /ˈɔfən/ *adv* (*more ~, most ~* is more usual than -er, -est) many times; frequently: *We ~ go there. We've been there quite ~.* ***every so often,*** from time to time. ***once too often,*** once more than is wise, safe, etc: *You've let me down once too ~ and I won't ever believe you again.*

ogle /ˈougəl/ *vi,vt* look at in a flirtatious way; stare at in an offensive manner: *ogling all the pretty girls.*

ogre /ˈougər/ *n* [C] **1** (in fables) cruel man-eating giant. **2** someone who is greatly feared.

ogress /ˈougrɪs/ *n* [C] female ogre.

oh[1] /ou/ *int* exclamation of surprise, fear, etc.

OH[2] *postal abbr* = Ohio. ⇨ App 6.

ohm /oum/ *n* [C] unit of electrical resistance.

oil /ˈɔiəl/ *n* **1** [C,U] (kinds of) liquid not mixing readily with water, obtained from animals, plants, or minerals. ***burn the midnight oil,*** sit up late at night to study, etc. **2** [U] petroleum. **3** (*pl*) paints made with oil. **4** [U] painting made with oil colors. □ *vt* (*pres p* oiling /ˈɔilɪŋ/) put oil on or into (eg to make a machine run smoothly).

oil·cloth /ˈɔiəlˌklɔθ/ *n* [C] cloth made waterproof by a coating of paint or oil.

oil color /ˈɔiəl ˌkələr/ *n* [C] paint made by mixing coloring matter with oil.

oil painting /ˈɔiəl ˌpeintɪŋ/ *n* **1** [U] art of painting in oil colors. **2** [C] picture painted in oil colors.

oil·skin /ˈɔiəlˌskɪn/ *n* **1** [U] cloth treated with oil to make it waterproof. **2** (*pl*) suit of clothes made of this material, as worn by sailors, etc.

oil well /ˈɔiəl ˌwel/ *n* [C] well from which crude petroleum is obtained.

oily /ˈɔili/ *adj* (-ier, -iest) **1** of or like oil: *an ~ liquid.* **2** covered or soaked with oil: *~ fingers.* **3** unpleasantly smooth: *~ compliments.*

oint·ment /ˈɔintmənt/ *n* [C,U] (kinds of) thick oily or waxy substance used on the skin (as a medication or as a cosmetic).

OK[1]**, okay** /ˌouˈkei/ *adj, adv* (*informal*) all right; fine. □ *vt* (*pt,pp* OK'd, okayed /ouˈkeid/; *pres p* OK'ing, okaying /ouˈkeiɪŋ/) agree to; approve. □ *n* [C] approval: *Have they given you their OK?*

OK[2] *postal abbr* = Oklahoma ⇨ App 6.

okra /ˈoukrə/ *n* [C,U] (tropical and semitropical plant with) edible green seed pods used as a vegetable.

old /ould/ *adj* (-er, -est) ⇨ also elder[1], eldest. **1** of (a certain) age: *He's forty years old. How old are you?* What age are you? **2** (contrasted with *young*) having lived a long time; no longer young; advanced in age: *He's far too old for the job. What will he do when he grows/is/gets old?* **3** (contrasted with *new, modern, up-to-date*) belonging to or dating from past times; having been in existence or use for a long time: *old clothes; old customs/families/civilizations/times.* ***of the ˈold school,*** conservative; old-fashioned. **4** of long standing: *an old friend of mine,* a friend for a long time (but not necessarily old in years). **5** former; previous (but not necessarily old in years): *his old teacher.* **6** having much experience or practice. ***old hand,*** person with a great deal of experience: *He's an old hand at organizing.* **7** (*informal*) dear; familiar: *Good old John!* **8** (*sl*) (used to intensify) at all: *Any old thing will do.* □ *n* **1 (the) old,** old people: *He helps (the) young and (the) old.* **2 *of old,*** (*liter*) in, from, the past: *in days of old; the men of old.*

olden /ˈouldən/ *adj* (*liter*) of a former age: *in the olden days.*

old-ˈfas·hioned *adj* **(a)** out-of-date; belonging or characteristic of an earlier period. **(b)** keeping to the ways, customs, etc of a past era.

ˈold·ish /-ɪʃ/ *adj* rather old.

Old ˈGlory, flag of the US.

old ˈhat *adj* old-fashioned.

old ˈmaid, (a) (esp an older) woman who is not married. **(b)** (*informal*) prim, fussy person.

old ˈmaster, (a) outstanding European painter, esp one who lived before 1700. **(b)** painting by such an artist.

Old ˈNick, (*informal, dated*) the devil.

ˈ**old-time** *adj* belonging to former times: *old-time dancing*.
old-ˈtimer *n* [C] (*informal*) person having a long association with a place, job, group, etc.
Old ˈWorld, Europe, Asia and Africa.
ˈ**old-world** *adj* of or characteristic of the Old World, esp in former times.

oleagi·nous /ˌouliˈædʒənəs/ *adj* having properties of oil; producing oil; greasy.

oleo·mar·ga·rine /ˌoulioʊˈmardʒərən/ *n* [U] = margarine.

ol·fac·tory /alˈfæk(ə)tri, oul-/ *adj* of or relating to the sense of smell.

oligarch /ˈaləˌgark/ *n* [C] member of an oligarchy.

oli·garchy /ˈaləˌgarki/ *n* [C,U] (*pl* -ies) **1** (country with) government by a small group of persons. **2** such a group.

ol·ive /ˈalɪv/ *n* **1** [C] (evergreen tree common in southern Europe bearing a) small, oval, greenish or blackish fruit with a hard stone that is eaten as a relish or used to make oil: *Olive oil is used for cooking, in salads, etc*. **2** [U] yellow green color. □ *adj* yellowish-green.
ˈ**olive branch, (a)** branch of the olive tree, esp as a symbol of peace. **(b)** gesture of peace or goodwill.

Olym·pic /əˈlɪmpɪk/ *adj* (esp) of or relating to the Olympic Games.
Olympic Games (also **Olympics**) *n pl* **(a)** the contests held at Olympia in Greece in ancient times. **(b)** the international athletic and sports competitions of modern times, held every four years in a different country.

om·buds·man /ˈambədzmən/ *n* (*pl* -men /-men/) government official having authority to inquire into and judge the complaints of citizens against other officials of the government.

omega /ouˈmegə/ *n* [C] **1** the last letter (Ω ω) of the Greek alphabet. **2** (*fig*) last of a series.

om·elet, om·elette /ˈam(ə)lət/ *n* [C] eggs beaten together and fried, often folded over a filling of cheese, onion, herbs, etc.

omen /ˈoumən/ *n* [C] thing or event regarded as a sign of future good or evil fortune: *a good/bad* ~.

om·i·nous /ˈamənəs/ *adj* threatening: *an ~ silence*.
om·i·nous·ly *adv*

omis·sion /ouˈmɪʃən/ *n* **1** [U] act of omitting, leaving out; neglect. **2** [C] something that is omitted.

omit /ouˈmɪt/ *vt* (-tt-) **1** fail to do: *~ to say/~ saying who wrote it*. **2** fail to include; leave out: *This cost may be ~ted from the accounts*.

om·ni·bus /ˈamnəbəs/ *n* [C] (*pl* ~es) **1** former name for a bus. **2** book containing a collection of works on one subject or by one author.

om·nip·o·tence /amˈnɪpətəns/ *n* [U] unlimited power: *the ~ of God*.
om·nip·o·tent /-ənt/ *adj* having unlimited power. □ *n* **the Omnipotent,** God.

on[1] /an/ *adv* (For special uses with *on* in expressions such as *go on, go on something,* ⇨ the *verb* entries.) **1** (used to indicate progress or movement forward in space or time): *Come on! He's getting on in years*, growing old. ***later on,*** ⇨ late²(1). **2** (used to indicate repeated or continued action): *worked on through the night*. ***and ˈso on,*** ⇨ so²(1). ***ˌon and ˈon,*** without stopping: *We walked on and on*. ***off and on/on and off,*** ⇨ off²(5). **3** so as to be upon, in contact with, or covering: *Put your hat on straight. He climbed on (to) the table*. **4** (contrasted with off²(3)) in action; in use or operation: *The lights were all turned on. Someone has left the water on*, running. **5** ***have sth on,*** have plans, an appointment, etc: *Do you have anything on this evening*, any engagements, plans, etc? □ *adj* **1** operating: *The electricity is on*. **2** taking place or occurring: *Is the game on?*

on[2] /an/ *prep* **1** supported by; fastened or attached to; covering or forming part of (a surface); lying against; in contact with: *a carpet on the floor; the jug on the table; sit on the grass; write on paper; stick a stamp on the envelope; have lunch on the train. Do you have a match/any money on you*, ie in your pockets, etc? **2** (of time) **(a)** during; at: *on Sunday(s)/the 1st of May; on that day; on this occasion*. **(b)** at the time of: *on my arrival home; on (my) asking for information*. ***on time,*** punctual(ly). **3** about; concerning: *a lecture on Shakespeare*. **4** (used to indicate membership, association, etc): *He is on the committee/the jury/the staff*. **5** (used to indicate the object toward which an action is directed): *marching on the enemy's capital; turn one's back on her; put a tax on tobacco*. **6** (used to indicate the basis, ground or reason for something): *a story based on fact; act on your lawyer's advice; arrested on a charge of theft; be on one's oath/one's honor*. **7** close to; against: *a town on the coast; on both sides of the river; on my right/left*. **8** in the process, activity, action, or state of: *on business/vacation; on the way; on fire*, burning; *on sale/loan*. **9** added to: *suffer disaster on disaster*.

once /wəns/ *adv* **1** for one time, on one occasion, only: *I have been there ~. He goes to see his parents ~ a month*. ***once more,*** again; another time. ***once or twice; (every) once in a while,*** occasionally; a few times. **2** formerly: *He ~ lived in Iran*. ***once upon a time,*** (in story-telling style) at some indefinite time in the past: *Once upon a time there was a giant with two heads*. **3** ever; at all; even for one time: *He didn't ~/He never ~ offered to help*. □ *conj* as soon as: *Once you understand this rule, you will have no further difficulty*. □ *n* (*sing* only) one single time. ***all at once,*** suddenly. ***at once,*** **(a)** without delay; immediately: *I'm leaving for Rome at ~. Come here at ~!* **(b)** at the same time: *Don't all speak at ~! I can't do two things at ~*. ***(just) for once.*** on this one occasion only, as an exception.

once·over /ˈwənsˌouvər/ *n* (*sing* only) (*informal*) ***give sb/sth the onceover,*** examine him/it quickly.

on·com·ing /ˈanˌkəmɪŋ/ *adj* approaching; coming toward one: *~ traffic*.

one[1] /wən/ *adj* **1** being a single person or thing: *one pen, two pencils and three books; one thousand; one half*. ***one or two,*** a few: *I shall be away only one or two days*. ***be one up on sb,*** have an advantage over him. (*Note:* For use with other numbers ⇨ App 1.) **2** a certain: *one fine day/morning.* (used before a name, with or without a title) *I heard the news from one Mr. Smith.* **3** (always stressed; used for emphasis): *That's the ˈone piece of information he needs. Well, that's ˈone way of doing it, but I'm going to try something else.* ***for ˈone thing,*** for one reason (out of several or many): *I can't help you. For one thing, I don't have any money.* **4** (used as an *adjective*) the same: *They all went off in one direction.* ***all one,*** exactly the same: *It's all one to me whether you leave today or tomorrow.* **5** united; undivided: *The group was of one opinion.* □ *n* [C] **1** the number 1. **2** person or thing indicated or singled out from similar individuals or units: *I drew my chair nearer to the one on which she was sitting. He collects stamps and has some very rare ones.* **3** (*informal*) one-dollar bill.

one[2] /wən/ *pron* **1** single person or thing. **(a)** (used to indicate membership in a class or group): *He is not one of my close friends.* **(b)** (used to refer to an *indefinite noun*): *I don't have a pen. Can you lend me one?* ***one and all,*** everyone. ***one by one,*** one after another. **2** any person, including the speaker or the writer: *One doesn't like to have one's word doubted.* **3** ***one another,*** (used to indicate mutual action or relationship) each one of two or more: *They don't like one another. They borrowed one another's books.*

on·er·ous /ˈanərəs/ *adj* (*formal*) needing effort; burdensome: *~ duties.*

on·er·ous·ly *adv*

on·er·ous·ness /-nɪs/ *n* [U]

one·self /wənˈself/ *pron* **1** (used as a *reflexive*) one's own self: *wash/dress ~.* ***(all) by oneself,*** **(a)** alone. **(b)** without help. **2** (used for emphasis): *To be really sure one ought to look at it ~.*

one-sided /ˌwənˈsaidɪd/ *adj* **1** having one side only; occurring on one side only; unequal. **2** unfair: *a ~ argument.*

one·time /ˈwənˌtaim/ *adj* former: *a ~ politician.*

one-way /ˌwənˈwei/ *adj* moving or allowing movement in one direction only: *a ~ street.*

onion /ˈənyən/ *n* [C] (plant bearing an) edible, (usually) round bulb with a strong smell and flavor, that is used as a vegetable. ⇨ illus at vegetable.

on·look·er /ˈanˌlʊkər/ *n* [C] person who looks on; spectator.

only[1] /ˈounli/ *adj* **1** (used with a *sing noun*) that is the one specimen of its class; single: *Smith was the ~ person able to do it. Harry is an ~ child,* has no brothers or sisters. **2** (used with a *pl noun*) that are all the specimens or examples: *We were the ~ people wearing hats.* **3** best; most worth consideration: *He's the ~ man for me.*

only[2] /ˈounli/ *adv* **1** solely; and no one or nothing more: *I saw ~ Mary,* I saw Mary and no one else. **2** merely; just: *We've ~ half an hour to wait now.* ***if only,*** ⇨ if(7). **3** ***only too glad/happy/pleased, etc,*** very glad/happy/pleased, etc: *I shall be ~ too pleased to get home.*

only[3] /ˈounli/ *conj* but: *The book is likely to be useful, ~ it's rather expensive.*

ono·mato·poeia /ˌanəˌmætəˈpiə/ *n* [U] (formation of) words or names from sounds of the thing that is described (eg *buzz* for the sound made by a bee).

on·rush /ˈanˌrəʃ/ *n* [C] strong, onward rush or flow.

ˈon·rushing *adj* having rapid motion onward or toward one.

on·set /ˈanˌset/ *n* [C] **1** attack. **2** beginning; start: *at the first ~ of the disease.*

on·shore /ˈanˌʃɔr/ *adj, adv* toward the shore.

on·slaught /ˈanˌslɔt/ *n* [C] furious attack (*on*).

onto /antə, *emph form:* ˈanˌtu/ *prep* **1** to a position or place on or upon. **2** (*informal*) into a state of awareness about: *~ her and her schemes.*

onus /ˈounəs/ *n* (*sing* only) responsibility or burden: *The ~ of proof rests with you.*

on·ward /ˈanwərd/ *adj* forward: *an ~ march/movement.* □ *adv* (also **on·wards** /ˈanwərdz/) toward the front; forward: *move ~(s).*

onyx /ˈanɪks/ *n* [U] (kinds of) quartz in layers of different colors, used for ornaments, in jewelry, etc.

oodles /ˈudəlz/ *n pl* (*informal*) great amounts: *~ of money.*

ooze /uz/ *n* [U] soft liquid mud, esp on the bottom of a body of water. □ *vi,vt* **1** (of moisture, thick liquids) pass slowly (as) through small openings: *Blood was still oozing from the wound.* **2** give off: *He was oozing sweat.* (*fig*) *She ~d confidence.* **3** (*fig*) slowly go away as if by leaking: *Their courage was oozing away.*

opac·ity /ouˈpæsəti/ *n* [U] (quality of) being opaque.

opal /ˈoupəl/ *n* [C] precious stone which is changeable in color.

opaque /ouˈpeik/ *adj* **1** not allowing light to pass through. **2** dull; not reflecting light. **3** (*fig*) obscure; hard to understand.

opaque·ly *adv*

opaque·ness /-nɪs/ *n* [U]

op. cit. *abbr* (= *Lat* opere citato) in the work quoted. (*Note:* often spoken as /ˌapˈsɪt/.)

OPEC /ˈouˌpek/ *abbr* = Organization of Petroleum Exporting Countries.

open[1] /ˈoupən/ *adj* **1** not closed; allowing entrance and exit: *sleep with ~ windows; leave the door ~.* **2** not enclosed; permitting easy passage or view: *~ country; the ~ sea.* **3** not covered: *an ~ boat,* one without a deck; *an ~ carriage/car.* ***in the open air,*** outdoors. **4** spread out; unfolded: *The flowers were all ~. The book lay ~ on the table.* **5** public; free to all; not restricted: *an ~ competition/meeting.* **6** not filled or taken; available: *The position is still ~.* **7** not settled or decided: *leave a matter ~.* **8** unprejudiced; willing to consider new evidence, ideas, etc: *an ~ mind.* **9** ready for business; operating: *Are the stores ~ yet?* **10** known to all; not secret or disguised: *an ~ quarrel/scandal.* **11** frank; not secretive: *He was quite ~ with me.* **12** unprotected; unguarded; vulnerable: *~ to ridicule/attack.* □ *n* (*sing* only, with *the*) **1** outdoors. **2** public view or knowledge: *When did the scandal break into the ~?*

ˈopen-air *adj* outdoor: *an ~-air swimming pool.*

ˌ**open-ˈhanded** *adj* generous.
ˌ**open-ˈhearted** *adj* kind, generous.
ˌ**open ˈhouse, (a)** social event or party given for all who wish to attend. **(b)** occasion when a school, business, etc is open to the public for visiting.
open·ly *adv* without secrecy; frankly; publicly: *speak ~ly*.
ˌ**open-ˈminded** *adj* without prejudice.
open·ness /-nɪs/ *n* [U] frankness.
ˌ**open ˈshop** *n* [C] establishment in which it is not necessary to be a union member in order to hold a job.

open[2] /ˈoupən/ *vt,vi* **1** make or become open; unfasten: *~ a box. The door ~ed and a man came in.* **2** make an opening in or a passage through: *~ a new road through a forest.* **3** make accessible for development or use: *~ (up) a mine/a new territory to trade.* **4** spread out; unfold: *~ one's hand/a book/a newspaper/an envelope/a map. The flowers are ~ing.* **5** start: *~ an account*, eg at a bank, store; *~ a debate/a public meeting. The story ~s with a murder.* ***open fire (at/on),*** start shooting. **6** make or become ready for use, operation, business, etc: *~ a store/an office.* **7** give access to: *The windows ~ on (to) the garden.* **8** make or become sympathetic, understanding, etc: *~ed our hearts to the poor and the homeless.*
opener *n* [C] person or thing that opens: *a ˈcan ~er*.

open·ing /ˈoupənɪŋ/ *n* **1** [C] open space: *an ~ in a hedge.* **2** [C] **(a)** beginning: *the ~ of a book/speech.* **(b)** first performance of a play, musical, etc. **3** [U] process of becoming open: *the ~ of a flower.* **4** [C] position (in a business firm) which is open or vacant: *an ~ in the advertising department.* **5** [C] series of moves at the beginning of a game of checkers or chess. **6** [C] chance; opportunity. □ *adj* first: *his ~ remarks.*

open·work /ˈoupənˌwərk/ *n* [U] something made with a pattern of openings or spaces in the material.

op·era /ˈaprə/ *n* (*pl* ~s) [C] dramatic composition with music, in which the words are sung.
ˈ**opera glasses** *n pl* small binoculars for use in a theater.
ˈ**opera house,** theater for operas.
op·er·atic /ˌapəˈrætɪk/ *adj*

op·er·able /ˈapərəbəl/ *adj* **1** that can be treated by means of a surgical operation. **2** capable of being operated or put into use.

op·er·ate /ˈapəˌreit/ *vt,vi* **1** (cause to) work, be in action, have an effect; manage: *~ a machine/business. The elevator was not operating properly.* **2** perform a surgical operation: *The doctors decided to ~ at once.*
ˈ**operating room,** room in a hospital or clinic where surgical operations take place.

op·er·ation /ˌapəˈreiʃən/ *n* **1** [U] act, process, or way of operating or working. **2** [U] state of being at work, in use, or functional: *in ~. Is this rule in ~ yet?* **3** [C] military or naval mission, action, etc. **4** [C] (*math*) process (as addition or division) by which one mathematical expression is derived from others by means of a specific rule. **5** [C] procedure in which surgery is used to treat or cure a part of the body that is diseased, injured, etc: *an ~ to remove his appendix.*
op·er·ational /-əl/ *adj* **(a)** of, for, used in, operations. **(b)** ready for use: *When will the new airliner be ~al?*

op·er·at·ive /ˈapərətɪv/ *adj* **1** operating; having an effect: *This law became ~ on May 1.* **2** of surgical operations: *~ treatment.* □ *n* [C] **1** skilled worker. **2** secret agent; spy. **3** detective.

op·er·ator /ˈapəˌreitər/ *n* [C] **1** person who operates or works something: *ˈelevator ~*, (in control of a nonautomatic elevator). **2** person who handles calls which are not dialed directly. **3** (*informal*) shrewd person who gets what he wants by using methods which are very often tricky and unfair: *He's a smooth ~.*

op·er·etta /ˌapəˈretə/ *n* [C] (*pl* ~s) light, romantic opera with spoken dialogue.

oph·thal·mol·ogist /ˌafθælˈmalədʒɪst/ *n* [C] physician who is a specialist in ophthalmology.

oph·thal·mol·ogy /ˌafθælˈmalədʒi/ *n* [U] branch of medicine that deals with the structure, functions, and diseases of the eye.

opi·ate /ˈoupiɪt/ *n* [C,U] **1** drug prepared or derived from opium. **2** anything used as a sedative or narcotic.

opin·ion /əˈpɪnyən/ *n* **1** [C] belief or view not founded on positive knowledge: *political ~s. What's your ~ of the new President? In my ~, the scheme is unsound.* **2** [U] views, beliefs, of a group: *Opinion is shifting in favor of stiffer penalties for armed robbery.* **3** [C] judgment or estimate of the value of a person or thing. **4** [C] professional view or judgment: *get a lawyer's ~ on the question.*
opin·ion·ated /əˈpɪnyəˌneitɪd/ *adj* obstinate; dogmatic.

opium /ˈoupiəm/ *n* [U] narcotic drug made from a certain kind of poppy.

opos·sum, pos·sum /əˈpasəm, ˈpasəm/ *n* [C] small furry animal that lives in trees and carries its young around in a pouch on the body. ⇨ illus at animal.

opp. *abbr* = opposite.

op·po·nent /əˈpounənt/ *n* [C] person who opposes another in a fight, contest, etc.

op·por·tune /ˌapərˈtun/ *adj* timely; suitable: *arrive at an ~ moment; an ~ remark/speech.*
op·por·tune·ly *adv*

op·por·tun·ism /ˌapərˈtuˌnɪzəm/ *n* [U] practice of taking advantage of every available chance to achieve one's goal, without regard for right or wrong.

op·por·tun·ist /ˌapərˈtunɪst/ *n* [C] person who believes in or practices opportunism.

op·por·tun·ity /ˌapərˈtunəti/ *n* (*pl* -ies) [C,U] **1** favorable time or chance; suitable combination of circumstances: *to make/find/get an ~; have no/little/not much ~ for hearing good music.* **2** chance for advancement or progress.

op·pose /əˈpouz/ *vt* **1** contend or fight against: *~ the government/a scheme.* **2** place, set up, or be in opposition to: *~ your views to mine.* ***as opposed to,*** in contrast with.

op·po·site /ˈapəzɪt/ *adj* **1** facing; placed face to face or back to back: *on the ~ side of the road.* **2** entirely different; contrary: *in the ~ direction.*

□ *n* [C] something that is entirely contrary: *Black and white are ~s. I think the ~.* □ *prep* across from; facing: *Their house is ~ mine.*

op·po·si·tion /ˌapəˈzɪʃən/ *n* [U] **1** the state of being opposite or opposed: *worked in ~ to the program.* **2** resistance: *Our forces met with strong ~.*

op·press /əˈpres/ *vt* **1** govern or rule unjustly and harshly; crush or keep down by severe or cruel treatment. **2** (*fig*) burden; weigh heavily upon: *~ed with anxiety; feel ~ed with the heat.*

op·pres·sor /-sər/ *n* [C]

op·pres·sion /əˈpreʃən/ *n* **1** [U] oppressing or being oppressed: *victims of ~.* **2** [C] instance of this.

op·pres·sive /əˈpresɪv/ *adj* **1** unjust: *~ laws/rules.* **2** hard to endure: *~ weather/heat/taxes.*

op·pres·sive·ly *adv*

opt /apt/ *vi* make a choice: *Fewer students are opting for courses in the classics nowadays.*

op·tic /ˈaptɪk/ *adj* of the eye or the sense of sight.

optic ˈnerve, one of the two nerves that go from the eye to the brain. ⇨ illus at eye.

op·tics /ˈaptɪks/ *n* (used with a *sing verb*) science of light and the laws of light.

op·ti·cal /ˈaptɪkəl/ *adj* **1** of the sense of sight. **2** designed to help eyesight. **3** of the science of optics.

op·ti·cal·ly /-kli/ *adv*

op·ti·cian /apˈtɪʃən/ *n* [C] person who makes or supplies lenses, eyeglasses, and other optical instruments.

op·ti·mism /ˈaptəˌmɪzəm/ *n* [U] **1** belief that this world is the best one possible. **2** tendency to feel hopeful or cheerful.

op·ti·mist /-mɪst/ *n* [C] person who believes that all things happen for the best.

op·ti·mis·tic /ˌaptəˈmɪstɪk/ *adj* hoping for the best; cheerful: *an optimistic view of events.*

op·ti·mis·ti·cally /-kli/ *adv*

op·ti·mum /ˈaptəməm/ *adj* best or most favorable: *the ~ temperature for the growth of plants.*

op·tion /ˈapʃən/ *n* **1** [U] right or power of choosing: *I haven't much ~ in the matter,* cannot choose. **2** [C] thing that is or may be chosen: *None of the ~s is satisfactory.* ***leave one's options open,*** not commit oneself. **3** [C] (*business*) right to buy or sell at a certain price within a certain period of time: *have an ~ on a piece of land.*

op·tional /ˈapʃənəl/ *adj* which may be chosen or not; not compulsory: *~ subjects at school.*

opus /ˈoupəs/ *n* [C] (*pl* opera /ˈapərə/, rarely used, or ~es) work such as a musical composition or group of musical compositions.

or[1] /ɔr, in fast speech ər/ *conj* **1** (introducing an alternative): *Is it green or blue? Are you coming or not?* ***either... or,*** ⇨ either. ***or (else),*** otherwise; if not: *Hurry up or (else) you'll be late.* **2** (introducing all but the first of a series): *I'd like it to be black, (or) white or gray.* **3** (used to introduce a word or expression that means the same as another): *a half dollar, or fifty cents.*

OR[2] *postal abbr* = Oregon, ⇨ App 6.

or·acle /ˈɔrəkəl/ *n* [C] **1** place (as a shrine in ancient Greece) where questions about the future were asked of the gods. **2** person through whom the answers were given: *consult the ~.* **3** message or answer received. **4** person considered to be very wise.

oracu·lar /ɔˈrækyələr/ *adj*

oral /ˈɔrəl/ *adj* **1** spoken, not written: *an ~ examination.* **2** of or relating to the mouth: *~ medicine.* □ *n* [C] (*informal*) oral examination.

orally /ˈɔrəli/ *adv*

or·ange /ˈɔrɪndʒ, ˈar-/ *n* **1** [C] (evergreen tree bearing a) round, thick-skinned juicy fruit, of a color between yellow and red. ⇨ illus at fruit. **2** [U] reddish-yellow color of the ripe fruit. □ *adj* of the color orange.

orange·ade /ˌɔrɪndʒˈeid, ˌar-/ *n* [C,U] drink made of orange juice mixed with sugar and water.

orang·utan, orang·utang /əˈræŋəˌtæŋ/ *n* [C] large ape with long arms of Borneo and Sumatra. ⇨ illus at ape.

orate /ɔˈreit/ *vi* (*formal*) give an oration.

ora·tion /ɔˈreiʃən/ *n* [C] formal, dignified speech made on a public occasion: *a funeral ~.*

ora·tor /ˈɔrətər/ *n* [C] **1** person who gives an oration. **2** skilled public speaker.

ora·tori·cal /ˌɔrəˈtɔrɪkəl/ *adj* of oratory or orators.

ora·tory[1] /ˈɔrəˌtɔri/ *n* [U] (art of) making speeches.

ora·tory[2] /ˈɔrəˌtɔri/ *n* [C] (*pl* -ies) small chapel for private worship or prayer.

orb /ɔrb/ *n* [C] **1** ball; sphere; globe, as the sun, moon or one of the stars. **2** jeweled globe with a cross on top, a symbol of royal power.

or·bit /ˈɔrbɪt/ *n* [C] **1** path followed by one body, eg a planet, or a man-made satellite, around another body: *the earth's ~ around the sun. How many satellites have been put in ~ around the earth?* **2** range or sphere of activity, influence, etc. **3** socket or cavity in the skull for the eyeball. □ *vt,vi* (cause to) move or be in orbit: *When was the first satellite ~ed?*

or·bit·al /ˈɔrbɪtəl/ *adj*

or·chard /ˈɔrtʃərd/ *n* [C] **1** piece of land on which fruit trees grow. **2** group of such trees.

or·ches·tra /ˈɔrkɪstrə, ˈɔrkestrə/ *n* [C] (*pl* ~s) **1** (usually large) group of musicians playing together on musical instruments (esp stringed instruments): a *ˈsymphony ~.* **2** place in a theater, in front of the stage, where an orchestra sits. **3** (front section of seats on the) main floor of a theater.

or·ches·tral /ɔrˈkestrəl/ *adj* of, for, by, an orchestra: *~ instruments/performances.*

or·ches·trate /ˈɔrkəˌstreit/ *vt* compose or arrange music for orchestral performances.

or·ches·tra·tion /ˌɔrkəˈstreiʃən/ *n* [C,U]

or·chid /ˈɔrkɪd/ *n* **1** [C] (any of several plants bearing a) showy flower with petals of irregular shape. ⇨ illus at flower. **2** [U] light reddish-purple color. □ *adj* light reddish purple.

or·dain /ɔrˈdein/ *vt* **1** make (a person) a priest or minister by a special ceremony. **2** (*formal*) decree; order or establish by means of authority: *God has ~ed that all men shall die.*

or·deal /ɔrˈdiəl/ *n* [C] any severe test of character or endurance; painful or terrible experience: *pass through terrible ~s.*

or·der[1] /ˈɔrdər/ *n* **1** [U] way in which things are arranged one after another in space or time: *put names in alphabetical ~*. **2** [U] condition in which everything is systematically or properly arranged: *Please keep your room in ~*. **3** [U] working condition, esp of machines. ***out of order,*** (of a machine, etc) not functioning properly: *The phone is out of ~*. **4** [U] condition brought about by good government, observance of the law, etc: *It is the business of the police to keep/preserve ~*. ⇨ disorder. **5** [C] command: *Soldiers must obey ~s*. ***by order of,*** by the authority of: *by ~ of the Governor*. **6** [C] **(a)** request to supply goods, services, etc. **(b)** the goods, etc requested: *an ~ of groceries*. ***on order,*** requested but not yet supplied. **7** [C] written direction (as to a bank) to pay money: *a ˈmoney ~ for thirty dollars*. **8** ***in order to,*** for the purpose of: *We stood in the back in ~ to see clearly*. **9** [C] rank or class in society. **10** [C] group of people to which one is appointed by a government as an honor or reward. **11** [C] badge, emblem, etc worn by members of such a group: *the Order of Merit*. **12** (*pl*) rank or position of a priest or minister. **13** [C] group of persons living under religious rules, as a brotherhood of monks. **14** [C] club or association. **15** [C] style of architecture, esp with respect to the decorative elements and proportions used for the columns. **16** [C] (*biol*) grouping of related animals or plants, that ranks above the family and below the class: *The rose and the bean families belong to the same ~*. **17** [C] kind; sort: *intellectual ability of a high ~*.

or·der[2] /ˈɔrdər/ *vt* **1** give a command: *The doctor ~ed me to (stay in) bed*. **2** request to be supplied with: *I've ~ed lunch for 1:30*. **3** put in order. **4** arrange; manage: *~ one's life according to strict rules*.

or·der·ly /ˈɔrdərli/ *adj* **1** well arranged; in good order; tidy: *an ~ room/desk*. **2** methodical: *a man with an ~ mind*. **3** well behaved; obedient to discipline: *an ~ crowd*. □ *n* [C] (*pl* -ies) **1** soldier assigned to be an officer's messenger. **2** male attendant in a hospital.

or·der·li·ness /-nɪs/ *n* [U]

or·di·nal /ˈɔrdənəl/ *n* [C], *adj* (number) showing order or position in a series, eg *first, second, third*. ⇨ cardinal[1].

or·di·nance /ˈɔrdənəns/ *n* [C] order, rule, statute, esp one made by a city or town.

or·di·nary /ˈɔrdəˌneri/ *adj* normal; usual; average: *an ~ day's work; in ~ dress*.

or·di·nar·ily /ˌɔrdəˈnerəli/ *adv* **(a)** usually: *Ordinarily, she is a calm person*. **(b)** in the usual or normal way: *behave quite ordinarily*.

or·di·na·tion /ˌɔrdəˈneiʃən/ *n* **1** [C] ceremony of ordaining (a priest or minister). **2** [U] state of being ordained.

ord·nance /ˈɔrdnəns/ *n* [U] military supplies (as weapons, ammunition, etc).

ore /ɔr/ *n* [C,U] (kinds of) rock, earth, mineral, etc from which metal can be extracted: *iron ore*.

or·gan[1] /ˈɔrgən/ *n* [C] **1** any part of an animal or plant serving particular purpose: *the reproductive ~s*. **2** means of action; instrument: *Congress is one of the ~s of government*. **3** newspaper or other publication that expresses the view of a particular group, political party, etc.

or·gan[2] /ˈɔrgən/ *n* [C] **1** musical instrument from which sounds are produced by air forced through pipes, played by keys pressed with the fingers and pedals pressed with the feet. ⇨ illus at keyboard. **2** similar instrument which produces sounds like those of an organ: *an electronic ~*.

ˈor·gan·ist /-ɪst/ *n* [C] person who plays an organ.

or·gan·dy, or·gan·die /ˈɔrgəndi/ *n* [U] sheer, crisp muslin used for curtains, dresses, etc.

or·ganic /ɔrˈgænɪk/ *adj* **1** of an organ or organs of the body: *~ diseases*. **2** of or derived from living organism: *~ matter*. **3** (*chem*) of, relating to, or involving compounds of carbon: *~ chemistry*. ⇨ inorganic. **4** made of related parts; organized as a system: *an ~ structure*.

or·gani·cally /-kli/ *adv*

or·gan·ism /ˈɔrgəˌnɪzəm/ *n* [C] **1** living being (plant or animal) with parts which work together. **2** something like an organism, with parts dependent upon each other: *the social ~*.

or·gan·iz·ation /ˌɔrgənəˈzeiʃən/ *n* **1** [U] organizing or being organized: *He is engaged in the ~ of a new club*. **2** [U] condition or manner of being organized: *The human body has a very complex ~*. **3** [C] group of persons organized for a particular purpose.

or·gan·ize /ˈɔrgəˌnaiz/ *vt* **1** put into working order; arrange in a system: *~ one's work/oneself*. **2** form into a group for a particular purpose: *~d a skating club*. **3** cause (workers) to form or join a labor union: *spent years organizing the steel workers*.

organized ˈlabor, workers organized into or represented by a labor union.

organizer *n* [C] **(a)** wall shelf, desk-top filing cabinet, etc with compartments for organizing (1) supplies, papers, etc. **(b)** person who organizes(3) workers.

or·gasm /ˈɔrˌgæzəm/ *n* **1** [U] state of (esp erotic) excitement. **2** [C] instance of this, esp the climax of sexual intercourse.

orgy /ˈɔrdʒi/ *n* [C] (*pl* -ies) **1** wild, drunken party. **2** unrestrained indulgence in an activity: *an ~ of spending*.

Orient[1] /ˈɔriənt/ *n* **the Orient,** countries of the Far East.

orient[2] /ˈɔriˌent/ *vt* **1** place or determine the position of something with regard to the points of the compass. **2** (*fig*) make (a person) familiar with a new situation, surroundings, etc: *a program to ~ new members*. (*Note:* the variant *orientate* is not generally considered as correct as *orient*.)

orien·ta·tion /ˌɔriənˈteiʃən/ *n* [U]

orien·tal /ˌɔriˈentəl/ *adj* of the Orient: *~ civilization/art*. □ *n* [C] **Oriental,** native of the Orient, esp of China and Japan.

orien·tate /ˈɔriənˌteit/ *vt* ⇨ orient(2).

ori·fice /ˈɔrəfɪs/ *n* [C] outer opening; mouth; vent; hole.

orig. *abbr* = original.

ori·gin /ˈɔrədʒɪn/ *n* **1** [C] starting point or beginning: *the ~ of a quarrel; the ~(s) of civilization*. **2** [U] ancestry: *a man of Russian ~*. **3** point on a

graph at which the horizontal and vertical axes intersect.
orig·inal /əˈrɪdʒənəl/ *adj* **1** first or earliest: *the ~ inhabitants of the country*. **2** newly created; not copied or imitated: *an ~ design*. **3** able to produce new ideas, etc: *an ~ thinker/mind*. □ *n* something from which a copy, reproduction, or translation is made: *This picture is a copy; the ~ is in the National Gallery; read a novel in the ~*, read it in the language it was written in.
orig·i·nally /-nəli/ *adv*
orig·i·nal·ity /əˌrɪdʒəˈnæləti/ *n* [U] state or quality of being original(2,3): *work that lacks ~*.
orig·inate /əˈrɪdʒəˌneit/ *vi,vt* (cause to) come into being: *With whom did the scheme ~? ~ a new style of dancing*.
orig·in·ator /-tər/ *n* [C]
or·na·ment /ˈɔrnəmənt/ *n* [C] something that adorns or decorates: *~s for a Christmas tree*. □ *vt* /ˈɔrnəˌment/ decorate; make beautiful: *~ a dress with lace*.
or·na·men·tal /ˌɔrnəˈmentəl/ *adj* decorative.
or·nate /ɔrˈneit/ *adj* richly or elaborately ornamented.
or·nate·ly *adv*
or·nate·ness /-nɪs/ *n* [U]
or·ni·thol·ogist /ˌɔrnəˈθalədʒɪst/ *n* [C] expert in ornithology.
or·ni·thol·ogy /ˌɔrnəˈθalədʒi/ *n* [U] branch of science dealing with birds.
or·phan /ˈɔrfən/ *n* child whose parents are dead. □ *vt* cause to be an orphan: *~ed by war*.
or·phan·age /ˈɔrfənɪdʒ/ *n* [C] institution for the care of orphans.
or·tho·don·tist /ˌɔrθəˈdantɪst/ *n* [C] dentist who specializes in correcting irregular teeth.
or·tho·dox /ˈɔrθəˌdaks/ *adj* **1** having opinions, beliefs, etc which are generally accepted or approved: *an ~ member of the Church*. **2** conventional; usual: *~ behavior*. **3 Orthodox, (a)** of any of the Christian churches (eg of Greece, Russia, etc) which trace their origin to the time of the Byzantine Empire. **(b)** of the branch of Judaism that holds strictly to traditional customs and practices.
or·tho·doxy /ˈɔrθəˌdaksi/ *n* (*pl* -ies) **(a)** [U] being orthodox. **(b)** [C] orthodox belief, character, practice.
or·thogra·phy /ɔrˈθagrəfi/ *n* [U] **1** way of spelling. **2** correct or conventional spelling.
or·tho·pedics /ˌɔrθəˈpidɪks/ *n* (used with a *sing verb*) correction or prevention of bone deformities, disorders, injuries, etc.
or·tho·pedic *adj*
or·tho·ped·ist /ˌɔrθəˈpidɪst/ *n* [C] physician who is a specialist in orthopedics.
Oscar /ˈaskər/ *n* [C] small statue given as an award for outstanding acting, photography, etc in motion pictures.
os·cil·late /ˈasəˌleit/ *vi,vt* **1** swing backwards and forwards as the pendulum of a clock does. **2** (*fig*) change between extremes of opinion, etc.
os·cil·la·tion /ˌasəˈleiʃən/ *n* [C,U]
os·cil·lator /ˈasəˌleitər/ *n* [C] (esp) device for producing electromagnetic waves or alternating current.
os·mo·sis /azˈmousɪs, as-/ *n* [U] process in which a fluid solution passes through a membrane (eg of an animal or plant cell) until the level of concentration of the solution is the same on both sides of the membrane.
os·prey /ˈaspri/ *n* [C] (*pl* ~s) large kind of hawk that preys on fish.
oss·ify /ˈasəˌfai/ *vt,vi* (*pt,pp* -ied) **1** (*formal*) become bone; change into bone. **2** (*fig*) make or become rigid, conservative, or set in one's ways.
ossi·fi·ca·tion /ˌasəfəˈkeiʃən/ *n* [U]
os·ten·sible /aˈstensəbəl/ *adj* (*formal*) seeming to be, but not really so; pretended.
os·ten·sibly /-əbli/ *adv* outwardly; seemingly.
os·ten·ta·tion /ˌastənˈteiʃən/ *n* [U] showy display (of wealth, learning, skill, etc) for the purpose of impressing others.
os·ten·ta·tious /ˌastənˈteiʃəs/ *adj*
os·ten·ta·tious·ly *adv*
os·tra·cize /ˈastrəˌsaiz/ *vt* shut out or exclude from society: *She was ~ed by her neighbors after her imprisonment*.
os·trich /ˈɔstrɪtʃ/ *n* [C] (*pl* ~es) very large, fast-running bird, that is unable to fly, and whose long, soft feathers are often used for decoration, etc.
OTB /ˌou ˌti ˈbi/ *abbr* = off-track betting.
other /ˈəðər/ *adj* **1** being the one left of two or more: *Give me the ~ book. The post office is on the ~ side of the street*. ***on the ˈother hand (. . .),*** ⇨ hand[1](10b). **2** being the ones left of several: *All my ~ books are at home*. **3** second; alternate: *Write only on every ~ line*. **4** additional: *Do you have any ~ news?* **5** different: *Any ~ day but Tuesday will be fine*. □ *pron* **1** the remaining one(s): *Let's solve this problem first; then we can do the ~s*. **2** another or different person or thing (that is often indefinite or uncertain): *She was talking to someone or ~ on the phone when they arrived*. ***one after the other,*** in succession; not together. □ *adv* otherwise: *I can't do it ~ than slowly*.
other·wise /ˈəðərˌwaiz/ *adv* **1** in another or different way: *You evidently think ~*. **2** in other or different respects or conditions: *The rent is high, but ~ the house is satisfactory*. □ *conj* if not; or else: *Do what you've been told; ~ you will be punished*.
ot·ter /ˈatər/ *n* **1** [C] fur-covered, fish-eating aquatic animal with four webbed feet and a flat tail. **2** [U] its dark brown fur.
ouch /autʃ/ *int* (used to express sudden pain).
ought /ɔt/ *auxiliary verb* (no infinitive, no participles, no inflected forms) **1** (used to indicate duty or obligation): *He ~ to be grateful for their help. You ~ to have done that earlier*. **2** (used to indicate what is advisable or prudent): *There ~ to be more buses during the rush hours. You ~ to see that new movie at the Midtown Theater*. **3** (used to indicate likelihood or probability): *That ~ to be enough fish for three people*.
oughtn't /ˈɔtənt/ = ought not.
ounce /auns/ *n* [C] **1** (*abbr* **oz.**) unit of weight equal to one-sixteenth of a pound avoirdupois weight. **2** one-twelfth of a pound troy weight.
our /ar, *strong form* ˈauər/ *adj* of, relating to, or belonging to us: *We have done our share*.
ours /arz, *strong form* ˈauərz/ *possessive pron*

belonging to us: *This house is ~. Ours is larger than theirs.*

our·selves /ar'selvz/ *pron* **1** (used as a *reflexive*): *It's no use worrying ~ about that.* ***(all) by ourselves,*** **(a)** alone. **(b)** without help. **2** (used for emphasis): *We've often made that mistake ~.*

oust /aust/ *vt* force (a person) out of his job, position, etc: *~ a rival from the committee.*

out[1] /aut/ *adv* (For special uses of *out* in expressions such as *fall out, make out,* ⇨ the *verb* entries.) **1** away from the inside; away from the middle or center: *find one's way out.* **2** away from home, work, the usual or normal place: *The truckers went out on strike. They've gone out to lunch.* **3** at a distance away from a place or point: *He lives out in the country. The fishing boats sailed out to sea.* ***out West*** ⇨ West. **4** in(to) the open: *He let the secret out. The sun came out from behind a cloud.* **5** so as to be used up, completed, etc: *The fire's gone out. Put that cigarette out!* **6** (used as an intensifier): *I'm tired/worn out. He wrote out a description.* **7** loudly: *call/cry/shout out.* ***out loud,*** aloud. **8** ***out of,*** *prep* (contrasted with *in* and *into*) **(a)** from within to the outside: *She rushed out of her office.* **(b)** beyond or away from a place: *Fish cannot live out of water. He is out of town this week.* **(c)** (used to indicate cause, source, origin, basis, etc): *They helped us out of pity/kindness. The hut was made out of old planks.* **(d)** from among: *It happens in nine cases out of ten.* **(e)** not within the limits or range of: *out of fashion/control/order/danger.* **(f)** (used to indicate change from a state, attitude, intention, etc): *talked him out of running away.* **(g)** into a state of loss; no longer having or possessing: *cheat him out of his money.* ***out of it,*** not part of a group, activity, etc: *She felt out of it as she watched the others leave for the party.*

out[2] /aut/ *adj* **1** not in power. **2** not in fashion, use, operation, etc: *All the phones in this area are out.* **3** absent; missing. **4** (*baseball*) unsuccessful in reaching base. **5** not possible; not suitable: *Those two applicants are definitely out.* □ *n* [C] **1** person who is not in power. **2** means or way of escape: *I'll take any out to avoid going to that party.* **3** (*baseball*) play in which a batter or runner fails to reach base. □ *prep* out through: *out the window.*

out[3] /aut/ *vi* become known: *The truth will out.*

out- /aut/ *prefix* in a way that excels or surpasses: *outsmart.*

out-and-out /'aut-ən-'aut/ *adj* complete; thorough: *an ~ cheat.*

out·bid /aut'bɪd/ *vt* (-dd-; *pt* ~, *pp* ~, -bidden /-'bɪdən/) bid higher than (another person) at an auction, etc.

out·board mo·tor /ˌautˌbɔrd 'moutər/ *n* [C] removable engine that is mounted at the stern of a small boat.

out·bound /'aut ˌbaund/ *adj* (of a ship) outward bound; going away from a home port. ⇨ inbound.

out·break /'autˌbreik/ *n* [C] something that breaks out suddenly or violently: *an ~ of fever/hostilities.*

out·build·ing /'autˌbɪldɪŋ/ *n* [C] building, eg a shed or stable, separate from a main building.

out·burst /'autˌbərst/ *n* [C] outbreak.

out·cast /'autˌkæst/ *n* [C], *adj* (one who has been) driven out from home or society.

out·class /aut'klæs/ *vt* excel; surpass; do much better than: *He was ~ed from the start of the race.*

out·come /'autˌkəm/ *n* [C] result; consequence.

out·crop /'autˌkrap/ *n* [C] part of a layer or vein (of rock, etc) that comes above the surface of the ground.

out·cry /'autˌkrai/ *n* (*pl* -ies) **1** [C] loud shout or scream (of fear, alarm, etc). **2** [C,U] strong protest (*against*).

out·dated /aut'deitɪd/ *adj* made out-of-date by the passing of time.

out·dis·tance /aut'dɪstəns/ *vt* outrun(1).

out·do /aut'du/ *vt* (*3rd person sing pres* -does /-'dəz/, *pt* -did /-'dɪd/, *pp* -done /-'dən/) do more or better than: *Not to be outdone he tried again.*

out·door /'autˌdɔr/ *adj* done, existing, used, outdoors: *leading an ~ life; ~ sports.*

out·doors /aut'dɔrz/ *adv* in the open air; outside: *It's cold ~.*

outer /'autər/ *adj* **1** of or for the outside. ⇨ inner. **2** farther from the middle or center. **ˌouter 'space,** the universe beyond the limits of a heavenly body (as the earth) or a solar system.

outer·most /'autərˌmoust/ *adj* farthest from the inside or center.

out·field /'autˌfiəld/ *n* (*baseball*) **1** [U] outlying part of a baseball field. **2** [C] player (*left, center,* or *right fielder*) who plays in the outfield. ⇨ illus at baseball.

'out·fielder *n* [C] = outfield(2).

out·fight /aut'fait/ *vt* (*pt, pp* -fought) fight better than.

out·fit /'autˌfɪt/ *n* [C] **1** all the clothing or equipment needed for a particular purpose: *a camping ~.* **2** military unit or other group of persons working together. □ *vt* (-tt-) equip.

out·fitter *n* [C].

out·fox /aut'faks/ *vt* outsmart.

out·go·ing /'autˌgouɪŋ/ *adj* **1** going out; leaving: *the ~ tenant/tide.* **2** friendly and warm.

out·grow /aut'grou/ *vt* (*pt* -grew /-'gru/, *pp* -grown /-'groun/) **1** grow too large for, eg one's clothes. **2** grow faster than. **3** leave behind, as one grows older (bad habits, childish interests, opinions, etc).

out·growth /'autˌgrouθ/ *n* [C] **1** result, development or product. **2** that which grows out of something: *an ~ on a tree.*

out·house /'autˌhaus/ *n* [C] (*pl* ~s /-ˌhauzɪz/) outbuilding, esp one which is an outdoor toilet.

out·ing /'autɪŋ/ *n* [C] excursion; pleasure trip: *go for an ~ to the beach.*

out·land·ish /aut'lændɪʃ/ *adj* odd; strange; foreign: *~ dress/behavior/ideas.*

out·land·ish·ly *adv*

out·last /aut'læst/ *vt* last or exist longer than.

out·law /'autˌlɔ/ *n* [C] **1** person outside the protection of the law. **2** criminal; lawless person □ *vt* make illegal.

out·lay /'autˌlei/ *n* **1** [U] spending; providing money. **2** [C] sum of money that is spent: *a large*

~ *on/for scientific research.*

out·let /ˈautˌlet/ *n* [C] **1** opening or way out; exit: *an ~ for water.* **2** (*fig*) means of releasing feelings, energies, etc. **3** place (as a store) or means through which a product is sold. **4** (esp) wall socket connected to a wiring system, into which an electrical device may be plugged.

out·line /ˈautˌlain/ *n* [C] **1** line showing the shape or boundary of an object. **2** drawing that consists only of the outlines of a figure or object. **3** summary of the chief facts and points, usually arranged in numbered sections. □ *vt* **1** draw in outline. **2** give the main features of.

out·live /autˈlɪv/ *vt* live longer than: *~ one's wife.*

out·look /ˈautˌlʊk/ *n* [C] **1** view on which one looks out: *a pleasant ~ over the valley.* **2** what seems likely to happen: *a bright ~ for business.* **3** attitude; point of view: *a narrow ~.*

out·lying /ˈautˌlaiŋ/ *adj* far from the center: *~ towns.*

out·moded /autˈmoudɪd/ *adj* outdated.

out·num·ber /autˈnəmbər/ *vt* be greater in number than.

out-of-date /ˌaut-əv-ˈdeit/ *adj* outdated; obsolete: *an ~ set of figures* ⇨ date¹.

out-of-the-way /ˌaut-əv-ðə-ˈwei/ *adj* **1** remote; secluded: *an ~ cottage.* **2** unusual: *~ items of knowledge.*

out·patient /ˈautˌpeiʃənt/ *n* [C] person visiting a hospital for treatment but not remaining there overnight.

out·play /autˈplei/ *vt* play better than: *The Americans were ~ed by the Canadians.*

out·point /autˈpɔint/ *vt* (*sport*) score more points than.

out·post /ˈautˌpoust/ *n* [C] **1** (soldiers at a) post which is at some distance from the main body of troops. **2** any outlying settlement: *an ~ of the Roman Empire.*

out·put /ˈautˌpʊt/ *n* [U] **1** quantity of goods, etc produced, esp during a specified period of time: *the daily ~ of a gold mine/a factory.* **2** power, energy, etc produced by a system or device. **3** information produced from a computer. ⇨ input.

out·rage /ˈautˌreidʒ/ *n* [C,U] **1** wicked or cruel acts; grave offense or injury: *The use of H-bombs would be an ~ against humanity.* **2** great anger or resentment caused by such an act. □ *vt* **1** abuse; offend or injure greatly. **2** arouse great anger or resentment in.

out·rageous /autˈreidʒəs/ *adj* **1** shocking; very cruel. **2** shameful; offensive.

out·rage·ous·ly *adv*

out·rank /autˈræŋk/ *vt* rank higher than.

out·rider /ˈautˌraidər/ *n* [C] **1** person who rides ahead to mark the way, explore the countryside, etc. **2** mounted attendant or guard accompanying a wagon, coach, automobile, etc.

out·rig·ger /ˈautˌrɪgər/ *n* [C] **1** projecting frame attached to the side of a boat in order to keep it from upsetting. **2** boat equipped with such a framework.

out·right /ˈautˌrait/ *adj* thorough; complete: *an ~ denial.* □ *adv* **1** openly; with nothing held back: *tell a man ~ what one thinks of his behavior.* **2** completely: *gave them the house ~.* **3** immediately; without delay: *be killed ~.*

out·run /autˈrən/ *vt* (*pt* -ran /-ˈræn/, *pp* -run, *pres p* -nn-) **1** run faster than. **2** exceed: *His expenses are ~ning his income.*

out·set /ˈautˌset/ *n* (*sing* only) beginning.

out·shine /autˈʃain/ *vt* (*pt, pp* -shone /-ˈʃoun/) **1** shine more brightly than. **2** (*fig*) seem better than; surpass.

out·side /autˈsaid/ *n* (contrasted with *inside*) **1** [C] outer side or surface; the outer part(s): *The ~ of the house needs painting.* **2** ***at the (very) outside,*** at the most: *There were only fifty people there at the ~.* □ *adj* **1** of or on, nearer, the outside: *~ measurements of a box.* **2** greatest possible or probable: *an ~ estimate.* **3** not belonging to a group, organization, etc: *We shall need ~ help for this job.* **4** unlikely, small; *an ~ chance/possibility.* □ *adv* on or to the outside: *The car is waiting ~.* □ *prep* **1** at or on the outer side of: *~ the house.* **2** beyond the limits of: *~ the city.* **3** except: *He has no occupation ~ his office work.*

out·sider /autˈsaidər/ *n* [C] **1** person who is not, or who is not considered to be, a member of a group, society, etc. **2** horse that is thought to have little chance of winning a race.

out·skirts /ˈautˌskərts/ *n pl* outlying parts of a town, city, etc: *on the ~ of Tokyo.*

out·smart /autˈsmart/ *vt* get the better of by cleverness, or cunning.

out·spoken /autˈspoukən/ *adj* frank; saying freely what one thinks: *~ comments/delegates.*

out·spoken·ness /-nɪs/ *n* [C]

out·spread /autˈspred/ *adj* spread or stretched out.

out·stand·ing /autˈstændɪŋ/ *adj* **1** prominent; noticed, esp for excellence; distinguished: *The boy who won the scholarship was quite ~.* **2** not settled, still to be attended to: *~ debts; work that is still ~.*

out·stand·ing·ly *adv*

out·stay /autˈstei/ *vt* stay longer than: *~ the other guests.* ***outstay one's welcome,*** stay until one is no longer a welcome guest.

out·stretched /autˈstretʃt/ *adj* stretched or spread out: *lie ~ on the grass.*

out·strip /autˈstrɪp/ *vt* (-pp-) **1** outrun. **2** surpass.

out·ward /ˈautwərd/ *adj* **1** of or on the outside: *the ~ appearance of things.* **2** going out; moving away from a center: *during the ~ voyage.* □ *adv* (also **out·wards** /-wərdz/) toward the outside; away from home or the center: *The two ends must be bent ~s.*

out·ward·ly *adv* on the surface; apparently: *Though badly frightened she appeared ~ly calm.*

out·wear /autˈwer/ *vt* (*pt* -wore /-ˈwɔr/ *pp* -worn /-ˈwɔrn/) last longer than: *Good shoes will ~ cheaper ones.*

out·weigh /autˈwei/ *vt* be greater in weight, value or importance than: *Do the disadvantages ~ the advantages?*

out·wit /autˈwɪt/ *vt* (-tt-) outsmart.

out·wore, out·worn *pt,pp* of outwear.

ova *pl* of ovum.

oval /ˈouvəl/ *n* [C], *adj* (figure or object that is) shaped like an egg or ellipse.

ovary /ˈouvəri/ *n* [C] (*pl* -ies) **1** either of the two reproductive organs in females in which egg cells are produced. **2** part of a flowering plant in which the seeds are produced. ⇨ ovum. ⇨ illus at flower.

ova·tion /ouˈveiʃən/ *n* [C] enthusiastic expression (clapping, cheering) of welcome or approval.

oven /ˈəvən/ *n* [C] enclosed space (eg in a stove) heated for baking, roasting, etc: *Bread is baked in an* ~.

over[1] /ˈouvər/ *adv* (For special uses of *over* in expressions such as *turn over,* ⇨ the *verb* entries.) **1 (a)** from an upright position: *Don't knock that vase* ~. **(b)** so as to bring the downward or reverse side up: *turned the pancakes* ~. **2** upward and outward: *The milk boiled* ~. **3** from beginning to end; through: *You should think it* ~, consider the matter carefully. **4** again. ***over again,*** once more: *He did it so badly that I had to do it ~ again myself.* ***over and over*** repeatedly; many times: *I've warned you ~ and ~ not to do that.* **5** across a barrier, a street, an open space, a distance, etc: *Take these letters ~ to the post office.* **6** in addition; in excess; more: *children of fourteen and* ~. *Was any food left* ~? ⇨ over-. **7** from one person, party, etc to another: *He handed the plans ~ to the enemy.* **8** on the whole surface: *The pond was covered ~ with ice.* □ *adj* **1** done; finished: *The program is* ~. ***all over,*** ⇨ all². **2** in excess: *My estimate was ~ $500.*

over[2] /ˈouvər/ *prep* **1** upon and covering, partly or completely: *He spread his handkerchief ~ his face to keep the flies off.* **2** at a level higher than; above: *The sky is ~ our heads.* **3** above in rank, authority, etc: *He reigns ~ a great empire. He has no command ~ his students.* **4** in or across every part of; throughout: *Snow is falling ~ the Great Lakes region.* ***all over,*** ⇨ all²(3). **5** from one side to the other of; so as to be across and on the other side of: *He escaped ~ the frontier. climb ~ a wall; jump ~ a brook.* **6** more than: *He spoke for ~ an hour. The river is ~ fifty miles long. He's ~ fifty years old.* ***over and above,*** in addition to: *The waiters get good tips ~ and above their wages.* **7** in connection with; concerning: *He argued with her ~ his work.* **8** during: *Let's talk about it ~ lunch.*

over- /ˌouvər-/ *prefix* **1** across; above: *overland; overhead.* **2** too (much): *overactive; overabundance; overburden.* (*Note:* in *adjectives* of this type, *over* usually means *too;* in *nouns* and *verbs* of this type, *over* usually means *too much*).

over·abun·dance /ˌouvərəˈbəndəns/ *n* [U] too great a supply; excess.

over·abun·dant /-ənt/ *adj*

over·act /ˌouvərˈækt/ *vi,vt* act in an exaggerated way.

over·ac·tive /ˌouvərˈæktɪv/ *adj* too active; abnormally active.

over·all /ˌouvərˈɔl/ *adj* including everything; containing all: *the ~ measurements of a room.* □ *adv* as a whole; generally.

over·alls /ˈouvərˌɔlz/ *n pl* loose-fitting pants, usually made of heavy, strong material and having a piece that covers the chest, worn to protect other clothes from dirt, etc.

over·awe /ˌouvərˈɔ/ *vt* overcome or restrain by awe.

over·bal·ance /ˌouvərˈbæləns/ *vt* **1** cause to lose balance: *The boatman was ~d and fell into the water.* **2** have greater weight or importance than: *The gains ~ the losses.*

over·bear /ˌouvərˈber/ *vt* (*pt* -bore /-ˈbɔr/, *pp* -borne /-ˈbɔrn/) overcome (by strong arguments, force or authority).

over·bear·ing *adj* forcing others to one's will: *an ~ing manner.*

over·bear·ing·ly *adv*

over·board /ˈouvərˌbɔrd/ *adv* over the side of a ship or boat into the water: *fall/jump* ~. ***go overboard,*** (*informal*) go to extremes, esp of enthusiasm, approval, etc.

over·book /ˌouvərˈbʊk/ *vt, vi* book too many guests (at a hotel), passengers (for an aircraft flight), etc.

over·book·ing *n* [U]

over·bore, over·borne *pt,pp* of overbear.

over·bur·den /ˌouvərˈbərdən/ *vt* burden too heavily: *~ed with grief.*

over·cast /ˈouvərˌkæst/ *adj* **1** (of the sky) darkened (as) by clouds. **2** (*fig*) gloomy; sad. □ *n* [C] cloud-covered sky.

over·charge /ˌouvərˈtʃardʒ/ *vt,vi* **1** charge too high a price: *We were ~d for the eggs.* **2** fill or load too much: *~ an electric circuit.* □ *n* /ˈouvərˌtʃardʒ/ [C] load, price, etc that is too high or great.

over·cloud /ˌouvərˈklaud/ *vt,vi* cover, become covered, with clouds or shadows.

over·coat /ˈouvərˌkout/ *n* [C] long coat worn outdoors over other clothes in cold weather.

over·come /ˌouvərˈkəm/ *vt* (*pt* -came /-ˈkeim/, *pp* -come) **1** defeat; get the better of: *~ the enemy/a bad habit/temptation.* **2** exhaust; overpower: *be ~ by tiredness/sadness/whiskey/fumes.*

over·do /ˌouvərˈdu/ *vt* (*pt* -did /-ˈdɪd/, *pp* -done /-ˈdən/) **1** carry too far; exaggerate: **2** ***overdo it,*** **(a)** exaggerate: *He tried to show sympathy for us, but didn't he ~ it?* **(b)** work, etc too hard: *You should work hard, but don't ~ it and make yourself sick.* **3** cook too long: *~ne beef.*

over·dose /ˈouvərˌdous/ *n* [C] dose that is excessively large.

over·draft /ˈouvərˌdræft/ *n* [C] amount of money by which a bank account is overdrawn.

over·draw /ˌouvərˈdrɔ/ *vt,vi* (*pt* -drew /-ˈdru/, *pp* -drawn /-ˈdrɔn/) **1** draw more money from a bank account than one has in it. **2** exaggerate: *The characters in this novel are rather ~n,* are not true to life.

over·dress /ˌouvərˈdres/ *vt,vi* dress too richly or too formally.

over·due /ˌouvərˈdu/ *adj* **1** later than the time appointed or scheduled: *The train is* ~. **2** unpaid after the date set for payment: *These bills are all* ~.

over·eat /ˌouvərˈit/ *vi* (*pt* -ate /-ˈeit/, *pp* -eaten /-ˈitən/) eat too much.

over·esti·mate /ˌouvərˈestəˌmeit/ *vt* estimate or value too highly. □ *n* [C] /ˌouvərˈestəmɪt/ estimate that is too high.

over·ex·pose /ˌouvərɪkˈspouz/ *vt* **1** expose too much. **2** expose (a photographic film) to too much light.

over·ex·po·sure /-ˈspouʒər/ *n* [C,U]

over·flight /ˈouvərˌflait/ *n* [U] ⇨ overfly.

over·flow /ˌouvərˈflou/ *vt,vi* (*pt,pp* ~ed) **1** flow over the top or brim: *The river ~ed its banks.* **2** spread beyond the usual limits: *The crowds were so big that they ~ed into the street.* □ *n* /ˈouvərˌflou/ [C,U] **1** (act of) overflowing. **2** amount that overflows.

over·fly /ˌouvərˈflai/ *vt* (*pt* -flew /-ˈflu/, *pp* -flown /-ˈfloun/) fly over (a place).

over·flight /ˈouvərˌflait/ *n* [U] act, instant, of overflying.

over·grow /ˌouvərˈgrou/ *vt, vi* (*pt* -grew /-ˈgru/, *pp* -grown /-ˈgroun/) **1** grow too fast or too much. **2** cover with growth: *Weeds have ~n the path.*

over·hand /ˈouvərˌhænd/ *n* [C], *adj* (*sport*) stroke made with the hand raised above the shoulder and then brought forward and downward.

over·hang /ˌouvərˈhæŋ/ *vt,vi* (*pt,pp* -hung /-ˈhəŋ/) hang or project over, like a shelf: *The cliffs ~ the stream.* □ /ˈouvərˌhæŋ/ *n* [C] part that overhangs: *the ~ of a roof.*

over·haul /ˌouvərˈhɔl/ *vt* **1** examine thoroughly in order to learn about the condition of: *have the engine of a car ~ed.* **2** overtake; catch up with: *The fast cruiser soon ~ed the old cargo boat.* □ *n* /ˈouvərˌhɔl/ [C] act of overhauling.

over·head /ˌouvərˈhed/ *adv* above one's head; in the sky: *the people in the room ~; the stars ~.* □ *adj* /ˈouvərˌhed/ raised or located above one's head: *~ wires/cables.* □ *n* [U] /ˈouvərˌhed/ expenses of carrying on a business, that include rent, advertising, salaries, light, etc, but not labor or materials.

over·hear /ˌouvərˈhɪr/ *vt* (*pt,pp* ~d /-ˈhərd/) hear without the knowledge of the speaker(s) esp by chance.

over·joyed /ˌouvərˈdʒɔid/ *adj* very delighted: *~ by/at the news.*

over·land *adj* /ˈouvərlənd/, *adv* /ˈouvərˌlænd/ across or by land (as contrasted with the sea): *take the ~ route; travel ~.*

over·lap /ˌouvərˈlæp/ *vt,vi* (-pp-) **1** lie over and partly cover by extending beyond one edge: *tiles that ~ one another; ~ping boards.* **2** (*fig*) partly coincide; have some part in common: *His duties/authority and mine ~.* □ /ˈouvərˌlæp/ *n* [C,U]

over·load /ˌouvərˈloud/ *vt* put too great a load (of electric current, weight) on. □ /ˈouvərˌloud/ *n* [C,U] excessively large load.

over·look /ˌouvərˈlʊk/ *vt* **1** have a view of from above: *Our house ~s the lake.* **2** fail to see or notice: *His services have been ~ed by his employers.* **3** pass over; ignore: *~ a fault.*

over·much /ˌouvərˈmətʃ/ *adj, adv* too great(ly): *an author who has been praised ~.*

over·night /ˌouvərˈnait/ *adj,adv* **1** for, during, a single night: *stay ~ at a friend's house*, sleep there for the night. *an ~ journey.* **2** sudden(ly): *become rich ~; an ~ success.*

over·pass /ˈouvərˌpæs/ *n* [C] section of a road that crosses over a highway, railroad, etc. ⇨ underpass.

over·power /ˌouvərˈpauər/ *vt* **1** defeat by greater strength or numbers: *The criminals were easily ~ed by the police.* **2** overwhelm: *He was ~ed by the heat.*

over·pro·duce /ˌouvərprəˈdus/ *vt* produce too many or too much of.

over·pro·duc·tion /ˌouvərprəˈdəkʃən/ *n* [U]

over·rate /ˌouvərˈreit/ *vt* rate or value too highly: *~ her abilities; an ~d book.*

over·reach /ˌouvərˈritʃ/ *vt* **1** reach beyond or over. **2** ***overreach oneself,*** fail, damage one's own interests, by going too far.

over·ride /ˌouvərˈraid/ *vt* (*pt* -rode /-ˈroud/, *pp* -ridden /-ˈrɪdən/) **1** ride over; trample on. **2** be greater in force or influence than. **3** set aside; annul (a decision, claim, etc): *They overrode my wishes.* □ *n* [C] /ˈouvərˌraid/ act of overriding(3).

over·rule /ˌouvərˈrul/ *vt* **1** rule or decide against. **2** reverse or set aside: *The judge ~d the previous decision.*

over·run /ˌouvərˈrən/ *vt* (*pt* -ran /-ˈræn/, *pp* ~, *pres p* -nn-) **1** spread over in great numbers: *a country ~ by enemy troops; a garden ~ with weeds.* **2** extend or go beyond (a limit): *speakers who ~ the time allowed them.*

over·seas /ˌouvərˈsiz/ *adj* of, from, or across the sea: *~ trade.* □ *adv* across or beyond the sea; abroad: *go/live ~s*, abroad.

over·see /ˌouvərˈsi/ *vt* (*pt* -saw /-ˈsɔ/, *pp* -seen /-ˈsin/) watch over; direct; supervise.

over·seer /ˈouvərˌsɪr/ *n* [C] person in charge of workers, esp on a plantation.

over·shadow /ˌouvərˈʃædou/ *vt* **1** cast a shadow over. **2** (*fig*) cause to seem less important.

over·shoe /ˈouvərˌʃu/ *n* [C] outer shoe, often of rubber or plastic, worn for protection.

over·shoot /ˌouvərˈʃut/ *vt* (*pt,pp* -shot /-ˈʃat/) go over or beyond (a mark or limit): *The aircraft overshot the runway.*

over·sight /ˈouvərˌsait/ *n* **1** [C] unintentional error or omission: *Through an unfortunate ~ your letter was left unanswered.* **2** [U] supervision: *under the ~ of a nurse.*

over·sleep /ˌouvərˈslip/ *vi* (*pt,pp* -slept /-ˈslept/) sleep too long or after the intended time for waking: *He overslept and was late for work.*

over·state /ˌouvərˈsteit/ *vt* express or state too strongly; exaggerate: *Don't ~ your case.*

over·state·ment /ˌouvərˈsteitmənt/ *n* [C] exaggerated statement.

over·stay /ˌouvərˈstei/ *vt* stay beyond the time or limits of.

over·step /ˌouvərˈstep/ *vt* (-pp-) go beyond; exceed: *~ one's authority.*

over·stock /ˌouvərˈstak/ *vt* stock with more than is needed. □ *n* [U] /ˈouvərˌstak/ quantity of stock beyond what is needed.

over·strung /ˌouvərˈstrəŋ/ *adj* intensely nervous; easily excited; too sensitive.

overt /ouˈvərt/ *adj* open; not hidden: *~ hostility.*

overt·ly *adv*

over·take /ˌouvərˈteik/ *vt* (*pt* -took /-ˈtʊk/, *pp* -taken /-ˈteikən/) **1** catch up with. **2** catch up with and pass. **3** come upon suddenly or by surprise: *They were* ~*n by the storm.*

over·tax /ˌouvərˈtæks/ *vt* **1** tax too heavily. **2** put too heavy a burden or strain on: ~ *one's strength/her patience.*

over·throw /ˌouvərˈθrou/ *vt* (*pt* -threw /-ˈθru/, *pp* -thrown /-ˈθroun/) **1** overturn. **2** defeat; cause the downfall of: ~ *the government.* □ *n* [C] /ˈouvərˌθrou/ ruin; defeat; downfall.

over·time /ˈouvərˌtaim/ *n* [U], *adj, adv* (time) in excess of the usual hours: *working* ~; *be on* ~; ~ *pay.*

over·ture /ˈouvərtʃər/ *n* [C] **1** first approach or proposal made to another person, group, party, etc: *peace* ~*s; make* ~*s to the strikers.* **2** musical composition played as an introduction to an opera or other dramatic work, or as an independent work for performance.

over·turn /ˌouvərˈtərn/ *vt,vi* **1** (cause to) turn over; upset: *He* ~*ed the boat. The car* ~*ed.* **2** destroy; defeat.

over·weight /ˈouvərˌweit/ *n* [U] weight in excess of the normal or permitted weight. □ *adj* /ˌouvərˈweit/ weighing more than is allowed or normal: *If your luggage is* ~ *you'll have to pay extra.*

over·whelm /ˌouvərˈ(h)welm/ *vt* **1** submerge or cover over completely. **2** overpower; overcome: *be* ~*ed by the enemy.*

over·work /ˌouvərˈwərk/ *vt,vi* (cause to) work too hard or too long: ~ *a horse. It's foolish to* ~. □ *n* /ˈouvərˌwərk/ [U] too much work.

over·wrought /ˌouvərˈrɔt/ *adj* nervous; very excited.

ovi·duct /ˈouvəˌdəkt/ *n* [C] either of two tubes for the passage of ova from the ovary.

ovum /ˈouvəm/ *n* [C] (*pl* ova /ˈouvə/) female reproductive cell. ⇨ egg¹(2).

owe /ou/ *vt,vi* **1** be in debt (to a person) (for something): *He owes his father $50.* **2** be under an obligation to give or pay: *We owe a great deal to our parents and teachers.* **3** be obliged or indebted for: *He owes his success to good luck more than to ability.*

ow·ing /ˈouŋ/ *adj* still to be paid: *large sums still* ~. ***owing to,*** *prep* because of; on account of: *Owing to the rain they could not come.*

owl /aul/ *n* [C] bird of prey with a short, hooked bill and a large head and eyes, that is usually active at night. ⇨ illus at bird.

own[1] /oun/ *adj* (used with *possessive adjectives*) **1** belonging to oneself, itself: *She makes all her own clothes.* **2** (used for emphasis): *I saw it with my own eyes.* □ *pron* one(s) belonging to oneself or itself: *It's my own. This fruit has a flavor all its own.* ***on one's own,*** independently; without outside help: *I did it on my own.* ***come into one's own,*** receive the credit, fame, etc that is deserved. ***hold one's own,*** **(a)** maintain one's position against attack or criticism. **(b)** not lose strength: *The patient is holding her own.*

own[2] /oun/ *vt,vi* **1** possess; have as property; *This house is mine; I own it.* **2** admit; acknowledge: *own that a claim is justified.* **3** ***own up (to sth),*** confess fully and frankly.

owner /ˈounər/ *n* [C] person who owns something: *Who's the* ~ *of this house?*

ˈown·er·ship /-ˌʃɪp/ *n* [U] state of being an owner.

ox /aks/ *n* [C] (*pl* oxen /ˈaksən/) **1** any one of the common, large, domestic cattle, esp an adult, castrated male. **2** any of the larger, cud-chewing animals, such as the buffalo, that are related to domestic cattle.

ox·bow /ˈaksˌbou/ *n* [C] **1** U-shaped collar worn by an ox, with upper ends that fasten into a yoke. **2** U-shaped bend in a river.

ox·cart /ˈaksˌkart/ *n* [C] cart drawn by oxen.

ox·ford /ˈaksfərd/ *n* [C] men's laced shoe.

oxi·dize /ˈaksəˌdaiz/ *vt,vi* (cause to) combine with oxygen: *When iron* ~*s, it becomes rusty.*

oxi·da·tion /ˌaksəˈdeiʃən/ *n* [U]

oxy·acety·lene /ˌaksiəˈsetələn/ *adj* using a mixture of oxygen and acetylene: *an* ~ *torch.*

oxy·gen /ˈaksɪdʒən/ *n* [U] gaseous element (symbol **O**) without color, taste or smell, making up about one fifth of the atmosphere and necessary to the existence of all forms of life.

ˈoxygen mask, device worn over the nose and mouth, that is connected by a hose to a supply of oxygen.

ˈoxygen tent, enclosure to allow a patient to breathe air with a greater oxygen content.

oy·ster /ˈɔistər/ *n* [C] kinds of edible shellfish with a rough, grayish, double-hinged shell. ⇨ illus at bivalve.

ˈoyster bed, place where oysters breed or are bred.

oz. *abbr* = ounce(s).

o·zone /ˈouˌzoun/ *n* [U] poisonous, blue gas that is a form of oxygen with three atoms to a molecule instead of two.

p

P[1]**, p** /pi/ (*pl* P's, p's /piz/) the sixteenth letter of the English alphabet.
p.[2] *abbr* = **1** (*pl* pp.) page. **2** participle. **3** past. **4** per.
PA[1] *postal abbr* = Pennsylvania. ⇨ App 6.
P.A.[2] /ˌpi ˈei/ *abbr* = public address (usually as:) *P.A. system.*
p.a.[3] *abbr* = per annum.
pa[4] /pa/ *n* [C] (*informal*) father.
pab·lum /ˈpæbləm/ *n* [U] pabulum (⇨ next entry) especially prepared for infants.
pab·u·lum /ˈpæbyələm/ *n* [U] **1** soft food, easily digested. **2** (*fig*) food for thought.
pace /peis/ *n* [C] **1** (distance or length of a) single step. **2** rate of walking or moving; speed: *go at a good ~,* go fast. ***set the pace (for),*** set a speed for (eg runners in a race). ***keep pace (with)*** keep up with: *He finds it hard to keep ~ with all the developments in nuclear physics.* **3** gait of a horse in which both legs on the same side leave and return to the ground at the same time. □ *vi,vt* **1** walk, move, etc with slow or regular steps: *~ up and down.* **2** measure by paces: *~ off 30 feet.* **3** set the pace(2) for.
pace·maker /ˈpeisˌmeikər/ *n* [C] **1** one who sets the pace. **2** electronic device to correct weak or irregular heartbeats.
pachy·derm /ˈpækıˌdərm/ *n* [C] large, hoofed animal (as an elephant or rhinoceros) with a thick skin.
pa·cific /pəˈsıfık/ *adj* **1** peaceable; making or loving peace. **2** calm; serene.
pa·cifi·cally /-kli/ *adv*
Paˈcific ˌTime, one of the four official time zones of the continental US.
paci·fi·ca·tion /ˌpæsəfəˈkeiʃən/ *n* [U] pacifying or being pacified.
pa·ci·fi·er /ˈpæsəˌfaiər/ *n* [C] (esp) rubber or plastic device for a baby to bite or suck on.
paci·fism /ˈpæsəˌfızəm/ *n* [U] belief that war should be abolished; opposition to war.
paci·fist /ˈpæsəfist/ *n* [C] believer in pacifism.
pac·ify /ˈpæsəˌfai/ *vt* (*pt,pp* -ied) **1** calm or soothe; quiet. **2** bring or restore peace to.
pack[1] /pæk/ *n* [C] **1** bundle of things tied or wrapped up together; package. **2** group of similar animals, things, or persons: *a ~ of thieves/liars/lies; a ~ of wolves.* **3** complete set (usually 52) of playing cards. **4** pad of absorbent material used to put into a wound or opening, to apply medication to a part of the body, etc: *a hot ~ for aching muscles.* **5** small package: *a ~ of cigarettes.*
pack[2] /pæk/ *vt,vi* **1** put (things) into a box, bundle, bag, etc, for a trip, storage, etc: *~ed lunch for the children. Have you ~ed your trunk? You must begin ~ing your clothes at once.* **2** crush or crowd together; cram: *~ing people into a bus. She managed to ~ a lot of sightseeing into the short time she had in England.* **3** be suitable for packing: *Wool sweaters ~ well.* **4** ***pack sb off,*** cause to leave or go: *~ed her off to school.* ***send sb packing,*** send him away abruptly; get rid of him. **5** (*informal*) carry as equipment: *He ~s a gun.* **6** choose (the members of a committee, etc) dishonestly so that their decisions are likely to be favorable: *~ a jury.*
ˈpack·ing house, (a) slaughterhouse. **(b)** cannery.
pack·age /ˈpækıdʒ/ *n* [C] **1** parcel, bundle of things, packed together. **2** (*informal*) several conditions, services, etc offered or accepted together: *~ deal; ~ tour.* □ *vt* place in or make into a package.
packer /ˈpækər/ *n* [C] (esp) dealer that prepares and packs foods for transportation and sale.
packet /ˈpækıt/ *n* [C] **1** small package or bundle: *a ~ of letters.* **2** ship that carries passengers, mail, etc on a regular schedule.
pact /pækt/ *n* [C] compact; agreement: *a new peace ~.*
pad[1] /pæd/ *n* [C] **1** cushion; mass of soft material, used for protection, as stuffing, etc. **2** number of sheets of writing paper fastened together along one edge. **3** absorbent material used for inking rubber stamps. **4** soft, fleshy underpart of the toes and feet of some animals. **5** (*sl*) place to live. □ *vt* (-dd-) **1** supply with pads(1) as protection, stuffing, etc. **2** make (a sentence, essay, speech, etc) longer by using unnecessary material.
pad·ding /ˈpædıŋ/ *n* [U] material used to pad[1](1,2).
pad[2] /pæd/ *vi,vt* (-dd-) **1** travel on foot. **2** walk with a quiet step.
paddle[1] /ˈpædəl/ *n* **1** short oar with a broad, flat blade, used to propel a canoe or boat through the water. **2** instrument shaped like a paddle (eg one used for beating, stirring or mixing things). **3** short bat or racket, used to hit the ball in table tennis. **4** one of the broad boards set around the outer rim of a paddle wheel. □ *vt,vi* **1** move or row (as) by a paddle. ***paddle one's own canoe,*** depend on oneself alone. **2** beat with a paddle.
ˈpaddle boat, one propelled by a paddle wheel.
ˈpaddle wheel, steam-driven wheel, with boards or paddles around the rim, used to propel a paddle boat.
paddle[2] /ˈpædəl/ *vi* move the hands or feet in

shallow water.

pad·dock /ˈpædək/ *n* [C] **1** enclosed field, esp one used for exercising or grazing horses. **2** enclosure where horses are saddled and paraded before a race.

paddy /ˈpædi/ *n* [C] (*pl* -ies) marshy, wet field in which rice is grown.

pad·lock /ˈpædˌlak/ *n* [C] detachable lock with a hinged, U-shaped piece that can be snapped into a catch. □ *vt* lock up (as) with a padlock.

padre /ˈpadrei/ *n* [C] **1** (*informal*) military chaplain. **2** priest.

pae·an /ˈpiən/ *n* [C] hymn of praise, joy, triumph, etc.

pa·gan /ˈpeigən/ *n* [C], *adj* **1** (person who is) not a believer in any of the chief religions of the world. **2** (person who is) irreligious.

page¹ /peidʒ/ *n* [C] **1** one side of a leaf of paper in a book, periodical, etc. **2** entire leaf of a book, etc: *Several ~s have been torn out.* **3** material written or printed on a page. **4** record: *the ~s of history*. **5** memorable event. □ *vt* number the pages of.

page² /peidʒ/ *n* **1** attendant (as in a hotel, club, etc) employed to deliver messages, run errands, etc. **2** (in the Middle Ages) boy in training for knighthood and living in a knight's household. **3** boy or young man or woman acting as assistant to a person of high rank, esp elected representative: *congressional ~s.* □ *vt* summon (a person) by calling out his name: *~d him at the airport*.

pag·eant /ˈpædʒənt/ *n* [C] **1** entertainment in which scenes from legendary or historical events are presented. **2** celebration; colorful exhibition or spectacle.

pag·eantry /ˈpædʒəntri/ *n* [U] **(a)** rich and splendid ceremony or display. **(b)** pageants and the presentation of pageants.

pag·i·nate /ˈpædʒəˌneit/ *vt* number or order the pages of a book, report, etc.

pag·i·na·tion /ˌpædʒəˈneiʃən/ *n* [C,U]

pa·goda /pəˈgoudə/ *n* [C] (*pl* ~s) (in India, Sri Lanka, Burma, China, Japan, etc) temple or shrine built in the form of a tower with several stories, each story often having a roof that projects and turns upward.

paid *pt,pp* of pay².

pail /ˈpeiəl/ *n* [C] **1** usually cylindrical container with a handle, used for carrying: *a ~ of milk*. **2** = pailful.

ˈpail·ful /-ˌfʊl/ *n* [C] as much as a pail can hold.

pain /pein/ *n* **1** [U] suffering of mind or body: *be in (great) ~; feel some/no/not much/a great deal of ~.* **2** [C] particular or localized kind of bodily suffering: *a ~ in the knee; stomach ~s.* **3** [U] (*informal*) nuisance. ***a pain in the neck,*** (*informal*) troublesome person or thing. **4** (*pl*) trouble; effort: *work hard and get very little for all one's ~.* ***take (great) pains,*** make a great effort: *took ~s to do it neatly.* □ *vt* hurt; cause pain to: *My foot is still ~ing me.*

ˈpain-killer *n* [C] something, such as a drug, for lessening pain.

ˈpain·ful /-fəl/ *adj* causing or full of pain.

ˈpain·fully /-fəli/ *adv*

pain·less *adj* not painful; causing no pain.

pain·less·ly *adv*

pains·taking /ˈpeinzˌteikɪŋ/ *adj* very careful and thorough.

paint /peint/ *n* [U] **1** mixture of solid coloring matter and oil or other liquid that is used to color or decorate a surface: *give the doors two coats of ~.* **2** thin, dried film of this mixture. **3** cosmetics, such as rouge, used to color the skin. □ *vt,vi* **1** coat (as) with paint: *~ a door; ~ a cut with disinfectant.* ***paint the town red,*** (*informal*) go out and celebrate. **2** make a picture (of) with paint: *~ flowers; ~ in oils.* **3** (*fig*) describe vividly in words.

ˈpaint·brush *n* [C] brush for applying paint.

painter¹ /ˈpeintər/ *n* [C] person who paints.

painter² /ˈpeintər/ *n* [C] rope fastened to the bow of a boat by which it may be tied to a ship, pier, etc.

paint·ing /ˈpeintɪŋ/ *n* **1** [U] art or occupation of a painter. **2** [C] painted picture.

pair /per/ *n* [C] **1** two things of the same kind (to be) used together: *a ~ of shoes/gloves.* **2** single article with two parts always joined: *a ~ of trousers/tights/scissors/tongs.* **3** two persons closely associated, eg an engaged or married couple. ***in pairs,*** in twos. **4** two animals that are mated. **5** set of two persons, animals, or things considered together. □ *vt,vi* **1** form a pair. **2** make a pair or pairs of.

pais·ley /ˈpeizli/ *adj* with a colorful pattern of curved shapes.

pa·ja·mas /pəˈdʒaməz, -ˈdʒæm-/ *n pl* loose suit worn for sleeping or lounging.

pal /pæl/ *n* [C] (*informal*) comrade; friend. □ *vi* (-ll-) associate with as a friend.

pal·ace /ˈpælɪs/ *n* [C] **1** official residence of a sovereign. **2** any large and splendid house.

pal·at·able /ˈpælətəbəl/ *adj* **1** agreeable to the taste. **2** (*fig*) acceptable.

pal·ate /ˈpælɪt/ *n* **1** roof of the mouth. ⇨ illus at mouth. **2** sense of taste.

pa·la·tial /pəˈleiʃəl/ *adj* of or like a palace; splendid: *a ~ residence.*

pa·lav·er /pəˈlævər/ *vi* talk or chatter idly.

pale¹ /ˈpeiəl/ *adj* (-r, -st) **1** having little color: *He turned ~ at the news.* **2** not vivid or intense in color: *~ blue.* **3** not bright; dim. □ *vt,vi* (*pres p* paling /ˈpeilɪŋ/) make or become pale.

pale·ly /ˈpeiəlli/ *adv*

pale·ness /-nɪs/ *n* [U]

pale² /ˈpeiəl/ *n* [C] **1** pointed piece of wood used for fences; stake. ⇨ paling. **2** limit; boundary.

pale·face /ˈpeiəlˌfeis/ *n* [C] white person (term said to have been used by the North American Indians).

Paleo·lithic /ˌpeiliouˈlɪθɪk/ *adj* of the period marked by the use of primitive stone implements.

pale·on·tol·ogist /ˌpeilianˈtalədʒɪst/ *n* [C] scientist who specializes in paleontology.

pale·on·tol·ogy /ˌpeilianˈtalədʒi/ *n* [U] scientific study of fossils as a guide to the history of life on earth.

pal·ette /ˈpælɪt/ *n* [C] board (with a hole for the thumb) on which an artist mixes his colors.

pal·ing /ˈpeilɪŋ/ *n* [C,U] fence made of pales²(1).

pali·sade /ˌpæləˈseid/ *n* **1** [C] fence of strong,

pointed wooden stakes (eg as a defense). **2** (*pl*) line of high, steep cliffs (esp along a river).

pall[1] /pɔl/ *n* [C] **1** heavy cloth spread over a coffin. **2** (*fig*) any dark, heavy covering: *a ~ of smoke*.

ˈpall·bearer *n* [C] person who attends the coffin at a funeral.

pall[2] /pɔl/ *vi* become dull or boring: *pleasures that ~ after a time*.

pal·la·di·um /pəˈleidiəm/ *n* [U] silvery metallic element (symbol **Pa**) used in making alloys.

pal·let /ˈpælɪt/ *n* [C] **1** straw-filled mattress for sleeping on. **2** small, hard bed.

pal·lid /ˈpælɪd/ *adj* pale; lacking healthy color.

pal·lid·ly *adv*

pal·lid·ness /-nɪs/ *n* [U]

pal·lor /ˈpælər/ *n* [U] unhealthy paleness, esp of the face.

palm[1] /pam/ *n* [C] inner surface of the hand between the wrist and the fingers. ⇨ illus at arm. □ *vt* **1** hide in or pick up secretly with the hand, as when performing a trick. **2** ***palm sth off (on sb),*** get him to accept it by fraud, trickery, etc.

palm[2] /pam/ *n* [C] **1** kinds of tree growing in warm climates, with no branches and a mass of large wide leaves at the top: *ˈcoconut ~; ˈdate ~*. ⇨ illus at tree. **2** leaf of a palm, esp as a symbol of victory.

Palm ˈSunday, the Sunday before Easter, celebrated in memory of Christ's triumphal entry into Jerusalem.

pal·met·to /palˈmetou/ *n* [C] (*pl* ~s) kind of small palm tree.

pal·o·mino /ˌpæləˈminou/ *n* [C] (*pl* ~s) horse with a light tan coat and a lighter tail and mane.

pal·pable /ˈpælpəbəl/ *adj* **1** that can be felt or touched. **2** obvious: *a ~ error*.

pal·pably /-əbli/ *adv*

pal·pi·tate /ˈpælpəˌteit/ *vi* **1** beat rapidly and strongly. **2** shake; tremble; quiver.

pal·pi·ta·tion /ˌpælpəˈteiʃən/ *n* [C,U]

palsy /ˈpɔlzi/ *n* [U] **1** paralysis. **2** condition in which the trembling and shaking of (a part of) the body cannot be controlled. □ *vt* (*pt,pp* -ied) paralyze.

pal·try /ˈpɔltri/ *adj* (-ier, -iest) **1** worthless; of no importance. **2** mean; contemptible.

pam·pas /ˈpæmpəz, ˈpampəz/ *n pl* wide, treeless plains of South America.

pam·per /ˈpæmpər/ *vt* indulge too much; be excessively kind to: *a ~ed child/dog*.

pamph·let /ˈpæmflɪt/ *n* [C] small paper-covered book.

pamph·let·eer /ˌpæmfləˈtɪr/ *n* [C] writer of pamphlets.

pan[1] /pæn/ *n* [C] **1** usually shallow, open container, used for cooking and other domestic purposes. **2** any similar container, as used eg on a pair of scales or for washing gravel, etc to separate the gold. □ *vt,vi* (-nn-) **1** wash (gravel, etc) in a pan to separate the gold. **2** ***pan out,*** (*informal*) succeed; turn out: *How did things pan out?* **3** (*informal*) criticize harshly.

pan[2] /pæn/ *vi,vt* move a motion-picture or television camera to follow a moving object or to take in a wide view.

pan- *prefix* all: *Pan-African*.

pana·cea /ˌpænəˈsiə/ *n* [C] (*pl* ~s) remedy for all troubles, diseases, etc.

pan·cake /ˈpænˌkeik/ *n* [C] flat cake made of batter and cooked on both sides until brown.

PANCAKES OR FLAPJACKS

pan·chro·matic /ˌpænkrəˈmætɪk/ *adj* (in photography) sensitive to light of all colors: *~ film*.

pan·creas /ˈpæŋkriəs/ *n* [C] gland near the stomach, which secretes insulin and digestive juices.

pan·cre·atic /ˌpæŋkriˈætɪk/ *adj* of the pancreas.

panda /ˈpændə/ *n* [C] (*pl* ~s) bearlike mammal of Tibet and China, with black and white fur.

pan·de·mo·nium /ˌpændəˈmouniəm/ *n* [U] wild and noisy disorder.

pan·der /ˈpændər/ *n* [C] one that aids or encourages the low desires or weaknesses of others. □ *vi* act as a pander: *newspapers that ~ to the public interest in crime*.

pane /pein/ *n* [C] sheet of glass in (a division of) a window or door.

panel /ˈpænəl/ *n* [C] **1** separate part of the surface of a door, wall, ceiling, etc, raised above or sunk below the surrounding area. **2** piece of material inserted lengthwise in a dress. **3** board or other surface for controls and instruments: *the ˈinstrument ~ of an airplane*. **4** list of persons summoned to serve on a jury. **5** small group of persons chosen to discuss questions, take part in a quiz game, etc, often before an audience: *a ~ of experts*. □ *vt* (-l-, -ll-) furnish or decorate with panels(1,2): *a ~ed room/skirt*.

pan·el·ing *n* [U] **(a)** series of panels on a wall, etc. **(b)** material for panels.

ˈpanel truck, small, fully enclosed delivery truck. ⇨ illus at truck.

pang /pæŋ/ *n* [C] sudden, sharp feeling of pain, guilt, etc.

pan·han·dle /ˈpænˌhændəl/ *n* [C] narrow piece of territory sticking out from a larger territory like the handle of a pan: *The Texas ~*. □ *vt,vi* (*informal*) beg for money in the street.

pan·handler *n* [C] (*informal*) beggar.

panic /ˈpænɪk/ *n* [C,U] **1** sudden, uncontrolled fear: *There is always danger of* (*a*) *~ when a building catches fire*. **2** widespread alarm about financial matters, often causing a fall in prices. □ *vt,vi* (-ck-) (cause to) be affected with panic: *He ~ked and ran away*.

pan·icky /ˈpænɪki/ *adj* (*informal*) feeling or showing panic.

ˈpanic-stricken *adj* terrified; overcome by panic.

pan·nier /ˈpænyər/ *n* [C] one of a pair of baskets carried on either side of an animal or bicycle.

pan·or·ama /ˌpænəˈræmə/ *n* [C] (*pl* ~s) **1** wide,

uninterrupted view. **2** complete view or presentation of a subject. **3** wide picture that is unrolled one part at a time before the spectator.
pan·or·amic /ˌpænəˈræmɪk/ *adj*
pan·pipes /ˈpænˌpaips/ *n pl* musical instrument made of a series of reeds or pipes of different lengths, played by blowing across the open ends.
pansy /ˈpænzi/ *n* [C] (*pl* -ies) **1** (plant bearing a) velvety flower with five petals. **2** (*sl*) effeminate man.
pant /pænt/ *vi,vt* **1** take short, quick breaths; gasp: *The dog ~ed along behind its master's horse.* **2** say with gasps: *He ~ed out his message.* **3** long for. □ *n* [C] short, quick breath; gasp.
pan·ta·lets, pan·ta·lettes /ˌpæntəˈlets/ *n pl* long underpants with a ruffle or frill at the bottom of each leg, that were formerly worn by women and girls.
pan·ta·loon /ˌpæntəˈlun/ *n* **1 Pantaloon,** clown. **2** (*pl*) trousers.
pan·the·ism /ˈpænθiˌɪzəm/ *n* [U] **1** belief that God and nature are one and the same. **2** belief in and worship of all gods.
pan·the·ist /-ɪst/ *n* [C]
pan·the·is·tic /ˌpænθiˈɪstɪk/ *adj*
pan·ther /ˈpænθər/ *n* [C] **1** leopard. **2** cougar. **3** jaguar. ⇨ illus at cat.
pan·ties /ˈpæntiz/ *n pl* (*informal*) woman's or child's close-fitting short underpants.
pan·to·mime /ˈpæntəˌmaim/ *n* **1** [U] acting without speech, that uses gestures, facial expressions, etc to convey meaning. **2** [C] play or dramatic performance acted in this way.
pan·try /ˈpæntri/ *n* [C] (*pl* -ies) small room or closet, usually near a kitchen, in which silver, glass, china, food, etc are kept.
pants /pænts/ *n pl* (often ***a pair of pants***) two-legged outer clothing usually reaching from the waist to the ankles.
panty hose /ˈpænti ˌhouz/ *n* (used with a *pl verb*) one-piece garment which combines stockings and underpants.
papa /ˈpapə/ *n* [C] (*informal*) father.
pa·pacy /ˈpeipəsi/ *n* [C] (*pl* -ies) **1** position or authority of the pope. **2** period of a pope's reign. **3** system of church government by popes.
pa·pal /ˈpeipəl/ *adj* of the pope or the papacy.
pa·paw, paw·paw /ˈpɔˌpɔ/ = papaya.
pa·paya /pəˈpaiə/ *n* [C] (tropical American tree bearing a) large, yellow, melonlike fruit.
pa·per /ˈpeipər/ *n* **1** [U] substance manufactured from wood, rags, etc usually in the form of thin sheets, that is used for writing, printing, drawing, wrapping, packing, etc. **2** [C] piece or sheet of paper. **3** [C] newspaper: *the evening ~.* **4** (*pl*) official documents showing who a person is, what authority he has, etc. **5** [C] document. **6** [C] report; essay: *a ~ on currency reform.* **7** [U] wallpaper. □ *vt* cover with paper, esp wallpaper: *~ the dining room.*
paper·back /ˈpeipərˌbæk/ *n* [C] book with a flexible paper binding or cover (contrasted with *hardback*).
pa·per·weight /ˈpeiperˌweit/ *n* [C] small, heavy object used to hold down loose papers.
pa·poose /pæˈpus/ *n* [C] North American Indian baby.
pap·rika /pæˈprikə, pə-/ *n* [U] seasoning made from sweet red peppers that have been dried and ground.
pa·py·rus /pəˈpairəs/ *n* (*pl* ~es, papyri /pəˈpaiˌrai/) **1** [U] (paper made in ancient Egypt from a) tall water plant or reed. **2** [C] manuscript written on this paper.
par[1] /par/ *n* [U] **1** average or normal amount, degree, value, etc. ***above/below par,*** above/below the average or normal. **2** level of equality. ***on a par (with),*** equal (to). **3** number of strokes considered standard for completing a hole or course in golf.
Par.[2] *abbr* = Parish.
par.[3] *abbr* = paragraph.
par·able /ˈpærəbəl/ *n* [C] simple story designed to teach a moral lesson.
pa·rab·ola /pəˈræbələ/ *n* [C] (*pl* ~s) plane curve formed by the intersection of a cone with a plane that is parallel to one of its sides.
para·bolic /ˌpærəˈbalɪk/ *adj*
para·chute /ˈpærəˌʃut/ *n* [C] umbrella-shaped apparatus used for a safe jump from an aircraft or for dropping supplies, etc. □ *vt,vi* drop, descend, by means of a parachute.
para·chut·ist /-ɪst/ *n* [C]
pa·rade /pəˈreid/ *vt,vi* **1** (cause to) march in a procession. **2** make a display of; show off: *~ one's wealth.* □ *n* [C] **1 (a)** ceremonial parading of troops. **(b)** (also **parade ground**) area on which such parades are held. **2** festive procession with music, colorful costumes, etc: *the circus ~.* **3** crowd of people walking or strolling by: *the Easter ~.* **4** showy display or exhibition.
para·dise /ˈpærəˌdais/ *n* **1 Paradise,** the Garden of Eden, home of Adam and Eve in some religious traditions. **2 Paradise,** Heaven. **3** (with *a*) place or condition of perfect happiness.
para·dox /ˈpærəˌdaks/ *n* [C] statement that seems to be contradictory or false, but which may be seen to be true after some thought (eg "There is honor among thieves.")
para·doxi·cal /ˌpærəˈdaksɪkəl/ *adj*
para·doxi·cally /-kli/ *adv*
par·af·fin /ˈpærəfɪn/ *n* [U] waxy substance used for making candles, sealing and lubricating materials, etc.
para·gon /ˈpærəˌgan/ *n* [C] model of excellence; perfect example: *a ~ of virtue.*
para·graph /ˈpærəˌgræf/ *n* [C] **1** division of a piece of writing consisting of one or more sentences on one point or idea, that usually begins on a new line. **2** small item of news in a newspaper. □ *vt* divide into paragraphs.
para·keet /ˈpærəˌkit/ *n* [C] small, parrotlike bird. ⇨ illus at bird.
par·al·lel /ˈpærəˌlel/ *adj* **1** extending in the same direction and always at the same distance from one another: *~ lines; in a direction ~ with/to the main road.* **2** similar; corresponding: *Their situation is ~ to ours.* □ *n* [C] **1** parallel line or surface. **2** one of the imaginary circles around the earth, that is parallel to the equator and marks latitude. **3** match; person or thing that is the equal of another: *a brilliant career without*

(*a*) ~ *in modern times.* **4** comparison that shows a likeness or similarity: *draw a ~ between....* ◻ *vt* **1** (cause to) be or run parallel to. **2** draw or make a comparison to. **3** correspond to: *His experiences ~ mine in many instances.*

par·al·lelo·gram /ˌpærəˈleləˌgræm/ *n* [C] four-sided flat figure whose opposite sides are parallel and equal. ⇨ illus at geometry.

par·al·ysis /pəˈræləsɪs/ *n* [U] **1** loss of feeling or power to move in any part of the body. **2** (*fig*) inability to move or function.

para·lyt·ic /ˌpærəˈlɪtɪk/ *adj* of, causing, or suffering from paralysis(1). ◻ *n* [C] person suffering from paralysis.

para·lyze /ˈpærəˌlaiz/ *vt* **1** affect with paralysis. **2** (*fig*) make helpless: *~d with fear.*

para·me·cium /ˌpærəˈmisiəm/ *n* [C] (*pl* -cia /-siə/, ~s) very small, one-celled organism that moves about by means of hairlike projections.

para·mount /ˈpærəˌmaunt/ *adj* (*formal*) supreme; superior to all others; primary: *of ~ importance.*

para·noia /ˌpærəˈnɔiə/ *n* [U] mental disorder marked by delusions, eg of persecution or of one's importance.

para·noid /ˈpærəˌnɔid/, **para·noiac** /ˌpærəˈnɔiˌæk/ *n* [C], *adj* (person) suffering from paranoia.

para·pet /ˈpærəpɪt/ *n* [C] **1** low wall along the edge of a flat roof, side of a bridge, etc. **2** low wall or bank of earth, stone, etc to protect soldiers from enemy fire.

para·pher·nalia /ˌpærəfə(r)ˈneilyə/ *n* [U] (used with a *sing* or *pl verb*) **1** personal possessions. **2** equipment; gear.

para·phrase /ˈpærəˌfreiz/ *vt* restate; give the meaning of in different words. ◻ *n* [C] restatement.

para·ple·gia /ˌpærəˈplidʒə/ *n* [U] paralysis of the lower part of the body, including both legs.

para·plegic /ˌpærəˈplidʒɪk/ *n* [C], *adj* (person) suffering from paraplegia.

para·site /ˈpærəˌsait/ *n* [C] **1** organism living on or in another kind of organism, usually to the injury of its host. **2** person who lives off another and gives nothing in return.

para·sitic /ˌpærəˈsɪtɪk/ *adj*

para·sol /ˈpærəˌsɔl/ *n* [C] light umbrella carried for protection from the sun.

para·troops /ˈpærəˌtrups/ *n pl* troops trained and equipped for parachuting from aircraft.

para·trooper /ˈpærəˌtrupər/ *n* [C]

par·boil /ˈparˌbɔiəl/ *vt* (*pres p* ~ing /-ˌbɔilɪŋ/) boil (food) until partially cooked.

par·cel /ˈparsəl/ *n* [C] **1** package; bundle. ***part and parcel,*** ⇨ part¹ (1). **2** section or plot of land. **3** group; lot: *a ~ of idiots.* ◻ *vt* (-l-, -ll-) **1** divide into portions and distribute: *~ out the food.* **2** make into a parcel: *~ the books.*

parch /partʃ/ *vt* **1** make dry, esp with heat: *the ~ed deserts of North Africa.* **2** toast and dry: *~ed corn.*

parch·ment /ˈpartʃmənt/ *n* **1** [U] writing material prepared from the skin of a sheep or goat. **2** [U] kind of paper resembling parchment. **3** [C] document written on parchment.

par·don /ˈpardən/ *n* **1** [U] forgiveness: *ask for ~.* ***beg sb's pardon,*** ask forgiveness of him for a social error or omission. **2** [C] official release from punishment or penalty for an offense. ◻ *vt* **1** forgive; excuse: *~ her for doing wrong.* **2** release or free from punishment.

par·don·able /-əbəl/ *adj* that can be forgiven, etc.

pare /pær/ *vt* **1** cut away the outer part, edge or skin of: *~ apples for a pie.* **2** (*fig*) reduce as if by paring: *~ down one's expenses.*

paren¹ /pəˈren, ˈpærən/ *n* [C] (*informal*) (short for) parenthesis (compare the following entry).

paren.² *abbr* = parenthesis (compare the preceding entry).

par·ent /ˈpærənt/ *n* [C] **1** father or mother; ancestor. **2** (*fig*) source or originator.

ˈpar·ent·age /-ɪdʒ/ *n* [U] lineage; ancestry.

pa·rental /pəˈrentəl/ *adj* of a parent: *showing ~al care.*

pa·ren·the·sis /pəˈrenθəsɪs/ *n* [C] (*pl* -eses /-ˌsiz/) **1** word, phrase, or sentence placed within sentence, as an explanation, comment, etc. **2** one of two curved lines () used for this purpose or for grouping elements in a mathematical expression.

par·en·thetic /ˌpærənˈθetɪk/, **par·en·theti·cal** /-ɪkəl/ *adj*

par·en·theti·cally /-kli/ *adv*

par·ent·hood /ˈpærəntˌhʊd/ *n* [U] state of being a parent.

pari-mu·tuel /ˌpærəˈmyutʃuəl/ *n* [U] system of betting in which the winners are paid from the bets placed by the losers.

par·ish /ˈpærɪʃ/ *n* [C] **1** division or part of a diocese with its own church and clergymen. **2** persons living in such an area who attend the church. **3** district in the state of Louisiana which is equivalent to a county.

par·ish·ioner /pəˈrɪʃənər/ *n* [C] member or inhabitant of a parish.

par·ity /ˈpærəti/ *n* [U] equality in value, importance, etc.

park /park/ *n* [C] **1** public garden or public recreation ground in a town. **2** large area of grassland, trees, etc kept for public use and enjoyment. **3** stadium: *a ball ~.* **4** place for leaving or storing motor vehicles: *a trailer ~.* ◻ *vt,vi* **1** place or leave (a motor vehicle) temporarily: *Where can we ~ (the car)?* **2** (*informal*) put and leave (a person or thing) temporarily: *Where can I ~ my luggage?*

ˈparking lot, area for parking motor vehicles.

ˈparking meter, coin-operated meter which measures the time a vehicle may be parked in the space served by the meter.

parka /ˈparkə/ *n* [C] warm jacket with a hood.

Par·ker House roll /ˌparkər ˌhaus ˈroul/ *n* [C] soft luncheon or dinner roll, made by folding the dough before baking.

Parkinson's disease /ˈparkɪnsənz dɪˌziz/ *n* [U] chronic progressive disease of the nervous system, marked by muscular tremors and general weakness.

park·way /ˈparkˌwei/ *n* [C] broad, landscaped highway or thoroughfare.

par·ley /ˈparli/ *n* [C] (*pl* ~s) conference, esp between enemies or hostile parties. ◻ *vi* hold a parley.

par·lia·ment /ˈparləmənt/ *n* [C] **1** supreme law-making council or assembly of some countries. **2 Parliament,** national law making body of Great Britain, Canada, etc.

par·lia·men·tar·ian /ˌparləmənˈteriən/ *n* [C] person skilled in parliamentary rules and procedures.

par·lia·men·tary /ˌparləˈmentəri/ *adj*

par·lor /ˈparlər/ *n* [C] **1** room in a private house, hotel, club, etc, used for conversation, entertaining visitors, etc. **2** place for a special kind of business: *a ˈbeauty ~.*

par·ochial /pəˈroukiəl/ *adj* **1** of a parish. **2** (*fig*) limited, narrow: *a ~ mind/attitude.*

par·ochi·ally /-kiəli/ *adv*

parˈochial school, school maintained by a church parish or religious organization.

par·ody /ˈpærədi/ *n* (*pl* -ies) **1** [C,U] imitation of a person, literary work, musical composition, etc in which characteristics, features and styles are usually exaggerated for comic effect. **2** [C] poor or bad imitation: *a ~ of justice.* □ *vt* (*pt, pp* -ied) make a parody of.

pa·role /pəˈroul/ *n* [U] release of a prisoner before his full sentence has been served on condition of good behavior. □ *vt* set (a prisoner) free on parole.

par·ox·ysm /ˈpærəkˌsɪzəm/ *n* [C] **1** sudden attack or fit. **2** outburst (of pain, anger, laughter, etc).

par·quet /parˈkei/ *n* [C] **1** floor made of wood fitted together to make a pattern. **2** main floor of a theater.

par·ri·cide /ˈpærəˌsaid/ *n* **1** [U] murder of one's father, mother, or close relative. **2** [C] person guilty of this.

par·rot /ˈpærət/ *n* [C] **1** tropical bird with a short hooked bill and usually brightly colored feathers, which sometimes can be trained to imitate human speech. **2** person who repeats something without understanding it. □ *vt* repeat something without understanding it.

parry /ˈpæri/ *vt* (*pt,pp* -ied) **1** turn aside or block (a blow). **2** (*fig*) evade (a question). □ *n* [C] act of parrying, esp in fencing and boxing.

parse /pars/ *vt* **1** identify the part of speech, the form, and the grammatical function of a word in a phrase or sentence. **2** break down a sentence or phrase into its parts and explain how these parts are related to each other.

Par·si, Par·see /ˈparˌsi/ *n* [C] member of a religious sect in India descended from Persians who settled in India in the 8th century.

par·si·moni·ous /ˌparsəˈmouniəs/ *adj* stingy; miserly.

par·si·mo·ny /ˈparsəˌmouni/ *n* [U] stinginess.

pars·ley /ˈparsli/ *n* [U] herb with aromatic leaves, used to flavor or garnish food.

pars·nip /ˈparˌsnɪp/ *n* [C] (plant with a) long, white or pale-yellow root, used as a vegetable.

par·son /ˈparsən/ *n* [C] **1** minister in charge of a parish. **2** clergyman.

ˈpar·son·age /-ɪdʒ/ *n* [C] house provided for a minister by a church.

part[1] /part/ *n* [C] **1** (often *sing* without *a*) portion of a larger thing; something less than the whole: *We spent (a) ~ of our holiday in France. Parts of the book are interesting.* ***for the ˈmost part,*** in most cases; generally. ***in part,*** to some degree; partly. ***part and parcel,*** essential or inseparable part. **2** (*pl*) region; district: *in these/those ~s.* **3** any one of a number of equal divisions or units making up a whole: *A minute is the sixtieth ~ of an hour.* **4** division of an animal or plant body; organ. **5** person's share in some activity: *did her ~ to make the meeting a success.* ***take part,*** have a share in; participate: *Are you going to take ~ in the discussion?* **6** side in a dispute, conflict, etc. ***take sb's part,*** support him: *He always takes his brother's ~.* ***for ˈmy part,*** as far as I am concerned: *For my ~ I am quite happy about the division of the money.* **7** actor's lines or role: *played the ~ of Lady Macbeth.* **8** piece of a machine, instrument, etc: *spare ~s for a tractor.* **9** (*pl*) talent; natural abilities: *a man of ~s.* **10** (*music*) **(a)** melody for a particular voice or instrument. **(b)** musical score for this. **11** line where the hair is divided in combing. □ *adv* partly: *made ~ of iron and ~ of wood.*

part·ly *adv* to some extent.

ˌpart of ˈspeech *n* [C] (*gram*) class of words (eg *noun, verb, adjective*) which is determined by use or function.

ˌpart-ˈtime *adj, adv* for only a part of the working day or week: *be employed ~-time; ~-time teaching.*

part[2] /part/ *vt,vi* **1** (cause to) become separated: *We tried to ~ the two fighters. Let's ~ friends.* **2** depart; go away. **3** ***part with,*** give up possession; let go: *He hates to ~ with his money.* **4** divide into parts. **5** divide one's hair by combing or brushing.

par·take /parˈteik/ *vi,vt* (*pt* -took /-ˈtʊk/, *pp* -taken /-ˈteikən/) (*formal*) **1** take a share of: *They partook of our simple meal.* **2** take part in: *~ in the celebration.* **3** have some of the nature or characteristics of: *His political views ~ of an almost unbelievable naiveté.*

par·tial /ˈparʃəl/ *adj* **1** forming only a part; not complete: *a ~ success; a ~ eclipse of the sun.* **2** biased; favoring one person or side over another. **3** having a liking for: *~ to French wines.*

par·ti·ally /ˈparʃəli/ *adv*

par·ti·al·ity /ˌparʃiˈæləti/ *n* **1** [U] bias; being partial(2) in treatment of people, etc. **2** [C] fondness; special liking: *a ~ity for moonlight walks.*

par·tici·pant /parˈtɪsəpənt/ *n* [C] one who takes part in something.

par·tici·pate /parˈtɪsəˌpeit/ *vi* have a share or take part in: *~ in a plot.*

par·ti·ciple /ˈpartəˌsɪpəl/ *n* [C] (*gram*) (esp) verbal which can modify a noun but which retains some of the characteristics of a verb, such as tense and the ability to take an object: *"Hurrying" and "hurried" are the present and past ~s of "hurry."*

par·ti·cip·ial /ˌpartəˈsɪpiəl/ *adj*

par·ticle /ˈpartɪkəl/ *n* [C] **1** very small bit: *~s of dust.* **2** (*gram*) word (as an article or preposition) which serves to connect or express relationships.

par·ticu·lar /pər'tɪkyələr/ *adj* **1** relating to one as distinct from others: *in this ~ case*. **2** of or connected with a single person or thing. **3** special; exceptional; outstanding: *for no ~ reason. He took ~ trouble to get it right*. **4** very exact: *a full and ~ account of what we saw*. **5** difficult to satisfy: *She's very ~ about what she wears*. □ *n* [C] detail. ***in particular,*** especially: *I remember the color in ~*.

par·ticu·lar·ly *adv* **(a)** especially: *He was ~ly noticeable*. **(b)** specifically.

part·ing /'partɪŋ/ *n* [C] **1** departure. **2** (place of) separation or division.

par·ti·san /'partəzən/ *n* [C] **1** person devoted to a party, group or cause. **2** (esp) member of an armed resistance movement in a country occupied by enemy forces: *~ troops*. □ *adj* biased; uncritically devoted to a cause: *His loyalties are too ~*.

par·ti·tion /par'tɪʃən/ *n* **1** [U] division into parts: *the ~ of India in 1947*. **2** [C] thin wall or structure which divides a room or space. □ *vt* divide into sections, esp by using a partition(2): *~ off a room*.

part·ner /'partnər/ *n* [C] **1** person who takes part with another or others in some activity, esp in a business partnership. **2** either of two persons dancing together, playing a game together, etc. **3** husband or wife.

'part·ner·ship *n* **(a)** [U] state of being a partner. **(b)** [C] business organization in which two or more persons share the profits and losses: *enter/go into ~ship (with her)*.

par·took *pt* of partake.

par·tridge /'partrɪdʒ/ *n* [C] (*pl* ~, ~s) kinds of game bird of the same family as the quail.

party /'parti/ *n* (*pl* -ies) [C] **1** group of persons sharing the same political principles and beliefs, who work together to advance their policies and usually to nominate and support candidates for election to public office. **2** one of the persons or sides in a legal matter or dispute. **3** small group of persons traveling or working together, or on duty together: *a ~ of tourists*. **4** social gathering for pleasure: *a 'dinner/'birthday ~*. **5** person taking part in and approving of a matter or action: *be a ~ to the decision*. **6** (*informal*) person: *They arrested the wrong ~*.

'party-crasher *n* [C] (*informal*) person who attends a party without having been invited.

'party line, (a) telephone line shared by two or more persons. **(b)** official policy of a political party.

'party-pooper *n* [C] (*informal*) person who, by some act, lessens the general enjoyment at a party.

pas·chal /'pæskəl/ *adj* **1** of the Jewish Passover. **2** of Easter.

pass[1] /pæs/ *n* **1** [C] act of passing. **2** [C] movement or motion over something, made with the hand(s). **3** (*sing* only) situation; condition. ***bring to pass,*** cause to happen. ***come to pass,*** happen. ***reach/come to a fine/sad/pretty pass,*** reach a distressing state or condition. **4** [C] usually written permission or authority to travel, enter or leave a place, occupy a free seat, etc. **5** [C] (*sport*) act of kicking, throwing, or hitting a ball or puck to another player (of the same team). **6** [C] narrow way, esp over or through mountains. **7** [C] attempt; effort: *made a ~ at cleaning up, but couldn't finish it*. ***make a pass at,*** (*informal*) make an amorous or sexual approach. **8** [C] (in card games) act of passing (15).

pass[2] /pæs/ *vi,vt* (compare past[1]) **1** (cause to) move or proceed (*along, through, down, etc*): *~ through a small town. He ~ed his fingers through his hair*. **2** move or go by and beyond: *Turn right after ~ing the Post Office. The two ships ~ed (by) each other during the night*. **3** catch up with and go beyond: *She left an hour later, but her car ~ed ours on the road*. **4** go or cause to go through, across, over or between: *No complaints ~ed her lips*. **5** give by handing: *Please ~ (me) the butter. The letter was ~ed around to all the members of the family*. **6** change ownership or possession: *The estate ~ed to his niece*. **7** (of time) go by; elapse: *Six months ~ed and still we had no news of them*. **8** spend time: *How shall we ~ the evening?* ***pass the time,*** occupy a period of (spare) time pleasantly. **9** change from one state to another: *Water ~es from a liquid to a solid state when it freezes*. **10** be considered or accepted as: *He can easily ~ for an adult*. **11** enact; be enacted: *Congress ~ed the bill. The bill ~ed and became law*. **12** take place; happen: *Tell me everything that ~ed between you*. **13(a)** complete or go through successfully an examination, course of study, etc: *He finally ~ed French*. **(b)** allow (a student) to go through a course, etc successfully: *~ed all the seniors*. **14** give an opinion, judgment, etc: *~ sentence on an accused man. I can't ~ on the quality of your work without seeing it*. **15** (in card games) let one's turn go by without playing, betting, or making a bid. **16** (*sport*) throw, kick, hit, etc (a ball or puck) to a teammate. **17** discharge bodily wastes. ***pass water,*** urinate. **18** (special uses with *adverbial particles* and *prepositions*):

pass away, die: *He ~ed away peacefully*.

pass sth/sb off as, represent a person or thing falsely: *He tried to ~ himself off as a qualified doctor. She ~ed it off as a joke*.

pass on, die.

pass out, (*informal*) faint.

pass sb/sth over, fail to notice or consider: *~ over an important mistake. They ~ed me over in favor of a younger man*.

pass sth up, (*informal*) neglect it; not take advantage of something: *~ up an opportunity*.

pass.[3] *abbr* = **1** passenger(s). **2** passive.

pass·able /'pæsəbəl/ *adj* **1** that can be passed or crossed: *Are the roads ~ yet?* **2** fairly good but not excellent: *a ~ knowledge of German*.

pass·ably /-əbli/ *adv*

pas·sage /'pæsɪdʒ/ *n* **1** [U] passing; act of going past, through or across: *the ~ of time*. **2** [C] journey, esp by sea: *a rough ~ to Marseille*. **3** right to travel or pass. **4** [C] way through: *force a ~ through a crowd*. **5** [C] narrow way (as a path, channel, or corridor) through which something may pass. **6** [C] usually short piece taken from a speech, piece of writing, musical composition, etc. **7** enactment or passing of a bill by a legislature.

ˈ**pass·age·way** *n* = passage(4).

pass·book /ˈpæsˌbʊk/ *n* [C] book in which the deposits and withdrawals of a bank account are recorded for the customer.

passé /pæˈsei/ *adj* outdated.

pas·sen·ger /ˈpæsəndʒər/ *n* [C] person driven or conveyed in a bus, taxi, train, ship, aircraft, etc.

passer·by /ˌpæsərˈbai/ *n* [C] (*pl* passersby) person who passes by.

pas·sing /ˈpæsɪŋ/ *adj* going by; not lasting: *the ~ years*. □ *n* [U] **1** the act of going by: *the ~ of the old year*, ie on New Year's Eve. **2** death.

passion /ˈpæʃən/ *n* **1** [U] strong feeling or emotion, as love, hate or anger. **2(a)** [U] enthusiasm; strong liking: *a ~ for salted peanuts*. **(b)** [C] object of such liking: *His ~s are music and art*. **3 Passion,** the suffering and death of Jesus.

passion·less *adj*

ˈ**Passion play,** drama about the Passion of Christ.

ˌ**Passion** ˈ**Sunday,** the fifth Sunday in Lent.

passion·ate /ˈpæʃənɪt/ *adj* filled with or showing passion: *a ~ nature; ~ language*.

passion·ate·ly *adv*

pas·sive /ˈpæsɪv/ *adj* **1** acted upon but not acting. **2** submissive; not actively resisting.

pas·sive·ly *adv*

pas·sive·ness /-nɪs/ *n* [U]

ˌ**passive** ˈ**voice,** (*gram*) verb form which indicates that its subject is acted upon: *"The cake was eaten by the children"* is in the passive voice. ⇨ active.

pass·key /ˈpæsˌki/ *n* [C] skeleton key; master key.

Pass·over /ˈpæˌsouvər/ *n* Jewish religious festival commemorating the liberation of the Jews from slavery in Egypt.

pass·port /ˈpæsˌpɔrt/ *n* [C] **1** official document issued to a citizen, which identifies him and gives him permission to leave his country for travel abroad. **2** (*fig*) anything that enables one to win or obtain something: *Is flattery a ~ to success with that teacher?*

pass·word /ˈpæsˌwərd/ *n* [C] secret word or phrase that must be spoken in order to pass a guard or sentry.

past[1] /pæst/ *adj* gone by in time: *during the ~ week; in times ~; ~ generations*. □ *n* [U] **1 the past,** past or former time: *We cannot change the ~*. **2** person's past life or experiences: *We know nothing of his ~*. **3** = past tense.

ˌ**past** ˈ**tense,** (*gram*) verb tense that expresses an action or state in the past.

past[2] /pæst/ *prep* **1** beyond in time; after: *half ~ two; a woman ~ middle age*. **2** beyond in space; up to and farther than: *He walked ~ the house*. **3** beyond the limits, power or range of: *That old house is ~ saving*, is too old, etc. ***not put sth past sb,*** consider him capable of any action, esp a dishonest one: *I wouldn't put it ~ him to run off with the money*. □ *adv* so as to go or pass by: *walk/march/go/run/hurry ~*.

pasta /ˈpastə/ *n* **1** [U] dough made of flour, water, and sometimes eggs, mixed and formed or cut into various shapes. **2** [C] dish of cooked pasta.

paste /peist/ *n* [U] **1** soft mixture of flour, shortening, etc, used for making pastry. **2** food that has been ground into a soft, moist mass: *tomato ~*. **3** mixture used for sticking things together: *wallpaper ~*. **4** glassy material used in making artificial gems. □ *vi* **1** stick together with paste (3). **2** cover with something which is pasted on. **3** (*sl*) punch or hit hard.

ˈ**paste·board** *n* [U] = cardboard.

pas·tel /pæˈstel/ *n* [C] **1** crayon made of a dried paste of ground color. **2** picture drawn with such a crayon or crayons. **3** soft, light, delicate color.

pas·tern /ˈpæstərn/ *n* [C] part of a horse's leg between the fetlock and the joint at the hoof.

pas·teur·ize /ˈpæstʃəˌraiz/ *vt* heat (milk, etc) in order to destroy disease-producing and other unwanted bacteria.

pas·teur·iz·ation /ˌpæstʃərəˈzeiʃən/ *n* [U]

pas·time /ˈpæsˌtaim/ *n* [C] activity that makes time pass pleasantly: *Flirting was her favorite ~*.

pas·tor /ˈpæstər/ *n* [C] minister or priest who is in charge of a church or parish.

pas·toral /ˈpæstərəl/ *adj* **1** of or relating to shepherds or country life: *~ poetry*. **2** of or relating to a pastor.

pas·tra·mi /pəˈstrami/ *n* [U] seasoned, smoked beef, made usually from a shoulder cut.

pas·try /ˈpeistri/ *n* (*pl* -ies) **1** [U] rich dough made of flour, shortening, etc used to make pies, tarts, etc. **2** [C] something made with this.

pas·ture /ˈpæstʃər/ *n* [U] **1** piece of land suitable for grazing animals. **2** grass and other plants for grazing cattle, horses, etc. □ *vt,vi* **1** put an animal to graze. **2** (of animals) graze.

pasty /ˈpeisti/ *adj* (-ier, -iest) like paste(1), esp in having a white and unhealthy color: *a ~ complexion*.

pat[1] /pæt/ *vt,vi* (-tt-) **1** stroke or tap gently with the open hand, esp as a sign of affection: *pat a dog*. ***pat sb/oneself on the back,*** give praise or approval to. **2** smooth or flatten by patting. □ *n* [C] **1** tap or stroke made with the open hand, eg as a caress. **2** small mass of something, esp butter, formed by patting(2). **3** light sound made by patting.

pat[2] /pæt/ *adj* (-tter, -ttest) **1** ready and suitable for use: *a pat answer to the problem*. **2 *have sth down/know sth pat,*** know it perfectly. **3 *stand pat,*** stick firmly to one's position.

pat.[3] *abbr* = **1** patent. **2** patented.

patch[1] /pætʃ/ *n* [C] **1** piece of material used to cover a hole, tear, or worn place: *a coat with ~es on the elbows; a ~ on the inner tube of a tire*. **2** bandage or pad worn to protect an injured eye. **3** small, irregular area or part that differs from its surroundings: *a dog with a white ~ on its neck*. **4** small area: *a ~ of ground*.

patch[2] /pætʃ/ *vt* **1** put a patch on; mend with a patch. **2** make out of scraps or patches of material. **3 *patch up,*** repair; settle; mend: *~ up a quarrel*, end it.

patch ˈ**pocket,** pocket made by sewing a patch of (usually different) material on a garment.

patch·work /ˈpætʃˌwərk/ *n* [U] **1** something

made up of pieces of cloth of various sizes, shapes and colors, sewn together usually in a pattern: (as an *adjective*) *a ~ quilt*. ⇨ illus at quilt. **2** (*fig*) something made up of various different parts.

pate /peit/ *n* [C] head, esp the top of the head.

pa·tel·la /pəˈtelə/ *n* [C] (*pl* ~s) kneecap. ⇨ illus at skeleton.

pat·ent[1] /ˈpætənt/ *adj* **1** evident, easily seen: *It was ~ to everyone that he disliked the idea.* **2** protected by a patent[2].

pat·ent·ly *adv* clearly; obviously.

pat·ent[2] /ˈpætənt/ *n* [C] government authority giving an inventor the exclusive right to make, use or sell a new invention. □ *vt* **1** obtain a patent for. **2** give a patent to.

pat·ent leather /ˌpætənt ˈleðər/ *n* [U] leather with a very smooth, shiny surface, used for making shoes, handbags, etc.

pat·ent medi·cine /ˌpætənt ˈmedəsən/ *n* [C,U] medicine made and packaged by the manufacturer for use and purchase without a doctor's prescription.

pa·ter·nal /pəˈtərnəl/ *adj* **1** of or like a father: *~ care*. **2** related through the father: *my ~ grandfather*.

pa·ter·nal·ism /-ˌlızəm/ *n* [U] principle or practice of governing people in a fatherly way which limits their freedom or responsibility.

pa·ter·nally /-nəli/ *adv*

pa·ter·nity /pəˈtərnəti/ *n* [U] **1** fatherhood; being a father. **2** ancestry or origin on the father's side.

pater·nos·ter /ˈpætərˌnastər/ *n* the Lord's Prayer.

path /pæθ/ *n* [C] (*pl* ~s /pæðz/) **1** way made esp by walking: *Keep to the ~ or you may lose your way*. ⇨ footpath. **2** line along which something or somebody moves: *the ˈflight ~ of a spacecraft*. **3** way of life, conduct, etc.

path·less *adj* having no paths: *~less jungles*.

ˈpath·way *n* [C] path.

pa·thetic /pəˈθetık/ *adj* **1** arousing pity or sorrow: *a ~ sight; ~ ignorance*. **2** melancholy; sad.

pa·theti·cally /-kli/ *adv*

path·o·logical /ˌpæθəˈladʒıkəl/ *adj* **1** of or caused by disease. **2** of or relating to pathology.

path·o·logi·cally /-kli/ *adv*

path·ol·ogist /pəˈθalədʒıst/ *n* [C] physician who specilizes in pathology.

pa·thol·ogy /pəˈθalədʒi/ *n* [U] scientific study of diseases.

pa·thos /ˈpeiˌθas/ *n* [U] quality in life or in a work of art, which arouses a feeling of pity, sympathy or tenderness.

pa·tience /ˈpeiʃəns/ *n* [U] **1** ability to endure trouble, suffering, inconvenience, etc, calmly and without complaining. **2** self-control and perseverance in spite of opposition or difficulties. **3** absence of haste, rashness.

pa·tient[1] /ˈpeiʃənt/ *adj* having, showing, or requiring patience: *be ~ with a child*.

pa·tient·ly *adv*

pa·tient[2] /ˈpeiʃənt/ *n* [C] person under medical treatment.

patio /ˈpætiou/ *n* [C] (*pl* ~s) **1** courtyard, open to the sky. **2** often paved area near a house or apartment, used for recreation.

pa·tri·arch /ˈpeitriˌark/ *n* [C] **1** venerable old man. **2** male head of a large family or tribe. **3** high-ranking bishop in some churches.

pa·tri·archal /ˌpeitriˈarkəl/ *adj*

pa·tri·cian /pəˈtrıʃən/ *n* [C] **1** member of the nobility in ancient Rome. **2** person of aristocratic birth or refined tastes.

pat·ri·cide /ˈpætrəˌsaid/ *n* **1** [U] killing of one's own father. **2** [C] person guilty of this.

pat·ri·mony /ˈpætrəˌmouni/ *n* [C] (*pl* -ies) **1** property inherited from one's father or ancestors. **2** heritage. **3** endowment of a church, etc.

pat·ri·mo·nial /ˌpætrəˈmouniəl/ *adj*

pa·triot /ˈpeitriət/ *n* [C] person who loves and defends his country.

pa·tri·otic /ˌpeitriˈatık/ *adj* having, showing, the qualities of a patriot.

pa·tri·oti·cally /-kli/ *adv*

pa·triot·ism /ˈpeitriəˌtızəm/ *n* [U] love and devotion for one's country.

pa·trol /pəˈtroul/ *vt,vi* (-ll-) go around (an area) to see that all is well and to look out for trouble. □ *n* **1** [U] the act of patrolling: *soldiers on ~*. **2** [C] person(s), ship(s) or aircraft on patrol.

pa·trol·man /-mən/ *n* [C] (*pl* ~men /-men/) policeman who patrols an area.

pa·tron /ˈpeitrən/ *n* [C] **1** person who encourages and supports a person, cause, activity, etc: *a ~ of the arts*. **2** regular customer or client.

ˈpa·tron·ess /-ıs/ *n* [C] woman patron(1).

ˌpatron ˈsaint, saint regarded as the special protector of a church, town, person, profession, etc.

pa·tron·age /ˈpeitrənıdʒ/ *n* [U] **1** support, encouragement, given by a patron. **2** power to appoint people to government positions: *owes his job to ~*. **3** trade given by customers to a store, restaurant, etc.

pa·tron·ize /ˈpeitrəˌnaiz/ *vt* **1** act as patron toward; support: *~ a young musician*. **2** do business with as a regular customer. **3** treat (a person) in a condescending way.

pat·ron·iz·ing *adj*

pat·ron·iz·ing·ly *adv*

pat·ter[1] /ˈpætər/ *n* [U] rapid, easy speech used by a salesman, magician, comedian, etc.

pat·ter[2] /ˈpætər/ *n* [U] sound of quick, light taps or footsteps: *the ~ of rain on a roof; the ~ of tiny feet*. □ *vi* **1** tap or strike lightly. **2** move with quick, light steps: *~ed around in slippers*.

pat·tern /ˈpætərn/ *n* [C] **1** excellent example: *She's a ~ of all the virtues*. **2** something used as a model or guide: *a paper ~ for making a dress*. **3** decorative or ornamental design, eg on a carpet, on wallpaper, or cloth: *a ~ of roses; geometrical ~s*. **4** set of elements, features, etc making a repeated or regular arrangement: *new ~s of family life*. □ *vt* model; design or make according to a pattern.

pat·ty /ˈpæti/ *n* [C] (*pl* -ies) small, flat cake of food.

pau·city /ˈpɔsəti/ *n* [U] (*formal*) smallness of number or quantity.

paunch /pɔntʃ/ *n* [C] belly, esp one that is large or sticks out.

paunchy *adj* (-ier, -iest)

pau·per /ˈpɔpər/ *n* [C] very poor person, esp one who is supported by charity.

pause /pɔz/ *n* [C] **1** short interval or stop (while doing or saying something): *during a ~ in the conversation.* **2** (*music*) sign over or under a note, rest, etc to show that it is to be lengthened. □ *vi* stop for a short time: *~ to look around.*

pave /peiv/ *vt* cover with stones, bricks, concrete, etc to make a smooth surface for walking or driving: *a path ~d with brick.* ***pave the way,*** make the way easy or smooth: *His discovery ~ed the way for many new inventions.*

pave·ment /ˈpeivmənt/ *n* [C] hard, paved surface, as of a street or sidewalk.

pa·vil·ion /pəˈvɪlyən/ *n* [C] **1** light building in a park, athletic field, etc. used for shelter, or recreation. **2** large, ornate tent.

paw /pɔ/ *n* [C] animal's foot, esp of an animal that has claws or nails. □ *vt* **1** strike or touch with the paw(s). **2** strike (the ground) with a hoof. **3** handle awkwardly, rudely or too familiarly.

pawn[1] /pɔn/ *n* [C] **1** least valuable piece in the game of chess. **2** person used or controlled by another.

pawn[2] /pɔn/ *vt* leave or deposit (clothing, jewelry, etc) as security for money borrowed: *The medical student ~ed his microscope to pay his rent.* □ *n* [U] state of being pawned: *My watch is in ~.*

pawn·broker /ˈpɔnˌbroukər/ *n* [C] person licensed to lend money at interest on the security of goods left with him.

paw·paw = papaw.

pay[1] /pei/ *n* [U] **1** money paid for regular work or services: *get an increase in pay.* **2** state of being employed. ***in the pay of,*** employed by (often with a suggestion of dishonor): *in the pay of the enemy.*

ˈpay·check *n* [C] check in payment of salary or wages.

ˈpay·day *n* [C] regular day on which wages, salaries, etc are (to be) paid.

ˈpay·phone *n* [C] coin-operated telephone.

ˈpay·roll *n* [C] **(a)** list of persons to be paid and the amounts due to each. **(b)** total amount of wages, salaries, etc to be paid.

pay ˈtelevision, pay T.ˈV. *n* **(a)** [U] system of closed-circuit television programs obtainable for a monthly fee. **(b)** [C] coin-operated television set.

pay[2] /pei/ *vt,vi* (*pt,pp* paid /peid/) **1** give (a person) money for goods, services, etc: *You must pay me what you owe. I paid you last week. He paid $600 to a dealer for that car.* **2** settle (debts, etc): *Have you paid all your taxes?* **3** be profitable: *He says that sheep farming doesn't pay.* **4** give or yield as a return: *His work pays well.* **5** give or offer: *Please pay more attention to your work. He seldom pays his wife any compliments.* ***pay through the nose,*** ⇨ nose[1](1). ***pay a visit,*** visit. **6** (special uses with *adverbial particles* and *prepositions*):

pay sth back, return (money, etc) that has been borrowed. ***pay sb back (for sth),*** punish him; have one's revenge: *I've paid him back for the trick he played on me.*

pay for, **(a)** give money that is due or owed: *pay for the use of the room.* **(b)** suffer pain or punishment for: *He'll pay for this foolish behavior.*

pay off, pay one's obligations in full: *pay off a mortgage.*

pay out, (*naut*) slacken and allow (rope) to run out freely.

pay up, pay in full what is owing: *If you don't pay up, I'll take legal action.*

payer /ˈpeiər/ *n* [C]

pay·able /ˈpeiəbəl/ *adj* which must or may be paid.

payee /peiˈ(y)i/ *n* [C] person to whom money is (to be) paid.

pay·ment /ˈpeimənt/ *n* **1** [U] paying: *demand prompt ~.* **2** [C] sum of money (to be) paid: *$50 now and ten monthly ~s of $5.* **3** [C,U] (*fig*) something given in return, as reward or punishment.

pay·off /ˈpeiˌɔf/ *n* [C] (*informal*) **1** (time of) full and final settlement or of revenge. **2** climax of a story, incident, or series of events.

pc(s). *abbr* = piece(s).

PD[1] *abbr* = Police Department.

pd.[2] *abbr* = paid.

P.D.Q. /ˌpi ˌdi ˈkyu/ *abbr* (*sl*) = pretty damned quick.

PDST *abbr* = Pacific Daylight Saving Time.

PE /ˌpi ˈi/ *abbr* = physical education.

pea /pi/ *n* [C] (plant bearing) round, edible seeds in long, green pods. ⇨ illus at vegetable. ***as alike as two peas (in a pod),*** exactly alike.

peace /pis/ *n* [U] **1** state of freedom from war: *be at ~ with neighboring countries. After a brief ~* (= a brief period of peace) *war broke out again.* **2** treaty of ~ to end a war: *Peace was signed between the two countries.* **3** freedom from civil disorder. ⇨ Justice of the Peace. **4** rest; quiet; calm: *the ~ of the countryside.* ***at peace (with),*** **(a)** in a state of calm or harmony. **(b)** not at war. ***in peace,*** peacefully: live in ~ with one's neighbors.

ˈpeace·maker *n* [C] person who settles an argument or conflict.

ˈpeace pipe, (a) pipe(5a) smoked by North American Indians as a sign of peace and friendship. **(b)** (*fig*) any token of a desire to end a quarrel, etc. ***smoke a/the peace pipe,*** end a conflict, argument, etc.

peace·ful /ˈpisfəl/ *adj* **1** inclined to peace; not violent or warlike: *~ nations.* **2** calm; quiet: *a ~ evening.*

peace·ful·ly /-fəli/ *adv*

peace·ful·ness /-nɪs/ *n* [U]

peach /pitʃ/ *n* **1** [C] (tree with) juicy, round fruit with delicate yellowish-pink skin and a rough stone-like seed. ⇨ illus at fruit. **2** [U] yellowish-pink color. **3** [C] (*informal*) person or thing greatly admired or liked: *Our new teacher is a ~!*

pea coat /ˈpi ˌkout/ *n* [C] = pea jacket.

pea·cock /ˈpiˌkak/ *n* [C] male peafowl noted for its brilliant blue and green feathers and fine tail feathers which can be spread out like a fan.

pea·fowl /ˈpiˌfaul/ *n* [C] (*pl* ~, ~s) large bird of Asia and the East Indies, that is related to the pheasant.

pea·hen /ˈpiˌhen/ *n* [C] female of the peacock.

pea jacket /ˈpi ˌdʒækɪt/ *n* [C] heavy, double-breasted jacket, esp as worn by sailors.

peak /pik/ *n* [C] **1** projecting point. **2** (pointed top of a) mountain. **3** visor of a cap; projecting brim (to shade the eyes). **4** highest level, height, or intensity: *~ hours of traffic*, times when the traffic is heaviest.

peaked[1] /pikt/ *adj* having a peak: *a ~ cap/roof*.

peaked[2] /ˈpikɪd/ *adj* pale or sickly in appearance.

peal /piəl/ *n* [C] **1** loud ringing of a bell or of a set of bells. **2** set of bells tuned to each other. **3** loud sound or series of sounds: *a ~ of thunder; ~s of laughter*. □ *vi,vt* (*pres p* ~ing /ˈpilɪŋ/) ring or sound loudly.

pea·nut /ˈpiˌnət/ *n* [C] **1** trailing plant of the pea family bearing edible seeds in pods which ripen underground. **2** one of these pods. **3** oily, nut-like seed of this plant. **4** (*sl*, usually *pl*) very small or trivial amount.

ˈpeanut brittle, hard candy containing peanuts.

ˈpeanut butter, paste of ground roasted peanuts.

pear /per/ *n* [C] (tree with) sweet, juicy fruit, usually tapering toward the stalk. ⇨ illus at fruit.

pearl /pərl/ *n* **1** [C] silvery-white or bluish-white rounded body that is formed inside the shells of some oysters and is used as a gem: *a necklace of ~s; a ~ necklace*. **2** [U] mother-of-pearl. **3** [C] something that resembles a pearl. **4** [C] person or thing that is highly valued: *~s of wisdom. She's a ~ among women*.

peas·ant /ˈpezənt/ *n* [C] (in Europe) member of the class of farm laborers or of small farmers who rent or own their land.

peas·ant·ry /ˈpezəntri/ *n* peasants of a country or as a class.

peat /pit/ *n* [U] plant material partly decomposed by the action of water, used as a fuel: *a ˈ~ bog*, a marshy place where peat is found.

pebble /ˈpebəl/ *n* [C] small, rounded stone.

peb·bly /ˈpeb(ə)li/ *adj* (-ier, -iest)

pe·can /pɪˈkan, pɪˈkæn/ *n* [C] (nut of a) kind of hickory tree growing in the southern region of the US.

pec·ca·ry /ˈpekəri/ *n* [C] (*pl* -ies) wild, piglike animal native to tropical America.

peck[1] /pek/ *n* [C] unit of dry measure equal to 2 gallons or ¼ of a bushel.

peck[2] /pek/ *vi,vt* **1** pick up or strike with the beak: *hens ~ing at the corn/each other*. **2** make by this means: *~ing a hole in the sack*. **3** tap or strike: *~ing away at the typewriter*. **4** eat only small amounts: *~ at one's food*. □ *n* [C] **1** strike with the beak. **2** mark made by this. **3** (*informal*) hurried kiss.

pec·tin /ˈpektɪn/ *n* [U] any of certain substances found in ripe fruits, that are used in preparing jellies.

pec·toral /ˈpektərəl/ *adj* of or relating to the chest or breast: *a ~ muscle/fin*.

pe·cu·liar /pɪˈkyulyər/ *adj* **1** distinctively belonging to or characteristic of one person, thing, etc: *customs ~ to these tribes*. **2** strange; unusual; odd: *There's something ~ about him*.

pe·cu·liar·ly *adv*

pe·cu·liar·ity /pɪˌkyuliˈærəti/ *n* (*pl* -ies) **1** [U] the quality of being peculiar. **2** [C] something distinctive or characteristic. **3** [C] something odd or strange.

pe·cuni·ary /pɪˈkyuniˌeri/ *adj* (*formal*) of money: *~ reward*.

peda·gog·ic, peda·gogi·cal /ˌpedəˈgadʒɪk, -ɪkəl/ *adj* of pedagogy.

peda·gogue /ˈpedəˌgag/ *n* [C] (esp a pedantic) teacher.

peda·gogy /ˈpedəˌgadʒi/ *n* [U] (*formal*) art or science of teaching.

pedal /ˈpedəl/ *n* [C] lever (eg on a bicycle, sewing machine, organ or piano) worked by the foot or feet. □ *vi,vt* (-l-, -ll-) use, operate by using, a pedal or pedals.

ped·ant /ˈpedənt/ *n* [C] **1** person who puts too much stress on formal rules and trivial details. **2** person who makes a tiresome show of his knowledge.

pe·dan·tic /pɪˈdæntɪk/ *adj* of or like a pedant.

pe·danti·cally /-kli/ *adv*

ped·ant·ry /ˈpedəntri/ *n* [U] **(a)** tiresome and unnecessary display of knowledge. **(b)** too much insistence on formal rules.

peddle /ˈpedəl/ *vi,vt* **1** go from house to house trying to sell small articles. **2** (*fig*) spread; give out: *She is always peddling gossip*.

ped·dler *n* [C]

ped·estal /ˈpedəstəl/ *n* [C] **1** base of a column, or support for a statue, vase, or other work of art. **2** position of esteem or high regard: *placed him on a ~*.

pe·des·trian /pɪˈdestriən/ *n* [C] person walking in a street, etc. □ *adj* **1** connected with walking. **2** on foot. **3** uninteresting; unimaginative and ordinary.

pedia·tric·ian /ˌpidiəˈtrɪʃən/ *n* [C] physician who specializes in pediatrics.

pedi·at·rics /ˌpidiˈætrɪks/ *n* (used with a *sing verb*) branch of medicine concerned with children, their care, and their illnesses.

pedi·cure /ˈpedəˌkyʊr/ *n* [C] beauty treatment and care of the feet and toe nails.

pedi·gree /ˈpedəˌgri/ *n* **1** [C] list of ancestors. **2** [U] ancestry; lineage. **3** record of ancestors of esp a purebred animal.

ped·i·greed *adj*

pe·dom·eter /pɪˈdamətər/ *n* [C] device that measures the distance a person covers in walking.

peek /pik/ *vi* look or show briefly: *~ed through the window; violets ~ing through the leaves*. □ *n* [C] quick look: *have a ~ at the answers before doing the exercises*.

peel /piəl/ *vt,vi* (*pres p* ~ing /ˈpilɪŋ/) **1** take the skin off (fruit, etc): *~ a banana; ~ potatoes*. **2** come off in strips or flakes: *The wallpaper is ~ing off. After a day in the hot sun my skin began to ~/my face ~ed*. □ *n* [U] skin of fruit, some vegetables, etc ⇨ illus at fruit.

peeler /ˈpilər/ *n* [C] device used for peeling fruit and vegetables.

peep[1] /pip/ *n* [C] short, quick look, often made secretly or cautiously: *have a ~ at her through* *the keyhole.* □ *vi* **1** take a peek: *neighbors ~ing at us from behind curtains.* **2** show slightly.

peep[2] /pip/ *n* [C] weak, shrill sound made by mice, young birds, etc. □ *vi* make this sound.

peer[1] /pɪr/ *n* [C] person equal in rank, merit or quality: *It will not be very easy to find his ~.*

peer[2] /pɪr/ *vi* **1** look closely, as if unable to see well: *~ into dark corners; ~ing at her over his spectacles.* **2** peep(2).

peer·less /ˈpɪrlɪs/ *adj* unmatched; having no equal.

peeve /piv/ *n* [C] something that irritates or annoys: *Carelessness is my pet ~,* carelessness is the thing that annoys me most. □ *vt* irritate.

peev·ish *adj* irritable; fretful.

pee·wee /ˈpiˌwi/ *n* [C] very small person or thing.

peg[1] /peg/ *n* [C] **1** usually cylindrical pin often made of wood, used to fasten things or to plug a hole: *a tent peg.* ***a square peg in a round hole,*** a person or thing that is unsuitable for a purpose. **2** projecting hook used to hang clothing on. **3** wooden screw for tightening or loosening the strings of a musical instrument in order to raise or lower the pitch. **4** degree; step. ***take sb 'down a peg (or two),*** make him feel less important.

peg[2] /peg/ *vt,vi* (-gg-) **1** fasten with pegs: *peg a tent down.* **2** mark, eg by means of pegs. **3** keep or hold to a certain level.

pe·king·ese /ˌpikɪˈniz/ *n* [C] (*pl* ~) small Chinese breed of dog with a broad, flat face and long, silky hair.

peli·can /ˈpelɪkən/ *n* [C] large waterbird with a large bill under which hangs a pouch for storing food.

pel·let /ˈpelɪt/ *n* [C] **1** small ball of food, bread, etc. **2** small shot, eg as used in an air gun.

pell-mell, pell·mell /ˌpel-ˈmel/ *adv* in a hurrying, disorderly manner.

pelt[1] /pelt/ *n* [C] animal's skin with the fur or hair on it.

pelt[2] /pelt/ *vt,vi* **1** hurl or throw at: *~ them with stones/snowballs/mud.* **2** (of rain, etc) fall heavily; beat: *The rain was ~ing down.* □ *n* [C] pelting. ***at full pelt,*** as fast as possible.

pel·vic /ˈpelvɪk/ *adj* of the pelvis.

pel·vis /ˈpelvɪs/ *n* [C] (*pl* ~es, pelves /ˈpelˌviz/) (*anat*) basin-shaped structure formed by the hip bones and the lower part of the backbone. ⇨ illus at skeleton.

pen[1] /pen/ *n* [C] instrument for writing with ink: *a ballpoint/quill/fountain pen.* □ *vt* (-nn-) write (a letter, etc) with a pen.

pen[2] /pen/ *n* [C] small, usually fenced enclosure, esp for animals. □ *vt* (-nn-) ***pen up/in,*** shut up (as) in a pen.

pen[3] /pen/ *n* [C] (*sl*) penitentiary.

penal /ˈpinəl/ *adj* connected with punishment: *~ laws.*

pe·nal·ize /ˈpinəˌlaiz, ˈpenə-/ *vt* give a penalty to.

pen·alty /ˈpenəlti/ *n* (*pl* -ies) **1** [U] punishment for doing wrong, for failure to obey rules, etc. **2** [C] something (such as imprisonment, payment of a fine, etc) imposed as punishment: *The ~ for theft used to be death.* **3** disadvantage, suffering, or loss: *The ~ for not working will be failing the exam.* **4** (*sport*) punishment given to a player or team for breaking a rule: *The referee gave the other team a ~ of 5 yards.*

pen·ance /ˈpenəns/ *n* [U] **1** act performed to show repentance. **2** in some Christian churches, a sacrament which includes confession, repentance, punishment, and absolution.

pence /pens/ *n pl* ⇨ penny(2).

pen·cil /ˈpensəl/ *n* [C] **1** instrument for drawing or writing, esp one made of graphite encased in wood or fixed in a holder. **2** something that is shaped or used like a pencil: *an eyebrow ~.* □ *vt* (-l-, -ll-) write, draw, mark, with a pencil.

pend. *abbr* = pending.

pen·dant /ˈpendənt/ *n* [C] ornament which hangs down, esp one attached to a necklace, bracelet, etc.

pend·ing /ˈpendɪŋ/ *adj* waiting to be decided or settled: *The lawsuit was still ~.* □ *prep* until: *~ his acceptance of the offer.*

pen·du·lum /ˈpendʒələm/ *n* [C] weight hung from a fixed point so that it swings freely, esp one that regulates the movement of a clock. ***the swing of the pendulum,*** (*fig*) reaction or movement from one extreme to the opposite extreme: *the swing of the ~ from love to hate.*

pen·etrable /ˈpenətrəbəl/ *adj* (*formal*) that can be penetrated.

pen·etrate /ˈpenəˌtreit/ *vt,vi* **1** make a way into or through: *The cat's sharp claws ~d my skin.* **2** enter and spread through: *The smell ~d (into) the room.* **3** see into or through: *Our eyes could not ~ the darkness.* **4** (*fig*) understand.

pen·etrat·ing *adj* **(a)** able to see and understand quickly and well. **(b)** piercing; sharp.

pen·etrat·ing·ly *adv*

pen·etra·tion /ˌpenəˈtreiʃən/ *n* [U] **1** penetrating. **2** ability to understand.

pen·guin /ˈpengwɪn/ *n* [C] seabird of the Antarctic with webbed feet and flipperlike wings that are used for swimming.

peni·cil·lin /ˌpenəˈsɪlɪn/ *n* [U] antibiotic drug that prevents germs from surviving or multiplying.

pen·in·sula /pəˈnɪnsələ/ *n* [C] (*pl* ~s) area of land almost surrounded by water or projecting into the sea.

pen·in·su·lar /-lər/ *adj*

pe·nis /ˈpinɪs/ *n* [C] male organ of copulation.

peni·tence /ˈpenətəns/ *n* [U] sorrow and regret for doing wrong.

peni·tent /ˈpenətənt/ *adj* feeling or showing regret or remorse. □ *n* [C] person who is penitent.

peni·tent·ly *adv*

peni·ten·tiary /ˌpenəˈtenʃ(ə)ri/ *n* [C] (*pl* -ies) prison for persons convicted of serious crimes.

pen·knife /ˈpenˌnaif/ *n* [C] (*pl* -knives /-ˌnaivz/) small pocketknife with one or more folding blades.

pen·man·ship /ˈpenmənˌʃɪp/ *n* [U] **1** art or skill of handwriting. **2** style or manner of handwriting.

pen name /ˈpen ˌneim/ *n* [C] name used by an author instead of his real name.

pen·nant /ˈpenənt/ *n* [C] **1** flag (usually long and

narrow) used on a ship for signaling, identification, etc. **2** (*sport*) flag which is the emblem of championship in professional baseball.

pen·ni·less /ˈpenɪlɪs, ˈpenəlɪs/ *adj* without any money: *I'm ~ until payday.*

pen·non /ˈpenən/ *n* [C] **1** long, narrow (usually triangular) flag, as carried on a lance. **2** any flag or banner.

Penn·syl·va·nia Dutch /ˌpensəlˌveinyə ˈdətʃ/ *n* [U] **1** people who are descended from German and Swiss immigrants to the US, who settled in Pennsylvania in the 18th century. **2** dialect of German spoken by them.

penny /ˈpeni/ *n* [C] **1** (*pl* -ies) (*informal*) cent coin of the US and Canada. ⇨ App 4. **2** (*pl* pence /pens/) British coin (1/240 of a pound sterling before 1971 and 1/100 of a pound since then).

penny·weight /ˈpeniˌweit/ *n* [C] 24 grains, one-twentieth of a troy ounce.

pen·sion /ˈpenʃən/ *n* [C] regular payment made to a person, after retirement. □ *vt* **1** grant or pay a pension to. **2** dismiss or allow to retire with a pension.

pen·sion·er *n* [C] person receiving a pension.

pen·sive /ˈpensɪv/ *adj* seriously thoughtful.

pen·sive·ly *adv*

pen·sive·ness /-nɪs/ *n* [U]

pen·ta·gon /ˈpentəˌgan/ *n* **1** [C] flat figure with five (esp equal) sides and five angles. **2 the Pentagon,** building in Arlington, Virginia, headquarters of the US Armed Forces and of the US Department of Defense.

U.S. PENTAGON

pen·tag·onal /penˈtægənəl/ *adj* five-sided.

pen·tath·lon /penˈtæθlən/ *n* [C] athletic contest in which each competitor takes part in five different events.

Pente·cost /ˈpentɪˌkast/ *n* **1** Jewish holiday, fifty days after Passover, the day on which Moses received the Ten Commandments. **2** the seventh Sunday after Easter, commemorating the descent of the Holy Ghost upon the disciples of Christ.

Pente·costal, *adj* **(a)** of or relating to Pentecost. **(b)** of or relating to Pentecostalism.

Pente·costal·ism, *n* [U] form of Christian worship featuring faith healing, revival meetings, etc.

pent·house /ˈpentˌhaus/ *n* [C] (*pl* ~s /-ˌhauzɪz/) apartment built on the roof of a tall building.

pent-up /ˈpentˌəp/ *adj* shut up; not expressed: *~ feelings/anger.*

pen·ul·ti·mate /pɪˈnəltəmɪt/ *adj* next to the last.

pen·ury /ˈpenyʊri/ *n* [U] (*formal*) extreme poverty.

pe·on /ˈpiˌan/ *n* [C] **1** farm laborer of Latin America. **2** person forced to do work in order to pay off a debt.

peony /ˈpiəni/ *n* [C] (*pl* -ies) garden plant with large round pink, red or white flowers.

people /ˈpipəl/ *n* (*Note:* For senses 1 to 4 below, use *man, woman, boy,* or *girl,* as appropriate, to refer to a single human being) **1** (*pl*) persons; human beings: *streets crowded with ~.* **2** (*pl*) persons belonging to a community, nation, region, social class, etc. **3** (*pl*) ordinary persons; persons without high rank, position, etc: *took the side of the ~ against the nobility.* **4** (*pl*) family; relatives. **5** [C] ethnic group united by a common culture, language, religion, etc: *the nomadic ~s of Asia; a brave and intelligent ~.* □ *vt* fill with people.

pep /pep/ *n* [U] (*informal*) vigor; high spirits. □ *vt* (-pp-) ***pep up,*** give energy or life to.

ˈpep talk, speech given (eg by a coach, to players on a team) to arouse enthusiasm.

pep·per /ˈpepər/ *n* **1** [U] hot-tasting seasoning made from the dried and ground berries of an East Indian vine. **2** [C] (garden plant with a) red or green fleshy, hollow fruit which is used as a vegetable: *stuffed ~s* ⇨ illus at vegetable.□ *vt* **1** put pepper(1) on (food). **2** spray or shower with small objects.

pep·pery *adj* **(a)** tasting of pepper; hot; spicy. **(b)** (*fig*) hot-tempered.

pep·per·corn /ˈpepərˌkɔrn/ *n* [C] the dried, black berry of the East Indian pepper vine.

pep·per·mint /ˈpepərˌmɪnt/ *n* **1** [U] kind of mint with a sharp, pleasant taste, used as a flavoring. **2** candy flavored with peppermint.

ˈpeppermint stick, stick of peppermint candy.

per /pər/ *prep* **1** for each: *30 miles per gallon.* **2** according to: *per instructions.*

per. *abbr* = **1** period. **2** person.

per annum /ˌpər ˈænəm/ *adj, adv* for each year.

per cap·i·ta /ˌpər ˈkæpətə/ *adj, adv* by or for each person.

per·ceive /pərˈsiv/ *vt* (*formal*) become aware of, through the senses or the mind.

per·cent /pərˈsent/ *adj, adv* of, for, or out of each hundred: *a ten ~ increase; supported him 100 ~.* □ *n* [C] (*pl* ~) **1** hundredth. **2** percentage: *What ~ of the total order can you send me?*

per·cent·age /pərˈsentɪdʒ/ *n* [C] **1** rate or number out of each hundred. **2** proportion: *What ~ of his income is paid in income tax?*

per·cep·tible /pərˈseptəbəl/ *adj* (*formal*) that can be perceived.

per·cep·tibly /-əbli/ *adv*

per·cep·tion /pərˈsepʃən/ *n* (*formal*) **1** [U] process or act of perceiving. **2** [U] ability to perceive. **3** [C] something that is perceived.

per·cep·tive /pərˈseptɪv/ *adj* (*formal*) **1** having, connected with, perception. **2** showing perception or keen observation: *~ remarks.*

per·cep·tive·ly *adv*

perch[1] /pərtʃ/ *n* [C] (*pl* ~) kinds of freshwater fish with spiny fins, used as food.

perch[2] /pərtʃ/ *n* [C] **1** bird's resting place, eg a branch, bar or rod. **2** (*informal*) high seat or position. □ *vi,vt* **1** alight or settle: *The birds ~ed*

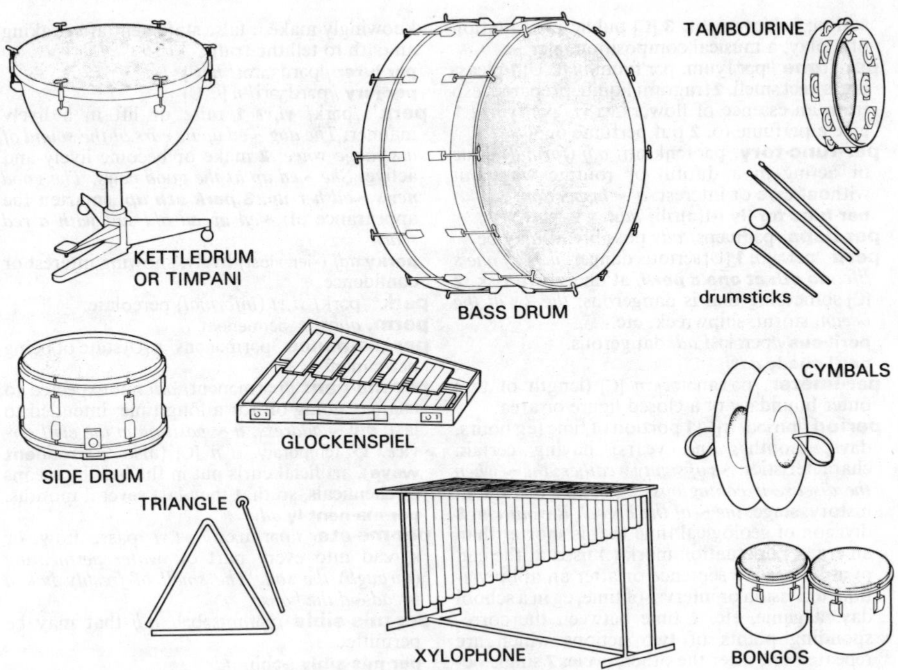

PERCUSSION INSTRUMENTS

on the roof. **2** sit (as) on a perch: *~ed on stools at the bar.* **3** place high up: *a castle ~ed on a rock.*

per·co·late /ˈpərkəˌleit/ *vi,vt* **1** (of liquid) (cause to) pass through a filter, coffee grounds, etc. **2** (*fig*) permeate.

per·co·lator /-tər/ *n* [C] (esp) kind of coffee pot in which boiling water percolates through coffee.

per·cus·sion /pərˈkəʃən/ *n* [U] **1** the striking together of two (usually hard) objects. **2 the percussion,** (*music*) percussion instruments of a band or orchestra.

perˈcussion instrument, musical instrument (such as a drum or piano) in which sound is produced by striking.

per·cus·sion·ist /-ɪst/ *n* [C] player of a percussion instrument.

per·emp·tory /pəˈremptəri/ *adj* (*formal*) **1** (of commands) not to be disobeyed or questioned. **2** (of a person, his manner) (too) commanding; arrogant.

per·emp·tor·ily /-tərəli/ *adv*

per·en·nial /pəˈreniəl/ *adj* **1** continuing throughout the whole year. **2** lasting for a very long time. **3** (of plants) living for many years. □ *n* [C] perennial plant.

per·en·nially /-niəli/ *adv*

per·fect[1] /ˈpərfikt/ *adj* **1** complete; possessing everything that is essential. **2** without fault; excellent: *a ~ wife.* **3** exact; accurate: *a ~ circle.* **4** completely trained or qualified: *a ~ teacher.* **5** complete: *a ~ stranger/fool; ~ nonsense.* **6** absolute: *~ silence.* **7** (*gram*) of, being, or relating to a verb form which expresses an action completed before the time of speaking or before the time spoken of. □ *n* [C] **1** perfect tense. **2** verb form in the perfect tense.

per·fect·ly *adv* completely: *~ happy.*

per·fect[2] /pərˈfekt/ *vt* make perfect or complete.

per·fect·ible /-əbəl/ *adj* that can be perfected.

per·fec·tion /pərˈfekʃən/ *n* [U] **1** perfecting or being perfected: *The craftsman spends much time in the ~ of his work.* **2** perfect person or thing: *He thought her face was ~ itself.* **3** best possible state or quality: *beef roasted/done to ~.*

per·fec·tion·ist /-ɪst/ *n* [C] person who is satisfied with nothing less than what he thinks to be perfect.

per·fidi·ous /pərˈfidiəs/ *adj* (*formal*) treacherous; faithless.

per·fidi·ous·ly *adv*

per·fo·rate /ˈpərfəˌreit/ *vt,vi* **1** make a hole or holes in. **2** make rows of tiny holes (in paper) so that it may be torn easily along the row: *a ~d sheet of postage stamps.*

per·fo·ration /ˌpərfəˈreiʃən/ *n* [C,U]

per·form /pərˈfɔrm/ *vt,vi* **1** do or carry out (a piece of work, an order, a promise, etc): *~ a task.* **2** execute and present (a play, a piece of music, a dance, etc) before an audience: *~ "Death of a Salesman." Do you enjoy seeing ~ing animals?* **3** function; act: *She ~s well even when she's tired.*

per·former *n* [C]

per·form·ance /pərˈfɔrməns/ *n* **1** [U] performing: *faithful in the ~ of his duties.* **2** [C] notable action; achievement. **3** [C] public presentation of a play, a musical composition, etc.

per·fume /ˈpərˌfyum, pərˈfyum/ *n* [C,U] **1** pleasing, sweet smell. **2** fragrant liquid, prepared, esp from an essence of flowers. □ *vt* /pərˈfyum/ **1** give a perfume to. **2** put perfume on.

per·func·tory /pərˈfəŋktəri/ *adj* (*formal*) done or acting in a dutiful or routine way, but without care or interest: *a ~ inspection.*

per·func·tor·ily /-t(ə)rɪli/ *adv*

per·haps /pərˈhæps/ *adv* possibly; it may be.

peril /ˈperəl/ *n* **1** [U] serious danger: *in ~ of one's life.* ***do sth at one's peril,*** at one's own risk. **2** [C] something that is dangerous: *the ~s of the ocean*, storm, shipwreck, etc.

peril·ous /ˈperələs/ *adj* dangerous.

peril·ous·ly *adv*

per·imeter /pəˈrɪmətər/ *n* [C] (length of the) outer boundary of a closed figure or area.

period /ˈpɪriəd/ *n* [C] **1** portion of time (eg hours, days, months, and years) having certain characteristics: *~s of sunny weather; the ~ when the disease is contagious.* **2** portion of time in history; stage: *the ~ of the French Revolution.* **3** division of geological time that is shorter than an era. **4** punctuation mark (.) used at the end of a declarative sentence or after an abbreviation. **5** division or interval of time, eg in a school day, a game, etc. **6** time between the corresponding points of two actions which are repeated one after the other; cycle. **7** single occurrence of menstruation.

peri·odic /ˌpɪriˈadɪk/ *adj* **1** occurring or appearing at regular intervals: *~ headaches.* **2** occurring from time to time.

ˌperiodic ˈtable, (*chem*) chart of the elements (1) in order of their increasing atomic numbers.

peri·od·ical /pɪriˈadɪkəl/ *adj* = periodic. □ *n* [C] magazine or other publication which appears at regular intervals, eg monthly, quarterly.

peri·od·ically /-kli/ *adv*

peri·pa·tetic /ˌperɪpəˈtetɪk/ *adj* going about from place to place; wandering.

pe·riph·eral /peˈrɪfərəl/ *adj* of or relating to a periphery.

pe·riph·ery /pəˈrɪfəri/ *n* [C] (*pl* -ies) **1** external boundary or surface. **2** outermost part within a boundary. **3** area immediately outside the limits or boundary of something.

peri·scope /ˈperəˌskoup/ *n* [C] instrument, as used in submarines, with mirrors and lenses arranged to reflect a view down a tube, etc so that the user may see things which are above his eye level.

per·ish /ˈperɪʃ/ *vi* pass away; come to an end; die: *Hundreds of people ~ed in the earthquake.*

per·ish·able /-əbəl/ *adj* (esp of food) quickly or easily going bad. □ *n pl* (esp) goods, eg fish, fresh fruit, etc, which spoil or go bad easily.

per·ito·ni·tis /ˌperɪtəˈnaitɪs/ *n* [U] inflammation of the membrane lining the cavity of the abdomen.

per·i·winkle[1] /ˈperiˌwɪŋkəl/ *n* [C] trailing, evergreen vine with small blue or white flowers.

per·i·winkle[2] /ˈperiˌwɪŋkəl/ *n* [C] small, edible sea snail. ⇨ illus at mollusk.

per·jure /ˈpərdʒər/ *vt* (*reflex*) ***perjure oneself,*** knowingly make a false statement after taking an oath to tell the truth.

per·jurer /ˈpərdʒərər/ *n* [C]

per·jury /ˈpərdʒəri/ *n* [C,U]

perk[1] /pərk/ *vi,vt* **1** raise or lift in a lively manner: *The dog ~ed up its ears at the sound of a strange voice.* **2** make or become lively and active: *She ~ed up at the good news. The good news ~ed her up.* **3** ***perk sth up,*** smarten the appearance of: *~ed up an old suit with a red scarf.*

perky *adj* (-ier, -iest) lively; showing interest or confidence.

perk[2] /pərk/ *vi,vt* (*informal*) percolate.

perm. *abbr* = permanent.

per·ma·nence /ˈpərmənəns/ *n* [U] state of being permanent.

per·ma·nent /ˈpərmənənt/ *adj* not expected to change; going on for a long time; intended to last: *my ~ address; a ~ position in the civil service.* ⇨ temporary. □ *n* [C] (also **ˈpermanent wave**), artificial curls put in the hair by means of chemicals, so that they last several months.

per·ma·nent·ly *adv*

per·me·ate /ˈpərmiˌeit/ *vt,vi* pass, flow or spread into every part of: *water permeating (through) the soil. The smell of freshly baked bread ~d the house.*

per·mis·sible /pərˈmɪsəbəl/ *adj* that may be permitted.

per·mis·sibly /-əbli/ *adv*

per·mis·sion /pərˈmɪʃən/ *n* [U] **1** act of allowing or permitting. **2** consent: *Has he given you ~ to leave?*

per·miss·ive /pərˈmɪsɪv/ *adj* tending to give permission.

per·miss·ive·ness /-nɪs/ *n* [U]

per·mit[1] /ˈpərmɪt/ *n* [C] written authority to go somewhere, do something, etc: *You won't get into the atomic research station without a ~.*

per·mit[2] /pərˈmɪt/ *vt,vi* (-tt-) **1** allow; authorize: *I can't ~ you to do that. Smoking is not ~ted in the library.* **2** make possible: *The seriousness of the situation does not ~ any delay.*

per·mu·ta·tion /ˌpərmyəˈteiʃən/ *n* [C] (*math*) **1** change in the order of a set of things arranged in an ordered group. **2** any one such arrangement: *The ~s of x, y and z are xyz, xzy, yxz, yzx, zxy, zyx.*

per·ni·cious /pərˈnɪʃəs/ *adj* harmful, injurious: *~ gossip.*

per·ni·cious·ly *adv*

per·ox·ide /pəˈrakˌsaid/ *n* [U] (also **hydrogen peroxide**) colorless liquid used as an antiseptic and a bleach. □ *vt* bleach (hair) with hydrogen peroxide.

per·pen·dicu·lar /ˌpərpənˈdɪkyələr/ *adj* **1** at an angle of 90°: *~ to the table top.* **2** upright; crossing the horizontal at an angle of 90°. □ *n* [C] perpendicular line or plane.

per·pe·trate /ˈpərpəˌtreit/ *vt* commit (a crime, an error).

per·pe·tra·tion /ˌpərpəˈtreiʃən/ *n* [U]

per·pe·tra·tor /-tər/ *n* [C]

per·pet·ual /pərˈpetʃuəl/ *adj* going on for a long time or without stopping.

per·pet·ually /-tʃuəli/ *adv*

per·petu·ate /pərˈpetʃuˌeit/ *vt* make last for a long time: *~ his memory by erecting a statue of him.*

per·petu·ation /pərˌpetʃuˈeiʃən/ *n* [U]

per·petu·ity /ˌpərpəˈtuəti/ *n* [U] state of being perpetual. ***in perpetuity,*** for ever.

per·plex /pərˈpleks/ *vt* **1** puzzle; bewilder: *~ her with questions.* **2** make more complicated.

per·plexed *adj*

per·plex·ed·ly /pərˈpleksədli/ *adv*

per·plex·ity /-əti/ *n* (*pl* -ies) **(a)** [U] state of being confused, eg because of doubt: *He looked at us in ~.* **(b)** [C] perplexing thing.

per se /ˌpər ˈsei, ˌpər ˈsi/ *adv* (*Lat*) by or of itself.

per·se·cute /ˈpərsəˌkyut/ *vt* **1** punish, treat cruelly, esp because of political or religious beliefs. **2** cause repeated trouble to: *~ a man with questions.*

per·se·cu·tion /ˌpərsəˈkyuʃən/ *n* [C,U]

per·se·cu·tor /-tər/ *n* [C]

per·se·ver·ance /ˌpərsəˈvɪrəns/ *n* [U] constant effort to achieve something.

per·se·vere /ˌpərsəˈvɪr/ *vi* keep at or continue with something in spite of difficulties, opposition, etc: *~ with/in one's studies.*

per·se·ver·ing *adj*

per·se·ver·ing·ly *adv*

per·sim·mon /pərˈsɪmən/ *n* [C] (tree bearing a) bright orange fruit

per·sist /pərˈsɪst/ *vi* **1** refuse to change (what one is doing, one's beliefs, etc) in spite of argument, opposition, etc: *She ~s in wearing that old coat.* **2** continue to exist: *The fog is likely to ~ in most areas.*

per·sist·ence /-əns/ *n* [U]

per·sist·ent /-ənt/ *adj* **(a)** continuing or existing for a long time: *~ent denials/attacks of malaria.* **(b)** refusing to give up; persevering: *a ~ent salesman.*

per·sist·ent·ly *adv*

per·son /ˈpərsən/ *n* [C] (*Note: people* is most often used as the *plural.*) **1** human being (*Note: person* in this sense occurs usually in formal contexts; otherwise its use to refer to a single individual is sometimes considered to be derogatory): *Who is this ~?* **2** individual character or personality of a human being: *He is a generous ~.* **3** living body of a human being. ***in person,*** physically present: *He'll collect his certificate in ~,* will be there himself. **4** (*gram*) any one of the three classes esp of personal pronouns which indicate the speaker, the one spoken to, or the one spoken about: *the first ~* (I, we), *the second ~* (you), *and the third ~* (he, she, it, they).

per·son·able /ˈpərsənəbəl/ *adj* good-looking and pleasant.

per·son·age /ˈpərsənɪdʒ/ *n* [C] (important) person.

per·sonal /ˈpərsənəl/ *adj* **1** private; individual; of a particular person: *My ~ affairs/needs/opinions; your ~ rights.* **2** done or made by a person himself: *The President made a ~ appearance at the meeting.* **3** done for or directed to a particular person: *He did me a ~ favor,* one directed to me. **4** of the body: *Personal cleanliness is important to health.* **5** of or about a person, esp in a critical or hostile way: *I object to such ~ remarks.* □ *n* [C] personal item or advertisement in a newpaper, magazine, etc.

per·son·ally /-nəli/ *adv* **1** in person, not through a representative: *He showed me around the exhibition ~ly.* **2** speaking for oneself: *Personally I have no objection to your joining us.* **3** as a person: *Do you know him ~ly?*

ˌpersonal ˈpronoun *n* [C] pronoun which refers to a person(4).

per·son·al·ity /ˌpərsəˈnæləti/ *n* (*pl* -ies) **1** [U] person considered as an individual. **2** [U] qualities that make up a person's character: *a woman with a strong ~.* **3** [U] pleasing or appealing qualities of character: *has more ~ than brains.* **4** [C] person who is famous or distinguished: *a TV ~.*

per·son·al·ize /ˈpərsənəˌlaiz/ *vt* **1** personify. **2** make personal, esp by marking: *~d stationery.*

per·son·ify /pərˈsanəˌfai/ *vt* (*pt,pp* -ied) **1** regard or represent an inanimate object or an idea as a person: *Time is often personified as an old man with a beard.* **2** be an example of (a quality): *That man is greed personified.*

per·soni·fi·ca·tion /pərˌsanəfɪˈkeiʃən/ *n* **(a)** [U] personifying. **(b)** (usually *sing* with *the*) excellent example of a quality: *He's the personification of every virtue.*

per·son·nel /ˌpərsəˈnel/ *n* [U,C] **1** (used with a *sing* or *pl verb*) group of persons employed eg in a business, the armed forces, etc: *Five airline ~ died in the plane crash.* **2** part of a business, etc that deals with employees, their hiring, training, etc.

per·spec·tive /pərˈspektɪv/ *n* **1** [U] the art of drawing solid objects on a flat surface so as to give an impression of their relative height, width, depth, distance, etc. **2** [U] ability to see the relations between different aspects of a problem: *He has the ~ needed to make the right decision.* **3** [C] (*liter, fig*) view; prospect: *a ~ of the nation's history.*

per·spi·ca·cious /ˌpərspəˈkeiʃəs/ *adj* (*formal*) able to see and understand clearly.

per·spi·cac·ity /ˌpərspɪˈkæsəti/ *n* [U]

per·spire /pərˈspaiər/ *vi* sweat.

per·spir·ation /ˌpərspəˈreiʃən/ *n* [U] sweat; sweating.

per·suade /pərˈsweid/ *vt* convince (a person) to believe or to do something by arguments, reasoning, requests, etc: *How can I ~ you of my sincerity/that I am sincere? We ~d him to try again. Can you ~ her not to interfere?*

per·suad·able /-əbəl/ *adj*

per·sua·sion /pərˈsweiʒən/ *n* **1** [U] persuading or being persuaded. **2** [U] power of persuading. **3** [U] belief (the usual word): *It is my ~ that...* **4** [C] group of people holding a particular belief: *various political ~s.*

per·sua·sive /pərˈsweisɪv/ *adj* able to persuade: *She has a ~ manner/voice.*

per·sua·sive·ly *adv*

per·sua·sive·ness /-nɪs/ *n* [U]

pert /pərt/ *adj* **1** impudent; not showing proper respect: *a ~ child/answer.* **2** lively.

pert·ly *adv*

pert·ness /-nɪs/ *n* [U]

per·tain /pərˈtein/ *vi* (*formal*) **1** belong as a part or accessory: *the farm and the lands ~ing to it.* **2** have reference; relate to: *His questions did not ~ to the subject we were discussing.*

per·ti·na·cious /ˌpərtəˈneiʃəs/ *adj* (*formal*) determined; persistent.

per·ti·na·cious·ly *adv*

per·ti·nac·ity /ˌpərtəˈnæsəti/ *n* [U] determination.

per·ti·nent /ˈpərtənənt/ *adj* (*formal*) relating to or relevant to a specific matter: *a ~ reply.*

per·ti·nent·ly *adv*

per·turb /pərˈtərb/ *vt* (*formal*) cause concern to; make anxious: *a man who is never ~ed.*

per·tur·ba·tion /ˌpərtərˈbeiʃən/ *n* [U]

pe·rusal /pəˈruzəl/ *n* [C,U] act of reading carefully.

pe·ruse /pəˈruz/ *vt* (*formal*) read carefully.

per·vade /pərˈveid/ *vt* (*formal*) spread through every part of; permeate.

per·va·sive /pərˈveisɪv/ *adj* tending to pervade: *~ influences.*

per·va·sive·ly *adv*

per·va·sive·ness /-nɪs/ *n* [U]

per·verse /pərˈvərs/ *adj* **1** morally bad or wrong. **2** stubborn; obstinate; willfully opposed.

per·verse·ly *adv*

per·verse·ness /-nɪs/ *n* [U]

per·ver·sion /pərˈvərʒən/ *n* **1** [U] perverting or being perverted. **2** [C] (esp) abnormal sexual behavior or act.

per·ver·sity /pərˈvərsəti/ *n* (*pl* -ies) **1** [U] being perverse. **2** [C] perverse act.

per·vert[1] /ˈpərˌvərt/ *n* [C] person whose sexual behavior is considered abnormal.

per·vert[2] /pərˈvərt/ *vt* **1** turn (something) to a wrong use. **2** cause (a person) to turn away from right behavior, beliefs, etc: *~ (the mind of) a child.*

pes·ky /ˈpeski/ *adj* (-ier, -iest) (*informal*) irritating; troublesome.

pe·so /ˈpeisou/ *n* [C] (*pl* ~s) unit of money used in many Latin American countries and in the Philippines.

pes·si·mism /ˈpesəˌmɪzəm/ *n* [U] **1** tendency to believe that the worst thing is most likely to happen. **2** belief that evil is more common than good.

pes·si·mist /-ɪst/ *n* [C] believer in pessimism.

pes·si·mis·tic /ˌpesəˈmɪstɪk/ *adj*

pessi·mis·ti·cally /-kli/ *adv*

pest /pest/ *n* [C] **1** troublesome or destructive thing, animal, etc: *garden ~s,* eg insects. **2** person who is a nuisance: *You little ~!*

pes·ter /ˈpestər/ *vt* annoy; trouble: *be ~ed with flies/with requests for help.*

pes·ti·cide /ˈpestəˌsaid/ *n* [C,U] substance used to destroy pests.

pes·ti·lence /ˈpestələns/ *n* [C,U] fatal epidemic disease, eg bubonic plague.

pestle /ˈpes(t)əl/ *n* [C] stick with a thick, rounded end used in a mortar for pounding or crushing things.

pet /pet/ *n* [C] **1** animal, etc kept as a companion, and treated with care and affection, eg a cat or a dog. **2** favorite: *Mary is the teacher's pet.* □ *vt* (-tt-) stroke gently; caress.

petal /ˈpetəl/ *n* [C] one of the (often brightly colored) leaflike parts of a flower: *ˈrose ~s.* ⇨ illus at flower.

peter /ˈpitər/ *vi* ***peter out,*** come gradually to an end.

pe·tite /pəˈtit/ *adj* trim and slender.

pe·ti·tion /pəˈtɪʃən/ *n* [C] **1** prayer; earnest request. **2** written request or appeal made to an authority, often signed by a large number of people. □ *vt,vi* **1** make an appeal to, eg the authorities. **2** ***petition for,*** make a formal, written request: *~ for a retrial.*

pe·ti·tioner *n* [C]

pet·rel /ˈpetrəl/ *n* [C] long-winged black and white seabird.

pet·rify /ˈpetrəˌfai/ *vt,vi* (*pt,pp* -ied) **1** (cause to) change into stone. **2** (*fig*) paralyze or make numb through fear, surprise, etc.

pe·tro·leum /pɪˈtrouliəm/ *n* [U] thick, oily liquid found chiefly underground, that consists of hydrocarbons and is used in various forms (such as gasoline, kerosene, etc) for lighting, heating and driving machines.

pet·ti·coat /ˈpetiˌkout/ *n* [C] loose, sleeveless undergarment, worn under a dress or skirt.

petty /ˈpeti/ *adj* (-ier, -iest) **1** small; unimportant. **2** on a small scale: *~ larceny,* theft of articles of little value. **3** having or showing a narrow mind; mean: *~ spite.*

ˌpetty ˈcash, (*business*) small amount of money for minor expenses.

pet·tily /ˈpetəli/ *adv*

pet·ti·ness /ˈpetinɪs/ *n* [U]

ˈpetty officer, officer in the US navy or coastguard below commissioned rank.

petu·lant /ˈpetʃələnt/ *adj* peevish; unreasonably impatient or irritable.

petu·lance /ˈpetʃələns/ *n* [U]

petu·lant·ly *adv*

pe·tu·nia /pəˈtunyə/ *n* (*pl* ~s) [C] garden plant with funnel-shaped flowers of various colors.

pew /pyu/ *n* [C] church bench with a back. ⇨ illus at church.

pe·wee /ˈpiˌwi/ *n* [C] small greenish bird that feeds on insects.

pe·wit /ˈpiwɪt/ *n* [C] pewee.

pew·ter /ˈpyutər/ *n* [U] (objects made of a) gray alloy of lead and tin.

phal·anx /ˈfeiˌlæŋks/ *n* [C] (*pl* ~es or phalanges /fəˈlænˌdʒiz/) **1** (in ancient Greece) body of soldiers in close formation for fighting. **2** any compact body of persons or troops. **3** (*anat*) bone in a finger or toe. ⇨ illus at skeleton.

phal·lic /ˈfælɪk/ *adj* of a phallus: *~ symbols/emblems.*

phal·lus /ˈfæləs/ *n* [C] (*pl* phalli, /ˈfæˌlai/, ~es) (image or symbol of) the penis.

phan·tasy /ˈfæntəsi/ *n* = fantasy.

phan·tom /ˈfæntəm/ *n* [C] **1** ghost. **2** something seen as in a dream or vision. **3** something that exists only in appearance: *only a ~ of power.*

Phar·aoh /ˈfærou/ *n* [C] title of the kings of ancient Egypt.

Phari·see /ˈfærəˌsi/ *n* [C] **1** member of an ancient Jewish sect known for strict obedience to written laws. **2** **pharisee,** hypocritical and self-righteous person.

phar·ma·ceuti·cal /ˌfarməˈsutɪkəl/ *adj* of pharmacy or pharmacists: *the ~ industry.*

phar·ma·cist /ˈfarməsɪst/ *n* [C] person skilled in preparing drugs; druggist.

phar·ma·col·ogist /ˌfarməˈkalədʒɪst/ *n* [C] expert in pharmacology.

phar·ma·col·ogy /ˌfarməˈkalədʒi/ *n* [U] science of drugs, and esp of their medicinal use.

phar·macy /ˈfarməsi/ *n* (*pl* -ies) **1** [U] preparation and dispensing of medicines and drugs. **2** [C] place where drugs are sold or prepared; drugstore.

phar·ynx /ˈfærɪŋks/ *n* [C] (*pl* pharynges /fəˈrɪnˌdʒiz/, ~es) cavity extending from the back of the mouth to the esophagus. ⇨ illus at head.

phase /feiz/ *n* [C] **1** stage of development: *the critical ~ of an illness.* **2** (of the moon or a planet) apparent shape of the illuminated surface at any given time in a cycle. □ *vt* plan, carry out, by phases: *The presidential candidate hired an adviser to help ~ the new campaign plan.* ***phase in/out,*** introduce/withdraw one stage at a time: *The factory is phasing in new equipment.*

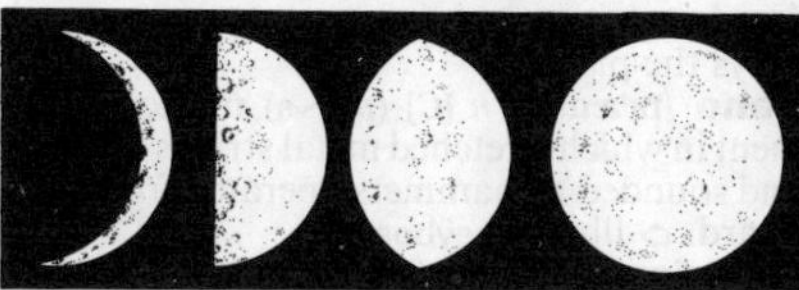

PHASES OF THE MOON

Ph.D. /ˌpi ˌeitʃ ˈdi/ *abbr* = Doctor of Philosophy (degree). □ *n* [C] (*pl* Ph.D.'s) one who has such a degree.

pheas·ant /ˈfezənt/ *n* [C] long-tailed game bird usually having brightly colored feathers.

phe·nom·enal /fɪˈnamənəl/ *adj* **1** of, relating to, or being a phenomenon or phenomena. **2** enormous; extraordinary.

phe·nom·enally /-nəli/ *adv*

phe·nom·enon /fɪˈnaməˌnan/ *n* (*pl* -na /-nə/) **1** thing that can be perceived by the senses: *the phenomena of nature.* **2** remarkable or unusual person, thing, happening, etc.

phew /fyu/ *int* used to express astonishment, impatience, discomfort, disgust, etc.

phial /ˈfaiəl/ *n* [C] small bottle, esp one for liquid medicine; vial.

phil·an·thropic /ˌfɪlənˈθrapɪk/ *adj* benevolent; kind and helpful; charitable.

phil·an·thropi·cally /-kli/ *adv*

phil·an·thro·pist /fɪˈlænθrəpɪst/ *n* [C] person who helps others, esp those who are poor or in trouble.

phil·an·thropy /fɪˈlænθrəpi/ *n* (*pl* -ies) **1** [U] love of mankind. **2** [C] charitable act or gift. **3** [C] institution, charity, etc devoted to promoting human welfare.

Phi·lis·tine /ˈfɪləˌstin/ *n* [C] **1** (in the Bible) one of the warlike people in Palestine who were the enemies of the Israelites. **2** (sometimes **philistine**) uncultured person, esp one who is materialistic, or uninterested in literature, art, etc.

philo·logi·cal /ˌfɪləˈladʒɪkəl/ *adj* of philology.

phil·ol·ogist /fɪˈlalədʒɪst/ *n* [C] student of, expert in, philology.

phil·ol·ogy /fɪˈlalədʒi/ *n* [U] study of the development of language, or of particular languages.

phil·os·opher /fɪˈlasəfər/ *n* [C] **1** student or teacher of philosophy. **2** person who faces misfortune or hardship with reason, patience, and calm.

philo·sophi·cal /ˌfɪləˈsafɪkəl/ *adj* **1** of, relating to, or guided by philosophy. **2** calm; patient; reasonable.

philo·sophi·cally /-kli/ *adv*

phil·os·ophize /fɪˈlasəˌfaiz/ *vi* **1** think or reason like a philosopher. **2** moralize.

phil·os·ophy /fɪˈlasəfi/ *n* (*pl* -ies) **1** [U] study of the persistent problems concerning the nature of man and the world in which he lives, man's knowledge of the world, and the principles of value. **2** [C] set of personal opinions, beliefs, or principles about life: *a man with a practical ~.* **3** [U] calmness, good judgment, and patience in the face of unhappiness, danger, difficulty, etc.

phil·ter /ˈfɪltər/ *n* [U] magic potion.

phlegm /flem/ *n* [U] **1** thick mucus produced in the throat, the nose, and other respiratory passages. **2** quality of being phlegmatic.

phleg·matic /flegˈmætɪk/ *adj* being slow to act or to show feeling or interest.

phleg·mat·i·cally /-kli/ *adv*

phlox /flaks/ *n* [C] (*pl* ~, ~es) (plant bearing a) reddish, purple, or white flower growing in clusters.

pho·bia /ˈfoubiə/ *n* [C] (*pl* ~s) strong, abnormal fear or dislike.

phoe·be /ˈfibi/ *n* [C] small, grayish bird of the eastern US, whose call sounds like the name.

phone[1] /foun/ *n* [C], *vt,vi* (*informal*) (short for) telephone.

ˈphone booth *n* [C] (*informal*) telephone booth.

phone[2] /foun/ *n* [C] (*ling*) single speech sound.

pho·neme /ˈfouˌnim/ *n* [C] (*ling*) smallest unit of sound in a language, which can distinguish one word from another.

pho·nemic /fəˈnimɪk/ *adj*

pho·netic /fəˈnetɪk/ *adj* **1** of or relating to phonetics. **2** representing the sounds of speech.

pho·neti·cally /-kli/ *adv*

pho·net·ics *n* (used with a *sing verb*) study and science of speech sounds, their production, and the signs used to represent them.

pho·neti·cian /ˌfounəˈtɪʃən/ *n* [C] expert in phonetics.

phon·ic /ˈfanɪk/ *adj* of or relating to sounds, esp speech sounds.

phon·ics /ˈfanɪks/ *n* [U] (used with a *sing verb*) method of teaching reading by using a simplified phonetic system.

pho·no·graph /ˈfounəˌgræf/ *n* [C] device that reproduces sounds recorded on a grooved disk; record player.

pho·ny, phoney /ˈfouni/ *adj* (-ier, -iest) (*informal*) fake; not genuine or sincere. □ *n* [C] (*pl* -ies) phony person: *He's a complete ~.*

phooey /ˈfui/ *int* used to express disgust, disbelief, etc.

phos·pho·rescence /ˌfasfəˈresəns/ *n* [U] **1** process of giving out light without heat. **2** process of emitting light after exposure to radiation.

phos·pho·rescent /-sənt/ *adj*

phos·phorus /ˈfasf(ə)rəs/ *n* [U] yellowish, non-metallic, poisonous waxy element (symbol **P**) which catches fire easily and gives out a faint light in the dark.

photo /ˈfoutou/ *n* [C] (*informal*) (short for) photograph.

photo- /ˌfoutou-/ (*combined form*) **1** of light: *photoelectric*. **2** of photography: *photogenic*.

photo·copy /ˈfoutouˌkapi/ *vt* (*pt, pp* -ied) make a copy of (a document, etc) by a photographic method. □ *n* [C] (*pl* -ies) such a copy.

pho·to·elec·tric cell /ˌfoutouɪˌlektrɪk ˈsel/ *n* [C] cell which converts changes in the amount of light falling on it to changes in electric current, used eg to cause a door to open when someone approaches it or to set off a burglar alarm.

photo finish /ˌfoutou ˈfɪnɪʃ/ *n* [C] finish of a contest which is so close that it is difficult to decide the winner.

photo·genic /ˌfoutouˈdʒenɪk/ *adj* likely to be photographed well or effectively.

photo·graph /ˈfoutəˌgræf/ *n* [C] picture or likeness made from an image produced by the action of light rays on the film or plates in a camera. □ *vt* take a photograph of.

pho·tog·ra·pher /fəˈtagrəfər/ *n* [C] person who takes photographs, esp as a profession.

pho·to·graphic /ˌfoutəˈgræfɪk/ *adj* of, related to, used in, taking photographs.

photo·graphi·cally /-kli/ *adv*

pho·tog·ra·phy /fəˈtagrəfi/ *n* [U] art or process of taking photographs.

phr. *abbr* = phrase.

phrase /freiz/ *n* [C] **1** (*gram*) group of two or more words which have meaning, but do not form a complete sentence, eg in the garden, in order to. **2** short, clever expression. **3** (*music*) short passage from a longer composition. □ *vt* express in words: *a neatly ~d compliment*.

ˈphras·al *adj* in the form of a phrase: *phrasal expression*.

ˌphrasal ˈverb (*gram*) verb, often having a special or idiomatic meaning, that consists of a verb with an adverb or a preposition, eg *make out, blow up*.

phra·seol·ogy /ˌfreiziˈalədʒi/ *n* [U] choice of words; manner of expression; style.

PHS *abbr* = Public Health Service.

phys. *abbr* = **1** physical. **2** physician. **3** physics.

physic /ˈfɪzɪk/ *n* [U] medicine, esp a laxative.

physi·cal /ˈfɪzɪkəl/ *adj* **1** of material things (contrasted with mental or spiritual things): *the ~ world*. **2** of the body: *~ exercise*, eg running. **3** of the laws of nature: *a ~ impossibility*. **4** of the natural features of the world: *~ geography*. **5** of or relating to physics.

physi·cally /-kli/ *adv*

physi·cal ed·u·ca·tion /ˌfɪzɪkəl ˌedʒəˈkeiʃən/ *n* [U] instruction in the care and training of the body, esp through exercise and sports.

physi·cal ther·a·py /ˌfɪzɪkəl ˈθerəpi/ *n* [U] treatment of injury or disease by physical means such as exercise, massage, baths, etc. rather than by means of drugs.

phys·ician /fɪˈzɪʃən/ *n* [C] (esp) doctor of medicine.

physi·cist /ˈfɪzəsɪst/ *n* [C] specialist in physics.

phys·ics /ˈfɪzɪks/ *n pl* (used with a *sing verb*) science dealing with matter and energy, that includes the study of eg heat, light, sound, mechanics, and electricity, but usually excludes chemistry and biology.

physio·logi·cal /ˌfɪziəˈladʒɪkəl/ *adj* of physiology.

physi·ol·ogist /ˌfɪziˈalədʒɪst/ *n* [C] expert in physiology.

physi·ol·ogy /ˌfɪziˈalədʒi/ *n* [U] **1** science of the normal functions of living things. **2** all the activities and functions of a living thing or of any of its parts.

physio·thera·pist /ˌfɪziouˈθerəpɪst/ *n* [C] person trained to give physical therapy.

physio·ther·apy /ˌfɪziouˈθerəpi/ *n* [U] physical therapy.

phy·sique /fɪˈzik/ *n* [U] structure and development of the body: *a strong ~*.

pia·nist /piˈænɪst, ˈpiənɪst/ *n* [C] person who plays the piano.

pi·ano /pɪˈænou/ *n* [C] (*pl ~s*) musical instrument in which stretched metal strings are struck and sounded by hammers operated from a keyboard. ⇨ illus at keyboard.

piano·forte /piˈænəˌfɔrt(i)/ *n* [C] (*formal*) = piano.

pi·az·za /piˈæzə/ *n* [C] (*pl ~s*) **1** open square in an Italian town. **2** porch.

pic·a·yune /pɪkəˈyun/ *adj* **1** of small or little value. **2** petty.

pic·ca·lilli /ˈpɪkəlɪli/ *n* [U] relish made of chopped vegetables, spices, vinegar, etc.

pic·colo /ˈpɪkəlou/ *n* [C] (*pl ~s*) small flute which is an octave higher than an ordinary flute. ⇨ illus at brass.

pick[1] /pɪk/ *n* [C] **1** choice; selection. **2** the best or the choicest one.

pick[2] /pɪk/ *n* [C] **1** = pickax. **2** small, sharp-pointed instrument. **3** plectrum.

pick[3] /pɪk/ *vt,vi* **1** take up, remove, or pull away, (as) by plucking with the fingers: *~ flowers/fruit*. ***pick sb's brains,*** get ideas and information from him. ***pick sb's pocket,*** steal from it. **2** strike or dig at (as) with a pointed instrument to clean, etc: *~ one's teeth*, get bits of food from the spaces between them, etc by using a *ˈtoothpick*. ***pick a lock,*** unlock it without a key. ***have a ˈbone to pick with sb,*** ⇨ bone(2). ***pick a quarrel with sb,*** provoke or start quarrel intentionally. ***pick holes in an argument,*** find mistakes or weak points in it. **3** choose; select: *~ a team*, choose players. **4** eat in a fussy way or in small amounts: *She only ~ed at her food*. **5** pluck (the strings of) a musical instrument: *~ a banjo*. **6** (special uses with *adverbial particles* and *prepositions*):

pick at sb, (*informal*) find fault with: *Why are you always ~ing at the poor child?*

pick on sb, (*informal*) single out for punishment, criticism, etc: *You're always ~ing on me.*

pick sb/sth out, **(a)** choose. **(b)** distinguish from a group of persons, objects, etc: ~ *out a friend in a crowd.* **(c)** play the notes of slowly or one by one: ~ *out a tune.* ***pick sth over,*** examine and make a selection from: ~ *over a basket of grapes*, eg to throw out any that are bad. ***pick sth up,*** **(a)** take hold of and lift: ~ *up one's hat/parcels, etc.* **(b)** gain or get casually: ~ *up a foreign language*, learn it without taking lessons or studying; ~ *up bits of information;* ~ *up a bargain at a sale.* **(c)** succeed in seeing or hearing (by means of apparatus): *enemy planes ~ed up by our searchlights/radar, etc.* ***pick sb up,*** **(a)** make the acquaintance of casually: *a girl he ~ed up on the street.* **(b)** take a person into one's vehicle as a passenger: *He stopped the car to ~ up a hitchhiker.* **(c)** arrest: *The escaped prisoner was ~ed up by the police at his sister's house.* ***pick oneself up,*** raise (oneself): *She slipped and fell, but quickly ~ed herself up.* ***pick up,*** improve: *Business ~ed up during the sale.*

pick·ax, pick·axe /ˈpɪkˌæks/ *n* [C] heavy tool with an iron head that is pointed at one or both ends, used for breaking up earth, roads, etc.

picket /ˈpɪkɪt/ *n* [C] **1** pointed stick, etc set upright in the ground (as part of a fence, etc). **2** small group of soldiers placed as guard against enemy attack. **3** worker stationed at a factory, business, etc during a strike. **4** person stationed for the purpose of a demonstration or protest. □ *vt,vi* **1** put pickets(1) around. **2** station (men) as pickets(2). **3** place a picket(3,4): ~ *a factory.*

pickle /ˈpɪkəl/ *n* **1** [U] brine or vinegar solution for preserving meat, vegetables, etc. **2** [C] article of food preserved in such a solution: *cucumber ~s.* **3** [C] (*informal*) difficult situation. □ *vt* preserve in a vinegar or brine solution: *~d onions.*

pick·pock·et /ˈpɪkˌpakɪt/ *n* [C] person who steals from pockets and purses.

pick·up /ˈpɪkˌəp/ *n* (*pl* ~s) **1** [C] part of a phonograph that holds the stylus. **2** [C] small light truck, open and with low sides. **3** [C] (*informal*) person (esp a sexual partner) whose acquaintance is made casually. **4** [C,U] acceleration: *an engine/car with (a) good ~.* **5** (*sing* only) (*informal*) improvement.

picky /ˈpɪki/ *adj* (-ier, -iest) (*informal*) fussy.

pic·nic /ˈpɪkˌnɪk/ *n* [C] **1** pleasure trip on which food is carried to be eaten outdoors. **2** (*informal*) something easy and enjoyable: *It's no ~,* is not an easy job. □ *vi* (-ck-) take part in a picnic: *~king in the woods.*

pic·tor·ial /pɪkˈtɔriəl/ *adj* of, resembling, represented in, pictures: *a ~ record of the wedding.*

pic·ture /ˈpɪktʃər/ *n* [C] **1** painting, drawing, or similar image. **2** likeness: *She's the ~ of her mother.* **3** type or example: *the ~ of health.* **4** (*fig*) vivid account or description. **5** state of affairs; situation. **6** motion picture. **7** image on a screen. □ *vt* **1** make a picture of. **2** imagine: *Can you ~ me as a doctor?*

pic·tur·esque /ˌpɪktʃəˈresk/ *adj* **1** having the quality of being similar to, or suitable for, the subject of a painting; quaint; attractive: *a ~ village.* **2** vivid; expressive: *~ language.*

pic·tur·esque·ly *adv*

pid·dling /ˈpɪdlɪŋ/ *adj* insignificant: *~ jobs.*

pidgin /ˈpɪdʒɪn/ *n* [C] **1** form of simplified speech used for communication between groups of people speaking different languages. **2** jargon.

pie /pai/ *n* [C,U] pastry crust baked with a filling of meat or fruit: *apple pie.* ***have a finger in every pie,*** be (too) concerned in all that is going on. ***as easy as pie,*** (*sl*) very easy. ***pie in the sky,*** unrealistic hopes.

pie·bald /ˈpaiˌbɔld/ *adj* having white and dark patches of irregular shape.

piece[1] /pis/ *n* [C] **1** part or bit broken off or separated from a whole: *a ~ of paper/string. Will you have another ~ of cake? The vase fell and was broken to ~s.* ***go (all) to pieces,*** (*informal*) break down; have a physical or mental collapse. **2** separate instance or example: *a ~ of news/luck/advice/information/furniture.* ***give sb a piece of one's mind,*** criticize strongly; scold. **3** single composition (in art, music, etc): *a fine ~ of work/music/poetry.* **4** one item out of a set: *a dinner service of 50 ~s.* **5** one of the objects moved on a board in such games as chess. **6** coin: *a gold ~.* **7** firearm.

piece[2] /pis/ *vt* repair or make by joining or adding (pieces) together: *~ together odds and ends of cloth.*

piece·meal /ˈpisˌmiəl/ *adv* one part at a time; gradually: *work done ~.* □ *adj* made, done, etc piecemeal.

piece·work /ˈpisˌwərk/ *n* [U] work which is paid for by the number of items produced.

pied /paid/ *adj* having patches of two or more colors.

pier /pɪr/ *n* [C] **1** platform of wood, iron, etc built out from the shore and extending over the water, used as a landing place, for walking on, etc. **2** pillar or structure supporting the span of a bridge, etc. **3** supporting structure between two windows or other openings.

pierce /pɪrs/ *vt,vi* **1** go into or through (as) with a pointed instrument: *The arrow ~d his shoulder. Her screams ~d the air.* **2** force or make a way through or into: *Our forces ~d through the enemy's lines.* **3** make an opening or hole in: *The drill ~d through the wood.* **4** see through or understand.

pierc·ing *adj* penetrating; sharp: *a piercing wind.*

pierc·ing·ly *adv*

piety /ˈpaiəti/ *n* (*pl* -ies) (*formal*) **1** [U] devotion to God and good actions. **2** [C] act, etc that shows piety.

pig /pɪg/ *n* **1** [C] domestic or wild animal with short, bristly hair and a broad snout. ⇨ illus at animal. **2** [U] its flesh as meat. ⇨ bacon, ham, pork. **3** dirty, greedy or ill-mannered person. ***make a pig of oneself,*** eat or drink too much.

ˈpig·gish /-ɪʃ/ *adj* dirty or greedy.

pi·geon /ˈpɪdʒən/ *n* [C] **1** bird with smooth feathers, a plump body, and usually short legs. **2** easily deceived person.

pi·geon·hole /ˈpɪdʒənˌhoul/ *n* [C] one of a number of small open compartments in a desk for keeping papers in. ▫ *vt* **1** put (papers, etc) in or as in a pigeonhole. **2** classify or put into a group.

pi·geon-toed /ˈpɪdʒənˌtoud/ *adj* having the toes turned inwards.

pig·gy·back /ˈpɪgiˌbæk/ *adj, adv* on the back or shoulders of another person.

pig·gy bank /ˈpɪgi ˌbæŋk/ *n* [C] child's bank, made in the shape of a pig.

pig-head·ed /ˈpɪg-ˌhedɪd/ *adj* stubborn.

pig·let /ˈpɪglɪt/ *n* [C] young pig.

pig·ment /ˈpɪgmənt/ *n* **1** [C,U] coloring matter for making dyes, paint, etc. **2** [U] the natural coloring matter in plant or animal tissues.

pigmy /ˈpɪgmi/ *n* [C] = pygmy.

pig·skin /ˈpɪgˌskɪn/ *n* **1** [U] (leather made of a) pig's skin. **2** (*informal*) football.

pig·sty /ˈpɪgˌstai/ *n* [C] (*pl* -ies) **1** small building for pigs. **2** dirty home.

pig·tail /ˈpɪgˌteiəl/ *n* [C] braid of hair at the back of the head.

pike[1] /paik/ *n* [C] long wooden shaft with a spearhead, formerly used by soldiers fighting on foot.

pike[2] /paik/ *n* [C] large, fierce, freshwater fish.

pike[3] /paik/ *n* [C] turnpike.

pike[4] /paik/ *n* [C] sharp point or spike.

pile[1] /ˈpaiəl/ *n* [C] **1** number of things lying one on another: *a ~ of books.* **2** (*pl*) (*informal*) large amount: *I've got ~s of work to do.* **3** (*informal*) large amount of money. ***make a/one's pile,*** earn a lot of money.

pile[2] /ˈpaiəl/ *n* [C] long column of timber, steel, concrete, etc driven into the ground, as a foundation for a building, a support for a bridge, etc.

pile[3] /ˈpaiəl/ *n* [U] **1** soft, thick, hairlike surface of velvet, carpets, etc. **2** soft, fine hair or fur.

pile[4] /ˈpaiəl/ *vt,vi* (*pres p* piling /ˈpailɪŋ/) **1** make or stack into a pile(1): *~ (up) dishes on a table.* **2** load or heap in abundance: *~ food on one's plate/~ one's plate with food.* **3** accumulate; form (as) into a heap: *My work keeps piling up.* **4** move in a crowd or in a disorderly group: *They all ~d into/out of the car.*

piles /ˈpaiəlz/ *n* [U] = hemorrhoids.

pil·fer /ˈpɪlfər/ *vt,vi* steal, esp in small quantities.

pil·grim /ˈpɪlgrɪm/ *n* [C] **1** person who travels to a sacred place as an act of religious devotion. **2** **Pilgrims,** (also **Pilgrim Fathers**), English Puritans who went to America in 1620 and founded the colony of Plymouth, Massachusetts.

pil·grim·age /ˈpɪlgrɪmɪdʒ/ *n* [C] journey of a pilgrim.

pill /pɪl/ *n* [C] **1** small ball or tablet of medicine for swallowing whole. **2** **the pill,** oral contraceptive. ***on the pill,*** taking such pills regularly. **3** (*sl*) something distasteful as a pill. **4** (*sl*) disagreeable or boring person.

pil·lar /ˈpɪlər/ *n* [C] **1** upright column, of stone, wood, metal, etc as a support or ornament. ***from pillar to post,*** (*fig*) to and fro. **2** (*fig*) strong support: *a ~ of the Church.* **3** something in the shape of a pillar, eg a column of fire, smoke.

pil·lion /ˈpɪlyən/ *n* [C] **1** saddle for a passenger behind the driver of a motorcycle. **2** seat for a second rider behind the rider of a horse.

pil·lo·ry /ˈpɪləri/ *n* [C] (*pl* -ies) wooden frame with holes for the head and arms, formerly used as a punishment for offenders who were locked in and exposed to public shame. ▫ *vt* (*pt, pp* -ied) **1** put in the pillory. **2** (*fig*) expose to public ridicule or shame.

pil·low /ˈpɪlou/ *n* [C] soft cushion for the head, esp when lying in bed. ▫ *vt* rest, support, on or as on a pillow.

ˈpil·low·case *n* [C] removable, washable cover for a pillow.

pi·lot /ˈpailət/ *n* [C] **1** person trained and licensed to take ships into or out of a harbor, along a river, through a canal, etc. **2** person trained to operate an aircraft. **3** guide or leader. ▫ *adj* experimental; used as a model to test how something will work, how it may be improved, etc: *a ˈ~ project.* ▫ *vt* act as a pilot to.

pi·lot fish /ˈpailət ˌfɪʃ/ *n* [C] small fish which often swims in company with sharks.

pi·lot light /ˈpailət ˌlait/ *n* [C] small flame, as in a stove, which lights large burners, etc when the gas is turned on.

pi·mien·to, pi·men·to /pɪˈmentou/ *n* [C] (*pl* ~s) mild-flavored, sweet red pepper(2).

pim·per·nel /ˈpɪmpərˌnel/ *n* [C] small wild plant, with scarlet, blue or white flowers that close in rainy or cloudy weather.

pimple /ˈpɪmpəl/ *n* [C] small, inflamed swelling on the skin, often containing pus.

pim·pled *adj* having pimples.

pim·ply /ˈpɪmpli/ *adj* (-ier, -iest)

pin[1] /pɪn/ *n* [C] **1** short, thin piece of stiff wire with a sharp point and a round head, used for fastening things together. ***pins and needles,*** tingling feeling in a part of the body that has been numb because of poor circulation. ***on pins and needles,*** very tense or anxious: *on pins and needles waiting for his call.* **2** ornament, eg a brooch, fastened with a pin. **3** article of wood or metal used for fastening: *clothespin; hairpin; safety pins.* **4** one of the pegs around which the strings of a musical instrument are fastened. **5** bottle-shaped wooden piece at which a bowling ball is aimed. **6** (*dated*) something that is worthless or of little value: *I don't care two pins about him.*

ˈpin·cush·ion /ˈpɪnˌkʊʃən/ *n* [C] pad for keeping pins(1) ready for use.

pin[2] /pɪn/ *vt* (-nn-) **1** fasten with a pin or pins: *pin papers together; pin up a notice*, eg with push pins on a bulletin board. ***pin sth on sb,*** make him appear responsible or deserving of blame. ***pin one's hopes on,*** rely completely on a person, a decision, etc. **2** make unable to move: *He was pinned under the wrecked car. He pinned me against the wall*, held me there and prevented me from moving. ***pin down***, establish; determine. ***pin sb down,*** (*fig*) get him to commit himself, to decide, etc.

pin·a·fore /ˈpɪnəˌfɔr/ *n* [C] article of clothing, similar to an apron, that is worn over a dress to keep it clean.

pin·cers /ˈpɪnsərz/ *n pl* **1** instrument with a pair of jaws and two handles, used for gripping things. **2** pincer-shaped claws of eg a lobster or a crab. ⇨ illus at crustacean.

pinch /pɪntʃ/ *vt,vi* **1** squeeze between the thumb and finger or between two hard things which are pressed together: *He ~ed himself to keep awake. I ~ed my fingers in the door,* let the door close on them. **2** be too tight; hurt by squeezing: *These shoes ~ (me).* **3** (*sl*) steal: *Who ~ed my dictionary?* **4** live economically: *~ and scrape in order to save money.* **5** (*sl*) arrest: *be ~ed for stealing.* □ *n* [C] **1** painful squeeze: *His fingers got a bad ~ in the door.* **2** (*fig*) stress: *feel the ~ of poverty.* **3** amount which can be taken up with the thumb and finger: *a ~ of salt.* **4** emergency; difficult situation: *We can get six people round the table in a ~.* **5** (*sl*) theft. **6** (*sl*) arrest.

pine[1] /pain/ *n* **1** [C] kinds of evergreen tree with cones and needle-shaped leaves. ⇨ illus at tree. **2** [U] the wood of this tree.

pine[2] /pain/ *vi* **1** waste away through sorrow, grief, etc. **2** long for; have a strong desire: *exiles pining for home/to return home.*

pine·apple /ˈpaiˌnæpəl/ *n* [C] (tropical plant bearing a) sweet, juicy fruit with an oval shape and a cluster of stiff leaves at the top. ⇨ illus at fruit.

ping /pɪŋ/ *n* [C] short, sharp, ringing sound. □ *vi* make this sound.

ping-pong /ˈpɪŋˌpɔŋ/ *n* (*P* = Ping-Pong) table tennis.

pin·ion[1] /ˈpɪnyən/ *n* [C] **1** bird's wing. **2** feather of a bird. □ vt **1** cut off a pinion of (a bird) to hamper flight. **2** bind the limb(s) of (a person) to prevent movement.

pin·ion[2] /ˈpɪnyən/ *n* [C] small gear with teeth fitting into those of a larger gear.

pink[1] /pɪŋk/ *n* **1** [U] pale red color. **2** [C] garden plant related to the carnation, with sweet-smelling white, pink, crimson or variegated flowers. **3** [U] highest degree: *in the ~ of condition.* □ *adj* **1** of pale red color. **2** having somewhat leftist political views. ⇨ red(2).

ˈpink·ish /-ɪʃ/ *adj* rather pink.

pink[2] /pɪŋk/ *vt* **1** pierce with a sword. **2** decorate (leather, cloth) with small holes, etc. **3** cut (cloth) so that it has a notched or scalloped edge.

pink·eye /ˈpɪŋkˌai/ *n* [U] contagious disease of the eyelid and eyeball, which makes them pinkish and inflamed.

pinky /ˈpɪŋki/ *n* [C] (*informal*) the little finger.

ˈpinky ring, one worn on the little finger.

pin·nacle /ˈpɪnəkəl/ *n* [C] **1** small spire or turret. **2** high, slender mountain peak. **3** (*fig*) highest point: *at the ~ of his fame.*

pi·nochle, pi·nocle /ˈpiˌnəkəl/ *n* [U] card game played with two packs from which the low-valued cards have been left out.

pin·point /ˈpɪnˌpɔint/ *n* [C] **1** point of a pin. **2** something very small. □ *vt* locate with extreme accuracy or precision: *~ a target.*

pin·stripe /ˈpɪnˌstraip/ *n* [C,U] **1** very thin strip, esp on cloth. **2** cloth with pinstripes, esp for men's suits.

pint /paint/ *n* [C] unit of measure for liquids equal to one half of a quart or about .473 of a liter: *a ~ of milk/beer.*

pin·to /ˈpɪntou/ *n* [C] (*pl* ~s, ~es) horse with irregular markings of two or more colors. □ *adj* pied; mottled.

pin-up /ˈpɪˌnəp/ *n* [C] picture, esp of an attractive girl, that is for hanging or pinning on a wall.

pi·on·eer /ˌpaiəˈnɪr/ *n* [C] **1** person who goes into a new or undeveloped country to settle or work there. **2** person who goes first into a new branch of study, uses a new method etc. □ *vi,vt* **1** act as a pioneer. **2** explore or open up.

pi·ous /ˈpaiəs/ *adj* having, showing, deep devotion to religion.

pi·ous·ly *adv*

pip[1] /pɪp/ *n* [C] **1** small seed, esp of a lemon, orange, apple or pear. ⇨ illus at fruit. **2** (*sl*) someone or something that is a very good example.

pip[2] /pɪp/ *n* [U] disease of birds.

pip[3] /pɪp/ *vt* break through (the shell of an egg) in hatching.

pip[4] /pɪp/ *n* [C] **1** spot on playing cards, dice, or dominoes. **2** (one kind of) spot on a radar screen.

pipe[1] /paip/ *n* [C] **1** tube through which liquids or gases can flow: *ˈgas ~s.* **2(a)** musical instrument consisting of a single tube that is played by blowing. **(b)** tube from which sound is produced in an organ. **(c)** (*pl*) bagpipes. **3** song or note of some birds. **4** tubular organ in the body: *the ˈwind~.* **5(a)** tube with a bowl and a mouthpiece, used for smoking tobacco. **(b)** quantity of tobacco held in the bowl.

ˌpipe of ˈpeace, = peace pipe.

pipe[2] /paip/ *vi,vt* **1** convey (water, etc) through pipes: *~ water into a house.* **2** play as on a pipe. ***pipe down,*** (*sl*) be less noisy. **3** speak in a high, shrill voice. ***pipe up,*** begin to speak. **4** trim or ornament something with piping(2).

pipe·dream, pipe dream /ˈpaipˌdrim/ *n* [C] hope or plan which has little chance of being achieved.

pipe·line /ˈpaipˌlain/ *n* [C] **1** system of pipes, often underground, for conveying liquids, gases, etc to distant places. **2** channel for goods or information.

piper /ˈpaipər/ *n* [C] one who plays on a pipe or bagpipes.

pip·ette /paiˈpet/ *n* [C] slender tube for transferring small quantities of liquid, esp in a laboratory.

pip·ing /ˈpaipɪŋ/ *n* [U] **1** length of pipe(1); system of pipes. **2** narrow cord used for decorating or edging. **3** action of playing on a pipe. **4** sound produced from a pipe. □ *adj* shrill like the sound from a pipe(2): *in a ~ voice.* □ *adv* ***piping hot,*** (of food) very hot.

pip·it /ˈpɪpɪt/ *n* [C] small songbird like a lark.

pip·pin /ˈpɪpɪn/ *n* [C] apple used in cooking.

pip·squeak /ˈpɪpˌskwik/ *n* [C] small, insignificant person.

pi·quancy /ˈpikənsi/ *n* [U] the quality of being piquant.

pi·quant /ˈpikənt/ *adj* **1** pleasantly sharp to the taste: *a ~ sauce.* **2** stimulating.

pi·quant·ly *adv*

pique /pik/ *vt* **1** irritate. **2** arouse. □ *n* [U] resentment: *go away in a fit of* ~.

pi·qué /pɪˈkei/ *n* [U] ribbed fabric, usually of cotton.

pi·racy /ˈpairəsi/ *n* (*pl* -ies) **1** [U] robbery on the high seas. **2** [U] pirating of a book, invention, etc. **3** [C] act of piracy.

pi·ra·nha /pɪˈranyə/ *n* [C] (kind of) flesh-eating, tropical American freshwater fish, noted for attacking and eating live animals.

pi·rate[1] /ˈpairɪt/ *n* [C] person who commits piracy. □ *vt* commit piracy.

pi·rati·cal /ˌpaiˈrætɪkəl/ *adj*

pi·rati·cally /-kli/ *adv*

pi·rate[2] /ˈpairɪt/ *vt* **1** violate the copyrights on a book, etc by (re)publishing it without permission. **2** violate radio or television broadcasting rights by transmitting on an assigned wavelength without permission.

pir·ou·ette /ˌpɪruˈet/ *n* [C] full turn of the body on the ball of the foot or the toe, as in dancing. □ *vi* perform a pirouette.

Pis·ces /ˈpaiˌsiz/ *n* the Fish, twelfth sign of the zodiac. ⇨ illus at zodiac.

piss /pɪs/ *vt, vi* ⚠ pass urine; urinate. ***pissed off*** (*sl,* ⚠) angry. □ *n* (avoided in polite use) urine.

pis·ta·chio /pɪˈstæʃ(i)ou/ *n* (*pl* ~s) **1** [C] (tree bearing a) nut with an edible green kernel. **2** [U] light green color.

pis·til /ˈpɪstjl/ *n* [C] seed-producing, female reproductive organ of a flower.

pis·tol /ˈpɪstjl/ *n* [C] small firearm held and fired in one hand.

pis·ton /ˈpɪstjn/ *n* [C] disk or short cylinder (as in an engine, pump, etc) which moves back and forth inside a hollow cylinder or tube.

ˈpiston valve, sliding valve in a brass musical instrument, which lowers the pitch when pressed.

pit[1] /pɪt/ *n* [C] **1** cavity or large hole in the ground. **2** covered hole as a trap for wild animals, etc. **3** hollow in an animal or plant body: *the pit of the stomach* (where the breastbone ends); *ˈarmpit* (underneath the arm where it joins the body). **4** scar or depression in the skin. **5** place, usually in front of the stage, for the orchestra in a theater. **6** sunken area in the floor of a garage from which the underside of a motor vehicle can be examined and repaired. **7** enclosed place in which animals are kept or put to fight. □ *vt* (-tt-) **1** mark with pits or with holes. **2** place in competition with: *pitted the two champions against each other.*

pit[2] /pɪt/ *n* [C] hard, stonelike seed of such fruits as cherries, plums, peaches, etc. □ *vt* (-tt-) remove pits from.

pitch[1] /pɪtʃ/ *n* [C] **1** act or example of pitching. **2** (*baseball*) single throw of a ball by a pitcher to a batter. **3** amount of slope, esp of a roof. **4** distance between one point on a gear tooth or screw thread and the corresponding point on the next gear tooth or screw thread. **5** distance which a propeller moves forward in one complete revolution. **6** degree of highness or lowness of a sound: *the* ~ *of a voice.* **7** degree of intensity: *The noise made by the crowd reached such a* ~ *that we could not hear the speaker.* **8** (*informal*) very persuasive sales talk, arguments, etc.

pitch[2] /pɪtʃ/ *n* [U] sticky black substance made from coal tar, petroleum, etc, used for paving, roofing, waterproofing, etc.

ˌpitch-ˈblack *adj* very black.

ˌpitch-ˈdark *adj* very dark.

ˈpitch·man /-mən/ *n* [C] (*pl* ~men /-men/) hawker; salesman who gives a pitch(8) for his wares.

pitch[3] /pɪtʃ/ *vt,vi* **1** set up, erect: ~ *camp/a tent.* **2** throw, toss (a ball, etc): ~ *hay.* **3** (*music*) set in a particular key: *This song is* ~*ed too low for me.* **4** (cause to) fall headlong: *The boat overturned and the passengers were* ~*ed out.* **5** (of a ship) move up and down as the bow rises and falls. ⇨ roll[2](6). **6** ***pitch in,*** **(a)** set to work with energy. **(b)** give or contribute to a common task, fund, etc: *We* ~*ed in $5 each to buy the food.* **7** (*baseball*) throw (the ball) to the batter. **8** (*baseball*) play (a game) as pitcher; act as pitcher.

pitch·blende /ˈpɪtʃˌblend/ *n* [U] mineral that is the source of uranium and radium.

pitch·er[1] /ˈpɪtʃər/ *n* [C] open container for serving cold liquids (water, milk, etc) with a single handle and a pouring spout or lip.

pitch·er[2] /ˈpɪtʃər/ *n* [C] (*baseball*) player who throws the ball to the batter. ⇨ illus at baseball.

pitch·fork /ˈpɪtʃˌfɔrk/ *n* [C] large, long-handled fork for pitching or lifting hay.

pit·eous /ˈpɪtiəs/ *adj* arousing pity.

pit·eous·ly *adv*

pit·fall /ˈpɪtˌfɔl/ *n* [C] **1** covered pit as a trap for animals. **2** (*fig*) hidden trap or danger.

pith /pɪθ/ *n* [U] **1** soft substance that fills the stems of some plants (eg reeds). **2** (*fig*) essential part: *the* ~ *of his argument/speech, etc.*

pith·ily /-əli/ *adv*

pithy *adj* (-ier, -iest) **(a)** of, like, full of, pith. **(b)** short and full of meaning: ~ *remarks.*

piti·able /ˈpɪtiəbəl/ *adj* pitiful.

piti·ably /-əbli/ *adv*

piti·ful /ˈpɪtifəl, ˈpɪtəfəl/ *adj* **1** causing pity: *a* ~ *sight.* **2** arousing contempt: *his* ~ *behavior.*

piti·fully /-f(ə)li/ *adv*

piti·less /ˈpɪtilɪs, ˈpɪtəlɪs/ *adj* without pity.

piti·less·ly *adv*

piti·less·ness /-nɪs/ *n* [U]

pit·tance /ˈpɪtəns/ *n* [C] very small amount, esp of money: *work all day for a mere* ~.

pit·ter-pat·ter /ˈpɪtərˌpætər/ *n* [U] rapid succession of light, tapping sounds: *the* ~ *of rain.*

pi·tu·itary /pɪˈtuəˌteri/ *n* [C] (*pl* -ies) (also **pituitary gland**) small ductless gland at the base of the brain, secreting hormones that influence growth, etc.

pity /ˈpɪti/ *n* **1** [U] feeling of sorrow for the troubles, sufferings, etc of another person: *be filled with/feel* ~ *for her.* ***for pity's sake,*** (used when making an earnest request): *For* ~*'s sake try to save him!* **2** (only in the *sing*) cause for regret or sorrow: *What a* ~ (= How unfortunate) (*that*) *you can't come with us!* □ *vt* (*pt,pp* -ied) feel pity for: *He is to be pitied for his unhappiness.*

piv·ot /ˈpɪvət/ *n* [C] **1** central pin or shaft on which something turns. **2** (*fig*) central part or point. **3** □ *vt,vi* turn (as) on a pivot.

piv·otal /-təl/ *adj*
pixie, pixy /ˈpɪksi/ *n* [C] (*pl* -ies) small elf or fairy.
pizza /ˈpitsə/ *n* [C,U] thin layer of bread dough baked with a topping of tomatoes, cheese, etc. **ˈpizza parlor,** pizzeria.
piz·ze·ria /ˌpitsəˈriə, pɪtsə-/ *n* [C] (*pl* ~s) place where pizzas are made and sold.
PJ's /ˈpiˌdʒeiz/ *n pl* (*informal*) pajamas.
pk. *abbr* = **1** pack. **2** park. **3** peak.
pkg. *abbr* = **1** package. **2** parking.
pkwy. *abbr* = parkway.
pl. *abbr* = **1** place. **2** plural.
plac·ard /ˈplæˌkard/ *n* [C] notice or printed announcement (to be) publicly displayed; poster. ◻ *vt* post a placard on or in.
pla·cate /ˈpleiˌkeit/ *vt* pacify; soothe.
place¹ /pleis/ *n* [C] **1** space (to be) occupied by a person or thing: *I can't be in two ~s at once.* ***in/out of place,*** in/not in the right or proper place: *I like to have everything in ~.* ***out of place*** (*fig*) unsuitable: *his remarks were out of ~.* ***in place of,*** instead of. ***take the place of,*** substitute for: *Plastics have taken the ~ of many natural materials.* ***take place,*** happen. **2** particular location, as a city, town, etc. ***ˈgo places,*** (*informal*) have increasing success. **3** building, location, or area of land used for some particular purpose: *a ~ of worship,* a church, mosque etc; *a ~ of business.* **4** particular part: *a sore ~ on my neck.* **5** particular part reached in reading: *I've lost my ~.* **6** rank or position. **7** suitable or proper position, situation, etc: *It's not his ~ to make that decision.* **8** (*math*) position of a figure in a series or in a numeral. **9** job. **10** seat or accommodation for one person: *set a ~ at the table; found a ~ in the theater.* **11** house or other residence: *He has a nice little ~ in the country. Come over to my ~ some evening.* **12** street, square, etc in a town: *They rented a house in Laura Place.*
place² /pleis/ *vt* **1** put in a particular place or position: *Place them in the right order.* **2** appoint to a position: *He was ~d in command of the Second Army.* **3(a)** invest money (constructed with *in*): *~ $2,000 in municipal bonds.* **(b)** bet money (constructed with *on*): *He ~ $10 on his favorite horse in the second race.* **4** put; give: *~ an order for books.* **5** recognize or remember a person: *I know that man's face, but I can't ~ him.* **6** (also *vi*) finish in a particular position or rank in a contest, race, etc: *We (were) ~d third in our division.*
place·ment *n* [C,U] (instance of) placing.
place·kick *n* (*football*) one in which the ball is placed on the ground before it is kicked.
pla·cen·ta /pləˈsentə/ *n* [C] (*pl* ~s) organ lining the uterus during pregnancy, by which the fetus is nourished.
placer /ˈpleisər/ *n* [C] bed of sand or gravel containing gold.
ˈplacer mine, one at which gold is mined by washing the sand or gravel.
pla·cid /ˈplæsɪd/ *adj* calm; peaceful.
pla·cid·ly *adv*
pla·gia·rism /ˈpleidʒəˌrɪzəm/ *n* **1** [U] plagiarizing. **2** [C] instance of this.
pla·gia·rist /-ɪst/ *n* [C] person who plagiarizes.
pla·gia·rize /ˈpleidʒəˌraiz/ *vt* take and use somebody else's ideas, words, etc as if they were one's own.
plague /pleig/ *n* [C,U] **1** contagious, usually fatal disease which spreads quickly: *bubonic ~.* **2** (*fig*) cause of serious trouble or annoyance: *a ~ of locusts/flies.* ◻ *vt* **1** cause trouble or suffering. **2** annoy: *Stop plaguing me with your questions!*
plaid /plæd/ *n* **1** [C] long piece of woolen cloth worn over one shoulder by Scottish Highlanders. **2** [C] pattern of stripes of different widths and colors which cross to form squares; tartan. **3** [U] cloth with a tartan pattern, as used for this article of dress.
plain¹ /plein/ *adj* (-er, -est) **1** easy to see, hear or understand: *in ~ sight. The meaning is quite ~.* **2** simple; ordinary; without luxury or ornament: *~ cooking; a ~ blue dress,* without a pattern on it, or without trimmings, etc. ***in plain clothes,*** in ordinary clothes, not in police uniform. **3** straightforward; frank: *~ speaking.* **4** not pretty or handsome: *It's a pity his wife is so ~.* ◻ *adv* **1** clearly: *learn to speak ~.* **2** completely: *just ~ foolish.*
ˈplain·clothes *n pl* civilian or ordinary clothes when worn instead of a uniform by a policeman.
ˈplain·clothes·man /-mən/ (*pl* ~clothesmen /-men/) policeman (eg a detective) who does not wear a uniform.
plain·ly *adv*
plain·ness /-nɪs/ *n* [U]
plain² /plein/ *n* [C] area of level land: *the ~s of Kansas.*
plain-spo·ken /ˌplein-ˈspoukən/ *adj* frank in speech.
plain·tiff /ˈpleintɪf/ *n* [C] person who brings an action at law. ⇨ defendant.
plain·tive /ˈpleintɪv/ *adj* sounding sad.
plait /pleit, plæt/ *n* [C] **1** braid, esp of hair. **2** pleat. ◻ *vt* **1** braid. **2** pleat.
plan /plæn/ *n* [C] **1** diagram or drawing (eg of a building, machine, model, etc) showing the relative size, positions, etc of the parts: *~(s) for a new school.* **2** arrangement for doing or using something, considered in advance: *make ~s for the vacation.* ◻ *vt* (-nn-) make a plan: *~ a house/vacation/a military campaign. We're ~ning to go to England this summer.*
plan·ner *n* [C]
plane¹ /plein/ *n* [C] one of several kinds of tree, such as the sycamore, with spreading branches, broad leaves and thin bark.
plane² /plein/ *n* [C] tool for smoothing and leveling the surface of wood by taking shavings from it. ◻ *vt,vi* use a plane.
plane³ /plein/ *n* [C] **1** flat or level surface. **2** (*geom*) surface such that a straight line joining any two points on it lies wholly within the surface. **3** airplane. **4** level or stage (of development, etc): *on a higher social ~.* ◻ *adj* **1** flat; level. **2** of or relating to planes: *~ geometry.*
planet /ˈplænɪt/ *n* [C] one of the heavenly bodies (eg *Mars, Venus*) which move around a star such as the sun.
plan·e·tary /ˈplænəˌteri/ *adj*

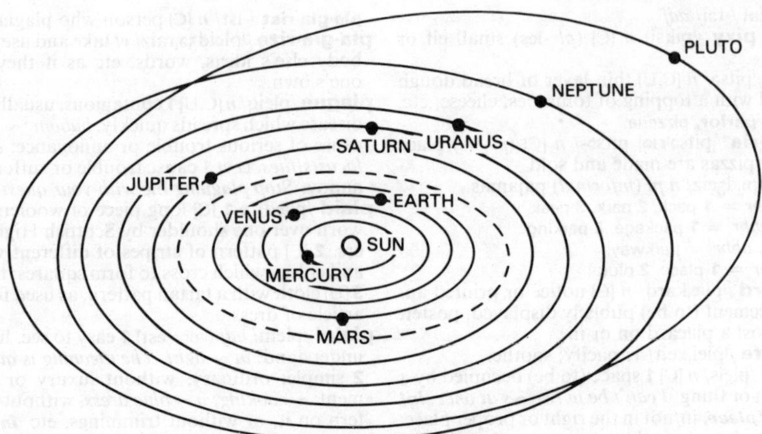

PLANETS OF OUR SOLAR SYSTEM

plan·e·tar·i·um /ˌplænəˈteriəm/ *n* [C] **1** optical device that projects the images of heavenly bodies on the ceiling of a dome. **2** place in which such a device is housed or operated.

plank /plæŋk/ *n* [C] **1** wide, flat board. **2** basic principle in a political platform. ⇨ platform(2). □ *vt* cover (a floor, etc) with planks.

plank·ton /ˈplæŋktən/ *n* [U] the minute forms of animal and plant life that drift in or float on the water of oceans, lakes, rivers, etc.

plant¹ /plænt/ *n* [C] **1** living organism which differs from an animal by lacking the ability to move itself, by having cell walls of cellulose, and by having the ability to make its own food with the aid of sunlight. **2** such an organism of a kind that is smaller than trees and shrubs, and that lacks a woody stem. **3** factory. **4** buildings and equipment of an institution.

plant² /plænt/ *vt* **1** put plants, bushes, trees, etc in the ground for growing: *~ a garden with rose bushes/plant rose bushes in a garden*. **2** (*fig*) cause to form and develop: *~ doubt in the minds of the members*. **3** place firmly in position; take up a position or attitude: *~ed himself in my chair*. **4** establish, found (a community, colony, etc). **5** deliver (a blow, etc) with deliberate aim: *~ a blow on his ear*. **6** place so as to mislead or trap: *He ~ed the stolen pen in my room*.

plan·tain¹ /ˈplæntən/ *n* [C] (tropical plant bearing a) fruit similar to the banana.

plan·tain² /ˈplæntən/ *n* [U] common wild plant with broad leaves and spokes of tiny seeds.

plan·ta·tion /plænˈteiʃən/ *n* [C] **1** area of land planted with trees: *~s of fir and pine*. **2** large farm or estate on which a cash crop is cultivated, usually by resident workers.

plant·er /ˈplæntər/ *n* [C] **1** person who grows crops on a plantation. **2** machine for planting. **3** ornamental container for growing plants.

plaque /plæk/ *n* **1** [C] flat plate used as an ornament or memorial. **2** [U] film or crust which sometimes forms on the teeth.

plasma /ˈplæzmə/ *n* [U] clear, yellowish liquid part of blood in which the blood cells are carried.

plas·ter /ˈplæstər/ *n* **1** [U] soft mixture of lime, sand, water, etc that hardens to a smooth coating for walls and ceilings. **2** [C] piece of fabric spread with a medicinal substance, used eg to heal an injury. □ *vt* **1** cover (a wall, etc) with plaster(1). **2** put a plaster(2) on (the body). **3** cover thickly, as with plaster: *hair ~ed with oil*.

plas·terer *n* [C]

ˌplaster of ˈParis, white paste that becomes very hard when dry, used for making molds, casts, etc.

plas·tic /ˈplæstɪk/ *adj* **1** easily shaped or molded: *Clay is a ~ substance*. **2** made of plastic: *~ raincoats/curtains*. **3** of the shaping or modeling of materials: *the ~ arts*. □ *n* [C,U] (kinds of) manmade material which can be shaped, molded, or drawn into threads.

plas·tic·ity /plæˈstɪsəti/ *n* [U] state or quality of being plastic (1).

ˌplastic ˈsurgery, surgery for the restoration of deformed or diseased parts of the body (by grafting skin, etc).

plate¹ /pleit/ *n* **1** [C] **(a)** shallow, usually circular dish from which food is served or eaten: *a ˈdinner ~*. **(b)** contents of this: *a ~ of meat and vegetables*. **(c)** food and service for one person: *dinner at $10 a ~*. **2** [U] a thin coating of metal on (usually) another metal: *silver ~,* a coating of silver. **3** [U] (*collect*) gold or silver household articles, eg spoons, dishes, etc. **4** [C] flat, thin sheet of metal or other material. **5** [C] sheet of glass with a coating sensitive to light, that is used for photography. **6** [C] flat piece of metal on which something is stamped, engraved, etc: *a license ~*. **7** [C] sheet of metal, plastic, rubber, etc from which the pages of a book are printed. **8** [C] book illustration, esp one printed separately from the text. **9** [C] thin piece of plastic or metal fitted to the shape of the mouth, with false teeth attached to it: *upper and lower ~s*. **10** [C] (*baseball*) (also **home play**) base at which a batter stands, which must be touched by a player after he touches the other three bases in order to score a home run. ⇨ illus at baseball.

plate·ful /-ˌfʊl/ *n* [C] amount that a plate(1) holds.

plate² /pleit/ *vt* cover with a thin coating of metal. ⇨ plate¹(2).

pla·teau /plæˈtou/ *n* [C] (*pl* ∼s or ∼x /-ˈtouz/) **1** expanse of level land higher than the surrounding land. **2** level or state, esp one which is stable.

plate glass /ˌpleit ˈglæs/ *n* [U] thick, very clear glass made in sheets for large windows, mirrors, etc.

plate·let /ˈpleitlɪt/ *n* [C] flat body found in the blood, that assists in clotting.

plat·form /ˈplætˌfɔrm/ *n* [C] **1** flat surface which is at a higher level than the surrounding area or floor: *Which ∼ does your train leave from? She led the speaker to the ∼.* **2** statement of principles, esp of a political party.

plat·ing /ˈpleitɪŋ/ *n* [U] (esp) thin coating of gold, silver, etc. ⇨ plate¹(2).

plat·i·num /ˈplætənəm/ *n* [U] gray metal (symbol **Pt**) used for jewelry and in industry.

plati·tude /ˈplætəˌtud/ *n* [C] statement that is obviously true, but trite and ordinary.

plati·tudi·nous /ˌplætəˈtudənəs/ *adj*

pla·toon /pləˈtun/ *n* [C] **1** body of soldiers, subdivision of a company, usually commanded by a lieutenant. **2** (*football*) group of players sent into or taken out of a game in a body.

plat·ter /ˈplætər/ *n* [C] **1** large, shallow dish for serving food, esp meat and fish. **2** (*sl*) phonograph record.

plat·y·pus /ˈplætəpəs/ *n* [C] ⇨ duckbilled platypus.

plau·dit /ˈplɔdɪt/ *n* [C] (usually *pl*) (*formal*) approval: *gratified at the ∼s of the audience.*

plaus·ible /ˈplɔzəbəl/ *adj* seeming to be true or reasonable: *a ∼ excuse/explanation.*

plaus·ibly /-əbli/ *adv*

play¹ /plei/ *n* **1** [C] (performance of a) drama, story, etc on the stage, TV, etc. **2** [U] (activity done for) amusement: recreation: *The children are at ∼*, playing. ***a play on words,*** pun. **3** [U] the (manner of) playing: *rough ∼ in a football game.* ***in/out of play,*** (of a ball) in/not in legitimate use according to the rules of the game. ***fair play,*** ⇨ fair¹ (1). **4** (*sing* only) turn or move in a game: *It's your ∼.* **5** [U] gambling: *lose $50 in one evening's ∼.* **6** [U] light, quick, movement: *the ∼ of sunlight on water.* **7** [U] (space for) free and easy movement; scope for activity: *give free ∼ to one's emotions; a knot with too much ∼*, one that is not tight enough. **8** [U] activity; operation: *the ∼ of natural forces.* ***come into play,*** begin to operate or be active. ***bring sth into play,*** make use of it; bring it into action.

play² /plei/ *vt, vi* (*pt, pp* ∼ed /pleid/) **1** (contrasted with *work*) have fun; do things to pass the time pleasantly, as children do: *Let's go out and ∼. She was ∼ing with the kitten.* **2** pretend, for fun, to be or do: *Let's ∼ (at being) pirates.* **3** practice; do: *He has ∼ed a trick on me.* ***play the market,*** ⇨ market¹ (4). ***play for time,*** ⇨ time¹ (3). **4** take part in a game or sport: *He ∼s cards/football/tennis.* ***play fair,*** act fairly or in accordance with the rules. ***play the game,*** **(a)** observe the rules of the game. **(b)** (*fig*) be fair and honest. **5** compete against: *Who's ∼ing the Celtics next week?* ***play ball (with),*** (*informal*) cooperate. **6** put into action or use in a game: *∼ the ace of hearts.* ***play one's cards right,*** (*fig*) make good use of one's opportunities. **7(a)** perform on (a musical instrument): *∼ the piano.* **(b)** perform (a musical composition): *∼ a Beethoven sonata.* **8** (cause to) produce sounds from a broadcast, recorded material, etc: *∼ed the radio until I was ready to scream.* ***play second fiddle (to),*** ⇨ fiddle. **9(a)** perform or act (a part) in a drama: *∼ the hero in a romantic comedy.* **(b)** be performed or presented in front of an audience: *What's ∼ing at the opera this week?* **10** act in a certain way. ***play the fool,*** act foolishly. **11** move in a free, rapid, lively manner: *sunlight ∼ing on the water. They ∼ed colored lights over the dance floor.* **12** operate continuously; discharge in a steady stream: *The firemen ∼ed their hoses on the burning building.* **13** ***play a fish,*** (when angling with a rod and line) allow a fish to exhaust itself by pulling against the line. **14** treat lightly, idly, or casually: *∼ed with the idea of going into business.* **15** toy with; handle lightly or casually: *She's always ∼ing with her bracelets.* **16** (special uses with *adverbial particles* and *prepositions*):

play sth back (of a recording of speech, music, etc) play it for review, esp just after it has been made.

play sth down, deliberately treat it as unimportant.

play one person off against another, encourage rivalry or disagreement between them, esp for one's own advantage.

play on/upon sth, try to make use of (a person's feelings, trust, etc) for one's own advantage: *He tried to ∼ on her sympathies.*

play sth out, (*fig*) play it to the finish: *The long struggle between the strikers and their employers is not yet ∼ed out.*

play sth up, make the most of or exaggerate it: *His account ∼s up his importance.* ***play up to sb,*** (*informal*) flatter a person to win his favor: *He always ∼s up to the boss.*

play·boy /ˈpleiˌbɔi/ *n* [C] rich, pleasure-loving man.

player /ˈpleiər/ *n* [C] **1** person who plays a game. **2** actor. **3** person who plays a musical instrument. **4** mechanical device for producing musical sounds: *a ˈrecord ∼.*

play·fel·low /ˈpleiˌfelou/ *n* [C] playmate.

play·ful /ˈpleifəl/ *adj* **1** in a mood for play; fond of playing: *as ∼ as a kitten.* **2** humorous; joking: *in a ∼ manner.*

play·ful·ly /-fəli/ *adv*

play·ful·ness /-nɪs/ *n* [U]

play·ground /ˈpleiˌgraund/ *n* [C] area of ground at a school, etc for children to play.

play·house /ˈpleiˌhaus/ *n* [C] (*pl* ∼es /-ˌhauzɪz/) **1** = theater. **2** small house for children to play in.

play·ing card /ˈpleiɪŋ ˌkard/ *n* [C] any one of a set of cards which is marked to show its rank and suit, and is used for playing games. ⇨ illus at card.

play·mate /ˈpleiˌmeit/ *n* [C] friend a child plays

with.
play·off /ˈpleiˌɔf/ *n* [C] game or series of games played to break a tie or determine a championship.
play·pen /ˈpleiˌpen/ *n* [C] portable enclosure a baby can be left to play in.
play·thing /ˈpleiˌθɪŋ/ *n* [C] toy; thing to play with.
play·wright /ˈpleiˌrait/ *n* [C] person who writes plays.
plaza /ˈplæzə, ˈplazə/ *n* [C] (*pl* ~s) open square (esp in a town or city).
plea /pli/ *n* [C] **1** (*legal*) answer made by or for a defendant charged in a law court. **2** request: *~s for mercy*. **3** reason or excuse offered for doing wrong or failing to do something, etc.
plead /plid/ *vt,vi* (*pt,pp* ~ed, or pled /pled/) **1** (*legal*) address a court of law on behalf of either the plaintiff or the defendant: *~ for/against her*. **2** admit or deny that one is guilty: *Did you ~ not guilty?* **3** offer as an explanation or excuse: *The thief ~ed poverty*. **4** ask earnestly: *He ~ed with his son to be less trouble to his mother*. **5** argue in favor of; give reasons for (a cause, etc): *~ the cause of political freedom*.
pleas·ant /ˈplezənt/ *adj* giving pleasure; agreeable; delightful: *a ~ afternoon/taste/wine/surprise/companion*.
pleas·ant·ly *adv*
pleas·ant·ness /-nɪs/ *n* [U]
pleas·ant·ry /ˈplezəntri/ *n* (*pl* -ies) (*formal*) **1** [U] playfulness. **2** [C] humorous or joking remark.
please /pliz/ *vi,vt* **1** (used as a polite form of request): *Come in, ~. Please come in. Two coffees, ~. Please don't do that*. **2** give satisfaction to: *It's difficult to ~ everybody. Are you ~d with your new clothes?* **3** wish; choose; prefer: *I shall do as I ~. Take as many as you ~*.
pleased /plizd/ *adj* glad; feeling or showing satisfaction: *He looked ~d with himself. I'm very ~d to see you looking so fit. They seemed ~ that so many of their friends were there*.
pleas·ing /ˈplizɪŋ/ *adj* giving pleasure (*to*); agreeable.
pleas·ure /ˈpleʒər/ *n* **1** [U] feeling of enjoyment, of being happy or satisfied: *It gave me such ~ to hear of your success. May we have the ~ of your company for lunch? Some boys take great ~ in teasing their little sisters*. **2** [U] (*formal*) will; desire: *You may go or stay at your ~*, as you wish. **3** [C] something that gives happiness: *the ~s of friendship*.
ˈ**pleasure-boat/-craft,** one used for enjoyment only.
pleas·ur·able /ˈpleʒərəbl/ *adj* giving enjoyment.
pleas·ur·ably /-əblɪ/ *adv*
pleat /ˈplit/ *n* [C] fold made by doubling cloth on itself. □ *vt* make pleats in: *a ~ed skirt*.
plebi·scite /ˈplebɪsait/ *n* [C] (decision made about a political question by) the votes of all qualified citizens.
plec·trum /ˈplektrəm/ *n* [C] small piece of metal, plastic, etc attached to the finger for plucking the strings of some instruments, eg the guitar.
pled /pled/ *pt,pp* of plead.
pledge /pledʒ/ *n* **1** [C] something left with a person to be kept until the giver has done whatever he has to do. **2** [U] state of being left on these conditions: *put/hold goods in ~*. **3** [C] something given as a sign of love, approval, etc. **4** [U] agreement; promise: *under ~ of secrecy*. ***take/sign the pledge,*** (esp) make a written promise not to take alcoholic drink. □ *vt* **1** give as security; put in pawn. **2** make an undertaking: *be ~d to secrecy; ~ one's word/honor*.
ple·na·ry /ˈplinəri, ˈplen-/ *adj* **1** (of powers, authority) unlimited; absolute. **2** (of meetings) attended by all who have a right to attend: *a ~ session*.
plen·i·po·ten·tia·ry /ˌplenəpəˈtenʃəri/ *n* [C] (*pl* -ries) diplomatic representative having full power to act, make decisions, etc (on behalf of his government, etc).
plen·te·ous /ˈplentiəs/ *adj* (*liter*) plentiful.
plen·ti·ful /ˈplentɪfəl/ *adj* existing in large quantities or numbers.
plen·ti·fully /-fəli/ *adv*
plenty /ˈplenti/ *n* [U] **1** as much as or more than is needed or desired: *We'll get to the station in ~ of time. Six will be ~*, as many as I need. **2** a large number or quantity: *There are ~ of eggs*.
pleur·isy /ˈplʊrəsi/ *n* [U] serious illness marked by inflammation of the delicate membrane of the chest cavity and the lungs.
plexus /ˈpleksəs/ *n* [C] (*pl* ~es /-səsɪz/, ~) (*anat*) network of nerves or blood vessels in the body.
pli·able /ˈplaiəbəl/ *adj* **1** easily bent, shaped or twisted. **2** easily influenced.
pli·a·bil·ity /ˌplaiəˈbɪləti/ *n* [U]
pli·ant /ˈplaiənt/ *adj* = pliable.
pli·ers /ˈplaiərz/ *n pl* (also ***a pair of pliers***) pincers with long, flat jaws, used for holding, bending or cutting.
plight[1] /plait/ *n* [C] serious and difficult condition: *in a terrible ~*.
plight[2] /plait/ *vt* (*formal*) **1** promise or pledge solemnly. **2** engage (to be married).
plinth /plɪnθ/ *n* [C] square base or block on which a column or statue stands.
plod /plad/ *vi,vt* (-dd-) **1** walk slowly or heavily. **2** work with great effort: *~ away at a dull task*.
plop /plap/ *n* [C] sound (as) of an object dropping into water. □ *adv* with a plop. □ *vt,vi* (-pp-) **1** make, fall with, a plop. **2** sink heavily: *~ down in a comfortable chair*.
plot[1] /plat/ *n* [C] (usually small) piece of ground: *a* ˈ*building ~; a ~ of vegetables*. □ *vt,vi* (-tt-) **1** make a plan, map or diagram of. **2** mark on a map, diagram, graph.
plot[2] /plat/ *n* [C] **1** secret plan (good or bad): *a ~ to overthrow the government*. **2** main story of a novel, drama, etc. □ *vt,vi* (-tt-) make or take part in, a secret plan.
plot·ter *n* [C]
plover /ˈpləvər, ˈplouvər/ *n* [C] any of several long-legged, short-tailed shore birds with short, stout bills.
plow /plau/ *n* [C] **1** implement for cutting, lifting, or turning up soil. **2** any kind of implement resembling a plow. □ *vt,vi* **1** break up (land) with a plow: *~ a field*. **2** make or force a way through, like a plow: *~ through the mud/a dull textbook*. **3** ***plow into,*** (*informal*) run into or

against with force: *The truck ~ed right into a brick wall.*

plow·man /ˈplaumən/ *n* [C] (*pl* -men /-men/) man who operates a plow.

plow·share /ˈplauˌʃer/ *n* [C] broad cutting blade of a plow.

ploy /plɔi/ *n* [C] trick for gaining an advantage: *crying as a ~ to gain sympathy.*

pluck /plək/ *vt,vi* **1** pull the hair or feathers off: *Has this chicken been ~ed?* **2** pick (flowers, fruit, etc). **3** take hold of and pull: *He was ~ing at his mother's skirt.* □ *n* **1** [U] courage; spirit: *a boy with plenty of ~.* **2** [C] short, sharp pull.

plucky *adj* (-ier, -iest) brave.

plug /pləg/ *n* [C] **1** piece of wood, rubber, etc used to stop up a hole (eg in a sink, bathtub, etc). **2** device for making a connection with a supply of electric current: *put the ~ in the socket.* **3** spark plug. **4** cake of pressed or twisted tobacco. **5** (*informal*) piece of favorable publicity (eg on a radio or TV program). ⇨ 4 below. □ *vt,vi* (-gg-) **1** stop or fill with a plug: *~ (up) a leak.* **2** ***plug (sth) in,*** make a connection with a plug(2): *~ in the TV set.* **3** ***plug away at (sth),*** (*informal*) work hard at it: *He ~ed away at his assignment.* **4** (*informal*) advertise or recommend (something): *~ a new song,* eg on radio or TV. **5** ***plug sb,*** (*sl*) shoot him.

plug ˈnickel, (only in:) ***not worth a plug nickel,*** (*informal*) worthless.

plum /pləm/ *n* **1** [C] (tree having a) soft round, smooth-skinned fruit with a stone like a seed. ⇨ illus at fruit. **2** [C] raisin in a cake, pudding, etc. **3** [C] something (eg a job) considered good and desirable. **4** [U] dark reddish purple color. □*adj* dark reddish purple.

plum·age /ˈplumɪdʒ/ *n* [U] bird's feathers: *brightly colored ~.*

plumb /pləm/ *n* [C] weight hung on the end of a cord or rope, used for finding the depth of water or testing whether a wall is vertical. □ *adv* **1** straight up and down. **2** (*informal*) completely: *~ crazy.* □ *vt* (*fig*) **1** test (as) with a plumb. **2** get to the bottom of: *~ the depths of a mystery.*

plumber /ˈpləmər/ *n* [C] workman who installs and repairs pipes.

plumb·ing /ˈpləmɪŋ/ *n* [U] **1** the work of a plumber. **2** the water pipes, fixtures, etc connected with the use of water in a building.

plume /plum/ *n* [C] **1** feather, esp a large one used as a decoration. **2** something suggesting a feather by its shape: *a ~ of smoke.* □ *vt* **1** (of a bird) smooth (its own) feathers. **2** ***plume oneself,*** show or take pride: *~d himself on his cleverness.*

plum·met /ˈpləmɪt/ *n* [C] plumb. □ *vi* fall; plunge: *Stock prices have ~ed.*

plump[1] /pləmp/ *adj* rounded and fat in a pleasant-looking way: *a baby with ~ cheeks.* □ *vt,vi* make or become rounded: *She ~ed up the pillows.*

plump[2] /pləmp/ *vi,vt* (cause to) fall or drop, suddenly and heavily: *~ (oneself) down in a chair; ~ down a heavy bag.* □ *adv* suddenly, abruptly: *fall ~ into the hole.* □ *n* [C] abrupt, heavy fall.

plun·der /ˈpləndər/ *vt,vi* rob, as in wartime; pillage: *~ a conquered town.* □ *n* [U] **1** act of plundering. **2** goods plundered.

plunge /pləndʒ/ *vt,vi* **1** put or thrust (something) suddenly and with force into: *~ one's hand into cold water/a hole.* **2** move forward and downward quickly; fall. **3** (cause to) enter suddenly: *~d into the water; ~ the family into gloom.* □ *n* [C] act of plunging (eg from a diving board into water).

plunger *n* [C] **(a)** part of a mechanism that moves with a plunging motion, eg the piston of a pump. **(b)** suction device for clearing a blocked pipe.

plunk /pləŋk/ *vt,vi* **1** drop suddenly or heavily: *~ed a silver dollar on the counter; ~ down on a bed.* **2** pluck the strings of a musical instrument. **3** make a harsh, metallic sound. □ *n* [C] sound that is harsh and metallic.

plu·ral /ˈplʊrəl/ *n* [C], *adj* (form of a word) used to refer to more than one: *The ~ of "child" is "children."*

plus /pləs/ *adj* **1** positive; greater than zero: *a ~ quantity.* **2** slightly more than: *a grade of C ~.* □ *prep* **1** with the addition of: *Two ~ five is seven.* **2** (*informal*) with. □ *n* [C] (*pl* ~ses) **1** (also ˈ**plus sign**) sign (+) used to indicate addition. **2** advantage: *Great height is a ~ in basketball.*

plush /pləʃ/ *n* [U] fabric like velvet, with a longer and deeper pile. □ *adj* (*informal*) (also **plushy**) luxurious: *a ~(y) restaurant.*

Pluto /ˈplutou/ *n* (*astron*) planet farthest from the sun. ⇨ illus at planet.

plu·to·cracy /pluˈtakrəsi/ *n* [C,U] (*pl* -ies) (government by a) rich and powerful class.

plu·to·crat /ˈplutəˌkræt/ *n* [C] person who is powerful because of his wealth.

plu·to·cratic /ˌplutəˈkrætɪk/ *adj*

plu·to·nium /pluˈtouniəm/ *n* [U] radioactive element (symbol **Pu**) used in nuclear reactors and weapons.

ply[1] /plai/ *n* [C] (*pl* -ies) **1** layer of wood or thickness of cloth. **2** one strand in wool, rope, etc: *four-ply wool for knitting socks.*

ply[2] /plai/ *vt,vi* (*pt,pp* plied, *present part* plying) **1** (*formal*) work (esp with an instrument, eg a needle). ***ply a trade,*** work at it skillfully. **2** (of ships, buses, etc) go or travel regularly to and from: *ships that ply between Glasgow and New York.* **3** ***ply sb with sth,*** keep him constantly supplied with: *ply one's guests with food and drink; plied her with questions.*

ply·wood /ˈplaiˌwʊd/ *n* [U] material made by gluing together thin layers of wood.

PM, pm /ˌpi ˈem/ *abbr* (= *Lat* post meridiem) (in the) afternoon; between noon and midnight. ⇨ App 2.

pmt. *abbr* = payment.

pneu·matic /nuˈmætɪk/ *adj* **1** of or relating to air or other gases. **2** worked or driven by compressed air: *~ drills.* **3** filled with compressed air: *~ tires.*

pneu·mati·cally /-kli/ *adv*

pneu·monia /nuˈmounyə/ *n* [U] serious illness marked by inflammation of one or both lungs.

P.O. *abbr* = post office. (*Note:* this *abbr* is often retained in speech as /ˌpi ˈou/ in **P.O. Box.**)

poach[1] /poutʃ/ *vt* cook (an egg, fish, etc) in

simmering liquid.

poach[2] /poutʃ/ *vt,vi* (go on another's property and) hunt or fish illegally.

poacher *n* [C]

pock /pak/ *n* [C] **1** small swelling on the skin caused by smallpox or other disease. **2** pockmark.

pock·et /ˈpakɪt/ *n* [C] **1** small bag attached to an article of clothing, for carrying things in. ***have sb in one's pocket,*** have him under one's control. ***pick sb's pocket.*** ⇨ pick³(1). **2** money; means. ***in/out of pocket,*** rich(er)/poor(er). **3** (esp) small cavity in the ground or in rock, containing gold or ore. **4** (also **ˈair pocket**) downward current of air which can cause an aircraft to drop or lose altitude suddenly. **5** small, isolated area or group: *~s of resistance; ~s of unemployment in the South.* **6** (as an *adjective*) like a pocket in appearance or use: *~book.* **7** (as an *adjective*) suitable for carrying in a pocket: *~ calculator.* □ *vt* **1** put into one's pocket: *He ~ed the money.* **2** keep for oneself (often dishonestly): *He ~ed half the profits.*

pocket·ful /-ˌfʊl/ *n* [C] amount which a pocket holds.

pock·et·book /ˈpakɪtˌbʊk/ *n* [C] **1** container for money, papers, etc. **2** handbag. **3** income; means: *My ~ can't stand the expense.* **4** (also **pocket book**) small, paperback book.

pock·et·knife /ˈpakɪtˌnaif/ *n* [C] (*pl* -knives /-ˌnaivz/) small knife with a folding blade or blades, to be carried in the pocket.

pock·mark /ˈpakˌmark/ *n* [C] scar or mark on the skin (as) left after smallpox.

pod /pad/ *n* [C] seed case of various plants, eg peas and beans. ⇨illus at vegetable.

po·di·um /ˈpoudiəm/ *n* [C] (*pl* -ia /-iə/, ~s) raised platform for a speaker, conductor of an orchestra, etc.

po·em /ˈpouɪm/ *n* [C] literary composition (often in verse form) which expresses deep feeling in beautiful and vivid language.

po·et[1] /ˈpouɪt/ *n* [C] writer of poems.

poet.[2] *abbr* = **1** poetic(al). **2** poetry.

po·et·ess /ˈpouɪtɪs/ *n* [C] (*rare*) woman poet.

po·et·ic /pouˈetɪk/ (also **po·et·i·cal** /-ɪkəl/) *adj* of poets and poetry.

po·et·i·cally /-kli/ *adv*

po·et·ry /ˈpouɪtri/ *n* [U] **1** the art of a poet; poems. **2** quality (such as beauty or gracefulness) that produces feelings like those produced by poems: *the ~ of motion.*

po·grom /pəˈgrəm/ *n* [C] organized killing of a group or class of people.

poig·nancy /ˈpɔinyənsi/ *n* [U] (*formal*) state or quality of being poignant.

poign·ant /ˈpɔinyənt/ *adj* (*formal*) causing sad or painful feelings: *~ memories.*

poign·ant·ly *adv*

poin·set·tia /pɔinˈsetiə/ *n* [C] (*pl* ~s) tropical plant with usually red, petallike leaves growing around its small, yellow flowers.

point[1] /pɔint/ *n* **1** [C] sharp tip (as of a pin, pencil, knife, etc). **2** [C] tapering piece of land that stretches out into the sea, a lake, etc. **3** dot or period: *decimal ~.* **4** [C] **(a)** locality or position, in space or time: *the highest ~.* ***at this point,*** at this place or moment. ***point of view,*** position from which something is viewed or considered. ***be at/on the point of doing sth,*** be about to do it. **(b)** geometric element having position but not size. **5** [C] particular degree or stage of development: *the ˈboiling ~ of water; a turning ~ in his career.* **6(a)** [C] unit of measurement. **(b)** unit of scoring in some games, sports and competitions. **7** [C] one of the thirty-two marks or divisions indicating direction on a compass. **8** [C] single item, detail, idea, etc: *There are ~s on which we differ.* **9** [C] chief idea or thought. ***come to/get to the point,*** come to what is essential or most important. ***get/miss the point of sth,*** understand/fail to understand: *She missed the ~ of the joke.* ***make a point of doing sth,*** take particular care to do it. ***off/to the point,*** irrelevant/relevant. **10** [U] purpose; aim: *There's very little ~ in protesting,* It won't help much. **11** [C] characteristic: *What are her best ~s as a secretary?*

point[2] /pɔint/ *vt,vi* **1** direct attention to; show the position or direction of; be a sign of: *He ~ed to the door. All the evidence ~s to his guilt.* **2** aim or direct (something): *~ing a gun at him.* **3** ***point sth out,*** show; call or direct attention to: *~ out a mistake. Can you ~ out the man you suspect? I must ~ out that the price is too high.* **4** make a point on (eg a pencil; sharpen). **5** ***point up,*** emphasize; stress. **6** ***point off,*** mark off or separate, esp with a decimal point. **7** (of a dog) take up a position with the body steady and the head pointing in the direction of game. ⇨ pointer(3).

pointed *adj* **(a)** (*fig*) directed toward a particular person: *Jack was showing ~ed attentions to the glamorous teacher.* **(b)** apt, relevant. **(c)** having a point.

point·ed·ly *adv*

point-blank /ˌpɔintˈblæŋk/ *adj* **1** (esp of a shot) at very close range: *fired at ~ range.* **2** (*fig*) blunt; leaving no room for doubt: *a ~ refusal.* □ *adv* **1** straight. **2** bluntly; straightforwardly: *ask him ~ whether he intends to help.*

pointer /ˈpɔintər/ *n* [C] **1** stick used to point to things on a map, etc. **2** indicator on a dial or balance. **3** short-haired hunting dog, trained to indicate the location of game by facing toward it.

point·less /ˈpɔintlɪs/ *adj* **1** (*fig*) with little or no sense, aim or purpose: *It seemed ~ to argue.* **2** without a point.

point·less·ly *adv*

poise /pɔiz/ *vt,vi* **1** be or keep balanced: *~d in mid air.* **2** hold or support in a particular position: *Note the way the dancer ~s his head.* □ *n* [U] **1** balance, equilibrium. **2** self-confidence; composure.

poi·son /ˈpɔizən/ *n* [C,U] **1** substance causing death or harm if absorbed by a living thing (animal or plant): *~ for killing weeds; commit suicide by taking ~.* **2** (*fig*) anything considered harmful or destructive. □ *vt* **1** kill or injure with poison: *~ rats.* **2** put poison on or in: *~ the food.* **3** (*fig*) have a harmful or injurious influence on: *~ somebody's mind against another person.*

pois·oner *n* [C]

pois·on·ous /ˈpɔizənəs/ *adj* **(a)** causing death or injury: *~ous plants.* **(b)** harmful; malicious: *a man with a ~ous tongue.*
pois·on·ous·ly *adv*

poi·son ivy /ˌpɔizən ˈaivi/ *n* [U] plant with greenish berries and leaflets arranged in groups of three, that can cause an itching skin rash when touched.

poi·son oak /ˌpɔizən ˈouk/ *n* [U] plant related to poison ivy and capable of causing the same kind of skin rash.

poke[1] /pouk/ *vt,vi* **1** push sharply, jab (with a stick, one's finger, etc): *~ a man in the ribs.* **2** thrust or push forward: *Don't let him ~ his head out of the (train) window — it's dangerous!* ***poke fun at sb,*** try to make him look foolish. **3** search: *Who's that poking about in the garden?* **4** make (a hole) by poking. **5** move slowly: *~ along.* □ *n* [C] act of poking.

poker[1] /ˈpoukər/ *n* [C] strong metal rod or bar for stirring a fire.

poker[2] /ˈpoukər/ *n* [U] card game for two or more persons in which the players gamble on the value of the cards they hold.
ˈpoker face, facial expression which does not reveal one's true feelings.
ˈpoker-faced *adj*

poky, pok·ey /ˈpouki/ *adj* (-ier, -iest) **1** crowded; too small: *a ~ little room.* **2** slow.

po·lar /ˈpoulər/ *adj* **1** of or relating to a pole, esp the North or South Pole. **2** directly opposite.

po·lar bear /ˈpoulər ˌber/ *n* [C] large white bear living in the north polar regions.

po·lar·ity /pouˈlærəti/ *n* [U] **1** possession of two contrasted or opposite qualities, principles or tendencies. **2** condition of being polar or having poles. **3** orientation (in a battery, etc) with respect to the positive and negative poles: *causing it to reverse ~,* causing the positive pole to become the negative and vice versa.

po·lar·ize /ˈpouləˌraiz/ *vt,vi* **1** make or become polar. **2** divide or separate into two opposite extremes.
po·lar·iz·ation /ˌpoulərəˈzeiʃən *n* [U]

pole[1] /poul/ *n* [C] **1** either of the two ends of the earth's axis: *the North Pole; the South Pole.* **2** = magnetic pole. **3** (*astron*) either of two points in the heavens about which the stars appear to turn. **4** either of the two ends of a magnet or the terminal points of an electric battery: *the negative/positive ~.* **5** (*biol*) either of two opposed regions at the extreme end of the axis of a nucleus, cell, or organism.

pole[2] /poul/ *n* [C] **1** long, slender, rounded piece of wood or metal, such as a support for a tent, as a handle for a broom, etc. **2** measure of length equal to $5\frac{1}{2}$ yds. or about 5 meters.

pole·cat /ˈpoulˌkæt/ *n* [C] **1** skunk. **2** small, dark-brown, fur-covered European animal related to the weasel.

po·lem·ic /pəˈlemɪk/ *n* **1** [C] (*formal*) dispute; argument. **2** (*pl*) (used with a *sing* or *plural verb*) art or practice of arguing. □ *adj* (also **po·lemi·cal** /-ɪkəl/) of polemics.
pol·emi·cally /-kli/ *adv*

pole·star /ˈpoulˌstar/ *n* [C] the North Star, almost coinciding with true north.

pole vault /ˈpoul ˌvɔlt/ *n* [C] (athletic contest consisting of a) jump for height over a crossbar, with the aid of a long pole.
ˈpole-vault *vi* make a jump of this kind.
ˈpole-vaulter *n* [C]

po·lice /pəˈlis/ *n* (always *sing* in form, used with *the* and a *pl verb*) **1** department of a government concerned with the keeping of public order. **2** **(the) police,** the members of such a department; policemen: *Several hundred ~ were on duty at the demonstration. The ~ have not made any arrests.* □ *vt* keep order in (a place) (as) with police: *United Nations forces ~d the area for a long time.*

po·lice·man/·woman /pəˈlismən, -ˌwʊmən/ *n* [C] (*pl* ~men /-men/, ~women /-ˌwɪmɪn/) male/female member of a police force.

POLICE OFFICERS

pol·i·cy[1] /ˈpaləsi/ *n* (*pl* -ies) [C] principle, method, or plan of action of a government, political party, business company, etc: *Is honesty the best ~?*

pol·i·cy[2] /ˈpaləsi/ *n* [C] (*pl* -ies) written statement of the terms of a contract of insurance.

po·lio /ˈpouliˌou/ *n* [U] (*informal*) (short for) poliomyelitis.

po·lio·my·e·li·tis /ˌpoulioujmaiəˈlaitɪs/ *n* [U] infectious disease marked by inflammation of the nerves cells of the spinal cord, often resulting in physical disablement.

pol·ish /ˈpalɪʃ/ *vt,vi* **1** make or become smooth and shiny by rubbing (with or without a chemical substance): *~ furniture/shoes.* **2** refine or improve in behavior, speech, intellectual interests, etc. **3** ***polish off,*** finish quickly: *~ off a large meal.* □ *n* **1** [U] (surface, etc obtained by) polishing: *shoes/tables with a good ~.* **2** [C,U] substance used for polishing: *ˈshoe/ˈfurniture ~.* **3** [U] (*fig*) refinement; elegance.

po·lite /pəˈlait/ *adj* having, showing, good manners, courteous: *a ~ boy; a ~ remark.*
po·lite·ly *adv*
po·lite·ness /-nɪs/ *n* [U]

poli·tic /ˈpalətɪk/ *adj* having or showing shrewdness or good judgment: *a ~ remark.*

po·liti·cal /pəˈlɪtɪkəl/ *adj* **1** of government or

governmental affairs: *a ~ decision.* **2** of politics or politicians: *a ~ campaign.*

po·liti·cally /-kli/ *adj*

po·lit·i·cal sci·ence /pəˌlɪtɪkəl ˈsaiəns/ *n* [U] study of government and of governmental institutions.

pol·i·ti·cian /ˌpaləˈtɪʃən/ *n* [C] person taking part in politics or very experienced in politics.

pol·i·tics /ˈpaləˌtɪks/ *n pl* (used with a *sing* or *pl verb*) **1** the science or art of government; political science. **2** political affairs, activities, or business. **3** competition for power within a group. **4** person's political opinions or position.

pol·i·ty /ˈpaləti/ *n* (*pl* -ies) **1** [U] form or process of government. **2** [C] community or society organized under a particular form of government.

pol·ka /ˈpoulkə/ *n* [C] (piece of music for a) lively dance of Eastern European origin.

poll[1] /poul/ *n* [C] **1** casting and recording of votes in an election. **2** (*pl*) place where voting takes place. **3** survey of public opinion made by questioning a representative selection of persons. **4** (top of the) head.

ˈpoll tax, payment, formerly required in some localities, in order to vote in an election.

poll[2] /poul/ *vt* **1** receive votes: *He ~ed over 3,000 votes.* **2** question (persons) in a poll or survey.

pol·len /ˈpalən/ *n* [U] fine powder (usually yellow) formed on flowers which fertilizes the seeds of other flowers when carried to them by the wind, insects, etc.

pol·li·nate /ˈpaləˌneit/ *vt* fertilize with pollen.

pol·li·na·tion /ˌpaləˈneiʃən/ *n* [U]

pol·li·wog /ˈpaliˌwag,-ˌwɔg/ *n* [C] tadpole.

poll·ster /ˈpoulstər/ *n* [C] person who conducts public opinion polls.

pol·lute /pəˈlut/ *vt* make dirty or impure: *rivers ~d with waste from factories; (fig) ~ young minds.*

pol·lu·tant /-ənt/ *n* [C] anything that pollutes, eg waste material dumped in a river.

pol·lu·tion /pəˈluʃən/ *n* [C,U]

polo /ˈpoulou/ *n* [U] ball game played by riders on horseback, who use mallets to drive a wooden ball.

pol·o·naise /ˌpaləˈneiz, ˌpou-/ *n* [C] (piece of music for a) slow processional dance of Polish origin.

po·lo·ni·um /pəˈlouniəm/ *n* [U] radioactive metallic element (symbol **Po**) produced by the disintegration of radium.

po·ly·ga·mist /pəˈlɪgəmɪst/ *n* [C] man who practices polygamy.

po·ly·gamy /pəˈlɪgəmi/ *n* [U] practice of having more than one wife at the same time. ⇨ monogamy.

po·ly·ga·mous /pəˈlɪgəməs/ *adj* of, relating to, or practicing polygamy.

pol·y·glot /ˈpaliˌglat/ *adj* knowing or speaking many languages. □ *n* [C] polyglot person.

poly·gon /ˈpalɪˌgan/ *n* [C] plane figure or shape with three or more straight sides.

Poly·ne·sian /ˌpaləˈniʒən/ *n, adj* **1** (of) a group of peoples native to certain islands of the Pacific, including Hawaii. **2** of their language(s), customs, area of settlement, etc.

pol·y·no·mi·al /ˌpalɪˈnoumiəl/ *n* [C] algebraic expression with two or more terms.

pol·yp /ˈpalɪp/ *n* [C] **1** small organism (such as a coral) having a hollow, tubelike body and a mouth surrounded by tentacles. **2** abnormal growth arising from a mucous membrane.

pol·y·the·ism /ˈpalɪθiˌɪzəm/ *n* [C] belief in or worship of more than one god.

pol·y·the·is·tic /ˌpalɪθiˈɪstɪk/ *adj*

po·made /pəˈmeid/ *n* [U] perfumed ointment, esp for the hair.

pome·gran·ate /ˈpam(ə)ˌgrænɪt/ *n* [C] (tree with) thick-skinned round fruit having many small seeds enclosed in a juicy red pulp.

pom·mel /ˈpəməl/ *n* [C] **1** raised part at the front of a saddle. **2** knob on the hilt of a sword. □ *vt* (-ll-, -ll-) = pummel.

pomp /pamp/ *n* [U] splendid display; magnificence: *the ~ and ceremony of a military parade.*

pom·pa·dour /ˈpampəˌdɔr/ *n* [C] (arrangement of) hair puffed high over the forehead.

pom·pon /ˈpamˌpan/ *n* [C] **1** rounded tuft of material, used as an ornament on a hat, garment, etc. **2** small, rounded chrysanthemum.

pom·pous /ˈpampəs/ *adj* full of, showing (too much) self-importance: *a pop official.*

pom·pous·ly *adv*

pon·cho /ˈpantʃou/ *n* [C] (*pl* ~s) **1** cloak made by a large piece of cloth with a slit in the middle for the head. **2** waterproof garment made like this.

pond /pand/ *n* [C] body of water, smaller than a lake.

pon·der /ˈpandər/ *vt,vi* think about at length: *He ~ed (over) the matter for days.*

pon·der·ous /ˈpandərəs/ *adj* **1** heavy: *the ~ movements of a fat man.* **2** difficult; dull; labored: *a ~ writing style.*

pon·der·ous·ly *adv*

pon·tiff /ˈpantɪf/ *n* [C] **1** pope. **2** bishop.

pon·tif·i·cal /panˈtɪfəkəl/ *adj* of or relating to a pope or a bishop.

pon·tif·i·cate /panˈtɪfəˌkeit/ *n* [C] office or term of a pope. □ *vi* speak pompously.

pon·toon /panˈtun/ *n* [C] **1** flat-bottomed boat. **2** float used to support a bridge. **3** float on a sea plane, supporting it on water.

po·ny /ˈpouni/ *n* [C] (*pl* -ies) **1** small breed of horse. **2** (*informal*) translation used by students to avoid work in preparing a foreign-language lesson.

pooch /putʃ/ *n* [C] (*informal*) dog.

poodle /ˈpudəl/ *n* [C] kind of dog with thick curling hair. ⇨ illus at dog.

pooh /pu/ *int* used to express impatience or disapproval.

pool[1] /pul/ *n* [C] **1** small, deep body of water (smaller than a pond). **2** quantity of standing liquid; puddle: *He was lying in a ~ of blood.* **3** swimming pool.

pool[2] /pul/ *n* [C] **1** total amount of money bet in a card game, horse race, etc. **2** game played usually with fifteen balls on a billiard table having six pockets at the sides and corners. **3** arrangement for sharing a common supply of resources, services, etc: *a ˈtyping ~.* □ *vt* contribute (money, resources, etc) to a com-

mon fund for the use of all: *They ~ed their savings and bought a car.*
poop[1] /pup/ *n* [C] raised structure at the stern of a ship.
poop[2] /pup/ *vt,vi* (*sl*) tire: *I'm ~ed (out).*
poor /pʊr/ *adj* (-er, -est) **1** having little money; needy. **2** unfortunate; deserving or needing help or sympathy: *The ~ little puppy had been abandoned.* **3** small in quantity; scanty: *a ~ supply of well-qualified science teachers.* **4** low in quality: *~ soil; in ~ health.*
poor·house /ˈpʊrˌhaus/ *n* [C] (*pl* ~es /-ˌhauzɪz/) (*dated*) place for maintaining poor people at public expense.
poor·ly /ˈpʊrli/ *adv* in a poor(4) manner; badly: *~ lit streets.*
pop[1] /pap/ *n* [C] **1** short, sharp, explosive sound: *the pop of a cork.* **2** carbonated drink: *soda pop.* □ *adv* suddenly or with the sound of popping: *I heard it go pop.* □ *vt,vi* (-pp-) **1** (cause to) make a sharp, quick sound (as when a cork comes out of a bottle). **2** (cause to) burst with a pop. **3** (*informal*) shoot: *They were popping away at the pigeons.* **4** (cause to) go or move quickly or unexpectedly: *He popped his head in at the door. She popped the whiskey bottle into the cupboard as her mother entered the room.* ***pop the question,*** propose marriage. **5** bulge or stick out: *His eyes almost popped out of his head when he saw that he had won.* **6** (*baseball*) hit (a ball) high into the air.
pop[2] /pap/ (sometimes **pops** /paps/) *n* [C] (*informal*) father.
pop[3] /pap/ *adj* (*informal*) (short for) popular: *ˈpop music; ˈpop singers.*
pop·corn /ˈpapˌkɔrn/ *n* [U] **1** kind of Indian corn having kernels which burst open into white puffs when heated. **2** these puffs, as a snack.
pope /poup/ *n* **the Pope,** head of the Roman Catholic Church.
pop·gun /ˈpapˌgən/ *n* [C] toy gun that shoots corks or pellets, or makes a popping sound.
pop·lar /ˈpaplər/ *n* **1** [C] tall, straight, fast-growing tree. **2** [U] its wood.
pop·lin /ˈpaplɪn/ *n* [U] strong fabric with a plain weave.
pop·pa /ˈpapə/ *n* [C] (*informal*) father.
pop·py /ˈpapi/ *n* [C] (*pl* -pies) (kinds of plant, wild and cultivated, bearing a) large, often red flower: *ˈopium ~*, kind from which opium is obtained.
pop·py·cock /ˈpapiˌkak/ *n* [U] (*informal*) nonsense.
pop·u·lace /ˈpapyəlɪs/ *n* [C] (*formal*) the general public; common people.
pop·u·lar /ˈpapyələr/ *adj* **1** of or for the people or the general public: *~ government.* **2** suited to the tastes, needs, educational level, etc of the general public: *entertainment at ~ (= low) prices.* **3** liked and admired: *a man who is ~ with his neighbors.* **4** widespread; generally accepted.
pop·u·lar·ly *adv*
pop·u·lar·ity /ˌpapyəˈlærəti/ *n* [U] quality of being popular(3).
pop·u·lar·ize /ˈpapyələˌraiz/ *vt* make popular: *~ a new book.*
pop·u·lar·iz·ation /ˌpapyələrəˈzeiʃən/ *n* [U]
pop·u·late /ˈpapyəˌleit/ *vt* **1** supply with people. **2** inhabit; form the population of.
pop·u·la·tion /ˌpapyəˈleiʃən/ *n* [C] (total number of) all the people living in a place, country, or area: *the ~ of Los Angeles; a city with a ~ of three million.*
pop·u·lous /ˈpapyələs/ *adj* densely populated.
por·ce·lain /ˈpɔrs(ə)lən/ *n* [U] (object, such as a dish, made of a) hard, white, translucent material.
porch /pɔrtʃ/ *n* [C] **1** covered entrance to a building. **2** veranda.
por·cu·pine /ˈpɔrkyəˌpain/ *n* [C] small animal covered with long sharp spines for protection.
pore[1] /pɔr/ *n* [C] tiny opening (as in the skin) through which fluids (eg sweat) may pass.
pore[2] /pɔr/ *vi* study or examine something with close attention: *~ over a letter/book.*
por·gy /ˈpɔrgi/ *n* [C] (*pl* -ies, ~) any one of several kinds of edible saltwater fish.
pork /pɔrk/ *n* [U] flesh of a pig or hog used as food. ⇨ bacon, ham(1).
pork·er /ˈpɔrkər/ *n* [C] pig raised for food.
por·nog·ra·phy /pɔrˈnagrəfi/ *n* [U] writings or pictures dealing with sexual matters and intended to arouse sexual excitement.
por·no·graph·ic /ˌpɔrnəˈgræfɪk/ *adj*
po·rous /ˈpɔrəs/ *adj* **1** having pores. **2** allowing liquid to pass through: *Sandy soil is ~.*
por·poise /ˈpɔrpəs/ *n* [C] blunt-snouted sea animal related to the whale, but smaller.
por·ridge /ˈpɔrɪdʒ, ˈpar-/ *n* [U] soft food made by boiling meal in water or milk: *a bowl of ~.*
port[1] /pɔrt/ *n* [C] **1** harbor. **2** town or city with a harbor, where ships load and unload cargo. **3** (*fig*) refuge.
port[2] /pɔrt/ *n* [C] **1** (*naut*) porthole. **2** opening through which a gun may be fired.
port[3] /pɔrt/ *n* [U] left side of a ship or aircraft as one faces forward. □ *adj* on the left side: *on the ~ bow/quarter.* ⇨ starboard.
port[4] /pɔrt/ *n* [U] rich, usually sweet wine.
port·able /ˈpɔrtəbəl/ *adj* that can be carried about: *~ radios/typewriters.*
port·abil·ity /ˌpɔrtəˈbɪləti/ *n* [U] being portable.
port·age /ˈpɔrtɪdʒ/ *n* **1** [C,U] (cost of) carrying goods overland between two rivers. **2** [C] route by which this is done.
por·tal /ˈpɔrtəl/ *n* [C] doorway, esp a large, elaborate one.
por·tend /pɔrˈtend/ *vt* (*formal*) be a sign or warning of (a future event, etc): *This ~s war.*
por·tent /ˈpɔrˌtent/ *n* [C] (*formal*) omen.
por·ten·tous /pɔrˈtentəs/ *adj* (*formal*) **(a)** ominous; threatening. **(b)** marvelous; extraordinary.
por·ten·tous·ly *adv*
por·ter[1] /ˈpɔrtər/ *n* [C] **1** person whose work is to carry loads, baggage, etc, esp at stations, airports, hotels, etc. **2** attendant on a train.
por·ter[2] /ˈpɔrtər/ *n* [U] dark-brown beer.
por·ter·house /ˈpɔrtərˌhaus/ *n* [C] (also **porterhouse steak**) beefsteak with a T-shaped bone and a large piece of tenderloin.
port·folio /pɔrtˈfouliou/ *n* [C] (*pl* ~s) **1** flat case for keeping papers, documents, drawings, etc. **2** office and duties of a minister of state: *He is*

minister without ~, not in charge of any particular department. **3** securities and investments (as stocks, bonds, etc) owned by an individual, a bank, etc.

port·hole /ˈpɔrtˌhoul/ *n* [C] small opening or window in the side of a ship or aircraft.

por·ti·co /ˈpɔrtɪkou/ *n* [C] (*pl* ~es or ~s) roof supported by columns, esp at the entrance of a building.

por·tion /ˈpɔrʃən/ *n* [C] **1** part or share of a whole. **2** single helping of food: *a generous* ~ *of roast duck.* □ *vt* ***portion sth out (among/between),*** give out in portions.

port·ly /ˈpɔrtli/ *adj* (-ier, -iest) having a stout body; fat.

port·man·teau /pɔrtˈmæntou/ *n* [C] (*pl* ~s or ~x /-touz/) traveling bag that opens into two equal parts.

Por·to Ri·can /ˌpɔrtou ˈrikən, ˌpɔrtə-/ *n, adj* = Puerto Rican.

por·trait /ˈpɔrtrɪt/ *n* [C] **1** painted picture, drawing, photograph, of a person, esp one that shows the face. **2** vivid description in words.

por·trai·ture /ˈpɔrtrətʃər/ *n* [U] art of making portraits.

por·tray /pɔrˈtrei/ *vt* **1** make a picture of. **2** describe vividly in words. **3** act the part of (as in a play).

por·tray·al /pɔrˈtreiəl/ *n* [C] act of portraying.

Por·tu·guese man-of-war /ˌpɔrtʃuˌgiz ˌmæn-əv-ˈwɔr/ *n* [C] (*pl* -men-of-war /-ˌmen-əv-ˈwɔr/) (kinds of) large floating jellyfish with stinging tentacles.

pos. *abbr* = positive.

pose /pouz/ *vt,vi* **1** put (a person) in a position before making a portrait, taking a photograph, etc. **2** take up a certain position (as for a photograph, etc): *Will you* ~ *for me?* **3** put forward; create; cause: *The increase in student numbers* ~*s many problems for the universities.* **4** ***pose as,*** pretend to be: ~ *as an expert on old coins.* □ *n* [C] **1** position taken, as for a portrait, photograph, etc: *an unusual* ~. **2** pretense; attitude taken for effect: *His sympathy is a mere* ~.

poser *n* [C] awkward or difficult question or problem.

posh /paʃ/ *adj* (*informal*) elegant; stylish: *a* ~ *hotel;* ~ *clothes.*

po·si·tion /pəˈzɪʃən/ *n* **1** [C] place where a person or thing is located: *find a* ~ *where one will get a good view of the procession.* ***in/out of position,*** in/not in the right place. **2** [U] advantageous location or place: *They were maneuvering for* ~. **3** [C] attitude or posture: *sit/lie in a comfortable* ~. **4** [C] person's place or rank in relation to others, in employment, in society, etc: *a pupil's* ~ *in class; a high/low* ~ *in society.* **5** [C] job; employment: *apply for the* ~ *of assistant manager.* **6** [C] condition; circumstances: *I'm sorry but I am not in a* ~ (= am unable) *to help you.* **7** [C] opinion; attitude: *What's your* ~ *on this problem?* □ *vt* place in proper position.

pos·i·tive /ˈpazətɪv/ *adj* **1** definite; clearly stated: *I gave you* ~ *instructions.* **2** sure; certain: *Are you* ~ (*that*) *it was after midnight?* **3** constructive; helpful: *a* ~ *suggestion;* ~ *criticism.* **4** favorable; affirmative: *a* ~ *response.* **5** (*math*) numerically greater than zero. **6** of or characterized by an electric charge that is lacking in electrons: *a* ~ *charge.* **7** (*photo*) showing light and shadows as in nature, not reversed (as in a *negative*). **8** (*gram*) (of *adjectives* and *adverbs*) of the simple form, not the comparative or superlative. **9** indicating the presence of a suspected disease, organism, etc: *the blood tests were* ~. □ *n* [C] **1** positive degree, adjective, quantity, etc. **2** positive photograph.

pos·i·tive·ly *adv* definitely; certainly.

positive sign, the sign +.

pos·sess /pəˈzes/ *vt* **1** own, have: ~ *nothing; lose all that one* ~*es.* **2** control the mind of; influence: *What* ~*ed you to do that?*

pos·ses·sor /-sər/ *n* [C] owner.

pos·ses·sion /pəˈzeʃən/ *n* **1** [U] possessing; ownership: *How did it come into your* ~*? How did you get* ~ *of it? The information in my* ~ *is strictly confidential.* **2** [C] (often *pl*) something owned; property: *lose all one's* ~*s.* **3** [C] territory that is ruled or controlled by a nation, but that is not part of it.

pos·ses·sive /pəˈzesɪv/ *adj* **1** eager to possess or control: *She has a* ~ *nature.* **2** (*gram*) showing possession: *the* ~ *case,* eg Tom's, the boy's, the boys'; *a* ~ *pronoun,* eg yours, his. □ *n* [C] **1** possessive case. **2** word in the possessive case.

pos·ses·sive·ly *adv*

pos·si·bil·ity /ˌpasəˈbɪləti/ *n* (*pl* -ies) **1** [U] state, degree, of being possible: *Is there any/much* ~ *of your getting to Boston this week?* **2** [C] something that is possible: *I see great possibilities for this scheme.*

pos·sible /ˈpasəbəl/ *adj* **1** that can be done; that can exist or happen: *Come as quickly as* ~. *It is* ~ *that he has already solved the problem. Will it be* ~ *to get the books for her tomorrow?* **2** that is reasonable or satisfactory: *He is the only* ~ *man for the position.*

pos·sibly /-əbli/ *adv* **(a)** by any possibility: *I will come as soon as I possibly can.* **(b)** perhaps: *"Will they increase your salary?" — "Possibly."*

pos·sum /ˈpasəm/ *n* [C] = opossum.

post[1] /poust/ *n* [C] **1** place where a soldier is stationed: *The sentries are all at their* ~*s.* **2** place to which soldiers are assigned, as a military base or camp. **3** local branch of a veterans' organization. **4** position or appointment; job: *be given the* ~ *as general manager.* □ *vt* **1** send to a post or position: ~ *an officer to a unit; be* ~*ed at the gates; be* ~*ed as an ambassador to Paris.* **2** put forward as security: ~ *bail.* **3** mail (the usual word). **4** in bookkeeping, transfer (figures or items) to a ledger. **5** ***keep sb posted,*** (*fig*) keep him informed.

post exchange (*abbr* **PX,** which is more usual) store at a military base for the personnel stationed there.

post[2] /poust/ *n* upright piece of wood, metal, etc supporting or marking something: ˈ*gate*~*s; the* ˈ*starting* ~, post marking the starting point in a race. □ *vt* announce or make known publicly by putting up a notice, placard, etc: *The announcement was* ~*ed up on the wall of the town hall.*

post- /poust-/ *prefix* after: *postscript; postgraduate.*

post·age /ˈpoustɪdʒ/ *n* [U] payment for the carrying of letters, etc: *What is the ~ for a letter to Australia?*

ˈpostage meter, machine that prints postage on an envelope.

ˈpostage stamp, stamp (to be) stuck on mail showing that the postage has been paid.

postal /ˈpoustəl/ *adj* of or relating to the post office or the mails.

post·card /ˈpoustˌkard/ *n* [C] oblong card (usually with a picture on one side) used for sending short messages.

post·date /ˌpoustˈdeit/ *vt* put a date (on a letter, check, etc) later than the date of writing.

poster /ˈpoustər/ *n* [C] large notice, often illustrated, (to be) displayed in a public place (announcing or advertising something).

pos·te·rior /paˈstɪriər/ *adj* **1** later in time or order. **2** placed behind; at the back. □ *n* [C] (esp) buttocks

pos·ter·ity /paˈsterəti/ *n* [U] **1** descendants of one person. **2** future generations: *plant trees for the benefit of ~.*

post·grad·u·ate /ˌpoustˈgrædʒuɪt/ *adj* of courses taken after the bachelor's degree. □ *n* [C] person taking such courses.

post·haste /ˌpoustˈheist/ *adv* with great speed.

post·hu·mous /ˈpastʃəməs/ *adj* **1** (of a child) born after the death of its father. **2** coming or happening after death: *~ fame.*

post·hu·mous·ly *adv*

post·man /ˈpoustmən/ *n* [C] (*pl* -men /-men/) mailman; person who carries and delivers mail.

post·mark /ˈpoustˌmark/ *n* [C] official mark stamped on letters, canceling the postage stamp(s) and giving the place, date, and time of dispatch. □ *vt* mark (an envelope, etc) with this.

post·mas·ter /ˈpoustˌmæstər/ *n* [C] male official in charge of a post office.

post·mis·tress /ˈpoustˌmɪstrɪs/ *n* [C] female official in charge of a post office.

post·mor·tem /ˌpoustˈmɔrtəm/ *n* [C], *adj* **1** (also **postmortem examination**) medical examination made after death to establish the cause of death: *A ~ showed that the man had been poisoned.* **2** review of an event, etc after it has occurred. □ *adj* occurring after death.

post of·fice /ˈpoust ˌɔfɪs/ *n* [C] **1** government department responsible for the collection and delivery of mail. **2** place serving as a local branch of a post office department.

ˈpost office box (*abbr* **P.ˈO. Box**) numbered box in a post office where letters are kept for collection by an individual or company.

post·paid /ˌpoustˈpeid/ *adj, adv* with postage (eg of merchandise) paid by the sender.

post·pone /pousˈpoun/ *vt* change or put off to a later time: *~ a meeting.*

post·pone·ment *n* [C,U]

post·script /ˈpousˌskrɪpt/ *n* [C] sentence(s) added to a letter after the signature.

pos·tu·late /ˈpastʃəˌleit/ *vt* put forward or assume as true. □ *n* /ˈpastʃəlɪt/ [C] something assumed to be true.

pos·ture /ˈpastʃər/ *n* [C] **1** way of holding the body; bearing: *Fashion models must have good ~.* **2** attitude; position: *The government's ~ of peaceful intentions was shattered when it invaded its neighbor.* □ *vt,vi* put or arrange in a position.

posy /ˈpouzi/ *n* [C] (*pl* -ies) **1** flower. **2** small bunch of cut flowers.

pot /pat/ *n* **1** [C] round vessel of earthenware, metal or glass, for holding liquids or solids, for cooking or growing things in, etc: *a ˈtea/ˈcoffee/flowerpot.* **2** [C] contents of a pot: *a pot of soup.* **3** [C] potbelly. **4** ***go to pot,*** go to ruin. **5** [C] trap for fish or lobster. **6** (*sing* only) total amount of the bets made on one hand in a card game. **7** [C] (*informal*) large sum: *make a pot/pots of money.* **8** [U] (*sl*) = marijuana. □ *vt,vi* (-tt-) **1** preserve (meat, fish, etc) in a pot or jar. **2** plant in a flowerpot.

pot·ash /ˈpatˌæʃ/ *n* [U] one of several compounds containing potassium, esp such a material obtained from wood ashes.

po·tas·si·um /pəˈtæsiəm/ *n* [U] soft, white metallic element (symbol **K**).

po·tato /pəˈteitou/ *n* [C] (*pl* ~es) (plant bearing a) rounded tuber eaten as a vegetable: *baked ~es.* ⇨ sweet potato. ⇨ illus at vegetable.

pot·belly /ˈpatˌbeli/ *n* [C] (*pl* -ies) **1** abdomen that sticks out or sags. **2** (usually wood-burning or coal-burning) stove with a rounded body.

ˈpot·bellied *adj* having a large, round belly.

po·tent /ˈpoutənt/ *adj* **1** strong; powerful. **2** effective.

po·tency /ˈpoutənsi/ *n* [U]

po·tent·ly *adv*

po·ten·tial /pəˈtenʃəl/ *adj* possible: *~ wealth; the ~ sales of a new book.* □ *n* **1** [C] possibility. **2** [U] capability for development, growth, etc: *He/It hasn't much ~.*

po·ten·ti·ally /-ʃəli/ *adv*

po·ten·ti·al·ity /pəˌtenʃiˈæləti/ *n* (*pl* -ies) **1** [C] power or quality which is possible, and needs development: *a country with great potentialities.* **2** [U] = potential(2).

pot·hole /ˈpatˌhoul/ *n* [C] hole in a road or street.

po·tion /ˈpouʃən/ *n* [C] dose of liquid medicine, poison, etc.

pot·luck /ˈpatˌlək/ *n* [U] whatever food is available for a meal: *dropped in and took ~ with us.*

pot·pie /ˈpatˌpai/ *n* [C] pie consisting of meat and vegetables covered with a pastry crust: *chicken ~.*

pot roast /ˈpatˌroust/ *n* [C] cut of beef, etc browned and then cooked slowly with a very little liquid in a covered pot.

pot·shot /ˈpatˌʃat/ *n* [C] shot fired carelessly or at an easy target.

pot·ter[1] /ˈpatər/ *vi* = putter[2].

pot·ter[2] /ˈpatər/ *n* [C] person who makes pottery.

ˈpotter's ˌwheel, horizontal revolving disc on which pots are shaped.

pot·tery /ˈpatəri/ *n* (*pl* -ies) **1** [U] dishes, pots, etc made from moist clay and hardened by heat. **2** [C] place where pottery is made.

pouch /pautʃ/ *n* [C] **1** small bag or sack: *a toˈbacco ~.* **2** baglike body structure, eg that in which a female kangaroo carries her young.

poul·tice /ˈpoultɪs/ *n* [C] soft heated mass of often medicated material (eg linseed, mustard), spread on a cloth, and put on the skin to relieve pain, etc.

poul·try /ˈpoultri/ *n* (*collect*) **1** (used with a *pl verb*) domestic birds, as hens, ducks, geese, etc: *The ~ are being fed.* **2** (used with a *sing verb*) flesh of these birds as food: *Poultry is expensive this year.*

pounce /pauns/ *vi* **1** seize suddenly by jumping or swooping down on: *The hawk ~d on its prey.* **2** (*fig*) seize: *He ~d at the first chance for a vacation.* □ *n* [C] such an attack.

pound[1] /paund/ *n* [C] **1** unit of weight equal to 16 ounces avoirdupois or 12 ounces troy. **2** unit of money (symbol £) used in various countries, eg Great Britain, Israel, Syria, Turkey, etc.

ˌpound ˈsterling, ⇨ sterling *n* (2).

pound[2] /paund/ *n* [C] place for keeping stray dogs and cats.

pound[3] /paund/ *vt,vi* **1** strike or beat heavily and repeatedly: *Someone was ~ing at/on the door with his fist. He ~ed the nails into the wood. She could feel her heart ~ing as she finished the 100 meter race.* **2** crush to powder; break to pieces: *~ crystals in a mortar.*

pour /pɔr/ *vt,vi* **1** (cause to) flow in a continuous stream: *Pour yourself another cup of coffee. The sugar came ~ing out of a hole in the side of the bag.* **2** (*fig*): *The crowds were ~ing out of the football stadium. Letters of complaint ~ed in.* **3** rain heavily: *It ~ed for three days.* **4** speak or express freely: *He ~ed out his story of the plane crash.*

pout /paut/ *vt,vi* push out the lips as a sign of annoyance. □ *n* such an act.

pov·er·ty /ˈpavərti/ *n* [U] **1** state of being poor: *live in ~.* **2** lack; deficiency: *an essay which shows ~ of ideas.*

ˈpoverty-stricken *adj* very poor.

P.O.W. /ˌpi ˌou ˈdəbəlyu/ *abbr n* (*pl* P.O.W.'s) = prisoner of war.

pow·der /ˈpaudjr/ *n* [C,U] **1** (kind of) substance that has been crushed, rubbed or worn to very fine particles: *ˈface ~; ˈsoap ~.* **2** gunpowder. □ *vt,vi* **1** make or turn into powder. **2** cover or dust (as) with powder. **3** apply cosmetic powder.

pow·dered *adj* reduced to powder: *~ed milk/eggs.*

pow·dery *adj* of, like, covered with, powder: *~y snow.*

power /ˈpaujr/ *n* **1** [U] ability to do or act: *I will do everything in my ~ to help.* **2** (*pl*) particular ability of the body or mind: *He's a man of great intellectual ~s.* **3** [U] strength; force: *the ~ of a blow.* **4** [U] energy or force that can be used to do work: *eˈlectric ~.* **5** [U] control; authority: *the ~ of the law; the ~ of Congress.* ***have power over sb,*** be in authority, control. ***in power,*** having control, esp political control. **6** [C] (in *sing* or *pl*) legal authority or right: *The President has exceeded his ~(s),* has done more than he has authority to do. **7** [C] someone or something (esp a nation) having great authority and influence. **8** [C] (*math*) **(a)** number of times a number or expression is (to be) multiplied by itself. **(b)** result obtained by multiplying a number or expression by itself a specified number of times: *the second, third, fourth, etc ~ of x* (= x^2, x^3 x^4, etc); *the fourth ~ of 3* (= 3 × 3 × 3 × 3 = 81). **9** [U] capacity to magnify: *the ~ of a lens; a telescope of high ~.* □ *vt* supply with power.

power·boat /ˈpauərˌbout/ *n* [C] motorboat.

power·ful /ˈpauərfəl/ *adj* having or producing great power: *a ~ enemy; a ~ drug.*

power·fully /-fli/ *adv*

power·house /ˈpauərˌhaus/ *n* [C] **1** place where electric power is generated. **2** powerful group, organization, etc. **3** person of great force or energy.

power·less /ˈpauərlɪs/ *adj* without power or force to act: *be ~ to resist.*

power·less·ly *adv*

power·plant /ˈpauərˌplænt/ *n* [C] = powerhouse(1).

pow·wow /ˈpauˌwau/ *n* [C] **1** North American Indian ceremony in which magic spells, dances, etc are performed to assure victory in war, success in hunting, etc. **2** meeting of or with North American Indians. **3** (*informal*) any meeting or gathering, esp one that is noisy.

pox /paks/ *n* [U] disease (eg chicken pox) causing eruptions on the skin.

PP[1] *abbr* = prepositional phrase.

pp.[2] *abbr* = pages.

p.p.[3] *abbr* = past participle.

PR[1] /ˌpi ˈar/ *abbr* = public relations.

PR[2] *postal abbr* = Puerto Rico.

pr.[3] *abbr* = **1** pair(s). **2** present. **3** pronoun.

prac·ti·cable /ˈpræktɪkəbəl/ *adj* capable of being put into effect: *ideas that are not ~.*

prac·ti·ca·bil·ity /ˌpræktɪkəˈbɪləti/ *n* [U]

prac·ti·cably /-əbli/ *adv*

prac·ti·cal /ˈpræktɪkəl/ *adj* **1** concerned with practice or actual use rather than ideas or theory: *a suggestion/proposal with little ~ value.* **2** realistic; sensible; better at doing things rather than thinking about them: *a ~ husband/mind.* **3** useful; workable: *Your invention is clever, but not very ~.*

prac·ti·cal·ity /ˌpræktɪˈkæləti/ *n* [U]

ˌpractical ˈjoke, trick played on a person so that he appears ridiculous.

prac·ti·cally /-kli/ *adv* **(a)** in a practical manner. **(b)** almost: *We've had ~ly no sunshine this month.*

prac·tice[1], **prac·tise** /ˈpræktɪs/ *n* **1** [U] actual use or performance; the doing of something: *The idea would never work in ~,* would never work if carried out. **2** [C] something done regularly or as a custom: *the ~ of closing stores on Sundays.* ***make a practice of (sth),*** do it habitually: *boys who make a ~ of cheating in examinations.* **3** [U] systematic, repeated exercise for the purpose of gaining a skill: *Piano playing needs a lot of ~. It takes years of ~ to become an expert.* ***out of practice,*** unskillful because of lack of practice. **4** [U] work of following a profession: *the ~ of law.* **5** [C] business which is a result of this, esp persons who regularly consult a doctor or lawyer: *a doctor with a large ~.*

prac·tice[2], **prac·tise** /ˈpræktɪs/ *vt,vi* **1** do

something repeatedly or regularly in order to acquire or improve a skill: ~ *the piano;* ~ *for two hours every day*. **2** make a habit of: ~ *economy*. ***practice what one preaches,*** make a habit of doing what one advises others to do. **3** work at or engage in (a profession, etc): ~ *medicine/law*, work as a doctor/lawyer.

prac·ticed, prac·tised *adj* skilled; having had much practice.

prac·ti·tion·er /præk'tɪʃənər/ *n* [C] one who practices a skill, profession, or art esp in medicine or law.

prag·mat·ic /præg'mætɪk/ *adj* **1** concerned with practical results, reasons and values. **2** of or relating to pragmatism.

prag·mat·i·cally /-kli/ *adv*

prag·ma·tism /'prægmə,tɪzəm/ *n* [U] philosophical belief that the truth or value of a theory depends on its practical results.

prag·ma·tist /-tɪst/ *n* [C] believer in pragmatism.

prairie /'preri/ *n* [C] wide area of level land with grass but no trees, esp in North America.

prairie dog /'preri ,dɔg/ *n* [C] small, burrowing animal of the plains of North America.

prairie schooner /'preri ,skunər/ *n* [C] covered wagon.

praise /preiz/ *vt* **1** say that one admires or approves of: ~ *a man for his kindness*. **2** give honor and glory to (God). □ *n* [U] **1** act of praising: *His heroism is worthy of great* ~. **2** honor; glory: *Praise be to God*.

'praise·wor·thy /-,wərði/ *adj* deserving praise.

prance /præns/ *vi* **1** (of a horse) spring forward, by raising the forelegs and jumping with the hind legs. **2** (*fig*) move proudly or boldly; swagger. **3** dance or jump happily and gaily. □ *n* [C] prancing movement.

prank /præŋk/ *n* [C] playful or mischievous trick.

prattle /'prætəl/ *vi* talk in a simple, childish way. □ *n* [U] such talk.

prawn /prɔn/ *n* [C] edible shellfish resembling a large shrimp.

pray /prei/ *vi* **1** address God in order to offer thanks, make requests, etc: ~ *to God for help. They knelt down and* ~*ed*. **2** ask earnestly; entreat.

prayer /prer/ *n* **1** [U] act of praying to God: *He knelt down in* ~. **2** [U] form of church worship: *Morning/Evening Prayer*. **3** [C] form of words used in praying: *the Lord's Prayer*. **4** [C] earnest request.

pre- /pri-/ *prefix* before; beforehand: *prearrange; premature*.

preach /pritʃ/ *vt,vi* **1** deliver a sermon; give a talk about religion or morals: ~ *the gospel*. **2** urge; recommend (as right or desirable): *The dictator* ~*ed war as a means of making the country great*.

preacher *n* [C]

pre·amble /pri'æmbəl/ *n* [C] introductory statement (esp to a formal document).

pre·arrange /,priə'reindʒ/ *vt* arrange in advance.

pre·arrange·ment *n* [C,U]

pre·cari·ous /prɪ'kæriəs/ *adj* (*formal*) uncertain; unsafe; insecure: *make a* ~ *living as an author*.

pre·cari·ous·ly *adv*

pre·cau·tion /prɪ'kɔʃən/ *n* **1** [U] care taken in advance to avoid a risk. **2** [C] instance of this: *take an umbrella as a* ~.

pre·cau·tion·ary /prɪ'kɔʃəneri/ *adj*

pre·cede /prɪ'sid/ *vt,vi* come or go before (in time, place or order): *Spring* ~*s summer*.

pre·ced·ing *adj* existing or coming before.

prec·e·dence /'presədəns/ *n* [U] (*formal*) (right to a) priority because of rank or importance. ***have/take precedence (over),*** have the right to be considered first.

prec·e·dent /'presədənt/ *n* [C] (*formal*) previous event, decision, etc taken as an example or rule to be followed later: *set/create/establish a* ~.

pre·cept /'pri,sept/ *n* (*formal*) [C] rule or guide, esp for behavior.

pre·cinct /'pri,sɪŋkt/ *n* [C] **1** space enclosed by outer walls or boundaries, eg of a cathedral, college, etc: *within the* ~*s of the university*. **2** subdivision of a county, city, etc: *an e'lection* ~*; a po'lice* ~. **3** (*pl*) neighborhood.

pre·cious /'preʃəs/ *adj* **1** of great value or high price: *my* ~ *possessions;* ~ *metals/stones*. **2** highly prized; dear: *Her children are very* ~ *to her*. □ *adv* (used for emphasis): *I have* ~ *little* (= very little) *money left*.

pre·cious·ly *adv*

pre·cious·ness /-nɪs/ *n* [C]

prec·i·pice /'presəpɪs/ *n* [C] overhanging or very steep face of a rock, cliff or mountain.

pre·cipi·tate /prɪ'sɪpə,teit/ *vt* **1** (*formal*) throw or send violently down from a height. **2** cause (an event) to happen suddenly, quickly, or abruptly: ~ *a crisis*. **3** (*chem*) separate out from a solution in the form of a solid. **4** condense (vapor) and fall as rain, dew, etc. □ *n* [C] /prɪ'sɪpətɪt/ usually solid substance which is precipitated from a solution. □ *adj* /prɪ'sɪpətət/ rash; hasty; acting or done without enough thought.

pre·cipi·tate·ly *adv*

pre·cipi·ta·tion /prɪ,sɪpə'teiʃən/ *n* **1** [C] (esp) deposit of rain, sleet, snow or hail. **2** amount of this: *What is the annual* ~ *in Seattle?* **3** [U] haste; impulsiveness: *act with* ~. **4** [U] act or process of precipitating.

pre·cipi·tous /prɪ'sɪpətəs/ *adj* (*formal*) very steep.

pre·cipi·tous·ly *adv*

pré·cis /'prei,si/ *n* [C] (*pl* ~ /'prei,siz/) summary of the chief ideas, points, etc of a speech or piece of writing.

pre·cise /prɪ'sais/ *adj* **1** exact; correctly and clearly stated. **2** very accurate; free from error: ~ *measurements*. **3** distinct; correct: ~ *speech*. **4** strict about observing rules, customs, etc: *prim and* ~ *in his manner*.

pre·cise·ly *adv*

pre·cise·ness /-nɪs/ *n* [U]

pre·ci·sion /prɪ'sɪʒən/ *n* [U] state of being precise: (as an *adjective*) ~ *instrument/tool*, used in technical work, very precise (for measuring, etc).

pre·clude /prɪ'klud/ *vt* (*formal*) prevent; make

impossible: *His explanation ~d any misunderstanding.*

pre·co·cious /prɪˈkouʃəs/ *adj* **1** showing skills, intelligence, etc at an earlier age than is normal. **2** (of actions, knowledge, etc) showing such development.

pre·co·cious·ly *adv*

pre·co·cious·ness /-nɪs/ *n* [U]

pre·con·ceive /ˌprikənˈsiv/ *vt* form (ideas, opinions) in advance (before getting knowledge or experience): *visit a foreign country with ~d ideas.*

pre·con·cep·tion /ˌprikənˈsepʃən/ *n* [C] preconceived idea, opinion.

pre·cur·sor /prɪˈkərsər/ *n* [C] (*formal*) person or thing coming before; forerunner.

pred·ator /ˈpredətər/ *n* [C] (esp) predatory animal.

preda·tory /ˈpredəˌtori/ *adj* (*formal*) **1** living by or inclined to plundering and robbery: *~ tribesmen.* **2** preying on other animals.

pred·e·ces·sor /ˈpredəˌsesər/ *n* [C] **1** former holder of any office or position: *I was his ~ on the Board.* **2** something which has gone before: *Is the new proposal any better than its ~?*

pre·des·ti·na·tion /priˌdestəˈneiʃən/ *n* [U] **1** belief or doctrine that God has determined beforehand that some persons will have eternal happiness and some eternal punishment. **2** doctrine that God has decreed in advance everything that happens. **3** destiny.

pre·des·tine /priˈdestɪn/ *vt* (often *passive*) decide or determine beforehand, (as) by divine decree: *Everything took place as if it had been ~d.*

pre·de·ter·mine /ˌpridɪˈtərmɪn/ *vt* (*formal*) decide or determine in advance.

pre·de·ter·mi·na·tion /ˌpridɪˌtərməˈneiʃən/ *n* [U]

pre·dic·a·ment /prɪˈdɪkəmənt/ *n* [C] difficult or unpleasant situation: *be in an awkward ~.*

predi·cate[1] /ˈpredɪkɪt/ *n* [C] (*gram*) part of a sentence which says something about the subject, eg "is short" in "Life is short."

predicate adjective *n* [C] (*gram*) one used in the predicate, eg *asleep, alive.*

predi·cate[2] /ˈpredəˌkeit/ *vt* (*formal*) **1** declare or assert to be true: *~ a motive to be good.* **2** found; base: *His faith in them was ~d on a belief in their honesty.*

pre·dict /prɪˈdɪkt/ *vt* say or make known in advance; foretell: *~ a good harvest/that there will be an earthquake.*

pre·dict·able /-əbəl/ *adj* that can be predicted.

pre·dic·tion /prɪˈdɪkʃən/ *n* **(a)** [U] predicting. **(b)** [C] something predicted.

pre·dis·pose /ˌpridɪsˈpouz/ *vt* (*formal*) cause (somebody) to have an interest or inclination beforehand: *The old man's frailty ~d him to serious illnesses.*

pre·dis·po·si·tion /ˌpriˌdɪspəˈzɪʃən/ *n* [C] (*formal*) tendency or inclination to: *a ~ to arthritis.*

pre·dom·i·nant /prɪˈdamənənt/ *adj* (*formal*) having more strength, numbers, influence, etc than others: *Her ~ characteristic is her friendliness.*

pre·dom·i·nance /-nəns/ *n* [U]

pre·domi·nant·ly *adv* for the most part: *a ~ly brown-eyed race.*

pre·dom·i·nate /prɪˈdaməˌneit/ *vi* (*formal*) **1** have control or power (over). **2** be superior in numbers, strength, influence, etc: *a forest in which oak trees ~.*

pre·em·i·nent /priˈemənənt/ *adj* superior to all; outstanding: *~ above all his rivals.*

pre·em·i·nence /-nəns/ *n* [U]

pre·em·i·nent·ly *adv*

pre·empt /priˈempt/ *vt* (*formal*) take for oneself before anyone else can.

preen /prin/ *vt* **1** (of a bird) smooth (itself, its feathers) with its beak. **2** (*fig*) (of a person) dress with great care. **3** take great pride in (oneself).

pref. *abbr* = **1** preface. **2** preferred. **3** prefix.

pre·fab /ˈpriˌfæb/ *n* [C] prefabricated structure.

pre·fab·ri·cate /ˌpriˈfæbrɪˌkeit/ *vt* manufacture the parts (eg roofs, walls, of a building) at a factory for putting together easily on the site: *~d houses.*

pre·fab·ri·ca·tion /ˌpriˌfæbrɪˈkeiʃən/ *n* [U]

pref·ace /ˈprefɪs/ *n* [C] author's explanatory remarks at the beginning of a book. □ *vt* provide with a preface; introduce (as) with a preface: *He ~d his remarks with a very funny joke.*

prefa·tory /ˈprefəˌtori/ *adj* acting as a preface or introduction.

prefect /ˈpriˌfekt/ *n* [C] **1** (in France) administrative official. **2** official of high rank in ancient Rome.

pre·fer /prɪˈfər/ *vt* (-rr-) **1** choose over another or others; like better: *Which would you ~, coffee or tea? I ~ walking to riding.* **2** present; put forward: *~ charges against a motorist.*

pref·er·able /ˈpref(ə)rəbəl/ *adj* more desirable; worthy of being preferred: *an idea ~ to his.* (*Note:* not used with *more.*)

pref·er·ably /-əbli/ *adv*

pref·er·ence /ˈpref(ə)rəns/ *n* **1** [C,U] act of preferring: *have a ~ for modern jazz.* **2** [C] something which is preferred: *What are your ~s?* **3** [U] the favoring of one person, country, etc more than another.

pref·er·en·tial /ˌprefəˈrenʃəl/ *adj* of or showing preference: *get ~ treatment.*

pre·fer·ment /prɪˈfərmənt/ *n* [U] **1** advancement or promotion in rank, position, etc. **2** position which brings dignity or profit.

pre·fix /ˈpriˌfɪks/ *n* [C] **1** word or syllable, eg pre-, co-, placed in front of a word to add to or change its meaning. **2** title used before a person's name, eg Mr., Dr. **3** (*telephone*) the first three digits (not including the *area code*) of a seven-digit telephone number. ⇨ App 1. □ *vt* add a prefix to or in front of.

preg·nan·cy /ˈpregnənsi/ *n* (*pl* -ies) **1** [U] the state of being pregnant. **2** [C] instance of this.

preg·nant /ˈpregnənt/ *adj* **1** (of a woman or female animal) having a fetus in the uterus. **2** (*fig*) (of words, actions) filled with meaning; significant: *words ~ with meaning; a ~ pause in a play.*

pre·hen·sile /priˈhensəl/ *adj* adapted or suitable for seizing and holding.

pre·his·tor·ic, pre·his·tor·i·cal /ˌpri(h)ɪsˈtɔrɪk, -ɪkəl/ *adj* of the time before recorded history.

pre·judge /ˌpriˈdʒədʒ/ *vt* make a decision or form an opinion before learning all the facts.

pre·judg·ment *n* [C,U]

prej·u·dice /ˈpredʒədɪs/ *n* **1** [U] opinion, like or dislike, formed before learning the facts. **2** [C] instance of this: *Her ~s kept her from making a sensible decision.* **3** hostility or dislike for a person, race, religious group, etc: *racial ~,* against members of other races. **4** [U] (*legal*) injury that may or does arise from some action or judgment. □ *vt* **1** cause a person to have a prejudice (1). **2** injure or harm: *He ~d his claim by asking too much.*

prej·u·di·cial /ˌpredʒəˈdɪʃəl/ *adj* tending to cause harm or injury.

prel·ate /ˈprelɪt/ *n* [C] high-ranking clergyman, such as a bishop.

pre·limi·nary /prɪˈlɪməneri/ *adj* coming first and preparing for what follows: *after a few ~ remarks.* □ *n* [C] (*pl* -ries) (usually *pl*) something which is preliminary.

prel·ude /ˈprelˌyud, ˈpriˌlud/ *n* [C] **1** action, event, etc that serves as an introduction to (another). **2** (*music*) (usually /ˈpreiˌlud/) introductory movement to a larger work. □ *vt* serve as a prelude to.

pre·ma·ture /ˌpriməˈtʊr/ *adj* done, happening, or appearing before the right or usual time: *~ birth.*

pre·ma·ture·ly *adv*

pre·med·i·cal /ˌpriˈmedɪkəl/ *adj* preparing for the study of medicine.

pre·med·i·tate /ˌpriˈmedəˌteit/ *vt* plan or think about (something) in advance: *a ~d murder.*

pre·med·i·ta·tion /ˌpriˌmedəˈteiʃən/ *n* [U]

pre·miere /prɪˈmɪr/ *n* [C] first performance of a play, motion picture, etc.

prem·ise /ˈpremɪs/ *n* [C] **1** statement on which reasoning is based. **2** (*pl*) house or building with its grounds: *Students should not leave the ~s of the school without permission.* □ *vt* postulate.

pre·mi·um /ˈprimiəm/ *n* [C] (*pl* ~s) **1** (installment) payment for an insurance policy. **2** reward; bonus or extra benefit. **3** addition to ordinary charges: *He had to pay the agent a ~ before he could rent the house.* **4** high or unusual value: *put a ~ on loyalty.* ***at a premium,*** very valuable.

pre·mo·ni·tion /ˌpreməˈnɪʃən/ *n* [C] feeling of uneasiness considered as a warning (of approaching danger, etc): *have a strong ~ of failure.*

pre·mon·i·tory /prɪˈmanɪˌtori/ *adj*

pre·na·tal /ˌpriˈneitəl/ *adj* before birth.

pre·oc·cu·pa·tion /ˌpriˌakyəˈpeiʃən/ *n* **1** [U] state of being preoccupied. **2** [C] subject which preoccupies a person.

pre·oc·cu·py /priˈakyəˌpai/ *vt* (*pt,pp* -ied) take all the attention; absorb: *preoccupied with family problems.*

pre·or·dain /ˌpriɔrˈdein/ *vt* determine in advance.

prep /prep/ *n* [C] (*informal*) student in a preparatory school.

ˈprep school, ⇨ preparatory.

prep·a·ra·tion /ˌprepəˈreiʃən/ *n* **1** [U] preparing or being prepared: *The book is in ~.* **2** [C] (usually *pl*) things done to get ready: *~s for war; make ~s for a voyage.* **3** [C] something prepared for a special use: *chemical ~s.*

pre·par·a·tory /prɪˈpærəˌtori, ˈprep(ə)rəˌtori/ *adj* preparing or serving to prepare: *~ measures/training.*

preˈparatory ˌschool (often shortened in *informal* usage to **prep school** /ˈprep ˌskul/) *n* [C] usually private school that prepares students for college.

pre·pare /prɪˈpær/ *vt,vi* **1** ***prepare (for),*** get or make ready: *~ the family for a surprise. Are they preparing to leave town?* **2** put together; make: *~d dinner.*

pre·pay /ˌpriˈpei/ *vt* (*pt,pp* -paid /-ˈpeid/) pay in advance.

pre·pon·der·ance /priˈpandərəns/ *n* [U] (*formal*) greater amount, weight, etc.

pre·pon·der·ant /prɪˈpandərənt/ *adj* (*formal*) greater in weight, number, importance, etc.

pre·pon·der·ant·ly *adv*

prep·o·si·tion /ˌprepəˈzɪʃən/ *n* [C] word or group of words (eg *at, in front of, from, to*) occurring before a noun or pronoun to show a relation (such as location, direction, source, method, etc) to another word.

prep·o·si·tional /-ʃənəl/ *adj* of, containing, a preposition.

prepositional phrase, phrase made up of a preposition and its object, eg in the night; on the beach.

pre·pos·sess /ˌpripəˈzes/ *vt* (*formal*) influence (a person) in advance, esp favorably.

pre·pos·sess·ing *adj* attractive; making a good impression: *a girl of ~ing appearance.*

pre·pos·ses·sion /ˌpripəˈzeʃən/ *n* [U]

pre·pos·ter·ous /prɪˈpastərəs/ *adj* contrary to reason or sense; absurd; ridiculous.

pre·pos·ter·ous·ly *adv*

preppy /ˈprepi/ *n* [C] (*sl*) person attending an expensive private school or affecting the conservative appearance of such a person: *He looks like a ~ with his short hair and dark-blue blazer;* (as an *adj*) *~ clothes.*

pre·re·cord /ˌpririˈkɔrd/ *vt* record, eg a radio or TV program, in advance for later use.

pre·req·ui·site /prɪˈrekwɪzɪt/ *n* [C], *adj* (something) required beforehand as a condition for something else: *A college degree is a ~ for that position.*

pre·rog·a·tive /priˈragətɪv/ *n* [C] special right or privilege, esp one that is attached to a certain position, rank, etc.

Pres.[1] *abbr* = President.

pres.[2] *abbr* = present.

Pres·by·te·rian /ˌprezbəˈtɪriən/ *adj* of or relating to a Protestant church governed by elders, all of equal rank. □ *n* [C] member of this church.

pre·scribe /prɪˈskraib/ *vt,vi* **1** advise or order the use of, esp as a remedy: *~d a new medicine for the patient.* **2** direct; order: *penalties which are ~d by the law.*

pre·scrip·tion /prɪˈskrɪpʃən/ *n* **1** [U] act of prescribing. **2** [C] that which is prescribed. **3** [C] doctor's written order or direction for the making up and use of a medicine. **4** [C] the medicine itself.

pre·scrip·tive /prɪˈskrɪptɪv/ *adj* giving orders or directions.

pres·ence /ˈprezəns/ *n* [U] **1** being present in a place, etc: *in the ~ of his friends*, with his friends there. ***presence of mind,*** ⇨ mind[1](1). **2** person's way of standing, moving, etc, esp as they affect other people: *a man of great ~.*

pres·ent[1] /ˈprezənt/ *adj* **1** being at hand or in view at a certain place: *The Smiths were ~ at the ceremony*. **2** now being considered. **3** existing now: *the ~ Administration*. □ *n* **1 the present,** now; this time: *the past, the ~, and the future*. ***at present,*** now: *We don't need any more at ~.* **2** (*gram*) present tense.

ˌpresent ˈparticiple (*gram*) verb that expresses present action or state, eg *coming, being*.

ˌpresent ˈtense (*gram*) tense expressing an action or state in the present or at the time of speaking.

pres·ent[2] /ˈprezənt/ *n* [C] gift; something presented: *ˈbirthday ~s.*

pre·sent[3] /prɪˈzent/ *vt* **1** give; offer: *the watch that was ~ed to me when I retired*. **2** (*reflex*) appear; come forward: *~ oneself for trial/for examination*. **3** show; display: *The old house ~ed a fine appearance*. **4** bring (a play, film, radio or television program, etc) before the public: *The Civic Players will ~ the musical "Oklahoma"*.

pre·sent·able /prɪˈzentəbəl/ *adj* fit to appear or be seen: *made himself ~.*

pre·sent·ably /-əbli/ *adv*

pre·sen·ta·tion /ˌprizenˈteiʃən/ *n* **1** [U] presenting or being presented. **2** [C] something presented: *the ~ of a new play*.

pre·sen·ti·ment /prɪˈzentəmənt/ *n* [C] (*formal*) vague feeling that something (esp unpleasant or undesirable) is about to happen.

pres·ent·ly /ˈprezəntli/ *adv* **1** soon: *I'll be with you ~.* **2** at the present time: *The Secretary of State is ~ in Africa.*

pres·er·va·tion /ˌprezərˈveiʃən/ *n* [U] preserving or being preserved.

pre·serv·ative /prɪˈzərvətɪv/ *n* [C], *adj* (substance) capable of preserving (eg food).

pre·serve /prɪˈzərv/ *vt* **1** keep safe from harm or danger: *preserving both his life and his honor*. **2** preserve (food) and keep it from decay (by pickling, canning, freezing, etc): *~ fruit*. **3** keep or maintain in perfect condition: *~ one's eyesight*. □ *n* [C] **1** (usually *pl*) fruit cooked with sugar. **2** place where animals, natural resources, etc are protected: *a ˈwildlife ~.*

pre·server *n* [C]

pre·shrunk /ˌpriˈʃrəŋk/ *adj* (of cloth) shrunk before being made into garments. ⇨ shrink.

pre·side /prɪˈzaid/ *vi* occupy position of authority at a meeting, esp as chairman: *The city council is ~d over by the mayor.*

pres·i·den·cy /ˈprezədənsi/ *n* [C] (*pl* -ies) **1** the office of president. **2** term of office as a president: *during the ~ of Lincoln*.

pres·i·dent /ˈprezədənt/ *n* [C] **1** head of the government in the US and other modern republics. **2** chief officer of some business companies, colleges, societies, etc.

pres·i·den·tial /ˌprezəˈdenʃəl/ *adj* of a president or presidency.

press[1] /pres/ *n* [C] **1** act of pressing. **2** machine or apparatus for pressing: *a ˈwine ~.* **3 the press (a)** printed periodicals and newspapers generally. **(b)** journalists: *The book was favorably noticed by the ~.* **4** comment or notice in the press: *His speech got a good ~.* **5** business establishment for printing. **6** printing press. **7** = pressure (the usual word): *the ~ of modern life.*

ˈpress agent, person whose work is to get favorable publicity for his employer.

ˈpress conference, meeting with journalists arranged for the purpose of giving an interview, giving out news, etc.

ˈpress release, item of news prepared by a concerned organization, individual, etc and given to the press for their use.

press[2] /pres/ *vt,vi* **1** push steadily or bear down on: *~ (on) a button; ~ one's thumb into the clay*. **2** smooth or flatten, esp by ironing: *~ a suit/skirt*. **3** squeeze: *~ the juice out of an orange*. **4** push forward or carry out vigorously an attack, carry it out with determination: *~ on with one's work/journey*. **5** make repeated requests; urge; insist or demand: *~ for an investigation into a question; ~ him for an answer*. **6** push, crowd, with weight or force: *crowds ~ing against the barriers*. **7** embrace; clasp as a sign of affection or sympathy: *He ~ed her to his side. She ~ed his hand*. **8** weigh heavily on; oppress: *The new taxes ~ed down heavily on the people.*

press·ing /ˈpresɪŋ/ *adj* urgent; requiring or demanding immediate attention: *~ing business.*

pres·sure /ˈpreʃər/ *n* **1** [U] pressing. **2** [U] (amount of) force exerted on or against something: *air ~.* **3** [U] force or influence: *the union ~ on him to vote for the bill*. **4** [C] something that is difficult to bear: *the ~ of taxation*. □ *vt* force by means of persuasion, influence, etc: *He was ~d into buying a new suit.*

ˈpressure cooker, airtight saucepan for cooking quickly with steam under pressure.

pres·sur·ize /ˈpreʃəˌraiz/ *vt* maintain normal air pressure, eg in an aircraft.

pres·sur·ized /ˈpreʃəˌraizd/ *adj*

pres·tige /preˈstiʒ/ *n* [U] respect, reputation, or influence coming from achievements, power, wealth, etc.

pres·tig·ious /preˈstɪdʒəs/ *adj* producing ~.

pres·to /ˈprestou/ *adj, adv* **1** (*music*) very quick(ly). **2** (*informal*) at once; suddenly.

pre·sum·able /prɪˈzuməbəl/ *adj* that may be presumed.

pre·sum·ably /-əbli/ *adv*

pre·sume /prɪˈzum/ *vt,vi* **1** suppose to be true: *An accused man is ~d (to be) innocent until he is proved guilty*. **2** (*formal*) take the liberty; dare: *I won't ~ to disturb you.*

pre·sump·tion /prɪˈzəmpʃən/ *n* **1** [C] something which seems likely although there is no proof: *on the ~ that he was drowned*. **2** [U] arrogance: *What ~ to say that he is better than me!*

pre·sump·tu·ous /prɪˈzəmptʃuəs/ *adj* too forward or self-confident; arrogant.

pre·sump·tu·ous·ly *adv*

pre·sup·pose /ˌprisəˈpouz/ *vt* **1** assume beforehand. **2** require as a condition: *Sound sleep ~s a peaceful mind.*

pre·sup·po·si·tion /ˌpriˌsəpəˈzɪʃən/ *n* **(a)** [C] something presupposed. **(b)** [U] presupposing.

pre·tech·no·logi·cal /ˌpriˌteknəˈladʒɪkəl/ *adj* of a stage (eg of cultural or economic development) which existed before the advent of technology.

pre·tend /prɪˈtend/ *vt,vi* **1** make believe: *~ to be asleep. They ~ed that they were pioneers.* **2** claim falsely (as an excuse or reason, to avoid danger, difficulty, etc): *~ sickness.*

pre·tend·er *n* [C] **(a)** person who pretends. **(b)** one who puts forward a claim (to a throne, etc).

pre·tense /prɪˈtens, ˈpriˌtens/ *n* **1** [U] pretending; make believe. **2** [U] false appearance or show: *Under the ~ of friendship, he learned all their secrets.* **3** [C] pretext or excuse. **4** [C] false claim, act, or purpose. ***false pretenses,*** acts intended to deceive: *obtain money under false ~s.* **5** [U] affectation; pretentiousness.

pre·ten·sion /prɪˈtenʃən/ *n* **1** [C] claim: *He makes no ~s to expert knowledge of the subject.* **2** [U] being pretentious: *Pretension is his worst fault.*

pre·ten·tious /prɪˈtenʃəs/ *adj* claiming (without justification) great merit or importance: *a ~ student/speech; use ~ language.*

pre·ten·tious·ly *adv*

pre·ten·tious·ness /-nɪs/ *n* [U]

pre·text /ˈpriˌtekst/ *n* [C] reason or excuse that is given to hide the real reason for an action, etc: *find a ~ for refusal/refusing the invitation.*

pretty /ˈprɪti/ *adj* (-ier, -iest) **1** pleasing and attractive without being beautiful or magnificent: *a ~ girl/garden/picture/piece of music.* **2** considerable: *That's a ~ mess you've made of it! He returned with a ~ catch of fish.* ▫ *adv* to a certain extent; rather: *The situation seems ~ hopeless. It's ~ cold outside.* ***pretty much/nearly/well,*** almost: *We've ~ nearly/well finished the work.* ***sitting pretty,*** (*informal*) in a favorable or advantageous position.

pret·tily /ˈprɪtəli/ *adv*

pret·ti·ness /ˈprɪtinɪs/ *n* [U]

pret·zel /ˈpretsəl/ *n* [C] often salted crisp cracker baked in the form of a knot or a thin stick.

pre·vail /prɪˈveiəl/ *vi* (*pres p* ~ing /prɪˈveilɪŋ/) **1** gain victory (over); fight successfully (against): *Truth will ~.* **2** be generally seen, done, etc; predominate: *the conditions now ~ing in Africa.* **3** persuade: *~ on/upon a friend to lend you $100.*

pre·vail·ing /prɪˈveilɪŋ/ *adj* most frequent or usual: *the ~ing winds/fashions.*

prev·a·lent /ˈprevələnt/ *adj* (*formal*) commonly existing or occurring, seen or done everywhere (at the time in question): *Is malaria still ~ in that country?*

prev·a·lence /ˈprevələns/ *n* [U]

pre·var·i·cate /prɪˈværəˌkeit/ *vi* (*formal*) make untrue or partly untrue statements; evade telling the (whole) truth.

pre·var·i·ca·tion /prɪˌværəˈkeiʃən/ *n* [C,U]

pre·vent /prɪˈvent/ *vt* stop or hinder: *Who can ~ us from getting married/~ our marriage?*

pre·vent·able /-əbəl/ *adj* that can be prevented.

pre·ven·tion /prɪˈvenʃən/ *n* [U] act of preventing: *Prevention is better than cure.*

pre·ven·tive /prɪˈventɪv/ *adj* serving or designed to prevent.

pre·view /ˈpriˌvyu/ *n* [C] showing of a motion picture, play, etc before it is shown to the general public. ▫ *vt,vi* have or give a preview of.

pre·vi·ous /ˈpriviəs/ *adj* earlier: *on a ~ occasion.* ***previous to,*** before.

pre·vi·ous·ly *adv*

prey /prei/ *n* (*sing* only) **1** animal, bird, etc hunted by another for food: *The eagle was devouring its ~.* **2** victim. ▫ *vi* **1** take, hunt, as prey: *hawks ~ing on small birds.* **2** steal from; plunder: *Our ships were ~ed on/upon by pirates.* **3** produce a harmful effect: *anxieties/losses that ~ on my mind.*

price /prais/ *n* **1** [C] sum of money for which something is (to be) sold or bought: *What ~ are you asking?* **2** [U] value; worth: *a pearl of great ~.* **3** [C] cost of obtaining something: *Loss of independence is a high ~ to pay for peace!* ▫ *vt* **1** find out the price of. **2** set a price for. ***price oneself/one's goods out of the market,*** set prices so high that people cannot afford to buy.

price·less *adj* too valuable to be priced: *~less paintings.*

prick[1] /prɪk/ *n* [C] **1** small mark or hole caused by pricking: *~s made by a needle.* **2** pain caused by pricking: *I can still feel the ~.*

prick[2] /prɪk/ *vt,vi* **1** make a hole or a mark in (something) with a sharp point. **2** (cause to) feel sharp pain: *My fingers ~.* **3** (*fig*) cause a feeling of guilt: *His conscience ~ed him.* **4** ***prick up one's ears,*** (esp) listen intently.

prickle /ˈprɪkəl/ *n* [C] pointed growth such as a thorn or a spine. ▫ *vt,vi* (cause to) feel a pricking sensation.

prick·ly /ˈprɪkli/ *adj* (-ier, -iest) **1** covered with prickles. **2** tingling. **3** easily irritated or annoyed: *You're a bit ~ today!*

prickly ˈpear, cactus covered with prickles and having pear-shaped fruit.

pride /praid/ *n* **1** [U] feeling of satisfaction or pleasure in one's achievements, possessions, etc: *look with ~ at one's garden.* **2** [U] self-respect; knowledge of one's worth and character: *Don't say anything that may wound his ~.* **3** (*sing* only) object of pride(1): *a girl who is her mother's ~ and joy.* **4** [U] too high an opinion of oneself, one's position, possessions, etc: *be puffed up with ~.* **5** [C] group: (esp) *a ~ of lions/peacocks.* ▫ *vt* (*reflex*) be pleased and satisfied about: *He ~s himself on his skill as a pianist.*

priest /prist/ *n* [C] **1** clergyman in the Roman Catholic and Eastern Orthodox churches, esp one who has the authority to administer the sacrament to give absolution. **2** in non-Christian religions, person who performs special acts of religion.

priest·ess /ˈpristɪs/ *n* [C] woman priest.

ˈpriest·hood /-ˌhʊd/, *n* [U] **(a)** (*collect*) the whole body of priests of a church. **(b)** office and duties of a priest.

priest·ly *adj* of, for or like a priest.

prig /prɪg/ *n* [C] person who shows too much

self-satisfaction.

prim /prɪm/ *adj* (-mmer, -mmest) very correct and formal in behavior, dress, etc: *a very ~ and proper old lady.*

prim·ly *adv*

prim·ness /-nɪs/ *n* [U]

pri·ma don·na /ˌprimə ˈdanə/ **1** leading woman singer in opera. **2** temperamental or vain person.

pri·mal /ˈpraiməl/ *adj (formal)* **1** original; first in time. **2** first in importance.

pri·mar·ily /praiˈmerəli/ *adv* in the first place; above all.

pri·mary /ˈpraiˌmeri/ *adj* leading in time, order or development: *of ~* (= chief) *importance; a ˈ~ school,* school which includes the first three or four grades. □ *n* [C] (*pl* -ies) election in which voters select party candidates for a coming election.

ˈprimary colors, red, blue and yellow, from which all other colors can be derived.

pri·mate /ˈpraiˌmeit/ *n* [C] **1** bishop or archbishop who holds the highest rank in a country, province, etc. **2** member of one of the highest order of mammals that includes men, apes, monkeys, lemurs, etc.

prime[1] /praim/ *adj* **1** chief; most important: *his ~ motive.* **2** excellent; first in quality: *~ (cuts of) beef.* **3** original; primary. **4** of or relating to a prime number.

prime ˈminister, (a) chief executive of a parliamentary government. **(b)** chief minister of a ruler.

prime ˈnumber, one which can be divided exactly only by itself and the number 1 (eg 7, 17, 41).

prime ˈtime, period of the day (about 8:00 to 10:30 pm) when esp television broadcasting reaches the largest audience, and for which the highest advertising rates are charged.

prime[2] /praim/ *n* [U] **1** state of highest perfection; the best part: *in the ~ of life.* **2** first or earliest part: *the ~ of the year*, spring.

prime[3] /praim/ *vt* **1** get ready for use or action by charging or filling: *~ a pump with water.* **2** supply with facts, etc: *The witness had been ~d by a lawyer.* **3** cover (a surface) with the first coat of paint, oil, varnish, etc.

primer[1] /ˈprɪmər/ *n* [C] simple textbook for teaching elementary reading.

primer[2] /ˈpraimər/ *n* [C] **1** substance for igniting the powder in a cartridge, bomb, etc. **2** special paint used for priming(3).

pri·me·val /praiˈmivəl/ *adj* of the earliest time in the world's existence.

prim·ing /ˈpraimɪŋ/ *n* [U] **1** gunpowder used to fire the charge of a gun, bomb, mine, etc. **2** = primer[2](2).

prim·i·tive /ˈprɪmətɪv/ *adj* **1** of the earliest times; of an early stage of esp human development: *~ man*, early man; *~ culture*, pretechnological culture. **2** simple; crude; having undergone little development: *~ weapons*, eg bows and arrows, spears. □ *n* [C] member of a pretechnological culture.

prim·i·tive·ly *adv*

prim·i·tive·ness /-nɪs/ *n* [U]

prim·rose /ˈprɪmˌrouz/ *n* [C] plant bearing a pale yellow flower.

prince /prɪns/ *n* [C] **1** ruler, esp of a small state. **2** male member of a royal family, esp a son of the sovereign.

prince·ly *adj* (-ier, -iest) worthy of a prince; splendid; generous: *a ~ly gift.*

prin·cess /ˈprɪnsɪs, -ˌses/ *n* [C] **1** wife of a prince. **2** daughter of a sovereign.

prin·ci·pal /ˈprɪnsəpəl/ *adj* highest in order of importance: *the ~ rivers of Europe.* □ *n* [C] **1** head of school. **2** chief participant in a business deal for whom another acts as agent: *I must consult my ~.* **3** sum of money lent, invested, etc on which interest is payable. **4** person directly responsible for a crime.

prin·ci·pally /-pli/ *adv* for the most part; chiefly.

prin·ci·pal·ity /ˌprɪnsəˈpæləti/ *n* [C] (*pl* -ies) country ruled by a prince.

prin·ciple /ˈprɪnsəpəl/ *n* [C] **1** basic truth; fundamental law: *the (first) ~s of geometry.* **2** guiding rule for behavior: *moral ~s.* ***in principle,*** with respect to basic or fundamental rules. ***on principle,*** from a moral motive: *He refuses on ~ to avoid paying taxes.* **3** scientific fact or law explaining how something works: *These machines work on the same ~.*

print[1] /prɪnt/ *n* **1** [C] mark made on a surface by pressure: *ˈfinger ~s; ˈfoot ~s.* **2** [U] **(a)** letters made by printing. **(b)** printed matter. **3** [C] picture, design, etc made by printing on paper, etc: *old Japanese ~s.* **4** [C] photograph printed from a negative.

print[2] /prɪnt/ *vt,vi* **1** press or stamp (letters, a design, etc) onto or into paper, fabric, etc. **2** make books, pictures, etc in this way. **3** publish; cause to be printed: *~ a magazine.* **4** write in printed characters (instead of ordinary, connected handwriting). **5** make (a photograph) from a negative film or plate: *How many copies shall I ~ for you?*

printer *n* [C] **(a)** person who owns or operates a printing business. **(b)** device that prints.

ˈprinting press, machine for printing books, etc.

print·out /ˈprɪntˌaut/ *n* [C,U] printed record or material, as from a computer.

prior[1] /ˈpraiər/ *adj* earlier in time, order or importance: *have a ~ claim (to the money).* ***prior to*** *prep* before: *The house was sold ~ to auction,* before the day of the auction.

prior[2] /ˈpraiər/ *n* [C] head of a monastery, ranking next below an abbot.

prioress /ˈpraiərɪs/ *n* [C] head of a convent, ranking next below an abbess.

pri·or·ity /praiˈɔrəti, -ˈar-/ *n* (*pl* -ies) **1** [U] condition of coming before others in importance, order, etc: *I have ~ over you in my claim.* **2** [C] something which holds a high place among competing claims: *Road building is a top ~.*

pri·ory /ˈpraiəri/ *n* [C] (*pl* -ies) monastery or convent governed by a prior or prioress.

prism /ˈprɪzəm/ *n* [C] **1** solid figure with similar, equal and parallel ends, and with sides which are parallelograms. **2** solid of this form, usually triangular and made of glass, which breaks up white light into the colors of the rainbow.

pris·matic /prɪzˈmætɪk/ *adj* **1** like, having the shape of, a prism. **2** (of colors) brilliant and varied.

pris·on /ˈprɪzən/ *n* **1** [C] place in which a criminal is confined. **2** [C] any place where a person is confined against his will. **3** [U] confinement.

pris·on·er /ˈprɪzənər/ *n* [C] **1** person kept in prison for crime or until trial for a crime. **2** person who has been arrested (esp for a serious crime): *Officer Smith brought his ~ to the station.* ***take sb prisoner,*** arrest or capture him. **3** person, animal, kept in confinement: *political ~s.*

pri·va·cy /ˈpraivəsi/ *n* [U] **1** state of being away from others, alone and undisturbed: *I don't want my ~ disturbed.* **2** secrecy; seclusion: *They were married in strict ~.*

pri·vate /ˈpraivɪt/ *adj* **1** (opposite of *public*) of, for the use of, concerning, one person or group of persons, not people in general: *a ~ letter; ~ property.* **2** secret: *have ~ information about it.* **3** secluded; isolated: *a ~ spot.* **4** having no official position; not holding any public office: *a ~ citizen* □ *n* **1** [C] (esp) enlisted member of the US army or marine corps holding the lowest rank. **2** ***in private,*** not in public.

private·ly *adv*

private ˈschool *n* [C] one which is not controlled or operated by the state.

pri·va·tion /praiˈveiʃən/ *n* (*formal*) [C] lack of the necessities of life; destitution: *fall ill through ~; suffering many ~s.*

privet /ˈprɪvɪt/ *n* [U] shrub with dark green leaves, often used for garden hedges.

pri·vi·lege /ˈprɪvəlɪdʒ/ *n* [C] right or advantage available only to a person, group, etc or attached to a certain position.

priv·i·leged *adj* having, granted, a privilege.

privy /ˈprɪvi/ *adj* (*archaic; liter*) **1** secret; private. **2** ***privy to,*** having secret knowledge of: *~ to the plot against the President.* □ *n* [C] (*pl* -ies) outhouse.

prize[1] /praiz/ *n* [C] **1** something (to be) awarded to one who succeeds in a competition, etc: *win first ~.* **2** (*fig*) anything worth having or struggling for: *the ~s of life.* □ *vt* value highly: *my most ~d possessions.*

prize[2] /praiz/ *vt* force, lever: *~ open/up/off the cover of a box.*

pro- /ˌprou-/ *prefix* **1** supporting; in favor of: *pro-Chinese.* **2** acting for: *pronoun.*

pro[1] /prou/ *n* [C] (*pl* pros) (*informal*) (short for) professional, esp in sports: *a ˈtennis pro.* □ *adj: pro basketball.* ***go ˈpro,*** turn professional.

pro[2] /prou/ *n* [C] (*pl* pros) argument in favor of something. □ *adv* in favor of; for. ***pro and con*** /ˌprouənˈkan/, for and against: *argue the matter pro and con.*

the ˌpros and ˈcons *n pl* the arguments for and against.

prob·a·bil·ity /ˌprabəˈbɪləti/ *n* (*pl* -ies) **1** [U] quality of being probable; likelihood: *There is not much ~ that he will succeed.* **2** [C] something which is probable: *What are the probabilities?*

prob·able /ˈprabəbəl/ *adj* likely to happen or to prove true or correct: *the ~ result; a ~ winner. It's very ~ that he'll be elected.*

prob·ably /-əbli/ *adj*

pro·bate /ˈprouˌbeit/ *n* (*legal*) [U] the official process of proving the validity of a will. □ *vt* establish the validity of a will.

pro·ba·tion /prouˈbeiʃən/ *n* [U] **1** testing of a person's conduct, abilities, qualities, etc before he is finally accepted for a position, admitted into a society, etc. **2** system by which convicted offenders are released under supervision on condition of good behavior.

probationer *n* [C] **(a)** student nurse. **(b)** offender who is on probation(2).

proˈbation officer, official who supervises offenders who are on probation.

probe /proub/ *n* [C] **1** slender instrument, used by doctors for learning about the depth and direction of a wound, etc. **2** investigation. □ *vt* **1** examine (as) with a probe. **2** investigate or examine thoroughly.

prob·lem /ˈprabləm/ *n* [C] **1** question, situation, etc which is troublesome and difficult. **2** question to be solved in mathematics.

prob·lem·atic /ˌprabləˈmætɪk/ *adj* uncertain; doubtful; puzzling.

prob·lem·ati·cally /-kli/ *adv*

pro·bos·cis /prəˈbasɪs/ *n* [C] (*pl* ~es) **1** elephant's trunk. **2** long tubelike part of the mouth of some insects. ⇨ illus at insect.

pro·ce·dure /prəˈsidʒər/ *n* [C,U] (the regular) order of doing things: *the usual ~ at committee meetings.*

pro·ce·dur·al /prəˈsidʒərəl/ *adj*

pro·ceed /prəˈsid/ *vi* **1** go forward or continue, esp after an interruption: *Let us ~ to business/to the next item on the agenda.* **2** come, arise (from): *famine, plague and other evils ~ing from war.* **3** begin and carry on an action: *He ~ed to tell me all his troubles.*

pro·ceed·ing /prəˈsidɪŋ/ *n* **1** [U] course of action: *a cautious ~.* **2** [C] event: *There have been suspicious ~s in committee meetings.* **3** [C] legal action. **4** (*pl*) official records (of the activities of a society, etc).

pro·ceeds /ˈprouˌsidz/ *n pl* financial results, profits, of an undertaking: *All the ~ go to charity.*

pro·cess /ˈpraˌses/ *n* **1** [C] connected series of actions, operations, steps, etc leading to a certain result: *the ~es of digestion, reproduction and growth; the ~ of manufacturing steel.* **2** [U] progress: *a building in the ~ of construction.* **3** [C] (*legal*) **(a)** course of an action at law. **(b)** writ or summons to appear in a court of law. **4** [C] growth which projects from (a part of) the body. □ *vt* treat (material, food, etc) by means of a process.

pro·ces·sion /prəˈseʃən/ *n* **1** [C] number of persons, vehicles, etc moving forward and following each other in an orderly way: *a ˈfuneral ~.* **2** [U] act of moving forward in this way.

pro·ces·sional /-nəl/ *adj* of, for, used in, processions: *~al music.*

pro·claim /prouˈkleim/ *vt* **1** make known publicly or officially; declare: *~ war/peace; ~ a man (to be) a traitor/that he is a traitor.* **2** show; indicate: *His accent ~ed that he was a Southerner.*

proc·la·ma·tion /ˌprakləˈmeiʃən/ *n* **1** [U] proclaiming: *by public* ∼. **2** [C] something which is proclaimed: *issue/make a* ∼.

pro·con·sul /ˌprouˈkansəl/ *n* [C] **1** administrator of a province in ancient Rome. **2** governor of a colony or dominion.

pro·cras·ti·nate /prouˈkræstəˌneit/ *vi* (*formal*) delay action, esp repeatedly: *He* ∼*d until it was too late.*

pro·cras·ti·na·tion /prouˌkræstəˈneiʃən/ *n* [U]

pro·create /ˈproukriˌeit/ *vt* (*formal*) give birth to.

pro·cre·ation /ˌproukriˈeiʃən/ *n* [C,U]

pro·cure /prəˈkyʊr/ *vt* (*formal*) **1** obtain, esp with care or effort: ∼ *rare and beautiful paintings.* **2** bring about; cause: ∼ *his death by poison.*

prod /prad/ *vt,vi* (-dd-) **1** push or poke with something pointed. **2** (*fig*) urge or stir to action: *I was always* ∼*ding her to see her doctor.* □ *n* [C] something used for prodding.

prod·i·gal /ˈpradɪgəl/ *adj* (*formal*) **1** spending or using too much; wasteful. **2** lavish.

pro·di·gious /prəˈdɪdʒəs/ *adj* **1** enormous: *a* ∼ *sum of money.* **2** amazing; wonderful: ∼ *feats of strength.*

pro·di·gious·ly *adv*

prod·igy /ˈpradədʒi/ *n* [C] (*pl* -ies) **1** something wonderful or extraordinary. **2** person who has unusual or remarkable abilities.

pro·duce[1] /ˈpraˌdus/ *n* [U] that which is produced, esp by farming: *garden/farm/agricultural* ∼.

pro·duce[2] /prəˈdus/ *vt,vi* **1** put or bring forward to be looked at or examined: ∼ *one's ticket when asked to do so.* **2** manufacture; make; grow; create: *We must* ∼ *more food and import less.* **3** give birth to; bring forth. **4** cause; bring about: *a movie that* ∼*d a sensation.* **5** present (a play, motion picture, etc) to the public.

pro·ducer /prəˈdusər/ *n* [C] **1** person who manufactures goods. **2** person responsible for presenting a play, a movie, or a radio or TV program.

prod·uct /ˈpradəkt, -ˌdəkt/ *n* [C] **1** thing produced (by nature or by man): *metal* ∼*s from Germany.* **2** result; outcome: *The plan was the* ∼ *of many hours of careful thought.* **3** (*math*) quantity obtained by multiplication. **4** (*chem*) substance obtained by chemical reaction.

pro·duc·tion /prəˈdəkʃən/ *n* **1** [U] process of producing: *the* ∼ *of crops/manufactured goods.* **2** [U] quantity produced: *a fall/increase in* ∼. **3** [C] thing produced: *his early* ∼*s as a writer,* his first novels, plays, etc.

pro·duc·tive /prəˈdəktɪv/ *adj* **1** able to produce; fertile: ∼ *land.* **2** resulting in: ∼ *of happiness.* **3** producing things economically: ∼ *methods.*

pro·duc·tive·ly *adv*

pro·duc·tiv·ity /ˌproudəkˈtɪvəti, ˌpradək-/ *n* [U] being productive; power of being productive: *a* ∼ *bonus for workers.*

Prof.[1] *abbr* = Professor.

prof[2] /praf/ *n* [C] (*pl* ∼s) (*informal*) (short for) professor.

pro·fane /prouˈfein/ *adj* **1** (*formal*) (contrasted with *sacred, holy*) worldly: ∼ *literature.* **2** having or showing contempt for God and sacred things: ∼ *language.* □ *vt* treat (sacred or holy places, things) with contempt, without proper reverence.

pro·fane·ly *adv*

pro·fan·ity /prouˈfænəti/ *n* (*pl* -ies) **1** [U] profane conduct, speech or language. **2** (*pl*) profane language.

pro·fess /prəˈfes/ *vt,vi* **1** declare that one has (beliefs, likes, ignorance, interests, etc): *He* ∼*ed a great interest in my welfare.* **2** declare one's faith in (a religion): ∼ *Islam/Christ.* **3** claim; represent oneself: *I don't* ∼ *to be an expert on that subject.*

pro·fessed *adj* self-confessed; openly declared: *a* ∼*ed Christian.*

pro·fes·sion /prəˈfeʃən/ *n* [C] **1** occupation, esp one needing advanced education and special training, eg the law, teaching, medicine. **2** statement or declaration (of belief, feeling, etc): ∼*s of faith/loyalty.*

pro·fes·sion·al /prəˈfeʃənəl/ *adj* **1** of a profession(1): ∼ *skill;* ∼ *men,* eg doctors, lawyers. **2** doing or practicing something for payment or to make a living: ∼ *football;* ∼ *musicians.* ***turn professional,*** become professional. □ *n* [C] **1** (*abbr* = **pro** /prou/) person who teaches or engages in some kind of sport for money. **2** person who does something for payment that others do (without payment) for pleasure. **3** (*abbr* = **pro** /prou/) person who shows professional skill at something: *That player/chairman/carpenter is a real* ∼*!* ⇨ amateur.

pro·fes·sion·al·ly /-nəli/ *adv*

prof·es·sor /prəˈfesər/ *n* [C] college or university teacher of the highest rank.

prof·es·sor·ial /ˌproufəˈsɔriəl, ˌprafə-/ *adj*

prof·es·sor·ship /prəˈfesərˌʃɪp/ *n* [C] post, office, or duties of a professor.

prof·fer /ˈprafər/ *vt* (*formal*) offer.

pro·fi·ciency /prəˈfɪʃənsi/ *n* [U] being skilled: *a certificate of* ∼ *in English.*

pro·fi·cient /prəˈfɪʃənt/ *adj* skilled: ∼ *in using a calculator.*

pro·fi·cient·ly *adv*

pro·file /ˈprouˌfaiəl/ *n* [C] **1** side view, esp of the head. **2** edge or outline of something seen against a background. **3** brief biography, as given in a periodical or on TV. □ *vt* (*pres p* profiling /-ˌfailɪŋ/) draw, show, in profile.

prof·it[1] /ˈprafɪt/ *n* **1** [U] advantage or good obtained from something: *gain* ∼ *from one's studies.* **2** [C,U] money gained in business, etc: *sell a bike at a* ∼.

prof·it[2] /ˈprafɪt/ *vt,vi* (of persons) gain or be helped: *I have* ∼*ed by your advice.*

prof·it·able /ˈprafɪtəbəl/ *adj* **1** bringing profit: ∼ *investments.* **2** (*fig*) useful: *a deal that was* ∼ *to all of us.*

prof·it·ably /-əbli/ *adv*

profi·teer /ˌprafəˈtɪr/ *vi* make large profits, esp by taking advantage in times of difficulty, eg in war. □ *n* [C] person who does this.

prof·li·gate /ˈprafləˌgeit/ *adj* (*formal*) **1** shamelessly immoral. **2** very extravagant; wasteful. □ *n* [C] profligate person.

pro·found /prəˈfaund/ *adj* **1** (*formal*) deep: *a* ∼

sleep. **2** needing, showing, having, great knowledge: *a man of ~ learning*. **3** needing much thought to understand: *~ mysteries*.

pro·found·ly *adv* deeply: *~ly grateful*.

pro·fun·dity /prəˈfəndəti/ *n* (*formal*) [U] depth: *the ~ of his knowledge*.

pro·fuse /prəˈfyus/ *adj* (*formal*) **1** very plentiful: *~ gratitude*. **2** extravagant: *He was ~ in his apologies*, apologized almost too much.

pro·fuse·ly *adv*

pro·fu·sion /prəˈfyuʒən/ *n* [U] (*formal*) great supply: *flowers in ~*.

pro·geni·tor /prouˈdʒenɪtər/ *n* [C] (*formal*) = ancestor.

prog·eny /ˈpradʒəni/ *n* (*collect sing*) (*formal*) offspring; descendants.

prog·no·sis /pragˈnousɪs/ *n* [C] (*pl* -es) (*med*) forecast of the probable course of a disease or illness.

prog·nos·tic /pragˈnastɪk/ *adj* (*formal*) predictive (*of*). □ *n* [C] omen; sign: *a ~ of failure*.

prog·nos·ti·cate /pragˈnastəˌkeit/ *vt* (*formal*) predict.

prog·nos·ti·ca·tion /ˌpragˌnastəˈkeiʃən/ *n* [C,U]

pro·gram /ˈprouˌgræm/ *n* [C] **1** list of items, events, etc, eg for a concert, for radio or TV or for a sports meeting; list of names of singers at a concert, actors in a play, etc. **2** plan of what is to be done: *a political ~. What's the ~ for tomorrow?* What are we/you going to do? **3** coded collection of information, data, etc fed into a computer. □ *vt* (-mm-, -m-) make a program of or for; plan.

pro·gram·mer *n* [C] person who prepares a computer program.

prog·ress[1] /ˈpragrɪs, ˈpraˌgres/ *n* [U] forward movement; improvement; development: *making fast ~*. ***in progress,*** being made, done. ***make good progress,*** **(a)** (of health) improve satisfactorily. **(b)** (of a task) do it well.

pro·gress[2] /prəˈgres/ *vi* make progress: *The work is ~ing steadily. She is ~ing in her studies*.

pro·gres·sion /prəˈgreʃən/ *n* [U] moving forward; improvement.

pro·gres·sive /prəˈgresɪv/ *adj* **1** making continuous forward movement. **2** increasing by regular amounts: *~ taxation*. **3** improving; supporting or favoring improvement, modernization: *a ~ political party*. □ *n* [C] person supporting a progressive (political) policy.

pro·gres·sive·ly *adv*

pro·hib·it /prouˈhɪbɪt/ *vt* **1** forbid: *Smoking is strictly ~ed*. **2** prevent or make impossible.

pro·hi·bi·tion /ˌprouəˈbɪʃən/ *n* **1** [U] prohibiting. **2** [C] law or order that forbids: *a ~ against smoking*. **3 Prohibition,** period in US history (1920-33) when the manufacture and consumption of alcoholic beverages was nationally prohibited.

pro·hib·i·tive /prouˈhɪbətɪv/ *adj* tending to prohibit: *~ prices*.

proj·ect[1] /ˈpraˌdʒekt/ *n* [C] (plan for a) scheme or undertaking: *a ~ to study community welfare*.

pro·ject[2] /prəˈdʒekt/ *vt,vi* **1** make plans for: *~ a new dam/waterworks*. **2** cause a shadow, an outline, a picture from a film, slide, etc to fall on a surface, etc: *~ a beam of light on to a wall*. **3** imagine that another person has feelings (such as guilt, inferiority) that one has oneself. **4** make known; convey: *She ~ed her tension and anxiety*. **5** throw; send: *to ~ missiles into space*. **6** stand out beyond the surface nearby: *a balcony that ~s over the street*.

pro·jec·tile /prəˈdʒektəl/ *n* [C] something (to be) sent forward, esp from a gun or launching pad.

pro·jec·tion /prəˈdʒekʃən/ *n* **1** [U] the act of projecting. **2** [C] something that projects or has been projected.

pro·jec·tion·ist /-ɪst/ *n* [C] person who operates a motion picture projector.

pro·jec·tor /prəˈdʒektər/ *n* [C] apparatus for projecting pictures by rays of light on to a screen: *a ˈslide ~*.

pro·let·ar·iat /ˌprouləˈteriət/ *n* [C] (*collect*) the class of workers (as contrasted with the owners of industry and capital).

pro·let·ar·ian /-iən/ *n* [C], *adj* (member) of the proletariat.

pro·lif·er·ate /prəˈlɪfəˌreit/ *vi,vt* (*formal*) **1** reproduce, by rapid multiplication of cells, new parts, etc. **2** (*fig*) increase rapidly.

pro·lif·er·ation /prəˌlɪfəˈreiʃən/ *n* [U]

pro·lific /prəˈlɪfɪk/ *adj* (*formal*) producing much or many: *a ~ author*.

pro·logue /ˈprouˌlɔg, -ˌlag/ *n* [C] **1** introductory (part of a) poem: *the "Prologue" to the "Canterbury Tales."* **2** (*fig*) first of a series of events.

pro·long /prəˈlɔŋ, prou-/ *vt* make longer: *~ a visit*.

pro·longed *adj* continuing for a long time: *a ~ed discussion*.

pro·lon·ga·tion /ˌproulɔŋˈgeiʃən/ *n* [C,U]

prom /pram/ *n* [C] (often formal) dance held by a class in high school or college.

prom·e·nade /ˌpraməˈneid, -ˈnad/ *n* **1** (place suitable for, made for, a) walk taken in public, for exercise or pleasure. **2** formal dance or ball. □ *vi,vt* go, take, on a promenade.

promi·nence /ˈpramənəns/ *n* **1** [U] the state of being prominent. **2** [C] prominent(1) part or place: *a ~ in the middle of a plain*.

promi·nent /ˈpramənənt/ *adj* **1** standing out; easily seen: *~ cheekbones; the most ~ feature in the landscape*. **2** (of persons) distinguished: *~ politicians*. **3** important: *play a ~ part in public life*.

promi·nent·ly *adv*

prom·is·cu·ity /ˌpraməˈskyuəti/ *n* [U] (state of) being promiscuous.

pro·mis·cu·ous /prəˈmɪskyuəs/ *adj* (esp) indiscriminate; casual (esp in sexual relationships).

pro·mis·cu·ous·ly *adv*

prom·ise[1] /ˈpramɪs/ *n* **1** [C] written or spoken undertaking to do, or not to do, give, something, etc: *make/give/keep/carry out/break a ~*. **2** [C] that which one undertakes to do, etc. **3** [U] indication or hope of success or good results: *a writer who shows much ~*, seems likely to succeed.

prom·ise[2] /ˈpramɪs/ *vt,vi* **1** make a promise(1) to: *He ~d (me) to be here/that he would be here at 6 o'clock*. **2** give cause for expecting: *The clouds ~ rain*.

prom·is·ing *adj* seeming likely to succeed, have good results, etc.

prom·on·tory /ˈpramənˌtɔri/ *n* [C] (*pl* -ies) high point of land standing out from the coastline.

pro·mote /prəˈmout/ *vt* **1** give (a person) higher position or rank: *He was ~d sergeant/to sergeant/to the rank of sergeant.* **2** help to organize and start; help the progress of: *try to ~ good feelings (between...).*

pro·mot·er *n* [C] (esp) person who supports with money, etc new companies, professional sports, etc.

pro·mo·tion /prəˈmouʃən/ *n* **1** [U] promoting or being promoted. **2** [C] instance of promoting or being promoted: *He resigned because ~s were few.* **3** advertising using publicity, etc: *sales ~.*

prompt[1] /prampt/ *adj* acting, done, sent, given, without delay: *a ~ reply.*

prompt·ly *adv*

prompt·ness /-nɪs/ *n* [U]

prompt[2] /prampt/ *vt* **1** move or inspire (a person to do something): *He was ~ed by patriotism.* **2** remind or tell (eg an actor) what to say if he forgets. □ *n* [C] action of prompting(2).

prompt·er *n* [C] person who prompts actors.

prom·ul·gate /ˈpraməlˌgeit/ *vt* (*formal*) **1** make public, announce officially (a decree, a new law, etc). **2** make known beliefs, knowledge.

prom·ul·ga·tion /ˌpraməlˈgeiʃən/ *n* [U]

pron. *abbr* = **1** pronoun. **2** pronunciation.

prone /proun/ *adj* **1** (stretched out, lying) face downwards: *in a ~ position.* **2** ***prone to,*** have a tendency: *~ to illness. Some people seem to be ˈaccident-~.*

prong /prɔŋ, praŋ/ *n* [C] (something like) one of the long, pointed parts of a fork.

pro·noun /ˈprouˌnaun/ *n* [C] word used in place of a *noun* or *noun phrase*, eg he, it, hers, me, them.

pro·nounce /prəˈnauns/ *vt,vi* **1** make the sound of (a word, etc): *The "b" in "debt" is not ~d.* **2** declare, announce (esp formally, solemnly or officially): *Has judgment been ~d yet?* **3** (*formal*) declare as one's opinion: *He ~d himself in favor of the plan.*

pro·nounce·able /-əbəl/ *adj* (of sounds, words) that can be pronounced.

pro·nounced *adj* definite; easy to notice: *a man of ~d opinions.*

pro·nounce·ment *n* [C] formal statement or declaration.

pro·nun·ci·ation /prəˌnənsiˈeiʃən/ *n* [U] act or way of pronouncing: *Has her English ~ improved?*

proof[1] /pruf/ *adj* ***proof (against),*** giving safety or protection; able to resist: *~ against bullets; ˈwater~; ˈsound~; (fig) ~ against temptation.*

proof[2] /pruf/ *n* **1** [U] evidence (in general), or [C] a particular piece of evidence, that is sufficient to show, or helps to show, that something is a fact: *Is there any ~ that the accused man was at the scene of the crime?* **2** [U] demonstrating; testing of whether something is true, a fact, etc: *He produced documents in ~ of his claim.* **3** [C] test, trial, examination. **4** [C] trial copy of something printed or engraved, for approval before other copies are printed. **5** [U] standard of strength of distilled alcoholic liquors: *This rum is 30 percent below ~.*

prop[1] /prap/ *n* **1** support used to keep something up. **2** (*fig*) person who supports another person: *He is the ~ of his parents in their old age.* □ *vt* (-pp-) **1** support; keep in position: *Use this box to ~ the door open.* **2** (*fig*) support: *He can't always expect his friends to ~ him up.*

prop[2] /prap/ *n* [C] object, used esp in stage or film studio settings, to add realism to scenes.

propa·ganda /ˌprapəˈgændə/ *n* [U] (means of, methods for the) spreading of information, doctrines, ideas, etc: *political ~.*

propa·gan·dize /-ˌdaiz/ *vi* engage in propaganda.

propa·gate /ˈprapəˌgeit/ *vt,vi* (*formal*) **1** increase the number of (plants, animals, diseases) by natural process from the parent stock: *Trees ~ themselves by seeds.* **2** spread more widely: *~ news/knowledge.* **3** (of animals and plants) reproduce.

propa·ga·tion /ˌprapəˈgeiʃən/ *n* [U] propagating: *the propagation of disease by insects.*

pro·pel /prəˈpel/ *vt* (-ll-) drive forward: *a boat ~led by oars.*

pro·pel·lant, -lent /-ənt/ *n* [C,U] something used to produce forward motion, eg fuel that burns to fire a rocket, etc.

pro·pel·ler *n* [C] device with two or more blades which turn to move a ship, helicopter, etc. ⇨ illus at aircraft.

pro·pen·sity /prəˈpensəti/ *n* [C] (*pl* -ies) (*formal*) natural tendency: *a ~ to exaggerate.*

proper /ˈprapər/ *adj* **1** right, correct, fitting, suitable: *Are you doing it the ~ way? Is this the ~ tool for the job?* **2** in conformity with, paying regard to, the conventions of society: *~ behavior.* **3** (placed after the *noun*) strictly limited to what has been specified: *the city ~*, excluding its suburbs, etc.

ˌproper ˈfraction, (*math*) (eg $\frac{1}{2}$, $\frac{3}{4}$) one in which the number above the line is smaller than that below the line.

proper·ly *adv*

ˌproper ˈnoun, (*gram*) noun which is the name of an individual person, town, etc, eg Mary, Prague.

prop·erty /ˈprapərti/ *n* (*pl* -ies) **1** [U] (*collect*) things owned; possessions: *Don't take my bike —it's not your ~.* **2** [C] land or land and buildings: *He owns a business ~ in town.* **3** [U] ownership; the fact of owning or being owned: *Property has its obligations*, eg you must look after it. **4** [C] special quality that belongs to something: *the chemical properties of iron.*

proph·ecy /ˈprafəsi/ *n* (*pl* -ies) **1** [U] power of telling what will happen in the future: *have the gift of ~.* **2** [C] statement that tells what will happen: *His ~ came true.*

proph·esy /ˈprafəˌsai/ *vt,vi* (*pt,pp* -ied) **1** say what will happen: *~ war/that war will break out.* **2** speak as a prophet.

prophet /ˈprafɪt/ *n* [C] **1** person who teaches religion and claims that his teaching comes to him directly from God. **2** pioneer of a new theory, cause, etc: *Ralph Waldo Emerson was an early American ~ of transcendentalism.* **3** person who tells, or claims to tell, what will happen in the future.

prophet·ess /ˈprafɪtɪs/ *n* [C] woman prophet.

pro·phetic /prəˈfetɪk/ *adj* of a prophet or prophecy: *Her dreams were ~.*

pro·pheti·cally /-kli/ *adv*

pro·pi·ti·ate /prəˈpɪʃiˌeit/ *vt* (formal) do something to take away the anger of; appease: *offer a sacrifice to ~ the gods.*

pro·pi·ti·ation /prəˌpɪʃiˈeiʃən/ *n* [U]

pro·pi·ti·atory /prəˈpɪʃəˌtɔri/ *adj*

pro·pi·tious /prəˈpɪʃəs/ *adj* (*formal*) favorable: *~ weather.*

pro·pi·tious·ly *adv*

pro·po·nent /prəˈpounənt/ *n* [C] one who advances and defends a doctrine, claim, etc.

pro·por·tion /prəˈpɔrʃən/ *n* **1** [U] relation of one thing to another in quantity, size, etc; relation of a part to the whole: *The ~ of imports to exports is worrying the government.* ***in proportion to,*** relative to: *payment in ~ to work done.* ***out of proportion (to),*** out of balance: *When you're angry, you often get things out of ~,* think things are more important than they really are. **2** [C] part; share: *You have not done your ~ of the work.* **3** (often *pl*) the correct relation of parts or of the sizes of the several parts: *a room of good ~s.* **4** (*pl*) size; measurements: *export trade of substantial ~s.* **5** (*math*) equality of relationship between two sets of numbers; statement that two ratios are equal (eg 4 is to 8 as 6 is to 12). □ *vt* (*formal*) put into a correct relationship: *Do you ~ your expenditure to your income?*

pro·por·tional /prəˈpɔrʃənəl/ *adj* (*formal*) corresponding in degree or amount (to): *payment ~ to the work done.*

pro·por·tion·ally /-nəli/ *adv*

pro·por·tion·ate /prəˈpɔrʃənɪt/ *adj* (*formal*) = proportional.

pro·por·tion·ate·ly *adv*

pro·pos·al /prəˈpouzəl/ *n* **1** [U] proposing. **2** [C] plan or scheme: *a ~ for peace.* **3** [C] offer (esp of marriage): *five ~s in one week.*

pro·pose /prəˈpouz/ *vt,vi* **1** offer or put forward for consideration, as a suggestion, plan or purpose: *I ~ starting early/an early start/that we should start early.* **2** offer (marriage). **3** put forward (somebody's name) for an office, for membership, etc: *I ~ Mr. Smith for chairman.*

pro·posed *adj*

prop·osi·tion /ˌprapəˈzɪʃən/ *n* [C] **1** statement; assertion: *a ~ stated so well that it needs no explanation.* **2** undertaking: *Tunneling under the English Channel is a big ~.* **3** suggestion, esp something immoral or illegal, such as an indecent suggestion made to a girl. □ *vt* make a proposition(3) to.

pro·pound /prəˈpaund/ *vt* (*formal*) offer for consideration or solution: *~ a theory.*

pro·pri·etary /prəˈpraiəˌteri/ *adj* owned or controlled by somebody; held as property.

pro·pri·etor /prəˈpraiətər/ *n* [C] owner, esp of a hotel, store, land or patent.

pro·pri·etress /prəˈpraiətrɪs/ *n* [C] woman proprietor.

pro·pri·ety /prəˈpraiəti/ *n* (*pl* -ies) (*formal*) **1** [U] state of being correct in behavior and morals: *a breach of ~.* **2** (*pl*) rules of correct social behavior: *observe the proprieties.*

pro·pul·sion /prəˈpəlʃən/ *n* [U] propelling force.

pro·saic /prouˈzeiɪk/ *adj* (*formal*) dull; uninteresting; commonplace: *a ~ husband.*

pro·sai·cally /-kli/ *adv*

pro·scribe /prouˈskraib/ *vt* **1** denounce (a person, practice, etc) as dangerous. **2** publicly put (a person) out of the protection of the law.

pro·scrip·tion /prouˈskrɪpʃən/ *n* **(a)** [U] proscribing or being proscribed. **(b)** [C] instance of this.

prose /prouz/ *n* [U] ordinary language, as contrasted with verse.

pros·ecute /ˈprasɪˌkyut/ *vt* **1** start or carry on legal proceedings against: *Trespassers will be ~d.* **2** carry on determinedly.

pros·ecu·tion /ˌprasɪˈkyuʃən/ *n* (*legal*) **1** [U] prosecuting or being prosecuted: *make oneself liable to ~.* **2** [C] instance of this. **3** (*collect*) person and his advisers who prosecute(1).

pros·ecutor /ˈprasɪˌkyutər/ *n* [C]

pros·pect[1] /ˈpraˌspekt/ *n* **1** [C] wide view over land or sea. **2** (*fig*) broad view before the mind, in the imagination. **3** (*pl*) something expected, hoped for, looked forward to: *There are bright ~s for me if I accept the position.* **4** [U] expectation; hope: *I see no/little/not much ~ of his recovery.* **5** [C] possible customer or client: *He's a good ~.* **6** [C] location at which gold or valuable ore is found.

pros·pect[2] /ˈpraˌspekt/ *vi* search (for): *~ing for gold.*

pro·spec·tive /prəˈspektɪv/ *adj* hoped for; looked forward to: *a ~ buyer; the ~ candidate.*

pros·pec·tor /ˈpraˌspektər/ *n* [C] person who explores a region looking for gold or other valuable ores, etc.

pro·spec·tus /prəˈspektəs/ *n* [C] (*pl* ~es) printed account giving details of and advertising something, eg a book about to be published.

pros·per /ˈpraspər/ *vi,vt* succeed; do well: *The business ~ed.*

pros·per·ity /praˈsperəti/ *n* [U] state of being successful; good fortune: *a life of happiness and ~; live in ~.*

pros·per·ous /ˈpraspərəs/ *adj* successful; rich: *a ~ business; ~ years.*

pros·per·ous·ly *adv*

pros·ti·tute /ˈprastəˌtut/ *n* [C] person who performs sexual acts for payment. □ *vt* **1** (*reflex*) make a prostitute of (oneself). **2** put to wrong or unworthy uses.

pros·ti·tu·tion /ˌprastəˈtuʃən/ *n* [U] practice of prostituting.

pros·trate /ˈpraˌstreit/ *adj* **1** lying stretched out on the ground, usually face downward, eg because exhausted, or to show submission or deep respect. **2** (*fig*) overcome (with grief, etc); conquered. □ *vt* **1** make oneself, cause to be, prostrate: *trees ~d by the gale.* **2** make helpless: *She is ~d with grief.*

pros·tra·tion /praˈstreiʃən/ *n* [C,U]

pro·tag·on·ist /prouˈtægənɪst/ *n* [C] (*formal*) chief person in a drama, novel, story, etc.

pro·tect /prəˈtekt/ *vt* keep safe (from danger, enemies; against attack): *well ~ed from the cold/*

against the weather.

pro·tec·tion /prəˈtekʃən/ *n* **1** [U] protecting or being protected: *These plants need ~ against the sun.* **2** [U] system of protecting home industry against foreign competition. **3** [C] person or thing that protects: *wearing a heavy coat as a ~ against the cold.*

pro·tec·tive /prəˈtektɪv/ *adj* **1** giving protection: *a ~ covering.* **2 protective (toward),** (of persons) with a wish to protect: *A mother naturally feels ~ toward her children.*

pro·tec·tive·ly *adv*

pro·tec·tor /prəˈtektər/ *n* [C] person or thing that protects.

pro·tec·tor·ate /prəˈtektərɪt/ *n* [C] country under the protection of another, stronger nation.

pro·tégé /ˈproutəˌʒei/ *n* [C] person to whom another gives protection and help (usually over a long period).

pro·tein /ˈprouˌtin/ *n* [C,U] body-building substance essential to good health, in such foods as milk, eggs, meat.

pro·test[1] /ˈprouˌtest/ *n* **1** [C,U] (statement of) disapproval or objection: *He paid without ~*, without making any objection. **2** [C] public gathering for the purpose of expressing protest: (as an *adj*) *a ˈ~ march.*

pro·test[2] /prəˈtest/ *vt,vi* **1** affirm strongly; assert against opposition: *He ~ed his innocence/that he was innocent.* **2** raise an objection, say something (*against*): *I ~ against being called an old fool.*

pro·test·er *n* [C]

pro·test·ing·ly *adv*

Prot·es·tant /ˈpratəstənt/ *n,adj* [C] (member) of any of the Christian sects which descend from those that separated from the Roman Catholic Church of Rome in the 16th century.

prot·esta·tion /ˌpratɪˈsteiʃən/ *n* [C] (*formal*) serious declaration: *~s of innocence.*

pro·to·col /ˈproutəˌkɔl/ *n* **1** [C] first or original draft of an agreement (esp between states), signed by those making it, in preparation for a treaty. **2** [U] code of behavior as practiced on diplomatic occasions: *Was the seating arranged according to ~?*

pro·ton /ˈprouˌtan/ *n* [C] positively charged particle forming part of an atomic nucleus. ⇨ illus at atom.

pro·to·type /ˈproutəˌtaip/ *n* [C] first or original example, eg of an aircraft, from which others have been or will be copied or developed.

pro·to·zoa /ˌproutəˈzouə/ *n pl* (division of the animal kingdom consisting of) animals of the simplest type formed of a single cell.

pro·tract /prouˈtrækt/ *vt* lengthen the time taken by: *a ~ed visit/argument.*

pro·trac·tion /prouˈtrækʃən/ *n* [U] lengthening out.

pro·trac·tor /prouˈtræktər/ *n* [C] instrument, usually a semicircle, marked (0° to 180°) for measuring and drawing angles.

pro·trude /prouˈtrud/ *vi,vt* (cause to) stick out or project: *protruding eyes/teeth.*

pro·tru·sion /prouˈtruʒən/ *n* **1** [U] protruding. **2** [C] something that protrudes.

pro·tu·ber·ance /prouˈtubərəns/ *n* **1** [U] bulging. **2** [C] bulge or swelling.

pro·tu·ber·ant /prouˈtubərənt/ *adj* curving or swelling outwards; bulging.

proud /praud/ *adj* (-er, -est) **1** having or showing a proper pride or dignity: *~ of their success/of being so successful.* **2** having or showing too much pride: *He was too ~ to join our party.* **3** magnificent; splendid: *It was a ~ day for the school when its team won the championship.*

proud·ly *adv*

prov. *abbr* = proverb.

prov·able /ˈpruvəbəl/ *adj* that can be proved.

prove /pruv/ *vt,vi* (*pp* ~d, or ~n /ˈpruvən/) **1** supply proof of; show beyond doubt to be true: *~ that he is guilty. Can you ~ it (to me)?* ***The exception proves the rule,*** shows that the rule is valid in most cases. **2** establish the genuineness, quality or accuracy of: *~ a man's worth.* **3** turn out (to be): *The new typist ~d (to be) excellent. Our wood supply ~d (to be) insufficient.*

prov·erb /ˈpraˌvərb/ *n* [C] popular short saying, with words of advice or warning, eg "It takes two to make a quarrel."

pro·verb·ial /prəˈvərbiəl/ *adj* widely known and talked about: *His stupidity is ~ial.*

pro·verbi·ally /-əli/ *adv*

pro·vide /prəˈvaid/ *vi,vt* **1** do what is necessary: *We have had many visitors to ~ food for.* **2** give, supply (what is needed, esp what a person needs in order to live): *providing the children with food and clothes/food and clothes for the family.* **3** state: *The agreement ~s that the tenant shall pay for repairs to the building.*

pro·vid·er *n* [C]

pro·vid·ed /prəˈvaidɪd/ *conj* on condition (that): *I'll come ~ that he stays away.*

provi·dence /ˈpravədəns/ *n* **1 Providence, (a)** God. **(b)** God's care and protection. **2** [U] prudence; being provident.

provi·dent /ˈpravədənt/ *adj* (*formal*) (careful in) providing for future needs or events, esp in old age.

provi·dent·ly *adv*

pro·vid·ing /prəˈvaidɪŋ/ *conj* = provided.

prov·ince /ˈpravɪns/ *n* [C] **1** large administrative division of a country. **2** area of learning or knowledge; department of activity: *That is outside my ~*, not something with which I can or need deal. **3 the provinces,** areas of a country away from the large cities, cultural centers, etc.

prov·in·cial /prəˈvɪnʃəl/ *adj* **1** of a province(1): *~ government.* **2** having, typical of, the unsophisticated speech, manners, views, etc of a person living in the provinces: *a ~ accent.* □ *n* [C] person from the provinces.

prov·in·ci·ally /-ʃəli/ *adv*

pro·vi·sion /prəˈvɪʒən/ *n* **1** [U] providing, preparation (esp for future needs): *make ~ for one's old age*, eg by saving money. **2** [C] amount provided: *issue a ~ of meat to the troops.* **3** (*pl*) food; food supplies: *have a good supply of ~s.* **4** [C] condition in a legal document, eg a clause in a will. □ *vt* supply with food and stores.

pro·vi·sional /prəˈvɪʒənəl/ *adj* for the present time only; temporary.

pro·vi·sion·ally /-nəli/ *adv*

pro·vo·ca·tion /ˌpravəˈkeiʃən/ *n* **1** [U] provoking or being provoked: *She shouts at/on the slightest* ~. **2** [C] something that provokes or annoys.
pro·voca·tive /prəˈvakətɪv/ *adj* causing, likely to cause, anger, argument, interest, etc: ~ *remarks; a* ~ *dress.*
pro·voca·tive·ly *adv*
pro·voke /prəˈvouk/ *vt* **1** make angry: *If you* ~ *the dog, it will attack you.* **2** cause: ~ *laughter/a smile/a riot. His suggestion* ~*d her into slapping his face.*
pro·vok·ing *adj* annoying.
pro·vok·ing·ly *adv*
pro·vost /ˈprouˌvoust/ *n* [C] (title of) a high-level administrator in some US universities.
prow /prau/ *n* [C] pointed front of a ship or boat.
prow·ess /ˈprauɪs/ *n* [U] (*liter*) **1** bravery; valor. **2** unusual skill or ability.
prowl /praul/ *vi,vt* go about quietly looking for a chance to get food (as wild animals do), or to steal, etc. □ *n* ***on the prowl,*** prowling.
prowl·er *n* [C]
prox·im·ity /prakˈsɪməti/ *n* [U] nearness: *in* (*close*) ~ *to*, (very) near to (the more usual phrase).
proxy /ˈpraksi/ *n* (*pl* -ies) **1** [C,U] (document giving) authority to represent or act for another (esp in voting at an election). **2** [C] person given a proxy.
prude /prud/ *n* [C] person who is often exaggeratedly or affectedly moral in behavior or speech.
pru·dery /ˈprudəri/ *n* (*pl* -ies) **(a)** [U] quality of being prudish. **(b)** [C] prudish act or remark.
pru·dence /ˈprudəns/ *n* [U] careful forethought.
pru·dent /ˈprudənt/ *adj* acting only after careful thought or planning: *a* ~ *housewife.*
pru·dent·ly *adv*
pru·den·tial /pruˈdenʃəl/ *adj* of, relating to, or marked by prudence.
prud·ish /ˈprudɪʃ/ *adj* easily shocked; extremely moral.
prud·ish·ly *adv*
prud·ish·ness /-nɪs/ *n* [U]
prune[1] /prun/ *n* [C] dried plum.
prune[2] /prun/ *vt* **1** cut away parts of (trees, bushes, etc) in order to control growth or shape: ~ *the rose bushes.* **2** (*fig*) take out unnecessary parts from: ~ *a report of unnecessary detail.*
pry[1] /prai/ *vi* (*pt,pp* pried /praid/) inquire or look too inquisitively (into other people's affairs).
pry·ing·ly *adv*
pry[2] /prai/ *vt* (*pt,pp* pried /praid/) **1** move or force open (as) with a lever; prize[2]. **2** extract with difficulty.
P.S. /ˌpi ˈes/ *abbr* = **1** postscript. **2** Public School.
psalm /sam/ *n* [C] sacred song or hymn, esp (**the Psalms**) in the Bible.
pseud(o)- /ˌsudou-, ˌsudə-/ *prefix* false; fake: *pseudonym.*
pseu·do·nym /ˈsudəˌnɪm/ *n* [C] name taken, esp by an author, instead of his real name.
PST *abbr* = Pacific Standard Time.
psych. *abbr* = psychology.
psyche /ˈsaiki/ *n* [C] **1** human soul or spirit. **2** human mind.
psyche·delic /ˌsaikəˈdelɪk/ *adj* of, causing, hallucinations, altered mental states, etc: ~ *drugs.*
psy·chi·atric /ˌsaikiˈætrɪk/ *adj* of or relating to psychiatry.
psy·chia·trist /sɪˈkaiətrɪst, sai-/ *n* [C] physician who is a specialist in psychiatry.
psy·chia·try /sɪˈkaiətri, sai-/ *n* [U] branch of medicine dealing with the study and treatment of mental illness.
psy·chic /ˈsaikɪk/ *adj* **1** of the soul or mind. **2** of phenomena and conditions which appear to be outside physical or natural laws, eg telepathy.
psy·chi·cal /ˈsaikɪkəl/ *adj*
psy·cho- /ˌsaikou-, ˌsaikə-/ *prefix* of the mind: *psychopath.*
psy·cho·an·aly·sis /ˌsaikouəˈnæləsɪs/ *n* [U] method of treating mental illnesses by having the patient talk freely about his behavior, his dreams, and his memories of childhood events.
psy·cho·anal·yst /ˌsaikouˈænəlɪst/ *n* [C] person who practices psychoanalysis.
psy·cho·an·a·lytic /ˌsaikouˌænəˈlɪtɪk/ *adj* relating to psychoanalysis.
psy·cho·an·a·lyze /ˌsaikouˈænəˌlaiz/ *vt* treat (a person) by psychoanalysis.
psy·cho·log·i·cal /ˌsaikəˈladʒɪkəl/ *adj* **1** of or relating to psychology. **2** of the mind; mental. **3** influencing the mind or the emotions: ~ *warfare.*
psy·cho·log·i·cal·ly /-kli/ *adv*
psy·chol·ogist /saiˈkalədʒɪst/ *n* [C] student of, expert in, psychology.
psy·chol·ogy /saiˈkalədʒi/ *n* [U] science, study, of the mind and its processes.
psy·cho·path /ˈsaikəˌpæθ/ *n* [C] person suffering from a severe emotional disorder, esp one who is aggressive and antisocial.
psy·cho·pathic /ˌsaikəˈpæθɪk/ *adj*
psy·cho·sis /saiˈkousɪs/ *n* [C] (*pl* -choses /-ˈkouˌsiz/) very serious mental disorder.
psy·cho·ther·apy /ˌsaikouˈθerəpi/ *n* [U] treatment by psychological methods of mental, emotional and nervous disorders.
pt[1] *abbr* = **1** part. **2** pint. **3** point. **4** port.
p.t.[2] *abbr* = past tense.
PTA /ˌpi ˌti ˈei/ *abbr* = Parent-Teacher Association.
pub. *abbr* = **1** public. **2** publication.
pu·berty /ˈpyubərti/ *n* [U] stage at which a person becomes physically able to become a parent.
pu·bic /ˈpyubɪk/ *adj* of the lower front part of the abdomen: ~ *hair.*
pub·lic /ˈpəblɪk/ *adj* (opposite of *private*) of, for, connected with, owned by, done for or done by, known to, people in general: *a* ~ *library/park.* ***be in the public eye,*** having much publicity. □ *n* **1 the public,** people; community in general: *The* ~ *is not admitted.* ***in public,*** openly, not in private. **2** particular group of people: *the reading* ~.
public address system, electronic system of microphone, loudspeakers, etc for addressing large audiences.
pub·lic·ly /-kli/ *adv*

ˌ**public reˈlations** *n pl* the promotion of good will between an organization, etc and the general public.

ˈ**public school** *n* [C] elementary or secondary school providing free education from public funds.

public ˈspirited, ready to do things that are for the good for the community.

pub·li·ca·tion /ˌpəbləˈkeiʃən/ *n* **1** [U] act of making known to the public, by publishing something. **2** [C] something published, eg a book or a periodical.

pub·lic·ity /pəˈblɪsəti/ *n* [U] **1** the state of being known to, seen by, everyone: *an actress who seeks/avoids* ~. **2** (business of) providing information to interest people in general: *a* ˈ~ *campaign*.

pub·li·cize /ˈpəbləˌsaiz/ *vt* bring to the attention of the public.

pub·lish /ˈpəblɪʃ/ *vt* **1** have (a book, periodical, etc) printed and announce that it is for sale. **2** make known to the public: *~ the news*.

pub·lisher *n* [C] person, company, whose business is publishing books.

puck /pək/ *n* [C] hard rubber disc used like a ball in ice hockey.

pucker /ˈpəkər/ *vt,vi* draw or come together into small folds or wrinkles: *~ up one's lips*.

pud·ding /ˈpʊdɪŋ/ *n* [C,U] (dish of) food, usually a soft, sweet mixture, served as part of a meal, eaten after the meat or fish course.

puddle /ˈpədəl/ *n* [C] small, temporary pool of water, esp on a flat surface.

pudgy /ˈpədʒi/ *adj* (-ier, -iest) short, thick and fat: *~ fingers*.

pueblo /ˈpweblou/ *n* [C] community dwelling of some Indians of the southwestern US, made up of one large or several small stone or adobe buildings.

puer·ile /ˈpyʊrəl/ *adj* childish; immature.

Puer·to Ri·can /ˌpwertouˈrikən, ˌpwertə-/ *n, adj* **1** (native) of Puerto Rico. **2** (in continental US) US-born Spanish-speaker of Puerto Rican ancestry.

puff[1] /pəf/ *n* [C] **1** (sound of a) short, quick sending out of breath, air, etc: *have a ~ at a pipe*. **2** pad for applying cosmetic powder. **3** full, gathered mass of material on a dress, etc. **4** light pastry, often with a filling of cream, jam, etc.

puffy *adj* (-ier, -iest) **(a)** short of breath (by running, climbing, etc). **(b)** swollen: *~y under the eyes*.

puff[2] /pəf/ *vi,vt* **1** breathe quickly (as after running); (of smoke, steam, etc) come out in puffs: *He was ~ing hard when he jumped on the bus. He was ~ing (away) at his cigar*. **2** send out in puffs. **3** ***puff sth out,*** cause to swell: *He ~ed out his chest with pride*.

puf·fin /ˈpəfɪn/ *n* [C] North Atlantic sea bird with a large bill.

pug /pəg/ *n* [C] breed of small dog with a flat nose.

pug·na·cious /ˌpəgˈneiʃəs/ *adj* (*formal*) fond of fighting; quarrelsome.

puke /pyuk/ *vi,vt* (*informal*) vomit.

Pu·litzer /ˈpʊlɪtsər/ (also ˌ**Pulitzer** ˈ**Prize**) *n* [C] any of several prizes given each year for outstanding work in American literature, journalism, etc.

pull[1] /pʊl/ *n* **1** [C] act of pulling: *give a ~ at a rope*. **2** [U] force or effort: *It was a long ~ to the top of the mountain*. **3** [U] (*informal*) special influence, eg with people in high positions: *He has a great deal of ~ with the City Council*.

pull[2] /pʊl/ *vt,vi* **1** (contrasted with *push*) use force on (a person or thing) so as to draw it toward or in the direction of the force exerted: *The horse was ~ing a heavy cart. Would you rather push or ~ the wagon?* ***pull sth to pieces,*** **(a)** use force to separate its parts or to break it up into parts. **(b)** (*fig*) criticize severely by pointing out the weak points or faults: *He ~ed my theory to pieces*. **2** move: *The men ~ed for the shore. She ~ed her car out of the parking space*. ***pull together,*** (*fig*) work together; cooperate. **3** ***pull at/on sth,*** **(a)** give a tug: *~ at/on a rope*. **(b)** draw or suck: *~ing at his pipe*. **4** ***pull a muscle,*** strain it. **5** (*informal*) perform: *~ed a trick on me*. **6** draw out (eg a gun). **7** attract. **8** (special uses):

pull sth down, destroy or demolish, eg an old building.

pull in, arrive: *The express bus from Los Angeles ~ed in on time*.

pull sb's leg ⇨ leg.

pull sth off, succeed in; accomplish in spite of difficulties: *~ off a deal*.

pull out (of), leave a place; withdraw from: *Troops are ~ing out of these troubled areas*.

pull (sth) over, (cause a vehicle to) move to one side of the road and stop.

pull one's punch(es), **(a)** strike with less force than one could apply. **(b)** (*fig*) speak with less than complete frankness.

pull through, come or bring successfully through difficulties, dangers, illness, etc.

pull oneself together, get control of oneself, of one's feelings, etc.

pull (sth) up, bring to a stop: *The rider ~ed (his horse) up when he reached the stream*.

pul·let /ˈpʊlɪt/ *n* [C] young hen, esp one that is less than one year old.

pul·ley /ˈpʊli/ *n* [C] (*pl* ~s) grooved wheel(s) for ropes or chains, used for lifting things.

Pull·man /ˈpʊlmən/ *n* [C] (also ˌ**Pullman** ˈ**car**) railroad sleeping car of a type in use until World War II. □ *adj* of or for such a car: *~ conductor/porter*.

pull·over /ˈpʊˌlouvər/ *n* [C] knitted garment pulled on over the head.

pul·mon·ary /ˈpʊlməˌneri/ *adj* (*anat*) of, in, connected with, the lungs: *~ diseases; the ~ arteries*, carrying blood to the lungs.

pulp /pəlp/ *n* [U] **1** soft, fleshy part of fruit. **2** soft mass of other material, esp of wood fiber as used for making paper. □ *vt* make into pulp.

pulpy *adj* (-ier, -iest)

pul·pit /ˈpʊlpɪt, ˈpəlpɪt/ *n* [C] raised and enclosed structure in a church, used by a clergyman, esp when preaching.

pul·sate /ˈpəlˌseit/ *vt,vi* beat or throb; expand and contract rhythmically.

pul·sa·tion /pəlˈseiʃən/ *n* [C,U]

pulse /pəls/ *n* [C] **1** the regular beat of the

arteries, eg as felt at the wrist, as the blood is pumped through them by the heart. **2** (*fig*) any rhythmical beat: *the ~ of life in a big city.* □ *vi* beat; throb: *news that sent the blood pulsing through his veins.*

pul·ver·ize /ˈpəlvəˌraiz/ *vt,vi* **1** grind to a powder; smash completely. **2** become powder or dust.

puma /ˈp(y)umə/ *n* [C] (*pl* ~s) large brown American animal of the cat family also called a *cougar, mountain lion,* or *panther*. ⇨ illus at cat.

pum·ice /ˈpəmɪs/ *n* [U] (also **pumice ˈstone**) light, porous stone (from lava) used for cleaning and polishing.

pum·mel /ˈpəməl/ *vt* (-l-, -ll-) beat; pound.

pump /pəmp/ *n* [C] machine or device for forcing liquid, gas or air into, out of or through something, eg water from a well, air into a tire: *a ˈbicycle ~.* □ *vt,vi* **1** force, eg water, air, into, from, something using a pump: *~ gas.* **2** (*fig*) obtain by repeated questioning: *~ information out of her|~ her for information.*

pum·per·nickel /ˈpəmpərˌnɪkəl/ *n* [U] (kind of) heavy, dark rye bread.

pump·kin /ˈpəmpkɪn/ *n* [C,U] (plant, a trailing vine, with a) large, round orange-yellow fruit, used as a vegetable and as a filling for pies: *~ ˌpie.*

pun /pən/ *n* [C] (also *a play on words*) humorous use of words which sound the same or of two meanings of the same word, eg "Can you canoe?" □ *vi* (-nn-) make a pun or puns.

punch¹ /pəntʃ/ *n* [C] **1** tool or machine for cutting holes in leather, metal, paper, etc. **2** tool for stamping designs on surfaces. □ *vt* **1** make a hole (in something) with a punch: *~ a train ticket.* ***punch in/out,*** **(a)** record one's arrival at/departure from work by means of a clock which punches the exact time on a card. **(b)** (*fig*) arrive at/depart from work. **2** force (nails, etc) in or out with a punch.

ˈpunch card, one on which information is recorded for computer use by punching holes in it.

punch² /pəntʃ/ *n* [U] drink made of wine or spirits mixed with hot water, sugar, lemons, spice, etc.

punch³ /pəntʃ/ *vt* hit hard with the fist: *~ a man on the chin.* □ *n* **1** [C] blow given with the fist: *a ~ on the nose.* ***pull one's punch(es),*** ⇨ pull²(8). **2** [U] (*fig*) energy: *a speech with plenty of ~ in it.*

ˈpunch line, the (usually last) line of a joke or funny story which creates the humorous effect.

punc·tili·ous /pəŋkˈtɪliəs/ *adj* (*formal*) very careful to carry out correctly duties, etc.

punc·tili·ous·ly *adv*

punc·tual /ˈpəŋktʃuəl/ *adj* neither early nor late; coming, doing something, at the time fixed: *be ~ for the lecture|in the payment of one's rent.*

punc·tu·al·ity /ˌpəŋktʃuˈæləti/ *n* [U] being punctual.

punc·tu·ally /-uəli/ *adv*

punc·tu·ate /ˈpəŋktʃuˌeit/ *vt* **1** put periods, commas, etc, into a piece of writing. **2** interrupt from time to time: *a speech ~d with cheers.*

punc·tu·ation /ˌpəŋktʃuˈeiʃən/ *n* [U]

punc·ture /ˈpəŋktʃər/ *n* [C] small hole, esp one made accidentally in a tire. □ *vt,vi* **1** make a puncture in: *~ an abscess.* **2** experience a puncture: *Two of my tires ~ed while I was on that stony road.*

pun·dit /ˈpəndɪt/ *n* [C] knowledgeable person, esp one regarded as an authority on some subject.

pun·gent /ˈpəndʒənt/ *adj* (*formal*) **1** (of smells, tastes) sharp; stinging: *a ~ sauce.* **2** (*fig*) (of remarks) hurting: *~ criticism.*

pun·ish /ˈpənɪʃ/ *vt* **1** cause (a person) suffering or discomfort for doing wrong: *~ a man with/by a fine.* **2** treat roughly; hit: *The champion ~ed his opponent severely.*

ˈpun·ish·able /-əbəl/ *adj* that can be punished (by law).

pun·ish·ment *n* **(a)** [U] punishing or being punished: *escape without ~.* **(b)** [C] penalty for doing wrong: *severe ~ment for murder.*

pu·ni·tive /ˈpyunətɪv/ *adj* (intended for) punishing.

pun·ster /ˈpənstər/ *n* [C] person who makes puns.

punt¹ /pənt/ *n* [C] flat-bottomed, shallow boat with square ends, moved by pushing the end of a long pole against the riverbed. □ *vt,vi* move, carry in, a punt.

punt² /pənt/ *vt,vi* kick (eg a football) before it touches the ground after it is dropped from the hands. □ *n* [C] kick performed in this manner.

punt·er /ˈpəntər/ *n* [C]

puny /ˈpyuni/ *adj* (-ier, -iest) small and weak: *What a ~ little man!*

pun·ily /ˈpyunəli/ *adv*

pup /pəp/ *n* [C] (*informal*) puppy.

pupa /ˈpyupə/ *n* [C] (*pl* ~s, or ~e /-pi/) stage in the development of an insect (eg a moth) which is between the larva and the adult form.

pu·pil¹ /ˈpyupəl/ *n* [C] young student in school.

pu·pil² /ˈpyupəl/ *n* [C] (*anat*) round opening in the center of the iris of the eye, regulating the passage of light. ⇨ illus at eye.

pup·pet /ˈpəpɪt/ *n* [C] **1** doll, small figure of an animal, etc with jointed limbs moved by the hand or by wires or strings. **2** person, group of persons, whose behavior is completely controlled by another: (as an *adjective*) *a ~ government.*

puppy /ˈpəpi/ *n* [C] (*pl* -ies) young dog.

ˈpuppy love, love between young people.

pup tent /ˈpəp ˌtent/ *n* [C] small tent, holding one or two persons, for military or camping use.

pur·chase¹ /ˈpərtʃəs/ *n* **1** [U] buying. **2** [C] (*formal*) something bought: *I have some ~s to make.*

pur·chase² /ˈpərtʃəs/ *vt* buy (which is much more usual): *~d a diamond ring.*

pur·chaser *n* [C] = buyer (the usual word).

pure /pyʊr/ *adj* (-r, -st except 5,6 below) **1** unmixed with any other substance, etc: *~ air,* free from smoke, fumes, etc. **2** of unmixed race or breed: *a ~ poodle.* **3** without evil or sin: *~ in body and mind.* **4** (of sounds) clear and distinct: *a ~ note.* **5** dealing with, studied for the sake of, theory only (not *applied*): *~ mathematics|*

science. **6** complete: *a ~ waste of time.*

pure·ly *adv* (esp) entirely; completely: *~ly by accident.*

pu·rée /pyʊˈrei/ *n* [C,U] pulp made of food that has been pressed through a sieve: *raspberry ~.*

pur·ga·tive /ˈpərgətɪv/ *n, adj* (substance) having the power to purge or act as a laxative.

pur·ga·tory /ˈpərgəˌtɔri/ *n* [C] (*pl* -ies) (esp in Roman Catholic doctrine) place or condition in which the soul is to be purified after death by temporary suffering.

pur·ga·tor·ial /ˌpərgəˈtɔriəl/ *adj*

purge /ˈpərdʒ/ *vt* **1** make clean or free, esp of sin or guilt. **2** empty (the bowels) of waste matter by means of medicine. **3** rid (eg a political party, etc) of members who are considered undesirable. □ *n* [C] **1** act of purging : *the political ~s that followed the revolution.* **2** something that purges.

pu·rify /ˈpyʊrəˌfai/ *vt* (*pt,pp* -ied) make pure; cleanse: *~ing the air in a factory.*

pu·ri·fi·ca·tion /ˌpyʊrəfəˈkeiʃən/ *n* [U]

puri·tan /ˈpyʊrətən/ *n* [C] **1 Puritan,** (16th and 17th centuries in England, 17th and 18th centuries in New England) member of a division of the Protestant Church which wanted simpler forms of church ceremony. **2** person who is strict in morals and religion, who considers some kinds of fun and pleasure as sinful. □ *adj* of or like a Puritan or a puritan.

puri·tani·cal /ˌpyʊrəˈtænəkəl/ *adj* esp of puritan (2).

puri·tani·cally /ˌpyʊrəˈtænəkli/ *adv*

pu·rity /ˈpyʊrəti/ *n* [U] state or quality of being pure.

purl /pərl/ *n* [C] (in knitting) stitch made backward, which produces a ribbed appearance when it alternates with the plain stitch. □ *vt,vi* knit in this way.

pur·loin /pərˈlɔin/ *vt* (*formal*) steal.

purple /ˈpərpəl/ *n* [U], *adj* (color) of red and blue mixed together.

pur·port /ˈpərˌpɔrt/ *n* [C] (*formal*) general meaning or intention of something said or written; likely explanation of a person's actions: *the ~ of what he said.* □ *vt* /pərˈpɔrt/ claim: *It's ~ed to be an original but it is really a fake.*

pur·pose /ˈpərpəs/ *n* **1** [C] that which one means to do, get, be, etc; plan; design; intention: *This van is used for various ~s.* **2** [U] (*formal*) determination; power of forming plans and keeping to them: *weak of ~.* **3 *on purpose,*** by intention, not by chance: *She sometimes does things on ~ just to annoy me.* □ *vt* (*formal*) have as one's purpose: *They ~ a further attempt/~ to make/~ making a further attempt.*

pur·pose·ful /-fəl/ *adj*

pur·pose·fully /-fəli/ *adv*

pur·pose·less *adj* having no plan, design, reason.

pur·pose·less·ly *adv.*

purr /pər/ *vi,vt* **1** (of a cat) make a low, continuous vibrating sound expressing pleasure. **2** make a similar vibrating sound. □ *n* [C] purring sound.

purse /pərs/ *n* [C] **1** small bag for money. **2** money; funds. **3** handbag. □ *vt* draw together in tiny folds or wrinkles.

purser /ˈpərsər/ *n* [C] officer responsible for a ship's accounts and stores, esp in a passenger liner.

pur·su·ance /pərˈsuəns/ *n* ***in pursuance of,*** (*formal*) in the carrying out or performance of (one's duties, a plan, etc).

pur·su·ant /-ənt/ *adj* ***pursuant to,*** (*formal*) in accordance with: *pursuant to your instructions.*

pur·sue /pərˈsu/ *vt* **1** go after in order to catch up with, capture or kill: *They were pursuing a robber/a bear. Make sure that you are not being ~d.* **2** (*fig*) (of consequences, penalties, etc) persistently attend: *His record as a criminal ~d him wherever he went.* **3** go on with: *~ one's studies after leaving school.* **4** have as an aim or purpose: *~ pleasure.*

pur·su·er *n* [C]

pur·suit /pərˈsut/ *n* **1** [U] act of pursuing: *a dog in ~ of rabbits.* **2** [C] something at which one works or to which one gives one's time: *scientific/literary ~s.*

pur·vey /pərˈvei/ *vt,vi* (*formal*) provide; supply; furnish.

pur·veyor /-ər/ *n* [C]

pus /pəs/ *n* [U] thick yellowish-white liquid formed in an inflamed or infected place in the body.

push¹ /pʊʃ/ *n* **1** [C] act of pushing: *Give the door a hard ~.* **2** [C] great effort: *We must make a ~ to finish the job this week.* **3** [U] drive; determination: *He hasn't enough ~ to succeed as a salesman.*

ˈpush pin, tack with a knob, used for pinning up notices on boards, walls etc.

push² /pʊʃ/ *vt,vi* **1** (contrasted with *pull*) press against or use force on (a person or thing) to cause movement forward or away: *Please ~ the table nearer to the wall. We had to ~ our way through the crowd.* **2** promote vigorously: *Unless you ~ your claim you'll get no satisfaction.* **3** sell (illicit drugs). **4** put pressure on: *We're ~ing them for payment/an answer.* **5** urge on or forward: *She'll ~ him to succeed.* **6** press: *~ a button,* eg to ring a bell. **7 *pushing fifty, etc,*** (*informal*) nearing the age mentioned: *She wouldn't like you to think so, but she's ~ing thirty.* **8** (special uses with *adverbial particles* and *prepositions*):

push sb around, (*informal*) treat him roughly or unfairly: *I'm not going to be ~ed around by you or anybody else!*

push off, (*informal*) leave; go away: *I told him to ~ off!*

push on, go on resolutely; continue: *We must ~ on with our work.*

push·cart /ˈpʊʃˌkart/ *n* [C] small cart pushed by hand.

push·er /ˈpʊʃər/ *n* [C] **1** something or someone that pushes. **2** (*informal*) seller of illicit drugs.

push·over /ˈpʊʃˌouvər/ (*sl*) **1** something very easy to do. **2** person who is easily defeated, influenced, etc.

puss /pʊs/ *n* [C] **1** (*sl*) face: *He has an ugly ~.* **2** (*informal*) cat.

pussy /ˈpʊsi/ *n* [C] (*pl* -ies) (also **pussy·cat** /ˈpʊsiˌkæt/) (*informal*) cat.

pussy wil·low /ˌpʊsiˈwɪlou/ *n* [C] (kinds of) willow tree with tuft-like flowers.

put /pʊt/ *vi,vt* (*pt,pp* put, *present part* putting) **1** move into a certain place or position: *He put the book down on the table. He put his hands in(to) his pockets. Did you put cream in my coffee? They've put men on the moon.* ***put one's foot in it,*** ⇨ foot[1](1). **2** cause to be in a state, relation, etc: *Let's put these papers in order. His speech put everyone to sleep.* ***put sb at his ease,*** make him feel relaxed. ***put an end/a stop to sth,*** end or abolish it. ***put sth right,*** settle it properly or correctly: *A short note put the matter right.* ***put sb in his place,*** remind him of his inferior position, authority, etc. ***put oneself in sb's/sb else's place/position,*** imagine oneself in his position. **3** cause to undergo or suffer: *They're ~ting great pressure on him to resign.* ***put sb to death,*** execute him. ***put sb/sth to the test,*** test him/it. **4** set or apply to an action or activity: *put the enemy to flight; put the students to work; put one's mind to solving a puzzle.* **5** propose; offer for consideration: *put a proposal to the Board of Directors.* **6** express: *She put her thoughts into words.* **7** translate: *How would you put this in Spanish?* **8** set a value (on): *The experts refused to put a price on the Rubens painting.* **9** impose: *put a high tax on gasoline.* **10** (special uses with *adverbial particles* and *prepositions*):

put sth across (to sb), communicate it successfully: *a teacher who quickly puts his ideas across to his students.*

put sth aside, **(a)** lay it down: *put one's work aside.* **(b)** save: *He has put aside a good sum of money.*

put sth away, kill a sick or old animal. ***put sb away,*** (*informal*) put into confinement, eg in a mental home: *He acted so strangely that he had to be put away.*

put sth by, ⇨ put aside (b).

put sth down, **(a)** suppress it: *put down a rebellion.* **(b)** write down; make a note of: *Here's my address — put it down before you forget it.* ***put sb down,*** criticize or belittle.

put sth forward, suggest for consideration: *put forward a new theory.*

put in/into, (*naut*) (of a boat) enter eg a port: *The boat put in at Malta/put into Malta for repairs.* ***put in for sth,*** apply formally for: *put in for the position of manager; put in for leave,* request permission to be absent from duty, work, etc. ***put sth in,*** do, perform: *put in an hour's work before breakfast.*

put sth off, **(a)** postpone: *put off going to the dentist.* **(b)** get rid of: *You must put off your doubts and fears.* ***put sb off,*** **(a)** repel: *His formality puts most people off.* **(b)** escape; avoid: *I won't be put off with such silly excuses,* won't accept them.

put sth on, **(a)** (opposite = *take off*) clothe oneself with: *put one's hat/shoes on.* **(b)** pretend to have: *Her modesty is all put on,* she's only pretending to be modest. ***put sb on,*** mock; fool: *She didn't mean it — she was just putting you on.*

put sth out, **(a)** extinguish; cause to stop burning: *put out the lights/the gas/the fire.* **(b)** produce: *The firm puts out 1,000 bales of cotton sheeting every week.* ***put sb out,*** **(a)** cause to be annoyed or worried: *She was very much put out by your rudeness.* **(b)** inconvenience: *He was put out by the late arrival of his guests.* **(c)** (*baseball*) cause (a player) to be out. **(d)** force to leave.

put sth through, carry it out successfully: *put through a business deal.* ***put sb through,*** connect (by telephone): *Please put me through to the manager.*

put sth to sb/put it to sb (that), express; offer: *put a proposal to the Board of Directors.* ***put sth to sth,*** submit: *put a proposal/question to a vote.*

put sb up, provide lodging and food (for): *We can put you up for the weekend.* ***put sb up to sth,*** urge him to do something mischievous or wrong: *Who put you up to all these tricks?* ***put sth up,*** **(a)** raise; hold up: *put up one's hands; put up a flag/a sail.* **(b)** build: *put up a shed.* **(c)** prepare for later use, esp by canning: *put up tomatoes.* **(d)** supply or contribute (a sum of money): *I will supply the skill and knowledge if you will put up the $2,000 capital.* ***put up with sb/sth,*** endure or bear patiently: *There are many inconveniences that have to be put up with when you are camping.*

pu·trefy /ˈpyutrəˌfai/ *vt,vi* (*pt,pp* -ied) (cause to) become decayed.

pu·tre·fac·tion /ˌpyutreˈfækʃən/ *n* [C,U]

pu·tres·cent /pyuˈtresənt/ *adj* in the process of decaying.

pu·trid /ˈpyutrɪd/ *adj* having become decayed; decomposed and smelling bad.

putt /pət/ *vi,vt* strike (a golf ball) gently with a club so that it rolls across the ground towards or into a hole.

put·ter[1] /ˈpətər/ *n* [C] specially-shaped club used in golf for putting the ball.

put·ter[2] /ˈpətər/ (sometimes **potter** /ˈpatər/) *vi* do things without concentration or effort, primarily to occupy one's time: *He ~ed (around) in the garden.*

putty /ˈpəti/ *n* [U] soft substance used for fixing glass in window frames, etc. □ *vt* (*pt,pp* -ied) fill or fix with putty: *~ up a hole.*

puzzle /ˈpəzəl/ *n* [C] **1** question or problem difficult to understand or answer. **2** problem (eg: *a ˈcrossword ~*) or toy (eg: *a ˈjigsaw ~*) designed to test a person's knowledge, skill, patience. **3** (*sing* only) state of feeling confused, thinking hard about a problem: *be in a ~ about this refusal.* □ *vt,vi* **1** cause (a person) to be confused, worried, (about the solution to a problem): *This letter ~s me.* **2** ***puzzle over sth,*** think very much about it. ***puzzle sth out,*** (try to) find the answer or solution by thinking hard.

puzzle·ment *n* [U] state of being puzzled.

pvt., Pvt. *abbr* = private; Private.

PW /ˌpi ˈdəbəlyu/ *abbr* = prisoner of war.

PX /ˌpi ˈeks/ *abbr* = post exchange. ⇨ post[1].

pygmy /ˈpɪgmi/ *n* [C] (*pl* -ies) **1 Pygmy,** member of a dwarf race in Equatorial Africa. **2** very small person or thing; dwarf.

py·lon /ˈpaiˌlan/ *n* [C] **1** tower (steel framework) for supporting high-tension electric cables. **2** framework for attaching an external engine, fuel tank, etc to an airplane.

py·or·rhea /ˌpaiəˈriə/ *n* [U] inflammation of the gums that causes loosening of the teeth.

pyra·mid /ˈpɪrəˌmɪd/ *n* [C] **1** solid with a polygon as a base and sloping, triangular sides meeting at a point. **2** structure with such a shape, built as a monument in ancient Egypt.

pyre /ˈpaiər/ *n* [C] large pile of wood for burning, esp a funeral pile for a corpse.

py·thon /ˈpaiˌθan/ *n* [C] large snake that kills its prey by twisting itself around it and crushing it.

q

Q[1], q /kyu/ (*pl* Q's, q's /kyuz/) the seventeenth letter of the English alphabet.

Q[2] *abbr* = question.

Q.E.D. /ˌkyu ˌi ˈdi/ *abbr* (= *Lat* quod erat demonstrandum) that which was to be proved.

QM *abbr* = Quartermaster.

qt. *abbr* = quart(s).

q.t. *abbr* (*sl*) ***on the q.t.,*** on the quiet; in confidence.

quack[1] /kwæk/ *vi, n* [C] (make the) cry of a duck.

quack[2] /kwæk/ *n* [C] person dishonestly claiming to have (esp medical) knowledge and skill.

quad /kwad/ *n* [C] (short for) **1** quadrangle. **2** quadruplet.

quad·rangle /ˈkwaˌdræŋgəl/ *n* [C] **1** flat shape with four sides, such as a square or a rectangle. **2** space in the form of a rectangle, (nearly) surrounded by buildings.

quad·ran·gu·lar /kwaˈdræŋgyələr/ *adj*

quad·rant /ˈkwadrənt/ *n* [C] **1** quarter of a circle or its circumference. ⇨ illus at circle. **2** graduated strip of metal, etc shaped like a quarter of a circle, for use in measuring altitude in astronomy and navigation.

quad·ri·lat·eral /ˌkwadrɪˈlætərəl/ *adj, n* [C] (of a) quadrangle(1).

quad·ru·ped /ˈkwadrəˌped/ *n* [C] four-footed animal.

quad·ruple /kwaˈdrupəl/ *adj* **1** made up of four parts. **2** multiplied by four. □ *n* [C] number or amount four times as great as another: *20 is the ~ of 5.* □ *vt,vi* multiply by four: *He has ~d his income/His income has ~d in the last year.*

quad·ru·plet /kwaˈdruplɪt/ *n* [C] any of four children or animals born at the same time of the same mother.

quag·mire /ˈkwægˌmaiər/ *n* [C] area of soft, wet land.

qua·hog /ˈkwɔˌhɔg/ *n* [C] thick-shelled clam of the Atlantic coast of North America.

quail[1] /ˈkweiəl/ *n* [C] small game bird eaten as food.

quail[2] /ˈkweiəl/ *vi* (*pres p* ~ing /ˈkweilɪŋ/) cower: *He ~ed at the prospect before him.*

quaint /kweint/ *adj* (-er, -est) attractive or pleasing because unusual or old-fashioned: *Visitors to western North Carolina admire the mountaineers' ~ dress and speech.*

quaint·ly *adv*

quaint·ness /-nɪs/ *n* [U]

quake /kweik/ *vi* **1** (of the earth) shake: *The ground ~d under his feet.* **2** (of persons) tremble: *quaking with fear/cold.* □ *n* [C] (esp) earthquake.

Quaker /ˈkweikər/ *n* member of the Society of Friends, a Christian group that holds meetings and is opposed to the use of violence or resort to war.

quali·fi·ca·tion /ˌkwaləfəˈkeiʃən/ *n* **1** [U] qualifying or being qualified. **2** [C] something which restricts, modifies or limits: *You can accept his statement without ~/with certain ~s.* **3** [C] training, test, diploma, degree, etc that qualifies(1) a person.

qual·ify /ˈkwaləˌfai/ *vt,vi* (*pt,pp* -ied) **1** (cause to) be competent, eg by training, education, experience, etc: *He's qualified/His training qualifies him as a teacher of English. He's the manager's son but that does not ~ him to criticize my work.* **2** limit the meaning of; make less general: *The statement "Boys are lazy" needs to be qualified*, eg by saying "Some boys" or "Many boys." **3** (*gram*) modify: *Adjectives ~ nouns.*

quali·fied /-ˌfaid/ *adj* **(a)** having the necessary qualifications. **(b)** limited: *give a scheme one's qualified approval.*

ˈquali·fier /-ˌfaiər/ *n* [C] (*gram*) qualifying word, eg an adjective or adverb.

quali·tat·ive /ˈkwaləˌteitɪv/ *adj* relating to quality(2) (in contrast to *quantity*): *~ analysis*, (of a chemical compound) to determine the basic elements which make it up.

qual·ity /ˈkwaləti/ *n* (*pl* -ies) **1** [U] degree or grade of excellence: *good/poor ~.* **2** [U] goodness or worth: *We aim at ~ rather than quantity*, aim to produce superior goods, not large quantities. **3** [C] characteristic of a person or thing: *One ~ she has is honesty.*

qualm /ˈkwam/ *n* [C] **1** feeling of doubt (esp about whether one is doing or has done right): *He felt no ~s about borrowing money from friends.* **2** temporary feeling of sickness in the stomach: *~s which spoiled his appetite.*

quan·dary /ˈkwand(ə)ri/ *n* [C] (*pl* -ies) state of doubt or confusion: *be in a ~ about what to do next.*

quan·ti·tat·ive /ˈkwantəˌteitɪv/ *adj* relating to quantity(1) (in contrast to *quality*): *~ analysis*, (of a chemical compound) to determine the relative amounts of the elements which make it up.

quan·tity /ˈkwantəti/ *n* (*pl* -ies) **1** [U] the property of things which can be measured, eg size, weight, number: *I prefer quality to ~.* **2** [C] amount, total or number: *There's only a small ~* (ie not much or not many) *left.* **3** (often *pl*) large amount or number: *He buys things in large quantities.* **4** something, eg a number, which can be the subject of a mathematical operation. ***an unknown quantity,*** **(a)** (*math*) symbol (usually *x*) representing an unknown value in an equation. **(b)** (*fig*) person or thing whose ability, etc is not known.

quar·an·tine /ˈkwɔrənˌtin/ *n* [C,U] (period of) separation from others until it is known that there is no danger of spreading disease: *be in/out of* ~. □ *vt* put in quarantine.

quar·rel /ˈkwɔrəl/ *n* [C] **1** angry argument; strong disagreement: *have a* ~ *with him about the weather*. **2** cause for being angry; reason for protest or complaint: *I have no* ~ *with/against him*. ***pick a quarrel (with sb),*** find or invent some occasion or excuse for disagreement, etc. □ *vi* (-l-, -ll-) **1** have, take part in, a quarrel: *The thieves* ~*ed with one another about how to divide the loot*. **2** disagree (with); find fault with: *It's not the fact of examinations I'm* ~*ing with; it's the way they're conducted.*

ˈquar·rel·some /-səm/ *adj* inclined to argue.

quarry[1] /ˈkwɔri, ˈkwæri/ *n* [C] (*pl* -ies) (usually *sing*) animal, bird, etc which is hunted.

quarry[2] /ˈkwɔri, ˈkwæri/ *n* [C] (*pl* -ies) open excavation (not underground like a mine) where stone, slate, etc is obtained (for buildings, roads, etc). □ *vt,vi* get from a quarry[2].

quart /kwɔrt/ *n* [C] measure of capacity equal to two pints or about .946 of a liter.

quar·ter /ˈkwɔrtər,ˈkwɔrdər, ˈkɔrdər/ *n* [C] **1** fourth part ($\frac{1}{4}$); one of four equal or corresponding parts: *a* ~ *of a mile; a mile and a* ~*; a* ~ *of an hour*, 15 minutes; *an hour and a* ~*; the first* ~ *of this century*, ie 1901-25. ➪ App 1. **2** point of time 15 minutes before or after any hour: *a* ~ *to/of two; a* ~ *past six*. ➪ App 2. **3** period of three months. **4** coin worth 25 cents. ➪ App 4. **5** part of an animal that includes a leg and the parts near it: *a* ~ *of beef*. **6** person, group, etc that is not specified: *He could expect no help from any* ~. **7(a)** region; part. **(b)** division of a town, esp one containing a particular group of people: *the Chinese* ~ *of San Francisco*. **8** one-fourth of a lunar month: *the moon at the first* ~*/in its last* ~. **9** (*pl*) place for living: *found comfortable* ~*s in the town*. **10** ***at close quarters,*** close together. **11** place for duty by sailors on a ship, esp for fighting: *Officers and men at once took up their* ~*s*. **12** [U] mercy: *gave no* ~ *to the enemy*. □ *vt* **1** divide into quarters. **2** place (troops) in lodgings: ~ *troops on the villagers.*

quar·ter·back /ˈkwɔrtərˌbæk,ˈkwɔrdər-, ˈkɔrdər-/ *n* [C] (*football*) player who calls the signals, directs the offense, and usually does the passing.

quar·ter·mas·ter /ˈkwɔrtərˌmæstər, ˈkwɔrdər-, ˈkɔrdər-/ *n* [C] **1** (*army*) officer in charge of the equipment, clothing, etc of troops. **2** (*navy*) petty officer in charge of steering the ship, signals, etc.

quar·ter·ly /ˈkwɔrtərli, ˈkwɔrdərli, ˈkɔrdərli/ *adj, adv* (happening) once in each three months: ~ *payments; to be paid* ~.

quar·tet /kwɔrˈtet, kɔrˈtet/ *n* [C] (piece of music for) four players or singers: *a string* ~, for (usually) two violins, viola and cello; *a piano* ~, for piano and three stringed instruments.

quartz /ˈkwɔrts, ˈkɔrts/ *n* [U] clear, hard mineral (esp crystallized silica), found in rocks, and in agate and other semiprecious stones.

qua·sar /ˈkweiˌzar/ *n* [C] source of intense radio wave emission in other space, thought to be a kind of star.

quash /kwaʃ/ *vt* put an end to, annul, reject as not valid (by legal procedure): ~ *a verdict/decision*.

quasi /ˈkweiˌzai, ˈkwaˌsi/ *adj, adv* almost; seeming(ly): *a* ~*-official position*.

qua·ver /ˈkweivər/ *vt,vi* **1** shake; tremble: *in a* ~*ing voice*. **2** say or sing in a shaking voice. □ *n* [C] trembling sound.

quay /ki, kwei/ *n* [C] landing place usually built of stone or iron, alongside which ships can be tied up for loading and unloading.

queasy /ˈkwizi/ *adj* (-ier, -iest) **1** causing a feeling of sickness in the stomach. **2** easily nauseated. **3** easily troubled or upset.

queas·ily /-əli/ *adv*

queen /kwin/ *n* [C] **1** woman ruler in her own right: *Annapolis, Maryland was named after Queen Anne*. **2** wife of a king. **3** woman regarded as first of a group: *a ˈbeauty* ~. **4** most powerful piece for attack or defense in the game of chess. **5** playing card with the picture of a queen that ranks below the king: *the* ~ *of spades/hearts*. **6** fertile, egg-producing, female of bees, ants, etc.

queen·ly *adj* (-ier, -iest) like, fit for, a queen.

queer /kwɪr/ *adj* (-er, -est) **1** strange; unusual: *a* ~ *way of talking*. **2** causing doubt or suspicion: ~ *noises in the attic*. **3** unwell: *feel very* ~.

quell /kwel/ *vt* suppress (a rebellion, rebels, opposition).

quench /kwentʃ/ *vt* **1** put out (flames, fire). **2** satisfy (thirst). **3** put an end to; destroy.

queru·lous /ˈkwerələs/ *adj* (*formal*) expressing or given to complaints: *in a* ~ *tone*.

query /ˈkwɪri/ *n* [C] (*pl* -ies) question, esp one raising a doubt about the truth of something: *raise a* ~. □ *vt* **1** ask questions of: *I queried my teacher on this point*. **2** express doubt about: ~ *a person's instructions*.

quest /kwest/ *n* [C] (*formal*) search: *the* ~ *for gold*. □ *vt* (*formal*) search (for): ~*ing for further evidence*.

ques·tion[1] /ˈkwestʃən/ *n* **1** [C] sentence which asks for information, an answer, etc. **2** [C] something which needs to be decided; inquiry; problem: *economic* ~*s. Success is only a* ~ *of time*, will certainly come sooner or later. **3** [C] subject under discussion: *The* ~ *is*. . ., what we want to know/what we must decide, is. . .. ***in question,*** being talked about or considered: *Where's the man in* ~? ***out of the question,*** impossible: *We can't go out in this weather; it's out of the* ~. **4** [U] doubt, uncertainty: *There is no* ~ *about/some* ~ *as to his honesty*. ***beyond (all)/without question,*** certain(ly); without doubt: *His honesty is beyond all* ~. *Without* ~, *he's the best man for the job.*

ˈquestion mark, the mark (?) at the end of a written question.

ques·tion[2] /ˈkwestʃən/ *vt* **1** ask a question; examine: *He was* ~*ed by the police*. **2** express or

feel doubt about: ~ *her honesty;* ~ *the value/importance of games at school.*
ˈques·tion·able /-əbəl/ *adj* doubtful.
ˈques·tion·ably /-əbli/ *adv*
ques·tioner *n* [C]
ques·tion·naire /ˌkwestʃəˈner/ *n* [C] printed list of questions to be answered by a group of people, esp to get facts or information, or for a survey.
quibble /ˈkwɪbəl/ *n* [C] use of vague language to avoid the real issue (in an argument). □ *vi* argue about small points or differences: ~ *over nothing of importance.*
quick /kwɪk/ *adj* (-er, -est) **1** moving fast; able to move fast and do things in a short time; done in a short time: *a* ~ *train/worker; have a* ~ *meal. Be* ~ *about it!* Hurry up! **2** alert; bright; prompt to understand: ~ *to seize an opportunity;* ~ *to learn.* **3** easily aroused: *a* ~ *temper.* □ *n* [U] tender or sensitive flesh below the skin, esp the nails: *bite one's nails to the* ~. ***cut/touch sb to the quick,*** hurt his feelings deeply. □ *adv* (-er, -est) (*Note:* always placed after the *verb*): *Can't you run* ~*er? He wants to get rich* ~.
quick·ly *adv*
quick·ness /-nɪs/ *n* [U]
quicken /ˈkwɪkən/ *vt,vi* **1** make or become quick(er): *We* ~*ed our pace. Our pace* ~*ed.* **2** make or become more lively, vigorous or active: *His pulse* ~*ed.*
quick·sand /ˈkwɪkˌsænd/ *n* [C] (area of) loose, wet, deep sand which sucks down men, animals, vehicles, etc on its surface.
quick·sil·ver /ˈkwɪkˌsɪlvər/ *n* [U] = mercury.
quid /kwɪd/ *n* [C] wad (eg of tobacco) for chewing.
quiet /ˈkwaiɪt/ *adj* (-er, -est) **1** making little or no movement or sound: *a* ~ *sea/evening.* **2** peaceful: *live a* ~ *life in the country.* **3** gentle; not rough (in disposition, etc). **4** not bright or showy. □ *n* [U] state of being quiet (all senses): *live in peace and* ~. □ *vt,vi* make or become quiet: ~ *the children/fears/suspicions. The city* ~*ed/*~*ed down after the riots.*
quill /kwɪl/ *n* [C] **1** large wing or tail feather of a bird. **2** (hollow stem of) such a feather formerly used for writing with: *a* ~ *pen.* **3** long, sharp, stiff spine of a porcupine.
quilt /kwɪlt/ *n* [C] thick bed-covering of two layers of cloth padded with soft material kept in place by crossed lines of stitches. □ *vt* make in the form of a quilt, ie with soft material between layers of cloth: *a* ~*ed bathrobe.*

PATCHWORK QUILT

quin·ine /ˈkwaiˌnain/ *n* [U] bitter drug used esp for treating malaria.
quin·tes·sence /kwɪnˈtesəns/ *n* [C] (*formal*) perfect example: *the* ~ *of virtue/politeness.*
quin·tet /kwɪnˈtet/ *n* [C] (piece of music for) five players or singers: *a string* ~, string quartet and an additional cello or viola; *a piano* ~, string quartet and piano; *a wind* ~, bassoon, clarinet, flute, horn and oboe.
quin·tu·plet /kwɪnˈtəplɪt/ *n* [C] any of five children or animals born at the same time of the same mother.
quip /kwɪp/ *n* [C] clever, witty or sarcastic remark. □ *vi* (-pp-) make quips.
quire /ˈkwaiər/ *n* [C] group of 24 or 25 sheets of paper of the same size and quality.
quirk /kwərk/ *n* [C] **1** sudden twist or turn. **2** peculiarity of behavior.
quit[1] /kwɪt/ *adj* free, clear: *We are well* ~ *of him,* fortunate to be rid of him.
quit[2] /kwɪt/ *vt,vi* (*pt,pp* ~, ~ted, *pres p* -tt-) **1** stop or give up doing something; cease (from): *The athlete will never* ~ *until he wins. Quit pestering me!* **2** go away from; leave: *The enemy soldiers* ~ *the town. The club made too many demands on his time, so he* ~.
quit·ter *n* [C] (*informal*) person who does not finish what he has started.
quite /kwait/ *adv* **1** completely; altogether: *I* ~ *agree/understand. She was* ~ *alone. That's* ~ *another* (ie a completely different) *story.* **2** to a certain extent; rather: ~ *a good player. It's* ~ *warm today.* **3** really; truly: *She's* ~ *beautiful.*
quits /kwɪts/ *adj* ***be quits (with sb),*** be on even terms (by repaying a debt of money, punishment, etc): *We're* ~ *now.* ***call it quits,*** agree that things are even, that a dispute or quarrel is over.
quiver[1] /ˈkwɪvər/ *n* [C] sheath for carrying arrows.
quiver[2] /ˈkwɪvər/ *vt,vi* shake or tremble slightly: *a* ~*ing leaf.* □ *n* [C] quivering sound or movement.
quix·otic /kwɪkˈsatɪk/ *adj* (*formal*) idealistic and romantic.
quiz /kwɪz/ *vt* (-zz-) ask questions of, as a test of knowledge. □ *n* [C] short test.
ˈquiz show, radio or television contest in which participants are asked difficult questions.
quiz·zi·cal /ˈkwɪzɪkəl/ *adj* (*formal*) **1** questioning; puzzled. **2** teasing: *a* ~ *smile.*
quiz·zi·cally /-kli/ *adv*
quoit /kwɔit/ *n* [C] **1** ring (of metal, rubber, rope) to be thrown at a peg so as to encircle it. **2** (*pl*) game played with quoits.
quo·rum /ˈkwɔrəm/ *n* [C] (*pl* ~s) number of persons who must, by the rules, be present at a meeting (of a committee, etc) in order for its proceedings to be valid: *have/form a* ~.
quota /ˈkwoutə/ *n* [C] (*pl* ~s) limited share, amount or number, eg of goods to be manufactured, sold, etc or, of immigrants allowed to enter a country: *The* ~ *of trainees for this year has already been filled.*
quo·ta·tion /kwouˈteiʃən/ *n* **1** [U] quoting(1). **2** [C] something quoted(1): ~*s from Shakespeare.* **3** [C] (statement of the) current price of an article, etc: *the latest* ~*s from the Stock Exchange.*

4 quotation mark. ***(put) in quotes,*** (write) between quotation marks.
quo'tation marks, either of the two sets of marks " " or ' ' used to enclose an exact quotation.
quote /kwout/ *vt* **1** repeat, write (words used by another, from a book, an author, etc): *~ from the newspaper; ~ the Chairman.* **2** give (a reference, etc) to support a statement: *Can you ~ (me) a recent instance?* **3** state (a price): *This is the best price I can ~ you.*
quot·able /-əbəl/ *adj* that can be, or deserves to be, quoted.
quoth /kwouθ/ *vt* (*archaic*) (1st and 3rd person *sing, pt* only) said: *~ I/he/she.*
quo·tient /ˈkwouʃənt/ *n* [C] (*math*) number obtained by dividing one number by another.
q.v. *abbr* (= *Lat* quod vide, but usually read /ˌkyu ˈvi/) which see (ie, the reader should look up the cited reference, word, etc).

r

R[1], **r** /ar/ (*pl* R's, r's /arz/) the eighteenth letter of the English alphabet.

R.[2] *abbr* = River.

r.[3] *abbr* = right.

rabbi /ˈræˌbai/ *n* [C] (*pl* ~s) **1** (*Biblical*) teacher of the Jewish law. **2** (title of a) spiritual leader of a Jewish congregation.

rab·bini·cal /rəˈbɪnɪkəl/ *adj*

rab·bit /ˈræbɪt/ *n* [C] small burrowing animal of the hare family, with long ears and a short, fluffy tail.

rabble /ˈræbəl/ *n* [C] (used as a term of contempt) disorderly crowd; mob.

ˈrabble-rouser *n* [C] person who incites the passions of the mob.

rabid /ˈræbɪd/ *adj* **1** affected with rabies. **2** (*fig*) furious; fanatical: *The old man is a ~ Democrat.*

ra·bies /ˈreibiz/ *n* [U] usually fatal disease of the nervous system, transmitted by the bite of an infected dog or other animal.

rac·coon /ræˈkun/ *n* **1** [C] small, flesh-eating animal of North America with a bushy, ringed tail. ⇨ illus at animal. **2** [U] its fur.

race[1] /reis/ *n* [C] **1** contest or competition in speed, eg in running, swimming, etc: *a ˈhorse ~.* ***a race against time,*** an effort to finish something before a certain time. **2** any contest to reach a certain end or goal. **3** strong, fast current of water in the sea, a river, etc. □ *vi,vt* **1** take part in a race: *boys racing home from school.* **2** enter (horses, etc) in a race or races. **3** (cause to) move at full speed: *He ~d me to the station in his car.*

ˈrace horse, special breed for running in races.

ˈrace·track *n* [C] usually oval track prepared for races.

race[2] /reis/ *n* **1** [C,U] any of several subdivisions of mankind sharing certain physical characteristics, as color of skin, color and type of hair, shape of eyes and nose, etc: *people of the same ~ but of different cultures.* **2** [C] (*dated*) group of people having a common culture, history or language: *the German ~.* **3** [C] group of plants or animals within a species, forming a distinct type and capable of breeding with each other. **4** [C] mankind: *the human ~.*

ra·cial /ˈreiʃəl/ *adj* relating to race²(1,2): *~ conflict/minorities/discrimination.*

ra·cial·ism *n* [U] racism.

ra·cial·ist *adj* racist.

ra·cially /-ʃəli/ *adv*

ra·cily, ra·ci·ness ⇨ racy.

ra·cism /ˈreɪˌsɪzəm/ *n* [U] discrimination or prejudice because of race.

ra·cist /-ɪst/ *n* **(a)** [C] person who believes in or practices racism. **(b)** (as an *adjective*) of racism or a racist: *~ beliefs.*

rack[1] /ræk/ *n* [C] **1** wooden or metal framework for holding food for animals (in a stable or in the fields). **2** framework with bars, pegs, etc for hanging things on, etc: *a ˈclothes ~.* **3** shelf or shelves, eg over the seats of a train, plane, bus, etc: *a ˈbaggage ~.* **4** rod, bar or rail with teeth or cogs which mesh with the teeth on a gearwheel or pinion. **5** rib section (of an animal used for food): *~ of lamb.*

rack[2] /ræk/ *n* [C] (usually **the rack**) instrument of torture consisting of a frame with rollers to which a person's wrists and ankles were tied so that his joints were stretched when the rollers were turned. □ *vt* **1** torture by placing on the rack. **2** (*fig*) inflict torture on: *~ed with pain.* **3** ***rack one's brains (for),*** make great mental efforts (for, in order to find, an answer, method, etc).

racket[1] /ˈrækɪt/ *n* **1** (*sing* only, with *a, an*) loud noise: *The drunken men in the street made a ~,* were very noisy. **2** [C] (*informal*) dishonest scheme for getting money (by deceiving or threatening people, selling worthless goods, etc).

rack·et·eer /ˌrækəˈtɪr/ *n* [C] person who is engaged in a criminal racket(2).

racket[2] /ˈrækɪt/ *n* [C] light, stringed bat used for hitting the ball in tennis, etc. ⇨ illus at tennis.

rac·oon = raccoon.

rac·quet /ˈrækɪt/ *n* [C] **1** = racket². **2** (*pl*) ball game for two or four players in a court with four walls.

racy /ˈreisi/ *adj* (-ier, -iest) **1** (of speech or writing) full of activity; spirited; vigorous: *a ~ style/novel.* **2** slightly improper: *a ~ story.*

ra·cily /-əli/ *adv*

ra·ci·ness /ˈreisinɪs/ *n* [U]

ra·dar /ˈreiˌdar/ *n* [U] (the use of) apparatus for determining the position, speed, etc of a distant object (eg an automobile, aircraft, etc) by means of radio waves reflected from the object: *follow an aircraft by ~.*

ˈradar·scope, ˈradar screen, visual display screen of a radar set.

ˈradar set, apparatus for sending and receiving radar signals.

ˈradar trap, radar set, used by police along a highway, for detecting speeding motorists.

ra·dial /ˈreidiəl/ *adj* **1** relating to a ray, rays or a radius. **2** from a common center; arranged like rays or radii.

ra·di·ally /-iəli/ *adv*
radial ˈtire, one strengthened with steel or nylon radial cords.
ra·di·ance /ˈreidiəns/ *n* [U] radiant quality.
ra·di·ant /ˈreidiənt/ *adj* **1** sending out rays of light; shining: *the ~ sun.* **2** (of a person, his looks, eyes) showing great joy or love: *a ~ face.* **3** (*phys*) transmitted by radiation: *~ heat/energy.*
ra·di·ant·ly *adv*
ra·di·ate /ˈreidiˌeit/ *vt,vi* **1** send out rays of (light or heat). **2** (*fig*) send out: *a bride who ~s happiness.* **3** come or go out (as) in rays: *heat that ~s from a fireplace; the happiness that ~s from her eyes.* **4** spread out like radii: *In Washington, D.C., many streets and avenues ~ from the Capitol building.*
ra·di·ation /ˌreidiˈeiʃən/ *n* **1** [U] radiating. **2** [U] (*phys*) the sending out of energy, heat, light, etc in rays. **3** [C] something radiated: *~s emitted by an X-ray apparatus.*
ra·di·ator /ˈreidiˌeitər/ *n* [C] **1** apparatus (in a room) for radiating heat, esp heat from hot water or steam. **2** device for cooling in the engine of a motor vehicle: *This car has a fan-cooled ~.*
rad·ical /ˈrædıkəl/ *adj* **1** of or from the root; fundamental: *~ changes.* **2** (esp *politics*) favoring complete and drastic changes. □ *n* [C] **1** person with radical(2) opinions. **2** root of a mathematical expression, esp as indicated by the radical sign.
radi·cally /-kli/ *adv*
ra·dii /ˈreidiˌai/ *pl* of radius.
ra·dio /ˈreidiou/ *n* (*pl* ~s) **1** [U] (communication by) radio telegraphy or by telephone: *send a message by ~.* **2** [U] broadcasting by this means: *hear something on the ~;* (as an *adjective*) *a ~ program.* **3** [C] apparatus for transmitting or receiving radio waves: *a transistor ~.*
radioman /-mən/ (*pl* -men /-men/) person who operates a radio (esp on a ship or at a military installation).
ˈradio station, (a) station set up for radio broadcasting on an assigned frequency, including studios, sending apparatus, etc. **(b)** (esp commercial) organization for doing this.
ˈradio waves, electromagnetic impulses, as transmitted by a radio or some natural sources.
radio- /ˌreidiou-/ *combined form* (esp) of radiation: *radioactive.*
ra·dio·ac·tive /ˌreidiouˈæktıv/ *adj* of or showing radioactivity.
ˌra·dio·acˈtiv·ity *n* [U] property or process by which some elements (such as uranium) send out radiation as the result of disintegration of atomic nuclei.
ra·di·ogra·phy /ˌreidiˈagrəfi/ *n* [U] production of X-ray photographs.
ˌra·diˈogra·pher *n* [C] person trained in radiography.
ra·dio·iso·tope /ˌreidiouˈaisəˌtoup/ *n* [C] radioactive form of an element, used in medicine, industry, etc.
ra·dio tele·scope /ˌreidiou ˈteləˌskoup/ *n* [C] apparatus that detects radio waves from outer space.
ra·dio·ther·apy /ˌreidiouˈθerəpi/ *n* [U] treatment of disease by means of X-rays or other forms of radiation.
ˌra·dio·ˈther·apist *n* [C] expert in radiotherapy.
rad·ish /ˈrædıʃ/ *n* [C] plant used in salad, with a white or red root.
ra·dius /ˈreidiəs/ *n* [C] (*pl* radii /-diˌai/) **1** (length of a) straight line from the center of a circle or sphere to any point on the circumference or surface. ⇨ illus at circle. **2** circular area determined by its radius: *The police searched all the fields and woods within a ~ of two miles.* **3** (*anat*) bone in the forearm on the thumb side. ⇨ illus at skeleton
raf·fia /ˈræfiə/ *n* [U] fiber from the leaf stalks of a kind of palm tree, used for making baskets, hats, mats, etc.
raffle /ˈræfəl/ *n* [C] lottery, often for a charitable purpose. □ *vt* (*pres p* raffling /ˈræflıŋ/) sell in a raffle: *raffling (off) a television set.*
raft /ræft/ *n* [C] number of logs fastened together to be floated down a river. □ *vt,vi* carry, move, go, on a raft.
raf·ter /ˈræftər/ *n* [C] one of the sloping beams on which a roof is supported.
rag[1] /ræg/ *n* [C] **1** frayed, worn piece of cloth: *a rag to polish the car with.* ***chew the rag,*** (*sl*) engage in (usually idle) conversations. **2** (*pl*) shabby, worn clothing: *dressed in rags.*
rag[2] /ˈræg/ *n* **1** [U] (short for) ragtime. **2** [C] piece of music in ragtime.
raga·muf·fin /ˈrægəˌməfın/ *n* [C] (esp) dirty, poorly-clothed child.
rage /reidʒ/ *n* **1** [C,U] (outburst of) furious anger: *shouting with ~; the ~ of the sea,* its violence during a storm. ***be in/fly into a rage,*** be, become, very angry. **2** [C] fad; craze; temporary enthusiasm: *Long hair on men was all the ~ that summer.* □ *vi* **1** be very angry: *He ~d and fumed against me for not letting him have his own way.* **2** continue violently or uncontrollably: *The storm ~d all day.*
rag·ged /ˈrægıd/ *adj* **1** (with clothes) badly torn or in rags: *a ~ coat/old man.* **2** having rough or irregular edges or outlines or surfaces: *a dog with a ~ coat of hair; a sleeve with ~ edges.* **3** (of work, etc) lacking smoothness or uniformity: *a ~ performance,* eg of an actor, a piece of music.
rag·ged·ly *adv*
rag·time /ˈrægˌtaim/ *n* [U] form of popular music in which a melody with irregularly accented notes is played against an accompaniment having a regular beat.
raid /reid/ *n* [C] **1** surprise attack made by troops, ship(s) or aircraft: *make a ~ on the enemy's camp.* **2** sudden visit by police to make arrests: *a ~ on a casino.* **3** sudden attack for the purpose of stealing: *a ~ on a bank by armed men.* □ *vt,vi* carry out a raid: *Boys have been ~ing my orchard,* visiting it to steal fruit.
raider *n* [C]
rail[1] /ˈreiəl/ *n* [C] **1** usually horizontal bar or rod supported at both ends, as in a fence, as a protection against contact or falling over: *He was leaning over the (ship's) ~.* **2** steel bar or continuous line of such bars, laid as a track for trains. **3** railroad. □ *vt* (*pres p* ~ing /ˈreilıŋ/) ***rail***

off/in, put rails(1) around: *fields that are ~ed off from the road.*

rail·ing /ˈreiliŋ/ *n* [C] fence made with rails.

rail[2] /ˈreiəl/ *vi* (*pres p* ~ing /ˈreiliŋ/) criticize. ***rail against,*** find fault with.

rail·road /ˈreiəlˌroud/ *n* [C] **1** track made of rails, on which trains run: *build a new ~.* **2** system of such tracks, with the locomotives, cars, etc and the organization controlling the system: (as an *adjective*) *a ˈ~ station/bridge.*

rai·ment /ˈreimənt/ *n* [U] (*liter*) clothing.

rain[1] /rein/ *n* **1** [U] water condensed from the moisture of the atmosphere falling in separate drops: *It looks like ~*, as if there will be a fall of *~. Don't go out in the ~.* ***(come) ˌrain or ˈshine,*** whether the weather is wet or sunny. **2** [C] (with *a* and an *adjective*) fall or shower of rain: *There was a heavy ~ last night.* **3** (usually *sing* with *a*) fall of something like rain: *a ~ of arrows/bullets.* **4** (*pl*) the season in tropical countries when there is heavy and continuous rain.

ˈrain·bow *n* [C] arch of different colors, formed in the sky by sunlight on mist or raindrops.

ˈrain·coat *n* [C] light coat of waterproof or tightly-woven material.

ˈrain·drop *n* [C] single drop of rain.

ˈrain·fall *n* [U] amount of rain falling within a given area in a given time.

ˈrain·storm *n* [C] storm with much rain.

rain[2] /rein/ *vi,vt* **1** fall as rain: *It was ~ing.* ***It never rains but it pours,*** (*prov*) things, usually unwelcome, do not come singly but in numbers, eg if one disaster happens, another will follow. **2** fall in a stream: *Tears ~ed down her cheeks.* **3** send or come down (on): *The people ~ed gifts on/upon the heroes returning from the war.*

rain check /ˈrein ˌtʃek/ *n* [C] (*informal*) (ticket, etc given as a) promise that goods or services not available when paid for will be supplied at a later date. ***take a rain check (on an offer),*** decline it, with a promise to claim the same offer at a later date.

rainy /ˈreini/ *adj* (-ier, -iest) having much rain: *~ weather; a ~ day/climate; the ˈ~ season.* ***save/put away/keep sth for a rainy day,*** save, etc, sth for a time of need.

raise[1] /reiz/ *vt* **1** lift up; move from a low(er) to a high(er) level; cause to rise: *~ a sunken ship to the surface of the sea; ~ one's glass to one's lips; ~ prices; ~* (= build, erect) *a monument.* ***raise sb's hopes,*** make him more hopeful. ***raise one's voice,*** speak more loudly or in a higher tone: *voices ~d in anger.* **2** cause to be upright: *~ a man from his knees; ~ the standard of revolt.* **3** cause to rise or appear: *~ a cloud of dust; shoes that ~ blisters on my feet; a long, hot walk that ~d a good thirst,* caused the walker to be thirsty. ***raise sb from the dead,*** restore him to life. ***raise a laugh,*** do something to cause laughter. ***raise Cain/hell/the devil/the roof,*** (*sl*) start a big row or disturbance. **4** bring up for discussion or attention: *~ a new point/a question/a protest/an objection.* **5** grow or produce (crops); breed (sheep, etc); rear, bring up (a family). **6** get or bring together; manage to get: *~ an army; ~ a loan; ~ money for a new swimming pool.*

raise[2] /reiz/ *n* **1** act of raising or increasing. **2** increase in salary.

raisin /ˈreizən/ *n* [C] dried sweet grape, as used in cakes, etc.

ra·jah /ˈradʒə/ *n* [C] Indian prince; Malayan chief.

rake[1] /reik/ *n* [C] long-handled tool with prongs used for drawing together straw, dead leaves, etc, and for smoothing soil or gravel, etc. □ *vt,vi* **1** smooth or gather with a rake: *~ garden paths; ~ together dead leaves.* ***rake it/the money in,*** (*fig*) earn or make a great deal of money: *The firm is very successful—they're raking it in/raking in the money.* **2** search for facts, etc: *~ through old manuscripts for information.* ***rake sth up,*** (esp) bring to people's knowledge (something unpleasant): *~ up old quarrels/the past.* **3** scratch, esp in long strokes, with some object like a rake: *The tiger ~ed him with its claws.* **4** fire at with guns, from end to end: *~ a ship.*

ˈrake-off *n* (*informal*) (usually dishonest) commission or share of profits.

rake[2] /reik/ *n* [C] (*dated*) immoral man.

rake[3] /reik/ *vi,vt* slant or slope. □ *n* [C] degree of slope.

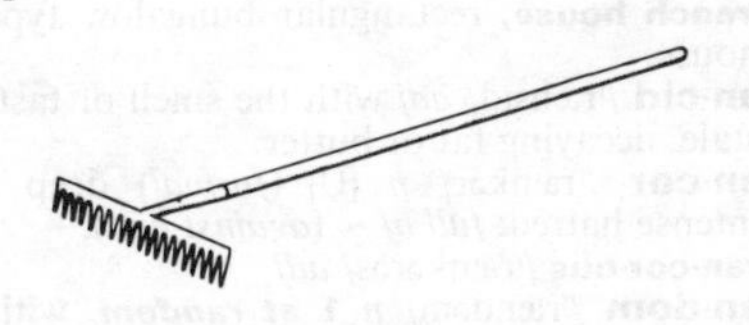

RAKE

rak·ish /ˈreikiʃ/ *adj* smart or stylish in appearance.

rak·ish·ly *adv*

rally /ˈræli/ *vt,vi* (*pt,pp* -lied) **1** (cause to) come together or unite for a common cause, esp after defeat or disappointment: *The troops rallied around their leader. The leader rallied his men. They rallied to the support of the mayor.* **2** give new strength to; (cause to) recover health, strength, firmness: *~ one's strength/spirits; ~ from an illness. The boy rallied his wits. The market rallied,* eg of the Stock Exchange, prices stopped dropping and became firm. □ *n* [C] (*pl* -ies) **1** (act or process of) rallying. **2** gathering or assembly, esp to encourage fresh effort: *a poˈlitical ~.*

ram /ræm/ *n* [C] **1** male sheep. **2** one of various implements or devices for striking or pushing with great force. **3** battering ram. □ *vt* (-mm-) **1** strike and push heavily: *ram piles into a river bed.* **2** crash into.

Rama·dan /ˈræməˌdan/ *n* ninth month of the Moslem year, when Moslems fast between sunrise and sunset.

ramble /ˈræmbəl/ *vi* **1** walk for pleasure, with no special destination. **2** (*fig*) wander in one's talk, not keeping to the subject. **3** (of plants) grow with long shoots that trail or straggle: *rambling roses.* □ *n* [C] rambling walk: *go for a ~ in the country.*

ram·bler *n* [C]

ram·bling *adj* **(a)** (esp of buildings, streets, towns), extending in various directions irregularly, as if built without planning. **(b)** (of a speech, essay, etc) disconnected.

ramp /ræmp/ *n* [C] sloping way from one level to another, eg instead of stairs or steps.

ram·page /ˈræmˌpeidʒ/ *vi* rush about in excitement or violent rage. □ *n* ***be/go on a/the rampage,*** be/go rampaging.

ram·pant /ˈræmpənt/ *adj* **1** growing or spreading beyond control: *Disease was ~ in the town.* **2** (of animals, esp of a lion in heraldry) on the hind legs.

ram·pant·ly *adv*

ram·part /ˈræmˌpart/ *n* [C] wide bank of earth, often with a wall, built to defend a fort, etc.

ram·rod /ˈræmˌrad/ *n* [C] metal rod for ramming the charge into a muzzle-loading gun.

ram·shackle /ˈræmˌʃækəl/ *adj* almost collapsing: *a ~ house/old bus.*

ran *pt* of run².

ranch /ræntʃ/ *n* [C] large farm, esp one with extensive lands for cattle, but also for fruit, chickens, etc.

rancher *n* [C] person who owns, manages or works on a ranch.

ˈranch house, rectangular bungalow type of house.

ran·cid /ˈrænsɪd/ *adj* with the smell or taste of stale, decaying fat or butter.

ran·cor /ˈræŋkər/ *n* [U] (*formal*) deep and intense hatred: *full of ~* (*against him*).

ran·cor·ous /ˈræŋkərəs/ *adj*

ran·dom /ˈrændəm/ *n* **1** ***at random,*** without reason, aim or purpose: *choosing children at ~ to help in the class.* **2** (as an *adjective*) done, made, taken, at random: *a ~ remark/sample/selection.*

rang *pt* of ring².

range¹ /reindʒ/ *n* [C] **1** row, line or series of things: *a magnificent ~ of mountains; a ˈmountain ~.* **2** area for practicing shooting: *a ˈrifle ~.* **3** maximum distance which a missile or vehicle can travel: *a ~ of 50 miles.* **4** distance at which one can see or hear, or to which sound will carry. **5** extent, limits: *the annual ~ of temperature,* eg from −10°C to 40°C; *cotton in a wide ~ of colors.* **6** (*fig*) extent: *a wide ~ of interests.* **7** open ground used for grazing livestock. **8** area over which plants are found growing or in which animals are found living: *What is the ~ of the elephant in Africa?* **9** type of stove, with ovens, a surface for pans, kettles, etc: *a gas/electric ~.*

range² /reindʒ/ *vt,vi* **1** place or arrange in a row or rows: *The general ~d his men along the river bank.* **2** go, move, wander: *animals ranging through the forests/over the hills.* **3** (*fig*) extend: *researches that ~d over a wide field; a wide-ranging discussion.* **4** extend, run in a line: *a boundary that ~s north and south/from A to B.* **5** vary between limits: *prices ranging from $7 to $10/between $7 and $10.* **6** classify; put in an order, class or group.

ranger /ˈreindʒər/ *n* [C] **1** person employed to protect (part of) a forest. **2** one of a body of armed men employed as police (eg in thinly populated areas): *the Texas ~s.*

rank /ræŋk/ *n* **1** [C] line of persons or things. **2** number of soldiers placed side by side. **3** (*pl*) ordinary soldiers, ie privates and corporals, contrasted with officers. **4** [C,U] official position, eg in the armed forces: *promoted to the ~ of captain.* **5** (*pl*) body of individuals classed together: *be in the ~s of the unemployed.* □ *vt,vi* **1** put or arrange in a rank; put in a class: *Would you ~ him among the world's great statesmen?* **2** have a certain position or value: *Does he ~ among/with the failures? A major ~s above a captain.*

rankle /ˈræŋkəl/ *vi* continue to be a painful or annoying memory: *The insult ~d in his mind.*

ran·sack /ˈrænˌsæk/ *vt* **1** search (a place) thoroughly and roughly: *~ a drawer for money/to find money.* **2** rob: *The house had been ~ed of all that was worth anything.*

ran·som /ˈrænsəm/ *n* **1** [U] release of a person who has been kidnapped in exchange for payment. **2** [C] sum of money, etc, paid for this. ***hold sb ransom,*** keep him as a prisoner and ask for money. ***a king's ransom,*** a very large sum of money. □ *vt* obtain the freedom of (a person), set (a person) free, in exchange for ransom: *~ a kidnapped diplomat.*

rant /rænt/ *vi,vt* use extravagant, boasting, loud language: *~ing and raving on the stage.*

rap /ræp/ *n* [C] **1** (sound of a) light, quick blow: *I heard a rap on the door.* **2** (*informal*) blame; consequences. ***take the rap (for sth),*** be punished, etc (esp when innocent). □ *vt,vi* (-pp-) give a rap to; make the sound of a rap: *rap (at) the door.*

ra·pa·cious /rəˈpeiʃəs/ *adj* (*formal*) greedy (esp for money).

ra·pa·cious·ly *adv*

rape /reip/ *vt* force (a woman) to have sexual intercourse against her will. □ *n* [C] act of raping.

ra·pist /ˈreipɪst/ *n* [C] person who rapes.

rapid /ˈræpɪd/ *adj* **1** quick; moving, happening, with great speed: *a ~ decline in sales; ~ questions,* in a quick succession. **2** (of a slope) steep; descending steeply.

ra·pid·ity /rəˈpɪdəti/ *n* [U]

rap·id·ly *adv*

rapid ˈtransit, special kind(s) of public transportation, esp in and around the cities, designed for speed (eg subways, buses in special lanes, etc).

rap·ids /ˈræpɪdz/ *n pl* place in a river where a steep slope causes the water to flow fast.

rapier /ˈreipiər/ *n* [C] light sword used for thrusting in duels.

rapt /ræpt/ *adj* so deep in thought, so deeply moved, that one is unaware of other things: *listening with ~ attention; ~ in a book.*

rap·ture /ˈræptʃər/ *n* [U] great delight; ecstasy: *gazing with ~ at the face of the girl he loved.*

rap·tur·ous /ˈræptʃərəs/ *adj*

rap·tur·ous·ly *adv*

rare¹ /rær/ *adj* (-r, -st) unusual; uncommon: *a ~ animal. It is very ~ for her to arrive late.*

rare·ly *adv* not often: *~ly seen.*

rare·ness /-nɪs/ *n* [U]

rare² /rær/ *adj* (of meat) cooked so that the redness and juices are kept: *a ~ steak.*
rarefy /ˈrærəˌfai/ *vt,vi* (*pt,pp* -ied) make or become less dense; purify: *the rarefied air on the mountain.*
rar·ing /ˈrærɪŋ/ *adj* (*informal*) full of eagerness: *They're ~ to go.*
rar·ity /ˈrærəti/ *n* (*pl* -ies) **1** [U] rareness. **2** [C] something uncommon or unusual (and so valuable): *The person who is always happy is a ~.*
ras·cal /ˈræskəl/ *n* [C] **1** dishonest person. **2** mischievous child.
rash¹ /ræʃ/ *n* [C] **1** eruption of tiny red spots on the skin: *a ˈheat ~.* **2** (*fig*) sudden outbreak or spread: *a ~ of new red brick homes on a country road.*
rash² /ræʃ/ *adj* too hasty; reckless: *a ~ act/statement/man.*
rash·ly *adv*
rash·ness /-nɪs/ *n* [U]
rasher /ˈræʃər/ *n* [C] **1** slice of bacon or ham (to be) fried. **2** serving of (several slices of) fried bacon.
rasp /ræsp/ *n* [C] **1** metal tool like a coarse file with a surface or surfaces having sharp points, used for scraping. **2** rough, grating sound produced by this tool. □ *vt,vi* **1** scrape with a rasp. **2** (*fig*) irritate: *~ing my nerves.* **3** say with a grating sound: *~ out orders/insults.* **4** make a harsh, grating sound.
rasp·ing·ly *adv*
rasp·berry /ˈræzˌberi/ *n* [C] (*pl* -ies) **1** (bush with a) small, sweet yellow or red berry: (as an *adjective*) *~ jam.* **2** (*sl*) noise made with the tongue and lips to show dislike or disapproval.
rat /ræt/ *n* [C] **1** animal like, but larger than, a mouse. ***smell a rat,*** suspect that something wrong is being done. **2** (*fig*) cowardly traitor or deserter. □ *vt* (-tt-) **1** (esp of a cat or dog) hunt rats: *go ratting.* **2** (*sl*) ***rat (on a friend),*** betray or desert him.
ˈrat race, (*informal*) task or job which is intensely demanding or competitive but gives no sense of satisfaction.
rate¹ /reit/ *n* **1** [C] quantity or amount measured in proportion to another amount: *walk at the ~ of 3 miles an hour.* **2** charge, etc per unit: *What is the ~ per ounce for air mail?* ***at ˈthis/ˈthat rate,*** if this/that is true; if this/that state of affairs continues. ***at ˈany rate,*** in any case; whatever happens. **3** (with ordinal numbers) class or grade: *a first-~ ˈteacher,* one of high quality. *second-~,* mediocre.
rate² /reit/ *vt,vi* **1** estimate the value or quality of: *What do you ~ his wealth at?* **2** consider: *He was ~d as kind and hospitable.* **3** have a certain rating or rank: *She ~d fourth.*
rather /ˈræðər/ *adv* **1** more willingly; by preference or choice: *I'd ~ you came tomorrow than today. A: "Will you join us in a game of cards?" — B: "Thank you, but I'd ~ not,"* prefer not to. **2** more truly, accurately or precisely: *He arrived very late last night or ~ in the early hours this morning.* **3** in a certain degree or measure; somewhat: *a ~ surprising result;* (with *nouns*) *It's ~ a pity;* (with *verbs*) *We were all ~ exhausted when we got to the top of the mountain.*
rat·ify /ˈrætəˌfai/ *vt* (*pt,pp* -ied) confirm (an agreement) by signature or other formality.
rati·fi·ca·tion /ˌrætəfəˈkeiʃən/ *n* [U]
rat·ing /ˈreitɪŋ/ *n* [C] **1** class, classification, eg of quality, capacity, etc. **2** popularity of radio or TV programs as estimated by asking a selected group.
ratio /ˈreiʃ(ɪ)ou/ *n* [C] (*pl* ~s) (*math*) relation between two amounts determined by the number of times one contains the other: *The ~s of 1 to 5 and 20 to 100 are the same.*
ra·tion /ˈræʃən/ *n* **1** [C] fixed quantity, esp of food, allowed to one person. **2** (*pl*) fixed allowance served out to, eg members of the armed forces: *go and draw ~s.* □ *vt* **1** limit (a person) to a fixed ration. **2** limit (food, water, etc): *We'll have to ~ the water.*
ra·tion·al /ˈræʃənəl/ *adj* **1** able to reason; having the faculty of reasoning. **2** sensible; logical; based on reasoning: *~ conduct/explanations.*
ra·tion·al·ity /ˌræʃəˈnæləti/ *n* [U]
ra·tion·ally /-ʃənəli/ *adv*
ra·tion·ale /ˌræʃəˈnæl/ *n* [C] fundamental reason, logical basis (of something).
ra·tion·al·ize /ˈræʃənəˌlaiz/ *vt* **1** make reasonable. **2** explain in a seemingly rational manner: *~ one's fears/behavior.*
ration·al·iz·ation /ˌræʃənələˈzeiʃən/ *n* [C,U]
rattle /ˈrætəl/ *vt,vi* **1** (cause to) make short, sharp sounds quickly, one after the other: *The windows were rattling in the wind. The wind ~d the windows.* **2** talk, say or repeat (something) quickly and in a thoughtless way: *The boy ~d off the poem he had learned.* **3** upset; disturb: *His questions obviously ~d her.* □ *n* **1** [U] rattling sound: *the ~ of bottles in a milkman's van.* **2** [C] device, eg a toy, for producing a rattling sound. **3** [C] dry, horny rings on the tail of a rattlesnake, which rattle when shaken. ⇨ illus at snake.
rattler /ˈrætlər/ *n* [C] (*informal*) rattlesnake.
ˈrattle·trap *n* (*sl*) dilapidated old car.
rattle·snake /ˈrætəlˌsneik/ *n* [C] poisonous snake that makes a rattling noise with its tail. ⇨ illus at snake.
rau·cous /ˈrɔkəs/ *adj* **1** (of sounds) harsh; rough; hoarse: *the ~ cries of the crows.* **2** disorderly and noisy.
rau·cous·ly *adv*
rav·age /ˈrævɪdʒ/ *vt,vi* **1** destroy; damage badly: *forests ~d by fire.* **2** (of armies, etc) rob, plunder, with violence: *They had ~d the countryside.* □ *n* **1** [U] destruction. **2** (*pl*) destructive effects: *the ~s of time,* eg on a woman's looks.
rave /reiv/ *vi* **1** talk wildly or violently, often without making sense: *He was raving about their carelessness.* **2** (of the sea, wind, etc) roar; rage. **3** talk with (often) excessive enthusiasm or praise: *She ~d about the food she had had in France.* □ *n* [C] (*informal*) (often as an *adjective*) enthusiastic praise: *a ~ review,* eg of a book.
ravel /ˈrævəl/ *vt,vi* (-l-, -ll-) (of knitted or woven things) separate into threads; fray.
raven /ˈreivən/ *n* [C] large, black bird like a crow.
rav·en·ous /ˈrævənəs/ *adj* **1** very hungry. **2** greedy: *a ~ appetite.*
rav·en·ous·ly *adv*

ra·vine /rəˈvin/ *n* [C] deep, narrow valley or gorge.

ravi·oli /ˌræviˈouli/ *n pl (I)* small, square pieces of pasta filled with chopped meat, cheese, etc.

rav·ish /ˈrævɪʃ/ *vt* **1** carry away by violent means. **2** rape. **3** plunder. **4** fill with delight: *~ed by the view.*

rav·ish·ing /ˈrævɪʃɪŋ/ *adj* unusually beautiful or enchanting: *a ~ smile.*

rav·ish·ing·ly *adv*

raw /rɔ/ *adj* **1** uncooked: *raw meat.* **2** in the natural state, not manufactured or prepared for use: *the raw materials of industry*, eg coal, ores. ***in the raw,*** **(a)** in the natural state. **(b)** naked. **3** (of persons) untrained; unskilled; inexperienced: *raw recruits*, for the army, etc. **4** (of the weather) damp and cold: *a raw February morning.* **5** (of a place on the flesh) with the skin rubbed off; sore and painful. **6** ***a raw deal,*** harsh or unjust treatment.

raw·hide /ˈrɔˌhaid/ *adj,n* [U] (of) untanned hide.

ray[1] /rei/ *n* [C] **1** line, beam, of radiant light, heat, energy: *the rays of the sun.* **2** *(fig)* small sign: *a ray of hope.* **3** any one of a number of lines coming out from a center. □ *vi,vt* send out or come out in rays.

ray[2] /rei/ *n* [C] kinds of large ocean fish with a broad, flat body.

rayon /ˈreiˌan/ *n* [U] synthetic material made from cellulose.

raze /reiz/ *vt* destroy (towns, buildings) completely, esp by making them level with the ground: *a city ~d by an earthquake.*

razor /ˈreizər/ *n* [C] instrument with a sharp blade used for shaving hair from the skin.

razor·back /ˈreizərˌbæk/ *n* [C] hog of the southern US, with a spinal ridge on the back.

razzle-dazzle /ˌræzəl-ˈdæzəl/ *n* [U] *(informal)* glitter; excitement.

Rd. *abbr* = Road.

re[1] /rei/ *n* [C] *(music)* syllable used for the second note of a scale.

re[2] /rei, ri/ *prep (Lat)* with regard to; concerning.

re-[3] /ri-, rɪ-/ *prefix* **1** again: *reappear, replay.* **2** back: *recall.*

reach /ritʃ/ *vt,vi* **1** stretch (out): *He ~ed (out his hand) for the knife.* **2** stretch out the hand for and grasp: *Can you ~ that book?* **3** arrive at: *~ the airport/San Franciso; ~ the end of the chapter.* **4** extend; go; pass: *My land ~es as far as the river.* □ *n* **1** *(sing* only) act of stretching out (a hand, etc). **2** [U] extent to which a hand, etc can be reached out: *This boxer has a long ~. I like to have my reference books within my ~/within easy ~*, so near that I can get them quickly and easily. **3** [U] attainment (through ability or understanding): *It is beyond/within his ~.* **4** [C] continuous unbroken expanse.

re·act /riˈækt/ *vi* **1** have a return influence or effect (on the person or thing): *Force often ~s on/upon the user.* **2** behave in response: *Do children ~ to kind treatment by becoming more self-confident?* **3** respond to in opposition: *The audience ~ed against the poor play by booing.* **4** *(chem)* take part in or undergo a change: *How do acids ~ on metals?*

re·ac·tion /riˈækʃən/ *n* [C,U] **1** action or state resulting from, in response to, something: *He had a ~ to the drug.* **2** opposition to progress: *The forces of ~ made reform difficult.* **3** attitude, action or opinion as a response to something: *What was his ~ to your proposal?* **4** *(chem)* action set up by one substance in another; change or transformation.

re·ac·tion·ary /riˈækʃəˌneri/ *n* [C] *(pl* -ies), *adj* (person) opposing progress or reform.

re·ac·tor /riˈæktər/ *n* [C] (also **nuclear reactor**) apparatus for producing nuclear energy.

read /rid/ *vt,vi (pt,pp* read /red/) **1** look at and (be able to) understand (something written or printed): *Can you ~ French/a musical score?* **2** speak aloud the words of (an author, book, etc): *She was ~ing the letter to the children.* **3** study (a subject): *He's ~ing up on physics.* **4** interpret mentally; learn the significance of: *~ a person's thoughts.* **5** learn by reading: *~ in the newspaper that the sale would be held on Thursday.* **6** find implications in (what is read, etc): *Silence mustn't always be ~ as consent.* ***read between the lines,*** look for or discover meanings that are not actually expressed. ***read into sth,*** add more than is justified: *You have ~ into her letter more sympathy than she probably feels.* **7** (of instruments) show: *What does the thermometer ~?* □ *adj* having knowledge gained from books, etc: *a ˌwell-~ ˈman.*

read·abil·ity /ˌridəˈbɪləti/ *n* [U]

read·able /ˈridəbəl/ *adj* easy or pleasant to read.

reader /ˈridər/ *n* [C] **1** person who reads, esp one who spends much time in reading. **2** textbook for reading in class; book with selections for reading by students of a language: *a Latin Reader.*

read·ily, readi·ness ⇨ ready.

read·ing /ˈridɪŋ/ *n* **1** [U] activity of reading. **2** [U] material for reading. **3** [C] way in which something is interpreted or understood: *My ~ of the situation is...* **4** [C] figure of measurement, etc as shown on a dial, scale, etc: *The ~s on my thermometer last month were well above the average.*

re·ad·just /ˌriəˈdʒəst/ *vt,vi* adjust or adapt again: *It's sometimes difficult to ~ after working abroad.*

re·ad·just·ment *n* [C,U]

ready /ˈredi/ *adj* (-ier, -iest) (*Note:* in senses (1) and (2), *ready* does not occur before the word it modifies.) **1** in the condition needed for use; prepared: *~ for work.* ***make ready,*** prepare. **2** willing: *~ to help.* **3** quick; prompt: *He always has a ~ answer.* **4** within reach; easily obtained: *~ cash.* □ *vt (pt,pp* -ied) prepare; get ready.

read·ily /ˈredəli/ *adv* **(a)** without showing hesitation or unwillingness. **(b)** without difficulty.

readi·ness /ˈredinɪs/ *n* [U] **(a)** condition of being prepared: *have everything in readiness for an early start.* **(b)** willingness: *a surprising readiness to accept the proposal.*

ˌready-ˈmade *adj* prepared and ready for use: *~-made clothes.*

real /ˈriəl/ *adj* **1** existing in fact; not imagined or supposed; actual: *Was it a ~ man you saw or a ghost? Things that happen in ~ life are sometimes stranger than in stories. Who is the ~*

owner of the business? **2** not made up or artificial: *Tell me the* ~ (= true) *reason for your absence from work. Are those flowers* ~*?* **3** of or being immovable property.

ˈreal estate, land and buildings as property.

real·ism /ˈriəˌlɪzəm/ *n* [U] **1** (in art and literature) showing of real life, facts, etc in a true way, omitting nothing that is ugly or painful, and idealizing nothing. **2** behavior based on facing the facts and disregarding sentiment and convention.

real·ist /-ɪst/ *n* [C] person who believes or practices realism.

real·is·tic /ˌriəˈlɪstɪk/ *adj* **(a)** showing the true form. **(b)** practical: *realistic policies*.

real·is·ti·cally /-kli/ *adv*

re·al·ity /riˈæləti/ *n* (*pl* -ies) **1** [U] the quality of being real; real existence: *belief in the* ~ *of miracles.* ***in reality,*** in actual fact. **2** [C] someone or something that is real: *the grim realities of war*. **3** [U] (in art, etc) truth; lifelike resemblance to the original: *The TV broadcast described what was happening with extraordinary* ~.

real·ize /ˈriəˌlaiz/ *vt* **1** be fully conscious of; understand: *Does he* ~ *his mistake yet? She* ~*d that he lied.* **2** make real; accomplish: ~ *one's hopes/ambitions/dreams*. **3** obtain or bring in as a profit: *How much did you* ~ *on the paintings you sent to the sale?*

real·iz·able /-əbəl/ *adj*

real·iz·ation /ˌriələˈzeiʃən/ *n* [C,U]

really /ˈri(ə)li/ *adv* **1** in fact; actually: *What do you* ~ *think about it? I'm* ~ *sorry.* **2** truly: *a* ~ *difficult book*.

realm /relm/ *n* [C] **1** (*poetic*) kingdom: *in Nature's Realm.* **2** (*fig*) region: *the* ~ *of the imagination*.

re·alty /ˈriəlti/ *n* [U] real estate.

ream[1] /rim/ *n* [C] **1** measure for paper equal to 480, 500, or 516 sheets of the same size and quality. **2** (*pl*) (*informal*) great quantity (of writing): *She has written* ~*s of verse*.

ream[2] /rim/ *vt* widen, shape, or clean out a hole with a pointed tool.

reamer *n* [C]

reap /rip/ *vt,vi* **1** cut or gather (grain, etc). **2** gather in a crop of grain from (a field, etc): ~ *a field of barley*. **3** (*fig*) gain: ~ *the reward of virtue*.

reaper *n* [C]

re·appear /ˌriəˈpɪr/ *vi* appear again.

re·appear·ance /-rəns/ *n* [C,U]

rear[1] /rɪr/ *n* [C] **1** back part: *The kitchen is in the* ~ *of the house.* **2** (*informal*) buttocks: *gave him a kick in the* ~. **3** part farthest from the fighting part of an army, fleet, etc. □ *adj* located in the rear.

ˌrear ˈadmiral, commissioned officer in the US navy or coast guard who ranks above a captain and below a vice admiral.

rear-view ˈmirror, one placed in a vehicle so that the driver can see rearward through it.

ˈrear·ward(s) *adj* toward the rear.

rear[2] /rɪr/ *vt,vi* **1** cause or help to grow; bring up: ~ *poultry/cattle;* ~ *children.* ⇨ raise(5). **2** (esp of a horse) rise on the hind legs. **3** lift up: *The snake* ~*ed its head*.

rea·son[1] /ˈrizən/ *n* **1** [C,U] (fact as a) cause of or explanation for something: *Is there any* ~ *why you are late? The* ~ *why he's late is that/because there was a breakdown on the railroad.* ***with reason,*** rightly. ***by reason of,*** because of: *He was excused by* ~ *of his age.* **2** [U] power of the mind to understand, form opinions, etc: *Only man has* ~. ***lose one's reason,*** go crazy. **3** [U] good judgment; common sense. ***without rhyme or reason,*** ⇨ rhyme(1).

rea·son[2] /ˈrizən/ *vi,vt* **1** make use of one's reason (2); exercise the power of thought: *Man's ability to* ~ *makes him different from the animals.* **2** ***reason with sb,*** argue in order to convince him: *She* ~*ed with me for an hour.* **3** say by way of argument: *He* ~*ed that if we started at dawn, we could arrive before noon.* **4** express logically or in the form of an argument: *a well-*~*ed statement/manifesto.* ***reason sth out,*** find an answer by considering successive arguments, etc. **5** persuade by argument (not) to do something: ~ *a person out of his fears*.

reason·ing *n* [U] process of reaching conclusions by using one's reason: *There's no* ~*ing with that woman*, She won't listen to sensible advice, arguments.

rea·son·able /ˈrizənəbəl/ *adj* **1** having ordinary common sense; able to reason; willing to listen to reason. **2** not excessive; moderate: *a* ~ *price/offer*. **3** logical; in accordance with reason: *a* ~ *explanation*.

rea·son·ably /-əbli/ *adv*

re·as·sure /ˌriəˈʃʊr/ *vt* assure again; restore confidence to: *She felt* ~*d after her teacher told her she would pass the examination*.

re·as·sur·ance /-rəns/ *n* [U]

re·as·sur·ing·ly *adv*

re·bate /ˈriˌbeit/ *n* [C] return of part of a payment; reduction: *There is a* ~ *of $15.00 if the account is settled before December 31.* □ *vt,vi* give (money as) a rebate.

rebel[1] /ˈrebəl/ *n* [C] person who rebels or participates in a rebellion.

re·bel[2] /rɪˈbel/ *vi* (-ll-) **1** take up arms to fight (against the government). **2** show resistance; protest strongly: *The children* ~*led against having to do three hours' homework each evening*.

re·bel·lion /rɪˈbelyən/ *n* **1** [U] rebelling, eg against a government: *rise in* ~ (*against the Union*). **2** [C] instance of this: *a* ~ *against the dictator*.

re·bel·li·ous /rɪˈbelyəs/ *adj* **1** taking part in a rebellion: ~ *members/behavior*. **2** inclined to disobey: *a child with a* ~ *temper*.

re·bel·li·ous·ly *adv*

re·birth /ˌriˈbərθ, ˈriˌbərθ/ *n* [C] revival: *the* ~ *of learning*.

re·born /ˌriˈbɔrn/ *adj* born again.

re·bound /ˌriˈbaund/ *vi* **1** spring or bounce back after hitting something: *The ball* ~*ed from the wall.* **2** recover from a disappointment or setback. □ /ˈriˌbaund/ *n* [C] action, instance of rebounding. ***on the rebound,*** **(a)** while bouncing back: *hit a ball on the* ~. **(b)** (*fig*) while still reacting to a disappointment: *She quarreled with Paul and then married Peter on the* ~.

re·buff /rɪˈbəf/ *vt* refuse in an unkind or unfriendly way; show indifference to (an offer of or request for help, friendship, etc). □ /ˈrɪˌbəf/ *n* [C] action, instance of rebuffing.

re·build /ˌriˈbɪld/ *vt* (*pt,pp* -built /-ˈbɪlt/) build or put together again.

re·buke /rɪˈbyuk/ *vt* (*formal*) scold or speak severely to: *~ an employee for being rude.* □ *n* [C] scolding.

re·buk·ing·ly *adv*

re·but /rɪˈbət/ *vt* (-tt-) prove (a charge, piece of evidence, etc) to be false by presenting evidence which opposes it.

re·but·tal /-təl/ *n* [C] act of rebutting; evidence that rebuts.

rec. *abbr* = **1** receipt. **2** record. **3** recording. **4** recreation.

re·cal·ci·trant /rɪˈkælsətrənt/ *adj* (*formal*) defiant; resisting authority or discipline.

re·cal·ci·trance /rɪˈkælsətrəns/ *n* [U] (*formal*)

re·call /rɪˈkɔl/ *vt* **1** ask to come back: *~ an ambassador* (*from his post/to his own country*). **2** bring back to the mind; remember: *I don't ~ his name/face/meeting him/where I met him.* **3** take back; cancel. □ /ˈriˌkɔl/ *n* **1** [C] request to return. **2** [U] ability to remember. **3** [C] act or procedure of removing an official from public office by the vote of the people.

re·cant /ˌriˈkænt/ *vt,vi* give up (an opinion, a belief); take back (a statement) as being false: *The torturers could not make him ~.*

re·can·ta·tion /ˌrikænˈteiʃən/ *n* [C,U]

re·cap /ˌriˈkæp/ *vt,vi* **1** replace the rubber tread on a (esp automobile) tire. **2** (*informal*) (short for) recapitulate. □ /ˈriˌkæp/ *n* [C] **1** tread replacement on a tire. **2** (*informal*) (short for) recapitulation.

re·cap·itu·late /ˌrikəˈpɪtʃəˌleit/ *vt,vi* repeat, in shorter form, the chief points of (something that has been said, discussed, argued about, etc); summarize.

re·cap·itu·la·tion /ˌrikəˌpɪtʃəˈleiʃən/ *n* [C,U]

re·cap·ture /ˌriˈkæptʃər/ *vt* **1** capture again. **2** recall: *try to ~ the past.*

re·cast /ˌriˈkæst/ *vt* **1** cast or fashion again: *~ a gun/a bell; ~* (= rewrite) *a sentence/paragraph/chapter.* **2** change the cast of a play.

recd. *abbr* = received.

re·cede /rɪˈsid/ *vi* **1** mó back or away (from an earlier position): *As the tide ~d we were able to explore the beach. As our ship steamed out to sea the coast slowly ~d.* **2** slope backward: *a receding chin.*

re·ceipt /rɪˈsit/ *n* **1** [U] receiving or being received: *on ~ of the news.* **2** (*pl*) money received (in a business, etc) (contrasted with *expenditure*). **3** [C] written statement that something (money or goods) has been received: *get a ~ for money spent; sign a ~.* **4** [C] recipe. □ *vt* write out and sign or stamp a receipt(3): *~ a hotel bill.*

re·ceiv·able /rɪˈsivəbəl/ *adj* **1** that can be received. **2** (*comm*) (of bills, accounts, etc) on which money is to be received.

re·ceive /rɪˈsiv/ *vt,vi* **1** acquire, get (something offered, sent, etc): *When did you ~ the letter/news/telegram? He has ~d a good education.* **2** welcome: *~d him with open arms.* **3** transform incoming radio waves into sound or images.

re·ceiver /rɪˈsivər/ *n* [C] **1** person who receives. **2** person appointed to take charge of the property and affairs of another. **3** part of an apparatus for receiving and converting an incoming signal, eg that part of a telephone that is held to the ear: *a ˈradio ~.*

re·cent /ˈrisənt/ *adj* (having existed, been made, happened) not long before; begun not long ago: *~ news; a ~ event; within ~ memory.*

re·cent·ly *adv*

re·cep·tacle /rɪˈseptəkəl/ *n* [C] container or holder in which things may be put.

re·cep·tion /rɪˈsepʃən/ *n* **1** [U] receiving or being received: *prepare rooms for the ~ of guests.* **2** [C] formal occasion on which guests are received: *There was a ~ after the wedding ceremony.* **3** [U] receiving of radio, etc signals; degree of efficiency of this: *Is radio ~ good in your locality?*

re·cep·tion·ist /-ɪst/ *n* [C] person employed in an office to receive clients.

re·cep·tive /rɪˈseptɪv/ *adj* quick or ready to receive suggestions, new ideas, etc: *~ to new ideas.*

re·cep·tive·ly *adv*

re·cess /ˈriˌses, ˌriˈses/ *n* [C] **1** (usually brief) period of time when school, work or business is stopped. **2** part of a room where the wall is set back from the main part. **3** secret place; place difficult to get in: *the dark ~es of a cave.* **4** (*fig*) deep, inner part: *in the ~es of the mind.* □ *vt,vi* **1** take, call a recess(1). **2** place in, provide with, a recess(2).

re·ces·sion /rɪˈseʃən/ *n* **1** [U] withdrawal; act of receding. **2** [C] slowing down of business and industrial activity: *Did the recent ~ cause a lot of unemployment?*

re·ces·sional /rɪˈseʃənəl/ *n* [C] hymn sung while the clergy and choir withdraw after a church service.

re·ces·sive /rɪˈsesɪv/ *adj* **1** tending to recede or go back. **2** (*biol*) (such as hair color) which is present but not apparent when a dominant and opposing gene for that trait is also present in the organism: *Blue eyes and blond hair are ~ traits.*

recipe /ˈresəpi/ *n* [C] direction for preparing (a cake, a dish of food, a medical remedy) or for getting (any result): *a ~ for a fruit cake. Have you a ~ for happiness?*

re·cipi·ent /rɪˈsɪpiənt/ *n* [C] (*formal*) person who receives something.

re·cip·ro·cal /rɪˈsɪprəkəl/ *adj* **1** given and received in return: *~ affection/help.* **2** mutually corresponding.

re·cip·ro·cally /-kli/ *adv*

re·cip·ro·cate /rɪˈsɪprəˌkeit/ *vt,vi* **1** give in return; give and receive, each to and from each: *He ~d by wishing her a pleasant journey.* **2** (of parts of a machine) (cause to) move backward and forward alternately (eg the piston of an engine): *a reciprocating engine/saw.*

re·cip·ro·ca·tion /rɪˌsɪprəˈkeiʃən/ *n* [U]

reci·proc·ity /ˌresɪˈprasəti/ *n* [U] (*formal*) principle or practice of making mutual concessions; the granting of privileges in return for similar privileges: *~ in trade* (*between two countries*).

re·cital /rɪˈsaitəl/ *n* [C] **1** detailed account of a number of connected events, etc: *We were bored by the long* ~ *of his adventures.* **2** performance of music by a soloist or small group, or of the works of one composer: *a piˈano* ~.

reci·ta·tion /ˌresəˈteiʃən/ *n* **1** [U] the act of reciting. **2** [U] public delivery of passages of prose or poetry. **3** [C] student's oral responses to questions on a lesson, assignment, etc.

re·cite /rɪˈsait/ *vt,vi* **1** say (esp poems) aloud from memory: *The little girl refused to* ~ *at the party.* **2** give a detailed account esp after preparation: ~ *the names of all the state capitals.*

reck·less /ˈrekləs/ *adj* not thinking or caring about the consequences: *a* ~ *spender/driver.*

reck·less·ly *adv*

reck·less·ness /-nɪs/ *n* [U]

reckon /ˈrekən/ *vt,vi* **1** calculate; compute: ~ *the cost of a vacation.* **2** ***reckon with sb/sth,*** **(a)** deal with; settle with: *When the fighting is over, we'll* ~ *with the enemy's sympathizers.* **(b)** take into account; consider: *He is certainly a man to be* ~*ed with,* a man who cannot be ignored. **3** depend (on): *I am* ~*ing on your help.* **4** consider as being: *One-fourth of the country is* ~*ed to be/as unproductive. Do you still* ~ *him among/as one of your friends?* **5** (*informal*) suppose; assume: *I* ~ *we'll go next week.*

reck·oner /ˈrekənər/ *n* [C]

reck·on·ing /ˈrekənɪŋ/ *n* **(a)** [C] (*old use*) (totaled) account of items to be paid for: *pay the* ~*ing.* ***day of reckoning,*** time when one must be punished for doing something. **(b)** [U] calculation.

re·claim /rɪˈkleim/ *vt* **1** return (waste land, etc) to a useful condition, a state of cultivation, etc. **2** (*formal*) reform (a person): *a* ~*ed drunkard.* **3** recover extract from waste material.

rec·la·ma·tion /ˌrekləˈmeiʃən/ *n* [U]

re·cline /rɪˈklain/ *vi,vt* lie back or down: *reclining on a couch/in a chair.*

re·cluse /ˈreˌklus, ˌriˈklus/ *n* [C] person who lives alone and avoids other people.

rec·og·ni·tion /ˌrekəgˈnɪʃən/ *n* [U] **1** recognizing or being recognized: *Recognition of the new state is unlikely,* it is unlikely that diplomatic relations will be established with it. **2** act of acknowledgment. **3** favorable attention or notice.

rec·og·nize /ˈrekəgˌnaiz/ *vt* **1** know, (be able to) identify again (a person or thing) that one has seen, heard, etc before: ~ *a tune/an old friend.* **2** be willing to accept the status or existence of: *refuse to* ~ *a new government.* **3** be prepared to admit; acknowledge: *He* ~*d that he was not qualified for the post/*~*d his lack of qualifications. Everyone* ~*d him to be the greatest living poet.* **4** acknowledge as an acquaintance. **5** acknowledge as a person who is permitted to speak at a meeting.

rec·og·niz·able /-əbəl/ *adj* that can be identified.

rec·og·niz·ably /-əbli/ *adv*

re·coil /rɪˈkɔiəl/ *vi* (*pres p* ~ing /rɪˈkɔilɪŋ/) **1** draw or shrink back from: ~ *from doing something* (in fear, horror, disgust, etc). **2** move or spring back. **3** (*fig*) return: *Revenge may* ~ *on the person who takes it.* □ /ˈriˌkɔiəl/ *n* [C] act of recoiling.

rec·ol·lect /ˌrekəˈlekt/ *vt,vi* remember: ~ *childhood days; as far as I* ~.

rec·ol·lec·tion /ˌrekəˈlekʃən/ *n* **1** [U] act or power of recollecting: *to the best of my* ~, if I remember correctly. **2** [U] time over which the memory goes back: *Such a problem has never arisen within my* ~. **3** [C] that which is remembered: *The old letters brought many* ~*s of my father.*

rec·om·mend /ˌrekəˈmend/ *vt* **1** speak favorably of; say that one thinks something is good (for a purpose) or that a person is suitable (for a post, etc as): *I can* ~ *this soap. He has been* ~*ed as a typist.* **2** suggest as wise or suitable; advise: *Do you* ~ *lowering the voting age?* **3** make pleasing or acceptable: *Behavior of that sort will not* ~ *you.*

rec·om·men·da·tion /ˌrekəmenˈdeiʃən/ *n* **(a)** [U] recommending: *buy it on the* ~*ation of a friend.* **(b)** [C] something recommended: *The jury brought in a verdict of guilty, with a* ~*ation of mercy.* **(c)** [C] something which recommends: *Will he get a* ~*ation for that job?*

rec·om·pense /ˈrekəmˌpens/ *vt* **1** reward or pay. **2** make up for: ~ *a person for losing his pen.* □ *n* [C,U] **1** reward; payment: *work hard without* ~. **2** repayment.

rec·on·cile /ˈrekənˌsaiəl/ *vt* (*pres p* reconciling /-ˌsailɪŋ/) **1** cause (persons) to become friends after they have quarreled: *He refused to become* ~*d with his brother.* **2** settle, end (a quarrel, difference of opinion, etc). **3** cause to agree with: *I can't* ~ *what you say with the facts of the case.* **4** overcome one's objections to; resign oneself to: *You must* ~ *yourself to a life of hardship and poverty.*

rec·on·cil·able /ˈrekənˌsailəbəl/ *adj*

rec·on·cili·ation /ˌrekənˌsɪliˈeiʃən/ *n* **(a)** [U] reconciling or being reconciled. **(b)** [C] instance of this: *bring about a reconciliation between friends who have quarreled.*

re·con·di·tion /ˌrikənˈdɪʃən/ *vt* put into good condition again: *a car with a* ~*ed engine.*

re·con·nais·sance /rɪˈkanəsəns/ *n* [C] preliminary survey of an area, made esp to get information about an enemy's position, activity, etc.

re·con·noiter /ˌrekəˈnɔitər/ *vt,vi* make reconnaissance of: ~ *the area.*

re·con·struct /ˌrikənˈstrəkt/ *vt* **1** construct again. **2** build up a complete structure or description of (something of which one has only a few parts or only partial evidence): *The detective tried to* ~ *the crime,* picture to himself how it had been committed.

re·con·struc·tion /ˌrikənˈstrəkʃən/ *n* [C,U] **1** act, result of reconstructing. **2** **Reconstruction,** the period (1865-77) of Federal occupation and radical reform in the states of the former Confederacy following the US Civil War.

rec·ord[1] /ˈrekərd/ *n* **1** [C] written account of facts, events, etc: *a* ~ *of school attendances/of road accidents.* **2** [U] state of being recorded or preserved in writing, esp as authentic evidence:

a matter of ~, something that is established as fact. ***off the record,*** (*informal*) not for publication: *What the President said at his press conference was off the* ~, not to be repeated by the newspaper men there, and not to be used in their reports or articles. **3** [C] facts known about the past of a person or something: *He has an honorable* ~ *of service/a good* ~. *That airline has a bad* ~, eg has had many accidents to its aircraft. **4** [C] something that provides evidence or information: *Our museums are full of* ~*s of past history*. **5** [C] disc on which sound has been registered: *ˈphonograph* ~*s*. ⇨ recording. **6** [C] limit, score, point, mark, etc (high or low), not reached before; (esp in sports) the best yet done: *Which country holds the* ~ *for the 5,000 meters race?* (as an *adjective*) *There was a* ~ *rice crop in Thailand that year*. ***break/beat the record,*** do better than has been done before.

ˈrecord-breaking *adj* surpassing previous accomplishments.

ˈrecord player, instrument for reproducing sound from discs.

re·cord[2] /rɪˈkɔrd/ *vt* **1** preserve for use or for reference, by writing or in other ways, eg on tape, film, etc: *This volume* ~*s the history of the regiment. The program was* ~*ed*. **2** (of an instrument) mark or show on a scale: *The thermometer* ~*ed 40°C*.

re·corder /rɪˈkɔrdər/ *n* [C] **1** apparatus that records: *a ˈtape recorder*. **2** wooden musical instrument resembling a flute. ⇨ illus at brass.

re·cord·ing /rɪˈkɔrdɪŋ/ *n* [C] something recorded on a disc, magnetic tape, film, etc for reproduction: *made a* ~ *of the performance*.

re·count[1] /rɪˈkaunt/ *vt* (*formal*) give a description of; tell: *He* ~*ed to them the story of his adventures in Mexico*.

re·count[2] /ˌriˈkaunt/ *vt* count again: ~ *the votes*. □ *n* [C] /ˈriˌkaunt/ another count: *One of the candidates demanded a* ~.

re·coup /rɪˈkup/ *vt* **1** make up for: ~ *one's losses*. **2** repay.

re·course /ˈriˌkɔrs/ *n* (*formal*) [U] **1** turning to for help: *I still have* ~ *to the law*. **2** source of help: *Your only* ~ *is legal action against them*.

re·cover /rɪˈkəvər/ *vt,vi* **1** get back (something lost, etc); get back the use of: ~ *what was lost;* ~ *consciousness* (after fainting); ~ *one's sight/hearing*. **2** become well; get back to a former position of prosperity, state of health, mental condition, etc: *He is slowly* ~*ing from his illness. Has the country* ~*ed from the effects of the war yet?* **3** get control of oneself again; become calm or normal: *He almost fell, but quickly* ~*ed* (*himself*).

re·cover·able /-əbəl/ *adj* that can be recovered (1): *Is the deposit I've paid* ~*able?*

re·cov·ery *n* [C,U] (*pl* -ies) (instance of) recovering: *make a quick recovery*, get well again quickly or quickly regain one's position after losing for a time in a game, athletic match, etc.

re-cover /ˌriˈkəvər/ *vt* supply with a new cover: *This chair needs to be* ~*ed*.

recpt. *abbr* = receipt.

rec·re·ation /ˌrekriˈeiʃən/ *n* [C,U] (form of) play or amusement; refreshment of body and mind; something that pleasantly occupies one's time after work is done: *walk and climb mountains for* ~.

rec·re·ational /-nəl/ *adj*

re·crimi·nate /rɪˈkrɪməˌneit/ *vi* accuse (a person) in return: ~ *against my sister*.

re·crimi·na·tion /rɪˌkrɪməˈneiʃən/ *n* [C,U] (act of) recriminating.

re·crimi·na·tory /rɪˈkrɪmənəˌtɔri/ *adj* of recrimination.

re·cruit /rɪˈkrut/ *n* [C] new member of a society, group, etc, esp a soldier in the early days of his training: *gain a few* ~*s to one's political party*. □ *vt,vi* get new members for: *a ˈ*~*ing officer*.

rec·tal /ˈrektəl/ *adj* (*anat*) of the rectum.

rec·tangle /ˈrekˌtæŋgəl/ *n* [C] flat shape with four sides and four right angles, esp one with adjacent sides unequal. ⇨ illus at geometry.

rec·tangu·lar /rekˈtæŋgyələr/ *adj*

rec·tify /ˈrektəˌfai/ *vt* (*pt,pp* -ied) **1** put right; take out mistakes from: *mistakes that cannot be rectified*. **2** purify or refine by repeated distillation or other process: *rectified spirits*.

rec·ti·lin·ear /ˌrektəˈlɪniər/ *adj* in or forming a straight line; bounded by, characterized by, straight lines.

rec·tor /ˈrektər/ *n* [C] **1** clergyman in charge of a parish in the Protestant Episcopal Church. **2** head of certain universities, colleges, schools or religious institutions.

rec·tory /ˈrektəri/ *n* [C] (*pl* -ies) rector's residence.

rec·tum /ˈrektəm/ *n* [C] (*pl* ~s) (*anat*) lower and final part of the large intestine.

re·cum·bent /rɪˈkəmbənt/ *adj* (*formal*) (esp of a person) lying down: *a* ~ *figure on a tomb*.

re·cu·per·ate /rɪˈkupəˌreit/ *vt,vi* make or become strong again after illness, exhaustion or loss: ~ *one's health; go to the seashore in order to* ~.

re·cu·per·ation /rɪˌkupəˈreiʃən/ *n* [U] recuperating.

re·cu·per·at·ive /rɪˈkupəˌreitɪv/ *adj* helping, relating to, recuperation.

re·cur /rɪˈkər/ *vi* (-rr-) **1** come, happen, again; be repeated: *a problem which* ~*s frequently*. **2** come back to the mind: *My first meeting with her often* ~*s to me/my memory*.

re·cur·rence /rɪˈkərəns/ *n* [C,U] repetition: *Let there be no* ~*rence of this error*.

re·cur·rent /-ənt/ *adj* (of events, fevers etc) happening again frequently or regularly.

re·cycle /ˌriˈsaikəl/ *vt* treat (substances already used for industry, waste materials, etc) so that further use is possible: ~ *waste paper*.

red /red/ *adj* (-dder, -ddest) **1** of the color of fresh blood or rubies: *red with anger/embarrassment*, flushed in the face; *eyes red with weeping*. ***paint the town ˈred,*** go on a spree. ***see red,*** become angry. **2 Red** (*informal, dated*) **(a)** Russian; Soviet. **(b)** Communist. □ *n* **1** [C,U] (shade of) red color: *the reds and browns of the woods in autumn*. **2 Red** [C] (*informal, dated*) (esp) person favoring or supporting Communism. **3** ***in the red,*** in debt; at a loss.

ˈred·breast *n* [C] bird, such as a robin having a red breast.

ˈ**red·cap** *n* railroad porter.
ˌ**red ˈcent** (only in) ***not worth a red cent,*** (*informal*) worthless.
ˈ**red·coat** *n* [C] (*informal*) (name for) British soldiers, during the American Revolution.
ˌ**Red ˈCross,** (emblem of the) international organization concerned with the relief of suffering caused by natural disasters, etc and for helping the sick and wounded and those taken prisoner in war.
red ˈdeer (*pl* ~) kind of deer native to the forests of Europe and Asia.
ˌ**red-ˈhanded** *adv* in the act of doing something wrong.
ˈ**red·head** *n* [C] person having red hair.
ˌ**red ˈherring,** (esp) something irrelevant used to take attention from the subject being discussed.
ˌ**red-ˈhot** *adj* **(a)** glowing with heat. **(b)** highly excited, furious. **(c)** (*informal*) very fresh or recent.
ˌ**red-ˈletter** *adj* memorable because something good happened: *a red-letter day.*
red-ˈlight district, area, in city, where many brothels are located.
ˈ**red·neck,** (esp narrow-minded) rural white of southern US.
ˌ**red ˈpepper** *n* [U] cayenne pepper.
ˈ**red·skin** *n* [C] (*informal, old use*) North American Indian.
ˌ**red ˈtape** *n* [U] excessive use of formalities in public business; too much attention to rules and regulations: *red tape in government offices.*
ˌ**red ˈtide,** seawater colored red by toxic algae.
red·den /ˈredən/ *vt,vi* make or become red; blush.
red·dish /ˈredɪʃ/ *adj* rather red.
re·deem /rɪˈdim/ *vt* **1** get (something) back by payment or by doing something: *~ a mortgage; ~ one's honor.* **2** perform (a promise or obligation). **3** set free by payment: *~ a slave/prisoner.* **4** compensate: *his ~ing feature,* the feature or quality that balances his faults, etc.
re·deem·able /-əbəl/ *adj*
the Redeemer *n* (in the Christian religion) Jesus Christ.
re·demp·tion /rɪˈdempʃən/ *n* [U] (*formal*) redeeming or being redeemed: *the ~ of a promise; past/beyond ~,* too bad to be rescued from being evil.
re·do /ˌriˈdu/ *vt* (*pt* -did /-ˈdɪd/, *pp* -done /-ˈdən/) do again, esp redecorate.
redo·lent /ˈredələnt/ *adj* (*formal*) having a strong smell, esp one that recalls something: *bed sheets ~ of lavender.*
re·double /ˌriˈdəbəl/ *vt,vi* make or become twice as great: *They ~d their efforts.*
re·dress /rɪˈdres/ *vt* set (a wrong) right again; make up for, do something that compensates for (a wrong): *You should confess and ~ your errors.* ***redress the balance,*** make things equal again. □ *n* [U] /rɪˈdres, ˈriˌdres/ **1** redressing. **2** compensation or satisfaction for a wrong.
re·duce /rɪˈdus/ *vt,vi* **1** make less; make smaller in weight, size, number, degree, price, etc: *reducing speed/pressure/costs; ~ one's expenses/weight.* **2** bring or get to a certain condition, way of living, etc: *~ a class of noisy children to order; ~ him to silence,* cause him to stop talking. *They were ~d to begging,* They became so poor that they had to beg. **3** (*math*) change to a simpler form without changing value: *~ a fraction.*
re·duc·ible /-əbəl/ *adj*
re·duc·tion /rɪˈdəkʃən/ *n* **1** [U] reducing or being reduced. **2** [C] instance of this: *a ~ in numbers; price ~s.* **3** [C] copy, on a smaller scale, of a picture, map, etc.
re·dun·dancy /rɪˈdəndənsi/ *n* (*pl* -ies) **1** [U] being redundant. **2** [C] instance of this: *a great many redundancies in his instructions.*
re·dun·dant /rɪˈdəndənt/ *adj* **1** more than is needed. **2** containing more words than is necessary.
reed /rid/ *n* [C] **1** (tall, firm stem or stalk of) kinds of coarse grasses growing in or near water. **2** (in some wind instruments, eg the oboe, bassoon, clarinet and in some organ pipes) strip of metal, etc that vibrates to produce sound. ⇨ illus at brass.
reef[1] /rif/ *n* [C] that part of a sail which can be rolled up or folded so as to reduce its area. □ *vt* reduce the area of (a sail) by rolling up or folding a part.
reef[2] /rif/ *n* [C] ridge of rock, coral, etc just below or above the surface of the sea: *a coral ~.*
reefer /ˈrifər/ *n* [C] (*sl*) marijuana cigarette.
reek /rik/ *n* [U] strong, bad smell: *the ~ of stale tobacco smoke.* □ *vi* smell unpleasantly: *He ~s of whiskey/garlic.*
reel[1] /ˈriəl/ *n* [C] **1** cylinder, roller or similar device on which thread, wire, photographic film, magnetic tape, hose (for water, etc), etc is wound. **2** amount, eg of film, rolled on one reel. □ *vt* (*pres p* ~ing /ˈrilɪŋ/) **1** roll or wind (thread, a fishing line, etc) on to, or with the help of, a reel: *~ in the fish.* **2** ***reel sth off,*** tell, say or repeat something without pause or apparent effort: *~ off a list of names.*
reel[2] /ˈriəl/ *vi* (*pres p* ~ing /ˈrilɪŋ/) **1** be shaken (physically or mentally) by a blow, a shock, rough treatment, etc: *His mind ~ed when he heard the news.* **2** walk or stand unsteadily, moving from side to side; sway: *He ~ed like a drunken man.* **3** appear to move, sway or shake: *The street ~ed before his eyes when the bike hit him.*
reel[3] /ˈriəl/ *n* [C] (music for a) lively country dance, usually for two or more couples.
re·en·try /ˌriˈentri/ *n* [C] (*pl* -ies) act of entering again, eg return of a spacecraft into the earth's atmosphere.
ref.[1] *abbr* = **1** referee. **2** reference.
ref[2] /ref/ *n* [C] (*informal*) referee. □ *vt, vi* (-ff-) (*informal*) referee.
re·fec·tory /rɪˈfektəri/ *n* [C] (*pl* -ies) dining hall (in a monastery or college).
re·fer /rɪˈfər/ *vt,vi* (-rr-) **1** send, take, hand over (to, back to, a person or thing) for help, information, etc: *The dispute was ~red to the United Nations. I was ~red to the Manager.* **2** speak about; apply to: *When I said that some people are stupid I wasn't ~ring to you. Does that remark ~ to me?* **3** turn to, go to, for information, etc: *The speaker often ~red to his notes.* **4**

credit, attribute (the more usual words): *He ~red his success to the good teaching he'd had.*
ref·er·able /ˈref(ə)rəbəl, rɪˈfərəbəl/ *adj*

ref·eree /ˌrefəˈri/ *n* [C] **1** person to whom disputes, eg in industry, between workers and employers, are referred for decision. **2** (*sport*) person who enforces the rules, judges points in dispute, etc. ⇨ umpire. □ *vt,vi* act as a referee: *~ a football game.*

ref·er·ence /ˈrefrəns/ *n* **1** [C,U] (instance of) referring: *The book is full of ~s to places that I know well.* **2** [C] (person who can give a) statement about a person's character or abilities: *The clerk has excellent ~s from former employers.* **3** [C] note, direction, etc telling where certain information may be found: *He dislikes history books that are crowded with ~s to earlier authorities.* **4** [U] ***in/with reference to,*** concerning; about.
ˈreference book, one that is not read through but consulted for information, eg a dictionary or encyclopedia.

ref·er·en·dum /ˌrefəˈrendəm/ *n* [C] (*pl* ~s, -da /-də/) the referring of a political question to a direct vote of the electorate.

re·fill /ˌriˈfɪl/ *vt* fill again. □ *n* [C] /ˈriˌfɪl/ something that refills: *two ~s for a ballpoint pen.*

re·fine /rɪˈfain/ *vt,vi* **1** free from other substances; make or become pure: *~ sugar/oil/ores.* **2** cause to become more cultured or polished: *~d language/manners/speech/taste.*

re·fine·ment /rɪˈfainmənt/ *n* **1** [U] refining or being refined. **2** [U] purity of feeling, taste, language, etc. **3** [C] feature which refines.

re·finer /rɪˈfainər/ *n* [C] **1** person whose business is to refine something: *ˈsugar ~.* **2** machine for refining metals, sugar, etc.
re·finery /-nəri/ *n* [C] place, building, etc where something is refined: *a ˈsugar ~y.*

re·flect /rɪˈflekt/ *vt,vi* **1** (of a surface) throw back (light, heat, sound). **2** send back an image of: *Look at the trees ~ed in the lake. The sight of my face ~ed in the mirror never pleases me.* **3** show; reveal: *Her sad looks ~ed the thoughts passing through her mind.* **4** (of actions, results) bring (credit or discredit on): *The results ~ the greatest credit on all concerned. Your rude behavior ~s only on yourself,* you are the only person whose reputation is hurt by it. **5** consider; think: *I must ~ on/upon what answer to give/how to answer that question.*

re·flec·tion /rɪˈflekʃən/ *n* **1** [U] reflecting or being reflected: *the ~ of heat.* **2** [C] something reflected, esp an image reflected in a mirror or in water. **3** [U] thought (the usual word): *be lost in ~.* ***on reflection,*** after reconsidering the matter. **4** [C] expression of a thought in speech or writing: *~s on the pleasures of being idle.* **5** [C] something that brings discredit: *This is a ~ on your honor.*

re·flec·tor /rɪˈflektər/ *n* [C] something that reflects heat, light or sound, esp a piece of glass or metal for reflecting light, etc in a required direction.

re·flex[1] /ˈriˌfleks/ *n* [C] **1** reflection, esp an image made by reflection. **2** (power of) involuntary response to a stimulation of the nerves, eg sneezing: *test one's ~es.*
reflex angle *n* [C] one that is bigger than 180°.

re·flex.[2] *abbr* = reflexive.

re·flex·ive /rɪˈfleksɪv/ *adj, n* [C] (*gram*) (of a) word or form showing that the subject's action is on himself or itself: *a ~ pronoun,* eg myself, themselves; *a ~ verb,* showing that the subject and object are the same, as in: *He cut himself.*

re·form /rɪˈfɔrm/ *vt,vi* make or become better by removing or putting right what is bad or wrong: *~ a sinner/one's character/the world.* □ *n* **1** [U] reforming; removal of vices, imperfections, etc: *demonstrate for social or political ~.* **2** [C] instance of reform: *a ~ in teaching methods.*
re·former *n* [C]

ref·or·ma·tion /ˌrefərˈmeiʃən/ *n* **1** [U] reforming or being reformed. **2** [C] radical change for the better in social, political or religious affairs. **3** **the Reformation,** the 16th-century movement for reform of the Roman Catholic Church, resulting in the establishment of the Protestant Churches.

re·fract /rɪˈfrækt/ *vt* cause (a ray of light) to bend when it enters a different medium: *Light is ~ed when it passes through a prism.*
re·frac·tion /rɪˈfrækʃən/ *n* [U]

re·frain[1] /rɪˈfrein/ *n* [C] (*formal*) = chorus(2).

re·frain[2] /rɪˈfrein/ *vi* (*formal*) hold oneself back from doing something: *Please ~ from smoking/swearing.*

re·fresh /rɪˈfreʃ/ *vt* **1** revive; make fresh again: *~ oneself with a warm bath.* **2** ***refresh one's memory,*** remember by referring to notes, etc.
re·fresh·ing *adj* **1** strengthening; giving rest and relief: *a ~ing breeze/sleep.* **2** welcome and interesting because rare or unexpected: *The news that the children were doing things to help the old man was ~ing.*

re·fresh·ment /rɪˈfreʃmənt/ *n* **1** [U] refreshing or being refreshed: *feel ~ of mind and body.* **2** (*pl*) food and drink: *Refreshments were provided for the volunteers.*

re·frig·er·ate /rɪˈfrɪdʒəˌreit/ *vt* make cool or cold; keep (food) in good condition by making and keeping it cold.
re·frig·er·ation /rɪˌfrɪdʒəˈreiʃən/ *n* [U]
re·frig·er·ator /rɪˈfrɪdʒəˌreitər/ *n* [C] apparatus in which food and drinks are kept cold.

re·fuel /ˌriˈfyuəl/ *vt* (-l-, -ll-) supply with, take on, more fuel.

ref·uge /ˈreˌfyudʒ/ *n* [C,U] (place giving) shelter or protection from trouble, danger, pursuit, etc: *seek ~ from the floods.*

refu·gee /ˈrefyəˌdʒi/ *n* [C] (esp) person who has been forced to flee from his country because of war, political persecution, etc.

re·fund /ˌriˈfənd/ *vt* pay back (money): *~ the cost of postage.* □ *n* /ˈriˌfənd/ [C] repayment: *obtain a ~ of a deposit/of $20.*

re·fur·bish /ˌriˈfərbɪʃ/ *vt* make clean or bright again, (as if) like new.

re·fusal /rɪˈfyuzəl/ *n* **1** [U] act of refusing. **2** [C] instance of this: *We were surprised at his ~ to do what I asked.*

ref·use[1] /ˈreˌfyus/ *n* [U] waste or worthless objects, materials, etc (to be burned, etc).

re·fuse[2] /rɪˈfyuz/ *vt,vi* **1** say "no" to (a request);

deny: ~ *permission. I* ~! **2** show unwillingness to accept (something offered); reject: ~ *a gift*. **3** decline to do (something): ~ *to help*.

re·fute /rɪˈfyut/ *vt* prove (a person, statements, opinions, etc) to be wrong or mistaken: ~ *an argument/an opponent*.

refu·ta·tion /ˌrefyəˈteiʃən/ *n* [U]

reg. *abbr* = **1** regiment. **2** region. **3** register. **4** regular. **5** regulation.

re·gain /ˌriˈgein/ *vt* **1** get possession of again: ~ *consciousness;* ~ *one's freedom*. **2** get back to (a place or position): ~ *one's footing*, recover one's balance after slipping or falling.

re·gal /ˈrigəl/ *adj* of, for, fit for, by, a monarch; ~ *dignity/splendor/power*.

re·gally /-gəli/ *adv*

re·gale /rɪˈgeiəl/ *vt* (*pres p* regaling /-ˈgeilɪŋ/) (*formal*) entertain or treat (as by a feast): *regaling themselves on caviar and champagne*.

re·galia /rɪˈgeiəlyə, rɪˈgeiliə/ *n pl* (often used with a *sing verb*) **1** emblems (crown, orb, scepter, etc) of royalty. **2** emblems or decorations of rank, office, etc. **3** special or fancy clothes.

re·gard[1] /rɪˈgard/ *n* **1** [U] attention; concern; consideration: *He has very little* ~ *for the feelings of others. More* ~ *must be paid to safety on the roads*. **2** [U] esteem; respect: *hold a person in high/low* ~. **3** (*pl*) kindly thoughts and wishes: *Please give my kind* ~*s to your brother* (eg at the end of a letter). **4** gaze; look: *He turned his* ~ *on the accused man*. ***5 in/with regard to,*** with respect to; concerning.

re·gard·less *adj* paying no attention: ~*less of expense*.

re·gard[2] /rɪˈgard/ *vt* **1** look at steadily: ~ *her with interest*. **2** consider (a person) to be: *He is* ~*ed as a fool*. **3** esteem. **4** pay attention to: *He never* ~*s my advice*. ***as regards,*** with reference to; about.

re·gard·ing *prep* concerning.

re·gatta /rɪˈgætə/ *n* [C] (*pl* ~s) boat race or series of boat races.

re·gency /ˈridʒənsi/ *n* [C] (*pl* -ies) (period of) office of a regent.

re·gen·er·ate /rɪˈdʒenəˌreit/ *vt,vi* **1** reform spiritually or morally. **2** give new strength or life to. **3** grow again.

re·gen·er·ation /rɪˌdʒenəˈreiʃən/ *n* [U]

re·gent /ˈridʒənt/ *n* [C] **1** member of a governing board (eg of a state university). **2** person appointed to perform the duties of a ruler who is unable to rule because of youth, illness, absence, etc.

re·gime, ré·gime /reiˈʒim, ˌreˈʒim/ *n* [C] **1** method or system of government or of administration: *under the old* ~, before the changes were made, etc. **2** = regimen.

regi·men /ˈredʒəmən/ *n* [C] set of rules for diet, exercise, etc for improving one's health and physical well-being.

regi·ment /ˈredʒəmənt/ *n* [C] military unit made up of several battalions and usually commanded by a colonel. □ *vt* organize rigidly for the sake of conformity.

regi·men·tal /ˌredʒəˈmentəl/ *adj* of a regiment: *a* ~ *badge*. □ *n* (*pl*) military uniform.

re·gion /ˈridʒən/ *n* [C] **1** area or division with or without definite boundaries or characteristics: *the ˈArctic* ~*s; the densely populated* ~*s of the United States*. **2** area or part of the body: *a pain in the* ~ *of the abdomen*.

re·gional /-nəl/ *adj* of a region or regions.

re·gion·ally /-nəli/ *adv*

reg·is·ter[1] /ˈredʒɪstər/ *n* [C] **1** (book containing a) record or list. **2** (part of the) range of the human voice or of a musical instrument: *the lower* ~ *of the clarinet*. **3** mechanical device for indicating and recording speed, force, numbers, etc: *a cash* ~. **4** device with shutters, for regulating the flow of air.

reg·is·ter[2] /ˈredʒɪstər/ *vt,vi* **1** make an official record of, in a list: ~ *one's car*. **2** enter or cause (a name) to be entered on a register, eg at a hotel. **3** (of instruments) indicate; record: *The thermometer* ~*ed only two degrees above freezing-point*. **4** show (emotion, etc): *Her face* ~*ed surprise*. **5** make an impression: *The name just doesn't* ~. **6** record (a piece of mail) with the post office by paying an extra charge, in order to protect against loss: *Send cash by* ~*ed mail*.

reg·is·trar /ˈredʒɪˌstrar/ *n* [C] official whose duty is to keep records or registers, eg for a university.

reg·is·tra·tion /ˌredʒɪˈstreiʃən/ *n* **1** [U] registering; recording. **2** number of persons registered. **3** [C] entry in a register. **4** document which certifies registration: *an automobile* ~.

reg·is·try /ˈredʒɪstri/ *n* (*pl* -ies) **1** [C] (sometimes **register**) place where registers are kept. **2** [U] = registration(1).

re·gress /rɪˈgres/ *vi* return to an earlier state: ~ *mentally/culturally*.

re·gres·sion /rɪˈgreʃən/ *n* [C,U]

re·gret[1] /rɪˈgret/ *n* **1** [U] feeling of sorrow or sadness; sense of loss or disappointment: *hear with* ~ *that a friend is ill. Much to my* ~ *I am unable to accept your kind invitation*. **2** (*pl*) polite refusal of an invitation: *sent her* ~*s*.

re·gret·ful /-fəl/ *adj* sad; sorry.

re·gret·fully /-fəli/ *adv* sadly; with regret.

re·gret[2] /rɪˈgret/ *vt* (-tt-) **1** be sorry for the loss of: ~ *lost opportunities*. **2** feel sorry for; be sorry: *I* ~ *(to say) that I cannot help*.

re·gret·table /-əbəl/ *adj* to be regretted: ~*table failures*.

re·gret·tably /-əbli/ *adv*

reg·ular /ˈregyələr/ *adj* **1** evenly arranged; symmetrical; systematic: ~ *teeth; a* ~ *design*. **2** coming, happening, done, again and again at fixed intervals: *keep* ~ *hours*, eg leaving and returning home, getting up and going to bed, at the same times every day. *He has no* ~ *work*, no steady occupation. **3** properly qualified or trained. **4** belonging to a full-time or standing army: ~ *soldiers*, not volunteers; *the* ~ *army*, made up of professional soldiers. **5** according to correct procedure or behavior: *I doubt whether your methods would be considered* ~ *by the Customs officials*. **6** (*gram*) (of *verbs, nouns*, etc) having normal inflections: *The verb "go" is not* ~. **7** (*informal*) thorough; complete: *He's a* ~ *nuisance*. **8** (*informal*) agreeable; likable: *a* ~ *fellow*. □ *n* [C] **1** soldier of the regular army. **2** (*informal*) frequent or steady customer or client, eg at a restaurant.

regu·lar·ity /ˌregyəˈlærəti/ *n* [U] state of being regular.

reg·ular·ly *adv*

regu·lar·ize /ˈregyələˌraiz/ *vt* make regular.

regu·lar·iz·ation /ˌregyələrəˈzeiʃən/ *n* [U]

regu·late /ˈregyəˌleit/ *vt* **1** control using rules; cause to obey a rule or standard: *~ one's expenditure; ~ the traffic.* **2** adjust (an apparatus, mechanism) so that it works properly: *~ the speed of a machine.*

regu·la·tion /ˌregyəˈleiʃən/ *n* **1** [U] regulating or being regulated: *the ~ of affairs/of a clock.* **2** [C] rule; order; authoritative direction: *ˈsafety ~s,* eg in factories; *ˈtraffic ~s,* made by the police for drivers of vehicles. □ *adj* as required by rules: *~ dress/size.*

re·gur·gi·tate /rɪˈgərdʒəˌteit/ *vi,vt* bring (swallowed food) up through the mouth; vomit.

re·gur·gi·tation /rɪˌgərdʒəˈteiʃən/ *n* [U]

re·ha·bili·tate /ˌri(h)əˈbɪləˌteit/ *vt* **1** restore (eg old buildings) to a good condition. **2** restore (a person) to former rank, position or reputation: *He has been ~d in public esteem.* **3** bring back (a person who is physically or mentally disabled) to a (more) normal life by special treatment.

re·ha·bili·ta·tion /ˌri(h)əˌbɪləˈteiʃən/ *n* [U]

re·hash /ˌriˈhæʃ/ *vt* slightly alter the form of something old or commonplace to make it appear novel. □ *n* [C] /ˈriˌhæʃ/ act or result of rehashing.

re·hearsal /rɪˈhərsəl/ *n* **1** [U] rehearsing: *put a play into ~.* **2** [C] act of rehearsing: *a ˈdress ~,* one in which the actors wear the costumes and use the props as for public performances.

re·hearse /rɪˈhərs/ *vt,vi* practice (a play, program, etc) for public performance: *rehearsing (the parts in) a play.*

reign /rein/ *n* [C] (period of) sovereignty, rule: *during five successive ~s; The American Revolution took place during the ~ of King George III.* □ *vi* **1** hold office as a monarch: *The king ~ed over the country for ten years.* **2** be predominant: *the ~ing beauty among the students. Silence ~ed everywhere.*

re·im·burse /ˌriɪmˈbərs/ *vt* pay back: *You will be ~d for your expenses.*

re·im·burse·ment *n* [C,U]

rein /rein/ *n* [C] **1** long, narrow strap fastened to the bit of a bridle for controlling a horse. **2** (*fig*) any means of restraint or control. ***give (free) rein to sb/sth,*** allow freedom to: *give free ~ to one's imagination.* ***hold/take the reins,*** (*fig*) have/take control: *hold the ~s of government.* ***keep a tight rein on sb/sth,*** allow little freedom to. □ *vt* control (as) with reins: *~ in a horse,* restrain it.

re·in·car·na·tion /ˌriɪnˌkarˈneiʃən/ *n* **1** [U] rebirth after death, in another (human or animal) body. **2** [C] instance of this.

rein·deer /ˈreinˌdɪr/ *n* [C] (*pl* ~) kind of large deer with branched antlers, native to Greenland and northern Europe, used for transport, food etc. ⇨ illus at animal.

re·in·force /ˌriɪnˈfɔrs/ *vt* **1** make stronger by adding or supplying more men or material: *~ an army/a fleet.* **2** strengthen by increasing the size, thickness, etc of something: *~ a bridge.*

re·in·force·ment *n* **(a)** [U] reinforcing or being reinforced. **(b)** [C] (often *pl*) (esp) soldiers, ships, etc sent to reinforce.

re·in·state /ˌriɪnˈsteit/ *vt* restore (a person) to a former position or condition: *~ him as the chairman.*

re·in·state·ment *n* [C,U]

re·iter·ate /riˈɪtəˌreit/ *vt* say or do over again: *~ a command.*

re·iter·ation /ˌriˌɪtəˈreiʃən/ *n* [C,U]

re·ject[1] /rɪˈdʒekt/ *vt* **1** put aside, throw away, as not good enough to be kept: *~ fruit that is over-ripe.* **2** refuse to accept: *~ an offer of help/of marriage. The army doctors ~ed him,* would not accept him as medically fit.

re·jec·tion /rɪˈdʒekʃən/ *n* **(a)** [U] rejecting or being rejected. **(b)** [C] instance of this. **(c)** [C] something rejected.

re·ject[2] /ˈriˌdʒekt/ *n* [C] person or thing rejected.

re·joice /rɪˈdʒɔis/ *vt,vi* **1** feel great joy or happiness: *rejoicing over a victory; ~ at her success.* **2** (*liter*) make glad; cause to be happy: *The boy's success ~d his mother's heart.*

re·joic·ing *n* [U] happiness; joy.

re·join[1] /rɪˈdʒɔin/ *vt,vi* (*formal*) answer; reply.

re·join·der /-dər/ *n* [C] something said in reply.

re·join[2] /ˌriˈdʒɔin/ *vt* **1** join the company of again: *~ one's regiment/ship.* **2** join (together) again.

re·ju·ven·ate /rɪˈdʒuvəˌneit/ *vt,vi* make young or youthful again in nature or appearance.

re·ju·ven·ation /rɪˌdʒuvəˈneiʃən/ *n* [U]

re·kindle /ˌriˈkɪndəl/ *vt,vi* kindle again: *~ a fire.* (*fig*) *Our hopes ~d.*

rel. *abbr* = **1** related. **2** relating. **3** relative. **4** religion.

re·laid *pt, pp* of relay[2].

re·lapse /rɪˈlæps/ *vi* fall back again (into bad ways, error, heresy, illness, silence etc). □ *n* [C] /ˈriˌlæps/ relapsing, esp after recovering from illness: *The patient has had a major ~.*

re·late /rɪˈleit/ *vt,vi* **1** (*formal*) tell (a story); give an account of (facts, adventures etc): *He ~d to his wife some amusing stories about his employer.* **2** have or show a connection: *It is difficult to ~ these results with/to any known cause.* **3** ***relate to,*** have reference (to): *She is a girl who notices nothing except what ~s to herself.*

re·lated *adj* **(a)** connected. **(b)** connected by blood or marriage: *She says she is ~d to the president of the company.*

re·la·tion /rɪˈleiʃən/ *n* **1** [U] the act of relating (1,2) or telling: *the ~ of his adventures.* **2** [C] that which is told; tale or narrative. **3** [U] connection; association: *There was little ~ between the effort that was made and the result that was obtained.* ***in/with relation to,*** as regards; concerning. **4** (usually *pl*) dealings; affairs; what one person, group, country, etc has to do with another: *have business ~s with a firm in Stockholm; the friendly ~s between my country and yours; diplomatic ~s.* **5** [C] relative(2): *All his poor ~s came to spend their holidays at his home.* ⇨ distant(2), near[1](2).

re·la·tion·ship /rɪˈleiʃənˌʃɪp/ *n* **1** [C] association or connection between two persons, groups, etc: *a purely business ~; a lasting ~*. **2** [U] condition of belonging to the same family; being connected by birth or marriage. **3** [C] (instance of) being related: *the ~ between cause and effect*.

rela·tive /ˈrelətɪv/ *adj* **1** comparative: *the ~ advantages of gas and electricity for cooking. They are living in ~ comfort*, ie compared with other people. **2** ***relative to,*** relating to; having a connection with: *the facts ~ to this problem*. **3** (*gram*) referring to an antecedent: *a ~ pronoun*. □ *n* [C] **1** relative word, esp a pronoun. **2** person to whom one is related by blood or marriage, eg an uncle or aunt, a cousin, a nephew or niece.

relative ˈclause, one joined by a relative pronoun.

rela·tive·ly *adv* comparatively: *The matter is ~ly unimportant*.

relative ˈpronoun, pronoun which refers to an antecedent, eg "whom" in "the man whom we saw."

re·lax /rɪˈlæks/ *vt,vi* **1** (cause or allow to) become less tight, stiff, strict or rigid: *~ one's grip/hold on something; ~ing the muscles. His face ~ed in a smile*. **2** take recreation: *Let's stop working and ~ for an hour*.

re·lax·ation /ˌrilækˈseiʃən/ *n* **(a)** [U] relaxing or being relaxed: *~ation of the muscles*. **(b)** [C,U] (something done for) recreation: *Fishing is his favorite ~ation*.

re·lay[1] /ˈriˌlei/ *n* [C] **1** fresh supply, eg of men, to replace tired or worn ones: *working in/by ~s*. **2** device (as a switch) which operates another in turn. **3** (short for a) relay race. **4** act of passing (something) on. □ *vt* /rɪˈlei/ (*pt,pp* ~ed) send or pass on (as) by relays: *~ a message*.

relay race /ˈriˌlei ˌreis/ *n* [C] one between two teams, each member of the team running a certain section of the total distance.

re·lay[2] /ˌriˈlei/ *vt* (*pt,pp* -laid /-ˈleɪd/) lay (a cable, carpet, etc) again.

re·lease /rɪˈlis/ *vt* **1** allow to go; set free: *~ one's grip/a man from prison*. **2** relieve, as from a promise or obligation. **3** make available for publication, exhibition, or sale: *recently ~d films/news*. **4** give up or surrender (a right, debt, property) to another. □ *n* **1** [U] releasing or being released. **2** [C] instance of this: *an order for his ~ from prison; a ˈpress ~*, ie of a news item to the newspapers; *the newest ~es*, eg records. **3** [C] handle, lever, catch, etc that releases part of a machine: *the ˈcarriage ~ on a typewriter*.

rel·egate /ˈreləˌgeit/ *vt* **1** hand over (a duty, task, etc) to someone else. **2** dismiss to a lower position or condition: *Will our team be ~d to the second division?*

re·lent /rɪˈlent/ *vi* become less severe or strict: *At last mother ~ed and let us stay up to watch TV*.

re·lent·less *adj* without pity: *~less persecution*.

re·lent·less·ly *adv*

rel·evance /ˈreləvəns/ *n* [U] state of being relevant: *What ~ does your theory have to the facts?*

rel·evant /ˈreləvənt/ *adj* pertinent; connected with what is being considered: *have all the ~ documents ready; supply the facts ~ to the case*.

rel·evant·ly *adv*

re·li·able /rɪˈlaiəbəl/ *adj* that may be relied or depended on: *~ tools/assistants/information/witnesses*.

re·lia·bil·ity /rɪˌlaiəˈbɪləti/ *n* [U]

re·li·ably /-əbli/ *adv*

re·li·ance /rɪˈlaiəns/ *n* **1** [U] trust; confidence: *Do you place much ~ on/upon your doctor?* **2** person or thing depended on.

re·li·ant /-ənt/ *adj* trusting; relying.

relic /ˈrelɪk/ *n* [C] **1** object which is treasured or revered because it is associated with a saint or martyr. **2** something from the past that has survived: *a ~ of early civilization*.

re·lief[1] /rɪˈlif/ *n* [U] (used with the *a, an* as in examples, but not normally in the *pl*) **1** lessening, ending or removal of pain, distress, anxiety, etc: *The doctor's treatment gave/brought some/not much ~. It was a great ~ to find the children safe*. **2** help given to those in need; food, clothes, money, etc for persons in trouble: *a fund for the ~ of refugees; a ~ fund*. **3** something that makes a change from monotony or that relaxes tension: *Shakespeare introduced comic scenes into his tragedies by way of ~*. **4** help given to a besieged town; raising (of a siege): *The general hastened to the ~ of the fortress*. **5(a)** release from duty. **(b)** person or persons appointed to go on duty in place of another: (as an *adjective*) *a ~ pitcher*.

re·lief[2] /rɪˈlif/ *n* **1** [U] method of carving or molding in which a design stands out from a flat surface: *a profile carved in ~*. **2** [C] design or carving made in this way. **3** [U] (in drawing, etc) appearance of being done in relief by the use of shading, color, etc. **4** [U] vividness; distinctness of outline.

reˈlief map, map showing hills, valleys, etc by shading or other means, not only by contour lines.

re·lieve /rɪˈliv/ *vt* **1** give or bring relief[1] to; lessen or remove (pain or distress): *We were ~d to hear that you had arrived safely. The fund is for relieving distress among the flood victims*. **2** release from duty: *~ the guard/the watch/a sentry*. **3** take something from somebody: *Let me ~ you of your suitcase*. **4** make less boring: *took a walk to ~ the monotony*.

re·lig·ion /rɪˈlɪdʒən/ *n* **1** [U] belief in the existence of a supernatural power which created and controls the universe. **2** [C] one of the various systems of faith and worship based on such belief: *the great ~s of the world*, (esp) Christianity, Islam, Judaism, Hinduism, Buddhism.

re·lig·ious /rɪˈlɪdʒəs/ *adj* **1** of religion. **2** (of a person) devout; having faith. **3** of a monastic order: *a ~ house*, a monastery or convent. **4** conscientious: *do one's work with ~ care*.

re·lig·ious·ly *adv*

re·lin·quish /rɪˈlɪŋkwɪʃ/ *vt* **1** give up: *~ a hope/a habit/a belief*. **2** surrender: *~ one's rights/shares to a partner*.

rel·ish /ˈrelɪʃ/ *n* **1** [C,U] (something used to give, or which has, a) special flavor or attractive quality: *Olives and sardines are ~es. Some pastimes lose their ~ when one grows old*. **2** [U] liking (*for*): *I have no further ~ for active pursuits now that I am 90*. □ *vt* enjoy; get pleasure out of: *She won't ~ having to get up before dawn to catch* *that train.*

re·live /ˌriˈlɪv/ *vt* live through, undergo, again: *It's an experience I don't want to* ~.

re·lo·cate /ˌriˈlouˌkeit/ *vt,vi* establish, become established, in a new place or area.

re·lo·ca·tion /ˌrilouˈkeiʃən/ *n* [U]

re·luc·tance /rɪˈləktəns/ *n* [U] being reluctant.

re·luc·tant /rɪˈləktənt/ *adj* (slow to act because) unwilling or not wanting to: *He seemed* ~ *to join us.*

re·luc·tant·ly *adv*

rely /rɪˈlai/ *vi* (*pt,pp* -lied) depend (on) with confidence, trust: *He can always be relied on/upon for help.*

re·main /rɪˈmein/ *vi* **1** be still present after a part has gone or has been taken away: *After the fire, very little* ~*ed of my house. If you take 3 from 8, 5* ~*s.* **2** continue in some place or condition; continue to be: *How many weeks will you* ~ (= stay) *here? He* ~*ed silent.*

re·main·der /rɪˈmeindər/ *n* **1** [C,U] that which remains; part that is left over: *Twenty people came in and the* ~ (= the rest, the others) *stayed outside.* **2** (*math*) **(a)** in subtraction, the difference. **(b)** in division, number which is left over and cannot be divided.

re·mains /rɪˈmeinz/ *n pl* **1** what is left: *the* ~ *of a meal; ancient* ~ *of Rome.* **2** dead body; corpse: *His mortal* ~ *are buried in the churchyard.*

re·make /ˌriˈmeik/ *vt* (*pt,pp* -made /-ˈmeid/) make again. □ /ˈriˌmeik/ *n* [C] something made again: *a* ~ *of a motion picture.*

re·mand /rɪˈmænd/ *vt* send (a prisoner) back into custody until trial or for further imprisonment. □ *n* [U] remanding or being remanded.

re·mark /rɪˈmark/ *vt,vi* **1** (*formal*) notice; see: *Did you* ~ *the similarity between them?* **2** say (*that*): *He* ~*ed that he would be absent the next day.* **3** say something by way of comment: *It would be rude to* ~ *on/upon her appearance.* □ *n* **1** [U] notice; attention: *There was nothing worthy of* ~ *at the Flower Show.* **2** [C] comment: *pass rude* ~*s about her; make a few* ~*s*, give a short talk.

re·mark·able /-əbəl/ *adj* out of the ordinary; deserving or attracting attention: *a* ~*able event/boy.*

re·mark·ably /-əbli/ *adv*

re·marry /ˌriˈmæri/ *vt,vi* (*pt,pp* -ied) marry again.

re·medi·able /rɪˈmidiəbəl/ *adj* that can be remedied.

re·medial /rɪˈmidiəl/ *adj* intended to improve or remedy: ~ *reading.*

re·me·di·a·tion /rɪˌmidiˈeiʃən/ *n* [U] process of remedying.

rem·edy /ˈremədi/ *n* [C,U] (*pl* -ies) cure (for a disease, evil, etc), method of, something used for, putting right something that is wrong: *a good* ~ *for colds. Your only* ~ (= way to get satisfaction) *is to sue them.* □ *vt* (*pt,pp* -ied) put right; provide a cure for (evils, defects): *Those mistakes in your pronunciation can be remedied.*

re·mem·ber /rɪˈmembər/ *vt,vi* **1** call back to mind: *Can you* ~ *where you were? I* ~*ed* (= did not forget). **2** have, keep in the mind as a memory: *I shall always* ~ *her as a slim young girl.* **3** make a present to: *I hope you'll* ~ *me in your will*, leave me something. **4** convey greetings: *Please* ~ *me to your brother.*

re·mem·brance /rɪˈmembrəns/ *n* **1** [U] remembering or being remembered; memory: *have no* ~ *of an event; a service in* ~ *of those killed in the war.* **2** [C] something given or kept in memory of a person or thing: *He sent us a small* ~ *of his visit.* **3** (*pl*) regards; (greetings the usual words): *Give my kind* ~*s to your parents.*

re·mind /rɪˈmaind/ *vt* cause (a person) to remember to do (something, etc); cause (a person) to think of (something): *Please* ~ *me to answer that letter. He* ~*s me of his brother; that* ~*s me*, what you have just said makes me remember, I've just remembered. . ., etc.

re·minder *n* [C]

remi·nisce /ˌreməˈnɪs/ *vi* think or talk (about past events and experiences).

remi·nis·cence /ˌreməˈnɪsəns/ *n* **1** [U] recalling of past experiences. **2** (*pl*) remembered experiences (thought, spoken or written): ~*s of my days in the Navy.*

remi·nis·cent /ˌreməˈnɪsənt/ *adj* reminding one of, recalling, to the mind.

remi·nis·cent·ly *adv*

re·miss /rɪˈmɪs/ *adj* (*formal*) **1** careless: *You have been* ~ *in your duties.* **2** negligent: *That was very* ~ *of you.*

re·mis·sion /rɪˈmɪʃən/ *n* **1** [U] pardon or forgiveness (of sins). **2** [U] freeing (from debt, punishment, etc). **3** [C] instance of this. **4** [U] temporary lessening of pain, of the effects of a disease, etc.

re·mit /rɪˈmɪt/ *vt,vi* (-tt-) **1** pardon or forgive (sins). **2** excuse payment (of a debt, a punishment). **3** send (money, etc) by mail. **4** make or become less: ~ *one's efforts.* **5** lessen in intensity.

re·mit·tance /-təns/ *n* **(a)** [U] the sending of money. **(b)** [C] sum of money sent.

rem·nant /ˈremnənt/ *n* [C] **1** small part that remains: ~*s of a banquet;* ~*s of former glory.* **2** (esp) length of cloth offered at a reduced price after the greater part has been sold.

re·mon·strate /rɪˈmanˌstreit/ *vi* (*formal*) speak or argue in protest: ~ *against cruelty to children.*

re·morse /rɪˈmɔrs/ *n* [U] deep, bitter regret for doing wrong: *feel/be filled with* ~ *for one's failure to help her; in a fit of* ~*; without* ~, merciless(ly).

re·morse·ful /-fəl/ *adj* feeling remorse.

re·morse·fully /-fəli/ *adv*

re·morse·less *adj* without mercy.

re·morse·less·ly *adv*

re·mote /rɪˈmout/ *adj* (-r, -st) **1** far away in space or time: *in the* ~ *past; live in a house* ~ *from any town or village.* **2** distant in relationship: *Some of your statements are too* ~ *from the subject we are discussing.* **3** distant in manner. **4** (often in the *superlative*) slight: *a* ~ *possibility. I haven't the* ~*st idea of what you mean.*

remote conˈtrol, control of apparatus, eg an aircraft, a rocket, from a distance.

re·mote·ly *adv*

re·mote·ness /-nɪs/ *n* [U]

re·mount /ˌriˈmaunt/ *vt,vi* (esp) get on (a horse,

bicycle, etc) again.

re·moval /rɪˈmuvəl/ *n* **1** [U] act of removing. **2** [C] instance of removal.

re·move /rɪˈmuv/ *vt,vi* **1** take off or away (from the place occupied): ~ *the cloth from the table.* **2** get rid of: ~ *doubts/fears. What do you advise for removing grease/ink stains from clothes?* **3** dismiss from office: ~ *a judge.* □ *n* [C] distance or degree of separation.

re·mov·able /-əbəl/ *adj* that can be removed.

re·mun·er·ate /rɪˈmyunəˌreit/ *vt* (*formal*) pay (a person) (for work or services); reward.

re·mun·er·ation /rɪˌmyunəˈreiʃən/ *n* [C,U] (*formal*) payment; reward.

re·mun·er·ative /rɪˈmyunəˌreitɪv/ *adj* profitable (the usual word).

re·nais·sance /ˈrenəˌsans/ *n* **1 the Renaissance,** (period of the) revival of classical art and literature in Europe in the 14th, 15th and 16th centuries: (as an *adjective*) ~ *art.* **2** [C] any similar revival.

re·nal /ˈrinəl/ *adj* (*anat*) of or in the (region of the) kidneys: ~ *artery.*

re·nas·cent /rɪˈnæsənt/ *adj* reviving; being reborn.

rend /rend/ *vt* (*pt,pp* rent /rent/) (*liter*) **1** pull or tear apart forcibly: *a country rent* (*in two*) *by civil war.* (*fig*) *Loud cries rent the air.* **2** remove by force: *Children were rent from their mothers' arms by the brutal soldiers.*

ren·der /ˈrendər/ *vt* **1** give in return or exchange: ~ *thanks to God;* ~ *good for evil.* **2** give; contribute: ~ *help to those in need;* ~ *a service to him/*~ *him a service.* **3** present; offer; send in (an account for payment): *You will have to* ~ *an account of your expenditure.* **4** hand down: ~ *a judgment.* **5** cause to be or become: *be* ~*ed helpless by an accident.* **6** give a performance of: *The piano solo was well* ~*ed.* **7** translate: *There are many English idioms that cannot be* ~*ed into other languages.* **8** melt down: ~ *down fat/lard.*

ren·dez·vous /ˈrandɪˌvu/ *n* (*pl* ~ /-ˌvuz/) [C] **1** (place decided on for a) meeting at a time agreed on. **2** place where people often meet: *This café is a* ~ *for writers and artists.* □ *vi* meet at a rendezvous.

ren·di·tion /renˈdɪʃən/ *n* [C] (*formal*) interpretation or performance (*of* a song, etc).

ren·egade /ˈrenəˌgeid/ *n* [C] person who deserts a faith, cause, political party, etc; traitor.

re·new /rɪˈnu/ *vt* **1** make (as good as) new; put new life and vigor into; restore to the original condition: ~ *acquaintance with an old friend; begin again with* ~*ed enthusiasm.* **2** get, make, say or give, again: ~ *an offer.* **3** continue in force: ~ *a lease/contract;* ~ *one's subscription to a periodical.* **4** replace (with the same sort of thing, etc): *We must* ~ *our supplies of coal.*

re·new·able /-əbəl/ *adj* that can be renewed: *Is the lease* ~*able?*

re·newal /-əl/ *n* **(a)** [U] renewing or being renewed: *urban* ~*al,* eg the provision of better housing, etc. **(b)** [C] something renewed, eg an insurance policy.

re·nounce /rɪˈnauns/ *vt* **1** declare formally that one will give up, resign, or abandon: ~ *one's faith/one's family;* ~ *one's claim to an inheritance.* **2** refuse to recognize: *He* ~*d his sons because they were criminals.*

reno·vate /ˈrenəˌveit/ *vt* restore to a good or strong condition.

reno·va·tion /ˌrenəˈveiʃən/ *n* [C,U]

re·nown /rɪˈnaun/ *n* [U] fame: *win* ~*; a man of high* ~.

re·nowned *adj* famous; celebrated: *He was* ~*ed for his skill.*

rent[1] /rent/ *n* [C,U] regular payment for the use of land, a building, a room or rooms, machinery, etc; sum of money paid in this way: *You owe me three weeks'* ~. □ *vt,vi* **1** occupy or use (land, buildings, etc) for rent: *We don't own our house, we* ~ *it.* **2** allow (land, buildings, etc) to be used or occupied in return for rent: *He* ~*s this office to us for $100 a week.* **3** be for rent.

rent·able /-əbəl/ *adj*

rent·al /ˈrentəl/ *n* [C] amount of rent paid or received.

rent[2] /rent/ *n* [C] **1** torn place in cloth, etc: *a* ~ *in the shirt.* **2** (*fig*) division or split (in a political party, etc).

rent[3] *pt,pp* of rend.

re·nunci·ation /rɪˌnənsiˈeiʃən/ *n* [U] renouncing.

re·open /ˌriˈoupən/ *vt,vi* open again after closing or being closed: ~ *a shop;* ~ *a discussion; School* ~*s on Monday.*

re·or·gan·ize /riˈɔrgəˌnaiz/ *vt,vi* organize again or in a new way.

Rep. *abbr* = **1** Representative. **2** Republican.

re·pair[1] /rɪˈper/ *vt* **1** restore (something worn or damaged) to good condition: ~ *the roads/a watch.* **2** put right again: ~ *an error.* □ *n* **1** [U] repairing or being repaired: *road under* ~. **2** (*sing* or *pl* but not with *a, an*) work or process of repairing: *The shop will be closed during* ~*s.* **3** [U] condition for using or being used: *The machine is in a bad state of* ~*/in good* ~.

re·pair·able /-əbəl/ *adj* that can be repaired.

re·pair·man /rɪˈperˌmæn/ *n* [C] (*pl* ~men /-ˌmen/) one who works at repairing things.

re·pair[2] /rɪˈper/ *vi* (*formal*) (esp) go: ~ *to the seaside for the summer.*

rep·a·ration /ˌrepəˈreiʃən/ *n* **1** [U] act of compensating for loss or damage. **2** (*pl*) compensation for war damages demanded from a defeated enemy.

rep·ar·tee /ˌreparˈti/ *n* **1** [C] witty, clever reply. **2** [U] the making of such remarks.

re·past /rɪˈpæst/ *n* [C] (*formal*) meal: *a luxurious* ~ *in the elegant restaurant.*

re·pa·tri·ate /ˌriˈpeitriˌeit/ *vt* send or bring (a person) back to his own country: ~ *refugees after a war.* □ *n* /ˌriˈpeitriɪt/ [C] repatriated person.

re·pat·ri·ation /riˌpeitriˈeiʃən/ *n* [U]

re·pay /rɪˈpei/ *vt,vi* (*pt,pp* -paid /-ˈpeid/) **1** pay back (money): *If you'll lend me a dollar, I'll* ~ *you next week.* **2** give in return: *How can I* ~ *him for his kindness?*

re·pay·able /-əbəl/ *adj* that can or must be repaid.

re·pay·ment *n* **(a)** [U] repaying. **(b)** [C] instance of this.

re·peal /rɪˈpiəl/ *vt* (*pres p* ~ing /rɪˈpilɪŋ/) cancel, annul, (a law, etc). □ *n* [C,U] repealing.

re·peat /rɪˈpit/ *vt,vi* **1** say or do again: ~ *word/a mistake.* **2** say (what somebody else has said or what one learned by heart): *You must not ~ what I've told you; it's very confidential.* □ *n* [C] something repeated: *There will be a ~ of the program on Friday.*

re·peat·ed·ly *adv* again and again.

re·pel /rɪˈpel/ *vt* (-ll-) **1** drive back or away: ~ *the enemy/temptation.* **2** cause a feeling of dislike in: *His long, rough beard ~led her.* **3** reject: *~led his offer.*

re·pel·lent /-ənt/ *adj* unattractive; uninviting: *~lent work/food/manners.* □ *n* [C] (esp) preparation that repels insects.

re·pent /rɪˈpent/ *vi,vt* think with regret or sorrow of; be full of regret; wish one had not done (something): *Don't you ~ of your foolishness?*

re·pent·ance /-əns/ *n* [U] regret or remorse for doing wrong: *show ~ance for one's sins.*

re·pent·ant /-ənt/ *adj* feeling or showing regret.

re·pent·ant·ly *adv*

re·per·cus·sion /ˌripərˈkəʃən/ *n* [C,U] **1** echoing sound. **2** (usually *pl*) far-reaching and indirect effect (of an event, etc): *The assassination of the President was followed by ~s throughout the whole country.*

rep·er·toire /ˈrepərˌtwar/ *n* [C] all the plays, songs, pieces, etc which a company, actor, musician, etc is prepared to perform: *She has a large ~ of songs.*

rep·er·tory /ˈrepərˌtɔri/ *n* [C] (*pl* -ies) = repertoire.

rep·eti·tion /ˌrepəˈtɪʃən/ *n* **1** [U] repeating or being repeated. **2** [C] instance of this: *Let there be no ~ of this,* don't do it again.

rep·eti·tious /ˌrepəˈtɪʃəs/ *adj* characterized by repetition, esp dull and tedious repetition: *a repetitious lecture.*

re·place /rɪˈpleis/ *vt* **1** put back in its place: *replacing a dictionary on the shelf.* **2** take the place of: *Can anything ~ a mother's love and care?* **3** supply as a substitute for: ~ *oil by/with coal.*

re·place·able /-əbəl/ *adj* that can be replaced.

re·place·ment *n* **(a)** [U] replacing or being replaced. **(b)** [C] person or thing that replaces: *get a ~ment while one is away on vacation.*

re·plen·ish /rɪˈplenɪʃ/ *vt* (*formal*) fill up again; get a new supply.

re·plete /rɪˈplit/ *adj* (*formal*) filled with; holding as much as possible: ~ *with food; feeling ~.*

re·ple·tion /rɪˈpliʃən/ *n* [U] (*formal*) state of being replete.

rep·lica /ˈreplɪkə/ *n* [C] (*pl* ~s) exact copy (esp one made by the original artist) of a work of art.

re·ply /rɪˈplai/ *vi,vt* (*pt, pp* -ied) give as an answer to: *He failed to ~ (to my question). He replied that he would do whatever we asked.* □ *n* (*pl* -ies) **1** [U] act of replying. **2** [C] what is replied: *He made no ~.*

re·port¹ /rɪˈpɔrt/ *n* **1** [C] detailed account of something heard, seen, done, etc: *the annual ~ of a business company; newspaper ~s.* **2** [U] rumor. **3** [C] sound of an explosion: *the loud ~ of a gun.*

reˈport card, report containing a student's school grades, sent regularly to the student's parents or guardian.

re·port² /rɪˈpɔrt/ *vt,vi* **1** give an account of (something seen, heard, done, etc); give as news: ~ *on/upon a meeting. The discovery of a new planet has been ~ed. He ~ed that a new planet has been discovered.* **2** provide (news) for newspapers, etc: ~ *for a television network.* **3** present oneself for work, duty, etc: ~ *for duty at the office; ~ to the Manager.* **4** make a complaint against a person (esp to authorities): *I shall have to ~ your lateness.*

re·por·ter *n* [C] (esp) person who supplies news to a newspaper, or for radio or TV.

re·pose¹ /rɪˈpouz/ *vt* (*formal*) place (trust, confidence, etc) in: *Don't ~ too much confidence in his honesty.*

re·pose² /rɪˈpouz/ *vt,vi* (*formal*) **1** rest; (cause to) lie at rest: *a girl reposing on a cushion; ~d herself on the couch.* **2** rest for support on. □ *n* [U] (*formal*) **1** rest; sleep. **2** peace, calm: *His attitude lacked ~,* ease of manner.

re·posi·tory /rɪˈpazəˌtɔri/ *n* [C] (*pl* -ies) (*formal*) place where things are or may be stored: *Desks are repositories for all sorts of useless papers.*

rep·re·hend /ˌreprɪˈhend/ *vt* (*formal*) reprove; voice disapproval of: ~ *his conduct.*

rep·re·hen·sible /ˌreprɪˈhensəbəl/ *adj* deserving blame or disapproval.

rep·re·sent /ˌreprɪˈzent/ *vt* **1** be, give, or serve as, a picture, sign, symbol or example of: *Phonetic symbols ~ sounds. This painting ~s a hunting scene.* **2** declare to be; describe (*as*): *He ~ed himself as an expert.* **3** act or speak for; be an agent for: *delegates ~ing the large cities.*

rep·re·sen·ta·tion /ˌreprɪˌzenˈteiʃən/ *n* **(a)** [U] representing or being represented. **(b)** [C] that which represents.

rep·re·sen·ta·tive /ˌreprɪˈzentətɪv/ *adj* **1** serving as an example of a class or group; containing examples of a number of classes or groups: *a ~ collection of French Impressionist paintings.* **2** consisting of elected deputies; based on representation by such elected deputies: ~ *government/institutions.* □ *n* [C] **1** example; typical specimen (*of*). **2** person elected or appointed to represent or act for others: *send a ~ to a conference.* **3 Representative,** title of a member of the House of Representatives (the lower house of the US Congress or of a state legislature).

re·press /rɪˈpres/ *vt* **1** keep or put down or under; prevent from finding an outlet: *~ed emotions.* **2** subdue, esp by force: ~ *an uprising.*

re·pres·sion /rɪˈpreʃən/ *n* [U]

re·pres·sive /rɪˈpresɪv/ *adj* serving or tending to repress: *~ive legislation.*

re·prieve /rɪˈpriv/ *vt* **1** postpone or delay punishment (esp the execution of a person condemned to death). **2** (*fig*) give relief for a short time (from danger, trouble, etc). □ *n* [C] (order giving authority for the) postponement or canceling of punishment (esp by death): *grant a ~.*

rep·ri·mand /ˈreprəˌmænd/ (also /ˌreprəˈmænd/) *vt* express disapproval to (a person) severely and officially (because of a fault, etc). □ *n* [C] serve an official expression of disapproval.

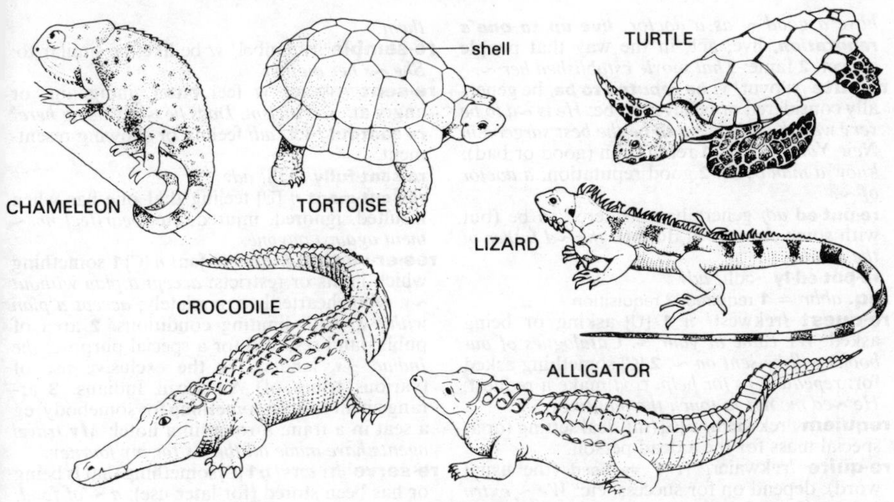

REPTILES

re·print /ˌriˈprɪnt/ *vt* print again. □ *n* [C] /ˈriˌprɪnt/ book, etc printed again.

re·pri·sal /rɪˈpraizəl/ *n* **1** [U] paying back injury with injury: *do something by way of ~*. **2** [C] such an act, esp by one country against another during a war.

re·proach /rɪˈproutʃ/ *vt* blame or find fault with (a person): *~ one's wife for being late with the dinner*. □ *n* **1** [U] reproaching: *a term/look of ~*. **2** [C] instance, word, phrase, etc of reproach. ***above/beyond reproach,*** perfect, blameless: *She/Her behavior is beyond ~*. **3** [C] something that brings disgrace or discredit (*to*): *slums that are a ~ to the city council.*

re·proach·ful /-fəl/ *adj* full of, expressing, reproach: *a ~ful look*.

re·proach·fully /-fəli/ *adv*

re·pro·duce /ˌriprəˈdus/ *vt,vi* **1** cause to be seen, heard, exist, etc again: *~ music from magnetic tape*. **2** make a copy or image of: *~ a painting*. **3** bring forth offspring: *~ one's kind; plants that ~ easily*.

re·pro·duc·er *n* [C]

re·pro·duc·ible /-əbəl/ *adj* that can be reproduced.

re·pro·duc·tion /ˌriprəˈdəkʃən/ *n* **(a)** [U] process of reproducing. **(b)** [C] something reproduced, esp a work of art.

re·pro·duc·tive /ˌriprəˈdəktɪv/ *adj* reproducing; for, relating to, reproduction: *reproductive organs*.

re·proof /rɪˈpruf/ *n* **1** [U] blame (the more usual word); disapproval: *a glance of ~; conduct deserving of ~*. **2** [C] expression of blame or disapproval.

re·prove /rɪˈpruv/ *vt* give a reproof to; scold: *The priest ~d the people for not attending church services.*

rep·tile /ˈreptəl, ˈrepˌtaiəl/ *n* [C] cold-blooded egg-laying animal with a backbone, and usually covered with scales or horny plates, eg a lizard, tortoise, crocodile, snake.

rep·til·ian /repˈtɪliən/ *adj* of, or like a reptile.

re·pub·lic /rɪˈpəblɪk/ *n* [C] (country with a) system of government in which the elected representatives of the people are supreme, and usually with an elected head (the president): *a constitutional ~*, eg the US.

re·pub·li·can /rɪˈpəblɪkən/ *adj* of, relating to, supporting the principles of, a republic. □ *n* [C] **1** person who favors republican government. **2** **Republican,** member or supporter of the Republican Party.

the Reˈpublican Party, one of the two main political parties in the US ⇨ democratic.

re·pudi·ate /rɪˈpyudiˌeit/ *vt* (*formal*) **1** say that one will have nothing more to do with; disown: *~ a wicked son*. **2** refuse to accept or acknowledge: *~ the authorship of an article*, declare that one did not write it. **3** refuse to pay (a debt).

re·pudi·ation /rɪˌpyudiˈeiʃən/ *n* [U]

re·pug·nance /rɪˈpəgnəns/ *n* [U] (*formal*) strong dislike or distaste; aversion.

re·pug·nant /rɪˈpəgnənt/ *adj* (*formal*) causing a feeling of dislike or disgust: *I find his views/proposals ~*.

re·pulse /rɪˈpəls/ *vt* **1** drive back (the enemy); resist (an attack) successfully. **2** refuse to accept (a person's help, friendly offers, etc); discourage (a person) by unfriendly treatment. □ *n* [U] repulsing or being repulsed.

re·pul·sion /rɪˈpəlʃən/ *n* [U] **(a)** feeling of dislike or distaste: *feel repulsion for him*. **(b)** repulsing or being repulsed.

re·pul·sive /rɪˈpəlsɪv/ *adj* **1** causing a feeling of disgust: *a ~ sight*. **2** tending to repulse or repel.

re·pul·sive·ly *adv*

repu·table /ˈrepyətəbəl/ *adj* respected; of good reputation: *~ dealers*.

repu·tably /-əbli/ *adv*

repu·ta·tion /ˌrepyəˈteiʃən/ *n* [U] (used with *a, an* as in examples) **1** the general opinion about the character, qualities, etc of a person or thing:

have a good ~ *as a doctor.* ***live up to one's reputation,*** live, act, in the way that people expect. **2** fame: *That movie established her* ~.

re·pute /rɪˈpyut/ *vt* ***be reputed to be,*** be generally considered or believed to be: *He is* ~*d to be very wealthy. He is* ~*d to be the best surgeon in New York.* □ *n* [U] **1** reputation (good or bad): *know a man by* ~. **2** good reputation: *a doctor of* ~.

re·put·ed *adj* generally considered to be (but with some element of doubt): *the* ~*d father of the child.*

re·put·ed·ly /-ədli/ *adv*

req. *abbr* = **1** required. **2** requisition.

re·quest /rɪˈkwest/ *n* **1** [U] asking or being asked: *We came at your* ~. *Catalogues of our books will be sent on* ~. **2** [C] something asked for: *repeated* ~*s for help.* □ *vt* make a request: *He* ~*ed me not to touch the paintings.*

requiem /ˈrekwiəm/ *n* [C] (musical setting for a) special mass for the a dead person.

re·quire /rɪˈkwaiər/ *vt* **1** = need (the usual word); depend on for success, etc: *We* ~ *extra help.* **2** (*formal*) order; demand; insist on as a right or by authority: *Students are* ~*d to take three science courses. I have done all that is* ~*d by law.*

re·quire·ment *n* [C] something required or needed: *meet his* ~*ments,* do what he wants done.

requi·site /ˈrekwəzɪt/ *n* [C], *adj* (thing) needed or required by circumstances or for success: *We supply every* ~ *for travel.*

requi·si·tion /ˌrekwəˈzɪʃən/ *n* **1** [U] act of requiring or demanding. **2** [C] formal, written demand: *a* ~ *for supplies.* □ *vt* make a requisition for: ~ *supplies.*

re·run /ˌriˈrən/ *vt* (-nn-) show a motion picture or recorded television program again. □ *n* [C] /ˈriˌrən/ showing of a motion picture, etc again.

res. *abbr* = **1** reserved. **2** residence.

re·sale /ˈriˌseiəl/ *n* [C] sale of something previously bought.

re·sal·able /ˌriˈseiləbəl/ *adj* capable of being resold.

re·scind /rɪˈsɪnd/ *vt* repeal, cancel (a law, contract, etc).

res·cue /ˈreskyu/ *vt* deliver, make free (from danger, etc): ~ *a child* (*from drowning*). □ *n* **1** [U] rescuing or being rescued: *John came to my* ~. **2** [C] instance of this: *three* ~*s from drowning in one afternoon.*

res·cu·er *n* [C]

re·search /rɪˈsərtʃ, ˈriˌsərtʃ/ *n* [C,U] (sometimes with *a, an,* and in the *pl*, but not usually with *many* or numerals) investigation undertaken in order to discover new facts, get additional information, etc: *be engaged in* ~; *be busy with* ~ *work; carry out a* ~/~*es into/on the causes of cancer. His* ~*es have been successful.* □ *vi* do research on (a problem, etc): ~ *into/on the causes of cancer.*

re·search·er *n* [C]

re·sell /ˌriˈsel/ *vt, vi* (*pt, pp* resold /ˌriˈsould/) sell something previously bought.

re·sem·blance /rɪˈzembləns/ *n* [C,U] (point of) likeness, similarity: *There's very little* ~ *between them.*

re·semble /rɪˈzembəl/ *vt* be like; be similar to: *She* ~*s her mother.*

re·sent /rɪˈzent/ *vt* feel bitter, indignant, or angry at: ~ *criticism. Does he* ~ *my being here?*

re·sent·ful /-fəl/ *adj* feeling or showing resentment.

re·sent·fully /-fəli/ *adv*

re·sent·ment *n* [U] feeling that one has when insulted, ignored, injured, etc: *bear/feel no* ~*ment against anyone.*

res·er·va·tion /ˌrezərˈveiʃən/ *n* [C] **1** something which limits or restricts: *accept a plan without* ~*s,* wholeheartedly, completely; *accept a plan with* ~*s,* with limiting conditions. **2** area of public land reserved for a special purpose: *the Indian* ~*s,* land(s) for the exclusive use of (various tribes of) American Indians. **3** arrangement to keep something for somebody, eg a seat in a train, a room in a hotel: *My travel agents have made all the* ~*s for my journey.*

re·serve[1] /rɪˈzərv/ *n* **1** [C] something that is being or has been stored (for later use): *a* ~ *of food; the bank's* ~*s,* ie of money. **2** (*sing* or *pl*) (*mil*) military forces kept back for use when needed. **3** [U] ***in reserve,*** kept back unused, but available if needed: *have/hold a little money in* ~. **4** [C] place or area reserved for some special use or purpose: *a* ˈ*game* ~, eg in Africa, for the preservation of wild animals. **5** [C,U] (instance of) limitation or restriction; condition that limits or restricts: *We accept your statement without* ~, believe it completely. **6** [U] self-control in speech and behavior: *break through his* ~, get him to talk and be sociable.

re·serve[2] /rɪˈzərv/ *vt* **1** store, keep back, for a later occasion: *Reserve your strength for the climb. The judge* ~*d his decision,* deferred announcing it until a future time. **2** keep for the special use of, or for a special purpose: *We are reserving these seats for special guests.* **3** order in advance: ~ *rooms at a hotel.*

re·served *adj* (of a person, his character) slow to show feelings or opinions: *He is too* ~*d to be popular.*

re·serv·ed·ly /-ədli/ *adv*

res·er·voir /ˈrezə(r)ˌvwar/ *n* [C] **1** place (often an artificial lake) where water is stored, eg for supplying a town. **2** (*fig*) extra supply (of facts, knowledge, etc).

re·side /rɪˈzaid/ *vi* (*formal*) **1** live (the more usual word), have one's home: ~ *abroad.* **2** (of power, rights, etc) be the property of, be present in: *The supreme authority* ~*s in the President.*

resi·dence /ˈrezədəns/ *n* **1** [U] residing: *take up* ~ *in a new house.* **2** place where one lives.

resi·dent /ˈrezədənt/ *adj* residing in a particular place: *the* ~ *population of the town* (contrasted with visitors, tourists, etc). □ *n* [C] **1** person who resides in a place (contrasted with a visitor). **2** (also **resident physician**) one who lives in a hospital while he receives specialized training.

resi·den·tial /ˌrezɪˈdenʃəl/ *adj* **1** of or relating to residence: *the* ~ *requirements for voters.* **2** of, with, private houses: ~ *parts of the town* (contrasted with business or industrial parts).

re·sid·ual /rɪˈzɪdʒuəl/ *adj* remaining: ~ *income*

after tax.

resi·due /ˈrezəˌdu/ *n* [C] that which remains after a part is taken or used.

re·sign /rɪˈzain/ *vt,vi* **1** give up (a post, office, etc): *~ one's job; ~ from the Committee.* **2** (*formal*) hand over: *I ~ my children to your care.* **3** be ready to put up with or accept without complaining: *be ~ed to one's fate.*

re·signed *adj* having or showing patient acceptance: *with a ~ed look.*

re·sign·ed·ly /-ədli/ *adv*

res·ig·na·tion /ˌrezɪgˈneiʃən/ *n* **1** [U] resigning (1). **2** [C] letter or written notice stating this: *offer/send in/hand in one's ~.* **3** [U] state of being resigned to, accepting, conditions, etc: *accept failure with ~.*

re·sil·ience /rɪˈzɪliəns/, **re·sil·iency** /-iənsi/ *n* [U] **1** quality or property of quickly recovering the original shape or condition after being pulled, pressed, crushed, etc: *the ~ of rubber.* **2** (*fig*) power of recovering quickly: *the ~ of the human body.*

re·sil·ient /-ənt/ *adj* having or showing resilience.

resin /ˈrezən/ *n* [C,U] **1** sticky substance that flows out from most plants when cut or injured, esp from fir and pine trees, hardening in air, used in making varnish, lacquer, etc. **2** kind of similar substance made chemically, widely used in industry.

re·sist /rɪˈzɪst/ *vt,vi* **1** oppose; use force against in order to prevent the advance of: *~ the enemy/an attack/authority/the police.* **2** be undamaged or unaffected by: *a kind of glass that ~s heat,* eg that does not break or crack in a hot oven. **3** keep from yielding to: *~ temptation. She can't ~ chocolates.*

re·sist·er *n* [C]

re·sis·tance /rɪˈzɪstəns/ *n* **1** [U] (power of) resisting: *make/offer no/not much ~ to the enemy's advance.* **2** often **Resistance,** (in a country occupied by an enemy) group of people organized to oppose the invaders. **3** [U] opposing force: *An aircraft has to overcome the ~ of the air.* ***line of least resistance,*** **(a)** direction in which a force meets least opposition. **(b)** (*fig*) easiest way or method. **4** [U] opposition which a body offers to the passage of an electric current.

re·sis·tant /rɪˈzɪstənt/ *adj* offering resistance: *insects that have become ~ to DDT.*

re·sis·tor /rɪˈzɪstər/ *n* [C] device used to provide resistance in an electric circuit.

res·ol·ute /ˈrezəˌlut/ *adj* (*formal*) determined; firm: *a ~ man.*

re·sol·ute·ly *adv*

re·sol·ute·ness /-nɪs/ *n* [U]

res·ol·ution /ˌrezəˈluʃən/ *n* **1** [U] quality of being resolute or determined: *show great ~; a man who lacks ~.* **2** [C] something that is decided; formal expression of opinion by a legislative body or a public meeting; proposal for this: *pass/carry/adopt/reject a ~ (for/against/in favor of/that...).* **3** [C] something one makes up one's mind to do: *a New Year's ~,* something one resolves to do in a new year, eg to give up smoking. **4** [U] resolving, solution (of a doubt, question, etc). ⇨ resolve(3).

re·solve /rɪˈzalv/ *vt,vi* **1** decide; determine: *He ~d that nothing should prevent him from succeeding. He ~d to succeed.* **2** (of a committee, public meeting, legislative body) pass by formal vote the decision (*that*): *The legislature ~d that...* **3** put an end to (doubts, difficulties, etc) by supplying an answer. **4** break up, separate (into parts); convert, be converted: *~ a problem into its elements.* □ *n* [C] something that has been decided: *keep one's ~.*

res·on·ance /ˈrezənəns/ *n* [U] quality of being resonant.

res·on·ant /ˈrezənənt/ *adj* **1** capable of continuing to sound; echoing. **2** rich, vibrating quality: *a deep, ~ voice.*

res·on·ate /ˈrezəˌneit/ *vi* produce or show resonance.

re·sort /rɪˈzɔrt/ *vi* **1** turn to for help or to gain one's purpose, etc: *If other means fail, we shall ~ to force.* **2** go to: *The police watched the cafés to which the wanted man was known to ~.* □ *n* **1** [U] resorting(1): *Can we do it without ~ to force?* ***in the/as a last resort,*** when all else has failed, as a last means of finding help or relief. **2** [C] person or thing that is resorted(1) to: *An expensive taxi was the only ~ left.* **3** [C] place often visited for a particular purpose: *ˈski/ˈhealth ~.*

re·sound /rɪˈzaund/ *vi,vt* **1** (of a voice, instrument, sound, etc) echo; sound loudly: *The organ ~ed.* **2** be or become filled with sound: *The room ~ed with music.* **3** (*fig*) be much talked of.

re·sound·ing *adj* **(a)** ringing; echoing. **(b)** striking: *The movie was a ~ing success.*

re·sound·ing·ly *adv*

re·source /ˈriˌsɔrs, rɪˈsɔrs/ *n* **1** (*pl*) wealth, supplies of goods, raw materials, etc which a person, country, etc has or can use: *the natural ~s of our country,* its mineral wealth, potential water power, the productivity of the soil, etc. **2** [C] something which helps in doing something, that can be turned to for support, help, consolation: *Leave him to his own ~s,* to amuse himself, find his own way of passing the time. **3** [U] skill in finding resources(2): *a man of ~.*

re·source·ful /rɪˈsɔrsfəl/ *adj* good or quick at finding resources(2).

re·source·fully /-fəli/ *adv*

re·spect[1] /rɪˈspekt/ *n* **1** [U] honor; high opinion or esteem: *Children should show ~ for their teachers.* **2** [U] consideration; regard: *We must have ~ for the rights of others.* **3** [U] reference; relation. ***with respect to,*** concerning. **4** [C] detail; particular aspect. *They resemble one another in some/a few ~s.* **5** (*pl*) regards; polite greetings: *My father sends you his ~s.* ***pay one's respects (to sb),*** greet him in a polite and formal way.

re·spect[2] /rɪˈspekt/ *vt* show respect for; treat with consideration: *He is ~ed by everyone. We must ~ his wishes. Do you ~ the laws of your country?*

re·spect·able /rɪˈspektəbəl/ *adj* **1** deserving respect. **2** good or proper in character, appearance, behavior, etc: *Is she/her appearance ~?* **3** of moderate size; fairly good: *He earns a*

~ *income.*

re·spect·abil·ity /rɪˌspektəˈbɪləti/ *n* [U] quality of being socially respectable.

re·spect·ably /-əbli/ *adv* in a respectable manner: *respectably dressed.*

re·spect·ful /rɪˈspektfəl/ *adj* showing respect: *They stood at a ~ distance from the President.*

re·spect·fully /-fəli/ *adv*

re·spect·ive /rɪˈspektɪv/ *adj* for, belonging to, each in the order mentioned: *The three men were given work according to their ~ abilities.*

re·spect·ive·ly *adv* separately or in turn, and in the order mentioned: *Rooms for men and women are on the first and second floors ~ly*, ie for men on the first floor and for women on the second.

res·pi·ration /ˌrespəˈreiʃən/ *n* **1** [U] breathing. **2** [C] single act of breathing in and breathing out.

res·pir·ator /ˈrespəˌreitər/ *n* [C] **1** breathing apparatus that filters the air of harmful fumes. **2** device for giving artificial respiration.

res·pir·at·ory /ˈresp(ə)rəˌtɔri/ *adj* of breathing: *~ diseases,* eg bronchitis, asthma.

lend you my camera if you will take full ~ for it. **2** [C] something for which a person is responsible; duty: *the heavy responsibilities of the President.*

re·spon·sible /rɪˈspansəbəl/ *adj* **1** (of a person) legally or morally in a position where one may be blamed for loss, failure, etc: *The pilot of an airliner is ~ for the safety of the passengers. Who is ~ to the parents for the education of children?* **2** having obligations and duties: *I've made you ~ for buying all the necessary supplies.* **3** to be relied on; trustworthy: *Give the task to a ~ man.* **4** ***be responsible for sth,*** be the cause or source of: *Negligence is ~ for many accidents.*

re·spon·sibly /-əbli/ *adv*

re·spon·sive /rɪˈspansɪv/ *adj* **1** answering: *a ~ gesture.* **2** answering easily or quickly: *~ to affection/treatment.*

re·spon·sive·ly *adv*

rest[1] /rest/ *n* **1** [U] condition of being free from activity, movement, disturbance; quiet; sleep: *Rest is necessary after hard work. She had a good night's ~,* sleep. **2** absence of motion.

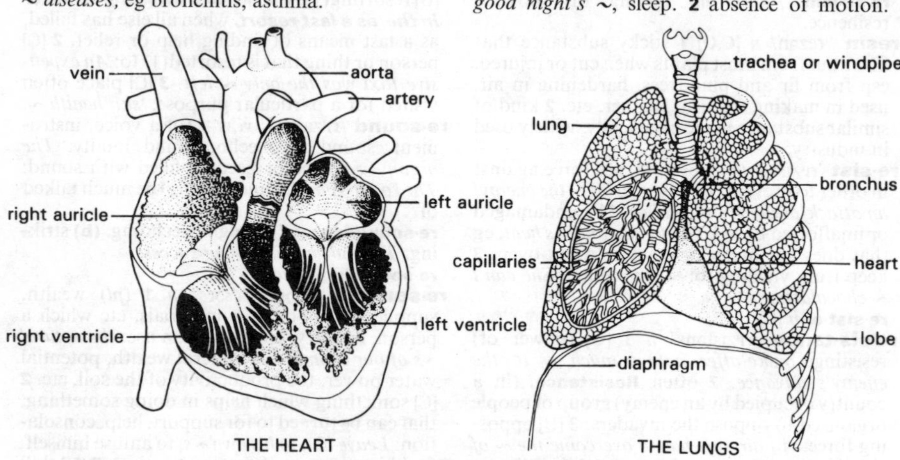

RESPIRATORY SYSTEM

re·spire /rɪˈspaiər/ *vi* (*formal*) = breathe (the usual word).

res·pite /ˈrespɪt/ *n* [C] **1** time of relief or rest (from toil, suffering, anything unpleasant): *work without (a) ~.* **2** temporary postponement or delay.

re·splen·dent /rɪˈsplendənt/ *adj* very brilliant; rich and splendid: *a ~ exhibition by the Metropolitan Museum.*

re·splen·dent·ly *adv*

re·spond /rɪˈspand/ *vi* **1** answer: *~ to a speech of welcome.* **2** act in answer to, or because of, the action of another: *The referee ~ed to their insults by ordering them off the field.* **3** react (to); be affected (by): *The patient quickly ~ed to treatment.*

re·sponse /rɪˈspans/ *n* **1** [C] answer: *My letter of inquiry brought no ~.* **2** [C,U] reaction to stimulation.

re·spon·si·bil·ity /rɪˌspansəˈbɪləti/ *n* (*pl* -ies) **1** [U] being responsible; being accountable: *I'll*

come to rest, (of a moving body) stop moving. **3** [C] that on which something is supported: *an ˈarm~.* **4** [C] (*music*) (sign marking an) interval of silence. ⇨ illus at notation.

rest·ful /-fəl/ *adj* quiet; peaceful; giving (a feeling of) rest: *a ~ful scene; colors that are ~ful to the eyes.*

rest·less *adj* **(a)** never still or quiet; unable to rest: *the ~less waves.* **(b)** without rest or sleep: *spend a ~less night.*

rest·less·ly *adv*

rest·less·ness /-nɪs/ *n* [U]

ˈrest room, public lavatory.

rest[2] /rest/ *n* **1** **the rest,** what remains; the remainder: *Take what you want and throw the ~ away. Her hat was red, like the ~ of her clothes.* **2** (used with a *pl verb*) the others: *John and I are going to play tennis; what are the ~ of you going to do?*

rest[3] /rest/ *vi,vt* **1** be still or quiet; refrain from activity, movement, etc: *We ~ed (for) an hour* *after lunch.* **2** lie dead: *May he ~ in peace.* **3** give rest or relief to: *He stopped to ~ his horse. These dark glasses ~ my eyes.* **4** (cause to) be supported (*on/against* something): *She ~ed her elbows/Her elbows were ~ing on the table. Rest the ladder against the wall.* **5** ***rest with,*** be left in the hands or charge of: *It ~s with you to decide,* it is your responsibility. **6** depend, rely: *His fame ~s on/upon his plays more than his novels.* **7** (*legal*) finish offering evidence in a court trial: *the prosecution ~s.* ***rest a case,*** allow it to be judged on the evidence already given: *The defense ~ed its/the case at that point.*

re·state /ˌriˈsteit/ *vt* state again or in a different way.

re·state·ment *n* [C,U] (instance of) restating.

res·taur·ant /ˈrest(ə)rənt, -ˌrant/ *n* [C] place where meals can be bought and eaten.

res·ti·tu·tion /ˌrestəˈtuʃən/ *n* [U] **1** restoring (of something stolen, etc) to its owner: *~ of property.* **2** = reparation(1).

res·tive /ˈrestɪv/ *adj* **1** hard to manage or control. **2** restless; uneasy.

res·tive·ly *adv*

res·tive·ness /-nɪs/ *n* [U]

res·to·ra·tion /ˌrestəˈreiʃən/ *n* **1** [U] restoring or being restored: *~ to health and strength; ~ of stolen property.* **2 the Restoration,** (the period of) the reestablishment of the monarchy in England in 1660, when Charles II returned to the throne. **3** [C] model representing the supposed original form of an extinct animal, ruined building, etc; building formerly ruined and now rebuilt.

re·store /rɪˈstɔr/ *vt* **1** give back: *restoring stolen property/borrowed books.* **2** bring back into use; reintroduce: *~ old customs.* **3** make well or normal again; bring back (to a former condition): *quite ~d to health; feel completely ~d. Law and order have been ~d.* **4** repair; rebuild as before: *~ an old theater.* **5** place in or bring back to the former position, etc: *~ an employee to his old post/an officer to his command.*

re·stor·er *n* [C]

re·strain /rɪˈstrein/ *vt* hold back; keep under control; prevent (a person or thing from doing something): *~ a child from (doing) mischief; ~ one's anger.*

re·strained *adj* (esp) not emotional or wild; kept under control.

re·straint /rɪˈstreint/ *n* **1** [U] restraining or being restrained. ***without restraint,*** freely; without control. **2** [U] moderation; avoidance of excess or exaggeration. **3** [C] that which restrains; check; controlling influence: *the ~s of poverty.*

re·strict /rɪˈstrɪkt/ *vt* limit; keep within limits: *Discussion at the meeting was ~ed to the agenda. We are ~ed to 30 miles an hour in residential areas.*

re·stric·tion /rɪˈstrɪkʃən/ *n* **(a)** [U] restricting or being restricted. **(b)** [C] something, eg a rule, that restricts.

re·stric·tive /rɪˈstrɪktɪv/ *adj* restricting or tending to restrict.

re·stric·tive·ly *adv*

re·sult /rɪˈzəlt/ *vi* **1** come about, happen, as an effect or consequence: *Any damage ~ing from negligence must be paid for by the borrower.* **2** end in a specified manner: *Their efforts ~ed in a defeat for the proposal.* □ *n* [C,U] that which is produced by an activity or cause; outcome; effect: *work without (much) ~; announce the ~s of an election.*

re·sult·ant /-ənt/ *adj* coming as a result or outcome.

re·sume /rɪˈzum/ *vt* **1** go on after stopping for a time: *~ one's work/a story.* **2** take or occupy again: *~ one's seat.*

ré·su·mé /ˈrezəˌmei/ *n* [C] summary.

re·sump·tion /rɪˈzəmpʃən/ *n* **1** [U] resuming. **2** [C] instance of this.

re·sur·gence /rɪˈsərdʒəns/ *n* [U] revival; return of energy, activity, etc.

res·ur·rect /ˌrezəˈrekt/ *vt* **1** raise from the dead. **2** bring back into use; revive the practice of: *~ an old word/custom.*

res·ur·rec·tion /ˌrezəˈrekʃən/ *n* [U] **1 the Resurrection,** (in the Christian religion) **(a)** the rising of Jesus from the dead. **(b)** the rising of all the dead for the final judgment. **2** revival from disuse, inactivity, etc: *the ~ of hope.*

re·sus·ci·tate /rɪˈsəsəˌteit/ *vt,vi* bring or come back to life or consciousness: *~ a person who has been nearly drowned.*

re·sus·ci·ta·tion /rɪˌsəsəˈteiʃən/ *n* [U]

ret. *abbr* = **1** retired. **2** return.

re·tail /ˈriˌteiəl/ *n* [U] sale of goods to the general public, not for resale: *sell goods at ~.* (as an *adj*) of or relating to retail: *a ~ store.* □ *adv* at retail: *Do you buy wholesale or ~?* □ *vt,vi* (*pres p* ~ing /ˈriˌteilɪŋ/) **1** sell or be sold retail: *an article that is ~ed at/that ~s at $40.* **2** (also /rɪˈteiəl/; *pres p* ~ing /rɪˈteilɪŋ/) repeat (what one has heard, esp gossip): *~ gossip.*

re·tail·er /ˈriˌteilər/ *n* [C]

re·tain /rɪˈtein/ *vt* **1** keep in place: *This dike was built to ~ the flood waters.* **2** continue to have: *She ~s a clear memory of her schooldays.* **3** hire the services of (esp a lawyer) by paying a fee.

re·tain·er *n* [C] fee paid to retain the services of, eg a lawyer.

re·take /ˌriˈteik/ *vt* (*pt* -took /-ˈtʊk/, *pp* -taken /-ˈteikən/) **1** recapture (a fort, prisoner, etc). **2** repeat, redo the photographing of a subject, scene, etc. □ *n* [C] /ˈriˌteik/ act, instance of rephotographing.

re·tali·ate /rɪˈtæliˌeit/ *vi* return the same sort of ill treatment that one has received: *He ~d by kicking the other boy on the ankle. If we raise our import duties on their goods, they may ~ against us.*

re·tali·ation /rɪˌtæliˈeiʃən/ *n* [U] retaliating: *in retaliation for being critical.*

re·tali·at·ory /rɪˈtæliəˌtɔri/ *adj* returning ill treatment for ill treatment; of or for retaliation: *retaliatory acts.*

re·tard /rɪˈtard/ *vt* check; hinder: *~ progress/development; a ~ed child,* one who is mentally deficient.

retch /retʃ/ *vi* (strain to) vomit.

re·ten·tion /rɪˈtenʃən/ *n* [U] retaining or being retained: *the ~ of funds for emergency use.*

re·ten·tive /rɪˈtentɪv/ *adj* having the power of retaining(2) things: *a ~ memory.*

re·ten·tive·ly *adv*
re·ten·tive·ness /-nɪs/ *n* [U]
reti·cence /ˈretəsəns/ *n* [U] being reticent; [C] instance of this.
reti·cent /ˈretəsənt/ *adj* in the habit of saying little; reserved: *She was ~ about/on what Tom had said to her.*
re·ti·cent·ly *adv*
ret·ina /ˈret(ə)nə/ *n* [C] (*pl* ~s or -nae /-ni/) layer of membrane that lines the eyeball, and is connected to the brain by the optic nerve. ⇨ illus at eye.
reti·nue /ˈretəˌnu/ *n* [C] group of persons (staff, attendants, etc) traveling with a person of high rank.
re·tire /rɪˈtaiər/ *vi,vt* **1** withdraw; go away: *He ~d to his cabin.* **2** (*formal*) go to bed: *My wife usually ~s at 10 o'clock.* **3** withdraw; go back: *Our forces ~d to prepared positions.* **4** give up one's work, position, business, etc: *He will ~ at 65.* **5** cause (a person) to retire (4). **6** (*baseball*) put out a batter, side, etc.
re·tired *adj* having retired (4): *a ~d civil servant.*
re·tire·ment *n* [U]
re·tir·ing *adj* shy; avoiding attention or notice: *a girl of a retiring nature.*
re·tort /rɪˈtɔrt/ *vt,vi* answer back quickly, cleverly or angrily (esp to an accusation or challenge): *"It's entirely your fault," he ~ed.* □ *n* **1** [U] retorting: *say something in ~.* **2** [C] quick or clever answer: *make an insolent ~.*
re·touch /ˌriˈtətʃ/ *vt* improve or alter (a photograph, painting, etc).
re·trace /ˌriˈtreis/ *vt* go back over or along: *~ one's steps.*
re·tract /rɪˈtrækt/ *vt,vi* **1** take back or withdraw (a statement, offer, opinion, etc): *Even when confronted with proof the accused man refused to ~ his statement.* **2** draw in or back: *A cat can ~ its claws.*
re·tract·able /-əbəl/ *adj* that can be retracted.
re·trac·tion /rɪˈtrækʃən/ *n* [C,U]
re·tread /ˌriˈtred/ *vt* (*pt,pp* ~ed) put a new tread (3) on (an old tire). □ *n* [C] /ˈriˌtred/ tire that has been retreaded.
re·treat /rɪˈtrit/ *vi* (esp of an army) go back; withdraw: *force the enemy to ~.* □ *n* **1** [U] act of retreating: *The army was in full ~.* **2** [C] signal for this: *sound the ~*, eg on a bugle. **3** [C] instance of retreating: *after many advances and ~s.* **4** [C,U] quiet and restful place: *a quiet country ~.*
re·trial /ˈriˌtraiəl/ *n* [C] second trial.
ret·ri·bu·tion /ˌretrəˈbyuʃən/ *n* [U] deserved punishment: *Is the death penalty just ~ for the crime of murder?*
re·trib·u·tive /rɪˈtrɪbyətɪv/ *adj* inflicted or coming as a penalty for doing wrong.
re·triev·able /rɪˈtrivəbəl/ *adj* that may be retrieved.
re·triev·al /rɪˈtrivəl/ *n* [U] **1** act of retrieving: *the ~ of one's fortunes.* **2** possibility of recovery: *beyond/past ~.*
re·trieve /rɪˈtriv/ *vt,vi* **1** get possession of again: *~ a lost umbrella.* **2** put or set right; make good for: *~ an error/a loss/disaster/defeat.* **3** rescue (from); restore: *~ a person from ruin; ~ one's honor/fortunes.* **4** (of specially trained dogs) find and bring in (killed or wounded game).
re·triev·er *n* [C] breed of dog used for retrieving (4).
retro·ac·tive /ˌretrouˈæktɪv/ *adj* (of laws, etc) applying to or taking effect on a date before enactment: *a ~ pay increase.*
retro·ac·tive·ly *adv*
retro·grade /ˈretrəˌgreid/ *adj* **1** directed backwards: *~ motion.* **2** deteriorating; likely to cause worse conditions: *a ~ policy.* □ *vi* **1** go back. **2** decline; grow worse.
retro·gress /ˌretrəˈgres/ *vi* (*formal*) go or move backwards.
retro·gres·sion /ˌretrəˈgreʃən/ *n* [U] return to a less advanced state.
retro·gres·sive /ˌretrəˈgresɪv/ *adj* returning, tending to return, to a less advanced state; becoming worse.
retro·rock·et /ˈretrouˌrakɪt/ *n* [C] rocket engine used to slow down or alter the course of a missile, spacecraft, etc.
retro·spect /ˈretrəˌspekt/ *n* ***in retrospect,*** looking back at past events, etc.
retro·spec·tion /ˌretrəˈspekʃən/ *n* (*formal*) [U] action of looking back at past events, scenes, etc.
retro·spec·tive /ˌretrəˈspektɪv/ *adj* looking back on past events, etc.
retro·spec·tive·ly *adv*
re·turn[1] /rɪˈtərn/ *n* **1** [C,U] coming, going, giving, sending, putting, back: *on my ~*, when I got/get back; *the ~ of spring.* **2** [C] something returned. **3** [C] profit on an investment or undertaking: *a quick ~.* **4** [C] official report or statement: *make out one's tax ~; election ~s.*
re·turn[2] /rɪˈtərn/ *vi,vt* **1** come or go back (to a place, condition, etc): *~ home; ~ to California from the East. I shall ~ to this point later in my lecture. He has ~ed to his old habits.* **2** give, put, send, pay, carry, back: *When will you ~ the book I lent you?* **3** make as an answer or reply. **4** elect (a person) to public office. **5** state or report officially: *The jury ~ed a verdict of guilty.*
re·turn·able /-əbəl/ *adj* that may be sent, given back.
returnee /ˌriˌtərˈni/ *n* [C] person who returns from military service abroad, esp after a war.
return enˈgagement, repeat showing of a movie, staging of a play, etc at a particular location.
reˈturn game, = return match.
reˈturn match, second game, fight, etc between opposing teams, boxers, etc.
return ˈticket, ticket to return from a trip.
re·un·ion /riˈyunyən/ *n* **1** [U] reuniting or being reunited. **2** [C] (esp) gathering of old friends, former colleagues, etc after separation: *a family ~ at Christmas.*
re·unite /ˌriyuˈnait/ *vt,vi* bring or come together again: *~d after long years of separation.*
Rev.[1] *abbr* = Reverend.
rev.[2] *abbr* = **1** reverse. **2** review. **3** revised. **4** revision. **5** revolution(s).
rev[3] /rev/ *vt,vi* (-vv-) (*informal*) increase the speed of an idling engine: *Don't rev up (the*

engine) so hard.

re·vamp /ˌriˈvæmp/ *vt* (*informal*) reconstruct; renew; revise: ~ *an old book with new illustrations.*

re·veal /rɪˈviəl/ *vt* (*pres p* ~ing /rɪˈvilɪŋ/) **1** allow or cause to be seen; display: *Fear was ~ed in her face.* **2** make known: *One day the truth about these events will be ~ed. The doctor did not ~ to him that his condition was hopeless.*

re·veal·ing /rɪˈvilɪŋ/ *adj*

re·veal·ing·ly *adv*

re·veille /ˈrevəli/ *n* [C] (in the armed forces) bugle signal to men to get up in the morning: *sound the ~.*

revel /ˈrevəl/ *vi* (-l-, -ll-) **1** have a gay, festive time: *They ~ed until dawn.* **2** ***revel in,*** take great delight in: ~ *in one's success; people who ~ in gossip.* □ *n* [C] (occasion of) joyous festivity.

rev·el·er, rev·el·ler /ˈrevələr/ *n* [C] person who revels.

rev·el·ation /ˌrevəˈleiʃən/ *n* **1** [U] act of revealing. **2** [C] that which is revealed, esp something that causes surprise: *It was a ~ to John when Mary said she had married him only for his money.*

rev·elry /ˈrevəlri/ *n* [C,U] (*pl* -ies) (occasion of) noisy, joyous festivity and merrymaking: *when the ~/revelries ended.*

re·venge /rɪˈvendʒ/ *vt* **1** do something to get satisfaction for (an offense, etc to oneself or another): ~ *an injustice/insult.* **2** get satisfaction by deliberately inflicting injury in return for injury inflicted on a person or oneself: ~ *a friend; be ~ed on a persecutor.* ⇨ avenge. □ *n* [U] **1** deliberate infliction of injury on the person(s) from whom injury has been received: *thirsting for ~; take revenge on somebody (for something); have/get one's ~ (on somebody) (for something); do something in/out of ~ (for something).* **2** revenging.

re·venge·ful /-fəl/ *adj* feeling or showing a desire for revenge.

re·venge·fully /-fəli/ *adv*

rev·enue /ˈrevən(y)u/ *n* [U] **1** income of a government department collected for public expenses. **2** income from investment or other sources.

re·ver·ber·ate /rɪˈvərbəˌreit/ *vt,vi* echo back; resound: *The roar of the train ~d/was ~d in the tunnel.*

re·ver·ber·ation /rɪˌvərbəˈreiʃən/ *n* [C,U]

re·vere /rɪˈvɪr/ *vt* have deep respect for; regard as sacred: *He ~d his grandfather.*

rev·er·ence /ˈrev(ə)rəns/ *n* [U] deep respect; feeling of wonder and awe: *a bishop who was held in ~ by everyone.* □ *vt* treat or regard with reverence.

rev·er·end /ˈrev(ə)rənd/ *adj* **1** deserving to be treated with respect or reverence. **2 the Reverend,** used as a title for a clergyman: *the Reverend John Smith.*

rev·er·ent /ˈrev(ə)rənt/ *adj* feeling or showing reverence.

rev·er·ent·ly *adv*

rev·erie /ˈrevəri/ *n* [C] (instance of, occasion of a) condition of being lost in daydreamy thoughts.

re·ver·sal /rɪˈvərsəl/ *n* **1** [U] reversing or being reversed. **2** [C] instance of this: *a ~ of procedure.*

re·verse[1] /rɪˈvərs/ *adj* **1** contrary or opposite in character or order; inverted: *the ~ side of a coin.* **2** causing backward or reverse movement: ~ *gear.*

re·verse[2] /rɪˈvərs/ *n* **1** [U] (with *the*) opposite; contrary: *do the ~ of what one is expected to do.* **2** [C] reverse side (of a coin, medal, record, etc): *The title is on this side of the page; what is on the ~?* **3** mechanism or device that reverses: *Most cars have four forward gears and (a) ~. Put the car into ~.* **4** [C] (esp) change to a worse condition or state: *Our forces/My finances have suffered a slight ~.*

re·verse[3] /rɪˈvərs/ *vt,vi* **1** turn (something) the other way around or up or inside out: ~ *a procedure; ~ one's policy.* **2** (cause to) go in the opposite direction: ~ *one's car into the garage.* **3** change the order or position of: *Their positions are now ~d; Tom is poor and Ben is rich.* **4** cancel, annul: ~ *the decision of a lower court; ~ a decree.* **5** make (the charge for a telephone call) payable by the person who receives it: ~ *the charges.*

re·vers·ible /-əbəl/ *adj* **(a)** that can be reversed. **(b)** capable of being worn or used with either side out.

re·ver·sion /rɪˈvərʒən/ *n* **1** [U] reverting (of property, etc). ⇨ revert(2). **2** [C] right to future possession of property in certain circumstances.

re·vert /rɪˈvərt/ *vi* **1** return (to a former state, condition, topic, etc): *The committee gave up the new proposal and ~ed to its original plan.* **2** (*legal*) (of property, rights, etc) return at some named time or under certain conditions (*to* the original owner, the state, etc): *If he dies without an heir, his property will ~ to the State.*

re·view /rɪˈvyu/ *vt,vi* **1** consider or examine again; go over again: ~ *last week's lesson.* **2** look back on: ~ *one's achievements.* **3** inspect formally (troops, a fleet, etc). **4** write a criticism of (eg a book, or play) for newspapers and other periodicals: *His new novel has been favorably ~ed.* □ *n* **1** [U] act of reviewing (1). **2** [C] instance of this; survey: *a ~ of the year's sporting events.* **3** [C] inspection of military, naval, etc forces. **4** [C] article that discusses and evaluates a new book, etc: *write ~s for the monthly magazines.* **5** [C] going over or further study of material covered earlier.

re·view·er *n* [C]

re·vile /rɪˈvaiəl/ *vt,vi* (*pres p* reviling /rɪˈvailɪŋ/) (*formal*) swear at; use abusive language: ~ *one's persecutors.*

re·vise /rɪˈvaiz/ *vt* reconsider; read carefully through, esp in order to correct and improve: ~ *one's estimates; ~ one's opinions of her.*

re·vi·sion /rɪˈvɪʒən/ *n* **(a)** [U] revising or being revised. **(b)** [C] (esp) that which has been revised; corrected version: *Several revisions have been made.*

re·viv·al /rɪˈvaivəl/ *n* **1** [C,U] (instance of) reviving or being revived: **2** [C] something (eg a play) that is revived. *a ~ of trade.* **3** [C] (series of meetings intended to produce an) increase or renewal of interest in religion: *a religious ~; ~ meetings*.

re·viv·al·ist *n* [C] person who conducts religious revival meetings.

re·vive /rɪˈvaiv/ *vi,vt* **1** come or bring back to consciousness, strength, health or an earlier state: *~ a person who has fainted; ~ an old play*, present it again after many years. **2** come or bring into use again: *customs which have been ~d*.

revo·cable /ˈrevəkəbəl, rɪˈvoukəbəl/ *adj* that can be revoked.

revo·ca·tion /ˌrevəˈkeiʃən/ *n* **1** [U] revoking or being revoked. **2** [C] instance of this.

re·voke /rɪˈvouk/ *vt,vi* repeal; cancel; withdraw (a decree, consent, permission, etc): *~ a driver's license*.

re·volt /rɪˈvoult/ *vi,vt* **1** rise in rebellion: *The people ~ed against the dictator*. **2** fill with disgust or horror: *scenes that ~ed all who saw them*. □ *n* [C] act or state of revolting; rebellion: *~s against authority*.

re·volt·ing /rɪˈvoultɪŋ/ *adj* disgusting.

re·volt·ing·ly *adv*

rev·o·lu·tion /ˌrevəˈluʃən/ *n* **1** [C] act of revolving or going around: *the ~ of the earth round the sun*. **2** [C] complete turn of a wheel, record, etc. **3** [C] sudden and complete change in a political system, esp the overthrow of a government by those governed: *the Russian Revolution*. **4 the (American) Revolution,** the war of independence of the British colonies in North America. **5** any sudden and radical change: *the industrial ~*.

rev·ol·u·tion·ary /ˌrevəˈluʃəˌneri/ *adj* **1** of, relating to, or tending to promote political revolution: *~ ideas*. **2** radical. **3 the Revolutionary War,** = the American Revolution. ⇨ revolution(4). □ *n* [C] (*pl* -ies) person who supports or takes part in a (political) revolution.

rev·o·lu·tion·ize /ˌrevəˈluʃəˌnaiz/ *vt* make a complete change in; cause to be entirely different: *The use of computers promises to ~ the lives of coming generations*.

re·volve /rɪˈvalv/ *vt,vi* **1** (cause to) go around in a circle: *The earth ~s around the sun*. **2** think about all sides of (a problem, etc): *revolving a problem in one's mind*.

revolving ˈdoor, one having four panels revolving around a central post, designed to keep much-used buildings sealed from outside weather.

re·volv·er /rɪˈvalvər/ *n* [C] pistol with a revolving bullet chamber that makes it possible to fire a number of times without reloading.

re·vue /rɪˈvyu/ *n* [C] theatrical entertainment which consists of sketches, dances and songs, usually making fun of current events, people etc.

re·vul·sion /rɪˈvəlʃən/ *n* [U] **1** (often with *a, an*) sudden withdrawal or turning away: *There was an obvious ~ of public feeling against capital punishment*. **2** feeling of disgust.

re·ward /rɪˈwɔrd/ *n* **1** [U] something given in return for service or merit: *work without hope of any ~*. **2** [C] (esp) money which is offered or given in return for eg the restoration of lost or stolen property, the capture of a criminal, etc: *offer a large ~ for information about a stolen necklace*. □ *vt* give a reward to: *~ a man for his honesty*.

rhap·sody /ˈræpsədi/ *n* [C] (*pl* -ies) **1** enthusiastic expression of delight: *Everyone went into rhapsodies over his performance as Othello*. **2** (*music*) composition in free or irregular form: *Liszt's Hungarian Rhapsodies*.

rhet·oric /ˈretərɪk/ *n* [U] **1** (study or art of) using words effectively in speech and writing. **2** affected or exaggerated language: *the ~ of politicians*.

rhe·tori·cal /rɪˈtɔrɪkəl *adj* **1** in, using, a style designed to impress or persuade. **2** artificial or exaggerated in language.

rhe·tori·cally /-kli/ *adv*

rhetorical ˈquestion, question asked for the sake of effect, no answer being needed or expected.

rheu·matic /ruˈmætɪk/ *adj* relating to or suffering from rheumatism. □ *n* [C] person who suffers from rheumatism.

rheu·ma·tism /ˈruməˌtɪzəm/ *n* [U] (kinds of) painful disease with stiffness and inflammation of the muscles and joints.

rhino /ˈrainou/ *n* [C] (*pl* ~s, or, collectively, ~) (short for) rhinoceros.

rhi·noc·eros /raiˈnasərəs/ *n* [C] (*pl* ~es, ~) thick-skinned, heavy animal of Africa and Asia with one or two horns on the snout.

rho·di·um /ˈroudiəm/ *n* [U] hard, silvery-white metallic element (symbol **Rh**).

rhom·bus /ˈrambəs/ *n* [C] (*pl* ~es) four-sided figure with equal sides, and angles which are not right angles (eg diamond or lozenge shape). ⇨ illus at geometry.

rhu·barb /ˈruˌbarb/ *n* [U] **1** (garden plant with) thick, juicy, pink stalks which are cooked and used in pies, puddings, etc. **2** (*sl*) noisy quarrel.

rhyme /raim/ *n* **1** [U] sameness of sound of the endings of two or more words or lines of verse, eg say, play; measure, pleasure; puff, rough. ***without rhyme or reason,*** senseless. **2** [C] word which provides a rhyme: *Is there a ~ for "hiccups"?* **3** [C] verse or verses with rhyme. □ *vt,vi* **1** put together to form a rhyme: *Can we ~ "hiccups" with "pick-ups"?* **2** (of words or lines of verse) be in rhyme: *"Ship" doesn't ~ with "sheep."*

rhythm /ˈrɪðəm/ *n* **1** [U] regular pattern of stresses, accents, or beats (in speech, poetry, music, etc). **2** [U] regular recurrence of events, processes, etc: *the ~ of the tides*, their regular rise and fall. **3** [C] particular kind of such a regular pattern succession or recurrence.

rhyth·mic /ˈrɪðmɪk/, **rhyth·mi·cal** /ˈrɪðmɪkəl/ *adj* marked by, having, rhythm: *the ~ical noise of a typewriter*.

RI *postal abbr* = Rhode Island. ⇨ App 6.

rib /rɪb/ *n* [C] **1(a)** any one of the 12 pairs of curved bones extending from the backbone around the chest to the front of the body in man. ⇨ illus at skeleton. **(b)** corresponding bone in an animal. **2** cut of meat which includes a rib. **3** something which functions like a rib by giving support to a structure. **4** main vein of a leaf. **5** ridge or raised line in knitted or woven fabric. □ *vt* (-bb-) **1** supply with, mark off in, ribs: *ribbed patterns.* **2** (*informal*) tease.

rib·ald /ˈrɪbəld/ *adj* indecent; crude; coarse: ~ *jests/songs.*

ri·baldry /-dri/ *n* [U] such language.

rib·bon /ˈrɪbən/ *n* **1** [C,U] long, narrow, woven strip or band, eg of silk or velvet, used for ornamenting, for tying things, etc: *She had a ~ in her hair. Typewriter ~s* (for inking the keys) *may be all black or black and red.* **2** [C] piece of ribbon of a special design, color, etc worn to show membership of an order, as a military decoration (when medals are not worn). **3** [C] (*pl*) long, narrow strip: *His clothes were hanging in ~s,* were very torn or worn.

rice /rais/ *n* [U] (grass bearing a) starchy grain used as food. ⇨ illus at cereal.

rich /rɪtʃ/ *adj* (-er, -est) **1** having much money or property: ~ *people.* **2** (of clothes, jewels, furniture, etc) costly; luxurious. **3** very productive: ~ *soil.* ***rich in,*** having an abundant supply: *a country ~ in minerals.* **4** (of food) containing a large proportion of fat, sugar, etc: *a ~ fruit cake.* **5** (of colors, sounds, etc) full; deep; mellow; strong: *the ~ colors of the national flags; the ~ voice of the baritone.* **6** (*informal*) very amusing. □ *n* **the rich,** rich people.

rich·ly *adv* **(a)** in a rich manner: *~ly dressed.* **(b)** thoroughly; fully: *He ~ly deserved the punishment he received.*

rich·ness /-nɪs/ *n* [U] quality or state of being rich (but not in the sense of 1 above).

riches /ˈrɪtʃɪz/ *n pl* wealth; being rich: *from rags to ~,* from poverty to great wealth.

rick /rɪk/ *n* [C] stack or pile of hay, straw, corn, etc (in a field).

rick·ets /ˈrɪkɪts/ *n pl* (used with a *sing* or *pl verb*) disease marked by softening and malformation of the bones, caused by deficiency of vitamin D.

rick·ety /ˈrɪkɪti/ *adj* likely to break and collapse: *~ furniture.*

rick·sha, rick·shaw /ˈrɪkˌʃɔ/ *n* [C] two-wheeled carriage for one or two passengers, pulled by a man.

rico·chet /ˈrɪkəˌʃei/ *n* [C] rebound (of a stone, bullet, etc) after hitting a surface. □ *vi* (*pt,pp* -cheted /-ˌʃeid/) (of a shot, etc) rebound or move away sharply: *The bullet ~ed off his helmet.*

rid /rɪd/ *vt* (*pt, pp* rid) make free: *rid oneself of debt/a country of bandits.* ***be/get rid of,*** be/become free of: *We were glad to be rid of our overcoats. They are difficult to get rid of,* eg of articles in a store, difficult to sell.

rid·dance /ˈrɪdəns/ *n* [U] state of being rid of; removal of something unwanted or undesirable: *Good ~ to bad rubbish,* (said of the welcome removal or departure of something or somebody undesirable).

riddle[1] /ˈrɪdəl/ *n* [C] **1** puzzling question, statement or description, intended to make a person think hard in order to know the answer or meaning: *know the answer to a ~.* **2** person, thing, situation, etc which is hard to understand: *the ~ of the universe.*

riddle[2] /ˈrɪdəl/ *n* [C] coarse sieve (for stones, earth, gravel, cinders etc). □ *vt* **1** pass (soil, ashes, etc) through a riddle. **2** make many holes in (something): ~ *a man with bullets.* **3** damage or weaken as if by making holes: *a government department ~d by corruption.*

ride[1] /raid/ *n* [C] **1** act or period of riding on horseback, on a bicycle, bus, etc: *It's a short ~ on the bus.* ***take sb for a ride,*** (*informal*) deceive him. **2** road or track for the use of persons on horseback and not for vehicles.

ride[2] /raid/ *vi,vt* (*pt* rode /roud/, *pp* ridden /ˈrɪdən/) **1** sit on the back of an animal, in a vehicle, etc and go or be carried along: *He jumped on his horse and rode off/away. He was riding in a bus/taxi.* **2** sit on and control or drive: ~ *a horse/pony/bicycle.* **3** compete or take part in, on horseback, etc: ~ *a race.* **4** (cause to) be carried or conveyed: *The boy was riding on his father's shoulders.* **5** float on: *a ship riding the waves.* **6** be supported by or carried on: *a bird riding (on) the wind.* **7** ***ride out,*** (*fig*) come through safely: ~ *out a storm.* **8** ***let sth ride,*** take no action on it; leave things to take their natural course. **9** ***ride up,*** eg of an article of clothing, shift or move upwards.

rider /ˈraidər/ *n* [C] **1** person who rides, esp one who rides a horse: *A superb horsewoman, Miss White is one of the best ~s in Kentucky.* **2** additional clause (often on an unrelated subject) attached to a legislative bill.

rider·less *adj* without a rider.

ridge /rɪdʒ/ *n* [C] **1** raised line where two sloping surfaces meet: *the ~ of a roof.* **2** chain of hills or mountains. **3** raised, narrow part on the body: *the ~ of the spine.* **4** narrow, raised part between two furrows.

ridi·cule /ˈrɪdɪˌkyul/ *n* [U] being made fun of; derision: *She has become an object of ~.* ***hold a man up to ridicule,*** make fun of him. □ *vt* make fun of; cause to appear foolish: *Why do you ~ my proposal?*

ri·dicu·lous /rɪˈdɪkyələs/ *adj* deserving to be laughed at; absurd: *You look ~ in that old hat. What a ~ idea!*

rid·icu·lous·ly *adv*

rife /raif/ *adj* widespread; common: *Is superstition still ~ in the country?*

riffle /ˈrɪfəl/ *vt,vi* **1** way of shuffling playing-cards. **2** turn over (the pages of a book, etc) quickly.

riff·raff /ˈrɪfˌræf/ *n* [U] disreputable persons.

rifle[1] /ˈraifəl/ *n* [C] gun having a long barrel with spiral grooves, to be fired from the shoulder.

ˈrifle·man /-mən/ (*pl* ~men /-men/) *n* [C] soldier of a rifle regiment.

rifle[2] /ˈraifəl/ *vt* search thoroughly in order to steal from: *The thief ~d every drawer in the room.*

rift /rɪft/ *n* [C] **1** split or crack: *a ~ in the clouds.* **2** (*fig*) disagreement, quarrel (eg between two friends or friendly groups, etc).

rig[1] /rɪg/ *vt* (-gg-) **1** supply (a ship) with masts, rigging, sails, etc. **2** provide (a person) with necessary clothes, equipment, etc: *rig the children out with rainwear.* **3** ***rig sth up,*** make, put together, quickly or with any materials that may be available: *They rigged up some scaffolding for the workmen.* □ *n* [C] **1** way in which a ship's masts, sails, etc are arranged. **2** equipment or clothing for a special purpose.

rig·ging *n* [U] all the ropes, chains, etc which support a ship's masts and sails.

rig[2] /rɪg/ *vt* (-gg-) manage or control by dishonest means: *rig an election.*

right[1] /rait/ *adj* (1,2,3 contrasted with *wrong*) **1** just; morally correct: *Always do what is ~ and honorable.* **2** true; correct: *What's the ~ time? Have you got the ~ fare?* **3** most suitable; fitting; appropriate: *He is the ~ man for the job.* **4** physically or mentally healthy: *She doesn't look ~.* ***right as rain,*** (*informal*) perfectly sound or healthy. **5** meant to be facing outward: *the fabric should be ~ side out.*

right·ly *adv* **(a)** justly; justifiably: *She was angry, and ~ly so.* **(b)** properly.

right·ness /-nɪs/ *n* [U]

right[2] /rait/ *adv* **1** exactly: *Put it ~ in the middle.* ***right away/now,*** at once, without any delay. **2** (used for emphasis) *Go ~ to the end of this road, and then turn left. There's a fence ~ around the building. The pear was rotten ~ through.* **3** correctly; properly: *if I remember ~.* ***It serves him right,*** it is what he deserves, etc.

right[3] /rait/ *n* **1** [U] that which is good, just, morally correct, etc: *know the difference between ~ and wrong.* **2** [C] something which one may justly or legally claim: *What gives you the ~ to say that?* ***by right(s),*** if justice were done: *The property is not mine by ~(s).* ***ˌright of ˈway,*** **(a)** right of the general public to use a path, road, etc area over which such a right exists. **(b)** (in road traffic) right to proceed before others.

right[4] /rait/ *vt* **1** put, bring or come back, into the right or an upright condition: *The ship ~ed herself after the big wave had passed.* **2** correct: *~ the wrongs of the world.*

right[5] /rait/ *adj* (contrasted with *left*) of the side of the body which is toward the east when a person faces north: *my ~ hand/leg. In the US traffic keeps to the ~ side of the road.* □ *adv* to the right hand or side: *He looked neither ~ nor left.* ***right and left,*** everywhere. □ *n* **1** [C] side or direction on one's right hand: *Take the first turn to the ~.* **2 the Right,** group holding more conservative political views: (as an *adj*) *the ~ wing of the party.*

ˌright–ˈhand *adj* of, situated on, the right side: *a house on the ~-hand side of the street.*

ˌright-ˈhanded *adj* **(a)** (of a person) using the right hand more, or with more ease, than the left. **(b)** (of a blow, etc) given with the right hand. **(c)** having a clockwise turn or twist.

right·ist /-ɪst/ *n* [C], *adj* supporter of a right wing political party: *~ist sympathizers.*

right angle /ˈrait ˌæŋgəl/ *n* [C] angle of 90° formed by two lines which are perpendicular to each other.

right·eous /ˈraitʃəs/ *adj* morally right; *~ anger.*

right·eous·ly *adv*

right·eous·ness /nɪs/ *n* [U]

right·ful /ˈraitfəl/ *adj* **1** according to right and justice: *the ~ owner of the land.* **2** (of actions, etc) fair; justifiable.

right·fully /-fəli/ *adv*

right·ness /-nɪs/ *n* [U]

rig·id /ˈrɪdʒɪd/ *adj* **1** stiff; that cannot be bent: *a ~ support for a tent.* **2** firm; strict; not changing; not to be changed: *a ~ disciplinarian; practice ~ economy.*

rig·id·ly *adv*

ri·gid·ity /rɪˈdʒɪdəti/ *n* [U] **1** inflexibility: *the ~ of his religious beliefs.* **2** strictness.

rig·ma·role /ˈrɪgməˌroul/ *n* [C] **1** composed, incoherent speech. **2** complicated procedure.

rig·or /ˈrɪgər/ *n* **1** [U] sternness; strict enforcement (of rules, etc): *use the ~ of the law.* **2** [U] hardship; severe conditions: *the ~s of prison life.*

rig·or·ous /ˈrɪgərəs/ *adj* **1** stern; strict; determined: *a ~ search for drugs.* **2** harsh; severe: *a ~ climate.*

rig·or·ous·ly *adv*

rile /ˈraiəl/ *vt* (*pres p* riling /ˈrailɪŋ/) annoy; cause anger in: *It ~d him that no one would believe his story.*

rim /rɪm/ *n* [C] **1** circular edge of the framework of a wheel. **2** outer edge, border or margin of something circular: *the rim of a cup/bowl.* □ *vt* (-mm-) **1** provide with a rim. **2** be a rim for.

rind /raind/ *n* [C] hard, outside skin or covering (of some fruits, eg melons, or of bacon and cheese). ⇨ illus at fruit.

ring[1] /rɪŋ/ *n* [C] **1** circular band worn round a finger as an ornament, or as a token: *an enˈgagement ~; a ˈwedding ~.* **2** circular band of any kind of material, eg metal, wood, ivory: *a ˈnapkin ~.* **3** circle: *a ~ of light round the moon; the ~s of a tree,* seen in wood when the trunk is cut across, showing the tree's age. ***make/run rings around sb,*** do things better than he does. **4** group of persons (traders, politicians, etc) working together, often illicitly for their own advantage, eg to keep prices up or down, to control policy: *a ~ of dealers at a public auction.* **5** (also **ˈcircus ring**) circular enclosure or space for performances in a circus. **6** roped area for a boxing match. □ *vt,vi* (*pt,pp* ~ed) **1** surround: *~ed about with enemies.* **2** provide with a ring.

ˈring·master *n* [C] man who directs performances in a circus.

ˈring·side *n* [C] place just outside the ring at a circus, a boxing match, etc: *have a ~side seat,* be favorably placed for seeing an event, etc.

ring[2] /rɪŋ/ *vt,vi* (*pt* rang /ræŋ/, *pp* rung /rəŋ/) **1** (cause to) give out a clear, musical sound as when metal vibrates: *How long has that telephone (bell) been ~ing? She rang the bell.* **2** produce a certain effect when heard. *His words rang true,* seemed sincere. **3** call or summon by a bell: *~ the bell for the steward.* ***ring a bell,*** (*informal*) bring something back to mind: *Ah! That name ~s a bell!* **4** resound; echo: *The children's playground rang with happy shouts.* **5** be filled with: *The town is still ~ing with the scandal.* **6** ***ring up,*** record, as on a cash register: *~ up a sale.* **7** give a signal by ringing a bell, etc: *Did he ~ the fire alarm?* □ *n* **1** (*sing* only) sound produced by a bell or piece of metal when it is struck: *This coin has a good ~.* **2** (*sing* only) loud and clear sound: *the ~ of happy voices.* **3** (*sing* only) sound or effect of a particular quality: *There was a ~ of truth in his statement.* **4** [C] **(a)**

act of ringing; sound of a bell: *There was a ~ at the door.* **(b)** telephone call: *I'll give you a ~ this evening.*

ringer /ˈrɪŋər/ *n* [C] **1** ***be a (dead) ringer for sb,*** (*sl*) resemble him exactly. **2 (a)** (*sl*) athlete or horse entered in a competition by fraudulent means: *The winning horse was a ~* (= had falsified papers) *and was later disqualified.* **(b)** (*sl*) person who is not what he claims to be: *The man we thought was a business executive was really a ~ planted by the KGB.*

ring·let /ˈrɪŋlɪt/ *n* [C] small curl of hair: *She arranged her hair in ~s.*

ring·worm /ˈrɪŋˌwərm/ *n* [U] contagious disease of the skin, esp of children, producing round, red patches.

rink /rɪŋk/ *n* [C] specially prepared area of ice for skating or hockey, or floor for roller skating.

rinse /rɪns/ *vt* wash with clean water in order to remove unwanted substances, etc: *rinsing soap out of the clothes; ~ the clothes; ~ (out) the mouth,* eg while being treated by a dentist. □ *n* [C] **1** act of rinsing: *Give your hair a good ~ after you've had your shampoo.* **2** liquid used for rinsing. **3** solution for tinting the hair.

riot /ˈraiət/ *n* [C] **1** (*legal*) violent disturbance of the peace by three or more persons assembled together: *Riots during the election were dealt with by the police.* **2** noisy, uncontrolled behavior **3** (*sing* only, with *a, an*) profuse or bright display: *The flower beds in the park were a ~ of color.* **4** person or thing that is very amusing. □ *vi* take part in a riot(1,2).

riot·er *n* [C]

riot·ous /-əs/ *adj* **(a)** of or taking part in a riot. **(b)** disorderly; boisterous.

riot·ous·ly *adv*

rip[1] /rɪp/ *vt,vi* (-pp-) **1** pull, tear or cut (something) quickly and with force (to get it off, out, open, etc): *rip open a letter; rip the cover off; rip the seams of a dress.* **2** saw (wood, etc) with the grain. **3** ***rip off,*** (*sl*) steal. **4** go or move fast; rush along. ***Let her rip!*** (*informal*, and always unstressed *her*, pronounced /ər/, regardless of real *subject*) let (something) occur at full speed or force. □ *n* [C] torn place; long cut: *bad rips in my tent.*

ˈrip cord, cord which is pulled to release a parachute from its pack.

ˈrip current, = rip tide.

ˈrip tide, strong, narrow current running out from the shore.

RIP[2], **R.I.P.** *abbr* (= *Lat* requiescat in pace) (may he/she) rest in peace.

ripe /raip/ *adj* (-r, -st) **1** (of fruit, grain, etc) ready to be gathered and used: *~ fruit; cherries not ~ enough to eat.* **2** aged and ready for use: *~ cheese.* **3** fully developed and mature: *a ~ old age.* **4** ***ripe for,*** ready, fit, prepared: *land that is ~ for development*, eg for building houses or factories.

ripe·ly *adv*

ripe·ness /-nɪs/ *n* [U]

ripen /ˈraipən/ *vt,vi* make or become ripe.

ri·poste /rɪˈpoust/ *n* [C] **1** quick return or thrust in fencing. **2** (*formal*) quick, sharp reply or retort. □ *vi* deliver a riposte.

ripple /ˈrɪpəl/ *n* [C] (sound of) small movement(s) on the surface of water, etc, eg made by a gentle wind, or of the rise and fall of soft voices or laughter: *A long ~ of laughter passed through the audience.* □ *vt,vi* (cause to) move in ripples; (cause to) rise and fall gently: *The wheat ~d in the breeze.*

rip·saw /ˈrɪpˌsɔ/ *n* [C] saw with coarse teeth, used for cutting wood along the grain.

rise[1] /raiz/ *n* [C] **1** small hill or upward slope: *on the ~ of a hill; a ~ in the ground.* **2** increase (in value, temperature, etc): *a ~ in prices.* **3** upward progress: *a ~ in social position; the ~ and fall of the tide.* **4** (*informal*) emotional reaction: *get a ~ out of a person.* **5** origin; start: *The river has/takes its ~ among the hills.* ***give rise to,*** be the cause of; suggest: *Such conduct might give ~ to misunderstandings.*

rise[2] /raiz/ *vi* (*pt* rose /rouz/, *pp* risen /ˈrɪzən/) **1** (of the sun, moon, stars) appear above the horizon: *The sun ~s in the East.* ⇨ set[2] (1). **2** get up from a lying, sitting or kneeling position: *The wounded man fell and was too weak to ~. The horse rose on its hind legs.* **3** get out of bed; get up (which is more usual): *He ~s very early.* **4** come to life (again): *He looked as though he had ~n from the dead/the grave.* **5** go, come, up or higher; reach a high(er) level or position: *The river/flood, etc has ~n two feet. Prices continue to ~. The temperature is rising. New buildings are rising in our town.* **6** come to the surface: *Bubbles rose from the bottom of the lake.* **7** slope upwards: *rising ground.* **8** have as a starting point; originate: *Where does the Nile ~?* **9** become or be visible above the surroundings: *A range of hills rose on our left.* **10** develop greater intensity, volume, or pitch: *The wind is rising. His voice rose in anger/excitement, etc.* **11** reach a higher position in society; make progress (in one's profession, etc): *~ in the world; ~ from the ranks,* ie to be an officer; *a rising young politician/lawyer.* **12** become more cheerful: *Our spirits rose when we heard the good news.* **13** ***rise to an occasion/a challenge,*** prove oneself able to deal with an unexpected problem, a difficult task, etc. **14** (often with *up*) rebel; revolt: *~ (up) against the government.*

ris·ing *n* [C] (esp) armed rebellion. ⇨ uprising.

ris·er /ˈraizər/ *n* [C] **1** person who rises, esp from sleep; *early/late ~.* **2** vertical part of a step, connecting the treads of a staircase.

risk /rɪsk/ *n* **1** [U] possibility or chance of danger, loss, injury, etc: *There's no/not much ~ of injury if you obey the rules.* ***at one's own risk,*** accepting responsibility, agreeing to make no claims, for loss, injury, etc. ***at the risk of,*** with the possibility of loss, etc: *He was determined to get there even at the ~ of his life.* **2** situation or instance of risk. ***run/take risks/a risk/the risk of sth,*** put oneself in a position where there is risk: *She's too sensible to take ~s when she's driving. He was ready to run the ~ of being taken prisoner by the enemy.* **3** [C] person or thing considered as a possibility for loss: *He's a good/poor ~.* □ *vt* **1** expose to risk: *~ one's health in the jungle.* **2** take the chance of: *We mustn't ~ getting caught in a storm.*

risky *adj* (-ier, -iest) full of danger: *a ~y undertaking.*

ris·qué /rɪˈskei/ *adj* slightly improper; likely to be considered indecent.

rite /rait/ *n* [C] **1** act or ceremony (esp in religious services): *ˈburial ~s.* **2** form prescribed for such a ceremony.

rit·ual /ˈrɪtʃuəl/ *n* **1** [U] all the rites or forms connected with a ceremony; way of conducting a religious service: *the ~ of the Catholic Church.* **2** [C] any procedure regularly followed, as if it were a ritual: *He went through his usual ~ of cutting and lighting his cigar.* **3** [C] group of ceremonial observances. □ *adj* of or according to rites or ritual: *the ~ dances of an African tribe.*

ritzy /ˈrɪtsi/ *adj* (*informal, dated*) posh; high-class, esp in a showy or exaggerated way; *a ~ hotel.*

riv. *abbr* = river.

ri·val /ˈraivəl/ *n* [C] person who competes with another (because he wants the same thing, or to be or do better than the other): *ˈbusiness ~s; ~s in love;* (as an *adjective*) *~ business firms.* □ *vt* (-l-, -ll-) **1** be a rival of. **2** equal; be as good as: *Can baseball ~ football in excitement?*

ri·valry /ˈraivəlri/ *n* [C,U] (*pl* -ies) (instance of) being rivals.

river /ˈrɪvər/ *n* [C] **1** large natural stream of water flowing in a channel to the sea or to a lake, etc or joining another river: *the Mississippi River.* ***sell sb down the river,*** (*fig*) betray him. ***send sb up the river,*** (*sl*) send him to prison. **2** great flow: *a ~ of lava; ~s of blood,* great bloodshed (as in war).

ˈriver basin, area drained by a river and its tributaries.

ˈriver·bed *n* [C] ground over which a river flows.

ˈriver·side *n* [C] ground along a river bank.

rivet /ˈrɪvɪt/ *n* [C] metal pin or bolt for fixing metal plates (eg in a ship's sides), the plain end being hammered flat to prevent slipping. □ *vt* **1** fasten with rivets; flatten (the end of a bolt) to make it secure. **2** (*fig*) fix or concentrate (one's eyes, attention) on: *He ~ed his eyes on the scene.* **3** take up, hold (attention, etc): *Some television documentaries are ~ing.*

rivu·let /ˈrɪvyəlɪt/ *n* [C] small stream.

rm. *abbr* = **1** ream. **2** room.

RN, R.N. *abbr* = registered nurse.

rnd. *abbr* = round.

roach /routʃ/ *n* [C] **1** (*informal*) = cockroach. **2** (*sl*) marijuana cigarette.

road /roud/ *n* [C] **1** clear, level way between (usually remote) places, for the use of vehicles, pedestrians, etc: (as an *adjective*) *ˈ~ junctions; ˈ~ map of California; ˈ~ sign.* ***hit the road,*** **(a)** (*informal*) go on a trip. **(b)** (*sl*) leave a place: *Hit the ~!* Get out! ***(be) on the road,*** (be) traveling (esp in connection with one's occupation). **2** one's way or route: *You're in the/my ~,* obstructing me. **3** ***the road to,*** way of getting: *Is too much drinking the ~ to ruin?*

ˈroad·block *n* [C] barricade built across a road to stop or slow down traffic (eg by police to catch an escaped prisoner).

ˈroad hog, (*sl*) inconsiderate driver.

ˈroad·side *n* [C] ground along the side of a road.

ˈroad test, test of a vehicle's performance under actual driving conditions.

roam /roum/ *vi,vt* travel without any definite aim or destination over or through (a country, etc); roam: *~ about the world/~ the seas.*

roar /rɔr/ *n* [C] loud, deep sound as of a wild animal, of thunder, of a person in pain, etc: *the ~s of a tiger; the ~ of traffic; ~s of laughter.* □ *vt,vi* **1** make such loud, deep sounds: *lions ~ing in the distance. Several trucks ~ed past; ~ with laughter/pain.* **2** say, sing, loudly: *~ out an order/a drinking song; ~ oneself hoarse,* make oneself hoarse by roaring.

roar·ing *adj* **(a)** unruly; noisy: *The~ing twenties,* the wild decade of the 1920s. **(b)** lively; thriving: *do a ~ing business.* □ *adv* wildly; extremely: *~ing drunk.*

roast /roust/ *vt,vi* **1** cook, be cooked, in a hot oven, or over or in front of a hot fire: *The meat was ~ing in the oven.* **2** prepare certain kinds of seeds (eg coffee and cacao beans) for consumption by means of heat. **3** (*fig*) suffer from the heat: *We were ~ing in the overheated room.* □ *adj* roasted: *~ beef/pork.* □ *n* [C] **1** piece of meat for roasting or that has been roasted. **2** outdoor meal at which food is roasted.

roast·er *n* [C] **(a)** (esp) kind of pan for roasting. **(b)** chicken, etc suitable for roasting.

rob /rab/ *vt* (-bb-) **1** take property from (a person or a place) unlawfully (and often by force): *The bank was robbed last night. I was robbed of my watch.* **2** deprive a person of (what is due to him, etc): *be robbed of the rewards of one's labor.*

rob·ber *n* [C]

rob·bery /ˈrabəri/ *n* [C,U] (*pl* -ries) (instance of) robbing.

robe /roub/ *n* [C] **1** long, loose outer garment. **2** bathrobe. **3** (often *pl*) long, loose garment often worn as a sign of rank or office: *magistrates/judges in their black ~s.* □ *vt* put a robe on: *professors ~d in their academic gowns.*

robin /ˈrabɪn/ *n* [C] large, brownish bird with red breast-feathers.

ro·bot /ˈrouˌbat/ *n* [C] machine which can perform human tasks.

ro·bust /rouˈbəst/ *adj* strong, active; healthy: *a ~ young man; a ~ appetite.*

ro·bust·ly *adv*

ro·bust·ness /-nɪs/ *n* [U]

rock[1] /rak/ *n* **1** [U] solid stony part of the earth's crust: *a house built on ~.* **2** [C,U] large mass of rock. **3** [C] stone: *~s rolling down the side of a mountain.* **4** [C] someone or something that is very reliable. **5** ***on the rocks,*** (*fig*) **(a)** in or into a state of failure or ruin. **(b)** (of alcoholic drinks) served over ice, with no water, soda, etc.

ˌrock-ˈbottom *adj* down to the lowest point: *~-bottom prices.*

ˈrock crystal, pure natural transparent quartz.

rock[2] /rak/ *vt,vi* **1** (cause to) sway or swing backwards and forwards, or from side to side: *~ a baby to sleep.* **2** shake violently: *The town was ~ed by an earthquake.* ***rock the boat,*** (*fig*) do something that upsets the smooth progress of an undertaking, etc.

rock·er *n* [C] **(a)** one of the curved pieces of

wood on which something, eg a chair or cradle, rocks. **(b)** = rocking chair. **(c)** ***off one's rocker,*** (*sl*) crazy.

ˈ**rocking chair,** one fitted with rockers on which it rests.

ˈ**rocking horse,** toy horse with rockers for a child to ride on.

rock[3] /rak/ *n* **1** [C] swaying movement. **2** [U] popular music with a highly stressed beat, containing elements derived from blues, folk and country music.

rock-'n-roll /ˌrak-ən-ˈroul/ *n* [U] (also **rock and roll**) = rock[3] (2).

rocket /ˈrakɪt/ *n* [C] **1** device which is filled with fast-burning material, which launches itself into the air (as a firework, as a signal of distress) and explodes in a shower of sparks. **2** jet engine which carries its own oxygen for burning fuel in order to produce a forward or upward thrust: *~ propulsion; ˈ~-propelled.* **3** spacecraft or missile propelled by such an engine: □ *vi* travel or go up fast (as) in a rocket: *Prices are ~ing.*

rock·etry /-tri/ *n* [U] (science of) using rockets for space missiles, etc.

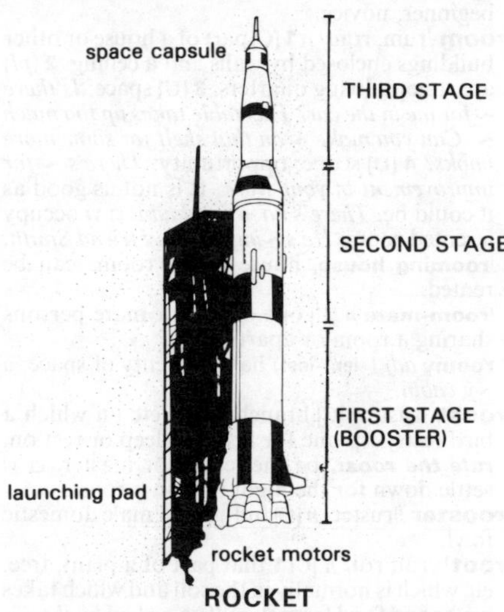

ROCKET

Rockies /ˈrakiz/ *n pl* = Rocky Mountains.

rocky[1] /ˈraki/ *adj* (-ier, -iest) **1** of rock, full of rocks: *a ~ road; ~ soil.* **2** hard and firm like rock.

ˌ**Rocky** ˈ**Mountains,** principal mountain system in the western US and Canada.

rocky[2] *adj* (-ier, -iest) **1** unstable; shaky: *a ~ table.* **2** difficult: *a ~ career.*

rod /rad/ *n* [C] **1** thin, straight piece of wood or metal: *a ˈfishing rod.* **2** stick used for punishing. **3** (*sl*) revolver. **4** measure of length equal to $5\frac{1}{2}$ yds. **5** rod-shaped cell in the retina of the eye, which is sensitive to dim light.

rode *pt* of ride[2].

ro·dent /ˈroudənt/ *n* [C] animal, eg a rat, rabbit, squirrel or beaver, which has large front teeth specially adapted for gnawing.

ro·deo /ˈroudiˌou, rouˈdeiou/ *n* [C] (*pl* ~s) **1** (on the plains of Western US) rounding up of cattle. **2** exhibition of skill in lassoing cattle, riding untamed horses, etc.

roe[1] /rou/ *n* [C,U] (mass of) eggs in a female fish, esp with the membrane in which they are held.

roe[2] /rou/ *n* [C] (*pl* roes, roe) small kind of European and Asiatic deer.

ˈ**roe·buck** *n* [C] male roe.

rogue /roug/ *n* [C] **1** (*old use*) vagabond. **2** scoundrel; rascal. **3** person fond of playing tricks, teasing people.

ro·guery /ˈrougəri/ *n* (*pl* -ies) **(a)** [C,U] (instance or example of the) conduct of a rogue. **(b)** [U] mischievousness.

ro·guish /ˈrougɪʃ/ *adj*

role, rôle /roul/ *n* [C] **1** actor's part in a play: *play the ˈtitle ~ in "Hamlet,"* play the part of Hamlet. **2** proper task or function: *What is your new ~ on the Committee?*

roll[1] /roul/ *n* [C] **1** something made into the shape of a cylinder by being rolled: *a ~ of carpet/photographic film; a jelly ~,* cake spread with jelly and then rolled up. **2** (esp) small, rounded piece of bread dough which has been shaped and baked. **3** act of rolling or rolling movement: *The slow, steady ~ of the ship made us sick.* **4** official list or record, esp of names. ***call the roll,*** read out a list of names (to check who is present and who absent). **5** rolling sound: *the distant ~ of thunder/drums.*

ˈ**roll call,** action of calling the roll.

roll[2] /roul/ *vt,vi* **1** (cause to) move along by turning over and over: *The coin fell and ~ed under the table. The bicycle hit me and sent me ~ing/~ed me over. He ~ed* (= wrapped by turning over) *himself* (*up*) *in the blanket.* **2** make into the shape of a ball or a cylinder: *Roll the string into a ball. The campers ~ed up their sleeping bags.* **3** move steadily or smoothly: *The clouds ~ed away as the sun rose higher. The years ~ed on/by,* passed. *The smoke ~ed up the chimney. The tears were ~ing* (= flowing) *down her cheeks.* **4** turn over and over: *a dog ~ing on the ground.* **5** make smooth or flat, (as) with a rolling pin, etc: *~ a lawn; ~ out pastry for a pie.* **6** (cause to) sway or move from side to side: *The ship was ~ing heavily. The drunken man ~ed as he walked.* **7** have surfaces that rise and fall: *miles and miles of ~ing country.* **8** move, be moved, on wheels or rollers: *The car ~ed down the hill. We ~ed the piano into the corner.* **9** make or send out, long, deep, vibrating or echoing sounds: *The thunder ~ed in the distance.* ***roll one's r's,*** utter them with the tongue making a rapid succession of taps against the palate. **10** (of the eyes) (cause to) move around in the socket: *His eyes ~ed strangely. Don't ~ your eyes at me.* **11** (*informal*) enjoy a great abundance: *simply ~ing in money.* **12** (special uses with *adverbial particles* and *prepositions*):

roll in, come, arrive, in large numbers or quantities: *Offers of help are ~ing in.*

roll up, **(a)** increase; accumulate: *He ~ed up a large number of votes.* **(b)** arrive (in a vehicle): *Two or three latecomers ~ed up.*

roller /ˈroulər/ *n* [C] **1** cylinder-shaped object of wood, metal, rubber, etc, for pressing, smoothing, shaping, etc: *put her hair up in* ~*s to make it curly*. **2** cylinder of wood, metal, around which something may be rolled: ~ *for a window shade*. **3** small wheel. **4** cylinder for applying paint or ink. **5** long, rolling wave.

ˈroller skate, skate with small wheels for use on a smooth surface.

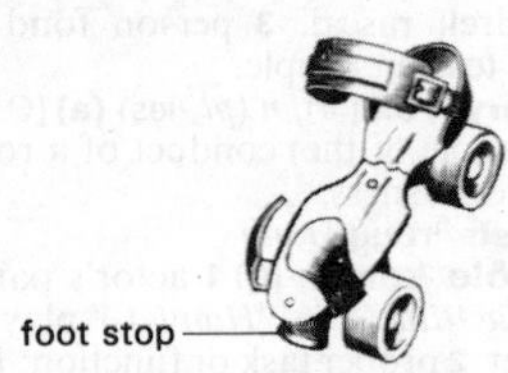

ROLLER SKATES

roll·ing pin /ˈroulɪŋ ˌpɪn/ *n* [C] cylinder of wood for rolling pastry, etc.

roly-poly /ˌrouli-ˈpouli/ *n* [C] (*pl* roly-polies), *adj* person or thing that is short and plump.

Ro·man /ˈroumən/ *adj* **1** of Rome, esp ancient Rome: *the* ~ *Empire*. **2** Roman Catholic, of or relating to the Church. □ *n* citizen or inhabitant of ancient Rome.

ˌroman ˈletter/ˈtype, upright kind, not italic.

ˌroman ˈnumeral, numeral, as I, IV, XL, M, etc (as in the system of the ancient Romans), used esp on clock faces and public monuments, and to indicate the number in a series (of volumes in a set, of descendants or successors with the same name, etc).

ro·mance /rouˈmæns/ *n* **1** [C] **(a)** story or novel of adventure. **(b)** love story. **2** [C] medieval story, often in verse, relating the adventures of some hero of chivalry. **3** [C] love affair: *Their* ~ *is over*. **4** [U] qualities characteristic of stories of love and adventure: *travel abroad in search of* ~.

Ro·mance lan·guage /rouˌmæns ˈlæŋwɪdʒ/ *n* [C] language, eg French, Italian, Spanish, Portuguese, Rumanian, etc, developed from Latin.

ro·man·tic /rouˈmæntɪk/ *adj* **1** not practical; remote from experience and real life: *a* ~ *schoolboy;* ~ *notions of saving the world*. **2** of, like, suggesting, romances or romance: ~ *music/situations/adventures/tales/scenes; a* ~ *old castle*. **3** of or relating to love. **4** (in art, literature and music) of or characteristic of romanticism: *the* ~ *poets*, eg Shelley, Keats. □ *n* [C] person with romantic(1, 3) ideals.

ro·man·ti·cally /-kli/ *adv*

ro·man·ti·cism /rouˈmæntəˌsɪzəm/ *n* [U] movement in art, literature and music marked by an emphasis on imagination, feeling, and freedom from conventional constraints.

ro·man·ti·cist /-təsɪst/ *n* [C] follower of romanticism.

romp /ramp/ *vi* **1** (esp of children) play about, esp running, jumping and being rather rough. **2** win, succeed, quickly or without apparent effort: *John just* ~*s through his examinations*, passes them easily. □ *n* [C] period of romping: *have a* ~.

rom·pers *n pl* child's garment with loose, full legs.

roof /ruf, rʊf/ *n* [C] (*pl* ~s) **1** top covering of a building, tent, bus, car, etc: *a slate* ~. ***raise the roof,*** (*informal*) create an uproar or fuss. **2** anything like a roof: *the* ~ *of heaven*, the sky; *the* ~ *of the mouth*, the palate. □ *vt* (*pp* ~ed /ruft, rʊft/) supply or cover with a roof: *a shed* ~*ed over with strips of bark*.

roof·ing *n* [U] material used for roofs (eg slates, tiles).

rook[1] /rʊk/ *n* [C] large black bird like a crow.

rook·ery /-əri/ *n* [C] (*pl* -ies) **(a)** place (a group of trees) where many rooks have their nests. **(b)** breeding place or colony of some other birds or animals, eg penguins or seals.

rook[2] /rʊk/ *vt* cheat.

rook[3] /rʊk/ *n* [C] chess piece (also called a *castle*) which can move across any number of unoccupied squares in a vertical or horizontal direction.

rook·ie /ˈrʊki/ *n* [C] (*informal*) **1** recruit, undergoing training in the Army, police force, etc. **2** athlete in his first year as a professional player, eg on a major baseball or football team. **3** beginner; novice.

room /rum, rʊm/ *n* **1** [C] part of a house or other buildings enclosed by walls and a ceiling. **2** (*pl*) apartment; living quarters: **3** [U] space: *Is there* ~ *for me in the car? This table takes up too much* ~. *Can you make* ~ *on that shelf for some more books?* **4** [U] scope; opportunity: *There's* ~ *for improvement in your work*, It is not as good as it could be. *There's no* ~ *for doubt*. □ *vi* occupy a rented room: *He's* ~*ing with my friend Smith*.

ˈrooming house, house where rooms can be rented.

ˈroom-mate *n* [C] one of two or more persons sharing a room or apartment.

roomy *adj* (-ier, -iest) having plenty of space: *a* ~*y cabin*.

roost /rust/ *n* [C] branch, pole, etc on which a bird rests, esp one for hens to sleep or rest on. ***rule the roost,*** be the leader or master. □ *vi* settle down for the night (as) on a roost.

rooster /ˈrustər/ *n* [C] full-grown male domestic fowl.

root[1] /rut, rʊt/ *n* [C] **1** that part of a plant, tree, etc which is normally in the soil and which takes water and food from it: *pull up a plant by the* ~*s*. ⇨ illus at vegetable. ***take root,*** **(a)** (eg of a cutting) send out roots and start to grow. **(b)** (*fig*) become established. **2** that part of a hair, tooth, the tongue, a fingernail, etc that is like a root in position, function, etc. **3** (*fig*) basis or source: *Is money the* ~ *of all evil?* ***get at/to the root of sth,*** deal with (the problem) at its source. **4** (*pl*) ties or feelings of attachment to a community, group, etc: *pull up one's* ~*s,* move from a settled home, job, etc; *put down new* ~*s,* establish new ties in another place. **5** (*gram*) word from which other words are formed, eg by adding affixes: *"Walk" is the* ~ *of "walks," "walked," "walking," and "walker."* **6** (*math*) quantity which, when multiplied by itself an indicated number of times, produces a specified product: *4 is the square* ~ *of 16 and the cube* ~ *of 64*.

ˈroot beer, non-alcoholic drink flavored with

roots.

root[2] /rut, rʊt/ *vt,vi* **1** (of plants, cuttings, etc) (cause to) send out roots and begin to grow: *Some cuttings ~ easily.* **2** cause to stand fixed and unmoving: *He stood there ~ed to the spot.* **3** ***root sth out,*** remove (as) by pulling out the roots.

root[3] /rut, rʊt/ *vi,vt* **1** dig or turn up the ground with the snout: *pigs ~ing across from the ground in search of food.* **2** poke about; turn things over when searching: *~ing around among piles of papers for a missing document.*

root[4] /rut/ *vi* (*informal*) encourage or support (as) by cheering: *~ing for the baseball team.*

rope /roup/ *n* **1** [C,U] (piece or length of) thick strong cord or wire cable made by twisting finer cords or wires together. ***give sb (plenty of) rope,*** (*fig*) freedom of action. ***give sb enough rope to hang himself,*** leave him to bring about his own ruin. **2** ***know/learn the ~s,*** the conditions, the rules, the procedure (in some sphere of an action). **3** [C] number of things twisted, strung or threaded together: *a ~ of flowers.* □ *vt* fasten or bind with rope: *~ climbers together*, connect them with a rope for safety. ***rope sth off,*** separate with a rope: *Part of the field was ~d off.* ***rope sb in,*** persuade him to help in some activity.

ro·sary /ˈrouzəri/ *n* [C] (*pl* -ies) **1** series of prayers used in the Roman Catholic Church. **2** string of beads for counting prayers.

rose[1] *pt* of rise[2].

rose[2] /rouz/ *n* **1** [C] (shrub or bush with prickles or thorns on its stems and bearing a) colorful and usually sweet-smelling flower. ⇨ illus at flower. ***a ˌbed of ˈroses,*** a pleasant, easy condition of life. **2** [U] deep pinkish-red color. ***see things through rose-colored glasses,*** be very optimistic.

ˈrose·bud *n* [C] bud of a rose.

rose·mary /ˈrouzˌmeri/ *n* [U] evergreen shrub with fragrant leaves used as a herb and in making perfumes.

ro·sette /rouˈzet/ *n* [C] small rose-shaped badge, ornament or carving in stone.

rose·wood /ˈrouzˌwʊd/ *n* [U] hard, dark red wood obtained from several varieties of tropical tree.

Rosh Hashanah /ˌrouʃəˈʃanə, ˌraʃə-, ˌrɔʃə-, -ˈʃounə/ *n* [C] (*Hebrew*) Jewish New Year.

rosin /ˈrazən/ *n* [U] resin, esp in solid form, as used on the bows of string instruments. □ *vt* rub with rosin.

ros·ter /ˈrastər/ *n* [C] list of names esp of persons available for duty.

ros·trum /ˈrastrəm/ *n* [C] (*pl* ~s or -tra /-trə/) platform for public speaking.

rosy /ˈrouzi/ *adj* (-ier, -iest) **1** of a reddish or deep pink color: *~ cheeks.* **2** (*fig*) good, bright, cheerful: *~ prospects.*

rot /rat/ *n* [U] **1** decay; condition of rotting or of being rotten: *Rot has set in*, decay has begun. **2** (*informal*) nonsense. □ *vt,vi* (-tt-) (cause to) deteriorate, decay, or decompose because of the action of bacteria: *The wood rotted away.*

ro·ta·ry /ˈroutəri/ *adj* relating to, causing, moving in, rotation: *~ movement.* □ *n* [C] (*pl* -ies) **1** rotary machine. **2** one-way road in the form of a circle at the junction of several streets or roads.

ro·tate /ˈrouˌteit/ *vt,vi* **1** (cause to) turn around on axis or center point. **2** (cause to) take turns or come in succession: *~ players on a team.*

ro·ta·tion /rouˈteiʃən/ *n* **1 (a)** [U] rotating or being rotated: *the ~ of the earth.* **(b)** [C] complete turning: *five ~s an hour.* **2** [C,U] regular coming round of things or events in succession: *ˈcrop ~*, varying the crops grown each year on the same land to avoid exhausting the soil. ***in rotation,*** in turn; in regular succession.

ro·tis·serie /rouˈtɪsəri/ *n* [C] revolving spit for cooking food directly over a fire.

ro·tor /ˈroutər/ *n* [C] assembly of horizontally rotating blades of a helicopter propellor.

rot·ten /ˈratən/ *adj* **1** decayed; having gone bad: *~ eggs.* **2** (*informal*) very bad; terrible: *She's had a ~ day at work.*

ro·tund /rouˈtənd/ *adj* **1** plump; rounded. **2** rich and full: *~ tones.*

ro·tunda /rouˈtəndə/ *n* [C] circular domed (part of a) building.

rouge /ruʒ/ *n* [U] **1** cosmetic for coloring the cheeks or lips. **2** powder used for polishing metal, glass, etc. □ *vt* apply rouge to.

rough[1] /rəf/ *adj* (-er, -est) **1** having a surface that is not level, smooth or polished: *~ paper; a ~ skin.* **2** not calm or gentle; moving or acting violently: *~ children; ~ behavior; a ~* (= stormy) *sea.* ***give sb/have a rough time,*** (cause him to) experience hardship, to be treated severely, etc (according to context). ***rough and tumble,*** disorderly. **3** made or done without attention to detail, esp as a first attempt: *a ~ sketch/translation; a ~ draft*, eg of a letter. ***rough-and-ready,*** good enough for ordinary or general purposes, occasions, etc; not particularly efficient, etc: *ˌ~-and-ready ˈmethods.* **4** (of sounds) harsh: *a ~ voice.*

rough·ly *adv* **(a)** in a rough manner: *treat somebody ~ly.* **(b)** approximately: *at a cost of ~ly $5.* **(c)** ***roughly speaking,*** with no claim to accuracy.

rough[2] /rəf/ *adv* in a rough manner: *play ~*, be (rather) violent (in games, etc).

rough[3] /rəf/ *n* [U] uneven, uncleared ground.

roughen /ˈrəfən/ *vt,vi* make or become rough.

rough·house /ˈrəfˌhaus, -ˌhauz/ *vt, vi* (*informal*) **1** act boisterously. **2** handle roughly. □ *n* (*informal*) boisterous disturbance: (as an *adj*): *~ behavior.*

rough·neck /ˈrəfˌnek/ *n* [C] (*informal*) noisy, ill-mannered person.

rou·lette /ruˈlet/ *n* [U] gambling game in which a small ball falls by chance into one of the numbered compartments of a revolving wheel.

round[1] /raund/ *adj* (-er, -est) **1 (a)** having a shape like a circle, a ball, or a column. **(b)** curved. **2** plump: *a short, ~ body.* **3** done with or involving a circular movement. ***round trip,*** trip made to a place and then back to the starting point. **4** complete; full: *a ~ dozen.* **5** ***round number,*** number that is approximately correct as the result of rounding off to the nearest tenth, ten, hundred, etc.

round·ness *n* [U]

round[2] /raund/ *adv* = around.

round[3] /raund/ *n* [C] **1** something round in shape: *a ~ of toast* (esp). **2** ***in the round,*** with the audience on all sides of a center stage. **3** habitual route; customary series of visits: *The doctor makes his ~s of the wards every evening.* **4** (in games, contests, etc) one unit of play: *a boxing match of ten ~s.* **5** one of a set or series of recurring actions or events: *a ~ of drinks,* one drink for every member of the group; *another ~ of price increases.* **6** (ammunition for) one discharge of a weapon, by a single person or by a group: *have only three ~s of ammunition left,* enough to fire three times. **7** song for several persons or groups, the second singing the first line while the first is singing the second line, etc. **8** dance in which the dancers are arranged in a circle.

round[4] /raund/ *vt,vi* **1** make or become round: *stones ~ed by the action of water.* **2** go around: *He ~ed the corner on two wheels.* **3** ***round off,*** **(a)** finish; complete: *~ed off her job by writing a report.* **(b)** adjust a number to the nearest tenth, ten, hundred, etc: *~ off 2.8 to 3.* **4** ***round sb/sth up,*** drive, bring or collect, together: *He ~ed up the tourists and took them back to the bus. The cowboy ~ed up the cattle.*

round·about /ˈraundəˌbaut/ *adj* indirect: *I heard the news in a ~ way. What a ~ way of doing things!*

round·ly /ˈraundli/ *adv* **1** in the form of a curve, circle, etc. **2** completely; thoroughly. **3** bluntly.

round·up /ˈraunˌdəp/ *n* [C] **1** act of bringing or gathering cattle together. **2** act of gathering together a group of persons or things.

rouse /rauz/ *vt,vi* (usually *formal*) **1** wake up: *I was ~ed by the ringing of a bell.* **2** cause (a person) to be or become more active, interested, etc: *politicians rousing the masses; be ~d to anger by insults.*

roust·a·bout /ˈraustəˌbaut/ *n* [C] deck hand, dock worker, esp one who loads and unloads ships.

rout[1] /raut/ *n* [C] **1** disastrous defeat. **2** disorderly retreat after a defeat. □ *vt* **1** defeat completely. **2** put to flight.

rout[2] /raut/ *vt* **1** get (a person) up/out from a place, out of bed, etc: *We were ~ed out of our cabins before breakfast.* **2** dig up; root.

route /rut, raut/ *n* [C] **1** way or road from one place to another. **2** itinerary for a particular carrier to deliver mail, newspapers, milk, etc. **3** (*fig*) way or means: *the ~ to victory.* □ *vt* send by a certain route: *We were ~d through Chicago.*

rou·tine /ruˈtin/ *n* [C,U] fixed and regular way of doing things: *the dull ~ of housework.* □ *adj* having the character of a routine.

rou·tine·ly *adv*

rove /rouv/ *vt,vi* wander aimlessly over; roam: *~ the desert. His eyes were roving about the room.*

rover *n* [C]

row[1] /rou/ *n* [C] number of persons or things in a usually straight line: *a row of houses/plants/desks; take a seat at the end of the row.* ***have a hard row to hoe,*** (*informal*) have a difficult task.

row[2] /rou/ *vt,vi* **1** propel a boat with oars. **2** carry or transport in this way: *Shall I row you up the river?* □ *n* [C] act or instance of rowing.

row·er *n* [C]

row[3] /rau/ *n* [C,U] loud quarrel or disturbance: *have a row with the neighbors; make a row rushing down the stairs.* □ *vi* quarrel noisily: *He rowed with his wife all evening.*

row·boat /ˈrouˌbout/ *n* [C] small boat propelled by oars.

row·dy /ˈraudi/ *adj* (-ier, -iest) noisy and disorderly in behavior. □ *n* [C] (*pl* -ies) person who is rowdy.

row·dily /-əli/ *adv*

row·di·ness /ˈraudinɪs/ *n* [U]

royal /ˈrɔiəl/ *adj* of, like, suitable for, supported by, or relating to, a king or queen: *the ~ family.*

roy·al·ist /-ɪst/ *n* [C] **(a)** supporter of government by a king or queen. **(b) Royalist,** supporter of the royal side, as in a civil war or revolt, esp a supporter of the British Crown during the American Revolution.

roy·ally /ˈrɔiəli/ *adv*

roy·alty /ˈrɔiəlti/ *n* (*pl* -ies) **1** [U] royal persons: *The play was performed in the presence of ~.* **2** [U] position, rank, dignity, or power, of a monarch. **3** (*pl*) money paid to an author, inventor, etc from the profits made by the sale or use of his work.

rpm /ˌarˌpi ˈem/ *abbr* = revolution(s) per minute.

rpt. *abbr* = report.

RR *abbr* = railroad.

R.S.V.P. /ˌar ˌes ˌvi ˈpi/ *abbr* (= *F* Répondez s'il vous plaît) (at the end of a formal invitation) please reply.

rt. *abbr* = right.

Rte. *abbr* = route.

rub[1] /rəb/ *vt,vi* (-bb-) **1** press and move (something) back and forth on the surface (eg of a body or object): *The dog rubbed its head against my legs. She asked me to rub her shoulder. He was rubbing his hands together.* **2** put on or spread by rubbing: *rub liniment on aching legs; rub polish on a table.* **3** bring to a certain state by rubbing: *rub the table top to a high polish.* **4** chafe or make sore by rubbing: *The new shoes rubbed her heel.* ***rub sb the wrong way,*** irritate or annoy him: *Her criticism rubbed me the wrong way.* **5** (special uses with *adverbial particles* and *prepositions*):

rub sb/sth down, massage or rub vigorously.

rub sth in/into sth, force it in by rubbing: *Rub the ointment well in/into the skin.* ***rub it in,*** remind a person repeatedly of a fault, failure, etc: *I know I behaved foolishly but you needn't rub it in.*

rub sth off, remove it by rubbing.

rub sth out, remove (marks, writing, etc) by rubbing: *rub out a word/pencil marks/mistakes.*

rub[2] /rəb/ *n* [C] **1** act of rubbing. **2** remark that hurts someone's feelings. **3** difficulty: *I'd like to go to the theater; the rub is I don't have enough money.*

rub·ber[1] /ˈrəbər/ *n* **1** [U] tough elastic substance made from the milky liquid that flows from certain trees when the bark is cut, used for making tires, tennis balls, etc: (as an *adjective*) *'~ trees; ~ bands*, elastic bands for keeping things together. **2** [U] synthetic material similar to this. **3** [C] piece of rubber material for rubbing out pencil marks, etc. **4** (*pl*) low overshoe made of rubber.

rub·ber[2] /ˈrəbər/ *n* [C] (in such card-games as whist and bridge) **1** three successive games between the same sides or persons. **2** the winning of two games out of three; the third game when each side has won one.

rub·bish /ˈrəbɪʃ/ *n* [U] **1** waste material; that which is, or is to be, thrown away as worthless. **2** nonsense; worthless ideas: *This book is ~.*

rubble /ˈrəbəl/ *n* [U] bits of broken stone, rock or brickwork: *build roads with a foundation of ~.*

rub·down /ˈrəbˌdaun/ *n* [C] massage or vigorous rubbing.

ruby /ˈrubi/ *n* **1** [C] (*pl* -ies) deep red precious stone. **2** [U] (often as an *adj*) deep red color.

ruck·sack /ˈrəkˌsæk/ *n* [C] knapsack.

ruck·us /ˈrəkəs/ *n* [C] (*informal*) noisy disturbance.

rud·der /ˈrədər/ *n* [C] **1** flat, broad piece of wood or metal hinged vertically at the stern of a boat or ship for steering. **2** similar structure attached to the tail of an aircraft.

ruddy /ˈrədi/ *adj* (-ier, -iest) **1** having a healthy red color: *~ cheeks*. **2** red or reddish: *a ~ glow in the sky*.

rude /rud/ *adj* (-r, -st) **1** discourteous; impolite; not showing respect or consideration: *It's ~ to interrupt/to point at people. Don't be ~ to your teacher.* **2** startling; violent; abrupt: *get a ~ shock*. **3** roughly made; crude: *the ~ prehistoric implements*.

rude·ly *adv* in a rude manner.

rude·ness /-nɪs/ *n* [U]

ru·di·ment /ˈrudəmənt/ *n* **1** (*pl*) basic principles: *learn the ~s of chemistry/grammar*. **2** [C] something which is incompletely formed or developed: *A newborn chick has only the ~s of wings.*

ru·di·men·tary /ˌrudəˈment(ə)ri/ *adj* **1** elementary: *a ~ knowledge of German*. **2** undeveloped: *~ tail*.

rue /ru/ *vt* (*archaic; liter*) feel remorse or regret: *You'll rue your unkindness some day.*

rue·ful /ˈrufəl/ *adj* showing, feeling, expressing, regret.

rue·fully /ˈrufəli/ *adv*

ruff /rəf/ *n* [C] **1** ring of differently colored or marked feathers around a bird's neck, or of hair around an animal's neck. **2** wide, stiff frill worn as a collar in the 16th century.

ruf·fian /ˈrəfiən/ *n* [C] violent, brutal young man.

ruffle /ˈrəfəl/ *vt,vi* **1** disturb the peace, calm or smoothness of: *The bird ~d up its feathers. Who's been ruffling your hair?* **2** trouble; annoy: *Anne is easily ~d.* **3** gather into a ruffle or frill. □ *n* **1** [C] frill used to ornament a garment, eg at the wrist or neck. **2** [U] ruffling or being ruffled (1).

rug /rəg/ *n* [C] **1** mat of thick material for covering all or part of a floor: *a ˈhearth rug*. **2** thick covering or blanket.

rug·ged /ˈrəgɪd/ *adj* **1** rough; uneven: *a ~ coast*. **2** having furrows or wrinkles: *a ~ face*. **3** hardy; full of endurance: *~ pioneers*. **4** difficult; severe: *a ~ test*.

rug·ged·ly *adv*

rug·ged·ness /-nɪs/ *n* [U]

ruin /ˈruɪn/ *n* **1** [U] destruction; overthrow; serious damage: *the ~ of her hopes*. **2** [U] state of being damaged, destroyed, worthless: *The castle has fallen into ~.* **3** [C] something which has decayed, been destroyed, etc: *The building is a ~/in ~s.* **4** (*sing* only) cause of ruin: *Gambling was his ~.* □ *vt* cause the ruin of: *The storm ~ed the crops.*

ruin·ation /ˌruɪˈneiʃən/ *n* [U] being ruined; bringing to ruin: *These debts will be the ~ation of him.*

ruin·ous /-əs/ *adj* causing or likely to cause ruin: *~ous expenditure*.

ruin·ous·ly *adv*: *~ously expensive*.

rule /rul/ *n* **1** [C] law or regulation which guides or controls behavior or action: *obey the ~s of the game. It's against the ~s to handle the ball in soccer.* ***rule of thumb,*** ⇨ thumb. **2** [C] habit: *He makes it a ~ to do an hour's work in the garden every day.* ***as a rule,*** usually; more often than not. **3** [U] government; authority: *countries that were once under French ~.* **4** [C] strip of wood, metal, etc, used to measure: *a ˈslide ~.* □ *vi,vt* **1** govern; have authority (over): *Is it true that she tries to ~ the office?* **2** control, guide, or influence: *Don't be ~d by your passions/by hatred.* **3** give as a decision: *The chairman ~d the motion out of order/that the motion was out of order.* ***rule sth out,*** declare that it cannot be considered, that it is out of the question: *That's a possibility that can't be ~d out*, it is something we must consider. **4** make (a line or lines) on paper (with a ruler): *~d notepaper*. ***rule sth off,*** separate it, end it, by ruling a line.

ruler /ˈrulər/ *n* [C] **1** person who rules or governs. **2** straight length of wood, plastic, metal, etc used in drawing straight lines or for measuring.

rul·ing /ˈrulɪŋ/ *adj* **1** having control; governing. **2** chief; predominant: *his ~ passion*. □ *n* [C] (esp) decision made by a person in authority, eg a judge.

rum /rəm/ *n* [C,U] alcoholic drink made from sugar cane or molasses.

rumble /ˈrəmbəl/ *vi,vt* **1** make, move with, a deep, heavy, continuous sound: *thunder/gunfire rumbling in the distance*. **2** make, say, in a deep voice: *~ out a few comments*. □ *n* [U] deep, heavy, continuous sound: *the ~ of a motor*.

ru·mi·nant /ˈrumənənt/ *n* [C], *adj* (animal) which chews the cud, eg cows, deer.

ru·mi·nate /ˈruməˌneit/ *vi* **1** meditate: *~ over/about/on recent events*. **2** (of animals) chew the cud.

ru·mi·na·tion /ˌruməˈneiʃən/ *n* [U]

ru·mi·na·tive /ˈrumənətɪv/ *adj* inclined to meditate.

rum·mage /ˈrəmɪdʒ/ *vi,vt* **1** search thoroughly by turning things over, moving things about, etc: *~ (about) in a desk drawer*. **2** find by searching thoroughly: *~ up some old letters*. □ *n* [U] thorough search.

ru·mor /ˈrumər/ *n* **1** [U] general talk, gossip: *Rumor has it that she will be promoted.* **2** [C] statement, report, or story which is of uncertain origin and doubtful accuracy: *There is a ~ that there will be a coal strike this winter.* □ *vt* report by way of rumor: *He is ~ed to have escaped to Mexico.* (*Note:* usually *passive.*)

rump /rəmp/ *n* [C] (cut of meat from the) fleshy back part of an animal's body, above the hind legs.

rumple /ˈrəmpəl/ *vt* crease; crumple; disorder: *Don't sit on my lap or you'll ~ my dress.*

rum·pus /ˈrəmpəs/ *n* [C] disturbance; noise: *What's all this ~ about?* ***kick up/make a rumpus,*** cause a rumpus.

run[1] /rən/ *n* **1** [C] act of running: *go for a short run across the fields.* ***at a run,*** running: *He started off at a run but soon got tired and began to walk.* ***on the run,*** **(a)** running away: *He's on the run from the police.* **(b)** continuously active and moving about: *I've been on the run all day.* ***a run for one's money,*** strong competition: *We must give him a good run for his money.* **2** [C] trip or journey in a car, train, etc: *Can we have a trial run in the new car?* **3** [C] distance traveled during such a trip: *a run of 40 miles.* **4** (*sing* only) route taken by vehicles, ships, etc: *The bus was taken off its usual run.* **5** (*sing* only) series of performances: *The play had a long run/a run of six months.* **6** (*sing* only) unbroken succession or series of events: *a run of bad luck.* **7** sudden series of demands by many customers on a bank or depositors. **8** (enclosed) space for domestic animals, fowls, etc: *a ˈchicken run.* **9** (*baseball*) when a player reaches home base safely. **10** common, average or ordinary type or class: *the common run of mankind,* ordinary, average people. **11** permission to make free use (of): *I have the run of his library.* **12** way in which things tend to move; general direction or trend: *The run of events is rather puzzling.* ***in the ˈlong run,*** in the end: *It pays in the long run to buy goods of high quality.* **13** (*music*) series of notes sung or played quickly and in the order of the scale. **14** large movement or migration of fish, esp to spawn: *a run of salmon,* eg on their way upstream. **15(a)** period of operation, production, processing, etc, eg in a factory. **(b)** amount or quantity produced in such a period. **16** unraveled length in knitted fabric: *a run in my stockings.*

ˌrun-of-the-ˈmill *adj* ordinary; average.

run[2] /rən/ *vi,vt* (*pt* ran /ræn/, *pp* run; -nn-) **1** (of men and animals) move with quick steps, faster than when walking: *run three miles; run fast; run upstairs. We ran to help him. Don't run across the road until you're sure it's safe.* **2** escape or flee (as) by running: *ran for his life.* **3** enter (a horse, etc) or compete in a race: *Is he running in the Boston Marathon? Are you running your horse in the Kentucky Derby?* ***run a race,*** take part in one. ***also-ran,*** ⇨also. **4** ***run for,*** compete for (an elected office): *run for President.* **5** present or put forward (for an office): *How many candidates is the Democratic Party running in the election?* **6** finish a race or contest in a certain position: *He ran second in the race.* **7** (cause to) move or go quickly, smoothly, or freely, to the end of, through, or over (eg something): *run one's fingers/a comb through one's hair; run one's eyes over a page. The thought kept running through my head. The pain ran up my arm. A shiver ran down his spine. The news ran like wildfire. A whisper ran through the crowd.* **8** expose or subject oneself to. ***run the chance/danger of sth:*** *You run the chance of being suspected of theft.* ***run risks/a risk/the risk of sth,*** ⇨ risk(2). **9** (of ships, etc) sail or steer; (of fish) swim: *The ship ran aground/on the rocks/ashore.* **10** travel in large numbers: *The salmon are running,* swimming upstream. **11** go forward with a sliding, smooth or continuous motion: *Sledges run well over frozen snow. The train ran past the signal.* **12** (cause to) function or operate: *He ran the machine at top speed. Don't leave the engine of your car running.* **13** travel or go back and forth: *The buses run every ten minutes.* **14** organize; manage: *run a business/a theater.* **15** convey; transport: *I'll run you back home,* drive you there in my car. ***run errands/messages (for sb),*** perform errands, carry messages, etc. **16** smuggle: *run liquor.* **17** cause (something) to penetrate or come into contact with: *run a splinter into one's finger. The drunken driver ran his car into a tree.* **18** (cause to) flow, drip: *The tears ran down my cheeks. Who has left the water running? She ran some hot water into the pan. Your nose is running.* **19** (of colors, dyes) spread: *Will the colors run if the dress is washed?* **20** become; pass into (a specified condition): *Supplies are running short/low. I have run short of money. Feelings/Passions ran high,* became stormy or violent. *My blood ran cold,* I was filled with horror. ***run wild,*** be without control, discipline, etc: *The garden is running wild. She lets her children run wild.* ***run a temperature,*** become feverish. **21** (cause to) extend, reach, or continue in a certain direction, to a certain limit etc: *shelves running round the walls; a scar that runs across his left cheek: a road that runs across the fields. He has run a wire to the lamp. The play ran* (*for*) *six months,* was kept on the stage, was performed, during this period of time. *The lease of my house has only a year to run.* **22** have a tendency or common characteristic: *Yellow hair runs in the family. These shoes run large.* **23** be in or take a certain form: *So the story ran,* that is what was told or said. **24** (of woven or knitted material) become unwoven or unravel: *Nylon stockings sometimes run.* **25** (special uses with *adverbial particles* and *prepositions*):

run across sb/sth, meet or find by chance: *I ran across her in Paris last week.*

run after sb/sth, chase; try to catch: *The dog was running after a rabbit.* ***run after sb,*** (*informal*) try to gain the attention and company of: *He's always running after women.*

run away, flee; escape: *The boy ran away to sea,* left home and became a sailor.

run down, **(a)** slow down and stop. **(b)** become weak or exhausted: *The battery is/has run down.* □ (*adj*) (of a person) become exhausted or weak from overwork, mental strain, etc. ***run sb***

down, **(a)** knock him down or collide with him: *He was run down by a truck.* **(b)** say unkind things about: *That man doesn't like me; he's always running me down.* **(c)** chase and overtake: *run down an escaped prisoner.*

run for it, run for safety, shelter, etc: *It's raining; let's run for it.*

run into sb/sth, **(a)** meet unexpectedly: *run into an old friend in the street; ran into difficulties.* **(b)** collide with: *The bus got out of control and ran into a wall.*

run off, go away; flee: *His daughter has run off with a married man/with all the funds.* ***run sth off,*** print; produce: *run off a hundred copies on the duplicating machine.*

run on, **(a)** talk continuously: *He will run on for an hour if you don't stop him.* **(b)** elapse: *Time ran on.*

run out, **(a)** go out: *The tide is running out.* **(b)** (of a period of time) come to an end: *When does the lease of the house run out?* **(c)** (of stocks, supplies) come to an end, be exhausted: *Our provisions are running out. Her patience is running out.* ***run 'out on sb,*** abandon, desert: *Poor Jane! Her husband has run out on her.*

run over sth, review or read through quickly: *Let's run over our parts again,* eg when learning and rehearsing parts in a play. *He ran over his notes before starting his lecture.* ***run over sb/run sb over,*** drive, pass over (a person, etc) in a vehicle: *He was run over and had to be taken to the hospital.*

run sth up, **(a)** raise; hoist: *run up a flag on the mast.* **(b)** erect, make quickly: *run up a dress; The builder ran up the house in only a few months.* **(c)** cause to increase or grow quickly in amount: *run up a big bill at a hotel.*

'run·away *adj, n* [C] **(a)** fugitive. **(b)** (horse, machine, etc which is) out of control.

'run·down *n* [C] item-by-item or point-by-point review.

'run·off *n* **(a)** [U] drainage. **(b)** [C] final contest between the most successful preliminary contestants in a race, election, etc.

rung[1] /rəŋ/ *n* [C] **1** rounded crosspiece between the legs of a chair. **2** crosspiece forming a step in a ladder. **3** (*fig*) particular level in society, one's employment, etc: *start on the lowest/reach the highest ~ (of the ladder).*

rung[2] *pp* of ring[2].

run·ner /ˈrənər/ *n* [C] **1** person, animal, etc that runs: *How many ~s were there in the race?* **2** messenger. **3** part on which something slides or moves along: *the ~s of a sledge.* **4** long narrow carpet, eg for stairs. **5** stem of a plant that puts forth roots along its length and so produces new plants.

runner·up /ˌrənərˈəp/ *n* [C] person, animal, taking second place in a race.

run·ning /ˈrənɪŋ/ *n* [U] competition. ***in/out of the running,*** (of competitors) having some/no chance of winning. □ *adj* **1** done, made, carried on, or started while running: *a ~ kick/jump.* **2** continuous; uninterrupted: *a ~ fire of questions,* coming in a continuous stream. **3** in succession: *win three times ~.* **4** flowing: *All bedrooms in this hotel have hot and cold ~ water.* **5** (of sores, etc) with liquid or pus coming out.

runny /ˈrəni/ *adj* (-ier, -iest) tending to run or flow: *a ~ nose.*

runt /rənt/ *n* [C] (*informal*) very small person or animal.

run·way /ˈrənˌwei/ *n* [C] **1** usually paved surface along which aircraft take off and land. **2** way or track on which something runs.

rup·ture /ˈrəptʃər/ *n* [C] **1** act of breaking apart or bursting. **2** split or tear. **3** (instance of) ending of friendly relations. **4** hernia. □ *vt,vi* **1** break or burst. **2** break off or end (a connection, etc).

ru·ral /ˈrʊrəl/ *adj* in, of, characteristic of, suitable for, the country: *~ scenery/life.*

ruse /ruz/ *n* [C] deception; trick.

rush[1] /rəʃ/ *n* **1** [U] rapid movement toward; sudden advance. **2** [C] movement or migration to a new place: *the ~ of settlers to California.* **3** [C,U] (period of) excitement, hurry, or hasty activity: *the Christmas ~,* the period before Christmas when crowds of people go shopping.

'rush hour, time when business and traffic are at their highest level.

rush[2] /rəʃ/ *n* [C] (tall stem of one of numerous varieties of) marsh plant with slender leafless stems, often dried and used for weaving into mats, baskets, etc.

rush[3] /rəʃ/ *vi,vt* **1** (cause to) go or come, do something, with haste or speed: *The children ~ed out of the school gates. They ~ed more soldiers to the front.* ***rush to conclusions,*** form them (too) hastily. ***rush sth through,*** get it done at high speed: *The new bill was ~ed through Congress.* **2** attack or charge suddenly: *~ the gates of the stadium.* **3** force into hasty action: *I must think things over, so don't ~ me.* **4** (*football*) advance the ball by running with it.

rusk /rəsk/ *n* [C] piece of bread or biscuit baked hard and crisp.

rus·set /ˈrəsɪt/ *n* **1** [U] reddish-brown color. **2** [C] kind of apple. □ *adj* reddish-brown.

rust /rəst/ *n* [U] **1** reddish-brown coating formed on iron, steel, etc by the action of water and air. **2** (plant disease marked by rust-colored spots caused by) kinds of fungus. **3** reddish brown color. □ *vt,vi* (cause to) become covered with rust.

rusti·ness /ˈrəstinɪs/ *n* [U]

rusty /ˈrəsti/ *adj* (-ier, -iest) **(a)** covered with rust: *~y needles.* **(b)** poor or inadequate from lack of practice: *My German is rather ~y.*

rus·tic /ˈrəstɪk/ *adj* **1** plain and simple in a way that is characteristic of country people: *~ charm.* **2** rough; unrefined: *~ speech/manners.* □ *n* [C] person who lives in the country.

rustle /ˈrəsəl/ *vi,vt* **1** make a gentle, light sound (like dry leaves blown by the wind); move along making such a sound: *Did you hear something rustling in the hedge?* **2** cause to make this sound: *I wish people wouldn't ~ their programs while the band is playing.* **3** ***rustle up,*** (*informal*) get together: *~ up some food for an unexpected guest.* **4** steal cattle. □ *n* [U] gentle light sound as of dry leaves blown by the wind: *the ~ of paper.*

rus·tler /ˈrəslər/ *n* [C] (esp) person who steals cattle.

rut /rʌt/ *n* [C] **1** line or track made by wheel(s) in soft ground. **2** (*fig*) habitual way of doing something, behaving, living, etc that is often boring: *be in/get into a rut.* □ *vt* (-tt-) (usually in *pp*) mark with ruts: *a deeply rutted road.*

ruth·less /ˈruθlɪs/ *adj* cruel; without pity; showing no mercy.

ruth·less·ly *adv*

ruth·less·ness /-nɪs/ *n* [U]

rye /raɪ/ *n* [U] **1** (plant with) grain used for making flour. ⇨ illus at cereal. **2** kind of whiskey made from rye.

S

S¹, s /es/ (*pl* S's, s's /ˈesɪz/) the nineteenth letter of the English alphabet.

S.² *abbr* = **1** saint. **2** south. **3** sentence.

-s /s after p, t, k, f, θ, otherwise z/ *suff* (-es /ɪz/ after -s, -z, -x, -ch, -sh) **1** (used to form the *pl* of a *n*.) **2** (used to form the *3rd pers sing pres t* of a *v*.) **3** (used to form an *adv*: *towards*.)

-'s /s after p, t, k, f, θ; ɪz after s, z, ʃ, ʒ; otherwise z/ *suff* **1** (used to form the *possessive* of a *n*.) **2** (contracted form of *is*. ⇨ be.) **3** (contracted form of *has*. ⇨ have¹.)

Sab·bath /ˈsæbəθ/ *n* day of rest and worship, observed on Saturday by Jews and some Christians, and on Sunday by most Christians.

sab·bati·cal /səˈbætɪkəl/ *adj* of or like the Sabbath. □ *n* time of freedom from routine duties given to some college teachers to enable them to travel or study.

sa·ber /ˈseibər/ *n* [C] heavy cavalry sword with a curved blade.

sable /ˈseibəl/ *n* **1** [U] black color. **2** [C] small animal valued for its beautiful dark fur. **3** [U] fur of this animal.

sa·bot /sæˈbou, ˈsabət/ *n* [C] shoe hollowed out of a single piece of wood.

sab·otage /ˈsæbəˌtaʒ/ *n* [U] the willful damaging of machinery, materials, etc or the hindering of work, by workmen, during a strike, or by enemy agents during war. □ *vt* perform an act of sabotage against.

sab·oteur /ˌsæbəˈtər/ *n* [C] person who commits sabotage.

sac¹ /sæk/ *n* [C] baglike part in an animal or plant.

SAC² /ˌes ˌei ˈsi, sæk/ *abbr* = Strategic Air Command.

sachet /sæˈʃei/ [C] small bag filled with a sweet-smelling substance, used to scent the contents of drawers, closets, etc.

sack¹ /sæk/ *n* **1** [C] (quantity held by a) large bag of strong material for storing and carrying goods: *two ~s of potatoes*. **2** (*sl*) bed. ***hit the sack,*** go to bed. **3 the sack,** (*sl*) dismissal from a job: *He got the ~ for petty thieving*. □ *vt* **1** put in a sack. **2** (*sl*) dismiss from employment.

ˈsack·cloth *n* [U] coarse material made of flax or hemp.

sack·ing *n* [U] sackcloth.

sack² /sæk/ *vt* (of a victorious army) steal from, loot (a captured city, etc). □ *n* (usually *sing* with *the*) sacking of a captured town, etc: *The citizens lost everything they had during the ~ of the town*.

sac·ra·ment /ˈsækrəmənt/ *n* [C] solemn religious ceremony in the Christian Church, eg Baptism, Confirmation, Matrimony, believed to be accompanied by great spiritual benefits.

sac·ra·men·tal /ˌsækrəˈmentəl/ *adj*

sacred /ˈseikrɪd/ *adj* **1** holy; connected with God, a god, or religion: *a ~ building*, eg a church, mosque, synagogue or temple. **2** solemn; (to be) treated with great respect or reverence: *a ~ trust*.

sac·ri·fice /ˈsækrəˌfais/ *n* **1 (a)** [U] the offering of something precious to a god: *the ~ of an ox to Jupiter*. **(b)** [C] the thing offered: *kill a sheep as a ~*. **2(a)** [C,U] the giving up of something of great value to oneself for a special purpose, or to benefit another person. **(b)** [C] something given up in this way: *Parents often make ~s* (eg go without things) *for their children*. □ *vt,vi* **1** make a sacrifice(1): *sacrificing a lamb to the gods*. **2** give up as a sacrifice(2): *He ~d his life to save the drowning child*.

sac·ri·fi·cial /ˌsækrəˈfɪʃəl/ *adj* of or like a sacrifice.

sac·ri·lege /ˈsækrəlɪdʒ/ *n* [U] act of violence or disrespect to something that is sacred.

sac·ri·legious /ˌsækrɪˈlɪdʒəs/ *adj*

sac·ro·sanct /ˈsækrouˌsæŋkt/ *adj* extremely sacred or holy, and therefore not to be violated.

sad /sæd/ *adj* (-dder, -ddest) **1** unhappy; filled with sorrow: *Why is he looking so sad?* **2** causing sadness or sorrow: *sad thoughts of the past*. **3** unfortunate; to be regretted: *a sad state of affairs*.

sad·ly *adv*

sad·ness /nɪs/ *n* [U]

sad·den /ˈsædən/ *vt,vi* make or become sad.

saddle /ˈsædəl/ *n* [C] **1** leather seat for a rider esp on a horse, donkey, etc. **2** cut of meat that includes part of the backbone and both loins: *a ~ of lamb*. **3** line or ridge of high land rising at each end to a high point. □ *vt* **1** put a saddle on (a horse). **2** ***saddle sb with sth,*** put a heavy responsibility or burden on: *be ~d with a wife and ten children*.

ˈsaddle·bag *n* [C] **(a)** one of a pair of bags placed over the back of a horse or donkey. **(b)** bag at the back of a bicycle or motorcycle seat.

sa·dism /ˈseiˌdɪzəm, ˈsæˌdɪzəm/ *n* [U] **1** mental disorder in which a person gets pleasure and satisfaction (esp sexual) from cruelty to another person. **2** (pleasure in) excessive cruelty.

sa·dist /-ɪst/ *n* [C] person guilty of sadism.

sa·dis·tic /səˈdɪstɪk/ *adj* of sadism.

sa·fari /səˈfari/ *n* [C] hunting expedition, or journey of exploration, esp in eastern Africa.

safe[1] /seif/ *adj* (-r, -st) **1** free from, protected from, danger: *~ from attack.* ***play (it) safe,*** avoid taking risks. **2** unhurt and undamaged: *a ~ journey.* **ˌsafe and ˈsound,** secure and unharmed: *return ~ and sound from a dangerous expedition.* **3** not causing or likely to cause harm or danger: *Is 55 miles an hour ~ on this road? Are these toys ~ for small children?* **4** (of a place, etc) giving security: *Keep it in a ~ place.* **5** (in elections) that can be counted on: *Is this a ~ seat for the Republicans?* Is it certain that the Republican candidate will be elected? **6** cautious; not taking risks: *They appointed a ~ man as school principal.* ***it is safe to say,*** it can be said without risk of being proved wrong, etc. ***be on the ˈsafe side,*** take more precautions than may be necessary: *He took his umbrella to be on the ~ side.* ***better ˌsafe than ˈsorry,*** it is better to be cautious than to take risks.

ˌsafe-ˈconduct *n* (document giving the) right to visit or pass through a district without the risk of being arrested or harmed (esp in time of war).

ˈsafe-deposit *n* building containing strongrooms and safes which persons may rent separately for storing valuables.

ˈsafe-deposit ˌbox, rentable individual safe in a safe-deposit.

ˈsafe·guard *n* [C] condition, circumstance, etc that tends to prevent harm, give protection: *a ~guard against death.* □ *vt* protect, guard.

ˌsafe-ˈkeeping *n* [U] care; custody: *Leave your jewels in the bank for ~keeping while you are on vacation.*

safe·ly *adv*

ˈsafe period, (in the menstrual cycle) when conception is least likely.

safe[2] /seif/ *n* [C] **1** fireproof and burglar-proof box in which money and other valuables are kept. **2** cool cupboard used to protect food from flies, etc: *a ˈmeat ~,* eg in a butcher shop.

safety /ˈseifti/ *n* **1** [U] being safe; freedom from danger: *do nothing that might endanger the ~ of other people.* **2** [C] = safety catch. ***put (a gun) on safety,*** set the safety catch so that it cannot be fired.

ˈsafety belt = seat belt.

ˈsafety catch/lock, device that gives safety against a possible danger (eg to prevent a gun from being fired by accident or a door being opened without the proper key).

ˈsafety curtain, fireproof screen that can be lowered between the stage and auditorium of a theater.

ˌsafety ˈfirst, motto used to warn that safety is important.

ˈsafety glass, glass that does not splinter.

ˈsafety match, one that lights only when rubbed on the side of a matchbox.

ˈsafety net, used to catch an acrobat, etc if he falls.

ˈsafety pin, one with a guard for the point which is bent back to the head.

ˈsafety razor, razor with a guard to prevent the blade from cutting the skin.

ˈsafety valve, (a) valve which releases pressure (in a steam boiler, etc) when it becomes too great. **(b)** (*fig*) way of releasing feelings of anger, excitement, etc harmlessly.

saf·fron /ˈsæfrən, ˈsæˌfran/ *n* [U], *adj* orange-yellow coloring obtained from flowers of the autumn crocus, used as a dye and for flavoring.

sag /sæg/ *vi* (-gg-) sink or curve down under weight or pressure: *a sagging roof. Sales are sagging,* falling (as shown on a graph). □ *n* [C] (degree of) sagging: *There is a bad sag in the seat of this chair.*

saga /ˈsagə/ *n* [C] (*pl* ~s) **1** old story of heroic deeds, esp of Icelandic or Norwegian heroes. **2** long narrative, eg a number of connected books (esp novels) about a family, social group, etc: *The Forsyte Saga.* **3** (*modern use*) long account (of troubles, bad experiences, etc): *I had to listen to boring ~s about her vacation.*

sa·ga·cious /səˈgeiʃəs/ *adj* (*formal*) showing good judgment, common sense or (of animals) intelligence.

sa·ga·cious·ly *adv*

sa·gac·ity /səˈgæsəti/ *n* [U] (*formal*) wisdom of a practical kind.

sage[1] /seidʒ/ *n* [C] wise man; man who is believed to be wise. □ *adj* wise; having the wisdom of experience.

sage[2] /seidʒ/ *n* [U] **1** herb with dull grayish-green leaves, used to flavor food. **2** kind of wild shrub common throughout the southwestern US which looks and smells something like sage(1).

ˈsage·brush *n* = sage(2).

ˌsage-ˈgreen *n* [U], *adj* color of sage(1) leaves.

Sag·it·ta·rius /ˌsædʒiˈtæriəs/ *n* the Archer, the ninth sign of the zodiac. ⇨ illus at zodiac.

said *pt,pp* of say.

sail[1] /seiəl/ *n* **1** [C,U] sheet of canvas spread to catch the wind and move a boat or ship forward: *hoist/lower the ~s.* ***under sail,*** (moving) with sails spread. ***set sail (from/to/for),*** begin a voyage. **2** [C] set of boards attached to the arm of a windmill to catch the wind. **3** (*pl* unchanged) ship: *a fleet of twenty ~.* **4** [C] (rarely *pl*) voyage or excursion on water for pleasure: *go for a ~;* sea voyage of a specified duration: *How many days' ~ is it from Rhode Island to the Bahamas?*

ˈsail·boat *n* [C] boat moved by sails. ⇨ illus at ship.

ˈsail·fish *n* (kinds of) sea fish with a large sail-like fin.

ˈsail·plane *n* [C] aircraft that uses air currents, etc instead of engines.

sail[2] /seiəl/ *vi,vt* (*pres p* ~ing /ˈseilıŋ/) **1** move forward across the sea, a lake, etc by using sails or engine power, move forward (in sport) across ice or a sandy beach, by means of a sail or sails: *~ up/along the coast; ~ into harbor; go ~ing.* **2** (of a ship or persons on board) begin a voyage; travel on water by use of sails or engines: *When does the ship ~? He has ~ed for Europe.* **3** travel across or on: *~ the sea/the Pacific.* **4** (be able to) control (a boat): *He ~s his own yacht. Do you ~?* **5** move smoothly like a ship with sails: *The moon/clouds ~ed across the sky.*

ˈsail·ing boat, = sailboat. ⇨ sail[1].

ˈsail·ing ship/vessel, boat, etc moved by sails.

sailor /ˈseilər/ *n* [C] seaman; member of a ship's crew.

saint /seint/ *n* [C] **1** holy person. **2** person who, having died, is held to be among the blessed in Heaven. **3** (*abbr* **St.**) person who has been declared by the (esp Roman Catholic) Church to have won by holy living on earth a place in Heaven and veneration on earth. **4** unselfish or patient person: *What a ~ my wife is!*

saint·ly *adj* very holy or good; like, of, a saint: *a ~ly expression on his face.*

St. Bernard /ˌseint bərˈnard/, large, powerful breed of dog, originally bred by monks in the Swiss Alps, trained to rescue travelers lost in snowstorms.

St. ˈPatrick's Day, March 17 (patron saint of Ireland).

St. ˈValentine's Day, ⇨ Valentine.

sake /seik/ *n* ***for the sake of sb/sth; for ˈmy/ˈyour/the ˈcountry's, etc sake,*** for the welfare or benefit of; because of an interest in or desire for: *We must be patient for the ~ of peace. He argues for the ~ of arguing*, only because he likes arguing.

sa·laam /səˈlam, səˈlæm/ *n* **1** Muslim greeting (from an Arabic word) meaning "Peace." **2** [C] low bow. □ *vi* make a low bow.

sal·able, sale·able /ˈseiləbəl/ *adj* fit for sale; likely to find buyers.

sa·la·cious /səˈleiʃəs/ *adj* (*formal*) (of speech, books, pictures, etc) obscene; indecent.

sa·la·cious·ly *adv*

sa·la·cious·ness /-nɪs/ *n* [U]

salad /ˈsælɪd/ *n* **1** [C,U] (cold dish of) sliced (and usually uncooked) vegetables such as lettuce, or cold cooked potatoes or macaroni, seasoned with oil, vinegar, etc eaten with, or including, cheese, cold meat, etc: *a chicken ~; potato ~; cold beef and ~.* ⇨ fruit salad. **2** lettuce or other green vegetables for eating raw.

ˈsalad days *n pl* period of inexperienced youth.

ˈsalad dressing, mixture of oil, vinegar, cream, etc used with salad.

ˈsalad oil, superior quality of oil (olive, etc) for salad dressing.

sa·lami /səˈlami/ *n* [U] sausage salted and flavored with garlic.

sal·ary /ˈsæləri/ *n* [C] (*pl* -ies) (weekly, monthly) payment for employment based on a total amount for a year: *a ~ of $15,000 per annum.* ⇨ wage[1].

sal·ar·ied *adj* receiving a salary; (of employment) paid for by means of a salary.

sale /ˈseiəl/ *n* **1** [U] exchange of goods or property for money; act of selling: *The ~ of his old home made him sad.* ***for sale,*** intended to be sold: *Is the house for ~?* ***on sale,*** (of goods in shops, etc) offered for purchase. ***make a sale,*** succeed in selling something. ***put sth up for sale,*** announce that it may be bought. **2** [C] instance of selling something: *Sales are up/down this month*, more/fewer goods have been sold. **3** [C] the offering of goods at low prices for a period (to get rid of old stock, etc): *the winter/summer ~s.* ***on sale,*** reduced in price: *ˈ~ price*, low price at a sale. **4** occasion when goods, property, etc are put up for sale by auction: *get bargains at ~s.*

ˈsales department, that part of a business company that is concerned with selling goods (contrasted with manufacture, delivery, etc).

ˈsales·man/·woman /-mən, -wʊmən/ *n* [C] (*pl* ~smen/-men/, ~swomen /-ˌwɪmɪn/) person selling goods in a store or (on behalf of wholesalers) to storekeepers.

ˈsales·man·ship /-mənˌʃɪp/ *n* [U] skill in selling goods.

ˈsales pitch = sales talk.

ˈsales·room, room where goods, etc are sold by public auction.

ˈsales talk, talk (to a prospective customer) to sell goods.

ˈsales tax, tax payable on the sum received for articles sold by retail.

sa·li·ent /ˈseiliənt/ *adj* (*formal*) **1** most significant; easily noticed: *the ~ points of a speech.* **2** (of an angle) pointing outwards.

sa·line /ˈseiˌlin/ *adj* containing salt; salty: *a ~ solution*, eg as is used for gargling. □ *n* [U] solution of salt and water.

sal·iva /səˈlaivə/ *n* [U] the natural liquid present in the mouth.

sali·vary /ˈsæləˌveri/ *adj* of or producing saliva: *the ˈ~ry glands.*

sali·vate /ˈsæləˌveit/ *vi* secrete (too much) saliva.

sal·low /ˈsælou/ *adj* (-er, -est) (of the human skin or complexion) of an unhealthy yellow color. □ *vt,vi* make or become sallow: *a face ~ed by years of living in the tropics.*

sally /ˈsæli/ *n* [C] (*pl* -ies) **1** sudden breaking out by soldiers who are surrounded by the enemy. **2** lively, witty remark. □ *vi* **1** make a sally(1). **2** ***sally forth,*** go out on a journey or for a walk.

salmon /ˈsæmən/ *n* **1** [C] (*pl* unchanged) large fish, valued for food and the sport of catching it with rod and line. ⇨ illus at fish. **2** [U] its flesh as food. **3** the color of its flesh, orange-pink.

salon /səˈlan/ *n* [C] **1** assembly, as a regular event, of notable persons at the house of a lady of fashion (esp in Paris); reception room of a kind used for this purpose. **2** business offering services connected with fashion, etc: *a ˈbeauty ~.*

sa·loon /səˈlun/ *n* [C] **1** room for social use in a ship, hotel, etc: *the ship's ˈdining ~.* **2** (*dated*) room or establishment in which alcoholic drinks are sold and consumed; bar(3).

salt[1] /sɔlt/ *n* **1** [U] white substance obtained from mines, present in seawater and obtained from it by evaporation, used to flavor and preserve food: *ˈtable ~*, powdered for convenient use at table. ***rub salt in the wound,*** (*fig*) make humiliation, suffering, worse. ***take (a statement, etc) with a grain/pinch of salt,*** feel some doubt whether it is altogether true. ***the ˌsalt of the ˈearth,*** person(s) with very high qualities. **2** [C] (*chem*) chemical compound of a metal and an acid. **3** [C] experienced sailor: *He's an old ~.* **4** (*pl*) medicine used to empty the bowels: *take a dose of (Epsom) ~s.* **5** [U] (*fig*) something that gives flavor or appeal: *Adventure is the ~ of life to some men.* □ *vt* put salt on or in (food) to season it or preserve it: *~ed meat.*

□ *adj* **1** (opp. of *fresh*(6)) containing, tasting of, preserved with, salt: ~ *water*. **2** (of land) containing salt: ~ *marshes*.

ˈsalt·cellar *n* [C] small container for salt at table.

salti·ness /-nɪs/ *n* [U]

ˌsalt·ˈwater *adj* of the sea: *ˌ~water ˈfish*.

salty *adj* (-ier, -iest) containing, tasting of, salt.

SALT[2] /sɔlt/ *abbr* = Strategic Arms Limitation Talks.

salt·peter /sɔltˈpitər/ *n* [U] potassium nitrate; white powder used in making gunpowder, for preserving food and as medicine.

sa·lu·bri·ous /səˈlubriəs/ *adj* (*formal*) (esp of climate) health-giving: *the ~ air of Switzerland.*

salu·tary /ˈsælyəˌteri/ *adj* having a good effect (on body or mind): ~ *exercise/advice*.

salu·ta·tion /ˌsælyəˈteiʃən/ *n* [C,U] (*formal*) (act or expression of) greeting or goodwill (eg a bow or a kiss): *He raised his hat in ~.*

sa·lute /səˈlut/ *n* [C] **1** something done to welcome a person or to show respect or honor, esp (eg in the armed forces) the raising of the hand to the forehead, the firing of guns, the lowering and raising of a flag: *give a ~; fire a ~ of ten guns*. **2** friendly greeting such as a bow or wave. □ *vt,vi* **1** give a salute (to): *The soldier ~d smartly*. **2** greet.

sal·vage /ˈsælvɪdʒ/ *n* [U] **1** the saving of property from loss (by fire or other disaster, eg a wrecked ship): *a ˈ~ company*, one whose business is to bring wrecked ships to port, raise valuables from a ship that has sunk, etc. **2** property so saved. **3** payment given to those who save property. **4** (saving of) waste material that can be used again after being processed. □ *vt* save from loss, fire, wreck, etc.

sal·va·tion /sælˈveiʃən/ *n* [U] **1** the act of saving, the state of having been saved, from sin and its consequences. **2** that which saves a person from loss, disaster, etc: *Government loans have been the ~ of several shaky business companies.*

Salˌvation ˈArmy, Christian religious and missionary organization on a military model for the revival of religion among the masses and for helping the poor everywhere.

salve /sæv/ *n* **1** [C,U] (kinds of) oily medicinal substance used on wounds, sores or burns: *ˈlip ~*. **2** (*fig*) something that comforts wounded feelings or soothes an uneasy conscience. □ *vt* soothe: *It is pointless trying to ~ one's conscience by giving stolen money to charity.*

sal·ver /ˈsælvər/ *n* [C] (usually silver) tray on which servants hand letters, drinks, etc.

salvo /ˈsælvou/ *n* [C] (*pl* ~s, ~es) the firing of a number of guns together as a salute.

SAM /sæm/ *abbr* = surface-to-air missile.

Sa·mari·tan /səˈmærɪtən/ *n* person who pities and gives practical help to persons in trouble.

same /seim/ *adj, pron* (*Note:* always with *the* except as noted in 5 below.) **1** identical; unchanged; not different: *He is the ~ age as his wife. We have lived in the ~ house for fifty years.* **2** ***the same... that/as***: *He uses the ~ books that you do/the ~ books as you.* **3** (used with a clause introduced by *that, where, who*, etc): *Put the book back in the ~ place where you found it.* **4** (used as a *pronoun*) the same thing: *We must all say the ~. And I would do the ~ again.* ***same ˈhere,*** (*informal*) the same applies to me. ***And the same to you,*** I hope you experience the same thing. ***at the same time,*** **(a)** together: *Don't all speak at the ~ time.* **(b)** (introducing a fact, etc that is to be borne in mind) still; nevertheless: *At the ~ time you must not forget that...* ***ˌone and the ˈsame,*** absolutely the same: *Jekyll and Hyde were one and the ~ person.* ***be all/just the same to,*** make no difference to: *You can do it now or leave it till later; it's all the ~ to me.* ***come/amount to the ˌsame ˈthing,*** have the same result, meaning, etc: *You may pay in cash or by check; it comes to the ~ thing.* **5** (with *this, that, these, those*) already thought of, mentioned or referred to: *On Monday I didn't go to work. On that ~ day, the office was bombed.* □ *adv* in the same way: *Old people do not feel the ~ about these things as the younger generation.* ***all the same,*** = nevertheless.

same·ness /-nɪs/ *n* [U] the condition of being the same, (and so being uninteresting through lack of variety).

samo·var /ˈsæməˌvar/ *n* [C] metal urn used (originally in Russia) for boiling water for tea.

sam·pan /ˈsæmˌpæn/ *n* [C] small, flat-bottomed boat used in the Far East.

sample /ˈsæmpəl/ *n* [C] specimen; one of a number, part of a whole, taken to show what the rest is like. □ *vt* take a sample of; test a part of: *sampling the quality of the wine.*

sam·urai /ˈsæmʊˌrai/ *n* (*pl* unchanged) **1 the samurai,** the military caste in feudal Japan. **2** [C] member of this caste. **3** (as an *adjective*) of (the members of) this caste: *a ~ sword.*

sana·tor·ium /ˌsænəˈtɔriəm/ *n* [C] (*pl* ~s) = sanitarium.

sanc·tify /ˈsæŋktəˌfai/ *vt* (*pt,pp* -ied) make holy; observe as sacred.

sanc·ti·fi·ca·tion /ˌsæŋktəfɪˈkeiʃən/ *n* [U]

sanc·ti·moni·ous /ˌsæŋktəˈmouniəs/ *adj* making a show (often insincere) of sanctity.

sanc·ti·moni·ous·ly *adv*

sanc·tion /ˈsæŋkʃən/ *n* **1** [U] right or permission given by authority to do something: *translate a book without the ~ of the author*. **2** [U] approval, encouragement (of behavior, etc), by general custom or tradition. **3** [C] penalty, esp as adopted by several nations together against a country violating international law: *apply economic ~s against a country*. **4** [C] reason for obeying a rule, etc: *The best moral ~ is that of conscience.* □ *vt* give sanction(2) to: *Torture should never be ~ed.*

sanc·tity /ˈsæŋktəti/ *n* (*pl* -ies) **1** [U] holiness; sacredness; saintliness: *break the ~ of an oath.* **2** (*pl*) sacred obligations, feelings, etc.

sanc·tu·ary /ˈsæŋktʃuˌeri/ *n* (*pl* -ies) **1** [C] holy or sacred place, esp a church, temple or mosque. **2** [C] sacred place (eg the altar of a church) where, in former times, a person running away from the law, etc could, by Church law, take refuge: *The English-speaking countries have always been sanctuaries for political refugees from many parts of the world.* **3** [U] (right of offering such) freedom from arrest: *to seek/be offered ~.*

4 [C] area where by law it is forbidden to kill birds, rob their nests, etc to shoot animals, etc: *a ˈbird ~*.

sand /sænd/ *n* **1** [U] (mass of) finely crushed rock as seen on the seashore, in riverbeds, deserts, etc. **2** (often *pl*) expanse of sand (on the seashore or a desert). □ *vt* **1** cover, sprinkle, with sand. **2** make smooth by using sandpaper.

ˈsand·bag *n* [C] bag filled with sand used in groups as a defensive wall (in war, against rising flood-water, etc).

ˈsand·bank *n* [C] bank of sand in a river or the sea.

ˈsand bar, sand·bar *n* [C] long bank of sand, esp at the mouth of a river or harbor.

ˈsand·blast *vt* send a jet of sand against, eg stonework, to clean it, or against glass to make a design on it.

ˈsand·box *n* [C] enclosure with sand for children to play in.

ˈsand dune, hill of sand (as on a beach or in the desert).

ˈsand flea, kind commonly living in the sand on seashores.

ˈsand fly, kind found on seashores.

ˈsand·glass *n* glass with two bulbs containing enough sand to take a definite time in passing from one bulb to the other.

sand·man, sand man /ˈsændˌmæn/ *n* mythical being who makes children sleepy by putting sand in their eyes.

ˈsand·paper *n* [U] strong paper with sand glued to it, used for rubbing rough surfaces smooth. □ *vt* make smooth with sandpaper.

ˈsand·piper *n* [C] small bird living in wet, sandy places near streams.

ˈsand·stone *n* [U] type of rock formed of sand.

ˈsand·storm *n* [C] storm in a sandy desert with clouds of sand raised by the wind.

sandy *adj* (-ier, -iest) **(a)** covered with, of, sand: *a ~y beach.* **(b)** (of hair, etc) yellowish-red.

san·dal /ˈsændəl/ *n* [C] (also ***a pair of sandals***) kind of shoe made of a sole with straps to hold it on the foot.

san·dal·wood /ˈsændəlˌwʊd/ *n* [U] hard, sweet-smelling wood; its perfume.

sand·wich /ˈsænwɪtʃ/ *n* [C] two slices of bread with meat, salad, etc between: *ham/chicken/cheese ~es.* □ *vt* put (one thing or person) between two others, esp when there is little space: *I was ~ed between two fat men on the bus.*

ˈsandwich board, structure with two boards hung over the shoulders displaying advertisements.

sane /sein/ *adj* (-r, -st) **1** mentally healthy; not mad. **2** sensible: *a ~ policy; ~ judgment.*

sane·ly *adv*

sang *pt* of sing¹.

san·gui·nary /ˈsæŋgwɪˌneri/ *adj* (*formal*) **1** with much killing or wounding: *a ~ battle.* **2** delighting in cruel acts: *a ~ ruler.*

san·guine /ˈsæŋgwɪn/ *adj* (*formal*) **1** hopeful; optimistic: *He is very ~ in his outlook.* **2** having a red complexion.

sani·tar·ium /ˌsænəˈteriəm/ *n* [C] (*pl* ~s) establishment for the treatment of sick people, esp convalescents.

sani·tary /ˈsænəˌteri/ *adj* **1** clean; free from dirt which might cause disease: *~ conditions.* **2** of, concerned with, the protection of (public) health: *a ˈ~ inspector.*

ˈsanitary napkin, absorbent pad used during menstruation.

sani·ta·tion /ˌsænəˈteiʃən/ *n* [U] arrangements to protect public health, esp the disposal of sewage.

san·ity /ˈsænəti/ *n* [U] **1** health of mind. **2** soundness of judgment.

sank *pt* of sink².

san·skrit /ˈsænskrɪt/ *adj, n* (of the) ancient language of India; (of the) literary language of Hinduism.

Santa Claus /ˈsæntə ˌklɔz/ (sometimes shortened to **Santa**) *n* the person who, small children are told, brings them toys by night at Christmas.

sap¹ /sæp/ *n* [C] tunnel or covered trench made to get nearer to the enemy. □ *vt,vi* (-pp-) **1** make a sap or saps. **2** (*fig*) destroy or weaken (a person's health, strength, energy, faith, confidence, etc): *The climate sapped his health. The criticism sapped his determination.*

sap² /sæp/ *n* [U] **1** liquid in a plant, carrying food to all parts. **2** (*fig*) (anything that provides) strength or energy.

sap·less *adj* without sap or energy.

sap·ling *n* [C] young tree.

sap·phire /ˈsæˌfaiər/ *n* **1** [C] bright blue precious stone. **2** [U] (often as an *adjective*) bright blue color.

sa·ra·pe = serape.

sar·casm /ˈsarˌkæzəm/ *n* [U] (use of) remarks intended to hurt the feelings; [C] such a remark.

sar·cas·tic /sarˈkæstɪk/ *adj* of, using, sarcasm.

sar·cas·ti·cally /-kli/ *adv*

sar·copha·gus /sarˈkafəgəs/ *n* [C] (*pl* -gi /-gai/, ~es) stone coffin.

sar·dine /ˌsarˈdin/ *n* [C] small fish (usually preserved and canned in oil or tomato sauce). ***packed like sardines,*** closely crowded together.

sar·donic /sarˈdanɪk/ *adj* scornful; cynical: *a ~ smile.*

sar·doni·cally /-kli/ *adv*

sari /ˈsari/ *n* [C] (*pl* ~s) length of cotton or silk cloth draped around the body, worn by Hindu women.

sa·rong /səˈrɔŋ/ *n* [C] long strip of cotton or silk material worn round the middle of the body by Malays and Javanese.

sar·sa·pa·rilla /ˌsæs(ə)pəˈrɪlə, ˌsars(ə)-/ *n* [U] **1** (plant with a) root used in flavoring drinks, etc. **2** drink made with this root.

sash /sæʃ/ *n* [C] long strip of cloth worn around the waist or over one shoulder for ornament or as part of a uniform.

sash win·dow /ˈsæʃ wɪndou/ *n* [C] one with a frame that slides up and down on ropes.

sass /sæs/ *n* [U] (*informal*) impudence: *None of your ~!* □ *vt, vi* talk impudently (to); respond impudently.

sas·sa·fras /ˈsæsəˌfræs/ *n* [U] (wood of a) sweet smelling tree, used in scenting soap, etc and in tea as a tonic.

SAT[1] /sæt/ *abbr* = Scholastic Aptitude Test.
Sat.[2] *abbr* = Saturday.
sat[3] *pt,pp* of sit.
Satan /ˈseitən/ *n* the Devil.
Sa·tanic /seiˈtænɪk/ *adj* of, like, the Devil.
satchel /ˈsætʃəl/ *n* [C] bag with a long strap for carrying school books.
sate /seit/ *vt* = satiate.
sat·el·lite /ˈsætəˌlait/ *n* [C] **1** small body moving in orbit around a planet; moon. **2** artificial object, eg a spacecraft, put in orbit around a celestial body: *comˌmuniˈcations ~*, for sending back to the earth telephone messages, radio and TV signals. **3** (*fig*) (often as an *adjective*) person, state, depending on and taking the lead from another.
sati·able /ˈseiʃəbəl/ *adj* (*formal*) that can be fully satisfied.
sati·ate /ˈseiʃiˌeit/ *vt* (*formal*) satisfy fully or too much: *be ~d with food/pleasure.*
sati·ety /səˈtaiəti/ *n* [U] (*formal*) condition of being satiated.
satin /ˈsætən/ *n* [U] silk material shiny on one side: (as an *adjective*) *~ ribbons.* □ *adj* smooth like satin.
sat·ire /ˈsæˌtaiər/ *n* **1** [U] form of writing, drama, etc making a person, idea, appear foolish or absurd. **2** [C] piece of writing that does this.
sa·tiri·cal /səˈtɪrɪkəl/ *adj*
sa·tiri·cally /-kli/ *adv*
sat·ir·ist /ˈsætərɪst/ *n* [C] person who writes or uses satire.
sat·ir·ize /ˈsætəˌraiz/ *vt* attack with satire; describe satirically.
sat·is·fac·tion /ˌsætɪsˈfækʃən/ *n* **1** [U] the state of being satisfied, pleased or contented; act of satisfying: *have the ~ of being successful in life.* **2** [C] (with *a, an*, but rarely *pl*) something that satisfies: *It is a great ~ to know that he is well again.* **3** [U] (opportunity of getting) revenge or compensation for an injury or insult: *The angry man demanded ~ but the other refused it*, would neither apologize nor fight.
sat·is·fac·tory /ˌsætɪsˈfækt(ə)ri/ *adj* **1** giving pleasure or satisfaction: *a ~ holiday.* **2** good enough for a purpose: *Will these shoes be ~ for a long walk?*
sat·is·fac·tor·ily /-əli/ *adv*
sat·isfy /ˈsætɪsˌfai/ *vt,vi* (*pt,pp* -ied) **1** make contented; give (a person) what he wants or needs: *Nothing satisfies him; he's always complaining.* **2** be enough for (one's needs); be equal to (what one hopes for or desires): *~ one's hunger.* **3** make free from doubt: *He satisfied me that he could do the work well.*
sat·is·fy·ing *adj* giving satisfaction: *a ~ing meal.*
satu·rate /ˈsætʃəˌreit/ *vt* **1** make thoroughly wet; soak with moisture: *We were caught in the rain and came home ~d.* **2** cause to absorb like water: *be ~d with sunshine.* **3** be unable to take any more: *The market for used cars is ~d.* **4** (*chem*) cause (one substance) to absorb the greatest possible amount of another: *a ~d solution of salt.*
satu·ra·tion /ˌsætʃəˈreiʃən/ *n* [U] state of being saturated.
ˌsatuˈration point, the stage beyond which no more can be absorbed.
Sat·ur·day /ˈsætərdi, -ˌdei/ *n* seventh and last day of the week.
Sat·urn /ˈsætərn/ *n* (*astron*) large planet encircled by rings, sixth in order from the sun. ⇨ illus at planet.
satyr /ˈsætər/ *n* (*Greek and Roman myth*) god of the woods, half man and half animal.
sauce /sɔs/ *n* [C,U] (kind of) (semi-)liquid preparation served with food to give flavor: *spaghetti and tomato ~.*
sauce·pan /ˈsɔsˌpæn/ *n* [C] deep metal cooking pot with a lid and a handle.
saucer /ˈsɔsər/ *n* [C] small curved dish on which a cup stands. ⇨ flying saucer.
sauer·kraut /ˈsauərˌkraut/ *n* [U] (*G*) chopped, pickled cabbage.
sauna /ˈsaunə/ *n* [C] (*pl* ~s) (building for a) steam bath.
saun·ter /ˈsɔntər/ *vi* walk in a leisurely way: *~ along Main Street windowshopping.* □ *n* [C] quiet, unhurried walk or pace.
saus·age /ˈsɔsɪdʒ/ *n* [U] chopped-up meat, etc flavored and stuffed into a casing or tube of thin skin; [C] one section of such a tube.
ˈsausage meat, meat minced for making sausages.
sauté /səˈtei, sou-/ *adj* (*F*) (of food) quickly fried in a little fat: *~ potatoes.* □ *vt* fry food in this way.
sav·age /ˈsævɪdʒ/ *adj* **1** in a primitive or uncivilized state: *~ people/tribes/countries.* **2** fierce; cruel: *a ~ dog/attack; ~ criticism.* □ *n* [C] member of a primitive tribe living by hunting and fishing. □ *vt* attack, bite, etc: *a lion savaging its trainer.*
sav·age·ly *adv*
sav·agery /ˈsævɪdʒri/ *n* [U] the state of being savage; savage behavior.
sa·vanna(h) /səˈvænə/ *n* [C] treeless plain, eg in southeastern US and parts of West Africa. (*Note:* compare *prairie*, north and central US.)
save[1] /seiv/ *vt,vi* **1** make or keep safe (from loss, injury, etc): *~ her from drowning; ~ his life.* ***save face,*** ⇨ face[1](2). ***save one's skin,*** ⇨ skin(1). **2** keep for future use: *~ (up) money for a vacation; ~ some of the meat for tomorrow. He is saving himself/saving his strength for the heavy work he'll have to do this afternoon.* ***save for a rainy day,*** ⇨ rainy. **3** free (a person) from the need of using: *That will ~ you a dollar a day/a lot of trouble.* **4** (in the Christian religion) set free from the power of (or the eternal punishment for) sin: *Jesus Christ came into the world to ~ sinners.*
saver *n* [C] **(a)** person who saves (money). **(b)** means of saving: *This device is a useful ˈtime-~r.*
sav·ing *adj* (esp) that compensates. □ *n* **(a)** [C] way of saving; amount saved: *a useful saving of time and money.* **(b)** (*pl*) money saved up: *keep one's savings in the bank.*
saving ˈgrace, good quality in a person whose other qualities are not all good.
ˈsavings account, (with a bank) on which interest is paid.

ˈsavings bank, bank which holds, and gives interest on, small savings.
ˈsavings bond, nontransferable US Treasury bond.
save[2] /seiv/ (*pres p* saving /ˈseiviŋ/) *prep* (*dated*) except: *all ~ him.*
sav·ior /ˈseivyər/ *n* **1** [C] person who rescues or saves a person from danger. **2 The/Our Savior,** (in the Christian religion) Jesus Christ.
sa·vor /ˈseivər/ *n* [C,U] **1** taste or flavor (of something): *soup with a ~ of garlic.* **2** (*fig*) quality (of): *His political views have a/the ~ of fascism.* □ *vi* have the quality (of): *His speech ~s of a humane approach.*
sa·vory /ˈseivəri/ *adj* **1** having an appetizing taste or smell. **2** having a salt or sharp, not a sweet, taste: *a ~ omelette.* □ *n* [U] kind of herb used as a seasoning in cooking food: *summer ~, winter ~.*
sa·voy /səˈvɔi/ (also **savoy cabbage**) *n* [C,U] (kind of) winter cabbage with wrinkled leaves.
savvy /ˈsævi/ *n* [U] (*informal*) know-how.
saw[1] *pt* of see[1].
saw[2] /sɔ/ *n* [C] (kinds of) tool with a sharp-toothed edge, for cutting wood, metal, □ *vt,vi* (*pt* sawed, *pp* sawed, sawn /sɔn/) **1** cut with, use, a saw: *saw wood; saw a log in two.* ***saw sth off,*** cut off with a saw: *saw a branch off a tree.* ***saw sth up,*** cut into pieces with a saw. **2** capable of being sawed: *This wood saws easily.* **3** move backward and forward: *sawing at his violin,* using his bow as if it were a saw.

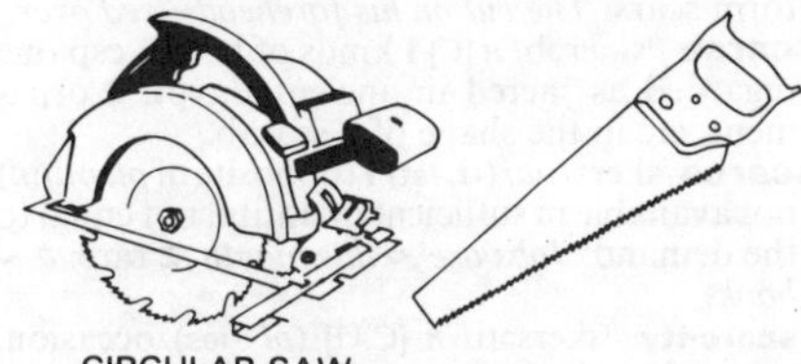

SAW

ˈsaw·dust *n* [U] tiny bits of wood falling off when wood is being sawed.
ˈsaw mill, factory with power-operated saws.
saw·yer /ˈsɔyər/ *n* [C] man whose work is sawing wood.
saxo·phone /ˈsæksəˌfoun/ *n* [C] musical wind instrument with a reed in the mouthpiece and keys for the fingers, made of brass. ⇨ illus at brass.
sax·ophon·ist /ˈsæksəˌfounɪst/ *n* [C] saxophone player.
say /sei/ *vt,vi* (*3rd person, present tense* says /sez/, *pt,pp* said /sed/) **1** make (a word or remark); use one's ordinary voice (not singing, etc) to produce (words, sentences): *Did you say anything? He said that his friend's name was Smith. The boy was saying his prayers.* ***that is to say,*** or to use other words: *He's 15, that is to say, he's very young.* ***What do you say to...?*** What do you think about...? *What do you say to a walk/to playing tennis?* ***When all is said and done,*** after all (the effort to convince a person): *He thinks he is brilliant but when all is said and done, he's only an ordinary student.* ***You can say ˈthat again!*** (*informal*) I agree. ***You don't say!*** (*informal*) (once commonly used to express surprise when hearing news, etc, but now mostly used as a sarcastic response to an apparent lie or unnecessary statement of obvious fact). ***go without saying,*** ⇨ go[1](25). ***say no more,*** you need not add anything because I agree. ***say so,*** **(a)** say what you think, feel: *If you think I have lied to you, say so.* **(b)** give permission: *I'll go if you say so.* **2** state: *It says here that he was killed.* ***They say/It is said (that),*** (used to introduce rumors): *They say/It's said that he's a thief.* **3** make known information: *She spoke for an hour but didn't say much.* **4** form and give an opinion concerning: *There is no saying when peace will be achieved.* ***and so say all of us,*** that is the opinion of us all. **5** estimate: *You could speak English in, I'd say/let's say, six weeks.* ***be hard to say,*** be difficult to estimate. □ *n* (only in the following) ***have/say one's say,*** express one's opinion; state one's views: *Let him have his say.* ***have/be allowed a/no/not much, etc say in the matter,*** have some/no/not much right or opportunity to share in a discussion, express one's opinions, etc: *He wasn't allowed much say in choosing his vacation.*
ˈsay-so *n* [U] (*informal*) authority: *I'll do it on your say-so.*
say·ing /ˈseiɪŋ/ *n* [C] remark often made; well-known phrase, proverb, etc: *"More haste, less speed," as the ~ goes.*
sb. *abbr* = somebody.
SC *postal abbr* = South Carolina ⇨ App 6.
scab /skæb/ *n* [C] **1** dry crust formed over a wound or sore. **2** (*informal*) workman who refuses to join a strike, or his trade union, or who takes a striker's place.
scabby *adj* (-ier, -iest) having scabs(1).
scab·bard /ˈskæbəd/ *n* [C] sheath for the blade of a sword, etc.
sca·bies /ˈskeibiz/ *n* [U] kind of skin disease causing itching.
scaf·fold /ˈskæfould/ *n* [C] **1** structure put up for workmen and materials around a building which is being erected or repaired. **2** platform on which criminals are executed: *go to the ~,* be executed.
scaf·fold·ing /ˈskæfəldɪŋ/ *n* [U] (materials for a) scaffold(1) (eg poles and planks).
scal·a·wag /ˈskæləˌwæg/ *n* [C] (*informal, dated*) dishonest or good-for-nothing person.
scald /skɔld/ *vt* **1** burn with hot liquid or steam: *~ one's hand with boiling water.* **2** clean (instruments, etc) with boiling water or steam. □ *n* [C] injury to the skin from hot liquid or steam.
scale[1] /ˈskeiəl/ *n* **1** [C] one of the thin overlapping pieces of hard material that cover the skin of many fish, etc: *scrape the ~s off a bass.* ⇨ illus at fish. **2** [C] piece like a scale, eg a flake of skin that loosens and comes off the body in some diseases, a flake of rust on iron. **3** [U] chalky deposit inside boilers, kettles, waterpipes, etc (from the lime in hard water). **4** [U] deposit of tartar on teeth. □ *vt,vi* (*pres p* scaling /ˈskeilɪŋ/) **1** cut or scrape scales from (eg fish). **2** ***scale off,*** come off in flakes: *paint/plaster scaling off a*

wall.

scaly /ˈskeili/ *adj* (-ier, -iest) covered with, coming off in, scales: *a kettle scaly with rust.*

scale[2] /ˈskeiəl/ *n* [C] **1** series of marks at regular intervals for the purpose of measuring (as on a ruler or a thermometer): *This ruler has one ~ in centimeters and another in inches.* **2** ruler or other tool or instrument marked in this way. **3** system of units for measuring: *the ˈdecimal ~.* **4** arrangement in steps or degrees: *a ~ of wages; a person who is high in the social ~.* ⇨ sliding scale. **5** proportion between the size of something and the map, diagram, etc which represents it: *a map on the ~ of ten miles to the inch.* ***drawn to scale,*** with a uniform reduction or enlargement. **6** relative size, extent, etc: *They are preparing for war on a large ~.* **7** (*music*) series of tones arranged in order of pitch, esp a series of eight starting on a keynote: *practice ~s on the piano.* □ *vt* (*pres p* scaling /ˈskeilıŋ/) **1** make a copy or representation of, according to a certain scale: *~ a map/building.* **2** ***scale up/down,*** increase/decrease by a certain proportion: *All wages/marks were ~d up by 10%.*

scale[3] /ˈskeiəl/ *n* [C] **1** one of the two pans on a balance. **2** (*pl*, or ***a pair of scales***) simple balance or instrument for weighing. **3** any machine for weighing: *bathroom ~s,* for measuring one's weight.

scale[4] /ˈskeiəl/ *vt* climb up (a wall, cliff, etc).

scal·lop /ˈskaləp, ˈskæləp/ *n* [C] **1** kind of shellfish with a hinged double shell divided into grooves. ⇨ illus at bivalve. **2** (*pl*) dish made from shelled scallops.

scalp /skælp/ *n* [C] **1** skin and hair of the head, excluding the face. **2** this skin, etc from an enemy's head as a trophy of victory. □ *vt* cut the scalp off.

scal·pel /ˈskælpəl/ *n* [C] small, light knife used by surgeons.

scamp /skæmp/ *n* [C] (*dated*) (used playfully of a child) rascal.

scam·per /ˈskæmpər/ *vi* (of small animals, eg mice, rabbits, when frightened, or of children and dogs at play) run quickly. □ *n* [C] short, quick run.

scampi /ˈskæmpi/ *n pl* (used with a *sing verb*) (dish made of) large prawns.

scan /skæn/ *vt,vi* (-nn-) **1** look at attentively or over every part of: *The shipwrecked sailor ~ned the horizon anxiously every morning.* **2** (*modern use*) glance at quickly but not very thoroughly: *He ~ned the newspaper while having his breakfast.* **3** test the rhythm of (a line of verse). **4** (of verse) be composed so that it can be scanned: *This line does not/will not ~. The verses ~ well.* **5** (*television*) prepare (a picture) for transmission (by separating its elements of light and shade). **6** (*radar*) pass electronic beams across an area in search of something.

scan·sion /ˈskænʃən/ *n* [U] scanning of verse; the way verse scans.

scan·dal /ˈskændəl/ *n* **1** [C,U] (action, behavior, etc that causes) general shock, anger, opposition; [C] shameful or disgraceful action: *The way they treat the poor is a ~.* **2** [U] careless or unkind talk which damages a person's reputation: *Most of us enjoy a bit of ~.*

ˈscan·dal·ize /-ˈskændəˌlaiz/ *vt* offend the moral feelings of: *~ize the neighbors by sunbathing in the nude.*

ˈscandal·monger /-ˌməŋgər/ *n* [C] person who gossips.

ˈscan·dal·ous /-əs/ *adj* **(a)** disgraceful; shocking. **(b)** (of reports, rumors) containing scandal. **(c)** (of persons) fond of gossiping.

scan·dal·ous·ly *adv* in a scandalous way.

scan·sion /ˈskænʃən/ ⇨ scan.

scant /skænt/ *adj* (having) hardly enough: *pay ~ attention to her advice.*

scant·ily /-əli/ *adv* in a scanty manner: *~ily dressed.*

scanty *adj* (-ier, -iest) (opposite of *ample*) small in size or amount; only just large enough: *a ~y bikini.*

-scape /-ˌskeip/ *suff* (*n* + ~ = *n* [C]) a stretch of scenery: *landscape; moonscape.*

scape·goat /ˈskeipˌgout/ *n* [C] person blamed or punished for the mistake(s) or wrong acts of another or others.

scap·ula /ˈskæpyələ/ *n* [C] (*pl* ~s) = shoulder blade. ⇨ illus at skeleton.

scar /skar/ *n* [C] **1** mark remaining on the surface (of skin, furniture, etc) as the result of injury or damage. **2** (*fig*) mark or effect of suffering, bad planning, etc: *Mining that leaves a ~ on the countryside.* □ *vt,vi* (-rr-) **1** mark with a scar: *a face ~red by smallpox.* **2** (*fig*) mark with effects of suffering, etc: *The city was scarred by war.* **3** form scars: *The cut on his forehead ~red over.*

scarab /ˈskærəb/ *n* [C] **1** kinds of beetle, esp one regarded as sacred in ancient Egypt. **2** ornament, etc in the shape of a scarab.

scarce /skers/ *adj* (-r, -st) **1** (opposite of *plentiful*) not available in sufficient quantity; not equal to the demand: *Jobs are ~ this month.* **2** rare: *a ~ book.*

scarc·ity /ˈskersəti/ *n* [C,U] (*pl* -ies) occasion, state of being scarce; smallness of supply compared with demand: *The scarcity of fruit was caused by the drought.*

scarce·ly /ˈskersli/ *adv* barely; not quite; almost not: *There were ~ a hundred people present. I ~ know him.*

scare /sker/ *vt,vi* frighten; become afraid: *The dogs ~d the thief away. He was ~d by the thunder. He ~s easily/is easily ~d. She's ~ed of the dark.* ***be scared stiff (of sth),*** (*informal*) be very afraid, frightened by: *He's ~d stiff of women.* ***scare sb out of his wits,*** make him extremely frightened: *The sound of footsteps outside the door ~d her out of her wits.* □ *n* [C] feeling, state, of alarm: *The news caused a war ~,* a fear that war might break out.

ˈscare·crow *n* [C] figure of a man dressed in old clothes, set up to scare birds away from crops.

ˈscare·monger /-ˌməŋgər/ *n* [C] person who spreads alarming news.

scary /ˈskeri/ *adj* (-ier, -iest) (*informal*) causing alarm.

scarf /skarf/ *n* [C] (*pl* scarves /skarvz/ or ~s) long strip of material (silk, wool, etc) worn over the shoulders, around the neck or (by women) over the hair.

scar·ify /ˈskærəˌfai/ *vt* (*pt,pp* -ied) **1** (in surgery) make small cuts in, cut off skin, from. **2** make scars on the skin, especially as a tribal marking.

scar·let /ˈskarlət/ *n* [U], *adj* bright red. ***go scarlet,*** blush.

ˌscarlet ˈfever, infectious disease causing red marks on the skin.

ˌscarlet ˈrunner, kind of bean plant.

scarp /skarp/ *n* [C] steep slope.

scat /skæt/ *int* (*dated sl*) go away.

scath·ing /ˈskeiðɪŋ/ *adj* (of criticism, etc) severe; harsh: *a* ~ *review of a new book.*

scath·ing·ly *adv*

scat·ter /ˈskætər/ *vt,vi* **1** send, go, in different directions: *The police* ~*ed the crowd. The crowd* ~*ed.* **2** throw or put in various directions: ~ *seed.* □ *n* [C] that which is scattered; sprinkling: *a* ~ *of hailstones.*

ˈscatter·brain *n* person who is unable to concentrate or organize things in a systematic way.

ˈscatter·brained *adj*

scat·tered *adj* not situated together: *a few* ~*ed villages.*

scav·enge /ˈskævɪndʒ/ *vt,vi* act as a scavenger.

scav·en·ger /ˈskævɪndʒər/ *n* [C] **1** animal or bird, eg a vulture, that lives on decaying flesh. **2** person who looks among rubbish for food, useful things.

scen·ario /sɪˈnæriˌou/ *n* [C] (*pl* ~s) written outline of a play, an opera, a film, with details of the scenes, etc.

scene /sin/ *n* [C] **1** place of an actual or imagined event: *the* ~ *of a great battle. The* ~ *of the novel is set in Scotland.* **2** description of an incident, or of part of a person's life; incident in real life suitable for such a description: *There were distressing* ~*s when the earthquake occurred.* **3** (incident characterized by an) emotional outburst: *She made a* ~*/We had a* ~ *when I arrived late.* **4** view; something seen: *The boats in the harbor make a beautiful* ~. ***change of scene,*** new surroundings. **5** (*abbr* **Sc**) one of the parts, shorter than an act, into which some plays and operas are divided; episode within such a part: *"Macbeth," Act II, Sc 1.* **6** place represented on the stage of a theater; the painted background, woodwork, canvas, etc representing such a place: *The* ~*s are changed during the intermission.* ***behind the scenes,*** **(a)** out of sight of the audience; behind the stage. **(b)** (*fig*) (of a person) influencing events secretly; having private or secret information and influence. ***come on the scene,*** (usually *fig*) appear. **7** (*informal*) area of what is currently fashionable or notable: *the ˈdrug* ~ *in big cities.*

ˈscene painter, person who paints scenery(2).

ˈscene·shifter *n* [C] person who changes the scenes(6).

scen·ery /ˈsinəri/ *n* [U] **1** general natural features of a district, eg mountains, plains, valleys, forests: *mountain* ~*; stop to admire the* ~. **2** the furnishings, painted canvas, etc used on the stage of a theater.

scenic /ˈsinɪk/ *adj* of scenery: *a* ~ *highway across the Virginia mountains;* ~ *effects*, eg in a film.

sceni·cally /-kli/ *adv*

scent /sent/ *n* **1** [U] smell, esp of something pleasant: *a rose that has no* ~. **2** [C] particular kind of smell: ~*s of lavender and rosemary.* **3** [U] perfume: *a bottle of* ~*; a ˈ*~*-bottle.* **4** [C] (usually *sing*) smell left by (the track of) an animal: *follow/lose/recover the* ~. ***off/on the scent,*** not having/having the right clue. ***put/throw sb off the scent,*** (*fig*) mislead him by giving false information. **5** [U] sense of smell (in dogs): *hunt by* ~. □ *vt* **1** learn the presence of by smell: *The dog* ~*ed a rat.* **2** begin to suspect the presence or existence of: ~ *a crime;* ~ *treachery/trouble.* **3** put scent on; make fragrant: ~ *a handkerchief; roses that* ~ *the air.*

scent·less *adj* having no scent: ~*less flowers.*

scepter /ˈseptər/ *n* [C] rod or staff carried by a ruler as a symbol of power or authority.

sch. *abbr* = school.

sched·ule /ˈskedʒul, -dʒəl/ *n* [C] list or statement of details, especially of times for doing things; program or timetable for work: *a proˈduction* ~, eg in a factory; *a full* ~, a busy program. ***on/behind schedule,*** on/not on time: *The train arrived on* ~. ***(according) to schedule,*** as planned. □ *vt* **1** make, put in, a schedule: ~*d flights*, (eg of aircraft) flying according to announced timetables. ⇨ charter(2). **2** enter in a list of arrangements: *The President is* ~*d to make a speech tomorrow.*

sche·matic /skiˈmætɪk/ *adj* **1** of the nature of a scheme or plan. **2** (shown) in a diagram or chart.

sche·mati·cally /-kli/ *adv*

scheme /skim/ *n* [C] **1** arrangement; ordered system: *a ˈcolor* ~, eg for a room, so that colors of walls, rugs, curtains, etc match. **2** plan or design (for work or activity): *a* ~ *for manufacturing paper from straw.* **3** secret and dishonest plan: *a* ~ *to avoid paying taxes.* □ *vi,vt* **1** make a (esp dishonest) scheme: *They* ~*d to defeat/for the overthrow of the government.* **2** make plans for (esp something dishonest): *a scheming* (= crafty) *young man.*

schemer *n* [C] person who schemes.

schism /ˈskɪzəm *or* ˈsɪzəm/ *n* [U] (offense of causing the) division of an organization (esp a Church) into two or more groups; [C] instance of such separation.

schis·matic /skɪzˈmætɪk, sɪzˈmætɪk/ *adj*

schizo /ˈskɪtsou/ *adj, n* (*pl* ~s) (*informal*) (short for) schizophrenic.

schizo·phrenia /ˌskɪtsəˈfriniə/ *n* [U] type of mental disorder marked by lack of association between the intellectual processes and actions.

schizo·phrenic /ˌskɪtsəˈfrenɪk/ *adj* of, suffering from, schizophrenia. □ *n* [C] person suffering from schizophrenia.

scholar /ˈskalər/ *n* [C] **1** (*dated*) boy or girl at school. **2** student who, after a competitive examination or other means of selection, is awarded money or other help so that he may attend school or college: *Fulbright* ~*s.* **3** person with much learning (usually of a particular subject): *Professor X, the famous ˈGreek ˌ*~, specialist in Greek. (*Compare: ˌGreek ˈscholar*, scholar who is a Greek.) **4** (*informal*) person able to read and write well: *I'm not much of a* ~.

schol·ar·ly *adj* having or showing much learning; of or suitable for a scholar(3); fond of learning: *a ~ly translation; ~ly young woman.*

schol·ar·ship /ˈskalərˌʃɪp/ *n* **1** [U] learning or knowledge obtained by study; proper concern for scholarly methods. **2** [C] payment of money, eg a yearly grant to a scholar(2) so that he may continue his studies: *win a ~ to the university.*

schol·as·tic /skəˈlæstɪk/ *adj* **1** (*dated*) of schools and education: *the ~ profession*, teaching. **2** connected with the learning of the Middle Ages, esp when scholars argued over small points of dogma.

school[1] /skul/ *n* **1** [C] institution for educating children and young people: *ˈprimary and ˈsecondary ~s.* **2** (not with *the, a* or *an*) process of being educated in a school: *ˈ~ age*, between the ages of starting and finishing school. *Is he old enough for ~/to go to ~? He left ~ when he was fifteen.* **3** (not with *the, a* or *an*) time when teaching is given; lessons: *School begins at 9am. There will be no ~* (= no lessons) *tomorrow.* **4** (with *the*) all the pupils in a school: *The whole ~ hopes that its football team will win.* **5** [C] department or division of a university for the study of a particular subject: *the ˈLaw/ˈMedical School; the School of Dentistry.* **6** [C] (*fig*) circumstances or occupation that provides discipline or instruction: *the hard ~ of experience.* **7** [C] group of persons who are followers or imitators of an artist, a philosopher, etc: *the ˈDutch ~ of painting.* ***the same school of thought,*** the same way of thinking; agreement. **8** [C] group of persons having the same characteristics: *of the ˈold ~*, having traditional attitudes. □ *vt* train; control; discipline: *~ a horse; ~ one's temper.*

ˈschool·bag *n* [C] for carrying school books, equipment.

ˈschool·boy *n* [C] boy at school: (as an *adjective*) *~boy pranks.*

ˈschool children, children at school.

ˈschool days, time of being at school: *look back on one's ~ days with pleasure.*

ˈschool·fellow *n* [C] boy of the same school.

ˈschool·girl *n* [C] girl at school.

ˈschool·house *n* [C] building of a school in a small town or rural area.

school·ing *n* [U] = education (the usual word): *He had very little ~ing.*

ˈschool·master/mistress *n* [C] teacher (esp in a private school or old-fashioned grammar school).

ˈschool·mate *n* [C] boy, girl, of the same school.

ˈschool·teacher *n* [C] person who teaches in a school.

ˈschool·time *n* lesson time at school.

school[2] /skul/ *n* [C] large number of fish swimming together.

schoo·ner /ˈskunər/ *n* [C] **1** kind of sailing ship with two or more masts. **2** tall drinking glass.

schwa /ʃwa/ *n* [C] (*pl* ~s) the symbol /ə/ as used in the phonetic notation for *above* /əˈbəv/.

sci. *abbr* = science.

science /ˈsaiəns/ *n* **1** [U] knowledge arranged in an orderly manner, esp knowledge obtained by observation and the testing of facts; effort to find such knowledge: *Science is an exact discipline,* demands complete accuracy and precision. **2** [C,U] branch of such knowledge, eg physics: *study ~/the ~s at school.* ⇨ social science.

ˌscience ˈfiction, fiction dealing with recent or imagined scientific discoveries and advances.

scien·ti·fic /ˌsaiənˈtɪfɪk/ *adj* of, for, connected with, used in, science; guided by the rules of science: *~ methods; ~ instruments.*

scien·ti·fi·cally /-kli/ *adv*

scien·tist /ˈsaiəntɪst/ *n* [C] student of, expert in, one of the natural or physical sciences.

scimi·tar /ˈsɪmɪtər, -ˌtar/ *n* [C] oriental curved sword.

scin·til·late /ˈsɪntəˌleit/ *vi* **1** sparkle. **2** (*fig*) talk cleverly: *scintillating conversation.*

scin·til·la·tion /ˌsɪntəˈleiʃən/ *n* [U]

scis·sors /ˈsɪzərz/ *n pl* (often ***a pair of scissors***) instrument with two blades which cut as they come together: *Where are my ~?*

scoff /skɔf/ *vi* say disrespectful things, eg about religion. □ n [C] **1** scoffing remark. **2** object of ridicule.

scoffer *n* [C] person who scoffs.

scold /skould/ *vt,vi* **1** blame with angry words: *~ a child for being lazy.* **2** complain: *She's always ~ing.* □ *n* [C] woman who scolds.

scold·ing *n* [C] complaint using angry words: *get/give her a ~ing for being late.*

scoop /skup/ *n* [C] **1** (sorts of) short-handled tool like a shovel for taking up and moving quantities of grain, flour, sugar, etc. **2** motion of, or as of, using a scoop: *at one ~*, in one single movement of a scoop. **3** (*informal*) piece of news obtained and published by one newspaper before its competitors. **4** (*comm*) large profit from sudden luck. □ *vt* **1** ***scoop sth out/up,*** lift with, or as with, a scoop. **2** make (a hole, groove, etc) with, or as with, a scoop: *~ out a hole in the sand.* **3** (*informal*) get (news, a profit, etc) as a scoop(3,4): *He ~ed the market.*

scoot /skut/ *vi* (*informal*) = scram.

scooter /ˈskutər/ *n* [C] **1** (also **ˈmotor scooter**) low-built motorcycle with a small engine. **2** child's toy, an L-shaped vehicle with small wheels, one foot resting on it and the other being used to move it by pushing against the ground.

scope /skoup/ *n* [U] **1** opportunity: *work that gives ~ for one's abilities.* **2** range of action or observation: *Economics is beyond the ~ of a child's mind.*

-scope /-ˌskoup/ *suff* (forms a *n* [C]) instrument for observing or showing: *micro~; peri~.*

scorch /skɔrtʃ/ *vt,vi* **1** burn or discolor the surface of (something) by dry heat; cause to dry up (and die): *You ~ed my shirt when you ironed it. The long, hot summer ~ed the grass.* **2** become discolored, etc with heat. □ *n* [C] brown mark on the surface of something (esp cloth) made by dry heat.

scorcher *n* something that scorches: *Yesterday was a ~er*, a very hot day.

scorch·ing *adj* very hot. □ *adv: ~ing hot*, extremely hot.

score[1] /skɔr/ *n* [C] **1** cut, scratch or notch made on a surface: *~s on rock*. **2** mark made by whipping. **3** ***pay/settle an old score,*** get even with a person for past offenses; have one's revenge: *I have some old ~s to settle with him.* **4** (record of) points, goals, runs, etc made by a player or team in sport: *The ~ in the tennis final was 6-4, 3-6, 7-5. The half-time ~* (eg in football) *was 2-1.* ***keep the score,*** keep a record of the score as it is made. **5** reason; account. ***on 'that score,*** as far as that point is concerned: *You needn't have any anxiety on that ~.* **6** copy of orchestral, etc music showing what each instrument is to play, each voice to sing: *follow the ~ while listening to music.* **7** twenty; set of twenty: *a ~ of people; three ~ and ten,* 70, the normal length of human life according to the Bible. ⇨ App 1. ***scores of times,*** very often. **8** (*sl*) remark or act by which a person gains an advantage for himself in an argument, etc: *a politician who is clever at making ~s off opponents.*

'score·board/·book/·card *n* one on which the score is recorded.

score[2] /skɔr/ *vt,vi* **1** mark with scratches, cuts, lines, etc: *Don't ~ the floor by pushing heavy furniture around. The composition was ~d with corrections in red ink.* ⇨ score[1](1). **2** make or keep a record (esp for games): *Who's scoring?* **3** make as points in a game: *~ a goal; ~ tricks,* when playing card games. **4** obtain by hard work or effort: *The football team ~d a great victory.* **5** write instrumental or vocal parts for a musical composition: *~d for violin, viola and cello.* ⇨ score[1](6).

scorer *n* [C] **(a)** person who keeps a record of points, goals, runs, etc scored in a game. **(b)** player who scores runs, goals, etc.

scorn /skɔrn/ *n* [U] **1** feeling that a person or thing deserves no respect: *be filled with ~ for her; dismiss a suggestion with ~.* ***laugh sb/sth to scorn,*** laugh in a manner showing that he/it is inferior, worthless. **2** object of scorn: *He was the ~ of the neighborhood.* □ *vt* feel or show disrespect, disregard, for; refuse (to do something because it is unworthy): *He ~ed my advice. She ~s lying/telling lies/to tell a lie.*

scorn·ful /-fəl/ *adj* showing or feeling scorn: *a ~ful smile.*

scorn·fully /-fəli/ *adv*

Scor·pio /'skɔrpi,ou/ *n* the Scorpion, the eighth sign of the zodiac. ⇨ illus at zodiac.

scor·pion /'skɔrpiən/ *n* [C] small animal of the spider group with a poisonous sting in its long, jointed tail.

Scot /skat/ *n* [C] native of Scotland.

Scotch /skatʃ/ *adj* of Scotland: *~ whisky,* the kind distilled in Scotland. □ *n* [C,U] (portion of) Scotch whisky.

scot-free /,skat-'fri/ *adj* unharmed, unpunished: *He went/got off ~.*

Scots /skats/ *adj* Scottish.

'Scots·man/·woman /-mən, -,wumən/ *n* [C] (*pl* -men /-men/, ~women /-,wɪmɪn/) male/female native of Scotland.

Scot·tish /'skatɪʃ/ *adj* of Scotland or its people: *~ music.*

scoun·drel /'skaundrəl/ *n* [C] person who does wicked things.

scour[1] /'skauər/ *vt,vi* **1** make (a dirty surface) clean or bright by using a rough cloth, pad of wire, with soap, sand, etc: *~ the pots and pans; ~ out a saucepan,* clean the inside. **2** get rid of (rust, marks, etc) by rubbing, etc: *~ the rust off/away.* **3** clear out (a channel, etc) by flowing over or through it: *The torrent ~ed a channel down the hillside.* □ *n* [C] act of scouring.

scourer /'skaurər/ *n* [C] pad of stiff nylon or wire for cleaning pots and pans.

scour[2] /'skauər/ *vt,vi* look everywhere for: *The police ~ed the neighborhood for the thief/were ~ing about.*

scourge /skərdʒ/ *n* [C] **1** (*old use*) whip. **2** (*modern use*) (*fig*) cause of suffering: *After the ~ of war came the ~ of disease.* □ *vt* **1** (*old use*) whip. **2** (*fig*) cause suffering to.

scout /skaut/ *n* [C] **1** person, ship or small, fast aircraft, sent out to get information about the enemy. **2** (also **'boy scout** and **Scout**) member of an organization of boys intended to develop character and teach self-reliance, discipline and social awareness: *Boy Scouts of America.* **3** person employed to look out for talented performers (in sport, etc) and recruit them for his employer(s): *a 'talent ~.* □ *vi* ***scout about/around (for sb/sth),*** go about looking for.

'scout·master *n* [C] officer who leads a troop of Scouts.

scowl /skaul/ *n* [C] bad-tempered look (on the face). □ *vi* look in a bad-tempered way: *The prisoner ~ed at the judge.*

scrabble /'skræbəl/ *vi* ***scrabble (for sth),*** grope about to find or collect.

scrag /skræg/ *n* **1** [C] lean, skinny person or animal. **2** [U] (also **,scrag-'end**) bony part of a sheep's neck, used for making soup and stews.

scraggy *adj* (-ier, -iest) thin and bony.

scram /skræm/ *vi* (-mm-) (*sl*) go away quickly.

scramble /'skræmbəl/ *vi,vt* **1** climb (with difficulty) or crawl (over steep or rough ground): *~ up the side of a cliff/over a rocky hillside.* **2** struggle with others to get something: *The players were scrambling for possession of the ball.* **3** cook (eggs) by beating them and then heating them in a pan. **4** make a message sent by telephone, etc unintelligible. □ *n* [C] **1** walk, motorcycle competition or trial, over or through obstacles, rough ground, etc. **2** rough struggle: *There was a ~ for the best seats.*

scrap[1] /skræp/ *n* **1** [C] small (usually unwanted) piece: *~s of paper/broken glass.* **2** (*fig*) small amount: *not a ~ of truth in her statement.* **3** [U] waste or unwanted articles, especially those of value only for the material they contain: *He offers good prices for ~.* **4** (*pl*) bits of uneaten food: *Give the ~s to the dog.* **5** [C] picture or paragraph cut out from a periodical, etc for a collection. □ *vt* (-pp-) **1** throw away as useless or worn-out: *You ought to ~ that old bicycle and buy a new one.* **2** reject a plan, idea, etc: *This idea won't work, let's ~ it.*

'scrap·book *n* [C] book of blank pages on which to paste scraps(5).

'scrap heap, pile of waste or unwanted material or articles. ***throw sth/sb on the scrap heap,*** reject it/them as no longer wanted.

scrappy *adj* (-ier, -iest) **(a)** made up of bits or scraps. **(b)** not complete or properly organized: *a ~ idea.*

scrap[2] /skræp/ *n* [C] (*dated informal*) fight, quarrel (between children). □ *vi* (-pp-) fight; quarrel.

scrape /skreip/ *vt,vi* **1** make clean, smooth or level by drawing or pushing the hard edge of a tool, or something rough, along the surface; remove (mud, grease, paint, etc) in this way: *~ the rust off a nail; ~ paint from a door.* **2** injure or damage by rubbing, etc: *The boy fell and ~d (the skin off) his knee. He ~d the side of his car.* **3** make by scraping: *~ (out) a hole.* **4** go, get, pass along, touching or almost touching: *branches that ~ against the window.* ***scrape through (sth),*** only just pass: *The boy just ~d through (his exams).* ***ˌbow and ˈscrape,*** (*fig*) behave with exaggerated respect. **5** obtain by being careful, or with effort: *We managed to ~ together an audience of fifty people/enough money for a short vacation.* ***scrape a living,*** with difficulty make enough money for a living. □ *n* [C] **1** act or sound of scraping: *the ~ of a fork across a plate.* **2** place that is scraped; injury: *a bad ~ on the elbow*, eg as the result of a fall. **3** awkward situation resulting from foolish or thoughtless behavior: *That boy is always getting into ~s.*

scraper *n* [C] tool used for scraping, eg for scraping paint from woodwork.

scrappy /ˈskræpi/ *adj* ⇨ scrap[1].

scratch[1] /skrætʃ/ *n* **1** [C] mark, cut, injury, sound, made by scratching(1): *It's only a ~*, a very slight injury. *He escaped without a ~*, quite unhurt. **2** (*sing* only) act or period of scratching (5): *The dog enjoys having a good ~.* **3** (*sing* only without *the, a* or *an*) starting line for a race. ***start from scratch,*** (*fig*) **(a)** start at the beginning, without being allowed any advantage(s). **(b)** begin (something) without preparation. ***be/come/bring sb up to scratch,*** (*fig*) be ready/get him ready to do what is expected or required: *Will you be up to ~ for the examination?* **4** (as an *adjective*) brought together, done, made, with whatever or whoever is available: *a ~ team.*

scratch[2] /skrætʃ/ *vt,vi* **1** make lines on or in a surface with something pointed or sharp, eg fingernails, claws: *This cat ~es. Who has ~ed the paint?* ***scratch the surface,*** (*fig*) deal with a subject without getting deeply into it: *The teacher merely ~ed the surface of the subject.* **2** get (oneself, a part of the body) scratched by accident: *He ~ed his hands badly on a rosebush.* **3** draw a line or lines through a word or words, a name, etc: *~ out his name from the list.* **4** withdraw (a horse, a candidate, oneself) from a competition: *The horse was ~ed.* **5** scrape or rub (the skin), esp to stop itching: *~ mosquito bites. Stop ~ing (yourself).* ***scratch one's head,*** show signs of being puzzled. **6** make by scratching: *~ (out) a hole.* **7** make a scraping noise: *This pen ~es.* **8** tear or dig with the claws, fingernails, etc in search of something: *The chickens were ~ing around in the yard.*

scratchy *adj* (-ier, -iest) **(a)** (of writing, drawings) done carelessly. **(b)** (of a pen) making a scratching noise. **(c)** (of a phonograph record) full of interfering noise from scratches on the surface. **(d)** (of cloth, esp in clothes) coarse, irritating to the skin.

scrawl /skrɔl/ *vi,vt* write or draw quickly or carelessly; make meaningless marks: *He ~ed a few words on a postcard to his wife. Who has ~ed all over this wall?* □ *n* **1** [C] piece of bad writing; hurried note or letter. **2** (*sing* only) shapeless, untidy handwriting: *His signature was an illegible ~.*

scrawny /ˈskrɔni/ *adj* (-ier, iest) thin and bony.

scream /skrim/ *vi,vt* **1** (of humans, birds, animals) give a loud, sharp cry or cries of, or as of, fear or pain: *The baby has been ~ing for an hour.* **2** shout in a high voice: *She ~ed out that there was a burglar under the bed.* ***scream with laughter,*** laugh noisily. **3** (of the wind, machines, etc) make a loud, high noise: *The wind ~ed through the trees.* □ *n* [C] **1** loud, high, cry or noise: *~s of pain/laughter.* **2** (*informal*) person or thing that causes screams of laughter: *He/It was a ~.*

scree /skri/ *n* [C,U] (part of a mountainside covered with) small loose stones.

screech /skritʃ/ *vi,vt* **1** make a harsh, piercing sound: *The brakes ~ed as the car stopped.* **2** scream (as) in anger or pain: *monkeys ~ing in the trees.* □ *n* [C] screeching cry or noise: *the ~ of tires on wet roads.*

screen /skrin/ *n* [C] **1** (often movable) upright framework (some made so as to fold), used to divide a room, protect from draughts, etc. **2** (in a church) structure of wood or stone separating (but not completely) the main part of the church and the altar, or the nave of a cathedral and the choir. **3** anything that is or can be used to give shelter or protection from observation, the weather, etc: *a ~ of trees*, hiding a house from the road; *a ˈsmoke~*, used in war to hide ships, etc from the enemy. **4** white or silver surface on to which film transparencies, cinema films, etc are projected. **5** surface on which an image is seen on a cathode ray tube (as in a television set). **6** frame with fine wire netting (*ˈwindow ~, ˈdoor ~*) to keep out flies, mosquitoes, etc. □ *vt,vi* **1** shelter, hide, protect, with a screen: *The trees ~ our house from public view.* **2** (*fig*) protect from blame, discovery, punishment: *I'm not willing to ~ you from blame.* **3** investigate (a person's) past history, eg of a person applying for a position in government service, in order to judge his loyalty, dependability, etc. **4** show (a picture) on a screen(4, 5). **5** equip a house, windows, etc with screens(6).

ˈscreen·ing *n* **(a)** [U] wire netting for a screen (6). **(b)** [C] process of screening(4,5).

ˈscreen·play *n* [C] script of a film.

ˈscreen test, test of a person's suitability for acting in films.

ˈscreen·writer *n* [C] writer of scripts for films.

screw /skru/ *n* [C] **1** metal peg with slotted head and a spiral groove cut around its length, driven into wood, metal, etc by twisting under pressure, for fastening and holding things together. **2** something that is turned like a screw and is used for producing pressure, tightening, etc. ***put the screws on,*** (*informal*) use pressure, especially to intimidate. **3** action of turning; turn: *This isn't tight enough yet; give it another ~.* **4** (also ˈ**screw propeller**) propeller of a ship: *a twin-~ steamer.* ⇨ airscrew. **5** prison guard. **6** (*sl*) (instance of) sexual intercourse. □ *vt,vi* **1** fasten or tighten with a screw: *~ a lock on a door; ~ down the lid of a coffin.* ***have one's head screwed on (the right way),*** be sensible, have good judgment. **2** twist around; make tight, tense or more efficient: *~ a lid on/off a jar; ~ up one's face/features/eyes,* contract the muscles, eg when going out into bright sunshine from a dark room. **3** (*sl*) have sexual intercourse (with somebody). **4** ˌ***screwed*** ˈ***up,*** (*sl*) very confused; disorganized.

ˈ**screw·driver** *n* [C] **(a)** tool for turning a screw (1). **(b)** drink made with orange juice and vodka.

screwy *adj* (-ier, -iest) (*informal*) crazy; absurd.

scribble /ˈskrɪbəl/ *vt,vi* **1** write quickly or carelessly. **2** make meaningless marks on paper, etc. □ *n* [U] careless handwriting; [C] something scribbled.

scrib·bler /ˈskrɪblər/ *n* [C] person who scribbles.

scribe /skraib/ *n* [C] **1** person who, before the invention of printing, made copies of writings, eg in monasteries. **2** (among the Jews in Biblical times) maker and keeper of records; teacher of Jewish law (at the time of Jesus Christ).

scrim·mage /ˈskrɪmɪdʒ/ *n* [C,U] practice play between members of a single sports team. □ *vi* engage in scrimmage.

scrim·shaw /ˈskrɪmˌʃɔ/ *n* [U] artwork of (especially) nineteenth century American whalemen, made by engraving pictures or designs on whalebone, etc.

scrip /skrɪp/ *n* [U] certificate of money, goods, etc owed for the stated value, sometimes used as a substitute for currency: *The company was low on cash and wanted to pay its employees in/with ~.*

script /skrɪpt/ *n* **1** [U] handwriting; printed characters in imitation of handwriting. **2** [C] (short for) manuscript or typescript.

ˈ**script·writer** *n* [C] person who writes scripts for radio, TV, films.

scrip·ture /ˈskrɪptʃər/ *n* **1 The (Holy) Scriptures,** the Bible; (as an *adjective*) taken from, relating to, the Bible: *a* ˈ*~ lesson.* **2** sacred book of a religion other than Christianity.

scrip·tural /ˈskrɪptʃərəl/ *adj* based on the Bible.

scroll /skroul/ *n* [C] **1** roll of paper or parchment for writing on; ancient book written on a scroll. **2** ornamental design cut in stone like the curves of a scroll.

scro·tum /ˈskroutəm/ *n* [C] (*pl* ~s) pouch of skin enclosing the testicles in mammals.

scrounge /skraundʒ/ *vi,vt* (*informal*) get what one wants by taking it without permission, borrowing or by trickery. ***scrounge (around) for,*** search for (usually in an unplanned or disorganized way).

scrounger *n* [C] person who scrounges.

scrub[1] /skrəb/ *n* [U] (land covered with) trees and bushes of poor quality.

scrub[2] /skrəb/ *vt,vi* (-bb-) **1** clean by rubbing hard, esp with a stiff brush, soap and water: *~ the floor.* **2** (*informal*) cancel: *~ (out) an order.* □ *n* [C] act of scrubbing: *The floor needs a good ~.*

ˈ**scrub brush,** stiff brush for scrubbing floors, etc.

scruff /skrəf/ *n* (only in) ***the scruff of the neck,*** (clothes near) the back of the neck when used for grasping.

scruffy /ˈskrəfi/ *adj* (-ier, -iest) (*informal*) dirty, untended and untidy looking.

scruple /ˈskrupəl/ *n* [C,U] (feeling of doubt caused by a) troubled conscience: *Have you no ~s about borrowing things without permission?* □ *vi* hesitate owing to scruples: *He doesn't ~ to tell a lie if he thinks it useful.* (*Note:* usually *negative.*)

scru·pu·lous /ˈskrupyələs/ *adj* careful to do nothing morally wrong; paying great attention to small points (esp of conscience): *An attorney should act with ~ honesty.*

scru·pu·lous·ly *adv* in a scrupulous manner.

scru·ti·nize /ˈskrutəˌnaiz/ *vt* make a detailed examination of.

scru·tiny /ˈskrutəni/ *n* (*pl* -ies) [U] thorough and detailed examination; [C] instance of this.

scuff /skəf/ *vi,vt* **1** walk without properly lifting the feet from the ground. **2** wear out or scrape (shoes, etc) by walking in this way: *~ one's shoes.*

scuffle /ˈskəfəl/ *vi, n* [C] (take part in a) rough fight or struggle: *police scuffling with demonstrators.*

scull /skəl/ *n* [C] **1** one of a pair of oars used together by a rower, one in each hand. **2** oar worked at the stern of a boat with twisting strokes. □ *vt,vi* move, row, (a boat) with sculls.

scul·ler *n* [C] person who sculls.

sculpt /skəlpt/ *vt,vi* = sculpture.

sculp·tor /ˈskəlptər/ *n* [C] man who sculptures.

sculp·tress /ˈskəlptrɪs/ *n* [C] woman who sculptures.

sculp·ture /ˈskəlptʃər/ *n* **1** [U] art of making representations in stone, wood, metal, etc by carving or modeling. **2** [C,U] (piece of) such work. □ *vt,vi* **1** represent in, decorate with, sculpture: *~ a statue out of stone; ~d columns.* **2** be a sculptor.

scum /skəm/ *n* **1** [U] froth, etc which forms on the surface of some liquids. **2 the scum,** (*fig*) the worst, or seemingly worthless, section (of the population, etc).

scup·per /ˈskəpər/ *n* [C] opening in a ship's side to allow water to run off the deck. □ *vt* sink a ship deliberately.

scurf /skərf/ *n* [U] small bits of dead skin, esp on the scalp; dandruff (the usual word).

scurfy *adj* having, covered with, scurf.

scur·ri·lous /ˈskərələs/ *adj* using, full of, violent words of abuse: *~ attacks on the President.*

scurry /ˈskəri/ *vi* (*pt,pp* -ied) run with short, quick steps; hurry: *The rain sent everyone ~ing about/~ing for shelter.* □ *n* **1** [U] act or sound of scurrying: *There was a ~ toward the bar.* **2** [C] windy shower (of snow); cloud (of dust).

scurvy /ˈskərvi/ *n* [U] diseased state of the blood caused by eating too much salt meat and not enough fresh vegetables and fruit.

scuttle[1] /ˈskətəl/ *n* [C] (also **ˈcoalscuttle**) container for a supply of coal at the fireside.

scuttle[2] /ˈskətəl/ *vi* ***scuttle off/away,*** = scurry. ▫ *n* [C] hurried departure.

scuttle[3] /ˈskətəl/ *n* [C] small opening with a lid, in a ship's side or on deck or in a roof or wall. ▫ *vt* cut holes in, open valves in, a ship's sides or bottom to sink it: *The captain ~d his ship to avoid its being captured by the enemy.*

scythe /saið/ *n* [C] tool with a curved blade on a long wooden pole with two short handles, for cutting long grass, grain, etc. ▫ *vt* use a scythe.

SD[1] *postal abbr* = South Dakota. ⇨ App 6.

S.D.[2] *abbr* = **1** (degree of) Doctor of Science. **2** standard deviation.

SE *abbr* = southeast.

sea /si/ *n* **1 the sea,** expanse of salt water that covers most of the earth's surface; any part of this (in contrast to areas of fresh water and dry land): *Ships sail on the sea. The sea covers nearly three-quarters of the world's surface.* **2** (*pl*) same sense as 1 above. ***the high seas,*** ⇨ high[1]. ***the freedom of the seas,*** the right to carry on sea trade without interference. **3** (in proper names) particular area of sea which is smaller than an ocean: *the Caspian Sea; the Sea of Galilee.* **4** (in various phrases without *the, a* or *an*) ***at sea,*** away from, out of sight of, the land: *He was buried at sea.* ***all/completely at sea,*** (*fig*) puzzled: *He was all at sea when he began his new job.* ***by sea,*** in a ship: *travel by sea and land.* ***go to sea,*** become a sailor. ***put to sea,*** leave port or land. **5** (with *a, an* or in *pl*) local state of the sea swell of the ocean; big wave or billow: *There was a heavy sea,* large waves. ***half seas over,*** (*dated*) drunk. **6** large quantity or expanse (*of*): *a sea of upturned faces,* eg crowds of people looking upwards.

ˌsea ˈair, air at the seashore, considered to be good for health.

ˈsea anemone, popular name for a sea creature like a flower.

ˈsea·bed *n* floor of the sea.

ˈsea·bird *n* [C] any bird which lives close to the sea, ie on cliffs, islands, etc.

ˈsea·board *n* coastal region.

ˈsea·borne *adj* (of trade) carried in ships.

ˈsea breeze, breeze blowing inland from the sea.

ˈsea·faring /-ˌfærɪŋ/ *adj* of work or voyages on the sea: *a ˈseafaring man,* a sailor.

ˈsea·food *n* [U] edible fish or shellfish from the sea.

ˈsea·front *n* part of a town facing the sea.

ˈsea god, god living in or having power over the sea, eg Neptune.

ˈsea·going *adj* **(a)** (of ships) built for crossing the sea, not for coastal voyages only. **(b)** (of a person) seafaring.

ˌsea-ˈgreen *adj, n* [U] bluish-green as of the sea.

ˈsea gull, common seabird with long wings.

ˈsea horse, small fish with a head like a horse.

ˈsea legs, ability to walk on the deck of a rolling ship: *get/find one's sea legs.*

ˈsea level, level of sea halfway between high and low tide as the basis for measuring height of land and depth of sea: *500 feet above/below sea level.*

ˈsea lion, large seal of the northern Pacific Ocean.

ˈsea·man /-mən/ *n* [C] (*pl* seamen /-men/) **(a)** enlisted member of the US navy or coastguard holding the lowest rank. **(b)** person expert in nautical matters.

ˈsea·man·ship *n* [U] skill in managing a boat or ship.

ˈsea·plane *n* [C] aircraft constructed so that it can come down on and rise from water.

ˈsea·port *n* [C] town with a harbor used by seagoing ships.

ˈsea power, ability to control and use the seas (by means of naval strength).

ˈsea salt, (table) salt from the sea, containing minerals in addition to sodium chloride.

ˈsea·scape *n* picture of a scene at sea. ⇨ landscape.

ˈsea·shell *n* [C] shell of any shellfish living in the sea.

ˈsea·shore *n* (land close to) the shore.

ˈsea·sick *adj* (feeling) sick from the motion of a ship.

ˈsea·side *n* (often used as an *adjective*) place, town, etc by the sea, esp a vacation resort: *go to the seaside; a seaside town.*

ˈsea urchin, small sea animal with a shell covered with sharp points.

ˈsea·wall *n* [C] wall built to stop the sea from approaching the land.

ˈsea·ward /-wərd/ *adj* toward the sea; in the direction of the sea.

ˈsea·wards,/-wərdz/ *adv*

ˈsea·water *n* [U] water from the sea.

ˈsea·weed *n* [U] kinds of plant growing in the sea, esp on rocks washed by the sea.

ˈsea·worthy *adj* (of a ship) fit for a voyage.

seal[1] /ˈsiəl/ *n* [C] kinds of sea animal with flippers. ▫ *vi* (*pres p* ~ing /ˈsilɪŋ/) hunt seals.

ˈseal·skin *n* (leather made from the) skin of a seal.

SEAL

seal[2] /ˈsiəl/ *n* [C] **1** piece of wax, lead, etc stamped with a design, attached to a document to show that it is genuine, or to a letter, packet, box, bottle, door, etc to guard against its being opened by unauthorized persons. **2** something used instead of a seal(1), eg a paper disk stuck to, or an impression stamped on, a document. **3** piece of metal, etc with a design used to stamp the seal on wax, etc. **4 *seal of,*** (*fig*) act, event, etc regarded as a confirmation or guarantee or giving approval (of something): *the ~ of approval for spending the money.* **5** something that closes a thing tight to prevent leaks: *an airtight ~.* □ *vt* (*pres p* ~ing /ˈsilɪŋ/) **1** put a seal (1) on: *~ a letter.* **2** fasten or close tightly: *~ an envelope; ~ up a drawer.* **3** seal off, enclose to prevent entry or exit: *~ off an area of land.* **4** decide: *His fate is ~ed!*

seal·ing wax /ˈsilɪŋ ˌwæks/ kind of wax used to seal letters, etc.

seam /sim/ *n* [C] **1** line where two edges, eg of cloth, are turned back and sewn together. **2** line where two edges, eg of boards forming a ship's deck, meet. **3** layer of coal, etc between layers of other materials, eg rock, clay. **4** line or mark like a seam(1) (eg of folded paper).

seam·stress /ˈsimstrɪs/ (also **semp·stress** /ˈsempstrɪs/ in older use) *n* [C] woman who makes a living by sewing.

sé·ance /ˈseiˌæns, -ˌans/ *n* [C] meeting for communicating with the spirits of the dead through a medium(5).

sear, sere /sɪr/ *vt* **1** burn or scorch the surface of, esp with a heated iron. **2** (*fig*) make (a person, his conscience, etc) hard and without feeling: *His soul had been ~ed by injustice.*

search /sərtʃ/ *vt,vi* examine, look carefully at, through, or into (in order to find a person or thing): *He ~ed through all the drawers for the missing papers. I've ~ed my memory but can't remember that man's name.* ***Search ˈme!*** (*informal*) (in answer to a question) I haven't the slightest idea! □ *n* [C,U] **1** act of searching: *go in ~ of a missing child; a ~ for a missing aircraft.* **2** (*legal*) investigation (eg by lawyers) into prior patent applications, property claims, etc for a client.

searcher *n* [C] person who searches.

search·ing *adj* **(a)** (of a look) taking in all details. **(b)** (of a test, etc) thorough.

search·ing·ly *adv*

ˈsearch·light *n* [C] powerful light with a beam that can be turned in any direction to search for the enemy, escaped prisoners, etc.

ˈsearch party, number of persons looking for a person or thing that is lost.

ˈsearch warrant, official authority to enter and search a building (eg for stolen property).

sea·son /ˈsizən/ *n* [C] **1** one of the divisions of the year according to the weather, eg spring, summer, etc: *the ˈdry ~; the ˈrainy ~.* **2** period suitable or normal for something, or closely associated with it: *the ˈfootball ~; the ˈholiday/ˈtourist ~.* ***in/out of season,*** available/not available: *Oysters/Strawberries are out of ~ now.* □ *vt,vi* **1** make or become suitable for use: *Has this wood been well ~ed?,* dried and hardened? *The soldiers were not yet ~ed to the rigorous climate.* **2** flavor (food) (with salt, pepper, etc): *highly ~ed dishes.*

sea·son·ing *n* something used to season food: *Salt and pepper are ~ings.*

ˈseason ticket, ticket that gives the owner the right to attend a concert hall, etc during a certain period.

sea·son·able /ˈsizənəbəl/ *adj* **1** (of the weather) of the kind expected at the time of year. **2** (of help, advice, gifts, etc) coming at the right time.

sea·sonal /ˈsizənəl/ *adj* depending on a particular season; changing with the seasons: *~ occupations,* eg fruit picking.

sea·son·ally /-əli/ *adv*

seat /sit/ *n* [C] **1** something used or made for sitting on, eg a chair, box, bench: *The back ~ of the car is wide enough for three persons.* ***take a seat,*** sit: *Won't you take a seat?* ***take one's seat,*** sit down in one's place, eg in a hall or theater. ***take a back seat,*** ⇨ back seat. **2** that part of a chair, stool, bench, etc on which one sits (contrasted with the back, legs, etc): *a ˈchair ~.* **3** part of the body (the buttocks) on which one sits; part of clothing covering this: *He tore the ~ of his pants.* **4** place to sit in a movie house, theater, etc or in which one has a right to sit: *Mr. Smith is running for a ~ in the House of Representatives.* ***win a seat/lose one's seat,*** win/be defeated in a state or congressional election. **5** place where something is, or where something is carried on: *In the US, Washington is the ~ of government. A university is a ~ of learning.* **6** large house in the country: *He has a country ~ as well as a large house in the city.* □ *vt* **1** (*formal*) ***be seated,*** sit down: *Please/Kindly be ~ed, gentlemen.* **2** have seats for: *Our community hall ~s 500.*

ˈseat belt, strap for fastening across a seated passenger in a car or airplane.

-seater, (used in compounds after numerals to indicate the seating capacity of furniture, vehicles, etc): *My sportscar is a two-seater,* holds two people.

SEATO /ˈsitou/ *abbr* = Southeast Asia Treaty Organization.

SEC[1] *abbr* = Securities and Exchange Commission.

sec.[2] *abbr* = **1** second. **2** secretary. **3** section.

se·cede /sɪˈsid/ *vi* (of a group) withdraw (*from* membership of a state, federation, organization, etc).

se·ces·sion /sɪˈseʃən/ *n* [U] seceding; [C] instance of this (as in the US when eleven Southern States withdrew from the Federal Union in 1860-61).

se·ces·sion·ist /-ɪst/ *n* [C] supporter of secession.

se·clude /sɪˈklud/ *vt* keep (a person, oneself) away from the company of others: *~ oneself from society; keep a wife ~d in the kitchen.*

se·cluded *adj* (esp of a place) apart.

se·clu·sion /sɪˈkluʒən/ *n* [U] secluding or being secluded; solitary place: *live in ~; in the ~ of one's own home.*

sec·ond[1] /ˈsekənd/ *adj* (*abbr* **2nd**) **1** next after the first (in time, order, importance, etc): *February is the ~ month of the year. Tom is the ~ son—he has an elder brother.* ***ˌsecond to ˈnone,*** no other person, idea, etc is better. ***In the ˈsecond place...,*** = secondly. **2** additional; extra: *You will need a ~ pair of shoes.* ***play second fiddle (to),*** ⇨ fiddle. **3** of the same kind as one that has gone before: *This man seems to think he's a ~ Napoleon!* □ *adv* in the second place (in importance or in a race): *The Australian swimmer came (in) ~.*

ˌ**second ˈAdvent/ˈComing,** (in the Christian religion) return of Jesus Christ at the Last Judgment.

ˌ**second-ˈbest** *adj* next after the best: *my* ˌ*~-best* ˈ*suit.* □ *n, adv: I won't accept/put up with ~-best.* ***come off second-best,*** get the worst of it.

ˌ**second ˈchildhood,** period of old age when a person shows a weakening of mental powers: *He's in his ~ childhood.*

ˌ**second-ˈclass** *adj, n* **(a)** (of the) class next after the first: *a* ˌ*~-class hoˈtel.* **(b)** (regarded or treated as) inferior: ˌ*~-class ˈcitizens.* □ *adv: go/travel ~-class.*

ˌ**second ˈcousin,** child of a first cousin of either of one's parents.

ˌ**second ˈfloor,** the one above the first (in US one floor above the ground): (as an *adjective*) *a* ˌ*~-floor aˈpartment.*

ˌ**second** ˌ**geneˈration, (a)** having parents who were immigrants, etc. **(b)** second group (of members, etc) in time sequence: *the ~ generation of space technologists.*

ˈ**second·hand** *adj* **(a)** previously owned by someone else: ˌ*~hand ˈfurniture/ˈbooks.* **(b)** (of news, knowledge) obtained from others, not based on personal observation, etc: *get news ~hand.*

ˌ**second ˈhome, (a)** another home. **(b)** (*fig*) like one's house (because friendly, comfortable, etc).

second·ly *adv* and a second example is; in the next place; furthermore.

ˌ**second ˈname** = surname.

ˌ**second ˈnature,** tendency that has become instinctive like a habit: *Kindness is ~ nature to him.*

ˌ**second-ˈrate** *adj* not of the best quality; inferior: *a man with* ˌ*~-rate iˈdeas.*

ˌ**second ˈsight,** power to see future events, or events happening at a distance, as if present.

ˌ**second-ˈsighted** *adj* having this power.

ˌ**second ˈteeth,** those which grow after a child's first teeth are out.

ˈ**second thought, (a)** (in *sing*) opinion or resolution reached after reconsideration: *On ~ thought I will accept the offer.* **(b)** (in *pl*) doubts: *I'm having ~ thoughts* (= am not so sure) *about buying that house.*

ˌ**second ˈwind,** renewed strength, energy.

sec·ond[2] /ˈsekənd/ *n* **1** (*sing* only) person or thing that comes next to the first: *the ~ of May; Queen Elizabeth the Second* (or *II*). **2** (*sing* only) another person or thing besides the person or thing previously mentioned: *You are the ~ to ask me that question.* **3** (*pl*) goods below the best in quality: *There are many cheap ~s of china in the sale.* **4** [C] supporter of a boxer or wrestler; supporter in a duel.

sec·ond[3] /ˈsekənd/ *n* [C] **1** sixtieth part of a minute (indicated by the mark ″): *The winner's time was 1 minute and 5 ~s. 1° 6′ 10″ means one degree, six minutes, and ten ~s.* **2** moment; short time: *I shall be ready in a ~ or two/in a few ~s.*

ˈ**second hand,** extra hand on some watches and clocks recording seconds. ⇨ also secondhand.

se·cond[4] /ˈsekənd/ *vt* **1** support (esp a boxer, wrestler). **2** (a debate, etc) rise or speak formally in support of a motion to show that the proposer is not the only person in favor of it: *Mr. Smith proposed, and Mr. Green ~ed, a vote of thanks to the lecturer.*

se·conder *n* [C] person who supports a proposal or motion(3) at a meeting.

sec·ond·ary /ˈsekənˌderi/ *adj* **1** coming after: *~ education/schools,* for children over eleven. **2** less important or less strong: *~ symptoms.*

sec·ond·ar·ily /ˌsekənˈderəli/ *adv*

se·crecy /ˈsikrəsi/ *n* [U] keeping of secrets; ability to keep secrets; habit of keeping secrets; state of being kept secret: *I depend on your ~; prepare an escape in ~,* secretly; *do it with great ~.* ***swear sb to secrecy,*** ⇨ swear(2).

se·cret /ˈsikrɪt/ *adj* **1** (to be) kept from the knowledge or view of others; of which others have no knowledge: *a ~ marriage.* ***keep sth secret, (from),*** not tell it. **2** (of places) quiet and unknown. □ *n* **1** [C] something that is secret. ***keep a secret,*** not tell anyone else: *Can you keep a ~?* ***(be) an open secret,*** (of something thought to be secret) be (in fact) widely known. **2** [C] hidden cause; explanation, way of doing or getting something, that is not known to some or most people: *What is the ~ of his success?* **3** [U] ***in secret,*** secretly: *I was told about it in ~.* **4** [C] mystery: *the ~s of nature.*

ˌ**secret ˈagent,** member of the secret service.

ˌ**secret ˈballot,** when voters' choices are secret.

se·cret·ly *adv*

ˌ**secret poˈlice,** operating in secret (against political opposition).

the ˌ**secret ˈservice,** government department concerned with spying.

sec·re·tar·ial /ˌsekrəˈteriəl/ *adj* of (the work of) secretaries: *~ duties/training/colleges.*

sec·re·tary /ˈsekrəˌteri/ *n* [C] (*pl* -ies) **1** employee in an office, who deals with correspondence, keeps records, makes arrangements and appointments for a particular member of staff. **2** official who has charge of the correspondence, records, and other business affairs of a society, club or other organization. **3** cabinet-level chief of a department of the US Government: *Secretary of State/of the Interior,* chief of the Department of State/of the Interior.

ˌ**Secretary-ˈGeneral,** principal administrator (eg of the UNO).

se·crete /sɪˈkrit/ *vt* **1** produce by secretion(1). **2** put or keep in a secret place.

se·cre·tion /sɪˈkriʃən/ *n* **1** [U] process by which certain substances in a plant or animal body are separated (from sap, blood, etc); [C] substance so produced, eg saliva, bile. **2** [C] (*formal*) act of hiding: *the ~ of stolen goods.*

se·cret·ive /ˈsikrətɪv, sɪˈkritɪv/ *adj* having the habit of hiding one's actions, thoughts, feelings, intentions, etc.

se·cre·tive·ly *adv*

sect /sekt/ *n* [C] group of people united by (esp religious) beliefs or opinions.

sec·tar·ian /sekˈtæriən/ *n* [C], *adj* (member, supporter) of a sect or sects: *~ politics,* in which the advantage of a sect is considered more important than the public welfare.

sec·tion /ˈsekʃən/ *n* [C] **1** part cut off; one of the parts into which something may be divided: *the ~s of an orange*. **2** one of a number of parts which can be put together to make a structure: *glue the ~s of the model together*. **3** subdivision of an organized body of persons or of a piece of writing or of a town or community: *ˌresiˈdential/ˈshopping ~s* (*area* is the usual word). **4** view or representation of something seen as if cut straight through; thin slice suitable for examination under a microscope.

sec·tional /-əl/ *adj* **(a)** made or supplied in sections(2): *a ~al fishing rod*. **(b)** of one or more sections of a community, etc: *~al interests*, the different and often conflicting interests of various sections of a community.

sec·tion·al·ism /-ˌlɪzəm/ *n* [U] concern about sectional interests, not the community as a whole.

sec·tor /ˈsektər/ *n* [C] **1** part of a circle lying between two straight lines drawn from the center to the circumference. ⇨ illus at circle. **2** one of the parts into which an area is divided for the purpose of controlling (esp military) operations. **3** branch (of industry, etc): *the public and private ~s of industry*, those parts publicly owned and those privately owned.

secu·lar /ˈsekyələr/ *adj* **1** worldly or material, not religious or spiritual: *the ~ power*, the State contrasted with the Church. **2** living outside monasteries: *the ~ clergy*.

se·cure /sɪˈkyʊr/ *adj* (rarely -r, -st) **1** free from anxiety: *feel ~ about the future*. **2** certain; guaranteed: *He has a ~ position as a university lecturer*. **3** unlikely to involve risk; firm: *Are you sure the doors and windows are ~? Is that ladder ~?* **4** safe: *Are we ~ from attack?* □ *vt* **1** lock: *Secure all the doors and windows before leaving the house*. **2** make secure: *By strengthening the embankments they ~d the town against/from floods*. **3** succeed in getting (something for which there is a great demand): *She has ~d a good teaching job/job in teaching*.

se·cure·ly *adv*

se·cur·ity /sɪˈkyʊrəti/ *n* (*pl* -ies) **1** [C,U] (something that provides) safety, freedom from danger or anxiety: *children who lack the ~ of parental care*. **2** [C,U] something valuable, eg a life-insurance policy, given as a guarantee for the repayment of a loan or the fulfillment of a promise or undertaking: *lend money on ~; offer a house as (a) ~ for a loan*. **3** [C] document, certificate, etc showing ownership of property (esp bonds, stocks and shares): *government securities*, for money lent to a government.

sedan /sɪˈdæn/ enclosed car for four or more people.

se·date /sɪˈdeit/ *adj* (of a person, his behavior) calm; serious.

se·date·ly *adv*

se·da·tion /sɪˈdeiʃən/ *n* [U] treatment using sedatives; condition resulting from this. ***be under sedation,*** have taken sedatives: *He is under ~ and feels no pain*.

se·da·tive /ˈsedətɪv/ *n* [C], *adj* (medicine, drug) tending to calm the nerves and reduce stress: *After taking a ~ she was able to get to sleep*.

sed·en·tary /ˈsedənˌteri/ *adj* **1** (of work) done sitting down (at a desk, etc). **2** (of persons) spending much of their time seated: *lead a ~ life*.

sedi·ment /ˈsedəmənt/ *n* [U] matter (eg sand, dirt, gravel) that settles to the bottom of a liquid.

sedi·men·tary /ˌsedəˈmentəri/ *adj* of the nature of, formed from, sediment: *~ary rocks*, eg sandstone.

se·di·tion /sɪˈdɪʃən/ *n* [U] words or actions intended to make people rebel against authority, disobey the government, etc.

se·di·tious /sɪˈdɪʃəs/ *adj* of the nature of sedition: *seditious speeches/writings*.

se·duce /sɪˈdus/ *vt* **1** persuade (a person) to do wrong, to commit a crime or to sin: *be ~d by the offer of money into betraying one's country*. **2** persuade a person less experienced to have sexual intercourse: *How many women did Don Juan ~?*

se·ducer *n* person who seduces, esp(2).

se·duc·tion /sɪˈdəkʃən/ *n* **1** [U] seducing or being seduced; [C] instance of this. **2** something attractive that may lead a person to do something (but often with no implication of immorality): *surrender to the ~s of country life*.

se·duc·tive /sɪˈdəktɪv/ *adj* attractive; captivating: *seductive smiles; a seductive offer*.

se·duc·tive·ly *adv*

sedu·lous /ˈsedʒələs/ *adj* (*formal*) persevering; done with perseverance: *He paid her ~ attention*.

see[1] /si/ *vi,vt* (*pt* saw /sɔ/, *pp* seen /sin/) (For special uses with *adverbial particles* and *prepositions*, ⇨ 12 below.) **1** (often with *can, could;* not usually in the progressive tenses) have or use the power of sight: *If you shut your eyes you can't see. It was getting dark and I couldn't see to read. On a clear day we can see (for) miles.* ***seeing is believing,*** (*prov*) what we ourselves see is the most satisfactory evidence. ***be ˈseeing things,*** imagine that one can see things that are not there or that do not exist: *You're seeing things—there's nobody there!* **2** (often with *can, could,* esp when effort is needed; not in the progressive tenses) be aware of by using the power of sight: *I saw him put the key in the lock, turn it and open the door. The suspected man was seen to enter the building. If you watch carefully you will see how to do it/how I do it/how it is done. I looked for him but he was not to be seen,* I could not find him. ***see the last of sb/sth,*** have done with; see for the last time: *I'll be glad to see the last of this job,* get to the end of it. ***see the sights,*** visit notable places, etc as a tourist. ***see stars,*** have dancing lights before the eyes, eg as the result of a blow on the head. ***see one's way (clear) to doing sth,*** understand how to manage to do it, feel willing to do it: *He didn't see his way to lending me the money I needed.* **3** (in the *imperative*) look (at): *See, here he comes! See page 4.* **4** (not in the progressive tenses) understand; learn by search or inquiry or thinking: *He didn't see the joke/the point of the story. Do you see what I mean?* ***as ˈI see it,*** in my opinion. ***see for oneself,*** find out in order to be convinced or satisfied: *If you* *don't believe me, go and see for yourself!* **5** learn from the newspaper or other printed sources: *I see that the Secretary of State is in China.* **6** have knowledge or experience of: *He has seen a good deal in his long life. I never saw such rudeness.* ***have seen ˌbetter ˈdays,*** have now declined, lost former prosperity, etc. **7** give an interview to; visit; receive a call from: *The manager can see you for five minutes. You ought to see a doctor about that cough.* **8** allow; look on without protest or action: *You can't see people starve without trying to help them, can you?* **9** attend to; take care; make provision: *See that the windows and doors are locked/that the children have enough food.* **10** imagine: *He saw himself as the savior of his country.* **11** foresee; anticipate: *The war is seen lasting another year.* **12** (special uses with *adverbial particles* and *prepositions*):

see about sth, deal with: *He promised to see about my broken window.* ***see sb about sth,*** take advice: *I must see a builder about my roof.*

see sb across sth, guide, help, him across (a road, etc): *That man's blind—I'd better see him across the street.*

see sb back/home, accompany him: *Tom's had too much to drink—we'd better see him home.*

see sb off, go to a railway station, an airport, etc with a person about to start on a journey: *I was seen off by many of my friends.*

see sb out, accompany a person until he is out of a building: *My secretary will see you out.*

see through sb/sth, not be deceived by: *We all saw through him,* knew what kind of man he really was. ***see sb through (sth),*** give him support, encouragement during (it). ***ˌsee sth ˈthrough,*** not give up an undertaking until the end is reached: *Whatever happens, we'll see the struggle through.*

see to sth, attend to it: *The brake won't work; get a mechanic to see to it.*

see[2] /si/ *n* [C] district under a bishop; bishop's position, office, jurisdiction: *the See of Rome.*

seed /sid/ *n* [C] (*pl* ~s or unchanged) **1** flowering plant's element of life, from which another plant can grow: *a packet of ~(s).* ⇨ illus at flower, fruit. ***run/go to seed,*** **(a)** stop flowering as seed is produced. **(b)** (*fig*) become careless of one's appearance and manners. **2** cause, origin (*of* a tendency, development, etc): *sow the ~s of virtue in young children.* **3** = semen. **4** (*sport*) seeded player, eg in a tennis championship. ⇨ 4 below. □ *vi,vt* **1** (of a plant) produce seed when full grown. **2** sow with seed: *~ a field with wheat.* **3** remove seed from: *~ grapes.* **4** (esp in tennis) separate the best players from the rest when organizing competitions (in order to have good matches later in a tournament): *~ed players.*

ˈseed·bed *n* area of fine soil ready for sowing seed.

seed·less *adj* having no seed: *~less raisins.*

seed·ling /ˈsidlɪŋ/ *n* [C] young plant grown from a seed.

ˈseed money, money given to start an enterprise which is then expected to become self-supporting.

seedy /ˈsidi/ *adj* (-ier, -iest) **1** full of seed: *as ~ as a dried fig.* **2** (*informal*) looking worn, neglected, etc: *a ~ hotel; a ~-looking person.* **3** (*informal*) unwell: *feel ~.*

seed·ily /-əli/ *adv*

seek /sik/ *vt* (*pt,pp* sought /sɔt/) **1** look for; try to find: *~ shelter from the rain.* ***seek one's fortune,*** to try to become rich: *He's gone West to ~ his fortune.* **2** ask for: *I will ~ my doctor's advice.* **3** ***seek for,*** try to win: *~ing for glory in football.* ***(much) sought after,*** (much) in demand.

seem /sim/ *vi* have or give the impression or appearance of being or doing; appear to be: *What ~s easy to some people ~s difficult to others. He ~s to think so. The book ~s (to be) quite interesting.*

seem·ing *adj* apparent but perhaps not real or genuine: *In spite of his ~ing friendship he gave me no help.*

seem·ing·ly *adv* apparently.

seem·ly /ˈsimli/ *adj* (-ier, -iest) (of behavior) proper or correct (for the occasion or circumstances): *It isn't ~ to praise oneself.*

seen *pp* of see[1].

seep /sip/ *vi* (of liquids) come out or through: *water ~ing through the roof.*

seep·age /-ɪdʒ/ *n* [U] slow leaking through.

seer /siər/ *n* [C] person claiming to see into the future.

seer·sucker /ˈsɪrˌsəkər/ *n* **1** [U] kind of (usually striped) cloth. **2** [C] suit made of this.

see·saw /ˈsiˌsɔ/ *n* [C,U] **1** (game played on a) long plank with a person sitting on each end which can rise and fall alternately. **2** (*fig*) up-and-down or to-and-fro movement: *the ~ of bank interest charges.* □ *vi* **1** play on a seesaw. **2** move up and down or to and fro. **3** be uncertain: *~ between two opinions/points of view.*

seethe /sið/ *vi,vt* be very excited or agitated: *~ with anger; a country seething with discontent; streets seething with people.*

seg·ment /ˈsegmənt/ *n* [C] **1** part cut off or marked off by a line: *a ~ of a circle.* **2** section: *a ~ of an orange.* □ *vt,vi* /segˈment/ divide, become divided, into segments.

seg·men·ta·tion /ˌsegmənˈteiʃən/ *n* [U]

seg·re·gate /ˈsegrɪˌgeit/ *vt* put apart from the rest; isolate: *~ the boys from the girls.*

seg·re·ga·tion /ˌsegrɪˈgeiʃən/ *n* [U]

seis·mic /ˈsaizmɪk/ *adj* of earthquakes.

seis·mo·graph /ˈsaizməˌgræf/ *n* [C] instrument which records the strength, duration and distance away of earthquakes.

seis·mol·ogist /saizˈmalədʒɪst/ *n* [C] scientist studying earthquakes.

seis·mol·ogy /saizˈmalədʒi/ *n* [U] science of earthquakes.

seize /siz/ *vt,vi* **1** take possession of (property, etc) by law: *~ her house for payment of a debt.* **2** take hold of, suddenly and with force: *~ a thief by the collar.* **3** see clearly and use: *seizing (on) an idea/a chance/an opportunity.* **4** overpower; take control or possession of: *Panic ~d the audience when the theater caught fire.*

seiz·ure /ˈsiʒər/ *n* **1** [U] act of seizing or taking possession of by force or the authority of the law; [C] instance of this: *~ of drugs by Customs officers.* **2** [C] heart attack.

sel·dom /ˈseldəm/ *adv* not often; rarely: *She ~ goes out. She goes out very ~.*

se·lect /sɪˈlekt/ *vt* choose (as being the most suitable, etc): *~ a book/a present for a child. Who has been ~ed to speak at the meeting?* □ *adj* **1** carefully chosen: *~ passages from the Bible*. **2** of or for a particular group of persons, not for all: *shown to a ~ audience*.

se·lec·tion /sɪˈlekʃən/ *n* **1** [U] choosing. ⇨ natural selection. **2** [C] collection or group of selected things or examples; number of things from which to select: *That shop has a good ~ of handbags.*

se·lec·tive /sɪˈlektɪv/ *adj* **1** having the power to select; characterized by selection. **2** choosing only the best: *a ~ school*, that chooses its pupils.

se·lec·tive·ly *adv*

se·lec·tor /sɪˈlektər/ *n* [C] person who, that which, selects, eg a member of a committee choosing a national sports team, etc.

self /self/ *n* (*pl* selves /selvz/) **1** [U] person's nature, special qualities; one's own personality: *my former ~*, myself as I used to be. **2** one's own interests or pleasure: *She has no thought of ~* (*herself* is more usual), thinks only of others.

self- /ˌself-/ *prefix* of oneself or itself alone, independent: *ˌself-ˈtaught*, taught by oneself.

ˌself-aˈbasement *n* [U] degrading of oneself.

ˌself-abˈsorbed *adj* thinking of one's own interests only, unaware of other people.

ˌself-asˈsertion *n* [U] the putting forward of oneself or one's ideas in an effort to be noticed by everyone.

ˌself-asˈsurance *n* [U] confidence in oneself.

ˌself-asˈsured *adj*

ˌself-ˈcentered *adj* interested chiefly in oneself and one's own affairs.

ˌself-conˈfessed *adj* admitted by oneself: *a self-confessed ˈthief*.

ˌself-ˈconfidence *n* [U] belief in one's own abilities.

ˌself-ˈconfident *adj*

ˌself-ˈconscious *adj* **(a)** aware of one's own existence, thoughts and actions. **(b)** shy; embarrassed.

ˌself-ˈconsciousness *n* [U]

ˌself-conˈtained *adj* (of a person) not dependent on others.

ˌself-conˈtrol *n* [U] control of one's own feelings, behavior, etc: *exercise self-control; lose one's self-control.*

ˌself-deˈfense *n* [U] defense of one's own body, property, rights, etc: *kill a person in self-defense*, while defending oneself against attack.

ˌself-deˈnial *n* [U] going without things in order to help others.

ˌself-efˈfacing *adj* keeping oneself in the background (and avoiding praise, attention).

ˌself-emˈployed *adj* working, eg as a store-owner, as an owner of a business.

ˌself-eˈsteem *n* [U] good opinion (sometimes exaggerated) of oneself.

ˌself-ˈevident *adj* clear without proof or more evidence.

ˌself-ˈevidently *adv*

ˌself-exˈplanatory *adj* clear without (further) explanation.

ˌself-ˈgenerating *adj* produced from the thing itself or the person himself.

ˌself-ˈgovernment *n* [U] independent government (not a colony).

ˌself-imˈportance *n* [U] too high an opinion of oneself.

ˌself-imˈportant *adj*

ˌself-imˈposed *adj* (of a duty, task, etc) imposed on oneself.

ˌself-inˈdulgence *n* [U] giving way too easily to one's preferred comfort, pleasures, etc.

ˌself-inˈdulgent *adj*

ˌself-ˈinterest *n* [U] one's own interests and personal advantage.

ˌself-ˈmade *adj* successful in life through one's own efforts: *a ~-made man/woman.*

ˌself-ˈpity *n* [U] (exaggerated) pity for oneself.

ˌself-posˈsessed *adj* calm, confident: *a self-possessed young woman.*

ˌself-ˌpreserˈvation *n* [U] keeping oneself from harm or destruction: *the instinct of self-preservation.*

ˌself-reˈliance *n* [U] having or showing confidence in one's own powers, judgment, etc.

ˌself-reˈliant *adj*

ˌself-reˈspect *n* [U] feeling that one is behaving and thinking in ways that will not cause one to be ashamed of oneself: *lose all self-respect.*

ˌself-reˈspecting *adj* having self-respect: *No self-respecting man could agree to do such a thing.*

ˌself-ˈrighteous *adj* convinced of one's own goodness and that one is better than others.

ˌself-ˈrising *adj* (of flour) not needing the addition of baking powder for cakes, etc to rise.

ˌself-ˈrule *n* [U] = self-government.

ˌself-ˈsacrifice *n* [U] the giving up of one's own interests and wishes for the sake of other people.

ˌself-ˈsacrificing *adj*

ˈself·same *adj* very same; identical: *Tom and I reached Paris on the selfsame day.*

ˌself-ˈservice *n* [C] **(a)** (of eg a snack bar or restaurant), one at which persons collect their own food and drink from counters and carry it to tables. **(b)** (of a shop) one at which customers collect what they want from counters or shelves (in wire baskets) and pay as they leave. **(c)** (of a garage) one at which customers fill their own cars with gasoline, etc.

ˌself-ˈstyled *adj* using a name, title, etc which one has given oneself and to which one has no right: *a self-styled ˈexpert on music.*

ˌself-sufˈficient *adj* needing no help from others: *The country is now self-sufficient in oil*, no longer has to import it.

ˌself-supˈporting *adj* **(a)** (of a person) earning enough money to keep oneself: *now that my children are self-supporting*. **(b)** (of a business, etc) paying its way; not needing a subsidy.

ˌself-ˈtaught *adj* not taught or educated by others.

ˌself-ˈwill *n* [U] determination to do as one wishes and not be guided by others.

ˌself-ˈwilled *adj* obstinate; refusing advice or guidance.

ˌself-ˈwinding *adj* (of a wristwatch) wound automatically by the natural motions of the arm.

self·ish /ˈselfɪʃ/ *adj* chiefly thinking of one's self

and one's own affairs: *act from ~ motives.*
self·ish·ly *adv*
self·ish·ness /-nɪs/ *n* [U]

sell /sel/ *vt,vi* (*pt,pp* sold /sould/) **1** give in exchange for money: *~ books; ~ a car at a good price; ~ oranges at ten cents each. Will you ~ me your bike? I'll ~ it to you for $50.* ***sell sth off,*** sell (goods, etc) cheaply. ***sell sth out,*** sell all of one's stock of something: *We are sold out of small sizes.* ***sell out (to sb),*** go over to one's enemies, competitors, etc for a price. ***sell (sb) short,*** ⇨ short²(2). **2** keep stocks for sale; be a dealer in: *Do you ~ needles?* **3** (of goods) be sold; find buyers: *Your house ought to ~ for at least $75,000.* **4** cause to be sold: *It's the low prices which ~ our goods.* **5** ***ˈsell oneself,*** **(a)** present oneself to others in a convincing way (eg when applying for a job). **(b)** do something dishonorable for money or reward. **6** cheat; disappoint by failure to keep an agreement, etc: *I've been sold (out)!* ***sell sb down the river,*** ⇨ river(1). **7** ***be sold on sth,*** (*informal*) agree with it, believe that it is good, etc: *Is the company president sold on the idea of building a new factory?*
sel·ler *n* [C] person who sells: *a ˈbook~er.* ⇨ bestseller.
ˈsell·out *n* **(a)** event (a football game, concert, etc) for which all tickets have been sold. **(b)** (*informal*) betrayal: *government policies which are a ~out.*

sel·vage, sel·vedge /ˈselvɪdʒ/ *n* [C] edge of cloth woven so that threads do not come apart.

selves *pl* of self.

sem·an·tic /sɪˈmæntɪk/ *adj* relating to meaning in language.
se·man·tics *n pl* (used with a *sing verb*) branch of linguistics concerned with studying the meanings of words and sentences.

a circle.
ˈsemi·colon, *n* [C] the punctuation mark (;) used in writing and printing, between a comma and a full stop in value.
ˌsemi-ˈconscious *adj* partly conscious.
ˌsemi·deˈtached *adj* (of a house) joined to another on one side.
ˌsemi-ˈfinal *n* [C] match or round before the final (eg in football competitions).
ˌsemi-ˈfinalist *n* [C] player, team, in the semi-finals.
ˌsemi·ofˈficial *adj* (esp of announcements, etc made to newspapers) with the condition that they must not be considered as coming from an official source.
ˌsemi-ˈpre·cious *adj* of lesser value than a precious stone, gem, etc: *A garnet is a semiprecious stone.*
ˌsemi-ˈskilled *adj* having or needing some skill from training but less than skilled: *ˌsemiskilled ˈlabor.*
ˈsemi·trailer *n* [C] large trailer for carrying freight, with two wheels in back and front resting over the back wheels of the truck.
ˌsemi-ˈtropi·cal *adj* = subtropical.

sem·inar /ˈseməˌnar/ *n* [C] group studying a problem and meeting for discussion, often with a tutor or professor.

sem·inary /ˈseməˌneri/ *n* [C] (*pl* -ies) Roman Catholic training college for priests.

semo·lina /ˌseməˈlinə/ *n* [U] hard grains from wheat, used for making pasta, in puddings, etc.

semp·stress /ˈsempstrɪs/ = seamstress.

Sen. *abbr* = Senator.

sen·ate /ˈsenɪt/ *n* [C] **1** (in ancient Rome) highest council of state. **2** (*modern use*) upper house of the legislative assembly in various countries, eg US, France. **3** governing council of some universities.

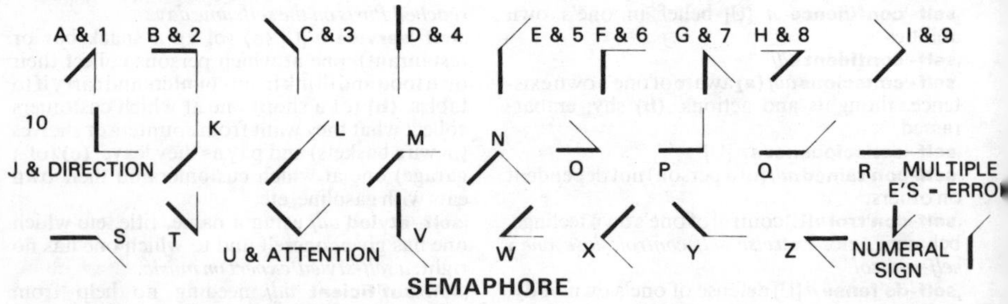

SEMAPHORE

sema·phore /ˈseməˌfɔr/ *n* [U] system (code) for sending signals, eg by using arms on a post or flags held in the hands, with various positions for the letters of the alphabet. □ *vt,vi* send (messages) by semaphore.

sem·blance /ˈsembləns/ *n* [C] appearance: *put on a ~ of gaiety.*

se·men /ˈsimən/ *n* [U] fertilizing fluid of male animals.

semi- /ˈsemi-, ˈseˌmai-/ *prefix* half of; partly; midway: *semicircle, semiliterate, semifinal.*
semi /ˈseˌmai/ (*informal*) = semitrailer.
ˈsemi·circle *n* [C] half a circle. ⇨ illus at circle.
ˌsemi-ˈcircular *adj* (having the shape of a) half

sena·tor /-tər/ *n* [C] member of a senate(1,2).
sena·tor·ial /ˌsenəˈtɔriəl/ *adj* of a senate or senator: *a senatorial district,* one entitled to elect a senator.

send /send/ *vt,vi* (*pt,pp* sent /sent/) (For special uses with *adverbial particles* and *prepositions,* ⇨ 4 below.) **1** cause a person or thing to go or be carried without going oneself: *~ a telegram; ~ a message to her/~ her a message. The children were sent to bed.* ⇨ take¹. **2** use force to cause a person or thing to move rapidly: *The wind sent the vase crashing to the ground.* **3** (*sl, dated*) cause to become ecstatic: *The music really ~s me.* **4** (special uses with *adverbial particles* and *prepositions*):

send sb away, dismiss, eg an employee. ***send away for sth,*** order (goods) to be delivered by rail, post, etc: *Shall we ~ away for this bargain in the newspaper?*

send sth down, cause to fall: *The excellent weather sent the price of food down.*

send for sb/sth (to do sth), ask or order a person/thing to come, for something to be delivered: *~ for a doctor/taxi.*

send sth in (for eg a competition, exhibition): *~ in one's entry for a competition.*

send sth on, **(a)** send it (eg luggage) in advance. **(b)** (of letters) readdress and post again (eg to previous occupants).

send sth out, **(a)** give out: *The sun ~s out light and warmth.* **(b)** produce: *The trees ~ out new leaves in spring.* **(c)** circularize.

send sb up, send him to prison. ***send sth up,*** cause to rise: *The heavy demand for beef sent the price up.*

sender /ˈsendər/ *n* [C] person or thing that sends: *Who was the ~ of the telegram?.*

Sen·e·ca /ˈsenɪkə/ *n, adj* (of) one of the Iroquoi Indian peoples of the Northeastern US.

se·nile /ˈsiˌnaiəl/ *adj* suffering from bodily or mental weakness because of old age; caused by old age: *~ decay.*

sen·il·ity /sɪˈnɪləti/ *n* [U] weakness (of body or mind) in old age.

sen·ior /ˈsinyər/ *adj* (opp of *junior*) **1** older in years; higher in rank, authority, etc: *He is ten years ~ to me. Smith is the ~ partner in* (= the head of) *the firm.* **2** (*abbr* **Sr.**) the father (used after a person's name esp when a father and his son have the same first and middle names). □ *n* [C] **1** senior person: *He is my ~ by ten years.* **2** student in the fourth year of high school or college.

ˌsenior ˈcitizen, person over the age of retirement.

sen·ior·ity /ˌsinˈyɔrəti/ *n* [U] condition of being senior (in age, rank, etc): *Should promotion be through merit or through ~?*

senna /ˈsenə/ *n* [U] dried leaves of a tropical tree, used as a laxative.

sen·sa·tion /senˈseiʃən/ *n* **1** [C,U] ability to feel; feeling: *lose all ~ in one's legs; have a ~ of warmth/dizziness/falling.* **2** [C,U] (instance of, something that causes, a) quick and excited reaction: *The news created a great ~.*

sen·sa·tional /-əl/ *adj* **(a)** causing a sensation (2): *a ~al murder.* **(b)** (of newspapers, etc) presenting news in a manner designed to cause sensation(2): *a ~al writer/newspaper.*

sen·sa·tion·al·ism /-əˌlɪzm/ *n* [U] the deliberate causing of sensation: *avoid ~alism during an election campaign.*

sen·sa·tion·al·ist /-əlɪst/ *n* [C] person causing sensation.

sen·sa·tion·ally /-əli/ *adv*

sense /sens/ *n* **1** [C] any one of the special powers of the body by which a person is conscious of things (ie sight, hearing, smell, taste and touch): *have a keen ~ of hearing.* ⇨ sixth sense. **2** (*pl*) normal state of mind: *in one's* (*right*) *~s*, sane; *out of one's ~s*, insane. ***bring sb to his senses,*** cause him to stop behaving foolishly or wildly: *Perhaps a month in prison will bring you to your ~s.* ***come to one's senses,*** stop behaving foolishly or wildly. ***have taken leave of one's ˈsenses,*** have become mad. **3** (with *a, an* or a *possessive pronoun* but not *pl*) appreciation or understanding of the value or worth (of): *a ~ of humor; my ~ of duty.* ⇨ direction(2). **4** (*sing* only) consciousness: *have no ~ of shame.* **5** [U] power of judging; good, practical, judgment: *Haven't you any ~? There's a lot of ~ in what he says. There's no ~ in doing that,* It's pointless. ⇨ common sense. **6** [C] meaning: *In what ~ are you using the word? using the widest ~ of the word,* the meaning which is the most general or the fullest. ***make sense,*** have a meaning that can be understood: *it just doesn't make ~,* seems to have no meaning. **7** [U] general feeling or opinion among a number of people: *take the ~ of a public meeting.* ⇨ consensus. □ *vt* have the opinion; be vaguely aware of; realize: *He ~d that his proposals were unwelcome.*

ˈsense organ, part of the body, eg ear, eye, used to experience a sense(1).

sense·less /ˈsenslɪs/ *adj* **1** foolish: *a ~ idea. What a ~ person he is!* **2** unconscious: *fall ~ to the ground.*

sense·less·ly *adv*

sense·less·ness /-nɪs/ *n* [U]

sen·si·bil·ity /ˌsensəˈbɪləti/ *n* (*pl* -ies) **1** [U] power of feeling, esp delicate emotional impressions: *the ~ of an artist or poet.* **2** (*pl*) sensitive(2) impressions (of what is right, in good taste, etc): *Her sensibilities are quickly injured.*

sen·sible /ˈsensəbəl/ *adj* **1** having or showing good sense(5); reasonable; practical: *a ~ woman; ~ clothes,* practical, not only for appearances or fashion. *That was ~ of you.* **2** (*science*) that can be known by the senses(1): *~ phenomena.*

sen·sibly /-əbli/ *adv* in a sensible way: *sensibly dressed for hot weather.*

sen·si·tive /ˈsensətɪv/ *adj* **1** quickly or easily receiving impressions: *The eyes are ~ to light.* **2** (of feelings) easily hurt or offended: *He is very ~ about his ugly appearance.* **3** (of instruments, and institutions thought of as measuring things) able to record or reproduce small changes: *a ~ record player. The Administration is ~ to public opinion.* **4** (of photographic film, etc) affected by light.

sen·si·tiv·ity /ˌsensəˈtɪvəti/ *n* [U] quality, degree, of being sensitive: *an injection to reduce sensitivity to the pain.*

sen·si·tize /ˈsensəˌtaiz/ *vt* make (photographic film, etc) sensitive to light.

sen·sory /ˈsensəri/ *adj* of the senses(1) or sensation: *~ nerves.*

sen·sual /ˈsenʃuəl/ *adj* **1** of, engaged in, the pleasures of the senses: *~ perception.* **2** enjoying, of, physical pleasures such as eating and drinking and sex: *~ enjoyment.*

sen·su·al·ity /ˌsenʃuˈæləti/ *n* [U] love of, pleasure in, sensual experiences.

sen·su·ous /ˈsenʃuəs/ *adj* affecting, noticed by, appealing to, the senses(1): *~ music/painting.*

sent *pt,pp* of send.
sen·tence /ˈsentəns/ *n* [C] **1** (statement by a judge, etc, of) punishment: *pass* ~ (*on him*), declare what the punishment is to be; *be under* ~ *of death*. **2** (*gram*) set of words complete in itself, used to express a statement, question, command, etc. □ *vt* state that (a person) is to have a certain punishment: ~ *a thief to six months' imprisonment*.
sen·ti·ment /ˈsentəmənt/ *n* **1** [C] mental feeling, the total of what one thinks and feels on a subject; [U] such feelings collectively as an influence: *The* ~ *of pity includes a feeling of sympathy and of a desire to help. What are your* ~*s toward my sister?* What do you feel toward her? **2** [U] (tendency to be affected by a) (display of) emotional feeling (contrasted with reason): *There's no place for* ~ *in business*. **3** expression of feeling; opinions or point of view: *The ambassador explained the* ~*s of his government*.
sen·ti·men·tal /ˌsentəˈmentəl/ *adj* **1** having to do with the feelings; emotional: *have a* ~ *attachment to one's birthplace. The bracelet had only* ~ *value*, eg because it belonged to one's mother. **2** (of things) producing, expressing, (often excessive) feelings: ~ *music;* (of persons) having such excessive feelings: *She's far too* ~ *about her cats*.
sen·ti·men·tal·ity /ˌsentəmenˈtæləti/ *n* [U] the quality of being very sentimental.
sen·ti·men·tally /-təli/ *adv*
sen·try /ˈsentri/ *n* [C] (*pl* -ies) soldier keeping watch or guard.
ˈsentry box, hut for a sentry.
sep. *abbr* = separate.
se·pal /ˈsipəl, ˈsepəl/ *n* [C] (*bot*) one of the divisions of the calyx of a flower. ⇨ illus at flower.
sep·ar·able /ˈsep(ə)rəbəl/ *adj* that can be separated.
sep·ar·ate¹ /ˈsep(ə)rɪt/ *adj* **1** divided; not joined or united: *Cut it into three* ~ *parts*. **2** not physically united but forming a distinct unit: *The children sleep in* ~ *beds*, Each of them has his own bed. *Mr. Green and his wife are living* ~ (= apart) *now*. □ *n* (*pl*) clothing which may be worn in a variety of combinations, eg jerseys, blouses and skirts.
sep·ar·ate·ly *adv* in a separate manner: *Tie them up* ~*ly*.
sep·ar·ate² /ˈsepəˌreit/ *vt,vi* **1** make, be, separate: ~ *the boys from the girls. Connecticut is* ~*d from Long Island by the Long Island Sound*. **2** (of two or more people) leave each other: *Mr and Mrs Brown* ~*d after ten years of marriage. We talked until midnight and then* ~*d*.
sep·ar·ation /ˌsepəˈreiʃən/ *n* **1** [U] (state of) being separated or separate; act of separating: *Separation from his friends made him sad*. **2** [C] instance of, period of, not being together: *after a* ~ *of five years*.
se·pia /ˈsipiə/ *n* [U], *adj* dark brown (ink or paint).
Sept. *abbr* = September.
Sep·tem·ber /sepˈtembər/ *n* the ninth month of the year.
sep·tet /sepˈtet/ *n* [C] (musical composition for a) group of seven voices or instruments.
sep·tic /ˈseptɪk/ *adj* causing, caused by, infection (with disease germs): *A dirty wound may become/turn* ~.
ˈseptic tank, tank outside a building in which sewage is disposed of and purified.
sep·ul·cher /ˈsepəlkər/ *n* [C] tomb, esp one cut in rock or built of stone.
sep·ul·chral /sɪˈpəlkrəl/ *adj* of a burial (in a tomb).
se·quel /ˈsikwəl/ *n* [C] **1** that which follows or arises out of (an earlier happening): *Famine has often been the* ~ *of war*. **2** story, film, etc continuing the plot, etc of an earlier one.
se·quence /ˈsikwəns, ˈsiˌkwens/ *n* [U] succession; [C] connected line of events, ideas, etc: *the* ~ *of events*, the order in which they occur.
se·ques·ter /sɪˈkwestər/ *vt* isolate, separate (somebody or something) for some reason or to perform some duty: ~ *a jury for deliberation*.
se·quin /ˈsikwɪn/ *n* [C] tiny shining disk sewn on to cloth as an ornament.
se·ra·pe, sa·ra·pe /səˈrapi/ *n* [C] (often bright colored) blanket worn as a cloak by men in Mexico and formerly in the southwestern US. ⇨ illus at sombrero.
sere /sɪr/ = sear.
ser·en·ade /serəˈneid/ *n* [C] (piece of) music (to be) sung or played outdoors at night. □ *vt* sing or play a serenade to (a person).
ser·ene /sɪˈrin/ *adj* clear and calm: *a* ~ *sky/look/smile*.
ser·ene·ly *adv*
ser·en·ity /sɪˈrenəti/ *n* [U]
serf /sərf/ *n* [C] (in former times) person who worked on the land and was sold with it like a slave.
serf·dom /-dəm/ *n* [U] **(a)** economic and social system using serfs. **(b)** serf's condition of life.
ser·geant /ˈsardʒənt/ *n* [C] **1** noncommissioned officer in the US army who ranks above a corporal. **2** police officer with rank below that of an inspector.
ˌsergeant ˈmajor (*pl* sergeants major) warrant officer (now the usual term), between commissioned and noncommissioned army officer.
ser·ial /ˈsɪriəl/ *adj* **1** of, in or forming a series: *the* ˈ~ *number of a banknote or check*. **2** (of a story, etc) appearing in parts (on radio, TV, in a magazine, etc). □ *n* [C] serialized play, story, etc.
ser·ial·ize /-ˌlaiz/ *vt* publish or produce in serial form.
series /ˈsɪriz/ *n* [C] (*pl* unchanged) number of things, events, etc each of which is related in some way to the others, esp to the one before it: *a* ~ *of stamps*, eg of different values, but issued at one time; *a* ˈ*television* ~, a number of programs, each complete in itself, linked by cast, theme, etc. ***in series,*** **(a)** in an orderly arrangement. **(b)** (of the parts of an electrical circuit) with the supply of current fed directly through each component.
seri·ous /ˈsɪriəs/ *adj* **1** thoughtful; not funny, silly or for pleasure: *a* ~ *attempt/appearance/face; look* ~. *Stop laughing and be* ~ *for a moment*. **2** important because of possible danger: *a* ~ *illness/mistake. The international situation*

looks ~. **3** in earnest; sincere: *a ~ worker. Please be ~ about your work.*

seri·ous·ly *adv* in a serious manner: *be ~ly ill.*

seri·ous·ness /-nɪs/ *n* [U] state of being serious: *the ~ness of inflation.* ***in all seriousness,*** very seriously: *I tell you this in all ~ness,* I am not joking, being insincere, etc.

ser·mon /ˈsərmən/ *n* [C] spoken or written speech on a religious or moral subject, esp one given from a pulpit in a church.

ser·mon·ize /ˈsərməˌnaiz/ *vt,vi* (*fig*) preach or talk seriously to: *Stop ~izing,* lecturing to me on my faults, etc.

ser·ous /ˈsɪrəs/ *adj* of or like serum.

ser·pent /ˈsərpənt/ *n* [C] **1** = snake (the more usual word). **2** (*fig*) sly, deceptive person.

ser·rated /ˈseˌreitɪd/ *adj* having notches on the edge like a saw.

ser·ried /ˈserid/ *adj* (of lines or ranks of persons) close together, shoulder to shoulder: *in ~ ranks.*

serum /ˈsɪrəm/ *n* (*pl* ~s) **1** [U] watery fluid in animal bodies; thin, transparent part of blood. **2** [C,U] (dose of) such a fluid taken from the blood of an animal and used for inoculations.

serv. *abbr* = service.

ser·vant /ˈsərvənt/ *n* [C] **1** person who works in a household for wages, food and lodging. **2** **ˌpublic ˈservant,** person who works for the public, eg a police officer, member of the fire department. ⇨ civil servant. **3** person devoted to a person or thing: *a ~ of Jesus Christ,* eg a Christian priest. **4** (*old southern US usage*) slave.

serve /sərv/ *vt,vi* **1** be a servant to, work for, (a person): *He ~s as gardener and also as chauffeur.* **2** perform duties (for): *~ one's country,* eg in Congress or in the armed forces. ***serve on sth,*** be a member of: *~ on a committee.* ***serve under sb,*** be in the armed forces (esp the Navy) under the command of: *My great-grandfather ~d under General Grant.* **3** attend to (customers in a shop, etc); supply (with goods and services); place (food, etc) on the table for a meal; give (food, etc) to people at a meal: *There was no one in the store to ~ me. Mint sauce is often ~d with lamb.* **4** be satisfactory for a need or purpose: *This box will ~ for a seat.* **5** act towards, treat (a person in a certain way): *I hope I'll never be ~d such a trick again,* have such a trick played on me. ***serve one right,*** experience failure, misfortune, etc which is deserved. **6** pass the usual or normal number of years (learning a trade, etc): *He's ~d his apprenticeship.* **7** go through a term of office: *He ~d as a manager for five years.* **8** undergo a period of imprisonment: *He has ~d five years of his sentence.* **9** (*legal*) deliver (a summons, etc) to the person named in it. **10** (in tennis, etc) put the ball into play by batting it to an opponent: *~ a ball; ~ well/badly.* □ *n* [C] (in tennis, etc) (turn for) striking and putting the ball into play: *Whose ~ is it?*

server *n* [C] **(a)** person who serves(3,10). **(b)** tray for dishes of food.

serv·ing *n* [C] quantity of food (to be) served to one person: *four servings of soup.*

ser·vice /ˈsərvɪs/ *n* **1** [U] being a servant; position as a servant: *Miss White has been in our ~ for five years.* **2** [C] department or branch of public work, government employment, etc: *the ˌDiploˈmatic Service.* ⇨ civil service. ***in the service,*** serving in the armed forces. ***on active service,*** performing duties as a member of the armed forces in time of war. **3** [C] something done to help or benefit another or others: *His ~ to the country has been immense. Do you need the ~s of a doctor/lawyer?* **4** [U] benefit, use, advantage: *Can I be of ~ to you,* help you in any way? *I am/My car is at your ~,* ready to help you. **5** [C,U] system or arrangement that supplies public needs, esp for communications: *ˈbus/ˈtrain ~; the ˈtelephone ~; (a) good ˈpostal ~.* **6** [C] form of worship and prayer to God: *three ~s every Sunday; the ˈmarriage ~.* **7** [C] complete set of plates, dishes, etc for use at meals: *a ˈtea/ˈdinner ~.* **8** [U] serving of food and drink (in hotels, etc); work done by hotel staff, etc: *The food is good at this hotel, but the ~ is poor.* **9** [U] maintenance given after the sale of an article: *send the car in for ~ every 3,000 miles,* eg for greasing, checking of brakes, etc. **10** (*legal*) serving of a writ, summons, etc. **11** (in tennis, etc) act of serving the ball; manner of doing this; person's turn to serve: *Her ~ is weak. Whose ~ is it?* □ *vt* maintain or repair (a car, radio, machine, etc) after sale (⇨ 9 above): *have the car ~d regularly.*

ser·vice·able /-əbəl/ *adj* **(a)** suited for ordinary wear and use; strong and durable: *~able clothes for children.* **(b)** capable of giving good service.

ˈservice charge, additional charge for service (8).

ˈservice industry, providing services, not making things.

ˈservice line, (in tennis, etc) from which the ball is served(10).

ˈservice road, branch off a main road giving access to houses, etc.

ˈservice station, place that retails gasoline, oil, etc for motor vehicles and provides repair and other services.

ser·vile /ˈsərvəl, ˈsərˌvaiəl/ *adj* **1** of or like slaves: *~ work.* **2** characteristic of a slave; not showing the spirit of independence: *~ to public opinion,* giving too much attention to it.

ser·vi·tude /ˈsərvəˌtud/ *n* [U] (*formal*) condition of being forced to work for others and having no freedom.

ses·ame /ˈsesəmi/ *n* **1** [U] plant with seeds used in various ways as food and giving an oil used in salads. **2** ***Open sesame!*** magic words said to cause a door to open.

ses·sion /ˈseʃən/ *n* [C] **1** (meeting of a) law court, law-making body, etc; time occupied by discussions at such a meeting: *the autumn ~* (= sitting) *of Congress; go into secret ~.* ***in session,*** meeting, active (not on holiday). **2** university term. **3** single, uninterrupted meeting for a purpose: *a reˈcording ~,* eg of music (being put on records or tapes).

set[1] /set/ *n* **1** [C] number of things of the same kind, that belong together because they are similar or complementary to each other: *a*

ˈ*coffee*/ˈ*tea set*, cups, saucers, etc; *a new set of false teeth; a set of stamps/of volumes.* **2** [C] number of persons who associate, or who have similar or identical tastes and interests: *the* ˈ*racing*/ˈ*literary*/ˈ*golfing set; the* ˈ*smart set*, those who consider themselves leaders in society; *the* ˈ*fast set*, those who gamble, etc; *the* ˈ*jet set*, rich people flying from one holiday resort to another. **3** [C] radio receiving apparatus: *a transistor set.* **4** (*sing* only) direction (of current, wind, etc); tendency (of opinion): *the set of the tide; the set of public opinion.* **5** (*sing* only) position or angle: *I recognize him by the set of his head/shoulders.* **6** [C] way in which clothing conforms to the shape of the body: *the set of a coat.* ⇨ set²(14). **7** [C] (in tennis, etc) group of games counting as a unit to the side that wins more than half the games in it. **8** setting of the hair: *have a shampoo and set.* **9** [C] scenery on the stage of a theater or in a studio or outside for filming: *everyone to be on the set by 7am.* **10** [C] young plant, cutting, bulb, etc ready to be planted: *onion sets.* **11** (*math*) collection of things of a similar type.

set² /set/ *vt,vi* (-tt-, *pt,pp* set) (For special uses with *adverbial particles* and *prepositions,* ⇨ 17 below.) **1** (of the sun, moon, stars) go down below the horizon: *It will be cooler when the sun has set.* **2** move or place something so that it is near to or touching something else: *set a glass to one's lips; set pen to paper*, begin to write. ***set a match/(a) light/fire to sth,*** cause it to begin burning. **3** cause (a person or thing) to be in, or reach, a specified state or relation. ***set sb/sth on his/its feet,*** **(a)** help him to get to his feet after a fall. **(b)** help him/it to gain strength, financial stability, etc: *Foreign aid set the country on its feet after the war.* ***set sb free,*** free (prisoners, etc). ***set sb's mind at ease/rest,*** help him to be free from worry, free him from anxiety. ***be all set/get set (for sth/to do sth),*** be/get ready (for the start of a race, etc). **4** cause a person or thing to begin to do something: *It's time we set the machinery going*, start operations. *The news set me (to) thinking.* ***set sth on fire,*** cause it to begin burning. **5** (usually with an *adverb* or *adverbial phrase;* ⇨ 17 below for combinations of *set* and *adverbial particles* with special meanings) put, place, lay, stand: *She set the food on the table.* **6** put forward as (material to be dealt with as a task, an example, etc): *I have set myself a difficult task.* ***set (sb) an example/a good example,*** offer a good standard for others to follow. ***set the fashion,*** start a fashion to be copied by others. ***set the pace,*** fix it by leading (in a race, etc). **7** give something (to a person/oneself) as a task: *He set his helper to chopping wood.* **8** (used with various grammatical objects, the *nouns* in alphabetical order) ***set eyes on sb,*** see him. ***set one's heart/hopes/mind on sth,*** be filled with strong desire for; direct one's hopes toward: *The boy has set his heart on becoming an engineer.* ***set a price on sth,*** declare what it will be sold for. ***set much/great/little/no store by sth,*** value it highly/little/not at all. **9** put in a certain state or condition for a particular purpose: *set a (broken) bone*, bring the parts together so that they may unite. ***set a clock/watch,*** put the hands to the correct time (or, for an alarm clock, to sound at the desired time). ***set one's hair,*** arrange it (when damp) so that when it is dried, it is waved: *She's having her hair set for the party.* ***set the scene,*** describe a place and the people taking part in an activity, eg in a play, novel or sporting event: *Our commentator will now set the scene in the stadium.* ***set sail (from/to/for),*** begin a voyage. ***set the table,*** lay it ready with plates, cutlery, etc. **10** put, fix, one thing firmly in another: *set a diamond in gold; a gold ring set with gems.* **11** (of tides, winds) move or flow along; gather force: *The current is setting in toward the shore. The wind sets from the west.* **12** ***set sth (to sth):*** *set words/a poem to music,* provide with music. **13** (of plants, fruit trees, their blossom) form or develop fruit as the result of fertilization: *The apple blossoms/The apples haven't set well this year.* **14** (of clothing) become adapted to the shape of the body. **15** (cause to) become firm, solid, rigid (from a liquid or soft state): *The gelatin is/has not set yet.* **16** (*pp*) **(a)** unmoving, fixed: *a set smile/look/purpose.* ***be set on/upon sth,*** be determined to be or get: *His heart* (= He) *is set on being a doctor.* **(b)** prearranged; *at a set time.* **(c)** unchanging: *set in one's ways*, having fixed habits; *a man of set opinions*, unable or unwilling to change them. **(d)** planned, learned; regular: *set phrases; a set speech; set forms of prayers.* **17** (special uses with *adverbial particles* and *prepositions*):

set about sth, start it: *I don't know how to set about this job*, how to make a start on it. ***set about sb,*** (*informal*) attack: *They set about each other in the park.*

set sb against sb, cause him to compete with, fight, him. ***set one thing against another,*** regard it as compensating for, balancing, another.

set sth apart/aside, **(a)** put on one side for future use. **(b)** disregard: *Let's set aside our personal feelings.* **(c)** (*legal*) reject: *set a claim aside.*

set sth back, **(a)** move back: *The horse set back its ears.* **(b)** be placed at a distance from: *The house is set back from the road.* ***set sb/sth back,*** **(a)** stop or reverse the progress of: *All our efforts at reform have been set back.* **(b)** (*sl*) cost: *That dinner party set me back $20.*

set sth down, **(a)** put down: *set down a load.* **(b)** write down on paper: *set it down for all to read.* ***set sb down,*** (of a vehicle, its driver) allow (a passenger) to get down or out: *The bus stopped to set down an old lady.*

set forth, = set out (which is more usual). ***set sth forth,*** (*formal*) make known: *set forth one's political views.*

set in, **(a)** start and seem likely to continue: *The rainy season has set in.* **(b)** (of tides, winds; ⇨ 11 above) begin to flow: *The tide is setting in*, flowing toward the shore.

set off, start (a journey, race, etc): *They've set off on a trip round the world.* ***set sth off,*** **(a)** explode a mine, firework, etc. **(b)** make more striking by comparison: *This gold frame sets off your painting very well.* **(c)** balance; compensate: *set off gains against losses.* **(d)** mark off: *set off a clause by a comma.* ***set sb off (doing sth),*** cause to start: *Don't set him off talking about football or he'll go on all evening.*

set on sb, attack: *She had been set on by muggers.*

set out, begin (a journey, etc): *They set out at dawn.* ***set out to do sth,*** have it as an aim or intention: *He set out to break the world record.*

set sth out, **(a)** make known: *set out one's reasons.* **(b)** arrange: *He sets out his ideas clearly in this essay.* **(c)** plan out.

set sb over sb, put him in control/command: *A younger man has been set over me.*

set 'to, begin doing something: *The engineers set to and repaired the bridge.*

set sth up, **(a)** place something in position: *set up a statue.* **(b)** establish (an institution, business, argument, etc): *set up an office.* ***set (oneself) up as,*** **(a)** go into business as: *He has set (himself) up as a bookseller.* **(b)** believe oneself to be: *I've never set myself up as perfect.* ***set sb up (as sth),*** get him started or established, eg by supplying money: *His father set him up in business.* ***set up house,*** start living in one. ***set sb up (for sth),*** (*informal*) put him in a position to be cheated, etc. ***set up house with sb/together,*** (of two persons) begin living together (as husband and wife).

'set·back *n* [C] (*pl* setbacks) reversal of one's progress; misfortune: *We suffered many setbacks.*

'set·up *n* [C] **(a)** (*informal*) arrangement of an organization: *What's the setup here?* **(b)** (*informal*) situation in which a person is put in a position to be cheated, etc.

set square /'set ˌskwer/ *n* [C] triangular plate of wood, plastic, metal, etc with angles of 90°, 60° and 30° (or 90°, 45°, 45°), used for drawing lines at these angles.

set·tee /se'ti/ *n* [C] seat like a sofa, with sides and back, for two or more persons.

set·ter /'setər/ *n* [C] **1** (breeds of) long-haired dog trained to stand motionless on scenting game. **2** (as a *suffix*) person who, thing which, sets (various meanings): *a 'pace~.*

set·ting /'setɪŋ/ *n* [C] **1** framework in which something is fixed or fastened: *the ~ of a jewel.* **2** surroundings: *a beautiful ~ for a picnic.* **3** music composed for a poem, etc. ⇨ set²(12). **4** descent (of the sun, moon, etc) below the horizon: (as an *adjective*) *the ~ sun.*

settle¹ /'setəl/ *n* [C] long, wooden seat with a high back and arms, the seat often being the lid of a chest.

settle² /'setəl/ *vt,vi* (For special uses with *adverbial particles* and *prepositions,* ⇨ 8 below.) **1** make one's home in (permanently): *~ in California/in town/in the country.* **2** come to rest (on); stay for some time (on): *The bird ~d on a branch. The dust ~d on everything.* **3** cause (a person) to become used to, or comfortable in, a new position (after a period of movement or activity): *The nurse ~d her patient for the night,* made him/her comfortable, etc. **4** make or become calm, untroubled: *We want a period of ~d weather for the harvest. Wait until the excitement has ~d.* **5** make an agreement about; decide: *It's time you ~d the dispute/argument. Nothing is ~d yet. The lawsuit was ~d out of court,* a decision was reached by the parties themselves (and their lawyers) instead of by the court. **6** pay: *~ a bill.* **7** (of dust, etc in the air, particles of solid substances in a liquid, etc) (cause to) sink; (of a liquid) become clear as solid particles sink: *We need a shower to ~ the dust.* **8** (special uses with *adverbial particles* and *prepositions*):

settle down, sit or lie comfortably (after a period of movement or activity): *He ~d down in his armchair to read.* ***settle (sb) down,*** make or become calm and peaceful: *Wait until the children have ~d down before you start your lesson.* ***settle down to sth,*** give one's attention to: *It's terrible—I can't ~ down to anything today,* am too restless to do my work, etc. ***settle down (to sth),*** become established (in a new way of life, new work, etc): *~ down in a new job.*

settle for sth, accept, although not altogether satisfactory: *I had hoped to get $500 for my old car but had to ~ for $250.* ***settle (sb) in,*** (help him to) move into a new house, apartment, job, etc and put things in order: *You must come and see our new house when we're/we've ~d in.*

settle sth on/upon sb, (*legal*) give him (property, etc) for use during his lifetime: *~ part of one's estate on one's son.* ⇨ settlement(2). ***settle on/upon sth,*** decide to have: *Which of the hats have you ~d on?*

settle (up) (with sb), pay what one owes: *I shall ~ (up) with you next month.*

settled /'setəld/ *adj* **1** fixed; unchanging; permanent: *a man of ~ opinions.* **2** (of a bill) paid.

settle·ment /'setəlmənt/ *n* **1** [U] the act of settling (a dispute, debt, etc); [C] instance of this: *The strikers have reached a ~ with the employers. I enclose a check in ~ of your account.* **2** [C] (statement of) property given to a person: *a 'marriage ~,* one made by a man in favor of his wife. **3** [U] process of settling people in a colony; [C] new colony: *empty lands awaiting ~; Dutch and English ~s in America.*

set·tler /'setlər/ *n* [C] person who has settled in a newly developed country: *white ~s in Kenya.*

seven /'sevən/ *adj, n* [C] (of) 7.

'seven·fold /-ˌfould/ *adj, adv* seven times as much, as great or as many.

seven·teen /ˌsevən'tin/ *adj, n* [C] (of) 17.

seven·teenth /ˌsevən'tinθ/ *adj, n* [C] (of) one of 17 (parts) or the next after 16.

sev·enth /'sevənθ/ *adj, n* [C] (of) one of 7 (parts) or the next after 6.

sev·enth·ly *adv* in the 7th place.

seven·ti·eth /'sevəntiəθ/ *adj, n* [C] (of) one of 70 (parts) or the next after 69.

sev·enty /'sevənti/ *adj, n* [C] (of) 70.

the seven·ties *n pl* **(a)** (of a person's age, temperature, etc) between 69 and 80. **(b)** (of a century) the years from 70 to 79 inclusive.

ˌseventy-'eight *n* [C] (*informal*) old-style phonograph record, playing at 78 revolutions per minute.

sever /ˈsevər/ *vt,vi* **1** = cut (the usual word): ~ *a rope*. **2** (*fig*) break off: ~ *one's connections with her*. **3** = break (the usual word): *The rope ~ed under the strain*.

sev·er·ance /ˈsev(ə)rəns/ *n* [U] : *~ance pay*, paid to an employee when his contract has ended.

sev·eral /ˈsevrəl/ *adj* **1** three or more; some but not many: *You will need ~ more. I've read it ~ times*. **2** separate; individual: *They went their ~ ways*, Each went his own way. □ *pron* a few; some: *Several of us refused*.

sev·er·ally /ˈsevrəli/ *adv* separately (the usual word).

se·vere /sɪˈvɪr/ *adj* **1** stern, strict: ~ *looks; be ~ with one's children*. **2** (of the weather, attacks of disease, etc) strong, extreme: *a ~ storm; ~ pain*. **3** making great demands on skill, ability, patience and other qualities: *The pace was too ~ to be kept up for long*.

sev·ere·ly *adv*

se·ver·ity /sɪˈverəti/ *n* (*pl* -ies) (*formal*) **1** [U] quality of being severe: *the ~* (= extreme cold) *of the winter in Canada*. **2** (*pl*) severe treatment or experiences: *the severities of the winter campaign*.

sew /sou/ *vt,vi* (*pt* sewed, *pp* sewn /soun/) work with a needle and thread; fasten with stitches; make (clothing) by stitching: *sew a button on. This dress is ˌhand-ˈsewn/sewn by hand*. ***sew sth up***, **(a)** join (at the edges) with stitches. **(b)** (*informal*) complete; arrange so as to obtain control: *We've got the market for dictionaries sewn up*.

sewer /ˈsouər/ *n* [C] person who sews.

sew·ing *n* [U] work (clothes, etc) being sewn. **ˈsewing machine**, machine for sewing.

sew·age /ˈsuɪdʒ/ *n* [U] waste organic matter, etc carried off in sewers.

sewer[1] /ˈsuər/ *n* [C] (system of) pipelines, etc to carry off sewage and rainwater.

sewer[2] *n* [C] ⇨ sew.

sewn *pp* of sew.

sex /seks/ *n* **1** [U] being male or female: *What is the cat's sex? Help them all, without distinction of race, age or sex*. **2** [C] males or females as a group: *the ˈfair sex*, women (*dated*). **3** [U] differences between males and females; consciousness of these differences: *ˈsex appeal*, attractiveness of a person of one sex to the other. **4** [U] sexual activity and everything connected with it.

sex·less /-lɪs/ *adj* neither male nor female.

sexy *adj* (-ier, -iest) (*informal*) sexually attractive.

sex·ism /ˈsekˌsɪzəm/ *n* [U] (behavior based on) belief that women are inferior to men.

sex·ist /ˈseksɪst/ *n* [C], *adj* (person who) considers women to be inferior to men.

sex·tant /ˈsekstənt/ *n* [C] instrument used for measuring the altitude of the sun, etc (in order to determine a ship's position, etc).

sex·ton /ˈsekstən/ *n* [C] man who takes care of a church building, digs graves in the churchyard, etc.

sex·ual /ˈsekʃuəl/ *adj* of sex or the sexes. **sexual ˈintercourse**, physical union of male and female persons or animals.

sexu·al·ity /ˌsekʃuˈæləti/ *n* [U] sex characteristics or appeal.

Sgt. *abbr* = Sergeant.

sh /ʃ/ (*int*) (sound made to call for silence): *Sh! You're making too much noise*.

shabby /ˈʃæbi/ *adj* (-ier, -iest) **1** in bad repair or condition; poorly dressed: *wearing a ~ hat. You look rather ~ in those clothes*. **2** (of behavior) mean; unfair.

shab·bily /ˈʃæbəli/ *adv*

shab·bi·ness /ˈʃæbinɪs/ *n* [U]

shack /ʃæk/ *n* [C] small, wooden shed, hut or house.

shackle /ˈʃækəl/ *n* [C] **1** one of a pair of iron rings joined by a chain for fastening a prisoner's wrists or ankles. **2** (*fig*) something that prevents freedom of action: *the ~s of convention*. □ *vt* put shackles on; prevent from acting freely.

shade /ʃeid/ *n* **1** [U or *sing* only] comparative darkness caused by the cutting off of direct rays of light: *a temperature of 95°(F) in the ~. The trees give a pleasant ~*. **2** (*fig*) comparative obscurity. ***put sb/sth in the shade***, cause to appear small, unimportant, etc by contrast: *You are so clever and brilliant that my poor efforts are put in the ~*. **3** [U] darker part(s) of a picture, etc; reproduction of the darker part of a picture: *There is not enough light and ~ in your drawing*. **4** [C] degree or depth of color: *dress materials in several ~s of blue*. **5** [C] degree of difference: *a word with many ~s of meaning*. **6** something that reduces light: *a ˈlamp~*. **7** [C] (*liter*) ghost, spirit. □ *vt,vi* **1** keep direct light from: *He ~d his eyes with his hands*. **2** screen (a light, lamp, etc) to reduce brightness. **3** darken (parts of a drawing, etc) to give the appearance of light and dark. **4** change by degrees: *scarlet shading off into pink*.

shad·ing *n* **(a)** [U] use of black, etc to give light and shade to a drawing. **(b)** [C] slight difference or variation.

shadow /ˈʃædou/ *n* **1** [C] area of shade, dark shape, thrown on the ground, a wall, floor, etc by something which cuts off the direct rays of light. **2** [C] something unsubstantial or unreal: *He is only the ~ of his former self*, is very thin and weak. **3** (*pl*) partial darkness: *the ~s of evening*. **4** [C] dark patch or area: *have ~s under/around the eyes*, such areas thought to be caused by lack of sleep, illness, etc. ***five o'clock shadow***, (*informal*) darkening of lower part of a man's face in late afternoon, caused by regrowth of hair removed by shaving. **5** (*sing* only) very small amount or degree: *without/beyond a ~ of doubt*. **6** person's inseparable friend or determined follower. □ *vt* **1** darken. **2** follow closely and watch the movements of: *The suspected spy was ~ed by detectives*.

shad·owy *adj*

shady /ˈʃeidi/ *adj* (-ier, -iest) **1** giving shade from sunlight; situated in shade: *the ~ side of the street*. **2** (*sl*) of doubtful honesty: *a ~ deal*.

shaft /ʃæft/ *n* [C] **1** (long, slender stem of an) arrow or spear. **2** long handle of an axe or other tool. **3** one of the pair of bars (wooden poles) between which a horse is harnessed to pull a cart, etc. **4** long part of a column (between the base and the top). **5** long, narrow space, usually vertical, eg for descending into a mine, for a lift in a building, or for ventilation. **6** bar or rod joining parts of a machine, or transmitting power. **7** ray (of light).

shag /ʃæg/ *n* [U] coarse kind of cut tobacco.

shaggy /ˈʃægi/ *adj* (-ier, -iest) **1** (of hair) rough, coarse and untidy. **2** covered with rough, coarse hair: *a ~ dog; ~ eyebrows.*

shake[1] /ʃeik/ *n* [C] shaking or being shaken: *a ~ of the head,* to indicate "no."

shake[2] /ʃeik/ *vt,vi* (*pt* shook /ʃʊk/, *pp* ~n /ˈʃeikən/) **1** (cause to) move from side to side, up and down etc: *~ a rug; ~ a man by the hand; ~ one's head,* to indicate "no," or doubt, disapproval, etc; *~ one's fist at him,* to show anger, defiance. *His sides were shaking with laughter. He was shaking with cold.* **2** shock; trouble; weaken: *They were badly ~n by the news.* **3** (of a person's voice) tremble; become weak: *Her voice shook with emotion.* **4** (special uses with *adverbial particles* and *prepositions*):

shake down, become adjusted to a new environment, new conditions, etc: *The new teaching staff is shaking down nicely.* ***shake sb down,*** (*sl*) extort money from him.

shake sth from/out of sth, get from/out of by shaking: *~ apples from a tree; ~ sand out of one's shoes.*

shake sb off, free oneself from: *The thief ran fast and soon shook off the police.* ***shake sth off,*** get rid of: *~ off a cold/a fit of depression.*

shake sth out, spread out by shaking: *~ out a tablecloth.*

shake sth up, **(a)** mix well by shaking: *~ up a bottle of medicine.* **(b)** restore something to shape by shaking: *~ up a cushion.* ***shake sb up,*** **(a)** restore from apathy or laziness: *Some of these managers need shaking up—they're asleep on the job.* **(b)** (*informal*) unnerve; cause mental upset: *That news really shook me up.*

ˈ**shake·down** *n* **(a)** breaking-in period. **(b)** (*sl*) extortion scheme.

ˈ**shake-up** *n* restoring from apathy: *We need a good ~-up in our office.*

Shaker /ˈʃeikər/ *n* [C] member of a Christian group believing in celibacy and communal living. □ *adj* of the Shakers, esp their style of dress, architecture, etc.

shak·ing /ˈʃeikɪŋ/ *n* = shake: *give a pillow a good ~,* shake it well.

shaky /ˈʃeiki/ *adj* (-ier, -iest) **1** (of a person, his movements, etc) weak; unsteady: *~ hands; speak in a ~ voice; feel very ~.* **2** unsafe; unreliable: *a ~ table. My French is rather ~.*

shak·ily /-əli/ *adv*

shale /ˈʃeiəl/ *n* [U] soft rock that splits easily into layers.

shall /ʃəl *strong form:* ʃæl/ *auxiliary verb* (shall not is sometimes shortened in *literary usage* to shan't /ʃænt/; *pt* should /ʃʊd; *weak form:* ʃəd/; should not is often shortened to shouldn't /ˈʃʊdənt/) **1** (used to express the future tense): *We ~/We'll arrive tomorrow. I'll see you soon.* (*Note: will* is often used instead, especially in *negative*). **2** (used to form a future or conditional statement expressing the speaker's will or intention; with stress on *shall, should,* it expresses obligation or compulsion; without special stress on *shall, should,* it expresses a promise or a threat): *You say you won't do it, but I say you ˈ~ do it. If you work well, you ~ have higher wages.* **3** (used to form statements or questions expressing the ideas of duty, command, obligation, conditional duty, and (in the *neg*) prohibition): *Shall I* (= Do you want me to) *open the window? I asked the man whether the boy should wait. You should* (= ought to) *have been more careful.* **4** (used in clauses expressing *may* or *might*): *I lent him the book so that he should study the subject.* **5** (*should* is used after *how, why*): *How should I know? Why should you/he think that?* **6** (*should* is used to express probability or expectation): *They should be there by now.*

shal·lot /ʃəˈlat/ *n* [C] sort of small onion.

shal·low /ˈʃælou/ *adj* (-er, -est) **1** of little depth: *~ water.* **2** (*fig*) not reasonable or serious: *a ~ argument; ~ talk.* □ *n* [C] (often *pl*) shallow place in a river or in the sea.

sham /ʃæm/ *vi,vt* (-mm-) pretend to be: *He ~med dead/death. He's only ~ming.* □ *n* **1** [C] person who shams; something intended to deceive: *His love was only a ~.* **2** [U] pretense: *What he says is all ~.* □ *adj* false; pretended: *~ pity.*

shamble /ˈʃæmbəl/ *vi* walk unsteadily as if unable to lift the feet properly: *The old man ~d up to me.* □ *n* [C] shambling walk.

shambles /ˈʃæmbəlz/ *n* (used with a *sing verb*) **1** scene of bloodshed: *The place became a ~.* **2** scene of muddle or confusion: *His apartment is a complete ~.*

shame /ʃeim/ *n* [U] **1** sad feeling, loss of self-respect, caused by wrong, dishonorable or foolish behavior, failure, etc (of oneself, one's family, etc): *feel ~ at having told a lie; hang one's head for/in ~.* **2** capacity for experiencing shame: *He has no ~/is without ~.* **3** dishonor. ***bring shame on sb/oneself,*** dishonor him/oneself. **4** (with *a, an* but not *pl*) something unworthy; something that causes shame; a person or thing that is wrong: *It's a ~ to take the money for doing such easy work. He's a ~ to his family.* □ *vt* **1** cause shame to; cause a person to feel shame; bring disgrace on: *~ one's family.* **2** frighten or force (a person to do/not to do something): *~ a man into apologizing.*

ˈ**shame·faced** *adj* looking ashamed.

shame·ful /-fəl/ *adj* causing or bringing shame: *~ful conduct.*

shame·fully /-fəli/ *adv*

shame·less *adj* without shame: *The ~less girl had no clothes on.*

sham·poo /ʃæmˈpu/ *n* [C,U] (special liquid, powder, etc for a) washing of the hair: *give her a ~ and set.* □ *vt* wash (the hair of the head): *Have you finished ~ing her hair?*

sham·rock /ˈʃæmˌrak/ *n* [C] plant with (usually) three leaves on each stem (the national emblem of Ireland).

shang·hai /ˈʃæŋˌhai/ *vt* (*pt, pp* ~ed, *present p* ~ing) press someone into service, esp as a sailor, by force or trickery.

shank /ʃæŋk/ *n* [C] **1** leg, esp the part between the knee and the ankle. **2** straight part of an anchor, etc.

shan't (*liter*) = shall not.

shanty /ˈʃænti/ *n* [C] (*pl* -ies) poorly made hut or house.

ˈshanty·town *n* area of a town with shanties.

shape¹ /ʃeip/ *n* **1** [C,U] outer form; total effect produced by the outlines of something: *There were clouds of different ~s. What's the ~ of his nose?* ***knock sth into/out of shape,*** put it into/out of the right shape. ***take shape,*** become definite in form or outline: *The new building/His plan is beginning to take ~.* **2** sort, description: *I've had no help from him in any ~ or form,* none of any sort. **3** condition: *He is in good ~,* is physically fit. *Her affairs are in good ~,* are controlled, organized. **4** [C] vague form: *I could see a ~ in the darkness.*

shape² /ʃeip/ *vt,vi* **1** give a shape or form to: *~ a pot on a wheel.* **2** (*pp*): *~d like a pear/ˈpear-~d,* having the shape of a pear. **3** (often used with *up*) give signs of future shape or development: *Our plans are shaping (up) well,* giving promise of success.

shape·less /-lɪs/ *adj* with no definite shape.

shape·ly /ˈʃeipli/ *adj* (-ier, -iest) (esp of a person) having a pleasing shape: *a ~ pair of legs.*

share¹ /ʃer/ *n* **1** [C] part or division which a person has in, receives from, or gives to, a stock held by several or many persons, or which he contributes to a fund, expenses, etc: *We shall all have a ~ in the profits.* ***go shares (with sb) (in sth),*** divide (profits, costs, etc) with others; become part owner (with others); pay (a part of an expense): *Let me go ~s with you in the repair costs.* **2** [U] part taken or received by a person in an action, etc, eg of responsibility, blame: *You must take your ~ of the blame.* **3** [C] one of the equal parts into which the capital of a company is divided with which the holder can have a part of the profits. □ *vt,vi* **1** give a share of to others; divide and distribute: *~ (out) $1,000 among/between five men,* eg by giving them *$200 each.* ***share sth with sb,*** give a part to somebody else: *He would ~ his last dollar with me.* **2** have or use (with): *He hated having to ~ the hotel bedroom with a stranger.* **3** have a share: *I will ~ (in) the cost with you.* ***ˌshare and ˌshare aˈlike,*** have equal shares with others in the use, enjoyment, expense, etc of something.

ˈshare·cropper *n* [C] farmer too poor to own land, who farms on another's land in exchange for a share of the crops.

ˈshare·holder *n* [C] owner of shares(3).

ˈshare-out *n* [C] distribution.

share² /ʃer *n* [C] blade of a plough.

shark /ʃark/ *n* [C] **1** ocean fish, often large and dangerous. ⇨ illus at fish. **2** (*fig*) person who cheats to gain money.

ˈloan ˌshark, one who lends money at excessive interest, often in order to claim the property offered as security.

sharp /ʃarp/ *adj* (-er, -est) **1** with a fine point or cutting edge: *a ~ knife; a ~ pin/needle.* **2** well-defined; distinct: *a ~ outline; a ~ image,* (in photography) one with clear contrasts between light and shade. **3** (of curves, slopes, bends) changing direction quickly: *a ~ bend in the road.* **4** (of sounds) shrill; piercing: *a ~ cry of distress.* **5** quickly aware of things: *a ~ intelligence/sense of smell.* ***keep a sharp lookout,*** look very carefully (for): *keep a ~ lookout for thieves.* **6** (of feelings, taste) producing a physical sensation like cutting or pricking: *a ~ pain.* **7** harsh; severe: *~ words; a ~ tongue,* of a person who criticizes, is easily angry, etc. **8** quick to take advantage: *a ~ lawyer.* **9** (*music*) (of a note) raised half a tone in pitch: *C ~,* ⇨ flat² (3). □ *n* [C] **1** (*music*) sharp note; the symbol # used to show this. ⇨ illus at notation. **2** = shark (2). □ *adv* **1** punctually: *at seven (o'clock) ~.* **2** suddenly; abruptly: *turn ~ to the left.*

sharpen /ˈʃarpən/ *vt,vi* make or become sharp: *~en a pencil.*

sharp·ener /ˈʃarpənər/ *n* [C] thing that sharpens: *a ˈpencil ~ener.*

sharp·ly *adv*

sharp·ness /-nɪs/ *n* [U]

sharp·shoot·er /ˈʃarpˌʃutər/ *n* [C] marksman.

shat·ter /ˈʃætər/ *vt,vi* **1** break suddenly into small pieces: *The explosion ~ed every window in the building.* **2** (*fig*) destroy; be destroyed: *Our hopes were ~ed.*

shave /ʃeiv/ *vt,vi* (*pt,pp* ~d or, as in (4) below, ~n /ˈʃeivən/) **1** cut (hair) off close to the skin with a razor: *He is shaving off his beard.* **2** take off (a thin layer, etc): *~ off a piece of wood.* **3** pass very close to, almost but not touching: *The bus ~d by me.* **4** (*pp*) (as an *adjective*): *ˌclean-ˈ~n,* without a beard. □ *n* [C] **1** shaving (of the face): *A sharp razor gives a good ~.* ***2 a close/narrow shave,*** a narrow escape from injury, danger, etc.

shaver *n* [C] **(a)** razor with an electric motor. **(b)** (*informal*) youngster.

ˈshaving brush, brush for spreading lather over the face before shaving.

ˈshaving cream, shaving soap in paste form or foam.

ˈshaving mug, mug for holding a cake of shaving soap and (sometimes) water for making lather.

shav·ings *n pl* thin pieces of wood which have been shaved(2) off.

ˈshaving soap, soap preparation for making lather with a brush for shaving.

shawl /ʃɔl/ *n* [C] large (usually square or oblong) piece of material worn around the shoulders or head of a woman, or wrapped around a baby.

she /ʃi/ *pron* female person, animal, etc previously referred to: *My sister says she is going for a walk.* □ *n* [C] (often used in compounds) female: *a ˈshe-goat. Is it a he or a she?* ⇨ her, object form.

sheaf /ʃif/ *n* [C] (*pl* sheaves /ʃivz/) **1** corn, barley, etc tied together after reaping. **2** arrows, etc tied together.

shear /ʃɪr/ *vt* (*pt,* ~ed, *pp* shorn /ʃɔrn/ or ~ed) **1** cut the wool off (a sheep) with shears. **2** (*fig*) take away completely from. ***shorn of,*** having lost completely: *The gambler came home shorn of his money.*

shears /ʃɪrz/ *n pl* (also ***a pair of shears***) large cutting instrument shaped like scissors, used to cut hedges, etc.
sheath /ʃiθ/ *n* [C] (*pl* ~s /ʃiðz/) cover for the blade of a weapon or tool: *Put the dagger back in its* ~.
ˈ**sheath knife,** knife, with a blade, that fits into a sheath.
sheathe /ʃið/ *vt* put into a sheath.
sheaves *pl* of sheaf.
shed[1] /ʃed/ *n* [C] small building, usually of wood, used for storing things (ˈ*tool* ~, ˈ*wood* ~, ˈ*coal* ~), for sheltering animals (ˈ*cattle* ~), for vehicles (ˈ*engine* ~, ˈ*bicycle* ~).
shed[2] /ʃed/ *vt* (*pt,pp* ~) (-dd-) **1** let (leaves, etc) fall; let come off: *Some trees* ~ *their leaves in autumn.* ***shed blood,*** **(a)** be wounded or killed. **(b)** cause the blood of others to flow: *The wicked ruler* ~ *rivers of blood.* ⇨ bloodshed. ***shed tears,*** = cry[1](2). **2** throw or take off; get rid of: *People on the beach began to* ~ *their clothes as it got hotter and hotter.* **3** spread or send out: *a fire that* ~*s warmth; a woman who* ~*s happiness.* ***shed light on sth,*** (*fig*) ⇨ light[3](5).
she'd = she had; she would.
sheen /ʃin/ *n* [U] brightness: *the* ~ *of silk.*
sheep /ʃip/ *n* [C] (*pl* unchanged) grass-eating animal kept for its flesh as food (mutton) and its wool. ⇨ ewe, lamb and ram.
ˈ**sheep·dog** *n* [C] dog trained to help a shepherd to look after sheep.
ˈ**sheep·fold** *n* [C] enclosure for sheep.
ˈ**sheep·ish** /-ɪʃ/ *adj* **(a)** awkwardly self-conscious: *a* ~*ish-looking boy.* **(b)** (feeling) foolish or embarrassed because of a fault.
sheep·ish·ly *adv*
sheep·ish·ness /-nɪs/ *n* [U]
ˈ**sheep·skin** *n* rug of a sheep's skin with the wool on it; clothing made of such skins.
sheer /ʃɪr/ *adj* **1** complete; thorough; absolute: ~ *nonsense; a* ~ *waste of time; by* ~ *chance.* **2** (of cloth, etc) finely woven and almost transparent: ~ *nylon.* **3** (almost) without a slope: *a* ~ *drop of 500 feet.* □ *adv* straight up or down: *He fell 500 feet* ~.
sheet[1] /ʃit/ *n* [C] **1** large rectangular piece of cotton, etc cloth, used in pairs for sleeping between: *put clean* ~*s on the bed.* **2** flat, thin piece (of a material): *a* ~ *of glass/notepaper.* **3** wide expanse (of water, ice, snow, flame, etc): *The rain came down in* ~*s,* very heavily.
sheet·ing *n* [U] material used for making sheets (1).
ˈ**sheet lightning,** lightning that comes in wide flashes of brightness (not in zigzags, etc).
ˈ**sheet music,** published on sheets of paper, not in a book.
sheet[2] /ʃit/ *n* [C] rope fastened at the lower corner of a sail to hold it and control the angle at which it is set. ⇨ illus at ship.
sheik(h) /ʃik/ *n* [C] Arab chieftain; head of an Arab village, tribe, etc.
sheik(h)·dom /-dəm/ *n* [C]
shelf /ʃelf/ *n* [C] (*pl* shelves /ʃelvz/) **1** flat piece of wood, metal, etc fastened at right angles to a wall or in a cupboard, etc, used to stand things on. ***on the shelf,*** (*informal*) **(a)** put aside as done with, eg of a person too old to continue working. **(b)** (of a woman) unmarried and considered as being unlikely to be asked to marry. **2** shelf-like piece of rock or earth along the edge of a cliff, mountainside, continent (as the *continental* ~, under the sea) etc.
shell /ʃel/ *n* [C] **1** hard outer covering of eggs, nuts, some seeds (eg peas) and fruits, and of some animals (eg snails) or parts of them. ⇨ illus at mollusk, crustacean, reptile. ***go/retire into/come out of one's shell,*** become/cease to be shy, reserved, quiet. **2** outside walls, etc of an unfinished building, ship, etc or of one of which the contents have been destroyed (eg by fire). **3** cartridge; metal case filled with explosive, to be fired from a gun. □ *vt,vi* **1** take out of a shell(1): ~*ing peas.* **2** remove the edible grains from the ear of Indian corn: ~*ed corn,* grains of corn separated from the ear. **3** fire shells(3) at: ~ *the enemy's trenches.* **4** ***shell out,*** (*informal*) pay up (money, a required sum): *Must I* ~ *out (the money) for the party?*
ˈ**shell·fish** *n* kinds of sea animal (crabs, lobsters, etc) with shells(1).
ˈ**shell shock,** nervous or mental disorder caused by the noise of shells(3).
she'll /ʃiəl/ = she will; she shall.
shel·ter /ˈʃeltər/ *n* **1** [U] condition of being kept safe, eg from rain, danger: *take* ~ *from the storm.* **2** [C] something that gives safety or protection: *a* ˈ*bus* ~, in which people wait for buses. □ *vt,vi* **1** give shelter to; protect: *trees that* ~ *a house from cold winds;* ~ (= hide, protect) *an escaped prisoner.* **2** take shelter: ~ *under the trees.*
shelve[1] /ʃelv/ *vt* **1** put (books, etc) on a shelf. **2** (*fig*) (of problems, plans, etc) postpone dealing with: ~ *a problem.*
shelve[2] /ʃelv/ *vi* (of land) slope gently: *The shore* ~*s down to the sea.*
shelves *pl* of shelf.
she·nan·i·gan /ʃɪˈnænɪgən/ *n* [C] (*informal*) (usually in *pl*) trickery.
shep·herd /ˈʃepərd/ *n* [C] man who takes care of sheep. □ *vt* **1** take care of. **2** guide or direct (people) like sheep: *The passengers were* ~*ed across the airport runway to the airliner.*
shep·herd·ess /ˈʃepərdɪs/ *n* [C] woman shepherd.
sher·iff /ˈʃerɪf/ *n* [C] chief law-enforcing officer of a county.
sherry /ˈʃeri/ *n* [U] yellow or brown wine from Southern Spain, Cyprus, etc.
she's /ʃiz/ = she is; she has.
shied *pt,pp* of shy[2].
shield /ˈʃiəld/ *n* [C] **1** piece of metal, leather, etc carried to protect the body when fighting. **2** representation of a shield showing a coat of arms. **3** (*fig*) person or thing that protects. **4** (in machinery, etc) piece of metal, etc designed to keep out dust, wind, etc. □ *vt* **1** protect; keep safe: ~ *one's eyes with one's hand.* **2** protect (a person) from suffering, etc: ~ *a friend from criticism.*
shift[1] /ʃɪft/ *n* [C] **1** change of place or character: *a* ~ *in emphasis.* **2** change of one thing for another: *a* ~ *from cars to bicycles.* **3** group of

workmen who start work as another group finishes; period for which such a group works: *on the ˈday/ˈnight* ~. **4** trick, way of avoiding a difficulty; clever way of getting something: *use clever ~s to get some money*. **5** woman's narrow dress without a waistline. **6** (*automotive*) mechanism for changing gear.

shift·less *adj* without ability to find ways of doing things.

shift[2] /ʃɪft/ *vt,vi* **1** change position or direction; transfer: *~ luggage from one hand to the other. Don't try to ~ the blame* (*on*) *to somebody else.* **2** (*automotive*) change (gears): *~ into second/third gear*. **3** ***shift for oneself,*** manage as best one can (to make a living, etc) without help: *When our father died we had to ~ for ourselves.*

shifty *adj* (-ier, -iest) not to be trusted: *a ~y customer; ~y behavior.*

shill /ʃɪl/ [C] (*sl*) secret partner of a pitchman, auctioneer or gambler, who attracts customers by pretending to be a customer himself.

shim·mer /ˈʃɪmər/ *vi, n* [U] (have a shine with a) wavering soft or faint light: *moonlight ~ing on the water*.

shin /ʃɪn/ *n* [C] front part of the leg below the knee. ⇨ illus at leg. □ *vi* (-nn-) ***shin up,*** climb up (using arms and legs to grip something): *~ up a tree.*

ˈshin·bone *n* inner and thicker of the two bones below the knee.

shin·dig /ˈʃɪnˌdɪg/ *n* [C] (*informal*) lively party, esp a rural dance.

shine /ʃain/ *vi,vt* (*pt,pp* shone /ʃoun/ but ⇨ 3 below) **1** give out or reflect light; be bright: *The moon is shining. His face shone with excitement.* **2** (*fig*) show particular ability or intelligence: *He didn't ~ in the exams. I don't ~ at tennis.* **3** (*informal*) (*pp* ~d) polish: *~ shoes.* □ *n* **1** (*sing only*) polish: *Give your shoes a good ~.* **2** [U] ***come rain or shine,*** **(a)** whatever the weather may be. **(b)** (*fig*) whatever may happen.

shiny *adj* (-ier, -iest) polished; bright: *shiny shoes.*

shingle /ˈʃɪŋgəl/ *n* **1** [C] flat piece of wood, etc for covering roofs by being placed in overlapping rows. **2** [U] gravel of small, rounded pebbles on the seashore.

shingles /ˈʃɪŋgəlz/ *n* (used with a *sing verb*) skin disease forming a band of inflamed, irritating spots (often around the waist).

ship[1] /ʃɪp/ *n* [C] **1** large boat that can travel on a sea: *a ˈsailing ~; a ˈmerchant ~; a ˈwar~.* **2** (*informal*) = spacecraft. **3** (*informal*) = aircraft.

ˈship·broker *n* [C] agent of a shipping company; one who buys, sells and charters ships; agent for marine insurance.

ˈship·builder *n* [C] person whose business is building ships.

ˈship·building *n* [U]

ˈship chandler, trader who sells equipment for ships.

ˈship·load *n* [C] as much cargo, or as many passengers, as a ship can carry.

ˈship·mate *n* [C] person belonging to the same crew: *Harry and I were ~mates in 1972.*

ˈship·owner *n* [C] person who owns a ship or ships.

ˈship·shape *adj* tidy; in good order.

ˈship·wreck *n* [U] loss or destruction of a ship at sea; [C] instance of this. □ *vt* destroy by shipwreck.

ˈship·wright *n* [C] shipbuilder.

ˈship·yard *n* [C] place where ships are built.

ship[2] /ʃɪp/ *vt,vi* (-pp-) **1** put, take, send, in a ship:

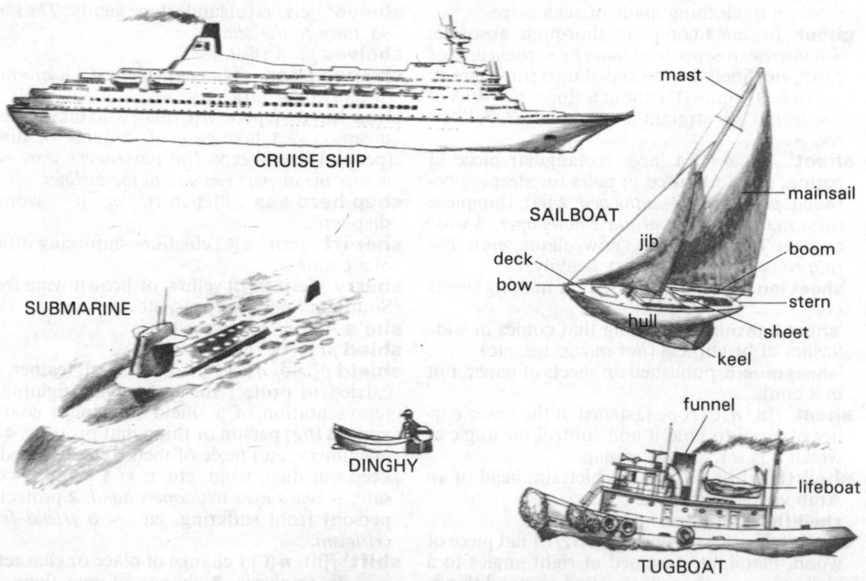

SHIPS AND BOATS

~ *oil to the US.* **2** take, send, by train, road, etc: ~ *goods by express train.* **3** ***ship oars,*** take them out of the water into the boat. **4** ***ship water,*** be flooded with water during a storm or through a hole in the side.

ship·per *n* [C] person who arranges for goods to be shipped.

ship·ping *n* [U] all the ships of a country, port, etc.

ˈship·ping agent, shipowner's representative at a port.

ship·ment *n* [U] putting of goods, etc on a ship; [C] quantity of goods shipped.

-ship /-ˌʃɪp/ *suffix* **1** state of being; status, office: *friendship; professorship.* **2** skill: *musicianship.*

shirk /ʃərk/ *vt,vi* try to avoid (doing something, responsibility, duty, etc): *He's ~ing (his duty).*

shirker, person who shirks.

shirt /ʃərt/ *n* [C] man's clothing for the upper part of the body (of cotton, nylon, etc) with sleeves. ***(be/go) in (one's) shirt-sleeves,*** ⇨ sleeve. ***keep one's shirt on,*** (*sl*) keep one's temper.

shiver /ˈʃɪvər/ *vi* tremble, esp from cold or fear: *~ing like a leaf.* □ *n* [C] trembling that cannot be controlled: *The sight sent cold ~s down my back.*

shoal[1] /ʃoul/ *n* [C] great number of fish swimming together: *a ~ of herring.* □ *vi* form shoals.

shoal[2] /ʃoul/ *n* [C] shallow place in the sea, esp where there are sandbanks. □ *vi* become shallow(er).

shock /ʃak/ *n* **1** [C] violent blow or shaking (eg as caused by a collision or explosion): *the ~ of a fall.* **2** [C] effect caused by the passage of an electric current through the body: *If you touch that live wire you'll get a ~.* **3** [C] sudden and strong disturbance of the feelings or the nervous system (caused by bad news, severe injury, etc); [U] condition caused by such a disturbance: *The news of her mother's death was a terrible ~ to her. She died of ~ following an operation on the brain.* □ *vt* cause shock(3) to: *I was ~ed at the news of her death.*

shocker *n* person or thing that shocks.

shock·ing *adj* **(a)** very bad or wrong: *~ing behavior.* **(b)** causing shock (3): *~ing news,* eg of a flood that causes great loss of life. **(c)** (*informal*) bad: *~ing handwriting.*

shock·ing·ly *adv*

ˈshock tactics, (a) sudden use of many troops to attack (in war). **(b)** (*fig*) similar show of force to attack.

ˈshock treatment/therapy, use of electric shocks to cure mental illness.

ˈshock wave, sudden change in air pressure in a region, eg behind a supersonic aircraft or a nuclear bomb.

shod *pt,pp* of shoe.

shoddy /ˈʃadi/ *adj* (-ier, -iest) of poor quality: *a ~ piece of work.*

shoe /ʃu/ *n* [C] **1** (often ***a pair of shoes***) outer covering of leather, etc for the foot, esp one which does not reach above the ankle. **2** = horseshoe. **3** part of a brake that presses against the wheel or drum (of a bicycle, motor vehicle, etc). □ *vt* (*pt,pp* shod /ʃad/) fit with shoes: *well shod for wet weather.*

ˈshoe·horn *n* [C] device with a curved blade for getting the heel easily into a shoe.

ˈshoe·lace *n* [C] cord for fastening a shoe.

ˈshoe·maker *n* [C] person who makes shoes and boots.

ˈshoe·shine *n* (*informal*) (act of) polishing shoes, (as an *adjective*) *ˈ~ stand,* where shoes are polished for a fee.

ˈshoe·string *n* [C] = shoelace. ***do sth on a shoestring,*** do it (eg start a business) with very little money.

shoestring poˈtatoes, potatoes cut into long, very thin strips and fried until crisp.

shone *pt,pp* of shine.

shoo /ʃu/ *int* cry used for telling children, pets, birds, etc to go away. □ *vt* (*pt,pp* ~ed) make them go away by making this cry.

ˈshoo-in *n* [C] (*informal*) easy or likely winner of a race, election, etc.

shook *pt* of shake².

shoot[1] /ʃut/ *n* [C] **1** new, young growth on a plant or bush. **2** party of people shooting for sport.

shoot[2] /ʃut/ *vi,vt* (*pt, pp* shot /ʃat/) **1** move, come, go, send, suddenly or quickly (*out, in, up,* etc): *Flames were ~ing up from the burning house. The meteor shot across the sky. Rents have shot up* (= risen suddenly) *in the last few months. Tom is ~ing up fast,* quickly growing tall. *She shot an angry look at him/shot him an angry look.* **2** (of plants, bushes) send out new twigs or branches from a stem. **3** (of pain) happen suddenly and go quickly: *The pain shot up his arm.* **4** (of boats) move, be moved, rapidly over, through, etc: *~ a bridge,* pass under it quickly. **5** aim and fire with a gun or revolver; aim with a bow and send an arrow at; hit with a shell, bullet, arrow, etc; wound or kill (a person, animal, etc) by doing this: *They were ~ing at a target. The soldier was shot* (= executed by shooting) *for desertion. The bomber was shot down in flames. He had his arm shot off.* **6** photograph (a scene): *a ˈ~ing script,* one to be used for a film (giving the order in which scenes are photographed, etc). **7** make an attempt to score a goal. **8** ***shoot off one's mouth,*** (*informal*) talk too much.

ˈshoot·ing gallery, (a) place where shooting is practiced with pistols or airguns. **(b)** (*sl*) (usually abandoned) building where drug addicts inject themselves.

ˌshoot·ing ˈstar, meteor seen as a moving star.

ˈshoot·ing stick, stick with a spiked end (to be pushed into the ground) and a handle which unfolds to form a seat.

ˈshoot-out, gunbattle involving a limited number of persons (less than for a *battle*), carried on until one side wins.

-shooter /-ˌʃutər/ *suffix* shooting implement: *a ˈsix-shooter,* revolver firing six shots without reloading.

shop /ʃap/ *n* **1** [C] (part of a) building where goods are shown and sold; (usually small) store: *a butcher's ~.* ***set up shop,*** set up in business as a retail trader. **2** [U] a person's profession, etc and things connected with it. ***talk shop,*** talk about one's work, profession, etc. **3** [C] = workshop: *a maˈchine ~; the men on the ~ floor*, the workers (not the management). □ *vi* (-pp-) go to shops to buy things (usually *go shopping*). ***shop around***, (*informal*) visit many shops or stores, markets, etc to obtain the best value for one's money, etc.

ˈshop·lifter *n* [C] person who steals things from stores.

ˈshop·lifting *n* [U]

shop·per *n* [C] person who is shopping.

shop·ping *n* [U]: *do one's ~ping; a ˈ~ping bag/basket*, in which to carry purchases.

ˈshop·ping center, part of a town where there are stores, markets, etc close together and often where cars are not allowed. ⇨ also window-shopping.

ˈshop steward, member of a branch committee of a labor union elected by the workers.

ˈshop·window *n* [C] window used for the display of things on sale.

shore[1] /ʃɔr/ *n* [C] stretch of land bordering on the sea or a large body of water: *a house on the ~(s) of a lake*.

shore[2] /ʃɔr/ *n* [C] wooden support or prop (as set against the side of a ship while it is being built). □ *vt* ***shore sth up,*** support, prop up, (with a wooden beam, etc).

shorn *pp* of shear.

short[1] /ʃɔrt/ *adj* (-er, -est) **1** (opposite of *long*) measuring little from end to end in space or time: *a ~ stick; ~ hair; a ~ way off*, not far away; *a ~ journey*. ***in the short run,*** over a short period of time; during the present time. ***short and sweet,*** brief and (therefore) pleasant. **2** (opposite of *tall*) below the average height: *a ~ man/mountain*. **3** not reaching the usual, stated or required number, amount, distance, etc: *have a ~ temper*, be easily made angry. *These goods are in ~ supply*, only a few are available. *The factory is on ~ time*, working fewer hours per day, or days per week, than usual. *You've given me ~ change*, less than the correct change. ***short of*** **(a)** not enough of: *~ of money/breath/time*. **(b)** distant from: *run out of gas(oline) five miles ~ of the garage*. ***little/nothing short of,*** almost: *Our escape was nothing ~ of a miracle*. ***short change*** (also ***ˈshortchange***) ***sb,*** give him less than is due, esp after a purchase. **4** (of a person) saying very little or saying much in a few words; (of what he says) using a few words: *He/His answer was ~ and to the point*. ***for short; short for,*** as an abbreviation: *Benjamin, called Ben for ~. Ben is ~ for Benjamin*. ***in short,*** briefly. ***the long and the short of it,*** ⇨ long[3]. **5** (of cake, pastry) easily breaking or crumbling. **6** (of vowels or syllables) taking a short time: *There is a ~ vowel in "ship" and a long vowel in "sheep."*

ˈshort·change, ⇨ short[1](3).

ˌshort ˈcircuit *n* [C] fault in the wiring so that an electric current flows without going through the resistance of a complete circuit. □ *vt,vi* **(a)** (also ***short sth out***) cause, make or take a short circuit in. **(b)** (*fig*) shorten or avoid by taking a more direct route.

ˈshort·coming *n* [C] instance of failure or inability to reach some standard of performance.

ˈshort·cut *n* [C] way of getting somewhere, doing something that is quicker than the usual way: *take a ~cut across the fields*.

ˈshort·fall *n* = deficit. ⇨ fall[2] (1).

ˈshort·hand *n* system of writing quickly using special symbols.

ˌshort-ˈhanded *adj* having not enough workers or helpers.

short-lived /ˌʃɔrtˈlaivd/ *adj* lasting for a short time: *a ~-lived success*.

short·ly *adv* **(a)** soon; in a short time: *~ly after(wards); ~ly before noon*. **(b)** briefly; in a few words. **(c)** sharply: *answer ~ly*.

short·ness /-nɪs/ *n* [U]

ˈshort-range *adj* **(a)** (of plans, etc) of use for a limited period. **(b)** (of missiles, etc) with a limited range[1](3): *ˌ~-range ˈbombers*.

ˌshort ˈshrift ⇨ shrift.

ˌshort ˈsight, (a) inability to see distant objects clearly. **(b)** (*fig*) inability to forecast the obvious (and act accordingly).

ˌshort-ˈsighted *adj: a ˌ~-sighted deˈcision to refuse help*. ⇨ near-sighted.

short·sight·ed·ness /-nɪs/ *n* [U]

ˈshort·stop *n* [C] (*baseball*) (position of) player between second and third base. ⇨ illus at baseball.

ˌshort-ˈtempered *adj* easily made angry.

ˈshort-term *adj* related to a short period of time: *ˌ~-term ˈloans*.

ˈshort·wave *n* radio wave of between 10 and 100 meters in length.

ˌshort-winded *adj* **(a)** quickly breathless after physical activity. **(b)** (*fig*) unable or unwilling to act or speak for a long time.

short[2] /ʃɔrt/ *adv* **1** abruptly; suddenly: *stop ~*. ***short of,*** except: *They would commit every crime ~ of murder*. **2** before the natural or expected time. ***come/fall short of,*** be insufficient, inadequate, disappointing (expectations, etc): *Your exam results fell ~ of my expectations*. ***cut sth/sb short,*** **(a)** interrupt; bring to an end before the usual or natural time: *The chairman had to cut ~ the discussion*. **(b)** make short(er). ***go short (of),*** do without: *I don't want you to go ~* (of money, etc) *in order to lend me what I need*. ***run short (of),*** reach the end: *We're running ~ of bread*. ***sell sb short,*** betray, cheat him.

short·age /ˈʃɔrtɪdʒ/ *n* [C,U] (amount of) deficiency; condition of not having enough: *ˈfood ~s; a ~ of staff*.

shorten /ˈʃɔrtən/ *vt,vi* make or become shorter: *Can you ~ my dress? The days are beginning to ~*, eg in autumn.

short·en·ing /ˈʃɔrt(ə)nɪŋ/ *n* [U] fat used for making pastry light and flaky. ⇨ short[1](5).

shorts /ʃɔrts/ *n pl* (often ***a pair of shorts***) short pants extending to or above the knees, as worn by children, by adults for games, etc.

shot[1] /ʃat/ *n* **1** [C] (sound of the) firing of a gun, etc: *hear ~s in the distance*. ***(do sth) like a shot,*** at once; without hesitation. **2** [C] (attempt at) hitting of something; attempt to do something, answer a question, etc; throw, stroke, hit, etc in certain games: *Good ~! That remark was a ~ at me*, was aimed at me. ***a ˌshot in the ˈdark,*** a guess. ***have a shot (at sth),*** try to do it: *Have a ~ at solving the problem. Let me have a ~ at it.* ***a 'long shot,*** an attempt to solve a problem, etc with little chance of success: *It's a long ~ but I think John must have stolen the bike.* ***not by a 'long shot,*** not even if circumstances were most favorable. **3** [C] that which is fired from a gun. ⇨ shell(3). **4** [C] heavy iron ball thrown in athletic competition called the *'~ put: putting the ~.* **5** [U] (also *lead ~*) quantity of tiny balls of lead contained in the cartridge of a sporting gun (instead of a single bullet). **6** [C] person who shoots, with reference to his skill: *He's a first-class/good/poor ~.* **7** [C] photograph, or one of a series of photographs taken with a movie camera: *The exterior ~s were taken in Bermuda.* **8** injection (of a drug). ***have/get/give sb a shot in the arm,*** have/give something that revives or restores, eg the economy. **9** ***a 'big shot,*** (*sl*) an important person, esp a conceited one.

'shot·gun *n* [C] sporting gun with a smooth bore firing cartridges containing shot(5).

'shot put, ⇨ 4 above.

shot² /ʃat/ *pt,pp* of shoot².

should ⇨ shall.

shoul·der /'ʃouldər/ *n* [C] **1** that part of the body of a human being or animal where an arm or foreleg is joined to the trunk, or where the wing of a bird joins its neck: *He has one ~ a little higher than the other.* ⇨ illus at arm, trunk. ***ˌshoulder to 'shoulder,*** (*fig*) united. ***give sb the cold shoulder,*** deliberately ignore him. ***stand head and shoulders above (others),*** **(a)** be considerably taller than. **(b)** (*fig*) be mentally or morally better than. ***straight from the shoulder,*** frankly. **2** (*pl*) part of the back between the shoulders: *give a child a ride on one's ~s.* **3** part of a bottle, tool, mountain, etc like a shoulder. □ *vt* **1** take the weight of responsibility: *~ a task/the responsibility for his debts.* **2** push with the shoulder: *be ~ed to one side.*

'shoulder blade, either of the flat bones of the upper back, behind and below the neck. ⇨ illus at skeleton.

'shoulder strap, (a) narrow strap on the shoulders of a military uniform. **(b)** similar strap on woman's underwear or a dress.

shouldn't /'ʃʊdənt/ = should not.

shout /ʃaut/ *n* [C] loud call or cry: *They greeted him with ~s of "Hurray for the President."* □ *vi,vt* **1** speak or call out in a loud voice: *Don't ~ at me! He ~ed to attract attention.* **2** say in a loud voice: *~ (out) one's orders. He ~ed to me/~ed for me to come. "Go back!" he ~ed.* ***shout sb down,*** shout to prevent him from being heard: *The crowd ~ed the speaker down.*

shout·ing *n* [U] shouts. ***It's/It was all over but the shouting,*** (said of a struggle, fight, etc) be finished except for the praise, cheers, etc to follow.

shove /ʃəv/ *vt,vi* (*informal*) push: *~ a boat into the water.* □ *n* [C] push: *Give it a ~.*

shovel /'ʃəvəl/ *n* [C] **1** spade-like tool, used for moving coal, sand, snow, etc. **2** large device used for the same purpose, mechanically operated from a crane in a vehicle. □ *vt* (-l-) lift, move, clear, using a shovel: *~ the snow away from the garden path; ~ a path through the snow.*

shovel·ful /-ˌfʊl/ as much as a shovel can hold.

show¹ /ʃou/ *n* **1** [U] showing (chiefly in): *by (a) ~ of hands,* (voting) by the raising of hands for or against (a proposal). **2** [C] collection of things publicly displayed, esp for competition, or as a public entertainment: *a 'flower/'horse/'cattle ~.* ***on show,*** exhibited. **3** [C] (*informal*) natural display: *Those trees make a fine ~.* **4** [C] kind of public entertainment, eg circus, theater, on radio, TV, etc: *Have you seen any good ~s lately?* **5** [C] (*informal*) performance (not theatrical, etc): *put up a good/poor ~,* do something well/badly. ***steal the show,*** attract all the attention. **6** [C] (*informal*) organization; business; something that is happening: *Who's running this ~?* Who is in control? **7** outward appearance; impression: *He didn't offer even a ~ of resistance.* **8** [U] something done to attract envy: *She does it for ~,* to make others envious. *They're fond of ~.*

'show·boat *n* [C] river steamboat on which theatrical performances were given (esp on the Mississippi).

'show business, business of entertaining the public.

'show·case *n* [C] **(a)** case with glass sides and (or) top, for displaying articles in a shop, museum, etc. **(b)** (*fig*) something intended largely for display: *The new public works project is a ~ for City Hall.*

'show·down *n* (*sl*) full and frank declaration of one's strength, intentions, etc.

'show·girl *n* [C] girl who sings or dances in a musical play, revue, etc.

'show·man /-mən/ (*pl* ~men /-men/) **(a)** organizer of public entertainments (esp circuses). **(b)** person (esp in public life) who uses publicity, etc to attract attention to himself: *Some politicians are great ~men and very little else.*

'show·place *n* [C] one that tourists go to see: *old palaces, castles and other ~places.*

showy *adj* (-ier, -iest) likely to attract attention because (too much) decorated or ornamented, or (too) brightly colored: *a ~y dress.*

show² /ʃou/ *vt,vi* (*pt* ~ed, *pp* ~n /ʃoun/) **1** cause to be seen: *You must ~ your ticket at the barrier. What films are they ~ing this week?* **2** allow to be seen: *A dark suit will not ~ the dirt. My shoes are ~ing signs of wear.* **3** be visible or noticeable: *Does the mark of the wound still ~? His fear ~ed in his eyes.* **4** be visible: *His annoyance ~ed itself in his looks.* ***show one's face,*** appear before people: *He's ashamed to ~ his face at the tennis club.* ***have nothing to show for it/sth,*** have nothing that is evidence of what one has achieved or tried to achieve. **5** give; grant: *He ~ed me great kindness.* **6** give evidence or proof of having or being: *She ~ed great courage. His new book ~s him to be a first-rate novelist.* **7** conduct a person into/out of a place: *Please ~ this gentleman out. We were ~n into the waiting-room.* **8** make clear; cause (a person) to understand: *He ~ed me how to do it/how he had done it. That ~s how little you know.* ***show sb the way,*** (*fig*) set an example. **9** ***show sb/sth off,*** display (him/it) to advantage: *a bikini that ~s* *off her figure well.* ***show off,*** make a display of one's wealth, learning, abilities, etc in order to impress people: *a man who is always ~ing off.* ***show sb/sth up,*** make the truth about (a dishonest, disreputable, etc person or thing) known: *~ up a fraud.* ***show sb up,*** attract criticism towards him: *Some children often ~ their mothers up by crying in the street.* ***show up,*** **(a)** be conspicuous, easily visible: *Her wrinkles ~ed up in the strong sunlight.* **(b)** (*informal*) put in an appearance; be present (*at*): *Three of our friends we invited to the party didn't ~ up.*

show·ing *n* (usually *sing*) (act of) displaying or pointing out; appearance: *a firm with a poor financial ~ing,* whose financial accounts do not appear to be good.

ˈshow-off *n* person who shows off: *He's a dreadful ~-off,* is always trying to attract attention, etc.

shower /ˈʃauər/ *n* [C] **1** brief fall of rain, sleet or hail; sudden sprinkle of water (as from a fountain). **2** (washing by using a) device which sprays water from above. **3** large number of things arriving together: *a ~ of stones/insults.* **4** party for a woman about to marry or have a baby, to which guests bring gifts: *Helen's friends gave her a bridal ~.* □ *vt,vi* **1** send or give, in a shower: *They ~ed the hero with honors.* **2** fall in a shower: *Good wishes ~ed* (*down*) *on the bride.* **3** have a shower (2): *I take a ~ every morning.*

show·ery *adj* (of the weather) with frequent showers.

shown *pp* of show².

shrank *pt* of shrink.

shrap·nel /ˈʃræpnəl/ *n* [U] fragments of shell or bullets packed inside a shell.

shred /ʃred/ *n* [C] **1** strip or piece scraped, torn or broken off something. **2** (*fig*) very small amount: *not a ~ of truth in what she says; not a ~ of evidence against me.* □ *vt* (-dd-) tear into shreds.

shred·der *n* [C] device for shredding food, paper etc.

shrew /ʃru/ *n* [C] **1** bad-tempered, scolding woman. **2** small animal like a mouse that feeds on insects.

shrew·ish /-ɪʃ/ *adj* scolding.

shrewd /ʃrud/ *adj* (-er, -est) **1** having, showing, sound judgment and common sense: *~ businessmen; ~ arguments.* **2** likely to be correct or effective: *make a ~ guess.*

shrewd·ly *adv*

shrewd·ness /-nɪs/ *n* [U]

shriek /ʃrik/ *vi,vt* **1** scream. **2** say, make, in a screaming voice: *~ out a warning; ~ with laughter.* □ *n* [C] scream: *~s of girlish laughter; the ~* (= whistle) *of a railroad engine.*

shrift /ʃrɪft/ *n* [U] ***get/give sb short shrift,*** get/give little attention to because not deserving: *They gave us/We got short ~.*

shrill /ʃrɪl/ *adj* (-er, -est) (of sounds, voices, etc) sharp; piercing; high-pitched: *a ~ voice/whistle.*

shrill·ness /-nɪs/ *n* [U]

shrimp /ʃrɪmp/ *n* [C] small shellfish used for food. ⇨ illus at crustacean. □ *vi* catch shrimps: *go ~ing.*

shrine /ʃrain/ *n* [C] **1** tomb or casket containing holy relics; altar or chapel with special associations or memory. **2** building or place associated with a person deeply respected or venerated.

shrink /ʃrɪŋk/ *vi,vt* (*pt* shrank /ʃræŋk/, or shrunk /ʃrəŋk/, *pp* shrunk, or, as an *adj* shrunken /ˈʃrəŋkən/) **1** make or become less, smaller (esp of cloth through wetting): *Will this soap ~ woolen clothes? They will ~ in the wash. Look at these shrunken jeans!* **2** ***shrink from/back,*** move back, show unwillingness to do something (from shame, dislike, etc): *A shy man ~s from meeting strangers.*

ˈshrink·age /-ɪdʒ/ *n* [U] process, degree, of shrinking: *The ~age in our export trade is serious.*

shrivel /ˈʃrɪvəl/ *vt,vi* (-l-, also -ll-) (cause to) become dried or curled (through heat, frost, dryness or old age): *The heat ~ed up the leaves. He has a ~ed face,* with the skin wrinkled.

shroud /ʃraud/ *n* [C] **1** cloth or sheet (to be) wrapped round a corpse. **2** something which covers and hides: *a ~ of mist.* **3** (*pl*) ropes supporting a ship's masts; ropes linking a parachute and the harness. □ *vt* **1** wrap (a corpse) in a shroud. **2** cover; hide: *~ed in darkness/mist; a crime ~ed in mystery.*

Shrove Tues·day /ˌʃrouv ˈtuzdi/ *n* (in the Christian religion) day before the beginning of Lent.

shrub /ʃrəb/ *n* [C] plant with a woody stem, lower than a tree, and (usually) with several separate stems from the root.

shrub·bery /ˈʃrəbəri/ *n* [C] (*pl* -ies) place, eg part of a garden, planted with shrubs.

shrug /ʃrəg/ *vt* (-gg-) lift (the shoulders) slightly (to show indifference, doubt, etc). ***shrug sth off,*** dismiss it as not deserving attention. □ *n* [C] such a movement: *with a ~ of the shoulders/a ~ of despair.*

shrunk, shrunken ⇨ shrink.

shuck[1] /ʃək/ *n* [C] **1** husk of an ear of Indian corn. **2** shell of a clam or oyster. □ *vt* **1** remove the husk from an ear of Indian corn. **2** open a clam or oyster and remove it from the shell.

shucks /ʃəks/ *int* used to express disappointment or suggest something is of little importance: *Shucks! Jean can't go to the movies with me.*

shud·der /ˈʃədər/ *vi* tremble as with fear or disgust: *~ with cold/horror; ~ at the sight of blood. He ~ed to think of it.* □ *n* [C] uncontrollable shaking.

shuffle /ˈʃəfəl/ *vi,vt* **1** walk without raising the feet properly. **2** move (playing cards, etc) one over the other to change their relative positions: *He ~d the papers together and put them in a drawer.* **3** do something in a careless way: *~ through one's work.* **4** (*fig*): *~ off responsibility onto others,* get rid of it by passing it to others. **5** keep shifting one's position; try to avoid giving an answer, a decision etc. □ *n* [C] **1** shuffling movement. **2** change of relative positions: *give the cards a ~.* **3** instance of dishonesty; misleading statement or action.

shun /ʃən/ *vt* (-nn-) avoid: *~ publicity/society.*

shunt /ʃənt/ *vt,vi* **1** send (railroad cars or

coaches, etc) from one track to another, esp to keep a track clear: *~ a train on to a siding.* **2** (of a train) be moved to a siding. **3** (*fig*) put aside (a project); leave (a person) unoccupied, or inactive.

shun·ter, (esp) railroad employee who shunts trains, etc.

shush /ʃəʃ/ *vi,vt* call for silence by saying "Sh!"

shut /ʃət/ *vt,vi* (*pt,pp* shut) (-tt-) (For special uses with *adverbial particles* and *prepositions,* ⇨ 4 below.) **1** move (a door, one's lips, etc) into position to stop an opening: *~ the doors and windows; ~ a drawer; ~ one's mouth.* ***shut/close one's ears/eyes to,*** deliberately ignore: *He ~ his eyes to her faults. He ~ his ears to all appeals for help.* ***shut the door on,*** refuse to consider: *Why have you ~ the door on further negotiations?* **2** become closed: *The door won't ~.* **3** bring the folding parts of (something) together: *~ a book.* (*Note: close* is more usual.) **4** (special uses with *adverbial particles* and *prepositions*):

shut (sth) down, (of a factory, etc) stop working; end activity: *The workshop has ~ down and the workers are unemployed.*

shut sb/sth in, keep or enclose: *We're ~ in by hills here,* surrounded by hills. *They ~ the boy in his bedroom,* kept him there.

shut sth off, stop the supply or flow of, eg gas, steam, water.

shut sb/sth out, keep out; exclude: *~ out immigrants/competitive goods.*

shut sth up, **(a)** close and secure all the doors and windows: *~ up a house before going away for a vacation.* **(b)** put away for safety: *~ up one's jewels in the safe.* ***shut sb up,*** (cause him to) stop talking: *Tell him to ~ up. Can't you ~ him up? Shut up!* Be quiet!

ˈshut·down *n* [C] (temporary or permanent) closing of a factory, etc.

shut·ter /ˈʃətər/ *n* [C] **1** movable cover (usually of wood and hinged) for a window, to keep out light or thieves. ***put up the shutters,*** (*fig*) stop doing business (for the day, or permanently). **2** device that opens to admit light through the lens of a camera. □ *vt* provide with, close with, shutters.

shuttle /ˈʃətəl/ *n* [C] **1** (in a loom) instrument with two pointed ends by which thread is carried between other threads. **2** (in a sewing-machine) sliding holder which carries the lower thread. □ *vt,vi* (cause to) move like a shuttle.

ˈshuttle·cock *n* [C] cork with feathers in it, hit across a net in the games of shuttlecock and badminton.

ˈshuttle service, frequent service (of trains, airlines, etc) between places not far apart.

shy[1] /ʃai/ *adj* (-er, -est) **1** (of persons) self-conscious and uncomfortable in the presence of others; (of behavior, etc) showing this: *He's not at all shy with women. She gave him a shy look/smile.* **2** (of animals, birds, fish, etc) easily frightened. **3** ***shy of,*** hesitating about: *Don't be shy of telling me what you want.* ***fight shy of,*** ⇨ fight[2](1).

shy·ly *adv*

shy·ness /-nɪs/ *n* [U]

shy[2] /ʃai/ *vi* (*pt,pp* shied /ʃaid/) (of a horse) turn aside from in fear or alarm: *The horse was shying at the hedge.*

shy[3] /ʃai/ *adv* (with or without *of* before a *noun*) short (of): lacking: *He was just shy (of) the price of admission.*

shyster /ˈʃaistər/ *n* [C] (also **shyster lawyer**) (*informal*) dishonest, petty lawyer.

Sia·mese /ˌsaiəˈmiz/ *adj, n* [C] **1** (also **Siamese twin**) (of) one of two persons joined together from birth. **2** (of an) oriental breed of cat with blue eyes and short cream, fawn or light gray hair.

sib·ling /ˈsɪblɪŋ/ *n* [C] brother or sister (the usual words).

sic /sɪk/ *adv* (*Lat*) thus (placed in brackets to show that the preceding word, statement, etc is correctly quoted, etc even though this seems unlikely or is incorrect).

sick /sɪk/ *adj* **1** *be ~,* throw up food from the stomach; *feel ~,* feel that one is about to do this. ⇨ seasick. **2** unwell; ill: *He has been ~ for six weeks.* ***sick at heart,*** very sad, disappointed. ***fall sick,*** become ill. **3** ***ˌsick (and ˈtired) of; ˌsick to ˈdeath of,*** (*informal*) very tired of, disgusted with: *I'm ~ and tired of being blamed for everything that goes wrong.* **4** ***feel sick at/about,*** (*informal*) unhappy, filled with regret: *feel ~ at failing the examination.* **5** ***sick for,*** filled with a longing for: *~ for home.* ⇨ homesick. **6** (*modern use*) perverted; basically sad: *~ humor/jokes.*

ˈsick bay, (*navy*) part of a ship for those who are ill.

ˈsick·bed, bed of a sick person.

ˈsick call, (*mil*) (daily) reporting of the sick for medical attention.

ˈsick leave, permission to be away from duty or work because of illness: *be/go on ~ leave.*

ˈsick pay, pay to an employee who is absent because ill.

sicken /ˈsɪkən/ *vi,vt* **1** get sick: *The child is starting to ~.* **2** cause to feel disgusted: *Torture is ~ing.* **3** feel sick to see: *They ~ed at the sight of so much slaughter.* **4** become tired of, disgusted with: *He ~ed of trying to bring about reforms.*

sick·en·ing /ˈsɪkənɪŋ/ *adj* disgusting; unpleasant: *~ing smells/news.*

sick·ish /ˈsɪkɪʃ/ *adj* a little sick or sickening: *feel ~; a ~ smell.*

sickle /ˈsɪkəl/ *n* [C] short-handled tool with a curved blade for cutting grass, grain, etc.

ˌsickle-cell aˈnemia, blood disease in which the red cells become sickle-like in shape.

sick·ly /ˈsɪkli/ *adj* (-ier, -iest) **1** often in poor health: *a ~ child.* **2** having the appearance of sickness or ill health: *These plants are/look rather ~.* **3** suggesting unhappiness: *a ~ smile.* **4** causing, or likely to cause, a feeling of sickness or distaste: *a ~ smell/taste.*

sick·ness /ˈsɪknɪs/ *n* **1** [U] illness; ill health. **2** [C,U] (an) illness or disease: *suffering from ˈsea ~.* **3** [U] tendency to vomit.

ˈsickness benefit, payment to a person absent from work through illness.

side[1] /said/ *n* [C] **1** one of the flat or fairly flat surfaces of a solid object: *the six ~s of a cube.*

Please carry the box with this ~ up, on top. **2** one of the surfaces which is not the top or the bottom: *A box has a top, a bottom, and four ~s.* **3** one of the surfaces which is not the top, bottom, front or back: (as an *adjective*) *the ~ entrance of the house* (not the *front* or *back* entrance). **4** (*math*) one of the lines of a figure such as a rectangle or triangle. **5** either of the two surfaces of a thin, flat object or of material such as paper: *Write on one ~ of the paper only. Which is the right ~ of the cloth,* the side intended to be seen? **6** inner or outer surface of something vertical, sloping, round or curved: *the ~ of a mountain.* **7** one of the two halves of a person on his left or right, esp from armpit to hip: *Come and sit by/at my ~.* ***ˌside by ˈside,*** close together. **8** one of the two halves of an animal from foreleg to hindleg, esp as part of a carcass: *a ~ of beef/bacon.* **9** part of an object, area, space, etc away from, at a distance from, a central line real or imaginary: *the left/right/shady/sunny ~ of the street; the east ~ of the town; the debit/credit ~ of an account.* ***on/from all sides; on/from every side,*** in/from all directions; everywhere. ***put sth on one side,*** **(a)** put it aside, apart. **(b)** postpone dealing with it. ***order sth on the side,*** (in a restaurant) a supplemental dish. **10** one of two groups or parties of people who are opposed (in games, politics, war, etc) or who hold different beliefs, opinions, etc: *be on the winning/losing ~; faults on both ~s; to pick* (= choose) *~s. The school has a strong ~,* eg a good football team. ***be on sb's side,*** be a supporter. ***let the side down,*** give an inferior performance and disappoint one's colleagues, teammates, etc. ***take sides (with),*** support (a person, a group) in a dispute. ⇨ side². **11** aspect or view that is not complete; aspect different from or opposed to other aspects: *look on the bright ~ of things/life; study all ~s of a question; a man with many ~s to his character. There are two ~s to the story,* two points of view. ***on the ˈhigh/ˈlow, etc side,*** rather high/low, etc: *Prices are on the high ~.* **12** line of descent through a parent: *a cousin on my father's ~.*

ˈside arms *n pl* **(a)** swords or bayonets, worn at the left side by soldiers. **(b)** pistol worn at the right side (usually in a holster).

ˈside·board *n* [C] table with drawers and cupboards, placed against the wall of a dining-room.

ˈside·burns *n pl* = side-whiskers.

ˈside dish, (a) food served as a supplement to the main course in a meal. **(b)** = side order.

ˈside effect, secondary or indirect effect, eg an undesirable effect of a drug used for a specific purpose.

ˈside-glance *n* [C] look to or from one side.

ˈside issue, question of less importance (in relation to the main one).

ˈside·kick *n* [C] (*informal*) companion.

ˈside·line *n* [C] **(a)** class of goods sold in addition to the chief class of goods; occupation which is not one's main work. **(b)** (*pl*) (space immediately outside either of) two lines marking the sides of a playing field, tennis court, etc.

ˈside·long *adj, adv* (directed) to or from one side: *a ˌ~long ˈglance.*

ˈside order, supplemental order of food in a restaurant, when not included with the main order: *a hamburger and a ~ order of french fries.*

ˈside road, minor road branching off a main road.

ˈside·saddle *n* [C] woman's saddle, made so that both feet may be on the same side of the horse. □ *adv* on a sidesaddle: *Not all women ride ~ saddle.*

ˈside·show *n* [C] **(a)** small show at a fair or exhibition. **(b)** activity of small importance in relation to the main activity.

ˈside·step *n* [C] step taken to one side (eg to avoid a blow in boxing). □ *vt,vi* (-pp-) **(a)** avoid (a blow, etc) by stepping to one side. **(b)** (*fig*) avoid answering (a question). **(c)** move, step, to one side.

ˈside street = side road.

ˈside·stroke *n* (kinds of) stroke used in swimming in which one side is above and the other below the water.

ˈside·swipe *vt* hit while passing: *Her car ~swiped the oncoming car on the narrow road.*

ˈside·track *n* [C] railroad siding. □ *vt* **(a)** turn (a train) into a siding. **(b)** (*fig*) turn (a person's attention) from his work.

ˈside view, view obtained from the side.

ˈside·walk *n* [C] hard, paved surface at the side of a street for people to walk on.

side·wards /-wərdz/, **sideways** /-ˌweiz/ *adv* to, toward, from, the side; with the edge first: *look ~ways at her; walk/carry a chair ~ways through a narrow opening.*

ˈside-whiskers *n pl* (of men) hair on the sides of the face near the ears.

ˈside·winder *n* [C] kind of small rattlesnake.

side² /said/ *vi* ***side with,*** take part, be on the same side (as a person in an argument or quarrel): *It is safer to ~ with the stronger party.*

-sided /-ˌsaidɪd/ *suffix* have a specified number of sides: *a ˈfive-sided shape.*

sid·ing /ˈsaidɪŋ/ *n* [C] short railroad track to and from which trains may be moved (from the main lines).

sidle /ˈsaidəl/ *vi* move (away from/up to a person) in a shy or nervous way: *The little girl ~d up to me.*

siege /sidʒ/ *n* [C,U] (period of) operations of armed forces who surround and blockade a town or fortress in order to capture it: *a ~ of 50 days.* ***lay siege to,*** attack: *lay ~ to a town.* ***raise a siege,*** end it by forcing the enemy's forces to withdraw.

si·enna /siˈenə/ *n* [U] kind of reddish-yellow earth used as a coloring matter.

sieve /sɪv/ *n* [C] utensil with wire network for separating finer grains, etc from coarse grains, etc or solids from liquids. ***have a head/memory like a sieve,*** be incapable of remembering anything. □ *vt* put through, sift with, a sieve: *sieving soil.*

sift /sɪft/ *vt,vi* **1** put, separate by putting, through a sieve: *~ the cinders.* **2** shake through a sieve: *~ flour.* **3** fall, pass, come through, as from a sieve. **4** (*fig*) examine carefully: *~ the evidence.*

sifter *n* [C] small sieve: *a* ˈ*flour ~er*.

sig. *abbr* = **1** signal. **2** signature.

sigh /sai/ *vi,vt* **1** take a deep breath that can be heard (showing sadness, tiredness, relief, etc). **2** (of the wind) make a sound like sighing. **3** feel a longing (for): *~ for the return of a lost friend.* **4** express with sighs: *~ out a prayer.* □ *n* [C] act of, sound of, sighing: *with a ~ of relief.*

sight[1] /sait/ *n* **1** [U] power of seeing: *lose one's ~*, become blind; *have long/short* or *far/near ~*, be able to see things well only at long/short range; *have good/poor ~* (= eyesight). ***know sb by sight,*** know him by his appearance only. **2** [U] seeing or being seen: *Their first ~ of land came after three days at sea.* ***catch sight of; have/get a sight of,*** begin to see; succeed in seeing: *If I ever catch ~ of him again, I'll ask for the money he owes me.* ***keep/lose sight of,*** see/no longer see; (not) forget about: *I've lost ~ of Smith. We must not lose ~ of the fact that...* ***at first sight,*** when first seen; without examination, etc: *He fell in love with her at first ~. At first ~ the problem seemed insoluble.* ***at (the) sight of,*** on seeing: *They all laughed at the ~ of the old man dancing with a girl of sixteen.* **3** [U] range of seeing; distance within which seeing is possible: *in/within/out of (one's) ~*, (of objects, etc) visible/invisible; *The train was still in ~/was not yet out of ~. Victory was not yet in ~,* not yet probable. ***in/within/out of sight of sth,*** (of the viewer) where it can/cannot be seen: *We are not yet within ~ of land,* can't see it. *We are now within ~ of finishing this job,* are near to the end. ***come into/go out of sight,*** come near enough/go too far away to be visible. ***keep out of sight,*** stay where one cannot be seen. ***not by a ˈlong ˌsight,*** by no means. ***Out of sight!*** (*sl*) marvelous! **4** [U] opinion: *All men are equal in the ~ of God.* **5** [C] something seen or worth seeing; (*pl*) noteworthy buildings, places, features, etc of a place or district: *Come and see the ~s of New York.* ***a ˌsight for ˌsore ˈeyes,*** person or thing one enjoys seeing. **6** (*sing* with *a, an*) (*informal*) person or thing that produces unfavorable comment: *What a ~ you are! She looks a ~!* **7** [C] device that helps to aim or observe when using a rifle, telescope, etc. ***draw a sight on sb/sth,*** take aim at him/it.

ˈ**sight-seeing** *n* [U] visiting sights(5) as a tourist.

ˈ**sight-seer** *n* [C] person who visits sights(5).

sight[2] /sait/ *vt* **1** get sight of, esp by coming near: *After many months at sea, Columbus ~ed land.* **2** observe (a star, etc) by using sights(7); adjust the sights(7) of a gun.

sight·ing *n* [C] occasion on which something is seen: *~ings of a new star.*

-sighted /-ˌsaitɪd/ *suffix* have the kind of sight (1) mentioned: ˈ*far-*/ˈ*long-sighted.*

sight·less /ˈsaitlɪs/ *adj* = blind (the usual word).

sign[1] /sain/ *n* [C] **1** mark, object, symbol, used to represent something: *mathematical ~s*, eg +, −, ×, ÷. **2** word or words, design, etc on a board or plate to give a warning, or to give directions: ˈ*traffic ~s*, eg for a speed limit, a bend in the road. **3** something that gives evidence, points to the existence or probability of something: *the ~s of suffering on his face. Are dark clouds a ~ of rain?* **4** movement of the hand, head, etc used with or instead of words; signal. **5** symbol and name (often painted on a board) displayed by traders and storekeepers (ˈ*shop ~s*), etc to advertise their business.

ˈ**sign·board** *n* [C] = sign(5).

ˈ**sign language,** language signed(2) by the hands, used by deaf persons, Trappist monks, and formerly by American Indians who spoke different languages.

ˈ**sign painter,** person who paints signboards.

ˈ**sign·post** *n* [C] post placed at a crossroads or road junction with signs on its arms giving directions to different places.

sign[2] /sain/ *vt,vi* **1** write one's name on (a letter, document, etc) to show that one is the writer or that one accepts or agrees with the contents: *~ a letter/a check; ~ one's name,* write it for this purpose. ***sign sb in/out,*** (at the point of entry to a building, etc) record his arrival/departure for purposes of timekeeping, etc. ***sign sth away,*** give up (rights, property, etc) by signing one's name. ***sign off,*** **(a)** end (a letter, etc) with a signature. **(b)** (radio, TV) end broadcasting (by saying goodnight, etc). ***sign sb on/up,*** (of an employer, etc) employ: *The firm ~ed on fifty more workers last week.* ***sign on/up,*** (of a worker, etc) sign an agreement about employment. **2** make known (to a person) an order or request by making signs(4): *He ~ed to me to be quiet.* (*Note: signal* is more usual.)

sig·nal /ˈsɪgnəl/ *n* [C] **1** (making of a) movement, (showing of a) light, (sending of a) message, device used, to give a warning, an order or information; order, warning, etc given in this way: ˈ*traffic ~s,* for cars, etc in the streets; ˈ*hand ~s,* made with the hand by the driver of a motor vehicle to show which way it will turn, etc. **2** event which is the immediate cause of general activity, etc: *The arrival of the President was the ~ for an outburst of cheering.* **3** electronic impulse in radio, TV, etc; sound or TV image, transmitted or received: *an area with a poor/excellent TV ~.* □ *vt,vi* (-l-) make a signal to; send by signal: *~ a message; ~ (to) the waiter to bring the menu; ~ that one is about to turn left.*

sig·naler /ˈsɪgnələr/ *n* [C] **(a)** person who signals. **(b)** signaling device.

ˈ**signal·man** /-mən/ *n* [C] (*pl* ~men /-men/) **(a)** person who operates signals on a railroad. **(b)** man who sends and receives signals (in the army and navy).

ˈ**signal tower,** building on a railroad from which signals and movements of trains are controlled.

sig·na·tory /ˈsɪgnəˌtɔri/ *n* [C] (*pl* -ies) (person, country, etc) that has signed an agreement: *the signatories to the Treaty.*

sig·na·ture /ˈsɪgnətʃər/ *n* [C] person's name signed by himself: *Can I have your ~ on these letters?*

ˈ**signature tune,** tune (a few bars of a piece of music) identifying a broadcasting station or a particular program or performer.

sig·net /ˈsɪgnɪt/ *n* [C] private seal used with or instead of a signature.

ˈsignet ring, finger ring with a signet set in it.

sig·ni·fi·cance /sɪgˈnɪfɪkəns/ *n* [U] meaning; importance: *a speech of great/little ~.*

sig·ni·fi·cant /sɪgˈnɪfɪkənt/ *adj* having a special or important meaning: *a ~ speech.*

sig·ni·fi·cant·ly *adv*

sig·ni·fi·ca·tion /ˌsɪgnɪfɪˈkeiʃən/ *n* [C] (*formal*) (intended) meaning (of a word, etc).

sig·nify /ˈsɪgnɪˌfai/ *vt,vi* (*pt,pp* -ied) (*formal*) **1** make known (one's views, intentions, purpose, etc); be a sign of; mean: *He signified his agreement/that he agreed by nodding. Does a high forehead ~ intelligence?* **2** (*formal*) be of importance: *It signifies much/little.*

Sikh /sik/ *n* member of an Indian sect believing in one God, founded in the 16th century.

si·lage /ˈsailɪdʒ/ *n* [U] kind of dry, green cattle food.

si·lence /ˈsailəns/ *n* [U] **1** condition of being quiet or silent; absence of sound: *the ~ of night/of the grave.* **2** condition of not speaking, answering (questions, spoken or written), or making comments, etc; (with *a, an*) period (of saying nothing): *Your ~ on recent events surprises me. There was a short ~ and then an uproar broke out.* ***in silence,*** silently: *listen in ~ to a speaker.* □ *vt* make (a person or thing) silent; cause to be quiet(er): *~ one's critics/the enemy's guns.*

si·lencer *n* [C] device that reduces the noise made by the exhaust of a gasoline engine, a gun, etc.

si·lent /ˈsailənt/ *adj* **1** making no or little sound; not accompanied by any sound: *a ~ prayer; with ~ footsteps.* **2** saying little or nothing; giving no answer, views, etc: *You'd better be ~ about what happened. Her husband is the strong, ~ type.* **3** written but not pronounced: *a ~ letter,* eg *b* in *doubt, w* in *wrong.*

silent ˈfilm, one without a sound track.

si·lent·ly *adv*

sil·hou·ette /ˌsɪluˈet/ *n* [C] picture in solid black showing only the outline; outline of a person or object seen against a light background: *~s of famous authors.* ***in silhouette,*** produced as a silhouette. □ *vt* (*passive*) shown, exhibited, in silhouette: *~ed against the sky.*

silk /sɪlk/ *n* **1** [U] fine, soft thread from the cocoons of certain insects; material made from this: (as an *adjective*) *~ scarves.* **2** (also as a *collective pl* in **ˈcorn·silk**) the soft tassel at the end of an ear of Indian corn.

ˈsilk·worm *n* [C] caterpillar that spins(2) silk to form a cocoon.

silken /ˈsɪlkən/ *adj* soft and smooth; soft and shining: *a ~ voice; ~ hair.*

silky /ˈsɪlki/ *adj* (-ier, -iest) soft, shiny, smooth, like silk: *a ~ voice.*

sill /sɪl/ *n* [C] flat shelf at the base of a window: *a vase of flowers on the ˈwindow ~.*

silly /ˈsɪli/ *adj* (-ier, -iest) (appearing to be) foolish: *say ~ things. How ~ of you to do that!* □ *n* [C] (*pl* -ies) (chiefly used as a term of address) silly person: *Stop worrying, ~!*

silt /sɪlt/ *n* [U] sand, mud, etc carried by moving water (and left at the mouth of a river, in a harbor, etc). □ *vt,vi* (cause to) become stopped with silt: *The sand has ~ed up the mouth of the river.*

sil·ver /ˈsɪlvər/ *n* [U] **1** shining white metal (symbol **Ag**) used for ornaments, coins, utensils, etc: *ˈtable ~,* spoons, forks, teapots, dishes, etc. **2** silver vessels, dishes, articles, eg candlesticks, trays: *have all one's ~ taken by burglars.* **3** (as an *adjective*) the color of silver: *the ~ moon.* ***Every cloud has a silver lining,*** ⇨ lining. **4** (of sounds) soft and clear: *He has a ~ tongue.* **5** silver(3) coins: *$50 in notes and $10 in ~.* □ *vt,vi* **1** coat with (something that looks like) silver: *The years have ~ed her hair.* **2** become white or silver color: *Her hair had ~ed.*

ˌsilver anniˈversary, 25th anniversary.

silver certificate, US paper currency against Treasury holdings in silver.

ˈsilver foil = tinfoil.

ˌsilver ˈmedal, medal of silver given as second prize.

ˈsilver paper, (a) = tinfoil. **(b)** paper with a metallic coating in imitation of silver sheeting or tinfoil.

ˈsilver plate, spoons, dishes, etc of silver or copper coated with silver.

ˈsilver·smith *n* [C] manufacturer of silver articles; merchant who sells these.

ˌsilver ˈwedding, 25th wedding anniversary.

sil·very *adj* like silver: *the ~y notes of a temple bell.*

simi·lar /ˈsɪmələr/ *adj* like; of the same sort: *My wife and I have ~ tastes in music. Your guitar is ~ to mine. They are ~.*

simi·lar·ly *adv*

simi·lar·ity /ˌsɪməˈlærəti/ *n* (*pl* -ies) [U] likeness; state of being similar; [C] point or respect in which there is likeness: *many ~s between the two men.*

sim·ile /ˈsɪməli/ *n* [C,U] (use of) comparison of one thing to another, eg He is as brave as a lion: *He uses interesting ~s. His style is rich in ~.*

sim·mer /ˈsɪmər/ *vi,vt* **1** be, keep (something), almost at boiling point: *Simmer the stew for an hour.* **2** be filled with anger, etc, which is only just kept under control: *~ with rage/annoyance.* ***simmer down,*** (*fig*) become calm (after being angry or excited).

sim·per /ˈsɪmpər/ *vi, n* [C] (give a) silly, self-conscious smile.

simple /ˈsɪmpəl/ *adj* (-r /ˈsɪmplər/, -st /ˈsɪmplɪst/) **1** not mixed; not divided into parts; having only a small number of parts: *a ~ machine.* **2** plain; not much decorated or ornamented: *~ food/cooking; a ~ design.* **3** not highly developed: *~ forms of life.* **4** easily done or understood; not needing great effort: *written in ~ English; a ~ task.* **5** innocent; straightforward: *as ~ as a child; ~ folk.* **6** inexperienced; easily deceived: *I'm not so ~ as to suppose you really like me.* **7** with nothing added; absolute: *a ~ fact.* ***ˌpure and ˈsimple,*** (*informal*) absolute(ly), unquestionably: *It's a case of kill or be killed, pure and ~.*

ˌsimple·ˈminded *adj* unsophisticated.

sim·ply /ˈsɪmpli/ *adv* **(a)** in a simple(2) manner:

dress simply; simply dressed. **(b)** completely; absolutely: *His pronunciation is simply terrible*, is very bad indeed. *She looks simply beautiful.* **(c)** nothing more nor less than: *He is simply a workman. It is simply a matter of working hard.*

simple·ton /ˈsɪmpəltən/ *n* [C] foolish person, esp one who is easily deceived.

sim·plic·ity /sɪmˈplɪsəti/ *n* [U] (*formal*) the state of being simple: *the ~ of the problem.* ***be simˌplicity itˈself,*** (*informal*) be extremely easy.

sim·plify /ˈsɪmpləˌfai/ *vt* (*pt,pp* -ied) make simple; make easy to do or understand: *a simplified reader/text.*

sim·pli·fi·ca·tion /ˌsɪmpləfəˈkeiʃən/ *n* [U] act or process of making simple; [C] instance of simplifying; thing simplified.

simu·late /ˈsɪmyəˌleit/ *vt* (*formal*) pretend to be; pretend to have or feel: *~d innocence/enthusiasm; insects that ~ dead leaves.*

simu·la·tion /ˌsɪmyəˈleiʃən/ *n* [U] pretense; imitation.

sim·ul·ta·neous /ˌsaiməlˈteiniəs/ *adj* happening or done at the same time: *~ signing of an agreement.*

sim·ul·ta·neous·ly *adv*

sin /sɪn/ *n* **1** [U] breaking of religious laws; behavior that is against the principles of morality. **2** [C] instance of this; immoral act such as telling a lie, stealing, adultery: *confess one's sins to a priest; ask for one's sins to be forgiven.* ***the seven deadly sins,*** pride, covetousness, lust, anger, gluttony, envy, sloth. **3** [C] (*informal*) offense against convention; something considered to be not common sense: *It's a sin to give the children so much candy. It's a sin to stay indoors on such a fine day.* □ *vi* (-nn-) commit sin; do wrong: *We are all liable to sin/capable of sinning.*

sin·ful /-fəl/ *adj* wrong; wicked.

sin·ful·ness /-nɪs/ *n* [U]

sin·ner /ˈsɪnər/ *n* [C] person who sins/has sinned.

since /sɪns/ *adv* **1** (with the perfect tenses) after a date, event, etc in the past; before the present time; between some time in the past and the present time, or the time referred to: *The town was destroyed by an earthquake ten years ago and has ~ been rebuilt. He left home in 1970 and has not been heard of ~.* ***ever since,*** throughout the whole of a period of time referred to and up to the present: *He went to Italy in 1970 and has lived there ever ~.* **2** (*dated*) (used with the simple tenses) ago (the usual word): *He did it many years ~.* □ *prep* (with perfect tenses in the main clause) after; during a period of time after: *She hasn't been home ~ her marriage.* □ *conj* **1** from the past time when: *Where have you been ~ I last saw you? How long is it ~ you were in the country?* **2** as: *Since we've no money, we can't buy it.*

sin·cere /sɪnˈsɪr/ *adj* **1** (of feelings, behavior) genuine; not pretended: *it is my ~ belief that.* **2** (of persons) not expressing feelings that are pretended.

sin·cere·ly *adv* in a sincere manner. ***Yours sincerely/Sincerely yours,*** (used before a signature at the end of a letter to a friend or informally in a business letter).

sin·cer·ity /sɪnˈserəti, -ˈsɪrəti/ *n* [U] the quality of being sincere: *speaking in all ~*, very sincerely and honestly.

sinew /ˈsɪnyu/ *n* [C] tendon (strong cord) joining a muscle to a bone.

sin·ewy /ˈsɪnyui/ *adj* tough; having strong sinews.

sing[1] /sɪŋ/ *vi,vt* (*pt* sang /sæŋ/, *pp* sung /səŋ/) **1** make musical sounds with the voice, produce words one after the other to a tune: *She ~s well. He was ~ing a French song. He was ~ing to the guitar. She sang the baby to sleep.* **2** make a humming, buzzing or ringing sound: *The kettle was ~ing (away) on the burner.* **3** celebrate in verse. ***sing sb's praises,*** praise him with enthusiasm. **4** ***sing out (for),*** shout (for).

singer *n* [C] person who sings, esp one who does this in public.

sing·ing *n* [U] (esp) art of the singer: *teach ~ing; take ˈ~ing lessons.*

sing.[2] *abbr* = singular.

singe /sɪndʒ/ *vt,vi* (*pres part* singeing) blacken the surface of by burning; burn slightly: *Careful! You're ~ing that dress!* □ *n* [C] slight burn (on cloth, etc).

single /ˈsɪŋgəl/ *adj* **1** one only; one and no more. ***in ˌsingle ˈfile,*** (moving, standing) one behind the other in a line. **2** not married: *~ men and women; remain ~.* **3** for the use of, used for, done by, one person: *a ~ bed; reserve* (at a hotel) *two ~ rooms and one double room.* □ *n* [C] **1** (*sport*) game with one person on each side. **2** unmarried man or woman (often used as an *adjective*): *a ~s bar*, a bar frequented by singles. **3** room or apartment designed for one person or family. □ *vt* ***single sb/sth out,*** select from others (for special attention, etc): *He ~d me out for criticism.*

ˌsingle-ˈbreasted *adj* (of a coat or waistcoat) having only one row of buttons down the front.

ˌsingle-ˈhanded *adj, adv* done by one person without help from others.

ˌsingle-ˈminded *adj* having, intent on, only one purpose.

sing·ly /ˈsɪŋgli/ *adv* one by one; by oneself.

sing·song /ˈsɪŋˌsɔŋ/ *n* [C] **1** (*dated*) composition in verse with a simple, repeated cadence. **2** (usually in *sing* only) monotonous cadence in speaking: *He gave the lecture in a ~.* □ *vi,vt* speak or recite something in a singsong.

sin·gu·lar /ˈsɪŋgyələr/ *adj* **1** (*dated*) uncommon; strange. **2** (*formal*) outstanding: *a man of ~ courage and honesty.* **3** (*gram*) of the form used in speaking or writing of one person or thing: *The ~ form of "children" is "child."* □ *n* [C] the singular form: *What is the ~ of "parties"?*

sin·gu·lar·ly *adv* (*formal*) strangely; peculiarly.

sin·gu·lar·ity /ˌsɪŋgyəˈlærəti/ *n* (*pl* -ies) (*formal*) [U] strangeness; [C] something unusual or strange.

sin·is·ter /ˈsɪnɪstər/ *adj* **1** suggesting evil or the likelihood of coming misfortune: *a ~ beginning.* **2** showing a bad temper; unkind: *a ~ face; ~ looks.* **3** (*formal*) of or on the left side.

sink[1] /sɪŋk/ *n* [C] **1** fixed basin (of china, steel, etc) with a drain for taking away water, usually in a kitchen or bathroom. **2** = cesspool.

sink[2] /sɪŋk/ *vi,vt* (*pt* sank /sæŋk/, *pp* sunk /səŋk/, and, as an *adjective,* sunken /ˈsəŋkən/) **1** go down, esp below the horizon or the surface of water or other liquid or a soft substance, eg mud: *The sun was ~ing in the west. Wood usually does not ~ in water, it floats. The ship sank,* went to the bottom. **2** slope downward; become lower or weaker: *The foundations have sunk.* **3** make by digging: *~ a well;* place (something) in a hole made by digging: *~ a post one foot deep in the ground.* **4** ***sink in/into,*** (of liquids, and fig) go down deep: *The rain sank into the dry ground.* **5** (*fig*) lose faith, hope, etc: *have a ~ing feeling,* feel all hope is lost. *His heart sank at the thought of failure.* **6** (*fig*) (of warnings, information) be understood, learned: *I've explained it to you often but nothing ~s in!* **7** come to a lower level or state (physical or moral): *~ into a deep sleep; ~ into crime. The old man has sunken cheeks. His voice sank to a whisper.* **8** cause or allow to sink: *~ a ship. He sank* (= lowered) *his voice to a whisper. Let us ~ our differences* (= put them out of our thoughts, forget them) *and work together.*

sink·able /-əbəl/ *adj* (of a boat, etc) that can be sunk.

sinu·ous /ˈsɪnyuəs/ *adj* (*formal*) full of curves and twists.

sinus /ˈsainəs/ *n* [C] (*pl* ~es) hollow in a bone, esp one of several air-filled cavities in the bones of the skull linked to the nostrils. ⇨ illus at skeleton.

-sion *suffix* ⇨ -tion.

Sioux /su/ *n* [C,U] (*pl* unchanged), *adj* **1** (member) of a tribe of North American Indians. ⇨ illus at Indian. **2** the language of these people.

sip /sɪp/ *vt,vi* (-pp-) drink, taking a very small quantity at a time: *sip one's coffee.* □ *n* [C] (quantity taken in a) sipping.

si·phon, syphon /ˈsaifən/ *n* [C] **1** bent or curved tube, pipe, etc so arranged (like an inverted U) that liquid will flow up through it and then down. **2** bottle from which soda water can be forced out by the pressure of gas in it. □ *vt,vi* ***siphon sth off/out,*** draw (liquid) out or off through or as if through a siphon.

sir /sər/ *n* **1** polite form used in addressing a man (esp an officer in the Armed Forces, by anyone of lesser rank) to whom one wishes to show respect: *Yes, sir.* **2** (used in letters): *My dear Sir; Dear Sir.* **3** prefix to the name of a British knight or baronet: *Sir ˌWinston ˈChurchill.*

sire /ˈsaiər/ *n* [C] **1** (*old use*) father or male ancestor. **2** male parent of an animal: *racehorses with pedigree ~s.* ⇨ dam[2]. □ *vt* (esp of horses) be the sire of: *a Kentucky Derby winner ~d by Pegasus.*

si·ren /ˈsairɪn/ *n* [C] **1** (*Greek myth*) one of a number of winged women whose songs charmed sailors and caused their destruction; (hence) woman who attracts and is dangerous to men. **2** ship's whistle for sending warnings and signals. **3** (also /ˌsaiˈrin/) device for producing a loud shrill noise (as a warning, etc): *an ambulance racing along with its ~s wailing.*

sir·loin /ˈsərˌlɔin/ *n* [C,U] best part of loin of beef.

si·sal /ˈsaisəl, ˈsɪsəl/ *n* [U] plant with leaves which provide strong fiber used for making rope.

sis·sy /ˈsɪsi/ *n* [C] (*informal*) effeminate or cowardly man or boy.

sis·ter /ˈsɪstər/ *n* [C] **1** daughter of the same parents as oneself or another person: *my/your/his ~.* ⇨ half sister, stepsister. **2** woman who behaves like a sister: *She was a ~ to him.* **3** member of a religious society; nun: *Sisters of Mercy.* **4** woman of the same society, profession, racial group etc as another.

sister·hood /-ˌhʊd/ *n* **(a)** [U] feeling as of a sister for a sister. **(b)** [C] society of women who live together in a religious order, belong to a socialist organization, do charitable works, etc.

sis·ter·ly *adj* of, like, a sister: *~ly love.*

ˈsister ship, of the same design, type, etc (as another).

sit /sɪt/ *vi,vt* (*pt,pp* sat /sæt/) (-tt-) (For special uses with *adverbial particles* and *prepositions,* ⇨ 11 below.) **1** take or be in a position in which the body is upright and supported by the buttocks (resting on the ground or on a seat): *sit on a chair/on the floor/in an armchair/at a table or desk/on a horse.* ***sit tight,*** **(a)** remain firmly in one's place, esp in the saddle. **(b)** (*informal*) hold firmly to one's opinions, not give in to opposition, etc. **2** cause to sit; place in a sitting position: *He lifted the child and sat* (= seated) *her at a little table.* **3** (of Congress, a law court, a committee, etc) hold meetings: *The Ways and Means Committee was still sitting at 3am.* **4** keep one's seat on (a horse, etc): *She sits her horse well.* **5** (of birds) rest (on a branch, fence, etc) with the body close to it: *sitting on a branch.* **6** (of domestic fowls) remain on the nest in order to hatch eggs: *That hen wants to sit.* **7** (*fig*) (of inanimate objects) occupy a position: *that clock has been sitting on the mantelpiece for over twenty years.* **8** (of clothes) suit, fit, hang: *The coat sits badly across the shoulders.* **9** act as a babysitter. **10** ***be a sitting duck,*** (*informal*) be an easy target. **11** (special uses with *adverbial particles* and *prepositions*):

sit back, **(a)** settle oneself comfortably back, eg in a chair. **(b)** (*fig*) rest (after great activity, etc). **(c)** take no (further) action.

sit down, take a seat: *Please sit down, all of you.*

sit for, **(a)** take (an examination). **(b)** pose (for one's portrait, photograph).

sit in on sth, attend (a discussion, etc) as an observer, not as a participant.

sit on sb, (*sl*) prevent him from interfering, opposing, etc. ***sit on sth,*** **(a)** be a member of (a jury, committee, etc). **(b)** (*informal*) neglect to deal with: *They've been sitting on my application for a month.*

sit out, sit outside: *sitting out in the garden.* ***sit out something*** (but ***sit it out***), **(a)** stay to the end of (a performance, etc): *Should I sit out this awful play? Yes, I'll sit it out.* **(b)** take no part in (esp a dance): *I think I'll sit out the next dance.*

sit up, not go to bed (until later than the usual time): *The nurse sat up with her patient all night.* ***sit (sb) up,*** (cause to) take a sitting position: *The patient is well enough to sit up in bed now. Sit up straight!* Don't lean back! ***(make sb) sit***

up (and take notice), (*informal*) alarm or frighten him; have one's interest (suddenly) stimulated.

ˈsit-down ˌstrike, strike by workers who refuse to leave the factory, etc until their demands are considered.

ˈsit-in *n* [C] demonstration by occupying (part of) a building.

ˈsit-up *n* [C] exercise in which one moves from a flat to a sitting-up position.

si·tar /sɪˈtar, ˈsɪˌtar/ *n* [C] kind of stringed musical instrument with a long neck. ➪ illus at string.

site /sait/ *n* [C] place where something was, is, or is to be: *a ~ for a new school; a ˈbuilding ~.* □ *vt* position; place: *Where have they decided to ~ the new factory?*

sit·ter /ˈsɪtər/ *n* [C] **1** person who is sitting for a portrait. **2** hen that sits(6): *a good/poor ~.* **3** bird or animal that is sitting and therefore easy to shoot. **4** = babysitter.

sit·ting /ˈsɪtɪŋ/ *n* [C] **1** time during which a court of law, Congress, etc is in session: *during a long ~.* **2** period of time during which one is engaged continuously in a particular occupation: *finish reading a book at one ~.* **3** act of posing for a portrait or photograph. **4** occasion of sitting down (for a meal, etc): *In this hotel 100 people can be served at one ~,* ie together. **5** collection of eggs on which a hen sits.

ˌsitting ˈduck, an easy target or victim.

situ·ated /ˈsɪtʃuˌeitɪd/ *adj* **1** (of a town, building, etc) placed: *The village is ~ in a valley.* **2** (of a person) in (certain) circumstances: *I'm badly ~ at the moment,* in difficult circumstances.

situ·ation /ˌsɪtʃuˈeiʃən/ *n* [C] **1** position (of a town, building, etc). **2** condition, state of affairs, esp at a certain time: *be in an embarrassing ~.* **3** work, employment, eg in domestic service: *Situations vacant, Situations wanted,* headings of newspaper advertisements of employment offered and asked for.

six /sɪks/ *adj, n* [C] (of) 6. ***six of one and half a dozen of the other,*** very little difference between the one and the other.

ˈsix·fold /-ˌfould/ *adj, adv* six times as much or as many or as great.

six·footer /ˌsɪksˈfʊtər/ *n* [C] person six feet tall or more.

ˈsix-gun *n* [C] (*informal*) revolver with six chambers.

ˈsix-pack *n* [C] (*informal*) package of six bottles or cans of beer, soda, etc.

ˈsix·shooter *n* [C] = six-gun.

six·teen /sɪkˈstin/ *adj, n* [C] (of) 16.

six·teenth /sɪkˈstinθ/ *adj, n* [C] (of) one of 16 (parts) or the next after 15.

sixth /sɪksθ/ *adj, n* (of) one of 6 (parts) or the next after 5.

sixth·ly *adv*

ˌsixth ˈsense, power to be aware of things independently of the five senses.

the six·ties *n pl* **(a)** of a person's age, temperature, etc) between 59 and 70. **(b)** (of a century) the years 60 to 69 inclusive.

six·ti·eth /ˈsɪkstiəθ/ *adj, n* [C] (of) one of 60 (parts) or the next after 59.

sixty /ˈsɪksti/ *adj, n* [C] (of) 60.

size[1] /saiz/ *n* **1** [U] degree of largeness or smallness: *about the ~ of* (= about as large as) *a duck's egg. They're both of a ~,* are the same size. ***cut sb down to size,*** reduce him to his correct level of (un)importance. **2** [C] one of the degrees of size in which articles of clothing, etc are made: *~ 5 shoes; three ~s too big. I take ~ 10.* □ *vt* **1** arrange according to size. **2 *size sb/sth up,*** (*informal*) form a judgment or opinion of.

siz·able /-əbəl/ *adj* fairly large.

size[2] /saiz/ *n* [U] thick substance used to glaze paper, stiffen cloth, etc. □ *vt* stiffen or treat with size.

sizing *n* = size[2].

-sized /-ˌsaizd/ *suffix* having a certain size: *ˌmedium-~ ˈeggs.*

sizzle /ˈsɪzəl/ *vi, n* [C] (*informal*) **1** (make the) hissing sound as of something cooking in fat: *sausages sizzling in the pan.* **2** (*fig*) be in a state of great heat: *a sizzling hot day.*

skate /skeit/ *n* [C] (also ***a pair of skates***) a sharp-edged steel blade to be fastened to a boot for moving smoothly over ice. ➪ roller skate. □ *vi* **1** move on skates. **2** (*fig*) ***skate over/around a difficulty/problem,*** make only passing and cautious reference to it.

ˈskate·board *n* [C] board on wheels, used to stand on and ride as a sport.

skater *n* [C] person who skates.

ˈskat·ing *n* [U] (sport of) moving on skates.

ˈskat·ing rink, specially prepared surface for skating.

ICE SKATING

ske·daddle /skɪˈdædəl/ *vi* (*informal*) leave quickly.

skein /skein/ *n* [C] length of silk or wool or thread coiled loosely into a bundle.

skel·eton /ˈskelətən/ *n* [C] **1** bony framework of an animal body; bones of an animal body in the same relative positions as in life. ***a skeleton in the closet,*** something of which a person is ashamed and which he tries to keep secret. **2** framework of a building, plan, to which details are to be added.

ˈskeleton key, one that will open a number of different locks.

ˈskeleton staff/crew/service, etc, one reduced to the smallest possible number needed.

skep·tic /ˈskeptɪk/ *n* [C] **1** person who doubts the truth of a particular claim, theory, belief, etc. **2** person who doubts the truth of a par-

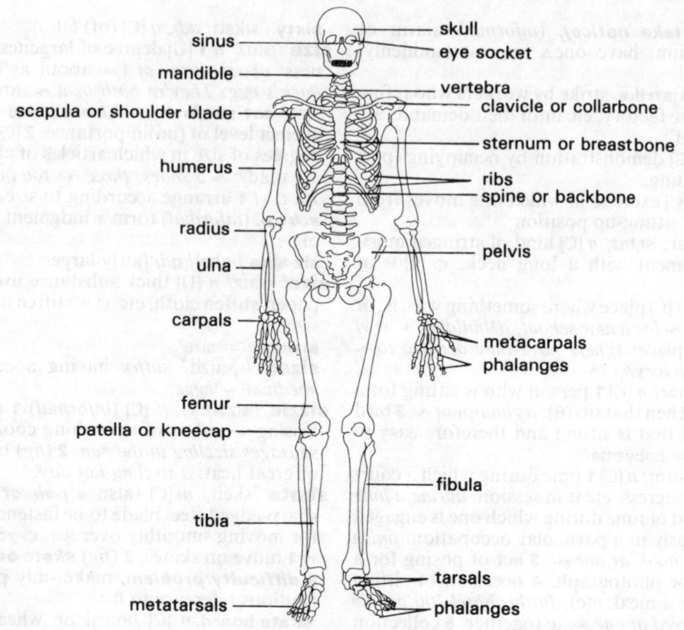

HUMAN SKELETON

ticular religion or of all religions.

skep·ti·cal /-kəl/ *adj* in the habit of not believing, of questioning the truth of claims, etc.

skep·ti·cally /-kli/ *adv*

skep·ti·cism /ˈskeptɪˌsɪzəm/ *n* [U] doubting state of mind, attitude.

sketch /sketʃ/ *n* [C] **1** rough, quickly made drawing: *make a ~ of a harbor*. **2** short account or description; general outline, without details: *He gave me a ~ of his plans for the expedition*. **3** short, humorous play or piece of writing. □ *vt,vi* **1** make a sketch of. ***sketch sth out,*** give a rough plan of; indicate without detail: *~ out plans for a new road*. **2** practice the art of making sketches: *My sister often goes into the country to ~*.

sketcher *n* [C] person who sketches(2).

sketchy *adj* (-ier, -iest) **(a)** done roughly and without detail or care. **(b)** incomplete: *He has a ~y knowledge of geography*.

skew /skyu/ *adj* twisted or turned to one side; not straight.

skewer /ˈskyuər/ *n* [C] pointed stick of wood or metal for holding meat together while cooking. □ *vt* fasten with a skewer.

ski /ski/ *n* [C] (*pl* ski or skis) one of a pair of long, narrow strips of wood, etc strapped under the feet for moving over snow. □ *vi* (*pt,pp* skied, *present participle* skiing) move over snow on skis: *go skiing*.

ˈski boot, especially made for use with skis.

skier /ˈskiər/ *n* [C] person using skis.

ˈski jump, steep slope before a sharp drop to let a skier leap through the air.

ˈski lift, seats on an overhead cable for carrying skiers uphill.

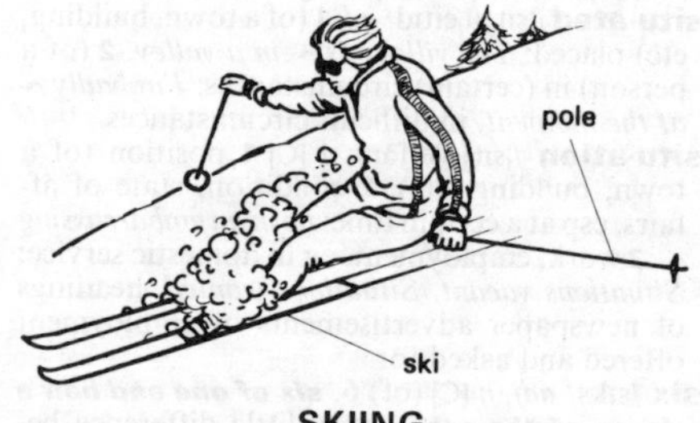

SKIING

ˈski pants, insulated pants closing at the ankles, for use with ski boots.

ˈski-plane *n* [C] aircraft fitted with skis instead of wheels, to enable it to land on snow.

ˈski suit, insulated suit for wearing while skiing.

skid /skɪd/ *n* [C] **1** slipping movement, often sideways, of the wheels of a car, etc on a slippery or icy road, or while turning a corner: *How would you get out of/correct a ~?* **2** piece of wood or metal fixed under the wheel of a cart, etc to prevent it from turning, to control the speed when going downhill. **3** log, plank, etc used to make a track over which heavy objects may be dragged or rolled. ***be on the skids,*** (*sl*) be slipping or have fallen from success in life to failure, esp as a result of chronic alcoholism. □ *vi* (-dd-) (of a car, etc) move or slip sideways, etc.

ˌskid ˈrow, (*informal*) rundown street or section of a town, esp one having cheap bars and frequented by vagrants and alcoholics.

ski·doo /skɪˈdu/ *vi* (*informal*) leave quickly.
skies *pl* of sky.
skiff /skɪf/ *n* [C] small, light, rowing boat.
skill /skɪl/ *n* **1** [U] ability to do something well. **2** [C] particular kind of skill.
skilled *adj* (needing a person who is) trained; experienced: *~ed workmen; ~ed work.*
skil·let /ˈskɪlɪt/ *n* [C] = frying pan. ⇨ fry.
skill·ful /ˈskɪlfəl/ *adj* having or showing skill.
skill·fully /-fəli/ *adv*
skim /skɪm/ *vt,vi* (-mm-) **1** remove floating matter from (the surface of a liquid): *~ milk; ~ off the grease from soup.* **2** move lightly over (a surface), not touching, or only lightly or occasionally touching (it): *The swallows were ~ming (over) the water.* **3** ***skim through sth,*** read quickly, noting only the chief points: *~ through a newspaper.*
skimp /skɪmp/ *vt,vi* supply, use, the minimum of what is needed: *They are so poor that they have to ~.*
skimpy *adj* (-ier, -iest)
skin /skɪn/ *n* **1** [U] (substance forming the) outer covering of the body of a person or animal: *We all got wet to the ~,* thoroughly wet (eg in heavy rain). ***by the ˌskin of one's ˈteeth,*** by a narrow margin. ***get under one's skin,*** (*fig*) **(a)** cause irritation or anger. **(b)** cause infatuation. ***have a thin/thick skin, be ˈthin-/ˈthick-skinned,*** (*fig*) be sensitive/insensitive; be easily hurt/not easily hurt by unkindness, criticism, swearing, etc. ***save one's skin,*** escape safely. **2** [C] animal's skin with or without the hair or fur: *ˈrabbit ~s.* **3** [C,U] outer covering of a fruit, or plant: *slip on a baˈnana ~.* ⇨ illus at fruit. **4** [C,U] thin layer that forms on boiled milk: *the ~ on a pudding.* □ *vt,vi* (-nn-) take the skin off: *~ a rabbit.*
ˌskin-ˈdeep *adj* (of beauty, feelings, etc) only on the surface; not deep or lasting.
ˈskin diver *n* [C] one who does skin diving.
ˈskin diving *n* [U] form of sport in which a person dives into and swims under the water without a diving suit, with a face mask to protect the eyes and a snorkel or aqualung to help breathing.
ˈskin·flint *n* [C] = miser.
ˈskin graft ⇨ graft[1](2).
ˈskinny *adj* (-ier, -iest) having little flesh, not fat.
ˌskin ˈtight *adj* (of clothing) fitting closely to the body.
skip[1] /skɪp/ *vi,vt* (-pp-) **1** jump lightly and quickly: *The lambs were ~ping around in the fields.* **2** jump over a rope which is turned over the head and under the feet as one jumps. **3** go from one place to another quickly: *~ over to Rome for the weekend. He ~ped off* (= left) *without saying anything to any of us.* **4** change from one subject to another when talking: *He ~s from one excuse to another.* **5** go from one part (of a book, etc) to another without reading, paying attention, etc: *We'll ~ the next chapter.* □ *n* [C] skipping movement: *a hop, a ~ and a jump.*
ˈskip rope, ˈskipping rope, length of rope with handles, used in the children's game of skipping.
skip[2] /skɪp/ *n* [C] **1** cage or bucket in which men or materials are raised and lowered in mines and quarries. **2** large metal container for carrying away builders' refuse, etc.
skip·per /ˈskɪpər/ *n* [C] captain, esp of a small merchant ship or fishing boat. □ *vt* act as captain: *~ a fishing boat.*
skir·mish /ˈskərmɪʃ/ *n* [C] fight between small parts of armies or fleets. □ *vi* engage in such a fight.
skirt /skərt/ *n* [C] **1** woman's clothing that hangs from the waist. **2** part of a dress, etc that hangs from the waist. **3** (*pl*) = outskirts (which is more usual). □ *vt,vi* be on, pass along, the edge of: *Our road ~ed the forest.*
skit /skɪt/ *n* [C] short piece of humorous writing making fun of a person, idea, style, etc: *They did a ~ on a television news broadcast.*
skit·tish /ˈskɪtɪʃ/ *adj* **1** (of horses) excitable; lively; difficult to control. **2** (*fig*) (of women) frivolous; excitable.
skit·tish·ly *adv*
skit·tish·ness /-nɪs/ *n* [U]
skulk /skəlk/ *vi* hide, move secretly, because afraid, or to avoid work or duty, or with an evil purpose: *~ing about in the corridors.*
skull /skəl/ *n* [C] **1** bony framework of the head. ⇨ illus at head, skeleton. ***have a thick skull,*** be stupid. **2** any conventionalized artistic representation of this, as a symbol of death.
skunk /skəŋk/ *n* [C] small, bush-tailed North American animal able to send out a strong disagreeable smell as a defense when attacked.
sky /skai/ *n* [C] (*pl* skies /skaiz/) the space we look up to from the earth, where we see clouds, the sun, moon and stars. (*Note:* usually *sing* with *the,* but with *a, an* when used with an *adj: a clear, blue sky,* and often *pl: The skies opened and the rain fell.*)
ˌsky-ˈblue *adj, n* [U] (of) the bright blue color of the sky on a cloudless day.
ˈsky·cap *n* porter in an airline terminal.
ˌsky-ˈhigh *adv* (*informal*) so as to reach the sky: *When the bomb exploded, the bridge was blown sky-high.*
ˈsky·lark *n* [C] small bird that sings as it flies up into the sky.
ˈsky·light *n* [C] window in a sloping roof.
ˈsky·line *n* [C] outline of hills, buildings, etc, defined against the sky: *the skyline of New York.*
ˈsky·rocket *vi* (of prices) rise quickly.
ˈsky·scraper *n* [C] very tall building.

SKYSCRAPERS: NEW YORK

sky·ward(s) /ˈskaiwərd(z)/ *adj, adv* toward the sky; upward.

sl. *abbr* = slang.

slab /slæb/ *n* [C] thick flat (usually square or rectangular) piece of stone, etc: *paved with ~s of stone; a ~ of chocolate.*

slack[1] /slæk/ *adj* (-er, -est) **1** giving little care or attention to one's work: *Don't get ~ in your work.* **2** inactive; with not much work to be done or business being done: *Trade/Business is ~ this week.* **3** loose, not tight: *a ~ rope.* **4** slow-moving: *periods of ~ water,* when the tide is neither ebbing nor flowing. □ *vi* **1** be lazy or careless in one's work: *Don't ~ off in your studies.* **2** reduce speed: *Slack up before you reach the crossroads.* **3** make (a rope, etc) loose.

slack·ly *adv*

slack·ness /-nɪs/ *n* [U]

slack[2] /slæk/ *n* **the slack,** that part of a rope, etc that hangs loosely.

slacken /ˈslækən/ *vt,vi* **1** make or become slower, less active, etc: *The ship's speed ~ed.* **2** make or become loose(r): *~ the ropes/reins.*

slacks /slæks/ *n pl* (*dated*) pants, not part of a suit, worn informally.

slag /slæg/ *n* [U] waste matter remaining when metal has been extracted from ore.

ˈslag heap, hill of slag (dumped from a mine).

slain *pp* of slay.

slake /sleik/ *vt* **1** satisfy or make less strong (thirst, desire for revenge). **2** change the chemical nature of (lime) by adding water.

sla·lom /ˈslaləm/ *n* [C] ski race along a zigzag course marked out by poles with flags.

slam /slæm/ *vt,vi* (-mm-) **1** shut violently and noisily: *~ the door (to); ~ the door in his face.* **2** be shut violently: *The door ~med.* **3** put, throw or knock with force: *She ~med the box down on the table.* □ *n* [C] **1** noise of something being slammed: *the ~ of a car door.* **2** (in whist, bridge): *a grand ~,* taking of 13 tricks; *a small ~,* taking of 12 tricks.

slan·der /ˈslændər/ *n* [C,U] (offense of making a) false statement that damages a person's reputation. □ *vt* use slander.

slan·derer *n* [C] person who uses slander.

slan·der·ous /-əs/ *adj* using or containing slander.

slang /slæŋ/ *n* [U] words, phrases, meanings of words, etc often used in conversation but not suitable for writing or for formal occasions.

slangy /ˈslæŋi/ *adj* (-ier, -iest) using slang.

slant /slænt/ *vi,vt* **1** slope: *His handwriting ~s from right to left.* **2** present information, etc so that it is seen from, and supports, a particular point of view (often prejudiced), eg in a newspaper. □ *n* [C] **1** slope. **2** (*informal*) point of view (sometimes prejudiced or biased) when thinking about something: *a new ~ on the political situation.*

slap /slæp/ *vt* (-pp-) **1** strike with the palm of the hand; smack: *She ~ped his face/~ped him on the face.* **2** put something down with a slapping noise: *He ~ped the book down on the table.* □ *n* [C] quick blow with the palm of the hand or with something flat. □ *adv* straight; directly: *The car ran ~ into the wall.*

ˈslap·dash *adj, adv* careless(ly): *a ~dash worker.*

ˈslap·happy *adj* carefree.

ˈslap·stick *n* [U] comedy with boisterous activities.

slash /slæʃ/ *vt,vi* **1** make a cut or cuts in (or at something) with sweeping strokes; strike with a whip: *His face had been ~ed with a razor blade.* **2** condemn with force and energy: *a ~ing attack on the government's policy.* **3** (*informal*) cut, reduce greatly: *~ prices/taxes/salaries.* □ *n* [C] act of slashing; long cut or gash.

slat /slæt/ *n* [C] thin narrow piece of wood, metal or plastic material, eg as in venetian blinds.

slate /sleit/ *n* **1** [U] kind of blue-gray or black stone that splits easily into thin, flat layers; [C] one of these layers, square or oblong, used for making roofs: *a ~ quarry.* **2** [C] sheet of slate in a wooden frame for writing on (as formerly used by school children). ***a clean slate,*** no cause for criticism, discredit, etc. ***wipe the slate clean,*** forgive all past offenses. **3** list of candidates running for election. □ *vt* **1** cover (a roof, etc) with slates. **2** schedule (an event, etc): *the game was ~d for the following week.*

slaty *adj* of or like slate.

slaugh·ter /ˈslɔtər/ *n* [U] **1** killing of animals (esp for food). **2** killing of many people at once: *the ~ on the roads,* the killing of people in road accidents. □ *vt* kill (animals, people) in large numbers.

slaugh·ter·er *n* [C] **(a)** person who kills animals for food. **(b)** person who kills many people.

ˈslaughter·house *n* [C] place where animals are butchered for food.

slave /sleiv/ *n* [C] **1** person who is the property of another and must serve him. **2** person compelled to work very hard for someone else: *You mustn't make ~s of your workers.* **3** person completely in the power of, under the control of, a habit, etc: *a ~ to duty/passion/convention/drink.* □ *vi* work hard: *Poor Jane! She's been slaving away (at her cooking) for three hours!*

ˈslave-driver *n* [C] (esp) person who makes those who are under him work very hard.

ˈslave ship, ship used in the slave trade.

ˈSlave States, southern states of the US in which slavery had not been abolished prior to the outbreak of the Civil War.

slav·ery /ˈsleiv(ə)ri/ *n* [U] **(a)** condition of being a slave: *sold into ~ry.* **(b)** custom of having slaves: *men who worked for the abolition of ~ry.* **(c)** hard or badly paid work.

ˈslave trade/traffic, capturing, transportation, buying and selling, of slaves.

slav·ish /ˈsleivɪʃ/ *adj* like, fit for, a slave.

slaver /ˈslævər/ *vi* let spit run from the mouth (*over*). □ *n* [U] saliva.

slaw /slɔ/ *n* [C] = coleslaw.

slay /slei/ *vt* (*pt* slew /slu/, *pp* slain /slein/) (*liter*) kill, murder.

sleazy /ˈslizi/ *adj* (-ier, -iest) (*informal*) uncared for, dirty, untidy: *a ~ hotel.*

sled /sled/ *n* [C] vehicle with runners (long, narrow strips of wood or metal) instead of wheels, used on snow, larger types (also *sleigh*) being pulled by horses or dogs and smaller types used in sport for traveling downhill at high speed. □

vi,vt (-dd-) travel or carry by sled: *go ~ding.*
sledge /sledʒ/ *n* = sled.
sledge hammer /ˈsledʒ ˌhæmər/ *n* [C] heavy hammer with a long handle, used for driving posts into the ground, and by blacksmiths.
sleek /slik/ *adj* (-er, -est) **1** (of hair, an animal's fur, etc) soft, smooth and glossy. **2** (of a person) having such hair. □ *vt* make sleek: *~ a cat's fur.*
sleep[1] /slip/ *n* **1** [U] condition of the body and mind at rest as happens regularly every night, in which the eyes are closed and the muscles, nervous system, etc are relaxed: *How many hours' ~ do you need?* **2** (with *a, an*) period of sleep: *have a short/good/restful ~.* **3** ***get to sleep,*** manage to fall asleep: *I couldn't get to ~ last night.* ***go to sleep,*** fall asleep. ***put sb to sleep,*** cause him to fall asleep.
sleep[2] /slip/ *vi,vt* (*pp,pt* slept /slept/) **1** rest in the condition of sleep, be or fall asleep: *We go to bed to ~. She slept (for) eight hours.* ***sleep like a top/log,*** very deeply, well. **2** provide beds for: *This hotel ~s 300 guests.* **3** (special uses with *adverbial particles* and *prepositions*):
sleep around, (*informal*) be promiscuous.
sleep sth off, recover from (a party, headache, etc) by sleeping: *~ off a bad headache/a hang-over.*
sleep ˈon, continue to sleep: *Don't wake him up — let him ~ on for another hour.* ***ˈsleep on sth,*** leave the answer, solution, to a problem, etc to the next day.
sleep through sth, not be woken up by (a noise, the alarm clock, etc).
sleep with sb, have sexual intercourse with.
sleeper /ˈslipər/ *n* [C] **1** person who sleeps: *a heavy/light ~,* one who is hard/easy to wake up. **2** heavy beam of wood (or similarly shaped piece of other material) to support flooring. **3** (bed or berth in a) sleeping car on a train. **4** children's sleeping garment, often one-piece pajamas with feet. **5** object or production (play, film, etc) which turns out to be more valuable or successful than expected.
ˈsleeping bag, warmly lined bag in which to sleep, eg in a tent.
ˈsleeping car, railroad coach fitted with beds or berths.
ˌsleeping ˈpartner, person who owns a share in a business but does not do any work in it.
ˈsleeping pill, one that contains a drug to encourage sleep.
ˈsleeping sickness, disease caused by the tsetse fly causing a weakening of the mental powers and (usually) death.
sleep·less /ˈsliplɪs/ *adj* without sleep: *pass a ~ night.*
sleep·less·ly *adv*
sleep·less·ness /-nɪs/ *n* [U]
sleepy /ˈslipi/ *adj* (-ier, -iest) **1** needing, ready for, sleep: *feel/look ~.* **2** (of places, etc) quiet; inactive: *a ~ little village.*
sleep·ily /-əli/ *adv*
sleet /slit/ *n* [U] falling snow or hail mixed with rain. □ *vi: It was ~ing,* sleet was falling.
sleety *adj* (-ier, -iest)
sleeve /sliv/ *n* [C] **1** part of clothing that covers all or part of the arm: *one's ˈshirt-~s.* ***(be/go) in (one's) ˈshirt-sleeves,*** wear a dress shirt without a jacket. ***have sth up one's sleeve,*** have an idea, plan, etc which one keeps secret for future use. ***laugh up one's sleeve,*** be secretly amused. **2** soft, paper envelope for a record.
sleeve·less /-lɪs/ *adj* without sleeves.
sleigh /slei/ *n* [C] sled, esp one drawn by a horse: *go for a ˈ~-ride/a ride in a ~.* □ *vi,vt* travel, carry (goods), by sleigh.
sleight /slait/ *n* (usually in) ***sleight of hand,*** great skill in using the hand(s) in performing tricks, juggling, etc.
slen·der /ˈslendər/ *adj* (-er, -est) **1** small in width or circumference compared with height or length: *~ fingers; a ~ waist.* **2** (of persons) slim: *a woman with a ~ figure.* **3** slight; inadequate: *have ~ means/hopes.*
slen·der·ness /-nɪs/ *n* [U]
slept *pt,pp* of sleep².
slew *pt* of slay.
slice /slais/ *n* [C] **1** thin, wide, flat piece cut off something, esp bread or meat. **2** part, share or price: *Smith took too big a ~ of the credit for our success.* **3** utensil with a wide, flat blade for cutting, serving or lifting (eg cooked fish, fried eggs); spatula. **4** (in games such as golf, tennis) stroke that causes the ball to go spinning off in a different direction. □ *vt,vi* **1** cut into slices: *~ (up) a loaf.* **2** (golf): *~ the ball,* ⇨ 4 above.
slick /slɪk/ *adj* (*informal*) **1** smooth; slippery: *The roads were ~ with wet mud.* **2** done smoothly and efficiently, perhaps with a little deceit: *a ~ business deal.* **3** (of a person) doing things in a slick way: *a ~ salesman.*
slide[1] /slaid/ *n* [C] **1** act of sliding(1); smooth stretch of ice, hard snow, etc on which to slide: *take a ~ on the ice.* **2** smooth slope down which persons or things can slide (eg a wooden or metal slope made for children to play on). **3** picture, diagram, etc on photographic film (and usually mounted in a frame). **4** glass plate on which is placed something to be examined under a microscope. **5** part of a machine, etc that slides (eg the U-shaped part of a trombone). **6** = landslide(1).
slide[2] /slaid/ *vi,vt* (*pt,pp* slid /slɪd/) **1** (cause to) move smoothly over, slip along, a polished surface: *children sliding on the ice. The drawers of this desk ~ in and out easily.* ***let things slide,*** not take care of, organize, do, them. **2** have, become, gradually, without being fully aware: *~ into dishonesty/bad habits.* **3** (cause to) move quickly, or so as to avoid observation: *The thief slid behind the curtains. She slid a coin into his hand.*
ˈslide rule, device of two rulers with logarithmic scales, one of which slides in a groove, used for calculating quickly.
slid·ing ˈdoor, one that is pulled across an opening (instead of turning on hinges).
ˈslid·ing scale, scale by which one thing, eg wages, goes up or down in relation to changes in something else, eg the cost of living.
slight[1] /slait/ *adj* (-er, -est) **1** slim; slender; frail-looking: *a ~ figure.* **2** small; not serious or important: *a ~ error; a ~ headache; without the ~est difficulty,* with no difficulty at all. *She takes*

offense at the ~est thing, is very easily offended.
slight·ly *adv* **(a)** slenderly: *a ~ly built boy.* **(b)** to a small degree: *The patient is ~ly better today. I know her ~ly.*
slight·ness /-nɪs/ *n* [U]

slight² /slaɪt/ *vt* treat without proper respect or courtesy: *She felt ~ed because no one spoke to her.* □ *n* [C] failure to show respect or courtesy: *suffer ~s.*

slim /slɪm/ *adj* (-mmer, -mmest) **1** slender: *a* ˌ*~-waisted* ˈ*girl.* **2** (*informal*) small; insufficient: *~ hopes/chances of success.* □ *vi* (-mm-) eat less, take exercise, etc in order to reduce one's weight and become thin: *~ming exercises.*
slim·ness /-nɪs/ *n* [U]

slime /slaɪm/ *n* [U] **1** soft, thick, sticky mud. **2** sticky substance from snails, etc: *a trail of ~.*
slimy /ˈslaɪmi/ *adj* (-ier, -iest) **(a)** of, like, covered with, slime. **(b)** (*fig*) disgustingly dishonest, flattering, etc: *That slimy boy gets everything he wants.*

sling /slɪŋ/ *n* [C] **1** band of material, length of rope, chain, etc looped around an object, eg a barrel, a broken arm, to support or lift it. **2** strip of leather (held in the hand in a loop) used to throw stones to a distance. **3** act of throwing. □ *vt,vi* (*pt,pp* slung /slən/) **1** throw with force; *young thugs ~ing stones at girls.* **2** support (something) so that it can swing, be lifted, etc: *~ a rope over the cliff; with his rifle slung over his shoulder.*
ˈ**sling·shot** *n* sling, powered by heavy rubber bands, fastened to a forked stick, for shooting pebbles, etc.

slink /slɪŋk/ *vi* (*pt,pp* slunk /slənk/) go or move (*off, away, in, out, by*) in a secret or sneaking way.

slip¹ /slɪp/ *n* [C] **1** act of slipping; false step; slight error caused by carelessness or inattention: *make a ~.* ***a* ˌ*slip of the* ˈ*tongue/*ˈ*pen,*** error in speaking/writing. ***give sb the slip,*** escape from, get away from him. **2** = pillowcase. **3** loose sleeveless women's undergarment worn under a dress or skirt. **4** young, slender person: *a* (*mere*) *~ of a boy/girl*, a slim boy/girl. **5** (usually *pl*) sloping way (of stone or timber) down to the water, on which ships are built, or pulled up out of the water for repairs. **6** stall, in or alongside a dock, at which a ship may be berthed. **7** [U] liquid clay for coating earthenware or making patterns on it.
ˈ**slip·cover** *n* [C] detachable cover for a piece of furniture.
ˈ**slip·knot** *n* [C] **(a)** knot which slips along the cord round which it is made to tighten or loosen the loop. **(b)** knot which can be undone by a pull.
ˈ**slip·stream** *n* stream of air from the propeller or jet engine of an aircraft.
ˈ**slip·way** *n* [C] = slip(5).

slip² /slɪp/ *vi,vt* (-pp-) **1** fall or almost fall as the result of losing one's balance: *He ~ped on the icy road and broke his leg.* **2** go or move quietly or quickly, esp without attracting attention: *She ~ped away/out/past without being seen. The years ~ped* (= passed) *by.* **3** move, get away, escape, fall, by being difficult to hold, or by not being balanced, fastened: *The fish ~ped out of my hand. The blanket ~ped off the bed.* ***let sth slip,*** **(a)** allow it to fall from one's hands, escape, or be neglected: *Don't let the opportunity ~ (by).* **(b)** accidentally reveal (a secret, etc). ***slip through one's fingers,*** (*fig*) fail to keep a hold on. ***slip one's mind,*** (of a name, address, message, etc) be forgotten (because one is in a hurry, busy, etc). **4** put, pull on or push off, with a quick, easy movement: *~ a coat on/off; ~ into/out of a dress.* **5** allow (small mistakes, etc) to enter, esp by carelessness: *errors that have ~ped into the text.* ***slip* ˈ*up,*** (*informal*) make a mistake. **6** move smoothly and effortlessly; go with a gliding motion: *The ship ~ped through the water.* **7** get free from; let go: *~ anchor*, detach a ship from the anchor; *~ a stitch*, (in knitting) move a stitch from one needle to the other without knitting it.
ˈ**slip-up** *n* [C] (*informal*) small mistake.

slip·per /ˈslɪpər/ *n* [C] (also ***a pair of slippers***) loose-fitting shoe worn in the house.

slip·pery /ˈslɪp(ə)ri/ *adj* (-ier, -iest) **1** (of a surface) smooth, wet, polished, etc so that it is difficult to hold, to stand on, or to move on: *~ roads.* **2** (*fig*) (of a subject) needing care: *We're on ~ ground when dealing with this subject.* **3** (*fig*) (of persons) unreliable; not to be trusted: *He's as ~ as an eel.*

slit /slɪt/ *n* [C] long, narrow cut, tear or opening. □ *vt* (*pt,pp* slit) (-tt-) **1** make a slit in; open (by slitting): *~ a man's throat; ~ an envelope open.* **2** be cut or torn lengthwise: *The shirt has ~ down the back.*

slither /ˈslɪðər/ *vi* slide or slip unsteadily: *~ down an ice-covered slope.*

sliver /ˈslɪvər/ *n* [C] **1** small, thin strip of wood; splinter. **2** thin piece cut off a large piece: *a ~ of cheese.* □ *vt,vi* break off, into, slivers.

slob /slab/ *n* [C] (*sl*) sloppy, unrefined person.

slob·ber /ˈslabər/ *vi,vt* **1** let saliva run from the mouth (as a baby does). **2** make wet with saliva: *The baby has ~ed (up) its bib.* □ *n* [U] saliva running from the mouth.

sloe /slou/ *n* [C] small, bluish-black wild plum, fruit of the blackthorn.

slog /slag, slɔg/ *vi,vt* (-gg-) **1** = slug³. **2** walk, work, etc long and hard: *~ging away at one's work; ~ging along the road.*
slog·ger *n* [C] person who slogs.

slo·gan /ˈslougən/ *n* [C] striking and easily remembered phrase used to advertise something, or to make clear the aim(s) of a group, organization, campaign, etc: *political ~s.*

sloop /slup/ *n* [C] small one-masted sailing ship.

slop /slap/ *vi,vt* (-pp-) **1** (of liquids) spill over the edge: *The tea ~ped (over) into the saucer.* **2** cause to spill: *~ beer over the counter in a bar.* **3** empty buckets containing urine, etc: *The prisoners had to ~ out every morning.* **4** make a mess with: *~ing paint all over the floor.* **5** splash: *Why do some children love ~ping around in puddles?* □ *n* **1** (*pl*) dirty waste water from the kitchen or from bedrooms (where there are no basins with running water and drains). **2** (*pl*) urine, excrement (in buckets, as in prison cell). **3** [U] liquid food, eg milk, soup, esp for people who are ill. **4** [U] swill (for pigs).

slope /sloup/ *n* **1** [C,U] slanting line; position or direction at an angle, less than 90°, to the earth's surface or to another flat surface: *the ~ of a roof; a hill with a ~ of 1 in 5.* **2** area of rising or falling ground: *ˈmountain ~s; ˈski ~s.* □ *vi,vt* **1** have a slope: *Our garden ~s (down) to the river.* **2** cause to slope. **3** (*informal*) ***slope off,*** go off or away (to avoid somebody, or escape doing something): *children sloping off after a meal to escape washing the dishes.*

sloppy /ˈslapi/ *adj* (-ier, -iest) **1** wet or dirty with rain, etc; full of puddles: *The melting snow made the roads ~.* **2** (*informal*) not done with or using care and thoroughness: *a ~ piece of work/workman.* **3** (*informal*) foolishly sentimental; weakly emotional: *~ talk about girlfriends and boyfriends.*

slop·pily /-əli/ *adv* in a careless manner: *sloppily* (= carelessly) *dressed.*

slop·pi·ness /ˈslapinɪs/ *n* [U]

slosh /slaʃ/ *vt,vi* **1** splash around in water or mud. **2** throw water or other liquid.

sloshed *adj* (*informal*) drunk.

slot /slat/ *n* [C] **1** narrow opening through which something is to be put, eg for a coin in a machine to buy something, eg tickets, cigarettes, candy. **2** slit, groove or channel into which something fits or along which it slides. **3** (*informal*) right or suitable place for something (in a broadcast program, scheme, etc): *too many advertising ~s.* □ *vt* (-tt-) make a slot in; place as if into a slot: *~ 30,000 graduates a year into jobs,* find jobs for them.

sloth /sloθ/ *n* **1** [U] laziness; idleness. **2** [C] South American mammal which lives in the branches of trees and moves very slowly.

sloth·ful /-fəl/ *adj* inactive; lazy.

slouch /slautʃ/ *vi* stand, sit or move, in a lazy, tired way: *boys who ~ around at street corners all day.* □ *n* [C] lazy attitude or way of walking: *walk with a ~.*

sloven /ˈsləvən/ *n* [C] person who is untidy, dirty.

sloven·ly /ˈsləvənli/ *adj* untidy, dirty, careless: *a ~ appearance*

slow[1] /slou/ *adj* (-er, -est) **1** not quick; taking a long time: *a ~ runner; a ~ journey.* **2** at less than the usual rate or speed. ***in slow motion,*** (of a moving picture) with the number of exposures per second greatly increased (so that when the film is shown at normal rate the action appears to be slow). **3** not quick to learn: *a ~ child.* **4** not acting immediately; acting only after a time; *~ poison. He is ~ to anger/~ to make up his mind.* **5** (of watches and clocks) showing a time behind the correct time (eg 1:55 when it is 2:00): *That clock is five minutes ~.* **6** not sufficiently interesting or lively: *We thought the party was rather ~.* **7** (of a surface) of such a nature that what moves over it (esp a ball) tends to do so at a reduced speed: *a ~ track.*

ˈslow·poke *n* [C] (*sl*) person who is slow in action.

slow[2] /slou/ *adv* (-er, -est) **1** at a low speed; slowly: *Tell the driver to go ~er.* ***go slow,*** be less active: *You ought to go ~ until you feel really well again.* **2** ˌ*~-ˈgoing/-ˈmoving/-ˈspoken,* going/moving/speaking slowly.

slow[3] /slou/ *vi,vt* (cause to) go, work, etc at a slower speed: *Slow up/down before you reach the crossroads. You should ~ up a bit* (= stop working so hard) *if you want to avoid a breakdown.*

ˈslow·down *n* [C] protest (by workers in a factory, etc to draw attention to demands, etc) carried out by working more slowly than normal.

sludge /slədʒ/ *n* [U] **1** thick, greasy mud. **2** thick, dirty oil or grease.

slug[1] /sləg/ *n* [C] slow-moving creature like a snail but without a shell. ⇨ illus at mollusk.

slug[2] /sləg/ *n* [C] **1** bullet. ***put a slug in sb,*** shoot him. **2** strip of metal with a line of type along one edge. **3** coin-size metal disk, esp one used as a makeshift substitute for a coin or token in a machine, turnstyle, etc. **4** (*sl*) small portion or mouthful of strong liquor.

slug[3] /sləg/ *vt,vi* (-gg-) (*informal*) hit hard (a ball, etc); punch.

slug·gish /ˈsləgɪʃ/ *adj* inactive; slow-moving: *a ~ river; feeling ~.*

sluice /slus/ *n* [C] **1** apparatus, device, for regulating the level of water by controlling the flow into or out of (a canal, lake, etc). **2** artificial water channel, eg one made by gold miners for rinsing gold from sand and dirt. **3** flow of water above, through or below a floodgate. □ *vt,vi* **1** send a stream of water over; wash with a stream of water: *~ ore,* to separate it from gravel, etc. **2** ***sluice out,*** (of water) rush out as from a sluice.

ˈsluice gate/valve = sluice(1).

ˈsluice·way *n* [C] = sluice(2).

slum /sləm/ *n* [C] street of dirty, crowded houses; such a house: *live in a ~.* □ *vi* (-mm-) (usually in ***go slumming***) frequent a lower-class neighborhood in search of entertainment, etc.

slummy *adj* of slums: *a ~my part of the town.*

slum·ber /ˈsləmbər/ *vi,vt* (*liter*) **1** sleep peacefully or comfortably. **2** pass (time) in sleep: *~ away a hot afternoon.* □ *n* sleep.

slump /sləmp/ *vi* **1** drop or fall heavily: *Tired from his walk, he ~ed into a chair.* **2** (of prices, trade, business activity) fall steeply or suddenly. □ *n* [C] general drop in prices, trade activity, etc; business depression.

slung *pt,pp* of sling.

slunk *pt,pp* of slink.

slur /slər/ *vt,vi* (-rr-) **1** join (sounds, letters, words) so that they are indistinct. **2** (*music*) sing or play a series of notes in a smooth or gliding manner. **3** deal quickly with in an attempt to conceal: *He ~red over the dead man's faults and spoke chiefly of his virtues.* □ *n* [C] **1** suggestion of having done wrong: *cast a ~ on her reputation; keep one's reputation free from (all) ~s.* **2** act of slurring sounds. **3** (*music*) mark used to show that two or more notes should be sung or played as one syllable or slurred (2). ⇨ illus at notation.

slush /sləʃ/ *n* [U] **1** melting, dirty snow. **2** (*fig*) foolish sentiment.

ˈslush fund, one used for bribes.

slut /slət/ *n* [C] slovenly or immoral woman.
slut·tish /-ɪʃ/ *adj*
sly /slai/ *adj* (-er, -est) deceitful; keeping or doing things secretly; seeming to have, suggesting, secret knowledge: *a sly look.* ***on the sly,*** secretly.
sly·ly *adv*
sly·ness /-nɪs/ *n* [U]
sm. *abbr* = small.
smack[1] /ˈsmæk/ *n* [C] (sound of a) blow given with the open hand; sound of the lips parted suddenly or of a whip: *with a ~ of the lips,* with this sound (suggesting enjoyment of food or drink). □ *vt* **1** strike with the open hand: *If you say that again, I'll ~ you in the face.* **2** part the lips with a smacking sound to show pleasure (at food or drink, etc). □ *adv* in a sudden and violent way: *It hit me ~ in the eye.*
smack·ing *n* act or occasion of hitting with the palm of the hand: *The child needs a good ~ing.*
smack[2] /ˈsmæk/ *n* [C] small sailing boat for fishing.
smack[3] /ˈsmæk/ *vi* have a slight flavor or suggestion (*of*): *opinions that ~ of heresy.*
small /smɔl/ *adj* (-er, -est) (opposite of *large*) **1** not large in degree, size, etc: *a ~ town/room/audience/sum of money.* ***on the ˈsmall side,*** a little too small. **2** not doing things on a large scale: *~ farmers/businessmen/shopkeepers.* **3** unimportant, trifling. **4** morally mean; ungenerous: *Only a ~ man/a man with a ~ mind would behave so badly.* **5** of low social position: *great and ~,* all classes of people. **6** ***in a ˈsmall way,*** modestly, unpretentiously: *He contributed to scientific progress in a ~ way.* **7** little or no: *have ~ cause for gratitude. He failed, and ~ wonder,* it is not surprising. □ *n* (with *the*) slenderest part: *the ~ of the back.*
ˈsmall arms *n pl* weapons light enough to be carried in the hand by a soldier.
small ˈchange, (a) coins of small value: *Can you give me ~ change for this dollar bill?* **(b)** (*fig*) insignificant matter(s).
ˈsmall-fry *n* person(s) of no importance.
the small hours *n pl* the three or four hours after midnight.
small ˈletters *n pl* not capitals.
ˌsmall-ˈminded *adj* mean; ungenerous.
small·ness /-nɪs/ *n* [U]
ˈsmall·pox *n* [U] serious contagious disease which leaves permanent marks on the skin.
ˈsmall talk, gossip about everyday and unimportant social matters.
ˈsmall·time *adj* (*informal*) of minor importance; third-rate.
smart[1] /smart/ *adj* (-er, -est) **1** bright; new-looking; clean; well-dressed: *a ~ dress/suit/car. You look very ~.* **2** fashionable; part of high society: *the ˈ~ set.* **3** clever; skillful; having a good, quick brain: *a ~ student/officer.* **4** quick; brisk: *walk at a ~ pace.* **5** severe: *a ~ rebuke; a ~ slap on the ear.*
ˈsmart aleck, (*informal*) conceited person; a know-it-all.
smart·ly *adv*
smart·ness /-nɪs/ *n* [U]
smarty /ˈsmarti/ (*informal*) = smart aleck.

smart[2] /smart/ *vt* feel or cause a sharp pain (of body or mind): *The smoke made my eyes ~. She was ~ing with anger.* □ *n* [U] sharp pain, bodily or mental: *The ~ of his wound kept him awake.*
smarten /ˈsmartən/ *vt, vi* make or become smart(1,4): *~ oneself up to see visitors.*
smash /smæʃ/ *vt,vi* **1** break, be broken, with force into small pieces: *~ a window. The firemen ~ed in/down the doors.* **2** rush, force a way (*into, through, etc*): *The car ~ed into a wall.* **3** defeat thoroughly: *~ the enemy.* ***smash a record,*** (in sport, etc) set up a far better record. **4** (*tennis*) hit (a ball) downward over the net with a hard, overhand stroke. **5** (of a business firm) go bankrupt. □ *n* [C] **1** breaking to pieces. **2** (*tennis, etc*) stroke in which the ball is brought swiftly down. □ *adv* with a smash: *go/run ~ into a wall.*
ˈsmash·up *n* [C] collision (of cars, trains, etc).
smat·ter·ing /ˈsmætərɪŋ/ *n* (usually *sing* with *a, an*) slight knowledge (*of* a subject): *a ~ of French.*
smear /smɪr/ *vt,vi* **1** cover or mark with something oily or sticky; spread (something oily, etc) on: *~ one's hands with grease; hands ~ed with blood.* **2** make dirty, greasy marks on. **3** (*fig*) defame (a person, his reputation). ***a ~ campaign,*** effort to discredit a person. □ *n* [C] mark made by smearing: *a ~ of paint.*
smell[1] /smel/ *n* **1** [U] that one of the five senses special to the nose: *Smell is more acute in dogs than in men.* **2** [C,U] that which is noticed by means of the nose; quality that affects this sense: *What a nice/horrible/unusual ~!* **3** (used without an *adj*) bad or unpleasant quality that affects the nose: *What a ~!* **4** (usually *sing* with *a, an*) act of breathing in through the nose to get the smell(2) of: *Have a ~ of this egg and tell me whether it's good.*
smell[2] /smel/ *vt,vi* (*pt,pp* smelt /smelt/) **1** (not used in the progressive tenses; often used with *can, could*) be aware of through the sense of smell: *Can/Do you ~ anything unusual? I can ~ something burning.* ***smell a rat,*** ⇨ rat(1). **2** (use with progressive tenses possible) use one's sense of smell in order to learn something: *Smell this and tell me what it is.* ***smell sth out,*** **(a)** discover by means of the sense of smell. **(b)** (*fig*) discover by intuition. **3** (not used in the progressive tenses) have the sense of smell: *Do/Can fishes ~?* **4** give out a smell (of the kind specified by an *adj* or *adv*); suggest or recall the smell (of): *The flowers ~ sweet. Your breath ~s of brandy.* (*Note:* if there is no *adj*, the suggestion is usually something unpleasant): *His breath/He ~s.*
ˈsmelling salts *n pl* sharp-smelling substances to be sniffed as a cure for faintness, etc.
smelly *adj* (-ier, -iest) (*informal*) having a bad smell: *~y feet.*
smelt[1] /smelt/ *vt* melt (ore); separate (metal) from ore by doing this.
smelt[2] /smelt/ *n* [C] (*pl* ~s or unchanged) kind of edible fish.
smelt[3] *pp,pt* of smell[2].
smidgen, smidgin /ˈsmɪdʒɪn/ *n* [C] (*informal*) small bit or portion.
smile /ˈsmaiəl/ *n* [C] pleased, happy, amused or other expression on the face, with (usually a

parting of the lips and) loosening of the face muscles: *There was a pleasant/amused ~ on her face. He was all ~s*, looked very happy. □ *vi,vt* (*pres p* smiling /ˈsmailıŋ/) **1** give a smile; show pleasure, amusement, sympathy, contempt, etc by this means: *He never ~s. What are you smiling at?* **2** express by means of a smile: *Father ~d his approval.* **3** give the kind of smile indicated: *~ sweetly.*

smirch /smərtʃ/ *vt* **1** make dirty. **2** (*fig*) dishonor. □ *n* [C] (*fig*) blot or stain.

smirk /smərk/ *vi, n* [C] (give a) silly, self-satisfied smile.

smite /smait/ *vt,vi* (*pt* smote /smout/, *pp* smitten /ˈsmıtən/) (*old use*) **1** strike; hit hard: *The sound of an explosion smote our ears.* **2** affect greatly: *He was smitten with guilt/smitten with that pretty girl.* **3** defeat utterly: *God will ~ our enemies.*

smith /smıθ/ *n* [C] worker in iron or other metals: *a ˈblack~.*

smithy /ˈsmıθi/ *n* [C] blacksmith's workshop.

smith·er·eens /ˌsmıðəˈrinz/ *n pl* small fragments: *broken into ~.*

smit·ten *pp* of smite.

smock /smak/ *n* [C] loose shirt (with smocking on it).

smock·ing *n* [U] kind of ornamentation on clothing made by gathering the cloth tightly with stitched patterns.

smog /smag, smɔg/ *n* [U] fog with smoke, exhaust fumes from motor vehicles, etc.

smoke[1] /smouk/ *n* **1** [U] visible vapor with particles of carbon, etc coming from a burning substance: *~ pouring from factory chimneys; ˌcigaˈrette ~.* ***go up in smoke,*** **(a)** be burned up. **(b)** (*fig*) be without result, leave nothing permanent or worth while behind. **2** [C] (act of smoking) a cigarette, etc: *stop working and have a ~.*

ˈsmoke screen, (a) clouds of smoke made to hide military operations. **(b)** (*fig*) explanation, etc designed to mislead people about one's real intentions, etc.

smoke·less *adj* that burns without smoke: *~less fuel.*

ˈsmoke·stack, (a) outlet for smoke and steam from a steamship. **(b)** tall chimney.

smoky *adj* (-ier, -iest) **(a)** full of smoke: *smoky chimneys/fires.* **(b)** like smoke in smell, taste or appearance.

smoke[2] /smouk/ *vi,vt* **1** give out smoke, or something thought to be like smoke, eg visible vapor or steam: *a smoking volcano.* **2** (of a fire or fireplace) send out smoke into the room (instead of up the chimney): *This fireplace ~s badly.* **3** draw in and let out the smoke of burning tobacco or other substance: *~ a pipe/cigar.* **4** bring (oneself) into a specific state by smoking tobacco: *He ~d himself sick.* **5** dry and preserve (meat, fish) with smoke (from wood fires). **6** stain, darken, dry, with smoke: *~d glass*, eg through which to look at the sun. **7** send smoke on to (plants, insects) (to kill pests). ***smoke sth out,*** force to leave by smoking: *~ out snakes from a hole.*

smoker *n* [C] person who habitually smokes tobacco.

smol·der /ˈsmouldər/ *vi* **1** burn slowly without flame. **2** (*fig*) (of feelings, etc) exist but be unseen, undetected, suppressed, etc: *~ing discontent/hatred.* □ *n* [U] slow burning: *The ~ became a blaze.*

smooth /smuð/ *adj* (-er, -est) **1** having a surface like that of glass; free from roughness: *~ paper/skin; ~ to the touch; a ~ sea*, calm, free from waves. ***take the ˌrough with the ˈsmooth,*** accept what is unpleasant with what is pleasant. **2** (of movement) free from shaking, bumping, etc: *a ~ ride in a car.* **3** (of a liquid mixture) free from lumps; well beaten or mixed: *mix to a ~ paste.* **4** free from harshness of sound or taste; flowing easily: *a ~ voice; ~ wine/whiskey.* **5** (of a person, his manner) flattering, polite (often with a suggestion of insincerity): *~ manners.* □ *vt,vi* **1** make smooth: *~ away/over obstacles/difficulties*, get rid of them. **2** become calm: *The sea has ~ed down.* □ *n* [C] act of smoothing: *give one's hair a ~.*

smooth·ly *adv* in a smooth manner: *Things are not going very ~ly*, There are troubles, obstacles, interruptions, etc.

smooth·ness /-nıs/ *n* [U]

smote *pt* of smite.

smother /ˈsməðər/ *vt* **1** cause the death of, by stopping the breath of or by keeping air from. **2** put out (a fire); keep (a fire) down (so that it burns slowly) by covering *with* ashes, sand, etc. **3** cover, wrap up: *~ a grave with flowers/a child with kisses/one's wife with kindness; be ~ed with/in dust by passing cars.* **4** suppress; hold back: *~ a yawn/one's anger.* □ *n* (usually *sing* with *a, an*) cloud of dust, smoke, steam, spray, etc.

smudge /smədʒ/ *n* [C] dirty mark: *You've got a ~ on your cheek.* □ *vt,vi* **1** make a smudge on. **2** (of ink, paint, etc) become blurred or smeared: *Ink ~s easily.*

smug /sməg/ *adj* (-gger, -ggest) having, showing, a character that is easily satisfied and without imagination, kindness for others, etc: *a ~ smile/young man.*

smug·ly *adv*

smug·ness /-nıs/ *n* [U]

smuggle /ˈsməgəl/ *vt* **1** get (goods) secretly and illegally (*into, out of*, a country, *through* the customs, *across* a frontier): *smuggling drugs into the US.* **2** take (a person or thing) secretly and in defiance of rules and regulations: *~ a letter/news into a prison.*

smug·gler /ˈsməglər/ *n* [C] person who smuggles.

smut /smət/ *n* **1** [C] (mark or stain made by a) bit of soot, dirt, etc. **2** [U] disease of corn, wheat, etc, that causes the ears to turn black. **3** [U] indecent or obscene words, topics: *Don't talk ~.* □ *vt* (-tt-) mark with smuts(1).

smutty *adj* (-ier, -iest) **(a)** dirty with smuts. **(b)** containing smut(3): *~ty stories.*

snack /snæk/ *n* [C] light meal (sandwiches, potato chips, etc).

ˈsnack bar, where snacks may be bought and eaten.

snag /snæg/ *n* [C] **1** rough or sharp object, root

of a tree, hidden rock, which may be a source of danger. **2** (*informal*) hidden, unknown or unexpected difficulty or obstacle: *There's a ~ in this plan somewhere.*

snail /ˈsneiəl/ *n* [C] kinds of animal with a soft body, no limbs and with a spiral shell. ⇨ illus at mollusk. ***at a ˈsnail's pace,*** very slowly.

snake /sneik/ *n* [C] **1** kinds of long, legless reptile, some of which are poisonous. **2** (*fig*) insincere, harmful person who pretends to be a friend. □ *vi* move in twists and glides: *The road ~s through the mountains.*

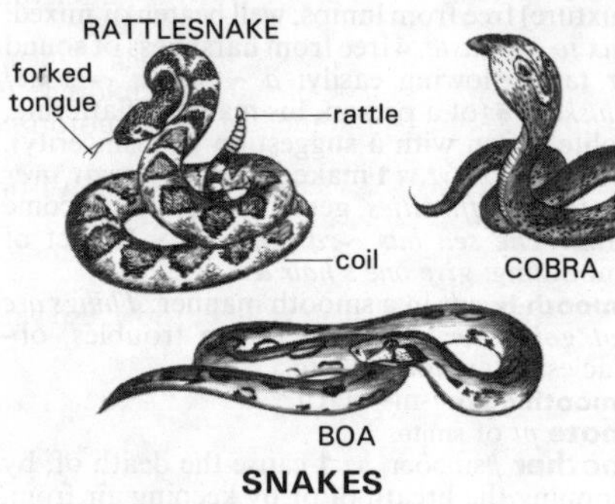

SNAKES

ˈsnake charmer, person who can control snakes with music.

snap /snæp/ *vt,vi* (-pp-) **1** (try to) catch with the teeth: *The dog ~ped at my leg.* **2** (*fig*) (try to) catch quickly: *They ~ped at the offer,* offered eagerly to accept it. ***snap sth up,*** buy eagerly: *The cheapest clothes were quickly ~ped up.* **3** break with a sharp crack; open or close with; make a sudden, sharp sound: *The rope ~ped. He ~ped down the lid of the box.* **4** say (something) quickly, sharply: *The sergeant ~ped out his orders.* ***snap at sb,*** speak to him in an angry, sharp voice. **5** take a photograph of. **6** ***snap out of it,*** get out of a mood, habit, etc. □ *n* [C] **1** act or sound of snapping: *The dog made a ~ at the meat. The lid shut with a ~.* **2** = cold snap. **3** kinds of small, crisp cookie: *ˈginger~s.* **4** = snapshot. **5** (*informal*) easy task: *It's a ~.* (also as an *adjective*) **(a)** quickly and easily done: *a ~ course.* **(b)** done with little or no warning: *a ~ decision.*

ˈsnap·dragon *n* [C] inds of plant with flowers that open when pressed.

snappy *adj* (-ier, -iest) bright; lively: *Make it ~py!* (*informal*) Hurry up!

ˈsnap·shot *n* [C] quickly taken photograph with a hand camera.

snare /snær/ *n* [C] **1** trap for catching small animals and birds. **2** (*fig*) something that tempts one to expose oneself to defeat, disgrace, loss, etc: *His promises are a ~ and a delusion.* □ *vt* catch in a snare: *~ a rabbit.*

snarl[1] /snarl/ *vi,vt* **1** (of dogs) show the teeth and growl (at). **2** (of persons) speak in an angry voice. □ *n* [C] act, sound, of snarling.

snarl[2] /snarl/ *n* [C] tangle; confused state: *the ˈtraffic ~s in a big town.* □ *vt,vi* (cause to) become jammed: *The traffic* (*was*) *~ed up.*

snatch /snætʃ/ *vt,vi* **1** put out the hand suddenly and take: *He ~ed the letter from me/~ed the letter out of my hand. He ~ed at* (ie tried to seize) *the letter but was not quick enough.* **2** get quickly or when a chance occurs: *~ an hour's sleep/meal; ~ a kiss.* □ *n* [C] **1** act of snatching: *make a snatch at the letter.* **2** (as an *adjective*): *a ~ decision,* made quickly. **3** short outburst or period: *overhear ~es of conversation.*

snatcher, person who snatches: *a purse ~er.*

sneak /snik/ *vi,vt* (*Note:* the only *pt, pp* considered fully correct is ~ed, though snuck /snək/ may often be heard in *informal* speech.) go quietly and secretly (*in, out, away, back, past,* etc). □ *n* [C] (*informal*) cowardly, harmful person.

sneak·ing *adj* **(a)** secret, sly: *have a ~ing respect/sympathy for him,* respect, etc which is not shown openly. **(b)** *a ~ing suspicion,* a vague, puzzling one.

sneak·ers /ˈsnikərz/ *n pl* (also ***a pair of sneakers***) canvas shoes soled with rope, rubber or some other substance; tennis shoes.

sneer /snɪr/ *vi* show contempt by using a wrinkled nose and an insincere smile (and perhaps despising words): *~ at religion.* □ *n* [C] sneering look, smile, etc.

sneer·ing·ly *adv*

sneeze /sniz/ *n* [C] sudden, uncontrollable outburst of air through the nose and mouth: *Coughs and ~s spread diseases.* □ *vi* make a sneeze: *sneezing into a handkerchief.* ***not to be sneezed at,*** (*informal*) worth having even though it is small: *A prize of $50 is not to be ~d at.*

snicker /ˈsnɪkər/ *n* [C] short giggle (esp at something improper, or in a cynical manner). □ *vi* laugh in this way.

snide /snaid/ *adj* sneering; slyly critical: *~ remarks about their friendship.*

sniff /snɪf/ *vi,vt* **1** draw air in through the nose so that there is a sound: *~ing and sneezing.* **2** sniff(1) to show disapproval or contempt. **3** draw in through the nose as one breathes: *~ the sea air; ~* (*at*) *a rose. The dog was ~ing* (*at*) *the lamppost.* □ *n* [C] act or sound of sniffing; breath (of air, etc): *One ~ of this stuff is enough to kill you.*

sniffle /ˈsnɪfəl/ *vi* make sniffing sounds; breathe noisily (as when the nose is partly stopped up). □ *n* [C] act or sound of sniffling.

snig·ger /ˈsnɪgər/ = snicker.

snip /snɪp/ *vt,vi* (-pp-) cut with scissors or shears, esp in short, quick strokes: *~ off the ends of the string.* □ *n* [C] cut made by snipping; thing cut off (something large).

snipe[1] /snaip/ *n* [C] (*pl* ~s or unchanged) bird with a long bill which lives in marshes.

snipe[2] /snaip/ *vi,vt* fire shots (at) from a hiding place, usually at long range; kill or hit in this way.

sniper *n* [C] person who snipes.

snip·pet /ˈsnɪpɪt/ *n* [C] **1** small piece cut off: *a ~ of cloth to use as a sample.* **2** (*pl*) bits (of information, news, etc): *catch only ~s of conversation.*

snitch /snɪtʃ/ *vt,vi* (*sl*) **1** steal (something of little or no value). **2** inform (*on* a person).

snivel /ˈsnɪvəl/ *vi* cry from insincere grief, sorrow or fear; complain, cry, in a miserable way: *a harassed woman with six ~ing children*.

snob /snab/ *n* [C] person who pays too much respect to social position or wealth, or who dislikes persons who are of lower social position: ˈ*~ appeal*, power to attract the interest of snobs.

snob·bery /ˈsnabəri/ *n* [U] state, quality, of being snobbish.

snob·bish /-ɪʃ/ *adj* of or like a snob.

snob·bish·ly *adv*

snooker /ˈsnukər/ *n* [U] game played with 15 red balls and 6 balls of other colors on a billiard table.

snoop /snup/ *vi* ***snoop into,*** enquire into matters one is not properly concerned with. ***snoop around,*** look for faults, breaking of laws, etc (to gain an advantage). □ *n* [C] = snooper.

snooper *n* [C] **(a)** one who snoops. **(b)** (*sl*) (esp private) detective.

ˈ**snooper·scope** *n* [C] device for seeing in the dark with infrared rays.

snooty /ˈsnuti/ *adj* (-ier, -iest) (*informal*) snobbish.

snoot·ily /-əli/ *adv*

snooze /snuz/ *vi, n* [C] (*informal*) (take a) short sleep (esp in the daytime): *have a ~ after lunch*.

snore /snɔr/ *vi* breathe roughly and noisily while sleeping. □ *n* sound of snoring: *His ~s woke me up*.

snorer *n* [C] person who snores.

snor·kel, schnor·kel /ˈsnɔrkəl, ˈʃn-/ *n* [C] **1** tube that enables a submarine to take in air while submerged. **2** short, bent tube held in the mouth, for a swimmer to take in air while under water.

snort /snɔrt/ *vi,vt* **1** force air violently out through the nose; do this to show impatience, contempt, etc: *~ with rage* (*at her/the idea*). **2** express by snorting: *~ out a reply*. *"Never!" he ~ed*. □ *n* [C] act or sound of snorting: *give a ~ of contempt*.

snot /snat/ *n* (*informal*) **1** [U] mucus of the nose. **2** [C] a rude person.

snotty *adj* (*informal*) **(a)** running with, wet with, mucus. **(b)** (esp of young people) rude.

ˈ**snot(ty)-nosed** *adj* unbearably arrogant and spiteful: *You ~(ty)-nosed little creep*.

snout /snaut/ *n* [C] **1** nose (and sometimes the mouth or jaws) of an animal (esp a dog or pig). ⇨ illus at dog, fish. **2** front of something, thought to be like a snout.

snow[1] /snou/ *n* [U] frozen water vapor falling from the sky in soft, white flakes; mass of such flakes on the ground, etc: *a heavy fall of ~*.

ˈ**snow·ball** *n* [C] **(a)** mass of snow pressed into a hard ball for throwing in play. **(b)** something that increases quickly in size as it moves forward. □ *vt,vi* **(a)** throw snowballs (at). **(b)** grow quickly in size, importance, etc: *Opposition to the war ~balled*.

ˈ**snow·blind** *adj* (temporarily) unable to see because the eyes are tired by the glare of the sun on snow.

ˈ**snow·bound** *adj* unable to travel because of heavy falls of snow.

ˈ**snow·drift** *n* [C] snow heaped up by the wind.

ˈ**snow·drop** *n* [C] bulb plant with small white flowers at the end of winter or in early spring. ⇨ illus at flower.

ˈ**snow·fall** *n* (esp) amount of snow that falls on one occasion or in a period of time.

ˈ**snow·flake** *n* [C] one of the collections of small crystals in which snow falls.

ˈ**snow job,** (*sl*) (attempt at) deception by obscuring one's perception with numerous details.

ˈ**snow·man** /-ˌmæn/ *n* [C] (*pl* ~men /-ˌmen/) figure of a man made of snow by children.

snow·mobile /ˈsnoumouˌbiəl/ *n* [C] motorized sled.

ˈ**snow·plow** *n* [C] device for pushing snow from highways and railroads.

ˈ**snow·shoes** *n pl* frames with leather straps for walking on deep snow without sinking in.

ˈ**snow·storm** *n* [C] heavy fall of snow, esp with strong wind.

ˌ**snow-ˈwhite** *adj* as white as snow.

snow[2] /snou/ *vi,vt* **1** (of snow) come down from the sky: *It ~ed all day*. ***be snowed in/up,*** be prevented by heavy snow from going out. **2** come in large numbers or quantities: *Gifts and messages ~ed in on her birthday. She was ~ed under with work/with invitations to dinner parties*. **3** (*sl*) deceive through the use of distracting details.

snowy *adj* (-ier, -iest) **(a)** covered with snow: *~y roofs*. **(b)** characterized by snow: *~y weather*.

snub /snəb/ *vt* (-bb-) ignore, treat with contempt (esp an inferior or less senior person); reject (an offer) in this way: *be/get ~bed by a head waiter*. □ *n* [C] snubbing words or behavior: *suffer a ~*.

snub-nose /ˈsnəbˌnouz/ *n* [C] short, turned up nose.

ˈ**snub-nosed** *adj*

snuck (*informal*) *pt,pp of* sneak.

snuff[1] /snəf/ *n* [U] powdered tobacco to be taken up into the nose by sniffing: *take a pinch of ~*.

ˈ**snuff·box** *n* [C] box for snuff.

snuff[2] /snəf/ *vt,vi* cut or pinch off the burned black end of the wick of (a candle).

snuffle /ˈsnəfəl/ = sniffle.

snug /snəg/ *adj* (-gg-) **1** sheltered from wind and cold; warm and comfortable: *~ in bed*. **2** neat and tidy; rightly or conveniently placed or arranged: *a ~ cabin*, on a ship. **3** closely fitting: *a ~ jacket*.

snug·ly *adv*

snuggle /ˈsnəgəl/ *vi,vt* lie or get (close to a person) for warmth, comfort or affection: *The child ~d up to its mother. She ~d down in bed*, made herself comfortable.

so[1] /sou/ *adv of degree* to such an extent: *It is not so big as I thought it would be. We didn't expect him to stay so long*, as, in fact, he did stay. *He is not so stupid as to do that. He was so ill that we had to send for a doctor. There were so many* *that we didn't know where to put them all. I'm ˈso glad to see you!* ***so far; So far, so good,*** ⇨ far²(2). ***so long as,*** ⇨ long²(1). ***so much for,*** all that can be said, done, etc, has been said, done, etc: *So much for that matter – let's just forget it for now.*

so² /sou/ *adv of manner* **1** in this (that) way; thus: *Stand just so. So it was* (= That is how) *I became a sailor. As you treat me, so I shall treat you.* ***and ˈso on,*** and other things of the same kind. **2** ***so that,*** **(a)** in order that: *Speak clearly, so that they may understand you.* **(b)** with the result that: *Nothing more was heard of him, so that people thought that he was dead.* ***so... that,*** **(a)** with the intent that: *We have so arranged matters that one of us is always on duty.* **(b)** with the result that; in a way that: *It so happened that I couldn't attend the meeting.* ***so as to,*** in order to; in such a way that: *I'll have everything ready so as not to keep you waiting.* **3** (used as a substitute for a word, phrase or situation): *I told you so!* That is what I told you! **4** (used to express agreement): *A: "It was cold yesterday." B: "So it was."* **5** also: *You are young and so am I,* ie I also am young.

so-and-so /ˈsou-ən-ˌsou/ *n* person not needing to be named: *Don't worry about what old so-and-so says.*

ˈso-called *adj* having this description but perhaps wrongly or doubtfully: *Your so-called friends won't help you in your troubles.*

ˈso-so *adj* (*informal*) not very good: *"How are you feeling?" "Only so-so."*

so³ /sou/ *conj* **1** therefore; that is why: *The shops were closed so I couldn't get any. She asked me to go, so I went.* **2** (used in exclamations) *So there you are! So what?* (*informal*) What of it?

soak /souk/ *vt,vi* **1** become completely wet by being in liquid or by absorbing liquid: *The clothes are ~ing in soapy water.* **2** cause something to absorb as much liquid as possible: *Soak the cloth in the dye for one hour.* **3** absorb; take in (liquid): *Blotting paper ~s up ink.* **4** ***soak oneself in sth,*** (*fig*) absorb: *~ oneself in the atmosphere of a place.* **5** (of rain, etc) make very wet: *We all got ~ed (through).* ***be ˌsoaked to the ˈskin,*** get wet right through one's clothes. **6** enter and pass through: *The rain had ~ed through the roof/his overcoat.* □ *n* [C] act of soaking: *Give the sheets a good ~.*

soap /soup/ *n* [U] substance made of fat or oil, etc, used for washing and cleaning: *a bar/cake of ~; use plenty of ~ and water.* ⇨ soft-soap. □ *vt* **1** apply soap: *~ oneself down.* **2** (*informal*) use flattery to try to please. ⇨ soft soap.

ˈsoap·box *n* [C] packing-case used by a speaker to stand on (in a street, park, etc).

ˌsoapbox ˈderby, children's race of vehicles, originally made of soapboxes or other crates, coasted downhill.

ˈsoap bubble, filmy ball of soapy water, full of air.

ˈsoap flakes/powder, used to wash clothes.

ˈsoap opera, serialized melodrama on radio or TV.

ˈsoap·suds *n pl* bubbly lather of soap and water.

soapy *adj* (-ier, -iest) **(a)** of or like soap: *This bread has a ~y taste.* **(b)** (*fig*) overanxious to please: *He has a ~y voice.*

soar /sɔr/ *vi* **1** (of birds, aircraft) fly or go up high in the air. **2** (*fig*) rise high up: *Prices ~ed when war broke out.*

sob¹ /sab/ *vi,vt* (-bb-) **1** draw in the breath sharply and irregularly from sorrow or pain, esp while crying: *She sobbed her heart out*, cried a great deal. **2** tell while sobbing: *She sobbed out the story of her son's death in a traffic accident.* □ *n* [C] act or sound of sobbing: *The child's sobs gradually died down.*

ˈsob story, (*informal*) sad story, intended to excuse a fault or mistake or to arouse sympathy.

S.O.B.² /ˌes ˌou ˈbi/ *abbr* (*informal*) = (*vulgar*) son of a bitch. (*Note:* the *abbr* is considered somewhat less offensive than the full form, which is a strong insult.)

so·ber /ˈsoubər/ *adj* **1** self-controlled; serious in thought, etc; calm: *make a ~ estimate of what is possible; ~ colors,* not bright. **2** avoiding drunkenness; not drunk: *Does he ever go to bed ~?* □ *vt,vi* **1** make or become sober(1): *The bad news ~ed all of us.* **2** make or become sober (2): *Leave him to ~ up.*

so·ber·ly *adv* in a controlled, serious manner.

so·bri·ety /səˈbraiəti/ *n* [U] (*formal*) quality or condition of being sober(1).

soc. *abbr* = **1** social. **2** society.

soc·cer /ˈsakər/ *n* [U] game in which the ball is moved by any part of the body but the arms and hands, played between two teams of eleven players.

SOCCER

so·ciable /ˈsouʃəbəl/ *adj* friendly; liking company.

so·ciably /-əbli/ *adv*

so·cia·bil·ity /ˌsouʃəˈbiləti/ *n* [U]

so·cial /ˈsouʃəl/ *adj* **1** living in groups, not separately: *~ ants. Man is a ~ animal.* **2** of people living in communities; of relations between persons and communities: *~ customs/reforms/welfare.* **3** of or in society: *one's ~ equals*, persons of the same class as oneself in society. **4** for companionship: *a ˈ~ club.* **5** = sociable. □ *n* [C] social gathering, eg one organized by a club.

so·cially /-ʃəli/ *adv*

ˌsocial seˈcurity, (also **Social Security**) government provisions for helping people who

are retired, ill, disabled, etc: *The family is on ~ security*, receiving such help.
ˌ**social ˈscience,** eg psychology, politics.
ˈ**social worker,** trained person who works to improve the social welfare of individuals.
so·cial·ism /ˈsouʃəˌlɪzəm/ *n* [U] philosophical, political and economic theory that land, transport, the chief industries, natural resources, eg coal, waterpower, etc should be owned and managed by the State and wealth equally distributed.
so·cial·ist /-ɪst/ *n* [C] supporter of, believer in socialism. □ *adj* of socialism.
so·cial·ize /ˈsouʃəˌlaiz/ **1** *vt* make socialist. **2** *vi* mix with others; engage in social activities.
so·cial·ite /ˈsouʃəˌlait/ *n* [C] person well-known in fashionable society.
so·ciety /səˈsaiəti/ *n* (*pl* -ies) **1** [U] social way of living; system whereby people live together in organized communities: *a danger to ~*, person, idea, etc that endangers the bodily or moral welfare of the members of a community. **2** [C] social community: *modern industrial societies*. **3** [U] company; companionship: *spend an evening in the ~ of one's friends*. **4** [U] people of fashion or distinction in a place, district, country, etc; the upper classes: *leaders of ~*. ⇨ high society. **5** [C] organization of persons formed with a purpose; club; association: *the school deˈbating ~; a co-ˈoperative ~; the Society of Friends*.
so·cio·logi·cal /ˌsousiəˈladʒɪkəl/ *adj* of sociology.
so·cio·logi·cally /-kli/ *adv*.
so·ci·ol·ogist /ˌsousiˈalədʒɪst/ *n* [C] student of, expert in, sociology.
so·ci·ol·ogy /ˌsousiˈalədʒi/ *n* [U] science of the nature and growth of society and social behavior.
sock[1] /sak/ *n* [C] (*pl* ~s or sox) (also ***a pair of socks/sox***) **1** woolen, cotton, etc covering for the foot and ankle. **2** cover for the head of a golf club.
sock[2] /sak/ *n* [C] (*sl*) blow given with the fist: *Give him a ~ on the jaw!* □ *vt* (*sl*) give (a person) such a blow: *Sock him on the jaw!* ***sock it to sb,*** (*sl*) assail somebody.
socket /ˈsakɪt/ *n* [C] natural or artificial hollow into which something fits or in which something turns: *the ˈeye ~s; a ~ for an electric light bulb*.
sod /sad/ *n* [U] upper layer of grassland including the grass with its roots and earth; [C] square or oblong piece of this pared off.
soda /ˈsoudə/ *n* [U] **1** common chemical substance used to make soap, manufacture glass, etc. **2** = soda water. **3** = soda pop.
ˈ**baking soda,** kind used as a leaven in baking some breads, etc.
ˌ**ice-cream ˈsoda,** drink of sweetened and flavored soda water with a scoop of ice cream floated in it.
ˈ**soda bread/cracker,** leavened with baking soda instead of yeast.
ˈ**soda fountain,** (part of a) store with a bar at which soda pop, ice cream, etc is served.
ˈ**soda jerk,** (*informal*) person who works at a soda fountain.
ˈ**soda pop,** sweetened and flavored soda water.
ˈ**soda water,** water containing carbon dioxide gas to make it bubble.
sod·den /ˈsadən/ *adj* **1** soaked through: *clothes ~ with rain*. **2** (of bread, etc) moist or sticky because undercooked.
so·dium /ˈsoudiəm/ *n* [U] silver-white metal (symbol **Na**) occurring naturally only in compounds: *~ chloride*, (symbol **NaCl**) common salt.
sod·omy /ˈsadəmi/ *n* [U] anal sexual intercourse, esp between males.
-so·ever /-souˈevər/ *suffix* (used with *relative pronouns, adverbs* and *adjectives*) any kind or extent of: *ˈhow~, ˈwho~*, etc.
sofa /ˈsoufə/ *n* [C] long seat with raised ends and back, on which several persons can sit or one person can lie.
soft /sɔft/ *adj* (-er, -est) **1** (opposite of *hard*) changing shape easily when pressed: *~ soil/ground/mud*. ***a soft landing,*** (eg of a spacecraft on the moon) one that avoids damage or destruction. **2** (of surfaces) smooth and delicate: *~ fur; ~ furnishings*, curtains, etc. **3** (of light, colors) restful to the eyes: *lampshades that give a ~ light*. **4** (of sounds) not loud: *~ music; in a ~ voice*. **5** (of outlines) indistinct. **6** (of answers, words, etc) mild; gentle; intended to please: *a ~ answer; have a ~ tongue*. **7** (of the air, weather) mild: *a ~ breeze/wind*. **8** (of water) free from mineral salts and therefore good for washing: *as ~ as rainwater*. **9** (of certain sounds): *C is ~ in "city" and hard in "cat." G is ~ in "gin" and hard in "get."* **10** easy: *have a ~ job*, an easy, well-paid job. **11** not having strength and determination: *Are the young people today getting ~?* **12** sympathetic; considerate: *have a ~ heart*. **13** (*informal*) easily affected, fooled: *He's not as ~ as he looks. Jack is ~* (= sentimentally silly) *on Anne*.
ˈ**soft-ˌboiled** *adj* (of eggs) boiled so that the yolk is liquid.
ˌ**soft ˈcurrency,** one that is not convertible to gold, or into certain other currencies which are more in demand.
ˈ**soft drink,** nonalcoholic (usually sweet and carbonated) cold drink.
ˌ**soft-ˈheaded** *adj* idiotic; foolish.
ˌ**soft-ˈhearted** *adj* sympathetic; kind.
soft·ly *adv*
soft·ness /-nɪs/ *n* [U]
ˌ**soft ˈoption,** alternative which is thought to involve little work.
ˌ**soft ˈpalate,** back part of the roof of the mouth. ⇨ illus at mouth.
ˌ**soft-ˈpedal** *vi,vt* (*fig*) make (a statement, etc) less definite or confident.
ˈ**soft soap** *n* **(a)** semi-liquid soap. **(b)** (*fig*) flattery. □ ˌ**soft-ˈsoap** *vt* flatter.
ˈ**soft-soled** *adj* (of shoes) having a sole made out of soft rubber or leather.
ˌ**soft-ˈspoken** *adj* having a gentle voice; saying pleasant, friendly things.
ˈ**soft·ware** *n* [U] data, programs, etc not forming parts of a computer but used for its operation. ⇨ hardware.
sof·ten /ˈsɔfən/ *vt,vi* **1** make or become soft:

curtains that ~ the light; people who are ~ed by luxurious living. **2** make (something) easier to bear: *Her gentle manner ~ed the effect of the news.*

soft·ener *n* [C] something used to soften water.

soggy /ˈsagi/ *adj* (-ier, -iest) (esp of ground) heavy with water.

sog·gi·ness /-nɪs/ *n* [U]

soil /ˈsɔiəl/ *n* [C,U] ground; earth, esp the upper layer of earth in which plants, trees, etc grow: *good/poor/sandy ~; a man of the ~,* one who works on the land (and likes to do so). □ *vt,vi* (*pres p* ~ing /ˈsɔilɪŋ/) **1** make dirty: *He refused to ~ his hands,* refused to do dirty work. **2** become soiled: *material that ~s easily.*

so·journ /ˈsouˌdʒərn/ *vi, n* [C] (*liter*) (make a) stay (*with* a person, *at* or *in*) for a time.

sol /sal/ *n* [C] (*music*) syllable used for the fifth note of a scale.

sol·ace /ˈsalɪs/ *n* [C,U] (*formal*) (that which gives) comfort or relief (when one is in trouble or pain): *The invalid found ~ in music.* □ *vt* give relief to: *The unhappy man ~d himself with whiskey.*

so·lar /ˈsoulər/ *adj* of the sun.

solar ˈcell, device (as used in satellites) which converts the energy of sunlight into electric energy.

solar ˈeclipse, eclipse of the sun by the moon.

solar ˈenergy, that obtained from sunlight.

solar ˈplexus /ˌsoulər ˈpleksəs/ group of nerves at the pit of the stomach.

the ˈsolar system, the sun and the planets which revolve round it. ⇨ illus at planet.

the solar ˈyear, time taken by the earth to complete one revolution round the sun, about 365 days, 5 hours, 48 minutes and 46 seconds.

sold *pt,pp* of sell.

sol·der /ˈsadər/ *n* [U] easily melted alloy used, when melted, to join harder metals, wires, etc. □ *vt* join with solder.

ˈsolder·ing iron, tool used for this work.

sol·dier /ˈsouldʒər/ *n* [C] member of an army: *three ~s, two sailors and one civilian.* □ *vi* serve as a soldier: *be tired of ~ing.* ***ˌsoldier ˈon,*** continue bravely with one's work, etc in the face of difficulties.

sol·dier·ly, ˈsoldier-like *adj* like a soldier; disciplined; brave.

sole[1] /soul/ *n* [C] flat ocean fish with a delicate flavor.

sole[2] /soul/ *n* [C] under surface of a human foot, or of a sock, shoe, etc. □ *vt* put a sole on (a shoe, etc): *send a pair of shoes to be ~d and heeled.*

-soled *suffix* (with the kind mentioned): *ˌrubber-soled ˈboots.*

sole[3] /soul/ *adj* **1** one and only; single: *the ~ cause of the accident.* **2** restricted to one person, company, etc: *We have the ~ right of selling the article.*

sole·ly /ˈsoul(l)i/ *adv* alone; only: *~ly responsible; ~ly because of you.*

sol·emn /ˈsaləm/ *adj* **1** done with religious or other ceremony; causing deep thought or respect: *a ~ silence as the coffin was carried out of the church; a ~ oath,* serious and important. **2** serious looking: *~ faces; look as ~ as a judge.*

sol·emn·ly *adv*

sol·emn·ness /-nɪs/ *n* [U]

sol·em·nity /səˈlemnəti/ *n* (*pl* -ies) (*formal*) **1** [U] seriousness; gravity. **2** solemn ceremony: *The President was inaugurated with all due ~/ with all the proper solemnities.*

sol·em·nize /ˈsaləmˌnaiz/ *vt* perform (a religious ceremony, esp a wedding) with the usual rites; make solemn.

sol·em·niz·ation /ˌsaləmnɪˈzeiʃən/ *n* [U]

sol·icit /səˈlɪsɪt/ *vt,vi* **1** ask (for) seriously; make determined requests (for): *Both the candidates ~ed my vote.* **2** (of a prostitute) make an immoral sexual offer (to), esp in a public place.

sol·ici·tor /səˈlɪsɪtər/ *n* [C] person who solicits trade, support, etc.

sol·ici·tous /səˈlɪsɪtəs/ *adj* (*formal*) anxious, concerned about (a person's welfare, etc) or to help somebody: *~ to please; ~ for her comfort.*

sol·ici·tous·ly *adv*

sol·ici·tude /səˈlɪsɪˌtud/ *n* [U] (*formal*) concern or anxiety: *my deep ~ for your welfare.*

solid /ˈsalɪd/ *adj* **1** not in the form of a liquid or gas: *~ food. When water freezes and becomes ~, we call it ice.* **2** firm; heavy: *a man with good ~ flesh on him.* **3** without holes or spaces; not hollow: *a ~ sphere.* **4** of strong material or construction; able to support weight or resist pressure: *~ buildings/furniture.* **5** that can be depended on: *~ arguments; a ~* (= financially sound) *business firm; a man of ~ character.* **6** of the same substance throughout: *made of ~ gold.* **7** unanimous; undivided: *There was a ~ vote in favor of the proposal.* **8** continuous; without a break: *wait for a ~ hour; sleep ten ~ hours/ten hours ~.* **9** (*math*) having length, breadth and thickness: *a ~ figure,* eg a cube. □ *n* [C] **1** body or substance which is solid, not a liquid or a gas. **2** (*math*) figure of three dimensions.

sol·id·ity /səˈlɪdəti/, **solid·ness** /ˈsalɪdnɪs/ *n* [U] quality of being solid: *the ~ity of a building/an argument.*

solid·ly *adv*

soli·dar·ity /ˌsaləˈdærəti/ *n* [U] unity because of common interests or feelings: *national ~ in the face of danger.*

sol·id·ify /səˈlɪdəˌfai/ *vt,vi* (*pt,pp* -ied) make or become solid, hard or firm.

sol·idi·fi·cation /səˌlɪdəfəˈkeiʃən/ *n* [U]

sol·il·oquy /səˈlɪləkwi/ *n* [C,U] (*pl* -ies) **1** (instance of) speaking one's thoughts aloud. **2** (in drama) speech in which a character speaks his thoughts without addressing a listener.

sol·il·oquize /səˈlɪləˌkwaiz/ *vi* talk to oneself; think aloud.

soli·taire /ˈsaləˌtær/ *n* [C] **1** (ornament such as an earring with a) single gem or jewel. **2** (also called *patience*) kinds of game for one player.

soli·tary /ˈsaləˌteri/ *adj* **1** (living) alone; without companions; lonely: *a ~ life; a ~ walk.* **2** only one: *not a ~ one/instance.* **3** seldom visited: *a ~ valley.*

soli·tar·ily /ˌsaləˈterəli/ *adv*

ˌsolitary conˈfinement, prison punishment by which a person is isolated in a separate cell.

soli·tude /ˈsaləˌtud/ *n* **1** [U] being without companions; solitary state: *live in ~; not fond of*

~. **2** [C] lonely place: *spend six months in the ~s of the Antarctic.*
solo /ˈsoulou/ *n* (*pl* ~s) **1** [C] piece of music (to be) performed by one person: *a violin/piano ~.* **2** [C] any performance by one person: (as an *adverb*) *fly ~*; (as an *adjective*) *his first ~ flight.* **3** [U] kind of whist in which one player opposes others.
ˈsolo·ist /-ɪst/ *n* [C] person who gives a solo(1).
sol·stice /ˈsalstɪs/ *n* [C] either time (*summer ~,* about June 21; *winter ~,* about December 22) at which the sun is farthest north or south of the equator.
sol·uble /ˈsalyəbəl/ *adj* **1** that can be dissolved. **2** = solvable.
solu·bil·ity /ˌsalyəˈbɪləti/ *n* [U]
sol·ution /səˈluʃən/ *n* **1** [C] answer (*to* a question, etc); way of dealing with a difficulty: *Perhaps economy is the ~ to/of your financial troubles.* **2** [U] process of finding an answer or explanation: *problems that defy ~,* cannot be solved. **3** [U] process of dissolving a solid or a gas in liquid: *the ~ of sugar in tea.* **4** [C,U] liquid that results from this process: *a ~ of salt in water; a salt ~.*
solv·able /ˈsalvəbəl/ *adj* that can be solved or explained.
solve /salv/ *vt* find the answer to (a problem, etc); explain (a difficulty): *~ a crossword puzzle.*
sol·vent /ˈsalvənt/ *adj* **1** of the power of dissolving or forming a solution: *the ~ action of water.* **2** having money enough to meet one's debts. □ *n* [C] substance (usually a liquid) able to dissolve another substance: *grease ~,* eg gasoline.
sol·vency /-nsi/ *n* [U] being solvent(2).
somber /ˈsambər/ *adj* dark-colored; gloomy: *a ~ January day; ~ clothes.*
somber·ly *adv*
somber·ness /-nɪs/ *n* [U]
som·brero /samˈbrerou/ *n* [C] (*pl* ~s) hat with a wide brim (as worn in the Southwest and in Latin American countries).

SOMBRERO, SERAPE

some¹ /ˈsəm; *weak form* səm/ *adj* **1** (used to show an amount or quantity, a certain degree or number (more than two)): *Please give me ~ milk. There are ~ children outside. Some* (= some people) *say that...* (*Note: some* is used in affirmative sentences; usually replaced by *any* in questions and negative sentences: *Have you any milk? We haven't any milk;* used in sentences where doubt or negation is implied. *Some* and *any* are *pl* equivalents of the numeral article *a, an,* of numeral *one,* and the *indefinite pron "one."*) **2** (used in questions if the speaker expects, or wishes to suggest, an affirmative answer): *Aren't there ~ stamps in that drawer?* **3** (used in questions which are really invitations or requests): *Will you have ~ cake?* **4** (used after *if,* introducing something supposed): *If we had ~/any money, we could buy it. If we find ~/any, we'll share them with you.* (*Note: some* or *any* can be used.) **5** (used with *more*): *Give me ~ more. Won't you have ~ more?* (*Compare: Do you want any more? I haven't any more.*) **6** (always /ˈsəm/) (contrasted with *the rest, other(s),* and *all*): *Some children learn languages easily (and others with difficulty). All work is not dull; ~ work is pleasant.* **7** (always /ˈsəm/) (used to show that the person, place, object, etc is unknown, or when the speaker does not wish to be specific): *He's living at ~ place in East Africa. I've read that story before in ~ book or other.* **8** (always /ˈsəm/) about; approximately: *That was ~ twenty years ago.* **9** (always /ˈsəm/) considerable quantity or number of: *I shall be away for ~ time,* a fairly long time. *The railway station is ~ distance* (= quite a long way) *from the town.* **10** (always /ˈsəm/) (used to suggest "to a certain extent"): *That is ~ help* (ie It helps to a certain extent) *toward understanding the problem.*
some² /ˈsəm/ *pron* (*Some* as a *pron* is used in the same ways as some, *adj,* 1,2,3 and 4. *Some of* and *any of* are equivalent to *a few of, a little of, part of*): *Some of these books are quite useful.* (*Compare: I don't want any of these (books). I don't want any of this (paper).*) *I agree with ~* (= part) *of what you say. Canada has ~ of the finest scenery in the world.* □ *adv* ⇨ some(8) above.
-some /-səm/ *suffix* (used to form an *adjective*) likely to, productive of: *quarrelsome.*
some·body /ˈsəmˌbədi/, **some·one** /ˈsəmˌwən/ *pron* **1** a person (unknown or unnamed): *There's ~ at the door.* (*Note:* replaced by *anybody* or *anyone* in questions, negative sentences: *Is there anyone at home? There isn't anybody at home.*) **2** (often with *a;* also in the *pl*) a person of some importance: *If you had studied harder at college you might have become ~. He's nobody here but he's a ~ in his own town.*
some·how /ˈsəmˌhau/ *adv* **1** in some way (or other); by one means or another: *We must find money for the rent ~ (or other). We shall get there ~.* **2** for some (vague) reason (or other): *Somehow I don't trust that man.*
some·one /ˈsəmˌwən/ *n* = somebody.
some·place /ˈsəmˌpleis/ *adv* (*informal*) = somewhere: *I've left my bag ~.*
som·er·sault /ˈsəmərˌsɔlt/ *n* [C] leap or fall in which one turns over completely before landing on one's feet: *turn/throw a ~.* □ *vi* turn a somersault.
some·thing /ˈsəmθɪŋ/ *pron* **1** a thing, object, event, etc (unknown, unnamed, etc): *There's ~ on the floor. I want ~ to eat. There's ~* (= some truth, some point) *in what he says.* (*Note:* replaced by *anything* in questions, negative sentences: *Is there anything in that box? There isn't anything to eat.*) ***2 or something,*** (used to show absence of precise information): *I hear he has*

broken an arm or ~, met with some sort of accident and has broken a limb, etc. □ *adv* ***something like,*** **(a)** having a little resemblance to: *The noise sounded ~ like an explosion.* **(b)** approximately: *It cost ~ like twenty dollars.*

some·time /ˈsəmˌtaim/ *adv* **1** at a point in time: *I saw him ~ in May. It was ~ last summer. I will speak to him about it ~.* (*Note:* do not confuse with *some ˈtime* meaning "for some period of time," as in: *I have been waiting some time.*) **2** former(ly): *Thomas Atkins, ~ professor at this University.*

some·times /ˈsəmˌtaimz/ *adv* now and then; from time to time: *I ~ have letters from him. I have ~ had letters from him.*

some·way /ˈsəmˌwei/ *adv* (*informal*) = somehow.

some·what /ˈsəmˌ(h)wət/ *adv* to some extent; in some degree: *I was ~ surprised/disappointed.*

some·where /ˈsəmˌ(h)wer/ *adv* in, at, to, a place (unknown, unnamed, etc): *It must be ~ near here. He lost it ~ between his office and the station.* (*Note:* replaced by *anywhere* in questions, negative sentences: *Is it anywhere near here? I didn't go anywhere yesterday.*)

son /sən/ *n* [C] **1** male child of a parent. **2** (used as a form of address, eg by an older man to a young man, a confessor to a penitent): *my son.* **3** person having the qualities, etc shown: *sons of freedom,* those who have inherited freedom from their ancestors.

ˈson-in-law *n* [C] (*pl* sons-in-law) husband of one's daughter.

ˌson-of-a-ˈgun, (*sl*) person. ***I'll be a son-of-a-gun!*** (*sl*) expression of surprise.

the Son of God/Man, (in the Christian religion) Jesus Christ.

so·nata /səˈnatə/ *n* [C] (*pl* ~s) musical composition for one instrument (eg the piano), or two (eg piano and violin), normally with three or four movements.

song /sɔŋ/ *n* **1** [U] singing; music for the voice: *burst into ~; the ~* (= musical sound) *of the birds.* **2** [U] (*poetic*) poetry; verse. **3** [C] short poem or number of verses set to music and intended to be sung: *pop ~s.*

ˈsong·bird *n* [C] bird (eg thrush) noted for its musical sound.

ˈsong·book *n* [C] collection of songs (with both words and music).

song·ster /-stər/ *n* [C] **(a)** singer. **(b)** songbird.

sonic /ˈsanɪk/ *adj* relating to sound, sound waves or the speed of sound. *a ~ boom,* noise made when an aircraft travels faster than the speed of sound ⇨ supersonic, ultrasonic.

son·net /ˈsanɪt/ *n* [C] kind of poem containing 14 lines, each of 10 syllables, and with a formal pattern of rhymes.

sonny /ˈsəni/ *n* [C] (*pl* -ies) familiar form of address to a young boy.

son·or·ous /ˈsanərəs/ *adj* (*formal*) **1** having a full, deep sound: *the ~ note of a large bell.* **2** (of language, words, etc) making a deep impression: *a ~ style.*

son·or·ous·ly *adv*

soon /sun/ *adv* (-er, -est) **1** not long after the present time or the time in question; in a short time: *We shall ~ be home. We shall be home quite ~ now. He'll be here very ~. It will ~ be five years since we came to live in America.* ***soon after,*** a short time after: *He arrived ~ after three.* (*Note:* the opposite of *soon after* is *a little before.*) **2** early: *How ~ can you be ready? Must you leave so ~?* **3** ***as/so soon as,*** at the moment that; when; not later than: *He started as ~ as he received the news. We didn't arrive so/as ~ as we had hoped.* ***no sooner...than,*** immediately when or after: *He had no ~er/No ~er had he arrived home than he was asked to go out again. No ~er said than done,* ie done immediately. **4** (used to show comparatives): *The ~er you begin the ~er you'll finish. The ~er the better.* ***as soon as not,*** more willingly: *I'd go there as ~ as not.* ***sooner or later,*** now or (much) later: *You'll get it back ~er or later.* ***sooner than,*** rather than: *He would ~er resign than take part in such dishonest business deals.*

soot /sʊt/ *n* [U] black powder in smoke, or left by smoke on surfaces. □ *vt* cover with soot.

sooty *adj* (-ier, -iest) black with, like, soot.

soothe /suð/ *vt* **1** make (a person, his nerves, passions) quiet or calm: *~ a crying baby; a soothing voice.* **2** make (pains, aches) less sharp or severe: *a soothing lotion for the skin,* eg against sunburn.

sooth·ing·ly *adv*

sooth·sayer /ˈsuθˌseiər/ *n* [C] (*old use*) fortune-teller.

sop /sap/ *n* [C] **1** piece of bread, etc soaked in milk, soup, etc. **2** something offered to prevent trouble or to give temporary satisfaction: *ask a tenant to give up a lease and offer money as a sop.* **3** weak-willed person. □ *vt* (-pp-) **1** soak (bread, etc in soup, etc). **2** absorb (liquid): *sop up the water with this towel.*

sop·ping *adj, adv* thoroughly (wet): *sopping wet.*

soph·is·ti·cated /səˈfɪstəˌkeitɪd/ *adj* **1** having lost natural simplicity through experience of the world; cultured: *a ~ girl; with ~ tastes.* **2** with the latest improvements and refinements: *~ modern weapons.* **3** (of mental activity) cultured, elaborate: *a ~ discussion/argument.*

soph·is·ti·ca·tion /səˌfɪstəˈkeiʃən/ *n* [U]

soph·o·more /ˈsafəˌmɔr/ *n* [C] student in the second year of high school or college.

sop·or·ific /ˌsapəˈrɪfɪk/ *n* [C], *adj* (substance, drink, etc) producing sleep.

sop·ping /ˈsapɪŋ/ *adj* ⇨ sop.

soppy /ˈsapi/ *adj* (-ier, -iest) very wet.

so·prano /səˈprænou/ *n* [C] (*pl* ~s), *adj* (musical part for, or singer having the) highest voice range of women and girls and boys.

sor·cerer /ˈsɔrsərər/ *n* [C] man who practices magic with the help of evil spirits.

sor·cer·ess /ˈsɔrsərɪs/ *n* [C] woman sorcerer.

sor·cery /ˈsɔrsəri/ *n* (*pl* -ies) **1** [U] witchcraft (the usual word). **2** (*pl*) evil acts done by sorcery.

sor·did /ˈsɔrdɪd/ *adj* **1** (of conditions) poor, dirty, uncomfortable: *a ~ slum; living in ~ poverty.* **2** (of persons, behavior, etc) without respect or honor.

sor·did·ly *adv*

sor·did·ness /-nɪs/ *n* [U]

sore /sɔr/ *adj* (-r, -st) **1** (of a part of the body) tender and painful; hurting when touched or used: *a ~ knee/throat*. ***a ˌsight for ˌsore ˈeyes,*** welcome, pleasant, person or thing. **2** filled with sorrow; sad: *a ~ heart*. **3** causing sorrow or annoyance. ***a sore point/subject,*** one that hurts the feelings when talked about. **4** (*informal*) hurt in one's feelings; angry: *feel ~ about not being invited to the party*. □ *n* [C] **1** sore place on the body (where the skin or flesh is injured). **2** (*fig*) painful subject or memory: *Let's not recall old ~s.*

sore·ly *adv* **(a)** (*formal*) severely: *~ly afflicted.* **(b)** greatly: *More financial help is ~ly needed.*

sore·ness /-nɪs/ *n* [U]

so·ror·ity /ˌsəˈrɔrəti/ *n* [C] (*pl* -ies) **1** society of women who are joined together esp by common interests. **2** society of women students, with branches in various colleges, usually with names made up of Greek letters. ⇨ fraternity.

sor·rel /ˈsɔrəl/ *adj* light orange-brown color. □ *n* [C] horse of this color.

sor·row /ˈsarou, ˈsɔrou/ *n* [C,U] (cause of) grief or sadness; regret: *express ~ for having done wrong; to my great ~.* □ *vi* feel grief (*at/for/over*): *~ing over her child's death.*

sor·row·ful /-fəl/ *adj* feeling, showing, causing, sorrow.

sor·row·fully /-f(ə)li/ *adv*

sorry /ˈsari, ˈsɔri/ *adj* **1** feeling regret or sadness: *We're ~ to hear of your father's death.* ***be/feel sorry (about/for sth),*** feel regret: *Aren't you ~ for/about what you've done?* ***be/feel sorry for sb,*** **(a)** feel sympathy: *I feel ~ for anyone who has to drive in weather like this.* **(b)** feel pity: *I'm ~ for you, but you've been rather foolish, haven't you?* **2** (used to express mild regret or an apology): *"Can you lend me five dollars?"—"Sorry, I can't."* **3** (-ier, -iest) pitiful.

sort[1] /sɔrt/ *n* [C] **1** group or class of persons or things which are alike in some way: *Pop music is the ~ (of music) she likes most. We can't approve of this ~ of thing/these ~ of things/things of this ~.* **2** ***a good sort,*** (esp) a person who is likable, who has good qualities. **3** ***ˌout of ˈsorts,*** (*informal*) feeling unwell, depressed. **4** ***sort of,*** (*informal*) rather; somewhat: *She's been ~ of nervous lately.*

sort[2] /sɔrt/ *vt,vi* arrange in groups; separate things of one sort from things of other sorts: *The boy was ~ing/~ing out/over the foreign stamps he had collected. We must ~ out the good apples from the bad.*

sor·ter *n* [C] one who sorts letters, fruit, etc.

SOS /ˌes ˌou ˈes/ *n* [C] letters of international code signal of distress; (*fig*) urgent appeal for help.

so-so /ˈsou-ˌsou/ *adj, adv* ⇨ so².

souf·flé /suˈflei/ *n* [C] (*F*) dish made with eggs, milk, etc.

soul /soul/ *n* [C] **1** nonmaterial part of a human, believed to exist for ever: *believe in the immortality of the ~. He eats hardly enough to keep body and ~ together,* to keep himself alive. *That man has no ~,* is unfeeling, selfish. **2** emotional and intellectual energy: *He put his heart and ~ into the work.* **3** person regarded as the ideal or personification of some virtue or quality: *He is the ~ of honor/discretion.* **4** departed spirit: *ˌAll ˈSouls' Day*, (in the Christian religious calendar) November 2. **5** person: *There wasn't a ~ to be seen.* No one was in sight. **6** (expressing familiarity, pity, etc according to context): *She's lost all her money, poor ~.* **7** (*informal*) all those qualities that enable a person to be in harmony with himself and others, used esp by Afro-Americans and expressed through their music and dancing.

ˈsoul brother/sister, fellow Afro-American.

ˈsoul-destroying *adj* killing the willpower or spirit: *ˌ~-destroying ˈwork.*

ˈsoul food, (originally Southern) Afro-American cuisine.

soul·ful /-fəl/ *adj* having, affecting, showing, deep feeling: *~ful eyes/music/glances.*

soul·fully /-fəli/ *adv*

soul·less *adj* without pity or deeper feelings.

soul·less·ly *adv*

sound[1] /saund/ *adj* (-er, -est) **1** healthy; in good condition; not hurt, injured or decayed: *~ fruit/teeth.* **2** dependable; based on logic, facts: *a ~ argument/policy; ~ advice.* **3** capable, careful: *a ~ tennis player.* **4** thorough; deep: *be a ~ sleeper; give him a ~ beating.* □ *adv* deeply: *be ~ asleep.*

sound·ly *adv* in a deep, thorough manner: *sleep ~ly; be ~ly beaten at tennis.*

sound·ness /-nɪs/ *n* [U]

sound[2] /saund/ *n* [C,U] **1** that which is or can be heard: *We heard the ~ of voices/footsteps.* **2** (*sing* only) mental impression produced by something stated (or read): *I don't like the ~ of it.*

ˈsound barrier, point at which an aircraft's speed equals that of sound waves, causing sonic booms.

ˈsound effects, sound (recorded on tape, film, etc) for use in broadcasts, in studio.

sound·less *adj* = silent (the usual word).

ˈsound track, (a) music, etc used in a cinema film. **(b)** film track on which the sound is recorded.

ˈsound wave, vibrations made in the air or other medium by which sound is carried.

sound[3] /saund/ *vt,vi* **1** produce sound from; make (something) produce sound: *~ a trumpet.* **2** produce: *~ a note of alarm/danger.* **3** pronounce: *Don't ~ the "h" in "hour" or the "b" in "dumb".* **4** give notice of: *~ the alarm*, eg by ringing a bell. **5** give forth sound: *The trumpet ~ed.* **6** test, examine (eg a person's lungs by tapping the chest). **7** give an impression when heard: *How sweet the music ~s!* **8** (*fig*) give an impression: *His explanation ~s all right*, seems reasonable enough.

sound[4] /saund/ *vt,vi* **1** test the depth of (the sea, etc) by letting down a weighted line (called a *ˈ~ing line* or *~ing apparatus*); find the depth of water in a ship's hold (with a *ˈ~ing rod*). **2** get records of temperature, pressure, etc in (the upper atmosphere) (by sending up instruments in a *ˈ~ing balloon*). **3** try (esp cautiously or in a reserved manner) to learn a person's views, sentiments, etc: *I will ~ out the manager about/*

on the question of holidays.

sound·ing *n* **(a)** (*pl*) place or area near enough to the shore to make it possible to sound⁴(1). **(b)** measurement obtained by sounding⁴(1).

sound⁵ /saund/ *n* [C] narrow passage of water joining two larger areas of water.

soup¹ /sup/ *n* [U] liquid food made by cooking meat, vegetables, etc in water: *chicken/pea/tomato* ~. ***in the soup,*** (*informal*) in trouble.

soup² /sup/ *vt* ***soup sth up,*** (*sl*) fit (a motor vehicle, its engine) with a supercharger (to increase its power and so its speed): *a ~ed-up car.*

sour /ˈsauər/ *adj* **1** having a sharp taste (like that of vinegar, a lemon or an unripe plum, apple, etc). **2** having a taste of having gone bad: ~ *milk.* **3** (*fig*) bad-tempered: *made ~ by disappointments.* □ *vt,vi* turn or become sour (all uses): *The hot weather has ~ed the milk. Her attitude toward him has ~ed.*

sour·dough *n* **(a)** [U] (bread made of) a kind of soured dough. **(b)** [C] outdoorsman, esp a prospector, in Alaska.

sour·ly *adv*

sour·ness /-nɪs/ *n* [U]

source /sɔrs/ *n* [C] **1** starting point of a river: *the ~s of the Nile. Where does the Mississippi have its ~?* **2** place from which something comes or is obtained: *The news comes from a reliable ~. Is that well the ~ of infection?* **3** (*pl*) original documents, etc for a study, eg of a period of history: (as an *adjective*) ~ *materials.*

souse /saus/ *n* **1** [U] jelly of pork trimmings cooked with vinegar, served cold and sliced. **2** [C] (*sl*) person who is always drunk. □ *vt* **1** throw into water; throw water on. **2** put (fish, etc) into salted water, vinegar, etc to preserve it: *~d herrings.*

soused *adj* (*sl*) drunk.

south /sauθ/ *n* **1 the south,** one of the four cardinal points of the compass, on the right of a person facing the sunrise. **2** (often **the South**) **(a)** part of any country, etc lying farther in this direction than other parts: *Mexico is to the ~ of the US.* **(b)** the southern part of the USA, esp the region including the states formerly belonging to the Confederacy. ***down South,*** to or in the southern part of the US: *We're moving down South.* □ *adj* in, of, from, the south: *South America; the South Pacific.* □ *adv* to or toward the south: *sailing ~.*

ˌsouth-ˈeast /ˌsauθˈist/) *n, adj, adv* (sometimes, esp *naut,* **sou'-east** /ˌsau-ˈist/) (regions) midway between south and east.

ˌsouth-ˈeaster·ly /-ˈistərli/ *adj* **(a)** (of wind) from the southeast. **(b)** (of direction) toward the southeast.

ˌsouth-ˈeastern /-ˈistərn/ *adj* of, from, or in the southeast.

south·er·ly /ˈsəðərli/ *adj, adv* from the south, toward the south, in or to the south.

south·ern /ˈsəðərn/ *adj* of, from, in the south part of the world, a country, etc: ~ *Europe; the ~ states of the USA.*

south·erner *n* person born in or living in the south of a country.

ˌsouthern ˈlights, = aurora australis.

ˈsouth·ern·most /-ˌmoust/ *adj* farthest south.

south·paw /ˈsauθˌpɔ/ *n* [C] **1** (*baseball*) left-handed pitcher. **2** (*informal*) left-handed person.

south·ward /ˈsauθwərd/ *adj, adv* toward the south: *in a ~ direction.*

sou·venir /ˌsuvəˈnɪr, ˈsuvəˌnɪr/ *n* [C] something taken, bought or received as a gift, and kept as a reminder of a person, place or event.

south·west /ˌsauθˈwest/ *n, adj, adv* (regions) midway between south and west.

ˌsouth-ˈwester·ly /-ˈwestərli/ *adj* **(a)** (of wind) from the southwest. **(b)** (of direction) toward the southwest.

ˌsouth-ˈwestern /-ˈwestərn/ *adj* of, from, or in the southwest.

sou'·wester /ˌsauˈwestər/ *n* [C] (esp) waterproof hat with a flap at the back to protect the neck.

sov·er·eign /ˈsavrən, ˈsəv-/ *adj* (of power) highest; without limit; (of a nation, state, ruler) having sovereign power: *become a ~ state,* fully self-governing and independent in foreign affairs. □ *n* [C] sovereign ruler, eg a king, queen or emperor.

sov·er·eignty /ˈsavrənti, ˈsəv-/ sovereign power.

so·viet /ˈsouviˌet/ *n* [C] council of workers, etc in a district of the USSR (*the Union of Soviet Socialist Republics*); any of the higher groups to which these councils give authority, forming part of the system of government (*the Supreme Soviet*) of the whole of the USSR: *Soviet Russia; the Soviet Union.*

sow¹ /sau/ *n* [C] fully grown female pig.

sow² /sou/ *vt,vi* (*pt* sowed, *pp* sown /soun/ or sowed) **1** put (seed) on or in the ground or in soil (in pots, seedboxes, etc); plant (land *with* seed): *sow seeds; sow a plot of land with grass.* **2** (*fig*) start, introduce: *sow the seeds of hatred.*

sower *n* [C] person who sows.

sox *pl* of sock¹.

soy /sɔi/ *n* [U] (also **ˈsoybean**) plant grown as food and for the oil obtained from its seeds: ~ *sauce,* from soybeans in brine.

soya /ˈsɔiə/ = soy.

spa /spa/ *n* [C] (*pl* spas) (place with a) spring of mineral water having medicinal properties.

space /speis/ *n* **1** [U] that in which all objects exist and move: *The universe exists in ~. Travel through ~ to other planets interests many people today.* **2** [C,U] interval or distance between two or more objects: *the ~s between printed words; separated by a ~ of ten feet.* **3** [C,U] area or volume: *open ~s,* (esp) land, in or near a town, not built on. **4** [U] limited or unoccupied place or area; room(3): *There isn't enough ~ in this classroom for thirty desks.* **5** (*sing* only) period of time: *a ~ of three years.* □ *vt* ***space sth out,*** set out with regular spaces between: *~ out the posts ten feet apart.*

ˈspace capsule/craft/helmet/rocket/ship/suit/vehicle, of the kind needed for travel beyond the earth's atmosphere.

spa·cious /ˈspeiʃəs/ *adj* having much space.

spa·cious·ly *adv*

spa·cious·ness /-nɪs/ *n* [U]

spade /speid/ *n* [C] **1** tool with flat blade having a sharp edge for digging. **2** one of the thirteen playing cards with black shapes like hearts upside down printed on them: *the five of ~s*. ⇨ illus at card. □ *vt* dig with a spade.

ˈspade·ful /-ˌfʊl/ *n* [C] (*pl* ~**fuls**) as much as a spade can hold.

ˈspade·work *n* [U] (*fig*) hard, basic, work: *He got all the credit for the research but I did all the ~work*.

spa·ghetti /spəˈgeti/ *n* [U] (*I*) pasta of narrow long strings or sticks, cooked by boiling.

span /spæn/ *n* [C] **1** distance between the tips of a persons's thumb and little finger when stretched out. **2** distance or part between the supports of an arch: *The arch has a ~ of 150 feet*. **3** length in time, from beginning to end: *for a short ~ of time*. □ *vt* (-nn-) **1** extend across (from side to side): *The river is ~ned by many bridges*. **2** (of time) from one period or point to another: *His life ~ned almost all of the 19th century*. **3** measure by spans(1).

spangle /ˈspæŋgəl/ *n* [C] tiny disc of shining metal, esp one of many, as used for ornament on a dress, etc. □ *vt* (esp as a *pp*) cover with, or as with, spangles.

Spaniard /ˈspænyərd/ *n* [C] native of Spain.

span·iel /ˈspænyəl/ *n* [C] sorts of dog with short legs and large, drooping ears.

Spanish /ˈspaniʃ/ *n* **1** the Spanish language. **2** (*pl*) (used with *the*) Spanish people. □ *adj* of Spain, its language or its people.

spank /spæŋk/ *vt,vi* punish (a child) by slapping him on the buttocks with the open hand or a slipper, etc.

spank·ing *n* **(a)** [U] punishment by slapping on the buttocks. **(b)** [C] instance of this.

spar[1] /spar/ *n* [C] strong wooden or metal pole used as a mast, boom, etc.

spar[2] /spar/ *vi* (-rr-) **1** make the motions of attack and defense with the fists (as in boxing). **2** (*fig*) quarrel or argue.

ˈspar·ring partner, man with whom a boxer spars as part of his training.

spare[1] /spær/ *adj* **1** additional to what is usually needed or used; in reserve for use when needed; (of time) leisure; unoccupied: *I have no/very little ~ time/money*, no time/money that I cannot use. *Is there a ~ tire in your car?* **2** (of persons) thin; lean: *a tall, ~ man*. □ *n* [C] spare part (for a machine, etc).

ˌspare ˈpart, part to replace a broken or worn-out part of a machine, an engine, etc.

spare·ribs /ˈspæ(r)ˌrɪbz/ *n pl* ribs of pork with most of the meat cut off.

spare[2] /spær/ *vt,vi* **1** (decide to) not hurt, damage or destroy; show mercy to: *~ a prisoner's life. He doesn't ~ himself*, makes great demands on himself (his energies, time, etc). ***spare sb's feelings,*** avoid hurting his feelings. **2** afford to, be able to, give (time, money, etc) to a person, or for a purpose: *Can you ~ an extra ticket for me? Can you ~ me a few minutes (of your time)? We haven't enough to ~*, are not able to give any away. ***spare a thought for sb,*** consider him when making a decision. **3** with no economy in money or effort: *I'm going to redecorate the house, no expense ~d*.

spar·ing *adj* ***sparing of,*** economical, careful (of): *You should be more sparing of your energy*.

spar·ing·ly *adv*

spark /spark/ *n* [C] **1** tiny glow from a burning substance or still present in ashes, etc or produced by hard metal and stone banging together, or by the breaking of an electric current: *The firework burst into a shower of ~s*. **2** (*fig*) sign of life, energy, etc: *He hasn't a ~ of generosity in him*. □ *vt,vi* **1** give out sparks. **2** ***spark sth off,*** (*fig*) be the immediate cause of: *His statement ~ed off a quarrel between them*.

ˈspark plug, device for firing the mixture of air and gasoline in an engine by means of an electric spark.

sparkle /ˈsparkəl/ *vi* **1** send out flashes of light: *Her diamonds ~d in the bright light*. **2** (*fig*) express brightly: *Her eyes ~d with excitement*. □ *n* [C] spark; glitter; gleam.

spark·ler *n* [C] something that sparkles, eg a kind of firework.

spark·ling /ˈsparklɪŋ/ *adj*

spar·row /ˈspærou/ *n* [C] very common, small brownish-gray bird.

sparse /spars/ *adj* **1** not crowded: *a ~ population*. **2** not dense, thick: *a ~ beard*.

sparsely *adv*: *a ~ly furnished room*, one with little furniture.

sparse·ness /-nɪs/ *n* [U]

spasm /ˈspæzəm/ *n* [C] **1** sudden and involuntary tightening of a muscle or muscles: *asthma ~s*. **2** sudden, convulsive movement: *in a ~ of pain/excitement; a coughing ~*. **3** sudden burst (of energy).

spas·modic /ˌspæzˈmadɪk/ *adj* **1** taking place, done, at irregular intervals. **2** caused by, affected by, spasms: *~ asthma*.

spas·modi·cally /-kli/ *adv*

spas·tic /ˈspæstɪk/ *n* [C], *adj* (person) physically disabled because of faulty links between the brain and motor nerves, causing difficulty in controlling voluntary muscles.

spat[1] /spæt/ *n* [C] brief but intensive quarrel or argument. □ *vi* engage in a spat.

spat[2] /spæt/ *n* (usually *pl*) buttoned or zippered covering for the ankles, worn over low shoes for protection or looks.

spat[3] *pt,pp* of spit².

spate /speit/ *n* [C,U] **1** strong current of water at abnormally high level (in a river). **2** sudden rush of business, etc: *a ~ of orders*.

spa·tial /ˈspeiʃəl/ *adj* of, in relation to, existing in, space.

spa·tially /-ʃəli/ *adv*

spat·ter /ˈspætər/ *vt,vi* **1** splash, scatter, in drips: *~ grease on one's clothes/~ one's clothes with grease*. **2** fall or spread out in drops: *rain ~ing down on the tent*. □ *n* [C] shower: *a ~ of rain/bullets*.

spat·ula /ˈspætʃələ/ *n* [C] (*pl* ~s) tool with a wide, flat, flexible blade used for mixing or spreading various substances, and for lifting or serving food.

spawn /spɔn/ *n* [U] eggs of fish and certain water animals, eg frogs. □ *vt,vi* **1** produce spawn. **2** (*fig*) produce in great numbers: *committees which ~ subcommittees*.

spay /spei/ *vt* remove the ovaries of a female (eg

a dog or cat) so that it cannot reproduce.

SPCA /ˌes ˌpi ˌsi ˈei/ *abbr* = Society for the Prevention of Cruelty to Animals.

speak /spik/ *vi,vt* (*pt* spoke /spouk/, *pp* spoken /ˈspoukən/) **1** use language in an ordinary, not a singing, voice: *Please ~ more slowly. I was ~ing to him about plans for the holidays.* ***speak for sb,*** **(a)** state the views, wishes, etc of. **(b)** give evidence on behalf of. ***nothing to speak of,*** nothing worth mentioning. ***speak out/up,*** **(a)** speak loud(er). **(b)** give one's opinions, etc without hesitation or fear. ***be on ˈspeaking terms with sb,*** **(a)** know him well enough to speak to him. **(b)** continue to speak to him (because there has not been a quarrel). ***so to speak,*** if I may use this expression, etc. **2** give evidence (of), express ideas (not necessarily in words): *Actions ~ louder than words.* **3** know and be able to use (a language): *He ~s several languages.* **4** address an audience; make a speech: *He spoke for forty minutes.* **5** make known: *~ the truth.* ***speak one's mind,*** express one's views. **6** ***strictly/roughly/generally speaking,*** using the word(s) in a strict/rough/general sense.

speaker *n* [C] **(a)** person who makes speeches (in the manner shown): *He's a good/poor ~er.* **(b)** (short for) loudspeaker. **(c) the Speaker,** presiding officer of the House of Representatives and other legislative assemblies.

spear /spɪr/ *n* [C] weapon with a metal point on a long shaft, used in hunting, or (formerly) by men fighting on foot. □ *vt* pierce, wound, make (a hole) in, with a spear, fork, etc.

ˈspear·head *n* [C] (*fig*) individual or group chosen to lead an attack. □ *vt* act as spearhead for: *~head the campaign for human rights.*

spear·mint /ˈspɪrˌmɪnt/ *n* [U] aromatic variety of mint used for flavoring.

spec.[1] *abbr* = **1** special. **2** specific. **3** specification.

spec[2] /spek/ *n* [C] (*informal*) specification: *What are the ~s of this design?*

ˈspec sheet, (*informal*) sheet listing specifications for a mechanical design, etc.

spe·cial /ˈspeʃəl/ *adj* **1** of a particular or certain sort; not common, usual or general; of or for a certain person, thing or purpose: *His painting is something ~,* particularly good. *He did it for her as a ~ favor. What are your ~ interests?* **2** exceptional in amount, degree, etc: *Why should we give you ~ treatment?* □ *n* [C] special train, edition of a newspaper, dish (of a restaurant), etc.

special deˈlivery, delivery of mail (a letter, package, etc) by a special messenger instead of by the usual postal services.

spe·cial·ist /-ʃəlɪst/, person who is an expert in a profession, esp medicine: *an ˈeye ~ist.*

spe·cially /-ʃəli/ *adv* particularly: *I came here ~ly to see you.*

spe·ci·al·ity /ˌspeʃiˈæləti/ *n* [C] (*pl* -ies) **1** special quality or characteristic. **2** = specialty.

spe·cial·ize /ˈspeʃəˌlaiz/ *vi,vt* **1** be or become a specialist; give special or particular attention to: *After his first degree he hopes to ~.* **2** (usually as a *pp*) for a particular purpose: *~d knowledge.*

spe·cial·iz·ation /ˌspeʃəlɪˈzeɪʃən/ *n* [C,U]

spe·cial·ty /ˈspeʃəlti/ *n* [C] (*pl* -ies) particular activity, product, operation, etc; thing to which a person (firm, etc) gives particular attention or for which a place is well known: *Embroidery is her ~.*

spe·cies /ˈspiˌʃiz/ *n* [C] (*pl* unchanged) **1** group of animals having similar characteristics, able to breed with each other but not with other groups: *the human ~,* mankind. **2** sort: *He's a rare ~,* rare type of person.

spe·ci·fic /spəˈsɪfɪk/ *adj* **1** detailed and precise: *~ orders.* **2** relating to one particular thing, etc, not general: *The money is to be used for a ~ purpose.*

spe·cifi·cally /-kli/ *adv* in a specific manner: *You were ~ally warned by your doctor not to smoke.*

spec·ifi·ca·tion /ˌspesəfɪˈkeiʃən/ *n* **1** [U] specifying. **2** [C] (often *pl*) details, instructions, etc for the design, materials, of something to be made or done: *~s for (building) a garage.*

spec·ify /ˈspesəˌfai/ *vt* (*pt,pp* -ied) name a particular one, type, etc: *~ which colors to use.*

speci·men /ˈspesəmɪn/ *n* [C] **1** one as an example of a class: *~s of rocks and ores.* **2** part taken to represent the whole. **3** something to be tested, etc for a special purpose: *supply the doctor with a ~ of urine.*

spe·cious /ˈspiʃəs/ *adj* (*formal*) appearing right or true, but not really so: *a ~ argument/person.*

spe·cious·ly *adv*

spe·cious·ness /-nɪs/ *n* [U]

speck /spek/ *n* [C] **1** small spot or particle (of dirt, etc): *~s of dust.* **2** (*fig*) small spot: *The ship was a ~ on the horizon.*

specked *adj* marked with specks: *~ed apples.*

speckle /ˈspekəl/ *n* [C] small mark or spot, esp one of many, distinct in color, on the skin, feathers, etc.

speckled *adj*

specs /speks/ *n pl* (*informal*) (short for) **1** spectacles(3): *Where are my ~?* **2** specifications.

spec·tacle /ˈspektəkəl/ *n* [C] **1** public display, procession, etc: *The Inauguration parade was a fine ~.* **2** something seen, esp something grand, remarkable: *The sunrise as seen from the top of the mountain was a tremendous ~.* **3** (*pl*) (also ***a pair of spectacles***) pair of lenses in a frame, resting on the nose and ears, to help the eyesight. (*Note: glasses* is more usual.)

spec·tacu·lar /ˌspekˈtækyələr/ *adj* making a fine spectacle(1,2).

spec·tacu·lar·ly *adv*

spec·ta·tor /ˈspekˌteitər/ *n* [C] person looking at (a show or game).

specter /ˈspektər/ *n* [C] **1** ghost (the usual word). **2** (*fig*) threat or fear of future trouble.

spec·tral /ˈspektrəl/ *adj* **(a)** of the spectrum: *spectral colors.* **(b)** of, like, a ghost.

spec·trum /ˈspektrəm/ *n* [C] (*pl* -tra /-trə/) **1** image of a band of colors (as seen in a rainbow and usually described as red, orange, yellow, green, blue, indigo and violet). **2** (*fig*) wide range or sequence: *the whole ~ of political opinion.*

specu·late /ˈspekyəˌleit/ *vi* **1** consider, form opinions (without having complete know-

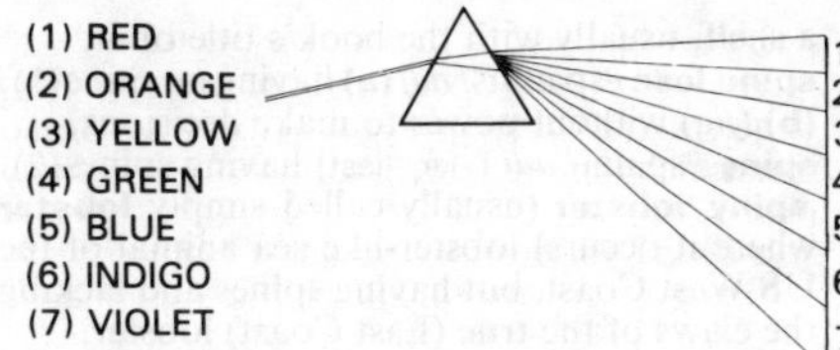

COLOURS OF THE SPECTRUM

ledge): ~ *about/on/upon the future of the human race*. **2** buy and sell goods, stocks and shares, etc with risk of loss and hope of profit through changes in their market value: ~ *in oil shares*.

specu·la·tor /-tər/ person who speculates(2).

specu·la·tion /ˌspekyəˈleiʃən/ *n* **1** [U] speculating(1); [C] opinion reached by this means. **2** [U] speculating(2): ~ *in rice;* [C] business deal of this kind.

specu·lat·ive /ˈspekyəˌleitɪv, ˈspekyələtɪv/ *adj* **1** concerned with speculation(1): ~ *philosophy*. **2** concerned with speculation(2): ~ *purchase of grain*.

specu·la·tive·ly *adv*

sped *pt,pp* of speed.

speech /spitʃ/ *n* **1** [U] power, act, manner, of speaking: *Man is the only animal that has the power of* ~. **2** [C] talk or address given in public: *make a* ~ *on/about human rights*.

speech·less *adj* **(a)** unable to speak, esp because of deep feeling: *Anger left him* ~*less*. **(b)** that causes a person to be unable to speak: ~*less rage*.

ˈspeech therapy, remedial treatment for defective speech, eg for stuttering.

speed /spid/ *n* **1** [U] quickness of movement. ***More ˌhaste, less ˈspeed/ The greater the hurry the less the speed,*** (*prov*) too much haste may result in delay. **2** [C,U] rate of motion or moving: *traveling at full/top* ~*; at a* ~ *of thirty miles an hour*. □ *vt,vi* (*pt,pp* sped but see 3 below) **1** move along, go quickly: *cars* ~*ing past the school*. **2** cause to move or go quickly: ~ *an arrow from the bow*. **3** (*pt,pp* sped or ~ed) increase the speed (of): *They have sped/*~*ed up production/the train service*.

speed·boat *n* [C] motorboat designed for high speeds.

speed·ing *n* [U] (of motorists) traveling at an illegal or dangerous speed: *fined $50 for* ~*ing*.

ˈspeed limit, fastest speed allowed, eg in a built-up area.

speed·o·meter /ˌspiˈdamətər/ *n* [C] instrument showing the speed of a motor vehicle, etc.

ˈspeed·way *n* **(a)** track, for fast driving and racing, esp by motorcycles. **(b)** road for fast traffic.

speedy *adj* (-ier, -iest) quick; coming, done, without delay: *I wish you a* ~*y recovery* (*from illness*).

spell[1] /spel/ *n* [C] **1** words used as a charm, supposed to have magic power: *cast a* ~ *over him; put a* ~ *on him; be under a* ~. **2** attraction, fascination, exercised by a person, occupation, etc: *the* ~ *of Mozart's music*.

ˈspell·bound /-ˌbaund/ *adj* with the attention held by a spell: *The speaker held his audience* ~*bound*.

spell[2] /spel/ *n* [C] **1** period of time: *a long* ~ *of warm weather*. **2** period of activity or duty, esp one at which two or more persons take turns: *take* ~*s at the wheel,* eg of two persons making a long journey by car.

spell[3] /spel/ *vt,vi* (*pt,pp* ~ed or spelt /spelt/) **1** name or write the letters of (a word): *How do you* ~ *your name? These children can't* ~. **2** (of letters) form when put together in a particular order: *C-A-T* ~*s cat*. **3** ***spell sth out,*** make clear and easy to understand; explain in detail: *My request seems simple enough—do you want me to* ~ *it out for you?* **4** have as a consequence: *Does laziness always* ~ *failure?*

speller *n* [C] **(a)** person who spells: *a good/poor* ~*er*. **(b)** spelling book.

spell·ing *n* [U] (knowledge of) the way words are spelled: *Are you good at* ~*ing?* Do you know how to spell words correctly?

ˈspelling book, book, for early school use, with word lists and exercises to teach spelling.

spelt *pt,pp* of spell[3].

spend /spend/ *vt,vi* (*pt,pp* spent /spent/) **1** pay out (money) for goods, services, etc: ~ *all one's money*. **2** use up: ~ *a lot of care/time cleaning the car. They went on firing until all their ammunition was spent*. **3** pass time: ~ *a weekend at the seashore*.

spender *n* [C] person who spends money (usually in the way shown by the *adjective*): *an extravagant* ~*er*.

ˈspend·thrift *n* [C] person who spends money extravagantly.

sperm /spərm/ *n* [U] fertilizing fluid of a man or a male animal.

spew /spyu/ *vt,vi* = vomit.

sphere /sfɪr/ *n* [C] **1** form of a globe; star; planet. ***music of the spheres,*** (*myth*) music produced by the movement of heavenly bodies which men cannot hear. **2** globe representing the earth or the night sky. **3** person's range of interests, activities, surroundings, etc: *gardening is outside the* ~ *of my activities*. **4** range, extent: *a* ~ *of influence*.

spheri·cal /ˈsfɪrɪkəl/ *adj* shaped like a sphere.

sphe·roid /ˈsfɪˌrɔid/ *n* solid that is almost spherical.

spice /spais/ *n* **1** [C,U] kinds of substance, eg ginger, nutmeg, cinnamon, cloves, used to flavor food. **2** [U] (and with *a, an*) (*fig*) interesting flavor, suggestion, or trace (of): *The novelist's use of slang gives real* ~ *to his writings. She has a* ~ *of malice in her character*. □ *vt* add flavor to (something) with: ~*d with humor*.

spicy *adj* (-ier, -iest) **(a)** of, flavored with, spice. **(b)** (*fig*) exciting or interesting because a little immoral: *spicy gossip about a pop star's love life*.

spick /spɪk/ *adj* (only in) ***ˌspick and ˈspan,*** bright, clean and tidy.

spi·der /ˈspaidər/ *n* [C] **1** (sorts of) creature with eight legs, many species of which spin webs for the capture of insects as food. **2** frying pan, esp one with legs for placing over coals.

spid·ery *adj* (of handwriting) with long, thin

strokes.

spied *pt,pp* of spy.

spigot /ˈspɪgət/ *n* [C] **1** plug or peg for the hole of a cask or barrel. **2** valve for controlling the flow of water, etc from a tank, etc.

spike /spaik/ *n* [C] **1** sharp point; pointed piece of metal, eg on iron railings or on running shoes. **2** long, pointed cluster of flowers or grain on a single stem: *~s of lavender*. □ *vt* **1** put spikes (on shoes, etc): *~d running shoes*. **2** pierce or injure with a spike. **3** (*sl*) add alcohol to a soft drink or punch to make it (more) intoxicating.

spiky *adj* (-ier, -iest) having sharp points.

spill /spɪl/ *vt,vi* **1** (of liquid or powder) (allow to) run over the side of the container: *Who has ~ed the milk?* **2** (of a horse, etc) cause (the rider, passenger, etc) to fall: *His horse ~ed him.* **3** (*informal*) give away information, esp sth not intended to be made known: *The government official ~ed the story to the press.* ***spill the beans,*** make known a secret. □ *n* [C] fall from a horse, motorcycle: *have a nasty ~.*

ˈspill·over *n* (often as an *adjective*) (of population) extra: *new suburbs for Miami's ~over (population).*

spilt /spɪlt/ *adj* (having been) spilled.

spin /spɪn/ *vt,vi* (*pt, pp* spun /spən/) (-nn-) **1** form (thread) by twisting wool, cotton, silk, etc; draw out and twist (wool, cotton, etc) into threads. **2** form by means of threads: *spiders ~ning their webs; silkworms ~ning cocoons.* **3** (*fig*) produce, compose (a story). ***spin sth out,*** make it last as long as possible: *He spun out his story, adding more fantastic details.* **4** cause (something) to go around and around: *~ a coin*, send it up in the air, revolving as it goes up, to decide something (by "heads or tails"). **5** move around quickly: *The top was ~ning merrily. The collision sent the car ~ning across the road.* □ *n* **1** [U] turning or spinning motion, esp as given to the ball in some games, eg baseball: *The pitcher gave (a) ~ to the ball.* **2** [C] short ride in a car, on a bicycle, etc; *have/go for a ~.* **3** [C] fast spinning movement of an aircraft during a diving descent: *get into/out of a ~.*

ˈspin·ning jenny, early kind of machine for spinning more than one thread at a time.

ˈspinning wheel, machine for spinning thread continuously on a spindle turned by a large wheel.

ˈspin-off *n* [C] advantage, benefit or product (often unexpected) (from a larger activity or process, or from research for it).

spin·ach /ˈspɪnɪtʃ/ *n* [U] plant with small green leaves, cooked and eaten as a vegetable.

spi·nal /ˈspainəl/ *adj* (*anat*) of or to the spine: *the ~ column*, the backbone.

spindle /ˈspɪndəl/ *n* [C] **1** (in spinning) thin rod for twisting and winding thread by hand. **2** bar or pin which turns round, or on which something turns (eg an axle or a shaft).

spin·dly /ˈspɪndli/ *adj* (-ier, -iest) long and thin; (too) tall and thin.

spine /spain/ *n* [C] **1** = backbone. ⇨ illus at skeleton. **2** sharp, pointed part on some plants, eg a cactus, and animals, eg a porcupine. **3** part of a book's cover that can be seen when it is on a shelf, usually with the book's title on it.

spine·less /ˈspainlɪs/ *adj* **(a)** having no spine(1). **(b)** (*fig*) without power to make decisions.

spiny /ˈspaini/ *adj* (-ier, -iest) having spines(2).

ˌspiny ˈlobster (usually called simply **lobster** where it occurs) lobster-like sea animal of the US West Coast, but having spines and lacking the claws of the true (East Coast) lobster.

spinet /ˈspɪnɪt/ *n* [C] **1** old type of keyboard instrument like a harpsichord. **2** small modern piano with the wires strung upright to save space. ⇨ illus at keyboard.

spin·na·ker /ˈspɪnɪkər/ *n* [C] large triangular sail on a racing yacht or dinghy.

spin·ster /ˈspɪnstər/ *n* [C] (*formal*) unmarried woman, esp after the conventional age for marrying. ⇨ bachelor.

ˈspin·ster·hood /-ˌhʊd/ *n* [U] state of being a spinster.

spi·ral /ˈspairəl/ *adj, n* [C] (in the form of an) advancing or ascending continuous curve winding around a central point: *A snail's shell is ~.* □ *vi* move in a spiral: *The smoke ~ed up.*

spire /ˈspaiər/ *n* [C] pointed structure rising above a tower (esp of a church).

spirit /ˈspɪrɪt/ *n* **1** [C,U] soul; immaterial, intellectual or moral part of man: *The ~ is willing but the flesh is weak*, One is willing (in theory) to do it, but physically (in practice) unable to do it. **2** [C] the soul thought of as separate from the body: *believe in ~s.* **3** [C] elf; goblin. **4** [U] life and consciousness not associated with a body: *God is pure ~.* **5** [C] (always with an *adjective*) person considered from the intellectual, moral or emotional point of view: *What a generous ~ he is!* **6** [U] quality of courage, strength, liveliness: *Put a little more ~ into your work.* **7** (*sing* only) mental or moral attitude: *Whether it was unwise or not depends on the ~ in which it was done.* **8** [U] real meaning or purpose underlying a law, etc (contrasted with the *letter* or apparent meaning of the words, etc): *obey the ~, not the letter, of the law.* **9** (*pl*) state of mind: *in high ~s*, cheerful; *in poor/low ~s, out of ~s*, depressed, unhappy. **10** [U] industrial alcohol. **11** (usually *pl*) strong alcoholic drink (eg whiskey, brandy, gin, rum). □ *vt* take a person or thing quickly, secretly or mysteriously: *She has disappeared as completely as if she had been ~ed away to another planet.*

spir·ited /ˈspɪrɪtɪd/ *adj* **(a)** full of spirit(6): *a ~ed attack/defense/reply.* **(b)** having the kind of spirits(9) shown: *ˌhigh-/ˌlow-ˈ~ed*, happy/depressed.

ˈspirit lamp, alcohol-burning device used for warming or heating small quantities of liquids, etc.

ˈspirit level, (piece of wood with a) glass tube partly filled with water or alcohol, with a bubble of air which, when centered, shows that a surface is horizontal.

spiri·tual /ˈspɪrɪtʃ(u)əl/ *adj* **1** of the spirit(1) or soul; of religion, not of material things; of, from, God; *concerned about one's ~ welfare.* **2** of spirits(2); supernatural. **3** caring much for things of the spirit(1). **4** of the church. □ *n* [C] kind of religious song sung esp by Negroes in the US.

spiri·tu·ally /-tʃəli/ *adv*

spiri·tu·al·ism /ˈspɪrɪtʃəˌlɪzəm/ *n* [U] belief in the possibility of receiving messages from the spirits of the dead; practice of attempting to do this.

spiri·tu·al·ist /-ɪst/ believer in spiritualism.

spiri·tu·al·is·tic /ˌspɪrɪtʃəˈlɪstɪk/ *adj*

spit[1] /spɪt/ *n* [C] **1** long thin metal spike on which to fix meat, etc for roasting. **2** small, narrow point of land running out into a sea, lake, etc. □ *vt* (-pp-) put a spit through (a chicken, piece of meat, etc).

spit[2] /spɪt/ *vt,vi* (*pt,pp* spat /spæt/ or unchanged) (-tt-) **1** send liquid (saliva) out from the mouth; do this as a sign of contempt or hatred: *He spat in the man's face/spat at him. The cat spat* (= made an angry spitting noise) *at the dog*. **2** send (out) from the mouth: *~ out a pit*. **3** (*fig*) say angrily or sharply: *She spat* (*out*) *curses at me*. **4** make the noise of spitting (while sending out something): *The frying pan was ~ting*. **5** (of rain or snow) fall lightly: *It's not raining heavily, only ~ting*. □ *n* **1** [U] = spittle (the usual word). **2** act of spitting. **3** ***the spit and/the spitting image of,*** exact replica or likeness of: *He's the ~ting image of his father*.

spite /spait/ *n* [U] desire to annoy, to cause pain or damage: *do something out of/from ~*. ***in spite of,*** not to be prevented by; although: *They went out in ~ of the rain. In ~ of all his efforts* (= Although he tried) *he failed*. □ *vt* injure or annoy because of spite: *The neighbors let their radio blare every afternoon just to ~ us*.

spite·ful /-fəl/ *adj* having, showing, spite.

spite·fully /-fəli/ *adv*

spite·ful·ness /-nɪs/ *n* [U]

spittle /ˈspɪtəl/ *n* [U] liquid of the mouth; saliva.

splash /splæʃ/ *vt,vi* **1** cause (a liquid) to be flung about in drops; make (a person or thing) wet by splashing: *Children love to ~ water over one another*. **2** (of a liquid) be flung about and fall in drops: *fountains ~ing in the park*. **3** move, fall, so that there is splashing: *The spacecraft ~ed down in the Pacific*. □ *n* [C] **1** (sound, spot, mark, made by) splashing: *He jumped into the swimming pool with a ~*. **2** patch of color: *Her dog is brown with white ~es*.

ˈsplash·down *n* [C] landing of a spacecraft in the sea.

splay /splei/ *vt,vi* make the distance between opposite sides (of an opening) wider; cause to slant or slope. □ *n* [C] sloping side (of a window opening, etc).

spleen /splin/ *n* [C] (*anat*) organ in the abdomen which causes changes in the blood.

splen·did /ˈsplendɪd/ *adj* **1** magnificent: *a ~ sunset/house/victory; ~ jewelry*. **2** (*formal*) excellent: *a ~ dinner/idea*.

splen·did·ly *adv*

splen·dor /ˈsplendər/ *n* [U] (sometimes *pl*) magnificence; brightness: *the ~ of the moonlight over the sea*.

splice /splais/ *vt* **1** join (two ends of rope) by twisting the threads of one into those of the other. **2** join (two pieces of wood, magnetic tape, film) by fastening them at the ends. □ *n* [C] joint made by splicing.

splint /splɪnt/ *n* [C] strip of wood, etc strapped to an arm, leg, etc to keep a broken bone in the right position.

splin·ter /ˈsplɪntər/ *n* [C] sharp piece of hard material (wood, metal, glass, etc) split, torn or broken off a larger piece: *have a ~ in one's finger*. □ *vt,vi* break into splinters.

ˈsplinter group/party, (*pol*) group of persons who have broken away from their party.

split /splɪt/ *vt,vi* (*pt,pp* split) (-tt-) **1** break, cause to break, be broken, into two or more parts, esp from end to end along the length or the line of natural division: *Some kinds of wood ~ easily. He can ~ a match in two*. **2** break open by bursting: *His coat has ~ at the seams*. ***a splitting headache,*** so severe that it feels that one's head may break. **3** (cause to) break into parts; divide: *The party ~ up into small groups*. ***split the difference,*** (when making a bargain) compromise (on the price, cost, etc). ***split hairs,*** make very fine distinctions (in an argument, etc). ***split one's sides laughing/with laughter,*** laugh a great deal about something. □ *n* [C] **1** (crack or tear made by splitting): *Will you sew up this ~ in my trousers?* **2** separation or division resulting from splitting: *a ~ in the Democratic Party*. **3** half-size bottle of wine. **4** acrobat's feat of sitting on the floor with legs stretched out in a line with the trunk upright: *do ~s*.

ˌsplit persoˈnality = schizophrenia.

ˌsplit ˈsecond, a brief moment.

splurge /ˈsplərdʒ/ *n* [C] brief but intense display of carefree activity, eg spending beyond one's means. □ *vt, vi* spend (money) wastefully.

splut·ter /ˈsplətər/ *vi,vt* speak quickly, confusedly (from excitement, etc): *~ out a few words/a threat*. □ *n* [U] spluttering sound.

spoil /ˈspɔiəl/ *vt,vi* (-ing /ˈspɔilɪŋ/) (*pt,pp* ~t, usually ~ed) **1** make useless or unsatisfactory: *fruit ~ed by insects; vacation ~ed by bad weather*. **2** harm the character or temperament of (somebody) by too much kindness or lack of discipline: *parents who ~ their children*. **3** pay great attention to the comfort and wishes of: *He likes having a wife who ~s him*. **4** (of food, etc) become bad, unfit for use: *Some kinds of food soon ~*. **5** ***be spoiling for sth,*** be eager for it: *Harry is ~ing for a fight*. □ *n* **1** (either [U] or *pl*, not with numerals) stolen goods: *The thieves divided up the ~(s)*. **2** (*pl*) profits, profitable positions, gained from political power: *the ~s of office*. **3** [U] earth, unwanted material, etc thrown or brought up in excavating, draining, etc.

ˈspoil·sport *n* [C] person who does things that interfere with the enjoyment of other people.

spoke[1] /spouk/ *n* [C] any one of the bars or wire rods connecting the hub (center) of a wheel with the rim (outer edge).

spoke[2]**, spoken** *pt,pp* of speak.

spokes·man /ˈspouksmən/ *n* [C] (*pl* -men /-men/) person speaking, chosen to speak, as the representative of a group.

sponge /spəndʒ/ *n* **1** [C] kinds of simple sea animal; its body made of elastic material full of holes and able to absorb water easily. **2** one of these, or something similar, used for washing, cleaning, etc. **3** piece of absorbent material, eg gauze, used in surgery. **4** = sponge cake. □ *vt,vi* **1** wash, wipe or clean with a sponge: *~ a wound/a child's face*. **2** take up (liquid) with a sponge: *~ up the mess*. **3** (*informal*) obtain money from a person, without giving, or intending to give, anything in return: *~ on one's friends*.

ˈsponge bath, substitute for a bath, when a tub cannot be used, by washing the body with a sponge.

ˈsponge boat, boat equipped and used for gathering sponges for market.

ˈsponge cake, soft cake like a sponge.

ˈsponge diver, professional diver for sponges.

sponger *n* [C] person who sponges(3).

spongy *adj* (-ier, -iest)

spon·sor /ˈspansər/ *n* [C] **1** person (eg a godfather) making himself responsible for another. **2** person who puts forward or guarantees a proposal. □ *vt* act as a sponsor for.

spon·ta·neous /ˌspanˈteiniəs/ *adj* done, happening, from natural impulse, not suggested: *He made a ~ offer of help.*

spon·ta·neity /ˌspantəˈneiəti/ *n* [U]

spon·ta·neous·ly *adv*

spoof /spuf/ *vt* parody, make fun of (esp in a movie or play). □ *n* [C] instance of this.

spook /spuk/ *n* [C] ghost. □ *vt* (*sl*) frighten.

spooky *adj* (-ier, -iest) of, suggesting, ghosts: *a ~y (=* haunted) *house*.

spool /spul/ *n* [C] reel (for thread, wire, photographic film, magnetic tape, etc).

spoon[1] /spun/ *n* [C] utensil with a shallow bowl on a handle, used for stirring, serving and taking up food (named according to use): *a desˈsert ~/ˈsoup ~/ˈtable~/ˈtea~*. □ *vt* take with a spoon: *~ up one's soup; ~ out the peas*, serve them.

ˈspoon-feed *vt* **(a)** feed (a baby, etc) from a spoon. **(b)** (*fig*) give (a person) too much help or teaching: *Some teachers ~-feed their pupils.*

ˈspoon·ful /-ˌfʊl/ *n* [C] (*pl* ~fuls) as much as a spoon can hold.

spoon[2] /spun/ *vi* (*dated*) behave in a way that shows that one is in love: *young couples ~ing on park seats.*

spor·adic /spəˈrædɪk/ *adj* occurring, seen, only here and there or occasionally: *~ raids/firing*.

spor·adi·cally /-kli/ *adv*

spore /spɔr/ *n* [C] germ, single cell, by which a flowerless plant (eg moss, a fern) reproduces itself.

sport /spɔrt/ *n* **1** [U] activity engaged in, esp outdoors, for amusement and exercise; [C] particular form of such activity: *fond of ~; athletic ~s*, eg running, jumping; *ˈ~s coverage/reporting on TV*. **2** unselfish, kind person: *Be a ~ and help me with this suitcase.* □ *vi,vt* **1** play about, amuse oneself: *seals ~ing about in the water.* **2** (*informal*) have or wear proudly: *~ a mustache/a diamond ring.*

sport·ing *adj* **(a)** connected with, interested in, sport: *a ~ing man.* **(b)** willing to take a risk of losing; involving a risk of losing: *give her a ~ing chance.*

sport·ing·ly *adv*

ˈsports car, small automobile designed for high speeds.

ˈsports·man /-mən/ (*pl* ~smen /-men/) **(a)** person who takes part in, is fond of, sport. **(b)** = sport(2).

sports·man·like *adj*

ˈsports·man·ship /-ˌʃɪp/ *n* [U] behavior suitable for a sportsman.

spot /spat/ *n* [C] **1** small (esp round) mark different in color from what it is on: *Which has ~s, the leopard or the tiger?* **2** dirty mark or stain: *~s of mud on your boots.* **3** small, red place on the skin: *This ointment won't clear your face of ~s.* **4** (*fig*) moral stain: *There isn't a ~ on her reputation.* **5** drop: *Did you feel a few ~s of rain?* **6** particular place or area: *the (very) ~ where he was murdered.* ***on the spot,*** **(a)** at the place where one is needed: *The police were on the ~ within a few minutes.* **(b)** immediately: *The bullet struck his head and he was killed on the ~.* ***find/put one's finger on sb's ˈweak spot,*** find the point (of character, etc) where he is most open to attack. ***hit the spot,*** (*sl*) (of food and drink) be very satisfying: *This lemonade really hits the ~!* □ *vt,vi* (-tt-) **1** mark, become marked, with spots: *a table ~ted with ink.* **2** pick out, recognize, see (one person or thing out of many): *~ a friend in a crowd.*

spot ˈcheck, check without warning: *~ checks by police on motor vehicles.*

spot·less *adj* free from spots; clean: *a ~less kitchen/reputation.*

spot·less·ly *adv: ~lessly clean.*

spot·ted *adj* marked with spots, eg of animal or material.

spotty *adj* (-ier, -iest) **(a)** marked with spots (on the skin): *a ~ty complexion.* **(b)** of varying quality: *a ~ty piece of work*, done unevenly.

spot·light /ˈspatˌlait/ *n* [C] (projector or lamp used for sending a) strong light directed onto a particular place or person, eg on the stage of a theater. ***be in/hold the spotlight,*** (*fig*) be the center of attention. □ *vt* direct a spotlight onto.

spouse /spaus/ *n* [C] (*legal*) husband or wife.

spout /spaut/ *n* [C] **1** pipe through or from which liquid pours, eg for tea from a teapot. **2** stream of liquid coming out with great force. ⇨ waterspout. □ *vt,vi* **1** (of liquid) come or send out with great force: *blood ~ing from a cut artery.* **2** (*informal*) speak, recite (verses, etc) pompously: *~ing political slogans.*

sprain /sprein/ *vt* injure (a joint, eg in the wrist or ankle) by twisting violently so that there is pain and swelling: *~ one's wrist.* □ *n* [C] injury so caused.

sprang *pt* of spring[2].

sprat /spræt/ *n* [C] small European ocean fish used as food.

sprawl /sprɔl/ *vi* **1** sit or lie with the arms and legs loosely spread out; fall so that one lies in this way: *~ing on the sofa; be sent ~ing in the mud.* **2** (of plants, handwriting) spread out loosely and irregularly. **3** (*fig*) (of towns) spread over much space: *suburbs that ~ out into the countryside.* □ *n* [C] sprawling position, movement or area.

spray[1] /sprei/ *n* [C] **1** small branch of a tree or plant, esp as an ornament. **2** ornament in a similar form: *a ~ of diamonds.*

spray² /sprei/ *n* **1** [U] liquid sent through the air in tiny drops (by the wind, or through an apparatus): *ˈsea ~.* **2** [C,U] kinds of liquid preparation, eg a perfume, disinfectant or insecticide, to be applied in the form of spray. **3** [C] device that sprays (perfume, etc). □ *vt* put spray on: *~ fruit trees.*

sprayer *n* **(a)** person who sprays. **(b)** apparatus for spraying.

ˈspray gun, apparatus using pressure to spread paint, varnish, etc over surfaces.

spread /spred/ *vt,vi* (*pt,pp* ~) **1** extend the surface or width of something by unfolding or unrolling it: *~ out a map; ~ (out) one's arms. The bird ~ its wings.* **2** cover by spreading: *~ a table with a cloth.* **3** put (a substance) on a surface and extend its area by flattening, etc; cover (a surface) by doing this: *~ butter on bread/a slice of bread with butter.* ***spread the table,*** place dishes, glasses, food, etc on it ready for a meal. **4** (cause to) become more widely extended or distributed: *~ knowledge. Flies ~ disease. The water ~ over the floor. The rumor quickly ~ through the village. The fire ~ from the factory to the houses next door.* **5** extend in space: *a desert ~ing for hundreds of miles.* **6** extend in time: *a course of studies ~ over three years; payments ~ over twelve months.* □ *n* [C] (rarely *pl*) **1** extent; breadth: *the ~ of a bird's wings.* **2** extension; spreading(4): *the ~ of disease/knowledge/education.* **3** (*informal*) table with good things to eat and drink on it: *What a superb ~!* **4** something that is spread(1) (usually in compounds): *a ˈbed~,* a cover spread over the bedclothes. **5** name used for various kinds of paste (to be) spread on bread, etc.

ˈspread-eagle *vt* (*reflexive*) take up a lying position with arms and legs extended to form a cross: *sunbathers were ~-eagled on the grass.*

spreader *n* [C] person who, that which, spreads, eg an implement used for spreading paste, etc on bread.

spree /spri/ *n* [C]: *have a ~,* have a lively, merry time; *a ˈspending/ˈbuying ~,* an occasion of (extravagant or unusual) spending of money. ***be on the spree/go out on a spree,*** be having/go out to enjoy, a spree.

sprig /sprɪg/ *n* [C] small twig (*of* a plant or bush) with leaves, etc: *a ~ of holly.*

spright·ly /ˈspraitli/ *adj* (-ier, -iest) lively; brisk.

spright·li·ness /-nɪs/ *n* [U]

spring¹ /sprɪŋ/ *n* **1** [C] act of springing or jumping up. **2** [C] (place where there is) water coming up from the ground: *a ˈhot ~; ˈmineral ~.* **3** [C] device of twisted, bent or coiled metal or wire which tends to return to its shape or position when pulled or pushed or pressed: *the ~ of a watch.* **4** [U] elastic quality: *rubber bands that have lost their ~.*

ˈspring balance, device that measures weight by how much the object pulls a spring down.

ˌspring ˈbinder, cover shaped like a book with a spring in the spine for holding papers.

ˈspring·board *n* [C] board to give a springing lift to a person jumping from it.

ˈspring clip, metal clip for holding papers, etc operated by a spring action.

springy *adj* (-ier, -iest) (of movement or substances) elastic; that springs: *walk with a youthful ~y step.*

spring² /sprɪŋ/ *vi,vt* (*pt* sprang /spræŋ/, *pp* sprung /sprəŋ/) **1** jump suddenly from the ground; move suddenly (*up, down, out,* etc) from being still, hidden, etc: *He sprang to his feet/sprang out of bed/sprang out from behind the bush/sprang up from his seat. The branch sprang back and hit me in the face.* **2** grow up quickly from the ground or from a stem: *Weeds were ~ing up everywhere.* **3** appear suddenly: *Where have you sprung from?* **4** (*fig*) occur suddenly: *A suspicion/doubt sprang up in her mind.* **5** cause suddenly: *He sprang a surprise on me.* **6** cause to operate by means of a mechanism: *~ a trap,* cause it to go off. **7** ***spring a leak,*** (of a ship, etc) crack or burst so that water enters.

spring³ /sprɪŋ/ *n* [C] season of the year in which vegetation begins; season between winter and summer: *in (the) ~;* (as an *adj*) *~ flowers/weather.*

ˌspring-ˈcleaning *n* [C] thorough cleaning of a house, room, etc (traditionally done once a year, in the spring).

ˈspring·like *adj: ~like weather.*

ˈspring·time (also (*formal*) **ˈspring·tide**) *n* season of spring.

sprinkle /ˈsprɪŋkəl/ *vt* direct, throw, a shower of (something) onto (a surface): *sprinkling water on a dusty path; ~ the floor with sand.*

sprink·ler /ˈsprɪŋklər/ *n* [C] (esp) apparatus or device for sprinkling water (eg onto a lawn) or (permanently installed in buildings) for fighting fire.

ˈsprinkler system, network of sprinklers buried in a lawn for watering or installed in a building to fight fire, placed so as to cover a large area with water.

sprink·ling /ˈsprɪŋklɪŋ/ *n* small quantity or number: *There was a sprinkling of young people in the audience.*

sprint /sprɪnt/ *vi* run a short distance at full speed: *He ~ed past his competitors just before reaching the tape.* □ *n* [C] **1** such a run. **2** short race, eg 100 yards.

sprin·ter *n* [C] person who sprints.

sprite /sprait/ *n* [C] fairy; elf.

sprout /spraut/ *vi,vt* **1** put out leaves; begin to grow: *Peter has really ~ed up in the past year.* **2** cause to grow: *The continuous wet weather has ~ed the wheat.* **3** develop, produce: *Tom has ~ed a mustache.* □ *n* [C] **1** new part of a plant. **2** = Brussels sprout.

spruce¹ /sprus/ *adj* neat and smart in dress and appearance. □ *vt,vi* make oneself smart: *Go and ~ yourself up.*

spruce·ly *adv*

spruce·ness /-nɪs/ *n* [U]

spruce² /sprus/ *n* [C,U] (also **ˈspruce fir**) kinds of fir tree grown in farms for its wood, used for making paper.

sprung *pp* of spring².

spry /sprai/ *adj* (-er, -est) lively: *still ~ at eighty.* ***look spry,*** be quick.

spud /spəd/ *n* [C] (*sl*) potato.

spume /spyum/ *n* [U] foam; froth.
spun *pp* of spin.
spunk /spəŋk/ *n* [U] (*informal*) courage: *a boy with plenty of* ~.
spur /spər/ *n* [C] **1** one of a pair of sharp-toothed wheels on the heels of a rider's boots and used to make the horse go faster. ⇨ illus at cowboy. **2** (*fig*) something that urges a person on to greater activity: *the* ~ *of poverty*. ***act on the spur of the moment,*** act on a sudden impulse. **3** ridge extending from a mountain or hill. □ *vt,vi* (-rr-) urge on with, or as with, spurs: *He was* ~*red on by ambition.*
spu·ri·ous /ˈspyʊriəs/ *adj* (*formal*) false; not genuine: *a* ~ *argument.*
spu·ri·ous·ly *adv*
spurn /spərn/ *vt* reject or refuse; have nothing to do with (an offer, a person or his advances).
spurt /spərt/ *vi* **1** (of liquids, flame, etc) come out in a sudden burst: *Blood* ~*ed* (*out*) *from the wound.* **2** make a sudden, short and violent effort, esp in a race or other contest: *The runner* ~*ed as he approached the winning post.* □ *n* [C] sudden bursting forth; sudden burst of energy: ~*s of water/flame/energy; put on a* ~ (= increase speed) *toward the end of a race.*
sput·ter /ˈspətər/ *vi,vt* **1** make a series of spitting sounds: *The sausages were* ~*ing in the frying pan.* **2** = splutter.
spu·tum /ˈspyutəm/ *n* [U] matter coughed up from the throat.
spy /spai/ *n* [C] (*pl* spies) **1** person who tries to get secret information, esp about the military affairs of other countries. **2** person who keeps a secret watch on the movements of others: *industrial spies,* employed to learn trade secrets, etc. □ *vi,vt* **1** act as a spy on, watch secretly: ~*ing on the enemy's movements;* ~ *out the land.* **2** observe; see; discover: *I* ~ *someone coming up the garden path.*
ˈspy·glass *n* [C] small telescope.
sq. *abbr.* = square.
squabble /ˈskwabəl/ *vi* take part in a small or noisy quarrel: *Tom was squabbling with his sister about who should use the bicycle.* □ *n* [C] noisy small quarrel.
squad /skwad/ *n* [C] small group of persons, eg of soldiers, working or being trained together.
ˈsquad car, police patrol car.
squad·ron /ˈskwadrən/ *n* [C] **1** sub-unit of a cavalry, armored or engineer regiment (120-200 men). **2** number of warships or military aircraft forming a unit.
squalid /ˈskwalɪd/ *adj* dirty, poor, uncared for: *living in* ~ *conditions/houses.*
squalid·ly *adv*
squall /skwɔl/ *n* [C] **1** loud cry of pain or fear (esp from a baby or child). **2** sudden violent wind, often with rain or snow. □ *vi* utter squalls (1): ~*ing babies.*
squalor /ˈskwalər/ *n* [U] squalid state: *born in* ~*; the* ~ *of the slums.*
squan·der /ˈskwandər/ *vt* waste (time, money).
square[1] /skwær/ *adj* **1** having the shape of a square(1): *a* ~ *table.* **2** having or forming (exactly or approximately) a right angle: ~ *corners; a* ~ *jaw/chin,* with angular, not curved, outlines. **3** level or parallel (*with*); balanced; settled: *get one's accounts* ~, settled. ***be (all) square,*** neither owing anything to the other; equal: *Let's call it all* ~*, shall we?* **4** connected with a number multiplied by itself: *a* ~ *yard/meter,* an area equal to that of a square surface which has sides of one yard/meter: *nine* ~ *centimeters. The* ~ *root of 9 is 3.* **5** ***a square meal,*** one with plenty of good, nutritious food. **6** fair, honest: ~ *dealings,* in business. **7** (*dated sl*) (of a person) formal, conventional, old-fashioned. □ *adv* **1** in a square(2) manner: *stand/sit* ~*; hit a man* ~ *on the jaw.* **2** ***ˌfair and ˈsquare,*** in an honest, fair manner.
ˌsquare-ˈbuilt *adj* (of a person) of comparatively broad shape.
ˈsquare dance, one in which the dancers face inwards from four sides.
ˈsquare knot, one tied so that the ends are parallel, giving it a square shape. ⇨ illus at knot.
square·ly *adv* **(a)** so as to form a right angle. **(b)** fairly; honestly: *act* ~*ly.* **(c)** directly opposite: *He faced me* ~*ly across the table.*
square·ness /-nɪs/ *n* [U]
ˌsquare-ˈshouldered *adj* with the shoulders at right angles to the neck, not sloping.
ˈsquare-toed *adj* (of shoes) having a square toe cap.
square[2] /skwær/ *n* [C] **1** flat shape with four equal sides and four right angles. ⇨ illus at geometry. ***back to square one,*** (*informal*) back to the starting point and forced to start again. **2** anything having the shape of a square. **3** four-sided open area, eg in a town, used as a garden or for recreation, or one enclosed by streets and buildings: *listening to the band playing in the* ~. **4** buildings and streets surrounding a square (3): *He lived at 95 Washington Square.* **5** block of buildings bounded by four streets; distance along one side. **6** result when a number or quantity is multiplied by itself: *The* ~ *of 7 is 49.* **7** L-shaped or (**ˈT-square**) T-shaped instrument for drawing or testing right angles. **8** (*dated sl*) person (considered to be) square(7).
square[3] /skwær/ *vt,vi* **1** make square; give a square shape to. **2** cause one line or side to make a right angle with another: ~ *timber.* **3** make straight or level: ~ *one's shoulders.* **4** multiply a number by itself: *Three* ~*d is nine.* **5** mark (*off*) in squares. **6** settle, balance (accounts): ~ *up on Friday.* **7** (*fig*) have one's revenge: ~ *accounts with an enemy.* **8** make or be consistent: *It would help if the facts* ~*d with the theory, but they do not.* **9** ***square off,*** take up the attitude of a boxer (ready to begin fighting).
squash[1] /skwaʃ/ *vt,vi* **1** press flat or into a small space: ~ *too many people into a bus.* **2** become squashed or pressed out of shape: *Soft fruits* ~ *easily.* **3** squeeze or crowd: *Don't all try to* ~ *into the elevator together.* **4** (*informal*) silence (a person) with a clever, sarcastic, etc reply, statement: *He was/felt completely* ~*ed.* **5** (*informal*) defeat (a rebellion). □ *n* [C] (rarely *pl*) **1** crowd of persons squashed together: *There was a terrible* ~ *at the gate.* **2** (sound of) something squashing or being squashed: *The ripe tomato hit the speaker in the face with a* ~.

squash[2] /skwaʃ/ *n* [U] (also ˈ**squash rackets**) game played with rackets and a rubber ball in a walled court.

squash[3] /skwaʃ/ *n* (*pl* unchanged) kinds of gourd, like a pumpkin, eaten as a vegetable. ⇨ illus at vegetable.

squat /skwat/ *vi* (-tt-) **1** sit on one's heels, or on the ground with the legs drawn up under or close to the body: *The old man ~ted in front of the fire.* **2** (of animals) crouch with the body close to the ground. **3** (*informal*) sit: *Find somewhere to ~.* **4** settle on land without permission, esp publicly owned and unoccupied land (in order to get ownership); occupy empty (usually deserted, derelict) buildings without authority. □ *adj* short and thick: *a ~ man.*

squat·ter *n* [C] **(a)** person who squats(1). **(b)** person who squats(4).

squaw /skwɔ/ *n* [C] North American Indian woman or wife.

squawk /skwɔk/ *vi, n* [C] **1** (chiefly of birds) (make a) loud, harsh cry, as when hurt or frightened. **2** (*informal*) (make a) loud complaint.

squeak /skwik/ *n* [C] **1** short, shrill cry, eg made by a mouse, or similar sound, eg from an unoiled hinge. **2** ***a narrow squeak,*** a narrow escape from danger or failure. □ *vi,vt* make a squeak: *These new shoes ~.*

squeaky *adj* (-ier, -iest) squeaking: *~y shoes.*

squeal /ˈskwiəl/ *n* [C] shrill cry or sound, longer and louder than a squeak, often showing terror or pain: *the ~ of brakes,* eg on trucks. □ *vi,vt* (-ing /ˈskwilɪŋ/) **1** make a squeal: *The pigs were ~ing. He ~ed like a pig.* **2** say in a squealing voice. **3** (*informal*) become an informer.

squealer /ˈskwilər/ *n* [C] **(a)** animal that squeals. **(b)** (*sl*) informer.

squeam·ish /ˈskwimɪʃ/ *adj* **1** having a delicate stomach and easily made sick; feeling sick. **2** too easily disgusted or offended.

squeam·ish·ly *adv*

squeam·ish·ness /-nɪs/ *n*

squee·gee /ˈskwiˌdʒi/ *n* [C] tool, with handle and (usually rubber) sponge, blade or roller for wiping excess water off window panes, photographic prints, etc. □ *vt* wipe off with a squeegee.

squeeze /skwiz/ *vt,vi* **1** press on from the opposite side or from all sides; change the shape, size, etc of something by doing this: *~ her hand; ~ a sponge; ~ one's fingers,* eg by catching them in a doorway. **2** get (water, juice, etc) out of something by pressing hard: *~ (the juice out of) a lemon; ~ the water out.* **3** force (a person, oneself) into or through a narrow passage or small space: *~ (one's way) into a crowded bus; ~ (oneself) through a gap in a hedge.* **4** get by force, demand, etc: *~ more money out of the public,* eg by increasing taxes. **5** give in to pressure: *Sponges ~ easily.* □ *n* **1** [C] act of squeezing; condition of being squeezed; something obtained by squeezing: *give her a hug and a ~.* ***a tight squeeze,*** **(a)** closely packed crowd. **(b)** a narrow victory, escape, etc. **2** [U] (*informal*) policy of high taxation, high interest rates, etc aimed at deflation. **3** [U] money obtained by squeezing(4).

squeezer *n* [C] person, thing, that squeezes, eg a device for squeezing out juice: *a ˈlemon-~r.*

squelch /skweltʃ/ *vi,vt* **1** make a sucking sound as when feet are lifted from stiff, sticky mud: *cows ~ing through the mud.* **2** crush something by stepping on it. **3** (*informal*) cause to be silent, esp by force or with authority. □ *n* [C] squelching sound or act.

squid /skwɪd/ *n* [C] kind of sea animal with ten long arms round the mouth. ⇨ illus at mollusk.

squiggle /ˈskwɪgəl/ *n* [C] small twisty line or scrawl: *Is this ~ supposed to be his signature?*

squint /skwɪnt/ *vi* **1** look at sideways or with half-shut eyes or through a narrow opening. **2** have eyes that do not turn together but look in different directions at once. □ *n* [C] squinting position of the eyelids or eyeballs: *a man with a ~.*

squire /ˈskwaiər/ *n* [C] **1** (*dated*) landowner in a country district. **2** (in olden times) young man who was a knight's attendant until he himself became a knight.

squirm /skwərm/ *vi* twist the body, wriggle (from discomfort, shame or embarrassment). □ *n* [C] squirming movement.

squir·rel /ˈskwərəl/ *n* [C] (kinds of) small, tree-climbing, bushy-tailed animal with red or gray fur.

squirt /skwərt/ *vt,vi* (of liquid, powder) force out, be forced out, in a thin stream or jet: *The water ~ed all over me.* □ *n* [C] **1** thin stream or jet (of liquid, powder, etc). **2** something from which liquid, etc can be squirted, eg a syringe. **3** (*informal*) insignificant, nasty person.

Sr. *abbr* = Senior.

S.R.O. /ˌes ˌar ˈou/ *abbr* = **1** single room occupancy. **2** standing room only.

SS *abbr* = **1** selective service. **2** social security.

SSA *abbr* = Social Security Administration.

SSS *abbr* = Selective Service System.

SST /ˌes ˌes ˈti/ *abbr* = supersonic transport (aircraft).

ST[1] *abbr* = standard time.

St.[2] *abbr* = **1** saint. **2** street.

sta. *abbr* = station.

stab /stæb/ *vt,vi* (-bb-) **1** pierce or wound with a sharp-pointed weapon or instrument, eg a knife: *~ a man in the back.* **2** produce a sensation of being stabbed: *~bing pains in the back.* □ *n* [C] **1** stabbing blow; pain caused by this. **2** (*informal*) try, attempt: *Let me have/take a ~ at it,* try to do it.

stab·ber *n* [C] person who stabs.

stable[1] /ˈsteibəl/ *adj* (-er, -est) firm; fixed; not likely to move or change: *What we need is a ~ Government. He needs a ~ job.*

sta·bil·ity /stəˈbɪləti/ *n* [U] quality of being stable.

sta·bil·iz·ation /ˌsteibəlɪˈzeiʃən/ *n* [U] making, becoming, stable.

sta·bil·ize /ˈsteibəˌlaiz/ *vt* make stable: *~ prices and wages.*

sta·bi·lizer *n* [C] person or thing that stabilizes.

stable[2] /ˈsteibəl/ *n* [C] **1** building in which horses are kept and fed. **2** (often *pl*) number of horses (esp commercial riding or racehorses) belonging to one particular owner and kept in one set of stables. □ *vt* put, keep, in a stable: *Where do you ~ your horse?*

stack[1] /stæk/ *n* [C] **1** pile of hay, straw, grain, etc usually with a sloping top, for storage in the open. **2** group of rifles arranged in the form of a pyramid. **3** pile or heap (of books, papers, wood, etc). ⇨ illus at pancake. **4** (*informal*) large amount: *I have ~s of work waiting to be done*. **5** (brickwork or stonework enclosing a) number of chimneys. **6** rack with shelves for books (in a library or bookshop). ***the stacks,*** area (esp in a library) where books are shelved. **7** number of aircraft circling at different heights while waiting for instructions to land.

stack[2] /stæk/ *vt* **1** make into a stack; pile up. **2** secretly arrange the order of playing cards in a deck in order to cheat. ***stack the cards/deck against sb,*** (*fig*) put (esp hidden) barriers in his way.

sta·dium /ˈsteidiəm/ *n* [C] (*pl* ~s) enclosed area of land for games, athletic competitions, etc, with seats, etc for spectators: *a new Olympic ~*.

staff /stæf/ *n* [C] **1** strong stick used as a support when walking or climbing, or as a weapon. **2** such a stick as a sign of office or authority: *a pastoral ~*, eg an ornamental one carried by or in front of a bishop, etc. **3** pole serving as a support: *a ˈflag~*. **4** group of assistants working together under a manager or head: *the principal and his ~*, ie the teachers; *ˈoffice ~*. **5** group of senior army officers engaged in planning and organization: *the General Staff*; (as an *adjective*) *ˈ~ officers*. **6** (*music*) (*pl* staves /ˈsteivz/) set of five parallel lines on or between which symbols for notes are placed. ⇨ illus at notation. □ *vt* provide with, act as, a staff(4): *a well-~ed hotel/hospital*.

stag /stæg/ *n* [C] male deer.

ˈstag party, (*informal*) party for men only, usually given for a man about to get married. ⇨ hen party.

stage /steidʒ/ *n* [C] **1** (in a theater) raised platform or structure of boards on which the actors appear. **2 the stage,** theatrical work; the profession of acting in theaters. ***be/go on the stage,*** be/become an actor or actress. **3** (*fig*) scene of action; place where events occur. **4** point, period or step in development: *at an early ~ in our history. The baby has reached the ˈtalking ~*, is learning to talk. **5** any of two or more successive periods on the journey of a spacecraft: *a ˌmulti-~ ˈrocket*. **6** journey, distance, between two stopping places along a road or route; such a stopping place: *travel by easy ~s*, for only a short distance at a time. **7** = stage coach. □ *vt,vi* **1** put on the stage(1); put before the public: *~ Eugene O'Neill's "Ah, Wilderness."* ***stage a comeback,*** come back (esp to a sport, eg to the boxing ring) from retirement or after having failed. **2** *~ well/badly*, (of a drama) be well/badly suited for the theater.

ˈstage·coach *n* [C] horse-drawn vehicle formerly carrying passengers (and often mail) along a regular route.

ˈstage·craft *n* [U] skill or experience in writing or directing plays.

ˈstage direction, printed direction in a play to actors about their positions, movements, etc.

ˌstage ˈdoor, entrance at the back of a theater, used by actors, etc.

ˈstage fright, nervousness felt when facing an audience.

ˌstage ˈmanager, person who organizes scenery and props, etc, supervises the rehearsals, etc.

ˈstage·struck *adj* having a strong desire to become an actor or actress.

ˌstage ˈwhisper, whisper that is meant to be overheard.

stag·fla·tion /ˌstægˈfleiʃən/ *n* [U] economic inflation occurring without increased productivity.

stag·ger /ˈstægər/ *vi,vt* **1** walk or move unsteadily (from weakness, a heavy burden, drunkenness, etc): *The man ~ed along/to his feet/across the room/from side to side on the pavement*. **2** (of a blow or shock) cause to walk or move unsteadily. **3** (of news, etc) shock deeply; cause worry or confusion to: *I was ~ed to hear/on hearing/when I heard that the firm was bankrupt*. **4** arrange (times of events) so that they do not all occur together: *~ office hours,* so that employees are not all using buses, trains, etc at the same time. □ *n* (*sing*) staggering movement.

stag·ing /ˈsteidʒɪŋ/ *n* **1** [C,U] (platform or working area on) scaffolding for men on constructional work, eg building. **2** [U] (method of) presenting a play on the stage of a theater.

stag·nant /ˈstægnənt/ *adj* **1** (of water) without current or tide: *water lying ~ in ponds and ditches*. **2** (*fig*) unchanging; inactive: *Business was ~ last week*.

stag·nancy /-nənsi/ *n* [U]

stag·nate /ˈstægˌneit/ *vi* **1** be or become stagnant. **2** (*fig*) be or become dull through disuse, inactivity, etc.

stag·na·tion /stægˈneiʃən/ *n* [U]

staid /steid/ *adj* (of persons, their appearance, behavior, etc) conservative, quiet and serious.

staid·ly *adv*

stain /stein/ *vt,vi* **1** (of liquids, other substances) change the color of; make colored patches or dirty marks on: *blood-~ed hands*. **2** color (wood, fabrics, etc) with a substance that soaks into the material: *He ~ed the wood brown*. **3** (of material) become discolored or soiled: *Does this material ~ easily?* □ *n* **1** [U] liquid used for staining wood, etc. **2** [C] stained place; dirty mark or patch of color: *ˈink-/ˈblood-~s*. **3** [C] (*fig*) blemish: *a ~ on your character*.

stained ˈglass, glass made by mixing into it transparent colors during the process of manufacture: *~ed glass windows in a church*.

stain·less *adj* **(a)** without a blemish: *a ~less reputation*. **(b)** (esp of a kind of steel alloy) that resists rust and corrosion: *~less steel cutlery*.

stair /ster/ *n* [C] (any one of a) series of fixed steps leading from one floor of a building to another: *The child was sitting on the bottom ~. She always runs up/down the ~s*. ***a flight of stairs,*** a set of stairs in a continuous line. ⇨ downstairs, upstairs.

ˈstair·case *n* [C] series of stairs (often with banisters) inside a building.
ˈstair rod, rod for keeping a carpet in position in the angle between two steps of a stair.
ˈstair·way *n* = staircase.
ˈstair·well *n* space in a building surrounded by a staircase.

stake[1] /steik/ *n* [C] **1** strong, pointed length of wood or metal (to be) driven into the ground as a post (eg for a fence) or as a support for something, eg plants, young trees. **2** post, as used in olden times, to which a person was tied before being burned to death as a punishment: *condemned to the ~; suffer at the ~.* **3** sum of money risked when gambling. ***at stake,*** to be won or lost; risked, depending, on the result of something: *His reputation/His life itself was at ~.* **4** interest or concern (*in* something); sum of money invested in an enterprise. **5** (*pl*) money to be contended for, esp in a horse race; such a race: *the ~s at the Kentucky Derby.*
ˈstake·holder *n* [C] person who keeps the stakes (3) until the result (of a race, etc) is known.

stake[2] /steik/ *vt* **1** support with a stake: *~ newly planted trees.* **2** mark (an area) with stakes: *~ out a claim* (to land in a new country, etc). **3** place (a location) under police surveillance: *The detectives ~d out the home of the suspect.* **4** risk (money, one's hopes, etc): *I'd ~ my life on it*, am very confident about it.
ˈstake·out *n* police surveillance of a location.

stal·ac·tite /stəˈlækˌtait/ *n* [C] length of lime hanging from the roof of a cave, created by dripping water.

stal·ag·mite /stəˈlægˌmait/ *n* [C] length of lime mounting upwards from the floor of a cave, created as water containing lime drips from the roof.

stale /ˈsteiəl/ *adj* **1** (of food) dry and unappetizing because not fresh: *~ bread.* **2** uninteresting because heard before: *~ news/jokes.* **3** (of athletes, musicians, etc) no longer able to perform really well because of too much playing, training, practice, etc: *become ~.* □ *vi* (*pres p* staling /ˈsteiliŋ/) become stale: *Are there any kinds of pleasure that never ~?*
stale·ness /-nɪs/ *n* [U]

stale·mate /ˈsteiəlˌmeit/ *n* [C,U] **1** (*chess*) position of the pieces from which no further move is possible. **2** (*fig*) any stage of a dispute at which further action by either side seems to be impossible. □ *vt* **1** (*chess*) reduce a player to a stalemate. **2** (*fig*) bring to a standstill.

stalk[1] /stɔk/ *n* [C] part of a plant that supports a flower or flowers, a leaf or leaves, or a fruit or fruits. ⇨ illus at flower, fruit.

stalk[2] /stɔk/ *vt,vi* **1** walk with slow, stiff strides, esp in a proud, self-important or serious way: *~ out of the room.* **2** move quietly and cautiously toward (wild animals, etc) in order to get near: *~ deer.*
stalker *n* [C] person who stalks animals.

stall /stɔl/ *n* [C] **1** compartment for one animal in a stable or cattle shed. **2** marked space (esp in a parking lot) for parking an automobile. **3** table or small, open shop, etc used by a trader in a market, on a street, in a railway station, etc: *a ˈbook~/ˈflower ~.* **4** condition of an aircraft when its speed has decreased to the point at which it no longer responds to the controls. □ *vt,vi* **1** place or keep (an animal) in a stall(1). **2** (eg of a car engine) fail to keep going through insufficient power or speed; (of a driver) cause an engine to stop from such a cause. **3** (of an aircraft) cause to be, become, out of control through loss of speed. **4** avoid giving a clear answer to a question, making a decision, (in order to get more time): *~ for time.*

stal·lion /ˈstælyən/ *n* [C] uncastrated fully grown male horse, esp used for breeding.

stal·wart /ˈstɔlwərt/ *adj* (*formal*) **1** tall and muscular; solidly built. **2** firm and determined: *~ supporters.* □ *n* [C] loyal supporter (of a political party, etc).

sta·men /ˈsteimɪn/ *n* [C] male part of a flower, bearing pollen. ⇨ illus at flower.

stam·ina /ˈstæmənə/ *n* [U] energy and physical, mental and moral strength, enabling a person or animal to work hard for a long time, to survive a serious illness, to deal with serious problems, etc.

stam·mer /ˈstæmər/ *vi,vt* **1** speak with a tendency to repeat rapidly the same sound or syllable, as in "G-g-give me that b-b-book." **2** say something in this way: *~ out a request.* □ *n* [C] (tendency to) stammering talk.
stam·merer *n* [C] person who stammers.

stamp[1] /stæmp/ *n* [C] **1** act of stamping with the foot: *a ~ of impatience.* **2** something used to make a mark or design on a surface: *a rubber ~*, one on which a design, words, etc are cut (used for printing dates, signatures, addresses, etc). **3** design, word(s), etc made by stamping on a surface. **4** (also **ˈpostage stamp**) piece of printed paper stuck on envelopes, documents, etc to show the postage paid, the insurance contribution, duty paid, etc. **5** (usually *sing*) characteristic mark or quality: *He bears the ~ of genius.* **6** (usually *sing*) kind; class: *men of that ~.*
ˈstamp album, one in which a collector of postage stamps keeps his specimens.
ˈstamp collector, person who collects postage stamps.

stamp[2] /stæmp/ *vt,vi* **1** put (one's foot) down with force (on something): *~ one's foot; ~ on the floor.* ***stamp sth out,*** crush, destroy, end: *~ out a fire in the grass/a rebellion/an epidemic disease.* **2** print (a design, lettering, the date, etc) on paper, cloth or other surface: *The girl forgot to ~ my library books*, stamp the date on which they were taken out (or should be returned). **3** put a stamp(4) on (a letter, etc): *I enclose a ~ed, self-addressed envelope for your reply.* **4** give shape to something (eg pieces of metal) with a die or cutter. **5** (*fig*) impress: *He ~ed his authority/personality on the game*, eg of a great football player.
ˈstamp·ing ground, (a) place where specified animals, eg elephants, may usually be found. **(b)** place where specified people often gather: *Monte Carlo, a ~ing ground of the very rich.*

stam·pede /stæmˈpid/ *n* [C] sudden rush of frightened people or animals. □ *vi,vt* **1** take part in a stampede; cause to do this. **2** force or frighten a person into action: *Don't be ~d into buying the house.*

stance /stæns/ *n* [C] **1** (in golf) position taken for a stroke. **2** person's intellectual attitude.

stanch /stæntʃ/ = staunch¹.

stan·chion /ˈstæntʃən/ *n* [C] (usually iron) post supporting an outdoor roof, awning, etc.

stand¹ /stænd/ *n* [C] **1** ***make a stand,*** be ready to resist or fight: *make a ~ against the enemy.* **2** position taken up: *He took his ~ near the window.* **3** small article of furniture, support, etc on or in which things may be placed: *a ˈmusic/ˈhat/umˈbrella ~.* **4** structure from which things are sold or exhibited: *a ˈnews~; the food ~s at the fair.* **5** place where vehicles may stand in line in a street, etc while waiting for passengers: *a ˈtaxi ~.* **6** structure, usually sloping, where people may stand or sit to watch races, sports events, etc: *a seat in the ~s.* ➪ grandstand. **7** engagement by a theatrical company when touring the country. ***a ˌone-night ˈstand,*** (*fig*) a social meeting or performance that will not be repeated. **8** witness box (in a law court): *take the ~.*

ˈstand·point *n* point of view: *from the ~point of the consumer.*

ˈstand·still *n* ***be at/come to/bring sth to a standstill,*** (of progress, motion) stop, be stopped.

stand² /stænd/ *vi,vt* (*pt,pp* stood /stʊd/) (For special uses with *adverbial particles* and *prepositions,* ➪ 10 below.) **1** have, take, keep, an upright position; balance, support, the body on the feet: *He was too weak to ~. Standing room only*, all seats are occupied, eg in a bus depot or theater. *His hair stood on end*, ie with terror. *He ~s six foot two*, is of this height when standing. **2** rise to the feet: *Stand up, please. Everyone stood (up) as the President entered.* **3** remain without change: *Let the words ~*, don't alter them or take them out. ***stand firm/fast,*** not give way, retreat, change one's views, etc. **4** be in a certain condition or situation: *As affairs now ~...*, As they are at present... *I ~ corrected*, accept that I was wrong, etc. *He ~s alone among his colleagues*, none of them equals him in ability, etc. *Stand clear of the gates*, eg as a warning when they are about to be closed. **5** have a certain place; be situated: *The house ~s on the hill. Where does Tom ~ in class*, What is his position (in order of ability, etc)? **6** cause to be placed in an upright position: *Stand the ladder against the wall. Stand the empty barrels on the floor.* **7** put up with; bear: *He can't ~ hot weather. I can't ~ that painting*, strongly dislike it. ***stand one's ground,*** (*fig*) not give way in an argument. ***stand trial,*** be tried (in a court of law). **8** provide at one's own expense: *~ a friend a good dinner.* **9** ***stand a (good/fair) chance (of),*** ➪ chance¹(3). ***stand to win/gain/lose something,*** be in a position where one is likely to win, etc: *What do we ~ to gain by the treaty?* **10** (special uses with *adverbial particles* and *prepositions*):

stand aside, **(a)** be inactive, do nothing: *He's a man who never ~s aside when there's something that needs doing.* **(b)** move to one side: *~ aside to let someone pass.*

stand at, be at a certain level (on a scale, etc): *The temperature stood at 30°C.*

stand back, **(a)** move back: *The policeman ordered us to ~ back.* **(b)** be situated away from: *The house ~s back from the road.*

stand by, **(a)** look on without doing anything: *How can you ~ by and see such cruelty?* ➪ bystander. **(b)** be ready for action: *The troops are ~ing by.* **(c)** wait for the chance to substitute for a confirmed passenger in a booked-up flight. ***stand by sb,*** support; show oneself to be a good friend: *I'll ~ by you whatever happens.* ***stand by sth,*** be faithful to (a promise, one's word, etc).

stand down, **(a)** leave a witness stand or similar position. **(b)** (of a candidate) withdraw.

stand for sth, **(a)** represent: *PO ~s for Post Office.* **(b)** (*informal*) tolerate: *She says she's not going to ~ for her children disobeying her.* ➪ 7 above.

stand in (for sb), take the place of, eg a musician who is ill.

stand off, remain at a distance; move away.

stand out, **(a)** be easily seen above or among others: *Does your work ~ out from that of others?* Is it obviously better? ➪ outstanding. ***stand out a mile,*** be obvious: *Her ability ~s out a mile.* **(b)** continue to resist: *The troops stood out against the enemy until their ammunition was exhausted.*

stand over sb, supervise, watch closely: *Unless I ~ over him he makes all sorts of mistakes.*

stand up, ➪ 2 above. ***stand sb up,*** (*informal*) not keep an appointment: *First she agreed to come out with me, then she stood me up.* ***stand up for sb,*** support; take the part of; defend. ***stand up to sth,*** (of materials) remain in good condition after long or hard use, etc: *metals that ~ up well to high temperatures.*

ˈstand·by *n* **(a)** state of readiness: *The troops are on 24-hour ~by*, ready to move at 24 hours' notice. **(b)** person or thing that one may depend on: *Aspirin is a good ~by for headaches.* **(c)** act of standing by to replace a confirmed passenger on a booked-up flight.

ˈstand·off *n* deadlock; tie.

ˌstand·ˈoff·ish *adj* cold and distant in behaviour.

ˈstand·up *adj* **(a)** (of food or drink served at certain places) consumed while standing: *a ˌ~up ˈbuffet* **(b)** (of comedian) one who performs alone, usually standing up.

stan·dard /ˈstændərd/ *n* [C] **1** distinctive flag, esp one to which loyalty is given or asked: *the regimental ~*, eg as carried by a particular regiment on parade or in battle. **2** (often as an *adjective*) something used as a test or measure for weights, lengths, qualities or for the required degree of excellence: *~ weights and measures; set a high ~ for candidates in an examination; a high ~ of living*, one with plenty of material comforts, etc; *~ authors*, accepted as good. ***be up to/below standard,*** be equal to, not so good as, normal, etc: *Their work is not up to ~.* ➪ gold standard. **3** (often as an *adjective*) upright support; pole or column.

ˈ**standard bearer,** **(a)** person carrying a standard(1). **(b)** (*fig*) prominent leader.
ˈ**Standard Time,** time officially adopted for (part of) a country. (*But note: Daylight Saving Time,* ⇨ daylight.)
stan·dard·ize /ˈstændərˌdaiz/ *vt* make of one size, shape, quality, etc according to fixed standards: *Automobile parts are usually* ~*d.*
stan·dard·iz·ation /ˌstændərdɪˈzeiʃən/ *n* [U]
stand·ing /ˈstændɪŋ/ *n* **1** [U] duration: *a debt of long* ~. **2** [C,U] position or reputation; (if there is no *adjective*) established position: *men of high* ~; *a member in full* ~. □ *adj* established and permanent; ready for use: *a* ~ *committee,* a permanent one that meets regularly; *a* ~ *order for newspapers and periodicals,* to be delivered regularly.
stank *pt* of stink.
stan·za /ˈstænzə/ *n* [C] (*pl* ~s) group of (usually) rhymed lines forming a division in some forms of poem.
staple[1] /ˈsteipəl/ *n* [C] **1** U-shaped metal pin hammered into a surface, to hold something in position. **2** piece of wire pushed through sheets of paper and bent to hold them together. □ *vt* fasten or fit with a staple.
sta·pler /ˈsteiplər/ *n* [C] device for fixing papers together with staples(2).
staple[2] /ˈsteipəl/ *n* **1** [C] chief sort of article or goods produced or traded in: *Cotton is one of the* ~*s of Egypt.* **2** [U] fiber of cotton, wool, etc (as determining its quality): *cotton of short/fine* ~. **3** (as an *adjective*) forming the chief part: *Is coffee still the* ~ *product of Brazil? Rice is the* ~ *diet* (= the principal food) *of many people in Asia.*
star /star/ *n* [C] **1** any one of the bodies seen in the sky at night as distant points of light. ***see stars,*** seem to see flashes of light, eg as the result of a hit on the head. **2** figure or design with points around it, suggesting a star by its shape; an asterisk (*): *a ˌfive-*~ *hoˈtel,* of the highest grade. **3** insignia of rank or office (worn on the shoulders by general officers in the US Army, Air Force and Marine Corps, as a badge by a sheriff, etc). **4** planet or heavenly body regarded as influencing a person's fortune, etc: *born under a lucky* ~. **5** person famous as a singer, actor, actress, etc: *the* ~*s of stage and screen;* ˈ*pop* ~*s.* □ *vi,vt* (-rr-) **1** mark or decorate with, or as with, stars. **2** mark with an asterisk, etc to direct attention to something; *I've* ~*red the important articles to read.* **3** be a star(5) (*in* a play, film, etc); present (a person) as a star(5).
ˈ**star·dom** /-dəm/ *n* [U] status of being a star(5).
ˈ**star·dust** *n* **(a)** (*poet*) appearance of heavenly dust created by masses of countless small stars. **(b)** (*informal*) excessively romantic feeling about somebody or something: *Get the* ~*dust out of your eyes,* by becoming more realistic in your judgment.
ˈ**star·fish** *n* [C] sea animal shaped like a star.
star·less *adj* with no stars to be seen: *a* ~*less sky/night.*
ˈ**star·let** /-lɪt/ *n* [C] young successful actress.
ˈ**star·light** *n* [U] light from the stars.
ˈ**star·lit** /-ˌlɪt/ *adj*
starry /ˈstari/ *adj* lighted by, shining like, stars: *a* ~*ry night;* ~*ry eyes.*
ˈ**starry-eyed** *adj* (*informal*) full of ideas but impractical: ˈ~*ry-eyed reˈformers.*
the ˌ**Stars and** ˈ**Bars,** (term for) the flag of the Confederacy during the Civil War, 1861-1865. ⇨ illus at flag.
the ˌ**Stars and** ˈ**Stripes,** (term for) the flag of the United States. ⇨ illus at flag.
the ˌ**Star-Spangled** ˈ**Banner,** **(a)** (poetic term for) the flag of the United States. **(b)** (title of and term for) the national anthem of the United States.
star·board /ˈstarbərd/ *n* [U] right side of a ship or aircraft as one faces forward. □ *adj* on the right side: *on the* ~ *bow.* ⇨ port[3].
starch /startʃ/ *n* [U] **1** white, tasteless food substance, as in potatoes, grain, etc. **2** this substance prepared in powdered form and used for stiffening cotton clothes, etc. **3** (*fig*) stiffness of manner; formality. □ *vt* make, eg shirt collars, stiff with starch.
starchy *adj* (-ier, -iest) of, like, containing, starch: ~*y foods.*
stare /stær/ *vi,vt* **1** look fixedly; (of eyes) be wide open: *Do you like being* ~*d at? She was staring into the distance. They all* ~*d with astonishment.* **2** ***stare one in the face,*** (*fig*) be obvious, be right in front of one: *The book I was looking for was staring me in the face.* □ *n* [C] staring look: *a rude* ~.
stark /stark/ *adj* **1** stiff, esp in death. **2** complete: ~ *madness.* □ *adv* completely: ~ *naked.*
star·ling /ˈstarlɪŋ/ *n* [C] common small bird (black with brown-spotted plumage).
starry /ˈstari/ ⇨ star.
start[1] /start/ *n* [C] **1** beginning of a journey, activity, etc: *make an early* ~; *the* ~ *of a race; from* ~ *to finish.* **2** (also **head start**) amount of time or distance by which one person starts in front of competitors: *They didn't give me* (*much of*) *a head* ~. *He got a good* ~ (= a position of advantage) *in life/business.* **3** sudden movement of surprise, fear, etc: *He sat up with a* ~. ***by fits and starts,*** in sudden short periods, not regularly.
start[2] /start/ *vi,vt* (*Note: begin* may replace *start* only as in 2 below.) **1** leave; set out: *We must* ~ (*out*) *early. We* ~*ed at six.* **2** begin: ~ *work. It* ~*ed raining. It's* ~*ing to rain.* **3** make a beginning: ~ (*on*) *one's journey home.* **4** make a sudden movement (from pain, surprise, fear, etc) or change of position: *He* ~*ed at the sound of my voice.* **5** set going; originate, bring into existence; cause or make able to begin: *This news* ~*ed me thinking. The smoke* ~*ed her coughing. A rich uncle* ~*ed him in business,* helped him, eg by supplying capital. **6** ***to start with,*** **(a)** in the first place: *To* ~ *with, we haven't enough money, and secondly we haven't enough time.* **(b)** at the beginning: *We had only six members to* ~ *with.* **7** (special uses with *adverbial particles* and *prepositions*):
start back, begin to return: *It's time we* ~*ed back* (eg said while out walking).
start off, begin to move: *The horse* ~*ed off at a steady trot.*

start out (to do sth), (*informal*) begin; take the first steps: *~ out to write a novel.* ***start sth up,*** put (an engine, etc) in motion: *We couldn't ~ up the car.*

star·ter *n* [C] **(a)** person, horse, etc that takes part in a race: *There were only five ~ers in the last race.* **(b)** person who gives the signal for a race to start. **(c)** device for causing an engine to start working. **(d)** (*informal*) first course of a meal.

ˈstarting gate, barrier where horses start a race.

ˈstarting point, place at which a start is made.

ˈstarting post, place from which competitors start in a race.

startle /ˈstartəl/ *vt* give a shock of surprise to; cause to move or jump: *be ~d out of one's sleep; be ~d out of one's wits,* suffer a sudden surprise or shock. *What startling news!*

starve /starv/ *vi,vt* **1** (cause to) suffer or die from hunger: *~ to death. They tried to ~ the soldiers out,* force them to surrender by preventing them from getting supplies of food. ***be starved for,*** (*fig*) be in great need of: *The motherless children were ~ed for affection.* **2** (*informal*) feel hungry: *What time's dinner? I'm starving!*

star·va·tion /starˈveiʃən/ *n* [U] suffering or death caused by lack of food: *die of starvation.*

stash /stæʃ/ *vt* (often used with *away*) (*informal*) hide away; store away.

state[1] /steit/ *n* **1** (*sing* only) condition in which a person or thing is (in circumstances, appearance, mind, health, etc): *The house was in a dirty ~. She's in a poor ~ of health.* **2** [C] (often **State**) organized political community with a government and its territory, either sovereign or forming part of a federal republic: *In some countries railways are owned/run by the State. How many ~s make up the United States of America?* **3** (as an *adjective*) of, for, concerned with, a state(2): *~ capital/legislature/park/university.* **4** [U] (often **State**) civil government: *Church and State; Chief of State,* head of a sovereign power; *Deˌpartment of ˈState, State Deˌpartment,* department (of the US Federal Government) concerned with relations with foreign powers. **5** [U] rank; dignity: *persons in every ~ of life.* **6** [U] ceremonial formality: *The President was received in ~.* **7** (as an *adjective*) of or for ceremony and formality: *a ~ dinner at the White House.* **8** ***lie in state,*** be placed on view in a public place before burial.

state·less *adj* (of a person) not recognized as a citizen or national of any country.

state·ly *adj* (-ier, -iest) impressive; dignified.

ˈstate·room *n* [C] private cabin (or sleeping compartment) on an ocean liner or in a railway car.

ˌstate's ˈevidence, (*legal*) evidence provided by an informer in a criminal case. ***turn state's evidence,*** (of an accused person) turn informer against others accused of the same crime in exchange for leniency.

ˌstate's ˈrights, (a) authority of an individual state to govern its own affairs. **(b)** belief that this authority should be strong.

state[2] /steit/ *vt* express in words, esp carefully, fully and clearly: *~ one's views.*

stated *adj* made known; announced: *at ~d times/intervals.*

state·ment *n* **(a)** [U] expression in words. **(b)** [C] stating of facts, views, a problem, etc (spoken or written); report: *a ˈbank ~ment; make a ~ment (in court),* give a formal account in a law court setting out the cause of a legal action or its defense.

states·man /ˈsteitsmən/ *n* [C] (*pl* -men /-men/) person taking an important part in the management of affairs of State.

ˈstates·manˌlike *adj* gifted with, showing, wisdom in public affairs.

ˈstates·manˌship *n* [U] skill and wisdom in managing public affairs.

static[1] /ˈstætɪk/ *adj* at rest; in a state of balance: *Sales are ~,* not increasing or decreasing.

static[2] /ˈstætɪk/ *n* [U] **1** (also **static electricity**) electric charges in the atmosphere, producing discharges in a storm, or on objects in dryness, producing shocks. **2** crackling noise in radio reception or the sound part of TV reception. **3** (*informal*) argument; complaint.

sta·tion /ˈsteiʃən/ *n* [C] **1** place, building, etc where a service is organized and provided: *a ˈbus/poˈlice ~.* **2** position, or relative position, to be taken up or maintained by a person or thing: *One of the cruisers was out of ~,* not in its correct position. **3** stopping place for railway trains. **4** social position, rank: *people in all ~s of life.* **5** military or naval base; those living there. **6** = service station. □ *vt* put (a person, oneself, etc) at or in a certain place: *The detective ~ed himself between the buildings,* hid there.

ˈstation master, person in charge of a railroad station.

ˈstation wagon, long automobile with tail gate.

sta·tion·ary /ˈsteiʃəˌneri/ *adj* **1** not intended to be moved from place to place: *a ~ crane/engine.* ⇨ mobile(1). **2** not moving or changing: *remain ~.*

sta·tioner /ˈsteiʃənər/ *n* [C] dealer in stationery.

sta·tion·ery /ˈsteiʃəˌneri/ *n* [U] paper, envelopes, etc for writing.

stat·is·ti·cian /ˌstætɪˈstɪʃən/ *n* [C] expert in statistics.

stat·is·tics /stəˈtɪstɪks/ *n* [U] **1** (used with a *pl verb*) collection of information shown in numbers: *Statistics suggest that the population of this country will be doubled in ten years' time.* **2** (used with a *sing verb*) the science of statistics.

stat·is·ti·cal /stəˈtɪstɪkəl/ *adj* of statistics: *statistical evidence.*

stat·is·ti·cally /-kli/ *adv*

statue /ˈstætʃu/ *n* [C] figure of a person, animal, etc in wood, stone, bronze, etc.

statu·ette /ˌstætʃuˈet/ *n* [C] small statue.

stat·ure /ˈstætʃər/ *n* [U] **1** (person's) natural bodily height. **2** (*fig*) mental or moral quality.

status /ˈsteitəs, ˈstætəs/ *n* [U] person's legal, social or professional position in relation to others: *have no official ~,* no official position.

ˈstatus symbol, something which is thought to be evidence of social rank, wealth, etc, eg a car.

stat·ute /ˈstætʃut/ *n* [C] (written) law passed by

STATUE OF LIBERTY

Congress or other law-making body.

ˈstatute book, book(s) containing statutes.

statu·tory /ˈstætʃəˌtɔri/ *adj* fixed, done, required, by statute: *statutory control of incomes.*

staunch¹ /stɔntʃ, stantʃ/ (also **stanch** /stæntʃ/) *vt* stop the flow of (esp blood).

staunch² /stɔntʃ, stantʃ/ *adj* (of a friend, supporter, etc) loyal; firm.

staunch·ly *adv*

staunch·ness /-nɪs/ *n* [U]

stave¹ /steiv/ *n* [C] **1** one of the curved pieces of wood used for the side of a barrel or tub. **2** (*music*) = staff(6). **3** stanza; verse.

stave² /steiv/ *vt,vi* (*pt,pp* ~d or stove /stouv/) **1** break, smash, make a hole *in: The side of the yacht was ~d in by the collision.* **2** ***stave sth off,*** keep off, delay (danger, disaster, bankruptcy, etc).

stay¹ /stei/ *vi,vt* **1** be, remain, in a place or condition: ~ *in the house/at home/in bed;* ~ (= be a guest) *at a hotel/with friends. I'm too busy to/I can't* ~, must leave now. ***stay ˈin,*** not go outdoors. ***stay ˈout,*** **(a)** remain outdoors: *Tell the children they shouldn't ~ out after dark.* **(b)** remain on strike: *The miners ~ed out for several weeks.* ***stay ˈup,*** not go to bed: *I ~ed up reading until midnight.* ***come to stay,*** (*informal*) become, or seem likely to be, permanent: *Has short hair for men come to ~?* **2** continue in a certain state: ~ *single,* not marry. *That fellow never ~s sober for long,* frequently gets drunk. ***stay ˈput,*** (*informal*) remain where placed. **3** stop, delay, postpone: ~ *the progress of a disease.* **4** be able to continue (work, etc); show endurance: *The horse lacks ˈ~ing power.* ***stay the course,*** **(a)** be able to continue to the end of the race. **(b)** (*fig*) continue the struggle, etc. □ *n* [C] **1** period of staying(1): *make a short ~ in Karachi.* **2** (*legal*) delay; postponement. ***a stay of execution,*** that an order of the court need not be carried out immediately.

stay² /stei/ *n* [C] **1** rope or wire supporting a mast, pole, etc. **2** (*pl*) (*dated*) kind of corset reinforced with strips of stiff material (bone or plastic). □ *vt* support by means of a wire, rope or prop.

stead·fast /ˈstedˌfæst/ *adj* firm and unchanging; keeping firm (*to*): *a ~ gaze.*

stead·fast·ly *adv*

steady /ˈstedi/ *adj* (-ier, -iest) **1** firmly fixed or supported; balanced; not likely to fall over: *make a table ~,* eg by repairing a leg; *not very ~ on one's legs,* eg of a person after a long illness. **2** regular in movement, speed, direction, etc: *a ~ speed/rate of progress.* **3** regular in behavior, habits, etc: *a ~ worker.* **4** constant, unchanging: *a ~ purpose.* □ *adv* = steadily. ***go steady,*** (*informal, dated*) go about regularly with a person of the opposite sex, though not yet engaged to marry: *Are Tony and Jane going ~?* □ *n* [C] (*pl* -ies) (*informal*) regular boyfriend or girlfriend. □ *vt,vi* make, become, keep, steady: *~ a boat; ~ oneself by holding on to the rail,* eg on the deck of a ship that is rolling.

stead·ily /ˈstedəli/ *adv* in a regular manner: *His health is getting steadily worse.*

steak /steik/ *n* [C,U] thick slice of meat or fish for frying, grilling, stewing, etc.

steal /ˈstiəl/ *vt,vi* (*pt* stole /stoul/, *pp* stolen /ˈstoulən/; *pres p* ~ing /ˈstilɪŋ/) **1** take (a person's property) secretly, without right: *Someone has stolen my watch.* **2** obtain by surprise or a trick: *~ a glance at her in the mirror.* **3** move, come, go (*in, out, away, etc*) secretly and quietly: *He stole into the room.*

steam /stim/ *n* [U] **1** gas or vapor which rises from boiling water: *clouds of ~.* **2** power or heat obtained from steam: *The ship was able to proceed under her own ~,* using her own engines and not needing to be towed. *They haven't turned on the ~* (= heat). ***ˌFull ˌsteam aˈhead!*** order (on a ship) to go forward at full speed. **3** (*fig*) (*informal*) energy. ***let off steam,*** release surplus energy or emotion; become less excited. ***run out of steam,*** become exhausted. ***under one's own ˈsteam,*** without help from others. □ *vi,vt* **1** give out steam or vapor: *~ing hot coffee.* **2** move, work, etc under (or as if under) the power of steam: *a ship ~ing up the Mississippi River.* **3** cook, soften, clean, by the use of steam: *~ fish.* **4** ***steam ˈup,*** become misty with condensed steam: *The windows ~ed up.*

ˈsteam·boat *n* [C] boat (esp on a river) driven by steam.

ˈsteam engine, one worked or driven by pressure of steam.

steamer *n* [C] **(a)** = steamship. **(b)** vessel(1) in which food is steamed.

ˌsteam ˈheat, heat given out by steam from radiators, pipes, etc. □ *vt: ~-heated buildings,* kept warm by steam heat.

ˈsteam·roller *n* [C] engine with a large, weighted roller for smoothing and leveling roadways, airport runways, etc.

ˈsteam·ship *n* [C] ship driven by steam.

ˈsteam·shovel *n* [C] large machine for digging and moving earth.

steamy *adj* (-ier, -iest) of, like, full of, steam: *the ~y heat of the tropics.*

steel /ˈstiəl/ *n* [U] hard alloy of iron and carbon or other elements, used for knives, tools, machinery, etc. □ *vt* (-ing /ˈstilɪŋ/) harden: *~ oneself/one's heart (against pity).*

steel ˈband, band of (West Indian) musicians who use old oil drums, etc as percussion instruments.

steel 'guitar, guitar with steel strings, used for playing certain kinds of music (eg Hawaiian).

steelie /ˈstili/ *n* steel marble(2).

steel 'wool, fine steel shavings (used for scouring and polishing).

'steel·works *n pl* (often used with a *sing verb*) factory where steel is made.

steep[1] /stip/ *adj* (-er, -est) **1** (of a slope) rising or falling sharply: *a ~ gradient/path/descent*. **2** (*informal*) (of a demand, price, etc) unreasonable; excessive.

steep·ly *adv*

steep·ness /-nɪs/ *n* [U]

steep[2] /stip/ *vt,vi* **1** soak in liquid: *Let the tea ~ for five minutes*. **2** (*fig*) become full of; get a thorough knowledge of: *~ed in ignorance; a scholar ~ed in Greek history*.

steeple /ˈstipəl/ *n* [C] high tower with a spire, rising above the roof of a church.

'steeple·chase *n* [C] race with obstacles such as fences, hedges and ditches.

'steeple·jack *n* [C] man who climbs steeples, tall chimney stacks, etc to do repairs.

steer[1] /stɪr/ *n* [C] (esp castrated) young male of any animal of the ox family, reared for meat.

steer[2] /stɪr/ *vt,vi* direct the course of (a boat, ship, car, etc): *~ north; ~ by the stars*. ***steer clear of,*** (*fig*) avoid.

'steering wheel, wheel used to control the direction of a car, boat, etc.

steer·age /ˈstɪrɪdʒ/ *n* [U] **1** (area containing the) steering equipment of a large ship. **2** area of a ship, belowdeck(s) and near the rudder, in which passengers might be given berths at low rates. **3** the cheapest class of service on (former) ocean-going passenger ships: *Many immigrants to America came over in ~*.

stein /stain/ (also **'beerstein**) *n* [C] heavy stoneware mug for drinking beer, usually decorated with German scenes and phrases and having a hinged metal top.

stel·lar /ˈstelər/ *adj* (*formal*) of stars: *~ light*.

stem[1] /stem/ *n* [C] **1** part of a plant coming up from the roots; part of a leaf, flower or fruit that joins it to the main stalk or twig. ⇨ illus at flower, fungus. **2** part like a stem, eg the narrow part of a wine glass or a tobacco pipe. **3** (*gram*) root or main part of a noun or verb from which other words are made by additions. □ *vi* (-mm-) ***stem from,*** have as origin: *His illness ~s from the period he lived in the tropics*.

'stem·ware *n* [U] glassware for the table of any type having stems, eg wine glasses.

stem[2] /stem/ *vt* (-mm-) **1** check, stop, dam up (a stream, a flow of liquid, etc). **2** make progress against the resistance of: *~ the tide*.

stench /stentʃ/ *n* [C] horrid smell.

sten·cil /ˈstensəl/ *n* [C] thin sheet of metal, cardboard, plastic, etc with letters or designs cut through it; lettering, design, etc printed through a stencil. □ *vt* (-l-, also -ll-) produce (a pattern, wording, etc) by using a stencil.

ste·nog·ra·phy /stɪˈnagrəfi/ *n* [U] (use of a) kind of shorthand.

ste·nog·ra·pher /-fər/ *n* [C] person skilled in stenography.

ste·no·graphic /stenəˈgræfɪk/ *adj*

steno·type /ˈstenəˌtaip/ *n* [C] machine, like a typewriter, for writing in (a kind of) shorthand. □ *vi, vt* write, transcribe with this machine.

steno·typist *n* [C] person skilled in using a stenotype.

steno·typy /ˈstenəˌtaipi/ *n* [U] kind of shorthand used on a stenotype.

step[1] /step/ *n* **1** act of stepping once; distance covered by doing this: *He was walking with slow ~s*. ***ˌstep by 'step,*** gradually. ***watch one's step,*** be careful or cautious. **2** sound made by somebody walking; way of walking (as seen or heard): *That's Lucy—I recognize her ~*. **3** ***be/get/fall in/out of step (with),*** **(a)** put/not put the right foot to the ground at the same time as others (in marching, dancing). **(b)** conform/not conform with other members of a group: *He's out of ~ with the official view*. ***keep step with,*** march in step with. **4** one action in a series of actions in order to do something: *take ~s to prevent the spread of influenza; a false ~*, a mistaken action. *What's the next ~?* What must I/we do next? **5** place for the foot when going from one level to another: *The child was sitting on the ~s/on the bottom ~*. ***flight (of steps),*** unbroken series of steps, leading from floor, landing, terrace, deck, etc to another. **6** grade, rank; promotion: *When do you get your next ~ up?* When will you be promoted?

'step·ladder *n* [C] portable folding ladder with steps, not rungs.

'step stool, combination stool and low stepladder, esp for kitchen use in reaching high shelves.

'step·up *n* increase.

'step·ping stone, (a) stone in a shallow stream, so that it can be crossed without getting wet. **(b)** (*fig*) means of getting something: *a first ~ping stone to success*.

step[2] /step/ *vi,vt* (-pp-) **1** move the foot, or one foot after the other (forward, or in the direction shown): *~ across a stream; ~ over a puddle; ~ into a boat*. **2** (special uses with *adverbial particles* and *prepositions*):

step a'side, **(a)** move to one side. **(b)** (*fig*) let another person take one's place.

step 'down, **(a)** (*fig*) resign (to make way for another person). **(b)** decrease.

step 'in, (*fig*) intervene (either to help or to obstruct).

Step on the 'gas!/'Step on it! (*informal*) Hurry up!

step sth 'up, increase: *~ up production; ~ up the campaign,* put more effort into it.

'step·down *n* decrease.

step- /step/ *prefix* (used to show a relationship not by blood but by a later marriage):

'step·brother/·sister, child of an earlier marriage of one's stepfather or stepmother.

'step·child/·son/·daughter, child of an earlier marriage of one's wife or husband.

'step·father/·mother, one's parent's later husband, wife.

stereo /ˈsteriou, ˈstɪr-/ *n* (*pl* ~s) **1** [U] (short for) stereophonic: *in ~* with stereophonic sound. **2** [C] stereophonic radio or record player.

stereo·phonic /ˌsteriəˈfanɪk, ˌstɪr-/ *adj* **1** (of broadcast and recorded sound, using two separately placed loudspeakers) giving the effect of naturally distributed sound: *a ~ recording.* **2** (of apparatus) designed for recording or reproducing sound in this way.

stereo·type /ˈsteriəˌtaip, ˈstɪr-/ *n* [C] (esp) fixed phrase, idea, belief. □ *vt* (of phrases, ideas, etc) used and repeated without change: *~d greetings,* eg "Good morning," "How d'you do?"

ster·ile /ˈsterəl/ *adj* **1** not producing, not able to produce, seeds or offspring. **2** (of land) barren. **3** (*fig*) having no result; producing nothing: *a ~ discussion.* **4** free from living germs.

ste·ril·ity /stəˈrɪləti/ *n* [U] state of being sterile.

ster·il·ize /ˈsterəˌlaiz/ *vt* make sterile.

ster·ili·za·tion /ˌsterəlɪˈzeiʃən/ *n* [U]

ster·ling /ˈstərlɪŋ/ *adj* **1** (of silver) of a high standard of value and purity. **2** (*fig*) of solid worth; genuine: *~ qualities.* □ *n* [U] **1** (*informal*) sterling silver: *This bracelet is made of ~.* **2** currency of the United Kingdom. ***pounds sterling,*** British (monetary) pounds: *payable in pounds ~.*

stern¹ /stərn/ *adj* (-er, -est) **1** demanding and enforcing obedience: *a ~ teacher.* **2** severe; strict: *a ~ face/look.*

stern·ly *adv*

stern·ness /-nɪs/ *n* [U]

stern² /stərn/ *n* [C] rear end of a ship or boat. ⇨ illus at ship.

ster·num /ˈstərnəm/ *n* [C] (*pl* ~s) (*anat*) narrow bone in the front of the chest (also called *ˈbreastbone*) connecting the collar bone and the top seven pairs of ribs. ⇨ illus at skeleton.

stetho·scope /ˈsteθəˌskoup/ *n* [C] instrument for listening to the beating of the heart, sounds of breathing, etc.

stet·son /ˈstetsən/ *n* [C] man's Western-style hat, with a high crown and a wide brim.

steve·dore /ˈstivəˌdɔr/ *n* [C] man whose work is loading and unloading ships.

stew /stu/ *vt,vi* cook, be cooked, in water or juice, slowly in a closed dish, pan, etc: *~ed chicken/fruit.* ***let a person ˌstew in his own ˈjuice,*** do nothing to help him (when he is in trouble for which he is himself responsible). □ *n* **1** [C,U] (dish of) stewed meat, etc: *lamb ~.* **2** ***be in/get into/a stew (about sth),*** (*informal*) a nervous, excited condition.

stew·ard /ˈstuərd/ *n* [C] **1** man who attends to the needs of passengers in a ship or airliner. **2** = shop steward.

stew·ard·ess /ˈstuərdɪs/ *n* [C] woman steward (1).

sth. *abbr* = something.

stick¹ /stɪk/ *n* [C] **1** thin branch broken, cut or fallen, from a bush, tree, etc. **2** such a branch cut to a convenient length, piece of cane cut, shaped, etc for a special purpose: *The old man cannot get around without a (ˈwalking) ~. We have only a few ~s of furniture,* furniture of the simplest kind. ***have/get hold of the wrong end of the stick,*** be confused; misunderstand things completely. **3** slender piece (of chalk, chewing gum, celery, etc).

stick² /stɪk/ *vt,vi* (*pt,pp* stuck /stək/) (For special uses with *adverbial particles* and *prepositions,* ⇨ 6 below.) **1** push (something pointed) (*into, through,* etc): *~ a fork into a potato.* **2** (of something pointed) be, remain, in a position by the point: *The needle stuck in my finger.* **3** (cause to) be or become joined or fastened with, or as with, paste, glue or other substance: *~ a stamp on a letter.* ***be/get stuck with (sb/sth),*** (*informal*) permanently involved with; unable to escape from: *It looks as if I'm stuck with the job of clearing up this mess.* **4** (*informal*) put (in some position or place), esp quickly or carelessly: *He stuck his pen behind his ear/his hands in his pockets/the papers in a drawer.* **5** be or become fixed; fail to work properly: *The key stuck in the lock,* could not be turned or taken out. **6** (special uses with *adverbial particles* and *prepositions*):

stick aˈround, (*informal*) stay in or near a place: *Stick around; we may need you.*

stick sth ˈon, fasten it with paste, etc: *~ on a label.*

stick sth ˈout, (cause to) project, stand out: *with his chest stuck out; a rude boy ~ing his tongue out at his sister. Don't ~ your head out of the window.* ***stick it ˈout,*** (*informal*) put up with hardship, etc until the end. ***stick one's neck out,*** ⇨ neck¹(1).

stick sth/two or more things toˈgether, **(a)** fasten together with paste. **(b)** assemble quickly or haphazardly.

stick to sb/sth, **(a)** be faithful to (one's ideals, a friend, etc). **(b)** remain determined: *~ to a resolution.* **(c)** continue at: *~ to a timetable,* do something in the time agreed.

stick toˈgether, (*informal*) (of persons) remain loyal or friendly to one another.

stick ˈup, project upward (and out of): *The branch was ~ing up out of the water.* ***stick sb/sth up,*** (*sl*) threaten to shoot in order to rob: *~ up a bank.*

stick up for sb/oneself/sth, defend, support: *~ up for one's friends.*

stick with sb/sth, remain loyal to, continue to support: *~ with a friend/an ideal.*

ˈstick·up *n* [C] (*sl*) robbery (esp of a bank) in which guns are used.

sticker /ˈstɪkər/ *n* [C] adhesive label.

stick-in-the-mud /ˈstɪk-ɪn-ðə-ˌməd/ *n* [C] conservative, stubborn person.

stick·ler /ˈstɪklər/ *n* [C] ***stickler for,*** person who insists on the importance of something (eg accuracy).

sticky /ˈstɪki/ *adj* (-ier, -iest) **1** that sticks or tends to stick to anything that touches it: *The table top feels ~/has a ~ feeling.* **2** (*sl*) ***have sticky fingers,*** (of a person) have a tendency to steal. **3** (*informal*) making, likely to make, objections, be unhelpful, etc: *be ~ about a late payment.*

stiff /stɪf/ *adj* (-er, -est) **1** not easily bent or changed in shape: *a sheet of ~ cardboard; have a ~ leg/back,* not easily bent. ***keep a stiff upper lip,*** not complain (when in pain, or trouble, etc). **2** hard to stir, work, move, etc: *a ~ paste.* **3** hard to do; difficult: *a ~ climb/examination.* **4** (of manners, behavior) formal, unfriendly: *be* *rather ~ with one's neighbors.* **5** great in degree: *a* ~ (= strong) *breeze; a* ~ (= high) *price.* □ *adv* to the point of stiffness; (hence) thoroughly: *It bored me ~,* bored me very much. *She was scared ~.* □ *n* [C] (*sl*) corpse.

stiff·ly *adv*

stiff·ness /-nɪs/ *n* [U]

stif·fen /ˈstɪfən/ *vt,vi* make or become stiff(1,2)

stiff·ener /ˈstɪf(ə)nər/ something used to stiffen, eg starch.

stiff·en·ing /ˈstɪf(ə)nɪŋ/ *n* [U] material used to stiffen a substance or an object.

stifle /ˈstaifəl/ *vt,vi* **1** give or have the feeling that breathing is difficult: *They were ~d by the heat. The heat was stifling.* **2** suppress; put down; keep back: *~ a yawn.*

stigma /ˈstɪgmə/ *n* [C] **1** (*pl* ~s) (*fig*) mark of shame or disgrace: *the ~ of imprisonment.* **2** (*pl* -mata /stɪgˈmatə/) marks (resembling those) made by the nails on the body of Jesus at the crucifixion. **3** (*pl* ~s) that part of the pistil of a flower which receives the pollen. ⇨ illus at flower.

stile /ˈstaiəl/ *n* [C] kind of step used to climb over a fence, gate, etc.

still[1] /stɪl/ *adj, adv* **1** without movement or sound: *Please keep ~ while I take your photograph.* **2** (of wines) not sparkling. □ *n* **1** (*poet*) deep silence: *in the ~ of the night.* **2** [C] one photograph from a motion picture film. □ *vt* cause to be still or at rest; make calm.

ˈstill·birth *n* [C] child or fetus dead at birth.

ˈstill·born *adj* **(a)** (of a child) dead at birth. **(b)** (*fig*) (of an idea, etc) never acted on.

ˈstill life *n* [U] representation of nonliving things (eg fruit, flowers, etc) in painting; [C] (*pl* ~s) painting of this kind.

still·ness /-nɪs/ *n* [U]

still[2] /stɪl/ *adv* **1** even to this or that time: *He is ~ busy. Will he ~ be here when I get back? In spite of his faults she ~ loved him/loved him ~. Is your brother ~ here,* hasn't he left? (*Note:* compare *Is your brother here yet,* has he arrived?) **2** (used with a *comparative*) even; yet; in a greater degree: *Tom is tall but Mary is ~ taller/taller ~.* **3** nevertheless; admitting that: *He has treated you badly; ~, he's your brother and you ought to help him.*

still[3] /stɪl/ *n* [C] apparatus for making liquors (brandy, whiskey, etc) by distilling.

stilted /ˈstɪltɪd/ *adj* (of written style, talk, behavior, etc) stiff and unnatural; too formal.

stilts /stɪlts/ *n pl* (also ***a pair of stilts***) poles with a support for the foot at some distance from the bottom, used to raise the user (eg a clown) from the ground: *walk on ~.*

stimu·lant /ˈstɪmyələnt/ *n* [C] **1** drink (eg coffee, brandy), drug, etc that increases bodily or mental activity. **2** something that encourages a person (eg praise, hope of gain).

stimu·late /ˈstɪmyəˌleit/ *vt* excite; increase; quicken thought or feeling: *stimulating him to make greater efforts.*

stimu·lat·ing *adj*

stimu·lus /ˈstɪmyələs/ *n* [C] (*pl* -li /-lai/) something that stimulates: *a ~ to make extra efforts.*

sting[1] /stɪŋ/ *n* **1** [C] sharp, often poisonous, pointed organ of some insects (eg bees). **2** hairs projecting from the surface of the leaves of plants (esp stinging nettles), which cause pain to the fingers, etc when touched. **3** [C] sharp pain caused by the sting of an insect or plant; wound made by a sting. **4** [C,U] any sharp pain of body or mind: *the ~ of a whip/of hunger.*

sting[2] /stɪŋ/ *vt,vi* (*pt,pp* stung /stəŋ/) **1** (have the power to) prick or wound with a sting or as with a sting: *A bee stung me on the cheek.* **2** cause sudden, strong physical or mental pain (to): *He was stung by his enemy's insults.* **3** (of parts of the body) feel strong pain: *His fingers were still ~ing from the cold.* **4** (*informal*) charge (a person) an excessive price: *He got stung for $500,* duped into paying this sum.

stinger /ˈstɪŋər/ *n* = sting[1](1).

ˈsting·ray *n* [C] (kinds of) ray[2] having a sting(1) on the tail.

stingy /ˈstɪndʒi/ *adj* (-ier, -iest) spending, using or giving unwillingly: *Don't be so ~ with the sugar!*

stin·gily /-əli/ *adv*

stin·gi·ness /-nɪs/ *n* [U]

stink /stɪŋk/ *vi,vt* (*pt* stank /stæŋk/ or stunk /stəŋk/, *pp* stunk) **1** have a foul and offensive smell: *Her breath stank of garlic.* **2** ***stink up,*** fill (a place) with a stink: *You'll ~ the place up with your cheap cigars!* □ *n* [C] foul smell. ***raise/kick up a stink (about sth),*** (*informal*) cause trouble or annoyance, eg by complaining.

ˈstink·bug *n* [C] (kinds of) bug which can give off a strong, foul odor if disturbed or injured.

stinker *n* [C] (*informal*) **(a)** disagreeable or mean person. **(b)** (*informal*) something difficult: *The biology paper* (ie in an examination) *was a ~er.*

ˈstink·weed *n* (kinds of) wild plant with an unpleasant smell.

stint /stɪnt/ *vt,vi* restrict (a person) to a small allowance: *Don't ~ yourself/the food.* □ *n* **1** (usually) ***without stint,*** without limit, without sparing any effort. **2** [C] fixed or allotted amount (of work): *do a ~ for /with the election campaign.*

stipple /ˈstɪpəl/ *vt* draw, paint, with dots.

stipu·late /ˈstɪpyəˌleit/ *vt,vi* state as a necessary condition: *It was ~d that the goods should be delivered within three days.*

stipu·la·tion /ˌstɪpyəˈleɪʃən/ *n* [C] condition: *on the stipulation that....*

stir[1] /stər/ *vi,vt* (-rr-) **1** be moving; cause to move: *A breeze ~red the leaves. Nobody was ~ring in the house,* Everyone was resting, in bed. ***not stir a finger,*** make no effort to help. **2** move a spoon, etc around and around in liquid, etc in order to mix it thoroughly: *~ one's coffee.* **3** excite: *The story ~red the boy's imagination.* □ *n* (usually *sing* with *a, an*) commotion; excitement: *The news caused quite a ~ in the town.*

stir·ring *adj* exciting: *~ring tales of adventure.*

stir·rup[1] /ˈstərəp/ *n* [C] footrest, hanging down from a saddle, for the rider of a horse.

stir·rup[2] /ˈstərəp/ *n* [C] (*anat*) bone in the ear. ⇨ illus at ear.

stitch /stɪtʃ/ *n* **1** [C] (in sewing) the passing of a needle and thread in and out of cloth, etc to join or decorate; (in knitting) one complete turn of the wool, etc over the needle. **2** the thread, etc seen between two consecutive holes made by a needle; result of a single movement with a knitting needle, etc: *drop a ~*, allow a loop to slip off the end of a knitting needle; *put ~es into/take ~es out of a wound*. ***A ˌstitch in ˌtime saves ˈnine,*** *(prov)* a small piece of work done now may save a lot of work later. **3** particular kind of stitch: *a ˈchain ~*. **4** (*sing* only) sharp pain in the side (as caused sometimes when running). □ *vt,vi* put stitches in or on.

stock[1] /stak/ *n* **1** [C,U] store of goods available for sale, distribution or use, esp goods kept by a trader or shopkeeper. ***(be) in/out of stock,*** be available/not available. ***take stock of,*** *(fig)* review (a situation); estimate (a person's abilities, etc). **2** (as an *adjective*) usually in stock (and therefore usually obtainable): *~ sizes; She's tired of her husband's ~ jokes*. **3** [C,U] supply of anything: *a good ~ of information; get in ~s of coal and fuel oil for the winter*. **4** [U] = livestock. **5** [C,U] money lent to a government in return for interest; shares in the capital of a business company. **6** [U] line of ancestry: *a woman of Irish/farming ~*. **7** [U] raw material ready for manufacture: *ˈpaper ~*. **8** [U] liquid in which bones, etc have been stewed, used for making soup, gravy, etc. **9** [C] base, support, or handle of an instrument, tool, etc: *the ~ of a rifle*. ***ˌlock, ˌstock and ˈbarrel,*** *(fig)* completely. **10** ***on the stocks,*** under construction; in preparation. **11** *(pl)* wooden framework with holes for the feet in which a person who had done something wrong was formerly locked. **12** [C] kind of garden plant with single or double brightly colored sweet-smelling flowers.

ˈstock·breeder/·raiser *n* [C] one who breeds, raises, cattle.

ˈstock·broker *n* [C] man who buys and sells stock(5).

ˈstock car, (a) railway car for transporting stock(4). **(b)** ordinary (not racing) car.

ˈstock-car racing, racing of ordinary (not racing) cars.

ˈstock exchange, place where stocks(5) and shares are bought and sold.

ˈstock·holder *n* [C] = shareholder.

ˌstock-in-ˈtrade *n* everything needed for a trade or occupation.

ˈstock market, (business at the) stock exchange.

ˈstock·pile *vi* reserve large quantities of materials, weapons, etc.

ˈstock·pot *n* [C] pot for stock(8).

ˈstock·room *n* [C] room for storing stock(1).

ˌstock-ˈstill *adv* motionless: *stand ~-still*.

ˈstock·taking *n* examining and recording stock (1).

ˈstock·yard *n* [C] enclosure for cattle (eg at a market).

stock[2] /stak/ *vt* supply or equip with stock; have, keep, a stock of: *~ a shop with goods. He is well ~ed with ideas*.

stock·ade /staˈkeid/ *n* [C] wall of upright stakes, built as a defense.

stock·ing /ˈstakıŋ/ *n* (usually *pl* or ***a pair of stockings***) **1** close-fitting wool, nylon or silk clothing covering the legs and feet, as worn by girls and women. **2** = sock[1].

stocky /ˈstaki/ *adj* (-ier, -iest) (of persons, animals, plants) short, strong and fat.

stock·ily /-əli/ *adv: stockily built*.

stodgy /ˈstadʒi/ *adj* **1** (of food) heavy and solid. **2** (of style) heavy, uninteresting. **3** (of persons) dull.

stoic /ˈstouık/ *n* [C] person who has great self-control, esp when suffering pain or misfortune.

sto·ical /-kəl/ *adj* of, like, a stoic.

sto·ically /-kli/ *adv*

sto·icism /ˈstouəˌsızəm/ *n* [U] patient and uncomplaining endurance of suffering, etc.

stoke /stouk/ *vt,vi* put (coal, etc) on the fire of (an engine, furnace, etc); attend to a furnace: *stoking (up) the furnace*.

stoker *n* [C] worker who stokes a furnace, etc.

stole[1] /stoul/ *n* [C] **1** strip of material worn (around the neck with the ends hanging down in front) by priests of some Christian Churches during services. **2** woman's wrap worn over the shoulders.

stole[2]**, stolen** *pt,pp* of steal.

stolid /ˈstalıd/ *adj* not easily excited.

stolid·ly *adv*

stom·ach /ˈstəmık/ *n* **1** [C] part (bag) of the alimentary canal into which food passes to be digested: *work on an empty ~*. ⇨ illus at trunk. **2** *(informal)* = abdomen. **3** [U] appetite. ***have no stomach for sth,*** dislike or disapprove of it: *have no ~ for bull fighting*. □ *vt* put up with; accept: *How can you ~ the violence in so many films today?*

ˈstomach·ache *n* pain in the belly.

stomp /stamp/ *vi* stamp, tread, heavily: *~ about the room in anger*.

stone /stoun/ *n* **1** [U] (often as an *adjective*) solid mineral matter which is not metallic; rock (often with a defining word as prefix, as *ˈsand~, ˈlime~*): *a wall made of ~; ~ walls/buildings*. ***have a ˌheart of ˈstone,*** be unsympathetic, hard. **2** [C] piece of stone: *a fall of ~s down a hillside*. ***leave ˌno ˌstone unˈturned,*** try every possible means. ***throw stones at,*** *(fig)* attack the character of. ***within a ˈstone's throw (of),*** very close (to). **3** [C] (also **ˈprecious stone**) = jewel(1). **4** [C] piece of stone of a definite shape, for a special purpose: *a ˈgrave~; a ˈstepping ~; a ˈtomb~*. **5** [C] something round and hard like a stone, esp **(a)** the hard shell and nut or seed of such fruits as the cherry. ⇨ illus at fruit. **(b)** hailstone. **(c)** small hard object that has formed in the gall bladder, etc. ⇨ gallstone. **6** (not *US*) (*pl* unchanged) unit of weight, 14 lb.: *I weigh 10 stone*. □ *vt* **1** throw stones at: *be ~d to death*. **2** take the stone(5a) out of (fruit): *~d dates*.

the ˈStone Age, prehistoric period when men used tools and weapons made of stone (before the Bronze Age and the Iron Age).

ˌstone-ˈblind/-ˈcold/-ˈdead/-ˈdeaf *adj* completely blind, etc.

ˈstone·mason *n* [C] person who cuts, prepares and builds with stone.

ˈstone·wall *vt (fig) (pol)* obstruct, cover misdeeds by firm denials, etc.

ˈstone·ware *n* [U] pottery made from clay and flint.

ˈstone·work *n* [U] masonry; part(s) of a building made of stone.

stoned /stound/ *adj* (*informal*) **1** under the influence of drugs. **2** drunk.

stony /ˈstouni/ *adj* (-ier, -iest) **1** having many stones: *~ soil/ground;* covered with stones: *a ~ path/road.* **2** hard, cold and unsympathetic: *a ~ stare.*

ston·ily /-əli/ *adv* in a stony(2) manner.

stood *pt,pp* of stand[2].

stooge /studʒ/ *n* [C] (*sl*) **1** lesser partner in a comedy routine, often taking the role of a stupid person. **2** = flunky. **3** = stool pigeon.

stool /stul/ *n* [C] **1** seat without a back or arms, usually for one person: *a piˈano ~.* **2** = footstool. **3** (*pl*) (*med*) solid excrement.

ˈstool pigeon, (*sl*) **(a)** person acting as a decoy eg a person used by the police to trap a criminal. **(b)** informer.

stoop[1] /stup/ *vi,vt* **1** bend the body forward and downward: *~ing with old age.* **2** (*fig*) lower oneself morally: *He's a man who would ~ to anything,* who would not hesitate to act immorally. □ *n* [C] (usually *sing*) stooping position of the body.

stoop[2] /stup/ *n* [C] platform (eg at the top of a stairway) at the entrance of a building.

stop[1] /stap/ *n* [C] **1** stopping or being stopped: *The train came to a sudden ~.* ***put a stop to sth,*** cause it to stop or end: *I'll put a ~ to this nonsense. Traffic was brought to a complete ~.* **2** place at which buses, streetcars, etc stop to take on passengers: *Where's the nearest ˈbus ~?* **3** (*music*) key or lever (eg in a flute) for regulating pitch; in an organ, knob or lever regulating the flow of air to a row of pipes. ⇨ illus at keyboard. ***pull out all the stops,*** (*fig*) make a great effort. **4** = period(4).

ˈstop·cock *n* [C] valve inserted in a pipe by which the flow of liquid or gas through the pipe can be regulated.

ˈstop·gap *n* [C] temporary substitute.

ˈstop·over *n* [C].

ˈstop·watch *n* [C] watch with a hand that can be started and stopped when desired, used to time events such as races.

stop[2] /stap/ *vt,vi* (-pp-) **1** put an end to (the movement or progress of a person, thing, activity, etc): *~ a car/a train.* **2** prevent: *What can ~ our going/~ us from going if we want to go?* **3** discontinue (doing something): *~ work. We ~ped talking.* **4** break off; discontinue: *The rain has ~ped. It has ~ped raining.* **5** halt: *Does this train ~ in Newark?* ***stop dead (in one's tracks),*** stop suddenly. **6** fill or close (a hole, opening, etc): *~ a leak in a pipe.* **7** cut off; keep back or refuse to give (something normally supplied): *~ (payment of) a check,* order the bank not to cash it. **8** ***stop off (at/in); stop over,*** break a journey and stay for a short period: *~ off/over in Paris.*

stop·page /ˈstapɪdʒ/ *n* [C] **1** obstruction. **2** stopping(7): *~ of pay.* **3** interruption of work (in a factory, etc as the result of strike action).

stop·per /ˈstapər/ *n* [C] object which fits into and closes an opening, esp the mouth of a bottle or pipe.

stor·age /ˈstɔrɪdʒ/ *n* [U] (space used for, money paid for) the storing of goods: *put one's furniture in ~;* (as an *adjective*) *ˈ~ tanks.*

ˈstorage battery, rechargeable battery(1).

store /stɔr/ *n* **1** [C] quantity or supply of something kept for use as needed: *have a good ~ of canned food in the house.* **2** [U] ***in store,*** **(a)** kept ready for use; for future use: *That's a treat in ~,* a pleasure still to come. **(b)** destined (*for*); coming to: *Who knows what the future has in ~ (for us)?* **3** (*pl*) goods, etc of a particular kind, or for a special purpose: *naval and military ~s.* **4** [C] = storehouse. **5** [C] commercial retail establishment where goods are sold: *Her parents manage a hardware ~. He opened a clothing ~.* **6** [U] ***set great/little/no/not much store by,*** consider of great/little, etc value or importance. □ *vt* **1** collect and keep for future use: *Do squirrels ~ up food for the winter?* **2** put (furniture, etc) in a warehouse, etc, for safe keeping. **3** equip, supply: *a mind well ~d with facts.*

ˈstore·front *n* frontage or facing of a (usually small) store(5) at street level.

ˌstorefront ˈchurch, small, independent (usually Pentecostal) house of worship occupying a store location in the city.

ˈstore·house *n* [C] place where goods are kept.

store·keeper *n* owner of a store.

ˈstore·room *n* [C] one in which household supplies are kept.

storey = story[2].

stork /stɔrk/ *n* [C] large, long-legged, usually white wading bird.

storm /stɔrm/ *n* **1** [C] occasion of violent weather conditions: *a ˈthunder/ˈrain/ˈdust/ˈsand-~.* **2** violent outburst of feeling: *a ~ of protests/cheering/applause/abuse.* **3** ***take by storm,*** capture by a violent and sudden attack. □ *vi,vt* **1** use violence and anger; shout angrily. **2** force (a way) into a building, etc; capture (a place) by sudden and violent attack: *The men ~ed (their way) into the fort/~ed the fort.*

ˈstorm·bound *adj* unable to continue a journey, voyage, etc, unable to go out, because of storms.

ˈstorm·cloud *n* [C] heavy gray cloud accompanying, or showing the likelihood of, a storm.

ˈstorm·proof *adj* able to resist storms.

ˈstorm-tossed *adj* damaged or blown about by storms.

ˈstorm troops, soldiers trained for violent attacks.

stormy *adj* (-ier, -iest) **(a)** marked by strong wind, heavy rain, snow or hail: *~y weather; a ~y night.* **(b)** marked by strong feelings of anger, etc: *a ~y discussion/meeting.*

story[1] /ˈstɔri/ *n* [C] (*pl* -ies) **1** account of past events: *stories of ancient Greece.* **2** account of imaginary events. **3** (esp by and to children) untrue statement: *Don't tell stories, Tom.*

ˈstory·book *n* [C] child's book of stories. ***a storybook ending,*** a happy one.

ˈstory·teller *n* [C] person who tells stories.

story[2] /ˈstɔri/ *n* [C] (*pl* -ies) (also **storey** (*pl* ~s)) floor or level in a building.

-stor·ied /-ˈstɔrid/ *suffix* having the number of stories shown: *a six-storied building.*

stout /staut/ *adj* (-er, -est) **1** strong, thick, not easily broken or worn out: *~ boots for mountain climbing.* **2** determined and brave: *a ~ heart.* ˌ***stout-ˈhearted,*** courageous. **3** (of a person) fat: *She's growing too ~ to walk far.* □ *n* [U] strongest kind of dark beer.

stout·ly *adv*

stout·ness /-nɪs/ *n* [U]

stove[1] /stouv/ *n* [C] closed apparatus burning wood, coal, gas, oil or other fuel, used for cooking, etc.

ˈ**stove·pipe** *n* [C] pipe for taking away smoke from a stove.

stove[2] *pt, pp* of stave[2].

stow /stou/ *vt* pack, esp carefully and closely: *~ cargo in a ship's holds; ~ things away in the attic.*

ˈ**stow·away** *n* [C] person who hides himself in a ship or aircraft (until after it starts) in order to make a journey without paying.

straddle /ˈstrædəl/ *vt,vi* sit or stand across (something) with the legs on either side: *~ a horse.*

strafe /streif/ *vt* rake a target or area with machine gun fire from low-flying aircraft.

straggle /ˈstrægəl/ *vi* **1** grow, spread, in an irregular or untidy manner: *vines straggling over the fences.* **2** be (far) behind (a group) while moving forward.

strag·gler *n* [C] person who straggles(2).

straight[1] /streit/ *adj* **1** without a bend or curve; extending in one direction only: *a ~ line/road; ~ hair,* with no curls in it. **2** level (esp horizontal): *Hang the picture ~.* **3** in good order; tidy: *get a room ~.* ***put the record straight,*** give a more accurate account of events, etc. **4** (of a person, his behavior, etc) honest, frank, upright: *give a ~ answer to a question.* ⇨ straight[2](4). **5** (*sl*) conventional with respect to social norms (eg not a homosexual, drug user, etc). **6** ***keep a straight face,*** refrain from smiling or laughing. **7** (of alcoholic drinks), without added mixers or soda water: *Two ~ whiskeys, please.*

straight·ness /-nɪs/ *n* [U]

straight play, an ordinary drama (contrasted with a musical, a show, etc.).

straight[2] /streit/ *adv* **1** directly; not in a curve or at an angle: *Keep ~ on. Look ~ ahead. Can you shoot ~,* aim accurately? **2** by a direct route; without going elsewhere; without delay: *Come ~ home. He flew ~ to New York without stopping in London.* ***come*** ˌ***straight to the*** ˈ***point,*** make a prompt and clear statement of what is meant, wanted, etc. **3** ˌ***straight a***ˈ***way***/ˈ***off,*** (*informal*) immediately. **4** ***go straight,*** (*fig*) live an honest life (esp after imprisonment).

straight[3] /streit/ *n* **1** (usually *sing* with *the*) condition of being straight: *the crooked and the ~.* **2** = stretch[2](3).

straight·jacket = straitjacket.

straighten /ˈstreitən/ *vt, vi* make or become straight[1](1,2,3).

straight·for·ward /ˌstreitˈfɔrwərd/ *adj* **1** honest; without avoiding anything: *a ~ explanation.* **2** easy to understand or do: *written in ~ language.*

straight·forward·ly *adv*

strain[1] /strein/ *n* **1** [C,U] condition of being stretched; the force used: *The rope broke under the ~.* **2** [C,U] something that tests one's powers; severe demand on one's strength, etc: *Do you suffer from the ~ of modern life? He has been under (a) severe ~.* **3** [U] exhaustion; fatigue: *suffering from mental/nervous ~; eye~.* **4** [C] = sprain. **5** (*pl*) (*poet*) music, song, verse (of the kind shown): *the ~s of a violin.* **6** [C] manner of speaking or writing: *in a cheerful ~.* **7** [C] tendency in a person's character: *There is a ~ of insanity in the family.* **8** [C] breed (of animals, insects, etc); line of descent: *~s of mosquitoes that are resistant to insecticides.*

strain[2] /strein/ *vt,vi* **1** stretch tightly by pulling (*at*): *a dog ~ing at its lead.* **2** make the greatest possible use of; use one's strength, etc: *~ every nerve (to do it),* do all one can; *I had to ~ my eyes to see it,* look with great effort. **3** injure or weaken by straining(2): *~ a muscle; ~ one's eyes,* by using them too much, or in poor light, etc. **4** make an intense effort: *The wrestlers ~ed and struggled.* **5** (*fig*) force beyond a limit or what is right: *~ the belief of one's listeners,* ask too much of it. **6** pass (liquid) through a cloth, or a network of fine wire, etc; separate solid matter in this way: *~ the soup; ~ off the water from the vegetables.* **7** (*pp*) (esp of feelings and behavior) unnatural; (as if) forced: *a ~ed laugh; ~ed relations,* showing loss of patience, risk of quarreling.

strainer *n* [C] sieve or other device for straining (6) liquid: *a* ˈ*tea ~er.*

strait /streit/ *n* [C] **1** narrow passage of water connecting two seas or two large bodies of water: *the Straits of Gibraltar; the Magellan Strait.* **2** (usually *pl*) trouble; difficulty: *be in financial ~s.*

strait·jacket, straight·jacket /ˈstreitˌdʒækɪt/ *n* [C] jacket with long sleeves tied around a mentally ill or violent person to prevent movement. □ *vt* **1** use a straitjacket on. **2** (*fig*) prevent growth or development.

strait·laced /ˈstreitˌleist/ *adj* strict, conservative, serious.

strand[1] /strænd/ *n* [C] (*poet*) sandy shore. □ *vi,vt* **1** (of a ship) (cause to) run aground. **2** ***be (left) stranded,*** (*fig*) (of a person) be (left) without means of transport, without money or friends, etc: *be ~ed in a foreign country.*

strand[2] /strænd/ *n* [C] **1** any of the threads, hairs, wires, etc twisted together into a rope, cable or cloth. **2** hair. **3** (*fig*) line of development (in a story, etc).

strange /streindʒ/ *adj* (-r, -st) **1** not previously known, seen, felt or heard of; (for this reason) surprising: *hear a ~ noise. Truth is ~r than fiction.* **2** ***strange to sth,*** fresh or new to: *The Kansas farm boy was ~ to city life.*

strange·ly *adv: behave/act ~ly; Strangely (enough)...,* It's hard to believe but. . .

strange·ness /-nɪs/ *n* [U]

stran·ger /ˈstreindʒər/ *n* [C] person one does not

know; person in a place where he is not known: *My dog always barks at ~s.*

strangle /ˈstræŋgəl/ *vt* kill by squeezing the throat of.

ˈstrangle·hold *n* (usually *fig*) tight grip: *The new laws have put a ~hold on our imports.*

strap /stræp/ *n* [C] strip of leather, cloth, plastic (usually with a buckle) to fasten things together or to keep something (eg a wristwatch) in place. □ *vt* (-pp-) **1** fasten or hold in place with a strap: *~ on a wristwatch. Is the baby ~ped in?* **2** hit with a belt.

strata *pl* of stratum.

strat·agem /ˈstrætɪdʒɪm/ *n* [C,U] (*pl* ~s) (use of a) trick or device to deceive a person.

stra·tegic /strəˈtidʒɪk/, **stra·tegi·cal** /-kəl/ *adj* of, by, serving the purpose of, strategy: *a ~ retreat.*

stra·tegi·cally /-kli/ *adv*

stra·tegics *n* [U] science, art, of strategy.

strat·egy /ˈstrætɪdʒi/ *n* **1** [U] the art of planning operations or actions, esp of the movements of armies and navies. **2** [U] skill in organizing and doing something. **3** [C] general plan of action.

strat·egist *n* [C] person skilled in strategy.

strat·ify /ˈstrætɪˌfai/ *vt,vi* (*pt,pp* -ied) **1** arrange in strata: *stratified rock.* **2** form into strata.

strat·ifi·ca·tion /ˌstrætəfɪˈkeiʃən/ *n* [U]

strato·sphere /ˈstrætəˌsfɪr/ *n* [C] layer of atmospheric air between about 10 and 60 km above the earth's surface.

stra·tum /ˈstreitəm, ˈstrætəm/ *n* [C] (*pl* -ta /-tə/) **1** horizontal layer of rock, etc in the earth's crust. **2** social class or division.

straw /strɔ/ *n* **1** [U] dry cut stalks of wheat, barley, rice and other grains, as material for making mats, etc or bedding for cattle, etc. **2** [C] single stalk or piece of straw. ***not worth a straw,*** worth nothing. ***a ˌstraw in the ˈwind,*** a slight hint that shows which way things may develop. ***the ˌlast ˈstraw,*** addition to a task, burden, etc, that makes it intolerable. **3** [C] thin tube of paper or plastic for sucking up liquid: *suck lemonade through a ~.*

ˈstraw boss, unofficial or assistant foremen.

ˈstraw-colored, pale yellow.

ˌstraw ˈman, (a) = scarecrow. **(b)** false enemy or issue, set up for convenience.

ˌstraw ˈvote, unofficial poll or vote to determine voters' sentiments.

straw·berry /ˈstrɔˌberi/ *n* [C] (*pl* -ies) (plant having) juicy red fruit with tiny yellow seeds on its surface. ⇨ illus at fruit.

ˌstrawberry ˈblonde, woman with hair of a color between red and blonde.

stray /strei/ *vi* (*pt,pp* ~ed) **1** move away (without realizing) (from the right path, from one's friends, etc). **2** (*fig*) lose one's line of argument, story, etc: *Don't ~ from the point.* □ *n* **1** strayed animal or person (esp a child). **2** (as an *adjective*) without a home: *~ cats.* **3** occasional: *a few ~ taxis/a ~ taxi now and then.*

streak /strik/ *n* [C] **1** long, thin, usually irregular line or band: *like a ~ of lightning*, very fast. **2** trace or touch (*of*): *There's a ~ of cruelty in his character.* **3** brief period: *The gambler had a ~ of good luck.* □ *vt,vi* **1** mark with streaks: *white fur ~ed with brown.* **2** (*informal*) move very fast (like a streak of lightning).

streaky *adj* (-ier, -iest) marked with, having, streaks: *~y bacon.*

stream /strim/ *n* [C] **1** small river or brook. **2** current: *go up/down stream,* move up/down the river. **3** steady flow (of liquid, persons, things, etc): *a ~ of blood/abuse. Streams of people were coming out of the stadium.* □ *vi* **1** flow freely; move continuously and smoothly in one direction: *Sweat was ~ing down his face.* **2** float or wave (in the wind): *Her long hair was ~ing in the wind.*

streamer *n* [C] long narrow flag; long narrow ribbon of paper.

ˈstream·line *vt* make more efficient (by simplifying, getting rid of, wasteful methods, etc): *~line production,* eg in a factory.

ˈstream·lined *adj* **(a)** having a shape that offers least resistance to the flow of air, water, etc: *~lined cars.* **(b)** having nothing likely to obstruct progress: *~lined controls.*

street /strit/ *n* [C] town or village road with houses on one side or both: *meet a friend in the ~; cross the ~; a ˈ~ map of New York City.* (*Note:* compare *a road map of New York State.*) ***the ˌman in the ˈstreet,*** typical citizen.

ˈstreet·car *n* [C] public transport powered by electricity, usually limited to service within or around a single city and running on rails in the street surface.

ˈstreet·wise *adj* (*sl*) experienced in the ways of a big city, esp those areas where vice and crime are prevalent.

strength /streŋθ/ *n* [U] **1** quality of being strong: *a man/horse of great ~. She hasn't the ~/hasn't ~ enough to walk upstairs. How is the ~ of alcoholic liquors measured?* ***on the strength of,*** encouraged by, relying on: *I employed the boy on the ~ of your recommendation.* **2** that which helps to make a person or thing strong: *God is our ~.* **3** power measured by numbers of persons present or persons who can be used: *The police force is 500 below ~*, needs 500 more persons. ***be/bring sth up to strength,*** the required number: *We must bring the police force up to ~.*

strengthen /ˈstreŋθən/ *vt,vi* make or become strong(er).

strenu·ous /ˈstrenyuəs/ *adj* using or needing great effort: *~ work; make ~ efforts; lead a ~ life.*

strenu·ous·ly *adv*

strenu·ous·ness /-nɪs/ *n* [U]

stress /stres/ *n* **1** [U] condition causing depression, mental illness, trouble etc: *times of ~,* of trouble and danger; *under the ~ of poverty/fear.* **2** [U] (also with *a, an*) emphasis: *a school that lays ~ on foreign languages.* **3** [C,U] (result of) extra force, used in speaking, on a particular word or syllable: *Stress and rhythm are important in speaking English.* **4** [C,U] (*mechanics*) force exerted between two bodies that touch, or between two parts of one body. □ *vt* put stress or emphasis on: *He ~ed the point that...*

ˈstress mark, mark (eg ˈ [principal or main

stress] and ˌ [secondary stress] as used in this dictionary) that shows the stress(3) on a syllable.

stretch[1] /stretʃ/ *vt,vi* **1** make wider, longer or tighter, by pulling; be or become wider, etc when pulled: ~ *a rope tight;* ~ *a rope across a path;* ~ *out one's arm for a book.* ***stretch one's legs,*** exercise by walking, eg after sitting. **2** lie at full length: *They were* ~*ed out on the lawn.* **3** make (a word, law, etc) include or cover more than is strictly right: ~ *the law/one's principles.* **4** use fully, strain: ~ *one's powers,* work very hard or too hard. **5** extend: *forests* ~*ing for hundreds of miles.*

stretch[2] /stretʃ/ *n* [C] **1** act of stretching or being stretched: *by a* ~ *of authority. The cat woke and gave a* ~. ***by ˈany/ˈno stretch of the imagination,*** however much one may try to imagine something. **2** unbroken or continuous period of time or extent of country, etc: *a beautiful* ~ *of land; working twelve hours at a* ~. **3** the final part of a track or racecourse: *The two horses were together as they entered the final* ~. **4** (*sl*) prison term: *The convicted burglar served a* ~ *of ten years in the penitentiary.*

stretcher *n* [C] **(a)** framework of poles, canvas, etc for carrying a sick, injured or wounded person. **(b)** device for stretching things (eg gloves, shoes).

strew /stru/ *vt* (*pt* ~ed, *pp* ~ed or ~n /strun/) scatter (things) over a surface; (partly) cover (a surface) (with things): ~ *flowers over a path;* ~ *a path with flowers.*

stricken /ˈstrɪkən/ *adj* affected or overcome: ~ *with malaria; ˈterror-*~, very frightened.

strict /strɪkt/ *adj* (-er, -est) **1** demanding obedience or exact observance: *a* ~ *father; be* ~ *with children.* **2** clearly and exactly defined; precisely limited: *I told her in* ~*est confidence; in the* ~ *sense of the word.*

strict·ly *adv* in a strict manner.

strict·ness /-nɪs/ *n* [U]

stride /straɪd/ *vi,vt* (*pt* strode /stroud/, *pp* (*rare*) stridden /ˈstrɪdən/) **1** walk with long steps: ~ *along the road;* ~ *off/away.* **2** pass over in one step: ~ *over a ditch.* □ *n* [C] (distance covered in) one long step. ***get into one's stride,*** settle down to the task. ***make great strides,*** make good and quick progress. ***take sth in one's stride,*** do it without effort.

strife /straɪf/ *n* [U] state of conflict: *industrial* ~ (between workers and employers).

strike[1] /straɪk/ *n* [C] **1** act of striking(5): *a* ~ *of bus drivers;* (as an *adjective*) *take* ~ *action.* ***be (out) on strike; come/go out on strike,*** be engaged in, start, a strike. **2** act of finding (oil, etc) in the earth: *a lucky* ~, a fortunate discovery. **3** (*baseball*) (count against the batter for) failure to hit the ball. **4** (*bowling*) successful knocking down of all ten pins with one ball.

ˈstrike benefit, union funds paid to a striking worker as compensation for loss of wages.

ˈstrike-bound *adj* unable to function because of a strike: *The docks were* ~*-bound for a week.*

ˈstrike·breaker *n* [C] worker hired to replace striking worker.

ˈstrike pay, strike benefit.

strike[2] /straɪk/ *vt,vi* (*pt,pp* struck /strək/) (For special uses with *adverbial particles* and *prepositions,* ⇨ 15 below.) **1** hit; aim a blow at: *He struck me on the chin. He struck the table with a heavy blow. The ship struck a rock. That tree was struck by lightning.* ***strike at the root of sth,*** attack trouble, evil, etc at its source. ***Strike while the ˌiron is ˈhot,*** (*prov*) act promptly while action is likely to get results. ***within ˈstriking distance,*** near enough to reach or attack easily. **2** produce (a light) by striking or scraping: ~ *a match.* **3** discover (by mining, drilling, etc): ~ *oil.* ***strike it rich,*** win wealth suddenly. **4** (cause to) sound: *The clock has struck (four).* ***strike a note of,*** give an impression (of the kind shown): *The President struck a note of warning against overoptimism.* **5** (of workers, etc) stop working for an employer (in order to get more pay, shorter hours, better conditions, etc or as a protest against something): ~ *for higher pay/against bad working conditions.* ⇨ strike[1](1). **6** impress; have an effect on the mind: *How does the idea/suggestion* ~ *you?* **7** have an effect on the body or mind: *The room* ~*s you as warm and comfortable when you enter.* **8** produce by stamping or punching: ~ *a coin/medal.* **9** achieve, arrive at, by reckoning or weighing: ~ *a balance between freedom and repression.* ***strike a bargain (with sb),*** reach an agreement. **10** set out, go (in a certain direction): *The boys struck out across the fields.* **11** cause (a person) to be, suddenly and as if by a single stroke: *be struck blind.* **12** fill, afflict, with fear, etc: *The bombing attack struck fear into their hearts.* **13** lower, take down, (flags, sails, tents). ***strike camp,*** pack up tents, etc. **14** hold or put the body in a certain way to show something: ~ *an attitude of defiance.* **15** (special uses with *adverbial particles* and *prepositions*):

strike sb down, **(a)** hit so that he falls to the ground. **(b)** (*fig*) kill: *He was struck down in the prime of life.*

strike sth off, cut off with a blow, eg of an axe.

strike sth off (sth), remove: *His name was struck off the list.*

strike out, **(a)** use the arms and legs vigorously in swimming: ~ *out for the shore.* **(b)** aim wild blows: *He lost his temper and struck out.* **(c)** follow a new or independent path, a new form of activity: ~ *out on one's own.* **(d)** (*baseball*) (of a batter) make three strikes[1](3), ending the turn at bat; (of a pitcher) put a batter out by making him have three strikes. ***strike sth out,*** cross out (a mistake etc). ⇨ cross[3](2).

strike (sth) up, begin to play: *The band struck up (a tune).* ***strike up sth (with sb),*** begin (perhaps casually) a friendship or acquaintance: *She struck up an acquaintance with him during the flight.*

striker /ˈstraɪkər/ *n* [C] **1** worker who strikes(5). **2** hammer which strikes the chimes on a clock.

strik·ing /ˈstraɪkɪŋ/ *adj* **1** attracting attention or great interest. **2** that strikes(4): *a* ~ *clock.*

strik·ing·ly *adv*

string[1] /strɪŋ/ *n* **1** [C,U] (piece or length of) fine cord for tying things, keeping things in place,

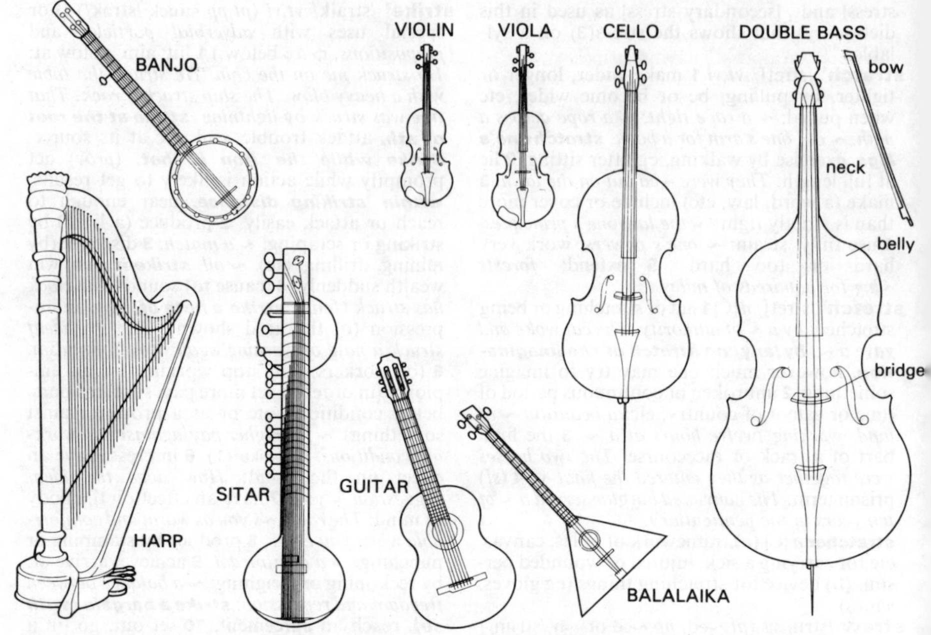

STRINGED INSTRUMENTS

etc: *a ball of ~; a piece of ~.* ***the first/second string,*** the first/the alternative person or thing relied on for achieving one's purpose. **2** [C] tightly stretched length of cord, gut or wire, eg in a violin or guitar, for producing musical sounds. **3** [C] (usually *pl*) string used for causing puppets to move. ***have/keep sb on a string,*** have/keep him under control. ***pull (the) strings,*** control the actions of other people (as if they were puppets). ***no strings (attached),*** (*informal*) (of help, esp of money) without conditions about how the help is to be used. **4** [C] series of things threaded on a string: *a ~ of beads.* **5** [C] repetition of types of things: *a ~ of abuses/curses/lies.*

ˈ**string bean,** kind of bean of which the long pod is used as a vegetable.

ˈ**stringed instrument,** musical instrument with strings(2), eg the violin, guitar, harp.

ˈ**string orchestra,** having only stringed instruments.

ˈ**string quartet,** for, with, four stringed instruments.

the strings, stringed instruments (in an orchestra).

stringy /ˈstrɪŋi/ *adj* (-ier, -iest) like string; having tough fibers: *~y meat.*

string² /strɪŋ/ *vt,vi* (*pt* strung /strʌŋ/, *pp* strung, or as *adj* in sense(1) stringed /strɪŋd/) **1** put a string or strings on (a bow, violin, tennis racket, etc). **2** ***strung (up),*** (of a person, his senses, nerves) made tense, ready, excited, etc. ***highly strung,*** very nervous, tense: *He is a very highly-strung/a very high-strung person.* **3** put (pearls, etc) on a string. **4** tie or hang on a string, etc: *~ (up) lamps across a street.* **5** (special uses with *adverbial particles* or *prepositions*):

string sb along, deliberately mislead a person into the belief that he/she will benefit, etc: *He doesn't intend to marry the girl—he's just ~ing her along.* ***string along with sb,*** maintain a relationship with a person for as long as it suits one, without making genuine commitments.

string out, be, become, spread out at intervals in a line. ***string sth out,*** cause this to happen: *horses strung out toward the end of a long race.*

string sb up, (*sl*) put him to death by hanging.

string sth up, ⇨ 4 above.

stringed ⇨ string²

strin·gent /ˈstrɪndʒənt/ *adj* (*formal*) **1** (of rules) strict, severe; that must be obeyed: *take ~ measures against smoking.* **2** (of the money market) difficult to operate because of scarcity of money.

strin·gent·ly *adv*

strip /strɪp/ *vt,vi* (-pp-) **1** take off (coverings, clothes, parts, etc): *They ~ped the house of all its furnishings. They ~ped off their clothes and jumped into the lake.* ***strip sth down,*** (eg of an engine) remove detachable parts (for servicing, etc). **2** deprive of property, etc: *~ a man of his possessions/titles.* □ *n* [C] long narrow piece (of material, land, etc): *a ~ of garden behind the house; a ~ of paper.* ⇨ airstrip, comic strip.

ˌ**strip-ˈtease** *n* stage or night club entertainment in which a person (usu a woman) takes off garments piece by piece.

stripe /straɪp/ *n* [C] **1** long, narrow band on a surface different in color, material, texture, etc: *a tiger's ~s.* **2** (often a V-shaped) badge worn on a uniform, showing rank, eg of a soldier: *How many ~s are there on the sleeve of a sergeant?*

striped /straipt/ *adj* having stripes(1).

stripy *adj* (*informal*) having stripes: *a stripy tie.*

strip·per /ˈstrɪpər/ *n* [C] person who performs a striptease.

strive /straiv/ *vi* (*pt* strove /strouv/, *pp* striven /ˈstrɪvən/) **1** struggle: *striving with/against poverty/opposition/the enemy.* **2** make great efforts: *~ for power/to win.*

strobe /stroub/ *n* [C] (*informal*) (short for) stroboscope.

stro·bo·scope /ˈstroubəˌskoup/ *n* [C] electronic light capable of extremely rapid flashes.

stro·bo·scopic /ˌstroubəˈskapɪk/ *adj* of a stroboscope.

strode *pt* of stride.

stroke[1] /strouk/ *n* [C] **1** (act of striking or dealing a) blow: *the ~ of a sword; 20 ~s of the whip.* **2** one of a series of regularly repeated movements, esp as a way of swimming or rowing: *swimming with a slow ~; the ˈbreast/ˈside/ˈback ~.* **3** (in a rowing crew) oarsman nearest the boat's stern who sets the rate of striking the oars. **4** single movement of the upper part of the body and arm(s), esp in games, eg golf. **5** single effort; result of this: *I haven't done a ~ of work today.* ***a ˌstroke of ˈluck,*** a piece of good fortune. ***at a/one stroke,*** with one effort and immediately. **6** (mark made by a) single movement of a pen or brush: *cross a name out with one ~ of the pen; thin/thick ~s.* **7** sound made by a bell striking the hours: *on the ~ of three,* at three o'clock. **8** sudden attack of illness in the brain, with loss of feeling, power to move, etc: *a paralytic ~.* ⇨ also sunstroke.

stroke[2] /strouk/ *vt* pass the hand along a surface, usually again and again: *~ a cat/one's beard.* □ *n* [C] act of stroking; stroking movement.

stroll /stroul/ *n* [C] quiet, unhurried walk: *have/go for a ~.* □ *vi* go for a stroll.

strol·ler *n* [C] **(a)** person who strolls. **(b)** folding chair on wheels, in which a small child can be pushed along.

strong /strɔŋ/ *adj* (-er, -est) **1** (opposite of *weak*) having power to resist; not easily hurt, injured, broken, captured, etc; having great power of body or mind: *a ~ stick,* not easily broken; *a ~ wind; a ~ will/imagination; feel quite ~ again,* in good health after an illness; *an army 500,000 ~,* numbering 500,000; *a ~ candidate,* one likely to be well supported, etc; *~* (= deeply held or rooted) *beliefs/convictions.* ***as ˌstrong as a ˈhorse,*** physically powerful. ***one's ˈstrong point,*** that which one does well. **2** (of drinks) having a large proportion of the flavoring element, or of alcohol: *~ coffee/tea.* **3** having a considerable effect on the mind or the senses: *a ~ smell of gas.* **4** (*adverbial* use) ***going strong,*** (*informal*) continuing (the race, activity, etc) with energy; continuing in good health: *aged 90 and still going ~.* **5** (*comm*) (of prices) rising steadily: *Prices/Markets are ~.*

ˈstrong-arm *adj* (of methods, tactics, etc) using physical force.

ˈstrong·box *n* [C] one strongly built for keeping valuables.

ˈstrong·hold *n* [C] **(a)** fort. **(b)** (*fig*) place where a cause or idea has a strong support: *a ~hold of Protestantism.*

strong ˈlanguage, with swear words, abuses, etc.

strong·ly *adv* in a strong manner: *I ~ly advise you to go.*

ˌstrong-ˈminded /-ˈmaindɪd/ *adj* having a mind that is capable and energetic.

ˈstrong room, one built with thick walls (eg in a bank) for storing valuables.

ˌstrong ˈverb, (*gram*) which forms the past tense with a vowel change, eg *sing, sang, sung.*

strove *pt* of strive.

struck *pt,pp* of strike[2].

struc·tural /ˈstrəktʃərəl/ *adj* of a structure, esp the framework: *~ alterations to a building,* eg combining two rooms into one.

struc·tur·ally /-rəli/ *adv*: *The building is ~ly sound.*

struc·ture /ˈstrəktʃər/ *n* **1** [U] way in which something is put together, organized, etc: *the ~ of the human body; sentence ~.* **2** [C] framework or essential parts of a building, etc: *The Parthenon was a magnificent marble ~.*

struggle /ˈstrəgəl/ *vi* fight, make great efforts: *~ against difficulties/with the accounts; ~ for power. The thief ~d to get free.* □ *n* [C] struggling; contest: *the ~ for freedom.*

strum /strəm/ *vi,vt* (-mm-) ***strum (on),*** play music (usually on a string instrument) (and esp without skill): *~ (on) the guitar.* □ *n* [C] sound of strumming.

strung *pt,pp* of string[2].

strut[1] /strət/ *n* [C] piece of wood or metal in a framework to strengthen it.

strut[2] /strət/ *vi* (-tt-) walk (*around, along, in, out, into a room, etc*) in a showy, deliberate way. □ *n* [C] such a way of walking.

strych·nine /ˈstrɪkˌnain/ *n* [U] strong poison.

stub /stəb/ *n* [C] **1** short remaining end of a pencil, cigarette or similar object: *a ~ of a tail,* a very short one. **2** counterfoil: *the ~s of a checkbook.* □ *vt* (-bb-) **1** *~ one's toe,* hit it against something. **2** extinguish (esp a cigarette) by pressing it against something hard: *~ out a cigar.*

stubble /ˈstəbəl/ *n* [U] **1** stalks of grain plants left in the ground after harvest. **2** something suggesting this, eg a short growth of beard.

stub·bly /ˈstəbli/ *adj*: *a stubbly beard.*

stub·born /ˈstəbərn/ *adj* obstinate; determined: *~ soil,* difficult to plough, etc. ***as ˌstubborn as a ˈmule*** ⇨ mule[1].

stub·born·ly *adv*

stub·born·ness /-nɪs/ *n* [U]

stubby /ˈstəbi/ *adj* (-ier, -iest) short and thick: *~ fingers.*

stuck *pt,pp* of stick[2].

stuck-up /ˌstək ˈəp/ *adj* (*informal*) conceited; snobbish.

stud[1] /stəd/ *n* [C] **1** small device put through buttonholes to fasten a collar, cuff, etc. **2** small projection (such as a knob or point) attached to a surface: *The cowboy wore a heavy belt decorated with brass studs.* **3** upright piece of wood, metal, etc, in the framework of a building, to which boards, panels, laths, etc are fastened. □ *vt* (-dd-) (usually *pp*) having (something) set in or scattered on the surface: *a crown ~ded with jewels; a sea ~ded with islands.*

stud[2] /stəd/ *n* [C] **1** number of horses kept by one owner for a special purpose (esp breeding or racing). **2** = studhorse.

'stud farm, place where horses are bred.

'stud·horse *n* [C] one kept for breeding purposes.

stud 'poker, kind of card game (⇨ poker[2]) in which the cards are dealt face up.

stud.[3] *abbr* = student.

stu·dent /'studənt/ *n* [C] **1** person who is studying at a college, institute, polytechnic or university: *'medical ~s; foreign ~s in the United States.* **2** boy or girl attending elementary or secondary school. **3** anyone who studies or who is devoted to learning: *a ~ of nature.*

stu·dio /'studiou/ *n* [C] (*pl* ~s) **1** workroom of a painter, sculptor, photographer, etc. **2** room(s) where films or plays are acted and photographed. **3** room from which radio or TV programs are broadcast or in which recordings are made.

,studio apartment, one-room apartment, with kitchen and bathroom.

'studio couch, couch that can be used as a bed.

stu·di·ous /'studiəs/ *adj* (*formal*) **1** having or showing the habit of learning. **2** painstaking: *with ~ politeness.*

stu·di·ous·ly *adv*

study[1] /'stədi/ *n* (*pl* -ies) **1** [U] (or as *pl*) devotion of time and thought to getting knowledge of, close examination of, a subject, esp from books: *fond of ~; My studies show that...* **2** [C] something that attracts investigation; that which is (to be) investigated: *social studies.* **3** [C] room used for reading, writing, etc: *You will find Mr. Green in the/his ~.* **4** [C] sketch, etc made for practice or experiment; piece of music played as a technical exercise.

study[2] /'stədi/ *vt,vi* (*pt,pp* -ied) **1** give time and attention to learning or discovering something: *~ medicine. He was ~ing to be a doctor.* **2** examine carefully: *~ the map.*

stuff[1] /stəf/ *n* **1** [C,U] material or substance of which something is made or which may be used for some purpose: *What ~ will you use to fill the cushions?* **2** [U] (*fig*) quality, type: *He is not the ~ heroes are made of.* **3** [U] (*informal*) material of which the name is uncertain, unknown or unimportant; material of poor quality: *Do you call this ~ beer?* **4** (*sl*) ***Do your stuff,*** show what you can do, etc. ***know one's stuff,*** be expert in what one claims to be able to do, etc.

stuff[2] /stəf/ *vt* **1** fill tightly with; press tightly into: *~ feathers into a bag; ~ oneself with food,* eat too much; *a head ~ed with silly ideas.* **2** put chopped up and specially flavored food into (a bird, etc) before cooking it: *a ~ed chicken.* **3** fill the carcass of (an animal, etc) with material to give it the original shape, eg for exhibition in a museum: *a ~ed tiger.* **4** put illegal or faked votes in (a ballot box).

stuff·ing *n* [U] material for stuffing cushions, birds, etc.

stuffy /'stəfi/ *adj* (-ier, -iest) **1** (of a room) badly ventilated. **2** (*informal*) (of a person) easily shocked or offended; too formal. **3** (of language, etc) dull; formal: *a ~ book.*

stuff·ily /-əli/ *adv*

stuffi·ness /-nɪs/ *n* [U]

stul·tify /'stəltɪ,fai/ *vt* (*pt,pp* -ied) (*formal*) cause to seem foolish or to be useless: *~ efforts to reach agreement.*

stumble /'stəmbəl/ *vi* **1** hit the foot against something and (almost) fall: *~ over the root of a tree. The child ~d and fell.* ***stumble across/on/upon sth,*** (*fig*) find it unexpectedly or by accident. **2** move or walk in an unsteady way: *stumbling along.* **3** speak in a hesitating way, with pauses and mistakes: *~ over one's words.* □ *n* [C] act of stumbling.

'stum·bling block, something that causes difficulties or prevents progress.

stump /stəmp/ *n* [C] **1** part of a tree remaining in the ground when the trunk has fallen or has been cut down. **2** anything remaining after the main part has been cut or broken off or has worn off, eg an amputated limb, the end of a pencil, etc. □ *vi,vt* **1** walk (*along, around,* etc) with stiff, heavy movements. **2** (*informal*) be too difficult for: *All the candidates were ~ed by the second question.*

stumpy /'stəmpi/ *adj* (-ier, -iest) short and thick: *a ~ little man; a ~ umbrella.*

stun /stən/ *vt* (-nn-) **1** make unconscious by a blow, esp one on the head. **2** shock; confuse the mind of: *He was ~ned by the news of his father's death.*

stun·ning *adj* (*informal*) extremely impressive: *a ~ning performance.*

stung *pt,pp* of sting[2].

stunk *pp* of stink.

stunt[1] /stənt/ *n* [C] (*informal*) something done to attract attention: *~ flying,* aerobatics.

'stunt man, person employed to perform stunts (involving risk, etc) as a stand-in for an actor in films, etc.

stunt[2] /stənt/ *vt* halt or slow down the growth or development of: *a ~ed mind.*

stu·pefy /'stupə,fai/ *vt* (*pt,pp* -ied) (*formal*) make clear thought impossible: *stupefied with drink/amazement.*

stu·pen·dous /stu'pendəs/ *adj* amazing (in size, degree): *a ~ achievement.*

stu·pen·dous·ly *adv*

stu·pid /'stupɪd/ *adj* **1** unintelligent; foolish: *Don't be ~ enough to believe that.* **2** in a state of stupor. □ *n* [C] (*informal*) foolish person: *I was only teasing, ~!*

stu·pid·ity /stu'pɪdəti/ *n* [C,U]

stu·pid·ly *adv*

stu·por /'stupər/ *n* [C,U] almost unconscious condition caused by shock, drugs, drink, etc: *in a drunken ~.*

sturdy /'stərdi/ *adj* (-ier, -iest) strong and solid: *~ children; offer a ~ resistance.*

stur·dily /-əli/ *adv*: *a sturdily built bicycle.*

stut·ter /'stətər/ *vi,vt, n* = stammer.

stut·terer *n* [C] person who stutters.

sty[1] /stai/ *n* [C] (*pl* sties) = pigsty.

sty[2], **stye** /stai/ *n* [C] (*pl* sties, styes) inflamed swelling on the edge of the eyelid.
style /ˈstaiəl/ *n* **1** [C,U] manner of writing or speaking (contrasted with the subject matter); manner of doing anything, esp when it is characteristic of an artist or of a period of art: *written in a delightful ~. What do you know about the ~s of architecture?* **2** [U] quality that marks something done or made as superior, fashionable or distinctive: *live in (grand) ~*, in a fashionable house, with luxuries, etc. *Did they live American-~ when they were in Japan?* **3** [C,U] (esp) fashion in dress, etc: *the latest ~s in shoes/in hairdressing.* **4** [C] general appearance, form or design; kind or sort: *made in all sizes and ~s.* **5** [C] right title (to be) used when addressing a person: *Has he any right to assume the ~ of Colonel?* **6** [C] (*bot*) part of the seed-producing part of a flower. ⇨ illus at flower. □ *vt* (*pres p* -ing /ˈstailɪŋ/) **1** describe by a specified title: *He styled himself "Dr." Smith, although he never completed work on his PhD.* **2** design: *new handbags ~d in Italy.*
styl·ish /ˈstailɪʃ/ *adj* having style(2,3); fashionable: *stylish clothes.*
sty·lish·ly *adv*: *stylishly dressed.*
sty·list /ˈstailɪst/ *n* [C] **1** person, esp a writer, with a good literary style. **2** person who is concerned with creating styles(3): *a ˈhair~.*
sty·lis·tic /ˌstaiˈlɪstɪk/ *adj* of style(1).
styl·is·ti·cally /-kli/ *adv*
sty·lize /ˈstaiˌlaiz/ *vt* represent or treat (art forms, etc) in the particular, conventional style.
sty·lus /ˈstailəs/ *n* [C] (*pl* ~es) part like a needle used to cut grooves in records or to reproduce sound from records.
suave /swav/ *adj* smooth and gracious (often insincerely) in manner.
suave·ly *adv*
sub[1] /səb/ *n* [C] (*informal*) (short for) submarine.
sub.[2] *abbr* = **1** substitute. **2** subscription.
sub- /səb-/ *prefix* (with or without-) **1** under: *subway.* **2** secondary, lower in rank: *subcommittee.* **3** not quite: *subtropical; subconscious.*
sub·com·mit·tee /ˈsəbkəˌmɪti/ *n* [C] committee formed from members of a main committee.
sub·con·scious /ˌsəbˈkanʃəs/ *adj* of those mental activites of which we are not (completely) aware: *the ~ self.* □ *n* **the subconscious,** subconscious thoughts, desires, etc.
sub·con·scious·ly *adv*
sub·con·scious·ness /-nɪs/ *n* [U]
sub·con·ti·nent /ˌsəbˈkantənənt/ *n* [C] mass of land large enough to be regarded as a separate continent but forming part of a larger mass.
sub·con·tract /ˌsəbˈkanˌtrækt/ *n* [C] contract which is for carrying out a previous contract or a part of it. □ *vt,vi* give or accept a subcontract.
sub·con·tractor /ˌsəbˈkanˌtræktər/ *n* [C] person who accepts a subcontract.
sub·cu·taneous /ˌsəbkyuˈteiniəs/ *adj* under the skin.
sub·di·vide /ˌsəbdɪˈvaid/ *vt,vi* divide into further divisions.
sub·di·vi·sion /ˌsəbdɪˈvɪʒən/ *n* [U] subdividing; [C] something produced by subdividing.
sub·due /səbˈdu/ *vt* **1** bring under control: *~ one's hatred.* **2** make quieter, softer, gentler (esp *pp*): *~d voices/lights.*
sub·hu·man /ˌsəbˈ(h)yumən/ *adj* more like an animal than a human being.
subj. *abbr* = subject.
sub·ject[1] /ˈsəbdʒɪkt/ *adj* ***subject to,*** **1** owing obedience (to): *We are ~ to the law of the land.* **2** having a tendency (to): *Are you ~ to colds?* **3** (*adj, adv*) conditional(ly) on: *The plan is ~ to confirmation.*
sub·ject[2] /ˈsəbdʒɪkt/ *n* [C] **1** any member of a State having a supreme ruler, except the supreme ruler: *British ~s.* (*Note:* compare *American citizens.*) **2** something (to be) talked or written about or studied: *an interesting ~ of conversation. What ~ are you studying?* ***change the subject,*** talk about something different. **3** person, animal or thing (to be) treated or dealt with, to be made to undergo or experience something: *a ~ for experiment.* **4** (*gram*) word(s) in a sentence which is described, which does, something, etc, eg *book* in "The book is green," and *they* in "Did they come early?" **5** (*music*) theme on which a composition is based.
ˈsubject matter, plot, topic, etc of a book or speech (contrasted with style).
sub·ject[3] /səbˈdʒekt/ *vt* **1** bring, get (a country, nation, person) under control: *The Romans ~ed most of Europe to their rule.* **2** cause to undergo or experience: *~ a man to torture.*
sub·jec·tion /səbˈdʒekʃən/ *n* [U]
sub·jec·tive /səbˈdʒektɪv/ *adj* **1** (opposite of *objective*) (of ideas, feelings, etc) existing in the mind, not produced by things outside the mind: *Did he really see a ghost or was it only a ~ impression?* **2** (of art and artists, writing, etc) giving the personal or individual point of view or feeling (opposite to *realistic*). **3** (*gram*) of the subject.
sub·jec·tive·ly *adv*
sub·jec·tiv·ity /ˌsəbˌdʒekˈtɪvəti/ *n* [U]
sub·ju·gate /ˈsəbdʒəˌgeit/ *vt* (*formal*) subdue; conquer.
sub·ju·ga·tion /ˌsəbdʒəˈgeiʃən/ *n* [U]
sub·junc·tive /səbˈdʒəŋktɪv/ *adj* (*gram*) expressing a condition, hypothesis, possibility, etc. □ *n* [C] the subjunctive mood; form of a verb in this mood.
sub·lease /ˌsəbˈlis/ *vt,vi* lease to another person. □ *n* [C] lease of this kind.
sub·let /ˌsəbˈlet/ *vt,vi* (-tt-) rent (a room, house, etc of which one is a tenant) to somebody else.
sub·li·mate /ˈsəbləˌmeit/ *vt* **1** (*psych*) direct (emotions, impulses) into higher or more desirable channels. **2** (*informal*) idealize.
sub·lime /səˈblaim/ *adj* **1** of the greatest and highest sort; causing wonder or reverence: *~ heroism.* **2** extreme (as of a person who does not fear the consequences): *What ~ indifference!* □ *n* **the sublime,** that which fills one with wonder or reverence.
sub·lime·ly *adv*
sub·lim·inal /ˌsəbˈlɪmɪnəl/ *adj* of which one is not consciously aware.
sub·mar·ine /ˈsəbməˌrin/ *adj* existing, designed for use, under the surface of the sea: *a ~ cable.* □ *n* [C] ship which can operate under water. ⇨

illus at ship.

ˌ**submarine ˈsandwich,** one made with a long roll, shaped like a submarine.

sub·merge /səbˈmərdʒ/ *vt,vi* **1** put under water; cover with a liquid. **2** sink out of sight; (of a submarine) go down under the surface. **3** (*fig*) inundate.

sub·merged *adj* **(a)** under the surface of the sea, etc: *~d rocks*. **(b)** (*fig*) overwhelmed.

sub·merg·ence /səbˈmərdʒəns/, **sub·mer·sion** /səbˈmərʒən/ *n* [U] submerging or being submerged.

sub·mis·sion /səbˈmɪʃən/ *n* **1** [U] act of submitting; acceptance of another's power or authority: *The enemy was starved into ~.* **2** [U] obedience; respect: *with all due ~.* **3** [C,U] (*legal*) theory, etc submitted to a judge or jury: *My ~ is that*...

sub·miss·ive /səbˈmɪsɪv/ *adj* yielding to the control or authority of another: *Marian is not a ~ wife.*

sub·miss·ive·ly *adv*

sub·miss·ive·ness /-nɪs/ *n* [U]

sub·mit /səbˈmɪt/ *vt,vi* (-tt-) **1** put (oneself) under the control of another: *~ oneself to discipline.* **2** put forward for opinion, discussion, decision, etc: *~ plans/proposals to a committee.* **3** (*legal*) suggest: *Counsel ~ted that there was no case against his client.* **4** surrender: *~ to separation from one's family.*

sub·nor·mal /ˌsəbˈnɔrməl/ *adj* below normal (esp intelligence).

sub·or·di·nate /səˈbɔrdənɪt/ *adj* junior in rank or position; less important: *in a ~ position.* □ *n* [C] person in a junior position. □ *vt* /səˈbɔrdəˌneit/ treat as junior.

subˌordinate ˈclause, (*gram*) dependent clause; clause which, introduced by a conjunction, serves as a *noun, adj* or *adv*.

sub·scribe /səbˈskraib/ *vi,vt* **1** (agree to) pay (a sum of money) with other persons (to a cause, for something): *He ~s liberally to charities.* **2** agree to take (a newspaper, periodical, etc) regularly. **3** agree with, share (an opinion, view, etc): *subscribing to the general view that*...

sub·scriber *n* [C] **(a)** person who agrees to donate money (esp to funds). **(b)** person, business, etc paying for having a telephone. **(c)** person agreeing to take a newspaper or periodical.

sub·scrip·tion /səbˈskrɪpʃən/ *n* **(a)** [U] subscribing or being subscribed: *paid for by public subscription.* **(b)** [C] sum of money paid (to charity, for receiving a newspaper, magazine, etc or for membership of a club).

sub·se·quent /ˈsəbsɪkwənt/ *adj* later; following: *~ events; ~ to this event.*

sub·se·quent·ly *adv* afterward.

sub·ser·vi·ent /səbˈsərviənt/ *adj* **1** giving too much respect (to authority): *~ junior staff.* **2** subordinate or subject.

sub·ser·vi·ent·ly *adv*

sub·side /səbˈsaid/ *vt* **1** (of flood water) sink to a lower or to the normal level. **2** (of land) sink, eg because of mining operations. **3** (of buildings) settle lower down in the ground. **4** (of winds, passions, etc) become quiet(er).

sub·sid·ence /səbˈsaidəns/ *n* [C,U] act or process of subsiding(2,3); instance of this.

sub·sidi·ary /səbˈsɪdiˌeri/ *adj* serving as a help or support but not of first importance: *a ~ company*, one that is controlled by a larger one. □ *n* [C] (*pl* -ies) subsidiary company, thing or person.

sub·si·dize /ˈsəbsəˌdaiz/ *vt* give a subsidy to.

sub·si·diz·ation /ˌsəbsədaiˈzeiʃən/ *n* [U]

sub·sidy /ˈsəbsədi/ *n* [C] (*pl* -ies) money granted, esp by a government or society, to an industry or other cause needing help, or (eg farm subsidies) to keep prices at a desired level.

sub·sist /səbˈsɪst/ *vi* (*formal*) exist; be kept in existence on: *~ on a vegetable diet.*

sub·sis·tence /-təns/ *n* [U] (means of) existing: *~ence crops*, those grown for consumption (contrasted with ˈ*cash crops*, sold for money).

sub·soil /ˈsəbˌsɔiəl/ *n* [U] layer of soil that lies immediately beneath the surface layer.

sub·sonic /ˌsəbˈsanɪk/ *adj* (at) less than the speed of sound.

sub·stance /ˈsəbstəns/ *n* **1** [C,U] (particular kind of) matter: *Water, ice and snow are the same ~ in different forms.* **2** [U] most important part, chief or real meaning, of something: *I agree in ~ with what you say, but differ on some small points.* **3** [U] firmness; solidity: *This material has some ~*, is fairly solid or strong. **4** [U] money; property: *a man of ~*, eg a property owner.

sub·stan·dard /ˌsəbˈstændərd/ *adj* below average standard; failing to measure up to some standard.

sub·stan·tial /səbˈstænʃəl/ *adj* **1** solidly or strongly built or made. **2** large; considerable: *a ~ meal/improvement/loan.* **3** possessing considerable property: *a ~ business firm.* **4** in essentials: *We are in ~ agreement.* **5** real: *Was what you saw something ~ or perhaps an illusion?*

sub·stan·tially /-ʃəli/ *adv: Your efforts contributed ~* (= a great deal) *to our success.*

sub·stan·ti·ate /səbˈstænʃiˌeit/ *vt* give facts to support (a claim, statement, charge, etc).

sub·stan·ti·ation /səbˌstænʃiˈeiʃən/ *n*

sub·sti·tute /ˈsəbstɪˌtut/ *n* [C] person or thing taking the place of, acting for or serving for another: *Substitutes for rubber can be made from petroleum.* □ *vt,vi* use, serve, as a substitute. *~ margarine for butter.*

sub·sti·tu·tion /ˌsəbstɪˈtuʃən/ *n* [U]

sub·stra·tum /ˌsəbˈstreitəm, -ˈstrætəm/ *n* [C] (*pl* -ta /-tə/) level lying below another: *a ~ of rock.*

sub·struc·ture /ˈsəbˌstrəktʃər/ *n* [C] foundation (the usual word).

sub·sume /səbˈsum/ *vt* (*formal*) include (an example, etc) under a rule or in a particular class.

sub·ter·fuge /ˈsəbtərˌfyudʒ/ *n* [C,U] (*formal*) trick; trickery.

sub·ter·ranean /ˌsəbtəˈreiniən/ *adj* (*formal*) = underground.

sub·title /ˈsəbˌtaitəl/ *n* [C] **1** secondary title (of a book). **2** (usually *pl*) translation of a foreign language film, printed on the film.

subtle /ˈsətəl/ *adj* **1** difficult to perceive or describe because fine or delicate: *a ~ distinction.* **2** clever; complex: *a ~ argument.* **3** quick and clever at seeing or describing small differences: *a ~ observer.*

subtlety *n* [C,U] (*pl* -ies)

sub·tly /ˈsətəli/ *adv*

sub·total /ˌsəbˈtoutəl/ *n* [C] sum of a part of a series of figures. □ *vt* add up part of a series of figures.

sub·tract /səbˈtrækt/ *vt* take (a number, quantity) away from (another number, etc): *~ 6 from 9.*

sub·trac·tion /səbˈtrækʃən/ *n* [C,U]

sub·tropi·cal /ˌsəbˈtrapɪkəl/ *adj* nearly tropical.

sub·urb /ˈsəˌbərb/ *n* [C] residential district around the outside of a town or city.

sub·ur·ban /səˈbərbən/ *adj* of or in a suburb.

sub·ur·ban·ite /səˈbərbəˌnait/ *n* [C] one who lives in the suburbs.

sub·ur·bia /səˈbərbiə/ *n* [U] (kind of life lived by, characteristic outlook of, people in) suburbs.

sub·ver·sion /səbˈvərʒən *n* [U] act of subverting.

sub·vers·ive /səbˈvərsɪv/ *adj* tending to subvert: *~ literature/speeches/policies.*

sub·vert /səbˈvərt/ *vt* destroy, overthrow (religion, a government) by weakening people's trust, confidence, belief.

sub·way /ˈsəbˌwei/ *n* [C] **1** underground passage or tunnel, eg used to get from one side of a street to another; underpass (the usual word). **2** underground electric railroad system, for rapid transportation within a large city (eg New York City). **3** subway train.

sub·zero, sub-zero /ˌsəb ˈzɪrou/ *adj* (of temperature) below zero.

suc·ceed /səkˈsid/ *vi,vt* **1** do what one is trying to do: *~ in passing an examination. The attack ~ed.* **2** come next after and take the place of: *Who ~ed Kennedy as President?*

suc·cess /səkˈses/ *n* **1** [U] succeeding; the gaining of what is aimed at: *meet with ~.* **2** [U] prosperity: *have great ~ in life.* **3** [C] person or thing that succeeds: *The plan/play/lecturer was a great ~.*

suc·cess·ful /-fəl/ *adj* having success: *~ful candidates.*

suc·cess·fully /-fəli/ *adv*

suc·ces·sion /səkˈseʃən/ *n* **1** [U] the coming of one thing after another in time or order: *the ~ of the seasons.* ***in succession,*** one after the other. **2** [C] number of things in succession: *a ~ of defeats.* **3** [U] (right of) succeeding to a title, throne, property, etc; person having this right: *Who is first in ~ to the British throne?*

suc·cess·ive /səkˈsesɪv/ *adj* coming one after the other in an uninterrupted sequence: *The Yankees won eleven ~ games.*

suc·cess·ive·ly *adv*

suc·ces·sor /səkˈsesər/ *n* [C] person or thing that succeeds another: *appoint a ~ to a superintendent of schools.*

suc·cinct /səkˈsɪŋkt/ *adj* expressed briefly and clearly.

suc·cinct·ly *adv*

suc·cinct·ness *n* [U]

suc·cor /ˈsəkər/ *n* [U] (*liter*) help given in time of need. □ *vt* give such help to.

suc·co·tash /ˈsəkəˌtæʃ/ *n* [U] dish consisting of corn and lima beans boiled together.

suc·cu·lent /ˈsəkyələnt/ *adj* **1** (of fruit and meat) juicy; tasting good: *a ~ steak.* **2** (of stems, leaves) thick and fleshy. □ *n* [C] succulent plant, eg a cactus.

suc·cumb /səˈkəm/ *vi* yield (to death, temptation, flattery, etc).

such /sətʃ/ *adj* (*Note:* there is no comparative or superlative; not placed between *a* and a *noun.*) **1** of the same kind or degree (as): *I've never heard of ~ a thing! all ~ people are respected; poets ~ as Pound and Eliot; ~ poets as Pound and Eliot; on ~ an occasion/on an occasion ~ as this.* ⇨ as²(10). ***2 such as it is,*** (used to suggest that something is of poor quality, of little value, etc): *You can use my bicycle, ~ as it is.* **3 *such (...) that:*** *His behavior was ~ that everyone disliked him. Such was the force of the explosion that all the windows were broken.* **4** (Compare the positions of *such* and *so* in these examples): *Don't be in ~ a hurry,* in so much of a hurry, in so great a hurry. *I haven't had ~ an enjoyable evening* (= so enjoyable an evening) *for months.* **5** (used in exclamatory sentences): *It was ~ a long time ago! We've had ~ a good time!* □ *pron* **1** this, that, these, those (as already stated, etc): *Such were his words. Such is life!* Life is like that. **2** person(s) or thing(s) of the same kind, etc: *I may have hurt his feelings but ~* (= that) *was certainly not my intention.* ***as such,*** as of that kind: *He is hardworking and as ~ should pass the exam.*

suck /sək/ *vt,vi* **1** draw (liquid) into the mouth by the use of the lip muscles: *~ the juice from an orange.* **2** hold (something) in the mouth and lick, move, squeeze, etc with the tongue: *The child still ~s its thumb.* **3 *suck sth up,*** absorb: *plants that ~ up moisture from the soil.* **4** (of a whirlpool, etc) pull in: *The canoe was ~ed (down) into the whirlpool.* □ *n* [C] act or process of sucking: *have/take a ~ at a lollipop.*

sucker /ˈsəkər/ *n* [C] **1** person who, that which, sucks. **2** organ of some animals so that they can rest on a surface by suction. **3** rubber device, eg a rubber disc, that can be used to fix an object to a surface by suction. **4** unwanted shoot from the roots of a tree, shrub, etc. **5** (*informal*) person foolish enough to be deceived by salesmen, advertisements, etc.

suckle /ˈsəkəl/ *vt* feed with milk from the breast or udder.

suc·tion /ˈsəkʃən/ *n* [U] **1** action of sucking. **2** removal of air, liquid, etc from a cavity so as to produce a partial vacuum and enable air pressure from outside to force in something (another liquid, etc): *Vacuum cleaners work by ~.* **3** similar process, eg in a rubber disc, a fly's foot, producing a vacuum that causes two surfaces to be held together.

sud·den /ˈsədən/ *adj* happening, coming, done, unexpectedly, quickly, without warning: *a ~ shower.* □ *n* (only in) ***all of a sudden,*** unexpectedly: *All of a ~ she screamed.*

sud·den·ly *adv*

sud·den·ness /-nɪs/ *n* [U]

suds /sədz/ *n pl* mass of tiny bubbles on soapy

water.

sudsy, *adj* having suds: *~y water.*

sue /su/ *vt,vi* ***sue for,*** **1** make a legal claim against: *sue a person for damages.* **2** beg (the usual word): *suing for mercy.*

suede, suède /sweid/ *n* [U] kind of soft leather without a shining surface.

suet /ˈsuɪt/ *n* [U] hard fat round the kidneys of sheep and oxen, used in cooking.

suf., suff. *abbr* = suffix.

suf·fer /ˈsəfər/ *vi,vt* **1** ***suffer (from),*** feel or have pain, loss, etc: *~ from* (= often have) *headaches. His business ~ed while he was ill,* His business did not do well. **2** experience (something unpleasant): *~ pain/defeat.* **3** put up with; allow: *How can you ~ such insolence?*

suf·ferer *n* [C] person who suffers.

suf·fer·ing *n* **(a)** [U] pain of body or mind. **(b)** (*pl*) feelings of pain, unhappiness, etc: *a prisoner's ~ings.*

suf·fer·ance /ˈsəfrəns/ *n* [U] with permission implied by the absence of objection: *He's here on ~.*

suf·fice /səˈfais/ *vi,vt* **1** be enough (the more usual words): *Will $10 ~ for your needs?* **2** meet the needs of: *One meal a day won't ~ a growing boy.*

suf·fi·ciency /səˈfɪʃənsi/ *n* (usually with *a*) sufficient quantity: *a ~ of fuel.*

suf·fi·cient /səˈfɪʃənt/ *adj* enough: *Have we ~ food for ten people?*

suf·fi·cient·ly *adv*

suf·fix /ˈsəfɪks/ *n* [C] letter(s), sounds or syllable(s) added at the end of a word to make another word (eg *-er* /-ər/ added to *sing* /sɪŋ/ to make *singer* /ˈsɪŋər/).

suf·fo·cate /ˈsəfəˌkeit/ *vt,vi* **1** cause or have difficulty in breathing: *The fumes were suffocating me.* **2** kill, choke, by making breathing impossible.

suf·fo·ca·tion /ˌsəfəˈkeiʃən/ *n* [U]

suf·frage /ˈsəfrɪdʒ/ *n* [U] the right to vote: *female/Negro ~.*

sugar /ˈʃʊgər/ *n* [U] sweet substance obtained from the juices of various plants, used in cooking and for sweetening drinks. □ *vt* sweeten or mix with sugar.

ˈsugar beet, root grown commercially as an alternative source of sugar to sugar cane.

ˈsugar bowl, (usually covered) bowl holding sugar for table use.

ˈsugar·cane *n* [U] kind of cane from which sugar is usually extracted.

ˈsugar daddy, (*sl*) rich, elderly man who is generous to a young woman.

sugary *adj* **(a)** tasting of sugar. **(b)** (*fig*) (of music, etc) too sweet.

sug·gest /səˈdʒest/ *vt* **1** put forward for consideration, as a possibility: *I ~ed a visit/~ed going/that we should go to the theater.* **2** bring (an idea, possibility, etc) into the mind: *That cloud ~s an old man.*

sug·ges·tion /səˈdʒestʃən/ *n* **(a)** [U] suggesting: *at the ~ of my brother; on your ~.* **(b)** [C] idea, plan, etc that is suggested: *What a silly ~ion!* **(c)** [C] slight indication: *a ~ion of a French accent.*

sug·ges·tive /səˈdʒestɪv/ *adj* **(a)** tending to bring ideas, etc into the mind: *~ive remarks.* **(b)** tending to suggest(2) something indecent: *~ive jokes.*

sug·ges·tive·ly *adv*

sui·cidal /ˌsuəˈsaidəl/ *adj* **1** of suicide. **2** very harmful: *~ economic policies.*

sui·cide /ˈsuəˌsaid/ *n* **1** [U] deliberate killing of oneself: *commit ~;* [C] instance of this: *three ~s last week;* [C] person who does this. **2** [U] action destructive to one's interests or welfare: *economic ~,* eg adoption of policies that will ruin the country's economy.

suit[1] /sut/ *n* [C] **1** set of articles of outer clothing of the same material: *a man's ~,* jacket (vest) and trousers. **2** (*formal*) request made to a superior, esp to a ruler: *press one's ~.* **3** = lawsuit. **4** any of the four sets of cards (spades, hearts, diamonds, clubs) used in many card games. ***follow suit,*** (*fig*) do what somebody else has done.

ˈsuit·case *n* [C] portable case with flat sides for clothes, used when traveling.

suit[2] /sut/ *vt,vi* **1** satisfy; meet the needs of; be convenient to or right for: *Does the climate ~ you/your health? Will Thursday ~ (you),* be convenient? ***suit oneself,*** act according to one's own wishes. **2** (esp of articles of dress, hair styles, etc) look well; be appropriate for: *Does this hat ~ me?* **3** ***be suited (to/for),*** be fitted, have the right qualities: *That man is not ~ed for teaching/to be a teacher.*

suit·able /ˈsutəbəl/ *adj* right for the purpose or occasion: *~ clothes for cold weather.*

suit·abil·ity /ˌsutəˈbɪləti/ *n* [U]

suit·ably /-əbli/ *adv: suitably dressed.*

suite /swit/ *n* [C] **1** group of personal attendants of an important person (eg a ruler). **2** complete set of matching articles of furniture: *a ˈbedroom ~.* **3** set of rooms (eg in a hotel): *the ˈbridal ~.* **4** (*music*) orchestral composition made up of three or more related parts.

suitor /ˈsutər/ *n* [C] **1** person bringing a lawsuit. **2** (*dated*) man courting a woman.

Suk·koth /ˈsʊkəs, -kəθ/ *n* (in Jewish religion) festival of thanksgiving for the sheltering of the Jews in the wilderness after leaving Egypt.

sul·fur /ˈsəlfər/ *n* [U] light-yellow nonmetal element (symbol **S**) that burns with a bright flame and a strong smell, used in medicine and industry.

sul·fu·ric /səlˈfyʊrɪk/ *adj*: *~ic acid.*

sulk /səlk/ *vi* be in a bad temper and show this by refusing to talk.

sulky *adj* (-ier, -iest) unsociable.

sul·len /ˈsələn/ *adj* **1** silent and angry: *~ looks.* **2** dark and gloomy: *a ~ sky.*

sul·len·ly *adv*

sul·tan /ˈsəltən/ *n* [C] Moslem ruler.

sul·tan·ate /ˈsəltəˌneit/ position, period of rule of, territory ruled by, a sultan.

sul·tana /ˈsəlˈtænə/ *n* [C] (*pl ~s*) **1** sultan's wife. **2** kind of small seedless raisin used in puddings and cakes.

sul·try /ˈsəltri/ *adj* (-ier, -iest) **1** (of the atmosphere, the weather) hot and oppressive. **2** (of a person's temper) passionate.

sul·trily /-trəli/ *adv*

sum /səm/ *n* [C] **1** (also **sum total**) total obtained by adding together items, numbers or amounts. **2** problem in arithmetic: *good at ~s*. **3** amount of money: *save a nice little ~ each week*. □ *vt,vi* (-mm-) ***sum (sb/sth) up,*** **1** give the total of. **2** express briefly (the chief points of what has been said): *The judge ~med up (the evidence)*. **3** form a judgment or opinion of: *He ~med up the situation at a glance*, realized it at once.

sum·mar·ize /ˈsəməˌraiz/ *vt* be or make a summary of.

sum·mary /ˈsəməri/ *adj* (*formal*) **1** brief; giving the chief points only: *a ~ account*. **2** done or given without delay or attention to small matters: *~ justice*. □ *n* [C] (*pl* -ies) brief account giving the chief points.

sum·mer /ˈsəmər/ *n* [C,U] (in countries outside the tropics) the warmest season of the year: *in (the) ~; this/next/last ~*; (as an *adjective*) *~ weather; the ~ vacation*.

ˈsummer school, (sessions of) school held in the summertime.

ˈsummer squash, (kinds of) squash which ripen in the summertime.

ˈsum·mer·time *n* the season of summer.

sum·mery *adj* like, suitable for, summer: *a ~y dress*.

sum·mit /ˈsəmɪt/ *n* [C] **1** highest point; top: *reach the ~*, of a mountain. **2** (*fig*): *the ~ of his power*.

ˈsummit conference/talk/meeting, (*modern use*) at the highest level (ie between heads of States).

sum·mon /ˈsəmən/ *vt* **1** call or send for: *~ a person to appear as a witness*, eg in a law court. **2** gather together: *~ up courage*.

sum·mons /ˈsəmənz/ *n* [C] (*pl* ~es) **1** order to appear before a judge or magistrate; document with such an order: *issue a ~*. **2** command to do something or appear somewhere. □ *vt* serve a summons(1) on.

sump·tu·ous /ˈsəmptʃuəs/ *adj* (*formal*) looking expensive: *~ clothes*.

sun[1] /sən/ *n* **1 the sun,** the heavenly body from which the earth gets warmth and light. ⇨ illus at planet. **2 the sun,** light and warmth from the sun: *sit in the sun*. ***under the sun,*** (anywhere) in the world: *the best wine under the sun*. **3** [C] any fixed star with satellites: *There are many suns larger than ours*. □ *vt* (-nn-) put in, expose (*oneself*) to, the rays of the sun: *The cat was sunning itself on the path*.

ˈsun·baked *adj* made hard by the heat of the sun: *sunbaked fields*.

ˈsun·bathe *vi* expose one's body to sunlight.

ˈsun·beam *n* [C] ray of sunshine.

ˈSun Belt, (*informal*) southern and southwestern regions of the US.

ˈsun·burn *n* [U] (place where there is a) reddening and blistering caused by too much exposure to the sun.

ˈsun·burnt *adj*

ˈsun·dial *n* [C] device that shows the time by the sun producing a shadow on a marked surface.

ˈsun·down *n* sunset.

ˈsun-drenched *adj* exposed to great light and heat from the sun: *ˌsun-drenched ˈbeaches*.

ˈsun-dried *adj* (of fruit, etc) dried naturally, by the sun, not by artificial heat.

ˈsun·fish *n* large fish almost spherical in shape.

ˈsun·flower *n* [C] kind of large yellow flower with edible seeds. ⇨ illus at flower.

ˈsun·glasses *n pl* with dark-colored glass to protect the eyes from bright sunshine.

ˈsun-god *n* the sun worshiped as a god.

ˈsun lamp, lamp that gives out ultraviolet rays used for artificial sunbathing.

sun·less *adj* receiving little or no sunlight.

ˈsun·light *n* the light of the sun.

ˈsun·lit *adj* lit by the sun: *a sunlit room*.

sunny *adj* (-ier, -iest) **(a)** bright with sunlight: *a sunny room*. **(b)** cheerful: *a sunny smile*. **(c)** ***sunny side up,*** (*informal*) (of eggs) fried only on one side, with the yolks remaining soft.

ˈsun·rise *n* (time of) the sun's rising.

ˈsun·set *n* (time of) the sun's setting.

ˈsun·shade *n* [C] shade (like an umbrella) to keep off the sun.

ˈsun·shine *n* [U] light of the sun.

ˈsun·spot *n* [C] (*astron*) dark patch on the sun.

ˈsun·stroke *n* [U] illness caused by too much exposure to the sun, esp on the head.

ˈsun·tan *n* browning of the skin from exposure to sunlight: *ˈsuntan lotion/oil*.

Sun.[2] *abbr* = Sunday.

sun·dae /ˈsəndei, ˈsəndi/ *n* [C] dish of ice cream topped with flavored syrup, fruit, etc.

Sun·day /ˈsəndi, ˈsəndei/ *n* first day of the week. ***(not in) a month of Sundays,*** (not for) a long period of time.

ˈSunday school, one for the religious instruction of children, usually held at church on Sunday.

sun·dries /ˈsəndriz/ *n pl* various small items.

sung *pp* of sing[1].

sunk, sunken *pp* of sink[2].

sup /səp/ *vt* (-pp-) (*formal*) eat supper.

super /ˈsupər/ *adj* (*informal*) excellent; splendid.

super- /ˌsupər-/ *prefix* **1** above, over: *superimpose*. **2** superior to: *superhuman*.

super·an·nu·ate /ˌsupərˈænyuˌeit/ *vt* give a pension to (an employee) when he is old or unable to work.

super·an·nu·ation /ˌsupərˌænyuˈeiʃən/ *n* [U] pension (the usual word).

su·perb /suˈpərb/ *adj* magnificent; first class: *a ~ meal/swimmer/result*.

su·perb·ly *adv*

super·cili·ous /ˌsupərˈsɪliəs/ *adj* (*formal*) snobbish and indifferent: *nose high in the air, looking ~*.

super·cili·ous·ly *adv*

super·cili·ous·ness /-nɪs/ *n* [U]

super·fi·cial /ˌsupərˈfɪʃəl/ *adj* **1** of or on the surface only: *a ~ wound*. **2** not thorough or deep: *have only a ~ knowledge of a subject*.

super·fi·cially /-ʃəli/ *adv*

su·per·flu·ous /suˈpərfluəs/ *adj* more than is needed or wanted.

su·per·flu·ous·ly *adv*

super·hu·man /ˌsupərˈ(h)yumən/ *adj* exceeding ordinary human power, size, knowledge, etc: *by a ~ effort*.

super·im·pose /ˌsupərɪmˈpouz/ *vt* put (one

thing) on top of something else.

super·in·tend /ˌsuparɪnˈtend/ *vt,vi* watch and direct (work, etc).

super·in·ten·dency /-ənsi/ *n* [U]

super·in·ten·dent /-ənt/ *n* [C] **(a)** person who superintends. **(b)** highest official of a public school system.

su·per·ior /səˈpɪriər/ *adj* **1** better than the average: *~ intelligence; ~ grades of coffee.* **2** greater in number: *The enemy attacked with ~ forces.* **3** ***superior to,*** **(a)** better than. **(b)** higher in rank or position than. **4** snobbish: *a ~ look.* □ *n* [C] **1** person of higher rank, authority, etc than another, or who is better, etc than another (in doing something): *Napoleon had no ~ as a general.* **2** (in titles): *the Father Superior*, abbot; *the Mother Superior*, abbess.

su·per·ior·ity /səˌpɪriˈɔrəti/ *n* [U] state of being superior: *the ~ity of one thing to another.*

su·per·la·tive /səˈpərlətɪv/ *adj* **1** of the highest degree or quality: *a man of ~ wisdom.* **2** (*gram*) (of the form of an *adjective* or *adverb*) expressing "most" as in *best, worst, highest, most foolish(ly).* □ *n* [C] superlative form of an *adjective* or *adverb.*

super·mar·ket /ˈsupərˌmarkɪt/ *n* [C] large self-service store selling food, household goods, etc.

super·natu·ral /ˌsupərˈnætʃ(ə)rəl/ *adj* spiritual; of that which is not controlled or explained by physical laws: *~ beings,* eg angels.

super·power /ˈsupərˌpauər/ *n* [C] country with great military, economic, and political power.

super·sede /ˌsupərˈsid/ *vt* take the place of; put or use a person or thing in the place of: *Expressways have ~d ordinary roads for long-distance travel.*

super·sonic /ˌsupərˈsanɪk/ *adj* **1** (of speeds) greater than that of sound. **2** (of aircraft) able to fly at supersonic speed.

super·star /ˈsupərˌstar/ *n* [C] very famous entertainer.

super·sti·tion /ˌsupərˈstɪʃən/ *n* [C,U] (idea, practice, etc based on) belief in magic, witchcraft, etc.

super·sti·tious /ˌsupərˈstɪʃəs/ *adj* of, showing, resulting from, believing in, superstitions: *superstitious beliefs/ideas/people.*

super·sti·tious·ly *adv*

super·struc·ture /ˈsupərˌstrəktʃər/ *n* [C] structure built on the top of something else.

super·vise /ˈsupərˌvaiz/ *vt,vi* watch and direct (work, workers, an organization).

super·vi·sion /ˌsupərˈvɪʒən/ *n* [U] supervising: *under the supervision of,* supervised by.

super·vi·sor /-zər/ *n* [C] person who supervises.

sup·per /ˈsəpər/ *n* [C,U] last meal of the day.

sup·plant /səˈplænt/ *vt* **1** supersede (the usual word). **2** take the place of (a person): *The Governor was ~ed by his rival.*

supple /ˈsəpəl/ *adj* (-r, -st) easily bent; not stiff: *the ~ limbs of a child.*

supple·ment /ˈsəpləmənt/ *n* [C] **1** something added later to improve or complete, eg a dictionary. **2** extra and separate addition to a newspaper or other periodical: *The Sunday Supplement,* (in a newspaper). □ *vt* /ˈsəpləˌment/ make an addition or additions to: *~ one's ordinary income by writing books.*

supple·men·tary /ˌsəpləˈment(ə)ri/ *adj* additional; extra: *~ estimates,* eg for additional expenditure.

supply /səˈplai/ *vt* (*pt,pp* -ied) **1** give or provide (something needed or asked for): *~ children with money for books.* **2** meet (a need): *Should the government ~ the need for more houses,* help to provide them (eg by making loans)? □ *n* **1** [U] supplying; [C] (*pl* -ies) that which is supplied; stock or amount of something which is obtainable: *Have you a good ~ of clothes for your vacation?* ***in short supply,*** scarce (the more usual word). **2** (*pl*) (esp) stores necessary for some public need: *ˈmedical supplies.*

sup·plier *n* [C] person or firm supplying goods, materials, etc.

sup·port /səˈpɔrt/ *vt* **1** bear the weight of; hold up or keep in place: *Is this bridge strong enough to ~ heavy trucks?* **2** provide a person or thing with what is necessary: *~ a political party,* agree with its policies; *a hospital ~ed by voluntary contributions; an accusation not ~ed by proofs.* **3** provide (money, etc) for: *He has a large family to ~.* □ *n* **1** [U] supporting or being supported: *I hope to have your ~ in the election. If you decide to oppose the decision, you have my full* (= total) *~. Representative X spoke in ~ of the motion. The divorced wife claimed ~* (ie a regular financial contribution) *for her children from her ex-husband.* **2** [C] person who, that which, supports: *Dick is the chief ~ of the family,* earns the money for the family.

sup·porter *n* [C] person who, device which, supports.

sup·pose /səˈpouz/ *vt* **1** let it be thought that; take it as a fact that: *Let us ~ (that) the news is true. Everyone is ~d to know the rules,* It is assumed that we all know the rules. **2** guess; think: *What do you ~ he wanted? "Will he come?"—"Yes, I ~ so"/"No, I ~ not"/"No, I don't ~ so."* **3** ***be supposed to,*** (*Note:* often pronounced /səˈpoustə/ in this and the following sense.) **(a)** be expected or required to (by customs, duty, etc): *Is he ~d to clean the outside of the windows or only the inside?* **(b)** (*informal*) (in the negative) not be allowed to: *We're not ~d to play football on Sundays.*

sup·pos·ed·ly /-ɪdli/ *adv* according to what is/was supposed(1,2).

sup·pos·ing *conj* if: *Supposing it rains, what shall you do?*

sup·po·si·tion /ˌsəpəˈzɪʃən/ *n* **1** [U] supposing: *This newspaper article is based on ~,* on what the writer thinks is true or correct, not on fact. **2** [C] guess: *Our ~s were fully confirmed.*

sup·posi·tory /səˈpazəˌtɔri/ *n* [C] (*pl* -ies) medical preparation (in a container which dissolves) put into the rectum or vagina.

sup·press /səˈpres/ *vt* **1** put an end to the activity or existence of: *~ a rebellion.* **2** prevent from being known or seen: *~ the truth/a yawn/one's feelings.*

sup·pres·sion /səˈpreʃən/ *n* [U]

sup·pres·sive *adj* tending to, designed to, suppress: *~ive action by the police.*

sup·pres·sor /-sər/, something that suppresses;

(esp) a device fitted to electric apparatus to prevent interference with radio and television reception.

su·prem·acy /sə'preməsi/ *n* [U] being supreme over; highest authority: *His ~ was unchallenged.*

su·preme /sə'prim/ *adj* **1** highest in rank or authority: *the Supreme (Allied) Commander; the Supreme Court*, highest in one of the States of the US or in the whole of the US; *the Supreme Being*, God. **2** most important; greatest: *make the ~ sacrifice*, die (eg in war).

su·preme·ly *adv* extremely: *~ly happy.*

sur·charge /'sərˌtʃardʒ/ *n* [C] **1** payment demanded in addition to the usual charge, eg for a letter with insufficient postage paid on it. **2** excessive or additional load. □ *vt* **1** overload. **2** demand a surcharge(1) on or in.

sure /ʃʊr/ *adj* **1** free from doubt; having confidence; knowing and believing; having, seeming to have, good reason for belief: *I think he's coming, but I'm not quite ~. You're ~ of* (= certain to receive) *a welcome. I'm not ~ why he wants it.* ***be/feel sure (about sth),*** have no doubts (about): *I think the answer's right, but I'm not ~ (about it).* ***be sure to,*** don't fail to: *Be ~ to write and give me all the news.* ***for sure,*** (*informal*) without doubt; without fail: *I'll be there for ~.* ***make sure that/of sth,*** **(a)** feel sure: *I made ~ he would be here.* **(b)** satisfy oneself; do what is necessary in order to feel sure, to get something, etc: *I think there's a train at 5 o'clock, but you'd better make ~*, eg by looking up trains in a timetable. **2** proved or tested; reliable: *a ~ cure for colds.* □ *adv* **1** ***sure e'nough,*** certainly: *I said it would happen, and ~ enough it did.* **2** ***as sure as,*** as certain as: *as ~ as my name's Bob.*

sure·ly /'ʃʊrli/ *adv* **1** with certainty: *He was working slowly but ~.* **2** if experience or probability can be trusted: *Surely this wet weather won't last much longer! You didn't want to hurt his feelings, ~!*

surety /'ʃʊr(ə)ti/ *n* [C,U] (*pl* -ies) **1** (something given as a) guarantee. **2** person who makes himself responsible for the conduct or debt(s) of another person: *stand ~ for a debtor.*

surf /sərf/ *n* [U] waves breaking in white foam on the seashore, on sandbanks or reefs. □ *vi* engage in surfing.

'surf·board *n* [C] board used for surfing.

surfing, 'surf-riding *n* [U] sport in which one balances oneself on a long narrow board while being carried along by heavy surf.

sur·face /'sərfɪs/ *n* [C] **1** the outside of any object, etc; any of the sides of an object: *Glass has a smooth ~. A cube has six ~s.* **2** top of a liquid: *The submarine rose to the ~.* **3** outward appearance; what is seen or learned from a quick view or consideration: *His faults are all on the ~. When you get below the ~, you find that he is generous.* **4** (as an *adjective*) of the surface only: *~ impressions*, received quickly or casually, with no depth of thought, observation, etc. ⇨ superficial. □ *vt,vi* **1** give a surface to: *~ a road with tarmac.* **2** (of a submarine, skin diver, etc) (cause to) come to the surface.

SURFING

'surface mail, sent by land or sea, not airmail.

sur·feit /'sərfɪt/ *n* [C] (usually with *a, an*) too much of anything, esp food and drink: *He had a ~ of turkey during Thanksgiving.* □ *vt* (cause to) take too much of anything: *be ~ed with pleasure.*

surge /sərdʒ/ *vi* move forward, roll on, in or like waves: *The floods ~d over the valley. The crowds were surging out of the sports stadium.* □ *n* [C] **1** forward or upward movement: *the ~ of the sea.* **2** (*fig*) (of feelings) grow suddenly: *a ~ of anger/pity.*

sur·geon /'sərdʒən/ *n* [C] doctor who performs medical operations.

sur·gery /'sərdʒəri/ *n* **1** [U] the science and practice of treating injuries and disease by operations: *qualified in both ~ and medicine.* **2** [C] room in which operations take place.

sur·gi·cal /'sərdʒɪkəl/ *adj* of, by, for, surgery: *~ instruments.*

sur·gi·cal·ly /-kli/ *adv*

sur·ly /'sərli/ *adj* (-ier, -iest) bad-tempered and unfriendly.

sur·mise /sər'maiz/ *vt,vi* guess (the usual word). □ *n* (also /'sərˌmaiz/) [C] guess.

sur·mount /sər'maunt/ *vt* **1** overcome (difficulties); get over (obstacles). **2** ***be surmounted by/with,*** have on or over the top: *a spire ~ed by a cross.*

sur·mount·able /-əbəl/ *adj* that can be overcome or conquered.

sur·name /'sərˌneim/ *n* [C] person's hereditary family name: *Smith is a very common American ~.* ⇨ first name, Christian name.

sur·pass /sər'pæs/ *vt* (*formal*) do or be better than: *~ him in speed/skill.*

sur·pass·ing *adj* (*formal*) excellent: *of ~ing beauty.*

sur·plice /'sərplɪs/ *n* [C] loose-fitting (usually white) gown with wide sleeves worn by priests (over a cassock) during (some) Christian church services.

sur·plus /'sərpləs, 'sərˌpləs/ *n* [C] **1** amount (of money) that remains after needs have been supplied. **2** amount (of anything) in excess of requirements: *Brazil had a ~ of coffee last year.* **3** (as an *adjective*) more than what is needed or used: *~ population*, for which there is not enough food, employment, etc.

sur·prise /sə(r)ˈpraiz/ *n* **1** [C,U] (feeling caused by) something sudden or unexpected: *What a horrible/wonderful ~! He looked up in ~.* **2** (as an *adjective*) unexpected; made, done, etc without warning: *a ~ visit/attack.* □ *vt* **1** give a feeling of surprise to: *She was more ~d than frightened.* **2** experience surprise: *We were ~d at the news/~d to hear the news.* **3** discover, see, suddenly or without warning: *~ a burglar in a house.*

sur·pris·ing *adj* causing surprise.

sur·pris·ing·ly *adv*

sur·ren·der /səˈrendər/ *vt,vi* **1** give up (oneself, a ship, a town, etc to the enemy, the police, etc): *We will never ~.* **2** give up under pressure or from necessity; abandon possession of: *We will never ~ our liberty.* **3** give way to (a habit, emotion, influence, etc): *He ~ed to despair and committed suicide.* □ *n* [U] surrendering or being surrendered: *demand the ~ of all weapons.*

sur·rep·ti·tious /ˌsərəpˈtɪʃəs/ *adj* (*formal*) (of actions) done secretly.

surrey /ˈsəri/ *n* [C] horse-drawn carriage with four wheels, front and back seats, and a flat roof.

sur·round /səˈraund/ *vt* be, go, all around, shut in on all sides: *a house ~ed with/by trees.*

sur·round·ing *adj* which is around about: *Nashville and the ~ing countryside.*

sur·round·ings *n* (*pl*) everything around and about a place; conditions that may affect a person: *living in pleasant ~ings. You don't see animals in their natural ~ings at a zoo.*

sur·veil·lance /sərˈveiləns/ *n* [U] close watch kept on persons suspected of doing wrong, etc: *under police ~.*

sur·vey /sərˈvei/ *vt* **1** take a general view of: *~ the countryside from the top of a hill.* **2** examine the general condition of: *The Secretary of State ~ed the international situation.* **3** measure and map out the position, size, boundaries, etc of (an area of land, a country, coast, etc): *~ land for development; ~ a new development.* **4** examine the condition of (a building, etc): *Have the house ~ed before you offer to buy it.* □ *n* /ˈsərˌvei/ [C] **1** general view: *make a general ~ of the situation/subject.* **2** (map, record of) surveying: *an aerial ~ of Africa,* made by photography from aircraft.

sur·vey·ing *n* [U] the work of surveying(3,4).

sur·veyor /sərˈveiər/ *n* [C] person who surveys (3,4).

sur·vival /sərˈvaivəl/ *n* [U] state of continuing to live or exist; surviving: *the ~ of the fittest,* the continuing existence of those animals and plants which are best adapted to their surroundings, etc; (as an *adjective*) *a ~ kit,* package of necessities for a person after a disaster, etc (eg at sea).

sur·vive /sərˈvaiv/ *vt,vi* continue to live or exist; live or exist longer than: *~ an earthquake/shipwreck. The old lady has ~d all her children/is still surviving.*

sur·vivor /-vər/ *n* [C] person who has survived: *Help was sent to the survivors of the air crash.*

sus·cep·tible /səˈseptəbəl/ *adj* **1** easily influenced by feelings: *a ~ nature.* **2** easily affected, influenced, by: *~ to pain.*

sus·cep·ti·bil·ity /səˌseptəˈbɪləti/ *n* (*pl* -ies) **(a)** [U] sensitiveness: *~ to colds.* **(b)** (*pl*) sensitive points of a person's nature: *We must avoid wounding their susceptibilities.*

sus·pect /səˈspekt/ *vt* **1** have an idea or feeling (concerning the possibility or likelihood of something): *She has more intelligence than we ~ed.* **2** feel doubt about: *~ the truth of an account.* **3** have a feeling that a person may be guilty (of): *He is ~ed of telling lies.* □ *n* /ˈsəˌspekt/ [C] person suspected of doing wrong, etc: *Are political ~s kept under police observation in your country?* □ *adj* /ˈsəˌspekt/ of doubtful character: *His statements are ~.*

sus·pend /səˈspend/ *vt* **1** hang up (from): *lamps ~ed from the ceiling.* **2** (of solid particles, in the air or other fluid medium) be or remain in place: *dust/smoke ~ed in the air.* **3** stop for a time; delay: *~ judgment,* postpone giving one. **4** announce that (a person) cannot be allowed to perform his duties, enjoy privileges, etc for a time: *~ a (professional) football player,* eg because of breaking the rules.

sus·penders /səˈspendərz/ *n pl* (also ***a pair of suspenders***) straps passing over the shoulders, sometimes used instead of a belt for keeping trousers up.

sus·pense /səˈspens/ *n* [U] uncertainty, anxiety (about news, events, decisions, etc): *We waited in ~ for the doctor's opinion.*

sus·pen·sion /səˈspenʃən/ *n* [U] suspending or being suspended(4): *the ~ of a student from school.*

susˈpension bridge, bridge hanging on steel cables supported from towers.

sus·pi·cion /səˈspɪʃən/ *n* **1** [C,U] feeling that a person has when he suspects; suspecting or being suspected; feeling that something is wrong: *I have a ~ that he may be right. He was arrested on (the) ~ of having stolen the money.* ***above suspicion,*** of such good reputation that suspicion is out of the question. ***under suspicion (of),*** being considered as possibly guilty (of). **2** (*sing* with *a* or *an*) slight taste or suggestion: *There was a ~ of sadness in her voice.*

sus·pi·cious /səˈspɪʃəs/ *adj* having, showing or causing suspicion: *The excuse is ~ to me. He's a ~ character,* there is reason to suspect that he is dishonest, etc. *Don't be so ~!*

sus·pi·cious·ly *adv*: *behave ~ly.*

sus·tain /səˈstein/ *vt* **1** keep from falling or sinking: *Will this light shelf ~ (the weight of) all these books?* **2** (enable to) keep up, maintain: *~ing food,* that gives strength; *~ an argument/attempt; ~ a note,* continue to sing or play the note without stopping; *make a ~ed effort.* **3** suffer; undergo: *~ a defeat/an injury.* **4** (*legal*) give a decision in favor of: *The court ~ed his claim.*

sus·ten·ance /ˈsəstənəns/ *n* [U] (*formal*) (nourishing quality of) food or drink: *There's more ~ in cocoa than in tea.*

SW *abbr* = southwest.

swab, swob /swab/ *n* [C] **1** mop or pad for cleaning, eg floors, decks. **2** piece of absorbent material, etc for medical use; specimen taken with a swab: *take throat ~s.* □ *vt* (-bb-) clean with a swab: *~ an injury*.

swag·ger /ˈswægər/ *vi* walk or behave in a self-important or self-satisfied manner. □ *n* [C] swaggering walk or way of behaving.

swal·low[1] /ˈswalou/ *n* [C] kinds of small bird with a forked tail.

ˈswallow-tailed *adj* (of butterflies, birds) with a deeply forked tail.

swal·low[2] /ˈswalou/ *vt,vi* **1** cause or allow to go down the throat: *~ one's food.* **2** take in; exhaust; cause to disappear; use up: *earnings that were ~ed up by lawyers' bills.* **3** (*fig*): *~ an insult*, accept it without complaining. ***swallow sth whole,*** believe it without argument, doubt. ***swallow one's words,*** express regret for them. □ *n* [C] act of swallowing; amount swallowed at one time.

swam *pt* of swim.

swamp /swamp/ *n* [C,U] (area of) soft wet land; marsh. □ *vt* **1** flood, soak, with water: *A big wave ~ed the boat.* **2** (*fig*) overwhelm: *We are ~ed with work. They ~ed us with orders.*

swampy *adj* (-ier, -iest) having swamps.

swan[1] /swan/ *n* [C] large, graceful, long-necked (and usually white) water bird.

ˈswan song, last performance, appearance, work before death or retirement of a poet, musician, etc.

swan[2] /swan/ *vi* (-nn-) (*dated informal*) state; declare: *I ~, he's the meanest man in town.*

swap, swop /swap/ *vt,vi* (-pp-) (*informal*) exchange, esp by bargaining: *~ foreign stamps.* ***swap places with sb,*** exchange seats, jobs, etc. □ *n* [C] exchange (by bargaining).

swarm /swɔrm/ *n* [C] large number, of insects, birds, etc moving around together: *a ~ of ants/locusts/bees.* □ *vi* **1** (of bees) move or go in large numbers, around a queen bee, for emigration to a new colony. **2** (of places) be crowded: *The beaches were ~ing with people.* **3** be present in large numbers: *The crowds ~ed into the buildings.*

swarthy /ˈswɔrði/ *adj* having a dark skin.

swas·ti·ka /ˈswastɪkə/ *n* [C] symbol (a + or × with arms turned at right angles) used by American Indians and the German Third Reich.

swat /swat/ *vt* (-tt-) slap with a flat object: *~ a fly.* □ *n* [C] slap of this kind: *Give that fly a ~.*

swatter, implement with a handle for swatting: *a ˈfly~ter.*

swathe /swað, sweið/ *vt* wrap: *~d in bandages.*

sway /swei/ *vi,vt* **1** (cause to) move, first to one side and then to the other: *The branches of the trees were ~ing in the wind.* **2** control or influence; govern the direction of: *a speech that ~ed the voters.* □ *n* [U] **1** swaying movement. **2** rule or control: *under the ~ of Rome* (in ancient times).

swear /swer/ *vt,vi* (*pt* swore /swɔr/, *pp* sworn /swɔrn/) **1** say solemnly or emphatically: *He swore to tell the truth/swore that he would tell the truth.* **2** (cause (a person) to) take an oath. ***swear sb in,*** cause him to take the oath of office. ***swear sb to secrecy,*** make him swear to keep a secret. **3** ***swear by sth,*** **(a)** appeal to as a witness or witnesses: *~ by all the gods that....* **(b)** (*informal*) use and have great confidence in: *He ~s by strictness for discipline.* **4** make an affirmation after having taken an oath: *sworn evidence/statements.* **5** use curses and bad language: *The captain swore at his crew.*

swearer *n* [C] person who swears(5).

ˈswear·word *n* [C] word used in swearing(5).

sweat /swet/ *n* **1** [U] moisture that is given off by the body through the skin: *wipe the ~ off one's brow.* **2** (with *a, an*) condition of a person or animal (esp a horse) when covered with sweat: *be in a ~.* □ *vt,vi* **1** give out sweat: *The long hot climb made him ~.* ***sweat sth out,*** (*sl*) hope for the best in a bad situation over which one has little or no control. **2** become covered with condensed moisture: *The glass of ice water began to ~ in the warm air.*

ˈsweat shirt *n* [C] loose-fitting, long-sleeved sweater of thick cotton, worn by athletes for warmth and to absorb sweat.

ˈsweat shop, factory, etc in which semiskilled workers (esp recent immigrants) must work long and hard for little pay.

ˈsweat suit, serving the same purpose as a sweat shirt, but sometimes designed with more style.

sweaty *adj* (-ier, -iest) (making) damp with sweat.

sweater /ˈswetər/ *n* [C] knitted jacket or jersey, usually of thick wool.

sweep[1] /swip/ *n* [C] **1** act of sweeping with, or as with, a broom, etc: *Give the room a good ~.* ***make a clean sweep of sth,*** **(a)** get rid of what is unwanted completely: *They made a clean ~ of the members of the committee.* **(b)** gain complete victory: *The tennis player made a clean ~ of the tournament.* (⇨ 6 below.) **2** sweeping movement: *with one ~ of his arm.* **3** space, range, covered by a sweeping movement: *The radar has a ~* (= range) *of 100 miles.* **4** long unbroken stretch, esp curved, on a road, river, coast, etc or of sloping land: *a fine ~ of country.* **5** steady uninterrupted flow: *the ~ of the tide.* **6** complete victory: *The basketball team made a ~ of the games last season.*

ˈsweep·stake *n* form of gambling on horse races, the money staked by those who take part being divided among the winners.

sweep[2] /swip/ *vt,vi* (*pt,pp* swept /swept/) **1** clear (dust, dirt, etc) away with, or as with, a brush or broom; clean by doing this: *~ the carpets/the floor; ~ up the crumbs; ~ a room clean/clear of dust.* **2** clean or move as with a broom: *The current swept the logs along.* ***sweep sb off his feet,*** ⇨ foot[1](1). **3** pass over or along, esp so as to overcome obstacles: *A huge wave swept over the deck.* **4** move in a dignified or stately manner: *She swept out of the room.* **5** extend in an unbroken line, curve or expanse: *The coast ~s northward in a wide curve.* **6** pass over (as if) to examine or survey: *The searchlights swept the sky.* **7** move over lightly and quickly: *Her dress swept the ground.* **8** win completely: *The President swept the election with a landslide victory.*

sweeper *n* [C] person or thing that sweeps: *ˈcarpet/street ~ers.*

sweep·ing *adj* far-reaching; taking in very much: *~ing changes/reforms; a ~ing statement,* making wild generalizations; *a ~ing* (= complete) *victory.*

sweet /swit/ *adj* (-er, -est) **1** (opposite of *sour*) tasting like sugar or honey: *It tastes ~,* has a sweet taste. ***have a sweet tooth,*** like things that taste sweet. **2** fresh and pure: *keep a room clean and ~; ~ breath.* **3** having a fragrant smell: *Don't the roses smell ~!* **4** pleasant or attractive: *a ~ face; a ~ voice. Isn't the baby ~!* ***4 be sweet on sb,*** (*sl*) be in love with him/her. □ *n* **1** (usually *pl*) something sweet; candy (the usual word). **2** [C] dish of sweet food (puddings, pies, etc) as one of the courses of a meal. **3** (*sing* only) (*dated*) (as a form of address) darling: *Yes, my ~.*

ˈsweet·bread *n* pancreas of a calf or lamb used as food.

ˈsweet·heart *n* [C] (*dated*) either of a pair of lovers: *David and his ~.*

sweetie /ˈswiti/, **ˈsweetie-pie,** (*informal*) *n* = sweetheart.

sweet·ly *adv*

ˈsweet·meat *n* (*dated*) piece of food tasting sweet (usually made of sugar or chocolate); candy.

sweet·ness /-nɪs/ *n* [U]

ˈsweet potato, tropical climbing plant with thick edible roots, cooked as a vegetable.

sweeten /ˈswitən/ *vt,vi* make or become sweet.

sweet·en·ing /ˈswitnɪŋ/ *n* [C,U] that which sweetens, eg food.

swell /swel/ *vi,vt* (*pt* ~ed /sweld/, *pp* swollen /ˈswoulən/) **1** (cause to) become greater in volume, thickness or force: *Wood often ~s when wet. His face began to ~,* eg from toothache. **2** have, cause to have, a curved surface: *The sails ~ed out in the wind. The wind ~ed the sails.* □ *n* [C] **1** gradual increase in the volume of sound: *the ~ of an organ.* **2** (*sing* only) slow rise and fall of the sea's surface after a storm: *There was a heavy ~ after the storm.* □ *adj* (*dated informal*) excellent; fashionable.

ˈswell·head *n* [C] (*informal*) conceited person.

ˈswell·headed *adj*

swell·ing *n* [C] (esp) swollen place on the body, eg the result of a toothache.

swel·ter /ˈsweltər/ *vi* be uncomfortably warm: *a ~ing hot day.*

swept *pt,pp* of sweep[2].

swerve /swərv/ *vi,vt* (cause to) change direction suddenly: *The car ~d to avoid knocking the boy down.* □ *n* [C] swerving movement.

swift[1] /swɪft/ *adj* (-er, -est) quick; fast; prompt: *a ~ revenge.*

swift·ly *adv*

swift·ness /-nɪs/ *n* [U]

swift[2] /swɪft/ *n* [C] kinds of small bird with long wings, similar to a swallow.

swig /swɪg/ *n* [C] (*informal*) **1** (of liquor) amount swallowed at a single lifting of the glass or bottle. **2** drink of liquor: *I need a ~.* □ *vt,vi* (*informal*) take a swallow (of liquor).

swill /swɪl/ *vt,vi* **1** rinse by pouring liquid into, over or through: *~ out a dirty tub.* **2** (*informal*) drink greedily: *The college students were ~ing beer at a fraternity party.* □ *n* [U] waste food, mostly liquid, eg as given to pigs.

swim /swɪm/ *vi,vt* (*pt* swam /swæm/, *pp* swum /swəm/) (-mm-) **1** move the body through water by using arms, legs, fins, the tail, etc: *Fishes ~. Let's go ~ming. He swam across the river.* **2** cross by swimming: *~ the English Channel;* take part in (a race) in this way; compete in this way: *~ a race; ~ two lengths of the pool.* **3** be covered (with), overflowing (with), or (as if) floating (in or on): *eyes ~ming with tears; meat ~ming in gravy.* **4** seem to be moving around and around; have a dizzy feeling: *The room swam before his eyes. His head swam.* □ *n* [C] act or period of swimming: *have/go for a ~.*

swim·mer *n* [C] person who swims.

ˈswim·ming hole, deep pool in a stream or pocket at the edge of a lake, used for swimming in rural areas.

ˈswim·ming pool, pool for swimming in.

ˈswim·ming suit, ˈswim·suit, one-piece garment worn by girls and women for swimming. ⇨ bikini.

ˈswim·ming trunks, shorts worn by boys and men for swimming.

swindle /ˈswɪndəl/ *vt,vi* cheat; get (money, etc) by cheating: *swindling money out of a brother; ~ a child out of his money.* □ *n* [C] piece, act of swindling, eg something sold, etc that is less valuable than it is described to be: *This new radio is a ~; the quality of the sound is bad.*

swin·dler /ˈswɪndlər/ *n* [C] person who gets money, etc by cheating.

swine /swain/ *n* [C] (*pl* unchanged) **1** pig. **2** (*sl*) disgusting person.

swing /swɪŋ/ *vi,vt* (*pt,pp* swung /swəŋ/) **1** (of something having one end or one side fixed and the other free) move, cause to move, forward and backward or in a curve: *His arms swung as he walked. The door swung shut.* **2** turn, cause to turn, in a curve: *He swung around* (= turned quickly) *and faced his accusers.* □ *n* [C] **1** swinging movement: *the ~ of the pendulum.* **2** syncopated rhythm. ***in full swing,*** active; in full operation. **3** seat held by ropes or chains for swinging on; act, period, of swinging on such a seat.

swipe /swaip/ *vt* (*informal*) **1** hit hard: *The car ~d the tree.* **2** steal. □ *n* [C] swinging blow: *have/take a ~ at the ball.*

swirl /swərl/ *vi,vt* (of water, air, etc) (cause to) move or flow at varying speeds, with twists and turns: *dust ~ing about the streets.* □ *n* [C] swirling movement: *the ~ of the current.*

swish /swɪʃ/ *vt,vi* **1** move (something) through the air with a hissing or brushing sound; cut (something off) in this way: *The horse ~ed its tail. He ~ed off the tops of the thistles with his whip.* **2** make, move with, a sound like that of something moving through the air: *Her long silk dress ~ed as she came in.* □ *n* [C] sound of, like, swishing.

switch /swɪtʃ/ *n* [C] **1** device for making and breaking a connection at railroad points (to allow trains to go from one track to another). **2** device for making and breaking an electric circuit: *a ˈlight ~.* **3** thin twig, etc, eg as used for urging a horse on. **4** bunch of false hair. **5** transfer; changeover: *a ~ from Republican to Democrat.* □ *vt,vi* **1** use a switch(2) to turn (electric current) on/off: *~ the light/radio on.* **2** move (a train, tram, etc) on to another track: *~ a train into a siding.* **3** shift; change: *He ~ed political parties, becoming a Democrat.* **4** use a switch(3).

ˈswitch·board *n* [C] apparatus for operating several telephone connections, eg in an office.

swivel /ˈswɪvəl/ *n* [C] device used to join two parts (eg a chain and hook) so that one part can turn without turning the other. □ *vt,vi* (-l-, also -ll-) turn on or as on a swivel: *He ~ed around in his chair.*

swob = swab.

swol·len *pp* of swell.

swoon /swun/ *vi* (*dated*) faint. □ *n* [C] fainting spell.

swoop /swup/ *vi* come down on with a rush: *The eagle ~ed down on the rabbit.* □ *n* [C] swooping movement; sudden attempt to snatch and carry off something.

swop = swap.

sword /sɔrd/ *n* [C] long steel blade fixed in a hilt, used as a weapon, or worn by army officers, etc as part of their dress uniform.

ˈsword dance, dance over swords put on the ground, or one in which they are waved or clashed.

ˈsword·fish *n* large ocean fish with a long, pointed upper jaw.

swore, sworn *pt,pp* of swear.

swum *pp* of swim.

swung *pt,pp* of swing.

syca·more /ˈsɪkəˌmɔr/ *n* **1** [C] large tree valued for its wood. **2** [U] its hard wood.

syl·labic /sɪˈlæbɪk/ *adj* of or in syllables.

syl·lable /ˈsɪləbəl/ *n* [C] minimum rhythmic unit of spoken or written language. *"Arithmetic" is a word of four ~s.*

syl·la·bus /ˈsɪləbəs/ *n* [C] (*pl* ~es) outline or summary of a course of studies; program of lessons.

syl·lo·gism /ˈsɪləˌdʒɪzm/ *n* [C] form of reasoning in which a conclusion is reached from two statements, eg: *All men must die; I am a man; therefore I must die.*

sym·bol /ˈsɪmbəl/ *n* [C] sign, mark, object, etc looked on as representing something: *mathematical ~s*, eg ×, ÷, +, −.

sym·bolic /sɪmˈbalɪk/ *adj* of, using, used as, a symbol.

sym·boli·cally /-kli/ *adv*

sym·bol·ize /ˈsɪmbəˌlaiz/ *vt* be a symbol of; make use of a symbol for.

sym·me·try /ˈsɪmətri/ *n* [U] (beauty resulting from the) correct correspondence of parts; quality of harmony or balance (in size, design, etc) between parts: *mathematical ~.*

sym·met·ric /sɪˈmetrɪk/, **sym·met·ri·cal** /-ɪkəl/ *adj* having symmetry; (of a design) having (usually two) exactly similar parts on either side of a dividing line.

sym·met·ri·cally /-kli/ *adv*

sym·path·etic /ˌsɪmpəˈθetɪk/ *adj* having or showing sympathy; caused by sympathy: *~ looks/words/smiles; be/feel ~ to/toward someone.*

sym·path·eti·cally /-kli/ *adv*

sym·path·ize /ˈsɪmpəˌθaiz/ *vi* feel or express sympathy (with): *Tom's parents do not ~ with his ambition to be an actor.*

sym·path·izer *n* [C] person who sympathizes, eg one who supports a political party.

sym·pathy /ˈsɪmpəθi/ *n* (*pl* -ies) **1** [U] (capacity for) sharing the feelings (troubles, pain) of others, feeling pity and tenderness: *send her a letter of ~; feel ~ for her.* **2** (*pl*): *My sympathies are with the miners, I agree with them.*

sym·phony /ˈsɪmfəni/ *n* [C] (*pl* -ies) (long) musical composition in (usually) three or four parts (called *movements*) for (usually a large) orchestra.

sym·phonic /sɪmˈfanɪk/ *adj* of, like a symphony.

symp·tom /ˈsɪmptəm/ *n* [C] **1** change in the body's condition that is a sign of illness: *~s of measles.* **2** sign of the existence of something: *~s of political discontent.*

symp·to·matic /ˌsɪmptəˈmætɪk/ *adj* serving as a symptom: *Headaches may be ~atic of many kinds of trouble.*

symp·to·mati·cally /-kli/ *adv*

syna·gogue, syna·gog /ˈsɪnəˌgag/ *n* [C] (building used for an) assembly of Jews for religious study and worship.

INSIDE A SYNAGOGUE

syn·chron·ize /ˈsɪŋkrəˌnaiz/ *vt,vi* (cause to) happen at the same time, agree in time, speeds, etc: *~ the clocks in a building.*

syn·chron·iz·ation /ˌsɪŋkrənɪˈzeiʃən/ *n* [U]

syn·co·pate /ˈsɪŋkəˌpeit/ *vt* change the rhythm of a piece of music by playing the notes slightly before or after the accented beat: *~d rhythm.*

syn·co·pa·tion /ˌsɪŋkəˈpeiʃən/ *n* [U]

syn·di·cate /ˈsɪndɪkɪt/ *n* [C] **1** business association that supplies articles, cartoons, etc to periodicals. **2** combination of commercial firms associated to forward a common interest. □ *vt* /ˈsɪndɪˌkeit/ publish (articles, cartoon strips, etc) in numerous periodicals through a syndicate (1).

syn·drome /ˈsɪnˌdroum/ *n* [C] (*med*) number of symptoms which indicate an illness, etc.

synod /ˈsɪnəd/ *n* [C] meeting of church officers to discuss and decide questions of policy, government, teaching, etc.

syn·onym /ˈsɪnəˌnɪm/ *n* [C] word that has the same general meaning as another but often with different implications and associations. ⇨ antonym.

syn·ony·mous /sɪˈnanəməs/ *adj*

syn·op·sis /sɪˈnapsɪs/ *n* [C] (*pl* -opses /-ˌsiz/) summary or outline (of a book, play, etc).

syn·op·tic /sɪˈnaptɪk/ *adj*

syn·tac·tic /sɪnˈtæktɪk/ *adj* of syntax.

syn·tac·ti·cally /-kli/ *adv*

syn·tax /ˈsɪnˌtæks/ *n* [U] (*ling*) (rules for) sentence building.

syn·thesis /ˈsɪnθəsɪs/ *n* [C,U] (*pl* -theses /-ˌsiz/) combination of separate parts, elements, substances, etc into a whole or into a system; that which results from this process: *produce rubber from petroleum by* ~.

syn·thetic /sɪnˈθetɪk/ *adj* **(a)** of or produced by synthesis. **(b)** produced by artificial rather than natural means: *synthetic rubber*.

syph·ilis /ˈsɪfəlɪs/ *n* [U] infectious venereal disease.

sy·phon *n* = siphon.

syr·inge /sɪˈrɪndʒ/ *n* [C] kinds of device for drawing in liquid by suction and forcing it out again in a fine stream, used for injecting liquids into the body, etc: *a hypodermic* ~. □ *vt* clean, inject liquid into, apply liquid, with a syringe.

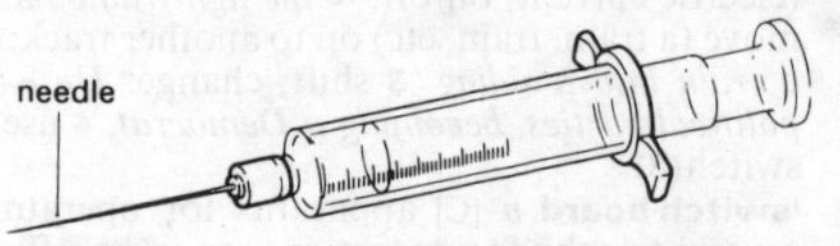

HYPODERMIC SYRINGE

syrup /ˈsərəp, ˈsɪrəp/ *n* [U] thick sweet liquid made from sugar cane juice or by boiling sugar with water.

sys·tem /ˈsɪstəm/ *n* **1** [C] group of things or parts working together in a regular relation: *the ˈnervous* ~; *the diˈgestive* ~; *a ˈrailroad* ~. **2** [C] ordered set of ideas, theories, principles, etc: *a* ~ *of government; a comˈputer* ~. **3** [U] organization: *You mustn't expect good results if you work without* ~.

sys·tem·atic /ˌsɪstəˈmætɪk/ *adj* methodical; based on a system: *a* ~*atic analysis*.

sys·tem·ati·cally /-kli/ *adv*

t

T, t /ti/ (*pl* T's, t's /tiz/) the twentieth letter of the alphabet.

ˌT-bone ˈsteak, loin steak, cut with a piece of bone in the shape of a T.

ˈT-junction *n* [C] place where two roads, pipes, wires, etc meet to form a T.

ˈT-shirt *n* [C] short-sleeved cotton shirt, worn as underwear or informally as a shirt.

ˈT-square *n* [C] T-shaped instrument for drawing right angles.

tab[1] /tæb/ *n* [C] **1** small piece or strip of cloth, etc fixed to clothing, etc as a badge or distinguishing mark or (as a loop) for hanging up a coat, etc. **2** (*informal*) account. ***keep tabs on sth/sb,*** keep under observation. ***pick up the tab,*** pay the bill, costs, etc.

tab[2] /tæb/ *n* [C] (*informal*) (short for) tabulator. ⇨ tabulate.

ˈtab key, key, on a typewriter, for setting the tabulator.

tab·er·nacle /ˈtæbərˌnækəl/ *n* **1 the Tabernacle,** the portable structure used by the Jews as a sanctuary during their wanderings before they settled in Palestine. **2** [C] place of worship, eg a Baptist church or Mormon temple.

table /ˈteibəl/ *n* [C] **1** piece of furniture consisting of a flat top with (usually four) supports (called *legs*): *a ˈdining ~; a ˈkitchen ~.* **2** (*sing* only) people seated at a table: *jokes that amused the whole ~.* **3** list, orderly arrangement, of facts, information, etc: *a ~ of contents,* summary of what a book contains; *a ˈtime~.* **4** ***turn the tables on sb,*** gain a position of superiority after having been defeated or in a position of inferiority. □ *vt* **1** put (a proposal, etc) aside for future discussion: *~ a motion/a Bill.* **2** put in the form of a table(3).

ˈtable·cloth *n* [C] one (to be) spread on a table.

ˈtable knife, knife for eating with.

ˈtable·spoon *n* [C] **(a)** large spoon for serving food from a dish, etc. **(b)** unit of measure in cooking.

ˈtable·spoon·ful /-ˌfʊl/ *n* [C] (*pl* ~spoonsful) as much as a tablespoon can hold.

ˈtable talk, conversation during a meal.

ˈtable tennis, game with paddles and a ball, similar to tennis but played on a table; ping-pong.

ˈtable·ware *n* [U] dishes, silver, cutlery, etc used for meals.

tab·let /ˈtæblɪt/ *n* [C] **1** flat surface with words cut or written on it, eg one fixed to a wall in memory of a person or thing. **2** number of sheets of writing paper fastened together along one edge. **3** piece of hard soap. **4** small, shaped piece of compressed medicine: *two ~s of aspirin.*

tab·loid /ˈtæˌblɔid/ *n* [C] newspaper with many pictures, strip cartoons, etc and with its news presented in a form easily understood.

ta·boo /təˈbu, tæˈbu/ *n* **1** [C,U] (among some primitive races) something which religion or custom regards as forbidden, not to be touched, spoken of, etc: *That tree is under (a) ~.* **2** [C] general agreement not to discuss or do something. □ *adj* under a taboo: *Unkind gossip ought to be ~.* □ *vt* forbid, esp on moral or religious grounds.

taˈboo word, one which convention prohibits, eg swearwords.

tabu·lar /ˈtæbyələr/ *adj* arranged in tables(3).

tabu·late /ˈtæbyəˌleit/ *vt* arrange (facts, figures, etc) in tables(3).

tabu·la·tion /ˌtæbyəˈleiʃən/ *n* [U]

tabu·lator /ˈtæbyəˌleitər/ *n* [C] mechanism on a typewriter to permit indenting to preset positions.

tacit /ˈtæsɪt/ *adj* understood without being put into words: *~ consent/agreement.*

tacit·ly *adv*

taci·turn /ˈtæsəˌtərn/ *adj* (*formal*) (in the habit of) saying very little.

tack /tæk/ *n* [C] **1** small, flat-headed nail (eg used for securing carpet to a floor). ⇨ thumbtack. **2** long, loose stitch used in fastening pieces of cloth together loosely or temporarily. **3** sailing ship's direction as fixed by the direction of the wind and the position of the sails. ***on the right/wrong tack,*** (*fig*) following a wise/unwise course of action. □ *vt,vi* **1** fasten with tacks(1): *~ down the carpet.* **2** fasten with tacks(2): *~ a hem.* **3** change the course of (a sailing ship).

tackle /ˈtækəl/ *n* **1** [C,U] set of ropes and pulleys for lifting weights, etc. **2** [U] equipment, apparatus, for doing something: *ˈfishing ~,* a rod, line, hooks, etc. **3** [C] act of seizing and bringing down an opponent with the ball (in football). □ *vt,vi* **1** deal with, attack (a problem, a piece of work): *I don't know how to ~ this problem,* how to start on it. **2** seize, eg a thief or a football player who has the ball: *He ~s fearlessly.*

tacky /ˈtæki/ *adj* lacking in good taste.

taco /ˈtakou/ *n* [C] (*pl* ~s) kind of (originally Mexican) sandwich made of meat or cheese and salad garnish folded inside a fried tortilla.

tact /tækt/ *n* [U] (use of) skill and understanding shown by a person who handles people and situations successfully and without causing offense: *show/have great ~.*

tact·ful /-fəl/ *adj* having or showing tact.
tact·fully /-fəli/ *adv*
tact·less *adj* lacking tact.
tact·less·ly *adv*

tac·tic /ˈtæktɪk/ *n* [C] **1** means of achieving an aim. **2** (*pl*) (often used with a *sing verb*) art of placing or moving fighting forces for or during battle. **3** (*pl*) (*fig*) plan(s) or method(s) for carrying out a policy: *These ~s are unlikely to help you.*
tac·ti·cal /-kəl/ *adj* of tactics: *a ~al error.*
tac·ti·cally /-kli/ *adv*

tac·ti·cian /tækˈtɪʃən/ *n* [C] expert in tactics.

tac·tile /ˈtæktəl/ *adj* of, experienced by, the sense of touch: *~ greetings,* eg kissing.

tad·pole /ˈtædˌpoul/ *n* [C] form of a frog or toad from the time it leaves the egg to the time when it takes its adult form.

tag /tæg/ *n* **1** [C] metal or plastic point at the end of a shoelace, string, etc. **2** [C] label (eg for showing prices, addresses) fastened to or stuck into something: *auto tag,* automobile license plate. **3** [C] any loose or ragged end. **4** [U] game in which one child chases and tries to touch another. □ *vt,vi* (-gg-) **1** fasten a tag(2) to. **2** ***tag along/behind/after,*** follow closely: *Tag along with us* (= Come with us) *if you like.*

tail /ˈteiəl/ *n* [C] **1** long movable part at the end of the body of a bird, some animals, fish or reptiles: *Dogs wag their ~s when they are pleased.* ***turn tail,*** run away. **2** something like a tail in position: *the ~ of a kite/aircraft.* ⇨ illus at aircraft. **3** (*pl*) side of a coin opposite to that in which there is the head (of a monarch, president, god, etc). **4** (*informal*) person employed to follow and watch another person, eg a suspected criminal: *put a ~ on him.* **5** (*sl*) buttocks. □ *vt,vi* (*pres p* ~ing /ˈteilɪŋ/) **1** ***tail after sb,*** follow close behind. **2** ***tail sb,*** follow him closely, eg because he is suspected to be a criminal. **3** ***tail off/away,*** **(a)** become smaller in number, size, etc. **(b)** (of remarks, etc) end in a hesitating or inconclusive way. **(c)** fall behind or away in a scattered line.
ˌtail ˈend, (usually with *the*) final part: *at the ~ end of the procession.*
ˈtail gate, door or flap at the rear of a motor vehicle which can be opened for loading and unloading.
ˈtail·gate *vt, vi* follow another car too closely for safety.
tail·less /ˈteiəl(l)ɪs/ *adj* having no tail: *a ~less cat.*
ˈtail·light *n* [C] light at the end of a train, bus or other vehicle.
ˈtail·spin *n* spiral dive of an aircraft.

-tailed /-teiəld/ *suffix*: *ˌlong-ˈtailed,* having a long tail.

tailor /ˈteilər/ *n* [C] maker of coats, suits, etc. □ *vt* **1** cut out and sew: *a well-~ed suit.* **2** adapt: *~ed for a particular age-group.*
ˌtailor-ˈmade *adj* **(a)** made by a tailor, with special attention to exact fit. **(b)** (*fig*) appropriate, suitable: *He seems ~-made for the job.*

taint /teint/ *n* [C,U] trace of some bad smell, decay or infection: *There was a ~ of insanity in the family.* □ *vt,vi* make or become infected: *~ed meat.*

take[1] /teik/ *vt,vi* (*pt* took /tʊk/, *pp* taken /ˈteikən/) (For use with a large number of *nouns* ⇨ the *noun* entries, eg account[1](5), care[1](1), effect(1), leave[2](4), notice(3), offense(2), part[1](5,6), place[1](1), stock[1](1), task, trouble(3). For special uses with *adverbial particles* and *prepositions* ⇨ 17 below.) **1** get or hold with the hand(s) or any other part of the body, eg the arms, teeth or with an instrument: *~ her hand; ~ a man by the throat; He took her in his arms,* embraced her. **2** capture; catch; win (in a contest, etc): *~ a town,* in war; *~ 500 prisoners; be ~n prisoner,* be caught and be made a prisoner. *Her horse took* (= was awarded) *the first prize.* ***take sb's fancy,*** please, delight: *The new play really took the public's fancy.* ***be taken ill,*** become ill. ***take sb unawares/by surprise,*** approach or discover him doing something when he does not know that one sees him, etc. **3** use without permission or by mistake; steal: *Who has ~n my bicycle?* **4** carry something, go (away) with somebody from a place: *~ letters to the post office; ~ a friend home in one's car. Take her some flowers.* **5** get, have; eat or drink; allow oneself: *~ a vacation/a walk/a bath/a quick look around/a deep breath. Do you ~ sugar in your coffee?* ***take a chair/a seat,*** sit down. **6** accept; receive: *Will you ~ $2000 for the car,* sell it for this sum? *I'm not taking any more of your insults,* I refuse to listen to them. ***take a chance (on sth),*** accept the possibility of not getting it: *I'll ~ a chance on finding him at home,* will call hoping to find him there. ***take it from me; take my word for it,*** believe me when I say: *Take it from me, there'll be some big changes made in the coming year.* ***be able to take it; can take it,*** be able to endure suffering, punishment, attack, etc without showing weakness, without admitting defeat, easily etc. **7** receive and pay for regularly: *Which newspapers do you ~?* **8** make a record of: *~ notes of a lecture; ~ a letter,* from dictation; *~ a photograph.* **9** need, require: *The work took four hours. These things ~ time.* ***take one's time (over sth),*** use as much time as one needs. **10** suppose; consider to be: *I took you to be an honest man. Do you ~ me for a fool?* ***take sth for granted,*** ⇨ grant, *v*(3). **11** find out (by inquiry, measurement, etc): *The doctor took my temperature.* **12** treat or act in a specified way: *~ it/things easy,* not work too hard or too fast. **13** be in charge and act: *~ a class,* give the class its lesson, etc. **14** be successful: *That smallpox injection did not ~.* **15** use as transport: *I always ~ the bus to work.* (*gram*) **16** occur with: *a transitive verb ~s a direct object.* **17** (special uses with *adverbial particles* and *prepositions*):
be taken aback (at/by sth), ⇨ aback.
take after sb, resemble (esp a parent or relation) in features or character: *Your daughter does not ~ after you in any way.*
take sth apart, separate it (machinery, etc) into its (component) parts.
take away, (*math*) minus: *4 ~ away 2 is 2.* ***take sth/sb away (from sth/sb),*** remove: *Not to be ~n away,* eg books from a library. *The child was ~n away from school,* not allowed to attend.

take sth back, **(a)** withdraw (what one has said) as an admission of error, as an apology, etc: *I ~ back what I said.* **(b)** agree to receive back: *Shops will not usually ~ back goods after they have been paid for.* ***take sb back (to),*** cause to think of an earlier period: *These stories took him back to his childhood days,* brought them back to his mind.
take sth down, **(a)** write down: *The reporters took down the speech.* **(b)** lower; get by lifting down from (a shelf, etc): *~ down a book from the top shelf; ~ down a mast.* **(c)** pull down; get into separate parts: *~ down the scaffolding around a building.*
take from, ⇨ take away above.
take sth in, **(a)** receive (work) to be done in one's own house for payment: *She earns money by taking in sewing.* **(b)** reduce the size, area, length or width of (clothes, a sail, etc): *This dress needs to be ~n in* (= made smaller) *at the waist.* **(c)** include, eg in one's journey or route: *a tour that ~s in six European capitals.* **(d)** understand: *They listened to my lecture, but how much did they ~ in?* **(e)** see at once: *She took in every detail of her clothes.* **(f)** listen to, watch, with excitement: *The children took in the whole spectacle open-mouthed.* ***take sb in,*** **(a)** receive, admit: *make a living by taking in guests.* **(b)** deceive: *Don't let yourself be ~n in by these politicians.*
take off, **(a)** make a start in jumping. **(b)** (of an aircraft) leave the ground and rise. **(c)** (*sl*) leave, depart (esp hurriedly). ***take sth off,*** **(a)** remove: *~ off one's hat.* **(b)** withdraw (from service): *The 7am express to Boston will be ~n off next month,* will not run. ***take sth off (sth),*** **(a)** lift and move to another position: *Take your hand off my shoulder.* **(b)** deduct: *~ 50 cents off the price.* ***take sb off,*** **(a)** lead away somewhere: *He was ~n off to prison.* **(b)** imitate: *Alice is clever at taking off the teacher.* ***not/never take one's eyes off sth/sb,*** look at constantly: *He never took his eyes off her,* looked at her all the time.
take sth on, **(a)** undertake: *~ on extra work/heavy responsibilities.* **(b)** put on (a quality, appearance): *The chameleon can ~ on the colors of its background.* ***take sb on,*** **(a)** accept as an opponent: *~ him on at golf.* **(b)** employ: *~ on twenty more workers.* **(c)** (of a vehicle) allow to enter: *The bus stopped to ~ on some children.*
take sth out, **(a)** extract; remove: *have a tooth ~n out.* **(b)** obtain: *~ out an insurance policy.* ***take sb out,*** **(a)** invite and go with a girlfriend, etc on a social outing. **(b)** lead, go with: *~ the children out for a walk.* ***take it out of sb,*** leave him weak and exhausted: *All that hard work has ~n it out of him.* ***take it out on sb,*** show one's disappointment, etc by being angry, etc with somebody else: *He was angry at losing his job and took it out on his wife.*
take sb over, carry from one place to another: *Mr. White took me over to the island in his launch.* ***take sth over,*** assume control of; succeed to the management or ownership of (a business, etc): *When Mr. Green retired his son took over the business.* ***take over (from sb),*** accept duties, responsibilities, etc: *The new president took over* (ie from his predecessor) *yesterday.*
take to sth, **(a)** adopt as a practice or hobby, etc; get into a habit: *~ to gardening when one retires.* **(b)** take refuge in; use as a means of escape: *~ to the woods,* go to the woods to avoid capture. ***take to sth/sb,*** have a liking for: *He will never ~ to baseball. I have really ~n to my mother-in-law.*
take sth up, **(a)** pick up; raise: *~ up one's pen/book/gun.* **(b)** interest oneself in: *~ up photography.* **(c)** continue (something unfinished): *Harry took up the tale at the point where John had left off.* **(d)** occupy (time, space): *This table ~s up too much space.* ***take sth up with sb,*** speak or write to: *I will ~ the matter up with the Department,* eg by asking for information, or by making a protest.
take sth upon oneself, assume responsibility; undertake: *You mustn't ~ upon yourself the right to make decisions.*
ˈtake·off *n* [C] **(a)** (of an athlete or an aircraft) place, act, of leaving the ground. **(b)** caricature: *a good ~off of the President.*
ˈtake·over *n* [C] change of control of a firm or company, eg after another has made a successful bid to buy its stock.

take[2] /teik/ *n* **1** [C] amount (of money) taken. **2** [C] (film industry) scene that has been or is to be photographed. **3** act of taking. ***be on the take,*** eager to take advantage of an opportunity, esp a dishonest one.

taker /ˈteikər/ *n* [C] person who, that which, takes, esp one who takes a bet: *There were no ~s,* no one willing to take bets.

talc /tælk/ *n* [U] **1** soft mineral, ground into powder as a lubricant. **2** talcum powder.

tal·cum powder /ˈtælkəm ˌpaudər/ *n* [C] powder for the skin.

tale /ˈteiəl/ *n* [C] **1** story: *~s of adventure.* **2** report; account. ***tell tales,*** tell something about another person, esp something he has done wrong.

tal·ent /ˈtælənt/ *n* **1** [C,U] (particular kind of) natural power to do something well: *a man of great ~; have a ~ for music/not much ~ for painting.* **2** [C] measure of weight, unit of money, used in ancient times among the Greeks, Romans, Assyrians, etc.
tal·ented *adj* having talent; skilled.

tal·is·man /ˈtælɪsmən/ *n* [C] lucky charm.

talk[1] /tɔk/ *n* **1** [C,U] conversation; discussion: *I've had several ~s with the principal about my boy.* ⇨ small talk. ***talk of the town,*** something or somebody that everyone is talking about. **2** [C] informal speech: *give a ~ on a vacation in Asia.*

talk[2] /tɔk/ *vi,vt* **1** say things; speak to give information; discuss something, etc: *He was ~ing with a friend. What are they ~ing about? Were they ~ing in Spanish or in Portuguese?* ***be/get oneself talked about,*** be made the subject of gossip. ***talk down to sb,*** talk in a way that suggests that the speaker is superior. ***Talking about...,*** While on the subject of: *Talking about travel, have you been to Munich yet?* ***talk***

sth over, discuss it. ***talk around sth,*** discuss a subject without reaching the point or a conclusion. **2** have the power of speech: *Can the baby ~ yet?* **3** be able to use (a language): *~ English/Spanish.* **4** discuss: *We ~ed music all evening.* ***talk turkey,*** (*informal*) discuss (eg a business deal) frankly: *Let's ~ turkey!* **5** express in words: *~ sense/nonsense/treason.* **6** bring into a certain condition by talking: *~ oneself hoarse,* talk until one's throat hurts. ***talk sb into/out of doing sth,*** persuade him to do/not to do it: *She ~ed her husband into going on vacation in France.* **7** (various uses): *Don't do anything indiscreet—you know how people ~,* gossip. *Has the accused man ~ed yet,* given information, eg under torture or threats?

talka·tive /ˈtɔkətɪv/ *adj* fond of talking.

talker *n* [C] (esp with an *adjective*) person who talks: *a good/poor ~er.*

ˈtalking point, topic that serves as an argument for or against something.

tall /tɔl/ *adj* (-er, -est) **1** (of persons) of more than average height: *She is ~er than her sister.* **2** (of objects such as a tree whose height is greater than its width) higher than the average or than surrounding objects: *a ~ apartment building.* **3** of a specified height: *Tom is six foot/feet ~.* **4** ***a tall order,*** an unreasonable request; a task difficult to perform. ***a tall story,*** one that it is difficult to believe.

tall·ish /-ɪʃ/ *adj* rather tall.

tal·low /ˈtælou/ *n* [U] hard (esp animal) fat used for making candles, etc.

tally /ˈtæli/ □ *vi* (*pt,pp* -ied) (of stories, amounts, etc) correspond; agree: *The two lists do not ~. Does your total ~ with mine?* □ *n* [C] score (of a game); comparative count (of more than one item).

Tal·mud /ˈtælməd, ˈtal-/ *n* collection of traditional Jewish writings on religion and law.

talon /ˈtælən/ *n* [C] claw of a bird, eg an eagle. ⇨ illus at bird.

ta·male /təˈmali/ *n* [C] (*pl* ~s) (originally Mexican) dish made of spiced meat and corn meal rolled in corn husks.

tamale ˈpie, one made with tamale ingredients.

tam·bour·ine /ˌtæmbəˈrin/ *n* [C] small, shallow drum with metal disks in the rim, played by striking with the knuckles and shaking it at the same time. ⇨ illus at percussion.

tame /teim/ *adj* (-r, -st) **1** (of animals) brought under control and/or accustomed to living with human beings; not wild or fierce: *a ~ monkey.* **2** (of a person) easily controlled or persuaded: *Her husband is a ~ little man.* **3** dull: *The story/film has a ~ ending.* □ *vt* make tame: *~ a lion.*

tame·ly *adv* (of a person) acting, speaking, without courage, strength, etc.

tame·ness /-nɪs/ *n* [U]

tamer *n* [C] (usually in compounds) person who tames animals: *a ˈlion ~r.*

tam·per /ˈtæmpər/ *vi* ***tamper with,*** interfere with: *Someone has been ~ing with the lock.*

tam·pon /ˈtæmˌpan/ *n* [C] plug of absorbent material used esp by menstruating women to control bleeding.

tan /tæn/ *n* [U], *adj* yellowish-brown; brown color of sunburned skin: *tan leather shoes/gloves; get a good tan* (on one's skin). □ *vt,vi* (-nn-) **1** (of an animal's skin) make, be made, into leather. ***tan sb's hide,*** (*informal*) give him a good beating. **2** make or become brown from exposure to the sun: *Some people tan quickly.*

tan·ner *n* [C] workman who tans skins.

tan·nery /ˈtænəri/ *n* [U] place where skins are tanned.

tan·dem /ˈtændəm/ *n* [C] bicycle made for two persons to ride on one behind the other, with pedals for both. □ *adv* (of horses in harness or two persons on a tandem) one behind the other: *drive/ride ~.*

tang /tæŋ/ *n* [C] sharp taste or flavor, esp one that is characteristic of something: *the salty ~ of the sea air.*

tan·ge·lo /ˈtændʒəˌlou/ *n* [C] hybrid tree and fruit between a tangerine and a grapefruit.

tan·gent /ˈtændʒənt/ *n* [C] straight line touching a curve. ⇨ illus at circle. ***go on/fly off at/on a tangent,*** (*fig*) change suddenly from one line of thought, action, etc to another.

tan·ger·ine /ˌtændʒəˈrin, ˈtændʒəˌrin/ *n* [C] small, sweet-scented, loose-skinned orange.

tan·ge·lo /ˈtændʒəˌlou/ *n* [C] hybrid tree and fruit between a tangerine and a grapefruit.

tan·gible /ˈtændʒəbəl/ *adj* **1** that can be known by touch. **2** clear and definite: *~ proof.*

tan·gibly /-əbli/ *adv*

tangle /ˈtæŋgəl/ *n* [C] **1** confused mass (of string, hair, etc): *brush the ~s out of a dog's hair.* **2** confused state: *The traffic was in an awful ~.* □ *vt,vi* **1** make or become confused, disordered: *~d hair.* ***(all) tangled up,*** (*informal*) **(a)** become mixed up in a tangle: *His fishing line got (all) ~d up/with the seaweed.* **(b)** involved (in the affairs of someone): *She's still ~d up with that no-good boyfriend.* **2** (*informal*) be/become involved in a fight or quarrel: *Don't ~ with Peter—he's bigger than you.*

ˈtangle·wood *n* [U] = thicket (the usual word).

tango /ˈtæŋgou/ *n* [C] (*pl* ~s) (music for a) South American dance with strongly marked rhythm and a variety of steps.

tank /tæŋk/ *n* [C] **1** (usually large) container for liquid or gas: *the ˈgas/gasoline ~ of a car; an ˈoil ~.* **2** armored fighting vehicle with guns, moving on endless belts instead of wheels. □ *vi* ***get tanked up,*** (*sl*) get drunk (on beer).

tan·ker *n* [C] **(a)** ship or aircraft for carrying petroleum. **(b)** heavy road vehicle with a large cylindrical tank for carrying oil, milk or other liquid.

tank·ard /ˈtæŋkərd/ *n* [C] large drinking mug, esp one for beer.

tan·ner, tan·nery ⇨ tan.

OIL TANKER

tan·ta·lize /ˈtæntəˌlaiz/ *vt* raise hopes that cannot (yet) be realized; keep just out of reach something that a person desires: *a tantalizing smell of food.*

tan·ta·mount /ˈtæntəˌmaunt/ *adj* ***tantamount to,*** equal in effect to: *The company president's request was ~ to a command.*

tan·trum /ˈtæntrəm/ *n* [C] (*pl* ~s) fit of temper or anger: *He's having one of his ~s again.*

tap[1] /tæp/ *n* **1** device for controlling the flow of liquid or gas from a pipe, barrel, etc. ***on tap,*** (*fig*) available when needed. **2** plug used to close the opening of a cask. □ *vt* (-pp-) **1** draw out liquid through the tap of a (barrel): *tap (off) cider from a cask or beer from a keg.* **2** cut (the bark of a tree) and get (the sap, etc): *tap rubber trees.* **3** extract or obtain: *tap a man for information; tap a telephone/wire/line,* listen in without permission to get information, etc.

tap[2] /tæp/ *n* [C] quick, light touch or blow: *a tap on the window/at the door.* □ *vt,vi* (-pp-) give a tap or taps (to): *tap a man on the shoulder.*

ˈtap dancing, with rhythmical tapping of the feet.

tape /teip/ *n* [C,U] **1** (piece, length of) narrow strip of material used for tying up parcels, etc or in dressmaking: *three meters/yards of linen ~.* ⇨ also magnetic tape, red tape. **2** length of tape stretched between the winning posts on a racetrack. □ *vt* **1** fasten, tie together, with tape. **2** record (sound) on magnetic tape.

ˈtape deck, ⇨ deck[1](5).

ˈtape measure, length of thin, flexible metal or of strengthened cloth, marked for measuring things with.

tape-record /ˈteip-riˌkɔrd/ *vt* record on a tape recorder.

ˈtape recorder, apparatus for recording sound on, and playing sound back from, magnetic tape.

ˈtape·worm *n* kinds of many-jointed, long, flat worm that live during the adult stage as parasites in the intestines of man and other animals.

taper[1] /ˈteipər/ *n* [C] length of string with a covering of wax, burned to give a light.

taper[2] /ˈteipər/ *vt,vi* make or become gradually narrower toward one end: *One end ~s/is ~ed (off) to a point.*

tap·es·try /ˈtæpɪstri/ *n* [C,U] (*pl* -ies) (piece of) cloth into which threads of colored wool are woven by hand to make designs and pictures, used for covering walls and furniture.

tapi·oca /ˌtæpiˈoukə/ *n* [U] food (hard, white grains) used to make a pudding.

ta·pir /ˈteipər/ *n* [C] pig-like animal of Central and South America with a long, flexible nose.

taps /tæps/ *n* [U] bugle call indicating that lights (in a military camp) should be extinguished, or (at a military funeral) that the soldier's life is ended.

tar /tar/ *n* [U] black substance, hard when cold, thick and sticky when warm, obtained from coal, etc used to preserve timber (eg in fences and posts), in making roads, etc. □ *vt* (-rr-) cover with tar. ***tar and feather sb,*** put tar on him and then cover him with feathers as a punishment. ***ˌtarred with the ˌsame ˈbrush,*** having the same faults.

ta·ran·tula /təˈræntʃələ/ *n* [C] large, hairy, poisonous spider.

tar·get /ˈtargɪt/ *n* **1** something to be aimed at in shooting practice; any object aimed at. ⇨ illus at archery. **2** thing, plan, etc against which criticism is directed: *This book will be the ~ of bitter criticism.* **3** objective (set for savings, production, etc); total which it is desired to reach.

tar·iff /ˈtærɪf/ *n* [C] **1** list of fixed charges, esp for meals, rooms, etc at a hotel. **2** list of taxes on goods imported or (less often) exported.

tarn /tarn/ *n* [C] small mountain lake.

tar·nish /ˈtarnɪʃ/ *vi,vt* **1** (esp of metal surfaces) lose, cause the loss of, brightness: *Brass ~es easily.* **2** (*fig*) lessen the quality of: *His reputation is ~ed.* □ *n* [U] dullness because of loss of polish: *Those old silver forks are black with ~.*

tar·pau·lin /tarˈpɔlɪn/ *n* [C,U] (sheet or cover of) canvas made waterproof, esp by being tarred.

tar·pon /ˈtarpən/ *n* [C] large game fish of the Gulf of Mexico.

tar·ra·gon /ˈtærəˌgan/ *n* [U] herb with sharp-tasting leaves.

tarry[1] /ˈtari/ *adj* covered, sticky, with tar.

tarry[2] /ˈtæri/ *vi* (*liter*) **1** stay, remain: *~ a few days.* **2** be slow in coming, going, appearing.

tar·sal /ˈtarsəl/ *adj* of the bones in the ankle. □ *n* bone in the ankle. ⇨ illus at skeleton.

tart[1] /tart/ *adj* **1** acid; sharp in taste: *a ~ flavor.* **2** (*fig*) bitter: *~ humor.*

tart·ly *adv*

tart·ness /-nɪs/ *n* [U]

tart[2] /tart/ *n* [C] circle of pastry cooked with fruit or jam on it.

tart[3] /tart/ *n* [C] girl or woman of immoral character.

tar·tan /ˈtartən/ *n* [U] Scottish woolen fabric woven with colored crossing stripes; [C] this pattern, eg of a Scottish clan.

tar·tar /ˈtartər/ *n* [U] **1** chalk-like substance deposited on the teeth. **2** substance deposited on the sides of casks from fermented wine.

task /tæsk/ *n* [C] piece of (esp hard) work (to be) done: *set a boy to a ~.* ***take sb to task (about/for sth),*** scold him: *It's wrong of you to take the child to ~ for such a silly offense.*

ˈtask force, specially organized unit (of police, etc) for a special purpose.

ˈtask·master/·mistress *n* [C] person who decides, esp strictly, on work to be done.

tas·sel /ˈtæsəl/ *n* [C] bunch of threads, etc tied together at one end and hanging (from a flag, hat, etc) as an ornament.

tas·seled *adj* having tassels.

taste[1] /teist/ *n* **1** [U] (with *the*) sense by which flavor is known: *sweet/sour to the ~.* **2** [C,U] quality of a substance made known by this sense, eg by putting some on the tongue: *Sugar has a sweet ~.* **3** (usually *sing* with *a, an*) small quantity (of something to eat or drink): *Won't you have a ~ of this cake/wine? Give him a ~ of the whip,* (*fig*) enough to be a sample of what it feels like to be whipped. **4** [C,U] liking or preference: *She has expensive ~s in clothes.* ***There's no accounting for tastes,*** we cannot

explain why different people like different things. **5** [U] ability to enjoy beauty, esp in art and literature; ability to form judgments about these; ability to choose and use the best kind of behavior: *She has excellent ~ in dress/dresses in perfect ~.*
taste·ful /-fəl/ *adj* showing good taste(5).
taste·fully /-fəli/ *adv* in a tasteful manner: *~fully decorated with flowers.*
taste·less *adj* **(a)** (of food) having no flavor. **(b)** without taste(5).
taste·less·ly *adv*
tasty *adj* (-ier, -iest) having a pleasant flavor.
taste[2] /teist/ *vt,vi* **1** be aware of the taste of something: *Can you ~ anything strange in this soup?* **2** have a particular taste or flavor: *~ sour/bitter/sweet.* **3** test the taste of: *She ~d the soup to see if she had put enough salt in it.* **4** experience: *~ happiness/the joys of freedom.*
tat ⇨ tit[2].
tat·ters /ˈtætərz/ *n pl* pieces of cloth, paper, etc torn off or hanging loosely from something: *in ~*, badly torn.
tattle /ˈtætəl/ *vi,vt* chatter, gossip. □ *n* [U] idle talk.
tattle-tale *n* child who informs on other children.
tat·too[1] /tæˈtu/ *n* [C] (*pl* ~s) **1** (*sing* only) beating of drum(s) to call soldiers back to quarters; hour at which this is sounded: *beat/sound the ~.* **2** continuous tapping: *He was beating a ~ on the table with his fingers.* **3** public entertainment, with music, marching, etc by soldiers.
tat·too[2] /tæˈtu/ *vt* mark (a person's skin) with permanent designs or patterns by pricking it and putting in dyes or stains: *The sailor had a ship ~ed on his arm.* □ *n* [C] (*pl* ~s) mark or design of this kind.
taught *pt,pp* of teach.
taunt /tɔnt/ *n* [C] remark intended to hurt a person's feelings: *listen to the ~s of a successful rival.* □ *vt* attack (a person) with taunts: *They ~ed the boy for being a coward.*
taunt·ing·ly *adv*
Taurus /ˈtɔrəs/ *n* the Bull, the second sign of the zodiac. ⇨ illus at zodiac.
taut /tɔt/ *adj* (of ropes, nerves, etc) tightly stretched: *pull a rope ~.*
taut·ly *adv*
taut·ness /-nɪs/ *n* [U]
tau·tog /ˈtɔˌtag/ *n* [C] kind of food fish of the Atlantic coast of the US.
tauto·logi·cal /ˌtɔtəˈladʒɪkəl/ *adj* of, containing, tautology.
taut·ol·ogy /tɔˈtalədʒi/ *n* [U] the saying of the same thing again in different ways without making one's meaning clearer or more forceful; [C] (*pl* -ies) instance of this.
tav·ern /ˈtævərn/ *n* [C] (*old use*) public house for the supply of food and drink (to be consumed on the premises).
taw·dry /ˈtɔdri/ *adj* (-ier, -iest) brightly colored or decorated, but cheap or in bad taste: *~ jewelry/dresses.*
taw·drily /-əli/ *adv*
tawny /ˈtɔni/ *adj* brownish-yellow.
tax /tæks/ *n* **1** [C,U] (sum of) money (to be) paid by citizens (according to income, value of purchases, etc) to the government for public purposes: *state/local taxes; direct taxes*, ie on income; *indirect taxes*, eg paid when one buys goods. **2** ***a tax on,*** (*sing* only) something that is a burden or strain: *a tax on one's strength/health/patience.* □ *vt* **1** put a tax on; require (a person) to pay a tax: *tax luxuries/incomes/rich and poor alike.* **2** be a tax on: *tax a person's patience*, eg by asking him many silly questions. **3** ***tax sb with sth,*** accuse: *tax her with neglect of/with having neglected her work.*
tax·able /-əbəl/ *adj* to be taxed: *taxable income.*
tax·ation /tækˈseiʃən/ *n* [U] (system of) raising money by taxes; taxes (to be) paid.
ˌtax-exˈempt, tax-ˈfree *adj* **(a)** not subject to taxation. **(b)** (of dividends or interest) on which tax has been deducted before distribution.
ˈtax·payer *n* [C] person who pays taxes.
taxi /ˈtæksi/ *n* [C] (*pl* ~s) automobile, esp one with a meter, which may be hired for journeys. □ *vi,vt* (of an aircraft) (cause to) move on wheels along the ground (or on floats, etc on the surface of water): *The plane ~ed/was ~ing across the runway.*
ˈtaxi·cab, (common *abbr* **cab**) = taxi.
ˈtaxi stand, place where taxis wait to be hired.
T.B. /ˌti ˈbi/ *abbr* (*informal*) = tuberculosis.
T-bone ⇨ T.
tbs., tbsp. *abbr* = tablespoon(s).
TCBM /ˌti ˌsi ˌbi ˈem/ *abbr* = transcontinental ballistic missile.
tea /ti/ *n* **1** [U] (dried leaves of an) evergreen shrub of eastern Asia, India, etc. **2** [C, U] drink made by pouring boiling water on these leaves: *a cup of tea; make tea*, prepare it. ***not my cup of tea,*** not the sort of thing I like.
ˈtea bag, small bag with enough tea leaves for one cup of tea.
ˈtea caddy, airtight box in which to keep a supply of tea for daily use.
ˈtea·cake *n* [C] flat, sweetened cake, usually eaten hot with butter.
ˈtea chest, large wooden box in which tea is packed for export.
ˈtea cozy, cover for keeping the contents of a teapot warm.
ˈtea·cup *n* [C] cup in which tea is served.
ˈtea·pot *n* [C] vessel in which tea is made. ***a tempest in a teapot,*** ⇨ tempest.
ˈtea·room *n* [C] restaurant which serves tea and light refreshments.
ˈtea service/set, set of cups, saucers, plates, with a teapot, etc.
ˈtea·spoon *n* [C] **(a)** small spoon for stirring tea. **(b)** unit of measure in cooking.
ˈtea·spoon·ful /-ˌfʊl/ *n* [C] (*pl* teaspoonsful) as much as a teaspoon can hold.
ˈtea strainer, device for sieving tea.
teach /titʃ/ *vt,vi* (*pt,pp* taught /tɔt/) give instruction to (a person); cause (a person) to know or be able to do something; give a person (knowledge, skill, etc); give lessons (at school, etc); do this for a living: *~ children; ~ French/history; ~ a child (how) to swim. She is ~ing the piano to children. He ~es for a living. I will ~ you (not) to...*, (*informal*) (used as a threat) I will punish

you, show you, the risk or penalty of....

teach·able /-əbəl/ *adj* that can be taught.

teacher *n* [C] person who teaches.

ˈ**teach-in** *n* [C] (*informal*) discussion of a subject of topical interest (as held in a college, with students, staff and other speakers).

teach·ing *n* **(a)** [U] work, profession of a teacher: *earn a living by ~ing*. **(b)** (usually *pl*) that which is taught: *the ~ings of Jesus*.

teak /tik/ *n* [C] tall, evergreen tree of India, Malaysia, etc; [U] its hard wood, used for making furniture, etc.

team /tim/ *n* [C] **1** two or more oxen, horses, etc pulling a cart, plough, etc together. **2** number of persons playing together and forming one side in some games, eg football, baseball, hockey and sports, eg relay races. **3** group of people working together: *a ~ of surgeons in the operating theater*. □ *vi* ***team up (with),*** (*informal*) make an effort in co-operation (with); work together (with).

ˈ**team·mate** *n* [C] fellow member of a team(2).

ˌ**team** ˈ**spirit,** spirit in which each member of a team thinks of the success, etc of the team and not of personal advantage, glory, etc.

ˈ**team·work** *n* [U] combined effort: organized co-operation: *succeed by means of good ~work*.

tear[1] /tɪr/ *n* [C] drop of salty water coming from the eye: *Her eyes filled with ~s. The sad story moved us to ~s*, made us cry. *The girl burst into ~s*, began to cry.

ˈ**tear·drop** *n* [C] single tear.

tear·ful /-fəl/ *adj* crying; wet with tears: *a ~ful face*.

tear·fully /-fəli/ *adv*

ˈ**tear gas,** gas that causes severe watering of the eyes (used by the police to disperse a mob of demonstrators, etc.)

ˈ**tear-jerker** *n* [C] (*sl*) sad story, song, movie, etc.

tear[2] /ter/ *vt,vi* (*pt* tore /tɔr/, *pp* torn /tɔrn/) **1** pull apart or to pieces; make a hole in something, damage, by pulling sharply: *~ a sheet of paper in two*/*~ it to pieces*/*to bits. He tore the parcel open*. ***tear sth up,*** tear it into small pieces. **2** cause (something) to be out of place (*down, off, away, etc*) by pulling sharply: *~ a page out of a book. She could scarcely ~ herself away from the scene,* found it difficult to leave. **3** destroy the peace of: *a country torn by civil war; a heart torn by grief*. ***torn between,*** unable to choose between (conflicting demands, wishes, etc). **4** become torn: *This material ~s easily*. **5** go in excitement or at great speed: *The children tore out of the school yard*. □ *n* [C] torn place.

tease /tiz/ *vt* **1** make fun of (a person) playfully or unkindly: *She ~d her father about his bald head. Molly was teasing the cat*, eg by pulling its tail. **2** separate, loosen, into separate fibers; fluff up the surface of (cloth, etc) by doing this: *~ flax*. ***tease sth out,*** separate something (eg the cause of a problem) from other things. □ *n* [C] person who is fond of teasing others: *What a ~ she is!*

teaser *n* [C] person who often teases.

teat /tit/ *n* [C] nipple(2).

tech. *abbr* = technical.

tech·ni·cal /ˈteknɪkəl/ *adj* **1** of, from, technique. **2** of, connected with, special to, one of the mechanical or industrial arts (eg printing, weaving) or with methods used by experts and artists: *a* ˈ*~ college*, for engineering, etc.

tech·ni·cally /-kli/ *adv*

tech·ni·cal·ity /ˌteknɪˈkæləti/ *n* [C] (*pl* -ies) technical word, phrase, point, etc: *The judge explained the legal technicalities of the case to the jury*.

tech·ni·cian /tekˈnɪʃən/ *n* [C] expert in the technique(s) of a particular art, etc; highly skilled craftsman or mechanic.

tech·nique /tekˈnik/ *n* **1** [U] technical or mechanical skill in art, music, etc. **2** [C] method of doing something expertly; method of artistic expression in music, painting, etc.

tech·noc·racy /tekˈnakrəsi/ *n* [C,U] (*pl* -ies) (state where there is) organization and management of a country's industrial resources by technical experts.

tech·no·crat /ˈteknəˌkræt/ *n* [C] supporter, member, of a technocracy.

tech·no·logi·cal /ˌteknəˈladʒɪkəl/ *adj* of technology: *~ problems*.

tech·nol·ogist /tekˈnalədʒɪst/ *n* [C] expert in, student of, technology.

tech·nol·ogy /tekˈnalədʒi/ *n* [U] **1** study, mastery and using of manufacturing methods and industrial arts. **2** systematic application of knowledge to practical tasks in industry: *study engineering at a college of ~*.

Teddy bear /ˈtedi ˌber/ *n* [C] stuffed toy bear.

tedi·ous /ˈtidiəs/ *adj* causing tiredness; uninteresting: *a ~ lecture*/*lecturer; ~ work*.

tedi·ous·ly *adv*

tedi·ous·ness /-nɪs/ *n* [U]

te·dium /ˈtidiəm/ *n* [U] (*informal*) boredom.

tee /ti/ *n* [C] **1** (*golf*) place from which a player starts at each hole; specially shaped piece of wood, plastic or rubber used for this. **2** mark aimed at in certain games, such as quoits. ***to a tee,*** perfectly; exactly: *She suits him to a tee*. □ *vt,vi* **1** ***tee (up),*** put the ball on a tee(1). **2** ***tee off,*** hit the ball from a tee.

teem[1] /tim/ *vi* **1** be present in large numbers: *Fish ~ in this river*. **2** ***teem with,*** have in great numbers: *His head is ~ing with bright ideas*.

teem[2] /tim/ *vi* (of rain) fall heavily; pour: *It was ~ing with rain*.

teen-age /ˈtinˌeidʒ/ *adj* for persons in their teens: *~ fashions*/*music*.

teen-ager /ˈtinˌeidʒər/ *n* [C] boy or girl in his or her teens or up to 21 years of age: *a club for ~s*.

teens /tinz/ *n pl* the ages 13 to 19: *girls in their ~*.

tee shirt /ˈti ˌʃərt/ *n* [C] = T-shirt.

tee·ter /ˈtitər/ *vi* stand or walk unsteadily: (*fig*) *~ing on the edge of disaster*.

teeth *pl* of tooth.

teethe /tið/ *vi* (of a baby) be getting its first teeth.

teeth·ing ring /ˈtiðɪŋ ˌrɪŋ/ rubber or plastic ring for a baby to bite on while teething.

tee·to·tal /tiˈtoutəl/ *adj* not drinking, opposed to the drinking of, alcoholic liquor.

tee·to·taler, tee·to·tal·ler /tiˈtout(ə)lər/ *n* [C] person who does not drink alcoholic beverages.

tel. *abbr* = telephone.

tele·com·muni·ca·tions /ˌteləkəˌmyunəˈkeiʃənz/ *n pl* communications by cable, telegraph, telephone, radio or TV.

tele·gram /ˈteləˌgræm/ *n* [C] message sent by telegraphy.

tele·graph /ˈteləˌgræf/ *n* [C] means of, apparatus for, sending messages by the use of electric current along wires or by radio. □ *vi,vt* send (news, etc) by telegraph.

tel·egra·pher /trˈlegrəfər/ *n* [C] operator who sends and receives messages by telegraph.

tele·graphic /ˌteləˈgræfɪk/ *adj* sent by, suitable for, of, the telegraph.

tel·egra·phy /trˈlegrəfi/ *n* [U] art, science, process, of sending and receiving messages by telegraph.

tel·epa·thy /trˈlepəθi/ *n* [U] transference of thoughts or ideas from one mind to another without using speech, signs, etc.

tele·pathic /ˌteləˈpæθɪk/ *adj*

tele·phone /ˈteləˌfoun/ *n* (usual *abbr* **phone** in speech) **1** [U] means, system, of transmitting the human voice by electric current, usually through wires. **2** [C] apparatus (with receiver and mouthpiece) for this purpose: *You're wanted on the ~.* □ *vt,vi* send (a message to a person) by telephone.

ˈtelephone booth, (*informal* = **ˈphone booth**) small enclosure with a coin-operated public telephone.

TELEPHONE BOOTH

ˈtelephone directory, (*informal* = **ˈphone book**) list of names with telephone numbers and addresses.

tele·scope /ˈteləˌskoup/ *n* [C] long instrument with lenses for making distant objects appear nearer and larger. □ *vt,vi* make or become shorter by means of or in the manner of sections that slide one within the other: *When the trains collided, the first two cars of one of the trains ~d/were ~d.*

tele·scopic /ˌteləˈskapɪk/ *adj* **(a)** of, containing, able to be seen with, a telescope: *a telescopic view of the moon,* seen through a telescope. **(b)** having sections which slide one within the other: *a telescopic aerial,* eg as part of a portable radio.

tele·vise /ˈteləˌvaiz/ *vt* send by television: *The Olympic Games were ~d.*

tele·vi·sion /ˈteləˌvɪʒən/ *n* (*abbr* **TV**) **1** [U] process of transmitting pictures by radio waves with sound at the same time: *Did you see the news on ~?* **2** [C] (also **ˈtelevision set**) apparatus for receiving and showing these pictures and sound.

tell /tel/ *vt,vi* (*pt,pp* told /tould/) **1** make known (in spoken or written words); give information concerning or a description of: *I told him my name. Tell me where you live. I can't ~ you how happy I am,* can't find words that are adequate. ***I told you so,*** I warned you that this would happen, etc and now you see that I'm right: *Things have gone wrong but please don't say "I told you so!"* **2** express with words: *~ a lie; ~ the children a story.* ***tell tales,*** ⇨ tale(2). **3** order; direct: *You must do as you're told. Tell him to wait.* **4** (esp with *can/could/be able to*) identify: *Can you ~ Tom from his twin brother? They look exactly the same; how can you ~ which is which?* **5** learn by observation; become aware (of something): *How do you ~ which of these keys to use?* ***tell the time,*** (be able to) read (or say) the time from a clock, etc: *Can Mary ~ the time yet?* ***there is/was, etc no telling,*** it is impossible or difficult to know: *There's no ~ing what may happen/where she's gone/what he's doing.* **6** ***tell sb off (for sth/for doing sth),*** (*informal*) criticize, blame, him with angry words: *He told me off for making so many careless mistakes.* **7** have a marked effect on; influence the result of: *All this hard work is ~ing on him,* is affecting his health. **8** (*informal*) inform against: *John told on his sister.* **9** tell a secret: *You promised not to ~ and now you have!*

tel·ler *n* [C] **(a)** person who receives and pays out money over a bank counter. **(b)** man who counts votes, eg in a legislature.

tell·ing *adj* impressive: *a ~ing argument/blow.*

ˌtelling-ˈoff *n* [C] ⇨ 6 above.

tell·tale /ˈtelˌteiəl/ *n* **1** [C] person who tells about another's private affairs, makes known a secret, etc. **2** (used as an *adjective*) circumstances, etc that reveal a person's thoughts, activities, etc: *a ~tale blush.*

te·mer·ity /təˈmerəti/ *n* [U] (*formal*) impudent speech or action: *have the ~ to go home early after arriving late.*

temp. *abbr* = **1** temperature. **2** temporary.

tem·per[1] /ˈtempər/ *n* **1** [C] state or condition of the mind: *in a good ~,* calm and pleasant; *in a bad ~,* angry, impatient, etc. ***keep/lose one's temper,*** keep/fail to keep one's temper under control. **2** [U] (of steel, etc) degree of strength, hardness, etc.

-tem·pered /ˈtempərd/ *suffix* having or showing a certain kind of temper: *a ˌbad-/ˌgood-/ˌhot-tempered ˈman.*

tem·per[2] /ˈtempər/ *vt,vi* **1** give, come to, the required temper(2) by heating and cooling. **2** soften or modify: *~ justice with mercy,* be merciful when giving a just punishment.

tem·pera·ment /ˈtemprəmənt/ *n* **1** [C,U] person's personality or nature, esp as this affects his way of thinking, feeling and behaving: *a girl with a nervous/an artistic ~.* **2** [U] (without an *adjective*) kind of personality that is easily excited.

tem·pera·men·tal /ˌtemprəˈmentəl/ *adj* **(a)** caused by temperament: *a ~al dislike for study*. **(b)** quickly changing moods: *a ~al tennis player*.

tem·pera·men·tally /-təli/ *adv*

tem·per·ance /ˈtemp(ə)rəns/ *n* [U] **1** self-control in speech, behavior and (esp) in the use of alcoholic drinks. **2** total abstinence from alcoholic drinks.

tem·per·ate /ˈtemp(ə)rɪt/ *adj* **1** showing, behaving with, self-control: *Be more ~ in your language, please*. **2** (of climate, parts of the world) free from extremes of heat and cold: *the north ˈ~ zone*, between the Tropic of Cancer and the Arctic zone.

tem·per·ate·ly *adv*

tem·pera·ture /ˈtempər(ə)tʃʊr/ *n* [C,U] degree of heat and cold: *The nurse took the ~s of all the patients*, measured their body temperatures with a thermometer. ***have/run a temperature,*** have a fever.

tem·pest /ˈtempɪst/ *n* **1** [C] violent storm. **2** (*fig*) violent agitation: *A ~ of anger swept through the crowd*. ***a ˌtempest in a ˈteapot,*** a lot of excitement about something unimportant.

tem·pes·tu·ous /temˈpestʃuəs/ *adj* (of the weather and *fig*) violent; stormy.

temple[1] /ˈtempəl/ *n* [C] **1** building used for the worship of a god. **2** (applied occasionally to a) place of Christian or Jewish worship (*church* or *chapel* and *synagogue* are the usual words). **3** any of the three successive religious centers of the Jews in ancient Jerusalem. **4** lodge(4) of certain societies.

temple[2] /ˈtempəl/ *n* [C] flat part of either side of the forehead. ⇨ illus at head.

tempo /ˈtempou/ *n* [C] (*pl* ~s or, in music, tempi /-pi/) (*I*) **1** rate of movement or activity: *the tiring ~ of city life*. **2** speed at which music is (to be) played.

tem·poral /ˈtempərəl/ *adj* (*formal*) **1** of, existing in, time. **2** of earthly human life; of this physical life only, not spiritual.

tem·por·ary /ˈtempəˌreri/ *adj* lasting for, designed to be used for, a short time only: *~ employment; a ~ bridge*. ⇨ permanent.

tem·por·ar·ily /ˌtempəˈrerəli/ *adv*

tempt /tempt/ *vt* **1** (try to) persuade (a person) to do something wrong or foolish: *Nothing could ~ him to agree that torture is a necessary evil*. **2** attract (a person) to have or do something: *The warm weather ~ed us to go for a swim*.

temp·ter *n* [C] person who tempts.

tempt·ing *adj* attractive: *a ~ing offer*.

temp·tress /-trɪs/ *n* [C] woman who tempts.

temp·ta·tion /tempˈteiʃən/ *n* **1** [U] tempting or being tempted: *yield/give way to ~. Don't put ~ in my way*. **2** [C] that which tempts or attracts: *Clever advertisements are ~s to spend money*.

ten /ten/ *n* [C], *adj* (of) the number 10. ***ˌten to ˈone,*** very probably: *Ten to one he'll arrive late*.

ten-cent store, five-and-ten-cent store ⇨ five.

ˈten·fold *adv* ten times as many or much.

ten-gallon ˈhat, (*informal*) with high crown and very wide brim, traditionally worn by cowboys in the southwestern US. ⇨ illus at cowboy.

tenth /tenθ/ *n* [C], *adj* (of) one of 10 (parts) or the next after 9.

tenth·ly *adv*

ten·able /ˈtenəbəl/ *adj* **1** that can be defended successfully: *His theory is hardly ~*. **2** (of an office or position) that can be held (by a person): *The lectureship is ~ for a period of three years*.

ten·acious /tɪˈneiʃəs/ *adj* (*formal*) holding tightly, refusing to let go: *a ~ memory; ~ of our rights*.

ten·acious·ly *adv*

ten·acious·ness, ten·ac·ity /tɪˈnæsəti/ *n* [U]

ten·ancy /ˈtenənsi/ *n* [U] **1** use of land, etc as a tenant: *during his ~ of the farm*. **2** (with *a, an*) length of time during which a tenant uses land, etc: *hold a life ~ of a house*.

ten·ant /ˈtenənt/ *n* [C] person who pays rent for the use of land, a building, a room, etc.

tend[1] /tend/ *vt* watch over; attend: *shepherds ~ing their flocks*.

tend[2] /tend/ *vi* be inclined to move; have as a characteristic or direction: *Prices are ~ing upward. He ~s to make too many mistakes*.

ten·dency /ˈtendənsi/ *n* [C] (*pl* -ies) turning or inclination: *Business is showing a ~ to improve*.

ten·den·tious /tenˈdenʃəs/ *adj* (*formal*) (of a speech, a piece of writing, etc) having an underlying purpose, aimed at helping a cause; not impartial: *Countries at war often send out ~ reports*, designed to win sympathy, etc.

ten·den·tious·ly *adv*

ten·der[1] /ˈtendər/ *adj* (-er, -est) **1** delicate; easily hurt or damaged; quickly feeling pain: *~ blossoms*, eg easily hurt by frosts. ***have a tender heart***, be easily moved to pity. **2** (of meat) easily chewed; not tough: *a ~ steak*. **3** kind, loving: *~ looks; ~ parents*.

ˈtender·hearted *adj* easily moved to pity.

ˈten·der·loin *n* tender part of the loin of beef or pork.

ten·der·ly *adv*

ten·der·ness /-nɪs/ *n* [U]

ten·der[2] /ˈtendər/ *n* [C] **1** person who looks after, watches over, something. ⇨ bartender. **2** small ship attending a larger one. **3** wagon for fuel and water usually behind a steam locomotive.

ten·der[3] /ˈtendər/ *vt,vi* **1** offer; present: *He ~ed his resignation to the President*. **2** make an offer (to carry out work, supply goods, etc) at a stated price: *~ for the construction of a new highway*. □ *n* [C] statement of the price at which one offers to supply goods or services, or to do something: *invite ~s for a new bridge*. ⇨ legal tender.

ten·der·ize /ˈtendəˌraiz/ *vt* make (esp meat) tender by pounding it or applying an enzyme.

ten·der·izer (also **ˈmeat tenderizer**) *n* **(a)** heavy tool for pounding meat to make it tender. **(b)** enzyme powder for tenderizing meat.

ten·don /ˈtendən/ *n* [C] tough, thick cord that joins muscle to bone.

ten·dril /ˈtendrəl/ *n* [C] part like a thread of a plant, eg a vine, that twists around any nearby support.

ten·ement /ˈtenəmənt/ *n* [C] **1** large house for the use of many families at low rents. **2** (*legal*) any dwelling house; any kind of permanent property.

tenet /ˈtenɪt/ *n* [C] (*formal*) principle; belief; doctrine.

ten·nis /ˈtenɪs/ *n* [U] game for two or four players who hit a ball backward and forward across a net.

TENNIS

ˈtennis court, marked area on which tennis is played.

ˈtennis elbow, inflammation of the elbow caused by playing tennis.

ˈtennis shoe, low shoe, with canvas top and rubber sole, worn esp when playing tennis.

tenon /ˈtenən/ *n* part that extends from a piece of wood, etc to form a joint by passing into the end of another piece (the *mortise*). □ *vt* **1** join or fasten in this way. **2** cut for insertion into a mortise.

tenor /ˈtenər/ *n* [C] **1** (musical part for, or singer having the) highest normal adult male voice: (as an *adjective*) *~ voice; the ~ part*. **2** instrument with the same range: *a ~ saxophone*.

tense[1] /tens/ *adj* (-r, -st) tightly stretched or strained: *~ nerves; a moment of ~ excitement/a ~ moment; look ~,* appear to be under strain. □ *vt,vi* make or become tense: *He ~d his muscles for the effort*.

tense·ly *adv*

tense·ness /-nɪs/ *n* [U]

tense[2] /tens/ *n* [C,U] (*gram*) verb form that shows time: *the present/past/future ~*.

ten·sion /ˈtenʃən/ *n* [U] **1** state of, degree of, being tense: *If you increase the ~ of the rope it will break*. **2** stretching or being stretched. **3** mental, emotional or nervous strain; condition when feelings are tense, when relations between persons, groups, states are strained: *political ~*. **4** voltage: *Keep away from those high ~ wires or you'll be electrocuted.*

tent /tent/ *n* [C] shelter made of canvas supported by poles and ropes, esp as used by campers, scouts, soldiers, etc. ⇨ oxygen tent.

ten·tacle /ˈtentəkəl/ *n* [C] long, slender, boneless growth on certain animals used for touching, feeling, holding, moving, etc. ⇨ illus at jellyfish, mollusk.

ten·ta·tive /ˈtentətɪv/ *adj* made or done as a trial, to test the effect: *make a ~ offer*.

ten·ta·tive·ly *adv*

tenth /tenθ/ *n, adj* ⇨ ten.

tenu·ous /ˈtenyuəs/ *adj* (*formal*) **1** thin; slender: *the ~ web of a spider*. **2** (of opinions, differences) without much meaning or value.

ten·ure /ˈtenyər/ *n* [C,U] **1** (period, time, condition of) holding (eg political office). **2** guarantee of a permanent position or employment (esp as a university professor) after a period of probation.

te·pee, ti·pi /ˈtipi/ *n* [C] tent, made of animal skins and shaped like a cone, used by Indians of the central plains of the US.

TEPEE

tepid /ˈtepɪd/ *adj* lukewarm.

term /tərm/ *n* [C] **1** fixed or limited period of time: *a long ~ of imprisonment; during his ~ of office as President*. **2** (of universities, etc) one of the periods (usually three) into which the academic year is divided: *end-of-~ examinations*. **3** (*legal*) period during which a court holds session. **4** (*pl*) conditions offered or agreed to: *~s of surrender*, eg offered to a defeated enemy. ***come to terms (with sb),*** reach an agreement. ***come to terms with sth,*** accept finally: *come to ~s with a difficult situation*. **5** (*pl*) ***be on good/friendly/bad terms (with sb),*** be friendly, etc with him. ⇨ also speak(1). **6** words used to express an idea, esp a specialized concept: *technical/scientific/legal ~s*. **7** (*pl*) mode of expression: *Why did you speak of her in such abusive ~s?* **8** (*math*) part of an expression joined to the rest by + or −: *The expression $a^2 + 2ab + b^2$ has three ~s*. □ *vt* name; apply a term(6) to: *He has no right to ~ himself a professor*.

ter·min·able /ˈtərmənəbəl/ *adj* that may be terminated.

ter·minal /ˈtərmənəl/ *adj* **1** of, taking place, each term(2,3): *~ examinations/accounts*. **2** of, forming, the point or place at the end: *~ cancer*, incurable; *the ˈ~ ward,* (in a hospital) for persons who cannot be cured and must soon die. □ *n* [C] **1** end of a railway line, bus route, etc; center (in a town) used by passengers departing for, or arriving from, an airport: *the ˌEast Side ˈAirlines Terminal* (in New York City). **2** point of connection in an electric circuit: *the ~s of a battery*.

ter·min·ally *adv*

ter·min·ate /ˈtərməˌneit/ *vt,vi* bring to an end; come to an end: *~ his contract*.

ter·mi·na·tion /ˌtərməˈneiʃən/ *n* **1** [C,U] ending: *the ~ of a contract*. **2** [C] final syllable or letter of a word.

ter·mi·nol·ogy /ˌtərməˈnalədʒi/ *n* [C,U] (*pl* -ies) (science of the) proper use of terms (6); terms used in a science or art: *medical/grammatical ~*.

ter·mi·no·logi·cal /ˌtərmənəˈladʒɪkəl/ *adj*
ter·mi·nus /ˈtərmənəs/ *n* [C] (*pl* -ni /-ˌnai/ or ~es) **1** (*formal*) finishing point of a journey or process. **2** station at the end of a railway line, bus route, etc.
ter·mite /ˈtərˌmait/ *n* [C] insect (popularly called *white ant*), which eats wood. ⇨ illus at insect.
terr. *abbr* = territory.
ter·race /ˈterəs/ *n* [C] **1** level(ed) area of ground with a vertical or sloping front or side; a series of these, separated by sloping banks, rising one above the other, eg as a method of irrigation on a hillside. **2** flight of wide, shallow steps (eg for spectators in an open theater). **3** continuous row of houses in one block. □ *vt* (usually as a *pp*) form into terraces: *a ~d lawn; ~d houses*, (long line of) houses joined together.
terra cotta /ˌterə ˈkatə/ *n* [U] hard, reddish-brown pottery; reddish-brown color.
ter·rain /təˈrein/ *n* [C] stretch of land, esp regarding its natural features: *difficult ~ for walking*.
ter·ra·pin /ˈterəpɪn/ *n* [C] (kinds of) fresh water turtle of the Eastern US.
ter·res·trial /təˈrestriəl/ *adj* **1** of, on, living on, the earth or land: *the ~ parts of the world*. **2** (opposite of *celestial*) of the earth.
ter·rible /ˈterəbəl/ *adj* **1** causing great fear or horror: *a ~ war/accident*. **2** causing great discomfort; extreme: *The heat is ~ in Baghdad during the summer*. **3** (*informal*) extremely bad: *What ~ food they gave us!*
ter·ribly /-əbli/ *adv* (*informal*) extremely: *How terribly boring he is!*
ter·rier /ˈteriər/ *n* [C] kinds of small and lively dog.
ter·rific /təˈrɪfɪk/ *adj* **1** causing fear. **2** (*informal*) very great; extreme: *driving at a ~ pace*.
ter·rifi·cally /-kli/ *adv* extremely.
ter·rify /ˈterəˌfai/ *vt* (*pt,pp* -ied) fill with fear: *The child was terrified of being left alone in the house. What a ~ing experience!*
ter·ri·torial /ˌterəˈtɔriəl/ *adj* **1** of land, esp land forming a division of a country: *~ possessions*. **2 Territorial,** of any of the US Territories: *Territorial laws*.
terriˌtorial ˈwaters, the sea near a country's coast, over which special rights are claimed, eg for fishing.
ter·ri·tory /ˈterəˌtɔri/ *n* (*pl* -ies) **1** [C,U] (area of) land, esp land under one ruler or Government: *Is this American ~?* **2 Territory** [C] land belonging to or forming a division of the US, but not a state: *the Territory of Hawaii* (from 1898 until 1959). **3** [C] land or district; [U] extent of such land, etc: *How much ~ can he cover* (= travel across) *in a day?*
ter·ror /ˈterər/ *n* **1** [U] great fear: *run away in ~*. **2** [C] instance of great fear; (person or thing that causes) great fear: *have a ~ of fire*.
ˈter·ror·ism /-ˌrɪzəm/ *n* [U] use of violence and intimidation, esp for political purposes.
ˈter·ror·ist /-rɪst/ *n* [C] supporter of, participant in, terrorism.
ˈter·ror·ize /-ˌraiz/ *vt* fill with terror by threats or acts of violence.
terse /tərs/ *adj* (of speech, style, speakers) brief and to the point.
terse·ly *adv*
terse·ness /-nɪs/ *n* [U]
ter·ti·ary /ˈtərʃiˌeri/ *adj* third in rank, order, occurrence, importance.
test /test/ *n* [C] (often as an *adjective*) examination or trial (of something) to find its quality, value, composition, etc; trial or examination (of a person, his powers, knowledge, skill, etc): *methods that have stood the ~ of time; a ˈblood ~*, eg at a hospital, for infection, etc; *a ˈdriving ~; an inˈtelligence ~*. □ *vt* examine; make a trial of: *have one's eyesight ~ed. The long climb ~ed* (= was a test of) *our strength*.
ˈtest case, (in law) one that shows the principle involved (even though it may not be important in itself).
ˈtest drive *n* [C] drive in a car one thinks of buying, to judge its qualities, worth, etc.
ˈtest-drive *vt*
ˈtest flight, flight to judge the performance of a new aircraft.
ˈtest-fly *vt*
ˈtest pilot, pilot who performs test flights.
ˈtest tube, slender glass tube, closed at one end, used in chemical experiments.
tes·ta·ment /ˈtestəmənt/ *n* **1** [C] (often *last Will and Testament*) statement in writing saying how a person wishes his property to be distributed after his death. **2 Old Testament, New Testament,** the two main divisions of the Bible.
tes·ticle /ˈtestɪkəl/ *n* [C] each of the two glands of the male sex organ that secrete sperm.
tes·tify /ˈtestəˌfai/ *vt,vi* (*pt,pp* -ied) **1** give evidence: *He testified under oath that he had not stolen the bicycle. The teacher testified to the boy's ability*. **2** serve as evidence of: *Her tears testified* (*to*) *her grief*.
tes·ti·mo·nial /ˌtestəˈmouniəl/ *n* [C] **1** written statement testifying to a person's merits, abilities, qualifications, etc. **2** something given to a person to show appreciation of services: *a ~ dinner*, for a retiree.
tes·ti·mony /ˈtestəˌmouni/ *n* [U] **1** declaration, esp in a law court, testifying that something is true: *The witness's ~ is false*. **2** declarations; statements: *According to the ~ of the medical profession, the health of the nation is improving*.
tes·tis /ˈtestɪs/ *n* [C] (*pl* -tes /-ˌtiz/) = testicle.
teta·nus /ˈtet(ə)nəs/ *n* [U] disease marked by tightening of voluntary muscles.
tether /ˈteðər/ *n* [C] rope or chain by which an animal is fastened while grazing. ***at the end of one's tether,*** (*fig*) at the end of one's patience, etc. □ *vt* fasten with a tether: *He ~ed his horse to the fence*.
Tex-Mex /ˈteks-ˌmeks/ *n* [C] (*pl* Tex-Mexes) **1** Mexican-American of long residence in Texas. **2** (as an *adjective*) of blended Mexican and Southwestern American culture: *~ food*.
text /tekst/ *n* **1** [U] printed words in a book (contrasted with notes, diagrams, illustrations, etc). **2** [C] original words of an author, apart from anything else in a book. **3** [C] short passage, sentence, esp of the Bible, etc, as the subject of a sermon or discussion.
ˈtext·book, book used to learn a subject: *an*

algebra ~book; a ~book on grammar.
tex·tual /ˈtekstʃuəl/ *adj* of, in, a text: *~ual errors.*
tex·tile /ˈtekˌstaiəl, ˈtekstəl/ *adj* of the making of cloth: *the ~ industry.* □ *n* [C] cloth.
tex·ture /ˈtekstʃər/ *n* [C,U] **1** the arrangement of the threads in a cloth: *cloth with a loose/close ~.* **2** arrangement of the parts that make up something: *the ~ of a mineral.*
than /ðən; *rarely heard strong form:* ðæn/ *conj* introducing the second part of a comparison: *John is taller ~ his brother. I know you better ~ he* (*does*), ie than he knows you. *I know you better ~ him,* ie than I know him. ***sooner than,*** ⇨ soon(3,4).
thank /θæŋk/ *vt* express gratitude: *~ a person for his help. There's no need to ~ me.* ***Thank you,*** formula for accepting something or expressing thanks. ***No, thank you,*** formula used to decline an offer. □ *n* (*pl*) (expression of) gratitude: *Thanks for the meal; kneel and give ~s to God.* ***No, thanks,*** (*informal*) No, thank you. ***thanks to,*** as the result of: *Thanks to you, we were successful/we failed.*
thank·ful /-fəl/ *adj* grateful: *You should be ~ful that you have escaped with minor injuries.*
thank·fully /-fəli/ *adv*
thank·less *adj* not feeling or expressing gratitude or winning appreciation: *a ~less task* with no appreciation or reward.
ˌthanks·ˈgiving *n* [U] **(a)** expression of gratitude, esp to God; form of prayer for this. **(b) Thanksgiving** (also **ˌThanksgiving ˈDay**) day set apart each year to thank God for His goodness (usually the fourth Thursday in November).
that[1] /ðæt/ *adj, pron* (*pl* those /ðouz/) (contrasted with *this, these*) **1** the person or thing pointed to or drawn attention to, named or understood to be known: *Look at ~ man/those men. What is ~? What are those? What was ~ noise? What noise was ~? This book is much better than ~* (*one*). *These are much better than those. Those who do not wish to do not need to go. Throw away all* (*of*) *those which are too old. I don't like ~ new secretary of his.* ***at ˈthat,*** even so, just the same: *The shirt was reduced to half-price, and expensive at ~.* **2** (used as a *collective sing*): *What about ~ twenty dollars you borrowed from me last month?* □ *adv* (*informal*) to such a degree; so: *I can't walk ~ far,* = as far as that. *It's about ~ high,* ie as high as that.
that[2] /ðet; *rarely heard strong form:* ðæt/ *conj* (*Note:* when *that* is in parentheses in examples, it is often omitted.) **1** (introducing *noun* clauses): *She said* (~) *she would come. The trouble is ~ we are short of money.* **2** ***so that; in order that,*** (introducing clauses of purpose): *Bring it nearer so* (~) *I can see it better.* **3** (introducing clauses of manner): *His behavior was so bad ~ we all refused to talk to him.* **4** (introducing clauses of condition): *on condition ~ . . .*
that[3] /ðet; *rarely heard strong form:* ðæt/ *relative pron* (*pl* unchanged) (*Note:* when *that* is in parentheses in examples, it is often omitted.) **1** (used as the subject of the *verb* in a clause): *The letter ~ came this morning is from my father.* **2** (*who* is usually preferred to *that* for a person, but *that* is preferred to *who* after superlatives, *only, all, any*, and *it is* or *it was*): *Newton was one of the greatest men ~ ever lived. You're the only person ~ can help me.* **3** (used as the object of the *verb* in the clause): *The pen* (~) *you gave me is very nice. Is this the best* (~) *you can do?* **4** (used after an expression of time): *the year* (~) *my father died.* **5** (used as the object of a *preposition*): *All the people* (~) *I wrote to agreed to come. Is this the book* (~) *you were looking for?*
thatch /θætʃ/ *n* [U] roof covering of dried straw, reeds, etc. □ *vt* cover (a roof, etc) with thatch.
thatching *n* = thatch.
that'd /ˈðætəd, ˈðætɪd/ = that had; that would.
that'll /ˈðætəl/ = that will; that shall.
that's /ðæts/ = that is; that has.
thaw /θɔ/ *vi,vt* **1** (of snow and ice) begin to melt. **2** (cause anything frozen to) become liquid or soft again: *leave frozen food to ~* (*out*) *before cooking it.* **3** (of persons, their behavior) (cause to) become less formal, more friendly: *After a good dinner he began to ~* (*out*). □ *n* (usually *sing*) (state of the weather causing) thawing: *Let's go skating before a ~ sets in.*
the /ðə; *before vowels and strong form:* ði/ *definite article* **1** (used as a less specific form of *this, these, that, those*, applied to person(s), thing(s), event(s), etc already referred to or being discussed. Note the changes from *a, an* to *the* in these sentences): *An old man lived in a small hut near a forest. One day the old man left the hut and went into the forest to gather wood.* **2** (used when the situation indicates who or what is referred to): *Please close the window*, ie the window that is open. **3** (used with a *noun* when it stands for something unique): *the sun; the moon; the year 1989; the universe.* **4** (used with *nouns* such as *sea, sky,* when there is no *adjective*): *The sea was calm. Isn't the wind strong!* **5** (used with a *noun* if it is shown by the context to be unique): *the back of the house.* (*Note:* in many phrases *the* is or may be omitted: *from beginning to end; from* (*the*) *top to* (*the*) *bottom; in* (*the*) *hospital.*) **6** (used with a superlative): *the best way to get there.* (*Note: the* is not needed after the *verb "be"* when the superlative is used without a *noun: It is wisest* (= The wisest plan is) *to avoid the center of the town.* When *most* means "very," *the* is not used: *The story was most exciting. This is a most useful dictionary.*) **7** (used before): **(a)** names of seas and oceans: *the Mediterranean, the Red Sea; the Atlantic* (*Ocean*). **(b)** names of rivers and canals: *the Missouri; the Panama Canal.* **(c)** most *pl* geographical names: *the Rockies; the Great Lakes.* **(d)** in a few *sing* geographical names: *the Sudan; the Sahara.* **8** (used to indicate all members of a class): *the rich; the dead.* **9** (used with musical instruments): *to play the piano/the violin/the guitar*, but not with names of games: *to play tennis/football.* **10** (used with *nouns* expressing a unit): *This car gets thirty miles to the gallon*, ie to each gallon of gasoline. **11** (used with numerals in titles): *Elizabeth the*

Second. □ *adv* by so much; by that amount: *The more he has the more he wants. The more he reads the less he understands.*

the·ater /ˈθiətər, θiˈeitər/ *n* [C] **1** building, etc for the performance of plays, for dramatic events, etc: *go to the ~ to see a Shakespeare play.* **2** hall or room with seats in rows rising one behind another for lectures, scientific demonstrations, surgical operations, etc: *operating theater.* **3** scene of important events: *a ~ of war.* **4** (usually *sing* with *the*) the writing and acting of plays, esp when connected with one author, country, period, etc: *a book about the Greek ~.*

ˈtheater·goer *n* [C] person who (often) visits theaters.

the·atri·cal /θiˈætrɪkəl/ *adj* **(a)** of, for, the theater: *theatrical costumes.* **(b)** (of behavior, manner, way of speaking, persons, etc) designed for effect; exaggerated, not natural.

the·atri·cally /-kli/ *adv*

thee /ði/ *personal pron* (*archaic*) (object form of *thou*) you (*sing*).

theft /θeft/ *n* [C,U] (the act of, an instance of) stealing.

their /ðer/ *adj* of, relating to, or belonging to them: *They have lost ~ dog. They have a house of ~ own. Good students do ~ best,* the best they can.

theirs /ðerz/ *possessive pron* belonging to them: *That dog is ~s, not ours. It's a habit of ~s,* one of their habits.

them /ðəm; *strong form:* ðem/ *personal pron* (used as the object form of *they*): *Give ~ to me. It was kind of ~.*

theme /θim/ *n* [C] **1** topic; subject of a talk or a piece of writing. **2** (*music*) short melody which is repeated, expanded, etc, eg in a sonata or symphony.

ˈtheme song, one that is often repeated in a musical play, film, etc.

them·selves /ðəmˈselvz/ *pron* **1** (used as a *reflexive*): *They hurt ~. They kept some for ~.* ***(all) by themselves,*** **(a)** without help: *They did the work by ~.* **(b)** alone: *They were by ~ when I called.* **2** (used for emphasis): *They ~ have often made that mistake.*

then /ðen/ *adv* **1** at the time (past or future): *I was still unmarried ~.* ***(every) ˌnow and ˈthen,*** ⇨ now²(2). **2** (used after a *preposition*): *from ~* (= from that time) *onward; until ~; since ~.* **3** next; after that; afterward: *We spent a week in Rome and ~ we went to Naples.* **4** in that case; that being so: *A: "It isn't here."—B: "Then it must be in the next room." You say you don't want to be a doctor.—Then what do you want to be?* **5** and also: *Then there's Mrs. Green—she must be invited to the wedding too.*

theo·lo·gian /ˌθiəˈloudʒən/ *n* [C] advanced student of theology.

theo·logi·cal /ˌθiəˈladʒɪkəl/ *adj* of theology.

theo·logi·cally /-kli/ *adv*

the·ol·ogy /θiˈalədʒi/ *n* [U] formation of a series of theories about the nature of God and of the foundations of religious belief.

the·orem /ˈθiərəm/ *n* [C] (*pl* ~s) **1** statement which logical reasoning shows to be true. **2** (*math*) statement for which a reasoned proof is required.

the·or·etic, -i·cal /ˌθiəˈretɪk, -ɪkəl/ *adj* based on theory, not on practice or experience.

theor·eti·cally /-kli/ *adv*

the·ory /ˈθiəri, ˈθɪri/ *n* (*pl* -ies) **1** [C,U] (explanation of the) general principles of an art or science (contrasted with practice): *Your plan is excellent in ~, but would it succeed in practice?* **2** [C] reasoned account offered to explain facts or events: *Darwin's ~ of evolution.* **3** [C] something offered as an opinion, not necessarily based on reasoning: *He has a ~ that wearing hats makes men bald.*

the·or·ist /-ɪst/ *n* [C] person who forms theories.

the·or·ize /ˈθiəˌraiz/ *vi* form theories.

thera·peutic /ˌθerəˈpyutɪk/ *adj* connected with the art of healing, the cure of disease.

thera·pist /ˈθerəpɪst/ *n* [C] specialist in therapy, esp psychotherapy.

ther·apy /ˈθerəpi/ *n* [U] curative treatment (esp of a kind shown by a preceding word): *occupational ~,* the curing of an illness by means of exercise. ⇨ psychotherapy.

there¹ /ðer/ *adv of place and direction* (contrasted with *here*) **1** in, at or to, that place: *We shall soon be ~. We're nearly ~,* have nearly arrived. *I've never been to Rome but I hope to go ~ next year.* **2** (used in exclamations; always stressed): *There goes the last bus! There they go!* **3** (used to call attention; always stressed): *There's the bell for lunch. There's gratitude for you!* Note how grateful/ungrateful he is! **4** at, in connection with, that point (in an action, story, argument, etc): *Don't stop ~! There* (on that point) *you are mistaken.* **5** (in phrases): ***here and there; here, there and everywhere,*** ⇨ here(3). ***there and back,*** to a place and back again: *Can I go ~ and back in one day?* ***over there,*** (of a place farther than is shown by using *there* alone): *I live here, Mr. Green lives ~, and Mr. Brown lives over ~, on the other side of the river.*

there² /ðer/ *adv* (always unstressed) (used as an introduction in a sentence of which the *verb*, esp *"be"* precedes the subject) **1** (used with *"be"*): *There's a man at the door.* **2** (used with other *verbs*, esp *seem* and *appear*): *There seems* (*to be*) *no doubt about it. There comes a time when* . . .

there³ /ðer/ *int* (always stressed) **1** (used to comfort): *There! There! You'll soon feel better.* **2** (used to suggest that the speaker was right, or to show triumph, dismay, etc according to the context): *There, now! What did I tell you?* You now see that I was right! *There! You've knocked over the flowerpot!*

there·about(s) /ˈðerəˌbaut(s)/ *adv* (usually preceded by *or*) near that place, number, quantity, degree, etc: *in 1978 or ~; $5/15 yards/3 o'clock or ~.*

there·after /ðerˈæftər/ *adv* (*formal*) = afterward.

there·by /ðerˈbai/ *adv* (*formal*) by that means; in that connection.

there·fore /ˈðerˌfɔr/ *adv* for that reason.

there·in /ðerˈɪn/ *adv* (*formal*) in that place.

there·of /ðerˈəv/ *adv* (*formal*) from that source.

there's /ðerz/ = there is; there has.

there·upon /ˈðerəˌpan/ *adv* (*formal*) as the

result of that.

therm /θərm/ *n* [C] unit for measuring heat, etc (= 100,000 British thermal units) in measuring the consumption of gas.

ther·mal /ˈθərməl/ *adj* of heat: ~ *springs*, of warm or hot water. □ *n* [C] rising current of warm air (as needed by a glider to gain height).

thermo- /ˌθərmou-/ *prefix* of heat, temperature.

ˌthermo·dyˈnamics *n pl* (usually used with a *sing verb*) science of the relations between heat and mechanical work.

ˌthermo·ˈnuclear *adj* (eg of weapons) of, using, the high temperatures released in nuclear fission: *the ˌ~nuclear ˈbomb*.

ˈthermo·stat /ˈθərməˌstæt/ *n* [C] device for automatically regulating temperature by cutting off and restoring the supply of heat (eg in central heating).

ther·mom·eter /θərˈmamətər/ *n* [C] instrument for measuring temperature.

ther·mos /ˈθərməs/ *n* [C] (*pl* ~es) (also **ˈthermos bottle**) = vacuum bottle.

the·sau·rus /θɪˈsɔrəs/ *n* [C] (*pl* ~es or -ri /-ˌrai/) (esp) a book or collection of words, phrases grouped together according to similarities in their meanings.

these /ðiz/ *pl* of this.

the·sis /ˈθisɪs/ *n* [C] (*pl* theses /-ˌsiz/) statement or theory (to be) put forward and supported by arguments, submitted (as part of the requirements) for a university degree.

they /ðei/ *personal pron* (subject form, *pl*, of *he, she, it*) people, animals or things previously referred to: *They* (= People in general) *say that the government will resign. What a lot of questions* ~ (= those in authority) *ask in this application!* ➪ them, object form.

they'd /ðeid/ = they had; they would.

they'll /ðeiəl/ = they will; they shall.

they're /ðer/ = they are.

they've /ðeiv/ = they have.

thick /θɪk/ *adj* (-er, -est) **1** (opposite of *thin*) of relatively great or a specified measurement in diameter, from one side to the other, or from the front to the back: *a ~ line; ice three feet ~*. **2** having a large number of units close together: *~ hair; a ~ forest*. **3** (of a hedge) with bushes, etc closely planted. **4** ***thick with,*** full of or packed with: *The air was ~ with dust*. **5** (of liquids) semisolid: *~ soup;* (of the air, etc) not clear; dense: *a ~ fog*. **6** (*informal*) stupid. **7** (*informal*) ***as ˌthick as ˈthieves,*** very friendly. **8** (*informal*) ***lay it on thick,*** be extravagant (with compliments, etc). □ *n* [U] **1** most crowded part; part where there is greatest activity: *We were in the ~ of it*. ***through ˌthick and ˈthin,*** under any kind of conditions, good or bad. **2** thick part of anything: *the ~ of the thumb*. □ *adv* thickly: *You spread the butter too ~*.

ˌthick·ˈheaded *adj* stupid.

thick·ly *adv*

thick·ness /-nɪs/ **(a)** [U] quality or degree of being thick: *four inches in ~ness* **(b)** [C] layer: *two ~nesses of woolen cloth*.

ˌthick·ˈset *adj* **(a)** (of a person) short and solid. **(b)** (of hedges, etc) closely planted.

ˌthick-ˈskinned *adj* (*fig*) not sensitive to criticism, insults, etc.

thicken /ˈθɪkən/ *vt, vi* make or become thick: ~ *the gravy*.

thicket /ˈθɪkɪt/ *n* [C] group of trees, shrubs, growing thickly together.

thief /θif/ *n* [C] (*pl* thieves /θivz/) person who steals, esp secretly and without violence. ➪ thick(7).

thieve /θiv/ *vi,vt* = steal (the usual word).

thigh /θai/ *n* [C] **1** part of the human leg between the knee and the hip. ➪ illus at leg. **2** corresponding part of the back legs of other animals.

thimble /ˈθɪmbəl/ *n* [C] cap (of metal, etc) used to protect the end of the finger when pushing a needle through cloth, etc.

thin /θɪn/ *adj* (-nner, -nnest) **1** (opposite of *thick*) having opposite surfaces close together; of small diameter: *a ~ sheet of paper; a ~ piece of string*. **2** not full or closely packed: *~ hair; a ~ audience*, with more seats empty than occupied. **3** (opposite of *fat*) having not much flesh: *rather ~ in the face*. **4** (of liquids) not having substance; watery: *~ soup; ~ blood*, as when weakened by illness, etc; (of the air, etc) not dense: *a ~ mist*. **5** not having some important ingredient; poor in quality: *a ~ excuse*, not very convincing; *a ~ disguise*, easily seen through. □ *adv* so as to be thin: *You've spread the butter very ~*. □ *vt,vi* (-nn-) make or become thin: *We had better wait until the fog ~s*, becomes less dense. *At last the crowd ~ned*.

thin·ly *adv* in a thin manner: *Sow the seed ~ly*, not close together.

thin·ness /ˈθɪnnəs/ *n* [U]

ˌthin-ˈskinned *adj* (*fig*) sensitive to criticism, insults, etc.

thine /ðain/ *adj, pron* (*archaic*) (possessive form of *thou*) of you (*sing*).

thing /θɪŋ/ *n* [C] **1** any material object: *What are those ~s on the table?* **2** (*pl*) belongings; articles of which the nature is clear (or thought to be clear) from the context: *Bring your swimming ~s* (= your bathing suit, towel, etc) *with you. Have you packed your ~s* (= clothes, etc) *for the vacation?* **3** subject: *There's another ~* (= something else) *I want to ask you about*. **4** ***be ˈseeing things,*** have hallucinations. **5** situation; event; course of action: *That only makes ~s worse. I must think ~s over*, consider what has happened, what has to be done, etc. *What's the next ~ to do?* What must be done next? ***for ˈone thing,*** (used to introduce a reason): *For one ~, I haven't any money; for another . . .* **6** (used of a person or an animal, expressing an emotion of some kind): *She's a sweet little ~/a dear old ~. Poor ~, he's been ill all winter*. **7** (*sing* with *the*) just what will be best in the circumstances: *A vacation will be just the ~ for you. He always says the right/wrong ~*, makes the most suitable/unsuitable remark or comment. **8** (phrases) ***the ˌthing ˈis,*** the question to be considered is: *The ~ is, can we get there in time?* ***first thing,*** before anything else; early: *We must do that first ~ in the morning*. ***a near thing,*** a narrow escape (from an accident, missing a train, etc). ***have a thing about,*** (*informal*) be obsessed by.

think[1] /θɪŋk/ *vi,vt* (*pt,pp* thought /θɔt/) (For special uses with *adverbial particles* and *prepositions*, ⇨ 7 below.) **1** use the mind in order to form opinions, come to conclusions: *What she said has set me ~ing. You should ~* (= not be hasty) *before doing that. Do you ~ in English when you speak English?* ***think aloud,*** say one's thoughts as they occur. **2** consider; be of the opinion: *Do you ~ it will rain? Yes, I ~ so. The child thought there was no harm in picking flowers in your garden. It will be better, don't you ~, to start early. I thought it would be better to stay away.* ***think fit.*** ⇨ fit[1](2). **3** (*negative* with *can/could*) imagine: *I can't ~ what you mean.* **4** have a vague intention: *I ~ I'll go for a swim.* **5** reflect: *She was ~ing* (*to herself*) *how strange the children were.* **6** expect, intend: *I thought as much,* that is what I expected or suspected. **7** (special uses with *adverbial particles* and *prepositions*):

think about sth, **(a)** examine, consider (esp a plan, idea, to see whether it is desirable, practicable, etc): *She's ~ing about buying a car.* **(b)** reflect on: *She was ~ing about her childhood days.*

think of sth, **(a)** consider; take into account: *We have a hundred and one things to ~ of before we can decide.* **(b)** consider (without reaching a decision or taking action): *We're ~ing of going to Italy this summer.* **(c)** imagine: *Just ~ of the cost/danger!* **(d)** have, entertain, the idea of (often with *could, would, should,* and *not* or *never,* with *dream* as a possible substitute for *think*): *He would never ~ of marrying a girl like you!* **(e)** remember: *I can't ~ of his name at the moment.* **(f)** suggest: *Can you ~ of a good place for a weekend vacation?* ***think highly/well/little, etc of sb/sth,*** have a high/good/poor, etc opinion of: *His work is highly thought of by the critics. He ~s the world of her,* loves her dearly. ***think nothing of,*** consider insignificant or unremarkable: *Barbara ~s nothing of walking 10 or 20 miles a day.*

think sth out, consider carefully and make a plan for: *It seems to be a well-thought-out scheme.*

think sth over, consider further (before reaching a decision, etc): *Please ~ over what I've said.*

think sth up, invent, devise (a scheme, etc): *There's no knowing what he'll ~ up next.*

think[2] /θɪŋk/ *n* (*informal*) occasion of, need for, thinking: *He's got another ~ coming,* will need to think again (because I refuse, etc).

ˈthink tank (*informal*) special quarters (at a university, institution, etc) where high-level scholars or scientists are brought to work on problems.

thinker /ˈθɪŋkər/ *n* [C] (with an *adjective*) person who thinks: *a great ~.*

think·ing /ˈθɪŋkɪŋ/ *adj* who thinks: *all ~ persons,* those people who think (about public affairs, etc). □ *n* [U] thought; way of reasoning: *do some hard ~,* think deeply.

third /θərd/ *adj, n* [C] (*abbr* **3rd**) (of) the next after two or one of three equal parts: *the ~ month of the year,* ie March; *on the ~ of April; every ~ day; a ~ of the cake; two-~s of a cup.*

ˌthird deˈgree, prolonged or hard questioning, use of torture (as used by the police in some countries to get confessions or information).

ˌthird-degree ˈburn, causing severe damage to the skin.

third·ly *adv*

ˌthird ˈparty, another person besides the two principals: (as an *adjective*) *ˌ~-party inˈsurance,* of/to a person other than the person insured, which the insurance company undertakes to meet.

ˌthird-ˈrate *adj* of poor quality.

the ˌThird ˈWorld, the developing countries not aligned with Communist or Western countries.

thirst /θərst/ *n* [U, and with *a* as in example] **1** feeling caused by a desire or need to drink; suffering caused by this: *They lost their way in the desert and died of ~.* **2** (*fig*) strong desire (*for*): *a ~ for knowledge.* □ *vt* **1** have thirst. **2** be eager (for): *~ for revenge.*

thirsty *adj* (-ier, -iest) having or causing thirst: *be/feel ~y.*

thir·teen /ˌθərˈtin/ *adj, n* [C] (of) 13.

thir·teenth /ˌθərˈtinθ/ *adj, n* [C] (of) one of thirteen (parts) or the next after twelve.

thirty /ˈθərti/ *adj, n* [C] (of) 30.

thir·ti·eth /ˈθərtiəθ/ *adj, n* [C] (of) one of thirty (parts) or the next after twenty-nine.

this /ðɪs/ *adj, pron* (*pl* these /ðiz/) (contrasted with *that, those*) **1** the person or thing nearby, touched, etc or drawn attention to, named or understood to be known: *Look at ~ box/these boxes. What's ~? What are these? This* (*one*) *is larger than that* (*one*). *These are better than those. This boy of yours seems very intelligent.* **2** (in narrative) a certain: *Then ~ funny little man came up to me.* □ *adv* (*informal*) so: *It's about ~ high. Now that we have come ~ far* (= as far as this).

thistle /ˈθɪsəl/ *n* [C] (kinds of) wild plant with prickly leaves and yellow, white or purple flowers.

tho' /ðou/ *adv, conj* = though.

thong /θɔŋ, θaŋ/ *n* [C] narrow strip of leather, eg as a fastening, the lash of a whip.

tho·rax /ˈθɔˌræks/ *n* [C] **1** part of an animal's body between the neck and the belly, eg in a man, the chest. **2** middle of the three main sections of an insect (with the legs and wings). ⇨ illus at insect.

thorn /θɔrn/ *n* **1** [C] pointed growth on the stem of a plant. ⇨ illus at flower. ***a thorn in one's flesh/side,*** (*fig*) constant source of irritation. **2** [C,U] kinds of shrub or tree with thorns.

thorny *adj* (-ier, -iest) **(a)** having thorns. **(b)** (*fig*) full of trouble and difficulty: *a ~y problem.*

thor·ough /ˈθərou/ *adj* complete in every way; not forgetting or overlooking anything; detailed: *a ~ worker; be ~ in one's work.*

ˈthorough·going *adj* complete: *a ˌ~going reˈvision.*

thor·ough·ly *adv*

thor·ough·ness /-nɪs/ *n* [U]

thor·ough·bred /ˈθərəˌbred/ *n* [C], *adj* (animal, esp a horse) of pure breed.

thor·ough·fare /ˈθərəˌfær/ *n* [C] road or street,

esp one much used by the traffic and open at both ends: *Broadway is New York's most famous ~.*

those /ðouz/ *pl* of that.

thou¹ /ðau/ *personal pron (archaic)* you (*sing*).

thou² /θau/ *adj, n (sl)* thousand.

though /ðou/ *conj* **1** (also **al·though** /ɔlˈðou/) in spite of the fact that: *Though they are poor, they are always neatly dressed. He passed the examination al~ he had been prevented by illness from studying.* **2** (introducing an independent statement) and yet; all the same: *I'll try to come, ~ I don't think I shall manage it.* ***as though,*** ⇨ as²(6). □ *adv* however: *He said he would come; he didn't ~.*

thought¹ *pt,pp* of think¹.

thought² /θɔt/ *n* **1** [U] (power, process of) thinking: *He was lost/deep in ~,* thinking so deeply as to be unaware of his surroundings, etc. **2** [U] way of thinking characteristic of a particular period, class, nation, etc: *scientific/Greek ~.* **3** [U] care, consideration: *He often acts without ~.* **4** [C,U] idea, opinion, intention, etc formed by thinking: *That boy hasn't a ~ in his head. He keeps his ~s to himself,* does not tell anyone what he thinks. *She says she can read my ~s. He had no ~* (= intention) *of hurting your feelings.* ***food for thought,*** ⇨ food(3). ***on second thought,*** after further consideration. ***give sb/sth a thought,*** think about before deciding, be sympathetic, etc according to context. ***have second thoughts about sb/sth,*** consider further, change one's mind about. ***spare a thought for sb,*** ⇨ spare²(2).

thought·ful /-fəl/ *adj* **(a)** full of, showing, thought: *~ful looks.* **(b)** considerate; thinking of the needs of others: *It was ~ful of you to warn me of your arrival.*

thought·fully /-fəli/ *adv*

thought·less *adj* **(a)** careless; unthinking: *Young people are often ~less of the future.* **(b)** selfish; inconsiderate (*of* others): *a ~less action.*

thought·less·ly *adv*

thou·sand /ˈθauzənd/ *adj, n* [C] **1** (of) 1,000. **2** great number: *A ~ thanks for your kindness. He made a ~ and one excuses.* ***a thousand to one (chance),*** a remote possibility. ***one in a thousand,*** a rare exception.

thousand·fold /-ˌfould/ *adj, adv* a thousand times (as much or many).

thou·sandth /ˈθauzənθ/ *adj, n* [C] (of) one of 1,000 (parts) or the next after 999.

thrash /θræʃ/ *vt,vi* **1** beat with a stick, whip, etc: *He threatened to ~ the boy,* beat him thoroughly. **2** (*informal*) defeat (a team, etc) in a contest. **3** ***thrash sth out,*** **(a)** clear up (a problem, etc) by discussion. **(b)** arrive at (the truth, a solution, etc) by discussion. **4** (cause to) toss, move violently: *The swimmer ~ed around in the water.*

thrash·ing *n* **(a)** beating: *give/get a good ~ing.* **(b)** defeat, eg in games.

thread /θred/ *n* **1** [C,U] (length of) spun cotton, silk, nylon, wool, etc esp for use in sewing and weaving: *a needle and ~.* **2** something like a thread: *A ~ of light came through the keyhole.* **3** [C] chain or line (connecting parts of a story, etc): *lose the ~ of one's argument.* **4** spiral ridge round a screw or bolt. □ *vt* **1** pass a thread through the eye of (a needle); put (beads, pearls, etc) on a thread. **2** ***thread one's way through,*** make one's way (through a crowd, etc). **3** (of hair) streak: *black hair ~ed with silver,* with streaks of silver hair in it.

ˈthread·bare /-ˌbær/ *adj* (of cloth) worn.

threat /θret/ *n* [C] **1** statement of an intention to punish or hurt a person, esp if he does not do as one wishes: *carry out a ~; be under the ~ of expulsion,* eg from a university. **2** sign or warning of coming trouble, danger, etc: *There was a ~ of rain in the dark sky.*

threaten /ˈθretən/ *vt,vi* **1** use threats: *~ an employee with dismissal.* **2** give warning of: *The clouds ~ed rain.* **3** seem likely to occur or come: *Knowing that danger ~ed, I kept an extra careful watch.*

threat·en·ing *adj: a ~ letter.*

threat·en·ing·ly *adv*

three /θri/ *adj, n* [C] (of) 3.

ˌthree-ˈcornered *adj* triangular: *a ˌ~-cornered ˈhat.*

ˌthree-ˈD *adj* (*informal*) = three-dimensional.

ˌthree-diˈmensional *adj* having, or appearing to have, three dimensions (length, breadth and depth).

ˌthree-ˈfigure *adj* (of numbers, amounts) between 100 and 999 (inclusive).

ˌthree-ˈpiece *n* [C], *adj* set of three articles of clothing (eg a suit); set of furniture (eg a sofa and two armchairs): *a ˌ~-piece ˈsuite.*

ˌthree-ˈply *adj* **(a)** (of wool, thread) having three strands. **(b)** (of wood) having three layers.

ˈthree-quarter(s) *adj* (consisting) of three-fourths (of something).

ˈthree·score *n* sixty.

ˈthree·some /-səm/ *n* [C] (game, dance, for) three persons.

ˌthree-way ˈbulb, electric light bulb controllable for giving three different degrees of light.

ˌthree-way ˈlamp, lamp built to use a three-way bulb.

thresh /θreʃ/ *vt,vi* beat (the grain out of) wheat, etc: *~ corn by hand.*

thresher *n* [C] person who, machine that, threshes.

ˈthresh·ing machine, one for threshing grain.

thresh·old /ˈθreʃˌhould/ *n* [C] **1** stone or plank under a doorway in a house, church, etc: *cross the ~.* **2** (*fig*) start, beginning: *He was on the ~ of his career.*

threw *pt* of throw¹.

thrice /θrais/ *adv* (*rare*) three times.

thrift /θrɪft/ *n* [U] care, economy, in the use of money or goods.

thrifty *adj* (-ier, -iest) = economical (the usual word).

thrill /θrɪl/ *n* [C] (experience causing an) excited feeling passing like a wave along the nerves: *a ~ of joy/pleasure/horror.* □ *vt,vi* **1** cause a thrill in: *The film ~ed the audience. We were ~ed with horror/joy.* **2** feel a thrill: *We ~ed at the good news.*

thril·ler *n* [C] novel, play or film in which excitement and emotional appeal are the essential elements.

thrive /θraiv/ *vi* (*pt* throve /θrouv/ or ~d *pp* thriven /ˈθrɪvən/) prosper; succeed; grow strong and healthy: *Children ~ on good food. He has a thriving business.*

throat /θrout/ *n* [C] **1** front part of the neck: *I gripped him by the ~.* ➪ illus at head. **2** passage in the neck through which food passes to the stomach and air to the lungs: *A bone has stuck in my ~.* ***cut one's own throat,*** cause one's own defeat. ***force/thrust sth down sb's throat,*** try to make him accept one's views, beliefs, etc. ***stick in one's throat,*** (*fig*) be unable to be accepted: *His words stuck in my ~.*

throb /θrab/ *vi* (-bb-) (of the heart, pulse, etc) beat, esp beat more quickly than usual: *His head ~bed,* he had a bad headache. □ *n* [C] throbbing or vibration: *~s of joy.*

throb·bing *adj* that throbs: *a ~bing pain/sound.*

throm·bo·sis /θramˈbousɪs/ *n* clot of blood in a blood vessel or in the heart. ➪ coronary.

throne /θroun/ *n* [C] **1** ceremonial chair or seat of a king, queen, bishop, etc. **2 the throne,** royal authority: *come to the ~,* become king or queen.

throng /θrɔŋ/ *n* [C] crowd. □ *vt,vi* make, be, a crowd: *People ~ed to see the new play.*

throttle /ˈθratəl/ *vt,vi* **1** seize (a person) by the throat and stop his breathing; strangle: *He ~d the guard and then robbed the bank.* **2** control the flow of steam, etc in an engine; lessen the speed of (an engine) by doing this. □ *n* [C] valve controlling the flow of steam, etc in an engine.

through[1] (also sometimes **thru**) /θru/ *adv* (For special combinations with *verbs,* eg *get ~,* ➪ the *verb* entries.) **1** from end to end, beginning to end, side to side: *They wouldn't let us ~,* eg pass the gate. *Did your brother get ~,* eg pass the examination? *He slept the whole night ~,* all night. *The nail went ~* (the wood) *easily.* ***all through,*** all the time (something was happening, etc): *I knew what the ending would be all ~ the film.* **2** to the very end. ***be through (with),*** **(a)** finish (with): *When will you be ~ with your work?* **(b)** (*informal*) have had enough of; be tired of: *I'm ~ with this job; I must find something more interesting.* **(c)** (*informal*) no longer be in love: *I'm ~ with her.* ***see sth through,*** continue to do it, etc until it is finished. ***ˌthrough and ˈthrough,*** in all parts; completely: *He's a reliable man ~ and ~.* **3** all the way to: *This train goes ~ to Chicago.* **4** (as an *adjective*) (used in the sense of 3): *a ~ train to Chicago; ~ traffic,* road traffic which is going through a place (contrasted with local traffic). **5 (a)** finished: *Are you ~ washing the dishes?* **(b)** (telephoning) connected: *I will put you ~ to the manager,* connect you.

through[2] (also sometimes **thru**) /θru/ *prep* (For combinations with *verbs,* eg *go through,* ➪ the *verb* entries.) **1** (of places) from end to end or side to side of; entering at one side, on one surface, etc and coming out at the other: *The James River flows ~ Richmond, Virginia. There is a path ~* (= across) *the fields. He was looking ~ a telescope.* **2** (*fig*): *He went ~/has come ~* (= experienced) *many hardships. We must go ~* (= examine) *the accounts.* **3** (of time) from beginning to end of: *He won't live ~ the night,* he will die before morning. **4** (showing the agency, means or cause) because of: *The accident happened ~ no fault of yours.* **5** without stopping for: *Don't drive ~ a red light.* **6** up to and including: *Monday ~ Friday.*

through·out /θruˈaut/ *adv* right through; in every part; in all ways or respects: *The house needs painting ~.* □ *prep* all or right through; from end to end of: *~ the country; ~ the war; ~ the year.*

throve *pt* of thrive.

throw[1] /θrou/ *vt,vi* (*pt* threw /θru/, *pp* thrown /θroun/) (For special uses with *adverbial particles* and *prepositions,* ➪ 11 below) **1** cause (something) to go through the air, usually with force, by a movement of the arm or by mechanical means: *Don't ~ stones at my dog! He threw the ball to his sister.* ***throw the book at sb,*** (*sl*) impose the maximum legal penalty on him. **2** put (articles of clothing) (*on, off, over,* etc) quickly or carelessly: *~ a coat over one's shoulders.* **3** move (one's arms, legs, etc) (*out, up, down, about*) energetically: *~ one's chest out; ~ one's head back.* **4 (a)** (of a horse) cause the rider to fall to the ground: *Two of the jockeys were ~n in the race.* **(b)** (of a wrestler) force (an opponent) to the floor. **5** (of dice) drop on to the table (after shaking them in something); get by doing this: *~ three sixes.* **6** (*fig*) cause to be noticed as if by throwing: *He threw me an angry look.* **7** shape (pottery) on a potter's wheel. **8** (*informal*) ***throw a party,*** give a (dinner, cocktail, etc) party. ***throw a fit,*** ➪ fit²(2). **9** ***throw sth open (to),*** make (eg a competition) open to all persons. **10** (used with *nouns*) ➪ gauntlet(1), light³(5), weight(2). **11** (special uses with *adverbial particles* and *prepositions*):

throw sth around, scatter: *Don't ~ waste paper around in the park.* ***throw money around,*** (*fig*) spend it carelessly.

throw sth away, **(a)** lose by foolishness or neglect: *~ away an opportunity.* **(b)** (of words spoken by actors, broadcasters, etc) say in a casual way, with conscious underemphasis.

throw oneself down, lie down at full length (eg to avoid danger).

throw sth in, **(a)** give something extra, without an addition to the price: *You can have the guitar for $20, with the case ~n in.* **(b)** put in (a remark, etc) casually. ***throw in the sponge/towel,*** (*informal*) admit defeat.

throw oneself into sth, begin to work hard at it.

throw sb/sth off, manage to get rid of; become free from: *~ off a cold/a pursuer.*

throw oneself on sb/sth, put one's trust in: *~ oneself on the mercy of the court.*

throw sth out, **(a)** say (esp casually): *~ out a hint/suggestion.* **(b)** reject (a case before a law court, etc).

throw sb over, desert, abandon: *~ over one's girlfriend.*

throw sth together, assemble (too) quickly: *That dress seems to have been ~n together.*

throw sth up, vomit (food). ***throw up one's***

hands (in horror), express horror by doing this. ***throw oneself upon sb/sth,*** = throw oneself on sb/sth.

ˈthrow·back *n* [C] person, animal, with characteristics of a remote ancestor.

throw² /θrou/ *n* [C] throwing; distance to which something is or may be thrown: *a ~ of 70 meters.* ***within a stone's throw (of).*** ⇨ stone(2).

thru = through.

thrush /θrəʃ/ *n* [C] kinds of songbird, such as the American robin, bluebird, etc.

thrust /θrəst/ *vt,vi* (*pt,pp* ~) push suddenly or violently; make a forward stroke with a sword, etc: *He ~ his hands into his pockets/a coin into my hand.* □ *n* **1** [C] act of thrusting. **2** [C] (in war) strong attempt to push forward into the enemy's positions. **3** [C] (in debate, etc) attack in words. **4** [U] force directed forward in a jet engine.

thud /θəd/ *n* [C] dull sound as of a blow on something soft: *He fell with a ~ to the carpet.* □ *vi* (-dd-) strike, fall, with a thud.

thug /θəg/ *n* [C] violent and dangerous person.

thumb /θəm/ *n* [C] short, thick finger set apart from the other four. ⇨ illus at arm. ***under sb's thumb,*** under his influence and control. ***rule of thumb,*** method or procedure based on experience and practice. □ *vt* **1** turn over (pages, etc); make dirty by doing this: *~ the pages of a dictionary; a ˌwell-~ed ˈbook.* **2** ***thumb a lift,*** = hitchhike.

ˈthumb·tack *n* [C] short pin with a wide head for pushing in with the thumb.

thump /θəmp/ *vt,vi* **1** strike heavily; hit with the fists: *He ~ed on the door. The two boys began to ~ one another. He was ~ing out a tune on the piano,* playing noisily. **2** beat(7) heavily: *His heart ~ed with excitement.* □ *n* [C] (noise of, or as of, a) heavy blow (esp one given with the fist): *Give him a friendly ~ on the back.*

thun·der /ˈθəndər/ *n* [U] **1** noise which usually follows a flash of lightning: *a loud crash/a long roll of ~.* **2** loud noise like thunder: *the ~ of the guns.* ***steal sb's thunder,*** spoil his attempt to be impressive by anticipating him. □ *vi,vt* **1** (impersonal): *It was ~ing and lightening.* **2** make a noise like thunder: *The guns were ~ing.* **3** speak in a loud voice, attack violently in words.

ˈthunder·bolt *n* [C] **(a)** flash of lightning with a crash of thunder. **(b)** (*fig*) unexpected and terrible event.

ˈthunder·clap *n* [C] sudden noise of thunder.

thun·der·ous /-əs/ *adj* making a noise like thunder: *~ous applause.*

ˈthunder·storm *n* [C] storm of thunder and lightning, usually with heavy rain.

ˈthunder·struck *adj* (*fig*) amazed.

Thurs. *abbr* = Thursday.

Thurs·day /ˈθərzdi, -ˌdei/ *n* fifth day of the week.

thus /ðəs/ *adv* in this way; so: *~ far,* to this point.

thwack /θwæk/ *vt, n* = whack.

thwart /θwɔrt/ *vt* obstruct (and so defeat): *be ~ed in one's ambitions/aims.*

thy /ðai/ *adj* (*archaic*) (possessive form of *thou*) belonging to you (*sing*).

thyme /taim/ *n* [U] kind of herb.

thy·roid /ˈθaiˌrɔid/ *n* [C] (also **ˈthyroid gland**) gland in the front part of the neck, producing a substance which affects the body's growth and activity. ⇨ illus at head.

ti /ti/ *n* [C] (*music*) syllable used for the seventh note of a scale.

ti·ara /tiˈarə/ *n* [C] (*pl* ~s) **1** coronet for a woman. **2** triple crown worn by the Pope.

tibia /ˈtɪbiə/ *n* [C] (*pl* ~e /-biˌ(y)i/) inner and thicker of the two bones between the knee and the foot. ⇨ illus at skeleton.

tic /tɪk/ *n* [C] involuntary twitching of the muscles (esp of the face).

tick¹ /tɪk/ *n* [C] **1** light, regularly repeated sound, esp of a clock or watch. **2** small mark (often) to show that something is correct. □ *vi,vt* **1** (of a clock, etc) make ticks(1): *The child put the watch to its ear and listened to it ~ing.* ***What makes him/it tick?*** (*informal*) What makes him/it act, behave, etc like that? **2** (of a clock): *~ away the hours.* **3** ***tick over,*** (of an internal-combustion engine) be operating with gears disconnected. **4** run, function (esp of a clockwork or other precision instrument): *Let's take this pencil sharpener apart and see what makes it ~,* see how it works. **5** put a tick(2) against: *~ off a name/the items on a list.*

tick² /tɪk/ *n* [C] small parasite that fastens itself on the skin and sucks blood.

ticker /ˈtɪkər/ *n* [C] **1** telegraphic machine which automatically prints news on paper tape. **2** (*sl*) heart.

ˈticker tape, paper tape used in a ticker.

ˌticker-tape paˈrade, one (traditional in New York City) in which ticker tape is showered on the guest of honor from skyscraper windows.

ticket /ˈtɪkɪt/ *n* [C] **1** written or printed piece of card or paper giving the holder the right to travel in a train, bus, ship, etc or to a seat in a theater, concert hall, etc: *Do you want a one-way or a round-trip ~?* **2** piece of card or paper, label, attached to something and giving information, eg about the price, size of clothing, etc. **3** printed notice of an offense against traffic regulations (eg a parking offense): *get a (ˈparking) ~.* **4** list (as on a blank ballot) of candidates for election nominated by a single party. ***on the ticket,*** nominated. **5** ***(just) the ticket,*** (*informal*) the proper thing to do. □ *vt* **1** put a ticket (2) on; mark with a ticket. **2** give a ticket(3) to.

ˈticket ˌagent, seller of tickets for a railroad, to the theater, etc.

ˈticket ˌoffice, in an agency, where tickets are sold.

tickle /ˈtɪkəl/ *vt,vi* **1** excite the nerves of the skin by touching lightly, esp at sensitive parts, often so as to cause laughter: *~ him in the ribs.* **2** please (one's sense of humor, etc). ***tickled pink/to death,*** very pleased, amused: *I was ~d pink at the praise given to me.* **3** have, feel, cause, an itching or tingling sensation: *My nose ~s.*

tick·lish /ˈtɪklɪʃ/ *adj* **(a)** (of a person) easily made to laugh when tickled. **(b)** (of a problem, piece of work, etc) needing delicate care or attention: *be in a ticklish situation.*

ti·dal /ˈtaidəl/ *adj* of a tide or tides: *a ~ river*, in which the tide rises and falls.

ˈtidal wave, great ocean wave, eg one that is (thought to be) caused by an earthquake.

tid·bit /ˈtidˌbit/ *n* [C] attractive bit (of food, news, gossip, etc).

tide /taid/ *n* **1** [C,U] regular rise and fall in the level of the sea, caused by the attraction of the moon: *at high/low ~*. **2** [C] flow or tendency (of public opinion, feeling, etc): *The Republicans hoped for a turn of the ~*, that public opinion might turn in their favor. □ *vt* ***tide sb over (sth),*** help him to get through or survive (a period of difficulty, etc): *Will $50 ~ you over until you're paid?*

ˈtide·mark *n* highest point reached by a tide on a beach.

ˈtide ˌpool, pool of seawater left in depressions at the shore when the tide falls.

tid·ings /ˈtaidɪŋz/ *n pl* (*liter*) (used with a *sing* or *pl verb*) news: *glad ~*.

tidy /ˈtaidi/ *adj* (-ier, -iest) **1** arranged neatly and in order; having the habit of placing and keeping everything in its right place: *a ~ room/boy*. **2** (*informal*) fairly large (esp of money): *a ~ sum of money*. □ *vt,vi* make tidy: *You'd better ~ (up) the room before the guests arrive*.

ti·dily /ˈtaidəli/ *adv*

ti·di·ness /ˈtaidinɪs/ *n* [U]

tie[1] /tai/ *n* [C] **1** something (rope, ribbon) used for fastening. **2** (often *pl*) (*fig*) something that keeps people united: *the ties of friendship; family ties*. **3** equal score in a game, etc: *The game ended in a tie, 2-2*. **4** band of material worn round the neck of a shirt and knotted in front. **5** (*music*) curved line joining two notes of the same pitch that are to be played or sung as one. ⇨ illus at notation.

tie[2] /tai/ *vt,vi* (*present participle* tying, *pt,pp* tied) **1** fasten or bind (with string, rope, wire, etc): *tie a man's feet together; tie up a parcel*. **2** fasten by means of the strings, etc of: *tie on a label*. **3** arrange (a ribbon, etc) in the form of a bow or knot: *tie one's shoelaces; tie a ribbon/scarf; tie the ribbon in(to) a bow*. **4** make by tying: *tie a knot in a piece of string*. **5** be fastened: *Does this dress tie in front or at the back?* **6** (of players, teams, candidates in a competitive examination) make the same score (as): *The two teams tied. They tied for first place (in the examination)*. **7** (special uses with *adverbial particles* and *prepositions*):

tie sb down, restrict his freedom: *He's not in a hurry to get married; he doesn't want to get tied down*. ***tie sb down to sth,*** restrict him to (the terms of a contract, etc).

tie (sth) in with sth, link, agree, with: *Doesn't this tie in with what we were told last week?*

tie sth up, **(a)** invest (capital) so that it is not easily available. **(b)** ensure that (property, eg land, buildings) can be used, sold, etc only under certain conditions. **(c)** block (traffic) because of a wrecked or stalled car, broken traffic light, etc. ***be/get tied up (with sth/sb),*** be, get, involved (with it/him) so that one has no time for other things: *I'm afraid I can't help you now—I'm too tied up with other things*.

ˈtie-up *n* [C] blockage of traffic, work, etc.

tier /tɪr/ *n* [C] row (esp of seats) parallel to and rising one above another, eg in a theater or stadium.

tiff /tɪf/ *n* [C] slight quarrel.

ti·ger /ˈtaigər/ *n* [C] large, fierce animal of the cat family with yellow fur with black stripes. ⇨ illus at cat.

ti·ger·ish /-ɪʃ/ *adj* like, cruel as, a tiger.

tight /tait/ *adj* (-er, -est) **1** fastened, fixed, fitting, held, closely: *a ~ knot. The drawer is so ~ that I can't open it*. **2** (esp in compounds) made so that something cannot get in or out: *ˈwater/ˈairˌ~*. **3** packed so as to occupy the smallest possible space or to get in as much as possible: *Make sure that the bags are filled/packed ~*. **4** (*informal*) having had too much alcoholic drink: *He gets ~ every payday*. **5** fully stretched: *a ~ rope*. **6** produced by pressure; causing difficulty. ***in a tight corner/spot,*** (*fig*) in a difficult or dangerous situation. ***a tight schedule,*** one that it is difficult to keep to. ***a tight squeeze,*** condition of being uncomfortably crowded: *We got everyone into the bus, but it was a ~ squeeze*. **7** (of money) not easily obtainable, eg on loan from banks: *Money is ~*. □ *adv* = tightly: *squeeze/hold it ~*. ***sit tight,*** ⇨ sit(1).

ˌtight-ˈfisted, miserly.

ˌtight-ˈlaced *adj* = strait-laced.

ˌtight-ˈlipped *adj* (*fig*) saying little or nothing.

tight·ly *adv*

tight·ness /-nɪs/ *n* [U]

ˈtight·rope *n* [C] one on which acrobats perform.

tighten /ˈtaitən/ *vt,vi* make or become tight(er): *~ (up) the screws; ~ the ropes of the tent*.

tights /taits/ *n pl* (often ***a pair of tights***) **1** close-fitting (usually nylon) clothing covering the hips, legs and feet, as worn by girls and women. **2** skintight clothing covering the legs and body, worn by acrobats, ballet dancers, etc.

tight·wad /ˈtaitˌwad/ *n* [C] (*sl*) miserly or stingy person.

ti·gress /ˈtaigrɪs/ *n* [C] female tiger.

tilde /ˈtɪldə/ *n* [C] **1** the mark (~) as used in this dictionary to replace the headword in the example sentences. **2** mark (~) placed over a vowel or consonant to indicate how it is to be sounded (as in Spanish *mañana*).

tile /ˈtaiəl/ *n* [C] (usually square or oblong) plate of baked clay for covering roofs, walls, etc, often painted with designs or pictures. □ *vt* (*pres p* tiling /ˈtailɪŋ/) cover (a roof, etc) with tiles.

til·ing /ˈtailɪŋ/ *n* [U] tile work.

till[1] /tɪl/ (also **until** /ˌənˈtɪl/) (*Note:* the choice between *till* and *until* is chiefly a matter of personal preference, though *until* is often considered more formal.) *conj* up to the time when: *Go straight on ~ you come to the post office and then turn left. She won't go away ~ you promise to help her*. □ *prep* up to the time when; up to; down to: *I shall wait ~ ten o'clock. He works from morning ~ night, day after day*.

till[2] /tɪl/ *n* [C] money drawer in a cash register.

till[3] /tɪl/ *vt* cultivate (land).

till·age /ˈtɪlɪdʒ/ *n* [U] act or process of tilling; tilled land.

tiller /ˈtɪlər/ *n* [C] lever (like a long handle) used to turn the rudder of a small boat.

tilt /tɪlt/ *vt,vi* (cause to) come into a sloping position (as by lifting one end); tip: *Don't ~ the table.* □ *n* [C] tilting; sloping position.

tim·ber /ˈtɪmbər/ *n* **1** [U] growing trees thought of as containing wood suitable for building, carpentry, etc: *The fire destroyed thousands of acres of ~.* **2** [C] large piece of shaped wood, beam, forming a support (eg in a roof or a ship).

tim·bered *adj* (of mountains, etc) covered with timber.

ˈtimber line, line of altitude in the high mountains above which trees do not grow.

time[1] /taɪm/ *n* **1** [U] all the days of the past, present and future: *past, present and future ~. The world exists in space and ~.* **2** [U] the passing of all the days, months and years, taken as a whole: *Time will show who is right.* **3** [U] (also with *a, an* and an *adjective*) portion or measure of time: *What a (long) ~ you have taken! Take your ~ over it,* Don't hurry. ***all the time,*** **(a)** during the whole period in question: *I looked all over the house for that letter, and it was in my pocket all the ~,* while I was searching. **(b)** at all times; first and last: *He's a businessman all the ~,* has no other interests in life. ***half the time,*** **(a)** as in: *He did the work in four hours; I could have done it in half the ~,* in two hours. **(b)** very often; nearly always: *He says he works hard, but he's asleep half the ~.* ***behind time,*** late: *The train is ten minutes behind ~.* ***for the time being,*** ⇨ be[1](7). ***on time,*** not late, punctual(ly): *The train is/came in on ~.* ***in no time,*** very soon; very quickly. ***stall for time,*** delay doing something in the hope that the situation will improve. **4** [U] point of time stated in hours and minutes of the day: *What ~ is it? What's the ~?* **5** [U] time measured in units (years, months, hours, etc): *The winner's ~ was 11 seconds.* ***pass the time of day (with...),*** exchange a greeting, say "Good morning!" etc. **6** [C,U] point or period of time associated with, or available or suitable for, a certain event, purpose, etc: *by the ~ we arrived home; every ~ I looked at her. It's ˈlunch ~. It's ~ I was going/~ for me to go,* I ought to leave now. ***at the same time,*** **(a)** together: *laugh and cry at the same ~.* **(b)** notwithstanding; nevertheless. ***from time to time; at times,*** occasionally; now and then. ***at all times,*** always. ***in time,*** **(a)** not late; early enough: *We were in ~ to catch the train.* **(b)** sooner or later: *You will learn how to do it in ~.* ***it's time (that)...*** (+ *verb* in *pt*), it is time to ...: *It's ~ we left,* time (for us) to leave. ***do/serve time,*** (*informal*) go to prison for a period. **7** [C] occasion: *this/that/next/another ~; the ~ before last; for the first/last ~.* ***time and again; times without number,*** again and again; repeatedly. **8** (*pl*) (used to show multiplication): *Three ~s five is/are fifteen,* 3 × 5 = 15. **9** [C] (often *pl*) period of time, more or less definite, associated with certain events, circumstances, persons, etc: *in ancient/prehistoric ~s.* **10** [C] (often *pl*) the conditions of life, the circumstances, etc of a period characterized by certain qualities, etc: *We lived through terrible ~s during the war years. Times are good/bad,* (often meaning that it is easy/difficult to make a living). ***behind the times,*** old-fashioned. ***have a ˌgood ˈtime,*** enjoy oneself. ***have the ˌtime of one's ˈlife,*** (*informal*) experience a period of exceptional happiness or enjoyment. **11** [U] **Greenwich/local/summer/standard time,** ⇨ these entries. **12** (*music*) measurement depending on the number of rhythmic beats in successive bars of a piece of music. ⇨ illus at notation. ***beat time,*** show the rhythm by movements made with the hand or a stick (called a *baton*).

ˈtime bomb, one designed to explode at some time after being dropped, placed in position.

ˈtime card/sheet, one for a record of workmen's hours of work.

ˈtime clock, one that records one's hours of work mechanically.

ˈtime-consuming *adj* (of a task) requiring a great deal of time to do.

ˈtime-honored *adj* respected because of its age.

ˈtime·keeper *n* [C] **(a)** one who, or that which, records the time spent by workers at their work. **(b)** (of a watch, etc) one that keeps time well, etc: *a good/bad ~keeper.*

ˈtime lag, interval of time between two connected events (eg between a flash of lightning and the thunder).

ˈtime limit, limited period of time; last moment of this: *set a ~ limit for the completion of a job.*

ˈtime·piece *n* [C] (*dated*) clock; watch.

ˈtime-saving *adj* serving to save time: *a ˌ~-saving iˈdea.*

ˈtime·server *n* [C] **(a)** person who conforms to the beliefs, tastes, etc of the times. **(b)** person who holds a job merely to earn retirement benefits. **(c)** (*informal*) convict.

ˈtime signal, signal (eg a series of pips) for telling the time (on a radio program, over the telephone, etc).

ˈtime signature, (music) indication (by numbers) of the time (12) in which a piece is to be played. ⇨ illus at notation.

ˈtime switch, switch set to operate at a desired time (eg to turn a heating system on or off).

ˈtime·table *n* [C] list showing the days or hours at which events will take place, work will be done, etc esp a list showing the times at which trains, buses, etc will arrive and depart.

ˈtime·worn *adj* **(a)** worn down by age: *a ~worn bridge.* **(b)** stale, overused: *a ~worn excuse.*

ˈtime ˌzone, one of the 24 zones of longitude, each of which is at a different hour of the day or night.

time[2] /taɪm/ *vt* **1** choose the time or moment for; arrange the time of: *He ~d his journey so that he arrived before dark.* **2** measure the time taken by or for (a race, runner, an action or event). **3** regulate: *~ the speed of a machine.*

timer /ˈtaɪmər/ *n* [C] **(a)** person who times races, etc. **(b)** instrument which times the operation of a machine, stove, etc by ringing a bell at the end of a set period. **(c)** = time switch.

tim·ing *n* [U] act of determining or regulating the (order of) occurrence of an action, event, etc to achieve the desired results: *The timing of last* *night's performance was excellent.*

time·ly /ˈtaimli/ *adj* (-ier, -iest) occurring at just the right time.

timid /ˈtɪmɪd/ *adj* easily frightened: *He's as ~ as a rabbit.*

tim·id·ity /tɪˈmɪdəti/ *n* [U]

timid·ly *adv*

tim·or·ous /ˈtɪmərəs/ *adj* timid.

tim·or·ous·ly *adv*

tim·pani /ˈtɪmpəni/ *n pl* set of kettledrums (eg of an orchestra). ⇨ illus at percussion.

tim·pan·ist /ˈtɪmpənɪst/ *n* [C] player of a kettledrum.

tin /tɪn/ *n* **1** [U] soft, white metal (symbol **Sn**) used in alloys and for coating iron sheets. **2** [U] sheet iron or steel coated with tin. ***have a tin ear,*** (*fig*) not good at distinguishing musical notes, the speech sounds of foreign languages, etc. **3** [C] (rare) = (tin)can. □ *vt* (-nn-) put a coating of tin on.

ˌtin ˈcan = can.

ˈtin·foil *n* [U] tin in thin, flexible sheets, used for wrapping and packing cigarettes, candy, etc.

tinny *adj* (-ier, -iest) of or like tin (eg in sound): *a tin piano.*

ˈtin·type *n* [C] old kind of photograph made on sheet iron.

tine /tain/ *n* [C] **1** point, prong (eg of a fork, etc). **2** branch of a deer's antler.

tinge /tɪndʒ/ *vt* **1** color slightly (with red, etc). **2** (*fig*) (esp in *pp*) affect slightly: *admiration ~d with envy.* □ *n* [C] slight coloring or mixture (*of*): *There was a ~ of sadness in her voice.*

tingle /ˈtɪŋgəl/ *vi* have a pricking or stinging feeling in the skin: *His fingers ~d with the cold. The children were tingling with excitement.* □ *n* [C] tingling feeling.

tin·ker /ˈtɪŋkər/ *n* [C] worker who repairs kettles, pans, etc. □ *vi* work in an inexpert way (at): *Please don't ~ with the engine of my car.*

tinkle /ˈtɪŋkəl/ *vi,vt* (cause to) make a succession of light, ringing sounds, eg of a small bell. □ *n* (*sing*) such sounds: *the ~ of a bell.*

tin·sel /ˈtɪnsəl/ *n* [U] **1** glittering metallic substance made in sheets, strips and threads, used for ornament: *trim a Christmas tree with ~.* **2** cheap, showy brilliance. □ *vt* (-l-) trim with tinsel.

tint /tɪnt/ *n* [C] (esp pale or delicate) shade or variety of color: *~s of green in the sky at dawn.* □ *vt* give a tint to; put a tint on.

tiny /ˈtaini/ *adj* (-ier, -iest) very small.

-tion /-ʃən/ (also **-sion** /-ʃən/, **-ation** /-eiʃən/, **-ition** /-ɪʃən/) *suffix* (*verb* + ~ = *noun*): *relation; confession; hesitation; competition.*

-tional /-ʃənəl/ *adj*

-tion·ally /-ʃənəli/ *adv*

tip[1] /tɪp/ *n* [C] **1** pointed or thin end of something: *the tips of one's fingers/the ˈfingertips.* ***(have sth) on the ˌtip of one's ˈtongue,*** (be) just going to say (it), just about to remember (it). **2** small piece put at the end of something: *cigarettes with filter tips.* □ *vt* (-pp-) supply with a tip(2): *filter-tipped cigarettes.*

ˈtip·toe *adv* ***on tiptoe,*** on the tips of one's toes: *be on tiptoe with excitement.* □ *vi* walk on tiptoe: *She tiptoed out of the bedroom.*

tip[2] /tɪp/ *vt,vi* (-pp-) ***tip (sth) up,*** (cause to) rise, lean or tilt on one side or at one end: *The table tipped up.* ***tip sth (over),*** (cause to) overbalance or overturn: *Careful! You'll tip the canoe over.* ***tip the scale (at),*** **(a)** be just enough to cause one scale or pan (of a balance) to go lower than the other. **(b)** (*fig*) be the deciding factor (for or against). **(c)** weigh: *He tipped the scale at 200 pounds.*

tip[3] /tɪp/ *vt* (-pp-) **1** touch or strike lightly: *His bat just tipped the ball.* **2** give a tip to (1,2 below): *tip the waiter.* ***tip sb off,*** (*informal*) give him a warning, information or a hint. □ *n* [C] **1** gift of money to a porter, waiter, etc for services: *leave a tip on the table*, eg in a restaurant. **2** piece of advice on something, eg information about the probable winner of a horse race, about a person wanted by the police, etc: *If you take my tip* (= advice) *you'll say you're sorry.* **3** ⇨ tap².

ˈtip-off *n* [C] hint of warning: *give the police a tip-off.*

ti·pi /ˈtipi/ = tepee.

tipple /ˈtɪpəl/ *n* [U] (usually alcoholic) drink: *My favorite ~ is sherry.*

tip·ster /ˈtɪpstər/ *n* [C] person who gives tips about races. ⇨ tip³(2).

tipsy /ˈtɪpsi/ *adj* (*informal*) slightly drunk.

tip·top, tip-top /ˈtɪpˌtap/ *adj* (*informal*) excellent, superb: *He's in ~ condition.*

ti·rade /taiˈreid/ *n* [C] long, angry or scolding speech.

tire[1] /ˈtaiər/ *n* [C] band of rubber on the rim of a wheel, esp (*pneumatic ~*) the kind on bicycle and automobile wheels.

tire[2] /ˈtaiər/ *vt,vi* make or become weary, in need of rest, etc: *The long walk ~d the child/~d him out/made him ~d.* ***be tired of,*** have had enough of: *be ~d of boiled eggs*, have had them too often.

tired /ˈtaiərd/ *adj* weary in body or mind: *feel ~d after a long climb.* ***tired out,*** completely exhausted.

tired·ness /-nɪs/ *n* [U]

tire·less *adj* **(a)** not easily tired: *a ~less worker.* **(b)** continuing a long time: *~less energy.*

ˈtire·some /-səm/ *adj* troublesome; tedious.

tis·sue /ˈtɪʃu/ *n* **1** [C,U] mass of cells and cell products in an animal body: *ˈmuscular ~.* **2** [C,U] (also **tissue paper**) thin, soft paper for wrapping things, protecting delicate articles, etc. **3** [C] a piece of soft paper for cosmetic and toilet use. **4** [C] (*fig*) series: *a ~ of lies.*

tit[1] /tɪt/ *n* [C] kinds of small bird.

tit[2] /tɪt/ *n* (only in) ***tit for tat,*** blow for blow.

tit[3] /tɪt/ *n* ⚠ (*vulgar sl*) nipple; woman's breast.

tit·bit /ˈtɪtbɪt/ = tidbit.

tit·il·late /ˈtɪtəˌleit/ *vt* stimulate or excite pleasantly.

tit·il·la·tion /ˌtɪtəˈleiʃən/ *n* [U]

titi·vate /ˈtɪtəˌveit/ *vt,vi* (*informal*) spruce up: *She was titivating herself in front of the mirror.*

title /ˈtaitəl/ *n* **1** [C] name of a book, poem, picture, etc. **2** [C] word used to show a person's rank, occupation, status, etc, eg President, Professor, Doctor, Miss. **3** [C,U] (*legal*) right or claim, esp right to the possession of a position, property: *Has he any ~ to the land?*

titled /ˈtaitəld/ *adj* having a title of nobility: *a ~d lady*, eg a duchess.

ˈtitle deed, document proving a title(3) to property.

ˈtitle role, part in a play that gives the play its name: *We went to the movie "Anna Christie" with Greta Garbo in the title role.*

tit·ter /ˈtɪtər/ *vt, n* [C] (give a) nervous or embarrassed little laugh.

titu·lar /ˈtɪtʃələr/ *adj* **1** held by virtue of a title: *~ possessions.* **2** existing in name but not having authority or duties: *the ~ head of the corporation.*

tizzy /ˈtɪzi/ *n* ***be in a tizzy,*** (*informal*) in a nervous state.

T-junction /ˈti ˌdʒəŋkʃən/ *n* [C] ⇨ T,t.

TKO /ˌti ˌkei ˈou/ *abbr* = technical knockout.

tkt. *abbr* = ticket.

TM *abbr* = trademark.

TN[1] *postal abbr* = Tennessee. ⇨App 6.

tn.[2] *abbr* = ton(s).

tnpk. *abbr* = turnpike.

TNT /ˌti ˌen ˈti/ *n* (*informal*) = trinitrotoluene.

to[1] /tu/ *adverbial particle* **1** to or in the usual or required position or state: *stand ˈto,* be alert. **2** ***to and fro,*** ⇨ fro. **3** ⇨ come(11), bring(5), and fall²(15).

to[2] /tə; *before vowels and strong form:* tu/ *participle* (marking the *infinitive*) **1** (used after many *verbs* but not after *can, do, may, must, shall, will*): *He wants to go.* **2** (used with *adverbs* of functions, purpose, result, outcome): *They came (in order) to help me. He turned out to be ninety.* **3** (limiting the meanings of *adjectives* and *adverbs*): *The book is easy to understand. He's old enough to go to school.* **4** (a subsequent fact): *The good old days have gone never to return,* and will never return. *He awoke to find himself* (= and found himself) *in a strange room.* **5** (used with an *infinitive* as a *noun*): *It is wrong to steal.* **6** (used as a substitute for the *infinitive*): *We didn't want to go home but we had to,* ie had to go home.

to[3] /tə; *before vowels and strong form:* tu/ *prep* **1** in the direction of; toward: *walk to work; point to it; hold it (up) to the light; turn to the right.* **2** (*fig*) toward (a condition, quality, etc): *a tendency to laziness; slow to anger.* **3** (introducing or referring back to the *indirect object*): *Who did you give it to? The man I gave it to has left.* **4** as far as: *from beginning to end; count (up) to ten.* **5** before: *a quarter to six.* **6** until: *from morning to night. I didn't stay to the end of the meeting.* **7** (of comparison, ratio, reference): *I prefer walking to climbing. We won by six to three.*

toad /toud/ *n* [C] animal like a frog that lives on land except when breeding.

ˈtoad·stool *n* [C] kinds of fungus, some of them poisonous. ⇨ illus at fungus.

toast[1] /toust/ *n* [U] (slice of) bread made brown and crisp by heating: *two slices of ~.* □ *vt,vi* **1** (of bread) make or become brown and crisp by heating. **2** warm (oneself, one's toes, etc) before a fire.

toaster *n* [C] electric device for toasting bread.

toast[2] /toust/ *vt* wish happiness, success, etc to (a person or thing) while raising a glass of wine: *~ the bride and bridegroom.* □ *n* [C] act of toasting; person, etc toasted: *propose/drink a ~.*

to·bacco /təˈbækou/ *n* [U] (*pl* for kinds of tobacco leaf) (plant having) leaves which are dried, cured and used for smoking (in pipes, cigars, cigarettes) or as snuff: *This is a mixture of the best ~s.*

to·bac·co·nist /təˈbækənɪst/ *n* [C] shop, person, selling tobacco, cigarettes, etc.

to·bog·gan /təˈbagən/ *n* [C] long, narrow sledge without runners for sliding on ice. □ *vi* go down a snow-covered or ice-covered slope on a toboggan.

to·day /təˈdei/ *adv, n* (*sing* only) **1** (on) this day: *Today is Sunday. Have you seen ~'s newspaper? We're leaving ~ week/a week from ~,* in one week's time. **2** (at) this present age or period: *the writers/the young people of ~.*

toddle /ˈtadəl/ *vi* walk with short, uncertain steps as a baby does.

tod·dler /ˈtadlər/ *n* [C] baby who can toddle.

tod·dy /ˈtadi/ *n* [C] (often **hot ˈtoddy**) sweet, spiced, alcoholic drink, heated when served.

toe /tou/ *n* [C] **1** each of the five divisions of the front part of the foot; similar part of an animal's foot. ⇨ illus at leg. ***tread/step on sb's toes,*** (*fig*) offend him. ***from ˌhead to ˈtoe,*** from head to foot, completely. ***on one's toes,*** (*fig*) alert, ready for action. ***on tiptoe,*** ⇨ tiptoe. **2** part of a sock, shoe, etc covering the toes. □ *vt* touch, reach, with the toes. ***toe the line,*** (*fig*) behave properly; obey orders given to one as a member of a group or party.

ˈtoe·cap *n* [C] outer covering of the toe of a shoe or boot, esp for reinforcement.

ˈtoe·nail *n* [C] nail of the toe of a human being.

tof·fee /ˈtɔfi/ *n* [C,U] (piece of) hard, brown sticky candy made by boiling sugar, butter, etc.

tog /tag/ *vt* (-gg-) (*informal*) put on smart clothes.

togs *n pl* (*informal*) clothes.

toga /ˈtougə/ *n* [C] (*pl* ~s) loose flowing outer clothing worn by men in ancient Rome.

to·gether /təˈgeðər/ *adv* **1** in company: *They went for a walk ~.* ***together with,*** as well as; in addition to; and also: *These new facts, ~ with the evidence you have already heard, prove the prisoner's innocence.* **2** so as to be in the same place, to be in contact, to be united: *Tie the ends ~. The leader called his men ~.* ***put your/our, etc heads together,*** consult with each other (to find a solution, make plans, etc). **3** at the same time: *All his troubles seemed to come ~.*

to·gether·ness /-nɪs/ *n* [C] friendship; feeling of unity.

tog·gle /ˈtagəl/ *n* [C] bar or pin attached (at center or end) to something so as to swivel.

ˈtoggle switch, electric switch worked by a lever with a swivel base.

toil /ˈtɔiəl/ *vi* (*pres p* toiling /ˈtɔilɪŋ/) work long or hard (at a task); move with difficulty and trouble: *The workmen ~ed in the hot sun.* □ *n* [U] hard work: *after long ~.*

toiler /ˈtɔilər/ *n* [C] hard worker.

toilet /ˈtɔilɪt/ *n* **1** [U] process of dressing, arranging the hair, etc: *She spent only a few minutes on her ~.* **2** (as an *adjective*): *a ˈ~ set, ˈ~ articles,* such things as a hairbrush, comb, etc. **3** (*informal*) lavatory; bathroom. **4** = toilet bowl.

ˈtoilet ˌbowl, (usually porcelain) water-flushed bowl, with swivel seat, for depositing human waste.

ˈtoilet paper, for use in a lavatory.

ˈtoilet ˌseat, swivel seat on toilet bowl.

to·ken /ˈtoukən/ *n* **1** [C] sign, evidence, guarantee or mark: *I am giving you this watch as a ~ of my affection.* **2** (as an *adjective*) acting as a preliminary or small-scale substitute: *The enemy offered only a ~ resistance,* did not resist seriously.

ˌtoken ˈpayment, payment of a small part of what is owed, made to show that the debt is recognized.

told *pt,pp* of tell.

tol·er·ance /ˈtalərəns/ *n* [U] quality of tolerating opinions, beliefs, customs, behavior, etc different from one's own: *religious/racial ~.*

tol·er·ant /ˈtalərənt/ *adj* having or showing tolerance: *Mr. X is not very ~ of criticism.*

tol·er·ant·ly *adv*

tol·er·ate /ˈtaləˌreit/ *vt* **1** put up with, allow, without protest: *I won't ~ your impudence/your doing that.* **2** put up with the company of: *How can you ~ that rude clerk?*

tol·er·able /ˈtalərəbəl/ *adj* (*formal*) that can be tolerated; fairly good: *tolerable food.*

tol·er·ably /-əbli/ *adv*

tol·er·ation /ˌtaləˈreiʃən/ tolerance, esp the practice of allowing religious freedom.

toll¹ /toul/ *n* [C] **1** payment required for the use of a road, bridge, harbor, etc. **2** (*fig*) something paid, lost or suffered: *The war took a heavy ~ of the nation's men.*

ˈtoll booth, booth for the man in charge of a toll gate.

ˈtoll gate, gate across a road at which a toll is payable.

toll² /toul/ *vt,vi* (of a bell) (cause to) ring with slow, regular strokes: *The funeral bell ~ed solemnly.* □ *n* (*sing* only) tolling stroke of a bell.

tom·a·hawk /ˈtaməˌhɔk/ *n* [C] hatchet with head of stone or metal, sometimes combined with a tobacco pipe, used for fighting and in ceremonies by North American Indians.

tom·ato /təˈmeitou/ *n* [C] (*pl* ~es) (plant with a) soft, juicy, (usually) red fruit: (as an *adjective*) *~ juice.* ⇨ illus at vegetable.

tomb /tum/ *n* [C] place dug in the ground, cut out of rock, etc for a dead body, usually with a monument over it.

ˈtomb·stone *n* [C] inscribed stone over a tomb.

tom·boy /ˈtamˌbɔi/ *n* [C] girl who likes rough, noisy games and play.

tom·cat /ˈtamˌkæt/ *n* [C] male cat.

tome /toum/ *n* [C] (*formal*) large, heavy book.

to·mor·row /təˈmarou, -mɔr-/ *adv, n* (*sing* only) (on) the day after today: *If today is Monday, ~ will be Tuesday and the day after ~ will be Wednesday. The announcement will appear in ~'s newspapers.*

tom·tom /ˈtamˌtam/ *n* [C] native (African, Asian, American, etc) drum, usually beaten with the hands.

ton /tən/ *n* [C] **1** measure of weight (2,000 lb in the US); *metric ton,* 2,204.6 lb or 1,000 kg. **2** (*informal*) large weight, quantity or number: *He has tons of money.*

to·nal /ˈtounəl/ *adj* (*music*) of tone or tones.

to·nal·ity /touˈnæləti/ *n* [C] (*pl* -ies) (*music*) character of a melody, depending on the scale in which it is written, etc.

tone¹ /toun/ *n* **1** [C] sound, esp with reference to its quality, pitch, duration, feeling, etc: *the sweet ~(s) of a violin; a serious ~ of voice; ˈdial ~,* signal that a telephone is ready for dialing. **2** [C] the pitch aspect of a (usually stressed) syllable; rise, fall, etc of the pitch of the voice in speaking: *In "Are you ill?" there is a rising ~ on "ill."* **3** (*sing* only) general spirit, character, morale, of a community, etc: *The ~ of the school is excellent.* **4** [C] shade (of color); degree (of light): *a carpet in ~s of brown.* **5** [C] (*music*) any one of the five larger intervals between one note and the next. **6** [U] proper and normal condition of (parts of) the body: *good muscular/muscle ~.*

tone·less *adj* not having color, spirit, etc; dull: *answer in a ~less voice.*

tone·less·ly *adv*

tone² /toun/ *vt,vi* **1** give a particular tone of sound or color to. **2** ***tone (sth) down,*** make or become less intense: *The artist ~d down the brighter colors. You'd better ~ down some of the offensive statements in your article.* **3** ***tone (sth) up,*** make or become more healthy, intense, brighter, etc: *Exercise ~s up the muscles.*

tongs /taŋz, tɔŋz/ *n pl* (also ***a pair of tongs***) one of various kinds of U-shaped tool for taking up and holding something: *ˈsugar ~.* ***be/go at it hammer and tongs,*** ⇨ hammer(1).

tongue /təŋ/ *n* **1** [C] movable organ in the mouth, used in talking, tasting, licking, etc: *Don't put your ~ out at me!* ⇨ illus at head, mouth. ***(have sth) on the tip of one's tongue,*** ⇨ tip¹(1). ***have one's tongue in one's cheek,*** say something that one does not intend to be taken seriously. ***have lost one's tongue,*** be too shy to speak. ***hold one's tongue,*** be silent, stop talking. **2** [C] language: *one's mother ~,* one's native language. **3** [C,U] animal's tongue as an article of food: *ham and ~ sandwiches.* **4** something like a tongue in shape or use, eg the strip of leather under the laces of a shoe, a flame.

ˈtongue lashing, (*informal*) scolding.

ˈtongue-tied *adj* silent; unable or unwilling to speak through shyness, fear, etc.

ˈtongue twister, word or succession or words difficult to say quickly and correctly.

tonic /ˈtanɪk/ *n* [C], *adj* **1** (something, eg, medicine) giving strength or energy: *get a bottle of ~ from the doctor. Praise can be a mental ~.* **2** (*music*) = keynote. **3** = tonic water: *a gin and ~.*

ˈtonic water, (bottled) water with quinine.

to·night /təˈnait/ *adv, n* (*sing* only) (on) the night of today: *last night, ~, and tomorrow night; ~'s news,* on the evening radio or TV.

ton·nage /ˈtənɪdʒ/ *n* [U] **1** internal cubic capacity of a ship. **2** total tonnage(1) of a country's merchant shipping. **3** charge per ton on cargo, etc for transport.

ton·sil /ˈtansəl/ *n* [C] either of two small oval masses of tissue at the sides of the throat, near the root of the tongue. ⇨ illus at head.

ton·sil·itis /ˌtansəlˈaitɪs/ *n* [U] inflammation of the tonsils.

too /tu/ *adv* **1** also; as well, in addition: *I, too, have been to Paris*, eg I, as well as he, you, etc. *I've been to Paris too*, eg to Paris as well as to Rome, Milan, etc. **2** moreover: *There was frost last night, and in May too!* **3** to, in, a higher degree than is allowable, required, etc: *We've had too much rain lately. You're driving too fast for safety. These shoes are much too small for me.* **4** (phrases) ***go/carry sth too far,*** ⇨ far²(2). ***all too soon/quickly, etc,*** sooner, more quickly, etc than is desired: *The holidays ended all too soon.* ***none too early, soon, etc,*** not at all too early, etc: *We were none too early for the train*, we caught the train with very little time to spare. ***one too many,*** ⇨ many(1). ***only too*** (+ *adj*) ⇨ only².

took *pt* of take¹.

tool /tul/ *n* [C] **1** instrument held in the hand(s) and used by workmen. **2** person used by another for dishonest purposes: *He was a mere ~ in the hands of the dictator*.

toot /tut/ *n* [C] short, sharp warning sound from a horn, whistle, trumpet, etc. □ *vi,vt* (cause to) give out a toot.

tooth /tuθ/ *n* [C] (*pl* teeth /tiθ/) **1** each of the hard, white, structures rooted in the gums, used for biting and chewing: *have a ~ pulled,* ie by a dentist. ⇨ illus at mouth. ***in the teeth of,*** against the full force of; in opposition to. ***armed to the teeth,*** completely and elaborately armed. ***long in the tooth,*** old; experienced. ***escape by the ˌskin of one's ˈteeth,*** have a narrow escape. ***fight ˌtooth and ˈnail,*** fiercely, with a great effort. ***get one's teeth into sth,*** attack (a job) vigorously. ***have a sweet tooth,*** ⇨ sweet(1). ***show one's teeth,*** take up a threatening attitude. **2** part of a comb, saw or rake like a tooth. ***go over/through sth with aˌfine-ˈtooth comb,*** examine it closely and thoroughly. **3** (*pl*) (*informal*) effective force: *When will the new legislation be given some teeth*, be made effective?

ˈtooth·ache *n* (*sing* only, with or without *a/the*) ache in a tooth or teeth.

ˈtooth·brush *n* [C] one for cleaning the teeth.

tooth·less *adj* without teeth: *a ~less grin*.

ˈtooth·paste/powder *n* [U] for cleaning the teeth.

ˈtooth·pick *n* [C] short, pointed piece of wood, etc, for removing bits of food from between the teeth.

tootle /ˈtutəl/ *vi, n* [C] toot softly or continuously, as on a flute.

top¹ /tap/ *n* **1** (usually *sing* with *the*) highest part or point: *at the top of the hill; the hilltop.* ***on top,*** above: *The green book is at the bottom of the pile and the red one is on top.* ***on (the) top of,*** **(a)** over, resting on: *Put the red book on (the) top of the others.* **(b)** in addition to: *He borrowed $100 from me for the trip and then, on top of that, asked me if he could borrow my car, too.* ***from ˌtop to ˈbottom,*** completely. ***blow one's top,*** (*informal*) explode in rage. **2** [C] upper surface, eg of a table: *polish the top of a table.* ***on ˌtop of the ˈworld,*** (*informal*) extremely happy, satisfied with everything: *I'm feeling on top of the world today!* ***on top of things/one's work,*** (*informal*) able to cope. **3** [C] highest rank, foremost (or most important) place: *He came out at the top of the list*, eg of examination results. ***come to the top,*** (*fig*) win fame, success, etc. ***reach/be at the top of the ladder/heap,*** the highest position in a profession, career, etc. **4** [C] greatest height or degree: ***shout at the top of one's ˈvoice,*** ⇨ voice(3). **5** (as an *adjective*) highest in position or degree: *on the top shelf; at top speed; charge top prices.*

ˌtop ˈbrass, (*informal*) senior management.

ˈtop·coat *n* [C] = overcoat (the usual word).

ˌtop ˈdog, (*sl*) master, winner, etc.

ˌtop-ˈflight/-ˈnotch *adj* (*informal*) first-rate; best possible: *top-flight French authors*.

ˌtop ˈhat, (a) tall silk hat. **(b)** (*informal*) the highest social class.

ˈtop-ˌheavy *adj* over-weighted at the top so as to be in danger of falling.

ˈtop·knot *n* knot of hair, bunch of feathers, etc on the top of the head.

top·less *adj* (of a woman's clothes) leaving the breasts bare: *a topless swimsuit*.

ˈtop·most /-ˌmoust/ *adj* highest.

ˌtop ˈpeople, those at the top of their profession, holding the highest positions, etc.

ˌtop-ˈranking *adj* of the highest rank.

ˌtop ˈsecret, needing to be secret because very important.

ˈtop soil, soil on the surface.

top² /tap/ *vt* (-pp-) **1** provide a top for; be a top for; be a top to: *a cake topped by/with icing.* **2** ***top sth off,*** finish; complete: *top off a skyscraper with a cornice; the hostess topped off dinner with homemade cherry pie.* **3** surpass, be taller or higher than: *Our exports have just topped the previous record.* ***to top it all,*** add the last (and surprising, etc) touch. **4** cut the tops off: *pull up and top carrots*, take them from the ground and cut off the leaves.

top³ /tap/ *n* [C] toy that spins and balances on a point. ***sleep like a top,*** sleep deeply.

to·paz /ˈtouˌpæz/ *n* [U] transparent yellow mineral; [C] gem cut from this.

topic /ˈtapɪk/ *n* [C] subject for discussion.

topi·cal /-kəl/ *adj* of interest now: *~al news.*

topi·cally /-kli/ *adv*

top·ogra·phy /təˈpagrəfi/ *n* [U] (description of the) features, eg rivers, valleys, roads, of a place or district.

topo·graphi·cal /ˌtapəˈgræfɪkəl/ *adj*

topo·graphi·cally /-kli/ *adv*

topple /ˈtapəl/ *vi,vt* (cause to) be unsteady and fall (over): *The pile of books ~d over/down. The dictator was ~d from power.*

tor /tɔr/ *n* [C] small hill; rocky peak.

torch /tɔrtʃ/ *n* [C] **1** piece of wood, etc soaked in oil, etc for carrying or using as a flaming light. **2** (*fig*) something that gives enlightenment: *the ~ of learning*.

ˈtorch·light *n* [U] light of a torch: (as an *adj*) *a ~light procession*.

tore *pt* of tear².
tor·ea·dor /ˈtɔriəˌdɔr/ *n* [C] bullfighter (usually on a horse).
tor·ment /ˈtɔrˌment/ *n* [U] (something that causes) severe bodily or mental pain or suffering: *be in ~; suffer ~ from an aching tooth.* □ *vt* /tɔrˈment/ cause severe suffering to; annoy: *~ed with pain/hunger.*
tor·men·tor /tɔrˈmentər/ *n* [C] person who, that which, torments.
torn *pp* of tear².
tor·nado /tɔrˈneidou/ *n* [C] (*pl* ~es) violent and destructive whirlwind.
tor·pedo /tɔrˈpidou/ *n* [C] (*pl* ~es) cigar-shaped self-propelling shell filled with explosives and traveling below the surface of the sea, used to attack ships. □ *vt* **1** attack or destroy with a torpedo. **2** (*fig*) attack (a policy, institution, etc) and make it ineffective: *Who ~ed the Disarmament Conference?*
torˈpedo boat, small, fast surface combat boat carrying and firing torpedoes.
tor·rent /ˈtɔrənt/ *n* [C] **1** violent, rushing stream of liquid (esp water): *mountain ~s; ~s of rain.* **2** (*fig*) violent outpouring: *a ~ of abuse/insults.*
tor·ren·tial /təˈrenʃəl/ *adj* of, like, caused by, a torrent: *~ial rain.*
torso /ˈtɔrsou/ *n* [C] (*pl* ~s) (statue of a) human body without head, arms and legs.
tor·tilla /tɔrˈti(y)ə/ *n* [C] (*pl* ~s) (originally Mexican) thin, round cake of unleavened corn meal.
tor·toise /ˈtɔrtəs/ *n* [C] slow-moving, four-legged land (and fresh-water) animal with a hard shell. ⇨ illus at reptile.
tor·tu·ous /ˈtɔrtʃuəs/ *adj* **1** full of twists and bends: *a ~ path.* **2** (*fig*) not straightforward: *a ~ argument/politician.*
tor·tu·ous·ly *adv*
tor·ture /ˈtɔrtʃər/ *vt* cause severe suffering to: *~ a man to make him confess; ~d with anxiety.* □ *n* **1** [U] infliction of severe bodily or mental suffering: *instruments of ~.* **2** [C,U] pain caused or suffered; method of torturing: *suffer ~ from the secret police.*
tor·turer *n* [C] person who tortures.
toss /tɔs/ *vt,vi* **1** throw up into or through the air: *He ~ed the beggar a coin/~ed a coin to the beggar. The horse ~ed its head.* ***toss a coin,*** send a coin spinning up in the air and guess which side will be on top when it falls. ***toss (sb) for sth,*** use the method of tossing a coin to decide something: *Who's going to pay for the drinks? Let's ~ for it.* **2** (cause to) move restlessly from side to side or up and down: *The ship (was) ~ed about on the stormy sea.* **3** ***toss sth off,*** produce it quickly and without much thought or effort: *~ off a letter.* □ *n* [C] **1** tossing movement: *a ~ of the head; take a ~,* (esp) be thrown from the back of a horse. **2** ***win/lose the toss,*** guess correctly/incorrectly when a coin is tossed.
ˈtoss-up *n* tossing of a coin; (hence) something about which there is doubt: *It's a ~-up whether he will get here in time.*
tot /tat/ *n* [C] (often **tiny tot**) very small child.
to·tal /ˈtoutəl/ *adj* complete; entire: *~ silence.* □ *n* [C] total amount: *Our expenses reached a ~ of $50.* □ *vt,vi* find, reach, the total of: *The visitors to the exhibition ~ed 15,000.*
to·tal·ity /touˈtæləti/ *n* [U] entirety.
to·tally /ˈtoutəli/ *adv* completely: *~ly blind.*
to·tali·tar·ian /ˌtouˌtæləˈteriən/ *adj* of a system in which only one political party and no rival loyalties are permitted.
tote /tout/ *vt* (*informal*) carry.
ˈtote bag, sturdy bag for carrying heavy things.
to·tem /ˈtoutəm/ *n* [C] natural object, esp an animal, considered in some primitive societies to have a close connection with a particular family or clan.
ˈtotem pole, (usually wooden) pole with a series of totems carved or painted on it, esp as found among the American Indians of the Northwest.
tot·ter /ˈtatər/ *vi* **1** walk with weak, unsteady steps; get up unsteadily: *The wounded man ~ed to his feet.* **2** be almost falling; seem to be about to collapse: *The tree ~ed and then fell.*
tou·can /ˈtukən/ *n* [C] kinds of tropical American bird with brightly colored feathers and a large beak.
touch¹ /tətʃ/ *n* **1** [C] act or fact of touching: *I felt a ~ on my arm.* **2** [U] (sense giving) feeling by touching: *soft/rough to the ~,* when touched. **3** [C] stroke made with a brush, pen, etc: *add a few finishing ~es* (to a drawing or any piece of work). **4** [C] slight quantity, trace: *a ~ of frost in the air; a ~ of sadness in his voice.* **5** [C] style or manner of playing a musical instrument, of workmanship (in art), etc: *have a light ~,* eg on a piano, a typewriter. **6** [U] communication. ***in/out of touch (with),*** in/not in regular communication (with); having/not having information about: *keep in ~ with old friends; be out of ~ with the political situation.* ***lose touch (with),*** be out of touch (with): *If we correspond regularly we shan't lose ~.* ***put the touch on sb,*** (*sl*) get money from (by begging): *He put the ~ on me for $5.*
ˌtouch and ˈgo *adj* risky; of uncertain result: *It was ~ and go whether the doctor would arrive in time.*
touch² /tətʃ/ *vt,vi* (For special uses with *adverbial particles* and *prepositions,* ⇨ 11 below.) **1** (cause to) be in contact with; bring a part of the body (esp the hand) into contact with: *One of the branches is ~ing the water. Can you ~* (= reach with your hand) *the top of the door? Visitors* (eg in a museum) *are requested not to ~ the exhibits.* ***touch bottom,*** **(a)** reach the bottom: *The water isn't deep here; I can just ~ bottom,* ie with my feet. **(b)** (*fig*) reach the lowest level of value, misfortune, etc. **2** apply a slight or gentle force to: *He ~ed the bell,* rang it by pressing the button. **3** (in the negative) compare with; be equal to: *No one can ~ him as an actor of tragic roles.* **4** (in the negative) take (food, drink): *He hasn't ~ed food for two days.* **5** affect (a person or his feelings); concern: *The sad story ~ed us/our hearts.* **6** have to do with: *As a pacifist I refuse to ~* (= invest money in) *shares of armament firms.* **7** injure slightly: *Luckily the paintings were not ~ed by the fire.* **8**

(*pp* ~ed) slightly mad or deranged: *He seems to be a bit ~ed.* **9** cause a painful or angry feeling in; wound: *The remark ~ed him deeply*; cause a feeling of gratitude: *I was so ~ed by your letter of sympathy*. ⇨ touching. **10** deal with; cope with; get a result from: *Nothing I have used will ~* (= get rid of) *these grease spots. She couldn't ~* (= even begin to answer) *the first two questions in the biology exam.* **11** (special uses with *adverbial particles* and *prepositions*):

touch down, (of aircraft) come down to land.

touch sth off, (*fig*) cause to start: *The arrest of the men's leaders ~ed off a riot.*

touch on sth, mention (a subject) briefly.

touch sth up, make small changes in (a picture, a piece of writing) to improve it.

ˈtouch·down *n* [C] **(a)** moment or point of contact of a landing aircraft with the ground. **(b)** (*football*) scoring (six points) by touching the ball down over the opponent's goal line.

touch·able /ˈtətʃəbəl/ *adj* that may be touched.

touch·ing /ˈtətʃɪŋ/ *adj* pathetic; causing gratitude, sympathy, etc: *a ~ request for help.* □ *prep* concerning.

touch·ing·ly *adv*

touchy /ˈtətʃi/ *adj* (-ier, -iest) easily or quickly offended.

tough /təf/ *adj* (-er, -est) **1** (of meat) hard to cut or get one's teeth into. **2** not easily cut, broken or worn out: *as ~ as leather.* **3** strong; able to endure hardships: *~ soldiers.* **4** (of persons) rough and violent: *a ~ criminal.* ***a tough customer,*** (*informal*) a difficult person to deal with. **5** stubborn; unyielding. ***be/get tough (with sb)***: *The employers got ~ with/adopted a ˌget-ˈ~ policy toward the workers.* **6** hard to carry out; difficult: *a ~ job/problem.*

ˌtough ˈluck, (*informal*) bad luck.

tough·ly *adv*

tough·ness /-nɪs/ *n* [U]

toughen /ˈtəfən/ *vt,vi* make or become tough.

tou·pee /tuˈpei/ *n* [C] false hair worn to cover a bald patch.

tour /tʊr/ *n* [C] **1** journey out and home again during which several or many places are visited: *a round-the-world ~; conducted ~s*, made by a group conducted by a guide. **2** brief visit to or through: *a ~ of the White House.* **3** period of duty or employment (overseas): *a one-year ~ in Africa with the Peace Corps.* **4** round of (official) visits to institutions, units, etc: *The Director leaves tomorrow on a ~ of overseas branches.* **5** number of visits to places made by a theatrical company, etc: *take a company on ~.* □ *vt,vi* make a tour (of): *~ western Europe. The play will ~ the West Coast this season.*

tour·ing *n, adj*: *a ˈ~ing party.*

tour·ism /ˈtʊˌrɪzəm/ *n* [U] organized touring: *foreign exchange from ~*, from the money brought in by tourists.

tour·ist /ˈtʊrɪst/ *n* **1** [C] person making a tour for pleasure: *Washington is full of ~s during the summer.* **2** (as an *adjective*) of or for tours: *a ˈ~ agency; ˈ~ class*, (ie, on airplanes) second class.

tour·na·ment /ˈtərnəmənt/ *n* [C] series of contests of skill between a number of players: *a ˈtennis/ˈchess ~.*

tour·ni·quet /ˈtərnɪkɪt/ *n* [C] device for stopping a flow of blood through an artery by twisting something tightly around a limb.

tousle /ˈtauzəl/ *vt* (*formal*) make (esp the hair) untidy: *a girl with ~d hair.*

tout /taut/ *n* [C] person who encourages others to buy something, use his services, etc. □ **1** *vi* act as a tout: *men outside the railroad station ~ing for the hotels.* **2** *vt* advertise wares for sale, propagate ideas, in a tasteless manner: *The man stood on the corner ~ing his wares. The amateur economist ~ed his arguments for/against free trade.*

tow /tou/ *vt* pull along by a rope or chain: *tow a damaged car to the nearest garage.* □ *n* [C,U] towing or being towed: *Can we give you a tow?* ***in tow,*** (*informal*) also with (a person). ***on tow,*** being towed.

to·ward(s) /tərd(z), təˈwərd(z)/ *prep* **1** approaching; in the direction of: *walking ~ the sea; first steps ~ the abolition of nuclear weapons.* **2** as regards; in relation to: *What will the Administration's attitude be ~ the plan?* **3** for the purpose of (helping): *We must save money ~ the children's education.* **4** (of time) near: *~ the end of the century.*

towel /ˈtauəl/ *n* [C] piece of cloth, etc for drying or wiping something wet (eg one's hands or body): *a ˈbath ~; a paper ~.* ***throw in the towel,*** ⇨ throw[1](11). □ *vt* (usually with *down*) dry or rub (oneself) with a towel.

towel·ing *n* [U] material for towels.

tower /ˈtauər/ *n* [C] **1** tall building, either standing alone or forming part of a church, castle or other large building (eg a college): *We visited Bok Tower in Florida; radio ~.* **2** ***a tower of strength,*** (*fig*) a person who can be relied on for protection, strength or comfort in time of trouble. **3** = water tower. □ *vi* rise to a great height, be very tall, esp in relation to the height of the surroundings: *the skyscrapers that ~ over New York.* ***tower above sb,*** (*fig*) (of persons) greatly exceed in ability, in intellectual or moral qualities: *a man who ~s above his contemporaries.*

town /taun/ *n* **1** [C] center of population smaller than a city; (*Note:* often used without *a* or *the*) towns and cities in general in contrast to the country(4): *Would you rather live in ~,* ie in a town or city, *or in the country? Farm workers are leaving the country in order to get better paying jobs in ~.* ***paint the town red,*** ⇨ paint. **2** [U] the business, shopping, etc part of a town (contrasted with the suburbs, etc): *go into ~ to do some shopping. He's in ~ today.* ⇨ downtown. ***go out on the town,*** go out and enjoy the entertainment facilities of a town (especially at night). ***go to town,*** (*informal*) act, behave, without hesitation or difficulty: *He really went to ~ on/with that sandwich,* ate it quickly and eagerly. **3** [U] the chief city or town in the neighborhood: *He's gone into ~ for the weekend.* **4** [U] (*sing* with *the*) the people of a town: *The whole ~ was talking about it.* ***the talk of the town,*** ⇨ talk[1](1).

ˌtown ˈclerk, official who keeps town or city records and advises on certain legal matters.

ˌ**town ˈhall,** building with offices of local government.

ˈ**town·house** *n* [C] house in town, of a particular style or belonging to a person who also has a house in the country.

ˌ**town ˈmeeting,** of taxpayers in a town to decide on local matters.

ˈ**town·ship** *n* [C] a town as an administrative unit.

toxic /ˈtaksɪk/ *adj* = poisonous (the usual word).

toxin /ˈtaksɪn/ *n* [C] poisonous substance.

toy /tɔi/ *n* **1** [C] something, eg a doll, for a child to play with. **2** (as an *adjective*): *toy soldier*, one made as a toy(1); *toy dog/spaniel,* small kinds kept as pets. □ *vi* **1** think not very seriously about: *He toyed with the idea of buying a new car.* **2** = fiddle(2): *toying with a pencil.*

ˈ**toy·shop** *n* [C] shop where toys are sold.

tr. *abbr* = transitive.

trace[1] /treis/ *n* [C] **1** mark, sign, etc showing that a person or thing has been present, that something has existed or happened: *~s of an ancient civilization. We've lost all ~ of them,* don't know where they are. **2** very small amount: *There were ~s of poison in his blood.*

trace[2] /treis/ *vt,vi* **1** draw, sketch, the course, outline, etc of: *tracing (out) one's route on a map.* **2** copy (something), eg by drawing on transparent paper the lines, etc on (a map, design, etc) placed underneath. **3** follow or discover (a person or thing) by looking at marks, tracks, evidence, etc: *I cannot ~* (= cannot find) *any letter from you dated June 1st.* ***trace (sth/sb) back (to sth),*** **(a)** find the origin of by going back in time: *He ~s his ancestors back to an old Scottish family.* **(b)** find the origin of by going back through evidence: *The rumor was ~d back to a journalist,* It was discovered that he had started it.

trace·able /-əbəl/ *adj* capable of being traced (*to*).

trac·ing *n* reproduction (of a map, design, etc) made by tracing(2).

tracery /ˈtreisəri/ *n* [C,U] (*pl* -ies) ornamental arrangement of designs (eg as made by frost on glass, or of stonework in a church window).

tra·chea /ˈtreikiə/ *n* [C] (*pl* ~e /-kiˌ(y)i/) (*anat*) = windpipe. ⇨ illus at respiratory.

track /træk/ *n* [C] **1** line or series of marks left by a vehicle, person, animal, etc in passing along; path made by persons, animals: *~s in the snow,* eg footprints; ˈ*sheep ~s across the moor.* ***be on sb's track/on the track of sb,*** be tracking: *The police are on the ~ of the thief.* ***cover up one's tracks,*** hide one's movements or activities. ***have a ˌone-track ˈmind,*** give all one's attention to one topic or thought. ***keep/lose track of sb/sth,*** keep in/lose touch with; follow/fail to follow the course or development of: *read the newspapers to keep ~ of current events.* ***off the track,*** (*fig*) following a wrong line of action. ⇨ beaten. **2** course; line taken by something (whether marked or not): *the ~ of a storm/spacecraft.* **3** set of rails for trains, etc: *The train left the ~,* was derailed. **4** path prepared for racing (eg made of cinders, etc). **5** either of two treaded belts on which a tank, caterpillar tractor, etc travels. **6** band for recording sound (on magnetized tape); section of something recorded (on a record or tape). □ *vt* follow the track of: *~ an animal to its den.* ***track sb/sth down,*** find by searching: *~ down a bear/a reference.*

tracker *n* [C] person, esp a hunter, who tracks wild animals.

ˈ**track event,** athletic contest, eg running, on a

FARM TRACTOR

DUMP TRUCK

TRACTOR-TRAILER

PANEL TRUCK

TRACTORS AND TRUCKS

track(4).

ˈ**track·ing station,** one which, by radar or radio, maintains contact with space vehicles, etc.

ˈ**track shoe,** with spikes on the sole, to grip the ground in running.

tract[1] /trækt/ *n* [C] **1** stretch or area (*of* forest, farmland, etc): *the wide ~s of desert in North Africa.* **2** system of related parts in an animal body: *the diˈgestive/ˈrespiratory ~.*

tract[2] /trækt/ *n* [C] short printed essay, esp on a moral or religious subject.

tract·able /ˈtræktəbəl/ *adj* (*formal*) easily controlled or guided.

trac·tion /ˈtrækʃən/ *n* [U] **1** (power used in) pulling or drawing something over a surface: *electric/steam ~.* **2** adhesive force that makes something move on a surface without slipping: *The chains gave the tires better ~ on the snow-covered road.*

trac·tor /ˈtræktər/ *n* [C] motor vehicle used for pulling agricultural machinery (ploughs, etc), or other heavy equipment, over rough ground.

tractor-trailer *n* [C] tractor with attached trailer unit.

trade[1] /treid/ *n* **1** [U] buying and selling of goods; exchange of goods for money or other goods: *The economist studies world ~.* **2** [C] particular branch of buying and selling: *He's in the ˈfurniture/ˈbook ~.* **3** [C,U] occupation; way of making a living, esp a handicraft: *He's a carpenter/tailor by ~. Shoemaking is a useful ~.*

ˈ**trade·mark** *n* [C] **(a)** design, special name, etc used to distinguish a manufacturer's goods from others. **(b)** (*fig*) distinguishing characteristics: *He leaves his ~mark on all his activities.*

ˈ**trade name,** name given to a manufactured article.

the Trades, = trade winds.

ˈ**trade wind,** strong wind blowing always toward the equator from the southeast and northeast.

trade[2] /treid/ *vi,vt* **1** engage in trade(1); buy and sell: *The US ~s with many other countries.* **2** exchange: *The boy ~d his skates for a baseball bat.* **3** ***trade sth in,*** give (a used article) in part payment for a new purchase: *He ~d in his car for a new one.* **4** take a wrong advantage of, use, in order to get something for oneself: *~ on her sympathy.*

ˈ**trade-in** *n* [C] something (to be) traded in. ⇨ trade[2](3).

trader *n* [C] person who trades(1).

tra·di·tion /trəˈdɪʃən/ *n* **1** [U] (handing down from generation to generation of) opinions, beliefs, customs, etc. **2** [C] opinion, belief, custom, etc handed down.

tra·di·tional /-nəl/ *adj*

tra·di·tion·ally /-nəli/ *adv*

traf·fic /ˈtræfɪk/ *n* [U] **1** (movement of) people and vehicles along roads and streets, of aircraft in the sky: *There was a lot of/not much ~ on the roads yesterday.* **2** transport business done by a railroad, steamship line, airline, etc. **3** illegal trading: *the ˈdrug ~.* □ *vi* (-ck-) trade: *trafficking in snakes.*

ˈ**traffic island,** platform in the center of a busy road, for pedestrians when crossing.

ˈ**traffic jam,** ⇨ jam[2]*n*(1).

ˈ**traffic light(s),** colored lights by the roadside controlling traffic.

ˈ**traffic signal(s)** = traffic light(s).

tra·gedy /ˈtrædʒədi/ *n* (*pl* -ies) **1** [C] play for film, the theater, TV, of a serious kind, with a sad ending. **2** [U] branch of the drama with this kind of play. **3** [C,U] very sad event, action, experience, etc in real life.

tra·gedian /trəˈdʒidiən/ *n* [C] writer of, actor in, tragedy.

tra·gedi·enne /trəˌdʒidiˈen/ *n* [C] writer of, actress in, tragedy.

tra·gic /ˈtrædʒɪk/ *adj* of tragedy: *a ~ actor/event.*

tragi·cally /-kli/ *adv*

trail /ˈtreiəl/ *n* [C] **1** line, mark or series of marks, drawn or left by a person or thing that has passed by: *a ~ of smoke,* (from a railway steam engine); *a ~ of destruction,* eg left by a violent storm. **2** track or scent followed in hunting. ***hot on the trail (of),*** close behind. **3** path through rough country. □ *vt,vi* (*pres p* ~ing /ˈtreilɪŋ/) **1** pull, be pulled, along: *Her long skirt was ~ing along the floor.* **2** = track[1]. **3** (of plants) grow over or along the ground, etc: *roses ~ing over the walls.*

trailer /ˈtreilər/ *n* [C] **(a)** transport vehicle hauled by a tractor or truck. **(b)** mobile home or cart drawn by an automobile. **(c)** trailing plant. **(d)** series of short extracts from a film to advertise it.

train[1] /trein/ *n* [C] **1** (locomotive and) number of railway cars joined together: *ˈpassenger/ˈgoods/ˈfreight ~s; travel by ~; get on/off a ~.* **2** number of persons, animals, carriages, etc moving in a line: *a ~ of camels.* **3** series or chain: *A knock at the door interrupted my ~ of thought.* **4** part of a long formal dress or robe that trails on the ground.

train[2] /trein/ *vt,vi* **1** give teaching and practice to (eg a child, a soldier, an animal) in order to bring to a desired standard of behavior, efficiency or physical condition: *~ a horse for a race/circus. There is a shortage of ~ed nurses.* **2** cause to grow in a required direction: *~ roses against/over a wall.* **3** point, aim: *~ a gun on the enemy.*

trainee /ˌtreiˈni/ *n* [C] person undergoing some form of (usually industrial) training.

trainer *n* [C] person who trains (esp athletes, race horses, etc).

train·ing *n* [U] ***in/out of training,*** in/not in good physical condition (eg for athletic contests).

traipse /treips/ *vi* (*informal*) walk wearily: *traipsing around from shop to shop.*

trait /treit/ *n* [C] distinguishing quality or characteristic: *Two good ~s in the American character are generosity and enthusiasm.*

trai·tor /ˈtreitər/ *n* [C] person who betrays a friend, is disloyal to a cause, his country, etc.

trai·tor·ous /-əs/ *adj* = treacherous (the usual word).

tramp /træmp/ *vi,vt* **1** walk with heavy steps: *He*

~*ed up and down the platform waiting for the train.* **2** walk through or over (esp for a long distance): ~ *through the mountains;* ~ *over the hills. They* ~*ed (for) miles and miles.* □ *n* **1 the tramp,** sound of heavy footsteps: *I heard the* ~ *of marching soldiers.* **2** [C] long walk: *go for a* ~ *in the country.* **3** [C] homeless person who goes from place to place and does no regular work: *There's a* ~ *at the door begging for food.*

ˈtramp steamer, cargo boat which goes to any port(s) where cargo can be picked up.

trample /ˈtræmpəl/ *vt,vi* **1** tread heavily on: *The children have* ~*d (down) the flowers/*~*d on the grass.* **2** (*fig*) affect badly and thoughtlessly: ~ *on his feelings.* □ *n* [C] sound, act, of trampling.

tram·po·line /ˈtræmpəˌlin/ *n* [C] strong canvas on a spring frame, used by gymnasts for acrobatic leaps.

trance /træns/ *n* [C] **1** condition like sleep: *be/fall/go into a* ~. **2** abnormal, hypnotic, state: *send her into a* ~.

tran·quil /ˈtræŋkwɪl/ *adj* (*formal*) calm; quiet: *a* ~ *life in the country.*

tran·quility /træŋˈkwɪləti/ *n* [U] calm, quiet state.

tran·quilly /-wəli/ *adv*

tran·quil·ize /ˈtræŋkwəˌlaiz/ *vt* make calm, quiet.

tran·quil·i·zer *n* [C] drug that produces a calm mental state.

trans. *abbr* = **1** transaction. **2** transitive. **3** translation. **4** transportation.

trans- /trænz-/ *prefix* **1** across: *transatlantic.* **2** to a changed state: *transform.*

trans·act /trænˈzækt/ *vt* (*formal*) conduct, do, (business, etc).

trans·ac·tion /trænˈzækʃən/ *n* **1** [U] (*sing* with *the*) transacting: *the* ~ *of business.* **2** [C] piece of business: *cash* ~*s.* **3** (*pl*) (records of the) proceedings of (esp a learned society, eg its meetings, lectures): *the* ~*s of the National Academy of Sciences.*

trans·at·lan·tic /ˌtrænzətˈlæntɪk/ *adj* **1** beyond, crossing, the Atlantic: *a* ~ *voyage/flight.* **2** concerning (countries on) both sides of the Atlantic: *a* ~ *treaty.*

tran·scend /trænˈsend/ *vt* go or be beyond or outside the range of (human experience, reason, belief, powers of description, etc).

tran·scen·den·tal /ˌtrænˌsenˈdentəl/ *adj* not based on experience or reason; going beyond human knowledge; that cannot be discovered or understood by practical experience: ~ *meditation.*

transcendentalism /-əˌlɪzəm/ *n* [U] transcendental philosophy.

transcendentalist /-əlɪst/ *n* [C] believer in transcendentalism.

transcendentally /-təli/ *adv*

trans·con·ti·nen·tal /ˌtrænzˌkantəˈnentəl/ *adj* crossing a continent: *a* ~ *railway.*

tran·scribe /trænˈskraib/ *vt* **1** copy in ordinary writing, esp from shorthand notes or from speech recorded on magnetic tape. **2** write in a special form: ~*d into phonetics.*

tran·script /ˈtrænˌskrɪpt/ *n* [C] something transcribed (esp (1)).

tran·scrip·tion /trænˈskrɪpʃən/ *n* [C,U] something transcribed (esp (2)).

tran·sept /ˈtrænˌsept/ *n* [C] (either end of the) transverse part of a cross-shaped church.

trans·fer[1] /ˈtrænzˌfər, ˈtræns-/ *n* **1** [C,U] (instance of) transferring. **2** [C] document that transfers a person or thing; drawing, plan, etc transferred from one surface to another. **3** [C] ticket that allows a traveler to change to a connecting bus line, etc without paying a full additional fare.

trans·fer[2] /trænzˈfər, træns-/ *vt,vi* (-rr-) **1** change position, move: *The head office has been* ~*red from New York to Houston.* **2** hand over the possession of (property, etc to): ~ *rights to a son.* **3** convey (a drawing, design, pattern, etc) from one surface to another (eg from a wooden surface to canvas). **4** change from one train, bus, etc to another. **5** move from one occupation (usually within the same profession), position, company, etc to another: *He has been* ~*red to the Sales Department.*

trans·fer·able /trænzˈfərəbəl, træns-/ *adj* that can be transferred: *These tickets are not* ~*able,* cannot be given to anyone else.

trans·fer·ence /trænzˈfərəns, træns-/ *n* [U]

trans·fix /trænzˈfɪks/ *vt* (*formal*) **1** pierce through: ~ *a leopard with a spear.* **2** cause (a person) to be unable to move, speak, think, etc: *He stood* ~*ed with horror.*

trans·form /trænzˈfɔrm, træns-/ *vt* change the shape, appearance, quality or nature of: *Success and wealth* ~*ed his character. A steam engine* ~*s heat into energy.*

trans·form·able /-əbəl/ *adj* that can be transformed.

trans·form·ation /ˌtrænzfərˈmeiʃən, ˌtræns-/ *n* **(a)** [U] transforming or being transformed. **(b)** [C] instance of this: *He has undergone a great* ~*ation since he was married.* **(c)** [C] (in grammar) a kind of rule indicating a change in word order, etc.

trans·for·mer *n* [C] person or thing that transforms, eg apparatus that increases or decreases the voltage of an electric power supply.

trans·fuse /trænzˈfyuz, træns-/ *vt* (esp) transfer the blood of one person to another.

trans·fusion /trænzˈfyuʒən, træns-/ *n* [U] act or process of transfusing; [C] instance of this: *The injured man was given a ˈblood transfusion.*

trans·gress /trænzˈgres/ *vt,vi* (*formal*) **1** go beyond (a limit or bound): ~ *the bounds of decency.* **2** break (a law, treaty, agreement). **3** sin.

trans·gres·sion /trænzˈgreʃən/ *n* [C,U] (instance of) transgressing.

trans·gres·sor /-sər/ *n* [C] person who transgresses; sinner.

tran·si·ent /ˈtrænʃənt/ *adj* (*formal*) lasting for a short time only: ~ *happiness.* □ *n* [C] occupant of a hotel, boarding house, etc staying only for a short time.

tran·sis·tor /trænˈzɪstər/ *n* [C] **1** small electronic device, used in radios, hearing aids and other kinds of electronic apparatus. **2** transistorized radio.

tran·sis·tor·ized /-ˌraizd/ *adj* having transistors, not valves: *a ~ized computer.*

tran·sit /ˈtrænsɪt, ˈtrænzɪt/ *n* [U] sending, carrying or being sent, across, over or through. ***in transit,*** while being carried or sent from one place to another.

ˈtransit visa, visa allowing passage through (but not a stay in) a country.

tran·si·tion /trænˈzɪʃən/ *n* [C,U] changing, change, from one condition or set of circumstances to another: *Adolescence is the period of ~ between childhood and adulthood.*

tran·si·tional /-nəl/ *adj*

tran·si·tive /ˈtrænsətɪv/ *adj* (*gram*) (of a verb) that can be used with a direct object. (*Note:* marked *vt* in this dictionary.)

tran·si·tive·ly *adv*

tran·si·tory /ˈtrænzəˌtɔri/ *adj* lasting for a short time only; transient: *Youth and beauty are ~.*

trans·late /trænzˈleit, ˈtrænzˌleit/ *vt* **1** give the meaning of (something said or written) in another language: *~ a book from English into French.* **2** interpret, explain (a person's behavior, etc): *How would you ~ his silence?* What do you think it means?

trans·la·tor /-tər/ *n* [C] person who translates.

trans·la·tion /trænzˈleiʃən/ *n* [U] translating: *errors in ~*; [C] something translated: *make/do a ~ into French.*

trans·lu·cent /trænzˈlusənt/ *adj* allowing light to pass through but not transparent: *Frosted glass is ~.*

trans·mis·sion /trænzˈmɪʃən/ *n* **1** [U] transmitting or being transmitted: *the ~ of news/a TV program.* **2** [C] clutch, gears and drive which help to send power from the engine to the wheels (of a motor vehicle).

trans·mit /trænzˈmɪt, træns-/ *vt* (-tt-) **1** pass or hand on; send on: *~ a message by radio; ~ a disease.* **2** allow through or along: *Iron ~s heat.*

trans·mit·ter *n* [C] person who, that which, transmits, esp (part of a) radio apparatus for sending out signals, messages, music, etc.

trans·mute /trænzˈmyut/ *vt* change the shape, nature or substance of: *We cannot ~ base metals into gold.*

trans·mu·tation /ˌtrænzmyuˈteiʃən/ *n* [U]

trans·par·ency /trænzˈpærənsi, træns-/ *n* (*pl* -ies) **1** [U] state of being transparent. **2** [C] framed diagram, picture, etc on photographic film (to be projected onto a screen).

trans·par·ent /trænzˈpærənt, træns-/ *adj* **1** allowing light to pass through so that objects (or at least their outlines) behind can be distinctly seen: *Ordinary glass is ~.* **2** about which there can be no mistake or doubt: *a man of ~ honesty.* **3** clear; easily understood: *a ~ style of writing.* **4** (*informal*) (of a person, his behavior) obviously lying, insincere, etc.

trans·par·ent·ly *adv*

tran·spire /trænˈspaiər/ *vi,vt* (*formal*) **1** (of an event, a secret) come to be known: *It ~d that the President had spent the weekend golfing.* **2** (*dated*) happen.

trans·plant /ˌtrænzˈplænt/ *vt,vi* **1** take up (plants, etc) with their roots and plant in another place. **2** transfer (tissue, or an organ, eg a heart or kidney) from one person to another. **3** (*fig*) (of people) move from one place to another. □ *n* /ˈtrænzˌplænt/ [C] instance of transplanting(2): *a ˈkidney ~.*

trans·port[1] /ˈtrænzˌpɔrt, ˈtræns-/ *n* **1** [U] carrying (to another place) or being carried; means of carrying: *the ~ of troops by air; road ~.* **2** (as an *adjective*) of or for carrying (to another place): *~ charges.*

trans·port[2] /ˌtrænzˈpɔrt, ˌtræns-/ *vt* **1** carry (goods, persons) from one place to another: *~ goods by truck.* **2** (in former times) send (a criminal) to a distant colony as a punishment: *~ed to Australia.*

trans·port·able /-əbəl/ *adj* that can be transported.

trans·por·ta·tion /ˌtrænzpərˈteiʃən, ˌtræns-/ *n* [U]

trans·porter /trænzˈpɔrtər, træns-/ *n* [C] person or thing that transports, eg a long vehicle for carrying several motor vehicles from a factory.

trans·pose /trænzˈpouz, træns-/ *vt* **1** cause (two or more things) to change places. **2** (*music*) put into another key.

trans·po·si·tion /ˌtrænzpəˈzɪʃən, ˌtræns-/ *n* [C,U]

tran·sub·stan·ti·ation /ˌtrænsəbˌstænʃiˈeiʃən/ *n* [U] **1** transmutation. **2** doctrine that the bread and wine in the Eucharist are changed into the body and blood of Christ.

trans·verse /ˈtrænzˌvərs/ *adj* lying or placed across.

trans·verse·ly *adv*

trap /træp/ *n* [C] **1** device for catching animals, etc: *a ˈmouse~.* **2** (*fig*) plan for deceiving a person; trick or device to make a person say or do something he does not wish to do or say: *The employer set a ~ for the man by putting marked money in the till.* **3** U-shaped or other section of a drainpipe which prevents the rising up of sewer gas (eg under a lavatory). **4** light, two-wheeled vehicle pulled by a horse or pony. **5** device (eg a box) from which an animal or object can be released, eg greyhounds at the start of a race. **6** (*sl*) mouth: *Shut your ~!* Be quiet! □ *vt* (-pp-) **1** catch in a trap. **2** capture by a trick.

trap·per *n* [C] person who catches animals, esp for their fur.

tra·peze /træˈpiz/ *n* [C] horizontal bar or rod supported by two ropes, used by acrobats and for gymnastic exercises.

tra·pezium /trəˈpiziəm/ *n* [C] (*pl* ~s) four-sided figure having no sides parallel.

trap·ezoid /ˈtræpəˌzɔid/ *n* [C] four-sided figure having two sides parallel. ⇨ illus at geometry.

trap·pings /ˈtræpɪŋz/ *n pl* (*fig*) ornaments or decorations, esp as a sign of public office: *He had all the ~ of high office but very little power.*

trash /træʃ/ *n* [U] **1** something worthless. **2** rubbish; refuse: *~ collector.* **3** (*informal*) worthless people.

trashy *adj* (*informal*) worthless: *~y novels.*

trauma /ˈtrɔmə/ *n* [C] (*pl* ~s or -mata /-mətə/) **1** diseased condition of the body produced by a wound or injury. **2** emotional shock.

trau·matic /trɔˈmætɪk/ *adj* **(a)** of or for (the treatment of) a wound or injury. **(b)** (of an experience) distressing and unforgettable.

travel /ˈtrævəl/ *vi,vt* **1** make (esp long) journeys:

~ *around the world;* ~ *(for) thousands of miles;* ~ *(over) the whole world.* **2** go from place to place as a salesman: *He* ~*s for a textbook publisher*. **3** move; go: *Light* ~*s faster than sound.* **4** pass from point to point: *Her mind* ~*ed over recent events.* □ *n* **1** [U] traveling: *He is fond of* ~. **2** (*pl*) journeys, esp abroad: *write a book about one's* ~*s.*

ˈtravel-agency/-bureau *n* [C]

ˈtravel agent, person who makes arrangements for travel, by selling tickets, reserving accommodation, etc.

trav·el·ed *adj* **(a)** having made many long journeys: *a* ~*ed man.* **(b)** used by people who travel: *a much* ~*ed part of the country*.

trav·eler *n* [C] **(a)** person who travels. **(b)** person on a journey. **(c)** = traveling salesman.

ˈtraveler's check, one issued by a bank or tourist agency for the convenience of travelers.

ˌtraveling ˈsalesman, one who goes from place to place selling goods.

trav·elogue, -log /ˈtrævəˌlɔg/ *n* [C] film or lecture describing travels.

tra·verse /trəˈvərs/ *vt* (*formal*) travel across; pass over: *Searchlights* ~*d the sky*. □ *n* /ˈtrævərs/ [C] **1** rod, screen, etc placed or moving crosswise. (*Note:* often used as an *adjective*) ~ *rod.* **2** zigzag changing of direction, eg of a ship sailing into the wind, of a trench (to prevent the enemy from firing along it). **3** (*mountaineering*) sideways movement across the face of a steep slope.

trav·esty /ˈtrævɪsti/ *n* [C] (*pl* -ies) imitation or description of something that is, often on purpose, unlike and inferior to the real thing: *His trial was a* ~ *of justice.* □ *vt* (*pt,pp* -ied) make or be a travesty of.

trawl /trɔl/ *vi,vt* fish (with a large net).

traw·ler *n* [C] boat, fisherman, that trawls.

tray /trei/ *n* [C] flat piece of wood, metal, etc with raised edges, for carrying light articles.

treach·er·ous /ˈtretʃərəs/ *adj* **1** false or disloyal (to a friend, cause, etc). **2** not to be relied on: ~ *weather*.

treach·er·ous·ly *adv*

treach·ery /ˈtretʃəri/ *n* (*pl* -ies) [U] being treacherous; (*pl*) treacherous acts.

tread /tred/ *vi,vt* (*pt* trod /trad/, *pp* trodden /ˈtradən/) **1** walk, put the foot or feet down (on): *Don't* ~ *on the flowers*. ***tread on sb's toes,*** (*fig*) offend him. **2** stamp or crush; push (down, etc) with the feet: ~ *out a fire in the grass;* ~ *grapes*, when making wine. **3** make by walking: *The cattle had trodden a path to the pond.* **4** walk along: ~ *a dangerous path,* (*fig*) follow a risky course of action. ***tread water,*** keep oneself afloat in deep water by moving the feet up and down (as if working the pedals of a bicycle). □ *n* [C] **1** way or sound of walking: *with a heavy/loud* ~. **2** part of a step or stair on which the foot is placed. **3** grooved part of a tire which touches the ground.

treadle /ˈtredəl/ *n* [C] pedal or lever that drives a machine, eg a lathe or sewing machine, worked by pressure of the foot or feet. □ *vi* work a treadle.

treas. *abbr* = treasurer.

trea·son /ˈtrizən/ *n* [U] betrayal of one's country or ruler; disloyalty.

trea·son·able /-əbəl/ *adj*

trea·son·ably /-əbli/ *adv*

treas·ure /ˈtreʒər/ *n* **1** [C,U] (store of) gold and silver, jewels, etc; wealth: *The pirates buried their* ~. **2** highly valued object or person: *The National Gallery has many priceless ˈart* ~*s. She says her new secretary is a real* ~. □ *vt* **1** store for future use: ~ *memories of one's youth.* **2** value highly: *He* ~*s the watch she gave him.*

ˈtreasure-house *n* [C] building where treasure is stored.

ˈtreasure trove, treasure found hidden in the earth and of unknown ownership.

treas·urer /ˈtreʒərər/ *n* [C] person in charge of money, etc belonging to a club or society.

treas·ury /ˈtreʒəri/ *n* (*pl* -ies) **1 the Treasury,** department of US Government controlling public revenue. **2** [C] (place for the) funds of a society, organization, etc: *The* ~ *of our tennis club is almost empty.* **3** [C] person, book, etc looked on as containing valuable information or as a valued source: *The book is a* ~ *of information.*

treat /ˈtrit/ *vt,vi* **1** act or behave toward: *He* ~*s his wife badly*. **2** consider: *We had better* ~ *it as a joke,* instead of taking it seriously. **3** discuss; deal with: *The lecturer* ~*ed his subject thoroughly*. **4** give medical or surgical care to: *Which doctors are* ~*ing her for her illness?* **5** put (a substance) through a process (in manufacture, etc): ~ *wood with a preservative.* **6** supply (food, drink, entertainment, etc) at one's own expense (to): *I shall* ~ *myself/you to a good weekend vacation.* □ *n* **1** [C] something that gives pleasure, esp not often enjoyed or unexpected: *It's a great* ~ *for her to go to the movies.* **2** act of treating(6): *This is to be my* ~, I'm going to pay.

treat·ise /ˈtritɪs/ *n* [C] book, etc that deals systematically with one subject.

treat·ment /ˈtritmənt/ *n* [C,U] (particular way of) treating a person or thing; what is done to obtain a desired result: *Is the* ~ *of political prisoners worse than it used to be? They are trying a new* ~ *for cancer.*

treaty /ˈtriti/ *n* (*pl* -ies) **1** [C] (*formal*) agreement made and signed between nations: *a ˈpeace* ~. **2** ***private treaty,*** agreement or negotiation between persons: *sell a house by private* ~.

treble[1] /ˈtrebəl/ *adj, n* [C] three times as much or as many (as): *He earns* ~ *my salary.* □ *vt,vi* make or become treble: *He has* ~*d his earnings/His earnings have* ~*d during the last few years.*

treble[2] /ˈtrebəl/ *n* [C], *adj* **1** (musical part for, or singer) having a voice in the range of that of a soprano. **2** instrument with the same range, taking the highest part in a piece of music. ⇨ illus at notation.

tree /tri/ *n* [C] **1** plant with a single self-supporting trunk of wood with (usually) no branches for some distance above the ground: *cut down* ~*s for timber*. **2** = family tree. **3** piece of wood for a special purpose: *a ˈshoe* ~, for keeping a shoe in shape while not being worn. □ *vt* corner an animal (in hunting) by forcing it to flee up a tree.

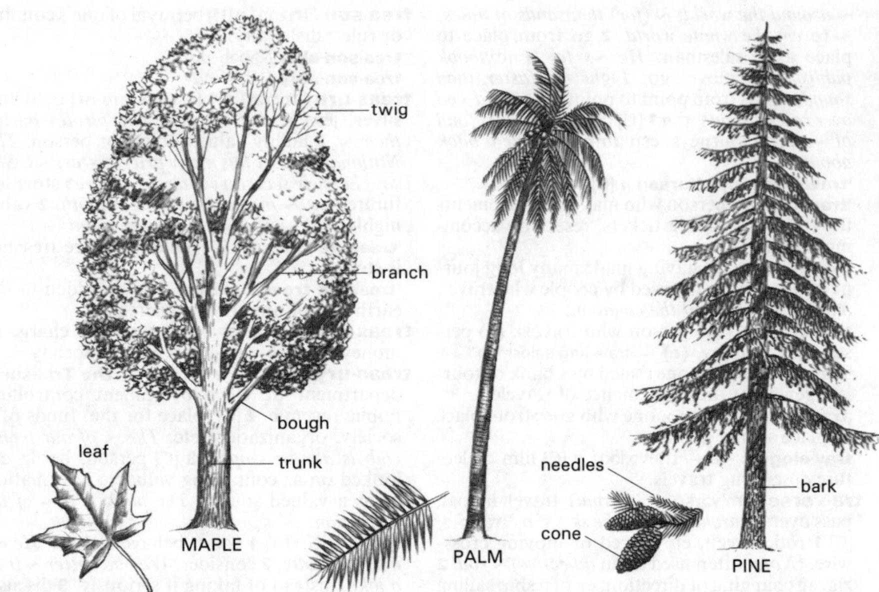

TREES

ˈtree farm, forest land with continuous, managed tree production for commercial purposes.

ˈtree house, child's playhouse built in the branches of a tree.

tree·less *adj* without trees.

ˈtree surgeon, specialist in tree surgery.

ˈtree surgery, corrective treatment of disease, etc in trees.

tre·foil /ˈtriˌfɔiəl/ *n* [C] **1** kinds of three-leaved plant, eg clover. **2** similar ornament or design.

trek /trek/ *vi* (-kk-) make a long journey, by wagon, horse or on foot. □ *n* [C] journey of this kind; any long, hard journey. ⇨ safari.

trel·lis /ˈtrelɪs/ *n* [C] light upright structure of strips of wood, etc esp as used for supporting climbing plants. □ *vt* furnish with, support on, a trellis.

tremble /ˈtrembəl/ *vi* **1** shake involuntarily (as from fear, anger, cold, physical weakness, etc): *His voice ~d with anger. We were trembling with cold/excitement.* **2** shake: *The bridge ~d as the heavy truck crossed it.* **3** be in a state of anxiety: *I ~ to think what has happened to him,* am deeply worried. □ *n* [C] uncontrollable shaking: *There was a ~ in his voice.*

tre·men·dous /trɪˈmendəs/ *adj* **1** very great; enormous; powerful: *a ~ explosion; traveling at a ~ speed.* **2** (*informal*) extraordinary: *He's a ~ eater/talker.* **3** (*informal*) first rate: *a ~ concert/performance/meal.*

tre·men·dously *adv* (esp *informal*) extremely: *~ly grateful.*

tremor /ˈtremər/ *n* [C] shaking or trembling: *ˈearth ~s,* as during an earthquake; *a ~ of fear.*

trench /trentʃ/ *n* [C] ditch dug in the ground, eg for the draining of water, for a latrine, as a protection for soldiers against enemy fire. □ *vt,vi* surround, strengthen, with a trench.

ˈtrench coat, double-breasted, military-style raincoat, usually tan and with shoulder loops.

trend /trend/ *n* [C] general direction; tendency: *The ~ of the coastline is to the south. The ~ of prices is still upward.* ***set the trend,*** start a style, etc which others follow. □ *vi* have a certain trend: *The road ~s toward the west.*

ˈtrend setter, one who sets a trend (style, etc) which others follow.

ˈtrend-setting *adj* (of a quality) which creates a trend.

trendy *adj* (-ier, -iest) (*informal*) showing, following, the latest fashion, etc.

trepi·da·tion /ˌtrepəˈdeiʃən/ *n* [U] (*formal*) alarm: *in fear and ~.*

tres·pass /ˈtrespəs, ˈtresˌpæs/ *vt* **1** go onto privately owned land without right or permission: *~ on someone's (private) property.* **2** make too much use of: *~ on my time/hospitality/privacy.* □ *n* [U] trespassing(1); [C] instance of this.

tres·pas·ser, person who trespasses(1): *Trespassers will be prosecuted.*

tress /tres/ *n* [C] (*poet* or *liter*) **1** (*pl*) hair (esp of a woman's or girl's head). **2** plait or braid of hair.

trestle /ˈtresəl/ *n* [C] horizontal beam of wood with two legs at each end, used in pairs to support planks, a table top, a workman's bench, etc.

ˈtrestle ˌtable, one made by laying planks on trestles.

tri- /trai-/ *prefix* three: *triangle.*

trial /ˈtraiəl/ *n* **1** [U] testing, trying, proving; [C] instance of this: *give a new typist a* ~, give her a chance to show her skill. ***on trial,*** **(a)** for the purpose of testing: *Take the machine on* ~ *and then, if you like it, buy it.* **(b)** when tested: *The new clerk was found on* ~ *to be incompetent.* ***ˌtrial and ˈerror,*** method of solving a problem by making tests until there are no more errors. **2** (as an *adjective*) for the purpose of testing: *a* ~ *flight*, eg of a new aircraft. **3** [C,U] examination in a law court before a judge (or judge and jury): *The* ~ *lasted a week.* ***be/go on trial (for sth),*** be tried in a court of law (for an offense). ***bring sb to trial; put sb on trial,*** cause him to be tried in a court of law. ***stand (one's) trial,*** be tried. **4** [C] troublesome or annoying person or thing, esp thought of as a test of one's patience: *Life is full of little* ~*s.*

ˈtrial balloon, **(a)** balloon sent up to test air currents. **(b)** plan publicized in order to test the reaction of the public or some special group to the idea.

tri·angle /ˈtraiˌæŋgəl/ *n* [C] **1** flat figure with three sides. ⇨ illus at geometry. **2** group of three. ***the eternal triangle,*** the situation existing when two persons are in love with the same person of the opposite sex. **3** (*music*) metal percussion instrument in the shape of a triangle. ⇨ illus at percussion.

tri·angu·lar /traiˈæŋgyələr/ *adj* **(a)** in the shape of a triangle. **(b)** in which there are three persons, etc: *a triangular contest in an election*, with three candidates.

tri·bal /ˈtraibəl/ *adj* of a tribe or tribes: ~ *dances.*

tri·bal·ism /-ˌlɪzəm/ *n* [U]

tribe /traib/ *n* [C] ethnic group, esp one united by language and customs, living as a community under one or more chiefs: *the Indian* ~*s of America.*

ˈtribes·man /-mən/ *n* [C] (*pl* ~smen /-men/) member of a tribe.

tribu·la·tion /ˌtrɪbyəˈleiʃən/ *n* [C,U] (*formal*) (cause of) trouble, grief: *trials and* ~*s.*

tri·bu·nal /traiˈbyunəl/ *n* [C] place of judgment; board of officials or judges appointed for special duty, eg to hear appeals against high rents.

tri·bune /ˈtrɪˌbyun, trɪˈbyun/ *n* [C] **1** official chosen by the common people of ancient Rome to protect their interests. **2** (later use) popular leader.

tribu·tary /ˈtrɪbyəˌteri/ *adj* (of a river) flowing into another. □ *n* [C] (*pl* -ies) (esp) tributary river.

trib·ute /ˈtrɪbyut/ *n* [C,U] **1** (regular) payment which one government or ruler demands from another: *Many conquered nations had to pay* ~ *to the rulers of ancient Rome.* **2** something done, said or given to show respect or admiration: *The actress received numerous floral* ~*s*, bunches of flowers.

trice /trais/ *n* ***in a trice,*** instantly.

trick /trɪk/ *n* [C] **1** something done in order to deceive or done to make a person appear ridiculous: *He got the money from me by a* ~. ***the tricks of the trade,*** ways of attracting customers, gaining advantages over rivals, etc. **2** practical joke: *The children are always up to amusing* ~*s.* ***play a trick on sb,*** ⇨ play²(3). **3** feat of skill with the hands, etc: *conjuring* ~*s. Are you clever at card* ~*s?* ***do the trick,*** (*sl*) make it possible to get something done, finished: *One more turn of the screwdriver should do the* ~, fasten the screw securely. **4** strange or characteristic habit, mannerism, etc: *He has a* ~ *of pulling his left ear when he is thinking out a problem.* **5** (cards played in) one round (of bridge, etc): *take/win/lose a* ~. □ *vt* deceive: *He* ~*ed the poor girl out of her money/*~*ed her into marrying him by pretending that he was rich.*

trick·ery /-əri/ deception; cheating.

tricky *adj* (-ier, -iest) **(a)** (of persons and their actions) deceptive: *a* ~*y politician.* **(b)** (of work, etc) having hidden or unexpected difficulties: *a* ~*y problem/job.*

trickle /ˈtrɪkəl/ *vi,vt* (cause to) flow in drops or in a thin stream: *The tears* ~*d down her cheeks.* □ *n* [C] weak or thin flow: ~ *of blood.*

tri·cycle /ˈtraisɪkəl/ *n* [C] three-wheeled cycle.

tried *pt, pp* of try¹.

tri·en·nial /traiˈeniəl/ *n* [C], *adj* (something) lasting for, happening, or done every three years.

trier /ˈtraiər/ *n* ⇨ try¹.

trifle /ˈtraifəl/ *n* **1** [C] thing, event, of little value or importance: *It's silly to quarrel over* ~*s.* **2** [C] small amount of money: *It cost me only a* ~. **3** ***a trifle,*** *adv* a little: *This dress is a* ~ *too short.* **4** [C,U] sweet dish made of cream, white of eggs, cake, jam, etc. □ *vi,vt* behave lightly or insincerely toward: *It's wrong to* ~ *with the girl's affections*, make her think that you love her when you don't.

trif·ling /ˈtraiflɪŋ/ *adj* unimportant: *a trifling error.*

trig·ger /ˈtrɪgər/ *n* [C] lever for releasing a spring, esp of a gun, rifle. □ *vt* ***trigger sth off,*** be the immediate cause of (something serious or violent): *Who/What* ~*ed off the rebellion?*

ˈtrigger-ˌhappy *adj* (*informal*) over-eager to fire a gun; irresponsible in using firearms.

trig·on·om·etry /ˌtrɪgəˈnamətri/ *n* [U] branch of mathematics that deals with the relations between the sides and angles of triangles.

tri·lat·eral /ˌtraiˈlætərəl/ *adj* **1** of, on, with, three sides. **2** (of an agreement, etc) made between three (persons, governments): *a* ~ *treaty.*

trill /trɪl/ *n* [C] **1** shaky or vibrating sound made by the voice or as in bird song. **2** (*music*) quick alternation of two notes a tone or a semitone apart. **3** vibrating speech sound (eg Spanish *"r"*). □ *vi,vt* sing or play (a musical note) with a trill.

tril·lion /ˈtrɪlyən/ *n* [C] *adj* million million. ⇨ App 1.

tril·ogy /ˈtrɪlədʒi/ *n* [C] (*pl* -ies) group of three plays, novels, operas, etc having a common subject.

trim /trɪm/ *adj* (-mmer, -mmest) in good order; neat and tidy: *a* ~ *little garden.* □ *n* [U] **1** trim state; readiness; fitness: *The swimmer kept in good* ~ *by exercising regularly.* **2** decoration or ornamentation: *The new car has chrome* ~ *along the sides.* □ *vt,vi* (-mm-) **1** make trim, esp by taking or cutting away uneven, irregular or unwanted parts: ~ *one's beard.* **2** decorate or ornament (a dress, etc): *a hat ~med with fur*. **3** make (a boat, ship, aircraft) evenly balanced by arranging the position of the cargo, passengers, etc; set (the sails) to suit the wind.

trim·ming *n* [C] **(a)** (*pl*) side dishes, garnishes, and other things that go with something: *For Christmas dinner we had Virginia ham and all the ~s*, pineapple slices, spiced pears, side dishes of mashed turnips, sweet potatoes, tomato pudding, etc. **(b)** (usually *pl*) something used for trimming(2): *lace ~mings*.

tri·nitro·tolu·ene /ˌtraiˌnaitrouˈtalyuˌin/ *n* [U] (usually **TNT**) powerful explosive.

trin·ity /ˈtrɪnəti/ *n* [C] (*pl* -ies) group of three. **the Trinity,** (in Christian belief) union of three persons, Father, Son and Holy Ghost, one God.

trin·ket /ˈtrɪŋkɪt/ *n* [C] ornament or jewel of small value.

trio /ˈtriou/ *n* [C] (*pl* ~s) **1** group of three. **2** (musical composition for a) group of three singers or players.

trip /trɪp/ *vi,vt* (-pp-) **1** ***trip on/over sth,*** catch one's foot, etc in an obstacle and fall: *He ~ped on/over the root of a tree.* ***trip (sb) up,*** **(a)** (cause to) fall or make a false step: *He ~ped up and nearly fell.* **(b)** (*fig*) cause to make an error: *The defense attorney's next question ~ped the witness up.* **2** (*poet*) walk, run or dance with quick, light steps: *She came ~ping down the garden path.* □ *n* [C] **1** journey, esp for pleasure: *a day ~ to the beach.* **2** fall. **3** (*sl*) experience resulting from taking a hallucinatory drug.

tri·par·tite /ˌtraiˈparˌtait/ *adj* **1** (of an agreement) in which three parties have a share. **2** having three parts.

tripe /traip/ *n* [U] **1** part of the wall of the stomach of an ox or cow used as food: *a dish of stewed ~ and onions.* **2** (*sl*) useless talk, writing, ideas, etc: *Stop talking ~!*

triple /ˈtrɪpəl/ *adj* made up of three (parts or parties): *the ~ crown,* the Pope's tiara. □ *vt,vi* multiply by three.

trip·let /ˈtrɪplɪt/ *n* [C] **1** any of three children or animals born at the same time of the same mother. **2** set of three.

trip·li·cate /ˈtrɪplɪkɪt/ *adj* of which three copies are made. □ *n* [C] one of three like things, esp documents: *drawn up in ~*, one original and two copies. □ *vt* /ˈtrɪplɪˌkeit/ make in triplicate.

tri·pod /ˈtraiˌpad/ *n* [C] three-legged support, eg for a camera.

trite /trait/ *adj* (of remarks, ideas, opinions) ordinary (and so dull).

trite·ly *adv*

trite·ness /-nɪs/ *n* [U]

tri·umph /ˈtraiəmf, -ˌəmf/ *n* [C,U] (joy or satisfaction at a) success or victory: *return home in ~; shouts of ~.* □ *vi* win a victory (over); show joy because of success: *~ over a defeated enemy.*

tri·um·phal /traiˈəmfəl/ *adj* of, for, expressing, triumph: *a ~al arch,* one built in memory of a victory.

tri·um·phant /traiˈəmfənt/ *adj* (celebrating at) having triumphed.

tri·um·phant·ly *adv*

tri·um·virate /traiˈəmvərɪt/ *n* [C] **1** ruling body of three individuals. **2** group of three (usually famous) persons, associated in some way.

trivet /ˈtrɪvɪt/ *n* [C] plate or stand of metal, wood, etc on which hot dishes are placed.

triv·ial /ˈtrɪviəl/ *adj* **1** of small value or importance: *a ~ offense.* **2** ordinary (and so dull): *a ~ speech.* **3** (of a person) superficial: *Don't marry a ~ young man.*

triv·ial·ity /ˌtrɪviˈæləti/ *n* [U] state of being trivial; [C] (*pl* -ies) trivial idea, event, etc: *talk/write ~ities.*

triv·ially *adv*

trod, trod·den *pt,pp* of tread.

troll /troul/ *n* [C] (in Scandinavian mythology) supernatural giant, or, in later tales, a mischievous but friendly dwarf.

trol·ley /ˈtrali/ *n* [C] (*pl* ~s) **1** = streetcar. **2** small truck running on rails, eg one used by workers on a railway.

trol·lop /ˈtraləp/ *n* [C] prostitute.

trom·bone /tramˈboun/ *n* [C] large brass musical instrument with a sliding tube. ⇨ illus at brass.

trom·bon·ist /tramˈbounɪst/ *n* [C] trombone player.

troop /trup/ *n* [C] **1** company of persons or animals, esp when moving: *a ~ of Scouts.* **2** (*pl*) soldiers. **3** unit of cavalry, armored vehicles or artillery (under the command of a lieutenant). □ *vi,vt* come or go together in a group: *children ~ing out of school.* (*Note:* used with a *pl* subject.)

ˈtroop carrier, ship or large aircraft for transporting troops.

trooper *n* [C] **(a)** soldier in a cavalry or armored regiment. ***swear like a trooper,*** swear a great deal. **(b)** member of the state (highway) police.

ˈtroop·ship *n* [C] ship for transporting troops.

trophy /ˈtroufi/ *n* [C] (*pl* -ies) **1** something kept in memory of a victory or success (eg in hunting, sport, etc). **2** prize, eg for winning a tournament: *ˈtennis trophies.*

tropic /ˈtrapɪk/ *n* **1** [C] line of latitude 23°27′ north (*Tropic of Cancer*) or south (*Tropic of Capricorn*) of the equator. **2 the tropics,** the parts of the world between these two latitudes.

tropi·cal /-kəl/ *adj* of, or as of, the tropics: *a ~al climate.*

tropi·cally /-kli/ *adv*

trot /trat/ *vi,vt* (-tt-) **1** (of horses, etc) go at a pace faster than a walk but not so fast as a gallop. **2** move with short steps. **3** ***trot sth out,*** (*informal*) produce; bring out for approval, inspection, etc: *They are always ~ting out the retired professor as an authority.* □ *n* (*sing* only) **1** trotting pace: *go at a steady ~.* **2** period of trotting: *go for a ~.*

trot·ter *n* [C] horse bred and trained to trot.

trouble /ˈtrəbəl/ *vt,vi* **1** cause worry, discomfort, anxiety or inconvenience to: *be ~d by bad news; ~d with a nasty cough.* **2** ask a person to do something inconvenient: *May I ~ you for a match?* **3** (esp *pp*) disturb: *~d looks.* □ *n* **1** [C,U] worry; unhappiness; difficulty: *She's always making ~ for her friends. He has been through much ~/has had many ~s. The ~ is that..*., The difficulty is that... ***in trouble,*** suffering, or likely to suffer, anxiety, punishment, etc eg because one has done wrong. ***ask/look for trouble,*** (*informal*) behave in such a way that trouble is likely: *It's asking for ~ to associate with criminals.* ***get into trouble,*** do something deserving punishment, etc. ***get sb into trouble,*** cause a person to be in trouble. ***get a girl into trouble,*** (*informal*) make her pregnant. **2** [C] nuisance: *I don't want to be any ~ to you.* **3** [U] (extra) work; inconvenience: *Did the work give you much ~? Thank you for all the ~ you've taken to help my son.* **4** [C,U] political or social unrest: *ˈLabor ~(s)* (eg strikes) *cost the country enormous sums last year.* **5** [C,U] illness: *ˈheart ~.*

ˈtrouble·maker *n* [C] person who causes trouble (eg in industry).

ˈtrouble·shooter *n* [C] expert on problems of a certain kind who is employed, or whose help is sought, in solving them.

ˈtrouble·some /-səm/ *adj* causing trouble: *a ~some child/headache/problem.*

trough /trɔf/ *n* [C] **1** long open box for animals to feed or drink from. **2** long open box in which a baker kneads dough for bread. **3** region of lower atmospheric pressure between two regions of higher pressure.

trounce /trauns/ *vt* (*dated*) defeat: *Our team was ~d on Saturday.*

troupe /trup/ *n* [C] company, esp of actors or of members of a circus.

trouper *n* [C] member of a theatrical troupe: *He's a good ~r*, a loyal and uncomplaining colleague.

trousers /ˈtrauzərz/ *n pl* = pants.

trous·seau /ˈtruˌsou/ *n* [C] (*pl* ~s) outfit of clothing, etc for a bride.

trout /traut/ *n* [C] (*pl* unchanged) freshwater fish valued as food and for the sport of catching it. ⇨ illus at fish.

trowel /ˈtrauəl/ *n* [C] **1** flat-bladed tool for spreading cement, etc. **2** tool with a curved blade for lifting plants, etc.

troy /trɔi/ *n* [U] system of weights, used for gold and silver, in which one pound = 12 ounces and one ounce = 20 pennyweights.

tru·ant /ˈtruənt/ *n* [C] child who stays away from school without permission. ***play truant,*** be a truant.

tru·ancy /ˈtruənsi/ *n* [C,U] (*pl* -ies) (instance of) playing truant.

truce /trus/ *n* [C] (agreement for the) stopping of fighting for a time.

truck[1] /trək/ *n* [C] **1** strong motor vehicle with carrying compartment built onto it, used for the transport of soil, goods, etc: *ˈtank ~,* for transporting milk, oil, etc. ⇨ illus at tractor. **2** motor vehicle like a truck(1), but with a swivel for pulling a detachable carrying compartment: *~ and trailer.*

trudge /trədʒ/ *vi* walk wearily or heavily: *trudging through the deep snow.* □ *n* [C] long, tiring walk.

true /tru/ *adj* (-r, -st) **1** according to, in agreement with, fact: *Is the news ~?* ***come true,*** (of a hope, dream) really happen, become fact. **2** loyal, faithful: *be ~ to one's word/promise*, do what one has promised to do. **3** in accordance with reason; genuine: *True friendship should last forever.* **4** ***true to type,*** being, behaving, etc as expected. ***ˌtried and ˈtrue,*** ⇨ try[1](3). **5** accurately fitted or placed: *Is the wheel ~?* **6** exact; accurate: *a ~ copy of a document.* □ *n* (only in) ***out of true,*** not in its exact or accurate position: *The door is out of ~.* □ *adv* (used with certain verbs involving accuracy) truly: *aim ~. He sketched it ~.*

ˌtrue-ˈblue *n* [C], *adj* (person who is) firmly loyal.

ˈtrue·love *n* (*dated*) (expression of love to a) boyfriend, girlfriend.

tru·ism /ˈtruˌɪzm/ *n* [C] statement that is obviously true and need not have been made: *It's a ~ to say that you are alive.*

truly /ˈtruli/ *adv* **1** truthfully: *speak ~.* **2** sincerely: *feel ~ grateful.* ***yours truly,*** (used at the end of a letter, before the signature). **3** genuinely; certainly: *a ~ brave action.*

trump /trəmp/ *n* [C] **1** (in card games such as whist, bridge) each card of a suit that has been declared as having higher value than the other three suits: *Hearts are ~s.* **2** (*informal*) good person; fine fellow: *He's a real ~, always there when you need a friend.* □ *vt,vi* **1** play a trump on: *~ the ace of clubs.* **2** invent (an excuse, a lie, etc) in order to deceive: *He was arrested on a ~ed-up charge.*

trum·pet /ˈtrəmpɪt/ *n* [C] **1** brass musical instrument played by blowing into it. ⇨ illus at brass. **2** sound (as) of a trumpet: *the ~ of an elephant.* **3** something like a trumpet in shape (eg a flower). □ *vt,vi* (esp of an elephant) make loud sounds.

trum·peter *n* [C] trumpet player.

trunk /trəŋk/ *n* [C] **1** main stem of a tree (contrasted with the branches). ⇨ illus at tree. **2** body (not the head, arms or legs). **3** main part of any structure. **4** large box with a hinged lid, for clothes, etc while traveling. **5** long nose of an elephant. **6** (*pl*) man's, boy's, clothing covering the lower part of the trunk(2), worn for swimming. **7** place for luggage, etc at the back of an automobile. **8** main connection line between two telephone switching stations or exchanges.

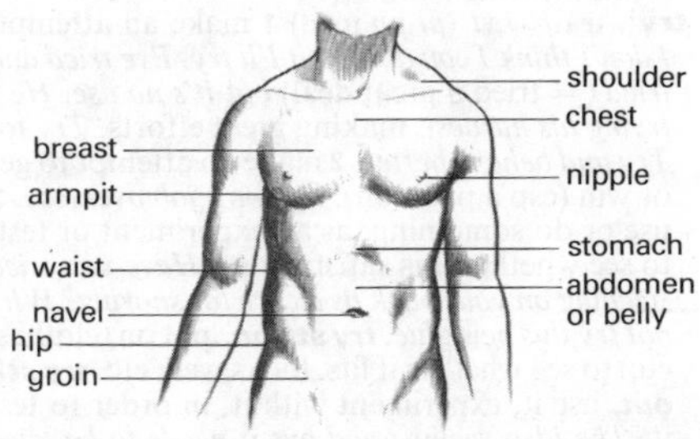

HUMAN TRUNK

ˈtrunk line, (a) main line of a railway. **(b)** = trunk(8).

truss /trəs/ *n* [C] **1** bundle. **2** framework supporting a roof, bridge, etc. **3** padded belt worn by a person suffering from hernia. □ *vt* **1** tie or fasten up: *~ up a chicken*, pin the wings to the body before boiling or roasting it. **2** support (a roof, bridge, etc) with a truss(2).

trust[1] /trəst/ *n* **1** [U] confidence, strong belief, in the goodness, strength, reliability of a person or thing: *A child usually has perfect ~ in its mother.* ***on trust,* (a)** without proof: *You'll have to take my statement on ~.* **(b)** on credit. **2** [U] responsibility: *a position of great ~.* **3** [C] (*legal*) property held and managed by one or more persons (*trustees*) for the benefit of another or others; [U] the legal relation between the trustee(s) and the property: *By his will he created ~s for his children.* **4** [C] association of business firms for eg reducing competition, maintenance of prices.

trust·ful /-fəl/, **trust·ing** *adj* ready to have trust in others; not suspicious.

trust·fully /-fəli/, **trust·ing·ly** *adv*

trust[2] /trəst/ *vt,vi* **1** believe in the honesty and reliability of: *He's not the sort of man to be ~ed/not a man I would ~.* **2** have confidence in: *~ in God.* **3** allow (a person) to do or have something, go somewhere, etc knowing that he will act sensibly, etc: *Do you ~ your young daughters to go out with any sort of men?*

trustee[1] /trəˈsti/ *n* [C] person who has charge of property in trust(3) or of the business affairs of an institution.

trus·tee·ship /-ˌʃɪp/ *n* [U] position of a trustee.

trustee[2] /ˈtrəsti/ *n* [C] = trusty.

trust·worthy /ˈtrəstˌwərði/ *adj* dependable.

trusty, trustee /ˈtrəsti/ *n* [C] convict considered trustworthy and given special privileges in prison.

truth /truθ/ *n* (*pl* ~s /truðz/) **1** [U] quality or state of being true: *There's no ~/not a word of ~ in what he says.* **2** [U] that which is true: *tell the ~.* ***to tell the truth...,*** (formula used when making a confession): *To tell the ~, I forgot all about it.* **3** [C] fact, belief, etc accepted as true: *scientific ~s.*

truth·ful /-fəl/ *adj* **(a)** (of persons) in the habit of telling the truth. **(b)** (of statements) true.

truth·fully /-fəli/ *adv*

truth·ful·ness /-nɪs/ *n* [U]

try[1] /trai/ *vi,vt* (*pt,pp* tried) **1** make an attempt: *I don't think I can do it, but I'll try. I've tried and tried* (= tried a great deal) *but it's no use. He's trying his hardest*, making great efforts. *Try to/Try and behave better.* **2** make an attempt to get or win (esp a position): *try for a job overseas.* **3** use or do something, as an experiment or test, to see whether it is satisfactory: *Have you tried sleeping on your back as a cure for snoring? Why not try this new glue.* ***try sth on,*** put on (clothes, etc) to see whether it fits, looks well, etc. ***try sth out,*** use it, experiment with it, in order to test it: *The idea seems good but it needs to be tried out.* ***ˌtried and ˈtrue,*** of proven worth or dependability. ***try one's hand at sth*** ⇨ hand[1](6). **4** submit a case or person to trial in a law court: *The case/accused was tried in Criminal Court.* **5** inquire into (a case) in a court of law: *He was tried and found guilty of murder.* **6** cause to be tired, exhausted, out of patience, etc: *His courage was severely tried.*

try·ing *adj* (⇨ 6 above) causing tiredness, exhaustion, impatience, etc: *have a trying day.*

ˈtry·out *n* [C] test of ability, qualification, etc, eg of an athlete.

try[2] /trai/ *n* [C] (*pl* tries) attempt: *He had three tries and failed each time.*

tsetse /ˈtetsi, ˈsetsi/ *n* [C] (also **ˈtsetse-fly**) blood-sucking fly (in tropical Africa) carrying and transmitting (often fatal) disease in cattle, horses, etc. ⇨ illus at insect.

T-shirt /ˈti ˌʃərt/ *n* ⇨ T, t.

tsp. *abbr* = teaspoon(s).

T-square /ˈtiˌskwær/ ⇨ T, t.

tub /təb/ *n* [C] **1** large open vessel, used for washing clothes, holding liquids, growing plants in, etc. **2** = tubful. **3** (*informal*) bathtub.

ˈtub·ful /-ˌfʊl/ *n* [C] as much as a tub can hold.

tuba /ˈtubə/ *n* [C] (*pl* ~s) large musical instrument of brass playing deep notes. ⇨ illus at brass.

tubby /ˈtəbi/ *adj* (-ier, -iest) (*informal*) fat and round: *a ~ little man.*

tube /tub/ *n* [C] **1** long hollow cylinder of metal, glass or rubber, esp for holding or carrying air, liquids, etc: *the ˈinner ~* (of a bicycle/automobile tire) of rubber, filled with air under pressure. **2** soft metal container with a screw cap, used for pastes, paints, etc: *a ~ of toothpaste.* **3** hollow cylindrical organ in the body: *the bronchial ~s.* **4** cathode-ray or vacuum tube. **the tube** (*sl*) television: *Children spend too much time with /watching the ~.*

tube·less *adj* having no inner tube: *~less tires.*

tub·ing *n* [U] material in the form of a tube: *copper tubing.*

tu·ber /ˈtubər/ *n* [C] enlarged part of an underground stem, eg a potato.

tu·ber·cu·lar /təˈbərkyələr/ *adj* of, affected by, tuberculosis.

tu·ber·cu·lo·sis /təˌbərkyəˈlousɪs/ *n* [U] (common *abbr* **TB**) disease affecting various parts of the body's tissues, esp the lungs.

tu·bu·lar /ˈtubyələr/ *adj* having, consisting of, tubes or tubing: *~ furniture*, with parts made of metal tubing.

tuck /tək/ *n* [C] flat, stitched fold of material in cloth, for shortening or for ornament. □ *vt,vi* draw together into a small space; put or push into a desired or convenient position: *Your shirt's hanging out; ~ it in to your trousers. He sat with his legs ~ed up under him. The map is ~ed away in a pocket at the end of the book. She ~ed him into/up in bed,* pulled the bed clothes up round him.

-tude /-ˌtud/ *suffix* (used to form a *noun*) condition: *magnitude.*

Tues. *abbr* = Tuesday.

Tues·day /ˈtuzdi, -ˌdei/ *n* third day of the week.

tuft /təft/ *n* [C] bunch of feathers, grass, etc growing closely together.

tufted *adj* having, growing in, tufts.

tug /təg/ *vt,vi* (-gg-) pull hard (*at*): *We tugged so*

hard that the rope broke. □ *n* [C] **1** sudden hard pull: *I felt a tug at my sleeve.* **2** (also ˈ**tugboat**) small powerful boat for towing ships, etc. ⇨ illus at ship.
ˌ**tug of ˈwar,** contest in which two teams pull against each other on a rope.
tu·ition /tuˈɪʃən/ *n* [U] (fee for) teaching or for enrollment in a school.
tu·lip /ˈtulɪp/ *n* [C] bulb plant with a large bell-shaped flower on a tall stem. ⇨ illus at flower.
tumble /ˈtəmbəl/ *vi,vt* **1** fall, esp quickly and end over end: *tumbling down the stairs/off a bicycle.* **2** move up and down, to and fro, in a restless or disorderly way: *The puppies were tumbling around on the floor.* ˈ***tumble*** ˌ***dry,*** dry (clothes, etc) in a tumble drier. **3** be in a weak state (as if ready to fall): *The old barn is tumbling down.* **4** cause to fall: *The accident ~d the riders out of the wagon.* □ *n* [C] **1** fall: *have a nasty ~.* **2** confused state: *Things were all in a ~.*
ˈ**tumble·down** *adj* dilapidated.
ˈ**tumble drier,** machine for drying washing by turning it in warm air.
tum·bler /ˈtəmblər/ *n* [C] **1** drinking glass without a handle or stem. **2** part of the mechanism of a lock which must be turned by a key before the lock will open.
tu·mes·cent /tuˈmesənt/ *adj* (*formal*) swelling; swollen.
tummy /ˈtəmi/ *n* [C] (*pl* -ies) (*informal*) (used by and to children) stomach; belly.
tu·mor /ˈtumər/ *n* [C] diseased growth in some part of the body.
tu·mult /ˈtuməlt/ *n* [C,U] **1** great disturbance: *the ~ of battle.* **2** confused and excited state of mind: *be in a ~.*
tu·mul·tu·ous /tuˈməltʃuəs/ *adj* (*formal*) noisy and energetic: *a ~ welcome.*
tu·mul·tu·ous·ly *adv*
tuna /ˈtunə/ *n* [C] (*pl ~ or ~s*) large seafish used as food. ⇨ illus at fish.
tun·dra /ˈtəndrə/ *n* [U] wide, treeless plain of the arctic regions (of Alaska, Canada, Russia.)
tune /tun/ *n* **1** [C] succession of notes forming a melody (of a song, etc). **2** [U] quality of having a strong melody: *music with very little ~ in it.* **3** [U] ***in/out of tune,*** at/not at the correct pitch: *sing/play in ~.* **4** [U] (*fig*) harmony: *be in/out of ~ with one's surroundings/companions.* ***change one's tune,*** change one's way of speaking, behavior, etc (eg from insolence or respect). ***to the tune of,*** to the amount of: *He was fined* (eg for a traffic violation) *to the ~ of $30.* □ *vt,vi* **1** adjust the strings, etc (of a musical instrument) to the right pitch: *~ a guitar.* **2** ***tune in (to),*** **(a)** adjust the controls of a radio or television to a particular frequency/station/channel/program. **(b)** (*fig*) be aware of what other people are saying, feeling, etc: *He's not very well ~d in to his surroundings.* **3** adjust an engine so that it gives its best, or a special, performance.
tune·ful /-fəl/ *adj* having a pleasing tune.
tune·fully /-fəli/ *adv*
ˈ**tune-up** *n* [C] adjustment of an engine to give good performance.
ˈ**tuning-fork,** small steel instrument like a fork which produces a musical note when struck.
tuner /ˈtunər/ *n* **1** person who tunes musical instruments: *a piˈano ~.* **2** (part of) a radio which receives the signals.
tu·nic /ˈtunɪk/ *n* [C] **1** sleeveless gown worn in ancient times (eg Greece and Rome). **2** = smock. **3** loose, pleated dress gathered at the waist with a belt.
tun·nel /ˈtənəl/ *n* [C] underground passage (esp through a hill or mountain, for a road, railway, etc). □ *vi,vt* (also -ll-) dig a tunnel (through/into something).
ˈ**tunnel vision, (a)** loss of sight at the edge of the normal field of vision. **(b)** (*fig*) unable to grasp the wider implications of something.
tunny /ˈtəni/ *n* [C] (*pl* -ies or unchanged) = tuna.
tur·ban /ˈtərbən/ *n* [C] **1** man's headdress made by winding a length of cloth round the head (as worn in some Asian countries). **2** similar woman's close-fitting hat.
tur·bine /ˈtərˌbain/ *n* [C] engine or motor whose driving wheel is turned by a current of water, steam or air.
tur·bu·lence /ˈtərbyələns/ *n* [C] state of being turbulent.
tur·bu·lent /ˈtərbyələnt/ *adj* violent; disorderly; uncontrolled: *~ waves/passions.*
tur·bu·lent·ly *adv*
turf /tərf/ *n* (*pl ~s* /tərfs/ or turves /tərvs/) **1** [U] soil with grass growing in it. **2** [C] piece of turf, esp for horse racing. □ *vt* cover or lay (a piece of land) with turf.
tur·key /ˈtərki/ *n* [C] (*pl ~s*) large bird valued as food, traditional at Thanksgiving; [U] its flesh.
Tur·kish bath /ˌtərkɪʃ ˈbæθ/ *n* [C] bath of hot air or steam, followed by a shower and massage.
tur·moil /ˈtərˌmɔiəl/ *n* [C,U] (instance of) trouble, disturbance: *The country was in (a) ~ during the election.*
turn[1] /tərn/ *n* [C] **1** act of turning; turning movement: *a few ~s of the handle.* ***done to a turn,*** cooked just enough, neither underdone nor overdone. **2** change of direction: *sudden ~s in the road.* ***at every turn,*** (*fig*) very frequently: *I've been coming across old friends at every ~ during my visit.* **3** change in condition: *The sick man/My affairs took a ~ for the better/worse.* **4** occasion or opportunity for doing something, esp in one's proper order among others: *It's your ~ to read now, John.* ***in turn,*** **(a)** (of two persons) one after the other. **(b)** (of more than two persons) in succession: *The boys were asked in ~ to see the examiner.* ***out of turn,*** before or after the permitted time: *You mustn't speak out of ~.* ***take turns at sth,*** do it in succession: *Mary and Helen took ~s at babysitting.* **5** action regarded as affecting a person: *do her a good ~,* be helpful, etc. **6** natural tendency: *a boy with a meˈchanical ~,* interested in, clever at, mechanical things. **7** short period of activity: *I'll take a ~ at the wheel if you want a rest (from driving).* **8** short performance on the stage.
ˈ**turn** ˌ**indicator,** flashing light on a motor vehicle showing the direction in which it is about to turn.
turn[2] /tərn/ *vt,vi* (For special uses with *adverbial particles* and *prepositions,* ⇨ 5 below.) **1** (cause to) move around a point; (cause to) move so as

to face in a different direction: *The earth ~s around the sun. He ~ed away from me. He ~ed to look at me. He ~ed (to the) left. When does the tide ~*, begin to flow in/out? ***turn the corner,*** ⇨ corner(1). ***turn a deaf ear (to),*** ⇨ ear¹(1). ***turn one's hand to sth,*** (be able to) do (a task, etc): *He can ~ his hand to most jobs around the house.* ***turn one's mind/thoughts/attention to sth,*** direct one's mind, etc to: *Please ~ your attention to something more important.* **2** (cause to) change in nature, quality, condition, etc: *Frost ~s water into ice. Caterpillars ~ into* (= become) *butterflies. His hair has ~ed grey.* ***turn sb's head,*** make him vain: *The excessive praise the young actor received ~ed his head.* **3** reach and pass: *He has ~ed* (= reach the age of) *fifty. It has just ~ed two*, is just after two o'clock. **4** shape (something) on a lathe, etc: *~ a bowl on a potter's wheel.* **5** (special uses with *adverbial particles* and *prepositions*):

turn (sb) against sb, (cause to) become hostile to: *He tried to ~ the children against their mother.*

turn (sb/sth) around, (cause to) face another way, be in another direction: *Turn around and let me see your new hairstyle.*

turn (sb) away, (cause to) turn in a different direction so as not to be facing; refuse to look at, welcome, help, admit (to a place): *She ~ed away in disgust. We had to ~ away hundreds of fans*, eg from a stadium, because all the seats were sold.

turn (sb/sth) back, (cause to) return the way one has come: *It's getting dark—we'd better ~ back.*

turn (sth) down, **(a)** (cause to) fold down: *~ down one's coat collar.* **(b)** reduce (the brilliance of a light, flow of water) by turning a dial or tap. ***turn sb/sth down,*** refuse to consider (an offer, a proposal, or the person who makes it): *He asked Jane to marry him but she ~ed him down.* ***turn 'in,*** (*informal*) go to bed. ***turn sb 'in,*** (*informal*) surrender him to the police. ***turn (sth) 'in,*** (cause to) fold or slant inward: *His toes ~ in.* ***turn (sth) ˌinside 'out,*** (cause to) become inside out: *The wind ~ed my old umbrella inside out.* ***turn 'off,*** change direction; leave (one road) for another: *Is this where we ~ off?* ***turn sth 'off,*** stop the flow of (liquid, gas, current) by turning a tap or other control: *~ off the water/lights/radio/TV.* ***turn (sb) 'off,*** (*sl*) (cause him to) lose interest, desire, etc: *He/This music really ~s me off!*

turn sth 'on, start the flow of (liquid, gas, current) by turning a tap, etc: *Turn the lights/radio on.* ***turn (sb) 'on*** (*sl*) have, give to him, great pleasure or excitement: *What kind of music ~s you on? Some psychedelic drugs ~ you on very quickly*, change your mental or emotional state. ***turn on sth,*** depend on: *The success of the debate ~s on the conservative vote.* ***turn on sb,*** attack: *The dog ~ed on me and bit me in the leg.* ***turn out (well, etc),*** prove to be; be in the end: *Everything ~ed out well/satisfactory. As it ~ed out...*, As it happened in the end... ***turn (sth) 'out,*** (cause to) point outward: *His toes ~ out.* ***turn sth out,*** **(a)** extinguish by turning a knob, etc: *Please ~ out the lights.* **(b)** empty (a drawer, one's pockets, a room, etc) when looking for something, etc: *~ out all the drawers in one's desk.* ***turn sb 'out (of/from sth),*** expel by force, threats, etc: *~ a tenant out* (= from his house) *for not paying the rent.* ***turn sb/sth 'out,*** produce: *Our new factory is ~ing out large quantities of goods. The school has ~ed out some first-rate athletes.* ***turn (sb) 'out,*** (cause people to) assemble for some event, or for duty: *Not many men ~ed out to watch the match.*

turn (sb/sth) 'over, (cause to) fall over, upset; change the position of: *He ~ed over in bed.* ***turn sth over in one's mind,*** think about it (before making a decision). ***turn sb/sth over (to sb),*** give the control or conduct of it or him to: *I've ~ed over the management of my affairs to my brother. The thief was ~ed over to the police.* ***turn sth over,*** do business to the amount of: *Mr. Smith says business ~s over $3,500 a week.* ***turn 'to,*** get busy: *The design staff ~ed to and produced a set of drawings in twenty-four hours.* ***turn to sb,*** go to: *The child ~ed to its mother for comfort.*

turn 'up, **(a)** make one's appearance; arrive: *He promised to come, but hasn't ~ed up yet.* **(b)** be found, esp by chance: *The book you've lost may ~ up one of these days.* **(c)** (of an opportunity, etc) happen: *He's still waiting for something* (eg a job, a piece of good luck) *to ~ up.* ***turn (sth) 'up,*** **(a)** (cause to) slope or face upward: *~* (= roll) *up one's shirt sleeves.* **(b)** expose; make visible: *He ~ed up some buried treasure on the beach.* ***turn up one's nose at sth,*** (*fig*) express a superior and critical attitude toward: *She ~ed up her nose at the suggestion.* ***turn upon sb/sth*** = turn on sb/sth.

turn·coat /ˈtərnˌkout/ *n* [C] person who deserts one group for another.

ˈturning point, (*fig*) point in place, time, development, etc which is critical: *reach a ~ point in history/in one's life.*

ˈturn·out *n* [C] assembly of persons turning out for something: *There was a good* (ie large) *~out for the meeting.*

ˈturn·over *n* [C] **(a)** amount of business done: *a profit of $1,000 on a ~ of $10,000.* **(b)** rate of replacement: *There is a higher ~ of teachers in big cities.*

tur·nip /ˈtərnɪp/ *n* [C] (plant with a) large round root used as a vegetable and as food for cattle.

turn·pike /ˈtərn ˌpaik/ *n* main public road, esp one supported by tolls: *We drove on the New Jersey Turnpike to reach New York.*

turn·stile /ˈtərnˌstaiəl/ *n* [C] revolving gate that allows one person through at a time.

tur·quoise /ˈtərˌkwɔiz/ *n* [C,U] (color of a) greenish-blue precious stone.

tur·ret /ˈtərɪt/ *n* [C] **1** small tower, esp at a corner of a building or defensive wall. **2** steel structure protecting gunners.

turtle /ˈtərtəl/ *n* [C] sea animal with a soft body protected by a hard shell like a tortoise. ⇨ at reptile.

tur·tle·neck /ˈtərtəlˌnek/ *n* [C] shirt or sweater with a high, round neck.

turves *pl* of turf.

tusk /təsk/ *n* [C] long-pointed tooth, esp one coming out from the closed mouth, as in the elephant, walrus or wild boar. ⇨ illus at walrus.
tussle /ˈtəsəl/ *n* [C], *vi* (have a) difficult struggle or fight (*with*).
tut /tət/, **tut-tut** /ˌtətˈtət/ *int* (*liter*) used to express impatience.
tu·te·lage /ˈtutəlɪdʒ/ *n* [U] (*formal*) guardianship.
tutor /ˈtutər/ *n* [C] private teacher of a single pupil or a very small class. □ *vt* teach as a tutor.
tu·tor·ial /tuˈtɔriəl/ *adj* of a tutor or his duties: *~ial classes.* □ *n* [C] teaching period for a small group of university students.
tux·edo /ˌtəkˈsidou/ *n* [C] (*pl* ~s) **1** evening attire for a man, usually black with silk or satin lapels on the jacket. **2** (also **tuxedo jacket**) semiformal dinner jacket.
TV /ˌti ˈvi/ *abbr* (*informal*) = television.
TV ˈdinner, meal for one person, cooked and frozen on a tinfoil tray, ready for quick heating.
TˈV guide, daily or weekly listing of television programs for a particular area.
twaddle /ˈtwadəl/ *n* [U] foolish talk.
twang /twæŋ/ *n* [C] **1** sound of a tight string or wire being pulled and released: *the ~ of a guitar.* **2** nasal tone of voice. **3** regional accent, esp of the southwest: *You can tell he's a Texan from his ~.* □ *vt,vi* (cause to) make a twang(1): *He was ~ing a banjo.*
'twas /twəz/ (*old use*) = it was.
tweak /twik/ *vt* pinch and twist: *~ a child's nose.* □ *n* [C] act of tweaking.
tweed /twid/ *n* **1** [U] (often as an *adjective*) thick woolen cloth of mixed colors: *a ~ coat.* **2** (*pl*) (suit of) clothes made of tweed: *dressed in Scottish ~s.*
tweet /twit/ *n* [C], *vi* (of a bird) = chirp.
tweez·ers /ˈtwizərz/ *n pl* (also *a pair of ~*) tiny pair of tongs for picking up or pulling out very small things, eg hairs from the eyebrows.
twelfth /twelfθ/ *n* [C], *adj* (of) one of 12 (parts) or the next after 11.
twelve /twelv/ *n* [C], *adj* (of) 12.
twen·ti·eth /ˈtwentiəθ/ *n* [C], *adj* (of) one of 20 parts or the next after 19.
twenty /ˈtwenti/ *n* [C], *adj* (of) 20.
twice /twais/ *adv* two times: *~ as much/as many. He's ~ the man he used to be,* healthier, stronger, more confident, more capable, etc. ***think twice about doing sth,*** hesitate, think carefully, before deciding to do it.
twiddle /ˈtwɪdəl/ *vt,vi* twist or turn idly: *~ one's thumbs; ~ a ring on one's finger.*
twig /twɪg/ *n* [C] small shoot on or at the end of a branch (tree, bush or plant). ⇨ illus at tree.
twi·light /ˈtwaiˌlait/ *n* [U] **1** faint light before sunrise or after sunset: *go for a walk in the ~.* **2** (*fig*) period about which little is known: *in the ~ of history.*
twill /twɪl/ *n* [U] strong cotton cloth.
twin /twɪn/ *n* **1** [C] either of two children or animals born at the same time of the same mother: (as an *adjective*) *ˌ~ ˈbrothers.* **2** (as an *adjective*) completely like, closely associated with, another: *ˌ~ ˈbeds,* two identical single beds.
twine /twain/ *n* [U] thin string made by twisting two or more yarns together. □ *vt,vi* twist; wind: *vines twining round a tree.*
twinge /twɪndʒ/ *n* [C] sudden, sharp sensation of pain, guilt, etc: *a ~ of pain from a bad tooth; a ~ of remorse.* □ *vi* produce this pain.
twinkle /ˈtwɪŋkəl/ *vi* **1** shine with a light that gleams unsteadily: *stars that ~ in the sky.* **2** (of eyes) sparkle: *Her eyes ~d with amusement/mischief.* □ *n* **1** [U] twinkling light: *the ~ of the stars.* **2** sparkle: *There was a mischievous ~ in her eyes.*
twink·ling /ˈtwɪŋklɪŋ/, (*sing* only) ***in a twinkling; in the twinkling of an eye,*** in an instant.
twirl /twərl/ *vt,vi* **1** (cause to) turn around and around quickly: *He sat ~ing his thumbs.* **2** curl: *He ~ed his mustache.* □ *n* [C] quick circular motion.
twist /twɪst/ *vt,vi* **1** wind or turn (a number of threads, strands, etc) one around the other: *~ pieces of straw into a rope.* **2** make (a rope, a garland, etc) by doing this. **3** turn, esp by the use of force; turn the two ends of (something) in opposite directions: *~ the cap off a tube of toothpaste. He fell and ~ed his ankle.* ***twist sb's arm,*** (*fig*) put (friendly or unfriendly) pressure on him to do something. ***twist sb around one's little finger,*** (*informal*) get him to do what one wants him to do. **4** force (a person's words) out of their true meaning: *The police tried to ~ his words into a confession of guilt.* **5** give a spiral form to (a rod, column, etc); receive, have, move or grow in, a spiral form: *~ed columns,* as in architecture. **6** turn and curve in different directions; change position or direction: *The road ~s and turns up the side of the mountain.* **7** pull out of the usual shape; distort: *He ~ed his face in a grimace.* **8** cause severe mental or emotional change: *The terrible shock must have ~ed his mind.* **9** dance the twist, ⇨ 5 below. □ *n* **1** [C] turning or being turned: *Give the rope a few more ~s. There are many ~s in the road.* **2** [C] something made by twisting: *a rope full of ~s.* **3** [C,U] thread, string, rope, etc made by twisting together two or more strands. **4** peculiar tendency of mind or character: *He has a criminal ~ in him.* **5** dance (popular in the 1960's) with twisting of the arms and hips.
twister *n* **(a)** difficult task, problem, etc. **(b)** (*informal*) = tornado. **(c)** = tongue twister.
twit /twɪt/ *n* [C] (*sl*) foolish person.
twitch /twɪtʃ/ *n* [C] **1** sudden, quick, usually uncontrollable movement of a muscle. **2** sudden quick pull: *I felt a ~ at my sleeve.* □ *vi,vt* (cause to) move in a twitch(1): *The horse ~ed its ears.*
twit·ter /ˈtwɪtər/ *vi* **1** (of birds) make a succession of soft short sounds. **2** (of persons) talk rapidly through excitement, nervousness, etc. □ *n* [C] chirping: *the ~ of sparrows.*
two /tu/ *adj, n* [C] (of) 2. ***break/cut sth in two,*** into two parts. ***put ˌtwo and ˌtwo toˈgether,*** infer something from what one sees, hears, learns, etc.
ˈtwo-bit *adj* (*informal*) cheap, inferior.
ˈtwo-ˌfaced /-ˌfeɪst/ *adj* (*fig*) insincere.
ˌtwo-ˈfacedly /-ˈfeisɪdli/ *adv*

ˌ**two-ˈfacedness** /-ˈfeisɪdnɪs/ *n* [U]
ˈ**two·fold** *adj, adv* double, doubly.
ˌ**two-ˈpiece** *n* set of clothes of similar or matching material, eg skirt and jacket, trousers and jacket: (as an *adjective*) *a* ˌ*two-piece* ˈ*bathing suit*.
ˈ**two-ply** *adj* of two strands or thicknesses: ˌ*two-ply* ˈ*wool*/ˈ*wood*.
ˌ**two-ˈseater** *n* [C] car, aircraft, etc with seats for two persons.
ˈ**two-time** *vt,vi* (*sl*) deceive.
ˈ**two-timing** *adj* (*sl*) deceitful.
ˈ**two-ˌway** *adj* **(a)** (of a switch) allowing current to be switched on or off from either of two points. **(b)** (of a road or street) in which traffic may move in both directions. **(c)** (of radio equipment, etc) for both sending and receiving.

TWX *abbr* = teletypewriter exchange.

TX *postal abbr* = Texas. ⇨ App 6.

ty·coon /taiˈkun/ *n* [C] (*informal*) wealthy and powerful business man or industrialist: ˈ*oil* ~*s*.

ty·ing *present participle* of tie²

tym·pa·num /ˈtɪmpənəm/ *n* (*pl* ~s or -na /-nə/) **1** middle ear. **2** eardrum. ⇨ illus at ear.

type¹ /taip/ *n* **1** [C] person, thing, event, etc considered as an example of a class or group: *You seldom see that ~ of house*. **2** [C] class or group considered to have common characteristics: *men of this ~*. ***true to type,*** ⇨ true(4). **3** [U] letters, etc cut from blocks of wood or cast in blocks of metal for use in printing; [C] one of these blocks.
ˈ**type·script** *n* [C] typewritten copy (prepared for printing, etc).
ˈ**type·write** *vt,vi* (*pt* -wrote /-ˌrout/, *pp* -written /-ˌrɪtən/) = type(1) (the usual word).
ˈ**type·writer** *n* [C] machine with which a person prints letters on paper, using the fingers on a keyboard.

type² /taip/ *vt,vi* **1** use, write with, a typewriter: ~ *a letter*. *She ~s well*. **2** determine the type(2) of something: ~ *a virus*.
typ·ing *n* [C] act, job, of using a typewriter.
ty·pist *n* [C] person who types(1).

type·cast /ˈtaipˌkæst/ *vt* (*pt,pp* typecast) cast (a person) for a part in a play, etc which seems to fit his/her own personality. □ *adj* (of a person) very suited to what he is doing.

ty·phoid /ˈtaiˌfɔid/ *n* [U] (also **typhoid ˈfever**) infectious disease which attacks the intestines.

ty·phoon /taiˈfun/ *n* [C] violent hurricane.

ty·phus /ˈtaifəs/ *n* [U] infectious disease with fever and purple spots on the body.

typi·cal /ˈtɪpɪkəl/ *adj* serving as a type; representative or characteristic.
typi·cally /-kli/ *adv*

typ·ify /ˈtɪpəˌfai/ *vt* (*pt,pp* -ied) be a symbol of; be representative of.

ty·pist *n* [C] ⇨ type².

ty·ran·ni·cal /tɪˈrænɪkəl/ *adj* of, like, a tyrant; acting like a tyrant.

tyr·an·nize /ˈtɪrəˌnaiz/ *vi,vt* rule cruelly and unjustly: ~ *(over) the weak*.

tyr·an·nous /ˈtɪrənəs/ *adj* = tyrannical.

tyr·anny /ˈtɪrəni/ *n* (*pl* -ies) **1** [U] cruel or unjust use of power; [C] instance of this. **2** [C,U] (instance of, country with, the) kind of government existing when a ruler has complete power, esp when this power has been obtained by force and is used unjustly: *live under (a) ~*.

ty·rant /ˈtairənt/ *n* [C] cruel or unjust ruler, esp one who has obtained complete power by force.

tzetze *n* [C] = tsetse.

U

U¹, u /yu/ (*pl* U's, u's /yuz/) the twenty-first letter of the English alphabet.

ˈU-ˌturn *n* [C] one of 180°: *No U-turns* (as a traffic notice on streets and highways).

ubi·qui·tous /yuˈbɪkwətəs/ *adj* (*formal*) present everywhere or in several places at the same time.

u.c. *abbr* = upper case.

ud·der /ˈədər/ *n* [C] part of a cow, goat or other animal, from which milk comes.

UFO /ˌyu ˌef ˈou/ *abbr* = unidentified flying object.

ugh /ˈə(h)/ *int* (used to show disgust).

ugly /ˈəgli/ *adj* (-ier, -iest) **1** unpleasant to look at: *~ men/furniture.* **2** threatening; unpleasant: *The situation looks ~.*

ug·li·ness /-nɪs/ *n* [U]

UK /yu ˈkei/ *abbr* = United Kingdom.

uku·lele /ˌyukəˈleili/ *n* [C] Hawaiian four-stringed guitar.

ul·cer /ˈəlsər/ *n* [C] **1** open sore (on the outside or inside surface of the body). **2** (*fig*) corrupting influence or condition.

ul·cer·ate /-ˌreit/ *vt,vi* form, convert into, an ulcer.

ul·cer·ous /-rəs/ *adj*

ulna /ˈəlnə/ *n* [C] (*pl* -nae /-ˌni/) inner of the two bones of the forearm. ⇨ illus at skeleton.

ul·ter·ior /ˌəlˈtɪriər/ *adj* beyond what is first seen or said.

ulˌterior ˈmotive, motive other than what is expressed or admitted.

ul·ti·mate /ˈəltəmɪt/ *adj* last, furthest, basic: *~ principles/truths; the ~ deterrent* (used of nuclear weapons).

ul·ti·mate·ly *adv* finally; in the end.

ul·ti·ma·tum /ˌəltəˈmeitəm/ *n* [C] (*pl* ~s) final statement of conditions to be agreed without discussion, eg one sent to a student threatening expulsion.

ultra- /ˈəltrə-/ *prefix* beyond, to excess: *~violet.*

ultra·sonic /ˌəltrəˈsanɪk/ *adj* of sound waves above normal human hearing.

ultra·vio·let /ˌəltrəˈvaiələt/ *adj* of the invisible part of the spectrum beyond the violet.

um·bili·cal /əmˈbɪlɪkəl/ *adj* **umbilical cord,** cord connecting a fetus at the navel with the placenta.

um·brella /əmˈbrelə/ *n* [C] (*pl* ~s) **1** folding frame covered with nylon, etc used to shelter the person holding it from rain. **2** (*fig*) protection: *under the ~ of the UN.*

um·laut /ˈʊmˌlaut/ *n* [C] (in Germanic languages) vowel change shown by two dots over the vowel (as in the German plural *Männer* of *Mann*).

um·pire /ˈəmˌpaiər/ *n* [C] person chosen to act as a judge in a dispute, to see that the rules are obeyed in baseball, tennis and other games. ⇨ illus at baseball. (*Note: referee* for football and boxing.) □ *vt,vi* act as an umpire: *~ a baseball game.*

ump·teen /ˌəmpˈtin/ *adj* (*sl*) many: *I've warned you ~ times.*

ump·teenth *adj: for the ~th time*, for I don't know how many times.

UN /ˌyu ˈen/ *abbr* = United Nations (Organization) ⇨ unite.

un- /ˌən-/ *prefix* **1** (used with an *adjective* or *noun*) not: *unable; untruth.* **2** (used with a *verb*) negative, reverse, opposite of: *uncover; unpack; undress.*

un·abated /ˌənəˈbeitɪd/ *adj* (of a storm, etc) (continuing) as strong, violent, etc as before.

un·able /ˌənˈeibəl/ *adj* ***unable to do sth,*** not able to.

un·accom·pan·ied /ˌənəˈkəmpənid/ *adj* **1** without a companion: *~ luggage*, sent separately. **2** (*music*) performed without an accompaniment.

un·ac·count·able /ˌənəˈkauntəbəl/ *adj* in a way that cannot be accounted for or explained.

un·ac·count·ably /-əbli/ *adv*

un·ac·cus·tomed /ˌənəˈkəstəmd/ *adj* **1** not accustomed to: *~ as I am to: ~ as I am to speaking in public.* **2** not usual: *his ~ silence*

un·ad·vised /ˌənədˈvaizd/ *adj* (esp) not discreet or wise

un·ad·vised·ly /ˌənədˈvaizɪdli/ *adv* rashly.

un·af·fec·ted /ˌənəˈfektɪd/ *adj* **1** sincere. **2** not affected.

un·alien·able /ˌənˈeiliənəbəl/ *adj* that cannot be taken away or separated: *~ rights.*

un·al·ter·ably /ˌənˈəltərəbli/ *adv* in a way that cannot be changed.

u·na·nim·ity /ˌyunəˈnɪməti/ *n* [U] complete agreement or unity.

u·nan·i·mous /yuˈnænɪməs/ *adj* in, showing, complete agreement: *He was elected by a ~ vote/with ~ approval.*

u·nan·i·mous·ly *adv*

un·an·nounced /ˌənəˈnaunst/ *adj* without having been announced.

un·an·swer·able /ˌənˈænsərəbəl/ *adj* (esp) against which no good argument can possibly be brought: *His case is ~.*

un·an·swered /ˌənˈænsərd/ *adj* not replied to:

~ *letters.*

un·ap·proach·able /ˌənəˈproutʃəbəl/ *adj* (esp, of a person) difficult to approach (because too stiff or formal).

un·armed /ˌənˈarmd/ *adj* without weapons or means of defense.

un·asked /ˌənˈæskt/ *adj* (esp) without being requested: *helping* ~.

un·as·sum·ing /ˌənəˈsumɪŋ/ *adj* not drawing attention to oneself; modest.

un·as·sum·ing·ly *adv*

un·at·tached /ˌənəˈtætʃt/ *adj* **1** not connected or associated with a particular person, group, organization, etc; independent. **2** not married or engaged to be married.

un·at·tended /ˌənəˈtendɪd/ *adj* not attended to; with no one to give care or attention to: *The teacher left the class* ~.

un·auth·or·ized /ˌənˈɔθəˌraizd/ *adj* not authorized; illegal.

un·avail·ing /ˌənəˈveilɪŋ/ *adj* without effect or success.

un·avoid·able /ˌənəˈvɔidəbəl/ *adj* that cannot be avoided.

un·a·void·ably /-əbli/ *adv: He was unavoidably absent.*

un·aware /ˌənəˈwær/ *adj* not knowing; not aware.

un·awares /-ˈwærz/ *adv* **(a)** by surprise: *He was taken ~s by the news.* **(b)** unconsciously: *She probably dropped the package ~s.*

un·bal·anced /ˌənˈbælənst/ *adj* (esp of a person, the mind) not sane or normal.

un·bear·able /ˌənˈberəbəl/ *adj* that cannot be borne or tolerated: *I find his rudeness* ~.

un·bear·ably /-əbli/ *adv* in a way that cannot be endured: *unbearably hot/rude.*

un·beaten /ˌənˈbitən/ *adj* (esp) not having been defeated or surpassed: *an ~ record for the 1,000 meters race.*

un·be·com·ing /ˌənbɪˈkəmɪŋ/ *adj* not appropriate.

un·be·liever /ˌənbɪˈlivər/ *n* [C] (esp) person who does not believe in God.

un·bend /ˌənˈbend/ *vi,vt* (*pt,pp* unbent /-ˈbent/) **1** behave in a way free from strain or formality: *After teaching I* ~. **2** relax: ~ *one's mind.*

un·bend·ing *adj* (esp) determined.

un·bi·ased /ˌənˈbaiəst/ *adj* impartial.

un·block /ˌənˈblak/ *vt* remove obstruction from.

un·born /ˌənˈbɔrn/ *adj* not yet born; future: ~ *generations.*

un·break·able /ˌənˈbreikəbəl/ *adj* that cannot be broken.

un·bro·ken /ˌənˈbroukən/ *adj* (esp) **1** (eg of a horse) not tamed. **2** not interrupted: *six hours of ~ sleep.* **3** (of records, etc) not beaten.

un·buckle /ˌənˈbəkəl/ *vt* undo the buckle(s) of.

un·built /ˌənˈbɪlt/ *adj* not (yet) built.

un·bur·den /ˌənˈbərdən/ *vt* relieve of a burden: ~ *one's conscience*, eg by making a confession.

un·called-for /ˌənˈkɔldˌfɔr/ *adj* not justified, desirable or necessary: *Such rude comments are* ~.

un·canny /ˌənˈkæni/ *adj* not natural, mysterious: *an ~ ability to predict disaster.*

un·cared-for /ˌənˈkærdˌfɔr/ *adj* neglected: ~ *children.*

un·ceas·ing /ˌənˈsisɪŋ/ *adj* going on, continuing, all the time.

un·ceas·ing·ly *adv*

un·cer·emo·ni·ous /ˌənˌserəˈmouniəs/ *adj* **1** informal. **2** lacking in courtesy.

un·cer·emo·ni·ous·ly *adv*

un·cer·tain /ˌənˈsərtən/ *adj* **1** not reliable: ~ *weather; a man with an ~ temper.* **2** not certainly knowing or known: *be/feel ~ (about) what to do next; ~ of/about/as to one's plans for the future.*

un·cer·tain·ly *adv*

un·cer·tain·ty /ˌənˈsərtənti/ *n* (*pl* -ies) **1** [U] state of being uncertain. **2** [C] something which is uncertain: *the uncertainties of employment in many countries.*

un·changed /ˌənˈtʃeindʒd/ *adj* staying, having stayed, the same: ~ *weather.*

un·chari·table /ˌənˈtʃærɪtəbəl/ *adj* (esp) severe or harsh (in making judgments of the conduct of others).

un·checked /ˌənˈtʃekt/ *adj* not kept under control: ~ *anger.*

un·christian /ˌənˈkrɪstʃən/ *adj* contrary to Christian principles.

un·civil /ˌənˈsɪvəl/ *adj* = impolite (the usual word).

un·claimed /ˌənˈkleimd/ *adj* that has or have not been claimed: ~ *letters/packages.*

uncle /ˈəŋkəl/ *n* [C] **1** brother of one's father or mother. **2** husband of one's aunt.

ˌUncle ˈSam, (*informal*) (personification of) the United States of America.

UNCLE SAM

ˌUncle ˈTom, (*informal*) Negro felt to be overly respectful to whites.

un·clouded /ˌənˈklaudɪd/ *adj* (*fig*) free from care: *a life of ~ happiness.*

un·colored /ˌənˈkələrd/ *adj* (*fig*) not exaggerated: *an ~ description of events.*

un·com·fort·able /ˌənˈkəmfərtəbəl/ *adj* not comfortable.

un·com·mit·ted /ˌənkəˈmɪtɪd/ *adj* not committed; free, independent.

un·com·mon /ˌənˈkamən/ *adj* unusual (and so remarkable).

un·com·mon·ly *adv* (esp) remarkably: *an ~ly intelligent child.*

un·com·pro·mis·ing /ˌənˈkamprəˌmaizɪŋ/ *adj* not prepared to make any compromise; firm: *an*

~ *member of the committee.*

un·con·cerned /ˌənkənˈsərnd/ *adj* **1** not involved (*in*); not (emotionally) concerned (*with*). **2** free from anxiety.

un·con·cern·ed·ly /ˌənkənˈsərnɪdli/ *adv*

un·con·di·tional /ˌənkənˈdɪʃənəl/ *adj* absolute; not subject to conditions: *We demanded ~ surrender.*

un·con·di·tion·ally /-nəli/ *adv*

un·con·di·tioned /ˌənkənˈdɪʃənd/ *adj* (esp): ~ *reflex*, instinctive response.

un·con·scious /ˌənˈkanʃəs/ *adj* not conscious (all senses). □ *n* **the unconscious,** (*psych*) that part of one's mental activity of which one is unaware, but which can be detected and understood through the skilled analysis of dreams, behavior, etc.

un·con·scious·ly *adv*

un·con·sid·ered /ˌənkənˈsɪdərd/ *adj* **1** (of words, remarks) spoken, made, thoughtlessly. **2** disregarded (as if of little value or worth).

un·cork /ˌənˈkɔrk/ *vt* take the cork from (a bottle).

un·couple /ˌənˈkəpəl/ *vt* unfasten: ~ *a locomotive from a train.*

un·couth /ˌənˈkuθ/ *adj* (of persons, their behavior) rough, awkward, uncultured.

un·couth·ly *adv*

un·cover /ˌənˈkəvər/ *vt* **1** remove a cover or covering from. **2** (*fig*) make known: *The police ~ed a plot against the President.*

un·cros·sed /ˌənˈkrɔst/ *adj* (esp, of a check) not crossed.

un·dated /ˌənˈdeitɪd/ *adj* not having a date: *an ~ check.*

un·daunted /ˌənˈdɔntɪd/ *adj* fearless.

un·de·cided /ˌəndɪˈsaidɪd/ *adj* not yet having made up one's mind.

un·de·fended /ˌəndɪˈfendɪd/ *adj* (esp of a lawsuit) in which no defense is offered.

un·de·mon·stra·tive /ˌəndɪˈmanstrətɪv/ *adj* not showing feelings of affection, interest, etc.

un·de·ni·able /ˌəndɪˈnaiəbəl/ *adj* undoubtedly true: *of ~ value.*

un·de·ni·ably /-əbli/ *adv: without doubt.*

un·der[1] /ˈəndər/ *adv* in or to a lower place, position, etc: *The ship went ~*, sank.

un·der[2] /ˈəndər/ *prep* **1** in or to a position lower than: *The cat was ~ the table.* ***There's nothing new under the sun,*** (*prov*), nothing new anywhere. **2** in and covered by: *He hid ~ the covers.* **3** less than; lower (in rank) than: *children ~ fourteen years of age; incomes ~ $7000; run a hundred meters in ~ ten seconds; no one ~* (*the rank of*) *captain.* (*Note:* opposites are *above* or *over.*) ***under age,*** ⇨ age[1](1). **4** (showing various conditions): *road ~ repair*, being repaired; *~ discussion*, being discussed; *be ~ the impression that*, have the idea or belief that.

under- /ˈəndər/ *prefix* **1** located beneath: *undergrowth.* **2** not enough: *undersized.* **3** lower in rank or importance: *understudy.*

under·act /ˌəndərˈækt/ *vt,vi* act with too little energy, enthusiasm.

under·arm /ˈəndərˌarm/ *adj, adv* (hitting or throwing a ball) with the hand kept below the level of the elbow.

under·bid /ˌəndərˈbɪd/ *vt* (*pt,pp* underbid) **1** make a lower bid than (another person). **2** (in card games) bid less on a hand of cards than its strength demands.

under·brush /ˈəndərˌbrəʃ/ *n* [U] (mass of) thick bushes growing on the ground among trees.

under·car·riage /ˈəndərˌkærɪdʒ/ *n* [C] (usually with *the*) = chassis.

under·charge /ˌəndərˈtʃardʒ/ *vt* charge too little for or to. □ *n* [C] /ˈəndərˌtʃardʒ/ charge that is too small.

under·clothes /ˈəndərˌklouz/ *n pl* clothing worn next to the skin.

under·cloth·ing /ˈəndərˌklouðɪŋ/ *n* [U] = underclothes.

under·cover /ˈəndərˌkəvər/ *adj* secret: *an ~ agent*, person who associates with suspected criminals, etc to get evidence against them.

under·cur·rent /ˈəndərˌkərənt/ *n* [U] **1** current of water flowing beneath the surface. **2** (*fig*) tendency (of thought or feeling) lying below what is apparent: *an ~ of hatred.*

under·cut /ˌəndərˈkət/ *vt* (*pt,pp* undercut) (-tt-) offer (goods, services) at a lower price than competitors.

under·de·vel·oped /ˌəndərdɪˈveləpt/ *adj* not yet fully developed: *~ muscles/countries.*

under·dog /ˈəndərˌdɔg/ *n* [C] (usually with *the*) (*fig*) person who is considered the poorest, weakest, the probable loser in a struggle, etc.

under·done /ˌəndərˈdən/ *adj* (esp of meat) not completely cooked throughout.

under·esti·mate /ˌəndərˈestəˌmeit/ *vt* form too low an estimate or opinion of: *~ the enemy's strength.* □ *n* /-ˈestəmɪt/ [C] estimate which is too low.

under·fed /ˌəndərˈfed/ *adj* having had too little food.

under·foot /ˌəndərˈfʊt/ *adv* under one's feet: *It is very stony ~.*

under·gar·ment /ˌəndərˈgarmənt/ *n* [C] article of clothing worn next to the skin.

under·go /ˌəndərˈgou/ *vt* (*pt* -went /-ˈwent/, *pp* -gone /-ˈgɔn/) experience: *The explorers had to ~ much suffering.*

under·grad·uate /ˌəndərˈgrædʒuɪt/ *n* [C] university student working for a bachelor's degree.

under·ground /ˈəndərˌgraund/ *adj* **1** under the surface of the ground: *~ passages/caves.* **2** secret (esp of political movement or one for resisting enemy forces in occupation of another country): *~ workers.* □ *adv*: *He went ~* (= into hiding) *when he heard the police were after him.* □ *n* resistance movement: *men of the French ~.* **ˌunderground ˈrailroad,** system of smuggling escaped slaves to the North prior to the Civil War.

under·growth /ˈəndərˌgrouθ/ *n* [U] shrubs, bushes, low trees, growing among taller trees.

under·handed /ˈəndərˌhændɪd/ *adj* deceitful.

under·hand·ed·ly *adv*

under·lay /ˈəndərˌlei/ *n* [U] material (felt, rubber, etc) laid under a carpet.

under·lie /ˌəndərˈlai/ *vt* form the basis of (a theory, of conduct, behavior, doctrine).

under·line /ˈəndərˌlain/ *vt* **1** draw a line under

(a word, etc). **2** (*fig*) emphasize. □ *n* [C] (also **under·lining** [U]) line drawn under a word or words.

under·ling /ˈəndərlɪŋ/ *n* [C] person in an unimportant position compared to others.

under·man·ned /ˌəndərˈmænd/ *adj* (of a ship, factory, etc) having not enough men to do all the work that needs to be done.

under·men·tioned /ˌəndərˈmenʃənd/ *adj* mentioned below or later (in an article, etc).

under·mine /ˌəndərˈmain/ *vt* **1** make a hollow or tunnel under: *cliffs ~d by the sea.* **2** weaken gradually: *His health was ~d by drink.*

under·neath /ˌəndərˈniθ/ *adv, prep* beneath; below; at or to a lower place.

under·nour·ished /ˌəndərˈnərɪʃt/ *adj* not provided with sufficient food for good health and normal growth.

under·pants /ˈəndərˌpænts/ *n pl* underwear covering (part of) the lower part of the body.

under·pass /ˈəndərˌpæs/ *n* [C] section of a road that goes under another road or railway.

under·pay /ˌəndərˈpei/ *vt* (*pt,pp* -paid /-ˈpeid/) pay (workmen, etc) inadequately.
under·pay·ment *n* [C,U]

under·pin /ˈəndərˌpɪn/ *vt* (-nn-) **1** place a support of stone, etc under (a wall, etc). **2** (*fig*) support, form the basis for (an argument, etc).
under·pin·ning *n* [U]

under·privi·leged /ˌəndərˈprɪvəlɪdʒd/ *adj* not having had the educational and social advantages enjoyed by more fortunate people, social classes, nations, etc.

under·rate /ˌəndərˈreit/ *vt* place too low a value or estimate on: *~ an opponent*, fail to realize his abilities, strength, etc.

under·sell /ˌəndərˈsel/ *vt* (*pt,pp* -sold /-ˈsould/) sell (goods) at a lower price than (competitors).

under·signed /ˈəndərˌsaind/ *pp: We, the ~...*, we whose signatures appear below...

under·sized /ˈəndərˌsaizd/ *adj* of less than the usual size.

under·skirt /ˈəndərˌskərt/ *n* [C] petticoat.

under·staffed /ˌəndərˈstæft/ *adj* having too small a staff.

under·stand /ˌəndərˈstænd/ *vt,vi* (*pt,pp* -stood /-ˈstʊd/) **1** know the meaning, nature, explanation, of (something): *~ him/French/a problem. He didn't ~ me/what I said.* **2** learn (from information received): *I ~ that you are married now.*
under·stand·able /-əbəl/ *adj* that can be understood: *His refusal to agree is ~able.*
under·stand·ing *adj* (good at) realizing other persons' feelings or points of view: *with an ~ing smile.* □ *n* **(a)** [U] power of clear thought, for seeing something from another's point of view, etc. **(b)** (often with *a, an*, but rarely *pl*) agreement; realization of another's views or feelings toward oneself: *reach/come to an ~ing with the bank manager.* ***on the understanding that...***, on condition that...

under·state /ˌəndərˈsteit/ *vt* fail to state fully or adequately: *They exaggerated the enemy's losses and ~d their own.*
under·state·ment /ˈəndərˌsteitmənt/ *n* [C,U]

under·stock /ˌəndərˈstak/ *vt* equip with less stock than is necessary.

under·study /ˈəndərˌstədi/ *n* [C] (*pl* -ies) person learning to, able to, take the place of another (esp an actor). □ *vt* (*pt,pp* -ied) study (a part in a play) for this purpose; act as an understudy to (an actor): *He is ~ing Willy Loman in "Death of a Salesman."*

under·take /ˌəndərˈteik/ *vt* (*pt* -took /-ˈtʊk/, *pp* -taken /-ˈteikən/) **1** make oneself responsible for; agree, promise, (to do something): *He undertook to finish the job by Friday.* **2** start (a piece of work).
under·tak·ing /ˈəndərˌteikɪŋ/ *n* [C] work that one has agreed to do.

under·taker /ˈəndərˌteikər/ *n* [C] person whose business is to prepare the dead for burial or cremation and manage funerals.

under·tone /ˈəndərˌtoun/ *n* [C] (*formal*) **1** low, quiet tone: *talk in ~s*, talk quietly. **2** underlying quality: *an ~ of sadness.*

under·took *pt* of undertake.

under·value /ˌəndərˈvælyu/ *vt* value at less than the true worth.
under·valu·ation /ˌəndərˌvælyuˈeiʃən/ *n* [U]

under·water /ˈəndərˌwɔtər/ *adj* below the surface of the water: *~ swimming.*

under·wear /ˈəndərˌwer/ *n* [U] underclothes.

under·went *pt* of undergo.

under·world /ˈəndərˌwərld/ *n* [C] **1** (*myth*) place of the departed spirits of the dead. **2** part of society that lives by vice and crime.

under·write /ˌəndərˈrait/ *vt* (*pt* -wrote /-ˈrout/, *pp* -written /-ˈrɪtən/) undertake to take responsibility for all or part of possible loss (by signing an agreement about insurance, esp of ships).
under·writer /ˈəndərˌraitər/ *n* [C] person who underwrites policies of (esp marine) insurance.

un·de·sir·able /ˌəndɪˈzairəbəl/ *adj* (esp of persons) of a kind not to be welcomed in society. □ *n* [C] undesirable person.

un·de·ter·red /ˌəndɪˈtərd/ *adj* not discouraged: *~ by the weather/by failure.*

un·de·vel·oped /ˌəndɪˈveləpt/ *adj* not developed: *~ land*, not yet used (for farming, etc).

un·did *pt* of undo.

un·dies /ˈəndiz/ *n pl* (*informal*) (short for) underclothes.

un·dis·charged /ˌəndɪsˈtʃardʒd/ *adj* **1** (of a cargo) not unloaded. **2** (of a debt) not paid.

undo /ˌənˈdu/ *vt* (*pt* undid /ˌənˈdɪd/, *pp* undone /ˌənˈdən/) **1** untie, unfasten, loosen (knots, buttons, etc): *My shoelace has come undone.* **2** destroy the result of: *He has undone the good work of his predecessor.*
un·do·ing *n* (cause of) ruin: *Drink was his ~ing.*
un·done *adj* not finished: *leave one's work undone.*

un·dom·es·ti·cated /ˌəndəˈmestɪˌkeitɪd/ *adj* **1** not tamed; wild: *The wildcat is an ~ animal.* **2** not trained or interested in household affairs: *His wife/Her husband is ~.*

un·doubted /ˌənˈdautɪd/ *adj* certain; accepted as true: *show an ~ improvement in health.*
un·doubted·ly *adv*

un·dreamed-of /ˌənˈdrimdˌəv/ *adj* not thought of or imagined: *~ wealth.*

un·dreamt-of /ˌənˈdremtˌəv/ *adj* = undreamed-of.
un·dress /ˌənˈdres/ *vt,vi* **1** remove the clothes of: *Jane ~ed her doll.* **2** take off one's clothes: *~ and get into bed/get ~ed and go to bed.* □ *n* ***in a state of undress,*** naked.
un·due /ˌənˈdu/ *adj* improper: *with ~ haste.*
un·duly /ˌənˈduli/ *adv* too: *unduly pessimistic.*
un·du·late /ˈəndʒəˌleit/ *vi* (of surfaces) have a wavy motion or look: *undulating land,* that rises and falls in gentle slopes.
un·du·la·tion /ˌəndʒəˈleiʃən/ *n* [C,U]
un·dy·ing /ˌənˈdaiŋ/ *adj* everlasting: *~ love.*
un·earned /ˌənˈərnd/ *adj* **1** not gained by work or service: *~ income,* eg inherited. **2** not deserved: *~ praise.*
un·earth /ˌənˈərθ/ *vt* discover and bring to light: *~ new evidence.*
un·earth·ly /ˌənˈərθli/ *adj* **1** supernatural. **2** mysterious; ghostly: *~ screams.* **3** (*informal*) unreasonable: *Why do you wake me up at this ~ hour?*
un·easy /ˌənˈizi/ *adj* (-ier, -iest) uncomfortable in body or mind: *have an ~ conscience.*
un·eas·ily /ˌənˈizəli/ *adv*
un·easi·ness /ˌənˈizinɪs/ *n* [U]
un·eaten /ˌənˈitən/ *adj* not eaten.
un·edu·cated /ˌənˈedʒəˌkeitɪd/ *adj* (suggesting a person is) not educated: *an ~ person.*
un·em·ploy·able /ˌənɪmˈplɔiəbəl/ *adj* that cannot be employed.
un·em·ployed /ˌənɪmˈplɔid/ *adj* **1** not working, not able to get work: *~ men.* **2** not being used: *~ capital.* □ *n* **the unemployed,** those who are (temporarily) without work.
un·em·ploy·ment /ˌənɪmˈplɔimənt/ *n* **1** [U] state of being unemployed: *Unemployment is a serious social evil.* **2** amount of unused labor: *There is more ~ now than there was six months ago.* **3** (as an *adjective*): *~ benefit,* money paid to a worker who cannot get employment.
un·end·ing /ˌənˈendɪŋ/ *adj* everlasting; continuous.
un·en·light·ened /ˌənɪnˈlaitənd/ *adj* uneducated; not well-informed.
un·equal /ˌənˈikwəl/ *adj* **1** not equal. **2** (esp of work such as writing) variable in quality. **3** not capable, strong, etc enough: *I feel ~ to the task.*
un·equally /-kwəli/ *adv*
un·equal·ed /ˌənˈikwəld/ *adj* unrivaled.
un·equivo·cal /ˌənɪˈkwɪvəkəl/ *adj* (*formal*) having one only possible meaning.
un·err·ing /ˌənˈərɪŋ/ *adj* (*formal*) accurate: *fire with ~ aim.*
UNESCO /yuˈneskou/ *abbr* = United Nations Educational, Scientific, and Cultural Organization.
un·ex·cep·tion·able /ˌənɪkˈsepʃənəbəl/ *adj* (*formal*) beyond criticism.
un·fail·ing /ˌənˈfeilɪŋ/ *adj* never coming to an end.
un·fail·ing·ly *adv* at all times: *~ly honest.*
un·fair /ˌənˈfær/ *adj* unjust: *~ remarks/competition.*
un·fair·ly *adv*
un·fair·ness /-nɪs/ *n* [U]
un·faith·ful /ˌənˈfeiθfəl/ *adj* **1** not true to one's duty, a promise, etc. **2** not faithful to marriage vows: *Her husband is ~ to her.*
un·faith·fully /-fəli/ *adv*
un·faith·ful·ness /-nɪs/ *n* [U]
un·fal·ter·ing /ˌənˈfɔltərɪŋ/ *adj* not hesitating: *with ~ courage.*
un·fam·il·iar /ˌənfəˈmɪlyər/ *adj* **1** not well known: *That face is not ~ to me,* I feel that I know it. **2** not acquainted with: *He is still ~ with this district.*
un·fath·om·able /ˌənˈfæðəməbəl/ *adj* **1** so deep that the bottom cannot be reached. **2** (*fig*) too strange or difficult to be understood.
un·fav·or·able /ˌənˈfeivərəbəl/ *adj* not favorable.
un·fit /ˌənˈfɪt/ *adj* not fit or suitable: *He is ~ for driving/~ to be a doctor/medically ~.*
un·fold /ˌənˈfould/ *vt,vi* **1** (of something folded) open out: *~ a newspaper.* **2** reveal, make known; become known or visible: *as the story ~s (itself).*
un·for·get·table /ˌənfərˈgetəbəl/ *adj* that cannot be forgotten: *an ~ experience.*
un·for·tu·nate /ˌənˈfɔrtʃənɪt/ *adj* **1** unlucky: *an ~ expedition.* **2** regrettable: *an ~ remark.*
un·founded /ˌənˈfaundɪd/ *adj* without proof: *~ rumors.*
un·fre·quented /ˌənfrɪˈkwentɪd/ *adj* visited rarely.
un·friend·ly /ˌənˈfrendli/ *adj* not friendly.
un·frock /ˌənˈfrak/ *vt* (of esp a priest guilty of bad conduct) dismiss from the priesthood.
un·fruit·ful /ˌənˈfrutfəl/ *adj* **1** not bearing fruit. **2** (*fig*) without results or success.
un·furl /ˌənˈfərl/ *vt,vi* unroll, spread out: *~ the sails.*
un·fur·nished /ˌənˈfərnɪʃt/ *adj* (esp) without furniture: *a house to rent ~.*
un·gain·ly /ˌənˈgeinli/ *adj* clumsy; awkward.
un·gen·er·ous /ˌənˈdʒen(ə)rəs/ *adj* not generous.
un·god·ly /ˌənˈgadli/ *adj* **1** not religious. **2** (*informal*) unreasonable: *Why did you phone me at this ~ hour?*
un·gov·ern·able /ˌənˈgəvərnəbəl/ *adj* that cannot be controlled: *an ~ temper.*
un·grate·ful /ˌənˈgreitfəl/ *adj* not showing gratitude.
un·guarded /ˌənˈgardɪd/ *adj* (esp of a person and what he says) careless; indiscreet.
un·happy /ˌənˈhæpi/ *adj* (-ier, -iest) not happy.
un·healthy /ˌənˈhelθi/ *adj* harmful to bodily or mental health.
un·heard /ˌənˈhərd/ *adj* **1** not heard. **2** not allowed a hearing. ***go unheard,*** (esp) have no one willing to listen: *Her request for help went ~.*
un·heard-of /ˌənˈhərdˌəv/ *adj* without an equal: *~-of wealth.*
un·hinged /ˌənˈhɪndʒd/ *adj* (*informal*) **1** temporarily out of control of one's emotions. **2** mentally ill.
un·hook /ˌənˈhʊk/ *vt* undo the hooks of (a dress, etc): *Please ~ my dress.*
un·hoped-for /ˌənˈhouptˌfɔr/ *adj* unexpected: *~ luck.*
uni- /yunə-/ *prefix* one; the same: *uniform.*
UNICEF /ˈyunɪˌsef/ *abbr* = United Nations (International) Children's (Emergency) Fund.

uni·corn /ˈyunɪˌkɔrn/ *n* [C] (in old stories) animal like a horse with one long horn.

un·iden·ti·fied /ˌənaiˈdentɪˌfaid/ *adj* which cannot be identified: *The victim is still ~.*

uniˌdentified ˌflying ˈobject, (*abbr* **UFO**) object seen in the sky and (claimed to have been) sent from another planet.

uni·form /ˈyunəˌfɔrm/ *adj* not varying in form, quality, etc: *~ temperature.* □ *n* [C,U] (style of) dress worn by all members of an organization, eg the police, the armed forces. ***in uniform,*** wearing such dress: *He looks handsome in* (*his*) *~.*

uni·form·ly *adv* without varying in quality, timing, etc.

uni·form·ity /ˌyunəˈfɔrməti/ *n* [U] condition of being the same throughout.

unify /ˈyunəˌfai/ *vt* (*pt,pp* -ied) **1** form into one; unite. **2** make uniform.

uni·fi·ca·tion /ˌyunəfəˈkeiʃən/ *n* [U]

uni·lat·eral /ˌyunəˈlætərəl/ *adj* (of an agreement, etc) of, on, affecting, done by, one side or party only: *a ~ declaration of independence* (*abbr* **UDI**); *~ repudiation of a treaty*, by one of the parties that signed it, without the consent of the other party or parties.

uni·lat·er·ally /-rəli/ *adv*

un·im·agin·ative /ˌənɪˈmædʒənətɪv/ *adj* (*formal*) not having, using, imagination.

un·im·peach·able /ˌənɪmˈpitʃəbəl/ *adj* that cannot be questioned or doubted: *news from an ~ source.*

un·in·formed /ˌənɪnˈfɔrmd/ *adj* (esp) not having, made without, adequate information: *~ criticism.*

un·in·hib·ited /ˌənɪnˈhɪbɪtɪd/ *adj* without inhibitions; unconventional.

un·in·spired /ˌənɪnˈspaiərd/ *adj* dull: *~ singing.*

un·in·ter·ested /ˌənˈɪntrɪstɪd/ *adj* **1** having, showing no interest. **2** having no personal concern in something.

union /ˈyunyən/ *n* **1** [U] uniting or being united; joining or being joined; [C] instance of this: *the ~ of the three towns into one.* **2** [U] state of being in agreement or harmony; [C] instance of this: *a happy ~*, eg a happy marriage. **3** [C] association formed by the uniting of persons, states, etc. ⇨ labor union.

union·ist, /-ɪst/ *n* **(a)** supporter of labor unions and the union movement. **(b)** member of a labor union. **(c) Unionist,** (esp) supporter of the Federal Government of the US during the Civil War.

union·ize *vt, vi* (get others) to join a labor union.

ˌunion ˈshop, business which employs only members of a labor union.

unique /yuˈnik/ *adj* having no like or equal; being the only one of its sort.

unique·ly *adv*

unique·ness /-nɪs/ *n* [U]

uni·sex /ˈyunəˌseks/ *adj* (of clothes, hair styling, etc) of a style designed for, or to be worn by, both sexes.

uni·son /ˈyunɪsən/ *n* ***in unison,*** together; in the same pitch: *sing in ~*

unit /ˈyunɪt/ *n* [C] **1** single person, thing or group regarded as complete in itself. **2** quantity or amount used as a standard of measurement: *The meter is a ~ of length.* **3** the number 1.

Uni·tar·ian /ˌyunəˈteriən/ *n* [C] member of a Christian church which rejects the doctrine of the Trinity and believes that God is one person. □ *adj* of the Unitarians: *the Unitarian Church.*

uni·tary /ˈyunəˌteri/ *adj* undivided.

unite /yuˈnait/ *vt,vi* **1** make or become one; join: *the interests that ~ our two countries*, that bring them together. **2** act or work together: *Let's ~ to fight for human rights.*

united *adj* **(a)** joined eg by love and sympathy: *a ~d family.* **(b)** resulting from association for a common purpose: *make a ~d effort.* **(c)** joined politically: *the United States.*

United Kingdom (*abbr* **UK**) Great Britain and Northern Ireland.

united·ly *adv*

United Nations (Organization) (*abbr* **UN(O)**) (since 1945) international organization for peace and mutual aid. (*Note:* usually used with *sing verb*).

United States (of America) (*abbr* **US(A)**) nation in North America. (*Note:* usually used with *sing verb*).

unity /ˈyunəti/ *n* (*pl* -ies) **1** [C,U] the state of being united; (an) arrangement of parts to form a complete or balanced whole: *The figure on the left spoils the ~ of the painting.* **2** [U] agreement (of aims, feelings, etc): *political ~.*

univ. *abbr* = university.

uni·ver·sal /ˌyunəˈvərsəl/ *adj* of, belonging to, done by, affecting, all: *War causes ~ misery.*

uni·ver·sally /-səli/ *adv*

uni·verse /ˈyunəˌvərs/ *n* **the Universe,** everything that exists everywhere; all the stars, planets, their satellites, etc.

uni·ver·sity /ˌyunəˈvərsəti/ *n* [C] (*pl* -ies) **1** (colleges, buildings, etc of an) institution for advanced teaching, conferring degrees and engaging in academic research. **2** members of such an institution collectively. **3** (as an *adjective*): *a ~ student.*

un·kempt /ˌənˈkempt/ *adj* = untidy (the usual word).

un·kind /ˌənˈkaind/ *adj* lacking in, not showing, kindness: *an ~ remark.*

un·kind·ly *adv* in an unkind manner.

un·know·ing /ˌənˈnouɪŋ/ *adj* unaware.

un·know·ing·ly *adv* unawares.

un·known /ˌənˈnoun/ *adj* not known or identified: *the tomb of the Unknown Soldier*, of an unknown serviceman buried in memory of those killed in World Wars I and II.

un·leash /ˌənˈliʃ/ *vt* (*fig*) set free (to attack): *~ one's temper.*

un·leav·ened /ˌənˈlevənd/ *adj* (of bread) made without yeast.

un·less /ənˈles/ *conj* if not: *You will fail ~ you work harder. Unless you work harder, you will fail.*

un·like /ˌənˈlaik/ *adj, prep* not like; different from.

un·like·ly /ˌənˈlaikli/ *adj* not likely to happen or be true: *an ~ event/story.*

un·load /ˌənˈloud/ *vt,vi* **1** remove a load, cargo

from: ~ *a ship. The ship is ~ing.* **2** get rid of (somebody, something not wanted): *Don't try to ~ all your boring girl friends on me!*

un·lock /ˌənˈlak/ *vt* use a key to open a lock.

un·looked-for /ˌənˈlʊktˌfɔr/ *adj* unexpected.

un·loose /ˌənˈlus/ *vt* let loose; make free.

un·lucky /ˌənˈləki/ *adj* (-ier, -iest) not lucky, not fortunate.

un·luck·ily /-əli/ *adv* unfortunately.

un·man·ly /ˌənˈmænli/ *adj* **1** weak; cowardly. **2** effeminate.

un·man·ned /ˌənˈmænd/ *adj* having no crew: *send an ~ spacecraft to Mars.*

un·mask /ˌənˈmæsk/ *vt,vi* **1** remove a mask (from). **2** (*fig*) show the true character or intentions of: ~ *a traitor.*

un·matched /ˌənˈmætʃt/ *adj* without an equal.

un·men·tion·able /ˌənˈmenʃənəbəl/ *adj* so bad, etc that it must not be spoken of. □ *n* (*pl*) (*dated, informal*) underclothes.

un·mind·ful /ˌənˈmaindfəl/ *adj* forgetful; oblivious: ~ *of the time.*

un·mis·tak·able /ˌənmɪˈsteikəbəl/ *adj* about which no mistake or doubt is possible: *Are black clouds an ~ sign of rain?*

un·mis·tak·ably /-əbli/ *adv*

un·miti·gated /ˌənˈmɪtɪˌgeitɪd/ *adj* (*formal*) complete; absolute: *an ~ rascal.*

un·moved /ˌənˈmuvd/ *adj* (esp) indifferent.

un·natu·ral /ˌənˈnætʃ(ə)rəl/ *adj* not natural or normal.

un·nec·ess·ary /ˌənˈnesəˌseri/ *adj* not necessary.

un·nec·ess·ar·ily /ˌənˌnesəˈserəli/ *adv*

un·nerve /ˌənˈnərv/ *vt* cause to lose self-control, power of decision, courage.

un·not·iced /ˌənˈnoutɪst/ *adj* not observed or noticed: *Her sadness went ~.*

un·num·bered /ˌənˈnəmbərd/ *adj* **1** more than can be counted. **2** having no number(s): ~ *tickets.*

UN(O) /ˌyu ˈen, ˌyu ˌen ˈou/ *abbr* = United Nations Organization. ⇨ unite.

un·ob·trus·ive /ˌənəbˈtrusɪv/ *adj* not too obvious or easily noticeable.

un·of·fi·cial /ˌənəˈfɪʃəl/ *adj* not official: *an ~ strike*, not authorized by the union.

un·or·tho·dox /ˌənˈɔrθəˌdaks/ *adj* not in accordance with what is orthodox, conventional, traditional: ~ *teaching methods.*

un·pack /ˌənˈpæk/ *vt,vi* take out (things packed): ~ *one's clothes/a suitcase.*

un·par·al·leled /ˌənˈpærəˌleld/ *adj* having no equal: *an ~ disaster.*

un·pleas·ant /ˌənˈplezənt/ *adj* not pleasant.

un·pleas·ant·ness /-nɪs/ *n* [U] unpleasant feeling (between persons); [C] quarrel.

un·prece·dented /ˌənˈpresəˌdentɪd/ *adj* never done or known before.

un·preju·diced /ˌənˈpredʒədɪst/ *adj* free from prejudice.

un·pre·ten·tious /ˌənprɪˈtenʃəs/ *adj* modest; not trying to seem important.

un·prin·cipled /ˌənˈprɪnsəpəld/ *adj* without moral principles; dishonest.

un·pro·fessional /ˌənprəˈfeʃənəl/ *adj* (esp of conduct) contrary to the rules or customs of a profession.

un·prompted /ˌənˈpramptɪd/ *adj* (of an answer, action) not said, done, etc as the result of a hint, suggestion, etc.

un·pro·voked /ˌənprəˈvoukt/ *adj* without provocation: ~ *aggression/attacks.*

un·quali·fied /ˌənˈkwaləˌfaid/ *adj* **1** not limited or restricted; absolute: ~ *praise.* **2** not qualified: ~ *to speak on the subject.*

un·ques·tion·able /ˌənˈkwestʃənəbəl/ *adj* beyond doubt; certain.

un·ques·tion·ably /-əbli/ *adv*

un·quote /ˈənˌkwout/ (*v*, imperative only) (in a telegram, a telephoned message, etc) end the quotation: *The rebel leader said* (*quote*) *"We will never surrender"* (~).

un·ravel /ˌənˈrævəl/ *vt,vi* **1** separate the threads of; pull or become separate: *The cat has ~ed the knitting.* **2** solve: ~ *a mystery.*

un·real /ˌənˈriəl/ *adj* imaginary; not real.

un·reas·on·able /ˌənˈrizənəbəl/ *adj* not reasonable.

un·re·lent·ing /ˌənrɪˈlentɪŋ/ *adj* not becoming less in intensity, etc: ~ *pressure/attacks.*

un·re·li·able /ˌənrɪˈlaiəbəl/ *adj* that cannot be relied on; not to be trusted.

un·re·mit·ting /ˌənrɪˈmɪtɪŋ/ *adj* (*formal*) unceasing: ~ *efforts.*

un·re·quit·ed /ˌənrɪˈkwaitɪd/ *adj* not returned or rewarded: ~ *love.*

un·re·serv·ed·ly /ˌənrɪˈzərvədli/ *adv* without reservation or restriction; openly: *speak ~.*

un·rest /ˌənˈrest/ *n* [U] (esp) disturbed condition(s): *political ~.*

un·re·strained /ˌənrɪˈstreind/ *adj* not kept under control: ~ *hatred/laughter.*

un·re·stricted /ˌənrɪˈstrɪktɪd/ *adj* without restriction(s); (esp of a road) not having a speed limit for traffic.

un·ri·valed /ˌənˈraivəld/ *adj* having no rival: ~ *in courage.*

un·ruffled /ˌənˈrəfəld/ *adj* calm; not upset or agitated: *He was ~ by all the criticisms.*

un·ruly /ˌənˈruli/ *adj* (-ier, -iest) not easily controlled; naughty: *an ~ child.*

un·said /ˌənˈsed/ *adj* not expressed: *Some things* (eg opinions) *are better left ~.*

un·sa·vory /ˌənˈseivəri/ *adj* (esp) nasty; disgusting: ~ *stories/scandals.*

un·scathed /ˌənˈskeiðd/ *adj* unharmed; unhurt.

un·scru·pu·lous /ˌənˈskrupyələs/ *adj* not guided by conscience (not to do wrong).

un·scru·pu·lous·ly *adv*

un·seas·oned /ˌənˈsizənd/ *adj* **1** (of wood) not matured. **2** (of food) not flavored with seasoning.

un·seat /ˌənˈsit/ *vt* **1** remove from office: *Mr. X was ~ed in the election*, lost his seat. **2** throw (the rider) from a horse.

un·seem·ly /ˌənˈsimli/ *adj* (of behavior, etc) not proper.

un·seen /ˌənˈsin/ *adj* not seen; invisible.

un·settle /ˌənˈsetəl/ *vt* make troubled, anxious or uncertain: *~d weather*, changeable weather.

un·sight·ly /ˌənˈsaitli/ *adj* unpleasant to look at: ~ *litter.*

un·skilled /ˌənˈskɪld/ *adj* **1** (of work) not needing special skill. **2** (of workers) not having special skill or special training.

un·soph·is·ti·cated /ˌənsəˈfɪstɪˌkeitɪd/ *adj* not sophisticated; inexperienced.

un·sound /ˌənˈsaund/ *adj* **1** unsatisfactory: *an ~ argument/building.* **2** ***of unsound mind,*** mentally disturbed.

un·spar·ing /ˌənˈspærɪŋ/ *adj* liberal; holding nothing back: *be ~ in one's efforts; ~ of praise.*

un·speak·able /ˌənˈspikəbəl/ *adj* that cannot be expressed or described in words: *~ joy/sadness.*

un·stuck /ˌənˈstək/ *adj* **1** not stuck or fastened: *The flap of the envelope has come ~.* **2** fail to work according to plan: *Our plan has come ~.*

un·suit·able /ˌənˈsutəbəl/ *adj* not suitable.

un·sung /ˌənˈsəŋ/ *adj* not celebrated (in poetry or song). ***go unsung,*** (*informal*) (of a person, his actions) be unknown, not thanked, praised.

un·swerv·ing /ˌənˈswərvɪŋ/ *adj* (esp of aims, purposes) not changing: *~ loyalty.*

un·think·able /ˌənˈθɪŋkəbəl/ *adj* not to be considered: *Such a possibility is ~!*

un·thought-of /ˌənˈθɔtˌəv/ *adj* unexpected.

un·tidy /ˌənˈtaidi/ *adj* (-ier, -iest) (of a room, desk, person etc) not tidy.

un·tie /ˌənˈtai/ *vt* (*present participle* untying, *pt,pp* untied) unfasten a knot, etc.

un·til /ənˈtɪl/ *prep, conj* ⇨ till¹.

un·tir·ing /ˌənˈtaiərɪŋ/ *adj* continuing to work without getting tired or causing tiredness: *his ~ efforts.*

un·told /ˌənˈtould/ *adj* (esp) too many or too much to be measured, etc: *~ wealth.*

un·truth /ˌənˈtruθ/ *n* **1** [U] lack of truth. **2** [C] (*pl* ~s /-ˈtruðz/) lie.

un·truth·ful /-fəl/ *adv*

un·truth·fully /-fəli/ *adv*

un·used¹ /ˌənˈyuzd/ *adj* never having been used.

un·used² /ˌənˈyust/ *adj* ***unused to,*** not accustomed to: *~ to city life.*

un·usual /ˌənˈyuʒuəl/ *adj* not usual; strange.

un·usu·ally *adv: ~ly hot.*

un·veil /ˌənˈveiəl/ *vt,vi* (*pres p* ~ing /ˌənˈveilɪŋ/) **1** remove a veil (from). **2** reveal.

un·wieldy /ˌənˈwiəldi/ *adj* awkward to move or control because of shape, size or weight.

un·wind /ˌənˈwaind/ *vt,vi* (*pt,pp* -wound /-ˈwaund/) **1** untwist (a ball of wool, etc); loosen (a spring, etc). **2** (*informal*) relax after a period of tension, exhausting work, etc. ⇨ wind³(6).

un·wrap /ˌənˈræp/ *vt,vi* (-pp-) remove the wrapping or cover.

un·zip /ˌənˈzɪp/ *vt* (-pp-) unfasten or open by pulling a zipper.

up¹ /əp/ *adverbial particle* (contrasted with *down*) (for special uses with *verbs,* eg *throw up,* ⇨ the *verb* entries.) **1** to or in an erect or vertical position (esp as suggesting readiness for activity): *He's already up,* out of bed. *It's time to get up,* out of bed. *Stand up!* ***up and about/around,*** out of bed and active (esp of a person recently ill). ***up at bat,*** (*baseball*) taking one's turn batting. ***on the up-and-up,*** honest; open and sincere: *He's always on the up-and-up in his dealings.* **2** to or in a high(er) place, position, degree, etc: *Lift your head up. Prices are still going up,* rising. **3** to a place, town in or to the north: *We're going up to Boston.* ***up North,*** in or to the Northern part of the US. **4** (used vaguely, in a way similar to the use of *down, around, over, across*) to the place in question, or in which the speaker is, was, will be: *He came up* (*to me*) *and asked the time.* **5** (used to show completeness, finality): *The stream has dried up,* has become completely dry. *We've eaten everything up. Lock/Tie/Fasten/Chain/Nail it up,* make it fast, secure, safe, etc by locking, tying, etc. **6** (used to show an increase in intensity, etc): *Speak up!* ie with more force. **7** ***ˈup against (it),*** faced with (difficulties, obstacles, etc). ***be up before,*** appear in court (before a magistrate, etc). ***ˌup and ˈdown,*** **(a)** forward and back: *walking up and down the station platform.* **(b)** so as to rise and fall: *The boat bobbed up and down on the water.* ***up for,*** **(a)** being tried (for an offense, etc): *up for exceeding the speed limit.* **(b)** being considered for; on offer: *The house is up for sale.* ***up to,*** **(a)** occupied or busy with: *What's he up to? He's up to no good.* **(b)** capable of: *I don't feel up to going to work.* **(c)** as far as: *up to now/then.* **(d)** required, looked on as necessary: *It's up to us* (= It is our duty) *to give them all the help we can.* □ *prep* (in the senses of the *adverb*): *climb up a mountain; walk up the stairs.*

ˌup-and-ˈcoming *adj* (of a person) making good progress, likely to succeed, in his profession, career, etc: *an up-and-coming young doctor.*

ˌups and ˈdowns, (*fig*) good and bad fortune.

UP² /ˌyu ˈpi/ *abbr* = United Press.

up- /ˈəp-, ˌəp-/ *prefix* to a higher or better state: *uphill; upgrade.*

up·beat /ˈəpˌbit/ *adj* lively.

up·bring·ing /ˈəpˌbrɪŋɪŋ/ *n* [U] training and education during childhood: *a good ~.*

up·coun·try /ˈəpˌkəntri/ *adj, adv* (esp in a large thinly populated country) toward the interior; inland.

up·date /ˌəpˈdeit/ *vt* bring up to date: *~ a dictionary.*

up·grade /ˌəpˈgreid/ *vt* raise to a higher grade. □ *n* /ˈəpˌgreid/ (esp) ***on the upgrade,*** making progress.

up·heaval /ˌəpˈhivəl/ *n* [C] great and sudden change: *political/social ~s.*

up·held *pt,pp* of uphold.

up·hill /ˌəpˈhɪl/ *adj* **1** sloping upward; ascending: *an ~ road.* **2** (*fig*) difficult; needing effort: *an ~ task.* □ *adv* up a slope: *walk ~.*

up·hold /əpˈhould/ *vt* (*pt,pp* upheld /-ˈheld/) **1** support or approve (a person, his conduct, a practice, etc): *I cannot ~ such conduct.* **2** confirm (a decision, a verdict).

up·hol·ster /əpˈhoulstər, əˈpoulstər/ *vt* provide (seats, etc) with padding, springs, covering material, etc.

up·hol·sterer *n* [C] person who upholsters.

up·hol·stery /-stri/ *n* [U] (materials used in, business of) upholstering.

up·keep /ˈəpˌkip/ *n* [U] (cost of) keeping something in good order and repair: *I can't afford the ~ of this large garden.*

up·land /ˈəplənd/ *n* (often *pl*) higher part(s) of a

region or country.
up·lift /ˌəpˈlɪft/ *vt* raise (spiritually or emotionally): *His soul was ~ed by the Bach cantatas.* □ *n* /ˈəpˌlɪft/ [U] moral or mental inspiration.
upon /əˈpan/ *prep* = on (which is more usual).
up·per /ˈəpər/ *adj* (contrasted with *lower*) higher in place; situated above: *the ~ lip; the ~ arm.* ***have/get the upper hand (of sb),*** have/get an advantage or control of. □ *n* [C] part of a shoe or boot over the sole.
ˈupper case, (in printing) capital letters.
the ˌupper ˈclass, top level of society.
ˈupper-class *adj*
the ˌUpper ˈHouse, (in Congress) the Senate.
ˈup·per·most *adj* highest: *Thoughts of the vacation were ~most in their minds.* □ *adv* on, to, at, the top or surface: *store this carton with the label ~most,* on top.
up·right /ˈəpˌrait/ *adj* **1** erect; placed vertically (at an angle of 90° to the ground): *an ~ post.* **2** honorable; straightforward in behavior: *an ~ man/judge.* □ *n* [C] upright support in a structure.
up·ris·ing /ˈəpˌraizɪŋ/ *n* [C] revolt; rebellion.
up·roar /ˈəpˌrɔr/ *n* [U] (also with *a, an*) (outburst of) noise and excitement: *The meeting ended in (an) ~.*
up·roari·ous /ˌəpˈrɔriəs/ *adj* very noisy, esp with loud laughter and great good humor: *~ious laughter.*
up·roari·ous·ly *adv*
up·root /ˌəpˈrut/ *vt* pull up with the roots: *The gale ~ed numerous trees.*
UPS /ˌyu ˌpi ˈes/ *abbr* = United Parcel Service.
up·set /ˌəpˈset/ *vt,vi* (*pt,pp* ~) (-tt-) **1** tip over; overturn: *Don't ~ the boat.* **2** trouble; cause (a person or thing) to be disturbed: *~ the enemy's plan; ~ one's stomach by eating too much rich food. She is easily ~ emotionally.* □ *n* /ˈəpˌset/ [C] **1** upsetting or being upset: *have a ˈstomach ~.* **2** (*sport*) unexpected result.
up·shot /ˈəpˌʃat/ *n* **the upshot,** outcome; result: *What will be the ~ of it all?*
up·side-down /ˌəpsaidˈdaun/ *adv* **1** with the upper side underneath or at the bottom. **2** (*fig*) in disorder: *The house was turned ~ by the burglars.*
up·stairs /ˌəpˈsterz/ *adv* **1** to or on a higher floor: *go/walk ~.* **2** (as an *adjective*) belonging to, situated on, an upper floor: *an ~ room.*
up·stand·ing /ˌəpˈstændɪŋ/ *adj* **1** standing erect; strong and healthy: *fine ~ children.* **2** honest.
up·start /ˈəpˌstart/ *n* [C] person who has suddenly risen to wealth, power or higher social position, esp one who is arrogant.
up·stream /ˈəpˌstrim/ *adv* up a river; in the opposite direction to the stream or current.
up·surge /ˈəpˌsərdʒ/ *n* [C] growth (of emotion): *an ~ of anger/indignation.*
up·tight, up tight /ˌəpˈtait/ *adj* (*sl*) extremely tense or nervous: *~ about an interview.*
up-to-date /ˌəp-tə-ˈdeit/ *adj* of the present time; of the newest sort: *~ methods.*
up-to-the minute /ˈəp-tə-ðə-ˌmɪnɪt/ *adj* very modern; latest: *~ reports.*
up·turn /ˈəpˌtərn/ *n* [C] **1** upward turn. **2** change for the better: *an ~ in profits.*
up·ward /ˈəpwərd/ *adj* moving or directed up: *an ~ glance.* □ *adv* (often **up·wards**) toward a higher place, level, etc.
ura·nium /yəˈreiniəm/ *n* [U] heavy white metal (symbol **U**) with radioactive properties, a source of atomic energy.
Ura·nus /yəˈreinəs/ *n* (*astron*) planet seventh in order from the sun. ⇨ illus at planet.
ur·ban /ˈərbən/ *adj* of or in a city or town: *~ areas.*
ˌurban guerˈrilla, member of a small armed group fighting against the established order in cities.
ur·ban·iz·ation /ˌərbənɪˈzeiʃən/ *n* [U] the change from a rural to an urban character.
ur·ban·ize /-ˌnaiz/ *vt*
ur·bane /ərˈbein/ *adj* (*formal*) polite; refined in manners.
ur·bane·ly *adv*
ur·chin /ˈərtʃɪn/ *n* [C] **1** mischievous small boy. **2** poor destitute child.
urge /ərdʒ/ *vt* **1** push or drive on: *The crowd ~d the tennis star on to win.* **2** request earnestly; try to persuade: *"Buy it now," he ~d. "Prices will soon rise."* **3** stress (the importance of) requests and arguments: *He ~d on his pupils the importance of hard work.* □ *n* [C] (rarely *pl*) strong desire: *He has/feels an ~ to travel.*
ur·gency /ˈərdʒənsi/ *n* [U] importance of, need for, haste or prompt action: *a matter of great ~.*
ur·gent /ˈərdʒənt/ *adj* **1** needing prompt decision or action: *It is most ~ that the patient be hospitalized.* **2** (of a person, his voice, etc) showing that something is urgent.
ur·gent·ly *adv*
uri·nary /ˈyʊrəˌneri/ *adj* of urine: *~ infection.*
uri·nate /ˈyʊrəˌneit/ *vi* discharge urine.
urine /ˈyʊrɪn/ *n* [U] waste liquid which collects in the bladder and is discharged from the body.
urn /ərn/ *n* [C] **1** vase with a stem as used for holding the ashes of a person whose body has been cremated. **2** large metal container in which a drink such as tea or coffee is made or kept hot, eg in coffee shops.
us[1] /əs *strong form:* ˈəs/ *personal pron* (used as the object form of *we*): *We hope you will visit us soon.*
US[2] /ˌyu ˈes/ *abbr* = United States.
USA *abbr* = **1** /ˌyu ˌes ˈei/ United States of America. **2** United States Army.
USAF *abbr* = United States Air Force.
usage /ˈyusɪdʒ/ *n* **1** [U] way of using something; treatment: *Machines soon wear out under rough ~.* **2** [C,U] conventions governing the use of a language (esp those not governed by grammatical rules): *Such ~s are not characteristic of educated speakers.*
USCG *abbr* = United States Coast Guard.
use[1] /yus/ *n* **1** [U] using or being used; condition of being used: *the use of electricity for cooking.* ***in use,*** being used. ***come into use,*** begin to be used: *When did the word "transistor" come into common use?* ***out of use,*** not being, no longer, used. **2** [C,U] purpose for which a person or thing is or may be employed; work that a person or thing is able to do: *a tool with many uses; find a use for it; have no further use for it.* **3** [U]

value; advantage: *Is this paper of any use to you?* **4** [U] power of using: *lose the use of one's legs*, become unable to walk. **5** [U] right to use: *You can have the use of my car.*

use·ful /ˈyusfəl/ *adj* helpful; producing good results: *Are you a useful member of society?*

use·fully /-fəli/ *adv*

use·ful·ness /-nɪs/ *n* [U]

use·less *adj* **(a)** of no use; worthless: *A car is useless without gasoline.* **(b)** without result; unrewarding: *It's useless to argue with them.*

use·less·ly *adv*

use·less·ness /-nɪs/ *n* [U]

use[2] /yuz/ *vt* (*pt,pp* used /yuzd/) **1** cause to act or serve for a purpose: *You use your legs when you walk. May I use* (= mention) *your name as a reference*, eg in an application for a job? **2** have the use of (until nothing is left): *How much coal did we use last winter? He has used up all his strength.* **3** behave toward: *Use others as you would like them to use you.*

used /yuzd/ *adj* no longer new: *used cars.*

user *n* [C] person or thing that uses: *There are more ˈtelephone users in the USA than in any other country.*

used /yus(t)/ *anomalous finite* (irregular *pt* and *pp* of use) (indicating a constant or frequent practice in the past, or, in the construction *there used to be*, the existence of something in the past): *That's where I ~ to live when I was a child. Life isn't so easy here as it ~ to be.*

used to /ˈyus(t) tə; *before vowel sounds:* tu/ *adj* having become familiar to by habit or custom: *You will soon be/get ~ it.*

usher /ˈəʃər/ *n* [C] person who shows people to their seats in theaters, etc. □ *vt* **1** lead, conduct: *The girl ~ed me to my seat* (in a theater). **2** produce: *The change of government ~ed in a period of prosperity.*

usher·ette /ˌəʃəˈret/ *n* [C] girl or woman usher.

USMC *abbr* = United States Marine Corps.

USN *abbr* = United States Navy.

USS /ˌyu ˌes ˈes/ *abbr* = United States ship.

USSR /ˌyu ˌes ˌes ˈar/ *abbr* = Union of Soviet Socialist Republics.

usu. *abbr* = **1** usual. **2** usually.

usual /ˈyuʒuəl/ *adj* such as commonly happens: *He arrived later than ~.*

usu·ally /ˈyuʒ(u)əli/ *adv* in the ordinary way: *What do you ~ly do on Sundays?*

usurer /ˈyuʒərər/ *n* [C] person who engages in usury.

usu·ri·ous /yuˈʒəriəs/, **usu·rous** /ˈyuʒərəs/ *adj* involving usury.

usurp /yuˈsərp/ *vt* wrongfully take (a person's power, authority, position): *~ the chairman's authority.*

usurper *n* [C] person who does this.

usury /ˈyuʒ(ə)ri/ *n* [U] (practice of) lending money, esp at a high rate of interest.

UT *postal abbr* = Utah. ⇨ App 6.

uten·sil /yuˈtensəl/ *n* [C] instrument, tool, etc, esp for use in the house: *ˈhousehold ~s*, eg pots, pans, brushes.

uterus /ˈyutərəs/ *n* [C] (*pl* ~es) (*anat*) = womb.

utili·tar·ian /yuˌtɪləˈteriən/ *adj* characterized by usefulness rather than by beauty, truth, goodness.

util·ity /yuˈtɪləti/ *n* (*pl* -ies) **1** [U] quality of being useful. **2** [C] public service such as the supply of water or telephone service. **3** (as an *adjective*): *ˈ~ pole*, one for telephone wires, etc.

util·ize /ˈyutəˌlaiz/ *vt* make use of; find a use for.

util·iz·ation /ˌyutəlɪˈzeiʃən/ *n* [U]

ut·most /ˈətˌmoust/ *adj* most extreme; greatest: *with the ~ care.* □ *n* (*sing* only) the most that is possible: *I shall do my ~ to see that justice is done.*

ut·ter[1] /ˈətər/ *adj* complete; total: *~ darkness.*

ut·ter·ly *adv* completely: *She's ~ly bored with him.*

ut·ter[2] /ˈətər/ *vt* **1** make (a sound or sounds) with the mouth: *~ a sigh/a cry of pain.* **2** say: *the last words he ~ed.* **3** (*formal*) put (counterfeit money, etc) into circulation.

ut·ter·ance /ˈətərəns/ *n* **1** (*sing* only) (*formal*) way of speaking: *a clear ~.* **2** [C] spoken word or words. **3** [U] ***give utterance to (one's feelings)***, express in words.

ut·ter·most /ˈətərˌmoust/ *adj, n* = utmost.

u·vu·la /ˈyuvyələ/ *n* [C] small fleshy extension of the soft palate. ⇨ illus at mouth.

u·vu·lar /ˈyuvyələr/ *adj* of or at the uvula.

V

V[1], v /vi/ *n* (*pl* V's, v's /viz/) **1** the twenty-second letter of the English alphabet. **2** Roman numeral for five.
V[2], v *abbr* = verb.
v.[3] *abbr* = versus.
VA[1] /ˌvi ˈei/ *abbr* = Veterans Administration.
VA[2] *postal abbr* = Virginia. ⇨ App. 6.
va·cancy /ˈveikənsi/ *n* (*pl* -ies) **1** [U] condition of being empty or unoccupied. **2** [C] unoccupied space: *There is a ~ in that building*, an apartment for rent. **3** [U] lack of ideas, intelligence or concentration. **4** [C] position in business, etc for which a person is needed: *vacancies for typists*.
va·cant /ˈveikənt/ *adj* **1** empty: *gaze into ~ space*. **2** not occupied by anyone: *a ~ room*, eg in a hotel; *apply for a ~ position*, eg in an office. **3** (of time) not filled with any activity. **4** (of the mind) without thought; (of the eyes) showing no signs of thought or interest: *a ~ expression*.
va·cant·ly *adv*
va·cate /ˈveiˌkeit/ *vt* **1** give up living in: *~ a house*. **2** leave unoccupied: *~ one's seat*.
va·ca·tion /veiˈkeiʃən/ *n* [C] **1** weeks during which schools, etc stop work: *the summer ~*. **2** period of rest from work: *we took a three-week ~ in February*.
vac·ci·nate /ˈvæksəˌneit/ *vt* protect (a person) (against smallpox, etc) by injecting vaccine.
vac·ci·na·tion /ˌvæksəˈneiʃən/ *n* [C,U] (instance of) vaccinating.
vac·cine /vækˈsin/ *n* [C,U] substance, usually from the blood of an animal, used to protect persons from a disease by causing them to have a slight, but not dangerous, form of the disease.
vac·il·late /ˈvæsəˌleit/ *vi* hesitate; be uncertain (in opinion, etc): *~ between hope and fear*.
vac·il·la·tion /ˌvæsəˈleiʃən/ *n* [C,U]
vac·uum /ˈvæky(u)əm, ˈvæˌkyum/ *n* [C] (*pl* ~s or, in science, vacua /-yuə/) **1** space completely empty of substance or gas(es). **2** space in a container from which the air has been pumped out. □ *vi,vt* clean (a rug, etc) with a vacuum cleaner.
ˈvacuum bottle, one having a vacuum between its inner and outer walls, keeping the contents at an unchanging temperature.
ˈvacuum cleaner, apparatus which takes up dust, dirt, etc by suction.
ˈvacuum tube, sealed glass or metal tube in which the flow of electrons is controlled for eg amplification in radios, etc.
vaga·bond /ˈvægəˌband/ *adj* having no fixed home: *live a ~ life*. □ *n* [C] vagabond person.
va·gary /ˈveigəri/ *n* [C] (*pl* -ies) (*formal*) strange, unusual act or idea, esp one for which there seems to be no good reason: *the vagaries of fashion*.
va·gina /vəˈdʒainə/ *n* [C] (*pl* ~s) passage (in a female mammal) from the external genital organs to the womb.
vag·inal /vəˈdʒainəl/ *adj*
va·grancy /ˈveigrənsi/ *n* [C,U] (instance of) being a vagrant.
va·grant /ˈveigrənt/ *adj* leading a wandering life: *~ tribes*. □ *n* [C] vagrant person.
vague /veig/ *adj* (-r, -st) **1** not clear or distinct: *I haven't the ~st idea what they want*. **2** (of persons, their looks, behavior) uncertain, suggesting uncertainty (about needs, intentions, etc).
vague·ly *adv*
vague·ness /-nɪs/ *n* [U]
vain /vein/ *adj* (-er, -est) **1** without use, value, meaning or result: *a ~ attempt; ~ hopes*. **2 *in vain,*** **(a)** without the desired result: *All our work was in ~*. **(b)** without due reverence, honor or respect: *take a person's name in ~*, use it disrespectfully. **3** having too high an opinion of one's looks, abilities, etc: *as ~ as a peacock*, very vain.
vain·ly *adv*
vale /ˈveiəl/ *n* [C] (*liter*) = valley.
val·en·tine /ˈvælənˌtain/ *n* [C] **1** letter, card, etc, sent on Saint Valentine's Day, February 14, to a sweetheart. **2** term used on Saint Valentine's Day for a sweetheart: *You're my ~*.
valet /væˈlei/ *n* [C] **1** member of (hotel) staff employed to dry-clean or press clothes. **2** stand of wood or metal for holding clothing.
val·iant /ˈvælyənt/ *adj* = brave (the usual word).
val·iant·ly *adv*
valid /ˈvælɪd/ *adj* **1** (*legal*) effective because made or done with the correct formalities: *a ~ claim/marriage*. **2** (of contracts, etc) having force in law: *a pass ~ for three months*. **3** (of arguments, reasons, etc) well based; sound: *raise ~ objections to a suggestion*.
va·lid·ity /vəˈlɪdəti/ *n* [U] state of being valid.
va·lid·ly *adv*
vali·date /ˈvæləˌdeit/ *vt* make valid: *~ a claim*.
vali·da·tion /ˌvæləˈdeiʃən/ *n* [C,U] (act of) validating.
va·lise /vəˈlis/ *n* [C] small leather case for clothes, etc during a journey.
val·ley /ˈvæli/ *n* [C] (*pl* ~s) stretch of land between hills or mountains, often with a river flowing through it.
val·or /ˈvælər/ *n* [U] (*formal*) bravery, esp in war.
valu·able /ˈvælyəbəl/ *adj* of great value, worth or use: *a ~ discovery*. □ *n* (usually *pl*) something of much value, eg jewels.

valu·ation /ˌvælyuˈeiʃən/ *n* **1** [U] process of deciding the value of a person or thing. **2** [C] the value that is decided on: *The surveyors arrived at widely different ~s.*

value /ˈvælyu/ *n* **1** [U] quality of being useful or desirable: *the ~ of walking as an exercise.* **2** [U] worth of something when compared with something else: *This book will be of great/little/some/no ~ to him in his studies.* **3** [C,U] worth of something in terms of money or other goods for which it can be exchanged: *Is the ~ of the American dollar likely to decline?* **4** [U] what something is considered to be worth (contrasted with the price obtainable): *I've been offered $700 for my car but its ~ is much higher.* **5** (in music) full time indicated by a note: *Give the note its full ~.* **6** (*pl*) standards: *moral/ethical ~s.* □ *vt* **1** estimate the money value of: *He ~d the house for me at $40,000.* **2** have a high opinion of: *Do you ~ her as a secretary?*

value·less *adj* worthless.

valve /vælv/ *n* [C] **1** (kinds of) mechanical device for controlling the flow of air, liquid, gas, etc in one direction only. **2** structure in the heart or in a blood vessel allowing the blood to flow in one direction only. **3** vacuum tube used in a radio, allowing the flow of electrons in one direction. **4** device in musical wind instruments, eg a cornet, for changing the pitch by changing the length of the column of air.

val·vu·lar /ˈvælvyələr/ *adj* of valves(2).

vam·pire /ˈvæmˌpaiər/ *n* [C] (in stories, etc) corpse that comes to life at night and sucks the blood of sleeping persons.

ˈvampire bat, kind of blood-sucking bat.

van[1] /væn/ *n* [C] roofed motor vehicle for carrying and delivering goods: *a ˈfurniture van.*

van[2] /væn/ *n* [U] **1** front or leading part of an army or fleet in battle. **2** those persons who lead a procession or (*fig*) a movement: *in the van of scientific progress.*

ˈvan·guard *n* **(a)** [C] advance party of an army, etc as a guard against surprise attack. **(b)** [U] = van²(2).

van·dal /ˈvændəl/ *n* [C] person who deliberately destroys works of art or public and private property.

van·dal·ism /-ˌlɪzəm/ *n* [U] behavior characteristic of vandals.

vane /vein/ *n* [C] **1** arrow or pointer on the top of a building, turning to show the direction of the wind. **2** blade of a propeller, or other flat surface acted on by wind or water.

van·guard /ˈvænˌgard/ *n* ⇨ van².

va·nilla /vəˈnɪlə/ *n* **1** [C] (pods or beans of) plant with sweet-smelling flowers. **2** [U] substance from vanilla beans or synthetic product used for flavoring: (as an *adjective*) *~ ice cream.*

van·ish /ˈvænɪʃ/ *vi* suddenly disappear; fade away gradually; go out of existence: *The thief ran into the crowd and ~ed.*

van·ity /ˈvænəti/ *n* (*pl* -ies) **1** [U] having too high an opinion of one's looks, abilities, etc: *do something out of ~.* **2** [U] quality of being unsatisfying, without true value: *the ~ of pleasure;* [C] vain, worthless thing or act: *the vanities of life.*

van·quish /ˈvæŋkwɪʃ/ *vt* = defeat (the usual word).

va·por /ˈveipər/ *n* [U] steam; mist; gas to which certain substances may be reduced by heat: *ˈwater ~.*

va·por·ize /ˈveipəˌraiz/ *vt,vi* change, be changed, into vapor.

vari·able /ˈværiəbəl/ *adj* varying; changeable: *~ winds; ~ standards.* □ *n* [C] variable thing or quantity; factor which may vary, eg in an experiment.

vari·abil·ity /ˌværiəˈbɪləti/ *n* [U]

vari·ably /-əbli/ *adv*

vari·ant /ˈværiənt/ *adj* different or alternative: *~ spellings of a word*—eg "honor" (*US*) and "honour" (*British*). □ *n* [C] variant form (eg of spelling).

vari·ation /ˌværiˈeiʃən/ *n* **1** [C,U] (degree of) varying or being variant: *~(s) of temperature.* **2** [C] (*music*) simple melody repeated in a different form: *~s on a theme by Mozart.* **3** [U] (*biol*) change in bodily structure or form caused by new conditions, environment, etc; [C] instance of such change.

vari·col·ored /ˈværɪˌkələrd/ *adj* of various colors.

vari·cose vein /ˌværəkous ˈvein/ *adj* vein that has become permanently swollen or enlarged.

var·ied /ˈværid/ *adj* **1** of different sorts: *the ~ scenes of life.* **2** full of changes or variety: *a ~ career.*

varie·gated /ˈværiəˌgeitɪd/ *adj* marked irregularly with differently colored patches: *The flowers of pansies are often ~.*

varie·ga·tion /ˌværiəˈgeiʃən/ *n* [U]

var·iety /vəˈraiəti/ *n* (*pl* -ies) **1** [U] quality of not being the same, or not being the same at all times: *a life full of ~.* **2** (*sing* only) number or range of different things: *for a ~ of reasons.* **3** [C] (*biol*) subdivision of a species. **4** [C] kind or sort which differs from others of the larger group of which it is a part: *rare varieties of early postage stamps.* **5** [U] kind of entertainment consisting of singing, dancing, comedy, etc: *a ~ act.*

vari·ous /ˈværiəs/ *adj* different; of a number of different sorts: *for ~ reasons; at ~ times.*

vari·ous·ly *adv*

var·nish /ˈvarnɪʃ/ *n* [C,U] (particular kind of) (liquid used to give a) hard, shiny, transparent coating on a surface. □ *vt* put a coating of varnish on: *Some women ~ their toenails.*

vars·ity /ˈvarsəti/ *n* [C] (*pl* -ies) university team.

vary /ˈværi/ *vi,vt* (*pt,pp* -ied) be, become, cause to become, different: *They ~ in weight from 5 to 10 pounds.*

vas·cu·lar /ˈvæskyələr/ *adj* (*anat*) of, made up of, containing, vessels or ducts through which blood, lymph, flows: *~ tissue.*

vase /veis, vaz/ *n* [C] vessel of glass, pottery, etc for holding cut flowers, or as an ornament.

va·sec·tomy /væˈsektəmi, -ˈzek-/ *n* [C,U] (*pl* -ies) surgical operation to make a man sterile.

vast /væst/ *adj* immense; extensive: *~ sums of money; a ~ expanse of desert.*

vast·ly *adv: ~ly improved,* greatly improved.

vast·ness /-nɪs/ *n* [U]

vat /væt/ *n* [C] large vessel for holding liquids, esp in brewing, dyeing.

vault[1] /vɔlt/ *n* [C] **1** arched roof; series of arches forming a roof. **2** underground room or cellar (with or without an arched roof) as a place of storage (ˈ*wine* ~*s*), or for burials (eg under a church), or for keeping valuables safe: *keep one's jewels in a* ˈ*bank* ~.

vault[2] /vɔlt/ *vi,vt* jump in a single movement, with the hand(s) resting on something, or with the help of a pole: ~ *(over) a fence*. □ *n* [C] jump made in this way. ⇨ pole vault.

vaulter *n* [C] person who vaults: *a* ˈ*pole-*~*er*.

VD /ˌvi ˈdi/ *abbr* = venereal disease.

veal /ˈviəl/ *n* [U] flesh of a calf eaten as food.

veer /vɪr/ *vi* change direction: *The wind* ~*ed around to the north. Opinion* ~*ed in our favor*.

veg·etable /ˈvedʒ(ə)təbəl/ *adj* of, from, relating to, plants or plant life: ~ *oils*. □ *n* [C] plant, esp one used for food, eg potatoes, cabbages, carrots.

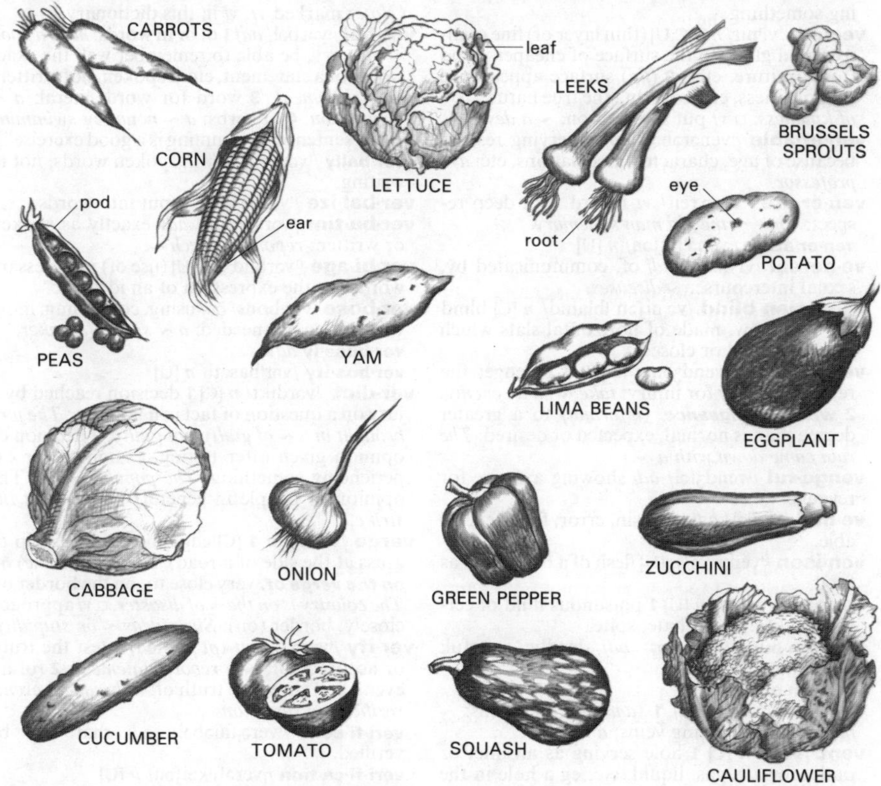

VEGETABLES

veg·etar·ian /ˌvedʒəˈteriən/ *n* [C] person who eats no meat: (as an *adjective*) *a* ~ *diet*.

veg·etate /ˈvedʒəˌteit/ *vi* lead a dull life with little activity, thought or interest.

veg·eta·tion /ˌvedʒəˈteiʃən/ *n* [U] plants generally and collectively: *a desert with no sign of* ~ *anywhere*.

ve·he·ment /ˈviəmənt/ *adj* (*formal*) **1** (of feelings) strong, eager. **2** (of persons, their speech, behavior, etc) filled with, showing, strong or eager feeling: ~ *passions*.

ve·he·ment·ly *adv*

ve·hicle /ˈvɪkəl, ˈviˌhɪkəl/ *n* [C] **1** (usually wheeled) means of moving goods or passengers on land (and in space). **2** means by which thought, feeling, etc can be carried: *Art may be used as a* ~ *for/of propaganda*.

ve·hicu·lar /viˈhɪkyələr/ *adj* related to, consisting of, carried by, vehicles: *The road is closed to vehicular traffic*.

veil /ˈveiəl/ *n* [C] **1** covering of fine net or other material to protect or hide a woman's face: *She lowered her* ~. **2** (*fig*) something that hides or disguises: *a* ~ *of mist*. □ *vt* (*pres p* ~ing /ˈveilɪŋ/) **1** put a veil over: *Not all Moslem women are* ~*ed*. **2** (*fig*) hide: *He could not* ~ *his distrust*.

veil·ing /ˈveilɪŋ/ *n* [U] light material used for veils.

vein /vein/ *n* [C] **1** blood vessel along which blood flows from all parts of the body to the heart. ⇨ illus at respiration. **2** one of the lines in some leaves or in the wings of some insects. **3** colored line or streak in some kinds of stone, eg marble. **4** (*fig*) characteristic: *There is a ~ of madness in him.* **5** crack in rock, filled with mineral or ore: *a ~ of gold.* **6** mood; train of thought: *in an imaginative ~.*

vel. *abbr* = velocity.

vel·oc·ity /vəˈlasəti/ *n* (*formal*) = speed.

ve·lour, ve·lours /vəˈlʊr/ *n* [U] fabric like velvet.

vel·vet /ˈvelvɪt/ *n* [U] cloth with a thick soft pile on one side.

vel·vety *adj* smooth and soft like velvet.

ve·nal /ˈvinəl/ *adj* **1** (of persons) ready to do something dishonest (eg using influence or position) for money: *~ politicians.* **2** (of conduct) influenced by, done for, (possible) payment: *~ practices.*

ve·nally /-nəli/ *adv*

vend /vend/ *vt, vi* sell.

ˈvend·ing machine, one which operates by the insertion of money to dispense articles of food, drinks, stamps, etc.

vendor /ˈvendər/ *n* [C] person or company selling something.

ve·neer /vɪˈnɪr/ *n* **1** [C,U] (thin layer of) fine quality wood glued to the surface of cheaper wood (for furniture, etc). **2** (*fig*) surface appearance (of politeness, etc) covering the true nature: *a ~ of kindness.* □ *vt* put a veneer on: *~ a desk.*

ven·er·able /ˈvenərəbəl/ *adj* deserving respect because of age, character, associations, etc: *a ~ professor.*

ven·er·ate /ˈvenəˌreit/ *vt* regard with deep respect: *They ~ the old man's memory.*

ven·er·ation /ˌvenəˈreiʃən/ *n* [U]

ve·nereal /vɪˈnɪriəl/ *adj* of, communicated by, sexual intercourse: *~ diseases.*

ve·ne·tian blind /vəˌniʃən ˈblaind/ *n* [C] blind for a window, made of horizontal slats which can be opened or closed.

ven·geance /ˈvendʒəns/ *n* [U] **1** revenge; the return of injury for injury: *take ~ on an enemy.* **2** ***with a vengeance,*** (*informal*) to a greater degree than is normal, expected or desired: *The rain came down with a ~.*

venge·ful /ˈvendʒfəl/ *adj* showing a desire for revenge.

ve·nial /ˈviniəl/ *adj* (of a sin, error, fault) excusable.

ven·ison /ˈvenəsən/ *n* [U] flesh of a deer eaten as food.

venom /ˈvenəm/ *n* [U] **1** poisonous fluid of certain snakes. **2** (*fig*) hate; spite.

ven·om·ous /ˈvenəməs/ *adj* deadly; spiteful: *~ous snakes/criticism.*

ven·om·ous·ly *adv*

ve·nous /ˈvinəs/ *adj* **1** (*anat*) of the veins: *~ blood.* **2** (*bot*) having veins: *a ~ leaf.*

vent /vent/ *n* [C] **1** hole serving as an inlet or outlet for air, gas, liquid, etc, eg a hole in the top of a barrel for air to enter as liquid is drawn out. **2** means of escape: *The floods found a ~ through the dikes.* **3** (*sing* only) outlet for one's feelings. ***give vent to,*** give free expression to: *He gave ~ to his feelings in an impassioned speech.* □ *vt* find or provide an outlet for: *He ~ed his anger on his long-suffering wife.*

ven·ti·late /ˈventəˌleit/ *vt* cause (air) to move in and out freely: *~ a room.*

ven·ti·la·tion /ˌventəˈleiʃən/ *n* [U]

ven·ti·la·tor /ˈventəˌleitər/ *n* [C] device for ventilating.

ven·tral /ˈventrəl/ *adj* of, on, near, the belly: *The scales of a fish are often smaller or absent around the ~ region.*

ven·tricle /ˈventrɪkəl/ *n* [C] hollow part of an organ, esp of the heart. ⇨ illus at respiratory.

ven·ture /ˈventʃər/ *n* [C,U] undertaking in which there is risk: *a ˈbusiness ~.* □ *vt,vi* **1** take the risk of, expose to, danger or loss: *~ too near the edge of a cliff.* **2** go so far as, dare: *~ (to put forward) an opinion; ~ a guess.*

Venus /ˈvinəs/ *n* (*astron*) planet second in order from the sun. ⇨ illus at planet.

ve·randa, ve·ran·dah /vəˈrændə/ *n* [C] roofed and floored open space along the side(s) of a house, sports pavilion, etc.

verb /vərb/ *n* [C] word showing what a person or thing does, what state he or it is in, what is becoming of him or it. ⇨ transitive, intransitive. (*Note:* marked *vt, vi* in this dictionary.)

ver·bal /ˈvərbəl/ *adj* **1** of or in words: *have a good ~ memory*, be able to remember well the exact words of a statement, etc. **2** spoken, not written: *a ~ statement.* **3** word for word, literal: *a ~ translation.* **4** of verbs: *a ~ noun* (eg *swimming* in the sentence "Swimming is a good exercise").

ver·bally /ˈvərbəli/ *adv* in spoken words, not in writing.

ver·bal·ize /ˈvərbəˌlaiz/ *vt* put into words.

ver·ba·tim /vərˈbeitɪm/ *adv* exactly as spoken or written: *report a speech ~.*

ver·bi·age /ˈvərbiɪdʒ/ *n* [U] (use of) unnecessary words for the expression of an idea, etc.

ver·bose /vərˈbous/ *adj* using, containing, more words than are needed: *a ~ speech/speaker.*

ver·bose·ly *adv*

ver·bos·ity /vərˈbasəti/ *n* [U]

ver·dict /ˈvərdɪkt/ *n* [C] **1** decision reached by a jury on a question of fact in a law case: *The jury brought in a ~ of guilty/not guilty.* **2** decision or opinion given after testing, examining or experiencing something: *The popular ~* (= The opinion of people in general) *was against the strike.*

verge /vərdʒ/ *n* **1** [C] edge; border (eg strip of grass at the side of a road). **2** (*sing* with *the*) ***be on the verge of,*** very close to, on the border of: *The country is on the ~ of disaster.* □ *vi* approach closely, border (on): *Such ideas ~ on stupidity.*

ver·ify /ˈverəˌfai/ *vt* (*pt,pp* -ied) **1** test the truth or accuracy of: *~ a report/statement.* **2** (of an event, etc) show the truth of: *Subsequent events verified my suspicions.*

veri·fi·able /ˈverəˌfaiəbəl/ *adj* that can be verified.

veri·fi·ca·tion /ˌverəfɪˈkeiʃən/ *n* [U]

veri·table /ˈverətəbəl/ *adj* rightly named: *a ~ liar.*

ver·mil·ion /vərˈmɪlyən/ *adj, n* [U] bright red (color).

ver·min /ˈvərmɪn/ *n* [U] (used with a *pl verb*, but not with numerals) **1** wild animals (eg rats, weasels, foxes) harmful to plants, birds and other animals. **2** parasitic insects (eg lice)

sometimes found on the bodies of human beings and other animals. **3** (*fig*) human beings who are harmful to society or who prey on others.
ver·min·ous /ˈvərmɪnəs/ *adj*
ver·nacu·lar /vərˈnækyələr/ *adj* (of a word, a language) of the country in question: *a ~ language,* native language; *a ~ poet*, one who uses a vernacular language. □ *n* [C] language or dialect of a country or district.
ver·sa·tile /ˈvərsəˌtaiəl/ *adj* interested in and clever at many different things; having various uses: *a ~ mind/invention.*
ver·sa·til·ity /ˌvərsəˈtɪləti/ *n* [U]
verse /vərs/ *n* **1** [U] (form of) writing arranged in lines, each conforming to a pattern of accented and unaccented syllables: *prose and ~.* ⇨ blank verse. **2** [C] group of lines of this kind forming a unit in a rhyme scheme: *a poem/hymn of five ~s.* **3** [C] one line of verse with a definite number of accented syllables: *a few ~s from Tennyson.* **4** one of the short numbered divisions of a chapter in the Bible.
versed /vərst/ *adj* ***versed in,*** skilled or experienced in: *well ~ in mathematics/the arts.*
ver·sion /ˈvərʒən/ *n* [C] **1** account of an event, etc from the point of view of one person: *There were three ~s of what happened/of what the accused had said.* **2** (of the Bible) translation: *a Cherokee ~ of the Gospels.*
ver·sus /ˈvərsəs/ *prep* (*Lat*) (in law and sport; often shortened to *v* or *vs* in print) against: *Robinson v Brown; the Yankees vs the Dodgers.*
ver·te·bra /ˈvərtəbrə/ *n* [C] (*pl* ~e /-ˌbri/) any one of the sections of the backbone. ⇨ illus at skeleton.
ver·te·brate /ˈvərtəbrɪt/ *n* [C], *adj* (animal, bird, etc) having a backbone.
ver·ti·cal /ˈvərtɪkəl/ *adj* (of a line or plane) at a right angle to the earth's surface or to another line or plane: *a ~-takeoff aircraft*, one that can rise vertically. □ *n* [C] vertical line, bar, etc. ⇨ horizontal.
ver·ti·cally /-kli/ *adv*
verve /vərv/ *n* [U] enthusiasm, spirit, vigor (esp in artistic or literary work).
very[1] /ˈveri/ *adj* **1** itself and no other; truly such: *At that ~ moment the phone rang. You're the ~ man I want to see.* **2** extreme: *at the ~ end/beginning; the letter at the ~ top of the pile.*
very[2] /ˈveri/ *adv* **1** (used to show intensity with *adverbs, adjectives*): *~ quickly/little.* ***very well,*** (often used to show agreement after persuasion or argument, or obedience to a command, request, etc): *Very well, doctor, I'll give up smoking.* **2** (with a *superlative*) in the highest possible degree: *at the ~ latest.*
vessel /ˈvesəl/ *n* [C] **1** hollow receptacle, esp for a liquid, eg a bucket, bowl, bottle, cup. **2** ship or large boat. ⇨ bloodvessel.
vest[1] /vest/ *n* [C] close-fitting sleeveless garment worn under a coat or jacket, buttoned down the front.
vest[2] /vest/ *vt* furnish or give as a fixed right: *~ a man with authority/rights in an estate.*
ves·tige /ˈvestɪdʒ/ *n* [C] **1** trace or sign; small remaining bit of evidence of what once existed: *There is not a ~ of truth in the report.* **2** (*anat*) organ, or part of one, which is a survival of something that once existed: *A human being has the ~ of a tail.*
vest·ment /ˈvestmənt/ *n* [C] ceremonial robe as worn by a priest in church.
ves·try /ˈvestri/ *n* [C] (*pl* -ies) **1** part of a church where vestments are kept. **2** room (in some kinds of church) used for Sunday School, prayer meetings, etc.
vet[1] /vet/ *n* [C] **1** (*informal*) (short for) veterinarian. **2** (*informal*) (short for) veteran.
vet.[2] *abbr* = veteran.
vet·eran /ˈvet(ə)rən/ *n* [C] **1** person who has had much or long experience, eg as a soldier: *a ~ teacher.* **2** any ex-serviceman.
ˈVeterans Day, US holiday, November 11, in honor of veterans(2), esp those who fought in wars.
vet·erin·arian /ˌvet(ə)rəˈneriən/ *n* [C] veterinary physician or surgeon.
vet·erin·ary /ˈvet(ə)rəˌneri/ *adj* of or concerned with the diseases and injuries of (esp farm and domestic) animals: *a ~ surgeon/college.*
veto /ˈviˌtou/ *n* [C] (*pl* ~es) constitutional right of a sovereign, president, legislative assembly or other body, or a member of the United Nations Security Council, to reject or forbid something; statement that rejects or prohibits something: *exercise a power of ~.* □ *vt* put a veto on: *The President ~ed the legislation.*
vex /veks/ *vt* (*formal*) annoy; distress: *He was vexed at his failure.*
vex·ation /vekˈseiʃən/ *n* [U] state of being vexed; [C] something that vexes.
VFW *abbr* = Veterans of Foreign Wars.
VI[1], **V.I.** *postal abbr* = Virgin Islands.
v.i.[2] *abbr* = verb, intransitive.
via /ˈvaiə/ *prep* (*Lat*) by way of: *travel from New York to Los Angeles via Chicago.*
vi·able /ˈvaiəbəl/ *adj* capable of existing, developing and surviving.
vi·abil·ity /ˌvaiəˈbɪləti/ *n* [U]
vi·aduct /ˈvaiəˌdəkt/ *n* [C] long bridge (usually with many arches) carrying a road or railway across a valley.
vial /ˈvaiəl/ *n* [C] small bottle (for medicine).
vibes /vaibz/ *n pl* (*sl*) **1** = vibrations(2). **2** = vibraphone.
vi·brant /ˈvaibrənt/ *adj* vibrating: *the ~ notes of a cello.*
vi·bra·phone /ˈvaibrəˌfoun/ *n* [C] instrument played by hitting metal bars of different lengths with a pair of sticks or mallets.
vi·brate /ˈvaiˌbreit/ *vi,vt* **1** (cause to) move quickly and continuously backwards and forwards: *The house ~s whenever a heavy truck passes.* **2** (of stretched strings, the voice) throb; quiver: *The strings of a piano ~ when the keys are struck.*
vi·bra·tion /vaiˈbreiʃən/ *n* [C,U] **1** vibrating movement: *We felt ~s as the train passed.* **2** (*pl*) (*informal*) sensation, influence: *good ~s from a Presidential candidate.*
vicar /ˈvɪkər/ *n* [C] (*RC Church*) deputy; representative: *the ~ of Christ*, the Pope.
vi·cari·ous /vaiˈkæriəs/ *adj* **1** (*formal*) done, ex-

perienced, by one person for another or others: *the ~ sufferings of Jesus.* **2** (of feelings or emotions) felt through sharing imaginatively in the feelings or activities of another person: *She derived much ~ pleasure from reading about the heroine's good fortune in the novel.*

vi·cari·ous·ly *adv*

vice /vais/ *n* [C,U] (any particular kind of) evil conduct or practice: *Gluttony is a ~.*

vice- /vais-/ *prefix* person who is next in rank to and may act for another: *vice-president.*

vice ad·miral /ˌvais ˈædmərəl/ *n* [C] commissioned officer in the US navy or coast guard who ranks above a rear admiral and below an admiral.

vice versa /ˌvais(ə) ˈvərsə/ *adj* (*Lat*) the other way around; with the terms or conditions reversed: *We gossip about them and ~,* and they gossip about us.

vi·cin·ity /vɪˈsɪnəti/ *n* (*pl* -ies) **1** [U] nearness; closeness of relationship: *in close ~ to the church.* **2** [C] neighborhood: *There isn't a good school in the ~.*

vi·cious /ˈvɪʃəs/ *adj* **1** evil (the usual word): *a ~ life.* **2** given or done with evil intent: *a ~ kick/look.*

ˌvicious ˈcircle, state of affairs in which a cause produces an effect which itself produces the original cause.

vi·cious·ly *adv*

vic·tim /ˈvɪktɪm/ *n* [C] **1** living creature killed and offered as a religious sacrifice. **2** person, animal, etc suffering injury, pain, loss, etc because of circumstances, an event, war, an accident, etc: *the ~s of the earthquake.*

vic·tim·ize /-ˌmaiz/ *vt* select for ill-treatment because of real or alleged misconduct, etc: *Labor union leaders claimed that some of their members had been ~ized,* eg by being dismissed.

vic·tim·iz·ation /ˌvɪktɪmɪˈzeiʃən/ *n* [U]

vic·tor /ˈvɪktər/ *n* [C] person who conquers or wins.

vic·tori·ous /vɪkˈtɔriəs/ *adj* having gained the victory.

vic·tori·ous·ly *adv*

vic·tory /ˈvɪkt(ə)ri/ *n* [C,U] (*pl* -ies) (instance, occasion, of) success (in war, a contest, game, etc): *gain/win a ~ over the enemy; lead the troops to ~;* (as an *adjective*) *a ~ march.*

video /ˈvɪdiou/ [C,U] *prefix* recording and reproducing vision: *~ cassettes.*

ˈvideo recorder, for using videotape.

ˈvideo·tape *n* magnetic tape for recording sound and vision, eg of television programs.

vie /vai/ *vi* ***vie with sb/for sth,*** rival or compete (the usual word): *The two boys vied with one another for the first place.*

view[1] /vyu/ *n* **1** [U] state of seeing or being seen; field of vision: *The speaker stood in full ~ of the crowd,* could see them and could be seen by them. ***in view of,*** considering, taking into account: *In ~ of the facts, it seems useless to continue.* ***on view,*** being shown or exhibited: *The latest summer fashions are now on ~ in the better stores.* ***come into view,*** become visible: *As we turned the corner the lake came into ~.* **2** [C] (picture, photograph, etc of) natural scenery, landscape, etc: *a house with a fine ~ of the mountains.* **3** [C] opportunity to see or inspect something: *a private ~,* eg of paintings, before public exhibition. **4** [C] personal opinion; mental attitude; thought or observation (on a topic, subject): *She had/expressed strong ~s on the subject of equal pay for men and women.* **5** aim; intention; purpose. ***with a/the view to/of,*** with the intention or hope: *with a ~ to saving trouble.*

ˈview·finder *n* device in a camera showing the area, etc that will be photographed.

ˈview·point = point of view. ⇨ point[1](3).

view[2] /vyu/ *vt* look at; examine; consider: *The subject may be ~ed in various ways. How do you ~ the situation?* What do you think about it?

viewer /ˈvyuər/ *n* [C] (esp): (*television*) *~er,* person watching a television program.

vigil /ˈvɪdʒəl/ *n* **1** [U] staying awake to keep watch or to pray: *keep ~ over a sick child.* **2** (*pl*) instances of this: *tired out by her long ~s.* **3** [C] eve of a religious festival, esp when observed with prayer and fasting.

vigi·lance /ˈvɪdʒələns/ *n* [U] watchfulness; keeping watch: *use ~.*

ˈvigilance committee, formed by citizens (esp in the early western US) to keep order in the absence of police and courts.

vigi·lant /ˈvɪdʒələnt/ *adj* watchful.

vigi·lant·ly *adv*

vigi·lante /ˌvɪdʒəˈlænti/ *n* [C] member of a vigilance committee.

vig·or /ˈvɪgər/ *n* [U] mental or physical strength; energy; forcefulness (of language).

vig·or·ous /ˈvɪgərəs/ *adj* strong; energetic.

vig·or·ous·ly *adv*

vile /ˈvaiəl/ *adj* (-r, -st) **1** shameful and disgusting: *~ habits/language.* **2** (*informal*) very bad: *~ weather.*

vile·ly /ˈvaiəl(l)i/ *adv*

vile·ness /-nɪs/ *n* [U]

vil·ify /ˈvɪləˌfai/ *vt* (*pt,pp* -ied) say evil things about (a person).

vil·ifi·ca·tion /ˌvɪləfəˈkeiʃən/ *n* [U]

villa /ˈvɪlə/ *n* [C] (*pl* ~s) country house with a large garden, esp in Italy or Southern France.

vil·lage /ˈvɪlɪdʒ/ *n* [C] place smaller than a town, where there are houses and stores, and usually a church and school: (as an *adjective*) *the ~ post office.*

vil·lager /ˈvɪlɪdʒər/ *n* [C] person who lives in a village.

vil·lain /ˈvɪlən/ *n* [C] (esp in drama) wicked person.

vil·lain·ous /ˈvɪlənəs/ *adj* evil: *~ous acts.*

vil·lainy *n* [U] evil conduct.

vin·di·cate /ˈvɪndəˌkeit/ *vt* show or prove the truth, justice, validity, etc (of something that has been attacked or disputed): *~ a claim. Events have ~d his judgment/actions.*

vin·di·ca·tion /ˌvɪndəˈkeiʃən/ *n* [C,U]

vin·dic·tive /vɪnˈdɪktɪv/ *adj* having or showing a desire for revenge.

vin·dic·tive·ly *adv*

vin·dic·tive·ness /-nɪs/ *n* [U]

vine /vain/ *n* [C] **1** climbing plant whose fruit is the grape. **2** any plant with slender stems that trails or climbs (eg melons, peas).

vin·ery /ˈvainəri/ *n* [C] (*pl* ~ries) greenhouse for vines.

vine·yard /ˈvɪnyərd/ *n* [C] area of land planted with grapevines.

vin·egar /ˈvɪnɪgər/ *n* [C] acid liquor (made from malt, wine, cider, etc) used in flavoring food and for pickling.

vin·egary /ˈvɪnɪg(ə)ri/ *adj* like vinegar.

vin·tage /ˈvɪntɪdʒ/ *n* **1** [C] (rarely *pl*) (period or season of) grape harvesting: *The ~ was later than usual last year*. **2** [C,U] (wine from) grapes of a particular year: *of the ~ of 1973; a ~ year*, one in which good wine was made. **3** (as an *adjective*) of a period in the past and having a reputation for high quality: *a ~ car*.

vint·ner /ˈvɪntnər/ *n* [C] wine merchant.

vi·nyl /ˈvainəl/ *n* [C,U] (kinds of) tough, flexible plastic, used for coverings, clothing, etc.

vi·ola /viˈoulə/ *n* [C] tenor violin, of larger size than the ordinary violin. ⇨ illus at string.

vi·ol·ate /ˈvaiəˌleit/ *vt* **1** break (an oath, a treaty, etc); act contrary to (what one's conscience tells one to do, etc). **2** act toward without proper respect: *~ a person's privacy*. **3** commit rape.

vi·ol·ation /ˌvaiəˈleiʃən/ *n* [C,U]

vi·ol·ence /ˈvaiələns/ *n* [U] state of being violent; violent conduct: *robbery with ~*.

vi·ol·ent /ˈvaiələnt/ *adj* **1** using, showing, accompanied by, great force: *a ~ wind/attack/temper*. **2** caused by a cruel attack: *meet a ~ death*. **3** severe: *~ toothache*.

vi·olent·ly *adv*

vi·olet /ˈvaiəlɪt/ *n* **1** [C] small wild or garden plant with sweet-smelling flowers. **2** [U] bluish-purple color (of wild violets).

vi·olin /ˌvaiəˈlɪn/ *n* [C] four-stringed musical instrument played with a bow. ⇨ illus at string.

vi·olin·ist /-ɪst/ *n* [C] violin player.

vi·olon·cello /ˌvaiələnˈtʃelou/ *n* [C] (*pl* ~s) (usual *abbr* **cello** /ˈtʃelou/) large bass violin held between the player's knees. ⇨ illus at string.

VIP /ˌvi ˌai ˈpi/ *abbr* (*informal*) = very important person.

vi·per /ˈvaipər/ *n* [C] kinds of poisonous snake, esp *the common ~*, the adder.

vir·gin /ˈvərdʒɪn/ *n* [C] person, esp a girl or woman, who has not experienced sexual intercourse. □ *adj* **1** pure and chaste. **2** pure and untouched: *~ snow*. **3** in the original condition; unused: *~ soil*, soil never before used for crops.

vir·gin·ity /vərˈdʒɪnəti/ *n* [U] state of being a virgin.

vir·ginal /ˈvərdʒɪnəl/ *adj* of, suitable for, a virgin.

Virgo /ˈvərgou/ *n* the Virgin, sixth sign of the zodiac. ⇨ illus at zodiac.

vir·ile /ˈvɪrɪl/ *adj* **1** having or showing strength, energy, manly qualities: *a ~ style* (*of writing*). **2** (of men) able to have sexual intercourse.

vir·il·ity /vɪˈrɪləti/ *n* [U] masculine strength and vigor; sexual power.

vir·tual /ˈvərtʃuəl/ *adj* being in fact, acting as, what is described, but not accepted openly or in name as such: *a ~ defeat/confession*.

vir·tu·ally /-tʃuəli/ *adv*

vir·tue /ˈvərtʃu/ *n* **1** [C,U] (any particular kind of) goodness or excellence: *Patience is a ~*. **2** [U] chastity, esp of women: *a woman of easy ~*, one who is promiscuous. **3** [U] ability to produce a definite result: *Have you any faith in the ~ of herbs to heal sickness?* **4** advantage: *The great ~ of the scheme is that it costs very little*. **5** ***by/in virtue of,*** by reason of; because of: *He claimed a pension in ~ of his long military service*.

vir·tu·ous /ˈvərtʃuəs/ *adj* having, showing, virtue(1).

vir·tu·ous·ly *adv*

vir·tu·os·ity /ˌvərtʃuˈasəti/ *n* [U] special artistic skill.

viru·lent /ˈvɪrələnt/ *adj* **1** (of poison) strong; deadly. **2** (of ill feeling, hatred) very strong. **3** (of words, etc) full of hatred. **4** (of diseases, etc) poisonous.

viru·lent·ly *adv*

vi·rus /ˈvairəs/ *n* [C] (*pl* ~es) any of various poisonous elements, smaller than bacteria, causing the spread of infectious disease.

visa /ˈvizə/ *n* [C] (*pl* ~s) stamp or signature put on a passport to show that it has been examined and approved by the officials of a foreign country which the owner intends to visit (ˈ*entrance* or ˈ*entry* ~) or leave (ˈ*exit* ~). □ *vt* put a visa in: *get one's passport ~ed* /ˈvizəd/ *before going to Poland*.

vis·count /ˈvaiˌkaunt/ *n* [C] nobleman higher in rank than a baron, lower than an earl.

vis·count·ess /-ɪs/ *n* [C] wife of a viscount; female viscount.

vise /vais/ *n* [C] apparatus with strong clamps in which things can be held tightly while being worked on.

vis·ible /ˈvɪzəbəl/ *adj* that can be seen; that is in sight: *The eclipse will be ~ to observers in the Pacific Northwest*.

vis·ibil·ity /ˌvɪzəˈbɪləti/ *n* [U] (esp) condition of the atmosphere for seeing things at a distance: *The aircraft returned because of poor visibility*.

vis·ibly /-əbli/ *adv* in a way that is obvious: *She was visibly annoyed*.

vi·sion /ˈvɪʒən/ *n* **1** [U] power of seeing or imagining, looking ahead, grasping the truth: *the field of ~*, all that can be seen from a certain point; *a man of ~*. **2** [C] something seen or imagined, dreamed, etc: *Have you ever had ~s of great wealth?*

vi·sion·ary /ˈvɪʒəˌneri/ *adj* **1** existing only in a vision or the imagination; unpractical: *~ schemes*. **2** (of persons) having grand ideas; dreamy. □ *n* [C] (*pl* -ies) visionary person.

visit /ˈvɪzɪt/ *vt,vi* **1** go to see (a person); go to (a place) for a time: *~ a friend; ~ Rome*. **2** go to in order to inspect or examine officially: *Restaurant and hotel kitchens are ~ed regularly by public health officers*. **3** (*informal*) chat: *Please stay and ~ with me for a while*. ***(be) visited upon,*** (be) inflicted on (esp as a punishment): *a plague was ~ed upon the people*. □ *n* [C] act, time, of visiting: *pay a ~ on a friend/a patient; a ~ of several hours*.

vis·it·ing *n* [U] paying visits: (as an *adj*) ˈ*~ing hours at a hospital*.

visi·ta·tion /ˌvɪzəˈteiʃən/ *n* [C] **1** appearance (esp to a person or group) of a ghost, spirit, etc. **2** official visit, eg one made by a church functionary. **3** disaster considered as a punishment from God: *The famine was a ~ of God for their sins.*

visi·tor /ˈvɪzɪtər/ *n* [C] person who visits; person who stays at a place: *summer ~s*, eg at a holiday resort.

vi·sor /ˈvaizər/ *n* [C] **1** (in former times) movable part of a helmet, covering the face. **2** peak of a cap or similar part of a crash helmet.

vista /ˈvɪstə/ *n* [C] (*pl* ~s) **1** long, narrow view: *a ~ of the church at the end of an avenue of trees.* **2** (*fig*) series of scenes, events, etc which one can look back on or forward to: *new ~s of scientific discovery.*

vis·ual /ˈvɪʒuəl/ *adj* concerned with, used in, seeing: *She has a ~ memory*, is able to remember well things she sees.

ˌvisual ˈaids, (eg in teaching) pictures, filmstrips, films, etc.

vis·ual·ize /-ˌlaiz/ *vt* imagine (as a picture): *I remember meeting the man two years ago but can't ~ize him*, remember what he looked like.

vis·ually /ˈvɪʒuəli/ *adv*

vi·tal /ˈvaitəl/ *adj* **1** of, connected with, necessary for, living: *Air is ~ for all animals.* **2** supreme; indispensable: *of ~ importance.*

vi·tally /ˈvaitəli/ *adv*

ˌvital staˈtistics, figures relating to the duration of life, and to births, marriages and deaths.

vi·tal·ity /vaiˈtæləti/ *n* [U] **1** capacity to endure, survive, perform functions: *Can an artificial language have any ~?* **2** energy, liveliness: *the ~ of young children.*

vi·tal·ize /ˈvaitəˌlaiz/ *vt* put energy, strength into.

vit·amin /ˈvaitəmɪn/ *n* [C] any of a number of organic substances which are present in certain foods and are essential to the health of man and other animals.

vit·reous /ˈvɪtriəs/ *adj* of or like glass: *~ rocks.*

vit·riolic /ˌvɪtriˈalɪk/ *adj* (of words, feelings) full of abuse.

vi·va·cious /vɪˈveiʃəs/ *adj* lively; high-spirited: *a ~ girl.*

vi·va·cious·ly *adv*

vi·vac·ity /vɪˈvæsəti/ *n* [U]

viva voce /ˌvaivə ˈvousi/ *adj, adv* oral(ly): *a ~ examination.* □ *n* [C] oral examination.

vivid /ˈvɪvɪd/ *adj* **1** (of colors, etc) intense; bright: *a ~ flash of lightning.* **2** lively; active: *a ~ imagination.* **3** clear and distinct: *have ~ recollections of a vacation in Italy.*

vivid·ly *adv*

viv·ify /ˈvɪvəˌfai/ *vt* (*pt, pp* -ied) (*formal*) give life to; animate.

vivi·sect /ˌvɪvəˈsekt/ *vt* operate or experiment on (living animals) for scientific research.

vivi·sec·tion /ˌvɪvəˈsekʃən/ *n* [C,U]

vivi·sec·tion·ist /-ɪst/ *n* [C] person who vivisects or considers vivisection justifiable.

vixen /ˈvɪksən/ *n* [C] **1** female fox. **2** bad-tempered woman.

vocab. *abbr* = vocabulary.

vo·cabu·lary /vəˈkæbyəˌleri/ *n* (*pl* -ies) **1** [C] total number of words which (with rules for combining them) make up a language: *No dictionary could list the total ~ of a language.* **2** [C,U] (range of) words known to, or used by, a person, in a profession, etc: *a writer with a large ~.* **3** [C] book containing a list of words; list of words used in a book, etc, usually with definitions or translations.

vo·cal /ˈvoukəl/ *adj* of, for, with or using, the voice: *the ~ organs,* lips, tongue, etc.

ˈvocal cords, folds of tissue in the larynx which vibrate to produce the voice. ⇨ illus at head.

vo·cal·ist /ˈvoukəlɪst/ *n* [C] singer.

vo·cal·ize /-ˌlaiz/ *vt* say or sing.

vo·cally /-əli/ *adv*

vo·ca·tion /vouˈkeiʃən/ *n* **1** (*sing* only) feeling that one is called to (and qualified for) a certain kind of work (esp social or religious): *"Nursing," said Florence Nightingale, "is a ~ as well as a profession."* **2** [U] special ability (*for*): *He has little or no ~ for teaching.* **3** [C] person's occupation or profession.

vo·ca·tional /-nəl/ *adj* of or for a vocation(3): *~al courses,* eg at a technical school.

vodka /ˈvadkə/ *n* [C,U] (portion of) strong Russian alcoholic drink distilled from rye, etc.

vogue /voug/ *n* [C but usually *sing*] **1** current fashion; something currently being done or used: *Were maxiskirts still the ~ then?* **2** popularity; popular use or acceptance: *The Beatles enjoyed a great ~ in the 1960's.* ***be in/come into vogue; be/go out of vogue,*** be/become (un)fashionable, (un)popular: *When did the miniskirt come into/go out of ~?*

voguish /ˈvougɪʃ/ *adj* very popular for a brief period.

voguish·ly *adv*

voice /vɔis/ *n* **1** [U] sounds made when speaking or singing: *He is not in good ~*, not speaking or singing as well as usual. **2** [C] power of making such sounds: *He has lost his ~*, cannot speak or sing properly, eg because of a bad cold. **3** [C,U] sounds made by a person, esp considered in relation to their quality: *in a loud/soft ~. They gave ~ to their indignation.* ***shout at the ˌtop of one's ˈvoice,*** shout as loudly as one can. **4** [U] ***have/demand a voice in sth,*** a right to express an opinion on: *I have no ~ in the matter.* **5** [C] anything which may be compared or likened to the human voice as expressing ideas, feelings, etc: *the inner ~*, conscience. **6** [U] (*gram*) the contrast between *active* and *passive* as shown in the sentences: *The dog ate the meat* and *The meat was eaten by the dog.* □ *vt* put into words: *The spokesman ~d the feelings of the crowd.*

void /vɔid/ *adj* **1** empty; vacant. **2** ***void of,*** without: *a subject ~ of interest.* **3** ***ˌnull and ˈvoid,*** (*legal*) without force; invalid: *The agreement, not having been signed, was null and ~.* □ *n* [C] space: *There was an aching ~ in his heart,* (*fig*) a feeling of sadness. □ *vt* (*legal*) make void (3).

vol. *abbr* = volume.

vol·atile /ˈvalətəl/ *adj* **1** (of a liquid) that easily changes into gas or vapor. **2** (of a person, his mood) changing quickly or easily from one mood or interest to another.

vol·atile·ness /-nɪs/ *n* [U] = volatility.

vol·atil·ity /ˌvaləˈtɪləti/ *n* [U]

vol·cano /valˈkeinou/ *n* [C] (*pl* ~es or ~s) hill or mountain with openings (⇨ crater) through which gases, lava, ashes, etc come up from below the earth's crust (in *an active* ~), or may come up after an interval (in *a dormant* ~), or have long stopped coming up (in *an extinct* ~).

vol·canic /val'kænɪk/ *adj* of, from, like, a volcano.

vole /voul/ *n* [C] animal like a mouse or rat, esp *a 'water* ~, large water rat.

vo·li·tion /vou'lɪʃən/ *n* [U] act, power, of using one's own will, of choosing, making a decision, etc: *do something of one's own* ~.

vol·ley /'vali/ *n* [C] **1** throwing or shooting of a number of stones, arrows, bullets, etc together. **2** succession of oaths, curses, questions. **3** (*tennis*) stroke which returns the ball to the sender before it touches the ground. □ *vt,vi* **1** (of guns) sound together. **2** return a tennis ball across the net before it touches the ground.

'volley·ball *n* **(a)** [U] game in which players on each side of a high net try to keep a ball in motion by hitting it with their hands back and forth over the net without letting it touch the ground. **(b)** [C] ball for this game.

volt /voult/ *n* [C] (*abbr* **v**) unit of electrical force.

volt·age /'voultɪdʒ/ *n* [C,U] electrical force measured in volts.

vol·uble /'valyəbəl/ *adj* talking, able to talk, very quickly and easily; (of speech) fluent.

vol·ubil·ity /ˌvalyə'bɪləti/ *n* [U]

vol·ubly /-yəbli/ *adv*

vol·ume /'valyəm/ *n* **1** [C] book, esp one of a set of books; number of sheets, papers, periodicals, etc bound together: *an encyclopedia in/of 20* ~*s*. **2** [U] amount of space (expressed in cubic feet, meters, etc) occupied by a substance, liquid or gas: *the* ~ *of wine in a magnum bottle*. **3** [C] large mass, amount or quantity: *the* ~ *of business/work*. **4** [C] (esp *pl*) masses of steam or smoke: ~*s of black smoke*. **5** [U] (of sound) loudness; strength: *Your radio has a '*~ *control*.

vol·umi·nous /və'lumənəs/ *adj* (*formal*) **1** (of writing) great in quantity: *a* ~ *work/history*. **2** (of an author) producing many books. **3** occupying much space: *a* ~ *tent*.

vol·un·tary /'valənˌteri/ *adj* **1** doing or ready to do things, willingly, without being forced; (something) done in this manner: ~ *work/helpers; a* ~ *confession*. **2** carried on, supported by, voluntary work and gifts. **3** (opposite = *involuntary*) (of bodily, muscular, movements) controlled by the will.

vol·un·tar·ily /ˌvalən'terəli/ *adv*

vol·un·teer /ˌvalən'tɪr/ *n* [C] **1** person who offers to do something, esp unpleasant or dangerous. **2** soldier who is not conscripted: (as an *adjective*) *a* ~ *corps*. □ *vt,vi* come forward as a volunteer; offer voluntarily: *He* ~*ed some information/*~*ed to get some information*.

vo·lup·tu·ous /və'ləptʃuəs/ *adj* of, for, causing or expressing, sensuous or sensual pleasures: ~ *beauty*.

vo·lup·tu·ous·ly *adv*

vomit /'vamɪt/ *vt,vi* **1** bring back from the stomach through the mouth: *He* ~*ed (up) everything he had eaten. He was* ~*ing blood*. **2** send out in large quantities: *factory chimneys* ~*ing smoke*. □ *n* [U] food that has been vomited.

voo·doo /'vuˌdu/ *n* [U] form of religion, with sorcery and witchcraft, practiced esp in New Orleans, the West Indies and Haiti.

voo·doo·ism /-ˌɪzəm/ *n* [U] this practice.

vo·ra·cious /və'reiʃəs/ *adj* (*formal*) very hungry or greedy: *a* ~ *appetite; a* ~ *reader*, one who reads many books.

vo·ra·cious·ly *adv* in a voracious manner.

vo·racity /və'ræsəti/ *n* [U]

vor·tex /'vɔrˌteks/ *n* [C] (*pl* ~es or vortices /-tɪˌsiz/) **1** mass of whirling fluid or wind, esp a whirlpool. **2** (*fig*) whirl of activity; system, pursuit, viewed as something that tends to absorb people or things: *the* ~ *of politics/war*.

vote /vout/ *n* [C] **1** (right to give an) expression of opinion or will by persons for or against a person or thing, esp by ballot or by putting up of hands: *I'm going to the polling booth to record/cast my* ~. *Mr. Smith proposed a* ~ *of thanks to the principal speaker*, asked the audience to show, by clapping their hands, that they thanked him. **2** total numbers of votes (to be) given (eg at a political election): *Will the black* ~ *increase or decrease in the next election?* □ *vi,vt* **1** ***vote for/against sb/sth,*** support/oppose by voting. ***vote on sth,*** express an opinion by voting. **2** (*informal*) declare, by general opinion: *He was* ~*d a fine teacher*, His students gave this as their opinion. **3** suggest, propose: *I* ~ *(that) we avoid him in the future*.

voter *n* [C] person who (by right) votes.

vouch /vautʃ/ *vi* ***vouch for sb/sth,*** be responsible for, express confidence in (a person, his honesty, etc): ~ *for him/his ability*.

voucher /'vautʃər/ *n* [C] receipt or document showing payment of money, correctness of accounts, etc.

vouch·safe /ˌvautʃ'seif/ *vt* (*formal*) be kind enough to give, to do (something): *He* ~*d to help*.

vow /vau/ *n* [C] solemn promise or undertaking: *'marriage vows; a vow of chastity; break a vow*, not do what one promised. □ *vt* make a vow; promise or declare solemnly: *He vowed to avenge/that he would avenge the insult*.

vowel /'vauəl/ *n* [C] **1** vocal sound made without audible stopping of the breath. **2** letter or symbol used to represent such a sound (eg the letters *a, e, i, o, u;* the phonetic symbols /i, ɪ, e, æ, a, o, ɔ, ʊ, u, ə/).

voy·age /'vɔiɪdʒ/ *n* [C] journey by water, esp a long one in a ship: *a* ~ *around the world; during the* ~ *out/home; on the outward/homeward* ~. □ *vi* go on a voyage: ~ *through the South Seas*.

voy·ager /'vɔiɪdʒər/ *n* [C] person who makes a voyage (esp of those who, in former times, explored unknown seas).

V.P. *abbr* = vice-president.

vs. *abbr* = **1** verse. **2** versus.

VT[1] *postal abbr* = Vermont. ⇨ App 6.

v.t.[2] *abbr* = verb, transitive.

vulg. *abbr* = vulgar.

vul·gar /'vəlgər/ *adj* **1** rude; showing bad manners: ~ *language/behavior/ideas; a* ~ *person*. **2** showing the absence of taste[1](5): ~ *decor of a restaurant*.

ˌvulgar 'fraction, one written in the traditional

way (eg $\frac{3}{4}$), contrasted with a decimal fraction.

vul·gar·ity /vəlˈgærəti/ *n* (*pl* -ies) **(a)** [U] vulgar behavior or taste[1](5). **(b)** (*pl*) vulgar acts, words, etc.

vul·gar·ly *adv*

vul·ner·able /ˈvəlnərəbəl/ *adj* that is capable of being damaged; not protected against attack: *a position* ~ *to attack;* ~ *to criticism.*

vul·ner·abil·ity /ˌvəlnərəˈbɪləti/ *n* [U]

vul·ture /ˈvəltʃər/ *n* [C] **1** kinds of large bird that live on the flesh of dead animals. **2** (*fig*) greedy person who profits from the misfortunes of others.

vy·ing *present participle* of vie.

W

W[1], **w** /ˈdəbəlˌyu/ (*pl* W's, w's) the twenty-third letter of the English alphabet.
W[2] *abbr* = **1** watt(s). **2** west.
w.[3] *abbr* = **1** wide. **2** width. **3** with.
w/ *abbr* = with.
WA *postal abbr* = Washington. ⇨ App 6.
wad /wad/ *n* [C] **1** lump of soft material for keeping things apart or in place, or to stop up a hole: *wads of absorbent cotton.* **2** collection of banknotes, documents, etc folded or rolled together. □ *vt* (-dd-) stop up, hold in place, with a wad.
waddle /ˈwadəl/ *vi* walk with slow steps as a duck does: *The baby ~d across the room.* □ *n* (usually *sing*) this kind of walk.
wade /weid/ *vi,vt* **1** walk with an effort (through water, mud or anything that makes progress difficult); walk across (something) in this way: *He ~d across the stream.* **2** ***wade in,*** make a strong attack. ***wade into sth,*** attack it with force.

wader *n* [C] **(a)** = wading bird. **(b)** = wading boot. **(c)** wading outfit, esp for fishing, with waterproof boots attached to waterproof trousers.

ˈ**wading bird,** long-legged water bird that wades (opposite to web-footed birds that swim).

ˈ**wading boot,** high waterproof boot worn esp for fishing.

wa·fer /ˈweifər/ *n* [C] **1** thin flat cookie (as eaten with ice cream). **2** small round piece of bread used in Holy Communion.
waffle[1] /ˈwafəl/ *n* [C] small cake made of batter baked in a special appliance.

ˈ**waffle iron,** special apparatus with two parts hinged together, for baking waffles.

WAFFLE IRON

waffle[2] /ˈwafəl/ *vi* (*informal*) respond weakly or uncertainly to a request, etc; vacillate, waver.
waft /wæft/ *vt* carry lightly and smoothly through the air or over water: *The scent of the flowers was ~ed to us by the breeze.* □ *n* [C] light breeze, smell: *~s of fresh air through the window.*
wag /wæg/ *vt,vi* (-gg-) (cause to) move from side to side or up and down: *The dog wagged its tail.* □ *n* [C] wagging movement: *with a wag of the tail.*
wage[1] /weidʒ/ *n* [C] payment made or received for work or services: *His ~s are $200 a week. The postal workers have asked for a* ˈ*~ increase/hike of $50 a week.* (*Note:* usually *pl* except when *wage* is used as an *adjective: a* ˈ*~ freeze.*) ⇨ fee(1), pay[1](1), salary.

ˈ**wage earner,** person who works for (usually hourly) wages (contrasted with one paid a salary).

ˈ**wage freeze,** official control of wage increases.

ˈ**wage hike** (*informal*) wage increase, esp a general one resulting from labor-management negotiation or government action.

wage[2] /weidʒ/ *vt* engage in (war, etc).
wa·ger /ˈweidʒər/ *n* [C], *vt,vi* bet (the usual word).
waggle /ˈwægəl/ *vt,vi* = wag.
wag·on /ˈwægən/ *n* [C] four-wheeled (usually open) vehicle for carrying passengers or goods, pulled by horses or oxen. ***covered wagon,*** one with a canvas cover, esp as used by settlers in the West. ⇨ station wagon.

ˈ**wagon train,** group of wagons traveling together.

waif /weif/ *n* [C] homeless child: *~s and strays,* homeless and abandoned children.
wail /ˈweiəl/ *vi,vt* (*pres p* ~ing /ˈweilɪŋ/) **1** cry or complain in a loud voice: *a ~ing child.* **2** make a similar sound (eg of a siren): *an ambulance racing through the streets with sirens ~ing.* **3** (of the wind) make similar sounds. □ *n* [C] wailing cry: *the ~s of a newborn child.*
wain·scot /ˈweinskət/ *n* [C] wooden paneling (on the lower half of the walls of a room).
waist /weist/ *n* [C] **1** part of the body between the ribs and the hips: *measure 24 inches around the ~.* ⇨ illus at trunk. **2** that part of clothing that goes round the waist. **3** middle and narrow part: *the ~ of a violin.*

ˈ**waist·band** *n* part of a skirt, etc that fits round the waist.

ˌ**waist-ˈdeep** *adj, adv* up to the waist: *~-deep in the mud.*

ˌ**waist-ˈhigh** *adj, adv* high enough to reach the waist: *The wheat was ~-high.*

ˈ**waist·line** *n* part of the body, a dress, etc at the smallest part of the waist: *a dress with a narrow*

~line.

wait[1] /ˈweit/ *n* **1** [C] act or time of waiting: *We had a long ~ for the bus.* **2** [U] ***lie in wait for,*** be in hiding in order to attack, etc: *The cat lay in ~ for the bird to fly down.*

wait[2] /ˈweit/ *vi,vt* **1** stay where one is, delay acting, until a person or thing comes or until something happens: *Please ~ a minute. How long have you been ~ing? We are ~ing for better weather. We ~ed (in order) to see what would happen.* ***keep sb waiting,*** fail to meet him or be ready at the appointed time: *His wife never keeps him ~ing.* ***wait sth out,*** do nothing or delay acting until something is over: *He ~ed out the thunderstorm in the barn.* ***wait up (for sb),*** (*informal*) stop in order to let someone catch up while walking, etc. **2** = await (the usual word): *He is ~ing his opportunity.* **3** ***wait on sb,*** **(a)** fetch and carry things for, eg as a waiter, clerk in a store, etc: *Her job is to ~ on customers at the store.* **(b)** (*informal*) stay in a place until a person or thing comes; wait for: *They ~ed on their friend nearly an hour.* ***wait on sb hand and foot,*** ⇨ hand[1](1).

waiter *n* [C] man who serves food, etc in a restaurant, hotel dining room, etc.

ˈwait·ing list, list of persons who will be served, treated, etc later, if possible: *Put me on a ~ing list for two concert tickets.*

ˈwait·ing room, (a) room in a railway station, etc used by people who are waiting for trains. **(b)** room (eg in a doctor's or dentist's house or office) where people wait until they can be attended to.

wait·ress /ˈweitrıs/ *n* [C] female waiter.

waive /weiv/ *vt* (say that one will) not insist on (a right or claim): *~ diplomatic immunity.*

waiver /ˈweivər/ *n* (*legal*) (written statement) waiving (a right, etc): *sign a ~r of claims against a person.*

wake[1] /weik/ *vi,vt* (*pt* woke /wouk/, *pp* woken /ˈwoukən/) **1** stop sleeping: *What time do you usually ~ (up)? He woke up with a start,* suddenly. **2** cause to stop sleeping: *Don't ~ the baby. The noise woke me (up).* **3** stir up from inactivity, inattention, etc: *He needs someone to ~ him up,* make him active, energetic.

waken /ˈweikən/ *vt,vi* (cause to) wake.

wak·ing *adj* being awake: *waking or sleeping,* while awake or asleep.

wake[2] /weik/ *n* [C] social gathering for all-night watch with a corpse before burial.

wake[3] /weik/ *n* [C] track left by a ship on smooth water, eg as made by propellers. ***in the wake of,*** after; following: *Traders arrived in the ~ of the explorers.*

walk[1] /wɔk/ *n* [C] **1** journey on foot, esp for pleasure or exercise: *go for a ~. The station is ten minutes' ~ from my house.* **2** manner or style of walking: *I recognized him at once by his ~.* **3** path or route for walking: *my favorite ~s in the neighborhood.* **4** ***walk of life,*** profession, occupation: *They interviewed people from all ~s of life.*

walk[2] /wɔk/ *vi,vt* (for special uses with *adverbial particles* and *prepositions,* ⇨ 5 below.) **1** (of persons) move by putting forward each foot in turn, not having both feet off the ground at once; (of animals) move at the slowest pace: *We ~ed five miles. He was ~ing up and down the station platform.* **2** cause to walk: *He ~ed his horse up the hill.* ***walk sb off his feet/sb's legs off,*** tire him out by making him walk far. **3** go over on foot: *I have ~ed this district for miles around.* **4** (used with various *nouns*): ***walk the streets,*** be a prostitute (*a ˈstreet-~er*). **5** (special uses with *adverbial particles* and *prepositions*):

walk away with sth, win (a prize or competition) easily: *The Russian team ~ed away with the gymnastics competition.*

walk in, enter.

walk into, meet with accidentally: *~ into an ambush.*

walk off with sth, take (either on purpose or unintentionally): *Someone has ~ed off with my umbrella.*

walk out, go on strike: *The workers ~ed out yesterday.* ***walk out on sb,*** (*informal*) desert him (at a time when he is expecting help, etc).

walk over sb, (*informal*) defeat him easily: *She ~ed all over the other competitors.*

walk up, **(a)** (*imperative*) (used as an invitation to enter (a circus, show, etc)). **(b)** walk along: *~ up Fifth Avenue.* **(c)** walk upstairs. **(d)** approach: *A stranger ~ed up (to me) and asked me the time.*

walker *n* [C] **(a)** person who walks (esp as a habit). **(b)** walking shoe. **(c)** device, consisting of a frame with wheels, to aid infants and invalids in walking.

ˈwalk-in *adj* large enough for one to walk into: *a ~-in closet.*

ˈwalk-out *n* [C] strike or protest involving walking out.

ˈwalk-over *n* [C] easy victory.

ˈwalk-up *n* [C] (esp apartment) building with several floors but no elevator.

walkie-talkie /ˌwɔki-ˈtɔki/ *n* [C] small, portable two-way radio.

wall /wɔl/ *n* [C] **1** continuous, usually vertical, solid structure of stone, brick, concrete, wood, etc forming one of the sides of a building or room, or used to enclose, divide or protect something (including land): *Hang the picture on that ~. Some old towns have ~s all the way around them.* ***have/with one's back to the wall,*** ⇨ back[1](1). ***be/go up against the wall,*** (*informal*) be put in a defensive position. ***be/go up the wall,*** (*informal*) be/become very angry. ***go to the wall,*** be defeated, especially financially. **2** (*fig*) something like a wall: *a ~ of fire; the abdominal ~.* □ *vt* **1** (usually *pp*) surround with walls: *a ~ed garden.* **2** ***wall sth up/off,*** fill or close up with bricks, etc: *~ up a window.*

ˈwall·flower *n* [C] **(a)** common garden plant with sweet-smelling flowers. **(b)** woman who does not dance because not asked.

ˈwall·paper *n* [U] paper, often with a printed design, for covering the walls of rooms.

wal·laby /ˈwaləbi/ *n* [C] (*pl* -ies) kinds of small kangaroos.

wal·let /ˈwalıt/ *n* [C] folding case of leather, etc for banknotes, credit cards, etc.

wal·lop /ˈwaləp/ *vt* (*informal*) beat severely; hit hard. □ *n* [C] heavy blow; crash: *Down he went with a ~!*

wal·low /ˈwalou/ *vi* **1** roll around (in mud, dirty water, etc): *pigs ~ing in the mud.* **2** (*fig*) take great delight in: *~ing in success.* □ *n* [C] place to which animals (eg water buffaloes) go regularly to wallow.

wal·nut /ˈwɔlnət, -ˌnət/ *n* **1** [C] (tree producing a) nut with a kernel that can be eaten. **2** [U] the wood, used for making furniture.

wal·rus /ˈwɔlrəs/ *n* [C] (*pl* ~es) large sea animal of the arctic regions with two long tusks.

WALRUS

walrus mustache, drooping style of mustache, similar in shape to the bristles of a walrus.

waltz /wɔlts/ *n* [C] (music for a) slow ballroom dance. □ *vi,vt* (cause to) dance a waltz: *She ~es beautifully.*

wam·pum /ˈwampəm/ *n* [U] American Indian bead work, made of shells, esp when used as money.

wan /wan/ *adj* (-nn-) **1** (of a person, his looks, etc) looking ill, sad, tired, anxious: *a wan smile.* **2** (of light, the sky) pale; not bright.

wan·ly *adv*

wand /wand/ *n* [C] slender stick or rod as used by a conjurer, fairy or magician.

wan·der /ˈwandər/ *vi,vt* **1** go from place to place without any special purpose or destination: *~ up and down the road; ~ (through/over) the world.* **2** leave the right path or direction: *Some of the sheep have ~ed away*, are lost. *We ~ed (for) miles and miles in the mist.* **3** allow the thoughts to go from subject to subject: *Don't ~ from the subject/point. His mind is ~ing.*

wan·derer *n* [C] person or animal that wanders.

wan·der·ings *n pl* **(a)** long travels; journeys: *tell the story of one's ~ings.* **(b)** confused speech during illness (esp high fever).

wan·der·lust /ˈwandərˌləst/ *n* [U] strong desire to travel.

wane /wein/ *vi* **1** (of the moon) show a gradually decreasing bright area after full moon. ⇨ wax². **2** become less or weaker: *His strength/reputation is waning.* □ *n* esp ***on the wane,*** waning.

wangle /ˈwæŋgəl/ *vt* (*informal*) get, arrange something, by using improper influence, by trickery, persuasion, etc: *~ an extra week's vacation.* □ *n* [C] act of wangling.

want[1] /want/ *n* **1** [U] scarcity; state of being absent: *The plants died from ~ of water. Your work shows ~ of thought/care.* **2** [U] need; absence of some necessary thing: *The house is in ~ of repair.* **3** [C] (usually *pl*) desire for something as necessary to life, happiness, etc; thing to be desired: *We can supply all your ~s.*

ˈwant ˌad, advertisement (eg in a newspaper) for something wanted.

want[2] /want/ *vt,vi* **1** be in need of: *That man ~s a wife to look after him*, needs to marry a woman who will look after him. *I don't ~* (= I object to having) *neighbors meddling in my affairs.* **2** wish for; have a desire for: *She ~s to go to Italy. She ~s me to go with her. He is ~ed by the police*, ie because he is suspected of having done wrong. (*Note: want* is used for something possible to get, *wish* is used for something impossible or unlikely.) **3** need, ought (as in the notes to the examples): *Your hair ~s cutting*, needs to be cut. *You ~* (= ought) *to talk to your teacher about that problem.* **4** (progressive tenses only) ***be wanting (in sth),*** (with human subject) be lacking: *He's ~ing in politeness*, is impolite. ***be found wanting***: *He was put to the test and found ~ing*, inadequate. **5** ***want for nothing,*** have all one needs.

wan·ton /ˈwantən/ *adj* **1** playful; irresponsible: *in a ~ mood.* **2** wild: *a ~ growth* (of weeds, etc). **3** deliberate: *~ destruction/damage.* **4** immoral: *a ~ woman.*

wanton·ly *adv* in a wanton manner.

war /wɔr/ *n* **1** [C,U] (state created by) the use of armed forces between countries or (*civil war*) rival groups in a nation: *We have had two world wars in this century.* ***at war,*** in a state of war. ***declare war (on),*** announce that a state of war exists (with another state). ***ˈgo to war (against),*** start fighting. **2** [U] science or art of fighting, using weapons, etc: *the art of war*, strategy and tactics. **3** (*fig*) any kind of struggle or conflict: *the war against poverty; a war of nerves/words.* □ *vi* (-rr-) fight; make war.

ˈwar cry, word or cry shouted as a signal in battle.

ˈwar dance, one by tribal warriors before going into battle, to celebrate a victory, or (in peace) to represent fighting.

war·fare /ˈwɔrˌfær/ *n* [U] making war; condition of being at war; fighting: *the horrors of modern warfare.*

ˈwar·head *n* [C] (of a torpedo, shell, etc) explosive head.

ˈwar-horse *n* [C] **(a)** (*old use*) horse used in military service. **(b)** (*fig*) veteran of military service, political campaigns, etc.

war·like /ˈwɔrˌlaik/ *adj* **(a)** ready for, suggesting, war: *warlike preparations.* **(b)** fond of war: *a cruel, warlike people.*

ˈwar·monger *n* [C] person who encourages war.

ˈwar·path *n* (only in) ***on the warpath,*** ready for, engaged in, a fight or quarrel.

ˈwar room, one, at a military headquarters, where strategy is worked out.

ˈwar·ship *n* [C] ship for use in war.

ˈwar·time *n* time when there is war: *in wartime;* (as an *adjective*) *wartime regulations.*

ˈwar-torn *adj* exhausted by, worn out in, war.

warble /ˈwɔrbəl/ *n* [C] vi,vt (esp of birds) sing with a gentle trilling note: *a bluebird warbling in a tree.* □ *n* [C] warbling.

war·bler /ˈwɔrblər/ *n* [C] (kinds of) bird that

warbles.

ward /wɔrd/ *n* [C] **1** division of, separate room in, a building, esp a hospital: *the children's ~.* **2** political division in an urban area, often subdivided into precincts. **3** person under the guardianship of an older person or of law authorities. □ *vt* ***ward sth off,*** keep away, avoid: *~ off a blow/danger.*

war·den /ˈwɔrdən/ *n* [C] person having control or authority: *a civil defense ~; ~ of a prison.*

ward·robe /ˈwɔrdˌroub/ *n* [C] **1** cupboard with pegs, shelves, etc for clothes. **2** stock of clothes: *My ~ needs to be renewed,* I must buy some new clothes. **3** stock of costumes of a theatrical company.

-ward(s) /-wərd(z)/ *suffix* in the direction of: *backward.*

ware /wær/ *n* **1** (as a *suffix*) manufactured goods: *ˈsilver~; ˈstem~; ˈhard~.* **2** (*pl*) articles offered for sale: *advertise one's ~s.*

ware·house /ˈwærˌhaus/ *n* [C] (*pl* /-ˌhauzɪz/) building for storing goods before distribution to retailers. □ *vt* /-ˌhauz/ store in a warehouse.

war·fare ⇨ war.

warm¹ /wɔrm/ *adj* (-er, -est) **1** having a medium degree of heat (between *cool* and *hot*): *Come and get ~ by the fire.* **2** (of clothing) serving to keep the body warm: *Put your ~est coat on.* **3** (of colors) suggesting warmth: *Red and yellow are ~ colors.* **4** enthusiastic, hearty: *give a speaker a ~ welcome.* **5** sympathetic; affectionate: *He has a ~ heart.*

ˌwarm-ˈblooded *adj* **(a)** (of animals) having warm blood. **(b)** (of a person) showing feelings, passion.

ˌwarm-ˈhearted *adj* kind and affectionate.

warm·ly *adv* in a warm manner: *~ly dressed; thank them ~ly.*

warm² /wɔrm/ *vt,vi* make or become warm or warmer: *~ oneself/one's hands by the fire. Please ~ (up) this milk.* ***warm to one's work/task, etc,*** become more interested and involved. ***warm up,*** get in physical condition for a game, contest, etc by exercising or practicing right before it.

ˈwarm-up *n* [C] exercise or practice right before a game or contest: (as an *adjective*) *~-up suit/session.*

warmth /wɔrmθ/ *n* [U] state of being warm: *He was pleased with the ~ of his welcome.*

warn /wɔrn/ *vt* inform (a person) of possible danger or unpleasant consequences; inform in advance of what may happen: *He was ~ed of the danger. He ~ed me that there were pickpockets in the crowd/~ed me against pickpockets.*

warn·ing /ˈwɔrnɪŋ/ *adj* that warns: *They fired some ~ shots.* □ *n* **1** [C] that which warns or serves to warn: *Let this be a ~ to you,* let this punishment, accident, misfortune, etc teach you to be careful in the future. **2** [U] action of warning; state of being warned: *The speaker sounded a note of ~,* spoke of possible danger.

warp /wɔrp/ *vt,vi* **1** (cause to) become bent or twisted from the usual or natural shape: *Some metals ~ in very hot weather.* **2** (*fig*) make evil; twist: *His judgment is ~ed,* biased because of possible advantage for himself. *He has a ~ed sense of humor,* eg that is cruel, evil, abnormal, etc. □ *n* **1** (*sing* only) twisted or bent condition in timber, etc caused by shrinking or expansion. **2 the warp,** threads over and under which other threads (the *weft* or *woof*) are passed when cloth is woven.

war·rant /ˈwɔrənt, ˈwar-/ *n* **1** [U] justification or authority: *He had no ~ for saying so/for what he did.* **2** [C] written order giving official authority: *a ~ to arrest a suspected criminal/for his arrest.* □ *vt* **1** be a warrant(1) for: *His interference was certainly not ~ed.* **2** = guarantee (the more usual word). **3** (usually *pp*) justified: *His anger is not ~ed.*

war·ran·tee /ˌwɔrənˈti, ˌwar-/ *n* person to whom a warranty is made.

ˈwarrant ˌofficer, officer in the US armed forces who receives a certificate of appointment instead of a commission.

war·ran·tor /ˈwɔrənˌtɔr, ˈwar-/ *n* person who makes a warranty.

war·ranty /ˈwɔrənti, ˈwar-/ *n* (written or printed) guarantee (eg to repair or replace defective goods): *The car is still under ~y.*

war·ren /ˈwɔrən, ˈwar-/ *n* [C] **1** area of land in which there are many burrows in which rabbits live and breed. **2** (*fig*) building or district in which it is difficult to find one's way around: *lose oneself in a ~ of narrow streets.*

war·rior /ˈwɔryər/ *n* [C] (*liter*) soldier; fighter: (as an *adjective*) *a ~ tribe.*

wart /wɔrt/ *n* [C] small, hard, dry growth on the skin.

wart·hog /ˈwɔrtˌhɔg/ *n* [C] kinds of African pig with two large tusks and growths like warts on the face.

wary /ˈwæri/ *adj* (-ier, -iest) in the habit of being careful about possible danger or trouble: *be ~ of giving offense/of strangers.*

war·ily /-əli/ *adv*

was ⇨ be¹.

wash¹ /wɔʃ, waʃ/ *n* **1** (*sing* only, usually with *a, an*) act of washing; being washed: *Will you give the car a ~, please.* **2** (*sing* only) clothing, sheets, etc (to be) washed or being washed: *When does the ~ come back from the laundry?* **3** (*sing* with *the*) movement or flow of water; sound made by moving water: *the ~ of the waves.* ⇨ also whitewash.

wash² /wɔʃ, waʃ/ *vt,vi* (for special uses with *adverbial particles* and *prepositions,* ⇨ 7 below.) **1** make clean with or in water or other liquid: *~ one's hands/clothes/the dishes. He never ~es* (ie washes himself) *in cold water.* ***wash one's hands of,*** ⇨ hand¹(3). **2** (of materials) be capable of being washed without damage or loss of color: *Does this material ~ well?* **3** (*fig*) be acceptable, bear examination: *That argument/excuse will not ~.* **4** (of the sea or a river) flow past or against: *The sea ~es the base of the cliffs.* **5** (of moving liquid) carry away, or in a specified direction: *He was ~ed overboard by a huge wave.* **6** go flowing, sweeping or splashing (*along, out, in, into, over,* etc): *We heard the waves ~ing against the sides of our boat. Huge waves ~ed over the deck.* **7** (special uses with

adverbial particles and *prepositions*):
wash sth away, remove by washing: *~ away stains.* ***be washed away,*** be removed by the movement of the sea, a river, etc: *The cliffs are gradually being ~ed away.*
wash sth down, clean by washing, eg with a hose: *~ down a car/the deck of a ship.* ***wash sth down (with),*** swallow (liquid) with: *bread and cheese ~ed down with beer.*
wash sth out, clean by washing: *~ out a dress.* ***washed out,*** **(a)** (*fig*) exhausted; pale: *feel ~ed out.* **(b)** (of games, sport) canceled because of heavy rain. **(c)** (of roads, etc) ruined by rain; flooded. **(d)** (of liquids) thin, watery. **(e)** (of colors) looking faded; pale. ⇨ washout below.
wash up, wash oneself, esp one's hands (eg before a meal). ***be washed up,*** carried on to the beach (by waves, etc): *The empty boat was ~ed up on the beach.* ***(all) washed up,*** (*informal*) ruined.

wash-[3] /wɔʃ, waʃ/ *prefix* (often used as a substitute for *washing*):
ˈwash·basin *n* [C] = washbowl.
ˈwash·bowl *n* [C] round, shallow container for holding water in which to wash one's face and hands.
ˈwash·cloth *n* [C] cloth for washing the face, etc.
ˈwash·out *n* [C] **(a)** place in a road, etc where a flood or heavy rain has carried away earth, etc and interrupted communications. **(b)** (*informal*) useless or unsuccessful person; complete failure.
ˈwash·rag *n* [C] (*informal*) = washcloth.
ˈwash·room *n* [C] toilet (esp in a public building, etc).
ˈwash·stand *n* [C] piece of furniture with a bowl, jug, etc formerly used for washing in a bedroom.
ˈwash·tub *n* [C] large wooden bowl in which to wash clothes.

wash·able /ˈwɔʃəbəl, ˈwaʃ-/ *adj* that can be washed without being spoiled.

washer /ˈwɔʃər, ˈwa-/ *n* [C] **1** machine for washing clothes, or (ˈ*dish~*) dishes. **2** small flat ring of metal, plastic, rubber or leather for making a joint or screw tight.

wash·ing /ˈwɔʃɪŋ, ˈwa-/ *n* [U] **1** washing or being washed. **2** clothes being washed or to be washed: *hang out the ~ on the line to dry.*
ˈwashing machine, machine for washing clothes.

wasn't /ˈwəzənt/ = was not.

WASP[1] /wasp/ *abbr* (*informal*) = white Anglo-Saxon Protestant.

wasp[2] /wasp/ *n* [C] kinds of flying insect with a powerful sting in the tail. ⇨ illus at insect.

wast·age /ˈweistɪdʒ/ *n* [U] amount wasted; loss by waste.

waste[1] /weist/ *adj* **1** (of land) that is not or cannot be used; no longer of use. ***lay sth waste,*** ⇨ lay[2](4). **2** useless; thrown away because not wanted: ˌ*~* ˈ*paper.*
ˈwaste·land *n* **(a)** barren, desolate or unused land. **(b)** land destroyed by war, etc. **(c)** (*fig*) life, society, looked on as culturally and spiritually barren.

waste[2] /weist/ *n* **1** [U] wasting or being wasted: *It's a ~ of time to wait any longer.* ***go/run to waste,*** be wasted: *What a pity to see so many ideas going to ~!* **2** [U] waste material; refuse. **3** [C] area of wasteland, etc: *the ~s of the Sahara.*
waste·ful /-fəl/ *adj* causing waste; using more than is needed: *~ful habits/processes.*
waste·fully /-fəli/ *adv*
ˈwaste·paper basket, basket or other container for scraps of paper, etc.

waste[3] /weist/ *vt, vi* **1** make no use of; use without a good purpose; use more of (something) than is necessary: *~ one's time and money. All his efforts were ~d,* had no result. **2** make (land) waste. **3** (cause to) lose strength by degrees: *He's wasting away.*

watch[1] /watʃ/ *n* **1** [U] act of watching, esp to see that all is well. ***be on the watch (for),*** be watching for (a person or thing, esp possible danger). **2** (usually *sing* with *the*) (in former times) body of men employed to go through the streets and protect people and their property, esp at night. **3** (on ships) period of duty (4 or 2 hours) for part of the crew. ***keep watch,*** be on watch or watching. ***stand watch,*** keep watch(3).
ˈwatch·dog *n* [C] dog kept to protect property.
watch·ful /-fəl/ *adj* (esp) wide-awake.
ˈwatch·man /-mən/ *n* [C] (*pl* ~men /-men/) man employed to guard a building (eg a bank, block of offices, factory) against thieves, esp at night.
watch·word /-ˌwərd/ *n* [C] **(a)** password. **(b)** slogan.

watch[2] /watʃ/ *vt,vi* look at; keep the eyes on: *Watch me carefully. Watch what I do and how I do it. We sat there ~ing the game. I'll ~ over* (= look after) *her while you go shopping.* ***watch one's step,*** (*fig*) be careful not to make an error, let a person win an advantage, etc, eg in negotiations.
watcher *n* [C] person who watches.

watch[3] /watʃ/ *n* [C] small instrument for telling the time that can be carried in the pocket or worn on the wrist.
ˈwatch·maker *n* [C] person who makes or repairs watches.

water[1] /ˈwɔtər, ˈwatər/ *n* (*pl* only as shown in examples below) **1** [U] liquid (symbol H_2O) as in rivers, lakes, seas and oceans: *Fish live in* (*the*) *~.* ***by water,*** by boat, ship, etc. ***in deep water(s),*** experiencing difficulty or misfortune. ***under water,*** flooded: *The fields were under ~ after the heavy rain.* ***like a fish out of water,*** feeling uncomfortable, behaving awkwardly, because of unfamiliar surroundings, an unfamiliar situation, etc. ***be in/get into hot water,*** have got/get into trouble (esp because of foolish behavior, etc). ***hold water,*** (of a theory) be sound when tested. ***keep one's head above water,*** avoid (esp financial) troubles or misfortunes. ***spend money, etc like water,*** extravagantly. ***throw cold water on (a plan, etc),*** discourage (it). ***tread water,*** ⇨ tread(4). **2** [U] the state of the tide: *at high/low ~.* **3** (*pl*) seas as shown by a preceding word: *Home ~s,* the seas near the country to which a ship belongs. **4** (usually *pl*) mass of water: *the* ˈ*head~s of the Nile,* the lake from which it flows. **5** [U] solution of a substance in water: ˈ*rose ~.*

ˈwater·bird *n* [C] kinds of bird that swim or wade in water.

ˈwater biscuit, thin, hard cracker eaten with butter and cheese.

ˈwater-borne *adj* **(a)** (of goods) carried by water. **(b)** (of diseases) passed on by the use of contaminated water.

ˈwater buffalo, the common domestic buffalo of India, Indonesia, etc.

ˈwater·color *n* **(a)** (*pl*) paints (to be) mixed with water, not oil. **(b)** [C] picture painted with watercolors. **(c)** (*pl* or *sing*) the art of painting such pictures.

ˈwater·cress *n* [U] creeping plant that grows in running water, with hot-tasting leaves used in salads.

ˈwater·fall *n* [C] fall of water, esp where a river falls over rocks or a cliff.

ˈwater·front *n* land at the water's edge, esp the part of a town facing the sea, the harbor, a lake, etc.

ˈwater heater, device installed in homes, etc for heating water for use.

ˈwater hole, shallow depression in which water collects (esp in the bed of a river otherwise dry, and to which animals go to drink).

ˈwater level, surface of water in a reservoir, etc esp as a measurement of depth.

ˈwater lily, kinds of plant with broad, flat leaves floating on the surface of the water.

ˈwater·logged *adj* **(a)** (of wood) so saturated with water that it will not float. **(b)** (of a ship) so full of water that it will not float. **(c)** (of land) thoroughly soaked with water.

ˈwater main, main pipe in a system of water supply.

ˈwater·mark *n* [C] **(a)** manufacturer's design in some kinds of paper, seen when the paper is held against light. **(b)** mark which shows how high water (eg the tide, a river) has risen or how low it has fallen.

ˈwater·melon *n* [C,U] (plant with) large, smooth-skinned melon with juicy pink or red flesh. ⇨ illus at fruit.

ˈwater·mill *n* [C] mill whose machinery is turned by waterpower.

ˈwater pipe, one for carrying water.

ˈwater polo, game played by two teams of swimmers who try to throw a ball into a goal.

ˈwater·power *n* [U] power obtained from flowing or falling water, used to drive machinery or generate electric current.

ˈwater·proof *adj* which does not let water through: *~proof material.* □ *vi* make waterproof.

ˈwater·proofing *n* [U] **(a)** process of making something waterproof. **(b)** substance for waterproofing.

ˈwater rat/vole, animal like a rat living in, near, water.

ˈwater-repellent *adj* capable of shedding water, though not fully waterproof.

ˈwater·shed *n* (a) line of high land separating river systems. **(b)** (*fig*) division between events which take different courses.

ˈwater·side *n* edge of the coast, a riverbank, etc: *go for a stroll along the ~side.*

ˈwater ski, one of a pair of skis used to water-ski.

ˈwater-ski *vi* ski on water (with water skis) while being towed at speed by a fast motorboat.

ˈwater-skiing *n* [U]

ˈwater·spout *n* (a) pipe or spout from which water is discharged, eg rainwater from a roof. **(b)** whirlwind over the sea which draws up a spinning column of water.

ˈwater supply, system of providing and storing water, amount stored, for a district, town, building, etc.

ˈwater·table *n* level below which the ground is filled with water: *The ~table has been lowered by drought.*

ˈwater·tight *adj* **(a)** so that water cannot get in or out: *~tight boots.* **(b)** (*fig*) (of an agreement, etc) so that there can be no escape from any of the provisions; leaving no possibility of misunderstanding.

ˈwater tower, one supporting a large tank which maintains the pressure for a water supply.

ˈwater·way *n* [C] navigable channel (eg a canal).

ˈwater·wheel, one turned by a flow of water, used to work machinery.

ˈwater·works *n pl* (used with a *sing* or *pl verb*) **(a)** system of reservoirs, pumping stations, for supplying water. **(b)** ornamental fountains.

ˈwater·worn *adj* (of rocks, etc) made smooth by the action of water.

water[2] /ˈwɔtər, ˈwatər/ *vt,vi* **1** put water on; sprinkle with water: *~ the lawn/the plants.* **2** give water to: *~ the horses.* **3** (of the eyes or mouth) fill with water; have much liquid: *The smoke made my eyes ~. The smell from the kitchen made my mouth ~,* made me feel hungry. **4** ***water (sth down),*** **(a)** add water to: *This whiskey has been ~ed (down).* **(b)** (*fig*) weaken: *The story was ~ed down.*

ˈwatering can, container with a long spout, used for watering plants.

ˈwatering hole/place, water hole.

wat·ery /ˈwɔtəri, watəri/ *adj* (-ier, -iest) **1** of or like water; (esp of cooked vegetables) containing, cooked in, too much water: *~ soup.* **2** (of color) pale. **3** (of the eyes or lips) covered with water.

WATS /wats/ *abbr* = wide area telephone service.

ˈWATS line, telephone service with long-distance calls covered by a fixed monthly charge.

watt /wat/ *n* [C] unit of electrical power: *a 60 ~ light bulb.*

watt·age /ˈwatɪdʒ/ *n* [U] electric power stated in watts.

wattle[1] /ˈwatəl/ *n* [U] structure of woven sticks or twigs used for fences, walls, etc.

wattle[2] /ˈwatəl/ *n* [C] red flesh hanging down from the head or throat of a bird, esp a turkey.

wave /weiv/ *vi,vt* **1** move to and fro, up and down: *flags/branches waving in the wind.* **2** cause (something) to move in this way (eg to make a signal or request, to give a greeting, etc): *~ one's hand/a flag. She ~d goodbye to us.* **3** cause (a person) to move in a certain direction by waving: *He* ~*d us away.* ***wave sth aside,*** (*fig*) dismiss: *My objections were* ~*d aside.* **4** (of a line or surface, of hair) be in a series of curves (~~~): *Her hair* ~*s beautifully.* **5** cause to be in a series of curves: *She's had her hair permanently* ~*d/permanent* ~*d.* □ *n* [C] **1** long ridge of water, esp on the sea, between two hollows; such a ridge curling over and breaking on the shore. ***in waves,*** in successive lines like waves: *The infantry attacked in* ~*s.* **2** act of waving(⇨2 above); waving movement: *with a* ~ *of his hand.* **3** curve like a wave of the sea: *the* ~*s in her hair.* **4** steady increase and spread: *a* ~ *of enthusiasm/hatred.* ⇨heat wave. **5** motion like a wave by which heat, light, sound or electricity is spread or carried.

'wave·length *n* distance between the highest point (the crest) of one wave(5) and that of the next. ***(not) on the same wavelength,*** (*fig*) (not) in agreement.

wavy *adj* (-ier, -iest) having curves: *a wavy line; wavy hair.*

wa·ver /ˈweivər/ *vi* **1** move uncertainly or unsteadily: ~*ing shadows/flames.* **2** be or become unsteady; begin to give way: *His courage* ~*ed.* **3** hesitate: ~ *between two opinions.*

wa·verer *n* [C] person who wavers.

wax[1] /wæks/ *n* [U] soft yellow substance produced by bees (ˈ*beeswax*) and used for making honeycomb cells; kinds of substance similar to beeswax (eg as obtained from petroleum), used for making candles, etc: (as an *adjective*) *a wax candle.* ⇨ sealing wax. □ *vt* cover, polish or treat with wax: *wax furniture/a wooden floor.*

wax[2] /wæks/ *vi* (of the moon) show a bright area which gradually increases until the moon is full. ⇨ wane(1).

way[1] /wei/ *n* **1** [C] road, street, path, etc: *a way across the fields. There's no way through.* ⇨ highway, pathway, etc. ***pave the way for,*** (*fig*) prepare for, prepare people to accept (reforms, etc). **2** [C] route, road (to be) used (*from* one place *to* another): *Which is the best/right/quickest/shortest way there? Can you find your way home? Which is the way in/out?* ***go one's way,*** depart. ***go out of one's way (to do sth),*** make a special effort: *He went out of his way to be rude to me/to help me.* ***lead the way,*** **(a)** go in front as leader. **(b)** show by example how something may be done. ***make one's way in life,*** succeed. ***pay one's way,*** **(a)** keep out of debt. **(b)** pay one's share of expenses instead of letting others pay. ***by way of,*** using a route over, on or through: *He came by way of the coastal highway.* ***out of the way,*** exceptional, uncommon: *He has done nothing out of the way yet.* **3** ***on the/one's way,*** being engaged in going or coming: *They're still on the/their way.* ***by the way,*** **(a)** during a journey. **(b)** (*fig*) incidentally (often used to introduce a remark not connected with the subject of conversation). ***on the way out,*** (*fig*) (*informal*) going out of fashion. **4** [C] method or plan; course of action: *the right/wrong/best way to do/of doing something. The work must be finished* (*in*) *one way or another.* ***Where there's a ˌwill there's a ˈway,*** (*prov*) if we want to do something, we will find a method of doing it. ***ˈNo ˈway!*** (*informal*) by no means/under no conditions (will something happen/be done). ***ˌways and ˈmeans,*** methods, esp of providing money. ***have/get one's own way,*** get/do what one wants. ***go one's own way,*** act independently, esp against advice. **5** (*sing* only) distance between two points; distance (to be) traversed: *It's a long way off/a long way from here. This will go a long way* (= will be very helpful) *in overcoming the difficulty.* **6** [C] direction: *He went this/that/the other way. Look this* ~, *please. Such opportunities never come my way*, come to me. **7** [U] advance in some direction; progress (esp of a ship or boat). ***be under way,*** (of a ship) be moving through the water. ***get under way,*** start to move forward. **8** [U] space for forward movement, for passing ahead; freedom to go forward: *Don't stand in the/my way.* ***be/put sth out of harm's way,*** in a safe place. ***get sth out of the way,*** settle it, dispose of it. ***give way (to sth/sb),*** ⇨ give[1](9). ***make way (for),*** allow space or a free passage: *All traffic has to make way for an ambulance.* ***see one's way (clear) to doing sth,*** (esp) feel justified in doing something: *I don't see my way clear to helping you.* **9** [C] custom; manner of behaving; personal peculiarity: *American/Chinese way of living; the way of the world*, what appears to be justified by custom. *I don't like the way* (= manner in which) *he looks at me.* ***mend one's ways,*** improve one's manners, behavior, etc. ***to ˈmy way of thinking,*** in my opinion. **10** [C] respect; point or detail: *He's a clever man in some ways. He's a nice man in his* (*own*) *way.* **11** [C] condition, state, degree: *Things are/She's in a bad way.* ***in a small way,*** on a small scale: *help in a small way.* ***have it ˈboth ways,*** choose first one and then the other of alternatives in order to suit one's convenience, argument, etc. **12** [C] ordinary course: *do something in the way of business.* **13** ***by way of,*** **(a)** as a substitute for or as a kind of: *say something by way of an introduction.* **(b)** for the purpose of, with the intention of: *ask questions by way of learning the facts.* **(c)** in the course of: *by way of business.* ⇨ also 2 above.

way[2] (sometimes **'way**) /wei/ *adv* (*informal*) away; far (away): *The eagle looks like a small bird way up in the sky.* **ˈway ˈout** (*sl*) (of behavior, fashions, events, etc) extreme. *Those clothes are way out.*

way·farer /ˈweiˌfærər/ *n* [C] (*liter*) traveler, esp on foot.

ˈway·faring /-ˌfærɪŋ/ *adj* traveling: *a wayfaring man.*

way·lay /ˈweiˌlei/ *vt* (*pt,pp* -laid /-ˌleid/) (wait somewhere to) attack, rob (a person), approach (a person) unexpectedly (with a request): *He waylaid me with a request for a loan.*

way·side *n* [C] side of a road: *by the* ~; (as an *adjective*) ~ *flowers.*

way·ward /ˈweiwərd/ *adj* not easily controlled or guided: *a* ~ *child.*

we /wi/ *personal pron* used by a speaker or writer referring to himself and another or others: *Can we all come to visit you?* **2**

sometimes formally used by an editor, author, or by a royal person instead of *I*. ⇨ us, object form.

weak /wik/ *adj* (-er, -est) **1** (opposite of *strong*) lacking in strength; easily broken; unable to resist strong use, opposition, etc: *too ~ to walk; ~ in the legs; a ~ team; the ~ points of an argument/plan.* **2** (of health, etc) below the usual standard: *a ~ heart; ˌ~-ˈsighted, ˌ~-ˈminded, ˌ~-ˈheaded.* **3** (of mixed liquids or solutions) having little of some substance in relation to the water, etc: *~ tea/beer.* **4** not good; not efficient: *~ in spelling/grammar.*

ˈweak form (of the pronunciation of some words) form occurring in an unstressed position, usually by the use of a different vowel sound or by the absence of a vowel sound or consonant (eg /ən/ for *and*).

ˌweak-ˈkneed *adj* (*fig*) weak in character.

weak·ling *n* [C] weak person or animal.

weak·ly *adv* in a weak manner.

weak·ness /-nɪs/ *n* **(a)** [U] state of being weak: *the ~ness of old age.* **(b)** [C] fault or defect of character: *We all have our little ~nesses.* **(c)** ***have a weakness for,*** a special or foolish liking for: *He has a ~ness for ice cream/blondes.*

ˌweak ˈverb, (*gram*) one inflected by additions to the stem, not by vowel change (eg walk, walked).

weaken /ˈwikən/ *vt,vi* make, become, weak(er).

weal /ˈwiəl/ *n* [C] mark on the skin made by a blow from a whip, etc.

wealth /welθ/ *n* **1** [U] (possession of a) great amount of property, money, etc: *a man of ~.* **2** (*sing* only with *a, an* or *the*) great amount or number of: *a book with a ~ of illustrations; the ~ of phrases and sentences to illustrate meanings in this dictionary.*

wealthy *adj* (-ier, -iest) rich.

wean /win/ *vt* **1** accustom (a baby, a young animal) to food other than its mother's milk. **2** (*fig*) cause (a person) to turn away (from a habit, bad companions, etc): *~ a person off/away from drugs.*

weapon /ˈwepən/ *n* [C] something designed for, or used in, fighting or struggling (eg swords, guns, fists, a strike by workers).

weapon·less *adj* = unarmed (the usual word).

weap·onry /-ri/ *n* [U] weapons collectively.

wear[1] /wer/ *n* [U] **1** wearing or being worn; use as clothing: *This coat is beginning to look the worse for ~*, shows signs of having been worn for a long time, so that it is no longer in a good or useful condition. **2** damage or loss of quality from use: *The carpet is showing signs of ~.* ***wear and tear,*** damage, loss in value, because used. **3** capacity for keeping in good condition: *There's not much ~ left in these shoes*, they cannot be worn much longer. **4** (used chiefly in compounds or in terms used by tradesmen) things to wear: *ˈunder~; ˈladies'/ˈmen's/ˈchildren's ~.*

wear[2] /wer/ *vt,vi* (*pt* wore /wɔr/, *pp* worn /wɔrn/) **1** have on the body, carry on one's person or on some part of it: *He was ~ing spectacles/heavy shoes/a ring on his finger. She never ~s green,* ie green clothes. *She used to ~ her hair long*, used to have long hair. **2** (of expressions) have on the face: *~ a smile.* **3** (cause to) become less useful or to be in a certain condition, by being used: *I have worn my socks into holes. This material has worn thin. The stones were worn by the constant flow of water.* **4** make (a hole, groove, etc) in by rubbing or attrition: *~ holes in a rug/one's socks. In time a path was worn across the field.* **5** remain in a certain condition (after use): *Good leather will ~ for years. This cloth has worn well/badly. Old Mr. Smith is ~ing well*, still looks well in spite of his advanced age. **6** (special uses with *adverbial particles* and *prepositions*):

wear away, **(a)** become broken, thin, weak, as the result of constant use: *The inscription on the stone had worn away*, the words were difficult to read. **(b)** (of time) pass slowly: *as the evening wore away.* ***wear sth away,*** use up or damage something by constant use, etc: *The footsteps of thousands of visitors had worn away the stones.*

wear down, become gradually smaller, thinner, weaker, etc: *The heels of these shoes are ~ing down.* ***wear sth down,*** cause to wear down. ***wear sb/sth down,*** weaken by constant attack, nervous strain, etc: *These noisy children certainly ~ me down!*

wear off, pass away: *The novelty will soon ~ off.*

wear on, (of time) pass: *Evening wore on.*

wear (sth) out, (cause to) become useless, worn thin, exhausted: *Cheap shoes soon ~ out. His patience had/was at last worn out.* ***wear sb out,*** exhaust, tire out: *I'm worn out by all this hard work.*

ˌworn-ˈout *adj*: *a ˌworn-out ˈcoat.*

wear·able /ˈwerəbəl/ *adj* that can be, or is fit to be, worn.

weary /ˈwɪri/ *adj* (-ier, -iest) **1** tired: *feel ~; be ~ of his constant grumbling.* **2** causing tiredness: *a ~ journey.* **3** showing tiredness: *a ~ sigh.* □ *vt,vi* make or become weary: *~ of living alone.*

wear·ily /-əli/ *adv*

weari·ness /ˈwɪrinɪs/ *n* [U]

weari·some /ˈwɪrisəm/ *adj* tiring; long and dull.

wea·sel /ˈwizəl/ *n* [C] small, fierce animal with red-brown fur.

weather[1] /ˈweðər/ *n* [U,C] conditions over a particular area and at a particular time with reference to sunshine, temperature, wind, rain, etc: *He stays indoors in wet ~. She goes out in all ~s* (*pl* here = all kinds of ~). (*Note: climate* is used when referring to a long period of time, eg a season.) ***be/feel under the weather,*** (*informal*) unwell.

ˈweather-beaten *adj* showing marks or signs which come from exposure to the sun, wind, rain, etc: *a ˌ~-beaten ˈface.*

ˈweather-bound *adj* unable to make or continue a journey because of bad weather.

ˈweather forecast, ⇨ forecast.

ˈweather·man /-ˌmæn/ (*pl* ~men /-ˌmen/) (*informal*) man who reports and forecasts the weather.

ˈweather map, diagram showing details of the weather over an area.

ˈweather·proof *adj* able to stand exposure to all types of weather.

ˈ**weather ship,** one at sea to make observations of the weather.

ˈ**weather station,** building where the weather is observed.

ˈ**weather vane** = vane(1).

weather² /ˈweðər/ *vt,vi* **1** (*lit* and *fig*) come through successfully: ~ *a storm/crisis.* **2** sail to the windward of: ~ *a cape.* **3** expose to the weather: ~ *wood,* leave it in the open air until it is properly shrunk and ready for use. **4** (cause to) discolor, become worn, by the weather: *rocks ~ed by wind and rain.*

weave /wiv/ *vt,vi* (*pt* wove /wouv/, *pp* woven /ˈwouvən/) **1** make (by hand or by machine) (threads) into cloth, etc; make (cloth, etc) from threads: ~ *cotton thread into cloth.* **2** make (garlands, baskets, etc) by a similar process: ~ *flowers into a wreath;* ~ *a garland of flowers.* **3** (*fig*) put together, compose (a story, romance, etc): ~ *a plot.* ***get weaving (on sth),*** (*sl*) make an energetic start (on a task, etc). **4** twist and turn: *The driver was weaving* (*his way*) *through the traffic.* □ *n* [C] style of weaving: *a loose/tight ~.*

weaver *n* [C] person who weaves cloth.

web /web/ *n* [C] **1** something made of threads by a spider or other spinning creature: *a spider's web.* ⇨ cobweb. **2** (usually *fig*): *a web of lies.* **3** skin joining the toes of some waterbirds, eg ducks, and some water animals, eg frogs.

web·bed *adj* having the toes joined by webs.

ˌ**web-ˈfooted** *adj*

wed¹ /wed/ *vt,vi* (*pt* wedded, *pp* wedded or *rare* wed) **1** marry. **2** unite: *simplicity wedded to beauty.* ***wedded to,*** devoted to; unable to give up: *He is wedded to his own opinions and nothing can change him.*

Wed.² *abbr* = Wednesday.

we'd /wid/ = we had; we would.

wed·ding /ˈwedɪŋ/ *n* [C] marriage ceremony (and festivities connected with it): *attend/invite one's friends to a ~; the ~ dress.*

ˈ**wedding ring,** ring placed on the bride's or groom's finger at a wedding.

wedge /wedʒ/ *n* [C] **1** V-shaped piece of wood or metal, used to split wood or rock (by being hammered), to widen an opening, or to keep two things separate. **2** something shaped like or used like a wedge: ~ *heels* (on shoes). □ *vt* fix tightly (as) with a wedge: ~ *a door open,* by placing a wedge under it; *be tightly ~d between two fat people on the bus.*

wed·lock /ˈwedˌlak/ *n* [U] condition of being married: *born out of ~,* illegitimate.

Wed·nes·day /ˈwenzdi, -ˌdei/ *n* fourth day of the week.

weed /wid/ *n* [C] **1** wild plant growing where it is not wanted (eg in a garden). **2** (*fig*) thin, tall, weak-looking person. □ *vt,vi* **1** take weeds out of (the ground): ~ *the garden.* **2** remove, get rid of (what is unwanted, or of lower value than the rest): ~ *out the lazy students.*

weedy *adj* (-ier, -iest) **(a)** full of, overgrown with, weeds. **(b)** tall, thin, weak: *a ~y young man.*

weeds /widz/ *n pl* (also ˈ**widow's weeds**) black clothes as (formerly) worn by a widow for mourning.

week /wik/ *n* [C] **1** any period of seven days; (esp) seven days from Saturday midnight to Saturday midnight: *this/last/next ~; this day a ~,* one week from today; *for the last/next six ~s; a six ~s' vacation; the work ~,* (usually) Monday to Friday or Saturday. ***week in, week out,*** for weeks in succession. **2** the working days of the week.

ˈ**week·day** *n* [C] any day except Saturday and Sunday: *I'm always busy on ~days.*

ˈ**week·end** *n* [C] Saturday and Sunday (as a period of rest or vacation): *spend the ~end with friends;* (as an *adjective*) *a ~end vacation.* □ *vi* spend a weekend: *I'm ~ending at Cape Cod.*

week·ly *adj, adv* (happening) once a week, every week; of, for or lasting a week: *a ~ly wage of $200; ~ly visits.* □ *n* [C] (*pl* -ies) periodical published once a week.

weep /wip/ *vi,vt* (*pt,pp* wept /wept/) cry; let tears fall from the eyes: ~ *for joy. She wept to see him in such a terrible state. She wept over her sad fate. She wept bitter tears.*

weep·ing *adj* (of trees, eg the birch and willow) having drooping branches.

wee·vil /ˈwiˌvəl/ *n* [C] small beetle with a hard shell, feeding on and infesting stores of grain, nuts and other seeds.

wee·wee /ˈwiˌwi/ *n* [U] (used by and to small children) urine. □ *vi* urinate.

weft /weft/ *n* [C] cross-threads taken over and under other threads (the *warp*) when cloth is woven.

weigh /wei/ *vt,vi* **1** measure (by means of a scale, balance, etc) how heavy something is: *He ~ed himself on the scales.* ***weigh sth out,*** distribute in defined quantities; take a definite quantity of: *She ~ed out flour, sugar and butter for a cake.* **2** show a certain measure when put on a scale, etc: ~ *25 pounds/a ton/nothing.* **3** (of a machine, etc) be capable of taking, designed to take, objects up to a specified weight: *This machine will ~ up to 2 tons.* **4** compare the importance, value, etc of (one thing and another): ~ *one plan against another.* ***weigh sth (up),*** consider carefully, assess: ~ (*up*) *the consequences of an action.* **5** ***weigh anchor,*** raise the anchor and start a voyage. **6** (special uses with *adverbial particles* and *prepositions*): ***weigh sth down,*** pull or bring down: *The fruit ~ed the branches down.* ***weigh sb down,*** make tired, depressed, troubled, etc: *~ed down with sorrow/cares/anxieties.*

weigh on sb/sth, cause concern, anxiety (because of importance, seriousness): *The problem/responsibility ~s heavily on him/his mind.*

ˈ**weighing machine,** machine for weighing objects that are too large for a simple balance or scale.

weight /weit/ *n* **1** [U] force with which a body tends toward the center of the earth. **2** [U] how heavy a thing is; this expressed in some scale (eg tons, kilograms) as measured on a scale, weighing machine, etc: *That man is twice my ~. My ~ is 150 pounds.* ***over/under weight,*** weighing too much/too little. ***put on weight,*** (of a person) become heavier. ***throw one's weight around,*** (*informal*) be conceited; try to bully people. **3** (not *pl*, but with *a, an* or *the*) load to be supported: *The pillars have a great ~ to bear/have to support the ~ of the roof. That's a great ~* (= problem) *off my mind.* **4** [U] (degree of) importance or influence: *opinions that carry ~; considerations that had great ~ with me.* **5** [C] piece of metal of known weight used in scales for weighing things: *one ounce/100 grams ~.* **6** [C] heavy object for various purposes: *keep papers down with a ˈpaper~.* **7** [U] system of units, scale or notation, for expressing weight: *troy/metric ~.* □ *vt* **1** put a weight(5) on; add weight to; make heavy: *~ a pendulum in a clock.* **2** (*fig*) give advantage: *Circumstances are ~ed in his favor.* **3** ***weight sb down,*** burden with: *He was ~ed down with suitcases.*

weight·less *adj* having no weight, eg because of absence of gravity.

ˈweight lifting, gymnastic feat of lifting great weights.

weighty *adj* (-ier, -iest) **(a)** very heavy. **(b)** (*fig*) influential; important: *~y considerations/arguments.*

weir /wɪr/ *n* [C] wall or barrier across a river or canal to control the flow of water or as a trap for catching fish.

weird /wɪrd/ *adj* **1** unnatural: *~ shrieks from the ruined castle.* **2** (*informal*) strange; difficult to understand or explain: *~ makeup on some rock stars.*

weird·ly *adv*

weird·ness /-nɪs/ *n* [U]

wel·come /ˈwelkəm/ *adj* **1** received with, giving, pleasure: *a ~ visitor/rest; ~ news; make a friend ~,* show him that his coming is welcome. **2** ***welcome to,*** **(a)** allowed with pleasure to: *You are ~ to borrow my bicycle.* **(b)** (*ironic*) allowed to have something burdensome or unwanted: *If anyone thinks he can do this job any better, he's ~ to it/~ to try!* **3** (used as an interjection): *Welcome home! Welcome to the United States!* □ *n* [C] greeting, response by word or action, when somebody arrives, when an offer is received, etc: *They gave us/We received a warm/cold/enthusiastic ~.* □ *vt* show pleasure or satisfaction at something, at the arrival of a person or thing: *~ a friend to one's home; ~ a suggestion warmly/coldly.*

weld /weld/ *vt,vi* **1** join (pieces of metal) by hammering or pressure (usually when the metal is softened by heat) or fusing; make by doing this: *~ (the pieces of) a broken axle; ~ parts together.* **2** (of iron, etc) be capable of being welded: *Some metals ~ better than others.* □ *n* [C] welded joint.

wel·der *n* [C] workman who welds.

wel·fare /ˈwelˌfær/ *n* [U] **1** condition of having good health, comfortable living and working conditions, etc: *work for the ~ of the nation; child/infant/social ~; ˈ~ work,* organized efforts to improve the welfare of those who need help. **2** program of US federal and local state finan-ial aid for the chronically unemployed: *He has ... on ~ for two years. She is a ~ mother,* a ... on welfare.

ˈWelfare ˌState, name applied to a country with State-financed social services, eg health, insurance, pensions.

well[1] /wel/ *n* [C] **1** shaft, usually lined with brick or stone, for obtaining water from an underground source: *drive/sink a ~.* **2** hole bored for petroleum: *the ˈoil ~s of Iran.* **3** space in a building for a staircase or elevator: *a ˈstair~.* □ *vi* flow, like water from a well: *The blood was ~ing out (from the wound).* ***well over,*** overflow. ***well up (in),*** rise, like water in a well: *Tears ~ed up in her eyes.*

ˈwell-water *n* [U] water from a well.

well[2] /wel/ *adj* (better, best) **1** in good health: *be/look/feel/get ~. I'm quite ~, thank you.* **2** in a satisfactory condition: *All's ~ that ends ~.* ***It's all very well...,*** (used ironically to show discontent, dissatisfaction, disagreement, etc): *It's all very ~ (for you) to suggest a vacation in Italy, but how am I to find the money?* **3** advisable; desirable: *It would be ~ to start early.*

well[3] /wel/ (better, best) *adv* **1** in a good, right or satisfactory manner: *The children behaved ~. They are ~-behaved children. Well done! I hope everything is going ~* (= satisfactorily) *with you. Does this color go ~ with that color?* ***do well,*** succeed; make progress; prosper: *Simon has done ~ at school this term.* ***be doing well,*** (in the progressive tense only) making a good recovery (from an operation, etc): *Both mother and baby are doing ~.* ***do well out of,*** make a profit from. **2** with praise or approval: *think/speak ~ of a person.* **3** fortunately. ***be well out of sth,*** be fortunate to be out of an undertaking, commitment, etc. ***ˌwell ˈoff,*** rich; fortunate: *He doesn't know when he is ~ off,* does not realize how fortunate he is. ***come off well,*** **(a)** (of a person) have good fortune; be lucky. **(b)** (of an event) have a satisfactory outcome. **4** with good reason, justice; fairly; advisably: *You may ~ be surprised. I couldn't very ~ refuse to help them,* It would have been difficult, unreasonable, etc to have done so. *It may ~ be that...,* It is likely or possible that... **5** ***may as well,*** ⇨ may[1](4). ***be just as well,*** with no loss of advantage, no need for regret: *It's just as ~ I didn't lend him the money.* **6** (end position) thoroughly; completely: *Examine the account ~ before you pay it.* **7** to a considerable extent: *His name is ~ up in the list,* near the top. *He must be ~ past forty/~ over forty years old.* **8** ***as well (as),*** in addition (to): *He gave me money as ~ as advice. Give me those as ~* = those too. **9** (used with another *adv*) ***pretty well,*** ⇨ pretty *adv.*

well[4] /wel/ *int* **1** (expressing astonishment): *Well, who would have thought he'd do that? Well, ~!* **2** (expressing relief): *Well, here we are at last!* **3** (expressing resignation): *Well, there's nothing we can do about it.* **4** (expressing understanding or agreement): *Very ~, then, we'll talk it over again tomorrow.* **5** (expressing concession): *Well, you may be right.* **6** (used to resume a story, etc): *Well, as I was saying,...*

well[5] /wel/ *n* [U] that which is good: *wish him ~,* wish him good fortune, success, etc. ***let well (-enough) alone,*** not change what is already satisfactory.

ˈ**well-wisher** *n* [C] person who wishes somebody well (eg at the start of a trip, business venture, etc).

well- /wel-/ *prefix* (~ + *pp* = *adjective*) fortunately, properly, thoroughly.

ˌ**well-adˈvised** *adj* wise: *You'd be well-advised to apologize.*

ˌ**well-ˈbalanced** *adj* sane, sensible.

ˌ**well-beˈhaved** *adj* behaving well.

ˈ**well-being** *n* welfare; health, happiness and prosperity: *the well-being of the nation.*

ˌ**well-ˈbred** *adj* of good upbringing.

ˌ**well-conˈducted** *adj* characterized by good organization and control: *a* ˌ*well-conducted* ˈ*meeting.*

ˌ**well-conˈnected** *adj* connected by blood or marriage with families of good social position or to rich or influential people.

ˌ**well-ˈearned** *adj* fully deserved: ˌ*well-earned* ˈ*praise; a* ˌ*well-earned* ˈ*rest.*

ˌ**well-ˈfounded** *adj* based on good evidence, having a foundation in fact: ˌ*well-founded susˈpicions.*

ˌ**well-ˈgrounded** *adj* **(a)** = well-founded. **(b)** having a good training in or knowledge of the groundwork of a subject.

ˌ**well-ˈheeled** *adj* (*sl*) rich.

ˌ**well-inˈformed** *adj* **(a)** having wide knowledge. **(b)** having access to reliable information: *in* ˌ*well-informed* ˈ*quarters.*

ˌ**well-inˈtentioned** *adj* showing good intentions.

ˌ**well-ˈknown** *adj* known by many.

ˌ**well-ˈmarked** *adj* definite; distinct.

ˌ**well-ˈmeaning** *adj* = well-intentioned.

ˌ**well-ˈmeant** *adj* done, said, etc with good intentions.

ˈ**well-nigh** *adv* almost: ˌ*well-nigh imˈpossible.*

ˌ**well-ˈread** *adj* having a mind full of ideas, information, as the result of reading much.

ˌ**well-ˈspoken** *adj* **(a)** speaking well, politely. **(b)** spoken well.

ˌ**well-ˈtimed** *adj* done, said, at the right or a suitable time.

ˌ**well-to-ˈdo** *adj* wealthy; from a high social class.

ˌ**well-ˈtried** *adj* (of methods, remedies) tested and proved useful.

ˌ**well-ˈturned** *adj* (of a compliment, phrase, verse) expressed well.

ˌ**well-ˈworn** *adj* **(a)** much used. **(b)** (*fig*) used, heard, often (and so dull).

we'll /ˈwiəl, wəl/ = we will; we shall.

wel·ling·ton /ˈwelɪŋtən/ *n* [C] (also ***a pair of wellingtons; a*** ˌ***wellington*** ˈ***boot***) waterproof boot reaching to the knee.

Welsh /welʃ/ *n* **1** the Welsh language. **2** (*pl*) (used with *the*) Welsh people. □ *adj* of Wales, its language or people.

ˈ**Welsh·man/·woman** /-mən, -ˌwʊmən/ *n* [C] (*pl* ~men /-men/, ~women /-ˌwɪmɪn/) male/female native of Wales.

wel·ter /ˈweltər/ *vi* be soaked or steeped (in blood, etc). □ *n* [C] general confusion; disorderly mixture or aimless conflict: *the* ~ *of political beliefs.*

wel·ter-weight /ˈweltərˌweit/ *n* [C] boxer weighing between 135 and 147 lb (61 and 66.6 kg).

went *pt* of go¹.

wept *pt,pp* of weep.

were *pt* of be¹.

we're /wɪr, wər/ = we are.

weren't /wərnt/ = were not.

were·wolf /ˈwɪrˌwʊlf, ˈwer-/ *n* [C] (*pl* -wolves /-ˌwʊlvz/) (in myths) human being turned into a wolf.

west /west/ *n* **1 the west,** point of the horizon where the sun sets. **2** part of any country, etc lying further in this direction than other parts: *Arizona is to the* ~ *of New Mexico.* **3 the West, (a)** Europe and the continent of America (contrasted with Asia). **(b)** (world politics) Western Europe and America (contrasted with the USSR and China). **(c)** western part of the US: *California is politically the most influential state in the West.* □ *adj* in, of, from or toward the west: *On the* ~ *coast.* □ *adv* to or toward the west: *to travel/face* ~. ***go west,*** die; become destroyed. ***out West,*** to, in the western US: *He's thinking of moving out West.*

west·er·ly /ˈwestərli/ *adj* in a western direction or position; (of the wind) coming from the west.

west·ern /ˈwestərn/ *adj* of, from, living in, the west part of the world, or the western US. □ *n* [C] film or novel dealing with life in the western part of the US in the times of the wars with the Indians, or one with cowboys, etc.

west·erner *n* [C] native or resident of the West, esp of the western US.

the ˌ**Western** ˈ**Hemisphere,** part of the world that includes North and South America.

west·ern·ize /-ˌnaiz/ *vt* introduce western civilization into.

ˈ**west·ern·most** /-ˌmoust/ *adj* farthest west.

Western saddle, kind with high front and back, originally used in the Western US and now throughout the country.

ˈ**Western** ˌ**time,** one of 4 standard time zones in the US.

west·ward(s) /ˈwestwərd(z)/ *adj,adv* toward the west: *in a* ~ *direction; travel* ~.

wet /wet/ *adj* (wetter, wettest) **1** covered or soaked with water or other liquid: *wet clothes/roads. Did you get wet*, eg in the rain? ˌ***wet*** ˈ***through,*** soaked: *Your coat is wet through.* **2** rainy: *wet weather.* **3** (*sl*) (of a state) not prohibiting the sale of alcoholic drink. □ *vt* (*pt,pp* wet or wetted) (-tt-) make wet: *The baby has wet its bed again.* ***wet one's whistle,*** ⇨ whistle, *n*(2).

ˌ**wet** ˈ**blanket,** (*informal*) person who prevents others from enjoying themselves by being gloomy or bad-tempered.

we've /wiv/ = we have.

whack /(h)wæk/ *vt* hit (a person or thing) with a hard blow, object. □ *n* [C] **1** (sound of a) hard blow. **2** (*sl*) share: *Have you had a* ~ *at it?*

whale /ˈ(h)weiəl/ *n* [C] **1** kinds of very large sea animal some of which are hunted for their oil and flesh. **2** ***have a whale of a (good) time,*** a very enjoyable time. □ *vi* (*pres p* whaling /ˈ(h)weilɪŋ/) hunt whales: *go whaling.*

WHALE

whaler /ˈ(h)weilər/ *n* [C] man, ship, engaged in whaling.

wharf /(h)wɔrf/ *n* [C] (*pl* ~s or wharves /(h)wɔrvz/) wooden or stone structure at which ships are moored for (un)loading cargo.

what /(h)wat, (h)wət/ *adj* **1** asking for a selection from an indefinite number or amount: *What books have you read on this subject? Tell me ~ books you have read recently. What time is it?* **2** (used in exclamations): *What a good idea!* **3** the... that; any... that; as much/many... as: *Give me ~ books* (= the books, any books, that) *you have on the subject. What few friends* (= The few friends that) *I have here have been very kind to me.* □ *pron* **1** what thing(s): *What happened? Tell me ~ happened.* ***what for,*** for what purpose: *What is this tool used for? What did you do that for?* Why did you do that? ***what... like,*** (used to ask for a description, for details, etc): *What's the weather like this morning?* ***what if,*** what will, would, be the result if: *What if it rains while we are out?* ***what about/of,*** **(a)** what news is there about... **(b)** ⇨ about³(1). **2** that which; the thing(s) which: *What he says is not important. Do ~ you think is right. It's a useful book and, ~ is more* (= also), *not an expensive one.*

what·ever /(h)watˈevər, (h)wət-/ *adj* **1** (emphatic for *what*) of any sort, degree, etc: *Whatever nonsense the newspapers print, some people always believe it.* **2** (placed after a *noun* in a negative context, giving emphasis to the negative): *There can be no doubt ~ about it.* □ *pron* **1** no matter what: *You are certainly right, ~ others may say. Keep calm, ~ happens.* **2** anything or everything that: *Do ~ you like.*

what'll /ˈ(h)wətəl/ = what will.

what's /ˈ(h)wəts/ = what is; what does; what has.

what·so·ever /ˌ(h)watsouˈevər, ˌ(h)wət-/ *adj* = whatever.

wheat /(h)wit/ *n* [U] (plant producing) grain from which flour (as used for bread) is made: *a field of ~.* ⇨ illus at cereal.

wheaten /ˈ(h)witən/ *adj* of wheat: *~en bread.*

wheedle /ˈ(h)widəl/ *vt* make oneself pleasant to a person, flatter, to get something one wants: *She ~d five dollars out of her father/~d her father into buying her a bicycle.*

wheel /ˈ(h)wiəl/ *n* [C] **1** circular frame or disc which turns on an axle (as on carts, cars, bicycles, etc and machines). ***put one's shoulder to the wheel,*** work hard when doing something. **2** motion like that of a wheel. □ *vt,vi* (-ing /ˈ(h)wilıŋ/) **1** push or pull (a vehicle with wheels): *~ a bike up a hill; ~ a barrow; ~ the rubbish out to the dump.* **2** (cause to) turn in a curve or circle: *The seagulls were ~ing in the air above me.*

ˈwheel·barrow *n* [C] small cart with one wheel and two handles for moving small loads.

WHEELBARROW

ˈwheel·base *n* distance between the axles of a motor vehicle.

ˈwheel·chair *n* [C] chair with large wheels for the use of invalids.

ˈwheel·wright *n* [C] person who makes and repairs wheels.

wheeze /(h)wiz/ *vi,vt* **1** breathe noisily, esp with a whistling sound in the chest (as when suffering from asthma). **2** say with such sounds: *The asthmatic man ~d out a few words.* □ *n* [C] sound of wheezing.

wheezy *adj* (-ier, -iest) breathing, speaking, with wheezes.

whelk /(h)welk/ *n* [C] kinds of sea animal (like a snail) with a spiral shell, some used as food. ⇨ illus at mollusk.

when /(h)wen/ *adv* **1** at what time; on what occasion: *When can you come? When did that happen? I don't know ~ that happened.* **2** (used after a *preposition*) what time: *Since ~ has he been missing?* □ *adv* (with *day, time*, etc) at or on which: *Sunday is the day ~ I am least busy. There are times ~ I could scream with rage.* □ *conj* **1** at or during the time that: *It was raining ~ we arrived. When ~ he spoke everyone listened.* **2** although: *He walks ~ he could take a taxi.* **3** since; considering that: *How can I help them to understand ~ they won't listen to me?* **4** at or during which time: *The Governor will visit the town in May, ~ he will open the new hospital.*

whence /(h)wens/ *adv* (*old use*) **1** (in questions) from what place or cause: *Do you know ~ she came?* **2** (in statements) from which place: *the land ~ they are come.* **3** to the place from which: *Return ~ you came.*

when·ever /(h)wenˈevər/ *adv* **1** at whatever time; no matter when: *I'll discuss it with you ~ you like to come.* **2** on any occasion; as often as; every time that: *Whenever that man says, "To tell the truth," he's about to tell a lie.* ***3 or whenever,*** (*informal*) or at any time: *He'll arrive on Monday, or Friday, or ~, and expect to be given a meal.*

when's /(h)wenz/ = when is; when does; when has.

where /(h)wer/ *adv* **1** in or to what place or position; in what direction; in what respect: *Where does he live? I wonder ~ he lives.* **2** (used with a *preposition* following the *verb*) what place: *Where does he come from? Where are you going to?* □ *adv* **1** (with *place*, etc) in or at which: *That's* *the place/corner ~ the accident occurred.* **2** in, at or to the place in which; in the direction in which: *I found my books ~ I had left them. That's ~* (ie the point in respect of which) *you are mistaken.*

ˌwhere·aˈbouts *adv* in or near what place: *Whereabouts did you find it?* □ *n* (ˈ*~abouts*) (used with a *sing* or *pl verb*) place where a person or thing is: *Her present ~abouts is/are unknown.*

where·ˈas *conj* **(a)** (esp *legal*) considering that. **(b)** but in contrast; while on the other hand: *Some people like fat meat, ~as others hate it.*

where·ˈby *adv* by what; by which: *He devised a plan ~by he might escape.*

ˈwhere·fore *conj* (*formal*) for which reason; why. □ *n* (*pl*): *the whys and the ~fores*, the reasons.

where·ˈin *adv* (*formal*) in what; in which; in what respect: *Wherein am I mistaken?*

where's /(h)werz/ = where is; where does; where has.

where·so·ever /ˌ(h)wersouˈevər/ *adv* (*old use*) = wherever.

wher·ever /(h)werˈevər/ *adv* in, to, at, whatever place; at those places: *Sit ~ you like.*

where·withal /ˈ(h)werwɪðˌɔl/ *adv* (*old use*) with which. □ *n* **the wherewithal,** (*informal*) money needed for a purpose: *I'd like to buy an automobile but haven't got the ~.*

whet /(h)wet/ *vt* (-tt-) **1** sharpen (a knife, axe, etc). **2** (*fig*) sharpen or excite (the appetite, a desire).

ˈwhet·stone *n* shaped stone used for sharpening tools, eg scythes.

whether /ˈ(h)weðər/ *conj* (introducing an indirect question expressing doubt or choice; often replaced by *if* in *informal* style): *I wonder ~/if it's large enough* (*or not*). *I wonder ~ we'll be in time for the last bus or ~ we'll have to walk home. I don't know ~ to accept or refuse. It's doubtful ~ we shall be able to come. The question was ~ to wait for the bus or* (*~*) *to walk. I am not interested in ~ you like the plan or not.*

whew /hwu, hyu/ *int* (used to express tiredness, etc.)

which /(h)wɪtʃ/ *adj* (asking for selection from two, or from a group, esp from possibilities thought of as limited in number): **1** *Which way shall we go — up the hill or along the river? Which languages can you speak?* **2** and this; and these: *Don't call between 1 o'clock and 2 o'clock, at ~ time I'm usually having lunch.* □ *pron* which thing(s), person(s): *Which of the boys is the tallest? I never know ~ is ~*, I cannot distinguish one from the other. □ *pron* (of things only, not of persons) **1** (in defining or restrictive clauses *which* is often replaced by *that*) **(a)** (with *which* as the subject of the *verb* in the clause): *Take the book ~ is lying on that table.* **(b)** (with *which* as the object of the *verb* in the clause): *Was the book* (*~/that*) *you were reading a novel?* **(c)** (with *which* as the object of a *preposition;* replaceable by *that*): *The photographs at ~ you were looking/The photographs* (*~/that*) *you were looking at were all taken by my brother.* **2** (in nondefining or nonrestrictive clauses *which* is not replaceable by *that*) **(a)** (with *which* as the subject of the clause): *The meeting, ~ was held in the park, was attended by five hundred people.* **(b)** (with *which* as the object of the *verb* in the clause): *This desk, ~ I bought second-hand, is made of oak.* **(c)** (with *which* as the object of a *preposition*): *His car, for ~ he paid $2,000, is very unreliable.* **(d)** (referring to a clause or sentence, not to a *noun*): *He said he had lost the book, ~* (= but this) *was untrue.*

which·ever /(h)wɪtʃˈevər/ *adj, pron* **1** the one which: *Take ~ you like best. Whichever* (*of you*) *comes in first will receive a prize.* **2** no matter which: *Does US foreign policy remain the same, ~ party is in power?*

whiff /(h)wɪf/ *n* [C] slight puff or breath (*of*): *a ~ of fresh air; the ~* (= smell) *of a cigar.* □ *vt,vi* **1** blow or puff lightly. **2** get a slight smell of.

while /(h)waiəl/ *n* [C] (period of) time: *Where have you been all this ~? I haven't seen him for a long ~.* ***(every) once in a while,*** occasionally. ***worth (one's) while,*** worth the time spent in doing it, etc: *It isn't worth ~ going there now. He will make it worth your ~*, ie will reward you. □ *vt* (-ing /ˈ(h)wailɪŋ/) (only in) ***while away,*** pass the time in a leisurely way: *whiling away the time.* □ *conj* **1** during the time that; for as long as; at the same time as: *He fell asleep ~* (*he was*) *reading his book.* **2** (used in contrasts) but: *Jane was dressed in brown ~ Mary was wearing blue.* **3** although: *While I admit that the problems are difficult, I don't agree that they cannot be solved.*

whilst /(h)waiəlst/ *conj* = while (which is more usual).

whim /(h)wɪm/ *n* [C] sudden desire or idea, often something unusual or unreasonable: *full of ~s.*

whim·per /ˈ(h)wɪmpər/ *vi,vt* **1** make weak, frightened or complaining sounds, eg like a baby when ill, a dog when frightened or hurt. **2** say, cry in this voice. □ *n* [C] sobbing sound.

whim·si·cal /ˈ(h)wɪmzɪkəl/ *adj* (*formal*) odd; quaint.

whim·si·cally /ˈ(h)wɪmzəkli/ *adv*

whimsy /ˈ(h)wɪmzi/ *n* [C] (*pl* -ies) whim.

whine /(h)wain/ *n* [C] long complaining cry or high-pitched sound (eg as made by a miserable dog, a child, a motor engine). □ *vi,vt* **1** make such cries: *The dog was whining to come into the room.* **2** complain, esp about trivial things: *a child that never stops whining.*

whinny /ˈ(h)wɪni/ *n* [C] (*pl* -ies) gentle cry of a horse. □ *vi* (*pt,pp* -ied) make such a sound.

whip[1] /(h)wɪp/ *n* [C] **1** strip (of cord, leather, etc) fastened to a handle, used for urging a horse on, or for punishing. **2** organizing secretary of a political party with authority over its members to maintain discipline and secure attendance at congressional debates; order given by such a secretary to members of his party to attend a debate and vote. **3** dish of eggs, cream, etc beaten or whipped(2): *strawberry ~.*

whip[2] /(h)wɪp/ *vt,vi* (-pp-) **1** beat with a whip: *~ a horse/a child.* **2** beat (eggs, cream, etc) with a fork or other utensil to mix thoroughly or to make stiff: *~ped cream.* **3** (*informal*) defeat (in a competition). **4** take, be taken, move, be moved, suddenly: *He ~ped out a knife.*

whip·ping *n* beating with a whip as a punishment.

ˈwhip·ping boy, person (being) punished for another's offense.

whip·poor·will /ˈ(h)wɪpərˌwɪl/ *n* [C] North American night bird having a call which sounds like its name.

whir, whirr /(h)wər/ *n* (*sing* only) sound (as) of a bird's wings moving quickly, or of wheels, etc turning fast: *the ~ of a helicopter's propellers.* □ *vi* (-rr-) make such sounds.

whirl /(h)wərl/ *vt,vi* **1** (cause to) move quickly around and around: *The wind ~ed the dead leaves around.* **2** (cause to) move or travel quickly (*away*, etc): *Our friends were ~ed away in Jack's sports car.* **3** (of the brain, the senses) seem to go around and around; (of thoughts) be confused: *His head ~ed.* □ *n* (*sing* only) **1** whirling movement: *a ~ of dust/of dead leaves.* **2** quick succession of activities, etc: *the ~ of modern life in a big city.*

ˈwhirl·pool *n* [C] place where there are circular currents in the sea, etc (drawing floating objects toward its center).

ˈwhirl·wind *n* [C] swift circling current of air.

whisk /(h)wɪsk/ *n* [C] **1** device (eg coiled wire) for whipping eggs, cream, etc. **2** light brushing movement (eg of a horse's tail). □ *vt,vi* **1** ***whisk sb/sth off/away,*** brush quickly and lightly: *~ the flies off.* **2** move with a whisk(2): *The cow ~ed her tail.* **3** take (a person) quickly and suddenly: *They ~ed him off to prison.* **4** = whip(2): *~ eggs.*

whisker /ˈ(h)wɪskər/ *n* **1** (*pl*) hair allowed to grow on the sides of a man's face. **2** one of the long, stiff hairs growing near the mouth of a cat, rat, etc.

whis·key /ˈ(h)wɪski/ *n* [C,U] (*pl* ~s) (portion of) strong alcoholic drink distilled from malted grain (esp barley or rye).

whis·per /ˈ(h)wɪspər/ *vi,vt* **1** speak, say (something), using the breath but no sound from the vocal cords: *~ (a word) to a person.* **2** tell privately or secretly: *It is ~ed that he is heavily in debt.* **3** (of leaves, the wind, etc) make soft sounds: *The wind was ~ing in the trees.* □ *n* [C] **1** whispering sound or speech: *He answered in a ~.* **2** whispered remark: *There are ~s that the firm is going bankrupt.*

whistle /ˈ(h)wɪsəl/ *n* [C] **1** (usually long) tuneful note made by forcing air or steam through a small opening (eg of the lips) or made by the wind; tuneful sound made by some kinds of bird (eg the Eastern meadowlark): *We heard the ~ of a steam-engine.* **2** instrument for producing such sounds: *the referee's ~* (in a football game). ***wet one's whistle,*** (*informal*) have a drink. □ *vi,vt* **1** make a whistle(1) (eg by blowing through rounded lips or by using a whistle (2)): *whistling at the girls.* ➪ wolf-whistle. ***(go) whistle for sth,*** wish for it but not get it: *I owe him $10, but he can (go) ~ for it.* **2** produce a tune in this way: *~ a tune.* **3** make a signal (to) by this means: *He ~d his dog back.* **4** pass swiftly with a whistling sound: *The bullets ~d past our ears.*

white[1] /(h)wait/ *adj* (-r, -st) of the color of fresh snow or common salt: *as ~ as a sheet,* very white. *His hair has turned ~. Her face went ~,* pale.

ˌwhite ˈAnglo-Saxon ˌProtestant (*abbr* **WASP**) US citizen having English Protestant ancestry, belonging to the group with greatest cultural, political, and economic influence.

ˈwhite ant, termite.

ˈwhite·cap *n* foam-crested wave, at sea.

white ˈChristmas, with snow on the ground.

ˌwhite-ˈcollar *adj* nonmanual: *ˌ~-collar ˈjobs/ˈworkers.* ➪ blue-collar.

ˌwhite ˈelephant, useless, troublesome possession.

ˌwhite ˈheat, temperature at which metals become white.

the ˈWhite House, the official residence of the President of the US, Washington, DC.

WHITE HOUSE

ˌwhite ˈlie, small lie considered to be harmless.

ˈwhite man, member of one of the races inhabiting, or from, Europe.

ˌwhite ˈmeat, poultry, veal, pork.

ˈwhite paper, report issued by a government stating its position on an issue.

ˈwhite·wash *n* [U] **(a)** mixture of powdered lime or chalk and water, used for coating walls, ceilings, etc. **(b)** (*fig*) means used to cover or hide errors, faults, etc. □ *vt* **(a)** put whitewash on (a wall, etc). **(b)** (*fig*) try to make (a person, his reputation, etc) appear blameless by covering up his faults, etc.

white[2] /(h)wait/ *n* **1** [U] white color: *dressed in ~.* **2** [C,U] colorless part, eg around the yolk of an egg or the white part of the eyeball.

white·ness /-nɪs/ *n* [U]

Whit·sun·day /ˈ(h)wɪtsənˌdei/ *n* [C] (also **ˌWhit ˈSunday**) 7th Sunday after Easter, the feast of the Pentecost.

whittle /ˈ(h)wɪtəl/ *vt,vi* shape (esp wood) by cutting away pieces from the surface. ***whittle sth away/down,*** **(a)** reduce the size of by cutting away slices, etc. **(b)** (*fig*) reduce gradually: *Our membership is being slowly ~d away/down.*

whiz[1], **whizz** /(h)wɪz/ *vi* (-zz-), *n* [U] (make the) sound of something rushing through the air: *The bullets ~zed by.*

ˈwhiz·gig, ˈwhizz·gig *n* toy which makes a whizzing sound when swung through the air.

ˈwhizz·bang, ˈwiz·bang *n* device (esp a kind of firecracker) which makes a whizzing sound before exploding.

whiz², whizz, wiz /(h)wɪz/ *n* [C] (*informal*) person who is brilliant in some area, esp one who thinks quickly: *He's a real ~ at mathematics.* (used as an *adjective*) *'~ kid,* brilliant young person.

who¹ /hu/ *pron* (used as the subject, and only of persons; object form = **whom** /hum/) **1** *Who is that man/are those men?* **2** (replaceable by *whom* in formal style): *Who(m) did you give it to? Who(m) did you see?* □ *pron* **1** (used in defining or restrictive clauses; *that* sometimes replaces *who*): *This is the man who/These are the men who wanted to see you.* **2** (*Whom* is often replaced by *that* except after a *preposition* and it can often be omitted): *That is the man (whom) I met in Europe last year. That's the man (that) we were speaking about. I know the man you mean.* **3** (used in nondefining clauses, not replaceable by *that*): *My wife, who has been abroad recently, hopes to see you soon.*

WHO² *abbr* = World Health Organization.

whoa /(h)wou, hou/ *int* (used to stop a horse).

who'd /hud/ = who had; who would.

who·ever /huˈevər/ *pron* any person who; the person who: *Whoever says that is wrong.*

whole /houl/ *adj* **1** not injured or damaged; unbroken: *She swallowed the candy ~. He ate the ~ loaf,* all of it. **2** entire; complete: *I waited for her a ~ half hour.* **3** (as an *adjective;* used with a *sing noun,* preceded by *the* or a *possessive*) all that there is of; complete: *I want to know the ~ truth about this matter. The ~ country* (= Everyone in the country) *was anxious for peace.* **4** (as an *adjective;* used with a *pl noun*) not less or fewer than; nothing less than: *It rained for three ~ days.* □ *n* (*sing* with *a, an* or *the*) thing that is complete in itself; all that there is of something: *Four quarters make a ~. He spent the ~ (of the) year in Pakistan.* ***as a whole,*** considered together. ***on the whole,*** having considered all the facts (and decided; for the most part: *On the ~ I agree with you.*

ˌwhole-ˈhearted(ly) *adj, adv* with complete attention, commitment, etc.

ˌwhole ˈnumber, undivided quantity; number without fractions.

ˈwhole-wheat *n* flour with all the parts of the grain.

wholly /ˈhou(l)li/ *adv* completely; entirely: *I wholly agree with you.*

whole·sale¹ /ˈhoulˌseiəl/ *n* [U] (usually as an *adjective*) selling of goods (esp in large quantities) to shopkeepers, for sale to the public. □ *adj, adv* **1** on the wholesale plan: *Our business is ~ only.* **2** (*fig*) on a large scale: *There was a ~ slaughter when the police opened fire.*

whole·sale² /ˈhoulˌseiəl/ *vt,vi* (*pres p* wholesaling /ˈhoulˌseilɪŋ/) sell goods wholesale.

ˈwhole·saler /-ˌseilər/ *n* [C] person who sells wholesale.

whole·some /ˈhoulsəm/ *adj* healthy; suggesting good health: *~ food/exercise; a ~ appearance.*

who'll /hul/ = who shall; who will.

whom /hum/ ⇨ who¹.

whoop /(h)wup, hup/ *n* [C] **1** loud cry: *~s of joy.* **2** gasping sound heard during a fit of coughing. □ *vi,vt* make a loud cry or yell: *to ~ with joy.*

ˈwhoop·ing-cough *n* children's disease with gasping coughs and long, noisy indrawing of breath.

who're /ˈhuər/ = who are.

whore /ˈhɔr/ *n* [C] prostitute.

whorl /(h)wərl/ *n* [C] **1** ring of leaves, petals, etc around a stem of a plant. **2** one turn of a spiral, eg as seen on the shell of a snail or on a fingerprint.

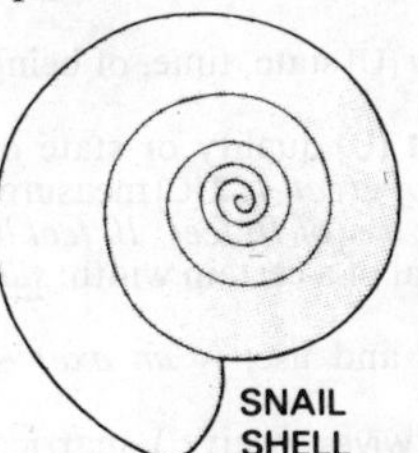

WHORLS

who's /huz/ = who is; who has.

whose /huz/ *possessive pron* (⇨ who¹, which) of whom; of which: *Whose house is that? I wonder ~ house that is. Is that the man ~ house was burned down last week? Members of the Fire Department, ~ work is often dangerous, are paid less than the Police Department.*

who·so·ever /ˌhusouˈevər/ *pron* (*old use*) = whoever.

why /(h)wai/ *adv* for what reason; with what purpose: *Why was he late? Do you know why he was late? That's (the reason) why I left.*

why'd /(h)waid/ = why did; why had; why would.

why's /(h)waiz/ = why is; why does; why has.

WI¹ *postal abbr* = Wisconsin. ⇨ App 6.

W.I.² *abbr* = West Indies.

wick /wɪk/ *n* [C,U] **1** (length of) string through a candle. **2** (strip of) woven material by which oil is drawn up in some cigarette lighters, an oil-lamp, etc.

wicked /ˈwɪkɪd/ *adj* **1** (of a person, his acts) wrong; immoral: *It was ~ of you to hit the old woman.* **2** spiteful; intended to injure: *a ~ blow.* **3** mischievous: *She gave me a ~ look.*

wick·ed·ly *adv*

wick·ed·ness /-nɪs/ *n* [U]

wicker /ˈwɪkər/ *adj* of twigs or canes woven together: *a ~ chair.*

wide /waid/ *adj* (-r, -st) **1** measuring much from side to side or in comparison with length: *a ~ river; a road twelve feet ~.* **2** (*fig*) of great extent; comprehensive: *a man with ~ interests,* interested in many subjects; *a ~ selection of new books; in the ~st sense of the word.* **3** fully opened: *Open your mouth ~.* **4** far from what is aimed at or from a specific point: *Your answer was ~ of the mark,* ⇨ mark¹(5). □ *adv* **1** far from the point aimed at: *The arrow fell ~ of the mark.* **2** fully: *He was ~ awake. The window was ~ open.* **3** over a large area: *travel far and ~.*

ˌwide-aˈwake *adj* (*fig*) alert, watchful: *a ~ -awake young woman,* one who realizes what is going on, etc and is not easily deceived.

wide·ly *adv* **(a)** at distant intervals: *~ly distributed.* **(b)** to a large extent or degree: *~ly different.* **(c)** over a large area; by many persons: *It is ~ly known that...*

ˈwide·spread *adj* (esp) found, distributed, over a large area.

widen /ˈwaidən/ *vt,vi* make or become wide(r).

widow /ˈwɪdou/ *n* [C] woman who has not married again after her husband's death.

wid·ower *n* [C] man who has not married again after his wife's death.

ˈwidow·hood /-ˌhʊd/ *n* [U] state, time, of being a widow.

width /wɪdθ, wɪtθ/ *n* **1** [U] quality or state of being wide: *a highway of great ~.* **2** [C] measurement from side to side: *a ~ of 10 feet; 10 feet in ~.* **3** [C] piece of material of a certain width: *silk of various ~s.*

wield /ˈwiəld/ *vt* have and use: *~ an axe; ~ power.*

wife /waif/ *n* [C] (*pl* wives /waivz/) married woman, esp in relation to her husband: *Smith and his ~; the baker's ~.*

wife·ly *adj* of, like, suitable for, a wife: *~ly duties.*

wig /wɪg/ *n* [C] head covering of false hair (as worn to hide baldness, etc.).

wiggle /ˈwɪgəl/ *vt,vi* (cause to) move with quick, short, side-to-side movements: *The baby was wiggling its toes.* □ *n* [C] wiggling movement.

wig·wam /ˈwɪgˌwam/ *n* [C] hut of animal skins, with a rounded top, as made by American Indians.

wild /ˈwaiəld/ *adj* (-er, -est) **1** (of animals) not tamed or domesticated; living in natural conditions (eg lions, giraffes, wolves); (of plants) growing in natural conditions; not cultivated: *~ flowers/birds.* **2** (of persons, tribes, etc) uncivilized; savage. **3** (of scenery, areas of land, etc) not lived in and perhaps dangerous: *~, mountainous areas.* **4** stormy: *You'd better stay indoors on a ~ night like this.* **5** excited; passionate: *There were sounds of ~ laughter. He was ~ with anger.* ***drive sb wild,*** make him angry, mad. **6** ***be wild about sth/sb,*** (*informal*) have a strong desire for; be madly enthusiastic about: *I'm still ~ about the Beatles.* **7** disorderly; out of control: *a state of ~ confusion; settle down after a ~ youth.* ***run wild,*** be without control or discipline: *They allow their children to run ~.* **8** done or said without thought or consideration: *a ~ guess.* □ *adv* in a wild manner: *shoot ~.*

ˌwild ˈboar, wild pig with tusks.

ˈwild·cat *n* **(a)** bobcat. **(b)** (*fig*) uncontrolled, hot-tempered woman. □ *adj* (of a strike) sudden and unofficial: *a ˌ~cat ˈstrike.*

ˈwild·fire *n* (in) ***spread like wildfire,*** (of rumors, etc) very fast.

ˈwild·fowl *n pl* game birds.

ˌwild-ˈgoose chase, hopeless, foolish search, etc.

ˈwild·life *n* wild animals, birds, insects, etc collectively.

wild·ly *adv* in a wild manner; *rush about ~ly; a ~ly* (= greatly) *exaggerated story.*

wild·ness /-nɪs/ *n* [U]

the wilds, uncultivated (and often uninhabited) areas: *the ~s of Africa.*

ˌWild ˈWest, western US in lawless and dangerous times of early settlement.

wil·der·ness /ˈwɪldərnɪs/ *n* [C] (rarely *pl*) **1** wild uncultivated land. **2** empty expanse: *a ~ of waters.*

wile /ˈwaiəl/ *n* [C] (usually *pl*) trick: *the ~s of the Devil.* □ *vt* (*pres p* wiling /ˈwailɪŋ/) (rare) **1** trick: *~ him away.* **2** (used for *while*): *wiling away the time.*

wil·ful *adj* = willful.

will¹ /wɪl/ *anomalous finite* (often shortened to 'll /(ə)l/ in speech; *negative* will not or won't /wount/; *pt conditional* would /wəd; *strong form* wʊd/ often shortened to 'd in speech; *negative* would not or wouldn't /ˈwʊdənt/) **1** (used to make the future tense): *If today is Monday, tomorrow ~ be Tuesday. You'll be in time if you hurry. I wonder whether it ~ be ready. I wondered whether it would be ready.* **2** (used with the first person (*I, we*) to express willingness, consent, an offer or a promise): *All right, I'll come. We won't do it again. We said we would help them.* **3** (used in questions, making requests, etc and often equivalent to *please*): *Will you come in? Pass the salt, ~ you?* Please pass the salt. **4** (used to show insistence or inevitability; always stressed): *He ˈ~ have his own way,* insists on this. *Accidents ˈ~ happen,* They are to be expected from time to time. *That's just what you ˈwould say,* what you might be expected to say. **5** (used in the negative to show refusal): *He won't/wouldn't help me.* **6** (used to show that something happens from time to time, that a person has the habit, that something is natural or to be expected): *He'll sit there hour after hour looking at the traffic go by.* **7** (used to show probability or likelihood): *This'll be the book you're looking for, I think.* **8** (*Would* is used with *I, we* to form conditional statements expressing the speaker's will or intention): *We would have come if it hadn't rained.*

will² /wɪl/ *vt* (*pt* would, no other forms used) (*old use*) **1** wish: *Let him do what he ~.* **2** (the subject *I* is often omitted) used to express wishes: *Would (that) it were otherwise!* **3** choose; desire: *the place where he would be.*

ˈwould-be *adj* (used to show what is desired, aspired to, or intended): *ˌwould-be ˈauthors.*

will³ /wɪl/ *vt,vi* (*pt,pp* ~ed) **1** make use of one's mental powers in an attempt to do or get something: *We cannot achieve success merely by ~ing it.* **2** use the will⁴(1): *Willing and wishing are not the same thing.* **3** intend unconditionally: *It's as if fate ~ed us to be happy.* **4** influence, control or compel, by exercising the will: *Can you ~ yourself to keep awake?* **5** leave (property, etc) (to a person) by means of a will⁴(6): *He ~ed most of his money to charities.*

will⁴ /wɪl/ *n* **1** ***the will,*** mental power by which a person can direct his thoughts and actions, and influence those of others: *the freedom of the ~.* **2** [C,U] (also **ˈwill-power**) control exercised over oneself, one's desires, etc: *He has no ~ of his own,* is easily influenced by others. *He has a strong/weak ~.* **3** (*sing* only) determination;

desire or purpose: *The ~ to live helps a patient to recover.* ***of one's own free will,*** without being required or compelled: *You did it of your own free ~.* **4** (*sing* with *a, an*) energy; enthusiasm: *work with a ~.* **5** [U] (used with a possessive) that which is desired or determined: *He has always had his ~* (or, *informal, his own way*). ⇨ illwill. **6** [C] (also ***last will and testament***) statement of how a person's property is to be owned after death.

will·ful /ˈwɪlfəl/ *adj* **1** (of a person) obstinate; determined to have one's own way: *a ~ child.* **2** intentional; for which compulsion, ignorance, or accident is no excuse: *~ murder/negligence.*

will·fully, wil·fully /-fəli/ *adv*

will·ful·ness, wil·ful·ness /-nɪs/ *n* [U]

will·ing /ˈwɪlɪŋ/ *adj* **1** ready, agreeing, to help, to do what is needed, asked, etc: *~ workers.* **2** done, given, etc quickly, without hesitation: *~ obedience.*

will·ing·ly *adv*

will·ing·ness /-nɪs/ *n* [U]: *show ~ness to help.*

wil·low /ˈwɪlou/ *n* [C] kinds of tree or shrub with thin, easily bent branches; [U] twigs of this tree used for weaving into baskets; its wood.

wilt /wɪlt/ *vi,vt* **1** (of plants, flowers) (cause to) droop, lose freshness (through dryness). **2** (*fig*) (of persons) lose energy: *~ in the hot weather.*

wily /ˈwaili/ *adj* (-ier, -iest) = cunning (the usual word).

win /wɪn/ *vt,vi* (*pt,pp* won /wən/) (-nn-) **1** get by means of hard work, perseverance, struggle, competition, gambling, etc: *win a race/a battle/a scholarship/second prize/fame and fortune.* ***win hands down,*** (*informal*) succeed easily. **2** persuade (a person) by argument; gain the favor of: *We won him over to our view.* **3** reach by effort: *win the summit/the shore.* □ *n* [C] success in a game, competition, etc: *Our team has had five wins this summer.*

win·ner *n* [C] person, animal, thing, that wins.

win·ning *adj* **(a)** that wins: *the winning horse.* **(b)** producing confidence and friendship: *a winning smile.*

win·nings *n pl* money won in betting, gambling, etc.

wince /wɪns/ *vt* show bodily or mental pain or distress (by a movement, sound or by loss of control): *He ~d at the insult.* □ *n* [C] wincing movement: *without a ~.*

winch /wɪntʃ/ *n* [C] machine for hoisting or pulling heavy objects. □ *vt* move by using a winch.

wind[1] /wɪnd/ *n* **1** [C,U] (often *sing* with *the;* with *much, little,* etc when the reference is to degree or force; with *a, an* or in *pl* when the reference is to the kind of wind) air in motion as the result of natural forces: *a north ~,* blowing from the north. *The ~ blew my hat off.* ***see/find out how the wind blows,*** what people are thinking, what is likely to happen. ***take the wind out of sb's sails,*** **(a)** prevent him from doing or saying something by doing it or saying it before him. **(b)** take away his advantage suddenly. **2** (*pl*) the cardinal points: *The house stands on a hilltop, exposed to the four ~s.* **3** [U] breath needed for running or continuous exercise: *The runner soon lost his ~,* became out of breath. ⇨ second wind. **4** [U] scent carried by the wind (showing where something is). ***get wind of,*** (*fig*) hear a rumor of, begin to suspect. **5** [U] empty words; meaningless or useless talk: *Don't listen to the politicians—they're all ~.* **6** [U] gas formed in the bowels and causing discomfort: *The baby is suffering from ~.* ***break wind,*** expel wind from the bowels. **7** (*sing* with *the*) orchestral wind instruments: *the ˈwood~,* eg flutes, oboes. ⇨ wood.

ˈwind·bag *n* (*informal*) person who talks a lot but says nothing important.

ˈwind·break *n* [C] hedge, fence, line of trees, etc to give protection from the wind.

ˈwind·breaker *n* [C] jacket designed to give protection against the wind.

ˈwind·fall *n* [C] **(a)** fruit (eg an apple) blown off a tree by the wind. **(b)** (*fig*) unexpected piece of good fortune, esp money coming to somebody.

wind·ily /ˈwɪndəli/ *adv*

windi·ness /ˈwɪndinɪs/ *n* [U]

ˈwind instrument, musical instrument in which sound is produced by a current of air (eg an organ, a flute, a cornet).

wind·less *adj* without wind: *a ~less day.*

ˈwind·mill *n* [C] mill worked by the action of the wind on sails(2) which revolve.

ˈwind·pipe *n* passage for air from the throat to the lungs. ⇨ illus at respiratory.

ˈwind·shield *n* [C] pane of glass at the front of a car, etc.

ˈwind·shield ˌwiper, apparatus for wiping rain from a windshield.

ˈwind·swept *adj* exposed to (and blown bare by) strong winds: *a ˌ~swept ˈhillside.*

ˈwind tunnel, structure through which air is forced (at controlled speeds) to study its effects on (models of) aircraft, etc.

wind·ward /-wərd/ *adj, adv, n* [U] (on or to the) side (esp of a ship) facing the wind (contrasted with *leeward*).

windy /ˈwɪndi/ *adj* (-ier, -iest) with a lot of wind: *a ~y day; ~y weather.*

wind[2] /wɪnd/ *vt* (from wind[1]) (*pt,pp* ~ed /ˈwɪndɪd/) **1** know the presence of by smell: *The hounds ~ed the fox.* **2** exhaust the wind(3) of: *He was quite ~ed by the long climb/by running to catch the bus.*

wind[3] /waind/ *vi,vt* (*pt,pp* wound /waund/) **1** go, (cause to) move, in a curving, spiral, or twisting manner: *The river ~s (its way) to the sea.* **2** twist (string, thread, etc) into a ball, or around or onto something: *~ (up) wool into a ball.* **3** fold or wrap closely (around): *~ a shawl around a baby. She wound her arms around the child.* **4** turn (a handle, eg of a winch); raise (something) by doing this: *~ a handle; ~ up a bucket from a well.* **5** tighten the spring of (a watch or clock), raise the weights that operate a clock: *If you forget to ~ (up) your watch it will stop.* **6** ***be wound up (to),*** be (emotionally) excited: *He was wound up to a high pitch of excitement.* ⇨ unwind(2). **7** ***wind (sth) up,*** come or bring to an end: *It's time for him to ~ up his speech. They wound up the evening by singing some folk songs.* □ *n* [C] single turn in winding string, winding up a clock, etc.

wind·lass /ˈwɪndləs/ *n* [C] machine for pulling or lifting things (eg water from a well) by means of a rope or chain which is wound around an axle.

win·dow /ˈwɪndoʊ/ *n* [C] opening (usually covered with glass) in a wall or roof of a building, the side of a ship, car, etc to let in light and air: *look out of the ~; break a ~.*

ˈwindow box, box fixed to a window sill for plants.

ˈwindow dresser, person whose profession is designing shop window displays.

ˈwindow dressing, (esp) (*fig*) giving a deliberately false or exaggerated image to hide the unpleasant truth.

ˈwindow·pane *n* [C] pane of glass for or in a window.

ˈwindow-shopping *n* [U] looking at goods displayed in shop windows.

ˈwindow sill, ⇨ sill.

windy /ˈwɪndi/ ⇨ wind[1].

wine /waɪn/ *n* **1** [U] alcoholic drink made from the fermented juice of grapes (and other fruit, vegetables): *a bottle/glass of ~.* **2** (*pl*) different kinds of wine: *French ~s.* □ *vt* (esp) ***wine and dine sb,*** entertain to a meal: *We were ~d and dined at the firm's expense.*

ˈwine·glass *n* [C] glass for drinking wine.

wing /wɪŋ/ *n* [C] **1** either of the two organs of a bird by which it flies; one of the similar organs of an insect; one of the surfaces by which an aircraft is supported in the air. ⇨ illus at aircraft, bird. ***clip a person's wings,*** limit his movements, power, expenditure, etc. ***take sb under one's wing,*** take him under one's protection; give him care and guidance. **2** part of a building, etc which projects or is extended from one of its sides: *add a new ~ to a hospital.* **3** those members of a political party holding more extreme views than those of the majority: *the left/right ~.* **4** (*pl*) unseen areas to the right and left of the stage of a theater. **5** ***on the wing,*** in flight. ***take wing,*** start flying. **6** something like a wing in appearance or position, eg certain types of screw, seeds (esp of the maple and sycamore). □ *vt,vi* **1** fly: *The planes ~ed (their way) over the Rockies.* **2** injure (a bird) in flight. **3** (*informal*) injure (a person) in the arm.

ˈwing chair, one with angled extensions on a high back.

wing ˈcollar, upright collar with corners turned down.

ˈwing span/spread, measurement across wings when extended.

ˈwing tip, outer edge of a wing.

wink /wɪŋk/ *vi,vt* **1** ***wink (at),*** close and open (one eye); *She ~ed at me,* eg as a private signal of some kind. **2** (of a star, light, etc) shine or flash at very short intervals: *A lighthouse was ~ing in the far distance.* □ *n* [C] **1** act of winking, esp as a signal or hint. **2** very short time: *I didn't sleep a ~/didn't have a ~ of sleep,* didn't sleep at all. ***have forty winks,*** a short sleep (esp during the day).

winkle /ˈwɪŋkəl/ *n* [C] sea snail used as food. □ *vt* extract, force or pull *out.*

win·ner, win·ning ⇨ win.

win·now /ˈwɪnoʊ/ *vt* use a stream of air to separate dry outer coverings from (grain).

win·some /ˈwɪnsəm/ *adj* (*formal*) (of a person, his appearance) attractive; pleasing.

win·ter /ˈwɪntər/ *n* [C] season between autumn and spring (November or December to February in the northern hemisphere): *a cold ~; have snow in ~; ~ sports,* eg ice skating, skiing. □ *vi* pass the winter: *~ in the south.*

win·tery, win·try /ˈwɪntri/ *adj* of or like winter: *a ~y sky/day.*

wipe[1] /waɪp/ *n* [C] **1** act of wiping. **2** something used for wiping (eg for cleaning wounds).

wipe[2] /waɪp/ *vt,vi* **1** clean or dry (something) by rubbing with a cloth, paper, the hands, etc: *~ one's hands on a towel; ~ plates dry.* **2** (special uses with *adverbial particles* and *prepositions*): ***wipe sth away,*** remove (eg tears) by wiping. ***wipe sth off,*** **(a)** remove by wiping: *~ off a drawing from the blackboard.* **(b)** get rid of: *~ off a debt.*

wipe sb/sth out, (*sl*) murder him. ***wipe sth out,*** **(a)** clean the inside of: *~ out a jug.* **(b)** get rid of; remove: *~ out an insult* (esp by revenge). **(c)** destroy completely: *a disease that almost ~d out the population.*

wipe sth up, take up (liquid, etc) by wiping: *~ up spilled milk; ~ up a mess.*

wire /ˈwaɪər/ *n* **1** [C,U] (piece or length of) metal in the form of a thread: *ˈtelephone ~(s); ~ netting,* made by weaving wire (used for fences, fruit cages, etc). ⇨ barbed wire. **2** [C] (*informal*) = telegram: *send off a ~.* □ *vt,vi* **1** fasten with wire: *~ two things together.* **2** install electrical circuits (in a building): *Has the house been ~d for electricity yet?* **3** (*informal*) = telegraph: *He ~d me that he would be delayed.*

ˈwire cutters, tool for cutting wire.

ˈwire-haired *adj* with stiff, wiry hair.

wir·ing *n* [U] (esp) system of wires for electric current.

wiry *adj* (-ier, -iest) **(a)** like wire. **(b)** (of persons) lean and with strong sinews.

wis·dom /ˈwɪzdəm/ *n* [U] **1** quality of being wise. **2** wise thoughts, sayings, etc: *the ~ of the ancients/our ancestors.*

ˈwisdom-tooth *n* [C] (*pl* ~teeth) back tooth, usually coming through after 20 years of age. ⇨ illus at mouth.

wise /waɪz/ *adj* (-r, -st) having or showing experience, knowledge, good judgment, etc: *~ men/acts. He was ~ enough not to drive when he was feeling ill.* ***be none the wiser,*** be no better informed: *After the lecture he was none the ~r,* knew no more than before.

wise·ly *adv*

wise·crack /ˈwaɪzˌkræk/ *n* [C] (*sl*) sarcastic comment. □ *vi* make sarcastic remarks.

wish /wɪʃ/ *vt,vi* **1** have a desire that is possible or impossible: *I ~ I knew what was happening. I ~ I were rich.* **2** have as a desire: *She ~ed herself home* (= wished that she was at home) *again.* **3** ***wish sb well/ill,*** hope that he may have good/ill fortune, etc: *He ~es me well. I ~ nobody ill.* **4** say that one hopes for: *I ~ you a pleasant journey.* **5** express as a greeting: *~ him good morning/goodbye.* **6** ***wish for,*** have a strong desire for (esp something unlikely to be obtained or achieved, or that can be obtained only by good fortune or in exceptional circumstances): *How he ~ed for an opportunity to go abroad! What more can you ~ for?* **7** express a desire: *Doing is better than ~ing.* **8** ***wish sb/sth on sb,*** (*informal*) transfer to a person (esp with the idea of getting rid of him or it): *I wouldn't ~ my father-in-law on anyone,* (suggesting that he is unpleasant). □ *n* **1** [C,U] desire; longing: *He ignored his father's ~es.* **2** [C] that which is wished for: *She got her ~.*

wish·ful /-fəl/ having or expressing a wish; desiring. ***wishful thinking,*** thinking or believing that something is true because one wishes it were true.

wish·fully /-fəli/ *adv*

wisp /wɪsp/ *n* [C] small bunch, amount: *a ~ of straw/hair/smoke.*

wispy *adj* (-ier, -iest) small, vague, slight.

wist·ful /ˈwɪstfəl/ *adj* sad and longing; having, showing disappointment: *a ~ expression.*

wist·fully /-fəli/ *adv* in a wistful manner: *She looked ~ly at the photographs of herself when she was young and beautiful.*

wit /wɪt/ *n* **1** (*sing* or *pl*) intelligence; understanding; quickness of mind: *He hadn't the wits/hadn't wit enough to realize what to do in the emergency.* ***at one's wit's end,*** not knowing what to do or say because of worry, etc. ⇨ also scare. ***have/keep one's wits about one,*** be alert and ready to act. ***live by one's wits,*** live by clever, not always honest, methods. **2** [U] clever and humorous expression of ideas; liveliness of spirit: *His writings sparkle with wit.* **3** [C] person noted for his wit(2).

wit·less /-lɪs/ *adj* stupid.

wit·ti·cism /ˈwɪtəˌsɪzəm/ *n* [C] witty remark.

wit·tily /-əli/ *adv*

witty *adj* (-ier, -iest) full of humor: *a witty girl/remark.*

witch /wɪtʃ/ *n* [C] **1** woman said to use magic, esp for evil purposes. **2** (*fig*) fascinating or persuasive woman.

ˈwitch·craft *n* [U] use of magic.

ˈwitch doctor, man believed to be able to cure disease by magic.

ˈwitch hunt, (*mod use, informal*) search and persecution (eg of persons said to be disloyal to the state).

with /wɪð, wɪθ/ *prep* **1** (equivalent to constructions with *have*) having; carrying; characterized by: *a coat ~ two pockets; a girl ~ blue eyes.* **2** (used to show what is used for filling, covering, etc): *Fill the box ~ sand. The hills were covered ~ snow.* **3** (used to show the means or method): *write ~ a pen; carry it ~ both hands; see it ~ your own eyes; ~ your help.* **4** (used to show accompaniment or relationship): *live ~ your parents; put one thing ~ others. Is there anyone ~ you or are you alone?* ***in with,*** mixed up with: *She's in ~ the wrong crowd,* eg of a girl whose companions are a bad influence. **5** (used to show antagonism, opposition): *fight/argue/struggle/quarrel ~ them.* ***fall out with,*** ⇨ fall²(15). ***have it out with sb,*** ⇨ have²(14). **6** (used to show cause) because of; owing to: *trembling ~ fear; shaking ~ cold.* **7** (used to show manner): *do it ~ an effort/~ pleasure; standing ~ his hands in his pockets; fight ~ courage,* courageously. **8** in the same way or direction as; at the same time as: *A tree's shadow moves ~ the sun. Do you rise ~ the sun,* ie at dawn? **9** (used to show care, charge or possession): *Leave the child ~* (= in the care of) *its aunt. I have no money ~ me.* **10** in regard to; concerning: *be patient ~ them; sympathize ~ her. What do you want ~ me? We can't do anything/can do nothing ~ him,* cannot influence, control, make use of, him. **11** (used to show separation): *He has broken ~ his best friend.* **12** (used to show agreement, harmony): *He who is not ~ me* (= on my side) *is against me. I (dis)agree ~ you.* ***be/get/ˈwith it,*** (*sl*) become aware of what is popular and up to date: (as an *adjective*) *ˈ~-it clothes.* **13** in spite of: *With all her faults he still liked her.*

with·draw /wɪðˈdrɔ, wɪθ-/ *vt,vi* (*pt* -drew /-ˈdru/, *pp* -drawn /-ˈdrɔn/) **1** pull or draw back; take out or away: *~ money from the bank. The workers threatened to ~ their labor,* to go on strike. **2** take back (a statement, an accusation, an offer): *He refused to ~ (the remark),* eg after calling a person a liar. **3** (cause to) move back or away: *~ troops from an exposed position; ~ from society.*

with·drawal /-əl/ *n* [U] withdrawing or being withdrawn; [C] instance of this.

with·drawn *adj* (of persons, their looks) shy; reserved and quiet.

wither /ˈwɪðər/ *vt,vi* **1** (cause to) become dry, faded or dead: *The hot summer ~ed (up) the grass. Her hopes ~ed (away).* **2** cause (a person) to be covered with shame or confusion: *She gave him a ~ing look.*

wither·ing·ly /ˈwɪðərɪŋli/ *adv*

with·ers /ˈwɪðərz/ *n pl* highest part of the back of a horse, etc between the shoulder blades.

with·hold /wɪðˈhould, wɪθ-/ *vt* (*pt,pp* -held /-ˈheld/) keep back; refuse to give: *He tried to ~ the truth from us. I shall ~ my consent.*

with·in /wɪðˈɪn/ *prep* inside; not beyond: *remain ~ call/reach,* near by; *live ~ one's income,* not spend more than one earns; *~ an hour,* in less than an hour: *~ a mile of the station.*

with·out /wɪðˈaut/ *prep* **1** not having; not with; free from: *You can't buy things ~ money. He was working ~ any hope of reward.* ***without doubt,*** admittedly; certainly. ***without fail,*** certainly. ***do without,*** ⇨ do²(13). **2** (uses before gerunds): *He can't speak German ~ making mistakes,* he speaks German incorrectly. ***it/that goes without saying,*** is too obvious, too well known, etc to need saying. □ *adv* (*old use*) to, at, or on, the outside.

with·stand /wɪðˈstænd, wɪθ-/ *vt* (*pt, pp* -stood /-ˈstʊd/) resist, hold out against (pressure, attack): *~ a siege; shoes that will ~ hard wear.*

wit·less /ˈwɪtlɪs/ *adj* ⇨ wit.

wit·ness /ˈwɪtnɪs/ *n* **1** [C] (often **ˈeye-witness**) person who was actually present at an event and should, for this reason, be able to describe it; person who gives evidence under oath in a law court. **2** [U] evidence; testimony; what is said about a person, an event, etc: *give ~ on* *behalf of an accused person at his trial.* ***bear witness to sth,*** be evidence of: *acts that bear ~ to her courage.* **3** [C] person who adds his own signature to a document to testify that another person's signature on it is genuine. **4** [C] person or thing that is a sign or proof: *My clothes are a ~ to my poverty.* □ *vt,vi* **1** be present at and see: *~ an accident.* **2** give evidence (in a law court): ~ (= testify) *to the truth of a statement.* **3** be a witness(3): *~ a signature.* **4** give evidence of; show: *Her pale face ~ed the pain she felt.*

ˈwitness stand, enclosure in a law court in which a witness gives evidence.

wit·ti·cism /ˈwɪtəˌsɪzəm/ ⇨ wit.

wit·ting·ly /ˈwɪtɪŋli/ *adv* knowingly; intentionally.

wives /waivz/ *pl* of wife.

wiz /wɪz/ *n* [C] **1** (*sl*) = wizard(2). **2** = whiz[2].

wiz·ard /ˈwɪzərd/ *n* [C] **1** magician. **2** person with amazing abilities: *a financial ~*, person able to make money with amazing ease.

wiz·bang /ˈwɪzˌbæŋ/ ⇨ whiz[1].

wiz·ened /ˈwɪzənd/ *adj* dried up, shriveled: *a ~ tree/apple.*

wk. *abbr* = week.

wobble /ˈwabəl/ *vi,vt* **1** (cause to) move unsteadily from side to side: *Jelly ~s.* **2** (*fig*) be uncertain (in opinions, in making decisions, etc): *I ~d between two opinions.*

wob·bly /ˈwabli/ *adj* (-ier, -iest) not firm or steady: *He's still a little wobbly on his legs after his long illness.*

woe /wou/ *n* (*poet*) **1** [U] sorrow; grief; distress: *a tale of woe.* **2** (*pl*) causes of woe; troubles: *poverty, illness and other woes.*

woe·ful /-fəl/ *adj* sorrowful; causing woe: *~ful ignorance.*

woe·fully /-fəli/ *adv*

wok /wɔk/ *n* [C] curved metal pan for quick frying in Chinese cooking.

woke, woken *pt,pp* of wake[1].

wolf /wʊlf/ *n* [C] (*pl* wolves /wʊlvz/) wild, flesh-eating animal of the dog family. ***cry wolf,*** raise false alarms. □ *vt* eat quickly and greedily: *~ down one's dinner.*

ˈwolf whistle, whistle or other sound (eg made by a man in the street) expressing admiration of a woman's beauty.

ˈwolf-whistle *vi* make the sound of a wolf whistle.

woman /ˈwʊmən/ *n* (*pl* women /ˈwɪmen, -mɪn/) **1** adult female human being: *men, women and children; a single* (= unmarried) *~; a ~ of the world,* one with experience of society, not young and innocent. **2** (used as an *adjective*): *a ~ driver/doctor.* **3** (without *a, an* or *the*) the female sex; any woman: *Woman is as capable as man.* **4** (*sing* with *the*) feminine emotions: *There is something of the ~ in his character.*

ˈwoman·hood /-ˌhʊd/ *n* **(a)** (*collect*) women in general. **(b)** the state of being a woman: *She had now grown to/reached ~hood.*

woman·ize /-ˌnaiz/ *vi* try to get a woman's friendship (esp for casual sexual relationships).

ˌwoman·ˈkind *n* women in general.

women·folk /ˈwɪmənˌfouk/ *n pl* women, esp of one's own family.

ˌwomen's ˈlib, (*informal*) (short for women's liberation) movement in support of equal rights for women.

womb /wum/ *n* [C] organ in a female mammal in which offspring is carried and nourished while developing before birth.

wom·bat /ˈwamˌbæt/ *n* [C] Australian animal (looking like a small bear), the female of which has a pouch for its young.

won *pt,pp* of win.

won·der /ˈwəndər/ *n* **1** [U] feeling caused by something unusual, surprising or that cannot be explained; surprise combined with admiration, etc: *They were filled with ~.* ***no/little/small wonder,*** it is not surprising: *No ~ you were so late.* **2** [C] thing or event that causes such feeling: *Walking on the moon is one of the ~s of our times.* ***work wonders,*** work with remarkable results. ***It is a wonder (that),*** it is surprising that: *It's a ~ (that) you didn't lose your way in the dark.* □ *vi,vt* **1** be filled with wonder(1); feel surprised: *I don't ~ at her refusing to marry him.* **2** feel curiosity; think: *I was ~ing about that. I was just ~ing. I ~ who he is.*

won·der·ful /-fəl/ *adj* causing wonder; surprising: *We've had ~ful weather.*

won·der·fully /-f(ə)li/ *adv*

ˈwon·der·land *n* **(a)** fairyland. **(b)** country that is remarkable in some way (eg because of many natural resources).

won·der·ment *n* [U] (*formal*) = surprise.

wont /wɔnt/ *n* (*sing* only) (*dated*) what a person is accustomed to doing: *He went to bed much earlier than was his ~,* than he usually did.

won't /wount/ = will not.

woo /wu/ *vt* (*pt,pp* wooed) **1** (*old use*) = court[2](1). **2** (*mod use*) try to win (fame, success): *woo voters.*

wooer /ˈwuər/ *n* [C] person who woos.

wood /wʊd/ *n* **1** [U] (with *a, an,* and *pl* only when meaning *kind, sort, variety*) hard solid substance of a tree below the bark: *Tables are usually made of ~. Put some more ~ on the fire. Teak is a hard (kind of) ~ and pine is a soft (kind of) ~.* **2** [C] (often *pl*) area of land covered with growing trees (not so extensive as a forest): *a house in the middle of a ~; go for a walk in the ~(s).* ***out of the woods,*** (*fig*) free from troubles or difficulties: *We're not yet out of the ~s,* still have difficulties to face. **3** (*sing* with *the*) ***in/from the wood,*** the cask or barrel: *wine in the ~.*

wood·chuck *n* burrowing North-American animal of the squirrel family, with grayish-brown or reddish-brown fur.

ˈwood·cut *n* [C] print from a design, drawing, picture, etc cut on a block of wood.

ˈwood·cutter *n* [C] man who cuts down trees.

wooded *adj* covered with trees: *a thickly ~ed country.*

wooden /ˈwʊdn/ *adj* **(a)** made of wood: *a ~en leg.* **(b)** stiff, clumsy, awkward (as if made of wood): *a ~en* (= inexpressive) *smile.*

wood·land /ˈwʊdlənd/ land covered with trees.

woods·man, wood·man /ˈwʊd(z)mən/ (*pl* ~(s)men /-men/) forester; woodcutter.

ˈwood·pecker *n* [C] kind of bird that clings to

the bark of trees and which taps or pecks it to find insects.

ˈ**wood·wind** *n* (often *pl*) wind instruments made of wood. ⇨ illus at brass.

ˈ**wood·work** *n* [U] **(a)** things made of wood, esp parts of a building. **(b)** carpentry.

woody *adj* (-ier, -iest) **(a)** wooded: *a ~y hillside.* **(b)** of or like wood: *the ~y stems of a plant.*

wooer *n* [C] ⇨ woo.

woof[1] /wʊf/ *n* [C] cry made by a dog.

woofer *n* [C] low frequency speaker on a high-fidelity player.

woof[2] /wuf, wʊf/ *n* [C] = weft.

wool /wʊl/ *n* [U] **1** soft hair of sheep, goats and some other animals; thread, yarn, cloth, clothing, made from this. ***pull the wool over sb's eyes,*** deceive or trick him. **2** material similar in appearance or texture to wool: *steel~,* fine steel pads for polishing, etc.

wool·en /ˈwʊlən/ *adj* made of wool: *~en cloth/blankets.*

wool·ens *n pl* woolen cloth, clothes, blankets, etc.

woolly, wooly /ˈwʊli/ *adj* (-ier, -iest) **(a)** covered with, made of, looking like, wool: *~ly hair; a ~ly coat.* **(b)** (*fig*) (of the mind, ideas, decisions) confused; not clear.

woozy /ˈwuzi/ *adj* (*informal*) dizzy, dazed: *~ from drinking too much wine.*

word /wərd/ *n* **1** [C] sound or combination of sounds (or the written or printed symbols) forming a unit of the grammar or vocabulary of a language: *When we speak we put our thoughts into ~s. I have no ~s to* (= cannot adequately) *express my gratitude.* ***a play on words,*** a pun. ***word for word,*** literally. ***in a/one word,*** briefly; to sum up. ***by word of mouth,*** in spoken, not written, words. **2** [C] something said; remark or statement: *He didn't say a ~ about it. I don't believe a ~ of the story.* ***eat one's words,*** admit that one was wrong. ***have a word with sb,*** speak to him. ***have words with sb,*** quarrel. ***have the last word,*** make the final remark in an argument. ***put words into sb's mouth,*** **(a)** tell him what to say. **(b)** suggest falsely that he has said something. ***say a few words,*** make a short speech. ***say/put in a good word (for sb),*** speak on his behalf (to support or defend). ***say the word,*** give the order. ***take the words out of sb's mouth,*** say what he was about to say. ***the last word (in sth),*** the latest, most up-to-date, etc in: *Our tours of Greece are the last ~ in comfort and convenience.* **3** (*sing*, without *the*) news; information: *Please send me ~ of your safe arrival. Word came that I was wanted at the office.* **4** (*sing* only) promise; assurance. ***be as good as one's word,*** do what one promises. ***give sb one's word (that...),*** promise: *The goods will arrive on time—I give you my ~.* ***take sb's word for it,*** believe what he says: *I have no proof, but you may take my ~ for it.* ***take sb at his word,*** believe that he is telling the truth, that he will keep a promise. **5** (*sing* only) command; order; spoken signal: *The officer gave the ~ to fire. His ~ is law,* His orders must be obeyed. ⇨ password. **6 the Word,** (in the Christian religion) the Scriptures, esp the Gospel. □ *vt* express in words: *a well-~ed letter.*

ˈ**word division,** dividing of the spelling of a word, eg at the end of a line of writing. (*Note:* correct places for word division are shown by (·) in this dictionary.)

word·ing *n* (*sing* only) way in which something is expressed; choice of words to express meaning: *A different ~ing might make the meaning clearer.*

ˌ**word** ˈ**processing,** electronic system of storing and editing the text of letters, reports, etc.

ˌ**word** ˈ**processor,** electronic equipment for word processing.

wordy *adj* (-ier, -iest) using, expressed in, a large number of words, esp unnecessary words: *a ~y telegram.*

wore *pt* of wear[2].

work[1] /wərk/ *n* **1** [U] use of bodily or mental powers with the purpose of doing or making something (esp contrasted with play or recreation): *Are you fond of hard ~? The ~ of building the new garage took six months. It was terribly hard ~ getting to the top of the mountain. This is the ~ of an enemy,* An enemy has done this. ***set/get to work (on sth/to do sth),*** begin; make a start. ***at work (on sth),*** busy or occupied with. ***all in a day's work,*** (used to show that something is) normal; what is usual or to be expected. **2** [U] what a person does to earn a living; employment: *What time do you get to (your) ~ every day? The men were on their way to ~.* ***in/out of work,*** having/not having employment. ***at work,*** at one's place of employment: *She's at ~ now, but she'll be back at six.* **3** [U] something to be done, not necessarily connected with a trade or occupation, not necessarily for payment: *I always find plenty of ~ that needs doing in my garden.* **4** [U] things needed or used for work: *She took her ~* (eg her sewing materials) *into the garden.* **5** [U] that which is produced by work: *The ~ of famous sculptors may be seen in museums.* ⇨ stonework, woodwork. **6** (*pl;* also *sing* with *a*) product of the intellect or the imagination: *the ~s of Hemingway; the ~s of Aaron Copland.* **7** [U] use of energy supplied by electricity, etc: *Many machines now do the ~ of men.* **8** (*pl*, and used with a *pl verb*) moving parts of a machine: *the ~s of a clock or watch. There's something wrong with the ~s.* **9** (*pl* in form but often treated as a *sing noun*) building(s) where industrial or manufacturing processes are carried on: *a* ˈ*gas~s; an* ˈ*iron~s; a water~s.*

ˌ**work of** ˈ**art,** (excellent) painting, piece of sculpture, etc.

ˈ**work·bench** *n* [C] table at which a carpenter, craftsman, hobbyist, etc, does work.

ˈ**work·book** *n* [C] book with outlines of a subject of study, with questions to be answered (in empty spaces provided), for notes, etc.

ˈ**work·day** *n* [C] day which is not a Sunday or a holiday.

ˈ**work force,** total number of men working in a factory, etc.

ˈ**work·man** /-mən/ *n* [C] (*pl* ~men /-men/) **(a)** man who earns a living by physical labor or at machines, etc. **(b)** person who works in a specified way: *a skilled ~man.*

ˈwork·man·like *adj* characteristic of a good workman.

ˈwork·man·ship /-mənʃɪp/ *n* quality as seen in something made: *articles of poor/excellent ~manship.*

ˈwork·room *n* [C] room in which work is done.

ˈwork·shop *n* [C] room or building in which things (esp machines) are made or repaired.

ˈwork-shy *adj* not liking to work; lazy.

ˈwork-study *n* study of how work may be done efficiently and economically.

ˈwork·table *n* [C] (esp) table with drawers for sewing materials, etc.

work² /wərk/ *vi,vt* (*pt,pp* ~ed) ⇨ wrought. (For special uses with *adverbial particles* and *prepositions,* ⇨ 9 below.) **1** do work; engage in physical or mental activity: *I've been ~ing hard all day. The men in this factory ~ 40 hours a week.* **2** (of a machine, apparatus, bodily organ, plan, method, etc) do what it is designed to do; have the desired result: *The elevator/telephone is not ~ing. This machine ~s by electricity. My brain doesn't seem to be ~ing well today. Will this new plan/method ~?* **3** cause to work; set in motion: *He ~s his wife/himself too hard. It ~s by electricity.* **4** produce or obtain as the result of effort: *~ wonders.* ***work one's way (through college, etc),*** have a paid job, while studying to meet costs: *He's ~ing his way through medical school.* ***work one's passage,*** pay for a journey on a ship by work: *He ~ed his passage to New York.* **5** operate; control; manage: *~ a mine.* **6** (cause to) move into, reach, a new state or position, usually by degrees or with a succession of small movements: *Your shirt has ~ed out,* has come out from above the top of your trousers. *One of the screws has ~ed loose.* **7** make or shape by hammering, mixing, squeezing, pressure, etc: *~ clay,* (when making pottery); *~ dough,* (when making bread). **8** make by sewing; embroider: *~ a design on a slipcover.* **9** (special uses with *adverbial particles* and *prepositions*):

work away (at sth), continue to work: *He's been ~ing away at this job since breakfast.*

work in/into, introduce; find a place for: *Can't you ~ in a few jokes/~ a few jokes into your lecture?*

work off, get rid of; dispose of; deal with: *~ off extra energy/excess weight.*

work on sb/sth, excite, influence: *The information about the treatment of prisoners ~ed on the consciences of the United Nations representatives.* ⇨ also 1 above: *~ on a novel.*

work out, **(a)** be capable of being solved: *This sum/problem doesn't ~ out.* **(b)** be, turn out, in the end: *The situation ~ed out quite well.* **(c)** ⇨ 6 above. **(d)** exercise, train (for a contest): *The champion is ~ing out in the gym this morning.*

work sth out, **(a)** calculate: *I've ~ed out your share of the expenses at $100.* **(b)** get results for: *I can't ~ out these algebra problems.* **(c)** devise; invent: *They've ~ed out a method of sending a spacecraft to Mars.* **(d)** solve: *He was ~ing out some coded messages.* **(e)** (*mod use*) solve problems in a relationship, marriage: *We can ~ it out,* solve our problems together. **(f)** (usually *passive*) exhaust by using, operating, etc: *That silver mine is now ~ed out,* has no more ore.

work up to sth, advance steadily to a high level: *The orchestra was ~ing up to a crescendo.* ***work sth up,*** excite; stir up: *~ up the feelings of an audience.* ***work sb/oneself up (into),*** encourage to a high point (of excitement, etc): *He ~ed himself/everyone up into a state of hysteria.*

work upon sb/sth, = work on sb/sth.

ˈwork·out *n* [C] **(a)** (of a person) period of physical exercise. **(b)** (of a machine) period of intense running, esp as a test.

work·able /ˈwərkəbəl/ *adj* that can be worked; that will work; practicable: *Is the proposed scheme ~,* feasible?

work·a·day /ˈwərkəˌdei/ *adj* common; ordinary.

worker /ˈwəkər/ *n* [C] person who works.

worker ant/bee, undeveloped female kind. ⇨ drone.

work·ing /ˈwərkɪŋ/ *n* **1** [C] the way something works, or the result of this: *the ~s of the human mind.* **2** (as an *adjective*) ***a working majority,*** one that is sufficient to be sure of winning when voting: *The Government has a ~ majority.* ***the working day,*** **(a)** workday (as opposed to a day of rest). **(b)** number of hours worked on a normal day: *a ~ day of eight hours.* ***in working order,*** able to function properly, do what is required; going smoothly: *put a machine in ~ order. Everything is in ~ order.* □ *adj* engaged in work.

ˌworking ˈclass, class of society engaged in manual work.

ˈworking-class *adj*

world /wərld/ *n* [C] **1** the earth, its countries and people; heavenly body that may look like it: *make a journey round the ~. The whole ~/All the ~ knows...,* it is widely or generally known... **2** (as an *adjective*) affecting, used by, intended for, extending over, the world: *We've had two ~ wars in this century.* **3** time, state or scene of existence: *this ~ and the next,* life on earth and existence after death. **4** the universe; everything: *Is this the best of all possible ~s?* ***in the world,*** in existence: *Nothing in the ~ would please me more.* ***for (all) the world,*** for any reason: *I wouldn't hurt her feelings for the ~.* ***think the world of sb,*** think very highly of him. ***be/feel on top of the world,*** elated (because of success, good health, etc). ***sth out of this world,*** something magnificent. ***a world of sth,*** a great number or quantity of; very much/many: *My vacation did me a ~ of good. There's often a ~ of difference between promise and achievement.* **5** the material things and occupations of life (contrasted with the spiritual). ***make the best of both worlds,*** the material and spiritual. **6** human affairs; active life: *know/see the ~,* have experience of life; *a man of the ~,* person who has had a great experience of life. **7** persons, institutions, etc connected with a special social class or special interests: *the ~ of sport/art; the racing/scientific ~.* **8** average society, fashionable society, their opinions, customs, etc: *What will the ~ think?* What will people think?

ˌworld-ˈfamous *adj* known throughout the world.

world·li·ness /-nɪs/ *n* [U]

world·ly *adj* **(a)** material: *my ~ly goods,* my property. **(b)** of the affairs of this life (esp the pursuit of pleasure, contrasted with *spiritual*). **(c)** concerned with, interested in, material things.

ˌworld ˈpower, nation influencing international politics.

ˈworld-weary *adj* tired of life.

ˈworld·wide *adj,adv* affecting, throughout, the world.

worm /wərm/ *n* [C] **1** kinds of small, boneless, limbless, creeping creature. ⇨ earthworm, tapeworm. **2** (used in compounds) name for larvae, insects, etc: *ˈsilk~; ˈglow~.* **3** (*fig*) insignificant or contemptible person. □ *vt* **1** move slowly, or by patience, or with difficulty: *He ~ed himself/his way through the undergrowth. He ~ed himself into her confidence.* ***worm sth out of sb,*** extract (by persistent questioning, etc): *He ~ed the secret out of me.* **2** rid of parasitic worms: *I think we'd better ~ the cat.*

worn *pp* of wear².

worri·some /ˈwərisəm/ *adj* causing worry.

worry /ˈwəri/ *vt,vi* (*pt,pp* -ied) **1** trouble; give (a person, oneself) no peace of mind; cause anxiety or discomfort to: *The noise of the traffic worried her. What's ~ing you? He'll ~ himself to death,* make himself ill by worrying. **2** be anxious, uneasy, troubled: *You have no cause to ~. What's the use of ~ing?* **3** (esp of dogs) seize with the teeth and shake: *The dog was ~ing the rat.* □ *n* (*pl* -ies) **1** [U] condition of being troubled: *show signs of ~.* **2** [C] (usually *pl*) something that worries; cause of anxiety: *Is your life full of worries? Money has always been a ~ to her.*

wor·ried *adj* troubled; anxious: *a worried look.*

worse /wərs/ *adj* (⇨ bad, worst) **1** more bad; more evil: *Your work is bad but mine is much ~. He escaped with nothing ~ than a broken arm.* ***the worse for wear,*** **(a)** badly worn as the result of long wear. **(b)** (*fig*) exhausted: *He looks the ~ for wear after only a year in office.* **2** in(to) less good health or condition or circumstances: *The doctor says she is much ~ today.* □ *adv* (⇨ badly, worst) **1** more badly: *He is behaving ~ than ever. He has been taken ~,* has become more seriously ill. ***none the worse,*** not less: *I like a man none the ~ for being outspoken.* ***worse off,*** in worse circumstances; poorer. **2** (used to intensify): *It's raining ~* (= more heavily) *than ever. She hates me ~* (= more strongly) *than before.* □ *n* worse thing(s): *I have ~ to tell. The first news was bad, but ~ followed.*

worsen /ˈwərsən/ *vt,vi* make, become, worse.

wor·ship /ˈwərʃɪp/ *n* [U] **1** reverence and respect paid to God: *places of ~,* churches and chapels. **2** admiration and respect shown to or felt for a person or thing: *the ~ of success; ˈhero ~.* □ *vt,vi* give worship to: *~ God.*

wor·shiper *n* [C] person who worships.

worst /wərst/ *adj* (⇨ bad, worse) the most bad, evil, ill: *the ~ storm for five years; the ~ behavior; the ~ condition.* □ *adv* (⇨ badly, worse) most badly: *Tom played badly, Harry played worse and I played ~.* □ *n* **the worst,** worst part, state, event, etc: *You must be prepared for the ~,* the worst possible news, outcome, etc. ***get the worst of,*** suffer most. □ *vt* (*rare*) get the better of: *He ~ed his enemy.*

worth /wərθ/ *adj* **1** having a certain value (money or ability, etc); of value equal to: *It's not ~ more than a few dollars.* ***worth (one's) while,*** ⇨ while. ***for what it is worth,*** without any guarantee or promise concerning it. **2** possessing; having property to the value of: *What's the old man ~?* ***for all one is worth,*** (*informal*) with all one's energy; making every effort: *He was running for all he was ~.* **3** giving a satisfactory or rewarding return for: *The book is well ~ reading. It's hardly ~ troubling about.* □ *n* [U] **1** value; what a person or thing is worth: *know a friend's ~.* **2** quantity of something of a specified value: *a ˈdollar's ~ of apples.*

worth·less *adj* having no value.

ˌworth·ˈwhile *adj* that is worth the time, etc needed: *a ~while experiment.* ⇨ while.

worthy /ˈwərði/ *adj* (-ier, -iest) **1** deserving: *a cause ~ of support; a man who is ~ of a place on the team/to be on the team.* **2** (often *ironic*) having merit; deserving respect: *a ~ gentleman.*

worth·ily /-əli/ *adv*

worthi·ness /ˈwərðinɪs/ *n* [U]

-worthy /-ˌwərði/ *suffix* deserving of: *praiseworthy.*

would ⇨ will¹·².

wouldn't /ˈwʊdənt/ = would not.

wound¹ /wund/ *n* [C] **1** hurt or injury to the living tissue of the body, caused by cutting, shooting, tearing, etc, esp as the result of attack (*injury* being more usually for the result of an accident): *a ˈbullet ~.* **2** injury to a plant, tree, etc in which the bark is cut or torn. **3** injury to a person's feelings: *a ~ to his pride/vanity.* □ *vt* give a wound to: *Ten soldiers were killed and thirty ~ed.*

wound² *pt,pp* of wind³.

wove, wo·ven *pt,pp* of weave.

wow /wau/ *int* (expressing wonder, admiration, etc): *Wow, what a girl!* □ *vt* (*sl*) cause wonder, admiration in someone: *This new pop singer is really wowing the audiences.*

wrangle /ˈræŋgəl/ *vi, n* [C] (take part in a) noisy or angry argument.

wrap /ræp/ *vt,vi* (-pp-) **1** put around; cover or roll up (in): *~ a child in a shawl; ~ up a present in tissue paper; ~ oneself in a blanket.* **2** wind or fold as a covering or protection: *Wrap plenty of paper around it.* **3** ***be wrapped up in,*** **(a)** (*fig*) be hidden in: *The affair is ~ped (up) in mystery.* **(b)** be deeply interested in: *He is ~ped up in his work/studies.* **(c)** be deeply devoted to: *She is ~ped up in her children,* devotes all her time, care, etc to them. □ *n* [C] outer clothing or covering (eg a scarf, cloak, fur or rug).

wrap·per *n* [C] **(a)** (esp) piece of paper (to be) wrapped around a newspaper or other periodical, a book etc (esp for mailing); cover of loose paper, etc for a book. **(b)** something used for covering or packing: ˈ*candy* ~*pers*.

wrap·ping *n* [U] material for covering or packing something: *Put plenty of* ~*ping around the cups*.

wrath /ræθ/ *n* [U] (*liter*) great anger (esp caused by misconduct, injustice).

wreak /rik/ *vt* give expression to: ~ *havoc/vengeance on her*.

wreath /riθ/ *n* [C] (*pl* ~s /riðz/) **1** flowers or leaves twisted or woven together into a circle (as placed on a casket, a grave, a memorial to the dead, etc). **2** curling line (*of* smoke, mist, etc).

wreathe /rið/ *vt,vi* **1** cover, encircle: ~*d with flowers; hills* ~*d in mist; a face* ~*d in smiles*. **2** ***wreathe sth into...,*** make (flowers, etc) (into a wreath). **3** (of smoke, mist, etc) move in the shape of a wreath.

wreck /rek/ *n* **1** [U] ruin or destruction, esp of a ship by storms: *save a ship from* ~*;* [C] instance of this: *The storm caused* ~*s all along the coast*. **2** [C] ship that has suffered wreck(1): *The fishermen explored the* ~*s off Cape Hatteras*. **3** [C] vehicle, building, etc that has been badly damaged or fallen into ruin: *The car was a worthless* ~ *after the collision*. **4** [U] (*fig*) ruin (of hopes, etc). **5** [C] person whose health has been destroyed: *If you worry too much, you'll become a nervous* ~. □ *vt* cause the wreck of: *The ship/train was* ~*ed*.

wreck·age /ˈrekɪdʒ/ *n* [U] wrecked object, material: *The* ~*age* (*of the aircraft*) *was scattered over a wide area*.

wren /ren/ *n* [C] kinds of small songbird.

wrench /rentʃ/ *n* [C] **1** sudden and violent twist or pull: *He gave his ankle a* ~, twisted it by accident. **2** (pain caused by a) sad parting or separation: *Separation from her children was a terrible* ~. **3** tool for gripping and turning nuts, bolts, etc; spanner. □ *vt* **1** twist or pull violently: ~ *the door open;* ~ *a door off its hinges*. **2** injure (eg one's ankle) by twisting.

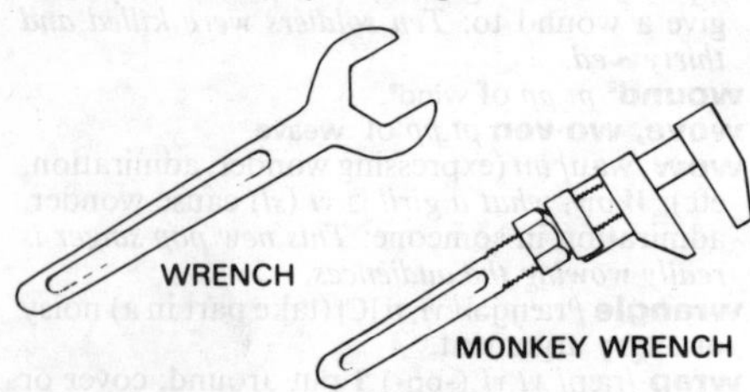

WRENCH

wrest /rest/ *vt* **1** take (something) away with force: ~ *a knife from him/*~ *it out of his hands*. **2** get by effort: ~ *a confession of guilt from a person*.

wrestle /ˈresəl/ *vi* **1** struggle with a person (as a sport) and try to throw him to the ground without hitting him. **2** (*fig*) struggle: ~ *with a problem/one's conscience*.

wres·tler /ˈreslər/ *n* [C] person who wrestles.

wretch /retʃ/ *n* [C] **1** unfortunate and miserable person. **2** contemptible, mean person.

wretched /ˈretʃɪd/ *adj* **1** miserable: *living in* ~ *poverty*. **2** causing misery: ~ *houses*. **3** (*informal*) of poor quality: ~ *weather/food*.

wretched·ly *adv*

wriggle /ˈrɪgəl/ *vi,vt* **1** move with quick, short, twistings; move along in this way: *Small children* ~ *in their seats when they are bored. The eel* ~*d out of my fingers*. **2** move with a wriggling motion: ~ *one's toes;* ~ *one's way out*. □ *n* [C] wriggling movement.

wring /rɪŋ/ *vt* (*pt,pp* wrung /rəŋ/) **1** twist; squeeze: ~ *a hen's neck,* to kill it. ***wring one's hands,*** squeeze them together (to show sorrow, etc). **2** twist and squeeze something tightly (to force out water): ~ *out wet clothes*. ***wringing wet,*** very wet. **3** (*fig*) force a person to confess, by persuasion, threats, etc: ~ *the truth out of him*. □ *n* [C] squeeze: *Give it another* ~.

wringer /ˈrɪŋər/ *n* [C] machine for wringing(2).

wrinkle /ˈrɪŋkəl/ *n* [C] small fold or line in the skin (esp of the kind produced by age) or on the surface of something: *She's beginning to get* ~*s around her eyes. She ironed out the* ~*s in her dress*. □ *vt,vi* make, get, have, wrinkles in: ~ *up one's forehead*, eg when worrying; ~*d with age*.

wrinkly /ˈrɪŋkli/ *adj*

wrist /rɪst/ *n* [C] joint between the hand and the arm: *He took me by the* ~. ⇨ illus at arm.

ˈ**wrist·band** *n* [C] band of cloth worn around the wrist, eg by tennis players.

ˈ**wrist·watch** *n* [C] watch worn on the wrist.

writ /rɪt/ *n* [C] **1** written order issued in the name of a ruler or an official to do or not to do something: *a* ~ *for the arrest of a suspected criminal*. **2 Holy Writ,** the Bible.

write /rait/ *vi,vt* (*pt* wrote /rout/, *pp* written /ˈrɪtən/) **1** make letters or other symbols (eg ideographs) on a surface, esp with a pen or pencil on paper: *learn to read and* ~. *I've been writing* (*for*) *three hours. Are we to* ~ *in ink or* (*in*) *pencil?* **2** put down (on paper) by means of words, etc: ~ *words/Chinese characters/shorthand;* ~ *one's name;* ~ *a check/a book;* ~ *an application* (by filling in the spaces with words, figures, etc). **3** do the work of an author; compose for publication: ~ *a novel;* ~ *for the newspapers; make a living by writing*. **4** write and send a letter (*to* or *informal,* without *to*): *He promised to* ~ (*to*) *me every week. He* ~*s home/*~*s to his parents regularly*. **5** (usually passive) show clear signs of: *He had pain/honesty written on his face*. **6** (special uses with *adverbial particles* and *prepositions*):

write sth down, put down (on paper) in words: *You'd better* ~ *the address down before you forget it*.

write in for sth, apply by letter for:

write off (for sth), order by mail: ~ *off for an application form*. ***write sth off,*** **(a)** compose quickly and easily: ~ *off a report*. **(b)** cancel; recognize that something is a loss or failure: ~ *off a debt. He has just written off a new car,* damaged it beyond repair, so that the insurers regard it as a loss.

write sth out, write the whole of; write in full: ~ *out a copy of an agreement;* ~ *out an abbreviation,* write the actual words. ***write out a check,*** fill one in.

write sth up, complete: *~ up one's diary. I must ~ up my notes of the lecture.*

ˈwrite-off *n* [C]: *The burned-out airliner was a complete ~-off,* had no value whatever.

ˈwrite-up *n* [C] written account of an event.

writer /ˈraitər/ *n* [C] **1** person who writes: *the ~ of this letter.* **2** author.

writer's cramp, cramp of the muscles in the hand, causing difficulty in writing.

writhe /raið/ *vi* twist or roll around (in pain) (mental or physical): *writhing under insults.*

writ·ing /ˈraitɪŋ/ *n* **1** [U] (in the senses of the verb *write*): *busy with his ~; put something down in ~.* **2** = handwriting. **3** (*pl*) literary work: *the ~s of Melville.*

ˈwriting paper, (esp) paper cut to the size usual for letters.

writ·ten *pp* of write.

wrong /rɔŋ/ *adj* (contrasted with *right*) **1** not morally right; unjust: *It is ~ to steal.* **2** mistaken; unsuitable; improper: *He has six ~ answers in his arithmetic. You've dialed the ~ number* (when telephoning). *Can you prove that I am/that my opinions are ~? We got into the ~ train. Go the ~ way.* **3** out of order; in a bad condition: *There's nothing ~ with the engine—perhaps there's no gas in the tank.* □ *adv* in a wrong manner: *guess ~. You've spelled my name ~. You've got it ~,* have misunderstood, miscalculated, etc. ***go wrong,*** **(a)** take the wrong path or road. **(b)** have a bad or poor result; fail: *All our plans went ~.* **(c)** (*informal*) (of a machine, etc) break down. **(d)** take to immorality: *What's the best way to help young girls who go ~?* □ *n* **1** [U] what is morally wrong; [C] wrong action: *know the difference between right and ~; do ~,* sin. *Two ~s don't make a right.* **2** [U] injustice; unjust treatment; [C] instance of this; unjust action: *suffer ~; do ~ to her.* **3** ***in the wrong,*** responsible for an error, for having caused a quarrel, etc: *He admitted that he was in the ~.* □ *vt* treat unjustly; be unfair to: *He ~ed me when he said that I was envious.*

wrong·ful /-fəl/ *adj* unjust; unlawful: *~ful dismissal* (from employment).

wrong·fully /-fəli/ *adv*

wrong·ly *adv* in a wrong manner (used esp before a *pp*): *~ly informed/directed/accused.*

wrong·doer /ˈrɔŋˌduər/ *n* [C] person who does wrong; criminal.

wrong·doing /ˈrɔŋˌduɪŋ/ *n* [U] criminal activity.

wrote *pt,pp* of write.

wrought /rɔt/ (*pt,pp* of work².) beaten into shape: *~ iron.*

ˌwrought-ˈup *adj* overexcited; extremely agitated.

wrung *pt,pp* of wring.

wry /rai/ *adj* (wrier, wriest) pulled or twisted out of shape: *a wry smile,* a forced smile that shows disappointment.

wry·ly *adv*

wt. *abbr* = weight.

WV *postal abbr* = West Virginia. ⇨ App 6.

WW *abbr* = World War.

WY *postal abbr* = Wyoming. ⇨ App 6.

X[1], **x** /eks/ (*pl* X's, x's /ˈeksɪz/) **1** the twenty-fourth letter of the English alphabet. **2** Roman numeral for ten. **3** (*alg*) first unknown quantity.

X[2] *abbr* = extension(3). ⇨ App 1.

xeno·phobia /ˌzenəˈfoubiə, ˌzinə-/ *n* [U] great hatred or fear of strangers or foreigners.

Xmas (common *abbr* for) Christmas.

X-ray /ˈeks-ˌrei/ *n* [C] (apparatus for using a) form of shortwave ray that penetrates solids and makes it possible to see into or through them; photograph taken by this means. □ *vt* examine, treat, photograph, with X-rays.

xylo·phone /ˈzailəˌfoun/ *n* [C] musical instrument of parallel wooden bars, of different lengths, which produce different notes when struck with small wooden hammers. ⇨ illus at percussion.

Y

Y[1], **y** /waɪ/ (*pl* Y's, y's /waɪz/) the twenty-fifth letter of the English alphabet.

Y[2] /waɪ/ *n* [C] (*pl* Y's /waɪz/) (*informal*) = **1** YMCA. **2** YMHA. **3** YWCA. **4** YWHA.

yacht /yat/ *n* [C] **1** light sailing boat built specially for racing. **2** (usually motor-driven) vessel kept by a wealthy person for pleasure cruising. □ *vi* travel or race in a yacht.

yacht·ing *n* [U] the art, sport, of sailing yachts.

yak /yæk/ *n* [C] long-haired ox, wild or domesticated, of Central Asia.

y'all /yɔl/ = you all. ⇨ you.

yam /yæm/ *n* [C,U] (edible tuber of) kinds of tropical climbing plant. ⇨ illus at vegetable.

yank /yæŋk/ *vt* give a sudden sharp pull to: *~ out a tooth.*

Yan·kee /ˈyæŋki/ *n* [C] (*informal*) (*Note:* sometimes shortened to **Yank** /yæŋk/.) **1** citizen of the US (contrasting with those of South America, etc). **2** inhabitant of the northern states of the US, esp New England (contrasting with those of the southern states).

yap /yæp/ *vi* (-pp-) **1** (esp of dogs) make short, sharp barks. **2** (*sl*) talk noisily or foolishly. □ *n* [C] **1** short, shrill bark. **2** (*sl*) mouth: *Shut your yap!* Be quiet!

yard[1] /yard/ *n* [C] **1** (usually unroofed) enclosed or partly enclosed space near or around a building or group of buildings: *a ˈfarm~.* **2** (usually in compounds) enclosure for a special purpose: *the ˈrailway ~, a ˈdock~.*

yard[2] /yard/ *n* [C] **1** unit of length, 3 feet or 36 inches: *Can you buy cloth by the ~?* **2** long piece of wood like a pole fastened to a mast for supporting and spreading a sail.

ˈyard·stick *n* [C] **(a)** marked stick or rod for measuring, one yard long. **(b)** (*fig*) standard of comparison.

yarn /yarn/ *n* **1** [U] fibers which have been spun for knitting, weaving, etc. **2** [C] (*informal*) story; traveler's tale. ***spin a yarn,*** tell a story (often untrue). □ *vi* tell yarns.

yawl /yɔl/ *n* [C] small fishing boat, with sails.

yawn /yɔn/ *vi* **1** (usually involuntarily) open the mouth wide and inhale as when sleepy or bored. **2** be wide open: *a ~ing gap.* □ *n* [C] act of yawning(1).

yaws /yɔz/ *n pl* contagious tropical skin disease.

yd. *abbr* = yard.

yeah /ˈyeə/ *adv* (*informal*) yes.

year /yɪr/ *n* [C] **1** time taken by the earth to make a revolution around the sun, about 365¼ days. **2** period from January 1 to December 31 (also **calendar year**): *in the ~ 1865; last ~; this ~; next ~; the ~ after next.* ***year ˌin, year ˈout,*** year after year. ***ˌall the ˌyear ˈround,*** at all times of the year. **3** any period of 365 days: *It is just a ~ since I arrived here. He's twenty ~s of age/twenty ~s old.* **4** period of one year associated with something: *the academic ~,* for schools, colleges and universities (beginning in the autumn); *the financial ~,* for making up accounts. **5** ***for years,*** for a long time: *We've been friends for ~s.*

year·ly *adj, adv* (taking place) every year; once a year.

year·ling /ˈyɪrlɪŋ/ *n* [C] animal between one and two years old.

yearn /yərn/ *vi* long for with great, tender feeling, affection, etc: *He ~ed for home.*

yearn·ing *n* [C,U] strong desire.

yeast /yist/ *n* [C] substance used in fermenting beer, wine and in making bread rise.

yeasty *adj*

yell /yel/ *vi,vt* **1** make a loud sharp cry or cries as of pain, excitement, etc: *~ with fright/laughter.* **2** say in a loud voice: *~ (out) an order.* □ *n* [C] loud, sharp cry: *a ~ of anger.*

yel·low /ˈyelou/ *n* [U], *adj* **1** (of) the color of gold or the yolk of a hen's egg. **2** (*informal*) cowardly: *He has a ~ streak in him.* □ *vt,vi* (cause to) become yellow: *The leaves of the book were ~ed/had ~ed with age.*

ˌyellow ˈfever, infectious tropical disease causing the skin to turn yellow.

yellow·ish /-ɪʃ/ *adj* a little yellow.

ˈyellow jacket, kind of wasp with yellow markings.

yellow·ness /-nɪs/ *n* [U]

yelp /yelp/ *vi, n* [C] (make a) short, sharp cry (of pain, anger, excitement, etc).

yeo·man /ˈyoumən/ *n* [C] (*pl* -men /-men/) **1** (old usage) independent farmer. **2** (*mod use*) petty officer in US Navy in charge of ship's stores.

yes /yes/ *adv* (contrasted with *no*) (used to express agreement, affirmation, consent, etc): *"Can you read this?" "Yes." "Don't you like it?" —"Yes."* (= "Yes, I do like it.") *"Isn't she beautiful!"—"Yes, isn't she?"* □ *n* [C]: *Answer with a plain "Yes" or "No."*

ye·shiva /yəˈʃivə/ *n* [C] Jewish seminary.

yes·ter·day /ˈyestərˌdei/ *adv, n* (*sing* only) (on) the day just past; (on) the day before today: *He arrived ~. Yesterday was Sunday. Where's ~'s newspaper?*

yes·ter·year /ˈyestərˌyɪr/ *adv, n* (*informal*) (in) times past.

yet /yet/ *adv* **1** by this or that time; up to now;

up to then: *They are not here yet/not yet here. At 2 o'clock they had not yet decided how to spend the afternoon.* **2** so far; up to this/that time: *Has your brother arrived yet? We needn't do it just yet.* ⇨ already, still². **3** still (the usual word): *Go at once while there is yet time,* while it is not too late. **4** at some future time; before all is over: *He may surprise us all yet.* **5** ***as yet,*** up to now or then: *As yet we have/had not made any plans for the vacation.* □ *conj* but at the same time: *He worked hard and yet he failed.*

yew /yu/ *n* [C] (also ˈ**yew-tree**) tree with dark-green leaves and red berries, often used for garden hedges; [U] wood of this tree.

Yid·dish /ˈyɪdɪʃ/ *n* [U] language, like German but with many Hebrew and Slavic words, spoken by Jews in Eastern Europe.

yield /ˈyiəld/ *vt,vi* **1** give a natural product, a result or profit: *trees that ~ fruit.* **2** give way (to); cease opposition: *We will never ~ to force. He ~ed to temptation.* □ *n* [C,U] amount produced: *a good ~ of wheat.*

yield·ing *adj* **(a)** easily giving way or bending. **(b)** (*fig*) not obstinate.

yip·pee /ˈyɪpi/ *int* expression of joy.

YMCA /ˌwai ˌem ˌsi ˈei/ *abbr* = Young Men's Christian Association.

YMHA /ˌwai ˌem ˌeitʃ ˈei/ *abbr* = Young Men's Hebrew Association.

yodel /ˈyoudəl/ *vt,vi* (also -ll-) sing (a song), make a musical call, with frequent changes from the normal voice to high falsetto notes, in the manner of Swiss mountaineers. □ *n* [C] such a song or call.

yodeler *n* [C] person who yodels.

yoga /ˈyougə/ *n* [U] Hindu system of meditation and self-control intended to produce mystical experience and the union of the individual soul with the universal spirit.

yogi /ˈyougi/ *n* [C] (*pl* ~s) teacher of, expert in, yoga.

yo·gurt, yo·ghurt, yo·ghourt /ˈyougərt/ *n* [U] semisolid food made from fermented milk.

yoke /youk/ *n* [C] **1** shaped piece of wood placed across the necks of oxen pulling a cart, plough, etc. **2** (*fig*) symbol of defeat, etc: *throw off the ~ of servitude,* rebel; refuse to obey. **3** shaped piece of wood to fit a person's shoulders and support a pail at each end. **4** (*dressmaking*) part of a dress, etc fitting around the shoulders from which the rest hangs. □ *vt,vi* **1** put a yoke on (oxen). **2** unite: *~d to an unwilling partner.*

yokel /ˈyoukəl/ *n* [C] simple countryman.

yolk /youk/ *n* [C,U] yellow part of an egg: *Beat up the ~s of three eggs.*

Yom Kippur /ˌyam ˈkɪpər, ˌyəm -/ *n* (in Jewish Religion) Day of Atonement.

yon /yan/ *adj, adv* (*liter* and *dial*) (short form of) yonder.

yon·der /ˈyandər/ *adj, adv* (*liter* and *dial*) (that is, that can be seen) over there.

you /yu, weak form yə/ *personal pron* **1** the person(s) addressed: *You are my friend. Does he know you?* **2** (*informal*) one; anyone: *It is much easier to cycle with the wind behind you.*

ˌ**you** ˈ**all** (contracted in speech to y'all /yɔl/) (*informal* and *dial*) you (*pl*).

you'd /yud/ = you had; you would.

you'll /yul/ = you will.

young /yəŋ/ *adj* (-er, -est) **1** (contrasted with *old*) not far advanced in life, growth, development, etc; of recent birth or origin: *a ~ woman/tree/animal/nation.* **2** still near its beginning: *The evening/century is still ~.* **3** (used before a person's name to distinguish, esp, a son from his father): *Young Jones is always ready to help his parents.* **4** (used as a form of address): *Now listen to me, ~ man/my ~ lady!* **5** having little practice or experience (in something): *~ in crime.* ⇨ old(2). □ *n* **1 the young,** young people; children: *books for the ~.* **2** [U] offspring; young animals, birds: *The cat fought to defend its ~.*

young·ish /ˈyəŋgɪʃ/ *adj* fairly young.

young·ster /ˈyəŋstər/ child, youth, esp a boy.

your /yʊr; *sometimes in rapid speech:* yər/ *adj* of, relating to, or belonging to you: *Show me ~ hands. You'll see the post office on your right,* ie the right side.

you're /yʊr; *sometimes in rapid speech:* yər/ = you are.

yours /yʊrz/ *adj, possessive pron* **1** belonging to you: *Is that book ~? I borrowed a book of ~.* **2** (used to end a letter). ⇨ affectionately/faithfully/sincerely/truly.

your·self /yʊrˈself/ *pron* (*pl* -selves /-ˈselvz/) **1** (used as a *reflexive*): *Did you hurt ~?* **2** (used for emphasis): *You ~ said so. You said so ~.* **3** your normal or healthy self: *You don't look ~ today.* ***(all) by yourself,*** **(a)** alone. **(b)** without help.

youth /yuθ/ *n* (*pl* ~s /yuðz/) **1** [U] the state or time of being young: *the friends of one's ~; in my ~,* when I was young. **2** [C] young man: *Half a dozen ~s were standing at the street corner.* **3** (*collect*) young men and women: *a ˈ~ center/club,* for the leisure time activities of young people.

youth·ful /-fəl/ *adj* young; having the qualities, etc of young people: *a ~ful appearance.*

youth·fully /-fəli/ *adv*

youth·ful·ness /-nɪs/ *n* [U]

you've /yuv/ = you have.

yowl /yaul/ *vi* howl.

yo-yo /ˈyou-ˌyou/ *n* [C] **1** wheel-like toy which spins up and down on a string attached to the hand. **2** (*sl*) stupid person.

yr. *abbr* = year.

yule /yul/ *n* (*dated*) Christmas.

YWCA /ˌwai ˌdəbəlyu ˌsi ˈei/ *abbr* = Young Women's Christian Association.

YWHA /ˌwai ˌdəbəlyu ˌeitʃ ˈei/ *abbr* = Young Women's Hebrew Association.

Z

Z[1], **z** /zi/ (*pl* Z's, z's /ziz/) the twenty-sixth and last letter of the English alphabet.

Z[2] *abbr* = zone.

zany /ˈzeini/ *adj* pleasantly foolish; odd.

zeal /ziəl/ *n* [U] great interest and effort: *work with great* ~.

zeal·ous /ˈzeləs/ *adj* enthusiastic (the usual word).

zebra /ˈzibrə/ *n* [C] (*pl* ~s) wild animal of Africa like a horse, with dark stripes on its body.

Zen /zen/ *n* [U] form of Buddhism, teaching that enlightenment comes from meditation and intuition, with less dependence on the scriptures.

zen·ith /ˈziniθ/ *n* [C] **1** part of the sky directly overhead. **2** (*fig*) highest point (of one's fame, fortunes, etc): *at the* ~ *of his career*.

zero /ˈzɪrou/ *n* [C] **1** the figure 0. ⇨ App 1. **2** the point between the positive (+) and negative (−) on a scale, esp on a thermometer: *The thermometer fell to* ~ *last night. It was ten degrees below* ~ (eg −10°C or −10°F). ⇨ absolute zero. □ *vi* ***zero* ˈin on,** aim or focus directly on (a target, etc).

ˈzero hour, time at which (military) operations are to begin: *Zero hour was 3am.*

zest /zest/ *n* [U] **1** great interest or pleasure: *He entered into our plans with* ~. **2** (often with *a, an*) pleasing or stimulating quality or flavor: *Garlic adds* ~ *to a stew.*

zig·zag /ˈzɪgˌzæg/ *n* [C] line or path which turns right and left alternately at sharp (equal or unequal) angles: (as an *adjective*) *a* ~ *path up the hillside.* □ *adv* in a zigzag. □ *vi* (-gg-) go in a zigzag: *The drunken man* ~*ged down the street.*

zil·lion /ˈzɪlyən/ *n* [C] (*sl*) extremely large number: *There seemed to be a* ~ *of them.* ⇨ App 1.

zinc /zɪŋk/ *n* [U] hard, bluish-white metal (symbol **Zn**) used in alloys and in coating iron sheets, etc to protect against rust.

zip /zɪp/ *n* [C] **1** sound as of a bullet going through the air, or of the sudden tearing of cloth. **2** = zipper □ *vt* (-pp-) open or close by means of a zipper.

zip code /ˈzɪp ˌkoud/ *n* postal code for speeding delivery of mail by means of numbered regions. ⇨ App 1.

zip·per /ˈzɪpər/ *n* [C] device for locking together two toothed metal or plastic edges by means of a sliding tab, used for fastening articles of clothing, bags, etc.

zither /ˈzɪðər/ *n* [C] musical instrument with many strings on a flat sounding-board, played with a plectrum or the fingers.

1
ARIES (the Ram)
MARCH 21-APRIL 20

2
TAURUS (the Bull)
APRIL 21-MAY 20

3
GEMINI (the Twins)
MAY 21-JUNE 20

4
CANCER (the Crab)
JUNE 21-JULY 20

5
LEO (the Lion)
JULY 21-AUGUST 19/22

6
VIRGO (the Virgin)
AUGUST 20/23-
SEPTEMBER 22

7
LIBRA (the Scales)
SEPTEMBER 23-
OCTOBER 22

8
SCORPIO (the Scorpion)
OCTOBER 23-
NOVEMBER 21

9
SAGITTARIUS (the Archer)
NOVEMBER 22-
DECEMBER 20

10
CAPRICORN (the Goat)
DECEMBER 21-
JANUARY 20

11
AQUARIUS
(the Water Carrier)
JANUARY 21-
FEBRUARY 19

12
PISCES (the Fish)
FEBRUARY 20-
MARCH 20

SIGNS OF THE ZODIAC

zo·diac /ˈzoudiˌæk/ *n* belt of the heavens extending about 8° on each side of the path followed by the sun and containing the path of the planets, divided into 12 equal parts known as the signs, named after 12 groups of stars: *the signs of the ~.*

zone /zoun/ *n* [C] **1** belt, band or stripe going around, and distinguished by color, appearance, etc. **2** one of the five parts into which the earth's surface is divided by imaginary lines parallel to the equator. **3** area with particular features, purpose or use: *the war ~; the ˈdanger ~.* **4** particular area in which certain postal, telephone, etc rates are charged. □ *vt* encircle, divide, mark, with, into, or as with a zone.

zonal /-nəl/ *adj* relating to, arranged in, zones.

zoo /zu/ *n* [C] (*pl* zoos) zoological gardens.

zo·ologi·cal /ˌzouəˈladʒɪkəl/ *adj* of zoology: *~ gardens*, place where many kinds of animals are kept for exhibition.

zo·ol·ogist /zouˈalədʒɪst/ *n* [C] student of, expert in, zoology.

zo·ol·ogy /zouˈalədʒi/ *n* [U] science of the structure, forms and distribution of animals.

zoom /zum/ *n* [U] (low, deep humming sound of the) sudden upward flight of an aircraft. □ *vi* **1** (of aircraft) move upward at high speed. **2** (of a camera with a zoom lens): *~ in/out*, cause the object being photographed to appear nearer/further.

ˈzoom lens, (on a camera), one with continuously variable focal length.

zuc·chini /zuˈkini/ (*pl* ~s or unchanged) (kind of) edible squash. ⇨ illus at vegetable.

Appendix 1 Numerical Expressions

1. Numbers

CARDINAL			ORDINAL		
1	one	/wən/	1st	first	/fərst/
2	two	/tu/	2nd	second	/ˈsekənd/
3	three	/θri/	3rd	third	/θərd/
4	four	/fɔr/	4th	fourth	/fɔrθ/
5	five	/faiv/	5th	fifth	/fɪfθ/
6	six	/sɪks/	6th	sixth	/sɪksθ/
7	seven	/ˈsevən/	7th	seventh	/ˈsevənθ/
8	eight	/eit/	8th	eighth	/eitθ/
9	nine	/nain/	9th	ninth	/nainθ/
10	ten	/ten/	10th	tenth	/tenθ/
11	eleven	/ɪˈlevən/	11th	eleventh	/ɪˈlevənθ/
12	twelve	/twelv/	12th	twelfth	/twelfθ/
13	thirteen	/ˌθərˈtin/	13th	thirteenth	/ˌθərˈtinθ/
14	fourteen	/ˌfɔrˈtin/	14th	fourteenth	/ˌfɔrˈtinθ/
15	fifteen	/ˌfɪfˈtin/	15th	fifteenth	/ˌfɪfˈtinθ/
16	sixteen	/ˌsɪkˈstin/	16th	sixteenth	/ˌsɪkˈstinθ/
17	seventeen	/ˌsevənˈtin/	17th	seventeenth	/ˌsevənˈtinθ/
18	eighteen	/ˌeiˈtin/	18th	eighteenth	/ˌeɪˈtinθ/
19	nineteen	/ˌnainˈtinθ	19th	nineteenth	/ˌnainˈtinθ/
20	twenty	/ˈtwenti/	20th	twentieth	/ˌtwentiəθ/
21	twenty-one	/ˌtwentiˈwən/	21st	twenty-first	/ˌtwentiˈfərst/
22	twenty-two	/ˌtwentiˈtu/	22nd	twenty-second	/ˌtwentiˈsekənd/
23	twenty-three	/ˌtwentiˈθri/	23rd	twenty-third	/ˌtwentiˈθərd/
30	thirty	/ˈθərti/	30th	thirtieth	/ˈθərtiəθ/
40	forty	/ˈfɔrti/	40th	fortieth	/ˈfɔrtiəθ/
50	fifty	/ˈfɪfti/	50th	fiftieth	/ˈfɪftiəθ/
60	sixty	/ˈsɪksti/	60th	sixtieth	/ˈsɪkstiəθ/
70	seventy	/ˈsevənti/	70th	seventieth	/ˈsevəntiəθ/
80	eighty	/ˈeiti/	80th	eightieth	/ˈeitiəθ/
90	ninety	/ˈnainti/	90th	ninetieth	/ˈnaintiəθ/

CARDINAL		
100	one hundred	/ˌwən ˈhəndrɪd/
200	two hundred	/ˌtu ˈhəndrɪd/
1,000	one thousand	/ˌwən ˈθauzənd/
5,000	five thousand	/ˌfaiv ˈθauzənd/
10,000	ten thousand	/ˌten ˈθauzənd/
100,000	one hundred thousand	/ˌwən ˌhəndrɪd ˈθauzənd/
1,000,000	one million	/ˌwən ˈmɪlyən/
10,000,000	ten million	/ˌten ˈmɪlyən/
100,000,000	one hundred million	/ˌwən ˌhəndrɪd ˈmɪlyən/
1,000,000,000	one billion	/ˌwən ˈbɪlyən/
1,000,000,000,000	one trillion	/ˌwən ˈtrɪlyən/

ORDINAL		
100th	hundredth	/ˈhəndrɪdθ/
200th	two hundredth	/ˌtu ˈhəndrɪdθ/
1,000th	thousandth	/ˈθauzənθ/
5,000th	five thousandth	/ˌfaiv ˈθauzənθ/
10,000th	ten thousandth	/ˌten ˈθauzənθ/
100,000th	hundred thousandth	/ˌhəndrɪd ˈθauzənθ/
1,000,000th	millionth	/ˈmɪlyənθ/
10,000,000th	ten millionth	/ˌten ˈmɪlyənθ/
100,000,000th	hundred millionth	/ˌhəndrɪd ˈmɪlyənθ/
1,000,000,000th	billionth	/ˈbɪlyənθ/
1,000,000,000,000th	trillionth	/ˈtrɪlyənθ/

EXAMPLES OF MORE COMPLEX CARDINAL AND ORDINAL NUMBERS

101 one hundred and one /ˌwən ˌhəndrɪd ən ˈwən/
101st one hundred and first /ˌwən ˌhəndrɪd ən ˌfərst/
334 three hundred and thirty-four /ˌθri ˌhəndrɪd ən ˌθərti ˈfɔr/
542nd five hundred and forty-second /ˈfaiv ˌhəndrɪd ən ˌfɔrti ˈsekənd/
1,234,753 one million, two hundred and thirty-four thousand, seven hundred and fifty-three /ˌwən ˈmɪlyən, ˌtu ˌhəndrɪd ən ˌθərti ˌfɔr ˈθauzənd, ˌsevən ˌhəndrɪd ən ˌfɪfti ˈθri/

COMMON FRACTIONS

½ one half /ˌwən ˈhæf/
⅓ one third /ˌwən ˈθərd/
¼ one fourth /ˌwən ˈfɔrθ/ or one quarter /ˌwən ˈkwɔrtər/

DECIMAL FRACTIONS

(0).5 (oh) point five /ˌou ˌpɔint ˈfaiv/
(0).33 (oh) point three three /ˌou ˌpɔint ˌθri ˈθri/
(0).25 (oh) point two five /ˌou ˌpɔint ˌtu ˈfaiv/

COLLECTIVE NUMBER WORDS

12 one dozen /ˌwən ˈdəzən/ (hence: 6 = half a dozen /ˌhæf ə ˈdəzən/ or a half dozen /ə ˌhæf ˈdəzən/)
20 one score /ˌwən ˈskɔr/
144 one gross /ˌwən ˈgrous/

Notes 1. A comma (not a decimal point, as in Europe) is used to set off thousands from hundreds, millions from thousands, etc., as in the preceding list of cardinal and ordinal numbers. But it is not used in numbers which are not read as thousands, etc., but rather as a series of small digits, e.g., identification numbers, telephone numbers, and dates: 1,776 for the number "one thousand, seven hundred and seventy-six," but 1776 for the date seventeen seventy-six; 2,100 for the number "two thousand, one hundred," but *Suite 2100* "twenty-one hundred" in a building.

2. In complex numbers listed above as starting with "one" (e.g., 100, 1,000, ½, the indefinite article *a* (or *an*) can be substituted for *one* if exactness is not intended. Thus *I own one thousand books* means "exactly or very close to 1,000," while *I own a thousand books* can imply "very roughly 1,000" or just "a great many." For this reason, only *a* is normally used with the slang mock-number *zillion* /ˈzɪlyən/ meaning "an uncountably large number (of)."

3. There is an informal way of saying (especially the lower) thousands as hundreds, especially when there are even hundreds in the number: e.g., 1,100 as "eleven hundred" (for the more formal "one thousand, one hundred"). This usage is often mirrored in writing (in letters, etc.) by omitting the comma.

4. Number names above *trillion* exist, but are rarely used. When larger numbers need to be expressed, e.g., in astronomy, this is usually done in terms of powers of 10: 4×10^{15} "four multiplied by ten to the fifteenth" =4,000,000,000,000,000. Another reason for this is that there are two systems of assigning number names to number values above the millions: the system used in the US and Canada in which *one billion* is 10^9 and *one trillion* is 10^{12}, and the British system in which these number names have the values 10^{12} and 10^{18} respectively.

5. For common fractions having denominators higher than 4, the spoken form of the denominator is always that of the corresponding ordinal number.

6. A point (called a *decimal point*) is used in writing decimal fractions (rather than a comma, as in Europe). The digits after the decimal point are read either by saying *point* and then each digit separately, or else the entire fraction is read as the decimal value, e.g., 2.03 is said either as "two point oh three" or as "two and three hundredths."

7. The cipher *0* is usually spoken as *oh* /ou/ or (more formally) as *zero* /ˈzɪrou/. Some people say *naught* /nɔt/ (also spelled *nought*), but this term is now considered dated in the U.S.

8. When followed by a *noun*, the collective number words *score* and *gross* are used with *of*: *a score of years*; *one gross of buttons*. With *dozen*, the *of* is omitted when dozen is qualified by the indefinite article or another number, e.g., *a dozen eggs*, but *of* is used when dozen appears without the indefinite article or another number, e.g., *dozens of applicants for the job*. All three of the collective number words remain unchanged in the plural when qualified by another number, e.g., *three dozen (eggs)*, *four score (of sheep)*, *two gross (of pencils)*, but have plurals formed in the usual way when used alone, e.g., *there were dozens/scores of them*.

2. House numbers and postal zip codes

A *house number* may be from one digit in length to five or more. It is always used *before* the street name in the US, and written *without* a comma or other punctuation. House numbers from 1 to 100 are spoken as the equivalent numbers in counting (see Appendix 1): 100 Main Street (spoken as) "one hundred Main Street." When the house number is above 100, either each digit is said as a separate number (with 0 as "oh" /ou/) or, where possible, by treating the last two or four digits as tens: 101 ("one oh one") Main Street; 123 ("one two three" or "one twenty-three") Main Street; 1234 ("one two three four" or "twelve thirty-four") Main Street. If the house number ends in 00 or 000, these are said as hundreds and thousands, respectively: 1200 ("twelve hundred") Main Street; 1000 ("one thousand") Main Street.

For addressing mail, the US Postal Service has assigned a five-digit *Zip Code* to each station and the area which it serves. The Zip Code is written after the name of the state (which in turn follows the name of the city), with a comma between city and state but not between state and Zip Code: Honolulu, Hawaii 96815. Zip Codes are spoken either by treating each digit as a separate number, or by treating the first and last two digits as tens: "nine six eight one five" or ninety-six eight fifteen."

Notes 1. Numbered streets and avenues are always spoken with ordinal numbers, though sometimes written with plain (cardinal) numbers: 19th Street/19 Street (both spoken as "Nineteenth Street"); 5th Avenue/5 Avenue (both as "Fifth Avenue"). If the number is written out, the ordinal form is of course the one used. In saying numbered streets and avenues, there is a difference in the use of stress; the number has primary stress with streets, but secondary stress with avenues: ˈFourth ˌStreet, but ˌFourth ˈAvenue.

2. Floors in buildings are numbered ordinally, beginning in the US with the ground floor, which accordingly is the ˈfirst ˌfloor, the one above it the ˈsecond ˌfloor, etc.

3. Telephone numbers

Telephones throughout the United States and Canada are reached by dialing a three-digit *Area Code*, indicating the region, plus a seven-digit number indicating the individual telephone. While the term *telephone number* (or *phone number* in *informal* usage) technically includes all ten digits, it is often used to refer to the seven-digit individual number alone. The Area Code is usually written separately from the seven-digit number, and often in parentheses as well, since it is only dialed when calling from one Area Code to another, i.e., when *calling long distance* or *making a long-distance* (*tele*)*phone call.* In writing the seven-digit number, the first three digits (called the *prefix*) are separated from the last four by a hyphen: (202) 234-5678.

The three digits of both the Area Code and the prefix are always spoken as a series of three separate numbers (with 0 usually said as "oh" /ou/), while the last four digits may be spoken as a series of four separate numbers or as two sets of tens: "Area Code two oh two, (number) two three four, five six seven eight" or "two three four, fifty-six seventy-eight." But if the last four digits end in 00 or 000, they are usually treated as hundreds and thousands, respectively: 234-5600 "two three four, five six-hundred"; 234-5000 "two three four, five-thousand."

Notes 1. Some individual telephone numbers are still found written in an older form in which the first two digits of the prefix are given as letters (A, B, or C for 2; D, E, or F for 3, etc.), separated from the third digit by a space: AD 4-5678 (=234-5678). These are spoken either as individual letters, "/ei di/ four, . . ." or as some established name starting with the two letters, e.g., "ADams four, . . ."

2. A telephone number may be that of a business switchboard with an internal operator who can connect an incoming call to a three- or four-digit *extension* number. On business cards, etc., the appropriate extension number is written, e.g., X246 and read "Extension two four six" or "two forty-six."

Appendix 2 Time of Day

TWELVE-HOUR CLOCK TIME

7:00	seven (o'clock)
7:05	seven oh five
	five (minutes) after/past seven
7:12	seven twelve
	twelve (minutes) after/past seven
7:15	seven fifteen
	fifteen (minutes) after/past seven
	a quarter after/past seven
7:30	seven thirty
	half past seven
7:35	seven thirty-five
	twenty-five (minutes) to/of eight
7:45	seven forty-five
	fifteen (minutes) to/of eight
	a quarter to/of eight

Notes 1. Where more than one version is given, the first (e.g., "seven oh five" for 7:05) is that generally used for reading from timetables, digital clocks, etc. It is becoming increasingly popular for time-telling in general in the US.

2. When necessary (e.g., on timetables) the ambiguity of twelve-hour clock time is removed by adding *AM/am* /ˌei ˈem/ or *PM/pm* /ˌpi ˈem/. When this is done, the first version of time-telling is preferred: *7:05 PM/7:05 pm* "seven oh five PM."

3. The terms *quarter* and *half* in the second and third versions are of course divisions of the hour. Note that while one can say either "a quarter after seven" or "a quarter past seven," one usually says only "half past seven." For *to/of*, the use of *to* is more formal.

TWENTY-FOUR HOUR CLOCK TIME

07:00	(oh) seven hundred (hours)	(=7:00 AM)
07:15	(oh) seven fifteen	(=7:15 AM)
07:30	(oh) seven thirty	(=7:30 AM)
07:45	(oh) seven forty-five	(=7:45 AM)
12:00	twelve hundred (hours)	(=midday/noon)
15:22	fifteen twenty-two	(=3:22 PM)
24:00	twenty-four hundred (hours)	(=midnight)

Appendix 3 **Dates**

When they are used, AD /ˌei ˈdi/ precedes the year number while BC /ˌbi ˈsi/ follows it: AD 55; 55 BC. AD is generally used only with the earlier (two-digit) years of the present era: AD 70, but simply 770 and 1770. The comma which is often used in regular numbers of more than three digits is never used in year numbers: 2000 BC (not 2,000 BC); 1776 (not 1,776).

Year numbers ending in 00 and 000 are spoken as hundreds and thousands, respectively: 700 "seven hundred"; 1700 "seventeen hundred"; 1000 "one thousand." Other three- and four-digit year numbers are read as hundreds plus tens, with the words "hundred and" usually omitted: 770 "seven (hundred and) seventy"; 1066 "ten (hundred and) sixty-six"; 1801 "eighteen (hundred and) one"; 1942 "nineteen (hundred and) forty-two." For year numbers ending in 01–09, these can be said as "oh /ou/ one" (etc.), in which case the words "hundred and" are never used: 1801 "eighteen (oh) one."

The numbers of days of the month are spoken as ordinals, even when written as plain or cardinal numbers: January 15th/15 (both said as) "January fifteenth."

Notes 1. In *informal* style, the hundreds referring to the century may be omitted when the context makes it obvious, with the omission marked by an apostrophe in writing: *He started out in the summer of '24* (". . . of twenty-four").

2. Decades may be referred to by pluralizing the 00, 20, etc., written as (')*s*: the 1900(')s "the nineteen hundreds"; the '20(')s "the twenties."

3. Dates are often written informally by assigning numbers 1 through 12 to the months, and writing month/day/year (last two digits) separated by slants (/): 9/8/72 = September 8, 1972. Note that, unlike the European system, the month is indicated first and that Roman numbers are not used for it.

Appendix 4 **Money**

Amounts in US currency are indicated by placing $ (the ˈ*dollar* ˌ*sign*) before the total amount, with a decimal point separating the dollars from the cents (100 cents = one dollar): $1 or $1.00 "one dollar"; $0.10 "ten cents"; $0.01 "one cent."

US currency occurs in coins and notes, with the following being the most common:

NAME OF COIN	VALUE OF COIN
a penny /ə ˈpeni/	$0.01 one cent /ˌwʌn ˈsent/
a nickel /ə ˈnɪkəl/	$0.05 five cents
a dime /ə ˈdaim/	$0.10 ten cents
a quarter /ə ˈkwɔrtər/	$0.25 twenty-five cents (See Notes 6 and 7 below.)
a half-dollar /ə ˈhæf-ˈdalər/ (or) a fifty-cent piece /ə ˌfifti-ˈsent ˌpis/	$0.50 fifty cents (See Notes 6 and 7 below.)
a silver dollar /ə ˌsɪlvər ˈdalər/	$1.00 one dollar /ˌwʌn ˈdalər/

NAME OF NOTE	VALUE OF NOTE
a dollar bill /ə ˌdalər ˈbɪl/ (or) a one /ə ˈwʌn/	$1.00 one dollar
a five (dollar bill)	$5.00 five dollars
a ten (dollar bill)	$10.00 ten dollars
a twenty (dollar bill)	$20.00 twenty dollars
a fifty (dollar bill)	$50.00 fifty dollars
a hundred (dollar bill)	$100.00 a/one hundred dollars

$325.42 "three hundred twenty-five dollars and forty-two cents"

Note 1. Note the use of *a* with *penny*, but *one* with *cent*.

2. With amounts betwen $100 and $199, both "a hundred" and "one hundred" are used with no difference in meaning: $165 "a hundred and sixty-five dollars" or "one hundred and . . .". The same is true for a/one thousand (dollars), a/one million (dollars), etc.

3. When it is clear that currency is referred to, the terms *dollar*(*s*) and *cent*(*s*) may be omitted (with the linking *and*) when saying amounts: $16.50 "sixteen fifty." Also, when they are combined with hundreds, the one-digit thousands may be said as hundreds: $1.500 "a/one thousand, five hundred (dollars)" or "fifteen hundred (dollars)."

4. US notes of higher value than $100 exist, but they are rarely used in everyday transactions.

5. When only amounts below $1.00 are being referred to, it is possible in informal writing to omit the dollar sign and decimal, and to write only the number of cents followed by ¢ (the ˈ*cent* ˌ*sign*): $0.10 or 10¢ "ten cents." (Note the difference in position of the dollar and cent signs: $10, but 10¢. The two signs are never used together.)

6. When the amounts $0.25 and $0.50 occur together with low numbers of dollars, they may be spoken in *informal* style as "and a quarter" and "and a half" respectively: $3.25 "three (dollars and) twenty-five (cents)" or "three (dollars) and a quarter". Alone, they may be "a quarter of/(a) half a dollar."

7. In *informal* usage, one sometimes hears ˌ*two* ˈ*bits* for $0.25, ˌ*four* ˈ*bits* for $0.50 and ˌ*six* ˈ*bits* for $0.75, though these terms are now becoming a little dated. But even those who still use them do so only when these amounts stand alone: $0.25 "two bits", but $1.25 (only) "a/one dollar and a quarter," "one (dollar) twenty-five."

Appendix 5 The Greek Alphabet

Many letters of the Greek alphabet are used as symbols in mathematics, in both the form of capitals and of small letters. Greek capitals are also used, in three-letter groupings, as the names of college fraternities, sororities, and honorary societies and sometimes (in *informal* usage) to refer to members of these. In speech, Greek letters are referred to by their names, as in the following list:

capitals	*small letters*	*name*	
Α	α	alpha	/ˈælfə/
Β	β	beta	/ˈbeitə/
Γ	γ	gamma	/ˈgæmə/
Δ	δ	delta	/ˈdeltə/
Ε	ε	epsilon	/ˈepsəˌlan/
Ζ	ζ	zeta	/ˈzeitə/
Η	η	eta	/ˈeitə/
Θ	θ	theta	/ˈθeitə/
Ι	ι	iota	/aiˈoutə/
Κ	κ	kappa	/ˈkæpə/
Λ	λ	lambda	/ˈlæmdə/
Μ	μ	mu	/myu/
Ν	ν	nu	/nu/
Ξ	ξ	xi	/zai, ksai/
Ο	ο	omicron	/ˈouməˌkran, ˈməˌkran/
Π	π	pi	/pai/
Ρ	ρ	rho	/rou/
Σ	σ	sigma	/ˈsɪgmə/
Τ	τ	tau	/tau/
Υ	υ	upsilon	/ˈyupsəˌlan, ˈʌpsəˌlan/
Φ	φ	phi	/fai/
Χ	χ	chi	/kai/
Ψ	ψ	psi	/sai, psai/
Ω	ω	omega	/ouˈmegə/

In most cases, these names may be used in place of the Greek letters themselves: *the value of* π */ of pi;* X^2 */ chi-square; ΦBK / Phi Beta Kappa.*

Appendix 6 Names and Postal Abbreviations of States

Alabama (AL) /ˌæləˈbæmə/
Alaska (AK) /əˈæskə/
Arizona (AZ) /ˌærəˈzounə/
Arkansas (AR) /ˈarkənˌsɔ/
California (CA) /ˌkæləˈfɔrnyə/
Colorado (CO) /ˌkaləˈrædou, -ˈra-/
Connecticut (CT) /kəˈnetɪkət/
Delaware (DE) /ˈdeləˌwær/
District of Columbia (DC) /ˌdɪstrɪkt əv kəˈləmbiə/
Florida (FL) /ˈflɔrədə/
Georgia (GA) /ˈdʒɔrdʒə/
Hawaii (HI) /həˈwai(y)i/
Idaho (ID) /ˈaidəˌhou/
Illinois (IL) /ˌɪləˈnɔi/
Indiana (IN) /ˌɪndiˈænə/
Iowa (IA) /ˈaiəwə/
Kansas (KS) /ˈkænzəs/
Kentucky (KY) /kɪnˈtəki/
Louisiana (LA) /luˌiziˈænə/
Maine (ME) /mein/
Maryland (MD) /ˈmerələnd/
Massachusetts (MA) /ˌmæsəˈtʃusɪts/
Michigan (MI) /ˈmɪʃɪgən/
Minnesota (MN) /ˌmɪnəˈsoutə/
Mississippi (MS) /ˌmɪsəˈsɪpi/
Missouri (MO) /mɪˈzʊri/
Montana (MT) /manˈtænə/
Nebraska (NE) /nəˈbræskə/
Nevada (NV) /nəˈvædə/
New Hampshire (NH) /ˌnuˈhæmpʃər/
New Jersey (NJ) /ˌnu ˈdʒərzi/
New Mexico (NM) /ˌnu ˈmeksɪkou/
New York (NY) /ˌnu ˈyɔrk/
North Carolina (NC) /ˌnɔrθ ˌkærəˈlainə/
North Dakota (ND) /ˌnɔrθ dəˈkoutə/
Ohio (OH) /ouˈhaiou/
Oklahoma (OK) /ˌoukləˈhoumə/
Oregon (OR) /ˈɔrɪgən, -ˌgan/
Pennsylvania (PA) /ˌpensəlˈveinyə/
Rhode Island (RI) /ˌroud ˈailənd/
South Carolina (SC) /ˌsauθ ˌkærəˈlainə/
South Dakota (SD) /ˌsauθ dəˈkoutə/
Tennessee (TN) /tenəˈsi/
Texas (TX) /ˈteksəs/
Utah (UT) /ˈyuˌtɔ/
Vermont (VT) /vərˈmant/
Virginia (VA) /vərˈdʒɪnyə/
Washington (WA) /ˈwɔʃɪŋtən, ˈwa-/
West Virginia (WV) /ˌwest vərˈdʒɪnyə/
Wisconsin (WI) /wɪsˈkansən/
Wyoming (WY) /waiˈoumɪŋ/